TIME
ALMANAC
2005

with **Information Please**®

BORGNA BRUNNER
EDITOR IN CHIEF

Editor Beth Rowen

Senior Contributing Editor
Christine Frantz

Contributing Editors Susan Hyde,
Holly Hartman

Production Director
Susan Hyde

Production Editor Christine Frantz

President George Kane

Proofreading and Fact-Checking
Susan Chicoski, Holly Hartman,
Ann-Marie Imbornoni, Elizabeth Olson

Editorial Assistant Shmuel Ross

Graphics Sean M. Dessureau

Technical Support Karl DeBisschop

Time Inc.
HOME ENTERTAINMENT

Contributing Editor Kelly Knauer

Design Anthony Kosner

Pictures Patricia Cadley

President Rob Gursha

Vice President, New Product Development
Richard Fraiman

Executive Director, Marketing Services
Carol Pittard

Director, Retail & Special Sales Tom Mifsud

Director of Finance Tricia Griffin

Marketing Director Ann Marie Doherty

Prepress Manager Emily Rabin

Book Production Manager Jonathan Polsky

Product Manager Kristin Walker

Special thanks to: Bozena Bannett, Alexandra Bliss, Bernadette Corbie, Robert Dente,
Anne-Michelle Gallero, Peter Harper, Suzanne Janso, Robert Marasco, Natalie McCrea,
Brook McGuire, Margarita Quiogue, Mary Jane Rigoroso, Steven Sandonato

The *TIME Almanac* welcomes comments and suggestions from readers. We prefer hearing from you
through email (ipa@infoplease.com), if possible. Although the editors carefully consider each suggestion,
because of the volume of correspondence we receive we cannot respond personally to each writer. The
TIME Almanac does not rule on bets or wagers.

Editorial Office
Information Please
Pearson Education
160 Gould Street
Needham, MA 02494
Email: ipa@infoplease.com

Customer Service
Attention: TIME Almanac
PO Box 11016
Des Moines, IA 50336-1016

ISBN: 1-932273-35-2 Paperback
ISBN: 1-932273-58-1 Hardcover
ISSN: 0073-7860

Keyword Index

Abbreviations of States........................442
Academy Awards.......................247–251
AIDS 547, 553–554
Animals....................................590–591
Architecture 443–450
Associations and Societies..............658–667
Astronomy.................................396–420
Aviation...................................435–439
Awards.....................................225–262
Biographies 58–75, 281–315, 955–959
Books..............241–245, 254–257, 266–269
Buildings and Structures.................443–450
Business and Economy 618–650
Cabinet, U.S................................84–89
Calendars 344–357
Chemical Elements.......................571–574
Cities, U.S. 181–210
Colleges and Universities...............321–343
Computers and the Internet.............563–568
Congress, U.S. 45–48
Constitution, U.S. 108–117
Consumer Resources.....................651–657
Copyrights, Trademarks, Patents 656–657
Countries of the World..................721–904
Crime Statistics..........................382–388
Crossword Puzzle Guide.................459–471
Current Events 32–42, 505–518, 1030–1039
Deaths...................................1035–1039
Declaration of Independence 106–107
Disasters, Great...........................211–224
Drugs 547–552, 557–558
Earthquakes 211–212, 490–492
Economic Figures........................618–650
Education..................................316–343
Elections....................................43–48
Embassies and Ambassadors 908–914
Emmy Awards 259
Endangered Species 591
Entertainment and Culture..............263–280
Environment and Nature.................585–596
Explorers 484–485
First Aid 561–562
Firsts in America 100
Flags of the World 519–522
Foreign Words and Phrases 477, 478–479
Gender Issues 371–374
Geography 483–504
Governors, U.S.....................48, 143–178
Grammar and Writing Guide 472–474
Grammy Awards 452–453
Health and Nutrition 537–560
History, U.S. 49–118
History, World..............................668–705
Holidays and Observances 344, 353–357
House of Representatives, U.S. 46–48
Hurricanes 211, 214–215, 597–599

International Relations 905–914
Internet.....................................563–567
Inventions and Discoveries 577–584
Law Enforcement and Crime...........382–388
Maps of the World 523–536
Mayors of 50 Largest U.S. Cities 181–204
Metric System 451, 454–456
Military Affairs...........................389–395
Mountains....................492–493, 502
Movies........................247–251, 279–280
Music 245, 252–253, 263–264, 271–274
Mythology.................................467–471
National Parks............................592–596
Newspapers and Magazines.......257, 277–278
Nobel Prizes........................42, 225–233
Obituaries 1035–1039
Olympics 915–931
Passports 610
People 281–315, 955–959, 1030–1039
Pictures, Year in.........................505–518
Population, U.S. 119–124
Population, World 706–710
Postal Regulations........................440–442
Presidents, U.S................56, 58–75
Pulitzer Prizes............................234–247
Race and Ethnicity 375–381
Religion....................................358–370
Science.....................................569–576
Senate, U.S. 45–46
Social Security 633–634
Societies and Associations...............658–667
Space Exploration 421–434
Sports.....................................915–1023
States, U.S. 143–180
Super Bowl................................939–941
Supreme Court 90–94
Taxes 1024–1028
Television 251, 258, 259–260
Temperatures.................610, 600–605
Terrorism..........211, 223–224, 716–718
TIME People of the Year....................1029
Time Zones 523
Tony Awards 251
Travel and Transportation...............606–617
United Nations 905–908
U.S. Geography 500–504
U.S. Government and History 49–118
U.S. Statistics............................119–142
Vice Presidents, U.S. 56–57
Volcanoes............211–212, 488–489
Weather and Climate....................597–605
Websites 565–566
Weights and Measures 451–458
World Series 1004–1007, 1021–1022
World Statistics............................706–720
Writing and Language 472–482

Section Index

ASTRONOMY **396**
   The Blueberries of Mars......................396
AVIATION **435**
AWARDS... **225**
BUSINESS AND ECONOMY **618**
   Is Your Job Going Abroad? 618
CALENDAR AND HOLIDAYS..................... **344**
COMPUTERS AND THE INTERNET **563**
   The Revolution in Radio 563
CONSUMER RESOURCES **651**
   Plastic That Pays Back 651
COUNTRIES OF THE WORLD **721**
CROSSWORD PUZZLE GUIDE **459**
CURRENT EVENTS **32**
   The News of 2004: Nation 32
   The News of 2004: World 34
   What Happened in 2004: Month by Month 35
DEATHS **1035**
EDUCATION **316**
ENTERTAINMENT AND CULTURE **263**
ENVIRONMENT AND NATURE.................... **585**
   The Tragedy of Tar Creek......................585
FIRST AID **561**
FLAGS **519**
GENDER ISSUES **371**
   A Primer on Same-Sex Marriages
     and Civil Unions.............................371
GEOGRAPHY.. **483**
   The Race to the North Pole.....................483
GREAT DISASTERS **211**
HEADLINE HISTORY **668**
HEALTH AND NUTRITION—TIME SPECIAL............ **537**
   The Secrets of Eating Smarter 537
   Welcome to America, a Low-Carb Nation 543
   America's Obesity Crisis 546
   A to Z Guide to Health and Medicine News ...547
INDEX, COMPREHENSIVE **6**
INTERNATIONAL RELATIONS **905**
INVENTIONS AND DISCOVERIES **577**
   Roundup of Recent Discoveries.................577
LAW ENFORCEMENT AND CRIME **382**
MAPS **523**
MILITARY AFFAIRS................................. **389**
   Iraq War Timeline..............................389
PEOPLE **281**
PEOPLE IN THE NEWS **1030**
POSTAL REGULATIONS **440**
RACE AND ETHNICITY **375**
   Civil Rights Timeline 380

RELIGION **358**
SCIENCE **569**
   Stem Cells: The Promise and the Paradox 569
SPACE EXPLORATION **421**
   Secrets of the Rings 421
SPORTS **915**
   Auto Racing 997
   Baseball 1001
   Baseball Hall of Fame 1002
   Baseball, Little League..........................1000
   Basketball, College...............................947
   Basketball, Professional.........................950
   Basketball, Women's Professional................954
   Bicycling 1000
   Bowling..964
   Boxing 972
   Figure Skating...................................969
   Football, College 932
   Football Hall of Fame, College 935
   Football Hall of Fame, Professional 944
   Football, Professional 939
   Golf 993
   Harness Racing..................................991
   Heisman Trophy 935
   Hockey..960
   Horse Racing 978
   Marathons 1000
   Olympic Games, Summer 915
   Olympic Games, Winter 928
   Personalities, Sports.............................955
   Skiing 966
   Soccer 1023
   Speed Skating...................................968
   Sullivan Award 959
   Swimming 970
   Tennis 985
   Track and Field 981
   World Series Records, Baseball 1004
STRUCTURES AND BUILDINGS.................... **443**
TAXES.. **1024**
TRAVEL AND TRANSPORTATION **606**
   Flying the Friendlier Skies 606
U.S. CITIES **181**
U.S. GOVERNMENT AND HISTORY..................... **49**
U.S. SOCIETIES AND ASSOCIATIONS **658**
U.S. STATES **140**
U.S. STATISTICS..................................... **119**
WEATHER AND CLIMATE.......................... **597**
WEIGHTS AND MEASURES **451**
WORLD STATISTICS **706**
WRITING AND LANGUAGE......................... **472**
YEAR IN PICTURES................................. **505**

Page numbers followed by "n" indicate information in footnotes.

A

Abacha, Sani, 836
Abbas, Mahmoud, 799, 840
Abbreviations:
  postal, 442
  state, 442
  of weights and measures, 453, 455
Abdullah II, King, 802–803
Abidjan, Côte d'Ivoire, 756
Abizaid, John, 389
Abortion, 556, 692, 693, 695, 697
Abscam, 99, 693
Absolute world records in aviation, 439
Absolute zero, 451, 454, 583
Abu Dhabi, United Arab Emirates, 882
Abu Ghraib scandal, 32, 37, 38, 41, 390, 795 506
Abuja, Nigeria, 835
Academy Awards (Oscars), 247–251
Acadia, 676, 745
Acadia National Park, 592, 596
Accidents. See also Disasters
  aircraft, 211, 219–221
  automobile, 613
  deaths from, 211–224
  drunk driving, 613
  fires and explosions, 217–218
  first aircraft fatality, 435
  holiday, 613
  railroad, 211, 221–222
  shipwrecks, 218–219
  space, 221
Accra, Ghana, 781
Aconcagua Peak, 487, 493, 725
Acre (measure), 453, 455
Acropolis, 443, 669
Actium, Battle of, 670
Actors and actresses:
  awards for, 247–252
  biographical information, 281–315
Adams, John, 51, 56, 59, 95, 104, 106. See also Presidents, U.S.
Adams, John Quincy, 51, 54, 56, 60, 95. See also Presidents, U.S.
Addis Ababa, Ethiopia, 769
Adenauer, Konrad, 281, 780
Administration, Office of, 81
Admirals (U.S.), first, 100
Adoption, 132, 133
Adrenaline, isolation of, 579
Adriatic Sea, 722, 800, 855
Advent (season), 344, 355
Advertising, 646
Aegean Sea, 878
Aerial combat, first, 436
Aerial photographers, first, 435
Aeschylus, 669
Affirmative action, 381, 704
Afghanistan, 33, 42, 43, 693, 703, 850
AFL-CIO, 658, 689
Africa. See also Continents; Countries
  area and elevation of, 487
  exploration of, 484
  map of, 532
  Portuguese territory in, 847
  southernmost point of, 865
African Americans. See Blacks in U.S.
African Union, 908
Age:
  at first marriage, 127
  life expectancy by, 135
  population by, 120, 122, 123, 124
Age limits, driving licenses, 614
Agencies, U.S., 81–84
Aggtelek Cavern, 497

Agincourt, Battle of, 673
Agnew, Spiro T., 57, 57n, 98, 692
Agriculture. See also Food
  ancient, 668
  economic statistics, 644
  farm index, 644
  number of farms by state, 644
  number of farms in U.S., 644
  production by state, 645
Agriculture, U.S. Dept. of (USDA):
  description, 81
  secretaries of, 81, 86–89
AIDS, 213, 547, 553–554, 554, 584
Air (atmosphere), 401
Air Force, U.S.. See also Armed forces, U.S.
  Secretary of, 82
Airlines:
  business, 606
  cargo carried by, 611
  consumer complaints, 611
  first scheduled passenger service, 436
  low-fare, 606
  passenger traffic, 611
  quality ratings, 606
Airmail:
  first, 100, 436
  international, 442
  rates, 442
Airplanes:
  accidents, 211, 219–221
  exports and imports, 641
  fatalities, 613
  invention of, 435
  passenger traffic, 611
Air pollutants, 588–589
Airports, world's busiest, 611
Airship, invention of, 579
Air transport company, first, 435
Akkadian civilization, 668, 669
Alabama, 143
Alabama-Coosa River, 500
Al-Aksa intifada, 799, 840
Alamo, The, 95, 173, 200, 679
Åland Islands, 771
Alaska, 144
  discovery of, 676
  exploration of, 144, 484
  mountain peaks, 502
  national parks in, 144, 592–593
  purchase of, 102, 144, 680
Albania, 722–723
Albany, N.Y., 165, 179
Albany Medical Center Prize, 262
Alberta, Canada, 745
Albert Canal, 450
Albright, Madeleine, 89, 699
Albums, top-selling, 272
Albuquerque, N.M., 164, 179, 181
Alcohol, 558
  Alcoholics Anonymous, 658
  drunk driving, 613, 614
Aldrin, Edwin E., Jr., 428, 691
Aleutian Islands, 677
Aleuts, 144
Alexander the Great, 281, 484, 670, 721, 765, 792
Alexandria, Egypt, 765
  Pharos of, 443
Alfred the Great, 671
Algeria, 723–724
  independence of, 688, 690, 773
Algiers, Algeria, 723
Alhambra, 444
Ali, Muhammad (Cassius Clay), 955, 973
Allawi, Iyad, 32, 38, 39, 41, 390, 507, 795, 1030

Allende, Salvador, 749
All Saints' Day, 344, 354
All-Star Game (baseball), 1001–1002
Al-Manámah, Bahrain, 731
Alpha Centauri, 400
Alps, 729, 771, 871
  tunnels under, 450
Altamaha-Ocmulgee River, 500
Altamira Cave, 497
Altiplano, 736
Altitudes. See Elevations
Aluminum, chemical properties of, 573
Alzheimer's, 547
Amazon River, 485, 495, 739, 752
Ambassadors, 912–914
Amendments to Constitution, 94, 96, 97, 98, 99, 113–117
  civil rights, 113
  right to bear arms, 113
  unreasonable search and seizure, 113
Armenian Massacre, 683
American Battle Monuments Commission, 83
American Federation of Labor, 658, 689
American Film Institute:
  best movies of all time, 279
  top movie songs, 280
American history. See United States history
American League. See Baseball; Football
American Library Association Awards, 255–257
American manual alphabet, 482
American Red Cross, 665
American Revolution. See Revolutionary War, American
American Samoa, 895
American Sign Language, 482
Amin, Idi, 881
Amman, Jordan, 802
Amperes, 454
Amsterdam, Netherlands, 831
Amsterdam-Rhine Canal, 450
Amtrak, 84
Amu Darya River, 495
Amur (Heilong) River, 495
Ancestry, U.S. population, 375
Anchorage, Alaska, 144, 179
Ancient empires, 668–670
Ancient history, events of, 668
Andaman Sea, 494
Andes, 492–493, 725, 749, 752, 843
Andorra, 724
Andorra la Vella, Andorra, 724
Andropov, Yuri V., 694, 850
Anesthetic, first use of, 579
Angel Falls, 496
Angkor Wat, 444
Angola, 724–725, 847
Angstrom, 455, 456n
Anguilla, 889
Animals:
  classification of, 570
  endangered species, 591
  farm, 645
  gestation, incubation, and longevity of, 590
  group terminology, 591
  names of, 590
  speed of, 590
Ankara, Turkey, 878
Annan, Kofi, 699, 905
Annapolis, Md., 156, 179
  Naval Academy, 156

Antananarivo, Madagascar, 817
Antarctica:
  area and elevation of, **487, 497**
  exploration of, **485, 685**
  Falkland Islands, **891**
  first flight over, **437**
  French Antarctica, **775**
Antarctic Circle, **351, 485, 486**
Antarctic icecap, **591**
Anthem, National, **105**
Anthony, Susan B., **372**
Anthrax, **703**
Antibiotics, **547, 579**
Anti-Comintern Treaty, **686, 779**
Antietam, Battle of, **680**
Antigua and Barbuda, **725**
Antimony, **572, 573**
Antiparos Cavern, **497**
Antiseptic, **579**
Antoinette Perry (Tony) Awards, **251**
Antwerp, Belgium, **733**
Anzio beachhead, **686**
Apalachicola-Chattahoochee River,
  500
Apartheid, **696, 865**
Apennine Mountains, **800, 855, 871**
Apennine Tunnel, **450**
Aphelion, **351, 397**
Apia, Samoa, **855**
Apollo space flights, **428**
  Apollo/Soyuz Test Project, **428, 431,
    692**
Apostrophe (punctuation), **474**
Apothecaries' fluid measure, **453**
Apothecaries' weight, **454**
Appalachian Regional Commission,
  83
Appalachian Trail, **596**
Appomattox surrender, **175, 680**
Aqaba, Gulf of, **766**
Aquino, Benigno, **694**
Aquino, Corazon C., **695**
Arabia, explored, **484.** See also
  specific Arab countries
Arabian Desert, **498**
Arab-Israeli conflict, **36, 39, 42, 689,
  691, 692, 693, 765–766, 797–799,
  803, 812, 857, 872, 878.** See also
  Egypt; Israel; Jordan; Lebanon;
  Saudi Arabia; Syria
Arab League, **794, 809, 857, 883, 908**
Arabs, **671**
Arafat, Yasir, **703, 799, 839–841**
Aral Lake, **494**
Arbor Day, **356**
Archaeozoic Eon, **575**
Archery, **927**
Architecture, **443–445.** See also
  Structures
  ancient, **443–445**
  tallest buildings, **445**
Arctic Circle, **351, 486**
  area and elevation of, **497**
  exploration of, **485**
  first flight over, **436**
Arctic Ocean, **494, 497**
Area:
  of cities of U.S., **181–205**
  of continents, **487**
  of countries, **709–710, 721–904**
  of deserts, **498**
  formulas for, **458**
  of islands, **496**
  largest countries, **707**
  measures of, **455**
  of oceans and seas, **494**
  smallest countries, **707**
  of states of U.S., **143–178, 179**
  territorial expansion of U.S., **102, 103**
  of territories of U.S., **893–896**
  of U.S., **119**
  world, **487**
Area codes, **209–210**
Argentina, **689, 693, 725–726**
Aristide, Jean-Bertrand, **34, 35, 511,
  698, 786, 1030**
Aristotle, **282, 670**

Arithmetic. *See* Mathematics
Arizona, **144–145**
Arkansas, **145**
Arkansas River, **484, 495, 500**
Arlington National Cemetery, **596n**
Armada, Spanish, **675, 866, 884**
Armed conflicts, worldwide, **715**
Armed forces, U.S. *See also* Defense,
  U.S. Dept. of; Selective Service
  System; Veterans
  active duty personnel, **393, 394**
  foreign countries, military personnel
    in, **393**
  gays in, **697**
  highest ranking officers, **392**
  Joint Chiefs of Staff, **82, 392**
  last living veterans, **395**
  Medal of Honor, **394**
  military spending, **392**
  prisoners of war, **391**
  ranks, **393**
  veterans, **391, 395**
  war casualties, **391**
  women in, **687**
Armenia, **726–727**
Armistice Day, **354**
Armstrong, Lance, **515, 955, 1000,
  1030**
Armstrong, Neil A., **428, 691**
Army, U.S. Dept. of. *See also* Armed
  forces, U.S.
  Secretary of, **82**
Arrests, **387.** *See also* Crime; Law
  Enforcement
Arsenic, **573**
Arson, arrests for, **387**
Artemis, Temple of, **443**
Arthur (king of the Britons), **671**
Arthur, Chester A., **52, 56, 57, 64, 96.**
  See also Presidents, U.S.
Articles of Confederation, **94, 101**
Art Ross Trophy, **962**
Arts and the Humanities, National
  Foundation on, **83**
Aruba, **832–833**
Ascension Day, **354, 355n, 355**
Ascension Island, **892**
ASEAN, **908**
Ashgabat, Turkmenistan, **879**
Ashmore and Cartier Islands, **728**
Ash Wednesday, **344, 353, 355**
Asia. *See also* Continents; Countries
  area and elevation of, **487**
  exploration of, **484–485**
  map of, **534–535**
Asian population, U.S., **378**
Asmara, Eritrea, **767**
Assad, Hafez, **872**
Assal, Lake, **487**
Assassinations and attempts, **118**
Assault, **387**
Assembly of the Eighth Day, **354,
  355n**
Assistance, public, **632–633**
Associations, **658–667**
Assyrian Empire, **669, 794**
Astana, Kazakhstan, **803**
Asteroids, **413–414**
Astoria, Ore., **607**
Astrological signs, **345**
Astronauts, **427–429**
  first women, **101**
Astronomical unit (A.U.), **399**
Astronomy, **396–420.** *See also* Space
  asteroids, **413–414**
  atmosphere, **401**
  auroras, **416**
  Big Bang theory, **398**
  comets, **414–415**
  conjunctions, **397, 417–420**
  constants, **399**
  constellations, **400, 415–416**
  earliest, **668**
  Hubble Space Telescope, **423, 696**
  measures, **399**
  meteors and meteorites, **405, 415**
  Milky Way, **577**

Moon, **400**
  Moon phases, **417–420**
  phenomena, **417–420**
  planets, **401–413, 417–420**
  seasons, **351, 402**
  stars, **398, 399–400**
  Sun, **398, 399–400, 417–420**
  terms, **397–398**
  universal time, **420**
  websites, **397**
  Zodiac, **416**
Asunción, Paraguay, **842**
Aswan Dam, **766**
Asylum seekers, **716**
Atacama Desert, **498, 749**
Athens, Greece, **669, 781**
Athletes. *See* Sports personalities
Atlanta, Ga., **149, 179, 181–182, 680**
Atlantic Charter, **686**
Atlantic Ocean, **494**
  islands of, **496**
  U.S. coastline, **502**
Atlas Mountains, **827**
Atmosphere, **401**
Atomic bomb, **686, 687, 802**
Atomic numbers, **572, 573–574**
Atomic theory, **579**
Atomic weights, **572, 573–574**
Atonement, Day of, **354, 355n**
Attila the Hun, **282, 671**
Attlee, Clement, **884**
Attorneys General:
  state, **143–178**
  U.S., **82, 84–89**
Augusta, Maine, **155, 179**
Augustus (Roman emperor), **282, 670**
Auroras, **416**
Auschwitz, **685**
Austerlitz, Battle of, **678**
Austin, Tex., **173, 179, 182**
Australasia. *See* Oceania
Australia, **727–728.** *See also*
  Continents
  area and elevation of, **487**
  dependencies, **706**
  desert, **498, 727**
  exploration of, **485**
  islands of, **496, 727–728**
  map of, **536**
Austria, **686, 728–729**
Authors. *See* People
Autogyro flight, **436**
Automobiles, **612, 613**
  accidents, **613**
  best-selling, **616**
  drunken driving arrests, **387**
  efficiency, **616**
  exports and imports, **641**
  fatalities, **613**
  holiday fatalities, **613**
  invention of, **579**
  most expensive, **615**
  most popular colors, **615**
  most stolen, **615**
  polluting, most and least, **616**
  quality ratings, **615, 616**
  speed limits, **614**
  state laws, **614**
  theft statistics, **387**
  traffic, **612**
Auto racing, **997–999**
Avalanches, **211, 213**
Average, mathematical, **452**
Aviation, **435–439.** *See also* Airlines;
  Airplanes
  accidents, **211, 219–221**
  airports, world's busiest, **611**
  ballooning, **435–439, 439**
  firsts in, **435–439**
  helicopter records, **439**
  inventions in, **435–439**
  records, **439**
  solar-powered, **438**
  traffic (passengers and freight), **611**
  women in, **435–439**
  world records, **439**
Avoirdupois weight, **451, 454, 456**

Awards, 225–262
Academy (Oscars), 247–251
Albany Medical Center Prize, 262
American Library Association, 255–257
Baseball Hall of Fame, 166, 1002–1004
Bollingen, 257
broadcasting, 258–260
Caldecott Medal, 255–256
Coretta Scott King, 257
Country Music, 253
Cy Young Award, 1014
Daytime Emmys, 259
Drama Desk Awards, 252
duPont–Columbia, 259
Eclipse, 981
Edwards, 257
Emmy, 259
Fermi, 260
Fields Medal, 261
Golden Globe, 251
Grammy, 252–253
Hart Trophy, 961
Heisman Trophy, 935
James E. Sullivan Memorial, 959
Kennedy Center Honors, 261–262
King, 257
MacArthur Foundation, 260
magazine, 257
Man Booker Prize, 254
Michael L. Printz, 257
Most Valuable Player (baseball), 1012
Most Valuable Player (basketball), 952
Most Valuable Player (hockey), 961
music, 245, 252–253, 258
NAACP Image, 258
National Book, 254
National Book Critics Circle, 254
National Magazine, 257
Newbery Medal, 255
Nobel Prizes, 225–233
Obie, 252
Peabody, 260
Presidential Medal of Freedom, 261
Printz, 257
Pulitzer Prizes, 234–247
Rookie of the Year (baseball), 1014
Spingarn Medal, 258
Tony (Antoinette Perry) Awards, 251
Truman Capote, 254
Tufts Poetry Prize, 257
Webby, 262
"Axis of evil", 389, 703, 793, 794, 807
Axis Powers, 686
Azerbaijan, 729–730
Aznar, José Maria, 1030
Azores, 847
Azov, Sea of, 494n
Aztecs, 673, 823

B

Babbage, Charles, 579, 679
Babylon, Hanging Gardens of, 443, 669
Babylonian Empire, 669, 794
Bach, Johann Sebastian, 282, 676
Bacteria, 579, 668
Baffin Bay, 484
Baffin Island, 496
Baghdad, 389, 793
Bahamas, 730
Bahrain, 731
Baikal, Lake, 494
Baker Island, 896
Bakke **case,** 381, 693
Baku, Azerbaijan, 729
Balaton, Lake, 787
Balearic Islands, 866
Balfour Declaration, 683
Bali, 791, 792
Balkan crisis, 737–738, 757, 858
Balkan Wars, 683

Balloons:
flights of, 435, 436, 438
invention of, 435
records, 439
Ball-point pen, 581
Baltic Sea, 494
Baltimore, Md., 156, 179, 182–183
Bamako, Mali, 820
Bandar Seri Begawan, Brunei Darussalam, 740
Bangkok, Thailand, 875
Bangladesh, 731–732, 732, 790, 838
Bangui, Central African Republic, 747
Banjul, Gambia, 777
Bank of North America, 100
Bankruptcies, 646
Banks and banking:
firsts in, 100
largest, 647
Banks Island, 496
Barak, Ehud, 700, 798, 799
Barbados, 732
Barbuda. *See* Antigua and Barbuda
Barometer, 579
Baseball, 1001–1023
2004 season, 1016–1019
All-Star Game, 1001–1002
American League statistics, 1017
batting statistics, 1008, 1008–1009, 1010, 1013, 1015, 1017
club standings, 1007, 1016
Cy Young Award, 1014
Hall of Fame, 166, 1002–1004
history of, 1001
home run statistics, 1008, 1008–1009, 1009, 1010–1011, 1015
Little League, 1000–1001
Most Valuable Player, 1012
National League statistics, 1017–1018
no-hit and perfect games, 1008
pennant winners, 1019–1021
pitching statistics, 1008, 1008–1009, 1013, 1017
records, 1008, 1008–1009, 1015
Rookie of the Year, 1014
World Series, 1004–1007, 1021–1022
Basketball, 946–949
college, 946–949
history of, 946
Most Valuable Players, 952
NBA finals, 515
Olympic Games, 927
women's professional, 954
Basse-Terre, Guadeloupe, 774
Basseterre, St. Kitts, 853
Bastille Day, 677
Basutoland. *See* Lesotho
Bataan surrender, 686
Baton Rouge, La., 154, 179
Battlefields, National, 594
Battles. *See* names of specific battles
Bay of Pigs invasion, 98, 689, 758
Beatles, The, 272, 274, 691
Beaumont-Port Arthur Canal, 450
Bechuanaland. *See* Botswana
Beef, 645
Beethoven, Ludwig van, 283, 677, 678
Begin, Menachem, 693, 766, 798
Beijing, China, 696, 749
Beirut, Lebanon, 798, 811
Belarus, 732–733
Belfast, Northern Ireland, 886
Belgian Congo. *See* Congo, Democratic Republic of
Belgium, 733–734
Belgrade, Yugoslavia, 858
Belize, 734–735
Bell, Alexander Graham, 283, 583, 681
Belmont Stakes, 980, 981
Belmopan, Belize, 734
Benelux, 816
Benin, 735

Bering, Vitus, 144
Bering Sea, 494
Bering Strait, 484
migrations across, 668
Berlin, Congress of, 681
Berlin, Germany, 778
airlift, 97, 687, 780
East Berlin uprising, 688
in World War II, 686
Berlin Wall, 689, 696
Berlusconi, Silvio, 800
Bermuda, 890
Bern, Switzerland, 871
Beslan hostage crisis, 33, 41, 852
Bessarabia, 848, 850
Bhutan, 735–736
Bhutto, Benazir, 695
Biafra, 691, 835
Biathlon, 931
Bible:
books of, 369
English translation of, 673
first printed, 673
King James Version, 675
New Testament, 360, 369
Old Testament, 360, 369, 465–467, 669, 670
Pentateuch, 670
Ten Commandments, 369, 669
Bicentennial, U.S., 692
Bicycles, 579. *See also* Cycling
Bifocal lens, 581
Big Bang theory, 398, 579
Bikini Atoll, 689, 821
Billings, Mont., 161, 179
Bill of Rights, 94, 113, 677
Bills (Congressional), procedures for, 80, 109
Bills (money), 452
Bin Laden, Osama, 74, 100, 703, 721, 722, 868
Biographies:
of people, 281
of U.S. presidents, 58–76
Bioko (formerly Fernando Po), 767
Birds, state, 143–178
Birendra (king of Nepal), 831
Birmingham, Ala., 143, 179
Birmingham, England, 883
Birth control, 132, 547, 683
Birth dates, of famous people, 281–315
Birth rates, world, 711
Births, U.S., 128–133
by age of mother, 128
cesarean births, 131
by race of mother, 128, 129
rates, 128, 129
sex ratios, 129
by state, 128
to teens, 130
to unmarried women, 130
Birthstones, 357
Bisexuality, 372
Bishkek (Frunze), Kyrgyzstan, 809
Bismarck, N.D., 166, 179
Bismarck, Otto von, 284, 779
Bissau, Guinea-Bissau, 784
Black Death, 673, 884
Black Friday panic, 680
Black Hills, 172
Black Hole of Calcutta, 676
Black holes, 397, 578
Blackout, Northeast (1965), 691
Black Sea, 848, 849
Blacks in U.S. *See also* Civil rights; Race and Ethnicity; Slavery
births and birth rates, 128, 129
civil rights timeline, 380–381
firsts by, 100
life expectancy, 136
population statistics, 120, 122, 123, 124, 377
Blair, Tony, 704, 883, 885
Blanc, Mont, 771
tunnel, 450
Blix, Hans, 389

Blizzards, 215
Blood, circulation of, 579
Blood pressure, 547, 558
Blood types, 559
Blue Grotto, 497
Blue Nile, 769
Bobsledding, 931
Body mass index, 560
Boers, 865
Boer War, 682, 865, 884
Bogotá (Santafé de Bogotá), Colombia, 752
Bohr, Niels, 227, 284, 582
Boiling points:
  of elements, 573–574
  of water, 451
Boise, Idaho, 150, 179
Bolivia, 736–737
Bollingen Prize, 257
Bolsheviks, 684, 849
Bolt and screw sizes, metric conversion of, 457
Bombay, India, 789
Bombing:
  of Afghanistan, 721
  embassy (1998), 700, 805, 875
  Sept. 11, 2001, 211, 220, 224, 703, 722, 857
  of Sudan, 868
Bonaire, 832
Bonaparte, Napoléon. See Napoleon Bonaparte
Bonds, Barry, 956, 1008, 1009, 1015
Booker Prize, 254
Books:
  awards for, 241–245, 254–257
  best of century, 267–268, 268–269
  best-selling adult, 266
  best-selling children's, 266, 267
  reading statistics, 265
Boone, Daniel, 154, 284
Booth, John Wilkes, 63, 96, 118, 284, 680
Borneo (island), 496, 791, 819
  Brunei Darussalam, 740
Boron, 572, 573
Boroughs of New York City, 195–196
Bosnia, 737–738. See also Balkan crisis
Boston, Mass., 157, 179, 183
  fire (1872), 217
Boston Massacre, 94, 676
Boston Tea Party, 94, 157, 676
Botanic garden, first, 100
Botanic Garden, U.S., 83
Botswana, 738–739
Bounty, H.M.S., 677, 892
Bourbon kings of France, 772, 773
Boutros-Ghali, Boutros, 905
Bowl games (football), 932–934
Bowling, 964–966
Boxer Rebellion, 682, 750
Boxing, 972–978
  bare-knuckle, 972
  heavyweight championship fights, 973–974
  history of, 972
  Olympic Games, 926
  professional, 973–977
  titleholders, 973–977
Boyne, Battle of the, 676
Boy Scouts of America, 660, 682
Brackets (punctuation), 474
Brahmaputra River, 495, 731, 789
Braille, 482, 579
Branch Davidian standoff, 99, 224
Brando, Marlon, 518, 1035
Brandt, Willy, 284
Brasília, Brazil, 739
Bratislava, Slovakia, 861
Brazil, 485, 739–740
Brazos River, 500
Brazzaville, Congo, 754
Breitling Orbiter 3 (Cameron Balloons R-650), 439
Bremer, L. Paul, 39, 42, 389, 507, 704, 1030

Brest-Litovsk, Treaty of, 850
Bretton Woods Conference, 687
Brezhnev, Leonid, 285, 694, 850
Bribery, 712
Bridgeport, Conn., 147, 179
Bridges, 447–448
Bridgetown, Barbados, 732
Brin, Sergey, 511, 1030
British Columbia, Canada, 745
British Guiana. See Guyana
British Honduras. See Belize
British Indian Ocean Territory, 890
British New Guinea. See Papua New Guinea
British Open Champions, 996
British Solomon Islands. See Solomon Islands
British Virgin Islands, 890
Broadcasting awards, 258–260
Broadway theater, longest runs, 271
Bronx, 195–196
Brooklyn, 195–196
Brooklyn Bridge, 445, 681
Brown, John, 95, 285, 679
Brown v. *Board of Education of Topeka*, 92, 380, 381, 688
Brunei Darussalam, 740
Brussels, Belgium, 733
Bryan, William Jennings, 52, 53, 86, 285, 682
Buchanan, James, 52, 54, 56, 62, 95.
  See also Presidents, U.S.
Bucharest, Romania, 848
Budapest, Hungary, 787
Buddha, 363–364, 669
Buddhism, 363–364
  founding of, 669
  introduced into China, 670
  in Japan, 671
Budget, federal, 635, 636, 637. See also Management and Budget, Office of
Buenos Aires, Argentina, 725
Buffalo, N.Y., 165
Buffalo Bill (William F. Cody), 285
Buildings, tallest, 445–446
Bujumbura, Burundi, 742
Bulganin, Nikolai A., 689
Bulgaria, 740–741
Bulge, Battle of the, 686
Bullet, 579
Bull Run, Battle of, 680
Burger, Warren E., 91
Burgesses, House of, 100
Burglary, 387
Burkina Faso, 741–742
Burlington, Vt., 174, 179
Burma. See also Myanmar
Burns, treatment of, 562
Burr, Aaron, 51, 56, 285, 678
Burundi, 742
Bush, Barbara Pierce, 58, 72
Bush, George H. W., 56, 57, 71–72, 99, 695. See also Presidents, U.S.
Bush, George W., 32–33, 35–42, 43, 44, 54–56, 74–75, 389–390, 508, 701, 702, 703, 704, 705, 794–796.
  See also Presidents, U.S.
Business and economy, 646–650.
  See also Industry; Retail trade; Wholesale trade
  largest businesses, 647–648
Busing to achieve school integration, 691
Byrd, Richard E., 285, 437, 685
Byzantine architecture, 443
Byzantium, 669, 671, 673

C

Cabinets, U.S., 81–82, 84–89
  first black member of, 100
  first woman member of, 101
Caesar, Julius, 285, 670, 771
Cairo, Egypt, 765, 766
Cairo Conference, 686

Calcium, 573
Calcutta, India, 789
Caldecott Medal, 255–256
Calder Trophy, 962
Calendars, 668, 670, 671
  Chinese, 352, 356
  Egyptian, 348
  Gregorian, 348
  Hindu, 352, 356
  history of, 348–349
  Islamic, 352, 355
  Jain, 356
  Jewish, 352, 355
  Julian, 348
  lunar, 348
  names of days and months, 350
  perpetual, 1800–2063, 346–347
  Roman, 348
  Sikh, 356
  years 2003, 2004, 2005, 344–345
Calgary, Canada, 744
Calhoun, John C., 51, 285
California, 146
  Gold Rush in, 146, 679
  mountain peaks, 502
Californium, 572, 573
Calvin, John, 286, 674
Cambodia, 43, 690, 692, 693, 742–743
  Angkor Wat, 444
Cambrian Mountains, 883, 889
Cambrian Period, 575
Camera, 681
Cameroon, 743–744
Camp Fire Boys and Girls, 660
Canada, 744–746
  economy of, 744
  geography of, 744
  government of, 745
  history of, 745–746
  latitudes and longitudes of, 504
  map of, 528
  Nunavut, 744
  population of, 745
  provinces of, 745
  territories of, 745
Canadian River, 500
Canals, 450
Canary Islands, 866
Canberra, Australia, 727
Cancer, 548, 555
  cancer rates, U.S., 554
  definition, 555
  mortality, leading causes, 557
Cancer, Tropic of, 351
Candela, 454
Canoe racing, 927
Cape Canaveral, 694
Cape Horn, 485, 749
Cape of Good Hope, 484, 865
Capetian Dynasty, 671, 771, 772
Cape Town, South Africa, 864
Cape Verde, 746–747
Capitalization, rules for, 472
Capital punishment, 101, 383, 384, 710. See also Death penalty; Executions
Capitals, foreign, 721–904
Capitals, of states, 143–178, 179
Capitals, of U.S.:
  early capitals, 101, 170
  Washington, DC, 204
Capone, Al, 685
Capote, Truman, literary award, 254
Capri, 497
Capriati, Jennifer, 956
Capricorn, Tropic of, 351
Caracas, Venezuela, 899
Carat (measure), 456
Carbohydrates, 543–545
Carbon, 573
Carbon emissions, 587
Carboniferous Period, 575
Carbon monoxide, 588
Cardiff, Wales, 889
Caribbean area. See also specific countries
  islands of, 496

map of, **525**
Caribbean Sea, **494, 496**
Carlsbad Caverns, **165, 497, 592**
Carnegie, Andrew, **286**
Carnival season, **353**
Carolingian Dynasty, **771, 772**
Carpathian Mountains, **845, 848**
Carpooling, **612**
Cars. See Motor vehicles
Cars, efficiency, **648**
Cars and trucks:
  best-selling, **616**
  most popular colors, **615**
Carson, Kit, **162**
Carson City, Nev., **162, 179**
CART champions, **999**
Carter, Jimmy (James E., Jr.), **53, 54, 56, 57, 70–71, 98.** See also Presidents, U.S.
Carthage, **669, 670, 671**
Cartoons, awards for, **235–236**
Carver, George Washington, **143, 160**
Casablanca, Morocco, **827**
Casablanca Conference, **686**
Caspian Sea, **487, 494n, 494**
Cassini-Huygens mission, **409, 421–422, 423**
Castries, St. Lucia, **854**
Castro, Fidel, **286, 689, 758**
Casualties, in U.S. wars, **391**
Caterpillar Club, **436**
Cathedrals, **443–445**
Catholic Church. See Roman Catholic Church
Cats, **139**
Cattle, **645**
Caucasus, **849**
Cavaliers, **675**
Caves and caverns, **497**
Cayenne, French Guiana, **774**
Cayman Islands, **890**
CDs, **272**
Ceasefires, recent, **715**
Celebes (Sulawesi), **791**
Celluloid, discovery of, **582**
Celsius (Centigrade) scale, **451, 454**
Cemeteries, National, **596**
  Arlington, **596n**
Cenozoic Era, **576**
Census:
  2000 census figures, **119, 120, 121, 122, 123**
  national censuses, **123**
Census of Marine Life, **578**
Centigrade (Celsius) scale, **451, 454**
Central African Republic, **747**
Central America. See also specific countries
Central America, map, **528**
Central Intelligence Agency (CIA), **82, 97, 697**
Central Powers, **683**
Cermak, Anton J., **118, 685**
Ceylon. See Sri Lanka
Chaco, **842**
Chad, **747–748**
Chad, Lake, **494, 748**
Chalabi, Ahmad, **1030**
Challenger (space shuttle), **99, 221, 429, 694**
Chamberlain, Neville, **286, 686, 884**
Channel Islands: Jersey and Guernsey, **891**
Charitable contributions, **141**
Charities, top U.S., **141**
Charlemagne, **286, 671, 771, 772, 779**
Charles, Ray, **1035**
Charles I (king of England), **156, 166, 171, 675, 884**
Charleston, W. Va., **176, 177, 179**
Charlotte, N.C., **166, 179, 183**
Chavez, Hugo, **33, 40, 703, 704, 705, 899, 900, 1030**
Chechnya, **701, 851**
Check Verification Companies, **653**
Chemicals:
  export and import of, **641**

Producer Price Index, **640**
Chemistry:
  discoveries and theories, **579–583**
  elements, **571, 572, 573–574**
  Nobel Prizes for, **228–230**
Cheney, Richard B., **36, 54, 57, 74, 508**
Chernenko, Konstantin U., **694, 850**
Chernobyl nuclear accident, **216, 695, 733, 850**
Chesapeake Bay, **156**
Chesapeake-Delaware Canal, **450**
Cheyenne, Wyo., **178, 179**
Chiang Kai-shek, **287, 686, 750, 873**
Chicago, Ill., **151, 179, 183–184**
  climate of, **604**
  fire (1871), **217, 680**
  St. Valentine's Day Massacre, **685**
Chickens, **590, 642**
Child, Julia, **518, 1035**
Child abuse and neglect, **133**
Children:
  abuse and neglect of, **133**
  best-selling books for, **266, 267**
  birth rates, **711**
  birth statistics, **128–133, 711**
  book awards, **255, 255–256**
  death rates, **711**
  in foster care, **133**
  killed by guns, **134**
  life expectancy of, **135, 136, 711**
Children's Crusade, **672**
Chile, **748–749**
China, **749–752.** See also Headline history
  Boxer Rebellion, **682, 750**
  Great Wall of, **444, 670, 750**
  history of, **750–751**
  and Japan, **681, 685, 686, 750, 802**
  Ming Dynasty, **673, 750**
  nuclear weapons testing by, **691**
  People's Republic established, **688**
  structures, **444**
  and U.S., **750**
  Yuan Dynasty, **673, 750**
China (Taiwan). See Taiwan
"China seat" (UN), **691, 751, 873**
Chinese:
  calendar, **352**
  New Year, **356**
Chinese civilization, ancient, **669**
Chinese-Japanese War (1894–95), **750, 802**
Chinese New Year, **353**
Chirac, Jacques, **703, 773**
Chisholm Trail, **182, 187, 204**
Chisinau, Moldova, **825**
Choking, **561**
Cholera, **213**
Chou En-lai. See Zhou Enlai
Christ. See Jesus Christ
Christian holidays, **353–355, 355**
Christianity:
  development of, **670**
  history of, **360–362**
  in Roman Empire, **360, 670**
  spread of, **671**
Christmas, **344, 355**
Christmas Island, **728, 861**
Chromium, **572, 573**
Chromosphere, **399**
Chronology:
  of civil rights, **380–381**
  of disasters, **211–224**
  of Iraq war, **389–390**
  of major Supreme Court cases, **92**
  of staffed space flights, **430–434**
  of U.S. history, **94–100**
  of unstaffed space flights, **425–427**
  women's rights movement, **372–373**
  of world history, **668–705**
Chrysler Building, **445**
Churches (buildings):
  famous, **443–445**
  in largest U.S. cities, **181–205**
Churches (organizations). See Religion

Churchill, Sir Winston, **287, 686, 687, 884**
Church of England, **674, 884**
CIA. See Central Intelligence Agency
Cicero, **670**
Cigarettes, **558**
Cimarron River, **500**
Cimmerian civilization, **669**
Cincinnati, Ohio, **167**
Circular measure, **454, 458**
Circumference, formula for, **458**
Citadel (Cairo), **444**
Cities, Canadian:
  latitude and longitude of, **504**
  time of day, **504**
Cities, U.S., **181–210.** See also specific cities
  bridges, **447–448**
  chambers of commerce, **181–205**
  climate of, **604–605**
  Consumer Price Index, **639**
  crime rates, **388**
  labor force, **181–205**
  largest, **181–205, 206**
  largest of each state, **179**
  latitudes and longitudes of, **504**
  mayors and managers of, **181–205**
  newspapers, **277**
  per capita income, **181–205**
  polluted, most, **588**
  population of, **143–178, 181–205, 207–209**
  ports, **646**
  same-sex households, **372**
  tallest buildings, **445–446**
  temperatures, **181–205**
  time of day, **504**
  tunnels, **450**
  unemployment, **181–205**
Cities, world, **708.** See also specific cities
  bridges, **447–448**
  capitals, **721–904**
  "distinctive destinations", **607**
  largest, by country, **721–904**
  latitudes and longitudes of, **499, 504**
  population of, **721–904**
  southernmost, **749**
  subway systems, **612**
  tallest buildings, **445–446**
  temperatures, **610**
  time of day in, **499**
  tunnels, **450**
City managers, U.S., **181–205**
Civilian labor force:
  characteristics of, **622**
  mothers in, **625**
  women in, **625**
Civil rights, **380–381**
  Bill of Rights, **113**
  Fourteenth Amendment, **115, 680**
  gay rights organization, **100**
  Montgomery boycott, **689**
  other constitutional provisions about, **112, 113, 115, 117**
  school desegregation, **688**
  timeline, **380–381**
  trial rights, **114**
Civil Rights, U.S. Commission on, **82**
Civil Rights Act, **98**
Civil Service Commission, U.S., **681.** See also Office of Personnel Management
Civil time, **349, 420**
Civil unions, **371**
Civil War, American, **96, 680**
  casualties, **394**
  chronology, **680**
  Confederate States, **102**
  Gettysburg Address, **118**
  last living widows, **395**
Civil War, English, **884**
Civil War, Russian, **684, 850**
Civil War, Spanish, **686, 866**
Clark, George Rogers, **676**
Clarke, Richard, **36**
Classification, scientific, **570**

Clay, Cassius. *See* Ali, Muhammad
Clay, Henry, 51, 52, 60, 287, 679
Cleopatra, 670, 765
Cleveland, Grover, 52, 54, 55, 56, 64, 96. *See also* Presidents, U.S.
Cleveland, Ohio, 167, 184
Climate. *See also* Weather
Clinton, Hillary Rodham, 45, 58, 72, 287, 701
Clinton, William Jefferson, 43, 54, 56, 72–74, 99, 287, 702, 1031. *See also* Presidents, U.S.
  impeachment of, 90, 99, 700
  sex scandal, 700
Clocks, pendulum, 580
Cloning, 569
Clothing:
  Consumer Price Index, 639
  export and import of, 641
  Producer Price Index, 640
Cloture rule, 80
Coal, export and import of, 641
Coastline of U.S., 502
Cobalt, 572, 573
Cocaine, 557
Cochise, 145
Cocos (Keeling) Islands, 728
Code of Hammurabi, 668
Coffee:
  export and import of, 641
  U.S. consumption of, 642
Coins, U.S., 453
Coldest weather, 599, 600
Cold war, 97, 697
Colleges and universities, 321–343
  costs, 319
  degrees granted, 316, 321
  endowments, 319–320
  enrollments, 317, 321–343
  firsts, 100
  in U.S., 321–343
Colombia, 752–753
Colombo, Sri Lanka, 867
Colon (punctuation), 474
Colonial population, 122
Colonial Williamsburg, 175
Colonies, 706
Colorado, 146–147, 502
Colorado Desert, 498
Colorado River (Colorado-Mexico), 484, 495, 500
Colorado River (Texas), 500
Colorado Springs, Colo., 146, 184–185
Colors, state, 143–178
Colosseum (Rome), 443, 670
Colossus at Rhodes, 443
Columbia (space shuttle), 221, 429, 431, 704, 705
Columbia, S.C., 171, 179
Columbia River, 495, 500
  Grand Coulee Dam, 176
Columbus, Christopher, 287, 484, 673, 762, 774, 801, 877
Columbus, Ohio, 167, 179, 185
Columbus Day, 344, 354
Colville River, 500
Combustion, 580
Comet Hale-Bopp, 699
Comets, 414–415
Comintern, 684
Comma (punctuation), 473
Commerce. *See* Foreign trade
Commerce, U.S. Dept. of:
  description of, 81
  secretaries of, 82, 86–89
Commission of Fine Arts, 83
Committees:
  Congressional, 76
  National, 50
Commodities, Producer Price Index, 640
Commodity Futures Trading Commission, 83
Common Market, 689, 694. *See also* European Economic Community
Commonwealth, Puritan, 884

Commonwealth of Independent States (CIS), 697, 849, 851, 908
Commonwealth of Nations, 908
Commune, Revolutionary (French), 677
Communism, 679, 683, 684
Communist Internationals, 681, 684
Communist Manifesto, 679
Communist Party, USSR, 689
Commuting characteristics, 612
Como, Lake, 686
Comoros, 753
Composers, awards for, 245, 252–253
Computers, 563–568
  game ratings, 567–568
  games, 568
  game software, 568
  inventions, 580
  software, 568
  statistics, 718
  usage, 567
Comstock Lode, 162
Conakry, Guinea, 784
Concentration camps, 685
Concord, N.H., 163, 179
Conditioned reflex, 580
Confederate Memorial Day, 356
Confederate States, 96, 102, 680
  secession and readmission dates of, 102
Conflicts, armed, 715
Confucianism, 365
Confucius, 287, 365, 669, 750
Congo:
  Democratic Republic of, 754–756, 754
  Republic of (Brazzaville), 754
Congo River, 484, 495, 754
Congress, U.S. *See also* House of Representatives; Senate
  adjournment of, 109
  assembling time of, 109, 116
  committees, 76
  compensation and privileges of members of, 109
  composition of, 45, 78–79
  conventions, political, 50
  first black members of, 100
  first sessions, 101
  first women members of, 101
  legislative powers of, 80, 109, 114, 116
  members of, 45–48
  powers and duties of, 109
  salaries of members of, 79, 109, 117
Congresses, Continental, 101, 106, 676
Congressional Medal of Honor, 394
Congress of Industrial Organizations, 689
Congress of Vienna, 678, 729, 772
Conjunctions (planetary), 397, 417–420
Connecticut, 147
Connecticut River, 147, 500
Constantine, Arch of, 443
Constantinople, 671, 673, 782, 878. *See also* Istanbul
Constantinople, Peace of, 674
Constellations, 400, 415–416
Constitution, U.S., 108–117, 170
  amendment procedure for, 113
  amendments to, 113–117
  drafting of, 94, 108
  ratification of, 101, 108, 113
  signing of, 677
  supremacy of, 113
Constitution, USS, 678
Constitutions, state:
  dates adopted, 143–178
  first, 101, 147
Consumer Price Index (CPI), 639
Consumer Product Safety Commission, 82
Consumers:
  credit, 629

organizations, 654–655
  price indexes, 639
  recalls, 655
  resource guide, 651–657
Consumption of food items, 642
Continental Congresses, 94, 101, 106, 676
Continental Divide, 161, 500
Continental drift, 401, 487
Continents. *See also* specific continents
  area and elevations of, 487
  exploration of, 484–485
Contraception, 132
Controllers of states, 143–178
Conventions, National, 49, 50
Conversion, weights and measures, 451, 453, 455–457, 457
Cook, Frederick, 483, 485n
Cook, James, 150, 169
Cook Islands, 833
Coolidge, Calvin, 53, 56, 66, 97. *See also* Presidents, U.S.
Copenhagen, Denmark, 760
Copernicus, Nicolaus, 674
Copper, 573
Coptic Christians, 361, 765, 769
Copyrights, 657
Coral Sea Islands, 728
Core (of Earth), 401
Corn, economic statistics, 645
Coronado, Francisco Vásquez de, 145, 153, 164, 168, 173
Corona of Sun, 399
Corporation for National Service, 82
Corporations, taxes on, 1025, 1028
Corpus Christi (holiday), 355n
Corregidor, 686
Corruption:
  leaders, 713
  prosecutions for, 384
  world, 712
Corruption index, countries, 712
Corsica, 771
Cortés, Hernando, 288, 484, 674, 823
Cosmetics, 580
Cosmonauts, 429
Costa Rica, 756
Côte d'Ivoire, 756–757
Cotton:
  economic statistics, 645
  export and import of, 641
Cotton Bowl, 934
Council of Economic Advisers, 81
Council of Nicaea, 360, 671
Council of Trent, 348, 674
Council on Environmental Quality, 81
Counterfeiting, 387
Counties, per state, 143–178
Countries of world, 721–904. *See also* Geography, world; History, world
  agriculture, 721–904
  areas of, 709–710, 721–904
  birth rates, 711, 721–904
  capitals of, 721–904
  cities, large, 721–904
  colonies, 706
  comparative statistics, 707
  corruption, 712, 713
  death rates, 711
  economic conditions, 721–904
  economics, 707, 719–720
  exploration of selected areas, 484–485
  exports, 721–904
  foreign trade, 721–904
  general statistics, 707
  governments of, 721–904
  gross domestic product, 719–720
  history of, 721–904
  holidays, 357
  imports, 721–904
  industry, 721–904
  infant mortality rate, 707
  inflation, 719–720, 721–904
  labor force, 721–904
  languages of, 721–904

life expectancy in, **711**
"livable," most and least, **713**
monetary units of, **721–904**
most populous, **708**
natural features of, **721–904**
political parties, **721–904**
poorest, **714**
population densities of, **721–904**
population of, **709–710**
premiers and prime ministers of, **721–904**
presidents of, **721–904**
race/ethnicity, **721–904**
rulers of, **721–904**
standard of living, **713, 714**
statistics, **706–720**
structures, **443–450**
taxes, **719**
unemployment, **721–904**
UN members, **907**
in World Wars I and II, **683, 686**
Country Music Association Awards, 253
Country Music Hall of Fame, 273
Courts, federal, 112. *See also* Supreme Court, U.S.
Cows, 645. *See also* Cattle
"Coxey's Army", 681
CPR, 561
Crater Lake National Park, 592
Craters, meteorite, 415
Credit, consumer, 629
Credit cards, 642, 651
Credit reporting bureaus, 653
Creed, Nicene, 360, 671
Cretaceous Period, 575
Crete, 668, 669, 671
Crime, 382–388. *See also* Law enforcement
 arrests, **387**
 assassinations and attempts, **118**
 by city, **388**
 corruption, prosecutions for, **384**
 hate crimes, **386**
 homicide rate, **385**
 index, **386**
 murder, **385, 387**
 rates, **387, 388**
 by states, **387**
 trial rights, **112**
 victims, **385**
 by weapon, **385**
Crimean War, 679, 879, 884
Croatia, 757–758
Crockett, Davy, 288, 679
Cro-Magnon man, 668
Cromwell, Oliver, 288, 675, 884
Crossbow, invention of, 580
Crossword puzzles:
 guide to, **459–471**
Crucifixion of Christ, 360, 670
Crusades, 672
Crust (of Earth), 401
Cuba, 758–759
 Bay of Pigs invasion, **98, 689, 758**
 island, **496**
Cuban missile crisis, 68, 98, 690, 758, 850
Cubic measure, 451, 453, 455
Cultural Revolution (China), 750
Cumberland River, 500
Cuneiform, 668
Curaçao, 832
Curie, Marie, 226, 229, 288, 682
Curie, Pierre, 226, 288, 682
Curling (sport), 931
Currency. *See* Money
Currency, U.S., 452
Current events, 32–42
 international, **33–42**
 people in the news, **1030**
 recent deaths, **1035**
 in U.S., **32–42**
Custer, George A., 96, 161, 288, 681
Cycling, 927
Cyclones, 214
Cyclotron, 580, 685

Cyprus, 759–760
 Greek-Turkish crisis, **759, 879**
Cy Young Award, 1014
Czechoslovakia, 686, 697
 separation of, **760**
 Warsaw Pact invasion of, **691**
Czech Republic, 760

D

da Gama, Vasco, 288, 484, 673, 789
Dahomey. *See* Benin
Dairy products, U.S. consumption of, 642
Dakar, Senegal, 857
Dalai Lama, 225, 288, 689
Dallas, Tex., 173, 185–186
 climate of, **604**
 Kennedy assassination in, **68, 118, 690**
Damascus, Syria, 872
Damavend, Mount, 792
Dams, 449
Dance companies, U.S., 264
Danish dependencies, 706
Danube River, 495, 729, 740, 779, 787, 848, 858
Dardanelles, 683, 878
Dare, Virginia, 100, 166
Dar es Salaam, Tanzania, 874
Darfur, Sudan, 34, 38, 39, 40, 41, 511, 869
Darling River, 495
Darrow, Clarence, 289, 684
Darwin, Charles, 289, 679
Dash (punctuation), 474
Da Silva, Lula, 739, 740
Date line, 350
Davis, Jefferson, 289, 680
 birthday, **356**
Davis Cup, 986
Daylight saving time, 344, 350–351
Days:
 names of, **350**
 sidereal and solar, **349, 399**
Daytime Emmy Awards, 259
D-Day, 686
Dead Sea, 797
Death and dying, 134–138. *See also* Infant mortality
 car accidents, **613**
 in disasters, **211–224**
 diseases, **136**
 of famous people, **281–315,** 1035
 fatalities, transportation, **613**
 by firearms, **137**
 leading causes of, **136, 137,** 557
 recent (2004), **1035**
 smoking-related, **558**
 suicide, **136, 138**
 U.S. death rates, **137**
Death penalty, 383, 384, 692, 710. *See also* Executions
Death rates, world, 711
Death Row, 383
Death Valley, 146, 487, 500, 503
Debs, Eugene V., 53, 289, 681
Debt, national, 635, 636
Decimals, fractions, 458
Declaration of Independence, 106–107, 179
Decoration Day. *See* Memorial Day
Deerfield Massacre, 676
Defense, U.S. Dept. of. *See also* Armed forces, U.S.
 description of, **82**
 secretaries of, **82, 87–89**
Defense of Marriage Act (DOMA), 33, 371
Defibrillator, 580
Deficit, national, 32, 40
de Gaulle, Charles, 289, 689, 773
Degrees, academic, first for women, 101
Degrees granted, 316, 321
Delaware, 148

Delaware River, 500
DeLay, Tom, 42, 1031
Democratic Party:
 members of Congress, **45–48**
 National Committee chairmen, **50**
 national conventions, **50, 682, 694,** 695
 presidential candidates, **51–54**
 Senate floor leaders, **77**
Demographics, 708
Denali National Park, 144, 592
Deng Xiaoping, 692, 696, 750–751
Denmark, 760–762
Densities of population:
 in countries, **721–904**
 in U.S., **123**
Denver, Colo., 146, 179, 186
 climate of, **604**
Dependent political entities, 706
Depression (economics), 685
Derrida, Jacques, 1036
Desegregation in schools, 688, 691
Deserts, 498
Des Moines, Iowa, 152, 153, 179
De Soto, Hernando, 143, 145, 149, 155, 159, 160, 172
Detroit, Mich., 157, 179, 186–187
Deuterium, 580
Devil's Hole, 497
Devonian Period, 575
Devon Island, 496
Dhaka, Bangladesh, 731
Diabetes, 548
Diamond mine (Arkansas), 145
Diamonds, 680, 865
Diana (Princess of Wales), 699
Diesel engine, 580, 681
Diet, 537–545, 548
Dili, East Timor, 763
Dionne quintuplets, 685
Diphtheria, antitoxin, 579
Diplomatic personnel, 912–914
 first black, **100**
Directory, French, 678, 772
Dirigibles, first flight of, 435
Disabled students, 317
Disasters, 211–224
 aircraft accidents, **211, 219–221**
 avalanches, **211, 213**
 blizzards, **211, 215**
 drought, **211, 216**
 earthquakes, **211–212**
 epidemics, **211, 213**
 explosions, **211, 217–218, 223–224**
 fires, **211, 217–218**
 floods, **211, 213**
 hurricanes, **211, 214–215**
 nuclear power plant accidents, **216**
 oil spills, **211, 222**
 railroad accidents, **211, 221–222**
 shipwrecks, **211, 218–219**
 space, **221**
 sports, **223**
 storms, **211, 214–215**
 terrorist attacks in U.S., **211, 223–224**
 tidal waves, **213**
 tornadoes, **211, 215–216**
 volcanic eruptions, **211–212**
 worst U.S., **211**
Discoveries, 577–584
 of chemical elements, **571, 573–574**
Diseases:
 deaths from, **136**
 medical discoveries, **579–583**
Disneyland, 146
Disney World, 149
Distance, airplane records, 439
District of Columbia, 204. *See also* Washington, DC
Diving. *See* Swimming
"Divorce capitals", 162
Divorce statistics, 127
Djibouti (city), Republic of Djibouti, 762
Djibouti, Republic of, 762
DNA, 230, 231, 580

crime exonerations, 383
Dnieper River, 495
Doctors, (physicians), first woman, 101
Dogs, 139
Doha, Qatar, 847
Dome of the Rock, 444
Dominica, 762
Dominican Republic, 763
Don River, 495
Dover, Del., 148, 179
Draft evaders, pardoning of, 692
Dram (measure), 454, 456
Drama, awards for, 245–246, 251–252
Drama Desk Awards, 252
Dred Scott v. *Sanford,* 92, 679
Dreyfus, Alfred, 290, 681
Drivers:
  arrests for drunkenness, 387
  licenses, 614, 617
  number of, 617
  state laws, 614
Dropout rates (high school), 317
Drought, 211, 216
Drug Control Policy, Office of National, 81
Drug use and abuse, 557
  alcohol, 557
  cocaine, 557
  heroin, 557
  marijuana, 557
  tobacco, 557, 558
Drunk driving, 387, 613
Drunkenness, arrests for, 387
Dry measures, 451, 454, 456
Duarte, José Napoleón, 767
Dublin, Ireland, 796
Du Bois, W.E.B., 682
Dukakis, Michael S., 54, 695
Dumbarton Oaks Conference, 687
Dunkerque evacuation, 686
Duomo (Florence), 444
duPont–Columbia University
  Broadcast-Awards, 259
Dushanbe, Tajikistan, 873
Dust bowl (1930s), 211, 216
Dutch dependencies, 706
Dutch East Indies. *See* Indonesia
Dutch Guiana. *See* Suriname
Duvalier, Jean-Claude, 695, 786
DVDs, 275
Dynamite, 580, 680
Dynamo. *See* Generator, electric
Dzaoudzi, Mayotte, 776

E

Earhart, Amelia, 290, 437, 685, 686
Earnings:
  by educational level, 319
  of government officials, 79
  median, 620
  minimum wages, 628
  by occupation, 620
  by race, 623
  wage gap, 373, 374
  women's, 374
Earth (planet), 401–402, 406. *See also*
  Planets
  astronomical constants, 399
  atmosphere, 401
  continental drift, 401
  formation of, 668
  geological periods, 575–576
  life on, 575–576, 668
  origin of, 401
Earthquakes, 211–212, 682, 695, 697, 698
  deaths from, 491, 492
  frequency worldwide, 491
  largest, worldwide, 490
  magnitude scales, 490
  major, 2004, 491
  Mercalli intensity scale, 491
  number, 491
  Richter magnitude, 490

severity measured, 490
East China Sea, 494
Easter Island, 749
Eastern Europe, map, 531
Eastern Front (World War I), 683
Eastern Orthodoxy, 361
Easter Rebellion, 683, 796
Easter Sunday, 344, 353, 355
East Germany. *See* Germany
East India Company, 675, 789
East Timor, 703, 763–764, 791
Ebert, Friedrich, 779
Eclipses, 420
Economic Advisers, Council of. *See*
  Council of Economic Advisors
Economic and Social Council, UN, 905–906
Economic Community, 692
Economics, Nobel Prizes for, 233
Economics, world statistics, 719–720
Economic statistics, U.S., 646–650
Economy:
  outlook through 2010, 621–622
  U.S. business and, 646–650
  world, 706
Ecuador, 764–765
Ecumenical councils:
  Council of Nicaea, 360, 671
  Counci of Trent, 674
  Vatican Council I, 362
  Vatican Council II, 362, 690, 694, 899
Eden, Sir Anthony, 290, 689, 884
Edinburgh, Scotland, 883, 888
Edison, Thomas A., 290, 580, 581, 681
Education, 119, 316–343. *See also*
  Colleges and universities
  attainment, 316
  civil rights, 380–381
  college costs, 319, 321–343
  degrees awarded, 316, 321
  disabled students, 317
  dropout rates, 317
  endowments, 319–320
  enrollments, 317, 321–343
  fundraising, 320
  General educational development
    (GED), 318
  government funding of, 318
  prayer in schools, 690
  pupil-teacher ratios, 318
  SAT scores, 318
  software, 568
  Supreme Court school decisions, 688, 690, 691, 693, 694
Education, U.S. Dept. of:
  description of, 82
  secretaries of, 82, 87–89
Edwards, John, 508, 1031
Edwards, Margaret A., book awards, 257
Edward VIII (king of England), 686, 884
Egypt, Arab Republic of, 765–766.
  See also Arab-Israeli conflict
  Great Sphinx, 443
  and Israel, 689, 692, 765–766, 797–799
  Pyramids, 443, 668
  Suez Canal, 450, 689, 765, 766, 798
Egyptian Empire, 668, 669
  mythology, 471
  structures, 443
Eichmann, Adolf, 689
Eid al-Adha, 353
Eid al-Fitr, 344, 354, 355
Eiffel Tower, 444, 681
Einstein, Albert, 227, 290, 682, 686
  Theorem, 458, 580, 582
Eire. *See* Ireland, Republic of
Eisenhower, Dwight D., 53, 56, 57, 67, 98, 154, 170, 173. *See also*
  Presidents, U.S.
Eisenhower Doctrine, 67, 689
Elbe River, 779
Elbert, Mount, 502

Elbrus, Russia, 487
Elderly, population characteristics, 124
Election, presidential (2004), 33, 35–42, 43, 44
Election Day, 344, 354, 355
Elections:
  closest presidential, 55
  congressional, 45–48
  facts about, 55
  presidential, 43, 44, 51–54
  presidential, procedure for, 49, 111, 114
  results (1789–2004), 43, 44, 51–54
  voter turnout, 55
Electoral College, 43, 44, 49, 114, 115
  votes, 49, 51–55
Electricity:
  average prices, 643
  electric current, 454
  inventions and discoveries, 579–583
Electricity consumption, 588
Electric lamp, invention of, 580
Electrocution, first, 100
Electrocution as death penalty, 384
Electromagnet, 580
Electron microscope, 581
Electrons, discovery of, 580
Elementary schools:
  enrollment, 317
  funding, 318
  pupil-teacher ratios, 318
Elements, chemical, 571, 572, 573–574
Elevations:
  of cities of U.S., 181–205
  of continents, 487
  of deserts, 498
  extremes of U.S., 500
  of mountain peaks, 492–493
  of states of U.S., 503
  of volcanoes, 488–489
Elizabeth I (queen of England), 674, 884
Elizabeth II (queen of England), 688, 883, 884
Elks (BPOE), 661
Ellesmere Island, 496
Ellice Islands. *See* Tuvalu
Ellington, Duke, 692
El Niño, 224
El Paso, Tex., 173, 187
El Salvador, 693, 694, 766–767
Email providers, 564
Embassies, foreign, 908–911
Embassy bombings (Kenya and Tanzania), 700
Embezzlement, arrests for, 387
Emmy Awards, 259
Empire, Second (French), 679, 772, 773
Empires, ancient, 668–670
Empire State Building, 445
Employment, 621–625. *See also*
  Cities, U.S.; Labor force
  by age, 624
  labor force, 622–624, 625
  median income, 620
  by occupation, 620, 624
  projections, 621–622
  by race, 623
  by sex, 624
  taxes, 1024–1025
  unions, 626
  wage gap, 373, 374
Endangered species, 591
Endowments, college and university, 319–320
Energy:
  consumption of, 587
  oil and gas reserves, 587
Energy, U.S. Dept. of:
  description of, 82
  secretaries of, 82, 88–89
Enewetak (Eniwetok) Atoll, 688, 821
Engels, Friedrich, 291, 679

Engines:
diesel, **580**
internal combustion, **580**
steam, **583, 677**
England:
poets laureate, **270**
rulers of, **885**
structures, **444**
English Channel, tunnel under, 450
English language development, 480
Enlightenment, The, 676
Enrollment:
in colleges and universities, **317,
321–343**
in elementary schools, **317**
in secondary schools, **317**
Enron, 703
Entebbe, 692
Entente Cordiale, 682
Entertainment, expenditures, 139
Entertainment and culture:
best-selling books, **266–267**
dance companies, **264**
expenditures, **139**
movie revenues, **279**
opera companies, **264**
symphonies, **263**
websites, **565**
Environment, 585–596
air pollutants, **588–589**
cities, most polluted, **588**
endangered species, **591**
issues and problems, **585–587**
National Park System, **592–596, 596**
pesticides, **586**
toxic-waste dumps, **585–587**
**Environmental Protection Agency
(EPA), 82, 585–587**
**Environmental Quality, Council on,
81**
Epidemics, 211, 213, 554
Epiphany, 344, 353
Episcopal Church, 362, 692
"E pluribus unum", 104
**Equal Employment Opportunity
Commission (EEOC), 82**
**Equal Rights Amendment (ERA), 373,
693**
Equator, 486
Equatorial Guinea, 767
Equestrian events, 927
Equinoxes, 351, 402, 417–420
Erie, Lake, 494
Battle of, **168, 678**
Erie Canal, **151, 165**
Erie Canal, 450
Eriksson, Leif, 484, 672, 745
Eritrea, 767–768
and Ethiopia, **769**
Eros (asteroid), 413–414
Eskimos, 144
Espionage, 694
Estonia, 687, 696, 768
Ether (anesthetic), 579, 679
Ethiopia, 685, 686, 769, 800
and Eritrea, **769**
Ethnicity, 375–381
Etruscans, 669
Euclid, 291, 581, 670
Euphrates River, 495, 794
Europe. See also Continents;
Countries of world
area and elevation of, **487**
exploration of, **484**
map of, **530, 531**
**European Economic Community,
689, 867, 884**
European Union (EU), 37, 908
**Everest, Mount, 224, 487, 492, 688,
830**
Everglades National Park, 149, 592
Evolution, human, 570, 668, 679, 684
Scopes trial, **684**
Exclamation point (punctuation), 473
Executions:
death row, **383**
exonerations, **383**

first state to abolish capital
punishment, **101**
methods by state, **384**
statistics, **383, 710**
**Executive departments and
agencies, U.S., 81–84**
Exercise, 559
Exosphere, 402
Expectation of life, 135, 136, 711
Expenditures:
education, **318**
by federal government, **636, 637**
gross domestic product, **635**
personal consumption, **643**
Explorations, 484–485
Explorer (satellite), 689
Explosions, 211, 217–218, 223–224
Explosives, inventions of, 580, 581
**Export-Import Bank of the United
States, 83**
Exports:
from countries, **721–904**
from U.S., **640, 641**
Extradition between states, 112
**Exxon Valdez (oil tanker), 72, 99, 211,
222**
Eyre, Lake, 487

F

Fabre, Henri, 436
Faeroe Islands, 761
Fahrenheit 9/11, 513, 1033
Fahrenheit scale, 451, 454
Falkland Islands, 693, 726, 884, 891
Falling bodies:
formulas for, **458**
law of, **580**
Falluja, Iraq, 36, 41
Families:
child abuse and neglect, **133**
credit card use by, **642**
income of, **627**
teen pregnancy, **130**
of U.S. presidents, **58**
**Famous people, 281–315, 955–959,
1029.** See also Awards; Headline
history
Faraday, Michael, 291, 580, 581
Fargo, N.D., 167, 179
Farm Credit Administration, 82
Farm Index, 644
Farms. See Agriculture
Farragut, Adm. David G., 100, 680
Fascists, 684, 800
Fatalities:
driving, **613**
earthquakes, **491, 492**
from firearms, **134, 137**
tornadoes, **599**
transportation, **613**
volcanic eruptions, **489**
Father's Day, 344, 354
Fatima, Portugal, 370
Fat intake, 560
Fats, 551
Fat Tuesday. See Shrove Tuesday
FBI. See Federal Bureau of
Investigation
Feasts, Jewish, 353–355, 355
Federal budget:
distribution by state, **637**
funding to states, **637**
outlays by agency, **635**
public debt, **635**
receipts and outlays, **636**
social welfare expenditure, **632, 634**
**Federal Bureau of Investigation
(FBI), 693**
director of, **82**
founding, **96, 97**
**Federal Communications
Commission (FCC), 82**
Federal courts, 112. See also
Supreme Court, U.S.

**Federal Deposit Insurance
Corporation (FDIC), 82**
Federal Election Campaign Act, 692
**Federal Election Commission (FEC),
82**
**Federal Emergency Management
Agency (FEMA), 83**
Federal Energy Administration. See
Energy, U.S. Dept. of
Federal government. See United
States government
Federal Housing Finance Board, 83
Federalist Papers, 59
Federalist Party, 51, 56n, 59
Federal Labor Relations Authority, 83
Federal Maritime Commission, 82
**Federal Mediation and Conciliation
Service (FMCS), 83**
Federal Power Commission. See
Energy, U.S. Dept. of
Federal Reserve System (FRS), 683
Board of Governors of, **83**
**Federal Trade Commission (FTC), 83,
683**
Feminist movement, 372–373
Fencing, 927
Fermentation, 580
Fermi, Enrico, 227, 260, 291, 581, 687
Fermi Award, 260
Fernando Po, Equatorial Guinea. See
Bioko
Fertility rates, U.S., 128
Festival of Lights, 355, 355n
**Fiction, awards for, 241, 254–257,
258**
Fields Medal, 261
Fifth Republic (French), 689, 772, 773
Figure skating, 928, 931, 969–970
Fiji, 770
Filibusters, 80
Fillmore, Millard, 52, 56, 62, 95. See
also Presidents, U.S.
Films. See Motion pictures
Fingal's Cave, 497
Finland, 712, 770–771
Firearms, 385, 387
deaths by, **134, 137**
inventions, **581, 582**
Fireballs, 415
Fires:
arson arrests, **387**
disastrous, **211, 217–218**
forest fires, **218**
First aid, 561–562
First Fruits, Feast of, 354, 355n
Firsts:
in aviation, **435–439**
in U.S. history, **100–101**
Fish, 541
export and import of, **641**
U.S. consumption of, **642**
Fitzgerald, Ella, 699
Five and dime store, first, 100
Flag Day, 344, 354
Flags:
adoption of first U.S., **94**
history of U.S., **104**
pledge of allegiance to, **104**
world, **519-522**
**Fleming, Alexander, 231, 291, 579,
685**
Flight Programs:
U.S. staffed, **427–429, 430–434**
Flights:
first, **435–439**
orbital, **850**
records, **439**
Floods, 211, 213
Johnstown, Pa. (1889), **211, 213, 681**
Floor leaders of Senate, 77
Florence, Italy, 444, 673
Florida, 148–149
exploration of, **484**
Spanish cession of, **676**
Flowers, state, 143–178
Flu, 549
Food. See also Agriculture

choking, treatment of, **561, 562**
Consumer Price Index, **639**
diet, **537-542**
  economic statistics, **645**
  export and import of, **641**
  prices, historical, **641**
  spending on, **631**
  U.S. consumption of, **642**
Food insecurity, **633**
Food pyramid, **538, 542**
Food stamps, **633**
Foot-and-mouth disease, **702**
Football, **932-946**
  American Conference Champions, **942-943**
  American League Champions, **942**
  bowl games, **932-934**
  college, **932-939**
  Hall of Fame (college), **935-939**
  Hall of Fame (professional), **944-946**
  Heisman Memorial Trophy, **935**
  history of, **932**
  National Conference champions, **941-942**
  National Football League, **939-946**
  National League champions, **941**
  professional, **939-946**
  records (professional), **943-944**
  Super Bowl, **939-940, 940**
Forbidden City (Beijing), **444**
Ford, Gerald R., **53, 56, 57, 69-70, 98.**
  See also Presidents, U.S.
  assassination attempts on, **118, 692**
Ford, Henry, **292, 682**
Foreign aid, from U.S., **639**
Foreign-born population, **376**
Foreign embassies, **908-911**
Foreign investment, **638-639**
Foreign languages studied, U.S., **475**
Foreign trade:
  U.S., **641**
  world, **721-904**
Foreign words and phrases, **477, 478-480**
Forests:
  resources of countries, **721-904**
  state, **143-178**
Forgery, **387**
Formosa. *See* Taiwan
Formulas, math and physics, **458**
Fort-de-France, Martinique, **774**
Fort Dodge, **153**
Fort Sumter, Battle of, **171, 680**
Fort Ticonderoga, **166, 175**
Fort Worth, Tex., **173, 187-188**
Fossett, Steve, **439**
Fossil hominids, earliest, **668**
Foster care, **133**
Fountain pen, **581**
Four Freedoms, **687**
Four Noble Truths, **364**
Fourth of July, **354**
Fox Quesada, Vicente, **702, 823-824**
Fractions, decimals, **458**
France, **771-776**
  in NATO, **773**
  overseas departments and territories of, **775-776**
  rulers of, **772**
  structures, **444**
Franco, Francisco, **292, 686**
Franco-Prussian War, **680, 773**
Frank, Anne, **687**
Frankfort, Ky., **154, 179**
Frankfurt, Germany, **778**
Franklin, Benjamin, **83, 104, 106, 292, 581, 676**
Fraternity, first, **100**
"Freedom March", **143**
Freedom of the press, **113, 676**
Freedoms, Constitutional, **113**
Freeman, Cathy, **920, 956**
Freetown, Sierra Leone, **860**
Frémont, John C., **146, 162**
French and Indian Wars, **94, 151, 158, 159, 167, 172, 175, 177, 676**
French dependencies, **706**

French Guiana, **773**
French Polynesia, **775**
French Revolution, **677, 772**
French Somaliland. *See* Djibouti
French Southern and Antarctic Lands, **775**
French Sudan. *See* Mali
French Territory of the Afars and Issas. *See* Djibouti
Fresno, Calif., **146, 188**
Freud, Sigmund, **292, 582, 682, 684**
Friedan, Betty, **373, 690**
Friendly Islands, **876**
Friends (Quakers), **362**
Frobisher Bay, **484**
Frost, Robert, **689**
Frostbite, treatment of, **562**
Fruit, **539**
  U.S. consumption of, **642**
  U.S. export and import of, **641**
Fuel. *See also* specific fuels
  average prices, **643**
  efficiency of vehicles, **648**
  export and import of, **641**
  Producer Price Index, **640**
Fujimori, Alberto, **843-844**
Funafuti, Tuvalu, **880**
Fundamental Orders of Connecticut, **101, 147**
Fundraising, preparatory schools and universities, **320**
Fur, export and import of, **641**
Furniture:
  export and import of, **641**
  Producer Price Index, **640**

G

Gabon, **776-777**
Gaborone, Botswana, **738**
Gadsden Purchase, **95, 102, 103, 145, 164**
Gagarin, Yuri A., **430, 689, 850**
Galápagos Islands, **485, 764**
Galaxy, **397**
Galena, Ill., **607**
Galilee, Sea of, **797**
Galileo (astronomer), **292, 398, 580, 583, 675**
Galileo space program, **427**
Gallo, Robert, **584**
Gambia, The, **777**
Gambia River, **484, 777**
Gambier Island, **775**
Gambling, **162, 164, 387, 825**
Game software, **568**
Gandhi, Indira, **292, 694, 789**
Gandhi, Mohandas K., **292, 684, 687, 789**
Gandhi, Sonia, **1031**
Ganges River, **495, 731, 789**
"Gang of Four", **692, 751**
Garfield, James A., **52, 54, 56, 64, 96.**
  See also Presidents, U.S.
  assassination of, **64, 96, 118, 681**
Gas, natural, **641**
Gas reserves, **587**
Gates, Bill, **292**
Gator Bowl, **934**
Gautama, Buddha, **363**
Gay rights organization, first, **100**
Gays, **33, 36, 38, 371, 372, 513, 701, 746**
Gaza Strip, **34, 35, 36, 37, 38, 41, 42, 691, 766, 798**
GDPs per capita, world's highest and lowest, **707**
Gemini space flights, **428**
Gemstones, **357**
Gender issues, **371-374**
General Assembly, UN, **905**
General educational development (GED), **318**
General Services Administration (GSA), **83**
Generator, electric, **580**

Genetics (heredity), **581, 680**
Geneva, Lake, **871**
Geneva, Switzerland, **684, 871**
Geneva Conference (1954), **690**
Genghis Khan, **292, 672, 721**
Genocide, **685**
Geographic centers:
  of states, **143-178**
  of U.S., **500**
Geographic Society, National, **662**
Geography, **483-504**
  caves and caverns, **497**
  coastline of U.S., **502**
  Continental Divide, **500**
  continents, **487**
  of countries, **721-904**
  deserts, **498**
  elevations, **487**
  explorations, **484-485**
  glossary of terms, **485**
  islands, **496**
  map projections, **486**
  mountain peaks, **492-493**
  national parks, **592-596, 596**
  oceans and seas, **494**
  rivers, **495, 500-501**
  volcanoes, **488-489**
  waterfalls, **496**
  world, **706**
Geological periods, **575-576**
Geometric formulas, **458**
Geometry, **581**
Georgetown, Guyana, **785**
Georgia (U.S. state), **149**
Georgia, Republic of, **777-778**
Germany, **778-780**
  history of, **779-780**
  Nazi regime, **684, 685, 779**
  reconstruction of, **687**
  reunification of, **696, 780**
  rulers of, **779**
  in World War I, **683, 779**
  in World War II, **686, 779**
Geronimo, **145, 164, 292, 681**
Gestation periods, animals, **590**
Gettysburg, Battle of, **118, 170, 680**
Gettysburg Address, **118**
Ghana, **780-781**
Ghent, Treaty of, **60, 678**
Gibbons v. *Ogden*, **92**
Gibraltar, **891**
Gibson, **513**
Gibson, Mel, **1031**
Gideon v. *Wainwright* , **92**
Gift taxes, federal, **1025, 1027**
Gilbert Islands, **805, 833.** *See also* Kiribati
Ginsburg, Ruth Bader, **91, 697**
Giotto probes, **426**
Girl Scouts of U.S.A., **662**
Giza, Great Pyramid, **668**
Glacier National Park, **161, 592**
Glasgow, Scotland, **883, 888**
Glass, export and import of, **641**
Glenn, John H., Jr., **98, 427, 428, 429, 690**
Glenwood Springs, Colo. , **607**
Globe, **486**
"Glorious Revolution", **675**
Gobi Desert, **498, 750**
Gods and goddesses, **467-471**
Godthaab, Greenland, **761**
Golan Heights, **691, 766, 798, 872**
Gold:
  chemical properties of, **572, 573**
  karat (measure of purity), **457**
  as monetary standard, **681**
  terminology, **457**
Gold Coast. *See* Ghana
Golden Gate Bridge, **146, 445, 447**
Golden Globe Awards, **251**
Golden Temple (India), **694, 790**
Gold Rush:
  in Alaska, **144**
  in California, **146, 201, 679**
  in Idaho, **151**
Golf, **993-996**

British Open Champions, **996**
  history of, **993**
  L.P.G.A. tour winners, **996**
  Masters Tournament winners, **515,
    993**
  other tour winners, **996**
  U.S. Amateur Champions, **994, 995**
  U.S. Open Champions, **993–994, 995**
  U.S. P.G.A. Champions, **995**
González, Elián, **701, 702**
Good Friday, **344, 353, 355n**
Good Friday Peace Accord, **700, 701,
  702, 797, 885, 887**
Good Hope, Cape of, **484, 865**
Google, **41, 512, 1030**
Gorbachev, Mikhail S., **225, 293, 694,
  696, 850**
Gore, Albert A., Jr., **54, 55, 57**
Gospels, **360, 670**
Goss, Porter, **42**
Göta Canal, **450**
Gothic architecture, **444**
Goths, **671**
Gotland, Sweden, **870**
Government Accountability Office
  (GAO), **83**
Government Printing Office (GPO),
  83
Governments:
  foreign heads of state, **721–904**
  of U.S. *See* United States
    government
  world, **721–904**
Governors, **48**
  first black, **100**
  first woman, **101, 178, 684**
  of Puerto Rico, **893**
  of U.S. states, **143–178**
  of U.S. territories, **893–896**
Grain, U.S. export and import of,
  641. *See also specific grains*
Grammy Awards, **252–253**
Grams (measure), **455, 457**
Grand Canal, **450**
Grand Canyon, **145**
Grand Canyon National Park, **592,
  596**
Grand Coulee Dam, **176**
Grand Prix (auto racing), **999**
Grand Teton National Park, **592, 596**
Grant, Ulysses S., **52, 56, 63, 96, 680.**
  See also Presidents, U.S.
Gravitation, law of, **581**
Great Arabian Desert, **498**
Great Bear Lake, **494**
Great Britain, **496**
Great Lakes, **494**
Great Salt Lake, **174, 494, 679**
Great Seal of U.S., **104**
Great Slave Lake, **494**
Great Smoky Mountains National
  Park, **166, 173, 592, 596**
Great Sphinx of Egypt, **443, 668**
Great Wall of China, **444, 670, 750**
Greece, **781–782**
Greece, ancient, **668, 670, 782, 915**
  mythology, **467–470**
  Persian Wars, **670**
  structures, **443**
Greek word elements, **480–481**
Greenback Party, **52**
Greeneville (submarine), **702**
Greenhouse gases, **589**
Greenland, **484, 496, 671, 761**
Green Mountain Boys, **175**
Green River (Ky.), **500**
Green River (Wyo.-Utah), **500**
Greenwich time, **350**
Gregorian calendar, **348**
Grenada, **782**
  U.S. military intervention in, **694, 783**
Griswold v. *Connecticut*, **373**
Gromyko, Andrei A., **294**
Gross domestic product, **635,
  721–904**
  by country, **719**
  world's highest and lowest, **707**

Groundhog Day, **344, 353**
Group of Eight, **908**
Guadalcanal, **863**
Guadalupe Hidalgo, Treaty of, **95**
Guadalupe Mountains National Park,
  173
Guadeloupe, **774**
Guam, **894**
Guatemala, **783–784**
Guatemala City, Guatemala, **783**
Guernsey, **891**
Guevara, Ché, **736, 758**
Guiana, British. *See* Guyana
Guiana, Dutch. *See* Suriname
Guiana, French, **773**
Guinea (Republic), **784**
Guinea, Portuguese. *See*
  Guinea-Bissau
Guinea, Spanish. *See* Equatorial
  Guinea
Guinea-Bissau, **784–785**
Gulf of Tonkin Resolution, **97, 690,
  691**
Gulf War, **99, 696, 698, 794, 809**
Gunpowder, invention of, **581**
Guns, **134, 137, 385, 387**
Gunter's chain (measure), **454**
Gupta dynasty, **671**
Gutenberg, Johann, **294, 582, 673**
Guthrie, Okla., **607**
Guthrie, Woody, **689**
Guyana, **785**
Gymnastics, **927**
Gyrocompass, **581**
Gyroscope, **581**

H

Habibie, B. J., **791**
Hague Conventions, **682**
Haider, Jörg, **729**
Haile Selassie I (emperor of
  Ethiopia), **294, 769**
Hailstone, largest, **599**
Haiti, **34, 35, 36, 511, 678, 697, 786**
  U.S. military intervention in, **786**
Haleakala National Park, **592**
Hale-Bopp comet, **699**
Halicarnassus, Mausoleum at, **443**
Halley's comet, **414, 695**
Hall of Fame:
  Baseball, **166, 1002–1004**
  Country Music, **273**
  Football (college), **935–939**
  Football (professional), **168, 944–946**
  Inventors, **584**
  Rock and Roll, **168, 274**
Halloween, **344, 354**
Hallucinogens, **557**
Hamas, **717**
Hambletonian, **991–992**
Hamburg, Germany, **778**
Hamilton, Alexander, **59, 84, 294, 678**
Hamilton, Lee, **1032**
Hammarskjöld, Dag, **294, 688, 905**
Hammurabi, Code of, **668**
Han dynasty, **671**
Hanging as death penalty, **384**
Hanging Gardens of Babylon, **443,
  669**
Hannibal, **294, 670**
Hanoi, Vietnam, **900**
Hanover, House of, **884**
Hanukkah, **344, 355**
Hapsburg, House of, **729, 787**
Harare, Zimbabwe, **904**
Harding, Warren G., **53, 56, 65–66,
  97.** *See also* Presidents, U.S.
Harness racing, **991–993**
Harper's Ferry raid, **679**
Harrisburg, Pa., **169, 179**
Harrison, Benjamin, **52, 54, 56, 64,
  96.** *See also* Presidents, U.S.
Harrison, William Henry, **51–52, 56,
  61, 95.** *See also* Presidents, U.S.
Hartford, Conn., **147, 179**

Hart Trophy, **961**
Harvard University, **100, 319**
Harvest, Feast of, **354, 355n**
Hashemite Kingdom. *See* Jordan
Hastings, Battle of, **672, 884**
Hate crime statistics, **386**
Havana, Cuba, **758**
Hawaii, **150**
  discovery of, **677**
  volcanoes in, **150**
Hawaiians, **378**
Hawaii Volcanoes National Park, **150,
  592**
Hawking, Stephen, **578**
Hayes, Rutherford B., **52, 54, 56,
  63–64, 96.** *See also* Presidents, U.S.
Haymarket Riots, **681**
Headline history, **668–705**
Health, **537–560**
  AIDS, **547, 553, 554**
  A-Z guide, **547–552**
  best hospitals, **555**
  blood pressure, **558**
  blood types, **559**
  body mass index, **560**
  cancer, **557**
  diet, **537–545**
  drug use, **557**
  exercise, **559**
  first aid, **561–562**
  insurance, **555, 556**
  obesity, **546, 560**
  organ transplants, **555**
  sexually transmitted diseases, **556**
  smoking, **558**
  TIME special, **537–560**
Health, Education, and Welfare, U.S.
  Dept. of. *See also* Education, U.S.
  Dept. of; Health and Human
  Services, U.S. Dept. of
  secretaries of, **88**
Health and Human Services, U.S.
  Dept. of:
  description of, **82**
  secretaries of, **82, 88–89**
Health insurance, **555**
Heaney, Seamus, **698**
Heard Island, **728**
Hearst, Patricia, **692**
Heart, human:
  first artificial, **690, 694**
  transplants, **691**
Heat cramps, treatment of, **562**
Heat exhaustion, treatment of, **562**
Heath, Edward, **884**
Heat stroke, treatment of, **562**
Heaven's Gate cult, **699**
Hebrew Pentecost, **354, 355n**
Hebrides, **888**
Hectares, **451, 455**
Hegira (Hijra), **362, 671**
Heimlich Maneuver, **562**
Heisman Memorial Trophy, **935**
Helena, Mont., **161, 179**
Helicopters:
  first flights of, **437**
  invention of, **437, 581**
  records, **439**
Helium:
  chemical properties of, **572, 573**
  discovered on sun, **581**
  first use in balloon, **436**
Helsinki, Finland, **770**
Hemisphere, **486**
Henry the Navigator (prince of
  Portugal), **673**
Heredity, **581, 680**
Heritage Areas, National, **596**
Heritage Corridors, National, **596**
Hermitage, The (Andrew Jackson's
  home), **173**
Heroin, **557**
Herschel Space Observatory, **425**
Herzegovina, **737–738**
Hezbollah, **717**
Hides:
  export and import of, **641**

Producer Price Index, **640**
Higher education, 319, 320, **321–343**
Highest points:
　U.S., **503**
　world, **487**:
High school:
　dropout rates, **317**
　enrollment, **317**
　funding, **318**
　percentage graduated, **316**
Hijackings, 692, **694**
Hijra. *See* Hegira
Hillary, Sir Edmund, 295, 492, **688**
Himalayas, 789, 790, **831**
Hindenburg (zeppelin), **219**
Hindenburg, Paul von, 295, 313, **779**
Hinduism, 363
　calendar, **352**
　festival dates, **356**
Hindu Kush range, **721**
Hippocrates, **670**
Hirohito (emperor of Japan), 295, **695**
Hiroshima, 686, 687, **802**
Hispanics:
　births, 128, **129**
　population, 375, **377**
Hispaniola, 496, 763, **786**
Hiss, Alger, **687**
Historical parks and sites, U.S., 593,
　594–595, **596**
Historic Area, National, **596**
Historic Trails, National, **596**
History, U.S. *See* United States history
History, world, **668–705**
　by country, **721–904**
　explorations, **484–485**
　Seven Wonders, **443**
History, Pulitzer Prizes for, **241–243**
Hitler, Adolf, 295, 684, 686, **779**
Hittite civilization, 668, **669**
HIV. *See* AIDS
Ho Chi Minh, 690, **901**
Ho Chi Minh City, Vietnam, **900**
Hockey, ice, **960–964**
　history of, **960**
　NHL trophy winners, **961–962**
　Olympic Games, **930**
　professional, **960–964**
Hokkaido, Japan, 496, **801**
Holidays, **353–355**
　Christian and secular, **355**
　Hindu, **356**
　Islamic, **353–355**
　Jain, **356**
　Jewish, **355**
　legal, U.S., **356**
　national, by country, **357**
　Orthodox, **355**
　religious and secular (2005), **353–355**
　Sikh, **356**
　state, **356**
　traffic accidents, **613**
Holland. *See* Netherlands
Hollywood, **146**
Holocaust, **685**
Holocene Period, **576**
Holy Roman Empire, 671, 674, **779**
Holy Saturday, **355n**
Holy sites, **370**
Homeland Security, U.S. Dept. of, 74,
　82
Homeownership, 125, **126**
Homer, 295, **669**
Home run records, 1008, 1008–1009,
　1009, 1010–1011, **1015**
Homestead Act, **96**
Homestead Strike, **681**
Homicide, 385. *See also* Murder
Hominids, 570, **578**
Homo erectus, **570**
Homo sapiens idaltu, **570**
Homo sapiens sapiens, **570**
Homosexuality, 371, **372**
　firsts in U.S., **100**
　same-sex unions, 33, 36, 38, 371,
　513, 701, **746**
　societies and associations, **662**

in U.S. armed forces, **697**
Honduras, **786–787**
Honduras, British. *See* Belize
Hong Kong, **751**
Honiara, Solomon Islands, **863**
Honolulu, Hawaii, 150, 179, **188**
Honshu, Japan, 496, **801**
Hood, Mount, 169, **503**
Hoover, Herbert, 53, 56, 57, 66, 97,
　153. *See also* Presidents, U.S.
Hoover Dam, 145, 163, **449**
　Lake Mead, **596**
Horace, **670**
Horn, Cape, 485, **749**
Horse racing, **978–981**. *See also*
　Harness racing
　Belmont Stakes, 980, **981**
　Eclipse Awards, **981**
　harness racing, **991–993**
　history of, **978**
　Kentucky Derby, 154, 681, 978, **981**
　Preakness Stakes, 979, **981**
　Triple Crown, 978, **981**
Hospitals, highest-rated, **555**
Hostages, American, 693, 694, 695,
　697
Hot-air balloons. *See* Balloons
Hot Springs National Park, 145, **592**
Hottest weather, 599, **600**
Households, **125**
　income, **628**
　by size, 1790–2002, **125**
　by type, 125, **126**
House of Burgesses, **100**
House of Representatives, U.S., 108,
　111. *See also* Congress, U.S.
　apportionment of, 79, 108, **115**
　committees of, **76**
　eligibility for, **108**
　first black member of, **100**
　first woman member of, **101**
　members, **46–48**
　salaries of representatives, **79**
　shooting on floor of, **688**
　Speakers of, **77**
**Housing and Urban Development,
　U.S. Dept. of:**
　description of, **82**
　secretaries of, 82, **88–89**
Houston, Tex., 173, 179, **189**
Houston Canal, **450**
Howland Island, **896**
Hsi River (Si Kiang). *See* Xi Jiang
Huang Ho (Yellow River), 495, **750**
Hubble Space Telescope, 423, 431,
　433, 434, **696**
Hudson, Henry, 148, **165**
Hudson Bay, 484, 494, **745**
Hudson River, 165, 196, **484**
Hudson's Bay Company, **745**
Huguenots, 674, **676**
Hu Jintao, 41, 704, **751**
Human ancestors, 570, 668, 679, **684**
Human development index (U.N.), **713**
Humphrey, Hubert H., **57**
"Hundred Days", **678**
Hundred Years' War, 771, **884**
Hungary, **787–788**
　1956 uprisings, **788**
Hunger, **633**
Huns. *See* Mongols
Hun Sen, **743**
Huron, Lake, 158, 494, **744**
Hurricanes, 211, **214–215**
　costliest, **597**
　deadliest, **597**
　Hurricane Charley, 41, **509**
　most intense, **597**
　names, Atlantic, **598**
　names, retired, **598**
Hus, Jan, **673**
Hussein (king of Jordan), 296, **803**
Hussein, Qusay and Uday, **389**
Hussein, Saddam, 39, 296, 389–390,
　507, 696, 705, 794–796, **809**
Hyde Park, N.Y., **165**
Hydrogen:

chemical properties of, **572, 573**
　first use in balloon, **435**
　heavy hydrogen, **580, 685**
　hydrogen bomb, 688, 689, **850**
Hyphen (punctuation), **474**

I

i.e./e.g., **477**
Ibn Batuta, **485**
Ice hockey. *See* Hockey
Iceland, 671, **788**
　area of, **496**
　exploration of, **484**
Ice skating. *See* Figure skating; Speed
　skating
Idaho, **150–151**
Ikhnaton, **669**
Iliad (Homer), **669**
Illinois, **151–152**
Illinois River, **500**
Immigration, 375, **376**
Impeachment, 89, 109, **112**
　of Andrew Johnson, 63, 89, **96**
　of Bill Clinton, 73, 90, 99, **700**
　of Richard Nixon, 69, **692**
Imperial gallon, **456**
Imports:
　of U.S., 640, **641**
　of world, **721–904**
Incas, 673, 674, 736, 749, 764, **843**
Income. *See also* Cities, U.S.
　by education, **319**
　family, **627**
　gap between men and women, **373**
　household, **628**
　median income, U.S., 627, **628**
　per capita, **629**
　per household, **628**
　by race, **628**
　by state, **629**
　weekly, **627**
Income inequality, world, **714**
Income tax, federal, **1024–1026**
　brackets, **1026**
　collection of, 1025, 1026, **1028**
　established, 115, 680, **1024**
　withholding for, **687**
Incubation periods, animals, **590**
Independence, Declaration of,
　106–107
Independence Day, 344, **354**
Independence Hall, 104, **170**
India, 731, 788–790, **838**
　British control of, 676, 679, **884**
　independence of, **687**
　Sikh rebellion in, 694, **790**
　structures, **444**
　Taj Mahal, **675**
Indiana, **152**
Indianapolis, Ind., 152, 179, **189**
Indianapolis "500", **997–998**
Indian Ocean, **494**
　islands, **496**
Indian Removal Act, **95**
Indians (American):
　Aztecs, 673, **823**
　Incas, 673, 736, 749, 764, **843**
　languages, **375**
　Mayans, **671**
　population of, **378**
　reservations, 145, **379**
　tribes, **378**
Indochina. *See* Cambodia; Laos;
　Vietnam
Indonesia, **790–792**
Indus River, 495, 789, **838**
Industrial Revolution, **677**
Indus Valley civilization, 668, **669**
IndyCar champions, **999**
Indy Racing League, **999**
Infantile paralysis. *See* Poliomyelitis
Infant mortality, 138, 557, 707, **711**
Inflation:
　by country, **719–720**
　world's highest and lowest, **707**

Influenza, 211, 213, 684
Information Marketplace. *See* Information technology
"Information Please" quiz show, 100
Ingathering, Feast of, 354, 355n
"In God We Trust", 118
Inini, 773
Inquisition, 673, 675
Institute of Medicine, U.S., 84
Insulin, 229, 231, 581, 692
Insurance:
  health, 555, 556
  life, 648
Intelligence failures, U.S., 32, 37, 39
Intelligence testing, 581
Inter-American Foundation, 83
Interior, U.S. Dept. of:
  description of, 82
  secretaries of, 82, 85–89
Internal Revenue Service, 1024–1025. *See also* Taxes
International adoptions, 133
International Court of Justice, UN, 905
International Date Line, 350, 486
International Monetary Fund, 687
International Organizations, 908
  U.S. contributions to, 639
International Relations, 905–914
International Space Station, 429, 433
International Trade Commission, U.S., 83
Internet:
  access, 564
  activities, 566
  advertisers, 566
  radio, 563
  top websites, 564–567
  usage worldwide, 567
  use, 564, 566
Internment, Japanese Americans, 686, 687
Interplanetary probes, 425–427
Interracial couples, 380
Inuit, 144
Inventions, 577–584
Inventors, Hall of Fame, 584
Investment, U.S. abroad, 638–639
Iolani Palace, 150
Ionosphere, 402
Iowa, 152–153
Iran, 34, 39, 792–793
  hostage crisis, 99, 693, 793
  Khomeini, Ayatollah Ruhollah, 793
  shah of (Mohammad Reza Pahlavi), 792
  war with Iraq, 693, 793, 794
Iran-Contra affair, 99, 695, 697
Iraq, 693, 696, 793–796
Iraq war, 32, 35–42, 75, 389–390, 391, 505–508, 704–705, 794–796
  intelligence failures, 33, 42, 728, 795, 796, 886
  Abu Ghraib scandal, 32, 37, 38, 41, 390, 506
Ireland, Northern, 796, 883, 886–888
Ireland, Republic of, 496, 683, 796–797
Irish Republican Army (IRA), 693, 698, 703, 797, 887
Iron:
  chemical properties of, 572, 573
  export and import of, 641
"Iron Curtain", 687
Irrawaddy River, 495, 828
Irtish River, 495
Islam, 362–363
  calendar, 352
  holidays, 353–355
  largest Muslim countries, 363
  Sunni and Shiite, 363
Islamabad, Pakistan, 837
Islands, 496
Isle of Man, 891
Isotopes of elements, 573–574, 581
Israel, 797–799
  ancient, 669, 797

Balfour Declaration, 683
Entebbe rescue, 692
Gaza, 34, 37, 38, 41
  independence of, 687, 798
  intifada, al-Aksa, 34, 799, 840
  invasion of Lebanon, 693, 812
  security barrier, 39, 510, 799
  wars with Arabs, 34, 689, 691, 692, 693, 703, 765–766, 794, 797–799, 803, 812, 857, 872, 878
Israel, ancient, 359
Israel, kings of, 466–467
Istanbul, Turkey, 878. *See also* Constantinople
Italicization, rules for, 473
Italy, 799–800. *See also* Roman Empire
  structures, 443–444
  unification of, 679
  in World War I, 683
  in World War II, 686
Ivan IV ("the Terrible"), 674
Ivory Coast. *See* Côte d'Ivoire

J

Jackson, Andrew, 51, 56, 60–61, 95, 171, 173. *See also* Presidents, U.S.
Jackson, Miss., 159, 179
Jacksonville, Fla., 148, 179, 189–190
Jack the Ripper, 681
Jain festival dates, 356
Jakarta, Indonesia, 790
Jamaica, 800–801
James River, 500
Jamestown, Va., 94, 175, 484, 675
Jammu, 789
Japan:
  and China, 681, 685, 686, 750, 802
  exploration of, 484
  islands of, 496, 801
  open to foreigners, 674, 679
  and Russia, 682, 802, 850
  space program, 424, 426
  structures, 444
  war trial, 687
  in World War I, 683, 802
  in World War II, 686
  World War II peace treaty of, 688
Japan, Sea of, 494, 801
Japanese-American internment, 686, 687
Japurá River, 495
Jarvis Island, 896
Java, 496, 791. *See also* Indonesia
Java man, 570
Jefferson, Thomas, 51, 55, 56, 59, 95, 104, 106, 677. *See also* Presidents, U.S.
  birthday, 356
Jefferson City, Mo., 160, 179
Jeffords, Jim, 702
Jenolan Caves, 497
Jersey (island), 891
Jerusalem, 359, 370, 669, 670, 671, 797, 803
Jesus Christ, 360, 670
Jet propulsion:
  first use in aviation, 437
  invention of, 581
Jewelry, birthstones, 357
Jewish holidays, 353–355, 355
Jewish New Year, 354, 355n
Jews. *See* Judaism
Jiang Zemin, 41, 704
Jin Mao Building (Shanghai), 445
Joan of Arc, 296, 673
Johnson, Andrew, 52, 56, 63, 89, 96. *See also* Presidents, U.S.
  impeachment of, 63, 89, 96
Johnson, Lyndon B., 53, 56, 57, 68, 98. *See also* Presidents, U.S.
Johnston Atoll, 896
Johnstown flood (1889), 211, 213, 681
Joint Chiefs of Staff, 82, 392

Joliet, Louis, 151, 153, 158, 172
Jones, Brian, 439
Jones, Marion, 920, 957
Jordan, 802–803
  and Israel, 803
Jordan, Michael, 951, 952, 957
Jordan, Vernon E., Jr., 118
Journalism:
  best American, 269–270
  Pulitzer Prizes for, 234–247
Juan Fernández Islands, 749
Judah, kings of, 466–467
Judaism, 359
  calendar, 352
  holidays, 353–355
Judiciary, U.S., 112. *See also* Supreme Court, U.S.
Judiciary Act of 1789, 100
Judo, 927
Julian calendar, 348
Juneau, Alaska, 144, 179
Jupiter (planet), 400, 405–408. *See also* Planets
  exploration of, 425–427
Jura Mountains, 575, 871
Jurassic Period, 575
Jury trial, 112, 114, 694
Justice, U.S. Dept. of:
  attorneys general, 82, 84–89
  description of, 82
Justices. *See* Supreme Court, U.S.
Justinian Code, 671
Justinian I ("the Great"), 671
Jutland, Battle of, 683

K

Kabbah, Ahmad Tejan, 860
Kabila, Laurent, 702, 755
Kabul, Afghanistan, 721
Kampala, Uganda, 880
Kanawha-New River, 500
Kansas, 153–154
Kansas City, Mo., 160, 179, 190
  climate of, 604
Kansas-Nebraska Act, 679
Kansas River, 500
Karafuto. *See* Sakhalin
Kara Kum Desert, 498
Karat (measure), 457
Karzai, Hamid, 33, 42, 721
Kashmir, 790, 838
Kathmandu, Nepal, 830
Kay, David, 390, 795
Kean, Thomas, 37, 1032
Keller, Helen, 143
Kellogg-Briand Pact, 685
Kelvin (scale), 454
Kennedy, Edward M., 70, 76, 691
Kennedy, John F., 53, 54, 56, 57, 67–68, 98, 689. *See also* Presidents, U.S.
  assassination of, 67, 98, 118, 690
  Warren Report, 691
Kennedy, Robert F., 88, 691
  assassination of, 98, 118
Kennedy Center Honors, 261–262
Kennedy International Airport, 165
Kennedy Space Center, 149
Kent's Cavern, 497
Kent State University, 691, 693
Kentucky, 154
Kentucky Derby, 154, 681, 978, 981
Kenya, 804–805
Kepler, Johannes, 297, 398, 414, 582, 583, 675
Kerry, John F., 33, 35–42, 35, 43, 44, 508, 1032
Key, Francis Scott, 95, 104, 105, 156, 182, 297
Khan, Abdul Qadeer, 34, 35, 839, 1032
Khartoum, Sudan, 681, 868
Khatami, Mohammad, 703, 792–793, 793
Khmer Republic. *See* Cambodia

Khmer Rouge, 42, 743
Khomeini, Ayatollah Ruhollah, 693, 695, 793
Khrushchev, Nikita, 68, 297, 689, 850
Kiel Canal, 450
Kiev (Kyiv), Ukraine, 881
Kigali, Rwanda, 852
Kilimanjaro, Mount, 487
Kilograms, 451, 454, 456, 457
Kilometers, 451, 455
Kim Jong Il, 806–807
King, Coretta Scott, book awards, 257
King, Rev. Martin Luther, Jr., 182, 298, 380, 689, 691
  assassination of, 98, 118
King, Rodney, 697
Kingdoms, 713
Kingman Reef, 896
Kings:
  contemporary, 713
  of England, 885
  of France, 772
  of Judah and Israel, 466–467
  of Russia, 851
Kingsley Tufts Poetry Prize, 257
Kingston, Jamaica, 801
Kingstown, St. Vincent and the Grenadines, 854
Kinshasa, Congo, 754
Kiribati, 805–806
Kissinger, Henry A., 88–89, 225, 298, 750, 766, 901
Kitty Hawk, N.C., 166, 435, 682
Kiwanis International, 663
Kjólen Mountains, 870
Knights of Columbus, 663
Know-Nothing Party, 54n
Knox, John, 298, 674
Kohl, Helmut, 780
Kohoutek (comet), 414
Koran (Qur'an), 362
Korea, North, 75, 806–807. See also Korean War
Korea, South, 807–808. See also Korean War
Korean Airlines Incident (1983), 694
Korean War, 97, 688, 806
  casualties, 394
Koror, Palau, 839
Kosciusko, Mount, 487, 727
Kosovo, 700, 859
Kosovo casualties, 391
Kostunica, Vojislav, 859
Kosygin, Aleksei N., 298, 850
Koyukuk River, 500
Kozlowski, L. Dennis, 704
Krakatau, 212
Kremlin (structure), 443
Kuala Lumpur, Malaysia, 819
  tallest buildings, 445
Kublai Khan, 298, 673, 750, 826
Ku Klux Klan, 684, 702
Kunlun Mountains, 750
Kuomintang, 750, 873
Kuril Islands, 801, 850
Kuskokwim River, 500
Kuwait, 808–809
Kuwait (city), Kuwait, 808
Kwanzaa, 355
Kyoto protocol, 702, 703
Kyrgyzstan, 809–810
Kyushu, Japan, 801
Kyzyl Kum Desert, 498

L

Labor. See also Employment
  civilian labor force in U.S. cities, 181–205
  farm and non-farm, 624
  historical figures, 623
  leading unions, 626
  National Labor Relations Board, 83
  organizations, 626
  statistics, 621–625

strikes, 625
women, 625
Labor, U.S. Dept. of:
  description of, 82
  secretaries of, 82, 86–88
Labor Day, 344, 354, 355
Labor force:
  characteristics of, 622
  civilian, 119
  fastest growing occupations, 620
  median age of, 626
  by occupation, 620
  persons in, 623
  projections, 621–622
  women in, 373, 625
Labrador, 484, 745
Labrador, Canada, 745
Lady Byng Trophy, 962
Lagos, Nigeria, 835
Lakes. See also specific lakes
Lakeshores, National, 595
"Lame Duck" Amendment, 97, 116
Lamps, electric incandescent, 580
Lancaster, House of, 884
Land area:
  of countries, 709–710, 721–904
  largest countries, 707
  smallest countries, 707
  of states, 143–178, 179
  of U.S. cities, 181–205
  world, 487
Land rush, 168
Languages:
  American Sign Language, 482
  basic phrases in other languages, 477
  Braille, 482
  foreign spoken, in U.S., 375
  foreign words and phrases, 478–480
  Latin and Greek roots, 480
  most studied, U.S., 475
  most widely spoken, 475
  use by country, 721–904
Lansing, Mich., 157, 179
Laos, 810
Lao-tse, 298, 669, 750
La Paz, Bolivia, 736
Larceny, 387
La Salle, Robert Cavelier, Sieur de, 152, 153, 155, 158, 160, 167, 172, 173
Laser, invention of, 581
Lassen Peak, 146
Last names, most common in U.S., 140
Las Vegas, Nev., 162, 179, 190–191
Lateran Treaty, 685, 899
Latin America. See also specific countries
Latinos, 375, 377
Latin word elements, 480–481
Latitude, definition, 485
Latitudes of cities, 499, 504
Latvia, 687, 696, 810–811
Lausanne, Switzerland, 871
Lava, 488
Law:
  codes of, 668, 671, 678
  first unconstitutional, 92, 100
Law, Cardinal Bernard, 704
Law enforcement, 382–388. See also Arrests; Crime; Prisoners
  corruption, prosecutions for, 384
  officers killed or assaulted, 384
Laws. See Bills (Congressional)
Lawyers, first woman, 101
Lay, Kenneth L., 511, 703
Lead, 572, 574
Lead poisoning, 589
League of Nations, 684, 685, 686, 687, 779, 871, 872
Leaning Tower of Pisa, 443
Leather, Producer Price Index, 640
Lebanon, 811–812
  civil war in, 812
  Israeli invasion of, 693, 812
  terrorism in, 693

U.S. military action in, 689
Lee, Robert E., 96, 299, 680
  birthday, 356
Leeward Islands. See British Virgin Islands; Montserrat
Lefkosia (Nicosia), Cyprus, 759
Legal holidays, 356
Legal Services Corporation, 84
Legionnaire's disease, 692
Legislatures, state:
  only unicameral, 162
Legislatures, world:
  by country, 721–904
  oldest, 788
Lena River, 495
Lend-Lease, 687
Length, units of, 453, 455
  metric system, 451, 455
Lenin, Vladimir, 299, 683, 684, 850
Leningrad, 849. See also St. Petersburg, Russia
Lens, bifocal, 581
Lent, 353
Leonardo da Vinci, 299, 673
Leopold-Loeb case, 684
Lepanto, Battle of, 674
Lesotho, 812–813
Lethal injection as death penalty, 384
Letters:
  postal rates since 1847, 442
  postal regulations, 440–442
Lewis and Clark expedition, 151, 153, 161, 167, 169, 172, 176, 484, 678
Lewisburg, W.Va., 607
Lexington-Concord, Battle of, 157, 676
Lexington-Fayette, Ky., 154, 179
Liberia, 813–814
Liberty, Statue of, 165, 681
Liberty Bell, 104, 170
Libraries:
  first circulating, 100
  presidential, 57
Libraries and Information Science, National Commission on, 83
Library of Congress, 83
Libreville, Gabon, 776
Libya, 34, 694, 814–815
Licenses, drivers, 614
Lidice, Czechoslovakia, 686
Lie, Trygve, 905
Liechtenstein, 815
Life expectancy, 135, 136
  highest and lowest, 707
  selected countries, 711
Life insurance, 648
Life on Earth, 575–576
Light:
  discoveries of, 581
  velocity of, 399, 581
Lightning, 597
Lightning rods, 581
Light-years, 399
Lilongwe, Malawi, 818
Lima, Peru, 843
Lincoln, Abraham, 52, 54, 56, 62–63, 96, 151. See also Presidents, U.S.
  assassination of, 63, 118, 680
  Gettysburg Address, 118
  home of, 151
  Lincoln-Douglas debates, 679
Lincoln, Neb., 161, 179
Lincoln's Birthday, 344, 353
Lindbergh, Charles A., 97, 299, 436, 684, 685
Lindh, John Walker, 703
Linear measures, 453, 455
Linotype machines, 582
Lions Clubs International, 663
Liquid measures, 451, 453, 456
Liquor. See also Prohibition
  export and import of, 641
  law violations, 387
  taxes, 1025
Lisbon, Portugal, 846
  earthquake in (1755), 211, 676
Literature:

authors. See People
prizes for, 226, 241–245, 254, 257, 258
Liters, 451, 455, 456, 457
Lithium, 572, 574
Lithography, 582
Lithuania, 687, 696, 815–816
Little Big Horn, Battle of, 96, 161, 681
Little Brown Jug (harness racing), 992
Little League (baseball), 1000–1001
Little Missouri River, 501
Little Rock, Ark., 145, 179
"Little White House", 149
Livestock, 641, 645
Ljubljana, Slovenia, 862
Locarno Conferences, 684
Locke, John, 676
Locomotives, 581
Logan, Mount, 744
Logarithms, 579
Lomé, Togo, 876
London, England, 883
   Great Fire of (1666), 217, 675
   Great Plague in, 675
   structures, 444
   subway system, 612
London, Tower of, 444
Long, Huey P., 300, 686
   assassination of, 300
Long Beach, Calif., 191
Longevity, 550
Longevity, of animals, 590
Long Island, Battle of, 676
Longitude, definition, 485
Longitudes of cities, 499, 504
Looms, 581
Lord's Prayer, 690
Los Angeles, Calif., 146, 179, 191–192
   climate of, 604
Lots, Feast of, 353, 355n
Lott, Trent, 704
Louis, Joe, 957, 973
Louisiana, 154–155
Louisiana Purchase, 59, 95, 102, 103, 145, 147, 153, 158, 160, 161, 167, 168, 172, 178, 678
Louisville, Ky., 154
Louis XIV (king of France), 772
Louis XVI (king of France), 677
Lourdes, France, 370
Louvre, 444
Low-carbohydrate diets, 543–545
Lowest points, U.S., 500, 503
Luanda, Angola, 724
"Lucy" (hominid), 570, 578
Luge (sport), 931
Lumber and wood. See also Forests
   export and import of, 641
   Producer Price Index, 640
Lunar flights, 425–428
Lunar Orbiter program, 425, 426
Lunar probes, 425–427
Lunation, 348
Luray Cavern, 497
Lusaka, Zambia, 903
Lusitania, 683
Luther, Martin, 300, 362, 674, 779
Lutherans, 362, 695
Luxembourg, 816
Luxembourg (city), Luxembourg, 816
Luzon, Philippines, 496, 844
Lydian civilization, 669
Lynch, Jessica, 389

M

Maastricht Treaty, 697
Macao, 752
MacArthur, Douglas, 300, 685, 688, 802, 806
MacArthur Foundation Awards, 260
Maccabean revolt, 670
MacDonald, Ramsay, 300

Macedonia, Greece, 781
Macedonia, Republic of, 702, 703, 816–817
Machine guns, 581
Machinery:
   export and import of, 641
   inventions, 579–583
   Producer Price Index, 640
Machu Picchu (Peru), 444, 671
Mackenzie River, 484, 495, 744
Mackinac Straits Bridge, 158, 447
Macmillan, Harold, 300, 884
Macon, Ga., 607
Madagascar, 496, 817–818
Mad cow, 550
Madeira, Portugal, 847
Madeira River, 495
Madison, James, 51, 56, 59–60, 95.
   See also Presidents, U.S.
Madison, Wis., 177, 179
Madrid, Spain, 866
Madrid bombing (2004), 33, 36, 37, 510
Magazines, 277–278
   awards for, 257
   circulation, 277–278
Magellan, Ferdinand, 300, 485, 674, 844
Magellan space project, 427
Maggiore, Lake, 871
Magna Carta, 672, 884
Magnesium, 572, 574
Magnitude, earthquakes, 490–491
Mahabharata, 363
Mail:
   first airmail route, 100, 436
   postal regulations, 440–442
Maine, 155–156
Maine (battleship), 681, 758
Major, John, 885
Majorca, 866
Majuro, Marshall Islands, 821
Malabo, Equatorial Guinea, 767
Malagasy, 818
Malawi, 818
Malaya. See Malaysia
Malaysia, 819
Malcolm X, 118, 381, 691
Maldives, 820
Malé, Maldives, 820
Malenkov, Georgi M., 688
Mali, 820–821
Mali Empire, 673
Malta, 821
Mammals:
   Age of, 576
   endangered, 591
Mammoth Cave, 154, 497, 592
Man, Isle of, 891
Management and Budget, Office of, 81
Managua, Nicaragua, 833
Man Booker Prize, 254
Manchester, N.H., 163, 179
Manchu Dynasty, 675, 682, 750, 802
Manchukuo, 750, 802
Manchuria, 685, 750, 802
Mandela, Nelson, 696, 698, 865
Manganese, 572, 574
Manhattan, 165, 195–196
Manhattan Project, 687
Manila, Philippines, 844
Manila Bay, Battle of, 681
Manitoba, Canada, 745
Manslaughter, 387n
Mantle (of Earth), 401
Manual Alphabet, American, 482
Manufacturing. See Business and economy
Mao Zedong (Tse-tung), 300, 688, 692, 750–751
Map projections, 486
Maps:
   of territorial expansion of U.S., 103
   time zones, 523
   world, 524–536
Maputo, Mozambique, 828
Marathon, Battle of, 670

Marathons, 1000
Marbury v. Madison, 92, 100
Marconi, Guglielmo, 301, 682
Marcos, Ferdinand, 694, 695, 844
Mardi Gras, 195, 353
Marie Antoinette, 301, 677
Marijuana, 557
Marine Corps, U.S.. See also Armed forces, U.S.
   actions, 683, 684, 689, 691, 694, 763, 834
   Commandant of, 82
Mariner space program, 425
Marne, Battles of the, 683
Marquesas Islands, 775
Marquette, Jacques, 151, 153, 158, 172
Marriage:
   median age at, 127
   mixed-race, 380
   percent never married, 127
   same-sex, 33, 36, 38, 371, 372, 513, 701, 746
   statistics, U.S., 127
Mars (planet), 396, 400, 404–405, 406.
   See also Planets
   exploration of, 35, 37, 396, 404–405, 423, 424, 514
Mars Global Surveyor, 423
Marshall, John, 90, 301
Marshall, Mich., 607
Marshall, Thurgood, 691
Marshall Islands, 821–822
Marshall Plan, 67, 97, 687
Mars Odyssey, 424
Martinique, 774
Martin Luther King, Jr.'s Birthday, 344, 353
Marx, Karl, 301, 679, 680
Mary, Queen of Scots, 301, 675
Maryland, 156
Maseru, Lesotho, 812
Masoud, Ahmed Shah, 722
Mass:
   chemical elements, 573–574
   metric system, 454
Massachusetts, 157
Mass-energy theorem, 458, 580
Massive, Mount, 502
Masters Tournament (golf), 993
Mata-Utu, Wallis and Futuna Islands, 775
Mathematics:
   averages, 452
   awards for, 261
   decimals and fractions, 458
   formulas, 458
   mean and median, 452
   metric and U.S. equivalents, 451, 455–457
   prefixes and multiples, 458
   prime numbers, 452
Matisse, Henri, 682
Mauna Kea, 150, 503
Mauna Loa, 150
Maundy Thursday, 355n
Mauritania, 822
Mauritius, 822–823
Mawlid an-Nabi, 354, 355
Maximilian (emperor of Mexico), 301, 680, 824
Maxwell, James Clerk, 301, 581, 582
Mayaguez incident, 692
Mayans, 670, 671
Mayflower (ship), 675
Mayors, U.S., 181–205
Mayotte, 776
Mbabane, Swaziland, 869
McCarthy (Joseph) hearings, 98, 688
McDonald Islands, 728
McGreevey, James, 40, 509, 1032
McGwire, Mark, 957, 1015
McHenry, Fort, 105, 678
McKinley, Mount (Denali), 487, 500, 502, 503, 592
McKinley, William, 52, 53, 56, 64, 96.
   See also Presidents, U.S.

assassination of, **118, 682**
McVeigh, Timothy, **224, 698, 699, 703**
Mean and median, **452**
Measures and weights, **451–458**
  capacities and volumes, **453, 455, 455–457**
  conversion factors, **451**
  cooking, **457**
Meat, **541, 641, 642, 645**
Mecca, Saudi Arabia, **362, 370, 671, 856**
Medal of Freedom, **261**
Medal of Honor, U.S., **394**
Mede civilization, **669**
Media:
  magazines, **277–278**
  newspapers, **277**
  statistics, world, **718**
Mediation and Conciliation Service (FMCS), Federal, **83**
Mediation Board, National, **83**
Medical care, Consumer Price Index, **639**
Medicare program, **634, 691**
Medicine, **553–560**
  best hospitals, **555**
  discoveries in, **579–583**
  Nobel Prizes for, **230–233**
Medina, Saudi Arabia, **362, 370, 671, 856**
Mediterranean Sea, **494, 670**
Medjugorje, Bosnia, **370**
Mein Kampf (Hitler), **684**
Mekong River, **495, 900**
Melting points, of elements, **573–574**
Memorial Day, **344, 354**
  Confederate, **356**
Memorials, National, **595**
Memphis, Tenn., **172, 179, 192**
Mendeleev, Dmitri, **571**
Mendelevium, **572, 574**
Mendelian Law, **581**
Mensk (Minsk), Belarus, **732**
Mercator projection, **486**
Mercury (element), **572, 574**
Mercury (planet), **402, 406.** *See also* Planets
  exploration of, **424**
Mercury, Project, **427**
Mercury-vapor lamp, **580**
Meredith, James H., **690**
Meridians, **485**
Merrimac (ship), **680**
Mesa, Ariz., **192–193**
Mesa Verde National Park, **147, 593**
Mesopause, **402**
Mesopotamia, **668, 669, 794**
Mesosphere, **402**
Mesozoic Era, **575**
Messner, Reinhold, **492**
Metals:
  as elements, **573–574**
  export and import of, **641**
  mineral wealth in countries, **721–904**
  Producer Price Index, **640**
Meteors and meteorites, **405, 415**
  showers, **415**
Meters (measure), **451, 455**
Methodism and Methodists, **362, 677**
Metric system, **454–457, 455–457**
  conversion tables, **451, 455–457**
Metropolitan Opera House, **681**
Mexican Cession, **102, 103, 679, 823**
Mexican War, **95, 145, 147, 162, 164, 173, 174, 178, 679, 823**
Mexico, **823–824**
  ancient civilizations of, **670, 671**
  conquest of, **484, 674, 823**
  pre-Columbian cultures of, **669**
  revolution in, **683, 824**
  U.S. military actions in, **683, 823**
Mexico, Gulf of, **494, 823**
Mexico City, Mexico, **823**
  subway system, **612**
Miami, Fla., **148, 193**
  climate of, **604**
Michelangelo, **673**

Michigan, **157–158**
Michigan, Lake, **152, 158, 484, 494**
Micronesia, **824**
Microscope, compound, **581**
Middle East, **692**
  Arab-Israeli conflicts, **34, 35, 36, 38, 75, 689, 691, 693, 701, 702, 704, 705, 765–766, 794, 797–799, 799, 812, 857, 872, 878**
  map of, **533**
  peace talks, **797–799, 799**
Midway Islands, **896**
Mile records, runners, **984**
Military, **389–395.** *See also* Armed forces, U.S.; National defense
Military budgets, world, **715**
Military forces. *See also* Armed forces, U.S.
Military Parks, National, **594**
Military spending, **392**
Milk, U.S. consumption of, **642**
Milk River, **501**
Milky Way, **397, 577**
Million Man March, **698**
Milosevic, Slobodan, **702, 703, 859**
Milton, John, **675**
Milwaukee, Wis., **177, 179, 193–194**
Mindanao, Philippines, **496, 844**
Mindszenty, József Cardinal, **788**
Mine disasters, **211, 217**
Minerals. *See* Coal
Ming Dynasty, **675, 750**
Minimum wage rates, **628**
Minneapolis, Minn., **158, 179, 194**
Minnesota, **158–159**
Minoan culture, **668, 669**
Minute Men, **157**
Miquelon. *See* St. Pierre and Miquelon
Mir (space station), **429, 431**
Miranda v. *Arizona*, **92**
Mispronounced words, commonly, **475**
Mississippi, **159–160**
  civil rights workers slain in, **691**
Mississippi-Missouri-Red Rock River, **495, 501**
Mississippi River, **155, 159, 484, 495, 501**
Missouri, **160**
Missouri (battleship), **686**
Missouri Compromise, **60, 95, 160, 678**
Missouri-Red Rock River, **501**
Missouri River, **495, 501**
Mistletoe, **355**
Mobile-Alabama-Coosa River, **501**
Mogadishu, Somalia, **863**
Mohammed, **856.** *See also* Muhammad
Mojave Desert, **498**
Moldova, **825**
Mole (measure), **454**
Moluccas Islands, **791**
Monaco, **825–826**
Monarchies, **466–467, 713, 772, 851, 885**
Mondale, Walter F., **54, 57**
Money:
  coins, new U.S., **453**
  of countries, **721–904**
  designs of U.S. bills, **452**
  portraits on U.S. bills, **452**
  value of dollar, **640**
Mongolia, **484, 826**
Mongols, **671, 673, 750, 849**
Monitor (ship), **680**
"Monkey Trial", **684**
Monroe, James, **51, 56, 60, 95, 105.** *See also* Presidents, U.S.
Monroe Doctrine, **60, 95, 105, 678**
Monrovia, Liberia, **813**
Montana, **161**
Mont Blanc tunnel, **450**
Monte Carlo, Monaco, **825**
Montenegro, **858–859**
Montevideo, Uruguay, **897**
Montgomery, Ala., **143, 179**

  bus boycott, **689**
Months:
  birthstones, **357**
  names of, **350**
  record high and low temperatures by, **603**
Monticello, Va., **59, 175**
Montpelier, Vt., **174, 179**
Montreal, Canada, **744**
Montserrat, **892**
"Monumental Mountain", **497**
Monuments, National, **593**
Moon (Earth's), **400**
  Apollo space program, **428**
  eclipses of, **420**
  first staffed landing, **428, 691**
  lunar probes, **425–427**
  perigee and apogee, **417–420**
  phases of, **417–420**
  phenomena, **417–420**
Moons (satellites), **400, 405–412**
  defined, **398**
  orbits defined, **397**
Moore, Michael, **513, 1033**
Moors, **673**
Mormons, **174, 679**
Moro, Aldo, **693**
Morocco, **827**
Moroni, Comoros, **753**
Morrison, Toni, **697**
Morse, Samuel F. B., **303, 583, 679**
Mortality, **557.** *See also* Death and dying
Mortality, infant, selected countries, **711**
Moscow, Russia, **849**
  subway system, **612**
Moses, **669**
Most Valuable Players:
  baseball, **1012**
  basketball, **952**
  hockey, **961**
"Mother of Presidents", **175**
Mother's Day, **344, 354**
Mother Teresa, **699**
Motion pictures:
  100 best, **279**
  awards for, **247–251, 258**
  inventions, **581**
  top grosses, **279**
Motorcycles, **581**
Motor vehicles, **612, 613**
  accidents, **613**
  best-selling, **616**
  export and import of, **641**
  fatalities, **613**
  holiday fatalities, **613**
  most popular colors, **615**
  speed limits, **614**
  state laws, **614**
  theft of, **387**
  traffic, **612**
Mottoes:
  national, **118**
  state, **143–178**
Mountains. *See also* names of mountains; Volcanoes
  "Seven Summits", **493**
  in U.S., **502, 503**
  world, **492–493**
Mount Everest, **224**
Mount Rainier National Park, **593**
Mount Vernon, Va., **58, 175**
Movies. *See* Motion pictures
Movie stars. *See* People
Mozambique, **827–828, 847**
Mozart, Wolfgang Amadeus, **303, 677**
Mubarak, Hosni, **766**
Mugabe, Robert, **904**
Muhammad, **303, 362, 671, 856**
Muharram, **352, 353, 355**
Mulroney, Brian, **694, 746**
Munich, Germany, **778**
  Beer Hall Putsch (1923), **684**
Munich Conference (1938), **686, 779**
Murder, **385, 387**
Murray River, **495**

Muscat, Oman, 837
Museum, first science, 101
Museveni, Yoweri, 881
Musharraf, Pervez, 34, 837, 838, 839
Music:
  awards for, 245, 252–253, 253, 258
  Country Music Hall of Fame, 273
  earliest written, 669
  Rock and Roll Hall of Fame, 274
  state songs, 143–178
  symphonies, 263
  top downloads, 272
  top-selling albums, 272
Musicians. *See* People
Muslim architecture, 444
Muslims. *See also* Black Muslims;
  Islam
Mussolini, Benito, 303, 684, 685, 686,
  800
Myanmar, 828–829
Mythology:
  Egyptian, 471
  Greek and Roman, 467–470
  Norse, 470–471

N

NAACP, 664, 682
  Image Awards, 258
Nagasaki, 686, 687, 802
NAIA football championships, 935
Nairobi, Kenya, 804
Names:
  of days, 350
  of months, 350
  most common in U.S., 140
  Old Testament, 465–467
  of states, origins of, 143–178
Namibia, 829–830
Nantes, Edict of, 674, 676
Napa, Calif., 607
Napoléon Bonaparte, 284, 677, 678,
  772
Napoleonic Code, 678
Napoleonic Wars, 678, 772, 849, 884
Narcotics:
  arrests for violations, 387
  use, 557
NASCAR, 998, 999
NASDAQ, 650
Nashville-Davidson, Tenn., 172, 179,
  194–195
Nassau, Bahamas, 730
Nasser, Gamal Abdel, 303, 766, 857
National Academy of Engineering, 84
National Academy of Sciences, 84
National Aeronautics and Space
  Administration (NASA). *See also*
  Space
  address, 83
  administrator, 83
National Anthem, 105
National Archives and Records
  Administration (NARA), 83
National Association for the
  Advancement of Colored People
  (NAACP), 664, 682
National Basketball Association
  (NBA), 950–954
National Book Awards, 254
National Book Critics Circle Awards,
  254
National Committees, 50
National Conventions, 49, 50
National Credit Union
  Administration, 83
National debt, 635
  constitutional validity of, 115
National Foundation on the Arts and
  the Humanities, 83
National Historical Parks, 593
National Historic Sites, 594
National Hockey League, 960–964
National holidays (by country), 357
National Labor Relations Board
  (NLRB), 83

National League. *See* Baseball;
  Football
National Magazine Awards, 257
National Mediation Board, 83
National Organization of Women, 373
National Park System, 592–596, 596
National Railroad Passenger
  Corporation (Amtrak), 84
National Republican Party, 51
National Research Council, 84
National Science Foundation (NSF),
  83
National Security Adviser, 81
National Security Council, 81
National Service, Corporation for, 82
National Transportation Safety
  Board, 83
National Trust for Historic
  Preservation, 607
Native Americans. *See* Indians
  (American)
NATO, 36, 908. *See also* North Atlantic
  Treaty Organization; North Atlantic
  Treaty Organization
Natural features, of countries,
  721–904. *See also* Geography
Natural resources:
  of countries, 721–904
  of states of U.S., 143–178
Nature, 590–596
Nautilus (submarine), 688
Naval Academy, U.S., 156
Navassa Island, 896
Navy, U.S.. *See also* Armed forces, U.S.
  first admiral of, 100
  secretaries of, 82, 87
Nazis, 684, 685, 687, 689, 779–780
NCAA basketball, 946–949
NCAA football championships, 935
N'Djamena, Chad, 747
Neanderthal man, 668
Neap tides, 401
Nebraska, 161–162
  Kansas-Nebraska Act, 679
Nebuchadnezzar, 443, 669
Negev Desert, 797
Nehru, Jawaharlal, 303, 789
Nelson River, 495
Neosho River, 501
Nepal, 830–831
Neptune (planet), 400, 406, 411–413.
  See also Planets
Neptunium, 572, 574, 581
Netherlands, 831–833
Netherlands Antilles, 832
Neutron, discovery of, 581
Neutron star, 397
Nevada, 162–163
Nevis, 853
New Amsterdam, 165, 675
Newark, N.J., 163, 179
Newbery Medal, 255
New Brunswick, Canada, 745
New Caledonia, 775
New Cornelia Tailings, 145
New Deal, 66, 685, 686
New Delhi, India, 789
Newfoundland, Canada, 496, 676, 745
New Freedom, 65
New Frontier, 68
New Guinea, 496. *See also* Papua
  New Guinea, Irian Jaya
New Hampshire, 163
New Hebrides. *See* Vanuatu
New Jersey, 163–164
New Mexico, 164–165
New Orleans, La., 154, 179, 195
  Battle of, 678
  climate of, 604
New Paltz, N.Y., 607
Newport, R.I., 607
News:
  deaths in 2004, 1035
  international, 33–42
  in U.S., 32–42
  people in the news, 1030
  websites, 565

Newsom, Gavin, 1033
Newspapers, 277
  awards for, 234–241
  circulation, 277
  first black, 100
  first in U.S., 676
  firsts in, 100
Newton (measure), 454
Newton, Sir Isaac, 303, 581, 583, 675,
  676
New Year:
  Chinese, 356
  Jewish, 354, 355n
New Year's Day, 344, 353
New York, 195–196
New York City, 165, 179, 195–196
  boroughs of, 195–196
  bridges, 447
  buildings and structures, 445,
    445–446
  climate, 604
  Kennedy Airport, 165
  Sept. 11 attacks, 100, 211, 224, 703,
    722, 857
  Statue of Liberty, 165
  subway commuters, 612
  subway system, 612, 682
  tunnels, 450
  Tweed Ring, 680
  U.N. Headquarters, 166
  World's Fairs, 686
New York State, 165–166
New York Stock Exchange, 649
New Zealand, 833
  exploration of, 485
New Zealand dependencies, 706
Niagara Falls, 165
Niamey, Niger, 834
Nicaea, Council of, 360, 671
Nicaragua, 833–834
  U.S. military actions in, 834
Nicene Creed, 360, 671
Nickel, 572
Nickel (element), 574
Nicknames of states, 143–178
Niger, 834–835
Nigeria, 691, 835–836
Niger River, 495, 834
Nightingale, Florence, 679
Nile River, 495, 765, 868
  Aswan Dam, 766
Niobrara River, 501
Nirvana, 364
Nitrogen, 572, 574
Nitrogen dioxide, 589
Nitroglycerin, 581
Niue Island, 833
Nixon, Richard M., 53, 54, 55, 56, 57,
  68–69, 98. *See also* Presidents, U.S.
  resignation of, 69, 692
Noatak River, 501
Nobel, Alfred, 303, 580, 680, 682
Nobel Prizes, 42, 225–233, 682
Nomenclature, binomial, 570
Nonfiction (general), awards for,
  244–245, 254
Nonfiction, best of 20th century,
  268–269
Nordic Combined, 931
Norfolk Island, 728
Normandy, House of, 884
Normandy Invasion, 686
Norris Trophy, 962
Norse mythology, 470–471
North, Oliver, Jr., 695
North America. *See also* Continents
  area and elevation of, 487
  exploration of, 484
  map of, 525
North American Free Trade
  Agreement (NAFTA), 697
North Atlantic Treaty Organization
  (NATO), 36, 97, 99, 688, 773, 879,
  908
North Canadian River, 501
North Carolina, 166
North Dakota, 166–167

Northeast Passage, 484
Northern Ireland, 796, 883, 886–888
  Good Friday Peace Accord, 700,
    701, 702, 797, 887
"Northern lights", 416
Northern Mariana Islands, 895–896
Northern Rhodesia. *See* Zambia
North Island (New Zealand), 496, 833
North Korea, 704
North Platte River, 501
North Pole, 483, 485, 497
  flights over, 436, 438
  reached, 682
North Sea, 494, 733, 831, 836, 883
Northwest Passage, 169, 484
Northwest Territories, Canada, 745
Norway, 836–837
Norwegian dependencies, 706
Notre-Dame de Paris, 444
Nouakchott, Mauritania, 822
Nouméa, New Caledonia, 775
Nova Scotia, Canada, 484, 745
Novelists. *See* People
Novels, best of 20th century, 267–
  268
Nuclear fission, 581
Nuclear physics, discoveries and
  theories, 579–583
Nuclear power, accidents, 216, 693,
  695
Nuclear-proliferation agreement, 693,
  696
Nuclear Regulatory Commission
  (NRC), 83
Nuclear weapons:
  countries with, 715
  India, 790
  Iran, 793
  North Korea, 807
  Pakistan, 838
  proliferation, 34
  testing of, 688, 691
Nuku'alofa, Tonga, 876
Numbers:
  cardinal, 452
  decimals and fractions, 458
  nominal, 452
  ordinal, 452
  prime, 452
  Roman, 452
Nunavut, Canada, 744
Nuremberg laws, 685
Nuremberg war crimes trial, 685, 687
Nutrition, 537–542
  obesity guidelines, 560
Nyasa, Lake, 494
Nyasaland. *See* Malawi
Nylon, invention of, 580

O

O.K. Corral, 145
Oakland, Calif., 146, 196
Oaths:
  constitutional, 111, 113
  presidential, 111
Oberlin, Ohio, 607
Obesity, 546, 550
Obie Awards, 252
Ob River, 495
Occupational Safety and Health
  Review Commission, 83
Occupations, 618–619, 620, 621,
  622–623, 626
Oceania. *See also* Continents
  area and elevation of, 487
  exploration of, 485
  map of, 536
Ocean liners. *See* Steamships
Oceans, 494
Odd Fellows, Independent Order of,
  665
Oder-Neisse Line, 780
Odyssey (Homer), 669
Office of Personnel Management
  (OPM), 83

Offices, Executive, 81–82
Ohio, 167–168
Ohio-Allegheny River, 495, 501
Ohio River, 501
Ohm's Law, 581
Oil (petroleum):
  export and import of, 641
  Exxon Valdez, 211, 222, 695, 697
  first commercial well in U.S., 100
  producers and consumers, top, 587
  reserves by country, 587
  spills, 211, 222
Okhotsk Sea, 494
Oklahoma, 168–169
Oklahoma City, Okla., 99, 168, 179, 197
  bombing (1995), 224, 698, 699, 700
Öland, Sweden, 870
Old North Church, 157
Old San Juan, Puerto Rico, 607
Old Testament names, 465–467
Olmecs, 669
Olympia, Wash., 176, 179
Olympic Games, 915–932
  ancient, 669
  Athens (2004), 41, 516, 782, 915–928
  first modern, 682
  history and sites, 915
  Munich Massacre, 692
  Soviet withdrawal from (1984), 694
  Summer Games, 915–928
  Winter Games, 928–932
Olympic National Park, 593, 596
Olympics (2004), 41, 516, 782,
  915–928
Omaha, Neb., 161, 179, 197
Oman, 837
Ontario, Canada, 745
Ontario, Lake, 494
OPEC, 908
Opera companies, U.S., 264
Operas, frequently produced, 264
Operation Iraqi Freedom, 795
Opium War, 679
Orange Bowl, 933
Orange River, 495
Oranjestad, Aruba, 832
Orbits:
  of comets, 397, 414–415
  defined, 397
  of Moon, 399, 400
  of planets, 397
Orchestras, symphony, 263
Ordovician Period, 575
Oregon, 169
Oregon Treaty, 95
Organization of American States, 687
Organization of Petroleum Exporting
  Countries (OPEC), 857
Organizations, 658–667
  consumers', 654–655
Organ transplants, 555
Orinoco River, 495, 752
Orkney Islands, 888
Orthodox:
  churches, 672
  Easter, 344, 354, 355
  holidays, 355
Osage River, 501
Oscars (Academy Awards), 247–251
Oslo, Norway, 836
Ostrogothic Kingdom, 671
Oswald, Lee Harvey, 68, 118, 690
Ottawa, Canada, 744
Ottoman Turks, 872, 878
Ouachita River, 501
Ouagadougou, Burkina Faso, 741
Outer Mongolia. *See* Mongolia
Outsourcing, 618–619
OxyContin, 557
Oxygen, 574
Ozone, 581
  atmospheric, 588, 589
  ozone-polluted cities, 588
Ozonosphere, 402

P

Pacific Islander, 378
Pacific Ocean, 494. *See also* Oceania
  islands, 496, 893–896
  sighted, 484
  U.S. coastline, 502
Page, Larry, 512, 1030
Pagodas, 444
Painted Desert, 498
Painters. *See* People
Paintings, most expensive, 278
Pakistan, 34, 687, 732, 789, 837–839
Palau, 839
Paleontology, 570
Paleozoic Era, 575
Palestine, 797
Palestine, ancient, 669
Palestine Liberation Organization
  (PLO), 693, 803, 812
  Achille Lauro hijacked, 694
Palestinian Authority, 703
Palestinian state (proposed), 34, 39,
  510, 799, 839–841
Palikir, Micronesia, 824
Palm Sunday, 344, 353, 355n
Palmyra Atoll, 896
Pamir Mountain Range, 493
Panama:
  U.S. military intervention in, 696
Panama Canal, 96, 98, 450, 683, 841
  treaties, 693, 841
Panama City, Panama, 841
Panay (gunboat), 686
Panmunjom, North Korea, 808
Pantheon (Rome), 443, 670, 671
Papal States, 899
Papeete, French Polynesia, 775
Paper:
  Chinese development of, 670
  export and import of, 641
  invention of, 581
  Producer Price Index, 640
Paper currency, 452
Papua New Guinea, 485, 496, 841–
  842
Parachutes, 581
Parachuting:
  Caterpillar Club, 436
  first jumps, 435, 436
Paraguay, 842–843
Paraguay River, 495, 739, 842
Parallels, 485
Paramaribo, Suriname, 869
Paraná River, 495, 739, 842
Parentheses, 474
Paris, France, 771
  structures, 444
  subway system, 612
  in World War I, 683
  in World War II, 686, 773
Paris, Peace of, 676
Paris, Treaty of:
  in 1898, 681
  in 1947, 687, 788
Parkinson's, 550
Parks:
  city-owned, 181–205
  most visited, 596
  National Park System, 592–596, 596
  state parks, 143–178
Parks, Rosa, 380
Parliament (Great Britain), 673, 675,
  678, 685, 883
Parole Commission, U.S., 83
Parsec (measure), 399
Parthenon, 443, 670
Parties, political (world), 721–904
Passion of the Christ, The, 513
Passover, 344, 354, 355
Passports, 610
Pasteur, Louis, 305, 580, 582, 680
Patents, 656–657
Paul, Alice, 372

Peabody Awards for Broadcasting, 260
Peace Corps, 83
Peacekeeping Operations, UN, 906
Peace Prizes, Nobel, 225
Peace River, 495
Peak Cavern, 497
Pearl, Daniel, 703
Pearl Harbor attack, 150, 188, 686, 687, 802
Pearl River, 501
Pearl River (Zhu Jiang), China, 750
Peary, Robert E., 305, 483, 484, 485, 682
Pecos River, 501
Pee Dee-Yadkin River, 501
Peking, China, 749. *See also* Beijing
Peloponnesian Wars, 670
PEN/Faulkner Award, 254
Pend Oreille-Clark Fork River, 501
Penicillin, 231, 579, 685
Penn, William, 148
Pennsylvania, 169–170
Pennyweight, 454, 456
Pension Benefit Guaranty Corporation, 83
Pentagon, 82
  bombing, 211, 224
Pentagon Papers, 690
Pentecost, 344, 354, 355
People, 281–315, 955–959, 1029, 1030
People's Party (Populists), 52
Per capita income, 629
  by countries, 721–904
  by states, 629
Pérez de Cuéllar, Javier, 905
Performers. *See* People
Pericles, 670
Perihelion, 351, 397
Period (punctuation), 473
Periodic law, 581
Periodic table, 571, 572
Periodic table, development of, 581
Permian Period, 575
Perón, Juan D., 305, 689, 726
Persia, ancient, 669
Persia, modern. *See* Iran
Persian Gulf States. *See* United Arab Emirates
Persian Gulf War, 99, 696, 698, 794, 809
Peru, 485, 843–844
Pesticides, 586
Petition, right of, 113
Petrified Forest National Park, 593
Petronas Towers, 445
Pets:
  names, 139
  ownership, 139
Pharos of Alexandria, 443
Phelps, Michael, 19, 1033
Philadelphia, Pa., 169, 179, 197–198, 677
  Continental Congresses in, 101
  Liberty Bell, 104, 170
Philippines, 694, 844–845
  as U.S. Territory, 96, 102
Philosophers. *See* People
Phnom Penh, Cambodia, 693, 742
Phoenician Empire, 669
Phoenix, Ariz., 144, 179, 198
  climate of, 605
Phoenix Islands, 805
Phonographs, invention of, 681
Photographic equipment, export and import of, 641
Photography:
  first aerial, 435
  inventions, 581, 681
  Pulitzer Prizes for, 236–237
Photosphere, 399
Phrases, foreign, 478–480
Phyrgian civilization, 669
Physical activity, 559
Physical Fitness and Sports, President's Council on, 83

Physics:
  inventions and discoveries, 579–583
  Nobel Prizes for, 226–228
Physiology, Nobel Prizes for, 230–233
Pi (measure), 458
Picasso, Pablo, 686
Piccard, Bertrand, 439
Pierce, Franklin, 52, 56, 62, 95. *See also* Presidents, U.S.
Pierre, S.D., 171, 172, 179
Pigs, 590, 591, 645
Pikes Peak, 147, 185, 502
Pilcomayo River, 495
Pilgrimage sites, 370
Pilgrims, 157, 183, 675
Pindus Mountains, 781
Pinochet, Augusto, 749
Pioneer space program, 425, 426
Pisa, Leaning Tower of, 443
Pitcairn Island, 677, 892
Pittsburgh, Pa., 169
Pizarro, Francisco, 305, 485, 674, 764, 843, 866
Plague, 671, 673, 675, 884
Planck, Max, 227, 305, 582
Planets, 401–413
  basic data, 406
  configurations of, 417–420
  conjunctions, 397, 417–420
  defined, 397
  exploration of, 423–427
  extrasolar, 397
  minor planets (asteroids), 413–414
  moons of, 400, 405–412
  origin of, 398
  visibility, 420
Plantagenet, House of, 884
Plants:
  classification of, 580
  endangered species, 591
Plastics, invention of, 582
Plata River, 739, 897
Plate-tectonics theory, 487
Plato, 305, 670
Platte River, 501
Plays, longest Broadway runs, 271
Playwrights. *See* People; Theater
Pledge of allegiance to flag, 104
Pleistocene Period, 576
Plessy v. *Ferguson*, 92
Plow, invention of, 582
Pluto (planet), 400, 406, 413, 577. *See also* Planets
Plutonium, 572, 574, 582
Plymouth Colony, 157, 675
Plymouth Rock, 675
Pocahontas, 675
Pocket veto, 80
Poetry, awards for, 244, 257
Poets. *See* People
Poets laureate:
  of England, 270
  of U.S., 271
Point Four Program, 688
Poisons, treatment of, 562
Poland, 683, 686, 845–846
  Kosciusko uprising (1794), 677
  partition of, 677
  Poznan uprising (1956), 689
  Solidarity Union, 846
  workers strikes in, 846
  in World War II, 686, 779
Polar flights, first, 436, 438
Polar regions, 497. *See also* Antarctica; Arctic Circle
Policemen, statistics, 384
Poliomyelitis, 213, 582, 688
Political parties:
  in U.S.. *See* specific parties
  world, 721–904
Polk, James Knox, 52, 54, 56, 61–62, 95. *See also* Presidents, U.S.
Poll tax, 117
Pollution, 585–589
  automobile, 616
  carbon dioxide, 587

cities, 588
greenhouse gases, 589
pesticides, 586
Polo, Marco, 305, 484, 673
Pol Pot, 693, 743, 901
Polynesia, French, 775
Pompeii, 211
Pompidou, Georges, 773
Ponce de León, Juan, 148
Pontiffs, Roman Catholic, 366–368
Pony Express, 160
Popes, 366–368
  John Paul I, 368, 693, 899
  John Paul II, 368, 693, 899
  John XXIII, 368, 690, 899
  Paul VI, 368, 690, 693, 899
Popular vote, 43, 44, 49, 52–54, 55
Population, U.S., 119–124, 143–178
  by age, 120, 122, 123, 124
  age 65 and over, 143–178
  of American Indians, 378, 379
  and ancestry, 375, 376
  and Asians, U.S., 377, 378
  black, 120, 122, 123, 143–178, 377
  census required by Constitution, 108
  in census years, 123
  cities: largest of each state, 143–178, 179
  colonial estimates, 122
  densities (1790–2000), 123
  distribution, 123
  ethnicity, 375–376, 377
  foreign-born, 123, 376
  growth of, 121, 123
  Hispanic origin, 120, 122, 143–178, 375, 377
  immigrants, 376
  languages spoken, 375
  and Pacific islanders, 378
  persons below poverty level, 630
  persons living alone, 126
  by race, 120, 122, 143–178, 377
  ratio of males to females, 122
  by region, 122
  by sex, 120, 122
  of states, 121
  of territories, 121, 893–896
  total U.S., 119, 120, 121
  urban, 207–209
Population, U.S. cities:
  by age, 181–205
  black, 181–205
  cities, largest, 181–205, 206
  Hispanic origin, 181–205
  by race, 181–205
Population, world, 706, 709–710, 721–904
  cities, 708
  cities, by countries, 721–904
  of countries, 709–710, 721–904
  densities, 721–904
  urban areas, 708
  world's highest and lowest densities, 707
Populists. *See* People's Party
Porcupine River, 501
Port-au-Français, French Southern and Antarctic Lands, 775
Port-au-Prince, Haiti, 786
Portland, Maine, 155, 179
Portland, Ore., 169, 179, 198–199
Port Louis, Mauritius, 822
Port Moresby, Papua New Guinea, 841
Port-of-Spain, Trinidad and Tobago, 877
Porto-Novo, Benin, 735
Ports, world sea, 646
Portsmouth, Treaty of, 163
Portugal, 846–847
Portuguese Guinea. *See* Guinea-Bissau
Portuguese West Africa. *See* Angola
Port Vila, Vanuatu, 898
Positron, 582
Post, Wiley, 306, 437
Postal Rate Commission, 83

Postal regulations, 440–442
Postal Service, U.S., 83, 676
  rates, 440–442
Postmasters General, 83, 88
Post Office. See Postal Service, U.S.
Postojna Grotto, 497
Potatoes, economic statistics, 645
Potomac River, 204, 501
Potsdam Conference, 686
Poultry, U.S. consumption of, 642
Poverty, 630–633
  level, 630
  people and families in, 630, 631
  population in, 630
  by state, 632
  thresholds, 630
  in U.S., 630
Poverty, worldwide, 714
Powder River, 501
Powell, Colin, 696
Power failure of 1965 (Ontario), 691
Power looms, 581
Prague, Czech Republic, 760
Praia, Cape Verde, 746
Preakness Stakes, 981

Preakness Stakes, 979
Precambrian, 575
Precipitation. See Rainfall
Preemptive strike, 389
Prefix, 480
Pregnancy:
  cigarette smoking during, 131
  teen, 130
Premiers and prime ministers:
  of Canada, 745
  of countries, 721–904
  of Great Britain, 886
  of Soviet Union, 851
Preparatory schools, fundraising,
  320
Presbyterian churches, 362, 674
Preserves, National, 594
Presidential Medal of Freedom, 261
Presidents, foreign, 721–904, 771–
  776
Presidents, U.S. See also Presidential
  candidates; Presidential elections
  assassinations and attempts on, 118
  biographies of, 58–76
  cabinets under, 84–89
  constitutional provisions about, 111
  of Continental Congresses, 101
  election (2004), 33, 35–42, 43, 44
  election of, 43, 44, 49, 51–54, 55
  election procedure for, 49, 111, 114
  families of, 58
  list of, 56
  minority (electoral), 54
  Mount Rushmore carvings, 172
  National Historic Sites, 594
  nomination of, 49
  oath of office of, 111
  powers and duties of, 111–112
  presidential libraries, 57
  qualifications of, 111
  religious affiliations of, 56
  salary of, 79, 111
  succession to, 81, 111, 116, 117
  tabulated data about, 56
  term of office of, 56, 111, 116
  vetoes, 80
  wives and children of, 58
President's Council on Physical
  Fitness and Sports, 83
Press, freedom of, 113, 676
Price indexes:
  consumer, 639
  farm, 644
  producer, 640
Prices, historical food, 641
Prime meridian, 486
Prime numbers, 452
Prince Edward Island, Canada, 745
Prince of Wales, 883n
Prince of Wales Trophy, 961
Princeton University, 319

Príncipe, 855–856
Printing, 582
Printz, Michael L., book awards, 257
Prisoners:
  federal prisons, 382
  jail inmates, 382
  under sentence of death, 383
  state prisons, 382
  statistics, 382
Prisoners of war, 391
Prizes. See Awards
Probes, lunar and deep space,
  425–427
Production indexes, U.S. industries,
  640. See also specific industries and
  products
Product recalls, 655
Professional Golfers Association
  (P.G.A.) Champions, 995
Profiles:
  of U.S., 119, 120
  of world, 706
Programming, computer, 579
Progressive Party:
  national conventions, 50
  presidential candidates, 53
Prohibition, 97, 115, 684, 685
Promontory Summit, 174
Propeller, screw, 582
Prostitution, arrests for, 387
Proterozoic Eon, 575
Protestant churches, U.S., 362
Protestantism, 358, 362
  Reformation, 362, 779
Proton, discovery of, 582
Providence, R.I., 170, 179
Prudhoe Bay, Alaska, 144
Prussia, 779
Psychoanalysis, development of, 582
Public assistance, 632
Public debt, 635
Publishing:
  best-selling books, 266
  magazines, 277–278
  newspapers, 277
Pueblo (ship), 691
Puerto Rico, 98, 893–894
  holidays in, 356
Pulitzer Prizes, 234–247
Pullman strike, 681
Pulsars, 397
Punctuation, rules for, 473–474
Punic Wars, 670
Punjab, 484, 838
Purim, 344, 353, 355
Puritan Commonwealth, 884
Puritans, 183
Purus River, 495
Putin, Vladimir, 35, 701, 849, 851,
  1033
Pyongyang, North Korea, 688, 806
Pyramids of Egypt, 443, 668
Pythagoras, 669

Q

Qaddafi, Muammar, 34, 510, 748, 814
Qaeda, al-, 100, 223, 224, 703, 704,
  717, 722, 827
Qatar, 847–848
Quakers. See Friends
Quantum theory, 582
Quart, 451, 453, 456, 457
Quarters, U.S., 453
Quasars, 397
Quayle, J. Danforth, 57
Quebec, Canada, 744–746
  city, 744
  province, 744
Queen Anne's War, 676
Queens (NYC), 195–196
Queensberry Rules, 972
Queens of England, 885
Question mark (punctuation), 473
Quisling, Maj. Vidkun, 837
Quito, Ecuador, 764

Quiz show, first panel, 100
Quotation marks (punctuation), 474
Qur'an. See Koran
Qurei, Amhed, 840

R

Rabat, Morocco, 827
Rabies, immunization, 582
Rabin, Yitzhak, 698
Race and ethnicity, 375–381
Racial statistics:
  arrests, 387
  educational attainment, 316, 317
  employment, 624
  hate crimes, 386
  life expectancy, 136
  population, 120, 122, 377, 378, 379
Racing. See Auto racing; Canoe
  racing; Harness racing
Radar, 582
Radiation, neutron-induced, 581
Radio:
  awards for, 259, 260
  first station licensed, 100
  Internet, 563
  inventions, 582
  most played songs, 272
  stations in U.S., 119, 181–205
Radioactivity, 582, 682
Radiocarbon dating, development of,
  582
Railroad Retirement Board, U.S., 83
Railroads:
  accidents and deaths, 211, 221–222
  fatalities, 613
  first passenger service, 678
  firsts in, 96, 100, 678
  ridership, 617
Railroad tunnels, 450
Rainfall:
  extremes, 599
  greatest, 600
  lowest precipitation, 600
  in U.S. cities, 604–605
Rainier, Mount, 176, 502, 503
Raleigh, N.C., 166, 179
Ramadan, 344, 354, 355
Ramakrishna, 363
Ramayana, 363
Ranger space program, 425
Rangoon (Yangon), Myanmar, 828
Rape, 387
Rather, Dan, 42, 1033
Reactors, nuclear, 216
Reading statistics, 265
Reagan, Nancy Davis, 58
Reagan, Ronald, 39, 54, 55, 57, 71,
  99, 517, 1038. See also Presidents,
  U.S.
  assassination attempt on, 71, 99,
  118, 693
  funeral, 517
Reaper, invention of, 582
Reconstruction, 681
Reconstruction Finance Corporation
  (1932), 685
Recording Industry Association of
  America, 272
Records, 272
  aviation, 439
  sports. See under specific sports
Recreation Areas, National, 596
Red Cross, American, 83, 665
Red Guards, 750
Red River (Minn.-Manitoba), 501
Red River (N.M.-La.), 501
Red Rock River, 495, 501
Red Sea, 494
Redwood National Park, 593
Reeve, Christopher, 1038
Reformation, 360, 362, 674, 779
Refugees, 716
Rehnquist, William H., 90–91, 695
Reichstag fire, 685
Reign of Terror (1793–94), 677

Relativity theories, 582, 682
Religion, 358–370. See also specific
  religions and churches
  churches in U.S., 181–205, 361
  freedom of religion, 113
  history of world, 359–365
  holidays, 353–355
  holy sites, 370
  largest religions, 359
  popes, 366–368
  practice by country, 721–904
  in U.S., 360, 366
Religious affiliations:
  of presidents, 56
  of Supreme Court justices, 90–91
Renaissance, 673, 674
  architecture, 444
Reparations (World War I), 684
Reporting, Pulitzer Prizes for,
  237–240
Representatives. See House of
  Representatives, U.S.
Reptiles, Age of, 575
Republic, oldest, 855
Republican Party:
  founding of, 679
  members of Congress, 45–48
  National Committee chairmen, 50
  national conventions, 50, 694, 695
  presidential candidates, 51–54
  Senate floor leaders, 77
Republican River, 501
Rescue breathing, 561
Reservations, U.S. Indian, 145, 379
Reserves, National, 594
Réunion, 774
Revenue:
  bills for raising of, 109
  national, 636
Revolutionary War, American, 94, 677
Revolvers, 582
Reykjavik, Iceland, 788
Rhine River, 771, 779, 831, 871
Rhode Island, 170–171
Rhodes, Cecil, 307, 865, 903, 904
Rhodes, Colossus at, 443
Rhodesia, 691. See also Zambia;
  Zimbabwe
Rhône River, 771
Ribbon Falls, 496
Rice, export and import of, 641
Richmond, Va., 175, 179
Richter scale, 490
Ride, Sally K., 101, 694
Riga, Latvia, 810
Rio de Janeiro, Brazil, 739
Rio de la Plata, 897
Rio Grande, 495, 501
Río Muni, 767
Rivers:
  U.S., 500–501
  world, 495
Rivers, National, 595
Riyadh, Saudi Arabia, 856
Riyadh bombing (2003), 857
Roanoke Island, 166
Roanoke River, 166, 501
Robbery, 387
Robinson projection, 486
Rock and Roll Hall of Fame, 168, 274
Rockefeller, John D., 307
Rockefeller, Nelson A., 57, 98
Rocket engine flight, first, 437
Rocky Mountain National Park, 593,
  596
Rocky Mountains, 147
Roebling, John, 584
Roentgen, Wilhelm Konrad, 226, 307,
  582, 681
Roe v. Wade, 92, 373
Roller bearing, 582
Roman Catholic Church:
  Council of Nicaea, 360, 671
  Council of Trent, 348, 674
  description of, 361–362
  Great Schism, 673
  hierarchy, 361

history of, 360–362
  Inquisition, 673, 675
  in Italy, 694
  membership in, 361
  popes, 361, 366–368, 899
  Vatican City, 444, 899
  Vatican Council I, 362
  Vatican Council II, 362, 690, 694,
    899
Roman Empire, 669, 670
  mythology, 467–470
  structures, 443
Romanesque architecture, 443–444
Romania, 848–849
Roman numerals, 452
Rome, Italy, 799
  architecture, 443, 443–444
  founding of, 669
  in World War II, 686
Rookie of the Year (baseball), 1014
Roosevelt, Eleanor, 58, 67, 308
Roosevelt, Franklin D., 53, 56, 57,
  66–67, 97, 149, 165, 166. See also
  Presidents, U.S.
  assassination attempt on, 118
  birthday, 356
Roosevelt, Theodore, 53, 56, 64–65,
  96, 225. See also Presidents, U.S.
  assassination attempt on, 118
Roots, word, 480–481
Roseau, Dominica, 762
Rose Bowl, 932
Rosenberg, Julius and Ethel, 98, 688
Roses, Wars of the, 673, 884
Rosh Hashanah, 344, 354, 355
Ross, Betsy, 308
Ross Trophy, 962
Rota (island), 895
Rotary International, 666
Rough Riders, 65
Rowing, 928
Rowley, Coleen, 703
Royalty, 673, 772, 851, 885
Rubber, vulcanized, 582
Ruby, Jack, 68, 118, 690
Rulers, 721–904
  monarchs, contemporary, 713
  monarchs, historical, 772, 851, 885
  most corrupt, 713
Rumania. See Romania
Rumsfeld, Donald, 42, 389, 705, 1033
Running. See Track and field
Rupert's Land, 745
Rushmore, Mount, 172
Russia, 33, 40, 849–852
  Beslan, 42, 852
  Chechen war, 851
  financial crisis (1998), 851
  history of, 849–852
  Kremlin (structure), 443
  Revolution, 683, 849
  rulers of, 851
  structures, 443
  in World War I, 683, 849
  in World War II, 686, 850
Russo-Finnish War, 686, 771, 850
Russo-Japanese War, 65, 163, 682,
  802, 849
Russo-Turkish War, 681, 879
Rwanda, 698, 699, 852–853
Ryukyu Islands, 801

S

Sabah, Malaysia, 740, 819
Sabine River, 501
Sabin vaccine, 582
Sacco-Vanzetti case, 684
Sacramento, Calif., 146, 179, 199
Sacramento River, 501
Sacred sites, 370
Sadat, Anwar el-, 308, 693, 765–766,
  798
Sadr, Moktada al-, 37, 39, 42, 390,
  795, 1033
Sahara, 484, 498, 723, 814, 878

Saigon, Vietnam. See Ho Chi Minh
  City
Sailing, 928
St. Bartholomew's Day Massacre,
  674
St. Christopher-Nevis. See St. Kitts
  and Nevis
St. Croix, V.I., 895
Saint-Denis, Réunion, 774
Saint Francis River, 501
St. George's, Grenada, 782
St. Helena, 678, 892
St. Helens, Mount, 176
St. John, V.I., 895
St. John's, Antigua and Barbuda, 725
St. John the Divine, Cathedral of,
  445
St. Kitts and Nevis, 853–854
St. Lawrence River, 484, 495, 744
St. Lawrence Seaway, 165, 450, 689
St. Louis, Mo., 160, 199–200
St. Lucia, 854
St. Mark's Cathedral, 443
St. Mihiel, Battle of, 683
St. Patrick's Day, 344, 353
St. Paul, Minn., 158, 179
St. Peter, Basilica of, 444, 674
St. Petersburg, Russia, 849. See also
  Leningrad
St. Pierre and Miquelon, 776
St. Thomas, V.I., 895
St. Valentine's Day, 344, 353
St. Valentine's Day Massacre, 685
St. Vincent and the Grenadines,
  854–855
Saipan, 896
Sakhalin, 496
Saladin, 672
Salamis, Battle of, 670
Salaries:
  of government officials, 79
  minimum wages, 628
  by occupation, 624
  wage gap, 373, 374
  women's, 620
Salem, Ore., 169, 179
Salisbury, Zimbabwe. See Harare,
  Zimbabwe
Salk vaccine, 582, 688
Salmon River, 501
SALT. See Strategic Arms Limitation
  Talks
Salt Lake City, Utah, 174, 179
Salvador, El. See El Salvador
Salvation Army, 666
Salween River, 495
Same-sex unions and marriages, 33,
  36, 38, 371, 372, 701, 746
Samoa, 855
Samoa, American, 895
Sanaá, Yemen, 902
San Antonio, Tex., 173, 200
San Diego, Calif., 146, 200–201
Sandinista guerrillas, 834
Sandwich Islands, 150
San Francisco, Calif., 146, 201
  climate, 605
  earthquakes, 96, 211, 212, 682
  Golden Gate Bridge, 445, 447
Sanger, Margaret, 372
San Jacinto, Battle of, 173, 679
San Joaquin River, 501
San Jose, Calif., 146, 201–202
San José, Costa Rica, 756
San Juan River, 501
San Marino, 855
San Salvador, El Salvador, 766
San Stefano, Treaty of, 681
Santa Claus, 355
Santa Fe, N.M., 164, 179
Santee-Wateree-Catawba River, 501
Santiago, Chile, 758
Santiago de Compostela, Spain, 370
Santiago de Cuba, 758
Santo Domingo, Dominican
  Republic, 763
São Francisco River, 495

São Tomé and Príncipe, 855–856
Sappho of Lesbos, 669
Sarajevo, Bosnia, 737
Saratoga, Battle of, 676
Sarawak, Malaysia, 740, 819
Sardinia, 671, 800
SARS, 551
Saskatchewan, Canada, 745
Saskatchewan River, 495
Satellite radio, 563
Satellites (moons), 400, 405–412
  defined, 398
  exploration of, 425–427
  orbits defined, 397
Satellites, scientific, 689
SAT scores, 318
"Saturday Night Massacre", 692
Saturn (planet), 400, 406, 408–410.
  See also Planets
  exploration of, 39, 421–422, 423,
    426, 514
Saudi Arabia, 33, 856–857
Sault Ste. Marie Canal, 158, 744
Savimbi, Jonas, 724
Savings bank, first in U.S., 100
Saxe-Coburg, House of, 884
Scalia, Antonin, 1034
Scenic Trails, National, 596
Schism, Great, 673
Schmidt, Helmut, 780
Schools. See also Colleges and
    universities; Education
  first public, 100
  and Supreme Court, 688, 690, 691,
    693, 694
Schröder, Gerhard, 700, 780
Schuman Plan (1951), 688
Schwarzenegger, Arnold, 705
Science, 569–576. See also
    Chemistry; Mathematics; Medicine;
    Physics
  branches of, 576
  chemical elements, 573–574
  classification, 570
  Fermi Award, 260
  human ancestors, 570
  inventions and discoveries, 577–583
  metric system, 454, 455–457
  Nobel Prizes, 225–233
  recent discoveries, 577–579
  transfermium elements, 573
  websites, 579
  weights and measures, 451–458
Science and Technology, Office of,
    81
Scientific classification, 570
Scientific instruments, export and
    import of, 641
Scopes Monkey Trial, 97, 684
Scotland, 676, 883, 888
Scott, Dred, 92, 679
Screw propeller, 582
Scythian civilization, 669
Seaborg, Glenn, 571
Seal of U.S., Great, 104
Sea ports, 646
Sears Tower, 445
Seas, 494
Seashores, National, 595
Seasons, 351, 402
Seat belts, 614
SEATO. See Southeast Asia Treaty
    Organization
Seattle, Wash., 176, 179, 202
  climate of, 605
Secondary schools, funding, 318
Secretaries-General, UN, 905
Securities and Exchange
    Commission (SEC), 83
Security Council, National, 81
Security Council, UN, 905
Sedna (planetoid), 577
Seine River, 771
Selassie, Haile. See Haile Selassie I
Selective Service System (SSS), 83,
    687
Seljuk Turks, 672

Selma, Ala., 143
Semicolon (punctuation), 474
Senate, U.S., 45–46, 108, 111. See
    also Congress, U.S.
  birthdates of members, 45–46
  committees of, 76
  eligibility for, 108
  first black member, 100
  first woman member, 101
  floor leaders of, 77
  impeachment cases heard by, 109
  members, 45–46
Seneca Falls convention, 166, 372
Senegal, 857–858
Senior citizens, population
    characteristics, 124
Seoul, South Korea, 807
  subway system, 612
Sepoy Mutiny, 679, 789
Sept. 11, 2001, attacks, 100, 211, 224,
    703, 722, 857
Sept. 11 commission, 36, 39, 509,
    1032
Serbia, 858
Serbia and Montenegro, 858–859
Service academies, 395
Seven Cities of Gold, 145
Seven Deadly Sins, 369
Seven summits, 493
Seven Weeks' War, 680
Seven Wonders of the World, 443
Seven Years' War, 676, 745
Seward, William H., 85, 118, 144
"Seward's Folly", 144
Sexes, distribution by:
  educational attainment, 316, 317
  life expectancy, 135, 136
  marriage statistics, 127
  median age at first marriage, 127
  sex ratios at birth, 129
  wages, 373, 374
Sex offenses, arrests for, 387
Sexual activity, U.S., 372
Sexual harassment, 698
Sexually transmitted diseases
    (STDs), 556
Sexual partners, 372
Seychelles, 860
Shah of Iran (Mohammad Reza
    Pahlavi), 693, 792
Shang Dynasty, 669
Shanghai, China, 749, 750
Shannon River, 796
Sharon, Ariel, 35, 37, 702, 704, 797,
    799, 1034
Shasta, Mount, 502
Shatt-al-Arab, 794
Shavuot, 344, 354, 355
Shays's Rebellion, 94
Shemini Atzeret, 354
Shenandoah (dirigible), 219
Shenandoah National Park, 175
Shepard, Alan B., Jr., 427, 428, 689
Sherman, William T., 149, 168
Sherman Antitrust Act, 681
Shetland Islands, 484, 888
Shiite, 363
Shikoku, Japan, 801
Shintoism, 365
Ship canals, 450
Shipping, commerce, 646
Ships. See Steamships
Shipwrecks, 211, 218–219
Shock, treatment of, 562
"Shock and awe", 389
Shooting stars, 415
Shoreline of U.S., 502
Shrove Tuesday, 353, 355n
Siam. See Thailand
Sicily, 671, 682, 800
Sidereal time, 349, 399
Sierra Leone, 484, 860–861
Sign language, 482
Sihanouk, Norodom, 743
Sikh festival dates, 356
Sikhism, 364
Sikh Rebellion (India), 694, 790

Sikkim, Kingdom of, 790
Silurian Period, 575
Silver, 574
Simchat Torah, 354, 355
Simplon Tunnels, 450
Simpson, O. J., 698
Sinai Peninsula, 689, 691, 765–766,
    798
Singapore, 686, 819, 861
Singers. See People
Singh, Manmohan, 38, 511, 1034
Singing Cave, 497
Sino-Japanese War (1894–95), 681,
    750
Sins, Seven Deadly, 369
Sioux Falls, S.D., 172, 179
Sirhan, Sirhan Bishara, 118, 691
Sistani, Ayatollah Ali al-, 389, 795
Sistine Chapel, 444, 674
Six-Day War, 691, 798. See also
    Arab-Israeli conflict
Skating, ice, 928, 931, 968–969,
    969–970
Skiing, 929, 966–968
Skopje, Macedonia, 816
Skylab, 428
Skyscrapers, 445–446
  first, 101
Slavery:
  abolished in British Empire, 679
  Dred Scott case, 679
  first slaves to America, 94, 101, 175,
    673
  first state to forbid, 175
  importation barred to U.S., 678
  Kansas-Nebraska Act, 679
  prohibited in U.S., 96, 114
Slovakia, 861–862
Slovenia, 862–863
Small Business Administration
    (SBA), 83
Smallpox, 551, 583, 677
Smith, Bessie, 684
Smith, John, 156, 163
Smith, Joseph, 151, 175
Smithsonian Institution, 84
Smoking, 551, 558
Smoky Hill River, 501
Snake River, 501
Snowdon, Mount, 889
Snowfalls, greatest, 599
Snyder-Gray case, 684
Soccer, 1023
  Major League, 1023
  World Cup, 1023
Socialist parties, U.S., 53
Social security, 633–634
  benefits, 634
  Social Security Act, 633–634
Societies and associations, 658–667
Society Islands, 775
Socrates, 310, 670
Sofia, Bulgaria, 740
Software, top-selling, 568
Solar-powered aircraft, 438
Solar system, 399–413, 583
Solar time, 349, 399
Solomon Islands, 863
Solon, 669
Solstices, 348, 402, 417–420
Somalia, 863–864
Somaliland, French. See Djibouti
Somme, Battle of the, 683
Somoza Debayle, Gen. Anastasio,
    693, 834
Songs:
  most downloaded, 272
  state, 143–178
  worst, 273
Sonoran Desert, 498
"Sooners", 168
Sophocles, 310, 670
Sorority, first, 101
Sosa, Sammy, 958, 1015
Sound:
  first flight faster than, 437
  speed of, 458

South Africa, Republic of, 682, 864–866
  Truth and Reconciliation Commission, 865
South America. *See also* Continents
  area and elevation of, 487
  exploration of, 485
  map of, 529
  southernmost point of, 749
South Carolina, 171
South China Sea, 494
South Dakota, 171–172
Southeast Asia Treaty Organization (SEATO), 688
Southeast Asia War. *See* Vietnam War
Southern Cameroons. *See* Nigeria
"Southern lights", 416
Southern Ocean, 494
Southern Rhodesia. *See* Zimbabwe
South Georgia, 892
South Island (New Zealand), 496, 833
South Platte River, 501
South Pole:
  exploration of, 485
  first flight over, 437
  geography of, 497
  reached, 682
South Sandwich Islands, 892
South West Africa. *See* Namibia
Soviet Union, 721, 850–851
  Afghanistan invasion, 693
  Germany, nonaggression pact with (1939), 686
  hydrogen bomb, 688, 689
  Korean Airlines incident, 694
  nuclear weapons testing, 688
  in World War II, 686
Soybeans, export and import of, 641
Soyuz space flights, 429, 430, 431, 434
Space. *See also* Astronomy
Space accidents, 221
Space exploration, 421–434
  astronauts, 427–429
  of Jupiter, 425–427
  of Mars, 423, 424
  of Mercury, 424
  Moon landings and explorations, 424, 425–427
  of Saturn, 423, 426
  Soviet space program, 429
  space shuttles, 429, 431, 694
  staffed flights, 430–434
  of the Sun, 423, 424, 425–427
  U.S. staffed flight programs, 427–429
  unstaffed flights, 425–427
  women in space program, 428
Space Needle (Seattle), 445
Spain, 866–867
  Arabs in, 671
  civil war in, 686, 866
  Cuban rebellion from, 681
  exploration by, 674
  French occupation of, 678
  loss of New World colonies, 676, 678
  Madrid bombing (2004), 36, 37, 510, 1032
  Phoenician colony in, 669
  republic in, 685
  revolution in, 680
  Spanish Armada defeated, 675, 866, 884
  structures, 444
Spanish-American War, 96, 681, 682
Spanish Armada, 675, 866, 884
Spanish Civil War, 686, 866
Spanish influenza, 211, 213
Spanish Succession, War of, 676
Sparta, 670
Spartacus, 670
Speakers of the House, 77
Species, endangered, 591
Speech, freedom of, 113
Speed:
  of animals, 590
  of light, 399
Speed limits, 614

Speed records:
  airplanes, 439
  sports. *See* under individual sports
Speed skating, 929, 931, 968–969
Spelling bee, 475
Spermatozoa, 583
Sphinx, Great, 443, 668
Spingarn Medal, 258
Spinning, inventions, 583
Spiral nebula, 397
Spirit of St. Louis (plane), 436
Spitsbergen Islands, 485, 837
Sports, 915–1023. *See also* individual sports
  disasters, 223
  Olympic Games, 915–932
  personalities, 955–959
Springfield, Ill., 151, 179
Spring tides, 401
Sputnik I (satellite), 689, 850
Sri Jayawardenepura Kotte, Sri Lanka, 867
Sri Lanka, 496, 867–868
Stalin, Joseph, 310, 684, 686, 687, 688, 850
Stalingrad, Battle of, 686
Stamp Act, 676
Stamps, postage, 100, 440–442
Standard of living, world, 713
Standard Oil Trust, 681
Standard time, 349–350
Stanford University, 319
Stanley Cup, 960, 963
Stanton, Elizabeth Cady, 96, 372
Stardust space mission, 424
Starr, Kenneth, 72–74
Stars, 398, 399–400
  birth and death of, 398
  brightest, 400
  constellations, 400, 415–416
  defined, 398
  neutron, 397
"Stars" of entertainment. *See* People
"Star-Spangled Banner", 95, 97, 104, 105, 182
START. *See* Strategic Arms Reduction Talks
State, Secretaries of (U.S. states), 143–178
State, U.S. Dept. of:
  description of, 82
  secretaries of, 82, 84–89, 101, 699
Staten Island, 195–196
States, Confederate, 96, 102
States of U.S., 143–180
  agricultural production of, 645
  births and birth rates, 128
  capitals, 143–178, 179
  cities: largest of each state, 143–178, 179
  coastlines, 502
  colleges and universities, 321–343
  Congress members, 45–48
  constitutional provisions about, 110, 112
  crime index, 387
  deaths and death rates, 134
  execution methods, 384
  first, 101, 102
  governors of, 48, 143–178
  health insurance, 555, 556
  holidays, 356
  land and water area of, 179
  motor vehicle laws, 614
  newspapers, 277
  order of entry into Union, 102
  per capita personal income, 629
  populations of, 121, 143–178
  poverty in, 632
  presidential election results (2004), 43, 44
  procedure for admitting new states to, 112
  Representatives, 46–48
  Senators, 45–46
  taxes. *See* Taxes

  taxes collected and spent, federal, 1028
  temperature highs and lows, 601–602
  thirteen original, 108
States' rights, 110, 112, 114
States' Rights Democratic Party, 53
Statistics, U.S., 119–142
Statistics, world, 706–720
Statue of Liberty, 165, 594, 681
Steam engines, 583, 677
Steam heat, first, 101
Steamships, 583
  disasters, 211, 218–219
Steel, export and import of, 641
Steinem, Gloria, 373
Stem cells, 569–570
Stewart, Martha, 37, 511, 1034
Stikine River, 501
Stimulants (drugs), 557
Stock-car racing, 998, 999
Stockholm, Sweden, 870
Stock market:
  most active stocks, 649, 650
  top stocks (by dollar value), 649
  top stocks (by market value), 650
Stolen identity, 652–653
Stonehenge, 668
Stone Mountain, 149
Storms, 214–215
Strategic Arms Limitation Talks (SALT), 693, 850
Strategic Arms Reduction Talks (START), 696, 697
Stratopause, 402
Stratosphere, 402
  first flight into, 437
Strikes (labor), 625
  first in U.S., 101
Structures, 445
  ancient, 443–445
  bridges, 447–448
  buildings, 445–446
  canals, 450
  dams, 449
  famous, 443–445
  museums, 444, 445
  Seven Wonders, 443
  towers, 446
  tunnels, 450
Stuart, House of, 884
Students, 316–343
  in educational institutions, 317
  with disabilities, 317
Style guide (writing), 472–474
Submarines, 683
  disasters, 211, 218–219
  first atomic powered, 688
Subways:
  commuter use, 612
  first in U.S., 101
  world's largest, 612
Sucre, Bolivia, 736
Sudan, 34, 868–869
  Darfur, 34, 38, 39, 40, 41, 484, 511, 869
Suez Canal, 450, 679, 680, 689, 765, 766, 798
Suffix, 480
Suffragists, 683
Sugar:
  export and import of, 641
  U.S. consumption of, 642
Sugar Bowl (football), 933
Suharto, 791
Suicide, 136, 138
Sukarno, 791
Sukkot, 354, 355
Sulawesi (Celebes), 496
Suleiman I ("the Magnificent"), 674
Sulfa drugs, 583
Sulfur dioxide, 589
Sumatra, 496, 791
Sumerian civilization, 669
Sun, 398, 399–400
  eclipses of, 420

exploration of, **423, 424, 425–427**
phenomena, **417–420**
seasons, **351**
time based on, **349**
Sungari River, **495**
Sunni, **363**
Sunspots, **399**
Sun Yat-sen, **311, 682, 750**
Super Bowl, **939, 940**
Superfund sites, **585–587**
Superior, Lake, **158, 494, 744**
Supernovas, **398**
Supersonic aircraft, **437, 438**
Supreme Court, U.S., **90–94, 94**
   constitutional provisions about, **112**
   first black member, **100, 691**
   first law declared unconstitutional, **92, 100**
   first woman member, **99, 101, 693**
   justices of, **90–91, 691, 693, 695, 697, 698**
   major decisions, **380–381**
   milestone cases, **92, 682, 688, 691**
   notable decisions (2003–2004), **93–94**
   salaries of justices, **79**
Surgery, first antiseptic, **680**
Suriname, **869**
Surveying measures, **454**
Surveyor space program, **425, 426**
Susquehanna River, **501**
Sutter's Mill, **95, 146**
Suu Kyi, Aung San, **829**
Suva, Fiji, **770**
Sverdrup Islands, **745**
Swaziland, **869–870**
Sweden, **870–871**
Swimming, **921–926, 928, 970–972**
   synchronized, **928**
Swine, economic statistics, **645**
Switzerland, **871**
Sydney, Australia, **727**
Symbols of chemical elements, **572, 573–574**
Symphonies, **263**
Syndicated TV programs, **276**
Synodic month, **399**
Syphilis, **583**
Syria, **872**
   and Israel, **798, 812, 872**

T

Tabernacles, Feast of, **354, 355n**
Tabloid newspaper, first, **101**
Taft, William Howard, **53, 56, 65, 91, 96.** *See also* Presidents, U.S.
Tahiti, **775**
Taipei, Taiwan, **873**
Taiwan (Republic of China), **751, 873**
Tajikistan, **873–874**
Taj Mahal, **444, 675**
Taliban, **699, 703, 721–722**
Tallahassee, Fla., **148, 179**
Tallinn, Estonia, **768**
Talmud, **359**
Tamerlane, **312, 721**
Tamil Tiger guerrillas, **867**
Tanana River, **501**
Tanganyika. *See* Tanzania
Tanganyika, Lake, **484, 494**
T'ang Dynasty, **750**
Tannenberg, Battle of, **683**
Tanzania, **874–875**
Taoism, **365, 669**
Tarawa, Kiribati, **805**
Tar Creek, Okla., **585–587**
Tashkent, Uzbekistan, **897**
Tasmania, **485, 496, 727**
Tax cuts, **75**
Taxes, **1024–1028**
   Bush tax cuts, **32, 42, 1024**
   collection of, **1028**
   constitutional provisions for, **109, 110, 115, 117**
   corporation, **1025, 1028**
   estate, **1025, 1027**

franchise, **1028**
gift, **1025, 1027**
income tax, federal, **1024–1026**
income tax, history of, **1024**
Internal Revenue Service, **1024–1025**
returns filed electronically, **1026**
state, **1027, 1028**
Taxonomy, **570**
Taylor, Charles, **705, 813–814**
Taylor, Zachary, **52, 54, 56, 62, 95.** *See also* Presidents, U.S.
Tbilisi, Georgia, **777**
Teapot Dome scandal, **66, 97, 684**
Technology. *See* Computers
Teen birth rates, **130**
Teen pregnancy, **130**
Tegucigalpa, Honduras, **786**
Teheran, Iran, **792**
Teheran Conference (1943), **686**
Tektites, **415**
Telegraph:
   first transatlantic cable, **679**
   invention of, **583, 679**
Telephones:
   Bell System broken up, **694**
   invention of, **583, 681**
Telephone statistics, world, **718**
Telescopes. *See also* Hubble Space Telescope
Telescopes, invention of, **583**
Television, **275–276**
   awards for, **251, 258, 259, 260**
   first color, **688**
   inventions, **583, 684**
   network programs, **276**
   set ownership, **275**
   specials, **276**
   sports shows, **276**
   stations in U.S., **119, 181–205**
   syndicated programs, **276**
   viewing, **275**
Temperatures:
   extremes, U.S., **599, 600**
   extremes, world, **599, 600**
   record highs and lows, **599, 601–602, 603**
   scales, **451, 454**
   in U.S. cities, **181–205, 604–605**
   wind chill factors, **605**
   in world cities, **610**
Ten Commandments, **369, 669**
Tenet, George, **40, 1034**
Tennessee, **172–173**
Tennessee-French River, **501**
Tennessee River, **501**
Tennessee Valley Authority (TVA), **83, 173**
Tennis, **985–991**
Tenzing Norgay, **492**
Teotihuacán, **443, 670**
Territorial expansion of U.S., **102, 103**
Territories, **706**
Territories of U.S., **893–896**
   acquisition of, **102**
   execution methods, **384**
   governors of, **893–896**
   land areas, **102, 893–896**
   population, **121, 893–896**
Terrorism, **33, 211, 223–224, 681, 692, 694, 695, 697, 703, 721, 805, 812, 868, 875, 887, 899**
   Sept. 11, 2001, attacks, **100, 211, 224, 703, 722, 857**
Terrorist organizations, **716–718**
Texas, **173–174, 679**
Textiles:
   export and import of, **641**
   Producer Price index, **640**
Thailand, **875–876**
Thames River, **883**
Thanksgiving Day, **344, 354, 355**
Thant, U, **905**
Thatcher, Margaret, **693, 694, 696, 884**
Theater:
   awards for, **245–246, 251–252**

first vaudeville, **101**
longest Broadway runs, **271**
Theft, **387**
The Hague, The Netherlands, **831**
Theories, scientific, **579–583**
Thermodynamics, **583**
Thermometer:
   invention, **583**
   scales, **583**
Thermopause, **402**
Thermopylae, Battles of, **670**
Thermosphere, **402**
Thieu, Nguyen Van, **690, 901**
Thimphu, Bhutan, **735**
Third Estate, **677**
Thirty Years' War, **675, 779, 870**
Thomas, Norman, **53, 55**
Thomas Aquinas, **673**
Thorshavn, Faeroe Islands, **761**
Three Gorges dam, **449n**
Three Mile Island, **216, 693**
Tibet, **484, 750**
Tidal shoreline of U.S., **502**
Tidal waves, **213**
Tides, **401**
Tien Shan Mountains, **750, 809**
Tierra del Fuego, **749**
Tigris River, **495, 794**
Time:
   kinds of, **349**
   time of day, cities, **504**
   universal and civil, **349, 420**
   in world cities, **499**
Timelines:
   of civil rights, **380–381**
   of Iraq war, **389–390**
   of staffed space flights, **430–434**
   of U.S. history, **94–100**
   of unstaffed space flights, **425–427**
   of women's rights movement, **372–373**
   of world history, **668–705**
TIME Man of the Year, **1029**
Time zones, **349–350**
   map, **523**
Timor, East, **701, 791**
Tin, **572, 574**
Tinian (island), **896**
Tippecanoe, Battle of, **61, 152**
Tirana, Albania, **722**
Tires, pneumatic: invention of, **681**
Titan (moon), **409, 421**
Titanic (ocean liner), **218, 683**
Titanium, **572, 574**
Titicaca, Lake, **494, 736**
Title IX, **373**
Tito (Josip Broz), **312, 687, 859**
Titus, Arch of, **443**
Tobacco:
   taxes, **1025**
   use of, **558**
Tobago. *See* Trinidad and Tobago
Tocantins River, **495**
Togo, **876**
Tojo, Hideki, **687**
Tokelau Island, **833**
Tokyo, Japan, **675, 801**
   subway system, **612**
Toledo, Ohio, **167**
Tombigbee River, **501**
Ton:
   gross or long, **451, 456**
   metric, **451, 455, 456**
   net or short, **451, 456**
Tonga, **876–877**
Tony Awards, **251**
Topeka, Kans., **153, 179**
Torah, **354, 359**
Tornadoes, **211, 215–216, 599**
Toronto, Canada, **744**
Toulouse, France, **771**
Tourism, **607, 608, 609, 610**
Tower, Leaning, of Pisa, **443**
Tower of London, **444**
Towers, tallest, **446**
Toxic air pollutants, **589**

Toxic-waste dumps, 585–587
Toys and games, export and import of, 641
Track and field, 981–985
 history of mile run, 984
 mile records, 984
 Olympic Games, 915–921
 world and U.S. records, 981–984
Tractor, invented, 583
Trade. *See* Foreign trade
Trade Commission, Federal, 83
Trade Commission, U.S. International, 83
Trademarks, 657
Trade Representative, Office of U.S., 81
Trade unions, 626
Trafalgar, Battle of, 678
Traffic, 612
Trail of Tears, 95
Trans-Alaska pipeline, 144
Transarctic flight, first, 437
Transatlantic flights, 435–439
Transcontinental flights, 436, 438
Transistor, 583
Transpacific flights, 435–439
Transplants, organ, 555
Transportation. *See also* Aviation
 airlines, 611
 commuting, 612
 driving, 613, 614, 615, 616
 fatalities, 613
 inventions, 579–583
 railroads, 617
 subways, 612
Transportation, U.S. Dept. of:
 description of, 82
 secretaries of, 82, 88–89
Travel:
 current travel warnings, 609
 diplomatic personnel, 912–914
 foreign embassies, 908–911
 National parks, most visited, 596
 National Trust for Historic Preservation, 607
 temperatures in tourist cities, 610
 top destinations, 608, 609
 top states and cities visited, 608, 609
 tourism, 607, 608, 609, 610
 U.S., to, 609
 U.S. tourists, 608
 warnings, 609
 websites, 565
 world travel statistics, 608
Treason, defined, 112
Treasurers, of states, 143–178
Treasury, U.S. Dept. of:
 description of, 82
 secretaries of, 82, 84–89
Trees, state, 143–178
Trent, Council of, 348, 674
Trenton, N.J., 163, 179
Triangle Shirtwaist Factory fire (1911), 217, 682
Triassic Period, 575
Tribes, Indian, 378
Trieste, 800
Trimble, David, 886, 888
Trinidad and Tobago, 877
Trinity River, 501
Trinity Sunday, 355n
Triple Alliance, 681
Triple Crown (horse racing), 978, 981
Tripoli, Libya, 814
Tristan da Cunha, 892
Trojan War, 669
Tropical year, 399
Tropic of Cancer, 351, 486
Tropic of Capricorn, 351, 486
Tropopause, 402
Troposphere, 401
Trotsky, Leon, 312, 683, 685, 687, 850
Trotting. *See* Harness racing
Troy, ancient, 669
Troy weight, 451, 454, 456
Trucial States. *See* United Arab Emirates

Trucks, best-selling, 616
Trucks, efficiency, 648
Trudeau, Pierre E., 312, 745
Truman, Harry S., 53, 54, 56, 57, 67, 97, 160, 688. *See also* Presidents, U.S.
 assassination attempt on, 118
Truman Doctrine, 67, 687
Trusteeship Council, UN, 906
Trusteeships, UN, 906
Tuberculosis, 681
Tubman, Harriet, 679
Tucson, Ariz., 202–203
Tudor, House of, 884
Tufts Poetry Prize, 257
Tugela Falls, 496
Tulsa, Okla., 168, 203
Tungsten filament, invention of, 580
Tunis, Tunisia, 877
Tunisia, 877–878
Tunnels, 450
Turbojet, first flight, 437
Turin, Italy, 370
Turkey, 878–879
Turkmenistan, 879–880
Turks and Caicos Islands, 893
Turner, Nat, 679
Tuskegee Institute, 143
Tutankhamen, 669
Tutu, Rev. Desmond, 225, 695
Tuvalu, 880
Tweed Ring, 680
Twelfth Night (holiday), 353
Tydings-McDuffie Act, 844
Tyler, John, 51–52, 56, 61, 95. *See also* Presidents, U.S.
Typhoons, 215

U

U-2 incident (1960), 689
Uganda, 880–881
Ukraine, 881–882
Ulaan Baatar, Mongolia, 826
Ulbricht, Walter, 780
Ulster, Northern Ireland, 887
Ulysses space mission, 423, 427
Uncertainty principle, 583
Unemployment. *See also* Cities, U.S.
 by occupation, 623
 by race, age, and sex, 624
 rate, 625
Union Islands. *See* Tokelau Island
Union Labor Party, 52
Unions, labor, 626
 labor organizations, 626
 membership by occupation, 626
 membership by state, 627
United Arab Emirates, 882–883
United Arab Republic, 689
United Kingdom, 883–893
 dependencies of, 706, 889
 formation of, 676
 prime ministers of, 886
 rulers of, 885
United Nations, 97, 905–908
 charter of, 905
 "China seat", 691, 751, 873
 established, 687
 events, 687, 691
 General Assembly, 905
 in Persian Gulf War, 794
 member nations of, 907
 peacekeeping operations, 906
 in Persian Gulf War, 696
 representatives to, U.S., 908
 Secretariat, 905
 Security Council, 905
United Nations Development Index, 713
United States. *See also* Foreign trade; United States government; United States history
 area of, 102
 armed forces of, 389–395
 birth statistics, 128–133

 bridges, 447–448
 canals, 450
 charities in, 141
 church membership in, 361
 cities, 181–205, 206
 city temperatures, 604–605
 climate extremes, 600
 coastline, 502
 colleges and universities, 321–343
 contributions to other countries, 639
 crime statistics, 119
 current events, 32–33
 dams, 449
 dance companies, 264
 death statistics, 134–138
 diplomatic personnel to and from, 912–914
 direct investment in other countries, 638–639
 disasters, 211–224
 divorce statistics, 119, 124, 127
 economic statistics, 646–650
 education statistics, 119
 epidemics, 211, 213
 exports from, 641
 extreme points of, 500
 family statistics, 627
 foreign-born population, 376
 foreign embassies in, 908–911
 geography, 119
 great seal of, 104
 growth of, 121, 122
 health statistics, 553–560
 highest points, 503
 holidays, 353–355
 immigration to, 375, 376
 imports of, 641
 labor force, 119, 621–625
 latitudes and longitudes, 504
 life expectancy in, 119, 135, 136
 lowest points, 503
 magazines, 277–278
 map of, 526-527
 marriage statistics, 127
 motor vehicle laws, 614
 national anthem, 105
 National Park System, 592–596, 596
 newspapers, 277
 opera companies, 264
 poets laureate, 271
 population, 119–124
 postal regulations, 440–442
 race and ethnicity, 375–381
 societies and associations, 658–667
 state profiles, 143–178
 state temperatures, 601–602
 statistical profile of, 119
 structures, 445
 symphonies of, 263
 tallest buildings, 445–446
 territories of, 102, 893–896
 top travel destinations, 609
 tunnels, 450
 weather and climate in, 600, 601–603, 604–605
United States dependencies, 706
United States government. *See also* individual agencies, offices, and subjects
 armed forces, 389–395
 budget of. *See* Federal budget
 cabinet, 84–89
 Congress, 45–48, 76–79
 Constitution (text), 108–117
 executive departments and agencies, 81–84
 expenditures and receipts of, 636
 foreign aid, 639
 House of Representatives, 46–48, 76, 79
 independent agencies, 83–84
 judicial powers, 112
 National Park System, 592–596, 596
 presidents of, 56, 58–76
 receipts and outlays of, 636
 salaries of U.S. officials, 79
 Senate, 45–46, 76

Speakers of the House, **77**
Supreme Court, **90–94, 112**
vice presidents, **56–57**
voting qualifications, **115, 117**
United States history, 49–118
armed services, **389–395**
Articles of Confederation, **94, 101**
assassinations and attempts in, **118**
Atlantic Charter, **686**
cabinets, **84–89**
chronology of, **676**
civil rights, **380–381**
Civil War, **680**
colonization, **675**
Continental Congresses, **94, 101, 676**
Declaration of Independence, **94, 106–107**
exploration, **484**
firsts in, **100–101**
Gettysburg Address, **118**
immigration, **375**
Indians, American, **378, 379**
Monroe Doctrine, **105**
national committee chairmen, **50**
national political conventions, **50**
presidential elections, **43, 44, 51–54**
presidents, **56, 58–76**
Pulitzer Prizes for, **241–243**
Revolutionary War period, **676**
"Star-Spangled Banner", **105**
territorial expansion, **102, 103**
timeline of, **94–100**
women's rights movement, **372–373**
Universal time, 420
Universe, origin of, 398
Universities, in U.S., 321–343. *See also* Colleges
Unleavened Bread, Feast of, 354, 355n
Upanishads, **363**
Upper Volta. *See* Burkina Faso
Ural River, 495
Uranium, chemical properties of, 572, 574
Uranus (planet), 400, 406, 410–411. *See also* Planets
Urban populations, world's largest, 708
Urey, Harold, 313, 580, 685
Uruguay, 897
Uruguay River, 739, 897
Ustinov, Peter, 1039
Utah, 174
Utrecht, Peace of, 676
Uzbekistan, 897–898

V

VA. *See* Veterans' Affairs (VA), U.S. Dept. of
Vacations, average length, 610
Vaccinations:
polio, **582, 688**
smallpox, **583, 677**
Vaccines, 551
Vacuum tube, 582
Vaduz, Liechtenstein, 815
Valdes Peninsula, Argentina, 487
Valentine's Day, 344, 353
Valletta, Malta, 821
Valley Forge, Pa., 170, 676
Valois, House of, 772
Van Allen Belt (layer), 416, 583
Van Buren, Martin, 51–52, 56, 61, 95. *See also* Presidents, U.S.
Vancouver, Canada, 744
Vandalism arrests, 387
Vandals, 671
Vanuatu, 898
Varanasi, India, 370
Vatican, 444
Vatican City (Holy See), 899. *See also* Roman Catholic Church
Vatican Council I, 362
Vatican Council II, 362, 690, 694, 899

Vaudeville theater, first, 101
Vedas, **363**
V-E Day (1945), 686
Vegetables and fruits:
export and import of, **641**
in diet, **539**
pesticides on, **586**
U.S. consumption of, **642**
Vehicles, efficiency, 648
Venera probes, 425–427
Venereal diseases, 556
Venezuela, 33, 899–900
Venus (planet), 400, 402–403, 406. *See also* Planets
Venus de Milo, 670
Vermont, 174–175
Verrazano-Narrows Bridge, 447
Versailles, Palace of, 444, 675, 779
Versailles, Treaty of, 684, 685, 686, 779
Vesuvius, Mount, 211
Veterans' Affairs (VA), U.S. Dept. of:
description of, **82**
secretaries of, **82, 89**
Veterans Day, 344, 354
Veterans from U.S. wars, 391, 395
Veto power, 80, 109
Vezina Trophy, 961
Vice presidential candidates, 51–54
Vice presidents, U.S.:
as acting president, **117**
election procedure for, **111, 114**
first woman candidate for, **101**
list of, **56–57**
nomination of, **49**
powers and duties of, **108**
salary of, **79**
succession to presidency, **81, 111, 116, 117**
Vichy, France, 772, 773, 901
Vicksburg, Battle of, 680
Victoria (island), 496
Victoria (queen of England), 679, 681, 682, 884
Victoria, Lake, 494, 874, 881
Victoria, Seychelles, 860
Victoria Falls, 484
Videocassettes, 275
Vieira de Mello, Sergio, 389
Vienna, Austria, 728
Vienna, Congress of, 678, 729, 772
Vientiane, Laos, 810
Viet Cong, 690, 901
Vietnam, 810, 900–901
Vietnam War, 97, 688, 690, 901. *See also* Cambodia; Laos; Thailand
Vikings, 761, 836
Viking space program, 425, 426
Vilnius, Lithuania, 815
Vinson Massif, 487
Violent crime, 382–388
Virgil, 670
Virginia, 175–176
Virginia Beach, Va., 175, 179, 203
Virgin Islands, British, 890
Virgin Islands, U.S., 683, 894–895
Vitamins, 552
Vitamins, discoveries, 583
V-J Day (1945), 686
Volcanoes, 488–489
current eruptions, **488**
deadliest eruptions, **489**
"Ring of Fire", **488**
significant eruptions, **211–212**
Volga River, 495
Volume:
formulas for, **458**
measure of, **453, 455**
Volunteer work, 142
Voskhod flights, 429
Vostok flights, 429
Voting:
by 18-year-olds, **117, 691**
in presidential elections, **43, 44, 49, 51–54, 55**
rights, **115, 117**
voter turnout, **55**

women's suffrage, **101, 116, 684**
Voting Rights Act, 98
Voyager space program, 423, 426, 694, 696

W

Wabash River, 501
Waco, Tex., 224
Wage gap, 373, 374
Wages and hours:
minimum wages, **628**
by occupation, **620**
Wake Island, 896
Waldheim, Kurt, 695, 729, 905
Wales, 883, 889
Wales, Prince of, 883n
Walesa, Lech, 225, 696, 846
Walking. *See* Track and field
Wallace, George, 692
assassination attempt on, **118**
Wallis and Futuna Islands, 775
Wall of China, Great, 444, 670, 750
Wannsee Conference, 685, 687
War, U.S. Dept. of, secretaries of, 84–87
War casualties, 391
War crimes, 685, 687, 694
War of 1812, 95, 678
Warren, Earl, 91
Warren Report (1964), 691
Wars. *See* specific wars
Wars, current, 715
Warsaw, Poland, 845
Warsaw Ghetto, 685
Warsaw Pact, 689, 696
Warsaw Treaty Organization, 788, 846, 848, 850
Wars of the Roses, 673, 884
War veterans, 391, 395
Washington (state), 176, 502
Washington, DC, 204
civil rights rally in (1963), **690**
established, **678**
march on, **381**
Twenty-third Amendment, **117**
U.S. capital moved to, **95**
in War of 1812, **678**
Washington Monument, **106**
Washington, George, 51, 56, 58, 94, 676, 677. *See also* Presidents, U.S.
Washington, Mount, 503
Washington Monument, 106
Washington's Birthday, 344, 353
Washita River, 501
Water, boiling and freezing points, 451
Waterfalls, 496
Watergate scandal, 69, 98, 692
Waterloo, Battle of, 678, 779, 884
Water supply of the world, 591
Watt, James, 314, 583, 677
Watts riots (1965, 1966), 98, 691
Weapons, 385, 387
Weapons of mass destruction, 32, 35, 40, 42, 75, 794
Weather and climate, 597–605
blizzards, **215**
disastrous storms, **211, 214–215**
El Niño, **224**
extremes, U.S., **600**
extremes, world, **599, 600**
floods, **213**
hail and hailstones, **599**
hurricanes, **214–215, 598**
lightning, **597**
snowfalls, **599**
tidal waves, **213**
tornadoes, **211, 215–216, 599**
tropical storms, **214–215**
of U.S. cities, **604–605**
of U.S. states, **601, 602**
Weaving, cloth, 581
Webby Awards, 262
Websites, 564–567
astronomy, **397**

entertainment and culture, **565**
science, **579**
travel, **565**
Weights, atomic, 573–574
Weights and measures, 451–458
capacities and volumes, **453, 455, 455–457**
conversion tables, **455–457**
Weimar Republic, 779
Welfare. See also Public assistance
social expenditures, **632**
Wellington, New Zealand, 833
Western Sahara (proposed state), 827, 901–902
Western Samoa. See Samoa
West Indies. See also specific islands
exploration of, **484**
West Irian. See Irian Jaya
Westminster Abbey, 444
West Papua, 791
West Point (U.S. Military Academy), 165
West Virginia, 176–177
Wheat, economic statistics, 645
Wheat flour. See Flour
Wheel, 583
Whig Party (U.S.), 51, 52, 60, 62
Whipple's theory (of comets), 414
Whiskey Rebellion, 677
White-collar crime, 384
White House, 81
White River, 501
Whitney, Mount, 146, 502, 503
Whitsunday, 354
Wichita, Kans., 153, 179, 204–205
Willemstad, Netherlands Antilles, 832
William II (kaiser of Germany), 779
Williams, Serena and Venus, 959, 987, 988, 989, 990
Williamsburg, Va., 175
William the Conqueror, 884
Wilmington, Del., 148, 179
Wilson, Harold, 315, 884
Wilson, Woodrow, 53, 54, 56, 65, 96.
See also Presidents, U.S.
Wimbledon champions, 988–990
Wind Cave National Park, 497
Wind chill factors, 605
Windhoek, Namibia, 829
Windmill, 583
Windward Islands. See St. Lucia; St. Vincent and the Grenadines
Winnie Mae (plane), **437**
Winnipeg, Lake, 494
Wisconsin, 177–178
Wisconsin River, 501
Wives of presidents, 58
Wollaston Islands, 749
Women:
in armed forces, **687**
firsts by, **101**
firsts in aviation, **435–439**
income, **374**
in labor force, **625**
life expectancy of, **135, 136**
marriage statistics, **127**
mothers, **128, 131**
mothers employed, **625**
political firsts by, **101**
presidents' wives, **58**
suffrage for, **97, 101, 116, 684**
Title IX, **373**
wage gap, **373, 374**
women's rights convention, **95**
women's rights movement, **372–373**
Women, famous. See People
Women's National Basketball Association, 954
Wonders of the World, Seven, 443
Wood. See Lumber and wood
Wood pulp, 640, 641
Woods, Tiger, 959, 993, 994, 995, 996

Words:
crossword puzzle guide, **459–471**
easily confused, **476–477**
foreign, **477, 478–480**
Latin and Greek, **480–481**
mispronounced, **475**
roots, **480**
Work stoppages, 625
World. See also Earth (planet)
area, **487**
bridges, **447–448**
canals, **450**
caves and caverns, **497**
cities. See Cities, world
climate extremes, **599, 600**
comparative statistics, **707**
corrupt leaders, most, **713**
countries of, **721–904**
current events, **33–34**
deserts, **498**
disasters, **211–224**
elevations, **487**
energy consumption, **588**
explorations, **484–485**
famous structures, **443–445**
flags of, **519–522**
governments. See Governments, foreign
highest mountain peaks, **492–493**
history, **668–705.** See also History, world
islands, **496**
maps of, **523–536**
military expenditures, **715**
national holidays, **357**
profile of, **706**
rivers, **495**
Seven Wonders of, **443**
statistics, **706–720**
subway systems, **612**
tallest buildings, **445–446**
tallest towers, **446**
time zones, **349–350**
tunnels, **450**
volcanoes, **488–489**
waterfalls, **496**
water supply, **591**
World Bank (IBRD), 687
World Court, International Court of Justice, 695
World Cup, Soccer, 1023
World history:
by country, **721–904**
timeline, **668–705**
World sea ports, 646
World Series, 1004–1007, 1021–1022
records and standing, **1004–1007**
World's Fair, New York (1939–40), 686
World statistics, 706–720
World Trade Center (New York), 99, 100, 211, 224
Sept. 11, 2001, bombing, **703, 722, 857**
World Trade Center bombings, 697, 699, 700, 703, 722
World War I, 96, 683
World War II, 97. See also specific countries
chronology, **686**
declarations of war, **686**
treaties, **686**
World Wide Web, 564, 566, 564–567, 583
Wrangell, Mount, 502, 564–567
Wrestling, 928
Wright, Orville and Wilbur, 96, 315, 435, 436, 682
Writers. See People
Writing and language, 472–482
American Sign Language, **482**
ancient, **668**

capitalization, **472**
easily confused words, **476–477**
foreign languages studied, **475**
foreign words and phrases, **477, 478–480**
italicization, **473**
Latin and Greek roots, **480**
mispronounced words, **475**
most widely spoken, **475**
punctuation, **473–474**
Wyandotte Cave, 152, 497
Wyoming, 178

X

Xavier, St. Francis, 484
Xenon, 574
Xerography, 583
Xi Jiang (Si Kiang), 495
X-rays, 582, 681

Y

Yale University, 319
Yalta Conference, 686
Yamoussoukro, Côte d'Ivoire, 756
Yangon (Rangoon), Myanmar, 828
Yangtze River (Chang Jiang), 495, 750
Yaoundé, Cameroon, 743
Yaren, Nauru, 830
Yawar, Ghazi, al-, 507
Yeager, Chuck, 437, 687
Year, defined, 349
Yeats, William Butler, 684
Yellow fever, 213, 583
Yellow River, 495, 750
Yellowstone National Park, 161, 178, 592, 593, 596
Yellowstone River, 501
Yeltsin, Boris, 696, 699, 850
Yemen, 902–903
Yenisei River, 495
Yerevan, Armenia, 726
YMCA, 667
Yom Kippur, 344, 354, 355
York, House of, 884
Yorktown, Battle of, 175, 676
Yosemite National Park, 146, 593, 596
Young, Brigham, 315, 679
Young Women's Christian Association (YWCA), 667
Yudhoyono, Susilo Bambang, 41, 792
Yugoslavia. See Serbia and Montenegro
Yukon River, 495, 501
Yukon Territory, Canada, 745

Z

Zagreb, Croatia, 757
Zaire. See Congo, Democratic Republic of
Zaire River, 484, 495
Zama, Battle of, 670
Zambezi River, 484, 495
Zambia, 903–904
Zanzibar. See Tanzania
Zarqawi, Sheik Abu Musab, al-, 43, 1034
Zenger, John Peter, 676
Zeppelin, first flight, 435
Zero, 583
Zeus, statue of, 443
Zhou Enlai, 315, 750
Zimbabwe, 904
Zinc, 574
ZIP codes, 207–209, 441
Zodiac, 416
Zugspitze Mountains, 779
Zwingli, Ulrich, 674

The News of 2004: Nation

Security and Reconstruction in Iraq

In 2004, the United States' major preoccupation was the ongoing war in Iraq. Hopes that Saddam Hussein's capture in Dec. 2003 would stem the country's turmoil faded with a dramatic upsurge in violence. By April, a number of separate uprisings had spread throughout the Sunni triangle and in the Shiite-dominated south. Suicide bombings, kidnappings, and beheadings targeted civilians, Iraqi security forces, foreign workers, and coalition soldiers. In September alone there were 2,300 attacks by insurgents. In October, U.S. officials estimated there were between 8,000 and 12,000 hardcore insurgents, and a total of more than 20,000 "active sympathizers." Loosely divided into Baathists, nationalists, and Islamists, all but about 1,000 were thought to be indigenous fighters. As of mid-October, more than 1,100 U.S. troops had died and 8,000 had been wounded in action. No official tally of Iraqi casualties exists, but most estimates range between 10,000 and 15,000 civilian deaths since the start of the war.

The deteriorating security situation was harshly criticized by Democrats and Republicans alike, who questioned whether the Pentagon had adequately prepared for an insurgency and deployed enough troops. Reconstruction efforts, hampered by bureaucracy and security concerns, had also fallen woefully short of expectations: by September, just 6% ($1 billion) of the reconstruction money approved by Congress in 2003 had in fact been used. Electricity and clean water were still below prewar levels, and half of Iraq's employable population was still without work. With few palpable signs of reconstruction to generate good will toward the U.S., American troops often faced a bitter and hostile populace. As a senior U.S. military officer put it, "We can either put Iraqis back to work, or we can leave them to shoot RPGs [rocket-propelled grenades] at us." A highly classified July 2004 national intelligence estimate offered pessimistic assessments of Iraq's future over the next year, ranging from "tenuous" stability at best to civil war at worst.

Signs of significant progress included the U.S.'s return of sovereignty to an interim Iraqi government on June 28, and a plan to hold national elections by Jan. 31, 2005. Shiite Iraqi Council member Iyad Allawi became prime minister, and Ghazi al-Yawar, a Sunni Muslim, was chosen president.

Abu Ghraib and Guantánamo

In April, worldwide outrage followed the release of photos in the American media depicting the appalling physical abuse and sexual degradation of Iraqi prisoners at Abu Ghraib prison, which a U.S. military report described as acts of "purposeless sadism." A July military report identified 94 more suspected or confirmed cases of abuse of prisoners in Iraq and Afghanistan, including the deaths of at least 39 prisoners. Further investigations are underway. In August, the Pentagon-sponsored Schlesinger report rejected the idea that the abuse was simply the work of a few aberrant soldiers, and asserted that there were "fundamental failures throughout all levels of command, from the soldiers on the ground to Central Command and to the Pentagon."

The controversial decision to classify detainees in the war in Afghanistan as enemy combatants, and not as prisoners of war subject to the Geneva Conventions, meant the U.S. could employ more coercive interrogation techniques, indefinitely detain prisoners, and deny them the rights to due process. White House Council Alberto Gonzales maintained that terrorism was "a new kind of war" that rendered portions of the Geneva Conventions "quaint." In June, the Supreme Court rejected the Bush administration's claim that the executive branch has unreviewable authority in time of war, ruling that detainees were legally entitled to challenge their imprisonment. By October, of the roughly 560 enemy combatants who had been held for three years at the U.S. naval base at Guantánamo Bay, Cuba, only four had been formally charged.

Intelligence Failures

On July 9, the Senate Intelligence Committee released a unanimous, bipartisan "Report on Pre-War Intelligence on Iraq," evaluating the intelligence assessments that formed the basis for the Bush administration's justifications for the war. It strongly criticized the CIA and other intelligence agencies, concluding that "most of the major key judgments" on Iraq's weapons of mass destruction were either "overstated, or were not supported by, the underlying intelligence report." It disputed the CIA's assertions that Iraq was reconstituting its nuclear, chemical, and biological weapons programs. It also concluded that there were "no operational links" between al-Qaeda and Saddam Hussein, another *casus belli* put forth by the Bush administration. In October, the Iraq Survey Group's final report confirmed that Iraq did not have weapons of mass destruction nor a formal plan to revive its WMD program. In response, President Bush began emphasizing that the removal of Iraq's repressive dictatorship was grounds enough for waging war, and contended that "America is safer today with Saddam Hussein in prison."

The Economy, Tax Cuts, and the Deficit

According to the Congressional Budget Office, the federal budget deficit reached a record $413 billion in 2004. The nonpartisan CBO also estimated that two-thirds of the 2004 deficit were the result of tax cuts. The Bush administration countered that the president's tax cuts had in fact kept the country's recession shallow and brief and were now stimulating the economy. In September, Congress renewed its faith in tax cuts by approving the extension of several cuts due to expire by 2006. Critics, including fiscally conservative Republicans, argued that it was unsound to offer tax cuts while the country was in the midst of an expensive war, a jobless recovery, and an unprecedented deficit.

In August, the Census Bureau reported that the number of Americans living in poverty had increased by 1.3 million in 2003, while the ranks of those without health insurance had increased by 1.4 million, the third straight annual increase in both categories.

Defining Marriage

On May 17, same-sex marriages became legal in Massachusetts after the state's supreme court ruled in Nov. 2003 that barring gays and lesbians from marrying violated the state constitution. A strong backlash around the country followed, with conservatives vowing to undo the work of "activist judges." Although there was little support for a proposed federal consititutional amendment to ban gay marriage, all 11 state referendums banning gay marriage passed in November elections. Thirty-eight states already had Defense of Marriage laws in place.

2004 Presidential Election

The 2004 presidential campaign between President Bush and Democratic senator John Kerry was one of the most closely followed and contentious races in recent history. Terrorism, the war in Iraq, tax cuts, health care, and the economy, were the major issues. Kerry accused the president of mismanaging the war in Iraq and the fight against terrorism and promised to roll back the Bush tax cuts for the wealthiest Americans. The president accused his opponent of being a "flip-flopper" on issues, and of not having the resolute leadership needed to fight the war on terror. President Bush won reelection, with 51% of the popular vote. Republicans also expanded their majorities in the Senate and in the House. (*See* pp. 43–48 for complete election results.)

The News of 2004: World

Global Terrorism

Spain. On March 11, 2004, Spain's most horrific terrorist attack occurred: 202 people were killed and 1,400 were injured in bombings at Madrid's railway station. The government at first blamed ETA, the Basque terrorist organization, but evidence quickly surfaced implicating al-Qaeda. In presidential elections just days later, Prime Minister Aznar's Popular Party suffered a stinging defeat, and José Luis Rodríguez Zapatero of the Socialist Party became the new prime minister. Many Spaniards blamed Aznar's staunch support of the U.S.-led war in Iraq for making Spain an al-Qaeda target. Others were angered by what they saw as the government's politically motivated insistence that ETA was to blame for the attacks at the same time that links to al-Qaeda were emerging. By April, a dozen al-Qaeda suspects, most of them Moroccan, were arrested; several suspects blew themselves up during a police raid to avoid capture. In May, the new prime minister made good on his campaign promise, recalling Spain's 1,300 soldiers from Iraq, much to the displeasure of the United States, which said Spain was appeasing terrorists.

Russia. Before and after August elections in Russia's autonomous, largely Muslim state of Chechnya, terrorists blew up two planes, killing all 90 passengers, and killed nine at a Moscow subway stop. An even more barbaric act followed: on Sept. 1–3, dozens of guerrillas seized a school in Beslan, near Chechnya, and held about 1,100 young schoolchildren, teachers, and parents hostage. At least 335 hostages were killed, including about 156 children, and more than 550 were wounded. Chechen warlord Shamil Basayev claimed responsibility. In the aftermath, prime minister Vladimir Putin announced that he would radically restructure the government to fight terrorism more effectively, raising alarms that his consolidation of power would roll back Russian democracy.

Saudi Arabia. The monarchy has suffered a variety of terrorist attacks since May 2003, many attributed to al-Qaeda. The attacks have caused the deaths of about 100, mostly foreign workers, but for the first time, some attacks were also aimed at Saudi government targets. While the government has arrested a sizeable number of suspected terrorists in 2003 and 2004, little has been done to quell Islamic militancy in the kingdom, which is now beginning to turn its wrath against the regime itself.

Democracy Under Duress

Afghanistan. In 2004, attacks on American-led forces intensified in Afghanistan as the Taliban and al-Qaeda continued to regroup. President Hamid Karzai's hold on power remained tenuous, as entrenched warlords continued to exert regional control. Remarkably, however, Afghanistan's first democratic presidential elections in Oct. 2004 were a success. Ten million Afghans, more than a third of the country, registered to vote, including more than 40% of eligible women. Despite the Taliban's threats to kill anyone who participated, the polls were reasonably peaceful and the elections deemed fair by international observers. Karzai won amid a field of 18 presidential candidates.

Venezuela. After years of bridling under Venezuelan president Hugo Chávez's autocratic rule, and having failed in 2003 to oust him through a nine-week national strike, opposition groups (primarily made up of business, media, and labor groups) pursued a recall referendum. In Aug. 2003, a petition with 3.2 million signatures was delivered to the country's election commission, which was ruled invalid. Almost a year later, after the Chávez government challenged several subsequent petitions, the electoral board finally scheduled the referendum in Aug. 2004. Chávez, who had been shoring up his standing with the Venezuelan poor during the delays, won the referendum with an overwhelming 58% of the vote. The opposition alleged fraud, but international observers confirmed that there had been no irregularities. While Chávez's hand was clearly strengthened, the results were likely to fracture the divided country even further.

Haiti. Jean-Bertrand Aristide, once a charismatic champion of democracy in Haiti, grew corrupt and authoritarian as his country's president (1991, 1994–1996, 2001–2004), despite significant support from the U.S. and other countries. Failing to improve the lot of his people, among the poorest in the Western hemisphere, he was finally ousted from power on Feb. 29, just a month after the country celebrated its bicentennial as the world's first independent black republic. The rebels turned the country over to an interim government.

Sudan

In 2004, after two years of troubled negotiations and cease-fires, Sudan's brutal, 20-year-long civil war seemed at an end. The war had pitted the Arab-Muslim government of the North against the black Christian and animist South. Two million people had died in the conflict, primarily through starvation and disease, and another four million had been displaced. In addition to the staggering death toll, the war had led to a resurgence of slavery, with Arab raiders from the north enslaving thousands of black southerners. In May, a near-final peace agreement was signed between the Khartoum government and the major rebel group, the Sudan People's Liberation Army (SPLA), with both sides agreeing to a power-sharing government for six years, to be followed by a referendum on self-determination for the south—a hard-won agreement given that 75% of Sudan's oil wealth is located in the south.

But just as Africa's longest war was ending, another murderous conflict in Sudan's western Darfur region intensified. After the Khartoum government crushed a small-scale rebellion in Darfur in Feb. 2003, it permitted pro-government Arab militias called Janjaweed to carry out massacres against black villagers and rebels in the region. While the civil war had pitted Arab Muslims against black non-Muslims, the Darfur crisis pitted Arab and black Muslims against each other. By Oct. 2004, the Janjaweed, surreptitiously armed by Khartoum, had massacred more than 70,000 Darfuris and displaced another 1.5 million. Deemed the world's worst humanitarian disaster by the UN, the Darfur crisis has been labeled genocide by the U.S., and much of the international community has vowed never to repeat the global-scale moral failure of Rwanda. But worldwide outrage, combined with several toothless UN resolutions and the deployment of a few hundred African peacekeeping forces, was the extent of the international response as of late Oct. 2004. Khartoum continued to react with defiant impunity.

Israeli-Palestinian Conflict

Approximately 2,800 Palestinians and 1,000 Israelis have now died in the four-year-old al-Aksa intifada, and nearly 27,200 Palestinians and 5,700 Israelis have been wounded. Frequent military incursions into the Palestinian territories, the assassinations of several dozen militant leaders (including Hamas leader Sheik Ahmed Yassin and his successor), and the construction of the massive security barrier in the West Bank have resulted in dramatically fewer Palestinian suicide bombings: 13 in the first 9 months of 2004, compared to 44 in 2003, and 61 in 2002. While Israel's increased militarism under Prime Minister Ariel Sharon has measurably saved Israeli lives, the toll on Palestinians has been devastating. Since the beginning of the intifada, Israel has razed more than 2,751 Palestinian homes, almost 40% of them in 2004. In May, Israel launched its largest military operation in Gaza in a decade, and in October, in retaliation for Palestinian rocket attacks, carried out its deadliest incursion.

In 2004, Sharon introduced a startling proposal to withdraw unilaterally from the Gaza Strip, while at the same time permanently retaining large blocks of land in the West Bank for Israel and rejecting the "right of return" for Palestinian refugees. Given that last year's "road map" peace plan had been virtually abandoned by all parties, including its U.S. and European sponsors, Sharon found it an opportune moment to end diplomatic stagnation while securing advantages for Israel. By conceding the lesser territory of Gaza, he planned to shore up Israel's hold on the West Bank—an intention confirmed by his approval of additional West Bank housing construction and pushing ahead with the West Bank security barrier. Although two-thirds of Israelis supported his plan, Sharon's own Likud party repeatedly rejected it, viewing it as a dangerous unravelling of Israel's territorial claims. The far right opposed the dismantling of settlements of any kind. The Labor party gingerly embraced the withdrawal, but remained uncertain whether it was meant to serve as a prelude to future talks or as a means of circumventing negotiations indefinitely. Although the Knesset approved the withdrawal on Oct. 26, a crucial step towards its implementation, Sharon's gamble to push ahead with a plan his party largely rejected threatened to bring down his government.

Nuclear Proliferation

In 2004, a global nuclear black market was uncovered when A. Q. Khan, the father of Pakistan's nuclear bomb, was exposed in Feb. 2004 for having sold nuclear secrets to North Korea, Iran, and Libya in the 1980s and 1990s. While much of the world reviled his incalculable damage to global security, Prime Minister Pervez Musharraf swiftly pardoned him—Khan remains such a national hero in Pakistan that Musharraf did not risk a stronger rebuke. Also convenient for Musharraf was Khan's claim that he alone and not Pakistan's military or government was involved in the selling of these ultra-classified secrets. The claim was met with widespread skepticism outside Pakistan.

Khan's nuclear trafficking was revealed after an illegal shipment of centrifuge parts to Libya was intercepted in Oct. 2003. Libya's Qaddafi quickly admitted his clandestine pursuit of weapons of mass destruction and submitted to full UN weapons inspections. The International Atomic Energy Agency (IAEA) concluded that Libya had been in the very nascent stages of building a nuclear bomb. Libya's nuclear confession, as well as its admission of guilt and offers of compensation for its sponsorship of terrorist acts, including the 1988 Lockerbie bombing, allowed it to shed its decades-old pariah status—years of international sanctions were lifted.

Despite Iran's promises in 2003 to fully cooperate with nuclear inspections after traces of highly enriched uranium were found in one of its nuclear facilities, the IAEA censured the country once again in June 2004 for failing to fully cooperate with nuclear inspections. Neither U.S. threats nor Europe's coaxing managed to halt Iran's alarming defiance. North Korea—which many believe now has a minimum of one or two nuclear weapons and perhaps as many as eight—continued to issue taunts and threats to the West in lieu of negotiations.

—Borgna Brunner, Nov. 3, 2004

What Happened in 2004: Month by Month

Below are highlights of key events of the year, organized month by month, in three categories for easy reference. For the year's major Supreme Court decisions, *see* p. 149. "Countries of the World" covers specific international events, country by country. *See also* "People in the News," pp. 1030–1034, and "2004 Deaths," pp. 1035–1039, for more current-events coverage. Go to www.infoplease.com/ipa/A0920845.html for additional events.

January

WORLD

Georgia Elects New President (Jan. 4): Mikhail Saakashvili, a 36-year-old lawyer, wins in a landslide.

Afghan Leaders Approve New Constitution (Jan. 4): Delegates to grand council agree to charter that will rename country the Islamic Republic of Afghanistan, establish a presidential system and a national assembly, and grant equal rights to women. **(Jan. 26):** President Hamid Karzai signs the new constitution

Iran's Religious Council Disqualifies Candidates (Jan. 11): Council bars more than 3,600 reformist candidates from running in parliamentary elections. **(Jan. 30):** Council reinstates more than 1,160 candidates.

Palestinian Suicide Bomber Strikes in Gaza Strip (Jan. 14): Member of the militant group Hamas kills herself and four Israelis. First time Hamas has used a woman suicide bomber.

U.S. Office Attacked in Iraq (Jan. 18): Suicide bomber attacks American occupation headquarters in Baghdad, killing at least 20 people, mostly Iraqi citizens.

Iraq Weapons Investigator Steps Down (Jan. 23): CIA chief weapons inspector David Kay says his 1,400-member team failed to find any evidence of chemical, biological, or nuclear weapons in Iraq. **(Jan. 28):** Kay calls for an independent investigation into the intelligence gathered before the U.S.-led war in Iraq.

Report Exonerates Blair (Jan. 28): British judge Lord Hutton says Prime Minister Tony Blair did not intentionally exaggerate intelligence on Iraq's weapons.

NATION

U.S. Begins Fingerprinting Foreign Visitors (Jan. 5): New security system, U.S. Visitor and Immigrant Status Indicator Technology, or US-VISIT, requires international travelers to be fingerprinted and photographed.

Former Cabinet Member Speaks Out (Jan. 11): Paul O'Neill, former treasury secretary, says on *60 Minutes* that the Bush administration had been planning an attack against Iraq since the first days of Bush's presidency.

Bush Proposes Journey to the Moon (Jan. 14): President sets sights on another flight to the Moon by 2020 and a launching base there for a trip to Mars and beyond.

Bush Appoints Controversial Judge (Jan. 16): During the Congressional recess, Bush gives Charles Pickering, Sr., a seat on the U.S. Court of Appeals.

Kerry Takes Iowa (Jan. 19): Massachusetts senator John Kerry stages surprise win in Iowa caucuses, taking 38% of the vote. Former Vermont governor and recent Democratic front-runner Howard Dean takes third, behind Sen. John Edwards.

Bush Delivers State of the Union (Jan. 20): President defends action in Iraq and tax cuts and highlights the urgency to continue fighting terrorism.

Kerry Prevails in First Primary (Jan. 27): Massachusetts senator John Kerry places first in New Hampshire primary, taking 39% of the vote.

Bush Administration Revises Cost of Drug Plan (Jan. 29): Reports Medicare prescription drug benefit will cost $534 billion, up from initial pricetag of $395 billion.

BUSINESS / SCIENCE / SOCIETY

Rover Lands on Mars (Jan. 3): *Spirit* sends back images of the planet. The images show a flat but rocky surface. **(Jan. 25):** Second rover, *Opportunity*, lands on Mars and sends pictures back to Earth.

Job Growth Stalled in December (Jan. 9): Labor Department announces thousands of unemployed people stopped looking for employment in December 2003. Department had forecast creation of 150,000 jobs, but reported only 1,000 for December.

Former Enron CFO Pleads Guilty (Jan. 13): Andrew Fastow admits to covering up Enron's financial woes and defrauding the company. His wife, Lea, pleads guilty to a tax felony.

Jackson Appears in Court (Jan. 16): Pop star Michael Jackson pleads not guilty to nine felony counts—seven for allegedly engaging in lewd acts with a child under age 14 and two of giving an intoxicant to a child.

February

WORLD

Iranian Politicians Resign (Feb. 1): About one third of Iran's Parliament steps down to protest move by Guardian Council that barred more than 2,000 reformists from running in parliamentary elections.

Suicide Bomber Kills Dozens of Kurds (Feb. 1): Several top Kurdish leaders slain in northern Iraq.

Sharon Says He May Have Settlers Leave Gaza (Feb. 2): Israeli prime minister indicates he plans to order the evacuation of several settlements in the Gaza Strip.

Pakistani Scientist Admits to Selling Weapons Technology (Feb. 4): Abdul Qadeer Khan admits that he had sold designs and technology for nuclear weapons to other countries, including North Korea, Iran, and Libya. **(Feb. 5):** President Musharraf pardons Khan.

Protests Rock Haiti (Feb. 5): Armed rebels take control of Gonaïves. Violent protests against President Jean-Bertrand Aristide's government overwhelm the Haitian military and police. **(Feb. 9):** Violence spreads to about a dozen towns. **(Feb. 17):** Prime Minister Yvon Neptune appeals for international help after rebels attack a police station in central Haiti, killing the police chief. **(Feb. 22):** Rebels take control of Cap Haitien, Haiti's second-largest city. **(Feb. 29):** Under U.S. pressure, Aristide resigns and goes into exile.

Suicide Bombs Kill Dozens in Iraq (Feb. 10): At least 54 people, mostly civilians lined up applying for jobs, die outside a police station in Iskandariyah. **(Feb. 11):** Bomber in Baghdad kills nearly 50 people seeking employment with Iraq's new army.

Halliburton Accused of Overcharging for Gas (Feb. 12): Two ex-employees say the oil services company, which secured no-bid contracts for reconstruction projects in Iraq, "routinely overcharged" the U.S. military. Company, formerly headed by Dick Cheney, is under investigation by several government agencies.

Train Explosion Kills Hundreds in Iran (Feb. 18): About 300 people die when a train crashes in the northeast.

Hardliners Dominate Elections (Feb. 20): Religious conservatives breeze to victory in Iranian elections, taking a clear majority in parliament.

Russian President Sacks Prime Minister and Government (Feb. 24): Russian president Vladimir Putin unexpectedly fires his entire cabinet and premier.

NATION

Bush Releases Budget (Feb. 2): Bush's proposed $2.4 trillion plan would boost military funding by 7.1%, increase domestic security expenditures by 9.7%, and attempt to cut the deficit.

Poison Found in Senate Office (Feb. 3): Three office buildings closed when ricin is found in the office of Senate majority leader Bill Frist.

Kerry Prevails in Five States (Feb. 3): Sen. John Kerry takes contests in Missouri, Delaware, Arizona, New Mexico, and North Dakota. Sen. Joe Lieberman drops out of the race.

Massachusetts Court Supports Gay Marriage (Feb. 4): State's supreme judicial court rules that only full marriage complies with its Nov. 2003 ruling that said barring gays from marrying violates the state constitution.

Bush Creates Panel to Investigate Intelligence (Feb. 6): President calls for independent commission to study the country's intelligence-gathering operations.

Bush Defends Action in Iraq and Economy (Feb. 8): On NBC's *Meet the Press,* president says that although inspectors have not found banned weapons in Iraq, the war in Iraq was justified because Saddam Hussein had the ability to produce such weapons.

Kerry Prevails in the South, Clark Quits (Feb. 10): John Kerry continues his winning streak, sweeping both the Virginia and Tennessee primaries. **(Feb. 11):** Retired general Wesley Clark drops out of the race.

Gay Couples Marry in San Francisco (Feb. 12): More than 85 couples tie the knot after Mayor Gavin Newsom orders the city clerk's office to issue marriage licenses to same-sex couples.

Dean Drops Out of Race (Feb. 18): Howard Dean quits the race for the Democratic presidential nomination.

Election Commission Greenlights Advocacy Groups (Feb. 18): Permits groups, called "527 committees," to spend unlimited sums on political ads.

Bush Appoints Second Judge During Congressional Recess (Feb. 20): President gives William Pryor, Jr., a seat on the U.S. Court of Appeals.

Nader Announces Candidacy (Feb. 22): Ralph Nader says he will run for president as an independent.

Education Secretary Under Fire for Comment (Feb. 23): Rod Paige, secretary of education, compares the National Education Association to a terrorist organization. He later apologizes for the remark.

Bush Endorses Constitutional Amendment Banning Gay Marriage (Feb. 24): President says marriage between a man and a woman is "the most fundamental institution of civilization."

BUSINESS/SCIENCE/SOCIETY

Researchers Report New Elements (Feb. 1): Scientists create two new chemical elements, named Ununtrium (Element 113) and Ununpentium (Element 115).

Scientists Say They Have Cloned Human Embryos (Feb. 12): Scientists in South Korea announce that they have created 30 human embryos by cloning and have removed embryonic stem cells from them.

Greenspan Urges Measures to Cut Deficit (Feb. 25): Federal Reserve chairman recommends cutting spending on Social Security and Medicare rather than increasing taxes to rein in deficit.

Investigation Reveals Thousands of Priests Abused Children (Feb. 26): Study by the John Jay College of Criminal Justice reports 10,667 children were abused by 4,392 priests between 1950 and 2002.

March

WORLD

Putin Appoints Prime Minister (March 1): Russian president names Mikhail Fradkov as premier. **(March 14):** Putin overwhelmingly reelected to a second term.

Suicide Bombers Hit Iraqi Mosques (March 2): About 170 Shiite Muslims observing *ashoura* killed in attacks in Baghdad and Karbala.

New Leaders Take Office in Haiti (March 8): Boniface Alexandre, Haiti's chief justice, sworn in as interim president. **(March 10):** Gérard Latortue, a lawyer and economist, appointed interim prime minister.

Iraqi Governing Council Signs Interim Constitution (March 8): Charter to take effect when U.S.-led coalition forces end their occupation.

Spain Rocked by Terrorist Attacks (March 11): At least 10 bombs explode on four commuter trains in Madrid during rush hour, killing 202 people and wounding about 1,400. An Arabic newspaper reports it received a fax alleging that al-Qaeda was behind the attack. **(March 14):** Spanish officials say they have found a videotape on which al-Qaeda takes responsibility for the bombings. Police arrest three Moroccans and two Indians in connection with the attacks. **(March 14):** Governing Popular Party upset by opposition Socialists, led by incoming prime minister José Luis Rodríguez Zapatero.

South Korean President Impeached (March 12): National Assembly votes, 193–2, to impeach President Roh Moo Hyun for allegedly violating election laws.

Fighting Erupts in Pakistan (March 16): Pakistani troops attack foreign militants in the South Waziristan region, which borders Afghanistan. The operation begins amid rumors that Ayman al-Zawahiri, second-in-command of the terrorist group al-Qaeda, is in the area. **(March 26):** Eight Pakistani soldiers taken hostage by the militants are found dead, believed to have been executed.

Taiwanese President Shot on Eve of Elections (March 19): President Chen Shui-bian and Vice President Annette Lu shot. Neither sustain life-threatening injuries. **(March 20):** Chen reelected, beating Nationalist Party candidate Lien Chen 50.1% to 49.9%.

Violence Spreads in Kosovo (March 20): Dozens die in clashes between Serbs and ethnic Albanians. **(March 18):** NATO deploys 1,000 peacekeepers to help the 18,000 already there.

Israeli Forces Kill Hamas Leader (March 22): Sheik Ahmed Yassin, the leader and founder of the militant group Hamas, and seven others hit by missile in Gaza City. **(March 23):** Hamas appoints Dr. Abdel Aziz Rantisi as its leader in the Gaza Strip.

NATO Expands Eastward (March 29): North Atlantic Treaty Organization formally admits 7 new countries. New members are Bulgaria, Estonia, Latvia, Lithuania, Romania, Slovakia, and Slovenia.

Iraqi Mob Mutilates Four Americans (March 31): Civilian contract workers shot and then dragged through the streets of Falluja.

NATION

Kerry Wraps Up Nomination (March 2): John Kerry wins nine of ten states in the Super Tuesday primaries and caucuses, effectively sealing his nomination as the Democratic presidential candidate. **(March 3):** Sen. John Edwards drops out of the race.

Snipers Sentenced (March 9): John Muhammad sentenced to death for his role in the 2002 sniper shootings in the Washington, DC, area. **(March 10):** Accomplice Lee Malvo sentenced to life without parole.

San Francisco Ordered to Stop Gay Marriages (March 11): California Supreme Court orders city to halt issuance of marriage licenses to same-sex couples.

Current and Former Officials Testify Before 9/11 Commission (March 23): Secretary of State Colin Powell and Secretary of Defense Donald Rumsfeld appear before a federal commission investigating the Sept. 11, 2001, terrorist attacks. Officials in Clinton administration also testify. **(March 24):** Richard Clarke, the Bush administration's former counterterrorism chief, testifies and criticizes the Bush administration's handling of al-Qaeda. He also apologizes to the families of victims of the attacks.

Former Counterterrorism Official Criticizes Bush (March 24): Appearing on *60 Minutes,* Richard Clarke says that throughout 2001, Bush's inner circle failed to heed his warnings of an imminent attack by al-Qaeda.

Senate Approves Legislation to Outlaw Injuring a Fetus (March 25): Votes, 61–38, for measure that makes it a crime to harm a fetus while committing a federal crime against a pregnant woman.

Massachusetts Approves Amendment to Ban Gay Marriage (March 29): Legislature votes, 105–92, in favor of amendment to create civil unions and bar same-sex marriage. The legislature must pass it again during the 2005–2006 session and voters must approve the amendment in a 2006 referendum.

BUSINESS/SCIENCE/SOCIETY

NASA Cites Evidence of Water on Mars (March 2): Robot explorer *Opportunity* has detected signs that water had once covered a small crater. **(March 23):** Rover *Opportunity* explores sedimentary rocks that appear to have been formed under flowing saltwater.

Martha Stewart Found Guilty (March 5): Convicted of four counts of obstruction of justice. Charges stem from her Dec. 2001 sale of shares of the stock ImClone.

U.S. Trade Deficit Increases (March 10): Commerce Department reports January deficit reached $43.1 billion, the highest monthly shortfall ever.

Scientists Report New Planetoid (March 15): NASA reports discovery of a distant object in our solar system that closely resembles a planet. Object called Sedna.

European Commission Rules Against Microsoft (March 24): Fines the software giant $603 million and orders the company to stop bundling its products, such as Windows Media Player, with its operating system.

April

WORLD

Madrid Bombing Suspect Kills Himself (April 3): Three others die in blast in Madrid during a police raid.

U.S. Troops Under Attack (April 4): Eight Americans die in coordinated attacks ordered by radical Shiite cleric Moktada al-Sadr. **(April 5):** U.S. troops raid Falluja in response to killing and mutilation on March 31 of four U.S. civilian contractors. **(April 6):** About a dozen U.S. Marines in Ramadi in battle with Sunni insurgents. **(April 7):** U.S. reports evidence that Shiites and Sunnis, former enemies, are uniting against the U.S.-led occupation. **(April 11):** U.S. orders cease-fire in Falluja. Two members of Iraqi Governing Council resign in protest of American offensive in Falluja. **(April 19):** U.S. officials say they will end the offensive in Falluja if insurgents agree to surrender their weapons.

Forces Loyal to Afghan Warlord Take Over Province (April 8): Governor of Faryab Province steps down and flees when armed faction loyal to Gen. Abdul Rashid Dostrum takes control of several districts.

Hostages Taken in Iraq (April 8): Iraqi militants say they will kill the hostages, three Japanese civilians, unless Japan withdraws troops from Iraq. Militants have also kidnapped nine other foreigners. **(April 9):** American contract worker Thomas Hamill taken hostage. **(April 17):** Number of hostages reaches about 40.

Sharon Announces Settlement Plan (April 12): Israeli prime minister says that as part of his proposal to unilaterally separate from Palestinians in the Gaza Strip he plans to keep five West Bank settlements under Israeli control. **(April 14):** In a move that outrages Arab world, President Bush endorses Sharon's unilateral strategy.

U.S. Accepts UN Proposal for Iraq (April 15): Bush administration agrees to a plan to replace the Iraqi Governing Council with a caretaker government when the U.S. returns sovereignty to Iraqis.

ANC Sweeps Election (April 15): As expected, the African National Congress wins South Africa's general election, taking about 70% of the vote. Thabo Mbeki retains presidency.

Hamas Leader Killed in Gaza (April 17): Israelis kill Dr. Abdel Aziz Rantisi.

New Spanish Prime Minister Recalls Troops (April 18): One day after being sworn in as premier, José Luis Rodríguez Zapatero orders soldiers back from Iraq as

soon as possible. Leaders of Honduras and Dominican Republic later announce plans to withdraw troops.

Car Bombs Kill Dozens in Iraq (April 21): Five coordinated suicide attacks in Basra kill 68 people.

U.S. Rethinks Policy on Iraq Baath Party Officials (April 22): U.S. says that some Iraqi officials who were forced out of their jobs after the fall of Saddam Hussein will be allowed to resume their positions.

Train Ignites Massive Explosion in North Korea (April 22): Hundreds feared dead in Ryongchon blast.

Abuse Reported at Iraqi Prison (April 30): CBS's *60 Minutes II* broadcasts graphic photos, taken in late 2003, of American soldiers grinning as they abuse Iraqis in the Abu Ghraib prison. Images spark outrage around the world, especially in the Middle East.

NATION

White House Admits to Withholding Documents (April 1): Bush administration admits that it failed to give the commission investigating the Sept. 11, 2001, terrorist attacks thousands of pages of national security papers from the Clinton administration. **(April 2):** White House says it will allow the commission to review the documents.

Rice Testifies Before 9/11 Commission (April 8): National Security Adviser Condoleezza Rice tells the committee that President Bush was warned of suspicious activity by terrorists in the U.S. before the attacks.

Bush Administration Releases Top-Secret Document (April 10): The President's Daily Briefing from Aug. 6, 2001, titled "Bin Laden Determined to Attack Inside the United States," says that members of al-Qaeda had been in the U.S. for several years and were thought to have been conducting surveillance of federal buildings in New York.

U.S. Intelligence Agencies Harshly Criticized (April 13): Thomas Kean, chairman of the independent commission investigating the Sept. 11, 2001, terrorist attacks, says the FBI "is an agency that does not work." Former acting director of the FBI Thomas Pickard testifies that Attorney General John Ashcroft failed to make counterterrorism a priority for the FBI and that Ashcroft told Pickard that he did not want to hear briefings about terrorist threats. Ashcroft denies he made such statements. **(April 14):** In its preliminary report, commission says CIA failed to follow up on several important leads.

Air Pollution Violates Federal Standards (April 15): The Environmental Protection Agency tells 31 governors that the air pollution in their states does not meet federal health standards.

Hundreds of Thousands Rally for Abortion Rights (April 25): Demonstrators in Washington, DC, protest Bush administration's policy on reproductive rights.

Bush and Cheney Appear Before Commission (April 29): In a closed-door meeting, president and vice president are interviewed by members of the committee investigating the Sept. 11, 2001, terrorist attacks.

BUSINESS/SCIENCE/SOCIETY

Economy Posts Big Gain in Job Creation (April 2): Labor Department reports addition of 308,000 jobs in March.

Tornadoes Tear Through Midwest (April 21): At least 8 people die when 14 twisters hit Illinois, Indiana, Iowa, Nebraska, and Oklahoma. Illinois hit hardest.

World War II Memorial Opens (April 29): Memorial to 16 million Americans who served in the war opens in Washington, DC.

May

WORLD

European Union Expands (May 1): Ten countries join, bringing number of member nations to 25.

Foreigners Killed in Saudi Arabia (May 1): Two Americans, two Britons, and an Australian die when gunmen open fire in an engineering office in Cairo.

Likud Party Rejects Sharon's Gaza Plan (May 3): Israeli prime minister's party votes down his proposal to withdraw settlers and soldiers from the Gaza Strip.

Shiites Demand Rebel Cleric Withdraw Forces (May 4): About 150 influential leaders meet in Baghdad and urge Moktada al-Sadr to hand over weapons and remove his militia from Najaf and Karbala. **(May 27):** U.S. agrees to withdraw from Najaf and suspend the arrest warrant for al-Sadr, who agrees to pull his militia off the streets.

Bush Addresses Prison Abuse (May 5): In interviews on Arab television, president calls abuse and deaths of Iraqi prisoners "abhorrent." Bush upbraids Secretary of Defense Donald Rumsfeld for not informing him about the photos earlier.

American Decapitated in Iraq (May 8): Videotape broadcast on an Islamist website shows murder of Nicholas Berg, a 26-year-old businessman. Jordanian militant Abu Musab al-Zarqawi believed to be responsible.

Bomb Kills Chechen President (May 9): Akhmad Kadyrov, a former rebel leader who was elected in late 2003, and 13 others die in Grozny.

Israeli Troops Raid Gaza (May 11): Palestinian attack on an armored vehicle kills six Israeli soldiers searching for weapons facilities. Israelis return fire, killing several Palestinian militants. Israelis confiscate body parts of slain Israelis. **(May 13):** In Egyptian-brokered deal, Palestinians return remains of Israeli soldiers in exchange for Israeli withdrawal of troops. **(May 18):** In pursuit of Palestinian militants and weapons, Israeli troops raid Palestinian neighborhood in Gaza Strip, killing about 20.

India's Prime Minister Resigns (May 13): Indian National Congress Party prevails in parliamentary elections. Premier Atal Bihari Vajpayee steps down.

Court Dismisses Impeachment of South Korean President (May 14): Constitutional Court ruling reinstates Roh Moo Hyun as president.

Iraqi Leader Killed (May 17): Ezzidin Salim, president of the Iraqi Governing Council, is killed by a suicide bomber in Baghdad.

Gandhi Refuses to Become Prime Minister (May 18): Sonia Gandhi, leader of the Indian National Congress Party, announces she will not become premier. Former finance minister Manmohan Singh is named to the post.

U.S. Soldier Sentenced in Abuse Scandal (May 19): In the first court-martial in the prisoner abuse scandal in Iraq, Spc. Jeremy Sivits pleads guilty to several charges.

Israelis Open Fire on Protest (May 20): Nearly 40 killed—many of them civilians and children—when helicopter gunship attacks protest march in Gaza Strip. Israeli tanks bulldoze more than 100 homes in a Gaza neighborhood. UN Security Council passes a resolution condemning actions.

U.S. Raids Office of Former Iraqi Ally (May 20): U.S. troops and Iraqis confiscate computers and ransack headquarters of Ahmad Chalabi, a member of the Iraqi Governing Council who had been receiving a monthly stipend from the U.S. government.

Roof Collapses at Airport in France (May 23): At least five killed at new terminal at the Charles de Gaulle airport near Paris. Authorities blame faulty construction.

Army Report Reveals Widespread Prison Abuse (May 25): Document, dated May 5, indicates abuse started in Afghanistan in late 2002 and lasted until April 2004.

Sudan Rebels and Government Reach Accord (May 26): Islamic government and Sudan People's Liberation Army agree to end civil war that has lasted more than 20 years and claimed about two million people. However, war in western Darfur region between Arab militias and black Africans continues unabated.

Prime Minister of Iraq Chosen (May 28): Former exile and member of the Iraqi Governing Council Iyad Allawi will serve as interim premier.

Militants Attack Residential Area of Saudi Arabia (May 29): Gunmen open fire on Khobar complex that houses Americans and other foreigners and take several hostages. **(May 30):** Saudi commandos free most of the hostages and capture several militants.

NATION

White House Requests More Money for Iraq (May 5): Administration seeks an additional $25 billion for the military budget.

FDA Rejects Morning-After Pill (May 6): Food and Drug Administration disregards the opinion of its expert advisory panel and bans over-the-counter sale of emergency contraception drug.

FEC Allows Campaign Spending (May 13): Federal Election Commission refuses to limit spending by independent political committees, known as 527 organizations.

Bush Administration Alters AIDS Drug Policy (May 16): Changes expedite process for approving generic and combination antiretroviral drugs. Plan will allow countries in Africa and the Caribbean to buy drugs at lower prices.

Gay Marriages Begin in Massachusetts (May 17): Dozens of same-sex couples marry in Massachusetts, the first state in the country to legalize such unions.

Sept. 11 Panel Criticizes New York's Infrastructure (May 18): Commission investigating the attacks reports that efforts of police and fire departments were compromised by interagency communication problems and rivalries.

Bush Outlines Iraq Plan (May 24): Five-step plan to build a secure and democratic Iraq includes handing over authority to a sovereign government; helping to establish stability and security; continuing to rebuild infrastructure; encouraging more international support; and moving toward free elections.

Court Upholds Assisted Suicide Law (May 27): Saying the federal government can't intervene in state law, a federal appeals court rules that the justice department does not have the authority to penalize doctors who help terminally ill patients commit suicide.

BUSINESS/SCIENCE/SOCIETY

Picasso Work Sold for Record Price (May 5): Pablo Picasso's *Boy with a Pipe* sells for $104.1 million at a Sotheby's auction.

Economy Adds Jobs (May 7): Labor Department reports creation of 288,000 jobs in April. Unemployment rate drops to 5.6% from 5.7% in March.

Bush Renominates Greenspan (May 18): President asks chairman of the Federal Reserve to serve a fifth four-year term. Senate confirmation expected.

Violent Crime Decreased in 2003 (May 24): FBI's annual report indicates violent crimes dropped by 3.2%. Murder, however, increased by 1.3%.

Floods Devastate Caribbean Island (May 26): Death toll reaches 1,950 from floods caused by days of heavy rains in Haiti and the Dominican Republic.

June

WORLD

New Government Formed in Iraq (June 1): Cabinet of 36 Iraqis assumes power from the Iraqi Governing Council. Interim government is led by Prime Minister Iyad Allawi. Ghazi al-Yawar is named president.

Pentagon Proposes Troop Withdrawal (June 3): Plan includes removing two Army divisions from Germany. **(June 7):** Defense Department intends to withdraw about 12,500 troops from South Korea.

Iraqi Militias Agree to Dissolve (June 7): Nine groups agree to disband. The two largest, the Mahdi Army and the Falluja Brigade, however, do not commit to the agreement.

Security Council Passes Iraq Resolution (June 8): Votes, 15–0, in favor of American and British resolution to transfer power to an interim Iraqi government on June 30. It also calls for elections by Jan. 31, 2005.

Rebel Iraqi Cleric Endorses Government (June 11): Moktada al-Sadr urges his followers to observe cease-fire. **(June 12):** Al-Sadr says he plans to form a political party and participate in elections in 2005. **(June 16):** Al-Sadr orders his followers to lay down arms.

American Kidnapped in Saudi Arabia (June 12): Paul Johnson, Jr., held by members of an al-Qaeda cell. **(June 18):** Militants decapitate Johnson. Hours later, Saudi security officials kill four top leaders of the cell.

Iraqi Officials Fatally Shot (June 12): Deputy Foreign Minister Bassam Salih Kubba shot in northwest Baghdad. **(June 13):** Ministry official killed by insurgents in western Baghdad. **(June 16):** Oil ministry official killed in Kirkuk.

Dozens of Colombian Coca Farmers Killed (June 15): Officials blame FARC, a group of Marxist rebels. Farmers were working for right-wing paramilitary group that has been fighting FARC for control of coca fields.

UN Agency Reprimands Iran (June 18): International Atomic Energy Agency resolution criticizes Iran for not being forthcoming about its nuclear activity. Iran declares it will continue to produce equipment for its nuclear centrifuges.

South Korean Beheaded in Iraq (June 22): Terrorists linked to al-Zaraqawi kill Kim Sun Il, an interpreter.

U.S. Reaches Out to North Korea (June 23): U.S. offers delivery of fuel oil and a "provisional security guarantee" if North Korea agrees to disclose details of its weapons program, allow inspections, and begin to dismantle its nuclear program. **(June 24):** North Korea threatens to test one of its nuclear weapons.

Iraqi Insurgents Launch Deadly Attacks (June 24): More than 100 people die and hundreds more are wounded in a series of coordinated attacks in Falluja, Ramadi, Baquba, Mosul, and Baghdad.

U.S. Hands Over Power to Iraqis (June 28): L. Paul Bremer III, the U.S. administrator in Iraq, formally transfers sovereignty to Iraqi prime minister Iyad Allawi, who then formally takes oath of office. Ceremony held two days early in an attempt to thwart attacks by insurgents.

Canadian Prime Minister Reelected (June 29): Paul Martin narrowly reelected, but his Liberal party loses its majority in the House of Commons.

Israel Ordered to Remove Part of Barrier (June 30): Supreme Court tells army to dismantle a 20.5-mile portion of the security wall in the West Bank because it separates Palestinian landowners from their land and burdens an entire village.

Iraqis Take Custody of Hussein (June 30): Americans hand over legal custody of the former Iraqi dictator and 11 of his aides. The U.S. will, however, retain physical custody of the prisoners.

NATION

Judge Strikes Down Abortion Ban (June 1): Federal judge in San Francisco says 2003 Partial Birth Abortion Ban Act unconstitutional because it lacks a medical exception to save a woman's life and it places an unnecessary burden on women who seek abortions.

Army Extends Service for Soldiers (June 2): Active-duty and reserve troops heading for service in Iraq and Afghanistan face extended tours. **(June 29):** Pentagon announces it will call up 5,600 former soldiers for service in Iraq and Afghanistan.

CIA Director Tenet Says He Will Resign (June 3): George Tenet unexpectedly announces he will step down after serving seven years.

President Reagan Dies (June 5): Ronald Reagan, the 40th president, dies at age 93. He had been suffering from Alzheimer's disease. World leaders gather in Washington, DC, for Reagan's funeral.

Bush Nominates UN Ambassador (June 4): Selects former senator John Danforth to replace John Negroponte as American representative to the UN. Negroponte is the new U.S. ambassador to Iraq.

Ashcroft Grilled by Judiciary Committee (June 8): Attorney general faces harsh questioning from senators about memos from 2002 and 2003 that said that during wartime, in the interest of national security, the Bush administration was exempt from complying with the Geneva Convention and other treaties that ban torture.

Sept. 11 Panel Contradicts White House (June 16): Committee investigating terrorist attacks against the U.S. reports no link between al-Qaeda and Iraq. Report suggests White House reaction to the attacks was chaotic. Panel also finds no evidence that the Saudi government or officials financed al-Qaeda, a contradiction of an earlier report by a joint Congressional committee.

Connecticut Governor Resigns (June 21): John Rowland announces he will step down on July 1. He's the subject of a federal corruption investigation and an impeachment inquiry.

House Committee Criticizes CIA (June 24): Intelligence Committee report is highly critical of agency's spying operations, and says mismanagement led to intelligence failure on Iraq's weapons program.

BUSINESS/SCIENCE/SOCIETY

Economy Adds Jobs (June 4): Labor Department reports creation of 248,000 jobs in May. Unemployment rate remains at 5.6%.

Civilian Reaches Space (June 21): Michael Melvil pilots *SpaceShipOne* into space, becoming the first person to do so in a privately developed aircraft.

Federal Reserve Raises Rate (June 30): For the first time in four years, Fed chairman Alan Greenspan raises key rate to 1.25% from 1%.

Spacecraft Transmits Photos of Saturn's Rings (June 30): Black-and-white photos from the *Cassini* spacecraft reveal details of Saturn's ice and rock rings.

July

WORLD

Powell Visits Sudan (July 1): U.S. secretary of state and Kofi Annan, secretary-general of the UN, urge government to rein in the Arab militias in Darfur.

Hussein Appears in Court (July 1): Former Iraqi president and 11 codefendants are arraigned on charges of crimes against humanity.

Pentagon Sets Up Tribunal for Prisoners (July 7): Combat Status Review Tribunal will allow nearly 600 prisoners at Guantánamo Bay to challenge their status as enemy combatants.

World Court Rules Against Israeli Barrier (July 9): International Court of Justice says portion of the fence that cuts into occupied Palestinian land in the West Bank is illegal and advises Israel to remove it.

Afghanistan Postpones Parliamentary Elections (July 9): Elections, scheduled for late 2004, put off until April 2005 because of country's continuing instability.

Violence Rocks Iraq (July 14): Car bomb explodes outside American compound in Baghdad, killing 10 people. **(July 18):** Defense ministry official assassinated.

British Report Critical of Intelligence on Iraq (July 14): Report says government relied on "seriously flawed" intelligence to make its case for the war in Iraq.

Palestinian Premier Submits Resignation (July 17): Ahmed Qurei tells Palestinian leader Yasir Arafat he plans to step down. **(July 27):** Qurei withdraws resignation after Arafat agrees to hand over some control of security agencies to Qurei.

Kidnappings Follow Philippine Troop Withdrawal (July 20): Angelo dela Cruz released after Philippine president Gloria Macapagal Arroyo accedes to kidnappers' demands and pulls troops from Iraq. **(July 21):** Insurgents kidnap seven other foreign workers and threaten to behead them.

Former Mexican President Charged (July 23): Prosecutor accuses Luis Echeverría, president of Mexico from

1970 to 1976, of genocide in the 1971 massacre of 25 student protesters. **(July 24):** A federal judge dismisses the case.

Iraq Wracked by Violence (July 28): At least 70 people die when suicide bomb explodes outside a police station in Baquba. Iraqi forces and foreign troops attack insurgent stronghold south of Baghdad, killing 35 militants.

Aid Agency to Withdraw from Afghanistan (July 28): Doctors Without Borders announces plans to leave Afghanistan after 24 years of service because of dangerous conditions.

UN Adopts Resolution on Sudan (July 30): Security Council demands Sudanese government move to disarm militias in Darfur.

NATION

Panel Highly Critical of Intelligence Agencies (July 5): Senate Intelligence Committee reports that information on Iraq's weapons programs that was used to justify the war in Iraq was flawed.

Kerry Names Running Mate (July 6): Presumptive Democratic presidential nominee selects Sen. John Edwards as his pick for vice president.

Senate Kills Effort to Ban Same-Sex Marriages (July 14): Votes, 50–48, against proposed constitutional amendment to ban gay marriage.

Los Alamos Shut Down (July 16): Director of nuclear weapons laboratory halts most operations after a series of security and safety lapses. **(July 26):** Secretary of Energy Spencer Abraham orders a halt in classified operations at all of the Energy Department's labs.

September 11 Panel Harshly Critical of Government (July 22): Bipartisan commission completes 19-month investigation with the release of a report that calls for sweeping changes in country's intelligence agencies and the creation of a cabinet-level intelligence director.

Army Report Blames Rogue Soldiers for Abu Ghraib Scandal (July 22): U.S. Army inspector general contradicts other reports when he concludes that the prison abuse was not a systemic problem.

Democratic National Convention Begins (July 26): Delegates gather in Boston to nominate Sen. John Kerry as their presidential candidate. Speakers include Bill Clinton, Jimmy Carter, Al Gore, and Sen. Hillary Clinton. **(July 27):** Barack Obama delivers keynote address. Ron Reagan, son of former President Ronald Reagan, urges voters to support stem-cell research. **(July 29):** Sen. Kerry accepts the Democratic nomination.

BUSINESS/SCIENCE/SOCIETY

Jobs Growth Slows (July 2): Labor Dept. reports gain of 112,000 jobs in June. Jobless rate stays at 5.6%.

Cholesterol Targets Changed (July 12): Federal health agencies reduce target levels of LDL cholesterol by about 30%.

Stewart Sentenced (July 16): Martha Stewart sentenced to five months in prison and fined $30,000 after being found guilty of four counts of obstruction of justice and lying to federal investigators.

Bush Administration Predicts Record Budget Shortfall (July 30): White House projects $445 billion deficit for current fiscal year, or 3.8% of GDP, largest dollar amount in history.

Economic Growth Stalls (July 31): Commerce Department reports GDP grew at annual rate of 3% in the second quarter, down from 4.5% in the first quarter.

August

WORLD

British Arrest Senior al-Qaeda Member (Aug. 3): Authorities detain Abu Issa al-Hindi, who authorities believe surveyed potential targets in New York in 2000 and 2001. Several other terror suspects also arrested. **(Aug. 17):** Eight of the men are charged with conspiracy to commit murder and other terrorism-related charges.

Violence Flares in Najaf and Baghdad (Aug. 5): Shiite cleric al-Sadr orders an uprising against American and allied troops. His Mahdi Army sets up a base at the Imam Ali Shrine. Violence kills hundreds of Iraqis. **(Aug. 26):** Al-Sadr agrees to deal brokered by Grand Ayatollah Ali al-Sistani to end the siege of Najaf and Kufa. **(Aug. 27):** Mahdi Army withdraws from Imam Ali Shrine.

Iraqi Leader Asserts Control (Aug. 8): Prime Minister Allawi reinstates death penalty for a wide range of crimes.

Iraqi Magistrate Issues Warrant for Chalabi (Aug. 8): Ahmad Chalabi, Iraqi exile leader, wanted on counterfeiting charges.

Dozens Killed at UN Camp in Burundi (Aug. 13) More than 150 people, mostly women and children, massacred by rebel group, the National Liberation Forces.

Delegates Elect Iraqi Congress (Aug. 16): More than 1,000 delegates select 100-member committee to oversee elections. Assembly will also has veto power over decrees enacted by interim government.

Venezuelan President Survives Recall (Aug. 16): Venezuela votes, 58% to 42%, to keep Hugo Chávez in office.

Russia Rocked by Terrorism (Aug. 25): Two passenger planes go down within minutes of each other, killing 90 people. **(Aug. 29):** Russian officials confirm they found traces of explosives on the planes and declare the crashes acts of terrorism. **(Aug. 31):** Woman suicide bomber detonates a bomb outside a Moscow subway station, killing 9 others and wounding more than 50.

Chechen General Wins Election (Aug. 30): Alu Alkhanov, choice of the Kremlin, takes presidency in a landslide.

Nepalese Hostages Killed in Iraq (Aug. 31): A dozen laborers are executed by Iraqi insurgents.

Two Buses Blow Up in Israel (Aug. 31): In the worst violence in months, 16 people are killed in twin blasts in Beersheba. Militant group Hamas takes responsibility.

NATION

Administration Raises Terror Alert (Aug. 1): Intelligence indicates financial-institutions in New York City; Washington, DC; and Newark, New Jersey, are vulnerable. **(Aug. 2):** Officials say much of the intelligence that prompted the terror alert was years old.

Bush Calls for National Intelligence Director (Aug. 2): Supports overall recommendation of the commission that investigated the Sept. 11, 2001, terrorist attacks, but indicates power and influence of the intelligence official will be limited.

Missourians Approve Gay Marriage Ban (Aug. 3): Voters favor amendment to state constitution to bar same-sex marriage. First state to put question on ballot.

Bush Nominates Intelligence Chief (Aug. 10): Selects Florida representative Porter Goss as director of the CIA. Senate must confirm the nomination.

New Jersey Governor to Resign (Aug. 12): Democrat James McGreevey announces that he had an affair with another man and plans to resign in November.

California Annuls Gay Marriages (Aug. 12): State supreme court voids about 4,000 gay marriages performed in February and March.

Bush Calls for End to Independent Ads (Aug. 23): Says political ads paid for by third-party groups, called 527s, should be banned. **(Aug. 25):** National counsel for Bush resigns after he admits that he advised the Swift Boat Veterans for Truth, a 527 group critical of John Kerry.

Cheney Defends Gay Marriage (Aug. 24): Vice president parts with Bush administration, saying people should be free to enter into "any kind of relationship."

Officers Faulted in Reports on Prison Abuse (Aug. 24): Panel, led by former Secretary of Defense James Schlesinger, investigating the abuse at the Abu Ghraib prison in Iraq says that failures reached as high as the Pentagon. Panel also states that interrogation techniques used at Abu Ghraib violated military rules. **(Aug. 25):** Army investigation, headed by Maj. Gen. George

Fay, rejects earlier claim that the abuse was isolated to a few military police guards, stating that military intelligence soldiers and officers were culpable.

Judge Says Abortion Ban Unconstitutional (Aug. 26): Federal judge rules law prohibiting dilation and extraction is unconstitutional because it does not contain an exemption for women whose health could be in danger without the procedure.

Poor and Uninsured Increased in 2003 (Aug. 26): Census Bureau reports that poverty rate increased to 12.5% in 2003, up from 12.1% in 2002. Rate of uninsured rose to nearly 16% in 2003, from 14.2% in 2000.

Thousands of Bush Foes Gather in New York (Aug. 29): About a half-million people march in midtown Manhattan on the eve of the Republican National Convention.

Republican Convention Opens in New York (Aug. 30): Delegates meet to nominate President Bush. Speakers include Rudolph Giuliani, who recalls Bush's leadership after Sept. 11 attacks. **(Aug. 31):** More than 1,100 protesters are arrested at several Manhattan locations. **(Aug. 31):** Arnold Schwarzenegger and Laura Bush portray the president as a compassionate conservative.

BUSINESS/SCIENCE/SOCIETY

Hundreds Die in Store Fire (Aug. 1): More than 400 people die in inferno near Asunción, Paraguay.

Job Growth Slows (Aug. 6): Labor Department reports increase of only 32,000 jobs in July, far fewer than predicted. Unemployment rate drops to 5.5% from 5.6%.

Federal Reserve Raises Rate (Aug. 10): Fed chairman Alan Greenspan raises key rate to 1.5% from 1.25%.

Florida Pounded by Storms (Aug. 12): Tropical storm Bonnie pounds the Florida Panhandle. **(Aug. 13):** At least 13 people die as Hurricane Charley tears into the state's west coast, with winds of 145 miles an hour.

Summer Olympics Open in Athens (Aug. 13): The XXVII games open amid heightened security and sluggish ticket sales. **(Aug. 29):** Games close after more than 10,000 athletes from about 200 countries competed.

Google Goes Public (Aug. 18): Number of shares offered to public in auction is reduced, with demand lower than expected. Price of shares is $85, lower than the $108–$135 range initially targeted.

Munch Paintings Stolen (Aug. 22): *The Scream* and *Madonna* taken from Oslo's crowded Munch Museum.

Bush Administration Changes Position on Global Warming (Aug. 25): Report to Congress says scientific evidence suggests climate change is caused by emissions of carbon dioxide and other heat-trapping gases.

September

WORLD

Russian Insurgents Take Over School (Sept. 1): Armed Islamic guerrillas, most of them Chechen, take about 1,200 schoolchildren, parents, and teachers hostage in Beslan. **(Sept. 3):** Standoff ends in tragedy, as about 340 people die as the militants detonate explosives inside the school. **(Sept. 17):** Guerrilla leader Shamil Basayev claims responsibility for the recent terrorist attacks.

Little Progress Reported in Sudan (Sept. 1): UN Secretary General Kofi Annan says government has failed to disarm Arab militias, called the Janjaweed, or stop attacks on civilians in Darfur. **(Sept. 9):** Secretary of State Colin Powell testifies that rapes and mass killings in Darfur qualify as genocide.

South Korea Reports Scientist Produced Uranium (Sept. 2): Tells International Atomic Energy Agency that in 2000, a group of rogue scientists produced small amount of near weapons-grade uranium.

Several U.S. Troops Killed in Bombing (Sept. 6): Seven marines killed outside Falluja when a car bomb explodes near a convoy of American and Iraqi soldiers. Deadliest attack on American soldiers in months.

Car Bomb Explodes at Embassy in Indonesia (Sept. 7): Suicide bombers attack Australian Embassy in Jakarta, killing nine people and wounding nearly 200.

American Death Toll in Iraq Reaches Milestone (Sept. 7): Number of casualties reaches 1,000, as violence between Mahdi Army, led by Moktada al-Sadr, and U.S. and Iraqi troops resumes.

Governor Removed From Power in Afghanistan (Sept. 11): President Hamid Karzai dismisses Herat's powerful warlord Ismail Khan.

Widespread Fighting Erupts in Iraq (Sept. 12): Nearly 60 people are killed in suicide bombings and attacks by insurgents. **(Sept. 14):** Suicide bomber kills nearly 50 men applying for jobs in Baghdad.

Putin Calls for Drastic Changes in Government (Sept. 13): International community criticizes broad overhaul as a consolidation of power that will roll back democracy.

UN Leader Condemns War in Iraq (Sept. 15): UN Secretary General Kofi Annan says the war was illegal and violated the UN charter.

Atomic Energy Agency Tells Iran to Stop Enriching Uranium (Sept. 18): Passes resolution that requires Iran to cease all uranium-enrichment activities.

Chinese President Takes Control of the Military (Sept. 19): At the annual meeting of the Central Committee of the Communist Party, former president Jiang Zemin steps down as China's military chief, thus completing the transfer of power to President Hu.

Indonesia Elects New President (Sept. 20): Retired general Susilo Bambang Yudhoyono soundly defeats incumbent president Megawati Sukarnoputri.

Iraqi Prime Minister Addresses U.S. Congress (Sept. 23): Iyad Allawi reports progress in security, stability, and economy in Iraq.

Pakistani Militant Killed (Sept. 26): Officials say they have killed Amjad Hussain Farooqi, a terrorist linked to al-Qaeda and believed to have organized two assassination attempts on President Pervez Musharraf.

***Cole* Bombers Sentenced (Sept. 29):** Yemeni judge sentences Abd al-Rahim al-Nashiri and Jamal al-Badawi to death for plotting the 2000 attack on the American destroyer.

Car Bombs Kill Dozens in Iraq (Sept. 30): Two bombs explode at the opening of a sewer plant, killing 41 people, including at least 34 children.

Israeli Troops Attack Gaza Camp (Sept. 30): Soldiers battle with Palestinian militants in refugee camp. Nearly 30 Palestinians and 3 Israelis die in the fighting, the worst in two years.

NATION

Democrat Gives Keynote Address at RNC (Sept. 1): Democratic senator Zell Miller delivers keynote address harshly critical of Kerry. **(Sept. 2):** President Bush accepts the Republican presidential nomination.

Medicare Premiums to Increase (Sept. 3): Government announces 17% increase in 2005 premiums.

CBS Claims Bush Received Special Treatment (Sept. 8): Memos, written by Bush's former squadron commander and revealed on *60 Minutes,* suggest president received preferential treatment in joining the National Guard and later when he served in it. **(Sept. 20):** CBS News and Dan Rather, who reported on the memos, acknowledge that they were not able to prove the documents are authentic.

Weapons Ban Expires (Sept. 13): Law banning 19 types of semiautomatic weapons lapses.

Intelligence Report Painted Grim Picture of Iraq (Sept. 15): U.S. official says that highly classified National Intelligence Estimate prepared for President Bush and released in July predicted bleak future for Iraq.

Bush Proposes Shifting Iraq Funds (Sept. 15): Administration requests that the Senate divert $3.4 billion of the $18.4 billion Iraq reconstruction budget to improving security in the country.

Senate Confirms Intelligence Chief (Sept. 22): Votes, 77–17, to make Florida representative Porter Goss director of the CIA.

Congress Extends Tax Cuts (Sept. 23): House votes, 339–65, to extend several tax cuts that were to expire at the end of 2005. Cost of cuts totals about $146 billion over 10 years. Senate passes legislation, 92–3.

DeLay Rebuked by Ethics Committee (Sept. 30): House majority leader chastised for pressuring another representative to vote in favor of the Medicare bill.

Bush and Kerry Meet in First Debate (Sept. 30): Two presidential candidates discuss foreign affairs, focusing on the war in Iraq, in first of three debates.

BUSINESS/SCIENCE/SOCIETY

Bryant Case Dismissed (Sept. 1): Prosecution drops rape charges against the Los Angeles Lakers basketball star when his accuser says she will no longer cooperate.

Jobless Rate Drops (Sept. 3): Unemployment rate declines to 5.4% from 5.5% the previous month, and 144,000 jobs were added to the economy in August.

Florida Hit Hard by Hurricane (Sept. 4): Enormous, slow-moving Frances pounds state, causing about $40 billion in damage.

Clinton Has Heart Procedure (Sept. 7): Former president undergoes quadruple coronary bypass surgery to clear four blocked arteries. Full recovery expected.

Space Probe Crashes (Sept. 8): Capsule with samples of the Sun crashes after its parachutes fail to open.

Airline Files for Bankruptcy (Sept. 12): US Airways seeks bankruptcy protection for the second time.

Advisory Panel Recommends Warning for Antidepressants (Sept. 14): Group advising the FDA urges drug manufacturers to strongly warn parents and doctors that prescribing antidepressants to teenagers and children may increase suicidal behavior.

Storms Ravage South (Sept. 15): Ivan hits Alabama and Florida, causing tornadoes and the evacuation of more than 2 million people. Nearly 100 people die in the hurricane: 70 in the Caribbean and 27 in the U.S. **(Sept. 26):** Jeanne hits Florida, causing five deaths and severe flooding. Florida's fourth hurricane of season.

Hundreds Killed in Haiti (Sept. 20): Floods and mudslides caused by Tropical Storm Jeanne claim more than 550.

Fed Raises Rates (Sept. 21): Federal Reserve raises short-term interest rates a quarter of a percentage point, to 1.75%.

October

WORLD

U.S. and Iraqi Troops Attack Insurgents (Oct. 1): More than 5,000 soldiers attempt to take over Samarra, held by militants. As many as 125 insurgents killed. **(Oct. 3):** U.S. and Iraqi troops take control of Samarra.

Report Concludes No Illicit Weapons in Iraq (Oct. 6): Final report by chief weapons inspector Charles Duelfer says Iraq "essentially destroyed" all illicit weapons by the end of 1991 and had no such programs underway. Report also says Saddam Hussein had intended to resume weapons program.

Cambodian King Abdicates (Oct. 7): Move by King Norodom Sihanouk casts confusion over country as there's no clear successor. **(Oct. 11):** Throne Council names his son Prince Norodom Sihamoni king.

Israelis Targeted in Egypt (Oct. 8): At least 30 people die in three bombings at three resorts in the Sinai Peninsula.

Afghanistan Holds Elections (Oct. 9): Turnout high for presidential election. President Hamid Karzai and 17 other candidates on ballot. Karzai's rivals allege corruption and fraud. **(Oct. 24):** Karzai wins election, taking 55.3% of the vote, according to preliminary results.

Rebel Army Gives Up Weapons (Oct. 11): Moktada al-Sadr's Mahdi Army begins to surrender heavy weapons. Results deemed a "mixed success."

Bombs Explode in Baghdad's Guarded Site (Oct. 14): Insurgents detonate two bombs in the Green Zone, home to Iraqi officials and the American Embassy.

Israeli Troops Withdraw from Gaza (Oct. 16): Move ends deadly 17-day offensive to stop Palestinians from firing rockets into Israeli settlements; 109 Palestinians killed.

Dozens of Iraqi Soldiers Killed (Oct. 24): Fifty new soldiers executed by insurgents loyal to Abu Musab al-Zarqawi.

Tons of Explosives Missing in Iraq (Oct. 25): *New York Times* reports that about 380 tons of powerful explosives disappeared from military installation called Al Qaqaa sometime after the U.S.-led war began in 2003.

Israeli Parliament Approves Sharon Plan (Oct. 26): Votes, 67–45, in favor of prime minister's proposal to remove settlements and soldiers from the Gaza Strip and parts of the West Bank.

NATION

Rumsfeld Plays Down Iraq–al-Qaeda Link (Oct. 4): Tells Council on Foreign Relations that he sees no "strong, hard evidence" of a connection.

Former Iraq Administrator Critical of Troop Deployment (Oct. 4): Paul Bremer says that President Bush failed to send enough soldiers to secure Iraq.

Candidates Debate Issues (Oct. 5): Vice President Dick Cheney and Sen. John Edwards aggressively attack each other's records in their first and only debate. War in Iraq dominates session. **(Oct. 8):** President Bush and Sen. John Kerry field questions from undecided voters in a town-hall-style debate. **(Oct. 14):** In final debate, candidates attack each other's domestic policies.

Ethics Committee Criticizes DeLay (Oct. 6): House majority leader Tom DeLay faulted for questionable fund-raising tactics and for asking federal officials to intervene in state issue regarding gerrymandering.

Chief Justice Has Cancer (Oct. 25): Supreme Court announces that William Rehnquist is undergoing treatment for thyroid cancer.

BUSINESS/SOCIETY/SCIENCE

Mt. St. Helens Erupts (Oct. 1): After almost two decades of dormancy, the Washington volcano erupts in a small explosion of steam and ash. No deaths, damage, or injuries reported.

Flu Vaccine Contaminated (Oct. 5): Half of the country's flu vaccine to be destroyed because its maker, Chiron Corp., had its manufacturing license suspended.

Economy Adds Jobs (Oct. 9): Labor Department reports employment increased by less than 100,000 jobs. Jobless rate remains at 5.4%.

For online updates of 2004 events, see www.infoplease.com/ipa/A0920845.html.

2004 Nobel Prize Winners

Peace: Wangari Maathai (Kenya) "for her contribution to sustainable development, democracy, and peace."

Literature: Elfriede Jelinek (Austria) "for her musical flow of voices and counter-voices in novels and plays that with extraordinary linguistic zeal reveal the absurdity of society's clichés and their subjugating power."

Physics: David J. Gross, H. David Politzer, and Frank Wilczek (all U.S.) "for the discovery of asymptotic freedom in the theory of the strong interaction."

Chemistry: Aaron Ciechanover (Israel), Avram Hershko (Israel), and Irwin Rose (U.S.) "for the discovery of ubiquitin-mediated protein degradation."

Physiology or Medicine: Richard Axel and Linda Buck (both U.S.) "for their discoveries of odorant receptors and the organization of the olfactory system."

Economics: Finn E. Kydland (Norway) and Edward C. Prescott (U.S.) "for their contributions to dynamic macroeconomics: the time consistency of economic policy and the driving forces behind business cycles."

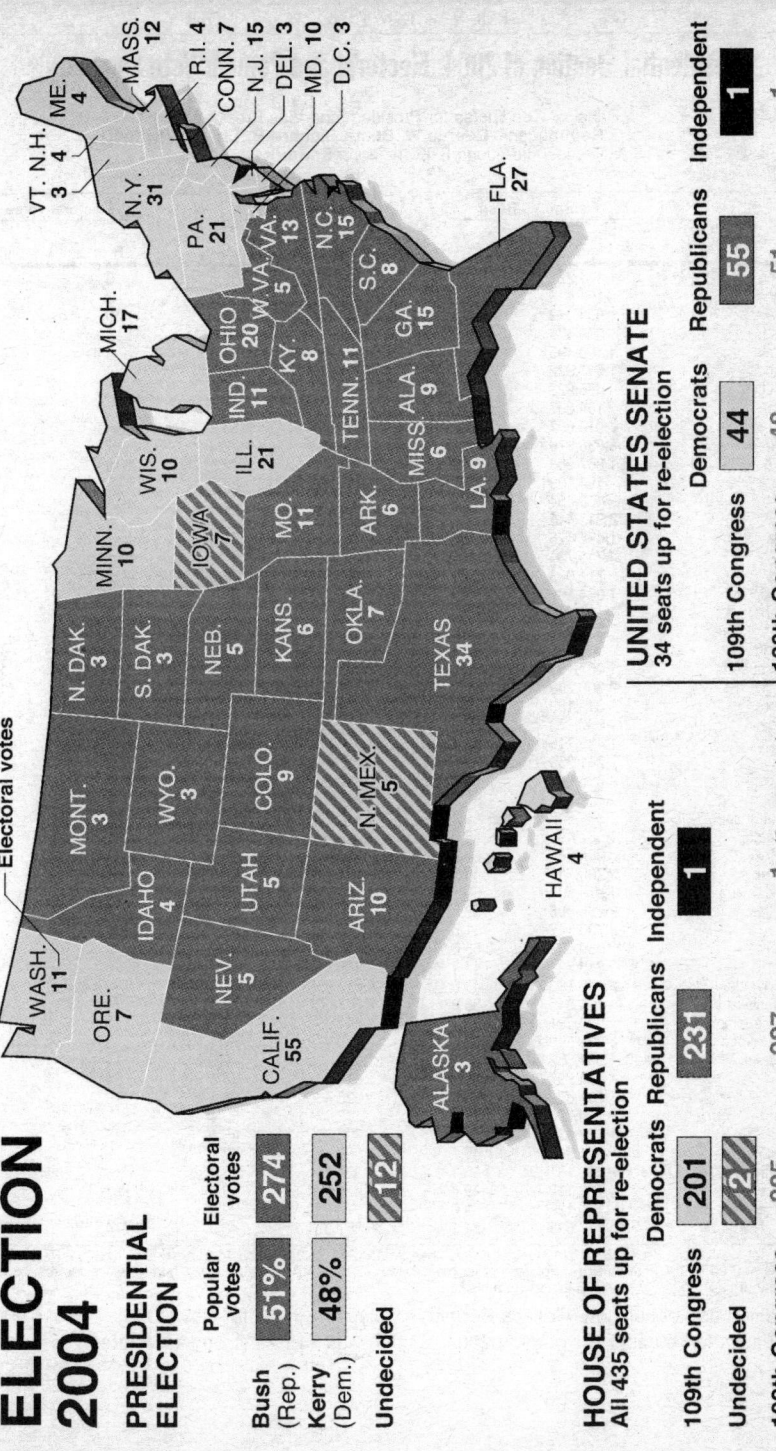

ELECTION 2004

PRESIDENTIAL ELECTION

	Popular votes	Electoral votes
Bush (Rep.)	51%	274
Kerry (Dem.)	48%	252
Undecided		12

— Electoral votes

WASH. 11
ORE. 7
CALIF. 55
NEV. 5
IDAHO 4
MONT. 3
WYO. 3
UTAH 5
ARIZ. 10
COLO. 9
N. DAK. 3
S. DAK. 3
NEB. 5
KANS. 6
OKLA. 7
N. MEX. 5
TEXAS 34
MINN. 10
IOWA 7
MO. 11
ARK. 6
LA. 9
WIS. 10
ILL. 21
IND. 11
MICH. 17
OHIO 20
KY. 8
TENN. 11
MISS. 6
ALA. 9
GA. 15
S.C. 8
N.C. 15
W.VA. 5
VA. 13
PA. 21
N.Y. 31
VT. 3
N.H. 4
ME. 4
MASS. 12
R.I. 4
CONN. 7
N.J. 15
DEL. 3
MD. 10
D.C. 3
FLA. 27
ALASKA 3
HAWAII 4

HOUSE OF REPRESENTATIVES
All 435 seats up for re-election

	Democrats	Republicans	Independent
109th Congress	201	231	1
Undecided	2		
108th Congress	205	227	1 (2 vacancies)

UNITED STATES SENATE
34 seats up for re-election

	Democrats	Republicans	Independent
109th Congress	44	55	1
108th Congress	48	51	1

KERRY CONCEDES: Sen. John Kerry conceded the election to President George W. Bush at mid-day on Nov. 3, choosing not to contest Bush's narrow margin of victory in Ohio. As of early Nov. 4, Iowa and New Mexico were too close to call in the presidential race, and two Louisiana seats in the House were undecided.

Presidential Election of 2004, Electoral and Popular Vote Summary

Principal Candidates for President and Vice President:
Republican—George W. Bush; Richard B. Cheney (winner)
Democratic—John F. Kerry; John Edwards

| | George W. Bush | | John F. Kerry | | Electoral votes | |
	Popular vote	%	Popular vote	%	R	D
Alabama	1,174,278	62.5%	691,830	36.8%	9	
Alaska	151,498	61.9	85,819	35.0	3	
Arizona	905,379	55.2	724,589	44.2	10	
Arkansas	566,676	54.3	464,156	44.5	6	
California	4,403,495	44.3	5,427,055	54.6		55
Colorado	1,017,322	52.4	898,566	46.3	9	
Connecticut	686,923	44.0	847,666	54.3		7
Delaware	164,807	45.8	191,870	53.3		3
DC	19,007	9.3	183,876	89.5		3
Florida	3,838,376	52.2	3,460,867	47.0	27	
Georgia	1,867,988	58.6	1,302,703	40.9	15	
Hawaii	194,109	45.3	231,318	54.0		4
Idaho	408,254	68.5	180,920	30.4	4	
Illinois	2,313,415	44.7	2,826,757	54.7		21
Indiana	1,474,475	60.1	960,899	39.2	11	
Iowa[1]	745,734	50.1	732,483	49.2		
Kansas	711,083	62.2	416,905	36.5	6	
Kentucky	1,064,504	59.6	709,072	39.7	8	
Louisiana	1,101,710	56.8	818,211	42.2	9	
Maine	308,997	45.0	364,153	53.0		4
Maryland	936,505	43.2	1,209,827	55.8		10
Massachusetts	1,067,163	37.0	1,793,916	62.1		12
Michigan	2,306,259	47.8	2,471,402	51.2		17
Minnesota	1,345,168	47.6	1,443,564	51.1		10
Mississippi	657,920	59.7	435,584	39.5	6	
Missouri	1,452,715	53.4	1,253,879	46.1	11	
Montana	261,939	59.2	170,172	38.4	3	
Nebraska	486,025	66.6	234,303	32.1	5	
Nevada	414,939	50.5	393,372	47.9	5	
New Hampshire	330,848	49.0	340,019	50.3		4
New Jersey	1,587,494	46.5	1,799,320	52.7		15
New Mexico[1]	364,569	50.2	353,788	48.7		
New York	2,780,749	40.5	3,967,047	57.8		31
North Carolina	1,919,903	56.1	1,488,278	43.5	15	
North Dakota	195,998	62.9	110,662	35.5	3	
Ohio	2,796,147	51.0	2,659,664	48.5	20	
Oklahoma	959,655	65.6	504,077	34.4	7	
Oregon	818,792	47.5	888,544	51.5		7
Pennsylvania	2,748,900	48.6	2,870,358	50.8		21
Rhode Island	161,345	38.9	247,071	59.6		4
South Carolina	920,321	58.0	647,998	40.9	8	
South Dakota	232,545	59.9	149,225	38.4	3	
Tennessee	1,381,852	56.8	1,033,030	42.5	11	
Texas	4,495,797	61.2	2,816,501	38.3	34	
Utah	608,851	71.0	226,456	26.4	5	
Vermont	120,710	38.9	183,621	59.1		3
Virginia	1,662,439	54.0	1,396,233	45.3	13	
Washington	921,543	45.7	1,068,762	53.0		11
West Virginia	418,151	56.1	321,641	43.2	5	
Wisconsin	1,477,122	49.4	1,488,935	49.8		10
Wyoming	167,129	69.0	70,620	29.1	3	
Total	59,117,523	51.1	55,557,584	48.0	274	252

NOTE: Total electoral votes = 538. Total electoral votes needed to win = 270. As of 8:44 a.m. ET, Nov. 4, 2004. Percentages may not add up to 100% due to rounding and other candidates. 1. As of Nov. 4, 2004, Iowa and New Mexico results were too close to call. *Source:* Federal Election Commission.

Voting age population (Census Bureau Population Survey for Nov. 2000): 205,815,000
Estimated number of voters in 2004 election was 115.7 million (Associated Press).

The One Hundred Ninth Congress

Composition of the 108th and 109th Congresses

109th Congress	Rep.	Dem.	Ind.	Undecided	108th Congress	Rep.	Dem.	Ind.	Vacancies
Senate	55	44	1	—	Senate	51	48	1	—
House	231	201	1	2	House	227	205	1	2

The Senate

Dates in left column indicate term in office; birth dates are given in parentheses after party affiliation. All terms are for six years and expire in January. Senators listed in italics were elected or reelected in 2004.

Alabama
1987–2011 *Richard Shelby (R) (1934)*
1997–2009 Jeff Sessions (R) (1946)
Alaska
1969–2009 Ted Stevens (R) (1923)
2002–2011 *Lisa Murkowski (R) (1957)*
Arizona
1987–2011 *John McCain (R) (1936)*
1995–2007 Jon Kyl (R) (1942)
Arkansas
2003–2009 Mark Pryor (D) (1963)
1999–2011 *Blanche Lincoln (D) (1960)*
California
1993–2007 Dianne Feinstein (D) (1933)
1993–2011 *Barbara Boxer (D) (1940)*
Colorado
1997–2009 Wayne Allard (R) (1943)
2005–2011 *Ken Salazar (D) (1955)*
Connecticut
1981–2011 *Christopher J. Dodd (D) (1944)*
1989–2007 Joseph I. Lieberman (D) (1942)
Delaware
1973–2009 Joseph R. Biden, Jr. (D) (1942)
2001–2007 Thomas R. Carper (D) (1947)
Florida
2001–2007 Bill Nelson (D) (1942)
2005–2011 *Mel Martinez (R) (1946)*
Georgia
2003–2009 Saxby Chambliss (R) (1943)
2005–2011 *Johnny Isakson (R) (1944)*
Hawaii
1963–2011 *Daniel K. Inouye (D) (1924)*
1990–2007 Daniel K. Akaka (D) (1924)
Idaho
1991–2009 Larry E. Craig (R) (1945)
1999–2011 *Mike Crapo (R) (1951)*
Illinois
1997–2009 Richard J. Durbin (D) (1944)
2005–2011 *Barack Obama (D) (1961)*
Indiana
1977–2007 Richard G. Lugar (R) (1932)
1999–2011 *Evan Bayh (D) (1955)*
Iowa
1981–2011 *Charles E. Grassley (R) (1933)*
1985–2009 Tom Harkin (D) (1939)
Kansas
1997–2011 *Sam Brownback (R) (1956)*
1997–2009 Pat Roberts (R) (1936)
Kentucky
1985–2009 Mitch McConnell (R) (1942)
1999–2011 *Jim Bunning (R) (1931)*
Louisiana
1997–2009 Mary L. Landrieu (D) (1955)
2005–2011 *David Vitter (R) (1961)*
Maine
1995–2007 Olympia J. Snowe (R) (1947)
1997–2009 Susan M. Collins (R) (1952)

Maryland
1977–2007 Paul S. Sarbanes (D) (1933)
1987–2011 *Barbara A. Mikulski (D) (1936)*
Massachusetts
1963–2007 Edward M. Kennedy (D) (1932)
1985–2009 John F. Kerry (D) (1943)
Michigan
1979–2009 Carl Levin (D) (1934)
2001–2007 Debbie A. Stabenow (D) (1950)
Minnesota
2003–2009 Norm Coleman (R) (1949)
2001–2007 Mark Dayton (D) (1947)
Mississippi
1979–2009 Thad Cochran (R) (1937)
1989–2007 Trent Lott (R) (1941)
Missouri
1987–2011 *Christopher S. Bond (R) (1939)*
2003–2009 James M. Talent (R) (1956)
Montana
1978–2009 Max Baucus (D) (1941)
1989–2007 Conrad Burns (R) (1935)
Nebraska
1997–2009 Charles Hagel (R) (1946)
2001–2007 Ben Nelson (D) (1941)
Nevada
1987–2011 *Harry Reid (D) (1939)*
2001–2007 John Ensign (R) (1958)
New Hampshire
1993–2011 *Judd Gregg (R) (1947)*
2003–2009 John E. Sununu (R) (1964)
New Jersey
2001–2007 Jon Corzine (D) (1947)
2003–2009 Frank R. Lautenberg (D) (1924)
New Mexico
1973–2009 Pete V. Domenici (R) (1932)
1983–2007 Jeff Bingaman (D) (1943)
New York
1999–2011 *Charles E. Schumer (D) (1950)*
2001–2007 Hillary Rodham Clinton (D) (1947)
North Carolina
2003–2009 Elizabeth Dole (R) (1936)
2005–2011 *Richard Burr (R) (1955)*
North Dakota
1987–2007 Kent Conrad (D) (1948)
1993–2011 *Byron L. Dorgan (D) (1942)*
Ohio
1995–2007 Mike DeWine (R) (1947)
1999–2011 *George Voinovich (R) (1936)*
Oklahoma
1989–2005 Don Nickles (R) (1948)
2005–2011 *Tom Coburn (R) (1948)*
Oregon
1996–2011 *Ron Wyden (D) (1949)*
1997–2009 Gordon H. Smith (R) (1952)
Pennsylvania
1981–2011 *Arlen Specter (R) (1930)*
1995–2007 Rick Santorum (R) (1958)

Rhode Island
1997–2009 Jack Reed (D) (1949)
1999–2007 Lincoln Chafee (R) (1953)
South Carolina
2003–2009 Lindsey Graham (R) (1955)
2005–2011 Jim DeMint (R) (1951)
South Dakota
2005–2011 John R. Thune (R) (1961)
1997–2009 Tim Johnson (D) (1946)
Tennessee
1995–2007 William Frist (R) (1952)
2003–2009 Lamar Alexander (R) (1940)
Texas
1995–2007 Kay Bailey Hutchison (R) (1943)
2003–2009 John Cornyn (R) (1952)
Utah
1977–2007 Orrin G. Hatch (R) (1934)
1993–2011 Robert Bennett (R) (1933)

Vermont
1975–2011 Patrick J. Leahy (D) (1940)
1989–2007 James M. Jeffords (I)
Virginia
1979–2009 John Warner (R) (1927)
2001–2007 George Allen (R) (1952)
Washington
1993–2011 Patty Murray (D) (1950)
2001–2007 Maria Cantwell (D) (1958)
West Virginia
1959–2007 Robert C. Byrd (D) (1917)
1985–2009 John D. "Jay" Rockefeller IV (D) (1937)
Wisconsin
1989–2007 Herbert Kohl (D) (1935)
1993–2011 Russ Feingold (D) (1953)
Wyoming
1995–2007 Craig Thomas (R) (1933)
1997–2009 Michael B. Enzi (R) (1944)

The House of Representatives

In the following lists, the numeral indicates the congressional district represented; AL is for representatives at large. All terms run from Jan. 2005 to Jan. 2007.

Alabama
1. Jo Bonner (R)
2. Terry Everett (R)
3. Mike Rogers (R)
4. Robert B. Aderholt (R)
5. Robert E. "Bud" Cramer, Jr. (D)
6. Spencer Bachus (R)
7. Artur Davis (D)

Alaska
AL Don Young (R)

Arizona
1. Rick Renzi (R)
2. Trent Franks (R)
3. John Shadegg (R)
4. Ed Pastor (D)
5. J. D. Hayworth (R)
6. Jeff Flake (R)
7. Raul Grijalva (D)
8. Jim Kolbe (R)

Arkansas
1. Marion Berry (D)
2. Vic Snyder (D)
3. John Boozman (R)
4. Mike Ross (D)

California
1. Mike Thompson (D)
2. Wally Herger (R)
3. Dan Lungren (R)
4. John T. Doolittle (R)
5. Robert T. Matsui (D)
6. Lynn C. Woolsey (D)
7. George Miller (D)
8. Nancy Pelosi (D)
9. Barbara Lee (D)
10. Ellen O. Tauscher (D)
11. Richard W. Pombo (R)
12. Tom Lantos (D)
13. Fortney Pete Stark (D)
14. Anna G. Eshoo (D)
15. Michael M. Honda (D)
16. Zoe Lofgren (D)
17. Sam Farr (D)
18. Dennis Cardoza (D)
19. George P. Radanovich (R)
20. Jim Costa (D)
21. Devin Nunes (R)
22. Bill Thomas (R)
23. Lois Capps (D)
24. Elton Gallegly (R)
25. Howard P. McKeon (R)
26. David Dreier (R)
27. Brad Sherman (D)
28. Howard L. Berman (D)
29. Adam B. Schiff (D)
30. Henry A. Waxman (D)
31. Xavier Becerra (D)
32. Hilda L. Solis (D)
33. Diane Watson (D)
34. Lucille Roybal-Allard (D)
35. Maxine Waters (D)
36. Jane Harman (D)
37. Juanita Millender-McDonald (D)
38. Grace F. Napolitano (D)
39. Linda T. Sanchez (D)
40. Ed Royce (R)
41. Jerry Lewis (R)
42. Gary G. Miller (R)
43. Joe Baca (D)
44. Ken Calvert (R)
45. Mary Bono (R)
46. Dana Rohrabacher (R)
47. Loretta Sanchez (D)
48. Christopher Cox (R)
49. Darrell Issa (R)
50. Randy Cunningham (R)
51. Bob Filner (D)
52. Duncan Hunter (R)
53. Susan Davis (D)

Colorado
1. Diana DeGette (D)
2. Mark Udall (D)
3. John T. Salazar (D)
4. Marilyn Musgrave (R)
5. Joel Hefley (R)
6. Thomas G. Tancredo (R)
7. Bob Beauprez (R)

Connecticut
1. John B. Larson (D)
2. Robert R. Simmons (R)
3. Rosa L. DeLauro (D)
4. Christopher Shays (R)
5. Nancy L. Johnson (R)

Delaware
AL Michael N. Castle (R)

Florida
1. Jeff Miller (R)
2. Allen Boyd (D)
3. Corrine Brown (D)
4. Ander Crenshaw (R)
5. Virginia Brown-Waite (R)
6. Cliff Stearns (R)
7. John L. Mica (R)
8. Ric Keller (R)
9. Michael Bilirakis (R)
10. C. W. Bill Young (R)
11. Jim Davis (D)
12. Adam Putnam (R)
13. Katherine Harris (R)
14. Connie Mack (R)
15. Dave Weldon (R)
16. Mark Foley (R)
17. Kendrick Meek (D)
18. Ileana Ros-Lehtinen (R)
19. Robert Wexler (D)
20. Debbie Wasserman Schultz (D)
21. Lincoln Diaz-Balart (R)
22. E. Clay Shaw, Jr. (R)
23. Alcee L. Hastings (D)
24. Tom Feeney (R)
25. Mario Diaz-Balart (R)

Georgia
1. Jack Kingston (R)
2. Sanford D. Bishop, Jr. (D)
3. Jim Marshall (D)
4. Cynthia McKinney (D)
5. John Lewis (D)
6. Tom Price (R)
7. John Linder (R)
8. Lynn A. Westmoreland (R)
9. Charlie Norwood (R)
10. Nathan Deal (R)
11. Phil Gingrey (R)
12. John Barrow (D)
13. David Scott (D)

Hawaii
1. Neil Abercrombie (D)
2. Ed Case (D)

Idaho
1. C. L. Otter (R)
2. Mike Simpson (R)

Illinois
1. Bobby L. Rush (D)
2. Jesse L. Jackson, Jr. (D)
3. Dan Lipinski (D)
4. Luis V. Gutierrez (D)
5. Rahm Emanuel (D)
6. Henry J. Hyde (R)
7. Danny K. Davis (D)
8. Melissa L. Bean (D)
9. Janice Schakowsky (D)
10. Mark Steven Kirk (R)
11. Jerry Weller (R)
12. Jerry F. Costello (D)

13. Judy Biggert (R)
14. J. Dennis Hastert (R)
15. Timothy V. Johnson (R)
16. Donald Manzullo (R)
17. Lane Evans (D)
18. Ray LaHood (R)
19. John Shimkus (R)

Indiana
1. Peter J. Visclosky (D)
2. Chris Chocola (R)
3. Mark E. Souder (R)
4. Steve Buyer (R)
5. Dan Burton (R)
6. Mike Pence (R)
7. Julia Carson (D)
8. John Hostettler (R)
9. Mike Sodrel (R)

Iowa
1. Jim Nussle (R)
2. Jim Leach (R)
3. Leonard L. Boswell (D)
4. Tom Latham (R)
5. Steve King (R)

Kansas
1. Jerry Moran (R)
2. Jim Ryun (R)
3. Dennis Moore (D)
4. Todd Tiahrt (R)

Kentucky
1. Edward Whitfield (R)
2. Ron Lewis (R)
3. Anne M. Northup (R)
4. Geoff Davis (R)
5. Harold Rogers (R)
6. Ben Chandler (D)

Louisiana
1. Bobby Jindal (R)
2. William J. Jefferson (D)
3. Vacant[1]
4. Jim McCrery (R)
5. Rodney Alexander (R)
6. Richard H. Baker (R)
7. Vacant[1]

Maine
1. Thomas H. Allen (D)
2. Mike Michaud (D)

Maryland
1. Wayne T. Gilchrest (R)
2. C. A. "Dutch" Ruppersberger (D)
3. Benjamin L. Cardin (D)
4. Albert R. Wynn (D)
5. Steny H. Hoyer (D)
6. Roscoe G. Bartlett (R)
7. Elijah E. Cummings (D)
8. Chris Van Hollen (D)

Massachusetts
1. John W. Olver (D)
2. Richard E. Neal (D)
3. Jim McGovern (D)
4. Barney Frank (D)
5. Marty Meehan (D)
6. John F. Tierney (D)
7. Edward J. Markey (D)
8. Michael E. Capuano (D)
9. Stephen F. Lynch (D)
10. William Delahunt (D)

Michigan
1. Bart Stupak (D)
2. Peter Hoekstra (R)

1. Seat to be decided in a Dec. 4 run-off election.

3. Vernon J. Ehlers (R)
4. Dave Camp (R)
5. Dale Kildee (D)
6. Fred Upton (R)
7. Joe Schwarz (R)
8. Mike Rogers (R)
9. Joseph Knollenberg (R)
10. Candice Miller (R)
11. Thaddeus McCotter (R)
12. Sander M. Levin (D)
13. Carolyn C. Kilpatrick (D)
14. John Conyers, Jr. (D)
15. John D. Dingell (D)

Minnesota
1. Gil Gutknecht (R)
2. John Kline (R)
3. Jim Ramstad (R)
4. Betty McCollum (D)
5. Martin Olav Sabo (D)
6. Mark Kennedy (R)
7. Collin C. Peterson (D)
8. James L. Oberstar (D)

Mississippi
1. Roger Wicker (R)
2. Bennie Thompson (D)
3. Charles Pickering (R)
4. Gene Taylor (D)

Missouri
1. William Lacy Clay (D)
2. Todd Akin (R)
3. Russ Carnahan (D)
4. Ike Skelton (D)
5. Emanuel Cleaver (D)
6. Sam Graves (R)
7. Roy Blunt (R)
8. Jo Ann Emerson (R)
9. Kenny Hulshof (R)

Montana
AL Denny Rehberg (R)

Nebraska
1. Jeff Fortenberry (R)
2. Lee Terry (R)
3. Tom Osborne (R)

Nevada
1. Shelley Berkley (D)
2. James A. Gibbons (R)
3. Jon C. Porter (R)

New Hampshire
1. Jeb Bradley (R)
2. Charles Bass (R)

New Jersey
1. Robert E. Andrews (D)
2. Frank A. LoBiondo (R)
3. Jim Saxton (R)
4. Christopher H. Smith (R)
5. Scott Garrett (R)
6. Frank Pallone, Jr. (D)
7. Michael A. Ferguson (R)
8. Bill Pascrell, Jr. (D)
9. Steven R. Rothman (D)
10. Donald M. Payne (D)
11. Rodney Frelinghuysen (R)
12. Rush D. Holt (D)
13. Robert Menendez (D)

New Mexico
1. Heather Wilson (R)
2. Steve Pearce (R)
3. Tom Udall (D)

New York
1. Tim Bishop (D)
2. Steve J. Israel (D)
3. Peter King (R)

4. Carolyn McCarthy (D)
5. Gary L. Ackerman (D)
6. Gregory W. Meeks (D)
7. Joseph Crowley (D)
8. Jerrold Nadler (D)
9. Anthony D. Weiner (D)
10. Edolphus Towns (D)
11. Major R. Owens (D)
12. Nydia Velázquez (D)
13. Vito J. Fossella (R)
14. Carolyn Maloney (D)
15. Charles B. Rangel (D)
16. José E. Serrano (D)
17. Eliot L. Engel (D)
18. Nita M. Lowey (D)
19. Sue W. Kelly (R)
20. John E. Sweeney (R)
21. Michael R. McNulty (D)
22. Maurice Hinchey (D)
23. John McHugh (R)
24. Sherwood L. Boehlert (R)
25. James T. Walsh (R)
26. Thomas Reynolds (R)
27. Brian M. Higgins (D)
28. Louise McIntosh Slaughter (D)
29. John "Randy" Kuhl (R)

North Carolina
1. G. K. Butterfield (D)
2. Bob Etheridge (D)
3. Walter Jones (R)
4. David E. Price (D)
5. Virginia Foxx (R)
6. Howard Coble (R)
7. Mike McIntyre (D)
8. Robin Hayes (R)
9. Sue Myrick (R)
10. Patrick McHenry (R)
11. Charles H. Taylor (R)
12. Melvin L. Watt (D)
13. Brad Miller (D)

North Dakota
AL Earl Pomeroy (D)

Ohio
1. Steve Chabot (R)
2. Rob Portman (R)
3. Michael Turner (R)
4. Michael G. Oxley (R)
5. Paul E. Gillmor (R)
6. Ted Strickland (D)
7. David Hobson (R)
8. John A. Boehner (R)
9. Marcy Kaptur (D)
10. Dennis J. Kucinich (D)
11. Stephanie Tubbs Jones (D)
12. Patrick J. Tiberi (R)
13. Sherrod Brown (D)
14. Steven C. LaTourette (R)
15. Deborah Pryce (R)
16. Ralph Regula (R)
17. Tim Ryan (D)
18. Bob Ney (R)

Oklahoma
1. John Sullivan (R)
2. Dan Boren (D)
3. Frank D. Lucas (R)
4. Tom Cole (R)
5. Ernest Istook (R)

Oregon
1. David Wu (D)
2. Greg Walden (R)
3. Earl Blumenauer (D)
4. Peter A. DeFazio (D)
5. Darlene Hooley (D)

Pennsylvania
1. Robert A. Brady (D)
2. Chaka Fattah (D)
3. Philip S. English (R)
4. Melissa A. Hart (R)
5. John E. Peterson (R)
6. Jim Gerlach (R)
7. Curt Weldon (R)
8. Mike Fitzpatrick (R)
9. Bill Shuster (R)
10. Don Sherwood (R)
11. Paul E. Kanjorski (D)
12. John P. Murtha (D)
13. Allyson Y. Schwartz (D)
14. Mike Doyle (D)
15. Charles W. Dent (R)
16. Joseph R. Pitts (R)
17. Tim Holden (D)
18. Timothy F. Murphy (R)
19. Todd R. Platts (R)

Rhode Island
1. Patrick J. Kennedy (D)
2. James R. Langevin (D)

South Carolina
1. Henry E. Brown, Jr. (R)
2. Joe Wilson (R)
3. J. Gresham Barrett (R)
4. Bob Inglis (R)
5. John M. Spratt (D)
6. James E. Clyburn (D)

South Dakota
AL Stephanie Herseth (D)

Tennessee
1. William L. Jenkins (R)
2. John J. Duncan (R)
3. Zach Wamp (R)
4. Lincoln Davis (D)
5. Jim Cooper (D)
6. Bart Gordon (D)

7. Marsha Blackburn (R)
8. John Tanner (D)
9. Harold E. Ford, Jr. (D)

Texas
1. Louie Gohmert (R)
2. Ted Poe (R)
3. Sam Johnson (R)
4. Ralph M. Hall (R)
5. Jeb Hensarling (R)
6. Joe Barton (R)
7. John A. Culberson (R)
8. Kevin P. Brady (R)
9. Al Green (D)
10. Michael McCaul (R)
11. Mike Conaway (R)
12. Kay Granger (R)
13. William Thornberry (R)
14. Ron E. Paul (R)
15. Rubén E. Hinojosa (D)
16. Silvestre Reyes (D)
17. Chet Edwards (D)
18. Sheila Jackson-Lee (D)
19. Randy Neugebauer (R)
20. Charles A. Gonzalez (D)
21. Lamar S. Smith (R)
22. Tom DeLay (R)
23. Henry Bonilla (R)
24. Kenny Marchant (R)
25. Lloyd Doggett (D)
26. Michael C. Burgess (R)
27. Solomon P. Ortiz (D)
28. Henry Cuellar (D)
29. Gene Green (D)
30. Eddie Bernice Johnson (D)
31. John R. Carter (R)
32. Pete Sessions (R)

Utah
1. Rob Bishop (R)
2. Jim Matheson (D)
3. Chris Cannon (R)

Vermont
AL Bernard Sanders (I)

Virginia
1. Jo Ann S. Davis (R)
2. Thelma D. Drake (R)
3. Bobby Scott (D)
4. Randy Forbes (R)
5. Virgil H. Goode, Jr. (R)
6. Bob Goodlatte (R)
7. Eric I. Cantor (R)
8. James P. Moran (D)
9. Rick Boucher (D)
10. Frank R. Wolf (R)
11. Thomas M. Davis (R)

Washington
1. Jay Inslee (D)
2. Rick Larsen (D)
3. Brian Baird (D)
4. Doc Hastings (R)
5. Cathy McMorris (R)
6. Norman D. Dicks (D)
7. Jim McDermott (D)
8. Dave Reichert (R)
9. Adam Smith (D)

West Virginia
1. Alan B. Mollohan (D)
2. Shelley Moore Capito (R)
3. Nick J. Rahall II (D)

Wisconsin
1. Paul D. Ryan (R)
2. Tammy Baldwin (D)
3. Ron J. Kind (D)
4. Gwen S. Moore (D)
5. F. James Sensenbrenner, Jr. (R)
6. Thomas E. Petri ((R)
7. David R. Obey (D)
8. Mark Green (R)

Wyoming
AL Barbara Cubin (R)

The Governors of the Fifty States

State	Governor	Current term[1]	State	Governor	Current term[1]
Ala.	Robert Riley (R)	2003–2007	*Mont.*	*Brian Schweitzer (D)*	*2005–2009*
Alaska	Frank H. Murkowski (R)	2002–2006[2]	Nebr.	Mike Johanns (R)	2003–2007
Ariz.	Janet Napolitano (D)	2003–2007	Nev.	Kenny Guinn (R)	2003–2007
Ark.	Mike Huckabee (R)	2003–2007	*N.H.*	*John Lynch (D)*	*2005–2007*
Calif.	Arnold Schwarzenegger (R)[3]	2003–2007	N.J.	Richard Codey (D)[5]	2002–2006
Colo.	Bill Owens (R)	2003–2007	N.M.	Bill Richardson (D)	2003–2007
Conn.	M. Jodi Rell (R)[4]	2004–2007	N.Y.	George E. Pataki (R)	2003–2007
Del.	*Ruth Ann Minner (D)*	*2005–2009*	*N.C.*	*Mike F. Easley (D)*	*2005–2009*
Fla.	Jeb Bush (R)	2003–2007	*N.D.*	*John Hoeven (R)*	*2004–2008[2]*
Ga.	Sonny Perdue (R)	2003–2007	Ohio	Bob Taft (R)	2003–2007
Hawaii	Linda Lingle (R)	2002–2006[2]	Okla.	Brad Henry (D)	2003–2007
Idaho	Dirk Kempthorne (R)	2003–2007	Ore.	Ted Kulongoski (D)	2003–2007
Ill.	Rod R. Blagojevich (D)	2003–2007	Pa.	Ed Rendell (D)	2003–2007
Ind.	*Mitchell Daniels (R)*	*2005–2009*	R.I.	Don Carcieri (R)	2003–2007
Iowa	Tom Vilsack (D)	2003–2007	S.C.	Mark Sanford (R)	2003–2007
Kans.	Kathleen Sebelius (D)	2003–2007	S.D.	Mike Rounds (R)	2003–2007
Ky.	Ernie Fletcher (R)	2003–2007[2]	Tenn.	Phil Bredesen (D)	2003–2007
La.	Kathleen Blanco (D)	2004–2008	Tex.	Rick Perry (R)	2003–2007
Maine	John Baldacci (D)	2003–2007	*Utah*	*Jon Huntsman (R)*	*2005–2009*
Md.	Robert L. Ehrlich, Jr. (R)	2003–2007	*Vt.*	*James H. Douglas (R)*	*2005–2007*
Mass.	Mitt Romney (R)	2003–2007	Va.	Mark Warner (D)	2002–2006
Mich.	Jennifer Granholm (D)	2002–2007	*Wash.*	(6)	*2005–2009*
Minn.	Tim Pawlenty (R)	2003–2007	*W. Va.*	*Joe Manchin (D)*	*2005–2009*
Miss.	Haley Barbour (R)	2004–2008	Wis.	Jim Doyle (D)	2003–2007
Mo.	*Matt Blunt (R)*	*2005–2009*	Wyo.	Dave Freudenthal (D)	2003–2007

NOTE: Governors listed in italics were elected or reelected in 2004. 1. Except where indicated, all terms begin and end in January. 2. Term begins and ends in December. 3. Gray Davis (D) was voted out of office in a recall election Oct. 7, 2003. 4. John Rowland resigned in June 2004 under the threat of an impeachment inquiry, but could still face criminal charges of corruption. Rell was the lieutenant governor. 5. Jim McGreevey announced on Aug. 12, 2004, that he would resign effective Nov. 15. Senate president Richard Codey became acting governor. 6. Close race between Christine Gregoire (D) and Dino Rossi (R) undecided as of Nov. 4, 2004.

How a President Is Nominated and Elected

The Conventions

The national conventions of both major parties are held during the summer of a presidential election year. Earlier, each party selects delegates by primaries, conventions, committees, etc.

At each convention, a temporary chairman is chosen. After a credentials committee seats the delegates, a permanent chairman is elected. The convention then votes on a platform, drawn up by the platform committee.

By the third or fourth day, presidential nominations begin. The chairman calls the roll of states alphabetically. A state may place a candidate in nomination or yield to another state.

Voting, again alphabetically by roll call of states, begins after all nominations have been made and seconded. A simple majority is required in each party, although this may require many ballots.

Finally, the vice-presidential candidate is selected. Although there is no law saying that the candidates *must* come from different states, it is, practically, necessary for this to be the case. Otherwise, according to the Constitution (*see* the 12th Amendment), electors from that state could vote for only one of the candidates and would have to cast their other vote for some person of another state. This could result in a presidential candidate's receiving a majority electoral vote and his or her running mate's failing to do so.

The Electoral College

The next step in the process is the nomination of electors in each state, according to its laws. These electors must not be federal office holders. In the November election, the voters cast their votes for electors, not for president. In some states, the ballots include only the names of the presidential and vice-presidential candidates; in others, they include only names of the electors. Nowadays, it is rare for electors to be split between parties. The last such occurrence was in North Carolina in 1968; the last before that, in Tennessee in 1948. On four occasions (1824, 1876, 1888, and 2000), the presidential candidate with the largest popular vote failed to obtain an electoral vote majority.

Each state has as many electors as it has senators and representatives. For the 2000 election, the total electors were 538, based on 100 senators and 435 representatives, plus 3 electoral votes from the District of Columbia as a result of the 23rd Amendment to the Constitution.

On the first Monday after the second Wednesday in December, the electors cast their votes in their respective state capitols. Constitutionally they may vote for someone other than the party candidate but usually they do not since they are pledged to one party and its candidate on the ballot. Should the presidential or vice-presidential candidate die between the November election and the December meetings, the electors pledged to vote for him or her could vote for whomever they pleased. However, it seems certain that the national committee would attempt to get an agreement among the state party leaders for a replacement candidate.

The votes of the electors, certified by the states, are sent to Congress, where the president of the Senate opens the certificates and has them counted in the presence of both houses on Jan. 6. The new president is inaugurated at noon on Jan. 20.

Should no candidate receive a majority of the electoral vote for president, the House of Representatives chooses a president from among the three highest candidates, voting, not as individuals, but as states, with a majority (now 26) needed to elect. Should no vice-presidential candidate obtain the majority, the Senate, voting as individuals, chooses from the highest two.

Electoral College Votes by State, 2004 Presidential Elections

(total electoral votes: 538; majority needed to elect: 270)

State	Votes	State	Votes	State	Votes
Alabama	9	Kentucky	8	North Dakota	3
Alaska	3	Louisiana	9	Ohio	20
Arizona	10	Maine	4	Oklahoma	7
Arkansas	6	Maryland	10	Oregon	7
California	55	Massachusetts	12	Pennsylvania	21
Colorado	9	Michigan	17	Rhode Island	4
Connecticut	7	Minnesota	10	South Carolina	8
Delaware	3	Mississippi	6	South Dakota	3
District of Columbia	3	Missouri	11	Tennessee	11
Florida	27	Montana	3	Texas	34
Georgia	15	Nebraska	5	Utah	5
Hawaii	4	Nevada	5	Vermont	3
Idaho	4	New Hampshire	4	Virginia	13
Illinois	21	New Jersey	15	Washington	11
Indiana	11	New Mexico	5	West Virginia	5
Iowa	7	New York	31	Wisconsin	10
Kansas	6	North Carolina	15	Wyoming	3

National Political Conventions Since 1856

Opening date	Party	Where held	Opening date	Party	Where held
June 17, 1856	Republican	Philadelphia	June 27, 1932	Democratic	Chicago
June 2, 1856	Democratic	Cincinnati	June 9, 1936	Republican	Cleveland
May 16, 1860	Republican	Chicago	June 23, 1936	Democratic	Philadelphia
April 23, 1860	Democratic	Charleston and Baltimore	June 24, 1940	Republican	Philadelphia
June 7, 1864	Republican[1]	Baltimore	July 15, 1940	Democratic	Chicago
Aug. 29, 1864	Democratic	Chicago	June 26, 1944	Republican	Chicago
May 20, 1868	Republican	Chicago	July 19, 1944	Democratic	Chicago
July 4, 1868	Democratic	New York City	June 21, 1948	Republican	Philadelphia
June 5, 1872	Republican	Philadelphia	July 12, 1948	Democratic	Philadelphia
June 9, 1872	Democratic	Baltimore	July 17, 1948	(3)	Birmingham
June 14, 1876	Republican	Cincinnati	July 22, 1948	Progressive	Philadelphia
June 28, 1876	Democratic	St. Louis	July 7, 1952	Republican	Chicago
June 2, 1880	Republican	Chicago	July 21, 1952	Democratic	Chicago
June 23, 1880	Democratic	Cincinnati	Aug. 20, 1956	Republican	San Francisco
June 3, 1884	Republican	Chicago	Aug. 13, 1956	Democratic	Chicago
July 11, 1884	Democratic	Chicago	July 25, 1960	Republican	Chicago
June 19, 1888	Republican	Chicago	July 11, 1960	Democratic	Los Angeles
June 6, 1888	Democratic	St. Louis	July 13, 1964	Republican	San Francisco
June 7, 1892	Republican	Minneapolis	Aug. 24, 1964	Democratic	Atlantic City
June 21, 1892	Democratic	Chicago	Aug. 5, 1968	Republican	Miami Beach
June 16, 1896	Republican	St. Louis	Aug. 26, 1968	Democratic	Chicago
July 7, 1896	Democratic	Chicago	July 10, 1972	Democratic	Miami Beach
June 19, 1900	Republican	Philadelphia	Aug. 21, 1972	Republican	Miami Beach
July 4, 1900	Democratic	Kansas City	July 12, 1976	Democratic	New York City
June 21, 1904	Republican	Chicago	Aug. 16, 1976	Republican	Kansas City, Mo.
July 6, 1904	Democratic	St. Louis	Aug. 11, 1980	Democratic	New York City
June 16, 1908	Republican	Chicago	July 14, 1980	Republican	Detroit
July 7, 1908	Democratic	Denver	Aug. 20, 1984	Republican	Dallas
June 18, 1912	Republican	Chicago	July 16, 1984	Democratic	San Francisco
June 25, 1912	Democratic	Baltimore	July 18, 1988	Democratic	Atlanta
June 7, 1916	Republican	Chicago	Aug. 15, 1988	Republican	New Orleans
June 14, 1916	Democratic	St. Louis	July 13, 1992	Democratic	New York City
June 8, 1920	Republican	Chicago	Aug. 17, 1992	Republican	Houston
June 28, 1920	Democratic	San Francisco	Aug. 10, 1996	Republican	San Diego
June 10, 1924	Republican	Cleveland	Aug. 26, 1996	Democratic	Chicago
June 24, 1924[2]	Democratic	New York City	July 29, 2000	Republican	Philadelphia
June 12, 1928	Republican	Kansas City	Aug. 14, 2000	Democratic	Los Angeles
June 26, 1928	Democratic	Houston	July 26, 2004	Democratic	Boston
June 14, 1932	Republican	Chicago	Aug. 30, 2004	Republican	New York City

1. The convention adopted name Union Party to attract War Democrats and others favoring prosecution of war. 2. In session until July 10, 1924. 3. States' Rights delegates from 13 southern states.

National Committee Chairs Since 1944

Chairman and (state)—Republican	Term	Chairman and (state)—Democratic	Term
Herbert Brownell, Jr. (N.Y.)	1944–1946	Robert E. Hannegan (Mo.)	1944–1947
Carroll Reece (Tenn.)	1946–1948	J. Howard McGrath (R.I.)	1947–1949
Hugh D. Scott, Jr. (Pa.)	1948–1949	William M. Boyle, Jr. (Mo.)	1949–1951
Guy G. Gabrielson (N.J.)	1949–1952	Frank E. McKinney (Ind.)	1951–1952
Arthur E. Summerfield (Mich.)	1952–1953	Stephen A. Mitchell (Ill.)	1952–1954
Wesley Roberts (Kan.)	1953	Paul M. Butler (Ind.)	1955–1960
Leonard W. Hall (N.Y.)	1953–1957	Henry M. Jackson (Wash.)	1960–1961
Meade Alcorn (Conn.)	1957–1959	John M. Bailey (Conn.)	1961–1968
Thruston B. Morton (Ky.)	1959–1961	Lawrence F. O'Brien (Mass.)	1968–1969
William E. Miller (N.Y.)	1961–1964	Fred R. Harris (Okla.)	1969–1970
Dean Burch (Ariz.)	1964–1965	Lawrence F. O'Brien (Mass.)	1970–1972
Ray C. Bliss (Ohio)	1965–1969	Jean Westwood (Utah)	1972
Rogers C. B. Morton (Md.)	1969–1971	Robert S. Strauss (Tex.)	1972–1977
Robert Dole (Kan.)	1971–1973	Kenneth M. Curtis (Me.)	1977
George H. Bush (Tex.)	1973–1974	John C. White (Tex.)	1977–1981
Mary Louise Smith (Iowa)	1974–1977	Charles T. Manatt (Calif.)	1981–1985
William E. Brock III (Tenn.)	1977–1981	Paul G. Kirk, Jr. (Mass.)	1985–1989
Richard Richards (Utah)	1981–1983	Ronald H. Brown (D.C.)	1989–1993
Frank J. Fahrenkopf, Jr. (Nevada)	1983–1989	David Wilhelm (Ill.)	1993–1994
Lee Atwater (S.C.)	1989–1991	Christopher J. Dodd (Conn.)	1995–1996
Clayton K. Yeutter (Neb.)	1991–1992	Steven Grossman (Mass.)	1996–1999
Richard Bond (N.Y.)	1992–1993	Joe Andrew (Ind.)	1999–2001
Haley Barbour (Miss.)	1993–1997	Terry McAuliffe (Va.)	2001–
Jim Nicholson (Colo.)	1997–2001		
Jim Gilmore (Va.)	2001–2002		
Marc Racicot (Mont.)	2002–2003		
Ed Gillespie (DC)	2003–		

Republican National Committee: 310 First St., SE, Washington, DC 20003. *Democratic National Committee:* 430 South Capitol St., SE, Washington, DC 20003.

Presidential Elections, 1789–2000

For the original method of electing the president and the vice president (elections of 1789, 1792, 1796, and 1800), *see* Article II, Section 1, of the Constitution. The election of 1804 was the first one in which the electors voted for president and vice president on separate ballots. (See Amendment XII to the Constitution.)

Year	Presidential candidate	Party	Electoral votes
1789[1]	George Washington	(no party)	69
	John Adams	(no party)	34
	Scattering	(no party)	35
	Votes not cast		8
1792	George Washington	Federalist	132
	John Adams	Federalist	77
	George Clinton	Anti-Federalist	50
	Thomas Jefferson	Anti-Federalist	4
	Aaron Burr	Anti-Federalist	1
	Votes not cast		6

Year	Presidential candidate	Party	Electoral votes
1796	John Adams	Federalist	71
	Thomas Jefferson	Dem.-Rep.	68
	Thomas Pinckney	Federalist	59
	Aaron Burr	Dem.-Rep.	30
	Scattering		48
1800[2]	Thomas Jefferson	Dem.-Rep.	73
	Aaron Burr	Dem.-Rep.	73
	John Adams	Federalist	65
	Charles C. Pinckney	Federalist	64
	John Jay	Federalist	1

Year	Presidential candidate	Party	Electoral votes	Vice-presidential candidate	Party	Electoral votes
1804	Thomas Jefferson	Dem.-Rep.	162	George Clinton	Dem.-Rep.	162
	Charles C. Pinckney	Federalist	14	Rufus King	Federalist	14
1808	James Madison	Dem.-Rep.	122	George Clinton	Dem.-Rep.	113
	Charles C. Pinckney	Federalist	47	Rufus King	Federalist	47
	George Clinton	Dem.-Rep.	6	John Langdon	Ind. (no party)	9
	Votes not cast		1	James Madison	Dem.-Rep.	3
				James Monroe	Dem.-Rep.	3
				Votes not cast		1
1812	James Madison	Dem.-Rep.	128	Elbridge Gerry	Dem.-Rep.	131
	De Witt Clinton	Federalist	89	Jared Ingersoll	Federalist	86
	Votes not cast		1	Votes not cast		1
1816	James Monroe	Dem.-Rep.	183	Daniel D. Tompkins	Dem.-Rep.	183
	Rufus King	Federalist	34	John E. Howard	Federalist	22
	Votes not cast		4	James Ross	Ind (no party)	5
				John Marshall	Federalist	4
				Robert G. Harper	Ind. (no party)	3
				Votes not cast		4
1820	James Monroe	Dem-Rep	231	Daniel D. Tompkins	Dem.-Rep.	218
	John Quincy Adams	Ind. (no party)	1	Richard Stockton	Ind. (no party)	8
	Votes not cast		3	Daniel Rodney	Ind. (no party)	4
				Richard Rush	Ind. (no party)	1
				Robert G. Harper	Ind. (no party)	1
				Votes not cast		3
1824[3]	John Quincy Adams	(no party)	84	John C. Calhoun	(no party)	182
	Andrew Jackson	(no party)	99	Nathan Sanford	(no party)	30
	William H. Crawford	(no party)	41	Nathaniel Macon	(no party)	24
	Henry Clay	(no party)	37	Andrew Jackson	(no party)	13
				Martin Van Buren	(no party)	9
				Henry Clay	(no party)	2
				Votes not cast		1
1828	Andrew Jackson	Democratic	178	John C. Calhoun	Democratic	171
	John Quincy Adams	Natl. Rep.	83	Richard Rush	Natl. Rep.	83
				William Smith	Democratic	7
1832	Andrew Jackson	Democratic	219	Martin Van Buren	Democratic	189
	Henry Clay	Natl. Rep.	49	John Sergeant	Natl. Rep.	49
	John Floyd	Ind. (no party)	11	Henry Lee	Ind. (no party)	11
	William Wirt	Antimasonic[4]	7	Amos Ellmaker	Antimasonic	7
	Votes not cast		2	William Wilkins	Ind. (no party)	30
				Votes not cast		2
1836	Martin Van Buren	Democratic	170	Richard M. Johnson[5]	Democratic	147
	William H. Harrison	Whig	73	Francis Granger	Whig	77
	Hugh L. White	Whig	26	John Tyler	Whig	47
	Daniel Webster	Whig	14	William Smith	Ind. (no party)	23
	W. P. Mangum	Ind. (no party)	11			

Year	Presidential candidate	Party	Electoral votes	Vice-presidential candidate	Party	Electoral votes
1840	William H. Harrison[6]	Whig	234	John Tyler	Whig	234
	Martin Van Buren	Democratic	60	Richard M. Johnson	Democratic	48
				L. W. Tazewell	Ind. (no party)	11
				James K. Polk	Democratic	1
1844	James K. Polk	Democratic	170	George M. Dallas	Democratic	170
	Henry Clay	Whig	105	Theo. Frelinghuysen	Whig	105
1848	Zachary Taylor[7]	Whig	163	Millard Fillmore	Whig	163
	Lewis Cass	Democratic	127	William O. Butler	Democratic	127
1852	Franklin Pierce	Democratic	254	William R. King	Democratic	254
	Winfield Scott	Whig	42	William A. Graham	Whig	42
1856	James Buchanan	Democratic	174	John C. Breckinridge	Democratic	174
	John C. Fremont	Republican	114	William L. Dayton	Republican	114
	Millard Fillmore	American[8]	8	A. J. Donelson	American[8]	8
1860	Abraham Lincoln	Republican	180	Hannibal Hamlin	Republican	180
	John C. Breckinridge	Democratic	72	Joseph Lane	Democratic	72
	John Bell	Const. Union	39	Edward Everett	Const. Union	39
	Stephen A. Douglas	Democratic	12	H. V. Johnson	Democratic	12
1864	Abraham Lincoln[9]	Union[10]	212	Andrew Johnson	Union[10]	212
	George B. McClellan	Democratic	21	G. H. Pendleton	Democratic	21
1868	Ulysses S. Grant	Republican	214	Schuyler Colfax	Republican	214
	Horatio Seymour	Democratic	80	Francis P. Blair, Jr.	Democratic	80
	Votes not counted[11]		23	Votes not counted[11]		23

NOTE: Due to the communications constrictions of the time and the lack of formal political party organizations, the framers of the Constitution specified that the president and vice president be chosen based upon the votes cast by members of an electoral college rather than by a direct popular vote. Eventually, states began to change the method by which electors cast their votes. Today, all but two states, Maine and Nebraska, have a winner-take-all system in which a popular vote decides which candidates will be given all of a given state's electoral votes. The number of popular votes won by each presidential candidate are listed here for elections beginning in 1872.

Year	Presidential candidate	Party	Electoral votes	Popular votes	Vice-presidential candidate and party
1872	Ulysses S. Grant	Republican	286	3,597,132	Henry Wilson—R
	Horace Greeley	Dem., Liberal Rep.	(12)	2,834,125	B. Gratz Brown—D, LR—(47)
	Thomas A. Hendricks	Democratic	42		Scattering—(19)
	B. Gratz Brown	Dem., Liberal Rep.	18		Vote not counted—(14)
	Charles J. Jenkins	Democratic	2		
	David Davis	Democratic	1		
	Votes not counted		17		
1876[13]	Rutherford B. Hayes	Republican	185	4,033,768	William A. Wheeler—R
	Samuel J. Tilden	Democratic	184	4,285,992	Thomas A. Hendricks—D
	Peter Cooper	Greenback	0	81,737	Samuel F. Cary—G
1880	James A. Garfield[14]	Republican	214	4,449,053	Chester A. Arthur—R
	Winfield S. Hancock	Democratic	155	4,442,035	William H. English—D
	James B. Weaver	Greenback	0	308,578	B. J. Chambers—G
1884	Grover Cleveland	Democratic	219	4,911,017	Thomas A. Hendricks—D
	James G. Blaine	Republican	182	4,848,334	John A. Logan—R
	Benjamin F. Butler	Greenback	0	175,370	A. M. West—G
	John P. St. John	Prohibition	0	150,369	William Daniel—P
1888	Benjamin Harrison	Republican	233	5,440,216	Levi P. Morton—R
	Grover Cleveland	Democratic	168	5,538,233	A. G. Thurman—D
	Clinton B. Fisk	Prohibition	0	249,506	John A. Brooks—P
	Alson J. Streeter	Union Labor	0	146,935	Charles E. Cunningham—UL
1892	Grover Cleveland	Democratic	277	5,556,918	Adlai E. Stevenson—D
	Benjamin Harrison	Republican	145	5,176,108	Whitelaw Reid—R
	James B. Weaver	People's[15]	22	1,041,028	James G. Field—Peo
	John Bidwell	Prohibition	0	264,133	James B. Cranfill—P
1896	William McKinley	Republican	271	7,035,638	Garret A. Hobart—R
	William J. Bryan	Dem., People's[15]	176	6,467,946	Arthur Sewall—D—(149)
					Thomas E. Watson—Peo—(27)
	John M. Palmer	Natl. Dem.	0	133,148	Simon B. Buckner—ND
	Joshua Levering	Prohibition	0	132,007	Hale Johnson—P

Year	Presidential candidate	Party	Electoral votes	Popular votes	Vice-presidential candidate and party
1900	William McKinley[16]	Republican	292	7,219,530	Theodore Roosevelt—R
	William J. Bryan	Dem., People's[15]	155	6,358,071	Adlai E. Stevenson—D, Peo
	Eugene V. Debs	Social Democratic	0	94,768	Job Harriman—SD
1904	Theodore Roosevelt	Republican	336	7,628,834	Charles W. Fairbanks—R
	Alton B. Parker	Democratic	140	5,084,491	Henry G. Davis—D
	Eugene V. Debs	Socialist	0	402,400	Benjamin Hanford—S
1908	William H. Taft	Republican	321	7,679,006	James S. Sherman—R
	William J. Bryan	Democratic	162	6,409,106	John W. Kern—D
	Eugene V. Debs	Socialist	0	402,820	Benjamin Hanford—S
1912	Woodrow Wilson	Democratic	435	6,286,214	Thomas R. Marshall—D
	Theodore Roosevelt	Progressive	88	4,126,020	Hiram Johnson—Prog
	William H. Taft	Republican	8	3,483,922	Nicholas M. Butler—R[17]
	Eugene V. Debs	Socialist	0	897,011	Emil Seidel—S
1916	Woodrow Wilson	Democratic	277	9,129,606	Thomas R. Marshall—D
	Charles E. Hughes	Republican	254	8,538,221	Charles W. Fairbanks—R
	A. L. Benson	Socialist	0	585,113	G. R. Kirkpatrick—S
1920	Warren G. Harding[18]	Republican	404	16,152,200	Calvin Coolidge—R
	James M. Cox	Democratic	127	9,147,353	Franklin D. Roosevelt—D
	Eugene V. Debs	Socialist	0	917,799	Seymour Stedman—S
1924	Calvin Coolidge	Republican	382	15,725,016	Charles G. Dawes—R
	John W. Davis	Democratic	136	8,385,586	Charles W. Bryan—D
	Robert M. LaFollette	Progressive, Socialist	13	4,822,856	Burton K. Wheeler—Prog, S
1928	Herbert Hoover	Republican	444	21,392,190	Charles Curtis—R
	Alfred E. Smith	Democratic	87	15,016,443	Joseph T. Robinson—D
	Norman Thomas	Socialist	0	267,420	James H. Maurer—S
1932	Franklin D. Roosevelt	Democratic	472	22,821,857	John N. Garner—D
	Herbert Hoover	Republican	59	15,761,841	Charles Curtis—R
	Norman Thomas	Socialist	0	884,781	James H. Maurer—S
1936	Franklin D. Roosevelt	Democratic	523	27,751,597	John N. Garner—D
	Alfred M. Landon	Republican	8	16,679,583	Frank Knox—R
	Norman Thomas	Socialist	0	187,720	George Nelson—S
1940	Franklin D. Roosevelt	Democratic	449	27,244,160	Henry A. Wallace—D
	Wendell L. Willkie	Republican	82	22,305,198	Charles L. McNary—R
	Norman Thomas	Socialist	0	99,557	Maynard C. Krueger—S
1944	Franklin D. Roosevelt[19]	Democratic	432	25,602,504	Harry S. Truman—D
	Thomas E. Dewey	Republican	99	22,006,285	John W. Bricker—R
	Norman Thomas	Socialist	0	80,518	Darlington Hoopes—S
1948	Harry S. Truman	Democratic	303	24,179,345	Alben W. Barkley—D
	Thomas E. Dewey	Republican	189	21,991,291	Earl Warren—R
	J. Strom Thurmond	States' Rights Dem.	39	1,176,125	Fielding L. Wright—SR
	Henry A. Wallace	Progressive	0	1,157,326	Glen Taylor—Prog
	Norman Thomas	Socialist	0	139,572	Tucker P. Smith—S
1952	Dwight D. Eisenhower	Republican	442	33,936,234	Richard M. Nixon—R
	Adlai E. Stevenson	Democratic	89	27,314,992	John J. Sparkman—D
1956	Dwight D. Eisenhower	Republican	457	35,590,472	Richard M. Nixon—R
	Adlai E. Stevenson	Democratic	73[20]	26,022,752	Estes Kefauver—D
1960	John F. Kennedy[21]	Democratic	303	34,226,731	Lyndon B. Johnson—D
	Richard M. Nixon	Republican	219[22]	34,108,157	Henry Cabot Lodge—R
1964	Lyndon B. Johnson	Democratic	486	43,129,484	Hubert H. Humphrey—D
	Barry M. Goldwater	Republican	52	27,178,188	William E. Miller—R
1968	Richard M. Nixon	Republican	301	31,785,480	Spiro T. Agnew—R
	Hubert H. Humphrey	Democratic	191	31,275,166	Edmund S. Muskie—D
	George C. Wallace	American Independent	46	9,906,473	Curtis F. LeMay—AI
1972	Richard M. Nixon[23]	Republican	520[24]	47,169,911	Spiro T. Agnew—R
	George McGovern	Democratic	17	29,170,383	Sargent Shriver—D
	John G. Schmitz	American	0	1,099,482	Thomas J. Anderson—A
1976	Jimmy Carter	Democratic	297	40,830,763	Walter F. Mondale—D
	Gerald R. Ford	Republican	240[25]	39,147,973	Robert J. Dole—R
	Eugene J. McCarthy	Independent	0	756,631	None

Year	Presidential candidate	Party	Electoral votes	Popular votes	Vice-presidential candidate and party
1980	Ronald Reagan	Republican	489	43,899,248	George Bush—R
	Jimmy Carter	Democratic	49	36,481,435	Walter F. Mondale—D
	John B. Anderson	Independent	0	5,719,437	Patrick J. Lucey—I
1984	Ronald Reagan	Republican	525	54,455,075	George Bush—R
	Walter F. Mondale	Democratic	13	37,577,185	Geraldine A. Ferraro—D
1988	George H. Bush	Republican	426	48,886,097	J. Danforth Quayle—R
	Michael S. Dukakis	Democratic	111[26]	41,809,074	Lloyd Bentsen—D
1992	William J. Clinton	Democratic	370	44,909,889	Albert A. Gore, J.—D
	George H. Bush	Republican	168	39,104,545	J. Danforth Quayle—R
	H. Ross Perot	Independent	0	19,742,267	James B. Stockdale—I
1996	William J. Clinton	Democratic	379	47,402,357	Albert A. Gore, Jr.—D
	Robert J. Dole	Republican	159	39,198,755	Jack F. Kemp—R
	H. Ross Perot	Reform Party[27]	0	8,085,402	Pat Choate—RP[27]
2000	George W. Bush	Republican	271	50,456,002	Richard B. Cheney—R
	Albert A. Gore	Democratic	266[28]	50,999,897	Joseph I. Lieberman—D
	Ralph Nader	Green Party	0	2,882,955	Winona LaDuke—GP

1. Only 10 states participated in the election. The New York legislature chose no electors, and North Carolina and Rhode Island had not yet ratified the Constitution. 2. As Jefferson and Burr were tied, the House of Representatives chose the president. In a vote by states, 10 votes were cast for Jefferson, 4 for Burr; 2 votes were not cast. 3. As no candidate had an electoral-vote majority, the House of Representatives chose the president from the first three. In a vote by states, 13 votes were cast for Adams, 7 for Jackson, and 4 for Crawford. 4. The Antimasonic Party on Sept. 26, 1831, was the first party to hold a nominating convention to choose candidates for president and vice president. 5. As Johnson did not have an electoral-vote majority, the Senate chose him 33–14 over Granger, the others being legally out of the race. 6. Harrison died April 4, 1841, and Tyler succeeded him April 6. 7. Taylor died July 9, 1850, and Fillmore succeeded him July 10. 8. Also known as the Know-Nothing Party. 9. Lincoln died April 15, 1865, and Johnson succeeded him the same day. 10. Name adopted by the Republican National Convention of 1864. Johnson was a War Democrat. 11. 23 Southern electoral votes were excluded. 12. Greeley died Nov. 29, 1872, before his 66 electors voted; 63 of Greeley's votes were scattered among four of the other candidates. 13. Hayes was chosen by a special electoral commission since initially neither candidate had the requisite 185 electoral votes. 14. Garfield died Sept. 19, 1881, and Arthur succeeded him Sept. 20. 15. Members of People's Party were called Populists. 16. McKinley died Sept. 14, 1901, and Roosevelt succeeded him the same day. 17. James S. Sherman, Republican candidate for vice president, died Oct. 30, 1912, and the Republican electoral votes were cast for Butler. 18. Harding died Aug. 2, 1923, and Coolidge succeeded him Aug. 3. 19. Roosevelt died April 12, 1945, and Truman succeeded him the same day. 20. One electoral vote from Alabama was cast for Walter B. Jones. 21. Kennedy died Nov. 22, 1963, and Johnson succeeded him the same day. 22. Sen. Harry F. Byrd received 15 electoral votes. 23. Nixon resigned Aug. 9, 1974, and Gerald R. Ford succeeded him the same day. 24. One electoral vote from Virginia was cast for John Hospers, Libertarian Party. 25. One electoral vote from Washington was cast for Ronald Reagan. 26. One electoral vote from West Virginia was cast for Lloyd Bentsen. 27. Perot helped establish the Reform Party following his defeat in the 1992 election. 28. One elector from the District of Columbia left her ballot blank to protest the city's lack of representation in Congress, leaving Gore with 266 electoral votes instead of 267.

Plurality and Majority

In order to win a plurality, a candidate must receive a greater number of votes than anyone running against him. If he receives 50 votes, for example, and two other candidates receive 49 and 2, he will have a plurality of one vote over his closest opponent.

However, a candidate does not have a majority unless he receives more than 50% of the total votes cast. In the example above, the candidate does not have a majority, because his 50 votes are less than 50% of the 101 votes cast.

Presidents Elected Without a Majority

Fifteen candidates (three of them twice) have become president of the United States with a popular vote less than 50% of the total cast. It should be noted, however, that in elections before 1872, presidential electors were not chosen by popular vote in all states. Adams's election in 1824 was by the House of Representatives, which chose him over Jackson, who had a plurality of both electoral and popular votes, but not a majority in the electoral college.

The "minority" presidents are listed below.

Year	President	Electoral percent	Popular percent
1824	John Q. Adams	31.8%	29.8%
1844	James K. Polk (D)	61.8	49.3
1848	Zachary Taylor (W)	56.2	47.3
1856	James Buchanan (D)	58.7	45.3
1860	Abraham Lincoln (R)	59.4	39.9
1876	Rutherford B. Hayes (R)	50.1	47.9
1880	James A. Garfield (R)	57.9	48.3
1884	Grover Cleveland (D)	54.6	48.8
1888	Benjamin Harrison (R)	58.1	47.8

Year	President	Electoral percent	Popular percent
1892	Grover Cleveland (D)	62.4%	46.0%
1912	Woodrow Wilson (D)	81.9	41.8
1916	Woodrow Wilson (D)	52.1	49.3
1948	Harry S. Truman (D)	57.1	49.5
1960	John F. Kennedy (D)	56.4	49.7
1968	Richard M. Nixon (R)	56.1	43.4
1992	William J. Clinton (D)	68.8	43.0
1996	William J. Clinton (D)	70.4	49.0
2000	George W. Bush (R)	50.3	47.8

The Closest Presidential Races

Although the 2000 presidential race was extremely close, there have been others that were also too close to call immediately after the election. Indeed, the results of the Nov. 7 election in 1876 were not known until March 2, 1877, just three days before the inauguration. More recently, John F. Kennedy's defeat of Richard M. Nixon in 1960 wasn't official until noon the following day.

President	Electoral votes	Popular votes
1800[1]		
Thomas Jefferson (Dem.-Rep.)	73	—
Aaron Burr (Dem.-Rep.)	73	—
John Adams (Federalist)	65	—
Charles C. Pinckney (Federalist)	64	—
John Jay (Federalist)	1	—
1824[2]		
John Quincy Adams (no party)	84	—
Andrew Jackson (no party)	99	—
William H. Crawford (no party)	41	—
Henry Clay (no party)	37	—
1876		
Rutherford B. Hayes (R)	185	4,033,768
Samuel J. Tilden (D)	184	4,285,992
1880		
James A. Garfield (R)	214	4,449,053
Winfield S. Hancock (D)	155	4,442,035

President	Electoral votes	Popular votes
1916		
Woodrow Wilson (D)	277	9,129,606
Charles E. Hughes (R)	254	8,538,221
1960		
John F. Kennedy (D)	303	34,226,731
Richard M. Nixon (R)	219	34,108,157
1968		
Richard M. Nixon (R)	301	31,785,480
Hubert H. Humphrey (R)	191	31,275,166
George C. Wallace (American Independent)	46	9,906,473
1976		
Jimmy Carter (D)	297	40,830,763
Gerald R. Ford (R)	240	39,147,973
2000		
George W. Bush (R)	271	50,455,156
Albert A. Gore (D)	266[3]	50,992,335

1. As Jefferson and Burr were tied, the House of Representatives chose the president. In a vote by states, 10 votes were cast for Jefferson, 4 for Burr; 2 votes were not cast. For the original method of electing the president and vice president (elections of 1789, 1792, 1796, and 1800), see Article II, Section 1, of the Constitution. 2. As no candidate had an electoral vote majority, the House of Representatives chose the president from the first three. In a vote by states, 13 votes were cast for Adams, 7 for Jackson, and 4 for Crawford. 3. One elector from the District of Columbia left her ballot blank to protest the city's lack of representation in Congress, leaving Gore with 266 electoral votes instead of 267.

National Voter Turnout in Federal Elections: 1964–2000

Year	Voting-age population	Voter registration	Voter turnout	Turnout of voting-age population (percent)
2000	**205,815,000**	**156,421,311**	**105,586,274**	**51.3%**
1998	200,929,000	141,850,558	73,117,022	36.4
1996	**196,511,000**	**146,211,960**	**96,456,345**	**49.1**
1994	193,650,000	130,292,822	75,105,860	38.8
1992	**189,529,000**	**133,821,178**	**104,405,155**	**55.1**
1990	185,812,000	121,105,630	67,859,189	36.5
1988	**182,778,000**	**126,379,628**	**91,594,693**	**50.1**
1986	178,566,000	118,399,984	64,991,128	36.4
1984	**174,466,000**	**124,150,614**	**92,652,680**	**53.1**
1982	169,938,000	110,671,225	67,615,576	39.8
1980	**164,597,000**	**113,043,734**	**86,515,221**	**52.6**
1978	158,373,000	103,291,265	58,917,938	37.2
1976	**152,309,190**	**105,037,986**	**81,555,789**	**53.6**
1974	146,336,000	96,199,020[1]	55,943,834	38.2
1972	**140,776,000**	**97,328,541**	**77,718,554**	**55.2**
1970	124,498,000	82,496,747[2]	58,014,338	46.6
1968	**120,328,186**	**81,658,180**	**73,211,875**	**60.8**
1966	116,132,000	76,288,283[3]	56,188,046	48.4
1964	**114,090,000**	**73,715,818**	**70,644,592**	**61.9**

n.a. = not available. NOTE: Presidential election years are in boldface. 1. Registrations from Iowa not included. 2. Registrations from Iowa and Mo. not included. 3. Registrations from Iowa, Kans., Miss., Mo., Nebr., and Wyo. not included. D.C. did not have independent status. *Source:* Federal Election Commission. Data drawn from Congressional Research Service reports, Election Data Services Inc., and State Election Offices.

Facts About Elections

Candidate with highest popular vote: Reagan (1984), 54,455,075.

Candidate with highest electoral vote: Reagan (1984), 525.

Candidate carrying most states: Nixon (1972) and Reagan (1984), 49.

Candidate running most times: Norman Thomas (Socialist Party), six (1928, 1932, 1936, 1940, 1944, 1948).

Candidate elected, defeated, then reelected: Cleveland (1884, 1888, 1892).

Presidents

	Name and (party)[1]	Term	State of birth	Born	Died	Religion	Age at inaug.	Age at death
1.	Washington (F)[2]	1789–1797	Va.	2/22/1732	12/14/1799	Episcopalian	57	67
2.	J. Adams (F)	1797–1801	Mass.	10/30/1735	7/4/1826	Unitarian	61	90
3.	Jefferson (DR)	1801–1809	Va.	4/13/1743	7/4/1826	Deist	57	83
4.	Madison (DR)	1809–1817	Va.	3/16/1751	6/28/1836	Episcopalian	57	85
5.	Monroe (DR)	1817–1825	Va.	4/28/1758	7/4/1831	Episcopalian	58	73
6.	J. Q. Adams (DR)	1825–1829	Mass.	7/11/1767	2/23/1848	Unitarian	57	80
7.	Jackson (D)	1829–1837	S.C.	3/15/1767	6/8/1845	Presbyterian	61	78
8.	Van Buren (D)	1837–1841	N.Y.	12/5/1782	7/24/1862	Reformed Dutch	54	79
9.	W. H. Harrison (W)[3]	1841	Va.	2/9/1773	4/4/1841	Episcopalian	68	68
10.	Tyler (W)	1841–1845	Va.	3/29/1790	1/18/1862	Episcopalian	51	71
11.	Polk (D)	1845–1849	N.C.	11/2/1795	6/15/1849	Methodist	49	53
12.	Taylor (W)[3]	1849–1850	Va.	11/24/1784	7/9/1850	Episcopalian	64	65
13.	Fillmore (W)	1850–1853	N.Y.	1/7/1800	3/8/1874	Unitarian	50	74
14.	Pierce (D)	1853–1857	N.H.	11/23/1804	10/8/1869	Episcopalian	48	64
15.	Buchanan (D)	1857–1861	Pa.	4/23/1791	6/1/1868	Presbyterian	65	77
16.	Lincoln (R)[4]	1861–1865	Ky.	2/12/1809	4/15/1865	Liberal	52	56
17.	A. Johnson (U)[5]	1865–1869	N.C.	12/29/1808	7/31/1875	([6])	56	66
18.	Grant (R)	1869–1877	Ohio	4/27/1822	7/23/1885	Methodist	46	63
19.	Hayes (R)	1877–1881	Ohio	10/4/1822	1/17/1893	Methodist	54	70
20.	Garfield (R)[4]	1881	Ohio	11/19/1831	9/19/1881	Disciples of Christ	49	49
21.	Arthur (R)	1881–1885	Vt.	10/5/1829	11/18/1886	Episcopalian	50	56
22.	Cleveland (D)	1885–1889	N.J.	3/18/1837	6/24/1908	Presbyterian	47	71
23.	B. Harrison (R)	1889–1893	Ohio	8/20/1833	3/13/1901	Presbyterian	55	67
24.	Cleveland (D)[7]	1893–1897	N.J.	3/18/1837	6/24/1908	Presbyterian	55	71
25.	McKinley (R)[4]	1897–1901	Ohio	1/29/1843	9/14/1901	Methodist	54	58
26.	T. Roosevelt (R)	1901–1909	N.Y.	10/27/1858	1/6/1919	Reformed Dutch	42	60
27.	Taft (R)	1909–1913	Ohio	9/15/1857	3/8/1930	Unitarian	51	72
28.	Wilson (D)	1913–1921	Va.	12/28/1856	2/3/1924	Presbyterian	56	67
29.	Harding (R)[3]	1921–1923	Ohio	11/2/1865	8/2/1923	Baptist	55	57
30.	Coolidge (R)	1923–1929	Vt.	7/4/1872	1/5/1933	Congregationalist	51	60
31.	Hoover (R)	1929–1933	Iowa	8/10/1874	10/20/1964	Quaker	54	90
32.	F. D. Roosevelt (D)[3]	1933–1945	N.Y.	1/30/1882	4/12/1945	Episcopalian	51	63
33.	Truman (D)	1945–1953	Mo.	5/8/1884	12/26/1972	Baptist	60	88
34.	Eisenhower (R)	1953–1961	Tex.	10/14/1890	3/28/1969	Presbyterian	62	78
35.	Kennedy (D)[4]	1961–1963	Mass.	5/29/1917	11/22/1963	Roman Catholic	43	46
36.	L. B. Johnson (D)	1963–1969	Tex.	8/27/1908	1/22/1973	Disciples of Christ	55	64
37.	Nixon (R)[8]	1969–1974	Calif.	1/9/1913	4/22/1994	Quaker	56	81
38.	Ford (R)	1974–1977	Neb.	7/14/1913	—	Episcopalian	61	—
39.	Carter (D)	1977–1981	Ga.	10/1/1924	—	Southern Baptist	52	—
40.	Reagan (R)	1981–1989	Ill.	2/6/1911	6/5/2004	Disciples of Christ	69	93
41.	G.H.W. Bush (R)	1989–1993	Mass.	6/12/1924	—	Episcopalian	64	—
42.	Clinton (D)	1993–2001	Ark.	8/19/1946	—	Baptist	46	—
43.	G. W. Bush (R)	2001–	Conn.	7/6/46	—	Methodist	54	—

1. F—Federalist; DR—Democratic-Republican; D—Democratic; W—Whig; R—Republican; U—Union. 2. No party for first election. The party system in the U.S. made its appearance during Washington's first term. 3. Died in office. 4. Assassinated in office. 5. The Republican National Convention of 1864 adopted the name Union Party. It renominated Lincoln for president; for vice president it nominated Johnson, a War Democrat. Although frequently listed as a Republican vice president and president, Johnson undoubtedly considered himself strictly a member of the Union Party. When that party broke apart after 1868, he returned to the Democratic Party. 6. Johnson was not a professed church member; however, he admired the Baptist principles of church government. 7. Second nonconsecutive term. 8. Resigned Aug. 9, 1974.

Vice Presidents

	Name and (party)[1]	Term	State of birth	Birth and death dates	President served under
1.	John Adams (F)[2]	1789–1797	Massachusetts	1735–1826	Washington
2.	Thomas Jefferson (DR)	1797–1801	Virginia	1743–1826	J. Adams
3.	Aaron Burr (DR)	1801–1805	New Jersey	1756–1836	Jefferson
4.	George Clinton (DR)[3]	1805–1812	New York	1739–1812	Jefferson and Madison
5.	Elbridge Gerry (DR)[3]	1813–1814	Massachusetts	1744–1814	Madison
6.	Daniel D. Tompkins (DR)	1817–1825	New York	1774–1825	Monroe
7.	John C. Calhoun[4]	1825–1832	South Carolina	1782–1850	J. Q. Adams and Jackson
8.	Martin Van Buren (D)	1833–1837	New York	1782–1862	Jackson
9.	Richard M. Johnson (D)	1837–1841	Kentucky	1780–1850	Van Buren
10.	John Tyler (W)[5]	1841	Virginia	1790–1862	W. H. Harrison
11.	George M. Dallas (D)	1845–1849	Pennsylvania	1792–1864	Polk
12.	Millard Fillmore (W)[5]	1849–1850	New York	1800–1874	Taylor
13.	William R. King (D)[3]	1853	North Carolina	1786–1853	Pierce

	Name and (party)[1]	Term	State of birth	Birth and death dates	President served under
14.	John C. Breckinridge (D)	1857–1861	Kentucky	1821–1875	Buchanan
15.	Hannibal Hamlin (R)	1861–1865	Maine	1809–1891	Lincoln
16.	Andrew Johnson (U)[5]	1865	North Carolina	1808–1875	Lincoln
17.	Schuyler Colfax (R)	1869–1873	New York	1823–1885	Grant
18.	Henry Wilson (R)[3]	1873–1875	New Hampshire	1812–1875	Grant
19.	William A. Wheeler (R)	1877–1881	New York	1819–1887	Hayes
20.	Chester A. Arthur (R)[5]	1881	Vermont	1829–1886	Garfield
21.	Thomas A. Hendricks (D)[3]	1885	Ohio	1819–1885	Cleveland
22.	Levi P. Morton (R)	1889–1893	Vermont	1824–1920	B. Harrison
23.	Adlai E. Stevenson (D)	1893–1897	Kentucky	1835–1914	Cleveland
24.	Garret A. Hobart (R)[3]	1897–1899	New Jersey	1844–1899	McKinley
25.	Theodore Roosevelt (R)[5]	1901	New York	1858–1919	McKinley
26.	Charles W. Fairbanks (R)	1905–1909	Ohio	1852–1918	T. Roosevelt
27.	James S. Sherman (R)[3]	1909–1912	New York	1855–1912	Taft
28.	Thomas R. Marshall (D)	1913–1921	Indiana	1854–1925	Wilson
29.	Calvin Coolidge (R)[5]	1921–1923	Vermont	1872–1933	Harding
30.	Charles G. Dawes (R)	1925–1929	Ohio	1865–1951	Coolidge
31.	Charles Curtis (R)	1929–1933	Kansas	1860–1936	Hoover
32.	John N. Garner (D)	1933–1941	Texas	1868–1967	F. D. Roosevelt
33.	Henry A. Wallace (D)	1941–1945	Iowa	1888–1965	F. D. Roosevelt
34.	Harry S. Truman (D)[5]	1945	Missouri	1884–1972	F. D. Roosevelt
35.	Alben W. Barkley (D)	1949–1953	Kentucky	1877–1956	Truman
36.	Richard M. Nixon (R)	1953-1961	California	1913–1994	Eisenhower
37.	Lyndon B. Johnson (D)[5]	1961–1963	Texas	1908–1973	Kennedy
38.	Hubert H. Humphrey (D)	1965–1969	South Dakota	1911–1978	L. B. Johnson
39.	Spiro T. Agnew (R)[6]	1969–1973	Maryland	1918–1996	Nixon
40.	Gerald R. Ford (R)[7]	1973–1974	Nebraska	1913–	Nixon
41.	Nelson A. Rockefeller (R)[8]	1974–1977	Maine	1908–1979	Ford
42.	Walter F. Mondale (D)	1977–1981	Minnesota	1928–	Carter
43.	George Bush (R)	1981–1989	Massachusetts	1924–	Reagan
44.	J. Danforth Quayle (R)	1989–1993	Indiana	1947–	G.H.W. Bush
45.	Albert A. Gore, Jr. (D)	1993–2001	Washington, D.C.	1948–	Clinton
46.	Richard B. Cheney (R)	2001–	Nebraska	1941–	G. W. Bush

1. F—Federalist; DR—Democratic-Republican; D—Democratic; W—Whig; R—Republican; U—Union. 2. No party for first election. The party system in the U.S. made its appearance during Washington's first term as president. 3. Died in office. 4. Democratic-Republican with J. Q. Adams; Democratic with Jackson. Calhoun resigned in 1832 to become a U.S. senator. 5. Succeeded to presidency on death of president. Prior to the passage of the 25th Amendment (ratified Feb. 10, 1967), there were no provisions for filling a vacancy in the vice presidency. In the event of a vacancy, the president pro tempore took over most of the vice president's duties. 6. Resigned Oct. 10, 1973, after pleading no contest to federal income tax evasion charges. 7. Nominated by Nixon on Oct. 12, 1973, under provisions of 25th Amendment. Confirmed by Congress on Dec. 6, 1973, and was sworn in same day. He became president Aug. 9, 1974, upon Nixon's resignation. 8. Nominated by Ford Aug. 20, 1974; confirmed by Congress on Dec. 19, 1974, and was sworn in same day.

Presidential Libraries

These are not traditional libraries, but rather repositories for preserving and making available the papers, records, and other historical materials of the presidents since Herbert Hoover. The presidential library system formally began in 1939, when President Franklin Roosevelt donated his personal and presidential papers to the federal government.

Hoover Library
210 Parkside Drive
P.O. Box 488
West Branch, IA 52358-0488
http://hoover.archives.gov

Roosevelt Library
4079 Albany Post Road
Hyde Park, NY 12538-1999
http://www.fdrlibrary.marist.edu/

Truman Library
500 West U.S. Highway 24
Independence, MO 64050-1798
http://www.trumanlibrary.org

Eisenhower Library
200 SE 4th Street
Abilene, KS 67410-2900
http://www.eisenhower.utexas.edu

Kennedy Library
Columbia Point
Boston, MA 02125-3398
http://www.jfklibrary.org

Johnson Library
2313 Red River Street
Austin, TX 78705-5702
http://www.lbjlib.utexas.edu

The Nixon Project[1]
National Archives at College Park
8601 Adelphi Road
College Park, MD 20740-6001
http://www.nixon.archives.gov/

Ford Library
1000 Beal Avenue
Ann Arbor, MI 48109-2114
http://www.ford.utexas.edu

Carter Library
441 Freedom Parkway
Atlanta, GA 30307-1498
http://www.jimmycarterlibrary.org/

Reagan Library
40 Presidential Drive
Simi Valley, CA 93065-0666
http://www.reagan.utexas.edu

George H. W. Bush Library
1000 George Bush Drive West
College Station, TX 77845
http://bushlibrary.tamu.edu/

Clinton Library
1200 President Clinton Ave.
Little Rock, AK 72201
http://www.clintonpresidentialcenter.org

1. The Nixon Project is not affiliated with the Richard Nixon Library and Birthplace in Yorba Linda, Calif., a private institution that was established by Nixon in 1990. *Source:* National Archives and Records Administration. Web: www.archives.gov/.

Wives and Children of the Presidents

President	Wife's name	Year and place of wife's birth	Married	Wife died	Children[1] Sons	Children[1] Daughters
Washington	Martha Dandridge Custis	1732, Va.	1759	1802	—	—
John Adams	Abigail Smith	1744, Mass.	1764	1818	3	2
Jefferson[2]	Martha Wayles Skelton	1748, Va.	1772	1782	1	5
Madison	Dorothy "Dolley" Payne Todd	1768, N.C.	1794	1849	—	—
Monroe	Elizabeth "Eliza" Kortright	1768, N.Y.	1786	1830	—	2
J. Q. Adams	Louisa Catherine Johnson	1775, England	1797	1852	3	1
Jackson	Rachel Donelson Robards	1767, Va.	1791	1828	—	—
Van Buren	Hannah Hoes	1788, N.Y.	1807	1819	4	—
W. H. Harrison	Anna Symmes	1775, N.J.	1795	1864	6	4
Tyler	Letitia Christian	1790, Va.	1813	1842	3	5
	Julia Gardiner	1820, N.Y.	1844	1889	5	2
Polk	Sarah Childress	1803, Tenn.	1824	1891	—	—
Taylor	Margaret Smith	1788, Md.	1810	1852	1	5
Fillmore	Abigail Powers	1798, N.Y.	1826	1853	1	1
	Caroline Carmichael McIntosh	1813, N.J.	1858	1881	—	—
Pierce	Jane Means Appleton	1806, N.H.	1834	1863	3	—
Buchanan	(Unmarried)	—	—	—	—	—
Lincoln	Mary Todd	1818, Ky.	1842	1882	4	—
A. Johnson	Eliza McCardle	1810, Tenn.	1827	1876	3	2
Grant	Julia Dent	1826, Mo.	1848	1902	3	1
Hayes	Lucy Ware Webb	1831, Ohio	1852	1889	7	1
Garfield	Lucretia Rudolph	1832, Ohio	1858	1918	5	2
Arthur	Ellen Lewis Herndon	1837, Va.	1859	1880	2	1
Cleveland	Frances Folsom	1864, N.Y.	1886	1947	2	3
B. Harrison	Caroline Lavinia Scott	1832, Ohio	1853	1892	1	1
	Mary Scott Lord Dimmick	1858, Pa.	1896	1948	—	1
McKinley	Ida Saxton	1847, Ohio	1871	1907	—	2
T. Roosevelt	Alice Hathaway Lee	1861, Mass.	1880	1884	—	1
	Edith Kermit Carow	1861, Conn.	1886	1948	4	1
Taft	Helen Herron	1861, Ohio	1886	1943	2	1
Wilson	Ellen Louise Axson	1860, Ga.	1885	1914	—	3
	Edith Bolling Galt	1872, Va.	1915	1961	—	—
Harding	Florence Kling DeWolfe	1860, Ohio	1891	1924	—	—
Coolidge	Grace Anna Goodhue	1879, Vt.	1905	1957	2	—
Hoover	Lou Henry	1875, Iowa	1899	1944	2	—
F. D. Roosevelt	(Anna) Eleanor Roosevelt	1884, N.Y.	1905	1962	5	1
Truman	Bess Wallace	1885, Mo.	1919	1982	—	1
Eisenhower	Mamie Geneva Doud	1896, Iowa	1916	1979	2	—
Kennedy	Jacqueline Lee Bouvier	1929, N.Y.	1953	1994	2	1
L. B. Johnson	Claudia Alta "Lady Bird" Taylor	1912, Tex.	1934	—	—	2
Nixon	Thelma Catherine "Pat" Ryan	1912, Nev.	1940	1993	—	2
Ford	Elizabeth "Betty" Bloomer Warren	1918, Ill.	1948	—	3	1
Carter	Rosalynn Smith	1928, Ga.	1946	—	3	1
Reagan	Jane Wyman	1914, Mo.	1940[3]	—	1[4]	1
	Nancy Davis	1921, N.Y.	1952	—	1	1
G.H.W. Bush	Barbara Pierce	1925, N.Y.	1945	—	4	2
Clinton	Hillary Rodham	1947, Ill.	1975	—	—	1
G. W. Bush	Laura Welch	1946, Tex.	1977	—	—	2

1. Includes children who died in infancy. 2. Number of children listed here reflects only children Jefferson had with Martha Wayles Skelton. Scientists and historians agree, based on DNA evidence, that Jefferson may have fathered at least one child with slave Sally Hemings. 3. Divorced in 1948. 4. Adopted.

Biographies of the Presidents

GEORGE WASHINGTON was born on Feb. 22, 1732 (Feb. 11, 1731/2, old style) in Westmoreland County, Va. While in his teens, he trained as a surveyor, and at the age of 20 he was appointed adjutant in the Va. militia. For the next three years, he fought in the wars against the French and Indians, serving as Gen. Edward Braddock's aide in the disastrous campaign against Ft. Duquesne. In 1759, he resigned from the militia, married Martha Dandridge Custis, a widow with children, and settled down as a gentleman farmer at Mount Vernon, Va.

As a militiaman, Washington had been exposed to the arrogance of the British officers, and his experience as a planter with British commercial restrictions increased his anti-British sentiment. He opposed the Stamp Act of 1765 and after 1770 became increasingly prominent in organizing resistance. A delegate to the Continental Congress, Washington was selected as commander in chief of the Continental Army and took command at Cambridge, Mass., on July 3, 1775.

Inadequately supported and sometimes covertly sabotaged by the Congress, in charge of troops who were inexperienced, badly equipped, and impatient of discipline, Washington conducted the war on the policy of avoiding major engagements with the British and wearing them down by harassing tactics. His able generalship, along with the French alliance and the growing weariness within Britain, brought the war to a conclusion with the surrender of Cornwallis at Yorktown, Va., on Oct. 19, 1781.

The chaotic years under the Articles of Confederation led Washington to return to public life in the hope of promoting the formation of a strong central government. He presided over the Constitutional Convention and yielded to the universal demand that he serve as first president. He was inaugurated on April 30, 1789, in New York, the first national capital. In office, he sought to unite the nation and establish the authority of the new government at home and abroad. Greatly distressed by the emergence of the Hamilton-Jefferson rivalry, Washington worked to maintain neutrality but actually sympathized more with Hamilton. Following his unanimous reelection in 1792, his second term was dominated by the Federalists. His Farewell Address on Sept. 17, 1796 (published but never delivered) rebuked party spirit and warned against "permanent alliances" with foreign powers.

He died at Mount Vernon on Dec. 14, 1799.

JOHN ADAMS born on Oct. 30 (Oct. 19, old style), 1735, at Braintree (now Quincy), Mass. A Harvard graduate, he considered teaching and the ministry but finally turned to law and was admitted to the bar in 1758. Six years later, he married Abigail Smith. He opposed the Stamp Act, served as lawyer for patriots indicted by the British, and by the time of the Continental Congresses, was in the vanguard of the movement for independence. In 1778, he went to France as commissioner. Subsequently he helped negotiate the peace treaty with Britain, and in 1785 became envoy to London. Resigning in 1788, he was elected vice president under Washington and was reelected in 1792.

Though a Federalist, Adams did not get along with Hamilton, who sought to prevent his election to the presidency in 1796 and thereafter intrigued against his administration. In 1798, Adams's independent policy averted a war with France but completed the break with Hamilton and the right-wing Federalists; at the same time, the enactment of the Alien and Sedition Acts, directed against foreigners and against critics of the government, exasperated the Jeffersonian opposition. The split between Adams and Hamilton resulted in Jefferson's becoming the next president. Adams retired to his home in Quincy. He and Jefferson died on the same day, July 4, 1826, the 50th anniversary of the adoption of the Declaration of Independence.

His *Defence of the Constitutions of Government of the United States* (1787) contains original and striking, if conservative, political ideas.

THOMAS JEFFERSON was born on April 13 (April 2, old style), 1743, at Shadwell in Goochland (now Albemarle) County, Va. A William and Mary graduate, he studied law, but from the start showed an interest in science and philosophy. His literary skills and political clarity brought him to the forefront of the revolutionary movement in Virginia. As delegate to the Continental Congress, he drafted the Declaration of Independence. In 1776, he entered the Virginia House of Delegates and initiated a comprehensive reform program for the abolition of feudal survivals in land tenure and the separation of church and state.

In 1779, he became governor, but constitutional limitations on his power, combined with his own lack of executive energy, caused an unsatisfactory administration, culminating in Jefferson's virtual abdication when the British invaded Virginia in 1781. He retired to his beautiful home at Monticello, Va., to his family. His wife, Martha Wayles Skelton, whom he married in 1772, died in 1782.

Jefferson's *Notes on Virginia* (1784–85) illustrate his many-faceted interests, his limitless intellectual curiosity, his deep faith in agrarian democracy. Sent to Congress in 1783, he helped lay down the decimal system and drafted basic reports on the organization of the western lands. In 1785 he was appointed minister to France, where the Anglo-Saxon liberalism he had drawn from John Locke, the British philosopher, was stimulated by contact with the thought that would soon ferment in the French Revolution. In 1789, Washington appointed him secretary of state. While favoring the Constitution and a strengthened central government, Jefferson came to believe that Hamilton contemplated the establishment of a monarchy. Growing differences resulted in Jefferson's resignation on Dec. 31, 1793.

Elected vice president in 1796, Jefferson continued to serve as spiritual leader of the opposition to Federalism, particularly to the repressive Alien and Sedition Acts. He was elected president in 1801 by the House of Representatives as a result of Hamilton's decision to throw the Federalist votes to him rather than to Aaron Burr, who had tied him in electoral votes. He was the first president to be inaugurated in Washington, which he had helped to design.

The purchase of Louisiana from France in 1803, though in violation of Jefferson's earlier constitutional scruples, was the most notable act of his administration. reelected in 1804, with the Federalist Charles C. Pinckney opposing him, Jefferson tried desperately to keep the United States out of the Napoleonic Wars in Europe, employing to this end the unpopular embargo policy.

After his retirement to Monticello in 1809, he developed his interest in education, founding the University of Virginia and watching its development with never-flagging interest. He died at Monticello on July 4, 1826. Jefferson had an enormous variety of interests and skills, ranging from education and science to architecture and music.

JAMES MADISON was born in Port Conway, Va., on March 16, 1751 (March 5, 1750/1, old style). A Princeton graduate, he joined the struggle for independence on his return to Virginia in 1771. In the 1770s and 1780s he was active in state politics, where he championed the Jefferson reform program, and in the Continental Congress. Madison was influential in the Constitutional Convention as leader of the group favoring a strong central government and as recorder of the debates; and he subsequently wrote, in collaboration with Alexander Hamilton and John Jay, the *Federalist* papers to aid the campaign for the adoption of the Constitution.

Serving in the new Congress, Madison soon emerged as the leader in the House of the men who opposed Hamilton's financial program and his pro-British leanings in foreign policy. Retiring from Congress in 1797, he continued to be active in Virginia and drafted the Virginia Resolution protesting the Alien and Sedition Acts. His intimacy with Jefferson made him the natural choice for secretary of state in 1801.

In 1809, Madison succeeded Jefferson as president, defeating Charles C. Pinckney. His wife, Dolley Payne Todd, whom he married in 1794, brought a new social sparkle to the executive mansion. In the meantime, increasing tension with Britain culminated in the War of 1812—a war for which the United States was unprepared and for which Madison lacked the executive talent to clear out incompetence and mobilize the nation's energies. Madison was reelected in 1812, running against the Federalist De Witt Clinton. In 1814, the British actually captured Washington and forced Madison to flee to Virginia.

Madison's domestic program capitulated to the Hamiltonian policies that he had resisted 20 years before and he now signed bills to establish a United States Bank and a higher tariff.

After his presidency, he remained in retirement in Virginia until his death on June 28, 1836.

JAMES MONROE was born on April 28, 1758, in Westmoreland County, Va. A William and Mary graduate, he served in the army during the first years of the Revolution and was wounded at Trenton. He then entered Virginia politics and later national politics under the sponsorship of Jefferson. In 1786, he married Elizabeth (Eliza) Kortright.

Fearing centralization, Monroe opposed the adoption of the Constitution and, as senator from Virginia, was highly critical of the Hamiltonian program. In 1794, he was appointed minister to France, where his ardent sympathies with the Revolution exceeded the wishes of the State Department. His troubled diplomatic career ended with his recall in 1796. From 1799 to 1802, he was governor of Virginia. In 1803, Jefferson sent him to France to help negotiate the Louisiana Purchase and for the next few years he was active in various negotiations on the Continent.

In 1808, Monroe flirted with the radical wing of the Republican Party, which opposed Madison's candidacy; but the presidential boom came to naught and, after a brief term as governor of Virginia in 1811, Monroe accepted Madison's offer to become secretary of state. During the War of 1812, he vainly sought a field command and instead served as secretary of war from September 1814 to March 1815.

Elected president in 1816 over the Federalist Rufus King, and reelected without opposition in 1820, Monroe, the last of the Virginia dynasty, pursued the course of systematic tranquilization that won for his administrations the name "the era of good feeling." He continued Madison's surrender to the Hamiltonian domestic program, signed the Missouri Compromise, acquired Florida, and with the able assistance of his secretary of state, John Quincy Adams, promulgated the Monroe Doctrine in 1823, declaring against foreign colonization or intervention in the Americas. He died in New York City on July 4, 1831, the third president to die on the anniversary of Independence.

JOHN QUINCY ADAMS was born on July 11, 1767, at Braintree (now Quincy), Mass., the son of John Adams, the second president. He spent his early years in Europe with his father, graduated from Harvard, and entered law practice. His anti-Paine newspaper articles won him political attention. In 1794, he became minister to the Netherlands, the first of several diplomatic posts that occupied him until his return to Boston in 1801. In 1797, he married Louisa Catherine Johnson.

In 1803, Adams was elected to the Senate, nominally as a Federalist, but his repeated displays of independence on such issues as the Louisiana Purchase and the embargo caused his party to demand his resignation and ostracize him socially. In 1809, Madison rewarded him for his support of Jefferson by appointing him minister to St. Petersburg. He helped negotiate the Treaty of Ghent in 1814, and in 1815 became minister to London. In 1817 Monroe appointed him secretary of state where he served with great distinction, gaining Florida from Spain without hostilities and playing an equal part with Monroe in formulating the Monroe Doctrine.

When no presidential candidate received a majority of electoral votes in 1824, Adams, with the support of Henry Clay, was elected by the House in 1825 over Andrew Jackson, who had the original plurality. Adams had ambitious plans of government activity to foster internal improvements and promote the arts and sciences, but congressional obstructionism, combined with his own unwillingness or inability to play the role of a politician, resulted in little being accomplished. After being defeated for reelection by Jackson in 1828, he successfully ran for the House of Representatives in 1830. There, though nominally a Whig, he pursued as ever an independent course. He led the fight to force Congress to receive antislavery petitions and fathered the Smithsonian Institution.

Adams had a stroke while on the floor of the House, and died two days later on Feb. 23, 1848. His long and detailed *Diary* gives a unique picture of the personalities and politics of the times.

ANDREW JACKSON was born on March 15, 1767, in what is now generally agreed to be Waxhaw, S.C. After a turbulent boyhood as an orphan and a British prisoner, he moved west to Tennessee, where he soon qualified for law practice but found time for such frontier pleasures as horse racing, cockfighting, and dueling. His marriage to Rachel Donelson Robards in 1791 was complicated by subsequent legal uncertainties about the status of her divorce. During the 1790s, Jackson served in the Tennessee Constitutional Convention, the United States House of Representatives and Senate, and on the Tennessee Supreme Court.

After some years as a country gentleman, living at the Hermitage near Nashville, Jackson in 1812 was given command of Tennessee troops sent against the Creeks. He defeated the Indians at Horseshoe Bend in 1814; subsequently he became a major general and won the Battle of New Orleans over veteran British troops, though after the treaty of peace had been signed at Ghent. In 1818, Jackson invaded Florida, captured Pensacola, and hanged two

Englishmen named Arbuthnot and Ambrister, creating an international incident. A presidential boom began for him in 1821, and to foster it, he returned to the Senate (1823–25). Though he won a plurality of electoral votes in 1824, he lost in the House when Clay threw his strength to Adams. Four years later, he easily defeated Adams.

As president, Jackson greatly expanded the power and prestige of the presidential office and carried through an unprecedented program of domestic reform, vetoing the bill to extend the United States Bank, moving toward a hard-money currency policy, and checking the program of federal internal improvements. He also vindicated federal authority against South Carolina with its doctrine of nullification and against France on the question of debts. The support given his policies by the workingmen of the East as well as by the farmers of the East, West, and South resulted in his triumphant reelection in 1832 over Clay.

After watching the inauguration of his handpicked successor, Martin Van Buren, Jackson retired to the Hermitage, where he maintained a lively interest in national affairs until his death on June 8, 1845.

MARTIN VAN BUREN was born on Dec. 5, 1782, at Kinderhook, N.Y. After graduating from the village school, he became a law clerk, entered practice in 1803, and soon became active in state politics as state senator and attorney general. In 1820, he was elected to the United States Senate. He threw the support of his efficient political organization, known as the Albany Regency, to William H. Crawford in 1824 and to Jackson in 1828. After leading the opposition to Adams's administration in the Senate, he served briefly as governor of New York (1828–1829) and resigned to become Jackson's secretary of state. He was soon on close personal terms with Jackson and played an important part in the Jacksonian program.

In 1832, Van Buren became vice president; in 1836, president. The Panic of 1837 overshadowed his term. He attributed it to the overexpansion of the credit and favored the establishment of an independent treasury as repository for the federal funds. In 1840, he established a 10-hour day on public works. Defeated by Harrison in 1840, he was the leading contender for the Democratic nomination in 1844 until he publicly opposed immediate annexation of Texas, and was subsequently beaten by the Southern delegations at the Baltimore convention. This incident increased his growing misgivings about the slave power.

After working behind the scenes among the antislavery Democrats, Van Buren joined in the movement that led to the Free-Soil Party and became its candidate for president in 1848. He subsequently returned to the Democratic Party while continuing to object to its pro-Southern policy. He died in Kinderhook on July 24, 1862. His *Autobiography* throws valuable sidelights on the political history of the times.

His wife, Hannah Hoes, whom he married in 1807, died in 1819.

WILLIAM HENRY HARRISON was born in Charles City County, Va., on Feb. 9, 1773. Joining the army in 1791, he was active in Indian fighting in the Northwest, became secretary of the Northwest

Territory in 1798 and governor of Indiana in 1800. He married Anna Symmes in 1795. Growing discontent over white encroachments on Indian lands led to the formation of an Indian alliance under Tecumseh to resist further aggressions. In 1811, Harrison won a nominal victory over the Indians at Tippecanoe and in 1813 a more decisive one at the Battle of the Thames, where Tecumseh was killed.

After resigning from the army in 1814, Harrison had an obscure career in politics and diplomacy, ending up 20 years later as a county recorder in Ohio. Nominated for president in 1835 as a military hero whom the conservative politicians hoped to be able to control, he ran surprisingly well against Van Buren in 1836. Four years later, he defeated Van Buren but caught pneumonia and died in Washington on April 4, 1841, a month after his inauguration. Harrison was the first president to die in office.

JOHN TYLER was born in Charles City County, Va., on March 29, 1790. A William and Mary graduate, he entered law practice and politics, serving in the House of Representatives (1817–21), as governor of Virginia (1825–27), and as senator (1827–36). A strict constructionist, he supported Crawford in 1824 and Jackson in 1828, but broke with Jackson over his United States Bank policy and became a member of the Southern state-rights group that cooperated with the Whigs. In 1836, he resigned from the Senate rather than follow instructions from the Virginia legislature to vote for a resolution expunging censure of Jackson from the Senate record.

Elected vice president on the Whig ticket in 1840, Tyler succeeded to the presidency on Harrison's death. His strict-constructionist views soon caused a split with the Henry Clay wing of the Whig party and a stalemate on domestic questions. Tyler's more considerable achievements were his support of the Webster-Ashburton Treaty with Britain and his success in bringing about the annexation of Texas.

After his presidency he lived in retirement in Virginia until the outbreak of the Civil War, when he emerged briefly as chairman of a peace convention and then as delegate to the provisional Congress of the Confederacy. He died on Jan. 18, 1862. He married Letitia Christian in 1813 and, two years after her death in 1842, Julia Gardiner.

JAMES KNOX POLK was born in Mecklenburg County, N.C., on Nov. 2, 1795. A graduate of the University of North Carolina, he moved west to Tennessee, was admitted to the bar, and soon became prominent in state politics. In 1825, he was elected to the House of Representatives, where he opposed Adams and, after 1829, became Jackson's floor leader in the fight against the Bank. In 1835, he became Speaker of the House. Four years later, he was elected governor of Tennessee, but was beaten in tries for reelection in 1841 and 1843.

The supporters of Van Buren for the Democratic nomination in 1844 counted on Polk as his running mate, but when Van Buren's stand on Texas alienated Southern support, the convention swung to Polk on the ninth ballot. He was elected over Henry Clay, the Whig candidate. Rapidly disillusioning those who thought that he would not run his own administration, Polk proceeded steadily and precisely to achieve four major objectives—the acquisition of California, the settlement of the Oregon question, the reduction of the tariff, and the establishment of the independent treasury. He also enlarged the Monroe Doctrine to exclude all non-American intervention in American affairs, whether forcible or not, and he forced Mexico into a war that he waged to a successful conclusion.

His wife, Sarah Childress, whom he married in 1824, was a woman of charm and ability. Polk died in Nashville, Tenn., on June 15, 1849.

ZACHARY TAYLOR was born at Montebello, Orange County, Va., on Nov. 24, 1784. Embarking on a military career in 1808, Taylor fought in the War of 1812, the Black Hawk War, and the Seminole War, meanwhile holding garrison jobs on the frontier or desk jobs in Washington. A brigadier general as a result of his victory over the Seminoles at Lake Okeechobee (1837), Taylor held a succession of Southwestern commands and in 1846 established a base on the Rio Grande, where his forces engaged in hostilities that precipitated the war with Mexico. He captured Monterrey in Sept. 1846 and, disregarding Polk's orders to stay on the defensive, defeated Santa Anna at Buena Vista in Feb. 1847, ending the war in the northern provinces.

Though Taylor had never cast a vote for president, his party affiliations were Whiggish and his availability was increased by his difficulties with Polk. He was elected president over the Democrat Lewis Cass. During the revival of the slavery controversy, which was to result in the Compromise of 1850, Taylor began to take an increasingly firm stand against appeasing the South; but he died in Washington on July 9, 1850, during the fight over the Compromise. He married Margaret Mackall Smith in 1810. His bluff and simple soldierly qualities won him the name Old Rough and Ready.

MILLARD FILLMORE was born at Locke, Cayuga County, N.Y., on Jan. 7, 1800. A lawyer, he entered politics with the Anti-Masonic Party under the sponsorship of Thurlow Weed, editor and party boss, and subsequently followed Weed into the Whig Party. He served in the House of Representatives (1833–35 and 1837–43) and played a leading role in writing the tariff of 1842. Defeated for governor of New York in 1844, he became state comptroller in 1848, was put on the Whig ticket with Taylor as a concession to the Clay wing of the party, and became president upon Taylor's death in 1850.

As president, Fillmore broke with Weed and William H. Seward and associated himself with the pro-Southern Whigs, supporting the Compromise of 1850. Defeated for the Whig nomination in 1852, he ran for president in 1856 as candidate of the American, or Know-Nothing, Party, which sought to unite the country against foreigners in the alleged hope of diverting it from the explosive slavery issue. Fillmore opposed Lincoln during the Civil War. He died in Buffalo on March 8, 1874.

He was married in 1826 to Abigail Powers, who died in 1853, and in 1858 to Caroline Carmichael McIntosh.

FRANKLIN PIERCE was born at Hillsboro, N.H., on Nov. 23, 1804. A Bowdoin graduate, lawyer, and Jacksonian Democrat, he won rapid political advancement in the party, in part because of the prestige of his father, Gov. Benjamin Pierce. By 1831 he was Speaker of the New Hampshire House of Representatives; from 1833 to 1837, he served in the federal House and from 1837 to 1842 in the Senate. His wife, Jane Means Appleton, whom he married in 1834, disliked Washington and the somewhat dissipated life led by Pierce; in 1842 Pierce resigned from the Senate and began a successful law practice in Concord, N.H. During the Mexican War, he was a brigadier general.

Thereafter Pierce continued to oppose antislavery tendencies within the Democratic Party. As a result, he was the Southern choice to break the deadlock at the Democratic convention of 1852 and was nominated on the 49th ballot. In the election, Pierce overwhelmed Gen. Winfield Scott, the Whig candidate.

As president, Pierce followed a course of appeasing the South at home and of playing with schemes of territorial expansion abroad. The failure of his foreign and domestic policies prevented his renomination. He died in Concord on Oct. 8, 1869, in relative obscurity.

JAMES BUCHANAN was born near Mercersburg, Pa., on April 23, 1791. A Dickinson graduate and a lawyer, he entered Pennsylvania politics as a Federalist. With the disappearance of the Federalist Party, he became a Jacksonian Democrat. He served with ability in the House (1821–31), as minister to St. Petersburg (1832–33), and in the Senate (1834–45), and in 1845 became Polk's secretary of state. In 1853, Pierce appointed Buchanan minister to Britain, where he participated with other American diplomats in Europe in drafting the expansionist Ostend Manifesto.

He was elected president in 1856, defeating John C. Frémont, the Republican candidate, and former President Millard Fillmore of the American Party. The growing crisis over slavery presented Buchanan with problems he lacked the will to tackle. His appeasement of the South alienated the Stephen Douglas wing of the Democratic Party without reducing Southern militancy on slavery issues. While denying the right of secession, Buchanan also denied that the federal government could do anything about it. He supported the administration during the Civil War and died in Lancaster, Pa., on June 1, 1868.

The only president to remain a bachelor throughout his term, Buchanan used his charming niece, Harriet Lane, as White House hostess.

ABRAHAM LINCOLN was born in Hardin (now Larue) County, Ky., on Feb. 12, 1809. His family moved to Indiana and then to Illinois, and Lincoln gained what education he could along the way. While reading law, he worked in a store, managed a mill, surveyed, and split rails. In 1834, he went to the Illinois legislature as a Whig and became the party's floor leader. For the next 20 years he practiced law in Springfield, except for a single term (1847–49) in Congress, where he denounced the Mexican War. In 1855, he was a candidate for senator and the next year he joined the new Republican Party.

A leading but unsuccessful candidate for the vice-presidential nomination with Frémont, Lincoln gained national attention in 1858 when, as Republican candidate for senator from Illinois, he engaged in a series of debates with Stephen A. Douglas, the

Democratic candidate. He lost the election, but continued to prepare the way for the 1860 Republican convention and was rewarded with the presidential nomination on the third ballot. He won the election over three opponents.

From the start, Lincoln made clear that, unlike Buchanan, he believed the national government had the power to crush the rebellion. Not an abolitionist, he held the slavery issue subordinate to that of preserving the Union, but soon perceived that the war could not be brought to a successful conclusion without freeing the slaves. His administration was hampered by the incompetence of many Union generals, the inexperience of the troops, and the harassing political tactics both of the Republican Radicals, who favored a hard policy toward the South, and the Democratic Copperheads, who desired a negotiated peace. The Gettysburg Address of Nov. 19, 1863, marks the high point in the record of American eloquence. Lincoln's long search for a winning combination finally brought generals Ulysses S. Grant and William T. Sherman to the top; and their series of victories in 1864 dispelled the mutterings from both Radicals and Peace Democrats that at one time seemed to threaten Lincoln's reelection. He was reelected in 1864, defeating Gen. George B. McClellan, the Democratic candidate. His inaugural address urged leniency toward the South: "With malice toward none, with charity for all . . . let us strive on to finish the work we are in; to bind up the nation's wounds . . ." This policy aroused growing opposition on the part of the Republican Radicals, but before the matter could be put to the test, Lincoln was shot by the actor John Wilkes Booth at Ford's Theater, Washington, on April 14, 1865. He died the next morning.

Lincoln's marriage to Mary Todd in 1842 was often unhappy and turbulent, in part because of his wife's pronounced instability.

ANDREW JOHNSON was born at Raleigh, N.C., on Dec. 29, 1808. Self-educated, he became a tailor in Greeneville, Tenn., but soon went into politics, where he rose steadily. He served in the House of Representatives (1843–54), as governor of Tennessee (1853–57), and as a senator (1857–62). Politically he was a Jacksonian Democrat and his specialty was the fight for a more equitable land policy. Alone among the Southern Senators, he stood by the Union during the Civil War. In 1862, he became war governor of Tennessee and carried out a thankless and difficult job with great courage. Johnson became Lincoln's running mate in 1864 as a result of an attempt to give the ticket a nonpartisan and nonsectional character. Succeeding to the presidency on Lincoln's death, Johnson sought to carry out Lincoln's policy, but without his political skill. The result was a hopeless conflict with the Radical Republicans who dominated Congress, passed measures over Johnson's vetoes, and attempted to limit the power of the executive concerning appointments and removals. The conflict culminated with Johnson's impeachment for attempting to remove his disloyal secretary of war in defiance of the Tenure of Office Act, which required senatorial concurrence for such dismissals. The opposition failed by one vote to get the two thirds necessary for conviction.

After his presidency, Johnson maintained an interest in politics and in 1875 was again elected to the Senate. He died near Carter Station, Tenn., on July 31, 1875. He married Eliza McCardle in 1827.

ULYSSES SIMPSON GRANT was born (as Hiram Ulysses Grant) at Point Pleasant, Ohio, on April 27, 1822. He graduated from West Point in 1843 and served without particular distinction in the Mexican War. In 1848 he married Julia Dent. He resigned from the army in 1854, after warnings from his commanding officer about his drinking habits, and for the next six years held a wide variety of jobs in the Middle West. With the outbreak of the Civil War, he sought a command and soon, to his surprise, was made a brigadier general. His continuing successes in the western theaters, culminating in the capture of Vicksburg, Miss., in 1863, brought him national fame and soon the command of all the Union armies. Grant's dogged, implacable policy of concentrating on dividing and destroying the Confederate armies brought the war to an end in 1865. The next year, he was made full general.

In 1868, as Republican candidate for president, Grant was elected over the Democrat, Horatio Seymour. From the start, Grant showed his unfitness for the office. His cabinet was weak, his domestic policy was confused, and many of his intimate associates were corrupt. The notable achievement in foreign affairs was the settlement of controversies with Great Britain in the Treaty of London (1871), negotiated by his able secretary of state, Hamilton Fish.

Running for reelection in 1872, he defeated Horace Greeley, the Democratic and Liberal Republican candidate. The Panic of 1873 graft scandals close to the presidency created difficulties for his second term.

After retiring from office, Grant toured Europe for two years and returned in time to accede to a third-term boom, but was beaten in the convention of 1880. Illness and bad business judgment darkened his last years, but he worked steadily at the *Personal Memoirs,* which were to be successful when published after his death at Mount McGregor, near Saratoga, N.Y., on July 23, 1885.

RUTHERFORD BIRCHARD HAYES was born in Delaware, Ohio, on Oct. 4, 1822. A graduate of Kenyon College and the Harvard Law School, he practiced law in Lower Sandusky (now Fremont) and then in Cincinnati. In 1852 he married Lucy Webb. A Whig, he joined the Republican party in 1855. During the Civil War he rose to major general. He served in the House of Representatives from 1865 to 1867 and then confirmed a reputation for honesty and efficiency in two terms as governor of Ohio (1868–72). His election to a third term in 1875 made him the logical candidate for those Republicans who wished to stop James G. Blaine in 1876, and he was nominated.

The result of the election was in doubt for some time and hinged upon disputed returns from South Carolina, Louisiana, Florida, and Oregon. Samuel J. Tilden, the Democrat, had the larger popular vote but was adjudged by the strictly partisan decisions of the Electoral Commission to have one fewer electoral vote, 185 to 184. The national acceptance of this result was due in part to the general understanding that Hayes would pursue a conciliatory policy toward the South. He withdrew the troops from the South, took a conservative position on financial and labor issues, and urged civil service reform.

Hayes served only one term by his own wish and spent the rest of his life in various humanitarian endeavors. He died in Fremont on Jan. 17, 1893.

JAMES ABRAM GARFIELD, the last president to be born in a log cabin, was born in Cuyahoga County, Ohio, on Nov. 19, 1831. A Williams graduate, he taught school for a time and entered Republican politics in Ohio. In 1858, he married Lucretia Rudolph. During the Civil War, he had a promising career, rising to major general of volunteers; but he resigned in 1863, having been elected to the House of Representatives, where he served until 1880. His oratorical and parliamentary abilities soon made him the leading Republican in the House, though his record was marred by his unorthodox acceptance of a fee in the DeGolyer paving contract case and by suspicions of his complicity in the Crédit Mobilier scandal.

In 1880, Garfield was elected to the Senate, but instead became the presidential candidate on the 36th ballot as a result of a deadlock in the Republican convention. In the election, he defeated Gen. Winfield Scott Hancock, the Democratic candidate. Garfield's administration was barely under way when he was shot by Charles J. Guiteau, a disappointed office seeker, in Washington on July 2, 1881. He died in Elberton, N.J., on Sept. 19.

CHESTER ALAN ARTHUR was born at Fairfield, Vt., on Oct. 5, 1829. A graduate of Union College, he became a successful New York lawyer. In 1859, he married Ellen Herndon. During the Civil War, he held administrative jobs in the Republican state administration and in 1871 was appointed collector of the Port of New York by Grant. This post gave him control over considerable patronage. Though not personally corrupt, Arthur managed his power in the interests of the New York machine so openly that President Hayes in 1877 called for an investigation and the next year Arthur was suspended.

In 1880 Arthur was nominated for vice president in the hope of conciliating the followers of Grant and the powerful New York machine. As president upon Garfield's death, Arthur, stepping out of his familiar role as spoilsman, backed civil service reform, reorganized the cabinet, and prosecuted political associates accused of post office graft. Losing machine support and failing to gain the reformers, he was not nominated for a full term in 1884. He died in New York City on Nov. 18, 1886.

(STEPHEN) GROVER CLEVELAND was born at Caldwell, N.J., on March 18, 1837. He was admitted to the bar in Buffalo, N.Y., in 1859 and lived there as a lawyer, with occasional incursions into Democratic politics, for more than 20 years. He did not participate in the Civil War. As mayor of Buffalo in 1881, he carried through a reform program so ably that the Democrats ran him successfully for governor in 1882. In 1884 he won the Democratic nomination for president. The campaign contrasted Cleveland's spotless public career with the uncertain record of James G. Blaine, the Republican candidate, and Cleveland received enough Mugwump (independent Republican) support to win.

As president, Cleveland pushed civil service reform, opposed the pension grab and attacked the high tariff rates. While in the White House, he married Frances Folsom in 1886. Renominated in 1888, Cleveland was defeated by Benjamin Harrison, polling more popular but fewer electoral votes. In 1892, he was elected over Harrison. When the Panic of 1893 burst upon the country, Cleveland's attempts to solve it by sound-money measures alienated the free-silver wing of the party, while his tariff policy alienated the protectionists. In 1894, he sent troops to break the Pullman strike. In foreign affairs, his firmness caused Great Britain to back down in the Venezuela border dispute.

In his last years Cleveland was an active and much-respected public figure. He died in Princeton, N.J., on June 24, 1908.

BENJAMIN HARRISON was born in North Bend, Ohio, on Aug. 20, 1833, the grandson of William Henry Harrison, the ninth president. A graduate of Miami University in Ohio, he took up the law in Indiana and became active in Republican politics. In 1853, he married Caroline Lavinia Scott. During the Civil War, he rose to brigadier general. A sound-money Republican, he was elected senator from Indiana in 1880. In 1888, he received the Republican nomination for president on the eighth ballot. Though behind on the popular vote, he won over Grover Cleveland in the electoral college by 233 to 168.

As president, Harrison failed to please either the bosses or the reform element in the party. In foreign affairs he backed Secretary of State Blaine, whose policy foreshadowed later American imperialism. Harrison was renominated in 1892 but lost to Cleveland. His wife died in the White House in 1892 and Harrison married her niece, Mary Scott (Lord) Dimmick, in 1896. After his presidency, he resumed law practice. He died in Indianapolis on March 13, 1901.

WILLIAM MCKINLEY was born in Niles, Ohio, on Jan. 29, 1843. He taught school, then served in the Civil War, rising from the ranks to become a major. Subsequently he opened a law office in Canton, Ohio, and in 1871 married Ida Saxton. Elected to Congress in 1876, he served there until 1891, except for 1883–85. His faithful advocacy of business interests culminated in the passage of the highly protective McKinley Tariff of 1890. With the support of Mark Hanna, a shrewd Cleveland businessman interested in safeguarding tariff protection, McKinley became governor of Ohio in 1892 and Republican presidential candidate in 1896. The business community, alarmed by the progressivism of William Jennings Bryan, the Democratic candidate, spent considerable money to assure McKinley's victory.

The chief event of McKinley's administration was the war with Spain, which resulted in the United States' acquisition of the Philippines and other islands. With imperialism an issue, McKinley defeated Bryan again in 1900. On Sept. 6, 1901, he was shot at Buffalo, N.Y., by Leon F. Czolgosz, an anarchist, and he died there eight days later.

THEODORE ROOSEVELT was born in New York City on Oct. 27, 1858. A Harvard graduate, he was early interested in ranching, in politics, and in writing picaresque historical narratives. He was a Republican member of the New York Assembly in 1882–84, an unsuccessful candidate for mayor of

New York in 1886, a U.S. civil service commissioner under Benjamin Harrison, police commissioner of New York City in 1895, and assistant secretary of the Navy under McKinley in 1897. He resigned in 1898 to help organize a volunteer regiment, the Rough Riders, and take a more direct part in the war with Spain. He was elected governor of New York in 1898 and vice president in 1900, in spite of lack of enthusiasm on the part of the bosses.

Assuming the presidency of the assassinated McKinley in 1901, Roosevelt embarked on a wide-ranging program of government reform and conservation of natural resources. He ordered antitrust suits against several large corporations, threatened to intervene in the anthracite coal strike of 1902, which prompted the operators to accept arbitration, and, in general, championed the rights of the "little man" and fought the "malefactors of great wealth." He was also responsible for such progressive legislation as the Elkins Act of 1903, which outlawed freight rebates by railroads; the bill establishing the Department of Commerce and Labor; the Hepburn Act, which gave the I.C.C. greater control over the railroads; the Meat Inspection Act; and the Pure Food and Drug Act.

In foreign affairs, Roosevelt pursued a strong policy, permitting the instigation of a revolt in Panama to dispose of Colombian objections to the Panama Canal and helping to maintain the balance of power in the East by bringing the Russo-Japanese War to an end, for which he won the Nobel Peace Prize, the first American to achieve a Nobel prize in any category. In 1904, he decisively defeated Alton B. Parker, his conservative Democratic opponent.

Roosevelt's increasing coldness toward his successor, William Howard Taft, led him to overlook his earlier disclaimer of third-term ambitions and to reenter politics. Defeated by the machine in the Republican convention of 1912, he organized the Progressive Party (Bull Moose) and polled more votes than Taft, though the split brought about the election of Woodrow Wilson. From 1915 on, Roosevelt strongly favored intervention in the European war. He became deeply embittered at Wilson's refusal to allow him to raise a volunteer division. He died in Oyster Bay, N.Y., on Jan. 6, 1919. He was married twice: in 1880 to Alice Hathaway Lee, who died in 1884, and in 1886 to Edith Kermit Carow.

WILLIAM HOWARD TAFT was born in Cincinnati on Sept. 15, 1857. A Yale graduate, he entered Ohio Republican politics in the 1880s. In 1886 he married Helen Herron. From 1887 to 1890, he served on the Ohio Superior Court; 1890–92, as solicitor general of the United States; 1892–1900, on the federal circuit court. In 1900 McKinley appointed him president of the Philippine Commission and in 1901 governor general. Taft had great success in pacifying the Filipinos, solving the problem of the church lands, improving economic conditions, and establishing limited self-government. His period as secretary of war (1904–08) further demonstrated his capacity as administrator and conciliator, and he was Roosevelt's hand-picked successor in 1908. In the election, he polled 321 electoral votes to 162 for William Jennings Bryan, who was running for the presidency for the third time.

Though he carried on many of Roosevelt's policies, Taft got into increasing trouble with the progressive wing of the party and displayed mounting irritability and indecision. After his defeat in 1912, he became professor of constitutional law at Yale. In 1921 he was appointed chief justice of the United States Supreme Court. He died in Washington, DC, on March 8, 1930.

(THOMAS) WOODROW WILSON was born in Staunton, Va., on Dec. 28, 1856. A Princeton graduate, he turned from law practice to post-graduate work in political science at Johns Hopkins University, receiving his Ph.D. in 1886. He taught at Bryn Mawr, Wesleyan, and Princeton, and in 1902 was made president of Princeton. After an unsuccessful attempt to democratize the social life of the university, he welcomed an invitation in 1910 to be the Democratic gubernatorial candidate in New Jersey, and was elected. His success in fighting the machine and putting through a reform program attracted national attention.

In 1912, at the Democratic convention in Baltimore, Wilson won the nomination on the 46th ballot and went on to defeat Roosevelt and Taft in the election. Wilson proceeded under the standard of the New Freedom to enact a program of domestic reform, including the Federal Reserve Act, the Clayton Antitrust Act, the establishment of the Federal Trade Commission, and other measures designed to restore competition in the face of the great monopolies. In foreign affairs, while privately sympathetic with the Allies, he strove to maintain neutrality in the European war and warned both sides against encroachments on American interests.

Reelected in 1916 as a peace candidate, he tried to mediate between the warring nations; but when the Germans resumed unrestricted submarine warfare in 1917, Wilson brought the United States into what he now believed was a war to make the world safe for democracy. He supplied the classic formulations of Allied war aims and the armistice of Nov. 11, 1918, was negotiated on the basis of Wilson's Fourteen Points. In 1919 he strove at Versailles to lay the foundations for enduring peace. He accepted the imperfections of the Versailles Treaty in the expectation that they could be remedied by action within the League of Nations. He probably could have secured ratification of the treaty by the Senate if he had adopted a more conciliatory attitude toward the mild reservationists; but his insistence on all or nothing eventually caused the diehard isolationists and diehard Wilsonites to unite in rejecting a compromise.

In Sept. 1919 Wilson suffered a paralytic stroke that limited his activity. After leaving the presidency he lived on in retirement in Washington, dying on Feb. 3, 1924. He was married twice—in 1885 to Ellen Louise Axson, who died in 1914, and in 1915 to Edith Bolling Galt.

WARREN GAMALIEL HARDING was born in Morrow County, Ohio, on Nov. 2, 1865. After attending Ohio Central College, Harding became interested in journalism and in 1884 bought the *Marion* (Ohio) *Star*. In 1891 he married a wealthy widow, Florence Kling De Wolfe. As his paper prospered, he entered Republican politics, serving as state senator (1899–1903) and as lieutenant governor (1904–06). In 1910, he was defeated for governor, but in 1914 was elected to the Senate. His reputation as an orator made him the keynoter at the 1916 Republican convention.

When the 1920 convention was deadlocked between Leonard Wood and Frank O. Lowden, Harding became the dark-horse nominee on his solemn affirmation that there was no reason in his past that he should not be. Straddling the League question, Harding was easily elected over James M. Cox, his Democratic opponent. His cabinet contained some able men, but also some manifestly unfit for public office. Harding's own intimates were mediocre when they were not corrupt. The impending disclosure of the Teapot Dome scandal in the Interior Department and illegal practices in the Justice Department and Veterans' Bureau, as well as political setbacks, profoundly worried him. On his return from Alaska in 1923, he died unexpectedly in San Francisco on Aug. 2.

(JOHN) CALVIN COOLIDGE was born in Plymouth, Vt., on July 4, 1872. An Amherst graduate, he went into law practice at Northampton, Mass., in 1897. He married Grace Anna Goodhue in 1905. He entered Republican state politics, becoming successively mayor of Northampton, state senator, lieutenant governor and, in 1919, governor. His use of the state militia to end the Boston police strike in 1919 won him a somewhat undeserved reputation for decisive action and brought him the Republican vice-presidential nomination in 1920. After Harding's death Coolidge handled the Washington scandals with care and finally managed to save the Republican Party from public blame for the widespread corruption.

In 1924, Coolidge was elected without difficulty, defeating the Democrat, John W. Davis, and Robert M. La Follette running on the Progressive ticket. His second term, like his first, was characterized by a general satisfaction with the existing economic order. He stated that he did not choose to run in 1928.

After his presidency, Coolidge lived quietly in Northampton, writing an unilluminating autobiography and a syndicated column. He died there on Jan. 5, 1933.

HERBERT CLARK HOOVER was born at West Branch, Iowa, on Aug. 10, 1874, the first president to be born west of the Mississippi. A Stanford graduate, he worked from 1895 to 1913 as a mining engineer and consultant throughout the world. In 1899, he married Lou Henry. During World War I, he served with distinction as chairman of the American Relief Committee in London, as chairman of the Commission for Relief in Belgium, and as U.S. Food Administrator. His political affiliations were still too indeterminate for him to be mentioned as a possibility for either the Republican or Democratic nomination in 1920, but after the election he served Harding and Coolidge as secretary of commerce.

In the election of 1928, Hoover overwhelmed Gov. Alfred E. Smith of New York, the Democratic candidate and the first Roman Catholic to run for the presidency. He soon faced the worst depression in the nation's history, but his attacks upon it were hampered by his devotion to the theory that the forces that brought the crisis would soon bring the revival and then by his belief that there were too many areas in which the federal government had no power to act. In a succession of vetoes, he struck down measures proposing a national employment system or national relief, he reduced income tax rates, and only at the end of his term did he yield to popular pressure and set up agencies such as the Reconstruction Finance Corporation to make emergency loans to assist business.

After his 1932 defeat, Hoover returned to private business. In 1946, President Truman charged him with various world food missions; and from 1947 to 1949 and 1953 to 1955, he was head of the Commission on Organization of the Executive Branch of the Government. He died in New York City on Oct. 20, 1964.

FRANKLIN DELANO ROOSEVELT was born in Hyde Park, N.Y., on Jan. 30, 1882. A Harvard graduate, he attended Columbia Law School and was admitted to the New York bar. In 1910, he was elected to the New York State Senate as a Democrat. Reelected in 1912, he was appointed assistant secretary of the navy by Woodrow Wilson the next year. In 1920, his radiant personality and his war service resulted in his nomination for vice president as James M. Cox's running mate. After his defeat, he returned to law practice in New York. In Aug. 1921, Roosevelt was stricken with infantile paralysis while on vacation at Campobello, New Brunswick. After a long and gallant fight, he recovered partial use of his legs. In 1924 and 1928, he led the fight at the Democratic national conventions for the nomination of Gov. Alfred E. Smith of New York, and in 1928 Roosevelt was himself induced to run for governor of New York. He was elected, and was reelected in 1930.

In 1932, Roosevelt received the Democratic nomination for president and immediately launched a campaign that brought new spirit to a weary and discouraged nation. He defeated Hoover by a wide margin. His first term was characterized by an unfolding of the New Deal program, with greater benefits for labor, the farmers, and the unemployed, and the progressive estrangement of most of the business community.

At an early stage, Roosevelt became aware of the menace to world peace posed by totalitarian fascism, and from 1937 on he tried to focus public attention on the trend of events in Europe and Asia. As a result, he was widely denounced as a warmonger. He was reelected in 1936 over Gov. Alfred M. Landon of Kansas by the overwhelming electoral margin of 523 to 8, and the gathering international crisis prompted him to run for an unprecedented third term in 1940. He defeated Wendell L. Willkie.

Roosevelt's program to bring maximum aid to Britain and, after June 1941, to Russia was opposed, until the Japanese attack on Pearl Harbor restored national unity. During the war, Roosevelt shelved the New Deal in the interests of conciliating the business community, both in order to get full production during the war and to prepare the way for a united acceptance of the peace settlements after the war. A series of conferences with Winston Churchill and Joseph Stalin laid down the bases for the postwar world. In 1944 he was elected to a fourth term, running against Gov. Thomas E. Dewey of New York.

On April 12, 1945, Roosevelt died of a cerebral hemorrhage at Warm Springs, Ga., shortly after his return from the Yalta Conference. His wife, (Anna) Eleanor Roosevelt, whom he married in 1905, was a woman of great ability who made significant contributions to her husband's policies.

HARRY S. TRUMAN was born on a farm near Lamar, Mo., on May 8, 1884. During World War I, he served in France as a captain with the 129th Field Artillery. He married Bess Wallace in 1919. After engaging briefly and unsuccessfully in the haberdashery business in Kansas City, Mo., Truman entered local politics. Under the sponsorship of Thomas Pendergast, Democratic boss of Missouri, he held a number of local offices, preserving his personal honesty in the midst of a notoriously corrupt political machine. In 1934, he was elected to the Senate and was reelected in 1940. During his first term he was a loyal but quiet supporter of the New Deal, but in his second term, an appointment as head of a Senate committee to investigate war production brought out his special qualities of honesty, common sense, and hard work, and he won widespread respect.

Elected vice president in 1944, Truman became president upon Roosevelt's sudden death in April 1945 and was immediately faced with the problems of winding down the war against the Axis and preparing the nation for postwar adjustment. Germany surrendered on May 8, and in July Truman attended the Potsdam Conference to discuss the settlement plans for postwar Europe. To end the war with Japan, he authorized the dropping of atomic bombs on Hiroshima and Nagasaki on Aug. 6 and Aug. 9, 1945. Japan surrendered on Aug. 14. Although the action undoubtedly saved many American lives by bringing the war to an end, the morality of the decision is still debated.

The years 1947–48 were distinguished by civil-rights proposals, the Truman Doctrine to contain the spread of Communism, and the Marshall Plan to aid in the economic reconstruction of war-ravaged nations. Truman's general record, highlighted by a vigorous Fair Deal campaign, brought about his unexpected election in 1948 over the heavily favored Thomas E. Dewey.

Truman's second term was primarily concerned with the cold war with the Soviet Union, the implementing of the North Atlantic Pact, the United Nations police action in Korea, and the vast rearmament program with its accompanying problems of economic stabilization.

On March 29, 1952, Truman announced that he would not run again for the presidency. After leaving the White House, he returned to his home in Independence, Mo., to write his memoirs. He further busied himself with the Harry S. Truman Library there. He died in Kansas City, Mo., on Dec. 26, 1972.

DWIGHT DAVID EISENHOWER was born in Denison, Tex., on Oct. 14, 1890. His ancestors lived in Germany and emigrated to America, settling in Pennsylvania, early in the 18th century. His father, David, had a general store in Hope, Kans., which failed. After a brief time in Texas, the family moved to Abilene, Kan.

After graduating from Abilene High School in 1909, Eisenhower did odd jobs for almost two years. He won an appointment to the Naval Academy at Annapolis, but was too old for admittance. Then he received an appointment in 1910 to West Point, from which he graduated as a second lieutenant in 1915.

He did not see service in World War I, having been stationed at Fort Sam Houston, Tex. There he met Mamie Geneva Doud, whom he married in Denver on July 1, 1916, and by whom he had two sons: Doud Dwight (died in infancy) and John Sheldon Doud.

Eisenhower served in the Philippines from 1935 to 1939 with Gen. Douglas MacArthur. Afterward, Gen. George C. Marshall, the army chief of staff, brought him into the War Department's General Staff and in 1942 placed him in command of the invasion of North Africa. In 1944, he was made Supreme Allied Commander for the invasion of Europe.

After the war, Eisenhower served as army chief of staff from Nov. 1945 until Feb. 1948, when he was appointed president of Columbia University.

In Dec. 1950, President Truman recalled Eisenhower to active duty to command the North Atlantic Treaty Organization forces in Europe. He held his post until the end of May 1952.

At the Republican convention of 1952 in Chicago, Eisenhower won the presidential nomination on the first ballot in a close race with Sen. Robert A. Taft of Ohio. In the election, he defeated Gov. Adlai E. Stevenson of Illinois.

Through two terms, Eisenhower hewed to moderate domestic policies. He sought peace through Free World strength in an era of new nationalisms, nuclear missiles, and space exploration. He fostered alliances pledging the United States to resist "Red" aggression in Europe, Asia, and Latin America. The Eisenhower Doctrine of 1957 extended commitments to the Middle East.

At home, the popular president lacked Republican congressional majorities after 1954, but he was reelected in 1956 by 457 electoral votes to 73 for Stevenson.

While retaining most Fair Deal programs, he stressed "fiscal responsibility" in domestic affairs. A moderate in civil rights, he sent troops to Little Rock, Ark., to enforce court-ordered school integration.

With his wartime rank restored by Congress, Eisenhower returned to private life and the role of elder statesman, with his vigor hardly impaired by a heart attack, an ileitis operation, and a mild stroke suffered while in office. He died in Washington, DC, on March 28, 1969.

JOHN FITZGERALD KENNEDY was born in Brookline, Mass., on May 29, 1917. His father, Joseph P. Kennedy, was ambassador to Great Britain from 1937 to 1940.

Kennedy was graduated from Harvard University in 1940 and joined the navy the next year. He became skipper of a PT boat that was sunk in the Pacific by a Japanese destroyer. Although given up for lost, he swam to a safe island, towing an injured enlisted man.

After recovering from a war-aggravated spinal injury, Kennedy entered politics in 1946 and was elected to Congress. In 1952, he ran against Sen. Henry Cabot Lodge, Jr., of Massachusetts, and won.

Kennedy was married on Sept. 12, 1953, to Jacqueline Lee Bouvier, by whom he had three children: Caroline, John Fitzgerald, Jr. (died in a 1999 plane crash), and Patrick Bouvier (died in infancy).

In 1957 Kennedy won the Pulitzer Prize for a book he had written earlier, *Profiles in Courage.*

After strenuous primary battles, Kennedy won the Democratic presidential nomination on the first ballot at the 1960 Los Angeles convention. With a plurality of only 118,574 votes, he carried the election over Vice President Richard M. Nixon and became the first Roman Catholic president.

Kennedy brought to the White House the dynamic idea of a "New Frontier" approach in dealing with problems at home, abroad, and in the dimensions of space. Out of his leadership in his first few months in office came the 10-year Alliance for Progress to aid Latin America, the Peace Corps, and accelerated programs that brought the first Americans into orbit in the race in space.

Failure of the U.S.-supported Cuban invasion in April 1961 led to the entrenchment of the Communist-backed Castro regime, only 90 mi from United States soil. When it became known that Soviet offensive missiles were being installed in Cuba in 1962, Kennedy ordered a naval "quarantine" of the island and moved troops into position to eliminate this threat to U.S. security. The world seemed on the brink of a nuclear war until Soviet premier Khrushchev ordered the removal of the missiles.

A sudden "thaw," or the appearance of one, in the cold war came with the agreement with the Soviet Union on a limited test-ban treaty signed in Moscow on Aug. 6, 1963.

In his domestic policies, Kennedy's proposals for medical care for the aged and aid to education were defeated, but on minimum wage, trade legislation, and other measures he won important victories.

Widespread racial disorders and demonstrations led to Kennedy's proposing sweeping civil rights legislation. As his third year in office drew to a close, he also recommended an $11-billion tax cut to bolster the economy. Both measures were pending in Congress when Kennedy, looking forward to a second term, journeyed to Texas for a series of speeches.

While riding in an automobile procession in Dallas on Nov. 22, 1963, he was shot to death by an assassin firing from an upper floor of a building. The alleged assassin, Lee Harvey Oswald, was killed two days later in the Dallas city jail by Jack Ruby, owner of a strip-tease club.

At 46 years of age, Kennedy became the fourth president to be assassinated and the eighth to die in office.

LYNDON BAINES JOHNSON

LYNDON BAINES JOHNSON was born in Stonewall, Tex., on Aug. 27, 1908. On both sides of his family he had a political heritage mingled with a Baptist background of preachers and teachers. Both his father and his paternal grandfather served in the Texas House of Representatives.

After his graduation from Southwest Texas State Teachers College, Johnson taught school for two years. He went to Washington in 1932 as secretary to Rep. Richard M. Kleberg. During this time, he married Claudia Alta Taylor, known as "Lady Bird." They had two children: Lynda Bird and Luci Baines.

In 1935, Johnson became Texas administrator for the National Youth Administration. Two years later,

he was elected to Congress as an all-out supporter of Franklin D. Roosevelt, and served until 1949. He was the first member of Congress to enlist in the armed forces after the attack on Pearl Harbor. He served in the navy in the Pacific and won a Silver Star.

Johnson was elected to the Senate in 1948 after he had captured the Democratic nomination by only 87 votes. He was 40 years old. He became the Senate Democratic leader in 1953. A heart attack in 1955 threatened to end his political career, but he recovered fully and resumed his duties.

At the height of his power as Senate leader, Johnson sought the Democratic nomination for president in 1960. When he lost to John F. Kennedy, he surprised even some of his closest associates by accepting second place on the ticket.

Johnson was riding in another car in the motorcade when Kennedy was assassinated in Dallas on Nov. 22, 1963. He took the oath of office in the presidential jet on the Dallas airfield.

With Johnson's insistent backing, Congress finally adopted a far-reaching civil-rights bill, a voting-rights bill, a Medicare program for the aged, and measures to improve education and conservation. Congress also began what Johnson described as "an all-out war" on poverty.

Amassing a record-breaking majority of nearly 16 million votes, Johnson was elected president in his own right in 1964, defeating Sen. Barry Goldwater of Arizona.

The double tragedy of a war in Southeast Asia and urban riots at home marked Johnson's last two years in office. Faced with disunity in the nation and challenges within his own party, Johnson surprised the country on March 31, 1968, with the announcement that he would not be a candidate for reelection. He died of a heart attack suffered at his LBJ Ranch on Jan. 22, 1973.

RICHARD MILHOUS NIXON

RICHARD MILHOUS NIXON was born in Yorba Linda, Calif., on Jan. 9, 1913, to Midwestern-bred parents, Francis A. and Hannah Milhous Nixon, who raised their five sons as Quakers.

Nixon was a high school debater and was undergraduate president at Whittier College in California, where he was graduated in 1934. As a scholarship student at Duke University Law School in North Carolina, he graduated third in his class in 1937.

After five years as a lawyer, Nixon joined the navy in August 1942. He was an air transport officer in the South Pacific and a legal officer stateside before his discharge in 1946 as a lieutenant commander.

Running for Congress in California as a Republican in 1946, Nixon defeated Rep. Jerry Voorhis. As a member of the House Un-American Activities Committee, he made a name as an investigator of Alger Hiss, a former high State Department official, who was later jailed for perjury. In 1950, Nixon defeated Rep. Helen Gahagan Douglas, a Democrat, for the Senate. He was criticized for portraying her as a Communist dupe.

Nixon's anti-Communism ideals, his Western roots, and his youth figured into his selection in 1952 to run for vice president on the ticket headed by Dwight D. Eisenhower. Demands for Nixon's withdrawal followed disclosure that California businessmen had paid some of his Senate office expenses. His televised rebuttal, known as "the

Checkers speech" (named for a cocker spaniel given to the Nixons), brought him support from the public and from Eisenhower. The ticket won easily in 1952 and again in 1956.

Eisenhower gave Nixon substantive assignments, including missions to 56 countries. In Moscow in 1959, Nixon won acclaim for his defense of U.S. interests in an impromptu "kitchen debate" with Soviet premier Nikita S. Khrushchev.

Nixon lost the 1960 race for the presidency to John F. Kennedy.

In 1962, Nixon failed in a bid for California's governorship and seemed to be finished as a national candidate. He became a Wall Street lawyer, but kept his old party ties and developed new ones through constant travels to speak for Republicans.

Nixon won the 1968 Republican presidential nomination after a shrewd primary campaign, then made Gov. Spiro T. Agnew of Maryland his surprise choice for vice president. In the election, they edged out the Democratic ticket headed by Vice President Hubert H. Humphrey by 510,314 votes out of 73,212,065 cast.

Committed to winding down the U.S. role in the Vietnamese War, Nixon pursued "Vietnamization"—training and equipping South Vietnamese to do their own fighting. American ground combat forces in Vietnam fell steadily from 540,000 when Nixon took office to none in 1973 when the military draft was ended. But there was heavy continuing use of U.S. air power.

Nixon improved relations with Moscow and reopened the long-closed door to mainland China with a good-will trip there in Feb. 1972. In May of that same year, he visited Moscow and signed agreements on arms limitation and trade expansion and approved plans for a joint U.S.–Soviet space mission in 1975.

Inflation was a campaign issue for Nixon, but he failed to master it as president. On Aug. 15, 1971, with unemployment edging up, Nixon abruptly announced a new economic policy: a 90-day wage-price freeze, stimulative tax cuts, a temporary 10% tariff, and spending cuts. A second phase, imposing guidelines on wage, price, and rent boosts, was announced Oct. 7.

The economy responded in time for the 1972 campaign, in which Nixon played up his foreign-policy achievements. Played down was the burglary on June 17, 1972, of Democratic national headquarters in the Watergate apartment complex in Washington. The Nixon–Agnew reelection campaign cost a record $60 million and swamped the Democratic ticket headed by Sen. George McGovern of South Dakota with a plurality of 17,999,528 out of 77,718,554 votes. Only Massachusetts, with 14 electoral votes, and the District of Columbia, with 3, went for McGovern.

In Jan. 1973, hints of a cover-up emerged at the trial of six men found guilty of the Watergate burglary. With a Senate investigation under way, Nixon announced on April 30 the resignations of his top aides, H. R. Haldeman and John D. Ehrlichman, and the dismissal of White House counsel John Dean III. Dean was the star witness at televised Senate hearings that exposed both a White House cover-up of Watergate and massive illegalities in Republican fund-raising in 1972.

The hearings also disclosed that Nixon had routinely tape-recorded his office meetings and telephone conversations.

On Oct. 10, 1973, Agnew resigned as vice president, then pleaded no-contest to a negotiated federal charge of evading income taxes on alleged bribes. Two days later, Nixon nominated the House minority leader, Rep. Gerald R. Ford of Michigan, as the new vice president. Congress confirmed Ford on Dec. 6, 1973.

In June 1974, Nixon visited Israel and four Arab nations. Then he met in Moscow with Soviet leader Leonid I. Brezhnev and reached preliminary nuclear arms limitation agreements.

But, in the month after his return, Watergate ended the Nixon regime. On July 24 the Supreme Court ordered Nixon to surrender subpoenaed tapes. On July 30, the Judiciary Committee referred three impeachment articles to the full membership. On Aug. 5, Nixon bowed to the Supreme Court and released tapes showing he halted an FBI probe of the Watergate burglary six days after it occurred. It was in effect an admission of obstruction of justice, and impeachment appeared inevitable.

Nixon resigned on Aug. 9, 1974, the first president ever to do so. A month later, President Ford issued an unconditional pardon for any offenses Nixon might have committed as president, thus forestalling possible prosecution.

In 1940, Nixon married Thelma Catherine (Pat) Ryan. They had two daughters, Patricia (Tricia) and Julie, who married Dwight David Eisenhower II, grandson of the former president.

He died on April 22, 1994, in New York City of a massive stroke.

GERALD RUDOLPH FORD was born Leslie King Jr. in Omaha, Neb., on July 14, 1913, the only child of Leslie and Dorothy Gardner King. His parents were divorced in 1915. His mother moved to Grand Rapids, Mich., and married Gerald R. Ford. The boy was renamed for his stepfather.

Ford captained his high school football team in Grand Rapids, and a football scholarship took him to the University of Michigan, where he starred as varsity center before his graduation in 1935. A job as assistant football coach at Yale gave him an opportunity to attend Yale Law School, from which he graduated in the top third of his class in 1941.

He returned to Grand Rapids to practice law, but entered the Navy in April 1942. He saw wartime service in the Pacific on the light aircraft carrier *Monterey* and was a lieutenant commander when he returned to Grand Rapids early in 1946 to resume law practice and dabble in politics.

Ford was elected to Congress in 1948 for the first of his 13 terms in the House. He was soon assigned to the influential Appropriations Committee and rose to become the ranking Republican on the subcommittee on Defense Department appropriations.

As a legislator, Ford described himself as "a moderate on domestic issues, a conservative in fiscal affairs, and a dyed-in-the-wool internationalist." He carried the ball for Pentagon appropriations, was a hawk on the war in Vietnam, and kept a low profile on civil-rights issues.

Ford was also dependable and hard-working and popular with his colleagues. In 1963, he was elected chairman of the House Republican Conference. He served in 1963–1964 as a member of the Warren Commission, which investigated the assassination of John F. Kennedy. A revolt by dissatisfied younger Republicans in 1965 made him minority leader.

On Oct. 12, 1973, Nixon nominated Ford to fill the vice presidency left vacant by Agnew's resignation under fire. It was the first use of the procedures for filling vacancies in the vice presidency laid down in the 25th Amendment to the Constitution, which Ford had helped enact. Once in office, he said he did not believe Nixon had been involved in the Watergate scandals, but he criticized Nixon's stubborn court battle against releasing tape recordings of Watergate-related conversations for use as evidence. The scandals led to Nixon's unprecedented resignation on Aug. 9, 1974, and Ford was sworn in immediately as the 38th president, the first to enter the White House without winning a national election.

Ford assured the nation when he took office that "our long national nightmare is over" and pledged "openness and candor" in all his actions. He won a warm response from the Democratic 93rd Congress when he said he wanted "a good marriage" rather than a honeymoon with his former colleagues. In Dec. 1974 congressional majorities backed his choice of former New York governor Nelson A. Rockefeller as his vice president.

The cordiality was chilled by Ford's announcement on Sept. 8, 1974, that he had granted an unconditional pardon to Nixon for any crimes he might have committed as president. Although no formal charges were pending, Ford said he feared "ugly passions" would be aroused if Nixon were brought to trial. The pardon was widely criticized.

To fight inflation, the new president first proposed fiscal restraints and spending curbs and a 5% tax surcharge that got nowhere in the Senate and House. Congress again rebuffed Ford in the spring of 1975 when he appealed for emergency military aid to help the governments of South Vietnam and Cambodia resist massive Communist offensives.

Politically, Ford's fortunes improved steadily in the first half of 1975. Badly divided Democrats in Congress were unable to muster votes to override his vetoes of spending bills that exceeded his budget. He faced some right-wing opposition in his own party, but moved to preempt it with an early announcement—on July 8, 1975—of his intention to be a candidate in 1976. During the election campaign, Ford was regarded as a caretaker president lacking in strength and vision. He was defeated in November by Jimmy Carter.

In 1948, Ford married Elizabeth Anne (Betty) Bloomer. They had four children, Michael Gerald, John Gardner, Steven Meigs, and Susan Elizabeth.

JAMES EARL CARTER, JR., was born in the tiny village of Plains, Ga., Oct. 1, 1924, and grew up on the family farm at nearby Archery. Both parents were fifth-generation Georgians. His father, James Earl Carter, was known as a segregationist, but treated his black and white workers equally. Carter's mother, Lillian Gordy, was a matriarchal presence in home and community and opposed the then-prevailing code of racial inequality. The future president was baptized in 1935 in the conservative Southern Baptist Church and spoke often of being a "born again" Christian, although committed to the separation of church and state.

Carter married Rosalynn Smith, a neighbor, in 1946. Their first child, John William, was born a year later in Portsmouth, Va. Their other children are James Earl III, born in Honolulu in 1950; Donnel Jeffrey, born in New London, Conn., in 1952; and Amy Lynn, born in Plains in 1967.

In 1946 Carter was graduated from the U.S. Naval Academy at Annapolis and served in the nuclear-submarine program under Adm. Hyman G. Rickover. In 1954, after his father's death, he resigned from the Navy to take over the family's flourishing warehouse and cotton gin, with several thousand acres for growing seed peanuts.

Carter was elected to the Georgia Senate in 1962. In 1966 he lost the race for governor, but was elected in 1970. His term brought a state government reorganization, sharply reduced agencies, increased economy and efficiency, and new social programs, all with no general tax increase. In 1972 the peanut farmer–politician set his sights on the presidency and in 1974 built a base for himself as he criss-crossed the country as chairman of the Democratic Campaign Committee, appealing for revival and reform. In 1975 he won the support of most of the old Southern civil-rights coalition after endorsement by Rep. Andrew Young, black Democrat from Atlanta, who had been the closest aide to the Rev. Martin Luther King, Jr. Having won 19 out of 31 primaries with a broad appeal to conservatives and liberals, black and white, poor and well-to-do, he defeated Gerald R. Ford in Nov. 1976.

In his one term, Carter fought hard for his programs against resistance from an independent-minded Democratic Congress that frustrated many pet projects although it overrode only two vetoes. Public dissatisfaction with the "stagflation" economy, staff problems, friction with Congress, long gasoline lines, and the months-long Iranian crisis, including the abortive sally in April 1980 to free the hostages also proved problematic for the administration. Yet, assessments of his record have noted many positive elements. There was, for one thing, peace throughout his term, with no American combat deaths and with a brake on the advocates of force. Regarded as perhaps his greatest personal achievements were the Camp David accords between Israel and Egypt and the resulting treaty—the first between Israel and an Arab neighbor. The treaty with China and the Panama Canal treaties were also major achievements. Carter worked for nuclear-arms control. His concern for international human rights was credited with saving lives and reducing torture, and he supported the British policy that ended internecine warfare in Rhodesia, now Zimbabwe. Domestically, his environmental record was a major accomplishment. His judicial appointments won acclaim, with 265 choices for the federal bench that included minority members and women.

In 1980 Carter was renominated on the first ballot after vanquishing Sen. Edward M. Kennedy of Massachusetts in the primaries. In the election campaign, he attacked his rivals, Ronald Reagan and John B. Anderson, independent, with the warning that a Reagan Republican victory would heighten the risk of war and impede civil rights and economic opportunity. In November Carter lost to Reagan, who won 489 electoral college votes and 51% of the popular tally, to 49 electoral votes and 41% for Carter. He was awarded the 2002 Nobel Peace Prize.

RONALD WILSON REAGAN rode to the presidency in 1980 on a tide of resurgent right-wing sentiment among an electorate longing for a distant, simpler era. He left office in Jan. 1989 with two-thirds of the American people approving his performance during his two terms. It was the highest rating for any retiring president since World War II.

Reagan, an actor turned politician, a New Dealer turned conservative, came to films and politics from a thoroughly Middle-American background—middle class, Middle West, and small town. He was born in Tampico, Ill., Feb. 6, 1911, the second son of John Edward Reagan and Nelle Wilson Reagan; the family later moved to Dixon, Ill. His father was a shop clerk and merchant with Democratic sympathies. It was an impoverished family; young Ronald sold homemade popcorn at high school games and worked as a lifeguard to earn money for his college tuition. When his father got a New Deal WPA job, the future president became an ardent Roosevelt Democrat.

Reagan earned a BA degree in 1932 from Eureka (Ill.) College, where a photographic memory aided in his studies and in debating and college theatricals. During the Depression, he made $100 a week as a sports announcer for radio station WHO in Des Moines, Iowa. His career as a film and TV actor stretched from 1937 to 1966, and his salary climbed to $3,500 a week. As a World War II captain in army film studios, Reagan recoiled from what he saw as the laziness of civil service workers, and moved to the Right. As president of the Screen Actors Guild, he resisted what he considered a Communist plot to subvert the film industry. With advancing age, Reagan left leading-man roles and became a television spokesman for the General Electric Company.

With oratorical skill as his trademark, Reagan became an active Republican. In 1966, at the behest of a small group of conservative businessmen, he ran for governor of California with a pledge to cut spending; he was elected by almost a million votes over the political veteran, Democratic governor Edmund G. Brown. Reelected to a second term, he served as governor until 1975.

In the 1980 election battle against Jimmy Carter, Reagan broadened his appeal by espousing moderate policies, gaining much of his support from disaffected Democrats and blue-collar workers. The incoming administration immediately set out to "turn the government around" with a new economic program. Over strenuous congressional opposition, Reagan pushed through his "supply side" economic program to stimulate production and control inflation through tax cuts and sharp reductions in government spending. However, in 1982, as the economy declined into the worst recession in 40 years, the president's popularity slipped and support for supply-side economics faded.

Barely three months into his first term, Reagan was the target of an assassin's bullet; his courageous comeback won public admiration. The president also won high acclaim for his nomination of Sandra Day O'Connor as the first woman on the Supreme Court. His later nominations met increasing opposition and did much to tilt the Court's orientation to the Right.

Internationally, Reagan confronted numerous problems in his first term. In an effort to establish order on the Caribbean island of Grenada and eliminate the Cuban military presence there, Reagan ordered an invasion of the tiny nation on Oct. 25, 1983. The troops met strong resistance from Cuban military personnel on the island but soon occupied it. Another military effort, in Lebanon, ended in failure, however. U.S. Marines engaged as part of a multinational peacekeeping force in Beirut were forced to withdraw in 1984 after a disastrous terrorist attack left 241 marines dead.

With the economy improving and inflation under control, the popular president won reelection in a landslide in 1984. Domestically, a tax reform bill that Reagan backed became law. But the constantly growing budget deficit remained an irritant, with the president and Congress persistently at odds over priorities in spending for defense and domestic programs. Congress was also increasingly reluctant to increase spending for the Nicaraguan "Contras." But even severe critics praised Reagan's restrained but decisive handling of the crisis following the hijacking of an American plane in Beirut by Muslim extremists. The attack on Libya in April 1986 galvanized the nation, although it drew scathing disapproval from the NATO alliance.

Reagan's popularity with the public dipped sharply in 1986 when the Iran-Contra scandal broke, shortly after the Democrats gained control of the Senate. The weeks-long congressional hearings in the summer of 1987 heard an array of administration officials, present and former, reveal a web of deceit and undercover maneuvering in the White House. Yet the president's personal reputation remained untouched; on Aug. 12, 1987, he told the nation that he had not known of questionable activities but agreed that he was ultimately accountable.

Reagan's place in history will rest, perhaps, on the short- and intermediate-range missile treaty consummated on a cordial visit to the Soviet Union that he had once reviled as an "evil empire." Its provisions, including a ground-breaking agreement on verification inspection, were formulated in four days of summit talks in Moscow in May 1988 with the Soviet leader, Mikhail S. Gorbachev. Reagan could point to numerous domestic achievements as well: sharp cuts in income tax rates, creating economic growth without inflation, and reducing the unemployment rate, among others. He failed, however, to win the "Reagan Revolution" on such issues as abortion and school prayer.

Reagan married his wife, Nancy, four years after his divorce from the screen actress Jane Wyman. The children from his first marriage are Maureen, his daughter by Wyman, and Michael, an adopted son. He had two children by Nancy: Patricia and Ron. Reagan suffered from Alzheimer's disease, which he developed in the years following his presidency.

GEORGE HERBERT WALKER BUSH was born June 12, 1924, in Milton, Mass., to Prescott and Dorothy Bush. The family later moved to Connecticut. The youth studied at the elite Phillips Academy in Andover, Mass.

The future president joined the Navy after war broke out and at 18 became the Navy's youngest commissioned pilot, serving from 1942 to 1945, and was awarded the Distinguished Flying Cross. He fought the Japanese on 58 missions and was shot down once.

After the war, Bush earned an economics degree and a Phi Beta Kappa key in two and a half years at Yale University.

In 1945 Bush married Barbara Pierce of Rye, N.Y., daughter of a magazine publisher. With his bride, Bush moved to Texas instead of entering his father's investment banking business. There he founded his oil company and by 1980 reported an estimated wealth of $1.4 million.

Throughout his whole career, Bush had the backing of an established family, headed by his father, Prescott Bush, who was elected to the Senate from Connecticut in 1952. The family helped the young patrician become established in his early business ventures, a rich uncle raising most of the capital required for founding the oil company.

In the 1960s, Bush won two contests for a Texas Republican seat in the House of Representatives, but lost two bids for a Senate seat. After Bush's second race for the Senate, President Nixon appointed him U.S. delegate to the United Nations and he later became Republican National Committee chairman. He headed the U.S. liaison office in Beijing before becoming Director of Central Intelligence. In 1980 Bush became Reagan's running mate despite earlier criticism of Reagan "voodoo economics" and by the 1984 election had won acclaim for his devotion to Reagan's conservative agenda.

The vice president entered the 1988 presidential campaign and easily defeated Democrat Michael Dukakis. Bush's choice of Sen. Dan Quayle of Indiana as a running mate provoked criticism and ridicule that continued even after the administration was in office. Nonetheless Bush strongly defended his choice. George Herbert Walker Bush became president on Jan. 20, 1989, with his theme harmony and conciliation after the often-turbulent Reagan years.

Bush's early Cabinet choices reflected a pragmatic desire for an efficient, nonideological government. And with his usual cautious instinct, in 1990 he nominated to the Supreme Court the scholarly David H. Souter, with broadly conservative views.

In his first year, Bush was confronted with the Lebanese hostage crisis, the *Exxon Valdez* oil spill in Alaska, and the ongoing war against drug trafficking. His public approval soared following the invasion of Panama in late 1989. But a staggering budget deficit and the savings and loan crisis caused the president's popularity to dip sharply in his second year. This plunge followed Bush's recantation of his campaign "no new taxes" pledge as he sat down with congressional leaders to tame the budget deficit and deal with a faltering economy.

In 1991, the president emerged as the leader of an international coalition of Western democracies, Japan, and even some Arab states that came together to free Kuwait following an invasion of the country by Iraq in Aug. 1990. The coalition forces defeated Iraq in only a little more than a month after Operation Desert Storm was launched on Jan. 16–17, 1991, and a nation grateful at feeling the end of the "Vietnam syndrome" gave the president an 89% approval rating. However, the high rating fell as the year went on, as doubts persisted about the war's outcome—Iraqi president Saddam Hussein remained in power and persistently avoided complying with the terms of the peace treaty—and as concerns began to grow about the faltering U.S. economy and other domestic problems.

A major Bush accomplishment in 1991 was the Strategic Arms Reduction Treaty (START), signed in July with Soviet president Mikhail S. Gorbachev at their fourth summit conference, marking the end of the long weapons buildup.

In the 1992 presidential election, Bush was defeated by Gov. Bill Clinton of Arkansas.

The Bushes have four sons, George, Jeb, Neil, and Marvin, and a daughter, Dorothy. Another daughter, Robin, died at age three from leukemia. Son George served as governor of Texas from 1995 to 2000, when he was elected the 43rd U.S. president. Jeb Bush was elected governor of Florida in 1998.

WILLIAM JEFFERSON CLINTON was born William Jefferson Blythe IV in Hope, Ark., on Aug. 19, 1946. He was named for his father, who was killed in an automobile accident before Clinton's birth. Virginia Kelley, his mother, eventually married Roger Clinton, a car dealer, whose surname the future president later adopted.

In high school in Hot Springs, Ark., Clinton considered becoming a doctor, but politics beckoned after a meeting with President John F. Kennedy in Washington, DC, on a Boys' Nation trip. He earned a BS in international affairs in 1968 at Georgetown University, having spent his junior year working for Arkansas senator J. William Fulbright. He was a Rhodes scholar at Oxford between 1968 and 1970. He then attended Yale Law School, where he met his future wife, Hillary Rodham, a Wellesley graduate. The couple has one child, Chelsea.

Clinton taught at the University of Arkansas (1974–1976), was elected state attorney general (1976), and in 1979 became the nation's youngest governor. But he was defeated for reelection in 1980 by voters irate at a rise in the state's automobile license fees. In 1982 he was elected again. This time he reined in liberal tendencies to accommodate the conservative bent of the voters.

Clinton became the 42nd U.S. president following a turbulent political campaign. He overcame vigorous personal attacks on his character and on his actions during the Vietnam War, which he actively opposed. The "character issue" stemmed from allegations of infidelity, which Clinton refuted in a television interview in which he and Hillary avowed their relationship was solid. Throughout his term in office, Clinton was dogged by allegations relating to the Whitewater real estate deal in which he and Hillary were involved prior to the 1992 election. Though the Clintons were never accused of any wrongdoing, partners in the venture were convicted of fraud and conspiracy in a trial in 1996.

The problems faced by the new president were as daunting as they were varied. In Jan. 1993 he became embroiled with the military leadership over his campaign pledge to allow homosexuals to serve openly in the armed services. He ultimately agreed to a compromise, dubbed the "don't ask, don't tell" policy. Clinton's first year also saw him wrangling with Congress over the federal budget and economic policy.

In his second year, Clinton was faced with acrimonious battles over health care, welfare reform, and crime prevention. A health care reform package crafted by his wife failed to gain sufficient support. Clinton had to reduce his objective from massive overhaul to incremental reform. \

Clinton won major victories with the passage of the North American Free Trade Agreement (NAFTA), which took effect Jan. 1, 1994, and the Global Agreement on Tariffs and Trade (GATT), which led to the establishment in 1995 of the World Trade Organization (WTO). Congress also approved a deficit reduction bill, rules allowing abortion counseling in federally funded clinics, a waiting period for handgun purchases (the Brady Bill), and a national service program.

Foreign affairs became a proving ground for Clinton, since he has been elected primarily on a domestic economic agenda. He improved his international image when the Israel–Jordan peace agreement was signed at the White House in the summer of 1994 by Israeli prime minister Yitzhak Rabin and Jordan's King Hussein. In the fall of that year, the administration succeeded in restoring Haiti's ousted president, Jean-Bertrand Aristide, to power. Clinton scored again by bolstering Russian president Boris Yeltsin's popularity with promises of economic aid.

The problems in Eastern Europe were Clinton's next big challenge. Though he wanted desperately to end the brutal ethnic cleansing in Bosnia, he did not want to commit American ground troops to do so. A peace accord involving American peacekeeping troops was ultimately signed in Dayton, Ohio, in Nov. 1995.

The 1994 elections resulted in a Republican-controlled Congress, and 1995 was largely a tug-of-war between the White House and Capitol Hill over budget-balancing and other key points of the GOP's "Contract with America," crafted by Speaker of the House Newt Gingrich.

In 1996, aided by a booming economy, Clinton won reelection to a second term, becoming the first Democratic president since Franklin D. Roosevelt to do so. The country's general prosperity also made it possible in 1997 for Clinton and the Republicans to reach an agreement to balance the federal budget in three decades.

However, the character issues that had followed Clinton for years soon began to emerge once again. A series of investigations was begun to determine whether Clinton and Vice President Gore had participated in questionable fund-raising practices in their 1996 campaign.

As his tenure wore on, Clinton came under increasing pressure from Kenneth Starr, the independent counsel who in 1994 took over the investigation of the Clintons' involvement in the Whitewater land deal. Over time, Starr's brief was expanded to include other matters, such as the death of White House lawyer Vincent Foster, the handling of firings in the White House travel office, and shocking allegations of sexual misconduct by Clinton.

In Jan. 1998, Clinton was called to testify in a long-pending sexual harassment suit brought against him by Paula Corbin Jones, a former Arkansas state employee. In his testimony, Clinton denied that he had had a sexual relationship with a young White House intern, Monica Lewinsky, and that he had attempted to cover it up. Although a federal judge in Arkansas threw out the Jones sexual harassment suit in April 1998, by this time the Lewinsky affair had become the focus of Kenneth Starr's investigation as well as a national obsession.

Finally, on Aug. 17, 1998, after relentless media attention, leaks, and news of Lewinsky's upcoming testimony, Clinton made history by becoming the first U.S. president to testify in front of a grand jury in an investigation of his own possibly criminal conduct. In an address to the nation that evening, he admitted to having had an "inappropriate relationship" with Lewinsky, but reaffirmed that he did not ask anyone to lie about or cover up the affair.

Paradoxically, however, in spite of the scandalous outcome of events, Clinton's overall popularity among Americans remained high. The country seemed willing to ignore his weaknesses in character, much as they did in the 1992 elections, as long as the economy was good, his policies were popular, and the United States remained strong abroad.

On Sept. 9, Starr—a conservative Republican whose investigation was seen by Clinton supporters as a politically inspired vendetta—delivered his report to the House of Representatives. While the report outlined 11 possible grounds for impeachment, none stemmed from the initial subjects of the investigation, including the Whitewater real estate deal. The real focus of the accusations seemed to be Clinton's moral conduct, and the "Starr Report" graphically detailed his sexual affair.

Despite the American population's general disapproval of a trial (which was reflected in poll after poll), Congress moved forward in its highly partisan impeachment proceedings and on Dec. 19, Clinton became the second president in American history to be impeached. Two of the four articles of impeachment passed (Article I, grand jury perjury, and Article III, obstruction of justice), the votes drawn along party lines. After a Senate trial in Jan.–Feb. 1999, Clinton was acquitted on both counts.

While the impeachment trial overshadowed all other activity in Washington for a good portion of 1998, Clinton was forced to respond to continued problems with Iraq at the end of the year. In December, Saddam Hussein blocked a weapons inspection by the United Nations. The UN responded with airstrikes that would continue on a nearly daily basis for the next three months, and then off and on through the spring and summer, as Iraq taunted the U.S. and its allies further by shooting at jets patrolling the no-fly zones set up after the Persian Gulf war.

In the spring of 1999, reports of continued ethnic cleansing in the Serbian province of Kosovo were growing. Clinton and his British counterpart, Tony Blair, led the push for NATO intervention, which resulted in a 78-day bombing campaign against Serbia that began in March. Although Clinton received some sharp criticism for holding back on the deployment of NATO ground troops, he was ultimately justified, as Serbian president Slobodan Milosevic finally agreed to a peace treaty, signed June 9.

In his final year of office, the president maintained a relatively low profile but took several major trips overseas, to South Asia, Europe, and Africa. He also prepared for the 2000 elections, lending his support not only to presidential hopeful Al Gore, but also to his wife, Hillary Clinton, who successfully ran for U.S. senator from New York.

On Jan. 19, 2001, the day before he left office, Clinton agreed to a five-year suspension of his Arkansas law license and his paying of a $25,000 fine to the Arkansas Bar Association. In exchange, Kenneth Starr's successor, Robert Ray, agreed to close the Whitewater probe, ending the threat of criminal liability for Mr. Clinton after he left office.

GEORGE WALKER BUSH

GEORGE WALKER BUSH was born on July 6, 1946, in New Haven, Conn., the first child of future president George H. W. Bush. In 1948, the family moved to Odessa, Tex., where the senior Bush went to work in the oil business. George W. grew up mainly in Midland, Tex., and Houston, and later attended two of his father's alma maters, Phillips Academy in Andover, Mass., and Yale.

After graduating from Yale with a history degree in 1968, Bush joined the Texas Air National Guard, where he served as a part-time fighter pilot until 1973. After receiving an MBA from Harvard Business School in 1975, he returned to Texas, where he established his own oil and gas business. In 1977 he met and married his wife, Laura Welch, a librarian. The couple has twin daughters, Jenna and Barbara, born in 1981.

Coming from a prominent political family—his grandfather Prescott Bush had been a senator from Connecticut and his father a U.S. congressman and political appointee—George W. had been immersed in politics since childhood. In 1977 he entered the fray himself, unsuccessfully running for U.S. Congress from the West Texas district that included his hometown of Midland.

Following his defeat, Bush returned to the oil business. In 1985, however, oil prices fell sharply, and Bush's company verged on collapse until it was acquired by a Dallas firm. Bush then headed to Washington to become a paid adviser to his father's successful 1988 presidential campaign. After the election, Bush returned to Texas and assembled a group of investors to buy the Texas Rangers.

Bush again entered politics in 1993, running for the Texas governorship. Although he had a tough opponent in the immensely popular incumbent Ann Richards, he created a clear agenda focused on issues such as education and juvenile justice and won with 53% of the vote. He was reelected in 1998, not long before he announced plans to run for president.

During the 2000 campaign, Bush characterized himself as a "compassionate conservative," a somewhat vague description meant to evoke a kinder, gentler Republican. On the core issues, Bush adhered closely to the traditional conservative line, favoring small government, tax cuts, a strong military, and opposing gun control and abortion. His choice of running mate, Dick Cheney, former secretary of defense during his father's administration, provided his campaign with seasoned Washington political experience.

With the country in a state of general prosperity and the candidates divided along only narrowly differentiated ideological lines, the 2000 election between George W. Bush and Vice President Al Gore was perceived to be one of the least dynamic on issues. As it turned out, the race was one of the closest in the country's history. By early evening on election night, it was apparent that whoever won

Florida would win the election. Bush's razor thin margin of about 1,200 votes prompted an automatic recount. The case ultimately ended up in the U.S. Supreme Court. Bush officially became the president-elect on Dec. 13, after the Supreme Court reversed a decision by the Florida Supreme Court to allow manual recounts of ballots in some Florida counties, contending that such a partial recount violated the Constitution's equal protection and due process guarantees. With Florida in his column, Bush won the presidency with 271 electoral votes, just one more than he needed, although he lost the popular vote by half a million. The Supreme Court decision generated enormous controversy, with critics asserting that the Supreme Court, and not the electorate, had effectively determined the outcome of the presidential election.

The top item on Bush's domestic agenda—a $1.35 trillion tax cut over 11 years—was swiftly enacted in June 2001. In his first year in office, President Bush also championed an antimissile defense system, meant to intercept long-range missiles lobbed at U.S. shores. Opponents of the plan argued that it was technologically unfeasible and astronomically expensive. Bush's early foreign policy was defined by the rejection of a number of international treaties that the White House felt were detrimental to American interests, including the Kyoto treaty on global warming, the biological weapons convention banning germ warfare, and a treaty to establish an international war-crimes court. Bush also withdrew from the 1972 Antiballistic Missile Treaty, the basis for three decades of nuclear stability with the Soviet Union, but at the same time succeeded in persuading Russia to agree to a landmark treaty that would cut U.S. and Russian nuclear weapons stockpiles by two-thirds over the next decade.

The terrorist attacks on the World Trade Center and the Pentagon on Sept. 11, 2001, irrevocably altered the direction of the Bush presidency; his primary focus became the war on international terrorism. Bush shored up enormous support from the international community to fight terrorism worldwide through intelligence-sharing, freezing financial assets of suspected terrorists, and apprehending al-Qaeda members and other terrorist suspects, and in the case of Afghanistan, military action. On Oct. 7, the U.S. and Britain began air strikes against Afghanistan, after the Taliban government repeatedly refused to surrender Osama bin Laden, the mastermind of the Sept. 11 attacks. The Taliban collapsed on Dec. 9, but despite this outstanding military success, bin Laden remained at large.

National security efforts included creating the White House Department of Homeland Security, a cabinet-level domestic security agency that consolidated 20 federal agencies in a massive government reorganization. More controversial was the passage of the USA Patriot Act, anti-terrorism legislation that has presented law enforcement officials with sweeping new powers to conduct searches without warrants, and to detain and deport individuals in secret.

President Bush's broad characterizations of the terrorist threat led him to expand the scope of his foreign policy from al-Qaeda and other terrorist organizations to other regimes hostile to the United States, regardless of their connection to the Sept. 11 attacks. Following the war in Afghanistan, Bush designated Iraq as the primary new threat to American security.

He famously labeled Iraq, along with North Korea and Iran, as part of an "axis of evil." Over the course of 2002, President Bush announced that the U.S. foreign strategy of containment and deterrence was an outdated cold war policy. In an age of terrorism, he maintained, the United States could no longer wait by defensively until a potential threat to its security grew into an actual one—a preemptive strike was called for. In Sept. 2002, Bush addressed the UN, challenging the organization to swiftly enforce its own resolutions against Iraq, or else the U.S. would have no choice but to act on its own. Many world leaders expressed alarm at this shift in U.S. policy, which stressed unilateralism rather than international consensus. The alleged existence of weapons of mass destruction, Iraq's links to terrorism, and Saddam Hussein's despotism and human rights abuses were cited as the casus belli for "regime change." The UN Security Council unanimously approved a resolution imposing tough new arms inspections on Iraq, but after three months of inspections that resulted in modest Iraqi cooperation, U.S. patience ran out: on March 19, President Bush declared war on Iraq and U.S. troops, along with their British allies, began bombing Baghdad. By April 9, Baghdad had fallen, and by May 1, combat was officially declared over.

The official phase of the war was swift, but the post-war reconstruction period proved far more difficult. The country was enveloped in violence and chaos, its infrastructure in ruins, and coalition forces continued to meet greater and greater Iraqi resistance. As American casualties grew and costs mounted (the Pentagon estimated $1 billion per week), the U.S.'s hasty go-it-alone policy began to haunt them: only about 10,000 foreign troops came to the aid of American and British soldiers in Iraq. While the Bush administration successfully turned over sovereignty to an interim Iraqi government in June 2004, and scheduled elections for Jan. 2005, by the fall of 2004, pockets of Iraq were essentially under the control of insurgents. Not only was security an issue, but progress on rebuilding Iraq was dismal: by fall 2004, just 6% ($1 billion) of the funds approved by Congress in 2003 had in fact been used on reconstruction projects. President Bush assured the country that despite these difficulties, the United States would stay the course until Iraq emerged as a free and democratic country.

More than a year-and-a-half of searching for Iraq's weapons of mass destruction—one of the prime reasons the Bush and Blair administrations cited for launching the war—yielded no hard evidence, and both administrations and their intelligence agencies came under fire. There were also mounting allegations that the existence of these weapons and their imminent threat to American security was exaggerated or distorted as a pretext to justify the war. The Senate Intelligence Committee's unanimous, bipartisan "Report on Pre-War Intelligence on Iraq," harshly criticized the CIA: "most of the major key judgments" on Iraq's weapons of mass destruction were "either overstated, or were not supported by, the underlying intelligence report." The report disputed the CIA's assertions that Iraq was reconstituting its nuclear program and that it had chemical and biological weapons, and also concluded that there was no "established formal relationship" between al-Qaeda and Saddam Hussein. With the justifications for the war evaporating, the Bush administra-

tion began emphasizing that the removal of the belligerent and repressive Saddam Hussein, perpetrator of countless human rights violations, was grounds enough for waging war, and that the United States was more secure as a result of it.

Critics of the administration's policy in Iraq described it as a distraction from the war on terror, preventing the United States from effectively battling the war on its genuine fronts. Osama bin Laden was still at large, and despite the U.S. intervention in Afghanistan, the country remained rife with warlords, Taliban, and al-Qaeda operatives. Since the start of the U.S. war in Iraq, the two remaining countries in the "axis of evil," North Korea and Iran, had grown into alarming nuclear threats. The Bush administration's diplomatic efforts made little headway against Iran and North Korea's defiance and evasion.

Early in his presidency, Bush disengaged the U.S. from the Palestinian-Israeli crisis, but following the war in Iraq, which had been fought in part to introduce democracy to the Middle East, Bush presented a "road map" for peace to Israel and the Palestinians in May 2003. But within months, the escalating violence on both sides made it clear that the road map was going nowhere.

On the domestic front, President Bush promoted an "ownership society" that would give Americans more control over health care, education, and retirement. In Jan. 2002, he passed the No Child Left Behind Act, a federal program dedicated to improving schools across the country. In June 2003 he signed into law the largest expansion of Medicare since its creation. The law provided a prescription drug coverage under Medicare for the first time, at an estimated cost of $400 billion over the next 10 years.

In early 2003, President Bush unveiled a sweeping economic stimulus plan that characteristically centered around tax cuts. The plan, in its original form, would have cut taxes by $670 billion over ten years; Congress approved a $350 billion version. Although all workers were to benefit from the tax plan, it strongly favored two groups: two-parent households with several children and the wealthy—nearly half the proposed tax benefits were reserved for the richest 10% of American taxpayers. Critics of the plan, including fiscally conservative Republicans, argued that it was unsound to offer tax cuts while the country was involved in an expensive war and in the midst of a jobless recovery (nearly 600,000 jobs had been lost since Bush came to office). The federal budget deficit, according to the nonpartisan Congressional Budget Office, was expected to reach a record $300 billion in 2004. The White House countered that the Bush tax cuts had kept the recession remarkably shallow and brief and were in fact stimulating the economy.

The 2004 presidential campaign between the president and Democratic senator John Kerry was one of the most closely followed and heated races in recent history. Terrorism, the war in Iraq, tax cuts, health care, the economy, and the deficit were the major issues. Kerry accused the president of mismanaging the war on Iraq and the fight against terrorism and promised to roll back the Bush tax cuts for the wealthiest Americans. The president accused his opponent of being a "flip-flopper" on issues and of not having the leadership to fight the war on terror.

Senate and House Standing Committees, 108th Congress

Committees of the Senate

Agriculture, Nutrition, and Forestry (21 members)
Chairman: Thad Cochran (Miss.)
Ranking Dem.: Tom Harkin (Iowa)

Appropriations (29 members)
Chairman: Ted Stevens (Alaska)
Ranking Dem.: Robert C. Byrd (W.Va.)

Armed Services (25 members)
Chairman: John Warner (Va.)
Ranking Dem.: Carl Levin (Mich.)

Banking, Housing, and Urban Affairs (21 members)
Chairman: Richard C. Shelby (Ala.)
Ranking Dem.: Paul S. Sarbanes (Md.)

Budget (23 members)
Chairman: Don Nickles (Okla.)
Ranking Dem.: Kent Conrad (N.D.)

Commerce, Science, and Transportation (23 members)
Chairman: John McCain (Ariz.)
Ranking Dem.: Ernest F. Hollings (S.C.)

Energy and Natural Resources (23 members)
Chairman: Pete V. Domenici (N.M.)
Ranking Dem.: Jeff Bingaman (N.M.)

Environment and Public Works (19 members)
Chairman: James M. Inhofe (Okla.)
Ranking Member: James Jeffords (Vt.)

Finance (21 members)
Chairman: Charles E. Grassley (Iowa)
Ranking Dem.: Max Baucus (Mont.)

Foreign Relations (19 members)
Chairman: Richard G. Lugar (Ind.)
Ranking Dem.: Joseph R. Biden, Jr. (Del.)

Governmental Affairs (17 members)
Chairman: Susan Collins (Maine)
Ranking Dem.: Joseph Lieberman (Conn.)

Health, Education, Labor, and Pensions (21 members)
Chairman: Judd Gregg (N.H.)
Ranking Dem.: Edward M. Kennedy (Mass.)

Judiciary (19 members)
Chairman: Orrin G. Hatch (Utah)
Ranking Dem.: Patrick J. Leahy (Vt.)

Rules and Administration (19 members)
Chairman: Trent Lott (Miss.)
Ranking Dem.: Christopher Dodd (Conn.)

Small Business (19 members)
Chairman: Olympia J. Snowe (Maine)
Ranking Dem.: John Kerry (Mass.)

Veterans' Affairs (15 members)
Chairman: Arlen Specter (Pa.)
Ranking Dem: Bob Graham (Fla.)

Senate Special or Select Committees

Aging (21 members)
Chairman: Larry Craig (Idaho)
Ranking Dem.: John B. Breaux (La.)

Ethics (6 members)
Chairman: George V. Voinovich (Ohio)
Ranking Dem.: Harry Reid (Nev.)

Indian Affairs (15 members)
Chairman: Ben Nighthorse Campbell (Colo.)
Ranking Dem.: Daniel K. Inouye (Hawaii)

Intelligence (17 members)
Chairman: Pat Roberts (Kans.)
Ranking Dem.: John D. Rockefeller IV (W. Va.)

Committees of the House

Agriculture (51 members)
Chairman: Bob Goodlatte (Va.)
Ranking Dem.: Charles W. Stenholm (Tex.)

Appropriations (65 members)
Chairman: C. W. Bill Young (Fla.)
Ranking Dem.: David R. Obey (Wis.)

Armed Services (60 members)
Chairman: Duncan Hunter (Calif.)
Ranking Dem.: Ike Skelton (Mo.)

Budget (43 members)
Chairman: Jim Nussle (Iowa)
Ranking Dem.: John M. Spratt, Jr. (S.C.)

Education and the Workforce (49 members)
Chairman: John A. Boehner (Ohio)
Ranking Dem.: George Miller (Calif.)

Energy and Commerce (57 members)
Chairman: Joe Barton (Tex.)
Ranking Dem.: John D. Dingell (Mich.)

Financial Services (70 members)
Chairman: Michael G. Oxley (Ohio)
Ranking Dem.: Barney Frank (Mass.)

Government Reform (44 members)
Chairman: Tom Davis (Va.)
Ranking Dem.: Henry A. Waxman (Calif.)

House Administration (9 members)
Chairman: Robert W. Ney (Ohio)
Ranking Dem.: John B. Larson (Conn.)

International Relations (49 members)
Chairman: Henry J. Hyde (Ill.)
Ranking Dem.: Tom Lantos (Calif.)

Judiciary (37 members)
Chairman: F. James Sensenbrenner, Jr. (Wis.)
Ranking Dem.: John Conyers, Jr. (Mich.)

Resources (52 members)
Chairman: Richard Pombo (Calif.)
Ranking Dem.: Nick J. Rahall II (W. Va.)

Rules (13 members)
Chairman: David Dreier (Calif.)
Ranking Dem.: Martin Frost (Tex.)

Science (47 members)
Chairman: Sherwood L. Boehlert (N.Y.)
Ranking Dem.: Bart Gordon (Tenn.)

Small Business (36 members)
Chairman: Donald A. Manzullo (Ill.)
Ranking Dem.: Nydia M. Velázquez (N.Y.)

Standards of Official Conduct (10 members)
Chairman: Joel Hefley (Colo.)
Ranking Dem.: Alan B. Mollohan (W. Va.)

Transportation and Infrastructure (75 members)
Chairman: Don Young (Alaska)
Ranking Dem.: James L. Oberstar (Minn.)

Veterans' Affairs (31 members)
Chairman: Christopher H. Smith (N.J.)
Ranking Dem.: Lane Evans (Ill.)

Ways and Means (41 members)
Chairman: William M. Thomas (Calif.)
Ranking Dem.: Charles B. Rangel (N.Y.)

Speakers of the House of Representatives

Dates served	Congress	Name and state	Dates served	Congress	Name and state
1789–1791	1	Frederick A. C. Muhlenberg (Pa.)	1869–1875	41–43	James G. Blaine (Maine)
1791–1793	2	Jonathan Trumbull (Conn.)	1875–1876	44	Michael C. Kerr (Ind.)[6]
1793–1795	3	Frederick A. C. Muhlenberg (Pa.)	1876–1881	44–46	Samuel J. Randall (Pa.)
1795–1799	4–5	Jonathan Dayton (N.J.)[1]	1881–1883	47	J. Warren Keifer (Ohio)
1799–1801	6	Theodore Sedgwick (Mass.)	1883–1889	48–50	John G. Carlisle (Ky.)
1801–1807	7–9	Nathaniel Macon (N.C.)	1889–1891	51	Thomas B. Reed (Maine)
1807–1811	10–11	Joseph B. Varnum (Mass.)	1891–1895	52–53	Charles F. Crisp (Ga.)
1811–1814	12–13	Henry Clay (Ky.)[2]	1895–1899	54–55	Thomas B. Reed (Maine)
1814–1815	13	Langdon Cheves (S.C.)	1899–1903	56–57	David B. Henderson (Iowa)
1815–1820	14–16	Henry Clay (Ky.)[3]	1903–1911	58–61	Joseph G. Cannon (Ill.)
1820–1821	16	John W. Taylor (N.Y.)	1911–1919	62–65	Champ Clark (Mo.)
1821–1823	17	Philip P. Barbour (Va.)	1919–1925	66–68	Frederick H. Gillett (Mass.)
1823–1825	18	Henry Clay (Ky.)	1925–1931	69–71	Nicholas Longworth (Ohio)
1825–1827	19	John W. Taylor (N.Y.)	1931–1933	72	John N. Garner (Tex.)
1827–1834	20–23	Andrew Stevenson (Va.)[4]	1933–1934	73	Henry T. Rainey (Ill.)[7]
1834–1835	23	John Bell (Tenn.)	1935–1936	74	Joseph W. Byrns (Tenn.)[8]
1835–1839	24–25	James K. Polk (Tenn.)	1936–1940	74–76	William B. Bankhead (Ala.)[9]
1839–1841	26	Robert M. T. Hunter (Va.)	1940–1947	76–79	Sam Rayburn (Tex.)
1841–1843	27	John White (Ky.)	1947–1949	80	Joseph W. Martin, Jr. (Mass.)
1843–1845	28	John W. Jones (Va.)	1949–1953	81–82	Sam Rayburn (Tex.)
1845–1847	29	John W. Davis (Ind.)	1953–1955	83	Joseph W. Martin, Jr. (Mass.)
1847–1849	30	Robert C. Winthrop (Mass.)	1955–1961	84–87	Sam Rayburn (Tex.)[10]
1849–1851	31	Howell Cobb (Ga.)	1963–1971	87–91	John W. McCormack (Mass.)[11]
1851–1855	32–33	Linn Boyd (Ky.)	1971–1977	92–94	Carl Albert (Okla.)[12]
1855–1857	34	Nathaniel P. Banks (Mass.)	1977–1987	95–99	Thomas P. O'Neill, Jr. (Mass.)[13]
1857–1859	35	James L. Orr (S.C.)	1987–1989	100–101	James C. Wright, Jr. (Tex.)[14]
1859–1861	36	Wm. Pennington (N.J.)	1989–1995	101–103	Thomas S. Foley (Wash.)
1861–1863	37	Galusha A. Grow (Pa.)	1995–1999	104–105	Newt Gingrich (Ga.)[15]
1863–1869	38–40	Schuyler Colfax (Ind.)	1999–	106–	Dennis Hastert (Ill.)
1869–1869	40	Theodore M. Pomeroy (N.Y.)[5]			

1. George Dent (Md.) was elected Speaker pro tempore for April 20 and May 28, 1798. 2. Resigned during second session of 13th Congress. 3. Resigned between first and second sessions of 16th Congress. 4. Resigned during first session of 23rd Congress. 5. Elected Speaker and served the day of adjournment. 6. Died between first and second sessions of 44th Congress. During first session, there were two Speakers pro tempore: Samuel S. Cox (N.Y.), appointed for Feb. 17, May 12, and June 19, 1876, and Milton Sayler (Ohio) appointed for June 4, 1876. 7. Died in 1934 after adjournment of second session of 73rd Congress. 8. Died during second session of 74th Congress. 9. Died during third session of 76th Congress. 10. Died between first and second sessions of 87th Congress. 11. Not a candidate in 1970 election. 12. Not a candidate in 1976 election. 13. Not a candidate in 1986 election. 14. Resigned during first session of 101st Congress. 15. Resigned Jan. 3, 1999, three days before the first session of the 106th Congress. *Source: Congressional Directory.*

Floor Leaders of the Senate

Democratic	Republican
Gilbert M. Hitchcock, Neb. (Min. 1919–20)	Charles Curtis, Kan. (Maj. 1925–29)
Oscar W. Underwood, Ala. (Min. 1920–23)	James E. Watson, Ind. (Maj. 1929–33)
Joseph T. Robinson, Ark. (Min. 1923–33, Maj. 1933–37)	Charles L. McNary, Ore. (Min. 1933–44)
Alben W. Barkley, Ky. (Maj. 1937–46, Min. 1947–48)	Wallace H. White, Jr., Maine (Min. 1944–47, Maj. 1947–48)
Scott W. Lucas, Ill. (Maj. 1949–50)	
Ernest W. McFarland, Ariz. (Maj. 1951–52)	Kenneth S. Wherry, Neb. (Min. 1949–51)
Lyndon B. Johnson, Tex. (Min. 1953–54, Maj. 1955–60)	Styles Bridges, N.H. (Min. 1951–52)
Mike Mansfield, Mont. (Maj. 1961–77)	Robert A. Taft, Ohio (Maj. 1953)
Robert C. Byrd, W. Va. (Maj. 1977–81, Min. 1981–86, Maj. 1987–88)	William F. Knowland, Calif. (Maj. 1953–54, Min. 1955–58)
	Everett M. Dirksen, Ill. (Min. 1959–69)
George John Mitchell, Maine (Maj. 1989–1994)	Hugh Scott, Pa. (Min. 1969–1977)
Thomas A. Daschle, S.D. (Min. 1995–2001, Maj. 2001–2002, Min. 2003–)	Howard H. Baker, Jr., Tenn. (Min. 1977–81, Maj. 1981–84)
	Robert J. Dole, Kan. (Maj. 1985–86, Min. 1987–94, Maj. 1995–96)
	Trent Lott, Miss. (Maj. 1996–2001, Min. 2001–2002)
	Bill Frist, Tenn. (Maj. 2003–)

NOTE: Min. = Minority Leader; Maj. = Majority Leader. *Source:* United States Senate, Secretary for the Majority.

Composition of Congress, by Political Party, 1855–2003

Congress	Years	Senate					House				
		Total	Dems	Reps	Others	Vacant	Total	Dems	Reps	Others	Vacant
34th	1855–1857	62	42	15	5	—	234	83	108	43	—
35th	1857–1859	64	39	20	5	—	237	131	92	14	—
36th	1859–1861	66	38	26	2	—	237	101	113	23	—
37th	1861–1863	50	11	31	7	1	178	42	106	28	2
38th	1863–1865	51	12	39	—	—	183	80	103	—	—
39th	1865–1867	52	10	42	—	—	191	46	145	—	—
40th	1867–1869	53	11	42	—	—	193	49	143	—	1
41st	1869–1871	74	11	61	—	2	243	73	170	—	—
42nd	1871–1873	74	17	57	—	—	243	104	139	—	—
43rd	1873–1875	74	19	54	—	1	293	88	203	—	2
44th	1875–1877	76	29	46	—	1	293	181	107	3	2
45th	1877–1879	76	36	39	1	—	293	156	137	—	—
46th	1879–1881	76	43	33	—	—	293	150	128	14	1
47th	1881–1883	76	37	37	2	—	293	130	152	11	—
48th	1883–1885	76	36	40	—	—	325	200	119	6	—
49th	1885–1887	76	34	41	—	1	325	182	140	2	1
50th	1887–1889	76	37	39	—	—	325	170	151	4	—
51st	1889–1891	84	37	47	—	—	330	156	173	1	—
52nd	1891–1893	88	39	47	2	—	333	231	88	14	—
53rd	1893–1895	88	44	38	3	3	356	220	126	10	—
54th	1895–1897	88	39	44	5	—	357	104	246	7	—
55th	1897–1899	90	34	46	10	—	357	134	206	16	1
56th	1899–1901	90	26	53	11	—	357	163	185	9	—
57th	1901–1903	90	29	56	3	2	357	153	198	5	1
58th	1903–1905	90	32	58	—	—	386	178	207	—	1
59th	1905–1907	90	32	58	—	—	386	136	250	—	—
60th	1907–1909	92	29	61	—	2	386	164	222	—	—
61st	1909–1911	92	32	59	—	1	391	172	219	—	—
62nd	1911–1913	92	42	49	—	1	391	228	162	1	—
63rd	1913–1915	96	51	44	1	—	435	290	127	18	—
64th	1915–1917	96	56	39	1	—	435	231	193	8	3
65th	1917–1919	96	53	42	1	—	435	210[1]	216	9	—
66th	1919–1921	96	47	48	1	—	435	191	237	7	—
67th	1921–1923	96	37	59	—	—	435	132	300	1	2
68th	1923–1925	96	43	51	2	—	435	207	225	3	—
69th	1925–1927	96	40	54	1	1	435	183	247	5	—
70th	1927–1929	96	47	48	1	—	435	195	237	3	—
71st	1929–1931	96	39	56	1	—	435	163	267	1	4
72nd	1931–1933	96	47	48	1	—	435	216[2]	218	1	—
73rd	1933–1935	96	59	36	1	—	435	313	117	5	—
74th	1935–1937	96	69	25	2	—	435	322	103	10	—
75th	1937–1939	96	75	17	4	—	435	333	89	13	—
76th	1939–1941	96	69	23	4	—	435	262	169	4	—
77th	1941–1943	96	66	28	2	—	435	267	162	6	—
78th	1943–1945	96	57	38	1	—	435	222	209	4	—
79th	1945–1947	96	57	38	1	—	435	243	190	2	—
80th	1947–1949	96	45	51	—	—	435	188	246	1	—
81st	1949–1951	96	54	42	—	—	435	263	171	1	—
82nd	1951–1953	96	48	47	1	—	435	234	199	2	—
83rd	1953–1955	96	46	48	2	—	435	213	221	1	—
84th	1955–1957	96	48	47	1	—	435	232	203	—	—
85th	1957–1959	96	49	47	—	—	435	234	201	—	—
86th	1959–1961	98	64	34	—	—	436[3]	283	153	—	—
87th	1961–1963	100	64	36	—	—	437[4]	262	175	—	—
88th	1963–1965	100	67	33	—	—	435	258	176	—	1
89th	1965–1967	100	68	32	—	—	435	295	140	—	—
90th	1967–1969	100	64	36	—	—	435	248	187	—	—
91st	1969–1971	100	58	42	—	—	435	243	192	—	—
92nd	1971–1973	100	54	44	2	—	435	255	180	—	—
93rd	1973–1975	100	56	42	2	—	435	242	192	1	—
94th	1975–1977	100	61	37	2	—	435	291	144	—	—
95th	1977–1979	100	61	38	1	—	435	292	143	—	—
96th	1979–1981	100	58	41	1	—	435	277	158	—	—
97th	1981–1983	100	46	53	1	—	435	242	192	1	—
98th	1983–1985	100	46	54	—	—	435	269	166	—	—
99th	1985–1987	100	47	53	—	—	435	253	182	—	—
100th	1987–1989	100	55	45	—	—	435	258	177	—	—
101st	1989–1991	100	55	45	—	—	435	260	175	—	—

Congress	Years	Senate					House				
		Total	Dems	Reps	Others	Vacant	Total	Dems	Reps	Others	Vacant
102nd	1991–1993	100	56	44	—	—	435	267	167	1	—
103rd	1993–1995	100	57	43	—	—	435	258	176	1	—
104th	1995–1997	100	48	52	—	—	435	204	230	1	—
105th	1997–1999	100	45	55	—	—	435	207	226	2	—
106th	1999–2001	100	45	55	—	—	435	211	223	1	—
107th	2001–2003	100	50	50	—	—	435	212	221	2	—
108th	2003–2005	100	48	51	1	—	435	205	229	1	—

NOTE: All figures reflect immediate results of elections. 1. Democrats organized House with help of other parties. 2. Democrats organized House due to Republican deaths. 3. Proclamation declaring Alaska a state issued Jan 3., 1959. 4. Proclamation declaring Hawaii a state issued Aug. 21, 1959. *Source:* Office of the Clerk of the House of Representatives. Web: http://clerkweb.house.gov/histrecs/history.htm.

Salaries of the President, Vice President, and Other U.S. Officials, 2004

(per year)

Position	Salary	Position	Salary
President		Vice President	$202,900[2]
1789	$ 25,000	Senator	158,000
1873	50,000	Representative	158,000
1909	75,000	Majority and Minority Leaders	175,600
1949	100,000[1]	Speaker of the House	202,900
1969	200,000[1]	Chief Justice, U.S. Supreme Court	202,900
2001	400,000[1]	Assoc. Justice, U.S. Supreme Court	194,200

1. Plus $50,000 non-taxable expense allowance to assist in defraying expenses relating to or resulting from the discharge of his official duties. 2. Plus $10,000 taxable expense allowance. *Source:* Office of Personnel Management. Web: www.opm.gov/.

Congressional Apportionment, 2000

Source: U.S. Census Bureau

Apportionment is the process of dividing the 435 seats in the House of Representatives among the 50 states. The number of seats, or representatives, each state is entitled to is apportioned according to the new census figures that are compiled every 10 years. States with larger populations have more representatives than states with smaller populations. Each state must have at least one representative.

Once the number of seats is assigned to each state, it is up to the individual state legislatures to redraw new congressional districts. Each representative is elected by voters from a congressional district within their state.

Who Counts?

The population figure used to calculate the apportionment of House seats is based on the total resident population of the United States, including citizens and noncitizens, plus U.S. military personnel and federal civilian employees and their dependents living overseas. It excludes the populations of the District of Columbia, Puerto Rico, and other U.S. territories that do not have voting seats in the House of Representatives. The Census 2000 apportionment population was 281,424,177.

Congressional District Size

The number of representatives in the U.S. House of Representatives has remained constant at 435 since 1911, except for a temporary increase to 437 at the time of admission of Alaska and Hawaii as states in 1959. However, the apportionment based on the 1960 census, which took effect for the election of 1962, reverted to 435 seats.

The average size of a congressional district based on the Census 2000 apportionment population will be 646,952, more than triple the average district size of 193,167 based on the 1900 census apportionment, and about 74,486 more than the average size of 572,466 based on the 1990 census.

Congressional Seats Gained/Lost in the 108th Congress[1]

Seats gained		Seats lost	
+ 2 seats	**+1 seat**	**–1 seat**	**–2 seats**
Arizona (8)	California (53)	Connecticut (5)	New York (29)
Florida (25)	Colorado (7)	Illinois (19)	Pennsylvania (19)
Georgia (13)	Nevada (3)	Indiana (9)	
Texas (32)	North Carolina (13)	Michigan (15)	
		Mississippi (4)	
		Ohio (18)	
		Oklahoma (5)	
		Wisconsin (8)	

NOTE: The number of representatives based on Census 2000 is given in parentheses after each state. 1. Based on Census 2000. *Source:* U.S. Census Bureau, Census 2000. Web: www.census.gov.

How a Bill Becomes a Law

When a senator or a representative introduces a bill, he or she sends it to the clerk of his house, who gives it a number and title. This is the *first reading*, and the bill is referred to the proper committee.

The committee may decide the bill is unwise or unnecessary and *table* it, thus killing it at once. Or it may decide the bill is worthwhile and hold hearings to listen to facts and opinions presented by experts and other interested persons. After members of the committee have debated the bill and perhaps offered amendments, a vote is taken; and if the vote is favorable, the bill is sent back to the floor of the house.

The clerk reads the bill sentence by sentence to the house, and this is known as the *second reading*. Members may then debate the bill and offer amendments. In the House of Representatives, the time for debate is limited by a *cloture rule,* but there is no such restriction in the Senate for cloture, where 60 votes are required. This makes possible a *filibuster,* in which one or more opponents hold the floor to defeat the bill.

The *third reading* is by title only, and the bill is put to a vote, which may be by voice or roll call, depending on the circumstances and parliamentary rules. Members who must be absent at the time but who wish to record their vote may be paired if each negative vote has a balancing affirmative one.

The bill then goes to the other house of Congress, where it may be defeated, or passed with or without amendments. If the bill is defeated, it dies. If it is passed with amendments, a joint congressional committee must be appointed by both houses to iron out the differences.

After its final passage by both houses, the bill is sent to the president. If he approves, he signs it, and the bill becomes a law. However, if he disapproves, he *vetoes* the bill by refusing to sign it and sending it back to the house of origin with his reasons for the veto. The objections are read and debated, and a roll-call vote is taken. If the bill receives less than a two-thirds vote, it is defeated and goes no further. But if it receives a two-thirds vote or greater, it is sent to the other house for a vote. If that house also passes it by a two-thirds vote, the president's veto is *overridden,* and the bill becomes a law.

Should the president desire neither to sign nor to veto the bill, he may retain it for ten days, Sundays excepted, after which time it automatically becomes a law without signature. However, if Congress has adjourned within those ten days, the bill is automatically killed, that process of indirect rejection being known as a *pocket veto*.

Presidential Vetoes, 1789–2003

President	Coincident Congresses	Regular vetoes	Pocket vetoes	Total vetoes	Vetoes overridden
Washington	1st–4th	2	—	2	—
Adams	5th–6th	—	—	—	—
Jefferson	7th–10th	—	—	—	—
Madison	11th–14th	5	2	7	—
Monroe	15th–18th	1	—	1	—
J. Q. Adams	19th–20th	—	—	—	—
Jackson	21st–24th	5	7	12	—
Van Buren	25th–26th	—	1	1	—
W. H. Harrison	27th	—	—	—	—
Tyler	27th–28th	6	4	10	1
Polk	29th–30th	2	1	3	—
Taylor	31st	—	—	—	—
Fillmore	31st–32nd	—	—	—	—
Pierce	33rd–34th	9	—	9	5
Buchanan	35th–36th	4	3	7	—
Lincoln	37th–39th	2	5	7	—
A. Johnson	39th–40th	21	8	29	15
Grant	41st–44th	45	48	93	4
Hayes	45th–46th	12	1	13	1
Garfield	47th	—	—	—	—
Arthur	47th–48th	4	8	12	1
Cleveland	49th–50th	304	110	414	2
B. Harrison	51st–52nd	19	25	44	1
Cleveland	53rd–54th	42	128	170	5
McKinley	55th–57th	6	36	42	—
T. Roosevelt	57th–60th	42	40	82	1
Taft	61st–62nd	30	9	39	1
Wilson	63rd–66th	33	11	44	6
Harding	67th	5	1	6	—
Coolidge	68th–70th	20	30	50	4
Hoover	71st–72nd	21	16	37	3
F. D. Roosevelt	73rd–79th	372	263	635	9
Truman	79th–82nd	180	70	250	12
Eisenhower	83rd–86th	73	108	181	2
Kennedy	87th–88th	12	9	21	—
L. B. Johnson	88th–90th	16	14	30	—
Nixon	91st–93rd	26	17	43	7

President	Coincident Congresses	Regular vetoes	Pocket vetoes	Total vetoes	Vetoes overridden
Ford	93rd–94th	48	18	66	12
Carter	95th–96th	13	18	31	2
Reagan	97th–100th	39	39	78	9
G.H.W. Bush[1]	101st–102nd	29	15	44	1
Clinton	103rd–106th	36	1	37	2
G. W. Bush	107th–108th	—	—	—	—
Total		1,484	1,066	2,550	106

1. President Bush attempted to pocket veto two bills during intrasession recess periods. Congress considered the two bills enacted into law because of the president's failure to return the legislation. The bills are not counted as pocket vetoes in this table. *Source:* Office of the Clerk of the House. Web: http://clerk.house.gov.

Order of Presidential Succession

According to the Presidential Succession Act of 1792, the Senate president pro tempore[1] was next in line after the vice president to succeed to the presidency, followed by the Speaker of the House.

In 1886, however, Congress changed the order of presidential succession, replacing the president pro tempore and the Speaker with the cabinet officers. Proponents of this change argued that the congressional leaders lacked executive experience, and none had served as president, while six former secretaries of state had later been elected to that office.

The Presidential Succession Act of 1947, signed by President Harry Truman, changed the order again

to what it is today. The cabinet members are ordered in the line of succession according to the date their offices were established.

Prior to the ratification of the 25th Amendment in 1967, there was no provision for filling a vacancy in the vice presidency. When a president died in office, the vice president succeeded him, and the vice presidency then remained vacant. The first vice president to take office under the new procedure was Gerald Ford, who was nominated by Nixon on Oct. 12, 1973, and confirmed by Congress the following Dec. 6.

1. The Vice President
2. Speaker of the House
3. President pro tempore of the Senate[1]
4. Secretary of State
5. Secretary of the Treasury
6. Secretary of Defense
7. Attorney General
8. Secretary of the Interior
9. Secretary of Agriculture
10. Secretary of Commerce
11. Secretary of Labor
12. Secretary of Health and Human Services
13. Secretary of Housing and Urban Development
14. Secretary of Transportation
15. Secretary of Energy
16. Secretary of Education
17. Secretary of Veterans Affairs
18. Secretary of Homeland Security[2]

NOTE: An official cannot succeed to the Presidency unless that person meets the Constitutional requirements. 1. The president pro tempore presides over the Senate when the vice president is absent. By tradition the position is held by the senior member of the majority party. 2. May move to number 8 on the list pending legislation.

Executive Departments and Agencies

Source: United States Government Manual, 2002–2003

Unless otherwise indicated, addresses shown are in Washington, DC. ZIP codes are in parentheses.

White House Offices and Agencies

Office of Administration
Eisenhower Executive Office Bldg., 725 17th St., NW (20503)
   Established: Dec. 12, 1977
   Director: Timothy A. Campen
Office of National Drug Control Policy
Executive Office of the President (20503)
   Established: Jan. 29, 1989
   Director: John P. Walters
Council of Economic Advisers (CEA)
Old Executive Office Bldg. (20502)
   Members: 3
   Established: Feb. 20, 1946
   Chair: Dr. N. Gregory Mankin
Council on Environmental Quality
722 Jackson Place, NW (20503)
   Established: 1969
   Chair: James Connaughton
Office of Management and Budget
Executive Office Bldg. (20503)
   Established: July 1, 1939
   Director: Joshua B. Bolten

Office of Science and Technology Policy
Eisenhower Executive Office Building (20502)
   Established: May 11, 1976
   Director: John H. Marburger III
National Security Council (NSC)
Eisenhower Executive Office Bldg. (20504)
   Members: 4
   Established: July 26, 1947
   Chair: The President
   National Security Adviser: Condoleezza Rice
   Other members: Vice President; Secretary of State; Secretary of Defense
Office of the United States Trade Representative
600 17th St., NW (20508)
   Established: Jan. 15, 1963
   Trade Representative: Robert Zoellick

Executive Departments

Department of Agriculture
1400 Independence Ave., SW (20250)
   Established: May 15, 1862. Administered by Commissioner of Agriculture until 1889, when it was made executive department.
   Secretary: Ann Veneman
Department of Commerce
1401 Constitution Ave., NW (20230)

Established: Department of Commerce and Labor was created Feb. 14, 1903. On March 4, 1913, all labor activities were transferred out of Department of Commerce and Labor and it was renamed Department of Commerce.
Secretary: Donald L. Evans

Department of Defense
Office of the Secretary, The Pentagon (20301-1155)
Established: July 26, 1947, as National Military Establishment; name changed to Department of Defense on Aug. 10, 1949. Subordinate to Secretary of Defense are Secretaries of Army, Navy, Air Force.
Secretary: Donald H. Rumsfeld
Deputy Secretary: Paul D. Wolfowitz
Secretary of Army: Les Brownlee (acting)
Secretary of Navy: Gordon R. England
Secretary of Air Force: James G. Roche
Commandant of Marine Corps: Gen. Michael W. Hagee
Joint Chiefs of Staff: Gen. Richard B. Myers, Air Force, Chairman; Gen. Peter Pace, Marine Corps, Vice Chairman; Vice Adm. Timothy J. Keating, Director; Gen. Peter J. Schoomaker, Army; Adm. Vernon E. Clark, Navy; Gen. John P. Jumper, Air Force.

Department of Education
400 Maryland Ave., SW (20202)
Established: Oct. 17, 1979
Secretary: Roderick R. Paige

Department of Energy
1000 Independence Ave., SW (20585)
Established: Oct. 1, 1977
Secretary: Spencer Abraham

Department of Health and Human Services
200 Independence Ave., SW (20201)
Established: Formed April 11, 1953, replacing Federal Security Agency created in 1939. On Oct. 17, 1979, the Department of Education became a separate department.
Secretary: Tommy G. Thompson
Surgeon General: Dr. Richard Carmona

Department of Homeland Security
Washington DC (20528)
Established: The most significant transformation of the U.S. government since 1947 was formed in the aftermath of Sept. 11, 2001, when 22 separate agencies were combined to become the cabinet-level Department of Homeland Security. It became an official cabinet department Jan. 24, 2003
Secretary: Tom Ridge

Department of Housing and Urban Development
451 7th St., SW (20410)
Established: Nov. 9, 1965, replacing Housing and Home Finance Agency created in 1947
Secretary: Alphonso Jackson

Department of the Interior
1849 C St., NW (20240)
Established: March 3, 1849
Secretary: Gale A. Norton

Department of Justice
950 Pennsylvania Ave., NW (20530)
Established: Office of Attorney General was created Sept. 24, 1789. Although one of the original cabinet members, the attorney general was not an executive department head until June 22, 1870, when the Department of Justice was established.
Attorney General: John Ashcroft
Solicitor General: Paul D. Clement (acting)
Director of FBI: Robert S. Mueller, III

Department of Labor
200 Constitution Ave., NW (20210)
Established: Bureau of Labor was created in 1884 under Department of the Interior; later became independent department without executive rank. Returned to bureau status in Department of Commerce and Labor, but on March 4, 1913, became independent executive department under its present name.
Secretary: Elaine L. Chao

Department of State
2201 C St., NW (20520)
Established: 1781 as Department of Foreign Affairs; reconstituted, 1789, following adoption of Constitution; name changed to Department of State Sept. 15, 1789.
Secretary: Colin L. Powell
UN Ambassador: John D. C. Danforth
Deputy UN Ambassador: Anne W. Patterson

Department of Transportation
400 7th St., SW (20590)
Established: Oct. 15, 1966, as result of Department of Transportation Act, which became effective April 1, 1967.
Secretary: Norman Y. Mineta

Department of the Treasury
1500 Pennsylvania Ave., NW (20220)
Established: Sept. 2, 1789
Secretary: John Snow
Treasurer of the U.S.: Vacant

Department of Veterans' Affairs
810 Vermont Ave., NW (20420)
Established: March 15, 1989, replacing Veterans Administration created in 1930
Secretary: Anthony J. Principi

Major Independent Agencies

Central Intelligence Agency (CIA)
Washington, DC (20505)
Established: 1947
Director of Central Intelligence: Porter J. Goss

U.S. Commission on Civil Rights
624 9th St., NW (20425)
Established: 1957
Staff Director: Les Jin

Consumer Product Safety Commission
East West Towers, 4330 East West Highway, Bethesda, Md. 20814
Established: Oct. 27, 1972
Chair: Harold D. Stratton

Corporation for National and Community Service
1201 New York Ave., NW (20525)
Established: Sept. 1993
CEO: David Eisner

Environmental Protection Agency (EPA)
1200 Pennsylvania Ave., NW (20460)
Established: Dec. 2, 1970
Administrator: Michael O. Leavitt

Equal Employment Opportunity Commission (EEOC)
1801 L St., NW (20507)
Members: 5
Established: July 2, 1965
Chair: Cari M. Dominguez

Farm Credit Administration (FCA)
1501 Farm Credit Dr., McLean, Va. 22102-5090
Members: 13
Established: March 27, 1933
Chair: Nancy C. Pellett

Federal Communications Commission (FCC)
445 Twelfth Street, SW (20554)
Established: 1934
Chair: Michael Powell

Federal Deposit Insurance Corporation (FDIC)
550 17th St., NW (20429)
Established: June 16, 1933
Chair: Donald E. Powell

Federal Election Commission (FEC)
999 E St., NW (20463)
Members: 6
Established: 1975
Chair: Bradley A. Smith

Federal Maritime Commission
800 North Capitol St., NW (20573-0001)
Members: 5
Established: Aug. 12, 1961
Chair: Steven R. Blust

Federal Mediation and Conciliation Service (FMCS)
2100 K St., NW (20427)
  Established: 1947
  Director: Peter J. Hurtgen
Federal Reserve System (FRS), Board of Governors of
20th St. & Constitution Ave., NW (20551)
  Members: 7
  Established: Dec. 23, 1913
  Chair: Alan Greenspan
Federal Trade Commission (FTC)
600 Pennsylvania Ave., NW (20580)
  Members: 5
  Established: Sept. 26, 1914
  Chair: Deborah Platt Majoras
General Services Administration (GSA)
1800 F St., NW (20405)
  Established: July 1, 1949
  Administrator: Stephen A. Perry
U.S. International Trade Commission
500 E St., SW (20436)
  Members: 6
  Established: Sept. 8, 1916
  Chair: Stephen Koplan
National Aeronautics and Space Administration (NASA)
300 E St., SW (20546)
  Established: 1958
  Administrator: Sean O'Keefe
National Archives and Records Administration (NARA)
8601 Adelphi Road, College Park, Md. 20740-6001
  Established: Oct. 19, 1984. NARA is the successor agency to the National Archives Establishment, which was created in 1934 and later incorporated into the General Services Administration as the National Archives and Records Service in 1949.
  Archivist of the U.S.: John W. Carlin
National Foundation on the Arts and the Humanities
1100 Pennsylvania Ave., NW (20506-0001)
  Established: 1965
  Chairs: National Endowment for the Arts, Chair, Dana Gioia; National Endowment for the Humanities, Chair, Bruce Cole
National Labor Relations Board (NLRB)
1099 14th St., NW (20570)
  Members: 5
  Established: July 5, 1935
  Chair: Robert J. Battista
National Mediation Board
Suite 250 East, 1301 K St., NW (20572)
  Established: June 21, 1934
  Chair: Harry R. Hoglander
National Science Foundation (NSF)
4201 Wilson Blvd., Arlington, Va. 22230
  Established: 1950
  Director: D. Arden L. Bement, Jr. (acting)
National Transportation Safety Board
490 L'Enfant Plaza, SW (20594)
  Members: 5
  Established: April 1, 1967, as an independent agency supported by the Dept. of Transportation. Ties with Dept. of Transportation officially ended in 1975.
  Chair: Ellen Engleman Conners
Nuclear Regulatory Commission (NRC)
Washington, DC 20555
  Members: 5
  Established: Jan. 19, 1975
  Chair: Nils J. Diaz
Office of Personnel Management (OPM)
1900 E St., NW (20415-0001)
  Established: Jan. 1, 1979
  Director: Kay Coles James
U.S. Postal Service
475 L'Enfant Plaza West, SW (20260-0010)
  Established: In 1775 with the appointment of Benjamin Franklin as the first postmaster general under the Conti-

nental Congress. In 1970 became independent agency headed by 11-member board of governors.
  Postmaster General: John E. Potter
Securities and Exchange Commission (SEC)
450 5th St., NW (20549)
  Members: 5
  Established: July 2, 1934
  Chair: William H. Donaldson
Selective Service System (SSS)
National Headquarters, Arlington, Va., 22209-2425
  Established: Sept. 16, 1940
  Director: Jack Martin (acting)
Small Business Administration (SBA)
409 3rd St., SW (20416)
  Established: July 30, 1953
  Administrator: Hector V. Barreto
Tennessee Valley Authority (TVA)
400 West Summit Hill Drive, Knoxville, Tenn. 37902. Washington office: One Massachusetts Ave., NW (20444-0001)
  Members of Board of Directors: 3
  Established: May 18, 1933
  Chairman: Glenn L. McCullough, Jr.

Other Independent Agencies

American Battle Monuments Commission—Courthouse Plaza II, Suite 500, 2300 Clarendon Blvd., Arlington, Va. (22201)
Appalachian Regional Commission—1666 Connecticut Ave., NW, Suite 700 (20009-1068)
Commission of Fine Arts—441 F St., NW, Ste. 312 (20001)
Commodity Futures Trading Commission—1155 21st St., NW (20581)
Export-Import Bank of the United States—811 Vermont Ave., NW (20571)
Federal Emergency Management Agency—500 C St., SW (20472)
Federal Housing Finance Board—1777 F St., NW (20006)
Federal Labor Relations Authority—607 14th St., NW (20424-0001)
Inter-American Foundation—901 N. Stuart St., Arlington, Va. 22203
National Commission on Libraries and Information Science—1110 Vermont Ave., NW, Ste. 820 (20005-3552)
National Credit Union Administration—1775 Duke St., Alexandria, Va. 22314-3428
Occupational Safety and Health Review Commission—1120 20th St., NW (20036-3419)
U.S. Parole Commission—Dept. of Justice, 5550 Friendship Blvd., Ste. 420, Chevy Chase, Md. 20815
Peace Corps—1111 20th St., NW (20526)
Pension Benefit Guaranty Corporation—1200 K St., NW (20005-4026)
Postal Rate Commission—1333 H St., NW (20268-0001)
President's Council on Physical Fitness and Sports—Dept. W, 200 Independence Ave., SW, Room 738-H (20201-0004)
Railroad Retirement Board (RRB)—844 N. Rush St., Ninth Floor, Chicago, Ill. 60611-2092; Office of Legislative Affairs: 1310 G St., N.W, Ste. 500 (20005-3004).

Legislative Department

Architect of the Capitol—U.S. Capitol Building (20515)
Government Accountability Office (GAO)—441 G St., NW (20548)
Government Printing Office (GPO)—732 North Capitol St., NW (20401)
Library of Congress—101 Independence Ave., SE (20540)
United States Botanic Garden—Office of Executive Director, 245 1st St., SW (20024)

Quasi-Official Agencies

American National Red Cross—2025 E St., NW (20006)

Legal Services Corporation—3333 K St., NW 3rd Fl. (20007-3522)

National Academy of Sciences, National Academy of Engineering, National Research Council, Institute of Medicine—500 Fifth St., NW (20001)

National Railroad Passenger Corporation (Amtrak)—60 Massachusetts Ave., NE (20002)

Smithsonian Institution—PO Box 37012 SI Bldg., Rm. 153, MRC 010 (20013–7012)

Government Officials

Cabinet Members with Dates of Appointment

Although the Constitution made no provision for a president's advisory group, the heads of the three executive departments (State, Treasury, and War) and the attorney general were organized by Washington into such a group; and by about 1793, the name "cabinet" was applied to it. With the exception of the attorney general up to 1870 and the postmaster general from 1829 to 1872, cabinet members have been heads of executive departments.

Cabinet members are appointed by the president, subject to the confirmation of the Senate; and as their terms are not fixed, they may be replaced at any time by the president. At a change in administration, it is customary for cabinet members to resign, but they remain in office until successors are appointed.

The table of cabinet members lists only those members who actually served after being duly commissioned. The dates shown are those of appointment. "Cont." indicates that the term continued from the previous administration for a substantial amount of time.

Washington

Secretary of State	Thomas Jefferson, 1789
	Edmund Randolph, 1794
	Timothy Pickering, 1795
Secretary of the Treasury	Alexander Hamilton, 1789
	Oliver Wolcott, Jr., 1795
Secretary of War	Henry Knox, 1789
	Timothy Pickering, 1795
	James McHenry, 1796
Attorney General	Edmund Randolph, 1789
	William Bradford, 1794
	Charles Lee, 1795

J. Adams

Secretary of State	Timothy Pickering (Cont.)
	John Marshall, 1800
Secretary of the Treasury	Oliver Wolcott, Jr. (Cont.)
	Samuel Dexter, 1801
Secretary of War	James McHenry (Cont.)
	Samuel Dexter, 1800
Attorney General	Charles Lee (Cont.)
Secretary of the Navy	Benjamin Stoddert, 1798

Jefferson

Secretary of State	James Madison, 1801
Secretary of the Treasury	Samuel Dexter (Cont.)
	Albert Gallatin, 1801
Secretary of War	Henry Dearborn, 1801
Attorney General	Levi Lincoln, 1801
	Robert Smith, 1805
	John Breckinridge, 1805
	Caesar A. Rodney, 1807
Secretary of the Navy	Benjamin Stoddert (Cont.)
	Robert Smith, 1801

Madison

Secretary of State	Robert Smith, 1809
	James Monroe, 1811
Secretary of the Treasury	Albert Gallatin (Cont.)
	George W. Campbell, 1814
	Alexander J. Dallas, 1814
	William H. Crawford, 1816
Secretary of War	William Eustis, 1809
	John Armstrong, 1813
	James Monroe, 1814
	William H. Crawford, 1815
Attorney General	Caesar A. Rodney (Cont.)
	William Pinckney, 1811
	Richard Rush, 1814
Secretary of the Navy	Paul Hamilton, 1809
	William Jones, 1813
	B. W. Crowninshield, 1814

Monroe

Secretary of State	John Quincy Adams, 1817
Secretary of the Treasury	William H. Crawford (Cont.)
Secretary of War	John C. Calhoun, 1817
Attorney General	Richard Rush (Cont.)
	William Wirt, 1817
Secretary of the Navy	B. W. Crowninshield (Cont.)
	Smith Thompson, 1818
	Samuel L. Southard, 1823

J. Q. Adams

Secretary of State	Henry Clay, 1825
Secretary of the Treasury	Richard Rush, 1825
Secretary of War	James Barbour, 1825
	Peter B. Porter, 1828
Attorney General	William Wirt (Cont.)
Secretary of the Navy	Samuel L. Southard (Cont.)

Jackson

Secretary of State	Martin Van Buren, 1829
	Edward Livingston, 1831
	Louis McLane, 1833
	John Forsyth, 1834
Secretary of the Treasury	Samuel D. Ingham, 1829
	Louis McLane, 1831
	William J. Duane, 1833
	Roger B. Taney[1], 1833
	Levi Woodbury, 1834
Secretary of War	John H. Eaton, 1829
	Lewis Cass, 1831
Attorney General	John M. Berrien, 1829
	Roger B. Taney, 1831
	Benjamin F. Butler, 1833
Postmaster General[2]	William T. Barry, 1829
	Amos Kendall, 1835
Secretary of the Navy	John Branch, 1829
	Levi Woodbury, 1831
	Mahlon Dickerson, 1834

1. Not confirmed by the Senate. 2. The postmaster general did not become a cabinet member until 1829. Earlier postmasters general were: Samuel Osgood (1789), Timothy Pickering (1791), Joseph Habersham (1795), Gideon Granger (1801), Return J. Meigs, Jr. (1814), and John McLean (1823).

Van Buren

Secretary of State	John Forsyth (Cont.)
Secretary of the Treasury	Levi Woodbury (Cont.)
Secretary of War	Joel R. Poinsett, 1837
Attorney General	Benjamin F. Butler (Cont.)
	Felix Grundy, 1838
	Henry D. Gilpin, 1840

Postmaster General	Amos Kendall (Cont.)
	John M. Niles, 1840
Secretary of the Navy	Mahlon Dickerson (Cont.)
	James K. Paulding, 1838

W. H. Harrison

Secretary of State	Daniel Webster, 1841
Secretary of the Treasury	Thomas Ewing, 1841
Secretary of War	John Bell, 1841
Attorney General	John J. Crittenden, 1841
Postmaster General	Francis Granger, 1841
Secretary of the Navy	George E. Badger, 1841

Tyler

Secretary of State	Daniel Webster (Cont.)
	Abel P. Upshur, 1843
	John C. Calhoun, 1844
Secretary of the Treasury	Thomas Ewing (Cont.)
	Walter Forward, 1841
	John C. Spencer[1], 1843
	George M. Bibb, 1844
Secretary of War	John Bell (Cont.)
	John C. Spencer, 1841
	James M. Porter[1], 1843
	William Wilkins, 1844
Attorney General	John J. Crittenden (Cont.)
	Hugh S. Legaré, 1841
	John Nelson, 1843
Postmaster General	Francis Granger (Cont.)
	Charles A. Wickliffe, 1841
Secretary of the Navy	George E. Badger (Cont.)
	Abel P. Upshur, 1841
	David Henshaw[1], 1843
	Thomas W. Gilmer, 1844
	John Y. Mason, 1844

1. Not confirmed by the Senate.

Polk

Secretary of State	James Buchanan, 1845
Secretary of the Treasury	Robert J. Walker, 1845
Secretary of War	William L. Marcy, 1845
Attorney General	John Y. Mason, 1845
	Nathan Clifford, 1846
	Isaac Toucey, 1848
Postmaster General	Cave Johnson, 1845
Secretary of the Navy	George Bancroft, 1845
	John Y. Mason, 1846

Taylor

Secretary of State	John M. Clayton, 1849
Secretary of the Treasury	William M. Meredith, 1849
Secretary of War	George W. Crawford, 1849
Attorney General	Reverdy Johnson, 1849
Postmaster General	Jacob Collamer, 1849
Secretary of the Navy	William B. Preston, 1849
Secretary of the Interior	Thomas Ewing, 1849

Fillmore

Secretary of State	Daniel Webster, 1850
	Edward Everett, 1852
Secretary of the Treasury	Thomas Corwin, 1850
Secretary of War	Charles M. Conrad, 1850
Attorney General	John J. Crittenden, 1850
Postmaster General	Nathan K. Hall, 1850
	Samuel D. Hubbard, 1852
Secretary of the Navy	William A. Graham, 1850
	John P. Kennedy, 1852
Secretary of the Interior	Thos. M. T. McKennan, 1850
	Alex. H. H. Stuart, 1850

Pierce

Secretary of State	William L. Marcy, 1853
Secretary of the Treasury	James Guthrie, 1853
Secretary of War	Jefferson Davis, 1853
Attorney General	Caleb Cushing, 1853

Postmaster General	James Campbell, 1853
Secretary of the Navy	James C. Dobbin, 1853
Secretary of the Interior	Robert McClelland, 1853

Buchanan

Secretary of State	Lewis Cass, 1857
	Jeremiah S. Black, 1860
Secretary of the Treasury	Howell Cobb, 1857
	Philip F. Thomas, 1860
	John A. Dix, 1861
Secretary of War	John B. Floyd, 1857
	Joseph Holt, 1861
Attorney General	Jeremiah S. Black, 1857
	Edwin M. Stanton, 1860
Postmaster General	Aaron V. Brown, 1857
	Joseph Holt, 1859
	Horatio King, 1861
Secretary of the Navy	Isaac Toucey, 1857
Secretary of the Interior	Jacob Thompson, 1857

Lincoln

Secretary of State	William H. Seward, 1861
Secretary of the Treasury	Salmon P. Chase, 1861
	William P. Fessenden, 1864
	Hugh McCulloch, 1865
Secretary of War	Simon Cameron, 1861
	Edwin M. Stanton, 1862
Attorney General	Edward Bates, 1861
	James Speed, 1864
Postmaster General	Montgomery Blair, 1861
	William Dennison, 1864
Secretary of the Navy	Gideon Welles, 1861
Secretary of the Interior	Caleb B. Smith, 1861
	John P. Usher, 1863

A. Johnson

Secretary of State	William H. Seward (Cont.)
Secretary of the Treasury	Hugh McCulloch (Cont.)
Secretary of War	Edwin M. Stanton (Cont.)
	John M. Schofield, 1868
Attorney General	James Speed (Cont.)
	Henry Stanbery, 1866
	William M. Evarts, 1868
Postmaster General	William Dennison (Cont.)
	Alexander W. Randall, 1866
Secretary of the Navy	Gideon Welles (Cont.)
Secretary of the Interior	John P. Usher (Cont.)
	James Harlan, 1865
	Orville H. Browning, 1866

Grant

Secretary of State	Elihu B. Washburne, 1869
	Hamilton Fish, 1869
Secretary of the Treasury	George S. Boutwell, 1869
	William A. Richardson, 1873
	Benjamin H. Bristow, 1874
	Lot M. Morrill, 1876
Secretary of War	John A. Rawlins, 1869
	William W. Belknap, 1869
	Alphonso Taft, 1876
	James D. Cameron, 1876
Attorney General	Ebenezer R. Hoar, 1869
	Amos T. Akerman, 1870
	George H. Williams, 1871
	Edwards Pierrepont, 1875
	Alphonso Taft, 1876
Postmaster General	John A. J. Creswell, 1869
	Marshall Jewell, 1874
	James N. Tyner, 1876
Secretary of the Navy	Adolph E. Borie, 1869
	George M. Robeson, 1869
Secretary of the Interior	Jacob D. Cox, 1869
	Columbus Delano, 1870
	Zachariah Chandler, 1875

Hayes

Secretary of State	William M. Evarts, 1877
Secretary of the Treasury	John Sherman, 1877
Secretary of War	George W. McCrary, 1877
	Alexander Ramsey, 1879
Attorney General	Charles Devens, 1877
Postmaster General	David M. Key, 1877
	Horace Maynard, 1880
	Richard W. Thompson, 1877
	Nathan Goff, Jr., 1881
Secretary of the Interior	Carl Schurz, 1877

Garfield

Secretary of State	James G. Blaine, 1881
Secretary of the Treasury	William Windom, 1881
Secretary of War	Robert T. Lincoln, 1881
Attorney General	Wayne MacVeagh, 1881
Postmaster General	Thomas L. James, 1881
Secretary of the Navy	William H. Hunt, 1881
Secretary of the Interior	Samuel J. Kirkwood, 1881

Arthur

Secretary of State	James G. Blaine (Cont.)
	F. T. Frelinghuysen, 1881
Secretary of the Treasury	William Windom (Cont.)
	Charles J. Folger, 1881
	Walter Q. Gresham, 1884
	Hugh McCulloch, 1884
Secretary of War	Robert T. Lincoln (Cont.)
Attorney General	Wayne MacVeagh (Cont.)
	Benjamin H. Brewster, 1881
Postmaster General	Thomas L. James (Cont.)
	Timothy O. Howe, 1881
	Walter Q. Gresham, 1883
	Frank Hatton, 1884
Secretary of the Navy	William H. Hunt (Cont.)
	William E. Chandler, 1882
Secretary of the Interior	Samuel J. Kirkwood (Cont.)
	Henry M. Teller, 1882

Cleveland

Secretary of State	Thomas F. Bayard, 1885
Secretary of the Treasury	Daniel Manning, 1885
	Charles S. Fairchild, 1887
Secretary of War	William C. Endicott, 1885
Attorney General	Augustus H. Garland, 1885
Postmaster General	William F. Vilas, 1885
	Don M. Dickinson, 1888
Secretary of the Navy	William C. Whitney, 1885
Secretary of the Interior	Lucius Q. C. Lamar, 1885
	William F. Vilas, 1888
Secretary of Agriculture	Norman J. Colman, 1889

B. Harrison

Secretary of State	James G. Blaine, 1889
	John W. Foster, 1892
Secretary of the Treasury	William Windom, 1889
	Charles Foster, 1891
Secretary of War	Redfield Proctor, 1889
	Stephen B. Elkins, 1891
Attorney General	William H. H. Miller, 1889
Postmaster General	John Wanamaker, 1889
Secretary of the Navy	Benjamin F. Tracy, 1889
Secretary of the Interior	John W. Noble, 1889
Secretary of Agriculture	Jeremiah M. Rusk, 1889

Cleveland

Secretary of State	Walter Q. Gresham, 1893
	Richard Olney, 1895
Secretary of the Treasury	John G. Carlisle, 1893
Secretary of War	Daniel S. Lamont, 1893
Attorney General	Richard Olney, 1893
	Judson Harmon, 1895
Postmaster General	Wilson S. Bissell, 1893
	William L. Wilson, 1895

Secretary of the Navy	Hilary A. Herbert, 1893
Secretary of the Interior	Hoke Smith, 1893
	David R. Francis, 1896
Secretary of Agriculture	Julius Sterling Morton, 1893

McKinley

Secretary of State	John Sherman, 1897
	William R. Day, 1898
	John Hay, 1898
Secretary of the Treasury	Lyman J. Gage, 1897
Secretary of War	Russell A. Alger, 1897
	Elihu Root, 1899
Attorney General	Joseph McKenna, 1897
	John W. Griggs, 1898
	Philander C. Knox, 1901
Postmaster General	James A. Gary, 1897
	Charles E. Smith, 1898
Secretary of the Navy	John D. Long, 1897
Secretary of the Interior	Cornelius N. Bliss, 1897
	Ethan A. Hitchcock, 1898
Secretary of Agriculture	James Wilson, 1897

T. Roosevelt

Secretary of State	John Hay (Cont.)
	Elihu Root, 1905
	Robert Bacon, 1909
Secretary of the Treasury	Lyman J. Gage (Cont.)
	Leslie M. Shaw, 1902
	George B. Cortelyou, 1907
Secretary of War	Elihu Root (Cont.)
	William H. Taft, 1904
	Luke E. Wright, 1908
Attorney General	Philander C. Knox (Cont.)
	William H. Moody, 1904
	Charles J. Bonaparte, 1906
Postmaster General	Charles E. Smith (Cont.)
	Henry C. Payne, 1902
	Robert J. Wynne, 1904
	George B. Cortelyou, 1905
	George von L. Meyer, 1907
Secretary of the Navy	John D. Long (Cont.)
	William H. Moody, 1902
	Paul Morton, 1904
	Charles J. Bonaparte, 1905
	Victor H. Metcalf, 1906
	Truman H. Newberry, 1908
Secretary of the Interior	Ethan A. Hitchcock (Cont.)
	James R. Garfield, 1907
Secretary of Agriculture	James Wilson (Cont.)
Secretary of Commerce and Labor	George B. Cortelyou, 1903
	Victor H. Metcalf, 1904
	Oscar S. Straus, 1906

Taft

Secretary of State	Philander C. Knox, 1909
Secretary of the Treasury	Franklin MacVeagh, 1909
Secretary of War	Jacob M. Dickinson, 1909
	Henry L. Stimson, 1911
Attorney General	George W. Wickersham, 1909
Postmaster General	Frank H. Hitchcock, 1909
Secretary of the Navy	George von L. Meyer, 1909
Secretary of the Interior	Richard A. Ballinger, 1909
	Walter L. Fisher, 1911
Secretary of Agriculture	James Wilson (Cont.)
Secretary of Commerce and Labor	Charles Nagel, 1909

Wilson

Secretary of State	William J. Bryan, 1913
	Robert Lansing, 1915
	Bainbridge Colby, 1920
Secretary of the Treasury	William G. McAdoo, 1913
	Carter Glass, 1918
	David F. Houston, 1920
Secretary of War	Lindley M. Garrison, 1913
	Newton D. Baker, 1916

Attorney General	James C. McReynolds, 1913
	Thomas W. Gregory, 1914
	A. Mitchell Palmer, 1919
Postmaster General	Albert S. Burleson, 1913
Secretary of the Navy	Josephus Daniels, 1913
Secretary of the Interior	Franklin K. Lane, 1913
	John B. Payne, 1920
Secretary of Agriculture	David F. Houston, 1913
	Edwin T. Meredith, 1920
Secretary of Commerce	William C. Redfield, 1913
	Joshua W. Alexander, 1919
Secretary of Labor	William B. Wilson, 1913

Harding

Secretary of State	Charles E. Hughes, 1921
Secretary of the Treasury	Andrew W. Mellon, 1921
Secretary of War	John W. Weeks, 1921
Attorney General	Harry M. Daugherty, 1921
Postmaster General	Will H. Hays, 1921
	Hubert Work, 1922
	Harry S. New, 1923
Secretary of the Navy	Edwin Denby, 1921
Secretary of the Interior	Albert B. Fall, 1921
	Hubert Work, 1923
Secretary of Agriculture	Henry C. Wallace, 1921
Secretary of Commerce	Herbert Hoover, 1921
Secretary of Labor	James J. Davis, 1921

Coolidge

Secretary of State	Charles E. Hughes (Cont.)
	Frank B. Kellogg, 1925
Secretary of the Treasury	Andrew W. Mellon (Cont.)
Secretary of War	John W. Weeks (Cont.)
	Dwight F. Davis, 1925
Attorney General	Harry M. Daughtery (Cont.)
	Harlan F. Stone, 1924
	John G. Sargent, 1925
Postmaster General	Harry S. New (Cont.)
Secretary of the Navy	Edwin Denby (Cont.)
	Curtis D. Wilbur, 1924
Secretary of the Interior	Hubert Work (Cont.)
	Roy O. West, 1928
Secretary of Agriculture	Henry C. Wallace (Cont.)
	Howard M. Gore, 1924
	William M. Jardine, 1925
Secretary of Commerce	Herbert Hoover (Cont.)
	William F. Whiting, 1928
Secretary of Labor	James J. Davis (Cont.)

Hoover

Secretary of State	Frank B. Kellogg (Cont.)
	Henry L. Stimson, 1929
Secretary of the Treasury	Andrew W. Mellon (Cont.)
	Ogden L. Mills, 1932
Secretary of War	James W. Good, 1929
	Patrick J. Hurley, 1929
Attorney General	William D. Mitchell, 1929
Postmaster General	Walter F. Brown, 1929
Secretary of the Navy	Charles F. Adams, 1929
Secretary of the Interior	Ray Lyman Wilbur, 1929
Secretary of Agriculture	Arthur M. Hyde, 1929
Secretary of Commerce	Robert P. Lamont, 1929
	Roy D. Chapin, 1932
Secretary of Labor	James J. Davis (Cont.)
	William N. Doak, 1930

F. D. Roosevelt

Secretary of State	Cordell Hull, 1933
	E. R. Stettinius, Jr., 1944
Secretary of the Treasury	William H. Woodin, 1933
	Henry Morgenthau, Jr., 1934
Secretary of War	George H. Dern, 1933
	Harry H. Woodring, 1936
	Henry L. Stimson, 1940

Attorney General	Homer S. Cummings, 1933
	Frank Murphy, 1939
	Robert H. Jackson, 1940
	Francis Biddle, 1941
Postmaster General	James A. Farley, 1933
	Frank C. Walker, 1940
Secretary of the Navy	Claude A. Swanson, 1933
	Charles Edison, 1940
	Frank Knox, 1940
	James Forrestal, 1944
Secretary of the Interior	Harold L. Ickes, 1933
Secretary of Agriculture	Henry A. Wallace, 1933
	Claude R. Wickard, 1940
Secretary of Commerce	Daniel C. Roper, 1933
	Harry L. Hopkins, 1938
	Jesse H. Jones, 1940
	Henry A. Wallace, 1945
Secretary of Labor	Frances Perkins, 1933

Truman

Secretary of State	E. R. Stettinius, Jr. (Cont.)
	James F. Byrnes, 1945
	George C. Marshall, 1947
	Dean Acheson, 1949
Secretary of the Treasury	Henry Morgenthau, Jr. (Cont.)
	Frederick M. Vinson, 1945
	John W. Snyder, 1946
Secretary of Defense	James Forrestal, 1947
	Louis A. Johnson, 1949
	George C. Marshall, 1950
	Robert A. Lovett, 1951
Attorney General	Francis Biddle (Cont.)
	Tom C. Clark, 1945
	J. Howard McGrath, 1949
	James P. McGranery, 1952
Postmaster General	Frank C. Walker (Cont.)
	Robert E. Hannegan, 1945
	Jesse M. Donaldson, 1947
Secretary of the Interior	Harold L. Ickes (Cont.)
	Julius A. Krug, 1946
	Oscar L. Chapman, 1949
Secretary of Agriculture	Claude R. Wickard (Cont.)
	Clinton P. Anderson, 1945
	Charles F. Brannan, 1948
Secretary of Commerce	Henry A. Wallace (Cont.)
	W. Averell Harriman, 1946
	Charles Sawyer, 1948
Secretary of Labor	Frances Perkins (Cont.)
	Lewis B. Schwellenbach, 1945
	Maurice J. Tobin, 1948
Secretary of War[1]	Henry L. Stimson (Cont.)
	Robert P. Patterson, 1945
	Kenneth C. Royall, 1947
Secretary of the Navy[1]	James Forrestal, 1945

1. On July 26, 1947, the Departments of War and of the Navy were incorporated into the Department of Defense.

Eisenhower

Secretary of State	John Foster Dulles, 1953
	Christian A. Herter, 1959
Secretary of the Treasury	George M. Humphrey, 1953
	Robert B. Anderson, 1957
Secretary of Defense	Charles E. Wilson, 1953
	Neil H. McElroy, 1957
	Thomas S. Gates, Jr., 1959
Attorney General	Herbert Brownell, Jr., 1953
	William P. Rogers, 1958
Postmaster General	Arthur E. Summerfield, 1953
Secretary of the Interior	Douglas McKay, 1953
	Frederick A. Seaton, 1956
Secretary of Agriculture	Ezra Taft Benson, 1953
Secretary of Commerce	Sinclair Weeks, 1953
	Lewis L. Strauss[1], 1958
	Frederick H. Mueller, 1959

Secretary of Health, Education, and Welfare	Oveta Culp Hobby, 1953
	Marion B. Folsom, 1955
	Arthur S. Flemming, 1958
Secretary of Labor	Martin P. Durkin, 1953
	James P. Mitchell, 1953

1. Not confirmed by the Senate.

Kennedy

Secretary of State	Dean Rusk, 1961
Secretary of the Treasury	C. Douglas Dillon, 1961
Secretary of Defense	Robert S. McNamara, 1961
Attorney General	Robert F. Kennedy, 1961
Postmaster General	J. Edward Day, 1961
	John A. Gronouski, 1963
Secretary of the Interior	Stewart L. Udall, 1961
Secretary of Agriculture	Orville L. Freeman, 1961
Secretary of Commerce	Luther H. Hodges, 1961
Secretary of Labor	Arthur J. Goldberg, 1961
	W. Willard Wirtz, 1962
Secretary of Health, Education, and Welfare	Abraham A. Ribicoff, 1961
	Anthony J. Celebrezze, 1962

L. B. Johnson

Secretary of State	Dean Rusk (Cont.)
Secretary of the Treasury	C. Douglas Dillon (Cont.)
	Henry H. Fowler, 1965
	Joseph W. Barr[1], 1968
Secretary of Defense	Robert S. McNamara (Cont.)
	Clark M. Clifford, 1968
Attorney General	Robert F. Kennedy (Cont.)
	N. de B. Katzenbach, 1965
	Ramsey Clark, 1967
Postmaster General	John A. Gronouski (Cont.)
	Lawrence F. O'Brien, 1965
	W. Marvin Watson, 1968
Secretary of the Interior	Stewart L. Udall (Cont.)
Secretary of Agriculture	Orville L. Freeman (Cont.)
Secretary of Commerce	Luther H. Hodges (Cont.)
	John T. Connor, 1964
	A. B. Trowbridge, 1967
	C. R. Smith, 1968
Secretary of Labor	W. Willard Wirtz (Cont.)
Secretary of Health, Education, and Welfare	Anthony J. Celebrezze (Cont.)
	John W. Gardner, 1965
	Wilbur J. Cohen, 1968
Secretary of Housing and Urban Development	Robert C. Weaver, 1966
	Robert C. Wood[1], 1969
Secretary of Transportation	Alan S. Boyd, 1966

1. Recess appointment.

Nixon

Secretary of State	William P. Rogers, 1969
	Henry A. Kissinger, 1973
Secretary of the Treasury	David M. Kennedy, 1969
	John B. Connally, 1971
	George P. Shultz, 1972
	William E. Simon, 1974
Secretary of Defense	Melvin R. Laird, 1969
	Elliot L. Richardson, 1973
	James R. Schlesinger, 1973
Attorney General	John N. Mitchell, 1969
	Richard G. Kleindienst, 1972
	Elliot L. Richardson, 1973
	William B. Saxbe, 1974
Postmaster General[1]	William M. Blount, 1969
Secretary of the Interior	Walter J. Hickel, 1969
	Rogers C. B. Morton, 1971
Secretary of Agriculture	Clifford M. Hardin, 1969
	Earl L. Butz, 1971
Secretary of Commerce	Maurice H. Stans, 1969
	Peter G. Peterson, 1972
	Frederick B. Dent, 1973
Secretary of Labor	George P. Shultz, 1969
	James D. Hodgson, 1970
	Peter J. Brennan, 1973

Secretary of Health, Education, and Welfare	Robert H. Finch, 1969
	Elliot L. Richardson, 1970
	Caspar W. Weinberger, 1973
Secretary of Housing and Urban Development	George Romney, 1969
	James T. Lynn, 1973
Secretary of Transportation	John A. Volpe, 1969
	Claude S. Brinegar, 1973

1. The postmaster general is no longer a cabinet member.

Ford

Secretary of State	Henry A. Kissinger (Cont.)
Secretary of the Treasury	William E. Simon (Cont.)
Secretary of Defense	James R. Schlesinger (Cont.)
	Donald H. Rumsfeld, 1975
Attorney General	William B. Saxbe (Cont.)
	Edward H. Levi, 1975
Secretary of the Interior	Rogers C. B. Morton (Cont.)
	Stanley K. Hathaway, 1975
	Thomas S. Kleppe, 1975
Secretary of Agriculture	Earl L. Butz (Cont.)
	John Knebel, 1976
Secretary of Commerce	Frederick B. Dent (Cont.)
	Rogers C. B. Morton, 1975
	Elliot L. Richardson, 1976
Secretary of Labor	Peter J. Brennan (Cont.)
	John T. Dunlop, 1975
	William J. Usery, Jr., 1976
Secretary of Health, Education, and Welfare	Caspar W. Weinberger (Cont.)
	F. David Mathews, 1975
Secretary of Housing and Urban Development	James T. Lynn (Cont.)
	Carla A. Hills, 1975
Secretary of Transportation	Claude S. Brinegar (Cont.)
	William T. Coleman, Jr., 1975

Carter

Secretary of State	Cyrus R. Vance, 1977
	Edmund S. Muskie, 1980
Secretary of the Treasury	W. Michael Blumenthal, 1977
	G. William Miller, 1979
Secretary of Defense	Harold Brown, 1977
Attorney General	Griffin B. Bell, 1977
	Benjamin R. Civiletti, 1979
Secretary of the Interior	Cecil D. Andrus, 1977
Secretary of Agriculture	Bob S. Bergland, 1977
Secretary of Commerce	Juanita M. Kreps, 1977
	Philip M. Klutznick, 1979
Secretary of Labor	F. Ray Marshall, 1977
Secretary of Health and Human Services[1]	Joseph A. Califano, Jr., 1977
	Patricia Roberts Harris, 1979
Secretary of Housing and Urban Development	Patricia Roberts Harris, 1977
	Moon Landrieu, 1979
Secretary of Transportation	Brock Adams, 1977
	Neil E. Goldschmidt, 1979
Secretary of Energy	James R. Schlesinger, 1977
	Charles W. Duncan, Jr., 1979
Secretary of Education	Shirley Mount Hufstedler, 1979

1. Known as Department of Health, Education, and Welfare until May 1980.

Reagan

Secretary of State	Alexander M. Haig, Jr., 1981
	George P. Shultz, 1982
Secretary of the Treasury	Donald T. Regan, 1981
	James A. Baker 3rd, 1985
	Nicholas F. Brady, 1988
Secretary of Defense	Caspar W. Weinberger, 1981
	Frank C. Carlucci, 1987
Attorney General	William French Smith, 1981
	Edwin Meese 3rd, 1985
	Richard L. Thornburgh, 1988
Secretary of the Interior	James G. Watt, 1981
	William P. Clark, 1983
	Donald P. Hodel, 1985
Secretary of Agriculture	John R. Block, 1981
	Richard E. Lyng, 1986

Secretary of Commerce	Malcolm Baldrige, 1981
	C. William Verity, Jr., 1987
Secretary of Labor	Raymond J. Donovan, 1981
	William E. Brock, 1985
	Ann Dore McLaughlin, 1987
Secretary of Health and	Richard S. Schweiker, 1981
Human Services	Margaret M. Heckler, 1983
	Otis R. Bowen, 1985
Secretary of Housing and	Samuel R. Pierce, Jr., 1981
Urban Development	
Secretary of Transportation	Andrew L. Lewis, Jr., 1981
	Elizabeth H. Dole, 1983
	James H. Burnley 4th, 1987
Secretary of Energy	James B. Edwards, 1981
	Donald P. Hodel, 1983
	John S. Herrington, 1985
Secretary of Education	T. H. Bell, 1981
	William J. Bennett, 1985
	Lauro F. Cavazos, 1988

G. H. W. Bush

Secretary of State	James A. Baker 3d, 1989
	Lawrence S. Eagleburger, 1992
Secretary of the Treasury	Nicholas F. Brady (Cont.)
Secretary of Defense	Richard Cheney, 1989
Attorney General	Richard L. Thornburgh (Cont.)
	William P. Barr, 1992
Secretary of the Interior	Manuel Lujan Jr., 1989
Secretary of Agriculture	Clayton K. Yeutter, 1989
	Edward Madigan, 1991
Secretary of Commerce	Robert A. Mosbacher Sr., 1989
	Barbara H. Franklin, 1992
Secretary of Labor	Elizabeth H. Dole, 1989
	Lynn Martin, 1991
Secretary of Health and	Louis W. Sullivan, 1989
Human Services	
Secretary of Housing and	Jack F. Kemp, 1989
Urban Development	
Secretary of Transportation	Samuel K. Skinner, 1989
	Andrew Card, 1992
Secretary of Energy	James D. Watkins, 1989
Secretary of Education	Lauro F. Cavazos (Cont.)
	Lamar Alexander, 1991
Secretary of Veterans'	Edward J. Derwinski, 1989
Affairs	

Clinton

| Secretary of State | Warren M. Christopher, 1993 |
| | Madeleine Albright, 1996 |

Secretary of the Treasury	Lloyd Bentsen, 1993
	Robert E. Rubin, 1995–1999
	Lawrence H. Summers, 1999
Secretary of Defense	Les Aspin, 1993
	William J. Perry, 1994
	William S. Cohen, 1997
Attorney General	Janet Reno, 1993
Secretary of the Interior	Bruce Babbitt, 1993
Secretary of Agriculture	Mike Espy, 1993
	Dan Glickman, 1995
Secretary of Commerce	Ronald H. Brown, 1993
	Mickey Kantor, 1996
	William M. Daley, 1997
	Norman Y. Mineta, 2000
Secretary of Labor	Robert B. Reich, 1993
	Alexis Herman, 1997
Secretary of Health and	Donna E. Shalala, 1993
Human Services	
Secretary of Housing and	Henry G. Cisneros, 1993
Urban Development	Andrew M. Cuomo, 1997
Secretary of Transportation	Federico F. Pena, 1993
	Rodney Slater, 1997
Secretary of Energy	Hazel R. O'Leary, 1993
	Frederico F. Pena, 1997
	Bill Richardson, 1998
Secretary of Education	Richard W. Riley, 1993
Secretary of Veterans'	Jesse Brown, 1993
Affairs	Togo D. West, Jr., 1998

G. W. Bush

Secretary of State	Gen. Colin L. Powell, 2001
Secretary of the Treasury	Paul H. O'Neill, 2001–2002
	John Snow, 2003
Secretary of Defense	Donald H. Rumsfeld, 2001
Attorney General	John Ashcroft, 2001
Secretary of the Interior	Gale A. Norton, 2001
Secretary of Agriculture	Ann M. Veneman, 2001
Secretary of Commerce	Donald L. Evans, 2001
Secretary of Labor	Elaine L. Chao, 2001
Secretary of Health and	Tommy G. Thompson, 2001
Human Services	
Secretary of Homeland	Tom Ridge, 2003
Security	
Secretary of Housing and	Melquiades R. Martinez, 2001
Urban Development	Alphonso Jackson, 2003
Secretary of Transportation	Norman Y. Mineta, 2001
Secretary of Energy	Spencer Abraham, 2001
Secretary of Education	Roderick R. Paige, 2001
Secretary of Veterans'	Anthony Principi, 2001
Affairs	

Impeachments of Federal Officials

Source: Congressional Directory

The procedure for the impeachment of federal officials is detailed in Article I, Section 3, of the Constitution. The Senate has sat as a court of impeachment in the following cases:

William Blount, senator from Tennessee; charges dismissed for want of jurisdiction, Jan. 14, 1799.

John Pickering, judge of the U.S. District Court for New Hampshire; removed from office March 12, 1804.

Samuel Chase, associate justice of the Supreme Court; acquitted March 1, 1805.

James H. Peck, judge of the U.S. District Court for Missouri; acquitted Jan. 31, 1831.

West H. Humphreys, judge of the U.S. District Court for the middle, eastern, and western districts of Tennessee; removed from office June 26, 1862.

Andrew Johnson, president of the United States; acquitted May 26, 1868.

William W. Belknap, secretary of war; acquitted Aug. 1, 1876.

Charles Swayne, judge of the U.S. District Court for the northern district of Florida; acquitted Feb. 27, 1905.

Robert W. Archbald, associate judge, U.S. Commerce Court; removed Jan. 13, 1913.

George W. English, judge of the U.S. District Court for eastern district of Illinois; resigned Nov. 4, 1926; proceedings dismissed.

Harold Louderback, judge of the U.S. District Court for the northern district of California; acquitted May 24, 1933.

Halsted L. Ritter, judge of the U.S. District Court for the southern district of Florida; removed from office April 17, 1936.

Harry E. Claiborne, judge of the U.S. District Court for the district of Nevada; removed from office Oct. 9, 1986.

Alcee L. Hastings, judge of the U.S. District Court for the southern district of Florida; removed from office Oct. 20, 1988.

Walter L. Nixon, judge of the U.S. District Court for Mississippi; removed from office Nov. 3, 1989.

William J. Clinton, president of the United States; acquitted Feb. 12, 1999.

Members of the Supreme Court of the United States

Mailing address for the Supreme Court: U.S. Supreme Court Building, 1 First Street NE Washington, DC 20543

| Name, state | Service | | | Birth | | | |
	Assoc. Justice	Chief Justice	Yrs	Place	Date	Died	Religion
John Jay , N.Y.		1789–1795	5	N.Y.	1745	1829	Episcopal
James Wilson, Pa.	1789–1798		8	Scotland	1742	1798	Episcopal
John Rutledge, S.C.*	1790–1791	1795	1	S.C.	1739	1800	Church of England
William Cushing, Mass.	1790–1810		20	Mass.	1732	1810	Unitarian
John Blair, Va.	1790–1796		5	Va.	1732	1800	Presbyterian
James Iredell, N.C.	1790–1799		9	England	1751	1799	Episcopal
Thomas Johnson, Md.	1792–1793		0	Md.	1732	1819	Episcopal
William Paterson, N.J.	1793–1806		13	Ireland	1745	1806	Protestant
Oliver Ellsworth, Conn.		1796–1800	4	Conn.	1745	1807	Congregational
Samuel Chase, Md.	1796–1811		15	Md.	1741	1811	Episcopal
Bushrod Washington, Va.	1799–1829		30	Va.	1762	1829	Episcopal
Alfred Moore, N.C.	1800–1804		3	N.C.	1755	1810	Episcopal
John Marshall, Va.		1801–1835	34	Va.	1755	1835	Episcopal
William Johnson, S.C.	1804–1834		30	S.C.	1771	1834	Presbyterian
Brockholst Livingston, N.Y.	1807–1823		16	N.Y.	1757	1823	Presbyterian
Thomas Todd, Ky.	1807–1826		18	Va.	1765	1826	Presbyterian
Gabriel Duval, Md.	1811–1835		23	Md.	1752	1844	French Protestant
Joseph Story, Mass.	1812–1845		33	Mass.	1779	1845	Unitarian
Smith Thompson, N.Y.	1823–1843		20	N.Y.	1768	1843	Presbyterian
Robert Trimble, Ky.	1826–1828		2	Va.	1777	1828	Protestant
John McLean, Ohio	1830–1861		31	N.J.	1785	1861	Methodist-Epis.
Henry Baldwin, Pa.	1830–1844		14	Conn.	1780	1844	Trinity Church
James M. Wayne, Ga.	1835–1867		32	Ga.	1790	1867	Protestant
Philip P. Barbour, Va.	1836–1841		4	Va.	1783	1841	Episcopal
Roger B. Taney, Md.		1836–1864	28	Md.	1777	1864	Roman Catholic
John Catron, Tenn.	1837–1865		28	Pa.	1786	1865	Presbyterian
John McKinley, Ala.	1837–1852		14	Va.	1780	1852	Protestant
Peter V. Daniel, Va.	1841–1860		18	Va.	1784	1860	Episcopal
Samuel Nelson, N.Y.	1845–1872		27	N.Y.	1792	1873	Protestant
Levi Woodbury, N.H.	1845–1851		5	N.H.	1789	1851	Protestant
Robert C. Grier, Pa.	1846–1870		23	Pa.	1794	1870	Presbyterian
Benjamin R. Curtis, Mass.	1851–1857		5	Mass.	1809	1874	(2)
John A. Campbell, Ala.	1853–1861		8	Ga.	1811	1889	Episcopal
Nathan Clifford, Maine	1858–1881		23	N.H.	1803	1881	(1)
Noah H. Swayne, Ohio	1862–1881		18	Va.	1804	1884	Quaker
Samuel F. Miller, Iowa	1862–1890		28	Ky.	1816	1890	Unitarian
David Davis, Ill.	1862–1877		14	Md.	1815	1886	(4)
Stephen J. Field, Calif.	1863–1897		34	Conn.	1816	1899	Episcopal
Salmon P. Chase, Ohio		1864–1873	8	N.H.	1808	1873	Episcopal
William Strong, Pa.	1870–1880		10	Conn.	1808	1895	Presbyterian
Joseph P. Bradley, N.J.	1870–1892		21	N.Y.	1813	1892	Presbyterian
Ward Hunt, N.Y.	1872–1882		9	N.Y.	1810	1886	Episcopal
Morrison R. Waite, Ohio		1874–1888	14	Conn.	1816	1888	Episcopal
John M. Harlan, Ky.	1877–1911		33	Ky.	1833	1911	Presbyterian
William B. Woods, Ga.	1880–1887		6	Ohio	1824	1887	Protestant
Stanley Matthews, Ohio	1881–1889		7	Ohio	1824	1889	Presbyterian
Horace Gray, Mass.	1882–1902		20	Mass.	1828	1902	(3)
Samuel Blatchford, N.Y.	1882–1893		11	N.Y.	1820	1893	Presbyterian
Lucius Q. C. Lamar, Miss.	1888–1893		5	Ga.	1825	1893	Methodist

Name, state	Assoc. Justice	Chief Justice	Yrs	Place	Date	Died	Religion
Melville W. Fuller, Ill.		1888–1910	21	Maine	1833	1910	Episcopal
David J. Brewer, Kan.	1889–1910		20	Asia Minor	1837	1910	Protestant
Henry B. Brown, Mich.	1890–1906		15	Mass.	1836	1913	Protestant
George Shiras, Jr., Pa.	1892–1903		10	Pa.	1832	1924	Presbyterian
Howell E. Jackson, Tenn.	1893–1895		2	Tenn.	1832	1895	Baptist
Edward D. White, La.*	1894–1910	1910–1921	26	La.	1845	1921	Roman Catholic
Rufus W. Peckham, N.Y.	1895–1909		13	N.Y.	1838	1909	Episcopal
Joseph McKenna, Calif.	1898–1925		26	Pa.	1843	1926	Roman Catholic
Oliver W. Holmes, Mass.	1902–1932		29	Mass.	1841	1935	Unitarian
William R. Day, Ohio	1903–1922		19	Ohio	1849	1923	Protestant
William H. Moody, Mass.	1906–1910		3	Mass.	1853	1917	Episcopal
Horace H. Lurton, Tenn.	1909–1914		4	Ky.	1844	1914	Episcopal
Charles E. Hughes, N.Y.*	1910–1916	1930–1941	16	N.Y.	1862	1948	Baptist
Willis Van Devanter, Wyo.	1910–1937		26	Ind.	1859	1941	Episcopal
Joseph R. Lamar, Ga.	1910–1916		4	Ga.	1857	1916	Ch. of Disciples
Mahlon Pitney, N.J.	1912–1922		10	N.J.	1858	1924	Presbyterian
James C. McReynolds, Tenn.	1914–1941		26	Ky.	1862	1946	Disciples of Christ
Louis D. Brandeis, Mass.	1916–1939		22	Ky.	1856	1941	Jewish
John H. Clarke, Ohio	1916–1922		5	Ohio	1857	1945	Protestant
William H. Taft, Conn.		1921–1930	8	Ohio	1857	1930	Unitarian
George Sutherland, Utah	1922–1938		15	England	1862	1942	Episcopal
Pierce Butler, Minn.	1923–1939		16	Minn.	1866	1939	Roman Catholic
Edward T. Sanford, Tenn.	1923–1930		7	Tenn.	1865	1930	Episcopal
Harlan F. Stone, N.Y.*	1925–1941	1941–1946	20	N.H.	1872	1946	Episcopal
Owen J. Roberts, Pa.	1930–1945		15	Pa.	1875	1955	Episcopal
Benjamin N. Cardozo, N.Y.	1932–1938		6	N.Y.	1870	1938	Jewish
Hugo L. Black, Ala.	1937–1971		34	Ala.	1886	1971	Baptist
Stanley F. Reed, Ky.	1938–1957		19	Ky.	1884	1980	Protestant
Felix Frankfurter, Mass.	1939–1962		23	Austria	1882	1965	Jewish
William O. Douglas, Conn.	1939–1975		36	Minn.	1898	1980	Presbyterian
Frank Murphy, Mich.	1940–1949		9	Mich.	1890	1949	Roman Catholic
James F. Byrnes, S.C.	1941–1942		1	S.C.	1879	1972	Episcopal
Robert H. Jackson, Pa.	1941–1954		13	N.Y.	1892	1954	Episcopal
Wiley B. Rutledge, Iowa	1943–1949		6	Ky.	1894	1949	Unitarian
Harold H. Burton, Ohio	1945–1958		13	Mass.	1888	1964	Unitarian
Frederick M. Vinson, Ky.		1946–1953	7	Ky.	1890	1953	Methodist
Tom C. Clark, Tex.	1949–1967		17	Tex.	1899	1977	Presbyterian
Sherman Minton, Ind.	1949–1956		7	Ind.	1890	1965	Roman Catholic
Earl Warren, Calif.		1953–1969	15	Calif.	1891	1974	Protestant
John M. Harlan, N.Y.	1955–1971		16	Ill.	1899	1971	Presbyterian
William J. Brennan, Jr., N.J.	1956–1990		33	N.J.	1906	1997	Roman Catholic
Charles E. Whittaker, Mo.	1957–1962		5	Kan.	1901	1973	Methodist
Potter Stewart, Ohio	1958–1981		23	Mich.	1915	1985	Episcopal
Byron R. White, Colo.	1962–1993		31	Colo.	1917	2002	Episcopal
Arthur J. Goldberg, Ill.	1962–1965		2	Ill.	1908	1990	Jewish
Abe Fortas, Tenn.	1965–1969		3	Tenn.	1910	1982	Jewish
Thurgood Marshall, N.Y.	1967–1991		24	Md.	1908	1993	Episcopal
Warren E. Burger, Va.		1969–1986	17	Minn.	1907	1995	Presbyterian
Harry A. Blackmun, Minn.	1970–1994		24	Ill.	1908	1999	Methodist
Lewis F. Powell, Jr., Va.	1972–1987		15	Va.	1907	1998	Presbyterian
William H. Rehnquist, Ariz.*	1972–1986	1986–	—	Wis.	1924	—	Lutheran
John Paul Stevens, Ill.	1975–		—	Ill.	1920	—	Protestant
Sandra Day O'Connor, Ariz.	1981–		—	Tex.	1930	—	Episcopal
Antonin Scalia, DC	1986–		—	N.J.	1936	—	Roman Catholic
Anthony M. Kennedy, Calif.	1988–		—	Calif.	1936	—	Roman Catholic
David H. Souter, N.H.	1990–		—	Mass.	1939	—	Episcopal
Clarence Thomas, DC	1991–		—	Ga.	1948	—	Roman Catholic
Ruth Bader Ginsburg, DC	1993–		—	N.Y.	1933	—	Jewish
Stephen G. Breyer, Mass.	1994–		—	Calif.	1938	—	Jewish

NOTE: **Bold=Chief Justice** *Served as both chief justice and associate justice. 1. Congregational; later Unitarian. 2. Unitarian; then Episcopal. 3. Unitarian or Congregational. 4. Not a member of any church.

Milestone Cases in Supreme Court History

1803   *Marbury* v. *Madison* was the first instance in which a law passed by Congress was declared unconstitutional. The decision greatly expanded the power of the Court by establishing its right to overturn acts of Congress, a power not explicitly granted by the Constitution. Initially the case involved Secretary of State James Madison, who refused to seat four judicial appointees although they had been confirmed by the Senate.

1824   *Gibbons* v. *Ogden* defined broadly Congress's right to regulate commerce. Aaron Ogden had filed suit in New York against Thomas Gibbons for operating a rival steamboat service between New York and New Jersey ports. Ogden had exclusive rights to operate steamboats in New York under a state law, while Gibbons held a federal license. Gibbons lost the case and appealed to the U.S. Supreme Court, which reversed the decision. The Court held that the New York law was unconstitutional, since the power to regulate interstate commerce, which extended to the regulation of navigation, belonged exclusively to Congress. In the 20th century, Chief Justice John Marshall's broad definition of commerce was used to uphold civil rights.

1857   *Dred Scott* v. *Sandford* was a highly controversial case that intensified the national debate over slavery. The case involved Dred Scott, a slave, who was taken from a slave state to a free territory. Scott filed a lawsuit claiming that because he had lived on free soil he was entitled to his freedom. Chief Justice Roger B. Taney disagreed, ruling that blacks were not citizens and therefore could not sue in federal court. Taney further inflamed antislavery forces by declaring that Congress had no right to ban slavery from U.S. territories.

1896   *Plessy* v. *Ferguson* was the infamous case that asserted that "equal but separate accommodations" for blacks on railroad cars did not violate the "equal protection under the laws" clause of the 14th Amendment. By defending the constitutionality of racial segregation, the Court paved the way for the repressive Jim Crow laws of the South. The lone dissenter on the Court, Justice John Marshall Harlan, protested, "The thin disguise of 'equal' accommodations . . . will not mislead anyone."

1954   *Brown* v. *Board of Education of Topeka* invalidated racial segregation in schools and led to the unraveling of de jure segregation in all areas of public life. In the unanimous decision spearheaded by Chief Justice Earl Warren, the Court invalidated the Plessy ruling, declaring "in the field of public education, the doctrine of 'separate but equal' has no place" and contending that "separate educational facilities are inherently unequal." Future Supreme Court justice Thurgood Marshall was one of the NAACP lawyers who successfully argued the case.

1963   *Gideon* v. *Wainwright* guaranteed a defendant's right to legal counsel. The Supreme Court overturned the Florida felony conviction of Clarence Earl Gideon, who had defended himself after having been denied a request for free counsel. The Court held that the state's failure to provide counsel for a defendant charged with a felony violated the Fourteenth Amendment's due process clause. Gideon was given another trial, and with a court-appointed lawyer defending him, he was acquitted.

1964   *New York Times* v. *Sullivan* extended the protection offered the press by the First Amendment. L.B. Sullivan, a police commissioner in Montgomery, Ala., had filed a libel suit against the *New York Times* for publishing inaccurate information about certain actions taken by the Montgomery police department. In overturning a lower court's decision, the Supreme Court held that debate on public issues would be inhibited if public officials could sue for inaccuracies that were made by mistake. The ruling made it more difficult for public officials to bring libel charges against the press, since the official had to prove that a harmful untruth was told maliciously and with reckless disregard for truth.

1966   *Miranda* v. *Arizona* was another case that helped define the due process clause of the 14th Amendment. At the center of the case was Ernesto Miranda, who had confessed to a crime during police questioning without knowing he had a right to have an attorney present. Based on his confession, Miranda was convicted. The Supreme Court overturned the conviction, ruling that criminal suspects must be warned of their rights before they are questioned by police. These rights are: the right to remain silent, to have an attorney present, and, if the suspect cannot afford an attorney, to have one appointed by the state. The police must also warn suspects that any statements they make can be used against them in court. Miranda was retried without the confession and convicted.

1973   *Roe* v. *Wade* legalized abortion and is at the center of the current controversy between "pro-life" and "pro-choice" advocates. The Court ruled that a woman has the right to an abortion without interference from the government in the first trimester of pregnancy, contending that it is part of her "right to privacy." The Court maintained that right to privacy is not absolute, however, and granted states the right to intervene in the second and third trimesters of pregnancy.

1978   *Regents of the University of California* v. *Bakke* imposed limitations on affirmative action to ensure that providing greater opportunities for minorities did not come at the expense of the rights of the majority. In other words, affirmative action was unfair if it lead to reverse discrimination. The case involved the University of Calif., Davis, Medical School and Allan Bakke, a white applicant who was rejected twice even though there were minority applicants admitted with significantly lower scores than his. A closely divided Court ruled that while race was a legitimate factor in school admissions, the use of rigid quotas was not permissible.

2003 *Grutter* v. *Bollinger* upheld the University of Michigan Law School's consideration of race and ethnicity in admissions. In her majority opinion, Justice O'Connor said that the law school uses a "highly individualized, holistic review of each applicant's file." Race, she said, is not used in a "mechanical way." Therefore, the university's program is consistent with the requirement of "individualized consideration" set in 1978's *Bakke* case. "In order to cultivate a set of leaders with legitimacy in the eyes of the citizenry, it is necessary that the path to leadership be visibly open to talented and qualified individuals of every race and ethnicity," O'Connor said. However, the court, in *Gratz* v. *Bollinger*, ruled that the University of Michigan's undergraduate admissions system, which awards 20 points to black, Hispanic, and American-Indian applicants, is "nonindividualized, mechanical," and thus unconstitutional.

Notable Decisions of the U.S. Supreme Court, 2003–2004 Term

Court Upholds Campaign Finance Laws (December 10, 2003): Court, 5–4, upholds major aspects of the 2001 law intended to thwart corruption—or the appearance of such—in political elections. In *McConnell v. The Federal Election Commission,* the justices vote that the ban on unlimited donations to political parties, known as soft money, does not violate free speech. However, the court acknowledges that the ruling will not end the flow of enormous sums of money in campaigns. "Money, like water, will always find an outlet," write Justices John Paul Stevens and Sandra Day O'Connor.

States Can Deny Aid to Divinity Students (February 25, 2004): Voting 7–2, the court upholds the provisions of Washington state's Promise Scholarship program, which offers taxpayer-funded scholarships to low-income college students enrolled in secular studies. The justices rule in *Locke v. Davey* that states are not violating the First Amendment's guarantee of religious freedom if they choose not to subsidize students studying for the ministry.

Court Upholds Redistricting Plan (April 28, 2004): In *Vieth v. Jubelirer,* court rules, 5–4, that it is impossible to objectively determine if Pennsylvania's Republican-controlled legislature violated Democrats' right of equal treatment under the state constitution when it redrew congressional districts to eliminate seats held by Democratic incumbents.

Disabled Have Right to Sue States (May 17, 2004): Justices rule, 5–4, in *Tennessee v. Lane* that private citizens can sue states that violate the Americans with Disabilities Act by failing to make their courthouses accessible to the disabled.

"Under God" to Remain in Pledge (June 14, 2004): In a unanimous 8–0 decision (Justice Scalia recused himself in the case), the court in *Elk Grove v. Newdow* overturns a federal appeals court ruling that said the term "under God" in the Pledge of Allegiance is unconstitutional because it violates the separation of church and state. Justices O'Connor and Thomas and Chief Justice Rehnquist say the words "under God" are constitutional and were added in 1954 to set the U.S. apart from "godless Communism." The other five justices, however, say the plaintiff, Michael Newdow, did not have the legal standing to bring the case because he and the girl's mother, who opposed the suit, are in a custody battle.

Court Strikes Down Patients' Rights Law (June 21, 2004): Court rules, 9–0, that states cannot allow individuals to sue managed-care companies for damages when the company refuses to cover a medical procedure that a doctor has determined necessary and injury or death occur as a result. In *Aetna v. Davila,* the court strikes down a Texas patients' rights law, saying it conflicts with a federal law, the Employee Retirement Income Security Act of 1974, which allows patients to sue managed-care companies for reimbursement for cost of treatments that were denied, but not for damages.

Suspects Must Identify Themselves to Police (June 21, 2004): Court, 5–4, rejects the argument of a Nevada rancher in *Hiibel v. The Sixth Judicial District Court* that the Fourth Amendment's protection against unreasonable search and seizure and the Fifth Amendment's right against self-incrimination do not allow a person suspected of being involved in a crime to refuse to identify himself to the police.

Court Invalidates Sentencing Guidelines (June 24, 2004): Ruling, 5–4, states that under the Sixth Amendment's guarantee of a trial by jury, only juries—not judges—may take into account other factors when increasing sentences beyond the maximum set forth by Washington state's sentencing guidelines. The court says in *Blakely v. Washington* that Washington's sentencing rules granted judges unconstitutional power.

Death Penalty Ban Not Retroactive (June 24, 2004): In *Schriro v. Summerlin,* justices rule, 5–4, that a 2002 decision to invalidate the death penalty in five states could not be retroactively applied to those sentenced to death before the decision.

Court Rules in Favor of Vice President (June 24, 2004): Court rules, 7–2, to send a case involving Dick Cheney back to a federal court of appeals. In the politically charged case, *Cheney v. U.S. District Court for the District of Columbia,* the court says the appeals court acted "prematurely" when it denied Cheney's request to keep confidential the details of his energy-task force meetings. The Sierra Club and Judicial Watch sued Cheney and his task force, which was made up of government officials and advised by executives in the energy industry, to try to make them reveal details about the group's meetings. Cheney said the group was shielded by the Federal Advisory Committee Act, which allows groups made up of government officials to keep the proceedings secret. The Sierra Club and Judicial Watch, however, said the executives were active enough in the group to be considered de facto members.

Detainees Have Right to Appear in Court (June 28, 2004): In *Rasul v. Bush,* court rules, 6–3, that foreign detainees held at the U.S. naval base in Guantánamo Bay, Cuba, are legally entitled to file petitions for writs of habeas corpus when they believe they are being held illegally because the base falls under the jurisdiction of federal courts. The ruling says Guantánamo Bay is "territory over which the United States exercises exclusive jurisdiction and control."

Court Declares Detention of U.S. Citizen Invalid (June 28, 2004) In an 8–1 ruling in the case *Hamdi v. Rumsfeld,* justices say the detention of Yaser Esam Hamdi, a U.S. citizen held for two years as an enemy combatant, is invalid. Justices O'Connor, Kennedy, and Breyer, as well as Chief Justice William Rehnquist, say Hamdi has the right to a "fair opportunity to rebut the government's factual assertions before a neutral decisionmaker." Justices Souter and Ginsberg rule that Congress did not authorize such a detention. Finally, Justices Scalia and Stevens say that Hamdi must either be tried for a specific crime or released. The court rejects the Bush administration's claim that the executive branch has unreviewable authority in time of war.

Justices Invalidate Questioning Tactic (June 28, 2004): Court, 5–4, rejects police tactic of questioning suspects twice, first before advising them of their *Miranda* rights—with the intention of elicting a confession—and again after. The ruling in *Missouri v.*

Seibert says the strategy intentionally avoids informing suspects of their right to remain silent before questioning undermines *Miranda.*

Court Extends Ban on Child Pornography Law (June 29, 2004): The court rules, 5–4, that Congress's attempts to protect children from Internet pornography threaten free speech. It sends the case, *Ashcroft v. the American Civil Liberties Union,* back to a lower court, charging the government with proving that the criminal penalties imposed under the Child Online Protection Act (COPA) on certain sexually explicit websites are the only way to prevent children from accessing sexually explicit content on the Web.

U.S. History Timeline

NOTES: o.s. = old style (according to the Julian calendar). *See also,* States by Order of Entry into the Union; Presidential Elections 1789–2000; the Confederate States of America; National Censuses; Milestone Cases in Supreme Court History; World History; and Current Events.

c. 12,000 B.C. North American Indian cultures flourish.

A.D. 1000 Norse seaman Leif Ericsson lands in Newfoundland, which he calls Vinland.

1492 Christopher Columbus, financed by Spain, makes the first of four voyages to the New World. He lands in the Bahamas (**Oct. 12**).

1513 Spanish explorer Juan Ponce de León lands on the coast of Florida.

1565 Saint Augustine, Florida, settled by the Spanish, becomes the first permanent European colony in North America.

1607 Jamestown, the first permanent English settlement in America, is established by the London Company in southeast Virginia (**May 14 o.s.**).

1619 The House of Burgesses, the first representative assembly in America, meets for the first time in Virginia (**July 30 o.s.**). The first African slaves are brought to Jamestown (**summer**).

1620 The Plymouth Colony in Massachusetts is established by Pilgrims from England (**Dec. 11 o.s.**). Before disembarking from their ship, the *Mayflower,* 41 male passengers sign the Mayflower Compact, an agreement that forms the basis of the colony's government.

1650 Colonial population is estimated at 50,400.

1752 Britain and the British colonies switch from the Julian to the Gregorian calendar (**Sept. 2**).

1754–1763 French and Indian War: Final conflict in the ongoing struggle between the British and French for control of eastern North America. The British win a decisive victory over the French on the Plains of Abraham outside Quebec (**Sept. 13, 1759**) and, by the Treaty of Paris (signed **Feb. 10, 1763**), formally gain control of Canada and all the French possessions east of the Mississippi.

1770 Boston Massacre: British troops fire into a mob, killing five men and leading to intense public protests (**March 5**).

1773 Boston Tea Party: Group of colonial patriots disguised as Mohawk Indians board three ships in Boston harbor and dump more than 300 crates of tea overboard as a protest against the British tea tax (**Dec. 16**).

1774 First Continental Congress meets in Philadelphia, with 56 delegates representing every colony except Georgia. Delegates include

Patrick Henry, George Washington, and Samuel Adams (**Sept. 5–Oct. 26**).

1775–1783 American Revolution: War of independence fought between Great Britain and the 13 British colonies on the eastern seaboard of North America. Battles of Lexington and Concord, Mass., between the British Army and colonial minutemen, mark the beginning of the war (**April 19, 1775**). Battle-weary and destitute Continental army spends brutally cold winter and following spring at Valley Forge, Pa. (**Dec. 19, 1777–June 19, 1778**). British general Charles Cornwallis surrenders to Gen. George Washington at Yorktown, Va. (**Oct. 19, 1781**). Great Britain formally acknowledges American independence in the Treaty of Paris, which officially brings the war to a close (**Sept. 3, 1783**).

1776 Continental Congress adopts the Declaration of Independence in Philadelphia (**July 4**).

1777 Continental Congress approves the first official flag of the United States (**June 14**). Continental Congress adopts the Articles of Confederation, the first U.S. constitution (**Nov. 15**).

1786 Shays's Rebellion erupts (**Aug.**); farmers from New Hampshire to South Carolina take up arms to protest high state taxes and stiff penalties for failure to pay.

1787 Constitutional Convention, made up of delegates from 12 of the original 13 colonies, meets in Philadelphia to draft the U.S. Constitution (**May–Sept.**).

1789 George Washington is unanimously elected president of the United States in a vote by state electors (**Feb. 4**). U.S. Constitution goes into effect, having been ratified by nine states (**March 4**). U.S. Congress meets for the first time at Federal Hall in New York City (**March 4**). Washington is inaugurated as president at Federal Hall in New York City (**April 30**).

1790 U.S. Supreme Court meets for the first time at the Merchants Exchange Building in New York City (**Feb. 2**). The court, made up of one chief justice and five associate justices, hears its first case in 1792. The nation's first census shows that the population has climbed to nearly 4 million.

1791 First ten amendments to the Constitution, known as the Bill of Rights, are ratified (**Dec. 15**).

1793 Washington's second inauguration is held in Philadelphia (**March 4**). Eli Whitney's invention of the cotton gin greatly increases the demand for slave labor.

1797 John Adams is inaugurated as the second president in Philadelphia (**March 4**).

1800 The U.S. capital is moved from Philadelphia to Washington, DC (**June 15**). U.S. Congress meets in Washington, DC, for the first time (**Nov. 17**).

1801 Thomas Jefferson is inaugurated as the third president in Washington, DC (**March 4**).

1803 Louisiana Purchase: United States agrees to pay France $15 million for the Louisiana Territory, which extends west from the Mississippi River to the Rocky Mountains and comprises about 830,000 sq mi (treaty signed **May 2**). As a result, the U.S. nearly doubles in size.

1804 Lewis and Clark set out from St. Louis, Mo., on expedition to explore the West and find a route to the Pacific Ocean. (**May 14**).

1805 Jefferson's second inauguration (**March 4**). Lewis and Clark reach the Pacific Ocean (**Nov. 15**).

1809 James Madison is inaugurated as the fourth president (**March 4**).

1812–1814 War of 1812: U.S. declares war on Britain over British interference with American maritime shipping and westward expansion (**June 18, 1812**). Madison's second inauguration (**March 4, 1813**). British capture Washington, DC, and set fire to White House and Capitol (**Aug. 1814**). Francis Scott Key writes *Star-Spangled Banner* as he watches British attack on Fort McHenry at Baltimore (**Sept. 13–14, 1814**). Treaty of Ghent is signed, officially ending the war (**Dec. 24, 1814**).

1817 James Monroe is inaugurated as the fifth president (**March 4**).

1819 Spain agrees to cede Florida to the United States (**Feb. 22**).

1820 Missouri Compromise: In an effort to maintain the balance between free and slave states, Maine (formerly part of Massachusetts) is admitted as a free state so that Missouri can be admitted as a slave state; except for Missouri, slavery is prohibited in the Louisiana Purchase lands north of latitude 36°30′ (**March 3**).

1821 Monroe's second inauguration (**March 5**).

1823 Monroe Doctrine: In his annual address to Congress, President Monroe declares that the American continents are henceforth off-limits for further colonization by European powers (**Dec. 2**).

1825 John Quincy Adams is inaugurated as the sixth president (**March 4**). Erie Canal, linking the Hudson River to Lake Erie, is opened for traffic (**Oct. 26**).

1828 Construction is begun on the Baltimore and Ohio Railroad, the first public railroad in the U.S. (**July 4**).

1829 Andrew Jackson is inaugurated as seventh president (**March 4**).

1830 President Jackson signs the Indian Removal Act, which authorizes the forced removal of Native Americans living in the eastern part of the country to lands west of the Mississippi River (**May 28**). By the late 1830s the Jackson administration has relocated nearly 50,000 Native Americans.

1833 Jackson's second inauguration (**March 4**).

1836 Texas declares its independence from Mexico (**March 1**). Texan defenders of the Alamo are all killed during siege by the Mexican Army (**Feb. 24–March 6**). Texans defeat Mexicans at San Jacinto (**April 21**).

1837 Martin Van Buren is inaugurated as the eighth president (**March 4**).

1838 More than 15,000 Cherokee Indians are forced to march from Georgia to Indian Territory in present-day Oklahoma. Approximately 4,000 die from starvation and disease along the "Trail of Tears."

1841 William Henry Harrison is inaugurated as the ninth president (**March 4**). He dies one month later (**April 4**) and is succeeded in office by his vice president, John Tyler.

1845 U.S. annexes Texas by joint resolution of Congress (**March 1**). James Polk is inaugurated as the 11th president (**March 4**). The term "manifest destiny" appears for the first time in a magazine article by John L. O'Sullivan (**July–August**). It expresses the belief held by many white Americans that the United States is destined to expand across the continent.

1846 Oregon Treaty fixes U.S.-Canadian border at 49th parallel; U.S. acquires Oregon territory (**June 15**). The Wilmot Proviso attempts to ban slavery in territory gained in the Mexican War. The proviso is blocked by Southerners, but continues to enflame the debate over slavery.

1846–1848 Mexican War: U.S. declares war on Mexico in effort to gain California and other territory in Southwest (**May 13, 1846**). War concludes with signing of Treaty of Guadalupe Hidalgo (**Feb. 2, 1848**). Mexico recognizes Rio Grande as new boundary with Texas and, for $15 million, agrees to cede territory comprising present-day California, Nevada, Utah, most of New Mexico and Arizona, and parts of Colorado and Wyoming.

1848 Gold is discovered at Sutter's Mill in California (**Jan. 24**); gold rush reaches its height the following year. Women's rights convention is held at Seneca Falls, N.Y. (**July 19–20**).

1849 Zachary Taylor is inaugurated as the 12th president (**March 5**).

1850 President Taylor dies (**July 9**) and is succeeded by his vice president, Millard Fillmore. The continuing debate whether territory gained in the Mexican War should be open to slavery is decided in the Compromise of 1850.

1853 Franklin Pierce is inaugurated as the 14th president (**March 4**). Gadsden Purchase treaty is signed; U.S. acquires border territory from Mexico for $10 million (**Dec. 30**).

1854 Congress passes the Kansas-Nebraska Act, establishing the territories of Kansas and Nebraska (**May 30**). The legislation repeals the Missouri Compromise of 1820 and renews tensions between anti- and proslavery factions.

1857 James Buchanan is inaugurated as the 15th president (**March 4**).

1858 Abraham Lincoln comes to national attention in a series of seven debates with Sen. Stephen A. Douglas during Illinois state election campaign (**Aug.–Oct.**).

1859 Abolitionist John Brown and 21 followers capture federal arsenal at Harpers Ferry, Va. (now W. Va.), in an attempt to spark a slave revolt (**Oct. 16**).

1860 Abraham Lincoln is elected president (**Nov. 6**). South Carolina secedes from the Union (**Dec. 20**).

1861 Mississippi, Florida, Alabama, Georgia, and Louisiana secede (**Jan.**). Confederate States of America is established (**Feb. 8**). Jefferson Davis is elected president of the Confederacy (**Feb. 9**). Texas secedes (**March 2**). Abraham Lincoln is inaugurated as the 16th president (**March 4**).

1861–1865 Civil War: Conflict between the North (the Union) and the South (the Confederacy) over the expansion of slavery into western states. Confederates attack Ft. Sumter in Charleston, S.C., marking the start of the war (**April 12, 1861**). Virginia, Arkansas, North Carolina, and Tennessee secede (**April–June**). Emancipation Proclamation is issued, freeing slaves in the Confederate states (**Jan. 1, 1863**). Gen. William T. Sherman captures Atlanta (**Sept. 2, 1864**). Lincoln's second inauguration (**March 4, 1865**). Gen. Ulysses S. Grant captures Richmond, Va., the capital of the Confederacy (**April 3**). Confederate general Robert E. Lee surrenders to Ulysses S. Grant at Appomattox Courthouse, Va., (**April 9**).

1863 Homestead Act becomes law, allowing settlers to claim land (160 acres) after they have lived on it for five years (**Jan. 1**).

1865 Lincoln is assassinated (**April 14**) by John Wilkes Booth in Washington, DC, and is succeeded by his vice president, Andrew Johnson. Thirteenth Amendment to the Constitution is ratified, prohibiting slavery (**Dec. 6**).

1867 U.S. acquires Alaska from Russia for the sum of $7.2 million (treaty concluded **March 30**).

1868 President Johnson is impeached by the House of Representatives (**Feb. 24**), but he is acquitted at his trial in the Senate (**May 26**). Fourteenth Amendment to the Constitution is ratified, defining citizenship (**July 9**).

1869 Ulysses S. Grant is inaugurated as the 18th president (**March 4**). Central Pacific and Union Pacific railroads are joined at Promontory, Utah, creating first transcontinental railroad (**May 10**).

1870 Fifteenth Amendment to the Constitution is ratified, giving blacks the right to vote (**Feb. 3**).

1871 Chicago fire kills 300 and leaves 90,000 people homeless (**Oct. 8–9**).

1872 Crédit Mobilier scandal breaks, involving several members of Congress (**Sept.**).

1873 Grant's second inauguration (**March 4**).

1876 Lt. Col. George A. Custer's regiment is wiped out by Sioux Indians under Sitting Bull at the Little Big Horn River, Mont. (**June 25**).

1877 Rutherford B. Hayes is inaugurated as the 19th president (**March 5**). The first telephone line is built from Boston to Somerville, Mass.; the following year, President Hayes has the first telephone installed in the White House.

1881 James A. Garfield is inaugurated as the 20th president (**March 4**). He is shot (**July 2**) by Charles Guiteau in Washington, DC, and later dies from complications of his wounds in Elberon, N.J. (**Sept. 19**). Garfield's vice president, Chester Alan Arthur, succeeds him in office.

1882 U.S. adopts standard time (**Nov. 18**).

1885 Grover Cleveland is inaugurated as the 22nd president (**March 4**).

1886 Statue of Liberty is dedicated (**Oct. 28**). American Federation of Labor is organized (**Dec.**).

1889 Benjamin Harrison is inaugurated as the 23rd president (**March 4**). Oklahoma is opened to settlers (**April 22**).

1890 National American Woman Suffrage Association (NAWSA) is founded, with Elizabeth Cady Stanton as president. Sherman Antitrust Act is signed into law, prohibiting commercial monopolies (**July 2**). Last major battle of the Indian Wars occurs at Wounded Knee, S.D. (**Dec. 29**). In reporting the results of the 1890 census, the Census Bureau announces that the West has been settled and the frontier is closed.

1892 Ellis Island becomes chief immigration station of the U.S. (**Jan. 1**).

1893 Grover Cleveland is inaugurated a second time, as the 24th president (**March 4**). He is the only president to serve two nonconsecutive terms.

1897 William McKinley is inaugurated as the 25th president (**March 4**).

1898 Spanish-American War: USS *Maine* is blown up in Havana harbor (**Feb. 15**), prompting U.S. to declare war on Spain (**April 25**). Treaty of Paris is signed, ending the Spanish-American War (**Dec. 10**); Spain gives up control of Cuba, which becomes an independent republic, and cedes Puerto Rico, Guam, and (for $20 million) the Philippines to the U.S.

1898 U.S. annexes Hawaii by an act of Congress (**July 7**).

1899 U.S. acquires American Samoa by treaty with Great Britain and Germany (**Dec. 2**).

1900 Galveston hurricane leaves an estimated 6,000 to 8,000 dead (**Sept. 8**). According to the census, the nation's population numbers nearly 76 million.

1901 McKinley's second inauguration (**March 4**). He is shot (**Sept. 6**) by anarchist Leon Czolgosz in Buffalo, N.Y., and later dies from his wounds (**Sept. 14**). He is succeeded by his vice president, Theodore Roosevelt.

1903 U.S. acquires Panama Canal Zone (treaty signed **Nov. 17**). Wright brothers make the first controlled, sustained flight in heavier-than-air aircraft at Kitty Hawk, N.C. (**Dec. 17**).

1905 Theodore Roosevelt's second inauguration (**March 4**).

1906 San Francisco earthquake leaves 500 dead or missing and destroys about 4 sq mi of the city (**April 18**).

1908 Bureau of Investigation, forerunner of the FBI, is established (**July 26**).

1909 William Howard Taft is inaugurated as the 27th president (**March 4**).

1913 Woodrow Wilson is inaugurated as the 28th president (**March 4**). Seventeenth Amendment to the Constitution is ratified, providing for the direct election of U.S. senators by popular vote rather than by the state legislatures (**April 8**).

1914–1918 World War I: U.S. enters World War I, declaring war on Germany (**April 6, 1917**) and Austria-Hungary (**Dec. 7, 1917**) three years after conflict began in 1914. Armistice ending World War I is signed (**Nov. 11, 1918**).

1914 Panama Canal opens to traffic (**Aug. 15**).

1915 First long distance telephone service, between New York and San Francisco, is demonstrated (**Jan. 25**).

1916 U.S. agrees to purchase Danish West Indies (Virgin Islands) for $25 million (treaty signed **Aug. 14**). Jeannette Rankin of Montana is the first woman elected to the U.S. House of Representatives (**Nov. 7**).

1917 Wilson's second inauguration (**March 5**). First regular airmail service begins between Washington, DC, and New York (**May 15**).

1918 Worldwide influenza epidemic strikes; by 1920, nearly 20 million are dead. In U.S., 500,000 perish.

1919 League of Nations meets for the first time; U.S. is not represented (**Jan. 13**). Eighteenth Amendment to the Constitution is ratified, prohibiting the manufacture, sale, and transportation of liquor (**Jan. 16**). It is later repealed by the Twenty-First Amendment in 1933. Nineteenth Amendment to the Constitution is ratified, granting women the right to vote (**Aug. 18**). President Wilson suffers a stroke (**Sept. 26**). Treaty of Versailles, outlining terms for peace at the end of World War I, is rejected by the Senate (**Nov. 19**).

1921 Warren G. Harding is inaugurated as the 29th president (**March 4**). He signs resolution declaring peace with Austria and Germany (**July 2**).

1923 President Harding dies suddenly (**Aug. 2**). He is succeeded by his vice president, Calvin Coolidge. Teapot Dome scandal breaks, as Senate launches an investigation into improper leasing of naval oil reserves during Harding administration (**Oct.**)

1925 Coolidge's second inauguration (**March 4**). Tennessee passes a law against the teaching of evolution in public schools (**March 23**), setting the stage for the Scopes Monkey Trial (**July 10–25**).

1927 Charles Lindbergh makes the first solo nonstop transatlantic flight in his plane *The Spirit of St. Louis* (**May 20–21**).

1929 Herbert Hoover is inaugurated as the 31st president (**March 4**). Stock market crash precipitates the Great Depression (**Oct. 29**).

1931 *The Star-Spangled Banner* is adopted as the national anthem (**March 3**).

1932 Hattie Wyatt Caraway of Arkansas is the first woman elected to the U.S. Senate, to fill a vacancy caused by the death of her husband (**Jan. 12**). She is reelected in 1932 and 1938. Amelia Earhart completes first solo nonstop transatlantic flight by a woman (**May 21**).

1933 Twentieth Amendment to the Constitution, sometimes called the "Lame Duck Amendment," is ratified, moving the president's inauguration date from March 4 to Jan. 20 (**Jan. 23**). Franklin Roosevelt is inaugurated as the 32nd president (**March 4**). New Deal recovery measures are enacted by Congress (**March 9–June 16**). Twenty-First Amendment to the Constitution is ratified, repealing Prohibition (**Dec. 5**).

1935 Works Progress Administration is established (**April 8**). Social Security Act is passed (**Aug. 14**). Bureau of Investigation (established 1908) becomes the Federal Bureau of Investigation under J. Edgar Hoover.

1937 F. Roosevelt's second inauguration (**Jan. 20**).

1938 Fair Labor Standards Act is passed, setting the first minimum wage in the U.S. at 25 cents per hour (**June 25**).

1939–1945 World War II: U.S. declares its neutrality in European conflict (**Sept. 5, 1939**). F. Roosevelt's third inauguration (**Jan. 20, 1941**). He is the first and only president elected to a third term. Japan attacks Hawaii, Guam, and the Philippines (**Dec. 7, 1941**). U.S. declares war on Japan (**Dec. 8**). Germany and Italy declare war on the United States; U.S. reciprocates by declaring war on both countries (**Dec. 11**). Allies invade North Africa (**Oct.–Dec. 1942**) and Italy (**Sept.–Dec. 1943**). Allies invade France on D-Day (**June 6, 1944**). F. Roosevelt's fourth inauguration (**Jan. 20, 1945**). President Roosevelt, Churchill, and Stalin meet at Yalta in the USSR to discuss postwar occupation of Germany (**Feb. 4–11**). President Roosevelt dies of a stroke (**April 12**) and is succeeded by his vice president, Harry Truman. Germany surrenders unconditionally (**May 7**). First atomic bomb is detonated at Alamogordo, N.M. (**July 16**). President Truman, Churchill, and Stalin meet at Potsdam, near Berlin, Germany, to demand Japan's unconditional surrender and to discuss plans for postwar Europe (**July 17–Aug. 2**). U.S. drops atomic bomb on Hiroshima, Japan (**Aug. 6**). U.S. drops atomic bomb on Nagasaki, Japan (**Aug. 9**). Japan agrees to unconditional surrender (**Aug. 14**). Japanese envoys sign surrender terms aboard the USS *Missouri* in Tokyo harbor (**Sept. 2**).

1945 United Nations is established (**Oct. 24**).

1946 The Philippines, which had been ceded to the U.S. by Spain at the end of the Spanish-American War, becomes an independent republic (**July 4**).

1947 Central Intelligence Agency is established.

1948 Congress passes foreign aid bill including the Marshall Plan, which provides for European postwar recovery (**April 2**). Soviets begin blockade of Berlin in the first major crisis of the cold war (**June 24**). In response, U.S. and Great Britain begin airlift of food and fuel to West Berlin (**June 26**).

1949 Truman's second inauguration (**Jan. 20**). North Atlantic Treaty Organization (NATO) is established (**April 4**). Soviets end blockade of Berlin (**May 12**), but airlift continues until Sept. 30.

1950–1953 Korean War: Cold war conflict between Communist and non-Communist forces on Korean Peninsula. North Korean communists invade South Korea (**June 25, 1950**). President Truman, without the approval of Congress, commits American troops to battle (**June 27**). Armistice agreement is signed (**July 27, 1953**).

1950–1975 Vietnam War: Prolonged conflict between Communist forces of North Vietnam, backed by China and the USSR, and non-Communist forces of South Vietnam, backed by the United States. President Truman authorizes $15 million in economic and military aid to the French, who are fighting to retain control of French Indochina, including Vietnam. As part of the aid package, Truman also sends 35 military advisers (**May 1950**). North Vietnamese torpedo boats allegedly attack U.S. destroyer in Gulf of Tonkin off the coast of North Vietnam (**Aug. 2, 1964**). Congress approves Gulf of Tonkin resolution, authorizing President Johnson to take any measures necessary to defend U.S. forces and prevent further aggression (**Aug. 7**). U.S. planes begin bombing raids of

North Vietnam **(Feb. 1965)**. First U.S. combat troops arrive in South Vietnam **(March 8–9)**. North Vietnamese army and Viet Cong launch Tet Offensive, attacking Saigon and other key cities in South Vietnam **(Jan.–Feb. 1968)**. American soldiers kill 300 Vietnamese villagers in My Lai massacre **(March 16)**. U.S. troops invade Cambodia **(May 1, 1970)**. Representatives of North and South Vietnam, the Viet Cong, and the U.S. sign a cease-fire agreement in Paris **(Jan. 27, 1973)**. Last U.S. troops leave Vietnam **(March 29)**. South Vietnamese government surrenders to North Vietnam; U.S. embassy Marine guards and last U.S. civilians are evacuated **(April 30, 1975)**.

1951 Twenty-Second Amendment to the Constitution is ratified, limiting the president to two terms **(Feb. 27)**. President Truman speaks in first coast-to-coast live television broadcast **(Sept. 4)**.

1952 Puerto Rico becomes a U.S. commonwealth **(July 25)**. First hydrogen bomb is detonated by the U.S. on Eniwetok, an atoll in the Marshall Islands **(Nov. 1)**.

1953 Dwight Eisenhower is inaugurated as the 34th president **(Jan. 20)**. Julius and Ethel Rosenberg are executed for passing secret information about U.S. atomic weaponry to the Soviets **(June 19)**.

1954 Sen. Joseph R. McCarthy accuses army officials, members of the media, and other public figures of being Communists during highly publicized hearings **(April 22–June 17)**.

1957 Eisenhower's second inauguration **(Jan. 21)**. President sends federal troops to Central High School in Little Rock, Ark., to enforce integration of black students **(Sept. 24)**.

1958 *Explorer I*, first American satellite, is launched **(Jan. 31)**.

1959 Alaska becomes the 49th state **(Jan. 3)** and Hawaii becomes the 50th **(Aug. 21)**.

1961 U.S. severs diplomatic relations with Cuba **(Jan. 3)**. John F. Kennedy is inaugurated as the 35th president **(Jan. 20)**. Bay of Pigs invasion of Cuba fails **(April 17–20)**. A mixed-race group of volunteers sponsored by the Committee on Racial Equality—the so-called Freedom Riders—travel on buses through the South in order to protest racially segregated interstate bus facilities **(May)**.

1962 Lt. Col. John Glenn becomes first U.S. astronaut to orbit Earth **(Feb. 20)**. Cuban Missile Crisis: President Kennedy denounces Soviet Union for secretly installing missile bases on Cuba and initiates a naval blockade of the island **(Oct. 22–Nov. 20)**.

1963 Rev. Martin Luther King, Jr., delivers his "I Have a Dream" speech before a crowd of 200,000 during the civil rights march on Washington, DC **(Aug. 28)**. President Kennedy is assassinated in Dallas, Tex. **(Nov. 22)**. He is succeeded in office by his vice president, Lyndon B. Johnson.

1964 President Johnson signs the Civil Rights Act **(July 2)**.

1965 In his annual state of the Union address, President Johnson proposes his Great Society program **(Jan. 4)**. L. Johnson's second inauguration **(Jan. 20)**. State troopers attack peaceful demonstrators led by Rev. Martin Luther King, Jr., as they try to cross bridge in Selma, Ala. **(March 7)**. President Johnson signs the Voting Rights Act, which prohibits discriminatory voting practices **(Aug. 6)**. In six days of rioting in Watts, a black section of Los Angeles, 35 people are killed and 883 injured **(Aug. 11–16)**.

1967 Twenty-Fifth Amendment to the Constitution is ratified, outlining the procedures for filling vacancies in the presidency and vice presidency **(Feb. 10)**.

1968 Rev. Martin Luther King, Jr., is assassinated in Memphis, Tenn. **(April 4)**. Sen. Robert F. Kennedy is assassinated in Los Angeles, Calif. **(June 5–6)**.

1969 Richard Nixon is inaugurated as the 37th president **(Jan. 20)**. Astronauts Neil Armstrong and Edwin Aldrin, Jr., become the first men to land on the Moon **(July 20)**.

1970 Four students are shot to death by National Guardsmen during an antiwar protest at Kent State University **(May 1)**.

1971 The Twenty-Sixth Amendment to the Constitution is ratified, lowering the voting age from 21 to 18 **(July 1)**.

1972 Nixon makes historic visit to Communist China **(Feb. 21–27)**. U.S. and Soviet Union sign strategic arms control agreement known as SALT I **(May 26)**. Five men, all employees of Nixon's reelection campaign, are caught breaking into rival Democratic headquarters at the Watergate complex in Washington, DC **(June 17)**.

1973 Nixon's second inauguration **(Jan. 20)**. Senate Select Committee begins televised hearings to investigate Watergate cover-up **(May 17–Aug. 7)**. Vice President Spiro T. Agnew resigns over charges of corruption and income tax evasion **(Oct. 10)**. President Nixon nominates Gerald R. Ford as vice president **(Oct. 12)**. Ford is confirmed by Congress and sworn in **(Dec. 6)**.

1974 House Judiciary Committee recommends to full House that Nixon be impeached on grounds of obstruction of justice, abuse of power, and contempt of Congress **(July 27–30)**. Nixon resigns; he is succeeded in office by his vice president, Gerald Ford **(Aug. 9)**. Nixon is granted an unconditional pardon by President Ford **(Sept. 8)**. Five former Nixon aides go on trial for their involvement in the Watergate cover-up **(Oct. 15)**; H. R. Haldeman, John D. Ehrlichman, and John Mitchell eventually serve time in prison. Nelson Rockefeller is confirmed and sworn in as vice president **(Dec. 19)**.

1977 Jimmy Carter is inaugurated as the 39th president **(Jan. 20)**. President Carter signs treaty **(Sept. 7)** agreeing to turn control of Panama Canal over to Panama on Dec. 31, 1999.

1978 President Carter meets with Egyptian president Anwar Sadat and Israeli prime minister Menachem Begin at Camp David **(Sept. 6)**; Sadat and Begin sign Camp David Accord, ending 30-year conflict between Egypt and Israel **(Sept. 17)**.

1979 U.S. establishes diplomatic ties with mainland China for the first time since Communist takeover in 1949 **(Jan. 1)**. Malfunction at Three Mile Island nuclear reactor in Pennsylvania causes near meltdown **(March 28)**. Panama takes control of the Canal Zone, formerly administered by U.S. **(Oct. 1)**. Iranian students storm U.S. embassy in Teheran and hold 66 people hostage **(Nov. 4)**; 13 of the hostages are released **(Nov. 19–20)**.

1980 President Carter announces that U.S. athletes will not attend Summer Olympics in Moscow unless Soviet Union withdraws from Afghanistan **(Jan. 20)**. FBI's undercover bribery investigation, code named Abscam, implicates a U.S. senator, seven members of the House, and 31 other public officials **(Feb. 2)**. U.S. mission to rescue hostages in Iran is aborted after a helicopter and cargo plane collide at the staging site in a remote part of Iran and 8 servicemen are killed **(April 25)**.

1981 Ronald Reagan is inaugurated as the 40th president **(Jan. 20)**. U.S. hostages held in Iran are released after 444 days in captivity **(Jan. 20)**. President Reagan is shot in the chest by John Hinckley, Jr. **(March 30)**. Sandra Day O'Connor is sworn in as the first woman Supreme Court justice **(Sept. 25)**.

1982 Deadline for ratification of the Equal Rights Amendment to the Constitution passes without the necessary votes **(June 30)**.

1983 U.S. invades Caribbean island of Grenada after a coup by Marxist faction in the government **(Oct. 25)**.

1985 Reagan's second inauguration **(Jan. 21)**.

1986 Space shuttle *Challenger* explodes 73 seconds after liftoff, killing all seven crew members **(Jan. 28)**. It is the worst accident in the history of the U.S. space program. U.S. bombs military bases in Libya in effort to deter terrorist strikes on American targets **(April 14)**. Iran-Contra scandal breaks when White House is forced to reveal secret arms-for-hostages deals **(Nov.)**.

1987 Congress holds public hearings in Iran-Contra investigation **(May 5–Aug. 3)**. In a speech in Berlin, President Reagan challenges Soviet leader Mikhail Gorbachev to "tear down this wall" and open Eastern Europe to political and economic reform **(June 12)**. Reagan and Gorbachev sign INF treaty, the first arms-control agreement to reduce the superpowers' nuclear weapons **(Dec. 8)**.

1989 George H. W. Bush is inaugurated as the 41st president **(Jan. 20)**. Oil tanker *Exxon Valdez* runs aground in Prince William Sound, spilling more than 10 million gallons of oil **(March 24)**. It is the largest oil spill in U.S. history. President Bush signs legislation to provide for federal bailout of nearly 800 insolvent savings and loan institutions **(Aug. 9)**. U.S. forces invade Panama in an attempt to capture Gen. Manuel Noriega, who previously had been indicted in the U.S. on drug trafficking charges **(Dec. 20)**.

1991 Persian Gulf War: U.S. leads international coalition in military operation (code named "Desert Storm") to drive Iraqis out of Kuwait **(Jan. 16–Feb. 28)**. Iraq accepts terms of UN ceasefire, marking an end of the war **(April 6)**.

1991 U.S. and Soviet Union sign START I treaty, agreeing to further reduce strategic nuclear arms **(July 31)**. Senate Judiciary Committee conducts televised hearings to investigate allegations of past sexual harassment brought against Supreme Court nominee Clarence Thomas by Anita Hill, a law professor at the University of Oklahoma **(Oct. 11–13)**.

1992 Following the breakup of the Soviet Union in Dec. 1991, President Bush and Russian president Boris Yeltsin meet at Camp David and formally declare an end to the cold war **(Feb. 1)**. The acquittal of four white police officers charged in the 1991 beating of black motorist Rodney King in Los Angeles sets off several days of rioting, leading to more than 50 deaths, thousands of injuries and arrests, and $1 billion in property damage **(April 29)**. President Bush authorizes sending U.S. troops to Somalia as part of UN relief effort **(Dec. 4)**. President Bush grants pardons to six officials convicted or indicted in the Iran-Contra scandal, leading some to suspect a cover-up **(Dec. 24)**.

1993 Bill Clinton is inaugurated as the 42nd president **(Jan. 20)**. Bomb explodes in basement garage of World Trade Center, killing 6, injuring 1,000, and causing more than $500 million in damage **(Feb. 26)**. After 51-day standoff with federal agents, Branch Davidian compound in Waco, Tex., burns to the ground, killing 80 cult members **(April 19)**. President Clinton orders missile attack against Iraq in retaliation for alleged plot to assassinate former President Bush **(June 26)**. Eighteen U.S. soldiers are killed in ambush by Somali militiamen in Mogadishu **(Oct. 3–4)**. President Clinton signs North American Free Trade Agreement into law **(Dec. 8)**.

1994 Paula Jones, a former Arkansas state employee, files a federal lawsuit against President Clinton for sexual harassment **(May 6)**.

1995 Bombing of federal office building in Oklahoma City kills 168 people **(April 19)**. U.S. establishes full diplomatic relations with Vietnam **(July 11)**. President Clinton sends first 8,000 of 20,000 U.S. troops to Bosnia for 12-month peacekeeping mission **(Dec.)**. Budget standoff between President Clinton and Congress results in partial shutdown of U.S. government **(Dec. 16–Jan. 6)**.

1997 Clinton's second inauguration **(Jan. 20)**.

1998 President Clinton denies having had a sexual relationship with a White House intern named Monica Lewinsky **(Jan. 17)**. President Clinton releases 1999 federal budget plan; it is the first balanced budget since 1969 **(Feb. 2)**. In televised address, President Clinton admits having had a sexual relationship with Monica Lewinsky **(Aug. 17)**. U.S. launches missile attacks on targets in Sudan and Afghanistan following terrorist attacks on U.S. embassies in Kenya and Tanzania **(Aug. 20)**. U.S. and Britain launch air strikes against weapons sites in Iraq **(Dec. 16)**. House of Representatives votes to impeach President Clinton on charges of perjury and obstruction of justice **(Dec. 19)**.

1999 Senate acquits Clinton of impeachment charges **(Feb. 12)**. NATO wages air campaign against Yugoslavia over killing and deportation of ethnic Albanians in Kosovo **(March 24–June 10)**. School shooting at Columbine High School in Littleton, Colo., leaves 14 students (including the 2 shooters) and 1 teacher dead and 23 others wounded **(April 20)**.

2000 According to the census, the nation's population numbers more than 280 million **(April 1)**. No clear winner is declared in the close presidential election contest between Vice President

Al Gore and Texas governor George W. Bush (**Nov. 7**). More than a month after the presidential election, the U.S. Supreme Court rules against a manual recount of ballots in certain Florida counties, which it contends would violate the Constitution's equal protection and due process guarantees. The decision provokes enormous controversy, with critics maintaining that the court has in effect determined the outcome of the election (**Dec. 12**). Bush formally accepts the presidency, having won a slim majority in the electoral college but not a majority of the popular vote (**Dec. 13**).

2001   George W. Bush is inaugurated as the 43rd president (**Jan. 20**). Two hijacked jetliners ram twin towers of World Trade Center in worst terrorist attack against U.S.; a third hijacked plane flies into the Pentagon, and a fourth crashes in rural Pennsylvania. More than 3,000 people die in the attacks (**Sept. 11**). U.S. and Britain launch air attacks against targets in Afghanistan after Taliban government fails to hand over Saudi terrorist Osama bin Laden, the suspected mastermind behind the Sept. 11 attacks (**Oct. 7**). Following air campaign and ground assault by Afghani opposition troops,

the Taliban regime topples (**Dec. 9**); however, the hunt for bin Laden and other members of al-Qaeda terrorist organization continues.

2002   In his first State of the Union address, President Bush labels Iran, Iraq, and North Korea an "axis of evil" and declares that U.S. will wage war against states that develop weapons of mass destruction (**Jan. 29**). President Bush signs legislation creating a new cabinet department of Homeland Security. (**Nov. 25**).

2003   Space shuttle *Columbia* explodes upon reentry into Earth's atmosphere, killing all seven astronauts on board (**Feb. 1**). War waged by the U.S. and Britain against Iraq begins (**March 19**). President Bush signs $350 billion tax-cut bill (**May 28**).

2004   The U.S. returns sovereignty to an interim government in Iraq, but maintains roughly 135,000 troops in the country to fight a growing insurgency (**June 28**). Four hurricanes devastate Florida and other parts of the southern United States (**Aug. and Sept.**).

See What Happened in 2004: Month-by-Month, National News, pp. 35–42.

Firsts in America

This selection is based on our editorial judgment. Other sources may list different firsts.

Admiral in U.S. Navy: David Glasgow Farragut, 1866.

Airmail route, first transcontinental: Between New York City and San Francisco, 1920.

Assembly, representative: House of Burgesses, founded in Virginia, 1619.

Bank established: Bank of North America, Philadelphia, 1781.

Birth in America to English parents: Virginia Dare, born Roanoke Island, N.C., 1587.

Black newspaper: *Freedom's Journal,* 1827, edited by John B. Russworm.

Black U.S. diplomat: Ebenezer D. Bassett, 1869, minister-resident to Haiti.

Black elected governor of a state: L. Douglas Wilder, Virginia, 1990.

Black elected to U.S. Senate: Hiram Revels, 1870, Mississippi.

Black elected to U.S. House of Representatives: Jefferson Long, Georgia, 1870.

Black associate justice of U.S. Supreme Court: Thurgood Marshall, Oct. 2, 1967.

Black secretary of state: Gen. Colin Powell, appointed Dec. 2000.

Black U.S. cabinet minister: Robert C. Weaver, 1966, Secretary of the Department of Housing and Urban Development.

Botanic garden: Established by John Bartram in Philadelphia, 1728, and is still in existence in its original location.

College: Harvard, founded 1636.

College to establish coeducation: Oberlin College (Ohio), 1833.

Electrocution of a criminal: William Kemmler in Auburn Prison, Auburn, N.Y., Aug. 6, 1890.

Five and Dime store: Founded by Frank Woolworth, Utica, N.Y., 1879 (moved to Lancaster, Pa., same year).

Fraternity, Greek-letter: Phi Beta Kappa; founded Dec. 5, 1776, at College of William and Mary.

Gay and lesbian civil rights advocacy organization, national: National Gay and Lesbian Task Force, founded in New York City, 1973.

Lesbian, acknowledged, elected to high local office: Kathy Kozachenko, 1974, Ann Arbor City Council.

Gay man, acknowledged, elected to high local office: Harvey Milk, 1977, San Francisco Board of Supervisors.

Law to be declared unconstitutional by U.S. Supreme Court: Judiciary Act of 1789. Case: *Marbury* v. *Madison*, 1803.

Library, circulating: Philadelphia, 1731.

Newspaper, illustrated daily: *New York Daily Graphic,* 1873.

Newspaper published daily: *Pennsylvania Packet and General Advertiser,* Philadelphia, Sept. 1784.

Newspaper published over a continuous period: *The Boston News-Letter,* April 1704.

Oil well, commercial: Titusville, Pa., 1859.

Panel quiz show on radio: *Information Please,* May 17, 1938.

Postage stamps issued: 1847.

Public school: Boston Latin School, Boston, 1635.

Radio station licensed: KDKA, Pittsburgh, Pa., Oct. 27, 1920.

Railroad, transcontinental: Central Pacific and Union Pacific railroads, joined at Promontory, Utah, May 10, 1869.

Savings bank: The Provident Institute for Savings, Boston, 1816.

Science museum: Founded by Charleston (S.C.) Library Society, 1773.

Skyscraper: Home Insurance Co., Chicago, 1885 (10 floors, 2 added later).

Slaves brought into America: At Jamestown, Va., 1619, from a Dutch ship.

Sorority: Alpha Delta Pi, at Wesleyan Female College, 1851.

State to abolish capital punishment: Michigan, 1847.

State to enter Union after original 13: Vermont, 1791.

Steam-heated building: Eastern Hotel, Boston, 1845.

Steam railroad (carried passengers and freight): Baltimore & Ohio, 1830.

Strike on record by union: Journeymen Printers, New York City, 1776.

Subway: Opened in Boston, 1897.

"Tabloid" picture newspaper: *The Illustrated Daily News* (now *The Daily News*), New York City, 1919.

Vaudeville theater: Gaiety Museum, Boston, 1883.

Woman astronaut appointed shuttle commander: Lt. Col. Eileen Collins, *Columbia,* launched July 1999.

Woman astronaut to ride in space: Dr. Sally K. Ride, 1983.

Woman astronaut to walk in space: Dr. Kathryn D. Sullivan, 1984.

Woman cabinet member: Frances Perkins, Secretary of Labor, 1933.

Woman candidate for president: Victoria Claflin Woodhull, nominated by National Woman's Suffrage Assn. on ticket of Nation Radical Reformers, 1872.

Woman candidate for vice president: Geraldine A. Ferraro, nominated on a major party ticket, Democratic Party, 1984.

Woman doctor of medicine: Elizabeth Blackwell; M.D. from Geneva Medical College of Western New York, 1849.

Woman elected governor of a state: Nellie Tayloe Ross, Wyoming, 1925.

Woman elected to U.S. Senate: Hattie Caraway, Arkansas; elected Nov. 1932.

Woman graduate of law school: Ada H. Kepley, Union College of Law, Chicago, 1870.

Woman member of U.S. House of Representatives: Jeannette Rankin (Mont.); elected Nov. 1916.

Woman member of U.S. Senate: Rebecca Latimer Felton (Ga.); appointed Oct. 3, 1922.

Woman member of U.S. Supreme Court: Sandra Day O'Connor; appointed July 1981.

Woman secretary of state: Madeleine Albright, appointed Dec. 1996.

Woman suffrage granted: Wyoming Territory, 1869.

Written constitution: *Fundamental Orders of Connecticut,* 1639.

The Early Congresses

At the urging of Massachusetts and Virginia, the First Continental Congress met in Philadelphia on Sept. 5, 1774, and was attended by representatives of all the colonies except Georgia. Patrick Henry of Virginia declared: "The distinctions between Pennsylvanians, New Yorkers, and New Englanders are no more. I am not a Virginian but an American." This Congress, which adjourned Oct. 26, 1774, passed intercolonial resolutions calling for extensive boycott by the colonies against British trade.

The following year, most of the delegates from the colonies were chosen by popular election to attend the Second Continental Congress, which assembled in Philadelphia on May 10. As war had already begun between the colonies and England, the chief problems before the Congress were the procuring of military supplies, the establishment of an army and proper defenses, the issuing of continental bills of credit, etc. On June 15, 1775, George Washington was elected to command the Continental army. Congress adjourned Dec. 12, 1776.

Other Continental Congresses were held in Baltimore (1776–1777), Philadelphia (1777), Lancaster, Pa. (1777), York, Pa. (1777–1778), and Philadelphia (1778–1781).

In 1781, the Articles of Confederation, although establishing a league of the thirteen states rather than a strong central government, provided for the continuance of Congress. Known thereafter as the Congress of the Confederation, it held sessions in Philadelphia (1781–1783), Princeton, N.J. (1783), Annapolis, Md. (1783–1784), and Trenton, N.J. (1784). Five sessions were held in New York City between the years 1785 and 1789.

The Congress of the United States, established by the ratification of the Constitution, held its first meeting on March 4, 1789, in New York City. Several sessions of Congress were held in Philadelphia, and the first meeting in Washington, DC, was on Nov. 17, 1800.

Presidents of the Continental Congresses

Name	Elected	Birth and death dates	Name	Elected	Birth and death dates
Peyton Randolph, Va.	9/5/1774	c.1721–1775	John Hanson, Md.	11/5/1781	1715–1783
Henry Middleton, S.C.	10/22/1774	1717–1784	Elias Boudinot, N.J.	11/4/1782	1740–1821
Peyton Randolph, Va.	5/10/1775	c.1721–1775	Thomas Mifflin, Pa.	11/3/1783	1744–1800
John Hancock, Mass.	5/24/1775	1737–1793	Richard Henry Lee, Va.	11/30/1784	1732–1794
Henry Laurens, S.C.	11/1/1777	1724–1792	John Hancock, Mass.[1]	11/23/1785	1737–1793
John Jay, N.Y.	12/10/1778	1745–1829	Nathaniel Gorham, Mass.	6/6/1786	1738–1796
Samuel Huntington, Conn.	9/28/1779	1731–1796	Arthur St. Clair, Pa.	2/2/1787	1734–1818
Thomas McKean, Del.	7/10/1781	1734–1817	Cyrus Griffin, Va.	1/22/1788	1748–1810

1. Resigned May 29, 1786, never having served, because of continued illness.

States by Order of Entry into Union

State	Entered Union	Year settled	State	Entered Union	Year settled
1. Delaware	Dec. 7, 1787	1638	26. Michigan	Jan. 26, 1837	1668
2. Pennsylvania	Dec. 12, 1787	1682	27. Florida	Mar. 3, 1845	1565
3. New Jersey	Dec. 18, 1787	1660	28. Texas	Dec. 29, 1845	1682
4. Georgia	Jan. 2, 1788	1733	29. Iowa	Dec. 28, 1846	1788
5. Connecticut	Jan. 9, 1788	1634	30. Wisconsin	May 29, 1848	1766
6. Massachusetts	Feb. 6, 1788	1620	31. California	Sept. 9, 1850	1769
7. Maryland	Apr. 28, 1788	1634	32. Minnesota	May 11, 1858	1805
8. South Carolina	May 23, 1788	1670	33. Oregon	Feb. 14, 1859	1811
9. New Hampshire	June 21, 1788	1623	34. Kansas	Jan. 29, 1861	1727
10. Virginia	June 25, 1788	1607	35. West Virginia	June 20, 1863	1727
11. New York	July 26, 1788	1614	36. Nevada	Oct. 31, 1864	1849
12. North Carolina	Nov. 21, 1789	1660	37. Nebraska	Mar. 1, 1867	1823
13. Rhode Island	May 29, 1790	1636	38. Colorado	Aug. 1, 1876	1858
14. Vermont	Mar. 4, 1791	1724	39. North Dakota	Nov. 2, 1889	1812
15. Kentucky	June 1, 1792	1774	40. South Dakota	Nov. 2, 1889	1859
16. Tennessee	June 1, 1796	1769	41. Montana	Nov. 8, 1889	1809
17. Ohio	Mar. 1, 1803	1788	42. Washington	Nov. 11, 1889	1811
18. Louisiana	Apr. 30, 1812	1699	43. Idaho	July 3, 1890	1842
19. Indiana	Dec. 11, 1816	1733	44. Wyoming	July 10, 1890	1834
20. Mississippi	Dec. 10, 1817	1699	45. Utah	Jan. 4, 1896	1847
21. Illinois	Dec. 3, 1818	1720	46. Oklahoma	Nov. 16, 1907	1889
22. Alabama	Dec. 14, 1819	1702	47. New Mexico	Jan. 6, 1912	1610
23. Maine	Mar. 15, 1820	1624	48. Arizona	Feb. 14, 1912	1776
24. Missouri	Aug. 10, 1821	1735	49. Alaska	Jan. 3, 1959	1784
25. Arkansas	June 15, 1836	1686	50. Hawaii	Aug. 21, 1959	1820

Source: Compiled from various sources by the editors.

The Confederate States of America

	State	Seceded from Union	Readmitted to Union[1]		State	Seceded from Union	Readmitted to Union[1]
1.	South Carolina	Dec. 20, 1860	July 9, 1868	7.	Texas	March 2, 1861	March 30, 1870
2.	Mississippi	Jan. 9, 1861	Feb. 23, 1870	8.	Virginia	April 17, 1861	Jan. 26, 1870
3.	Florida	Jan. 10, 1861	June 25, 1868	9.	Arkansas	May 6, 1861	June 22, 1868
4.	Alabama	Jan. 11, 1861	July 13, 1868	10.	North Carolina	May 20, 1861	July 4, 1868
5.	Georgia	Jan. 19, 1861	July 15, 1870[2]	11.	Tennessee	June 8, 1861	July 24, 1866
6.	Louisiana	Jan. 26, 1861	July 9, 1868				

NOTE: Four other slave states—Delaware, Maryland, Kentucky, and Missouri—remained in the Union. The latter two were actually represented on the Confederate flag, which, like the Stars and Stripes, featured a star for every state. 1. Date of readmission to representation in U.S. House of Representatives. 2. Second readmission date. First date was July 21, 1868, but the representatives were unseated March 5, 1869.

Territorial Expansion

Accession	Date	Area[1]	Accession	Date	Area[1]
United States	—	3,717,796	Other territory		
Territory in 1790	—	891,364	Philippines[2]	1898	115,600
Louisiana Purchase	1803	831,321	Puerto Rico	1899	3,508
Florida	1819	69,866	Guam	1899	217
Texas	1845	384,958	American Samoa	1900	90
Oregon	1846	283,439	Canal Zone[3]	1904	553
Mexican Cession	1848	530,706	Virgin Islands of U.S.	1917	171
Gadsden Purchase	1853	29,640	Trust Territory of Pacific Islands[4]	1947	241
Alaska	1867	591,004	Northern Mariana Islands	1986	189
Hawaii	1898	6,471	All other	—	16
			Total, 1990	—	**3,722,228**

1. Total area (land and water), in square miles. 2. Became independent in 1946. 3. Reverted to Panama in 1979. 4. Palau, the last remaining trust territory, became a sovereign state in 1994. *Source:* U.S. Bureau of the Census, Web: www.census.gov.

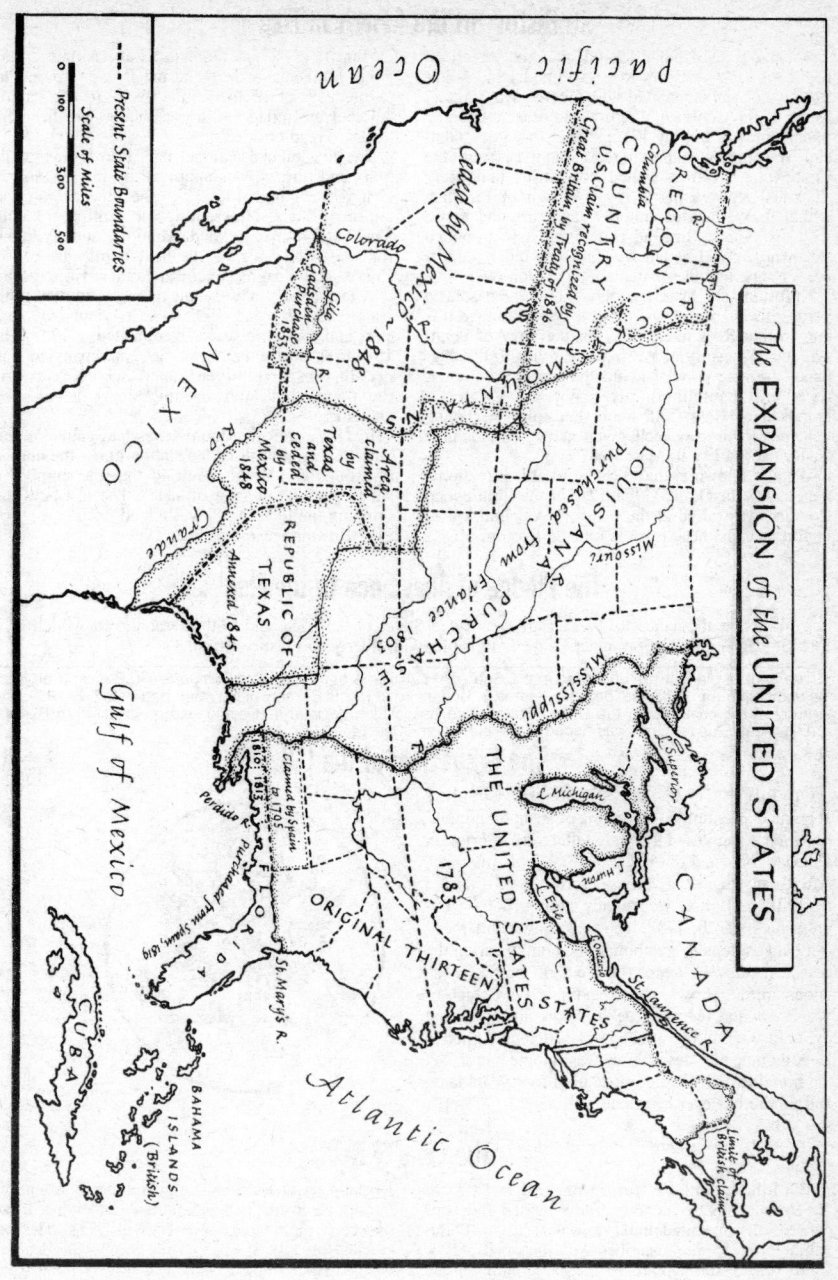

The EXPANSION of the UNITED STATES

History of the American Flag

According to popular legend, the first American flag was made by Betsy Ross, a Philadelphia seamstress who was acquainted with George Washington, leader of the Continental Army, and other influential Philadelphians. In May 1776, so the story goes, General Washington and two representatives from the Continental Congress visited Ross at her upholstery shop and showed her a rough design of the flag. Although Washington initially favored using a star with six points, Ross advocated for a five-pointed star, which could be cut with just one quick snip of the scissors, and the gentlemen were won over.

Unfortunately, historians have never been able to verify this charming version of events, although it is known that Ross made flags for the navy of Pennsylvania. The story of Washington's visit to the flagmaker became popular about the time of the country's first centennial, after William Canby, a grandson of Ross, told about her role in shaping U.S. history in a speech given at the Philadelphia Historical Society in March 1870.

What is known is that the first unofficial national flag, called the Grand Union Flag or the Continental Colours, was raised at the behest of General Washington near his headquarters outside Boston, Mass.,

on Jan. 1, 1776. The flag had 13 alternating red and white horizontal stripes and the British Union Flag (a predecessor of the Union Jack) in the canton. Another early flag had a rattlesnake and the motto "Don't Tread on Me."

The first official national flag, also known as the Stars and Stripes, was approved by the Continental Congress on June 14, 1777. The blue canton contained 13 stars, representing the original 13 colonies, but the layout varied. Although nobody knows for sure who designed the flag, it may have been Continental Congress member Francis Hopkinson.

After Vermont and Kentucky were admitted to the Union in 1791 and 1792, respectively, two more stars and two more stripes were added in 1795. This 15-star, 15-stripe flag was the "star-spangled banner" that inspired lawyer Francis Scott Key to write the poem that later became the U.S. national anthem.

In 1818, after five more states had gained admittance, Congress passed legislation fixing the number of stripes at 13 and requiring that the number of stars equal the number of states. The last new star, bringing the total to 50, was added on July 4, 1960, after Hawaii became a state.

The Pledge of Allegiance to the Flag[1]

I pledge allegiance to the Flag of the United States of America, and to the Republic for which it stands, one Nation under God,[2] indivisible, with liberty and justice for all.

1. The original pledge was published in the Sept. 8, 1892, issue of *The Youth's Companion* in Boston. For years, the authorship was in dispute between James B. Upham and Francis Bellamy of the magazine's staff. In 1939, after a study of the controversy, the United States Flag Association decided that authorship be credited to Bellamy.
2. The phrase "under God" was added to the pledge on June 14, 1954.

The Great Seal of the U.S.

On July 4, 1776, the Continental Congress appointed a committee consisting of Benjamin Franklin, John Adams, and Thomas Jefferson "to bring in a device for a seal of the United States of America." After many delays, a verbal description of a design by William Barton was finally approved by Congress on June 20, 1782. The seal shows an American bald eagle with a ribbon in its mouth bearing the device *E pluribus unum* (One out of many). In its talons are the arrows of war and an olive branch of peace. On the reverse side it shows an unfinished pyramid with an eye (the eye of Providence) above it. Although this description was adopted in 1782, the first drawing was not made until four years later, and no die has ever been cut.

The Liberty Bell

The Liberty Bell was cast in England in 1752 for the Pennsylvania Statehouse (now named Independence Hall) in Philadelphia. It was recast in Philadelphia in 1753. It is inscribed with the words, "Proclaim liberty throughout all the land unto all the inhabitants thereof" (Lev. 25:10). The bell was rung on July 8, 1776, for the first public reading of the Declaration of Independence. Hidden in Allentown during the British occupation of Philadelphia, it was re-placed in Independence Hall in 1778. The bell cracked on July 8, 1835, while tolling the death of Chief Justice John Marshall. In 1976 the Liberty Bell was moved to a special exhibition building near Independence Hall.

The Star-Spangled Banner

Francis Scott Key, 1814

O say, can you see, by the dawn's early light,
What so proudly we hail'd at the twilight's last gleaming?
Whose broad stripes and bright stars, thro' the perilous fight,
O'er the ramparts we watch'd, were so gallantly streaming?
And the rockets' red glare, the bombs bursting in air,
Gave proof thro' the night that our flag was still there.
O say, does that star-spangled banner yet wave
O'er the land of the free and the home of the brave?

On the shore dimly seen thro' the mists of the deep,
Where the foe's haughty host in dread silence reposes,
What is that which the breeze, o'er the towering steep,
As it fitfully blows, half conceals, half discloses?
Now it catches the gleam of the morning's first beam,
In full glory reflected, now shines on the stream:
'Tis the star-spangled banner: O, long may it wave
O'er the land of the free and the home of the brave!

And where is that band who so vauntingly swore
That the havoc of war and the battle's confusion,
A home and a country should leave us no more?
Their blood has wash'd out their foul footsteps' pollution.
No refuge could save the hireling and slave
From the terror of flight or the gloom of the grave:
And the star-spangled banner in triumph doth wave
O'er the land of the free and the home of the brave.

O thus be it ever when free-men shall stand
Between their lov'd home and the war's desolation;
Blest with vict'ry and peace, may the heav'n-rescued land
Praise the Pow'r that hath made and preserv'd us a nation!
Then conquer we must, when our cause it is just,
And this be our motto: "In God is our trust!"
And the star-spangled banner in triumph shall wave
O'er the land of the free and the home of the brave!

On Sept. 13, 1814, Francis Scott Key visited the British fleet in Chesapeake Bay to secure the release of Dr. William Beanes, who had been captured after the burning of Washington, DC. The release was secured, but Key was detained on ship overnight during the shelling of Fort McHenry, one of the forts defending Baltimore. In the morning, he was so delighted to see the American flag still flying over the fort that he began a poem to commemorate the occasion. First published under the title "Defense of Fort M'Henry," the poem soon attained wide popularity as sung to the tune "To Anacreon in Heaven." The origin of this tune is obscure, but it may have been written by John Stafford Smith, a British composer born in 1750. "The Star-Spangled Banner" was officially made the national anthem by Congress in 1931, although it already had been adopted as such by the army and the navy.

The Monroe Doctrine

The Monroe Doctrine was announced in President James Monroe's message to Congress, during his second term on Dec. 2, 1823, in part as follows:

"In the discussions to which this interest has given rise, and in the arrangements by which they may terminate, the occasion has been deemed proper for asserting as a principle in which rights and interests of the United States are involved, that the American continents, by the free and independent condition which they have assumed and maintain, are henceforth not to be considered as subjects for future colonization by any European power. . . . We owe it, therefore, to candor and to the amicable relations existing between the United States and those powers to declare that we should consider any attempt on their part to extend their system to any portion of this hemisphere as dangerous to our peace and safety. With the existing colonies or dependencies of any European power we have not interfered and shall not interfere. But with the governments who have declared their independence and maintain it, and whose independence we have, on great consideration and on just principles, acknowledged, we could not view any interposition for the purpose of oppressing them or controlling in any other manner their destiny by any European power in any other light than as the manifestation of an unfriendly disposition toward the United States."

Washington Monument

Construction of this magnificent Washington, DC, monument took nearly a century of planning, building, and controversy. Provision for a large equestrian statue of George Washington was made in the original city plan, but the project was soon dropped. After Washington's death it was taken up again, and a number of false starts and changes of design were made. Finally, in 1848, work was begun on the monument that stands today. The design, by architect Robert Mills, then featured an ornate base. In 1854, however, political squabbling and a lack of money brought construction to a halt. Work was resumed in 1880, and the monument was completed in 1884 and opened to the public in 1888. The tapered shaft, faced with white marble and rising from walls 15 ft (4.6 m) thick at the base, was modeled after the obelisks of ancient Egypt. The monument, one of the tallest masonry constructions in the world, stands just over 555 ft (169 m). Memorial stones from the 50 states, foreign countries, and organizations line the interior walls. The top, reached only by elevator, commands a panoramic view of the city.

The Declaration of Independence

On April 12, 1776, the legislature of North Carolina authorized its delegates to the Continental Congress to join with others in a declaration of separation from Great Britain; the first colony to instruct its delegates to take the actual initiative was Virginia on May 15. On June 7, 1776, Richard Henry Lee of Virginia offered a resolution to the Congress to the effect "that these United Colonies are, and of right ought to be, free and independent States. . . ." A committee consisting of Thomas Jefferson, John Adams, Benjamin Franklin, Robert R. Livingston, and Roger Sherman was organized to "prepare a declaration to the effect of the said first resolution." The Declaration of Independence was adopted on July 4, 1776. Most delegates signed the Declaration August 2, but George Wythe (Va.) signed August 27; Richard Henry Lee (Va.), Elbridge Gerry (Mass.), and Oliver Wolcott (Conn.) in September; Matthew Thornton (N.H.), not a delegate until September, in November; and Thomas McKean (Del.), although present on July 4, not until 1781 by special permission, having served in the army in the interim.

In Congress, July 4, 1776
The unanimous Declaration of the thirteen United States of America

When in the Course of human events it becomes necessary for one people to dissolve the political bands which have connected them with another, and to assume among the powers of the earth, the separate and equal station to which the Laws of Nature and of Nature's God entitle them, a decent respect to the opinions of mankind requires that they should declare the causes which impel them to the separation.

We hold these truths to be self-evident, that all men are created equal, that they are endowed by their Creator with certain unalienable Rights, that among these are Life, Liberty and the pursuit of Happiness.—That to secure these rights, Governments are instituted among Men, deriving their just powers from the consent of the governed.—That whenever any Form of Government becomes destructive of these ends, it is the Right of the People to alter or to abolish it, and to institute new Government, laying its foundation on such principles and organizing its powers in such form, as to them shall seem most likely to effect their Safety and Happiness. Prudence, indeed, will dictate that Governments long established should not be changed for light and transient causes; and accordingly all experience hath shewn that mankind are more disposed to suffer, while evils are sufferable, than to right themselves by abolishing the forms to which they are accustomed. But when a long train of abuses and usurpations, pursuing invariably the same Object evinces a design to reduce them under absolute Despotism, it is their right, it is their duty, to throw off such Government, and to provide new Guards for their future security.—Such has been the patient sufferance of these Colonies; and such is now the necessity which constrains them to alter their former Systems of Government. The history of the present King of Great Britain is a history of repeated injuries and usurpations, all having in direct object the establishment of an absolute Tyranny over these States. To prove this, let Facts be submitted to a candid world.

He has refused his Assent to Laws, the most wholesome and necessary for the public good.

He has forbidden his Governors to pass Laws of immediate and pressing importance, unless suspended in their operation till his Assent should be obtained; and when so suspended, he has utterly neglected to attend to them.

He has refused to pass other Laws for the accommodation of large districts of people, unless those people would relinquish the right of Representation in the Legislature, a right inestimable to them and formidable to tyrants only.

He has called together legislative bodies at places unusual, uncomfortable, and distant from the depository of their Public Records, for the sole purpose of fatiguing them into compliance with his measures.

He has dissolved Representative Houses repeatedly, for opposing with manly firmness his invasions on the rights of the people.

He has refused for a long time, after such dissolutions, to cause others to be elected; whereby the Legislative Powers, incapable of Annihilation, have returned to the People at large for their exercise; the State remaining in the mean time exposed to all the dangers of invasion from without, and convulsions within.

He has endeavoured to prevent the population of these States; for that purpose obstructing the Laws for Naturalization of Foreigners; refusing to pass others to encourage their migrations hither, and raising the conditions of new Appropriations of Lands.

He has obstructed the Administration of Justice, by refusing his Assent to Laws for establishing Judiciary Powers.

He has made Judges dependent on his Will alone, for the tenure of their offices, and the amount and payment of their salaries.

He has erected a multitude of New Offices, and sent hither swarms of Officers to harass our people, and eat out their substance.

He has kept among us, in times of peace, Standing Armies without the Consent of our legislatures.

He has affected to render the Military independent of and superior to the Civil Power.

He has combined with others to subject us to a jurisdiction foreign to our constitution, and unacknowledged by our laws; giving his Assent to their Acts of pretended Legislation:

For quartering large bodies of armed troops among us:

For protecting them, by a mock Trial, from punishment for any Murders which they should commit on the Inhabitants of these States:

For cutting off our Trade with all parts of the world:

For imposing Taxes on us without our Consent:

For depriving us in many cases, of the benefits of Trial by Jury:

For transporting us beyond Seas to be tried for pretended offences:

For abolishing the free System of English Laws in a neighbouring Province, establishing therein an Arbitrary government, and enlarging its Boundaries so as to render it at once an example and fit instrument for introducing the same absolute rule into these Colonies:

For taking away our Charters, abolishing our most valuable Laws and altering fundamentally the Forms of our Governments:

For suspending our own Legislatures, and declaring themselves invested with power to legislate for us in all cases whatsoever.

He has abdicated Government here, by declaring us out of his Protection and waging War against us.

He has plundered our seas, ravaged our Coasts, burnt our towns, and destroyed the lives of our people.

He is at this time transporting large Armies of foreign Mercenaries to compleat the works of death, desolation, and tyranny, already begun with circumstances of Cruelty & Perfidy scarcely paralleled in the most barbarous ages, and totally unworthy the Head of a civilized nation.

He has constrained our fellow Citizens taken Captive on the high Seas to bear Arms against their Country, to become the executioners of their friends and Brethren, or to fall themselves by their Hands.

He has excited domestic insurrections amongst us, and has endeavoured to bring on the inhabitants of our frontiers, the merciless Indian Savages, whose known rule of warfare, is an undistinguished destruction of all ages, sexes and conditions.

In every stage of these Oppressions We have Petitioned for Redress in the most humble terms: Our repeated Petitions have been answered only by repeated injury. A Prince, whose character is thus marked by every act which may define a Tyrant, is unfit to be the ruler of a free people.

Nor have We been wanting in attentions to our British brethren. We have warned them from time to time of attempts by their legislature to extend an unwarrantable jurisdiction over us. We have reminded them of the circumstances of our emigration and settlement here. We have appealed to their native justice and magnanimity, and we have conjured them by the ties of our common kindred to disavow these usurpations, which would inevitably interrupt our connections and correspondence. They too have been deaf to the voice of justice and of consanguinity. We must, therefore, acquiesce in the necessity, which denounces our Separation, and hold them, as we hold the rest of mankind, Enemies in War, in Peace Friends.

We, therefore, the Representatives of the United States of America, in General Congress, Assembled, appealing to the Supreme Judge of the world for the rectitude of our intentions, do, in the Name, and by Authority of the good People of these Colonies, solemnly publish and declare, That these United Colonies are, and of Right ought to be Free and Independent States; that they are Absolved from all Allegiance to the British Crown, and that all political connection between them and the State of Great Britain, is and ought to be totally dissolved; and that as Free and Independent States, they have full Power to levy War, conclude Peace, contract Alliances, establish Commerce, and to do all other Acts and Things which Independent States may of right do.—And for the support of this Declaration, with a firm reliance on the protection of Divine Providence, we mutually pledge to each other our Lives, our Fortunes and our sacred Honor.

—John Hancock

New Hampshire
Josiah Bartlett
Wm. Whipple
Matthew Thornton

Rhode Island
Step. Hopkins
William Ellery

Connecticut
Roger Sherman
Sam'el Huntington
Wm. Williams
Oliver Wolcott

New York
Wm. Floyd
Phil. Livingston
Frans. Lewis
Lewis Morris

New Jersey
Richd. Stockton
Jno. Witherspoon
Fras. Hopkinson
John Hart
Abra. Clark

Pennsylvania
Robt. Morris
Benjamin Rush
Benj. Franklin
John Morton
Geo. Clymer
Jas. Smith
Geo. Taylor
James Wilson
Geo. Ross

Massachusetts-Bay
Saml. Adams

John Adams
Robt. Treat Paine
Elbridge Gerry

Delaware
Caesar Rodney
Geo. Read
Tho. M'Kean

Maryland
Samuel Chase
Wm. Paca
Thos. Stone
Charles Carroll of
  Carrollton

Virginia
George Wythe
Richard Henry Lee
Th. Jefferson

Benj. Harrison
Ths. Nelson, Jr.
Francis Lightfoot Lee
Carter Braxton

North Carolina
Wm. Hooper
Joseph Hewes
John Penn

South Carolina
Edward Rutledge
Thos. Heyward, Junr.
Thomas Lynch, Junr.
Arthur Middleton

Georgia
Button Gwinnett
Lyman Hall
Geo. Walton

Constitution of the United States of America

(Historical text has been edited to conform to contemporary American usage. The bracketed words are designations for your convenience; they are not part of the Constitution.)

The oldest federal constitution in existence was framed by a convention of delegates from twelve of the thirteen original states in Philadelphia in May 1787, Rhode Island failing to send a delegate. George Washington presided over the session, which lasted until September 17, 1787. The draft (originally a preamble and seven Articles) was submitted to all thirteen states and was to become effective when ratified by nine states. It went into effect on the first Wednesday in March 1789, having been ratified by New Hampshire, the ninth state to approve, on June 21, 1788. The states ratified the Constitution in the following order:

Delaware	December 7, 1787	South Carolina	May 23, 1788
Pennsylvania	December 12, 1787	New Hampshire	June 21, 1788
New Jersey	December 18, 1787	Virginia	June 25, 1788
Georgia	January 2, 1788	New York	July 26, 1788
Connecticut	January 9, 1788	North Carolina	November 21, 1789
Massachusetts	February 6, 1788	Rhode Island	May 29, 1790
Maryland	April 28, 1788		

[Preamble]

We the people of the United States, in order to form a more perfect Union, establish justice, insure domestic tranquility, provide for the common defence, promote the general welfare, and secure the blessings of liberty to ourselves and our posterity, do ordain and establish this Constitution for the United States of America.

Article I

Section 1

[**Legislative powers vested in Congress.**] All legislative powers herein granted shall be vested in a Congress of the United States, which shall consist of a Senate and House of Representatives.

Section 2

[**Composition of the House of Representatives.—1.**] The House of Representatives shall be composed of members chosen every second year by the people of the several States, and the electors in each State shall have the qualifications requisite for electors of the most numerous branch of the State Legislature.

[**Qualifications of Representatives.—2.**] No Person shall be a Representative who shall not have attained to the age of twenty-five years, and been seven years a citizen of the United States, and who shall not, when elected, be an inhabitant of that State in which he shall be chosen.

[**Apportionment of Representatives and direct taxes—census.[1]—3.**] (Representatives and direct taxes shall be apportioned among the several States which may be included within this Union, according to their respective numbers, which shall be determined by adding to the whole number of free persons, including those bound to service for a term of years, and excluding Indians not taxed, three fifths of all other persons.) The actual enumeration shall be made within three years after the first meeting of the Congress of the United States, and within every subsequent term of ten years, in such manner as they shall by law direct. The number of Representatives shall not exceed one for every thirty thousand, but each State shall have at least one Representa-

tive; and until such enumeration shall be made, the State of New Hampshire shall be entitled to choose three, Massachusetts eight, Rhode-Island and Providence Plantations one, Connecticut five, New York six, New Jersey four, Pennsylvania eight, Delaware one, Maryland six, Virginia ten, North Carolina five, South Carolina five, and Georgia three.

[**Filling of vacancies in representation.—4.**] When vacancies happen in the representation from any State, the Executive Authority thereof shall issue writs of election to fill such vacancies.

[**Selection of officers; power of impeachment.—5.**] The House of Representatives shall choose their Speaker and other officers; and shall have the sole power of impeachment.

Section 3[2]

[**The Senate.—1.**] The Senate of the United States shall be composed of two Senators from each State, chosen by the Legislature thereof, for six years; and each Senator shall have one vote.

[**Classification of Senators; filling of vacancies.—2.**] Immediately after they shall be assembled in consequence of the first election, they shall be divided as equally as may be into three classes. The seats of the Senators of the first class shall be vacated at the expiration of the second year, of the second class at the expiration of the fourth year, and of the third class at the expiration of the sixth year, so that one-third may be chosen every second year; and if vacancies happen by resignation, or otherwise, during the recess of the Legislature of any State, the Executive thereof may make temporary appointments (until the next meeting of the Legislature, which shall then fill such vacancies).

[**Qualification of Senators.—3.**] No person shall be a Senator who shall not have attained to the age of thirty years, and been nine years a citizen of the United States, and who shall not, when elected, be an inhabitant of that State for which he shall be chosen.

[**Vice President to be President of Senate.—4.**] The Vice President of the United States shall be President of the Senate, but shall have no vote, unless they be equally divided.

[**Selection of Senate officers; President pro tempore.—5.**] The Senate shall choose their other

---

1. The clause included in parentheses is amended by the 14th Amendment, Section 2. 2. The first paragraph of this section and the part of the second paragraph included in parentheses are amended by the 17th Amendment.

officers, and also a President pro tempore, in the absence of the Vice President, or when he shall exercise the office of President of the United States.

[Senate to try impeachments.—6.] The Senate shall have the sole power to try all impeachments. When sitting for that purpose, they shall be on oath or affirmation. When the President of the United States is tried, the Chief Justice shall preside: and no person shall be convicted without the concurrence of two thirds of the members present.

[Judgment in cases of Impeachment.—7.] Judgment in cases of impeachment shall not extend further than to removal from office, and disqualification to hold and enjoy any office of honor, trust, or profit under the United States: but the party convicted shall nevertheless be liable and subject to indictment, trial, judgment and punishment, according to Law.

Section 4

[Control of congressional elections.—1.] The times, places, and manner of holding elections for Senators and Representatives, shall be prescribed in each State by the Legislature thereof; but the Congress may at any time by law make or alter such regulations, except as to the places of choosing Senators.

[Time for assembling of Congress[3]—2.] The Congress shall assemble at least once in every year, and such meeting shall be on the first Monday in December, unless they shall by law appoint a different day.

Section 5

[Each house to be the judge of the election and qualifications of its members; regulations as to quorum.—1.] Each House shall be the judge of the elections, returns, and qualifications of its own members, and a majority of each shall constitute a quorum to do business; but a smaller number may adjourn from day to day, and may be authorized to compel the attendance of absent members, in such manner, and under such penalties as each House may provide.

[Each house to determine its own rules.—2.] Each House may determine the rules of its proceedings, punish its members for disorderly behavior, and, with the concurrence of two thirds, expel a member.

[Journals and yeas and nays.—3.] Each House shall keep a journal of its proceedings, and from time to time publish the same, excepting such parts as may in their judgment require secrecy; and the yeas and nays of the members of either House on any question shall, at the desire of one fifth of those present, be entered on the journal.

[Adjournment.—4.] Neither House, during the session of Congress, shall, without the consent of the other, adjourn for more than three days, nor to any other place than that in which the two Houses shall be sitting.

Section 6

[Compensation and privileges of members of Congress.—1.] The Senators and Representatives shall receive a compensation for their services, to be ascertained by law, and paid out of the Treasury of the United States. They shall in all cases, except treason, felony, and breach of the peace, be privileged from arrest during their attendance at the session of their respective Houses, and in going to and returning from the same; and for any speech or debate in either House, they shall not be questioned in any other place.

[Incompatible offices; exclusions.—2.] No Senator or Representative shall, during the time for which he was elected, be appointed to any civil office under the authority of the United States, which shall have been created, or the emoluments whereof shall have been increased during such time; and no person holding any office under the United States shall be a member of either House during his continuance in office.

Section 7

[Revenue bills to originate in House.—1.] All bills for raising revenue shall originate in the House of Representatives; but the Senate may propose or concur with amendments as on other bills.

[Manner of passing bills; veto power of President.—2.] Every bill which shall have passed the House of Representatives and the Senate, shall, before it becomes a law, be presented to the President of the United States; if he approve he shall sign it, but if not he shall return it, with his objections to that House in which it shall have originated, who shall enter the objections at large on their journal, and proceed to reconsider it. If after such reconsideration two thirds of that House shall agree to pass the bill, it shall be sent, together with the objections, to the other House, by which it shall likewise be reconsidered, and if approved by two thirds of that House, it shall become a law. But in all such cases the votes of both Houses shall be determined by yeas and nays, and the names of the persons voting for and against the bill shall be entered on the journal of each house, respectively. If any bill shall not be returned by the President within ten days (Sundays excepted) after it shall have been presented to him, the same shall be a law, in like manner as if he had signed it, unless the Congress by their adjournment prevent its return, in which case it shall not be a law.

[Concurrent orders or resolutions, to be passed by President.—3.] Every order, resolution, or vote to which the concurrence of the Senate and House of Representatives may be necessary (except on a question of adjournment) shall be presented to the President of the United States; and before the same shall take effect, shall be approved by him, or being disapproved by him, shall be repassed by two thirds of the Senate and House of Representatives, according to the rules and limitations prescribed in the case of a bill.

Section 8

[General powers of Congress.[4]]

[Taxes, duties, imposts, and excises.—1.] The Congress shall have power to lay and collect taxes, duties, imposts and excises, to pay the debts and provide for the common defense and general welfare of the United States; but all duties, imposts and excises shall be uniform throughout the United States;

---

3. Amended by the 20th Amendment, Section 2. 4. By the 16th Amendment, Congress is given the power to lay and collect taxes on income.

[**Borrowing of money.—2.**] To borrow money on the credit of the United States;

[**Regulation of commerce.—3.**] To regulate commerce with foreign nations, and among the several States, and with the Indian tribes;

[**Naturalization and bankruptcy.—4.**] To establish a uniform rule of naturalization, and uniform laws on the subject of bankruptcies throughout the United States;

[**Money, weights and measures.—5.**] To coin money, regulate the value thereof, and of foreign coin, and fix the standard of weights and measures;

[**Counterfeiting.—6.**] To provide for the punishment of counterfeiting the securities and current coin of the United States;

[**Post offices.—7.**] To establish post offices and post roads;

[**Patents and copyrights.—8.**] To promote the progress of science and useful arts, by securing for limited times to authors and inventors the exclusive right to their respective writings and discoveries;

[**Inferior courts.—9.**] To constitute tribunals inferior to the Supreme Court;

[**Piracies and felonies.—10.**] To define and punish piracies and felonies committed on the high seas, and offences against the law of nations;

[**War; marque and reprisal.—11.**] To declare war, grant letters of marque and reprisal, and make rules concerning captures on land and water;

[**Armies.—12.**] To raise and support armies, but no appropriation of money to that use shall be for a longer term than two years;

[**Navy.—13.**] To provide and maintain a navy;

[**Land and naval forces.—14.**] To make rules for the government and regulation of the land and naval forces;

[**Calling out militia.—15.**] To provide for calling forth the militia to execute the laws of the Union, suppress insurrections, and repel invasions;

[**Organizing, arming, and disciplining militia. —16.**] To provide for organizing, arming, and disciplining, the militia, and for governing such part of them as may be employed in the service of the United States, reserving to the States, respectively, the appointment of the officers, and the authority of training the militia according to the discipline prescribed by Congress;

[**Exclusive legislation over District of Columbia.—17.**] To exercise exclusive legislation in all cases whatsoever, over such district (not exceeding ten miles square) as may, by cession of particular States, and the acceptance of Congress, become the seat of the Government of the United States, and to exercise like authority over all places purchased by the consent of the Legislature of the State in which the same shall be, for the erection of forts, magazines, arsenals, dock-yards, and other needful buildings;—And

[**To enact laws necessary to enforce Constitution.—18.**] To make all laws which shall be necessary and proper for carrying into execution the foregoing powers, and all other powers vested by this Constitution in the Government of the United States, or in any department or officer thereof.

Section 9

[**Migration or importation of certain persons not to be prohibited before 1808.—1.**] The migration or importation of such persons as any of the States now existing shall think proper to admit, shall not be prohibited by the Congress prior to the year one thousand eight hundred and eight, but a tax or duty may be imposed on such importation, not exceeding ten dollars for each person.

[**Writ of habeas corpus not to be suspended; exception.—2.**] The privilege of the writ of habeas corpus shall not be suspended, unless when in cases of rebellion or invasion the public safety may require it.

[**Bills of attainder and ex post facto laws prohibited.—3.**] No bill of attainder or ex post facto law shall be passed.

[**Capitation and other direct taxes.—4.**] No capitation, or other direct, tax shall be laid, unless in proportion to the census or enumeration herein before directed to be taken.[5]

[**Exports not to be taxed.—5.**] No tax or duty shall be laid on articles exported from any State.

[**No preference to be given to ports of any States; interstate shipping.—6.**] No preference shall be given by any regulation of commerce or revenue to the ports of one State over those of another: nor shall vessels bound to, or from, one State, be obliged to enter, clear, or pay duties in another.

[**Money, how drawn from treasury; financial statements to be published.—7.**] No money shall be drawn from the Treasury, but in consequence of appropriations made by law; and a regular statement and account of the receipts and expenditures of all public money shall be published from time to time.

[**Titles of nobility not to be granted; acceptance by government officers of favors from foreign powers.—8.**] No title of nobility shall be granted by the United States: and no person holding any office of profit or trust under them, shall, without the consent of the Congress, accept of any present, emolument, office, or title, of any kind whatever, from any king, prince, or foreign state.

Section 10

[**Limitations of the powers of the several States.—1.**] No State shall enter into any treaty, alliance, or confederation; grant letters of marque and reprisal; coin money; emit bills of credit; make any thing but gold and silver coin a tender in payment of debts; pass any bill of attainder, ex post facto law, or law impairing the obligation of contracts, or grant any title of nobility.

[**State imposts and duties.—2.**] No State shall, without the consent of the Congress, lay any imposts or duties on imports or exports, except what may be absolutely necessary for executing its inspection laws; and the net produce of all duties and imposts, laid by any State on imports or exports, shall be for the use of the Treasury of the United States; and all such laws shall be subject to the revision and control of the Congress.

[**Further restrictions on powers of States.—3.**] No State shall, without the consent of Congress, lay any duty of tonnage, keep troops, or ships of war in time of peace, enter into any agreement or compact

---

5. *See* the 16th Amendment.

with another state, or with a foreign power, or engage in war, unless actually invaded, or in such imminent danger as will not admit of delay.

Article II

Section 1

[The president; the executive power.—1.] The executive power shall be vested in a President of the United States of America. He shall hold his office during the term of four years, and, together with the Vice President, chosen for the same term, be elected, as follows

[Appointment and qualifications of presidential electors.—2.] Each State shall appoint, in such manner as the Legislature thereof may direct, a number of electors, equal to the whole number of Senators and Representatives to which the State may be entitled in the Congress: but no Senator or Representative, or person holding an office of trust or profit under the United States, shall be appointed an elector.

[Original method of electing the president and vice president.[6]] (The electors shall meet in their respective States, and vote by ballot for two persons, of whom one at least shall not be an inhabitant of the same State with themselves. And they shall make a list of all the persons voted for, and of the number of votes for each; which list they shall sign and certify, and transmit sealed to the seat of the Government of the United States, directed to the President of the Senate. The President of the Senate shall, in the presence of the Senate and House of Representatives, open all the certificates, and the votes shall then be counted. The person having the greatest number of votes shall be the President, if such number be a majority of the whole number of electors appointed; and if there be more than one who have such majority, and have an equal number of votes, then the House of Representatives shall immediately choose by ballot one of them for President; and if no person have a majority, then from the five highest on the list the said House shall in like manner choose the President. But in choosing the President, the votes shall be taken by States, the representation from each State having one vote; A quorum for this purpose shall consist of a member or members from two thirds of the States, and a majority of all the states shall be necessary to a choice. In every case, after the choice of the President, the person having the greatest number of votes of the electors shall be the Vice President. But if there should remain two or more who have equal votes, the Senate should choose from them by ballot the Vice President.)

[Congress may determine time of choosing electors and day for casting their votes.—3.] The Congress may determine the time of choosing the electors, and the day on which they shall give their votes; which day shall be the same throughout the United States.

[Qualifications for the office of president.[7]—4.] No person except a natural born citizen, or a citizen of the United States, at the time of the adoption of this Constitution, shall be eligible to the office of President; neither shall any person be eligible to that office who shall not have attained to the age of thirty-five years, and been fourteen years a resident within the United States.

[Filling vacancy in the office of president.[8]—5.] In case of the removal of the President from office, or of his death, resignation, or inability to discharge the powers and duties of the said office, the same shall devolve on the Vice President, and the Congress may by law provide for the case of removal, death, resignation or inability, both of the President and Vice President, declaring what officer shall then act as President, and such officer shall act accordingly, until the disability be removed, or a President shall be elected.

[Compensation of the president.—6.] The President shall, at stated times, receive for his services, a compensation, which shall neither be increased nor diminished during the period for which he shall have been elected, and he shall not receive within that period any other emolument from the United States, or any of them.

[Oath to be taken by the president.—7.] Before he enter on the execution of his office, he shall take the following oath or affirmation:—"I do solemnly swear (or affirm) that I will faithfully execute the office of President of the United States, and will to the best of my ability, preserve, protect, and defend the Constitution of the United States."

Section 2

[The president to be commander in chief of army and navy and head of executive departments; may grant reprieves and pardons.—1.] The President shall be Commander in Chief of the Army and Navy of the United States, and of the militia of the several States, when called into the actual service of the United States; he may require the opinion, in writing, of the principal officer in each of the executive departments, upon any subject relating to the duties of their respective offices, and he shall have power to grant reprieves and pardons for offences against the United States, except in cases of impeachment.

[President may, with concurrence of Senate, make treaties, appoint ambassadors, etc.; appointment of inferior officers, authority of Congress over.—2.] He shall have power, by and with the advice and consent of the Senate, to make treaties, provided two thirds of the Senators present concur; and he shall nominate, and by and with the advice and consent of the Senate, shall appoint ambassadors, other public ministers and consuls, judges of the Supreme Court, and all other officers of the United States, whose appointments are not herein otherwise provided for, and which shall be established by law: but the Congress may by law vest the appointment of such inferior officers, as they think proper, in the President alone, in the courts of law, or in the heads of departments.

[President may fill vacancies in office during recess of Senate.—3.] The President shall have power to fill up all vacancies that may happen during the recess of the Senate, by granting commissions which shall expire at the end of their session.

---

6. This clause has been superseded by the 12th Amendment. 7. For qualifications of the vice president, *see* the 12th Amendment. 8. Amended by the 20th Amendment, Sections 3 and 4.

Section 3

[President to give advice to Congress; may convene or adjourn it on certain occasions; to receive ambassadors, etc.; have laws executed and commission all officers.] He shall from time to time give to the Congress information of the state of the Union, and recommend to their consideration such measures as he shall judge necessary and expedient; he may, on extraordinary occasions, convene both Houses, or either of them, and in case of disagreement between them, with respect to the time of adjournment, he may adjourn them to such time as he shall think proper; he shall receive ambassadors and other public ministers: he shall take care that the laws be faithfully executed, and shall commission all the officers of the United States.

Section 4

[All civil officers removable by impeachment.] The President, Vice President, and all civil officers of the United States shall be removed from office on impeachment for, and conviction of, treason, bribery, or other high crimes and misdemeanors.

Article III

Section 1

[Judicial powers; how vested; term of office and compensation of judges.] The judicial Power of the United States, shall be vested in one Supreme Court, and in such inferior courts as the Congress may from time to time ordain and establish. The judges, both of the supreme and inferior courts, shall hold their offices during good behavior, and shall, at stated times, receive for their services, a compensation, which shall not be diminished during their continuance in office.

Section 2

[Jurisdiction of federal courts[9]—1.] The judicial power shall extend to all cases, in law and equity, arising under this Constitution, the laws of the United States, and treaties made, or which shall be made, under their authority; to all cases affecting ambassadors, other public ministers and consuls; to all cases of admiralty and maritime jurisdiction; to controversies to which the United States, shall be a party; to controversies between two or more States; between a State and citizens of another State; between citizens of different States; between citizens of the same State claiming lands under grants of different states, and between a State, or the citizens thereof, and foreign states, citizens, or subjects.

[Original and appellate jurisdiction of Supreme Court.—2.] In all cases affecting ambassadors, other public ministers and consuls, and those in which a State shall be party, the Supreme Court shall have original jurisdiction. In all the other cases before mentioned, the Supreme Court shall have appellate jurisdiction, both as to law and fact, with such exceptions, and under such regulations, as the Congress shall make.

[Trial of all crimes, except impeachment, to be by jury.—3.] The trial of all crimes, except in cases of impeachment, shall be by jury; and such trial shall be held in the State where the said crimes shall have been committed; but when not committed within any State, the trial shall be at such place or places as the Congress may by law have directed.

Section 3

[Treason defined; conviction of.—1.] Treason against the United States, shall consist only in levying war against them, or, in adhering to their enemies, giving them aid and comfort. No person shall be convicted of treason unless on the testimony of two witnesses to the same overt act, or on confession in open court.

[Congress to declare punishment for treason; proviso.—2.] The Congress shall have power to declare the punishment of treason, but no attainder of treason shall work corruption of blood, or forfeiture except during the life of the person attained.

Article IV

Section 1

[Each state to give full faith and credit to the public acts and records of other states.] Full faith and credit shall be given in each State to the public acts, records, and judicial proceedings of every other State. And the Congress may by general laws prescribe the manner in which such acts, records, and proceedings shall be proved, and the effect thereof.

Section 2

[Privileges of citizens.—1.] The citizens of each State shall be entitled to all privileges and immunities of citizens in the several States.

[Extradition between the several states.—2.] A person charged in any State with treason, felony, or other crime, who shall flee from justice, and be found in another State, shall on demand of the Executive authority of the State from which he fled, be delivered up, to be removed to the State having jurisdiction of the crime.

[Persons held to labor or service in one state, fleeing to another, to be returned.—3.] No person held to service or labor in one State, under the laws thereof, escaping into another, shall, in consequence of any law or regulation therein, be discharged from such service or labor, but shall be delivered up on claim of the party to whom such service or labor may be due.

Section 3

[New states.—1.] New States may be admitted by the Congress into this Union; but no new State shall be formed or erected within the jurisdiction of any other State; nor any State be formed by the junction of two or more States, or parts of States, without the consent of the Legislatures of the States concerned as well as of the Congress.

[Regulations concerning territory.—2.] The Congress shall have power to dispose of and make all needful rules and regulations respecting the territory or other property belonging to the United States; and nothing in this Constitution shall be so construed as to prejudice any claims of the United States, or of any particular State.

Section 4

[Republican form of government and protection guaranteed the several states.] The United States shall guarantee to every State in this Union a Republican form of government, and shall protect each of them against invasion; and on application of the Legislature, or of the Executive (when the Legislature cannot be convened) against domestic violence.

---

9. This section is abridged by the 11th Amendment.

Article V

[Ways in which the Constitution can be amended.] The Congress, whenever two thirds of both Houses shall deem it necessary, shall propose amendments to this Constitution, or, on the application of the Legislatures of two thirds of the several States shall call a convention for proposing amendments, which, in either case, shall be valid to all intents and purposes, as part of this Constitution, when ratified by the Legislatures of three fourths of the several States, or by conventions in three fourths thereof, as the one or the other mode of ratification may be proposed by the Congress; provided that no amendment which may be made prior to the year one thousand eight hundred and eight shall in any manner affect the first and fourth clauses in the ninth Section of the first Article; and that no State, without its consent, shall be deprived of its equal suffrage in the Senate.

Article VI

[Debts contracted under the confederation secured.—1.] All debts contracted and engagements entered into, before the adoption of this Constitution, shall be as valid against the United States under this Constitution, as under the Confederation.

[Constitution, laws, and treaties of the United States to be supreme.—2.] This Constitution, and the laws of the United States which shall be made in pursuance thereof; and all treaties made, or which shall be made, under the authority of the United States, shall be the supreme law of the land; and the judges in every State shall be bound thereby, any thing in the Constitution or laws of any State to the contrary notwithstanding.

[Who shall take constitutional oath; no religious test as to official qualification.—3.] The Senators and Representatives before mentioned, and the members of the several State Legislatures, and all executive and judicial officers, both of the United States and of the several States, shall be bound, by oath or affirmation, to support this Constitution; but no religious test shall ever be required as a qualification to any office or public trust under the United States.

Article VII

[Constitution to be considered adopted when ratified by nine states.] The ratification of the conventions of nine States shall be sufficient for the establishment of this Constitution between the States so ratifying the same.

Done in convention by the unanimous consent of the States present the seventeenth day of September in the year of our Lord one thousand seven hundred and eighty seven and of the independence of the United States of America the Twelfth. In witness whereof we have hereunto subscribed our names.

George Washington
President and Deputy from Virginia

New Hampshire	David Brearley	John Dickinson	**South Carolina**
John Langdon	Jona. Dayton	Richard Bassett	J. Rutledge
Nicholas Gilman		Jaco. Broom	Charles Cotesworth
Massachusetts	**Pennsylvania**	**Maryland**	Pinckney
Nathaniel Gorham	B. Franklin	James McHenry	Charles Pinckney
Rufus King	Thomas Mifflin	Dan. of St. Thos. Jenifer	Pierce Butler
Connecticut	Robt. Morris	Danl. Carroll	**Georgia**
Wm. Saml. Johnson	Geo. Clymer	**Virginia**	William Few
Roger Sherman	Thos. FitzSimons	John Blair	Abr. Baldwin
New York	Jared Ingersoll	James Madison, Jr.	Attest: William Jackson,
Alexander Hamilton	James Wilson	**North Carolina**	Secretary
New Jersey	Gouv. Morris	Wm. Blount	
Wil. Livingston	**Delaware**	Richd Dobbs Spaight	
Wm. Paterson	Geo. Read	Hu. Williamson	
	Gunning Bedford Jun.		

Amendments to the Constitution of the United States

(Amendments I to X inclusive, popularly known as the Bill of Rights, were proposed and sent to the states by the first session of the First Congress. They were ratified Dec. 15, 1791.)

Amendment I

[Freedom of religion, speech, of the press, and right of petition.] Congress shall make no law respecting an establishment of religion, or prohibiting the free exercise thereof; or abridging the freedom of speech, or of the press; or the right of the people peaceably to assemble, and to petition the Government for a redress of grievances.

Amendment II

[Right of people to bear arms not to be infringed.] A well regulated militia, being necessary to the security of a free State, the right of the people to keep and bear arms, shall not be infringed.

Amendment III

[Quartering of troops.] No soldier shall, in time of peace be quartered in any house, without the consent of the owner, nor in time of war, but in a manner to be prescribed by law.

Amendment IV

[Persons and houses to be secure from unreasonable searches and seizures.] The right of the people to be secure in their persons, houses, papers, and effects, against unreasonable searches and seizures, shall not be violated, and no warrants shall issue, but upon probable cause, supported by oath or affirmation, and particularly describing the place to be searched, and the persons or things to be seized.

Amendment V

[Trials for crimes; just compensation for private property taken for public use.] No person shall be held to answer for a capital, or otherwise infamous crime, unless on a presentment or indictment of a Grand Jury, except in cases arising in the land or naval forces, or in the militia, when in actual service in time of war or public danger; nor shall any person be subject for the same offence to be twice put in jeopardy of life or limb; nor shall be compelled in any criminal case to be a witness, against himself, nor be deprived of life, liberty, or property, without due process of law; nor shall private property be taken for public use, without just compensation.

Amendment VI

[Civil rights in trials for crimes enumerated.] In all criminal prosecutions, the accused shall enjoy the right to a speedy and public trial, by an impartial jury of the State and district wherein the crime shall have been committed, which district shall have been previously ascertained by law, and to be informed of the nature and cause of the accusation; to be confronted with the witnesses against him; to have compulsory process for obtaining witnesses in his favor, and to have the assistance of counsel for his defense.

Amendment VII

[Civil rights in civil suits.] In suits at common law, where the value in controversy shall exceed twenty dollars, the right of trial by jury shall be preserved, and no fact tried by a jury, shall be otherwise re-examined in any court of the United States, than according to the rules of the common law.

Amendment VIII

[Excessive bail, fines, and punishments prohibited.] Excessive bail shall not be required, nor excessive fines imposed, nor cruel and unusual punishments inflicted.

Amendment IX

[Reserved rights of people.] The enumeration in the Constitution, of certain rights, shall not be construed to deny or disparage others retained by the people.

Amendment X

[Powers not delegated, reserved to states and people respectively.] The powers not delegated to the United States by the Constitution, nor prohibited by it to the States, are reserved to the States, respectively, or to the people.

Amendment XI

(The proposed amendment was sent to the states Mar. 5, 1794, by the Third Congress. It was ratified Feb. 7, 1795.)
[Judicial power of United States not to extend to suits against a state.] The judicial power of the United States shall not be construed to extend to any suit in law or equity, commenced or prosecuted against one of the United States by citizens of another State, or by citizens or subjects of any foreign state.

Amendment XII

(The proposed amendment was sent to the states Dec. 12, 1803, by the Eighth Congress. It was ratified July 27, 1804.)
[Present mode of electing president and vice president by electors.[1]]
The electors shall meet in their respective states, and vote by ballot for President and Vice President, one of whom, at least, shall not be an inhabitant of the same state with themselves; they shall name in their ballots the person voted for as President, and in distinct ballots the person voted for as Vice President, and they shall make distinct lists of all persons voted for as President, and of all persons voted for as Vice President, and of the number of votes for each, which lists they shall sign and certify, and transmit sealed to the seat of the government of the United States, directed to the President of the Senate; the President of the Senate shall, in the presence of the Senate and House of Representatives, open all the certificates and the votes shall then be counted; the person having the greatest number of votes for President, shall be the President, if such number be a majority of the whole number of electors appointed; and if no person have such majority, then from the persons having the highest numbers not exceeding three on the list of those voted for as President, the House of Representatives shall choose immediately, by ballot, the President. But in choosing the President, the votes shall be taken by states, the representation from each State having one vote; a quorum for this purpose shall consist of a member or members from two thirds of the states, and a majority of all the states shall be necessary to a choice. And if the House of Representatives shall not choose a President whenever the right of choice shall devolve upon them, before the fourth day of March next following, then the Vice President shall act as President, as in the case of the death or other constitutional disability of the President. The person having the greatest number of votes as Vice President, shall be the Vice President, if such number be a majority of the whole number of electors appointed, and if no person have a majority, then from the two highest numbers on the list, the Senate shall choose the Vice President; a quorum for the purpose shall consist of two thirds of the whole number of Senators, and a majority of the whole number shall be necessary to a choice. But no person constitutionally ineligible to the office of President shall be eligible to that of Vice President of the United States.

Amendment XIII

(The proposed amendment was sent to the states Feb. 1, 1865, by the Thirty-eighth Congress. It was ratified Dec. 6, 1865.)

Section 1

[Slavery prohibited.] Neither slavery nor involuntary servitude, except as a punishment for crime whereof the party shall have been duly convicted, shall exist within the United States, or any place subject to their jurisdiction.

Section 2

[Congress given power to enforce this article.] Congress shall have power to enforce this article by appropriate legislation.

1. Amended by the 20th Amendment, Sections 3 and 4.

Amendment XIV

(The proposed amendment was sent to the states June 16, 1866, by the Thirty-ninth Congress. It was ratified July 9, 1868.)

Section 1

[Citizenship defined; privileges of citizens.] All persons born or naturalized in the United States, and subject to the jurisdiction thereof, are citizens of the United States and of the State wherein they reside. No State shall make or enforce any law which shall abridge the privileges or immunities of citizens of the United States; nor shall any State deprive any person of life, liberty, or property, without due process of law; nor deny to any person within its jurisdiction the equal protection of the laws.

Section 2

[Apportionment of Representatives.] Representatives shall be apportioned among the several States according to their respective numbers, counting the whole number of persons in each State, excluding Indians not taxed. But when the right to vote at any election for the choice of electors for President and Vice President of the United States, Representatives in Congress, the executive and judicial officers of a State, or the members of the Legislature thereof, is denied to any of the male inhabitants of such State, being twenty-one years of age, and citizens of the United States, or in any way abridged, except for participation in rebellion, or other crime, the basis of representation therein shall be reduced in the proportion which the number of such male citizens shall bear to the whole number of male citizens twenty-one years of age in such State.

Section 3

[Disqualification for office; removal of disability.] No person shall be a Senator or Representative in Congress, or elector of President and Vice President, or hold any office, civil or military, under the United States, or under any State, who, having previously taken an oath, as a member of Congress, or as an officer of the United States, or as a member of any State Legislature, or as an executive or judicial officer of any State, to support the Constitution of the United States, shall have engaged in insurrection or rebellion against the same, or given aid or comfort to the enemies thereof. But Congress may, by a vote of two thirds of each House, remove such disability.

Section 4

[Public debt not to be questioned; payment of debts and claims incurred in aid of rebellion forbidden.] The validity of the public debt of the United States, authorized by law, including debts incurred for payment of pensions and bounties for services in suppressing insurrection or rebellion, shall not be questioned. But neither the United States nor any State shall assume or pay any debt or obligation incurred in aid of insurrection or rebellion against the United States, or any claim for the loss or emancipation of any slave; but all such debts, obligations, and claims shall be held illegal and void.

Section 5

[Congress given power to enforce this article.] The Congress shall have power to enforce, by appropriate legislation, the provisions of this article.

Amendment XV

(The proposed amendment was sent to the states Feb. 27, 1869, by the Fortieth Congress. It was ratified Feb. 3, 1870.)

Section 1

[Right of certain citizens to vote established.] The right of citizens of the United States to vote shall not be denied or abridged by the United States or by any State on account of race, color, or previous condition of servitude.

Section 2

[Congress given power to enforce this article.] The Congress shall have power to enforce this article by appropriate legislation.

Amendment XVI

(The proposed amendment was sent to the states July 12, 1909, by the Sixty-first Congress. It was ratified Feb. 3, 1913.)

[Taxes on income; Congress given power to lay and collect.] The Congress shall have power to lay and collect taxes on incomes, from whatever source derived, without apportionment among the several States, and without regard to any census or enumeration.

Amendment XVII

(The proposed amendment was sent to the states May 16, 1912, by the Sixty-second Congress. It was ratified April 8, 1913.)

[Election of U.S. senators; filling of vacancies; qualifications of electors.] The Senate of the United States shall be composed of two Senators from each State, elected by the people thereof, for six years; and each Senator shall have one vote. The electors in each State shall have the qualifications requisite for electors of the most numerous branch of the State Legislatures.

When vacancies happen in the representation of any State in the Senate, the executive authority of such State shall issue writs of election to fill such vacancies: Provided, that the legislature of any State may empower the executive thereof to make temporary appointment until the people fill the vacancies by election as the legislature may direct.

This amendment shall not be so construed as to affect the election or term of any Senator chosen before it becomes valid as part of the Constitution.

Amendment XVIII[2]

(The proposed amendment was sent to the states Dec. 18, 1917, by the Sixty-fifth Congress. It was ratified by three quarters of the states by Jan. 16, 1919, and became effective Jan. 16, 1920.)

Section 1

[Manufacture, sale, or transportation of intoxicating liquors, for beverage purposes, prohibited.] After one year from the ratification of this

2. Repealed by the 21st Amendment.

article the manufacture, sale, or transportation of intoxicating liquors within, the importation thereof into, or the exportation thereof from the United States and all territory subject to the jurisdiction thereof for beverage purposes is hereby prohibited.

Section 2

[**Congress and the several states given concurrent power to pass appropriate legislation to enforce this article.**] The Congress and the several States shall have concurrent power to enforce this article by appropriate legislation.

Section 3

[**Provisions of article to become operative, when adopted by three fourths of the states.**] This article shall be inoperative unless it shall have been ratified as an amendment to the Constitution by the legislatures of the several States, as provided in the Constitution, within seven years from the date of the submission hereof to the States by Congress.

Amendment XIX

(**The proposed amendment was sent to the states June 4, 1919, by the Sixty-sixth Congress. It was ratified Aug. 18, 1920.**)

[**The right of citizens to vote shall not be denied because of sex.**] The right of citizens of the United States to vote shall not be denied or abridged by the United States or by any State on account of sex.

[**Congress given power to enforce this article.**] Congress shall have power to enforce this article by appropriate legislation.

Amendment XX

(**The proposed amendment, sometimes called the "Lame Duck Amendment," was sent to the states Mar. 3, 1932, by the Seventy-second Congress. It was ratified Jan. 23, 1933; but, in accordance with Section 5, Sections 1 and 2, did not go into effect until Oct. 15, 1933.**)

Section 1

[**Terms of president, vice president, senators, and representatives.**] The terms of the President and Vice President shall end at noon on the twentieth day of January, and the terms of Senators and Representatives at noon on the third day of January, of the years in which such terms would have ended if this article had not been ratified; and the terms of their successors shall then begin.

Section 2

[**Time of assembling Congress.**] The Congress shall assemble at least once in every year, and such meeting shall begin at noon on the third day of January, unless they shall by law appoint a different day.

Section 3

[**Filling vacancy in office of president.**] If, at the time fixed for the beginning of the term of the President, the President-elect shall have died, the Vice President-elect shall become President. If a President shall not have been chosen before the time fixed for the beginning of his term, or if the President-elect shall have failed to qualify, then the Vice President shall have qualified; and the Congress may by law provide for the case wherein neither a President-elect nor a Vice President-elect shall have qualified, declaring who shall then act as President, or the manner in which one who is to act shall be selected, and such person shall act accordingly until a President or Vice President shall have qualified.

Section 4

[**Power of Congress in presidential succession.**] The Congress may by law provide for the case of the death of any of the persons from whom the House of Representatives may choose a President whenever the right of choice shall have devolved upon them, and for the case of the death of any of the persons from whom the Senate may choose a Vice President whenever the right of choice shall have devolved upon them.

Section 5

[**Time of taking effect.**] Sections 1 and 2 shall take effect on the 15th day of October following the ratification of this article.

Section 6

[**Ratification.**] This article shall be inoperative unless it shall have been ratified as an amendment to the Constitution by the legislatures of three fourths of the several States within seven years from the date of its submission.

Amendment XXI

(**The proposed amendment was sent to the states Feb. 20, 1933, by the Seventy-second Congress. It was ratified Dec. 5, 1933.**)

Section 1

[**Repeal of Prohibition Amendment.**] The eighteenth article of amendment to the Constitution of the United States is hereby repealed.

Section 2

[**Transportation of intoxicating liquors.**] The transportation or importation into any State, territory, or possession of the United States for delivery or use therein of intoxicating liquors, in violation of the laws thereof, is hereby prohibited.

Section 3

[**Ratification.**] This article shall be inoperative unless it shall have been ratified as an amendment to the Constitution by convention in the several States, as provided in the Constitution, within seven years from the date of the submission thereof to the States by the Congress.

Amendment XXII

(**The proposed amendment was sent to the states Mar. 21, 1947, by the Eightieth Congress. It was ratified Feb. 27, 1951.**)

Section 1

[**Limit to number of terms a president may serve.**] No person shall be elected to the office of the President more than twice, and no person who has held the office of President, or acted as President, for more than two years of a term to which some other person was elected President shall be elected to the office of the President more than once. But this article shall not apply to any person holding the office of President when this article was proposed by the Congress, and shall not prevent any person who may be holding the office of President, or acting as President, during the term within which this article becomes operative from holding the office of President or acting as President during the remainder of such term.

Section 2

[Ratification.] This article shall be inoperative unless it shall have been ratified as an amendment to the Constitution by the legislatures of three fourths of the several States within seven years from the date of its submission to the States by the Congress.

Amendment XXIII

(The proposed amendment was sent to the states June 16, 1960, by the Eighty-sixth Congress. It was ratified March 29, 1961.)

Section 1

[Electors for the District of Columbia.] The District constituting the seat of Government of the United States shall appoint in such manner as the Congress may direct: A number of electors of President and Vice President equal to the whole number of Senators and Representatives in Congress to which the District would be entitled if it were a State, but in no event more than the least populous State; they shall be in addition to those appointed by the States, but they shall be considered, for the purposes of the election of President and Vice President, to be electors appointed by a State; and they shall meet in the District and perform such duties as provided by the twelfth article of amendment.

Section 2

[Congress given power to enforce this article.] The Congress shall have the power to enforce this article by appropriate legislation.

Amendment XXIV

(The proposed amendment was sent to the states Aug. 27, 1962, by the Eighty-seventh Congress. It was ratified Jan. 23, 1964.)

Section 1

[Payment of poll tax or other taxes not to be prerequisite for voting in federal elections.] The right of citizens of the United States to vote in any primary or other election for President or Vice President, for electors for President or Vice President, or for Senator or Representative in Congress, shall not be denied or abridged by the United States or any State by reasons of failure to pay any poll tax or other tax.

Section 2

[Congress given power to enforce this article.] The Congress shall have the power to enforce this article by appropriate legislation.

Amendment XXV

(The proposed amendment was sent to the states July 6, 1965, by the Eighty-ninth Congress. It was ratified Feb. 10, 1967.)

Section 1

[Succession of vice president to presidency.] In case of the removal of the President from office or of his death or resignation, the Vice President shall become President.

Section 2

[Vacancy in office of vice president.] Whenever there is a vacancy in the office of the Vice President, the President shall nominate a Vice President who shall take office upon confirmation by a majority vote of both Houses of Congress.

Section 3

[Vice president as acting president.] Whenever the President transmits to the President pro tempore of the Senate and the Speaker of the House of Representatives his written declaration that he is unable to discharge the powers and duties of his office, and until he transmits to them a written declaration to the contrary, such powers and duties shall be discharged by the Vice President as Acting President.

Section 4

[Vice president as acting president.] Whenever the Vice President and a majority of either the principal officers of the executive departments or of such other body as Congress may by law provide, transmit to the President pro tempore of the Senate and the Speaker of the House of Representatives their written declaration that the President is unable to discharge the powers and duties of his office, the Vice President shall immediately assume the powers and duties of the office as Acting President.

Thereafter, when the President transmits to the President pro tempore of the Senate and the Speaker of the House of Representatives his written declaration that no inability exists, he shall resume the powers and duties of his office unless the Vice President and a majority of either the principal officers of the executive department or of such other body as Congress may by law provide, transmit within four days to the President pro tempore of the Senate and the Speaker of the House of Representatives their written declaration that the President is unable to discharge the powers and duties of his office. Thereupon Congress shall decide the issue, assembling within forty-eight hours for that purpose if not in session. If the Congress, within twenty-one days after receipt of the latter written declaration, or, if Congress is not in session, within twenty-one days after Congress is required to assemble, determines by two thirds vote of both Houses that the President is unable to discharge the powers and duties of his office, the Vice President shall continue to discharge the same as Acting President; otherwise, the President shall resume the powers and duties of his office.

Amendment XXVI

(The proposed amendment was sent to the states Mar. 23, 1971, by the Ninety-second Congress. It was ratified July 1, 1971.)

Section 1

[Voting for 18-year-olds.] The right of citizens of the United States, who are 18 years of age or older, to vote shall not be denied or abridged by the United States or by any state on account of age.

Section 2

[Congress given power to enforce this article.] The Congress shall have power to enforce this article by appropriate legislation.

Amendment XXVII

(Ratified May 7, 1992.)

[Congressional raises.] No law, varying the compensation for the services of the Senators and Representatives, shall take effect, until an election of Representatives shall have intervened.

Lincoln's Gettysburg Address

The Battle of Gettysburg, one of the most noted battles of the Civil War, was fought on July 1–3, 1863. On Nov. 19, 1863, the field was dedicated as a national cemetery by President Lincoln in a two-minute speech that was to become immortal. At the time of its delivery the speech was relegated to the inside pages of the papers, while a two-hour address by Edward Everett, the leading orator of the time, caught the headlines.

Four score and seven years ago our fathers brought forth on this continent a new nation conceived in liberty and dedicated to the proposition that all men are created equal. Now we are engaged in a great civil war testing whether that nation, or any nation so conceived and so dedicated, can long endure. We are met on a great battlefield of that war. We have come to dedicate a portion of that field as a final resting-place for those who here gave their lives that that nation might live. It is altogether fitting and proper that we should do this. But, in a larger sense, we cannot dedicate, we cannot consecrate, we cannot hallow this ground. The brave men, living and dead, who struggled here have consecrated it far above our poor power to add or detract. The world will little note nor long remember what we say here, but it can never forget what they did here. It is for us the living rather to be dedicated here to the unfinished work which they who fought here have thus far so nobly advanced. It is rather for us to be here dedicated to the great task remaining before us—that from these honored dead we take increased devotion to that cause for which they gave the last full measure of devotion—that we here highly resolve that these dead shall not have died in vain, that this nation under God shall have a new birth of freedom, and that government of the people, by the people, for the people shall not perish from the earth.

Assassinations and Attempts in U.S. Since 1865

Lincoln, Abraham (president of U.S.): Shot April 14, 1865, in Washington, DC, by John Wilkes Booth; died April 15.

Seward, William H. (secretary of state): Escaped assassination (though injured) April 14, 1865, in Washington, DC, by Lewis Powell (or Paine), accomplice of John Wilkes Booth.

Garfield, James A. (president of U.S.): Shot July 2, 1881, in Washington, DC, by Charles J. Guiteau; died Sept. 19.

McKinley, William (president of U.S.): Shot Sept. 6, 1901, in Buffalo by Leon Czolgosz; died Sept. 14.

Roosevelt, Theodore (ex-president of U.S.): Escaped assassination (though shot) Oct. 14, 1912, in Milwaukee while campaigning for president.

Cermak, Anton J. (mayor of Chicago): Shot Feb. 15, 1933, in Miami by Giuseppe Zangara, who attempted to assassinate Franklin D. Roosevelt; Cermak died March 6.

Roosevelt, Franklin D. (president-elect of U.S.): Escaped assassination unhurt Feb. 15, 1933, in Miami.

Long, Huey P. (U.S. senator from Louisiana): Shot Sept. 8, 1935, in Baton Rouge by Dr. Carl A. Weiss; died Sept. 10.

Truman, Harry S. (president of U.S.): Escaped assassination unhurt Nov. 1, 1950, in Washington, DC, as 2 Puerto Rican nationalists attempted to shoot their way into Blair House.

Kennedy, John F. (president of U.S.): Shot Nov. 22, 1963, in Dallas, Tex., allegedly by Lee Harvey Oswald; died same day. Injured was Gov. John B. Connally of Texas. Oswald was shot and killed two days later by Jack Ruby.

Malcolm X, also known as El-Hajj Malik El-Shabazz (black activist): Shot and killed in a New York City auditorium, Feb. 21, 1965; his killer(s) were never positively identified.

King, Martin Luther, Jr. (civil rights leader): Shot April 4, 1968, in Memphis by James Earl Ray; died same day.

Kennedy, Robert F. (U.S. senator from New York): Shot June 5, 1968, in Los Angeles by Sirhan Bishara Sirhan; died June 6.

Wallace, George C. (governor of Alabama): Shot and critically wounded in assassination attempt May 15, 1972, at Laurel, Md., by Arthur Herman Bremer. Wallace paralyzed from waist down.

Ford, Gerald R. (president of U.S.): Escaped assassination attempt Sept. 5, 1975, in Sacramento, Calif., by Lynette Alice (Squeaky) Fromme, who pointed but did not fire .45-caliber pistol. Escaped assassination attempt in San Francisco, Calif., Sept. 22, 1975, by Sara Jane Moore, who fired one shot from a .38-caliber pistol that was deflected.

Jordan, Vernon E., Jr. (civil rights leader): Shot and critically wounded in assassination attempt May 29, 1980, in Fort Wayne, Ind.

Reagan, Ronald (president of U.S.): Shot in left lung in Washington by John W. Hinckley, Jr., on March 30, 1981; three others also wounded.

'In God We Trust'

"In God We Trust" first appeared on U.S. coins after April 22, 1864, when Congress passed an act authorizing the coinage of a 2-cent piece bearing this motto. Thereafter, Congress extended its use to other coins. On July 30, 1956, it became the national motto.

Profile of the United States

This profile was created by the editors of the almanac from many data sources. Most figures are approximate. For additional details about the U.S., please refer to the appropriate sections of the almanac.

Geography

Number of states: 50
Territories: 15
Area (2000): total: 3,794,083 sq mi (9,826,675 sq km), land only: 3,537,438 sq mi (9,161,964 sq km), water: 256,645 sq mi (664,711 sq km). Share of world land area (1990): 6.2%
Northernmost point: Point Barrow, Alaska
Easternmost point: West Quoddy Head, Maine
Southernmost point: Ka Lae (South Cape), Hawaii
Westernmost point: Cape Wrangell, Alaska[1]
Geographic center (50 states): in Butte County, S.D. (44′ 58′ N. lat., 103′ 46′ W. long.)
Highest point: Mt. McKinley, Alaska (20,320 ft)
Lowest point: Death Valley, Calif. (282 ft below sea level)

1. The extreme points are measured from the geographic center of the United States (incl. Alaska and Hawaii), west of Castle Rock, S.D., 44° 58′ N. lat., 103° 46′ W. long. If measured from the prime meridian in Greenwich, England, Cape Wrangell, Alaska, would be the easternmost point.

Population

(Based on Census 2000 data unless otherwise noted.)

Total Resident Pop. (Oct. 2004 est.)[1]: 294,451,983
Population density: 79.6 people per sq mi
Mean center of population: 3 mi east of Edgar Springs in Phelps County, Mo.
Males: 138,053,563 (49.1% of pop.)
Females: 143,368,343 (50.9% of pop.)
White: 211,460,626 (75.1% of pop.)
Black: 34,658,190 (12.3% of pop.)
Asian: 10,242,998 (3.6% of pop.)
American Indian and Alaska Native: 2,475,956 (0.9% of pop.)
Hispanic/Latino[2]: 35,305,818 (12.5% of pop.)
Native Hawaiian and Other Pacific Islander: 398,835 (0.1% of pop.)
Median age: 35.3
Metropolitan population: 225,981,679
Nonmetropolitan population: 55,440,227
Families: 71,787,347
Average family size: 3.14
Homeownership: 67.4% of pop.
Married couples: 56,497,000
Never married: 48,200,000
Divorced: 19,800,000
Widowed: 13,700,000

1. Excludes the U.S. Armed Forces overseas. 2. People of Hispanic or Latino origin may be of any race.

Vital Statistics

Births (2002): 4,021,726 (13.9 per 1,000 pop.)
Deaths (2001): 2,417,798 (8.5 per 1,000 pop.)
Marriages (2003): 2,187,000 (7.5 per 1,000 pop.)
Divorces (2003): 3.8 per 1,000 pop.[1]
Infant mortality rate (2001): 6.8 per 1,000 live births
Legal abortions (2000): 857,475
Life expectancy (2001): Total U.S., both sexes, 77.2; total men, 74.4; total women, 79.8; white men, 75.0; white women, 80.2; black men, 68.6; black women, 75.5

1. U.S. totals no longer available.

Civilian Labor Force

All (2003): 146,510,000 (6.0% unemployed)
Men (2003): 78,238,000 (6.3% unemployed)
Women (2003): 68,272,000 (5.7% unemployed)
Work at home (2001 est.): 19.8 million
Farms (2003): 2,126,860; total acres (2003): 938,750,000
Avg. weekly earnings of workers (2003): $620
Avg. weekly hours of workers (2000): 34.5

Income and Credit

GDP (2003): $10,987.9 billion
Fed. Budget (2003): total receipts, $1,782.3 billion; total outlays, $2,157.6 billion; (2004 est.): total receipts, $1,798.1 billion; total outlays, $2,318.8 billion
Personal income per capita (2003): $31,632
Median four-person family income (2002): $62,732
Consumer credit outstanding (2003): $2,025.5 billion
Number below poverty level (2003): total, 35,861,000; white, 24,272,000; black, 8,781,000; Hispanic, 9,051,000; Asian, 1,401,000

Education

Public elementary school pupils, pre-K–grade 8 (2002):[1] 33,942,000
Public secondary school pupils, grades 9–12 (2002):[1] 13,976,000
Private elementary school pupils, K–grade 8 (2002):[1] 4,885,000
Private secondary school pupils, grades 9–12 (2002):[1] 1,356,000
High school dropout rate, ages 16–24 (2001): 10.7%
Total 2- and 4-year colleges and universities (2002): 4,168
Total higher education enrollment (2002): 15,927,987
  Undergraduate (2002): 13,715,610
  Graduate (2002): 1,903,730
  Professional (2002): 308,647

1. Estimated

Conveniences

Radio stations (Sept. 2003): AM, 4,802; FM, 8,648
Television stations (Sept. 2003): 1,730
Registered automobiles (2002): 135,920,677
Daily newspaper circulation (2002): 55,186,157
Total TV households (2003): 106,700,000
Percent households with a TV set (2003): 98%
Avg. number TV sets per household (2000): 2.4
Cable TV households (2003): 70%
Avg. number TV households with VCRs (2003): 92%
Percent households with a computer (2001): 56.5%
Percent households with Internet access (2001): 50.5%
Number of books sold (2000): 2,500,000,000

Crime

Total arrests (2002): 13.7 million
State, federal, and local prison inmates (2003): 2,078,570
Prisoners under sentence of death (2002): 3,557
Persons executed under civil authority (2003): 65
Law enforcement officers killed (2001): 220
Total murder victims (2002): 14,054
Violent crimes per 100,000 people (2002): 494.6
Property crimes per 100,000 people (2002): 3,624.1
Homicides per 100,000 people (2002): 5.6
Hate crime victims (2002): 7,642

Profile of General Demographic Characteristics, Census 2000

Subject	Number	Percent
Total population	**281,421,906**	**100.0%**
Sex and age		
Male	138,053,563	49.1
Female	143,368,343	50.9
Under 5 years	19,175,798	6.8
5 to 9 years	20,549,505	7.3
10 to 14 years	20,528,072	7.3
15 to 19 years	20,219,890	7.2
20 to 24 years	18,964,001	6.7
25 to 34 years	39,891,724	14.2
35 to 44 years	45,148,527	16.0
45 to 54 years	37,677,952	13.4
55 to 59 years	13,469,237	4.8
60 to 64 years	10,805,447	3.8
65 to 74 years	18,390,986	6.5
75 to 84 years	12,361,180	4.4
85 years and over	4,239,587	1.5
Median age (years)	35.3	n.a.
18 years and over	209,128,094	74.3
Male	100,994,367	35.9
Female	108,133,727	38.4
21 years and over	196,899,193	70.0
62 years and over	41,256,029	14.7
65 years and over	34,991,753	12.4
Male	14,409,625	5.1
Female	20,582,128	7.3
Race		
One race	274,595,678	97.6
White	211,460,626	75.1
Black or African American	34,658,190	12.3
American Indian and Alaska Native	2,475,956	0.9
Asian	10,242,998	3.6
Asian Indian	1,678,765	0.6
Chinese	2,432,585	0.9
Filipino	1,850,314	0.7
Japanese	796,700	0.3
Korean	1,076,872	0.4
Vietnamese	1,122,528	0.4
Other Asian[1]	1,285,234	0.5
Native Hawaiian and Other Pacific Islander	398,835	0.1
Native Hawaiian	140,652	—
Guamanian or Chamorro	58,240	—
Samoan	91,029	—
Other Pacific Islander[2]	108,914	—
Some other race	15,359,073	5.5
Two or more races	6,826,228	2.4
Race alone or in combination with one or more other races:[3]		
White	216,930,975	77.1
Black or African American	36,419,434	12.9
American Indian and Alaska Native	4,119,301	1.5
Asian	11,898,828	4.2
Native Hawaiian and Other Pacific Islander	874,414	0.3
Some other race	18,521,486	6.6

Subject	Number	Percent
Hispanic or Latino and race		
Total population	**281,421,906**	**100.0%**
Hispanic or Latino (of any race)	35,305,818	12.5
Mexican	20,640,711	7.3
Puerto Rican	3,406,178	1.2
Cuban	1,241,685	0.4
Other Hispanic or Latino	10,017,244	3.6
Not Hispanic or Latino	246,116,088	87.5
White alone	194,552,774	69.1
Relationship		
Total population	**281,421,906**	**100.0%**
In households	273,643,273	97.2
Householder	105,480,101	37.5
Spouse	54,493,232	19.4
Child	83,393,392	29.6
Own child under 18	64,494,637	22.9
Other relatives	15,684,318	5.6
Under 18	6,042,435	2.1
Nonrelatives	14,592,230	5.2
Unmarried partner	5,475,768	1.9
In group quarters	7,778,633	2.8
Institutionalized pop.	4,059,039	1.4
Noninstitutionalized pop.	3,719,594	1.3
Household by type		
Total households	**105,480,101**	**100.0**
Family households (families)	71,787,347	68.1
With own children under 18	34,588,368	32.8
Married-couple family	54,493,232	51.7
With own children under 18	24,835,505	23.5
Female householder, no husband present	12,900,103	12.2
With own children under 18	7,561,874	7.2
Nonfamily households	33,692,754	31.9
Householder living alone	27,230,075	25.8
Householder 65 and over	9,722,857	9.2
Households with individuals under 18	38,022,115	36.0
Households with individuals 65 and over	24,672,708	23.4
Average household size	2.59	n.a.
Average family size	3.14	n.a.
Housing occupancy		
Total housing units	**115,904,641**	**100.0**
Occupied housing units	105,480,101	91.0
Vacant housing units	10,424,540	9.0
For seasonal, recreational, or occasional use	3,578,718	3.1
Homeowner vacancy rate (%)	1.7	n.a.
Rental vacancy rate (%)	6.8	n.a.
Housing tenure		
Occupied housing units	**105,480,101**	**100.0**
Owner-occupied housing units	69,815,753	66.2
Renter-occupied housing units	35,664,348	33.8
Average household size of owner-occupied units	2.69	n.a.
Average household size of renter-occupied units	2.40	n.a.

NOTES: (—) represents zero or rounds to zero; n.a. = not applicable. 1. Other Asian alone, or two or more Asian categories. 2. Other Pacific Islander alone, or two or more Native Hawaiian and Other Pacific Islander categories. 3. In combination with one or more of the other races listed. The six numbers may add to more than the total population and the six percentages may add to more than 100% because individuals may report more than one race. *Source:* U.S. Census Bureau, Census 2000. Web: www.census.gov.

Population by State

State	July 2003 pop.	2000	1990	1950	1900	1790
Alabama	4,500,752	4,447,100	4,040,587	3,061,743	1,828,697	—
Alaska	648,818	626,932	550,043	128,643	63,592	—
Arizona	5,580,811	5,130,632	3,665,228	749,587	122,931	—
Arkansas	2,725,714	2,673,400	2,350,725	1,909,511	1,311,564	—
California	35,484,453	33,871,648	29,760,021	10,586,223	1,485,053	—
Colorado	4,550,688	4,301,261	3,294,394	1,325,089	539,700	—
Connecticut	3,483,372	3,405,565	3,287,116	2,007,280	908,420	237,946
Delaware	817,491	783,600	666,168	318,085	184,735	59,096
DC	563,384	572,059	606,900	802,178	278,718	—
Florida	17,019,068	15,982,378	12,937,926	2,771,305	528,542	—
Georgia	8,684,715	8,186,453	6,478,216	3,444,578	2,216,331	82,548
Hawaii	1,257,608	1,211,537	1,108,229	499,794	154,001	—
Idaho	1,366,332	1,293,953	1,006,749	588,637	161,772	—
Illinois	12,653,544	12,419,293	11,430,602	8,712,176	4,821,550	—
Indiana	6,195,643	6,080,485	5,544,159	3,934,224	2,516,462	—
Iowa	2,944,062	2,926,324	2,776,755	2,621,073	2,231,853	—
Kansas	2,723,507	2,688,418	2,477,574	1,905,299	1,470,495	—
Kentucky	4,117,827	4,041,769	3,685,296	2,944,806	2,147,174	73,677
Louisiana	4,496,334	4,468,976	4,219,973	2,683,516	1,381,625	—
Maine	1,305,728	1,274,923	1,227,928	913,774	694,466	96,540
Maryland	5,508,909	5,296,486	4,781,468	2,343,001	1,188,044	319,728
Massachusetts	6,433,422	6,349,097	6,016,425	4,690,514	2,805,346	378,787
Michigan	10,079,985	9,938,444	9,295,297	6,371,766	2,420,982	—
Minnesota	5,059,375	4,919,479	4,375,099	2,982,483	1,751,394	—
Mississippi	2,881,281	2,844,658	2,573,216	2,178,914	1,551,270	—
Missouri	5,704,484	5,595,211	5,117,073	3,954,653	3,106,665	—
Montana	917,621	902,195	799,065	591,024	243,329	—
Nebraska	1,739,291	1,711,263	1,578,385	1,325,510	1,066,300	—
Nevada	2,241,154	1,998,257	1,201,833	160,083	42,335	—
New Hampshire	1,287,687	1,235,786	1,109,252	533,242	411,588	141,885
New Jersey	8,638,396	8,414,350	7,730,188	4,835,329	1,883,669	184,139
New Mexico	1,874,614	1,819,046	1,515,069	681,187	195,310	—
New York	19,190,115	18,976,457	17,990,455	14,830,192	7,268,894	340,120
North Carolina	8,407,248	8,049,313	6,628,637	4,061,929	1,893,810	393,751
North Dakota	633,837	642,200	638,800	619,636	319,146	—
Ohio	11,435,798	11,353,140	10,847,115	7,946,627	4,157,545	—
Oklahoma	3,511,532	3,450,654	3,145,585	2,233,351	790,391[1]	—
Oregon	3,559,596	3,421,399	2,842,321	1,521,341	413,536	—
Pennsylvania	12,365,455	12,281,054	11,881,643	10,498,012	6,302,115	434,373
Rhode Island	1,076,164	1,048,319	1,003,464	791,896	428,556	68,825
South Carolina	4,147,152	4,012,012	3,486,703	2,117,027	1,340,316	249,073
South Dakota	764,309	754,844	696,004	652,740	401,570	—
Tennessee	5,841,748	5,689,283	4,877,185	3,291,718	2,020,616	35,691
Texas	22,118,509	20,851,820	16,986,510	7,711,194	3,048,710	—
Utah	2,351,467	2,233,169	1,722,850	688,862	276,749	—
Vermont	619,107	608,827	562,758	377,747	343,641	85,425
Virginia	7,386,330	7,078,515	6,187,358	3,318,680	1,854,184	747,610[2]
Washington	6,131,445	5,894,121	4,866,692	2,378,963	518,103	—
West Virginia	1,810,354	1,808,344	1,793,477	2,005,552	958,800	—
Wisconsin	5,472,299	5,363,675	4,891,769	3,434,575	2,069,042	—
Wyoming	501,242	493,782	453,588	290,529	92,531	—
Total U.S.	**290,809,777**	**281,421,906**	**248,709,873**	**151,325,798**	**76,212,168**	**3,929,214**

1. Includes population of Indian Territory, 1900: 392,960. 2. Until 1863, Virginia included what is now West Virginia. *Source:* U.S. Bureau of the Census. Web: www.census.gov.

Total U.S. Population

Area	2000	1990	1980	Area	2000	1990	1980
50 states[1]	281,421,906	248,709,873	226,545,805	N. Mariana Is.[3]	69,221	43,345	([4])
48 coterminous[1]	279,583,437	247,051,601	225,179,263	Puerto Rico	3,808,610	3,522,037	3,196,520
Alaska	626,932	550,043	401,851	Trust Ter. of Pac. Is.	([7])	15,122[6]	132,929[5]
Hawaii	1,211,537	1,108,229	964,691	Virgin Is. of U.S.	108,612	101,809	96,569
American Samoa	57,291	46,773	32,297	Wake Island	([2])	([2])	302
Guam	154,805	133,152	105,979	Population abroad	576,367[8]	922,819	995,546
Johnston Atoll	([2])	([2])	327	Armed forces	n.a.	910,611	515,408
Midway	([2])	([2])	453	**Total**	**286,196,812**	**253,451,585**	**231,106,727**

NOTE: n.a. = not available. 1. Includes the District of Columbia. 2. No indigenous population. 3. The Commonwealth of the Northern Mariana Islands (CNMI) became part of the United States in 1986. 4. Included under the territory of the Pacific Islands. 5. Includes Northern Mariana Islands. 6. Palau only trust territory remaining. 7. Palau, the last remaining trust territory, became an independent country in 1994. 8. Includes overseas U.S. military and federal civilian employees and their dependents living with them. *Source:* U.S. Bureau of the Census. Web: www.census.gov.

Colonial Population Estimates
(in round numbers)

Year	Population	Year	Population	Year	Population	Year	Population
1610	350	1660	75,100	1710	331,700	1760	1,593,600
1620	2,300	1670	111,900	1720	466,200	1770	2,148,100
1630	4,600	1680	151,500	1730	629,400	1780	2,780,400
1640	26,600	1690	210,400	1740	905,600		
1650	50,400	1700	250,900	1750	1,170,800		

Covers years before the establishment of the U.S. Census in 1790.

U.S. Population by Region, 1990–2003

	Population			Change, 1990–2000	
Area	April 1, 1990	April 1, 2000	July 1, 2003	Number	Percent
United States	**248,709,873**	**281,421,906**	**290,809,777**	**32,712,033**	**13.2%**
Region[1]					
Northeast	50,809,229	53,594,378	54,399,446	2,785,149	5.5
Midwest	59,668,632	64,392,776	65,406,134	4,724,144	7.9
South	85,445,930	100,236,820	104,538,348	14,790,890	17.3
West	52,786,082	63,197,932	66,465,849	10,411,850	19.7

1. The Northeast region includes Conn., Maine, Mass., N.H., N.J., N.Y., Pa., R.I., and Vt. The Midwest includes Ill., Ind., Iowa, Kans., Mich., Minn., Mo., Neb., N.D., Ohio, S.D., and Wis. The South includes Ala., Ark., Del., D.C., Fla., Ga., Ky., La., Md., Miss., N.C., Okla., S.C., Tenn., Tex., Va., and W.Va.. The West includes Alaska, Ariz., Calif., Colo., Hawaii, Idaho, Mont., Nev., N.M., Ore., Utah, Wash., and Wyo. *Source:* U.S. Census Bureau, Census 2000; 1990 Census. Web: www.census.gov.

Resident Population—Selected Characteristics, 1790–2003
(in thousands)

						Other			
Date	Male	Female	White	Black	Total	American Indian, Eskimo, Aleut	Asian and Pacific Islanders	Two or more races	Hispanic origin[1]
1790 (Aug. 2)	n.a.	n.a.	3,172	757	n.a.	n.a.	n.a.	n.a.	n.a.
1800 (Aug. 4)	n.a.	n.a.	4,306	1,002	n.a.	n.a.	n.a.	n.a.	n.a.
1850 (June 1)	11,838	11,354	19,553	3,639	n.a.	n.a.	n.a.	n.a.	n.a.
1900 (June 1)	38,816	37,178	66,809	8,834	351	n.a.	n.a.	n.a.	n.a.
1910 (Apr. 15)	47,332	44,640	81,732	9,828	413	n.a.	n.a.	n.a.	n.a.
1920 (Jan. 1)	53,900	51,810	94,821	10,463	427	n.a.	n.a.	n.a.	n.a.
1930 (Apr. 1)	62,137	60,638	110,287	11,891	597	n.a.	n.a.	n.a.	n.a.
1940 (Apr. 1)	66,062	65,608	118,215	12,866	589	n.a.	n.a.	n.a.	n.a.
1950 (Apr. 1)[2]	74,833	75,864	134,942	15,042	713	n.a.	n.a.	n.a.	n.a.
1950 (Apr. 1)	75,187	76,139	135,150	15,045	1,131	n.a.	n.a.	n.a.	n.a.
1960 (Apr. 1)	88,331	90,992	158,832	18,872	1,620	n.a.	n.a.	n.a.	n.a.
1970 (Apr. 1)	98,926	104,309	178,098	22,581	2,557	n.a.	n.a.	n.a.	n.a.
1980 (Apr. 1)	110,053	116,493	194,713	26,683	5,150	1,420	3,729	n.a.	14,609
1990 (Apr. 1)	121,271	127,494	208,727	30,511	9,527	2,065	7,462	n.a.	22,372
2000 (Apr. 1)[3]	138,054	143,368	228,104	35,704	17,613	2,664	11,052	3,898	35,306
2003 (July 1)[4]	143,037	147,773	234,196	37,099	19,514	2,787	12,420	4,308	39,899

NOTES: n.a. = not available. 1. Persons of Hispanic origin may be of any race. 2. Excludes Alaska and Hawaii. 3. Total population count has been revised, as have the sex, race, and Hispanic origin numbers. 4. June 2004 estimate. *Source:* U.S. Census Bureau. Web: www.census.gov.

Ratio of Males to Females, by Age Group, 1950–2003
(number of males per 100 females, total resident population)

Age	1950	1960	1970	1980	1990[1]	2000	2003[2]
All ages	**98.6**	**97.1**	**94.8**	**94.5**	**95.1**	**96.3**	**96.8**
Under 14 years	103.7	103.4	103.9	104.6	104.9	104.9	104.8
14 to 24 years	98.2	98.7	98.7	101.9	104.6	105.1	105.7
25 to 44 years	96.4	95.7	95.5	97.4	98.9	100.2	101.1
45 to 64 years	100.1	95.7	91.6	90.7	92.5	94.8	95.0
65 years and over	89.6	82.8	72.1	67.6	67.2	70.8	71.3

NOTES: As of April 1 for all years except 2003. 1. The April 1, 1990, census count (248,765,170) includes count resolution corrections processed through August 1997, and does not include adjustments for census coverage errors except for adjustments estimated for the 1995 Census Test in Oakland, Calif.; Paterson, N.J.; and six Louisiana parishes. These adjustments amounted to a total of 55,297 persons. 2. As of July 1; June 2004 estimate. *Source:* U.S. Census Bureau, *Current Population Reports,* P25-1095 and P25-1130; and unpublished data. From *Statistical Abstract of the United States 1999.* 2000 data are from Census 2000; 2003 data are from NC-EST2003-02.

National Censuses, 1790–2000[1]

Year	Resident population[2]	Land area, sq mi	Pop. per sq mi	Year	Resident population[2]	Land area, sq mi	Pop. per sq mi
1790	3,929,214	864,746	4.5	1900	75,994,575	2,969,834	25.6
1800	5,308,483	864,746	6.1	1910	91,972,266	2,969,565	31.0
1810	7,239,881	1,681,828	4.3	1920	105,710,620	2,969,451	35.6
1820	9,638,453	1,749,462	5.5	1930	122,775,046	2,977,128	41.2
1830	12,866,020	1,749,462	7.4	1940	131,669,275	2,977,128	44.2
1840	17,069,453	1,749,462	9.8	1950	150,697,361	2,974,726	50.7
1850	23,191,876	2,940,042	7.9	1960	179,323,175	3,540,911	50.6
1860	31,443,321	2,969,640	10.6	1970	203,302,031	3,540,023	57.4
1870	39,818,449	2,969,640	13.4	1980	226,545,805	3,539,289	64.0
1880	50,155,783	2,969,640	16.9	1990	248,709,873	3,536,278	70.3
1890	62,947,714	2,969,640	21.2	2000	281,421,906	3,537,441	79.6

1. Beginning with 1960, figures include Alaska and Hawaii. 2. Excludes armed forces overseas. *Source:* U.S. Bureau of the Census. Web: www.census.gov.

Population Distribution by Age, Race, Nativity, and Sex Ratio, 1860–2003

	Age						Race and nativity				
							White[1]				
Year	Total	Under 5	5–19	20–44	45–64	65 and over	Total	Native born	Foreign born	Black	Other races[1]
Percent distribution											
1860[2]	100.0%	15.4%	35.8%	35.7%	10.4%	2.7%	85.6%	72.6%	13.0%	14.1%	0.3%
1870[2]	100.0	14.3	35.4	35.4	11.9	3.0	87.1	72.9	14.2	12.7	0.2
1880[2]	100.0	13.8	34.3	35.9	12.6	3.4	86.5	73.4	13.1	13.1	0.3
1890[3]	100.0	12.2	33.9	36.9	13.1	3.9	87.5	73.0	14.5	11.9	0.3
1900	100.0	12.1	32.3	37.7	13.7	4.1	87.9	74.5	13.4	11.6	0.5
1910	100.0	11.6	30.4	39.0	14.6	4.3	88.9	74.4	14.5	10.7	0.4
1920	100.0	10.9	29.8	38.4	16.1	4.7	89.7	76.7	13.0	9.9	0.4
1930	100.0	9.3	29.5	38.3	17.4	5.4	89.8	78.4	11.4	9.7	0.5
1940	100.0	8.0	26.4	38.9	19.8	6.8	89.8	81.1	8.7	9.8	0.4
1950	100.0	10.7	23.2	37.6	20.3	8.1	89.5	82.8	6.7	10.0	0.5
1960	100.0	11.3	27.1	32.2	20.1	9.2	88.6	83.4	5.2	10.5	0.9
1970[2]	100.0	8.4	29.5	31.7	20.6	9.8	87.6	83.4	4.3	11.1	1.4
1980	100.0	7.2	24.8	37.1	19.6	11.3	83.1	—	—	11.7	5.2
1990	100.0	7.6	21.3	40.1	18.6	12.5	83.9	—	—	12.3	3.8
2000	100.0	6.8	21.8	37.0	22.0	12.4	75.1[4]	—	—	12.3[4]	10.1[5]
2003[6]	100.0	6.8	21.1	36.1	23.6	12.4	80.5	—	—	12.8[4]	6.7[5]
Males per 100 females											
1860[2]	104.7	102.4	101.2	107.9	111.5	98.3	105.3	103.7	115.1	99.6	260.8
1870[2]	102.2	102.9	101.2	99.2	114.5	100.5	102.8	100.6	115.3	96.2	400.7
1880[2]	103.6	103.0	101.3	104.0	110.2	101.4	104.0	102.1	115.9	97.8	362.2
1890[3]	105.0	103.6	101.4	107.3	108.3	104.2	105.4	102.9	118.7	99.5	165.2
1900	104.4	102.1	100.9	105.8	110.7	102.0	104.9	102.8	117.4	98.6	185.2
1910	106.0	102.5	101.3	108.1	114.4	101.1	106.6	102.7	129.2	98.9	185.6
1920	104.0	102.5	100.8	102.8	115.2	101.3	104.4	101.7	121.7	99.2	156.6
1930	102.5	103.0	101.4	100.5	109.1	100.5	102.9	101.1	115.8	97.0	150.6
1940	100.7	103.2	102.0	98.1	105.2	95.5	101.2	100.1	111.1	95.0	140.5
1950	98.6	103.9	102.5	96.2	100.1	89.6	99.0	98.8	102.0	93.7	129.7
1960	97.1	103.4	102.7	95.6	95.7	82.8	97.4	97.6	94.2	93.3	109.7
1970[2]	94.8	104.0	103.3	95.1	91.6	72.1	95.3	95.9	83.8	90.8	100.2
1980	94.5	104.7	104.0	98.1	90.7	67.6	94.8	—	—	89.6	100.3
1990	95.1	104.8	105.0	99.8	92.5	67.2	95.9	—	—	89.8	96.5
2000	96.3	104.8	105.3	101.0	94.8	70.0	96.4[4]	—	—	90.5[4]	102.2[5]
2003[6]	96.8	104.6	105.2	102.1	95.0	71.3	97.8	—	—	91.0[4]	95.7[5]

NOTES: Data exclude armed forces overseas. (—) Data not available. 1. The racial census data for 1980 and all years following are not directly comparable to those of other years because of changes in the way some persons reported their race, as well as changes in procedures relating to racial classification. 2. Excludes persons for whom age is not available. 3. Excludes persons enumerated in the Indian Territory and on Indian reservations. 4. Includes only those claiming one race only. 5. Includes American Indian and Alaska Native, Asian, Native Hawaiian and other Pacific Islander, and those claiming more than one race. 6. June 2004 estimate. *Source:* U.S. Bureau of the Census. Web: www.census.gov.

Population Explosion Among Older Americans

The United States saw a rapid growth in its elderly population during the 20th century. The number of Americans aged 65 and older climbed above 34.9 million in 2000, compared with 3.1 million in 1900. For the same years, the ratio of elderly Americans to the total population jumped from 1 in 25 to 1 in 8. The trend is guaranteed to continue in the coming century as the baby-boom generation grows older. Between 1990 and 2020, the population aged 65 to 74 is projected to grow 74%.

The elderly population explosion is a result of impressive increases in life expectancy. When the nation was founded, the average American could expect to live to the age of 35. Life expectancy at birth had increased to 47.3 by 1900 and in 2000 stood at 76.9.

Along with the growth of the general elderly population has come a remarkable increase in the number of Americans reaching age 100. In 2000 there were 50,454 centenarians (people aged 100 or over), representing 1 out of every 5,578 people. In 1990 centenarians numbered 37,306 people, or 1 out of every 6,667 people.

Source: Based on U.S. Census Bureau data.

Persons 65 Years Old and Over—Characteristics by Sex, 1980–2000

Characteristic	Total			Male			Female		
	1980	1990	2000	1980	1990	2000	1980	1990	2000
Total[1] (million)	24.2	29.6	32.6	9.9	12.3	13.9	14.2	17.2	18.7
White (million)	21.9	26.5	n.a.	9.0	11.0	n.a.	12.9	15.4	n.a.
Black (million)	2.0	2.5	n.a.	0.8	1.0	n.a.	1.2	1.5	n.a.
Percent below poverty level[2]	15.2%	11.4%	9.7%	11.1%	7.8%	6.9%	17.9%	13.9%	11.8%
Percent distribution									
Marital status:									
Single	5.5%	4.6%	3.9%	4.9%	4.2%	4.2%	5.9%	4.9%	3.6%
Married	55.4	56.1	57.2	78.0	76.5	75.2	39.5	41.4	43.8
Spouse present	53.6	54.1	54.6	76.1	74.2	72.6	37.9	39.7	41.3
Spouse absent	1.8	2.0	2.6	1.9	2.3	2.6	1.7	1.7	2.5
Widowed	35.7	34.2	32.1	13.5	14.2	14.4	51.2	48.6	45.3
Divorced	3.5	5.0	6.7	3.6	5.0	6.1	3.4	5.1	7.2
Years of school completed:									
8 years or fewer	43.1%	28.5%	16.7%	45.3%	30.0%	17.8%	41.6%	27.5%	15.9%
1 to 3 years of high school	16.2	16.1	13.8[3]	15.5	15.7	12.7[3]	16.7	16.4	14.7[3]
4 years of high school	24.0	32.9	35.9[4]	21.4	29.0	30.4[4]	25.8	35.6	39.9[4]
1 to 3 years of college	8.2	10.9	18.0[5]	7.5	10.8	17.8[5]	8.6	11.0	18.2[5]
4 years or more of college	8.6	11.6	15.6[6]	10.3	14.5	21.4[6]	7.4	9.5	11.4[6]
Labor force participation[7]:									
Employed	12.2%	11.5%	12.4%	18.4%	15.9%	16.9%	7.8%	8.4%	9.1%
Unemployed	0.4	0.4	0.4	0.6	0.5	0.6	0.3	0.3	0.3
Not in labor force	87.5	88.1	87.2	81.0	83.6	82.5	91.9	91.3	90.6

NOTES: n.a. = not available. 1. Includes other races, not shown separately. 2. Poverty status based on income in preceding year. 3. Represents those who completed 9th to 12th grade, but have no high school diploma. 4. High school graduate. 5. Some college or associate degree. 6. Bachelor's or advanced degree. 7. Annual averages of monthly figures (from U.S. Bureau of Labor Statistics, *Employment and Earnings*, January issues). Data beginning 1994 not directly comparable with earlier years). *Source:* Except as noted, U.S. Bureau of the Census, *Current Population Reports.* From *Statistical Abstract of the United States 2001.*

10 Places of 100,000 or More Population with the Highest Proportion of Population 65 and Over, 2000

Place[1]	Total population	Population 65 and over	Percent 65 and over
Clearwater, Fla.	108,787	23,357	21.5%
Cape Coral, Fla.	102,286	20,020	19.6
Honolulu, Hawaii[2]	371,657	66,257	17.8
St. Petersburg, Fla.	248,232	43,173	17.4
Hollywood, Fla.	139,357	24,159	17.3
Warren, Mich.	138,247	23,871	17.3
Miami, Fla.	362,470	61,768	17.0
Livonia, Mich.	100,545	16,988	16.9
Scottsdale, Ariz.	202,705	33,884	16.7
Hialeah, Fla.	226,419	37,679	16.6

1. Census 2000 showed 245 places in the United States with 100,000 or more population. They included 238 incorporated places (including 4 city-county consolidations) and 7 census designated places that were not legally incorporated. For a list of these places by state, see www.census.gov/population/www/cen2000/phc-t6.html. 2. Honolulu, Hawaii, is a census designated place and is not legally incorporated. Source: U.S. Census Bureau. Web: www.census.gov

Household and Family Statistics

Households by Size, 1790–2002

		Percent distribution of number of households							
Year	Number of households (in thousands)	1 person	2 persons	3 persons	4 persons	5 persons	6 persons	7 or more persons	Avg. pop. per household
1790 (Mar.)	558	3.7%	7.8%	11.7%	13.8%	13.9%	13.2%	35.8%	—
1890 (June)	12,690	3.6	13.2	16.7	16.8	15.1	11.6	23.0	4.93
1900 (Mar.)	15,964	5.1	15.0	17.6	16.9	14.2	10.9	20.4	—
1930 (Apr.)	29,905	7.9	23.4	20.8	17.5	12.0	7.6	10.9	4.11
1940 (Apr.)	34,949	7.1	24.8	22.4	18.1	11.5	6.8	9.3	3.67
1950 (Apr.)[1]	43,468	10.9	28.8	22.6	17.8	10.0	5.1	4.9	3.37
1955 (Mar.)	47,788	10.9	28.5	20.4	18.9	11.1	5.4	4.9	3.33
1960 (Mar.)	52,610	13.1	27.8	18.9	17.6	11.5	5.7	5.4	3.35
1965 (Mar.)	57,251	15.0	28.1	17.9	16.1	11.0	5.8	6.1	3.32
1970 (Mar.)	62,874	17.0	28.8	17.3	15.8	10.4	5.6	5.1	3.14
1975 (Mar.)	71,120	19.6	30.6	17.4	15.6	9.0	4.3	3.5	2.94
1980 (Mar.)	80,776	22.7	31.3	17.5	15.7	7.5	3.1	2.2	2.76
1985 (Mar.)	86,789	23.7	31.6	17.8	15.7	7.0	2.6	1.5	2.69
1990 (Mar.)	93,347	24.6	32.2	17.2	15.5	6.7	2.3	1.4	2.63
1995 (Mar.)	98,990	25.0	32.1	17.0	15.5	6.7	2.3	1.4	2.65
2000 (Mar.)	104,705	25.5	33.1	16.4	14.6	6.7	2.3	1.4	2.62
2002 (Mar.)[2]	109,297	28.8	36.2	17.7	15.8	6.9	2.4	1.4	2.58

1. Covers related persons only; therefore, not strictly comparable with other years. 2. Based on Census 2000 and an expanded sample of households. *Source:* U.S. Census Bureau. Web: www.census.gov.

Households by Type, 1980–2002

	Households					
	Number				Percent distribution	
Type of household	1980	1990	2000	2002	1990	2000
Total households	80,776,000	93,347,000	104,705,000	109,297,000	100%	100%
Family households	59,550,000	66,090,000	72,025,000	74,329,000	71	69
Married couple family	49,112,000	52,317,000	55,311,000	56,747,000	56	53
Male householder, no spouse present	1,733,000	2,884,000	4,028,000	4,438,000	3	4
Female householder, no spouse present	8,705,000	10,890,000	12,687,000	13,143,000	12	12
Nonfamily households	21,226,000	27,257,000	32,680,000	34,969,000	29	31
Living alone	18,296,000	22,999,000	26,724,000	28,775,000	25	26
Male householder	8,807,000	11,606,000	14,641,000	15,579,000	12	14
Living alone	6,966,000	9,049,000	11,181,000	12,004,000	10	11
Female householder	12,419,000	15,651,000	18,039,000	19,390,000	17	17
Living alone	11,330,000	13,950,000	15,543,000	16,771,000	15	15

Source: U.S. Census Bureau, *Current Population Reports.* From *Statistical Abstract of the United States, 2002.*

Homeownership Rates by Race and Ethnicity of Householder

	1995	1996	1997	1998	1999	2000	2002	2003
U.S. total	64.7	65.4	65.7	66.3	66.8	67.4	67.9	68.3
White, total	68.7	69.1	69.3	70.0	70.5	71.1	71.8	72.1
White, non-Hispanic	70.9	71.7	72.0	72.6	73.2	73.8	74.5	75.4
Black, total	42.7	44.1	44.8	45.6	46.3	47.2	47.3	48.1
Other race[1]	47.2	51.0	52.5	53.0	53.7	53.5	54.7	56.0
American Indian, Aleut, Eskimo	55.8	51.6	51.7	54.3	56.1	56.2	54.6	54.3
Asian or Pacific Islander	50.8	50.8	52.8	52.6	53.1	52.8	54.7	56.3
Other	37.4	n.a.	n.a.	n.a.	n.a.	n.a.	n.a.	n.a.
Hispanic	42.1	42.8	43.3	44.7	45.5	46.3	48.2	46.7
Non-Hispanic	66.7	67.4	67.8	68.3	68.9	69.5	70.0	70.8

NOTE: n.a. = not applicable. 1. Beginning in 1996, those answering "other" for race were allocated to one of the four race categories—white; black; American Indian, Aleut, or Eskimo (one category); or Asian or Pacific Islander. *Source:* U.S. Census Bureau. Web: www.census.gov.

Homeownership by State, 1990 and 2003

State	Homeownership rate (%) 1990	2003	State	Homeownership rate (%) 1990	2003	State	Homeownership rate (%) 1990	2003
U.S. total	63.9%	68.3%	Kentucky	65.8%	74.4%	Ohio	68.7%	72.8%
Alabama	68.4	76.2	Louisiana	67.8	67.5	Oklahoma	70.3	69.1
Alaska	58.4	70.0	Maine	74.2	73.7	Oregon	64.4	68.0
Arizona	64.5	67.0	Maryland	64.9	71.6	Pennsylvania	73.8	73.7
Arkansas	67.8	69.6	Massachusetts	58.6	64.3	Rhode Island	58.5	59.9
California	53.8	58.9	Michigan	72.3	75.6	South Carolina	71.4	75.0
Colorado	59.0	71.3	Minnesota	68.0	77.2	South Dakota	66.2	70.9
Connecticut	67.9	73.0	Mississippi	69.4	73.4	Tennessee	68.3	70.8
Delaware	67.7	77.2	Missouri	64.0	74.0	Texas	59.7	64.5
DC	36.4	43.0	Montana	69.1	71.5	Utah	70.1	73.4
Florida	65.1	69.5	Nebraska	67.3	69.5	Vermont	72.6	71.4
Georgia	64.3	71.4	Nevada	55.8	64.8	Virginia	69.8	75.0
Hawaii	55.5	58.3	New Hampshire	65.0	74.4	Washington	61.8	65.9
Idaho	69.4	74.4	New Jersey	65.0	66.9	West Virginia	72.0	78.1
Illinois	63.0	70.7	New Mexico	68.6	70.3	Wisconsin	68.3	72.8
Indiana	67.0	74.4	New York	53.3	54.3	Wyoming	68.9	72.9
Iowa	70.7	73.4	North Carolina	69.0	70.0			
Kansas	69.0	70.3	North Dakota	67.2	68.7			

Source: U.S. Census Bureau. Web: www.census.gov.

Persons Living Alone, by Sex and Age
(in thousands)

	1990 Number	%	2000 Number	%	2002 Number	%
Both sexes	22,999	100	26,724	100	28,775	100
15 to 24 years old	1,210	5	1,144	4	1,292	4
25 to 34 years old	3,972	17	3,848	14	3,923	14
35 to 44 years old	3,138	14	4,109	15	4,103	14
45 to 64 years old	5,502	24	7,842	29	8,992	31
65 to 74 years old	4,350	19	4,091	15	4,279	15
75 years old and over	4,825	21	5,692	21	6,187	22
Male.	9,049	39	11,181	42	12,004	42
15 to 24 years old	674	3	556	2	601	2
25 to 34 years old	2,395	10	2,279	9	2,322	8
35 to 44 years old	1,836	8	2,569	10	2,613	9
45 to 64 years old	2,203	10	3,422	13	3,904	14
65 to 74 years old	1,042	5	1,108	4	1,225	4
75 years old and over	901	4	1,247	5	1,339	5
Female.	13,950	61	15,543	58	16,771	58
15 to 24 years old	536	2	588	2	691	2
25 to 34 years old	1,578	7	1,568	6	1,601	6
35 to 44 years old	1,303	6	1,540	6	1,490	5
45 to 64 years old	3,300	14	4,420	17	5,087	18
65 to 74 years old	3,309	14	2,983	11	3,054	11
75 years old and over	3,924	17	4,444	17	4,848	17

Source: U.S. Census Bureau, *Current Population Reports*, P20-547, and earlier reports; and unpublished data.

Married-Couple and Unmarried-Partner Households for the U.S. and Regions, 2000

Area	Total number of coupled households[1]	Coupled households (% of all households)	Married couples (% of coupled households)	Unmarried partners (% of coupled households)	Opposite sex unmarried partners (% of coupled households)	Same-sex unmarried partners (% of coupled households)
United States	59,969,000	56.9%	90.9%	9.1%	8.1%	1.0%
Region						
Northeast	11,205,641	55.2	90.4	9.6	8.6	1.1
Midwest	14,222,533	57.5	91.1	8.9	8.1	0.7
South	21,549,582	56.7	91.6	8.4	7.4	1.0
West	12,991,244	57.9	89.8	10.2	9.0	1.2

NOTE: Totals may not add up due to rounding. 1. Coupled households represent total of married-couple and unmarried-partner households. *Source:* U.S. Census Bureau, Census 20000 Summary File 1.

Marital Status
Marriages and Divorces, 1900–2003

Year	Marriage Number	Rate[2]	Divorce[1] Number	Rate[2]	Year	Marriage Number	Rate[2]	Divorce[1] Number	Rate[2]
1900	709,000	9.3	55,751	0.7	1960	1,523,000	8.5	393,000	2.2
1910	948,166	10.3	83,045	0.9	1970	2,158,802	10.6	708,000	3.5
1920	1,274,476	12.0	170,505	1.6	1980	2,406,708	10.6	1,182,000	5.2
1930	1,126,856	9.2	195,961	1.6	1990	2,448,000	9.8	1,175,000	4.7
1940	1,595,879	12.1	264,000	2.0	2000	2,329,000	8.5	—	4.1
1950	1,667,231	11.1	385,144	2.6	2003	2,187,000	7.5	—	3.8

NOTE: (—) Data not available. Marriage and divorce figures for most years include some estimated data. Alaska is included beginning 1959, Hawaii beginning 1960. 1. Includes annulments. 2. Per 1,000 population. *Source:* U.S. Dept. of Health and Human Services, National Center for Health Statistics. Web: www.cdc.gov/nchs/.

Median Age at First Marriage

Year	Males	Females	Year	Males	Females	Year	Males	Females
1890	26.1	22.0	1940	24.3	21.5	1990	26.1	23.9
1900	25.9	21.9	1950	22.8	20.3	1995	26.9	24.5
1910	25.1	21.6	1960	22.8	20.3	2000	26.8	25.1
1920	24.6	21.2	1970	23.2	20.8	2001	26.9	25.1
1930	24.3	21.3	1980	24.7	22.0	2002	26.9	25.3

Source: U.S. Bureau of the Census; Web: www.census.gov.

Percent Never Married

Age	1970	1999	2000	2002	Age	1970	1999	2000	2002
Male:					**Female:**				
20 to 24 years	35.8%	83.2%	83.7%	85.4%	20 to 24 years	54.7%	72.3%	72.8%	74.0%
25 to 29 years	10.5	52.1	51.7	53.7	25 to 29 years	19.1	38.9	38.9	40.4
30 to 34 years	6.2	30.7	30.0	34.0	30 to 34 years	9.4	22.1	21.9	23.0
35 to 39 years	5.4	21.1	20.3	21.1	35 to 39 years	7.2	15.2	14.3	14.7
40 to 44 years	4.9	15.8	15.7	16.7	40 to 44 years	6.3	10.9	11.8	11.5

NOTE: Data apply to the U.S. *Source:* U.S. Bureau of the Census. From *Statistical Abstract of the United States 2001.*

Marital Status of the Population by Sex, 1900–2002
(numbers are in thousands)

	Males Total	Never married	Married	Widowed	Divorced	Females Total	Never married	Married	Widowed	Divorced
1900	25,493.0	10,262.0	13,919.0	1,173.0	84.0	24,176.0	7,549.0	13,781.0	2,706.0	114.0
1910	32,311.0	12,521.0	18,065.0	1,467.0	156.0	29,993.0	8,918.0	17,664.0	3,167.0	185.0
1920	36,828.0	12,940.0	21,820.0	1,754.0	234.0	35,122.0	9,601.0	21,295.0	3,909.0	273.0
1930	43,829.0	14,938.0	26,311.0	2,023.0	489.0	42,795.0	11,294.0	26,156.0	4,728.0	572.0
1940	49,336.0	16,377.0	30,191.0	2,144.0	624.0	49,362.0	12,752.0	30,087.0	5,700.0	823.0
1950	53,511.0	13,319.0	36,859.0	2,262.0	1,070.0	56,055.0	10,379.0	37,570.0	6,734.0	1,373.0
1960	59,913.0	13,919.0	42,623.0	2,072.0	1,299.0	63,616.0	10,990.0	42,891.0	7,880.0	1,855.0
1970	69,349.0	18,315.0	46,981.0	2,128.0	1,925.0	75,861.0	15,604.0	47,644.0	9,610.0	3,002.0
1980	83,836.0	25,132.0	52,009.0	2,156.0	4,539.0	91,420.0	21,027.0	52,497.0	11,318.0	6,577.0
1990	93,817.0	28,805.0	55,678.0	2,378.0	6,957.0	101,325.0	23,755.0	55,821.0	12,122.0	9,627.0
2000	107,027.0	32,381.0	62,692.0	2,699.0	9,255.0	114,121.0	27,532.0	62,309.0	11,975.0	12,305.0
2002	106,819.0	34,229.0	61,268.0	2,636.0	8,686.0	114,639.0	28,861.0	62,103.0	11,408.0	12,268.0
Percent distribution										
1900	100.0%	40.3%	54.6%	4.6%	0.3%	100.0%	31.2%	57.0%	11.2%	0.5%
1910	100.0	38.8	55.9	4.5	0.5	100.0	29.7	58.9	10.6	0.6
1920	100.0	35.1	59.2	4.8	0.6	100.0	27.3	60.6	11.1	0.8
1930	100.0	34.1	60.0	4.6	1.1	100.0	26.4	61.1	11.0	1.3
1940	100.0	33.2	61.2	4.3	1.3	100.0	25.8	61.0	11.5	1.7
1950	100.0	24.9	68.9	4.2	2.0	100.0	18.5	67.0	12.0	2.4
1960	100.0	23.2	71.1	3.5	2.2	100.0	17.3	67.4	12.4	2.9
1970	100.0	26.4	67.7	3.1	2.8	100.0	20.6	62.8	12.7	4.0
1980	100.0	30.0	62.0	2.6	5.4	100.0	23.0	57.4	12.4	7.2
1990	100.0	30.7	59.3	2.5	7.4	100.0	23.4	55.1	12.0	9.5
2000	100.0	30.3	58.6	2.5	8.6	100.0	24.1	54.6	10.5	10.8
2002	100.0	32.0	57.4	2.5	8.1	100.0	25.2	54.2	10.0	10.7

Source: Statistical Abstract of the United States 2003.

Births

Births, Birth Rates, and Fertility Rates by State, 2002

State	Number of births	Birth rate[1]	Fertility rate[2]	State	Number of births	Birth rate[1]	Fertility rate[2]
United States[3]	4,021,726	13.9	64.8	Nevada	32,571	15.0	72.5
Alabama	58,967	13.1	61.2	New Hampshire	14,442	11.3	52.4
Alaska	9,938	15.4	73.5	New Jersey	114,751	13.4	63.5
Arizona	87,837	16.1	77.8	New Mexico	27,753	15.0	70.7
Arkansas	37,437	13.8	66.6	New York	251,415	13.1	59.8
California	529,357	15.1	68.3	North Carolina	117,335	14.1	65.4
Colorado	68,418	15.2	69.3	North Dakota	7,757	12.2	58.7
Connecticut	42,001	12.1	58.8	Ohio	148,720	13.0	61.7
Delaware	11,090	13.7	62.2	Oklahoma	50,387	14.4	68.8
District of Columbia	7,498	13.1	52.9	Oregon	45,192	12.8	61.9
Florida	205,579	12.3	62.5	Pennsylvania	142,850	11.6	56.4
Georgia	133,300	15.6	68.4	Rhode Island	12,894	12.1	54.6
Hawaii	17,477	14.0	68.6	South Carolina	54,570	13.3	60.7
Idaho	20,970	15.6	73.8	South Dakota	10,698	14.1	68.3
Illinois	180,622	14.3	66.1	Tennessee	77,482	13.4	62.2
Indiana	85,081	13.8	64.8	Texas	372,450	17.1	77.1
Iowa	37,559	12.8	61.7	Utah	49,182	21.2	90.6
Kansas	39,412	14.5	68.7	Vermont	6,387	10.4	48.9
Kentucky	54,233	13.3	60.5	Virginia	99,672	13.7	61.9
Louisiana	64,872	14.5	65.4	Washington	79,028	13.0	60.2
Maine	13,559	10.5	49.8	West Virginia	20,712	11.5	57.0
Maryland	73,323	13.4	60.6	Wisconsin	68,560	12.6	59.0
Massachusetts	80,645	12.5	56.7	Wyoming	6,550	13.1	63.6
Michigan	129,967	12.9	60.7	Puerto Rico	52,747	13.7	61.6
Minnesota	68,025	13.6	62.0	Virgin Islands	1,634	15.0	71.1
Mississippi	41,518	14.5	65.7	Guam	3,212	19.9	88.3
Missouri	75,251	13.3	62.1	American Samoa	1,627	28.2	126.7
Montana	11,049	12.1	60.3	Northern Marianas	1,290	17.4	45.1
Nebraska	25,383	14.7	69.5				

NOTE: Data by place of residence. 1. Birth rates are live births per 1,000 estimated population in each area. 2. Fertility rates are live births per 1,000 women aged 15–44 years estimated in each area. 3. Excludes data for Puerto Rico, Virgin Islands, Guam, American Samoa, and Northern Marianas. *Source:* National Center for Health Statistics, *National Vital Statistics Reports,* vol. 52, no. 10, Dec. 17, 2003. Web: www.cdc.gov/nchs.

Live Births by Age and Race of Mother, 1940–2002

Year[1]/race	Total	Age of mother							
		Under 15	15–19	20–24	25–29	30–34	35–39	40–44	45–49[2]
1940	2,558,647	3,865	332,667	799,537	693,268	431,468	222,015	68,269	7,558
1945	2,858,449	4,028	298,868	832,746	785,299	554,906	296,852	78,853	6,897
1950	3,631,512	5,413	432,911	1,155,167	1,041,360	610,816	302,780	77,743	5,322
1955	4,014,112	6,181	493,770	1,290,939	1,133,155	732,540	352,320	89,777	5,430
1960	4,257,850	6,780	586,966	1,426,912	1,092,816	687,722	359,908	91,564	5,182
1965	3,760,358	7,768	590,894	1,337,350	925,732	529,376	282,908	81,716	4,614
1970	3,731,386	11,752	644,708	1,418,874	994,904	427,806	180,244	49,952	3,146
1975	3,144,198	12,642	582,238	1,093,676	936,786	375,500	115,409	26,319	1,628
1980	3,612,258	10,169	552,161	1,226,200	1,108,291	550,354	140,793	23,090	1,200
1985	3,760,561	10,220	467,485	1,141,320	1,201,350	696,354	214,336	28,334	1,162
1990	4,158,212	11,657	521,826	1,093,730	1,277,108	886,063	317,583	48,607	1,638
1995	3,899,589	12,242	499,873	965,547	1,063,539	904,666	383,745	67,250	2,727
1998	3,941,553	9,462	484,895	965,122	1,083,010	889,365	424,890	81,027	3,782[2]
1999	3,959,417	9,054	476,050	981,929	1,078,252	892,400	434,294	83,090	4,348[2]
2000	4,058,814	8,519[3]	468,990	1,017,806	1,087,547	929,278	452,057	90,013	4,604[2]
2001	4,025,933	7,781[3]	445,944	1,021,627	1,058,265	942,697	451,723	92,813	5,083[2]
2002	4,021,726	7,315	425,493	1,022,106	1,060,391	951,219	453,927	95,788	5,487[2]
White	3,174,760	3,884	305,988	783,000	851,142	779,535	369,833	76,928	4,450[2]
Black	593,691	3,188	103,795	194,704	136,591	95,006	48,388	11,443	576[2]
American Indian[4]	42,368	133	7,707	14,343	10,139	6,338	2,976	701	31[2]
Asian or Pacific Islander	210,907	110	8,003	30,059	62,519	70,340	32,730	6,716	430[2]
Hispanic origin[5]	876,642	2,421	127,900	265,235	236,143	157,887	71,480	14,809	767[2]

NOTE: Data refer only to births occurring within the U.S. 1. Data for 1940–1955 are adjusted for under-registration. Beginning 1960, only registered births are shown. Data for 1960–1970 based on a 50% sample of births. For 1972–1984, based on 100% of births in selected states and on 50% sample in all other states. Beginning 1989, births are tabulated by race of mother; previously based on race of child. 2. Beginning 1998, ages 45–54. 3. Ages 10–14. 4. Includes births to Aleuts and Eskimos. 5. Persons of Hispanic origin may be any race. *Source:* National Center for Health Statistics, *National Vital Statistics Reports,* vol. 52, no. 10, Dec. 17, 2003. Web: www.cdc.gov/nchs.

Live Births by Sex and Sex Ratio

	Total[1,2]			White			Black		
Year	Male	Female	Males per 1,000 females	Male	Female	Males per 1,000 females	Male	Female	Males per 1,000 females
1985	1,927,983	1,832,578	1,052	1,536,646	1,454,727	1,056	308,575	299,618	1,030
1986	1,924,868	1,831,679	1,051	1,523,914	1,446,525	1,053	315,788	305,433	1,034
1987	1,951,153	1,858,241	1,050	1,535,517	1,456,971	1,054	325,259	316,308	1,028
1988	2,002,424	1,907,086	1,050	1,562,675	1,483,487	1,053	341,441	330,535	1,033
1989	2,069,490	1,971,468	1,050	1,606,757	1,525,234	1,053	360,131	349,264	1,031
1990	2,129,495	2,028,717	1,050	1,654,928	1,570,415	1,054	367,455	357,121	1,029
1991	2,101,518	2,009,389	1,046	1,659,077	1,582,196	1,049	346,455	336,147	1,031
1992	2,082,097	1,982,917	1,050	1,641,811	1,559,867	1,053	342,726	330,907	1,036
1993	2,048,861	1,951,379	1,050	1,616,332	1,533,501	1,054	333,984	324,891	1,028
1994	2,022,589	1,930,178	1,048	1,599,803	1,521,401	1,051	322,554	313,837	1,028
1995	1,996,355	1,930,234	1,049	1,588,427	1,510,458	1,052	308,115	297,024	1,031
1996	1,990,480	1,901,014	1,047	—	—	1,050	—	—	1,028
1997	1,985,596	1,895,298	1,048	—	—	1,052	—	—	1,031
1998	2,016,205	1,925,348	1,047	—	—	1,052	—	—	1,034
1999	2,026,854	1,932,563	1,049	—	—	1,052	—	—	1,031
2000	2,076,969	1,981,845	1,048	—	—	1,050	—	—	1,031
2001	2,057,922	1,968,011	1,046	—	—	1,047	—	—	1,032
2002	2,057,979	1,963,747	1,048	—	—	1,054	—	—	1,032

NOTE: (—) Data not available. 1. Excludes births to nonresidents of U.S. 2. Includes races other than white and black. *Source:* National Center for Health Statistics, *National Vital Statistics Reports,* vol. 52, no. 10, Dec. 17, 2003. Web: www.cdc.gov/nchs.

Selected Characteristics of Births by Race of Mother, 2002

Characteristic	All races	White	Black	American Indian[1]	Asian or Pacific Islander	Hispanic origin[2]
Percentage of mothers who:						
Had prenatal care beginning in the first trimester	83.7%	85.4%	75.2%	69.8%	84.8%	76.7%
Had late or no prenatal care	3.6	3.1	6.2	8.0	3.1	5.5
Were tobacco users[3]	11.4	12.3	8.7	19.7	2.5	3.0
Were alcohol users[3]	0.8	0.8	0.9	2.5	0.3	0.5
Gained less than 16 lbs[3]	12.2	11.3	17.6	17.0	9.3	15.1
Median weight gain[4]	30.5	30.6	30.0	30.0	30.2	28.7
Had cesarean births	26.1	25.9	27.6	23.1	25.0	25.2
Percentage of infants who:						
Were born prior to 37 full weeks	12.1	11.1	17.5	13.1	10.4	11.6
Weighed less than 1,500 grams (3 lb 4 oz.)	1.5	1.2	3.1	1.3	1.1	1.2
Weighed less than 2,500 grams (5 lb 8 oz.)	7.8	6.8	13.3	7.2	7.8	6.5
Weighed 4,000 grams (8 lb 14 oz.) or more	9.2	10.2	5.0	11.2	5.5	8.5
Had five-minute Apgar scores of less than 7[5]	1.4	1.2	2.3	1.4	1.0	1.1

1. Includes births to Aleuts and Eskimos. 2. Hispanic origin may be of any race. 3. Excludes data for Calif. 4. Excludes data for Calif. Median weight gain shown in pounds. 5. Excludes data for Calif. and Tex. Apgar scores on birth certificate. Apgar scores are derived from evaluations of five major signs at one minute and five minutes after birth. Each sign is given a score of 0–2 for a total of ten possible points; scores of 7–10 are considered normal, 4–7 may require resuscitative measures, and 0–3 require immediate resuscitation. The signs and scores (0-1-2) are as follows: Activity or muscle tone (absent—arms and legs flexed—active movement); Pulse (absent—below 100 bpm—above 100 bpm); Grimace or reflex irritability (no response—grimace—sneeze, cough, pulls away); Appearance or skin color (blue-gray, pale all over—normal, except for extremities—normal over entire body); Respiration (absent—slow, irregular—good, crying). *Source:* National Center for Health Statistics, *National Vital Statistics Reports,* vol. 52, no. 10, Dec. 17, 2003. Web: www.cdc.gov/nchs.

Gestational Age and Birthweight Characteristics by Plurality: United States, 2002

	Singletons	Twins	Triplets	Quadruplets	Quintuplets/+
Number	3,889,191	125,134	6,898	434	69
Percent very preterm[1]	1.6	11.9	36.1	59.9	78.3
Percent preterm[2]	10.4	58.2	92.4	96.8	91.3
Mean gestational age (weeks)	38.8	35.3	32.2	29.9	28.5
Percent very low birthweight[3]	1.1	10.2	34.5	61.1	83.8
Percent low birthweight[4]	6.1	55.4	94.4	98.8	94.1
Mean birthweight (grams)	3,332	2,347	1,687	1,309	1,105

1. Very preterm is less than 32 completed weeks of gestation. 2. Preterm is less than 37 completed weeks of gestation. 3. Very low birthweight is less than 1,500 grams. 4. Low birthweight is less than 2,500 grams. *Source:* National Center for Health Statistics, *National Vital Statistics Reports,* vol. 52, no. 10, Dec. 17, 2003. Web: www.cdc.gov/nchs.

Teen Birth Rates Continue to Decline

Source: Centers for Disease Control, National Center for Health Statistics, *National Vital Statistics Reports,* vol. 52, no. 10, Dec. 7, 2003.

Teenage childbearing has been on a long-term decline in the United States since the late 1950s, except for a brief, but steep, upward climb in the late 1980s through 1991. The 2002 rate (43.0 births per 1,000 for teens ages 15–19) has plunged 53% from the peak rate recorded in 1957 (96 per 1,000). The declining teenage birth rate has had an impressive impact on the number of babies born to teenagers. If the birth rates by age had remained at 1991 levels throughout the 1990s instead of declining as they

did, there would have been an additional 546,000 births to teenagers over the decade. Possible factors accounting for the decline include decreased sexual activity reflecting changing attitudes toward premarital sex, an increase in condom use, and the adoption of newly available hormonal contraception, implants, and injectables.

Despite the rates' reaching record lows in 2002, U.S. teenage birth rates remain substantially higher than rates for other developed countries.   □

Teen Birth Rates in the U.S., Selected Years

(rates per 1,000 females in specified group)

Age	1980	1985	1990	1991	1993	1995	1998	2000	2001	2002
All races										
10–14 years	1.1	1.2	1.4	1.4	1.4	1.3	1.0	0.9	0.8	0.7
15–19 years	53.0	51.0	59.9	62.1	59.6	56.8	51.1	47.7	45.8	43.0
White, total										
10–14 years	—	—	0.7	0.8	0.8	0.8	0.6	0.6	0.5	0.5
15–19 years	—	—	50.8	52.8	51.1	50.1	45.4	43.2	41.2	39.4
White, non-Hispanic										
10–14 years	0.4	—	0.5	0.5	0.5	0.4	0.3	0.3	0.3	—
15–19 years	41.2	—	42.5	43.4	40.7	39.3	35.2	32.6	30.3	—
Black										
10–14 years	4.3	4.5	4.9	4.8	4.6	4.2	2.9	2.3	2.0	1.8
15–19 years	97.8	95.4	112.8	115.5	108.6	96.1	85.4	77.4	71.8	66.6
American Indian[1]										
10–14 years	1.9	1.7	1.6	1.6	1.4	1.8	1.6	1.1	1.0	0.9
15–19 years	82.2	79.2	81.1	85.0	83.1	78.0	72.1	58.3	56.3	53.8
Asian/Pacific Islander										
10–14 years	0.3	0.4	0.7	0.8	0.6	0.7	0.4	0.3	0.2	0.3
15–19 years	26.2	23.8	26.4	27.4	27.0	26.1	23.1	20.5	19.8	18.3
Hispanic[2]										
10–14 years	1.7	—	2.4	2.4	2.7	2.7	2.1	1.7	1.6	1.4
15–19 years	82.2	—	100.3	106.7	106.8	106.7	93.6	87.3	86.4	83.4

NOTE: (—) = Data not available. 1. Includes births to Aleuts and Eskimos. 2. Persons of Hispanic origin may be of any race. *Source:* Centers for Disease Control, National Center for Health Statistics, *National Vital Statistics Reports,* vol. 52, no. 10, Dec. 17, 2003.

Births to Teenagers and to Unmarried Women, 1940–2002

	Teen childbearing			Nonmarital childbearing		
Year	Total number of births to women 15–19 years	Birth rate per 1,000 women 15–19 years	Percent of teen births to unmarried women	Total number of births to unmarried women	Birth rate per 1,000 unmarried women 15–44 years	Percent of all births to unmarried women
1940	300,747	54.1	13.6%	89,500	7.1	3.8%
1950	419,535	81.6	13.4	141,600	14.1	4.0
1960	586,966	89.1	14.8	224,300	21.6	5.3
1970	644,708	68.3	29.5	398,700	26.4	10.7
1980	552,161	53.0	47.6	665,747	29.4	18.4
1990	521,826	59.9	67.1	1,165,384	43.8	28.0
2000	468,990	48.5	78.8	1,347,043	45.2	33.2
2002[1]	424,670	42.9	n.a.	n.a.	n.a.	33.8

1. Preliminary data. *Source:* U.S. National Center for Health Statistics, *Nonmarital Childbearing in the United States, 1940-99, National Vital Statistics Reports,* vol. 48, no. 16; *Births to Teenagers in the United States, 1940–2000, National Vital Statistics Reports,* vol. 49, no. 10; and Births: *Final Data for 2001, National Vital Statistics Reports,* vol. 51, no. 2. From U.S. Census Bureau, *Statistical Abstract of the United States: 2003.*

Births: Other Data for 2002

The source for the data on U.S. births, birth rates, and fertility rates in this section is the *National Vital Statistics Reports* series published by the National Center for Health Statistics, a part of the Centers for Disease Control and Prevention. The report issued on Dec. 17, 2003, showing final birth data for 2002 also highlighted these findings:

Births in the United States decreased slightly for 2002, to 4,021,726, from 4,025,933 in 2001. This marks the second consecutive decline in the number of births following three consecutive years of increases. Births to non-Hispanic white and non-Hispanic black women were down, but births to Hispanic, American Indian, and Asian or Pacific Islander women increased. The 2002 U.S. **birth rate** fell to the lowest rate ever recorded for the United States, 13.9 per 1,000 total population. The **general fertility rate** declined 1% for 2001–2002 to 64.8 births per 1,000 women ages 15–44 years.

The **birth rate for teenagers** reached another historic low in 2002, falling to 43.0 births per 1,000 women ages 15–19 years, a record low for the nation.

The birth rate for **women 20–24 years** declined 2%, to 103.6 per 1,000, whereas the rate for women 25–29 years was stable at 113.6. After rising steadily for a decade, the birth rate for women 30–34 years declined to 91.5 per 1,000 in 2002. The rate for women 35–39 years, however, rose to 41.4, the highest level in more than three decades. The birth rate for women 40–44 years increased to the highest level since 1969 (8.3 per 1,000). The number of births to women 50–54 years increased to 263, 10% higher than in 2001.

The **mean or average age at first birth** was 25.1 years, an all-time high for the nation. This average has risen from 21.4 years since 1970.

Unmarried childbearing has changed very little since 1995. The birth rate for 2002 was stable at 43.7 births per 1,000 unmarried women aged 15–44

years. The number of births rose 1% to 1,365,966, the highest number ever reported, while the percent of births to unmarried women increased from 33.5% to 34.0%.

Cigarette smoking during pregnancy dropped to 11.4% of all mothers in 2002, a decline of 42% from 1989. Smoking rates declined for all age groups and most race and Hispanic origin groups in 2002. Infant health can be seriously compromised by prenatal smoking; 12.2% of mothers who smoked had a low birthweight child in 2002 compared with 7.5% of nonsmokers.

The **cesarean delivery rate** increased 7% to 26.1% of all births from 2001 to 2002, the highest rate ever reported in the United States. The cesarean rate fell between 1989 and 1996, but has risen 26% since 1996. The escalation in the total cesarean rate is fueled by both the rise in the primary cesarean rate and the steep decline in the rate of vaginal birth after cesarean (VBAC) delivery. The primary rate rose 7% in 2002, and the rate of VBAC delivery plunged 23%.

The **preterm birth rate,** or percentage of infants born after less than 37 completed weeks of gestation, increased again in 2002 to 12.1% of all births. Preterm delivery is a leading cause of neonatal mortality and birth-related morbidity. Influenced in part by the rising rate of multiple births (multiples are more likely to be born early), the proportion of preterm infants has risen 14% since 1990. Over this same period, the preterm rate for singleton births only has risen 7%, from 9.7% to 10.4%.

The **twin birth rate** continued its steady climb, rising 3% for 2002 to 31.1 per 1,000. The twinning rate has risen 38% since 1990, and 65% since 1980. The rate of triplet and higher multiple births (triplet/+) declined slightly to 184.0. The decline in the triplet/+ rate in 3 of the last 4 years may signal an end to the steep hike (more than 400% between 1980 and 1998) in these high-risk births.

Live Births by Method of Delivery and Rates of Caesarean Delivery, 1989–2002

	All births	Vaginal	Caesarean	Caesarean rate		All births	Vaginal	Caesarean	Caesarean rate
1989	3,798,734	2,793,463	826,955	22.8	2000	4,058,814	3,108,188	923,991	22.9
1990	4,110,563	3,111,421	914,096	22.7	2002	4,021,726	2,958,423	1,043,846	26.1
1995	3,899,589	3,063,724	806,722	20.8					

Source: National Center for Health Statistics, *National Vital Statistics Reports,* vol. 52, no. 10, Dec. 17, 2003. Web: www.cdc.gov/nchs.

Live Births and Birth Rates, 1910–2001

Year	Births[1] (thousands)	Birth rate per 1,000 population[1]	Year	Births[1] (thousands)	Birth rate per 1,000 population[1]
1910	2,777	30.1	1970	3,731	18.4
1920	2,950	27.7	1980	3,612	15.9
1930	2,618	21.3	1990	4,158	16.7
1940	2,559	19.4	1995	3,900	14.6
1950	3,632	24.1	2000	4,059	14.4
1960	4,258	23.7	2001	4,026	14.1

NOTE: n.a. = not available. 1. Prior to 1960 data adjusted for under registration. *Source:* 1900-1970, U.S. Public Health Service, *Vital Statistics of the United States,* annual, Vol. I and Vol II; 1971-2001, U.S. National Center for Health Statistics, *Vital Statistics of the United States,* annual; *National Vital Statistics Report* (NVSR) (formerly *Monthly Vital Statistics Report*); and unpublished data. From *Statistical Abstract of the United States: 2003.*

Contraceptive Use by Women, 15 to 44 Years Old

Contraceptive status and method	All women	Age 15–24 years	Age 25–34 years	Age 35–44 years	Marital status Never married	Marital status Currently married	Marital status Formerly married
All women (in thousands)	60,201	18,002	20,758	21,440	22,679	29,673	7,849
Percent distribution							
Pill	17.3%	23.1%	23.7%	6.3%	20.4%	15.6%	14.6%
IUD	0.5	0.1	0.6	0.8	0.3	0.7	0.4
Diaphragm	1.2	0.2	1.2	2.0	0.5	1.8	0.9
Condom	13.1	13.9	15.0	10.7	13.9	13.3	10.1
Periodic abstinence	1.5	0.5	1.8	2.0	0.6	2.3	0.7
Withdrawal	2.0	1.6	2.3	1.9	1.5	2.3	1.8
Other methods[3]	3.9	5.6	4.2	2.1	4.6	3.3	3.9

1. Total sterile includes male sterile for unknown reasons. 2. Persons sterile from illness, accident, or congenital conditions. 3. Includes implants, injectables, morning-after-pill, suppository, Today™ sponge, and less frequently used methods. *Source:* U.S. National Center for Health Statistics, special tabulations from the 1995 National Survey of Family Growth. From *Statistical Abstract of the United States: 2003.*

Adoption Trends

Background

Although adoption is mentioned in the legal codes and writings of many ancient peoples, including the Romans and Hebrews, no such laws existed in England or her colonies prior to the middle of the 19th century. Instead, indigent children were generally sent to public institutions known as almshouses until the age of six or seven, when they could be "put out" as indentured servants or apprentices. Families also sometimes took in children informally, especially in rural areas to help on the farm.

In the United States, these practices worked well enough until the early 19th century, when changes in economic conditions and the size of the population produced numbers of children the system couldn't cope with. At the same time, largely through the efforts of certain social reformers, society's attitude toward adoption began to change. Private agencies were established to place children in homes where they would be treated as members of the family rather than servants. And families who took in children increasingly petitioned state legislatures for private adoption acts to ensure the legal status and inheritance rights of adopted children.

Finally, as a result of pressure from individual families and to provide better care for destitute children, the state legislatures were prompted to take action. Between 1851 and 1873, 17 states enacted adoption legislation, and by 1929 all states had such laws. (England did not enact general adoption laws until 1926.) Under these new statutes, adoptions had to be approved by a judge, after which the adopted child assumed the same rights accorded any natural, legitimate child of the petitioners.

Adoption in the 20th Century

Despite the legislation, foundling homes continued to exist, and legal adoption was still relatively infrequent. Many people feared that poor, abandoned, or illegitimate children were doomed to grow into troubled adults. Infants in particular were undesirable because of high mortality rates and the lack of readily available breast milk.

Following World War I, however, the demand for babies began to grow. This was partly a response to the sharp drop in population caused by the war and the influenza epidemic of 1918, and partly also due to the development of a successful feeding formula. The number of adoptions exploded, and "closed" adoptions became the norm. In closed adoptions, the identities of the birth parents and adoptive parents were kept a secret because, it was thought, this helped the child bond to its new family and avoid the stigma of illegitimacy.

By the mid-1950s the demand for healthy infants began to exceed the number available. Agencies began screening prospective parents more selectively, and by 1975 many had stopped accepting applications for nondisabled white children altogether. Other agencies were obliged to put prospective parents on waiting lists, usually for an average of three to five years. Factors contributing to the decline in available infants included the increased availability of effective contraception, a rise in the abortion rate following *Roe* v. *Wade* in 1973, and an increase in the number of unmarried women keeping their babies rather than giving them up for adoption.

It was also during the 1970s that "open" adoption, in which adoptive and birth parents were known to each other, became more accepted. A growing number of prospective parents adopted through private placement, contacting a birth mother directly through an advertisement or through the services of a lawyer or other professional specializing in adoption.

More Recent Trends

Since the end of the 20th century, infertile couples and single people have increasingly turned to transracial and international adoptions, as well as new advanced medical techniques for treating infertility and providing alternative methods of reproduction. Meanwhile, the number of older special needs children waiting adoption has skyrocketed. These children often come from backgrounds of abuse and neglect, and finding appropriate placements for them is one of the most pressing concerns in child welfare today.

Source: Columbia Encyclopedia, 6th Edition. Web: www.infoplease.com. Sokoloff, Burton Z., "Antecedents of American Adoption" in *The Future of Children: Adoption,* vol. 3, no. 1. (David and Lucile Packard Foundation: Los Altos, Calif.) Spring 1993. Web: www.futureofchildren.org.

Top Countries of Origin for U.S. International Adoptions

Rank	2003 Country of origin	Number[1]	2002 Country of origin	Number[1]	Rank	2003 Country of origin	Number[1]	2002 Country of origin	Number[1]
1.	China (mainland)	6,859	China (mainland)	5,053	11.	Philippines	214	Cambodia	254
					12.	Romania	200	Philippines	221
2.	Russia	5,209	Russia	4,939	13.	Bulgaria	198	Haiti	187
3.	Guatemala	2,328	Guatemala	2,219	14.	Belarus	191	Belarus	169
4.	South Korea	1,790	South Korea	1,779	15.	Ethiopia	135	Romania	168
5.	Kazakhstan	825	Ukraine	1,106	16.	Cambodia	124	Ethiopia	105
6.	Ukraine	702	Kazakhstan	819	17.	Poland	97	Poland	101
7.	India	472	Vietnam	766	18.	Thailand	72	Thailand	67
8.	Vietnam	382	India	466	19.	Azerbaijan	62	Peru	65
9.	Colombia	272	Colombia	334	20.	Mexico	61	Mexico	61
10.	Haiti	250	Bulgaria	260		Total[2]	21,616	Total[2]	20,099

1. Figures based on number of immigrant visas issued to orphans. 2. Figures for fiscal year. *Source:* U.S. State Department. Web: http://travel.state.gov/orphan_numbers.html.

Children in Foster Care

	Percent	Number		Percent	Number
Total		542,000	**Race/ethnicity**		
Ages			White, non-Hispanic	37%	203,222
Under 1 year	4%	22,957	Black, non-Hispanic	38	204,973
1–5 years	24	130,857	Hispanic[1]	17	89,785
6–10 years	24	127,711	American Indian/Alaskan Native, non-Hispanic	2	10,106
11–15 years	30	160,419			
16–18 years	17	89,632	Asian, non-Hispanic	1	3,649
19 years and over	2	10,424	Hawaiian/Pacific Islander, non-Hispanic	0	1,551
Gender			Unknown/unable to determine	3	17,235
Male	52	283,854	Two or more races non-Hispanic	2	11,479
Female	48	258,146			

NOTE: Preliminary FY 2001 estimates as of March 2003. Percentages may not add up to 100% and numbers may not add up to totals due to rounding. 1. Hispanic can be of any race. *Source:* U.S. Dept. of Health and Human Services, Admin. for Children and Families, Adoption and Foster Care Analysis and Reporting System (AFCARS) Report #5. Web: www.acf.dhhs.gov/programs/cb.

Child Abuse and Neglect

Item	1990 Number	Percent	1995 Number	Percent	2000 Number	Percent	2001 Number	Percent
Types of substantiated maltreatment								
Victims, total[1]	690,658	—	970,285	—	862,455	—	903,141	—
Neglect	338,770	49.1%	507,015	52.3%	515,792	59.8%	516,646	57.2%
Physical abuse	186,801	27.0	237,840	24.5	166,232	19.3	168,284	18.6
Sexual abuse	119,506	17.3	122,964	12.7	87,480	10.1	86,834	9.6
Emotional maltreatment	45,621	6.6	42,051	4.3	66,293	7.7	61,779	6.8
Medical neglect	n.a.	n.a.	28,541	2.9	25,450	3.0	17,664	2.0
Sex of victim								
Victims, total	742,519	100.0	809,634	100.0	862,455	100.0	903,141	100.0
Male	323,339	43.5	381,075	47.1	412,074	47.8	433,108	48.0
Female	369,919	49.8	425,193	52.5	444,793	51.6	465,433	51.5
Age of victim								
Victims, total	731,282	100.0	808,575	100.0	862,455	100.0	903,141	100.0
1 year and younger	97,101	13.3	103,335	12.8	132,267	15.3	140,786	15.6
2 to 5 years old	172,791	23.6	215,303	26.6	204,367	23.7	215,745	23.9
6 to 9 years old	157,681	21.6	195,400	24.2	210,463	24.4	217,803	24.1
10 to 13 years old	135,130	18.5	154,682	19.1	174,854	20.3	189,262	21.0
14 to 17 years old	103,383	14.1	121,548	15.0	125,370	14.5	134,099	14.9
18 years and over	4,880	0.7	7,506	0.9	995	0.1	1,556	0.2

NOTE: n.a. = not available. (—) = not applicable. 1. More than one type of maltreatment may be substantiated per child. Therefore, totals for this category will add up to more than 100 percent. Victim totals and maltreatment types are based on subset of states that reported both the number of child victims and maltreatment incidences by type for that year. *Source: Statistical Abstract of the United States, 2003.*

Mortality

Deaths, by State

(number in thousands; rates per 100,000 population in each area)

Area	2001 number	Rate	Area	2001 number	Rate	Area	2001 number	Rate
United States[1]	2,417	8.5	Maine	12	9.7	Rhode Island	10	9.5
Alabama	45	10.1	Maryland	44	8.1	South Carolina	37	9.0
Alaska	3	4.7	Massachusetts	57	8.9	South Dakota	7	9.1
Arizona	41	7.7	Michigan	86	8.6	Tennessee	55	9.6
Arkansas	28	10.3	Minnesota	38	7.6	Texas	153	7.1
California	234	6.8	Mississippi	28	9.9	Utah	13	5.6
Colorado	28	6.4	Missouri	55	9.8	Vermont	5	8.5
Connecticut	30	8.7	Montana	8	9.1	Virginia	56	7.8
Delaware	7	8.9	Nebraska	15	8.8	Washington	45	7.4
District of Columbia	6	10.4	Nevada	16	7.8	West Virginia	21	11.6
Florida	167	10.2	New Hampshire	10	7.8	Wisconsin	47	8.6
Georgia	64	7.7	New Jersey	75	8.8	Wyoming	4	8.2
Hawaii	8	6.8	New Mexico	14	7.7			
Idaho	10	7.4	New York	159	8.3	Puerto Rico	29	7.6
Illinois	105	8.4	North Carolina	71	8.6	Virgin Islands	1	5.6
Indiana	55	9.0	North Dakota	6	9.5	Guam	1	4.2
Iowa	28	9.5	Ohio	108	9.5	American Samoa	n.a.	4.2
Kansas	25	9.1	Oklahoma	35	10.0	Northern Marianas	n.a.	2.1
Kentucky	40	9.8	Oregon	30	8.7			
Louisiana	42	9.3	Pennsylvania	130	10.5			

1. Excludes data for Puerto Rico, Virgin Islands, Guam, American Samoa, and Northern Marianas. *Source:* U.S. National Center for Health Statistics, *National Vital Statistics Report.* From *Statistical Abstract of the United States, 2003.*

Deaths, 1900–2001

Year	Total number of deaths (thousands)	Total deaths per 1,000 population	Year	Total number of deaths (thousands)	Total deaths per 1,000 population
1900	343	17.2	1960	1,712	9.5
1910	697	14.7	1970	1,921	9.5
1920	1,118	13.0	1980	1,990	8.8
1930	1,327	11.3	1990	2,148	8.6
1940	1,417	10.8	2000	2,403	8.7
1950	1,452	9.6	2001	2,417	8.5

Source: U.S. National Center for Health Statistics, *Vital Statistics of the United States,* annual; *National Vital Statistics Reports NVSR)* (formerly *Monthly Vital Statistics Report).* From *Statistical Abstract of the United States, 2003.*

Death Rates by Cause of Death, 1900–2001

(per 100,000 population)

Year	Tuberculosis, all forms	Malignant neoplasms (cancer)	Major cardio-vascular/renal diseases	Influenza and pneumonia	Motor vehicle accidents
1900	194.4	64.0	345.2	202.2	n.a.
1910	153.8	76.2	371.9	155.9	1.8
1920	113.1	83.4	364.9	207.3	10.3
1930	71.1	97.4	414.4	102.5	26.7
1940	45.9	120.3	485.7	70.3	26.2
1950	22.5	139.8	510.8	31.3	23.1
1960	6.1	149.2	521.8	37.3	21.3
1970	2.6	162.8	496.0	30.9	26.9
1980	0.9	183.9	436.4	24.1	23.5
1990	0.7	203.2	368.3	32.0	18.8
2000	0.3	200.5	340.4	24.3	15.2
2001	0.3	194.4	323.9	21.8	15.4

Source: 1900-1970, U.S. Public Health Service, *Vital Statistics of the United States,* annual, Vol. I and Vol II; 1971-2001, U.S. National Center for Health Statistics, *Vital Statistics of the United States,* annual; *National Vital Statistics Report (NVSR)* (formerly *Monthly Vital Statistics Report);* and unpublished data. From *Statistical Abstract of the United States: 2003.*

Children Killed by Guns: In 1999, there were 3,385 firearms-related deaths for children ages 0–19 years. They break down as follows: 214 unintentional, 1,078 suicides, 1,990 homicides, 83 for which the intent could not be determined, and 20 due to legal intervention. Source: 2002 edition of *Injury Facts*®.

Life Expectancy by Age, 1850–2001

The expectation of life at a specified age is the average number of years that members of a hypothetical group of people of the same age would continue to live if they were subject throughout the remainder of their lives to the same mortality rate.

Calendar period	Age								
	0	10	20	30	40	50	60	70	80
White males									
1850[1]	38.3	48.0	40.1	34.0	27.9	21.6	15.6	10.2	5.9
1890[1]	42.50	48.45	40.66	34.05	27.37	20.72	14.73	9.35	5.40
1900–1902[2]	48.23	50.59	42.19	34.88	27.74	20.76	14.35	9.03	5.10
1909–1911[2]	50.23	51.32	42.71	34.87	27.43	20.39	13.98	8.83	5.09
1919–1921[3]	56.34	54.15	45.60	37.65	29.86	22.22	15.25	9.51	5.47
1929–1931	59.12	54.96	46.02	37.54	29.22	21.51	14.72	9.20	5.26
1939–1941	62.81	57.03	47.76'	38.80	30.03	21.96	15.05	9.42	5.38
1949–1951	66.31	58.98	49.52	40.29	31.17	22.83	15.76	10.07	5.88
1959–1961[5]	67.55	59.78	50.25	40.98	31.73	23.22	16.01	10.29	5.89
1969–1971[6]	67.94	59.69	50.22	41.07	31.87	23.34	16.07	10.38	6.18
1979–1981	70.82	61.98	52.45	43.31	34.04	25.26	17.56	11.35	6.76
1990	72.7	63.5	54.0	44.7	35.6	26.7	18.7	12.1	7.1
2000	74.8	65.4	55.7	46.4	37.1	28.2	20.0	13.0	7.6
2001	75.0	65.6	56.0	46.6	37.3	28.4	20.2	13.2	7.7
White females									
1850[1]	40.5	47.2	40.2	35.4	29.8	23.5	17.0	11.3	6.4
1890[1]	44.46	49.62	42.03	35.36	28.76	22.09	15.70	10.15	5.75
1900–1902[2]	51.08	52.15	43.77	36.42	29.17	21.89	15.23	9.59	5.50
1909–1911[2]	53.62	53.57	44.88	36.96	29.26	21.74	14.92	9.38	5.35
1919–1921[3]	58.53	55.17	46.46	38.72	30.94	23.12	15.93	9.94	5.70
1929–1931	62.67	57.65	48.52	39.99	31.52	23.41	16.05	9.98	5.63
1939–1941	67.29	60.85	51.38	42.21	33.25	24.72	17.00	10.50	5.88
1949–1951	72.03	64.26	54.56	45.00	35.64	26.76	18.64	11.68	6.59
1959–1961[5]	74.19	66.05	56.29	46.63	37.13	28.08	19.69	12.38	6.67
1969–1971[6]	75.49	66.97	57.24	47.60	38.12	29.11	20.79	13.37	7.59
1979–1981	78.22	69.21	59.44	49.76	40.16	30.96	22.45	14.89	8.65
1990	79.4	70.1	60.3	50.6	41.0	31.6	23.0	15.4	9.0
2000	80.0	70.5	60.7	50.9	41.3	32.0	23.2	15.5	9.1
2001	80.2	70.8	60.9	51.2	41.6	32.3	23.5	15.7	9.3
All other males[4]									
1900–1902[2]	32.54	41.90	35.11	29.25	23.12	17.34	12.62	8.33	5.12
1909–1911[2]	34.05	40.65	33.46	27.33	21.57	16.21	11.67	8.00	5.53
1919–1921[3]	47.14	45.99	38.36	32.51	26.53	20.47	14.74	9.58	5.83
1929–1931	47.55	44.27	35.95	29.45	23.36	17.92	13.15	8.78	5.42
1939–1941	52.33	48.54	39.74	32.25	25.23	19.18	14.38	10.06	6.46
1949–1951	58.91	52.96	43.73	35.31	27.29	20.25	14.91	10.74	7.07
1959–1961[5]	61.48	55.19	45.78	37.05	28.72	21.28	15.29	10.81	6.87
1969–1971[6]	60.98	53.67	44.37	36.20	28.29	21.24	15.35	10.68	7.57
1979–1981	65.63	57.40	47.87	39.13	30.64	22.92	16.54	11.36	7.22
1990	67.0	58.5	49.0	40.3	31.9	23.9	17.0	11.4	7.0
2000	68.3	59.6	50.0	41.1	32.3	24.3	17.5	11.8	7.4
2001	68.6	59.8	50.3	41.4	32.5	24.4	17.5	11.7	7.3
All other females[4]									
1900–1902[2]	35.04	43.02	36.89	30.70	24.37	18.67	13.60	9.62	6.48
1909–1911[2]	37.67	42.84	36.14	29.61	23.34	17.65	12.78	9.22	6.05
1919–1921[3]	46.92	44.54	37.15	31.48	25.60	19.76	14.69	10.25	6.58
1929–1931	49.51	45.33	37.22	30.67	24.30	18.60	14.22	10.38	6.90
1939–1941	55.51	50.83	42.14	34.52	27.31	21.04	16.14	11.81	8.00
1949–1951	62.70	56.17	46.77	38.02	29.82	22.67	16.95	12.29	8.15
1959–1961[5]	66.47	59.72	50.07	40.83	32.16	24.31	17.83	12.46	7.66
1969–1971[6]	69.05	61.49	51.85	42.61	33.87	25.97	19.02	13.30	9.01
1979–1981	74.00	65.64	55.88	46.39	37.16	28.59	20.49	14.44	9.17
1990	75.2	66.6	56.8	47.3	38.1	29.2	21.3	14.5	8.8
2000	75.0	66.2	56.4	46.8	37.6	29.0	21.0	14.1	8.7
2001	75.5	66.6	56.8	47.2	38.0	29.3	21.5	14.7	9.2

1. Massachusetts only; white and nonwhite combined, the latter being about 1% of the total. *Source:* U.S. Dept. of Commerce, Bureau of the Census, *Historical Statistics of the United States.* 2. Original Death Registration States. 3. Death Registration States of 1920. 4. Data for periods 1900–1902, 1929–1931, and 2000 and 2001 relate to blacks only. 5. Alaska and Hawaii included beginning in 1959. 6. Deaths of nonresidents of the United States excluded starting in 1970. *Sources:* Department of Health and Human Services, National Center for Health Statistics; *National Vital Statistics Reports,* vol 52., no. 3, Sept. 18, 2003. Web: www.dhhs.gov.

Life Expectancy at Birth by Race and Sex, 1940–2001

	All races			White			Black		
Year	Both sexes	Male	Female	Both sexes	Male	Female	Both sexes	Male	Female
2001	77.2	74.4	79.8	77.7	75.0	80.2	72.2	68.6	75.5
2000[1]	77.0	74.3	79.7	77.6	74.9	80.1	71.9	68.3	75.2
1999	76.7	73.9	79.4	77.3	74.6	79.9	71.4	67.8	74.7
1998	76.7	73.8	79.5	77.3	74.5	80.0	71.3	67.6	74.8
1997	76.5	73.6	79.4	77.2	74.3	79.9	71.1	67.2	74.7
1996	76.1	73.1	79.1	76.8	73.9	79.7	70.2	66.1	74.2
1995	75.8	72.5	78.9	76.5	73.4	79.6	69.6	65.2	73.9
1994	75.7	72.4	79.0	76.5	73.3	79.6	69.5	64.9	73.9
1993	75.5	72.2	78.8	76.3	73.1	79.5	69.2	64.6	73.7
1992	75.8	72.3	79.1	76.5	73.2	79.8	69.6	65.0	73.9
1991	75.5	72.0	78.9	76.3	72.9	79.6	69.3	64.6	73.8
1990	75.4	71.8	78.8	76.1	72.7	79.4	69.1	64.5	73.6
1989	75.1	71.7	78.5	75.9	72.5	79.2	68.8	64.3	73.3
1988	74.9	71.4	78.3	75.6	72.2	78.9	68.9	64.4	73.2
1987	74.9	71.4	78.3	75.6	72.1	78.9	69.1	64.7	73.4
1986	74.7	71.2	78.2	75.4	71.9	78.8	69.1	64.8	73.4
1985	74.7	71.1	78.2	75.3	71.8	78.7	69.3	65.0	73.4
1984	74.7	71.1	78.2	75.3	71.8	78.7	69.5	65.3	73.6
1983	74.6	71.0	78.1	75.2	71.6	78.7	69.4	65.2	73.5
1982	74.5	70.8	78.1	75.1	71.5	78.7	69.4	65.1	73.6
1981	74.1	70.4	77.8	74.8	71.1	78.4	68.9	64.5	73.2
1980	73.7	70.0	77.4	74.4	70.7	78.1	68.1	63.8	72.5
1979	73.9	70.0	77.8	74.6	70.8	78.4	68.5	64.0	72.9
1978	73.5	69.6	77.3	74.1	70.4	78.0	68.1	63.7	72.4
1977	73.3	69.5	77.2	74.0	70.2	77.9	67.7	63.4	72.0
1976	72.9	69.1	76.8	73.6	69.9	77.5	67.2	62.9	71.6
1975	72.6	68.8	76.6	73.4	69.5	77.3	66.8	62.4	71.3
1974	72.0	68.2	75.9	72.8	69.0	76.7	66.0	61.7	70.3
1973	71.4	67.6	75.3	72.2	68.5	76.1	65.0	60.9	69.3
1972[2]	71.2	67.4	75.1	72.0	68.3	75.9	64.7	60.4	69.1
1971	71.1	67.4	75.0	72.0	68.3	75.8	64.6	60.5	68.9
1970	70.8	67.1	74.7	71.7	68.0	75.6	64.1	60.0	68.3
1960	69.7	66.6	73.1	70.6	67.4	74.1	—	—	—
1950	68.2	65.6	71.1	69.1	66.5	72.2	—	—	—
1940	60.8	60.8	65.2	64.2	62.1	66.6	—	—	—

(—) Data not available. 1. Figures are revised. 2. Deaths based on a 50% sample. *Source:* National Center for Health Statistics, *National Vital Statistics Reports,* vol. 52, no. 3, Sept. 18, 2003. Web: www.cdc.gov/nchs.

15 Leading Causes of Death in the U.S., 2001

Leading causes of death differ somewhat by age, sex, and race. In 2001, as in previous years, accidents were the leading cause of death for those under 34 years, while in older age groups chronic diseases such as cancer and heart disease were the leading causes. The top three causes for males and females—heart disease, cancer, and stroke—are exactly the same. However, suicide and chronic liver disease ranked 8th and 10th for males but were not ranked among the ten leading causes for females. Similarly, Alzheimer's disease ranked 7th for females but was not among the top ten for males. For white males aged 15–34, the top two causes were accidents and suicide, while for black males in the same age group, the top two causes of death were homicide and accidents.

Rank[1]	Causes of death	Number	Deaths per 100,000 population
	All causes	**2,416,425**	**848.5**
1.	Diseases of heart	700,142	245.8
2.	Malignant neoplasms (cancer)	553,768	194.4
3.	Cerebrovascular diseases	163,538	57.4
4.	Chronic lower respiratory diseases	123,013	43.2
5.	Accidents (unintentional injuries)	101,537	35.7
6.	Diabetes mellitus	71,372	25.1
7.	Influenza and pneumonia	62,034	21.8
8.	Alzheimer's disease	53,852	18.9
9.	Nephritis, nephrotic syndrome, and nephrosis	39,480	13.9
10.	Septicemia	32,238	11.3
11.	Suicide	30,622	10.8
12.	Chronic liver disease and cirrhosis	27,035	9.5
13.	Homicide	20,308	7.1
14.	Hypertension and hypertensive renal disease	19,250	6.8
15.	Pneumonitis due to solids and liquids	17,301	6.1
	All other causes	400,935	140.8

1. Rank based on number of deaths. *Source:* U.S. National Center for Health Statistics, *National Vital Statistics Report,* vol. 52, no. 3, Sept. 18, 2003. Web: www.cdc.gov/nchs.

U.S. Annual Death Rates per 1,000 Population

Year	Rate	Year	Rate	Year	Rate	Year	Rate	Year	Rate	Year	Rate	Year	Rate
1900	17.2	1942	10.3	1952	9.6	1963	9.6	1973	9.3	1983	8.6	1993	8.8
1905	15.9	1943	10.9	1953	9.6	1964	9.4	1974	9.1	1984	8.6	1994	8.8
1910	14.7	1944	10.6	1954	9.2	1965	9.4	1975	8.8	1985	8.7	1995	8.8
1915	13.2	1945	10.6	1955	9.3	1966	9.5	1976	8.8	1986	8.7	1996	8.8
1920	13.0	1946	10.0	1956	9.4	1967	9.4	1977	8.6	1987	8.7	1997	8.6
1925	11.7	1947	10.1	1957	9.6	1968	9.7	1978	8.7	1988	8.8	1998	8.6
1930	11.3	1948	9.9	1958	9.5	1969'	9.5	1979	8.5	1989	8.7	1999	8.8
1935	10.9	1949	9.7	1959	9.4	1970[1]	9.5	1980	8.7	1990	8.6	2000	8.7
1940	10.8	1950	9.6	1960	9.5	1971	9.3	1981	8.6	1991	8.5	2001	8.5
1941	10.5	1951	9.7	1962	9.5	1972	9.4	1982	8.5	1992	8.5		

NOTES: Includes only deaths occurring within the registration states. Beginning with 1933, area includes entire U.S.; with 1959 includes Alaska, and with 1960 includes Hawaii. Excludes fetal deaths. Rates as of April 1 for 1940, 1950, 1960, 1970, and 1980, and estimated as of July 1 for all other years. 1. First year for which deaths of nonresidents are excluded. *Sources:* Department of Health and Human Services, National Center for Health Statistics; *National Vital Statistics Reports,* vol. 52, no. 3, Sept. 18, 2003. Web: www.dhhs.gov.

Deaths by Major Causes, 1960 to 2001

(age-adjusted death rates per 100,000 population)

Year	Heart disease	Cancer	Cerebro-vascular diseases	Chronic lower respiratory diseases	Accidents	Diabetes mellitus	Influenza and pneumonia	Suicide	Chronic liver disease and cirrhosis	Homicide
1960	559.0	193.9	177.9	12.5	63.1	22.5	53.7	12.5	13.3	5.2
1965	542.5	195.6	166.4	18.3	65.8	22.9	46.8	13.0	14.9	6.1
1970	492.7	198.6	147.7	21.3	62.2	24.3	41.7	13.1	17.8	9.0
1975	431.2	200.1	123.5	23.7	50.8	20.3	34.9	13.6	16.7	10.2
1980	412.1	207.9	96.4	28.3	46.4	18.1	31.4	12.2	15.1	10.5
1985	375.0	211.3	76.6	34.5	38.5	17.4	34.5	12.5	12.3	8.0
1990	321.8	216.0	65.5	37.2	36.3	20.7	36.8	12.5	11.1	9.5
1995	296.3	211.7	63.9	40.5	34.9	23.4	33.8	12.0	10.0	8.6
2000	257.6	199.6	60.9	44.2	34.9	25.0	23.7	10.4	9.5	5.9
2001	247.8	196.0	57.9	43.7	35.7	25.3	22.0	10.7	9.5	7.1

Source: U.S. National Center for Health Statistics, *Vital Statistics of the United States,* annual. From *Statistical Abstract of the United States: 2003.*

Deaths by Firearms, 1979–2001

(per 100,000 population in specified group)

Year	All races[1]		White		Black	
	Number of deaths	Death rate[2]	Number of deaths	Death rate[2]	Number of deaths	Death rate[2]
1979	33,019	14.7	24,234	12.5	8,304	31.6
1980	33,780	14.9	24,849	12.8	8,505	31.9
1981	34,050	14.8	25,237	12.8	8,324	30.7
1982	32,957	14.2	25,071	12.7	7,415	27.0
1983	31,099	13.3	24,038	12.1	6,589	23.6
1984	31,331	13.3	24,419	12.2	6,449	22.9
1985	31,566	13.3	24,507	12.1	6,565	23.0
1986	33,373	13.9	25,339	12.5	7,494	25.9
1987	32,895	13.6	24,789	12.1	7,586	25.9
1988	33,989	13.9	24,892	12.1	8,475	28.5
1989	34,776	14.1	25,023	12.1	9,077	30.1
1990	37,155	14.9	26,299	12.6	10,175	33.4
1991	38,317	15.2	26,455	12.5	11,025	35.4
1992	37,776	14.8	26,120	12.3	10,906	34.5
1993	39,595	15.4	26,948	12.5	11,763	36.6
1994	38,505	14.8	26,403	12.2	11,223	34.4
1995	35,957	13.7	25,438	11.7	9,643	29.1
1996	34,040	12.8	24,114	11.0	9,175	27.4
1997	32,436	12.1	23,270	10.5	8,389	24.7
1998	30,708	11.4	22,480	10.1	7,503	21.8
1999	28,874	10.6	21,143	9.4	7,017	20.1
2000	28,663	10.4	20,945	9.3	7,054	20.0
2001	29,573	10.4	21,760	9.4	7,184	19.3

1. Includes races other than black or white. 2. On an annual basis, per 100,000 population in specified group. *Source:* Centers for Disease Control and Prevention, *National Vital Statistics Reports,* vol. 52, no. 3, Sept. 18, 2003.

Infant Mortality Rates, 1950–2001

		Deaths per 1,000 live births				
		Neonatal			Fetal	Late fetal
Year	Infant	Under 28 days	Under 7 days	Postneonatal	mortality rate[1]	mortality rate[2]
All races						
1950[3]	29.2	20.5	17.8	8.7	18.4	14.9
1960[3]	26.0	18.7	16.7	7.3	15.8	12.1
1970	20.0	15.1	13.6	4.9	14.0	9.5
1980	12.6	8.5	7.1	4.1	9.1	6.2
1985	10.6	7.0	5.8	3.7	7.8	4.9
1990	9.2	5.8	4.8	3.4	7.5	4.3
1995	7.6	4.9	4.0	2.7	7.0	3.6
2000	6.9	4.6	3.7	2.3	6.6	3.3
2001	6.8	4.5	3.6	2.3	6.5	3.3
Race of child: white						
1950	26.8	19.4	17.1	7.4	16.6	13.3
1960	22.9	17.2	15.6	5.7	13.9	10.8
1970	17.8	13.8	12.5	4.0	12.3	8.6
1980	11.0	7.5	6.2	3.5	8.1	5.7
Race of mother: white						
1980	10.9	7.4	6.1	3.5	8.1	5.7
1985	9.2	6.0	5.0	3.2	6.9	4.5
1990	7.6	4.8	3.9	2.8	6.4	3.8
1995	6.3	4.1	3.3	2.2	5.9	3.3
2000	5.7	3.8	3.0	1.9	5.6	2.9
2001	5.7	3.8	3.0	1.9	5.5	2.9
Race of child: black						
1950	43.9	27.8	23.0	16.1	32.1	—
1960	44.3	27.8	23.7	16.5	—	—
1970	32.6	22.8	20.3	9.9	23.2	—
1980	21.4	14.1	11.9	7.3	14.4	8.9
Race of mother: black						
1980	22.2	14.6	12.3	7.6	14.7	9.1
1985	19.0	12.6	10.8	6.4	12.8	7.2
1990	18.0	11.6	9.7	6.4	13.3	6.7
1995	15.1	9.8	8.2	5.3	12.7	5.7
2000	14.1	9.4	7.6	4.7	12.4	5.4
2001	14.0	9.2	7.6	4.8	12.1	5.3

NOTES: "Infant" is defined as under 1 year of age; "neonatal" is under 28 days; "postneonatal" is 28 days–11 months. 1. Number of fetal deaths of 20 weeks or more gestation per 1,000 live births plus fetal deaths. 2. Number of fetal deaths of 28 weeks or more gestation per 1,000 live births plus late fetal deaths. 3. Includes birth and deaths of persons who were not residents of the 50 states and the District of Columbia. *Sources:* Centers for Disease Control and Prevention, National Center for Health Statistics. From *Health, United States, 2003.*

Death Rates for Suicide, 1950–2001

(deaths per 100,000 resident population)

	1950	1960	1970	1980	1990	1995	2000	2001
All ages, age adjusted	13.2	13.2	13.2	13.2	12.5	11.8	10.4	10.7
5–14 years	0.2	0.3	0.3	0.4	0.8	0.9	0.7	0.7
15–24 years	4.5	5.2	8.8	12.3	13.2	13.0	10.2	9.9
15–19 years	2.7	3.6	5.9	8.5	11.1	10.3	8.0	7.9
20–24 years	6.2	7.1	12.2	16.1	15.1	15.8	12.5	12.0
25–44 years	11.6	12.2	15.4	15.6	15.2	15.1	13.4	13.8
25–34 years	9.1	10.0	14.1	16.0	15.2	15.0	12.0	12.8
35–44 years	14.3	14.2	16.9	15.4	15.3	15.1	14.5	14.7
45–64 years	23.5	22.0	20.6	15.9	15.3	13.9	13.5	14.4
45–54 years	20.9	20.7	20.0	15.9	14.8	14.4	14.4	15.2
55–64 years	26.8	23.7	21.4	15.9	16.0	13.2	12.1	13.1
65 years and over	30.0	24.5	20.8	17.6	20.5	17.9	15.2	15.3
65–74 years	29.6	23.0	20.8	16.9	17.9	15.7	12.5	13.3
75–84 years	31.1	27.9	21.2	19.1	24.9	20.6	17.6	17.4
85 years and over	28.8	26.0	19.0	19.2	22.2	21.3	19.6	17.5
Male, all ages, age adjusted	21.2	20.0	19.8	19.9	21.5	20.3	17.7	18.2
Female, all ages	5.6	5.6	7.4	5.7	4.8	4.3	4.0	4.0

Sources: Centers for Disease Control and Prevention, National Center for Health Statistics. From *Health, United States, 2003.*

Miscellaneous

Expenditure per Consumer Unit for Entertainment and Reading

	Total	Percent of total expenditures	Fees and admissions	Television, radios, and sound equipment	Other equipment and services[1]	Reading
1985	$1,311	5.6%	$320	$371	$ 479	$141
1990	1,575	5.6	371	454	597	153
1995	1,775	5.5	433	542	637	163
2000	2,009	5.3	515	622	727	146
2001	2,094	5.3	526	660	767	141
Age[2]						
Under 25 years old	1,212	5.2	289	506	356	60
25 to 34 years old	2,112	5.4	492	698	810	111
35 to 44 years old	2,644	5.6	707	787	1,014	136
45 to 54 years old	2,405	5	635	781	817	172
55 to 64 years old	2,520	6.1	588	642	1,107	183
65 to 74 years old	1,455	4.5	379	500	417	159
75 years old and over	950	4.1	207	361	254	128
Origin of reference person[2]						
Hispanic	1,305	3.8	277	593	376	59
Non-Hispanic	2,170	5.4	550	666	805	149
Race of reference person[2]						
White and other	2,237	5.5	573	671	841	152
Black	1,050	3.6	188	575	225	62
Region of residence[2]						
Northeast	2,023	4.9	561	681	611	169
Midwest	2,382	6	587	680	953	162
South	1,753	4.8	410	614	628	101
West	2,400	5.5	620	693	928	159

1. Other equipment and services includes pets, toys, and playground equipment; sports, exercise, and photographic equipment; and recreational vehicles. 2. Figures are for 2001. *Source:* U.S. Bureau of Labor Statistics, *Consumer Expenditure Survey,* annual. From *Statistical Abstract of the United States, 2003.*

Household Pet Ownership, 2001

Item	Dog	Cat	Pet bird	Horse
Percent of households owning companion pets[1]	36.1%	31.6%	4.6%	1.7%
Average number owned	1.6	2.1	2.1	3.0
Households obtaining veterinary care[2]	85.0%	66.8%	12.9%	56.7%
Average visits per household per year	2.8	1.9	0.3	2.2
Percent of households owning pets				
Annual household income:				
Under $20,000	29.7%	28.1%	5.1%	1.0%
$20,000 to $34,999	33.9	30.9	4.5	1.3
$35,000 to $54,999	37.9	32.2	4.8	2.0
$55,000 to $84,999	40.5	34.3	4.4	2.1
$85,000 and over	39.7	33.7	4.2	2.1
Household size:[1]				
One person	20.8	23.5	2.8	0.7
Two persons	34.3	31.3	4.0	1.6
Three persons	46.2	37.4	5.9	2.2
Four persons	50.6	38.2	6.3	2.3
Five or more persons	53.0	39.7	8.3	3.2

NOTE: Based on a sample survey of 80,000 households in 2001. 1. As of Dec. 31, 2001. 2. During 2001. *Source:* American Veterinary Medical Association, Schaumburg, Ill., *U.S. Pet Ownership and Demographics Sourcebook, 2002.* Reprinted with permission.

Most Popular Pet Names

The American Society for the Prevention of Cruelty to Animals (ASPCA) has conducted a veterinarian survey to find out which pet names are most popular in the United States today. Here are the top 30:

1. Max	7. Kitty	13. Misty	19. Samantha	25. Sheba
2. Sam	8. Molly	14. Missy	20. Lucky	26. Rocky
3. Lady	9. Buddy	15. Pepper	21. Muffin	27. Patches
4. Bear	10. Brandy	16. Jake	22. Princess	28. Tigger
5. Smokey	11. Ginger	17. Bandit	23. Maggie	29. Rusty
6. Shadow	12. Baby	18. Tiger	24. Charlie	30. Buster

Top Ten Dog Breeds

Source: The American Kennel Club www.akc.org

Rank	Breed	Number*
1.	Labrador Retriever	154,616
2.	Golden Retriever	56,124
3.	German Shepherd	46,963
4.	Beagle	44,610
5.	Dachshund	42,571
6.	Yorkshire Terrier	37,277
7.	Boxer	34,340
8.	Poodle	33,917
9.	Chihuahua	28,466
10.	Shih Tzu	28,294

*"Number" refers to the number of dogs of that breed registered in 2002.

Top Ten Cat Breeds

Source: Cat Fanciers' Association www.cfainc.org

Rank*	Breed
1.	Persian
2.	Maine Coon
3.	Exotic
4.	Siamese
5.	Abyssinian
6.	Oriental
7.	Birman
8.	American Shorthair
9.	Tonkinese
10.	Burmese

*Based on registration statistics for the year 2002.

Most Popular Given Names, 1880–2003

Boys

1880: John, William, Charles, George, James, Joseph, Frank, Henry, Thomas, Harry

1890: John, William, James, George, Charles, Joseph, Frank, Harry, Henry, Edward

1900: John, William, James, George, Charles, Joseph, Frank, Henry, Robert, Harry

1910: John, William, James, Robert, Joseph, Charles/George (tie), Edward, Frank, Henry

1920: John, William, James, Robert, Joseph, Charles, George, Edward, Thomas, Frank

1930: Robert, James, John, William, Richard, Charles, Donald, George, Joseph, Edward

1940: James, Robert, John, William, Richard, Charles, David, Thomas, Donald, Ronald

1950: John, James, Robert, William, Michael, David, Richard, Thomas, Charles, Gary

1960: David, Michael, John, James, Robert, Mark, William, Richard, Thomas, Steven

1970: Michael, David, John, James, Robert, Christopher, William, Mark, Richard, Brian

1980: Michael, Jason, Christopher, David, James, Matthew, John, Joshua, Robert, Daniel

1990: Michael, Christopher, Joshua, Matthew, David, Daniel, Andrew, Joseph, Justin, James

2000: Jacob, Michael, Matthew, Joshua, Christopher, Nicholas, Andrew, Joseph, Daniel, Tyler

2002: Jacob, Michael, Joshua, Matthew, Ethan, Joseph, Andrew, Christopher, Daniel, Nicholas

2003: Jacob, Michael, Joshua, Matthew, Andrew, Joseph, Ethan, Daniel, Christopher, Anthony

Girls

1880: Mary, Anna, Elizabeth, Margaret, Minnie, Emma, Martha, Alice, Marie, Annie/Sarah (tie)

1890: Mary, Anna, Elizabeth, Emma, Margaret, Rose, Ethel, Florence, Ida, Bertha/Helen (tie)

1900: Mary, Helen, Anna, Margaret, Ruth, Elizabeth, Marie, Rose, Florence, Bertha

1910: Mary, Helen, Margaret, Dorothy, Ruth, Anna, Mildred, Elizabeth, Alice, Ethel

1920: Mary, Dorothy, Helen, Margaret, Ruth, Virginia, Elizabeth, Anna, Mildred, Betty

1930: Mary, Betty, Dorothy, Helen, Barbara, Margaret, Maria, Patricia, Doris, Joan/Ruth (tie)

1940: Mary, Barbara, Patricia, Carol, Judith, Betty, Nancy, Maria, Margaret, Linda

1950: Linda, Mary, Patricia, Barbara, Susan, Maria, Sandra, Nancy, Deborah, Kathleen

1960: Mary, Susan, Maria, Karen, Lisa, Linda, Donna, Patricia, Debra, Deborah

1970: Jennifer, Lisa, Kimberly, Michelle, Angela, Maria, Amy, Melissa, Mary, Tracy

1980: Jennifer, Jessica, Amanda, Melissa, Sarah, Nicole, Heather, Amy, Michelle, Elizabeth

1990: Jessica, Ashley, Brittany, Amanda, Stephanie, Jennifer, Samantha, Sarah, Megan, Lauren

2000: Emily, Hannah, Madison, Ashley, Sarah, Alexis, Samantha, Jessica, Taylor, Elizabeth

2002: Emily, Madison, Hannah, Emma, Alexis, Ashley, Abigail, Sarah, Samantha, Olivia

2003: Emily, Emma, Madison, Hannah, Olivia, Abigail, Alexis, Ashley, Elizabeth, Samantha

NOTE: Represents the most frequently used given names for births, based on a sampling of Social Security Number card applications. *Source:* Social Security Administration. Web: www.ssa.gov/cgi-bin/babynames.cgi.

Most Common Last Names in the U.S.

Rank	Name	Frequency[1]	Rank	Name	Frequency[1]	Rank	Name	Frequency[1]
1.	Smith	1.01%	11.	Anderson	0.31%	21.	Clark	0.23%
2.	Johnson	0.81	12.	Thomas	0.31	22.	Rodriguez	0.23
3.	Williams	0.70	13.	Jackson	0.31	23.	Lewis	0.23
4.	Jones	0.62	14.	White	0.28	24.	Lee	0.22
5.	Brown	0.62	15.	Harris	0.28	25.	Walker	0.22
6.	Davis	0.48	16.	Martin	0.27	26.	Hall	0.20
7.	Miller	0.42	17.	Thompson	0.27	27.	Allen	0.20
8.	Wilson	0.34	18.	Garcia	0.25	28.	Young	0.19
9.	Moore	0.31	19.	Martinez	0.23	29.	Hernandez	0.19
10.	Taylor	0.31	20.	Robinson	0.23	30.	King	0.19

NOTE: Based on 1990 Census data. Numbers are rounded. 1. Percent of U.S. population sample. *Source:* U.S. Census Bureau. Web: www.census.gov/genealogy/names/dist.all.last.

2003 Charitable Contributions by Type of Recipient Organization
(in billions)

Type of organization	Amount contributed	Percent	Type of organization	Amount contributed	Percent
Total	$240.72	100.0%	Human services	$18.89	7.8%
Religion	86.39	35.9	Arts, culture, and humanities	13.11	5.4
Education	31.59	13.1			
Unallocated giving	24.03	10.0	Public-society benefit	12.13	5.0
Foundations[1]	21.44	8.9	Environment/animals	6.95	2.9
Health	20.89	8.7	International affairs	5.30	2.2

NOTE: All figures are rounded. Total may not be 100%. 1. Estimate. Source: AAFRC Trust for Philanthropy/Giving USA 2004.

2003 Charitable Contributions by Source of Contributions
(in billions)

Source	Amount contributed	Percent	Source	Amount contributed	Percent
Total	$240.72	100.0%	Bequests	$21.60	9.0%
Individuals	179.36	74.5	Corporations	13.46	5.6
Foundations	26.30	10.9			

NOTE: All figures are rounded. Total may not be 100%. Source: AAFRC Trust for Philanthropy/Giving USA 2004.

U.S. Charities Receiving Highest Donations in 2003

Rank	Organization	Private support	Total income	Total expenses
1.	American National Red Cross (Washington, D.C.)	$1,736,354,705	$4,087,431,368	$3,541,137,732
2.	Salvation Army (Alexandria, Va.)	1,371,964,000	2,147,427,000	2,491,745,000
3.	Gifts In Kind International (Alexandria, Va.)	793,151,513	795,653,227	751,734,307
4.	American Cancer Society (Atlanta)	765,000,000	789,398,000	832,297,000
5.	Fidelity Investments Charitable Gift Fund (Boston)	735,454,143	758,194,427	768,642,979
6.	Lutheran Services in America (Baltimore)	723,253,495	8,030,780,248	6,959,844,547
7.	YMCA of the USA (Chicago)	713,854,000	4,271,651,000	4,164,153,000
8.	Nature Conservancy (Arlington, Va.)	628,339,364	972,368,622	632,518,625
9.	University of Southern California (Los Angeles)	585,161,932	n.a.	n.a.
10.	Feed the Children (Oklahoma City)	546,983,436	553,397,898	579,068,632
11.	United Way of New York City	497,959,872	523,138,906	370,243,465
12.	America's Second Harvest (Chicago)	485,147,423	487,872,272	479,776,539
13.	Harvard University (Cambridge, Mass.)	477,617,144	2,362,169,932	2,314,507,723
14.	Stanford University (Palo Alto, Calif.)	454,769,878	2,511,828,809	2,240,714,974
15.	Boys & Girls Clubs of America (Atlanta)	453,657,870	1,079,440,769	1,001,834,303
16.	American Heart Association (Dallas)	437,531,420	525,681,616	505,662,147
17.	World Vision (Federal Way, Wash.)	437,110,000	553,049,000	541,562,000
18.	AmeriCares Foundation (New Canaan, Conn.)	412,689,073	413,490,531	421,989,820
19.	Habitat for Humanity International (Americus, Ga.)	411,944,000	718,392,000	716,984,000
20.	Cornell University (Ithaca, N.Y.)	363,031,766	1,876,031,000	1,750,021,000
21.	Campus Crusade for Christ International (Orlando, Fla.)	346,681,000	386,820,000	381,058,000
22.	Goodwill Industries International (Bethesda, Md.)	337,800,000	2,055,200,000	1,981,900,000
23.	Food for the Poor (Deerfield Beach, Fla.)	320,765,464	351,899,592	351,381,851
24.	University of Pennsylvania (Philadelphia)	319,742,070	2,714,353,089	2,579,382,327
25.	The Johns Hopkins University (Baltimore)	318,687,392	2,412,934,000	2,231,521,000
26.	University of Wisconsin at Madison	307,213,842	1,697,873,943	1,586,520,621
27.	Boy Scouts of America (Irving, Tex.)	291,285,000	664,969,000	700,490,000
28.	University of California at Los Angeles	282,343,369	n.a.	n.a.
29.	Shriners Hospitals for Children (Tampa, Fla.)	272,635,000	272,635,000	512,108,000
30.	American Lebanese Syrian Associated Charities/St. Jude Children's Research Hospital (Memphis)	271,395,825	324,615,022	387,158,503

Source: The Chronicle of Philanthropy, 2003. Reprinted with permission.

Percent of Adult Population Doing Volunteer Work, 2000

Age, sex, race, and Hispanic origin	Percent of population volunteering	Average hours volunteered per month	Educational attainment and household income	Percent of population volunteering	Average hours volunteered per month
Total	44.0%	15.1	Less than high school graudate	20.0%	17.1
			High-school graduate	36.1	12.3
21–24 years	32.3	12.1	Technical, trade, or business school	46.9	16.3
25–34 years	40.5	15.9	4-year college degree	60.3	15.3
35–44 years	50.9	16.1	Some graduate school	58.4	16.7
45–54 years	47.9	14.7			
55–64 years	42.9	12.1	Under $10,000	23.8	8.3
65–74 years	41.4	14.1	$10,000–19,999	27.2	13.1
75 years and over	39.0	19.5	$20,000–29,999	32.3	17.4
			$30,000–39,999	37.3	12.5
Male	41.2	14.6	$40,000–49,999	40.4	13.7
Female	45.9	15.5	$50,000–59,999	48.3	13.0
			$60,000–74,999	58.6	14.6
White	46.7	14.6	$75,000–99,999	57.0	16.5
Black	36.9	18.4	$100,000 or more	55.5	18.6
Hispanic[1]	33.4	13.6			

Type of activity	Percent of population involved in activity	Type of activity	Percent of population involved in activity
Arts, culture, humanities	2.1%	Private, community foundations	2.2%
Education	7.7	Public and societal benefit	4.0
Environment	2.1	Recreation—adults	1.5
Health	7.9	Religion	19.1
Human services	6.8	Work-related organizations	1.0
International, foreign	0.4	Youth development	6.6
Political organizations	1.3		

1. Hispanic persons may be of any race. NOTE: Covers persons 21 years and over. Volunteers are persons who worked in some way to help others for no monetary pay during the previous year. Based on a sample survey conducted during the spring of the following year and subject to sampling variability. *Source: Statistical Abstract of the United States: 2002.*

Personal Consumption Expenditures for Recreation: 1990 to 2001

Type of product or service	1990	1995	2000	2001	Type of product or service	1990	1995	2000	2001
Total recreation expenditures	284.9	401.6	564.7	593.9	Radio and television repair	3.7	3.6	4.1	4.2
Percent of total personal consumption	7.4	8.1	8.4	8.5	Flowers, seeds, and potted plants	10.9	13.8	17.5	18.5
Books and maps	16.2	23.1	33.2	35.1	Admissions to specified spectator amusements	14.8	19.2	27.1	29.4
Magazines, newspapers, and sheet music	21.6	26.2	34.2	35.2	Motion picture theaters	5.1	5.5	7.8	8.7
Nondurable toys and sport supplies	32.8	47.2	62.7	66.7	Legitimate theaters and opera, and entertainments of nonprofit institutions [2]	5.2	7.6	9.9	10.6
Wheel goods, sports and photographic equipment[1]	29.7	38.5	55.3	60.8	Spectator sports[3]	4.5	6.1	9.5	10.1
Video and audio products, computer equipment, and musical instruments	52.9	77.0	106.3	105.6	Clubs and fraternal organizations except insurance[4]	8.7	12.7	16.7	17.3
Video and audio goods, including musical instruments	43.9	55.9	71.8	72.7	Commercial participant amusements[5]	24.6	43.9	68.4	73.3
					Pari-mutuel net receipts	3.5	3.5	4.7	4.8
Computers, peripherals, and software	8.9	21.0	34.5	32.9	Other[6]	65.4	93.1	134.4	142.9

1. Includes boats and pleasure aircraft. 2. Except athletic. 3. Consists of admissions to professional and amateur athletic events and to racetracks, including horse, dog, and auto. 4. Consists of dues and fees excluding insurance premiums. 5. Consists of billiard parlors; bowling alleys; dancing, riding, shooting, skating, and swimming places; amusement devices and parks; golf courses; sightseeing buses and guides; private flying operations; casino gambling; and other commercial participant amusements. 6. Consists of net receipts of lotteries and expenditures for purchases of pets and pet care services, cable TV, film processing, photographic studios, sporting and recreation camps, video cassette rentals, and recreational services, elsewhere classified. *Source:* U.S. Department of Commerce, Bureau of Economic Analysis, *National Income and Product Accounts, Volume 1, 1929–97,* and *Survey of Current Business,* May 2003. *See also* www.bea.gov/bea/dn/ nipaweb/selecttable.asp (released as of 30 May 2003). From *Statistical Abstracts of the United States, 2003.*

States

Data for state populations are the latest available from the U.S. Census Bureau. NOTE: Persons of Hispanic origin can be any race. "American Indian" includes American Indians, Eskimos, and Aleuts. "Asian" includes Asian Indians, Chinese, Filipino, Japanese, Korean, and Vietnamese. Largest cities include incorporated places only, as defined by the U.S. Census Bureau. They do not include adjacent or suburban areas. Population data for U.S. cities are also the latest available from the U.S. Census Bureau.

For secession and readmission dates of the former Confederate states, *see* U.S. Government & History: The Confederate States of America. For a separate list of governors, and lists of senators and representatives elected to terms beginning in 2003, *see* U.S. Government & History: The Governors of the Fifty States, The Senate, and The House of Representatives. For U.S. Territories, *see* Countries of the World: United States.

Alabama

Capital: Montgomery
Governor: Bob Riley, R (to Jan. 2007)
Lieut. Governor: Lucy Baxley, D (to Jan. 2007)
Senators: Jeff Sessions, R (to Jan. 2009); Richard C. Shelby, R (to Jan. 2005)
Secy. of State: Nancy Worley, D (to Jan. 2007)
Treasurer: Kay Ivey, R (to Jan. 2007)
Atty. General: Troy King, R (to Jan. 2007)
Organized as territory: March 3, 1817
Entered Union (rank): Dec. 14, 1819 (22)
Present constitution adopted: 1901
Motto: *Audemus jura nostra defendere* (We dare defend our rights)
State Symbols: flower, camellia (1959); **bird,** yellowhammer (1927); **song,** "Alabama" (1931); **tree,** Southern longleaf pine (1949, 1997); **salt water fish,** fighting tarpon (1955); **fresh water fish,** largemouth bass (1975); **horse,** racking horse (1975); **mineral,** hematite (1967); **rock,** marble (1969); **game bird,** wild turkey (1980); **dance,** square dance (1981); **nut,** pecan (1982); **fossil,** species *Basilosaurus Cetoides* (1984); **official mascot and butterfly,** eastern tiger swallowtail (1989); **insect,** monarch butterfly (1989); **reptile,** Alabama red-bellied turtle (1990); **gemstone,** star blue quartz (1990); **shell,** *scaphella junonia johnstoneae* (1990)
Nickname: Yellowhammer State
Origin of name: May come from Choctaw meaning "thicket-clearers" or "vegetation-gatherers"
10 largest cities (2003 est.): Birmingham, 236,620; Montgomery, 200,123; Mobile, 193,464; Huntsville, 164,237; Tuscaloosa, 79,294; Hoover, 65,070; Dothan, 60,036; Decatur, 54,239; Auburn, 46,923; Gadsden, 37,619
Land area: 50,744 sq mi. (131,427 sq km)
Geographic center: In Chilton Co., 12 mi. SW of Clanton
Number of counties: 67
Largest county by population and area: Jefferson, 659,743 (2001); Baldwin, 1,596 sq mi.
State forests: 21 (48,000 ac.)
State parks: 22 (45,614 ac.)
Residents: Alabamian, Alabaman
2003 resident population est.: 4,500,752
2000 resident census population (rank): 4,447,100 (23). **Male:** 2,146,504 (48.3%); **Female:** 2,300,596 (51.7%). **White:** 3,162,808 (71.1%); **Black:** 1,155,930 (26.0%); **American Indian:** 22,430 (0.5%); **Asian:** 31,346 (0.7%); **Other race:** 28,998 (0.7%); **Two or more races:** 44,179 (1.0%); **Hispanic/Latino:** 75,830 (1.7%). **2000 percent population 18 and over:** 74.7; **65 and over:** 13.0; **median age:** 35.8.

Spanish explorers are believed to have arrived at Mobile Bay in 1519, and the territory was visited in 1540 by the explorer Hernando de Soto. The first permanent European settlement in Alabama was founded by the French at Fort Louis de la Mobile in 1702. The British gained control of the area in 1763 by the Treaty of Paris but had to cede almost all the Alabama region to the U.S. and Spain after the American Revolution. The Confederacy was founded at Montgomery in Feb. 1861, and, for a time, the city was the Confederate capital.

During the later 19th century, the economy of the state slowly improved with industrialization. At Tuskegee Institute, founded in 1881 by Booker T. Washington, Dr. George Washington Carver carried out his famous agricultural research.

In the 1950s and '60s, Alabama was the site of such landmark civil-rights actions as the bus boycott in Montgomery (1955–56) and the "Freedom March" from Selma to Montgomery (1965).

Today paper, chemicals, rubber and plastics, apparel and textiles, primary metals, and automobile manufacturing constitute the leading industries of Alabama. Continuing as a major manufacturer of coal, iron, and steel, Birmingham is also noted for its world-renowned medical center. The state ranks high in the production of poultry, soybeans, milk, vegetables, livestock, wheat, cattle, cotton, peanuts, fruits, hogs, and corn.

Points of interest include the Helen Keller birthplace at Tuscumbia, the Space and Rocket Center at Huntsville, the White House of the Confederacy, the restored state Capitol, the Civil Rights Memorial, the Rosa Parks Museum & Library, and the Shakespeare Festival Theater Complex in Montgomery; the Civil Rights Institute and the McWane Center in Birmingham; the Russell Cave near Bridgeport; the Bellingrath Gardens at Theodore; the USS *Alabama* at Mobile; Mound State Monument near Tuscaloosa; and the Gulf Coast area.

Selected famous natives and residents: Hank Aaron, baseball player; Ralph Abernathy, civil rights activist; Tallulah Bankhead, actress; Hugo L. Black, jurist; George Washington Carver, educator, agricultural chemist; Nat "King" Cole, entertainer; Lionel Hampton, jazz musician; W. C. Handy, composer; Courtney Cox-Arquette, actress; Helen Keller, author and educator; Coretta Scott King, civil rights leader; Harper Lee, writer; Joe Louis, boxer; Willie Mays, baseball player; Jim Nabors, actor; Jesse Owens, athlete; Rosa Parks, civil rights activist; Wayne Rogers, actor; Tascaluza, Choctaw chief; George Wallace, governor; William Weatherford (Red Eagle), Creek leader; Heather Whitestone, Miss America (1995).

Alaska

Capital: Juneau
Governor: Frank H. Murkowski, R (to Dec. 2006)
Lieut. Governor: Loren Leman, R (to Dec. 2006)
Senators: Lisa Murkowski, R (to Jan. 2005); Ted Stevens, R (to Jan. 2009)
Atty. General: Gregg D. Renkes, R (apptd. by gov.)
Organized as territory: 1912
Entered Union (rank): Jan. 3, 1959 (49)
Constitution ratified: April 24, 1956
Motto: North to the Future
State Symbols: flower, forget-me-not (1949); **tree,** sitka spruce (1962); **bird,** willow ptarmigan (1955); **fish,** king salmon (1962); **song,** "Alaska's Flag" (1955); **gem,** jade (1968); **marine mammal,** bowhead whale (1983); **fossil,** woolly mammoth (1986); **mineral,** gold (1968); **sport,** dog mushing (1972)
Nickname: The state is commonly called "The Last Frontier" or "Land of the Midnight Sun"
Origin of name: Corruption of Aleut word meaning "great land" or "that which the sea breaks against"
10 largest cities (2003 est.): Anchorage, 270,951; Juneau, 31,187; Fairbanks, 30,970; Sitka, 8,876; Ketchikan, 7,453; Kenai, 7,347; Wasilla, 7,084; Kodiak, 6,302; Bethel, 5,983; Palmer, 5,742
Land area: 571,951 sq mi. (1,4 81,353 sq km)
Geographic center: 60 mi. NW of Mt. McKinley
Number of boroughs (counties): 27
Largest borough by population and area: Anchorage, 264,937 (2001); Yukon-Koyukuk, 157,121 sq mi.
State parks: more than 100 (3.5 million acres)
Residents: Alaskan
2003 resident population est.: 648,818
2000 resident census population (rank): 626,932 (48). **Male:** 324,112 (51.7%); **Female:** 302,820 (48.3%). **White:** 434,534 (69.3%); **Black:** 21,787 (3.5%); **American Indian and Alaska Native:** 98,043 (15.6%); **Asian:** 25,116 (4.0%); **Other race:** 9,997 (1.6%); **Two or more races:** 34,146 (5.4%); **Hispanic/Latino:** 25,852 (4.1%). **2000 percent population 18 and over:** 69.6; **65 and over:** 5.7; **median age:** 32.4.

Vitus Bering, a Dane working for the Russians, and Alexei Chirikov discovered the Alaskan mainland and the Aleutian Islands in 1741. The tremendous land mass of Alaska—equal to one-fifth of the continental U.S.—was unexplored in 1867 when Secretary of State William Seward arranged for its purchase from the Russians for $7,200,000. The transfer of the territory took place on Oct. 18, 1867. Despite a price of about two cents an acre, the purchase was widely ridiculed as "Seward's Folly." The first official census (1880) reported a total of 33,426 Alaskans, all but 430 being of aboriginal stock. The Gold Rush of 1898 resulted in a mass influx of more than 30,000 people. Since then, Alaska has contributed billions of dollars' worth of products to the U.S. economy.

In 1968, a large oil and gas reservoir near Prudhoe Bay on the Arctic Coast was found. The Prudhoe Bay reservoir, with an estimated recoverable 10 billion barrels of oil and 27 trillion cubic feet of gas, is twice as large as any other oil field in North America. The Trans-Alaska pipeline was completed in 1977 at a cost of $7.7 billion. Oil flows through the 800-mile-long pipeline from Prudhoe Bay to the port of Valdez.

Other important industries are fisheries, wood and wood products, furs, and tourism.

Denali National Park and Mendenhall Glacier in North Tongass National Forest are of interest, as is the large totem pole collection at Sitka National Historical Park. The Katmai National Park includes the "Valley of Ten Thousand Smokes," an area of active volcanoes.

The Alaska Native population includes Eskimos, Indians, and Aleuts. About half of all Alaska Natives are Eskimos. (*Eskimo* is used for Alaska Natives; *Inuit* is used for Eskimos living in Canada.) The two main Eskimo groups, Inupiat and Yupik, are distinguished by their language and geography. The former live in the north and northwest parts of Alaska and speak Inupiaq, while the latter live in the south and southwest and speak Yupik.

About a third of Alaska Natives are American Indians. The major tribes are the Alaskan Athabaskan in the central part of the state, and the Tlingit, Tsimshian, and Haida in the southeast.

The Aleuts, native to the Aleutian Islands, Kodiak Island, the lower Alaska and Kenai Peninsulas, and Prince William Sound, are physically and culturally related to the Eskimos. About 15% of Alaska Natives are Aleuts.

Selected famous natives and residents: Clarence L. Andrews, author; Aleksandr Baranov, first governor of Russian America; Margaret Elizabeth Bell, author; Benny Benson, designed state flag at age 13; Vitus Bering, explorer; Charles E. Bunnell, educator; Susan Butcher, sled-dog racer; William A. Egan, first state governor; Carl Ben Eielson, pioneer pilot; Henry E. Gruennig, political leader; B. Frank Heintzleman, territorial governor; Walter J. Hickel, governor; Sheldon Jackson, educator and missionary; Joe Juneau, prospector; Austin Lathrop, industrialist; Sydney Lawrence, painter; Ray Mala, actor; Virgil F. Partch, cartoonist; Joe Redington, Sr., sled-dog musher and promoter; Peter Trinble Rowe, first Episcopal bishop; Ivan Popov-Veniaminov (St. Innocent), Russian Orthodox missionary; Ferdinand Wrangel, educator; Samuel Hall Young, founder of first American church.

Arizona

Capital: Phoenix
Governor: Janet Napolitano, D (to Jan. 2007)
Senators: Jon Kyl, R (to Jan. 2007); John McCain, R (to Jan. 2005)
Secy. of State: Jan Brewer, R (to Jan. 2007)
Atty. General: Terry Goddard, D (to Jan. 2007)
Treasurer: David Petersen, R (to Jan. 2007)
Organized as territory: Feb. 24, 1863
Entered Union (rank): Feb. 14, 1912 (48)
Present constitution adopted: 1911
Motto: *Ditat Deus* (God enriches)
State Symbols: flower, flower of saguaro cactus (1931); **bird,** cactus wren (1931); **colors,** blue and old gold (1915); **song,** "Arizona" (1919); **tree,** palo verde (1954); **neckwear,** bola tie (1971); **fossil,** petrified wood (1988); **gemstone,** turquoise (1974); **mammal,** ringtail (1986); **reptile,** Arizona ridgenose rattlesnake (1986); **fish,** Arizona trout (1986); **amphibian,** Arizona tree frog (1986); **butterfly,** two-tailed swallowtail (2001)
Nickname: Grand Canyon State
Origin of name: From the Indian "Arizonac," meaning "little spring" or "young spring"
10 largest cities (2003 est.): Phoenix, 1,388,416; Tucson, 507,658; Mesa, 432,376; Glendale, 232,838; Scottsdale, 217,989; Chandler, 211,299; Tempe, 158,880; Gilbert, 145,250; Peoria, 127,580; Yuma, 81,605
Land area: 113,635 sq mi. (294,315 sq km)
Geographic center: In Yavapai Co., 55 mi. ESE of Prescott
Number of counties: 15
Largest county by population and area: Maricopa, 3,194,798 (2001); Coconino, 18,562 sq mi.
State parks: 28

Residents: Arizonan, Arizonian
2003 resident population est.: 5,580,811
2000 resident census population (rank): 5,130,632 (20). **Male:** 2,561,057 (49.9%); **Female:** 2,569,575 (50.1%). **White:** 3,873,611 (75.5%); **Black:** 158,873 (3.1%); **American Indian:** 255,879 (5.0%); **Asian:** 92,236 (1.8%); **Other race:** 596,774 (11.6%); **Two or more races:** 146,526 (2.9%); **Hispanic/Latino:** 1,295,617 (25.3%). **2000 percent population 18 and over:** 73.4; **65 and over:** 13.0; **median age:** 34.2.

Marcos de Niza, a Spanish Franciscan friar, was the first European to explore Arizona. He entered the area in 1539 in search of the mythical Seven Cities of Gold. Although he was followed a year later by another gold seeker, Francisco Vásquez de Coronado, most of the early settlement was for missionary purposes. In 1775 the Spanish established Fort Tucson. In 1848, after the Mexican War, most of the Arizona territory became part of the U.S., and the southern portion of the territory was added by the Gadsden Purchase in 1853.

Arizona history is rich in legends of America's Old West. It was here that the great Indian chiefs Geronimo and Cochise led their people against the frontiersmen. Tombstone, Ariz., was the site of the West's most famous shoot-out—the gunfight at the O.K. Corral. Today, Arizona has one of the largest U.S. Indian populations; more than 14 tribes are represented on 20 reservations.

Manufacturing has become Arizona's most important industry. Principal products include electrical, communications, and aeronautical items. The state produces over half of the country's copper. Agriculture is also important to the state's economy. Top commodities are cattle and calves, dairy products, and cotton. In 1973 one of the world's most massive dams, the New Cornelia Tailings, was completed near Ajo.

State attractions include the Grand Canyon, the Petrified Forest, the Painted Desert, Hoover Dam, Lake Mead, Fort Apache, and the reconstructed London Bridge at Lake Havasu City.

Selected famous natives and residents: Apache Kid, Indian outlaw; Erma Bombeck, humorist and writer; Glen Campbell, singer; Lynda Carter, actress; Cesar Chavez, labor leader; Cochise, Apache chief; Alice Cooper, singer and songwriter; Wyatt Earp, marshall; Max Ernst, painter; Geronimo (Goyathlay), Apache chief; Barry Goldwater, politician; Zane Grey, novelist; Carl Trumbull Hayden, politician; George W. P. Hunt, first state governor; Bill Keane, cartoonist; Eusebio Kino, missionary; Percival Lowell, astronomer; Frank Luke, Jr., WWI fighter ace; Charles Mingus, jazz musician and composer; Carlos Montezuma, doctor and Indian spokesman; Stevie Nicks, singer; Sandra Day O'Connor, jurist; William O'Neill, frontier sheriff; Alexander M. Patch, general; William H. Pickering, astronomer; Linda Ronstadt, singer; Paolo Soleri, architect; Clyde W. Tombaugh, astronomer; Tanya Tucker, singer; Stewart Udall, secretary of the Interior; Frank Lloyd Wright, architect.

Arkansas

Capital: Little Rock
Governor: Mike Huckabee, R (to Jan. 2007)
Lieut. Governor: Winthrop Rockefeller, R (to Jan. 2007)
Senators: Mark Pryor, D (to Jan. 2009);
Blanche Lambert Lincoln, D (to Jan. 2005)
Secy. of State: Charlie Daniels, D (to Jan. 2007)
Atty. General: Mike Beebe, D (to Jan. 2007)
Treasurer: Gus Wingfield, D
(to Jan. 2007)
Organized as territory: March 2, 1819
Entered Union (rank): June 15, 1836 (25)

Present constitution adopted: 1874
Motto: *Regnat populus* (The people rule)
State Symbols: flower, apple blossom (1901); **tree,** pine (1939); **bird,** mockingbird (1929); **insect,** honeybee (1973); **song,** "Arkansas" (1963)
Nickname: The Natural State
Origin of name: From the Quapaw Indians
10 largest cities (2003 est.): Little Rock, 184,053; Fort Smith, 81,562; Fayetteville, 62,078; North Little Rock, 59,687; Jonesboro, 57,435; Pine Bluff, 53,905; Springdale, 52,471; Conway, 47,840; Rogers, 42,795; Hot Springs, 36,770
Land area: 52,068 sq mi. (134,856 sq km)
Geographic center: In Pulaski Co., 12 mi. SW of Little Rock
Number of counties: 75
Largest county by population and area: Pulaski, 361,967 (2001); Union, 1,039 sq mi.
State parks: 50
Residents: Arkansan
2003 resident population est.: 2,725,714
2000 resident census population (rank): 2,673,400 (33). **Male:** 1,304,693 (48.8%); **Female:** 1,368,707 (51.2%). **White:** 2,138,598 (80.0%); **Black:** 418,950 (15.7%); **American Indian:** 17,808 (0.7%); **Asian:** 20,220 (0.8%); **Other race:** 40,412 (1.5%); **Two or more races:** 35,744 (1.3%); **Hispanic/Latino:** 86,866 (3.2%). **2000 percent population 18 and over:** 74.6; **65 and over:** 14.0; **median age:** 36.0.

Spaniard Hernando de Soto was among the early European explorers to visit the territory in the mid-16th century, but it was a Frenchman, Henri de Tonti, who in 1686 founded the first permanent white settlement—the Arkansas Post. In 1803 the area was acquired by the U.S. as part of the Louisiana Purchase.

Part of the Territory of Missouri from 1812, the area became a separate entity in 1819 after the first large wave of settlers arrived. The next several decades were marked by the development of the cotton industry and the spread of the Southern plantation system west into Arkansas. Arkansas joined the Confederacy in 1861, but from 1863 the northern part of the state was occupied by Union troops.

Food products are the state's largest employing sector, with lumber and wood products a close second. Arkansas is also a leader in the production of cotton, rice, and soybeans. It also has the country's only active diamond mine; located near Murfreesboro, it is operated as a tourist attraction.

Hot Springs National Park and Buffalo National River in the Ozarks are major state attractions. Blanchard Springs Caverns, the Historic Arkansas Museum at Little Rock, the William J. Clinton Birthplace in Hope, and the Arkansas Folk Center in Mountain View are also of interest.

Selected famous natives and residents: Maya Angelou, author and poet; Daisy Bates, social reformer; Dee Brown, author; Helen Gurley Brown, editor; Dale Bumpers, governor and senator; Glen Campbell, singer; Hattie Caraway, first elected woman senator; Johnny Cash, singer; Eldridge Cleaver, social activist; William Jefferson Clinton, former president; William Darby, founder of the Darby Rangers Dizzy Dean, baseball player; Orval Faubus, governor; John Gould Fletcher, poet; J. William Fulbright, former senator; John Grisham, author; Tess Harper, actress; John H. Johnson, publisher; E. Fay Jones, architect; Scott Joplin, composer; Douglas MacArthur, general; Patsy Montana, singer; Isaac C. Parker, judge; Albert Pike, pioneer teacher and lawyer; Mary Steenburgen, actress; Billy Bob Thornton, actor; Sam Walton, founder of Wal-Mart; William C. Warfield, concert singer and actor.

California

Capital: Sacramento
Governor: Arnold Schwarzenegger,[1] R (to Jan. 2007)
Lieut. Governor: Cruz M. Bustamante, D (to Jan. 2007)
Senators: Barbara Boxer, D (to Jan. 2005);
  Dianne Feinstein, D (to Jan. 2007)
Secy. of State: Kevin Shelley, D (to Jan. 2007)
Atty. General: Bill Lockyer, D (to Jan. 2007)
Treasurer: Phil Angelides, D (to Jan. 2007)
Entered Union (rank): Sept. 9, 1850 (31)
Present constitution adopted: 1879
Motto: *Eureka* (I have found it)
State Symbols: flower, golden poppy (1903); **tree,**
  California redwoods (*Sequoia sempervirens &*
  Sequoiadendron giganteum) (1937, 1953); **bird,**
  California valley quail (1931); **animal,** California grizzly
  bear (1953); **fish,** California golden trout (1947);
  colors, blue and gold (1951); **song,** "I Love You,
  California" (1951)
Nickname: Golden State
Origin of name: From a book, *Las Sergas de Espland-*
  ián, by Garcia Ordóñez de Montalvo, c. 1500
10 largest cities (2003 est.): Los Angeles, 3,819,951;
  San Diego, 1,266,753; San Jose, 898,349; San
  Francisco, 751,682; Long Beach, 475,460; Fresno,
  451,455; Sacramento, 445,335; Oakland, 398,844;
  Santa Ana, 342,510; Anaheim, 332,361
Land area: 155,959 sq mi. (403,934 sq km)
Geographic center: In Madera Co., 38 mi. E of Madera
Number of counties: 58
Largest county by population and area: Los Angeles,
  9,637,494 (2001); San Bernardino, 20,062 sq mi.
National forests: 18
State parks and beaches: 264
Residents: Californian
2003 resident population est.: 35,484,453
2000 resident census population (rank): 33,871,648
  (1). **Male:** 16,874,892 (49.8%); **Female:** 16,996,756
  (50.2%). **White:** 20,170,059 (59.5%); **Black:**
  2,263,882 (6.7%); **American Indian:** 333,346 (1.0%);
  Asian: 3,697,513 (10.9%); **Other race:** 5,682,241
  (16.8%); **Two or more races:** 1,607,646 (4.7%);
  Hispanic/Latino: 10,966,556 (32.4%). **2000 percent
  population 18 and over:** 72.7; **65 and over:** 10.6;
  median age: 33.3.

1. Gray Davis (D) was voted out of office in a recall election Oct. 7, 2003.

Although California was sighted by Spanish navigator Juan Rodríguez Cabrillo in 1542, its first Spanish mission (at San Diego) was not established until 1769. California became a U.S. territory in 1847 when Mexico surrendered it to John C. Frémont. On Jan. 24, 1848, James W. Marshall discovered gold at Sutter's Mill, starting the California Gold Rush and bringing settlers to the state in large numbers. By1964, California had surpassed New York to become the most populous state. One reason for this was that more immigrants settle in California than any other state—more than one-third of the nation's total in 1994. Asians and Pacific Islanders led the influx.

Leading industries include agriculture, manufacturing (transportation equipment, machinery, and electronic equipment), biotechnology, aerospace-defense, and tourism. Principal natural resources include timber, petroleum, cement, and natural gas.

Death Valley, in the southeast, is 282 ft below sea level, the lowest point in the nation. Mt. Whitney (14,491 ft) is the highest point in the contiguous 48 states. Lassen Peak is one of two active U.S. volca-

noes outside of Alaska and Hawaii; its last eruptions were recorded in 1917.

Other points of interest include Yosemite National Park, Disneyland, Hollywood, the Golden Gate Bridge, Sequoia National Park, San Simeon State Park, and Point Reyes National Seashore.

Selected famous natives and residents: Gertrude Atherton, author; David Belasco, playwright and producer; Shirley Temple Black, actress, ambassador; Dave Brubeck, musician; Luther Burbank, horticulturalist; Julia Child, chef; Joe DiMaggio, baseball player; James H. Doolittle, air force general; Isadora Duncan, dancer; John Frémont, explorer; Robert Frost, poet; Henry George, economist; George E. Hale, astronomer; Bret Harte, writer; William Randolph Hearst, publisher; Helen Hunt Jackson, writer; Robinson Jeffers, poet; Anthony M. Kennedy, jurist; Jack London, author; James W. Marshall, first discovered gold; Aimee Semple McPherson, evangelist; Marilyn Monroe, actress; John Muir, naturalist; Richard M. Nixon, president; Isamu Noguchi, sculptor; Kathleen Norris, novelist; George S. Patton, Jr., general; Robert Redford, actor; Sally K. Ride, astronaut; William Saroyan, author; Junípero Serra, missionary; Upton Sinclair, novelist; Leland Stanford, railroad magnate; Lincoln Steffens, journalist, author; John Steinbeck, author; Adlai Stevenson, statesman; Johann Sutter, pioneer; Michael Tilson Thomas, conductor; Earl Warren, jurist.

Colorado

Capital: Denver
Governor: Bill Owens, R (to Jan. 2007)
Lieut. Governor: Jane Norton, R (to Jan. 2007)
Senators: Wayne A. Allard, R (to Jan. 2009);
  Ben Nighthorse Campbell, R (to Jan. 2005)
Secy. of State: Donetta Davidson, R (to Jan. 2007)
Treasurer: Mike Coffman, R (to Jan. 2007)
Atty. General: Ken Salazar, D (to Jan. 2007)
Organized as territory: Feb. 28, 1861
Entered Union (rank): Aug. 1, 1876 (38)
Present constitution adopted: 1876
Motto: *Nil sine Numine* (Nothing without Providence)
State Symbols: flower, Rocky Mountain columbine
  (1899); **tree,** Colorado blue spruce (1939); **bird,** lark
  bunting (1931); **animal,** Rocky Mountain bighorn
  sheep (1961); **gemstone,** aquamarine (1971); **colors,**
  blue and white (1911); **song,** "Where the Columbines
  Grow" (1915); **fossil,** stegosaurus (1991)
Nickname: Centennial State
Origin of name: From the Spanish, "ruddy" or "red"
10 largest cities (2003 est.): Denver, 557,478; Colorado
  Springs, 370,448; Aurora, 290,418; Lakewood,
  142,474; Fort Collins, 125,740; Pueblo, 103,648;
  Westminster, 103,391; Arvada, 101,972; Centennial,
  98,586; Thornton, 96,584
Land area: 103,717 sq mi. (268,627 sq km)
Geographic center: In Park Co., 30 mi. NW of
  Pikes Peak
Number of counties: 63
Largest county by population and area: Denver,
  554,446 (2001); Las Animas, 4,773 sq mi.
State forests: 1 (71,000 ac.)
State parks: 44 (160,000 ac.)
Residents: Coloradan, Coloradoan
2003 resident population est.: 4,550,688
2000 resident census population (rank): 4,301,261
  (24). **Male:** 2,165,983 (50.4%); **Female:** 2,135,278
  (49.6%). **White:** 3,560,005 (82.8%); **Black:** 165,063
  (3.8%); **American Indian:** 44,241 (1.0%); **Asian:**
  95,213 (2.2%); **Other race:** 309,931 (7.2%); **Two or
  more races:** 122,187 (2.8%); **Hispanic/Latino:**
  735,601 (17.1%). **2000 percent population 18 and
  over:** 74.4; **65 and over:** 9.7; **median age:** 34.3.

First visited by Spanish explorers in the 1500s, the territory was claimed for Spain by Juan de

Ulibarri in 1706. The U.S. obtained eastern Colorado as part of the Louisiana Purchase in 1803, the central portion in 1845 with the admission of Texas as a state, and the western part in 1848 as a result of the Mexican War.

Colorado has the highest mean elevation of any state, with more than 1,000 Rocky Mountain peaks over 10,000 ft high and 54 towering above 14,000 ft. Pikes Peak, the most famous of these mountains, was discovered by U.S. Army lieutenant Zebulon M. Pike in 1806.

Once primarily a mining and agricultural state, Colorado's economy is now driven by the service industries, including medical providers and other business and professional services. Colorado's economy also has a strong manufacturing base. The primary manufactures are food products, printing and publishing, machinery, and electrical instruments. The state is also a communications and transportation hub for the Rocky Mountain region.

The farm industry, which is primarily concentrated in livestock, is also an important element of the state's economy. The primary crops in Colorado are corn, hay, and wheat.

Breathtaking scenery and world-class skiing make Colorado a prime tourist destination. The main tourist attractions in the state include Rocky Mountain National Park, Mesa Verde National Park, the Great Sand Dunes and Dinosaur National Monuments, Colorado National Monument, and the Black Canyon of the Gunnison National Monument.

Selected famous natives and residents: Tim Allen, actor and comedian; William Bent, fur trader and pioneer; Charles F. Brannan, lawyer and public official; M. Scott Carpenter, astronaut; Lon Chaney, actor; Mary Coyle Chase, playwright; Jack Dempsey, boxer; John Evans, physician, educator; Douglas Fairbanks, actor; Eugene Fodor, violinist; Gene Fowler, writer; Erick Hawkins, choreographer; Helen Hunt Jackson, novelist and Indian rights activist; Ted Mack, TV host; Ouray, Ute Indian chief; Anne Parrish, writer; Barbara Rush, actress; Horace A. Tabor, silver king and lieut. governor; Lowell Thomas, commentator and author; Dalton Trumbo, screenwriter, novelist; Amy Van Dyken, athlete; Byron R. White, jurist; Paul Whiteman, conductor; Don Wilson, announcer.

Connecticut

Capital: Hartford
Governor: M. Jodi Rell,[1] R (to Jan. 2007)
Lieut. Governor: Kevin Sullivan,[2] D (to Jan. 2007)
Senators: Christopher J. Dodd, D (to Jan. 2005); Joseph I. Lieberman, D (to Jan. 2007)
Secy. of the State: Susan Bysiewicz, D (to Jan. 2007)
Treasurer: Denise Nappier, D (to Jan. 2007)
Atty. General: Richard Blumenthal, D (to Jan. 2007)
Entered Union (rank): Jan. 9, 1788 (5)
Present constitution adopted: Dec. 30, 1965
Motto: *Qui transtulit sustinet* (He who transplanted still sustains)
State Symbols: flower, mountain laurel (1907); **tree,** white oak (1947); **animal,** sperm whale (1975); **bird,** American robin (1943); **hero,** Nathan Hale (1985); **heroine,** Prudence Crandall (1995); **insect,** praying mantis (1977); **mineral,** garnet (1977); **song,** "Yankee Doodle" (1978); **ship,** USS *Nautilus* (1983); **shellfish,** eastern oyster (1989); **fossil,** *Eubrontes Giganteus* (1991); **composer,** Charles Edward Ives (1991)
Nickname: Constitution State (official, 1959); Nutmeg State
Origin of name: From an Indian word (Quinnehtukqut) meaning "beside the long tidal river"
10 largest cities (2003 est.): Bridgeport, 139,664; New Haven, 124,512; Hartford, 124,387; Stamford, 120,107; Waterbury, 108,130; Norwalk, 84,170; Danbury, 77,353; New Britain, 71,572; Greenwich, 61,972; West Hartford, 61,424
Land area: 4,844 sq mi. (12,545 sq km)
Geographic center: In Hartford Co., at East Berlin
Number of counties: 8
Largest county by population and area: Fairfield, 885,368 (2001); Litchfield, 920 sq mi.
State forests: 30 (149,352 ac.)
State parks: 93 (32,960 ac.)
Residents: Connecticuter; Nutmegger
2003 resident population est.: 3,483,372
2000 resident census population (rank): 3,405,565 (29). **Male:** 1,649,319 (48.4%); **Female:** 1,756,246 (51.6%). **White:** 2,780,355 (81.6%); **Black:** 309,843 (9.1%); **American Indian:** 9,639 (0.3%); **Asian:** 82,313 (2.4%); **Other race:** 147,201 (4.3%); **Two or more races:** 74,848 (2.2%); **Hispanic/Latino:** 320,323 (9.4%). **2000 percent population 18 and over:** 75.3; **65 and over:** 13.8; **median age:** 37.4.

1. John Rowland resigned in June 2004 under the threat of an impeachment inquiry, but could still face criminal charges of corruption. Rell was the lieutenant governor. 2. Sullivan was the Connecticut Senate president.

The Dutch navigator, Adriaen Block, was the first European of record to explore the area, sailing up the Connecticut River in 1614. In 1633, Dutch colonists built a fort and trading post near present-day Hartford but soon lost control to English Puritans from the Massachusetts Bay Colony. English settlements established in the 1630s at Windsor, Wethersfield, and Hartford united in 1639 to form the Connecticut Colony under the *Fundamental Orders*, the first modern constitution.

Connecticut played a prominent role in the Revolutionary War, serving as the Continental Army's major supplier. Sometimes called the "Arsenal of the Nation," the state became one of the most industrialized in the nation.

Today, Connecticut factories produce weapons, sewing machines, jet engines, helicopters, motors, hardware and tools, cutlery, clocks, locks, silverware, and submarines. Hartford has the oldest U.S. newspaper still being published—the *Hartford Courant,* established 1764—and is the insurance capital of the nation.

Connecticut leads New England in the production of eggs, pears, peaches, and mushrooms, and its oyster crop is the nation's second largest. Poultry and dairy products also account for a large portion of farm income.

Connecticut is a popular resort area with its 250-mile Long Island Sound shoreline and many inland lakes. Among the major points of interest are Yale University's Gallery of Fine Arts and Peabody Museum. Other famous museums include the P. T. Barnum, Winchester Gun, and American Clock and Watch. The town of Mystic features a re-created 19th-century New England seaport and the Mystic Marinelife Aquarium.

Selected famous natives and residents: Dean Acheson, statesman; Ethan Allan, American Revolutionary soldier; Benedict Arnold, American Revolutionary general; P. T. Barnum, showman; John Brown, abolitionist; Prudence Crandall, educator and reformer; Charles Goodyear, inventor; Nathan Hale, American Revolutionary officer; Dorothy Hamill, ice skater; Katharine Hepburn, actress; Charles Ives, composer; John Pierpont Morgan, financier; Frederick Law Olmsted, landscape designer; Rosa Ponselle, soprano; Adam Clayton Powell, Jr., congressman; Benjamin Spock, pediatrician; Harriet Beecher Stowe, author; Noah Webster, lexicographer.

Delaware

Capital: Dover
Governor: Ruth Ann Minner, D (to Jan. 2005)
Lieut. Governor: John C. Carney, Jr., D (to Jan. 2005)
Senators: Joseph R. Biden, Jr., D (to Jan. 2009);
    Thomas R. Carper, D (to Jan. 2007)
Secy. of State: Harriet Smith Windsor, D (to Jan. 2007)
Treasurer: Jack Markell, D (to Jan. 2007)
Atty. General: M. Jane Brady, R (to Jan. 2007)
Entered Union (rank): Dec. 7, 1787 (1)
Present constitution adopted: 1897
Motto: Liberty and independence
State Symbols: colors, colonial blue and buff; **flower,**
peach blossom (1895); **tree,** American holly (1939);
bird, blue hen chicken (1939); **insect,** ladybug (1974);
butterfly, tiger swallowtail (1999); **fish,** weakfish,
cynoscion regalis (1981); **song,** "Our Delaware";
beverage, milk; **fossil,** belemnite
Nicknames: Diamond State; First State; Small Wonder
Origin of name: From Delaware River and Bay; named
in turn for Sir Thomas West, Baron De La Warr
10 largest cities (2003 est.): Wilmington, 72,051; Dover,
32,808; Newark, 29,821; Milford, 6,991; Seaford, 6,948;
Middletown, 6,496; Smyrna, 6,207; Elsmere, 5,764;
Georgetown, 4,811; New Castle, 4,787
Land area: 1,954 sq mi. (5,161 sq km)
Geographic center: In Kent Co., 11 mi. S of Dover
Number of counties: 3
Largest county by population and area: New Castle,
505,829 (2001); Sussex, 938 sq mi.
State forests: 3 (over 15,000 ac.)
State parks: 14
Residents: Delawarean
2003 resident population est.: 817,491
2000 resident census population (rank): 783,600 (45).
Male: 380,541 (48.6%); **Female:** 403,059 (51.4%).
White: 584,773 (74.6%); **Black:** 150,666 (19.2%);
American Indian: 2,731 (0.3%); **Asian:** 16,259 (2.1%);
Other race: 15,855 (2.0%); **Two or more races:**
13,033 (1.7%); **Hispanic/Latino:** 37,277 (4.8%). **2000
percent population 18 and over:** 75.2; **65 and over:**
13.0; **median age:** 36.0.

Henry Hudson, sailing under the Dutch flag, is
credited with Delaware's discovery in 1609. The
following year, Capt. Samuel Argall of Virginia
named Delaware for his colony's governor, Thomas
West, Baron De La Warr. An attempted Dutch settlement failed in 1631. Swedish colonization began at
Fort Christina (now Wilmington) in 1638, but New
Sweden fell to Dutch forces led by New Netherlands' governor Peter Stuyvesant in 1655.

England took over the area in 1664, and it was
transferred to William Penn as the lower Three
Counties in 1682. Semiautonomous after 1704,
Delaware fought as a separate state in the American
Revolution and became the first state to ratify the
Constitution in 1787.

During the Civil War, although a slave state,
Delaware did not secede from the Union.

In 1802, Éleuthère Irénée du Pont established a
gunpowder mill near Wilmington that laid the foundation for Delaware's huge chemical industry. Delaware's manufactured products now also include vulcanized fiber, textiles, paper, medical supplies, metal
products, machinery, machine tools, and automobiles.

Delaware also grows a great variety of fruits and
vegetables and is a U.S. pioneer in the food-canning
industry. Corn, soybeans, potatoes, and hay are
important crops. Delaware's broiler-chicken farms
supply the big Eastern markets, and fishing and
dairy products are other important industries.

Points of interest include the Fort Christina
Monument, Hagley Museum, Holy Trinity Church
(erected in 1698, the oldest Protestant church in the
United States still in use), and Winterthur Museum,
in and near Wilmington; central New Castle, an
almost unchanged late 18th-century capital; and the
Delaware Museum of Natural History.

Popular recreation areas include Cape Henlopen,
Delaware Seashore, Trap Pond State Park, and
Rehoboth Beach.

Selected famous natives and residents: Richard Allen,
founder of the African Methodist Episcopal Church; Henry
S. Canby, editor and author; Annie Jump Cannon,
astronomer; Elizabeth Margaret Chandler, author; Felix
Darley, artist; John Dickinson, statesman; E. I. du Pont,
industrialist; Thomas Garrett, abolitionist; Henry Heimlich,
surgeon, inventor; William Julius "Judy" Johnson, baseball
player; J. P. Marquand, novelist; Howard Pyle, artist and
author; George Read, jurist, signer of Declaration of
Independence; Caesar Rodney, patriot, signer of
Declaration of Independence; Estelle Taylor, actress;
George Alfred Townsend, journalist and author.

District of Columbia

See Washington, DC, listing in U.S. Cities.

Florida

Capital: Tallahassee
Governor: Jeb Bush, R (to Jan. 2007)
Lieut. Governor: Toni Jennings, R (to Jan. 2007)
Senators: Bob Graham, D (to Jan. 2005); Bill Nelson, D
(to Jan. 2007)
Secy. of State: Glenda Hood, R (to Jan. 2007)
Atty. General: Charlie Crist, R (to Jan. 2007)
Chief Financial Officer: Tom Gallagher, R
(to Jan. 2007)
Organized as territory: March 30, 1821
Entered Union (rank): March 3, 1845 (27)
Present constitution adopted: 1969
Motto: In God we trust (1868)
State Symbols: flower, orange blossom (1909); **bird,**
mockingbird (1927); **song,** "Suwannee River" (1935)
Nickname: Sunshine State (1970)
Origin of name: From the Spanish, meaning "feast of
flowers" (Easter)
10 largest cities (2003 est.): Jacksonville, 773,781;
Miami, 376,815; Tampa, 317,647; St. Petersburg,
247,610; Hialeah, 226,401; Orlando, 199,336; Fort
Lauderdale, 162,917; Tallahassee, 153,938; Pembroke
Pines, 148,927; Hollywood, 143,408
Land area: 53,927 sq mi. (139,671 sq km)
Geographic center: In Hernando Co., 12 mi. NNW of
Brooksville
Number of counties: 67
Largest county by population and area: Miami-Dade,
2,289,683 (2001); Palm Beach, 2,034 sq mi.
State forests: 31 (more than 890,000 ac.)
State parks: 151 (523,920 ac.)
Residents: Floridian, Floridan
2003 resident population est.: 17,019,068
2000 resident census population (rank): 15,982,378
(4). **Male:** 7,797,715 (48.8%); **Female:** 8,184,663
(51.2%). **White:** 12,465,029 (78.0%); **Black:**
2,335,505 (14.6%); **American Indian:** 53,541 (0.3%);
Asian: 266,256 (1.7%); **Other race:** 477,107 (3.0%);
Two or more races: 376,315 (2.4%); **Hispanic/
Latino:** 2,682,715 (16.8%). **2000 percent population
18 and over:** 77.2; **65 and over:** 17.6; **median age:**
38.7.

In 1513, Ponce de León, seeking the mythical
"Fountain of Youth," discovered and named Florida,
claiming it for Spain. Later, Florida would be held

at different times by Spain and England until Spain finally sold it to the United States in 1819. (Incidentally, France established a colony named Fort Caroline in 1564 in the state that was to become Florida.)

Florida's history in the early 19th century was marked by wars with the Seminole Indians, which did not end until 1842.

Florida's economy rests on a solid base of tourism, manufacturing, and agriculture. Leading the manufacturing sector are electrical equipment and electronics, printing and publishing, transportation equipment, food processing, and machinery. Oranges, grapefruit, and other citrus fruits lead Florida's agricultural products list, followed by potatoes, melons, strawberries, sugar cane, peanuts, dairy products, and cattle.

Major tourist attractions are Miami Beach, Palm Beach, St. Augustine (founded in 1565, thus the oldest permanent city in the U.S.), Daytona Beach, and Fort Lauderdale on the East Coast; Sarasota, Tampa, and St. Petersburg on the West Coast; and Key West off the southern tip of Florida. The Orlando area, where Disney World is located on a 27,000-acre site, is Florida's most popular tourist destination. Also drawing many visitors are the NASA Kennedy Space Center's Spaceport USA, Everglades National Park, and the Epcot Center.

Selected famous natives and residents: Julian "Cannonball" Adderley, jazz saxophonist; Pat Boone, singer; Fernando Bujones, ballet dancer; Steve Carlton, baseball player; Faye Dunaway, actress; Stepin Fetchit (Lincoln Theodore Perry), comedian; Lue Gim Gong, horticulturist; Dwight Gooden, baseball player; Zora Neale Hurston, writer; Daniel James, air force general; James Weldon Johnson, author and educator; Frances Langford, singer; Butterfly McQueen, actress; Jim Morrison, singer; Osceola, Seminole Indian leader; Sidney Poitier, actor; A. Philip Randolph, labor leader; Marjorie Kinnan Rawlings, author; Burt Reynolds, actor; Charles and John Ringling, circus entrepreneurs; Joseph W. Stilwell, army general; Norman E. Thargard, astronaut; Clarence Thomas, jurist; Ben Vereen, actor.

Georgia

Capital: Atlanta
Governor: Sonny Perdue, R¹(to Jan. 2007)
Lieut. Governor: Mark Taylor, D (to Jan. 2007)
Senators: Saxby Chambliss, R (to Jan. 2009); Zell Miller, D (to Jan. 2005)
Secy. of State: Cathy Cox, D (to Jan. 2007)
Atty. General: Thurbert Baker, D (to Jan. 2007)
Entered Union (rank): Jan. 2, 1788 (4)
Present constitution adopted: 1983
Motto: Wisdom, justice, and moderation
State Symbols: flower, Cherokee rose (1916); **tree,** live oak (1937); **bird,** brown thrasher (1935); **song,** "Georgia on My Mind" (1922)
Nicknames: Peach State, Empire State of the South
Origin of name: In honor of George II of England
10 largest cities (2003 est.): Atlanta, 423,019; Augusta-Richmond County,¹ 193,316; Columbus,¹ 185,702; Savannah, 127,573; Athens-Clarke County,¹ 102,498; Macon, 95,267; Roswell, 78,229; Albany, 76,202; Marietta, 61,282; Warner Robins, 54,264
Land area: 57,906 sq mi. (149,977 sq km)
Geographic center: In Twiggs Co., 18 mi. SE of Macon
Number of counties: 159
Largest county by population and area: Fulton, 816,638 (2001); Ware, 903 sq mi.
State forests: 25,258,000 ac. (67% of total state area)
State parks: 53 (42,600 ac.)
Residents: Georgian
2003 resident population est.: 8,684,715

2000 resident census population (rank): 8,186,453 (10). **Male:** 4,027,113 (49.2%); **Female:** 4,159,340 (50.8%). **White:** 5,327,281 (65.1%); **Black:** 2,349,542 (28.7%); **American Indian:** 21,737 (0.3%); **Asian:** 173,170 (2.1%); **Other race:** 196,289 (2.4%); **Two or more races:** 114,188 (1.4%); **Hispanic/Latino:** 435,227 (5.3%). **2000 percent population 18 and over:** 73.5; **65 and over:** 9.6; **median age:** 33.4.

1. The city is part of a consolidated city-county government; the city and county are coextensive.

Hernando de Soto, the Spanish explorer, first traveled parts of Georgia in 1540. British claims later conflicted with those of Spain. After obtaining a royal charter, Gen. James Oglethorpe established the first permanent settlement in Georgia in 1733 as a refuge for English debtors. In 1742, Oglethorpe defeated Spanish invaders in the Battle of Bloody Marsh.

A Confederate stronghold, Georgia was the scene of extensive military action during the Civil War. Union general William T. Sherman burned Atlanta and destroyed a 60-mile-wide path to the coast, where he captured Savannah in 1864.

The largest state east of the Mississippi, Georgia is typical of the changing South with an ever-increasing industrial development. Atlanta, largest city in the state, is the communications and transportation center for the Southeast and the area's chief distributor of goods.

Georgia leads the nation in the production of paper and board, tufted textile products, and processed chicken. Other major manufactured products are transportation equipment, food products, apparel, and chemicals.

Important agricultural products are corn, cotton, tobacco, soybeans, eggs, and peaches. Georgia produces twice as many peanuts as the next leading state. From its vast stands of pine come more than half of the world's resins and turpentine and 74.4 percent of the U.S. supply. Georgia is a leader in the production of marble, kaolin, barite, and bauxite.

Principal tourist attractions in Georgia include the Okefenokee National Wildlife Refuge, Andersonville Prison Park and National Cemetery, Chickamauga and Chattanooga National Military Park, the Little White House at Warm Springs where Pres. Franklin D. Roosevelt died in 1945, Sea Island, the enormous Confederate Memorial at Stone Mountain, Kennesaw Mountain National Battlefield Park, and Cumberland Island National Seashore.

Selected famous natives and residents: Conrad Aiken, poet; James Bowie, soldier; James Brown, singer; Jim Brown, actor and athlete; Erskine Caldwell, writer; James E. Carter, former president; Ray Charles, singer; Lucius D. Clay, banker and general; Ty Cobb, baseball player; Ossie Davis, actor and writer; James Dickey, poet; Melvyn Douglas, actor; Rebecca Latimer Felton, first appointed woman U.S. senator; Roosevelt Grier, entertainer and former athlete; Oliver Hardy, comedian; Joel Chandler Harris, journalist and author; Larry Holmes, boxer; Miriam Hopkins, actress; Alan Jackson, singer; Harry James, trumpeter; Jasper Johns, painter and sculptor; Bobby Jones, golfer; Stacy Keach, actor; DeForest Kelley, actor; Martin Luther King, Jr., civil rights leader; Gladys Knight, singer; Joseph R. Lamar, jurist; Little Richard, singer; Juliette Gordon Low, U.S. Girl Scouts founder; Carson McCullers, novelist; Johnny Mercer, songwriter; Margaret Mitchell, novelist; Elijah Muhammad, religious leader; Jessye Norman, soprano; Otis Redding, singer; Burt Reynolds, actor; Jackie Robinson, baseball player; Dean Rusk, former secretary of state; Nipsey Russell, comedian; Travis Tritt, singer; Alice Walker, author; Joanne Woodward, actress. Trisha Yearwood, singer;

Hawaii

Capital: Honolulu (on Oahu)
Governor: Linda Lingle, R (to Dec. 2006)
Lieut. Governor: James "Duke" Aiona, R (to Dec. 2006)
Senators: Daniel K. Akaka, D (to Jan. 2007); Daniel K. Inouye, D (to Jan. 2005)
Atty. General: Mark J. Bennett, R (to Dec. 2006)
Organized as territory: 1900
Entered Union (rank): Aug. 21, 1959 (50)
Motto: *Ua Mau Ke Ea O Ka Aina I Ka Pono* (The life of the land is perpetuated in righteousness)
State Symbols: flower, hibiscus (yellow) (1988); **song,** "Hawaii Ponoi" (1967); **bird,** nene (Hawaiian goose) (1957); **tree,** kukui (candlenut) (1959)
Nickname: Aloha State (1959)
Origin of name: Uncertain. The islands may have been named by Hawaii Loa, their traditional discoverer. Or they may have been named after Hawaii or Hawaiki, the traditional home of the Polynesians.
10 largest cities[1] (2000): Honolulu, 371,657; Hilo, 40,759; Kailua, 36,513; Kaneohe, 34,970; Waipahu, 33,108; Pearl City, 30,976; Waimalu, 29,371; Mililani Town, 28,608; Kahului, 20,146; Kihei, 16,749
Land area: 6,423 sq mi. (16,637 sq km)
Geographic center: Between islands of Hawaii and Maui
Number of counties: 5 (Kalawao non-functioning)
Largest county by population and area: Honolulu, 881,295 (2001); Hawaii, 4,028 sq mi.
State parks and historic sites: 69
Residents: Hawaiian, also kamaaina (native-born nonethnic Hawaiian), malihini (newcomer)
2003 resident population est.: 1,257,608
2000 resident census population (rank): 1,211,537 (42). **Male:** 608,671 (50.2%); **Female:** 602,866 (49.8%). **White:** 294,102 (24.3%); **Black:** 22,003 (1.8%); **American Indian:** 3,535 (0.3%); **Asian:** 503,868 (41.6%); **Native Hawaiian and Other Pacific Islander:** 113,539 (9.4%); **Other race:** 15,147 (1.3%); **Two or more races:** 259,343 (21.4%); **Hispanic/Latino:** 87,699 (7.2%). **2000 percent population 18 and over:** 75.6; **65 and over:** 13.3; **median age:** 36.2.

1. Census Designated Places.

First settled by Polynesians sailing from other Pacific islands between A.D. 300 and 600, Hawaii was visited in 1778 by British captain James Cook, who called the group the Sandwich Islands.

Hawaii was a native kingdom throughout most of the 19th century, when the expansion of the sugar industry (pineapple came after 1898) meant increasing U.S. business and political involvement. In 1893, Queen Liliuokalani was deposed, and a year later the Republic of Hawaii was established with Sanford B. Dole as president. Following annexation (1898), Hawaii became a U.S. territory in 1900.

The Japanese attack on the naval base at Pearl Harbor on Dec. 7, 1941, was directly responsible for U.S. entry into World War II.

Hawaii, 2,397 mi west-southwest of San Francisco, is a 1,523-mile chain of islets and eight main islands—Hawaii, Kahoolawe, Maui, Lanai, Molokai, Oahu, Kauai, and Niihau. The Northwestern Hawaiian Islands, other than Midway, are administratively part of Hawaii.

The temperature is mild, and cane sugar, pineapple, and flowers and nursery products are the chief products. Hawaii also grows coffee beans, bananas, and macadamia nuts. The tourist business is Hawaii's largest source of outside income.

Hawaii's highest peak is Mauna Kea (13,796 ft). Mauna Loa (13,679 ft) is the largest volcanic mountain in the world by volume.

Among the major points of interest are Hawaii Volcanoes National Park (Hawaii), Haleakala National Park (Maui), Puuhonua o Honaunau National Historical Park (Hawaii), Polynesian Cultural Center (Oahu), the USS *Arizona* and USS *Missouri* Memorial at Pearl Harbor, The National Memorial Cemetery of the Pacific (Oahu), and Iolani Palace (the only royal palace in the U.S.), Bishop Museum, and Waikiki Beach (all in Honolulu).

Selected famous natives and residents: Salevaa Atisanoe (Konishiki), sumo wrestler; George Ariyoshi, first Japanese-American elected governor; Angela Perez Baraquio, Miss America (2001); Tia Carrere, singer, actress; Steve Case, business executive; Father Damien, priest; Hiram L. Fong, first Chinese-American senator; Don Ho, entertainer; Kaahumanu, Hawaiian queen; Duke Paoa Kahanamoku, Olympic swimming champion; Kamehameha I, first Hawaiian king; Kamehameha V, last of the dynasty; Liliuokalani, queen, last Hawaiian monarch; Bette Midler, singer; Ellison Onizuka, astronaut; Chad Rowan (Akebono), sumo wrestler; Carolyn Suzanne Sapp, Miss America (1991); John Waihee, first Hawaiian elected governor.

Idaho

Capital: Boise
Governor: Dirk Kempthorne, R (to Jan. 2007)
Lieut. Governor: Jim Risch, R (to Jan. 2007)
Senators: Larry E. Craig, R (to Jan. 2009); Mike Crapo, R (to Jan. 2005)
Secy. of State: Ben Ysursa, R (to Jan. 2007)
Atty. General: Lawrence Wasden, R (to Jan. 2007)
Treasurer: Ron G. Crane, R (to Jan. 2007)
Organized as territory: March 3, 1863
Entered Union (rank): July 3, 1890 (43)
Present constitution adopted: 1890
Motto: *Esto perpetua* (It is forever)
State Symbols: flower, syringa (1931); **tree,** white pine (1935); **bird,** mountain bluebird (1931); **horse,** Appaloosa (1975); **gem,** star garnet (1967); **song,** "Here We Have Idaho"; **folk dance,** square dance; **fish,** cutthroat trout (1990); **fossil,** Hagerman horse fossil (1988)
Nickname: Gem State
Origin of name: Though popularly believed to be an Indian word, it is an invented name whose meaning is unknown.
10 largest cities (2003 est.): Boise, 190,117; Nampa, 64,269; Idaho Falls, 51,507; Pocatello, 51,009; Meridian, 41,127; Coeur d'Alene, 37,262; Twin Falls, 36,742; Caldwell, 31,041; Lewiston, 30,937; Rexburg, 21,862
Land area: 82,747 sq mi. (214,315 sq km)
Geographic center: In Custer Co., at Custer, SW of Challis
Number of counties: 44, plus small part of Yellowstone National Park
Largest county by population and area: Ada, 312,337 (2001); Idaho, 8,485 sq mi.
State forests: 881,000 ac.
State parks: 27 (43,000+ ac.)
Residents: Idahoan
2003 resident population est.: 1,366,332
2000 resident census population (rank): 1,293,953 (39). **Male:** 648,660 (50.1%); **Female:** 645,293 (49.9%). **White:** 1,177,304 (91.0%); **Black:** 5,456 (0.4%); **American Indian:** 17,645 (1.4%); **Asian:** 11,889 (0.9%); **Other race:** 54,742 (4.2%); **Two or more races:** 25,609 (2.0%); **Hispanic/Latino:** 101,690 (7.9%). **2000 percent population 18 and over:** 71.5; **65 and over:** 11.3; **median age:** 33.2.

The region was explored by Meriwether Lewis and William Clark in 1805–1806. It was then a part of the Oregon country, held jointly by the United States and Great Britain. Boundary disputes with Great Britain were settled by the Oregon Treaty in 1846, and the first permanent U.S. settlement in Idaho was established by the Mormons at Franklin in 1860.

After gold was discovered at Orofino Creek in 1860, prospectors swarmed into the territory, but they left little more than a number of ghost towns.

In the 1870s, growing white occupation of Indian lands led to a series of battles between U.S. forces and the Nez Percé, Bannock, and Sheepeater tribes.

Mining and lumbering have been important for years. Idaho ranks high among the states in silver, antimony, lead, cobalt, garnet, phosphate rock, vanadium, zinc, and mercury.

Agriculture is a major industry: The state produces about one fourth of the nation's potato crop, as well as wheat, apples, corn, barley, sugar beets, and hops.

The 1990s saw a remarkable growth in the high technology industries, concentrated in the metropolitan Boise area.

With the growth of winter sports, tourism now outranks other industries in revenue. Idaho's many streams and lakes provide fishing, camping, and boating sites. The nation's largest elk herds draw hunters from all over the world, and the famed Sun Valley resort attracts thousands of visitors to its swimming, golfing, and skiing facilities.

Points of interest are the Craters of the Moon National Monument; Nez Percé National Historic Park, which includes many sites visited by Lewis and Clark; and the State Historical Museum in Boise. Other attractions are the Snake River Birds of Prey National Conservation Area south of Boise, Hells Canyon on the Idaho-Oregon border, and the Sawtooth National Recreation Area in south-central Idaho.

Selected famous natives and residents: Joe Albertson, grocery chain founder; Cecil Andrus, governor; T. H. Bell, educator; Ezra Taft Benson, secretary of Agriculture, pres. LDS church, marketing specialist; William E. Borah, senator; Gutzon Borglum, Mt. Rushmore sculptor; Carol R. Brink, author; Frank F. Church, senator; Fred Dubois, senator; Vardis Fisher, novelist; Lawrence H. Gipson, historian; Ernest Hemingway, author; Mariel Hemingway, actress; Chief Joseph, Nez Percé chief; Harmon Killebrew, baseball player; Jerry Kramer, football player, author; Ezra Pound, poet; Sacagawea, Shoshonean guide; J. R. Simplot, industrialist; Robert E. Smylie, political leader; Henry Spalding, missionary; Frank Steunenberg, governor; Picabo Street, skier; David Tompson, founded first trading post; Lana Turner, actress.

Illinois

Capital: Springfield
Governor: Rod R. Blagojevich, D (to Jan. 2007)
Lieut. Governor: Patrick Quinn, D (to Jan. 2007)
Senators: Richard J. Durbin, D (to Jan. 2009); Peter G. Fitzgerald, R (to Jan. 2005)
Atty. General: Lisa Madigan, D (to Jan. 2007)
Secy. of State: Jesse White, D (to Jan. 2007)
Treasurer: Judith Barr Topinka, R (to Jan. 2007)
Organized as territory: Feb. 3, 1809
Entered Union (rank): Dec. 3, 1818 (21)
Present constitution adopted: 1970
Motto: State sovereignty, national union
State Symbols: flower, violet (1908); **tree,** white oak (1973); **bird,** cardinal (1929); **animal,** white-tailed deer (1982); **fish,** bluegill (1987); **insect,** monarch butterfly (1975); **song,** "Illinois" (1925); **mineral,** fluorite (1965)
Nickname: Prairie State
Origin of name: Algonquin for "tribe of superior men"
10 largest cities (2003 est.): Chicago, 2,869,121; Aurora, 162,184; Rockford, 151,725; Naperville, 137,894; Joliet, 123,570; Springfield, 113,586; Peoria, 112,907; Elgin, 97,117; Waukegan, 91,452; Cicero, 83,029
Land area: 55,584 sq mi. (143,963 sq km)
Geographic center: In Logan Co., 28 mi. NE of Springfield
Number of counties: 102
Largest county by population and area: Cook, 5,350,269 (2001); McLean, 1,184 sq mi.
Public use areas: 186 (275,000 ac.), incl. state parks, memorials, forests and conservation areas
Residents: Illinoisan
2003 resident population est.: 12,653,544
2000 resident census population (rank): 12,419,293 (5). **Male:** 6,080,336 (49.0%); **Female:** 6,338,957 (51.0%). **White:** 9,125,471 (73.5%); **Black:** 1,876,875 (15.1%); **American Indian:** 31,006 (0.2%); **Asian:** 423,603 (3.4%); **Other race:** 722,712 (5.8%); **Two or more races:** 235,016 (1.9%); **Hispanic/Latino:** 1,530,262 (12.3%). **2000 percent population 18 and over:** 73.9; **65 and over:** 12.1; **median age:** 34.7.

French explorers Jacques Marquette and Louis Joliet, in 1673, were the first Europeans of record to visit the region. In 1699 French settlers established the first permanent settlement at Cahokia, near present-day East St. Louis. Great Britain obtained the region at the end of the French and Indian Wars in 1763. The area figured prominently in frontier struggles during the Revolutionary War and in Indian wars during the early 19th century.

Significant episodes in the state's early history include the influx of settlers following the opening of the Erie Canal in 1825; the Black Hawk War, which virtually ended the Indian troubles in the area; and the rise of Abraham Lincoln from farm laborer to president.

Today, Illinois stands high in manufacturing, coal mining, agriculture, and oil production. The state's manufactures include food and agricultural products, transportation equipment, chemicals, industrial machinery, and computer equipment. The sprawling Chicago district (including a slice of Indiana) is a great iron and steel producer, meat packer, grain exchange, and railroad center. Chicago is also famous as a Great Lakes port.

Illinois is a leading producer of soybeans, corn, and hogs. Other agricultural commodities include cattle, wheat, oats, sorghum, and hay.

Central Illinois is noted for shrines and memorials associated with the life of Abraham Lincoln. In Springfield are the Lincoln Home, the Lincoln Tomb, and the restored Old State Capitol. Other points of interest are the home of Mormon leader Joseph Smith in Nauvoo and, in Chicago: the Art Institute, Field Museum, Museum of Science and Industry, Shedd Aquarium, Adler Planetarium, Merchandise Mart, and Chicago Portage National Historic Site.

Selected famous natives and residents: Franklin Pierce Adams, author; Jane Addams, social worker; Mary Astor, actress; Jack Benny, comedian; Black Hawk, Sauk Indian chief; Harry A. Blackmun, jurist; Ray Bradbury, author; William Jennings Bryan, orator and politician; Edgar Rice Burroughs, novelist; Gower Champion, choreographer; John Chancellor, TV commentator; Raymond Chandler, writer; Jimmy Connors, tennis champion; James Gould Cozzens, novelist; Richard J. Daley, mayor of Chicago; Miles Davis, musician; Peter

DeVries, novelist; Everett Dirksen, senator; Walt Disney, film animator and producer; John Dos Passos, author; James T. Farrell, novelist; Dan Fogelberg, singer and songwriter; Betty Friedan, feminist; Benny Goodman, musician; John Gunther, author; Ernest Hemingway, author; Charlton Heston, actor; Wild Bill Hickok, scout; William Holden, actor; Rock Hudson, actor; Burl Ives, singer; James Jones, novelist; John Jones, civil rights leader; Quincy Jones, composer; Keokuk (Watchful Fox), chief of the Sac and Fox Indians; Walter Kerr, drama critic; Archibald MacLeish, poet; David Mamet, playwright; Robert A. Millikan, physicist; Sherrill Milnes, baritone; Bill Murray, actor; Bob Newhart, actor and comedian; William S. Paley, broadcasting executive; Drew Pearson, columnist; Richard Pryor, comedian and actor; Ronald Reagan, former president and actor; Carl Sandburg, poet; Sam Shepard, playwright; William L. Shirer, author and historian; John Paul Stevens, jurist; McLean Stevenson, actor; Preston Sturges, director; Gloria Swanson, actress; Carl Van Doren, writer and educator; Melvin Van Peebles, playwright; Irving Wallace, novelist; Alfred Wallenstein, conductor; Raquel Welch, actress; Oprah Winfrey, television talk show host and actress; Florenz Ziegfield, theatrical producer.

Indiana

Capital: Indianapolis
Governor: Joseph E. Kernan,[1] D (to Jan. 2005)
Lieut. Governor: Katherine Davis, D (to Jan. 2005)
Senators: Evan Bayh, D (to Jan. 2005); Richard
  G. Lugar, R (to Jan. 2007)
Secy. of State: Todd Rokita, R (to Dec. 2004)
Treasurer: Tim Berry, R (to Feb. 2007)
Atty. General: Stephen Carter, R (to Jan. 2005)
Organized as territory: May 7, 1800
Entered Union (rank): Dec. 11, 1816 (19)
Present constitution adopted: 1851
Motto: The Crossroads of America
State Symbols: flower, peony (1957); **tree,** tulip tree
  (1931); **bird,** cardinal (1933); **song,** "On the Banks of
  the Wabash, Far Away" (1913); **river,** Wabash; **stone,**
  limestone
Nickname: Hoosier State
Origin of name: Meaning "land of Indians"
Official language: English
10 largest cities (2003 est.): Indianapolis, 783,438; Fort
  Wayne, 219,495; Evansville, 117,881; South Bend,
  105,540; Gary, 99,961; Hammond, 80,547;
  Bloomington, 70,642; Muncie, 66,521; Lafayette,
  61,229; Anderson, 58,394
Land area: 35,867 sq mi. (92,896 sq km)
Geographic center: In Boone Co., 14 mi. NNW of India-
  napolis
Number of counties: 92
Largest county by population and area: Marion,
  856,938 (2001); Allen, 657 sq mi.
State parks: 23 (56,409 ac.)
State historic sites: 17 (2,007 ac.)
Residents: Indianan, Indianian, Hoosier
2003 resident population est.: 6,195,643
2000 resident census population (rank): 6,080,485
  (14). **Male:** 2,982,474 (49.0%); **Female:** 3,098,011
  (51.0%); **White:** 5,320,022 (87.5%); **Black:** 510,034
  (8.4%); **American Indian:** 15,815 (0.3%); **Asian:**
  59,126 (1.0%); **Other race:** 97,811 (1.6%); **Two or
  more races:** 75,672 (1.2%); **Hispanic/Latino:**
  214,536 (3.5%). **2000 percent population 18 and
  over:** 74.1; **65 and over:** 12.4; **median age:** 35.2.

1. Lt. Gov. Kernan was sworn in as governor in Sept. 2003, after Frank O'Bannon's death.

First explored for France by Robert Cavelier, Sieur de la Salle, in 1679–1680, the region figured importantly in the Franco-British struggle for North America that culminated with British victory in 1763. George Rogers Clark led American forces against the British in the area during the Revolutionary War and, prior to becoming a state, Indiana was the scene of frequent Indian uprisings until the victories of Gen. Anthony Wayne at Fallen Timbers in 1794 and Gen. William Henry Harrison at Tippecanoe in 1811.

During the 19th century, Indiana was the site of several experimental communities, including those established by George Rapp and Robert Owen at New Harmony.

Indiana's 41-mile Lake Michigan waterfront—one of the world's great industrial centers—turns out iron, steel, and oil products. Products include automobile parts and accessories, mobile homes and recreational vehicles, truck and bus bodies, aircraft engines, farm machinery, and fabricated structural steel. Wood office furniture and pharmaceuticals are also manufactured.

The state is a leader in agriculture with corn the principal crop. Hogs, soybeans, wheat, oats, rye, tomatoes, onions, and poultry also contribute heavily to Indiana's agricultural output.

Much of the building limestone used in the U.S. is quarried in Indiana, which is also a large producer of coal. Other mineral commodities include crushed stone, cement, and sand and gravel.

Wyandotte Cave, one of the largest in the U.S., is located in Crawford County in southern Indiana, and West Baden and French Lick are well known for their mineral springs. Other attractions include Indiana Dunes National Lakeshore, Indianapolis Motor Speedway, Lincoln Boyhood National Memorial, and the George Rogers Clark National Historical Park.

Selected famous natives and residents: George Ade, humorist; Leon Ames, actor; Anne Baxter, actress; Albert J. Beveridge, political leader; Larry Bird, basketball player; Bill Blass, fashion designer; Frank Borman, astronaut; Hoagy Carmichael, songwriter; James Dean, actor; Eugene V. Debs, Socialist leader; Theodore Dreiser, writer; Bernard F. Gimbel, merchant; Virgil Grissom, astronaut; Phil Harris, actor and band leader; John Milton Hay, statesman; James R. Hoffa, labor leader; Michael Jackson, singer; Buck Jones, actor; Alfred C. Kinsey, zoologist; David Letterman, TV host and comedian; Carole Lombard, actress; Shelley Long, actress; Marjorie Main, actress; James McCracken, tenor; Joaquin Miller, poet; Paul Osborn, playwright; Cole Porter, songwriter; Gene Stratton Porter, naturalist and author; Ernest Taylor Pyle, journalist; J. Danforth Quayle, former vice president; James Whitcomb Riley, poet; Knute Rockne, football coach; Ned Rorem, composer; Red Skelton, comedian; Rex Stout, mystery writer; Booth Tarkington, author; Twyla Tharp, dancer and choreographer; Forrest Tucker, actor; Harold C. Urey, physicist; Kurt Vonnegut, Jr., author; Robert Wise, director; Jessamyn West, novelist; Wendell Willkie, lawyer; Wilbur Wright, inventor.

Iowa

Capital: Des Moines
Governor: Tom Vilsack, D (to Jan. 2007)
Lieut. Governor: Sally Pederson, D (to Jan. 2007)
Senators: Chuck Grassley, R (to Jan. 2005);
  Tom Harkin, D (to Jan. 2009)
Secy. of State: Chet Culver, D (to Jan. 2007)
Treasurer: Michael L. Fitzgerald, D (to Jan. 2007)
Atty. General: Tom Miller, D (to Jan. 2007)
Organized as territory: June 12, 1838
Entered Union (rank): Dec. 28, 1846 (29)
Present constitution adopted: 1857
Motto: Our liberties we prize and our rights we
  will maintain
State Symbols: flower, wild rose (1897); **bird,** eastern
  goldfinch (1933); **colors,** red, white, and blue (in state
  flag); **song,** "Song of Iowa"
Nickname: Hawkeye State
Origin of name: Probably from an Indian word meaning
  "this is the place" or "the Beautiful Land"

10 largest cities (2003 est.): Des Moines, 196,093; Cedar Rapids, 122,542; Davenport, 97,512; Sioux City, 83,876; Waterloo, 67,054; Iowa City, 63,807; Council Bluffs, 58,656; Dubuque, 57,204; Ames, 53,284; West Des Moines, 51,699
Land area: 55,869 sq mi. (144,701 sq km)
Geographic center: In Story Co., 5 mi. NE of Ames
Number of counties: 99
Largest county by population and area: Polk, 379,029 (2001); Kossuth, 973 sq mi.
State forests: 8 (40,706 ac.)
State parks: 83 (53,000 ac.)
Residents: Iowan
2003 resident population est.: 2,944,062
2000 resident census population (rank): 2,926,324 (30). **Male:** 1,435,515 (49.1%); **Female:** 1,490,809 (50.9%). **White:** 2,748,640 (93.9%); **Black:** 61,853 (2.1%); **American Indian:** 8,989 (0.3%); **Asian:** 36,635 (1.3%); **Other race:** 37,420 (1.3%); **Two or more races:** 31,778 (1.1%); **Hispanic/Latino:** 82,473 (2.8%). **2000 population 18 and over:** 74.9; **65 and over:** 14.9; **median age:** 36.6.

The first Europeans to visit the area were the French explorers Jacques Marquette and Louis Joliet in 1673. The U.S. obtained control of the area in 1803 as part of the Louisiana Purchase, and during the first half of the 19th century, there was heavy fighting between white settlers and Indians. Lands were taken from the Indians after the Black Hawk War in 1832 and again in 1836 and 1837.

When Iowa became a state in 1846, its capital was Iowa City; the more centrally located Des Moines became the new capital in 1857. At that time, the state's present boundaries were also drawn.

Although Iowa produces a tenth of the nation's food supply, the value of Iowa's manufactured products is twice that of its agriculture. Major industries are food and associated products, non-electrical machinery, electrical equipment, printing and publishing, and fabricated products.

Iowa stands in a class by itself as an agricultural state. Its farms sell over $10 billion worth of crops and livestock annually. Iowa leads the nation in all corn, soybean, and hog marketings, and comes in third in total livestock sales. Iowa's forests produce hardwood lumber, particularly walnut, and its mineral products include cement, limestone, sand, gravel, gypsum, and coal.

Tourist attractions include the Herbert Hoover birthplace and library near West Branch; the Amana Colonies; Fort Dodge Historical Museum, Fort, and Stockade; the Iowa State Fair at Des Moines in August; and the Effigy Mounds National Monument, a prehistoric Indian burial site at Marquette.

Selected famous natives and residents: Bix Beiderbecke, jazz musician; Norman Borlaug, plant pathologist, geneticist, and Nobel Peace Prize winner; William "Buffalo Bill" F. Cody, scout; Johnny Carson, TV entertainer; Gardner Cowles, Jr., publisher; Simon Estes, bass-baritone; William Frawley, actor; George H. Gallup, poll taker; Susan Glaspell, writer; Herbert Hoover, president; MacKinlay Kantor, novelist; Charles A. Kettering, inventor; Ann Landers, columnist; Cloris Leachman, actress; John L. Lewis, labor leader; Glenn L. Martin, aviator and manufacturer; Elsa Maxwell, writer; Frederick L. Maytag, inventor and manufacturer; Glenn Miller, bandleader; Kate Mulgrew, actress; Harriet Nelson, actress; Nathan M. Pusey, educator; David Rabe, playwright; Harry Reasoner, TV commentator; Donna Reed, actress; Lillian Russell, soprano; Robert Schuller, evangelist; Wallace Stegner, novelist and critic; Billy Sunday, evangelist; James A. Van Allen, space physicist; Abigail Van Buren, columnist; Henry A. Wallace, statesman and vice president; John Wayne, actor; Andy Williams, singer; Meredith Willson, composer; Grant Wood, painter.

Kansas

Capital: Topeka
Governor: Kathleen Sebelius, D (to Jan. 2007)
Lieut. Governor: John E. Moore, D (to Jan. 2007)
Senators: Sam Brownback, R (to Jan. 2005); Pat Roberts, R (to Jan. 2009)
Secy. of State: Ron Thornburgh, R (to Jan. 2007)
Treasurer: Lynn Jenkins, R (to Jan. 2007)
Atty. General: Phill Kline, R (to Jan. 2007)
Organized as territory: May 30, 1854
Entered Union (rank): Jan. 29, 1861 (34)
Present constitution adopted: 1859
Motto: *Ad astra per aspera* (To the stars through difficulties)
State Symbols: flower, sunflower (1903); **tree,** cottonwood (1937); **bird,** western meadowlark (1937); **animal,** buffalo (1955); **song,** "Home on the Range" (1947)
Nicknames: Sunflower State; Jayhawk State
Origin of name: From a Sioux word meaning "people of the south wind"
10 largest cities (2003 est.): Wichita, 354,617; Overland Park, 160,368; Kansas City, 145,757; Topeka, 122,008; Olathe, 105,274; Lawrence, 82,120; Shawnee, 54,093; Salina, 45,833; Manhattan, 44,733; Lenexa, 41,995
Land area: 81,815 sq mi. (211,901 sq km)
Geographic center: In Barton Co., 15 mi. NE of Great Bend
Number of counties: 105
Largest county by population and area: Johnson, 465,058 (2001); Butler, 1,428 sq mi.
State parks: 22 (14,394 ac.)
Residents: Kansan
2003 resident population est.: 2,723,507
2000 resident census population (rank): 2,688,418 (32). **Male:** 1,328,474 (49.4%); **Female:** 1,359,944 (50.6%). **White:** 2,313,944 (86.1%); **Black:** 154,198 (5.7%); **American Indian:** 24,936 (0.9%); **Asian:** 46,806 (1.7%); **Other race:** 90,725 (3.4%); **Two or more races:** 56,496 (2.1%); **Hispanic/Latino:** 188,252 (7.0%). **2000 percent population 18 and over:** 73.5; **65 and over:** 13.3; **median age:** 35.2.

Spanish explorer Francisco de Coronado, in 1541, is considered the first European to have traveled this region. Sieur de la Salle's extensive land claims for France (1682) included present-day Kansas. Ceded to Spain by France in 1763, the territory reverted to France in 1800 and was sold to the U.S. as part of the Louisiana Purchase in 1803.

Lewis and Clark, Zebulon Pike, and Stephen H. Long explored the region between 1803 and 1819. The first permanent white settlements in Kansas were outposts—Fort Leavenworth (1827), Fort Scott (1842), and Fort Riley (1853)—established to protect travelers along the Santa Fe and Oregon Trails.

Just before the Civil War, the conflict between the pro- and anti-slavery forces earned the region the grim title of Bleeding Kansas.

Today, wheat fields, oil-well derricks, herds of cattle, and grain-storage elevators are chief features of the Kansas landscape. A leading wheat-growing state, Kansas also raises corn, sorghum, oats, barley, soybeans, and potatoes. Kansas stands high in petroleum production and mines zinc, coal, salt, and lead. It is also the nation's leading producer of helium.

Wichita is one of the nation's leading aircraft-manufacturing centers, ranking first in production of private aircraft. Kansas City is an important transportation, milling, and meat-packing center.

Points of interest include the Kansas History Center at Topeka, the Eisenhower boyhood home and the Eisenhower Memorial Museum and Presidential Library at Abilene, John Brown's cabin at Osawatomie, re-created Front Street in Dodge City, Fort Larned (an important military post on the Santa Fe Trail), Fort Leavenworth, and Fort Riley.

Selected famous natives and residents: Roscoe "Fatty" Arbuckle, actor; Clarence D. Batchelor, political cartoonist; Gwendolyn Brooks, poet; Walter P. Chrysler, auto manufacturer; Clark M. Clifford, secretary of defense; John Steuart Curry, painter; Charles Curtis, vice president; Robert Dole, senator; Amelia Earhart, aviator; Dwight D. Eisenhower, general and president; Milton S. Eisenhower, educator; Gary Hart, politician; William Inge, playwright; Walter Johnson, baseball pitcher; Osa L. Johnson, documentary film producer; Buster Keaton, comedian; Emmett Kelly, clown; Stan Kenton, jazz musician; James Lehrer, broadcast journalist; Edgar Lee Masters, poet; Hattie McDaniel, actress; Karl Menninger, psychiatrist; Carry A. Nation, temperance leader; Gordon Parks, film director; ZaSu Pitts, actress; Samuel Ramey, opera singer; Charles Robinson, statesman and first governor; Charles (Buddy) Rogers, actor; Damon Runyon, journalist; Gale Sayers, football player; Eugene W. Smith, photojournalist; Milburn Stone, actor; John Cameron Swayze, news commentator; William Allen White, journalist; Charles E. Whittaker, jurist; Jess Willard, boxer.

Kentucky

Capital: Frankfort
Governor: Ernie Fletcher, R (to Dec. 2007)
Lieut. Governor: Stephen B. Pence, R (to Dec. 2007)
Senators: Jim Bunning, R (to Jan. 2005);
  Mitch McConnell, R (to Jan. 2009)
Secy. of State: C.M. "Trey" Grayson, R (to Dec. 2007)
Treasurer: Jonathan Miller, D (to Dec. 2007)
Atty. General: Gregory D. Stumbo, D (to Dec. 2007)
Entered Union (rank): June 1, 1792 (15)
Present constitution adopted: 1891
Motto: United we stand, divided we fall
State Symbols: tree, tulip poplar (1994); **flower,** goldenrod; **bird,** Kentucky cardinal; **song,** "My Old Kentucky Home"
Nickname: Bluegrass State
Origin of name: From an Iroquoian word "Ken-tah-ten" meaning "land of tomorrow"
10 largest cities (2003 est.): Lexington-Fayette,[1] 266,798; Louisville, 248,762; Owensboro, 54,312; Bowling Green, 50,663; Covington, 42,687; Richmond, 29,080; Hopkinsville, 28,678; Henderson, 27,468; Frankfort, 27,408; Jeffersontown, 26,331
Land area: 39,728 sq mi. (102,896 sq km)
Geographic center: In Marion Co., 3 mi. NNW of Lebanon
Number of counties: 120
Largest county by population and area: Jefferson, 692,910 (2001); Pike, 787 sq mi.
State forests: 4 (30,200 ac.)
State parks: 59
Residents: Kentuckian
2003 resident population est.: 4,117,827
2000 resident census population (rank): 4,041,769 (25). **Male:** 1,975,368 (48.9%); **Female:** 2,066,401 (51.1%). **White:** 3,640,889 (90.1%); **Black:** 295,994 (7.3%); **American Indian:** 8,616 (0.2%); **Asian:** 29,744 (0.7%); **Other race:** 22,623 (0.6%); **Two or more races:** 42,443 (1.1%); **Hispanic/Latino:** 59,939 (1.5%). **2000 percent population 18 and over:** 75.4; **65 and over:** 12.5; **median age:** 35.9.

1. Coextensive with Fayette County.

Kentucky was the first region west of the Allegheny Mountains to be settled by American pioneers. James Harrod established the first permanent settlement at Harrodsburg in 1774; the following year Daniel Boone, who had explored the area in 1767, blazed the Wilderness Trail through the Cumberland Gap and founded Boonesboro.

Politically, the Kentucky region was originally part of Virginia, but statehood was gained in 1792. Gen. Anthony Wayne's victory in 1794 at Fallen Timbers in Ohio marked the end of Native American resistance in the area and secured the Kentucky frontier.

As a slaveholding state with a considerable abolitionist population, Kentucky was caught in the middle during the Civil War, supplying both Union and Confederate forces with thousands of troops.

Kentucky prides itself on producing some of the nation's best tobacco, horses, and whiskey. Corn, soybeans, wheat, fruit, hogs, cattle, and dairy products are among the agricultural items produced.

Among the manufactured items produced in the state are motor vehicles, furniture, aluminum ware, brooms, apparel, lumber products, machinery, textiles, and iron and steel products. Kentucky also produces significant amounts of petroleum, natural gas, fluorspar, clay, and stone. However, coal accounts for 85% of the total mineral income.

Louisville is famous for the Kentucky Derby at Churchill Downs, and the Bluegrass country around Lexington is the home of some of the world's finest race horses. Other attractions are Mammoth Cave, the George S. Patton, Jr., Military Museum at Fort Knox, and Old Fort Harrod State Park.

Selected famous natives and residents: John Adair, pioneer and political leader; Muhammad Ali, boxer; Alben W. Barkley, vice president; Louis D. Brandeis, jurist; John Mason Brown, critic; Kit Carson, scout; Champ Clark, politician; George Clooney, actor; Rosemary Clooney, singer; Irvin S. Cobb, humorist; Jefferson Davis, president of the Confederacy; Johnny Depp, actor; Irene Dunne, actress; Crystal Gayle, singer; David W. Griffith, film producer; John M. Harlan, jurist; Elizabeth Hardwick, writer; Casey Jones, locomotive engineer; Ashley Judd, actress; Naomi Judd, singer; Wynona Judd, singer; Barbara Kingsolver, writer; Abraham Lincoln, president; Loretta Lynn, singer; Bill Monroe, bluegrass musician; Carry A. Nation, temperance leader; Patricia Neal, actress; George Reeves, actor; Wiley B. Rutledge, jurist; Diane Sawyer, broadcast journalist; Phil Simms, football player; Adlai Stevenson, vice president; Allen Tate, poet and critic; Hunter Thompson, writer; Frederick M. Vinson, jurist; Robert Penn Warren, novelist.

Louisiana

Capital: Baton Rouge
Governor: Kathleen Blanco, D (to Jan. 2008)
Lieut. Governor: Mitch Landrieu, D (to Jan. 2008)
Senators: John B. Breaux, D (to Jan. 2005);
  Mary Landrieu, D (to Jan. 2009)
Secy. of State: W. Fox McKeithen, R (to Jan. 2008)
Treasurer: John Neely Kennedy, D (to Jan. 2008)
Atty. General: Charles C. Foti, Jr., D (to Jan. 2008)
Organized as territory: March 26, 1804
Entered Union (rank): April 30, 1812 (18)
Present constitution adopted: 1974
Motto: Union, justice, and confidence
State Symbols: flower, magnolia (1900); **tree,** bald cypress (1963); **bird,** eastern brown pelican (1958); **songs,** "Give Me Louisiana" and "You Are My Sunshine"
Nickname: Pelican State
Origin of name: In honor of Louis XIV of France
10 largest cities (2003 est.): New Orleans, 469,032; Baton Rouge, 225,090; Shreveport, 198,364; Lafayette, 111,667; Lake Charles, 70,735; Kenner, 70,202; Bossier City, 58,111; Monroe, 52,163; Alexandria, 45,649; New Iberia, 32,502

Land area: 43,562 sq mi. (112,826 sq km)
Geographic center: In Avoyelles Parish, 3 mi. SE of Marksville
Number of parishes (counties): 64
Largest parish by population and area: Orleans, 476,492 (2001); Vernon, 1,328 sq mi.
State forests: 1 (8,000 ac.)
State parks: 30 (13,932 ac.)
Residents: Louisianan, Louisianian
2003 resident population est.: 4,496,334
2000 resident census population (rank): 4,468,976 (22). **Male:** 2,162,903 (48.4%); **Female:** 2,306,073 (51.6%). **White:** 2,856,161 (63.9%); **Black:** 1,451,944 (32.5%); **American Indian:** 25,477 (0.6%); **Asian:** 54,758 (1.2%); **Other race:** 31,131 (0.7%); **Two or more races:** 48,265 (1.1%); **Hispanic/Latino:** 107,738 (2.4%). **2000 percent population 18 and over:** 72.7; **65 and over:** 11.6; **median age:** 34.0.

Louisiana has a rich, colorful historical background. Early Spanish explorers were Alvárez Piñeda, 1519; Álvar Núñez Cabeza de Vaca, 1528; and Hernando De Soto in 1541. Sieur de la Salle reached the mouth of the Mississippi and claimed all the land drained by it and its tributaries for Louis XIV of France in 1682.

Louisiana became a French crown colony in 1731 but was ceded to Spain in 1763 after the French and Indian Wars. (The portion east of the Mississippi came under British control in 1764.) Louisiana reverted to France in 1800 and was sold by Napoleon to the U.S. in 1803. The southern part, known as the territory of Orleans, became the state of Louisiana in 1812.

During the Civil War, Louisiana joined the Confederacy, but New Orleans was captured by Union Adm. David Farragut in April 1862. The state's economy suffered during Reconstruction; however, the situation improved at the turn of the 20th century, with the discovery of oil and natural gas and the growth of industry.

Louisiana is a leader in natural gas, salt, petroleum, and sulfur production. Much of the oil and sulfur comes from offshore deposits. The state also produces large crops of sweet potatoes, rice, sugar cane, pecans, soybeans, corn, and cotton. Leading manufactured items include chemicals, processed food, petroleum and coal products, paper, lumber and wood products, transportation equipment, and apparel.

The state has become a popular tourist destination. New Orleans is the major draw, known particularly for its picturesque French Quarter and the annual Mardi Gras celebration, held since 1838.

Other major points of interest include the Superdome in New Orleans, historic plantation homes near Natchitoches and New Iberia, Cajun country in the Mississippi Delta Region, Chalmette National Historic Park, and the state capital at Baton Rouge.

Selected famous natives and residents: Louis Armstrong, musician; Geoffrey Beene, fashion designer; Truman Capote, writer; Kitty Carlisle, singer and actress; Van Cliburn, concert pianist; Michael De Bakey, heart surgeon; Fats Domino, musician; Louis Moreau Gottschalk, pianist and composer; Bryant Gumbel, TV newscaster; Lillian Hellman, playwright; Al Hirt, trumpeter; Mahalia Jackson, gospel singer; Jean Laffite, privateer; Dorothy Lamour, actress; John A. Lejeune, Marine Corps general; Elmore Leonard, author; Jerry Lee Lewis, singer; Huey P. Long, politician; Wynton Marsalis, musician; Jelly Roll Morton, jazz musician and composer; Huey Newton, black activist; Paul Prudhomme, chef; Howard K. Smith, TV commentator; Ben Turpin, comedian; Ray Walston, actor; Edward Douglas White, jurist.

Maine

Capital: Augusta
Governor: John Baldacci, D (to Jan. 2007)
Lt. Governor/Senate President: Beverly C. Daggett, D (to Jan. 2005)
Senators: Susan Collins, R (to Jan. 2009); Olympia J. Snowe, R (to Jan. 2007)
Secy. of State: Dan A. Gwadosky, D (to Jan. 2007)
Treasurer: Dale McCormick (to Jan. 2007)
Atty. General: G. Steven Rowe, D (to Jan. 2007)
Entered Union (rank): March 15, 1820 (23)
Present constitution adopted: 1820
Motto: *Dirigo* (I lead)
State Symbols: flower, white pine cone and tassel (1895); **tree,** white pine tree (1945); **bird,** chickadee (1927); **fish,** landlocked salmon (1969); **mineral,** tourmaline (1971); **song,** "State of Maine Song" (1937); **animal,** moose (1979); **cat,** Maine coon cat (1985); **fossil,** *pertica quadrifaria* (1985); **insect,** honeybee (1975)
Nickname: Pine Tree State
Origin of name: First used to distinguish the mainland from the offshore islands. It has been considered a compliment to Henrietta Maria, queen of Charles I of England. She was said to have owned the province of Mayne in France.
10 largest cities (2003 est.): Portland, 63,635; Lewiston, 35,922; Bangor, 31,550; South Portland, 23,553; Auburn, 23,313; Biddeford, 21,685; Sanford, 21,666; Brunswick, 21,529; Augusta, 18,618; Scarborough, 18,459
Land area: 30,862 sq mi. (79,933 sq km)
Geographic center: In Piscataquis Co., 18 mi. N of Dover-Foxcroft
Number of counties: 16
Largest county by population and area: Cumberland, 266,988 (2001); Aroostook, 6,672 sq mi.
State forests: 1 (21,000 ac.)
State parks: 26 (247,627 ac.)
State historic sites: 18 (403 ac.)
Residents: Mainer
2003 resident population est.: 1,305,728
2000 resident census population (rank): 1,274,923 (40). **Male:** 620,309 (48.7%); **Female:** 654,614 (51.3%). **White:** 1,236,014 (96.9%); **Black:** 6,760 (0.5%); **American Indian:** 7,098 (0.6%); **Asian:** 9,111 (0.7%); **Other race:** 2,911 (0.2%); **Two or more races:** 12,647 (1.0%); **Hispanic/Latino:** 9,360 (0.7%); **2000 percent population 18 and over:** 76.4; **65 and over:** 14.4; **median age:** 38.6.

John Cabot and his son, Sebastian, are believed to have visited the Maine coast in 1498. However, the first permanent English settlements were not established until more than a century later, in 1623.

The first naval action of the Revolutionary War occurred in 1775 when colonials captured the British sloop *Margaretta* off Machias on the Maine coast. In that same year, the British burned Falmouth (now Portland).

Long governed by Massachusetts, Maine became the 23rd state as part of the Missouri Compromise in 1820.

Maine produces 98% of the nation's low-bush blueberries. Farm income is also derived from apples, potatoes, dairy products, and vegetables, with poultry and eggs the largest selling items.

The state is one of the world's largest pulp-paper producers. With almost 89% of its area forested, Maine turns out wood products from boats to toothpicks. Maine also leads the world in the production of the familiar flat tins of sardines, producing more than 75 million of them annually. In 2001, Maine lobstermen landed nearly 48 million pounds of lobster, compared with an estimated 53 million pounds in 2000.

A scenic seacoast, beaches, lakes, mountains, and resorts make Maine a popular vacationland. There are more than 2,500 lakes and 5,000 streams, plus 26 state parks to attract hunters, fishermen, skiers, and campers.

Major points of interest are Bar Harbor, Acadia National Park, Allagash National Wilderness Waterway, the Wadsworth-Longfellow House in Portland, Roosevelt Campobello International Park, and the St. Croix Island National Monument.

Selected famous natives and residents: F. Lee Bailey, defense attorney; Charles F. Browne (Artemus Ward), humorist; Cyrus Curtis, publisher; Dorothea Dix, civil rights reformer; John Ford, film director; Melville Fuller, jurist; Marsden Hartley, painter; Henry Wadsworth Longfellow, poet; Sarah Orne Jewett, author; Stephen King, writer; Linda Lavin, actress; Edna St. Vincent Millay, poet; Marston Morse, mathematician; Frank Munsey, publisher; Walter Piston, composer; George Putnam, publisher; Kenneth Roberts, historical novelist; Edwin Arlington Robinson, poet; Margaret Chase Smith, politician; Samantha Smith, peacemaker and actress; John Hay Whitney, publisher.

Maryland

Capital: Annapolis
Governor: Robert L. Ehrlich, Jr., R (to Jan. 2007)
Lieut. Gov.: Michael Steele, R (to Jan. 2007)
Senators: Barbara A. Mikulski, D (to Jan. 2005); Paul S. Sarbanes, D (to Jan. 2007)
Secy. of State: R. Karl Aumann, R (to Jan. 2007)
Treasurer: Nancy K. Kopp, D
Atty. General: J. Joseph Curran, Jr., D (to Jan. 2007)
Entered Union (rank): April 28, 1788 (7)
Present constitution adopted: 1867
Motto: *Fatti maschii, parole femine* (Manly deeds, womanly words)
State Symbols: bird, Baltimore oriole (1947); **boat,** skipjack (1985); **crustacean,** Maryland blue crab (1989); **dinosaur,** Astrodon johnstoni (1998); **dog,** Chesapeake Bay retriever (1964); **beverage,** milk (1998); **flower,** black-eyed susan (1918); **fish,** rockfish (1965); **folk dance,** square dance (1994); **fossil shell,** *ecphora gardnerae gardnerae* (Wilson) (1994); **insect,** Baltimore checkerspot butterfly (1973); **reptile,** Diamondback terrapin (1994); **song,** "Maryland! My Maryland!" (1939); **sport,** jousting (1962); **tree,** white oak (1941)
Nicknames: Free State; Old Line State
Origin of name: In honor of Henrietta Maria (queen of Charles I of England)
10 largest cities (2003 est.): Baltimore, 628,670; Gaithersburg, 57,365; Frederick, 56,128; Rockville, 55,213; Bowie, 53,660; Hagerstown, 36,953; Annapolis, 36,178; College Park, 25,329; Salisbury, 25,247; Greenbelt, 22,096
Land area: 9,774 sq mi. (25,315 sq km)
Geographic center: In Prince Georges Co., 4½ mi. NW of Davidsonville
Number of counties: 23, and 1 independent city
Largest county by population and area: Montgomery, 891,347 (2001); Frederick, 663 sq mi.
State forests: 13 (132,944 ac.)
State parks: 47 (87,670 ac.)
Residents: Marylander
2003 resident population est.: 5,508,909
2000 resident census population (rank): 5,296,486 (19). **Male:** 2,557,794 (48.3%); **Female:** 2,738,692 (51.7%). **White:** 3,391,308 (64.0%); **Black:** 1,477,411 (27.9%); **American Indian:** 15,423 (0.3%); **Asian:**

210,929 (4.0%); **Other race:** 95,525 (1.8%); **Two or more races:** 103,587 (2.0%); **Hispanic/Latino:** 227,916 (4.3%). **2000 percent population 18 and over:** 74.4; **65 and over:** 11.3; **median age:** 36.0.

In 1608, Capt. John Smith explored Chesapeake Bay. Charles I granted a royal charter for Maryland to Cecil Calvert, Lord Baltimore, in 1632, and English settlers, many of whom were Roman Catholic, landed on St. Clement's (now Blakistone) Island in 1634. Religious freedom, granted all Christians in the Toleration Act passed by the Maryland assembly in 1649, was ended by a Puritan revolt, 1654–1658.

From 1763 to 1767, Charles Mason and Jeremiah Dixon surveyed Maryland's northern boundary line with Pennsylvania. In 1791, Maryland ceded land to form the District of Columbia.

In 1814, during the British attempt to capture Baltimore, the bombardment of Fort McHenry inspired Francis Scott Key to write the words to "The Star-Spangled Banner." During the Civil War, Maryland was a slave state but remained in the Union. Consequently, Marylanders fought on both sides and many families were divided.

Maryland's Eastern Shore and Western Shore embrace the Chesapeake Bay, and the many estuaries and rivers create one of the longest waterfronts of any state. The Bay produces more seafood—oysters, crabs, clams, fin fish—than any comparable body of water. Important agricultural products are greenhouse and nursery products, chickens, dairy products, eggs, and soybeans. Stone, coal, sand, gravel, cement, and clay are the chief mineral products.

Manufacturing industries include food products, chemicals, computer and electronic products, transportation equipment, and primary metals. Baltimore, home of the Johns Hopkins University and Hospital, ranks as the nation's second port in foreign tonnage. The capital, Annapolis, is the site of the U.S. Naval Academy.

Among the popular attractions in Maryland are the Fort McHenry National Monument; Harpers Ferry and Chesapeake and Ohio Canal National Historic Parks; Antietam National Battlefield; National Aquarium, USS *Constellation,* and Maryland Science Center at Baltimore's Inner Harbor; Historic St. Mary's City; Jefferson Patterson Historical Park and Museum at St. Leonard; U.S. Naval Academy in Annapolis; Goddard Space Flight Center at Greenbelt; Assateague Island National Park Seashore; Ocean City beach resort; and Catoctin Mountain, Fort Frederick, and Piscataway parks.

Selected famous natives and residents: Benjamin Banneker, mathematician and astronomer; John Barth, writer; Eubie Blake, musician; John Wilkes Booth, actor and Lincoln assassin; Francis X. Bushman, actor; James M. Cain, writer; Samuel Chase, jurist; Frederick Douglass, abolitionist; John Fletcher Hurst, Methodist bishop and educator; Christopher Gist, frontiersman; Philip Glass, composer; John Hanson, president of Continental Congress; Matthew Henson, polar explorer; Billie Holiday, jazz-blues singer; Johns Hopkins, financier; Reverdy Johnson, lawyer and statesman; Thomas Johnson, political leader; Francis Scott Key, lawyer and poet; Thurgood Marshall, jurist; H. L. Mencken, writer; Hezekiah Niles, journalist; Charles Willson Peale, painter; Frank Perdue, farmer, businessman; James R. Randall, journalist and writer of the state song; Babe Ruth, baseball player; Upton Sinclair, novelist; Roger B. Taney, jurist; George Alfred Townsend (Gath), journalist; Harriet Tubman, abolitionist; Leon Uris, novelist; Frank Zappa, singer.

Massachusetts

Capital: Boston
Governor: Mitt Romney, R (to Jan. 2007)
Lieut. Governor: Kerry Healey, R (to Jan. 2007)
Senators: Edward M. Kennedy, D (to Jan. 2007);
  John F. Kerry, D (to Jan. 2009)
Secy. of the Commonwealth: William F. Galvin, D
  (to Jan. 2007)
Treasurer: Timothy P. Cahill, D (to Jan. 2007)
Atty. General: Thomas F. Reilly, D (to Jan. 2007)
Present constitution drafted: 1780 (oldest U.S. state
  constitution in effect today)
Entered Union (rank): Feb. 6, 1788 (6)
Motto: *Ense petit placidam sub libertate quietem*
  (By the sword we seek peace, but peace only
  under liberty)
State Symbols: flower, mayflower (1918); **tree,**
  American elm (1941); **bird,** chickadee (1941); **song,**
  "All Hail to Massachusetts" (1966); **beverage,**
  cranberry juice (1970); **insect,** ladybug (1974);
  cookie, chocolate chip (1997); **muffin,** corn muffin
  (1986); **dessert,** Boston cream pie (1996)
Nicknames: Bay State; Old Colony State
Origin of name: From Massachusett tribe of Native
  Americans, meaning "at or about the great hill"
10 largest cities (2003 est.): Boston, 581,616;
  Worcester, 175,706; Springfield, 152,157; Lowell,
  104,351; Cambridge, 101,587; Brockton, 95,090; New
  Bedford, 94,112; Fall River, 92,760; Lynn, 89,571;
  Quincy, 89,059
Land area: 7,840 sq mi. (20,306 sq km)
Geographic center: In the town of Rutland in Worcester
  Co.
Number of counties: 14
Largest county by population and area: Middlesex,
  1,463,454 (2001); Worcester, 1,513 sq mi.
State forests and parks: 144 (300,000 ac.)[1]
Residents: Bay Stater
2003 resident population est.: 6,433,422
2000 resident census population (rank): 6,349,097
  (13). **Male:** 3,058,816 (48.2%); **Female:** 3,290,281
  (51.8%). **White:** 5,367,286 (84.5%); **Black:** 343,454
  (5.4%); **American Indian:** 15,015 (0.2%); **Asian:**
  238,124 (3.8%); **Other race:** 236,724 (3.7%); **Two or
  more races:** 146,005 (2.3%); **Hispanic/Latino:**
  428,729 (6.8%). **2000 percent population 18 and
  over:** 76.4; **65 and over:** 13.5; **median age:** 36.5.

1. The Metropolitan District Commission, an agency of
the Commonwealth serving municipalities in the Boston
area, has about 20,000 acres of woodlands, wetlands,
and urban parks under its jurisdiction.

Massachusetts has played a significant role in
American history since the Pilgrims, seeking religious freedom, founded Plymouth Colony in 1620.
As one of the most important of the 13 colonies,
Massachusetts became a leader in resisting British
oppression. In 1773, the Boston Tea Party protested
unjust taxation. The Minute Men started the American Revolution by battling British troops at Lexington and Concord on April 19, 1775.

During the 19th century, Massachusetts was
famous for the intellectual activity of its writers and
educators and for its expanding commercial fishing,
shipping, and manufacturing interests. Massachusetts pioneered the manufacture of textiles and
shoes. Today, these industries have been replaced in
importance by the electronics and communications
equipment fields.

The state's cranberry crop is the nation's second-
largest (after Wisconsin). Also important are dairy
and poultry products, nursery and greenhouse produce, vegetables, and fruit.

Tourism has become an important factor in the
economy of the state because of its numerous recreational areas and historical landmarks. Cape Cod
has beaches, summer theaters, and an artists' colony
at Provincetown. The Berkshires, in the western part
of the state, is the site of Tanglewood, the summer
home of the Boston Symphony; art museums,
including Mass MoCA and the Clark Institute; and
Jacob's Pillow, a world renowned dance center.

Among the many other points of interest are Old
Sturbridge Village in Sturbridge, Minute Man
National Historical Park between Lexington and
Concord, and Plimoth Plantation in Plymouth. In
Boston there are many places of historical interest,
including Old North Church, Old State House,
Faneuil Hall, the USS *Constitution,* and the John F.
Kennedy Library and Museum.

Selected famous natives and residents: John Adams,
president; John Quincy Adams, president; Samuel Adams,
patriot; Bronson Alcott, educator and social reformer; Louisa
May Alcott, writer; Horatio Alger, novelist; Susan B.
Anthony, woman suffragist; Clara Barton, American Red
Cross founder; Leonard Bernstein, conductor; George H. W.
Bush, president; William Cullen Bryant, poet and editor;
Luther Burbank, horticulturalist; John Cheever, novelist;
John Singleton Copley, painter; e.e. cummings, poet;
Jacques d'Amboise, ballet dancer; Bette Davis, actress;
Cecil B. DeMille, film director; Emily Dickinson, poet; Ralph
Waldo Emerson, philosopher and poet; Geraldine Farrar,
soprano, actress; Benjamin Franklin, statesman and
scientist; Buckminster Fuller, architect and educator; Robert
Goddard, father of modern rocketry; John Hancock,
statesman; Nathaniel Hawthorne, novelist; Oliver Wendell
Holmes, jurist; Winslow Homer, painter; Elias Howe,
inventor; John F. Kennedy, president; Amy Lowell, poet;
James Russell Lowell, poet; Robert Lowell, poet; Horace
Mann, educator; Cotton Mather, clergyman; Herman
Melville, writer; Samuel F. B. Morse, painter and inventor;
Edgar Allan Poe, writer; Paul Revere, silversmith and
Revolutionary War figure; Norman Rockwell, artist; Dr.
Seuss (Theodore Geisel), author and illustrator; David
Souter, jurist; Lucy Stone, woman suffragist; Louis Henry
Sullivan, architect; Henry David Thoreau, author; Barbara
Walters, TV commentator; James McNeill Whistler, painter;
Eli Whitney, inventor; John Greenleaf Whittier, poet.

Michigan

Capital: Lansing
Governor: Jennifer Granholm, D (to Jan. 2007)
Lieut. Governor: John D. Cherry, D (to Jan. 2007)
Senators: Carl Levin, D (to Jan. 2009);
  Debbie A. Stabenow, D (to Jan. 2007)
Secy. of State: Terri Lynn Land, R (to Jan. 2007)
Atty. General: Mike Cox, R (to Jan. 2007)
Treasurer: Jay B. Rising (apptd. by governor)
Organized as territory: Jan. 11, 1805
Entered Union (rank): Jan. 26, 1837 (26)
Present constitution adopted: April 1, 1963, (effective
  Jan. 1, 1964)
Motto: *Si quaeris peninsulam amoenam circumspice*
  (If you seek a pleasant peninsula, look around you)
State Symbols: flower, apple blossom (1897); **bird,**
  robin (1931); **mammal,** white-tailed deer (1997);
  fishes, trout (1965), brook trout (1988); **gem,** isle
  royal greenstone (chlorastrolite) (1972); **stone,**
  petoskey stone (1965); **tree,** white pine (1955); **soil,**
  kalkaska soil series (1990); **reptile,** painted turtle
  (1995); **flag,** "Blue charged with the arms of the state"
  (1911); **wildflower,** Dwarf Lake iris (1998)
Nickname: Wolverine State
Origin of name: From Indian word "Michigana" meaning
  "great or large lake"
10 largest cities (2003 est.): Detroit, 911,402; Grand
  Rapids, 195,601; Warren, 136,016; Sterling Heights,
  126,182; Flint, 120,292; Lansing, 118,379; Ann Arbor,

114,498; Livonia, 99,487; Dearborn, 96,670; Westland, 85,707
Land area: 56,804 sq mi. (147,122 sq km)
Geographic center: In Wexford Co., 5 mi. NNW of Cadillac
Number of counties: 83
Largest county by population and area: Wayne, 2,045,473 (2001); Marquette, 1,821 sq mi.
State parks and recreation areas: 96 (265,000 ac.)
Residents: Michigander, Michiganite
2003 resident population est.: 10,079,985
2000 resident census population (rank): 9,938,444 (8). **Male:** 4,873,095 (49.0%); **Female:** 5,065,349 (51.0%). **White:** 7,966,053 (80.2%); **Black:** 1,412,742 (14.2%); **American Indian:** 58,479 (0.6%); **Asian:** 176,510 (1.8%); **Other race:** 129,552 (1.3%); **Two or more races:** 192,416 (1.9%); **Hispanic/Latino:** 323,877 (3.3%). **2000 percent population 18 and over:** 73.9; **65 and over:** 12.3; **median age:** 35.5.

Indian tribes were living in the Michigan region when the first European, Étienne Brulé of France, arrived in 1618. Other French explorers, including Jacques Marquette, Louis Joliet, and Sieur de la Salle, followed, and the first permanent settlement was established in 1668 at Sault Ste. Marie. France was ousted from the territory by Great Britain in 1763, following the French and Indian Wars.

After the Revolutionary War, the U.S. acquired most of the region, which remained the scene of constant conflict between the British and U.S. forces and their respective Indian allies through the War of 1812.

Bordering on four of the five Great Lakes, Michigan is divided into Upper and Lower peninsulas by the Straits of Mackinac, which link lakes Michigan and Huron. The two parts of the state are connected by the Mackinac Bridge, one of the world's longest suspension bridges. To the north, connecting lakes Superior and Huron, are the busy Sault Ste. Marie Canals.

While Michigan ranks first among the states in production of motor vehicles and parts, it is also a leader in many other manufacturing and processing lines, including prepared cereals, machine tools, airplane parts, refrigerators, hardware, and furniture.

The state produces important amounts of iron, copper, iodine, gypsum, bromine, salt, lime, gravel, and cement. Michigan's farms grow apples, cherries, beans, pears, grapes, potatoes, and sugar beets. Michigan's forests contribute significantly to the state's economy, supporting thousands of jobs in the wood-product, tourism, and recreation industries. With 10,083 inland lakes and 3,288 mi of Great Lakes shoreline, Michigan is a prime area for both commercial and sport fishing.

Points of interest are the automobile plants in Dearborn, Detroit, Flint, Lansing, and Pontiac; Mackinac Island; Pictured Rocks and Sleeping Bear Dunes National Lakeshores; Greenfield Village in Dearborn; and the many summer resorts along both the inland lakes and Great Lakes.

Selected famous natives and residents: Nelson Algren, novelist; Tim Allen, actor and comedian; Anita Baker, singer; William Boeing, Sr., airplane manufacturer; Ralph J. Bunche, statesman; Ellen Burstyn, actress; Bruce Catton, historian; Roger Chaffee, astronaut; Francis Ford Coppola, film director; Thomas E. Dewey, politician; Edna Ferber, novelist; Gerald Ford, former president; Henry Ford, industrialist; Ali Haji-Sheikh, football player; Julie Harris, actress; Earvin "Magic" Johnson, basketball player; Casey Kasem, radio personality; John Harvey Kellogg, surgeon and health reformer; Ring Lardner, writer; Charles A. Lindbergh, aviator; Madonna, singer; Dick Martin, comedian; Terry McMillan, author; John N. Mitchell, attorney general; Ted Nugent, singer; Chief Pontiac, Ottawa chief; Iggy Pop, musician; Gilda Radner, comedienne; Della Reese, singer; Jason Robards, Sr., actor; Diana Ross, singer; Steven Seagal, actor; Bob Seger, singer; Tom Selleck, actor; Thomas Schippers, conductor; Potter Stewart, jurist; Lily Tomlin, actress; Danny Thomas, entertainer; William E. Upjohn, pharmaceuticals manufacturer; Margaret Whiting, singer; Robin Williams, comedian and actor; Stevie Wonder, singer.

Minnesota

Capital: St. Paul
Governor: Tim Pawlenty, R (to Jan. 2007)
Lieut. Governor: Carol Molnau, R (to Jan. 2007)
Senators: Norm Coleman, R (to Jan. 2009)
   Mark Dayton, D (to Jan. 2007)
Secy. of State: Mary Kiffmeyer, R (to Jan. 2007)
Atty. General: Mike Hatch, D (to Jan. 2007)
Commissioner of Finance: Laura M. King
Organized as territory: March 3, 1849
Entered Union (rank): May 11, 1858 (32)
Present constitution adopted: 1858
Motto: L'Étoile du Nord (The North Star)
State Symbols: flower, lady slipper (1902); **tree,** red (or Norway) pine (1953); **bird,** common loon (also called great northern diver) (1961); **song,** "Hail Minnesota" (1945); **fish,** walleye (1965); **mushroom,** morel (1984)
Nicknames: North Star State; Gopher State; Land of 10,000 Lakes
Origin of name: From a Dakota Indian word meaning "sky-tinted water"
10 largest cities (2003 est.): Minneapolis, 373,188; St. Paul, 280,404; Rochester, 92,507; Duluth, 85,734; Bloomington, 83,080; Plymouth, 69,164; Brooklyn Park, 67,781; Eagan, 64,006; Coon Rapids, 62,310; Burnsville, 59,805
Land area: 79,610 sq mi. (206,190 sq km)
Geographic center: In Crow Wing Co., 10 mi. SW of Brainerd
Number of counties: 87
Largest county by population and area: Hennepin, 1,114,977 (2001); St. Louis, 6,226 sq mi.
State forests: 55
State parks: 66 (226,000 ac.)
Residents: Minnesotan
2003 resident population est.: 5,059,375
2000 resident census population (rank): 4,919,479 (21). **Male:** 2,435,631 (49.5%); **Female:** 2,483,848 (50.5%). **White:** 4,400,282 (89.4%); **Black:** 171,731 (3.5%); **American Indian:** 54,967 (1.1%); **Asian:** 141,968 (2.9%); **Other race:** 65,810 (1.3%); **Two or more races:** 82,742 (1.7%); **Hispanic/Latino:** 143,382 (2.9%). **2000 percent population 18 and over:** 73.8; **65 and over:** 12.1; **median age:** 35.4.

Following the visits of several French explorers, fur traders, and missionaries, including Jacques Marquette, Louis Joliet, and Robert Cavelier, Sieur de la Salle, the region was claimed for Louis XIV by Daniel Greysolon, Sieur Duluth, in 1679.

The U.S. acquired eastern Minnesota from Great Britain after the Revolutionary War and 20 years later bought the western part from France in the Louisiana Purchase of 1803. Much of the region was explored by U.S. Army lieutenant Zebulon M. Pike before the northern strip of Minnesota bordering Canada was ceded by Britain in 1818.

The state is rich in natural resources. A few square miles of land in the north in the Mesabi, Cuyuna, and Vermilion ranges produce more than 75% of the nation's iron ore. The state's farms rank high in yields of corn, wheat, rye, alfalfa, and sugar beets. Other leading farm products include butter, eggs, milk, potatoes, green peas, barley, soybeans, oats, and livestock.

Minnesota's factories produce nonelectrical machinery, fabricated metals, flour-mill products, plastics, electronic computers, scientific instruments, and processed foods. The state is also a leader in the printing and paper-products industries.

Minneapolis is the trade center of the Midwest, and the headquarters of the world's largest super-computer and grain distributor. St. Paul is the nation's biggest publisher of calendars and law books. These "twin cities" are the nation's third-largest trucking center. Duluth has the nation's largest inland harbor and now handles a significant amount of foreign trade. Rochester is home to the Mayo Clinic, a world-famous medical center.

Tourism is a major revenue producer in Minnesota, with arts, fishing, hunting, water sports, and winter sports bringing in millions of visitors each year.

Among the most popular attractions are the St. Paul Winter Carnival; the Tyrone Guthrie Theatre, the Institute of Arts, Walker Art Center, and Minnehaha Park, in Minneapolis; Boundary Waters Canoe Area; Voyageurs National Park; North Shore Drive; the Minnesota Zoological Gardens; and the state's more than 10,000 lakes.

Selected famous natives and residents: LaVerne, Maxene, and Patti Andrews, singers; Warren E. Burger, jurist; William E. Colby, CIA director; William Demarest, actor; William O. Douglas, jurist; Bob Dylan, singer and composer; F. Scott Fitzgerald, novelist; Judy Garland, singer and actress; J. Paul Getty, oil executive; Cass Gilbert, architect; Duane Hanson, sculptor; Hubert H. Humphrey, senator and vice president; Jessica Lange, actress; Sinclair Lewis, novelist; Cornell MacNeil, baritone; Roger Maris, baseball player; E. G. Marshall, actor; Charles H. Mayo, surgeon; William J. Mayo, surgeon; Eugene J. McCarthy, former senator; Kate Millett, feminist; Walter F. Mondale, former vice president; Gen. Lauris Norstad, NATO commander; Westbrook Pegler, columnist; John Sargent Pillsbury, businessman; Marion Ross, actress; Jane Russell, actress; Harrison E. Salisbury, journalist; Charles M. Schulz, cartoonist; Max Shulman, novelist; Maurice H. Stans, secretary of commerce; Harold E. Stassen, government official; Michael Todd, producer; Frederick Weyerhaeuser, businessman; Gig Young, actor.

Mississippi

Capital: Jackson
Governor: Haley Barbour, R (to Jan. 2008)
Lieut. Governor: Amy Tuck, R (to Jan. 2008)
Senators: Thad Cochran, R (to Jan. 2009); Trent Lott, R (to Jan. 2007)
Secy. of State: Eric Clark, D (to Jan. 2008)
Treasurer: Tate Reeves R (to Jan. 2008)
Atty. General: Jim Hood, D (to Jan. 2008)
Organized as territory: April 7, 1798
Entered Union (rank): Dec. 10, 1817 (20)
Present constitution adopted: 1890
Motto: *Virtute et armis* (By valor and arms)
State Symbols: flower, flower or bloom of the magnolia or evergreen magnolia (1952); **wildflower,** coreopsis (1991); **tree,** magnolia (1938); **bird,** mockingbird (1944); **song,** "Go, Mississippi" (1962); **stone,** petrified wood (1976); **fish,** largemouth or black bass (1974); **insect,** honeybee (1980); **shell,** oyster shell (1974); **water mammal,** bottlenosed dolphin or porpoise (1974); **fossil,** prehistoric whale (1981); **land mammal,** white-tailed deer (1974), red fox (1997);

waterfowl, wood duck (1974); **beverage,** milk (1984); **butterfly,** spicebush swallowtail (1991); **dance,** square dance (1995)
Nickname: Magnolia State
Origin of name: From an Indian word meaning "Father of Waters"
10 largest cities (2003 est.): Jackson, 179,599; Gulfport, 71,810; Biloxi, 48,972; Hattiesburg, 46,664; Meridian, 39,559; Greenville, 39,521; Tupelo, 35,297; Southhaven, 34,760; Vicksburg, 26,005; Pascagoula, 25,865
Land area: 46,907 sq mi. (121,489 sq km)
Geographic center: In Leake Co., 9 mi. WNW of Carthage
Number of counties: 82
Largest county by population and area: Hinds, 249,495 (2001); Yazoo, 920 sq mi.
State forests: 1 (1,760 ac.)
State parks: 29 (24,521 ac.)
Residents: Mississippian
2003 resident population est.: 2,881,281
2000 resident census population (rank): 2,844,658 (31). **Male:** 1,373,554 (48.3%); **Female:** 1,471,104 (51.7%). **White:** 1,746,099 (61.4%); **Black:** 1,033,809 (36.3%); **American Indian:** 11,652 (0.4%); **Asian:** 18,626 (0.7%); **Other race:** 13,784 (0.5%); **Two or more races:** 20,021 (0.7%); **Hispanic/Latino:** 39,569 (1.4%). **2000 percent population 18 and over:** 72.7; **65 and over:** 12.1; **median age:** 33.8.

First explored for Spain by Hernando De Soto, who discovered the Mississippi River in 1540, the region was later claimed by France. In 1699, a French group under Sieur d'Iberville established the first permanent settlement near present-day Ocean Springs.

Great Britain took over the area in 1763 after the French and Indian Wars, ceding it to the U.S. in 1783 after the Revolution. Spain did not relinquish its claims until 1798, and in 1810 the U.S. annexed West Florida from Spain, including what is now southern Mississippi.

For a little more than one hundred years, from shortly after the state's founding through the Great Depression, cotton was the undisputed king of Mississippi's largely agrarian economy. Over the last half-century, however, Mississippi has diversified its economy by balancing agricultural output with increased industrial activity.

Today, agriculture continues as a major segment of the state's economy. For almost four decades soybeans occupied the most acreage, while cotton remained the largest cash crop. In 2001, however, more acres of cotton were planted than soybeans, and Mississippi jumped to second in the nation in cotton production (exceeded only by Texas). The state's farmlands also yield important harvests of corn, peanuts, pecans, rice, sugar cane, and sweet potatoes as well as poultry, eggs, meat animals, dairy products, feed crops, and horticultural crops. Mississippi remains the world's leading producer of pond-raised catfish.

The state abounds in historical landmarks and is the home of the Vicksburg National Military Park. Other National Park Service areas are Brices Cross Roads National Battlefield Site, Tupelo National Battlefield, and part of Natchez Trace National Parkway. Pre–Civil War mansions are the special pride of Natchez, Oxford, Columbus, Vicksburg, and Jackson.

Selected famous natives and residents: Red Barber, sportscaster; Jimmy Buffett, singer and songwriter; Craig Claiborne, columnist and restaurant critic; Bo Diddley, guitarist; Charles Evers, civil rights leader; Medgar Evers, civil rights leader; William Faulkner, novelist; Brett Favre, football player; Shelby Foote, historian; Richard Ford, novelist; John Grisham, novelist; Barry Hannah, novelist; Beth Henley, playwright and actress; Jim Henson, puppeteer; James Earl Jones, actor; B. B. King, guitarist; Steve McNair, football player; Mary Ann Mobley, actress; Willie Morris, writer; Elvis Presley, singer and actor; Leontyne Price, soprano; William Raspberry, columnist; Jerry Rice, football player; Jimmie Rodgers, singer; Sela Ward, actress; Muddy Waters, singer and guitarist; Eudora Welty, novelist; Tennessee Williams, playwright; Oprah Winfrey, talk-show host and actress; Richard Wright, novelist; Tammy Wynette, singer.

Missouri

Capital: Jefferson City
Governor: Bob Holden, D (to Jan. 2005)
Lieut. Governor: Joe Maxwell, D (to Jan. 2005)
Senators: Christopher S. Bond, R (to Jan. 2005); James M. Talent, R (to Jan. 2009)
Secy. of State: Matt Blunt, R (to Jan. 2005)
Auditor: Claire C. McCaskill, D (to Jan. 2003)
Treasurer: Nancy Farmer, D (to Jan. 2005)
Atty. General: Jeremiah "Jay" W. Nixon, D (to Jan. 2005)
Organized as territory: June 4, 1812
Entered Union (rank): Aug. 10, 1821 (24)
Present constitution adopted: 1945
Motto: *Salus populi suprema lex esto* (The welfare of the people shall be the supreme law)
State Symbols: flower, hawthorn (1923); **bird,** bluebird (1927); **aquatic animal,** paddlefish (1997); **fish,** channel catfish (1997); **song,** "Missouri Waltz" (1949); **fossil,** crinoid (1989); **musical instrument,** fiddle (1987); **rock,** mozarkite (1967); **mineral,** galena (1967); **insect,** honeybee (1985); **tree,** flowering dogwood (1955); **tree nut,** eastern black walnut (1990); **animal,** mule (1995); **dance,** square dance (1995); **Missouri Day,** third Wednesday in October (1969)
Nickname: Show-me State
Origin of name: Named after the Missouri Indian tribe. "Missouri" means "town of the large canoes."
10 largest cities (2003 est.): Kansas City, 442,768; St. Louis, 332,223; Springfield, 150,867; Independence, 112,079; Columbia, 88,534; Lee's Summit, 77,052; St. Joseph, 72,663; O'Fallon, 63,677; St. Charles, 61,253; St. Peter's, 53,397
Land area: 68,886 sq mi. (178,415 sq km)
Geographic center: In Miller Co., 20 mi. SW of Jefferson City
Number of counties: 114, plus 1 independent city
Largest county by population and area: St. Louis, 1,015,417 (2001); Texas, 1,179 sq mi.
Conservation areas[1]: leased, 315 (197, 661 ac.); owned, 775 (770,574 ac.)
Conservation accesses: leased, 77; owned, 237
State parks and historic sites: 81
Residents: Missourian
2003 resident population est.: 5,704,484
2000 resident census population (rank): 5,595,211 (17). **Male:** 2,720,177 (48.6%); **Female:** 2,875,034 (51.4%). **White:** 4,748,083 (84.9%); **Black:** 629,391 (11.2%); **American Indian:** 25,076 (0.4%); **Asian:** 61,595 (1.1%); **Other race:** 45,827 (0.8%); **Two or more races:** 82,061 (1.5%); **Hispanic/Latino:** 118,592 (2.1%). **2000 percent population 18 and over:** 74.5; **65 and over:** 13.5; **median age:** 36.1.

1. Includes wildlife areas, natural history areas, state forests, and tower sites.

Hernando De Soto visited the Missouri area in 1541. France's claim to the entire region was based on Sieur de la Salle's travels in 1682. French fur traders established Ste. Genevieve in 1735, and St. Louis was first settled in 1764.

The U.S. gained Missouri from France as part of the Louisiana Purchase in 1803, and the territory was admitted as a state following the Missouri Compromise of 1820. Throughout the pre–Civil War period and during the war, Missourians were sharply divided in their opinions about slavery and in their allegiances, supplying both Union and Confederate forces with troops. However, the state itself remained in the Union.

Historically, Missouri played a leading role as a gateway to the West, St. Joseph being the eastern starting point of the Pony Express, while the much-traveled Santa Fe and Oregon trails began in Independence.

Missouri's economy is highly diversified. Service industries provide more income and jobs than any other segment, and include a growing tourism and travel sector. Wholesale and retail trade, manufacturing, and agriculture also play significant roles in the state's economy.

Missouri is a leading producer of transportation equipment (including automobile manufacturing and auto parts), beer and beverages, and defense and aerospace technology. Food processing is the state's fastest-growing industry.

Missouri mines produce 90% of the nation's principal (non-recycled) lead supply. Other natural resources include iron ore, zinc, barite, limestone, and timber.

The state's top agricultural products include grain, sorghum, hay, corn, soybeans, and rice. Missouri also ranks high among the states in cattle and calves, hogs, and turkeys and broilers. A vibrant wine industry also contributes to the economy.

Tourism draws hundreds of thousands of visitors to a number of Missouri points of interest: the country-music shows of Branson; Bass Pro Shops national headquarters (Springfield); the Gateway Arch at the Jefferson National Expansion (St. Louis); Mark Twain's boyhood home (Hannibal); the Harry S Truman home and library (Independence); the scenic beauty of the Ozark National Scenic Riverways; and the Pony Express and Jesse James museums (St. Joseph). The state's different lake regions also attract fishermen and sun-seekers from throughout the Midwest.

Selected famous natives and residents: Robert Altman, film director; Burt Bacharach, songwriter; Josephine Baker, singer and dancer; Wallace Beery, actor; Robert Russell Bennett, composer; Yogi Berra, baseball player; Thomas Hart Benton, painter; Bill Bradley, basketball player and N.J. senator; Omar N. Bradley, general; Grace Bumbry, soprano; William Burroughs, writer; Sarah Caldwell, opera director and conductor; Martha Jane Canary (Calamity Jane), frontierswoman; George Washington Carver, scientist; Don Cheadle, actor; Walter Cronkite, TV newscaster; Robert Cummings, actor; Jane Darwell, actress; Walt Disney, artist; T. S. Eliot, poet; Redd Foxx, actor and comedian; Betty Grable, actress; Dick Gregory, comic and activist; Jean Harlow, actress; Coleman Hawkins, jazz musician; George Hearn, actor; Edwin Hubble, astronomer; Langston Hughes, poet; John Huston, film director; Jesse James, outlaw; Scott Joplin, composer; Marianne Moore, poet; Geraldine Page, actress; James C. Penney, merchant; John Joseph Pershing, general; Vincent Price, actor; Joseph Pulitzer, journalist; Ginger Rogers, dancer and actress; Casey Stengel, baseball player; Gladys Swarthout, soprano; Sara Teasdale, poet; Virgil Thomson, composer; Harry S. Truman, president; Mark Twain, author; Dick Van Dyke, actor; Ruth Warrick, actress; Dennis Weaver, actor; Mary Wickes, actress; Laura Ingalls Wilder, author; Roy Wilkins, civil rights leader.

Montana

Capital: Helena
Governor: Judy Martz, R (to Jan. 2005)
Lieut. Governor: Karl Ohs, R (to Jan. 2005)
Senators: Max Baucus, D (to Jan. 2009);
  Conrad R. Burns, R (to Jan. 2007)
Secy. of State: Bob Brown, R (to Jan. 2005)
Auditor: John Morrison, D (to Jan. 2005)
Atty. General: Mike McGrath, D (to Jan. 2005)
Organized as territory: May 26, 1864
Entered Union (rank): Nov. 8, 1889 (41)
Present constitution adopted: 1972
Motto: *Oro y plata* (Gold and silver)
State Symbols: flower, bitterroot (1895); **tree,**
  ponderosa pine (1949); **stones,** sapphire and agate
  (1969); **bird,** Western meadowlark (1981); **song,**
  "Montana" (1945)
Nickname: Treasure State
Origin of name: Chosen from Latin dictionary by J. M.
  Ashley. It is a Latinized Spanish word meaning
  "mountainous."
10 largest cities (2003): Billings, 95,220; Missoula,
  60,722; Great Falls, 56,155; Butte-Silver Bow,[1] 32,519;
  Bozeman, 30,753; Helena, 26,718; Kalispell, 16,391;
  Havre, 9,448; Anaconda–Deer Lodge County, 8,953;
  Miles City, 8,242
Land area: 145,552 sq mi. (376,980 sq km)
Geographic center: In Fergus Co., 11 mi. W
  of Lewistown
Number of counties: 56
Largest county by population and area: Yellowstone,
  130,398 (2001); Beaverhead, 5,543 sq mi.
State forests: 7 (214,000 ac.)
State parks and recreation areas: 110 (18,273 ac.)
Residents: Montanan
2003 resident population est.: 917,621
2000 resident census population (rank): 902,195 (44).
  Male: 449,480 (49.8%); **Female:** 452,715 (50.2%).
  White: 817,229 (90.6%); **Black:** 2,692 (0.3%); **American Indian:** 56,068 (6.2%); **Asian:** 4,691 (0.5%);
  Other race: 5,315 (0.6%); **Two or more races:**
  15,730 (1.7%); **Hispanic/Latino:** 18,081 (2.0%). **2000
  percent population 18 and over:** 74.5; **65 and over:**
  13.4; **median age:** 37.5.

1. The city is part of a consolidated city-county government and is coextensive with Silver Bow County.

First explored for France by François and Louis-
Joseph Verendrye in the early 1740s, much of the
region was acquired by the U.S. from France as part
of the Louisiana Purchase in 1803. Before western
Montana was obtained from Great Britain in the
Oregon Treaty of 1846, American trading posts and
forts had been established in the territory.

The major Indian Wars (1867–1877) included the
famous 1876 Battle of the Little Big Horn, better
known as "Custer's Last Stand," in which Cheyenne
and Sioux defeated George A. Custer and more than
200 of his men in southeast Montana.

Much of Montana's early history was concerned
with mining, with copper, lead, zinc, silver, coal,
and oil as principal products. Butte is the center of
the area that once supplied half of the U.S. copper.

Fields of grain cover much of Montana's plains. It
ranks high among the states in wheat and barley,
with rye, oats, flaxseed, sugar beets, and potatoes as
other important crops. Sheep and cattle raising make
significant contributions to the economy.

Tourist attractions include hunting, fishing, skiing,
and dude ranching. Glacier National Park, on the
Continental Divide, has 60 glaciers, 200 lakes, and
many streams with good trout fishing. Other major
points of interest include the Little Bighorn Battlefield National Monument, Virginia City, Yellowstone National Park, Fort Union Trading Post and
Grant-Kohr's Ranch National Historic Sites, and the
Museum of the Plains Indians at Browning.

Selected famous natives and residents: Dorothy Baker,
author; Dirk Benedict, actor; W. A. (Tony) Boyle, labor union
official; Gary Cooper, actor; John Cowan, prospector and
founder of Last Chance Gulch (now Helena); Alfred Bertram
Guthrie, Pulitzer Prize–winning author; Chet Huntley, TV
newscaster; Will James, writer and artist; Dorothy Johnson,
author; Evel Knievel, daredevil motorcyclist; Myrna Loy,
actress; David Lynch, filmmaker; Mike Mansfield, senator;
George Montgomery, actor; Jeannette Rankin, first woman
elected to Congress; Martha Raye, actress; Charles M.
Russell, painter; Michael Smuin, choreographer; Lester C.
Thurow, economist and educator.

Nebraska

Capital: Lincoln
Governor: Mike Johanns, R (to Jan. 2007)
Lieut. Governor: David Heineman, R (to Jan. 2007)
Senators: Charles Hagel, R (to Jan. 2009);
  Ben Nelson, D (to Jan. 2007)
Secy. of State: John Gale, R (to Jan. 2007)
Atty. General: Jon Bruning, R (to Jan. 2007)
Treasurer: Ron Ross, R (to Jan. 2007)
Organized as territory: May 30, 1854
Entered Union (rank): March 1, 1867 (37)
Present constitution adopted: Oct. 12, 1875 (exten-
  sively amended 1919–20)
Motto: Equality before the law
State Symbols: flower, goldenrod (1895); **fish,** channel
  catfish (1997); **American folk dance,** square dance
  (1997); **ballad,** "A Place Like Nebraska" (1997); **tree,**
  cottonwood (1972); **bird,** Western meadowlark (1929);
  insect, honeybee (1975); **gemstone,** blue agate
  (1967); **rock,** prairie agate (1967); **fossil,** mammoth
  (1967); **song,** "Beautiful Nebraska" (1967); **soil,** typic
  argiustolls, holdreges series (1979); **mammal,** whitetail
  deer (1981); **grass,** little bluestem (1969); **beverage,**
  milk (1998)
Nicknames: Cornhusker State (1945); Beef State
Origin of name: From an Oto Indian word meaning
  "flat water"
10 largest cities (2003 est.): Omaha, 404,267; Lincoln,
  235,594; Bellevue, 46,734; Grand Island, 43,771;
  Kearney, 28,211; Fremont, 25,198; Norfolk, 24,061;
  North Platte, 23,924; Hastings, 23,536; Columbus,
  20,880
Land area: 76,872 sq mi. (199,098 sq km)
Geographic center: In Custer Co., 10 mi. NW of
  Broken Bow
Number of counties: 93
Largest county by population and area: Douglas,
  465,683 (2001); Cherry, 5,961 sq mi.
State parks: 85 areas, historical and recreational;
  8 major areas
Residents: Nebraskan
2003 resident population est.: 1,739,291
2000 resident census population (rank): 1,711,263
  (38). **Male:** 843,351 (49.3%); **Female:** 867,912
  (50.7%). **White:** 1,533,261 (89.6%); **Black:** 68,541
  (4.0%); **American Indian:** 14,896 (0.9%); **Asian:**
  21,931 (1.3%); **Other race:** 47,845 (2.8%); **Two or
  more races:** 23,953 (1.4%); **Hispanic/Latino:** 94,425
  (5.5%). **2000 percent population 18 and over:** 73.7;
  65 and over: 13.6; **median age:** 35.3.

French fur traders first visited Nebraska in the late
1600s. Part of the Louisiana Purchase in 1803, eastern Nebraska was explored by Lewis and Clark in
1804–1806. A few years later, Robert Stuart pioneered the Oregon Trail across Nebraska in 1812–

1813, and the first permanent white settlement was established at Bellevue in 1823.

Western Nebraska was acquired by treaty following the Mexican War in 1848. The Union Pacific began its transcontinental railroad at Omaha in 1865. In 1937, Nebraska became the only state in the Union to have a unicameral (one-house) legislature. Members are elected to it without party designation.

Nebraska is a leading grain-producer with bumper crops of sorghum, corn, and wheat. More varieties of grass, valuable for forage, grow in this state than in any other in the nation. The state's sizable cattle and hog industries make Dakota City and Lexington among the nation's largest meat-packing centers.

Manufacturing has become diversified: Firms making electronic components, auto accessories, pharmaceuticals, and mobile homes have joined such older industries as clothing, farm machinery, chemicals, and transportation equipment. Oil was discovered in 1939 and natural gas in 1949.

Among the principal attractions are Agate Fossil Beds, Homestead, and Scotts Bluff National Monuments; Chimney Rock National Historic Site; a recreated pioneer village at Minden; Boys Town; the Sheldon Memorial Art Gallery and the Lied Center for the Performing Arts at the University of Nebraska in Lincoln; the State Capitol in Lincoln; the Joslyn Art Museum in Omaha; the Henry Doorly Zoo in Omaha; Museum of Nebraska Art in Kearney; Museum of Nebraska History in Lincoln; and the University of Nebraska State Museum in Lincoln.

Selected famous natives and residents: Grace Abbott, social worker; Bess Streeter Aldrich, author; Grover Cleveland Alexander, baseball pitcher; Fred Astaire, dancer and actor; Max Baer, boxer; Bil Baird, puppeteer; George Beadle, geneticist; Marlon Brando, actor; William Jennings Bryan, political leader; Warren Buffett, investor; Johnny Carson, TV host; Willa Cather, author; Dick Cavett, TV entertainer; Richard B. Cheney, vice president; Montgomery Clift, actor; James Coburn, actor; William "Buffalo Bill" Cody, showman; Sandy Dennis, actress; Mignon Eberhart, author; Harold "Doc" Edgerton, inventor; Ruth Etting, singer and actress; Fr. Edward J. Flanagan, founder of Boys Town; Henry Fonda, actor; Gerald Ford, former president; Bob Gibson, baseball player; Howard Hanson, conductor; Leland Hayward, producer; Robert Henri, painter; David Janssen, actor; Francis La Flesche, ethnologist; Melvin Laird, politician; Frank W. Leahy, football coach; Harold Lloyd, actor; Malcolm X, civil rights advocate; Dorothy McGuire, actress; Julius Sterling Morton, politician and journalist; John G. Neihardt, epic poet; Nick Nolte, actor; George W. Norris, senator; John J. Pershing, army general; Nathan Roscoe Pound, educator and botanist; Red Cloud, Indian rights advocate; Mari Sandoz, author; Standing Bear, Indian rights advocate; Robert Taylor, actor; Susette La Flesche Tibbles, Omaha Indian activist; Paul Williams, singer, composer, and actor; Julie Wilson, singer and actress; Darryl F. Zanuck, film producer.

Nevada

Capital: Carson City
Governor: Kenny Guinn, R (to Jan. 2007)
Lieut. Governor: Lorraine Hunt, R (to Jan. 2007)
Senators: Harry Reid, D (to Jan. 2005);
   John Ensign, R (to Jan. 2007)
Secy. of State: Dean Heller, R (to Jan. 2007)
Treasurer: Brian Krolicki, R (to Jan. 2007)
Atty. General: Brian Sandoval, R (to Jan. 2003)
Organized as territory: March 2, 1861
Entered Union (rank): Oct. 31, 1864 (36)
Present constitution adopted: 1864
Motto: All for Our Country
State Symbols: flower, sagebrush (1959); **trees,**
   single-leaf pinon (1953) and bristlecone pine (1987);

bird, mountain bluebird (1967); **animal,** desert bighorn sheep (1973); **colors,** silver and blue (1983); **song,** "Home Means Nevada" (1933); **rock,** sandstone (1987); **precious gemstone,** virgin valley black fire opal (1987); **semiprecious gemstone,** Nevada turquoise (1987); **grass,** Indian ricegrass (1977); **metal,** silver (1977); **fossil,** ichthyosaur (1977); **fish,** lahontan cutthroat trout (1981); **reptile,** desert tortoise (1989); **state artifact,** tule duck decoy (1995)
Nicknames: Sagebrush State; Silver State; Battle Born State
Origin of name: Spanish: "snowcapped"
10 largest cities (2003 est.): Las Vegas, 517,017; Henderson, 214,852; Reno, 193,882; North Las Vegas, 144,502; Sparks, 77,295; Carson City, 55,311; Elko, 16,075; Boulder City, 15,314; Mesquite, 11,780; Fernley, 10,047
Land area: 109,826 sq mi. (284,449 sq km)
Geographic center: In Lander Co., 26 mi. SE of Austin
Number of counties: 16, plus 1 independent city
Largest county by population and area: Clark, 1,464,653 (2001); Nye, 18,147 sq mi.
State parks: 20 (150,000 ac., including leased lands)
Residents: Nevadan, Nevadian
2003 resident population est.: 2,241,154
2000 resident census population (rank): 1,998,257 (35). **Male:** 1,018,051 (50.9%); **Female:** 980,206 (49.1%). **White:** 1,501,886 (75.2%); **Black:** 135,477 (6.8%); **American Indian:** 26,420 (1.3%); **Asian:** 90,266 (4.5%); **Other race:** 159,354 (8.0%); **Two or more races:** 76,428 (3.8%); **Hispanic/Latino:** 393,970 (19.7%). **2000 percent population 18 and over:** 74.4; **65 and over:** 11.0; **median age:** 35.0.

Trappers and traders, including Jedediah Smith and Peter Skene Ogden, entered the Nevada area in the 1820s. In 1843–1845, John C. Frémont and Kit Carson explored the Great Basin and Sierra Nevada. The U.S. obtained the region in 1848 following the Mexican War, and the first permanent settlement was a Mormon trading post near present-day Genoa.

The driest state in the nation, with an average annual rainfall of only about 7 in., much of Nevada is uninhabited, sagebrush-covered desert. The wettest part of the state receives about 40 in. of precipitation per year, while the driest spot has less than 4 in. per year.

Nevada was made famous by the discovery of the Comstock Lode, the richest known U.S. silver deposit, in 1859, and its mines have produced large quantities of gold, silver, copper, lead, zinc, mercury, barite, and tungsten. Oil was discovered in 1954. Gold now far exceeds all other minerals in value of production.

In 1931, the state created two industries, divorce and gambling. For many years, Reno and Las Vegas were the "divorce capitals of the nation." More liberal divorce laws in many states have ended this distinction, but Nevada is still the gambling capital of the U.S. and a leading entertainment center. State gambling taxes account for 34.1% of general fund tax revenues.

The state's leading agricultural industry is cattle and calves. Agricultural crops consist mainly of hay, alfalfa seed, barley, wheat, and potatoes.

Nevada manufactures gaming equipment; lawn and garden irrigation devices; titanium products; seismic and machinery monitoring devices; and specialty printing.

Lake Tahoe, Reno, and Las Vegas are major resorts. Recreation areas include Pyramid Lake, Lake Tahoe, and Lake Mead and Lake Mohave, both in

Lake Mead National Recreation Area. Other attractions are Hoover Dam, Virginia City, and Great Basin National Park (includes Lehman Caves).

Selected famous natives and residents: Eva Adams, director of U.S. Mint; Andre Agassi, tennis player; Raymond T. Baker, director of U.S. Mint; Helen Delich Bentley, government official and newspaperwoman; Robert Caples, painter; Walter Van Tilburg Clark, writer; Henry Comstock, prospector; Abby Dalton, actress; Michele Greene, actress; Sarah Winnemucca Hopkins, author and Paiute interpreter and peacemaker; Jack Kramer, tennis player; Paul Laxalt, politician; Robert Laxalt, writer; William Lear, aviation inventor; Robert C. Lynch, surgeon; John W. Mackay, benefactor, one of Big Four of Comstock Lode; Emma Nevada, opera singer; Thelma "Pat" Nixon, first lady; James W. Nye, territory governor and senator; Lute Pease, cartoonist and Pulitzer Prize winner; Edna Purviance, actress; Patty Sheehan, golfer; Jack Wilson, Paiute Indian prophet; George Wingfield, mining millionaire.

New Hampshire

Capital: Concord
Governor: Craig Benson, R (to Jan. 2005)
Senators: Judd Gregg, R (to Jan. 2005); John E. Sununu, R (to Jan. 2009)
Treasurer: Michael Ablowich, R (to Dec. 2004)
Secy. of State: William M. Gardner, D (to Dec. 2004)
Atty. General: Peter Heed, R (to Jan. 2005)
Entered Union (rank): June 21, 1788 (9)
Present constitution adopted: 1784
Motto: Live free or die
State Symbols: flower, purple lilac (1919); **tree,** white birch (1947); **animal,** white-tailed deer (1983); **insect,** ladybug (1977); **saltwater fish,** striped bass (1994); **freshwater fish,** brook trout (1995); **amphibian,** spotted newt (1985); **butterfly,** karner blue (1992); **bird,** purple finch (1957); **songs,** "Old New Hampshire" (1949) and "New Hampshire, My New Hampshire" (1963)
Nickname: Granite State
Origin of name: From the English county of Hampshire
10 largest cities (2003 est.): Manchester, 108,871; Nashua, 87,285; Concord, 41,823; Derry, 34,471; Rochester, 29,654; Salem, 29,115; Dover, 28,216; Merrimack, 26,394; Londonderry, 24,201; Hudson, 23,839
Land area: 8,968 sq mi. (23,227 sq km)
Geographic center: In Belknap Co., 3 mi. E of Ashland
Number of counties: 10
Largest county by population and area: Hillsborough, 387,674 (2001); Coos, 1,801 sq mi.
State parks: 65 (50,000+ ac.)
Residents: New Hampshirite
2003 resident population est.: 1,287,687
2000 resident census population (rank): 1,235,786 (41). **Male:** 607,687 (49.2%); **Female:** 628,099 (50.8%). **White:** 1,186,851 (96.0%); **Black:** 9,035 (0.7%); **American Indian:** 2,964 (0.2%); **Asian:** 15,931 (1.3%); **Other race:** 7,420 (0.6%); **Two or more races:** 13,214 (1.1%); **Hispanic/Latino:** 20,489 (1.7%). **2000 percent population 18 and over:** 75.0; **65 and over:** 12.0; **median age:** 37.1.

Under an English land grant, Capt. John Smith sent settlers to establish a fishing colony at the mouth of the Piscataqua River, near present-day Rye and Dover, in 1623. Capt. John Mason, who participated in the founding of Portsmouth in 1630, gave New Hampshire its name.

After a 38-year period of union with Massachusetts, New Hampshire was made a separate royal colony in 1679. As leaders in the revolutionary cause, New Hampshire delegates received the honor of being the first to vote for the Declaration of Independence on July 4, 1776. New Hampshire gained a measure of international attention in 1905 when Portsmouth Naval Base played host to the signing of the treaty ending the Russo-Japanese War, known as the Treaty of Portsmouth.

Abundant water power turned New Hampshire into an industrial state early on, and manufacturing is the principal source of income. The most important industrial products are electrical and other machinery, textiles, pulp and paper products, and stone and clay products. Dairy and poultry, and growing fruit, truck vegetables, corn, potatoes, and hay are the major agricultural pursuits.

Because of New Hampshire's scenic and recreational resources, tourism now brings over $3.5 billion into the state annually.

Vacation attractions include Lake Winnipesaukee, largest of 1,300 lakes and ponds; the 724,000-acre White Mountain National Forest; Daniel Webster's birthplace near Franklin; and Strawbery Banke, restored buildings of the original settlement at Portsmouth. In 2003, the famous "Old Man of the Mountain" granite head profile, the state's official emblem, fell from its perch in Franconia.

Selected famous natives and residents: Sherman Adams, former governor and presidential advisor; Salmon P. Chase, jurist; Charles Anderson Dana, editor; Mary Baker Eddy, founder of the Christian Science Church; Dustin Farnum, actor; Thomas Green Fessenden, journalist and satirical poet; Daniel Chester French, sculptor; Robert Frost, poet; Horace Greeley, journalist and politician; Sarah J. Hale, editor; John Irving, writer; Benjamin F. Keith, theater entrepreneur; Jackson Hall Kelly, promoter of Oregon settlement; John Langdon, political leader; Sharon Christa McAuliffe, teacher and astronaut; Franklin Pierce, former president; Augustus Saint-Gaudens, sculptor; Alan Shepard, astronaut; Harlan F. Stone, jurist; Daniel Webster, statesman; Henry Wilson, politician and former vice president; Noah Worcester, clergyman and pacifist.

New Jersey

Capital: Trenton
Governor: Jim McGreevey,[1] D (to Jan. 2006)
President of the Senate: Richard J. Codey, D
Senators: Frank R. Lautenberg, D (to Jan. 2009); Jon Corzine, D (to Jan. 2007)
Secy. of State: Regena L. Thomas (to Jan. 2006)
Treasurer: John E. McCormac
Atty. General: Peter C. Harvey, I (to Jan. 2006)
Entered Union (rank): Dec. 18, 1787 (3)
Present constitution adopted: 1947
Motto: Liberty and prosperity
State Symbols: flower, purple violet (1913); **bird,** eastern goldfinch (1935); **insect,** honeybee (1974); **tree,** red oak (1950); **animal,** horse (1977); **colors,** buff and blue (1965); **folk dance,** square dance; **dinosaur,** hadrosaurus foulkii; **fish,** brook trout; **shell,** knobbed whelk
Nickname: Garden State
Origin of name: From the Channel Isle of Jersey
10 largest cities (2003 est.): Newark, 277,911; Jersey City, 239,097; Paterson, 150,782; Elizabeth, 123,215; Woodbridge, 100,866; Edison, 100,138; Dover, 93,671; Hamilton, 89,632; Trenton, 85,314; Camden, 80,089
Land area: 7,417 sq mi. (19,210 sq km)
Geographic center: In Mercer Co., 5 mi. SE of Trenton
Number of counties: 21
Largest county by population and area: Bergen, 886,680 (2001); Burlington, 805 sq mi.
State forests: 11
State parks: 35 (67,111 ac.)
Residents: New Jerseyite, New Jerseyan
2003 resident population est.: 8,638,396

2000 resident census population (rank): 8,414,350 (9). **Male:** 4,082,813 (48.5%); **Female:** 4,331,537 (51.5%). **White:** 6,104,705 (72.6%); **Black:** 1,141,821 (13.6%); **American Indian:** 19,492 (0.2%); **Asian:** 480,276 (5.7%); **Other race:** 450,972 (5.4%); **Two or more races:** 213,755 (2.5%); **Hispanic/Latino:** 1,117,191 (13.3%). **2000 percent population 18 and over:** 75.2; **65 and over:** 13.2; **median age:** 36.7.

1. Gov. McGreevey resigned in Aug. 2004, effective Nov. 15. Richard Codey, president of the Senate will become acting governor.

New Jersey's early colonial history was involved with that of New York (New Netherlands), of which it was a part. One year after the Dutch surrender to England in 1664, New Jersey was organized as an English colony under Gov. Philip Carteret.

In 1676 the colony was divided between Carteret and a company of English Quakers who had obtained the rights belonging to John, Lord Berkeley. New Jersey became a united crown colony in 1702, administered by the royal governor of New York. Finally, in 1738, New Jersey was separated from New York under its own royal governor, Lewis Morris. Because of its key location between New York City and Philadelphia, New Jersey saw much fighting during the American Revolution.

Today, New Jersey, an area of wide industrial diversification, is known as the Crossroads of the East. Products from over 15,000 factories can be delivered overnight to almost 60 million people, representing 12 states and the District of Columbia. The greatest single industry is chemicals; New Jersey is one of the foremost research centers in the world. Many large oil refineries are located in northern New Jersey. Other important manufactured items are pharmaceuticals, instruments, machinery, electrical goods, and apparel.

Productive farmland covers nearly one million acres, about 20% of New Jersey's land area. The state ranks high in the production of almost all garden vegetables, as well as cranberries, blueberries, and peaches. Poultry, dairy products, and seafood are also top commodities.

Tourism is the second-largest industry in New Jersey. The state has numerous resort areas on 127 mi of Atlantic coastline. In 1977, New Jersey voters approved legislation allowing legalized casino gambling in Atlantic City. Points of interest include the Delaware Water Gap, the Edison National Historic Site in West Orange, Princeton University, Liberty State Park, Jersey City, and the N.J. State Aquarium in Camden.

Selected famous natives and residents: Bud Abbott, comedian; Charles Addams, cartoonist; Edwin Aldrin, astronaut; Count Basie, band leader; Joan Bennett, actress; Jon Bon Jovi, musician; William J. Brennan, jurist; Aaron Burr, political leader; James Fenimore Cooper, novelist; Lou Costello, comedian; Stephen Crane, writer; Helen Gahagan Douglas, representative; Allen Ginsberg, poet; William Frederick Halsey, Jr., admiral; Alfred Joyce Kilmer, poet; Ernie Kovacs, comedian; Jerry Lewis, comedian and film director; Anne Morrow Lindbergh, author; Norman Mailer, novelist; Patricia McBride, ballerina; Richard Nixon, president; Dorothy Parker, author; Joe Piscopo, comedian and actor; Paul Robeson, singer and actor; Philip Roth, novelist; Ruth St. Denis, dancer and choreographer; Antonin Scalia, jurist; H. Norman Schwarzkopf, general; Frank Sinatra, singer and actor; Bruce Springsteen, musician; Alfred Stieglitz, photographer; Albert Payson Terhune, journalist and novelist; Sarah Vaughan, singer; William Carlos Williams, physician and poet; Bruce Willis, actor; Edmund Wilson, literary critic and author.

New Mexico

Capital: Santa Fe
Governor: Bill Richardson, D (to Jan. 2007)
Lieut. Governor: Diane Denish, D (to Jan. 2007)
Senators: Jeff Bingaman, D (to Jan. 2007); Pete V. Domenici, R (to Jan. 2009)
Secy. of State: Rebecca Vigil-Giron, D (to Jan. 2007)
Atty. General: Patricia A. Madrid, D (to Jan. 2007)
State Treasurer: Robert E. Vigil, D (to Jan. 2007)
Organized as territory: Sept. 9, 1850
Entered Union (rank): Jan. 6, 1912 (47)
Present constitution adopted: 1911
Motto: *Crescit eundo* (It grows as it goes)
State Symbols: flower, yucca (1927); **tree,** pinon (1949); **animal,** black bear (1963); **bird,** roadrunner (1949); **fish,** cutthroat trout (1955); **vegetables,** chili and frijol (1965); **gem,** turquoise (1967); **song,** "O Fair New Mexico" (1917); **Spanish-language song,** "Asi Es Nuevo Méjico" (1971); **poem,** A Nuevo México (1991); **grass,** blue gramma (1973); **fossil,** coelophysis (1981); **cookie,** bizcochito (1989); **insect,** tarantula hawk wasp (1989); **ballad,** "Land of Enchantment" (1989); **bilingual song,** "New Mexico—Mi Lindo Nuevo Mexico", (1995); **question,** "Red or Green?" (1999)
Nickname: Land of Enchantment (1999)
Origin of name: From the country of Mexico
10 largest cities (2003 est.): Albuquerque, 471,856; Las Cruces, 76,990; Santa Fe, 66,476; Rio Rancho, 58,981; Roswell, 44,228; Farmington, 41,420; Alamogordo, 35,551; Clovis, 32,815; Hobbs, 28,311; Carlsbad, 25,303
Land area: 121,356 sq mi. (314,312 sq km)
Geographic center: In Torrance Co., 12 mi. SSW of Willard
Number of counties: 33
Largest county by population and area: Bernalillo, 562,458 (2001); Catron, 6,928 sq mi.
State-owned forested land: 933,000 ac.
State parks: 31 (267,302 ac.)
Residents: New Mexican
2003 resident population est.: 1,874,614
2000 resident census population (rank): 1,819,046 (36). **Male:** 894,317 (49.2%); **Female:** 924,729 (50.8%). **White:** 1,214,253 (66.8%); **Black:** 34,343 (1.9%); **American Indian:** 173,483 (9.5%); **Asian:** 19,255 (1.1%); **Other race:** 309,882 (17.0%); **Two or more races:** 66,327 (3.6%); **Hispanic/Latino:** 765,386 (42.1%). **2000 percent population 18 and over:** 72.0; **65 and over:** 11.7; **median age:** 34.6.

Francisco Vásquez de Coronado, a Spanish explorer searching for gold, traveled the region that became New Mexico in 1540–1542. In 1598 the first Spanish settlement was established on the Rio Grande River by Juan de Onate; in 1610 Santa Fe was founded and made the capital of New Mexico.

The U.S. acquired most of New Mexico in 1848, as a result of the Mexican War, and the remainder in the 1853 Gadsden Purchase. Union troops captured the territory from the Confederates during the Civil War. With the surrender of Geronimo in 1886, the Apache Wars and most of the Indian conflicts in the area were ended.

Since 1945, New Mexico has been a leader in energy research and development with extensive experiments conducted at Los Alamos Scientific Laboratory and Sandia Laboratories in the nuclear, solar, and geothermal areas.

Minerals are the state's richest natural resource, and New Mexico is one of the U.S. leaders in output of uranium and potassium salts. Petroleum, natural gas, copper, gold, silver, zinc, lead, and molybdenum also contribute heavily to the state's income.

The principal manufacturing industries include food products, chemicals, transportation equipment, lumber, electrical machinery, and stone-clay-glass products. More than two-thirds of New Mexico's farm income comes from livestock products, especially sheep. Cotton, pecans, and sorghum are the most important field crops. Corn, peanuts, beans, onions, chilies, and lettuce are also grown.

Tourist attractions include the Carlsbad Caverns National Park, Inscription Rock at El Morro National Monument, the ruins at Fort Union, Billy the Kid mementos at Lincoln, the White Sands and Gila Cliff Dwellings National Monuments, Bandelier National Monument, and the Chaco Culture National Historical Park.

Selected famous natives and residents: Kathy Baker, actress; Notah Begay III, golfer; Judy Blume, author; Ernest L. Blumenshein, artist; William "Billy the Kid" Bonney, outlaw; Richard Bradford, author; Ralph Bunche, Nobel Peace Prize winner; Bruce Cabot, actor; Glen Campbell, singer; Kit Carson, army scout and trapper; Dennis Chavez, former senator; John Chisum, cattle king; Mangus Coloradas, Apache leader; Edward Condon, physicist; Bill Daily, actor; John Denver, singer; Bo Diddley, blues guitarist; Patrick Garrett, lawman; Greer Garson, actress; Sid Gutierrez, astronaut; William Hanna, animator; Neil Patrick Harris, actor; Carl Hatch, senator; Tony Hillerman, author; Conrad Hilton, hotel executive; Dennis Hopper, actor; Peter Hurd, artist; Preston Jones, playwright and actor; Ralph Kiner, baseball player and sportscaster; Nancy Lopez, golfer; Maria Martínez, San Ildefonso Pueblo potter; Demi Moore, actress; Jim Morrison, singer and songwriter; Bill Mauldin, political cartoonist; Popé, San Juan Pueblo medicine man and leader; Georgia O'Keeffe, painter; Harrison Schmitt, astronaut and representative; Kim Stanley, actress; Slim Summerville, actor; Clyde Tombaugh, astronomer; Al Unser, Bobby Unser, auto racers; Victorio, Apache chief; Linda Wertheimer, NPR correspondent; Kathy Whitworth, golfer.

New York

Capital: Albany
Governor: George E. Pataki, R (to Jan. 2007)
Lieut. Governor: Mary Donohue, R (to Jan. 2007)
Senators: Charles E. Schumer, D (to Jan. 2005); Hillary Rodham Clinton, D (to Jan. 2007)
Secy. of State: Randy A. Daniels, R (apptd. by governor)
Comptroller: Alan G. Hevesi, D (to Jan. 2007)
Atty. General: Eliot Spitzer, D (to Jan. 2007)
Entered Union (rank): July 26, 1788 (11)
Present constitution adopted: 1777 (last revised 1938)
Motto: *Excelsior* (Ever upward)
State Symbols: animal, beaver (1975); **fish,** brook trout (1975); **gem,** garnet (1969); **flower,** rose (1955); **tree,** sugar maple (1956); **bird,** bluebird (1970); **insect,** ladybug (1989); **song,** "I Love New York" (1980)
Nickname: Empire State
Origin of name: In honor of the Duke of York
10 largest cities (2003 est.): New York, 8,085,742; Buffalo, 285,018; Rochester, 215,093; Yonkers, 197,388; Syracuse, 144,001; Albany, 93,919; New Rochelle, 72,582; Mount Vernon, 68,404; Schenectady, 61,016; Utica, 59,485
Land area: 47,214 sq mi. (122,284 sq km)
Geographic center: In Madison Co., 12 mi. S of Oneida and 26 mi. SW of Utica
Number of counties: 62
Largest county by population and area: Kings, 2,465,286 (2001); St. Lawrence, 2,686 sq mi.
State forest preserves: Adirondacks, 2,500,000 ac.; Catskills, 250,000 ac.
State parks: 152
Residents: New Yorker

2003 resident population est.: 19,190,115
2000 resident census population (rank): 18,976,457 (3). **Male:** 9,146,748 (48.2%); **Female:** 9,829,709 (51.8%). **White:** 12,893,689 (67.9%); **Black:** 3,014,385 (15.9%); **American Indian:** 82,461 (0.4%); **Asian:** 1,044,976 (5.5%); **Other race:** 1,341,946 (7.1%); **Two or more races:** 590,182 (3.1%); **Hispanic/Latino:** 2,867,583 (15.1%). **2000 percent population 18 and over:** 75.3; **65 and over:** 12.9; **median age:** 35.9.

Giovanni da Verrazano, an Italian-born navigator sailing for France, discovered New York Bay in 1524. Henry Hudson, an Englishman employed by the Dutch, reached the bay and sailed up the river now bearing his name in 1609, the same year that northern New York was explored and claimed for France by Samuel de Champlain.

In 1624 the first permanent Dutch settlement was established at Fort Orange (now Albany). One year later Peter Minuit purchased Manhattan Island from the Indians for trinkets worth about 60 Dutch guilders and founded the Dutch colony of New Amsterdam (now New York City), which was surrendered to the English in 1664.

New York's extremely rapid commercial growth may be partly attributed to Gov. De Witt Clinton, who pushed through the construction of the Erie Canal (Buffalo to Albany), which was opened in 1825. Today, the 641-mile Gov. Thomas E. Dewey Thruway connects New York City with Buffalo and with Connecticut, Massachusetts, and Pennsylvania express highways. Two toll-free superhighways, the Adirondack Northway (linking Albany with the Canadian border) and the North-South Expressway (crossing central New York from the Pennsylvania border to the Thousand Islands), have been opened.

The great metropolis of New York City is the nerve center of the nation. It is a leader in manufacturing, foreign trade, commerce and banking, book and magazine publishing, and theatrical production. A leading seaport, its John F. Kennedy International Airport is one of the busiest airports in the world. New York is also home to the New York Stock Exchange, the largest in the world. The printing and publishing industry is the city's largest manufacturing employer, with the apparel industry second.

Nearly all the rest of the state's manufacturing is done on Long Island, along the Hudson River north to Albany, and through the Mohawk Valley, Central New York, and Southern Tier regions to Buffalo. The St. Lawrence seaway and power projects have opened the North Country to industrial expansion and have given the state a second seacoast.

The state ranks seventh in the nation in manufacturing, with 805,200 employees in 2002. The principal industries are printing and publishing, industrial machinery and equipment, electronic equipment, and instruments. The convention and tourist business is also an important source of income.

New York farms produce cattle and calves, corn and poultry, and vegetables and fruits. The state is a leading wine producer.

Major points of interest are Castle Clinton, Fort Stanwix, and Statue of Liberty National Monuments; Niagara Falls; U.S. Military Academy at West Point; National Historic Sites that include homes of Franklin D. Roosevelt at Hyde Park and Theodore Roosevelt in Oyster Bay and New York City; the Women's Rights National Historical Park in Seneca Falls; National Memorials, including Grant's Tomb and Federal Hall in New York City; Fort Ticonderoga; the Baseball Hall of Fame in Cooperstown; and the United Nations, skyscrapers, museums, theaters, and parks in New York City.

Selected famous natives and residents: Kareem Abdul-Jabbar, basketball player; Lucille Ball, actress; Humphrey Bogart, actor; James Cagney, actor; Maria Callas, opera singer; Benjamin N. Cardozo, jurist; Paddy Chayefsky, playwright; Peter Cooper, industrialist and philanthropist; Aaron Copland, composer; Tom Cruise, actor; Sammy Davis, Jr., actor and singer; Agnes de Mille, choreographer; Eamon De Valera, president of Ireland; George Eastman, inventor; Millard Fillmore, president; Lou Gehrig, baseball player; George Gershwin, composer; Learned Hand, jurist; Edward Hopper, painter; Julia Ward Howe, poet and reformer; Charles Evans Hughes, jurist; Washington Irving, author; Henry James, novelist; John Jay, jurist; Michael Jordan, basketball player; Jerome Kern, composer; Rockwell Kent, painter; Vince Lombardi, football coach; Chico, Groucho, Harpo, and Zeppo Marx, comedians; Herman Melville, author; Ethel Merman, singer and actress; Ogden Nash, poet; Rosie O'Donnell, comedian; Eugene O'Neill, playwright; Red Jacket, Seneca chief; John D. Rockefeller, industrialist; Norman Rockwell, painter and illustrator; Mickey Rooney, actor; Anna Eleanor Roosevelt, reformer and humanitarian; Franklin D. Roosevelt, president; Theodore Roosevelt, president; Jonas Salk, polio researcher; Margaret Sanger, birth control advocate; Beverly Sills, opera singer; Barbara Stanwyck, actress; Risë Stevens, opera singer; Joe Torre, baseball player and manager; Richard Tucker, tenor; Martin Van Buren, president; Mae West, actress; Walt Whitman, poet; Edith Wharton, novelist.

North Carolina

Capital: Raleigh
Governor: Mike Easley, D (to Jan. 2005)
Lieut. Governor: Beverly Perdue, D (to Jan. 2005)
Senators: John Edwards, D (to Jan. 2005);
   Elizabeth Dole, R (to Jan. 2009)
Secy. of State: Elaine F. Marshall, D (to Jan. 2005)
Treasurer: Richard H. Moore, D (to Jan. 2005)
Atty. General: Roy Cooper, D (to Jan. 2005)
Entered Union (rank): Nov. 21, 1789 (12)
Present constitution adopted: 1971
Motto: *Esse quam videri* (To be rather than to seem)
State Symbols: flower, dogwood (1941); **tree,** pine (1963); **bird,** cardinal (1943); **mammal,** gray squirrel (1969); **insect,** honeybee (1973); **reptile,** eastern box turtle (1979); **gemstone,** emerald (1973); **shell,** scotch bonnet (1965); **historic boat,** shad boat (1987); **beverage,** milk (1987); **rock,** granite (1979); **dog,** plott hound (1989); **song,** "The Old North State" (1927); **colors,** red and blue (1945); **fruit,** scuppernong grape (2001)
Nickname: Tar Heel State
Origin of name: In honor of Charles I of England
10 largest cities (2003 est.): Charlotte, 584,658; Raleigh, 316,802; Greensboro, 229,110; Durham, 198,376; Winston-Salem, 190,299; Fayetteville, 124,372; Cary, 99,824; High Point, 91,543; Wilmington, 91,137; Asheville, 69,045
Land area: 48,711 sq mi. (126,161 sq km)
Geographic center: In Chatham Co., 10 mi. NW of Sanford
Number of counties: 100
Largest county by population and area: Mecklenburg, 716,407 (2001); Robeson, 949 sq mi.
State forests: 6
State parks: 33 (125,000 ac.)
Residents: North Carolinian
2003 resident population est.: 8,407,248
2000 resident census population (rank): 8,049,313 (11). **Male:** 3,942,695 (49.0%); **Female:** 4,106,618 (51.0%). **White:** 5,804,656 (72.1%); **Black:** 1,737,545 (21.6%); **American Indian:** 99,551 (1.2%); **Asian:**

113,689 (1.4%); **Other race:** 186,629 (2.3%); **Two or more races:** 103,260 (1.3%); **Hispanic/Latino:** 378,963 (4.7%). **2000 percent population 18 and over:** 75.6; **65 and over:** 12.0; **median age:** 35.3.

English colonists, sent by Sir Walter Raleigh, unsuccessfully attempted to settle Roanoke Island in 1585 and 1587. Virginia Dare, born there in 1587, was the first child of English parentage born in America.

In 1653 the first permanent settlements were established by English colonists from Virginia near the Roanoke and Chowan rivers. The region was established as an English proprietary colony in 1663–1665 and in its early history was the scene of Culpepper's Rebellion (1677), the Quaker-led Cary Rebellion (1708), the Tuscarora Indian War (1711–1713), and many pirate raids.

During the American Revolution, there was relatively little fighting within the state, but many North Carolinians saw action elsewhere. Despite considerable pro-Union, antislavery sentiment, North Carolina joined the Confederacy during the Civil War.

North Carolina is the nation's largest furniture, tobacco, brick, and textile producer. Metalworking, chemicals, and paper are also important industries. The major agricultural products are tobacco, corn, cotton, hay, peanuts, and vegetable crops. The state is the country's leading producer of mica and lithium.

Tourism is also important, with visitors spending more than $1 billion annually. Sports include year-round golfing, skiing at mountain resorts, both fresh- and salt-water fishing, and hunting.

Among the major attractions are the Great Smoky Mountains, the Blue Ridge National Parkway, the Cape Hatteras and Cape Lookout National Seashores, the Wright Brothers National Memorial at Kitty Hawk, Guilford Courthouse and Moores Creek National Military Parks, Carl Sandburg's home near Hendersonville, and the Old Salem Restoration in Winston-Salem.

Selected famous natives and residents: David Brinkley, TV newscaster; Howard Cosell, sportscaster; Virginia Dare, first person born in America to English parents; Elizabeth Dole, government official; James B. Duke, industrialist; Donna Fargo, singer; Roberta Flack, singer; Ava Gardner, actress; Richard Gatling, inventor; Billy Graham, evangelist; Kathryn Grayson, singer and actress; Andy Griffith, actor; Jesse Helms, politician; O. Henry, writer; Barbara Howar, broadcaster and writer; Andrew Johnson, president; Charles Kuralt, TV journalist; Sugar Ray Leonard, boxer; Dolley Madison, first lady; Ronnie Milsap, singer; Thelonious Monk, pianist; Alfred Moore, jurist; Edward R. Murrow, commentator and government official; Walter Hines Page, journalist and ambassador; Floyd Patterson, boxer; Richard Petty, auto racer; James K. Polk, president; Soupy Sales, comedian; Earl Scruggs, bluegrass musician; Randy Travis, musician; John Scott Trotter, orchestra leader; Thomas Wolfe, novelist.

North Dakota

Capital: Bismarck
Governor: John Hoeven, R (to Dec. 15, 2004)
Lieut. Governor: Jack Dalrymple, R (to Dec. 15, 2004)
Senators: Kent Conrad, D (to Jan. 2007);
   Byron L. Dorgan, D (to Jan. 2005)
Secy. of State: Alvin A. Jaeger, R (to Dec. 31, 2004)
Treasurer: Kathi Gilmore, D (to Dec. 31, 2004)
Atty. General: Wayne Stenehjem, R (to Dec. 31, 2004)
Organized as territory: March 2, 1861
Entered Union (rank): Nov. 2, 1889 (39)
Present constitution adopted: 1889

Motto: Liberty and union, now and forever: one and inseparable

State Symbols: tree, American elm (1947); **bird,** western meadowlark (1947); **song,** "North Dakota Hymn" (1947); **fish,** northern pike (1969); **grass,** western wheatgrass (1977); **fossil,** teredo petrified wood (1967); **beverage,** milk (1983); **state march,** Spirit of the Land (1975); **flower,** wild prairie rose (1907); **equine,** Nokota horse (1993); **dance,** square dance (1995)

Nickname: Sioux State; Flickertail State; Peace Garden State; Rough Rider State

Origin of name: From the Sioux tribe, meaning "allies"

10 largest cities (2003 est.): Fargo, 91,484; Bismarck, 56,344; Grand Forks, 48,618; Minot, 35,424; Mandan, 16,781; West Fargo, 16,431; Dickinson, 15,683; Jamestown, 15,158; Williston, 12,224; Wahpeton, 8,443

Land area: 68,976 sq mi. (178,648 sq km)

Geographic center: In Sheridan Co., 5 mi. SW of McClusky

Number of counties: 53

Largest county by population and area: Cass, 124,021 (2001); McKenzie, 2,742 sq mi.

State parks: 20 (14,822 ac.)

Residents: North Dakotan

2003 resident population est.: 633,837

2000 resident census population (rank): 642,200 (47). **Male:** 320,524 (49.9%); **Female:** 321,676 (50.1%). **White:** 593,181 (92.4%); **Black:** 3,916 (0.6%); **American Indian:** 31,329 (4.9%); **Asian:** 3,606 (0.6%); **Other race:** 2,540 (0.4%); **Two or more races:** 7,398 (1.2%); **Hispanic/Latino:** 7,786 (1.2%). **2000 percent population 18 and over:** 75.0; **65 and over:** 14.7; **median age:** 36.2.

North Dakota was explored in 1738–1740 by French Canadians led by Sieur de la Verendrye. In 1803, the U.S. acquired most of North Dakota from France in the Louisiana Purchase. Lewis and Clark explored the region in 1804–1806, and the first settlements were made at Pembina in 1812 by Scottish and Irish families while this area was still in dispute between the U.S. and Great Britain. In 1818, the U.S. obtained the northeast part of North Dakota by treaty with Great Britain and took possession of Pembina in 1823. However, the region remained largely unsettled until the construction of the railroad in the 1870s and 1880s.

North Dakota is the most rural of all the states, with farms covering more than 90% of the land. North Dakota ranks first in the nation's production of spring and durum wheat; other agricultural products include barley, rye, sunflowers, dry edible beans, honey, oats, flaxseed, sugar beets, hay, beef cattle, sheep, and hogs.

Recently, manufacturing industries have grown, especially food processing and farm equipment. The state's coal and oil reserves are plentiful, and it also produces natural gas, lignite, clay, sand, and gravel.

The Garrison Dam on the Missouri River provides extensive irrigation and produces 400,000 kilowatts of electricity for the Missouri Basin areas.

Known for its waterfowl, grouse, pheasant, and deer hunting and bass, trout, and pike fishing, North Dakota has 20 state parks and recreation areas. Points of interest include the International Peace Garden near Dunseith, Fort Union Trading Post National Historic Site near Williston, Knife River Indian Villages National Historic Site in Stanton, the State Capitol at Bismarck, the Badlands, Theodore Roosevelt National Park, and Fort Abraham Lincoln State Park.

Selected famous natives and residents: Lynn Anderson, singer; Maxwell Anderson, playwright; Elizabeth Bodine, humanitarian; Dr. Anne Carlsen, educator; Warren Christopher, statesman; Ronald N. Davies, jurist; Angie Dickinson, actress; Ivan Dmitre, artist; Carl Ben Eielson, aviator; Phyllis Frelich, actress; Bertin C. Gamble, founder of Gamble-Skogmo; William H. Gass, writer and philosopher; Brynhild Haugland, state legislator; Phil D. Jackson, basketball player and coach; Dr. Leon O. Jacobson, researcher and educator; Harold K. Johnson, general; David C. Jones, general; Louis L'Amour, author; Peggy Lee, singer; William Lemke, representative; Roger Maris, baseball player; Marquis de Mores, cattleman who established Medora; Gerald P. Nye, senator; Casper Oimoen, skier; William A. Owens, admiral; Arthur Peterson, radio and TV actor; Cliff (Fido) Purpur, hockey player and coach; James Rosenquist, painter; Harold Schafer, founder of Gold Seal Co.; Eric Sevareid, TV commentator; Ann Sothern, actress; Dorothy Stickney, actress; Edward K. Thompson, editor; Era Bell Thompson, editor; Tommy Tucker, band leader; Lawrence Welk, band leader; Larry Woiwode, writer.

Ohio

Capital: Columbus

Governor: Bob Taft II, R (to Jan. 2007)

Lieut. Governor: Jennette Bradley, R (to Jan. 2007)

Senators: Mike DeWine, R (to Jan. 2007); George V. Voinovich, R (to Jan. 2005)

Secy. of State: J. Kenneth Blackwell, R (to Jan. 2007)

Treasurer: Joseph T. Deters, R (to Jan. 2007)

Atty. General: Jim Petro, R (to Jan. 2007)

Entered Union (rank): March 1, 1803 (17)

Present constitution adopted: 1851

Motto: With God all things are possible

State Symbols: flower, scarlet carnation (1904); **tree,** buckeye (1953); **bird,** cardinal (1933); **insect,** ladybug (1975); **gemstone,** flint (1965); **song,** "Beautiful Ohio" (1969); **beverage,** tomato juice (1965); **fossil,** trilobite (1985); **animal,** white-tailed deer (1988); **wildflower,** large white trillium (1987)

Nickname: Buckeye State

Origin of name: From an Iroquoian word meaning "great river"

10 largest cities (2003 est.): Columbus, 728,432; Cleveland, 461,324; Cincinnati, 317,361; Toledo, 308,973; Akron, 212,215; Dayton, 161,696; Parma, 83,861; Youngstown, 79,271; Canton, 79,255; Lorain, 67,955

Land area: 40,948 sq mi. (106,055 sq km)

Geographic center: In Delaware Co., 25 mi. NNE of Columbus

Number of counties: 88

Largest county by population and area: Cuyahoga, 1,380,421 (2001); Ashtabula, 703 sq mi.

State forests: 20 (more than 183,000 ac.)

State parks: 73 (more than 204,000 ac.)

Residents: Ohioan

2003 resident population est.: 11,435,798

2000 resident census population (rank): 11,353,140 (7). **Male:** 5,512,262 (48.6%); **Female:** 5,840,878 (51.4%). **White:** 9,645,453 (85.0%); **Black:** 1,301,307 (11.5%); **American Indian:** 24,486 (0.2%); **Asian:** 132,633 (1.2%); **Other race:** 88,627 (0.8%); **Two or more races:** 157,885 (1.4%); **Hispanic/Latino:** 217,123 (1.9%). **2000 percent population 18 and over:** 74.6; **65 and over:** 13.3; **median age:** 36.2.

First explored for France by Robert Cavelier, Sieur de la Salle, in 1669, the Ohio region became British property after the French and Indian Wars. Ohio was acquired by the U.S. after the Revolutionary War in 1783. In 1788, the first permanent settlement was established at Marietta, capital of the Northwest Territory.

The 1790s saw severe fighting with the Indians in Ohio; a major battle was won by Maj. Gen. Anthony

Wayne at Fallen Timbers in 1794. In the War of 1812, Commodore Oliver H. Perry defeated the British in the Battle of Lake Erie on Sept. 10, 1813.

Ohio is one of the nation's industrial leaders, ranking third in manufacturing employment nationwide. Important manufacturing centers are located in or near Ohio's major cities. Akron is known for rubber; Canton for roller bearings; Cincinnati for jet engines and machine tools; Cleveland for auto assembly, auto parts, and steel; Dayton for office machines, refrigeration, and heating and auto equipment; Youngstown and Steubenville for steel; and Toledo for glass and auto parts.

The state's fertile soil produces soybeans, corn, oats, greenhouse and nursery products, wheat, hay, and fruit, including apples, peaches, strawberries, and grapes. More than half of Ohio's farm receipts come from dairy farming and sheep and hog raising. Ohio ranks fourth among the states in lime production and also ranks high in sand and gravel and crushed stone production.

Tourism is a valuable revenue producer, bringing in $25.7 billion in 2000. Attractions include the Rock and Roll Hall of Fame, Indian burial grounds at Mound City Group National Monument, Perry's Victory International Peace Memorial, the Pro Football Hall of Fame at Canton, and the homes of presidents Grant, Taft, Hayes, Harding, and Garfield.

Selected famous natives and residents: Neil Armstrong, astronaut; Kathleen Battle, soprano; George Bellows, painter and lithographer; Ambrose Bierce, journalist; Erma Bombeck, columnist; Bill Boyd (Hopalong Cassidy), actor; Milton Caniff, cartoonist; Hart Crane, poet; George Armstrong Custer, army officer; Dorothy Dandridge, actress; Doris Day, singer and actress; Clarence Darrow, lawyer; Ruby Dee, actress; Rita Dove, poet; Hugh Downs, TV broadcaster; Thomas A. Edison, inventor; Clark Gable, actor; James A. Garfield, president; Lillian Gish, actress; John Glenn, astronaut and senator; Ulysses S. Grant, president; Warren G. Harding, president; Rutherford Hayes, president; Benjamin Harrison, president; William Dean Howells, novelist and critic; Zane Grey, author; Robert Henri, painter; Kenisaw Mountain Landis, first baseball commissioner; Dean Martin, singer and actor; William McKinley, president; Paul Newman, actor; Jack Nicklaus, golfer; Annie Oakley, markswoman; Norman Vincent Peale, clergyman; Tyrone Power, actor; Judith Resnik, astronaut; Eddie Rickenbacker, aviator; Roy Rogers, actor and singer; Arthur M. Schlesinger, Jr., historian; William Tecumseh Sherman, army general; Gloria Steinem, feminist; William H. Taft, president; Tecumseh, Shawnee Indian chief; Lowell Thomas, explorer and commentator; James Thurber, author and cartoonist; Orville Wright, inventor; Cy Young, baseball player.

Oklahoma

Capital: Oklahoma City
Governor: Brad Henry, D (to Jan. 2007)
Lieut. Governor: Mary Fallin, R (to Jan. 2007)
Senators: James M. Inhofe, R (to Jan. 2009);
    Don Nickles, R (to Jan. 2005)
Secy. of State: M. Susan Savage, D (to Jan. 2007)
Treasurer: Robert Butkin, D (to Jan. 2007)
Atty. General: W. A. Drew Edmondson, D (to Jan. 2007)
Organized as territory: May 2, 1890
Entered Union (rank): Nov. 16, 1907 (46)
Present constitution adopted: 1907
Motto: *Labor omnia vincit* (Labor conquers all things)
State Symbols: flower, mistletoe (1893); **tree,** redbud (1937); **bird,** scissor-tailed flycatcher (1951); **animal,** bison (1972); **reptile,** mountain boomer lizard (1969); **stone,** rose rock (barite rose) (1968); **colors,** green and white (1915); **song,** "Oklahoma" (1953); **beverage,** milk; **butterfly,** black swallowtail; **fish,**

white or sand bass; **folk dance,** square dance; **furbearer,** raccoon; **game animal,** white-tailed deer; **grass,** Indiangrass; **insect,** honeybee; **musical instrument,** fiddle; **poem,** "Howdy Folks," David Randolph Milsten; **waltz,** "Oklahoma Wind"; **wildflower,** Indian blanket
Nickname: Sooner State
Origin of name: From two Choctaw Indian words meaning "red people"
10 largest cities (2003 est.): Oklahoma City, 523,303; Tulsa, 387,807; Norman, 99,197; Lawton, 91,730; Broken Arrow, 83,607; Edmond, 71,643; Midwest City, 54,662; Enid, 46,436; Moore, 44,987; Stillwater, 41,320
Land area: 68,667 sq mi. (177,848 sq km)
Geographic center: In Oklahoma Co., 8 mi. N of Oklahoma City
Number of counties: 77
Largest county by population and area: Oklahoma, 662,153 (2001); Osage, 2,251 sq mi.
State parks: 51 (72,000 ac.)
Residents: Oklahoman
2003 resident population est.: 3,511,532
2000 resident census population (rank): 3,450,654 (27). **Male:** 1,696,895 (49.1%); **Female:** 1,754,759 (50.9%). **White:** 2,628,434 (76.2%); **Black:** 260,968 (7.6%); **American Indian:** 273,230 (7.9%); **Asian:** 46,767 (1.4%); **Other race:** 82,898 (2.4%); **Two or more races:** 155,985 (4.5%); **Hispanic/Latino:** 179,304 (5.2%). **2000 percent population 18 and over:** 74.1; **65 and over:** 13.2; **median age:** 35.5.

Francisco Vásquez de Coronado first explored the region for Spain in 1541. The U.S. acquired most of Oklahoma in 1803 in the Louisiana Purchase from France; the Western Panhandle region became U.S. territory with the annexation of Texas in 1845.

Set aside as Indian Territory in 1834, the region was divided into Indian Territory and Oklahoma Territory on May 2, 1890. The two were combined to make a new state, Oklahoma, on Nov. 16, 1907.

On April 22, 1889, the first day homesteading was permitted, 50,000 people swarmed into the area. Those who tried to beat the noon starting gun were called "Sooners," hence the state's nickname.

Oil made Oklahoma a rich state, but natural-gas production has now surpassed it. Oil refining, meat packing, food processing, and machinery manufacturing (especially construction and oil equipment) are important industries. Minerals produced in Oklahoma include helium, gypsum, zinc, cement, coal, copper, and silver.

Oklahoma's rich plains produce bumper yields of wheat, as well as large crops of sorghum, hay, cotton, and peanuts. More than half of Oklahoma's annual farm receipts are contributed by livestock products, including cattle, dairy products, swine, and broilers.

Tourist attractions include the National Cowboy Hall of Fame in Oklahoma City, the Will Rogers Memorial in Claremore, the Cherokee Cultural Center with a restored Cherokee village, the restored Fort Gibson Stockade near Muskogee, the Lake Texoma recreation area, pari-mutuel horse racing at Remington Park in Oklahoma City, and Blue Ribbon Downs in Sallisaw.

Selected famous natives and residents: Johnny Bench, baseball player; John Berryman, poet; Garth Brooks, singer; Iron Eyes Cody, Cherokee actor; L. Gordon Cooper, astronaut; Ralph Ellison, writer; James Garner, actor; Owen K. Garriott, astronaut; Vince Gill, singer; Chester Gould, cartoonist; Woody Guthrie, singer and composer; Roy Harris, composer; Paul Harvey, broadcaster; Van Heflin, actor; Ron Howard, actor and director; Ben Johnson, actor; Jennifer Jones, actress; Jeane Kirkpatrick, educator and public-affairs spokesperson; Shannon Lucid, astronaut; Wilma P. Mankiller, principal chief of the Cherokee Nation of Oklahoma; Mickey Mantle, baseball player; Reba McEntire, singer; Shannon Miller, Olympic gymnast; Bill Moyers, journalist; Daniel Patrick Moynihan, N.Y. senator; Patti Page, singer; Mary Kay Place, actress and writer; Tony Randall, actor; Oral Roberts, evangelist; Dale Robertson, actor; Will Rogers, humorist; Dan Rowan, comedian; Thomas P. Stafford, astronaut; Maria Tallchief, ballerina; Jim Thorpe, athlete; Alfre Woodard, actress.

Oregon

Capital: Salem
Governor: Ted Kulongoski, D (to Jan. 2007)
Senators: Gordon Smith, R (to Jan. 2009);
  Ron Wyden, D (to Jan. 2005)
Secy. of State: Bill Bradbury, D (to Jan. 2005)
Treasurer: Randall Edwards, D (to Jan. 2005)
Atty. General: Hardy Myers, D (to Jan. 2005)
Organized as territory: Aug. 14, 1848
Entered Union (rank): Feb. 14, 1859 (33)
Present constitution adopted: 1859
Motto: *Alis volat Propriis* (She flies with her own wings)
  (1987)
State Symbols: flower, Oregon grape (1899); **tree,**
  douglas fir (1939); **animal,** beaver (1969); **bird,**
  western meadowlark (1927); **fish,** chinook salmon
  (1961); **rock,** thunderegg (1965); **colors,** navy blue and
  gold (1959); **song,** "Oregon, My Oregon" (1927);
  insect, swallowtail butterfly (1979); **dance,** square
  dance (1977); **nut,** hazelnut (1989); **gemstone,**
  sunstone (1987); **seashell,** Oregon hairy triton (1991);
  beverage, milk (1997); **mushroom,** Pacific golden
  chanterelle (1999)
Nickname: Beaver State
Origin of name: Unknown. However, it is generally
  accepted that the name, first used by Jonathan Carver
  in 1778, was taken from the writings of Maj. Robert
  Rogers, an English army officer.
10 largest cities (2003 est.): Portland, 538,544; Salem,
  142,914; Eugene, 142,185; Gresham, 95,816;
  Beaverton, 80,520; Hillsboro, 77,709; Medford, 66,638;
  Bend, 59,779; Springfield, 54,773; Corvallis, 50,126
Land area: 95,997 sq mi. (248,632 sq km)
Geographic center: In Crook Co., 25 mi. SSE of
  Prineville
Number of counties: 36
Largest county by population and area: Multnomah,
  665,810 (2001); Harney, 10,135 sq mi.
State forests: 820,000 ac.
State parks: 240 (93,330 ac.)
Residents: Oregonian
2003 resident population est.: 3,559,596
2000 resident census population (rank): 3,421,399
  (28). **Male:** 1,696,550 (49.6%); **Female:** 1,724,849
  (50.4%). **White:** 2,961,623 (86.6%); **Black:** 55,662
  (1.6%); **American Indian:** 45,211 (1.3%); **Asian:**
  101,350 (3.0%); **Other race:** 144,832 (4.2%); **Two or
  more races:** 104,745 (3.1%); **Hispanic/Latino:**
  275,314 (8.0%). **2000 percent population 18 and
  over:** 75.3; **65 and over:** 12.8; **median age:** 36.3.

Spanish and English sailors are believed to have sighted the Oregon coast in the 1500s and 1600s. Capt. James Cook, seeking the Northwest Passage, charted some of the coastline in 1778. In 1792, Capt. Robert Gray, in the *Columbia*, discovered the river named after his ship and claimed the area for the U.S.

In 1805 the Lewis and Clark expedition explored the area. John Jacob Astor's fur depot, Astoria, was founded in 1811. Disputes for control of Oregon between American settlers and the Hudson Bay Company were finally resolved in the 1846 Oregon Treaty, in which Great Britain gave up claims to the region.

Oregon has a $3.3 billion lumber and wood products industry, and an $859 million paper and allied manufacturing industry. Its salmon-fishing industry is one of the world's largest.

In agriculture, the state leads in growing peppermint, cover seed crops, blackberries, boysenberries, loganberries, black raspberries, and hazelnuts. It is second in raising hops, red raspberries, prunes, snap beans, and onions.

With the low-cost electric power provided by dams, Oregon has developed steadily as a manufacturing state. Leading manufactured items are lumber and plywood, metalwork, machinery, aluminum, chemicals, paper, food packing, and electronic equipment.

Crater Lake National Park, Mount Hood, and Bonneville Dam on the Columbia are major tourist attractions. Other points of interest include the Oregon Dunes National Recreation Area, Oregon Caves National Monument, Cape Perpetua in Siuslaw National Forest, Columbia River Gorge between The Dalles and Troutdale, Hells Canyon, Newberry Volcanic National Monument, and John Day Fossil Beds National Monument.

Selected famous natives and residents: James Beard, food expert; Raymond Carver, writer and poet; Homer C. Davenport, political cartoonist; David Douglas, botanist; Abigail Scott Duniway, women's suffrage advocate; Robert Gray, sea captain and discoverer of Columbia River; Matt Groening, cartoonist; Mark Hatfield, senator; Donald P. Hodel, secretary of the Interior; Chief Joseph, Nez Percé chief; Dave Kingman, baseball player; Ursula LeGuin, writer; Edwin Markham, poet; Phyllis McGinley, author; Linus Pauling, chemist; Jane Powell, actress and singer; John Reed, poet and author; Harvey W. Scott, editor; Doc Severinsen, band leader; Norton Simon, business executive; Paul M. Simon, Illinois senator; William E. Stafford, poet; Sally Struthers, actress.

Pennsylvania

Capital: Harrisburg
Governor: Ed Rendell, D (to Jan. 2007)
Lieut. Governor: Catherine Baker Knoll, D (to Jan.
  2007)
Senators: Rick Santorum, R (to Jan. 2007);
  Arlen Specter, R (to Jan. 2005)
Secy. of the Commonwealth: Pedro Cortes, D (at the
  pleasure of the governor)
Treasurer: Barbara Hafer, R (to Jan. 2005)
Atty. General: Gerald J. Pappert, R (to Jan. 2005)
Entered Union (rank): Dec. 12, 1787 (2)
Present constitution adopted: 1968
Motto: Virtue, liberty, and independence
State Symbols: flower, mountain laurel (1933); **tree,**
  hemlock (1931); **bird,** ruffed grouse (1931); **dog,**
  Great Dane (1965); **colors,** blue and gold (1907);
  song, "Pennsylvania" (1990)
Nickname: Keystone State
Origin of name: In honor of Adm. Sir William Penn,
  father of William Penn. It means "Penn's Woodland."
10 largest cities (2003 est.): Philadelphia, 1,479,339;
  Pittsburgh, 325,337; Allentown, 105,958; Erie,
  101,373; Upper Darby, 80,556; Reading, 80,305;
  Scranton, 74,320; Lower Merion, 58,802; Bensalem,
  58,639; Abington, 56,064
Land area: 44,817 sq mi. (116,076 sq km)
Geographic center: In Centre Co., 2½ mi. SW
  of Bellefonte
Number of counties: 67
Largest county by population and area: Philadelphia,

1,491,812 (2001); Lycoming, 1,235 sq mi.
State forests: over 2 mil. ac.
State parks: 116
Residents: Pennsylvanian
2003 resident population est.: 12,365,455
2000 resident census population (rank): 12,281,054 (6).
Male: 5,929,663 (48.3%); **Female:** 6,351,391 (51.7%).
White: 10,484,203 (85.4%); **Black:** 1,224,612 (10.0%);
American Indian: 18,348 (0.1%); **Asian:** 219,813
(1.8%); **Other race:** 188,437 (1.5%); **Two or more
races:** 142,224 (1.2%); **Hispanic/Latino:** 394,088
(3.2%). **2000 percent population 18 and over:** 76.2;
65 and over: 15.6; **median age:** 38.0.

Rich in historic lore, Pennsylvania territory was disputed in the early 1600s among the Dutch, the Swedes, and the English. England acquired the region in 1664 with the capture of New York, and in 1681 Pennsylvania was granted to William Penn, a Quaker, by King Charles II.

Philadelphia was the seat of the federal government almost continuously from 1776 to 1800; there the Declaration of Independence was signed in 1776 and the U.S. Constitution drawn up in 1787. Valley Forge, of Revolutionary War fame, and Gettysburg, site of the pivotal battle of the Civil War, are both in Pennsylvania. The Liberty Bell is located in a glass pavilion across from Independence Hall in Philadelphia.

The nation's first oil well was dug at Titusville in 1859, and the mining of iron ore and coal led to the development of the state's steel industry. More recently Pennsylvania's industry has diversified, although the state still leads the country in the production of specialty steel. The service, retail trade, and manufacturing sectors provide the most jobs; Pennsylvania is a leader in the production of chemicals and pharmaceuticals, food products, and electronic equipment.

Pennsylvania's 59,000 farms (occupying nearly 8 million acres) are the backbone of the state's economy, producing a wide variety of crops. Leading commodities are dairy products, cattle and calves, mushrooms, greenhouse and nursery products, poultry and eggs, a variety of fruits, sweet corn, potatoes, maple syrup, and Christmas trees.

Pennsylvania's rich heritage draws billions of tourist dollars annually. Among the chief attractions are the Gettysburg National Military Park, Valley Forge National Historical Park, Independence National Historical Park in Philadelphia, the Pennsylvania Dutch region, the Eisenhower farm near Gettysburg, and the Delaware Water Gap National Recreation Area.

Selected famous natives and residents: Louisa May Alcott, novelist; Marian Anderson, contralto; Maxwell Anderson, dramatist; Samuel Barber, composer; John Barrymore, actor; Donald Barthelme, author; Stephen Vincent Benét, poet and story writer; Daniel Boone, frontiersman; Ed Bradley, TV anchorman; James Buchanan, former president; Alexander Calder, sculptor; Rachel Carson, biologist and author; Mary Cassatt, painter; Henry Steele Commager, historian; Bill Cosby, actor; Stuart Davis, painter; Jimmy and Tommy Dorsey, band leaders; W. C. Fields, comedian; Stephen Foster, composer; Robert Fulton, inventor; Grace, Princess of Monaco; Martha Graham, choreographer; Alexander Haig, secretary of state; Marilyn Horne, mezzo-soprano; Lee Iacocca, auto executive; Reggie Jackson, baseball player; Gene Kelly, dancer and actor; Gelsey Kirkland, ballerina; S. S. Kresge, merchant; Mario Lanza, actor and singer; George C. Marshall, general; George McClellan, general; Margaret Mead, anthropologist; Andrew Mellon, financier; Tom Mix, actor; Arnold Palmer, golfer; Robert E. Peary, explorer; Man Ray, painter; Mary Roberts Rinehart, novelist; Betsy Ross, flagmaker; B. F. Skinner, psychologist; John Sloan, painter; Gertrude Stein, author; James Stewart, actor; John Updike, novelist; Honus Wagner, baseball player; Fred Waring, band leader; Ethel Waters, singer and actress; Anthony Wayne, military officer; August Wilson, poet, writer, and playwright; Wallis Warfield, Duchess of Windsor; Andrew Wyeth, painter.

Rhode Island

Capital: Providence
Governor: Don Carcieri, R (to Jan. 2007)
Lieut. Governor: Charles J. Fogarty, D (to Jan. 2007)
Senators: Jack Reed, D (to Jan. 2009);
Lincoln Chafee, R (to Jan. 2007)
Secy. of State: Matt Brown, D (to Jan. 2007)
Atty. General: Patrick Lynch, D (to Jan. 2007)
General Treasurer: Paul J. Tavares, D (to Jan. 2007)
Entered Union (rank): May 29, 1790 (13)
Present constitution adopted: 1843
Motto: Hope
State Symbols: flower, violet (unofficial) (1968); **tree,**
red maple (official) (1964); **bird,** Rhode Island red hen
(official) (1954); **shell,** quahog (official); **mineral,**
bowenite (1966); **stone,** cumberlandite (1966); **colors,**
blue, white, and gold (in state flag); **song,** "Rhode
Island" (1946)
Nickname: The Ocean State
Origin of name: From the Greek Island of Rhodes
10 largest cities (2003 est.): Providence, 176,365;
Warwick, 87,365; Cranston, 81,679; Pawtucket,
74,330; East Providence, 49,906; Woonsocket,
44,654; Coventry, 34,910; Cumberland, 33,683; North
Providence, 33,403; West Warwick, 29,996
Land area: 1,045 sq mi. (2,706 sq km)
Geographic center: In Kent Co., 1 mi. SSW
of Crompton
Number of counties: 5
Largest county by population and area: Providence,
627,314 (2001); Providence, 413 sq mi.
State forests: 11 (20,900 ac.)
State parks: 14
Residents: Rhode Islander
2003 resident population est.: 1,076,164
2000 resident census population (rank): 1,048,319
(43). **Male:** 503,635 (48.0%); **Female:** 544,684
(52.0%). **White:** 891,191 (85.0%); **Black:** 46,908
(4.5%); **American Indian:** 5,121 (0.5%); **Asian:**
23,665 (2.3%); **Other race:** 52,616 (5.0%); **Two or
more races:** 28,251 (2.7%); **Hispanic/Latino:** 90,820
(8.7%). **2000 percent population 18 and over:** 76.4;
65 and over: 14.5; **median age:** 36.7.

From its beginnings, Rhode Island has been distinguished by its support for freedom of conscience and action: Clergyman Roger Williams founded the present state capital, Providence, after being exiled by the Massachusetts Bay Colony Puritans in 1636. Williams was followed by other religious exiles who founded Pocasset, now Portsmouth, in 1638 and Newport in 1639.

Rhode Island's rebellious, authority-defying nature was further demonstrated by the burnings of the British revenue cutters *Liberty* and *Gaspee* prior to the Revolution; by its early declaration of independence from Great Britain in May 1776; by its refusal to participate actively in the War of 1812; and by Dorr's Rebellion of 1842, which protested property requirements for voting.

Rhode Island, smallest of the fifty states, is densely populated and highly industrialized. It is a major center for jewelry manufacturing. Electronics, metal, plastic products, and boat and ship construction are other important industries. Non-manufacturing employment includes research in health, medicine, and the ocean environment. Providence is a wholesale distribution center for New England.

Fishing ports are at Galilee and Newport. Rural areas of the state support small-scale farming, including grapes for local wineries, turf grass, and nursery stock. Tourism generates over a billion dollars a year in revenue.

Newport became famous as the summer capital of high society in the mid-19th century. Touro Synagogue (1763) is the oldest in the U.S. Other points of interest include the Roger Williams National Memorial in Providence, Samuel Slater's Mill in Pawtucket, the General Nathanael Greene Homestead in Coventry, and Block Island.

Selected famous natives and residents: Harry Anderson, actor; George M. Cohan, actor and dramatist; Eddie Dowling, actor and stage producer; Nelson Eddy, baritone and actor; Ann Smith Franklin, printer and almanac publisher; Charles Gorham, silversmith; Spalding Gray, writer, performance artist; Bobby Hackett, trumpeter; David Hartman, TV newscaster; Ruth Hussey, actress; Anne Hutchinson, religious leader; Thomas H. Ince, film producer; Wilbur John, Quaker leader; Van Johnson, actor; Clarence King, first director of the U.S. Geological Survey; Galway Kinnell, poet; Oliver La Farge, writer; Irving R. Levine, news correspondent; H. P. Lovecraft, author; Ida Lewis, lighthouse keeper; John McLaughlin, political commentator, broadcaster; Dana C. Munro, educator and historian; Matthew C. Perry, naval officer; Oliver Hazard Perry, naval officer; King Philip (Metacomet), Indian leader; Anthony Quinn, actor; Gilbert Stuart, painter; Sarah Helen (Power) Whitman, poet; Jemima Wilkinson, religious leader; Roger Williams, clergyman and founder of Rhode Island; Leonard Woodcock, labor union official; James Woods, actor.

South Carolina

Capital: Columbia
Governor: Mark Sanford, R (to Jan. 2007)
Lieut. Governor: R. Andre Bauer, R (to Jan. 2007)
Senators: Ernest Hollings, D (to Jan. 2005);
    Lindsey Graham, R (to Jan. 2009)
Secy. of State: Mark Hammond, R (to Jan. 2007)
Treasurer: Grady L. Patterson, Jr. , D (to Jan. 2007)
Atty. General: Henry McMaster, R (to Jan. 2007)
Entered Union (rank): May 23, 1788 (8)
Present constitution adopted: 1895
Mottoes: *Animis opibusque parati* (Prepared in mind and resources) and *Dum spiro spero* (While I breathe, I hope)
State Symbols: flower, Carolina yellow jessamine (1924); **tree,** palmetto tree (1939); **bird,** Carolina wren (1948); **song,** "Carolina" (1911)
Nickname: Palmetto State
Origin of name: In honor of Charles I of England
10 largest cities (2003 est.): Columbia, 117,357; Charleston, 101,024; North Charleston, 81,577; Rock Hill, 56,114; Greenville, 55,926; Mount Pleasant, 54,788; Sumter, 39,790; Spartanburg, 38,718; Hilton Head Island, 34,407; Summerville, 31,734
Land area: 30,109 sq mi. (77,982 sq km)
Geographic center: In Richland Co., 13 mi. SE of Columbia
Number of counties: 46
Largest county by population and area: Greenville, 386,693 (2001); Horry, 1,134 sq mi.
State forests: 4 (124,052 ac.)
State parks: 50 (61,726 ac.)
Residents: South Carolinian
2003 resident population est.: 4,147,152
2000 resident census population (rank): 4,012,012 (26). **Male:** 1,948,929 (48.6%); **Female:** 2,063,083 (51.4%). **White:** 2,695,560 (67.2%); **Black:** 1,185,216

(29.5%); **American Indian:** 13,718 (0.3%); **Asian:** 36,014 (0.9%); **Other race:** 39,926 (1.0%); **Two or more races:** 39,950 (1.0%); **Hispanic/Latino:** 95,076 (2.4%). **2000 percent population 18 and over:** 74.8; **65 and over:** 12.1; **median age:** 35.4.

Following exploration of the coast in 1521 by Francisco de Gordillo, the Spanish tried unsuccessfully to establish a colony near present-day Georgetown in 1526, and the French also failed to colonize Parris Island near Fort Royal in 1562. The first English settlement was made in 1670 at Albemarle Point on the Ashley River, but poor conditions drove the settlers to the site of Charleston (originally called Charles Town).

South Carolina, officially separated from North Carolina in 1729, was the scene of extensive military action during the Revolution and again during the Civil War. The Civil War began in 1861 as South Carolina troops fired on federal Fort Sumter in Charleston Harbor, and the state was the first to secede from the Union.

Once primarily agricultural, South Carolina today has many large textile and other mills that produce several times the output of its farms in cash value. Charleston makes asbestos, wood, pulp, steel products, chemicals, machinery, and apparel.

Farms have become fewer but larger in recent years. South Carolina ranks third in peach production; it ranks fourth in overall tobacco production. Other top agricultural commodities include nursery and greenhouse products, watermelons, peanuts, broilers and turkeys, and cattle and calves. The only commercial tea plantation in America is 20 mi south of Charleston on Wadmalaw Island.

Points of interest include Fort Sumter National Monument, Fort Moultrie, Fort Johnson, and aircraft carrier USS *Yorktown* in Charleston Harbor; the Middleton, Magnolia, and Cypress Gardens in Charleston; Cowpens National Battlefield; the Hilton Head resorts; and the Riverbanks Zoo and Botanical Garden in Columbia.

Selected famous natives and residents: Bernard Baruch, statesman; Mary McLeod Bethune, educator; James F. Byrnes, senator, jurist and secretary of state; John C. Calhoun, statesman; Mark Clark, general; Joe Frazier, prize fighter; Althea Gibson, tennis champion; Dizzy Gillespie, jazz trumpeter; DuBose Heyward, poet, playwright, and novelist; Andrew Jackson, president; Jesse Jackson, civil rights leader; Eartha Kitt, singer; Francis Marion ("Swamp Fox"), Revolutionary general; Ronald McNair, astronaut; John Rutledge, jurist; Strom Thurmond, politician; Charles Townes, physicist; William Westmoreland, general; Vanna White, TV personality.

South Dakota

Capital: Pierre
Governor: Mike Rounds, R (to Jan. 2007)
Lieut. Governor: Dennis Daugaard, R (to Jan. 2007)
Senators: Thomas A. Daschle, D (to Jan. 2005);
    Tim Johnson, D (to Jan. 2009)
Atty. General: Larry Long, R (to Jan. 2007)
Secy. of State: Chris Nelson, R (to Jan. 2007)
Treasurer: Vernon L. Larson, R (to Jan. 2007)
Organized as territory: March 2, 1861
Entered Union (rank): Nov. 2, 1889 (40)
Present constitution adopted: 1889
Motto: Under God the people rule
State Symbols: flower, American pasqueflower (1903); **grass,** Western wheat grass (1970); **soil,** houdek (1990); **tree,** black hills spruce (1947); **bird,** ring-necked pheasant (1943); **insect,** honeybee

(1978); **animal,** coyote (1949); **mineral stone,** rose quartz (1966); **gemstone,** fairburn agate (1966); **colors,** blue and gold (in state flag); **song,** "Hail! South Dakota" (1943); **fish,** walleye (1982); **musical instrument,** fiddle (1989); **dessert,** kuchen (2000)
Nicknames: Mount Rushmore State; Coyote State
Origin of name: From the Sioux tribe, meaning "allies"
10 largest cities (2003 est.): Sioux Falls, 133,834; Rapid City, 60,876; Aberdeen, 24,086; Watertown, 20,191; Brookings, 18,464; Mitchell, 14,677; Pierre, 13,939; Yankton, 13,440; Huron, 11,377; Vermillion, 10,070
Land area: 75,885 sq mi. (196,542 sq km)
Geographic center: In Hughes Co., 8 mi. NE of Pierre
Number of counties: 66 (64 county governments)
Largest county by population and area: Minnehaha, 150,327 (2001); Meade, 3,471 sq mi.
State forests: None[1]
State parks: 12 plus 39 recreational areas (87,269 ac.)[2]
Residents: South Dakotan
2003 resident population est.: 764,309
2000 resident census population (rank): 754,844 (46). **Male:** 374,558 (49.6%); **Female:** 380,286 (50.4%). **White:** 669,404 (88.7%); **Black:** 4,685 (0.6%); **American Indian:** 62,283 (8.3%); **Asian:** 4,378 (0.6%); **Other race:** 3,677 (0.5%); **Two or more races:** 10,156 (1.3%); **Hispanic/Latino:** 10,903 (1.4%). **2000 percent population 18 and over:** 73.2; **65 and over:** 14.3; **median age:** 35.6.

1. No designated state forests; about 13,000 ac. of state land is forestland. 2. Acreage includes 39 recreation areas and 80 roadside parks, in addition to 12 state parks.

Exploration of this area began in 1743 when Louis-Joseph and François Verendrye came from France in search of a route to the Pacific.

The U.S. acquired the region as part of the Louisiana Purchase in 1803, and it was explored by Lewis and Clark in 1804–1806. Fort Pierre, the first permanent settlement, was established in 1817.

Settlement of South Dakota did not begin in earnest until the arrival of the railroad in 1873 and the discovery of gold in the Black Hills in 1874.

Agriculture is a cultural and economic mainstay, but it no longer leads the state in employment or share of gross state product. Durable-goods manufacturing and private services have evolved as the drivers of the economy. Tourism is also a booming industry in the state, generating over a billion dollars' worth of economic activity each year.

South Dakota is the second-largest producer of flaxseed and sunflower seed in the nation. It is the third-largest producer of hay and rye.

The Black Hills are the highest mountains east of the Rockies. Mt. Rushmore, in this group, is famous for the likenesses of Washington, Jefferson, Lincoln, and Theodore Roosevelt, which were carved in granite by Gutzon Borglum. A memorial to Crazy Horse is also being carved in granite near Custer.

Other tourist attractions include the Badlands; the World's Only Corn Palace, in Mitchell; and the city of Deadwood, where Wild Bill Hickok was killed in 1876 and where gambling was recently legalized.

Selected famous natives and residents: Sparky Anderson, baseball manager; Gertrude Bonnin (Zitkala-Sa), Sioux writer and pan-Indian activist; Tom Brokaw, TV newscaster; Robert Casey, writer; Myron Floren, accordionist; Joseph J. Foss, WW II Marine fighter ace; Mary Hart, TV host; Crazy Horse, Oglala chief; Oscar Howe, Sioux artist; Hubert H. Humphrey, vice president; Cheryl Ladd, actress; Ernest Orlando Lawrence, physicist; Russell Means, American Indian activist; George McGovern, politician; Arthur C. Mellette, first governor; Dorothy Provine, actress; Rain-in-the-Face, Hunkpapa Sioux chief; Red Cloud, chief of the Oglala Sioux; Ben Reifel, Brulé Sioux congressman; Ole Edvart Rølvaag, writer; Sitting Bull, chief of Hunkpappa Sioux; Norm Van Brocklin, football player; Mamie Van Doren, actress.

Tennessee

Capital: Nashville
Governor: Phil Bredesen, D (to Jan. 2007)
Lieut. Governor: John S. Wilder, D (to Jan. 2007)
Senators: Lamar Alexander, R (to Jan. 2009); William Frist, R (to Jan. 2007)
Secy. of State: Riley C. Darnell, D (to Jan. 2005)
Atty. General: Paul G. Summers, D (to Feb. 2007)
Treasurer: Dale Sims, D (to Jan. 2007)
Comptroller: John G. Morgan (to Jan. 2003)
Entered Union (rank): June 1, 1796 (16)
Present constitution adopted: 1870; amended 1953, 1960, 1966, 1972, 1978
Motto: Agriculture and Commerce (1987)
Slogan: Tennessee—America at its best! (1965)
State Symbols: flower, iris (1933); **tree,** tulip poplar (1947); **bird,** mockingbird (1933); **horse,** Tennessee walking horse; **animal,** raccoon (1971); **wild flower,** passion flower (1973); **songs,** "Tennessee Waltz" (1965); "My Homeland, Tennessee" (1925); "When It's Iris Time in Tennessee" (1935); "My Tennessee" (1955); "Rocky Top" (1982); "Tennessee" (1992).
Nickname: Volunteer State
Origin of name: Of Cherokee origin; the exact meaning is unknown
10 largest cities (2003 est.): Memphis, 645,978; Nashville-Davidson,[1] 544,765; Knoxville, 173,278; Chattanooga, 154,887; Clarksville, 107,953; Murfreesboro, 78,074; Jackson, 61,110; Johnson City, 57,394; Franklin, 46,528; Kingsport, 44,231
Land area: 41,217 sq mi. (106,752 sq km)
Geographic center: In Rutherford Co., 5 mi. NE of Murfreesboro
Number of counties: 95
Largest county by population and area: Shelby, 896,013 (2001); Shelby, 755 sq mi.
State forests: 5
State parks: 80
Residents: Tennessean, Tennesseean
2003 resident population est.: 5,841,748
2000 resident census population (rank): 5,689,283 (16). **Male:** 2,770,275 (48.7%); **Female:** 2,919,008 (51.3%). **White:** 4,563,310 (80.2%); **Black:** 932,809 (16.4%); **American Indian:** 15,152 (0.3%); **Asian:** 56,662 (1.0%); **Other race:** 56,036 (1.0%); **Two or more races:** 63,109 (1.1%); **Hispanic/Latino:** 123,838 (2.2%). **2000 percent population 18 and over:** 75.4; **65 and over:** 12.4; **median age:** 35.9.

1. The city is part of a consolidated city-county government and is coextensive with Davidson County.

First visited by the Spanish explorer Hernando de Soto in 1540, the Tennessee area would later be claimed by both France and England as a result of the 1670s and 1680s explorations of Jacques Marquette and Louis Joliet, Sieur de la Salle, and James Needham and Gabriel Arthur. Great Britain obtained the area after the French and Indian Wars in 1763.

During 1784–1787, the settlers formed the "state" of Franklin, which was disbanded when the region was allowed to send representatives to the North Carolina legislature. In 1790 Congress organized the territory south of the Ohio River, and Tennessee joined the Union in 1796.

Although Tennessee joined the Confederacy during the Civil War, there was much pro-Union sentiment in the state, which was the scene of extensive military action.

The state is now predominantly industrial; the majority of its population lives in urban areas. Among the most important products are chemicals, textiles, apparel, electrical machinery, furniture, and leather goods. Other lines include food processing, lumber, primary metals, and metal products. The state ranks high in the production of marble, zinc, pyrite, and ball clay.

Tennessee is a leading tobacco-producing state. Other farming income is derived from livestock and dairy products, as well as greenhouse and nursery products and cotton.

With six other states, Tennessee shares the extensive federal reservoir developments on the Tennessee and Cumberland River systems. The Tennessee Valley Authority operates a number of dams and reservoirs in the state.

Among the major points of interest are the Andrew Johnson National Historic Site at Greeneville, the American Museum of Atomic Energy at Oak Ridge, Great Smoky Mountains National Park, the Hermitage (home of Andrew Jackson near Nashville), Rock City Gardens near Chattanooga, and three National Military Parks.

Selected famous natives and residents: James Agee, writer; Eddy Arnold, singer; Chet Atkins, guitarist; Julian Bond, Georgia legislator; Davy Crockett, frontiersman; David G. Farragut, first American admiral; Lester Flatt, bluegrass musician; Tennessee Ernie Ford, singer; Abe Fortas, jurist; Aretha Franklin, singer; Nikki Giovanni, poet; Al Gore, Jr., vice president; Red Grooms, artist; Isaac Hayes, composer; Benjamin L. Hooks, civil rights activist; Cordell Hull, secretary of state; Andrew Jackson, president; Andrew Johnson, president; Estes Kefauver, legislator; Anita Kerr, singer; Grace Moore, soprano; Dolly Parton, singer; Minnie Pearl, singer and comedienne; James K. Polk, president; Grantland Rice, sportswriter; Carl Rowan, journalist; Wilma Rudolph, sprinter; Sequoyah, Cherokee scholar and educator; Cybil Shepherd, actress; Dinah Shore, actress and singer; Tina Turner, singer; Alvin York, World War I hero.

Texas

Capital: Austin
Governor: Rick Perry, R (to Jan. 2007)
Lieut. Governor: David Dewhurst, R (to Jan. 2007)
Senators: John Cornyn, R (to Jan. 2009);
    Kay Bailey Hutchison, R (to Jan. 2007)
Secy. of State: Geoffrey S. Connor, R (apptd. by gov.)
Comptroller: Carole Keeton Strayhorn, R (to Jan. 2007)
Atty. General: Greg Abbott, R (to Jan. 2007)
Entered Union (rank): Dec. 29, 1845 (28)
Present constitution adopted: 1876
Motto: Friendship
State Symbols: flower, bluebonnet (1901); **tree,** pecan (1919); **bird,** mockingbird (1927); **song,** "Texas, Our Texas" (1929); **fish,** guadalupe bass (1989); **seashell,** lightning whelk (1987); **dish,** chili (1977); **folk dance,** square dance (1991); **fruit,** Texas red grapefruit (1993); **gem,** Texas blue topaz (1969); **gemstone cut,** Lone Star cut (1977); **grass,** sideoats grass (1971); **reptile,** horned lizard (1993); **stone,** petrified palmwood (1969); **plant,** prickly pear cactus; **insect,** monarch butterfly; **pepper,** jalapeño pepper; **mammal,** longhorn; **small mammal,** armadillo; **flying mammal,** Mexican free-tailed bat
Nickname: Lone Star State
Origin of name: From an Indian word meaning "friends"
10 largest cities (2003 est.): Houston, 2,009,690; San Antonio, 1,214,725; Dallas, 1,208,318; Austin, 672,011; Fort Worth, 585,122; El Paso, 584,113; Arlington, 355,007; Corpus Christi, 279,208; Plano, 241,991; Garland, 218,027

Land area: 261,797 sq mi. (678,054 sq km)
Geographic center: In McCulloch Co., 15 mi. NE of Brady
Number of counties: 254
Largest county by population and area: Harris, 3,460,589 (2001); Brewster, 6,193 sq mi.
State forests: 5 (7,314 ac.)
State parks[1]: 125 (587,216 ac.)
Residents: Texan
2003 resident population est.: 22,118,509
2000 resident census population (rank): 20,851,820 (2). **Male:** 10,352,910 (49.6%); **Female:** 10,498,910 (50.4%). **White:** 14,799,505 (71.0%); **Black:** 2,404,566 (11.5%); **American Indian:** 118,362 (0.6%); **Asian:** 562,319 (2.7%); **Other race:** 2,438,001 (11.7%); **Two or more races:** 514,633 (2.5%); **Hispanic/Latino:** 6,669,666 (32.0%). **2000 percent population 18 and over:** 71.8; **65 and over:** 9.9; **median age:** 32.3.

1. Includes state parks and natural areas, two state fishing piers, and one county park.

Spanish explorers, including Álvar Núñez Cabeza de Vaca and Francisco Vásquez de Coronado, were the first to visit the region in the 16th and 17th centuries, settling at Ysleta near El Paso in 1682. In 1685, Robert Cavelier, Sieur de la Salle, established a short-lived French colony at Matagorda Bay.

Americans, led by Stephen F. Austin, began to settle along the Brazos River in 1821 when Texas was controlled by Mexico, recently independent from Spain. In 1836, following a brief war between the American settlers in Texas and the Mexican government, the Independent Republic of Texas was proclaimed with Sam Houston as president. This war was famous for the battles of the Alamo and San Jacinto. After Texas became the state in 1845, border disputes led to the Mexican War of 1846–1848.

Possessing enormous natural resources, Texas is a major agricultural state and an industrial giant. Second only to Alaska in land area, it leads all other states in such categories as oil, cattle, sheep, and cotton. Texas ranches and farms also produce poultry and eggs, dairy products, greenhouse and nursery products, wheat, hay, rice, sugar cane, and peanuts, and a variety of fruits and vegetables.

Sulfur, salt, helium, asphalt, graphite, bromine, natural gas, cement, and clays are among the state's valuable resources. Chemicals, oil refining, food processing, machinery, and transportation equipment are among the major Texas manufacturing industries.

Millions of tourists spend well over $20.6 billion annually visiting more than 100 state parks, recreation areas, and points of interest such as the Gulf Coast resort area, the Lyndon B. Johnson Space Center in Houston, the Alamo in San Antonio, the state capital in Austin, and the Big Bend and Guadalupe Mountains National Park.

Selected famous natives and residents: Alvin Ailey, choreographer; Mary Kay Ash, cosmetics entrepreneur; Stephen Fuller Austin, founding father of Texas; Gene Autry, singer and actor; Carol Burnett, comedienne; George W. Bush, president and governor; Cyd Charisse, actress and dancer; Denton A. Cooley, heart surgeon; Joan Crawford, actress; Dwight David Eisenhower, president and general; A. J. Foyt, auto racer; Ben Hogan, golfer; Sam Houston, general and statesman; Howard Hughes, industrialist and film producer; Jack Johnson, boxer; Lyndon B. Johnson, president; George Jones, singer; Tommy Lee Jones, actor; Janis Joplin, singer; Scott Joplin, composer; Trini Lopez, singer; Mary Martin, singer and actress; Spanky McFarland, actor; Audie Murphy, actor and war hero; Chester Nimitz, admiral; Sandra Day O'Connor, jurist; Buck Owens, singer; Selena Pérez, singer; Lou Diamond Phillips, actor; Katherine Anne Porter, novelist; Wiley Post, aviator; Dan

Rather, TV newscaster; Robert Rauschenberg, painter; Tex Ritter, singer; Rip Torn, actor and director; Tommy Tune, dancer and choreographer; Stevie Ray Vaughan, guitarist and singer; Lupe Velez, actress; Dooley Wilson, actor and musician; Babe Didrikson Zaharias, athlete and golfer.

Utah

Capital: Salt Lake City
Governor: Olene Walker,[1] R (to Jan. 2005)
Lieut. Governor: Gayle McKeachnie, R (to Jan. 2005)
Senators: Robert F. Bennett, R (to Jan. 2005);
  Orrin G. Hatch, R (to Jan. 2007)
Treasurer: Edward T. Alter, R. (Jan. 2005)
Atty. General: Mark Shurtleff, R (to Jan. 2005)
Organized as territory: Sept. 9, 1850
Entered Union (rank): Jan. 4, 1896 (45)
Present constitution adopted: 1896
Motto: Industry
State Symbols: flower, sego lily (1911); **tree,** blue spruce (1933); **bird,** California gull (1955); **emblem,** beehive (1959); **song,** "Utah, We Love Thee" (1953); **gem,** topaz; **animal,** Rocky Mountain elk (1971); **insect,** honeybee (1983); **grass,** Indian rice grass (1990); **fossil,** allosaurus (1988); **cooking pot,** dutch oven (1997); **fish,** Bonneville cutthroat trout (1997); **fruit,** cherry (1997); **mineral,** copper; **rock,** coal (1991)
Nickname: Beehive State
Origin of name: From the Ute tribe, meaning "people of the mountains"
10 largest cities (2003 est.): Salt Lake City, 179,894; West Valley City, 111,687; Provo, 105,410; Sandy, 89,319; Orem, 87,599; West Jordan, 84,701; Ogden, 78,293; Layton, 60,769; Taylorsville, 58,701; St. George, 56,382
Land area: 82,144 sq mi. (212,753 sq km)
Geographic center: In Sanpete Co., 3 mi. N. of Manti
Number of counties: 29
Largest county by population and area: Salt Lake, 904,331 (2001); San Juan, 7,821 sq mi.
National parks: 5
National monuments: 7
State parks/forests: 45 (64,097 ac.)
Residents: Utahan, Utahn
2003 resident population est.: 2,351,467
2000 resident census population (rank): 2,233,169 (34). **Male:** 1,119,031 (50.1%); **Female:** 1,114,138 (49.9%). **White:** 1,992,975 (89.2%); **Black:** 17,657 (0.8%); **American Indian:** 29,684 (1.3%); **Asian:** 37,108 (1.7%); **Other race:** 93,405 (4.2%); **Two or more races:** 47,195 (2.1%); **Hispanic/Latino:** 201,559 (9.0%). **2000 percent population 18 and over:** 67.8; **65 and over:** 8.5; **median age:** 27.1.

1. Assumed office when Michael O. Leavitt left in Nov. 2003 to become head of the Environmental Protection Agency.

The region was first explored for Spain by Franciscan friars Escalante and Dominguez in 1776. In 1824 the famous American frontiersman Jim Bridger discovered the Great Salt Lake.

Fleeing religious persecution in the East and Midwest, the Mormons arrived in 1847 and began to build Salt Lake City. The U.S. acquired the Utah region in the treaty ending the Mexican War in 1848, and the first transcontinental railroad was completed with the driving of a golden spike at Promontory Summit in 1869.

Mormon difficulties with the federal government about polygamy did not end until the Mormon Church renounced the practice in 1890, six years before Utah became a state.

Rich in natural resources, Utah has long been a leading producer of copper, gold, silver, lead, zinc,

and molybdenum. Oil has also become a major product. Utah shares rich oil shale deposits with Colorado and Wyoming. Utah also has large deposits of low sulphur coal.

The state's top agricultural commodities include cattle and calves, dairy products, hay, greenhouse and nursery products, and hogs.

Utah's traditional industries of agriculture and mining are complemented by increased tourism and growing aerospace, biomedical, and computer-related businesses.

Utah is a great vacationland with 11,000 mi of fishing streams and 147,000 acres of lakes and reservoirs. Among the many tourist attractions are Arches, Bryce Canyon, Canyonlands, Capitol Reef, and Zion National Parks; Cedar Breaks, Dinosaur, Hovenweep, Natural Bridges, Rainbow Bridge, Timpanogos Cave, and Grand Staircase (Escalante) National Monuments; the Mormon Tabernacle in Salt Lake City; and Monument Valley. Salt Lake City hosted the 2002 Winter Olympics.

Selected famous natives and residents: Maude Adams, actress; Roseanne, actress; Frank Borzage, film director and producer; John M. Browning, inventor; Butch Cassidy, outlaw; Laraine Day, actress; Bernard De Voto, writer; Avard Fairbanks, sculptor; Philo Farnsworth, television pioneer; Jake Garn, senator; John Gilbert, actor; J. Willard Marriott, restaurant and hotel chain founder; Peter Skene Ogden, fur trader and trapper; Merlin Olsen, football player; Donny Osmond, Marie Osmond, singers; Ivy Baker Priest, U.S. treasurer; Lee Greene Richards, painter; Leroy Robertson, composer; Brent Scowcroft, business executive and consultant; Reed Smoot, first Mormon elected to U.S. Senate; Mack Swain, actor; Everett Thorpe, painter; Robert Walker, actor; James Woods, actor; Brigham Young, territory governor and religious leader; Loretta Young, actress.

Vermont

Capital: Montpelier
Governor: Jim Douglas, R (to Jan. 2005)
Lieut. Governor: Brian Dubie, R (to Jan. 2005)
Senators: James M. Jeffords, I (to Jan. 2007);
  Patrick Leahy, D (to Jan. 2005)
Secy. of State: Deborah L. Markowitz, D (to Jan. 2007)
Treasurer: Jeb Spaulding, D (to Jan. 2007)
Atty. General: William Sorrell, D (to Jan. 2007)
Entered Union (rank): March 4, 1791 (14)
Present constitution adopted: 1793
Motto: Vermont, Freedom and Unity
State Symbols: flower, red clover (1894); **tree,** sugar maple (1949); **bird,** hermit thrush (1941); **animal,** Morgan horse (1961); **insect,** honeybee (1978); **song,** "These Green Mountains" (2000)
Nickname: Green Mountain State
Origin of name: From the French "vert mont," meaning "green mountain"
10 largest cities (2003 est.): Burlington, 39,148; Essex, 18,933; Colchester, 17,175; Rutland, 17,103; South Burlington, 16,285; Bennington, 15,637; Brattleboro, 11,996; Hartford, 10,610; Milton, 9,924; Barre, 9,166
Land area: 9,250 sq mi. (23,958 sq km)
Geographic center: In Washington Co., 3 mi. E of Roxbury
Number of counties: 14
Largest county by population and area: Chittenden, 147,591 (2001); Windsor, 971 sq mi.
State forests: 38 (167,769.5 ac.)
State parks: 59 (47,756.5 ac.)
Residents: Vermonter
2003 resident population est.: 619,107
2000 resident census population (rank): 608,827 (49). **Male:** 298,337 (49.0%); **Female:** 310,490 (51.0%).

White: 589,208 (96.8%); **Black:** 3,063 (0.5%); **American Indian:** 2,420 (0.4%); **Asian:** 5,217 (0.9%); **Other race:** 1,443 (0.2%); **Two or more races:** 7,335 (1.2%); **Hispanic/Latino:** 5,504 (0.9%). **2000 percent population 18 and over:** 75.8; **65 and over:** 12.7; **median age:** 37.7.

The Vermont region was explored and claimed for France by Samuel de Champlain in 1609, and the first French settlement was established at Fort Ste. Anne in 1666. The first English settlers moved into the area in 1724 and built Fort Dummer on the site of present-day Brattleboro. England gained control of the area in 1763 after the French and Indian Wars.

First organized to drive settlers from New York out of Vermont, the Green Mountain Boys, led by Ethan Allen, won fame by capturing Fort Ticonderoga from the British on May 10, 1775, in the early days of the Revolutionary War. In 1777 Vermont adopted its first constitution, abolishing slavery and providing for universal male suffrage without property qualifications.

Vermont leads the nation in the production of monument granite, marble, and maple syrup. It is also a leader in the production of talc. Vermont's rugged, rocky terrain discourages extensive agricultural farming, but is well suited to raising fruit trees and to dairy farming.

Principal industrial products include electrical equipment, fabricated metal products, printing and publishing, and paper and allied products.

Tourism is a major industry in Vermont. Vermont's many famous ski areas include Stowe, Killington, Mt. Snow, Bromley, Jay Peak, and Sugarbush. Hunting and fishing also attract many visitors to Vermont each year. Among the many points of interest are the Green Mountain National Forest, Bennington Battle Monument, the Calvin Coolidge Homestead at Plymouth, and the Marble Exhibit in Proctor.

Selected famous natives and residents: Chester A. Arthur, president; Orson Bean, actor; Calvin Coolidge, president; George Dewey, admiral; John Dewey, philosopher and educator; Stephen A. Douglas, politician; James Fisk, financial speculator; Willbur Fisk, clergyman and educator; Richard Morris Hunt, architect; William Morris Hunt, painter; Elisha Otis, inventor; Moses Pendleton, choreographer; Joseph Smith, religious leader; Ernest Thompson, actor and writer; Rudy Vallee, singer and band leader; Henry Wells, pioneer entrepreneur (Wells Fargo & Co.); Brigham Young, religious leader.

Virginia

Capital: Richmond
Governor: Mark Warner, D (to Jan. 2006)
Lieut. Governor: Tim Kaine, D (to Jan. 2006)
Senators: John Warner, R (to Jan. 2009);
George Allen, R (to Jan. 2007)
Secy. of the Commonwealth: Anita Rimler, D (apptd. by gov.)
Treasurer: Jody M. Wagner, R
Atty. General: Jerry W. Kilgore, R (to Jan. 2006)
Entered Union (rank): June 25, 1788 (10)
Present constitution adopted: 1970
Motto: *Sic semper tyrannis* (Thus always to tyrants)
State Symbols: flower, American dogwood (1918); **bird,** cardinal (1950); **dog,** American foxhound (1966); **shell,** oyster shell (1974); **tree,** dogwood (1956)
Nicknames: The Old Dominion; Mother of Presidents
Origin of name: In honor of Elizabeth "Virgin Queen" of England
10 largest cities (2003 est.): Virginia Beach, 439,467; Norfolk, 241,727; Chesapeake, 210,834; Richmond, 194,729; Arlington, 187,873; Newport News, 181,647; Hampton, 146,878; Alexandria, 128,923; Portsmouth, 99,617; Roanoke, 92,863
Land area: 39,594 sq mi. (102,558 sq km)
Geographic center: In Buckingham Co., 5 mi. SW of Buckingham
Number of counties: 95, plus 40 independent cities
Largest county by population and area: Fairfax, 985,161 (2001); Augusta, 972 sq mi.
State forests: 15 (50,869 ac.)
State parks: 34 (plus 33 natural areas)
Residents: Virginian
2003 resident population est.: 7,386,330
2000 resident census population (rank): 7,078,515 (12). **Male:** 3,471,895 (49.0%); **Female:** 3,606,620 (51.0%). **White:** 5,120,110 (72.3%); **Black:** 1,390,293 (19.6%); **American Indian:** 21,172 (0.3%); **Asian:** 261,025 (3.7%); **Other race:** 138,900 (2.0%); **Two or more races:** 143,069 (2.0%); **Hispanic/Latino:** 329,540 (4.7%). **2000 percent population 18 and over:** 75.4; **65 and over:** 11.2; **median age:** 35.7.

The history of America is closely tied to that of Virginia, particularly during the Colonial period. Jamestown, founded in 1607, was the first permanent English settlement in North America and slavery was introduced there in 1619. The surrenders ending both the American Revolution (Yorktown) and the Civil War (Appomattox) occurred in Virginia. The state is called the "Mother of Presidents" because eight U.S. presidents were born there.

Today, the service sector provides one-third of all jobs in Virginia, generating as much income as the manufacturing and retail industries combined in 1999 and accounting for 23% of gross state product. (The largest component of the service sector is business services, which includes computer and data processing services.)

Virginia has a large number of manufacturing industries, including transportation equipment, food processing, electronic and other electrical equipment, chemicals, textiles and apparel, lumber and wood products, and furniture.

Agriculture remains an important sector, and the state ranks among the top ten in a variety of agricultural products, including tomatoes, tobacco, peanuts, apples, summer potatoes, sweet potatoes, snap beans, and turkeys and broilers. Virginia also has a large dairy industry.

Virginia is one of the top ten coal producers in the U.S. Coal accounts for roughly 70% of Virginia's mineral value; crushed stone, sand and gravel, lime, and kyanite are also mined.

Points of interest include Mt. Vernon, home of George Washington; Monticello, home of Thomas Jefferson; Stratford, home of the Lees; Richmond, capital of the Confederacy and of Virginia; and Williamsburg, the restored Colonial capital.

Other attractions are the Shenandoah National Park, Colonial National Historical Park, Fredericksburg and Spotsylvania National Military Park, the Booker T. Washington birthplace near Roanoke, Arlington House (the Robert E. Lee Memorial), Luray Caverns, the Skyline Drive, and the Blue Ridge National Parkway.

Selected famous natives and residents: Richard Arlen, actor; Arthur Ashe, tennis player; Pearl Bailey, singer; Russell Baker, columnist; Warren Beatty, actor; George Bingham, painter; Richard E. Byrd, polar explorer; Willa Cather, novelist; Roy Clark, country music artist; William Clark, explorer; Henry Clay, statesman; Joseph Cotten, actor; Ella Fitzgerald, singer; William H. Harrison, president; Patrick Henry, statesman; Sam Houston, political leader;

Thomas Jefferson, president; Robert E. Lee, Confederate general; Meriwether Lewis, explorer; Shirley MacLaine, actress; James Madison, president; Moses Malone, basketball player; John Marshall, jurist; Cyrus McCormick, inventor; James Monroe, president; Opechancanough, Powhatan leader; John Payne, actor; Walter Reed, army surgeon; Matthew Ridgway, general; Bill "Bojangles" Robinson, dancer; George C. Scott, actor; Sam Snead, golfer; James "Jeb" Stuart, Confederate army officer; Thomas Sumter, general; Zachary Taylor, president; Nat Turner, leader of slave uprising; John Tyler, president; Booker T. Washington, educator; George Washington, first president; James E. West,, inventor; Woodrow Wilson, president; Tom Wolfe, journalist.

Washington

Capital: Olympia
Governor: Gary Locke, D (to Jan. 2005)
Lieut. Governor: Brad Owen, D (to Jan. 2005)
Senators: Patty Murray, D (to Jan. 2005);
    Maria Cantwell, D (to Jan. 2007)
Secy. of State: Sam Reed, R (to Jan. 2005)
Treasurer: Michael J. Murphy, D (to Jan. 2005)
Atty. General: Christine Gregoire, D (to Jan. 2005)
Auditor: Brian Sonntag, D (to Jan. 2005)
Organized as territory: March 2, 1853
Entered Union (rank): Nov. 11, 1889 (42)
Present constitution adopted: 1889
Motto: Al-Ki (Indian word meaning "by and by")
State Symbols: flower, coast rhododendron (1892); **tree,** western hemlock (1947); **bird,** willow goldfinch (1951); **fish,** steelhead trout (1969); **gem,** petrified wood (1975); **colors,** green and gold (1925); **song,** "Washington, My Home" (1959); **folk song,** "Roll On Columbia, Roll On" (1987); **dance,** square dance (1979); **grass,** bluebunch wheatgrass (1989); **insect,** blue darner dragonfly (1997); **fossil,** Columbian mammoth (1998); **fruit,** apple (1989)
Nicknames: Evergreen State
Origin of name: In honor of George Washington
10 largest cities (2003 est.): Seattle, 569,101; Tacoma, 196,790; Spokane, 196,624; Vancouver, 151,654; Bellevue, 112,344; Everett, 96,643; Federal Way, 81,711; Kent, 81,567; Yakima, 80,223; Bellingham, 71,289
Land area: 66,544 sq mi. (172,349 sq km)
Geographic center: In Chelan Co., 10 mi. WSW of Wenatchee
Number of counties: 39
Largest county by population and area: King, 1,741,785 (2001); Okanogan, 5,268 sq mi.
State forest lands: 2.1 million ac.
State parks: 215 (260,000 ac.)[1]
Residents: Washingtonian
2003 resident population est.: 6,131,445
2000 resident census population (rank): 5,894,121 (15). **Male:** 2,934,300 (49.8%); **Female:** 2,959,821 (50.2%). **White:** 4,821,823 (81.8%); **Black:** 190,267 (3.2%); **American Indian:** 93,301 (1.6%); **Asian:** 322,335 (5.5%); **Other race:** 228,923 (3.9%); **Two or more races:** 213,519 (3.6%); **Hispanic/Latino:** 441,509 (7.5%). **2000 percent population 18 and over:** 74.3; **65 and over:** 11.2; **median age:** 35.3.

1. Parks and undeveloped areas administered by State Parks and Recreation Commission. Dept. of Wildlife administers wildlife and recreation areas totaling 428,989.5 acres.

As part of the vast Oregon Country, Washington territory was visited by Spanish, American, and British explorers—Bruno Heceta for Spain in 1775, the American Capt. Robert Gray in 1792, and Capt. George Vancouver for Britain in 1792–1794. Lewis and Clark explored the Columbia River region and coastal areas for the U.S. in 1805–1806.

Rival American and British settlers and conflicting territorial claims threatened war in the early 1840s. However, in 1846 the Oregon Treaty set the boundary at the 49th parallel and war was averted.

Washington is a leading lumber producer. Its rugged surface is rich in stands of Douglas fir, hemlock, ponderosa and white pine, spruce, larch, and cedar. The state holds first place in apples, lentils, dry edible peas, hops, pears, red raspberries, spearmint oil, and sweet cherries, and ranks high in apricots, asparagus, grapes, peppermint oil, and potatoes. Livestock and livestock products make important contributions to total farm revenue and the commercial fishing catch of salmon, halibut, and bottomfish makes a significant contribution to the state's economy.

Manufacturing industries in Washington include aircraft and missiles, shipbuilding and other transportation equipment, lumber, food processing, metals and metal products, chemicals, and machinery.

Washington has over 1,000 dams, including the Grand Coulee, built for a variety of purposes including irrigation, power, flood control, and water storage. Its abundance of electrical power makes Washington one of the nation's major producers of refined aluminum.

Among the major points of interest: Mt. Rainier, Olympic, and North Cascades National Parks. Mount St. Helens, a peak in the Cascade Range, erupted in May 1980. Also of interest are Whitman Mission and Fort Vancouver National Historic Sites; and the Pacific Science Center and the Space Needle, in Seattle.

Selected famous natives and residents: Earl Anthony, professional bowler; Mildred Bailey, singer; Bob Barker, TV host; Dyan Cannon, actress; Raymond Carver, writer; Carol Channing, actress; Ray Charles, singer and musician; Kurt Cobain, rock musician; Judy Collins, singer; Chris Cornell, rock musician; Fred Couples, professional golfer; Bing Crosby, singer and actor; Bob Crosby, musician; Merce Cunningham, choreographer; Howard Duff, actor; Frances Farmer, actress; Kenny G., saxophonist; Bill Gates, software executive; Jimi Hendrix, guitarist; Frank Herbert, writer; Robert Joffrey, choreographer; Chuck Jones, animator; Quincy Jones, music producer; Hank Ketcham, cartoonist; Gary Larson, cartoonist; Gypsy Rose Lee, entertainer; Kenny Loggins, rock musician; Mary McCarthy, novelist; Guthrie McClintic, theatrical producer and director; John McIntire, actor; Steve Miller, rock musician; Robert Motherwell, artist; Patrice Munsel, soprano; Craig T. Nelson, actor; Ella Raines, actress; Ahmad Rashad, football player; Ann Reinking, dancer and actress; Tom Robbins, novelist; Ann Rule, writer; Francis Scobee, astronaut; Seattle, Suquamish chief; Smohalla, Indian prophet and chief; Hillary Swank, actress; Julia Sweeney, actress; Adam West, actor; Audrey Wurdemann, poet.

West Virginia

Capital: Charleston
Governor: Bob Wise, D (to Jan. 2005)
Lt. Governor/Senate President: Earl Ray Tomblin, D (to Jan. 2005)
Senators: Robert C. Byrd, D (to Jan. 2007);
    John D. "Jay" Rockefeller IV, D (to Jan. 2009)
Secy. of State: Joe Manchin, D (to Jan. 2005)
Treasurer: John D. Perdue, D (to Jan. 2005)
Atty. General: Darrell V. McGraw, Jr., D (to Jan. 2005)
Entered Union (rank): June 20, 1863 (35)
Present constitution adopted: 1872
Motto: Montani semper liberi (Mountaineers are always free)
State Symbols: flower, rhododendron (1903); **tree,** sugar maple (1949); **bird,** cardinal (1949); **animal,** black bear (1973); **colors,** blue and gold (official) (1863); **songs,** "West Virginia, My Home Sweet

Home," "The West Virginia Hills," and "This Is My West Virginia" (adopted by Legislature in 1947, 1961, and 1963 as official state songs);
Nickname: Mountain State
Origin of name: In honor of Elizabeth, "Virgin Queen" of England
10 largest cities (2003 est.): Charleston, 51,394; Huntington, 49,533; Parkersburg, 32,100; Wheeling, 30,096; Morgantown, 27,969; Weirton, 19,838; Fairmont, 18,984; Beckley, 16,994; Clarksburg, 16,425; Martinsburg, 15,309
Land area: 24,077 sq mi. (62,359 sq km)
Geographic center: In Braxton Co., 4 mi. E of Sutton
Number of counties: 55
Largest county by population and area: Kanawha, 197,338 (2001); Randolph, 1,040 sq mi.
State forests: 9 (79,502 ac.)
State parks: 37 (74,508 ac.)
Residents: West Virginian
2003 resident population est.: 1,810,354
2000 resident census population (rank): 1,808,344 (37). **Male:** 879,170 (48.6%); **Female:** 929,174 (51.4%). **White:** 1,718,777 (95.0%); **Black:** 57,232 (3.2%); **American Indian:** 3,606 (0.2%); **Asian:** 9,434 (0.5%); **Other race:** 3,107 (0.2%); **Two or more races:** 15,788 (0.9%); **Hispanic/Latino:** 12,279 (0.7%). **2000 percent population 18 and over:** 77.7; **65 and over:** 15.3; **median age:** 38.9.

West Virginia's early history from 1609 until 1863 is largely shared with Virginia, of which it was a part until Virginia seceded from the Union in 1861. The delegates of the 40 western counties who opposed secession formed their own government, which was granted statehood in 1863.

In 1731 Morgan Morgan established the first permanent white settlement on Mill Creek in present-day Berkeley County. Coal, a mineral asset that would figure significantly in West Virginia's history, was discovered in 1742. Other important natural resources are oil, natural gas, and hardwood forests, which cover about 75% of the state's area.

The state's rapid industrial expansion began in the 1870s, drawing thousands of European immigrants and African Americans into the region. Miners' strikes between 1912 and 1921 required the intervention of state and federal troops to quell the violence.

Today, the state ranks second in total coal production, with about 15% of the U.S. total. It is also a leader in steel, glass, aluminum, and chemical manufactures. Major agricultural commodities are poultry and eggs, dairy products, and apples.

Tourism is increasingly popular in mountainous West Virginia. More than a million acres have been set aside in 37 state parks and recreation areas and in 9 state forests and 2 national forests. Major points of interest include Harpers Ferry and New River Gorge National River, The Greenbrier and Berkeley Springs resorts, the scenic railroad at Cass, and the historic homes in the Eastern Panhandle.

Selected famous natives and residents: George Brett, baseball player; Pearl S. Buck, author; Phyllis Curtin, soprano; Martin R. Delany, first black army major; Billy Dixon, frontiersman and scout; Joanne Dru, actress; Thomas "Stonewall" Jackson, Confederate general; John S. Knight, publisher; Don Knotts, actor; Peter Marshall, TV host; Kathy Mattea, singer; Whitney D. Morrow, banker and diplomat; Mary Lou Retton, gymnast; Walter Reuther, labor leader; Eleanor Steber, soprano; Lewis L. Strauss, naval officer and scientist; Cyrus Vance, government official; Jerry West, basketball player; William Lyne Wilson, legislator and university president; Chuck Yeager, test pilot and Air Force general.

Wisconsin

Capital: Madison
Governor: Jim Doyle, D (to Jan. 2007)
Lieut. Governor: Barbara Lawton, D (to Jan. 2007)
Senators: Russell D. Feingold, D (to Jan. 2005); Herbert Kohl, D (to Jan. 2007)
Secy. of State: Douglas J. La Follette, D (to Jan. 2007)
State Treasurer: Jack C. Voight, R (to Jan. 2007)
Atty. General: Peg Lautenschlager, D (to Jan. 2007)
Superintendent of Public Instruction: Elizabeth Burmaster, Nonpartisan (to July 2005)
Organized as territory: July 4, 1836
Entered Union (rank): May 29, 1848 (30)
Present constitution adopted: 1848
Motto: Forward
State Symbols: flower, wood violet (1949); **tree,** sugar maple (1949); **grain,** corn (1990); **bird,** robin (1949); **animal,** badger; **wild life animal,** white-tailed deer (1957); **domestic animal,** dairy cow (1971); **insect,** honeybee (1977); **fish,** musky (muskellunge) (1955); **song,** "On Wisconsin"; **mineral,** galena (1971); **rock,** red granite (1971); **symbol of peace,** mourning dove (1971); **soil,** antigo silt loam (1983); **fossil,** trilobite (1985); **dog,** American Water Spaniel (1986); **beverage,** milk (1988); **dance,** polka (1994); **waltz,** "The Wisconsin Waltz" (2001); **ballad,** "Oh Wisconsin, Land of My Dreams" (2001)
Nickname: Badger State
Origin of name: French corruption of an Indian word whose meaning is disputed
10 largest cities (2003 est.): Milwaukee, 586,941; Madison, 218,432; Green Bay, 101,467; Kenosha, 92,871; Racine, 80,266; Appleton, 70,354; Waukesha, 66,840; Oshkosh, 63,237; Eau Claire, 62,496; Janesville, 61,145
Land area: 54,310 sq mi. (140,673 sq km)
Geographic center: In Wood Co., 9 mi. SE of Marshfield
Number of counties: 72
Largest county by population and area: Milwaukee, 932,012 (2001); Marathon, 1,545 sq mi.
State forests: 12 (493,975 ac.)
State parks & scenic trails: 43 parks, 14 trails (68,355 ac.)
Residents: Wisconsinite
2003 resident population est.: 5,472,299
2000 resident census population (rank): 5,363,675 (18). **Male:** 2,649,041 (49.4%); **Female:** 2,714,634 (50.6%). **White:** 4,769,857 (88.9%); **Black:** 304,460 (5.7%); **American Indian:** 47,228 (0.9%); **Asian:** 88,763 (1.7%); **Other race:** 84,842 (1.6%); **Two or more races:** 66,895 (1.2%); **Hispanic/Latino:** 192,921 (3.6%). **2000 percent population 18 and over:** 74.5; **65 and over:** 13.1; **median age:** 36.0.

The Wisconsin region was first explored for France by Jean Nicolet, who landed at Green Bay in 1634. In 1660 a French trading post and Roman Catholic mission were established near present-day Ashland.

Great Britain obtained the region in settlement of the French and Indian Wars in 1763; the U.S. acquired it in 1783 after the Revolutionary War. However, Great Britain retained actual control until after the War of 1812. The region was successively governed as part of the territories of Indiana, Illinois, and Michigan between 1800 and 1836, when it became a separate territory.

Wisconsin is a leading state in milk and cheese production. Other important farm products are peas, beans, beets, corn, potatoes, oats, hay, and cranberries.

The chief industrial products of the state are auto-mobiles, machinery, furniture, paper, beer, and pro-cessed foods. Wisconsin ranks second among the 47 paper-producing states. The state's mines produce copper, iron ore, lead, and zinc.

Wisconsin is a pioneer in social legislation, pro-viding pensions for the blind (1907), aid to depen-dent children (1913), and old-age assistance (1925). In labor legislation, the state was the first to enact an unemployment compensation law (1932) and the first in which a workman's compensation law actu-ally took effect. In 1984, Wisconsin became the first state to adopt the Uniform Marital Property Act.

The state has over 14,000 lakes, of which Win-nebago is the largest. Water sports, ice-boating, and fishing are popular, as are skiing and hunting. Pub-lic parks and forests take up one-seventh of the land, with 43 state parks, 12 state forests, 14 state trails, 3 recreational areas, and 2 national forests.

Among the many points of interest are the Apostle Islands National Lakeshore; Ice Age National Scientific Reserve; the Circus World Museum at Baraboo; the Wolf, St. Croix, and Lower St. Croix national scenic riverways; and the Wisconsin Dells.

Selected famous natives and residents: Don Ameche, actor; Roy Chapman Andrews, naturalist and explorer; Walter Annenberg, media tycoon and philanthropist; Carrie Catt, woman suffragist; John R. Commons, economist; Tyne Daly, actress; August Derleth, author; Jeanne Dixon, seer; Zona Gale, novelist; Eric Heiden, skater; Woody Herman, band leader; Hildegarde, singer; Harry Houdini, magician; Hans V. Kaltenborne, journalist; Pee Wee King, singer; George F. Kennan, diplomat; Robert La Follette, politician; William D. Leahy, admiral; Liberace, pianist; Charles Litel, actor; Allen Ludden, TV host; Alfred Lunt, actor; Frederic March, actor; Jackie Mason, comedian; John Ringling North, circus director; Pat O'Brien, actor; Georgia O'Keeffe, painter; Charlotte Rae, actress; William H. Rehnquist, jurist; Gena Rowlands, actress; Tom Snyder, newscaster; Spencer Tracy, actor; Thorstein Veblen, economist; Orson Welles, actor and producer; Thornton Wilder, author; Charles Winninger, actor; Frank Lloyd Wright, architect.

Wyoming

Capital: Cheyenne
Governor: Dave Freudenthal, D (to Jan. 2007)
Senators: Michael B. Enzi, R (to Jan. 2009); Craig Tho-mas, R (to Jan. 2007)
Secy. of State: Joe Meyer, R (to Jan. 2007)
Treasurer: Cynthia M. Lummis, R (to Jan. 2007)
Atty. General: Patrick Crank, D (to Jan. 2007)
Organized as territory: May 19, 1869
Entered Union (rank): July 10, 1890 (44)
Present constitution adopted: 1890
Motto: Equal rights (1955)
State Symbols: flower, Indian paintbrush (1917); **tree,** cottonwood (1947); **bird,** western meadowlark (1927); **dinosaur,** *Triceratops* (1994); **fish,** cutthroat trout (1987); **fossil,** *Knightia* (1987); **gemstone,** jade (1967); **insignia,** bucking horse (unofficial); **mammal,** bison (1985); **reptile,** horned toad (1993); **soil,** Forkwood series (unofficial); **song,** "Wyoming" (1955)
Nickname: Equality State
Origin of name: From the Delaware Indian word, mean-ing "mountains and valleys alternating"; the same as the Wyoming Valley in Pennsylvania
10 largest cities (2003): Cheyenne, 54,374; Casper, 50,632; Laramie, 26,956; Gillette, 21,840; Rock Springs, 18,400; Sheridan, 16,016; Green River, 11,541; Evanston, 11,375; Riverton, 9,314; Cody, 8,973
Land area: 97,100 sq mi. (251,501 sq km)
Geographic center: In Fremont Co., 58 mi. ENE of Lander

Number of counties: 23, plus Yellowstone National Park
Largest county by population and area: Laramie, 81,958 (2001); Sweetwater, 10,426 sq mi.
State parks and historic sites: 23 (58,498 ac.)
Residents: Wyomingite
2003 resident population est.: 501,242
2000 resident census population (rank): 493,782 (50). **Male:** 248,374 (50.3%); **Female:** 245,408 (49.7%). **White:** 454,670 (92.1%); **Black:** 3,722 (0.8%); **Ameri-can Indian:** 11,133 (2.3%); **Asian:** 2,771 (0.6%); **Other race:** 12,301 (2.5%); **Two or more races:** 8,883 (1.8%); **Hispanic/Latino:** 31,669 (6.4%). **2000 percent population 18 and over:** 73.9; **65 and over:** 11.7; **median age:** 36.2.

The U.S. acquired the land comprising Wyoming from France as part of the Louisiana Purchase in 1803. John Colter, a fur-trapper, is the first white man known to have entered the region. In 1807 he explored the Yellowstone area and brought back news of its geysers and hot springs.

Robert Stuart pioneered the Oregon Trail across Wyoming in 1812–1813 and, in 1834, Fort Laramie, the first permanent trading post in Wyoming, was built. Western Wyoming was obtained by the U.S. in the 1846 Oregon Treaty with Great Britain and as a result of the treaty ending the Mexican War in 1848.

When the Wyoming Territory was organized in 1869, Wyoming women became the first in the nation to obtain the right to vote. In 1925 Mrs. Nel-lie Tayloe Ross became the first woman governor in the United States.

Wyoming's towering mountains and vast plains provide spectacular scenery, grazing lands for sheep and cattle, and rich mineral deposits.

Mining, particularly oil and natural gas, is the most important industry. Wyoming has the world's largest sodium carbonate (natrona) deposits and has the nation's second largest uranium deposits.

In 2000 Wyoming ranked second among the states in wool production (exceeded only by Texas) and third in sheep and lambs (exceeded only by Texas and California); it also had 1,580,000 cattle. Princi-pal crops include wheat, oats, sugar beets, corn, bar-ley, and alfalfa.

Second in mean elevation to Colorado, Wyoming has many attractions for the tourist trade, notably Yellowstone National Park. Hikers, campers and skiers are attracted to Grand Teton National Park and Jackson Hole National Monument in the Teton Range of the Rockies. Cheyenne is famous for its annual "Frontier Days" celebration. Flaming Gorge, the Fort Laramie National Historic Site, and Devils Tower and Fossil Butte National Monuments are other points of interest.

Selected famous natives and residents: James Bridger, trapper, guide, and storyteller; Dick Cheney, vice president; Buffalo Bill Cody, scout; John Colter, trader and first white man to enter Wyoming; June E. Downey, educator; Thomas Fitzpatrick, mountain man and guide; Curt Gowdy, sportscaster; Tom Horn, detective; Isabel Jewell, actress; Velma Linford, writer; Esther Morris, first woman judge; Ted Olson, writer; John "Portugee" Phillips, frontiersman; Jackson Pollock, painter; Nellie Tayloe Ross, first woman elected governor of a state; Alan K. Simpson, senator; Jedediah S. Smith, mountain man and first American to reach California from the East; Alan Swallow, publisher and author; Willis Van Devanter, jurist; Francis E. Warren, first state governor; Chief Washakie, chief of the Shoshone; James G. Watt, secretary of the Interior.

Land and Water Area of States, 2000

(in square miles)

State	Rank (total area)	Land[1] area	Water[2] area	Total area	State	Rank (total area)	Land[1] area	Water[2] area	Total area
Alabama	30	50,744.00	1,675.01	52,419.02	Montana	4	145,552.43	1,489.96	147,042.40
Alaska	1	571,951.26	91,316.00	663,267.26	Nebraska	16	76,872.41	481.31	77,353.73
Arizona	6	113,634.57	363.73	113,998.30	Nevada	7	109,825.99	734.71	110,560.71
Arkansas	29	52,068.17	1,110.45	53,178.62	New				
California	3	155,959.34	7,736.23	163,695.57	Hampshire	46	8,968.10	381.84	9,349.94
Colorado	8	103,717.53	376.04	104,093.57	New Jersey	47	7,417.34	1,303.96	8,721.30
Connecticut	48	4,844.80	698.53	5,543.33	New Mexico	5	121,355.53	233.96	121,589.48
Delaware	49	1,953.56	535.71	2,489.27	New York	27	47,213.79	7,342.22	54,556.00
Dist. of					North Carolina	28	48,710.88	5,107.63	53,818.51
Columbia	—	61.4	6.94	68.34	North Dakota	19	68,975.93	1,723.86	70,699.79
Florida	22	53,926.82	11,827.77	65,754.59	Ohio	34	40,948.38	3,876.53	44,824.90
Georgia	24	57,906.14	1,518.63	59,424.77	Oklahoma	20	68,667.06	1,231.13	69,898.19
Hawaii	43	6,422.62	4,508.36	10,930.98	Oregon	9	95,996.79	2,383.85	98,380.64
Idaho	14	82,747.21	822.87	83,570.08	Pennsylvania	33	44,816.61	1,238.63	46,055.24
Illinois	25	55,583.58	2,330.79	57,914.38	Rhode Island	50	1,044.93	500.12	1,545.05
Indiana	38	35,866.90	550.83	36,417.73	South Carolina	40	30,109.47	1,910.73	32,020.20
Iowa	26	55,869.36	402.2	56,271.55	South Dakota	17	75,884.64	1,231.85	77,116.49
Kansas	15	81,814.88	461.96	82,276.84	Tennessee	36	41,217.12	926.15	42,143.27
Kentucky	37	39,728.18	680.85	40,409.02	Texas	2	261,797.12	6,783.70	268,580.82
Louisiana	31	43,561.85	8,277.85	51,839.70	Utah	13	82,143.65	2,755.18	84,898.83
Maine	39	30,861.55	4,523.10	35,384.65	Vermont	45	9,249.56	364.7	9,614.26
Maryland	42	9,773.82	2,632.86	12,406.68	Virginia	35	39,594.07	3,180.13	42,774.20
Massachusetts	44	7,840.02	2,714.55	10,554.57	Washington	18	66,544.06	4,755.58	71,299.64
Michigan	11	56,803.82	39,912.28	96,716.11	West Virginia	41	24,077.73	152.03	24,229.76
Minnesota	12	79,610.08	7,328.79	86,938.87	Wisconsin	23	54,310.10	11,187.72	65,497.82
Mississippi	32	46,906.96	1,523.24	48,430.19	Wyoming	10	97,100.40	713.16	97,813.56
Missouri	21	68,885.93	818.39	69,704.31	**U.S. total**		**3,537,438.44**	**256,644.62**	**3,794,083.06**

1. Dry land and land temporarily or partially covered by water, such as marshland, swamps, etc.; streams and canals under one-eighth statute mile wide; and lakes, reservoirs, and ponds under 40 acres. 2. Permanent inland water surface, such as lakes, reservoirs, and ponds having an area of 40 acres or more; streams, sloughs, estuaries, and canals one-eighth statute mile or more in width; deeply indented embayments and sounds, and other coastal waters behind or sheltered by headlands or islands separated by less than 1 nautical mile of water, and islands under 40 acres in area. Excludes areas of oceans, bays, sounds, etc. lying within U.S. jurisdiction but not defined as inland water. *Source:* Department of Commerce, Bureau of the Census.

State Capitals and Largest Cities

State	Capital	Largest city	State	Capital	Largest city
Alabama	Montgomery	Birmingham	**Montana**	Helena	Billings
Alaska	Juneau	Anchorage	**Nebraska**	Lincoln	Omaha
Arizona	Phoenix	Phoenix	**Nevada**	Carson City	Las Vegas
Arkansas	Little Rock	Little Rock	**New Hampshire**	Concord	Manchester
California	Sacramento	Los Angeles	**New Jersey**	Trenton	Newark
Colorado	Denver	Denver	**New Mexico**	Santa Fe	Albuquerque
Connecticut	Hartford	Bridgeport	**New York**	Albany	New York City
Delaware	Dover	Wilmington	**North Carolina**	Raleigh	Charlotte
Florida	Tallahassee	Jacksonville	**North Dakota**	Bismarck	Fargo
Georgia	Atlanta	Atlanta	**Ohio**	Columbus	Columbus
Hawaii	Honolulu	Honolulu	**Oklahoma**	Oklahoma City	Oklahoma City
Idaho	Boise	Boise	**Oregon**	Salem	Portland
Illinois	Springfield	Chicago	**Pennsylvania**	Harrisburg	Philadelphia
Indiana	Indianapolis	Indianapolis	**Rhode Island**	Providence	Providence
Iowa	Des Moines	Des Moines	**South Carolina**	Columbia	Columbia
Kansas	Topeka	Wichita	**South Dakota**	Pierre	Sioux Falls
Kentucky	Frankfort	Lexington	**Tennessee**	Nashville	Memphis
Louisiana	Baton Rouge	New Orleans	**Texas**	Austin	Houston
Maine	Augusta	Portland	**Utah**	Salt Lake City	Salt Lake City
Maryland	Annapolis	Baltimore	**Vermont**	Montpelier	Burlington
Massachusetts	Boston	Boston	**Virginia**	Richmond	Virginia Beach
Michigan	Lansing	Detroit	**Washington**	Olympia	Seattle
Minnesota	St. Paul	Minneapolis	**West Virginia**	Charleston	Charleston
Mississippi	Jackson	Jackson	**Wisconsin**	Madison	Milwaukee
Missouri	Jefferson City	Kansas City	**Wyoming**	Cheyenne	Cheyenne

Source: U.S. Bureau of the Census, 2000 figures.

Most Livable States, 2004

2004 rank	State	2003 rank	2004 rank	State	2003 rank	2004 rank	State	2003 rank
1.	New Hampshire	3.	18.	Delaware	18.	35.	Georgia	34.
2.	Minnesota	1.	19.	Utah	13.	36.	California	38.
3.	Vermont	7.	20.	Indiana	22.	37.	Florida	39.
4.	Iowa	2.	20.	Missouri	25.	38.	Arizona	45.
5.	New Jersey	12.	22.	Pennsylvania	27.	39.	Texas	36.
6.	Wyoming	14.	23.	Colorado	19.	40.	Oklahoma	34.
7.	Virginia	5.	24.	Rhode Island	26.	41.	New Mexico	40.
8.	Nebraska	4.	25.	Washington	23.	42.	Kentucky	37.
9.	Connecticut	11.	26.	Illinois	30.	43.	West Virginia	46.
10.	South Dakota	8.	27.	Montana	21.	44.	Arkansas	44.
11.	Kansas	6.	27.	Oregon	24.	45.	North Carolina	42.
12.	Maine	16.	29.	Ohio	29.	46.	Tennessee	48.
13.	Wisconsin	10.	30.	Nevada	31.	47.	Alabama	47.
14.	Maryland	14.	31.	Alaska	32.	48.	South Carolina	43.
15.	North Dakota	17.	32.	Hawaii	41.	49.	Louisiana	49.
16.	Massachusetts	9.	33.	New York	33.	50.	Mississippi	50.
17.	Idaho	20.	34.	Michigan	28.			

Methodology: To determine a state's livability rating, each state's rankings in 44 categories were averaged. Some of the positive factors included household income, homeownership, job growth, and educational attainment. The negative factors included crime rate, poverty rate, infant mortality rate, and unemployment rate. *Source:* Morgan Quitno Press. Web: www.morganquitno.com.

Healthiest States, 2004

2004 rank	State	2003 rank	2004 rank	State	2003 rank	2004 rank	State	2003 rank
1.	New Hampshire	2.	18.	Rhode Island	17.	35.	Alaska	36.
2.	Vermont	1.	19.	South Dakota	13.	36.	Tennessee	37.
3.	Hawaii	8.	20.	Idaho	21.	37.	Missouri	34.
4.	Iowa	4.	21.	Wisconsin	23.	38.	Arkansas	43.
5.	Minnesota	5.	22.	Virginia	22.	39.	Oklahoma	40.
6.	Utah	9.	23.	Montana	18.	40.	Arizona	41.
7.	Nebraska	3.	24.	Ohio	26.	41.	Florida	44.
8.	Massachusetts	6.	25.	Michigan	28.	42.	Georgia	42.
9.	Maine	7.	26.	Pennsylvania	24.	42.	Texas	39.
10.	Connecticut	11.	27.	Colorado	25.	44.	Delaware	38.
11.	New Jersey	16.	28.	Indiana	27.	45.	Nevada	45.
12.	North Dakota	10.	29.	Kentucky	31.	46.	South Carolina	48.
13.	Washington	12.	30.	North Carolina	29.	47.	Alabama	47.
14.	California	14.	31.	Illinois	32.	48.	Louisiana	49.
15.	Oregon	19.	32.	Maryland	35.	49.	New Mexico	46.
16.	Wyoming	20.	33.	New York	33.	50.	Mississippi	50.
17.	Kansas	15.	34.	West Virginia	30.			

Methodology: The Healthiest State designation is awarded on the basis of 21 factors selected from the 2004 edition of Morgan Quitno's annual reference book, *Health Care State Rankings*. These factors reflect access to health care providers, affordability of health care, and the general health of a state's population. *Source:* Morgan Quitno Press. Web: www.morganquitno.com.

Most Dangerous States, 2004

2004 rank	State	2003 rank	2004 rank	State	2003 rank	2004 rank	State	2003 rank
1.	Nevada	2.	18.	Alabama	20.	35.	Minnesota	34.
2.	Louisiana	1.	19.	Missouri	17.	36.	Kentucky	35.
3.	Arizona	3.	20.	Delaware	19.	37.	Virginia	38.
4.	Maryland	5.	21.	Washington	21.	38.	Utah	37.
5.	South Carolina	11.	22.	Ohio	22.	39.	Connecticut	36.
6.	New Mexico	7.	23.	Hawaii	26.	40.	Idaho	42.
7.	Florida	4.	24.	Colorado	25.	41.	Wisconsin	40.
8.	Tennessee	6.	25.	Arkansas	23.	42.	Iowa	43.
9.	Texas	10.	26.	Indiana	24.	43.	Wyoming	44.
10.	California	12.	27.	Massachusetts	31.	44.	Montana	41.
11.	Michigan	9.	28.	New York	29.	45.	West Virginia	45.
12.	Alaska	8.	29.	Rhode Island	27.	46.	South Dakota	47.
13.	Illinois	13.	30.	Pennsylvania	30.	47.	New Hampshire	46.
14.	Mississippi	14.	31.	Kansas	28.	48.	Maine	48.
15.	North Carolina	16.	32.	Oregon	33.	49.	Vermont	50.
16.	Oklahoma	18.	33.	New Jersey	32.	50.	North Dakota	49.
17.	Georgia	15.	34.	Nebraska	39.			

Methodology: To determine the most dangerous states, rates for six crime categories—murder, rape, robbery, aggravated assault, burglary, and motor vehicle theft—are compared to the national average for a given crime category. *Source:* Morgan Quitno Press. Web: www.morganquitno.com.

50 Largest Cities of the United States

Data supplied by U.S. Census Bureau and by the cities in response to questionnaires. Per capita personal income data are given for the Metropolitan Statistical Area (MSA), the Primary Metropolitan Statistical Area (PMSA), the New England County Metropolitan Area (NECMA), or the Consolidated Metropolitan Statistical Area (CMSA), as noted. NOTE: Persons of Hispanic origin may be of any race.

Albuquerque, N.M.

Mayor: Martin Chavez (to Nov. 2005)
2000 census population (rank): 448,607 (35); **% change:** 16.6; **Male:** 217,887 (48.6%); **Female:** 230,720 (51.4%); **White:** 321,179 (71.6%); **Black:** 13,854 (3.1%); **American Indian and Alaska Native:** 17,444 (3.9%); **Asian:** 10,068 (2.2%); **Other race:** 66,292 (14.8%); **Two or more races:** 19,318 (4.3%); **Hispanic/Latino:** 179,075 (39.9%). **2000 percent population 18 and over:** 75.5%; **65 and over:** 12.0%; **median age:** 34.9.
2003 population estimate (rank): 471,856 (33)
Land area: 181 sq mi. (469 sq km); **Alt.:** 4,958 ft.
Avg. daily temp.: Jan., 34.2° F; July, 78.5° F
Churches: 211; **City-owned parks:** 189; **Radio stations:** 43 (AM, 17; FM, 26); **Television stations:** 11
Civilian Labor Force (MSA) June 2004: 400,555; **Unemployed:** 22,116, **Percent:** 5.5; **Per capita personal income (MSA) 2002:** $28,471
Chamber of Commerce: Greater Albuquerque Chamber of Commerce, PO Box 25100, Albuquerque, N.M. 87125. Albuquerque Hispano Chamber of Commerce, 1309 Fourth St. S.W., Albuquerque, N.M. 87102

Albuquerque is the largest city in New Mexico and the seat of Bernalillo County. It is situated in west-central New Mexico on the upper Rio Grande.

Spanish settlers arrived in the mid-1600s, but they retreated from the area in 1680 after the Pueblo revolt. The old town was founded in 1706 by Don Francisco Cuervo y Valdés, the governor of New Mexico, and named after the Duke of Alburquerque, the viceroy of New Spain.

The opening of the Santa Fe Trail in the early 19th century brought an influx of settlers, and an army post was established following U.S. occupation in 1846. Albuquerque remained loyal to the Union during the Civil War, although it was briefly occupied by Confederate forces in 1862. The new town was laid out in 1880 after the Santa Fe Railroad was built one mile east of the original plaza. The Spanish old town and the mission church of San Felipe de Neri (1706) were soon enveloped by the new construction but survive today.

The city is noted as a center for health and medical services in the region, and government agencies, nuclear research, banking, and tourism are important to the economy. There is a growing high-tech center in Albuquerque, and Intel Corp.'s largest manufacturing facility is located there.

Albuquerque is the seat of the University of New Mexico (1889). Its numerous attractions include the Albuquerque Biological Park, the Indian Pueblo Cultural Center, the National Atomic Museum, Petroglyph National Monument, and the Sandia Mountain Wilderness.

Selected famous natives natives and residents: Annabeth Gish, actress; Fred Haney, baseball player; Ernie Pyle, war correspondent; Al and Bobby Unser, auto racers.

Atlanta, Ga.

Mayor: Shirley Franklin (to Jan. 2006)
2000 census population (rank): 416,474 (39); **% change:** 5.7; **Male:** 206,725 (49.6%); **Female:** 209,749 (50.4%); **White:** 138,352 (33.2%); **Black:** 255,689 (61.4%); **American Indian and Alaska Native:** 765 (0.2%); **Asian:** 8,046 (1.9%); **Other race:** 8,272 (2.0%); **Two or more races:** 5,177 (1.2%); **Hispanic/Latino:** 18,720 (4.5%). **2000 percent population 18 and over:** 77.7%; **65 and over:** 9.7%; **median age:** 31.9.
2003 population estimate (rank): 423,019 (41)
City land area: 132 sq mi. (341 sq km); **Alt.:** Highest, 1,050 ft.; lowest, 940 ft.
Avg. daily temp.: Jan., 41.0° F; July, 78.8° F
Churches: 1,500; **City-owned parks:** 277 (3,178 ac.); **Radio stations:** AM, 7; FM, 20; **Television stations:** 8 commercial; 2 PBS
Civilian Labor Force (MSA) June 2004: 2,447,235 **Unemployed:** 113,364, **Percent:** 4.6; **Per capita personal income (MSA) 2002:** $33,257[1]
Chamber of Commerce: Metro Atlanta Chamber of Commerce, 235 Andrew Young International Blvd., Atlanta, Ga. 30303

1. Atlanta-Sandy Springs–Marietta, Ga.

Atlanta, the largest city and capital of Georgia, is the seat of Fulton County. It is situated in the northwest part of the state at the base of the Blue Ridge Mountains near the Chattahoochee River. The first European settler was Hardy Ivy, who built a cabin there in 1833.

Founded as Terminus in 1837, the town served as the end of the Georgia railroad line (Western and Atlantic Railroad) and later became incorporated as Marthasville in 1843 in honor of ex-governor Lumpkin's daughter Martha. It was renamed Atlanta in 1845 and incorporated as a city in 1847. The name was suggested by the railroad's chief engineer, J. Edgar Thomson, and was derived from its location at the end of the Georgia and Atlantic railroad line. The city became the capital of Georgia in 1868.

During the Civil War, the city was burned and almost completely destroyed while occupied by Gen. William T. Sherman's troops in Nov. 1864. It was rebuilt after the war and grew rapidly due to the expansion of the railroads in the southwest.

Today, Atlanta is the major commercial and transportation hub of the southeast United States, and its international airport is one of the busiest in the world. The city's economy is led by the service, communications, retail trade, manufacturing, finance, and insurance industries. The convention business is also important, and Atlanta is home to many major corporations, including Coca-Cola, which was founded there in 1892.

Atlanta is also a major educational center, with many prestigious universities and colleges, including Emory University (1836), Georgia Institute of Technology (1885), and Georgia State University

(1913). Morehouse College (1867), Spelman College (1881), and Clark Atlanta University (1865; 1869) are important historically black colleges.

Major attractions include Martin Luther King, Jr., National Historic Site, Grant Park, and the Carter Presidential Center. The 1996 Summer Olympics were held in Atlanta.

Selected famous natives and residents: Hank Aaron, baseball player; Arrested Development, recording artists; Jimmy Carter, former president; Ray Charles, singer; James Dickey, poet; Mattiwilda Dobbs, soprano; Walt Frazier, basketball player; Oliver Hardy, comedian; Evander Holyfield, boxer; Alan Jackson, singer; Bobby Jones, golfer; DeForest Kelley, actor; Martin Luther King, Jr., civil rights leader and Nobel Peace Prize winner; Gladys Knight, singer; Kriss Kross, recording artists; Margaret Mitchell, novelist; Bert Parks, entertainer; Eric Roberts, actor; Julia Roberts, actress; Doug Stone, singer; Gwen Torrence, Olympic athlete; Lee Tracy, actor; Travis Tritt, singer; Ted Turner, TBS and CNN founder; Jane Withers, actress; Joanne Woodward, actress; Andrew Young, civil rights activist.

Austin, Tex.

Mayor: Will Wynn (to June 15, 2006)
2000 census population (rank): 656,562
   (16); **% change:** 41.0; **Male:** 337,569 (51.4%);
   Female: 318,993 (48.6%); **White:** 429,100 (65.4%);
   Black: 65,956 (10.0%); **American Indian and Alaska
   Native:** 3,889 (0.6%); **Asian:** 30,960 (4.7%); **Other
   race:** 106,538 (16.2%); **Two or more races:** 19,650
   (3.0%); **Hispanic/Latino:** 200,579 (30.5%). **2000 percent population 18 and over:** 77.5%; **65 and over:**
   6.7%; **median age:** 29.6
2003 population estimate (rank): 672,011 (16)
Land area: 252 sq mi. (653 sq km); **Alt.:** From 425 ft. to
   over 1000 ft.
Avg. daily temp.: Jan., 48.8° F; July, 84.5° F
Churches: 353 churches, representing 45 denominations; **City-owned parks and playgrounds:** 205
   (16,076 ac.); **Radio stations:** AM, 12; FM, 27;
   Television stations: 7 commercial; 1 PBS;
   1 independent
Civilian Labor Force (MSA) June 2004: 775,713,[1]
   Unemployed: 38,335,[1] **Percent:** 4.9;[1] **Per capita per-
   sonal income (MSA) 2002:** $31,677[2]
Chamber of Commerce: Greater Austin Chamber of
   Commerce, 210 Barton Springs Rd., Ste. 400, Aus-
   tin, Tex. 78704

1. Austin–San Marcos, Tex. 2. Austin–Round Rock, Tex.

Austin, the state capital of Texas and seat of Travis County, is the fourth-largest city in Texas. It is situated in the south-central part of the state on the Colorado River.

The site was called Waterloo in 1838, and in 1839 it was incorporated as a city and chosen as the capital of the independent Republic of Texas. Waterloo was renamed Austin in honor of Stephen F. Austin, the founder of the Texas Republic. It became the permanent capital of the state of Texas in 1870.

Austin's growth was spurred by several developments after the Civil War—the railroads reached the city in the 1870s; it was crossed by the important Chisholm cattle trail; and it became the seat of the state university in 1883.

Austin has a growing commercial and diversified manufacturing sector. Civilian government employment is 20% of the labor force and is important to the economy. As home to the University of Texas, Austin is a major center for research and development and is nationally recognized as a high-technology center.

Austin's visitor attractions include the Austin Museum of Art, the Lyndon B. Johnson Library and Museum, the Lady Bird Johnson Wildflower Center, and the Austin Zoo.

Selected famous natives and residents: Don Baylor, baseball player and manager; Earl Campbell, football player; Liz Carpenter, author; Dabney Coleman, actor; Ben Crenshaw, golfer; Michael Dell, founder Dell Computer Corp.; Tobe Hooper, film director; Lady Bird Johnson, former first lady; Tom Kite, golfer; James Michener, author; Willie Nelson, musician; Amado Pena, artist; Darrell Royal, football coach; Zachary Scott, actor; Jerry Jeff Walker, musician; Dalhart Windberg, artist.

Baltimore, Md.

Mayor: Martin O'Malley (to Dec. 2004)[1]
2000 census population (rank): 651,154
   (17); **% change:** –11.5; **Male:** 303,687 (46.6%);
   Female: 347,467 (53.4%); **White:** 205,982 (31.6%);
   Black: 418,951 (64.3%); **American Indian and
   Alaska Native:** 2,097 (0.3%); **Asian:** 9,985 (1.5%);
   Other race: 4,363 (0.7%); **Two or more races:** 9,554
   (1.5%); **Hispanic/Latino:** 11,061 (1.7%). **2000 percent population 18 and over:** 75.2%; **65 and over:**
   13.2%; **Median age:** 35.0.
2003 population estimate (rank): 628,670 (18)
Land area: 81 sq mi. (210 sq km); **Alt.:** Highest,
   490 ft.; lowest, sea level
Avg. daily temp.: Jan., 31.8° F; July, 77.0° F
Churches: Roman Catholic, 72; Jewish, 50; Protestant
   and others, 344; **City-owned parks:** 347 park areas
   and tracts (6,314 ac.); **Radio stations:** AM, 10; FM,
   11; **Television stations:** 7
Civilian Labor Force (PMSA) June 2004: 1,376,558;
   Unemployed: 66,566 **Percent:** 4.8; **Per capita per-
   sonal income (MSA) 2002:** $35,556[2]
Chamber of Commerce: Baltimore City Chamber of
   Commerce, 3 W. Baltimore St., Baltimore, Md. 21204

1. A change in Baltimore's election procedures changed the municipal elections to a presidential election year. O'Malley's term would have ended in 2003 had the old rules been in effect. 2. Baltimore–Towson, Md.

Baltimore, the largest city in Maryland, is situated in the northern part of the state on the Patapsco River estuary, an arm of Chesapeake Bay. The city is independent and does not fall within any county.

The site was settled in the early 17th century and founded as a town in 1729. The town was named after Lord Baltimore, the founder of Maryland, and was incorporated as a city in 1797. It has an excellent harbor and has been a principal port since the 18th century. Baltimore was a pioneer shipbuilding center, and the Baltimore clipper was used extensively in world trade.

The city has been greatly affected by the nation's wars. During the War of 1812, the British bombarded nearby Fort McHenry, inspiring Francis Scott Key to write the *Star-Spangled Banner*. And although Maryland never seceded from the Union, Baltimore was occupied by Union troops throughout the Civil War. The city was also an important shipbuilding and supply center during the World Wars.

Baltimore's economy is very diverse, with strong financial, legal, and nonprofit service industries. The city also leads in scientific research and development through two highly acclaimed medical institutions, Johns Hopkins Hospital and University of Maryland Hospital. There is also a significant tourist sector. Major attractions include the the National Aquarium, Harborplace, the Maryland Science Center, the Babe Ruth Museum, Fort McHenry National Monument, and Pimlico Race Course, site of the Preakness.

Selected famous natives and residents: Larry Adler, musician; John Astin, actor; Eubie Blake, pianist; Francis X. Bushman, actor; Charlie Chase, actor; Hans Conried, actor; Mildred Dunnock, actress; "Mama" Cass Elliot, singer; Barry Farber, broadcaster; Paul Ford, actor; Philip Glass, composer; Billie Holiday, singer; Barry Levinson, director; H. L. Mencken, writer; Babe Ruth, baseball player; Upton Sinclair, novelist; Leon Uris, novelist; John Waters, film director, writer, and actor; Frank Zappa, musician.

Boston, Mass.

Mayor: Thomas Menino (to Jan. 2006)
2000 census population (rank): 589,141 (20); **% change:** 2.6; **Male:** 283,588 (48.1%); **Female,** 305,553 (51.9%); **White:** 320,944 (54.5%); **Black:** 149,202 (25.3%); **American Indian and Alaska Native:** 2,365 (0.4%); **Asian:** 44,284 (7.5%); **Other race:** 46,102 (7.8%); **Two or more races:** 25,878 (4.4%); **Hispanic/Latino:** 85,089 (14.4%). **2000 percent population 18 and over:** 80.2%; **65 and over:** 10.4%; **median age:** 31.1.
2003 population estimate (rank): 581,616 (23)
Land area: 48 sq mi. (124 sq km); **Alt.:** Highest, 330 ft.; lowest, sea level
Avg. daily temp.: Jan., 28.6° F; July, 73.5° F
Churches: Protestant, 187; Roman Catholic, 70; Jewish, 13; others, 100; **City-owned parks, playgrounds, etc.:** 2,260 ac.; **Radio stations:**[1] AM, 24; FM, 22; **Television stations:**[1] 27
Civilian Labor Force (PMSA) June 2004: 1,875,179; **Unemployed:** 88,579, **Percent:** 4.7; **Per capita personal income (MSA) 2002:** $42,436[2]
Chamber of Commerce: Greater Boston Chamber of Commerce, 75 State St., 2nd Fl., Boston, Mass. 02109

1. Metropolitan area. 2. Boston–Cambridge–Quincy, Mass.–N.H.

Boston is the state capital, the seat of Suffolk County, and the largest city in Massachusetts. It is located in the eastern part of the state on Massachusetts Bay. It was incorporated as a city in 1822. No city in the U.S. is richer in historical associations than Boston, and no city has retained more of its original buildings as memorials to America's past.

The first European settler was Rev. William Blackstone, who arrived in 1623, just three years after the Pilgrims had landed at Plymouth in 1620. He was joined by Puritans from England in 1630. They named their new town Boston, after the former home of many of them in Lincolnshire, England. Fourteen years later, the pioneer Bostonians set aside the first public park in the U.S.—the Boston Common. The following year, 1635, they opened the first free public school in America. Today, the Boston area is home to 68 colleges and universities.

Boston is a major industrial, financial, and educational hub and has one of the finest ports in the world. The city's banking and financial services, insurance, and real estate sectors continue to drive Boston's economy. Boston is also a leading city in health care, with 25 inpatient hospitals and numerous community health centers. The city's unique cultural and historic heritage makes it a center of tourism, and its hotel industry ranks among the highest in the nation in occupancy. Boston's other businesses are in high technology, biotechnology, software, and electronics.

The city's tourist attractions include Faneuil Hall Marketplace, the JFK Library and Museum, the Museum of Fine Arts, the New England Aquarium, the USS *Constitution,* and many historic buildings and neighborhoods.

Selected famous natives and residents: Samuel Adams, patriot; Louisa May Alcott, author; John Singleton Copley, painter; Ralph Waldo Emerson, philosopher and poet; Arthur Fiedler, conductor; Benjamin Franklin, statesman and scientist; Edward Everett Hale, clergyman and author; Oliver Wendell Holmes, Supreme Court justice; Winslow Homer, painter; Joseph P. Kennedy, financier; Jack Lemmon, actor; Robert Lowell, poet; Edgar Allan Poe, writer; Paul Revere, patriot and silversmith; John L. Sullivan, boxer; Barbara Walters, TV journalist.

Charlotte, N.C.

Mayor: Pat McCrory (to Nov. 2005)
2000 census population (rank): 540,828 (26); **% change:** 36.6; **Male:** 264,978 (49.0%); **Female:** 275,850 (51.0%); **White:** 315,061 (58.3%); **Black:** 176,964 (32.7%); **American Indian and Alaska Native:** 1,863 (0.3%); **Asian:** 18,418 (3.4%); **Other race:** 19,242 (3.6%); **Two or more races:** 8,997 (1.7%); **Hispanic/Latino:** 39,800 (7.4%). **2000 percent population 18 and over:** 75.3%; **65 and over:** 8.8%; **median age:** 32.7.
2003 population estimate (rank): 584,658 (21)
Land area: 242 sq mi. (627 sq km); **Alt.:** 765 ft.
Avg. daily temp.: Jan., 39.3° F; July, 79.3° F
Churches: Protestant, over 500; Roman Catholic, 13; Jewish, 3; Greek Orthodox, 1; **City-owned parks and parkways:** 150+; **Radio stations:** AM, 10; FM, 19; **Television stations:** 6 commercial; 1 PBS
Civilian Labor Force (MSA) June 2004: 888,013;[1] **Unemployed:** 56,884,[1] **Percent:** 6.4;[1] **Per capita personal income (MSA) 2002:** $33,083[2]
Chamber of Commerce: Charlotte Chamber, P.O. Box 32785, Charlotte, N.C., 28232

1. Charlotte–Gastonia–Rock Hill, N.C.–S.C. 2. Charlotte–Gastonia–Concord, N.C.–S.C.

Charlotte, North Carolina's largest city and the seat of Mecklenburg County, is located in the southern part of the state near the South Carolina border. It was named for King George III of England's wife, Charlotte Sophia of Mecklenburg-Strelitz.

Settled about 1750, Charlotte was incorporated as a city in 1768 and made the county seat in 1774. From 1800 to 1848, Charlotte was the center of U.S. gold production. A branch of the U.S. mint operated there from 1837 to 1913. Charlotte was a leading Confederate city during the Civil War and was the last meeting place of the full Confederate cabinet.

Charlotte is the second-largest banking center in the United States, and two of the nation's top banks, Wachovia and Bank of America, are headquartered there. Other major employers are the education, health care, government, technology, and communications sectors. The city is a hub for US Airways.

Charlotte is the home of the University of North Carolina at Charlotte (1946) as well as the Carolina Panthers (football) and Lowe's Motor Speedway.

Selected famous natives and residents: Romare Bearden, artist; Billy Graham, evangelist; Charles Gwathmey, architect; Hamilton Jordan, government official; Randolph Scott, actor.

Chicago, Ill.

Mayor: Richard M. Daley (to April 2007)
2000 census population (rank): 2,896,016 (3); **% change:** 4.0; **Male:** 1,405,107 (48.5%); **Female:** 1,490,909 (51.5%); **White:** 1,215,315 (42.0%); **Black:** 1,065,009 (36.8%); **American Indian and Alaska Native:** 10,290 (0.4%); **Asian:** 125,974 (4.3%); **Other race:** 393,203 (13.6%); **Two or more races:** 84,437 (2.9%); **Hispanic/Latino:** 753,644 (26.0%). **2000 percent population 18 and over:** 73.8%; **65 and over:** 10.3%; **median age:** 31.5.

2003 population estimate (rank): 2,869,121 (3)
Land area: 227 sq mi. (588 sq km); **Alt.:** Highest, 672 ft.; lowest, 578.5 ft.
Avg. daily temp.: Jan., 22.4° F; July, 75.1° F
Churches: Protestant, 850; Roman Catholic, 252; Jewish, 51; **City-owned parks:** 552 (7,300 ac.) **Radio stations:** AM, 21; FM, 37; **Television stations:** 31
Civilian Labor Force (PMSA) June 2003: 4,321,242; **Unemployed:** 267,161, **Percent:** 6.2; **Per capita personal income (MSA) 2002:** $35,583[1]
Chamber of Commerce: Chicagoland Chamber of Commerce, One IBM Plaza, 330 N. Wabash, Suite 2800, Chicago, Ill. 60611

1. Chicago–Naperville–Joliet, Ill.–Ind.–Wis.

Chicago is the largest city in Illinois and the seat of Cook County. It stretches for 22 mi along the southwest shore of Lake Michigan in the northeast part of the state.

The first white men known to have visited the region were Louis Joliet and Jacques Marquette in 1673. The first permanent white settler was John Kinzie, who is sometimes called the Father of Chicago. He took over a trading post in 1796 that had been established in 1791 by Jean-Baptiste Point du Sable, a black fur trapper. Fort Dearborn, a blockhouse and stockade, was built in 1804 but was evacuated in 1812, at which time more than half of its garrison was massacred by Potawatomi and Ottawa Indians loyal to the British.

The name Chicago is thought to come from an Algonquian word meaning "onion" or "skunk."

Laid out in 1830, Chicago was incorporated as a village in 1833 and as a city in 1837. In the Great Chicago Fire of 1871, an area of the city about 4 mi long and nearly a mile wide—more than two thousand acres—was totally destroyed. However, much of the city, including the railroads and stockyards, survived intact, and from the ashes of the old wooden structures there arose more modern constructions in steel and stone.

Today, Chicago is a major Great Lakes port and the commercial, financial, industrial, and cultural center of the Midwest. The manufacturing industries dominate the wholesale and retail trade, and trade in agricultural commodities is important to the economy. The Chicago Board of Trade is the largest agricultural futures market in the world.

Among Chicago's many attractions are the Art Institute of Chicago, the Field Museum of Natural History, the Jane Addams–Hull House Museum, Navy Pier, and numerous architectural landmarks such as the Sears Tower and Frank Lloyd Wright's Robie House.

Selected famous natives and residents: Jack Benny, comedian; Edgar Rice Burroughs, author; Raymond Chandler, author; Hillary Rodham Clinton, U.S. senator, lawyer, and former first lady; Michael Crichton, author; Walt Disney, filmmaker; John Dos Passos, author; Bobby Fischer, chess player; Bob Fosse, choreographer and director; Benny Goodman, clarinetist; Dorothy Hamill, figure skater; Quincy Jones, composer; Gene Krupa, drummer; David Mamet, playwright; Bob Newhart, comedian; Kim Novak, actress; Donald O'Connor, actor; William L. Shirer, journalist and historian; Gloria Swanson, actress; Melvin Van Peebles, playwright; Alfred Wallenstein, conductor; Robin Williams, comedian and actor; Robert Young, actor.

Cleveland, Ohio

Mayor: Jane Campbell (to Jan. 2006)
2000 census population (rank): 478,403 (33); **% change:** –5.4; **Male:** 226,550 (47.4%); **Female:** 251,853 (52.6%); **White:** 198,510 (41.5%); **Black:**

243,939 (51.0%); **American Indian and Alaska Native:** 1,458 (0.3%); **Asian:** 6,444 (1.3%); **Other race:** 17,173 (3.6%); **Two or more races:** 10,701 (2.2%); **Hispanic/Latino:** 34,728 (7.3%). **2000 percent population 18 and over:** 71.5%; **65 and over:** 12.5%; **median age:** 33.0.
2003 population estimate (rank): 461,324 (35)
Land area: 78 sq mi. (202 sq km); **Alt.:** Highest, 1048 ft.; lowest, 573 ft.
Avg. daily temp.: Jan., 24.8° F; July, 71.9° F
Churches:[1] Protestant, 980; Roman Catholic, 187; Jewish, 31; Eastern Orthodox, 22; **City-owned parks:** 41 (1,930 ac.); **Radio stations:** AM, 9; FM, 19; **Television stations:** 22
Civilian Labor Force (PMSA) June 2004: 1,132,382;[1] **Unemployed:** 73,112,[1] **Percent:** 6.5;[1] **Per capita personal income (MSA) 2002:** $32,244[2]
Chamber of Commerce: Greater Cleveland Partnership, 50 Public Sq., Ste. 200, Cleveland, Ohio 44113

1. Cleveland–Lorain–Elyria, Ohio. 2. Cleveland–Elyria–Mentor, Ohio.

Cleveland is the second-largest city in Ohio and the seat of Cuyahoga County. It is located in the northeast part of the state on Lake Erie.

In the colonial era, the Cleveland area was known as the Connecticut Western Reserve, part of a land grant made to Connecticut by King Charles II in 1662. The city was founded in 1796 by Gen. Moses Cleaveland, who was the head surveyor of the Connecticut Land Company. This company had bought 3 million acres in what is now northern Ohio. A permanent settlement was founded in 1799, named after the general, and the spelling was shortened to Cleveland. The city was incorporated in 1836.

Cleveland's industrial growth was stimulated by the opening of the Ohio and Erie canals in 1832 and, later, by the advent of the Civil War, with the increasing demand for machinery, railroad equipment, ships, and other items. Today, the port of Cleveland is the largest overseas general cargo port on Lake Erie.

Greater Cleveland has long been famous as a durable goods manufacturing area. Following the national trend, however, Cleveland has been shifting to a more services-based economy. Greater Cleveland is a world corporate center for leading national and multinational companies in industries ranging from transportation, insurance, retailing, and utilities, to commercial banking and finance.

The city's cultural attractions include the Cleveland Museum of Art and the Cleveland Orchestra, one of the country's most highly acclaimed symphony orchestras. Jacobs Field, a new major league ballpark, and the Rock & Roll Hall of Fame also draw thousands of visitors to the city.

Selected famous natives and residents: Jim Backus, actor; Drew Carey, actor and comedian; Dorothy Dandridge, actress; Ruby Dee, actress; Phil Donahue, talk-show host; Joel Grey, actor; Arsenio Hall, talk-show host; Margaret Hamilton, actress; Philip Johnson, architect; Henry Mancini, composer; Burgess Meredith, actor; Paul Newman, actor; Carl Stokes, jurist.

Colorado Springs, Colo.

Mayor: Lionel Rivera (to April 2007)
2000 census population (rank): 360,890 (48); **% change:** 28.4; **Male:** 178,469 (49.5%); **Female:** 182,421 (50.5%); **White:** 291,095 (80.7%); **Black:** 23,677 (6.6%); **American Indian and Alaska Native:** 3,175 (0.9%); **Asian:** 10,179 (2.8%); **Other**

race: 18,091 (5.0%); **Two or more races:** 13,909 (3.9%); **Hispanic/Latino:** 43,330 (12.0%). **2000 percent population 18 and over:** 73.5%; **65 and over:** 9.6%; **median age:** 33.6.
2003 population estimate (rank): 370,448 (48)
Land area: 186 sq mi. (482 sq km); **Alt.:** 6,035 ft.
Avg. daily temp.: Jan., 28.8° F; July, 70.8° F
Churches: Protestant, 400+; Roman Catholic, 20; Jewish, 3; others, **City parks and playgrounds:** 156 (12,000+ ac.); **Radio stations:** AM, 7; FM, 17; **Television stations:** 7
Civilian Labor Force (MSA) June 2004: 292,677; **Unemployed:** 16,802, **Percent:** 5.7; **Per capita personal income (MSA) 2002:** $29,892
Chamber of Commerce: Colorado Springs Chamber of Commerce, 2 N. Cascade Ave., Suite 110, Colorado Springs, Colo. 80903

Colorado Springs is the second-largest city in Colorado, after Denver. It is the seat of El Paso County, making up about three-quarters of the county's population. It is located on the edge of the Rocky Mountains, with Pikes Peak (14,110 ft) towering beside it to the west. To the east begin the Great Plains.

The city was founded in 1871. Gen. William Jackson Palmer, a Pennsylvania-born Civil War veteran, came across the scenic spot in his railroad travels and was inspired to begin a new resort community there. The subsequent development of Colorado Springs was influenced in part by an influx of English tourists later in the 1870s and by the discovery of gold in nearby Cripple Creek in the 1890s. Millionaire businessmen and philanthropists, such as Spencer Penrose, Charles Tutt, and Winfield Scott Stratton, helped to establish the city's infrastructure and shape its popularity as a tourist destination.

During World War II, Colorado Springs sold a large amount of land just south of the city to the military. The U.S. Army established Fort Carson as a training facility. The military presence in Colorado Springs continued to grow with the establishment of the U.S. Air Force Academy there in the 1950s, and later, the construction of Peterson Air Force Base, Falcon Air Force Base, and Cheyenne Mountain Air Force Base. The bases are all home to space command centers (with Cheyenne Mountain housing the headquarters for the North American Aerospace Defense Command [NORAD]) and have collectively earned Colorado Springs its national reputation as the leading center for military space operations.

The city's economy is still based heavily on tourism, although in more recent years, Colorado Springs has gained a strong foothold in the electronics, high-technology, and manufacturing industries. The city is the headquarters of the U.S. Olympic Committee and Olympic Training Center facility.

Selected famous natives and residents: Bert Andrews, journalist; Kelly Bishop, actress; Spring Byington, actress; Lon Chaney, actor; Marjorie Daw, actress; Marceline Day, actress; Rich "Goose" Gossage, baseball player; Helen Hunt Jackson, writer and poet; Chase Masterson, actress; Sherry Stringfield, actress.

Columbus, Ohio

Mayor: Michael B. Coleman (to Nov. 2007)
2000 census population (rank): 711,470 (15);
% change: 12.4; **Male:** 345,878 (48.6%); **Female:** 365,592 (51.4%); **White:** 483,332 (67.9%); **Black:** 174,065 (24.5%); **American Indian and Alaska Native:** 2,090 (0.3%); **Asian:** 24,495 (3.4%); **Other**

race: 8,292 (1.2%); **Two or more races:** 18,829 (2.6%); **Hispanic/Latino:** 17,471 (2.5%). **2000 percent population 18 and over:** 75.8%; **65 and over:** 8.9%; **median age:** 30.6.
2003 population estimate (rank): 728,432 (15)
Land area: 210 sq mi. (544 sq km); **Alt.:** Highest, 902 ft.; lowest, 702 ft.
Avg. daily temp.: Jan., 26.4° F; July, 73.2° F
Churches: Protestant, 436; Roman Catholic, 62; Jewish, 5; Other, 8; **City-owned parks:** 203 (12,891 ac.); **Radio stations:** AM, 10; FM, 16; **Television stations:** 9 commercial, 3 PBS
Civilian Labor Force (MSA) June 2004: 899,912; **Unemployed:** 46,102, **Percent:** 5.1; **Per capita personal income (MSA) 2002:** $32,043
Chamber of Commerce: Columbus Area Chamber of Commerce, 37 N. High St., Columbus, Ohio 43215

Columbus, the largest city in Ohio, is the state capital and the seat of Franklin County. It is located in central Ohio on the Scioto River.

The first structures near the site of downtown Columbus were earthen mounds constructed by Indian tribes known as Mound Builders. Native Americans lived undisturbed in Central Ohio until the 1700s, when the first white explorers entered the Midwest. The first permanent white settlement in the area was founded by a surveyor from Kentucky, Lucas Sullivant, in 1797 and was named Franklinton. The state capital was laid out nearby in 1812 and named after Christopher Columbus. It became the capital in 1816. Columbus was chartered as a city in 1834 and annexed Franklinton in 1870. The city's growth was stimulated by the development of transportation facilities—a feeder to the Ohio Canal completed in 1832, the National Road in 1833, and the arrival of the railroad in 1850.

Columbus is a port of entry and a major commercial, distribution, and cultural center. It is the seat of Ohio State University (1870). The city has enjoyed steady growth over the years due to its economic diversity, and no single activity dominates the economy.

Selected famous natives and residents: Warner Baxter, actor; George Bellows, painter; Michael Feinstein, singer and pianist; Eileen Heckart, actress; Jack Nicklaus, golfer; Tom Poston, actor; Eddie Rickenbacker, aviator; Arthur M. Schlesinger, historian; James Thurber, writer and cartoonist; Nancy Wilson, singer.

Dallas, Tex.

Mayor: Laura Miller (to May 2007)
City Manager: Teodoro J. Benavides
2000 census population (rank): 1,188,580 (8);
% change: 18.0; **Male:** 598,991 (50.4%); **Female:** 589,589 (49.6%); **White:** 604,209 (50.8%); **Black:** 307,957 (25.9%); **American Indian and Alaska Native:** 6,472 (0.5%); **Asian:** 32,118 (2.7%); **Other race:** 204,883 (17.2%); **Two or more races:** 32,351 (2.7%); **Hispanic/Latino:** 422,587 (35.6%). **2000 percent population 18 and over:** 73.4%; **65 and over:** 8.6%; **median age:** 30.5.
2003 population estimate (rank): 1,208,318 (9)
Land area: 343 sq mi. (888 sq km); **Alt.:** Highest, 750 ft.; lowest, 375 ft.
Avg. daily temp.: Jan., 44.6° F; July, 85.9° F
Churches: 1,974 (in Dallas Co.); **City-owned parks:** 406 (21,000+ ac.); **Radio stations:** AM, 19; FM, 30; **Television stations:** 10 commercial, 1 PBS
Civilian Labor Force (PMSA) June 2004: 2,056,978; **Unemployed:** 136,468, **Percent:** 6.6; **Per capita personal income (MSA) 2002:** $33,816[1]

Chamber of Commerce: Greater Dallas Chamber of Commerce, 700 N. Pearl St., Ste. 1200, Dallas, Tex. 75201

1. Dallas–Fort Worth–Arlington, Texas.

Dallas is the second-largest city in Texas and the seat of Dallas County. It is situated 185 mi northeast of Austin on the Trinity River near the junction of its three forks.

Dallas was first settled by Tennessee lawyer John Neely Bryan as a trading post on the Trinity River in 1841. Many historians believe that Bryan named the city after George Mifflin Dallas, vice president under James K. Polk, but there is no official agreement on this. It was incorporated as a town in 1856 and as a city in 1871. Located in the chief cotton-producing region of Texas, the city developed as a cotton market in the 1870s.

The economy is highly diversified, and the city is the leading commercial, marketing, and industrial center of the southwest. The insurance business is important, and the service sector has experienced rapid growth. Dallas is also a popular tourist and convention city.

Selected famous natives and residents: Tex Avery, animator and director; Robby Benson, actor; Ernie Banks, baseball player; Bebe Daniels, actress; Linda Darnell, actress; Lee Elder, golfer; Morgan Fairchild, actress; Trini Lopez, singer; Aaron Spelling, producer; Stephen Stills, singer; Sharon Tate, actress; Lee Trevino, golfer.

Denver, Colo.

Mayor: John Hickenlooper (to June 30, 2007)
2000 census population (rank): 554,636 (25);
% change: 18.6; Male: 280,207 (50.5%); Female: 274,429 (49.5%); White: 362,180 (65.3%); Black: 61,649 (11.1%); American Indian and Alaska Native: 7,290 (1.3%); Asian: 15,611 (2.8%); Other race: 86,464 (15.6%); Two or more races: 20,794 (3.7%); Hispanic/Latino: 175,704 (31.7%); 2000 percent population 18 and over: 78.0%; 65 and over: 11.3%; median age: 33.1.
2003 population estimate (rank): 557,478 (26)
Land area: 155 sq mi. (401 sq km); Alt.: Highest, 5,672 ft.; lowest, 5,140 ft.
Avg. daily temp.: Jan., 29.7° F; July, 73.5° F
Churches:[1] Protestant, 859; Roman Catholic, 60; Jewish, 13; City-owned parks: 301 (5,100 ac.); City-owned mountain parks: 40 (13,600 ac.); Radio stations:[1] AM, 23; FM, 20; Television stations:[1] 10
Civilian Labor Force (PMSA) June 2004 1,278,315; Unemployed: 68,023, Percent: 5.3; Per capita personal income (MSA) 2002: $38,008[2]
Chamber of Commerce: Denver Metro Chamber of Commerce, 1445 Market Street, Denver, Colo. 80202

1. Metropolitan area. 2. Denver–Aurora, Colo.

Denver is the largest city in Colorado, the state capital, and the seat of Denver County. It lies at the foot of the Rocky Mountains at the junction of the South Platte River and Cherry Creek.

The city was born in 1858, when gold was discovered in the sands of Cherry Creek, at first just a tough village of cabins, shacks, and tents. It was incorporated as a city in 1861 and became the territorial capital in 1867. The city is named for James W. Denver, governor of the Kansas Territory, which included part of Colorado. The city prospered following the opening of the famous gold and silver mines of the 1870s and 1880s.

Today, Denver is an important communications, transportation, manufacturing, and agribusiness hub. Telecommunications and biomedical technology are

two of the largest industries; construction, real estate, and retail trade are among the fastest-growing industries. The city is also home to many environmental organizations, including federal government agencies such as the Environmental Protection Agency and the National Oceanic and Atmospheric Administration.

Denver International Airport, the first major new airport constructed in the U.S. in 21 years, opened to passenger traffic in 1995. At 53 sq mi, it is the largest airport in North America.

The city's tourist attractions include the Denver Zoo, the Six Flags Elitch Gardens amusement park, the Red Rocks Amphitheatre, the Coors Brewery, and nearby Rocky Mountain National Park.

Selected famous natives and residents: Tim Allen, comedian and actor; Ward Bond, actor; Douglas Fairbanks, Sr., actor; John Hart, newsman; Pat Hingle, actor; Ted Mack, TV host; Barbara Rush, actress; Alan K. Simpson, U.S. senator; Paul Whiteman, bandleader; Don Wilson, announcer.

Detroit, Mich.

Mayor: Kwame Kilpatrick (to Jan. 2006)
2000 census population (rank): 951,270 (10);
% change: –7.5; Male: 448,319 (47.1%); Female: 502,951 (52.9%); White: 116,599 (12.3%); Black: 775,772 (81.6%); American Indian and Alaska Native: 3,140 (0.3%); Asian: 9,268 (1.0%); Other race: 24,199 (2.5%); Two or more races: 22,041 (2.3%); Hispanic/Latino: 47,167 (5.0%). 2000 percent population 18 and over: 68.9%; 65 and over: 10.4%; median age: 30.9.
2003 population estimate (rank): 911,402 (10)
Land area: 139 sq mi. (360 sq km); Alt.: Highest, 685 ft.; lowest, 574 ft.
Avg. daily temp.: Jan., 24.7° F; July, 74.2° F
Churches:[1] Protestant, 1,165; Roman Catholic, 89; Jewish, 2; City-owned parks: 56 parks (3,843 ac.); 393 sites (5,838 ac.); Radio stations: AM, 27; FM, 30 (includes 3 in Windsor, Ont.); Television stations: 8[2] (includes 1 in Windsor, Ont.)
Civilian Labor Force (PMSA) June 2004: 2,287,717; Unemployed: 166,131, Percent: 7.3; Per capita personal income (MSA) 2002: $34,129[3]
Chamber of Commerce: Detroit Regional Chamber of Commerce, One Woodward Avenue, P.O. Box 33840, Detroit MI 48232-0840

1. Six-county metropolitan area. 2. Within four counties of Metro Detroit. 3. Detroit–Warren–Livonia, Mich.

Detroit, the largest city in Michigan, is situated in the southeast part of the state on the Detroit River. The seat of Wayne County, Detroit was incorporated as a city in 1815 and reincorporated in 1824.

Detroit is the oldest city of any size west of the seaboard colonies, having been founded by Antoine de la Mothe Cadillac on July 24, 1701, more than a century before Chicago was founded. The French were the first settlers, and they gave the city its name from their word meaning "strait," referring to the 27-mile-long Detroit River, which connects Lake Erie and Lake St. Clair. The river forms part of the international boundary, and marks the only point where Canada lies directly south of U.S. territory.

Because of its strategic location, Detroit was fought over by the French, the British, and the Indians during the French and Indian Wars. It was the headquarters for the British forces in the Northwest Territory during the American Revolutionary War.

The first steam vessel, the *Walk-in-the-Water*, made its appearance on the Great Lakes in 1818, and

Detroit was the western terminus for most of its voyages from Buffalo. Its link to all the important cities on the Great Lakes made it a major exporting center.

Detroit is one of the largest manufacturing cities in the U.S. and is the center of the automobile manufacturing industry, which has experienced a decline due to foreign competition in the past decade. The health and medical care sector is important to the economy, and employment in the finance, insurance, and real-estate industries has inched up in the Detroit metropolitan area since the early 1990s.

Selected famous natives and residents: Anita Baker, singer; Sonny Bono, congressman and singer; Ralph Bunche, statesman; Ellen Burstyn, actress; Francis Ford Coppola, director; Aretha Franklin, singer; Casey Kasem, radio personality; Charles Lindbergh, aviator; Madonna, singer and actress; John Mitchell, former U.S. attorney general; Harry Morgan, actor; Rosa Parks, activist; George Peppard, actor; Gilda Radner, comedian; Della Reese, singer; Smokey Robinson, singer; Sugar Ray Robinson, boxer; Diana Ross, singer; George C. Scott, actor; Tom Selleck, actor; Lily Tomlin, comedian and actress; Margaret Whiting, singer.

El Paso, Tex.

Mayor: Joe Wardy (to May 2005)
2000 census population (rank): 563,662 (23);
% change: 9.4; **Male:** 267,651 (47.5%); **Female:** 296,011 (52.5%); **White:** 413,061 (73.3%); **Black:** 17,586 (3.1%); **American Indian and Alaska Native:** 4,601 (0.8%); **Asian:** 6,321 (1.1%); **Other race:** 102,320 (18.2%); **Two or more races:** 19,190 (3.4%); **Hispanic/Latino:** 431,875 (76.6%). **2000 percent population 18 and over:** 69.0%; **65 and over:** 10.7%; **median age:** 31.1
2003 population estimate (rank): 584,113 (22)
Land area: 249 sq mi. (645 sq km); **Alt.:** 4,000 ft.
Avg. daily temp.: Jan., 42.8° F; July, 82.3° F
Churches: Protestant, 320; Roman Catholic, 39; Jewish, 3; others, 20; **City-owned parks:** 145 (2,150 ac.);[1] **Radio Stations:** AM, 18; FM, 17; **Television stations:** 6
Civilian Labor Force (MSA) June 2004: 295,120; **Unemployed:** 24,335, **Percent:** 8.2; **Per capita personal income (MSA) 2002:** $20,129
Chamber of Commerce: Greater El Paso Chamber of Commerce, 10 Civic Center Plaza, El Paso, Tex. 79944; Hispanic Chamber of Commerce, 201 E. Main, Ste. 100, Austin, Tex. 79901

1. Includes 129 developed and 16 undeveloped parks.

El Paso, the fifth-largest city in Texas and the seat of El Paso County, is located in the far western part of the state on the north bank of the Rio Grande, opposite the Mexican city of Ciudad Juárez on the south bank.

On April 30, 1598, Juan de Oñate took formal possession of the area for King Philip II of Spain. Subsequently he crossed the Rio Grande near a site west of present downtown El Paso, which he called "El Paso del Rio del Norte," meaning the crossing of the river—the first use of the name "El Paso." In 1659, the mission of Nuestra Señora de Guadalupe was founded on a site that is present-day downtown Ciudad Juárez; the mission is still in use today. In 1682, Spanish colonists from Mexico founded the settlement of Ysleta on the site of the present-day city. However, it wasn't until 1827 that the first permanent settlement at El Paso was established by Juan María Ponce de León. The city's real growth started with the arrival of the Southern Pacific Railroad in 1881. El Paso was incorporated as a city in 1873.

In 1888, Mexico changed the name of Paso del Norte to Ciudad Juárez in honor of Benito Juárez. Later, in 1967, the U.S. agreed to cede a long-disputed part of El Paso to Mexico due to changes in the course of the Rio Grande, which forms the international boundary between the two countries. El Paso and its sister city of Ciudad Juárez across the U.S./Mexico border are inexorably joined by culture and economy. El Paso and Juárez make up the largest international metroplex in the world.

El Paso is an important port of entry to the U.S. from Mexico. The high technology, medical device manufacturing, plastics, refining, automotive, food processing, and defense-related industries are important to the economy. El Paso's service sector has experienced healthy growth since the 1980s. El Paso is also a major tourist resort.

Selected famous natives and residents: Manuel Acosta, artist; Don Bluth, animation director; Vicki Carr, singer; Jose Cisneros, artist; Sam Donaldson, newsman; Albert Fall, government official; Judith Ivey, actress; Guy Kibbee, actor; Sandra Day O'Connor, Supreme Court justice; Debbie Reynolds, actress; Irene Ryan, actress.

Fort Worth, Tex.

Mayor: Mike Moncrief (to May 2005)
City Manager: Gary W. Jackson
2000 census population (rank): 534,694 (27);
% change: 19.5; **Male:** 263,720 (49.3%); **Female:** 270,974 (50.7%); **White:** 319,159 (59.7%); **Black:** 108,310 (20.3%); **American Indian and Alaska Native:** 3,144 (0.6%); **Asian:** 14,105 (2.6%); **Other race:** 75,100 (14.0%); **Two or more races:** 14,535 (2.7%); **Hispanic/Latino:** 159,368 (29.8%). **2000 percent population 18 and over:** 71.7%; **65 and over:** 9.6%; **median age:** 30.9
2003 population estimate (rank): 585,122 (20)
Land area: 293 sq mi. (759 sq km); **Alt.:** Highest, 780 ft.; lowest, 520 ft.
Avg. daily temp.: Jan., 43.4° F; July, 85.3° F
Churches: 1,032, representing 72 denominations; **City-owned parks:** 222 (10,380 ac.); **Radio stations:**[1] AM, 29; FM, 48; **Television stations:** 13
Civilian Labor Force (PMSA) June 2004: 976,327;[2] **Unemployed:** 59,383,[2] **Percent:** 6.1;[2] **Per capita personal income (MSA) 2001:** $33,816[3]
Chamber of Commerce: Fort Worth Chamber of Commerce, 777 Taylor Street, Suite 900, Fort Worth, Tex. 76102

1. Dallas–Fort Worth area. 2. Fort Worth–Arlington, Tex. 3. Dallas–Fort Worth–Arlington, Tex.

Fort Worth, seat of Tarrant County, is situated in the north-central part of Texas on the Trinity River.

The city was founded by Maj. Ripley Arnold in 1849 as a military outpost on the Trinity River to protect settlers moving westward from frequent Indian attacks. It was named after Gen. William J. Worth, the commander of the Texas army. Fort Worth was incorporated in 1873. Its growth was stimulated in the 1870s by its proximity to the Chisholm cattle trail. It prospered as a meat-packing and shipping center when the Texas and Pacific Railway arrived in 1876 and later experienced a new boom when oil was discovered nearby in 1917. The establishment of military installations in the area during both world wars also spurred the economy.

Fort Worth has traditionally been a diverse center of manufacturing and is not dependent on the oil or financial sectors. The city's industries range from clothing and food products to jet fighters, helicopters, computers, pharmaceuticals, and plastics. Fort

Worth is a national leader in aviation products, electronic equipment, and refrigeration equipment. It is home to a multitude of major corporate headquarters, offices, and distribution centers.

Selected famous natives and residents: Robert Bass, financier; Mark Brooks, golfer; Betty Buckley, singer and actress; Kate Capshaw, actress; Ornette Coleman, composer; Sandra Haynie, golfer; Patricia Highsmith, writer; Spanky McFarland, actor; R. Bruce Merrifield, Nobelist in chemistry; Roger Miller, singer; Fess Parker, actor; Bill Paxton, actor; Rex Reed, critic; Johnny Rutherford, auto racer; Liz Smith, columnist.

Fresno, Calif.

Mayor: Alan Autry (to Jan. 2005)
City Manager: Daniel G. Hobbs
2000 census population (rank): 427,652 (37);
% change: 20.7; **Male:** 210,107 (49.1%); **Female:** 217,545 (50.9%); **White:** 214,556 (50.2%); **Black:** 35,763 (8.4%); **American Indian and Alaska Native:** 6,763 (1.6%); **Asian:** 48,028 (11.2%); **Other race:** 99,898 (23.4%); **Two or more races:** 22,061 (5.2%); **Hispanic/Latino:** 170,520 (39.9%). **2000 percent population 18 and over:** 67.1%; **65 and over:** 9.3%; **median age:** 28.5.
2003 population estimate (rank): 451,455 (36)
Land area: 104 sq mi. (269 sq km); **Alt.:** 328 ft.
Avg. daily temp.: Jan., 45.7° F; July, 81.9° F
Churches: 450 (approximate); **City-owned parks:** 38 (690 ac.); **Radio stations:** AM, 11;[1] FM, 13;[1] Bilingual 1; **Television stations:** 8[1]
Civilian Labor Force (MSA) June 2004: 466,906;
Unemployed: 58,551, **Percent:** 12.5; **Per capita personal income (MSA) 2002:** $23,492
Chamber of Commerce: Fresno Chamber of Commerce, 2331 Fresno St., Fresno, Calif. 93721

1. Metropolitan area.

Fresno is located in central California, 184 mi southeast of San Francisco and 222 mi northwest of Los Angeles. It is the seat of Fresno County. Fresno was incorporated as a city in 1885.

Fresno began as a station for the Central Pacific Railroad in 1872 and was made the seat of Fresno County in 1874. The city's name is Spanish for the ash trees that the early explorers found in the area.

Fresno is a leading agribusiness hub, with 250 different crops produced by 7,500 farmers on 1.9 million irrigated acres, worth $3 billion a year. Fresno County's top agricultural products are grapes, cotton, tomatoes, cattle and calves, and turkeys.

The city is also a distribution and manufacturing center. Its diverse industries include agricultural chemicals, farm equipment, canned fruit and vegetables, clothing, computer software, electric wire, pumps, glass, and plastic products.

Selected famous natives and residents: Mike Connors, actor; Maynard Dixon, painter; Bruce Furniss, swimmer; Jon Hall, actor; Daryle Lamonica, football player; Sam Peckinpah, director; William Saroyan, novelist; Tom Seaver, baseball player.

Honolulu, Hawaii

Mayor: Jeremy Harris (to Jan. 2005)
2000 census population (rank):[1] 371,657 (46);
% change: 1.7; **Male:** 182,628 (49.1%); **Female:** 189,029 (50.9%); **White:** 73,093 (19.7%); **Black:** 6,038 (1.6%); **American Indian and Alaska Native:** 689 (0.2%); **Asian:** 207,588 (55.9%); **Native**

Hawaiian and Other Pacific Islander: 25,457 (6.8%); **Other race:** 3,318 (0.9%); **Two or more races:** 55,474 (14.9%); **Hispanic/Latino:** 16,229 (4.4%). **2000 percent population 18 and over:** 80.8%; **65 and over:** 17.8%; **median age:** 39.7
2003 population estimate (rank): 380,149 (45)
Land area: 85.7 sq mi. (221.9 sq km);[1] **Alt.:** Highest, 2,013 ft.;[1] lowest, sea level
Avg. daily temp.: Jan., 71.4° F; July, 78.9° F
Churches: Roman Catholic, 39; Buddhist, 51; Jewish, 2; Protestant and others, 402; **City-owned parks:**[1] 6,108 ac.; **Radio stations:**[1] AM, 17; FM, 11; **Television stations:**[1] 12
Civilian Labor Force (MSA) June 2004: 445,690;[2]
Unemployed: 13,395,[2] **Percent:** 3.0;[2] **Per capita personal income (MSA) 2002:** $31,707[2]
Chamber of Commerce: Chamber of Commerce of Hawaii, 1132 Bishop St., Suite 402, Honolulu, Hawaii 96813

1. Census Designated Place, approximately Salt Lake to Hawaii Kai. 2. City and county.

Honolulu is the capital and largest city of Hawaii, on the southeast coast of the island of Oahu. The city is legally coextensive with the county of Honolulu, which includes the entire island of Oahu and most of the Northwest Hawaiian Islands, from Nihoa to Kure Atoll, except Midway. The population of Oahu makes up 73% of the state's total population. It is situated in the central Pacific Ocean 2,397 mi west-southwest of San Francisco. Honolulu's name derives from the native words *hono,* meaning "a bay," and *lulu,* meaning "sheltered."

Honolulu's early history was one of turbulence and conflict. One of the last areas on the globe to be explored and exploited by Europeans (it was first visited by British captain James Cook in 1778), Hawaii was subject to strong pressures from many forces, including American missionaries, who arrived in 1820, and opportunistic whalers. These whalers were among those who built Honolulu originally, bringing trade, commerce, and prosperity that led to expansion into the sugar and pineapple industries.

As early as 1814, Russia tried to move in, and Russian soldiers built a bastion at the harbor's edge. The British flag was raised in 1843 and French forces occupied Honolulu in 1849. Each time control was returned to the independent native kingdom without bloodshed. In 1898, a group of Americans completed a project attempted at intervals during the previous 65 years—annexation to the United States. Honolulu was incorporated as a city in 1907.

The Honolulu area was bombed by Japan in a surprise attack on the unprepared U.S. naval base at Pearl Harbor on Dec. 7, 1941. This action forced the United States to enter World War II. "Remember Pearl Harbor" became a famous American wartime slogan.

Hawaiian statehood in 1959 and the viability of commercial air travel to the island brought boom times to Honolulu. Tourism is the city's principal industry, followed by federal defense expenditures and agricultural exports (chiefly pineapples).

Selected famous natives and residents: Hiram Bingham, explorer; Jean Erdman, dancer and choreographer; Hiram Fong, senator; Daniel Inouye, senator; Duke Kahanamoku, surfer and Olympian swimmer; Bette Midler, actress and singer; Kelly Preston, actress; Louise Morgan Sill, author; Don Stroud, actor; Merlin D. Tuttle, biologist and wildlife photographer.

Houston, Tex.

Mayor: Bill White (to Dec. 31, 2005)
2000 census population (rank): 1,953,631 (4);
% change: 19.8; **Male:** 975,551 (49.9%); **Female:**
978,080 (50.1%); **White:** 962,610 (49.3%); **Black:**
494,496 (25.3%); **American Indian and Alaska**
Native: 8,568 (0.4%); **Asian:** 103,694 (5.3%); **Other**
race: 321,603 (16.5%); **Two or more races:** 61,478
(3.1%); **Hispanic/Latino:** 730,865 (37.4%). **2000 per-**
cent population 18 and over: 72.5%; **65 and over:**
8.4%; **median age:** 30.9.
2003 population estimate (rank): 2,009,690 (4)
Land area: 579 sq mi. (1,500 sq km); **Alt.:** Highest, 120
ft.; lowest, sea level
Avg. daily temp.: Jan., 52.2° F; July, 83.5° F
Churches:[1] 1,750; **City-owned parks:** 293 (32,733 ac.);
Radio stations:[1] AM, 23; FM, 32; **Television sta-**
tions: 15 commercial, 1 PBS
Civilian Labor Force (PMSA) June 2004: 2,360,592;
Unemployed: 164,663, **Percent:** 7.0; **Per capita**
personal income (MSA) 2002: $34,969[2]
Chamber of Commerce: Greater Houston Partnership,
1200 Smith, Suite 700, Houston, Tex. 77002-4400

1. Harris County. 2. Houston–Baytown–Sugar Land, Tex.

Houston, the largest city in Texas and seat of Harris County, is located in the southeast part of the state near the Gulf of Mexico.

Sam Houston was the commander-in-chief of the Texas troops who fought a successful war of rebellion against Mexico, which had been in possession of Texas. On April 21, 1836, Houston's men won a decisive victory in which the Mexican dictator, Gen. Santa Anna, was taken prisoner and forced to sign the treaty that launched the Republic of Texas. In September, a constitution was ratified, and Houston was elected president. The Texas Republic was recognized by the U.S. and by the major European powers. The present city of Houston was incorporated in 1837 and named after Sam Houston; it was the Republic's first capital.

The port of Houston ranks high among U.S. ports in foreign tonnage handled. The city is a major business, financial, science, and technology center. Houston is outstanding in oil and natural-gas production and is the energy capital of the world. It is the home of one of the largest medical facilities in the world—the Texas Medical Center—and the focus of the aerospace industry. The Lyndon B. Johnson Space Center is the nation's headquarters for staffed spaceflight.

Among the city's many visitor attractions are Space Center Houston, the Houston Arboretum and Nature Center, Six Flags AstroWorld, George Ranch Historical Park, the Astrodome baseball stadium, and nearby San Jacinto Battlefield.

Selected famous natives and residents: Debbie Allen, choreographer; Lance Alworth, football player; Denton Cooley, heart surgeon; Jim Demaret, golfer; Allen Drury, novelist; Shelly Duvall, actress; A. J. Foyt, auto racer; Howard Hughes, industrialist and film producer; Barbara C. Jordan, educator, lawyer, and politician; Barbara Mandrell, singer; Annette O'Toole, actress; Dennis and Randy Quaid, actors; Kenny Rogers, singer; Patrick Swayze, actor and dancer.

Indianapolis, Ind.

Mayor: Bart Peterson (to Dec. 31, 2007)
2000 census population (rank): 781,870 (12);
% change: 6.7; **Male:** 378,310 (48.4%); **Female:**
403,560 (51.6%); **White:** 540,212 (69.1%); **Black:**
199,412 (25.5%); **American Indian and Alaska**
Native: 1,985 (0.3%); **Asian:** 11,161 (1.4%); **Other**
race: 15,921 (2.0%); **Two or more races:** 12,857
(1.6%); **Hispanic/Latino:** 30,636 (3.9%). **2000 per-**
cent population 18 and over: 74.3%; **65 and over:**
11.0%; **median age:** 33.5.
2003 population estimate (rank): 783,438 (12)
Land area: 366 sq mi. (948 sq km); **Alt.:** Highest, 840
ft.; lowest, 700 ft.
Avg. daily temp.: Jan., 25.5 F; July, 75.4° F
Churches:[1] 1,191; **City-owned parks:** 172 (10,174 ac.);
Radio stations:[2] AM, 8; FM, 17; **Television**
stations:[1] 7
Civilian Labor Force (MSA) June 2004: 915,993;
Unemployed: 39,736, **Percent:** 4.3 **Per capita per-**
sonal income (MSA) 2002: $32,916
Chamber of Commerce: Greater Indianapolis Chamber
of Commerce, 111 Monument Circle, Ste. 1950, Indianapolis, Ind. 46204

1. Marion County. 2. Metropolitan area.

Indianapolis, the largest city in Indiana and seat of Marion County, is located in the central part of the state on the West Fork of the White River. Its name derives from combining "Indiana" with "polis," the Greek word for city.

Indianapolis was settled in 1820, and five years later it was chosen as the state capital. It was incorporated as a city in 1832 and reincorporated in 1838. The city's growth began when the railroad reached it in 1847. Toward the end of the 19th century, the discovery of nearby natural gas and the start of the automobile industry hastened its industrial expansion. In 1970, Indianapolis merged with surrounding Marion County.

Indianapolis is at the center of a rich agricultural region and is a major grain and livestock market. It is also a focal point of commerce, transportation, and manufacturing for the region. Some leading industries are electronics, pharmaceuticals, and food processing. The financial sector and service and insurance industries are growing rapidly.

Indianapolis is the site of the world-famous 500-mile automobile race and the Indiana State Fair.

Selected famous natives and residents: Monte Blue, actor; David Letterman, TV host; Steve McQueen, actor; Jane Pauley, TV newscaster; Booth Tarkington, author; Kurt Vonnegut, Jr., author; Harry Von Zell, announcer; Clifton Webb, actor.

Jacksonville, Fla.

Mayor: John Peyton (to June 30, 2005)
2000 census population (rank): 735,617 (14);
% change: 15.8; **Male:** 356,284 (48.4%); **Female:**
379,333 (51.6%); **White:** 474,307 (64.5%); **Black:**
213,514 (29.0%); **American Indian and Alaska**
Native: 2,474 (0.3%); **Asian:** 20,427 (2.8%); **Other**
race: 9,816 (1.3%); **Two or more races:** 14,631
(2.0%); **Hispanic/Latino:** 30,594 (4.2%). **2000 per-**
cent population 18 and over: 73.3%; **65 and over:**
10.3%; **median age:** 33.8.
2003 population estimate (rank): 773,781 (13)
Land area: 758 sq mi. (1,963 sq km); **Alt.:** Highest,
71 ft.; lowest, sea level
Avg. daily temp.: Jan., 52.4° F; July, 81.6° F
Churches: Protestant, 794; Roman Catholic, 21; Jewish,
5; others, 22; **City-owned parks and playgrounds:**
337 (8,000+ ac.); **Radio stations:** AM, 14; FM, 16;
Television stations: 6 commercial, 1 PBS, 1 religious
Civilian Labor Force (MSA) June 2004: 618,529;
Unemployed: 36,210, **Percent:** 5.9; **Per capita per-**
sonal income (MSA) 2002: $30,037
Chamber of Commerce: Jacksonville Area Chamber of
Commerce, 3 Independent Dr., Jacksonville, Fla.
32202

Jacksonville, Florida's largest city, is located in Duval County in the northeast corner of Florida, on the banks of the St. Johns River and adjacent to the Atlantic Ocean. It is the largest metropolitan area in northeast Florida and southeast Georgia.

Starting in the 16th century, French, Spanish, and English explorers and colonists were attracted to the region by the St. Johns River. The site was settled by Lewis Hogans in 1816. Jacksonville was laid out in 1822 and was named after Gen. Andrew Jackson, the first military governor of Florida. It was incorporated as a city in 1832.

During the Civil War, much of the city was destroyed by Union forces, who occupied Jacksonville four times. The city was rebuilt and, following the development of its harbor and the railroads, quickly became the transportation hub and leading industrial city in Florida by the 1880s. In 1968, the city and county governments consolidated.

Jacksonville is the leading transportation and distribution hub in the state. However, the strength of the city's economy lies in its broad diversification. The area's economy is balanced among distribution, financial services, biomedical technology, consumer goods, information services, manufacturing, and other industries. Jacksonville has the largest deepwater port in the South Atlantic and is a leading port in the U.S. for automobile imports.

Selected famous natives and residents: Pat Boone, singer; Judy Canova, comedian; Harold Carmichael, football player; Billy Daniels, vocalist; Storm Davis, athlete; Bob Hayes, athlete; Wanda Hendrix, actress; James Weldon Johnson, author and educator; John Rosamond Johnson, musician and composer; Mark McCumber, pro golfer; Ray Mercer, boxer; Charles "Hoss" Singleton, songwriter; Bill Terry, baseball player and manager; Donnie Van Zant, rock musician; Ronnie Van Zant, rock musician; Leeroy Yarbrough, auto racer.

Kansas City, Mo.

Mayor: Kay Barnes (to April 2007)
City Manager: Wayne Cauthen (apptd. April 2003)
2000 census population (rank): 441,545 (36);
  % change: 1.5; **Male:** 213,141 (48.3%); **Female:** 228,404 (51.7%); **White:** 267,931 (60.7%); **Black:** 137,879 (31.2%); **American Indian and Alaska Native:** 2,122 (0.5%); **Asian:** 8,182 (1.9%); **Other race:** 14,158 (3.2%); **Two or more races:** 10,780 (2.4%); **Hispanic/Latino:** 30,604 (6.9%). **2000 percent population 18 and over:** 74.6%; **65 and over:** 11.7%; **median age:** 34.0.
2003 population estimate (rank): 442,768 (38)
Land area: 314 sq mi. (813 sq km); **Alt.:** Highest, 1,014 ft.; lowest, 722 ft.
Avg. daily temp.: Jan., 25.7° F; July, 78.5° F
Churches: 1,100 churches of all denominations;[1] **City-owned parks and playgrounds:** 211 (9,685 ac.); **Radio stations:**[1] AM, 14; FM, 19; **Television stations:**[1] 7
Civilian Labor Force (MSA) June 2004: 1,038,162;[2] **Unemployed:** 61,552,[2] **Percent:** 5.9;[2] **Per capita personal income (MSA) 2002:** $32,467[2]
Chamber of Commerce: Greater Kansas City Chamber of Commerce, 911 Main St., Kansas City, Mo. 64105

1. Metropolitan area. 2. Kansas City, Mo.–Kan.

Kansas City is the largest city in Missouri. It is located in the western part of the state, at the junction of the Missouri and Kansas rivers. Kansas City is located in Jackson, Clay, Platte, and Cass counties.

In 1821, the year Missouri entered the Union, French trader François Chouteau came from St. Louis to establish a trading post on the site of the present city to take advantage of the growing fur trade with the Kansa, Osage, Wyandotte, and other tribes. In 1833, a settlement called Westport Landing was laid out by John Calvin McCoy and developed. The community became the Town of Kansas and was incorporated as a city in 1850 and renamed Kansas City in 1889. The city's name reflects its Native American heritage—its site was within the territory of the Kansa, or Kaw, Indians.

The city grew rapidly in the mid-1880s as the starting point for gold prospectors and settlers heading westward. The coming of the Missouri-Pacific Railroad in 1865 and the spanning of the Missouri River by the Hannibal Bridge in 1869 also contributed to the city's growth. It also prospered as a center for the nation's cattle business.

The Kansas City metropolitan area, once known primarily for agriculture and manufacturing, has expanded its economic base to include strong growth in areas of telecommunications, banking and finance, and the service industry. A transportation hub since the 1800s, the area enjoys a national and regional prominence as a distribution and manufacturing center. Kansas City ranks nationally as first in greeting-card publishing (Hallmark Cards is located there), frozen food storage and distribution, and hard winter-wheat marketing; second in wheat flour production; and third in auto and truck assembly. The area is one of ten federal regional centers, and the federal, state, and local governments are among the top employers. The city is also a regional center for health care.

Selected famous natives and residents: Robert Altman, director; Edward Asner, actor; Burt Bacharach, composer; Noah and Wallace Beery, actors; Robert Russell Bennett, composer; Jeanne Eagels, actress; Jean Harlow, actress; Ted Shawn, dancer and choreographer; Casey Stengel, baseball player; Virgil Thompson, composer; Tom Watson, golfer.

Las Vegas, Nev.

Mayor: Oscar Goodman (to May 2007)
2000 census population (rank): 478,434 (32);
  % change: 85.2; **Male:** 243,077 (50.8%); **Female:** 235,357 (49.2%); **White:** 334,230 (69.9%); **Black:** 49,570 (10.4%); **American Indian and Alaska Native:** 3,570 (0.7%); **Asian:** 22,879 (4.8%); **Other race:** 46,643 (9.7%); **Two or more races:** 19,397 (4.1%); **Hispanic/Latino:** 112,962 (23.6%); **2000 percent population 18 and over:** 74.1%; **65 and over:** 11.6%; **median age:** 34.5.
2003 population estimate (rank): 517,017 (30)
Land area: 113 sq mi. (293 sq km); **Alt.:** 2,174 ft.
Avg. daily temp.: Jan., 45.5° F; July, 91.1° F
Churches: over 500 churches and synagogues; **Parks:** 50 (799 ac.) **Radio stations:** AM, 4; FM, 8; **Television stations:** 7
Civilian Labor Force (MSA) June 2004: 947,489;[1] **Unemployed:** 42,285,[1] **Percent:** 4.5;[1] **Per capita personal income (MSA) 2002:** $29,396[1]
Chamber of Commerce: 3720 Howard Hughes Parkway, Las Vegas, NV 89109

1. Las Vegas, Nev.–Ariz. 2. Las Vegas–Paradise, Nev.

Las Vegas, seat of Clark County in southeast Nevada, is the largest city in the state and one of the fastest-growing cities in the United States. Between April 1990 and April 2000, the Las Vegas metropolitan area population increased by 83%, growing from 852,737 to 1,563,282.

The area was discovered by Spanish explorers in 1829. The site of Las Vegas ("The Meadows" in

Spanish) was originally a watering place for travelers on their way to southern California. It was first settled by Mormons in 1855, who were attracted by its artesian springs. They abandoned their settlement two years later in 1857, and the U.S. Army established Fort Baker there in 1864. In 1867, Las Vegas was detached from the Arizona Territory and joined with Nevada.

The town was established and started to grow with the arrival of the railroad in 1905. However, its growth did not really take off until shortly after 1931, when the Nevada legislature legalized gambling in an effort to lift the state from the Great Depression. The construction of nearby Hoover Dam aided the area economically as well.

The Las Vegas that we know today basically began after World War II, when the idea of large hotels along the brand new "strip" was developed. Las Vegas is the "marriage capital" of America; there are 50 wedding chapels in the city. Tourism and the convention industry are the city's major sources of income. In addition, manufacturing, government, warehousing, and trucking are major sources of employment. Many high-technology companies are also located in Las Vegas.

Las Vegas has a favorable business climate: taxes are relatively low, and there are neither city nor state income taxes. This is because gambling and sales taxes, paid by tourists, have allowed the city and state governments to avoid personal and corporate income taxes.

Popular nearby tourist attractions are Hoover Dam and Lake Mead (the largest man-made lake in the U.S.), Lake Mojave, the Mt. Charleston Recreation Area, Red Rock Canyon, and the Death Valley National Monument.

Selected famous natives and residents: Andre Agassi, tennis player; Clara Bow, actress; Jack Kramer, tennis player; Phyllis McGuire, singer; Benjamin Siegel, hotel-casino promoter; Orson Welles, actor and producer; Joe Williams, jazz singer.

Long Beach, Calif.

Mayor: Beverly O'Neill (to April 2006)
City Manager: Gerald Miller
2000 census population (rank): 461,522 (34);
% change: 7.5; Male: 226,718 (49.1%); Female: 234,804 (50.9%); 1996 est. population breakdown: White: 208,410 (45.2%); Black: 68,618 (14.9%); American Indian and Alaska Native: 3,881 (0.8%); Asian: 55,591 (12.0%); Other race: 95,107 (20.6%); Two or more races: 24,310 (5.3%); Hispanic/Latino: 165,092 (35.8%). **2000 percent population 18 and over:** 70.8%; **65 and over:** 9.1%; **median age:** 30.8.
2003 population estimate (rank): 475,460 (32)
Land area: 50 sq mi. (130 sq km), **Alt.:** Highest, 170 ft.; lowest, sea level
Avg. daily temp.: Jan., 55.9° F; July, 73.1° F
Churches: 236; **City-owned parks:** 92 (plus 5 golf courses); **Radio stations:** AM, 2; FM, 2; **Television stations:** 8 (metro area)
Civilian Labor Force (PMSA) June 2004: 4,789,979;[1] **Unemployed:** 323,278,[1] **Percent:** 6.7;[1] **Per capita personal income (MSA) 2001:** $32,547[2]
Chamber of Commerce: Long Beach Area Chamber of Commerce, One World Trade Center, Suite 206, Long Beach, Calif. 90831-0350

1. Los Angeles–Long Beach, Calif. 2. Los Angeles–Long Beach–Santa Ana, Calif.

Long Beach is the fifth-largest city in California and is situated on San Pedro Bay, south of Los Angeles, in Los Angeles County.

The town was laid out and settled in 1881 by developer W. E. Willmore, who sold lots on the site as a seaside resort community called Willmore City. It was renamed Long Beach for its 8½-mile beach in 1884. The city was incorporated in 1888 and reincorporated in 1897.

Long Beach is a major industrial port, ranked second-busiest in the U.S. and tenth-busiest in the world. In addition to international trade through the port, high technology has also been an important economic engine for the Long Beach area. Major technology and aerospace corporations such Gulfstream and Raytheon have large facilities in Long Beach, and Boeing continues to be the top employer, with over 17,000 employees.

Tourism is also important to the economy. Major attractions are the RMS *Queen Mary*, the Aquarium of the Pacific, whale watching tours, and water sports.

Selected famous natives and residents: Jack Anderson, journalist; Jennifer Bartlett, artist; Barbara Britton, actress; Nicholas Cage, actor; Spike Jones, orchestra leader; Sally Kellerman, actress; Billie Jean King, tennis player; Martha Rae Watson, track star; Heather Watts, dancer.

Los Angeles, Calif.

Mayor: James K. Hahn (to June 2005)
2000 census population (rank): 3,694,820 (2);
% change: 6.0; Male: 1,841,805 (49.8%); Female: 1,853,015 (50.2%); White: 1,734,036 (46.9%); Black: 415,195 (11.2%); American Indian and Alaska Native: 29,412 (0.8%); Asian: 369,254 (10.0%); Other race: 949,720 (25.7%); Two or more races: 191,288 (5.2%); Hispanic/Latino: 1,719,073 (46.5%). **2000 percent population 18 and over:** 73.4%; **65 and over:** 9.7%; **median age:** 31.6.
2003 population estimate (rank): 3,819,951 (2)
Land area: 469 sq mi. (1,215 sq km), **Alt.:** Highest, 5,081 ft.; lowest, sea level
Avg. daily temp.: Jan., 58.3° F; July, 74.3° F
Churches: 2,000 of all denominations; **City-owned parks:** 387 (15,600 ac.); **Radio stations:** AM, 35; FM, 53; **Television stations:** 19
Civilian Labor Force (PMSA) June 2004: 4,789,979;[1] **Unemployed:** 323,278,[1] **Percent:** 6.7;[1] **Per capita personal income (MSA) 2002:** $32,547[2]
Chamber of Commerce: Los Angeles Chamber of Commerce, 350 S. Bixel St., Los Angeles, Calif. 90017

1. Los Angeles–Long Beach, Calif. 2. Los Angeles–Long Beach–Santa Ana, Calif.

Los Angeles is the largest city in California and the second-largest urban area in the nation. It is located in the southern part of the state on the Pacific Ocean. It is the seat of Los Angeles County. Geographically, it extends more than 40 mi from the mountains to the sea.

The Spanish explorer Gaspar de Portolá visited the site in 1769. On Sept. 4, 1781, the Mexican provincial governor, Filipe de Neve, founded "El Pueblo de Nuestra Señora la Reina de Los Angeles," meaning "The Village of Our Lady, the Queen of the Angels." The pueblo became the capital of the Mexican province, Alta California, and it was the last place to surrender to the United States at the time of the American occupation in 1847. By the Treaty of Guadalupe Hidalgo in 1848, Mexico ceded California to the United States, and Los Angeles was incorporated as a city in 1850.

The city's phenomenal growth was brought about by its equable climate, which attracted people and industry from all parts of the nation; the development of its citrus-fruit industry; the discovery of oil in the area during the early 1890s; the development of its man-made harbor—its port is one of the busiest in the United States; and the growth of the motion picture industry in the early 20th century. Today, Hollywood is a suburb of Los Angeles.

Los Angeles is a major hub of shipping, manufacturing, industry, and finance, and is world-renowned in the entertainment and communications fields. It is a favorite vacation destination and attracts millions of tourists to the area each year from all over the world. Apart from the movie studios and other landmarks associated with the movie industry, points of interest include the J. Paul Getty Museum, the Los Angeles County Museum of Art, the La Brea Tar Pits (famous for Ice Age fossils), Disneyland (Anaheim), and the Santa Anita and Hollywood racetracks.

Los Angeles County is the nation's largest manufacturing center, and the ports of Los Angeles and Long Beach are second only to New York as the largest customs district in the United States. Major employers in the Los Angeles Five-County area are in the business and management sector. Growth in the key wholesale industries—apparel and textiles, furniture, jewelry, and toys—and the boom in industrial trade were the trend for the region in the 1990s. Other important sectors are health services and international trade and investment. After some lean years, the aerospace industry is making a modest comeback as a result of increased federal defense spending.

Selected famous natives and residents: Busby Berkeley, choreographer and director; Marge Champion, dancer and choreographer; Jackie Coogan, actor; Jackie Cooper, actor; Linda Fratianne, figure skater; Jodie Foster, actress and director; John Gavin, actor and diplomat; Pancho Gonzalez, tennis player; Cynthia Gregory, ballerina; Jerome Hines, basso; Dustin Hoffman, actor; Theodore Harold Maiman, laser inventor; Marilyn Monroe, actress; Isamu Noguchi, sculptor; Leonard Slotkin, conductor; Duke Snider, baseball player; Adlai E. Stevenson, statesman; Madeleine Stowe, actress; Darryl Strawberry, baseball player.

Memphis, Tenn.

Mayor: W. W. Herenton (to Dec. 2007)
2000 census population (rank): 650,100 (18);
% change: 6.5; **Male:** 307,643 (47.3%); **Female:** 342,457 (52.7%); **White:** 223,728 (34.4%); **Black:** 399,208 (61.4%); **American Indian and Alaska Native:** 1,217 (0.2%); **Asian:** 9,482 (1.5%); **Other race:** 9,438 (1.5%); **Two or more races:** 6,788 (1.0%); **Hispanic/Latino:** 19,317 (3.0%). **2000 percent population 18 and over:** 72.1%; **65 and over:** 10.9%; **median age:** 31.9.
2003 population estimate (rank): 645,978 (17)
Land area: 279 sq mi. (723 sq km); **Alt.:** Highest, 417 ft.
Avg. daily temp.: Jan., 39.7° F; July, 82.6° F
Churches: 2000+; **Parks and playgrounds:** 187 (5,387 ac.); **Radio stations:** AM, 17; FM, 25; **Television stations:** 6
Civilian Labor Force (MSA) June 2004: 593,231;[1]
   Unemployed: 33,974;[1] **Percent:** 5.7;[1] **Per capita personal income (MSA) 2001:** $30,557[1]
Chamber of Commerce: Memphis Regional Chamber of Commerce, P.O. Box 224, Memphis, Tenn. 38103

1. Memphis, Tenn.–Miss.–Ark.

Memphis, the largest city in Tennessee and the seat of Shelby County, is located in the southwest corner of the state, on the Mississippi River near the borders of Arkansas and Mississippi.

The first settlers of Memphis were the Chickasaw Indians, who had a village named Chisca there on the bluffs overlooking the Mississippi River. Hernando de Soto, in 1541, is said to have had his first glimpse of the Mississippi from the site of Memphis; in the next century, Louis Joliet and Jacques Marquette stopped there to trade with the Indians. The French explorer Robert Cavelier, Sieur de La Salle, tried to claim the region for France in 1682 and built Fort Prudhomme on the site.

The area was ceded to the United States by the Chickasaw Indians in 1818. Memphis was officially established in 1819 by three enterprising businessmen from Nashville, James Winchester, John Overton, and future president Andrew Jackson. Jackson named it after the ancient Egyptian city because of its site on the Nile-like Mississippi River. Memphis was incorporated as a city in 1826 and became an important Mississippi River port.

During the Civil War, Memphis was a Confederate military center. In 1862, federal forces won a gunboat battle on the river at Memphis, and General Sherman was able to take the city. After the war, Memphis's population was devastated by several yellow-fever epidemics during the 1870s. As a result, the city fell into decline and went bankrupt, losing its charter in 1879. However, owing to its superior location, the city was able to recover economically, and a new city charter was granted in 1893.

Memphis is known as "America's Distribution Center," serving the northeast, southeast, and southwest regions of the country. The city has one of the country's largest inland ports and is the national headquarters for the Fed Ex air-courier company. Health care and related activities such as medical education and biomedical research are Memphis's largest industries, bringing over $5 billion a year to the local economy. Also important are high-technology communications.

Many of the city's tourist attractions are landmarks associated with the great Memphis music legends, such as Graceland, Elvis Presley's home.

Selected famous natives and residents: Kathy Bates, actress; Dixie Carter, actress; Rosalind Cash, singer; Abe Fortas, jurist; Aretha Franklin, singer; Morgan Freeman, actor; Al Green, singer; George Hamilton, actor; Anfernee "Penny" Hardaway, basketball player; Isaac Hayes, singer; Hal Holbrook, actor; Benjamin Hooks, organization official; Elvis Presley, singer and actor; Charlie Rich, singer; Cybill Shepherd, actress; Robert Siodmak, director; Fred Smith, business executive; Rufus Thomas, singer; Kemmons Wilson, business executive.

Mesa, Ariz.

Mayor: Keno Hawker (to June 2008)
City Manager: Mike Hutchinson
2000 census population (rank): 396,375 (42);
   % change: 37.6; **Male:** 196,378 (49.5%); **Female:** 199,997 (50.5%); **White:** 323,655 (81.7%); **Black:** 9,977 (2.5%); **American Indian and Alaska Native:** 6,552 (1.7%); **Asian:** 5,917 (1.5%); **Other race:** 38,271 (9.7%); **Two or more races:** 11,051 (2.8%); **Hispanic/Latino:** 78,281 (19.7%). **2000 percent population 18 and over:** 72.7%; **65 and over:** 13.3%; **median age:** 32.0
2003 population estimate (rank): 432,376 (40)
Land area: 125 sq mi. (324 sq km); **Alt.:** 1,241 ft.
Avg. daily temp.: Jan., 52.9° F; July, 91.2° F
City-owned parks: 55; **Radio stations:** AM, 23; FM, 12; **Television stations:** 7

Civilian Labor Force (MSA) June 2004: 1,855,927;[1]
   Unemployed: 77,892,[1] Percent: 4.2;[1] Per capita personal income (MSA) 2002: $28,481[2]
Chamber of Commerce: 120 N. Center St., P.O. Box 5820, Mesa, Ariz. 85201

1. Phoenix–Mesa, Ariz. 2. Phoenix–Mesa–Scottsdale, Ariz.

Mesa is the third-largest city in Arizona and is located in the south-central portion of the state in Maricopa County. Sitting atop a plateau overlooking the Valley of the Sun, the city gets its name from the Spanish word for "tabletop."

Prior to the arrival of Europeans, the area had been inhabited for centuries by native peoples, including the Hohokam and later the Pima. The Hohokam culture developed an extensive system of irrigation canals, some of which are still used today.

Controlled by Spain and then by Mexico, the area was ceded to the U.S. following the Mexican War (1846–1848). Mormon settlers arrived on the site in 1878 and used the old irrigation canals for farming in the Salt River valley. Mesa was incorporated as a town in 1883 and as a city in 1930.

Falcon Field Airport and Williams Air Force Base were built in 1941 to train fighter pilots during World War II. After the war, the city grew rapidly, as many military families decided to settle in Mesa permanently, and tourism also became a major force. Williams AFB closed in the early 1990s, but Falcon Field has become one of the ten largest U.S. airports in terms of based aircraft and supports more than 30 aviation-related businesses.

Currently Mesa is one of the fastest-growing cities in the United States, due to its excellent climate and strong local economy, which boasts some of the country's top manufacturers. Electronics, automotive testing, propulsion equipment, aerospace, and heavy machinery firms are among the most significant in the region.

With 313 days of sunshine a year, Mesa has been an ideal choice for several major-league baseball spring training camps.

Selected famous natives and residents: Danielle Fishel, actress; Liz Reney, actress; John J. Rhodes, politician; Keri Russell, actress.

Miami, Fla.

Mayor: Manuel A. Diaz (to Nov. 2005)
City Manager: Joe Arriola
2000 census population (rank): 362,470 (47);
   % change: 1.1; Male: 180,194 (49.7%); Female: 182,276 (50.3%); White: 241,470 (66.6%); Black: 80,858 (22.3%); American Indian and Alaska Native:, 810 (0.2%); Asian: 2,376 (0.7%); Other race: 19,644 (5.4%); Two or more races: 17,182 (4.7%); Hispanic/Latino: 238,351 (65.8%). 2000 percent population 18 and over: 78.3%; 65 and over: 17.0%; median age: 37.7.
2003 population estimate (rank): 376,815 (46)
Land area: 36 sq mi. (93 sq km); Water area: 19.5 sq mi.; Alt.: Average, 12 ft.
Avg. daily temp.: Jan., 67.2° F; July, 82.6° F
Churches:[1] Protestant, 850; Roman Catholic, 61; Jewish, 64; City-owned parks: 109; Radio stations:[1] 29; Television stations:[1] 9 TV, 1 Cable
Civilian Labor Force (PMSA) June 2004: 1,137,844;
   Unemployed: 81,237, Percent: 7.1; Per capita personal income (MSA) 2002: $32,373[2]
Chamber of Commerce: Greater Miami Chamber of Commerce, 1601 Biscayne Blvd., Miami, Fla. 33132

1. Dade County. 2. Miami–Fort Lauderdale–Miami Beach, Fla.

Miami, the second-largest city in Florida and seat of Miami-Dade County, is located in the southeast part of the state, on Biscayne Bay.

The area was once the home of the Tequesta Indians until they were nearly wiped out by European diseases and warfare brought on by two centuries of Spanish control of Florida. Miami was founded in 1870 near the site of Ft. Dallas, built in 1835 during the Seminole Indian wars. The city's name is probably derived from "Mayaimi," an Indian word for "big water."

Miami is the only U.S. city to have been planned by a woman. Julia Tuttle, a Clevelander, arrived there in 1891 and bought several hundred acres on the bank of the Miami River. She convinced New York financier Henry M. Flagler of the area's vast potential and persuaded him to extend his Florida East Coast Railroad to Miami in 1896, the year the city was incorporated. Flagler dredged Miami Harbor, built the renowned Royal Palm Hotel, and promoted the area as a winter playground. Tourists flocked there, and by 1910 the city was a thriving recreational area. Miami survived the collapse of a land speculation boom in the 1920s and severe hurricanes in 1926 and 1935 and continued to grow. It experienced a monumental population boost during the 1960s, when about 260,000 Cuban refugees arrived on its shore. They made a great impact on Miami, which is now a bilingual metropolis.

Miami is an international banking and finance center and has the greatest concentration of international and Edge Act banks (banks making only foreign loans and deposits) in North America; these constitute a major employment base. Greater Miami has a highly diversified economy with numerous multinational and Fortune 500 companies. It is a national leader in biomedical technology, and the health care sector is a major industry. Greater Miami is also part of an area known as the Computer Coast of Florida, and its growing technologies include computers, electrical engineering, and plastics manufacturing.

Miami is one of the world's leading year-round resort centers. The city is a major transportation hub, and the port of Miami is the world's largest cruise port and a major seaport for cargo. The famous island resort of Miami Beach, incorporated in 1915, is connected to Miami by four causeways.

Selected famous natives and residents: Fernando Bujones, dancer; Steve Carlton, baseball player; Debbie Harry, singer; Dick Howser, baseball player and manager; Sidney Poitier, actor; Janet Reno, former attorney general of the U.S.; Ben Vereen, actor; Ellen Zwilich, composer.

Milwaukee, Wis.

Mayor: Tom Barrett (to April 2008)
2000 census population (rank): 596,974 (19);
   % change: −5.0; Male: 285,363 (47.8%); Female: 311,611 (52.2%); White: 298,379 (50.0%); Black: 222,933 (37.3%); American Indian and Alaska Native: 5,212 (0.9%); Asian: 17,571 (2.9%); Other race: 36,428 (6.1%); Two or more races: 16,150 (2.7%); Hispanic/Latino: 71,646 (12.0%). 2000 percent population 18 and over: 71.4%; 65 and over: 10.9%; median age: 30.6.
2003 population estimate (rank): 586,941 (19)
Land area: 96 sq mi. (249 sq km); Alt.: 580.60 ft.
Avg. daily temp.: Jan., 19.9° F; July, 73.6° F

Churches: 411; **County-owned parks:** 140 (15,000+ ac.); **Radio stations:** AM, 6; FM, 13; **Television stations:** 11

Civilian Labor Force (PMSA) June 2004: 850,113;[1] **Unemployed:** 49,443;[1] **Percent:** 5.8;[1] **Per capita personal income (MSA) 2002:** $34,308[2]

Chamber of Commerce: Metropolitan Milwaukee Association of Commerce, 756 N. Milwaukee St., Milwaukee, Wis. 53202; Milwaukee Minority Chamber of Commerce, P.O. Box 1662, Milwaukee, Wis. 53201; Hispanic Chamber of Commerce, 816 W. National Ave., Milwaukee, Wis. 53204

1. Milwaukee–Waukesha, Wis. 2. Milwaukee–Waukesha–West Allis, Wis.

Milwaukee, the largest city in Wisconsin and seat of Milwaukee County, is located in the southeast part of the state on Lake Michigan.

French missionaries visited the site of Milwaukee in the 17th century, but it was not until 1795 that Jacques Vieau established a fur-trading post there. The first permanent white settler, Vieau's son-in-law, Solomon Juneau, an agent of the American Fur Company, made his home there in 1818. The settlement merged with several neighboring villages in 1838 to form Milwaukee, and the city was incorporated in 1846. A large wave of German immigrants arrived after 1848 and contributed greatly to the city's political, economic, and cultural development.

The origins of the word "Milwaukee" are disputed; it may come from the Potawatomi "Mahn-ah-wauk," meaning council grounds of the Potawatomi; "Mah-an-wauk-seepe," meaning gathering place of rivers; or the Algonquian "Milo-aki," meaning beautiful land.

Milwaukee is one of the great industrial centers in the country and one of the largest Great Lakes ports. Manufacturing remains strong, and Milwaukee manufacturers are national leaders in lithographic commercial printing and the production of medical diagnostic instruments, small gasoline engines, malt beverages, iron and steel forgings, mining machinery, and robotics. Milwaukee's high-tech manufacturing community is one of the largest among the nation's major metropolitan areas.

Though Milwaukee was once known as a "beer town," only a small percentage of its workforce is now involved in beer production. However, beer still plays an important role, and almost 11% of the nation's malt beverage is produced there.

Selected famous natives and residents: Donald Gramm, bass-baritone; Woody Herman, band leader; Al Jarreau, singer; Kristen Johnston, actress; George F. Kennan, diplomat; Alfred Lunt, actor; Douglas MacArthur, army general; Pat O'Brien, actor; Tom Snyder, TV personality; Speech, member of the rap group Arrested Development; Spencer Tracy, actor; Gene Wilder, actor; Jerry and David Zucker, film producers.

Minneapolis, Minn.

Mayor: R. T. Rybak (to Jan. 2006)

2000 census population (rank): 382,618 (45); **% change:** 3.9; **Male:** 192,232 (50.2%); **Female:** 190,386 (49.8%); **White:** 249,186 (65.1%); **Black:** 68,818 (18.0%); **American Indian and Alaska Native:** 8,378 (2.2%); **Asian:** 23,455 (6.1%); **Other race:** 15,798 (4.1%); **Two or more races:** 16,694 (4.4%); **Hispanic/Latino:** 29,175 (7.6%). **2000 percent population 18 and over:** 78.0%; **65 and over:** 9.1%; **median age:** 31.2

2003 population estimate (rank): 373,188 (47)

Land area: 55 sq mi. (142 sq km); **Alt.:** Highest, 945 ft.; lowest, 695 ft.

Avg. daily temp.: Jan., 11.8° F; July, 73.6° F

Churches: 419; **City-owned parks:** 170+ (6,400 ac.); **Radio stations:**[1] AM, 17; FM, 15; **Television stations:**[1] 6

Civilian Labor Force (MSA) June 2004: 1,880,904;[2] **Unemployed:** 87,421,[2] **Percent:** 4.6;[2] **Per capita personal income (MSA) 2002:** $37,787[3]

Chamber of Commerce: Minneapolis Regional Chamber of Commerce, Young Quinlan Building, 81 S. Ninth St., Suite 200, Minneapolis, Minn. 55402-3223

1. Metropolitan area. 2. Minneapolis–St. Paul, Minn.–Wis. 3. Minneapolis–St. Paul–Bloomington, Minn.–Wis.

Minneapolis, the largest city in Minnesota and the seat of Hennepin County, is located in the southeast central part of the state on the Mississippi River. It is adjacent to its "twin city" of St. Paul.

In 1680, Father Louis Hennepin visited the future site of Minneapolis and gave the Falls of St. Anthony their name. Lt. Zebulon Pike made a treaty with the Sioux Indians in 1805–1806, by which they ceded to the whites much land, including the Falls of St. Anthony and the site of Minneapolis. Fort Snelling was built in 1819–1820, and in 1823 the government built a lumber and flour mill. Flour milling became the major industry of early Minneapolis and made the city the milling capital of the world. The town of St. Anthony was established on the east bank of the Mississippi in 1848, and the town of Minneapolis grew up on the opposite bank of the river. The name Minneapolis is a combination of the Dakota Sioux word "minna," for water, and the Greek word "polis," for city. Minneapolis was incorporated as a city in 1867, and in 1872 the city of St. Anthony (chartered in 1860) was annexed to it. After the spread of the railroads in the 1870s, Minneapolis became the gateway to the Northern Great Plains.

Minneapolis is a center of industry and commerce serving a large agricultural region. During the 20th century, manufacturing, food processing, milling, computers, health services, and graphic arts developed as Minneapolis's major industries. Fifteen Fortune 500 companies are headquartered in the Minneapolis–St. Paul metropolitan area. The city is the headquarters of the Ninth Federal Reserve Bank.

The Twin Cities are known for their wide array of cultural attractions, and Minneapolis is home to many fine museums, including the Minneapolis Institute of Arts, the Walker Center, and the Frederick R. Weisman Art Museum at the University of Minnesota's Minneapolis campus.

Selected famous natives and residents: La Verne, Maxene, and Patti Andrews, singers; James Arness, actor; Lew Ayres, actor; Patty Berg, golfer; Virginia Bruce, actress; J. Paul Getty, oil executive; Peter Graves, actor; George Roy Hill, director; Cornell MacNeil, baritone; Ralph Meeker, actor; Westbrook Pegler, columnist; Prince, singer; Harrison Salisbury, journalist; Charles Schulz, cartoonist; Anne Tyler, writer; Bud Wilkinson, football coach; David Winfield, baseball player.

Nashville-Davidson, Tenn.

Mayor: Bill Purcell (to Oct. 2007)

2000 census population (rank):[1] 545,524 (22); **% change:** 11.6; **Male:** 264,095 (48.4%); **Female:** 281,429 (51.6%); **White:** 359,581 (65.9%); **Black:** 146,235 (26.8%); **American Indian and Alaska Native:** 1,639 (0.3%); **Asian:** 12,992 (2.4%); **Other race:** 13,677 (2.5%); **Two or more races:** 11,000 (2.0%); **Hispanic/Latino:** 25,774 (4.7%). **2000 percent population 18 and over:** 77.9%; **65 and over:** 11.0%; **median age:** 33.9.

2003 population estimate (rank): 544,765 (27)
Land area: 502 sq mi. (1,300 sq km); **Altitude:** Highest, 1,100 ft.; lowest, approx. 400 ft.
Avg. daily temp.: Jan., 36.2° F; July, 79.3° F
Churches: Protestant, 781; Roman Catholic, 18; Jewish, 3; **City-owned parks:** 100 (10,200 ac.); **Radio stations:** AM, 15; FM, 19; **Television stations:** 11
Civilian Labor Force (MSA) June 2004: 703,363;
    Unemployed: 26,298, **Percent:** 3.7; **Per capita personal income (MSA) 2002:** $32,026[2]
Chamber of Commerce: Nashville Area Chamber of Commerce, 211 Commerce Street, Suite 100, Nashville, Tenn. 37201

1. Nashville-Davidson city is consolidated with Davidson County. 2. Nashville–Davidson–Murfreesboro, Tenn.

Nashville-Davidson is the state capital and second-largest city in Tennessee and is located in the north-central part of the state on the Cumberland River. It is coextensive with Davidson County.

During the winter of 1779–1780, James Robertson and John Donelson founded a settlement at Big Salt Lick by the Cumberland River at the present site of the city. They built forts on both sides of the river, naming one of them Fort Nashborough in honor of Francis Nash, a Revolutionary War general. In 1784, the town was named Nashville, and it was incorporated as a city in 1806.

Nashville became the capital of Tennessee in 1843 and was the seat of Davidson County until 1963, when it merged with the county to become Nashville-Davidson.

The city is a port of entry and an important industrial and commercial center serving the Upper South. Its economy is based on a number of industries, including automobiles, apparel, publishing, insurance, and banking. Health care services are the largest sector, but Nashville is best known for its music industry. It is a major recording center, especially for country music.

Nashville is home to several religious organizations and is a major tourist attraction and convention center. Its many institutions of higher education include Vanderbilt University, Fisk University, and the University of Tennessee.

Selected famous natives and residents: Roy Acuff, singer; Gregg Allman, singer; Pat Boone, singer; Rita Coolidge, singer; Jeff Gordon, race car driver; Al Gore, former vice president; Red Grooms, artist; Alex Haley, author; Barbara Howar, hostess and writer; Brenda Lee, singer; Minnie Pearl, comedienne; Annie Potts, actress; Paula Robeson, flutist; Wilma Rudolph, athlete; Dinah Shore, actress and singer; Tina Turner, singer; Oprah Winfrey, entertainer.

New Orleans, La.

Mayor: C. Ray Nagin (to May 2006)
2000 census population (rank): 484,674 (31);
    % change: –2.5; **Male:** 227,094 (46.9%); **Female:** 257,580 (53.1%); **White:** 135,956 (28.1%); **Black:** 325,947 (67.3%); **American Indian and Alaska Native:** 991 (0.2%); **Asian:** 10,972 (2.3%); **Other race:** 4,498 (0.9%); **Two or more races:** 6,201 (1.3%); **Hispanic/Latino:** 14,826 (3.1%). **2000 percent population 18 and over:** 73.3%; **65 and over:** 11.7%; **median age:** 33.1.
2003 population estimate (rank): 469,032 (34)
Land area: 181 sq mi. (469 sq km); **Alt.:** Highest, 15 ft.; lowest, –4 ft.
Avg. daily temp.: Jan., 51.3° F; July, 81.9° F
Churches: 712; **City-owned parks:** 165; **Radio stations:** AM, 12; FM, 14; **Television stations:** 7

Civilian Labor Force (MSA) June 2004: 618,097;
    Unemployed: 38,735, **Percent:** 6.3; **Per capita personal income (MSA) 2002:** $28,995[1]
Chamber of Commerce: Greater New Orleans, Inc., 601 Poydras St., Suite 1700, New Orleans, La. 70130

1. New Orleans–Metairie–Kenner, La.

New Orleans, the largest city in Louisiana, is located in the southeast part of the state, between the Mississippi River and Lake Ponchartrain. It is coextensive with Orleans Parish.

One of the few cities of the nation that has been under three flags, New Orleans has belonged to Spain, France, and the United States. The French founded it in 1718 and named it in honor of the Duke of Orleans. In 1762, France ceded the city and the territory to Spain. In 1800, the territory was returned to France, but government authorities did not take over until 1803, just 20 days before the region became part of the United States in the Louisiana Purchase.

New Orleans is famous for its French Quarter, with its mixture of French, Spanish, and native architectural styles. The Mardi Gras—a week of carnival held in New Orleans before the beginning of Lent—is the most spectacular festival in the U.S. and is a popular tourist attraction. Tourism has grown rapidly in recent years, and New Orleans hosts more than seven million visitors annually.

New Orleans has one of the world's greatest international ports, one of the largest in the nation, and it is a major focus of the city's economy. New Orleans is home to the corporate offices of oil companies with major offshore operations in the Gulf of Mexico, as well as the distribution and service centers of offshore equipment suppliers and fabricators.

The manufacturing industry is a significant part of the economy, with petroleum, petrochemical, ship-building, and aerospace industries all playing a role. The New Orleans region also functions as a mining, processing, and transportation center for other minerals, principally sulfur. Service industries are playing a larger role, with health care and telecommunications leading the way. The New Orleans region is widely regarded as a leading center of medicine and health care in the South.

Selected famous natives and residents: Louis Armstrong, musician; Truman Capote, author; Fats Domino, musician; Louis Gottschalk, pianist and composer; Bryant Gumbel, TV personality; Lillian Hellman, playwright and author; Al Hirt, musician; Mahalia Jackson, singer; Dorothy Lamour, actress; Wynton Marsalis, musician; Huey Newton, activist; Marguerite Piazza, soprano; Rusty Staub, baseball player; Ben Turpin, comedian; Shirley Verrett, mezzo-soprano; Carl Weathers, actor; Del Williams, football player.

New York, N.Y.

Mayor: Michael R. Bloomberg (to Dec. 2005)
Borough Presidents: Bronx, Adolfo Carrion; Brooklyn, Marty Markowitz; Manhattan, C. Virginia Fields; Queens, Helen M. Marshall; Staten Island, James P. Molinaro
2000 census population (rank): 8,008,278 (1);
    % change: 9.4; **Male:** 3,794,204 (47.4%); **Female:** 4,214,074 (52.6%); **White:** 3,576,385 (44.7%); **Black:** 2,129,762 (26.6%); **American Indian and Alaska Native:** 41,289 (0.5%); **Asian:** 787,047 (9.8%); **Other race:** 1,074,406 (13.4%); **Two or more races:** 393,959 (4.9%); **Hispanic/Latino:** 2,160,554 (27.0%). **2000 percent population 18 and over:** 75.8%; **65 and over:** 11.7%; **median age:** 34.2.
2003 population estimate (rank): 8,085,742 (1)

Land area: 303 sq mi. (785 sq km) (Queens, 109; Brooklyn, 71; Staten Island, 58; Bronx, 42; Manhattan, 23); **Alt.:** Highest, 426 ft.; lowest, sea level
Avg. daily temp.: Jan., 31.5° F; July, 76.8° F
Churches: Protestant, 1,766; Jewish, 1,256; Roman Catholic, 437; Orthodox, 66; **City-owned parks:** 1,701 (28,312 ac.); **Radio stations:** AM, 13; FM, 18; **Television stations:** 6 commercial, 1 public
Civilian Labor Force (PMSA) June 2004: 4,371,770; **Unemployed:** 300,578, **Percent:** 6.9; **Per capita personal income (MSA) 2002:** $40,680[1]
Chamber of Commerce: Greater New York Chamber of Commerce and Industry, 172 Madison Ave., New York, N.Y. 10016

1. New York–Northern N.J.–Long Island, N.Y.–N.J.–Pa.

New York City is the largest city in the United States. It is located in the southern part of New York State, at the mouth of the Hudson River (also known as North River as it passes Manhattan Island).

In 1609, Henry Hudson, who worked for the Dutch East India Company, sailed up the river that now bears his name and went as far as Albany. Five years later, a permanent settlement was established at what is now New York, but it was originally called New Amsterdam by the Dutch governors. One of them, Peter Minuit, was said to have bought Manhattan Island from the Indians in exchange for beads, buttons, and trinkets. In 1664, Great Britain's Duke of York sent a fleet that quietly seized the settlement from the Dutch without bloodshed and rechristened the colony in honor of the duke.

Control of New York passed to the young U.S. at the end of the Revolutionary War, and George Washington was inaugurated president in New York's old City Hall. Congress met in New York from 1785 to 1790.

In 1898, when Greater New York was chartered, the city expanded to include the following five boroughs, which are also counties in New York State: Manhattan (New York County); Brooklyn (Kings County); Bronx (Bronx County); Queens (Queens County); and Staten Island (Richmond County).

"The Big Apple" is a major world capital and a world leader in finance, the arts, and communications. The port of New York is one of the finest in the world and ranks as the largest port complex on the East Coast. The city is the home of the United Nations and is headquarters for some of the world's largest corporations. The city is also the center of advertising, fashion, publishing, and radio broadcasting in the United States.

The city suffered incredible devastation in Sept. 2001, when terrorist hijackers crashed two commercial jets into the World Trade Center in lower Manhattan, causing the complete destruction of the twin towers and major loss of life.

Selected famous natives and residents: Kareem Abdul-Jabbar, basketball player; Woody Allen, actor and director; Lauren Bacall, actress; James Baldwin, novelist; Harry Belafonte, singer and actor; Humphrey Bogart, actor; James Cagney, actor; Maria Callas, soprano; Aaron Copland, composer; Sammy Davis, Jr., singer and actor; Agnes de Mille, choreographer; Robert De Niro, actor; Eamon De Valera, former president of Ireland; Gertrude Elion, Nobel Prize winner in medicine; Lou Gehrig, baseball player; George Gershwin, composer; Ira Gershwin, lyricist; Jackie Gleason, actor; Rita Hayworth, actress; Lena Horne, singer; Julia Ward Howe, poet and reformer; Washington Irving, author; Henry James, novelist; Michael Jordan, basketball player; Sandy Koufax, baseball player; Roy Lichtenstein, painter; Vince Lombardi, football player and coach; Chico, Groucho, Harpo, and Zeppo Marx, comedians; Herman Melville, novelist; Yehudi Menuhin, violinist; James Michener, novelist; Arthur Miller, playwright; Eugene O'Neill, playwright; J. Robert Oppenheimer, nuclear physicist; Al Pacino, actor; Jerome Robbins, choreographer; Eleanor Roosevelt, reformer and humanitarian; Theodore Roosevelt, former president; Jonas Salk, polio researcher; Beverly Sills, soprano; Neil Simon, playwright; Barbra Streisand, singer and actress; Ed Sullivan, TV personality; Mae West, actress; Edith Wharton, novelist.

Oakland, Calif.

Mayor: Jerry Brown (to Jan. 2007)
City Manager: Robert C. Bobb
2000 census population (rank): 399,484 (41); **% change:** 7.3; **Male:** 192,757 (48.3%); **Female:** 206,727 (51.7%); **White:** 125,013 (31.3%); **Black:** 142,460 (35.7%); **American Indian and Alaska Native:** 2,655 (0.7%); **Asian:** 60,851 (15.2%); **Other race:** 46,592 (11.7%); **Two or more races:** 19,911 (5.0%); **Hispanic/Latino:** 87,467 (21.9%). **2000 percent population 18 and over:** 75.0%; **65 and over:** 10.5%; **median age:** 33.3.
2003 population estimate (rank): 398,844 (43)
Land area: 56 sq mi. (145 sq km); **Alt.:** Highest, 1,700 ft.; lowest, sea level
Avg. daily temp.: Jan., 49.9° F; July, 62.1° F
Churches: 374, representing over 78 denominations in the city; over 500 churches in Alameda County; **City-owned parks:** 2,196 ac.; **Radio stations:** AM, 1; **Television stations:** 1 commercial, 1 government access, 2 education access, 1 local
Civilian Labor Force (PMSA) June 2004: 1,270,626; **Unemployed:** 70,998, **Percent:** 5.6; **Per capita personal income (MSA) 2002:** $46,920[1]
Chamber of Commerce: Oakland Chamber of Commerce, 475 Fourteenth St., Oakland, Calif. 94612

1. San Francisco–Oakland–Fremont, Calif.

Oakland is located in the west-central part of California on the east side of San Francisco Bay. It is the seat of Alameda County.

Don Luis Peralta first settled the site of Oakland in 1820 when he established the Rancho San Antonio. The gold rush of 1849 attracted more people to the area, and the city's population continued to grow after a ferry service to San Francisco was started in 1851. Oakland was incorporated as a town in 1852 and as a city in 1854. It was named after the numerous oak trees found in the area. Oakland became the western terminus of the Central Pacific Railroad in 1869 and the seat of Alameda County in 1873.

In the latter part of the 19th century and also in 1910, additional territory was annexed to Oakland and the city assumed its present size. In 1906, thousands of people fled to Oakland in the aftermath of the San Francisco earthquake and settled there permanently, furthering the city's growth. Oakland's economic development continued to rise with the opening of the San Francisco–Oakland Bay Bridge in 1936.

Oakland is a major center of culture and commerce. It is an important container shipping port and the terminus of three transcontinental railroads. Oakland's industries include food processing, transportation, software, telecommunications, pharmaceuticals, and electrical and high technology manufacturing. The city is the headquarters of many national and international corporations.

Selected famous natives and residents: Buster Crabbe, actor; Frederick Cottrell, inventor; Clint Eastwood, actor and director; Dennis Eckersley, athlete; Mark Hamill, singer, dancer, and songwriter; Hammer, actor; Tom Hanks, actor; Rod McKuen, singer and composer; Russ Meyer, producer and director; Eddie (Anderson) Rochester, actor; George Stevens, director; Amy Tan, writer; Jo Van Fleet, actress.

Oklahoma City, Okla.

Mayor: Mick Cornett (to April 2006)
City Manager: James D. Couch
2000 census population (rank): 506,132 (29);
   % change: 13.8; **Male:** 247,313 (48.9%); **Female:**
   258,819 (51.1%); **White:** 346,226 (68.4%); **Black:**
   77,810 (15.4%); **American Indian and Alaska Native:**
   17,743 (3.5%); **Asian:** 17,595 (3.5%); **Other race:**
   26,705 (5.3%); **Two or more races:** 19,693 (3.9%);
   Hispanic/Latino: 51,368 (10.1%). **2000 percent
   population 18 and over:** 74.5%; **65 and over:**
   11.5%; **median age:** 34.0.
2003 population estimate (rank): 523,303 (29)
Land area: 607 sq mi. (1,572 sq km); **Alt.:** Highest,
   1,320 ft.; lowest, 1,140 ft.
Avg. daily temp.: Jan., 35.9° F; July, 82.0° F
Churches: Roman Catholic, 25; Jewish, 4; Protestant and
   others, 741; **City-owned parks:** 144 (5,225 ac.); **Radio
   stations:** AM, 10; FM, 14; **Television stations:** 8
Civilian Labor Force (MSA) June 2004: 597,116;
   Unemployed: 29,058, **Percent:** 4.9; **Per capita personal income (MSA) 2002:** $27,877
Chamber of Commerce: Greater Oklahoma City Chamber of Commerce, 123 Park Ave., Oklahoma City, Okla.
   73102

Oklahoma City, the state capital and seat of Oklahoma County, is the largest city in Oklahoma. It is located in the central part of the state on the North Canadian River.

Oklahoma City sprang into being almost overnight. On April 22, 1889, the U.S. government opened the territory for settlement, and there was a rush across the border line to stake claims. A sprawling tent city sprang up near the Santa Fe railroad tracks, and within a short time Oklahoma City was a bustling town of 10,000. The city was incorporated in 1890 and replaced Guthrie as the state capital in 1910. Oil was discovered in the city in 1928, and petroleum production became a mainstay of the city's economy.

Oklahoma City is the wholesale and distributing center for the state, and the city's stockyards are the largest stocker and feeder cattle market in the world. Following the decline of the energy sector, Oklahoma City is fostering a private entrepreneurial environment and a more diversified economy. Within the service sector, health services are projected to grow, followed by retail trade and business services. Nearby Tinker Air Force Base, one of the world's largest air depots, is a major city employer.

In 1995 the city was the scene of a devastating terrorist bombing, which destroyed a federal office building and killed 168 people.

Selected famous natives and residents: Johnny Bench, baseball player; Lon Chaney, Jr., actor; Ralph Ellison, writer; Kay Francis, actress; Vince Gill, country singer; Dale Robertson, actor; Ted Shackleford, actor; Pamela Tiffin, actress.

Omaha, Neb.

Mayor: Michael Fahey (to June 2005)
2000 census population (rank): 390,007 (44);
   % change: 16.1; **Male:** 190,032 (48.7%); **Female:**
   199,975 (51.3%); **White:** 305,745 (78.4%); **Black:**
   51,917 (13.3%); **American Indian and Alaska Native:**
   2,616 (0.7%); **Asian:** 6,773 (1.7%); **Other race:**
   15,250 (3.9%); **Two or more races:** 7,478 (1.9%);
   Hispanic/Latino: 29,397 (7.5%). **2000 percent population 18 and over:** 74.4%; **65 and over:** 11.8%;
   median age: 33.5.
2003 population estimate (rank): 404,267 (42)

Land area: 116 sq mi. (300 sq km); **Alt.:** Highest,
   1,270 ft.
Avg. daily temp.: Jan., 21.1° F; July, 76.9° F
Churches: Protestant, 192; Roman Catholic, 44; Jewish,
   4; **City-owned parks:** 200+ (over 8,000 ac.); **Radio
   stations:** AM, 7; FM, 13; **Television stations:** 4
Civilian Labor Force (MSA) June 2004: 416,228;[1]
   Unemployed: 18,577,[1] **Percent:** 4.5;[1] **Per capita personal income (MSA) 2002:** $33,200[2]
Chamber of Commerce: Omaha Chamber of Commerce,
   1301 Harney St., Omaha, Neb. 68102

1. Omaha, Neb.–Iowa. 2. Omaha–Council Bluffs, Neb.–
Iowa.

Omaha, the largest city in Nebraska and the seat of Douglas County, is located in the eastern part of the state on the west bank of the Missouri River, opposite Council Bluffs, Iowa.

The Lewis and Clark expedition visited the area in 1804, and the U.S. Army built Ft. Atkinson nearby in 1819. Pierre Cabanne established a furtrading post at the site in 1825. The first Mormon migrants wintered there in 1846–1847 on their way to Utah. The city grew rapidly as the most northerly supply point for overland wagons to the Far West.

The city was officially founded in 1854 after the Nebraska Territory was opened for settlement. It was named for the Omaha Indians living nearby. Omaha was incorporated as a city in 1857 and was the capital of the Nebraska Territory from 1855 to 1867. The city continued to thrive as a point of entry and a major transportation center when the Union Pacific transcontinental railroad arrived in 1869.

Omaha is a major market for grain and livestock, food processing, telecommunications, and insurance. Other important industries include electrical equipment and finance as well as printing and publishing. It continues to be a major railroad hub.

Selected famous natives and residents: Fred Astaire, dancer and actor; Max Baer, boxer; Robert Boozer, basketball player; Marlon Brando, actor; Montgomery Clift, actor; Gerald Ford, former president; Bob Gibson, baseball player; Swoosie Kurtz, actress; Melvin Laird, former secretary of defense; Dorothy McGuire, actress; Nick Nolte, actor; Gale Sayers, football player; Malcolm X, political activist; Paul Williams, singer and composer.

Philadelphia, Pa.

Mayor: John F. Street (to Jan. 2008)
2000 census population (rank): 1,517,550 (5);
   % change: –4.3; **Male:** 705,107 (46.5%); **Female:**
   812,443 (53.5%); **White:** 683,267 (45.0%); **Black:**
   655,824 (43.2%); **American Indian and Alaska
   Native:** 4,073 (0.3%); **Asian:** 67,654 (4.5%); **Other
   race:** 72,429 (4.8%); **Two or more races:** 33,574
   (2.2%); **Hispanic/Latino:** 128,928 (8.5%). **2000 percent population 18 and over:** 74.7%; **65 and over:**
   14.1%; **median age:** 34.2.
2003 population estimate (rank): 1,479,339 (5)
Land area: 135 sq mi. (350 sq km); **Alt.:** Highest, 440
   ft.; lowest, sea level
Avg. daily temp.: Jan., 30.4° F; July, 76.7° F
Churches: Roman Catholic, 133; Jewish, 55; Protestant
   and others, 830; **City-owned parks:** 630 (10,252 ac.);
   Radio stations:[1] AM, 40; FM, 43; **Television
   stations:** 14
Civilian Labor Force (PMSA) June 2004: 2,665,612;[2]
   Unemployed: 147,308,[2] **Percent:** 5.5;[2] **Per capita
   personal income (MSA) 2002:** $35,753[3]
Chamber of Commerce: Philadelphia Chamber of Com-
   merce, 200 South Broad St., Suite 700, Philadelphia,
   Pa. 19102

1. Metropolitan area. 2. Philadelphia, Pa.–N.J.
3. Philadelphia–Camden–Wilmington, Pa–N.J.–Del.–Md.

Philadelphia, the largest city in Pennsylvania, is located in the southeast part of the state at the junction of the Schuylkill and Delaware Rivers. It is coextensive with Philadelphia County.

Philadelphia, the City of Brotherly Love, was settled in 1681 by Capt. William Markham, who, with a small band of colonists, had been sent out by his cousin, William Penn. Penn arrived the following year with the intention of creating a refuge for the Quakers.

In the period before the American Revolution, the city outstripped all others in the colonies in education, arts, science, industry, and commerce. In 1774–1776, the First and Second Continental Congresses met in Philadelphia, and, from 1781–1783, the city was the capital of the United States under the Articles of Confederation. In 1790, it became the nation's capital under the Constitution and remained so until the seat of the federal government moved to Washington in 1800.

Within a half-century of the founding of the nation at Independence Hall, Philadelphia had emerged as a leader in America's Industrial Revolution. Today the steam locomotives and hat factories of the 19th century have been replaced by diverse manufacturing specialties such as chemicals (including pharmaceuticals), medical devices, transportation equipment, and printing and publishing. In the services sector, Philadelphia leads in subsectors such as health services, insurance carriers, legal services, and architecture and engineering services. Philadelphia is also home to branches of the U.S. Mint, the Federal Reserve System, and the Internal Revenue Service.

The city's harbor, one of the largest freshwater ports in the world, is the centerpiece of the Ameri-Port facility in south Philadelphia, a major shipping center with rail links to the Midwest and Canada.

The city abounds in landmarks of early American history, including Independence Hall, where the Declaration of Independence was signed, and the Liberty Bell. Other significant tourist attractions are the Philadelphia Museum of Art, the Franklin Institute Science Museum, and the Philadelphia Zoological Gardens.

Selected famous natives and residents: Marian Anderson, contralto; Frankie Avalon, singer and actor; John, Lionel, and Ethel Barrymore, actors; Kevin Bacon, actor; Boyz II Men, R&B group; Mary Cassatt, artist; Wilt Chamberlain, basketball player; Chubby Checker, singer; Bill Cosby, actor; Stuart Davis, painter; Thomas Eakins, painter and sculptor; W. C. Fields, comedian; Benjamin Franklin, inventor and statesman; Grace (Kelly), actress and princess of Monaco; Walt Kelly, cartoonist; Patti LaBelle, singer; Mario Lanza, singer and actor; George McClellan, general; Margaret Mead, anthropologist; Edgar Allen Poe, author; Anna Quindlen, writer and Pulitzer Prize winner; Man Ray, painter; Betsy Ross, flagmaker; Will Smith, actor; Jacqueline Susann, novelist; Robert Venturi, architect.

Phoenix, Ariz.

Mayor: Phil Gordon (to Oct. 2007)
2000 census population (rank): 1,321,045 (6);
  % change: 34.3; **Male:** 671,760 (50.9%); **Female:** 649,285 (49.1%); **White:** 938,853 (71.1%); **Black:** 67,416 (5.1%); **American Indian and Alaska Native:** 26,696 (2.0%); **Asian:** 26,449 (2.0%); **Other race:** 216,589 (16.4%); **Two or more races:** 43,276 (3.3%); **Hispanic/Latino:** 449,972 (34.1%). **2000 percent population 18 and over:** 71.1%; **65 and over:** 8.1%; **median age:** 30.7.

2003 population estimate (rank): 1,388,416 (6)
Land area: 475 sq mi. (1,230 sq km); **Alt.:** Highest, 2,740 ft.; lowest, 1,017 ft.
Avg. daily temp.: Jan., 53.6° F; July, 93.5° F
City-owned parks: 200+ (25,235 ac.); **Radio stations:** AM, 20; FM, 20; **Television stations:** 9 commercial; 1 PBS
Civilian Labor Force (MSA) June 2004: 1,855,927;[1]
  Unemployed: 77,892,[1] **Percent:** 4.2;[1] **Per capita personal income (MSA) 2002** $28,481[2]
Chamber of Commerce: Phoenix Chamber of Commerce, 201 N. Central, Phoenix, Ariz. 85073

1. Phoenix–Mesa, Ariz. 2. Phoenix–Mesa–Scottsdale, Ariz.

Phoenix, the capital of Arizona and seat of Maricopa County, is the largest city in the state. It is located in the center of Arizona, on the Salt River.

The prehistoric Hohokam Indians first settled the area about 300 B.C. and dug a system of extensive irrigation canals for farming. The Indian culture mysteriously broke up in the 1400s.

The site was permanently resettled by Jack Swilling and "Lord Darrell" Duppa about 1867. Because the city was founded on the ruins of the ancient civilization, it was named Phoenix after the legendary bird that could regenerate itself. The irrigation canals were restored for farming, and ranching and prospecting began in the surrounding area. The city quickly grew as an important trading center. Phoenix was incorporated as a city in 1881 and was made the territorial capital in 1889. It became the state capital when Arizona was admitted to the Union in 1912.

Partly owing to its warm, dry climate, the city developed rapidly in the decades after World War II. Between 1950 and 1990 the population increased from 100,000 to 980,000. And Phoenix continues to be one of the fastest growing cities in the U.S.; between 1990 and 2000, its population increased another 34%, to 1.3 million.

Phoenix is a commercial and manufacturing center in an agricultural region. Major industries include government, agricultural products, aerospace technology, electronics, air-conditioning, leather goods, and Indian arts and crafts. Mining, timbering, and tourism also contribute to the economy.

Selected famous natives and residents: Lynda Carter, actress; Alice Cooper, musician; Arthur A. Fletcher, government official; Barry Goldwater, politician; Stevie Nicks, musician; Charles S. Robb, politician; Mare Winningham, actress.

Portland, Ore.

Mayor: Vera Katz (to Dec. 2004)
2000 census population (rank): 529,121 (28);
  % change: 21.0; **Male:** 261,565 (49.4%); **Female:** 267,556 (50.6%); **White:** 412,241 (77.9%); **Black:** 35,115 (6.6%); **American Indian and Alaska Native:** 5,587 (1.1%); **Asian:** 33,470 (6.3%); **Other race:** 18,760 (3.5%); **Two or more races:** 21,955 (4.1%); **Hispanic/Latino:** 36,058 (6.8%). **2000 percent population 18 and over:** 78.9%; **65 and over:** 11.6%; **median age:** 35.2.
2003 population estimate (rank): 538,544 (28)
Land area: 134 sq mi. (347 sq km); **Alt.:** Highest, 1073 ft.; lowest, sea level
Avg. daily temp.: Jan., 39.6° F; July, 68.2° F
Churches: Protestant, 450; Roman Catholic, 48; Jewish, 9; Buddhist, 6; other, 190; **City-owned parks:** 200 (over 10,000 ac.); **Radio stations:** AM: 14, FM: 14; **Television stations:** 5 commercial, 1 public
Civilian Labor Force (PMSA) June 2004: 1,084,938;[1]
  Unemployed: 73,427,[1] **Percent:** 6.8;[1] **Per capita personal income (MSA) 2002** $32,167[2]

Chamber of Commerce: Portland Business Alliance, 520 S.W. Yamhill St., Ste. 1000, Portland, Ore. 97204

1. Portland–Vancouver, Ore.–Wash. 2. Portland–Vancouver–Beaverton, Ore.–Wash.

Portland, the largest city in Oregon and seat of Multnomah County, is located in the northwest part of the state on the Willamette River.

Lewis and Clark camped at the site of Portland in 1805 on their expedition across the continent. Portland was founded in 1845 and was almost called Boston after the city in Massachusetts. Founders Amos Lovejoy from Massachusetts and Francis Pettygrove from Maine flipped a coin to decide the name of the new town. Pettygrove won the toss and named the place Portland after his hometown. Portland was incorporated as a city in 1851.

In the 1850s Portland served as a supply base for the California gold rush, and it grew with the development of its salmon and lumber industries and the arrival of the railroad in 1883. The city continued to grow from 1879 to 1900 as a supply point for the Alaska gold rush and as the site of the Lewis and Clark Centennial Exposition in 1905.

The port of Portland leads the West in grain exports and is among the top five auto-import centers in the United States.

Portland has a diverse economy with a broad base of manufacturing, distribution, wholesale and retail trade, regional government, and business services. Major manufacturing industries include machinery, electronics, metals, transportation equipment, and lumber and wood products. Technology is a thriving part of Portland's economy, with over 1,700 high-tech companies located in the metropolitan area. Tourism is also important to Portland's economy, drawing more than 7 million visitors annually.

Selected famous natives and residents: James Beard, food expert; Pietro Belluschi, architect; Richard Fosbury, high jumper; Matt Groening, cartoonist; Margaux Hemingway, actress; Phil Knight, founder of Nike; Terrance Knox, actor; Jeff Lorber, jazz musician; Linus Pauling, chemist; Jane Powell, singer and actress; Ahmad Rashad, football player and sportscaster; Susan Ruttan, actress; Doc Severinsen, band leader; Norton Simon, business executive; Sally Ann Struthers, actress; Gus Van Sant, film director; Lindsay Wagner, actress; Mitch Williams, baseball pitcher.

Sacramento, Calif.

Mayor: Heather Fargo (to Nov. 2004)
City Manager: Robert P. Thomas
2000 census population (rank): 407,018 (40); **% change:** 10.2; **Male:** 197,784 (48.6%); **Female:** 209,234 (51.4%); **White:** 196,549 (48.3%); **Black:** 62,968 (15.5%); **American Indian and Alaska Native:** 5,300 (1.3%); **Asian:** 67,635 (16.6%); **Other race:** 44,627 (11.0%); **Two or more races:** 26,078 (6.4%); **Hispanic/Latino:** 87,974 (21.6%). **2000 percent population 18 and over:** 72.7%; **65 and over:** 11.4%; **median age:** 32.8.
2003 population estimate (rank): 445,335 (37)
Land area: 97 sq mi. (251 sq km)
Avg. daily temp.: Jan., 45.2° F; July, 75.7° F
City park & recreational facilities: 160+ (2,000+ ac.); **Television stations:** 7
Civilian Labor Force (PMSA) June 2004: 886,622; **Unemployed:** 48,110, **Percent:** 5.4; **Per capita personal income (MSA) 2002** $31,069[1]
Chamber of Commerce: Sacramento Chamber of Commerce, 917 7th St., Sacramento, Calif. 95814

1. Sacramento–Arden–Arcade–Roseville, Calif.

Sacramento is the capital of California and the seat of Sacramento County. It is located in the north-central part of the state at the confluence of the Sacramento and American rivers.

In 1839, German-born Swiss citizen John Augustus Sutter obtained a grant from the Mexican governor to establish a colony for fellow Swiss emigrants on a large tract of land that he named New Helvetia (New Switzerland). He established Fort Sutter there as a trading post.

After gold was discovered on Sutter's property in 1848, the settlement rapidly expanded as the prominent supply point for gold prospectors coming from the East. Sacramento was laid out in 1848 and named after California's principal river, which ran beside it. The river's name in Spanish honors the Holy Sacrament. It became incorporated as a city in 1849 and was made the state capital in 1854. Sacramento was the terminus of the first railroad in 1856 and the western terminus of the Pony Express in 1860.

The city has always been a hub of river transportation and is a major deep-water port connected to the Pacific Ocean. Sacramento's economy is highly diversified and, along with state government and military installations, its industries include aerospace, high technology, furniture, chemicals, pharmaceuticals, meat packing, and food processing of crops from the Central Valley.

Selected famous natives and residents: Joan Didion, author; Mark Goodson, TV producer; Tom Hanks, actor; Henry Hathaway, director; Anthony M. Kennedy, Supreme Court justice; Molly Ringwald, actress.

St. Louis, Mo.

Mayor: Francis G. Slay (to April 2005)
2000 census population (rank): 348,189 (49); **% change:** –12.2; **Male:** 163,567 (47.0%); **Female:** 184,622 (53.0%); **White:** 152,666 (43.8%); **Black:** 178,266 (51.2%); **American Indian and Alaska Native:** 950 (0.3%); **Asian:** 6,891 (2.0%); **Other race:** 2,783 (0.8%); **Two or more races:** 6,539 (1.9%); **Hispanic/Latino:** 7,022 (2.0%). **2000 percent population 18 and over:** 74.3%; **65 and over:** 13.7%; **median age:** 33.7.
2003 population estimate (rank): 332,223 (53)
Land area: 62 sq mi. (161 sq km); **Alt.:** Highest, 616 ft.; lowest, 413 ft.
Avg. daily temp.: Jan., 28.4° F; July, 78.4° F
Churches: 900;[1] **City-owned parks:** 105 (3,136 ac.); **Radio stations:** AM, 21; FM 27;[1] **Television stations:** 6 commercial; 1 PBS
Civilian Labor Force (MSA) June 2004: 1,438,316;[2]; **Unemployed:** 85,914,[2] **Percent:** 6.0;[2] **Per capita personal income (MSA) 2002** $32,462[2]
Chamber of Commerce: St. Louis Regional Chamber and Growth Association, One Metropolian Square, Suite 1300, St. Louis, Mo. 63102

1. Metropolitan area. 2. St. Louis, Mo.–Ill.

St. Louis, the second-largest city in Missouri, is located in the east central part of the state on the Mississippi River. The city is independent and is not part of any county.

St. Louis was founded by the French in 1764 when Auguste Chouteau established a fur-trading post and Pierre Laclède Liguest, a New Orleans merchant, founded a town at the present site. They named it after King Louis XV of France and his patron saint, Louis IX. From 1770 to 1803, St. Louis was a Spanish possession, but it was ceded back to France in 1803 in accordance with the Treaty of San Ildefonso

(1800), only to be acquired by the U.S. as part of the Louisiana purchase later that year.

The town was incorporated in 1809. From 1812 to 1821, St. Louis was the capital of the Missouri Territory, and it was incorporated as a city in 1822.

John Jacob Astor opened the Western branch of the American Fur Company in 1819, and the city prospered during the early part of the 19th century as a commercial center for the fur trade. St. Louis continued to grow as a major transportation hub with the development of steamboat traffic and the later expansion of the railroads in the 1850s. The world-famous Louisiana Purchase Exposition was held here in 1904.

Manufacturing is important to the city's economy, and its highly developed industries include automobiles, aircraft and space technology, metal fabrication, beer, steelmaking, chemicals, food processing, and storage and distribution.

The giant stainless steel Gateway Arch, 630 ft high, standing on the banks of the Mississippi, symbolizes St. Louis as the Gateway to the West.

Selected famous natives and residents: Josephine Baker, singer; Yogi Berra, baseball player; Chuck Berry, singer and guitarist; Grace Bumbry, mezzo-soprano; T. S. Eliot, poet; Eugene Field, poet; Redd Foxx, comedian; Joe Garagiola, baseball player; John Goodman, actor; Betty Grable, actress; Dick Gregory, comedian; Al Hirschfeld, cartoonist; Kevin Kline, actor; David Merrick, producer; Vincent Price, actor; Judy Rankin, golfer; Leon Spinks, boxer; Herbert Bayard Swope, journalist; Sara Teasdale, poet; Helen Traubel, soprano; Roy Wilkins, civil rights leader.

San Antonio, Tex.

Mayor: Ed Garza (to May 2005)
City Manager: Terry M. Brechtel
2000 census population (rank): 1,144,646 (9);
% change: 22.3; **Male:** 553,245 (48.3%); **Female:** 591,401 (51.7%); **White:** 774,708 (67.7%); **Black:** 78,120 (6.8%); **American Indian and Alaska Native:** 9,584 (0.8%); **Asian:** 17,934 (1.6%); **Other race:** 221,362 (19.3%); **Two or more races:** 41,871 (3.7%); **Hispanic/Latino:** 671,394 (58.7%). **2000 percent population 18 and over:** 71.5%; **65 and over:** 10.4%; **median age:** 31.7.
2003 population estimate (rank): 1,214,725 (8)
Land area: 408 sq mi. (1,057 sq km); **Alt.:** 700 ft.
Avg. daily temp.: Jan., 49.3° F; July, 85.0° F
City-owned parks: 193 (15,546 ac.); **Radio stations:** AM, 20; FM, 22; **Television stations:** 9
Civilian Labor Force (MSA) June 2004: 846,048; **Unemployed:** 47,367, **Percent:** 5.6; **Per capita personal income (MSA) 2002** $27,368
Chamber of Commerce: Greater San Antonio Chamber of Commerce, 602 E. Commerce, San Antonio, Tex. 78296

San Antonio, the third-largest city in Texas and the seat of Bexar County, is located in the south-central part of the state, on the San Antonio River.

The site of San Antonio was first visited in 1691 by a Franciscan friar on the feast day of St. Anthony and was named San Antonio de Padua in his honor. San Antonio was permanently settled on May 1, 1718, when the Spanish governor of Coahuila and Texas, Martín de Alarcón, founded the presidio (a fort) of San Antonio de Bejar (Bexar) and the mission of San Antonio de Valero (later called the Alamo) on the site of a Coahuiltecan Indian village. San Antonio remained almost continuously under Spanish rule until 1812, when Mexico won its independence from Spain.

During the outbreak of the Texas revolution (1835) against the tyranny of Mexican dictator General Santa Anna, San Antonio was captured by a small band of rebels who occupied the fortified mission of the Alamo in Dec. 1835. The historic battle of the Alamo was fought there (Feb. 24 to March 6, 1836), and its 183 besieged defenders were massacred by Santa Anna's troops. Their heroism aroused the anger and fighting spirit of Texans and led them to shout their famous battle cry "Remember the Alamo!" and defeat the Mexicans six weeks later (April 21, 1836) at the battle of San Jacinto. Texas became an independent republic in 1836, and San Antonio was incorporated as a city on Jan. 5, 1837.

After the Civil War, with the arrival of the railroad in 1877, San Antonio prospered as a major shipping point for cattle. The city has been an important military center since World War II and is the home to five of the largest military installations in the nation, including Fort Sam Houston, constructed in 1876. San Antonio is a leading livestock center and one of the largest produce exchange markets. The city's industries are highly diversified, and tourism is also important to the economy.

Selected famous natives and residents: Carol Burnett, comedienne; George W. Bush, U.S. president; Cody Carlson, football player; Henry G. Cisneros, secretary of HUD; Joan Crawford, actress; Cito Gaston, baseball manager; Ann Harding, actress; Jesse James Leija, boxer; Emilio Navaira, Tejano music singer; Oliver North, military officer and government official; Suzy Parker, model and actress; Paula Prentiss, actress; Kyle Rote, football player; David R. Scott, astronaut; Patsy Torres, Tejano music singer; Edward H. White, astronaut.

San Diego, Calif.

Mayor: Dick Murphy (to Dec. 2004)
City Manager: P. Lamont Ewell (apptd. March 2004)
2000 census population (rank): 1,223,400 (7);
% change: 10.2; **Male:** 616,884 (50.4%); **Female:** 606,516 (49.6%); **White:** 736,207 (60.2%); **Black:** 96,216 (7.9%); **American Indian and Alaska Native:** 7,543 (0.6%); **Asian:** 166,968 (13.6%); **Other race:** 151,532 (12.4%); **Two or more races:** 59,081 (4.8%); **Hispanic/Latino:** 310,752 (25.4%). **2000 percent population 18 and over:** 76.0%; **65 and over:** 10.5%; **median age:** 32.5.
2003 population estimate (rank): 1,266,753 (7)
Land area: 324 sq miles (839 sq km); **Alt.:** Highest, 1,591 ft.; lowest, sea level
Avg. daily temp.: Jan., 57.4° F; July, 71.0° F
Churches: Roman Catholic, 39; Jewish, 9; Protestant, 334; Eastern Orthodox, 8; other, 18; **City park and recreation facilities:** 337 (36,300 ac.); **Radio stations:** AM, 14; FM, 25; **Television stations:** 9
Civilian Labor Force (MSA) June 2004: 1,518,300; **Unemployed:** 61,933, **Percent:** 4.1; **Per capita personal income (MSA) 2002** $34,872[1]
Chamber of Commerce: San Diego Chamber of Commerce, 402 West Broadway, Suite 1000, San Diego, Calif. 92101

1. San Diego–Carlsbad–San Marcos, Calif.

San Diego is the second-largest city in California. It is located in the southwest part of the state, on San Diego Bay.

Portuguese navigator Juan Rodríguez Cabrillo claimed the bay for Spain in 1542. The site was named San Miguel by Cabrillo. On Nov. 12, 1602, Don Sebastián de Viscaíno came ashore with his party on the day of St. Didacus (San Diego in Spanish) and celebrated a mass in the saint's honor. By coincidence, Viscaíno's flagship was named San

Diego. He renamed the place San Diego after the 15th-century saint.

In 1769, Franciscan father Junípero Serra established the first California mission there—San Diego del Alcala. In 1822, Mexico won control of the town after declaring its independence from Spain. In 1846, during the Mexican War, San Diego was seized by the U.S., and it was incorporated as a city in 1850, just after California joined the Union.

Today, San Diego's excellent natural harbor is a busy commercial port and a hub of U.S. naval operations (although the naval training center at San Diego has closed due to defense cutbacks). Other leading industries are electronics, aerospace and missiles, medical and scientific research, oceanography, and agriculture. Its magnificent climate and proximity to Mexico have made tourism a significant part of the city's economy.

Selected famous natives and residents: Billy Casper, golfer; Florence Chadwick, swimmer; Dennis Conner, yacht racer; Ted Danson, actor; Robert Duvall, actor; Nanette Fabray, actress; Margaret O'Brien, actress; Carol Vaness, soprano; Ted Williams, baseball player; Mickey Wright, golfer.

San Francisco, Calif.

Mayor: Gavin Newsom (to Jan. 2008)
2000 census population (rank): 776,733 (13);
% change: 7.3; **Male:** 394,828 (50.8%); **Female:** 381,905 (49.2%); **White:** 385,728 (49.7%); **Black:** 60,515 (7.8%); **American Indian and Alaska Native:** 3,458 (0.4%); **Asian:** 239,565 (30.8%); **Other race:** 50,368 (6.5%); **Two or more races:** 33,255 (4.3%); **Hispanic/Latino:** 109,504 (14.1%). **2000 percent population 18 and over:** 85.5%; **65 and over:** 13.7%; **median age:** 36.5.
2003 population estimate (rank): 751,682 (14)
Land area: 47 sq mi. (122 sq km); **Alt.:** Highest, 925 ft.; lowest, sea level
Avg. daily temp.: Jan., 51.1° F; July, 59.1° F
Churches: 540 of all denominations; **City-owned parks and squares:** 200+; **Radio stations:** 29; **Television stations:** 10
Civilian Labor Force (PMSA) June 2004: 896,369; **Unemployed:** 42,505, **Percent:** 4.7; **Per capita personal income (MSA) 2002:** $46,920[1]
Chamber of Commerce: San Francisco Chamber of Commerce, 235 Montgomery St., San Francisco, Calif. 94104

1. San Francisco–Oakland–Fremont, Calif.

San Francisco, the fourth-largest city in California, is coextensive with San Francisco County. It is located in the northern part of the state between the Pacific Ocean and San Francisco Bay on a narrow arm of land that embraces San Francisco Bay, the largest land-locked harbor in the world.

A Franciscan father who was sailing with Sebastián Rodríguez Cermeño named the bay San Francisco on Nov. 7, 1595. In 1776, the Spaniards established a presidio, or military post, and a Franciscan mission on the end of the beautiful peninsula. In the following year, a little town was founded around the mission. It was called Yerba Buena, Spanish for "Good Herb," because mint grew in abundance there. In 1846, during the Mexican War, Yerba Buena was taken over by the United States. It was renamed San Francisco in 1847 and became incorporated as a city in 1850.

When gold was discovered in California in 1848, the city's population jumped to 10,000, and it experienced turbulent years until order was established by Vigilance Committees, first in 1851, and again in

1856. Then followed a period of more orderly growth, and the foundations of the great commerce and industry of today were laid.

In 1906, San Francisco experienced the nation's most destructive earthquake, which, together with the fire that followed, practically destroyed the city. The city was quickly rebuilt and grew rapidly as a leading transportation, industrial, and cultural center. In the 19th century, the American explorer and soldier John C. Frémont, known as The Pathfinder, named the entrance to the bay the Golden Gate, and the famous bright orange Golden Gate Bridge was dedicated in May 1937.

A vital part of the economic and cultural fabric of northern California, the port of San Francisco covers 7½ mi of waterfront. The port is home to a broad range of commercial, maritime, and public activities. Its major shipping terminals serve shipping lines from around the world. Fisherman's Wharf, Alcatraz, Hyde St. Pier, and Pier 39 all make the port of San Francisco one of the world's leading visitor destinations.

The electronics and biotechnology industries are well represented throughout the Bay Area. With nearly 30% of the worldwide biotechnology labor force and 360 biotech firms, the Bay Area has been appropriately called "Bionic Bay."

Tourism is one of San Francisco's largest industries and the largest employer of city residents. In 2000, more than 17 million people visited San Francisco, and visitor spending was $7.6 billion, providing 82,000 jobs.

San Francisco is also the banking and financial center of the West and is home to a Federal Reserve Bank and a United States Mint. More than 60 foreign banks maintain offices there.

Selected famous natives and residents: Gracie Allen, comedienne; Luis Walter Alvarez, Nobel Prize winner in physics; David Belasco, dramatist and producer; Mel Blanc, actor and voice specialist; Rosemary Casals, tennis player; Isadora Duncan, dancer; Clint Eastwood, actor; Robert Frost, poet; Rube Goldberg, cartoonist; William Randolph Hearst, publisher; Bruce Lee, actor; Mervyn LeRoy, director; Jack London, novelist; Johnny Mathis, singer; Lloyd Nolan, actor; O. J. Simpson, football player; Robert G. Sproul, educator; Irving Stone, novelist; Natalie Wood, actress.

San Jose, Calif.

Mayor: Ron Gonzales (to March 2006)
City Manager: Del D. Borgsdorf
2000 census population (rank): 894,943 (11);
% change: 14.4; **Male:** 454,798 (50.8%); **Female:** 440,145 (49.2%); **White:** 425,017 (47.5%); **Black:** 31,349 (3.5%); **American Indian and Alaska Native:** 6,865 (0.8%); **Asian:** 240,375 (26.9%); **Other race:** 142,691 (15.9%); **Two or more races:** 45,062 (5.0%); **Hispanic/Latino:** 269,989 (30.2%). **2000 percent population 18 and over:** 73.6%; **65 and over:** 8.3%; **median age:** 32.6.
2003 population estimate (rank): 898,349 (11)
Land area: 175 sq mi. (453 sq km); **Alt.:** Highest, 4,372 ft.; lowest, sea level
Avg. daily temp.: Jan., 49.4° F; July, 69.5° F
Churches: 403; **City-owned parks and playgrounds:** 152 (3,136 ac.); **Radio stations:** 14; **Television stations:** 4
Civilian Labor Force (PMSA) June 2004: 874,357; **Unemployed:** 54,444, **Percent:** 6.2; **Per capita personal income (MSA) 2002:** $45,925[1]
Chamber of Commerce: San Jose Chamber of Commerce, 310 S. First St., San Jose, Calif. 95113

1. San Jose–Sunnyvale–Santa Clara, Calif.

San Jose, the third-largest city in California and seat of Santa Clara County, is located in the northern part of the state in the Santa Clara Valley, 50 mi south of downtown San Francisco.

San Jose was founded on Nov. 29, 1777, by Spanish colonizers who named the settlement Pueblo de San José de Guadalupe in honor of Saint Joseph and after the Guadalupe River on which the pueblo (town) was situated. San Jose was the first city to be established in California.

After California became a U.S. territory in 1847, San Jose was the state capital from 1849 to 1852 and was incorporated as a city in 1850. It developed commercially as a supply base for gold prospectors and, when the railroad connected it with San Francisco in 1864, it became the distribution point for agricultural products from the Santa Clara Valley.

Today, the city continues to be the distribution and food-processing center for the surrounding rich agricultural region, which produces seasonal fruits and grapes. More than 50 wineries grace the valley.

San Jose is the capital of Silicon (Santa Clara) Valley, where many high-tech companies are located. The area is also one of the world's leading centers for medical treatment and research. Heart transplants, gene splicing, and transportable baby incubators were developed there.

San Jose has healthy retail, transportation, and tourism industries and is the primary center for real estate and industrial development in the area. In 2001, it ranked second in the U.S. based on the median household income of $71,000.

Selected famous natives and residents: "Fatty" Arbuckle, actor; Cesar Chavez, labor leader; Peggy Fleming, figure skater; Farley Granger, actor; Edmund Lowe, actor; Jim Plunkett, football player.

Seattle, Wash.

Mayor: Greg Nickels (to Dec. 31, 2005)
2000 census population (rank): 563,374 (24);
   % change: 9.1; **Male:** 280,973 (49.9%); **Female:** 282,401 (50.1%); **White:** 394,889 (70.1%); **Black:** 47,541 (8.4%); **American Indian and Alaska Native:** 5,659 (1.0%); **Asian:** 73,910 (13.1%); **Other race:** 13,423 (2.4%); **Two or more races:** 25,148 (4.5%); **Hispanic/Latino:** 29,719 (5.3%). **2000 percent population 18 and over:** 84.4%; **65 and over:** 12.0%; **median age:** 35.4.
2003 population estimate (rank): 569,101 (24)
Land area: 84 sq mi. (218 sq km); **Alt.:** Highest, 521 ft.; lowest, sea level
Avg. daily temp.: Jan., 40.1° F; July, 65.2° F
Churches: Roman Catholic, 35; Jewish, 12; Protestant, 447; others, 42; **City-owned parks, playgrounds, etc.:** 400 (6,200 ac.); **Radio stations:** AM, 15; FM, 22; **Television stations:** 6
Civilian Labor Force (PMSA) June 2004: 1,423,145;[1]
   Unemployed: 84,560,[1] **Percent:** 5.9;[1] **Per capita personal income (MSA) 2002:** $38,037[2]
Chamber of Commerce: Greater Seattle Chamber of Commerce, 1301 5th Ave., Suite 2400, Seattle, Wash. 98101-2603

1. Seattle–Bellevue–Everett, Wash. 2. Seattle–Tacoma–Bellevue, Wash.

Seattle is the largest city in Washington and the seat of King County. A city of steep hills, Seattle lies in western Washington between two bodies of water—Puget Sound on the west and Lake Washington on the east. Its fine landlocked harbor has made Seattle one of the major ports in the United States.

Seattle was first settled by five pioneer families from Illinois at Alki Point at the south end of Elliott Bay in 1851. They moved in 1852 to the eastern shore of the bay and laid out a town in 1853. It was named Seattle after a friendly Suquamish Indian chief (Seattle is only an approximation of his name).

Seattle successfully withstood an Indian attack in 1856 and was incorporated as a city in 1869. A disastrous fire almost destroyed the entire business district in 1889. When the Great Northern Railway arrived in 1893, the city became a major rail terminus and it grew rapidly. It was a boom town during the Alaska gold rush of 1897 and continued to prosper as a major Pacific port of entry with the opening of the Panama Canal in 1914.

Seattle is the region's commercial and transportation hub and the center of manufacturing, trade, and finance. Its important diversified industries include aircraft, lumber and forest products, fishing, high technology, food processing, boat building, machinery, fabricated metals, chemicals, pharmaceuticals, and apparel.

Selected famous natives and residents: Chester Carlson, Xerox inventor; Carol Channing, actress; Judy Collins, singer; Fred Couples, golfer; Gail Devers, athlete; Frances Farmer, actress; William Gates, Microsoft founder; June Havoc, actress; Jimi Hendrix, guitarist; Robert Joffrey, choreographer; Gypsy Rose Lee, entertainer; Mary Livingstone, comedienne; Kevin McCarthy, actor; Mary McCarthy, novelist; Jeff Smith, food expert; Martha Wright, singer.

Tucson, Ariz.

Mayor: Bob Walkup (to Dec. 2007)
2000 census population (rank): 486,699 (30);
   % change: 20.1; **Male:** 238,408 (49.0%); **Female:** 248,291 (51.0%); **White:** 341,424 (70.2%); **Black:** 21,057 (4.3%); **American Indian and Alaska Native:** 11,038 (2.3%); **Asian:** 11,959 (2.5%); **Other race:** 81,988 (16.8%); **Two or more races:** 18,437 (3.8%); **Hispanic/Latino:** 173,868 (35.7%). **2000 percent population 18 and over:** 75.4%; **65 and over:** 11.9%; **median age:** 32.1.
2003 population estimate (rank): 507,658 (31)
Land area: 195 sq mi. (505 sq km); **Alt.:** 2,400 ft.
Avg. daily temp.: Jan., 51.3° F; July, 86.6° F
Churches: Protestant, 340; Roman Catholic, 42; other, 150; **City-owned parks and parkways:** (25,349 ac.); **Radio stations:** AM, 15; FM, 17; **Television stations:** 3 commercial; 1 educational; 3 other
Civilian Labor Force (MSA) June 2004: 432,258;
   Unemployed: 16,603, **Percent:** 3.8; **Per capita personal income (MSA) 2002:** $25,278
Chamber of Commerce: Tucson Metropolitan Chamber of Commerce, 465 W. St. Mary's Rd., Tucson, Ariz. 85701

Tucson is the second-largest city in Arizona and the seat of Pima County. It is located in the southeast part of the state on the Santa Cruz River.

The site was originally settled by the prehistoric Hohokam Indians (300 B.C.–A.D. 1400s). The first Europeans to visit the area were Spanish missionaries in the 17th century. In 1700, the Jesuit missionary explorer Father Eusebio Francisco Kino founded the mission of San Xavier del Bac close by the Papago Indian village of Stjukshon (later called Tucson). Stjukshon is an Indian word meaning "village of the dark spring at the foot of the mountain." The Papago Indians are descendants of the ancient Hohokam peoples.

In 1776, Spanish colonists from Mexico constructed a presidio (fort) at Tucson as protection against the hostile Apache Indians and also established the mission of San Jose de Tucson nearby. Tucson remained a military outpost under Spanish and later Mexican control until the area was sold to the United States as part of the Gadsden Purchase in 1853. Tucson was the capital of the Arizona Territory from 1867 to 1877. It was incorporated as a city in 1877. The town grew rapidly when the Southern Pacific Railroad arrived in 1880 and silver and copper deposits were discovered nearby.

Tucson is a popular vacation and health resort due to its sunny, mild, dry climate and unique desert location. Tourism is important to the city's economy. Major industries include aerospace and missile production, high technology, optics, biotechnology, environmental technology, software, and electronics. Tucson is also the commercial center for the surrounding area's agricultural and mining industries. The city is the home of the University of Arizona.

Selected famous natives and residents: Rose E. Bird, jurist; Dennis De Concini, senator; Barbara Eden, actress; Linda Ronstadt, singer.

Tulsa, Okla.

Mayor: Bill LaFortune (to April 2006)
2000 census population (rank): 393,049 (43); % change: 7.0; Male: 189,937 (48.3%); Female: 203,112 (51.7%); White: 275,488 (70.1%); Black: 60,794 (15.5%); American Indian and Alaska Native: 18,551 (4.7%); Asian: 7,150 (1.8%); Other race: 13,564 (3.5%); Two or more races: 17,300 (4.4%); Hispanic/Latino: 28,111 (7.2%). 2000 percent population 18 and over: 75.2%; 65 and over: 12.9%; median age: 34.5.
2003 population estimate (rank): 387,807 (44)
Land area: 183 sq mi. (474 sq km); Alt.: 674 ft.
Avg. daily temp.: Jan., 35.2° F; July, 83.3° F
Churches: Protestant, 290; Roman Catholic, 40; Jewish, 3; others, 4; City parks and playgrounds: 128 (5,987 ac.); Radio stations: AM, 10; FM, 16; Television stations: 7 commercial; 1 PBS; 123 cable
Civilian Labor Force (MSA) June 2004: 427,800; Unemployed: 21,155, Percent: 4.9; Per capita personal income (MSA) 2002: $30,627
Chamber of Commerce: Metropolitan Tulsa Chamber of Commerce, 2 West Second St., Ste. 150, Tulsa, Okla. 74103

Tulsa, the second-largest city in Oklahoma and seat of Tulsa County, is located in the northeast part of the state on the Arkansas River.

Tulsa was settled in the 1830s by Creek Indians from Alabama who were forcibly sent to the area (then part of Indian Territory) under the Indian Removal Act of 1830. Creek medicine men planted ashes from their old home at the new site, and the Creeks named their new village "Tulsy," meaning old town, in memory of their former home in Tallassee, Ala. In time, the village became the town of Tulsa.

The coming of the first railroad in 1882 attracted white settlers to Tulsa, and the town developed into a cattle-shipping center. When enormous oil deposits were discovered at nearby Red Fork in 1901 and at Glenn Pool in 1905, the city experienced rapid growth as a center of a booming petroleum industry. Tulsa was incorporated as a city in 1898 and chartered in 1908.

Tulsa is the center of the state's petroleum and telecommunications industries and has a diversified economy. Other important industries include aerospace, chemicals, computer parts, automobile glass, fabricated metals, and industrial machinery. The city became a major inland port when the Tulsa port of Catoosa opened in 1971.

Selected famous natives and residents: Garth Brooks, singer; Blake Edwards, director; Paul Harvey, commentator; Jennifer Jones, actress; Henry R. Kravis, investment banker; Daniel Patrick Moynihan, senator; Tony Randall, actor; Alfre Woodard, actress; Judy Woodruff, journalist.

Virginia Beach, Va.

Mayor: Meyera E. Oberndorf (to June 2008)
2000 census population (rank): 425,257 (38); % change: 8.2; Male: 210,524 (49.5%); Female: 214,733 (50.5%); White: 303,681 (71.4%); Black: 80,593 (19.0%); American Indian and Alaska Native: 1,619 (0.4%); Asian: 20,869 (4.9%); Other race: 6,402 (1.5%); Two or more races: 11,677 (2.7%); Hispanic/Latino: 17,770 (4.2%); 2000 percent population 18 and over: 72.5%; 65 and over: 8.4%; median age: 32.7.
2003 population estimate (rank): 439,467 (39)
Land area: 248 sq mi. (642 sq km); Alt.: 12 ft.
Avg. daily temp.: Jan., 39.1° F; July, 78.2° F
Churches: Protestant, 235; Catholic, 13; Jewish, 5; City-owned parks: 208 (4,000+ ac.); Radio stations: AM 13, FM 31; Television stations: 8 commercial, 1 PBS, 1 cable
Civilian Labor Force (MSA) June 2004: 818,440;[1] Unemployed: 36,760,[1] Percent: 4.5;[1] Per capita personal income (MSA) 2002: $28,365[1]
Chamber of Commerce: Hampton Roads Chamber of Commerce, 420 Bank St., Norfolk, Va. 23510

1. Norfolk–Virginia Beach–Newport News, Va.–N.C.

Virginia Beach, the most populous city in Virginia, is located in the southeast part of the state on the Atlantic coastline. It is independent and is not part of any county.

The first English settlers to set foot in America landed at Cape Henry at the tip of Virginia Beach on April 29, 1607. They were led by John Smith on his way to establishing Jamestown. The first permanent settlement within the city limits was made at Lynnhaven Bay in 1621. Cape Henry became an important port for British merchant ships calling on America, and it was here that the French fleet led by Admiral Comte de Grasse blockaded the British fleet during the American Revolution.

Virginia Beach gained its reputation as a famous vacation resort in the 19th century, following the building of a railroad connecting its oceanfront with Norfolk and the construction of its first hotel in 1883. Virginia Beach was incorporated as a town in 1906 and as a city in 1952.

Tourism is a mainstay of the economy; more than 3 million people visit Virginia Beach each year. Virginia Beach's economy is also supported by four military bases and diverse industries, including agriculture, computer software, engineering, and technical services.

Selected famous natives and residents: V. C. Andrews, novelist; D. J. Dozier, football and baseball player; George Eastman, inventor; Juice Newton, singer; Kenneth S. Reightler, Jr., astronaut; Pat Robertson, evangelist; Henry Walke, naval officer; Pernell "Sweet Pea" Whitaker, boxer; Skip Wilkins, wheelchair athlete.

Washington, DC

Created municipal corporation: Feb. 21, 1871
Mayor: Anthony Williams (to Jan. 2007)
Motto: *Justitia omnibus* (Justice to all)
Flower: American beauty rose; **Tree:** Scarlet oak
2000 census population (rank): 572,059 (21);
  % change: –5.7; **Male:** 269,366 (47.1%); **Female:**
  302,693 (52.9%); **White:** 176,101 (30.8%); **Black:**
  343,312 (60.0%); **American Indian and Alaska**
  Native: 1,713 (0.3%); **Asian:** 15,189 (2.7%); **Other**
  race: 21,950 (3.8%); **Two or more races:** 13,446
  (2.4%); **Hispanic/Latino:** 44,953 (7.9%); **2000 per-**
  cent population 18 and over: 79.9%; **65 and over:**
  12.2%; **median age:** 34.6.
2003 population estimate (rank): 563,384 (25)
Land area: 61 sq mi. (158 sq km); **Alt.:** Highest, 420 ft.;
  lowest, sea level
Avg. daily temp.: Jan., 34.6° F; July, 80.0° F
Churches: Protestant, 610; Roman Catholic, 132; Jewish, 9; **City parks:** 300 (800 ac.); **Radio stations:**
  AM, 9; FM, 38; **Television stations:** 19
Civilian Labor Force (MSA) June 2004: 2,947,529;[1]
  Unemployed: 98,443,[1] **Percent:** 3.3;[1] **Per capita per-**
  sonal income (MSA) 2002: $42,773[2]
Board of Trade: Greater Washington Board of Trade,
  1129 20th Street N.W., Washington, DC 20036
Chamber of Commerce: DC Chamber of Commerce,
  1213 K St. NW, Washington, DC 20005

1. Washington, DC–Md.–Va.–W.Va. 2. Washington–
Arlington–Alexandria, DC–Va.–Md.–W.Va.

The District of Columbia—identical with the city of Washington—is the capital of the United States. It is located between Virginia and Maryland on the Potomac River. The district is named after Columbus.

DC history began in 1790 when Congress directed selection of a new capital site, 100 sq mi, along the Potomac. When the site was determined, it included 30.75 sq mi on the Virginia side of the river. In 1846, however, Congress returned that area to Virginia, leaving the 68.25 sq mi ceded by Maryland in 1788. The seat of government was transferred from Philadelphia to Washington on Dec. 1, 1800, and President John Adams became the first resident in the White House.

The city was planned and partly laid out by Maj. Pierre Charles L'Enfant, a French engineer. This work was perfected and completed by Maj. Andrew Ellicott and Benjamin Banneker, a freeborn black man who was an astronomer and mathematician. In 1814, during the War of 1812, a British force burned the capital including the White House.

Until Nov. 3, 1967, the District of Columbia was administered by three commissioners appointed by the president. On that day, a government consisting of a mayor-commissioner and a 9-member council, all appointed by the president with the approval of the Senate, took office. On May 7, 1974, the citizens of the District of Columbia approved a Home Rule Charter, giving them an elected mayor and 13-member council—their first elected municipal government in more than a century. The district also has one nonvoting member in the House of Representatives and an elected Board of Education.

On Aug. 22, 1978, Congress passed a proposed constitutional amendment to give Washington, DC, voting representation in the Congress. The amendment had to be ratified by at least 38 state legislatures within seven years to become effective. It died in 1985. A petition asking for the district's admission to the Union as the 51st state was filed in Congress on Sept. 9, 1983, and new statehood bills were introduced in 1993. The district is continuing this drive for statehood.

The federal government and tourism are the mainstays of the city's economy, and many unions, business, professional, and nonprofit organizations are headquartered there. Among the city's many educational institutions are the Catholic University of America, Georgetown University, Howard University, and Gallaudet University. Cultural attractions include the National Gallery of Art, the Smithsonian Institution, the John F. Kennedy Center for the Performing Arts, and the Folger Shakespeare Library.

Selected famous natives and residents: Edward Albee, playwright; Billie Burke, comedienne; Ina Claire, actress; John Foster Dulles, statesman; Duke Ellington, musician; Jane Greer, actress; Goldie Hawn, actress; Helen Hayes, actress; J. Edgar Hoover, former director of the F.B.I.; William Hurt, actor; Noor al-Hussein, queen of Jordan; Michael Learned, actress; Roger Mudd, newscaster; Eleanor Holmes Norton, government official; Chita Rivera, dancer and actress; Leonard Rose, cellist; John Philip Sousa, composer; Frances Sternhagen, actress.

Wichita, Kans.

Mayor: Carlos Mayans (to April 2007)
City Manager: Cathy Holdeman (acting)
2000 census population (rank): 344,284 (50);
  % change: 13.2; **Male:** 169,604 (49.3%); **Female:**
  174,680 (50.7%); **White:** 258,900 (75.2%); **Black:**
  39,325 (11.4%); **American Indian and Alaska Native:**
  3,986 (1.2%); **Asian:** 13,647 (4.0%); **Other race:**
  17,566 (5.1%); **Two or more races:** 10,662 (3.1%);
  Hispanic/Latino: 33,112 (9.6%); **2000 percent popu-**
  lation 18 and over: 72.9%; **65 and over:** 11.9%;
  median age: 33.4.
2003 population estimate (rank): 354,617 (50)
Land area: 136 sq mi. (352 sq km); **Alt.:** 1,333 ft.
Avg. daily temp.: Jan., 29.5° F; July, 81.4° F
Churches: Protestant, 512; Roman Catholic, 20; Jewish,
  2; other, 66; **City parks:** 110 (4,388 ac.); **Radio sta-**
  tions: 22; **Television stations:** 7
Civilian Labor Force (MSA) June 2004: 293,738;
  Unemployed: 17,578, **Percent:** 6.0; **Per capita per-**
  sonal income (MSA) 2002 $29,587
Chamber of Commerce: Wichita Chamber of Commerce, 350 W. Douglas, Wichita, Kans. 67202

Wichita is the largest city in Kansas and the seat of Sedgwick County. It is located in the south-central part of the state, at the confluence of the Arkansas and Little Arkansas rivers. Incorporated as a city in 1870, Wichita is the chief commercial and industrial center of southern Kansas.

More or less uninhabited at the time of Kansas's entry into the Union in 1861, the area was first settled by Wichita Indians, who came north from Texas and Oklahoma during the Civil War. At about the same time (during the mid-1860s) a number of trading posts were established at or near the river junction. One of the traders, Jesse Chisholm, pioneered the Chisholm Trail, which passed through Wichita and was the main cattle-drive route from Texas to the railroad in Abilene. After the railroad was extended to Wichita in 1872, the city boomed first as a cow town and then later as the trading center in an agricultural and livestock region. Although the city experienced an economic slump at the end of the 19th century, oil was discovered nearby in 1915, and subsequently the population almost doubled.

Aircraft manufacturing began in the 1920s, and Wichita remains a center of the aircraft industry today. In addition, the city also has flour mills, meatpacking plants, and oil refineries. Major manufactures include camping equipment, heaters and air conditioners, and electronics. Wichita has a number of art and historical museums, a zoo, and a planetarium. It is the site of several universities, including Wichita State University (1895). McConnell Air Force Base is nearby.

Selected famous natives and residents: Kirstie Alley, actress; Alan Fudge, actor; Dan Glickman, former congressman and U.S. secretary of agriculture; Laurel Goodwin, actress; Stan Kenton, musician; Jim Lehrer, news anchor; Fred, Thomas, and Edwin McConnell, WWII pilots; Hattie McDaniel, actress; Barry Sanders, football player; Gale Sayers, football player; Arlen Specter, U.S. senator from Pennsylvania; Ron Wyden, U.S. senator from Oregon.

Population of the 15 Largest U.S. Cities, 1900–2003

	1900		1920		1940	
Rank	Place	Population	Place	Population	Place	Population
1.	New York, N.Y.	3,437,202	New York, N.Y.	5,620,048	New York, N.Y.	7,454,995
2.	Chicago, Ill.	1,698,575	Chicago, Ill.	2,701,705	Chicago, Ill.	3,396,808
3.	Philadelphia, Pa.	1,293,697	Philadelphia, Pa.	1,823,779	Philadelphia, Pa.	1,931,334
4.	St. Louis, Mo.	575,238	Detroit, Mich.	993,078	Detroit, Mich.	1,623,452
5.	Boston, Mass.	560,892	Cleveland, Ohio	796,841	Los Angeles, Calif.	1,504,277
6.	Baltimore, Md.	508,957	St. Louis, Mo.	772,897	Cleveland, Ohio	878,336
7.	Cleveland, Ohio	381,768	Boston, Mass.	748,060	Baltimore, Md.	859,100
8.	Buffalo, N.Y.	352,387	Baltimore, Md.	733,826	St. Louis, Mo.	816,048
9.	San Francisco, Calif.	342,782	Pittsburgh, Pa.	588,343	Boston, Mass.	770,816
10.	Cincinnati, Ohio	325,902	Los Angeles, Calif.	576,673	Pittsburgh, Pa.	671,659
11.	Pittsburgh, Pa.	321,616	Buffalo, N.Y.	506,775	Washington, DC	663,091
12.	New Orleans, La.	287,104	San Francisco, Calif.	506,676	San Francisco, Calif.	634,536
13.	Detroit, Mich.	285,704	Milwaukee, Wis.	457,147	Milwaukee, Wis.	587,472
14.	Milwaukee, Wis.	285,315	Washington, DC	437,571	Buffalo, N.Y.	575,901
15.	Washington, DC	278,718	Newark, N.J.	414,524	New Orleans, La.	494,537

	1960		1980		2003[1]	
Rank	Place	Population	Place	Population	Place	Population
1.	New York, N.Y.	7,781,984	New York, N.Y.	7,071,639	New York, N.Y.	8,085,742
2.	Chicago, Ill.	3,550,404	Chicago, Ill.	3,005,072	Los Angeles, Calif.	3,819,951
3.	Los Angeles, Calif.	2,479,015	Los Angeles, Calif.	2,966,850	Chicago, Ill.	2,869,121
4.	Philadelphia, Pa.	2,002,512	Philadelphia, Pa.	1,688,210	Houston, Texas	2,009,960
5.	Detroit, Mich.	1,670,144	Houston, Texas	1,595,138	Philadelphia, Pa.	1,479,339
6.	Baltimore, Md.	939,024	Detroit, Mich.	1,203,339	Phoenix, Ariz.	1,388,416
7.	Houston, Texas	938,219	Dallas, Texas	904,078	San Diego, Calif.	1,266,753
8.	Cleveland, Ohio	876,050	San Diego, Calif.	875,538	San Antonio, Texas	1,214,725
9.	Washington, DC	763,956	Phoenix, Ariz.	789,704	Dallas, Texas	1,208,318
10.	St. Louis, Mo.	750,026	Baltimore, Md.	786,775	Detroit, Mich.	911,402
11.	Milwaukee, Wis.	741,324	San Antonio, Tex.	785,880	San Jose, Calif.	898,349
12.	San Francisco, Calif.	740,316	Indianapolis, Ind.	700,807	Indianapolis, Ind.	783,438
13.	Boston, Mass.	697,197	San Francisco, Calif.	678,974	Jacksonville, Fla.	773,781
14.	Dallas, Tex.	679,684	Memphis, Tenn.	646,356	San Francisco, Calif.	751,682
15.	New Orleans, La.	627,525	Washington, DC	638,333	Columbus, Ohio	728,432

1. Populations for 1900–1980 are Census figures. 2003 figures are population estimates. *Source:* U.S. Census Bureau, *Statistical Abstract of the United States, 2003.* For 2000 Census figures, see Top 50 Cities in the U.S. by Population and Rank, 1990 and 2000 p. 206.

Safest and Most Dangerous U.S. Cities

(Population 75,000 and over)

	Safest				Most dangerous		
Rank	City	Rank	City	Rank	City	Rank	City
1.	Amherst, N.Y.	14.	Sterling Heights, Mich.	1.	St. Louis, Mo.	14.	Washington, DC
2.	Brick Township, N.J.	15.	Dover Township, N.J.	2.	Detroit, Mich.	15.	Dayton, Ohio
3.	Newton, Mass.	16.	Canton Township, Mich.	3.	Atlanta, Ga.	16.	Newark, N.J.
4.	Thousand Oaks, Calif.	17.	Parma, Ohio	4.	Gary, Ind.	17.	Kansas City, Mo.
5.	Sunnyvale, Calif.	18.	Greece, N.Y.	5.	Baltimore, Md.	18.	Trenton, N.J.
6.	Cary, N.C.	19.	Upper Darby Township, Pa.	6.	Camden, N.J.	19.	Youngstown, Ohio
7.	Orem, Utah	20.	Danbury, Conn.	7.	Compton, Calif.	20.	West Palm Beach, Fla.
8.	Clarkstown, N.Y.	21.	Fremont, Calif.	8.	Flint, Mich.	21.	Miami. Fla.
9.	Mission Viejo, Calif.	22.	Cheektowaga Town, N.Y.	9.	Tampa, Fla.	22.	Cleveland, Ohio
10.	Lake Forest, Calif.	23.	Simi Valley, Calif.	10.	Jackson, Miss.	23.	Dallas, Tex.
11.	Troy, Mich.	24.	Santa Clara, Calif.	11.	Memphis, Tenn.	24.	Chattanooga, Tenn.
12.	Irvine, Calif.	25.	Farmington Hills, Mich.	12.	New Orleans, La.	25.	Birmingham, Ala.
13.	Colonie, N.Y.			13.	Richmond, Va.		

NOTE: The rankings are based on a city's rate for six crime categories: murder, rape, robbery, aggravated assault, burglary, and motor vehicle theft. *Source:* Morgan Quitno Corporation. Web: www.morganquitno.com.

Top 50 Cities in the U.S. by Population and Rank, 1990, 2000, and 2003

	7/1/2003 population estimate	4/1/2000 census population	4/1/1990 census population	Size rank 1990	Size rank 2000	Size rank 2003
New York, N.Y.	8,085,742	8,008,278	7,322,564	1	1	1
Los Angeles, Calif.	3,819,951	3,694,820	3,485,398	2	2	2
Chicago, Ill.	2,869,121	2,896,016	2,783,726	3	3	3
Houston, Tex.	2,009,690	1,953,631	1,630,553	4	4	4
Philadelphia, Pa.	1,479,339	1,517,550	1,585,577	5	5	5
Phoenix, Ariz.	1,388,416	1,321,045	983,403	10	6	6
San Diego, Calif.	1,266,753	1,223,400	1,110,549	6	7	7
San Antonio, Tex.	1,214,725	1,144,646	935,933	9	9	8
Dallas, Tex.	1,208,318	1,188,580	1,006,877	8	8	9
Detroit, Mich.	911,402	951,270	1,027,974	7	10	10
San Jose, Calif.	898,349	894,943	782,248	11	11	11
Indianapolis, Ind.	783,438	791,926	741,952	13	12	12
Jacksonville, Fla.	773,781	735,617	635,230	15	14	13
San Francisco, Calif.	751,682	776,733	723,959	14	13	14
Columbus, Ohio	728,432	711,470	632,910	16	15	15
Austin, Tex.	672,011	656,562	465,622	25	16	16
Memphis, Tenn.	645,978	650,100	610,337	18	18	17
Baltimore, Md.	628,670	651,154	736,014	12	17	18
Milwaukee, Wis.	586,941	596,974	628,088	17	19	19
Fort Worth, Tex.	585,122	534,694	447,619	29	27	20
Charlotte, N.C.	584,658	540,828	395,934	33	26	21
El Paso, Tex.	584,113	563,662	515,342	22	23	22
Boston, Mass.	581,616	589,141	574,283	20	20	23
Seattle, Wash.	569,101	563,374	516,259	21	24	24
Washington, DC	563,384	572,059	606,900	19	21	25
Denver, Colo.	557,478	554,636	467,610	28	25	26
Nashville-Davidson, Tenn.[1]	544,765	569,891	510,784	26	22	27
Portland, Ore.	538,544	529,121	437,319	27	28	28
Oklahoma City, Okla.	523,303	506,132	444,719	30	29	29
Las Vegas, Nev.	517,017	478,434	258,295	63	32	30
Tucson, Ariz.	507,658	486,699	405,390	34	30	31
Long Beach, Calif.	475,460	461,522	429,433	32	34	32
Albuquerque, N.M.	471,856	448,607	384,736	40	35	33
New Orleans, La.	469,032	484,674	496,938	24	31	34
Cleveland, Ohio	461,324	478,403	505,616	23	33	35
Fresno, Calif.	451,455	427,652	354,202	48	37	36
Sacramento, Calif.	445,335	407,018	369,365	37	40	37
Kansas City, Mo.	442,768	441,545	435,146	31	36	38
Virginia Beach, Va.	439,467	425,257	393,069	39	38	39
Mesa, Ariz.	432,376	396,375	288,091	53	42	40
Atlanta, Ga.	423,019	416,474	394,017	38	39	41
Omaha, Neb.	404,267	390,007	335,795	47	44	42
Oakland, Calif.	398,844	399,484	372,242	35	41	43
Tulsa, Okla.	387,807	393,049	367,302	44	43	44
Honolulu CDP,[2] Hawaii	380,149	371,657	365,272	41	46	45
Miami, Fla.	376,815	362,470	358,548	46	47	46
Minneapolis, Minn.	373,188	382,618	368,383	43	45	47
Colorado Springs, Colo.	370,448	360,890	281,140	54	48	48
Arlington, Tex.	355,007	332,969	261,721	62	54	49
Wichita, Kans.	354,617	344,284	304,011	51	50	50
St. Louis, Mo.	332,223	348,189	396,685	42	49	53

1. Nashville-Davidson city is consolidated with Davidson County. 2. Honolulu Census Designated Place; by agreement with the State of Hawaii, the Census Bureau does not show data separately for the city of Honolulu, which is coextensive with Honolulu County. *Source:* U.S. Census Bureau. Web: www.census.gov. For 2003 population estimates, see Population of the 15 Largest U.S. Cities, 1900–2003, p. 205.

U.S. Cities with Population over 100,000

ZIP codes provided below indicate the primary ZIP code for each city. Consult a ZIP code directory to find the appropriate ZIP code for a particular address, or try the U.S. Postal Service's online "ZIP Code Lookup," www.usps.gov/zip4/.

City	2000 Pop.	2000 Rank*	ZIP Code	City	2000 Pop.	2000 Rank*	ZIP Code
Alabama				Santa Clarita	151,088	137	91355
Birmingham	242,820	72	35203	Santa Rosa	147,595	144	95402
Huntsville	158,216	130	35813	Simi Valley	111,351	206	93065
Mobile	198,915	94	36601	Stockton	243,771	71	95208
Montgomery	201,568	89	36119	Sunnyvale	131,760	165	94086
Alaska				Thousand Oaks	117,005	192	91362
Anchorage	260,283	66	99599	Torrance	137,946	159	90503
Arizona				Vallejo	116,760	193	94590
Chandler	176,581	116	85225	West Covina	105,080	224	91793
Gilbert	109,697	208	85296	**Colorado**			
Glendale	218,812	81	85302	Arvada	102,153	235	80004
Mesa	396,375	43	85201	Aurora	276,393	62	80017
Peoria	108,364	214	85381	Colorado Springs	360,890	49	80903
Phoenix	1,321,045	6	85026	Denver	554,636	25	80202
Scottsdale	202,705	88	85251	Fort Collins	118,652	189	80525
Tempe	158,625	129	85282	Lakewood	144,126	148	80202
Tucson	486,699	30	85726	Pueblo	102,121	236	81003
Arkansas				Westminster	100,940	239	80030
Little Rock	183,133	112	72202	**Connecticut**			
California				Bridgeport	139,529	156	06602
Anaheim	328,014	56	92803	Hartford	121,578	183	06101
Bakersfield	247,057	70	93380	New Haven	123,626	179	06511
Berkeley	102,743	231	94704	Stamford	117,083	191	06904
Burbank	100,316	243	91505	Waterbury	107,271	217	06702
Chula Vista	173,556	122	91910	**District of Columbia**			
Concord	121,780	181	94520	Washington[1]	572,059	21	20090
Corona	124,966	174	91718	**Florida**			
Costa Mesa	108,724	213	92628	Cape Coral	102,286	234	33909
Daly City	103,621	227	94015	Clearwater	108,787	212	33990
Downey	107,323	216	90241	Coral Springs	117,549	190	33075
El Monte	115,965	196	91734	Fort Lauderdale	152,397	134	33310
Escondido	133,559	164	92025	Hialeah	226,419	76	33010
Fontana	128,929	167	92335	Hollywood	139,357	157	33022
Fremont	203,413	87	94537	Jacksonville	735,617	14	32203
Fresno	427,652	37	93706	Miami	362,470	48	33152
Fullerton	126,003	173	92834	Orlando	185,951	107	32802
Garden Grove	165,196	127	92842	Pembroke Pines	137,427	161	33024
Glendale	194,973	100	91205	St. Petersburg	248,232	69	33730
Hayward	140,030	154	94544	Tallahassee	150,624	139	32301
Huntington Beach	189,594	103	92647	Tampa	303,447	58	33630
Inglewood	112,580	204	90301	**Georgia**			
Irvine	143,072	150	92619	Athens-Clarke County[2]	101,489	237	30608
Lancaster	118,718	188	93534	Atlanta	416,474	40	30304
Long Beach	461,522	34	90802	Augusta-Richmond County[3]	199,775	91	30901
Los Angeles	3,694,820	2	90052	Columbus	186,291	106	31908
Modesto	188,856	104	95350	Savannah	131,510	166	31402
Moreno Valley	142,381	152	92553	**Hawaii**			
Norwalk	103,298	229	90650	Honolulu CDP[4]	371,657	47	96820
Oakland	399,484	42	94612	**Idaho**			
Oceanside	161,029	128	92054	Boise	185,787	108	83708
Ontario	158,007	131	91761	**Illinois**			
Orange	128,821	168	92863	Aurora	142,990	151	60505
Oxnard	170,358	124	93030	Chicago	2,896,016	3	60607
Palmdale	116,670	194	93550	Joliet	106,221	221	60436
Pasadena	133,936	163	91103	Naperville	128,358	169	60540
Pomona	149,473	141	91769	Peoria	112,936	203	61601
Rancho Cucamonga	127,743	171	91729	Rockford	150,115	140	61125
Riverside	255,166	68	92507	Springfield	111,454	205	62703
Sacramento	407,018	41	95813	**Indiana**			
Salinas	151,060	138	93907	Evansville	121,582	182	47708
San Bernardino	185,401	110	92401	Fort Wayne	205,727	85	46802
San Buenaventura (Ventura)	100,916	240	93001	Gary	102,746	230	46401
San Diego	1,223,400	7	92199	Indianapolis	791,926	12	46206
San Francisco	776,733	13	94188	South Bend	107,789	215	46624
San Jose	894,943	11	95101	**Iowa**			
Santa Ana	337,977	52	92711	Cedar Rapids	120,758	185	52401
Santa Clara	102,361	232	95050	Des Moines	198,682	95	50318

City	2000 Pop.	2000 Rank*	ZIP Code	City	2000 Pop.	2000 Rank*	ZIP Code
Kansas				Akron	217,074	82	44309
Kansas City	146,866	146	66106	Cincinnati	331,285	55	45225
Overland Park	149,080	143	66204	Cleveland	478,403	33	44101
Topeka	122,377	180	66603	Columbus	711,470	15	43216
Wichita	344,284	51	67276	Dayton	166,179	126	45401
Kentucky				Toledo	313,619	57	43601
Lexington-Fayette	260,512	65	40511	**Oklahoma**			
Louisville	256,231	67	40231	Oklahoma City	506,132	29	73125
Louisiana				Tulsa	393,049	44	74107
Baton Rouge	227,818	75	70826	**Oregon**			
Lafayette	110,257	207	70509	Eugene	137,893	160	97401
New Orleans	484,674	31	70113	Portland	529,121	28	97208
Shreveport	200,145	90	71102	Salem	136,924	162	97309
Maryland				**Pennsylvania**			
Baltimore	651,154	17	21202	Allentown	106,632	219	18101
Massachusetts				Erie	103,717	226	16515
Boston	589,141	20	02205	Philadelphia	1,517,550	5	19104
Cambridge	101,355	238	02139	Pittsburgh	334,563	53	15290
Lowell	105,167	222	01853	**Rhode Island**			
Springfield	152,082	135	01101	Providence	173,618	121	02904
Worcester	172,648	123	01613	**South Carolina**			
Michigan				Columbia	116,278	195	29201
Ann Arbor	114,024	199	48104	**South Dakota**			
Detroit	951,270	10	48233	Sioux Falls	123,975	178	57104
Flint	124,943	175	48502	**Tennessee**			
Grand Rapids	197,800	96	49501	Chattanooga	155,554	132	37421
Lansing	119,128	187	48924	Clarksville	103,455	228	37043
Livonia	100,545	242	48150	Knoxville	173,890	119	37950
Sterling Heights	124,471	177	48311	Memphis	650,100	18	38101
Warren	138,247	158	48090	Nashville-Davidson[5]	569,891	22	37230
Minnesota				**Texas**			
Minneapolis	382,618	46	55401	Abilene	115,930	197	79604
St. Paul	287,151	60	55109	Amarillo	173,627	120	79120
Mississippi				Arlington	332,969	54	76004
Jackson	184,256	111	39205	Austin	656,562	16	78710
Missouri				Beaumont	113,866	200	77707
Independence	113,288	202	64052	Brownsville	139,722	155	78520
Kansas City	441,545	36	64108	Carrollton	109,576	209	75006
St. Louis	348,189	50	63155	Corpus Christi	277,454	61	78469
Springfield	151,580	136	65801	Dallas	1,188,580	8	75260
Nebraska				El Paso	563,662	23	79910
Lincoln	225,581	77	68501	Fort Worth	534,694	27	76161
Omaha	390,007	45	68108	Garland	215,768	83	75040
Nevada				Grand Prairie	127,427	172	75051
Henderson	175,381	118	89015	Houston	1,953,631	4	77201
Las Vegas	478,434	32	89199	Irving	191,615	102	75061
North Las Vegas	115,488	198	89030	Laredo	176,576	117	78041
Reno	180,480	114	89510	Lubbock	199,564	92	79402
New Hampshire				McAllen	106,414	220	78501
Manchester	107,006	218	03103	Mesquite	124,523	176	75149
New Jersey				Pasadena	141,674	153	77501
Elizabeth	120,568	186	07208	Plano	222,030	79	75074
Jersey City	240,055	73	07302	San Antonio	1,144,646	9	78284
Newark	273,546	64	07102	Waco	113,726	201	76702
Paterson	149,222	142	07510	Wichita Falls	104,197	225	76307
New Mexico				**Utah**			
Albuquerque	448,607	35	87101	Provo	105,166	223	84601
New York				Salt Lake City	181,743	113	84199
Buffalo	292,648	59	14240	West Valley City	108,896	211	84199
New York	8,008,278	1	10199	**Virginia**			
Rochester	219,773	80	14692	Alexandria	128,283	170	22314
Syracuse	147,306	145	13220	Chesapeake	199,184	93	23320
Yonkers	196,086	98	10701	Hampton	146,437	147	23670
North Carolina				Newport News	180,150	115	23607
Charlotte	540,828	26	28228	Norfolk	234,403	74	23501
Durham	187,035	105	27701	Portsmouth	100,565	241	23707
Fayetteville	121,015	184	28302	Richmond	197,790	97	23232
Greensboro	223,891	78	27420	Virginia Beach	425,257	38	23450
Raleigh	276,093	63	27613	**Washington**			
Winston-Salem	185,776	109	27102	Bellevue	109,569	210	98009
Ohio				Seattle	563,374	24	98108

City	2000 Pop.	2000 Rank*	ZIP Code	City	2000 Pop.	2000 Rank*	ZIP Code
Spokane	195,629	99	99201	Green Bay	102,313	233	54303
Tacoma	193,556	101	98413	Madison	208,054	84	53714
Vancouver	143,560	149	98668	Milwaukee	596,974	19	53203
Wisconsin							

*This list includes only cities within the 50 United States. San Juan, Puerto Rico is not included but is number 39. 1. Washington city is coextensive with the District of Columbia. 2. In 2000, Clarke County and the incorporated place of Athens-Clarke County are coextensive. 3. In 2000, Richmond County and the incorporated place of Augusta-Richmond County are coextensive. 4. Honolulu Census Designated Place; data are not given separately for the city of Honolulu, which is coextensive with Honolulu County. 5. Nashville-Davidson city is consolidated with Davidson County. *Source:* U.S. Census Bureau. Web: www.census.gov.

Area Codes: United States, Canada, Caribbean

Area codes	Selected cities
UNITED STATES	
Alabama	
205	Birmingham, Tuscaloosa
251	Jackson, Mobile
256	Huntsville, Florence
334	Montgomery, Dothan, Selma
Alaska	
907	Entire state
Arizona	
480	Chandler, Scottsdale
520	Tucson
602	Phoenix
623	Sun City, Peoria
928	Flagstaff, Yuma
Arkansas	
479	Fayetteville, Fort Smith
501	Hot Springs, Little Rock
870	Jonesboro, Texarkana
California	
209	Stockton, Modesto
213, 323	Los Angeles
310	Santa Monica, Beverly Hills, Torrance
408	San Jose
415	San Francisco, San Rafael
510	Oakland, Berkeley
530	Redding, Davis
559	Fresno
562	Long Beach, Whittier
619	San Diego
626	Pasadena, Azusa
650	Palo Alto, San Mateo
661	Bakersfield
707	Vallejo, Eureka, Santa Rosa
714	Orange, Anaheim, Huntington Beach
760	Barstow, Palm Springs
805	San Luis Obispo, Santa Barbara, Simi Valley
818	San Fernando, Burbank
831	Santa Cruz, Salinas
858	Poway
909	Pomona, San Bernardino
916	Sacramento
925	Concord, Walnut Creek
949	Irvine, Newport Beach
951	Riverside, San Jacinto
Colorado	
303, 720	Denver, Boulder
719	Colorado Springs, Pueblo
970	Aspen, Fort Collins
Connecticut	
203	Bridgeport, New Haven, Danbury

Area codes	Selected cities
860	Hartford, Norwich, New London
Delaware	
302	Entire state
District of Columbia	
202	Entire district
Florida	
239	Fort Myers, Naples
305	Miami, Key West
321	Orlando, Cape Canaveral
352	Gainesville, Ocala
386	Daytona Beach
407	Kissimmee, Orlando
561	West Palm Beach, Boca Raton
727	Clearwater, St. Petersburg
772	Fort Pierce, Port St. Lucie
786	Miami, Homestead
813	Tampa
850	Tallahassee, Pensacola
863	Lakeland, Winter Haven
904	Jacksonville
941	Port Charlotte, Sarasota
954, 754	Ft. Lauderdale
Georgia	
229	Albany, Valdosta
404	Atlanta
478	Macon
678, 770	Atlanta, Smyrna, Marietta
706	Athens, Augusta
912	Savannah
Hawaii	
808	Entire state
Idaho	
208	Entire state
Illinois	
217	Springfield, Champaign
224	Evanston, Schaumburg
309	Peoria, Bloomington
312, 773	Chicago
618	Carbondale, East St. Louis
630	Aurora, Naperville
708	Chicago Heights, Cicero
815	Rockford, Joliet
847	Waukegan, Skokie
Indiana	
219	Gary
260	Fort Wayne
317	Indianapolis
574	South Bend, La Porte
765	Lafayette, Muncie, Kokomo
812	Bloomington, Terre Haute
Iowa	
319	Cedar Rapids, Burlington
515	Des Moines, Ames
563	Dubuque, Davenport

Area codes	Selected cities
641	Mason City, Ottumwa
712	Sioux City, Council Bluffs
Kansas	
316	Wichita
620	Dodge City, Emporia
785	Topeka, Lawrence
913	Kansas City, Leavenworth
Kentucky	
270	Owensboro, Bowling Green
502	Frankfort, Louisville
606	Ashland
859	Lexington, Covington
Louisiana	
225	Baton Rouge
318	Shreveport
337	Lafayette, Lake Charles
504	New Orleans, Metairie
985	Houma, Slidell
Maine	
207	Entire state
Maryland	
240, 301	Frederick, Hagerstown, Bethesda
410, 443	Baltimore, Salisbury, Annapolis
Massachusetts	
413	Springfield, Northampton
508, 774	Worcester, New Bedford
617, 857	Boston, Cambridge
781, 339	Waltham, Lynn
978, 351	Lowell, Gloucester
Michigan	
231	Muskegon, Shelby
248, 947	Troy, Pontiac
269	Kalamazoo, Battle Creek
313	Detroit, Dearborn
517	Lansing, Jackson
586	Warren, St. Clair Shores
616	Grand Rapids, Holland
734	Ann Arbor, Monroe, Ypsilanti
810	Flint, Port Huron
906	Sault Ste. Marie
989	Saginaw, Midland
Minnesota	
218	Duluth, Moorhead
320	St.Cloud
507	Rochester, Mankato
612	Minneapolis
651	St. Paul
763	Maple Grove, Coon Rapids
952	Bloomington, Edina
Mississippi	
228	Gulfport, Biloxi
601	Jackson, Vicksburg
662	Tupelo, Greenville

Area codes	Selected cities
Missouri	
314	St. Louis, Webster Groves
417	Springfield, Joplin
573	Jefferson City, Columbia
636	Chesterfield, St. Charles
660	Sedalia
816	Kansas City, Independence
Montana	
406	Entire state
Nebraska	
308	Grand Island, Kearney
402	Lincoln, Omaha
Nevada	
702	Las Vegas, Henderson
775	Carson City, Reno
New Hampshire	
603	Entire state
New Jersey	
201, 551	Jersey City, Hackensack
609	Trenton, Atlantic City
732, 848	New Brunswick, Long Branch
856	Cherry Hill, Vineland, Camden
908	Elizabeth, Summit
973, 862	Newark, Paterson
New Mexico	
505	Entire state
New York	
212, 646	Manhattan
315	Syracuse, Utica
347, 718	Bronx, Brooklyn, Queens, Staten Island
516	Mineola, Hicksville
518	Albany, Troy
585	Rochester
607	Binghamton, Elmira
631	Riverhead, Islip
716	Buffalo, Niagara Falls
845	Poughkeepsie, Kingston
914	White Plains, Yonkers
917	Manhattan, Bronx, Queens, Staten Island, Brooklyn
North Carolina	
252	Greenville, Rocky Mount
336	Winston-Salem, Greensboro
704, 980	Charlotte, Gastonia
828	Asheville, Hickory
910	Fayetteville, Wilmington
919	Raleigh, Chapel Hill
North Dakota	
701	Entire state
Ohio	
216	Cleveland, Shaker Heights
234, 330	Akron, Youngstown
419, 567	Toledo, Sandusky
440	Ashtabula, Lorain
513	Cincinnati
614	Columbus
740	Chillicothe, Zanesville
937	Dayton, Xenia
Oklahoma	
405	Oklahoma City, Shawnee
580	Enid, Lawton
918	Tulsa, Muskogee
Oregon	
503, 971	Salem, Portland
541	Eugene, Corvallis

Area codes	Selected cities
Pennsylvania	
215, 267	Philadelphia, Levittown
412, 878	Pittsburgh, McKeesport
484, 610	Allentown, Reading
570	Scranton, Williamsport
717	Harrisburg, Lancaster
724, 878	Uniontown, New Castle
814	Erie, State College
Rhode Island	
401	Entire state
South Carolina	
803	Columbia, Aiken
843	Charleston, Myrtle Beach
864	Greenville, Spartanburg
South Dakota	
605	Entire state
Tennessee	
423	Chattanooga, Johnson City
615	Nashville, Gallatin
731	Jackson
865	Knoxville, Oak Ridge
901	Memphis
931	Columbia, Clarksville
Texas	
210	San Antonio
214,	
469, 972	Dallas, Plano
254	Waco, Killeen
281,	
713, 832	Houston
325	Abilene
361	Corpus Christi, Victoria
409	Galveston, Port Arthur
432	Midland, Odessa
512	Austin
682, 817	Fort Worth, Arlington
806	Lubbock, Amarillo
830	Uvalde, Seguin
903, 430	Tyler, Texarkana, Paris
915	El Paso
936	Huntsville, Nacogdoches
940	Wichita Falls, Denton
956	Laredo, Brownsville
979	Bryan, College Station
Utah	
435	Moab, St. George
801	Salt Lake City, Provo
Vermont	
802	Entire state
Virginia	
276	Abingdon, Wytheville
434	Danville, Lynchburg, Charlottesville
540	Roanoke, Harrisonburg
571, 703	Alexandria, Mount Vernon
757	Norfolk, Virginia Beach
804	Richmond, Hopewell
Washington	
206	Seattle, Bainbridge Island
253	Tacoma, Auburn
360	Olympia, Bellingham
425	Bellevue, Redmond
509	Spokane, Yakima
West Virginia	
304	Entire state

Area codes	Selected cities
Wisconsin	
262	Racine, Kenosha
414	Milwaukee, Wauwatosa
608	Madison, Beloit
715	Eau Claire, Wausau
920	Green Bay, Oshkosh
Wyoming	
307	Entire state
U.S. TERRITORIES	
684	American Samoa
671	Guam
670	Marianas Islands
787, 939	Puerto Rico
340	U.S. Virgin Islands
CANADA	
Alberta	
403	Calgary
780	Edmonton
British Columbia	
250	Victoria
604, 778	Vancouver
Manitoba	
204	Entire province
New Brunswick	
506	Entire province
Newfoundland	
709	Entire province
Nova Scotia	
902	Nova Scotia, Prince Edward Island
Ontario	
289, 905	Hamilton
416, 647	Toronto
519	Windsor
613	Ottawa
705	Sudbury
807	Thunder Bay
Quebec	
418	Quebec
450	Laval
514	Montreal
819	Trois-Rivieres
Saskatchewan	
306	Entire province
Yukon, Northwest Territories, & Nunavut	
867	All provinces
CARIBBEAN AND ATLANTIC ISLANDS	
264	Anguilla
268	Antigua and Barbuda
242	Bahamas
246	Barbados
441	Bermuda
284	British Virgin Islands
345	Cayman Islands
809	Dominican Republic
767	Dominica
473	Grenada
876	Jamaica
664	Montserrat
869	St. Kitts & Nevis
758	St. Lucia
784	St. Vincent & the Grenadines
868	Trinidad & Tobago
649	Turks & Caicos

The following lists are not all-inclusive due to space limitations. Only disasters involving great loss of life and/or property, historical interest, or unusual circumstances are listed. Data as of Sept. 2004. For other disasters *see* Current Events: What Happened in 2004, pp. 35–42.

WORST UNITED STATES DISASTERS

AIRCRAFT
1979 May 25, Chicago: American Airlines DC-10 crashed seconds after takeoff, killing all 272 people aboard and 3 on the ground.

AVALANCHE
1910 March 1, Wellington, Wash.: two trains snow-bound in Stevens Pass in Cascade Range swept off tracks into canyon 150 ft below, killing 96.

DROUGHT
1930s Many states: longest drought of 20th century. Peak periods were 1930, 1934, 1936, 1939, and 1940. During 1934, dry regions stretched solidly from N.Y. and Pa. across the Great Plains to the Calif. coast. A great "dust bowl" covered 50 million acres in south-central plains during winter of 1935–1936.

EARTHQUAKE
1906 April 18, San Francisco: earthquake accompanied by fire razed more than 4 sq mi; more than 500 dead or missing.

EPIDEMIC
1918 Nationwide: Spanish influenza killed over 500,000 Americans.

EXPLOSION
1947 April 16–18, Texas City, Tex.: a fire and subsequent explosion on the French freighter *Grandcamp* destroyed most of the city; 516 killed.

FIRE
1871 Oct. 8, Peshtigo, Wis.: over 1,500 lives lost and 3.8 million acres burned in forest fire.

FLOOD
1889 May 31, Johnstown, Pa.: collapse of South Fork Dam left more than 2,200 dead.

HURRICANE
1900 Sept. 8, Galveston, Tex.: an estimated 6,000–8,000 dead, mostly from devastation due to tidal surge.

MARINE
1865 April 27, Mississippi River, nr. Memphis, Tenn.: explosion on steamboat *Sultana* killed 1,547.

MINE
1907 Dec. 6, Monongah, W. Va.: coal mine explosion killed 362.

OIL SPILL
1989 March 24, Prince William Sound, Alaska: tanker *Exxon Valdez* hit an undersea reef and released 10 million plus gallons of oil into the waters.

RAILROAD
1918 July 9, Nashville, Tenn.: 101 killed in a two-train collision near Nashville.

SUBMARINE
1963 April 10, North Atlantic: atomic-powered submarine *Thresher* sank; 129 dead.

TERRORIST ATTACK
2001 Sept. 11, New York City, Arlington, Va., and Shanksville, Pa.: hijackers crashed two commercial jets into twin towers of World Trade Center; two more hijacked jets were crashed into the Pentagon and a field in rural Pa. Total dead numbered 2,992, including the 19 hijackers. Islamic al-Qaeda terrorist group blamed.

TORNADO
1925 March 18, Mo., Ill., and Ind.: great "Tri-State Tornado"; 689 dead; over 2,000 injured. Property damage estimated at $16.5 million.

WINTER STORM
1888 March 11–14, East Coast: the "Blizzard of 1888." 400 people died; as much as 5 ft of snow. Damage was estimated at $20 million.

EARTHQUAKES AND VOLCANIC ERUPTIONS

A.D. 79 Aug. 24, Italy: eruption of Mt. Vesuvius buried cities of Pompeii and Herculaneum, killing thousands.

856 Dec. 22, Damghan, Iran: earthquake killed 200,000.

893 March 23, Ardabil, Iran: earthquake killed about 150,000 people.

1138 Aug. 9, Aleppo, Syria: deadly earthquake claimed lives of 230,000 people.

1290 Sept., Chihli, China: earthquake killed about 100,000 people.

1556 Jan. 23, Shaanxi (Shensi) province, China: most deadly earthquake in history; 830,000 killed.

1667 Nov., Shemakha, Caucasia: earthquake killed about 80,000 people.

1727 Nov. 18, Tabriz, Iran: about 77,000 victims killed in deadly earthquake.

1755 Nov. 1, Portugal: earthquake leveled Lisbon and was felt as far away as southern France and North Africa; 70,000 killed.

1783 June 8, Iceland: eruption of Laki volcano lasted until Feb. 1784. Haze from eruption resulted in loss of island's livestock and widespread crop failure; 9,350 deaths, mostly due to starvation.

1792 May 21, Kyushu Island, Japan: collapse of old lava dome during eruption of Unzen volcano caused avalanche and tsunami that killed an estimated 14,300 people. (Most were killed by the tsunami.) Japan's greatest volcano disaster.

1811 Dec. 16, Mississippi Valley nr. New Madrid, Mo.: earthquake reversed the course of the Mississippi River. Fatalities unknown due to sparse population in area. Aftershocks and tremors continued into 1812. It has been estimated that three of the series of earthquakes had surface-wave magnitudes of 8.6, 8.4, and 8.8 on the Richter scale. It is the largest series of earthquakes known to have occurred in North America.

1815 April 5, 10–11, Netherlands Indies (Sumbawa, Indonesia): eruption of Tambora largest in historic times. An estimated 92,000 people were killed, about 10,000 directly as a result of explosions and ash fall and about 82,000 indirectly by starvation and disease.

1877 June 26, north-central Ecuador: eruption of Mt. Cotopaxi caused severe mudflows that wiped out surrounding cities and valleys; 1,000 deaths.

1883 Aug. 26–28, Netherlands Indies (Krakatau, Indonesia): eruption of Krakatau; violent explosions destroyed two-thirds of island, leaving an estimated 36,000 dead. Sea waves occurred as far away as Cape Horn and possibly England.

1886 Aug. 31, Charleston, S.C.: 60 people killed and extensive damage to city. Earthquake's magnitude was 7.7 on the Richter scale.

1902 May 8, Martinique, West Indies: Mt. Pelée erupted and wiped out city of St. Pierre; 40,000 dead.

1906 April 18, San Francisco: earthquake accompanied by fire razed more than 4 sq mi; more than 500 dead or missing.

1908 Dec. 28, Messina, Sicily: city totally destroyed by earthquake. Death toll 70,000–100,000 in Sicily and southern Italy.

1915 Jan. 13, Avezzano, Italy: earthquake left 29,980 dead.

1920 Dec. 16, Gansu province, China: magnitude 8.6 earthquake killed 200,000 in northwest China.

1923 Sept. 1, Japan: magnitude 8.3 earthquake destroyed one third of Tokyo and most of Yokohama. More than 140,000 killed.

1927 May 22, nr. Xining, China: magnitude 8.3 earthquake claimed approximately 200,000 victims.

1932 Dec. 25, Gansu, China: magnitude 7.6 earthquake killed approximately 70,000.

1935 May 30, Pakistan: earthquake at Quetta killed 30,000–60,000.

1939 Jan. 24, Chile: earthquake razed 50,000 sq mi; about 30,000 killed.

Dec. 27, northern Turkey: severe quakes destroyed city of Erzingan; about 100,000 casualties.

1950 Aug. 15, India: earthquake affected 30,000 sq mi in Assam; 20,000–30,000 believed killed.

1960 Feb. 29, Agadir, Morocco: 10,000–12,000 dead as earthquake set off tidal wave and fire, destroying most of city.

May 22, Chile: strongest earthquake ever recorded (9.5 magnitude) struck near the coast, killing more than 2,000, wounding 3,000.

1964 March 28[1], Alaska: strongest earthquake ever to strike North America (9.2 magnitude) hit 80 mi east of Anchorage; followed by seismic wave 50 ft high that traveled 8,445 mi at 450 mph; 117 killed.

1970 Jan. 5, Yunnan province, China: magnitude 7.7 quake killed 15,621.

May 31, Peru: earthquake left more than 50,000 dead, 17,000 missing.

1972 Dec. 22, Managua, Nicaragua: earthquake devastated city, leaving up to 6,000 dead.

1976 Feb. 4, Guatemala: quake left over 23,000 dead.

July 28, Tangshan, China: worst earthquake to hit China in 20th century; devastated 20 sq mi of city, leaving 242,000 dead (official). Estimated death toll as high as 655,000.

Aug. 17, Mindanao, Philippines: earthquake and tidal wave left up to 8,000 dead or missing.

1978 Sept. 16, Tabas, Iran: earthquake destroyed city in eastern Iran, leaving 25,000 dead.

1985 Sept. 19–20, Mexico: magnitude 8.1 earthquake devastated part of Mexico City and three coastal states; estimated 25,000 killed.

Nov. 14–16, Colombia: eruption of Nevada del Ruiz, 85 mi northwest of Bogotá. Mudslides buried most of the town of Armero and devastated Chinchiná; estimated 25,000 killed.

1988 Dec. 7, Armenia: earthquake measuring 6.9 in magnitude killed nearly 25,000, injured 15,000, and left at least 400,000 homeless.

1989 Oct. 17, San Francisco Bay area: earthquake measuring 7.1 in magnitude killed 67 and injured over 3,000. Over 100,000 buildings damaged or destroyed. Damage cost city billions of dollars.

1990 June 21, northwest Iran: earthquake measuring 7.7 in magnitude destroyed cities and villages in Caspian Sea area. At least 50,000 dead, over 60,000 injured, and 400,000 homeless.

July 16, northern Philippines: magnitude 7.7 quake killed nearly 2,000.

1991 July 15, Luzon Island, Philippines: eruption of Mt. Pinatubo buried over 300 sq mi under volcanic ash and resulted in more than 800 deaths.

1993 Aug. 8, Guam: earthquake measuring 8.1 in magnitude caused severe damage to many structures but no fatalities. Damages were estimated at nearly $300 million.

1994 Jan. 17, San Fernando Valley, Calif.: earthquake measuring 6.6 in magnitude killed 61 and injured over 8,000. Damage estimated at $13–20 billion.

1995 Jan. 17, Osaka, Kyoto, and Kobe, Japan: 5,100 killed and 26,800 injured; estimated damage $100 billion. Magnitude: 7.2.

1997 May 12, northeast Iran: severe earthquake measuring 7.1 in magnitude left more than 1,500 people dead and at least 4,460 injured.

June–Sept., southern Montserrat: ongoing eruption of Soufrière Hills volcano since July 1995; killed 20 people in major eruption on June 25, 1997, rendered southern two-thirds of Montserrat uninhabitable, and forced some 8,000 of the island's 12,000 residents to abandon the island.

1998 May 30, northern Afghanistan: magnitude 7.1 earthquake and aftershocks killed an estimated 5,000 and injured at least 1,500. A quake on Feb. 4 in same area had killed about 2,300.

1999 Jan. 25, Armenia, Colombia: 1,185 dead and more than 4,000 injured in magnitude 6.2 earthquake. More than 200,000 left homeless.

Aug. 17, northwest Turkey: magnitude 7.4 quake centered near Izmit killed over 17,000 and injured about 44,000. Damage estimated at $8.5 billion. Another severe 7.2 temblor killed more than 700 in Ducze and nearby towns in Nov.

Sept. 21, central Taiwan: severe 7.7 earthquake and aftershocks killed 2,295 and injured 8,729.

2001 Jan. 13, El Salvador: magnitude 7.7 earthquake set off some 185 landslides across El Salvador; at least 850 died and nearly 100,000 houses were destroyed.

Jan. 26, Bhuj, India: magnitude 7.7 earthquake rocked western Indian state of Gujarat, killing more than 20,000 people and leaving 600,000 homeless.

2003 May 21, Northern Algeria: magnitude 6.8 earthquake caused the collapse of numerous buildings, killed at least 2,266 people, and injured 10,000. The epicenter was 40 mi east of Algiers, the capital city.

Dec. 26, Bam, Iran: magnitude 6.6 earthquake devastated the ancient historic city of Bam in southeast Iran, killed more than 30,000 people, injured 30,000, and left 75,000 homeless, as mud-brick buildings collapsed.

1. March 28, 03:36:14 UT (March 27, 5:36 P.M. local time).

MAJOR U.S. EPIDEMICS

1793 **Philadelphia:** more than 4,000 residents died from yellow fever.

1832 **July–Aug., New York City:** over 3,000 people killed in a cholera epidemic.

Oct., New Orleans: cholera took the lives of 4,340 people.

1848 **New York City:** more than 5,000 deaths caused by cholera.

1853 **New Orleans:** yellow fever killed 7,790.

1867 **New Orleans:** 3,093 perished from yellow fever.

1878 **Southern states:** over 13,000 people died from yellow fever in lower Mississippi Valley.

1916 **Nationwide:** over 7,000 deaths occurred and 27,363 cases were reported of polio (infantile paralysis) in America's worst polio epidemic.

1918 **March–Nov., nationwide:** outbreak of Spanish influenza killed over 500,000 people in the worst single U.S. epidemic.

1949 **Nationwide:** 2,720 deaths occurred from polio, and 42,173 cases were reported.

1952 **Nationwide:** polio killed 3,300; 57,628 cases reported; worst epidemic since 1916.

1981-Dec. 2002: total estimated U.S. AIDS cases: 886,575; total estimated AIDS deaths: 501,669 (Centers for Disease Control); 2003 total world AIDS cases: 38 million; total world AIDS deaths: 20 million.

FLOODS, AVALANCHES, AND TIDAL WAVES

1228 **Holland:** 100,000 people reputedly drowned by sea flood in Friesland.

1642 **China:** rebels destroyed Kaifeng seawall; 300,000 drowned.

1889 **May 31, Johnstown, Pa.:** more than 2,200 died in flood after South Fork Dam collapsed.

1896 **June 15, Sanriku, Japan:** earthquake and tidal wave killed 27,000.

1910 **March 1, Wellington, Wash.:** avalanche in Cascade Range swept two trains into canyon, killing 96. Worst U.S. avalanche.

1928 **March 12, Santa Paula, Calif.:** collapse of St. Francis Dam left 450 dead.

1931 **July–Aug., China:** flood along Yangtze River left 3.7 million people dead from disease, starvation, or drowning.

1953 **Jan. 31–Feb. 5, northwest Europe:** storm followed by floods devastated North Sea coastal areas. Netherlands was hardest hit with 1,794 dead.

1954 **Aug., Teheran, Iran:** flood rains resulted in some 10,000 deaths.

1959 **Dec. 2, Fréjus, France:** flood caused by collapse of Malpasset Dam left 412 dead.

1962 **Jan. 10, Peru:** avalanche down extinct Huascaran volcano killed more than 3,000.

1963 **Oct. 9, Italy:** landslide into the Vaiont Dam; flood killed about 2,000.

1966 **Oct. 21, Aberfan, Wales:** avalanche of coal, waste, mud, and rocks killed 144 people, including 116 children in school.

1969 **Jan. 18–26, southern Calif.:** floods and mudslides from heavy rains caused widespread property damage; at least 100 dead.

1970 **Nov. 13, East Pakistan:** 200,000 killed by cyclone-driven tidal wave from Bay of Bengal. Over 100,000 missing.

1971 **Aug., Hanoi, North Vietnam:** heavy rains severely flooded the Red River Delta, killing 100,000.

1972 **Feb. 26, Man, W. Va.:** more than 118 died when slag-pile dam collapsed under pressure of torrential rains and flooded 17-mile valley.

June 9–10, Rapid City, S.D.: flash flood caused 237 deaths and $160 million in damage.

June 20, Eastern Seaboard: tropical storm Agnes, in ten-day rampage, caused widespread flash floods. Death toll 129; 115,000 left homeless; damage estimated at $3.5 billion.

1975 **Aug. 5, Yangtze River, China:** 63 dams failed, killing an estimated 80,000 to 200,000 people

from floods and subsequent famine. The Chinese government never acknowledged the event.

1988 **Aug.–Sept., Bangladesh:** heaviest monsoon in 70 years inundated three-fourths of country, killing more than 1,300 and leaving 30 million homeless.

1993 **June–Aug., Ill., Iowa, Kan., Ky., Minn., Mo., Neb., N.D., S.D., Wis.:** two months of heavy rain caused Mississippi River and tributaries to flood; 50 deaths and about $12 billion in damage. Almost 70,000 left homeless.

1997 **March, Ohio and Mississippi Valleys:** flooding and tornadoes plagued Ark., Mo., Miss., Tenn., Ill., Ind., Ky., Ohio, and W.Va. 67 were killed.

1998 **July 17, Papua New Guinea:** three tsunamis, possibly spurred by an undersea landslide following an earthquake, wiped out entire villages in the northwest province of Sepik. At least 2,000 found or presumed dead.

Summer, central and northeast China: heaviest flooding of Yangtze and other rivers since 1954. More than 3,000 killed and 14 million left homeless. Estimated damages exceeded $20 billion.

1999 **Oct., southwest Mexico:** over a week of heavy rains killed at least 360 people in mudslides and flood waters.

Nov. and Dec., Vietnam: devastating floods caused $285 million in damage and killed more than 700 people.

Dec. 15–16, northern Venezuela: heavy rains caused catastrophic flooding and mudslides, killing an estimated 5,000 to 20,000 people. Country's worst modern-day natural disaster.

2000 **Feb., southeast Africa:** weeks of rain resulted in deadly floods in Mozambique and Zimbabwe. About 700 people were killed and more than 280,000 were left homeless.

2002 **Sept. 20, Karmadon Gorge, North Ossetia, Russia:** an avalanche caused by a 500-foot chunk of glacier left 150 people dead.

Aug., Europe: record flooding across central and eastern Europe killed 108 people and caused billions of dollars of extensive infrastructure damage and deforestation.

2004 **May 18–26, Dominican Republic and Haiti:** torrential rains overflowed the Soliel River, causing floods and mudslides, destroying villages, and killing more than 2,000.

June–Aug., South Asia: annual monsoons left 5 million homeless and more than 1,800 dead in India, Nepal, and Bangladesh.

MAJOR STORMS

Cyclones, hurricanes, and typhoons are the same kind of tropical storm but are called by different names in different areas of the world.

CYCLONES

1864 Oct. 5, Calcutta, India: 70,000 killed.

1942 Oct. 16, Bengal, India: about 40,000 lives lost.

1960 Oct. 10, East Pakistan: cyclone and tidal wave killed about 6,000.

1963 May 28–29, East Pakistan: cyclone killed about 22,000 along coast.

1965 May 11–12 and June 1–2, East Pakistan: cyclones killed about 47,000.

Dec. 15, Karachi, Pakistan: about 10,000 killed.

1970 Nov. 12–13, East Pakistan: cyclone and tidal waves killed 200,000 and another 100,000 were reported missing.

1971 Sept. 29, Orissa state, India: cyclone and tidal wave killed as many as 10,000.

1974 Dec. 25, Darwin, Australia: cyclone destroyed nearly the entire city; 50 reported dead.

1977 Nov. 19, Andhra Pradesh, India: cyclone and tidal wave claimed lives of 20,000.

1991 April 30, southeast Bangladesh: cyclone killed over 131,000 and left as many as 9 million homeless.

1999 Oct. 29, Orissa state, India: supercyclone swept in from Bay of Bengal, killing at least 9,573 and leaving over 10 million homeless.

U.S. HURRICANES

(U.S. deaths only, except where noted. Damages are actual cost in U.S. dollars, followed in parentheses by dollar figures adjusted to the year 2000.)

1776 Sept. 2–9, N.C. to Nova Scotia: called the "Hurricane of Independence," it is believed that 4,170 in the U.S. and Canada died in the storm.

1856 Aug. 11, Last Island, La.: 400 died.

1893 Aug. 28, Savannah, Ga., Charleston, S.C., Sea Islands, S.C.: at least 1,000 died.

1900 Sept. 8, Galveston, Tex.: an estimated 6,000–8,000 died in hurricane and tidal surge. The "Galveston Hurricane" is considered the deadliest in U.S. history.

1909 Sept. 10–21, La. and Miss.: 350 deaths.

1915 Aug. 5–23, Galveston, Tex., and New Orleans, La.: 275 killed.

1919 Sept. 2–15, Fla. keys, La., and southern Tex.: more than 600 killed, mostly lost on ships at sea.

1926 Sept. 11–22, southeast Fla. and Ala.: 243 deaths.

1928 Sept. 6–20, Lake Okeechobee, southeast Fla.: 1,836 deaths. Second-deadliest U.S. hurricane on record.

1935 Aug. 29–Sept. 10, Fla. keys: "Labor Day Hurricane"; 408 deaths.

1938 Sept. 10–22, Long Island, N.Y., and southern New England: "New England Hurricane"; 600 deaths.

1944 Sept. 9–16, N.C. to New England: 390 deaths, 344 of which were at sea.

1954 Aug. 25–31, N.C. to New England: "Carol" killed 60 in Long Island–New England area.

Oct. 5–18, S.C. to N.Y.: "Hazel" killed 95 in U.S.; about 400–1,000 in Haiti; 78 in Canada.

1955 Aug. 7–21, N.C. to New England: "Diane" took 184 lives and cost $8.3 million ($5.5 billion).

1957 June 25–28, southwest La. and northern Tex.: "Audrey" wiped out Cameron, La., causing 390 deaths.

1960 Aug. 29–Sept. 13, Fla. to New England: "Donna" killed 50 in the U.S.; 115 deaths in Antilles.

1961 Sept. 3–15, Tex. coast: "Carla" devastated Tex. gulf cities, taking 46 lives.

1965 Aug. 27–Sept. 12, southern Fla. and La.: "Betsy" killed 75 and cost more than $1.4 ($8.5) billion.

1969 Aug. 14–22, Miss., La., Ala., Va., and W. Va.: 256 killed as a result of "Camille." Damages estimated at $1.4 ($6.9) billion.

1972 June 14–23, northwest Fla. to N.Y.: "Agnes" caused 117 deaths (50 in Pa.). Damages estimated at over $2.1 ($8.6) billion. Still the worst natural disaster ever in Pa.

1979 Aug. 29–Sept. 15, Ala. and Miss.: "Frederic" devastated Mobile, Ala., and caused $2.3 ($4.9) billion in damage overall.

1985 Oct. 6–Nov. 1: "Juan" struck La. and the Southeast. Though only a category 1 hurricane, it caused severe flooding and $1.5 ($2.4) billion in damages; 63 lives were lost.

1989 Sept. 10–22, Caribbean Sea, S.C., and N.C.: "Hugo" claimed 86 lives (57 U.S. mainland). With damages estimated at over $7 ($9.7) billion, it is the second most costly U.S. hurricanes.

1992 Aug. 22–26, Bahamas, southern Fla., and La.: Hurricane "Andrew" left 26 dead and more than 100,000 homes destroyed or damaged. With total U.S. damages estimated at $26.5 ($34.9) billion, it is the most costly U.S. hurricane.

1994 Nov. 8–21, Caribbean and southern Fla.: "Gordon" led to an estimated 1,122 deaths in Haiti. Eight died in Fla.

1995 Nov. 29, Fla. panhandle and Ala.: storm surge during "Opal" caused extensive damage; nine U.S. deaths and damages of $3 ($3.5) billion.

1996 Sept. 5, N.C. and Va.: "Fran" took 37 lives and caused more than $3.2 ($3.6) billion in damage.

1999 Sept. 14–18, Bahamas to New England: "Floyd" and associated flooding caused at least 57 deaths. Damage estimated at $4.5 ($4.6) billion.

2001 June 8–15, Gulf Coast to southern New England: tropical storm "Allison" caused severe flooding, damage estimated at $5 billion (actual cost); 41 deaths.

2003 Sept. 18, N.C. and Va.: "Isabel" took 50 lives and caused more than $3.7 billion in damage.

2004 Aug. 13–Sept. 26, Fl., Ala., and southern U.S.: Four major hurricanes in 6 weeks hit Florida. Aug. 13, "Charley," a category 4 hurricane killed 34, followed by "Frances" on Sept. 5, killing 33. "Ivan" swept from Grenada to Alabama and Florida on Sept. 16, killing 52 in the U.S., 66 in the Caribbean. On Sept. 26, "Jeanne" flooded Florida again, killing 8. Total U.S. damages from the 4 hurricanes estimated to exceed the cost of "Andrew."

OTHER HURRICANES

1780 Oct. 10–16, Barbados, West Indies: "The Great Hurricane of 1780" killed 20,000–22,000 people and completely flattened the islands of Barbados, Martinique, and St. Eustatius; is the deadliest western hemisphere hurricane on record.

1926 Oct. 20, Cuba: powerful hurricane killed 650.

1930 Sept. 3, Dominican Republic: hurricane killed about 8,000 people.

1955 Sept. 19, Mexico: "Hilda" took 200 lives.

Sept. 22–28, Caribbean: "Janet" killed 200 in Honduras and 300 in Mexico.

1961 Oct. 31, British Honduras: "Hattie" devastated capital Belize, killed at least 400.

1963 Oct. 2–7, Caribbean: "Flora" killed about 7,200 in Haiti and Cuba.

1966 Sept. 24–30, Caribbean area: "Inez" killed 293.

1974 Sept. 14–19, Honduras: "Fifi" struck northern part of country, leaving 8,000 dead and 100,000 homeless.

1988 Sept. 12–17, Caribbean Sea and Gulf of Mexico: "Gilbert" took at least 260 lives and caused some 39 tornadoes in Tex.

1997 Oct. 8–10, southern Mexico: "Pauline" devastated resort city of Acapulco, leaving 217 dead and 20,000 homeless.

1998 Sept. 20–29, Caribbean, Fla. Keys, and Gulf Coast: "Georges" killed about 600 people, mostly in Dominican Republic.

Oct. 26–Nov. 4, Honduras, Nicaragua, Guatemala: "Mitch" killed more than 11,000 people, becoming the deadliest Atlantic storm in 200 years. Two to three million people were left homeless; damages were more than $5 billion.

2004 Sept. 18, Haiti: Floods from tropical storm "Jeanne" killed more than 2,400 in Haiti and left 300,000 homeless.

TYPHOONS

1906 Sept. 18, Hong Kong: typhoon with tsunami killed an estimated 10,000 people.

1934 Sept. 21, Japan: typhoon killed more than 4,000 on Honshu.

1949 Dec. 5, off Korea: typhoon struck fishing fleet; several thousand men reported dead.

1958 Sept. 27, Honshu, Japan: "Vera" left nearly 5,000 dead and 1.5 million homeless.

1959 Aug. 20, Fukien province, China: "Iris" killed 2,334.

1960 June 9, Fukien province, China: "Mary" caused at least 1,600 deaths.

1984 Sept. 2–3, Philippines: "Ike" hit seven major islands, leaving 1,300 dead.

1991 Nov. 5, central Philippines: flash floods triggered by tropical storm "Thelma" killed about 3,000 people.

RECENT HURRICANE-LIKE STORMS

1999 Dec. 26–28, northern and western Europe: two back-to-back hurricane-force storms left 97 people dead. Winds reaching 120 mph uprooted trees, disrupted transportation, and left millions of homes without power.

BLIZZARDS

1888 Jan. 12, Dakota and Montana territories, Minn., Nebr., Kans., and Tex.: "Schoolchildren's Blizzard" resulted in 235 deaths, many of which were children on their way home from school.

March 11–14, East Coast: "Blizzard of 1888" resulted in 400 deaths and as much as 5 ft of snow. Damage was estimated at $20 million.

1949 Jan. 2–4, Nebr., Wyo., S.D., Utah, Colo., and Nev.: Although only 1 ft to 30 in. of snow fell, fierce winds of up to 72 mph created drifts as high as 30 ft. Tens of thousands of cattle and sheep perished.

1950 Nov. 25–27, eastern U.S.: "Storm of the Century" generated heavy snow and hurricane-force winds across 22 states and claimed 383 lives. Damages estimated at $70 million.

1978 Feb. 6–8, eastern U.S.: "Blizzard of 1978" battered the East Coast; claimed 54 lives and caused $1 billion in damage. Snowfall ranged from 2–4 ft in New England, plus nearly 2 ft of snow from an earlier storm.

1993 March 12–14, eastern U.S.: "Superstorm" paralyzed the eastern seaboard, causing the deaths of some 270 people. Record snowfalls (with rates of 2–3 in. per hour) and high winds caused $3 billion to $6 billion in damage.

1996 Jan. 6–8, eastern U.S.: heavy snow paralyzed the Appalachians, the mid-Atlantic, and the Northeast. 187 were killed in the blizzard and in the floods that resulted after a sudden warm-up. Damages reached $3 billion.

U.S. TORNADOES

1840 May 6, Natchez, Miss.: tornado struck heart of the city, killing 317 and injuring over 1,000.

1880 April 18, Marshfield, Mo.: series of 24 tornadoes demolished city, killing 99 people.

1884 Feb. 19, Miss., Ala., N.C., S.C., Tenn., Ky., Ind.: series of 60 tornadoes caused estimated 800 deaths.

1896 May 27, eastern Mo. and southern Ill.: series of 18 tornadoes; 1 tornado destroyed large section of St. Louis, Mo., killing 255.

1899 June 12, New Richmond, Wis.: tornado struck while circus was in town, causing 117 deaths.

1902 May 18, Goliad, Tex.: tornado killed 114.

1903 June 1, Gainesville, Holland, Ga.: twister caused 98 deaths.

1905 May 10, Snyder, Okla.: tornado killed 97.

1908 April 24–25, La., Miss., Ala., Ga.: 18 tornadoes resulted in 310 deaths (143 of these caused by 1 tornado that moved from Amite, La., to Purvis, Miss.).

April 24, Natchez, Miss.: twister struck, causing 91 deaths.

1913 March 23, eastern Nebr. and western Iowa: Easter Sunday, 8 tornadoes resulted in 181 deaths (94 in Omaha, Nebr.).

1917 May 26, Mattoon, Ill.: tornado smashed area, causing 101 deaths.

1925 March 18, Mo., Ill., Ind.: the "Tri-State Tornado" was the most violent single twister in U.S. history. It caused the deaths of 689 people and injured over 2,000. Property damage was estimated at $16.5 million.

1927 May 9, Poplar Bluff, Mo.: twister killed 98.

Sept. 29, St. Louis, Mo.: a five-minute tornado ripped through the city and caused 79 deaths.

1932 March 21–22, Ala., Miss., Ga., Tenn.: outbreak of 33 tornadoes killed 334 (268 in Ala.).

1936 April 5–6, Deep South: series of 17 tornadoes; 216 killed in Tupelo, Miss., and 203 killed in Gainesville, Ga.

1944 June 23, W.Va., Pa., Md.: 4 tornadoes caused 153 deaths.

1947 April 9, Woodward, Okla.: tornado demolished town, killing 181.

1952 March 21–22, Ark. and Tenn.: 28 tornadoes caused 204 deaths.

1953 May 11, Waco, Tex.: a single tornado killed 114.

June 8, Flint, Mich.: tornado killed 116.

June 9, Worcester, Mass.: tornado hit town, causing 90 deaths.

1955 May 25, Udall, Kans.: tornado killed 80.

1965 April 11–12, Midwest–Great Lakes region: tornadoes in Iowa, Ill., Ind., Ohio, Mich., and Wis. caused 256 deaths.

1967 April 21, northern Ill., also Mo., Iowa, lower Mich.: series of 52 tornadoes caused 58 deaths.

1971 Feb. 21, Miss., La., Ark., Tenn.: series of 10 tornadoes resulted in 121 deaths.

1974 April 3–4: a series of 148 twisters within 16 hours comprised the deadly "Super Tornado Outbreak" that struck 13 states in the East, South, and Midwest. Before it was over, 330 died and 5,484 were injured in a damage path covering more than 2,500 mi.

1979 April 10, northern Tex. and southern Okla.: 11 tornadoes caused 59 deaths.

1985 May 31, Pa. and Ohio: 27 tornadoes resulted in 756 deaths.

1992 Nov. 21–23, southeast Tex. to Mid-Atlantic and Ohio Valley: total of 94 tornadoes caused 26 deaths.

1994 March 27, Ala., Ga., and N.C.: Palm Sunday tornado outbreak resulted in 42 deaths, 320 injuries. Twenty people died and 90 were injured when a tornado caused the roof of a church near Piedmont, Ala., to collapse.

1999 May 3, Okla. and Kans.: unusually large twister, thought to have been a mile wide at times, killed 44 people and injured at least 748 others in Okla.

2002 Nov. 9–11, central and southeast U.S.: series of more than 70 tornadoes across 9 states from Miss. to Pa. killed 36 people.

2003 May 1–10, southern and midwestern U.S.: a record-breaking number of more than 400 tornadoes in 10 days killed 42.

DROUGHTS AND HEAT WAVES

1930s Many states: longest drought of the 20th century. Peak periods were 1930, 1934, 1936, 1939, and 1940. A great "dust bowl" covered some 50 million acres in the south-central plains during the winter of 1935–1936.

1955 Aug. 31–Sept. 7, Los Angeles: 8-day run of 100°-plus heat left 946 people dead.

1972 July 14–26, New York City: 891 people died in 14-day heat wave.

1980 June–Sept., central and eastern U.S.: an estimated 10,000 people were killed during the summer in a long heat wave and drought. Damages totaled about $20 billion.

1982–1983 worldwide: El Niño caused wildly unusual weather in the U.S. and elsewhere throughout 1983. Drought in the western Pacific region led to disastrous forest fires in Indonesia and Australia. Overall loss to world economy was over $8 billion. Similar event in 1997–1998 resulted in estimated loss of $25–33 billion.

1988 Summer, central and eastern U.S.: a severe drought and heat wave killed an estimated 5,000–10,000 people. Damages reached $40 billion.

1995 July 12–17, Chicago: 739 people died in record heat wave.

1998 Summer, southern U.S.: severe heat and drought spread across Tex. and Okla., all the way to N.C. and S.C. At least 200 were left dead .

1999 Summer, eastern U.S.: rainfall shortages resulted in worst drought on record for Md., Del., N.J., and R.I. The state of W.Va. was declared a disaster area. 3.81 million acres were consumed by fire as of mid-Aug. Record heat throughout the country resulted in 502 deaths nationwide.

2000 Spring–summer, southern U.S.: severe drought and heat killed an estimated 140 people.

2003 May–June, southern India: a month-long intense heat wave claimed more than 1,500 lives.

Aug., Europe: drought conditions and a heat wave, one of the worst in 150 years, covered Europe, broke temperature records from London to Portugal, fueled deadly forest fires, ruined crops, and caused thousands of deaths. (French fatalities estimated at more than 14,000.)

NUCLEAR POWER PLANT ACCIDENTS

1952 Dec. 12, Chalk River, nr. Ottawa, Canada: a partial meltdown of the reactor's uranium fuel core resulted after the accidental removal of four control rods. Although millions of gallons of radioactive water accumulated inside the reactor, there were no injuries.

1957 Oct. 7, Windscale Pile No. 1, north of Liverpool, England: fire in a graphite-cooled reactor spewed radiation over the countryside, contaminating a 200-square-mile area.

South Ural Mountains: explosion of radioactive wastes at Soviet nuclear weapons factory 12 mi from city of Kyshtym forced the evacuation of over 10,000 people from a contaminated area. No casualties were reported by Soviet officials.

1976 nr. Greifswald, East Germany: radioactive core of reactor in the Lubmin nuclear power plant nearly melted down due to the failure of safety systems during a fire.

1979 March 28, Three Mile Island, nr. Harrisburg, Pa.: one of two reactors lost its coolant, which caused overheating and partial meltdown of its uranium core. Some radioactive water and gases were released.

1986 April 26, Chernobyl, nr. Kiev, Ukraine: explosion and fire in the graphite core of one of four reactors released radioactive material that spread over part of the Soviet Union, eastern Europe, Scandinavia, and later western Europe. 31 claimed dead. Total casualties are unknown. Worst such accident to date.

1999 Sept. 30, Tokaimura, Japan: uncontrolled chain reaction in a uranium-processing nuclear fuel plant spewed high levels of radioactive gas into the air, killing two workers and seriously injuring one other.

2004 Aug. 9, Mihama, Japan: non-radioactive steam leaked from a nuclear power plant, killing four workers and severely burning seven others.

FIRES AND EXPLOSIONS

1666 **Sept. 2, England:** "Great Fire of London" destroyed St. Paul's Cathedral, etc. Damage £10 million.

1835 **Dec. 16, New York City:** 530 buildings destroyed by fire.

1871 **Oct. 8, Chicago:** the "Chicago Fire" burned 17,450 buildings and killed 250 people; $196 million in damage.

1872 **Nov. 9, Boston:** fire destroyed 800 buildings; $75 million in damage.

1876 **Dec. 5, New York City:** fire in Brooklyn Theater killed more than 300.

1881 **Dec. 8, Vienna:** at least 620 died in fire at Ring Theatre.

1900 **June 30, Hoboken, N.J.:** piers of North German Lloyd Steamship line burned; 326 dead.

1903 **Dec. 30, Chicago:** Iroquois Theatre fire killed 602.

1904 **Feb. 7, Baltimore, Md.:** blaze spread through downtown Baltimore. More than 1,500 buildings were destroyed

1906 **March 10, France:** explosion in coal mine in Courrières killed 1,060.

1907 **Dec. 6, Monongah, W. Va.:** coal mine explosion killed 362.

Dec. 19, Jacobs Creek, Pa.: explosion in coal mine left 239 dead.

1908 **Jan. 13, Boyertown, Pa.:** fire in Rhoads Opera House killed 170 people who were attending church-sponsored stage performance.

March 4, Collinwood, Ohio: fire in Collinwood school killed 176. Led to revision of fire codes for schools.

1909 **Nov. 13, Cherry, Ill.:** explosion in coal mine killed 259.

1911 **March 25, New York City:** fire in Triangle Shirtwaist Factory fatal to 145.

1913 **Oct. 22, Dawson, N.M.:** coal mine explosion left 263 dead.

1917 **Dec. 6, Halifax Harbor, Nova Scotia:** Belgian steamer collided with ammunition ship *Mont Blanc*, which was carrying over 2,500 tons of explosives. Explosion leveled part of Halifax and left about 1,600 people dead.

1921 **Sept. 21, Oppau, Germany:** ammonium nitrate exploded destroying the BASF plant, nearby houses, and killing 430 people.

1930 **April 21, Columbus, Ohio:** fire in Ohio State Penitentiary killed 320 convicts.

1937 **March 18, New London, Tex.:** explosion destroyed schoolhouse; 294 killed.

1942 **April 26, Manchuria:** explosion in Honkeiko Colliery killed 1,549.

Nov. 28, Boston, Mass.: Coconut Grove nightclub fire killed 491.

1944 **July 6, Hartford, Conn.:** fire and ensuing stampede in main tent of Ringling Brothers Circus killed 168, injured 487.

July 17, Port Chicago, Calif.: 322 killed when ammunition ships exploded.

1946 **Dec. 7, Atlanta:** fire in Winecoff Hotel killed 119.

1947 **April 16–18, Texas City, Tex.:** most of the city destroyed by a fire and subsequent explosion on the French freighter *Grandcamp*, which was carrying a cargo of ammonium nitrate. At least 516 were killed and over 3,000 injured.

1949 **Sept. 2, China:** fire on Chongqing (Chungking) waterfront killed 1,700.

1954 **May 26, off Quonset Point, R.I.:** explosion and fire aboard aircraft carrier *Bennington* killed 103 crewmen.

1956 **Aug. 7, Colombia:** about 1,100 reported killed when seven army ammunition trucks exploded at Cali.

Aug. 8, Belgium: 262 died in coal mine fire at Marcinelle.

1960 **Jan. 21, Coalbrook, South Africa:** coal mine explosion killed 437.

Nov. 13, Syria: 152 children killed in moviehouse fire.

1961 **Dec. 17, Niteroi, Brazil:** circus fire fatal to 323.

1962 **Feb. 7, Saarland, West Germany:** coal mine gas explosion killed 298.

1963 **Nov. 9, Japan:** explosion in coal mine at Omuta killed 447.

1965 **May 28, India:** coal mine fire in state of Bihar killed 375.

June 1, nr. Fukuoka, Japan: coal mine explosion killed 236.

1967 **May 22, Brussels, Belgium:** fire in L'Innovation department store left 322 dead.

July 29, off North Vietnam: fire on U.S. carrier *Forrestal* killed 134.

1972 **June 6, Wankie, Rhodesia:** explosion in coal mine killed 427.

1973 **Nov. 29, Kumamoto, Japan:** fire in Taiyo department store killed 101.

1975 **Dec. 27, Dhanbad, India:** explosion in coal mine followed by flooding from nearby reservoir left 372 dead.

1977 **May 28, Southgate, Ky.:** fire in Beverly Hills Supper Club; 167 dead.

1978 **Aug. 20, Abadan, Iran:** nearly 400 killed when arsonists set fire to crowded theater.

1986 **Dec. 31, San Juan, P.R.:** fire in Dupont Plaza Hotel set by three employees, killing 96 people.

1989 **June 3, Ural Mountains:** gas leaking from a pipeline alongside the Trans-Siberian railway exploded and destroyed two passing passenger trains, killing about 500 and injuring 723.

1990 **March 25, New York City:** arson fire in the illegal Happy Land Social Club killed 87 people.

1993 **May 10, nr. Bangkok, Thailand:** fire in doll factory killed at least 187 people and injured 500 others. World's deadliest factory fire.

1999 **March 24, Chamonix, France:** fire in Belgian truck in the Mont Blanc tunnel trapped dozens of cars. Death toll was at least 42.

2000 **Nov. 11, nr. Kaprun, Austria:** cable car transporting skiers broke into flames while moving through mountain tunnel. Final death toll reached 156 in what was termed Austria's worst Alpine disaster.

Dec. 25, Luoyang, China: at least 309 people were killed in fire at shopping center.

2002 **Jan. 27, Lagos, Nigeria:** explosions at military depot triggered a stampede from the surrounding neighborhoods. More than 1,000 killed.

June 20, Jixi, Heilongjian Province, China: gas explosion at a coal mine killed 111 people.

2003 **Feb. 18, Daegu, South Korea:** subway fire raced through two trains, killing 189 people and injuring more than 140.

Feb. 20, West Warwick, R.I.: fire, caused by a pyrotechnics display at a rock concert, engulfed a nightclub, killing 100 and injuring more than 150.

2004   **July 16, Southern India:** thatched roof of a private elementary school caught fire, killing 94 children.

Aug. 1, Asunción, Paraguay: fire, caused by a gas leak, swept through a supermarket, killing at least 400 people.

WORST U.S. FOREST FIRES

1871   **Oct. 8–14, Peshtigo, Wis:** over 1,500 lives lost and 3.8 million acres burned in nation's worst forest fire.

1889   **June 6, Seattle, Wash.:** fire destroyed 64 acres of the city and killed 2 people. Damage was estimated at $15 million.

1894   **Sept. 1, Minn.:** forest fires ravaged over 160,000 acres and destroyed 6 towns; 600 killed, including 413 in town of Hinckley.

1902   **Sept., Wash. and Ore.:** Yacoult fire destroyed 1 million acres and left 38 dead.

1910   **Aug. 10, Idaho and Mont.:** fires burned 3 million acres of woods and killed 85 people.

1918   **Oct. 13–15, Minn. and Wis.:** forest fire struck towns in both states; 1,000 died, including 400 in town of Cloquet, Minn. About $1 million in losses.

1947   **Oct. 25–27, Maine:** forest fire destroyed part of Bar Harbor and damaged Acadia National Park. In all, 205,678 acres burned and 16 lives were lost.

1949   **Aug. 5, Mann Gulch, Mont.:** 12 smokejumpers—firefighters who parachuted near the fire—and 1 forest ranger died after being overtaken by a 200-ft wall of fire at the top of a gulch near Helena, Mont. Three smokejumpers survived.

1970   **Sept. 26, Laguna, Calif.:** large-scale brush fire burned 175,425 acres and 382 structures.

1988   **Aug.–Sept., western U.S.:** fires destroyed over 1.2 million acres in Yellowstone National Park and damaged Alaska woodlands.

1990   **June, Santa Barbara, Calif.:** Painted Cave fire consumed 4,900 acres and destroyed 641 structures.

1991   **Oct. 20–23, Oakland–Berkeley, Calif.:** brush fire in drought-stricken area destroyed over 3,000 homes and apartments. At least 24 people died; damage estimated at $1.5 billion.

1994   **July 2–11, South Canyon, Colo.:** relatively small fire (2,000 acres) resulted in deaths of 14 firefighters.

2000   **April–May, northern N.M.:** prescribed fire started by National Park Service raged out of control, destroying 235 structures and forcing evacuation of more than 20,000 people.

Spring–Summer, western U.S.: dry conditions led to one of the most destructive forest fire seasons in U.S. history. About 7.2 million acres burned nationwide, nearly double the 10-year average. States hardest hit included Alaska, Idaho, Mont., N.M., Nev., and Ore.

2002   **June–early July, mainly western U.S.:** Hayman fire in Pike National Forest destroyed 137,760 acres and 600 structures, making it the worst wildfire in Colorado history. In central Ariz., the Rodeo fire, the worst in Arizona's history, merged with the Chediski fire to form an inferno that destroyed 468,638 acres and more than 400 structures.

2003   **Oct. 25–29, southern Calif.:** 15 devastating forest fires burned for two weeks, forcing more than 80,000 people to evacuate their homes and burning 800,000 acres. More than 15,500 firefighters battled the blazes that killed 24 people and destroyed 3,640 homes. The Cedar Fire in San Diego, which burned through 200,000 acres, was the largest fire in California's history.

2004   **July–Aug., Alaska:** wildfires in Alaska burned more than 5 million acres, the worst year for Alaska fires.

SHIPWRECKS

1833   **May 11, *Lady of the Lake:*** bound from England to Quebec, struck iceberg; 215 perished.

1853   **Sept. 29, *Annie Jane:*** emigrant vessel off coast of Scotland; 348 died.

1865   **April 27, *Sultana:*** boiler explosion on Mississippi River steamboat, near Memphis; 1,547 killed. Most of the dead were Union POWs finally heading home at the end of the Civil War.

1898   **Feb. 15, *Maine:*** U.S. battleship destroyed in Havana harbor by an explosion that killed 260 men. The incident led to the outbreak of the Spanish-American War in April 1898.

Nov. 26, *City of Portland:* 157 died nr. Cape Cod.

1904   **June 15, *General Slocum:*** excursion steamer burned in East River, N.Y.; 1,021 perished.

1912   **March 5, *Principe de Asturias:*** Spanish steamer struck rock off Sebastien Point; 500 drowned.

April 15, *Titanic:* supposedly unsinkable British ocean liner went down on maiden voyage after colliding with an iceberg. More than 1,500 people died.

1914   **May 29, *Empress of Ireland:*** sank after collision in St. Lawrence River; 1,024 died.

1915   **July 24, *Eastland:*** Great Lakes excursion steamer overturned in Chicago River; 812 died.

1934   **Sept. 8, *Morro Castle:*** 134 killed in fire off Asbury Park, N.J.

1945   **Jan. 30, *Wilhelm Gustloff:*** cruise ship carrying German refugees and soldiers sunk by Soviet submarine in Baltic. It is thought that as many as 10,000 people were aboard, of which only about 900 survived.

1949   **Sept. 17, *Noronic:*** Canadian Great Lakes cruise ship burned at Toronto dock; about 130 died.

1952   **April 26, *Hobson:*** minesweeper collided with aircraft carrier *Wasp* and sank during night maneuvers in mid-Atlantic; 176 people lost.

1953   **Jan. 9, *Chang Tyong-Ho:*** South Korean ferry foundered off Pusan; 249 reported dead.

1954   **Sept. 26, *Toya Maru:*** more than 1,000 killed when commercial ferry sank in Tsugaru Strait, Japan.

1956   **July 25, *Andrea Doria:*** Italian liner collided with Swedish liner *Stockholm* off Nantucket Island, Mass., and sank the next day. At least 52 died or were unaccounted for.

1962   **April 8, *Dara:*** British liner exploded and sank in Persian Gulf; 236 dead. Caused by time bomb.

1963   **April 10, *Thresher:*** atomic-powered U.S. submarine sank in North Atlantic; 129 dead.

1968   **Late May, *Scorpion:*** U.S. nuclear submarine sank in Atlantic 400 mi southwest of Azores; 99 dead.

1975   **Nov. 10, *Edmund Fitzgerald:*** cargo vessel carrying 26,000 long tons of iron ore pellets sank in eastern Lake Superior; all 29 crew lost.

1983   **May 25, *10th of Ramadan:*** Nile steamer caught fire and sank in Lake Nasser, near Aswan, Egypt; 272 dead and 75 missing.

1987 **March 6, *Herald of Free Enterprise:*** British ferry capsized after leaving Belgian port of Zeebrugge with 500 aboard; 134 drowned.

Dec. 20, *Dona Paz:* over 4,000 killed when passenger ferry collided with oil tanker *Victor* off Mindoro Is., south of Manila, Philippines.

1990 **April 7, *Scandinavian Star:*** suspected arson fire aboard Danish-owned North Sea ferry killed at least 110 passengers in Skagerrak Strait off Norway.

1991 **Dec. 15, *Salem Express:*** ferry carrying 569 passengers sank in Red Sea off coast of Safaga, Egypt, after hitting a coral reef. Over 460 people believed drowned.

1993 **Feb. 17, *Neptune:*** triple-deck ferry capsized off southern peninsula of Haiti during a squall. Over 1,000 passengers believed drowned. About 300 survived the sinking.

1994 **Sept. 28, *Estonia:*** passenger ferry capsized off coast of southwest Finland and sank in a stormy Baltic Sea. Only about 140 of the estimated 1,040 passengers aboard survived.

1996 **Jan. 21, *Gurita:*** overloaded ferry sank off the coast of northern Sumatra, killing 340.

1999 **Feb., *Harta Rimba:*** ship sank in the South China Sea, killing about 325 people. The ship had not been licensed for passenger use.

2000 **June 29, *Cahaya Bahari:*** ferry carrying refugees sank about 40 mi off the coast of Sulawesi. None of the 492 people aboard survived.

Aug. 12, *Kursk:* Russian nuclear submarine sank to bottom of Barents Sea following an explosion; 118 dead.

2001 **Feb. 9, *Ehime Maru:*** U.S. submarine *Greeneville* collided with Japanese fishing boat near Pearl Harbor, Hawaii. Twenty-six people aboard the *Ehime Maru* were rescued; nine others, including four students, were presumed dead.

2002 **Sept. 26, *Joola:*** overloaded Senegalese ferry capsized off the coast of Gambia, drowning 1,863 people. Only 64 passengers were rescued.

MYSTERIOUS DISAPPEARANCES

1872 **Mary Celeste:** the brigantine set sail from New York harbor for Genoa, Italy, on Nov. 5. A British brigantine, the *DeGratia,* discovered the ship derelict on Dec. 5 and boarded her. Everyone aboard the *Mary Celeste* had vanished—her captain, his family, and its 14-man crew. The ship was in perfect order with ample supplies and there was no sign of violence or trouble. The fate of the crew remains unknown.

1918 **USS Cyclops:** the navy coal ship, used to deliver fuel and other supplies to U.S. battlefleet during World War I, disappeared while en route from Brazil to Baltimore. The ship docked briefly at Barbados on March 3–4. When it failed to arrive in Baltimore on March 13, a search was made, but neither her wreck nor any of the 309 people aboard were ever found, and the cause of her loss remains unknown.

1928 **Köbenhavn:** five-masted Danish steel barque, a sail-training ship with a crew of 75 including 45 boy cadets, sailed from the River Plate for Melbourne, Australia, on Dec. 14. The last radio contact with the ship was made on Dec. 22 and all was well. The *Köbenhavn* and its crew disappeared without a trace and no one knows what happened to it.

AIRCRAFT CRASHES

(150 deaths or more, with exceptions. *See also* Terrorist Attacks, pp. 223–224.)

1921 **Aug. 24, England:** British dirigible *AR-2* broke in two on trial trip near Hull; 62 died.

1925 **Sept. 3, Caldwell, Ohio:** U.S. dirigible *Shenandoah* broke apart; 14 dead.

1930 **Oct. 5, Beauvais, France:** British dirigible *R 101* crashed, killing 47.

1933 **April 4, N.J.:** U.S. dirigible *Akron* crashed; 73 died.

1937 **May 6, Lakehurst, N.J.:** German zeppelin *Hindenburg* destroyed by fire at tower mooring; 36 killed.

1945 **July 28, New York City:** U.S. Army bomber B-25 crashed into Empire State Building; 13 dead.

1960 **Dec. 16, New York City:** United DC-8 and Trans World Super Constellation collided then crashed in two boroughs, killing 134 in air and on ground.

1961 **Feb. 15, nr. Brussels, Belgium:** 72 on board and farmer on ground killed in crash of Sabena plane; U.S. figure skating team wiped out.

1966 **Dec. 24, Binh Thai, South Vietnam:** crash of military-chartered CL-44 into village killed 129.

1971 **July 30, Morioka, Japan:** Japanese Boeing 727 and F-86 fighter collided in midair; 162 died.

1972 **Oct. 13, Moscow, Russia:** Aeroflot Ilyushin IL-14 crashed during landing due to pilot fatigue and 176 people perish.

1973 **Jan. 22, Kano, Nigeria:** 171 Nigerian Muslims returning from Mecca and 5 crewmen died in crash.

Feb. 21, Sinai: civilian Libyan Arab Airlines Boeing 727 shot down by Israeli fighters after it had strayed off course; 108 died, 5 survived.

Officials claimed that the pilot had ignored fighters' warnings to land.

1974 **March 3, Paris:** Turkish DC-10 jumbo jet crashed in forest shortly after takeoff; all 346 passengers and crew killed.

Dec. 4, Colombo, Sri Lanka: Dutch DC-8 carrying Muslims to Mecca crashed on landing approach, killing all 191 people aboard.

1975 **April 4, nr. Saigon, Vietnam:** Air Force Galaxy C-5A crashed after takeoff, killing 172, mostly Vietnamese children.

Aug. 3, Agadir, Morocco: chartered Boeing 707, returning Moroccan workers home after vacation in France, plunged into mountainside; all 188 aboard killed.

1976 **Sept. 10, Zagreb, Yugoslavia:** midair collision between British Airways Trident and Yugoslav charter DC-9 fatal to all 176 people aboard.

1977 **March 27, Santa Cruz de Tenerife, Canary Islands:** Pan American and KLM Boeing 747s collided on runway. All 249 on KLM plane and 333 of 394 aboard Pan Am jet killed. Total of 582 is highest for any type of aviation disaster.

1978 **Jan. 1, Bombay:** Air India 747 with 213 aboard exploded and plunged into sea minutes after takeoff.

Nov. 15, Colombo, Sri Lanka: chartered Icelandic Airlines DC-8, carrying 249 Muslim pilgrims from Mecca, crashed in thunderstorm during landing approach; 183 killed.

1979 **May 25, Chicago:** American Airlines DC-10 lost left engine upon takeoff and crashed seconds later, killing all 272 people aboard and 3 on the ground in worst U.S. air disaster.

Nov. 26, Jidda, Saudi Arabia: Pakistan International Airlines 707 carrying pilgrims returning from Mecca crashed on takeoff; all 156 aboard killed.

Nov. 28, Mt. Erebus, Antarctica: Air New Zealand DC-10 crashed on sightseeing flight; 257 killed.

1980 Aug. 19, Riyadh, Saudi Arabia: all 301 aboard Saudi Arabian jet killed when burning plane made safe landing but passengers were unable to escape.

1981 Dec. 1, Ajaccio, Corsica: Yugoslav DC-9 Super 80 carrying tourists crashed into mountain on landing approach, killing all 178 aboard.

1983 Aug. 30, nr. island of Sakhalin off Siberia: Korean Air Lines Boeing 747 shot down by Soviet fighter after it strayed off course into Soviet airspace. All 269 aboard killed. Secret Soviet documents released in Oct. 1992 reveal that the plane was flying a straight course for two hours with its navigational lights on and did not take evasive action. The Soviet fighter did not give a warning by firing tracer bullets as originally claimed.

Nov. 27, Madrid: Colombian Avianca Boeing 747 crashed near Mejorada del Campó Airport, killing 181 people aboard. Eleven people survived the accident.

1985 June 23, Atlantic Ocean: Air India 747 exploded over the ocean killing 329. The probable cause was a Sikh terrorist bomb.

Aug. 12, Japan: Japan Air Lines Boeing 747 crashed into a mountain, killing 520 of the 524 aboard. Highest death toll in a single-plane crash in aviation history.

Dec. 12, Gander, Newfoundland: a chartered Arrow Air DC-8 bringing American soldiers home for Christmas crashed on takeoff. All 256 aboard died.

1987 Aug. 16, Romulus, Mich.: Northwest Airlines McDonnell Douglas MD-80 crashed into a highway shortly after takeoff from Detroit Metropolitan Airport, killing 156 (including 2 on the ground). Girl, 4, only survivor.

Nov. 29, Burma: Korean Air Boeing 747 jetliner exploded from bomb planted by North Korean agents and crashed into sea, killing all 115 aboard.

1988 July 3, Persian Gulf: U.S. Navy cruiser *Vincennes* shot down Iran Air Airbus A-300 after mistaking it for an attacking jet fighter; 290 killed.

Aug. 28, Ramstein Air Force Base, West Germany: three jets from Italian Air Force acrobatic team collided in midair during air show and crashed, killing 70 people, including the pilots and spectators on the ground.

Dec. 21, Lockerbie, Scotland: N.Y.-bound Pan-Am Boeing 747 exploded in flight from a terrorist bomb and crashed into Scottish village, killing all 259 aboard and 11 on the ground. For terrorist attacks, *see* pp. 223–224.

1989 June 7, Paramaribo, Suriname: a Surinam Airways DC-8 carrying 174 passengers and 9 crew members crashed into the jungle while making a third attempt to land in a thick fog, killing 168 aboard.

1991 May 26, nr. Bangkok, Thailand: Austrian Lauda Air Boeing 767, en route to Vienna, crashed into jungle hilltop shortly after takeoff from Bangkok airport, killing all 223 aboard. Thailand's worst air disaster.

July 11, Jedda, Saudi Arabia: Canadian-chartered

DC-8 carrying pilgrims returning to Nigeria crashed after takeoff, killing 261 people.

1994 April 14, northern Iraq: two American F-15C fighter aircraft mistook two U.S. Army blackhawk helicopters for Russian-made Iraqi MI-24 helicopters and shot them down over no-fly zone, killing all 26 on board.

April 26, Nagoya, Japan: China Airlines Airbus A-300 from Taiwan crash-landed and exploded on the tarmac. Only 7 of the 271 passengers aboard survived.

1995 Dec. 20, nr. Cali, Colombia: 160 people killed when American Airlines Boeing 757 crashed in Andean Mountains.

1996 Jan. 8, Kinshasa, Zaire: Russian-built Antonov-32 cargo plane crashed after takeoff from Kinshasa into the center of the city, killing over 350 people and injuring at least 470.

Feb. 6, off coast of Puerto Plata, Dominican Republic: Dominican Alas Nacionales Boeing 737 crashed into Atlantic Ocean after takeoff, killing 189.

July 17, off coast of Long Island, N.Y.: TWA Boeing 747-100 bound for Paris from N.Y. exploded over waters of eastern L.I. and crashed into Atlantic Ocean, killing all 230 aboard.

Nov. 12, nr. New Delhi, India: shortly after takeoff, Saudi Arabian Airlines Boeing 747 collided in midair with Kazak Airlines Ilyushin 76 plane approaching the New Delhi airport. All 349 passengers and crew were killed; the world's worst midair collision.

1997 Aug. 6, Guam: Korean Air Boeing 747-300 from Seoul crashed into jungle near Agana International Airport, killing 228 people; 26 survived.

Sept. 26, nr. northern Indonesia: Indonesian Garuda Airlines A-300 Airbus jetliner crashed while approaching Medan Airport, Sumatra, killing all 234 people aboard.

1998 Feb. 16, Taipei, Taiwan: China Airlines Airbus A-300 jumbo jet crashed while trying to land in fog at Chiang Kai-shek International Airport, killing all 196 aboard and at least 6 people on the ground.

Sept. 2, off Nova Scotia, Canada: Swissair flight from N.Y. to Geneva crashed off Canadian coast, killing all 229 aboard. 136 Americans were on the McDonnell Douglas MD-11.

1999 Oct. 31, southeast of Nantucket Island: Egypt Air Boeing 767-300 on flight from N.Y. to Cairo crashed into the Atlantic Ocean, killing all 217 aboard.

2000 Jan. 30, off the Ivory Coast: Kenya Airways Airbus A-310, carrying 179 passengers and crew, crashed after takeoff from Abidjan into the Atlantic Ocean. Ten people survived.

July 25, Gonesse, France: Air France Concorde jet en route to N.Y. crashed into a hotel just after taking off from Charles de Gaulle airport near Paris; all 109 aboard and 4 on the ground were killed; first Concorde jet to crash since the plane went into commercial service in 1976.

2001 Sept. 11, New York City, Arlington, Va., and Shanksville, Pa.: For the attacks on the World Trade Center and the Pentagon, *see* p. 224.

Nov. 12, Queens, N.Y.: American Airlines Airbus A-300, bound for the Dominican Republic, crashed minutes after taking off from JFK International Airport. All 260 people aboard and 5 on the ground were killed.

2002 May 25, nr. Pescadores off western Taiwan: China Airlines Boeing 747, bound for Hong

Kong with 225 people aboard, broke apart in midair and plunged into sea 20 minutes after takeoff from Taipei. There were no survivors.

July 27, nr. Lviv, Ukraine: Russian-built Sukhoi-27 fighter jet crashed while performing an acrobatic maneuver during an air show. Eighty-three people were killed, including 23 children; the 2 pilots ejected to safety. It is the worst air show disaster in history.

2003 Feb. 19, nr. Shahdad, Iran: Iranian military airplane, Ilyushin Il-76MD, carrying members of Iran's Revolutionary Guards, crashed in the Sir-

ach Mountains, killing all 276 on board, making this Iran's worst air disaster.

Dec. 25, Cotonou, Benin: A chartered Boeing 727 jet bound for Beirut, Lebanon, crashed after hitting a building on takeoff, killing at least 140 people.

2004 Aug. 24, Moscow, Russia: two Russian planes, both departing from Moscow's airport, crashed within minutes of each other, killing a total of 89 people. Explosives were found on both flights.

SPACE ACCIDENTS

1967 Jan. 27, *Apollo 1*: a fire aboard the space capsule on the ground at Cape Kennedy, Fla., killed astronauts Virgil I. Grissom, Edward H. White, and Roger Chaffee.

April 23–24, *Soyuz 1*: Vladimir M. Komarov was killed when his craft crashed after its parachute lines, released at 23,000 ft for reentry, became snarled.

1971 June 6–30, *Soyuz 11*: three cosmonauts, Georgi T. Dolrovolsky, Vladislav N. Volkov, and Viktor I. Patsayev, found dead in the craft after its automatic landing. Apparent cause of death was loss of pressurization in the space craft during reentry into the earth's atmosphere.

1980 March 18, USSR: a Vostok rocket exploded on its launch pad while being refueled, killing 50 at the Plesetsk Space Center.

1986 Jan. 28, *Challenger* Space Shuttle: exploded 73 seconds after liftoff, killing all 7 crew members.

They were: Francis R. Scobee, Michael J. Smith, Judith A. Resnick, Ronald E. McNair, Ellison S. Onizuka, Gregory B. Jarvis, and schoolteacher Christa McAuliffe. A booster leak ignited the fuel, causing the explosion.

2003 Feb. 1, *Columbia* Space Shuttle: broke up on reentering Earth's atmosphere on its way to Kennedy Space Center, killing all seven crew members. They were: Rick D. Husband, William C. McCool, Michael P. Anderson, David M. Brown, Kalpana Chawla, Laurel Clark, and the first Israeli astronaut, Ilan Ramon. Foam insulation fell from the shuttle during launch, damaging the left wing. On reentry hot gases entered the wing, leading to the destruction of the space craft.

RAILROAD ACCIDENTS

NOTE: Very few passengers were killed in a single U.S. train wreck up until 1853. These early trains ran slowly and made short trips, night travel was rare, and there were not many of them in operation.

1831 June 17, nr. Charleston, S.C.: boiler exploded on America's first passenger locomotive, *The Best Friend of Charleston*, injuring the fireman and the engineer.

1833 Nov. 8, nr. Heightstown, N.J.: world's first train wreck and first passenger fatalities recorded. A 24-passenger Camden & Amboy train derailed due to a broken axle, killing 2 passengers and injuring all others. Former President John Quincy Adams and Cornelius Vanderbilt, who later made a fortune in railroads, were aboard the train.

1853 May 6, Norwalk, Conn.: New Haven Railroad train ran through an open drawbridge and plunged into the Norwalk River. Forty-six passengers were crushed to death or drowned. This was the first major drawbridge accident.

1856 July 17, Camp Hill, nr. Ft. Washington, Pa.: two Northern Penn trains crashed head-on. Approximately 50–60 people died, mostly children on their way to a Sunday school picnic.

1876 Dec. 29, Ashtabula, Ohio: Lake Shore train fell into the Ashtabula River when the bridge it was crossing collapsed; 92 people were killed.

1887 Aug. 10, nr. Chatsworth, Ill.: a burning railroad trestle collapsed while a Toledo, Peoria & Western train was crossing, killing 81 and injuring 372.

1904 Aug. 7, Eden, Colo.: train derailed on bridge during flash flood; 96 killed.

1910 March 1, Wellington, Wash.: two trains swept into canyon by avalanche; 96 dead.

1915 May 22, Gretna, Scotland: two passenger trains and troop train collided; 227 killed.

1917 Dec. 12, Modane, France: nearly 550 killed in derailment of troop train near mouth of Mt. Cenis tunnel.

1918 July 9, Nashville, Tenn.: 101 killed in a 2-train collision near Nashville.

Nov. 1, New York City: derailment of subway train in Malbone St. tunnel in Brooklyn left 92 dead.

1926 March 14, Virilla River Canyon, Costa Rica: an overcrowded train carrying pilgrims derailed while crossing the Colima Bridge, killing over 300 people and injuring hundreds more.

1939 Dec. 22, nr. Magdeburg, Germany: more than 125 killed in collision; 99 killed in another wreck near Friedrichshafen.

1943 Dec. 16, nr. Rennert, N.C.: 72 killed in derailment and collision of 2 Atlantic Coast Line trains.

1944 March 2, nr. Salerno, Italy: 521 suffocated when Italian train stalled in tunnel.

1949 Oct. 22, nr. Nowy Dwor, Poland: more than 200 reported killed in derailment of Danzig-Warsaw express.

1950 Nov. 22, Richmond Hill, N.Y.: 79 died when two Long Island Railroad commuter train crashed into rear of another.

1951 Feb. 6, Woodbridge, N.J.: 85 died when Pennsylvania Railroad commuter train plunged through temporary overpass.

1952 **Oct. 8, Harrow-Wealdstone, England:** two express trains crashed into commuter train; 112 dead.

1957 **Sept. 1, nr. Kendal, Jamaica:** about 175 killed when train plunged into ravine.

Sept. 29, nr. Montgomery, West Pakistan: express train crashed into standing oil train; nearly 300 killed.

Dec. 4, St. John's, England: 92 killed and 187 injured as one commuter train crashed into another in fog.

1960 **Nov. 14, Pardubice, Czechoslovakia:** two trains collided; 110 dead, 106 injured.

1962 **May 3, nr. Tokyo:** 163 killed and 400 injured when train crashed into wreckage of collision between inbound freight train and outbound commuter train.

1963 **Nov. 9, nr. Yokohama, Japan:** two passenger trains crashed into derailed freight train, killing 162.

1964 **July 26, Custoias, Portugal:** passenger train derailed; 94 dead.

1970 **Feb. 4, nr. Buenos Aires:** 236 killed when express train crashed into standing commuter train.

1972 **Oct. 6, nr. Saltillo, Mexico:** train carrying religious pilgrims derailed and caught fire, killing 204 and injuring over 1,000.

Oct. 30, Chicago: two Illinois Central commuter trains collided during morning rush hour; 45 dead and over 200 injured.

1974 **Aug. 30, Zagreb, Yugoslavia:** train entering station derailed, killing 153 and injuring over 60.

1981 **June 6, nr. Mansi, India:** driver of train carrying over 500 passengers braked to avoid hitting a cow, causing train to plunge off a bridge into the Baghmati River; 268 passengers were reported killed, but at least 300 more were missing.

1982 **July 11, Tepic, Mexico:** Nogales-Guadalajara train plunged down mountain gorge, killing 120.

1989 **Jan. 15, Maizdi Khan, Bangladesh:** train carrying Muslim pilgrims crashed head-on with a mail train, killing at least 110 people and injuring as many as 1,000.

Aug. 10, nr. Los Mochis, Mexico: a second-class passenger train traveling from Mazatlán to Mexicali, plunged off a bridge at Puente del Rio Bamoa into the river and killed an estimated 85 people and injured 107.

1990 **Jan. 4, Sangi village, Sindh province, Pakistan:** overcrowded 16-car passenger train rammed into a standing freight train. At least 210 people were killed and 700 were believed injured in what is said to be Pakistan's worst train disaster.

1993 **Sept. 22, nr. Mobile, Ala.:** Amtrak's *Sunset Limited,* en route to Miami, jumped rails on weakened bridge and plunged in Big Bayou Canot, killing 47 people.

1995 **Aug. 20, Firozabad, northern India:** a speeding passenger train rammed another train that was stalled after hitting a cow. About 300 people were killed and over 400 injured.

1997 **March 3, Punjab province, Pakistan:** passenger train crashed due to failed brakes, killing 119 and injuring at least 80 people.

1998 **June 3, nr. Eschede, Germany:** Inter City Express passenger train traveling at 125 mph crashed into support pier of overpass, killing 98. Is nation's worst postwar train accident.

1999 **Oct. 5, London:** out-bound Thames commuter train passed a red signal near Paddington Station and collided with London-bound Great Western express, killing 30 people and injuring 245.

2002 **Feb. 20, nr. Ayyat, Egypt:** 361 killed in fire after gas cylinder used for cooking exploded aboard crowded passenger train. Egypt's worst train disaster.

May 25, Muamba, Mozambique: 192 died and dozens more injured when passenger cars rolled for several miles at top speed into freight cars from which they had been disconnected because of mechanical problems.

June 24, nr. Msagali, central Tanzania: runaway passenger train collided with freight train on same track, leaving 200 dead.

2004 **Feb. 18, Neishabour, Iran:** runaway rail cars, loaded with fertilizer, petrol, and sulphur products, rolled 31 mi down the rails, caught fire, and exploded, killing more than 320 and devastating 5 villages.

April 22, Ryongchon, North Korea: two trains carrying flammable liquids collided, causing a huge explosion near the Chinese border, killing at least 161 and injuring more than 1,300.

OIL SPILLS

1967 **March 18, Cornwall, Eng.:** *Torrey Canyon* ran aground, spilling 38 million gallons of crude oil off the Scilly Islands.

1976 **Dec. 15, Buzzards Bay, Mass.:** *Argo Merchant* ran aground southeast of Nantucket Island, spilling 7.7 million gallons of fuel oil.

1977 **April, North Sea:** blowout of well in Ekofisk oil field leaked 81 million gallons.

1978 **March 16, off Portsall, France:** wrecked supertanker *Amoco Cadiz* spilled 68 million gallons, causing widespread environmental damage over 100 mi of Brittany coast.

1979 **June 3, Gulf of Mexico:** exploratory oil well Ixtoc 1 blew out, spilling an estimated 140 million gallons of crude oil into the open sea. Although it is one of the largest known oil spills, it had a low environmental impact.

July 19, Tobago: the *Atlantic Empress* and the

Aegean Captain collided, spilling 46 million gallons of crude. While being towed, the *Atlantic Empress* spilled an additional 41 million gallons off Barbados on Aug. 2.

1983 **Feb. 4, Persian Gulf, Iran:** Nowruz Field platform spilled 80 million gallons of oil.

Aug. 6, Cape Town, South Africa: the Spanish tanker *Castillo de Bellver* caught fire, spilling 78 million gallons of oil off the coast.

1989 **March 24, Prince William Sound, Alaska:** tanker *Exxon Valdez* hit an undersea reef and spilled 10 million plus gallons of oil into the waters, causing the worst oil spill in U.S. history.

1991 **Jan. 23–27, southern Kuwait:** during the Persian Gulf War, Iraq deliberately released 240–460 million gallons of crude oil into the Persian Gulf.

1992 **March 2, Fergana Valley, Uzbekistan:** 88 million gallons of oil spilled from an oil well.

SPORTS DISASTERS

1955 **June 11, Le Mans, France:** racing car in Grand Prix hurtled into grandstand, killing 82 spectators.

1964 **May 24, Lima, Peru:** more than 300 soccer fans killed and over 500 injured during riot and panic following unpopular ruling by referee in Peru vs. Argentina soccer game. It is worst soccer disaster on record.

1971 **Jan. 2, Glasgow, Scotland:** 66 killed in crush at Glasgow Rangers home stadium when soccer fans trying to leave encountered fans trying to return to stadium after hearing that a late goal had been scored.

1982 **Oct. 20, Moscow:** according to *Sovietsky Sport,* as many as 340 died in Lenin Stadium when exiting soccer fans collided with returning fans after final goal was scored. All the fans had been crowded into one section of stadium by police.

1985 **May 11, Bradford, England:** 56 burned to death and over 200 injured when fire engulfed main grandstand at Bradford's soccer stadium.

May 29, Brussels, Belgium: group of drunken British soccer fans supporting Liverpool club stormed stand filled with Italian supporters of Juventus team before European Champion's Cup final. While British fans attacked rival spectators at the Heysel Stadium, concrete retaining wall collapsed and 39 people were crushed or trampled to death, 32 of them Italians. More than 400 people were injured.

1988 **March 12, Katmandu, Nepal:** some 80 soccer fans seeking cover during a violent hail storm at the national stadium were trampled to death in a stampede because the stadium doors were locked.

1989 **April 15, Sheffield, England:** 96 people were killed at Hillsborough stadium during a semifinal match between Liverpool and Nottingham Forest. Most of the victims, who were Liverpool fans, were crushed when a barrier collapsed on an overcrowded pen behind one of the goals. It is Britain's worst soccer disaster.

1996 **Oct. 16, Guatemala City:** at least 84 killed and 147 injured by stampeding soccer fans before a 1998 World Cup qualifying match between Guatemala and Costa Rica held at Mateo Flores National Stadium.

2001 **May 9, Accra, Ghana:** at least 120 people were killed in a stampede at a soccer match. It was Africa's worst soccer-related disaster ever.

Suspected al-Qaeda Terrorist Acts

1993 (Feb.): Bombing of World Trade Center (WTC); six killed.

1993 (Oct.): Killing of U.S. soldiers in Somalia.

1996 (June): Truck bombing at Khobar Towers barracks in Dhahran, Saudi Arabia, killed 19 Americans.

1998 (Aug.): Bombing of U.S. embassies in East Africa; 224 killed, including 12 Americans.

1999 (Dec.): Plot to bomb millennium celebrations in Seattle foiled when customs agents arrest an Algerian smuggling explosives into the U.S.

2000 (Oct.): Bombing of the USS *Cole* in port in Yemen; 17 U.S. sailors killed.

2001 (Sept.): Destruction of WTC; attack on Pentagon. Total dead 2,992.

2002 (April): Explosion at historic synagogue in Tunisia left 21 dead, including 14 German tourists.

2002 (May): Car exploded outside hotel in Karachi, Pakistan, killing 14.

2002 (June): Bomb exploded outside American consulate in Karachi, Pakistan, killing 12.

2002 (Oct.): Boat crashed into oil tanker off Yemen coast, killing one.

2002 (Oct.): Nightclub bombings in Bali, Indonesia, killed 202, mostly Australian citizens.

2002 (Nov.): Suicide attack on a hotel in Mombasa, Kenya, killed 16.

2003 (May): Suicide bombers killed 34, including 8 Americans, at housing compounds for Westerners in Riyadh, Saudi Arabia.

2003 (May): Four bombs killed 33 people in Casablanca, Morocco.

2003 (Aug.): Suicide car-bomb killed 12, injured 150 at Marriott Hotel in Jakarta, Indonesia.

2003 (Nov.): Explosions rocked a Riyadh, Saudi Arabia housing compound, killing 17.

2003 (Nov.): Suicide car-bombers simultaneously attacked two synagogues in Istanbul, Turkey, killing 25 and injuring hundreds.

2003 (Nov.): Truck bombs detonated at London bank and British consulate in Istanbul, Turkey, killing 26.

2004 (March): Ten terrorists bombs exploded almost simultaneously during the morning rush hour in Madrid, Spain, killing 202 and injuring more than 1,400.

2004 (May): Terrorists attacked Saudi oil company offices in Khobar, Saudi Arabia, killing 22.

2004 (June): Terrorists kidnapped and executed American Paul Johnson, Jr., in Riyadh, Saudi Arabia.

2004 (Sept.): Car bomb outside the Australian embassy in Jakarta, Indonesia, killed nine.

TERRORIST ATTACKS

(within the United States or against Americans abroad)

1920 **Sept. 16, New York City:** TNT bomb planted in unattended horse-drawn wagon exploded on Wall Street opposite House of Morgan, killing 35 people and injuring hundreds more. Bolshevist or anarchist terrorists believed responsible, but crime never solved.

1975 **Jan. 24, New York City:** bomb set off in historic Fraunces Tavern killed 4 and injured more than 50 people. Puerto Rican nationalist group (FALN) claimed responsibility, and police tied 13 other bombings to the group.

1979 **Nov. 4, Tehran, Iran:** Iranian radical students seized the U.S. embassy, taking 66 hostages. Fourteen were later released. The remaining 52 were freed after 444 days.

1983 **April 18, Beirut, Lebanon:** U.S. embassy destroyed in suicide car-bomb attack; 63 dead, including 17 Americans.

Oct. 23, Beirut, Lebanon: Shiite suicide bombers exploded truck near U.S. military barracks at Beirut airport, killing 241 Marines. Minutes later a second bomb killed 58 French paratroopers in their barracks in West Beirut.

Dec. 12, Kuwait City, Kuwait Shiite truck bombers attacked the U.S. embassy and other targets, killing 5 and injuring 80.

1984 **Sept. 20, east Beirut, Lebanon:** truck bomb exploded outside the U.S. embassy annex, killing 24, including 2 U.S. military.

Dec. 3, Beirut, Lebanon: Kuwait Airways Flight 221, from Kuwait to Pakistan, hijacked and diverted to Tehran. Two Americans killed.

1985 **June 14, Beirut, Lebanon:** TWA flight 847 en route from Athens to Rome hijacked to Beirut by Hezbollah terrorists and held for 17 days. A U.S. Navy diver executed.

Oct. 7, Mediterranean Sea: gunmen attack Italian cruise ship, *Achille Lauro*. One U.S. tourist killed. Hijacking linked to Libya.

Dec. 18, Rome, Italy, and Vienna, Austria: airports in Rome and Vienna were bombed, killing 20 people, 5 of whom were Americans. Bombing linked to Libya.

1988 **Dec. 21, Lockerbie, Scotland:** N.Y.-bound Pan-Am Boeing 747 exploded in flight from a terrorist bomb and crashed into Scottish village, killing all 259 aboard and 11 on the ground. Passengers included 35 Syracuse University students and many U.S. military personnel. Libya formally admitted responsibility 15 years later (Aug. 2003) and offered $2.7 billion compensation to victims' families.

1993 **Feb. 26, New York City:** bomb exploded in basement garage of World Trade Center, killing 6 and injuring at least 1,040 others. In 1995, militant Islamist Sheik Omar Abdel Rahman and 9 others were convicted of conspiracy charges, and in 1998, Ramzi Yousef, believed to have been the mastermind, was convicted of the bombing. Al-Qaeda involvement is suspected.

1995 **April 19, Oklahoma City:** car bomb exploded outside federal office building, collapsing wall and floors. 168 people were killed, including 19 children. Over 220 buildings sustained damage. Timothy McVeigh and Terry Nichols later convicted in the antigovernment plot to avenge the Branch Davidian standoff in Waco, Tex., exactly two years earlier.

Nov. 13, Riyadh, Saudi Arabia: car bomb exploded at U.S. military headquarters, killing five U.S. military servicemen.

1996 **June 25, Dhahran, Saudi Arabia:** truck bomb exploded outside Khobar Towers military complex, killing 19 American servicemen and injuring hundreds of others.

1998 **Aug. 7, Nairobi, Kenya, and Dar es Salaam, Tanzania:** truck bombs exploded almost simultaneously near 2 U.S. embassies, killing 224 (213 in Kenya and 11 in Tanzania) and injuring about 4,500. Four men connected with al-Qaeda were convicted of the killings.

2000 **Oct. 12, Aden, Yemen:** U.S. Navy destroyer USS *Cole* heavily damaged when a small boat loaded with explosives blew up alongside it. Seventeen sailors killed. Linked to al-Qaeda terrorist network.

2001 **Sept. 11, New York City, Arlington, Va., and Shanksville, Pa.:** hijackers crashed two commercial jets into twin towers of World Trade Center; two more hijacked jets were crashed into the Pentagon and a field in rural Pa. Total dead and missing numbered 2,992: 2,749 in New York City, 184 at the Pentagon, 40 in Pa., and 19 hijackers. Islamic al-Qaeda terrorist group blamed.

2002 **June 14, Karachi, Pakistan:** bomb exploded outside American consulate in Karachi, Pakistan, killing 12. Linked to al-Qaeda.

2003 **May 12, Riyadh, Saudi Arabia:** suicide bombers killed 34, including eight Americans, at housing compounds for Westerners. Al-Qaeda suspected.

MISCELLANEOUS DISASTERS

1952 **Dec. 4–7, London, England:** high-pressure system settled over London, trapping pollution near the ground. Some 4,000 people died in "Great Smog," mostly from respiratory and cardiac distress.

1981 **July 18, Kansas City, Mo.:** suspended walkway in Hyatt Regency Hotel collapsed; 113 dead, 186 injured.

1982–1983 worldwide: El Niño caused wildly unusual weather in the U.S. throughout 1983, including severe winter storms in southern Calif., widespread flooding across the South, and unusually mild winter weather in the central and northern parts of the country. Warming ocean currents resulted in failed fishing harvests in Peru and Ecuador, and drought in the western Pacific region led to disastrous forest fires in Indonesia and Australia. Overall loss to world economy was over $8 billion. Similar event in 1997–1998 resulted in estimated loss of $25–33 billion.

1984 **Dec. 3, Bhopal, India:** toxic gas, methyl isocyanate, seeped from Union Carbide insecticide plant, killed more than 2,000, injured about 150,000.

1987 **Sept. 18, Goiânia, Brazil:** 244 people contaminated with cesium-137 that was removed from a steel cylinder taken from a cancer-therapy machine that had been sold as scrap. Four people died in worst radiation disaster in Western Hemisphere.

1988 **July 6, North Sea off Scotland:** 166 workers killed in explosion and fire on Occidental Petroleum's *Piper Alpha* rig in North Sea; 64 survivors. It is the world's worst offshore oil disaster.

1993 **April 19, Waco, Tex.:** 51-day stalemate between federal agents and members of Christian Branch Davidian cult ended in a fiery tragedy after federal agents botched their assault on the sect's compound. About 80 Branch Davidians, including at least 17 children, died when the compound burned to the ground in a suspicious blaze. Earlier, on Feb. 28, four agents were shot to death in failed attack on heavily armed compound.

1996 **May 10–11, Mt. Everest, Nepal:** 8 climbers died near summit during storm on mountain. A total of 15 climbers died that season, the worst single loss of life on Everest.

2004 **Feb. 1, Mecca, Saudi Arabia:** a stampede at the Hajj pilgrimage, during the stone-throwing ritual, killed 251 pilgrims.

Nobel Prizes

(For years not listed, no award was made. For 2004 awards, *see* p. 44.)

PEACE

1901 Henri Dunant (Switzerland); Frederick Passy (France)
1902 Elie Ducommun and Albert Gobat (Switzerland)
1903 Sir William R. Cremer (UK)
1904 Institut de Droit International (Belgium)
1905 Bertha von Suttner (Austria)
1906 Theodore Roosevelt (U.S.)
1907 Ernesto T. Moneta (Italy) and Louis Renault (France)
1908 Klas P. Arnoldson (Sweden) and Frederik Bajer (Denmark)
1909 Auguste M. F. Beernaert (Belgium) and Baron Paul H.B.B. d'Estournelles de Constant de Rebecque (France)
1910 Bureau International Permanent de la Paix (Switzerland)
1911 Tobias M. C. Asser (Holland) and Alfred H. Fried (Austria)
1912 Elihu Root (U.S.)
1913 Henri La Fontaine (Belgium)
1917 International Red Cross
1919 Woodrow Wilson (U.S.)
1920 Léon Bourgeois (France)
1921 Karl H. Branting (Sweden) and Christian L. Lange (Norway)
1922 Fridtjof Nansen (Norway)
1925 Sir Austen Chamberlain (UK) and Charles G. Dawes (U.S.)
1926 Aristide Briand (France) and Gustav Stresemann (Germany)
1927 Ferdinand Buisson (France) and Ludwig Quidde (Germany)
1929 Frank B. Kellogg (U.S.)
1930 Lars O. J. Söderblom (Sweden)
1931 Jane Addams and Nicholas M. Butler (U.S.)
1933 Sir Norman Angell (UK)
1934 Arthur Henderson (UK)
1935 Karl von Ossietzky (Germany)
1936 Carlos de S. Lamas (Argentina)
1937 Lord Cecil of Chelwood (UK)
1938 Office International Nansen pour les Réfugiés (Switzerland)
1944 International Red Cross
1945 Cordell Hull (U.S.)
1946 Emily G. Balch and John R. Mott (U.S.)
1947 American Friends Service Committee (U.S.) and British Society of Friends' Service Council (UK)
1949 Lord John Boyd Orr (Scotland)
1950 Ralph J. Bunche (U.S.)
1951 Léon Jouhaux (France)
1952 Albert Schweitzer (French Equatorial Africa)
1953 George C. Marshall (U.S.)
1954 Office of the UN High Commissioner for Refugees
1957 Lester B. Pearson (Canada)
1958 Rev. Dominique Georges Henri Pire (Belgium)
1959 Philip John Noel-Baker (UK)

1960 Albert John Luthuli (South Africa)
1961 Dag Hammarskjöld (Sweden)
1962 Linus Pauling (U.S.)
1963 Intl. Comm. of Red Cross; League of Red Cross Societies (both Switzerland)
1964 Rev. Dr. Martin Luther King, Jr. (U.S.)
1965 UNICEF (United Nations Children's Fund)
1968 René Cassin (France)
1969 International Labour Organization
1970 Norman E. Borlaug (U.S.)
1971 Willy Brandt (West Germany)
1973 Henry A. Kissinger (U.S.); Le Duc Tho (North Vietnam)[1]
1974 Eisaku Sato (Japan); Sean MacBride (Ireland)
1975 Andrei D. Sakharov (USSR)
1976 Mairead Corrigan and Betty Williams (both Northern Ireland)
1977 Amnesty International
1978 Menachem Begin (Israel) and Anwar el-Sadat (Egypt)
1979 Mother Teresa of Calcutta (India)
1980 Adolfo Pérez Esquivel (Argentina)
1981 Office of the UN High Commissioner for Refugees
1982 Alva Myrdal (Sweden) and Alfonso García Robles (Mexico)
1983 Lech Walesa (Poland)
1984 Bishop Desmond Tutu (South Africa)
1985 International Physicians for the Prevention of Nuclear War
1986 Elie Wiesel (U.S.)
1987 Oscar Arias Sánchez (Costa Rica)
1988 UN Peacekeeping Forces
1989 Dalai Lama (Tibet)
1990 Mikhail S. Gorbachev (USSR)
1991 Daw Aung San Suu Kyi (Burma)
1992 Rigoberta Menchú (Guatemala)
1993 F. W. de Klerk and Nelson Mandela (both South Africa)
1994 Yasir Arafat (Palestine), Shimon Peres, and Yitzhak Rabin (both Israel)
1995 Joseph Rotblat and Pugwash Conference on Science and World Affairs (UK)
1996 Carlos Filipe Ximenes Belo and José Ramos-Horta (East Timor)
1997 International Campaign to Ban Landmines and Jody Williams (U.S.)
1998 John Hume and David Trimble (both Northern Ireland)
1999 Doctors Without Borders (France)
2000 Kim Dae Jung (South Korea)
2001 United Nations and Kofi Annan
2002 Jimmy Carter (U.S.)
2003 Shirin Ebadi (Iran)

1. Le Duc Tho refused prize, charging that peace had not yet really been established in South Vietnam.

LITERATURE

1901 René F. A. Sully Prudhomme (France)
1902 Theodor Mommsen (Germany)
1903 Björnstjerne Björnson (Norway)
1904 Frédéric Mistral (France) and José Echegaray (Spain)
1905 Henryk Sienkiewicz (Poland)
1906 Giosuè Carducci (Italy)
1907 Rudyard Kipling (UK)
1908 Rudolf Eucken (Germany)
1909 Selma Lagerlöf (Sweden)
1910 Paul von Heyse (Germany)
1911 Maurice Maeterlinck (Belgium)
1912 Gerhart Hauptmann (Germany)
1913 Rabindranath Tagore (India)
1915 Romain Rolland (France)
1916 Verner von Heidenstam (Sweden)
1917 Karl Gjellerup and Henrik Pontoppidan (both Denmark)
1919 Carl Spitteler (Switzerland)
1920 Knut Hamsun (Norway)
1921 Anatole France (France)
1922 Jacinto Benavente (Spain)
1923 William B. Yeats (Ireland)
1924 Wladyslaw Reymont (Poland)
1925 George Bernard Shaw (Ireland)
1926 Grazia Deledda (Italy)
1927 Henri Bergson (France)
1928 Sigrid Undset (Norway)
1929 Thomas Mann (Germany)
1930 Sinclair Lewis (U.S.)
1931 Erik A. Karlfeldt (Sweden)
1932 John Galsworthy (UK)
1933 Ivan G. Bunin (Russia)
1934 Luigi Pirandello (Italy)
1936 Eugene O'Neill (U.S.)
1937 Roger Martin du Gard (France)
1938 Pearl S. Buck (U.S.)
1939 Frans Eemil Sillanpää (Finland)
1944 Johannes V. Jensen (Denmark)
1945 Gabriela Mistral (Chile)
1946 Hermann Hesse (Switzerland)
1947 André Gide (France)
1948 Thomas Stearns Eliot (UK)
1949 William Faulkner (U.S.)
1950 Bertrand Russell (UK)
1951 Pär Lagerkvist (Sweden)
1952 François Mauriac (France)
1953 Sir Winston Churchill (UK)
1954 Ernest Hemingway (U.S.)
1955 Halldór Kiljan Laxness (Iceland)
1956 Juan Ramón Jiménez (Spain)
1957 Albert Camus (France)
1958 Boris Pasternak (USSR) (declined)
1959 Salvatore Quasimodo (Italy)
1960 St. John Perse (Alexis Léger) (France)
1961 Ivo Andric (Yugoslavia)
1962 John Steinbeck (U.S.)
1963 Giorgios Seferis (Seferiades) (Greece)
1964 Jean-Paul Sartre (France) (declined)
1965 Mikhail Sholokhov (USSR)
1966 Shmuel Yosef Agnon (Israel) and Nelly Sachs (Sweden)
1967 Miguel Angel Asturias (Guatemala)
1968 Yasunari Kawabata (Japan)
1969 Samuel Beckett (Ireland)
1970 Aleksandr Solzhenitsyn (USSR)
1971 Pablo Neruda (Chile)
1972 Heinrich Böll (West Germany)
1973 Patrick White (Australia)

1974 Eyvind Johnson and Harry Martinson (both Sweden)
1975 Eugenio Montale (Italy)
1976 Saul Bellow (U.S.)
1977 Vicente Aleixandre (Spain)
1978 Isaac Bashevis Singer (U.S.)
1979 Odysseus Elytis (Greece)
1980 Czeslaw Milosz (U.S.)
1981 Elias Canetti (Bulgaria)
1982 Gabriel García Márquez (Colombia)
1983 William Golding (UK)
1984 Jaroslav Seifert (Czechoslovakia)
1985 Claude Simon (France)
1986 Wole Soyinka (Nigeria)
1987 Joseph Brodsky (U.S.)
1988 Naguib Mahfouz (Egypt)
1989 Camilo José Cela (Spain)
1990 Octavio Paz (Mexico)
1991 Nadine Gordimer (South Africa)
1992 Derek Walcott (Trinidad)
1993 Toni Morrison (U.S.)
1994 Kenzaburo Oe (Japan)
1995 Seamus Heaney (Ireland)
1996 Wislawa Szymborska (Poland)
1997 Dario Fo (Italy)
1998 José Saramago (Portugal)
1999 Günter Grass (Germany)
2000 Gao Xingjian (China)
2001 V. S. Naipaul (UK)
2002 Imre Kertész (Hungary)
2003 John M. Coetzee (South Africa)

PHYSICS

1901 Wilhelm K. Roentgen (Germany), for discovery of Roentgen rays
1902 Hendrik A. Lorentz and Pieter Zeeman (Netherlands), for work on influence of magnetism upon radiation
1903 A. Henri Becquerel (France), for work on spontaneous radioactivity; and Pierre and Marie Curie (France), for study of radiation
1904 John Strutt (Lord Rayleigh) (UK), for discovery of argon in investigating gas density
1905 Philipp Lenard (Germany), for work with cathode rays
1906 Sir Joseph Thomson (UK), for investigations on passage of electricity through gases
1907 Albert A. Michelson (U.S.), for spectroscopic and metrologic investigations
1908 Gabriel Lippmann (France), for method of reproducing colors by photography
1909 Guglielmo Marconi (Italy) and Ferdinand Braun (Germany), for development of wireless
1910 Johannes D. van der Waals (Netherlands), for work with the equation of state for gases and liquids
1911 Wilhelm Wien (Germany), for his laws governing the radiation of heat
1912 Gustaf Dalén (Sweden), for discovery of automatic regulators used in lighting lighthouses and light buoys
1913 Heike Kamerlingh-Onnes (Netherlands), for work leading to production of liquid helium
1914 Max von Laue (Germany), for discovery of diffraction of Roentgen rays passing through crystals
1915 Sir William Bragg and William L. Bragg (both UK), for analysis of crystal structure by X-rays

1917 Charles G. Barkla (UK), for discovery of Roentgen radiation of the elements

1918 Max Planck (Germany), for discoveries in connection with quantum theory

1919 Johannes Stark (Germany), for discovery of Doppler effect in Canal rays and decomposition of spectrum lines by electric fields

1920 Charles E. Guillaume (Switzerland), for discoveries of anomalies in nickel-steel alloys

1921 Albert Einstein (Germany), for discovery of the law of photoelectric effect

1922 Niels Bohr (Denmark), for investigation of structure of atoms and radiations emanating from them

1923 Robert A. Millikan (U.S.), for work on elementary charge of electricity and photoelectric phenomena

1924 Karl M. G. Siegbahn (Sweden), for investigations in X-ray spectroscopy

1925 James Franck and Gustav Hertz (Germany), for discovery of laws governing impact of electrons upon atoms

1926 Jean B. Perrin (France), for work on discontinuous structure of matter and discovery of the equilibrium of sedimentation

1927 Arthur H. Compton (U.S.), for discovery of Compton phenomenon; and Charles T. R. Wilson (UK), for method of perceiving paths taken by electrically charged particles

1928 In 1929, the 1928 prize was awarded to Sir Owen Richardson (UK), for work on the phenomenon of thermionics and discovery of the Richardson Law

1929 Prince Louis Victor de Broglie (France), for discovery of the wave character of electrons

1930 Sir Chandrasekhara Raman (India), for work on diffusion of light and discovery of the Raman effect

1932 In 1933, the prize for 1932 was awarded to Werner Heisenberg (Germany), for creation of quantum mechanics

1933 Erwin Schrödinger (Austria) and Paul A. M. Dirac (UK), for discovery of new fertile forms of the atomic theory

1935 James Chadwick (UK), for discovery of the neutron

1936 Victor F. Hess (Austria), for discovery of cosmic radiation; and Carl D. Anderson (U.S.), for discovery of the positron

1937 Clinton J. Davisson (U.S.) and George P. Thomson (UK), for discovery of diffraction of electrons by crystals

1938 Enrico Fermi (Italy), for identification of new radioactive elements and discovery of nuclear reactions effected by slow neutrons

1939 Ernest Orlando Lawrence (U.S.), for development of the cyclotron

1943 Otto Stern (U.S.), for detection of magnetic momentum of protons

1944 Isidor Isaac Rabi (U.S.), for work on magnetic movements of atomic particles

1945 Wolfgang Pauli (Austria), for work on atomic fissions

1946 Percy Williams Bridgman (U.S.), for studies and inventions in high-pressure physics

1947 Sir Edward Appleton (UK), for discovery of layer that reflects radio short waves in the ionosphere

1948 Patrick M. S. Blackett (UK), for improvement on Wilson chamber and discoveries in cosmic radiation

1949 Hideki Yukawa (Japan), for mathematical prediction, in 1935, of the meson

1950 Cecil Frank Powell (UK), for method of photographic study of atom nucleus, and for discoveries about mesons

1951 Sir John Douglas Cockcroft (UK) and Ernest T. S. Walton (Ireland), for work in 1932 on transmutation of atomic nuclei

1952 Edward Mills Purcell and Felix Bloch (U.S.), for work in measurement of magnetic fields in atomic nuclei

1953 Fritz Zernike (Netherlands), for development of "phase contrast" microscope

1954 Max Born (UK), for work in quantum mechanics; Walther Bothe (West Germany), for work in cosmic radiation

1955 Polykarp Kusch and Willis E. Lamb, Jr. (both U.S.), for atomic measurements

1956 William Shockley, Walter H. Brattain, and John Bardeen (all U.S.), for developing electronic transistor

1957 Tsung Dao Lee and Chen Ning Yang (both China), for disproving principle of conservation of parity

1958 Pavel A. Cherenkov, Ilya M. Frank, and Igor E. Tamm (all USSR), for work resulting in development of cosmic-ray counter

1959 Emilio Segre and Owen Chamberlain (both U.S.), for demonstrating the existence of the anti-proton

1960 Donald A. Glaser (U.S.), for invention of "bubble chamber" to study subatomic particles

1961 Robert Hofstadter (U.S.), for determination of shape and size of atomic nucleus; Rudolf Mössbauer (West Germany), for method of producing and measuring recoil-free gamma rays

1962 Lev D. Landau (USSR), for his theories about condensed matter

1963 Eugene Paul Wigner, Maria Goeppert Mayer (both U.S.), and J. Hans D. Jensen (West Germany), for research on structure of atom and its nucleus

1964 Charles Hard Townes (U.S.), Nikolai G. Basov, and Aleksandr M. Prochorov (both USSR), for developing maser and laser principle of producing high-intensity radiation

1965 Richard P. Feynman, Julian S. Schwinger (both U.S.), and Shinichiro Tomonaga (Japan), for research in quantum electrodynamics

1966 Alfred Kastler (France), for work on energy levels inside atom

1967 Hans A. Bethe (U.S.), for work on energy production of stars

1968 Luis Walter Alvarez (U.S.), for study of subatomic particles

1969 Murray Gell-Mann (U.S.), for study of subatomic particles

1970 Hannes Alfvén (Sweden), for theories in plasma physics; Louis Néel (France), for discoveries in antiferromagnetism and ferromagnetism

1971 Dennis Gabor (UK), for invention of holographic method of three-dimensional imagery

1972   John Bardeen, Leon N. Cooper, and John Robert Schrieffer (all U.S.), for theory of superconductivity, where electrical resistance in certain metals vanishes above absolute zero temperature

1973   Ivar Giaever (U.S.), Leo Esaki (Japan), and Brian D. Josephson (UK), for theories that have advanced and expanded the field of miniature electronics

1974   Antony Hewish (UK), for discovery of pulsars; Martin Ryle (UK), for using radiotelescopes to probe outer space with precision

1975   James Rainwater (U.S.), Ben Mottelson, and Aage N. Bohr (both Denmark), for showing that the atomic nucleus is asymmetrical

1976   Burton Richter and Samuel C. C. Ting (both U.S.), for discovery of subatomic particles known as J and psi

1977   Philip W. Anderson, John H. Van Vleck (both U.S.), and Nevill F. Mott (UK), for work underlying computer memories and electronic devices

1978   Arno A. Penzias and Robert W. Wilson (both U.S.), for work in cosmic microwave radiation; Piotr L. Kapitsa (USSR), for basic inventions and discoveries in low-temperature physics

1979   Steven Weinberg, Sheldon L. Glashow (both U.S.), and Abdus Salam (Pakistan), for developing theory that electromagnetism and the "weak" force, which causes radioactive decay in some atomic nuclei, are facets of the same phenomenon

1980   James W. Cronin and Val L. Fitch (both U.S.), for work concerning the asymmetry of subatomic particles

1981   Nicolaas Bloembergen, Arthur L. Schawlow (both U.S.), and Kai M. Siegbahn (Sweden), for developing technologies with lasers and other devices to probe the secrets of complex forms of matter

1982   Kenneth G. Wilson (U.S.), for analysis of changes in matter under pressure and temperature

1983   Subrahmanyam Chandrasekhar and William A. Fowler (both U.S.), for complementary research on processes involved in the evolution of stars

1984   Carlo Rubbia (Italy) and Simon van der Meer (Netherlands), for their role in discovering three subatomic particles, a step toward developing a single theory to account for all natural forces

1985   Klaus von Klitzing (West Germany), for developing an exact way of measuring electrical conductivity

1986   Ernst Ruska, Gerd Binnig (both West Germany), and Heinrich Rohrer (Switzerland), for work on microscopes

1987   K. Alex Müller (Switzerland) and J. Georg Bednorz (West Germany), for their discovery of high-temperature superconductors

1988   Leon M. Lederman, Melvin Schwartz, and Jack Steinberger (all U.S.), for research that improved the understanding of elementary particles and forces

1989   Norman F. Ramsey (U.S.), for work leading to development of the atomic clock; Hans G. Dehmelt (U.S.) and Wolfgang Paul (West Germany), for developing methods to isolate atoms and subatomic particles

1990   Richard E. Taylor (Canada), Jerome I. Friedman, and Dr. Henry W. Kendall (both U.S.), for their "breakthrough in our understanding of matter" that confirmed the reality of quarks

1991   Pierre-Gilles de Gennes (France), for his discoveries about the ordering of molecules in substances ranging from "super" glue to an exotic form of liquid helium

1992   George Charpak (France), for his inventions of particle detectors

1993   Joseph H. Taylor and Russell A. Hulse (both U.S.), for their discovery of a binary pulsar

1994   Clifford G. Shull (U.S.) and Bertram N. Brockhouse (Canada), for adapting beams of neutrons as probes to explore the atomic structure of matter

1995   Martin L. Perl and Frederick Reines (both U.S.), for their discoveries of "two of nature's most remarkable subatomic particles"—the tau and the neutrino

1996   David M. Lee, Robert C. Richardson, and Douglas I. Osheroff (all U.S.), for their discovery of superfluity in helium-3

1997   Steven Chu, William D. Phillips (both U.S.), and Claude Cohen-Tannoudji (France), for developing a method to cool and trap atoms using light from lasers

1998   Robert B. Laughlin (U.S.), Horst L. Störmer (Germany), and Daniel C. Tsui (U.S.), for their discovery of a new form of quantum fluid with fractionally charged excitations

1999   Gerardus 't Hooft (Netherlands) and Martinus J. G. Veltman (Netherlands), for their theory concerning the production of the Sun's energy

2000   Zhores I. Alferov (Russia), Herbert Kroemer, and Jack S. Kilby (both U.S.), for work in the development of transistors and microchip technology

2001   Wolfgang Ketterle (Germany), Eric A. Cornell, and Carl E. Wieman (both U.S.), for discovering Bose-Einstein condensate, a new state of matter

2002   Raymond Davis, Jr. (U.S.), and Masatoshi Koshiba (Japan), for the detection of cosmic neutrinos; Riccardo Giacconi (U.S.), for contributions to astrophysics, which have led to the discovery of cosmic X-ray sources

2003   Alexei A. Abrikosov (Russia, U.S.), Anthony J. Leggett (UK, U.S.), and Vitaly L. Ginzburg (Russia), for theories about superconductivity

CHEMISTRY

1901   Jacobus H. van't Hoff (Netherlands), for laws of chemical dynamics and osmotic pressure in solutions

1902   Emil Fischer (Germany), for experiments in sugar and purin groups of substances

1903   Svante A. Arrhenius (Sweden), for his electrolytic theory of dissociation

1904   Sir William Ramsay (UK), for discovery and determination of place of inert gaseous elements in air

1905   Adolf von Baeyer (Germany), for work on organic dyes and hydroaromatic combinations

1906   Henri Moissan (France), for isolation of fluorine and introduction of electric furnace

1907 Eduard Buchner (Germany), discovery of cell-less fermentation and investigations in biological chemistry

1908 Sir Ernest Rutherford (UK), for investigations into disintegration of elements

1909 Wilhelm Ostwald (Germany), for work on catalysis and investigations into chemical equilibrium and reaction rates

1910 Otto Wallach (Germany), for work in the field of alicyclic compounds

1911 Marie Curie (France), for discovery of the elements radium and polonium

1912 Victor Grignard (France), for reagent discovered by him; Paul Sabatier (France), for methods of hydrogenating organic compounds

1913 Alfred Werner (Switzerland), for linking up atoms within the molecule

1914 Theodore W. Richards (U.S.), for determining atomic weight of many chemical elements

1915 Richard Willstätter (Germany), for research into coloring matter of plants, especially chlorophyll

1918 Fritz Haber (Germany), for synthetic production of ammonia

1920 Walther Nernst (Germany), for work in thermochemistry

1921 Frederick Soddy (UK), for investigations into origin and nature of isotopes

1922 Francis W. Aston (UK), for discovery of isotopes in nonradioactive elements and for discovery of the whole-number rule

1923 Fritz Pregl (Austria), for method of microanalysis of organic substances discovered by him

1925 In 1926, the 1925 prize was awarded to Richard Zsigmondy (Germany), for work on the heterogeneous nature of colloid solutions

1926 Theodor Svedberg (Sweden), for work on disperse systems

1927 In 1928, the 1927 prize was awarded to Heinrich Wieland (Germany), for investigations of bile acids and kindred substances

1928 Adolf Windaus (Germany), for investigations on constitution of the sterols and their connection with vitamins

1929 Sir Arthur Harden (UK) and Hans K.A.S. von Euler-Chelpin (Sweden), for research on fermentation of sugars

1930 Hans Fischer (Germany), for work on coloring matter of blood and leaves and for his synthesis of hemin

1931 Karl Bosch and Friedrich Bergius (both Germany), for invention and development of chemical high-pressure methods

1932 Irving Langmuir (U.S.), for work in realm of surface chemistry

1934 Harold C. Urey (U.S.), for discovery of heavy hydrogen

1935 Frédéric and Irène Joliot-Curie (both France), for synthesis of new radioactive elements

1936 Peter J. W. Debye (Netherlands), for investigations on dipole moments and diffraction of X-rays and electrons in gases

1937 Walter N. Haworth (UK), for research on carbohydrates and vitamin C; Paul Karrer (Switzerland), for work on carotenoids, flavins, and vitamins A and B

1938 Richard Kuhn (Germany), for carotenoid study and vitamin research (declined)

1939 Adolf Butenandt (Germany), for work on sexual hormones (declined prize); Leopold Ruzicka (Switzerland), for work with polymethylenes

1943 Georg Hevesy De Heves (Hungary), for work on use of isotopes as indicators

1944 Otto Hahn (Germany), for work on atomic fission

1945 Artturi Illmari Virtanen (Finland), for research in the field of conservation of fodder

1946 James B. Sumner (U.S.), for crystallizing enzymes; John H. Northrop and Wendell M. Stanley (both U.S.), for preparing enzymes and virus proteins in pure form

1947 Sir Robert Robinson (UK), for research in plant substances

1948 Arne Tiselius (Sweden), for biochemical discoveries and isolation of mouse paralysis virus

1949 William Francis Giauque (U.S.), for research in thermodynamics, especially effects of low temperature

1950 Otto Diels and Kurt Alder (both West Germany), for discovery of diene synthesis, enabling scientists to study structure of organic matter

1951 Glenn T. Seaborg and Edwin H. McMillan (both U.S.), for discovery of plutonium

1952 Archer John Porter Martin and Richard Laurence Millington Synge (both UK), for development of partition chromatography

1953 Hermann Staudinger (West Germany), for research in giant molecules

1954 Linus C. Pauling (U.S.), for study of forces holding together protein and other molecules

1955 Vincent du Vigneaud (U.S.), for work on pituitary hormones

1956 Sir Cyril Hinshelwood (UK) and Nikolai N. Semenov (USSR), for parallel research on chemical reaction kinetics

1957 Sir Alexander Todd (UK), for research with chemical compounds that are factors in heredity

1958 Frederick Sanger (UK), for determining molecular structure of insulin

1959 Jaroslav Heyrovsky (Czechoslovakia), for development of polarography, an electrochemical method of analysis

1960 Willard F. Libby (U.S.), for "atomic time clock" to measure age of objects by measuring their radioactivity

1961 Melvin Calvin (U.S.), for establishing chemical steps during photosynthesis

1962 Max F. Perutz and John C. Kendrew (both UK), for mapping protein molecules with X-rays

1963 Karl Ziegler (West Germany) and Giulio Natta (Italy), for work in uniting simple hydrocarbons into large molecular substances

1964 Dorothy Mary Crowfoot Hodgkin (UK), for determining structure of compounds needed in combatting pernicious anemia

1965 Robert B. Woodward (U.S.), for work in synthesizing complicated organic compounds

1966 Robert Sanderson Mulliken (U.S.), for research on bond holding atoms together in molecule

1967   Manfred Eigen (West Germany), Ronald G. W. Norrish, and George Porter (both UK), for work in high-speed chemical reactions

1968   Lars Onsager (U.S.), for development of system of equations in thermodynamics

1969   Derek H. R. Barton (UK) and Odd Hassel (Norway), for study of organic molecules

1970   Luis F. Leloir (Argentina), for discovery of sugar nucleotides and their role in biosynthesis of carbohydrates

1971   Gerhard Herzberg (Canada), for contributions to knowledge of electronic structure and geometry of molecules, particularly free radicals

1972   Christian Boehmer Anfinsen, Stanford Moore, and William Howard Stein (all U.S.), for pioneering studies in enzymes

1973   Ernst Otto Fischer (West Germany) and Geoffrey Wilkinson (UK), for work that could solve problem of automobile exhaust pollution

1974   Paul J. Flory (U.S.), for developing analytic methods to study properties and molecular structure of long-chain molecules

1975   John W. Cornforth (Australia) and Vladimir Prelog (Switzerland), for research on structure of biological molecules such as antibiotics and cholesterol

1976   William N. Lipscomb, Jr. (U.S.), for work on the structure and bonding mechanisms of boranes

1977   Ilya Prigogine (Belgium), for contributions to nonequilibrium thermodynamics, particularly the theory of dissipative structures

1978   Peter Mitchell (UK), for contributions to the understanding of biological energy transfer

1979   Herbert C. Brown (U.S.) and Georg Wittig (West Germany), for developing a group of substances that facilitate very difficult chemical reactions

1980   Paul Berg, Walter Gilbert (both U.S.), and Frederick Sanger (UK), for developing methods to map the structure and function of DNA, the substance that controls the activity of the cell

1981   Roald Hoffmann (U.S.) and Kenichi Fukui (Japan), for applying quantum-mechanics theories to predict the course of chemical reactions

1982   Aaron Klug (UK), for research in the detailed structures of viruses and components of life

1983   Henry Taube (U.S.), for research on how electrons transfer between molecules in chemical reactions

1984   R. Bruce Merrifield (U.S.), for research that revolutionized the study of proteins

1985   Herbert A. Hauptman and Jerome Karle (both U.S.), for their outstanding achievements in the development of direct methods for the determination of crystal structures

1986   Dudley R. Herschback, Yuan T. Lee (both U.S.), and John C. Polanyi (Canada), for their work on "reaction dynamics"

1987   Donald J. Cram, Charles J. Pedersen (both U.S.), and Jean-Marie Lehn (France), for wide-ranging research that has included the creation of artificial molecules that can mimic vital chemical reactions of the processes of life

1988   Johann Deisenhofer, Robert Huber, and Hartmut Michel (all West Germany), for unraveling the structure of proteins that play a crucial role in photosynthesis

1989   Thomas R. Cech and Sidney Altman (both U.S.), for their discovery, independently, that RNA could actively aid chemical reactions in the cells

1990   Elias James Corey (U.S.), for developing new ways to synthesize complex molecules ordinarily found in nature

1991   Richard R. Ernst (Switzerland), for refinements he developed in nuclear magnetic-resonance spectroscopy

1992   Rudolph A. Marcus (U.S.), for his mathematical analysis of how the overall energy in a system of interacting molecules changes and induces an electron to jump from one molecule to another

1993   Kary B. Mullis (U.S.) and Michael Smith (Canada), for their contributions to the science of genetics

1994   George A. Olah (U.S.), for research that opened new ways to break apart and rebuild compounds of carbon and hydrogen

1995   F. Sherwood Rowland, Mario Molina (both U.S.), and Paul Crutzen (Netherlands), for their pioneering work in explaining the chemical processes that deplete the Earth's ozone shield

1996   Richard E. Smalley, Robert F. Curl, Jr. (both U.S.), and Harold W. Kroto (UK), for discovery of a new class of carbon molecule

1997   Paul D. Boyer (U.S.), Jens C. Skou (Denmark), and John E. Walker (UK), for discoveries about a molecule that allows the human body to store and transfer energy between cells

1998   Walter Kohn (U.S.) and John A. Pople (UK), for their developments in the study of the properties of molecules and the chemical processes in which they are involved

1999   Ahmed H. Zewail (Egypt and U.S.), for creating the world's fastest camera, which captures atoms in motion

2000   Alan J. Heeger, Alan G. MacDiarmid (both U.S.), and Hideki Shirakawa (Japan), for the discovery and development of conductive polymers

2001   William S. Knowles (U.S.) and Ryoji Noyori (Japan), for their work on chirally catalyzed hydrogenation reactions, and K. Barry Sharpless (U.S.), for his work on chirally catalyzed oxidation reactions

2002   John B. Fenn (U.S.) and Koichi Tanaka (Japan), for development of methods for analyses of biological macromolecules; Kurt Wüthrich (Switzerland), for determining the three-dimensional structure of biological macromolecules in solution

2003   Peter Agre and Roderick MacKinnon (both U.S.), for studies of channels in cell walls

PHYSIOLOGY OR MEDICINE

1901   Emil A. von Behring (Germany), for work on serum therapy against diphtheria

1902   Sir Ronald Ross (UK), for work on malaria

1903   Niels R. Finsen (Denmark), for his treatment of lupus vulgaris with concentrated light rays

1904   Ivan P. Pavlov (USSR), for work on the physiology of digestion

1905 Robert Koch (Germany), for work on tuberculosis

1906 Camillo Golgi (Italy) and Santiago Ramón y Cajal (Spain), for study of structure of the nervous system

1907 Charles L. A. Laveran (France), for work with protozoa in the generation of disease

1908 Paul Ehrlich (Germany) and Elie Metchnikoff (USSR), for work on immunity

1909 Theodor Kocher (Switzerland), for work on the thyroid gland

1910 Albrecht Kossel (Germany), for achievements in the chemistry of the cell

1911 Allvar Gullstrand (Sweden), for work on the dioptrics of the eye

1912 Alexis Carrel (France), for work on vascular ligature and grafting of blood vessels and organs

1913 Charles Richet (France), for work on anaphylaxy

1914 Robert Bárány (Austria), for work on physiology and pathology of the vestibular system

1919 Jules Bordet (Belgium), for discoveries in connection with immunity

1920 August Krogh (Denmark), for discovery of regulation of capillaries' motor mechanism

1922 In 1923, the 1922 prize was shared by Archibald V. Hill (UK), for discovery relating to heat-production in muscles, and Otto Meyerhof (Germany), for correlation between consumption of oxygen and production of lactic acid in muscles

1923 Sir Frederick Banting (Canada) and John J. R. Macleod (Scotland), for discovery of insulin

1924 Willem Einthoven (Netherlands), for discovery of the mechanism of the electrocardiogram

1926 Johannes Fibiger (Denmark), for discovery of the Spiroptera carcinoma

1927 Julius Wagner-Jauregg (Austria), for use of malaria inoculation in treatment of dementia paralytica

1928 Charles Nicolle (France), for work on typhus exanthematicus

1929 Christiaan Eijkman (Netherlands), for discovery of the antineuritic vitamins; Sir Frederick Hopkins (UK), for discovery of growth-promoting vitamins

1930 Karl Landsteiner (U.S.), for discovery of human blood groups

1931 Otto H. Warburg (Germany), for discovery of the character and mode of action of the respiratory ferment

1932 Sir Charles Sherrington (UK) and Edgar D. Adrian (U.S.), for discoveries of the function of the neuron

1933 Thomas H. Morgan (U.S.), for discoveries on hereditary function of the chromosomes

1934 George H. Whipple, George R. Minot, and William P. Murphy (all U.S.), for discovery of liver therapy against anemias

1935 Hans Spemann (Germany), for discovery of the organizer effect in embryonic development

1936 Sir Henry Dale (UK) and Otto Loewi (Germany), for discoveries on chemical transmission of nerve impulses

1937 Albert Szent-Györgyi von Nagyrapolt (Hungary), for discoveries on biological combustion

1938 Corneille Heymans (Belgium), for determining importance of sinus and aorta mechanisms in the regulation of respiration

1939 Gerhard Domagk (Germany), for antibacterial effect of prontocilate

1943 Henrik Dam (Denmark) and Edward A. Doisy (U.S.), for analysis of vitamin K

1944 Joseph Erlanger and Herbert Spencer Gasser (both U.S.), for work on functions of the nerve threads

1945 Sir Alexander Fleming, Ernst Boris Chain, and Sir Howard Florey (all UK), for discovery of penicillin

1946 Herman J. Muller (U.S.), for hereditary effects of X-rays on genes

1947 Carl F. and Gerty T. Cori (U.S.), for work on animal starch metabolism; Bernardo A. Houssay (Argentina), for study of the pituitary lobe

1948 Paul Mueller (Switzerland), for discovery of insect-killing properties of DDT

1949 Walter Rudolf Hess (Switzerland), for research on brain control of body; Antonio Caetano de Abreu Freire Egas Moniz (Portugal), for development of brain operation

1950 Philip S. Hench, Edward C. Kendall (both U.S.), and Tadeus Reichstein (Switzerland), for discoveries about hormones of adrenal cortex

1951 Max Theiler (South Africa), for development of vaccine against yellow fever

1952 Selman A. Waksman (U.S.), for discovery of streptomycin

1953 Fritz A. Lipmann (Germany, U.S.) and Hans Adolph Krebs (Germany, UK), for studies of living cells

1954 John F. Enders, Thomas H. Weller, and Frederick C. Robbins (all U.S.), for work with cultivation of polio virus

1955 Hugo Theorell (Sweden), for work on oxidation enzymes

1956 Dickinson W. Richards, Jr., André F. Cournand (both U.S.), and Werner Forssmann (West Germany), for new techniques in treating heart disease

1957 Daniel Bovet (Italy), for development of drugs to relieve allergies and relax muscles during surgery

1958 Joshua Lederberg (U.S.), for work with genetic mechanisms; George W. Beadle and Edward L. Tatum (both U.S.), for discovering how genes transmit hereditary characteristics

1959 Severo Ochoa and Arthur Kornberg (both U.S.), for discoveries related to compounds within chromosomes that play a vital role in heredity

1960 Sir Macfarlane Burnet (Australia) and Peter Brian Medawar (UK), for discovery of acquired immunological tolerance

1961 Georg von Bekesy (U.S.), for discoveries about physical mechanisms of stimulation within cochlea

1962 James D. Watson (U.S.), Maurice H. F. Wilkins, and Francis H. C. Crick (both UK), for determining structure of deoxyribonucleic acid (DNA)

1963 Alan Lloyd Hodgkin, Andrew Fielding Huxley (both UK), and Sir John Carew Eccles (Australia), for research on nerve cells

1964 Konrad E. Bloch (U.S.) and Feodor Lynen (West Germany), for research on mechanism and regulation of cholesterol and fatty-acid metabolism

1965 François Jacob, André Lwoff, and Jacques Monod (all France), for study of regulatory activities in body cells

1966 Charles Brenton Huggins (U.S.), for studies in hormone treatment of cancer of prostate; Francis Peyton Rous (U.S.), for discovery of tumor-producing viruses

1967 Haldan K. Hartline, George Wald (both U.S.), and Ragnar Granit (Sweden), for work on human eye

1968 Robert W. Holley, Har Gobind Khorana, and Marshall W. Nirenberg (all U.S.), for studies of genetic code

1969 Max Delbruck, Alfred D. Hershey, and Salvador E. Luria (all U.S.), for study of mechanism of virus infection in living cells

1970 Julius Axelrod (U.S.), Ulf S. von Euler (Sweden), and Sir Bernard Katz (UK), for studies of how nerve impulses are transmitted within the body

1971 Earl W. Sutherland, Jr. (U.S.), for research on how hormones work

1972 Gerald M. Edelman (U.S.), and Rodney R. Porter (UK), for research on the chemical structure and nature of antibodies

1973 Karl von Frisch, Konrad Lorenz (both Austria), and Nikolaas Tinbergen (Netherlands), for their studies of individual and social behavior patterns

1974 George E. Palade, Christian de Duve (both U.S.), and Albert Claude (Belgium), for contributions to understanding inner workings of living cells

1975 David Baltimore, Howard M. Temin, and Renato Dulbecco (all U.S.), for work in interaction between tumor viruses and genetic material of the cell

1976 Baruch S. Blumberg and D. Carleton Gajdusek (both U.S.), for discoveries concerning new mechanisms for the origin and dissemination of infectious diseases

1977 Rosalyn S. Yalow, Roger C. L. Guillemin, and Andrew V. Schally (all U.S.), for research in role of hormones in chemistry of the body

1978 Daniel Nathans, Hamilton Smith (both U.S.), and Werner Arber (Switzerland), for discovery of restriction enzymes and their application to problems of molecular genetics

1979 Allan McLeod Cormack (U.S.) and Godfrey Newbold Hounsfield (UK), for developing computed axial tomography (CAT scan) X-ray technique

1980 Baruj Benacerraf, George D. Snell (both U.S.), and Jean Dausset (France), for discoveries that explain how the structure of cells relates to organ transplants and diseases

1981 Roger W. Sperry, David H. Hubel (both U.S.), and Torsten N. Wiesel (Sweden), for studies vital to understanding the organization and functioning of the brain

1982 Sune Bergstrom, Bengt Samuelsson (both Sweden), and John R. Vane (UK), for research in prostaglandins, hormonelike substances involved in a wide range of illnesses

1983 Barbara McClintock (U.S.), for her discovery of mobile genes in the chromosomes of a plant that change the future generations of plants they produce

1984 Cesar Milstein (UK/Argentina), Georges J. F. Kohler (West Germany), and Niels K. Jerne (UK/Denmark), for their work in immunology

1985 Michael S. Brown and Joseph L. Goldstein (both U.S.), for their work, which has drastically widened our understanding of the cholesterol metabolism and increased our possibilities to prevent and treat atherosclerosis and heart attacks

1986 Rita Levi-Montalcini (dual U.S., Italy) and Stanley Cohen (U.S.), for their contributions to the understanding of substances that influence cell growth

1987 Susumu Tonegawa (Japan), for his discoveries of how the body can suddenly marshal its immunological defenses against millions of different disease agents that it has never encountered before

1988 Gertrude B. Elion, George H. Hitchings (both U.S.), and Sir James Black (UK), for their discoveries of important principles for drug treatment

1989 J. Michael Bishop and Harold E. Varmus (both U.S.), for their unifying theory of cancer development

1990 Joseph E. Murray and E. Donnall Thomas (both U.S.), for their pioneering work in transplants

1991 Erwin Neher and Bert Sakmann (both Germany), for their research, particularly for the development of a technique called patch clamp

1992 Edmond H. Fischer and Edwin G. Krebs (both U.S.), for their discovery of a regulatory mechanism affecting almost all cells

1993 Phillip A. Sharp (U.S.) and Richard J. Roberts (UK), for their independent discovery in 1977 of "split genes"

1994 Alfred G. Gilman and Martin Rodbell (both U.S.), for discovery of G-proteins that help cells respond to outside signals

1995 Edward B. Lewis, Eric F. Wieschaus (both U.S.), and Christiane Nüsslein-Volhard (Germany), for studies of the fruit fly that will help explain congenital malformations in humans

1996 Peter C. Doherty (Australia) and Rolf M. Zinkernagel (Switzerland), for discoveries about how the immune system recognizes virus-infected cells

1997 Stanley B. Prusiner (U.S.), for discovery of a new type of germ, called prions, that causes degenerative brain disorders

1998 Robert F. Furchgott, Louis J. Ignarro, and Ferid Murad (all U.S.), for discovering that nitric oxide acts as a signal in the cardiovascular system

1999 Günter Blobel (U.S.), for discovering that proteins have intrinsic signals that govern their transport and localization in the cell

2000 Arvid Carlsson (Sweden), Paul Greengard, and Eric R. Kandel (both U.S.), for discoveries concerning signal transduction in the nervous system

2001 Leland H. Hartwell (U.S.), R. Timothy Hunt, and Paul M. Nurse (both UK), for discoveries concerning control of the cell cycle, which may make new cancer treatments possible

2002 Sydney Brenner (UK), H. Robert Horvitz (U.S.), and John E. Sulston (UK), for discoveries concerning genetic regulation of organ development and programmed cell death

2003 Paul C. Lauterbur (U.S.) and Sir Peter Mansfield (UK), for discoveries concerning magnetic resonance imaging (MRI)

ECONOMIC SCIENCE

1969 Ragnar Frisch (Norway) and Jan Tinbergen (Netherlands), for work in econometrics (application of mathematics and statistical methods to economic theories and problems)

1970 Paul A. Samuelson (U.S.), for efforts to raise the level of scientific analysis in economic theory

1971 Simon Kuznets (U.S.), for developing concept of using a country's gross national product to determine its economic growth

1972 Kenneth J. Arrow (U.S.) and Sir John R. Hicks (UK), for theories that help to assess business risk and government economic and welfare policies

1973 Wassily Leontief (U.S.), for devising the input-output technique to determine how different sectors of an economy interact

1974 Gunnar Myrdal (Sweden) and Friedrich A. von Hayek (UK), for pioneering analysis of the interdependence of economic, social, and institutional phenomena

1975 Leonid V. Kantorovich (USSR) and Tjalling C. Koopmans (U.S.), for work on the theory of optimum allocation of resources

1976 Milton Friedman (U.S.), for work in consumption analysis and monetary history and theory, and for demonstration of complexity of stabilization policy

1977 Bertil Ohlin (Sweden) and James E. Meade (UK), for contributions to theory of international trade and international capital movements

1978 Herbert A. Simon (U.S.), for research into the decision-making process within economic organizations

1979 Sir Arthur Lewis (UK) and Theodore Schultz (U.S.), for work on economic problems of developing nations

1980 Lawrence R. Klein (U.S.), for developing models for forecasting economic trends and shaping policies to deal with them

1981 James Tobin (U.S.), for analyses of financial markets and their influence on spending and saving by families and businesses

1982 George J. Stigler (U.S.), for work on government regulation in the economy and the functioning of industry

1983 Gerard Debreu (U.S.), in recognition of his work on the basic economic problem of how prices operate to balance what producers supply with what buyers want

1984 Sir Richard Stone (UK), for his work to develop the systems widely used to measure the performance of national economics

1985 Franco Modigliani (U.S.), for his pioneering work in analyzing the behavior of household savers and the functioning of financial markets

1986 James M. Buchanan (U.S.), for his development of new methods for analyzing economic and political decision-making

1987 Robert M. Solow (U.S.), for seminal contributions to the theory of economic growth

1988 Maurice Allais (France), for his pioneering development of theories to better understand market behavior and the efficient use of resources

1989 Trygve Haavelmo (Norway), for his pioneering work in methods for testing economic theories

1990 Harry M. Markowitz, William F. Sharpe, and Merton H. Miller (all U.S.), whose work provided new tools for weighing the risks and rewards of different investments and for valuing corporate stocks and bonds

1991 Ronald Coase (U.S.), for his pioneering work in how property rights and the cost of doing business affect the economy

1992 Gary S. Becker (U.S.), for "having extended the domain of economic theory to aspects of human behavior which had previously been dealt with—if at all—by other social science disciplines"

1993 Robert W. Fogel and Douglass C. North (both U.S.), for their work in economic history

1994 John F. Nash, John C. Harsanyi (both U.S.), and Reinhard Selten (Germany), for their pioneering work in game theory

1995 Robert E. Lucas, Jr. (U.S.), for having had the greatest influence on macroeconomic research since 1970

1996 James A. Mirrlees (UK) and William Vickrey (U.S.), for their fundamental contributions to the economic theory of incentives

1997 Robert C. Merton and Myron S. Scholes (both U.S.), for developing a formula that determines the value of stock options and other derivatives

1998 Amartya Sen (India), for his contributions to welfare economics

1999 Robert A. Mundell (Canada), for his work on monetary dynamics and optimum currency areas

2000 James J. Heckman and Daniel L. McFadden (both U.S.), for developing methods used in statistical analysis of individual and household behavior

2001 George A. Akerlof, A. Michael Spence, and Joseph E. Stiglitz (all U.S.), for market analyses with asymmetric information

2002 Daniel Kahneman (U.S.), for having integrated insights from psychological research into economic science; Vernon L. Smith (U.S.), for having established laboratory experiments as a tool in empirical economic analysis

2003 Robert F. Engle (U.S.) and Clive W. J. Granger (UK), for developing statistical tools to improve analysis of stock prices and other data

Pulitzer Prizes

(For years not listed, no award was made.)

PULITZER PRIZES IN JOURNALISM

Meritorious Public Service

1918 *New York Times;* also special award to Minna Lewinson and Henry Beetle Hough
1919 *Milwaukee Journal*
1921 *Boston Post*
1922 *New York World*
1923 *Memphis Commercial Appeal*
1924 *New York World*
1926 Columbus (Ga.) *Enquirer Sun*
1927 Canton (Ohio) *Daily News*
1928 *Indianapolis Times*
1929 *New York Evening World*
1931 *Atlanta Constitution*
1932 *Indianapolis News*
1933 *New York World-Telegram*
1934 Medford (Ore.) *Mail Tribune*
1935 *Sacramento Bee*
1936 Cedar Rapids (Iowa) *Gazette*
1937 *St. Louis Post-Dispatch*
1938 Bismarck (N.D.) *Tribune*
1939 *Miami Daily News*
1940 Waterbury (Conn.) *Republican and American*
1941 *St. Louis Post-Dispatch*
1942 *Los Angeles Times*
1943 *Omaha World-Herald*
1944 *New York Times*
1945 *Detroit Free Press*
1946 Scranton (Pa.) *Times*
1947 *Baltimore Sun*
1948 *St. Louis Post-Dispatch*
1949 (Lincoln) *Nebraska State Journal*
1950 *Chicago Daily News* and *St. Louis Post-Dispatch*
1951 *Miami Herald* and *Brooklyn Eagle*
1952 *St. Louis Post-Dispatch*
1953 Whiteville (N.C.) *News Reporter* and Tabor City (N.C.) *Tribune*
1954 Newsday (Garden City, N.Y.)
1955 Columbus (Ga.) *Ledger* and *Sunday Ledger-Enquirer*
1956 Watsonville (Calif.) *Register-Pajaronian*
1957 *Chicago Daily News*
1958 (Little Rock) *Arkansas Gazette*
1959 Utica (N.Y.) *Observer Dispatch* and *Utica Daily Press*
1960 *Los Angeles Times*
1961 Amarillo (Tex.) *Globe-Times*
1962 Panama City (Fla.) *News-Herald*
1963 *Chicago Daily News*
1964 St. Petersburg (Fla.) *Times*
1965 Hutchinson (Kans.) *News*
1966 *Boston Globe*
1967 *Louisville Courier-Journal* and *Milwaukee Journal*
1968 Riverside (Calif.) *Press-Enterprise*
1969 *Los Angeles Times*
1970 Newsday (Garden City, N.Y.)
1971 Winston-Salem (N.C.) *Journal and Sentinel*
1972 *New York Times*
1973 *Washington Post*
1974 Newsday (Garden City, N.Y.)
1975 *Boston Globe*
1976 Anchorage (Alaska) *Daily News*
1977 Lufkin (Tex.) *News*
1978 *Philadelphia Inquirer*

1979 Point Reyes (Calif.) *Light*
1980 Gannett News Service
1981 Charlotte (N.C.) *Observer*
1982 *Detroit News*
1983 Jackson (Miss.) *Clarion-Ledger*
1984 *Los Angeles Times*
1985 *Fort Worth Star-Telegram*
1986 *Denver Post*
1987 *Pittsburgh Press,* for reporting by Andrew Schneider and Matthew Brelis
1988 Charlotte (N.C.) *Observer*
1989 *Anchorage Daily News*
1990 *Philadelphia Inquirer* and *Washington* (N.C.) *Daily News*
1991 *Des Moines Register,* for reporting by Jane Schorer
1992 *Sacramento Bee* for "The Sierra in Peril" series by Tom Knudson
1993 *Miami Herald*
1994 Akron (Ohio) *Beacon Journal*
1995 *Virgin Islands Daily News*
1996 *News and Observer* (Raleigh, N.C.)
1997 *Times-Picayune* (New Orleans, La.)
1998 Grand Forks (N.D.) *Herald*
1999 *Washington Post*
2000 *Washington Post*
2001 *Oregonian*
2002 *New York Times*
2003 *Boston Globe*
2004 *New York Times*

Editorial

1917 *New York Tribune*
1918 *Louisville Courier-Journal*
1920 Harvey E. Newbranch *(Omaha Evening World-Herald)*
1922 Frank M. O'Brien *(New York Herald)*
1923 William Allen White *(Emporia* [Kan.] *Gazette)*
1924 *Boston Herald;* special prize: Frank I. Cobb *(New York World)*
1925 Charleston (S.C.) *News and Courier*
1926 Edward M. Kingsbury *(New York Times)*
1927 F. Lauriston Bullard *(Boston Herald)*
1928 Grover Cleveland Hall *(Montgomery* [Ala.] *Advertiser)*
1929 Louis Isaac Jaffe *(Norfolk Virginian-Pilot)*
1931 Charles S. Ryckman *(Fremont* [Neb.] *Tribune)*
1933 Kansas City (Mo.) *Star*
1934 E. P. Chase *(Atlantic* [Iowa] *News Telegraph)*
1936 Felix Morley *(Washington Post);* George B. Parker (Scripps-Howard Newspapers)
1937 John W. Owens *(Baltimore Sun)*
1938 W. W. Waymack *(Des Moines Register and Tribune)*
1939 Ronald G. Callvert *(Portland Oregonian)*
1940 Bart Howard *(St. Louis Post-Dispatch)*
1941 Reuben Maury *(New York Daily News)*
1942 Geoffrey Parsons *(New York Herald Tribune)*
1943 Forrest W. Seymour *(Des Moines Register and Tribune)*
1944 Henry J. Haskell *(Kansas City* [Mo.] *Star)*
1945 George W. Potter *(Providence* [R.I.] *Journal-Bulletin)*
1946 Hodding Carter *(Delta Democrat-Times* [Greenville, Miss.])
1947 William H. Grimes *(Wall Street Journal)*
1948 Virginius Dabney *(Richmond Times-Dispatch)*

1949 John H. Crider (Boston Herald); Herbert Elliston (Washington Post)
1950 Carl M. Saunders (Jackson [Mich.] Citizen Patriot)
1951 William H. Fitzpatrick (New Orleans States)
1952 Louis LaCoss (St. Louis Globe-Democrat)
1953 Vermont C. Royster (Wall Street Journal)
1954 Don Murray (Boston Herald)
1955 Royce Howes (Detroit Free Press)
1956 Lauren K. Soth (Des Moines Register and Tribune)
1957 Buford Boone (Tuscaloosa [Ala.] News)
1958 Harry S. Ashmore (Arkansas Gazette)
1959 Ralph McGill (Atlanta Constitution)
1960 Lenoir Chambers (Virginian-Pilot)
1961 William J. Dorvillier (San Juan [P.R.] Star)
1962 Thomas M. Storke (Santa Barbara [Calif.] News-Press)
1963 Ira B. Harkey, Jr. (Pascagoula [Miss.] Chronicle)
1964 Hazel Brannon Smith (Lexington [Miss.] Advertiser)
1965 John R. Harrison (Gainesville [Fla.] Daily Sun)
1966 Robert Lasch (St. Louis Post-Dispatch)
1967 Eugene Patterson (Atlanta Constitution)
1968 John S. Knight (Knight Newspapers)
1969 Paul Greenberg (Pine Bluff [Ark.] Commercial)
1970 Phillip L. Geyelin (Washington Post)
1971 Horance G. Davis, Jr. (Gainesville [Fla.] Sun)
1972 John Strohmeyer (Bethlehem [Pa.] Globe Times)
1973 Roger Bourne Linscott (Berkshire Eagle [Pittsfield, Mass.])
1974 F. Gilman Spencer (Trenton [N.J.] Trentonian)
1975 John Daniell Maurice (Charleston [W. Va.] Daily Mail)
1976 Philip P. Kerby (Los Angeles Times)
1977 Warren L. Lerude, Foster Church, and Norman F. Cardoza (Reno [Nev.] Gazette and Nevada State Journal)
1978 Meg Greenfield (Washington Post)
1979 Edwin M. Yoder, Jr. (Washington Star)
1980 Robert L. Bartley (Wall Street Journal)
1982 Jack Rosenthal (New York Times)
1983 Editorial Board, Miami Herald
1984 Albert Scardino (Georgia Gazette)
1985 Richard Aregood (Philadelphia Daily News)
1986 Jack Fuller (Chicago Tribune)
1987 Jonathan Freedman (San Diego Tribune)
1988 Jane E. Healy (Orlando Sentinel)
1989 Lois Wille (Chicago Tribune)
1990 Thomas J. Hylton (Pottstown [Pa.] Mercury)
1991 Ron Casey, Harold Jackson, and Joey Kennedy (Birmingham [Ala.] News)
1992 Maria Henson (Lexington [Ky.] Herald-Leader)
1994 R. Bruce Dold (Chicago Tribune)
1995 Jeffrey Good (St. Petersburg [Fla.] Times)
1996 Robert B. Semple, Jr. (New York Times)
1997 Michael Gartner (Daily Tribune [Ames, Iowa])
1998 Bernard L. Stein (The Riverdale Press [Bronx, N.Y.])
1999 Editorial Board (Daily News [New York, N.Y.])
2000 John C. Bersia (The Orlando Sentinel [Orlando, Fla.])
2001 David Moats (Rutland Herald [Rutland, Vt.])
2002 Alex Raksin and Bob Sipchen (Los Angeles Times)
2003 Cornelia Grumman (Chicago Tribune)
2004 William Stall (Los Angeles Times)

Correspondence

1929 Paul Scott Mowrer (Chicago Daily News)
1930 Leland Stowe (New York Herald Tribune)
1931 H. R. Knickerbocker (Philadelphia Public Ledger and New York Evening Post)
1932 Walter Duranty (New York Times); Charles G. Ross (St. Louis Post-Dispatch)
1933 Edgar Ansel Mowrer (Chicago Daily News)
1934 Frederick T. Birchall (New York Times)
1935 Arthur Krock (New York Times)
1936 Wilfred C. Barber (Chicago Tribune)
1937 Anne O'Hare McCormick (New York Times)
1938 Arthur Krock (New York Times)
1939 Louis P. Lochner (Associated Press)
1940 Otto D. Tolischus (New York Times)
1941 Group award[1]
1942 Carlos P. Romulo (Philippines Herald)
1943 Hanson W. Baldwin (New York Times)
1944 Ernie Pyle (Scripps-Howard Newspaper Alliance)
1945 Harold V. (Hal) Boyle (Associated Press)
1946 Arnaldo Cortesi (New York Times)
1947 Brooks Atkinson (New York Times)

1. For the public services and the individual achievements of American news reporters in the war zones.

Editorial Cartooning

1922 Rollin Kirby (New York World)
1924 Jay Norwood Darling (New York Tribune)
1925 Rollin Kirby (New York World)
1926 D. R. Fitzpatrick (St. Louis Post-Dispatch)
1927 Nelson Harding (Brooklyn Eagle)
1928 Nelson Harding (Brooklyn Eagle)
1929 Rollin Kirby (New York World)
1930 Charles R. Macauley (Brooklyn Eagle)
1931 Edmund Duffy (Baltimore Sun)
1932 John T. McCutcheon (Chicago Tribune)
1933 H. M. Talburt (Washington Daily News)
1934 Edmund Duffy (Baltimore Sun)
1935 Ross A. Lewis (Milwaukee Journal)
1937 C. D. Batchelor (New York Daily News)
1938 Vaughn Shoemaker (Chicago Daily News)
1939 Charles G. Werner (Daily Oklahoman [Oklahoma City])
1940 Edmund Duffy (Baltimore Sun)
1941 Jacob Burck (Chicago Times)
1942 Herbert L. Block (NEA Service)
1943 Jay Norwood Darling (New York Herald Tribune)
1944 Clifford K. Berryman (Washington Evening Star)
1945 Bill Mauldin (United Features Syndicate)
1946 Bruce Alexander Russell (Los Angeles Times)
1947 Vaughn Shoemaker (Chicago Daily News)
1948 Reuben L. Goldberg (New York Sun)
1949 Lute Pease (Newark Evening News)
1950 James T. Berryman (Washington Evening Star)
1951 Reg (Reginald W.) Manning (Arizona Republic [Phoenix])
1952 Fred L. Packer (New York Mirror)
1953 Edward D. Kuekes (Cleveland Plain Dealer)
1954 Herbert L. Block (Washington Post and Times-Herald)
1955 Daniel R. Fitzpatrick (St. Louis Post-Dispatch)
1956 Robert York (Louisville Times)
1957 Tom Little (Nashville Tennessean)
1958 Bruce M. Shanks (Buffalo Evening News)
1959 Bill Mauldin (St. Louis Post-Dispatch)
1961 Carey Orr (Chicago Tribune)
1962 Edmund S. Valtman (Hartford Times)

1963 Frank Miller (*Des Moines Register*)
1964 Paul Conrad (formerly of *Denver Post,* later of *Los Angeles Times*)
1966 Don Wright (*Miami News*)
1967 Patrick B. Oliphant (*Denver Post*)
1968 Eugene Gray Payne (*Charlotte* [N.C.] *Observer*)
1969 John Fischetti (*Chicago Daily News*)
1970 Thomas F. Darcy (*Newsday* [Garden City, N.Y.])
1971 Paul Conrad (*Los Angeles Times*)
1972 Jeffrey K. MacNelly (*Richmond* [Va.] *News Leader*)
1974 Paul Szep (*Boston Globe*)
1975 Garry Trudeau (Universal Press Syndicate)
1976 Tony Auth (*Philadelphia Inquirer*)
1977 Paul Szep (*Boston Globe*)
1978 Jeffrey K. MacNelly (*Richmond* [Va.] *News Leader*)
1979 Herbert L. Block (*Washington Post*)
1980 Don Wright (*Miami News*)
1981 Mike Peters (*Dayton* [Ohio] *Daily News*)
1982 Ben Sargent (*Austin* [Tex.] *American-Statesman*)
1983 Richard Locher (*Chicago Tribune*)
1984 Paul Conrad (*Los Angeles Times*)
1985 Jeff MacNelly (*Chicago Tribune*)
1986 Jules Feiffer (*Village Voice*)
1987 Berke Breathed (*Washington Post* Writers Group)
1988 Doug Marlette (*Atlanta Constitution* and *Charlotte* [N.C.] *Observer*)
1989 Jack Higgins (*Chicago Sun-Times*)
1990 Tom Toles (*Buffalo News*)
1991 Jim Borgman (*Cincinnati Inquirer*)
1992 Signe Wilkinson (*Philadelphia Daily News*)
1993 Stephen R. Benson (*Arizona Republic*)
1994 Michael P. Ramirez (*Commercial Appeal,* Memphis)
1995 Mike Luckovich (*Atlanta Constitution*)
1996 Jim Morin (*Miami Herald*)
1997 Walt Handelsman (*Times-Picayune*)
1998 Stephen P. Breen (*Asbury Park* [N.J.] *Press*)
1999 David Horsey (*Seattle Post-Intelligencer*)
2000 Joel Pett (*Lexington* [Ky.] *Herald-Leader*)
2001 Ann Telnaes (*Los Angeles Times* Syndicate)
2002 Clay Bennett (*Christian Science Monitor*)
2003 David Horsey (*Seattle Post-Intelligencer*)
2004 Matt Davies (*The Journal News* [White Plains, N.Y.])

News Photography

1942 Milton Brooks (*Detroit News*)
1943 Frank Noel (Associated Press)
1944 Frank Filan (Associated Press); Earle L. Bunker (*Omaha World-Herald*)
1945 Joe Rosenthal (Associated Press)
1947 Arnold Hardy
1948 Frank Cushing (*Boston Traveler*)
1949 Nat Fein (*New York Herald Tribune*)
1950 Bill Crouch (*Oakland Tribune*)
1951 Max Desfor (Associated Press)
1952 John Robinson and Don Ultang (*Des Moines Register and Tribune*)
1953 William M. Gallagher (*Flint* [Mich.] *Journal*)
1954 Mrs. Walter M. Schau
1955 John L. Gaunt, Jr. (*Los Angeles Times*)
1956 *New York Daily News*
1957 Harry A. Trask (*Boston Traveler*)
1958 William C. Beall (*Washington Daily News*)
1959 William Seaman (*Minneapolis Star*)

1960 Andrew Lopez (United Press International)
1961 Yasushi Nagao (Mainichi Newspapers, Tokyo)
1962 Paul Vathis (Harrisburg [Pa.] bureau of Associated Press)
1963 Hector Rondon (*La Republica,* Caracas, Venezuela)
1964 Robert H. Jackson (*Dallas Times Herald*)
1965 Horst Faas (Associated Press)
1966 Kyoichi Sawada (United Press International)
1967 Jack R. Thornell (Associated Press)
1968 News: Rocco Morabito (*Jacksonville* [Fla.] *Journal*); features: Toshio Sakai (United Press International)
1969 Spot news: Edward T. Adams (Associated Press); features: Moneta Sleet, Jr.
1970 Spot news: Steve Starr (Associated Press); features: Dallas Kinney (*Palm Beach Post*)
1971 Spot news: John Paul Filo (*Valley Daily News* and *Daily Dispatch* [Tarentum and New Kensington, Pa.]); features: Jack Dykinga (*Chicago Sun-Times*)
1972 Spot news: Horst Faas and Michel Laurent (Associated Press); features: Dave Kennerly (United Press International)
1973 Spot news: Huynh Cong Ut (*Associated Press*); features: Brian Lanker (*Topeka Capital-Journal*)
1974 Spot news: Anthony K. Roberts (Associated Press); features: Slava Veder (Associated Press)
1975 Spot news: Gerald H. Gay (*Seattle Times*); features: Matthew Lewis (*Washington Post*)
1976 Spot news: Stanley J. Forman (*Boston Herald-American*); features: staff of *Louisville Courier-Journal* and *Times*
1977 Spot news: Neal Ulevich (Associated Press) and Stanley J. Forman (*Boston Herald-American*); features: Robin Hood (*Chattanooga News-Free Press*)
1978 Spot news: John Blair, freelance, Evansville, Ind.; features: J. Ross Baughman (Associated Press)
1979 Spot news: Thomas J. Kelly, 3rd (*Pottstown* [Pa.] *Mercury*); features: staff of *Boston Herald-American*
1980 Features: Erwin H. Hagler (*Dallas Times Herald*)
1981 Spot news: Larry C. Price (*Fort Worth Star-Telegram*); features: Taro M. Yamasaki (*Detroit Free Press*)
1982 Spot news: Ron Edmonds (Associated Press); features: John H. White (*Chicago Sun-Times*)
1983 Spot news: Bill Foley (Associated Press); features: James B. Dickman (*Dallas Times Herald*)
1984 Spot news: Stan Grossfeld (*Boston Globe*); features: Anthony Suau (*Denver Post*)
1985 Spot news: staff of *Register,* Santa Ana, Calif.; features: Stan Grossfeld (*Boston Globe*)
1986 Spot news: Michel duCille and Carol Guzy (*Miami Herald*); features: Tom Gralish (*Philadelphia Inquirer*)
1987 Spot news: Kim Komenich (*San Francisco Examiner*); features: David Peterson (*Des Moines Register*)
1988 Spot news: Scott Shaw (*Odessa* [Texas] *American*); features: Michel duCille (*Miami Herald*)

1989 Spot news: Ron Olshwanger *(St. Louis Post-Dispatch)*; features: Manny Crisostomo *(Detroit Free Press)*

1990 Spot news: *Oakland Tribune;* features: David C. Turnley *(Detroit Free Press)*

1991 Spot news: Greg Marinovich (Associated Press); features: William Snyder *(Dallas Morning News)*

1992 Spot news: Associated Press staff; features: John Kaplan *(Herald* [Monterey, Calif.] and *Pittsburgh Post-Gazette)*

1993 Spot news: William Snyder and Ken Geiger *(Dallas Morning News)*; features: Associated Press

1994 Spot news: Paul Watson *(Toronto Star)*; features: Kevin Carter, freelancer for *New York Times*

1995 Spot news: Carol Guzy *(Washington Post)*; features: Associated Press staff

1996 Spot news: Charles Porter IV, freelancer for Associated Press; features: Stephanie Walsh, freelancer for Newhouse News Service

1997 Spot news: Annie Wells *(Press Democrat* [Santa Rosa, Calif.]); features: Alexander Zemlianichenko (Associated Press)

1998 Spot news: Martha Rial *(Pittsburgh Post-Gazette)*; features: Clarence Williams *(Los Angeles Times)*

1999 Spot news: Associated Press photo staff; features: Associated Press photo staff

2000 Breaking news: photographic staff of *Denver Rocky Mountain News*; features: Carol Guzy, Michael Williamson, and Lucian Perkins *(Washington Post)*

2001 Breaking news: Alan Diaz (Associated Press); features: Matt Rainey *(Star-Ledger* [Newark, N.J.])

2002 Breaking news: *New York Times* staff; features: *New York Times* staff

2003 Breaking news: *Rocky Mountain News* staff; features: Don Bartletti *(Los Angeles News)*

2004 Breaking news: David Leeson and Cheryl Diaz Meyer *(Dallas Morning News)*; features: Carolyn Cole *(Los Angeles Times)*

National Telegraphic Reporting

1942 Louis Stark *(New York Times)*

1944 Dewey L. Fleming *(Baltimore Sun)*

1945 James Reston *(New York Times)*

1946 Edward A. Harris *(St. Louis Post-Dispatch)*

1947 Edward T. Folliard *(Washington Post)*

National Reporting

1948 Bert Andrews *(New York Herald Tribune)*; Nat S. Finney *(Minneapolis Tribune)*

1949 C. P. Trussell *(New York Times)*

1950 Edwin O. Guthman *(Seattle Times)*

1952 Anthony Leviero *(New York Times)*

1953 Don Whitehead (Associated Press)

1954 Richard Wilson (Cowles Newspapers)

1955 Anthony Lewis *(Washington Daily News)*

1956 Charles L. Bartlett *(Chattanooga Times)*

1957 James Reston *(New York Times)*

1958 Relman Morin (Associated Press) and Clark Mollenhoff *(Des Moines Register and Tribune)*

1959 Howard Van Smith *(Miami News)*

1960 Vance Trimble (Scripps-Howard Newspaper Alliance)

1961 Edward R. Cony *(Wall Street Journal)*

1962 Nathan G. Caldwell and Gene S. Graham *(Nashville Tennessean)*

1963 Anthony Lewis *(New York Times)*

1964 Merriman Smith (United Press International)

1965 Louis M. Kohlmeier *(Wall Street Journal)*

1966 Haynes Johnson *(Washington Evening Star)*

1967 Stanley Penn and Monroe Karmin *(Wall Street Journal)*

1968 Howard James *(Christian Science Monitor)*; Nathan K. (Nick) Kotz *(Des Moines Register* and *Minneapolis Tribune)*

1969 Robert Cahn *(Christian Science Monitor)*

1970 William J. Eaton *(Chicago Daily News)*

1971 Lucinda Franks and Thomas Powers (United Press International)

1972 Jack Anderson *(United Feature Syndicate)*

1973 Robert Boyd and Clark Hoyt *(Knight Newspapers)*

1974 Jack White *(Providence* [R.I.] *Journal-Bulletin)*; James R. Polk *(Washington Star-News)*

1975 Donald L. Barlett and James B. Steele *(Philadelphia Inquirer)*

1976 James Risser *(Des Moines Register)*

1977 Walter Mears (Associated Press)

1978 Gaylord D. Shaw *(Los Angeles Times)*

1979 James Risser *(Des Moines Register)*

1980 Bette Swenson Orsini and Charles Stafford *(St. Petersburg Times)*

1981 John M. Crewdson *(New York Times)*

1982 Rick Atkinson *(Kansas City* [Mo.] *Times)*

1983 *Boston Globe*

1984 John N. Wilford *(New York Times)*

1985 Thomas J. Knudson *(Des Moines Register)*

1986 Craig Flournoy and George Rodrigue *(Dallas Morning News)* and Arthur Howe *(Philadelphia Inquirer)*

1987 *Miami Herald* staff; *New York Times* staff

1988 Tim Weiner *(Philadelphia Inquirer)*

1989 Donald L. Barlett and James B. Steele *(Philadelphia Inquirer)*

1990 Ross Anderson, Bill Dietrich, Mary Ann Gwinn, and Eric Nalder *(Seattle Times)*

1991 Marjie Lundstrom and Rochelle Sharpe (Gannett News Service)

1992 Jeff Taylor and Mike McGraw *(Kansas City Star)*

1993 David Maraniss *(Washington Post)*

1994 Eileen Welsome *(Albuquerque* [N.M.] *Tribune)*

1995 Tony Horwitz *(Wall Street Journal)*

1996 Alix M. Freedman *(Wall Street Journal)*

1997 *Wall Street Journal* staff

1998 Russell Carollo and Jeff Nesmith *(Dayton* [Ohio] *Daily News)*

1999 *New York Times* staff

2000 *Wall Street Journal* staff

2001 *New York Times* staff

2002 *Washington Post* staff

2003 Alan Miller and Kevin Sack *(Los Angeles Times)*

2004 *Los Angeles Times* staff

International Telegraphic Reporting

1942 Laurence Edmund Allen (Associated Press)

1943 Ira Wolfert (North American Newspaper Alliance, Inc.)

1944 Daniel De Luce (Associated Press)

1945 Mark S. Watson *(Baltimore Sun)*

1946 Homer W. Bigart *(New York Herald Tribune)*

1947 Eddy Gilmore (Associated Press)

International Reporting

1948   Paul W. Ward *(Baltimore Sun)*
1949   Price Day *(Baltimore Sun)*
1950   Edmund Stevens *(Christian Science Monitor)*
1951   Keyes Beech and Fred Sparks *(Chicago Daily News);* Homer Bigart and Marguerite Higgins *(New York Herald Tribune);* Relman Morin and Don Whitehead (Associated Press)
1952   John M. Hightower (Associated Press)
1953   Austin C. Wehrwein *(Milwaukee Journal)*
1954   Jim G. Lucas (Scripps-Howard Newspapers)
1955   Harrison E. Salisbury *(New York Times)*
1956   William Randolph Hearst, Jr., and Frank Conniff (Hearst Newspapers); Kingsbury Smith (INS)
1957   Russell Jones (United Press)
1958   *New York Times*
1959   Joseph Martin and Philip Santora *(New York Daily News)*
1960   A. M. Rosenthal *(New York Times)*
1961   Lynn Heinzerling (Associated Press)
1962   Walter Lippmann *(New York Herald Tribune Syndicate)*
1963   Hal Hendrix *(Miami News)*
1964   Malcolm W. Browne (Associated Press); David Halberstam *(New York Times)*
1965   J. A. Livingston *(Philadelphia Bulletin)*
1966   Peter Arnett (Associated Press)
1967   R. John Hughes *(Christian Science Monitor)*
1968   Alfred Friendly *(Washington Post)*
1969   William Tuohy *(Los Angeles Times)*
1970   Seymour M. Hersh (Dispatch News Service)
1971   Jimmie Lee Hoagland *(Washington Post)*
1972   Peter R. Kann *(Wall Street Journal)*
1973   Max Frankel *(New York Times)*
1974   Hedrick Smith *(New York Times)*
1975   William Mullen and Ovie Carter *(Chicago Tribune)*
1976   Sydney H. Schanberg *(New York Times)*
1978   Henry Kamm *(New York Times)*
1979   Richard Ben Cramer *(Philadelphia Inquirer)*
1980   Joel Brinkley and Jay Mather *(Louisville Courier-Journal)*
1981   Shirley Christian *(Miami Herald)*
1982   John Darnton *(New York Times)*
1983   Thomas L. Friedman *(New York Times)*
1984   Karen E. House *(Wall Street Journal)*
1985   Josh Friedman, Dennis Bell, and Ozier Muhammad *(Newsday)*
1986   Lewis M. Simons, Pete Carey, and Katherine Ellison *(San Jose Mercury News)*
1987   Michael Parks *(Los Angeles Times)*
1988   Thomas L. Friedman *(New York Times)*
1989   Bill Keller *(New York Times);* Glenn Frankel *(Washington Post)*
1990   Nicholas D. Kristof and Sheryl WuDunn *(New York Times)*
1991   Caryle Murphy *(Washington Post);* Serge Schmemann *(New York Times)*
1992   Patrick J. Sloyan *(Newsday)*
1993   John F. Burns *(New York Times);* Roy Gutman *(Newsday)*
1994   *Dallas Morning News* team
1995   Mark Fritz (Associated Press)
1996   David Rohde *(Christian Science Monitor)*
1997   John F. Burns *(New York Times)*
1998   *New York Times* staff
1999   *Wall Street Journal* staff
2000   Mark Schoofs *(Village Voice)*

2001   Ian Johnson *(Wall Street Journal)* and Paul Salopek *(Chicago Tribune)*
2002   Barry Bearak *(New York Times)*
2003   Kevin Sullivan and Mary Jordan *(Washington Post)*
2004   Anthony Shadid *(Washington Post)*

Reporting

1917   Herbert B. Swope *(New York World)*
1918   Harold A. Littledale *(New York Evening Post)*
1920   John J. Leary, Jr. *(New York World)*
1921   Louis Seibold *(New York World)*
1922   Kirke L. Simpson (Associated Press)
1923   Alva Johnston *(New York Times)*
1924   Magner White *(San Diego Sun)*
1925   James W. Mulroy and Alvin H. Goldstein *(Chicago Daily News)*
1926   William Burke Miller *(Louisville Courier-Journal)*
1927   John T. Rogers *(St. Louis Post-Dispatch)*
1929   Paul Y. Anderson *(St. Louis Post-Dispatch)*
1930   Russell D. Owen *(New York Times);* special award: W. O. Dapping *(Auburn* [N.Y.] *Citizen)*
1931   A. B. MacDonald *(Kansas City* [Mo.] *Star)*
1932   W. C. Richards, D. D. Martin, J. S. Pooler, F. D. Webb, and J. N. W. Sloan *(Detroit Free Press)*
1933   Francis A. Jamieson (Associated Press)
1934   Royce Brier *(San Francisco Chronicle)*
1935   William H. Taylor *(New York Herald Tribune)*
1936   Lauren D. Lyman *(New York Times)*
1937   John J. O'Neill *(New York Herald Tribune);* William Leonard Laurence *(New York Times);* Howard W. Blakeslee (Associated Press); Gobind Behari Lal (Universal Service); David Dietz (Scripps-Howard Newspapers)
1938   Raymond Sprigle *(Pittsburg Post-Gazette)*
1939   Thomas L. Stokes *(New York World-Telegram)*
1940   S. Burton Heath *(New York World-Telegram)*
1941   Westbrook Pegler *(New York World-Telegram)*
1942   Stanton Delaplane *(San Francisco Chronicle)*
1943   George Weller *(Chicago Daily News)*
1944   Paul Schoenstein and associates *(New York Journal-American)*
1945   Jack S. McDowell *(San Francisco Call-Bulletin)*
1946   William Leonard Laurence *(New York Times)*
1947   Frederick Woltman *(New York World-Telegram)*
1948   George E. Goodwin *(Atlanta Journal)*
1949   Malcolm Johnson *(New York Sun)*
1950   Meyer Berger *(New York Times)*
1951   Edward S. Montgomery *(San Francisco Examiner)*
1952   George de Carvalho *(San Francisco Chronicle)*
1953   Editorial staff *(Providence Journal and Evening Bulletin);*[1] Edward J. Mowery *(New York World-Telegram and Sun)*[2]
1954   Editorial staff *Vicksburg* (Miss.) *Sunday Post-Herald;*[1] Alvin Scott McCoy *(Kansas City* [Mo.] *Star)*[2]
1955   Mrs. Caro Brown *(Alice* [Tex.] *Daily Echo);*[1] Roland Kenneth Towery *(Cuero* [Tex.] *Record)*[2]
1956   Lee Hills *(Detroit Free Press);*[1] Arthur Daley *(New York Times)*[2]
1957   *Salt Lake Tribune;*[1] Wallace Turner and William Lambert *(Portland Oregonian)*[2]

1958 Editorial staff *Fargo* [N.D.] *Forum;*[1] George Beveridge *(Washington* [D.C.] *Evening Star)*[2]

1959 Mary Lou Werner *(Washington* [DC] *Evening Star);*[1] John Harold Brislin *(Scranton* [Pa.] *Tribune & Scrantonian)*[2]

1960 Jack Nelson *(Atlanta Constitution);*[1] Miriam Ottenberg *(Washington* [DC] *Evening Star)*[2]

1961 Sanche de Gramont *(New York Herald Tribune);*[1] Edgar May *(Buffalo Evening News)*[2]

1962 Robert D. Mullins *(Deseret News* [Salt Lake City]);[1] George Bliss *(Chicago Tribune)*[2]

1963 Sylvan Fox, Anthony Shannon, and William Longgood *(New York World-Telegram and Sun);*[1] Oscar Griffin, Jr. (former editor of *Pecos* [Tex.] *Independent and Enterprise,* now on staff of *Houston Chronicle)*[2]

1. Reporting under pressure of edition deadlines.
2. Reporting not under pressure of edition deadlines.

General Local Reporting

1964 Norman C. Miller *(Wall Street Journal)*
1965 Melvin H. Ruder *(Hungry Horse News* [Columbia Falls, Mont.])
1966 *Los Angeles Times* staff
1967 Robert V. Cox *(Chambersburg* [Pa.] *Public Opinion)*
1968 *Detroit Free Press* staff
1969 John Fetterman *(Louisville Times and Courier-Journal)*
1970 Thomas Fitzpatrick *(Chicago Sun-Times)*
1971 *Akron* (Ohio) *Beacon* staff
1972 Richard Cooper and John Machacek *(Rochester* [N.Y.] *Times-Union)*
1973 *Chicago Tribune* staff
1974 Arthur M. Petacque and Hugh F. Hough *(Chicago Sun-Times)*
1975 *Xenia* (Ohio) *Daily Gazette* staff
1976 Gene Miller *(Miami Herald)*
1977 Margo Huston *(Milwaukee Journal)*
1978 Richard Whitt *(Louisville Courier-Journal)*
1979 *San Diego* (Calif.) *Evening Tribune* staff
1980 *Philadelphia Inquirer* staff
1981 *Longview* (Wash.) *Daily News* staff
1982 Staff of *Kansas City* (Mo.) *Star* and *Kansas City* (Mo.) *Times*
1983 *Fort Wayne* (Ind.) *News-Sentinel* staff
1984 *Newsday* staff

General News Reporting

1985 Thomas Turcol *(Virginian-Pilot and Ledger-Star)*
1986 Edna Buchanan *(Miami Herald)*
1987 *Akron Beacon Journal* staff
1988 *Alabama Journal* (Montgomery) staff; *Lawrence* (Mass.) *Eagle-Tribune* staff
1989 *Louisville Courier-Journal* staff
1990 *San Jose* (Calif.) *Mercury News* staff

Spot News Reporting

1991 *Miami Herald* staff
1992 *New York Newsday* staff
1993 *Los Angeles Times* staff
1994 *New York Times* staff
1995 *Los Angeles Times* staff
1996 Robert D. McFadden *(New York Times)*
1997 *Newsday* staff (Long Island, N.Y.)

Breaking News Reporting

1998 *Los Angeles Times* staff
1999 *Hartford Courant* staff

2000 *Denver Post* staff
2001 *The Miami Herald* staff
2002 *Wall Street Journal* staff
2003 *Eagle-Tribune* staff (Lawrence, Mass.)
2004 *Los Angeles Times* staff

Special Local Reporting

1964 James V. Magee, Albert V. Gaudiosi, and Frederick A. Meyer *(Philadelphia Bulletin)*
1965 Gene Goltz *(Houston Post)*
1966 John A. Frasca *(Tampa Tribune)*
1967 Gene Miller *(Miami Herald)*
1968 J. Anthony Lukas *(New York Times)*
1969 Albert L. Delugach and Denny Walsh *(St. Louis Globe-Democrat)*
1970 Harold Eugene Martin *(Montgomery Advertiser)*
1971 William Hugh Jones *(Chicago Tribune)*
1972 Timothy Leland, Gerard N. O'Neill, Stephen A. Kurkjian, and Ann DeSantis *(Boston Globe)*
1973 Sun Newspapers of Omaha, Neb.
1974 William Sherman *(New York Daily News)*
1975 *Indianapolis Star* staff
1976 *Chicago Tribune* staff
1977 Acel Moore and Wendell Rawls, Jr. *(Philadelphia Inquirer)*
1978 Anthony R. Dolan *(Stamford* [Conn.] *Advocate)*
1979 Gilbert M. Gaul and Elliot G. Jaspin *(Pottsville* [Pa.] *Republican)*
1980 Nils J. Bruzelius, Alexander B. Hawes, Jr., Stephen A. Kurkjian, Robert M. Porterfield, and Joan Vennochi *(Boston Globe)*
1981 Clark Hallas and Robert B. Lowe *(Arizona Daily Star,* Tucson)
1982 Paul Henderson *(Seattle Times)*
1983 Loretta Tofani *(Washington Post)*
1984 Kenneth Cooper, Joan FitzGerald, Jonathan Kaufman, Norman Lockman, Gary McMillan, Kirk Scharfenberg, and David Wessel *(Boston Globe)*

Investigative Reporting

1985 Lucy Morgan, Jack Reed *(St. Petersburg* [Fla.] *Times),* and William K. Marimow *(Philadelphia Inquirer)*
1986 Jeffrey A. Marx and Michael M. York *(Lexington* [Ky.] *Herald Leader)*
1987 Daniel R. Biddle, H. G. Bissinger, and Fredric N. Tulsky *(Philadelphia Inquirer)*
1988 Dean Baquet, William C. Gaines, and Ann Marie Lipinski *(Chicago Tribune)*
1989 Bill Dedman *(Atlanta Journal and Constitution)*
1990 Lou Kilzer and Chris Ison *(Minneapolis-St. Paul Star Tribune)*
1991 Joseph T. Hallinan and Susan M. Headden *(Indianapolis Star)*
1992 Lorraine Adams and Dan Malone *(Dallas Morning News)*
1993 Jeff Brazil and Steve Berry *(Orlando* [Fla.] *Sentinel)*
1994 *Providence* (R.I.) *Journal-Bulletin* staff
1995 Stephanie Saul and Brian Donovan *(Newsday)*
1996 *Orange County Register* staff (Santa Ana, Calif.)
1997 Eric Nalder, Deborah Nelson, and Alex Tizon *(Seattle Times)*
1998 Gary Cohn and Will Englund *(Baltimore Sun)*

1999 *Miami Herald* staff
2000 Sang-Hun Choe, Charles J. Hanley, and Martha Mendoza (Associated Press)
2001 David Willman *(Los Angeles Times)*
2002 Sari Horwitz, Scott Higham, and Sarah Cohen *(Washington Post)*
2003 Clifford J. Levy *(New York Times)*
2004 Michael D. Sallah, Mitch Weiss, and Joe Mahr *(The Blade* [Toledo, Ohio])

Feature Writing

1979 Jon D. Franklin *(Baltimore Evening Sun)*
1980 Madeleine Blais *(Miami Herald)*
1981 Teresa Carpenter *(Village Voice)*
1982 Saul Pett (Associated Press)
1983 Nan Robertson *(New York Times)*
1984 Peter M. Rinearson *(Seattle Times)*
1985 Alice Steinbach *(Baltimore Sun)*
1986 John Camp *(St. Paul Pioneer Press Dispatch)*
1987 Steve Twomey *(Philadelphia Inquirer)*
1988 Jacqui Banaszynski *(St. Paul Pioneer Press Dispatch)*
1989 David Zucchino *(Philadelphia Inquirer)*
1990 Dave Curtin *(Colorado Springs Gazette Telegraph)*
1991 Sheryl James *(St. Petersburg* [Fla.] *Times)*
1992 Howell Raines *(New York Times)*
1993 George Lardner, Jr. *(Washington Post)*
1994 Isabel Wilkerson *(New York Times)*
1995 Ron Suskind *(Wall Street Journal)*
1996 Rick Bragg *(New York Times)*
1997 Lisa Pollak *(Baltimore Sun)*
1998 Thomas French *(St. Petersburg* [Fla.] *Times)*
1999 Angelo B. Henderson *(Wall Street Journal)*
2000 J. R. Moehringer *(Los Angeles Times)*
2001 Tom Hallman, Jr. *(Oregonian)*
2002 Barry Siegel *(Los Angeles Times)*
2003 Sonia Nazario *(Los Angeles Times)*
2004 No award

Commentary

1970 Marquis W. Childs *(St. Louis Post-Dispatch)*
1971 William A. Caldwell *(Record* [Hackensack, N.J.])
1972 Mike Royko *(Chicago Daily News)*
1973 David S. Broder *(Washington Post)*
1974 Edwin A. Roberts, Jr. *(National Observer)*
1975 Mary McGrory *(Washington Star)*
1976 Walter W. (Red) Smith *(New York Times)*
1977 George F. Will *(Washington Post* Writers Group)
1978 William Safire *(New York Times)*
1979 Russell Baker *(New York Times)*
1980 Ellen H. Goodman *(Boston Globe)*
1981 Dave Anderson *(New York Times)*
1982 Art Buchwald *(Los Angeles Times* Syndicate)
1983 Claude Sitton *(Raleigh* [N.C.] *News and Observer)*
1984 Vermont Royster *(Wall Street Journal)*
1985 Murray Kempton *(Newsday)*
1986 Jimmy Breslin *(New York Daily News)*
1987 Charles Krauthammer *(Washington Post* Writers Group)
1988 Dave Barry *(Miami Herald)*
1989 Clarence Page *(Chicago Tribune)*
1990 Jim Murray *(Los Angeles Times)*
1991 Jim Hoagland *(Washington Post)*
1992 Anna Quindlen *(New York Times)*
1993 Liz Balmaseda *(Miami Herald)*
1994 William Raspberry *(Washington Post)*
1995 Jim Dwyer *(New York Newsday)*

1996 E. R. Shipp *(New York Daily News)*
1997 Eileen McNamara *(Boston Globe)*
1998 Mike McAlary *(New York Daily News)*
1999 Maureen Dowd *(New York Times)*
2000 Paul A. Gigot *(Wall Street Journal)*
2001 Dorothy Rabinowitz *(Wall Street Journal)*
2002 Thomas Friedman *(New York Times)*
2003 Colbert King *(Washington Post)*
2004 Leonard Pitts, Jr. *(Miami Herald)*

Criticism

1970 Ada Louise Huxtable *(New York Times)*
1971 Harold C. Schonberg *(New York Times)*
1972 Frank Peters, Jr. *(St. Louis Post-Dispatch)*
1973 Ronald Powers *(Chicago Sun-Times)*
1974 Emily Genauer *(Newsday* Syndicate)
1975 Roger Ebert *(Chicago Sun-Times)*
1976 Alan M. Kriegsman *(Washington Post)*
1977 William McPherson *(Washington Post)*
1978 Walter Kerr *(New York Times)*
1979 Paul Gapp *(Chicago Tribune)*
1980 William A. Henry, 3rd *(Boston Globe)*
1981 Jonathan Yardley *(Washington Star)*
1982 Martin Bernheimer *(Los Angeles Times)*
1983 Manuela Hoelterhoff *(Wall Street Journal)*
1984 Paul Goldberger *(New York Times)*
1985 Howard Rosenberg *(Los Angeles Times)*
1986 Donal Henahan *(New York Times)*
1987 Richard Eder *(Los Angeles Times)*
1988 Tom Shales *(Washington Post)*
1989 Michael Skube *(News and Observer* [Raleigh, N.C.])
1990 Allan Temko *(San Francisco Chronicle)*
1991 David Shaw *(Los Angeles Times)*
1993 Michael Dirda *(Washington Post)*
1994 Lloyd Schwartz *(Boston Phoenix)*
1995 Margo Jefferson *(New York Times)*
1996 Robert Campbell *(Boston Globe)*
1997 Tim Page *(Washington Post)*
1998 Michiko Kakutani *(New York Times)*
1999 Blair Kamin *(Chicago Tribune)*
2000 Henry Allen *(Washington Post)*
2001 Gail Caldwell *(Boston Globe)*
2002 Justin Davidson *(Newsday* [Long Island, N.Y.])
2003 Stephen Hunter *(Washington Post)*
2004 Dan Neil *(Los Angeles Times)*

Explanatory Reporting

1985 Jon Franklin *(Baltimore Evening Sun)*
1986 *New York Times* staff
1987 Jeff Lyon and Peter Gorner *(Chicago Tribune)*
1988 Daniel Hertzberg and James B. Stewart *(Wall Street Journal)*
1989 David Hanners, William Snyder, and Karen Blessen *(Dallas Morning News)*
1990 David A. Vise and Steve Coll *(Washington Post)*
1991 Susan C. Faludi *(Wall Street Journal)*
1992 Robert S. Capers and Eric Lipton *(Hartford Courant)*
1993 Mike Toner *(Atlanta Journal-Constitution)*
1994 Ronald Kotulak *(Chicago Tribune)*
1995 Leon Dash and Lucian Perkins *(Washington Post)*
1996 Laurie Garrett *(Newsday* [Long Island, N.Y.])
1997 Michael Vitez, Ron Cortes, and April Saul *(Philadelphia Inquirer)*
1998 Paul Salopek *(Chicago Tribune)*
1999 Richard Read *(Oregonian)*
2000 Eric Newhouse *(Great Falls* [Mont.] *Tribune)*

2001 *Chicago Tribune* staff
2002 *New York Times* staff
2003 *Wall Street Journal* staff
2004 Kevin Helliker and Thomas M. Burton *(Wall Street Journal)*

Specialized Reporting
1985 Randall Savage and Jackie Crosby *(Macon [Ga.] Telegraph and News)*
1986 Andrew Schneider and Mary Pat Flaherty *(Pittsburgh Press)*
1987 Alex S. Jones *(New York Times)*
1988 Walt Bogdanich *(Wall Street Journal)*
1989 Edward Humes *(Orange County Register)*
1990 Tamar Stieber *(Albuquerque* (N.M.) *Journal)*

Beat Reporting
1991 Natalie Angier *(New York Times)*
1992 Deborah Blum *(Sacramento Bee)*
1993 Paul Ingrassia and Joseph B. White *(Wall Street Journal)*
1994 Eric Freedman and Jim Mitzelfeld *(Detroit News)*
1995 David M. Shribman *(Boston Globe)*
1996 Bob Keeler *(Newsday* [Long Island, N.Y.])
1997 Byron Acohido *(Seattle Times)*
1998 Linda Greenhouse *(New York Times)*
1999 Chuck Philips and Michael A. Hiltzik *(Los Angeles Times)*
2000 George Dohrmann *(St. Paul Pioneer Press)*
2001 David Cay Johnston *(New York Times)*
2002 Gretchen Morgenson *(New York Times)*
2003 Diana K. Sugg *(Baltimore Sun)*
2004 Daniel Golden *(Wall Street Journal)*

PULITZER PRIZES IN LETTERS

Fiction[1]
1918 *His Family,* Ernest Poole
1919 *The Magnificent Ambersons,* Booth Tarkington
1921 *The Age of Innocence,* Edith Wharton
1922 *Alice Adams,* Booth Tarkington
1923 *One of Ours,* Willa Cather
1924 *The Able McLaughlins,* Margaret Wilson
1925 *So Big,* Edna Ferber
1926 *Arrowsmith,* Sinclair Lewis
1927 *Early Autumn,* Louis Bromfield
1928 *The Bridge of San Luis Rey,* Thornton Wilder
1929 *Scarlet Sister Mary,* Julia Peterkin
1930 *Laughing Boy,* Oliver La Farge
1931 *Years of Grace,* Margaret Ayer Barnes
1932 *The Good Earth,* Pearl S. Buck
1933 *The Store,* T. S. Stribling
1934 *Lamb in His Bosom,* Caroline Miller
1935 *Now in November,* Josephine Winslow Johnson
1936 *Honey in the Horn,* Harold L. Davis
1937 *Gone with the Wind,* Margaret Mitchell
1938 *The Late George Apley,* John Phillips Marquand
1939 *The Yearling,* Marjorie Kinnan Rawlings
1940 *The Grapes of Wrath,* John Steinbeck
1942 *In This Our Life,* Ellen Glasgow
1943 *Dragon's Teeth,* Upton Sinclair
1944 *Journey in the Dark,* Martin Flavin
1945 *A Bell for Adano,* John Hersey
1947 *All the King's Men,* Robert Penn Warren
1948 *Tales of the South Pacific,* James A. Michener
1949 *Guard of Honor,* James Gould Cozzens
1950 *The Way West,* A. B. Guthrie, Jr.
1951 *The Town,* Conrad Richter
1952 *The Caine Mutiny,* Herman Wouk

1953 *The Old Man and the Sea,* Ernest Hemingway
1955 *A Fable,* William Faulkner
1956 *Andersonville,* MacKinlay Kantor
1958 *A Death in the Family,* James Agee
1959 *The Travels of Jaimie McPheeters,* Robert Lewis Taylor
1960 *Advise and Consent,* Allen Drury
1961 *To Kill a Mockingbird,* Harper Lee
1962 *The Edge of Sadness,* Edwin O'Connor
1963 *The Reivers,* William Faulkner
1965 *The Keepers of the House,* Shirley Ann Grau
1966 *Collected Stories of Katherine Anne Porter,* Katherine Anne Porter
1967 *The Fixer,* Bernard Malamud
1968 *The Confessions of Nat Turner,* William Styron
1969 *House Made of Dawn,* N. Scott Momaday
1970 *Collected Stories,* Jean Stafford
1972 *Angle of Repose,* Wallace Stegner
1973 *The Optimist's Daughter,* Eudora Welty
1975 *The Killer Angels,* Michael Shaara
1976 *Humboldt's Gift,* Saul Bellow
1978 *Elbow Room,* James Alan McPherson
1979 *The Stories of John Cheever,* John Cheever
1980 *The Executioner's Song,* Norman Mailer
1981 *A Confederacy of Dunces,* John Kennedy Toole
1982 *Rabbit Is Rich,* John Updike
1983 *The Color Purple,* Alice Walker
1984 *Ironweed,* William Kennedy
1985 *Foreign Affairs,* Alison Lurie
1986 *Lonesome Dove,* Larry McMurtry
1987 *A Summons to Memphis,* Peter Taylor
1988 *Beloved,* Toni Morrison
1989 *Breathing Lessons,* Anne Tyler
1990 *The Mambo Kings Play Songs of Love,* Oscar Hijuelos
1991 *Rabbit at Rest,* John Updike
1992 *A Thousand Acres,* Jane Smiley
1993 *A Good Scent From a Strange Mountain,* Robert Olen Butler
1994 *The Shipping News,* E. Annie Proulx
1995 *The Stone Diaries,* Carol Shields
1996 *Independence Day,* Richard Ford
1997 *Martin Dressler: The Tale of an American Dreamer,* Steven Millhauser
1998 *American Pastoral,* Philip Roth
1999 *The Hours,* Michael Cunningham
2000 *Interpreter of Maladies,* Jhumpa Lahiri
2001 *The Amazing Adventures of Kavalier & Clay,* Michael Chabon
2002 *Empire Falls,* Richard Russo
2003 *Middlesex,* Jeffrey Eugenides
2004 *The Known World,* Edward P. Jones

1. Before 1948, award was for novels only.

History
1917 *With Americans of Past and Present Days,* J. J. Jusserand
1918 *A History of the Civil War, 1861–1865,* James Ford Rhodes
1920 *The War With Mexico,* Justin H. Smith
1921 *The Victory at Sea,* William Sowden Sims, in collaboration with Burton J. Hendrick
1922 *The Founding of New England,* James Truslow Adams
1923 *The Supreme Court in United States History,* Charles Warren
1924 *The American Revolution—A Constitutional Interpretation,* Charles Howard McIlwain
1925 *A History of the American Frontier,* Frederic L. Paxson

1926 *The History of the United States*, Edward Channing
1927 *Pinckney's Treaty*, Samuel Flagg Bemis
1928 *Main Currents in American Thought*, Vernon Louis Parrington
1929 *The Organization and Administration of the Union Army, 1861–1865*, Fred Albert Shannon
1930 *The War of Independence*, Claude H. Van Tyne
1931 *The Coming of the War: 1914*, Bernadotte E. Schmitt
1932 *My Experiences in the World War*, John J. Pershing
1933 *The Significance of Sections in American History*, Frederick J. Turner
1934 *The People's Choice*, Herbert Agar
1935 *The Colonial Period of American History*, Charles McLean Andrews
1936 *The Constitutional History of the United States*, Andrew C. McLaughlin
1937 *The Flowering of New England*, Van Wyck Brooks
1938 *The Road to Reunion, 1865–1900*, Paul Herman Buck
1939 *A History of American Magazines*, Frank Luther Mott
1940 *Abraham Lincoln: The War Years*, Carl Sandburg
1941 *The Atlantic Migration, 1607–1860*, Marcus Lee Hansen
1942 *Reveille in Washington*, Margaret Leech
1943 *Paul Revere and the World He Lived In*, Esther Forbes
1944 *The Growth of American Thought*, Merle Curti
1945 *Unfinished Business*, Stephen Bonsal
1946 *The Age of Jackson*, Arthur M. Schlesinger, Jr.
1947 *Scientists Against Time*, James Phinney Baxter III
1948 *Across the Wide Missouri*, Bernard DeVoto
1949 *The Disruption of American Democracy*, Roy Franklin Nichols
1950 *Art and Life in America*, Oliver W. Larkin
1951 *The Old Northwest, Pioneer Period 1815–1840*, R. Carlyle Buley
1952 *The Uprooted*, Oscar Handlin
1953 *The Era of Good Feelings*, George Dangerfield
1954 *A Stillness at Appomattox*, Bruce Catton
1955 *Great River: The Rio Grande in North American History*, Paul Horgan
1956 *The Age of Reform*, Richard Hofstadter
1957 *Russia Leaves the War: Soviet–American Relations, 1917–1920*, George F. Kennan
1958 *Banks and Politics in America: From the Revolution to the Civil War*, Bray Hammond
1959 *The Republican Era: 1869–1901*, Leonard D. White, assisted by Jean Schneider
1960 *In the Days of McKinley*, Margaret Leech
1961 *Between War and Peace: The Potsdam Conference*, Herbert Feis
1962 *The Triumphant Empire: Thunder-Clouds Gather in the West*, Lawrence H. Gipson
1963 *Washington, Village and Capital, 1800–1878*, Constance McLaughlin Green
1964 *Puritan Village: The Formation of a New England Town*, Sumner Chilton Powell
1965 *The Greenback Era*, Irwin Unger
1966 *Life of the Mind in America*, Perry Miller

1967 *Exploration and Empire: The Explorer and Scientist in the Winning of the American West*, William H. Goetzmann
1968 *The Ideological Origins of the American Revolution*, Bernard Bailyn
1969 *Origins of the Fifth Amendment*, Leonard W. Levy
1970 *Present at the Creation: My Years in the State Department*, Dean Acheson
1971 *Roosevelt: The Soldier of Freedom*, James McGregor Burns
1972 *Neither Black Nor White: Slavery and Race Relations in Brazil and the United States*, Carl N. Degler
1973 *People of Paradox: An Inquiry Concerning the Origin of American Civilization*, Michael Kammen
1974 *The Americans: The Democratic Experience, Vol. 3*, Daniel J. Boorstin
1975 *Jefferson and His Time*, Dumas Malone
1976 *Lamy of Santa Fe*, Paul Horgan
1977 *The Impending Crisis: 1841–1861*, David M. Potter
1978 *The Invisible Hand: The Managerial Revolution in American Business*, Alfred D. Chandler, Jr.
1979 *The Dred Scott Case: Its Significance in Law and Politics*, Don E. Fehrenbacher
1980 *Been in the Storm So Long*, Leon F. Litwack
1981 *American Education: The National Experience; 1783–1876*, Lawrence A. Cremin
1982 *Mary Chesnut's Civil War*, C. Vann Woodward, editor
1983 *The Transformation of Virginia, 1740–1790*, Rhys L. Isaac
1985 *The Prophets of Regulation*, Thomas K. McCraw
1986 *The Heavens and the Earth: A Political History of the Space Age*, Walter A. McDougall
1987 *Voyagers to the West: A Passage in the Peopling of America on the Eve of the Revolution*, Bernard Bailyn
1988 *The Launching of Modern American Science 1846–1876*, Robert V. Bruce
1989 *Parting the Waters*, Taylor Branch; *Battle Cry of Freedom*, James M. McPherson
1990 *In Our Image: America's Empire in the Philippines*, Stanley Karnow
1991 *A Midwife's Tale: The Life of Martha Ballard, Based on Her Diary 1785–1812*, Laurel Thatcher Ulrich
1992 *The Fate of Liberty: Abraham Lincoln and Civil Liberties*, Mark E. Neely, Jr.
1993 *The Radicalism of the American Revolution*, Gordon S. Wood
1995 *No Ordinary Time: Franklin and Eleanor Roosevelt: The Home Front in World War II*, Doris Kearns Goodwin
1996 *William Cooper's Town: Power and Persuasion on the Frontier of the Early American Republic*, Alan Taylor
1997 *Original Meanings: Politics and Ideas in the Making of the Constitution*, Jack N. Rakove
1998 *Summer for the Gods: The Scopes Trial and America's Continuing Debate Over Science and Religion*, Edward J. Larson
1999 *Gotham: A History of New York City to 1898*, Edwin G. Burrows and Mike Wallace

2000 *Freedom from Fear: The American People in Depression and War, 1929–1945*, David M. Kennedy

2001 *Founding Brothers: The Revolutionary Generation*, Joseph J. Ellis

2002 *The Metaphysical Club: A Story of Ideas in America*, Louis Menand

2003 *An Army at Dawn: The War in North Africa, 1942–1943*, Rick Atkinson

2004 *A Nation Under Our Feet*, Steven Hahn

Biography or Autobiography

1917 *Julia Ward Howe*, Laura E. Richards and Maude Howe Elliott, assisted by Florence Howe Hall

1918 *Benjamin Franklin, Self-Revealed*, William Cabell Bruce

1919 *The Education of Henry Adams*, Henry Adams

1920 *The Life of John Marshall*, Albert J. Beveridge

1921 *The Americanization of Edward Bok*, Edward Bok

1922 *A Daughter of the Middle Border*, Hamlin Garland

1923 *The Life and Letters of Walter H. Page*, Burton J. Hendrick

1924 *From Immigrant to Inventor*, Michael Idvorsky Pupin

1925 *Barrett Wendell and His Letters*, M. A. DeWolfe Howe

1926 *The Life of Sir William Osler*, Harvey Cushing

1927 *Whitman*, Emory Holloway

1928 *The American Orchestra and Theodore Thomas*, Charles Edward Russell

1929 *The Training of an American: The Earlier Life and Letters of Walter H. Page*, Burton J. Hendrick

1930 *The Raven*, Marquis James

1931 *Charles W. Eliot*, Henry James

1932 *Theodore Roosevelt*, Henry F. Pringle

1933 *Grover Cleveland*, Allan Nevins

1934 *John Hay*, Tyler Dennett

1935 *R. E. Lee*, Douglas S. Freeman

1936 *The Thought and Character of William James*, Ralph Barton Perry

1937 *Hamilton Fish*, Allan Nevins

1938 *Pedlar's Progress*, Odell Shepard; *Andrew Jackson*, Marquis James

1939 *Benjamin Franklin*, Carl Van Doren

1940 *Woodrow Wilson: Life and Letters*, Vols. VII and VIII, Ray Stannard Baker

1941 *Jonathan Edwards*, Ola E. Winslow

1942 *Crusader in Crinoline*, Forrest Wilson

1943 *Admiral of the Ocean Sea*, Samuel Eliot Morison

1944 *The American Leonardo: The Life of Samuel F. B. Morse*, Carleton Mabee

1945 *George Bancroft: Brahmin Rebel*, Russel Blaine Nye

1946 *Son of the Wilderness*, Linnie Marsh Wolfe

1947 *The Autobiography of William Allen White*

1948 *Forgotten First Citizen: John Bigelow*, Margaret Clapp

1949 *Roosevelt and Hopkins*, Robert E. Sherwood

1950 *John Quincy Adams and the Foundations of American Foreign Policy*, Samuel Flagg Bemis

1951 *John C. Calhoun: American Portrait*, Margaret Louise Coit

1952 *Charles Evans Hughes*, Merlo J. Pusey

1953 *Edmund Pendleton, 1721–1803*, David J. Mays

1954 *The Spirit of St. Louis*, Charles A. Lindbergh

1955 *The Taft Story*, William S. White

1956 *Benjamin Henry Latrobe*, Talbot F. Hamlin

1957 *Profiles in Courage*, John F. Kennedy

1958 *George Washington*, Douglas Southall Freeman (Vols. I–VI) and John Alexander Carroll and Mary Wells Ashworth (Vol. VII)

1959 *Woodrow Wilson, American Prophet*, Arthur Walworth

1960 *John Paul Jones*, Samuel Eliot Morison

1961 *Charles Sumner and the Coming of the Civil War*, David Donald

1963 *Henry James: Vol. II, The Conquest of London, 1870–1881; Vol. III, The Middle Years, 1881–1895*, Leon Edel

1964 *John Keats*, Walter Jackson Bate

1965 *Henry Adams* (3 Vols.), Ernest Samuels

1966 *A Thousand Days*, Arthur M. Schlesinger, Jr.

1967 *Mr. Clemens and Mark Twain*, Justin Kaplan

1968 *Memoirs, 1925–1950*, George F. Kennan

1969 *The Man From New York*, B. L. Reid

1970 *Huey Long*, T. Harry Williams

1971 *Robert Frost: The Years of Triumph, 1915–1938*, Lawrence Thompson

1972 *Eleanor and Franklin: The Story of Their Relationship Based on Eleanor Roosevelt's Private Papers*, Joseph P. Lash

1973 *Luce and His Empire*, W. A. Swanberg

1974 *O'Neill, Son and Artist*, Louis Sheaffer

1975 *The Power Broker: Robert Moses and the Fall of New York*, Robert A. Caro

1976 *Edith Wharton: A Biography*, Richard W. B. Lewis

1977 *A Prince of Our Disorder*, John E. Mack

1978 *Samuel Johnson*, Walter Jackson Bate

1979 *Days of Sorrow and Pain: Leo Baeck and the Berlin Jews*, Leonard Baker

1980 *The Rise of Theodore Roosevelt*, Edmund Morris

1981 *Peter the Great*, Robert K. Massie

1982 *Grant: A Biography*, William S. McFeely

1983 *Growing Up*, Russell Baker

1984 *Booker T. Washington*, Louis R. Harlan

1985 *The Life and Times of Cotton Mather*, Kenneth Silverman

1986 *Louise Bogan: A Portrait*, Elizabeth Frank

1987 *Bearing the Cross: Martin Luther King, Jr., and the Southern Christian Leadership Conference*, David J. Garrow

1988 *Look Homeward: A Life of Thomas Wolfe*, David Herbert Donald

1989 *Oscar Wilde*, Richard Ellmann

1990 *Machiavelli in Hell*, Sebastian de Grazia

1991 *Jackson Pollock: An American Saga*, Steven Naifeh and Gregory White Smith

1992 *Fortunate Son: The Healing of a Vietnam Vet*, Lewis B. Puller, Jr.

1993 *Truman*, David McCullough

1994 *W. E. B. Du Bois: Biography of a Race, 1868–1919*, David Levering Lewis

1995 *Harriet Beecher Stowe: A Life*, Joan D. Hedrick

1996 *God: A Biography*, Jack Miles

1997 *Angela's Ashes: A Memoir*, Frank McCourt

1998 *Personal History*, Katharine Graham

1999 *Lindbergh*, A. Scott Berg

2000 *Vera (Mrs. Vladimir Nabokov)*, Stacy Schiff

2001 *W. E. B. DuBois: The Fight for Equality and the American Century, 1919–1963*, David Levering Lewis

2002 *John Adams*, David McCullough

2003   *Master of the Senate*, Robert A. Caro
2004   *Krushchev: The Man and His Era*, William Taubman

Poetry[1]

1918   *Love Songs*, Sara Teasdale
1919   *Old Road to Paradise*, Margaret Widdemer; *Corn Huskers*, Carl Sandburg
1922   *Collected Poems*, Edwin Arlington Robinson
1923   *The Ballad of the Harp-Weaver; A Few Figs from Thistles;* eight sonnets in *American Poetry, 1922, A Miscellany*, Edna St. Vincent Millay
1924   *New Hampshire: A Poem With Notes and Grace Notes*, Robert Frost
1925   *The Man Who Died Twice*, Edwin Arlington Robinson
1926   *What's O'Clock*, Amy Lowell
1927   *Fiddler's Farewell*, Leonora Speyer
1928   *Tristram*, Edwin Arlington Robinson
1929   *John Brown's Body*, Stephen Vincent Benét
1930   *Selected Poems*, Conrad Aiken
1931   *Collected Poems*, Robert Frost
1932   *The Flowering Stone*, George Dillon
1933   *Conquistador*, Archibald MacLeish
1934   *Collected Verse*, Robert Hillyer
1935   *Bright Ambush*, Audrey Wurdemann
1936   *Strange Holiness*, Robert P. T. Coffin
1937   *A Further Range*, Robert Frost
1938   *Cold Morning Sky*, Marya Zaturenska
1939   *Selected Poems*, John Gould Fletcher
1940   *Collected Poems*, Mark Van Doren
1941   *Sunderland Capture*, Leonard Bacon
1942   *The Dust Which Is God*, William Rose Benét
1943   *A Witness Tree*, Robert Frost
1944   *Western Star*, Stephen Vincent Benét
1945   *V-Letter and Other Poems*, Karl Shapiro
1947   *Lord Weary's Castle*, Robert Lowell
1948   *The Age of Anxiety*, W. H. Auden
1949   *Terror and Decorum*, Peter Viereck
1950   *Annie Allen*, Gwendolyn Brooks
1951   *Complete Poems*, Carl Sandburg
1952   *Collected Poems*, Marianne Moore
1953   *Collected Poems, 1917–1952*, Archibald MacLeish
1954   *The Waking*, Theodore Roethke
1955   *Collected Poems*, Wallace Stevens
1956   *Poems—North & South*, Elizabeth Bishop
1957   *Things of This World*, Richard Wilbur
1958   *Promises: Poems, 1954–1956*, Robert Penn Warren
1959   *Selected Poems, 1928–1958*, Stanley Kunitz
1960   *Heart's Needle*, William Snodgrass
1961   *Times Three: Selected Verse From Three Decades*, Phyllis McGinley
1962   *Poems*, Alan Dugan
1963   *Pictures From Breughel*, William Carlos Williams
1964   *At the End of the Open Road*, Louis Simpson
1965   *77 Dream Songs*, John Berryman
1966   *Selected Poems*, Richard Eberhart
1967   *Live or Die*, Anne Sexton
1968   *The Hard Hours*, Anthony Hecht
1969   *Of Being Numerous*, George Oppen
1970   *Untitled Subjects*, Richard Howard
1971   *The Carrier of Ladders*, William S. Merwin
1972   *Collected Poems*, James Wright
1973   *Up Country*, Maxine Winokur Kumin
1974   *The Dolphin*, Robert Lowell
1975   *Turtle Island*, Gary Snyder

1976   *Self-Portrait in a Convex Mirror*, John Ashbery
1977   *Divine Comedies*, James Merrill
1978   *Collected Poems*, Howard Nemerov
1979   *Now and Then: Poems, 1976–1978*, Robert Penn Warren
1980   *Selected Poems*, Donald Rodney Justice
1981   *The Morning of the Poem*, James Schuyler
1982   *The Collected Poems*, Sylvia Plath
1983   *Selected Poems*, Galway Kinnell
1984   *American Primitive*, Mary Oliver
1985   *Yin*, Carolyn Kizer
1986   *The Flying Change*, Henry Taylor
1987   *Thomas and Beulah*, Rita Dove
1988   *Partial Accounts: New and Selected Poems*, William Meredith
1989   *New and Collected Poems*, Richard Wilbur
1990   *The World Doesn't End*, Charles Simic
1991   *Near Changes*, Mona Van Duyn
1992   *Selected Poems*, James Tate
1993   *The Wild Iris*, Louise Gluck
1994   *Neon Vernacular*, Yusef Komunyakaa
1995   *Simple Truth*, Philip Levine
1996   *The Dream of the Unified Field*, Jorie Graham
1997   *Alive Together: New and Selected Poems*, Lisel Mueller
1998   *Black Zodiac*, Charles Wright
1999   *Blizzard of One*, Mark Strand
2000   *Repair*, C. K. Williams
2001   *Different Hours*, Stephen Dunn
2002   *Practical Gods*, Carl Dennis
2003   *Moy Sand and Gravel*, Paul Muldoon
2004   *Walking to Martha's Vineyard*, Franz Wright

1. The poetry prize was established in 1922. The 1918 and 1919 awards were made from gifts provided by the Poetry Society.

General Nonfiction

1962   *The Making of the President, 1960*, Theodore H. White
1963   *The Guns of August*, Barbara W. Tuchman
1964   *Anti-Intellectualism in American Life*, Richard Hofstadter
1965   *O Strange New World*, Howard Mumford Jones
1966   *Wandering Through Winter*, Edwin Way Teale
1967   *The Problem of Slavery in Western Culture*, David Brion Davis
1968   *Rousseau and Revolution*, Will and Ariel Durant
1969   *So Human an Animal*, Rene Jules Dubos; *The Armies of the Night*, Norman Mailer
1970   *Gandhi's Truth*, Erik H. Erikson
1971   *The Rising Sun*, John Toland
1972   *Stilwell and the American Experience in China, 1911–1945*, Barbara W. Tuchman
1973   *Fire in the Lake: The Vietnamese and the Americans in Vietnam*, Frances FitzGerald; *Children of Crisis* (Vols. 1 and 2), Robert M. Coles
1974   *The Denial of Death*, Ernest Becker
1975   *Pilgrim at Tinker Creek*, Annie Dillard
1976   *Why Survive? Being Old in America*, Robert N. Butler
1977   *Beautiful Swimmers: Watermen, Crabs and the Chesapeake Bay*, William W. Warner
1978   *The Dragons of Eden*, Carl Sagan
1979   *On Human Nature*, Edward O. Wilson
1980   *Gödel, Escher, Bach: An Eternal Golden Braid*, Douglas R. Hofstadter
1981   *Fin-de-Siecle Vienna: Politics and Culture*, Carl E. Schorske

1982 *The Soul of a New Machine*, Tracy Kidder
1983 *Is There No Place on Earth for Me?*, Susan Sheehan
1984 *Social Transformation of American Medicine*, Paul Starr
1985 *The Good War: An Oral History of World War II*, Studs Terkel
1986 *Move Your Shadow: South Africa, Black and White*, Joseph Lelyveld; *Common Ground: A Turbulent Decade in the Lives of Three American Families*, J. Anthony Lukas
1987 *Arab and Jew: Wounded Spirits in a Promised Land*, David K. Shipler
1988 *The Making of the Atomic Bomb*, Richard Rhodes
1989 *A Bright Shining Lie*, Neil Sheehan
1990 *And Their Children After Them*, Dale Maharidge and Michael Williamson
1991 *The Ants*, Bert Holldobler and Edward O. Wilson
1992 *The Prize: The Epic Quest for Oil, Money and Power*, Daniel Yergin
1993 *Lincoln at Gettysburg: The Words That Remade America*, Garry Wills
1994 *Lenin's Tomb: The Last Days of the Soviet Empire*, David Remick
1995 *The Beak of the Finch: A Story of Evolution in Our Time*, Jonathan Weiner
1996 *The Haunted Land: Facing Europe's Ghosts After Communism*, Tina Rosenberg
1997 *Ashes to Ashes: America's Hundred-Year Cigarette War, the Public Health, and the Unabashed Triumph of Philip Morris*, Richard Kluger
1998 *Guns, Germs, and Steel: The Fates of Human Societies*, Jared Diamond
1999 *Annals of the Former World*, John McPhee
2000 *Embracing Defeat: Japan in the Wake of World War II*, John W. Dower
2001 *Hirohito and the Making of Modern Japan*, Herbert P. Bix
2002 *Carry Me Home: Birmingham, Alabama, the Climactic Battle of the Civil Rights Revolution*, Diane McWhorter
2003 *"A Problem from Hell:" America and the Age of Genocide*, Samantha Power
2004 *Gulag: A History*, Anne Applebaum

PULITZER PRIZES IN MUSIC

1943 *Secular Cantata No. 2, A Free Song*, William Schuman
1944 *Symphony No. 4 (Op. 34)*, Howard Hanson
1945 *Appalachian Spring*, Aaron Copland
1946 *The Canticle of the Sun*, Leo Sowerby
1947 *Symphony No. 3*, Charles Ives
1948 *Symphony No. 3*, Walter Piston
1949 *Louisiana Story* music, Virgil Thomson
1950 *The Consul*, Gian Carlo Menotti
1951 Music for opera *Giants in the Earth*, Douglas Stuart Moore
1952 *Symphony Concertante*, Gail Kubik
1954 *Concerto for Two Pianos and Orchestra*, Quincy Porter
1955 *The Saint of Bleecker Street*, Gian Carlo Menotti
1956 *Symphony No. 3*, Ernst Toch
1957 *Meditations on Ecclesiastes*, Norman Dello Joio
1958 *Vanessa*, Samuel Barber

1959 *Concerto for Piano and Orchestra*, John La Montaine
1960 *Second String Quartet*, Elliott Carter
1961 *Symphony No. 7*, Walter Piston
1962 *The Crucible*, Robert Ward
1963 *Piano Concerto No. 1*, Samuel Barber
1966 *Variations for Orchestra*, Leslie Bassett
1967 *Quartet No. 3*, Leon Kirchner
1968 *Echoes of Time and the River*, George Crumb
1969 *String Quartet No. 3*, Karel Husa
1970 *Time's Encomium*, Charles Wuorinen
1971 *Synchronisms No. 6 for Piano and Electronic Sound*, Mario Davidowsky
1972 *Windows*, Jacob Druckman
1973 *String Quartet No. 3*, Elliott Carter
1974 *Notturno*, Donald Martino
1975 *From the Diary of Virginia Woolf*, Dominick Argento
1976 *Air Music*, Ned Rorem
1977 *Visions of Terror and Wonder*, Richard Wernick
1978 *Déjà Vu for Percussion Quartet and Orchestra*, Michael Colgrass
1979 *Aftertones of Infinity*, Joseph Schwantner
1980 *In Memory of a Summer Day*, David Del Tredici
1982 *Concerto for Orchestra*, Roger Sessions
1983 *Three Movements for Orchestra*, Ellen T. Zwilich
1984 *Canti del Sole*, Bernard Rands
1985 *Symphony RiverRun*, Stephen Albert
1986 *Wind Quintet IV*, George Perle
1987 *The Flight Into Egypt*, John Harbison
1988 *12 New Etudes for Piano*, William Bolcom
1989 *Whispers Out of Time*, Roger Reynolds
1990 *Duplicates: A Concerto for Two Pianos and Orchestra*, Mel Powell
1991 *Symphony*, Shulamit Ran
1992 *The Face of the Night, The Heart of the Dark*, Wayne Peterson
1993 *Trombone Concerto*, Christopher Rouse
1994 *Of Reminiscences and Reflections*, Gunther Schuller
1995 *Stringmusic*, Morton Gould
1996 *Lilacs*, George Walker
1997 *Blood on the Field*, Wynton Marsalis
1998 *String Quartet No. 2, Musica Instrumentalis*, Aaron Jay Kernis
1999 *Concerto for Flute, Strings and Percussion*, Melinda Wagner
2000 *Life Is a Dream, Opera in Three Acts: Act II, Concert Version*, Lewis Spratlan
2001 *Symphony No. 2 for String Orchestra*, John Corigliano
2002 *Ice Field*, Henry Brant
2003 *On the Transmigration of Souls*, John Adams
2004 *Tempest Fantasy*, Paul Moravec

PULITZER PRIZES IN DRAMA

1918 *Why Marry?*, Jesse Lynch Williams
1920 *Beyond the Horizon*, Eugene O'Neill
1921 *Miss Lulu Bett*, Zona Gale
1922 *Anna Christie*, Eugene O'Neill
1923 *Icebound*, Owen Davis
1924 *Hell-Bent Fer Heaven*, Hatcher Hughes
1925 *They Knew What They Wanted*, Sidney Howard
1926 *Craig's Wife*, George Kelly
1927 *In Abraham's Bosom*, Paul Green

1928 *Strange Interlude*, Eugene O'Neill
1929 *Street Scene*, Elmer L. Rice
1930 *The Green Pastures*, Marc Connelly
1931 *Alison's House*, Susan Glaspell
1932 *Of Thee I Sing*, George S. Kaufman, Morrie Ryskind, and Ira Gershwin
1933 *Both Your Houses*, Maxwell Anderson
1934 *Men in White*, Sidney Kingsley
1935 *The Old Maid*, Zöe Akins
1936 *Idiot's Delight*, Robert E. Sherwood
1937 *You Can't Take It with You*, Moss Hart and George S. Kaufman
1938 *Our Town*, Thornton Wilder
1939 *Abe Lincoln in Illinois*, Robert E. Sherwood
1940 *The Time of Your Life*, William Saroyan
1941 *There Shall Be No Night*, Robert E. Sherwood
1943 *The Skin of Our Teeth*, Thornton Wilder
1945 *Harvey*, Mary Chase
1946 *State of the Union*, Russel Crouse and Howard Lindsay
1948 *A Streetcar Named Desire*, Tennessee Williams
1949 *Death of a Salesman*, Arthur Miller
1950 *South Pacific*, Richard Rodgers, Oscar Hammerstein II, and Joshua Logan
1952 *The Shrike*, Joseph Kramm
1953 *Picnic*, William Inge
1954 *The Teahouse of the August Moon*, John Patrick
1955 *Cat on a Hot Tin Roof*, Tennessee Williams
1956 *The Diary of Anne Frank*, Frances Goodrich and Albert Hackett
1957 *Long Day's Journey into Night*, Eugene O'Neill
1958 *Look Homeward, Angel*, Ketti Frings
1959 *J. B.*, Archibald MacLeish
1960 *Fiorello!*, George Abbott, Jerome Weidman, Jerry Bock, and Sheldon Harnick
1961 *All the Way Home*, Tad Mosel
1962 *How to Succeed in Business without Really Trying*, Frank Loesser and Abe Burrows
1965 *The Subject Was Roses*, Frank D. Gilroy
1967 *A Delicate Balance*, Edward Albee
1969 *The Great White Hope*, Howard Sackler
1970 *No Place to Be Somebody*, Charles Gordone
1971 *The Effect of Gamma Rays on Man-in-the-Moon Marigolds*, Paul Zindel
1973 *That Championship Season*, Jason Miller
1975 *Seascape*, Edward Albee
1976 *A Chorus Line*, conceived by Michael Bennett
1977 *The Shadow Box*, Michael Cristofer
1978 *The Gin Game*, Donald L. Coburn
1979 *Buried Child*, Sam Shepard
1980 *Talley's Folly*, Lanford Wilson
1981 *Crimes of the Heart*, Beth Henley
1982 *A Soldier's Play*, Charles Fuller
1983 *'Night, Mother*, Marsha Norman
1984 *Glengarry Glen Ross*, David Mamet
1985 *Sunday in the Park with George*, Stephen Sondheim and James Lapine
1987 *Fences*, August Wilson
1988 *Driving Miss Daisy*, Alfred Uhry
1989 *The Heidi Chronicles*, Wendy Wasserstein
1990 *The Piano Lesson*, August Wilson
1991 *Lost in Yonkers*, Neil Simon
1992 *The Kentucky Cycle*, Robert Schenkkan
1993 *Angels in America: Millennium Approaches*, Tony Kushner
1994 *Three Tall Women*, Edward Albee
1995 *The Young Man from Atlanta*, Horton Foote
1996 *Rent*, Jonathan Larson

1998 *How I Learned to Drive*, Paula Vogel
1999 *W;t*, Margaret Edson
2000 *Dinner with Friends*, Donald Margulies
2001 *Proof*, David Auburn
2002 *Topdog/Underdog*, Suzan-Lori Parks
2003 *Anna in the Tropics*, Nilo Cruz
2004 *I Am My Own Wife*, Doug Wright

SPECIAL CITATIONS

1938 *Edmonton* [Alberta] *Journal*, special bronze plaque for editorial leadership in defense of freedom of the press in province of Alberta
1941 *New York Times*, for the public educational value of its foreign news report
1944 Byron Price, director of the Office of Censorship, for the creation and administration of the newspaper and radio codes; Mrs. William Allen White, for her husband's interest and services during the past seven years as a member of the Advisory Board of the Graduate School of Journalism, Columbia University; Richard Rodgers and Oscar Hammerstein II, for their musical *Oklahoma!*
1945 The cartographers of the American press, for their war maps
1947 Columbia University and the Graduate School of Journalism, for their efforts to maintain and advance the high standards governing the Pulitzer Prize awards; the *St. Louis Post-Dispatch*, for its unswerving adherence to the public and professional ideals of its founder and its leadership in American journalism
1948 Dr. Frank D. Fackenthal, for his interest and service
1951 Cyrus L. Sulzberger *(New York Times)*, for his exclusive interview with Archbishop Stepinac in a Yugoslav prison
1952 *Kansas City Star*, for coverage of 1951 floods; Max Kase *(New York Journal-American)*, for exposures of bribery in basketball
1953 *New York Times*, for its 17-year publication of "Review of the Week," and Lester Markel, its founder
1957 Kenneth Roberts, for his historical novels
1958 Walter Lippmann *(New York Herald Tribune)*, for his "wisdom, perception and high sense of responsibility" in his commentary on national and international affairs
1960 Garrett Mattingly, for *The Armada*
1961 *American Heritage Picture History of the Civil War*, as a distinguished example of American book publishing
1964 Gannett Newspapers, Rochester, N.Y.
1973 James Thomas Flexner, for his biography *George Washington*
1974 Roger Sessions, for his "life's work in music"
1976 John Hohenberg, for "services for 22 years as Administrator of the Pulitzer Prizes"; Scott Joplin, for his contributions to American music
1977 Alex Haley, for his novel *Roots*
1978 E. B. White of *New Yorker* magazine and Richard L. Strout of *Christian Science Monitor*
1982 Milton Babbitt, "for his life's work as a distinguished and seminal American composer"
1984 Theodor Seuss Geisel (Dr. Seuss), for "books full of playful rhymes, nonsense words and strange illustrations"

1985 William Schuman, for "more than half a century of contribution to American music as a composer and educational leader"
1987 Joseph Pulitzer, Jr., "for extraordinary services to American journalism and letters during his 31 years as chairman of the Pulitzer Prize Board and for his accomplishments as an editor and publisher"

1992 *Maus*, Art Spiegelman
1996 Herb Caen *(San Francisco Chronicle)*, "for his extraordinary and continuing contribution as a voice and conscience of his city"
1998 George Gershwin
1999 Edward Kennedy "Duke" Ellington, who "made an indelible contribution to art and culture"

Academy Awards (Oscars)

1928
Picture: *Wings*, Paramount
Director: Frank Borzage, *Seventh Heaven*; Lewis Milestone, *Two Arabian Nights*
Actress: Janet Gaynor, *Seventh Heaven, Street Angel, Sunrise*
Actor: Emil Jannings, *The Way of All Flesh, The Last Command*

1929
Picture: *The Broadway Melody*, MGM
Director: Frank Lloyd, *The Divine Lady*
Actress: Mary Pickford, *Coquette*
Actor: Warner Baxter, *In Old Arizona*

1930
Picture: *All Quiet on the Western Front*, Universal
Director: Lewis Milestone, *All Quiet on the Western Front*
Actress: Norma Shearer, *The Divorcee*
Actor: George Arliss, *Disraeli*

1931
Picture: *Cimarron*, RKO Radio
Director: Norman Taurog, *Skippy*
Actress: Marie Dressler, *Min and Bill*
Actor: Lionel Barrymore, *A Free Soul*

1932
Picture: *Grand Hotel*, MGM
Director: Frank Borzage, *Bad Girl*
Actress: Helen Hayes, *The Sin of Madelon Claudet*
Actor: Fredric March, *Dr. Jekyll and Mr. Hyde*; Wallace Beery, *The Champ*

1933
Picture: *Cavalcade*, Fox
Director: Frank Lloyd, *Cavalcade*
Actress: Katharine Hepburn, *Morning Glory*
Actor: Charles Laughton, *The Private Life of Henry VIII*

1934
Picture: *It Happened One Night*, Columbia
Director: Frank Capra, *It Happened One Night*
Actress: Claudette Colbert, *It Happened One Night*
Actor: Clark Gable, *It Happened One Night*

1935
Picture: *Mutiny on the Bounty*, MGM
Director: John Ford, *The Informer*
Actress: Bette Davis, *Dangerous*
Actor: Victor McLaglen, *The Informer*

1936
Picture: *The Great Ziegfeld*, MGM
Director: Frank Capra, *Mr. Deeds Goes to Town*
Actress: Luise Rainer, *The Great Ziegfeld*
Actor: Paul Muni, *The Story of Louis Pasteur*
Supporting Actress: Gale Sondergaard, *Anthony Adverse*
Supporting Actor: Walter Brennan, *Come and Get It*

1937
Picture: *The Life of Emile Zola*, Warner Bros.
Director: Leo McCarey, *The Awful Truth*
Actress: Luise Rainer, *The Good Earth*
Actor: Spencer Tracy, *Captains Courageous*
Supporting Actress: Alice Brady, *In Old Chicago*
Supporting Actor: Joseph Schildkraut, *The Life of Emile Zola*

1938
Picture: *You Can't Take It with You*, Columbia
Director: Frank Capra, *You Can't Take It with You*
Actress: Bette Davis, *Jezebel*
Actor: Spencer Tracy, *Boys Town*
Supporting Actress: Fay Bainter, *Jezebel*
Supporting Actor: Walter Brennan, *Kentucky*

1939
Picture: *Gone with the Wind*, Selznick MGM
Director: Victor Fleming, *Gone with the Wind*
Actress: Vivien Leigh, *Gone with the Wind*
Actor: Robert Donat, *Goodbye, Mr. Chips*
Supporting Actress: Hattie McDaniel, *Gone with the Wind*
Supporting Actor: Thomas Mitchell, *Stagecoach*

1940
Picture: *Rebecca*, Selznick-United Artists
Director: John Ford, *The Grapes of Wrath*
Actress: Ginger Rogers, *Kitty Foyle*
Actor: James Stewart, *The Philadelphia Story*
Supporting Actress: Jane Darwell, *The Grapes of Wrath*
Supporting Actor: Walter Brennan, *The Westerner*

1941
Picture: *How Green Was My Valley*, 20th Century–Fox
Director: John Ford, *How Green Was My Valley*
Actress: Joan Fontaine, *Suspicion*
Actor: Gary Cooper, *Sergeant York*
Supporting Actress: Mary Astor, *The Great Lie*
Supporting Actor: Donald Crisp, *How Green Was My Valley*

1942
Picture: *Mrs. Miniver*, MGM
Director: William Wyler, *Mrs. Miniver*
Actress: Greer Garson, *Mrs. Miniver*
Actor: James Cagney, *Yankee Doodle Dandy*
Supporting Actress: Teresa Wright, *Mrs. Miniver*
Supporting Actor: Van Heflin, *Johnny Eager*

1943
Picture: *Casablanca*, Warner Bros.
Director: Michael Curtiz, *Casablanca*
Actress: Jennifer Jones, *The Song of Bernadette*
Actor: Paul Lukas, *Watch on the Rhine*
Supporting Actress: Katina Paxinou, *For Whom the Bell Tolls*
Supporting Actor: Charles Coburn, *The More the Merrier*

1944
Picture: *Going My Way*, Paramount
Director: Leo McCarey, *Going My Way*
Actress: Ingrid Bergman, *Gaslight*
Actor: Bing Crosby, *Going My Way*
Supporting Actress: Ethel Barrymore, *None but the Lonely Heart*
Supporting Actor: Barry Fitzgerald, *Going My Way*

1945

Picture: *The Lost Weekend,* Paramount
Director: Billy Wilder, *The Lost Weekend*
Actress: Joan Crawford, *Mildred Pierce*
Actor: Ray Milland, *The Lost Weekend*
Supporting Actress: Anne Revere, *National Velvet*
Supporting Actor: James Dunn, *A Tree Grows in Brooklyn*

1946

Picture: *The Best Years of Our Lives,* Goldwyn–RKO Radio
Director: William Wyler, *The Best Years of Our Lives*
Actress: Olivia de Havilland, *To Each His Own*
Actor: Fredric March, *The Best Years of Our Lives*
Supporting Actress: Anne Baxter, *The Razor's Edge*
Supporting Actor: Harold Russell, *The Best Years of Our Lives*

1947

Picture: *Gentleman's Agreement,* 20th Century–Fox
Director: Elia Kazan, *Gentleman's Agreement*
Actress: Loretta Young, *The Farmer's Daughter*
Actor: Ronald Colman, *A Double Life*
Supporting Actress: Celeste Holm, *Gentleman's Agreement*
Supporting Actor: Edmund Gwenn, *Miracle on 34th Street*

1948

Picture: *Hamlet,* Rank–Two Cities–UI
Director: John Huston, *Treasure of Sierra Madre*
Actress: Jane Wyman, *Johnny Belinda*
Actor: Laurence Olivier, *Hamlet*
Supporting Actress: Claire Trevor, *Key Largo*
Supporting Actor: Walter Huston, *Treasure of Sierra Madre*

1949

Picture: *All the King's Men,* Rossen-Columbia
Director: Joseph L. Mankiewicz, *A Letter to Three Wives*
Actress: Olivia de Havilland, *The Heiress*
Actor: Broderick Crawford, *All the King's Men*
Supporting Actress: Mercedes McCambridge, *All the King's Men*
Supporting Actor: Dean Jagger, *Twelve O'Clock High*

1950

Picture: *All About Eve,* 20th Century–Fox
Director: Joseph L. Mankiewicz, *All About Eve*
Actress: Judy Holliday, *Born Yesterday*
Actor: José Ferrer, *Cyrano de Bergerac*
Supporting Actress: Josephine Hull, *Harvey*
Supporting Actor: George Sanders, *All About Eve*

1951

Picture: *An American in Paris,* MGM
Director: George Stevens, *A Place in the Sun*
Actress: Vivien Leigh, *A Streetcar Named Desire*
Actor: Humphrey Bogart, *The African Queen*
Supporting Actress: Kim Hunter, *A Streetcar Named Desire*
Supporting Actor: Karl Malden, *A Streetcar Named Desire*

1952

Picture: *The Greatest Show on Earth,* DeMille-Paramount
Director: John Ford, *The Quiet Man*
Actress: Shirley Booth, *Come Back, Little Sheba*
Actor: Gary Cooper, *High Noon*
Supporting Actress: Gloria Grahame, *The Bad and the Beautiful*
Supporting Actor: Anthony Quinn, *Viva Zapata!*

1953

Picture: *From Here to Eternity,* Columbia
Director: Fred Zinnemann, *From Here to Eternity*
Actress: Audrey Hepburn, *Roman Holiday*
Actor: William Holden, *Stalag 17*
Supporting Actress: Donna Reed, *From Here to Eternity*
Supporting Actor: Frank Sinatra, *From Here to Eternity*

1954

Picture: *On the Waterfront,* Horizon-American Corp., Columbia
Director: Elia Kazan, *On the Waterfront*
Actress: Grace Kelly, *The Country Girl*
Actor: Marlon Brando, *On the Waterfront*

Supporting Actress: Eva Marie Saint, *On the Waterfront*
Supporting Actor: Edmond O'Brien, *The Barefoot Contessa*

1955

Picture: *Marty,* Hecht and Lancaster, United Artists
Director: Delbert Mann, *Marty*
Actress: Anna Magnani, *The Rose Tattoo*
Actor: Ernest Borgnine, *Marty*
Supporting Actress: Jo Van Fleet, *East of Eden*
Supporting Actor: Jack Lemmon, *Mister Roberts*

1956

Picture: *Around the World in 80 Days,* Michael Todd Co., Inc.–United Artists
Director: George Stevens, *Giant*
Actress: Ingrid Bergman, *Anastasia*
Actor: Yul Brynner, *The King and I*
Supporting Actress: Dorothy Malone, *Written on the Wind*
Supporting Actor: Anthony Quinn, *Lust for Life*

1957

Picture: *The Bridge on the River Kwai,* Horizon Films, Columbia
Director: David Lean, *The Bridge on the River Kwai*
Actress: Joanne Woodward, *The Three Faces of Eve*
Actor: Alec Guinness, *The Bridge on the River Kwai*
Supporting Actress: Miyoshi Umeki, *Sayonara*
Supporting Actor: Red Buttons, *Sayonara*

1958

Picture: *Gigi,* Arthur Freed Productions, Inc., MGM
Director: Vincente Minnelli, *Gigi*
Actress: Susan Hayward, *I Want to Live!*
Actor: David Niven, *Separate Tables*
Supporting Actress: Wendy Hiller, *Separate Tables*
Supporting Actor: Burl Ives, *The Big Country*

1959

Picture: *Ben-Hur,* MGM
Director: William Wyler, *Ben-Hur*
Actress: Simone Signoret, *Room at the Top*
Actor: Charlton Heston, *Ben-Hur*
Supporting Actress: Shelley Winters, *The Diary of Anne Frank*
Supporting Actor: Hugh Griffith, *Ben-Hur*

1960

Picture: *The Apartment,* Mirisch Co., Inc., United Artists
Director: Billy Wilder, *The Apartment*
Actress: Elizabeth Taylor, *Butterfield 8*
Actor: Burt Lancaster, *Elmer Gantry*
Supporting Actress: Shirley Jones, *Elmer Gantry*
Supporting Actor: Peter Ustinov, *Spartacus*

1961

Picture: *West Side Story,* Mirisch Pictures, Inc., and B and P Enterprises, Inc., United Artists
Director: Robert Wise and Jerome Robbins, *West Side Story*
Actress: Sophia Loren, *Two Women*
Actor: Maximillian Schell, *Judgment at Nuremberg*
Supporting Actress: Rita Moreno, *West Side Story*
Supporting Actor: George Chakiris, *West Side Story*

1962

Picture: *Lawrence of Arabia,* Horizon Pictures, Ltd.–Columbia
Director: David Lean, *Lawrence of Arabia*
Actress: Anne Bancroft, *The Miracle Worker*
Actor: Gregory Peck, *To Kill a Mockingbird*
Supporting Actress: Patty Duke, *The Miracle Worker*
Supporting Actor: Ed Begley, *Sweet Bird of Youth*

1963

Picture: *Tom Jones,* A Woodfall Production, United Artists–Lopert Pictures
Director: Tony Richardson, *Tom Jones*
Actress: Patricia Neal, *Hud*
Actor: Sidney Poitier, *Lilies of the Field*
Supporting Actress: Margaret Rutherford, *The V.I.P.s*
Supporting Actor: Melvyn Douglas, *Hud*

1964

Picture: *My Fair Lady,* Warner Bros.
Director: George Cukor, *My Fair Lady*
Actress: Julie Andrews, *Mary Poppins*
Actor: Rex Harrison, *My Fair Lady*
Supporting Actress: Lila Kedrova, *Zorba the Greek*
Supporting Actor: Peter Ustinov, *Topkapi*

1965

Picture: *The Sound of Music,* Argyle Enterprises
  Production, 20th Century–Fox
Director: Robert Wise, *The Sound of Music*
Actress: Julie Christie, *Darling*
Actor: Lee Marvin, *Cat Ballou*
Supporting Actress: Shelley Winters, *A Patch of Blue*
Supporting Actor: Martin Balsam, *A Thousand Clowns*

1966

Picture: *A Man for All Seasons,* Highland Films, Ltd.,
  Production, Columbia
Director: Fred Zinnemann, *A Man for All Seasons*
Actress: Elizabeth Taylor, *Who's Afraid of Virginia
  Woolf?*
Actor: Paul Scofield, *A Man for All Seasons*
Supporting Actress: Sandy Dennis, *Who's Afraid of
  Virginia Woolf?*
Supporting Actor: Walter Matthau, *The Fortune Cookie*

1967

Picture: *In the Heat of the Night,* Mirisch Corp.
  Productions, United Artists
Director: Mike Nichols, *The Graduate*
Actress: Katharine Hepburn, *Guess Who's Coming to Dinner*
Actor: Rod Steiger, *In the Heat of the Night*
Supporting Actress: Estelle Parsons, *Bonnie and Clyde*
Supporting Actor: George Kennedy, *Cool Hand Luke*

1968

Picture: *Oliver!,* Columbia Pictures
Director: Sir Carol Reed, *Oliver!*
Actress: Katharine Hepburn, *The Lion in Winter* and
  Barbra Streisand, *Funny Girl*
Actor: Cliff Robertson, *Charly*
Supporting Actress: Ruth Gordon, *Rosemary's Baby*
Supporting Actor: Jack Albertson, *The Subject Was Roses*

1969

Picture: *Midnight Cowboy,* Jerome Hellman–John
  Schlesinger Production, United Artists
Director: John Schlesinger, *Midnight Cowboy*
Actress: Maggie Smith, *The Prime of Miss Jean Brodie*
Actor: John Wayne, *True Grit*
Supporting Actress: Goldie Hawn, *Cactus Flower*
Supporting Actor: Gig Young, *They Shoot Horses, Don't
  They?*

1970

Picture: *Patton,* Frank McCarthy–Franklin J. Schaffner
  Production, 20th Century–Fox
Director: Franklin J. Schaffner, *Patton*
Actress: Glenda Jackson, *Women in Love*
Actor: George C. Scott, *Patton*
Supporting Actress: Helen Hayes, *Airport*
Supporting Actor: John Mills, *Ryan's Daughter*

1971

Picture: *The French Connection,* D'Antoni Productions,
  20th Century–Fox
Director: William Friedkin, *The French Connection*
Actress: Jane Fonda, *Klute*
Actor: Gene Hackman, *The French Connection*
Supporting Actress: Cloris Leachman, *The Last Picture
  Show*
Supporting Actor: Ben Johnson, *The Last Picture Show*

1972

Picture: *The Godfather,* Albert S. Ruddy Production,
  Paramount
Director: Bob Fosse, *Cabaret*
Actress: Liza Minnelli, *Cabaret*
Actor: Marlon Brando, *The Godfather*

Supporting Actress: Eileen Heckart, *Butterflies Are Free*
Supporting Actor: Joel Gray, *Cabaret*

1973

Picture: *The Sting,* Universal–Bill Phillips–George Roy Hill
  Production, Universal
Director: George Roy Hill, *The Sting*
Actress: Glenda Jackson, *A Touch of Class*
Actor: Jack Lemmon, *Save the Tiger*
Supporting Actress: Tatum O'Neal, *Paper Moon*
Supporting Actor: John Houseman, *The Paper Chase*

1974

Picture: *The Godfather, Part II,* Coppola Co. Production,
  Paramount
Director: Francis Ford Coppola, *The Godfather, Part II*
Actress: Ellen Burstyn, *Alice Doesn't Live Here Anymore*
Actor: Art Carney, *Harry and Tonto*
Supporting Actress: Ingrid Bergman, *Murder on the
  Orient Express*
Supporting Actor: Robert De Niro, *The Godfather, Part II*

1975

Picture: *One Flew Over the Cuckoo's Nest,* Fantasy Films
  Production, United Artists
Director: Milos Forman, *One Flew Over the Cuckoo's Nest*
Actress: Louise Fletcher, *One Flew Over the Cuckoo's Nest*
Actor: Jack Nicholson, *One Flew Over the Cuckoo's Nest*
Supporting Actress: Lee Grant, *Shampoo*
Supporting Actor: George Burns, *The Sunshine Boys*

1976

Picture: *Rocky,* Robert Chartoff–Irwin Winkler Production,
  United Artists
Director: John G. Avildsen, *Rocky*
Actress: Faye Dunaway, *Network*
Actor: Peter Finch, *Network*
Supporting Actress: Beatrice Straight, *Network*
Supporting Actor: Jason Robards, *All the President's Men*

1977

Picture: *Annie Hall,* Jack Rollins–Charles H. Joffe
  Production, United Artists
Director: Woody Allen, *Annie Hall*
Actress: Diane Keaton, *Annie Hall*
Actor: Richard Dreyfuss, *The Goodbye Girl*
Supporting Actress: Vanessa Redgrave, *Julia*
Supporting Actor: Jason Robards, *Julia*

1978

Picture: *The Deer Hunter,* Michael Cimino Film
  Production, Universal
Director: Michael Cimino, *The Deer Hunter*
Actress: Jane Fonda, *Coming Home*
Actor: Jon Voight, *Coming Home*
Supporting Actress: Maggie Smith, *California Suite*
Supporting Actor: Christopher Walken, *The Deer Hunter*

1979

Picture: *Kramer vs. Kramer,* Stanley Jaffe Production,
  Columbia Pictures
Director: Robert Benton, *Kramer vs. Kramer*
Actress: Sally Field, *Norma Rae*
Actor: Dustin Hoffman, *Kramer vs. Kramer*
Supporting Actress: Meryl Streep, *Kramer vs. Kramer*
Supporting Actor: Melvyn Douglas, *Being There*

1980

Picture: *Ordinary People,* Wildwood Enterprises
  Production, Paramount
Director: Robert Redford, *Ordinary People*
Actress: Sissy Spacek, *Coal Miner's Daughter*
Actor: Robert De Niro, *Raging Bull*
Supporting Actress: Mary Steenburgen, *Melvin and
  Howard*
Supporting Actor: Timothy Hutton, *Ordinary People*

1981

Picture: *Chariots of Fire,* Enigma Productions, Ladd
  Company/Warner Bros.
Director: Warren Beatty, *Reds*
Actress: Katharine Hepburn, *On Golden Pond*

Actor: Henry Fonda, *On Golden Pond*
Supporting Actress: Maureen Stapleton, *Reds*
Supporting Actor: John Gielgud, *Arthur*

1982

Picture: *Gandhi*, Indo-British Films Production/Columbia
Director: Richard Attenborough, *Gandhi*
Actress: Meryl Streep, *Sophie's Choice*
Actor: Ben Kingsley, *Gandhi*
Supporting Actress: Jessica Lange, *Tootsie*
Supporting Actor: Louis Gossett, Jr., *An Officer and a Gentleman*

1983

Picture: *Terms of Endearment*, Paramount
Director: James L. Brooks, *Terms of Endearment*
Actress: Shirley MacLaine, *Terms of Endearment*
Actor: Robert Duvall, *Tender Mercies*
Supporting Actress: Linda Hunt, *The Year of Living Dangerously*
Supporting Actor: Jack Nicholson, *Terms of Endearment*

1984

Picture: *Amadeus*, Orion
Director: Milos Forman, *Amadeus*
Actress: Sally Field, *Places in the Heart*
Actor: F. Murray Abraham, *Amadeus*
Supporting Actress: Dame Peggy Ashcroft, *A Passage to India*
Supporting Actor: Haing S. Ngor, *The Killing Fields*

1985

Picture: *Out of Africa*, Universal
Director: Sydney Pollack, *Out of Africa*
Actress: Geraldine Page, *The Trip to Bountiful*
Actor: William Hurt, *Kiss of the Spider Woman*
Supporting Actress: Anjelica Huston, *Prizzi's Honor*
Supporting Actor: Don Ameche, *Cocoon*

1986

Picture: *Platoon*, Orion
Director: Oliver Stone, *Platoon*
Actress: Marlee Matlin, *Children of a Lesser God*
Actor: Paul Newman, *The Color of Money*
Supporting Actress: Dianne Wiest, *Hannah and Her Sisters*
Supporting Actor: Michael Caine, *Hannah and Her Sisters*

1987

Picture: *The Last Emperor*, Columbia Pictures
Director: Bernardo Bertolucci, *The Last Emperor*
Actress: Cher, *Moonstruck*
Actor: Michael Douglas, *Wall Street*
Supporting Actress: Olympia Dukakis, *Moonstruck*
Supporting Actor: Sean Connery, *The Untouchables*

1988

Picture: *Rain Man*, United Artists
Director: Barry Levinson, *Rain Man*
Actress: Jodie Foster, *The Accused*
Actor: Dustin Hoffman, *Rain Man*
Supporting Actress: Geena Davis, *The Accidental Tourist*
Supporting Actor: Kevin Kline, *A Fish Called Wanda*

1989

Picture: *Driving Miss Daisy*, Warner Bros.
Director: Oliver Stone, *Born on the Fourth of July*
Actress: Jessica Tandy, *Driving Miss Daisy*
Actor: Daniel Day-Lewis, *My Left Foot*
Supporting Actress: Brenda Fricker, *My Left Foot*
Supporting Actor: Denzel Washington, *Glory*

1990

Picture: *Dances With Wolves*, Orion
Director: Kevin Costner, *Dances With Wolves*
Actress: Kathy Bates, *Misery*
Actor: Jeremy Irons, *Reversal of Fortune*
Supporting Actress: Whoopi Goldberg, *Ghost*
Supporting Actor: Joe Pesci, *Goodfellas*

1991

Picture: *The Silence of the Lambs*, Orion
Director: Jonathan Demme, *The Silence of the Lambs*

Actress: Jodie Foster, *The Silence of the Lambs*
Actor: Anthony Hopkins, *The Silence of the Lambs*
Supporting Actress: Mercedes Ruehl, *The Fisher King*
Supporting Actor: Jack Palance, *City Slickers*

1992

Picture: *Unforgiven*, Warner Bros.
Director: Clint Eastwood, *Unforgiven*
Actress: Emma Thompson, *Howards End*
Actor: Al Pacino, *Scent of a Woman*
Supporting Actress: Marisa Tomei, *My Cousin Vinny*
Supporting Actor: Gene Hackman, *Unforgiven*

1993

Picture: *Schindler's List*, Universal
Director: Steven Spielberg, *Schindler's List*
Actress: Holly Hunter, *The Piano*
Actor: Tom Hanks, *Philadelphia*
Supporting Actress: Anna Paquin, *The Piano*
Supporting Actor: Tommy Lee Jones, *The Fugitive*

1994

Picture: *Forrest Gump*, Paramount
Director: Robert Zemeckis, *Forrest Gump*
Actress: Jessica Lange, *Blue Sky*
Actor: Tom Hanks, *Forrest Gump*
Supporting Actress: Dianne Wiest, *Bullets Over Broadway*
Supporting Actor: Martin Landau, *Ed Wood*

1995

Picture: *Braveheart*, Paramount
Director: Mel Gibson, *Braveheart*
Actress: Susan Sarandon, *Dead Man Walking*
Actor: Nicolas Cage, *Leaving Las Vegas*
Supporting Actress: Mira Sorvino, *Mighty Aphrodite*
Supporting Actor: Kevin Spacey, *The Usual Suspects*

1996

Picture: *The English Patient*, Miramax
Director: Anthony Minghella, *The English Patient*
Actress: Frances McDormand, *Fargo*
Actor: Geoffrey Rush, *Shine*
Supporting Actress: Juliette Binoche, *The English Patient*
Supporting Actor: Cuba Gooding, Jr., *Jerry Maguire*

1997

Picture: *Titanic*, 20th Century–Fox and Paramount
Director: James Cameron, *Titanic*
Actress: Helen Hunt, *As Good As It Gets*
Actor: Jack Nicholson, *As Good As It Gets*
Supporting Actress: Kim Basinger, *L.A. Confidential*
Supporting Actor: Robin Williams, *Good Will Hunting*

1998

Picture: *Shakespeare in Love*, Miramax
Director: Steven Spielberg, *Saving Private Ryan*
Actress: Gwyneth Paltrow, *Shakespeare in Love*
Actor: Roberto Benigni, *Life Is Beautiful*
Supporting Actress: Judi Dench, *Shakespeare in Love*
Supporting Actor: James Coburn, *Affliction*

1999

Picture: *American Beauty*, DreamWorks SKG
Director: Sam Mendes, *American Beauty*
Actress: Hilary Swank, *Boys Don't Cry*
Actor: Kevin Spacey, *American Beauty*
Supporting Actress: Angelina Jolie, *Girl, Interrupted*
Supporting Actor: Michael Caine, *The Cider House Rules*

2000

Picture: *Gladiator*, DreamWorks and Universal
Director: Steven Soderbergh, *Traffic*
Actress: Julia Roberts, *Erin Brockovich*
Actor: Russell Crowe, *Gladiator*
Supporting Actress: Marcia Gay Harden, *Pollock*
Supporting Actor: Benicio Del Toro, *Traffic*

2001

Picture: *A Beautiful Mind*, Brian Grazer and Ron Howard, producers
Director: Ron Howard, *A Beautiful Mind*
Actress: Halle Berry, *Monster's Ball*

Actor: Denzel Washington, *Training Day*
Supporting Actress: Jennifer Connelly, *A Beautiful Mind*
Supporting Actor: Jim Broadbent, *Iris*

2002

Picture: *Chicago*, Martin Richards, producer
Director: Roman Polanski, *The Pianist*
Actress: Nicole Kidman, *The Hours*
Actor: Adrien Brody, *The Pianist*
Supporting Actress: Catherine Zeta-Jones, *Chicago*
Supporting Actor: Chris Cooper, *Adaptation*

2003

Picture: *The Lord of the Rings: The Return of the King*, Barrie M. Osborne, Peter Jackson, and Fran Walsh, producers
Director: Peter Jackson, *The Lord of the Return of the King*
Actress: Charlize Theron, *Monster*
Actor: Sean Penn, *Mystic River*
Supporting Actress: Renée Zellweger, *Cold Mountain*
Supporting Actor: Tim Robbins, *Mystic River*

Other Academy Awards for 2003

Art Direction: Grant Major, art direction; Dan Hennah and Alan Lee, set decoration, *The Lord of the Rings: The Return of the King*
Cinematography: Russell Boyd, *Master and Commander: The Far Side of the World*
Costume Design: Ngila Dickson and Richard Taylor, *The Lord of the Rings: The Return of the King*
Documentary (feature): *The Fog of War* (Errol Morris and Michael Williams)
Editing: Jamie Selkirk, *The Lord of the Rings: The Return of the King*
Foreign-Language Film: *The Barbarian Invasions* (Canada)
Makeup: Richard Taylor and Peter King, *The Lord of the Rings: The Return of the King*
Music (original score): Howard Shore, *The Lord of the Rings: The Return of the King*

Best Original Song: Fran Walsh, Howard Shore, and Annie Lennox, "Into the West," *The Lord of the Rings: The Return of the King*
Adapted Screenplay: Fran Walsh, Philippa Boyens, Peter Jackson, *The Lord of the Rings: The Return of the King*
Original Screenplay: Sofia Coppola, *Lost in Translation*
Short Subject (live action): *Two Soldiers* (Aaron Schneider and Andrew J. Sacks)
Sound: Christopher Boyes, Michael Semanick, Michael Hedges, and Hammond Peek, *The Lord of the Rings: The Return of the King*
Sound Editing: Richard King, *Master and Commander: The Far Side of the World*
Visual Effects: Jim Rygiel, Joe Letteri, Randall William Cook, and Alex Funke, *The Lord of the Rings: The Return of the King*
Honorary Award: Blake Edwards, director

2004 Golden Globe Awards

Film Awards

Best Motion Picture—Drama: *The Lord of the Rings: The Return of the King*
Best Actor in a Drama: Sean Penn, *Mystic River*
Best Actress in a Drama: Charlize Theron, *Monster*
Best Motion Picture—Musical or Comedy: *Lost in Translation*
Best Actor in a Musical or Comedy: Bill Murray, *Lost in Translation*
Best Actress in a Musical or Comedy: Diane Keaton, *Something's Gotta Give*
Best Supporting Actor: Tim Robbins, *Mystic River*
Best Supporting Actress: Renée Zellweger, *Cold Mountain*
Best Director: Peter Jackson, *The Lord of the Rings: The Return of the King*
Best Screenplay: Sofia Coppola, *Lost in Translation*
Best Original Score: Howard Shore, *The Lord of the Rings: The Return of the King*
Best Original Song: "Into The West," Howard Shore, Fran Walsh, and Annie Lennox, *The Lord of the Rings: The Return of the King*
Best Foreign Film: *Osama* (Afghanistan)
Cecil B. DeMille Award: Michael Douglas

Television Awards

Best Series—Drama: *24* (Fox)
Best Actor in a Drama: Anthony La Paglia, *Without a Trace*
Best Actress in a Drama: Frances Conroy, *Six Feet Under*
Best Series—Musical or Comedy: *The Office* (BBC America)
Best Actor in a Musical or Comedy Series: Ricky Gervais, *The Office*
Best Actress in a Musical or Comedy Series: Sarah Jessica Parker, *Sex and the City*
Best Miniseries or Movie Made for Television: *Angels in America* (HBO)
Best Actor in a Miniseries or Movie Made for Television: Al Pacino, *Angels in America*
Best Actress in a Miniseries or Movie Made for Television: Meryl Streep, *Angels in America*
Best Supporting Actor in a Series, Miniseries, or Movie Made for Television: Jeffrey Wright, *Angels in America*
Best Supporting Actress in a Series, Miniseries, or Movie Made for Television: Mary-Louise Parker, *Angels in America*

2004 Tony (Antoinette Perry) Awards

Play: *I Am My Own Wife*
Musical: *Avenue Q*
Revival—Play: *Henry IV*
Revival—Musical: *Assassins*
Actor—Play: Jefferson Mays, *I Am My Own Wife*
Actress—Play: Phylicia Rashad, *A Raisin in the Sun*
Actor—Musical: Hugh Jackman, *The Boy from Oz*
Actress—Musical: Idina Menzel, *Wicked*
Featured Actor—Play: Brían F. O'Byrne, *Frozen*
Featured Actress—Play: Audra McDonald, *A Raisin in the Sun*
Featured Actor—Musical: Michael Cerveris, *Assassins*
Featured Actress—Musical: Anika Noni Rose, *Caroline, or Change*

Director—Play: Jack O'Brien, *Henry IV*
Director—Musical: Joe Mantello, *Assassins*
Book—Musical: Jeff Whitty, *Avenue Q*
Score—Musical: Robert Lopez and Jeff Marx, *Avenue Q*
Orchestration: Michael Starobin, *Assassins*
Scenic Designer: Eugene Lee, *Wicked*
Costume Designer: Susan Hilferty, *Wicked*
Choreographer: Kathleen Marshall, *Wonderful Town*
Lighting Designer: Jules Fisher and Peggy Eisenhauer, *Assassins*
Regional Theater: Cincinnati Playhouse in the Park
Special Award: James M. Nederlander, for lifetime achievement

2003–2004 Drama Desk Awards

Outstanding Play: *I Am My Own Wife*
Outstanding Musical: *Wicked*
Outstanding Musical Revival: *Assassins*
Outstanding Play Revival: *Henry IV*
Best Actor in a Play: Kevin Kline, *Henry IV*
Best Actress in a Play (tie): Viola Davis, *Intimate Apparel;* Phylicia Rashad, *A Raisin in the Sun*
Best Featured Actor in a Play: Ned Beatty, *Cat on a Hot Tin Roof*
Best Featured Actress in a Play: Audra McDonald, *A Raisin in the Sun*
Best Actor in a Musical: Hugh Jackman, *The Boy From Oz*
Best Actress in a Musical: Donna Murphy, *Wonderful Town*
Best Featured Actor in a Musical: Raul Esparza, *Taboo*
Best Featured Actress in a Musical: Isabel Keating, *The Boy From Oz*
Best Director of a Play: Jack O'Brien, *Henry IV*
Best Director of a Musical: Joe Mantello, *Wicked*
Best Choreography: Kathleen Marshall, *Wonderful Town*

Best Book of a Musical: Winnie Holzman, *Wicked*
Best Music: Jeanine Tesori, *Caroline, or Change*
Best Lyrics: Stephen Schwartz, *Wicked*
Outstanding Orchestrations: Michael Starobin, *Assassins*
Outstanding Set Design of a Play: John Lee Beatty, *Twentieth Century*
Outstanding Set Design of a Musical: Eugene Lee, *Wicked*
Outstanding Costume Design: Susan Hilferty, *Wicked*
Outstanding Lighting Design: Jules Fisher and Peggy Eisenhauer, *Assassins*
Outstanding Sound Design: Dan Moses Schreier, *Assassins*
Outstanding Solo Performance: Jefferson Mayes, *I Am My Own Wife*
Unique Theatrical Experience: *Toxic Audio in Loud Mouth*
Special Awards: Dakin Matthews for his adaption of William Shakespeare's *Henry IV*, The Flea Theater, and The Classical Theatre of Harlem

2003–2004 Obie Awards

The Obie Awards, presented by *The Village Voice*, honor superior off-Broadway theater.

Best American Play: Craig Lucas, *Small Tragedy*
Direction: Lee Breuer, *Mabou Mines dollHouse;* Moisés Kaufman, *I Am My Own Wife*
Performance: Viola Davis, *Intimate Apparel;* Lisa Emery, *Iron;* Jayne Houdyshell, *Well;* Sarah Jones, *Bridge & Tunnel;* Jefferson Mays, *I Am My Own Wife;* Zilah Mendoza, *Living Out;* Maude Mitchell, *Mabou Mines dollHouse;* Brian F. O'Byrne, *Frozen;* Tonya Pinkins, *Caroline, or Change;* Lili Taylor, *Aunt Dan and Lemon;* Shannon Cochran, Michael Shannon, Michael Cullen, Amy Landecker, Reed Birney, *Bug;* Ana Reeder, Mary Shultz, Rob Campbell, Daniel Eric Gold, Lee Pace, Rosemarie DeWitt, *Small Tragedy*
Design: The design team of *Bug:* Lauren Helpern (sets), Tyler Micoleau (lights), Brian Ronan (sound), Kim Gill (costumes), Faye Armon (props); Derek McLane, set

design *I Am My Own Wife, Aunt Dan and Lemon,* and *Intimate Apparel*
Music: Robert Een *Hiroshima Maiden*
Special Citations: Pieter-Dirk Uys, *Foreign AIDS;* Tony Kushner and Jeanine Tesori, *Caroline, or Change;* Soho Rep, *Molly's Dream;* The Builders Association and motiroti, *Alladeen;* Kyle Jarrow and Alex Timbers, *A Very Merry Unauthorized Children's Scientology Pageant;* George C. Wolfe, for his stewardship of the Public Theater; Martin Moran, *The Tricky Part;* Terry Nemeth, Play Publishing, TCG
Lifetime Achievement: Mark Russell
Grants: The Civilians, Musicals Tonight, THAW (Theaters Against War)
Ross Wetzsteon Award: St. Ann's Warehouse (Susan Feldman, artistic director)

Major Grammy Awards for Recordings in 2003

Record: "Clocks," Coldplay
Album: *Speakerboxxx/The Love Below,* Outkast
Song: "Dance with My Father," Richard Marx, Luther Vandross, songwriters (Luther Vandross)
New Artist: Evanescence
Female Pop Vocal: "Beautiful," Christina Aguilera
Male Pop Vocal: "Cry Me a River," Justin Timberlake
Pop Duo or Group with Vocals: "Underneath It All," No Doubt
Pop Collaboration with Vocals: "Whenever I Say Your Name," Sting, Mary J. Blige
Pop Instrumental: "Marwa Blues," George Harrison
Pop Instrumental Album: *Mambo Sinuendo,* Ry Cooder, Manuel Galban
Pop Vocal Album: *Justified,* Justin Timberlake
Dance Recording: "Come Into My World," Kylie Minogue
Traditional Pop Vocal Album: *A Wonderful World,* Tony Bennett, k.d. lang
Female Rock Vocal: "Trouble," Pink
Male Rock Vocal: "Gravedigger," Dave Matthews
Rock Duo or Group with Vocals: "Disorder in the House," Warren Zevon, Bruce Springsteen
Hard Rock: "Bring Me To Life," Evanescence featuring Paul McCoy
Metal: "St. Anger," Metallica
Rock Instrumental: "Plan B," Jeff Beck

Rock Song: "Seven Nation Army," Jack White, songwriter (The White Stripes)
Rock Album: *One by One,* Foo Fighters
Alternative Music Album: *Elephant,* The White Stripes
Female R&B Vocal: "Dangerously in Love," Beyoncé
Male R&B Vocal: "Dance with My Father, " Luther Vandross
R&B Duo or Group with Vocals: "The Closer I Get to You," Beyoncé & Luther Vandross
Traditional R&B Vocal: "Wonderful, " Aretha Franklin
Urban/Alternative Vocal: "Hey Ya!," Outkast
R&B Song: "Crazy in Love," Shawn Carter, Rich Harrison, Beyoncé Knowles, Eugene Record, songwriters (Beyoncé featuring Jay-Z)
R&B Album: *Dance with My Father,* Luther Vandross
Contemporary R&B Vocal Album: *Dangerously in Love,* Beyoncé
Female Rap Solo: "Work It," Missy Elliott
Male Rap Solo: "Lose Yourself," Eminem
Rap Duo or Group: "Shake Ya Tailfeather," Nelly, P. Diddy, & Murphy Lee
Rap Sung/Collaboration: "Crazy in Love," Beyoncé featuring Jay-Z
Rap Song: "Lose Yourself," J. Bass, M. Mathers, L. Resto, songwriters (Eminem)
Rap Album: *Speakerboxxx/The Love Below,* Outkast

Female Country Vocal: "Keep on the Sunny Side," June Carter Cash
Male Country Vocal: "Next Big Thing," Vince Gill
Country Duo or Group with Vocals: "A Simple Life," Ricky Skaggs & Kentucky Thunder
Country Collaboration with Vocals: "How's the World Treating You," James Taylor, Alison Krauss
Country Instrumental: "Cluck Old Hen," Alison Krauss & Union Station
Country Song: "It's Five O'Clock Somewhere," Jim "Moose" Brown, Don Rollins, songwriters (Alan Jackson, Jimmy Buffett)
Country Album: *Livin', Lovin', Losin'—Songs of the Louvin Brothers,* various artists
Bluegrass Album: *Live,* Alison Krauss & Union Station
New Age Album: *One Quiet Night,* Pat Metheny
Contemporary Jazz Album: *34th N Lex,* Randy Brecker
Jazz Vocal Album: *A Little Moonlight,* Dianne Reeves
Jazz Instrumental, Solo: "Matrix," Chick Corea
Jazz Instrumental Album: *Alegria,* Wayne Shorter
Large Jazz Ensemble Album: *Wide Angles,* Michael Brecker Quindectet
Latin Jazz Album: *Live at the Blue Note,* Michel Camilo with Charles Flores & Horacio "El Negro" Hernandez
Rock Gospel Album: *Worldwide,* Audio Adrenaline
Pop/Contemporary Gospel Album: *Worship Again,* Michael W. Smith
Southern, Country, or Bluegrass Gospel Album: *Rise and Shine,* Randy Travis
Contemporary Soul Gospel Album: *. . . Again,* Donnie McClurkin
Gospel Album by a Choir or Chorus: *A Wing and a Prayer,* Bishop T. D. Jakes, choir director; The Potter's House Mass Choir
Latin Pop Album: *No Es Lo Mismo,* Alejandro Sanz
Latin Rock/Alternative Album: *Cuatro Caminos,* Café Tacuba
Tropical Latin Album: *Buenos Hermanos,* Ibrahim Ferrer
Salsa/Merengue Album: *Regalo Del Alma,* Celia Cruz
Mexican/Mexican-American Album: *Afortunado,* Joan Sebastian
Tejano Album: *Si Me Faltas Tu,* Jimmy Gonzalez y El Grupo Mazz
Traditional Blues Album: *Blues Singer,* Buddy Guy
Contemporary Blues Album: *Let's Roll,* Etta James
Traditional Folk Album: *Wildwood Flower,* June Carter Cash
Contemporary Folk Album: *The Wind,* Warren Zevon
Native American Music Album: *Flying Free,* Black Eagle
Reggae Album: *Dutty Rock,* Sean Paul
Traditional World Music Album: *Sacred Tibetan Chant,* The Monks of Sherab Ling Monastery
Contemporary World Music Album: *Voz D'Amor,* Cesaria Evora
Polka Album: *Let's Polka 'Round,* Jimmy Sturr
Musical Album for Children: *Bon Appetit!,* Cathy Fink and Marcy Marxer
Spoken Word Album for Children: *Prokofiev: Peter and the Wolf/Beintus: Wolf Tracks,* Bill Clinton, Mikhail Gorbachev, Sophia Loren
Spoken Word Album: *Lies and the Lying Liars Who Tell Them: A Fair and Balanced Look at the Right,* Al Franken
Comedy Album: *Poodle Hat,* Weird Al Yankovic
Musical Show Album: *Gypsy,* Jay David Saks, producer; Jule Styne, composer; Stephen Sondheim, lyricist
Best Compilation Soundtrack Album for a Motion Picture, Television, or Other Visual Media: *Chicago,* Various Artists
Best Score Soundtrack Album for a Motion Picture, Television, or Other Visual Media: *The Lord of the Rings: The Two Towers,* Howard Shore, composer
Song Written for a Motion Picture, Television, or Other Visual Media: "A Mighty Wind" (from *A Mighty Wind*), Christopher Guest, Eugene Levy, Michael McKean
Instrumental Composition: "Sacajawea," Wayne Shorter, composer (Wayne Shorter)
Instrumental Arrangement: "Timbuktu," Michael Brecker, Gil Goldstein, arrangers (Michael Brecker Orchestra)
Instrumental Arrangement with Accompanying Vocals: "Woodstock," Vince Mendoza, arranger (Joni Mitchell)
Historical Album: *Martin Scorsese Presents The Blues: A Musical Journey*
Producer, Non-Classical: The Neptunes
Classical Producer: Steven Epstein
Classical Album: *Mahler: Symphony No. 3; Kindertotenlieder,* Michael Tilson Thomas, conductor; Andreas Neubronner, producer
Orchestral Performance: *Mahler: Symphony No. 3,* Pierre Boulez, conducter (Vienna Philharmonic)
Opera Recording: *Janácek: Jenufa,* Bernard Haitink, conductor
Choral Performance: *Sibelius: Cantatas,* Paavo Järvi, conductor
Instrumental Soloist with Orchestra: *Britten: Violin Concerto/Walton: Viola Concerto,* Maxim Vengerov, violin & viola with the London Symphony Orchestra
Instrumental Soloist Without Orchestra: *Haydn: Piano Sonatas Nos. 29, 31, 34, 35 & 49,* Emanuel Ax, piano
Chamber Music: *Berg: Lyric Suite* Kronos Quartet & Dawn Upshaw, soprano
Small Ensemble Performance (with or Without Conductor): *Chavez: Suite for Double Quartet,* Jeff von der Schmidt, conductor; Southwest Chamber Music
Classical Vocal: *Schubert: Lieder with Orchestra,* Thomas Quasthoff, bass-baritone; Anne Sofie von Otter, mezzo soprano
Classical Contemporary Composition: *Argento: Casa Guidi,* Dominick Argento
Classical Crossover Album: *Obrigado Brazil,* Jorge Calandrelli, conductor; Yo-Yo Ma, cello
Music Video, Short Form: "Hurt" (Johnny Cash), Mark Romanek, director
Music Video, Long Form: *Legend* (Sam Cooke), Allen Klein, director
Lifetime Achievement Awards: Van Cliburn, The Funk Brothers, Ella Jenkins, Sonny Rollins, Artie Shaw, Doc Watson

2003 Country Music Association Awards

Entertainer of the Year: Alan Jackson
Male Vocalist of the Year: Alan Jackson
Female Vocalist of the Year: Martina McBride
Horizon Award: Joe Nichols
Vocal Group of the Year: Rascal Flatts
Vocal Duo of the Year: Brooks & Dunn
Single of the Year: "Hurt," Johnny Cash
Album of the Year: *American IV: The Man Comes Around,* Johnny Cash
Song of the Year: "Three Wooden Crosses," Doug Johnson and Kim Williams
Vocal Event of the Year: "It's Five O'Clock Somewhere," Alan Jackson and Jimmy Buffett
Musician of the Year: Randy Scruggs
Music Video of the Year: "Hurt," Johnny Cash

2003 National Book Awards

Fiction: *The Great Fire*, Shirley Hazzard (Farrar, Straus & Giroux)

Nonfiction: *Waiting for Snow in Havana: Confessions of a Cuban Boy*, Carlos Eire (Free Press/Simon & Schuster)

Poetry: *The Singing*, C. K. Williams (Farrar, Straus & Giroux)

Young People's Literature: *The Canning Season*, Polly Horvath (Farrar, Straus & Giroux)

Medal for Distinguished Contribution to American Literature: Stephen King

2003 National Book Critics Circle Awards

Fiction: *The Known World*, Edward P. Jones (Amistad/HarperCollins)

General Nonfiction: *Sons of Mississippi*, Paul Hendrickson (Knopf)

Biography or Autobiography: *Krushchev: The Man and His Era*, William Taubman (Norton)

Poetry: *Columbarium*, Susan Stewart (University of Chicago Press)

Criticism: *River of Shadows: Edweard Muybridge and the Technological Wild West*, Rebecca Solnit (Viking)

Ivan Sandrof Lifetime Achievement Award: Studs Terkel

Nona Balakian Citation for Excellence in Reviewing: Scott McLemme, *Chronicle of Higher Education*

PEN/Faulkner Award

The PEN/Faulkner award is the largest annual juried prize for fiction in the United States. The winner receives $15,000.

1981	Walter Abish, *How German Is It?*
1982	David Bradley, *The Chaneysville Incident*
1983	Toby Olson, *Seaview*
1984	John Edgar Wideman, *Sent for You Yesterday*
1985	Tobias Wolff, *The Barracks Thief*
1986	Peter Taylor, *The Old Forest*
1987	Richard Wiley, *Soldiers in Hiding*
1988	T. Coraghessan Boyle, *World's End*
1989	James Salter, *Dusk*
1990	E. L. Doctorow, *Billy Bathgate*
1991	John Edgar Wideman, *Philadelphia Fire*
1992	Don Delillo, *Mao II*
1993	E. Annie Proulx, *Postcards*
1994	Philip Roth, *Operation Shylock*
1995	David Guterson, *Snow Falling on Cedars*
1996	Richard Ford, *Independence Day*
1997	Gina Berriault, *Women in Their Beds*
1998	Rafi Zabor, *The Bear Comes Home*
1999	Michael Cunningham, *The Hours*
2000	Ha Jin, *Waiting*
2001	Philip Roth, *The Human Stain*
2002	Ann Patchett, *Bel Canto*
2003	Sabina Murray, *The Caprices*
2004	John Updike, *The Early Stories*

Man Booker Prize

Britain's most prestigious literary award, formerly called the Booker Prize, honors the best full-length novel written in English by a citizen of a current or former British Commonwealth country.

1969	*Something to Answer For*, P. H. Newby
1970	*The Elected Member*, Bernice Rubens
1971	*In a Free State*, V. S. Naipaul
1972	*G.: A Novel*, John Berger
1973	*The Siege of Krishnapur*, J. G. Farrell
1974	(tie) *The Conservationist*, Nadine Gordimer; *Holiday*, Stanley Middleton
1975	*Heat and Dust*, Ruth Prawer Jhabvala
1976	*Saville*, David Storey
1977	*Staying On*, Paul Scott
1978	*The Sea, The Sea*, Iris Murdoch
1979	*Offshore*, Penelope Fitzgerald
1980	*Rites of Passage*, William Golding
1981	*Midnight's Children*, Salman Rushdie
1982	*Schindler's List*, Thomas Keaneally
1983	*Life & Times of Michael K*, J. M. Coetzee
1984	*Hotel du Lac*, Anita Brookner
1985	*The Bone People*, Keri Hulme
1986	*The Old Devils*, Kingsley Amis
1987	*Moon Tiger*, Penelope Lively
1988	*Oscar and Lucinda*, Peter Carey
1989	*The Remains of the Day*, Kazuo Ishiguro
1990	*Possession: A Romance*, A. S. Byatt
1991	*The Famished Road*, Ben Okri
1992	(tie) *The English Patient*, Michael Ondaatje; *Sacred Hunger*, Barry Unsworth
1993	*Paddy Clarke, Ha Ha Ha*, Roddy Doyle
1994	*How Late It Was, How Late*, James Kelman
1995	*The Ghost Road*, Pat Barker
1996	*Last Orders*, Graham Swift
1997	*The God of Small Things*, Arundhati Roy
1998	*Amsterdam*, Ian McEwan
1999	*Disgrace*, J. M. Coetzee
2000	*The Blind Assassin*, Margaret Atwood
2001	*True History of the Kelly Gang*, Peter Carey
2002	*Life of Pi*, Yann Martel
2003	*Vernon God Little*, DBC Pierre

Truman Capote Award for Literary Criticism

The award is administered for the Truman Capote estate by the University of Iowa Writers' Workshop. The $50,000 award is the largest cash prize for literary criticism in the English language.

1996	Helen Vendler, *The Given and the Made*
1997	John Felstiner, *Paul Celan: Poet, Survivor, Jew*
1998	John Kerrigan, *Revenge Tragedy*
1999	Charles Rosen, *Romantic Poets, Critics, and Other Madmen*
2000	Elaine Scarry, *Dreaming by the Book;* Philip

	Fisher, *Still the New World*
2001	Malcolm Bowie, *Proust Among the Stars*
2002	Declan Kiberd, *Irish Classics*
2003	Seamus Heaney, *Finders Keepers: Selected Prose 1971–2001*
2004	Susan Stewart, *Poetry and the Fate of the Senses*

Newbery Medal

The Newbery Medal is awarded annually by the American Library Association for the most distinguished contribution to American literature for children.

2004 Newbery Medal and Honor Books
Newbery Medal for Best Book: *The Tale of Despereaux,* Kate DiCamillo (Candlewick Press)
Newbery Honor Books: *Olive's Ocean,* Kevin Henkes (Greenwillow Books); *An American Plague: The True and Terrifying Story of the Yellow Fever Epidemic of 1793,* Jim Murphy (Clarion Books)

1922–2003

1922   *The Story of Mankind,* Hendrick Willem Van Loon
1923   *The Voyages of Dr. Doolittle,* Hugh A. Lofting
1924   *The Dark Frigate,* Charles Boardman Hawes
1925   *Tales from Silver Lands,* Charles Joseph Finger
1926   *Shen of the Sea,* Arthur Bowie Chrisman
1927   *Smoky, the Cow Horse,* Will James
1928   *Gay-Neck, the Story of a Pigeon,* Dhan Gopal Mukerji
1929   *The Trumpeter of Krakow,* Eric P. Kelly
1930   *Hitty, Her First Hundred Years,* Rachel Field
1931   *The Cat Who Went to Heaven,* Elizabeth Jane Coatsworth
1932   *Waterless Mountain,* Laura Adams Armer
1933   *Young Fu of the Upper Yangtze,* Elizabeth Foreman Lewis
1934   *Invincible Louisa,* Cornelia Meigs
1935   *Dobry,* Monica Shannon
1936   *Caddie Woodlawn,* Carol Ryrie Brink
1937   *Roller Skates,* Ruth Sawyer
1938   *The White Stag,* Kate Seredy
1939   *Thimble Summer,* Elizabeth Enright
1940   *Daniel Boone,* James Henry Daugherty
1941   *Call It Courage,* Armstrong Sperry
1942   *The Matchlock Gun,* Walter Dumax Edmonds
1943   *Adam of the Road,* Elizabeth Janet Gray
1944   *Johnny Tremain,* Esther Forbes
1945   *Rabbit Hill,* Robert Lawson
1946   *Strawberry Girl,* Lois Lenski
1947   *Miss Hickory,* Carolyn Sherwin Bailey
1948   *The Twenty-One Balloons,* William Pène du Bois
1949   *King of the Wind,* Marguerite Henry
1950   *The Door in the Wall,* Marguerite de Angeli
1951   *Amos Fortune, Free Man,* Elizabeth Yates
1952   *Ginger Pye,* Eleanor Estes
1953   *Secret of the Andes,* Ann Nolan Clark
1954   *. . . And Now Miguel,* Joseph Krumgold
1955   *The Wheel on the School,* Meindert DeJong
1956   *Carry On, Mr. Bowditch,* Jean Lee Latham
1957   *Miracles on Maple Hill,* Virginia Eggertsen Sorensen
1958   *Rifles for Watie,* Harold Keith
1959   *The Witch of Blackbird Pond,* Elizabeth George Speare

1960   *Onion John,* Joseph Krumgold
1961   *Island of the Blue Dolphins,* Scott O'Dell
1962   *The Bronze Bow,* Elizabeth George Speare
1963   *A Wrinkle in Time,* Madeleine L'Engle
1964   *It's Like This, Cat,* Emily Cheney Neville
1965   *Shadow of a Bull,* Maia Wojciechowska
1966   *I, Juan de Pareja,* Elizabeth Borton de Treviño
1967   *Up a Road Slowly,* Irene Hunt
1968   *From the Mixed-Up Files of Mrs. Basil E. Frankweiler,* E. L. Konigsburg
1969   *The High King,* Lloyd Alexander
1970   *Sounder,* William H. Armstrong
1971   *Summer of the Swans,* Betsy Byars
1972   *Mrs. Frisby and the Rats of NIMH,* Robert C. O'Brien
1973   *Julie of the Wolves,* Jean Craighead George
1974   *The Slave Dancer,* Paula Fox
1975   *M. C. Higgins, the Great,* Virginia Hamilton
1976   *The Grey King,* Susan Cooper
1977   *Roll of Thunder, Hear My Cry,* Mildred D. Taylor
1978   *Bridge to Terabithia,* Katherine Paterson
1979   *The Westing Game,* Ellen Raskin
1980   *A Gathering of Days: A New England Girl's Journal, 1830–32,* Joan W. Blos
1981   *Jacob Have I Loved,* Katherine Paterson
1982   *A Visit to William Blake's Inn: Poems for Innocent and Experienced Travelers,* Nancy Willard
1983   *Dicey's Song,* Cynthia Voigt
1984   *Dear Mr. Henshaw,* Beverly Cleary
1985   *The Hero and the Crown,* Robin McKinley
1986   *Sarah, Plain and Tall,* Patricia MacLachlan
1987   *The Whipping Boy,* Sid Fleischman
1988   *Lincoln: A Photobiography,* Russell Freedman
1989   *Joyful Noise: Poems for Two Voices,* Paul Fleischman
1990   *Number the Stars,* Lois Lowry
1991   *Maniac Magee: a Novel,* Jerry Spinelli
1992   *Shiloh,* Phyllis Reynolds Naylor
1993   *Missing May,* Cynthia Rylant
1994   *The Giver,* Lois Lowry
1995   *Walk Two Moons,* Sharon Creech
1996   *The Midwife's Apprentice,* Karen Cushman
1997   *The View from Saturday,* E. L. Konigsburg
1998   *Out of the Dust,* Karen Hesse
1999   *Holes,* Louis Sachar
2000   *Bud, Not Buddy,* Christopher Paul Curtis
2001   *A Year Down Yonder,* Richard Peck
2002   *A Single Shard,* Linda Sue Park
2003   *Crispin: The Cross of Lead,* Avi

Caldecott Medal

The Caldecott Medal is awarded annually by the American Library Association for the most distinguished American picture book for children.

2004 Caldecott Medal and Honor Books
Caldecott Medal for Best Picture Book: *The Man Who Walked Between the Towers,* illustrated and written by Mordicai Gerstein (Roaring Brook Press)
Caldecott Honor Books: *Ella Sarah Gets Dressed,* illustrated and written by Margaret Chodos-Ivrine (Harcourt Inc.); *What Do You Do With a Tail Like This?,* illustrated and written by Steve Jenkins and Roger Page (Houghton Mifflin); *Don't Let the Pigeon Drive the Bus,* illustrated and written by Mo Willems (Hyperion)

1938–2003

1938 *Animals of the Bible, a Picture Book,* text selected by Helen Dean Fish, illustrated by Dorothy P. Lathrop

1939 *Mei Li,* written and illustrated by Thomas Handforth

1940 *Abraham Lincoln,* written and illustrated by Ingri and Edgar Parin D'Aulaire

1941 *They Were Strong and Good,* written and illustrated by Robert Lawson

1942 *Make Way for Ducklings,* written and illustrated by Robert McCloskey

1943 *The Little House,* written and illustrated by Virginia Lee Burton

1944 *Many Moons,* written by James Thurber, illustrated by Louis Slobodkin

1945 *Prayer for a Child,* written by Elizabeth Orton Jones

1946 *The Rooster Crows,* written and illustrated by Maud and Miska Petersham

1947 *The Little Island,* written by Golden MacDonald, illustrated by Leonard Weisgard

1948 *White Snow, Bright Snow,* written by Alvin Tresselt, illustrated by Roger Duvoisin

1949 *The Big Snow,* written and illustrated by Berta and Elmer Hader

1950 *Song of the Swallows,* written and illustrated by Leo Politi

1951 *The Egg Tree,* written and illustrated by Katherine Milhous

1952 *Finders Keepers,* written by William Lipkind, illustrated by Nicolas Mordvinoff

1953 *The Biggest Bear,* written and illustrated by Lynd Ward

1954 *Madeline's Rescue,* written and illustrated by Ludwig Bemelmans

1955 *Cinderella, or, The Little Glass Slipper,* translated and illustrated by Marcia Brown

1956 *Frog Went A-Courtin',* retold by John Langstaff, illustrated by Feodor Rojankovsky

1957 *A Tree Is Nice,* written by Janice May Udry, illustrated by Marc Simont

1958 *Time of Wonder,* written and illustrated by Robert McCloskey

1959 *Chanticleer and the Fox,* adapted and illustrated by Barbara Cooney

1960 *Nine Days to Christmas,* written by Marie Hall Ets and Aurora Labastida, illustrated by Marie Hall Ets

1961 *Baboushka and the Three Kings,* written by Ruth Robbins, illustrated by Nicolas Sidjakov

1962 *Once a Mouse,* retold and illustrated by Marcia Brown

1963 *The Snowy Day,* written and illustrated by Ezra Jack Keats

1964 *Where the Wild Things Are,* written and illustrated by Maurice Sendak

1965 *May I Bring a Friend?,* written by Beatrice Schenk de Regniers, illustrated by Beni Montresor

1966 *Always Room for One More,* written by Sorche Nic Leodhas, illustrated by Nonny Hogrogian

1967 *Sam, Bangs and Moonshine,* written and illustrated by Evaline Ness

1968 *Drummer Hoff,* written by Barbara Emberley, illustrated by Ed Emberley

1969 *The Fool of the World and the Flying Ship,* retold by Arthur Ransome, illustrated by Uri Shulevitz

1970 *Sylvester and the Magic Pebble,* written and illustrated by William Steig

1971 *A Story, A Story: An African Tale,* retold and illustrated by Gail E. Haley

1972 *One Fine Day,* written and illustrated by Nonny Hogrogian

1973 *The Funny Little Woman,* retold by Arlene Mosel, illustrated by Blair Lent

1974 *Duffy and the Devil,* retold by Harve Zemach, illustrated by Margot Zemach

1975 *Arrow to the Sun: A Pueblo Indian Tale,* adapted and illustrated by Gerald H. McDermott

1976 *Why Mosquitos Buzz in People's Ears (An African Tale),* retold by Verna Aardema, illustrated by Leo and Diane Dillon

1977 *Ashanti to Zulu: African Traditions,* written by Margaret Musgrove, illustrated by Leo and Diane Dillon

1978 *Noah's Ark,* written by Jacob Revius, illustrated by Peter Spier

1979 *The Girl Who Loved Wild Horses,* written and illustrated by Paul Goble

1980 *Ox-Cart Man,* written by Donald Hall, illustrated by Barbara Cooney

1981 *Fables,* written and illustrated by Arnold Lobel

1982 *Jumanji,* written and illustrated by Chris Van Allsburg

1983 *Shadow,* translated and illustrated by Marcia Brown

1984 *The Glorious Flight: Across the Channel with Louis Blériot,* written and illustrated by Alice and Martin Provensen

1985 *St. George and the Dragon,* retold by Margaret Hodges, illustrated by Trina Schart Hyman

1986 *The Polar Express,* written and illustrated by Chris Van Allsburg

1987 *Hey, Al,* written by Arthur Yorinks, illustrated by Richard Egielski

1988 *Owl Moon,* written by Jane Yolen, illustrated by John Schoenherr

1989 *Song and Dance Man,* written by Karen Ackerman, illustrated by Stephen Gammell

1990 *Lon Po Po: A Red-Riding Hood Story from China,* by Ed Young

1991 *Black & White,* written and illustrated by David Macaulay

1992 *Tuesday,* written and illustrated by David Wiesner

1993 *Mirette on the High Wire,* written and illustrated by Emily Arnold McCully

1994 *Grandfather's Journey,* written and illustrated by Allen Say

1995 *Smoky Night,* written by Eve Bunting, illustrated by David Diaz

1996 *Officer Buckle and Gloria,* written and illustrated by Peggy Rathmann

1997 *Golem,* written and illustrated by David Wisniewski

1998 *Rapunzel,* illustrated and retold by Paul O. Zelinsky

1999 *Snowflake Bentley,* written by Jacqueline Briggs Martin, illustrated by Mary Azarian

2000 *Joseph Had a Little Overcoat,* illustrated by Simms Taback

2001 *So You Want to Be President?,* by Judith St. George, illustrated by David Small

2002 *The Three Little Pigs,* written and illustrated by David Wiesner

2003 *My Friend Rabbit,* written and illustrated by Eric Rohmann

Other American Library Association Awards for Children's Books, 2004

Coretta Scott King Award, honoring black authors and illustrators: (author): *The First Part Last*, Angela Johnson (Simon & Schuster); **(illustrator):** *Beautiful Blackbird*, Ashley Bryan (Atheneum Books); **(John Steptoe new talent author):** *The Way a Door Closes*, Hope Anita Smith (Henry Holt); **(John Steptoe new talent illustrator):** *My Family Plays Music*, Elbrite Brown (Holiday House)

Michael L. Printz Award for excellence in young adult literature: *The First Part Last*, Angela Johnson (Simon & Schuster)

Robert F. Sibert Award for informational book: *An American Plague: The True and Terrifying Story of the Yellow Fever Epidemic of 1793*, Jim Murphy (Clarion Books)

Margaret A. Edwards Award for lifetime contribution in writing for young adults: Ursula K. LeGuin

Mildred L. Batchelder Award, for best book originally published in a foreign language in a foreign country: *Run, Boy, Run*, written by Uri Orlev in Hebrew and translated by Hillel Halkin (Walter Lorraine Books)

May Hill Arbuthnot Honor Lecture Award: Richard Jackson

Andrew Carnegie Medal for best children's video: *Giggle, Giggle, Quack*, based on the book written by Doreen Cronin and illustrated by Betsy Lewin, produced by Paul R. Gagne and Melissa Reilly of Weston Woods Studios

2004 Pura Belpré Awards, honoring Latino writers and illustrators (awarded biennially): (author): *Before We Were Free*, Julia Alvarez (Alfred A. Knopf); **(illustrator):** *Just a Minute: A Trickster Tale and Counting Book*, illustrated and written by Yuyi Moralees (Chronicle Books)

2004 National Magazine Awards

General Excellence:
Aperture (circulation less than 100,000)
Chicago Magazine (circulation 100,000 to 250,000)
Budget Living (circulation 250,000 to 500,000)
Gourmet (circulation 500,000 to 1,000,000)
Popular Science (circulation 1,000,000 to 2,000,000)
Newsweek (circulation more than 2,000,000)

Personal Service: *Men's Health*
Leisure Interests: *Consumer Reports*
Reporting: *Rolling Stone*
Public Interest: *The New Yorker*

Feature Writing: *The New Yorker*
Columns and Commentary: *New York Magazine*
Essays: *The New Yorker*
Reviews and Criticism: *Esquire*
Profiles: *Esquire*
Single-topic Issue: *The Oxford American*
Design: *Esquire*
Photography: *City*
Fiction: *Esquire*
General Excellence Online: *CNET News.com*

Bollingen Prize in Poetry

The Bollingen Prize in Poetry is administered by the Yale University Library.

1949	Ezra Pound	1969	John Berryman and Karl Shapiro
1950	Wallace Stevens	1971	Richard Wilbur and Mona Van Duyn
1951	John Crowe Ransom	1973	James Merrill
1952	Marianne Moore	1975	Archie Randolph Ammons
1953	Archibald MacLeish and William Carlos Williams	1977	David Ignatow
1954	W. H. Auden	1979	W. S. Merwin
1955	Léonie Adams and Louise Bogan	1981	Howard Nemerov and May Swenson
1956	Conrad Aiken	1983	Anthony Hecht and John Hollander
1957	Allen Tate	1985	John Ashbery and Fred Chappell
1958	e. e. cummings	1987	Stanley Kunitz
1959	Theodore Roethke	1989	Edgar Bowers
1960	Delmore Schwartz	1991	Laura Riding Jackson and Donald Justice
1961	Yvor Winters	1993	Mark Strand
1962	John Hall Wheelock and Richard Eberhart	1995	Kenneth Koch
1963	Robert Frost	1997	Gary Snyder
1965	Horace Gregory	1999	Robert Creeley
1967	Robert Penn Warren	2001	Louise Glück
		2003	Adrienne Rich

Kingsley Tufts Poetry Prize

1993	Susan Mitchell, *Rapture*	1999	B. H. Fairchild, *The Art of the Lathe*
1994	Yusef Komunyakaa, *Neon Vernacular*	2000	Robert Wrigley, *Reign of Snakes: Poems*
1995	Thomas Lux, *Split Horizon*	2001	Alan Shapiro, *The Dead Alive and Busy*
1996	Deborah Digges, *Rough Music*	2002	Carl Phillips, *The Tether*
1997	Campbell McGrath, *Spring Comes to Chicago*	2003	Linda Gregerson, *Waterborne*
1998	John Koethe, *Falling Water*	2004	Henri Cole, *Middle Earth*

2004 NAACP Image Awards

MOTION PICTURE

Outstanding Motion Picture: *The Fighting Temptations*
Outstanding Actress in a Motion Picture: Queen Latifah, *Bringing Down the House*
Outstanding Actor in a Motion Picture: Cuba Gooding, Jr., *Radio*
Outstanding Supporting Actress in a Motion Picture: Alfre Woodard, *Radio*
Outstanding Supporting Actor in a Motion Picture: Morgan Freeman, *Bruce Almighty*

TELEVISION

Outstanding Comedy Series: *The Bernie Mac Show*
Outstanding Actress in a Comedy Series: Mo'Nique, *The Parkers*
Outstanding Actor in a Comedy Series: Bernie Mac, *The Bernie Mac Show*
Outstanding Supporting Actress in a Comedy Series: Camille Winbush, *The Bernie Mac Show*
Outstanding Supporting Actor in a Comedy Series: Dorien Wilson, *The Parkers*
Outstanding Drama Series: *Soul Food*
Outstanding Actress in a Drama Series: Nia Long, *Third Watch*
Outstanding Actor in a Drama Series: Steve Harris, *The Practice*
Outstanding Supporting Actress in a Drama Series: Loretta Devine, *Boston Public*
Outstanding Supporting Actor in a Drama Series: Mekhi Phifer, *ER*
Outstanding Television Movie, Miniseries, or Dramatic Special: *D.C. Sniper: 23 Days of Fear*
Outstanding Actress in a Television Movie, Miniseries, or Dramatic Special: Whoopi Goldberg, *Good Fences*
Outstanding Actor in a Television Movie, Miniseries, or Dramatic Special: Charles S. Dutton, *D.C. Sniper: 23 Days of Fear*
Outstanding Actress in a Daytime Drama Series: Victoria Rowell, *The Young & the Restless*
Outstanding Actor in a Daytime Drama Series: Kristoff St. John, *The Young & the Restless*
Outstanding Variety Series/Special: *The 2003 Essence Awards*
Outstanding News, Talk, or Information Series or Special: *Judge Mathis*
Outstanding Performance in a Youth or Children's Series or Special: Raven, *That's So Raven*

RECORDING

Outstanding New Artist: Ruben Studdard
Outstanding Female Artist: Alicia Keyes
Outstanding Male Artist: Luther Vandross
Outstanding Duo or Group: OutKast
Outstanding Jazz Artist: Ramsey Lewis
Outstanding Gospel Artist: Donnie McClurkin
Outstanding Music Video: Luther Vandross, "Dance with My Father"
Outstanding Song: Luther Vandross, "Dance with My Father"
Outstanding Album: Luther Vandross, *Dance with My Father*

LITERARY WORK

Outstanding Literary Work, Fiction: *Love,* Toni Morrison
Outstanding Literary Work, Nonfiction: *Why I Love Black Women,* Michael Eric Dyson
Outstanding Literary Work, Children's: *My Brother Martin: A Sister Remembers Growing Up with the Rev. Dr. Martin Luther King, Jr.,* Christine King Farris

The Spingarn Medal

The Spingarn Medal is awarded annually by the National Association for the Advancement of Colored People for outstanding achievement by a black American.

1915	Ernest E. Just	1945	Paul Robeson	1975	Hank Aaron
1916	Charles Young	1946	Thurgood Marshall	1976	Alvin Ailey
1917	Harry T. Burleigh	1947	Percy Julian	1977	Alex Haley
1918	William Stanley Braithwaite	1948	Channing H. Tobias	1978	Andrew Young
1919	Archibald H. Grimke	1949	Ralph J. Bunche	1979	Rosa L. Parks
1920	W. E. B. Du Bois	1950	Charles Hamilton Houston	1980	Rayford W. Logan
1921	Charles S. Gilpin	1951	Mabel Keaton Staupers	1981	Coleman Young
1922	Mary B. Talbert	1952	Harry T. Moore	1982	Benjamin E. Mays
1923	George Washington Carver	1953	Paul R. Williams	1983	Lena Horne
1924	Roland Hayes	1954	Theodore K. Lawless	1984	Tom Bradley
1925	James Weldon Johnson	1955	Carl Murphy	1985	Bill Cosby
1926	Carter G. Woodson	1956	Jackie Robinson	1986	Benjamin L. Hooks
1927	Anthony Overton	1957	Martin Luther King, Jr.	1987	Percy Ellis Sutton
1928	Charles W. Chesnutt	1958	Daisy Bates and the Little Rock Nine	1988	Frederick Douglass Patterson
1929	Mordecai Wyatt Johnson			1989	Jesse Jackson
1930	Henry A. Hunt	1959	Edward Kennedy (Duke) Ellington	1990	L. Douglas Wilder
1931	Richard Berry Harrison			1991	Colin T. Powell
1932	Robert Russa Moton	1960	Langston Hughes	1992	Barbara Jordan
1933	Max Yergan	1961	Kenneth B. Clark	1993	Dorothy Irene Height
1934	William T. B. Williams	1962	Robert C. Weaver	1994	Maya Angelou
1935	Mary McLeod Bethune	1963	Medgar Evers	1995	John Hope Franklin
1936	John Hope	1964	Roy Wilkins	1996	A. Leon Higginbotham, Jr.
1937	Walter White	1965	Leontyne Price	1997	Carl Rowan
1938	No award	1966	John H. Johnson	1998	Myrlie Evers-Williams
1939	Marian Anderson	1967	Edward W. Brooke III	1999	Earl G. Graves, Sr.
1940	Louis T. Wright	1968	Sammy Davis, Jr.	2000	Oprah Winfrey
1941	Richard Wright	1969	Clarence M. Mitchell, Jr.	2001	Vernon E. Jordan, Jr.
1942	A. Philip Randolph	1970	Jacob Lawrence	2002	John Lewis
1943	William H. Hastie	1971	Leon Howard Sullivan	2003	Constance Baker Motley
1944	Charles Drew	1972	Gordon Parks	2004	Robert L. Carter
		1973	Wilson C. Riles		
		1974	Damon Keith		

2004 Major Emmy Awards

Drama Series: *The Sopranos* (HBO)
  Actress: Allison Janney, *The West Wing*
  Actor: James Spader, *The Practice*
  Supporting Actress: Drea De Matteo, *The Sopranos*
  Supporting Actor: Michael Imperioli, *The Sopranos*
  Guest Actor: William Shatner, *The Practice*
  Guest Actress: Sharon Stone, *The Practice*
  Directing: Walter Hill, *Deadwood:* "Pilot"
  Writing: Terence Winter, *The Sopranos:* "Long Term Parking"
Comedy Series: *Arrested Development* (Fox)
  Actress: Sarah Jessica Parker, *Sex and the City*
  Actor: Kelsey Grammer, *Frasier*
  Supporting Actress: Cynthia Nixon, *Sex and the City*
  Supporting Actor: David Hyde Pierce, *Frasier*
  Guest Actress: Laura Linney, *Frasier*
  Guest Actor: John Turturro, *Monk*
  Directing: Joe Russo and Anthony Russo, *Arrested Development:* "Pilot"
  Writing: Michael Hurwitz, *Arrested Development:* "Pilot"
Variety, Music, or Comedy Series: *The Daily Show with Jon Stewart* (Comedy Central)
Variety, Music, or Comedy Special: *Elaine Stritch: At Liberty* (HBO)
Individual Performance, Variety, or Music Program: Elaine Stritch, *Elaine Stritch: At Liberty*

Directing in a Variety, Music, or Comedy Program: Louis J. Horvitz, *The 76th Annual Academy Awards*
Writing in a Variety, Music, or Comedy Program: *The Daily Show with Jon Stewart*
Miniseries or Special: *Angels in America* (HBO)
  Actress: Meryl Streep, *Angels in America*
  Actor: Al Pacino, *Angels in America*
  Supporting Actress: Mary-Louise Parker, *Angels in America*
  Supporting Actor: Jeffrey Wright, *Angels in America*
  Directing: Mike Nichols, *Angels in America*
  Writing: Tony Kushner, *Angels in America*
Made-for-Television Movie: *Something the Lord Made* (HBO)
Outstanding Nonfiction Series: *American Masters* (PBS)
Outstanding Nonfiction Special: *The Forgetting: A Portrait of Alzeimher's* (PBS)
Outstanding Reality/Competition Program: *The Amazing Race* (CBS)
Outstanding Reality Program: *Queer Eye for the Straight Guy* (Bravo)
Outstanding Children's Program: *Happy to Be Nappy and Other Stories of Me* (HBO)
Outstanding Animated Program (one hour or less): *Samurai Jack:* "The Birth of Evil"

2003–2004 Daytime Emmy Awards

Outstanding Drama Series: *The Young and the Restless* (CBS)
Lead Actor in a Drama Series: Anthony Geary, *General Hospital*
Lead Actress in a Drama Series: Michelle Stafford, *The Young and the Restless*
Supporting Actor in a Drama Series: Benjamin Hendrickson, *As the World Turns*
Supporting Actress in a Drama Series: Cady McClain, *As the World Turns*
Younger Actor in a Drama Series: Chad Brannon, *General Hospital*
Younger Actress in a Drama Series: Jennifer Finnigan, *The Bold and the Beautiful*
Outstanding Preschool Children's Series: *Sesame Street* (PBS)
Outstanding Children/Youth/Family Special: *The Incredible Mrs. Ritchie* (Showtime)
Outstanding Children's Animated Program: *Little Bill* (Nick Jr.)
Outstanding Special Class Children's Animated Program: *Tutenstein* (NBC)
Performer in a Children's Series: Jeff Corwin, *Jeff Corwin Unleashed*

Performer in a Children's Special: Gena Rowlands, *The Incredible Mrs. Ritchie*
Performer in an Animated Program: Joe Alaskey, *Duck Dodgers*
Outstanding Children's Series: *Assignment Discovery* (Discovery Channel)
Outstanding Special Class Series: *When I Was a Girl* (WE)
Outstanding Special Class Special: *77th Annual Macy's Thanksgiving Day Parade* (NBC)
Outstanding Game/Audience Participation Show: *The Price Is Right* (CBS)
Outstanding Game-Show Host: Bob Barker, *The Price Is Right*
Outstanding Talk Show: *The Ellen DeGeneres Show* (syndicated)
Outstanding Talk-Show Host: Wayne Brady, *The Wayne Brady Show*
Outstanding Service Show: *Martha Stewart Living* (syndicated)
Outstanding Service-Show Host: Suze Orman, *Suze Orman: The Laws of Money, the Lessons of Life*

2004 Alfred I. du Pont–Columbia University Awards in Television and Radio

SILVER BATONS

ABC News and Ted Koppel for *Nightline: Tip of the Spear*
CBS NEWS, David Martin, and Mary Walsh for coverage of national security
PBS for *FRONTLINE: A Dangerous Business*
PBS for *FRONTLINE: Failure to Protect: The Taking of Logan Marr; The Caseworker Files;* and *A National Dialogue*
PBS for *FRONTLINE: Faith and Doubt at Ground Zero*
HBO and Maysles Films Inc., for *LaLee's Kin: The Legacy of Cotton*
KBCI-TV, Boise, for *Shake-Up at City Hall*

KHOU-TV, Houston, for *Evidence of Errors*
KMGH-TV, Denver, for *Honor and Betrayal: Scandal at the Academy*
National Public Radio (NPR) for coverage of the war in Iraq
P.O.V., Whitney Dow and Marco Williams (PBS) for *Two Towns of Jasper*
WESH-TV, Orlando, and Dan Billow for coverage of the *Columbia* space shuttle disaster
WTVF-TV, Nashville, for *Friends in High Places*

2003 George Foster Peabody Awards for Broadcasting

Honor and Betrayal: Scandal at the Academy:
KMGH-TV, Denver, Colo.

60 Minutes: All In the Family: CBS News, N.Y.

A Question of Fairness: NBC News, N.Y.

War Photographer: Christian Frei Filmproductions,
HBO/Cinemax Documentary Films, Swiss National
Television, Suisseimage, presented on HBO

The Elegant Universe with Brian Greene: NOVA/WGBH
(Boston) and Channel 4, presented on PBS

Flag Wars: P.O.V./American Documentary Inc., in
association with Independent Television Services (ITVS),
Zula Pearl Films, and National Black Programming
Consortium (NBPC), presented on PBS

Two Towns of Jasper: P.O.V./American Documentary
Inc., in association with Independent Television Service
(ITVS) and National Black Programming Consortium
(NBPC), presented on PBS

Chavez: Inside the Coup: ZDF German TV in association
with the Irish Film Board

Sisters in Pain: WEKU-FM, Down to Earth Productions

To Live Is Better Than to Die: Weijun Chen, HBO/
Cinemax Documentary Films, TV2 Denmark, BBC,
presented on Cinemax

*Know HIV/AIDS and Fight for Your Rights: Protect
Yourself Campaigns; A Walk in Your Shoes: Living
With HIV/AIDS; The Social History of HIV:* Viacom/
MTV and the Kaiser Family Foundation

Students Rising Above: KRON-TV, San Francisco, Calif.

Medicaid Dental Centers Investigation: WCNC-TV,
Charlotte, N.C.

FRONTLINE: A Dangerous Business: WGBH/Frontline,
The New York Times, and Canadian Broadcasting
Corporation, presented on PBS

Great Performances: Degas and the Dance: Thirteen/
WNET (New York), presented on PBS

American Mavericks: KSJN-FM/Minnesota Public Radio

Mother Flew Away As a Kite: TV Asahi Corporation

Soldier's Girl: Showtime

TRANSOM.ORG: Atlantic Public Media

The Murder of Emmett Till: American Experience/WGBH
(Boston), presented on PBS

Hoxie: The First Stand: University of Memphis, Memphis,
Tenn., presented on PBS

Evidence of Errors: KHOU-TV, Houston, Texas

Building Homes: Building Problems: WESH-TV, Winter
Park, Fla.

Israel's Secret Weapon: BBC2

Dora the Explorer: MTV Networks/Nickelodeon

The Wire: HBO

The Office: BBC America

Bill Moyers: Individual Peabody Award

2004 MacArthur Foundation Awards

The MacArthur Foundation awards $500,000 over five years to each MacArthur Fellow.

Angela Belcher, 37, nanotechnologist; Cambridge, Mass.

Gretchen Berland, 40, physician, filmmaker; New Haven,
Conn.

James Carpenter, 55, glass technologist; New York, N.Y.

Joseph DeRisi, 35, molecular biologist; San Francisco,
Calif.

Katherine Gottlieb, 52, Alaskan health-care leader;
Anchorage, Alaska

David Green, 48, technology transfer innovator; Berkeley,
Calif.

Aleksandar Hemon, 40, writer; Chicago, Ill.

Heather Hurst, 29, archaeological illustrator; New Haven,
Conn.

Edward P. Jones, 53, novelist; Arlington, Va.

John Kamm, 53, businessman, human-rights strategist;
San Francisco, Calif.

Daphne Koller, 36, computer scientist; Stanford, Calif.

Naomi Ehrich Leonard, 41, marine roboticist; Princeton,
N.J.

Tommie Lindsey, 53, high school debating coach; Union
City, Calif.

Rueben Martinez, 64, bookseller; Santa Ana, Calif.

Maria Mavroudi, 37, philologist; Berkeley, Calif.

Vamsi Mootha, 33, physician, researcher; Boston, Mass.

Judy Pfaff, 58, sculptor; Annandale-on-Hudson, N.Y.

Aminah Robinson, 64, folk artist; Columbus, Ohio

Reginald R. Robinson, 31, ragtime pianist and composer;
Chicago

Cheryl Rogowski, 43, farmer; Pine Island, N.Y.

Amy Smith, 41, inventor, instructor; Cambridge, Mass.

Julie Theriot, 36, microbiologist; Stanford, Calif.

C.D. Wright, 55, poet, professor; Providence, R.I.

Enrico Fermi Award

The $100,000 award is given in recognition of scientific and technical achievement in atomic energy.
Awarded by the president, it is the U.S. government's oldest science and technology award.

1954	Enrico Fermi	1982	Herbert Anderson and Seth Neddermeyer
1956	John von Neumann	1983	Alexander Hollaender and John Lawrence
1957	Ernest O. Lawrence	1984	Robert R. Wilson and Georges Vendryès
1958	Eugene P. Wigner	1985	Norman C. Rasmussen and Marshall N.
1959	Glenn T. Seaborg		Rosenblath
1961	Hans A. Bethe	1986	Ernest D. Courant and M. Stanley Livingston
1962	Edward Teller	1987	Luis W. Alvarez and Gerald F. Tape
1963	J. Robert Oppenheimer	1988	Richard B. Setlow and Victor F. Weisskopf
1964	Hyman G. Rickover	1990	George A. Cowan and Robley D. Evans
1966	Otto Hahn, Lise Meitner, and Fritz Strassman	1992	Leon M. Lederman, Harold Brown, and John S.
1968	John A. Wheeler		Foster, Jr.
1969	Walter H. Zinn	1993	Freeman J. Dyson and Liane B. Russell
1970	Norris E. Bradbury	1995	Ugo Fano and Martin Kamen
1971	Shields Warren and Stafford L. Warren	1996	Richard Garwin, Mortimer Elkind, and H. Rodney
1972	Manson Benedict		Withers
1976	William L. Russell	1998	Maurice Goldhaber and Michael E. Phelps
1978	Harold M. Agnew and Wolfgang K. H. Panofsky	2000	Sidney Drell, Sheldon Datz, and Herbert York
1980	Alvin M. Weinberg and Rudolf E. Peirls	2003	John N. Bahcall, Rayond Davis, Jr., and Seymour
1981	W. Bennett Lewis		Sack

Fields Medal Winners

The Fields Medal has been awarded quadrennially since 1936 by the International Congress of Mathematicians in Toronto to recognize outstanding mathematics achievement.

1936 Lars Valerian Ahlfors (Harvard University) and Jesse Douglas (Massachusetts Institute of Technology)
(Fields Medals were not awarded during World War II)
1950 Laurent Schwarts (University of Nancy) and Atle Selberg (Institute for Advanced Study, Princeton)
1954 Kunihiko Kodaira (Princeton University) and Jean-Pierre Serre (University of Paris)
1958 Klaus Friedrich Roth (University of London) and René Thom (University of Strasbourgh)
1962 Lars V. Hörmander (University of Stockholm) and John Willard Milnor (Princeton University)
1966 Michael Francis Atiyah (Oxford University), Paul Joseph Cohen (Stanford University), Alexander Grothendieck (University of Paris), and Stephen Smale (University of California, Berkeley)
1970 Alan Baker (Cambridge University), Heisuke Hironaka (Harvard University), Serge P. Novikov (Moscow University), and John Griggs Thompson (Cambridge University)
1974 Enrico Bombieri (University of Pisa) and David Bryant Mumford (Harvard University)
1978 Pierre René Deligne (Institut des Hautes Études Scientifiques), Charles Louis Fefferman (Princeton University), Gregori Alexandrovitch Margulis (Moscow University), and Daniel G. Quillen (Massachusetts Institute of Technology)

1982 Alain Connes (Institut des Hautes Études Scientifiques), William P. Thurston (Princeton University), and Shing-Tung Yau (Institute for Advanced Study, Princeton)
1986 Simon Donaldson (Oxford University), Gerd Faltings (Princeton University), and Michael Freedman (University of California, San Diego)
1990 Vladimir Drinfeld (Phys. Inst. Kharkov), Vaughan Jones (University of California, Berkeley), Shigefumi Mori (University of Kyoto), and Edward Witten (Institute for Advanced Study, Princeton)
1994 Pierre-Louis Lions (University of Paris–Dauphine), Jean-Christophe Yoccoz (University of Paris–Sud), Jean Bourgain (Institute for Advanced Study, Princeton), and Efim Zelmanov (University of Wisconsin)
1998 Richard E. Borcherds (Cambridge University), William T. Gowers (Cambridge University), Maxim Kontsevich (Institut des Hautes Études Scientifiques and Rutgers University), and Curtis T. McMullen (Harvard University)
2002 Laurent Lafforgue (Institut des Hautes Études Scientifiques) and Vladimir Voevodsky (Institute for Advanced Study, Princeton)

Presidential Medal of Freedom

The Presidential Medal of Freedom, the nation's highest civilian award, recognizes exceptional meritorious service. (These are the medals awarded during President Bush's administration.)

2002 Hank Aaron (baseball player), Bill Cosby (comedian and actor), Plácido Domingo (tenor), Peter Drucker (management theorist), Katharine Graham* (newspaper publisher), Dr. D. A. Henderson (leader in eradication of smallpox), Irving Kristol (author and editor), Nelson Mandela (former president of South Africa), Gordon Moore (Intel cofounder), Nancy Reagan (former first lady), Fred Rogers (children's television host), A. M. Rosenthal (editor and columnist)

2003 Jacques Barzun (writer and historian), Julia Child (chef), Roberto W. Clemente* (baseball player), Van Cliburn (pianist), Vaclav Havel (playwright and former president of Czech Republic), Charlton Heston (actor), Lord Robertson (secretary general of NATO),

Edward Teller (physicist), R. David Thomas* (Wendy's founder and adoption advocate), Byron R. White* (Supreme Court justice), James Q. Wilson (professor), John R. Wooden (basketball coach)

2004 Robert L. Bartley (editor), Edward Brooke III (politician), Doris Day (actress), Vartan Gregorian (historian), Gilbert Melville Grosvenor (president of the National Geographic Society), Gordon B. Hinckley (president of the Mormon Church), John Paul II (pope), Estee Lauder (founder of cosmetics company), Rita Moreno (dancer and actress), Arnold Palmer (golfer), Arnall Patz (ophthalmology researcher), Norman Podhoretz (journalist), Walter Wriston (economist and banker)

NOTE: An asterisk following a name denotes a posthumous award.

Recipients of Kennedy Center Honors

The Kennedy Center Honors recognize the lifetime achievements of selected American performing artists.

1978 Marian Anderson (contralto), Fred Astaire (dancer-actor), Richard Rodgers (Broadway composer), Arthur Rubinstein (pianist), George Balanchine (choreographer)
1979 Ella Fitzgerald (jazz singer), Henry Fonda (actor), Martha Graham (choreographer), Tennessee Williams (playwright), Aaron Copland (composer)
1980 James Cagney (actor), Leonard Bernstein (composer-conductor), Agnes de Mille (choreographer), Lynn Fontanne (actress), Leontyne Price (soprano)
1981 Count Basie (jazz composer-pianist), Cary Grant (actor), Helen Hayes (actress), Jerome Robbins (choreographer), Rudolf Serkin (pianist)

1982 George Abbott (Broadway producer), Lillian Gish (actress), Benny Goodman (jazz clarinetist), Gene Kelly (dancer-actor), Eugene Ormandy (conductor)
1983 Katherine Dunham (dancer-choreographer), Elia Kazan (director-author), James Stewart (actor), Virgil Thomson (music critic–composer), Frank Sinatra (singer)
1984 Lena Horne (singer), Danny Kaye (comedian-actor), Gian Carlo Menotti (composer), Arthur Miller (playwright), Isaac Stern (violinist)
1985 Merce Cunningham (dancer-choreographer), Irene Dunne (actress), Bob Hope (comedian), Alan Jay Lerner (lyricist-playwright), Frederick Loewe (composer), Beverly Sills (soprano)

1986 Lucille Ball (comedienne), Ray Charles (musician), Yehudi Menuhin (violinist), Antony Tudor (choreographer), Hume Cronyn and Jessica Tandy (husband-and-wife acting team)

1987 Perry Como (singer), Bette Davis (actress), Sammy Davis, Jr. (entertainer), Nathan Milstein (violinist), Alwin Nikolais (choreographer)

1988 Alvin Ailey (choreographer), George Burns (comedian-actor), Myrna Loy (actress), Alexander Schneider (violinist), Roger L. Stevens (theatrical producer and the Kennedy Center's founding chairman)

1989 Harry Belafonte (singer-actor), Claudette Colbert (actress), Alexandra Danilova (ballerina), Mary Martin (actress), William Schuman (composer)

1990 Dizzy Gillespie (jazz trumpeter), Katharine Hepburn (actress), Risë Stevens (mezzo soprano), Jule Styne (composer), Billy Wilder (director)

1991 Roy Acuff (country singer-songwriter), Betty Comden and Adolph Green (co-authors of books and lyrics of musicals), the brothers Fayard and Harold Nicholas (dancers), Gregory Peck (actor), Robert Shaw (choral director)

1992 Lionel Hampton (jazz musician), Paul Newman (actor), Joanne Woodward (actress), Ginger Rogers (dancer-actress), Mstislav Rostropovich (cellist-conductor), Paul Taylor (choreographer)

1993 Johnny Carson (talk-show host), Arthur Mitchell (dancer-choreographer), Georg Solti (conductor), Stephen Sondheim (composer-lyricist), Marion Williams (gospel singer)

1994 Kirk Douglas (actor), Aretha Franklin (singer), Morton Gould (composer), Harold Prince (producer-director), Pete Seeger (folk singer)

1995 Jacques d'Amboise (choreographer), Marilyn Horne (mezzo soprano), B. B. King (blues singer), Sidney Poitier (actor), Neil Simon (playwright)

1996 Edward Albee (playwright), Benny Carter (jazz musician), Johnny Cash (musician), Jack Lemmon (actor), Maria Tallchief (ballerina)

1997 Lauren Bacall (actress), Bob Dylan (singer-songwriter), Charlton Heston (actor), Jessye Norman (soprano), Edward Villella (ballet dancer–director)

1998 Bill Cosby (actor-comedian), John Kander and Fred Ebb (Broadway composer-and-lyricist team), Willie Nelson (singer-songwriter), André Previn (composer-conductor), Shirley Temple Black (actress)

1999 Victor Borge (comedian-pianist), Sean Connery (actor), Judith Jamison (dancer-teacher), Jason Robards (actor), Stevie Wonder (singer-songwriter)

2000 Mikhail Baryshnikov (dancer), Plácido Domingo (tenor), Angela Lansbury (actress), Chuck Berry (rock 'n' roll musician), Clint Eastwood (actor-director-producer)

2001 Julie Andrews (actress), Van Cliburn (pianist), Quincy Jones (music producer–composer), Jack Nicholson (actor), Luciano Pavarotti (singer)

2002 James Earl Jones (actor), James Levine (conductor), Chita Rivera (dancer-actress), Paul Simon (singer), Elizabeth Taylor (actress)

2003 James Brown (soul singer), Carol Burnett (comedian-actress), Loretta Lynn (country singer), Mike Nichols (film and theater director), Itzhak Perlman (violinist)

2004 Webby Awards

Activism: Tolerance.org: www.tolerance.org

Best Practices: Google: www.google.com

Broadband: P.O.V.—Borders: Environment: www.pbs.org/pov/borders/index_flash.html

Commerce: iTunes Music Store: www.apple.com/itunes/store/shop.html

Community: Wikipedia: www.wikipedia.org

Education: BBC—Human Body: www.bbc.co.uk/science/humanbody

Fashion: colette: www.colette.fr

Film: FOG OF WAR: www.sonyclassics.com/fogofwar/indexFlash.html

Finance: U.S. Securities and Exchange Commission: www.sec.gov

Games: Yohoho! Puzzle Pirates: www.puzzlepirates.com

Government and Law: HealthyOntario.com: www.healthyontario.com

Health: KidsHealth: http://KidsHealth.org

Humor: The Onion: www.theonion.com

Living: Epicurious.com: www.epicurious.com

Music: iTunes Music Store: www.apple.com/itunes/store

Net Art: Access: www.accessproject.net

News: BBC News: www.bbc.co.uk/news

Personal Website: RAKU-GAKI.COM: www.raku-gaki.com

Politics: Meetup: www.meetup.com

Print and Zines: {fray}: www.fray.com

Radio: KEXP Radio Online: www.kexp.org

Science: Exploratorium: www.exploratorium.edu

Services: Google: www.google.com

Spirituality: GraceCathedral.org: www.GraceCathedral.org

Sports: BBC Sport: http://news.bbc.co.uk/sport

Technical Achievement: Map24: www.map24.com

Travel: IgoUgo: www.igougo.com

TV: PBS.org: www.pbs.org

Weird: Car Stuck Girls: www.carstuckgirls.com

Youth: WIRETAP: www.wiretapmag.org

2004 Albany Medical Center Prize in Medicine and Biomedical Research

Each year the Albany Medical Center honors a physician, scientist, or group whose work has led to significant advances in the fields of health care and scientific research.

Dr. Stanley N. Cohen, distinguished professor at Stanford University, and Dr. Herbert W. Boyer, cofounder of the biotechnology company Genentech Inc. and professor emeritus at the University of California at San Francisco, for their groundbreaking research discovering recombinant DNA, known as gene cloning. Their work paved the way for the modern biotechnology industry.

U.S. Symphony Orchestras and Their Music Directors

Akron Symphony Orchestra: Ya-Hui Wang
Alabama Symphony Orchestra: Richard Westerfield
American Composers Orchestra: Steven Sloane
American Symphony Orchestra: Leon Botstein
Arkansas Symphony Orchestra: David Itkin
Aspen Chamber Symphony: David Zinman
Atlanta Symphony Orchestra: Robert Spano
Austin Symphony Orchestra: Peter Bay
Baltimore Symphony Orchestra: Yuri Temirkanov
Baton Rouge Symphony: Timothy Muffitt
Boston Philharmonic: Benjamin Zander
Boston Pops: Keith Lockhart
Boston Symphony Orchestra: James Levine
Boulder Philharmonic Orchestra: Theodore Kuchar
Brooklyn Philharmonic: Robert Spano
Buffalo Philharmonic Orchestra: JoAnn Falletta
Cedar Rapids Symphony: Christian Tiemeyer
Charleston Symphony Orchestra: David Stahl
Charlotte Pops: Christof Perick
Chattanooga Symphony & Opera: Robert Bernhardt
Chicago Sinfonietta: Paul Freeman
Chicago Symphony Orchestra: Daniel Barenboim
Cincinnati Symphony Orchestra: Paavo Järvi
Cleveland Orchestra: Franz Welser-Möst
Columbus Symphony Orchestra: Alessandro Siciliani
Dallas Symphony Orchestra: Andrew Litton
Dayton Philharmonic Orchestra: Neal Gittleman
Delaware Symphony Orchestra: David Amado
Des Moines Symphony: Joseph Giunta
Detroit Symphony Orchestra: Neeme Järvi
Elgin Symphony Orchestra: Robert Hanson
El Paso Symphony Orchestra: Gürer Aykal
Erie Philharmonic: Hugh Keelan
Evansville Philharmonic Orchestra: Alfred Savia
Florida Orchestra: Stefan Sanderling
Florida West Coast Symphony: Leif Bjaland[1, 2]
Fort Wayne Philharmonic: Edvard Tchivzhel
Fort Worth Symphony Orchestra: Miguel Harth-Bedoya
Fresno Philharmonic Orchestra: Theodore Kuchar
Grand Rapids Symphony: David Lockington
Grant Park Orchestra (Chicago): Carlos Kalmar[2]
Greensboro Symphony Orchestra: Dmitry Sitkovetsky
Greenville Symphony Orchestra: Edvard Tchivzhel
Handel & Haydn Society (Boston): Grant Llewellyn
Harrisburg Symphony Orchestra: Stuart Malina
Hartford Symphony Orchestra: Edward Cumming
Honolulu Symphony Orchestra: Samuel Wong
Houston Symphony: Hans Graf
Indianapolis Symphony: Mario Venzago
Jacksonville Symphony Orchestra: Fabio Mechetti
Kalamazoo Symphony Orchestra: Raymond Harvey
Kansas City Symphony: Timothy Hankewich[2]
Kennedy Center Opera House Orchestra: Heinz Fricke
Knoxville Symphony Orchestra: Lucas Richman
Little Orchestra Society of New York: Dino Anagnost
Long Beach Symphony Orchestra: Enrique Arturo Diemecke
Long Island Philharmonic: David Wiley
Los Angeles Chamber Orchestra: Jeffrey Kahane
Los Angeles Philharmonic: Esa-Pekka Salonen

Louisiana Philharmonic Orchestra: Klauspeter Seibel
Louisville Orchestra: Uriel Segal
Madison Symphony Orchestra: John DeMain
Memphis Symphony Orchestra: David Loebel
Milwaukee Symphony Orchestra: Andreas Delfs
Minnesota Orchestra: Osmo Vänskä
Mississippi Symphony Orchestra: Crafton Beck
Monterey Symphony: Max Bragado-Darman
Music of the Baroque (Chicago): Jane Glover
Naples Philharmonic Orchestra: Jorge Mester
Nashville Symphony: Kenneth Schermerhorn
National Symphony (DC): Leonard Slatkin
New Haven Symphony Orchestra: Jung-Ho Pak
New Jersey Symphony Orchestra: Neeme Järvi
New Mexico Symphony Orchestra: Guillermo Figueroa
New West Symphony: Boris Brott
New World Symphony (Fla.): Michael Tilson Thomas[1]
New York Philharmonic: Lorin Maazel
New York Pops: Skitch Henderson
North Carolina Symphony: Grant Llewellyn
Northeastern Pennsylvania Philharmonic: Clyde Mitchell
Oklahoma City Philharmonic: Joel Levine
Omaha Symphony: Victor Yampolsky
Omaha Symphony Chamber Orchestra: Victor Yampolsky
Oregon Symphony: Carlos Kalmar
Pacific Symphony Orchestra (Calif.): Carl St. Clair
Palm Beach Pops: Bob Lappin
Philadelphia Orchestra: Christoph Eschenbach
Philharmonia Baroque Orchestra: Nicholas McGegan
Phoenix Symphony: Hermann Michael
Pittsburgh Symphony: Mariss Jansons
Portland Symphony Orchestra: Toshiyuki Shimada
Quad City Symphony Orchestra: Donald Schleicher
Rhode Island Philharmonic: Larry Rachleff
Richmond Symphony: Mark Russell Smith
River City Brass Band: Denis Colwell
Rochester Philharmonic Orchestra: Christopher Seaman
St. Louis Symphony Orchestra: David Robertson
St. Paul Chamber Orchestra: Andreas Delfs
San Antonio Symphony: Larry Rachleff
San Francisco Symphony: Michael Tilson Thomas
Santa Barbara Symphony Orchestra: Gisèle Ben-Dor
Santa Rosa Symphony: Jeffrey Kahane
Seattle Symphony: Gerard Schwarz
Shreveport Symphony: Kermit Poling
Spokane Symphony: Eckart Preu
Springfield Symphony (Mass.): Kevin Rhodes
Stamford Symphony Orchestra: Roger Nierenberg
Syracuse Symphony Orchestra: Daniel Hege
Toledo Symphony: Stefan Sanderling[2]
Tucson Symphony Orchestra: George Hanson
Utah Symphony: Keith Lockhart
Virginia Symphony: JoAnn Falletta
Westchester Philharmonic: Paul Lustig Dunkel
West Virginia Symphony Orchestra: Grant Cooper[1, 2]
Wichita Symphony: Andrew Sewell
Winston-Salem Symphony: Peter Perret
Youngstown Symphony Orchestra: Isaiah Jackson

1. Artistic Director. 2. Principal Conductor.

U.S. Opera Companies

American Musical Theatre of San Jose: Stewart Slater, pres.
Arizona Opera Company: Joel Revzen, art. dir.
Aspen Opera Theater Center: Ed Berkeley, gen. dir.
Atlanta Opera: William Fred Scott, art. dir.
Austin Lyric Opera: Richard Buckley, art. dir.
Baltimore Opera Company: Michael Harrison, gen. dir.
Boston Lyric Opera Company: Janice Mancini Del Sesto, gen. dir.
Central City Opera: Pelham G. Pearce, gen. dir.
Cincinnati Opera Association: Nicholas Muni, art. dir.
Civic Light Opera: Jim Mercer, admin. dir.
Cleveland Opera: David Bamberger, gen. dir.
Dallas Opera: Karen Stone, gen. dir.
Florentine Opera Company: Dennis Hanthorn, gen. dir.
Florida Grand Opera: Robert M. Heuer, gen. dir.
Glimmerglass Opera: Joanne Cossa, gen. dir.
Goodspeed Musicals: Michael Price, exec. dir.
Hawaii Opera Theatre: George Sinclair, exec. dir.
Houston Grand Opera: David Gockley, gen. dir.
Kentucky Opera: Deborah Sandler, gen. dir.
Los Angeles Opera: Plácido Domingo, gen. dir.
Lyric Opera of Chicago: William Mason, gen. dir.
Lyric Opera of Kansas City: Evan R. Luskin, gen. dir.
Metro Lyric Opera: Era M. Tognoli, art. dir.
Metropolitan Opera: James Levine, art. dir.

Michigan Opera Theatre: David DiChiera, gen. dir.
Minnesota Opera: Dale Johnson, art. dir.
New York City Opera: Paul Kellogg, gen. dir. and art. dir.
Ohio Light Opera: Steven Daigle, art. dir.
Opera Colorado: Peter Russell, gen. dir.
Opera Company of Philadelphia: Robert B. Driver, producing art. dir.
Opera Pacific: John DeMain, art. dir.
Opera Theatre of St. Louis: Charles MacKay, gen. dir.
Orlando Opera Company: Robert Swedberg, gen. dir.
Palm Beach Opera: Joseph Barnette, gen. dir.
Pittsburgh Opera: Mark Weinstein, gen. dir.
Portland Opera: Christopher Mattaliano, gen. dir.
San Diego Civic Light Opera Association: Brian Wells, prod. art. dir.
San Diego Opera: Ian D. Campbell, gen. dir.
San Francisco Opera: Pamela Rosenberg, gen. dir.
San Francisco Opera Center: Sheri Greenawald, gen. dir.
Santa Fe Opera: Richard Gaddes, gen. dir.
Sarasota Opera Association: Victor DeRenzi, art. dir.
Seattle Opera Association: Speight Jenkins, gen. dir.
Utah Opera Company: Anne Ewers, gen. dir.
Virginia Opera: Peter Mark, art. dir.
Washington (DC) Opera: Plácido Domingo, gen. dir.

Most Frequently Produced Operas in North America

(through 2003–2004 season)

Opera	Composer	Opera	Composer
1. *La Traviata*	Verdi	11. *Carmen*	Bizet
2. *The Barber of Seville*	Rossini	12. *Così fan tutte*	Mozart
3. *Madama Butterfly*	Puccini	13. *Lucia di Lammermoor*	Donizetti
4. *Don Giovanni*	Mozart	14. *L'elisir d'amore*	Donizetti
5. *Rigoletto*	Verdi	15. *Pagliacci*	Leoncavallo
6. *Tosca*	Puccini	16. *Roméo et Juliette*	Gounod
7. *La bohème*	Puccini	17. *The Pirates of Penzance*	Sullivan
8. *The Magic Flute*	Mozart	18. *Faust*	Gounod
9. *Turandot*	Puccini	19. *Die Fledermaus*	Strauss, Jr.
10. *The Marriage of Figaro*	Mozart	20. *The Mikado*	Sullivan

Source: Opera America. Web: www.operaamerica.org.

U.S. Dance Companies

Alvin Ailey American Dance Theatre (1958): Judith Jamison, art. dir.
American Ballet Theatre (1940): Kevin McKenzie, art. dir.
Atlanta Ballet Company (1929): John McFall, art. dir.
Ballet Florida (1986): Marie Hale, art. dir.
BalletMet Columbus (1978): Gerard Charles, art. dir.
Ballet San Jose of Silicon Valley (1986): Dennis Nahat, art. dir.
Ballet West (1963): Jonas Kåge, art. dir.
Bill T. Jones/Arnie Zane Dance Company (1982): Bill T. Jones, art. dir.
Boston Ballet (1963): Mikko Nissinen, art. dir.
Cincinnati Ballet (1958): Victoria Morgan, art. dir.
Colorado Ballet (1961): Martin Fredmann, art. dir. and CEO
Dance Theater of Harlem (1969): Arthur Mitchell, art. dir.
Houston Ballet (1969): Stanton Welch, art. dir.

Joffrey Ballet of Chicago (1956): Gerald Arpino, art. dir.
José Limón Dance Company (1946): Carla Maxwell, art. dir.
Miami City Ballet (1986): Edward Villella, art. dir. and CEO
Milwaukee Ballet (1970): Michael Pink, art. dir.
Mark Morris Dance Group (1980): Mark Morris, art. dir.
Martha Graham Dance Company (1926): Terese Capucilli and Christine Dakin, art. dir.
Merce Cunningham Dance Company (1953): Merce Cunningham, art. dir.
New York City Ballet (1948): Peter Martins, ballet-master-in-chief
Pacific Northwest Ballet (1972): Kent Stowell and Francia Russell, art. dirs.
Paul Taylor Dance Company (1954): Paul Taylor, art. dir.
Pittsburgh Ballet Theater (1970): Terrence S. Orr, art. dir.
San Francisco Ballet (1933): Helgi Tomasson, art. dir.
Texas Ballet Theatre (1961): Ben Stevenson, art. dir.
Washington Ballet (1976): Septime Webre, art. dir.

NOTE: Year founded appears in parentheses after name.

Trends in Book and Literary Reading

The percentage of adult Americans reading literature has dropped dramatically over the past 20 years. "Literature" includes novels, short stories, plays, and poetry but not works of nonfiction.

	U.S. adult population			Rate of decline 1992–2002
	1982	1992	2002	
Number of literary readers (in millions)	**96**	**100**	**96**	
Percentage reading literature	56.9 %	54.0%	46.7%	−14%
Percentage reading any book	n.a.	60.9	56.6	−7

Source: National Endowment for the Arts, Reading at Risk: A Survey of Literary Reading in America, June 2004.

Demographic Characteristics of U.S. Adults Reading Literature[1]

(12-month period ending Aug. 2002)

Demographic characteristics	Percent reading literature	Number reading literature (in millions)	Demographic characteristics	Percent reading literature	Number reading literature (in millions)
Overall population	**46.7%**	**96**	**Education**		
Gender			Grade school	14.0%	2
Female	55.1	59	Some high school	23.4	5
Male	37.6	37	High school graduate	37.7	24
Ethnicity and race			Some college	52.9	30
Hispanic	26.5	6	College graduate	63.1	23
White	51.4	77	Graduate school	74.3	13
African American	37.1	9	**Family income**		
Other	43.7	4	$9,999 or less	32.1	5
Age			$10,000 to $19,999	37.5	8
18 to 24	42.8	11	$20,000 to $29,999	37.5	9
25 to 34	47.7	18	$30,000 to $39,999	44.1	11
35 to 44	46.6	21	$40,000 to $49,999	47.9	8
45 to 54	51.6	20	$50,000 to $74,999	52.3	18
55 to 64	48.9	13	$75,000 or more	60.8	28
65 to 74	45.3	8	Income not reported	39.8	9
75 or older	36.7	6			

1. "Literature" includes novels, short stories, plays, and poetry but not works of nonfiction. Source: National Endowment for the Arts, Reading at Risk: A Survey of Literary Reading in America, June 2004.

U.S. Adult Participation in Literary Activities

(12-month period ending Aug. 2002)

	Percent of population	Millions of people		Percent of population	Millions of people
Read any book	**56.6%**	**117**	**Did personal creative writing**	**7.0%**	**14**
Read literature[1]	**46.7**	**96**	Published	1.0	2
Read a novel or short story	45.1	93	Unpublished	6.1	13
Read poetry	12.1	25	**Took creative writing classes or lessons**		
Read a play	3.6	7	In past year	1.0	2
Listened to live or recorded readings of novels or books	**9.3**	**19**	Ever	13.3	27
Read or listened to poetry	**14.3**	**30**	**Used Internet to learn about, read, or discuss topics related to literature**	**9.2**	**19**
Read poetry	12.1	25			
Listened to live or recorded readings of poetry	5.9	12			

1. "Literature" includes novels, short stories, plays, and poetry but not works of nonfiction. Source: National Endowment for the Arts, Reading at Risk: A Survey of Literary Reading in America, June 2004.

Family Reading, 1993–2001

Percentage of children ages 3–5 who were read to every day in the last week by a family member

	1993	1995	1996	1999	2001
Percentage of U.S. children	53%	58%	57%	54%	58%

Source: U.S. Department of Education, National Center for Education Statistics, National Household Education Survey.

Best-Selling Books, 2003

Source: Publishers Weekly.

Hardcover Fiction

1. *The Da Vinci Code,* Dan Brown
2. *The Five People You Meet in Heaven,* Mitch Albom
3. *The King of Torts,* John Grisham
4. *Bleachers,* John Grisham
5. *Armageddon,* Tim LaHaye and Jerry B. Jenkins
6. *The Teeth of the Tiger,* Tom Clancy
7. *The Big Bad Wolf,* James Patterson
8. *Blow Fly,* Patricia Cornwell
9. *The Lovely Bones,* Alice Sebold
10. *The Wedding,* Nicholas Sparks
11. *Shepherds Abiding,* Jan Karon
12. *Dark Tower V: Wolves of the Calla,* Stephen King
13. *Safe Harbour,* Danielle Steel
14. *Babylon Rising,* Tim LaHaye and Greg Dinallo
15. *Trojan Odyssey,* Clive Cussler

Trade Paperback

1. *Dr. Atkins' New Carbohydrate Gram Counter,* Robert C. Atkins, M.D.
2. *The Secret Life of Bees,* Sue Monk Kidd
3. *East of Eden,* John Steinbeck
4. *Seabiscuit,* Laura Hillenbrand
5. *Dr. Atkins' New Diet Revolution,* Robert C. Atkins, M.D.
6. *Life of Pi,* Yann Martel
7. *Self Matters,* Dr. Phil McGraw
8. *The Nanny Diaries,* Emma McLaughlin and Nicola Kraus
9. *Ladies' Detective Agency,* Alexander McCall Smith
10. *Trading Spaces Behind the Scenes,* Meredith Books Editors
11. *What to Expect When You're Expecting,* Heidi Murkoff
12. *Fix-It and Forget-It Cookbook,* Dawn J. Ranck and Phyllis Pellman Good
13. *Cold Mountain,* Charles Frazier
14. *The Atkins Journal,* Robert C. Atkins, M.D.
15. *The Hours,* Michael Cunningham

Hardcover Nonfiction

1. *The Purpose-Driven Life,* Rick Warren
2. *The South Beach Diet,* Arthur Agatston, M.D.
3. *Atkins for Life,* Robert C. Atkins, M.D.
4. *The Ultimate Weight Solution,* Dr. Phil McGraw
5. *Living History,* Hillary Rodham Clinton
6. *Lies: And the Lying Liars Who Tell Them . . . ,* Al Franken
7. *Guinness World Records 2004,* Guinness World Records
8. *Who's Looking Out for You,* Bill O'Reilly
9. *Dude, Where's My Country?,* Michael Moore
10. *A Royal Duty,* Paul Burrell
11. *Good to Great,* Jim Collins
12. *Kate Remembered,* A. Scott Berg
13. *The Essential 55,* Ron Clark
14. *Treason,* Ann Coulter
15. *The World According to Mister Rogers,* Fred Rogers

Mass Market Paperback

1. *Dr. Atkins' New Diet Revolution,* Robert C. Atkins, M.D.
2. *The King of Torts,* John Grisham
3. *Seabiscuit,* Laura Hillenbrand
4. *Key of Light,* Nora Roberts
5. *Key of Knowledge,* Nora Roberts
6. *Key of Valor,* Nora Roberts
7. *Three Fates,* Nora Roberts
8. *Angels & Demons,* Dan Brown
9. *Red Rabbit,* Tom Clancy
10. *The Beach House,* James Patterson
11. *Prey,* Michael Crichton
12. *Daddy's Little Girl,* Mary Higgins Clark
13. *Four Blind Mice,* James Patterson
14. *Truly Madly Manhattan,* Nora Roberts
15. *Engaging the Enemy,* Nora Roberts

Children's Books

Hardcover

1. *Harry Potter and the Order of the Phoenix,* J. K. Rowling
2. *The Slippery Slope (A Series of Unfortunate Events #10),* Lemony Snicket; illustrated by Brett Helquist
3. *Eragon,* Christopher Paolini
4. *The English Roses,* Madonna; illustrated by Jeffrey Fulvimari
5. *Artemis Fowl: The Eternity Code,* Eoin Colfer
6. *Good Night, Sweet Butterflies,* Dawn Bentley; illustrated by Heather Cahoon
7. *Mr. Peabody's Apples,* Madonna; illustrated by Loren Long
8. *The Cat in the Hat Movie: Storybook,* Justine and Ron Fontes
9. *The Second Summer of the Sisterhood,* Ann Brashares
10. *Storybook Treasury of Dick and Jane and Friends,* Grosset & Dunlap

Paperback

1. *Pirates of the Caribbean,* Irene Trimble
2. *Disney/Pixar's Finding Nemo: Junior Novelization*
3. *Disney/Pixar's Finding Nemo: Best Dad in the Sea*
4. *Holes* (movie tie-in edition), Louis Sachar
5. *Disney's Winnie the Pooh: A Bear-y Good Neighbor,* Kathleen Weidner Zoehfeld; illustrated by Robin Cuddy
6. *The Rise and Fall of the Kate Empire (Lizzie McGuire #4)*
7. *Captain Underpants and the Big Bad Battle of the Bionic Booger Boy, Part 1,* Dav Pilkey
8. *High Tide in Hawaii (Magic Treehouse #28),* Mary Pope Osborne; illustrated by Sal Murdocca
9. *Captain Underpants and the Big Bad Battle of the Bionic Booger Boy, Part 2,* Dav Pilkey
10. *The Lizzie McGuire Movie* (Junior Novel)

All-Time Best-Selling Children's Books

Source: Publishers Weekly.
From the date of publication (in parentheses) through the end of 2000.

Hardcover

1. *The Poky Little Puppy*, Janette Sebring Lowrey (1942)
2. *The Tale of Peter Rabbit*, Beatrix Potter (1902)
3. *Tootle*, Gertrude Crampton (1945)
4. *Green Eggs and Ham*, Dr. Seuss (1960)
5. *Harry Potter and the Goblet of Fire*, J. K. Rowling (2000)
6. *Pat the Bunny*, Dorothy Kunhardt (1940)
7. *Saggy Baggy Elephant*, Kathryn and Byron Jackson (1947)
8. *Scuffy the Tugboat*, Gertrude Crampton (1955)
9. *The Cat in the Hat*, Dr. Seuss (1957)
10. *Harry Potter and the Chamber of Secrets*, J. K. Rowling (1999)

Paperback

1. *Charlotte's Web*, E. B. White; illustrated by Garth Williams (1974)
2. *The Outsiders*, S. E. Hinton (1968)
3. *Tales of a Fourth Grade Nothing*, Judy Blume (1976)
4. *Love You Forever*, Robert Munsch; illustrated by Sheila McGraw (1986)
5. *Where the Red Fern Grows*, Wilson Rawls (1973)
6. *Island of the Blue Dolphins*, Scott O'Dell (1971)
7. *Harry Potter and the Sorcerer's Stone*, J. K. Rowling (1999)
8. *Are You There, God? It's Me, Margaret*, Judy Blume (1972)
9. *Shane*, Jack Schaeffer (1972)
10. *The Indian in the Cupboard*, Lynne Reid Banks (1982)

The 100 Best English-Language Novels of the 20th Century

The Board of the Modern Library, a division of Random House, published its selections in July 1998.

1. *Ulysses*, James Joyce (1922)
2. *The Great Gatsby*, F. Scott Fitzgerald (1925)
3. *A Portrait of the Artist as a Young Man*, James Joyce (1916)
4. *Lolita*, Vladimir Nabokov (1958)
5. *Brave New World*, Aldous Huxley (1932)
6. *The Sound and the Fury*, William Faulkner (1929)
7. *Catch-22*, Joseph Heller (1961)
8. *Darkness at Noon*, Arthur Koestler (1941)
9. *Sons and Lovers*, D. H. Lawrence (1913)
10. *The Grapes of Wrath*, John Steinbeck (1939)
11. *Under the Volcano*, Malcolm Lowry (1947)
12. *The Way of All Flesh*, Samuel Butler (1903)
13. *1984*, George Orwell (1949)
14. *I, Claudius*, Robert Graves (1934)
15. *To the Lighthouse*, Virginia Woolf (1927)
16. *An American Tragedy*, Theodore Dreiser (1925)
17. *The Heart Is a Lonely Hunter*, Carson McCullers (1940)
18. *Slaughterhouse-Five*, Kurt Vonnegut (1969)
19. *Invisible Man*, Ralph Ellison (1952)
20. *Native Son*, Richard Wright (1940)
21. *Henderson the Rain King*, Saul Bellow (1959)
22. *Appointment in Samarra*, John O'Hara (1934)
23. *U.S.A.* (trilogy), John Dos Passos (1937—trilogy completed)
24. *Winesburg, Ohio*, Sherwood Anderson (1919)
25. *A Passage to India*, E. M. Forster (1924)
26. *The Wings of the Dove*, Henry James (1902)
27. *The Ambassadors*, Henry James (1903)
28. *Tender Is the Night*, F. Scott Fitzgerald (1934)
29. *The Studs Lonigan Trilogy*, James T. Farrell (1935)
30. *The Good Soldier*, Ford Madox Ford (1915)
31. *Animal Farm*, George Orwell (1946)
32. *The Golden Bowl*, Henry James (1904)
33. *Sister Carrie*, Theodore Dreiser (1900)
34. *A Handful of Dust*, Evelyn Waugh (1934)
35. *As I Lay Dying*, William Faulkner (1930)
36. *All the King's Men*, Robert Penn Warren (1946)
37. *The Bridge of San Luis Rey*, Thornton Wilder (1927)
38. *Howards End*, E. M. Forster (1910)
39. *Go Tell It on the Mountain*, James Baldwin (1953)
40. *The Heart of the Matter*, Graham Greene (1948)
41. *Lord of the Flies*, William Golding (1954)
42. *Deliverance*, James Dickey (1969)
43. *A Dance to the Music of Time* (series), Anthony Powell (1975—series completed)
44. *Point Counter Point*, Aldous Huxley (1928)
45. *The Sun Also Rises*, Ernest Hemingway (1926)
46. *The Secret Agent*, Joseph Conrad (1907)
47. *Nostromo*, Joseph Conrad (1904)
48. *The Rainbow*, D. H. Lawrence (1915)
49. *Women in Love*, D. H. Lawrence (1921)
50. *Tropic of Cancer*, Henry Miller (1934)
51. *The Naked and the Dead*, Norman Mailer (1948)
52. *Portnoy's Complaint*, Philip Roth (1969)
53. *Pale Fire*, Vladimir Nabokov (1962)
54. *Light in August*, William Faulkner (1932)
55. *On the Road*, Jack Kerouac (1957)
56. *The Maltese Falcon*, Dashiell Hammett (1930)
57. *Parade's End*, Ford Madox Ford (1950)
58. *The Age of Innocence*, Edith Wharton (1920)
59. *Zuleika Dobson*, Max Beerbohm (1911)
60. *The Moviegoer*, Walker Percy (1961)
61. *Death Comes for the Archbishop*, Willa Cather (1927)
62. *From Here to Eternity*, James Jones (1951)
63. *The Wapshot Chronicles*, John Cheever (1957)
64. *The Catcher in the Rye*, J. D. Salinger (1951)
65. *A Clockwork Orange*, Anthony Burgess (1962)
66. *Of Human Bondage*, W. Somerset Maugham (1915)
67. *Heart of Darkness*, Joseph Conrad (1902)
68. *Main Street*, Sinclair Lewis (1920)
69. *The House of Mirth*, Edith Wharton (1905)
70. *The Alexandria Quartet*, Lawrence Durrell (1960—series completed)
71. *A High Wind in Jamaica*, Richard Hughes (1929)
72. *A House for Mr. Biswas*, V. S. Naipaul (1961)
73. *The Day of the Locust*, Nathanael West (1939)
74. *A Farewell to Arms*, Ernest Hemingway (1929)
75. *Scoop*, Evelyn Waugh (1938)

76. *The Prime of Miss Jean Brodie*, Muriel Spark (1961)
77. *Finnegans Wake*, James Joyce (1939)
78. *Kim*, Rudyard Kipling (1901)
79. *A Room with a View*, E. M. Forster (1908)
80. *Brideshead Revisited*, Evelyn Waugh (1945)
81. *The Adventures of Augie March*, Saul Bellow (1953)
82. *Angle of Repose*, Wallace Stegner (1971)
83. *A Bend in the River*, V. S. Naipaul (1979)
84. *The Death of the Heart*, Elizabeth Bowen (1938)
85. *Lord Jim*, Joseph Conrad (1900)
86. *Ragtime*, E. L. Doctorow (1975)
87. *The Old Wives' Tale*, Arnold Bennett (1908)
88. *The Call of the Wild*, Jack London (1903)
89. *Loving*, Henry Green (1945)
90. *Midnight's Children*, Salman Rushdie (1981)
91. *Tobacco Road*, Erskine Caldwell (1933)
92. *Ironweed*, William Kennedy (1983)
93. *The Magus*, John Fowles (1966)
94. *Wide Sargasso Sea*, Jean Rhys (1966)
95. *Under the Net*, Iris Murdoch (1954)
96. *Sophie's Choice*, William Styron (1979)
97. *The Sheltering Sky*, Paul Bowles (1949)
98. *The Postman Always Rings Twice*, James M. Cain (1934)
99. *The Ginger Man*, J. P. Donleavy (1955)
100. *The Magnificent Ambersons*, Booth Tarkington (1918)

The 100 Best English-Language Nonfiction Books of the 20th Century

The Board of the Modern Library, a division of Random House, published its selections in April 1999.

1. *The Education of Henry Adams*, Henry Adams (1906)
2. *The Varieties of Religious Experience*, William James (1902)
3. *Up from Slavery*, Booker T. Washington (1901)
4. *A Room of One's Own*, Virginia Woolf (1929)
5. *Silent Spring*, Rachel Carson (1962)
6. *Selected Essays, 1917–1932*, T. S. Eliot (1932)
7. *The Double Helix*, James D. Watson (1968)
8. *Speak, Memory*, Vladimir Nabokov (1967)
9. *The American Language*, H. L. Mencken (1919)
10. *The General Theory of Employment, Interest, and Money*, John Maynard Keynes (1935–1936)
11. *The Lives of a Cell*, Lewis Thomas (1974)
12. *The Frontier in American History*, Frederick Jackson Turner (1920)
13. *Black Boy*, Richard Wright (1945)
14. *Aspects of the Novel*, E. M. Forster (1927)
15. *The Civil War*, Shelby Foote (1958–1974)
16. *The Guns of August*, Barbara Tuchman (1962)
17. *The Proper Study of Mankind*, Isaiah Berlin (1997)
18. *The Nature and Destiny of Man*, Reinhold Niebuhr (1941–1943)
19. *Notes of a Native Son*, James Baldwin (1955)
20. *The Autobiography of Alice B. Toklas*, Gertrude Stein (1933)
21. *The Elements of Style*, William Strunk and E. B. White (1959)
22. *An American Dilemma*, Gunnar Myrdal (1944)
23. *Principia Mathematica*, Alfred North Whitehead and Bertrand Russell (1910–1913)
24. *The Mismeasure of Man*, Stephen Jay Gould (1981)
25. *The Mirror and the Lamp*, Meyer Howard Abrams (1953)
26. *The Art of the Soluble*, Peter B. Medawar (1967)
27. *The Ants*, Bert Hoelldobler and Edward O. Wilson (1990)
28. *A Theory of Justice*, John Rawls (1971)
29. *Art and Illusion*, Ernest H. Gombrich (1961)
30. *The Making of the English Working Class*, E. P. Thompson (1963)
31. *The Souls of Black Folk*, W.E.B. Du Bois (1903)
32. *Principia Ethica*, G. E. Moore (1903)
33. *Philosophy and Civilization*, John Dewey (1927)
34. *On Growth and Form*, D'Arcy Thompson (1917)
35. *Ideas and Opinions*, Albert Einstein (1954)
36. *The Age of Jackson*, Arthur Schlesinger, Jr. (1945)
37. *The Making of the Atomic Bomb*, Richard Rhodes (1986)
38. *Black Lamb and Grey Falcon*, Rebecca West (1942)
39. *Autobiographies*, W. B. Yeats (1926)
40. *Science and Civilization in China*, Joseph Needham (1954–)
41. *Goodbye to All That*, Robert Graves (1929)
42. *Homage to Catalonia*, George Orwell (1938)
43. *The Autobiography of Mark Twain*, Mark Twain (1924)
44. *Children of Crisis*, Robert Coles (1967)
45. *A Study of History*, Arnold J. Toynbee (1934–1961)
46. *The Affluent Society*, John Kenneth Galbraith (1958)
47. *Present at the Creation*, Dean Acheson (1969)
48. *The Great Bridge*, David McCullough (1972)
49. *Patriotic Gore*, Edmund Wilson (1962)
50. *Samuel Johnson*, Walter Jackson Bate (1977)
51. *The Autobiography of Malcolm X*, Alex Haley and Malcolm X (1965)
52. *The Right Stuff*, Tom Wolfe (1979)
53. *Eminent Victorians*, Lytton Strachey (1918)
54. *Working*, Studs Terkel (1974)
55. *Darkness Visible*, William Styron (1990)
56. *The Liberal Imagination*, Lionel Trilling (1950)
57. *The Second World War*, Winston Churchill (1948–1953)
58. *Out of Africa*, Isak Dinesen (1937)
59. *Jefferson and His Time*, Dumas Malone (1948–1981)
60. *In the American Grain*, William Carlos Williams (1925)
61. *Cadillac Desert*, Marc Reisner (1986)
62. *The House of Morgan*, Ron Chernow (1990)
63. *The Sweet Science*, A. J. Liebling (1956)
64. *The Open Society and Its Enemies*, Karl Popper (1945)
65. *The Art of Memory*, Frances A. Yates (1966)
66. *Religion and the Rise of Capitalism*, R. H. Tawney (1926)
67. *A Preface to Morals*, Walter Lippmann (1929)
68. *The Gate of Heavenly Peace*, Jonathan D. Spence (1981)
69. *The Structure of Scientific Revolutions*, Thomas S. Kuhn (1962)
70. *The Strange Career of Jim Crow*, C. Vann Woodward (1955)
71. *The Rise of the West*, William H. McNeill (1963)
72. *The Gnostic Gospels*, Elaine Pagels (1979)
73. *James Joyce*, Richard Ellmann (1959)
74. *Florence Nightingale*, Cecil Woodham-Smith (1950)

75. *The Great War and Modern Memory,* Paul Fussell (1975)
76. *The City in History,* Lewis Mumford (1961)
77. *Battle Cry of Freedom,* James M. McPherson (1988)
78. *Why We Can't Wait,* Martin Luther King, Jr. (1964)
79. *The Rise of Theodore Roosevelt,* Edmund Morris (1979)
80. *Studies in Iconology,* Erwin Panofsky (1939)
81. *The Face of Battle,* John Keegan (1976)
82. *The Strange Death of Liberal England,* George Dangerfield (1935)
83. *Vermeer,* Lawrence Gowing (1952)
84. *A Bright Shining Lie,* Neil Sheehan (1988)
85. *West with the Night,* Beryl Markham (1942)
86. *This Boy's Life,* Tobias Wolff (1989)
87. *A Mathematician's Apology,* G. H. Hardy (1940)
88. *Six Easy Pieces,* Richard P. Feynman (1963)
89. *Pilgrim at Tinker Creek,* Annie Dillard (1974)
90. *The Golden Bough,* James George Frazer (1922) (1 vol. ed.)
91. *Shadow and Act,* Ralph Ellison (1964)
92. *The Power Broker,* Robert A. Caro (1974)
93. *The American Political Tradition,* Richard Hofstadter (1948)
94. *The Contours of American History,* William Appleman Williams (1966)
95. *The Promise of American Life,* Herbert Croly (1909)
96. *In Cold Blood,* Truman Capote (1965)
97. *The Journalist and the Murderer,* Janet Malcolm (1990)
98. *The Taming of Chance,* Ian Hacking (1990)
99. *Operating Instructions,* Anne Lamott (1994)
100. *Melbourne,* Lord David Cecil (1939 & 1954)

Best American Journalism of the 20th Century

The following works were chosen as the 20th century's best American journalism by a panel of experts assembled by New York University's journalism department.

1. **John Hersey:** "Hiroshima," *The New Yorker,* 1946
2. **Rachel Carson:** *Silent Spring,* book, 1962
3. **Bob Woodward and Carl Bernstein:** Investigation of the Watergate break-in, *The Washington Post,* 1972
4. **Edward R. Murrow:** *Battle of Britain,* CBS radio, 1940
5. **Ida Tarbell:** "The History of the Standard Oil Company," *McClure's,* 1902–1904
6. **Lincoln Steffens:** "The Shame of the Cities," *McClure's,* 1902–1904
7. **John Reed:** *Ten Days That Shook the World,* book, 1919
8. **H. L. Mencken:** Scopes "Monkey" trial, *The Sun* of Baltimore, 1925
9. **Ernie Pyle:** Reports from Europe and the Pacific during World War II, Scripps-Howard newspapers, 1940–1945
10. **Edward R. Murrow and Fred Friendly:** Investigation of Sen. Joseph McCarthy, CBS, 1954
11. **Edward R. Murrow, David Lowe, and Fred Friendly:** "Harvest of Shame," documentary, CBS television, 1960
12. **Seymour Hersh:** Investigation of massacre by American soldiers at My Lai in Vietnam, Dispatch News Service, 1969
13. *The New York Times:* Publication of the Pentagon Papers, 1971
14. **James Agee and Walker Evans:** *Let Us Now Praise Famous Men,* book, 1941
15. **W.E.B. Du Bois:** *The Souls of Black Folk,* collected articles, 1903
16. **I. F. Stone:** *I. F. Stone's Weekly,* 1953–1967
17. **Henry Hampton:** "Eyes on the Prize," documentary, 1987
18. **Tom Wolfe:** *The Electric Kool-Aid Acid Test,* book, 1968
19. **Norman Mailer:** *The Armies of the Night,* book, 1968
20. **Hannah Arendt:** *Eichmann in Jerusalem: A Report on the Banality of Evil,* collected articles, 1963
21. **William Shirer:** *Berlin Diary: The Journal of a Foreign Correspondent, 1939–1941,* collected articles, 1941
22. **Truman Capote:** *In Cold Blood,* book, 1965
23. **Joan Didion:** *Slouching Towards Bethlehem,* collected articles, 1968
24. **Tom Wolfe:** *The Kandy-Kolored Tangerine-Flake Streamline Baby,* collected articles, 1965
25. **Michael Herr:** *Dispatches,* book, 1977
26. **Theodore White:** *The Making of the President: 1960,* book, 1961
27. **Robert Capa:** Ten photographs from D-Day, 1944
28. **J. Anthony Lukas:** *Common Ground: A Turbulent Decade in the Lives of Three American Families,* book, 1985
29. **Richard Harding Davis:** Coverage of German march into Belgium, Wheeler Syndicate and magazines, 1914
30. **Dorothy Thompson:** Reports on the rise of Hitler, *Cosmopolitan* and *Saturday Evening Post,* 1931–1934
31. **John Steinbeck:** Reports on Okie migrant camp life, *The San Francisco News,* 1936
32. **A. J. Liebling:** *The Road Back to Paris,* collected articles, 1944
33. **Ernest Hemingway:** Reports on the Spanish Civil War, *The New Republic,* 1937–1938
34. **Martha Gellhorn:** *The Face of War,* collected articles, 1959
35. **James Baldwin:** *The Fire Next Time,* book, 1963
36. **Joseph Mitchell:** *Up in the Old Hotel and Other Stories,* collection of much older articles, 1992
37. **Betty Friedan:** *The Feminine Mystique,* book, 1963
38. **Ralph Nader:** *Unsafe at Any Speed: The Designed-In Dangers of the American Automobile,* book, 1965
39. **Herblock (Herbert Block):** Cartoons on McCarthyism, *The Washington Post,* 1950
40. **James Baldwin:** "Letter from the South: Nobody Knows My Name," *The Partisan Review,* 1959
41. **Nick Ut:** Photograph of a burning girl running from a napalm attack, The Associated Press, 1972
42. **Pauline Kael:** "Trash, Art, and the Movies," *Harper's,* 1969
43. **Gay Talese:** *Fame and Obscurity: Portraits by Gay Talese,* collected articles, 1970
44. **Randy Shilts:** Reports on AIDS, *The San Francisco Chronicle,* 1981–1985

45. **Janet Flanner (Genet):** *Paris Journals* chronicling Paris's emergence from the Occupation, *The New Yorker,* 1944–1945
46. **Neil Sheehan:** *A Bright Shining Lie: John Paul Vann and America in Vietnam,* book, 1988
47. **A. J. Liebling:** *The Wayward Pressman,* collected articles, 1947
48. **Tom Wolfe:** *The Right Stuff,* book, 1979
49. **Murray Kempton:** *America Comes of Middle Age: Columns 1950–1962,* collected articles, 1963
50. **Murray Kempton:** *Part of Our Time: Some Ruins and Monuments of the Thirties,* book, 1955
51. **Donald L. Barlett and James B. Steele:** "America: What Went Wrong?," *The Philadelphia Inquirer,* 1991
52. **Taylor Branch:** *Parting the Waters: America in the King Years, 1954–1963,* book, 1988
53. **Harrison Salisbury:** Reporting from the Soviet Union, *The New York Times,* 1949–1954
54. **John McPhee:** *The John McPhee Reader,* collected articles, 1976
55. **ABC:** Live television broadcast of Army-McCarthy hearings, 1954
56. **Frederick Wiseman:** *Titicut Follies,* documentary, 1967
57. **David Remnick:** *Lenin's Tomb: The Last Days of the Soviet Empire,* book, 1993
58. **Richard Ben Cramer:** *What It Takes: The Way to the White House,* book, 1992
59. **Jonathan Schell:** *The Fate of the Earth,* book, 1982
60. **Russell Baker:** "Francs and Beans," *The New York Times,* 1975
61. **Homer Bigart:** Account of being over Japan in a bomber when World War II came to an end, *The New York Herald-Tribune,* 1945
62. **Ben Hecht:** *1,001 Afternoons in Chicago,* collected articles, 1922
63. **Walter Cronkite:** Documentary on Vietnam, CBS television, 1968
64. **Walter Lippmann:** Early essays, *The New Republic,* 1914
65. **Margaret Bourke-White:** Photographs following the defeat of Germany, *Life* magazine, 1945
66. **Lillian Ross:** *Reporting,* collected articles, 1964
67. **Nicholas Lemann:** *The Promised Land: The Great Black Migration and How It Changed America,* book, 1991
68. **Joe Rosenthal:** Photograph of Marines raising an American flag on Mount Suribachi on the island of Iwo Jima, The Associated Press, 1945
69. **Hodding Carter Jr.:** "Go for Broke," editorial, Carter's *Delta Democrat-Times* (Greenville, Miss.), 1945
70. **The New Yorker:** *The New Yorker Book of War Pieces,* collected articles, 1947

71. **Meyer Berger:** Report on the murderer Howard Unruh, *The New York Times,* 1949
72. **Norman Mailer:** *The Executioner's Song,* book, 1979
73. **Robert Capa:** Spanish Civil War photos, *Life* magazine, 1936
74. **Susan Sontag:** "Notes on 'Camp'," *The Partisan Review,* 1964
75. **Bob Woodward and Carl Bernstein:** *All the President's Men,* book, 1974
76. **John Hersey:** *Here to Stay,* collected articles, 1963
77. **A. J. Liebling:** *The Earl of Louisiana,* book, 1961
78. **Mike Davis:** *City of Quartz: Excavating the Future in Los Angeles,* book, 1990
79. **Melissa Fay Greene:** *Praying for Sheetrock,* book, 1991
80. **J. Anthony Lukas:** "The Two Worlds of Linda Fitzpatrick," *The New York Times,* 1967
81. **Herbert Bayard Swope:** "Klan Exposed," *The New York World,* 1921
82. **William Allen White:** "To an Anxious Friend," *The Emporia* (Kan.) *Gazette,* 1922
83. **Edward R. Murrow:** Report of the liberation of Buchenwald, CBS radio, 1945
84. **Joseph Mitchell:** *McSorley's Wonderful Saloon,* collected articles, 1943
85. **Lillian Ross:** *Picture,* book, 1952
86. **Earl Brown:** Series of articles on race, *Harper's* and *Life* magazines, 1942–1944
87. **Greil Marcus:** *Mystery Train: Images of America in Rock 'n' Roll Music,* book, 1975
88. **Morley Safer:** Atrocities committed by American soldiers on the hamlet of Cam Ne in Vietnam, CBS television, 1965
89. **Ted Poston:** Coverage of the "Little Scottsboro" trial, *The New York Post,* 1949
90. **Leon Dash:** "Rosa Lee's Story," *The Washington Post,* 1994
91. **Jane Kramer:** *Europeans,* collected articles, 1988
92. **Eddie Adams and Vo Suu:** Associated Press photograph and NBC television footage of a Saigon execution, 1968
93. **Grantland Rice:** "Notre Dame's 'Four Horsemen'," *The New York Herald-Tribune,* 1924
94. **Jane Kramer:** *The Politics of Memory: Looking for Germany in the New Germany,* collected articles, 1996
95. **Frank McCourt:** *Angela's Ashes,* book, 1996
96. **Vincent Sheean:** *Personal History,* book, 1935
97. **W.E.B. Du Bois:** Columns on race during his tenure as editor of *The Crisis,* 1910–1934
98. **Damon Runyon:** Crime reporting, *The New York American,* 1926
99. **Joe McGinniss:** *The Selling of the President 1968,* book, 1969
100. **Hunter S. Thompson:** *Fear and Loathing on the Campaign Trail,* book, 1973

Poets Laureate of England

Edmund Spenser	1591–1599	Laurence Eusden	1718–1730	Alfred Austin	1896–1913
Samuel Daniel	1599–1619	Colley Cibber	1730–1757	Robert Bridges	1913–1930
Ben Jonson	1619–1637	William Whitehead	1757–1785	John Masefield	1930–1967
William Davenant	1638–1668	Thomas Warton	1785–1790	Cecil Day-Lewis	1967–1972
John Dryden[1]	1668–1689	Henry James Pye	1790–1813	Sir John Betjeman	1972–1984
Thomas Shadwell	1689–1692	Robert Southey	1813–1843	Ted Hughes	1984–1998
Nahum Tate	1692–1715	William Wordsworth	1843–1850	Andrew Motion	1999–
Nicholas Rowe	1715–1718	Alfred Lord Tennyson	1850–1892		

1. First to bear the title officially.

Poets Laureate of the United States

Robert Penn Warren	1986–1987	Robert Hass	1995–1997
Richard Wilbur	1987–1988	Robert Pinsky	1997–2000
Howard Nemerov	1988–1990	Stanley Kunitz	2000–2001
Mark Strand	1990–1991	Billy Collins	2001–2003
Joseph Brodsky	1991–1992	Louise Glück	2003–2004
Mona Van Duyn	1992–1993	Ted Kooser	2004–
Rita Dove	1993–1995		

NOTE: The post was established in 1985. Appointment is for a one-year term, but is renewable.

Longest Broadway Runs

Show	Dates	Performances[1]	Show	Dates	Performances[1]
1. Cats	10/82–9/2000	7,485	12. Life with Father	11/39–7/47	3,224
2. The Phantom of the Opera	1/88–present	6,781	13. Tobacco Road	12/33–5/41	3,182
3. Les Misérables	3/87–5/2003	6,680	14. Chicago (revival)	11/96–present	2,907
4. A Chorus Line	7/75–4/90	6,137	15. Hello, Dolly!	1/64–12/70	2,844
5. Oh! Calcutta! (revival)	9/76–8/89	5,959	16. My Fair Lady	3/56–9/62	2,717
			17. The Lion King	11/97–present	2,699
6. Beauty and the Beast	4/94–present	4,108	18. Annie	4/77–1/83	2,377
7. Miss Saigon	4/91–1/2001	4,092	19. Cabaret (revival)	3/98–1/04	2,377
8. 42nd Street	8/80–1/89	3,486	20. Man of La Mancha	11/65–6/71	2,328
9. Grease	2/72–4/80	3,388	21. Abie's Irish Rose	5/22–10/27	2,327
10. Rent	4/96–present	3,336	22. Oklahoma!	3/43–5/48	2,212
11. Fiddler on the Roof	9/64–7/72	3,242	23. Smokey Joe's Cafe	3/95–1/2000	2,036
			24. Pippin	10/72–6/77	1,944
			25. South Pacific	4/49–1/54	1,925

1. As of 5/3/04. Source: League of American Theatres and Producers, Inc.

2003 Top 20 Concert Tours

Rank	Gross in millions	Artist	Average ticket price	No. of cities/ shows	Rank	Gross in millions	Artist	Average ticket price	No. of cities/ shows
1.	$115.9	Bruce Springsteen & the E Street Band	$ 71.36	30/47	11.	$47.1	Dave Matthews Band	$ 44.09	41/53
2.	80.5	Celine Dion	135.81	1/145	12.	44.2	Toby Keith	37.95	104/104
3.	69.3	Eagles	107.57	47/55	13.	40.8	Shania Twain	60.56	39/43
4.	69.0	Fleetwood Mac	83.37	66/71	14.	38.5	The Rolling Stones	158.17	12/14
5.	68.2	Cher	65.91	98/102	15.	35.8	Phish	46.62	28/39
6.	64.5	Simon & Garfunkel	136.90	28/39	16.	34.5	Kenny Chesney	35.76	83/83
7.	64.0	Aerosmith/KISS	76.08	56/58	17.	32.7	Tim McGraw	52.25	50/52
8.	60.5	Dixie Chicks	56.00	56/65	18.	31.8	Justin Timberlake/ Christina Aguilera	61.59	40/44
9.	50.9	Billy Joel/Elton John	109.24	23/27	19.	29.3	Jimmy Buffett	52.10	26/28
10.	48.8	"Summer Sanitarium Tour"/Metallica	70.32	19/19	20.	29.1	Pearl Jam	37.62	50/59

NOTE: All figures are for North American dates only. Source: Pollstar.

Music Sales by Genre

(Percent of recordings sold[1])

	1995	2000	2003		1995	2000	2003
Rock	33.5%	24.8%	25.2%	Jazz	3.0%	2.9%	2.9%
Rap/Hip-Hop	6.7	12.9	13.3	Soundtracks	0.9	0.7	1.4
R&B/Urban	11.3	9.7	10.6	Oldies	1.0	0.9	1.3
Country	16.7	10.7	10.4	New Age	0.7	0.5	0.5
Pop	10.1	11.0	8.9	Children's	0.5	0.6	0.6
Religious	3.1	4.8	5.8	Other	7.0	8.3	7.6
Classical	2.9	2.7	3.0				

Source: The Recording Industry Association of America. 1. Includes CDs, cassettes, DVDs, and all other forms of recordings.

CD Sales, 1995, 2000, and 2003

(in millions)

CDs	1995	2000	2003
Units shipped	722.9	942.5	745.9
Dollar value[1]	$9,377.4	$13,214.5	$11,232.9

1. Dollar value reflects suggested retail price. Source: The Recording Industry Association of America.

Internet Music Sales, 2002 and 2003

(in millions)

	2003	2002
Internet album sales (units sold)	21.7	18.1
Digital single sales (units sold)	19.2	n.a.

Source: Nielsen Media Research. © 2004, Nielsen Media Research.

Top 10 Music Downloads, 2003

Rank Title	Number
1. "Hey Ya!," Outkast (Radio Mix)	111,000
2. "It's My Life," No Doubt	51,700
3. "Stacy's Mom," Fountains of Wayne	43,200
4. "Crazy in Love," Beyoncé	42,600
5. "Here Without You," 3 Doors Down	40,200
6. "Where Is the Love?," Black Eyed Peas	39,215
7. "First Cut Is the Deepest," Sheryl Crow	34,778
8. "Bad Boy," Beyoncé	30,636
9. "Harder to Breathe," Maroon 5	28,500
10. "Fallen," Sarah McLachlan (Album Mix)	26,361

Source: Nielsen Media Research. © 2004, Nielsen Media Research.

Top 10 Selling Albums, 2003

Rank Title	Units sold
1. *Get Rich or Die Tryin'*, 50 Cent	6,535,809
2. *Come Away with Me*, Norah Jones	5,137,468
3. *Meteora*, Linkin Park	3,478,361
4. *Fallen*, Evanescence	3,364,738
5. *Speakerboxx-Love*, Outkast	3,089,849
6. *Dangerously in Love*, Beyoncé	2,527,485
7. *Chocolate Factory*, R. Kelly	2,439,536
8. *Metamorphosis*, Hilary Duff	2,405,544
9. *Shock N Y'All*, Toby Keith	2,324,437
10. *Rush of Blood to the Head*, Coldplay	2,183,997

Source: Nielsen Media Research. © 2004, Nielsen Media Research.

The Recording Industry Association of America's Top-Selling Albums of All Time[*]

28 Million
Eagles Their Greatest Hits 1971–1975, Eagles (Elektra)

26 Million
Thriller, Michael Jackson (Epic)

23 Million
The Wall, Pink Floyd (Columbia)

22 Million
Led Zeppelin IV, Led Zeppelin (Swan Song)

21 Million
Greatest Hits Volumes I & II, Billy Joel (Columbia)

19 Million
Rumours, Fleetwood Mac (Warner Bros.)
Back in Black, AC/DC (Elektra)
The Beatles, The Beatles (Capitol)
Come On Over, Shania Twain (Mercury Nashville)

17 Million
Boston, Boston (Epic)
The Bodyguard (Soundtrack), Whitney Houston (Arista)

16 Million
Cracked Rear View, Hootie & the Blowfish (Atlantic)
Greatest Hits, Elton John (Rocket)
Hotel California, Eagles (Elektra)
The Beatles 1967–1970, The Beatles (Capitol)
No Fences, Garth Brooks (Capitol Nashville)
Jagged Little Pill, Alanis Morissette (Maverick)

15 Million
Born in the U.S.A., Bruce Springsteen (Columbia)
Physical Graffiti, Led Zeppelin (Swan Song)
Dark Side of the Moon, Pink Floyd (Capitol)
Saturday Night Fever (Soundtrack), Bee Gees (Polydor/ Atlas)
The Beatles 1962–1966, The Beatles (Capitol)
Appetite for Destruction, Guns 'N Roses (Geffen)
Double Live, Garth Brooks (Capitol Nashville)

14 Million
Supernatural, Santana (Arista)
Backstreet Boys, Backstreet Boys (Jive)
Ropin' the Wind, Garth Brooks (Capitol Nashville)
Bat Out of Hell, Meat Loaf (Epic)

13 Million
Purple Rain (Soundtrack), Prince and the Revolution (Warner Bros.)
Whitney Houston, Whitney Houston (Arista)
Bruce Springsteen & the E Street Band Live 1975–1985 (box set), Bruce Springsteen & the E Street Band (Columbia)
Greatest Hits 1974–1978, Steve Miller Band (Capitol)
Millennium, Backstreet Boys (Jive)
. . . Baby One More Time, Britney Spears (Jive)
Simon & Garfunkel's Greatest Hits, Simon & Garfunkel (Columbia)
Metallica, Metallica (Elektra)

12 Million
Wide Open Spaces, Dixie Chicks (Monument)
Yourself or Someone Like You, Matchbox Twenty (Atlantic)
No Jacket Required, Phil Collins (Atlantic)
Hysteria, Def Leppard (Mercury)
Slippery When Wet, Bon Jovi (Mercury)
II, Boyz II Men (Motown)
Abbey Road, The Beatles (Capitol)
Ten, Pearl Jam (Epic)
Led Zeppelin II, Led Zeppelin (Atlantic)
Breathless, Kenny G (Arista)
Forrest Gump (Soundtrack) (Epic)
Kenny Rogers' Greatest Hits, Kenny Rogers (Capitol Nashville)
Hot Rocks, The Rolling Stones (abkco)
The Woman in Me, Shania Twain (Mercury Nashville)

11 Million
James Taylor's Greatest Hits, James Taylor (Warner Bros.)
CrazySexyCool, TLC (LaFace)
Falling into You, Celine Dion (550 Music)
Dirty Dancing (Soundtrack) (RCA)
Houses of the Holy, Led Zeppelin (Atlantic)
Sgt. Pepper's Lonely Hearts Club Band, The Beatles (Capitol)
Eagles Greatest Hits, Vol. II, Eagles (Elektra)
Pieces of You, Jewel (Atlantic)
Titanic (Soundtrack) (Sony Classical)
Candle in the Wind 1997/Something About the Way You Look Tonight (Single), Elton John (Rocket)
Devil Without a Cause, Kid Rock (Lava)
No Strings Attached, 'N Sync (Jive)

[*]Through 6/25/2004.

Most Played Songs on Radio, 2003

Rank Title	Artist (Label)	Rank Title	Artist (Label)
1. "When I'm Gone"	3 Doors Down (Republic/ Universal)	6. "Get Busy"	Sean Paul (Atlantic)
2. "In Da Club"	50 Cent (Interscope)	7. "Crazy in Love"	Beyoncé (Columbia)
3. "Bring Me to Life"	Evanescence (Wind-Up)	8. "Shake Ya Tailfeather"	P. Diddy & Murphy Lee (Bad Boy/Universal)
4. "Unwell"	Matchbox Twenty (Atlantic)	9. "Headstrong"	Trapt (Warner Bros)
5. "Ignition"	R. Kelly (Jive)	10. "I'm with You"	Avril Lavigne (Arista)

Source: Nielsen Media Research. © 2004, Nielsen Media Research.

Country Music Hall of Fame

1961
Jimmie Rodgers
Fred Rose
Hank Williams

1962
Roy Acuff

1963
No candidate received
enough votes for induction.

1964
Tex Ritter

1965
Ernest Tubb

1966
Eddy Arnold
James R. Denny
George D. Hay
Uncle Dave Macon

1967
Red Foley
J. L. Frank
Jim Reeves
Stephen H. Sholes

1968
Bob Wills

1969
Gene Autry

1970
Bill Monroe
Original Carter Family

1971
Arthur Edward Satherley

1972
Jimmie H. Davis

1973
Chet Atkins
Patsy Cline

1974
Owen Bradley
Frank "Pee Wee" King

1975
Minnie Pearl

1976
Paul Cohen
Kitty Wells

1977
Merle Travis

1978
Grandpa Jones

1979
Hubert Long
Hank Snow

1980
Johnny Cash
Connie B. Gay
Original Sons of the Pioneers

1981
Vernon Dalhart
Grant Turner

1982
Lefty Frizzell
Roy Horton
Marty Robbins

1983
Little Jimmy Dickens

1984
Ralph Sylvester Peer
Floyd Tillman

1985
Lester Flatt and Earl Scruggs

1986
Whitey Ford
Wesley H. Rose

1987
Rod Brasfield

1988
Loretta Lynn
Roy Rogers

1989
Jack Stapp
Cliffie Stone
Hank Thompson

1990
Tennessee Ernie Ford

1991
Boudleaux and Felice Bryant

1992
George Jones
Frances Williams Preston

1993
Willie Nelson

1994
Merle Haggard

1995
Roger Miller
Jo Walker-Meador

1996
Patsy Montana
Buck Owens
Ray Price

1997
Harlan Howard
Brenda Lee
Cindy Walker

1998
George Morgan
Elvis Presley
E. W. "Bud" Wendell
Tammy Wynette

1999
Johnny Bond
Dolly Parton
Conway Twitty

2000
Charley Pride
Faron Young

2001
Bill Anderson
The Delmore Brothers
The Everly Brothers
Don Gibson
Homer & Jethro
Waylon Jennings
The Jordanaires
Don Law
The Louvin Brothers
Ken Nelson
Sam Phillips
Webb Pierce

2002
Bill Carlisle
Porter Wagoner

2003
Floyd Cramer
Carl Smith

The 50 Worst Songs Ever!

Blender magazine compiled a list of songs people love to hate. They range from one-hit wonders to chart-toppers.

1. "We Built This City," Starship (1985)
2. "Achy Breaky Heart," Billy Ray Cyrus, (1992)
3. "Everybody Have Fun Tonight," Wang Chung (1986)
4. "Rollin'," Limpbizkit (2000)
5. "Ice Ice Baby," Vanilla Ice (1990)
6. "The Heart of Rock & Roll," Huey Lewis and the News (1984)
7. "Don't Worry Be Happy," Bobby McFerrin (1988)
8. "Party All the Time," Eddie Murphy (1985)
9. "American Life," Madonna (2003)
10. "Ebony and Ivory," Paul McCartney and Stevie Wonder (1982)
11. "Invisible," Clay Aiken (2003)
12. "Kokomo," Beach Boys (1988)
13. "Illegal Alien," Genesis (1983)
14. "From a Distance," Bette Midler (1990)
15. "I'll Be There for You," The Rembrandts (1995)
16. "What's Up?," 4 Non Blondes (1993)
17. "Pumps and a Bump," Hammer (1994)
18. "You're the Inspiration," Chicago (1984)
19. "Broken Wings," Mr. Mister (1985)
20. "Dancing on the Ceiling," Lionel Richie (1986)
21. "Two Princes," Spin Doctors (1992)
22. "Courtesy of the Red, White and Blue (The Angry American)," Toby Keith (2002)
23. "Sunglasses at Night," Corey Hart (1984)
24. "Superman," Five for Fighting (2000)
25. "I'll Be Missing You," Puff Daddy featuring Faith Evans and 112
26. "The End," The Doors (1967)
27. "The Final Countdown," Europe (1987)
28. "Your Body Is a Wonderland," John Mayer (2001)
29. "Breakfast at Tiffany's," Deep Blue Something (1995)
30. "Greatest Love of All," Whitney Houston (1986)
31. "Mmm Mmm Mmm Mmm," Crash Test Dummies (1994)
32. "Will 2K," Will Smith (1999)
33. "Barbie Girl," Aqua (1997)
34. "Longer," Dan Fogelberg (1979)
35. "Shiny Happy People," R.E.M. (1991)
36. "Make Em Say Uhh!," Master P featuring Silkk, Fiend, Mia-X, and Mystikal (1998)
37. "Rico Suave," Gerardo (1991)
38. "Cotton Eye Joe," Rednex (1995)
39. "She Bangs," Ricky Martin (2000)
40. "I Wanna Sex You Up," Color Me Badd (1991)
41. "We Didn't Start the Fire," Billy Joel (1989)
42. "The Sound of Silence," Simon and Garfunkel (1965)
43. "Follow Me," Uncle Kracker (2000)
44. "I'll Do Anything for Love (But I Won't Do That)," Meat Loaf (1993)
45. "Mesmerize," Ja Rule featuring Ashanti (2002)
46. "Hangin' Tough," New Kids on the Block (1989)
47. "The Only Thing That Looks Good on Me Is You," Bryan Adams (1996)
48. "Ob-La-Di, Ob-La-Da," The Beatles (1968)
49. "I'm Too Sexy," Right Said Fred (1992)
50. "My Heart Will Go On," Celine Dion (1998)

Source: Blender, The Ultimate Music Magazine, 2004.

Rock and Roll Hall of Fame

1986
Chuck Berry
James Brown
Ray Charles
Sam Cooke
Fats Domino
The Everly Brothers
Buddy Holly
Jerry Lee Lewis
Elvis Presley
Little Richard
Nonperformers
Alan Freed
Sam Phillips
Early Influences
Robert Johnson
Jimmie Rodgers
Jimmy Yancey
Lifetime Achievement
John Hammond

1987
The Coasters
Eddie Cochran
Bo Diddley
Aretha Franklin
Marvin Gaye
Bill Haley
B.B. King
Clyde McPhatter
Ricky Nelson
Roy Orbison
Carl Perkins
Smokey Robinson
Joe Turner
Muddy Waters
Jackie Wilson
Nonperformers
Leonard Chess
Ahmet Ertegun
Jerry Leiber and Mike Stoller
Jerry Wexler
Early Influences
Louis Jordan
T-Bone Walker
Hank Williams

1988
The Beach Boys
The Beatles
The Drifters
Bob Dylan
The Supremes
Nonperformer
Berry Gordy, Jr.
Early Influences
Woody Guthrie
Leadbelly
Les Paul

1989
Dion
Otis Redding
The Rolling Stones
The Temptations
Stevie Wonder
Nonperformer
Phil Spector
Early Influences
The Ink Spots
Bessie Smith
The Soul Stirrers

1990
Hank Ballard
Bobby Darin
The Four Seasons
The Four Tops
The Kinks
The Platters
Simon and Garfunkel
The Who
Nonperformers
Gerry Goffin and Carole King
Brian Holland, Eddie Holland,
and Lamont Dozier
Early Influences
Louis Armstrong
Charlie Christian
Ma Rainey

1991
LaVern Baker
The Byrds
John Lee Hooker
The Impressions
Wilson Pickett
Jimmy Reed
Ike and Tina Turner
Nonperformers
Dave Bartholomew
Ralph Bass
Early Influence
Howlin' Wolf
Lifetime Achievement
Nesuhi Ertegun

1992
Bobby "Blue" Bland
Booker T. and the MG's
Johnny Cash
Jimi Hendrix Experience
Isley Brothers
Sam and Dave
The Yardbirds
Nonperformers
Leo Fender
Bill Graham
Doc Pomus
Early Influences
Elmore James
Professor Longhair

1993
Ruth Brown
Cream
Creedence Clearwater
Revival
The Doors
Etta James
Frankie Lymon and
the Teenagers
Van Morrison
Sly and the Family Stone
Nonperformers
Dick Clark
Milt Gabler
Early Influence
Dinah Washington

1994
The Animals
The Band
Duane Eddy

The Grateful Dead
Elton John
John Lennon
Bob Marley
Rod Stewart
Nonperformer
Johnny Otis
Early Influence
Willie Dixon

1995
The Allman Brothers Band
Al Green
Janis Joplin
Led Zeppelin
Martha and the Vandellas
Neil Young
Frank Zappa
Nonperformer
Paul Ackerman
Early Influence
The Orioles

1996
David Bowie
Jefferson Airplane
Little Willie John
Gladys Knight and the Pips
Pink Floyd
The Shirelles
The Velvet Underground
Nonperformer
Tom Donahue
Early Influence
Pete Seeger

1997
The Bee Gees
Buffalo Springfield
Crosby, Stills, and Nash
The Jackson Five
Joni Mitchell
Parliament-Funkadelic
The (Young) Rascals
Nonperformer
Syd Nathan
Early Influences
Mahalia Jackson
Bill Monroe

1998
The Eagles
Fleetwood Mac
Mamas and Papas
Lloyd Price
Santana
Gene Vincent
Nonperformer
Allen Toussaint
Early Influence
"Jelly Roll" Morton

1999
Billy Joel
Curtis Mayfield
Paul McCartney
Del Shannon
Dusty Springfield
Bruce Springsteen
The Staple Singers
Nonperformer
George Martin
Early Influences

Charles Brown
Bob Wills and His Texas
Playboys

2000
Eric Clapton
Earth, Wind, and Fire
Lovin' Spoonful
The Moonglows
Bonnie Raitt
James Taylor
Nonperformer
Clive Davis
Early Influences
Nat King Cole
Billie Holiday
Side-Men
Hal Blaine
King Curtis
James Jamerson
Scotty Moore
Earl Palmer

2001
Aerosmith
Solomon Burke
The Flamingos
Michael Jackson
Queen
Paul Simon
Steely Dan
Ritchie Valens
Nonperformer
Chris Blackwell
Side-Men
James Burton
Johnnie Johnson

2002
Isaac Hayes
Brenda Lee
Tom Petty and the
Heartbreakers
Gene Pitney
Ramones
Talking Heads
Nonperformer
Jim Stewart
Side-Men
Chet Atkins

2003
AC/DC
The Clash
Elvis Costello and the
Attractions
The Police
The Righteous Brothers
Nonperformer
Mo Ostin
Side-Men
Benny Benjamin
Floyd Cramer
Steve Douglas

2004
Jackson Browne
The Dells
George Harrison
Prince
Bob Seger
Traffic
ZZ Top

Top 10 DVD Sales, 2003

1. *Finding Nemo* (Buena Vista)
2. *Lord of the Rings: The Two Towers* (New Line/ Warner)
3. *Pirates of the Caribbean* (Buena Vista)
4. *Harry Potter and the Chamber of Secrets* (Warner)
5. *The Indiana Jones Collection* (Paramount)
6. *The Matrix Reloaded* (Warner)
7. *The Lion King Special Edition* (Buena Vista)
8. *My Big Fat Greek Wedding* (HBO/Warner)
9. *Signs* (Buena Vista)
10. *Bruce Almighty* (Universal)

Source: Video Business Research.

Top 10 DVD Rentals, 2003

1. *The Bourne Identity* (Universal)
2. *Catch Me if You Can* (DreamWorks/Universal)
3. *Old School* (DreamWorks/Universal)
4. *Bringing Down the House* (Buena Vista)
5. *Signs* (Buena Vista)
6. *How to Lose a Guy in 10 Days* (Paramount)
7. *The Ring* (DreamWorks/Universal)
8. *My Big Fat Greek Wedding* (HBO/Warner)
9. *Sweet Home Alabama* (Buena Vista)
10. *Phone Booth* (Fox)

Source: Rentrak Home Video Essentials.

Top 10 VHS Sales, 2003

1. *Finding Nemo* (Buena Vista)
2. *Harry Potter and the Chamber of Secrets* (Warner)
3. *My Big Fat Greek Wedding* (HBO/Warner)
4. *Sweet Home Alabama* (Buena Vista)
5. *101 Dalmatians 2: Patch's London Adventure* (Buena Vista)
6. *The Santa Clause 2* (Buena Vista)
7. *The Jungle Book 2* (Buena Vista)
8. *Treasure Planet* (Buena Vista)
9. *Stitch* (Buena Vista)
10. *Lord of the Rings: The Two Towers* (New Line/ Warner)

Source: Video Business Research.

Top 10 VHS Rentals, 2003

1. *Sweet Home Alabama* (Buena Vista)
2. *My Big Fat Greek Wedding* (HBO/Warner)
3. *Signs* (Buena Vista)
4. *The Bourne Identity* (Universal)
5. *Catch Me if You Can* (DreamWorks/Universal)
6. *The Ring* (DreamWorks/Universal)
7. *Maid in Manhattan* (Columbia)
8. *XXX* (Columbia)
9. *Two Weeks Notice* (Warner)
10. *How to Lose a Guy in 10 Days* (Paramount)

Source: Rentrak Home Video Essentials.

Weekly TV Viewing by Age
(in hours and minutes)

	Time per week				Time per week		
	Oct. 2003	Nov. 2002	Nov. 2001		Oct. 2003	Nov. 2002	Nov. 2001
Women 18–24	23 hr 11 min	23 hr 52 min	23 hr 11 min	Female teens 12–17	18 hr 08 min	21 hr 30 min	21 hr 20 min
Women 25–54	33 hr 46 min	33 hr 56 min	33 hr 56 min	Male teens 12–17	20 hr 28 min	22 hr 20 min	22 hr 20 min
Women 55+	42 hr 50 min	44 hr 52 min	44 hr 11 min	Children 2–5	23 hr 35 min	24 hr 32 min	24 hr 01 min
Men 18–24	21 hr 20 min	23 hr 31 min	22 hr 00 min	Children 6–11	19 hr 19 min	20 hr 10 min	20 hr 40 min
Men 25–54	30 hr 25 min	31 hr 05 min	30 hr 44 min				
Men 55+	38 hr 18 min	40 hr 29 min	39 hr 39 min				

Source: Nielsen Media Research. © 2004, Nielsen Media Research.

Television Set Ownership
Estimated total number of TV households: 108,400,000[1]

	1950	1955	1960	1965	1970	1975	1980	1985	1990	1995	2000	2001	2002
% of total households:													
TV households	10%	67%	87%	94%	96%	97%	98%	98%	98%	98%	98%	98%	98%
% of TV households:													
Multi-set	—	4	12	22	35	43	50	57	65	71	76	74	75
Color	—	—	—	7	41	74	83	91	98	99	99	100	100
VCR	—	—	—	—	—	—	—	14	66	79	86	91	92
Remote control	—	—	—	—	—	—	—	29	77	91	95	95	95
Wired pay cable	—	—	—	—	—	—	—	26	29	28	32	40	48
Wired cable	—	—	—	—	7	12	20	43	56	63	68	69	70

1. As of January 2004. *Source:* Nielsen Media Research. © 2003, Nielsen Media Research.

Top 10 Television Specials, 2003–2004[1]

Rank	Program name (network)	Rating (% of TV households)	Rank	Program name (network)	Rating (% of TV households)
1.	Super Bowl XXXVIII (CBS)	41.4%	6.	Friends Clip Show Special (NBC)	22.0%
2.	Super Bowl Post Gun (CBS)	39.5	7.	NFC Playoff (Fox)	20.5
3.	Super Bowl Post Game (CBS)	28.8	8.	Survivor All-Stars (CBS)	17.9
4.	Academy Awards (ABC)	26.0	9.	NFC Championship Gun (Fox)	17.6
5.	NFC Championship (Fox)	23.2	10.	Countdown to Oscars 2004 (ABC)	17.3

NOTES: Each rating point represents 1,084,000 households using television. Does not include sports telecasts. 1. Sept. 22, 2003–May 26, 2004. *Source:* Nielsen Media Research. © 2004, Nielsen Media Research.

Top 10 Syndicated TV Programs, 2003–2004[1]

Rank	Program name	Rating (% of TV households)	Rank	Program name	Rating (% of TV households)
1.	Wheel of Fortune	9.0%	6.	Friends (AT)	6.0%
2.	Jeopardy	7.3	7.	MMN Home Team Baseball	5.9
3.	ESPN NFL Regular Season	6.8	8.	Entertainment Tonight (AT)	5.6
4.	Oprah Winfrey Show (AT)	6.8	9.	Seinfeld (weekend) (AT)	5.6
5.	Seinfeld (AT)	6.1	10.	Everybody Loves Raymond (AT)	5.5

NOTES: Each rating point represents 1,084,000 households using television. (AT) = Additional Telecasts. 1. Sept. 22, 2003–May 26, 2004. *Source:* Nielsen Media Research. © 2004, Nielsen Media Research.

Top 10 Regularly Scheduled Network Programs, 2003–2004[1]

Rank	Program name (network)	Rating (% of TV households)	Rank	Program name (network)	Rating (% of TV households)
1.	CSI (CBS)	15.9%	6.	E.R. (NBC)	12.9%
2.	American Idol—Tuesday (Fox)	14.9	7.	Survivor: All-Stars (CBS)	12.4
3.	American Idol—Wednesday (Fox)	14.1	8.	Survivor: Pearl Islands (CBS)	12.1
4.	Friends (NBC)	13.6	9.	CSI: Miami (CBS)	11.9
5.	Apprentice (NBC)	13.0	10.	NFL Monday Night Football (ABC)	11.5

NOTE: Each rating point represents 1,084,000 households using television. 1. Through May 26, 2004. *Source:* Nielsen Media Research. © 2004, Nielsen Media Research.

Top 10 TV Movies, 2003–2004[1]

Rank	Movie (network)	Rating (% of TV households)	Rank	Movie (network)	Rating (% of TV households)
1.	10.5 (NBC)	12.4%	5.	Finding John Christmas (CBS)	10.4%
2.	10.5 Part II (NBC)	12.2	7.	Plainsong (CBS)	10.2
3.	Undercover Christmas (CBS)	11.5	8.	The Elizabeth Smart Story (CBS)	10.0
4.	Fallen Angel (CBS)	11.4	9.	It Must Be Love (CBS)	9.6
5.	Twelve Mile Road (CBS)	10.4	10.	Saving Jessica Lynch (NBC)	9.5

NOTE: Each rating point represents 1,084,000 households using television. 1. Sept. 22, 2003–May 26, 2004, 2003. *Source:* Nielsen Media Research. © 2004, Nielsen Media Research.

Top-Rated Series Finales

Rank	Date	Program	Rating	Number of homes	Number of persons
1.	2/28/83	M*A*S*H (CBS)	60.2	50,150,000	105,466,950
2.	8/29/67	The Fugitive (ABC)	45.9	25,700,000	n.a.
3.	5/20/93	Cheers (NBC)	45.5	42,361,000	80,401,000
4.	5/14/98	Seinfeld (NBC)	41.3	40,509,000	76,260,000
5.	5/1/88	CBS Sunday Movie: Magnum P.I.—Finale (CBS)	32.0	28,350,000	50,660,000
6.	5/6/04	Friends (NBC)	29.8	32,303,000	52,458,000
7.	4/30/92	The Cosby Show (NBC)	28.0	25,788,000	44,384,000
8.	4/8/79	All in the Family (CBS)	26.6	19,820,000	40,214,780
9.	3/19/77	Mary Tyler Moore (CBS)	25.5	18,160,000	n.a.
10.	5/3/91	Dallas (CBS)	22.0	20,480,000	33,259,520
11.	3/31/75	Gunsmoke (CBS)	20.4	13,970,000	30,901,640
12.	5/21/90	Newhart (CBS)	18.7	17,220,000	29,515,080
13.	3/23/71	The Beverly Hillbillies (CBS)	18.1	10,880,000	n.a.
14.	5/12/87	Hill Street Blues (NBC)	18.1	15,820,000	16,312,960
15.	5/25/88	St. Elsewhere (NBC)	17.0	15,060,000	22,514,700
16.	5/13/04	Frasier (NBC)	16.3	17,670,000	25,249,000
17.	1/16/73	Bonanza (NBC)	15.3	9,910,000	19,324,000
18.	5/20/97	Roseanne (ABC)	11.6	11,204,000	16,575,000

Source: Nielsen Media Research. © 2004, Nielsen Media Research.

Top 100 Daily Newspapers in the United States

Rank	Newspaper	Circulation	Rank	Newspaper	Circulation
1.	USA Today (Arlington, Va.)	2,136,068	51.	Daily Oklahoman (Oklahoma City)	199,581
2.	Wall Street Journal (New York, N.Y.)	1,800,607	52.	Virginian-Pilot (Norfolk, Va.)	195,866
3.	Times (New York, N.Y.)	1,113,000	53.	Pioneer Press (St. Paul, Minn.)	194,870
4.	Times (Los Angeles)	925,135	54.	Courant (Hartford, Conn.)	190,312
5.	Post (Washington, DC)	746,724	55.	World-Herald (Omaha, Neb.)	190,218
6.	Daily News (New York, N.Y.)	715,070	56.	Enquirer (Cincinnati)	189,084
7.	Tribune (Chicago)	679,327	57.	Times-Dispatch (Richmond, Va.)	187,409
8.	Post (New York, N.Y.)	590,061	58.	Democrat-Gazette (Little Rock, Ark.)	185,709
9.	Newsday (Long Island, N.Y.)	578,809	59.	Tennessean (Nashville)	184,106
10.	Chronicle (Houston)	552,052	60.	American-Statesman (Austin, Tex.)	183,288
11.	Chronicle (San Francisco)	512,129	61.	Contra Costa Times (Walnut Creek, Calif.)	182,196
12.	Morning News (Dallas)	505,724	62.	Press-Enterprise (Riverside, Calif.)	178,994
13.	Sun-Times (Chicago)	479,584	63.	Record (Bergen County, N.J.)	178,962
14.	Globe (Boston)	467,745	64.	Daily News (Los Angeles)	178,217
15.	Arizona Republic (Phoenix)	448,782	65.	Democrat and Chronicle (Rochester, N.Y.)	172,124
16.	Star-Ledger (Newark, N.J.)	408,557	66.	Asbury Park Press (Neptune, N.J.)	168,718
17.	Inquirer (Philadelphia)	373,892	67.	Times-Union (Jacksonville, Fla.)	168,558
18.	Journal-Constitution (Atlanta)	371,161	68.	Post (W. Palm Beach, Fla.)	167,531
19.	Free Press (Detroit)	368,839	69.	Journal (Providence, R.I.)	166,836
20.	Plain Dealer (Cleveland)	363,750	70.	Review-Journal (Las Vegas)	164,848
21.	Oregonian (Portland)	342,789	71.	News & Observer (Raleigh, N.C.)	163,460
22.	Star Tribune (Minneapolis)	342,780	72.	Bee (Fresno, Calif.)	158,286
23.	Union-Tribune (San Diego)	342,447	73.	Post-Intelligencer (Seattle)	157,558
24.	Times (St. Petersburg, Fla.)	333,557	74.	Commercial Appeal (Memphis)	156,513
25.	Herald (Miami)	315,340	75.	Register (Des Moines, Iowa)	152,633
26.	Post (Denver)	305,060	76.	Daily News (Philadelphia)	150,154
27.	Rocky Mountain News (Denver)	304,949	77.	Daily Herald (Chicago)	149,882
28.	Register (Orange County, Calif.)	300,888	78.	News (Birmingham, Ala.)	145,571
29.	Sun (Baltimore)	300,410	79.	Advertiser (Honolulu)	143,696
30.	Post-Dispatch (St. Louis)	287,424	80.	Blade (Toledo, Ohio)	140,628
31.	Bee (Sacramento, Calif.)	283,194	81.	Press (Grand Rapids, Mich.)	140,135
32.	Mercury News (San Jose, Calif.)	272,682	82.	World (Tulsa, Okla.)	139,383
33.	Star (Kansas City, Mo.)	269,188	83.	Journal News (Westchester Co., N.Y.)	139,170
34.	Investor's Business Daily (Los Angeles)	264,699	84.	Tribune (Salt Lake City)	134,777
35.	Sentinel (Orlando, Fla.)	256,520	85.	Beacon Journal (Akron, Ohio)	134,774
36.	Times-Picayune (New Orleans)	255,994	86.	Daily News (Dayton, Ohio)	131,435
37.	Star (Indianapolis)	254,624	87.	News Tribune (Tacoma, Wash.)	128,739
38.	Dispatch (Columbus, Ohio)	251,557	88.	La Opinion (Los Angeles, Calif.)	126,189
39.	Post-Gazette (Pittsburgh, Pa.)	243,091	89.	Post-Standard (Syracuse, N.Y.)	123,836
40.	Herald (Boston)	242,957	90.	Tribune-Review (Greensburg, Pa.)	119,338
41.	News (Detroit)	242,391	91.	News Journal (Wilmington, Del.)	119,163
42.	Journal Sentinel (Milwaukee)	242,234	92.	Morning Call (Allentown, Pa.)	118,859
43.	Sun-Sentinel (Fort Lauderdale, Fla.)	238,589	93.	State (Columbia, S.C.)	115,959
44.	Observer (Charlotte, N.C.)	235,759	94.	News-Sentinel (Knoxville, Tenn.)	112,017
45.	Times (Seattle)	224,140	95.	Herald-Leader (Lexington, Ky.)	108,892
46.	News (Buffalo, N.Y.)	223,957	96.	Journal (Albuquerque)	108,344
47.	Express-News (San Antonio, Tex.)	220,998	97.	Herald-Tribune (Sarasota, Fla.)	106,594
48.	Star-Telegram (Fort Worth, Tex.)	218,975	98.	Telegram & Gazette (Worcester, Mass.)	102,978
49.	Courier-Journal (Louisville, Ky.)	217,396	99.	Spokesman-Review (Spokane, Wash.)	102,805
50.	Tribune (Tampa, Fla.)	214,178	100.	Patriot-News (Harrisburg, Pa.)	101,598

NOTES: By circulation, as of Sept. 30, 2002. Most circulations are based on partial-week averages, therefore above circulations do not reflect full-week circulations. *Source: Editor & Publisher International Year Book 2003.* Web: www.editorandpublisher.com.

Top 100 Consumer Magazines, 2003

Rank	Magazine	Total paid circulation	Rank	Magazine	Total paid circulation
1.	AARP Bulletin	21,622,237	7.	Good Housekeeping	4,679,941
2.	AARP The Magazine	21,035,278	8.	Family Circle	4,615,536
3.	Reader's Digest	11,067,522	9.	Woman's Day	4,166,097
4.	TV Guide	9,018,212	10.	TIME	4,104,284
5.	Better Homes and Gardens	7,608,913	11.	Ladies' Home Journal	4,101,221
6.	National Geographic	6,644,167	12.	People	3,615,795

Rank	Magazine	Total paid circulation	Rank	Magazine	Total paid circulation
13.	Westways	3,477,257	58.	Fitness	1,407,612
14.	Home & Away	3,320,869	59.	American Rifleman	1,404,392
15.	Prevention	3,275,411	60.	Health	1,388,610
16.	Sports Illustrated	3,238,974	61.	Car and Driver	1,373,341
17.	Newsweek	3,148,379	62.	Self	1,330,960
18.	Playboy	3,100,093	63.	Game Informer Magazine	1,317,912
19.	Cosmopolitan	2,889,043	64.	Bon Appetit	1,302,180
20.	Guideposts	2,633,309	65.	Boys' Life	1,283,549
21.	Via Magazine	2,633,163	66.	Rolling Stone	1,277,041
22.	Southern Living	2,604,682	67.	Motor Trend	1,269,921
23.	O, The Oprah Magazine	2,592,572	68.	Stuff	1,262,483
24.	American Legion Magazine	2,591,965	69.	Cosmo Girl!	1,258,881
25.	Maxim	2,510,144	70.	Star Magazine	1,231,992
26.	Redbook	2,381,899	71.	Country Home	1,230,708
27.	Seventeen	2,372,261	72.	Popular Mechanics	1,230,658
28.	Martha Stewart Living	2,366,173	73.	US Weekly	1,229,737
29.	Glamour	2,286,429	74.	PC Magazine	1,226,265
30.	AAA Going Places	2,254,480	75.	Vogue	1,217,352
31.	YM	2,209,379	76.	Vanity Fair	1,153,651
32.	Parents	2,080,515	77.	Family Handyman	1,153,519
33.	Parenting Magazine	2,048,370	78.	FHM (For Him Magazine)	1,105,892
34.	Smithsonian	2,030,336	79.	PC World	1,103,769
35.	U.S. News & World Report	2,022,118	80.	Weight Watchers	1,073,867
36.	Money	1,998,136	81.	American Hunter	1,070,211
37.	Ebony	1,798,844	82.	Essence	1,069,734
38.	Entertainment Weekly	1,757,749	83.	Scouting	1,058,488
39.	Country Living	1,726,274	84.	Michigan Living	1,047,344
40.	ESPN The Magazine	1,726,216	85.	Kiplinger's Personal Finance	1,025,947
41.	Men's Health	1,686,195	86.	Elle	1,022,487
42.	In Style	1,675,493	87.	Home	1,008,968
43.	VFW Magazine	1,664,883	88.	Allure	1,007,059
44.	FamilyFun	1,661,559	89.	Businessweek (North America)	991,159
45.	Shape	1,638,069	90.	Gourmet	976,746
46.	Cooking Light	1,616,009	91.	New Yorker	972,409
47.	National Enquirer	1,604,494	92.	Travel + Leisure	968,721
48.	Woman's World	1,580,217	93.	This Old House	967,830
49.	Teen People	1,579,302	94.	Food & Wine	954,429
50.	Endless Vacation	1,575,644	95.	Child	937,164
51.	Golf Digest	1,569,695	96.	Outdoor Life	936,199
52.	Field & Stream	1,530,238	97.	Traditional Home	931,961
53.	Popular Science	1,468,418	98.	Forbes	921,502
54.	Real Simple	1,437,801	99.	Marie Claire	913,385
55.	Sunset	1,427,293	100.	Jet	912,061
56.	First for Women	1,425,082			
57.	Golf Magazine	1,412,896	**Top 100**		**246,435,609**

Source: Audit Bureau of Circulations, tabulated by Magazine Publishers of America.

The 10 Most Expensive Paintings Ever Sold

1. $104 million for Boy with a Pipe by Pablo Picasso (2004)

2. $82.5 million for Portrait du Dr. Gachet by Vincent van Gogh (1990)

3. $78.1 million for Au Moulin de la Galette by Pierre-Auguste Renoir (1990)

4. $76.7 million for The Massacre of the Innocents by Paul Rubens (2002)

5. $71.5 million for Portrait de L'Artiste Sans Barbe by Vincent van Gogh (1998)

6. $60.5 million for Rideau, Cruchon et Compotier by Paul Cézanne (1999)

7. $55 million for Femme aux Bras Croises by Pablo Picasso (2000)

8. $53.9 million for Irises by Vincent van Gogh (1987)

9. $51.7 million for Les Noces de Pierrette by Pablo Picasso (1989)

10. $49.5 million for Femme Assise Dans Un Jardin by Pablo Picasso (1999)

American Film Institute's 100 Greatest Movies of All Time

1. *Citizen Kane* (1941)
2. *Casablanca* (1942)
3. *The Godfather* (1972)
4. *Gone with the Wind* (1939)
5. *Lawrence of Arabia* (1962)
6. *The Wizard of Oz* (1939)
7. *The Graduate* (1967)
8. *On the Waterfront* (1954)
9. *Schindler's List* (1993)
10. *Singin' in the Rain* (1952)
11. *It's a Wonderful Life* (1946)
12. *Sunset Boulevard* (1950)
13. *The Bridge on the River Kwai* (1957)
14. *Some Like It Hot* (1959)
15. *Star Wars* (1977)
16. *All About Eve* (1950)
17. *The African Queen* (1951)
18. *Psycho* (1960)
19. *Chinatown* (1974)
20. *One Flew Over the Cuckoo's Nest* (1975)
21. *The Grapes of Wrath* (1940)
22. *2001: A Space Odyssey* (1968)
23. *The Maltese Falcon* (1941)
24. *Raging Bull* (1980)
25. *E.T.—The Extra-Terrestrial* (1982)
26. *Dr. Strangelove* (1964)
27. *Bonnie and Clyde* (1967)
28. *Apocalypse Now* (1979)
29. *Mr. Smith Goes to Washington* (1939)
30. *The Treasure of the Sierra Madre* (1948)
31. *Annie Hall* (1977)
32. *The Godfather Part II* (1974)
33. *High Noon* (1952)
34. *To Kill a Mockingbird* (1962)
35. *It Happened One Night* (1934)
36. *Midnight Cowboy* (1969)
37. *The Best Years of Our Lives* (1946)
38. *Double Indemnity* (1944)
39. *Doctor Zhivago* (1965)
40. *North by Northwest* (1959)
41. *West Side Story* (1961)
42. *Rear Window* (1954)
43. *King Kong* (1933)
44. *The Birth of a Nation* (1915)
45. *A Streetcar Named Desire* (1951)
46. *A Clockwork Orange* (1971)
47. *Taxi Driver* (1976)
48. *Jaws* (1975)
49. *Snow White and the Seven Dwarfs* (1937)
50. *Butch Cassidy and the Sundance Kid* (1969)
51. *The Philadelphia Story* (1940)
52. *From Here to Eternity* (1953)
53. *Amadeus* (1984)
54. *All Quiet on the Western Front* (1930)
55. *The Sound of Music* (1965)
56. *M*A*S*H* (1970)
57. *The Third Man* (1949)
58. *Fantasia* (1940)
59. *Rebel Without a Cause* (1955)
60. *Raiders of the Lost Ark* (1981)
61. *Vertigo* (1958)
62. *Tootsie* (1982)
63. *Stagecoach* (1939)
64. *Close Encounters of the Third Kind* (1977)
65. *The Silence of the Lambs* (1991)
66. *Network* (1976)
67. *The Manchurian Candidate* (1962)
68. *An American in Paris* (1951)
69. *Shane* (1953)
70. *The French Connection* (1971)
71. *Forrest Gump* (1994)
72. *Ben-Hur* (1959)
73. *Wuthering Heights* (1939)
74. *The Gold Rush* (1925)
75. *Dances with Wolves* (1990)
76. *City Lights* (1931)
77. *American Graffiti* (1973)
78. *Rocky* (1976)
79. *The Deer Hunter* (1978)
80. *The Wild Bunch* (1969)
81. *Modern Times* (1936)
82. *Giant* (1956)
83. *Platoon* (1986)
84. *Fargo* (1996)
85. *Duck Soup* (1933)
86. *Mutiny on the Bounty* (1935)
87. *Frankenstein* (1931)
88. *Easy Rider* (1969)
89. *Patton* (1970)
90. *The Jazz Singer* (1927)
91. *My Fair Lady* (1964)
92. *A Place in the Sun* (1951)
93. *The Apartment* (1960)
94. *GoodFellas* (1990)
95. *Pulp Fiction* (1994)
96. *The Searchers* (1956)
97. *Bringing Up Baby* (1938)
98. *Unforgiven* (1992)
99. *Guess Who's Coming to Dinner* (1967)
100. *Yankee Doodle Dandy* (1942)

Movie Revenues

	All-Time Box Office Grosses[1]			Top 25 Movies of 2003[1]	
1.	*Titanic* (1997)	$600,788,188	1.	*Lord of the Rings: The Return of the King* (New Line)	$376,716,328
2.	*Star Wars* (1977)[2]	460,998,007	2.	*Finding Nemo* (Disney/Pixar)	339,714,978
3.	*E.T.—The Extra-Terrestrial* (1982)[2]	434,949,459	3.	*Pirates of the Caribbean: The Curse of the Black Pearl* (Buena Vista)	305,411,224
4.	*Star Wars: Episode One— The Phantom Menace* (1999)	431,088,295	4.	*The Matrix Reloaded* (Warner Bros.)	281,519,061
5.	*Spider-Man* (2002)	403,706,375	5.	*Bruce Almighty* (Universal)	242,704,995
6.	*The Lord of the Rings: The Return of the King* (2003)	376,716,328[3]	6.	*X2: X-Men United* (Fox)	214,949,694
7.	*The Passion of the Christ* (2004)	368,027,248[3]	7.	*Elf* (New Line)	173,381,405
8.	*Jurassic Park* (1993)	357,067,947	8.	*Terminator 3: Rise of the Machines* (Warner Bros.)	150,358,296
9.	*Lord of the Rings: The Two Towers* (2002)	341,748,130	9.	*The Matrix Revolutions* (Warner Bros.)	139,259,759
10.	*Finding Nemo* (2003)	339,714,367	10.	*Cheaper by the Dozen* (Fox)	138,540,694
11.	*Forrest Gump* (1994)[2]	329,694,499	11.	*Bad Boys 2* (Sony)	138,396,624
12.	*The Lion King* (1994)[2]	328,539,505	12.	*Anger Management* (Sony)	134,403,613
13.	*Harry Potter and the Sorcerer's Stone* (2001)	317,575,550	13.	*Bringing Down the House* (Buena Vista)	132,541,238
14.	*The Lord of the Rings: The Fellowship of the Ring* (2001)	314,776,170	14.	*The Hulk* (Universal)	132,175,874
15.	*Star Wars: Episode II— Attack of the Clones* (2002)	310,676,740	15.	*2 Fast 2 Furious* (Universal)	127,145,654
16.	*Return of the Jedi* (1983)[2]	309,205,079	16.	*Something's Gotta Give* (Sony)	124,590,960
17.	*Independence Day* (1996)	306,169,255	17.	*Seabiscuit* (Universal)	120,170,960
18.	*Pirates of the Caribbean: The Curse of the Black Pearl* (2003)	305,411,224	18.	*S.W.A.T.* (Sony)	116,643,346
19.	*The Sixth Sense* (1999)	293,506,292	19.	*Spy Kids 3D: Game Over* (Dimension)	111,760,631
20.	*The Empire Strikes Back* (1980)[2]	290,271,960	20.	*The Last Samurai* (Warner Bros.)	111,110,575
21.	*Home Alone* (1990)	285,761,243	21.	*Freaky Friday* (Buena Vista)	110,222,438
22.	*The Matrix Reloaded* (2003)	281,519,061	22.	*Scary Movie 3* (Dimension)	110,000,082
23.	*Shrek* (2001)	267,665,011	23.	*The Italian Job* (Paramount)	106,128,601
24.	*Harry Potter and the Chamber of Secrets* (2002)	261,979,634	24.	*How to Lose a Guy in 10 Days* (Paramount)	106,094,499
25.	*Dr. Seuss' How the Grinch Stole Christmas* (2000)	260,031,035	25.	*American Wedding* (Universal)	104,440,899

1. As of May 9, 2004. 2. Including reissues. 3. Still tracking. *Source:* Exhibitor Relations Co. Inc.

American Film Institute's Top Movie Songs

Number	Song, Movie, Year
1.	"Over the Rainbow," *The Wizard of Oz*, 1939
2.	"As Time Goes By," *Casablanca*, 1942
3.	"Singin' in the Rain," *Singin' in the Rain*, 1952
4.	"Moon River," *Breakfast at Tiffany's*, 1961
5.	"White Christmas," *Holiday Inn*, 1942
6.	"Mrs. Robinson," *The Graduate*, 1967
7.	"When You Wish Upon a Star," *Pinocchio*, 1940
8.	"The Way We Were," *The Way We Were*, 1973
9.	"Stayin' Alive," *Saturday Night Fever*, 1977
10.	"The Sound of Music," *The Sound of Music*, 1965
11.	"The Man That Got Away," *A Star Is Born*, 1954
12.	"Diamonds Are a Girl's Best Friend," *Gentlemen Prefer Blondes*, 1953
13.	"People," *Funny Girl*, 1968
14.	"My Heart Will Go On," *Titanic*, 1997
15.	"Cheek to Cheek," *Top Hat*, 1935
16.	"Evergreen (Love Theme from *A Star is Born*)," *A Star Is Born*, 1976
17.	"I Could Have Danced All Night," *My Fair Lady*, 1964
18.	"Cabaret," *Cabaret*, 1972
19.	"Some Day My Prince Will Come," *Snow White and the Seven Dwarfs*, 1937
20.	"Somewhere," *West Side Story*, 1961
21.	"Jailhouse Rock," *Jailhouse Rock*, 1957
22.	"Everybody's Talkin'," *Midnight Cowboy*, 1969
23.	"Raindrops Keep Fallin' on My Head," *Butch Cassidy and the Sundance Kid*, 1969
24.	"Ol' Man River," *Show Boat*, 1936
25.	"High Noon (Do Not Forsake Me, Oh My Darlin')," *High Noon*, 1952
26.	"The Trolley Song," *Meet Me in St. Louis*, 1944
27.	"Unchained Melody," *Ghost*, 1990
28.	"Some Enchanted Evening," *South Pacific*, 1958
29.	"Born to Be Wild," *Easy Rider*, 1969
30.	"Stormy Weather," *Stormy Weather*, 1943
31.	"Theme from *New York, New York*," *New York, New York*, 1977
32.	"I Got Rhythm," *An American in Paris*, 1951
33.	"Aquarius," *Hair*, 1979
34.	"Let's Call the Whole Thing Off," *Shall We Dance*, 1937
35.	"America," *West Side Story*, 1961
36.	"Supercalifragilisticexpialidocious," *Mary Poppins*, 1964
37.	"Swinging on a Star," *Going My Way*, 1944
38.	"Theme from *Shaft*," *Shaft*, 1971
39.	"Days of Wine and Roses," *Days of Wine and Roses*, 1963
40.	"Fight the Power," *Do the Right Thing*, 1989
41.	"New York, New York," *On The Town*, 1949
42.	"Luck Be a Lady," *Guys and Dolls*, 1955
43.	"The Way You Look Tonight," *Swing Time*, 1936
44.	"Wind Beneath My Wings," *Beaches*, 1988
45.	"That's Entertainment," *The Band Wagon*, 1953
46.	"Don't Rain on My Parade," *Funny Girl*, 1968
47.	"Zip-a-Dee-Doo-Dah," *Song of the South*, 1947
48.	"Whatever Will Be, Will Be (Que Sera, Sera)," *The Man Who Knew Too Much*, 1956
49.	"Make 'Em Laugh," *Singin' in the Rain*, 1952
50.	"Rock Around the Clock," *Blackboard Jungle*, 1955
51.	"Fame," *Fame*, 1980
52.	"Summertime," *Porgy and Bess*, 1959
53.	"Goldfinger," *Goldfinger*, 1964
54.	"Shall We Dance," *The King and I*, 1956
55.	"Flashdance . . . What a Feeling," *Flashdance*, 1983
56.	"Thank Heaven for Little Girls," *Gigi*, 1958
57.	"The Windmills of Your Mind," *The Thomas Crown Affair*, 1968
58.	"Gonna Fly Now," *Rocky*, 1976
59.	"Tonight," *West Side Story*, 1961
60.	"It Had to Be You," *When Harry Met Sally*, 1989
61.	"Get Happy," *Summer Stock*, 1950
62.	"Beauty and the Beast," *Beauty and the Beast*, 1991
63.	"Thanks for the Memory," *The Big Broadcast of 1938*, 1938
64.	"My Favorite Things," *The Sound of Music*, 1965
65.	"I Will Always Love You," *The Bodyguard*, 1992
66.	"Suicide Is Painless," *M*A*S*H*, 1970
67.	"Nobody Does It Better," *The Spy Who Loved Me*, 1977
68.	"Streets of Philadelphia," *Philadelphia*, 1993
69.	"On the Good Ship Lollipop," *Bright Eyes*, 1934
70.	"Summer Nights," *Grease*, 1978
71.	"The Yankee Doodle Boy," *Yankee Doodle Dandy*, 1942
72.	"Good Morning," *Singin' in the Rain*, 1952
73.	"Isn't It Romantic?," *Love Me Tonight*, 1932
74.	"Rainbow Connection," *The Muppet Movie*, 1979
75.	"Up Where We Belong," *An Officer and a Gentleman*, 1982
76.	"Have Yourself a Merry Little Christmas," *Meet Me in St. Louis*, 1944
77.	"The Shadow of Your Smile," *The Sandpiper*, 1965
78.	"9 To 5," *9 To 5*, 1980
79.	"Arthur's Theme (Best That You Can Do)," *Arthur*, 1981
80.	"Springtime for Hitler," *The Producers*, 1968
81.	"I'm Easy," *Nashville*, 1975
82.	"Ding Dong the Witch Is Dead," *The Wizard of Oz*, 1939
83.	"The Rose," *The Rose*, 1979
84.	"Put the Blame on Mame," *Gilda*, 1946
85.	"Come What May," *Moulin Rouge!*, 2001
86.	"(I've Had) The Time of My Life," *Dirty Dancing*, 1987
87.	"Buttons and Bows," *The Paleface*, 1948
88.	"Do Re Mi," *The Sound of Music*, 1965
89.	"Puttin' on the Ritz," *Young Frankenstein*, 1974
90.	"Seems Like Old Times," *Annie Hall*, 1977
91.	"Let the River Run," *Working Girl*, 1988
92.	"Long Ago and Far Away," *Cover Girl*, 1944
93.	"Lose Yourself," *8 Mile*, 2002
94.	"Ain't Too Proud to Beg," *The Big Chill*, 1983
95.	"(We're Off on the) Road to Morocco," *Road to Morocco*, 1942
96.	"Footloose," *Footloose*, 1984
97.	"42nd Street," *42nd Street*, 1933
98.	"All That Jazz," *Chicago*, 2002
99.	"Hakuna Matata," *The Lion King*, 1994
100.	"Old Time Rock and Roll," *Risky Business*, 1983

PEOPLE

Many public figures not listed here may be found elsewhere in the almanac.

U.S. Presidents	British Prime Ministers
U.S. Vice Presidents	Rulers of England
Families of U.S. Presidents	Rulers of France
U.S. Governors	Rulers of Judah and Israel
U.S. Congress	Rulers of Prussia
U.S. Supreme Court Justices	Rulers of Russia
U.S. Government Officials	Sports Personalities

Names in parentheses indicate a person's original name or nickname. Locations in parentheses are the present-day name of the birthplace. Dates of birth appear as month/day/year. **Boldface** years in parentheses are dates of **(birth–death).**

Information has been gathered from many sources, including the individuals themselves. However, the almanac cannot guarantee the accuracy of every item.

A

Aalto, Alvar (architect); Kuortane, Finland **(1898–1976)**

Abbado, Claudio (orchestra conductor); Milan, Italy, 6/26/33

Abbott, Bud (William Abbott) (comedian); Asbury Park, N.J. **(1898–1974)**

Abbott, George (stage producer); Forestville, N.Y. **(1887–1995)**

Abelard, Peter (theologian); nr. Nantes, France **(1079–1142)**

Abernathy, Ralph (civil rights leader); Linden, Ala. **(1926–1990)**

Abraham, F(ahrid) Murray (actor); Pittsburgh, 10/24/39

Achebe, Chinua (writer); Ogidi, Nigeria, 11/16/30

Acheson, Dean (statesman); Middletown, Conn. **(1893–1971)**

Acuff, Roy Claxton (musician); nr. Maynardsville, Tenn. **(1903–1992)**

Adams, Abigail (First Lady, writer); Weymouth, Mass. **(1744–1818)**

Adams, Bryan (singer, songwriter); Kingston, Ont., Canada, 11/5/59

Adams, Charles Francis (diplomat); Boston **(1807–1886)**

Adams, Don (actor); New York City, 4/19/26

Adams, Edie (Edie Enke) (actress); Kingston, Pa., 4/16/29

Adams, Franklin Pierce (columnist, author); Chicago **(1881–1960)**

Adams, Gerry (political leader); West Belfast, Northern Ireland, 10/6/48

Adams, Henry Brooks (historian); Boston **(1838–1918)**

Adams, Joey (comedian); New York City **(1911–1999)**

Adams, John (2nd U.S. president); Braintree (Quincy), Mass. **(1735–1826)**

Adams,, John Quincy (6th U.S. president); Braintree (Quincy), Mass. **(1767–1848)**

Adams, Maude (Maude Kiskadden) (actress); Salt Lake City **(1872–1953)**

Adams, Samuel (American Revolutionary patriot); Boston **(1722–1803)**

Adams, Scott (cartoonist); Catskill, N.Y., 6/8/57

Adamson, Joy (naturalist, writer); Troppau, Silesia **(1910–1980)**

Addams, Charles (cartoonist); Westfield, N.J. **(1912–1988)**

Addams, Jane (social worker, Nobel laureate); Cedarville, Ill. **(1860–1935)**

Adderley, Julian "Cannonball" (jazz saxophonist); Tampa, Fla. **(1928–1975)**

Ade, George (humorist); Kentland, Ind. **(1866–1944)**

Adenauer, Konrad (statesman); Cologne, Germany **(1876–1967)**

Adler, Alfred (psychoanalyst); Vienna **(1870–1937)**

Adler, Larry (musician); Baltimore **(1914–2001)**

Adler, Richard (songwriter); New York City, 8/3/21

Aeschylus (dramatist); Eleusis, Greece **(525–456 B.C.)**

Aesop (fabulist); Samos?, Greece, fl. c. 500 B.C.

Agnew, Spiro (political figure); Baltimore **(1905–1996)**

Aiello, Danny (actor); New York City, 6/20/33

Aiken, Conrad (poet); Savannah, Ga. **(1889–1973)**

Ailey, Alvin (choreographer); Rogers, Tex. **(1931–1989)**

Akhmatova, Anna (poet); Odessa, Ukraine **(1889–1966)**

Akihito, Tsugunomiya (Emperor of Japan); Tokyo, 12/23/33

Albanese, Licia (operatic soprano); Bari, Italy, 7/22/13

Albee, Edward (playwright); Washington, D.C., 3/12/28

Albers, Josef (painter); Bottrop, Germany **(1888–1976)**

Albert, Eddie (Edward Albert Heimberger) (actor); Rock Island, Ill., 4/22/08

Albert, Edward (actor); Los Angeles, 2/20/51

Albertson, Jack (actor); Malden, Mass. **(1907–1981)**

Albright, Madeleine (diplomat, U.S. secretary of state); Prague, Czechoslovakia, 5/15/37

Alcott, Louisa May (novelist); Germantown, Pa. **(1832–1888)**

Alda, Alan (actor); New York City, 1/28/36

Alden, John (American Pilgrim); England **(c. 1599–1687)**

Alexander, Jane (Quigley) (actress); Boston, 10/28/39

Alexander, Jason (Jay Scott Greenspan) (actor); Newark, N.J., 9/23/59

Alexander the Great (monarch, conqueror); Pella, Macedonia, Greece **(356–323 B.C.)**

Alger, Horatio (author); Revere, Mass. **(1834–1899)**

Algren, Nelson (novelist); Detroit **(1909–1981)**

Allen, Debbie (dancer-choreographer, actress); Houston, 1/16/50

Allen, Ethan (American Revolutionary soldier); Litchfield, Conn. **(1738–1789)**

Allen, Fred (John Florence Sullivan) (comedian); Cambridge, Mass. **(1894–1956)**

Allen, Gracie (Grace Ethel Cecile Rosalie Allen) (comedienne); San Francisco **(1906–1964)**

Allen, Joan (actress); Rochelle, Ill., 8/20/56

Allen, Mel (Melvin Israel) (sportscaster); Birmingham, Ala. **(1913–1996)**

Allen, Peter (actor, songwriter); Tenterfield, Australia **(1944–1992)**

Allen, Steve (TV entertainer); New York City **(1921–2000)**

Allen, Woody (Allen Stewart Konigsberg) (actor, writer, director); Brooklyn, N.Y., 12/1/35

Allende, Isabel (novelist); Lima, Peru, 8/2/42

Alley, Kirstie (actress); Wichita, Kans., 1/12/55

Allison, Fran (actress); LaPorte City, Iowa **(1908?–1989)**

Allman, Gregg (singer); Nashville, Tenn., 12/8/47

Allyson, June (Ella Geisman) (actress); New York City, 10/7/17

Alonso, Alicia (ballet dancer); Havana, 12/21/21?

Alpert, Herb (band leader); Los Angeles, 3/31/35?

Alsop, Joseph W., Jr. (journalist); Avon, Conn. **(1910–1989)**

Alsop, Stewart (journalist); Avon, Conn. **(1914–1974)**

Alt, Carol (model); Flushing, New York, 12/1/60

Altman, Robert (director); Kansas City, Mo., 2/20/25

Amanpour, Christiane (broadcast journalist); London, 1958

Amati, Nicola (violin maker); Cremona, Italy **(1596–1684)**

Ambler, Eric (suspense writer); London **(1909–1998)**

Ambrose, Stephen (author, historian); Whitewater, Wis. **(1936–2002)**

Ameche, Don (Dominic Amici) (actor); Kenosha, Wis. **(1908–1993)**

Amis, Kingsley (novelist); London **(1922–1995)**

Amis, Martin (novelist); Oxford, England, 8/25/49

Amory, Cleveland (conservationist); Nahant, Mass. **(1917–1998)**

Amos, (Freeman F. Gosden) (radio comedian); Richmond, Va. **(1899–1982)**

Amos, John (actor); Newark, N.J., 12/27/41

Amos, Tori (singer); Newton, N.C., 8/22/63

Amsterdam, Morey (actor); Chicago **(1914–1996)**

Andersen, Hans Christian (author of fairy tales); Odense, Denmark **(1805–1875)**

Anderson, Eddie (Rochester) (actor); Oakland, Calif. **(1905–1977)**

Anderson, Gillian (actress); Chicago, 8/9/68

Anderson, Harry (actor); Newport, R.I., 10/14/52

Anderson, Ib (ballet dancer); Copenhagen, 12/14/54

Anderson, Jack (journalist); Long Beach, Calif., 10/19/22

Anderson, Dame Judith (actress); Adelaide, Australia **(1898–1992)**

Anderson, Lindsay (Gordon) (director); Bangalore, India **(1923–1994)**

Anderson, Loni (actress); St. Paul, Minn., 8/5/45

Anderson, Lynn (singer); Grand Forks, N.D., 9/26/47

Anderson, Marian (contralto); Philadelphia (1897–1993)
Anderson, Maxwell (dramatist); Atlantic, Pa. (1888–1959)
Anderson Lee, Pamela (Pamela Anderson) (model, actress); Ladysmith, B.C., Canada, 7/1/67
Anderson, Richard Dean (actor); Minneapolis, Minn., 1/23/50
Anderson, Robert (playwright); New York City, 4/28/17
Anderson, Sherwood (novelist); Camden, Ohio (1876–1941)
Andress, Ursula (actress); Bern, Switzerland, 3/19/38
Andrews, Julie (Julia Wells) (actress, singer); Walton-on-Thames, England, 10/1/35
Andrews, La Verne (singer); Minneapolis (1916–1967)
Andrews, Maxene (singer); Minneapolis (1918–1995)
Andrews, Patti (singer); Minneapolis, 2/16/20
Andy (Charles J. Correll) (radio comedian); Peoria, Ill. (1890–1972)
Angelico, Fra (Guido di Pietro; Giovanni de Fiesole) (painter); nr. Florence (c. 1400–1455)
Angelou, Maya (Marguerite Johnson) (poet, novelist); St. Louis, 4/4/28
Aniston, Jennifer (Jennifer Anistonapoulos) (actress); Sherman Oaks, Calif., 2/11/69
Anka, Paul (singer, composer); Ottawa, Ont., Canada, 7/30/41
Annan, Kofi (diplomat, UN secretary general); Kumasi, Ghana, 4/8/38
Ann-Margret (Ann-Margaret Olsson) (actress); Valsjobyn, Sweden, 4/28/41
Anouilh, Jean (playwright); Bordeaux, France (1910–1987)
Anthony, Susan Brownell (woman suffragist); Adams, Mass. (1820–1906)
Antonioni, Michelangelo (director); Ferrara, Italy, 9/29/12
Antony, Mark (Marcus Antonius) (statesman); Rome (c. 83–30 B.C.)
Anuszkiewicz, Richard (painter); Erie, Pa.; 5/23/30
Apple, Fiona (singer); New York City, 4/8/68
Applegate, Christina (actress); Los Angeles, Calif., 11/25/71
Aquinas, St. Thomas (philosopher); nr. Aquino, Italy (1225–1274)
Arafat, Yasir (Mohammed Abdel-Raouf Arafat al Qudwa al Husseini) (chairman of the Palestine Liberation Organization); Cairo, Egypt, 8/24/29
Arbuckle, Roscoe "Fatty" (actor, director); Smith Center, Kans. (1887–1933)
Archimedes (physicist, mathematician); Syracuse, Sicily (287–212 B.C.)
Archipenko, Alexandre (sculptor); Kiev, Ukraine (1887–1964)
Arden, Elizabeth (Florence Nightingale Graham) (cosmetics executive); Woodbridge, Canada (1878–1966)
Arden, Eve (Eunice Quedens) (actress); Mill Valley, Calif. (1912–1990)
Arendt, Hannah (historian); Hanover, Germany (1906–1975)
Aristophanes (dramatist); Athens (c. 448–c. 385 B.C.)
Aristotle (philosopher); Stagirus, Macedonia (384–322 B.C.)
Arkin, Adam (actor); New York City, 8/19/57
Arkin, Alan (actor, director); New York City, 3/26/34
Arledge, Roone (TV executive); Forest Hills, N.Y. (1931–2002)
Arlen, Harold (Hyman Arluck) (composer); Buffalo, N.Y. (1905–1986)
Armani, Georgio (fashion designer); Piacenza, Italy, 7/11/34
Armstrong, Louis ("Satchmo") (musician); New Orleans (1901–1971)
Arnaz, Desi (Desiderio Alberto Araz y de Acha III) (actor, producer); Santiago, Cuba (1917–1986)
Arness, James (James Aurness) (actor); Minneapolis, 5/26/23
Arno, Peter (cartoonist); New York City (1904–1968)
Arnold, Benedict (American Revolutionary War general, charged with treason); Norwich, Conn. (1741–1801)
Arnold, Matthew (poet, critic); Laleham, England (1822–1888)
Arp, Jean (sculptor, painter); Strasbourg, France (1887–1966)
Arquette, Cliff (actor); Toledo, Ohio (1905–1974)
Arquette, Patricia (actress); Chicago, 4/8/68
Arquette, Rosanna (actress); New York City, 8/10/59
Arrau, Claudio (pianist); Chillán, Chile (1903–1991)
Arroyo, Martina (soprano); New York City, 2/2/40
Arthur, Bea (Bernice Frankel) (actress); New York City, 5/13/23
Arthur, Chester Alan (21st U.S. president); Fairfield, Vt. (1829–1886)
Ashcroft, John (U.S. attorney general); Chicago, Ill., 5/9/42
Ashcroft, Dame Peggy (actress); Croydon, England (1907–1991)
Ashkenazy, Vladimir (concert pianist); Gorki, U.S.S.R., 7/6/37
Ashley, Elizabeth (actress); Ocala, Fla., 8/30/39
Ashton, Sir Frederick William Mallandaine (choreographer); Guayaquil, Ecuador (1904–1988)
Asimov, Isaac (author); Petrovichi, Russia (1920–1992)
Asner, Edward (actor); Kansas City, Mo., 11/15/29
Assante, Armand (actor); New York City, 10/4/49

Astaire, Fred (Frederick Austerlitz) (dancer, actor); Omaha, Neb. (1899–1987)
Astin, John (actor, director); Baltimore, 3/30/30
Astor, Brooke (socialite, philanthropist); Portsmouth, N.H., 3/30/1902
Astor, John Jacob (financier); Waldorf, Germany (1763–1848)
Astor, Mary (Lucile Langhanke) (actress); Quincy, Ill. (1906–1987)
Ataturk, Kemal (Mustafa Kemal) (Turkish soldier, statesman); Salonika, Greece (1881–1938)
Atkins, Chet (guitarist); nr. Luttrell, Tenn. (1924–2001)
Atkinson, Rowan (actor); Newcastle-Upon-Tyne, England, 1/6/55
Attenborough, Richard (actor, director); Cambridge, England, 8/29/23
Attila (King of Huns); (406?–453)
Attucks, Crispus (American Revolutionary patriot); Boston (c. 1723–1770)
Auberjonois, Rene (actor); New York City, 6/1/40
Auchincloss, Louis (author); Lawrence, N.Y., 9/27/17
Auden, W(ystan) H(ugh) (poet); York, England (1907–1973)
Audubon, John James (naturalist, painter); Haiti (1785–1851)
Auer, Leopold (violinist, teacher); Veszprém, Hungary (1845–1930)
Augustine, Saint (Aurelius Augustinus) (theologian); Tagaste, Numidia, Algeria (354–430)
Augustus (Gaius Octavius) (Roman emperor); Rome (63 B.C.– A.D. 14)
Aung San Suu Kyi (human rights activist); Rangoon, Burma, 6/19/45
Austen, Jane (novelist); Steventon, England (1775–1817)
Autry, Gene (singer, actor); Tioga, Tex. (1907–1998)
Avalon, Frankie (singer); Philadelphia, 9/18/39
Avedon, Richard (photographer); New York City, 5/15/23
Avery, Milton (artist); Altmar, N.Y. (1893–1965)
Ax, Emanuel (pianist); Lvov, Ukraine, 6/8/49
Axelrod, George (playwright); New York City (1922–2003)
Ayckbourn, Alan (playwright); London, 4/12/39
Aykroyd, Dan (actor); Ottawa, Ont., Canada, 7/1/52
Ayres, Lew (actor); Minneapolis (1908–1996)

B

Bacall, Lauren (Betty Joan Perske) (actress); New York City, 9/16/24
Bach, Carl Phillip Emanuel (composer); Weimar, Germany (1714–1788)
Bach, Johann Sebastian (composer); Eisenach, Germany (1685–1750)
Bacharach, Burt (songwriter); Kansas City, Mo., 5/12/29
Backus, Jim (actor); Cleveland (1913–1989)
Bacon, Francis (philosopher, essayist); London (1561–1626)
Bacon, Francis (painter); Dublin (1910–1992)
Bacon, Kevin (actor); Philadelphia, 7/8/58
Bacon, Roger (philosopher, scientist); Ilchester, England (c. 1214–1294?)
Badu, Erykah (Erykah Wright) (singer); Dallas, 1971
Baez, Joan (folk singer); Staten Island, N.Y., 1/9/41
Bailey, F. Lee (lawyer); Waltham, Mass., 6/10/33
Bailey, Pearl (actress); Newport News, Va. (1918–1990)
Bain, Conrad (actor); Lethbridge, Alba., Canada, 2/4/23
Baio, Scott (actor); Brooklyn, N.Y., 9/22/61
Baird, Bil (William B. Baird) (puppeteer); Grand Island, Neb. (1904–1987)
Baker, Anita (singer); Toledo, Ohio, 1958?
Baker, Carroll (actress); Johnstown, Pa., 5/28/31
Baker, Josephine (singer, dancer); St. Louis (1906–1975)
Baker, Russell (columnist); Loudoun County, Va., 8/14/25
Balanchine, George (choreographer); St. Petersburg, Russia (1904–1983)
Balboa, Vasco Nuñez de (explorer); Jerez de los Caballeros, Spain (1475–1517)
Baldwin, Alec (actor); Massapequa, N.Y., 4/3/58
Baldwin, James (novelist); New York City (1924–1987)
Bale, Christian (actor); Pembrokeshire, Wales, 1/30/74
Balenciaga, Cristóbal (fashion designer); Guetaria, Spain (1895–1972)
Ball, Lucille (Lucille Désirée Ball) (actress, producer); Celoron (nr. Jamestown), N.Y. (1911–1989)
Balsam, Martin (actor); Bronx, New York (1919–1996)
Balzac, Honoré de (novelist); Tours, France (1799–1850)
Bancroft, Anne (Annemarie Italiano) (actress); New York City, 9/17/31
Banderas, Antonio (José Antonio Dominguez Banderas) (actor, model); Málaga, Spain, 8/10/60
Bankhead, Tallulah (actress); Huntsville, Ala. (1903–1968)

Banks, Tyra (model); Los Angeles, 12/4/73

Banting, Fredrick Grant (physiologist); Alliston, Ont., Canada **(1891–1941)**

Bara, Theda (Theodosia Goodman) (actress); Cincinnati **(1890–1955)**

Barak, Ehud (former Israeli prime minister); Kibbutz Mishmar Hasharon, Israel, 2/12/42

Barbera, Joseph (animator, producer); New York City, 1911

Baraka, Imamu Amiri (LeRoi Jones) (playwright); Newark, N.J., 10/7/34

Baranski, Christine (actress); Buffalo, N.Y., 5/2/52

Barber, Red (Walter Lanier) (sportscaster); Columbus, Miss. **(1908–1992)**

Barber, Samuel (composer); West Chester, Pa. **(1910–1981)**

Barbie, Klaus (Nazi, "The Butcher of Lyon"); Bad Godesberg, Germany **(1913–1991)**

Bardem, Javier (actor); Gran Canaria, Spain, 5/1/69

Bardot, Brigitte (Camille Javal) (actress); Paris, 9/28/34

Barenboim, Daniel (concert pianist, conductor); Buenos Aires, 11/15/42

Barker, Bob (game-show host); Darrington, Wash., 12/12/23

Barkin, Ellen (actress); Bronx, N.Y., 4/16/54

Barnard, Christiaan N. (heart surgeon); Beauford West, South Africa **(1922–2001)**

Barnum, Phineas Taylor (showman); Bethel, Conn. **(1810–1891)**

Barrie, Sir James Matthew (author); Kirriemuir, Scotland **(1860–1937)**

Barry, John (naval officer); County Wexford, Ireland **(1745–1803)**

Barrymore, Diana (actress); New York City **(1921–1960)**

Barrymore, Drew (actress); Los Angeles, 2/22/75

Barrymore, Ethel (Ethel Blythe) (actress); Philadelphia **(1879–1959)**

Barrymore, Georgiana Drew (actress); Philadelphia **(1856–1893)**

Barrymore, John (John Blythe) (actor); Philadelphia **(1882–1942)**

Barrymore, Lionel (Lionel Blythe) (actor); Philadelphia **(1878–1954)**

Barrymore, Maurice (Herbert Blythe) (actor, playwright); Agra, India **(1847–1905)**

Barth, John (novelist); Cambridge, Md., 5/27/30

Barthelme, Donald (novelist); Philadelphia **(1931 –1989)**

Bartók, Béla (composer); Nagyszentmiklo, Hungary **(1881–1945)**

Barton, Clara (founder of American Red Cross); Oxford, Mass. **(1821–1912)**

Baruch, Bernard Mannes (statesman); Camden, S.C. **(1870–1965)**

Baryshnikov, Mikhail Nikolayevich (ballet dancer, artistic director); Riga, Latvia, 1/27/48

Basie, Count (William Basie) (band leader); Red Bank, N.J. **(1904–1984)**

Basinger, Kim (actress); Athens, Ga., 12/8/53

Bassett, Angela (actress); New York City, 8/16/58

Bassey, Shirley (singer); Cardiff, Wales, 1/8/37

Batchelor, Clarence Daniel (political cartoonist); Osage City, Kans. **(1888–1977)**

Bateman, Jason (actor); Rye, N.Y., 1/14/69

Bateman, Justine (actress); Rye, N.Y., 2/19/66

Bates, Alan (actor); Allestree, England **(1934–2003)**

Bates, Kathy (Kathleen Doyle Bates) (actress); Memphis, Tenn., 6/28/48

Battle, Kathleen (soprano); Portsmouth, Ohio, 8/13/48

Baudelaire, Charles Pierre (poet); Paris **(1821–1867)**

Baxter, Anne (actress); Michigan City, Ind. **(1923–1985)**

Baxter, Meredith (actress); Los Angeles, 6/21/47

Beardsley, Aubrey Vincent (illustrator); Brighton, England **(1872–1898)**

Beaton, Cecil (photographer, designer); London **(1904–1980)**

Beatty, Clyde (animal trainer); Bainbridge, Ohio **(1903–1965)**

Beatty, Warren (Henry Warren Beaty) (actor, producer); Richmond, Va., 3/30/37

Beaumont, Francis (dramatist); Grace-Dieu, England **(1584–1616)**

Becket, Thomas à (archbishop of Canterbury); London **(1118?–1170)**

Beckett, Samuel (playwright); Dublin **(1906–1989)**

Beckmann, Max (painter); Leipzig, Germany **(1884–1950)**

Bede, Saint ("The Venerable Bede") (scholar); Monkwearmouth, England **(673–735)**

Beecham, Sir Thomas (conductor); St. Helens, England **(1879–1961)**

Beecher, Henry Ward (clergyman); Litchfield, Conn. **(1813–1887)**

Beerbohm, Sir Max (author); London **(1872–1956)**

Beery, Noah (actor); Kansas City, Mo. **(1884–1946)**

Beery, Noah, Jr. (actor); New York City **(1913–1994)**

Beery, Wallace (actor); Kansas City, Mo. **(1886–1949)**

Beethoven, Ludwig van (composer); Bonn, Germany **(1770–1827)**

Begin, Menachem (Israeli prime minister); Brest-Litovsk, Belarus **(1913–1992)**

Begley, Ed (actor); Hartford, Conn. **(1901–1970)**

Beiderbecke, Bix (jazz musician); Davenport, Iowa **(1903–1931)**

Beineix, Jean-Jacques (director, producer, screenwriter) 1946

Belafonte, Harry (singer, actor); New York City, 3/1/27

Belafonte-Harper, Shari (actress); New York City, 9/22/54

Belasco, David (dramatist, producer); San Francisco **(1854–1931)**

Bel Geddes, Barbara (actress); New York City, 10/31/22

Bell, Alexander Graham (inventor); Edinburgh, Scotland **(1847–1922)**

Bell, Quentin (author, artist); England **(1910–1996)**

Bellamy, Edward (author); Chicopee Falls, Mass. **(1850–1898)**

Bellamy, Ralph (actor); Chicago **(1904–1991)**

Bellini, Giovanni (painter); Venice **(c. 1430–1516)**

Bellow, Saul (novelist); Lachine, Que., Canada, 6/10/15

Bellows, George Wesley (painter, lithographer); Columbus, Ohio **(1882–1925)**

Belushi, Jim (actor); Chicago, 6/15/54

Belushi, John (comedian, actor); Chicago **(1949–1982)**

Benchley, Peter Bradford (novelist); New York City, 5/8/40

Benchley, Robert Charles (humorist); Worcester, Mass. **(1889–1945)**

Bendix, William (actor); New York City **(1906–1964)**

Benedict, Ruth Fulton (anthropologist); New York City **(1887–1948)**

Benes, Eduard (statesman); Kozlany, former Czechoslovakia **(1884–1948)**

Benét, Stephen Vincent (poet, story writer); Bethlehem, Pa. **(1898–1943)**

Benét, William Rose (poet, novelist); Ft. Hamilton, Brooklyn, N.Y. **(1886–1950)**

Ben-Gurion, David (David Green) (statesman); Plónsk, Poland **(1886–1973)**

Benigni, Roberto (actor, director, screenwriter); Misericordia, Arezzo, Italy, 10/27/52

Bening, Annette (actress); Topeka, Kans., 5/29/58

Bennett, Enoch Arnold (novelist, dramatist); Hanley, England **(1867–1931)**

Bennett, James Gordon (editor); Keith, Scotland **(1795–1872)**

Bennett, Joan (actress); Palisades, N.J. **(1910–1990)**

Bennett, Robert Russell (composer); Kansas City, Mo. **(1894–1981)**

Bennett, Tony (Anthony Benedetto) (singer); Astoria, Queens, N.Y., 8/3/26

Benny, Jack (Benjamin Kubelsky) (comedian); Chicago **(1894–1974)**

Benson, Robby (Robert Segal) (actor); Dallas, 1/21/56

Bentham, Jeremy Heinrich (economist); London **(1748–1832)**

Benton, Thomas Hart (painter); Neosho, Mo. **(1889–1975)**

Berendt, John (writer); Syracuse, N.Y., 12/5/39

Berenger, Tom (actor); Chicago, 5/31/50

Berg, Alban (composer); Vienna **(1885–1935)**

Berg, Gertrude (writer, actress); New York City **(1899–1966)**

Bergen, Candice (actress); Beverly Hills, Calif., 5/9/46

Bergen, Edgar (ventriloquist); Chicago **(1903–1978)**

Bergen, Polly (Nellie Paulina Burgin) (actress, singer); Knoxville, Tenn., 7/14/30

Bergerac, Cyrano de (poet); Paris **(1619–1655)**

Bergman, Ingmar (film director); Uppsala, Sweden, 7/14/18

Bergman, Ingrid (actress); Stockholm **(1915–1982)**

Bergson, Henri (philosopher); Paris **(1859–1941)**

Berkeley, Busby (William Berkeley Enos) (choreographer, director); Los Angeles **(1895–1976)**

Berle, Milton (Milton Berlinger) (comedian); New York City **(1908–2002)**

Berlin, Irving (Israel Baline) (songwriter); Temum, Russia **(1888–1989)**

Berlioz, Louis Hector (composer); La Côte-Saint-André, France **(1803–1869)**

Berman, Lazar (concert pianist); Leningrad (St. Petersburg), Russia, 2/26/30

Bernardin, Joseph Cardinal (prelate); Columbia, S.C. **(1928–1996)**

Bernhard, Sandra (actress, comedian); Flint, Mich., 6/6/55

Bernhardt, Sarah (Rosine Bernard) (actress); Paris **(1844–1923)**

Bernini, Gian Lorenzo (sculptor, painter); Naples, Italy **(1598–1680)**

Bernoulli, Jacques (scientist); Basel, Switzerland **(1654–1705)**

Bernsen, Corbin (actor); North Hollywood, Calif., 9/7/54

Bernstein, Leonard (conductor); Lawrence, Mass. **(1918–1990)**

Berry, Chuck (Charles Edward Berry) (singer, guitarist); St. Louis, Mo., 10/19/26

Berry, Halle (actress, model); Cleveland, Ohio, 8/14/68

Berry, Ken (actor); Moline, Ill., 11/3/30

Berry, Richard (songwriter); Extension, S.C. **(1935–1997)**

Berryman, John (poet); McAlester, Okla. **(1914–1972)**
Bertinelli, Valerie (actress); Wilmington, Del., 4/23/60
Bertolucci, Bernardo (actor); Parma, Italy, 3/16/40
Bethune, Mary McLeod (educator); Mayesville, S.C. **(1875–1955)**
Betjeman, Sir John (poet laureate); London **(1906–1984)**
Bettelheim, Bruno (psychoanalyst); Vienna **(1903–1990)**
Bierce, Ambrose Gwinnett (journalist); Meigs County, Ohio **(1842–1914?)**
Bikel, Theodore (actor, folk singer); Vienna, 5/2/24
Bing, Sir Rudolf (opera manager); Vienna **(1902–1997)**
Bingham, George Caleb (painter); Augusta Co., Va. **(1811–1879)**
Binoche, Juliette (actress); Paris, 3/9/64
Bishop, Joey (Joseph Gottlieb) (comedian); New York City, 2/3/19
Bismarck-Schönhausen, Prince Otto Eduard Leopold von (statesman); Schönhausen, Germany **(1815–1898)**
Bisset, Jacqueline (actress); Weybridge, England, 9/13/44
Bixby, Bill (actor); San Francisco **(1934–1993)**
Bizet, Georges (Alexandre César Léopold Bizet) (composer); Paris **(1838–1875)**
Bjoerling, Jussi (tenor); Stora Tuna, Sweden **(1911–1960)**
Björk (Björk Gudmundsdottir) (pop musician, singer); Reykjavik, Iceland, 11/21/65
Black, Clint (singer, songwriter); Long Branch, N.J., 2/4/62
Black, Karen (Karen Ziegler) (actress); Park Ridge, Ill., 7/1/42
Black, Shirley Temple (child actress, former ambassador); Santa Monica, Calif., 4/23/28
Blackstone, Sir William (jurist); London **(1723–1780)**
Blackwell, Elizabeth (physician, educator); England **(1821–1910)**
Blades, Ruben (actor, musician, composer); Panama City, Panama, 7/16/48
Blair, Tony (British prime minister); Edinburgh, Scotland, 5/6/53
Blake, Amanda (Beverly Louise Neill) (actress); Buffalo, N.Y. **(1929–1989)**
Blake, Eubie (James Hubert) (pianist); Baltimore **(1883–1983)**
Blake, Robert (Michael Gubitosi) (actor); Nutley, N.J., 9/18/33
Blake, William (poet, artist); London **(1757–1827)**
Blanc, Mel (Melvin Jerome) (actor, voice specialist); San Francisco **(1908–1989)**
Blass, Bill (fashion designer); Fort Wayne, Ind. **(1922–2002)**
Bleeth, Yasmine (model, actress); New York City, 6/14/68
Blige, Mary J. (hip-hop singer); Bronx, N.Y., 1/11/71
Bloch, Ernest (composer); Geneva **(1880–1959)**
Bloom, Claire (actress); London, 2/15/31
Bloomberg, Michael (mayor of New York); Melrose, Mass., 2/14/1942
Bloomgarden, Kermit (producer); Brooklyn, N.Y. **(1904–1976)**
Blume, Judy (Judy Sussman) (young adult novelist); Elizabeth, N.J., 2/12/38
Bly, Nellie (pseud. for Elizabeth Seaman) (journalist); Cochrane Mills, Pa. **(1867–1922)**
Bly, Robert (poet, critic); Madison, Minn., 12/23/26
Boccaccio, Giovanni (author); Paris **(1313–1375)**
Boccherini, Luigi (Rodolfo) (composer); Lucca, Italy **(1743–1805)**
Boccioni, Umberto (painter, sculptor); Reggio di Calabria, Italy **(1882–1916)**
Bochco, Steven (TV producer, writer); New York City, 12/16/43
Bock, Jerry (composer); New Haven, Conn., 11/23/28
Bogarde, Dirk (Derek Van den Bogaerde) (film actor, director); London **(1921–1999)**
Bogart, Humphrey DeForest (actor); New York City **(1899–1957)**
Bogdanovich, Peter (producer, director); Kingston, N.Y., 7/30/39
Bogosian, Eric (playwright, screenwriter, actor, monologuist); Woburn, Mass., 4/24/53
Bohr, Niels (atomic physicist); Copenhagen **(1885–1962)**
Bok, Sissela (Sissela Ann Myrdal) (scholar); Stockholm, 12/2/34
Bolger, Ray (dancer, actor); Dorchester, Mass **(1904–1987)**
Bolívar, Simón (South American liberator); Caracas, Venezuela **(1783–1830)**
Bologna, Giovanni da (sculptor); Douai, France **(1529–1608)**
Bombeck, Erma (author, columnist); Dayton, Ohio **(1927–1996)**
Bonaparte, Napoléon (Emperor of the French); Ajaccio, Corsica, France **(1769–1821)**
Bond, Julian (Georgia legislator); Nashville, Tenn., 1/14/40
Bonet, Lisa (actress); San Francisco, 11/16/67
Bonham Carter, Helena (actress); London, 5/23/66
Bon Jovi, Jon (musician, songwriter); Sayreville, N.J., 3/2/62
Bonnard, Pierre (painter); Fontenayaux-Roses, France **(1867–1947)**
Bono (Paul Hewson) (singer, songwriter); Dublin, Ireland, 5/10/60
Bono, Sonny (Salvatore Bono) (singer, politician); Detroit **(1935–1998)**
Boone, Daniel (frontiersman); nr. Reading, Pa. **(1734–1820)**
Boone, Pat (Charles Boone) (singer); Jacksonville, Fla., 6/1/34

Boone, Richard (actor); Los Angeles **(1917–1981)**
Boorstin, Daniel (historian); Atlanta, 10/1/14
Booth, Edwin Thomas (actor); Bel Air, Md. **(1833–1893)**
Booth, Evangeline Cory (religious leader); London **(1865–1950)**
Booth, John Wilkes (actor; assassin of Lincoln); Harford County, Md. **(1838–1865)**
Booth, Shirley (Thelma Booth Ford) (actress); New York City **(1907–1992)**
Borden, Lizzie (Elizabeth Andrew Borden) (accused murderer); Fall River, Mass. **(1860–1927)**
Borge, Victor (pianist, comedian); Copenhagen **(1909–2000)**
Borgia, Cesare (nobleman, soldier); Rome **(1476–1507)**
Borgia, Lucrezia (Duchess of Ferrara); Rome **(1480–1519)**
Borgnine, Ernest (actor); Hamden, Conn., 1/24/17
Borromini, Francesco (architect); Bissone, Italy **(1599–1667)**
Bosch, Hieronymus (Hieronymus van Aeken) (painter); Hertogenbosch, Netherlands **(c. 1450–1516)**
Bosley, Tom (actor); Chicago, 10/1/27
Bostwick, Barry (actor); San Mateo, Calif., 2/24/45
Boswell, James (diarist, biographer); Edinburgh, Scotland **(1740–1795)**
Botticelli, Sandro (Alessandro di Mariano dei Filipepi) (painter); Florence, Italy **(1444–1510)**
Bottoms, Timothy (actor); Santa Barbara, Calif., 8/30/50
Boulez, Pierre (conductor); Montbrison, France, 3/26/25
Bourke-White, Margaret (photographer); New York City **(1906–1971)**
Boutros-Ghali, Boutros (ex-secretary general of the UN); Cairo, Egypt, 11/14/22
Bow, Clara (actress); Brooklyn, N.Y. **(1905–1965)**
Bowen, Catherine Drinker (biographer); Haverford, Pa. **(1897–1973)**
Bowie, David (David Robert Jones) (actor, musician); London, 1/8/47
Bowie, James (soldier); Burke County, Ga. **(1799–1836)**
Bowles, Chester (diplomat); Springfield, Mass. **(1901–1986)**
Boxleitner, Bruce (actor); Elgin, Ill., 5/12/50
Boyce, William (composer); London? **(1710–1779)**
Boyd, Bill ("Hopalong Cassidy") (actor); Cambridge, Ohio **(1895–1972)**
Boyd, Stephen (Stephen Millar) (actor); Belfast, Northern Ireland **(1928–1977)**
Boyer, Charles (actor); Figeac, France **(1897–1978)**
Boy George (George Alan O'Dowd) (singer); London, 6/14/61
Boyle, Peter (actor); Philadelphia, 10/18/33
Boyle, Robert (scientist); Lismore Castle, Munster, Ireland **(1627–1691)**
Bracken, Eddie (actor); Astoria, Queens, N.Y., 1920
Bradbury, Ray Douglas (science-fiction writer); Waukegan, Ill., 8/22/20
Bradlee, Benjamin C. (editor); Boston, 8/26/21
Bradley, Ed (broadcast journalist); Philadelphia, 6/22/41
Bradley, Omar N. (5-star general); Clark, Mo. **(1893–1981)**
Bradley, Thomas (mayor of Los Angeles); Calvert, Tex. **(1917–1998)**
Brady, Mathew (early photographer); Warren Co., N.Y. **(c. 1823–1896)**
Brahe, Tycho (astronomer); Knudstrup, Denmark **(1546–1601)**
Bragg, Billy (singer, songwriter); Barking, England, 12/20/57
Brahms, Johannes (composer); Hamburg, Germany **(1833–1897)**
Braille, Louis (teacher of blind); Coupvray, France **(1809–1862)**
Brailowsky, Alexander (pianist); Kiev, Ukraine **(1896–1976)**
Bramante, Donato D'Agnolo (architect); Monte Asdrualdo (now Fermignano), Italy **(1444–1514)**
Branagh, Kenneth (actor, director, writer, producer); Belfast, Northern Ireland, 12/10/60
Brancusi, Constantin (sculptor); Pestisansi, Romania **(1876–1957)**
Brandauer, Klaus Maria (Klaus Maria Steng) (actor); Bad Aussee, Steiermark, Austria , 6/22/44
Brando, Marlon (actor); Omaha, Neb. **(1924–2004)**
Brandt, Willy (Herbert Frahm) (ex-chancellor); Lübeck, Germany **(1913– 1992)**
Brandy (Brandy Norwood) (actress, singer); McComb, Miss., 2/11/79
Braque, Georges (painter); Argenteuil, France **(1882–1963)**
Bratt, Benjamin (actor); San Francisco, 12/16/63
Braugher, André (actor); Chicago, 7/1/62
Braxton, Toni (R&B singer); Severn, Maryland, 10/7/67
Brazelton, T(homas) Berry II (pediatrician, writer); Waco, Tex., 5/10/18
Brecht, Bertolt (dramatist, poet); Augsburg, Bavaria **(1898–1956)**
Brel, Jacques (singer, composer); Brussels **(1929–1978)**
Brennan, Walter (actor); Lynn, Mass. **(1894–1974)**

Brennan, William J., Jr. (Supreme Court justice); Newark, N.J. **(1906–1997)**
Breslin, Jimmy (journalist); Jamaica, Queens, N.Y., 10/17/30
Breton, André (writer); Tinchebray, France **(1896–1966)**
Breuer, Marcel (architect, designer); Pécs, Hungary **(1902–1981)**
Brewster, Kingman, Jr. (ex-president of Yale); Longmeadow, Mass. **(1919–1988)**
Brezhnev, Leonid I. (Communist Party secretary); Dneprodzerzhinsk, Ukraine **(1906–1982)**
Brice, Fanny (Fannie Borach) (comedienne); New York City **(1892–1951)**
Bridges, Beau (actor); Los Angeles, 12/9/41
Bridges, Jeff (actor); Los Angeles, 12/4/49
Bridges, Lloyd (actor); San Leandro, Calif. **(1913–1998)**
Brinkley, Christie (model, actress); Malibu, Calif., 2/2/54
Brinkley, David (TV newscaster); Wilmington, N.C. **(1920–2003)**
Britten, Benjamin (composer); Lowestoft, England **(1913–1976)**
Broderick, Matthew (actor); New York City, 3/21/62
Brodsky, Joseph Alexandrovitch (poet); St. Petersburg, Russia **(1940–1996)**
Brody, Jane (journalist); Brooklyn, N.Y., 5/19/41
Brokaw, Tom (TV newscaster); Webster, S.D., 2/6/40
Brolin, James (actor); Los Angeles, 7/18/40
Bromfield, Louis (novelist); Mansfield, Ohio **(1896–1956)**
Bronson, Charles (Charles Buchinsky) (actor); Ehrenfield, Pa. **(1921–2003)**
Brontë, Charlotte (novelist); Thornton, England **(1816–1855)**
Brontë, Emily Jane (novelist); Thornton, England **(1818–1848)**
Bronzino, Agnolo (painter); Monticelli, Italy **(1503–1572)**
Brook, Peter (director); London, 3/21/25
Brooke, Rupert (poet); Rugby, England **(1887–1915)**
Brooks, Albert (Albert Einstein) (actor, writer, director); Beverly Hills, Calif., 7/22/47
Brooks, Avery (actor) 4/18/49
Brooks, Gwendolyn (poet); Topeka, Kans. **(1917–2000)**
Brooks, James L. (film and television producer); New York City, 5/9/40
Brooks, Mel (Melvin Kaminsky) (writer, film director); Brooklyn, N.Y., 6/28/26
Brosnan, Pierce (actor); County Meath, Ireland, 5/16/52
Brothers, Joyce (Bauer) (psychologist, author, radio-TV personality); New York City, 9/20/28
Broun, Matthew Heywood Campbell (journalist); Brooklyn, N.Y. **(1888–1939)**
Brown, Charles Brockden (novelist); Philadelphia **(1771–1810)**
Brown, Helen Gurley (editor, author); Green Forest, Ark., 2/18/22
Brown, James (singer); Augusta, Ga., 5/3/34
Brown, Joe E. (comedian); Holgate, Ohio **(1892–1973)**
Brown, John (abolitionist); Torrington, Conn. **(1800–1859)**
Brown, Les (band leader); Reinerton, Pa. **(1912–2000)**
Brown, Margaret Wise (children's author); Brooklyn, N.Y. **(1910–1952)**
Brown, Trisha (choreographer); Aberdeen, Wash., 11/25/36
Browne, Jackson (singer, guitarist); Heidelberg, Germany, 10/9/48
Browning, Elizabeth Barrett (poet); Durham, England **(1806–1861)**
Browning, Robert (poet); London **(1812–1889)**
Brubeck, Dave (musician); Concord, Calif., 12/6/20
Bruce, Lenny (comedian); Long Island, N.Y. **(1926–1966)**
Bruce, Nigel (actor); Ensenada, Mexico **(1895–1953)**
Brueghel, Pieter (painter); nr. Breda, Flanders, Netherlands **(c. 1520–1569)**
Bruhn, Erik (Belton Evers) (ballet dancer); Copenhagen **(1928–1986)**
Brunelleschi, Filippo (architect); Florence, Italy **(1377–1446)**
Bruno, Giordano (philosopher); Nola, Italy **(1548–1600)**
Brutus, Marcus Junius (Roman politician) **(85–42 B.C.)**
Bryan, William Jennings (orator, politician); Salem, Ill. **(1860–1925)**
Bryant, Anita (singer); Barnsdall, Okla., 3/25/40
Bryant, William Cullen (poet, editor); Cummington, Mass. **(1794–1878)**
Brynner, Yul (Taidje Khan) (actor); Sakhalin Island, Russia **(1920–1985)**
Brzezinski, Zbigniew (ex-presidential adviser); Warsaw, 3/28/28
Buber, Martin (philosopher, theologian); Vienna **(1878–1965)**
Buchanan, James (15th U.S. president); near Mercersburg, Pa. **(1791–1868)**
Buchanan, Pat (politician); Washington, D.C., 11/2/38
Buchholz, Horst (actor); Berlin, 12/4/33
Büchner, Georg (dramatist); Goddelau, Germany **(1813–1837)**
Buchwald, Art (Arthur Buchwald) (columnist); Mount Vernon, N.Y., 10/20/25
Buck, Pearl S(ydenstricker) (author); Hillsboro, W. Va. **(1892–1973)**
Buckley, Christopher (writer); New York City, 1952

Buckley, Jeff (singer, songwriter); Orange County, Calif. **(1966–1997)**
Buckley, William F., Jr. (journalist); New York City, 11/24/25
Buffalo Bill (William Frederick Cody) (scout); Scott County, Iowa **(1846–1917)**
Buffett, Jimmy (singer, writer); Pascogoula, Miss., 12/25/46
Buffett, Warren (investment expert); Omaha, Neb., 8/30/30
Bujold, Geneviève (actress); Montreal, 7/1/42
Bujones, Fernando (ballet dancer); Miami, Fla., 3/9/55
Bulgakov, Mikhail (novelist); Kiev, Ukraine **(1891–1940)**
Bullins, Ed (playwright); Philadelphia, 7/2/35
Bullock, Sandra (actress); Washington D.C., 7/26/64
Bunche, Ralph J. (statesman); Detroit **(1904–1971)**
Bundy, McGeorge (educator); Boston **(1919–1996)**
Bundy, William Putnam (editor); Washington, D.C. **(1917–2000)**
Buñuel, Luis (film director); Calanda, Spain **(1900–1983)**
Bunyan, John (preacher, author); Elstow, England **(1628–1688)**
Burbank, Luther (horticulturist); Lancaster, Mass. **(1849–1926)**
Burke, Adm. Arleigh A. (ex-chief of Naval Operations); Boulder, Colo. **(1901–1996)**
Burke, Billie (Mary William Ethelbert Appleton Burke) (comedienne); Washington, D.C. **(1885–1970)**
Burke, Delta (actress); Orlando, Fla., 7/30/56
Burke, Edmund (statesman); Dublin **(1729–1797)**
Burne-Jones, Edward Coley (painter); Birmingham, England **(1833–1898)**
Burnett, Carol (comedienne); San Antonio, 4/26/33
Burney, Fanny (Frances) (writer); King's Lynn, England **(1752–1840)**
Burns, Edward (actor, film director, screenwriter, producer); Long Island, N.Y., 1/29/68
Burns, George (Nathan Birnbaum) (comedian); New York City **(1896–1996)**
Burns, Ken (documentary filmmaker); Brooklyn, N.Y., 7/29/53
Burns, Robert (poet); Alloway, Scotland **(1759–1796)**
Burr, Aaron (political leader); Newark, N.J. **(1756–1836)**
Burr, Raymond (William Stacey Burr) (actor); New Westminster, B.C., Canada **(1917–1993)**
Burroughs, Edgar Rice (novelist); Chicago **(1875–1950)**
Burroughs, William S. (writer); St. Louis **(1914–1997)**
Burrows, Abe (playwright, director); New York City **(1910–1985)**
Burstyn, Ellen (Edna Rae Gillooly) (actress); Detroit, 12/7/32
Burton, LeVar (actor, director); Landsthul, Germany, 2/16/57
Burton, Richard (Richard Jenkins) (actor); Pontrhydfen, Wales **(1925–1984)**
Burton, Tim (filmmaker); Burbank, Calif., 8/25/58
Buscemi, Steve (actor); Brooklyn, N.Y., 12/13/57
Bush, George Herbert Walker (41st U.S. president); Milton, Mass., 6/12/24
Butkus, Dick (NFL linebacker, actor); Chicago, 12/9/42
Butler, Samuel (author); Langar, England **(1835–1902)**
Butterworth, Charles (actor); South Bend, Ind. **(1896–1946)**
Buttons, Red (Aaron Chwatt) (actor); New York City, 2/5/19
Buzzi, Ruth (comedienne); Westerly, R.I., 7/24/36
Byrd, Richard Evelyn (polar explorer); Winchester, Va. **(1888–1957)**
Byrne, David (composer, musician, director, actor); Dumbarton, Scotland, 5/14/52
Byrne, Gabriel (actor); Dublin, 5/12/50
Byron, George Gordon (6th Baron Byron) (poet); London **(1788–1824)**

C

Caan, James (actor); Queens, N.Y., 3/26/39
Caballé, Montserrat (soprano); Barcelona, Spain, 4/12/33
Cabot, John (Giovanni Caboto) (navigator); Genoa **(1450–1498)**
Cabot, Sebastian (navigator); Venice **(c. 1476–1557)**
Cadmus, Paul (painter, etcher); New York City **(1904–1999)**
Caesar, Irving (lyricist); New York City **(1895–1996)**
Caesar, Gaius Julius (statesman); Rome **(100–44 B.C.)**
Caesar, Sid (comedian); Yonkers, N.Y., 9/8/22
Cage, Nicolas (Nicolas Coppola) (actor); Long Beach, Calif., 1/7/64
Cagney, James (actor); New York City **(1899–1986)**
Cahn, Sammy (songwriter); New York City **(1913–1993)**
Caine, Michael (Maurice J. Micklewhite) (actor); London, 3/14/33
Calder, Alexander (sculptor); Lawnton, Pa. **(1898–1976)**
Calderón del Barca, Pedro (dramatist); Madrid **(1600–1681)**
Caldwell, Erskine (novelist); White Oak, Ga. **(1903–1987)**
Caldwell, Sarah (opera director, conductor); Maryville, Mo., 3/6/24
Caldwell, Taylor (novelist); Manchester, England **(1900–1985)**
Caldwell, Zoe (actress); Hawthorn, Australia, 9/14/33
Calhoun, John Caldwell (statesman); nr. Calhoun Mills, S.C. **(1782–1850)**

Caligula Gaius Caesar (Roman emperor); Antium, Latium **(12–41)**

Calisher, Hortense (novelist); New York City, 12/20/11

Callas, Maria (Maria Calogeropoulos) (operatic soprano); New York City **(1923–1977)**

Calloway, Cab (Cabell Calloway) (band leader); Rochester, N.Y. **(1907–1994)**

Calvin, John (Jean Chauvin) (religious reformer); Noyon, Picardy **(1509–1564)**

Calvin, Melvin (chemist, Nobel laureate); St. Paul, Minn. **(1911–1997)**

Cambridge, Godfrey (comedian); New York City **(1933–1976)**

Cameron, James (director); Kapuskasing, Ont., Canada, 8/16/54

Cameron, Rod (Rod Cox) (actor); Calgary, Alba., Canada **(1912–1983)**

Campbell, Glen (singer); nr. Delight, Ark., 4/22/38

Campbell, Naomi (model); London, England, 5/22/70

Campbell, Neve (actress); Guelph, Ont., Canada, 10/3/73

Campion, Jane (director, screenwriter); Waikanae, New Zealand, 1954

Camus, Albert (author); Mondovi, Algeria **(1913–1960)**

Canaletto (Giovanni Antonio Canale) (painter); Venice **(1697–1768)**

Candy, John (actor, comedian); Toronto **(1950–1994)**

Caniff, Milton (cartoonist); Hillsboro, Ohio **(1907–1988)**

Cannon, Dyan (Samille Diane Friesen) (actress); Tacoma, Wash., 1/4/37

Cantinflas (Mario Moreno-Reyes) (comedian); Mexico City **(1911–1993)**

Cantor, Eddie (Edward Iskowitz) (actor); New York City **(1892–1964)**

Capone, Al(fonse) (gangster); Brooklyn, N.Y. **(1899–1947)**

Capote, Truman (Truman Streckfus Persons) (novelist); New Orleans **(1924–1984)**

Capp, Al (Alfred Gerald Caplin) (cartoonist); New Haven, Conn. **(1909–1979)**

Capra, Frank (film producer, director); Palermo, Italy **(1897–1991)**

Caputo, Phil (Philip Joseph Caputo) (author, journalist); Chicago, 6/10/41

Caravaggio, Michelangelo Merisi da (painter); Caravaggio, Italy **(1573–1610)**

Cardin, Pierre (fashion designer); nr. Venice, 7/7/22

Cardinale, Claudia (actress); Tunis, Tunisia, 4/15/39

Carey, Drew (actor, producer); Cleveland, 5/23/58

Carey, Harry (actor); New York City **(1878–1947)**

Carey, Macdonald (actor); Sioux City, Iowa **(1913–1994)**

Carlin, George (comedian); Bronx, N.Y., 5/12/37

Carlisle, Kitty (singer, actress); New Orleans, 9/3/15

Carlyle, Robert (actor); Glasgow, Scotland, 4/14/61

Carlyle, Thomas (essayist, historian); Ecclefechan, Scotland **(1795–1881)**

Carmichael, Hoagy (Hoagland Howard) (songwriter); Bloomington, Ind. **(1899–1981)**

Carne, Judy (Joyce Botterill) (singer, actress); Northampton, England, 4/27/39

Carnegie, Andrew (industrialist); Dunfermline, Scotland **(1835–1919)**

Carney, Art (actor); Mt. Vernon, N.Y. **(1918–2003)**

Caron, Leslie (actress); Paris, 7/1/31

Carpenter, Mary Chapin (singer, songwriter); Princeton, N.J., 2/21/58

Carr, Vikki (Florencia Bisenta de Casillas Martinez Cardona) (singer); El Paso, Tex., 7/19/41

Carracci, Annibale (painter); Bologna, Italy **(1560–1609)**

Carracci, Lodovico (painter); Bologna, Italy **(1555–1619)**

Carradine, David (actor); Hollywood, Calif., 12/8/36

Carradine, John (actor); New York City **(1906–1988)**

Carradine, Keith (actor); San Mateo, Calif., 8/8/49

Carreras, José (tenor); Barcelona, Spain, 12/5/46

Carroll, Diahann (Carol Diahann Johnson) (singer, actress); Bronx, N.Y., 7/17/35

Carroll, Leo G. (actor); Weedon, England **(1892–1972)**

Carroll, Lewis (Charles Lutwidge Dodgson) (author, mathematician); Daresbury, England **(1832–1898)**

Carson, Johnny (TV entertainer); Corning, Iowa, 10/23/25

Carson, Kit (Christopher Carson) (scout); Madison County, Ky. **(1809–1868)**

Carson, Rachel (biologist, author); Springdale, Pa. **(1907–1964)**

Carter, Betty (jazz singer, composer); Flint, Mich. **(1930–1998)**

Carter, Chris (television and film writer, director, producer); Bellflower, Calif., 10/13/57

Carter, Dixie (actress); McLemoresville, Tenn., 5/25/39

Carter, Jack (comedian); New York City, 6/24/23

Carter, James Earl, Jr. (39th U.S. president); Plains, Ga., 10/1/24

Carter, Lynda (actress); Phoenix, Ariz., 7/24/51

Cartier, Jacques (explorer); Saint-Malo, Brittany, France **(1491–1557)**

Cartier-Bresson, Henri (photographer); Chanteloup, France, 8/22/08

Cartland, Barbara (author); England **(1901–2000)**

Caruso, Enrico (Errico Caruso) (tenor); Naples, Italy **(1873–1921)**

Carver, George Washington (botanist); Diamond Grove, Mo. **(1864–1943)**

Cary, Arthur Joyce Lunel (novelist); Londonderry, Ireland **(1888–1957)**

Casals, Pablo (cellist); Vendrell, Spain **(1876–1973)**

Casanova de Seingalt, Giovanni Jacopo (adventurer); Venice **(1725–1798)**

Case, Steve (business executive); Honolulu, 8/21/58

Cash, Johnny (singer); nr. Kingsland, Ark. **(1932–2003)**

Cass, Peggy (Mary Margaret Cass) (comedienne); Boston **(1924–1999)**

Cassatt, Mary (painter); Allegheny, Pa. **(1844–1926)**

Cassavetes, John (director); New York City **(1929–1989)**

Cassidy, David (singer); New York City, 4/12/50

Cassidy, Jack (actor); Richmond Hill, Queens, N.Y. **(1927–1976)**

Cassidy, Shaun (actor, television producer, singer); Los Angeles, 9/27/58

Cassini, Oleg (Oleg Lolewski-Cassini) (fashion designer); Paris, 4/11/13

Castagno, Andrea del (painter); San Martino a Corella, Italy **(c. 1421–1457)**

Castaneda, Carlos (cultural anthropologist, author); São Paulo, Brazil **(1931–1998)**

Castle, Irene (Irene Foote) (actress, dancer); New Rochelle, N.Y. **(1893–1969)**

Castle, Vernon Blythe (dancer, aviator); Norwich, England **(1887–1918)**

Castro Ruz, Fidel (premier); Mayari, Oriente, Cuba, 8/13/26

Cather, Willa Sibert (novelist); Winchester, Va. **(1873?–1947)**

Cato, Marcus Porcius (called Cato the Elder) (statesman); Tusculum, Italy **(234–149 b.c.)**

Catt, Carrie Lane Chapman (woman suffragist); Ripon, Wis. **(1859–1947)**

Catton, Bruce (historian); Petoskey, Mich. **(1899–1978)**

Catullus, Gaius Valerius (poet); Verona **(c. 84–c. 54 b.c.)**

Cavallaro, Carmen (band leader); New York City **(1913–1989)**

Cavett, Dick (Richard Cavett) (TV entertainer); Gibbon, Neb., 11/19/36

Ceausescu, Nicolae (head of state); Scorniscesti, Romania **(1918–1989)**

Céline, Louis Ferdinand (pseud. of Louis Fuch Destouches) (novelist); Paris **(1894–1961)**

Cellini, Benvenuto (goldsmith, sculptor); Florence, Italy **(1500–1571)**

Cervantes Saavedra, Miguel de (novelist); Alcalá de Henares, Spain **(1547–1616)**

Cézanne, Paul (painter); Aix-en-Provence, France **(1839–1906)**

Chagall, Marc (painter); Vitebsk, Russia **(1887–1985)**

Chaliapin, Feodor Ivanovitch (operatic basso); Kazan, Russia **(1873–1938)**

Chamberlain, Arthur Neville (statesman); Edgbaston, England **(1869–1940)**

Chamberlain, Richard (actor, producer); Los Angeles, 3/31/35

Champion, Gower (choreographer); Geneva, Ill. **(1921–1980)**

Champion, Marge (Marjorie Celeste Belcher) (actress, dancer); Los Angeles, 9/2/23

Champlain, Samuel de (explorer); nr. Rochefort, France **(1567–1635)**

Chan, Jackie (Chan Kwong Sang) (actor); Hong Kong, 4/7/54

Chancellor, John (TV commentator); Chicago **(1927–1996)**

Chandler, Jeff (Ira Grossel) (actor); Brooklyn, N.Y. **(1918–1961)**

Chandler, Raymond (writer); Chicago **(1883–1959)**

Chanel, "Coco" (Gabriel Bonheur) (fashion designer); Issoire, France **(1883–1971)**

Chaney, Lon (actor); Colorado Springs, Colo. **(1883–1930)**

Channing, Carol (actress); Seattle, 1/31/23

Channing, Stockard (Susan Stockard) (actress); New York City, 2/13/44

Chaplin, Geraldine (actress); Santa Monica, Calif., 7/31/44

Chaplin, Sir Charles (actor); London **(1889–1977)**

Charisse, Cyd (Tula Finklea) (dancer, actress); Amarillo, Tex., 3/8/21

Charlemagne (Holy Roman Emperor); birthplace unknown **(742–814)**

Charles, Ray (Ray Charles Robinson) (pianist, singer, songwriter); Albany, Ga. **(1930–2004)**

Charo (Maria Rosario Pilar Martinez) (actress); Murcia, Spain, 1/15/51

Chase, Chevy (Cornelius Crane Chase) (comedian); New York City, 10/8/43

Chase, Lucia (founder Ballet Theatre [now American Ballet Theatre]); Waterbury, Conn. **(1907–1986)**

Chateaubriand, François René de (writer, statesman); St. Malo, France **(1768–1848)**

Chaucer, Geoffrey (poet); London **(c. 1340–1400)**

Chuan, Leekpai (prime minister of Thailand); Muang District, Thailand, 7/28/38

Chávez, Carlos (composer); nr. Mexico City **(1899–1978)**

Chavez, Cesar (labor leader); nr. Yuma, Ariz. **(1927–1993)**

Chayefsky, Paddy (Sidney Chayefsky) (playwright); New York City **(1923–1981)**

Checker, Chubby (Ernest Evans) (performer); Philadelphia, 10/3/41

Cheever, John (novelist); Quincy, Mass. **(1912–1982)**

Chekhov, Anton Pavlovich (dramatist, short-story writer); Taganrog, Russia **(1860–1904)**

Chen Shui-bian (president of Taiwan); Taiwan, 2/18/51

Cher (Cherilyn Sarkisian La Piere) (actress, singer); El Centro, Calif., 5/20/46

Cherubini, Luigi (composer); Florence **(1760–1842)**

Chesterton, Gilbert Keith (author); Kensington, England **(1874–1936)**

Chesnutt, Charles Waddell (author); Cleveland **(1858–1932)**

Chevalier, Maurice (entertainer); Paris **(1888–1972)**

Chiang Kai-shek (chief of state); Feng-hwa, China **(1887–1975)**

Child, Julia (food expert); Pasadena, Calif. **(1912–2004)**

Chippendale, Thomas (cabinet-maker); Otley, England **(1718–1779)**

Chirac, Jacques (president of France); Paris, 11/29/32

Chirico, Giorgio de (painter); Vólos, Greece **(1888–1978)**

Chisholm, Shirley Anita St. Hill (U.S. representative); Brooklyn, N.Y., 11/30/24

Chlumsky, Anna (actress); Chicago, 12/3/80

Chomsky, (Avram) Noam (linguist, educator, activist); Philadelphia, 12/7/28

Chopin, Frédéric François (composer); nr. Warsaw **(1810–1849)**

Chopin, Kate O'Flaherty (author); St. Louis **(1851–1904)**

Chow, Yun-Fat (actor); Hong Kong, 5/18/55

Chrétien, Jean Joseph-Jacques (prime minister of Canada); Shawinigan, Que., Canada, 1/11/34

Christie, Agatha (mystery writer); Torquay, England **(1890–1976)**

Christie, Julie (actress); Chukua, India, 4/14/41

Chung, Connie (broadcast journalist); Washington, D.C., 8/20/46

Churchill, Sir Winston Leonard Spencer (statesman); Blenheim Palace, Oxfordshire, England **(1874–1965)**

Cicero, Marcus Tullius (orator, statesman); Arpinum, Italy **(106–43 B.C.)**

Cid, El (Rodrigo [or Ruy] Díez de Bivar) (Spanish national hero); nr. Burgos, Spain **(c. 1043–1099)**

Cilento, Diane (actress); Queensland, Australia, 10/5/33

Cimabue, Giovanni (painter); Florence, Italy **(c. 1240–c. 1302)**

Cimino, Michael (director, writer, producer); New York City, 11/16/43

Claire, Ina (Ina Fagan) (actress); Washington, D.C. **(1895–1985)**

Clancy, Tom (novelist); Baltimore, 4/12/47

Clapton, Eric (singer, guitarist); Ripley, England, 3/30/45

Clark, Dick (TV personality); Mt. Vernon, N.Y., 11/30/29

Clark, Mary Higgins (writer); New York City, 12/24/31

Clark, Petula (singer); Epsom, England, 11/15/34

Clark, Roy (country music artist); Meherrin, Va., 4/15/33

Clark, William (explorer); Caroline County, Va. **(1770–1838)**

Clarke, Arthur C. (science fiction writer); Minehead, England, 12/16/17

Claude Lorrain (Claude Gellée) (painter); Champagne, France **(1600–1682)**

Clausewitz, Karl von (military strategist); Burg, Germany **(1780–1831)**

Clay, Henry (statesman); Hanover County, Va. **(1777–1852)**

Clay, Lucius D. (banker, ex-general); Marietta, Ga. **(1897–1978)**

Clayburgh, Jill (actress); New York City, 4/30/44

Cleary, Beverly (Beverly Atlee Bunn) (children's author); McMinnville, Ore., 1916

Cleaver, Eldridge (Leroy) (author, activist); Wabbaseka, Ark. **(1935–1998)**

Cleese, John (writer, actor); Weston-super-Mare, England, 10/27/39

Clemenceau, Georges (statesman); Mouilleron-en-Pareds, Vondée, France **(1841–1929)**

Cleopatra (queen of Egypt); Alexandria, Egypt **(69–30 B.C.)**

Cleveland, Stephen Grover (22nd & 24th U.S. president); Caldwell, N.J. **(1837–1908)**

Cliburn, Van (Harvey Lavan Cliburn, Jr.) (concert pianist); Shreveport, La., 7/12/34

Clift, Montgomery (actor); Omaha, Neb. **(1920–1966)**

Cline, Patsy (singer); Winchester, Va. **(1932–1963)**

Clinton, Hillary Rodham (ex-first lady, U.S. senator); Park Ridge, Ill., 10/26/47

Clinton, William Jefferson (42nd U.S. president); Hope, Ark., 8/19/46

Clooney, George (actor); Lexington, Ky., 5/6/61

Clooney, Rosemary (singer); Maysville, Ky. **(1928–2002)**

Close, Glenn (actress); Greenwich, Conn., 3/19/47

Cobain, Kurt (musician); Hoquiam, Wash. **(1967–1994)**

Cobb, Irvin Shrewsbury (humorist); Paducah, Ky. **(1876–1944)**

Cobb, Lee J. (Leo Jacob Cobb) (actor); New York City **(1911–1976)**

Coburn, Charles Douville (actor); Savannah, Ga. **(1877–1961)**

Coburn, James (actor); Laurel, Neb. **(1928–2002)**

Coca, Imogene (comedienne); Philadelphia **(1908–2001)**

Cocker, Jarvis (singer, songwriter); Sheffield, England, 9/19/63

Cocker, Joe (John Robert Cocker) (singer); Sheffield, England, 5/20/44

Coco, James (actor); New York City **(1929–1987)**

Cocteau, Jean (author); Maison-Lafitte, France **(1889–1963)**

Cohan, George Michael (actor, dramatist); Providence, R.I. **(1878–1942)**

Cohen, Leonard (composer); Montreal, Que., Canada, 9/21/34

Colbert, Claudette (Lily Chauchoin) (actress); Paris **(1903–1996)**

Cole, Nat "King" (singer); Montgomery, Ala. **(1919–1965)**

Cole, Natalie (singer); Los Angeles, 2/6/50

Cole, Thomas (painter); Lancashire, England **(1801–1848)**

Coleman, Dabney (actor); Austin, Tex., 1/3/32

Coleridge, Samuel Taylor (poet); Ottery St. Mary, England **(1772–1834)**

Colette (Sidonie-Gabrielle Colette) (novelist); St.-Sauveur, France **(1873–1954)**

Collingwood, Charles (TV commentator); Three Rivers, Mich. **(1917–1985)**

Collins, Joan (actress); London, 5/23/33

Collins, Judy (singer); Seattle, 5/1/39

Colman, Ronald (actor); Richmond, England **(1891–1958)**

Colonna, Jerry (comedian); Boston **(1905–1986)**

Coltrane, John (jazz musician); Hamlet, N.C. **(1926–1967)**

Columbus, Chris (director, screenwriter); Spangler, Pa., 9/10/58

Columbus, Christopher (Cristoforo Colombo) (explorer); Genoa, Italy **(1451–1506)**

Colvin, Shawn (folk singer); Vermillion, S.D., 1/10/58

Combs, Sean "Puffy" (singer, record producer); New York City, 11/9/69

Comden, Betty (writer); New York City, 5/3/19

Comenius, Johann Amos (educational reformer); Nivnice, Moravia, Czech Republic **(1592–1670)**

Commager, Henry Steele (historian); Pittsburgh **(1902–1998)**

Como, Perry (Pierino Como) (singer); Canonsburg, Pa. **(1912–2001)**

Compton, Karl Taylor (physicist); Wooster, Ohio **(1887–1954)**

Comte, Auguste (philosopher); Montpellier, France **(1798–1857)**

Conant, James B. (educator, statesman); Dorchester, Mass. **(1893–1978)**

Condon, Eddie (jazz musician); Goodland, Ind. **(1905–1973)**

Confucius (K'ung Fu-tzu) (philosopher); Shantung province, China **(c. 551–479 B.C.)**

Congreve, William (dramatist); nr. Leeds, England **(1670–1729)**

Connelly, Marc (playwright); McKeesport, Pa. **(1890–1980)**

Connery, Sean (actor); Edinburgh, Scotland, 8/25/30

Connick, Jr., Harry (musician, actor); New Orleans, La., 9/11/67

Conniff, Ray (band leader); Attleboro, Mass. **(1916–2002)**

Connors, Chuck (actor); Brooklyn, N.Y. **(1921–1992)**

Connors, Mike (Krekor Ohanian) (actor); Fresno, Calif., 8/15/25

Conrad, Joseph (Teodor Jozef Konrad Korzeniowski) (novelist); Berdichev, Ukraine **(1857–1924)**

Conrad, Robert (Conrad Robert Falk) (actor); Chicago, 3/1/35

Conrad, William (actor); Louisville, Ky. **(1920–1994)**

Conried, Hans Georg, Jr. (actor); Baltimore **(1917–1982)**

Conroy, Pat (author); Atlanta, 10/26/45

Constable, John (painter); East Bergholt, Suffolk, England **(1776–1837)**

Constantine II (ex-king of Greece); Athens, 6/2/40

Constantine, Michael (actor); Reading, Pa., 5/22/27

Conte, Richard (actor); New York City **(1916–1975)**

Conti, Tom (actor); Paisley, Scotland, 11/22/41

Convy, Bert (actor, host); St. Louis **(1933–1991)**

Conway, Tim (comedian); Chagrin Falls, Ohio, 12/15/33

Coogan, Jackie (actor); Los Angeles **(1914–1984)**

Cook, Peter (actor, writer); Torquay, England **(1937–1995)**

Cooke, Alistair (Alfred Alistair) (TV narrator, journalist); Manchester, England **(1908–2004)**

Cooke, Jack Kent (business executive); Hamilton, Ont., Canada **(1912–1997)**

Cooley, Denton A(rthur) (heart surgeon); Houston, 8/22/20

Coolidge, (John) Calvin (30th U.S. president); Plymouth, Vt. **(1872–1933)**

Coolidge, Rita (singer); Nashville, Tenn., 5/1/45

Coolio (Artis Ivey, Jr.) (rap artist); Los Angeles, Calif., 8/1/63

Cooper, Alice (Vincent Furnier) (rock musician); Detroit, 2/4/48

Cooper, Gary (Frank James Cooper) (actor); Helena, Mont. **(1901–1961)**

Cooper, Dame Gladys (actress); Lewisham, England **(1898–1971)**

Cooper, Jackie (actor, director); Los Angeles, 9/15/22

Cooper, James Fenimore (novelist); Burlington, N.J. **(1789–1851)**

Cooper, Peter (industrialist, philanthropist); New York City **(1791–1883)**

Copernicus, Nicolaus (Mikolaj Kopernik) (astronomer); Thorn, Poland **(1473–1543)**

Copland, Aaron (composer); Brooklyn, N.Y. **(1900–1990)**

Copley, John Singleton (painter); Boston **(1738–1815)**

Copperfield, David (David Kotkin) (illusionist); Metuchen, N.J., 9/16/56

Coppola, Francis Ford (film director); Detroit, 4/7/39

Corelli, Arcangelo (composer); Fusignano, Italy **(1653–1713)**

Corelli, Franco (operatic tenor); Ancona, Italy **(1923–2003)**

Corgan, Billy (musician); Elk Grove, Ill., 3/17/67

Corneille, Pierre (dramatist); Rouen, France **(1606–1684)**

Cornell, Katharine (actress); Berlin **(1893–1974)**

Corot, Jean Baptiste Camille (painter); Paris **(1796–1875)**

Corella, Angel (ballet dancer); Madrid, Spain, 11/8/75

Correggio, Antonio Allegri da (painter); Correggio, Italy **(1494–1534)**

Corsaro, Frank (opera director); New York harbor, 12/22/24

Cortés (or Cortez), Hernando (explorer); Medellin, Spain **(1485–1547)**

Cosby, Bill (actor); Philadelphia, 7/12/37

Cosell, Howard (Howard Cohen) (sportscaster); Winston-Salem, N.C. **(1918–1995)**

Costello, Elvis (Declan Patrick McManus) (singer, musician, songwriter); London, 1954

Costello, Lou (Louis Cristillo) (comedian); Paterson, N.J. **(1908–1959)**

Costner, Kevin (actor); Los Angeles, 1/18/55

Cotten, Joseph (actor); Petersburg, Va. **(1905–1994)**

Couperin, François (composer); Paris **(1668–1733)**

Courbet, Gustave (painter); Ornans, France **(1819–1877)**

Couric, Katie (TV host); Arlington, Va., 1/7/57

Courtenay, Tom (actor); Hull, England, 2/25/37

Cousins, Norman (publisher); Union Hill, N.J. **(1915–1990)**

Cousteau, Jacques-Yves (marine explorer); St. André-de-Cubzac, France **(1910–1997)**

Covey, Stephen R. (author); Salt Lake City, 10/24/32

Coward, Sir Noel (playwright, actor); Teddington, England **(1899–1973)**

Cowles, Gardner, Jr. (newspaper publisher); Algona, Iowa **(1903–1985)**

Cowper, William (poet); Great Berkhamstead, England **(1731–1800)**

Cox, Archibald (Watergate prosecutor); Plainfield, N.J. **(1912–2004)**

Cox, Courteney (actress); Birmingham, Ala., 6/15/64

Coyote, Peter (actor); New York City, 10/10/41

Cozzens, James Gould (novelist); Chicago **(1903–1978)**

Crabbe, Buster (Clarence Crabbe) (actor); Oakland, Calif. **(1908–1983)**

Cranach, Lucas, the elder (painter); Kronach, Germany **(1472–1553)**

Crane, Hart (poet); Garrettsville, Ohio **(1899–1932)**

Crane, Stephen (novelist, poet); Newark, N.J. **(1871–1900)**

Cranmer, Thomas (churchman); Aslacton, England **(1489–1556)**

Craven, Wes (director, producer, screenwriter); Cleveland, 8/2/39

Crawford, Broderick (actor); Philadelphia **(1911–1986)**

Crawford, Cheryl (stage producer); Akron, Ohio **(1902–1986)**

Crawford, Cindy (model, actress); De Kalb, Illinois, 2/20/66

Crawford, Joan (Lucille LeSueur) (actress, business executive); San Antonio **(1908–1977)**

Crazy Horse (Lakota Indian leader); nr. Bear Butte, S.D. **(1840?–1877)**

Crenna, Richard (actor); Los Angeles **(1927–2003)**

Crespin, Régine (operatic soprano); Marseilles, France, 1927

Crichton, (John) Michael (novelist, film producer); Chicago, 10/23/42

Crick, Francis Harry Compton (scientist, Nobel laureate); Northampton, England, 6/8/16

Crisp, Donald (actor); London **(1880–1974)**

Croce, Benedetto (philosopher); Peseasseroli, Aquila, Italy **(1866–1952)**

Croce, Jim (singer); Philadelphia **(1942–1973)**

Crockett, Davy (David) (frontiersman); Greene County, Tenn. **(1786–1836)**

Cromwell, Oliver (statesman); Huntingdon, England **(1599–1658)**

Cronenberg, David (film director); Toronto, Canada, 3/15/43

Cronin, A. J. (Archibald J. Cronin) (novelist); Cardross, Scotland **(1896–1981)**

Cronkite, Walter (TV newscaster); St. Joseph, Mo., 11/4/16

Cronyn, Hume (actor); London, Ont., Canada **(1911–2003)**

Crosby, Bing (Harry Lillis) (singer, actor); Tacoma, Wash. **(1904–1977)**

Crosby, Bob (musician); Spokane, Wash. **(1913–1993)**

Crosby, Cathy Lee (actress); Los Angeles, 12/2/48

Crosby, Norm (comedian); Boston, 9/15/27

Cross, Ben (Bernard) (actor); Paddington, England, 12/16/47

Cross, Milton (opera commentator); New York City **(1897–1975)**

Crouse, Russell (playwright); Findlay, Ohio **(1893–1966)**

Crow, Sheryl (musician, record producer); Kennett, Mo., 2/11/62

Crowe, Russell (actor, musician); Auckland, New Zealand, 4/7/64

Crudup, Billy (actor); Manhasset, N.Y., 7/8/68

Cruise, Tom (Thomas Mapother IV) (actor, producer); Syracuse, N.Y., 7/3/62

Crystal, Billy (comedian, actor); Long Beach, N.Y., 3/14/47

Cugat, Xavier (band leader); Barcelona, Spain **(1900–1990)**

Cukor, George (film director); New York City **(1899–1983)**

Culkin, Macaulay (actor); New York City, 8/26/80

Cullen, Bill (William Lawrence Cullen) (radio and TV entertainer); Pittsburgh **(1920–1990)**

Cullen, Countee (poet); New York City **(1903–1946)**

Culp, Robert (actor); Berkeley, Calif., 8/16/30

cummings, e. e. (Edward Estlin Cummings) (poet); Cambridge, Mass. **(1894–1962)**

Cummings, Robert (actor); Joplin, Mo. **(1908–1990)**

Cunningham, Merce (choreographer); Centralia, Wash., 4/16/19

Curie, Marie (Marja Sklodowska) (physical chemist, Nobel laureate); Warsaw **(1867–1934)**

Curie, Pierre (physicist); Paris **(1859–1906)**

Curtin, Jane (actress); Cambridge, Mass., 9/6/47

Curtin, Phyllis (soprano); Clarksburg, W. Va., 12/3/27

Curtis, Jamie Lee (actress); Los Angeles, 11/22/58

Curtis, Tony (Bernard Schwartz) (actor); Bronx, N.Y., 6/3/25

Curzon, Clifford (concert pianist); London **(1907–1982)**

Cusack, Joan (actress); New York City, 10/11/62

Cusack, John (actor); Chicago, 6/28/66

Custer, George Armstrong (army officer); New Rumley, Ohio **(1839–1876)**

D

Dafoe, Willem (William Dafoe, Jr.) (actor); Appleton, Wis., 7/22/55

da Gama, Vasco (explorer); Sines, Portugal **(1460–1524)**

Daguerre, Louis (photographic pioneer); nr. Paris **(1787–1851)**

Dahl, Arlene (actress); Minneapolis, 8/11/28

Dahl, Roald (writer); Llandaff, Wales **(1916–1990)**

Dalai Lama (Tenzin Gyatso) (spiritual and temporal head of Tibet); Taktser, China, 1935

Daley, Richard J. (mayor of Chicago); Chicago **(1902–1976)**

Dali, Salvador (painter); Figueras, Spain **(1904–1989)**

Dalton, John (chemist); nr. Cockermouth, England **(1766–1844)**

Dalton, Timothy (actor); Colwyn Bay, Wales, U.K., 3/21/46

Daly, Tyne (actress); Madison, Wis., 2/21/46

d'Amboise, Jacques (ballet dancer); Dedham, Mass., 7/28/34

Damone, Vic (Vito Farinola) (singer); Brooklyn, N.Y., 6/12/28

Damrosch, Walter Johannes (orchestra conductor); Breslau, Poland **(1862–1950)**

Dana, Charles Anderson (editor); Hinsdale, N.H. **(1819–1897)**

Dandridge, Dorothy (actress); Cleveland **(1923–1965)**

Danes, Claire (actress); New York City, 4/12/79

Dangerfield, Rodney (Jacob Cohen) (actor, comedian); Babylon, N.Y., 11/22/22

Daniels, Jeff (actor); Chelsea, Mich., 2/19/55

Daniels, William (actor); Brooklyn, N.Y., 3/31/27

Danilova, Alexandra (ballet dancer); Peterhof, Russia **(1904–1997)**

Dannay, Frederic (novelist, pseudonym Ellery Queen); Brooklyn, N.Y. **(1905–1982)**

Danner, Blythe (actress); Philadelphia, 2/3/43

D'Annunzio, Gabriele (soldier, author); Francaville at Mare, Pescara, Italy **(1863–1938)**

Danson, Ted (actor); San Diego, Calif., 12/29/47

Dante (or Durante) Alighieri (poet); Florence, Italy (1265–1321)

Danton, Georges Jacques (French Revolutionary leader); Arcis-sur-Aube, France (1759–1794)

Danza, Tony (actor); Brooklyn, N.Y., 4/21/51

Darren, James (actor); Philadelphia, 6/8/36

Darrow, Clarence Seward (lawyer); Kinsman, Ohio (1857–1938)

Darwin, Charles Robert (naturalist); Shrewsbury, England (1809–1882)

Dassin, Jules (film director); Middletown, Conn., 12/18/11

Daumier, Honoré (caricaturist); Marseilles, France (1808–1879)

David, Jacques-Louis (painter); Paris (1748–1825)

David (king of Israel and Judah); died c. 973 B.C.

Davidson, John (singer, actor); Pittsburgh, 12/13/41

Davies, Marion (Marion Douras) (actress); New York City (1897–1961)

Davies, (William) Robertson (writer); Thamesville, Ont., Canada (1913–1996)

Davis, Angela (social activist); Birmingham, Ala., 1/26/44

Davis, Ann B. (actress); Schenectady, N.Y., 5/5/26

Davis, Lt. Gen. Benjamin O., Jr. (Air Force general); Washington, D.C. (1912–2002)

Davis, Brig. Gen. Benjamin O., Sr. (U.S. Army general); Washington, D.C. (1877–1970)

Davis, Bette (actress); Lowell, Mass. (1908–1989)

Davis, Geena (Virginia Davis) (actress); Wareham, Mass., 1/21/57

Davis, Jefferson (president of the Confederacy); Christian (now Todd) County, Ky. (1808–1889)

Davis, Judy (actress); Perth, Australia, 1955

Davis, Mac (singer); Lubbock, Tex., 1/21/42

Davis, Miles (jazz trumpeter); Alton, Ill. (1926–1991)

Davis, Ossie (actor, writer); Cogdell, Ga., 12/18/17

Davis, Sammy, Jr. (actor, singer); New York City (1925–1990)

Davis, Stuart (painter); Philadelphia (1894–1964)

Dawson, Richard (actor, host); Gosport, Hampshire, England, 11/20/32

Day, Doris (Doris Kappelhoff) (singer, actress); Cincinnati, 4/3/24

Dayan, Moshe (ex-defense minister of Israel); Dagania, Palestine (1915–1981)

Day-Lewis, Daniel (actor); London, 4/29/58

Dean, James (actor); Marion, Ind. (1931–1955)

Dean, Jimmy (singer); Seth Ward, nr. Plainview, Tex., 8/10/28

De Bakey, Michael E. (heart surgeon); Lake Charles, La., 9/7/08

de Beauvoir, Simone (novelist, philosopher); Paris (1908–1986)

Debs, Eugene Victor (Socialist leader); Terre Haute, Ind. (1855–1926)

Debussy, Claude Achille (composer); St. Germain-en-Laye, France (1862–1918)

De Carlo, Yvonne (Peggy Yvonne Middleton) (actress); Vancouver, B.C., Canada, 9/1/22

Dee, Ruby (Ruby Ann Wallace) (actress); Cleveland, 10/27/24

Dee, Sandra (Alexandra Zuck) (actress); Bayonne, N.J., 4/23/42

Degas, Hilaire Germain Edgar (painter); Paris (1834–1917)

de Gaulle, Charles André Joseph Marie (soldier, statesman); Lille, France (1890–1970)

de Havilland, Olivia (actress); Tokyo, 7/1/16

de Kooning, Willem (artist); Rotterdam (1904–1997)

Delacroix, Eugène (painter); Charenton-St. Maurice, France (1798–1863)

Delany, Dana (actress); New York City, 3/15/56

de la Renta, Oscar (fashion designer); Santo Domingo, Dominican Republic, 7/22/32

Delaunay, Robert (painter); Paris (1885–1941)

De Laurentiis, Dino (film producer); Torre Annunziata, Bay of Naples, Italy, 8/8/18

della Robbia, Andrea (sculptor); Florence (1435–1525)

della Robbia, Luca (sculptor); Florence (1400–1482)

Delon, Alain (actor); Sceaux, France, 11/8/35

Del Toro, Benicio (actor); Santurce, Puerto Rico, 2/19/67

DeLuise, Dom (actor, comedian); Brooklyn, N.Y., 8/1/33

Demarest, William (actor); St. Paul, Minn. (1892–1983)

de Mille, Agnes (choreographer); New York City (1905–1993)

De Mille, Cecil Blount (film director); Ashfield, Mass. (1881–1959)

Demme, Jonathan·(director, producer, screenwriter); Baldwin, N.Y., 2/22/44

Demosthenes (orator); Athens (384?–322 B.C.)

Dench, Dame Judi (film and stage actress); York, England, 12/9/34

Deneuve, Catherine (actress); Paris, 10/22/43

Deng Xiaoping (Chinese leader); Sichuan province, China (1904–1997)

De Niro, Robert (actor, director); New York City, 8/17/43

Dennehy, Brian (actor); Bridgeport, Conn., 7/9/39

Dennis, Sandy (actress); Hastings, Neb. (1937–1992)

Denny, Reginald (actor); Richmond, England (1891–1967)

Denver, John (Henry John Deutschendorf, Jr.) (singer, actor); Roswell, N.M. (1943–1997)

De Palma, Brian (film director); Newark, N.J., 9/11/40

Depp, Johnny (actor); Owensboro, Ky., 6/9/63

Derain, André (painter); Chatou, Seine-et-Oise, France (1880–1954)

Derek, John (Derek Harris) (actor, director); Los Angeles (1926–1998)

Dern, Bruce (actor); Winnetka, Ill., 6/4/36

Dern, Laura (actress); Los Angeles, 2/10/67

Dershowitz, Alan (lawyer); Brooklyn, N.Y., 9/1/38

Derrida, Jacques (philosopher); El-Biar, Algeria, 7/15/30

Descartes, René (philosopher, mathematician); La Haye, France (1596–1650)

De Seversky, Alexander P. (aviator); Tiflis (Tbilisi), Georgia (1894–1974)

De Sica, Vittorio (film director); Sora, Italy (1901–1974)

Desmond, Johnny (singer, composer); Detroit (1921–1985)

De Soto, Hernando (explorer); Barcarrota, Spain (c. 1500–1542)

De Valera, Eamon (ex-president of Ireland); New York City (1882–1975)

Devane, William (actor); Albany, N.Y., 9/5/39

Devine, Andy (actor); Flagstaff, Ariz. (1905–1977)

DeVito, Danny (Daniel Michael DeVito) (actor, director, producer); Neptune, N.J., 11/17/44

de Vries, Peter (novelist); Chicago (1910–1993)

de Waart, Edo (conductor); Amsterdam, the Netherlands, 6/1/41

Dewey, George (admiral); Montpelier, Vt. (1837–1917)

Dewey, John (philosopher, educator); Burlington, Vt. (1859–1952)

Dewey, Thomas E. (political figure); Owosso, Mich. (1902–1971)

Dewhurst, Colleen (actress); Montreal (1926–1991)

Dey, Susan (actress); Pekin, Ill., 12/10/52

Diaghilev, Sergei (ballet impressario); Novgorod, Russia (1872–1929)

Diamond, Neil (singer); Brooklyn, N.Y., 1/24/41

Diaz, Cameron (actress, model); San Diego, Calif., 8/30/72

DiCaprio, Leonardo (actor); Los Angeles, 11/11/74

Dichter, Misha (pianist); Shanghai, 9/27/45

Dickens, Charles John Huffam (novelist); Portsea, England (1812–1870)

Dickey, James (writer); Atlanta (1923–1997)

Dickinson, Angie (Angeline Brown) (actress); Kulm, N.D., 9/30/31

Dickinson, Emily Elizabeth (poet); Amherst, Mass. (1830–1886)

Diddley, Bo (Elias McDaniel) (guitarist); McComb, Miss., 12/30/28

Diderot, Denis (encyclopedist); Langres, France (1713–1784)

Dietrich, Marlene (Maria Magdalena von Losch) (actress); Berlin (1901–1992)

DiFranco, Ani (singer, songwriter); Buffalo, N.Y., 9/23/70

Diller, Phyllis (Phyllis Driver) (comedienne); Lima, Ohio, 7/17/17

Dillon, Matt (actor); New Rochelle, N.Y., 2/18/64

Dine, Jim (painter); Cincinnati, 6/16/35

Dinesen, Isak (Karen Blixen) (author); Rungsted, Denmark (1885–1962)

Dinkins, David (ex-mayor of New York City); Trenton, N.J., 7/10/27

Diogenes (philosopher); Sinope, Turkey (c. 412–323 B.C.)

Dion (Dion DiMucci) (singer); Bronx, N.Y., 7/18/39

Dion, Celine (singer); Charlemagne, Que., Canada, 3/30/68

Dior, Christian (fashion designer); Granville, France (1905–1957)

Disney, Walt(er) Elias (film animator, producer); Chicago (1901–1966)

Disraeli, Benjamin (Earl of Beaconsfield) (statesman); London (1804–1881)

Dix, Dorothea (civil rights reformer); Hampden, Maine (1802–1887)

Dixon, Jeane (Pinckert) (seer); Medford, Wis. (1918–1997)

Dobbs, Mattiwilda (soprano); Atlanta, 7/11/25

Doctorow, E(dgar) L(aurence) (novelist); New York City, 1/6/31

Dogg, Snoop Doggy (Calvin Broadus) (musician); Long Beach, Calif., 10/20/72

Doherty, Shannen (actress); Memphis, Tenn., 4/21/71

Dole, Elizabeth Hanford (public official); Salisbury, N.C., 7/29/36

Dole, Robert (political figure); Russell, Kans., 7/22/23

Dolin, Anton (dancer); Slinfold, England (1904–1983)

Domingo, Placido (tenor); Madrid, 1/21/41

Domino, Fats (Antoine) (musician); New Orleans, 2/26/28

Donahue, Phil (TV host); Cleveland, 12/21/35

Donahue, Troy (Merle Johnson) (actor); New York City (1936–2001)

Donaldson, Sam (broadcast journalist); El Paso, Tex., 3/11/34

Donat, Robert (actor); Withington, England (1905–1958)

Donatello (Donato Niccolò di Betto Bardi) (sculptor); Florence (c. 1386–1466)

Donlevy, Brian (actor); Portadown, Ireland (1899–1972)

Donne, John (poet); London **(1573–1631)**

Donner, Richard (director, producer); New York City, 1939

D'Onofrio, Vincent (actor); Brooklyn, N.Y., 6/30/59

Donovan (Donovan Leitch) (singer, songwriter); Glasgow, Scotland, 2/10/46

Doolittle, James H. (ex-Air Force general); Alameda, Calif. **(1896–1993)**

Doohan, James (actor); Vancouver, B.C., 3/20/20

Dorati, Antal (orchestra conductor); Budapest **(1906–1988)**

Dorn, Michael (actor); Luling, Tex., 12/9/52

Dorris, Michael (anthropologist, writer); Louisville, Ky. **(1945–1997)**

Dorsey, Jimmy (band leader); Shenandoah, Pa. **(1904–1957)**

Dorsey, Thomas Andrew (father of gospel music); Villa Rice, Ga. **(1899–1993)**

Dorsey, Tommy (band leader); Mahanoy Plane, Pa. **(1905–1956)**

Dos Passos, John (author); Chicago **(1896–1970)**

Dostoevski, Fyodor Mikhailovich (novelist); Moscow **(1821–1881)**

Dotrice, Roy (actor); Guernsey, Channel Islands, England, 5/26/23

Douglas, Aaron (painter); Topeka, Kans. **(1900–1979)**

Douglas, Helen Gahagan (ex-representative); Boonton, N.J. **(1900–1980)**

Douglas, Kirk (Issur Danielovitch) (actor); Amsterdam, N.Y., 12/9/16

Douglas, Melvyn (Melvyn Hesselberg) (actor); Macon, Ga. **(1901–1981)**

Douglas, Michael (actor, producer); New Brunswick, N.J., 9/25/44

Douglas, Mike (Michael D. Dowd, Jr.) (TV host); Chicago, 8/11/25

Douglas, Stephen Arnold (politician); Brandon, Vt. **(1813–1861)**

Douglass, Frederick (abolitionist, author, orator); Tuckahoe, Md. **(1817–1895)**

Dow, Charles (financier); Sterling, Conn. **(1851–1902)**

Down, Lesley-Ann (actress); London, 3/17/54

Downey, Robert, Jr. (actor, director); New York City, 4/4/65

Downs, Hugh (broadcast journalist); Akron, Ohio, 2/14/21

Doyle, Sir Arthur Conan (novelist, spiritualist); Edinburgh, Scotland **(1859–1930)**

Doyle, David (actor); Lincoln, Neb. **(1929–1997)**

Drake, Sir Francis (navigator); Tavistock, England **(1545–1596)**

Dr. Dre (Andre Young) (rap singer); Los Angeles, 2/18/66

Dreiser, Theodore (writer); Terre Haute, Ind. **(1871–1945)**

Drescher, Fran (television and film actress); New York City, 9/30/57

Dreyfus, Alfred (French army officer); Mulhouse, France **(1859–1935)**

Dreyfuss, Richard (actor); Brooklyn, N.Y., 10/29/47

Drury, Allen (novelist); Houston **(1918–1998)**

Dryden, John (poet); Northamptonshire, England **(1631–1700)**

Dryer, Fred (ex-NFL player, actor); Hawthorne, Calif., 7/6/46

Dubček, Alexander (ex-president of Czechoslovakia); Uhrovek, Slovakia **(1921–1992)**

Dubinsky, David (David Dobnievski) (labor leader); Brest-Litovsk, Belarus **(1892–1982)**

Du Bois, W(illiam) E(dward) B(urghardt) (scholar, civil rights activist); Great Barrington, Mass. **(1868–1963)**

Duchamp, Marcel (painter); Blainville, France **(1887–1968)**

Duchin, Eddy (pianist, bandleader); Cambridge, Mass. **(1909–1951)**

Duchin, Peter (pianist, band leader); New York City, 7/28/37

Duchovny, David (actor); New York City, 8/7/60

Dufay, Guillaume (composer); Cambrai, France **(c. 1400–1474)**

Duffy, Julia (actress); Minneapolis, Minn., 6/27/50

Dufy, Raoul (painter); Le Havre, France **(1877–1953)**

Dukakis, Olympia (actress); Lowell, Mass., 6/20/31

Duke, James B. (industrialist); nr. Durham, N.C. **(1856–1925)**

Duke, Patty (Anna Marie Duke) (actress); New York City, 12/14/46

Dulles, Allen Welsh (ex-director of CIA); Watertown, N.Y. **(1893–1969)**

Dulles, John Foster (political figure); Washington, D.C. **(1888–1959)**

Dumas, Alexandre (called Dumas fils) (novelist); Paris **(1824–1895)**

Dumas, Alexandre (called Dumas père) (novelist); Villers-Cotterets, France **(1802–1870)**

du Maurier, Daphne (novelist); London **(1907–1989)**

du Maurier, George Louis Palmella Busson (novelist); Paris **(1834–1896)**

Dumont, Margaret (actress); Brooklyn, N.Y. **(1889–1965)**

Dunaway, Faye (actress); Bascom, Fla., 1/14/41

Dunbar, Paul Laurence (poet, novelist); Dayton, Ohio **(1872–1906)**

Duncan, Isadora (dancer); San Francisco **(1878–1927)**

Duncan, Michael Clarke (actor); Chicago, 12/10/57

Duncan, Sandy (actress); Henderson, Tex., 2/20/46

Dunham, Katherine (dancer, choreographer); Chicago, 6/22/09

Dunne, Irene (actress); Louisville, Ky. **(1898–1990)**

Duns Scotus, John (theologian); Duns, Scotland **(1265–1303)**

Dunst, Kirsten (actress); Point Pleasant, N.J., 4/30/82

Du Pont, Pierre S. (economist); Paris **(1739–1817)**

Durante, Jimmy (comedian); New York City **(1893–1980)**

Duras, Marguerite (Donnadieu) (novelist, dramatist); Gia Dinh, Vietnam **(1914–1996)**

Durbin, Deanna (Edna Mae) (actress); Winnipeg, Canada, 12/4/21

Dürer, Albrecht (painter, engraver); Nürnberg, Germany **(1471–1528)**

Durning, Charles (actor); Highland Falls, N.Y., 2/28/23

Durrell, Lawrence George (novelist); Julundur, India **(1912–1990)**

Duse, Eleonora (actress); Chioggia, Italy **(1859–1924)**

Dussault, Nancy (actress); Pensacola, Fla., 6/30/36

Duvall, Robert (actor, director, producer); San Diego, Calif., 1/5/31

Duvall, Shelley (actress); Houston, 7/7/49

Dvořák, Antonin (composer); Nelahozeves, Czechoslovakia **(1841–1904)**

Dylan, Bob (Robert Zimmerman) (singer, songwriter, guitarist); Duluth, Minn., 5/24/41

Dysart, Richard (actor); Brighton, Mass., 3/30/29

E

Eakins, Thomas (painter, sculptor); Philadelphia **(1844–1916)**

Earhart, Amelia (aviator); Atchison, Kans. **(1897–1937)**

Earp, Wyatt (Berry Stapp) (sheriff, gunfighter); Monmouth, Ill. **(1848–1929)**

Eastman, George (camera inventor); Waterville, N.Y. **(1854–1932)**

Eastwood, Clint (actor, director, producer); San Francisco, 5/31/30

Ebert, Roger (film critic); Urbana, Ill., 6/18/42

Ebsen, Buddy (Christian Ebsen, Jr.) (actor); Belleville, Ill. **(1908–2003)**

Eckstine, Billy (singer); Pittsburgh **(1914–1993)**

Eddy, Mary Baker (founder of Christian Science Church); Bow, N.H. **(1821–1910)**

Eddy, Nelson (baritone, actor); Providence, R.I. **(1901–1967)**

Edel, Leon (author); Pittsburgh **(1907–1997)**

Edelman, Marian Wright (social activist); Bennettsville, S.C., 6/6/39

Eden, Sir Anthony (Earl of Avon) (ex-prime minister); Durham, England **(1897–1977)**

Eden, Barbara (Barbara Huffman) (actress); Tucson, Ariz., 8/23/34

Edison, Thomas Alva (inventor); Milan, Ohio **(1847–1931)**

Edwards, Anthony (actor); Santa Barbara, Calif., 7/19/62

Edwards, Blake (film writer, producer); Tulsa, Okla., 7/26/22

Edwards, Jonathan (theologian); East Windsor, Conn. **(1703–1758)**

Edwards, Ralph (TV and radio producer); Merino, Colo., 6/13/13

Edwards, Vincent (Vincent Edward Zoino) (actor); Brooklyn, N.Y. **(1928–1996)**

Eglevsky, André (ballet dancer); Moscow **(1917–1977)**

Egoyan, Atom (film director, writer, editor); Cairo, 7/19/60

Ehrlich, Paul (bacteriologist); Strzelin, Poland **(1854–1915)**

Eichmann, (Karl) Adolf (Nazi, mass murderer); Solingen, Germany **(1906–1962)**

Eikenberry, Jill (actress); New Haven, Conn., 1/21/47

Einstein, Albert (physicist); Ulm, Germany **(1879–1955)**

Eisner, Michael (entertainment executive); Mt. Kisco, N.Y., 3/7/42

Eisenhower, Dwight David (34th U.S. president); Denison, Tex. **(1890–1969)**

Eisenhower, Milton S. (educator); Abilene, Kans. **(1899–1985)**

Eisenstaedt, Alfred (photographer, photojournalist); Dirschau (Prussia, now Tczew), Poland **(1898–1995)**

Ekland, Britt (Britt-Marie) (actress); Stockholm, 10/6/42

Electra, Carmen (Tara Patrick) (model, actress); Cincinnati, Ohio, 4/20/73

Elfman, Jenna (Jennifer Mary Butala) (actress); Los Angeles, 9/30/71

Elgar, Sir Edward (composer); Worcester, England **(1857–1934)**

Elgart, Larry (band leader); New London, Conn., 3/20/22

El Greco (Domenicos Theotocopoulos) (painter); Candia, Crete, Greece **(c. 1541–1614)**

Elion, Gertrude B. (chemist, Nobel laureate); New York City **(1918–1999)**

Eliot, George (Mary Ann Evans) (novelist); Chilvers Coton, England **(1819–1880)**

Eliot, Thomas Stearns (poet); St. Louis **(1888–1965)**

Elizabeth I (queen of England); Greenwich, England **(1533–1603)**

Elizabeth II (queen of England); London, 4/21/26

Elizondo, Hector (actor); New York City, 12/22/36

Ellington, Duke (Edward Kennedy) (jazz musician); Washington, D.C. **(1899–1974)**

Elliot, "Mama" Cass (Ellen Naomi Cohen) (singer); Baltimore **(1941–1974)**

Elliott, Sam (actor); Sacramento, Calif., 8/9/44

Ellison, Lawrence J. (computer industry executive); New York City, 1944

Ellison, Ralph (novelist); Oklahoma City, Okla. **(1914–1994)**
Ellsberg, Daniel (activist); Chicago, 4/7/31
Elman, Mischa (violinist); Stalnoye, Ukraine **(1891–1967)**
Emerson, Ralph Waldo (philosopher, poet); Boston **(1803–1882)**
Enesco, Georges (composer); Dorohoi, Romania **(1881–1955)**
Engels, Friedrich (Socialist writer); Barmen, Germany **(1820–1895)**
Englund, Robert (actor); Glendale, Calif., 6/6/49
Entremont, Philippe (concert pianist); Rheims, France, 6/7/34
Ephron, Nora (writer, director); New York City, 5/19/41
Epicurus (philosopher); Samos, Greece **(341–270 B.C.)**
Epstein, Sir Jacob (sculptor); New York City **(1880–1959)**
Erasmus, Desiderius (Gerhard Gerhards) (scholar); Rotterdam **(1469–1536)**
Erdrich, (Karen) Louise (writer); Little Falls, Minn., 7/6/54
Erickson, Leif (actor); Alameda, Calif. **(1911–1986)**
Ericsson, Leif (navigator) c. 10th century A.D.
Erikson, Erik H. (psychoanalyst); Frankfurt, Germany **(1902–1994)**
Ernst, Max (painter); Bruhl, Germany **(1891–1976)**
Erté (Romain de Tirtoff) (artist, designer); St. Petersburg, Russia **(1892–1990)**
Estevez, Emilio (actor, director, screenwriter); New York City, 5/12/62
Eszterhas, Joe (screenwriter); Csakanydoroslo, Hungary, 11/23/44
Euclid (mathematician); Megara, Greece, fl. 300 B.C.
Euler, Leonhard (mathematician); Basel, Switzerland **(1707–1783)**
Euripides (dramatist); Salamis, Greece **(c. 484–407 B.C.)**
Evangelista, Linda (model); St. Catharines, Ont., Canada, 5/10/65
Evans, Dale (born Lucille Wood Smith but raised as Frances Octavia Smith) (actress, singer); Uvalde, Tex. **(1912–2001)**
Evans, Dame Edith (actress); London **(1888–1976)**
Evans, Linda (actress); Hartford, Conn., 11/18/42
Evans, Maurice (actor); Dorchester, England **(1901–1989)**
Everett, Chad (Raymond Lee Cramton) (actor); South Bend, Ind., 6/11/36
Everett, Rupert (actor, model, musician); Norfolk, England, 5/29/59
Everhart, Angie (model, actress); Akron, Ohio, 9/7/69
Evers, Charles (civil rights leader); Decatur, Miss., 9/14/22
Evers, Medgar (civil rights leader); Decatur, Miss. **(1925–1963)**
Evers-Williams, Myrlie (civil rights leader); Vicksburg, Miss., 3/17/33

F

Fabares, Shelley (actress); Santa Monica, Calif., 1/19/44
Fabian (Fabian Anthony Forte) (singer); Philadelphia, 2/6/43
Fabray, Nanette (Nanette Fabarés) (actress); San Diego, Calif., 10/27/22
Fahrenheit, Gabriel (German physicist); Danzig, Poland **(1686–1736)**
Fairbanks, Douglas (Douglas Ulman) (actor); Denver **(1883–1939)**
Fairbanks, Douglas, Jr. (actor); New York City **(1909–2000)**
Fairchild, Morgan (Patsy Ann McClenny) (actress); Dallas, 2/3/50
Faith, Percy (conductor); Toronto **(1908–1976)**
Falk, Peter (actor); New York City, 9/16/27
Falla, Manuel de (composer); Cadiz, Spain **(1876–1946)**
Faludi, Susan (journalist, writer); New York City, 4/18/59
Falwell, Jerry (fundamentalist preacher); Lynchburg, Va., 8/11/33
Faraday, Michael (physicist); Newington, England **(1791–1867)**
Farentino, James (actor); Brooklyn, N.Y., 2/24/38
Farley, Chris (actor, comedian); Madison, Wis. **(1964–1997)**
Farmer, James (civil rights leader); Marshall, Tex. **(1920–1999)**
Farnsworth, Richard (actor); Los Angeles **(1920–2000)**
Farr, Jamie (Jameel Joseph Farah) (actor); Toledo, Ohio, 7/1/34
Farrar, Geraldine (soprano, actress); Melrose, Mass. **(1882–1967)**
Farrell, Eileen (operatic soprano); Willimantic, Conn. **(1920–2002)**
Farrell, James T. (novelist); Chicago **(1904–1979)**
Farrell, Mike (actor); St. Paul, Minn., 2/6/39
Farrell, Perry (Perry Bernstein) (lead singer); Queens, N.Y., 3/29/59
Farrell, Suzanne (Roberta Sue Ficker) (ballet dancer); Cincinnati, 8/16/45
Farrow, Mia (actress); Los Angeles, 2/9/45
Fasanella, Ralph (painter); New York City **(1914–1997)**
Fassbinder, Rainer Werner (film, stage director); Bad Wörishofen, Germany **(1946–1982)**
Fast, Howard (novelist); New York City **(1914–2003)**
Faubus, Orval E(ugene) (governor of Arkansas); Combs, Ark. **(1910–1994)**
Faulkner, William (novelist); New Albany, Miss. **(1897–1962)**
Fauré, Gabriel Urbain (composer); Pamiers, France **(1845–1924)**
Fawcett, Farrah (Mary Farrah Leni Fawcett) (actress); Corpus Christi, Tex., 2/2/47
Faye, Alice (Ann Leppert) (actress); New York City **(1912–1998)**
Feiffer, Jules (cartoonist); New York City, 1/26/29

Feininger, Lyonel (painter); New York City **(1871–1956)**
Feldman, Marty (actor, screenwriter, director); London **(1938–1982)**
Feldon, Barbara (actress); Pittsburgh, 3/12/41
Feliciano, José (singer); Larez, Puerto Rico, 9/10/45
Felker, Clay S. (editor, publisher); St. Louis, 10/2/25
Fell, Norman (actor); Philadelphia **(1923–1998)**
Fellini, Federico (film director); Rimini, Italy **(1920–1993)**
Fender, Freddie (Baldemar Huerta) (singer); San Benito, Tex., 6/4/37
Ferber, Edna (novelist); Kalamazoo, Mich. **(1885–1968)**
Ferguson, Maynard (jazz trumpeter); Verdun, Que., Canada, 5/4/28
Ferlinghetti, Lawrence (poet, writer, translator); Yonkers, N.Y., 3/24/19
Fermi, Enrico (atomic physicist); Rome **(1901–1954)**
Fernandel (Fernand Joseph Desire Contandin) (actor); Marseilles, France **(1903–1971)**
Ferraro, Geraldine Anne (political figure); New York City, 8/26/35
Ferrer, José (actor, director); Santurce, Puerto Rico **(1912–1992)**
Ferrer, Mel (actor); Elberon, N.J., 8/25/17
Fiedler, Arthur (conductor); Boston **(1894–1979)**
Field, Eugene (poet); St. Louis **(1850–1895)**
Field, Marshall (merchant); nr. Conway, Mass. **(1834–1906)**
Field, Sally (actress); Pasadena, Calif., 11/6/46
Fielding, Henry (novelist); nr. Glastonbury, England **(1707–1754)**
Fields, W. C. (William Claude Dukenfield) (comedian); Philadelphia **(1880–1946)**
Fiennes, Joseph (actor); Salisbury, England, 5/27/70
Fiennes, Ralph (actor); Suffolk, England, 12/22/62
Fierstein, Harvey (Forbes) (playwright, actor); Brooklyn, 6/6/54
Figgis, Mike (director, screenwriter, composer, actor); Carlisle, England, 2/28/48
Filene, Edward A. (merchant) **(1860–1937)**
Fillmore, Millard (13th U.S. president); Locke, Cayuga County, N.Y. **(1800–1874)**
Finch, Peter (actor); Kensington, England **(1916–1977)**
Finney, Albert (actor); Salford, England, 5/9/36
Fiorentino, Linda (Clorinda Fiorentino) (actress); Philadelphia, 3/9/60
Firkusny, Rudolf (pianist); Napajedia, former Czechoslovakia **(1912–1994)**
Firth, Colin (actor); Grayshot, England, 9/10/60
Fischer-Dieskau, Dietrich (baritone); Berlin, 5/28/25
Fishburne, Laurence (actor); Augusta, Ga., 7/30/61
Fisher, Carrie (actress); Los Angeles, 10/21/56
Fisher, Eddie (Edwin) (singer); Philadelphia, 8/10/28
Fitzgerald, Barry (William Joseph Shields) (actor); Dublin **(1888–1961)**
Fitzgerald, Ella (singer); Newport News, Va. **(1917–1996)**
Fitzgerald, F. Scott (Francis Scott Key Fitzgerald) (novelist); St. Paul, Minn. **(1896–1940)**
Fitzgerald, Geraldine (actress); Dublin, 11/24/14
Fitzgerald, Pegeen (radio broadcaster); Norcatur, Kans. **(1910–1989)**
Flack, Roberta (singer); Black Mountain, N.C., 2/10/40
Flagstad, Kirsten (Wagnerian soprano); Hamar, Norway **(1895–1962)**
Flatt, Lester Raymond (bluegrass musician); Overton County, Tenn. **(1914–1979)**
Flaubert, Gustave (novelist); Rouen, France **(1821–1880)**
Fleming, Sir Alexander (bacteriologist); Lochfield, Scotland **(1881–1955)**
Fletcher, John (dramatist); Rye, Sussex, England **(1579–1625)**
Flockhart, Calista (actress); Freeport, Ill., 11/11/64
Flynn, Errol (actor); Hobart, Tasmania **(1909–1959)**
Fodor, Eugene (violinist); Turkey Creek, Colo., 3/5/50
Fokine, Michel (dancer, choreographer); St. Petersburg, Russia **(1880–1942)**
Fonda, Bridget (actress); Los Angeles, 1/27/64
Fonda, Henry (actor); Grand Island, Neb. **(1905–1982)**
Fonda, Jane (actress); New York City, 12/21/37
Fonda, Peter (actor); New York City, 2/23/39
Fontaine, Frank (singer, comedian); Cambridge, Mass. **(1920–1979)**
Fontaine, Joan (Joan de Havilland) (actress); Tokyo, 10/22/17
Fontanne, Lynn (actress); London **(1887–1983)**
Fonteyn, Dame Margot (Margaret Hookham) (ballet dancer); Reigate, England **(1919–1991)**
Foote, Shelby (historian); Greenville, Miss., 11/17/16
Forbes, Malcolm S(tevenson) (publisher, sportsman); Brooklyn, N.Y. **(1919–1990)**
Ford, Gerald Rudolph (38th U.S. president); Omaha, Neb., 7/14/13
Ford, Glenn (Gwyllyn Ford) (actor); Ste.-Christine, Que., Canada, 5/1/16
Ford, Harrison (actor); Chicago, 7/13/42

Ford, Henry (industrialist); Greenfield, Mich. **(1863–1947)**
Ford, John (film director); Cape Elizabeth, Maine **(1895–1973)**
Ford, Tennessee Ernie (Ernie Jennings Ford) (singer); Bristol, Tenn. **(1919–1991)**
Foreman, George (boxer, actor); Marshall, Tex., 1/10/49
Forrester, Maureen (contralto); Montreal, 7/25/30
Forsythe, John (John Lincoln Freund) (actor); Penn's Grove, N.J., 1/29/18
Fosdick, Harry Emerson (clergyman); Buffalo, N.Y. **(1878–1968)**
Fosse, Bob (Robert Louis Fosse) (choreographer, director); Chicago **(1927–1987)**
Foster, Jodie (Alicia Christian Foster) (actress, director, producer); Los Angeles, 11/19/62
Foster, Stephen Collins (composer); nr. Pittsburgh **(1826–1864)**
Fountain, Pete (jazz musician); New Orleans, 7/3/30
Fox, Matthew (actor); Crowheart, Wyo., 7/14/66
Fox, Michael J. (actor, producer); Edmonton, Alta., Canada, 6/9/61
Foxx, Redd (John Elroy Sanford) (actor, comedian); St. Louis **(1922–1991)**
Foy, Eddie, Jr. (dancer, actor); New Rochelle, N.Y. **(1905–1983)**
Fracci, Carla (ballet dancer); Milan, Italy, 8/20/36
Fragonard, Jean Honoré (painter); Grasse, France **(1732–1806)**
Frakes, Jonathan (actor); Bethlehem, Pa., 8/19/52
Frampton, Peter (rock musician); Beckenham, England, 4/20/50
France, Anatole (Jacques Anatole François Thibault) (author); Paris **(1844–1924)**
Francescatti, Zino (violinist); Marseilles, France **(1902–1991)**
Franciosa, Anthony (Anthony Papaleo) (actor); New York City, 10/25/28
Francis, Anne (actress); Ossining, N.Y., 7/16/30
Francis, Connie (Concetta Franconero) (singer); Newark, N.J., 12/12/38
Francis, Genie (actress); Englewood, N.J., 5/26/62
Francis of Assisi, Saint (Giovanni Francesco Barnardone) (founder of Franciscans); Assisi, Italy **(1182–1226)**
Franck, César Auguste (composer); Liège, Belgium **(1822–1890)**
Franco Bahamonde, Francisco (chief of state); El Ferrol, Spain **(1892–1975)**
Frankenheimer, John (movie director, producer); New York City, 1930
Frankenthaler, Helen (artist); New York City, 12/12/28
Frankl, Victor E. (psychiatrist); Vienna **(1905–1997)**
Franklin, Aretha (singer); Memphis, Tenn., 3/25/42
Franklin, Benjamin (statesman, scientist); Boston **(1706–1790)**
Franklin, Bonnie (actress); Santa Monica, Calif., 1/6/44
Franklin, John Hope (historian); Rentiesville, Okla., 1/2/15
Frann, Mary (actress); St. Louis **(1943–1998)**
Franz, Dennis (Dennis Schlachta) (actor); Chicago, 10/28/44
Fraser, Brendan (actor); Indianapolis, Indiana, 12/3/67
Frazer, Sir James George (anthropologist); Glasgow, Scotland **(1854–1941)**
Freeman, Morgan (actor); Memphis, Tenn., 6/1/37
Freud, Sigmund (psychoanalyst); Moravia, Czech Repubic **(1856–1939)**
Frey, Glenn (musician); Detroit, 11/6/48
Frick, Henry Clay (industrialist); Westmoreland Co., Pa. **(1849–1919)**
Friedan, Betty (Betty Naomi Goldstein) (feminist, writer); Peoria, Ill., 2/4/21
Fromm, Erich (psychoanalyst); Frankfurt-am-Main, Germany **(1900–1980)**
Frost, David (TV entertainer); Tenterden, England, 4/7/39
Frost, Robert Lee (poet); San Francisco **(1874–1963)**
Fry, Christopher (playwright); Bristol, England, 12/18/07
Fugard, Athol (playwright); Middleburg, South Africa, 6/11/32
Fulbright, J. William (politician); Sumner, Mo. **(1905–1995)**
Fuller, Charles (playwright); Philadelphia, 3/5/39
Fuller, R(ichard) Buckminster (Jr.) (architect, educator); Milton, Mass. **(1895–1983)**
Fulton, Robert (inventor); Lancaster County, Pa. **(1765–1815)**
Funicello, Annette (actress); Utica, N.Y., 10/22/42
Funt, Allen (TV producer); Brooklyn, N.Y. **(1914–1999)**

G

Gabin, Jean (actor); Paris **(1904–1976)**
Gable, (William) Clark (actor); Cadiz, Ohio **(1901–1960)**
Gabo, Naum (sculptor); Briansk, Russia **(1890–1977)**
Gabor, Eva (actress); Budapest **(1920–1995)**
Gabor, Zsa Zsa (Sari) (actress); Budapest, 2/6/17
Gabriel, Peter (musician); Cobham, England, 2/13/50
Gabrieli, Giovanni (composer); Venice **(c. 1557–1612)**
Gaddis, William (novelist); New York City **(1922–1998)**

Gainsborough, Thomas (painter); Sudbury, Suffolk, England **(1727–1788)**
Galbraith, John Kenneth (economist); Iona Station, Ont., Canada, 10/15/08
Galilei, Galileo (astronomer, physicist); Pisa, Italy **(1564–1642)**
Gallico, Paul (novelist); New York City **(1897–1976)**
Gallup, George H. (poll taker); Jefferson, Iowa **(1901–1984)**
Galsworthy, John (novelist, dramatist); Coombe, England **(1867–1933)**
Galway, James (flutist); Belfast, Northern Ireland, 12/8/39
Gambling, John A. (radio broadcaster); New York City, 1930
Gandhi, Indira (Indira Nehru) (former prime minister); Allahabad, India **(1917–1984)**
Gandhi, Mohandas Karamchand (called Mahatma Gandhi) (Hindu leader); Porbandar, India **(1869–1948)**
Gannett, Frank E. (editor, publisher) **(1876–1957)**
Garagiola, Joe (Joseph Henry Garagiola) (sportscaster); St. Louis, 2/12/26
Garbo, Greta (Greta Gustafsson) (actress); Stockholm **(1905–1990)**
Garcia, Andy (Andres Arturo Garcia-Menendez) (actor); Havana, Cuba, 4/12/56
Garcia, Jerry (rock musician); San Francisco **(1942–1995)**
Garcia Lorca, Frederico (poet, dramatist); Fuente Vaqueros, Spain **(1898–1936)**
Garden, Mary (soprano); Aberdeen, Scotland **(1874–1967)**
Gardenia, Vincent (Vincente Scognamiglio) (actor); Naples, Italy **(1922–1992)**
Gardner, Ava (actress); Smithfield, N.C. **(1922–1990)**
Gardner, Erle Stanley (novelist); Malden, Mass. **(1889–1970)**
Garfield, James Abram (20th U.S. president); Cuyahoga County, Ohio **(1831–1881)**
Garfunkel, Art (Arthur) (singer); Newark, N.J., 11/5/41
Garibaldi, Giuseppe (Italian nationalist leader); Nice, France **(1807–1882)**
Garland, Judy (Frances Gumm) (actress, singer); Grand Rapids, Minn. **(1922–1969)**
Garner, Erroll (jazz pianist); Pittsburgh **(1921–1977)**
Garner, James (James Bumgarner) (actor); Norman, Okla., 4/7/28
Garofalo, Janeane (actress, comedienne); Newton, N.J., 9/28/64
Garr, Teri (actress); Lakewood, Ohio, 12/11/49
Garrison, William Lloyd (abolitionist); Newburyport, Mass. **(1805–1879)**
Garroway, Dave (TV host); Schenectady, N.Y. **(1913–1982)**
Garson, Greer (actress); County Down, Northern Ireland **(1903–1996)**
Garth, Jennie (actress); Urbana, Ill., 4/3/72
Garvey, Marcus Moziah (black nationalist leader); Jamaica **(1887–1940)**
Gassman, Vittorio (film actor, director); Genoa, Italy **(1922–2000)**
Gates, Bill (William Henry Gates III) (software pioneer); Seattle, 10/28/55
Gates, Henry Louis, Jr. (scholar); Keyser, W. Va., 9/16/50
Gaudí, Antonio (architect); Reus, Spain **(1852–1926)**
Gauguin, (Eugène Henri) Paul (painter); Paris **(1848–1903)**
Gautama Buddha (Prince Siddhartha) (philosopher); Kapilavastu, India **(c. 563–c. 483 B.C.)**
Gavin, John (actor, diplomat); Los Angeles, 4/8/35
Gavras, Konstantinos (Costa-Gavras) (film director); Loutra-Iraias, Greece, 2/13/33
Gaye, Marvin (singer); Washington, D.C. **(1939–1984)**
Gayle, Crystal (Brenda Gayle Webb) (singer); Paintsville, Ky., 1/9/51
Gaynor, Janet (actress); Philadelphia **(1906–1984)**
Gaynor, Mitzi (Francesca Mitzi Marlene de Czanyi von Gerber) (actress); Chicago, 9/4/31
Gazzara, Ben (Biagio Anthony Gazzara) (actor); New York City, 8/28/30
Gedda, Nicolai (tenor); Stockholm, 7/11/25
Gellar, Sarah Michelle (actress); New York City, 4/14/77
Genet, Jean (playwright); Paris **(1910–1986)**
Genghis Khan (Temujin) (conqueror); nr. Lake Baikal, Russia **(1162–1227)**
Gentry, Bobbie (Roberta Streeter) (singer); Chickasaw Co., Miss., 7/27/44
George, David Lloyd (statesman); Manchester, England **(1863–1945)**
George, Henry (economist, reformer); Philadelphia **(1839–1897)**
Gere, Richard (actor); Philadelphia, 8/31/49
Géricault, Jean Louis (painter); Rouen, France **(1791–1824)**
Geronimo (Goyathlay) (Apache chieftain); Arizona **(1829–1909)**
Gershwin, George (composer); Brooklyn, N.Y. **(1898–1937)**
Gershwin, Ira (lyricist); New York City **(1896–1983)**

Getty, J. Paul (oil executive); Minneapolis (1892–1976)

Getz, Stan (saxophonist); Philadelphia (1927–1991)

Ghiberti, Lorenzo (goldsmith, sculptor); Florence (1378–1455)

Ghostley, Alice (actress); Eve, Mo., 8/14/26

Giacometti, Alberto (sculptor); Switzerland (1901–1966)

Giannini, Giancarlo (actor); La Spezia, Italy, 8/1/42

Gibbon, Edward (historian); Putney, England (1737–1794)

Gibson, Charles Dana (illustrator); Roxbury, Mass. (1867–1944)

Gibson, Henry (actor, comedian); Germantown, Pa., 9/21/35

Gibson, Mel (actor, director, producer); Peekskill, N.Y., 1/3/56

Gide, André (author); Paris (1869–1951)

Gielgud, Sir John (actor); London (1904–2000)

Gifford, Kathie Lee (Kathie Lee Epstein) (talk show host); Paris, 8/16/53

Gilbert, Melissa (actress); Los Angeles, 5/8/64

Gilbert, Walter (chemist, Nobel laureate); Boston, 3/21/32

Gilbert, Sir William Schwenck (librettist); London (1836–1911)

Gilels, Emil (concert pianist); Odessa, Ukraine (1916–1985)

Gillespie, Dizzy (John Birks Gillespie) (jazz trumpeter); Cheraw, S.C. (1917–1993)

Gilligan, Carol (Friedman) (psychologist); New York City, 11/28/36

Gilpin, Peri (actress); Waco, Tex., 5/27/61

Gimbel, Bernard F. (merchant); Vincennes, Ind. (1885–1966)

Gingrich, Newt (politician); Harrisburg, Pa., 6/17/43

Ginsberg, Allen (poet); Newark, N.J. (1926–1997)

Giordano, Luca (painter); Naples, Italy (1632–1705)

Giorgione (painter); Castelfranco, Italy (c. 1477–1510)

Giotto di Bondone (painter); Vespignano, Italy (c. 1266–1337)

Giovanni, Nikki (poet); Knoxville, Tenn., 6/7/43

Giroud, Françoise (French government official); Geneva, 9/21/16

Gish, Dorothy (actress); Massillon, Ohio (1898–1968)

Gish, Lillian (Lillian de Guiche) (actress); Springfield, Ohio (1893–1993)

Giuliani, Rudolph (public official); Brooklyn, N.Y., 5/28/44

Givenchy, Hubert (fashion designer); Beauvais, France, 2/21/27

Gladstone, William Ewart (statesman); Liverpool, England (1809–1898)

Glaser, Paul Michael (actor, director); Cambridge, Mass., 3/25/43

Glass, Philip (composer); Baltimore, 1/31/37

Gleason, Jackie (comedian); Brooklyn, N.Y. (1916–1987)

Glenn, John (legislator, astronaut); Cambridge, Ohio, 7/18/21

Gless, Sharon (actress); Los Angeles, 5/31/43

Glover, Danny (actor); San Francisco, 7/22/47

Gluck, Christoph Willibald (composer); Erasbach, Germany (1714–1787)

Gobel, George (comedian); Chicago (1920–1991)

Godard, Jean Luc (film director); Paris, 12/3/30

Goddard, Paulette (Marion Levy) (actress); Great Neck, N.Y. (1911–1990)

Goddard, Robert Hutchings (father of modern rocketry); Worcester, Mass. (1882–1945)

Godfrey, Arthur (entertainer); New York City (1903–1983)

Goebbels, Joseph Paul (Nazi leader); Rheydt, Germany (1897–1945)

Goering, Hermann (Nazi leader); Rosenheim, Germany (1893–1946)

Goethals, George Washington (engineer); Brooklyn, N.Y. (1858–1928)

Goethe, Johann Wolfgang von (poet, playwright, novelist); Frankfurt-am-Main, Germany (1749–1832)

Gogol, Nikolai Vasilievich (novelist); nr. Mirgorod, Ukraine (1809–1852)

Goldberg, Rube (cartoonist); San Francisco (1883–1970)

Goldberg, Whoopi (Caryn Johnson) (actress); New York City, 11/13/49

Goldblum, Jeff (actor); Pittsburgh, 10/22/52

Golden, Harry (Harry Goldhurst) (author); New York City (1902–1981)

Goldman, Emma (anarchist); Kovno, Lithuania (1869–1940)

Goldsmith, Oliver (dramatist, poet); County Longford, Ireland (1728–1774)

Goldwyn, Samuel (Schmuel Gelbfisz) (film producer); Warsaw (1879–1974)

Gompers, Samuel (labor leader); London (1850–1924)

Goodall, Jane (Baroness van Lawick-Goodall) (ethologist); London, 4/3/34

Gooding, Jr., Cuba (actor); Bronx, New York, 1/2/68

Goodman, Benny (clarinetist); Chicago (1909–1986)

Goodman, John (actor); St. Louis, 6/20/52

Goodwin, Doris (Helen) Kearns (historian); Rockville Center, N.Y., 1/4/43

Goodyear, Charles (inventor); New Haven, Conn. (1800–1860)

Gorbachev, Mikhail Sergeyevich (former Soviet leader); Privolnoye, Russia, 3/2/31

Gordimer, Nadine (novelist, short-story writer); Springs, South Africa, 12/20/23

Gordon, Dexter (jazz musician); Los Angeles (1923–1990)

Gordon, Ruth (actress); Wollaston, Mass. (1896–1985)

Gore, Albert, Jr. (ex-vice president of the U.S.); Washington, D.C., 3/31/48

Gordy, Berry, Jr. (record company executive); Detroit, 11/28/29

Gorey, Edward (St. John) (illustrator, author); Chicago (1925–2000)

Gorki, Maxim (Alexei Maximovich Peshkov) (author); Nizhni Novgorod, Russia (1868–1936)

Gorky, Arshile (painter); Armenia (1904–1948)

Gormé, Eydie (singer); Bronx, N.Y., 8/16/32

Gorshin, Frank (actor); Pittsburgh, 4/5/34

Gossett, Louis, Jr. (actor); Brooklyn, N.Y., 5/27/36

Gottschalk, Louis Moreau (pianist, composer); New Orleans (1829–1869)

Gould, Chester (cartoonist); Pawnee, Okla. (1900–1985)

Gould, Elliott (Elliott Goldstein) (actor); Brooklyn, N.Y., 8/29/38

Gould, Glenn (concert pianist); Toronto (1932–1982)

Gould, Morton (composer); Richmond Hill, Queens, N.Y. (1913–1996)

Gould, Stephen Jay (paleontologist, science writer); New York City (1941–2002)

Goulet, Robert (singer); Lawrence, Mass., 11/26/33

Gounod, Charles François (composer); Paris (1818–1893)

Goya y Lucientes, Francisco José de (painter); Fuendetodos, Spain (1746–1828)

Grable, Betty (actress); St. Louis (1916–1973)

Grace, Princess of Monaco (Grace Kelly) (ex-actress); Philadelphia (1929–1982)

Graham, Bill (Wolfgang Grajonca) (rock impresario); Berlin (1930–1991)

Graham, Billy (William F. Graham) (evangelist); Charlotte, N.C., 11/7/18

Graham, Katharine Meyer (newspaper publisher); New York City (1917–2001)

Graham, Martha (choreographer); Pittsburgh (1894–1991)

Grainger, Percy Aldridge (pianist, composer); Melbourne, Australia (1882–1961)

Gramm, Donald (Grambach) (bass-baritone); Milwaukee (1927–1983)

Grammer, Kelsey (actor); St. Thomas, V.I., 2/21/55

Granger, Stewart (James Stewart) (actor); London (1913–1993)

Grant, Cary (Alexander Archibald Leach) (actor); Bristol, England (1904–1986)

Grant, Hugh (actor); London, England, 9/9/60

Grant, Lee (Lyova Haskell Rosenthal) (actress); New York City, 10/31/30

Grant, Ulysses Simpson (18th U.S. president); Point Pleasant, Ohio (1822–1885)

Grass, Günter (novelist); Danzig, Poland, 10/16/27

Graves, Nancy (Stevenson) (artist); Pittsfield, Mass. (1940–1996)

Graves, Peter (Peter Aurness) (actor); Minneapolis, 3/18/26

Graves, Robert (writer); London (1895–1985)

Gray, Linda (actress); Santa Monica, Calif., 9/12/40

Gray, Thomas (poet); London (1716–1771)

Greco, José (dancer); Montorio nei Frentani, Italy (1918–2000)

Greeley, Horace (journalist, politician); Amherst, N.H. (1811–1872)

Green, Adolph (actor, lyricist); New York City (1915–2002)

Green, Al (singer); Forrest City, Ark., 4/13/46

Greene, Graham (novelist); Berkhamsted, England (1904–1991)

Greene, Lorne (actor); Ottawa, Ont., Canada (1915–1987)

Greene, Shecky (comedian, actor); Chicago, 4/8/25

Greenstreet, Sydney (actor); Sandwich, England (1879–1954)

Greenspan, Alan (chairman of the Federal Reserve); New York City, 3/6/26

Greer, Germaine (feminist, writer); Melbourne, Australia, 1/29/39

Gregory, Cynthia (ballet dancer); Los Angeles, 7/8/46

Gregory, Dick (comedian); St. Louis, 10/12/32

Gregory, Lady (Isabella) Augusta (playwright); Roxborough, Ireland (1852–1932)

Greuze, Jean-Baptiste (painter); Tournus, France (1725–1805)

Grey, Joel (Joel Katz) (actor, dancer); Cleveland, 4/11/32

Grey, Zane (author); Zanesville, Ohio (1875–1939)

Grieg, Edvard Hagerup (composer); Bergen, Norway (1843–1907)

Grier, Pam (actress); Winston-Salem, N.C., 5/26/49

Griffin, Merv (TV host, producer); San Mateo, Calif., 7/6/25

Griffith, Andy (actor); Mount Airy, N.C., 6/1/26

Griffith, David Lewelyn Wark (film producer); La Grange, Ky. (1875–1948)

Griffith, Melanie (actress); New York City, 8/9/57

Grigorovich, Yuri (choreographer); Leningrad (St. Petersburg), Russia, 1/1/27

Grimes, Tammy (actress); Lynn, Mass., 1/30/34

Grimm, Jacob (author of fairy tales); Hanau, Germany (1785–1863)

Grimm, Wilhelm (author of fairy tales); Hanau, Germany (1786–1859)

Gris, Juan (José Victoriano González) (painter); Madrid (1887–1927)

Grisham, John (attorney, author); Jonesboro, Ark., 2/8/55

Grodin, Charles (actor); Pittsburgh, 4/21/35

Groening, Matt (animator, producer); Portland, Ore., 2/14/54

Gromyko, Andrei A. (diplomat); Starye Gromyki, Russia (1909–1989)

Gropius, Walter (architect); Berlin (1883–1969)

Gropper, William (painter, illustrator); New York City (1897–1977)

Gross, Michael (actor); 6/21/47

Grosz, George (painter); Germany (1893–1959)

Grove, Andrew (Andras Grof) (computer industry executive); Budapest, Hungary, 9/2/36

Grünewald, Matthias (Mathis Gothart Neithart) (painter); Würzburg, Germany (c. 1470–1528)

Guest, Christopher (Christopher Haden-Guest) (actor, writer, director); New York City, 2/5/48

Guggenheim, Meyer (capitalist); Langnau, Switzerland (1828–1905)

Guillaume, Robert (Robert Williams) (actor); St. Louis, 11/30/27

Guinness, Sir Alec (actor); London (1914–2000)

Guitry, Sacha (Alexandre Guitry) (actor, film director); St. Petersburg, Russia (1885–1957)

Gumbel, Bryant Charles (TV newscaster); New Orleans, 9/29/48

Gunther, John (author); Chicago (1901–1970)

Gutenberg, Johann (printer); Mainz, Germany (c. 1397–1468)

Guthrie, Arlo (singer); New York City, 7/10/47

Guthrie, Woody (folk singer, composer); Okemah, Okla. (1912–1967)

Gwenn, Edmund (actor); London (1875–1959)

Gwynne, Fred (actor); New York City (1926–1993)

H

Habibie, Bacharuddin, Jusuf (president of Indonesia); Pare-Pare, Indonesia, 6/25/36

Hackett, Bobby (trumpeter); Providence, R.I. (1915–1976)

Hackett, Buddy (Leonard Hacker) (comedian, actor); Brooklyn, N.Y. (1924–2003)

Hackman, Gene (actor); San Bernardino, Calif., 1/30/31

Hagen, Uta (actress); Göttingen, Germany (1919–2004)

Haggard, Merle (songwriter, singer); Bakersfield, Calif., 4/6/37

Hagman, Larry (Larry Hageman) (actor); Weatherford, Tex., 9/21/31

Haig, Alexander Meigs, Jr. (ex-secretary of state, ex-general); Bala-Cynwyd, Pa., 12/2/24

Haile Selassie (Ras Tafari Makonnen) (ex-emperor); Ethiopia (1892–1975)

Hailey, Arthur (novelist); Luton, England, 4/5/20

Halberstam, David (journalist); New York City, 4/10/34

Hale, Alan (actor, director); Washington, D.C. (1892–1950)

Hale, Barbara (actress); DeKalb, Ill., 4/18/21

Hale, Edward Everett (clergyman, author); Boston (1822–1909)

Hale, Nathan (American Revolutionary officer); Coventry, Conn. (1755–1776)

Halevi, Judah (Jewish poet); Toledo, Spain (1085–1140)

Haley, Alex (writer); Ithaca, N.Y. (1921–1992)

Haley, Jack (actor); Boston (1899–1979)

Hall, Anthony Michael (Michael Anthony Thomas Charles Hall) (actor, singer); Boston, 4/14/68

Hall, Arsenio (comedian, talk-show host); Cleveland, 2/12/58

Hall, Donald (Andrew, Jr.) (poet); New Haven, Conn., 9/20/28

Hall, Huntz (actor); New York City (1919–1999)

Hall, Jerry (model, actress); Mesquite, Texas, 7/2/56

Hall, Monty (TV personality); Winnipeg, Canada, 8/25/23

Halley, Edmund (astronomer); London (1656–1742)

Hals, Frans (painter); Antwerp, Netherlands (c. 1580–1666)

Halsey, William Frederick, Jr. (naval officer); Elizabeth, N.J. (1882–1959)

Hamel, Veronica (actress); Philadelphia, 11/20/43

Hamill, Mark (actor); Oakland, 9/25/52

Hamilton, Alexander (statesman); Nevis, British West Indies (1755–1804)

Hamilton, Alice (physician, reformer); New York City (1869–1970)

Hamilton, Edith (scholar); Dresden, Germany (1867–1963)

Hamilton, George (actor); Memphis, Tenn., 8/12/39

Hamlin, Harry (actor); Pasadena, Calif., 10/30/51

Hamlisch, Marvin (composer, pianist); New York City, 6/2/44

Hammarskjöld, Dag (UN secretary-general); Jönköping, Sweden (1905–1961)

Hammerstein, Oscar, II (librettist, stage producer); New York City (1895–1960)

Hampton, Lionel (vibraharpist, band leader); Birmingham, Ala. (1913–2002)

Hamsun, Knut (Knut Pedersen) (novelist); Lom, Norway (1859–1952)

Hancock, Herbie (jazz musician); Chicago, 4/12/40

Hancock, John (statesman); Braintree, Mass. (1737–1793)

Hand, Learned (jurist); Albany, N.Y. (1872–1961)

Handel, George Frideric (Georg Friedrich Händel) (composer); Halle, Germany (1685–1759)

Handy, William Christopher (blues composer); Florence, Ala. (1873–1958)

Hanks, Tom (actor, director, writer); Concord, Calif., 7/9/56

Hannah, Daryl (actress); Chicago, 12/19/60

Hannibal (Carthaginian general); North Africa (247–182 B.C.)

Hansberry, Lorraine (playwright); Chicago (1930–1965)

Hanson, Howard (conductor); Wahoo, Neb. (1896–1981)

Harburg, E. Y. "Yip" (songwriter); New York City (1896–1981)

Harden, Marcia Gay (actress); La Jolla, Calif., 8/14/59

Harding, Warren Gamaliel (29th U.S. president); Morrow County, Ohio (1865–1923)

Hardwicke, Sir Cedric (actor); Stourbridge, England (1893–1964)

Hardy, Oliver (comedian); Atlanta (1892–1957)

Hardy, Thomas (novelist); Dorsetshire, England (1840–1928)

Harkness, Edward S. (business executive); Cleveland (1874–1940)

Harlow, Jean (Harlean Carpenter) (actress); Kansas City, Mo. (1911–1937)

Harlow, Shalom (model, TV personality); Oshawa, Ontario, Canada, 12/5/73

Harmon, Mark (actor); Burbank, Calif., 9/2/51

Harnick, Sheldon (lyricist); Chicago, 4/30/24

Harper, Valerie (actress); Suffern, N.Y., 8/22/40

Harrell, Lynn (cellist); New York City, 1/30/44

Harrelson, Woody (actor); Midland, Tex., 7/23/61

Harriman, Pamela (ambassador); Farnborough, England (1920–1997)

Harriman, W. (William) Averell (ex-governor of New York); New York City (1891–1986)

Harrington, Pat, Jr. (actor, comedian); New York City, 8/13/29

Harris, Barbara (Sandra Markowitz) (actress); Evanston, Ill., 7/25/35

Harris, Ed (actor); Englewood, N.J., 11/28/50

Harris, Emmylou (singer); Birmingham, Ala., 4/2/47

Harris, Julie (actress); Grosse Pointe Park, Mich., 12/2/25

Harris, Phil (actor, band leader); Linton, Ind. (1906–1995)

Harris, Richard (actor); Limerick, Ireland (1930–2002)

Harris, Rosemary (actress); Ashby, England, 9/19/30

Harris, Roy (composer); Lincoln County, Okla. (1898–1979)

Harrison, Benjamin (23rd U.S. president); North Bend, Ohio (1833–1901)

Harrison, George (singer, songwriter); Liverpool, England (1943–2001)

Harrison, Gregory (actor); Avalon, Catalina Island, Calif., 5/31/50

Harrison, Sir Rex (Reginald Carey) (actor); Huyton, England (1908–1990)

Harrison, William Henry (9th U.S. president); Charles City County, Va. (1773–1841)

Harry, Deborah (Blondie) (musician); Miami, Fla., 7/1/45

Hart, Lorenz (lyricist); New York City (1895–1943)

Hart, Mary (Mary Johanna Harum) (host); Sioux Falls, S.D., 11/8/50

Hart, Melissa Joan (actress); Sayville, N.Y., 4/18/76

Hart, Moss (playwright); New York City (1904–1961)

Harte, Bret (Francis Brett Harte) (author); Albany, N.Y. (1836–1902)

Hartford, Huntington (George Huntington Hartford II) (A.&P. heir); New York City, 4/18/11

Hartford, John (singer, banjoist); New York City (1937–2001)

Hartley, Mariette (actress); New York City, 6/21/40

Hartman, David Downs (TV newscaster); Pawtucket, R.I., 5/19/35

Hartman, Phil (actor, comedian); Brantford, Ont., Canada (1948–1998)

Hartman Black, Lisa (actress); Houston, 6/1/56

Harvey, Laurence (Larushka Skikne) (actor); Joniskis, Lithuania (1928–1973)

Harvey, Polly Jean (PJ Harvey) (singer, songwriter); Yeovil, England, 10/9/69

Harvey, William (physician); Folkestone, England (1578–1657)

Hasselhoff, David (actor, producer); Baltimore, 7/17/52

Hatcher, Teri (actress); Sunnyvale, Calif., 12/8/64

Havel, Vaclav (political leader, dramatist, poet); Prague, 10/5/36

Havens, Richie (musician); Brooklyn, N.Y., 1/21/41

Hawke, Ethan (actor); Austin, Tex., 11/6/70
Hawking, Stephen (physicist, astronomer); Oxford, England, 1/8/42
Hawkins, Coleman (jazz musician); St. Joseph, Mo. **(1904–1969)**
Hawkins, Jack (actor); London **(1910–1973)**
Hawn, Goldie (actress, producer); Washington, D.C., 11/21/45
Haworth, Jill (actress); Sussex, England, 8/15/45
Hawthorne, Nathaniel (novelist); Salem, Mass. **(1804–1864)**
Hay, John Milton (statesman); Salem, Ind. **(1838–1905)**
Hayakawa, Sessue (actor); Honshu, Japan **(1890–1973)**
Hayden, Melissa (ballet dancer); Toronto, 4/25/23
Hayden, Sterling (Sterling Relyea Walter) (actor, writer); Montclair, N.J. **(1916–1986)**
Haydn, Franz Joseph (composer); Rohrau, Austria **(1732–1809)**
Hayek, Salma (actress); Coatzacoalcos, Mexico, 9/2/66
Hayes, Helen (Helen Hayes Brown) (actress); Washington, D.C. **(1900–1993)**
Hayes, Isaac (composer); Covington, Tenn., 8/20/42
Hayes, Peter Lind (comedian, singer); San Francisco **(1915–1998)**
Hayes, Rutherford Birchard (19th U.S. president); Delaware, Ohio **(1822–1893)**
Hayward, Leland (producer); Nebraska City, Neb. **(1902–1971)**
Hayward, Susan (Edythe Marrener) (actress); Brooklyn, N.Y. **(1918–1975)**
Hayworth, Rita (Margarita Cansino) (actress); New York City **(1918–1987)**
Head, Edith (costume designer); Los Angeles **(1907–1981)**
Heaney, Seamus (poet); Londonderry, Northern Ireland, 4/13/39
Hearst, Patricia (Campbell) (heiress); San Francisco, 2/20/54
Hearst, William Randolph (publisher); San Francisco **(1863–1951)**
Hearst, William Randolph, Jr. (publisher); New York City **(1908–1993)**
Heatherton, Joey (actress); Rockville Centre, N.Y., 9/14/44
Heche, Anne (actress); Aurora, Ohio, 5/25/69
Hecht, Ben (author); New York City **(1894–1964)**
Heckart, Eileen (actress); Columbus, Ohio **(1919–2001)**
Heflin, Van (Emmet Evan Heflin) (actor); Walters, Okla. **(1910–1971)**
Hefner, Hugh (publisher); Chicago, 4/9/26
Hegel, Georg Wilhelm Friedrich (philosopher); Stuttgart, Germany **(1770–1831)**
Heidegger, Martin (existentialist philosopher); Messkirch, Germany **(1889–1976)**
Heifetz, Jascha (concert violinist); Vilna, Russia **(1901–1987)**
Heine, Heinrich (Harry) (poet); Düsseldorf, Germany **(1797–1856)**
Heinemann, Gustav (ex-president of Germany); Schweim, Germany **(1899–1976)**
Heisenberg, Werner Karl (physicist); Würzburg, Germany **(1901–1976)**
Heller, Joseph (novelist); Brooklyn, N.Y. **(1923–1999)**
Hellman, Lillian (playwright); New Orleans **(1905–1984)**
Helmond, Katherine (actress); Galveston, Tex., 7/5/34
Helms, Jesse (politician); Monroe, N.C., 10/18/21
Helmsley, Harry Brakmann (business executive); New York City **(1909–1997)**
Hemingway, Ernest Miller (novelist); Oak Park, Ill. **(1899–1961)**
Hemingway, Margaux (actress); Portland, Ore. **(1955–1996)**
Hemmings, David (actor); Guilford, England, 11/2/41
Henderson, Florence (actress); Dale, Ind., 2/14/34
Henderson, Skitch (Lyle Russell Cedric) (conductor, pianist); Birmingham, England?, 1/27/18
Hendrix, Jimi (James Marshall Hendrix) (guitarist); Seattle **(1942–1970)**
Henley, Beth (playwright-actress); Jackson, Miss., 5/8/52
Henley, Don (musician); Linden, Tex., 7/22/47
Henner, Marilu (actress); Chicago, 4/6/52
Henning, Doug (magician, author); Winnipeg, Canada **(1947–2000)**
Henri, Robert (painter); Cincinnati **(1865–1926)**
Henriksen, Lance (actor, screenwriter); New York City, 5/4/40
Henry VIII (king of England); Greenwich, England **(1491–1547)**
Henry, O. (William Sydney Porter) (story writer); Greensboro, N.C. **(1862–1910)**
Henry, Patrick (statesman); Hanover County, Va. **(1736–1799)**
Henson, Jim (puppeteer); Greenville, Miss. **(1936–1990)**
Hepburn, Audrey (actress); Brussels **(1929–1993)**
Hepburn, Katharine (actress); Hartford, Conn. **(1907–2003)**
Hepplewhite, George (furniture designer); England **(?–1786)**
Hepworth, Barbara (sculptor); Wakefield, England **(1903–1975)**
Herbert, George (poet); Montgomery Castle, Wales **(1593–1633)**
Herbert, Victor (composer); Dublin **(1859–1924)**
Herblock (Herbert L. Block) (political cartoonist); Chicago **(1909–2001)**
Herman, Pee-wee (Paul Rubenfeld) (comedian); Peekskill, N.Y., 8/27/52

Herman, Woody (Woodrow Charles Herman) (band leader); Milwaukee **(1913–1987)**
Herod (called Herod the Great) (king of Judea) **(73–4 B.C.)**
Herodotus (historian); Halicarnassus, Asia Minor (Turkey) **(c. 484–425 B.C.)**
Herrick, Robert (poet); London **(1591–1674)**
Herschbach, Dudley Robert (chemist, Nobel laureate); San Jose, Calif., 6/18/32
Herschel, William (Frederich Wilhelm Herschel) (astronomer); Hannover, Germany **(1738–1822)**
Hershey, Barbara (Barbara Herzstein) (actress); Hollywood, Calif., 2/5/48
Herzog, Chaim (Israeli statesman); Belfast, Northern Ireland **(1918–1997)**
Hesburgh, Theodore M. (educator); Syracuse, N.Y., 5/25/17
Hesseman, Howard (actor); Salem, Ore., 2/27/40
Heston, Charlton (actor); Evanston, Ill., 10/4/24
Heyerdahl, Thor (ethnologist, explorer); Larvik, Norway **(1914–2002)**
Hill, Anita (lawyer, professor); Lone Tree, Okla., 7/30/56
Hill, Benny (comedian); Southampton, England **(1925–1992)**
Hill, Lauryn (actress, musician); South Orange, N.J., 5/25/75
Hillary, Sir Edmund (mountain climber); New Zealand, 7/20/19
Hiller, Wendy (actress); Bramhall, England **(1912–2003)**
Hillerman, John (actor); Denison, Tex., 12/20/32
Hilton, Conrad (hotelier); San Antonio, N.M. **(1887–1979)**
Hindemith, Paul (composer); Hanau, Germany **(1895–1963)**
Hindenburg, Paul von (Paul Ludwig Hans Anton von Hindenburg und Beneckendorff) (German field marshal, president); Poznan, Poland **(1847–1934)**
Hines, Earl "Fatha" (jazz pianist); Duquesne, Pa. **(1905–1983)**
Hines, Gregory (dancer, actor); New York City **(1946–2003)**
Hines, Jerome (Jerome Heinz) (basso); Los Angeles **(1921–2003)**
Hippocrates (physician); Cos, Greece **(c. 460–c. 377 B.C.)**
Hirohito (Emperor of Japan); Tokyo **(1901–1989)**
Hiroshige, Ando (painter); Edo, Tokyo **(1797–1858)**
Hirsch, Judd (actor); New York City, 3/15/35
Hirschfeld, Al (Albert) (cartoonist); St. Louis **(1903–2003)**
Hirschhorn, Joseph Herman (financier, speculator, art collector); Mitau, Latvia **(1899–1981)**
Hirt, Al (trumpeter); New Orleans **(1922–1999)**
Hiss, Alger (public official); Baltimore **(1904–1996)**
Hitchcock, Alfred J. (film director); London **(1899–1980)**
Hitler, Adolf (German dictator); Braunau, Austria **(1889–1945)**
Hobbes, Thomas (philosopher); Westport, England **(1588–1679)**
Hobson, Laura Z. (Laura K. Zametkin) (novelist); New York City **(1900–1986)**
Ho Chi Minh (Nguyen That Tranh) (Vietnamese nationalist leader); Kim Lien, Vietnam **(1890–1969)**
Hockney, David (artist); Bradford, England, 7/9/37
Hodgkin, Dorothy Mary Crowfoot (chemist, Nobel laureate); Cairo, Egypt **(1910–1994)**
Hoffa, "Jimmy" James R(iddle) (labor leader); Brazil, Ind. **(1913–1975?; presumed murdered.)**
Hoffman, Dustin (actor, director); Los Angeles, 8/8/37
Hoffman, Phillip Seymour (actor); Fairport, N.Y., 1968
Hofmann, Hans (painter); Germany **(1880–1966)**
Hoffmann, Roald (chemist, Nobel laureate); Zloczow, Poland, 7/18/37
Hofstadter, Richard (historian); Buffalo, N.Y. **(1916–1970)**
Hogan, Paul (actor); Lightning Ridge, N.S.W., Australia, 10/8/39
Hogarth, William (painter, engraver); London **(1697–1764)**
Hokusai, Katsushika (artist); Yedo, Japan **(1760–1849)**
Holbein, Hans (the Elder) (painter); Augsburg, Germany **(c. 1465–1524)**
Holbein, Hans (the Younger) (painter); Augsburg, Germany **(c. 1497–1543)**
Holbrook, Hal (actor); Cleveland, 2/17/25
Holden, William (William Franklin Beedle, Jr.) (actor); O'Fallon, Ill. **(1918–1981)**
Holder, Geoffrey (dancer); Port-of-Spain, Trinidad, 8/1/30
Holiday, Billie (Eleanora Fagan) (jazz-blues singer); Baltimore **(1915–1959)**
Holliman, Earl (Henry Earl Holliman) (actor); Delhi, La., 9/11/28
Holly, Buddy (singer); Lubbock, Tex. **(1936–1959)**
Holly, Lauren (actress); Geneva, N.Y., 10/28/63
Holm, Celeste (actress); New York City, 4/29/19
Holmes, Katie (actress); Toledo, Ohio, 12/18/78
Holmes, Oliver Wendell (jurist); Boston **(1841–1935)**
Home, Lord (Alexander Frederick Douglas-Home) (diplomat); London **(7/2/1903–10/9/1995)**
Homer, Winslow (painter); Boston **(1836–1910)**
Homer (Greek poet) fl. 850 B.C.

Honegger, Arthur (composer); Le Havre, France **(1892–1955)**
Hook, Sidney (philosopher); New York City **(1902–1989)**
Hooker, John Lee (blues guitarist, singer, songwriter); Clarksdale, Miss. **(1917–2001)**
Hoover, Herbert Clark (31st U.S. president); West Branch, Iowa **(1874–1964)**
Hoover, J. Edgar (FBI director); Washington, D.C. **(1895–1972)**
Hope, Bob (Leslie Townes Hope) (comedian); London **(1903–2003)**
Hopkins, Sir Anthony (actor); Port Talbot, Wales, 12/31/37
Hopkins, Gerald Manley (poet); Stratford, England **(1844–1899)**
Hopkins, Johns (financier); Anne Arundel County, Md. **(1795–1873)**
Hopper, Dennis (actor); Dodge City, Kans., 5/17/36
Hopper, Edward (painter); Nyack, N.Y. **(1882–1967)**
Horace (Quintus Horatius Flaccus) (poet); Venosa, Italy **(65– 8 B.C.)**
Horne, Lena (singer); Brooklyn, N.Y., 6/30/17
Horne, Marilyn (mezzo-soprano); Bradford, Pa., 1/16/34
Horowitz, Vladimir (pianist); Kiev, Ukraine **(1903–1989)**
Horsley, Lee (actor); Muleshoe, Tex., 5/15/55
Horton, Edward Everett (comedian); Brooklyn, N.Y. **(1887–1970)**
Hoskins, Bob (actor); Bury St. Edmunds, England, 10/26/42
Houdini, Harry (Ehrich Weiss) (magician); Budapest, Hungary **(1874–1926)**
Houseman, John (Jacques Haussmann) (producer, director, actor); Bucharest **(1902–1988)**
Housman, A(lfred) E(dward) (poet); Fockburg, England **(1859– 1936)**
Houston, Charles Hamilton (civil rights lawyer); Washington, D.C. **(1895–1950)**
Houston, Samuel (political leader); Rockbridge County, Va. **(1793– 1863)**
Houston, Whitney (singer); Newark, N.J., 8/9/63
Howard, Ken (actor); El Centro, Calif., 3/28/44
Howard, Leslie (Leslie Stainer) (actor); London **(1893–1943)**
Howard, Ron (actor, producer, director); Duncan, Okla., 3/1/54
Howard, Trevor (actor); Kent, England **(1916–1988)**
Howe, Elias (inventor); Spencer, Mass. **(1819–1867)**
Howe, Irving (literary critic); New York City **(1920–1993)**
Howe, Julia Ward (poet, reformer); New York City **(1819–1910)**
Hudson, Henry (English navigator); **(fl. 1607–1611)**
Hudson, Rock (born Roy Scherer, Jr.; took Roy Fitzgerald as legal name) (actor); Winnetka, Ill. **(1925–1985)**
Huggins, Nathan Irvin (historian); Chicago **(1927–1989)**
Hughes, Charles Evans (jurist); Glens Falls, N.Y. **(1862–1948)**
Hughes, Howard (industrialist, film producer); Houston **(1905–1976)**
Hughes, Langston (poet); Joplin, Mo. **(1902–1967)**
Hughes, Ted (poet); Mytholmroyd, England **(1930–1998)**
Hugo, Victor Marie (author); Besançon, France **(1802–1885)**
Hulce, Tom (actor); Detroit, 12/6/53
Hume, David (philosopher); Edinburgh, Scotland **(1711–1776)**
Hume, Kirsty (model); Glasgow, Scotland, 9/4/76
Humperdinck, Engelbert (composer); Siegburg, Germany **(1854– 1921)**
Humperdinck, Engelbert (Arnold Dorsey) (singer); Madras, India, 5/2/36
Hunt, Helen (actress); Los Angeles, 6/15/63
Hunt, Linda (actress); Morristown, N.J., 4/2/45
Hunter, Holly (actress); Atlanta, 3/20/58
Hunter, Kim (Janet Cole) (actress); Detroit **(1922–2002)**
Hunter, Tab (Arthur Andrew Gelien) (actor); New York City, 7/11/31
Hunter-Gault, Charlayne (activist, broadcast journalist); Due West, S.C., 2/27/42
Huntley, Chet (TV newscaster); Cardwell, Mont. **(1911–1974)**
Hurley, Elizabeth (actress, model); Backingstoke, England, 6/10/65
Hurok, Sol (Solomon Hurok) (impresario); Pogar, Russia **(1884– 1974)**
Hurst, Fannie (novelist); Hamilton, Ohio **(1889–1968)**
Hurston, Zora Neale (author); Eatonville, Fla. **(1901–1960)**
Hurt, John (actor); Shirebrook, England, 1/22/40
Hurt, William (actor); Washington, D.C., 3/20/50
Hus, Jan (Bohemian religious reformer); Husinetz, nr. Budweis, Czech Republic **(c. 1369–1415)**
Husing, Ted (sportscaster); New York City **(1901–1962)**
Hussein I (king); Jordan **(1935–1999)**
Hussein, Saddam (al-Tikriti) (Iraqi president); Tikrit, Iraq, 4/28/37
Huston, Anjelica (actress); Los Angeles, 7/8/51
Huston, John (actor, director, writer); Nevada, Mo. **(1906–1987)**
Huston, Walter (Walter Houghston) (actor); Toronto **(1884–1950)**
Hutchins, Robert M. (educator); Brooklyn, N.Y. **(1899–1977)**
Hutton, Betty (Betty Thornburg) (actress); Battle Creek, Mich., 2/26/21
Hutton, Lauren (actress, model); Charleston, S.C., 11/17/43
Hutton, Timothy (actor); Los Angeles, 8/16/60

Huxley, Aldous (author); Godalming, England **(1894–1963)**
Huxley, Sir Julian S. (biologist, author); London **(1887–1975)**
Huxley, Thomas Henry (biologist); Ealing, England **(1825–1895)**
Hynde, Chrissie (singer); Akron, Ohio, 9/7/51

I

Iacocca, Lee (Lido Anthony) (business executive); Allentown, Pa., 10/15/24
Ian, Janis (singer); New York City, 5/7/51
Ibsen, Henrik (dramatist); Skien, Norway **(1828–1906)**
Ice Cube (O'Shea Jackson) (musician, actor); Los Angeles, 6/15/69
Ice-T (Tracy Morrow) (rap musician, actor); Newark, N.J., 2/16/68
Inge, William (playwright); Independence, Kans. **(1913–1973)**
Ingres, Jean Auguste Dominique (painter); Montauban, France **(1780–1867)**
Inness, George (painter); nr. Newburgh, N.Y. **(1825–1894)**
Ionesco, Eugene (playwright); Slatina, Romania **(1912–1994)**
Ireland, Jill (actress); London **(1936–1990)**
Ireland, Kathy (model, actress); Glendale, Calif., 3/8/63
Ireland, Patricia (feminist, social activist); Oak Park, Ill., 10/19/45
Irons, Jeremy (actor); Cowes, Isle of Wight, England, 9/19/48
Irving, Amy (actress); Palo Alto, Calif., 9/10/53
Irving, John (Winslow) (writer); Exeter, N.H., 3/2/42
Irving, Washington (author); New York City **(1783–1859)**
Isaak, Chris (musician, actor); Stockton, Calif., 6/26/56
Isherwood, Christopher (novelist, playwright); nr. Dilsey and High Lane, England **(1904–1986)**
Iturbi, José (concert pianist); Valencia, Spain **(1895–1980)**
Ives, Burl (Icle Ivanhoe) (singer); Hunt, Ill. **(1909–1995)**
Ives, Charles E(dward) (composer); Danbury, Conn. **(1874–1954)**
Ivins, Molly (journalist); Monterey, Calif., 8/30/44
Ivory, James (director, producer); Berkeley, Calif., 6/7/28

J

Jackson, Andrew (7th U.S. president); Waxhaw, S.C. **(1767–1845)**
Jackson, Anne (actress); Millvale, Pa., 9/3/26
Jackson, Glenda (actress); Cheshire, England, 5/9/36
Jackson, Janet (singer); Gary, Ind., 5/16/66
Jackson, Rev. Jesse (civil rights leader); Greenville, S.C., 10/8/41
Jackson, Kate (actress); Birmingham, Ala., 10/29/49
Jackson, Mahalia (gospel singer); New Orleans **(1911–1972)**
Jackson, Maynard (mayor of Atlanta); Dallas **(1938–2003)**
Jackson, Michael (singer); Gary, Ind. 8/29/58
Jackson, Peter (director); Wellington, New Zealand, Oct. 31, 1961
Jackson, Samuel L. (actor); Washington, D.C., 12/21/48
Jackson, Thomas Jonathan ("Stonewall") (general); Clarksburg, Va. (now W. Va.) **(1824–1863)**
Jacobi, Derek (actor); Leytonstone, England, 10/22/38
Jacobs, Jane (urbanologist); Scranton, Pa., 5/1/16
Jagger, Mick (Michael Phillip Jagger) (singer); Dartford, England, 7/26/43
James, Harry (trumpeter); Albany, Ga. **(1916–1983)**
James, Henry (novelist); New York City **(1843–1916)**
James, Jesse Woodson (outlaw); Clay County, Mo. **(1847–1882)**
James, William (psychologist); New York City **(1842–1910)**
Jameson, (Margaret) Storm (novelist); Whitby, England **(1897– 1986)**
Janis, Byron (pianist); McKeesport, Pa., 3/24/28
Janis, Conrad (actor, musician); New York City, 2/11/28
Janssen, David (David Meyer) (actor); Naponee, Neb. **(1930–1980)**
Jaworkski, Leon (Watergate special prosecutor); Waco, Tex. **(1905–1982)**
Jay, John (statesman, jurist); New York City **(1745–1829)**
Jeanmaire, Renée (dancer); Paris, 4/29/24
Jefferson, Thomas (3rd U.S. president); Shadwell, Va. **(1743– 1826)**
Jemison, Mae C. (astronaut, physician); Decatur, Ala., 10/17/56
Jenner, Edward (physician); Berkeley, England **(1749–1823)**
Jennings, Peter (news anchor); Toronto, 7/29/38
Jennings, Waylon (singer); Littlefield, Tex. **(1937–2002)**
Jessel, George (entertainer); New York City **(1898–1981)**
Jessup, Philip C. (diplomat); New York City **(1897–1986)**
Jillian, Ann (Ann Jura Nauseda) (actress); Cambridge, Mass., 1/29/51
Joan of Arc (Jeanne d'Arc) (saint, patriot); Domremy-la-Pucelle, France **(1412–1431)**
Jobs, Steven Paul (computer industry pioneer); San Francisco, 1955
Joel, Billy (singer); New York City, 5/9/49
Joffrey, Robert (Abdullah Jaffa Bey Khan) (choreographer); Seattle **(1930–1988)**

John, Elton (Reginald Kenneth Dwight) (singer, pianist); Pinner, England, 3/25/47

Johns, Jasper (painter, sculptor); Augusta, Ga., 5/15/30

Johnson, Andrew (17th U.S. president); Raleigh, N.C. **(1808–1875)**

Johnson, Don (actor); Flatt Creek, Mo., 12/15/49

Johnson, James Weldon (author, educator); Jacksonville, Fla. **(1871–1938)**

Johnson, Lyndon Baines (36th U.S. president); Stonewall, Tex. **(1908–1973)**

Johnson, Philip Cortelyou (architect); Cleveland, 7/8/06

Johnson, Samuel (lexicographer, author); Lichfield, England **(1709–1784)**

Johnson, Van (actor); Newport, R.I., 8/20/16

Johnson, Virginia (human sexuality expert); Springfield, Mo., 2/11/25

Jolie, Angelina (actress); Los Angeles, 6/5/75

Joliot-Curie, Frédéric (chemist, Nobel laureate); Paris **(1900–1958)**

Joliot-Curie, Irène (Irène Curie) (chemist, Nobel laureate); France **(1897–1956)**

Jolliet, Louis (Louis Joliet) (explorer); Beaupré, Canada **(1645–1700)**

Jolson, Al (Asa Yoelson) (actor, singer); St. Petersburg, Russia **(1886–1950)**

Jones, Dean (actor); Morgan County, Ala., 1/25/35

Jones, George (singer); Saratoga, Tex., 9/12/31

Jones, Inigo (architect); London **(1573–1652)**

Jones, James (novelist); Robinson, Ill. **(1921–1977)**

Jones, James Earl (actor); Arkabutla, Miss., 1/17/31

Jones, Jennifer (Phylis Isley) (actress); Tulsa, Okla., 3/2/19

Jones, John Paul (John Paul) (naval officer); Scotland **(1747–1792)**

Jones, Quincy (composer); Chicago, 3/14/33

Jones, Shirley (singer, actress); Smithtown, Pa., 3/31/34

Jones, Spike (host, orchestra leader); Long Beach, Calif. **(1911–1965)**

Jones, Tom (Thomas Jones Woodward) (singer); Pontypridd, Wales, 6/7/40

Jones, Tommy Lee (actor); San Saba, Tex., 9/15/46

Jong, Erica (writer); New York City, 3/26/42

Jonson, Ben (Benjamin Jonson) (poet, dramatist); Westminster, England **(1572–1637)**

Joplin, Janis (singer); Port Arthur, Tex. **(1943–1970)**

Joplin, Scott (ragtime pianist, composer); Texarkansas, Tex. **(1868–1917)**

Jordan, Barbara (U.S. representative); Houston **(1936–1996)**

Jordan, Neil (film director, screenwriter); Sligo, Ireland, 2/25/50

Joseph (Chief Joseph) (Nez Perce Indian leader); eastern Ore. **(1841–1904)**

Josquin des Prés (usually known as Josquin) (composer); Condesur-L'Escaut?, Hainaut, Belgium **(c. 1445–1521)**

Jovovich, Milla (actress, model, singer); Kiev, Ukraine, 12/19/75

Joyce, James (novelist); Dublin **(1882–1941)**

Juárez, Benito Pablo (statesman); Guelatao, Mexico **(1806–1872)**

Judd, Ashley (actress); Los Angeles, 4/19/68

Julia, Raul (Raúl Rafael Carlos Julia y Arcelay) (actor); San Juan, P.R. **(1940–1994)**

Jung, Carl Gustav (psychoanalyst); Basel, Switzerland **(1875–1961)**

Jurado, Katy (Maria Christina Jurado Garcia) (actress); Guadalajara, Mexico **(1924–2002)**

K

Kabalevsky, Dmitri (composer); St. Petersburg, Russia **(1904–1987)**

Kafka, Franz (author); Prague **(1883–1924)**

Kádár, János (Communist Party leader); Hungary **(1912–1989)**

Kahn, Gus (songwriter); Coblenz, Germany **(1886–1941)**

Kahn, Louis I. (architect); Oesel Island, Estonia **(1901–1974)**

Kahn, Madeline (actress); Boston **(1942–1999)**

Kandinsky, Wassily (painter); Moscow **(1866–1944)**

Kanin, Garson (playwright); Rochester, N.Y. **(1912–1999)**

Kant, Immanuel (philosopher); Königsberg (Kaliningrad), Russia **(1724–1804)**

Kantor, MacKinlay (novelist); Webster City, Iowa **(1904–1977)**

Kaplan, Justin (writer, editor); New York City, 9/5/25

Karan, Donna (fashion designer); Forest Hills, N.Y., 10/2/48

Karloff, Boris (William Henry Pratt) (actor); London **(1887–1969)**

Kasdan, Lawrence (film director, writer, actor, producer); Miami, 1/14/49

Kasem, Casey (disc jockey); Detroit, 4/27/32

Kaufman, Andy (actor, comedian); New York City **(1949–1984)**

Kaufman, George S. (playwright); Pittsburgh **(1889–1961)**

Kavner, Julie (actress); Los Angeles, 9/7/51

Kaye, Danny (David Daniel Kominski) (comedian); Brooklyn, N.Y. **(1913–1987)**

Kaye, Sammy (band leader); Cleveland **(1910–1987)**

Kazan, Elia (director); Constantinople, Turkey **(9/7/09–Sept. 28, 2003)**

Kazan, Lainie (Levine) (singer); New York City, 5/15/40

Kazantzakis, Nikos (writer); Herakleion, Crete **(1883–1957)**

Keach, Stacy (actor); Savannah, Ga., 6/2/41

Keaton, Buster (Joseph Frank Keaton) (comedian); Piqua, Kans. **(1896–1966)**

Keaton, Diane (actress); Los Angeles, 1/5/46

Keaton, Michael (Michael Douglas) (actor); Robinson Township, Pa., 9/9/51

Keats, John (poet); London **(1795–1821)**

Keel, Howard (Harold Clifford Leek) (singer, actor); Gillespie, Ill., 4/13/19

Keeler, Ruby (Ethel Hilde Keeler) (actress, dancer); Halifax, N.S., Canada **(1910–1993)**

Keener, Catherine (actress); Miami, Fla., 1959(?)

Kefauver, Estes (legislator); Madisonville, Tenn **(1903–1963)**

Keitel, Harvey (actor); Brooklyn, N.Y., 5/13/39

Keith, Brian (Robert Brian Keith, Jr.) (actor); Bayonne, N.J. **(1921–1997)**

Keller, Helen Adams (author, educator); Tuscumbia, Ala. **(1880–1968)**

Kelley, DeForest (actor); Atlanta **(1920–1999)**

Kelly, Emmett (clown); Sedan, Kans. **(1898–1979)**

Kelly, Gene (dancer, actor); Pittsburgh **(1912–1996)**

Kelly, Grace (actress, Princess of Monaco); Philadelphia **(1929–1982)**

Kelly, R. (Robert Kelly) (singer, record producer, actor); Chicago, 1969

Kempis, Thomas à (mystic); Kempis, Prussia (Germany) **(1380–1471)**

Kendall, Henry W. (physicist, Nobel laureate); Boston **(1926–1999)**

Kennan, George F. (diplomat); Milwaukee, 2/16/04

Kennedy, Anthony (jurist); Sacramento, Calif., 7/23/36

Kennedy, Carolyn Bessette (socialite); White Plains, N.Y. **(1966–1999)**

Kennedy, George (actor); New York City, 2/18/25

Kennedy, John Fitzgerald (35th U.S. president); Brookline, Mass. **(1917–1963)**

Kennedy, John F., Jr. (publisher); Washington, D.C. **(1960–1999)**

Kennedy, Joseph P. (financier); Boston **(1888–1969)**

Kennedy, Robert Francis (legislator); Brookline, Mass. **(1925–1968)**

Kennedy, Rose Fitzgerald (president's mother); Boston **(1890–1995)**

Kent, Allegra (ballet dancer); Santa Monica, Calif., 8/11/38

Kent, Rockwell (painter); Tarrytown Heights, N.Y. **(1882–1971)**

Kenton, Stan (Stanley Newcomb) (jazz musician); Wichita, Kans. **(1912–1979)**

Kepler, Johannes (astronomer); Weil, Germany **(1571–1630)**

Kercheval, Ken (actor); Wolcottville, Ind., 7/15/35

Kerensky, Alexander Fedorovich (statesman); Simbirsk, Russia **(1881–1970)**

Kern, Jerome David (composer); New York City **(1885–1945)**

Kerns, Joanna (actress); San Francisco, 2/12/53

Kerouac, Jack (Jean-Louis Kerouac) (writer); Lowell, Mass. **(1922–1969)**

Kerr, Deborah (actress); Helensburgh, Scotland, 9/30/21

Kerry, John (U.S. senator); Denver, Colo., 12/11/43

Kettering, Charles F. (engineer, inventor); nr. Loudonville, Ohio **(1876–1958)**

Kevorkian, Jack (medical pathologist); Pontiac, Mich., 3/26/28

Key, Francis Scott (lawyer, author of national anthem); Frederick (Carroll) County, Md. **(1779–1843)**

Keyes, Frances Parkinson (novelist); Charlottesville, Va. **(1885–1970)**

Keynes, John Maynard (1st Baron of Tilton) (economist); Cambridge, England **(1883–1946)**

Khachaturian, Aram (composer); Tiflis, Russia **(1903–1978)**

Khomeini, Ayatollah Ruhollah (Islamic religious leader); Iran **(1900–1989)**

Khrushchev, Nikita S. (Soviet leader); Kalinovka, nr. Kursk, Ukraine **(1894–1971)**

Kidd, Michael (Milton Greenwald) (choreographer); Brooklyn, N.Y., 8/12/19

Kidd, William (called Captain Kidd) (pirate); Greenock, Scotland **(c. 1645–1701)**

Kidder, Margot (actress); Yellowknife, N.W.T., Canada, 10/17/48

Kidman, Nicole (actress); Honolulu, 6/20/67

Kiepura, Jan (tenor); Sosnowiec, Poland **(1902–1966)**

Kieran, John (writer); New York City **(1892–1981)**

Kierkegaard, Sören Aalys (philosopher); Copenhagen **(1813–1855)**

Kiesinger, Kurt Georg (diplomat); Ebingen, Germany **(1904–1988)**

Kiley, Richard (actor, singer); Chicago **(1922–1999)**

Kilmer, Alfred Joyce (poet); New Brunswick, N.J. **(1886–1918)**

Kilmer, Val (actor); Los Angeles,, 12/31/59

King, Alan (Irwin Alan Kniberg) (entertainer); Brooklyn, N.Y. **(1927–2004)**

King, B.B. (Riley King) (guitarist); Itta Bena, Miss., 9/16/25

King, Carole (singer, songwriter); Brooklyn, N.Y., 2/9/41

King, Coretta Scott (civil rights leader); Marion, Ala., 4/27/27

King, Larry (Lawrence Harvey Zeigler) (TV host); New York City, 11/19/33

King, Martin Luther, Jr. (civil rights leader); Atlanta **(1929–1968)**

King, Stephen (writer); Portland, Maine, 9/21/47

Kingsley, Ben (Krishna Bhanji) (actor); Snainton, England, 12/31/43

Kingsley, Sidney (Sidney Kirschner) (playwright); New York City **(1906–1995)**

Kingsolver, Barbara (writer); Annapolis, Md., 4/8/55

Kingston, Maxine Hong (novelist); Stockton, Calif., 10/27/40

Kinsey, Alfred Charles (human sexuality expert); Hoboken, N.J. **(1894–1956)**

Kinski, Nastassja (Nastassja Nakszynski) (actress); West Berlin, 1/24/61

Kipling, Rudyard (author); Bombay (Mumbai) **(1865–1936)**

Kipnis, Alexander (basso); Ukraine **(1891–1978)**

Kirby, George (comedian); Chicago **(1923–1995)**

Kirchner, Ernst Ludwig (painter); Aschaffenburg, Germany **(1880–1938)**

Kirk, Grayson (educator); Jeffersonville, Ohio **(1903–1997)**

Kirkland, Gelsey (ballet dancer); Bethlehem, Pa., 12/29/52

Kirkpatrick, Jeane Jordan (educator-public affairs); Duncan, Okla., 11/19/26

Kirkpatrick, Ralph (harpsichordist); Leominster, Mass. **(1911–1984)**

Kirstein, Lincoln (dance, theater executive); Rochester, N.Y. **(1907–1996)**

Kirsten, Dorothy (soprano); Montclair, N.J. **(1910–1992)**

Kissinger, Henry (Heinz Alfred Kissinger) (ex-U.S. secretary of state); Furth, Germany, 5/27/23

Kitt, Eartha (singer); North, S.C., 1/26/28

Klee, Paul (painter); Münchenbuchsee, nr. Bern, Switzerland **(1879–1940)**

Klein, Calvin (fashion designer); Bronx, N.Y., 11/19/42

Klein, Robert (comedian); New York City, 2/8/42

Kleist, Henrich von (poet); Frankfurt an der Oder, Germany **(1777–1811)**

Klemperer, Otto (conductor); Breslau, Poland **(1885–1973)**

Klemperer, Werner (actor); Cologne, Germany **(1920–2000)**

Klimt, Gustav (painter); Vienna **(1862–1918)**

Kline, Kevin (actor); St. Louis, 10/24/47

Klugman, Jack (actor); Philadelphia, 4/27/22

Knight, Gladys (singer); Atlanta, 5/28/44

Knight, John S. (publisher); Bluefield, W. Va. **(1894–1981)**

Knight, Ted (Tadeus Wladyslaw Konopka) (actor); Terryville, Conn. **(1923–1986)**

Knight, Wayne (actor); Cartersville, Ga., 8/7/55

Knopf, Alfred A. (publisher); New York City **(1892–1984)**

Knopfler, Mark (musician); Glasgow, Scotland, 8/12/49

Knotts, Don (actor); Morgantown, W. Va., 7/21/24

Knox, John (religious reformer); Haddington, East Lothian, Scotland **(1505–1572)**

Koch, Robert (physician); Klausthal, Germany **(1843–1910)**

Koenig, Walter (actor); Chicago, 9/14/36

Koestler, Arthur (novelist); Budapest **(1905–1983)**

Kokoschka, Oskar (painter); Póchlarn, Austria **(1886–1980)**

Kollwitz, Käthe (graphic artist, sculptor); Königsberg, Russia **(1867–1945)**

Koop, C. Everett (ex-surgeon general); Brooklyn, N.Y., 10/14/16

Kooper, Al (singer, pianist); Brooklyn, N.Y., 2/5/44

Kopell, Bernie (actor); New York City, 6/21/33

Koppel, Ted (broadcast journalist); Lancashire, England, 2/8/40

Korman, Harvey (actor); Chicago, 2/15/27

Kosciusko, Thaddeus (Tadeusz Andrzej Bonawentura Kosciuszko) (military officer and statesman) **(1746–1817)**

Kossuth, Lajos (patriot); Monok, Hungary **(1802–1894)**

Kostelanetz, André (orchestra conductor); St. Petersburg, Russia **(1901–1980)**

Kostunica, Vojislav (president of Yugoslavia); Belgrade, 3/24/44

Kosygin, Aleksei N. (premier); St. Petersburg, Russia **(1904–1980)**

Kotto, Yaphet (actor); New York City, 11/15/37

Koussevitzky, Serge (Sergei) Alexandrovitch (orchestra conductor); Vishni Volochek, Tver, Russia **(1874–1951)**

Kramer, Stanley E. (film producer, director); New York City **(1913–2001)**

Kraus, Lili (pianist); Budapest **(1905–1986)**

Kravitz, Lenny (musician); New York City, 5/26/64

Kreisler, Fritz (violinist, composer); Vienna **(1875–1962)**

Kresge, S. S. (merchant); Bald Mount, Pa. **(1867–1966)**

Krips, Josef (orchestra conductor); Vienna **(1902–1974)**

Kristofferson, Kris (singer); Brownsville, Tex., 6/22/36

Krupa, Gene (drummer); Chicago **(1909–1973)**

Krupp, Alfred (munitions magnate); Essen, Germany **(1812–1887)**

Kubelik, Rafael (conductor); Bychory, former Czechoslovakia **(1914–1996)**

Kublai Khan (Mongol conqueror) **(1216–1294)**

Kubrick, Stanley (film director, producer); New York City **(1928–1999)**

Kudrow, Lisa (actress); Encino, Calif., 7/30/63

Kuralt, Charles (TV journalist); Wilmington, N.C. **(1934–1997)**

Kurosawa, Akira (film director); Tokyo **(1910–1998)**

Kurtz, Efrem (conductor); St. Petersburg, Russia **(1900–1995)**

Kurtz, Swoosie (actress); Omaha, Neb., 9/6/44

L

LaBelle, Patti (singer, actress); Philadelphia, 5/24/44

Ladd, Cheryl (Cheryl Stoppelmoor) (actress); Huron, S.D., 7/12/51

Ladd, Diane (actress); Meridian, Miss., 11/29/42

Laden, Osama bin (terrorist); Riyadh, Saudi Arabia, c. 1957

Lafayette, Marquis de (Marie Joseph Paul Yves Roch Gilbert du Motier) (military officer); Auvergne, France **(1757–1834)**

Lafitte, Jean (pirate); Bayonne?, France **(1780–1826)**

La Follette, Robert Marin (politician); Primrose, Wis. **(1855–1925)**

La Fontaine, Jean de (poet); Château-Thierry, France **(1621–1695)**

La Guardia, Fiorello Henry (mayor of New York); New York City **(1882–1947)**

Lahti, Christine (actress, director); Birmingham, Mich., 4/4/50

Laine, Frankie (Frank Paul LoVecchio) (singer); Chicago, 3/30/13

Laird, Melvin (ex-secretary of defense); Omaha, Neb., 9/1/22

Lamarck, Chevalier de (Jean Baptiste Pierre Antoine de Monet) (naturalist); Bazantin, France **(1744–1829)**

Lamas, Lorenzo (actor); Los Angeles, 1/20/58

Lamb, Charles (Elia) (essayist); London **(1775–1834)**

L'Amour, Louis (author); Jamestown, N.D. **(1908–1988)**

Lancaster, Burt (actor); New York City **(1913–1994)**

Landau, Martin (actor); Brooklyn, N.Y., 6/20/31

Landers, Ann (Esther Pauline Friedman) (columnist); Sioux City, Iowa **(1918–2002)**

Landon, Michael (Eugene Maurice Orowitz) (actor, director, producer); Forest Hills, Queens, N.Y. **(1936–1991)**

Lane, Abbe (Abigail Francine Lassman) (singer); New York City, 1933

Lane, Burton (songwriter); New York City **(1912–1997)**

Lane, Nathan (Joseph Lane) (actor, singer); Jersey City, N.J., 2/3/56

Lang, Fritz (film director); Vienna **(1890–1976)**

Lange, Hope (actress); Redding Ridge, Conn. **(1933–2003)**

Lange, Jessica (actress); Cloquet, Minn., 4/20/49

Langella, Frank (actor); Bayonne, N.J., 1/1/40

Langmuir, Irving (chemist); Brooklyn, N.Y. **(1881–1957)**

Langtry, Lillie (Emily Le Breton) (actress); Island of Jersey **(1852–1929)**

Lansbury, Angela (actress, producer); London, 10/16/25

Lansing, Robert (Robert Howell Brown) (actor); San Diego, Calif. **(1928–1994)**

Lanza, Mario (Alfred Arnold Cocozza) (singer, actor); Philadelphia **(1921–1959)**

Lao-tse (Li Erh) (philosopher); Honan Province, China **(c. 604–531 B.C.)**

Lardner, Ring (Ringgold Wilmar Lardner) (story writer); Niles, Mich. **(1885–1933)**

La Rouchefoucauld, Francois duc de (author); Paris **(1613–1680)**

Larroquette, John (actor); New Orleans, 11/25/47

Larson, Gary (cartoonist); Tacoma, Wash., 8/14/50

La Salle, Eriq (actor); Hartford, Conn., 7/23/62

La Salle, Sieur de (Robert Cavelier) (explorer); Rouen, France **(1643–1687)**

Lasch, Christopher (historian, social critic); Omaha, Neb. **(1932–1994)**

La Tour, Georges de (painter); Vic-sur-Seille, France **(1593–1652)**

Lauer, Matt (TV host); New York City, 12/20/57

Laughton, Charles (actor); Scarborough, England **(1899–1962)**

Lauper, Cyndi (singer); New York City, 6/20/53

Laurel, Stan (Arthur Jefferson) (comedian); Ulverston, England **(1890–1965)**

Laurents, Arthur (playwright); New York City, 7/14/18

Laurie, Piper (Rosetta Jacobs) (actress); Detroit, 1/22/32

Lavin, Linda (actress); Portland, Maine, 10/15/37

Lavoisier, Antoine-Laurent (chemist); Paris **(1743–1794)**

Lawford, Peter (actor); London **(1923–1984)**

Lawless, Lucy (Lucy Ryan) (actress); Auckland, New Zealand, 3/29/68

Lawrence, David Herbert (novelist); Nottingham, England **(1885–1930)**

Lawrence, Jacob (painter); Atlantic City, N.J. **(1917–2000)**

Lawrence, Martin (actor); Frankfurt, Germany, 4/16/65

Lawrence, Sharon (actress); Charlotte, N.C., 6/29/62

Lawrence, Steve (Sidney Leibowitz) (singer); Brooklyn, N.Y., 7/8/35

Lawrence of Arabia (Thomas Edward Lawrence, later changed to Shaw) (author, soldier); Tremadoc, Wales **(1888–1935)**

Lawrence, Vicki (actress); Inglewood, Calif., 3/26/49

Leach, Penelope (Balchin) (child psychologist, writer); London, 11/19/37

Leach, Robin (host, producer); London, 8/29/41

Leachman, Cloris (actress); Des Moines, Iowa, 4/30/26

Leadbelly, (Huddie Ledbetter) (blues singer, guitarist); Mooringsport, La. **(1885–1949)**

Leakey, Louis Seymour Bazett (anthropologist); Kabete, Kenya **(1903–1972)**

Leakey, Mary (anthropologist); London **(1913–1996)**

Leakey, Richard (paleoanthropologist, wildlife conservationist); Kenya, 12/19/44

Lean, David (film director); Croydon, England **(1908–1991)**

Lear, Edward (nonsense poet); London **(1812–1888)**

Lear, Evelyn (Shulman) (soprano); Brooklyn, N.Y., 1/8/26

Lear, Norman (TV producer); New Haven, Conn., 7/27/22

Learned, Michael (actress); Washington, D.C., 4/9/39

Leary, Denis (actor, screenwriter, film director); Worcester, Mass., 8/18/57

Leary, Timothy (psychologist, LSD advocate); Springfield, Mass. **(1920–1996)**

Le Blanc, Matt (actor); Newton, Mass., 7/25/67

le Carré, John (David John Moore Cornwell) (novelist); Poole, England, 10/19/31

Le Corbusier (Charles Edouard Jeanneret) (architect); La Chaux-de-Fonds, Switzerland **(1887–1965)**

Lee, Ang (film director); Pingtung, Taiwan, 10/23/54

Lee, Christopher (actor); London, 5/27/22

Lee, Manfred B. (pseudonym Ellery Queen) (novelist); Brooklyn, N.Y. **(1905–1971)**

Lee, Peggy (Norma Engstrom) (singer); Jamestown, N.D. **(1920–2002)**

Lee, Robert E(dward) (Confederate general); Stratford Estate, Va. **(1807–1870)**

Lee, Spike (Shelton Jackson Lee) (actor, director, writer, producer); Atlanta, 3/20/57

Leeuwenhoek, Anton van (zoologist); Delft, Netherlands **(1632–1723)**

Lehár, Franz (composer); Komárom, Hungary **(1870–1948)**

Lehman, Herbert H. (governor, senator); New York City **(1878–1963)**

Lehmann, Lotte (soprano); Perleberg, Germany **(1888–1976)**

Lehrer, Jim (TV newscaster); Wichita, Kans., 5/19/34

Leibniz, Gottfried W. von (scientist); Leipzig, Germany **(1646–1716)**

Leibovitz, Annie (photographer); Westbury, Conn., 10/2/49

Leigh, Janet (Jeanette Helen Morrison) (actress); Merced, Calif., 7/6/27

Leigh, Jennifer Jason (Jennifer Morrow) (actress); Los Angeles, 2/5/62

Leigh, Mike (film director, screenwriter); Manchester, England, 2/20/43

Leigh, Vivien (Vivian Mary Hartley) (actress); Darjeeling, India **(1913–1967)**

Leinsdorf, Erich (conductor); Vienna **(1912–1993)**

Lemmon, Jack (actor); Boston **(1925–2001)**

Lenin, Vladimir (Vladimir Ilich Ulyanov) (Soviet leader); Simbirsk, Russia **(1870–1924)**

Lennon, John (singer, songwriter); Liverpool, England **(1940–1980)**

Leno, Jay (comedian, TV host); New Rochelle, N.Y., 4/28/50

Leonard, Sheldon (Sheldon Leonard Bershad) (actor, producer); New York City **(1907–1997)**

Leonardo da Vinci, (painter, scientist); Vinci, Tuscany, Italy **(1452–1519)**

Leoni, Téa (actress); New York City, 2/25/66

Lerner, Alan Jay (lyricist); New York City **(1918–1986)**

Lerner, Max (columnist); Minsk, Russia **(1902–1992)**

Lessing, Doris (novelist); Kermanshah, Iran, 10/22/19

Leto, Jared (actor); Bossier City, La., 12/26/71

Letterman, David (TV host, producer); Indianapolis, 4/12/47

Levant, Oscar (pianist); Pittsburgh **(1906–1972)**

Levenson, Sam (humorist); New York City **(1911–1980)**

Levi, Carlo (novelist); Turin, Italy **(1902–1975)**

Levine, James (artistic director, Metropolitan Opera); Cincinnati, 6/23/43

Levine, Joseph E. (film producer); Boston **(1905–1987)**

Levinson, Barry (screenwriter, director, producer, actor); Baltimore, 4/6/42

Lewis, C(live) S(taples) (author); Belfast, Northern Ireland **(1898–1963)**

Lewis, Gilbert Newton (chemist, Nobel laureate); Weymouth, Mass. **(1875–1946)**

Lewis, Jerry (Joseph Levitch) (comedian, film director); Newark, N.J., 3/16/26

Lewis, Jerry Lee (singer); Ferriday, La., 9/29/35

Lewis, John Llewellyn (labor leader); Lucas, Iowa **(1880–1969)**

Lewis, Juliette (actress); Los Angeles, 12/21/73

Lewis, Meriwether (explorer); Albemarle Co., Va. **(1774–1809)**

Lewis, (Percy) Wyndham (artist, writer); Bay of Fundy, Maine (at sea) **(1884–1957)**

Lewis, Shari (Shari Hurwitz) (puppeteer); New York City **(1934–1998)**

Lewis, Sinclair (novelist); Sauk Centre, Minn. **(1885–1951)**

Ley, Willy (science writer); Berlin **(1906–1969)**

Liberace (Wladziu Liberace) (pianist); West Allis, Wis. **(1919–1987)**

Lichtenstein, Roy (painter); New York City **(1923–1997)**

Lie, Trygve Halvdan (first U.N. secretary-general); Oslo **(1896–1968)**

Light, Judith (actress); Trenton, N.J., 2/9/49

Lightfoot, Gordon (singer, songwriter); Orillia, Ont., Canada, 11/17/38

Limbaugh, Rush (political commentator); Cape Girardeau, Mo., 1/12/51

Lin, Maya (architect, sculptor); Athens, Ohio, 10/5/59

Lin Yutang (author); Changchow, China **(1895–1976)**

Lincoln, Abraham (16th U.S. president); Hardin (Larue) County, Ky. **(1809–1865)**

Lind, Jenny (Johanna Maria Lind) (soprano); Stockholm **(1820–1887)**

Lindbergh, Anne Morrow (author); Englewood, N.J. **(1906–2001)**

Lindbergh, Charles A. (aviator); Detroit **(1902–1974)**

Linden, Hal (Harold Lipshitz) (actor); New York City, 3/20/31

Lindsay, Howard (playwright); Waterford, N.Y. **(1889–1968)**

Linkletter, Art (radio-TV personality); Moose Jaw, Sask., Canada, 7/17/12

Linnaeus, Carolus (Carl von Linné) (botanist); Råshult, Sweden **(1707–1778)**

Linney, Laura (actress); New York City, 2/5/64

Liotta, Ray (actor); Union, N.J., 12/18/55

Lipchitz, Jacques (sculptor); Druskieniki, Latvia **(1891–1973)**

Lippi, Fra Filippo (painter); Florence **(1406–1469)**

Lippmann, Walter (columnist, author, political analyst); New York City **(1889–1974)**

Lister, Joseph (1st Baron of Lyme Regis) (surgeon); Upton, England **(1827–1912)**

Liszt, Franz (composer, pianist); Raiding, Hungary **(1811–1886)**

Lithgow, John (actor); Rochester, N.Y., 6/6/45

Little, Rich (impressionist); Ottawa, Ont., Canada, 11/26/38

Livingstone, David (missionary, explorer); Lanarkshire, Scotland **(1813–1873)**

L. L. Cool J (James Todd Smith) (rap artist); New York City, 1/14/68

Llewellyn, Richard (novelist); St. David's, Wales **(1906–1983)**

Lloyd Webber, Andrew (composer); London, 3/22/48

Lloyd George, David (Earl of Dwyfor) (statesman); Manchester, England **(1863–1945)**

Lloyd, Jake (actor); Fort Collins, Colo., 3/5/89

Locke, Alain L. (philosopher); Philadelphia **(1886–1954)**

Locke, John (philosopher); Somersetshire, England **(1632–1704)**

Lockhart, June (actress); New York City, 6/25/25

Locklear, Heather (actress); Los Angeles, 9/25/61

Lodge, Henry Cabot (legislator); Boston **(1850–1924)**

Lodge, Henry Cabot, Jr. (diplomat); Nahant, Mass. **(1902–1985)**

Loesser, Frank (composer); New York City **(1910–1969)**

Loewe, Frederick (composer); Vienna **(1901–1988)**

Logan, Joshua (director, producer); Texarkana, Tex. **(1908–1988)**

Lollobrigida, Gina (Luigina Lollobrigida) (actress); Subiaco, Italy, 7/4/27

Lombard, Carole (Jane Alice Peters) (actress); Ft. Wayne, Ind. **(1908–1942)**

Lombardo, Guy (band leader); London, Ont., Canada **(1902–1977)**

London, George (baritone); Montreal **(1920–1985)**

London, Jack (John Griffith London) (novelist); San Francisco **(1876–1916)**

Long, Huey Pierce (politician); Winnfield, La. **(1893–1935)**
Long, Shelley (actress); Fort Wayne, Ind., 8/23/49
Longfellow, Henry Wadsworth (poet); Portland, Maine **(1807–1882)**
Longworth, Alice Roosevelt (social figure); New York City **(1884–1980)**
Loos, Anita (novelist); Sissons, Calif. **(1888–1981)**
Lopez, Jennifer (actress, singer); Bronx, N.Y., 7/24/70
Lopez, Trini (singer); Dallas, 5/15/37
Lopez, Vincent (band leader); Brooklyn, N.Y. **(1895–1975)**
Lord, Jack (John Joseph Ryan) (actor); New York City **(1920–1998)**
Loren, Sophia (Sofia Scicolone) (actress); Rome, 9/20/34
Lorenz, Konrad (ethologist); Vienna **(1903–1989)**
Lorre, Peter (Laszlo Löewenstein) (actor); Rosenberg, former Czechoslovakia **(1904–1964)**
Loudon, Dorothy (actress, singer); Boston, 9/17/33
Louis-Dreyfus, Julia (actress); New York City, 1/13/61
Louis XIV (King of France); St.-Germain-en-Laye, France **(1638–1715)**
Louise, Tina (actress); New York City, 2/11/37
Love, Susan (surgeon, oncologist, activist); Long Branch, N.J., 2/9/48
Lovecraft, Howard Phillips (author); Providence, R.I. **(1890–1937)**
Lovett, Lyle (country singer, songwriter); Klein, Tex., 11/1/56
Lowe, Rob (actor); Charlottesville, Va., 3/17/64
Lowell, Amy (poet); Brookline, Mass. **(1874–1925)**
Lowell, James Russell (poet); Cambridge, Mass. **(1819–1891)**
Lowell, Robert (poet); Boston **(1917–1977)**
Loy, Myrna (Myrna Williams) (actress); nr. Helena, Mont. **(1905–1993)**
Loyola, St. Ignatius of (Iñigo de Oñez y Loyola) (founder of Jesuits); Güipuzcoa Province, Spain **(1491– 1556)**
Lubitsch, Ernst (film director); Berlin **(1892–1947)**
Lucas, George (film director); Modesto, Calif., 5/14/44
Lucci, Susan (actress); Scarsdale, N.Y., 12/23/46
Luce, Clare Boothe (playwright, former ambassador); New York City **(1903–1987)**
Luce, Henry Robinson (editor, publisher); Tengchow, China **(1898–1967)**
Ludlum, Robert (author); New York City **(1927–2001)**
Lugosi, Béla (Béla Blasko) (actor); Lugos, Hungary **(1888–1956)**
Lukas, J. Anthony (author); New York City **(1933–1997)**
Lukas, Paul (actor); Budapest **(1895–1971)**
Lully, Jean Baptiste (French composer); Florence **(1639–1687)**
Lumet, Sidney (director); Philadelphia, 6/25/24
Lunden, Joan (TV host); Fair Oaks, Calif., 9/19/50
Lunt, Alfred (actor); Milwaukee **(1892–1977)**
Lupino, Ida (actress, director); London **(1918–1995)**
LuPone, Patti (actress, singer); Northport, N.Y., 4/21/49
Luther, Martin (religious reformer); Eisleben, East Germany **(1483–1546)**
Lynch, David (film director); Missoula, Mont., 1/20/46
Lynn, Loretta (singer); Butcher's Hollow, Ky., 4/14/35

M

Ma, Yo-Yo (cellist); Paris, 10/7/55
Maazel, Lorin (conductor); Neuilly, France, 3/5/30
MacArthur, Charles (playwright); Scranton, Pa. **(1895–1956)**
MacArthur, Douglas (five-star general); Little Rock Barracks, Ark. **(1880–1964)**
MacArthur, James (actor); Los Angeles, 12/8/37
Macaulay, Thomas Babington (author); Rothley Temple, England **(1800–1859)**
MacDermot, Galt (composer); Montreal, 12/19/28
MacDonald, James Ramsay (statesman); Lossiemouth, Scotland **(1866–1937)**
MacDonald, Jeanette (actress, soprano); Philadelphia **(1907–1965)**
Macdonald, Ross (Kenneth Millar) (mystery writer); Los Gatos, Calif. **(1915–1983)**
MacDowell, Edward Alexander (composer); New York City **(1861–1908)**
MacDowell, Andie (Rosalie Anderson MacDowell) (actress); Gaffney, S.C., 4/21/58
MacFadden, Bernarr (physical culturist); nr. Mill Spring, Mo. **(1868–1955)**
Machaut, Guillaume de (composer); Marchault, France **(1300–1377)**
Machiavelli, Niccolò (political philosopher); Florence, Italy **(1469–1527)**
Mackie, Bob (designer); Monterey Park, Calif., 3/24/40
MacLaine, Shirley (Shirley MacLean Beaty) (actress); Richmond, Va., 4/24/34
MacLeish, Archibald (poet); Glencoe, Ill. **(1892–1982)**

Macmillan, Harold (ex-prime minister); London **(1894–1986)**
MacMurray, Fred (actor); Kankakee, Ill. **(1908–1991)**
MacNeil, Cornell (baritone); Minneapolis, 9/24/22
MacNeil, Robert (TV newscaster); Montreal, 1/19/31
MacNicol, Peter (actor); Dallas, 4/10/54
Macpherson, Elle (Eleanor Gow) (model, actress); Sydney, Australia, 3/29/64
MacRae, Gordon (singer, actor); East Orange, N.J. **(1921–1986)**
MacRae, Sheila (comedienne); London, 9/24/24
Madison, James (4th U.S. president); Port Conway, Va. **(1751–1836)**
Madonna (Madonna Louise Ciccone) (singer, actress); Bay City, Mich., 8/16/58
Maeterlinck, Count Maurice (author); Ghent, Belgium **(1862–1949)**
Magellan, Ferdinand (Fernando de Magalhaes) (navigator); Sabrosa, Portugal **(c. 1480–1521)**
Magliozzi, Ray ("Car Talk" host); Cambridge, Mass., 3/30/49
Magliozzi, Tom ("Car Talk" host); Cambridge, Mass., 6/28/37
Magritte, René (painter); Belgium **(1898–1967)**
Magsaysay, Ramón (statesman); Iba, Luzon, Philippines **(1907–1957)**
Maguire, Tobey (actor); Santa Monica, Calif., 6/27/75
Mahan, Alfred Thayer (naval historian); West Point, N.Y. **(1840–1914)**
Mahler, Gustav (composer, conductor); Kalischt, Czechoslovakia **(1860–1911)**
Mahoney, John (actor); Manchester, England, 6/20/40
Mailer, Norman (novelist); Long Branch, N.J., 1/31/23
Maillol, Aristide (sculptor); Banyuls-sur-Mer, Rousillion, France **(1861–1944)**
Maimonides, Moses (Jewish philosopher); Cordoba, Spain **(1135–1204)**
Mainbocher (Main Rousseau Bocher) (fashion designer); Chicago **(1891–1976)**
Majors, Lee (Harvey Lee Yeary) (actor); Wyandotte, Mich., 4/23/40
Makarova, Natalia (ballet dancer); Leningrad (St. Petersburg), Russia, 11/21/40
Makeba, Miriam (singer); Johannesburg, South Africa, 3/4/32
Malamud, Bernard (novelist); Brooklyn, N.Y. **(1914–1986)**
Malcolm X (Malcolm Little; el Hajj Malik el-Shabazz) (Black nationalist, religious leader); Omaha, Neb. **(1925–1965)**
Malden, Karl (Karl Mladen Sekulovich) (actor); Chicago, 3/22/13
Malkovich, John (actor); Christopher, Ill., 12/9/53
Mallarmé, Stephane (poet, essayist); Paris **(1842–1898)**
Malle, Louis (director); Thumeries, France **(1932–1995)**
Malraux, André (author); Paris **(1901–1976)**
Malthus, Thomas Robert (economist); nr. Dorking, England **(1766–1834)**
Maltin, Leonard (film critic and historian); New York City, 12/18/50
Mamet, David (playwright); Chicago, 11/30/47
Manchester, Melissa (singer); Bronx, N.Y., 2/15/51
Manchester, William (writer); Attleboro, Mass. **(1922–2004)**
Mancini, Henry (composer, conductor); Cleveland **(1924–1994)**
Mandela, Nelson (Rolihlahla) (former president of South Africa); Umtata, Transkei, 7/18/18
Mandela, Winnie (Nomzamo) (South African political activist); Pondoland district of the Transkei, 1936?
Mandrell, Barbara (singer); Houston, 12/25/48
Manet, Edouard (painter); Paris **(1832–1883)**
Mangione, Chuck (hornist, pianist, composer); Rochester, N.Y., 11/29/40
Manheim, Camryn (actress); New York City, 3/8/61
Manilow, Barry (singer); Brooklyn, N.Y., 6/17/46
Mankiewicz, Frank F. (columnist); New York City, 5/16/24
Mankiewicz, Joseph L. (film writer, director); Wilkes-Barre, Pa. **(1909–1993)**
Mann, Horace (educator); Franklin, Mass. **(1796–1859)**
Mann, Thomas (novelist); Lübeck, Germany **(1875–1955)**
Mannes, Marya (writer); New York City **(1904–1990)**
Mansfield, Jayne (Jayne Palmer) (actress); Bryn Mawr, Pa. **(1933–1967)**
Mansfield, Katherine (story writer); Wellington, New Zealand **(1888–1923)**
Manson, Marilyn (Brian Warner) (rock musician); Canton, Ohio, 1/5/69
Mantegna, Andrea (painter); Isola di Carturo, Italy **(1431–1506)**
Mantegna, Joe (actor); Chicago, 11/13/47
Mantovani, Annunzio (conductor); Venice **(1905–1980)**
Mao Zedong (Tse-tung) (Chinese leader); Shao Shan, China **(1893– 1976)**
Mapplethorpe, Robert (photographer); Floral Park, Queens, N.Y. **(1946–1989)**

Marat, Jean Paul (French revolutionist); Boudry, Neuchâtel, Switzerland **(1743–1793)**

Marceau, Marcel (mime); Strasbourg, France, 3/22/23

Marceau, Sophie (actress); Paris, 11/17/66

March, Fredric (Frederick Bickel) (actor); Racine, Wis. **(1897–1975)**

Marchand, Nancy (actress); Buffalo, N.Y. **(1928–2000)**

Marconi, Guglielmo (inventor); Bologna, Italy **(1874–1937)**

Marcus Aurelius (Marcus Annius Verus) (Roman emperor); Rome **(121–180)**

Marcus, Rudolph Arthur (chemist, Nobel laureate); Montreal, 7/21/23

Marcuse, Herbert (philosopher); Berlin **(1898–1979)**

Margaret Rose (princess of England); Glamis Castle, Angus, Scotland, 8/21/30

Margrethe II (queen of Denmark); Copenhagen, 4/16/40

Margulies, Julianna (actress); Spring Valley, N.Y., 6/8/65

Marie Antoinette (Josephe Jeanne Marie Antoinette) (queen of France); Vienna **(1755 –1793)**

Marisol (Escobar) (Venezuelan-American sculptor); Paris, 1930

Markham, Edwin (poet); Oregon City, Ore. **(1852–1940)**

Markova, Dame Alicia (Lilian Alice Marks) (ballet dancer); London, 12/1/10

Marley, Bob (singer, songwriter); Kingston, Jamaica **(1945–1981)**

Marlowe, Christopher (dramatist); Canterbury, England **(1564–1593)**

Marquand, J(ohn) P(hillips) (novelist); Wilmington, Del. **(1893–1960)**

Marquette, Jacques (missionary, explorer); Laon, France **(1637–1675)**

Marriner, Neville (conductor); Lincoln, England, 4/15/24

Marsalis, Wynton (musician); New Orleans, 10/18/61

Marshall, E.G. (actor); Owatonna, Minn. **(1910–1998)**

Marshall, Garry (director, producer, screenwriter, actor); New York City, 11/13/34

Marshall, George Catlett (general); Uniontown, Pa. **(1880–1959)**

Marshall, Herbert (actor); London **(1890–1968)**

Marshall, John (jurist); nr. Germantown, Va. **(1755–1835)**

Marshall, Penny (Penny Marscharelli) (actress, director, producer); Bronx, N.Y., 10/15/42

Marshall, Thurgood (U.S. Supreme Court justice); Baltimore **(1908–1993)**

Martin, Dean (Dino Crocetti) (singer, actor); Steubenville, Ohio **(1917–1995)**

Martin, Mary (singer, actress); Weatherford, Tex. **(1913–1990)**

Martin, Steve (actor, writer, producer); Waco, Tex., 8/14/45

Martin, Tony (Alvin Morris) (singer); San Francisco, 12/25/12

Martinelli, Giovanni (tenor); Montagnana, Italy **(1885–1969)**

Martins, Peter (dancer, choreographer); Copenhagen, 10/27/45

Marvell, Andrew (poet); Winestead, England **(1621–1678)**

Marvin, Lee (actor); New York City **(1924–1987)**

Marx, Chico (Leonard) (comedian); New York City **(1887–1961)**

Marx, Groucho (Julius) (comedian); New York City **(1890–1977)**

Marx, Harpo (Arthur) (comedian); New York City **(1893–1964)**

Marx, Karl (Socialist writer); Treves, Germany **(1818–1883)**

Marx, Zeppo (Herbert) (comedian); New York City **(1901–1979)**

Mary Stuart (Mary, Queen of Scots) (queen of Scotland); Linlithgow, Scotland **(1542–1587)**

Masaccio, (Tommaso di Giovanni di Simone Cassai) (painter); San Giovanni Valdarno, Tuscany **(1401–c. 1428)**

Masaryk, Jan Garrigue (statesman); Prague **(1886–1948)**

Masaryk, Thomas Garrigue (statesman); Hodonin, Czech Republic **(1850–1937)**

Masefield, John (poet); Ledbury, England **(1878–1967)**

Masekela, Hugh (trumpeter); Wilbank, South Africa, 4/4/39

Mason, Jackie (Jacob Moshe Maza) (comedian); Sheboygan, Wis., 6/9/31

Mason, James (actor); Huddersfield, England **(1909–1984)**

Mason, Marsha (actress); St. Louis, 4/3/42

Massenet, Jules Emile Frédéric (composer); Montaud, France **(1842–1912)**

Massine, Léonide (choreographer); Moscow **(1896–1979)**

Masters, Edgar Lee (poet); Garnett, Kans. **(1869–1950)**

Masters, William (human sexuality expert); Cleveland **(1915–2001)**

Masterson, Mary Stuart (actress, writer, director); New York City, 6/28/66

Mastroianni, Marcello (actor); Fontana Liri, Italy **(1924–1996)**

Mather, Cotton (clergyman); Boston **(1663–1728)**

Mathis, Johnny (singer); Gilmer, Texas, 9/30/35

Matisse, Henri (painter); Le Cateau, France **(1869–1954)**

Matthau, Walter (Walter Matuschanskayasky) (actor); New York City **(1920–2000)**

Mature, Victor (actor); Louisville, Ky. **(1915–1999)**

Maugham, W(illiam) Somerset (author); Paris **(1874–1965)**

Mauldin, Bill (political cartoonist); Mountain Park, N.M. **(1921–2003)**

Maupassant, Henri René Albert Guy de (story writer); Normandy, France **(1850–1893)**

Maurois, André (Emile Herzog) (author); Elbauf, France **(1885–1967)**

Maximilian (Ferdinand Maximilian Joseph) (emperor of Mexico); Vienna **(** 1832–1867)

Maxwell, James Clerk (physicist); Edinburgh, Scotland **(1831–1879)**

Maxwell, (Ian) Robert (publisher); Selo Slatina, Czechoslavakia **(1923–1991)**

May, Elaine (Elaine Berlin) (entertainer, writer); Philadelphia, 4/21/32

May, Rollo (psychologist); Ada, Ohio **(1909–1994)**

Mayer, Louis B. (movie executive); Minsk, Russia **(1885–1957)**

Mayo, Charles H. (surgeon); Rochester, Minn. **(1865–1939)**

Mayo, Charles W. (surgeon); Rochester, Minn. **(1898–1968)**

Mayo, Virginia (Jones) (actress); St. Louis, 11/30/20

Mayo, William J. (surgeon); Le Sueur, Minn. **(1861–1939)**

Mayron, Melanie (actress); Philadelphia, 10/20/52

Mazzini, Giuseppe (patriot); Genoa **(1805–1872)**

McBride, Patricia (ballet dancer); Teaneck, N.J., 8/23/42

McCallum, David (actor); Glasgow, Scotland, 9/19/33

McCambridge, Mercedes (actress); Joliet, Ill. **(1918–2004)**

McCarthy, Eugene J. (ex-senator); Watkins, Minn., 3/29/16

McCarthy, Joseph Raymond (senator); Grand Chute, Wis. **(1908–1957)**

McCarthy, Mary (novelist); Seattle **(1912–1989)**

McCartney, Linda (photographer, singer); New York City **(1941–1998)**

McCartney, Paul (singer, songwriter); Liverpool, England, 6/18/42

McClanahan, Rue (actress); Healdton, Okla., 2/21/35

McClellan, George Brinton (general); Philadelphia **(1826–1885)**

McClintock, Barbara (geneticist, Nobel laureate) **(1902–1992)**

McCloy, John J. (lawyer, banker); Philadelphia **(1895–1989)**

McCormack, John (tenor); Athlone, Ireland **(1884–1945)**

McCormack, John W. (ex-Speaker of House); Boston **(1891–1980)**

McCormick, Cyrus Hall (inventor); Rockbridge County, Va. **(1809–1884)**

McCourt, Frank (writer); Brooklyn, N.Y., 8/19/30

McCracken, James (dramatic tenor); Gary, Ind. **(1926–1988)**

McCrea, Joel (actor); Los Angeles **(1905–1990)**

McCullers, Carson (novelist); Columbus, Ga. **(1917–1967)**

McCullough, David (author, historian); Pittsburgh, 7/7/33

McDermott, Dylan (actor); Waterbury, Conn., 10/26/62

McDormand, Frances (actress); Illinois, 6/23/57

McDowall, Roddy (actor); London **(1928–1998)**

McDowell, Malcolm (actor); Leeds, England, 6/15/43

McFadden, Gates (actress); Cuyahoga Falls, Ohio, 3/2/49

McGavin, Darren (actor); San Joaquin, Calif., 5/7/22

McGillis, Kelly (actress); Newport Beach, Calif., 7/9/57

McGinley, Phyllis (poet, writer); Ontario, Ore. **(1905–1978)**

McGoohan, Patrick (actor); Astoria, Queens, N.Y., 3/19/28

McGovern, Elizabeth (actress); Evanston, Ill., 7/18/61

McGovern, Maureen (singer); Youngstown, Ohio, 7/27/49

McGregor, Ewan (actor); Crieff, Scotland, 3/31/71

McKellen, Ian (actor); Burnley, England, 5/25/39

McKinley, William (25th U.S. president); Niles, Ohio **(1843–1901)**

McKuen, Rod (singer, composer); Oakland, Calif., 4/29/33

McLachlan, Sarah (singer, songwriter); Halifax, N.S., 1/28/68

McLaughlin, John (guitarist); Yorkshire, England, 1/4/42

McLean, Don (singer, songwriter); New Rochelle, N.Y., 10/2/45

McLuhan, Marshall (Herbert Marshall) (communications writer); Edmonton, Alta., Canada **(1911–1980)**

McMahon, Ed (TV personality); Detroit, 3/6/23

McMurtry, Larry (novelist); Wichita Falls, Tex., 6/3/36

McQueen, Butterfly (Thelma) (actress); Tampa, Fla. **(1911–1995)**

McQueen, Steve (Terence Stephen McQueen) (actor); Beech Grove, Indiana **(1930–1980)**

McRaney, Gerald (actor); Collins, Miss., 8/19/47

McTeer, Janet (actress); York, England, 1962

Mead, Margaret (anthropologist); Philadelphia **(1901–1978)**

Meadows, Audrey (actress); Wu Chang, China **(1924–1996)**

Meadows, Jayne (actress); Wu Chang, China, 9/27/26

Meaney, Colm (actor); Dublin, 5/30/53

Meany, George (labor leader); New York City **(1894–1980)**

Meara, Anne (actress); New York City, 9/20/29

Medici, Lorenzo de' (called Lorenzo the Magnificent) (Florentine ruler); Florence, Italy **(1449–1492)**

Mehta, Zubin (conductor); Bombay (Mumbai), 4/29/36

Meir, Golda (Golda Myerson, nee Mabovitz) (ex-premier of Israel); Kiev, Ukraine **(1898–1978)**

Melba, Dame Nellie (Helen Porter Mitchell) (soprano); nr. Melbourne, Australia **(1861–1931)**

Melchior, Lauritz (Lebrecht Hommel) (heroic tenor); Copenhagen **(1890–1973)**

Mellon, Andrew William (financier); Pittsburgh **(1855–1937)**

Melville, Herman (novelist); New York City **(1819–1891)**

Mencken, Henry Louis (writer); Baltimore **(1880–1956)**

Mendel, Gregor Johann (geneticist); Heinzendorf, Austrian Silesia **(1822–1884)**

Mendeleyev, Dmitri Ivanovich (chemist); Tobolsk, Russia **(1834–1907)**

Mendelssohn-Bartholdy, Jakob Ludwig Felix (composer); Hamburg **(1809–1847)**

Mendès-France, Pierre (ex-Premier); Paris **(1905–1982)**

Mengele, Josef (Nazi, "Angel of Death"); Günzberg, Germany **(1911–1979)**

Mennin, Peter (Peter Mennini) (composer); Erie, Pa. **(1923–1983)**

Menninger, William C. (psychiatrist); Topeka, Kans. **(1899–1966)**

Menotti, Gian Carlo (composer); Cadegliano, Italy, 7/7/11

Menuhin, Yehudi (violinist, conductor); New York City **(1916–1999)**

Menzies, Robert Gordon (ex-prime minister); Jeparit, Australia **(1894–1978)**

Mercer, Johnny (songwriter); Savannah, Ga. **(1909–1976)**

Mercer, Mabel (singer); Burton-on-Trent, England **(1900–1984)**

Merchant, Ismail (Ismail Noormohamed Abdul Rehman) (film producer); Bombay (Mumbai), 12/25/36

Merchant, Natalie (singer, songwriter); Jamestown, N.Y., 10/26/63

Mercury, Freddie (Farookh Bulsara) (musician, singer); Zanzibar **(1946–1991)**

Meredith, Burgess (actor); Cleveland **(1908–1997)**

Meredith, James (author, civil-rights leader); Kosciusko, Miss., 6/26/23

Merman, Ethel (Ethel Zimmerman) (singer, actress); Astoria, Queens, N.Y. **(1909–1984)**

Merrick, David (David Margulois) (stage producer); St. Louis **(1912–2000)**

Merton, Thomas (clergyman, writer); France **(1915–1968)**

Mesmer, Franz Anton (physician); Itzmang, nr. Constance, Germany **(1733–1815)**

Mesta, Perle (social figure); Sturgis, Mich. **(1889–1975)**

Metacom, (King Philip) (Wampanoag Indian sachem); southeastern Mass. **(1640–1676)**

Metternich, Prince Klemens Wenzel Nepomuk Lothar von (statesman); Coblenz, Germany **(1773–1859)**

Mfume, Kweisi (Frizzell Gray) (politician, NAACP leader); Baltimore, 10/24/48

Michaels, Lorne (producer); Toronto, 11/17/44

Michelangelo Buonarroti (painter, sculptor, architect); Caprese, Italy **(1475–1564)**

Michener, James A. (novelist); New York City **(1907–1997)**

Mickiewicz, Adam (Polish poet); Zozie, Belorussia (Belarus) **(1798–1855)**

Midler, Bette (singer, actress, producer); Honolulu, 12/1/45

Mielziner, Jo (stage designer); Paris **(1901–1976)**

Mifune, Toshiro (actor, film producer); Tsingtao, China **(1920–1997)**

Mies van der Rohe, Ludwig (architect, designer); Aachen, Germany **(1886–1969)**

Mikoyan, Anastas I. (diplomat); Sanain, Armenia **(1895–1978)**

Milano, Alyssa (actress); Brooklyn, New York, 12/19/72

Milhaud, Darius (composer); Aix-en-Provence, France **(1892–1974)**

Mill, John Stuart (philosopher); London **(1806–1873)**

Milland, Ray (Reginald Truscott-Jones) (actor); Neath, Wales **(1907–1986)**

Millay, Edna St. Vincent (poet); Rockland, Maine **(1892–1950)**

Miller, Ann (Lucille Ann Collier) (dancer, actress); Cherino, Tex. **(1923–2004)**

Miller, Arthur (playwright); New York City, 10/17/15

Miller, Glenn (band leader); Clarinda, Iowa **(1904–1944)**

Miller, Henry (novelist); New York City **(1891–1980)**

Miller, Jason (John Miller) (playwright, actor); New York City **(1939–2001)**

Miller, Mitch (Mitchell) (musician); Rochester, N.Y., 7/4/11

Miller, Roger (singer); Fort Worth **(1936–1992)**

Millet, Jean François (painter); Gruchy, France **(1814–1875)**

Millett, Kate (feminist, writer); St. Paul, Minn., 9/14/34

Millikan, Robert A. (physicist); Morrison, Ill. **(1869–1953)**

Mills, Donna (actress); Chicago, 12/11/41

Mills, Hayley (actress); London, 4/18/46

Mills, Juliet (actress); London, 11/21/41

Milne, A(lan) A(lexander) (author); London **(1882–1956)**

Milner, Martin (actor); Detroit, 12/28/31

Milnes, Sherrill (baritone); Downers Grove, Ill., 1/10/35

Milosevic, Slobodan (Yugoslav President); Pozarevac, Serbia, 8/29/41

Milstein, Nathan (concert violinist); Odessa, Ukraine **(1904–1992)**

Milton, John (poet); London **(1608–1674)**

Mingus, Charles (jazz composer); Nogales, Ariz. **(1922–1979)**

Minnelli, Liza (singer, actress); Hollywood, Calif., 3/12/46

Minnelli, Vincente (film director); Chicago **(1913–1986)**

Minuit, Peter (Governor of New Amsterdam); Wesel, Germany **(1580–1638)**

Miranda, Carmen (Maria do Carmo da Cunha) (singer, dancer); Lisbon **(1909–1955)**

Miró, Joan (painter); Barcelona **(1893–1983)**

Mirren, Helen (Ilynea Lydia Mironoff) (actress); London, 7/26/45

Mitchell, John N. (former Attorney General); Detroit **(1913–1988)**

Mitchell, Joni (Roberta Joan Anderson) (singer, songwriter); Ft. Macleod, Alb., Canada, 11/7/43

Mitchell, Margaret (novelist); Atlanta **(1900–1949)**

Mitchell, Maria (astronomer); Nantucket, Mass. **(1818–1889)**

Mitchum, Robert (actor); Bridgeport, Conn. **(1917–1997)**

Mitropoulos, Dimitri (orchestra conductor); Athens **(1896–1960)**

Mitterand, François (Maurice) (ex-prime minister of France); Jarnac, France **(1916–1996)**

Mix, Tom (actor); Mix Run, Pa. **(1880–1940)**

Mobutu Sese Seko (Zairean dictator); Lisala, Congo **(1930–1997)**

Modigliani, Amedeo (painter); Leghorn, Italy **(1884–1920)**

Moffo, Anna (soprano); Wayne, Pa., 6/27/34

Mohammed (prophet); Mecca, Saudi Arabia **(570–632)**

Molière (Jean Baptiste Poquelin) (dramatist); Paris **(1622–1673)**

Molina, Mario (chemist, Nobel laureate); Mexico City, 3/19/43

Moll, Richard (actor); Pasadena, Calif., 1/13/43?

Molnar, Ferenc (dramatist); Budapest **(1878–1952)**

Molotov, Vyacheslav M. (V. M. Skryabin) (diplomat); Kukarka, Russia **(1890–1986)**

Mondrian, Piet (painter); Amersfoort, Netherlands **(1872–1944)**

Monet, Claude (painter); Paris **(1840–1926)**

Monica Monica Arnold (singer); Atlanta, Ga., 10/24/80

Monk, Meredith (choreographer, composer, performing artist); Lima, Peru, 11/20/42

Monk, Thelonious (pianist); Rocky Mount, N.C. **(1918–1982)**

Monroe, James (5th U.S. president); Westmoreland County, Va. **(1758–1831)**

Monroe, Marilyn (Norma Jean Mortenson or Baker) (actress); Los Angeles **(1926–1962)**

Monsarrat, Nicholas (novelist); Liverpool, England **(1910–1979)**

Montaigne, Michel Eyquem de (essayist); nr. Bordeaux, France **(1533–1592)**

Montalban, Ricardo (actor); Mexico City, 11/25/20

Montand, Yves (Ivo Livi) (actor, singer); Florence, Italy **(1921–1991)**

Montesquieu, Charles-Louis de Secondat, baron de La Brède and de (philosopher); nr. Bordeaux, France **(1689–1755)**

Montessori, Maria (physician, educator); Chiaravalle, Italy **(1870–1952)**

Monteux, Pierre (conductor); Paris **(1875–1964)**

Monteverdi, Claudio (composer); Cremona Italy **(1567–1643)**

Montezuma II (Aztec emperor); Mexico **(1466–1520)**

Montgomery, Elizabeth (actress); Hollywood, Calif. **(1933–1995)**

Montgomery, Robert (Henry, Jr.) (actor); Beacon, N.Y. **(1904–1981)**

Montgomery of Alamein, 1st Viscount of Hindhead (Sir Bernard Law Montgomery) (military leader); London **(1887–1976)**

Montoya, Carlos (guitarist); Madrid **(1903–1993)**

Moore, Clayton (Jack Moore) (actor); Chicago **(1914–1999)**

Moore, Clement Clarke (author); New York City **(1779–1863)**

Moore, Demi (Demi Guynes) (actress); Roswell, N.M., 11/11/62

Moore, Dudley (actor, writer, musician); Dagenham, England **(1935–2002)**

Moore, Grace (soprano); Jellico, Tenn. **(1901–1947)**

Moore, Henry (sculptor); Castleford, England **(1898–1986)**

Moore, Julianne (actress); Fayetteville, N.C., 12/3/60

Moore, Marianne (poet); Kirkwood, Mo. **(1887–1972)**

Moore, Mary Tyler (actress); Brooklyn, N.Y., 12/29/36

Moore, Melba (Beatrice) (singer, actress); New York City, 10/27/45

Moore, Roger (actor); London, 10/14/27

Moore, Thomas (poet); Dublin **(1779–1852)**

Moorehead, Agnes (actress); Clinton, Mass. **(1906–1974)**

Moranis, Rick (actor); Toronto, 4/18/53

More, Henry (philosopher); Grantham, England **(1614–1687)**

More, Sir Thomas (statesman, author); London **(1478–1535)**

Moreno, Rita (Rosita Dolores Alverio) (actress); Humacao, P.R., 12/11/31

Morgan, Harry (Harry Bratsburg) (actor); Detroit, 4/10/15

Morgan, John Pierpont (financier); Hartford, Conn. **(1837–1913)**

Moriarty, Michael (actor); Detroit, 4/5/41

Morini, Erica (concert violinist); Vienna **(1904–1995)**

Morison, Samuel Eliot (historian); Boston **(1887–1976)**
Morita, Pat (Noriyuki Morita) (actor); Berkeley, Calif., 8/28/32
Morley, Christopher Darlington (novelist); Haverford, Pa. **(1890–1957)**
Morley, Robert (actor); Semley, England **(1908–1992)**
Morris, Mark (choreographer); Seattle, 8/29/56
Morris, William (poet, craftsman); Walthamstow, England **(1834–1896)**
Morrison, Jim (James Douglas Morrison) (singer, songwriter); Melbourne, Fla. **(1943–1971)**
Morrison, Toni (Chloe Anthony Wofford) (novelist); Lorain, Ohio, 2/18/31
Morrison, Van (singer); Belfast, Northern Ireland, 8/31/45
Morse, Marston (mathematician); Waterville, Maine **(1892–1977)**
Morse, Samuel Finley Breese (painter, inventor); Charlestown, Mass. **(1791–1872)**
Morton, Jelly Roll (Ferdinand Joseph La Menthe) (jazz composer); New Orleans **(1890–1941)**
Moseley-Braun, Carol (U.S. Senator); Chicago, 8/16/47
Moses, Grandma (Mrs. Anna Mary Robertson Moses) (painter); Greenwich, N.Y. **(1860–1961)**
Moses, Robert (urban planner); New Haven, Conn. **(1888–1981)**
Moss, Kate (model); London, England, 1/16/74
Mostel, Zero (Samuel Joel Mostel) (actor); Brooklyn, N.Y. **(1915–1977)**
Mother Teresa (Gonxha Agnes Bojaxhiu) (nun); Skopje, Macedonia **(1910–1997)**
Motherwell, Robert (artist, "action" painter); Aberdeen, Wash. **(1915–1991)**
Mott, Lucretia (Coffin) (feminist, reformer, abolitionist); Nantucket, Mass. **(1793–1880)**
Moussorgsky, Modest Petrovich (composer); Karev, Russia **(1839–1881)**
Moyers, Bill D. (Billy Don) (journalist); Hugo, Okla., 6/5/34
Moynihan, Daniel Patrick (New York senator); Tulsa, Okla. **(1927–2003)**
Mozart, Wolfgang Amadeus (Johannes Chrysostomus Wolfgangus Theophilus Mozart) (composer); Salzburg, Austria **(1756–1791)**
Mudd, Roger (TV newscaster); Washington, D.C., 2/9/28
Muggeridge, Malcolm (Thomas) (writer); Croydon, England **(1903–1990)**
Muhammad (founder of Islam); Mecca, Saudi Arabia **(c. 570–632)**
Muhammad, Elijah (Elijah Poole) (religious leader); Sandersville, Ga. **(1897–1975)**
Mulgrew, Kate (actress); Dubuque, Iowa, 4/29/55
Mulhare, Edward (actor); Ireland **(1923–1997)**
Mulliken, Robert Sanderson (chemist, Nobel laureate); Newburyport, Mass. **(1896–1986)**
Mulroney, Dermot (actor, musician, producer); Alexandria, Va., 10/31/63
Mumford, Lewis (cultural historian, city planner); Flushing, Queens, N.Y. **(1895–1990)**
Munch, Edvard (painter); Löten, Norway **(1863–1944)**
Munchhausen, Karl Friedrick Hieronymus, baron von (anecdotist); Hannover, Germany **(1720–1797)**
Muni, Paul (Muni Weisenfreund) (actor); Lemburg, Austria **(1895–1967)**
Muñoz Marin, Luis (ex-governor of Puerto Rico); San Juan, P.R. **(1898–1980)**
Munsel, Patrice (soprano); Spokane, Wash., 5/14/25
Murdoch, Iris (novelist); Dublin **(1919–1999)**
Murdoch, Rupert (publisher); Melbourne, Australia, 3/11/31
Murillo, Bartolome Esteban (painter); Seville, Spain **(1617–1682)**
Murphy, Audie (actor, war hero); Kingston, Tex. **(1924–1971)**
Murphy, Eddie (actor, comedian); Brooklyn, N.Y., 4/3/61
Murphy, George (actor, dancer, ex-senator); New Haven, Conn. **(1902–1992)**
Murray, Arthur (dance teacher); New York City **(1895–1991)**
Murray, Bill (actor, comedian); Wilmette, Ill., 9/21/50
Murray, Kathryn (dance teacher); Jersey City, N.J. **(1906–1999)**
Murrow, Edward R. (commentator, government official); Greensboro, N.C. **(1908–1965)**
Musil, Robert (novelist); Klagenfurt, Austria **(1880–1942)**
Muskie, Edmund (political figure); Rumford, Maine **(1914–1996)**
Mussolini, Benito (Italian dictator); Dovia, Forli, Italy **(1883–1945)**
Muti, Riccardo (orchestra conductor); Naples, Italy, 7/28/41
Mutter, Anne-Sophie (violinist); Rheinfelden, Germany, 6/29/63
Myers, Mike (actor, writer, comedian); Scarborough, Ont., Canada, 5/25/63
Myerson, Bess (consumer advocate); Bronx, N.Y., 7/16/24
Myrdal, Gunnar (sociologist, economist); Gustaf Parish, Sweden **(1898–1987)**

N

Nabokov, Vladimir (novelist); St. Petersburg, Russia **(1899–1977)**
Nabors, Jim (actor, singer); Sylacauga, Ala., 6/12/32
Nader, Ralph (consumer advocate); Winsted, Conn., 2/27/34
Nair, Mira (director, screenwriter); Bhubaneswar, India, 10/15/57
Nash, Graham (singer); Blackpool, England, 1942
Nash, Ogden (poet); Rye, N.Y. **(1902–1971)**
Nasser, Gamal Abdel (statesman); Beni Mor, Egypt **(1918–1970)**
Nast, Thomas (cartoonist); Landau, Germany **(1840–1902)**
Nation, Carry Amelia (temperance leader); Garrard County, Ky. **(1846–1911)**
Natta, Giulio (chemist, Nobel laureate); Imperia, Italy **(1903–1979)**
Natwick, Mildred (actress); Baltimore **(1905–1994)**
Neagle, Anna (Marjorie Robertson) (actress); London **(1908–1986)**
Neal, Patricia (actress); Packard, Ky., 1/20/26
Neeson, Liam (William John) (actor); Ballymena, Northern Ireland, 6/7/52
Negri, Pola (Apolina Mathias-Chalupec) (actress); Bromberg, Poland **(1899–1987)**
Nehru, Jawaharlal (first prime minister of India); Allahabad, India **(1889–1964)**
Neill, Sam (Nigel Neill) (actor); Omagh, Northern Ireland, 9/14/47
Nelligan, Kate (actress); London, Ont., Canada, 3/16/51
Nelson, Barry (Robert Haakon Nielsen) (actor); San Francisco, 4/16/20
Nelson, David (actor); New York City, 10/24/36
Nelson, Harriet Hilliard (Peggy Lou Snyder) (actress); Des Moines, Iowa **(1909–1994)**
Nelson, Ozzie (Oswald) (actor); Jersey City, N.J. **(1906–1975)**
Nelson, Ricky (Eric) (singer, actor); Teaneck, N.J. **(1940–1985)**
Nelson, Viscount Horatio (naval officer); Burnham Thorpe, England **(1758–1805)**
Nelson, Willie (singer); Waco, Tex., 4/30/33
Nenni, Pietro (Socialist leader); Faenza, Italy **(1891–1980)**
Nero (Nero Claudius Caesar Drusus Germanicus) (Roman emperor); Antium, Italy **(37–68)**
Nero, Peter (pianist); New York City, 5/22/34
Netanyahu, Benjamin (Binyamin) (former Israeli prime minister); Tel Aviv, Israel, 10/21/49
Neuwirth, Bebe (Beatrice Neuwirth) (actress); Newark, N.J., 12/31/58
Nevelson, Louise (sculptor); Kiev, Russia **(1899–1988)**
Neville, Aaron (singer); New Orleans, 1/24/41
Newhart, Bob (actor); Chicago, 9/5/29
Newhouse, Samuel I. (publisher); New York City **(1895–1979)**
Newley, Anthony (actor, songwriter); London **(1931–1999)**
Newman, Edwin (news commentator); New York City, 1/25/19
Newman, John Henry (prelate); London **(1801–1890)**
Newman, Paul (actor, director); Cleveland, 1/26/25
Newman, Randy (singer); Los Angeles, 11/28/43
Newton, Huey (black activist); New Orleans **(1942–1989)**
Newton, Sir Isaac (mathematician, scientist); nr. Grantham, England **(1642–1727)**
Newton, Wayne (singer); Norfolk, Va., 4/3/42
Newton-John, Olivia (singer); Cambridge, England, 9/26/48
Nichols, Nichelle (actress); Robbins, Ill., 12/28/33
Nichols, Mike (Michael Peschkowsky) (stage and film director); Berlin, 11/6/31
Nicholson, Jack (actor, director, writer); Neptune, N.J., 4/22/37
Nicks, Stevie (Stephanie Lynn Nicks) (singer, songwriter); Phoenix, Ariz., 5/26/48
Nielsen, Leslie (actor); Regina, Sask., Canada, 2/11/26
Nietzsche, Friedrich Wilhelm (philosopher); nr. Lützen, Saxony, Germany **(1844–1900)**
Nightingale, Florence (nurse); Florence, Italy **(1820–1910)**
Nijinsky, Vaslav (ballet dancer); Warsaw **(1890–1950)**
Nilsson, Birgit (soprano); West Karup, Sweden, 5/17/23
Nilsson, Harry (singer, songwriter); Brooklyn, N.Y. **(1941–1994)**
Nimitz, Chester W. (naval officer); Fredericksburg, Tex. **(1885–1966)**
Nimoy, Leonard (actor, director, writer, producer); Boston, 3/26/31
Nin, Anais (author, diarist); Neuilly, France **(1903–1977)**
Niven, David (actor); Kirriemuir, Scotland **(1910–1983)**
Nixon, Richard Milhous (37th U.S. president); Yorba Linda, Calif. **(1913–1994)**
Nizer, Louis (lawyer, author); London **(1902–1994)**
Nobel, Alfred Bernhard (industrialist); Stockholm **(1833–1896)**
Noguchi, Isamu (sculptor); Los Angeles **(1904–1988)**
Nolan, Lloyd (actor); San Francisco **(1902–1985)**
Nolte, Nick (actor); Omaha, Neb., 2/8/40

Norell, Norman (Norman Levinson) (fashion designer); Noblesville, Ind. **(1900–1972)**

Norman, Jessye (soprano); Augusta, Ga., 9/15/45

Norman, Marsha (Marsha Williams) (playwright); Louisville, Ky., 9/21/47

Normand, Mabel (actress); Boston **(1894–1930)**

Norris, Chuck (Carlos Ray Norris) (actor, athlete); Ryan, Oklahoma, 3/10/40

Norstad, Gen. Lauris (ex-commander of NATO forces); Minneapolis **(1907–1988)**

North, John Ringling (circus director); Baraboo, Wis. **(1903–1985)**

North, Oliver (ex-military officer); San Antonio, 10/7/43

North, Sheree (actress); Los Angeles, 1/17/33

Norton, Edward (actor); Columbia, Md., 8/18/69

Norton, Eleanor Holmes (New York City government official, lawyer); Washington, D.C., 6/13/37

Nostradamus (Michel de Notredame) (astrologer); St. Rémy, France **(1503–1566)**

Novaes, Guiomar (pianist); São João de Boa Vista, Brazil **(1895–1979)**

Novak, Kim (Marilyn Novak) (actress); Chicago, 2/13/33

Novarro, Ramon (Ramon Samaniegoes) (actor); Durango, Mexico **(1899–1968)**

Novello, Ivor (actor, playwright, composer); Cardiff, Wales **(1893–1951)**

Nugent, Elliott (actor, director); Dover, Ohio **(1899–1980)**

Nureyev, Rudolf (ballet dancer); Siberia **(1938–1993)**

Nyro, Laura (singer, songwriter); Bronx, N.Y. **(1947–1997)**

O

Oakie, Jack (actor); Sedalia, Mo. **(1903–1978)**

Oakley, Annie (Phoebe Anne Oakley Mozee) (markswoman); Darke County, Ohio **(1860–1926)**

Oates, Joyce Carol (novelist); Lockport, N.Y., 6/16/38

Oberon, Merle (Estelle Merle O'Brien Thompson) (actress); Bombay, India **(1911–1979)**

Oberth, Hermann (rocketry and space flight pioneer); Nagyszeben, Austria-Hungary (Sibiu, Romania) **(1894–1989)**

O'Brian, Hugh (Hugh J. Krampe) (actor); Rochester, N.Y., 4/19/25

O'Brien, Conan (TV personality); Brookline, Mass., 4/18/63

O'Brien, Edmond (actor); New York City **(1915–1985)**

O'Brien, Margaret (Angela Maxine O'Brien) (actress); San Diego, Calif., 1/15/37

O'Brien, Pat (William Joseph O'Brien, Jr.) (actor); Milwaukee **(1899–1983)**

O'Brien, Tim (novelist); Austin, Minn., 10/1/46

Obuchi, Keizo (former prime minister of Japan); Nakanojo, Japan **(1937–2000)**

O'Casey, Sean (playwright); Dublin **(1881–1964)**

Ochs, Adolph Simon (publisher); Cincinnati **(1858–1935)**

O'Connor, Carroll (actor); New York City **(1924–2001)**

Odets, Clifford (playwright); Philadelphia **(1906–1963)**

Odetta (Odetta Holmes) (folk singer, actress); Birmingham, Ala., 12/31/30

O'Donnell, Chris (actor); Winnetka, Ill., 6/26/70

O'Donnell, Rosie (actress, talk show host); Commack, N.Y., 3/21/62

Offenbach, Jacques (composer); Cologne, Germany **(1819–1880)**

O'Hara, John (novelist); Pottsville, Pa. **(1905–1970)**

O'Hara, Maureen (Maureen FitzSimons) (actress); Dublin, 8/17/20

Ohlsson, Garrick (pianist); Bronxville, N.Y., 4/3/48

Oistrakh, David (concert violinist); Odessa, Russia **(1908–1974)**

O'Keeffe, Georgia (painter); Sun Prairie, Wis. **(1887–1986)**

Oland, Warner (actor); Umea, Sweden **(1880–1938)**

Oldenburg, Claes (painter); Stockholm, 1/28/29

Oldman, Gary (actor; director); London, 3/21/58

Olin, Lena (actress); Stockholm, 3/22/55

Oliphant, Patrick B. (editorial cartoonist); Adelaide, Australia, 7/24/35

Olivier, Sir Laurence (actor); Dorking, England **(1907–1989)**

Olmos, Edward James (actor); East Los Angeles, 2/24/47

Olmsted, Frederick Law (landscape architect); Hartford, Conn. **(1822–1903)**

Olsen, Ole (John Sigvard Olsen) (comedian); Peru, Ind. **(1892–1963)**

Omar Khayyam (poet, astronomer); Nishapur, Iran (died c. 1123)

Onassis, Aristotle (shipping executive); Smyrna, Turkey **(1906–1975)**

Onassis, Christina (shipping executive); New York City **(1950–1988)**

Onassis, Jacqueline Kennedy (Jacqueline Bouvier) (first lady); Southampton, N.Y. **(1929–1994)**

O'Neal, Ryan (Patrick) (actor); Los Angeles, 4/20/41

O'Neal, Tatum (actress); Los Angeles, 11/5/63

O'Neill, Eugene Gladstone (playwright); New York City **(1888–1953)**

O'Neill, Jennifer (actress); Rio de Janeiro, 2/20/49

Oppenheimer, J. Robert (nuclear physicist); New York City **(1904–1967)**

Orbach, Jerry (actor); New York City, 10/20/35

Orff, Carl (composer); Munich, Germany **(1895–1982)**

Orlando, Tony (Michael Anthony Orlando Cassavitis) (singer); New York City, 4/3/44

Ormandy, Eugene (conductor); Budapest **(1899–1985)**

Ormond, Julia (actress); Epsom, Surrey, England, 1/4/65

Orozco, José Clemente (painter); Zapotlán, Jalisco, Mexico **(1883–1949)**

Orwell, George (Eric Arthur Blair) (British author); Motihari, India **(1903–1950)**

Osborn, Paul (playwright); Evansville, Ind. **(1901–1988)**

Osborne, John (playwright); London **(1929–1994)**

Osbourne, Ozzy (John Osbourne) (singer); Birmingham, England, 12/3/48

Osler, Sir William (physician); Bondhead, Ont., Canada **(1849–1919)**

Osmond, Donny (singer, actor); Ogden, Utah, 12/9/57

Osmond, Marie (Olive Marie) (singer, actress); Ogden, Utah, 10/13/59

O'Sullivan, Maureen (actress); County Roscommon, Ireland **(1911–1998)**

Oswald, Lee Harvey (presumed assassin); New Orleans **(1939–1963)**

Otis, Elisha (inventor); Halifax, Vt. **(1811–1861)**

O'Toole, Peter (actor); Connemara, Ireland, 8/2/32

Ovid (Publius Ovidius Naso) (poet); Sulmona, Italy **(43 B.C.–A.D. 17)**

Ovitz, Michael (entertainment executive); Chicago, 12/14/46

Owens, Buck (Alvis Edgar Owens) (singer); Sherman, Tex., 8/12/29

Ozawa, Seiji (orchestra conductor); Fentian (Shenyan), Manchuria, 9/1/35

P

Paar, Jack (TV personality); Canton, Ohio **(1918–2004)**

Pacino, Al (Alfred) (actor); New York City, 4/25/40

Packard, Vance (author); Granville Summit, Pa. **(1914–1996)**

Paderewski, Ignace Jan (pianist, statesman); Kurylowka, Russian Podolia **(1860–1941)**

Paganini, Nicolò (violinist); Genoa, Italy **(1782–1840)**

Page, Geraldine (actress); Kirksville, Mo. **(1924–1987)**

Page, Jimmy (musician); Heston, Ireland, 1/9/44

Page, Patti (Clara Ann Fowler) (singer, entertainer); Claremore, Okla., 11/8/27

Pagels, Elaine Hiesey (religious scholar); Palo Alto, Calif., 2/13/43

Paglia, Camille (writer, social critic); Endicott, N.Y., 4/2/47

Paine, Thomas (political philosopher); Thetford, England **(1737–1809)**

Pakula, Alan J. (film director); New York City **(1928–1998)**

Palance, Jack (Walter Palanuik) (actor); Lattimer, Pa., 2/18/19

Palestrina, Giovanni Pierluigi da (composer); Palestrina, Italy **(1526–1594)**

Paley, William S. (broadcasting executive); Chicago **(1901–1990)**

Palladio, Andrea (architect); Padua or Vicenza, Italy **(1508–1580)**

Palmer, Robert (rock musician); Batley, England **(1/19/49–9/26/2003)**

Palmerston, Henry John Templeton (3rd Viscount) (statesman); Broadlands, England **(1784–1865)**

Palminteri, Chazz (Calogero Lorenzo Palminteri) (actor, writer); Bronx, New York, 5/15/51

Paltrow, Gwyneth (actress); Los Angeles, 9/27/72

Papanicolaou, George N. (physician); Coumi, Greece **(1883–1962)**

Papas, Irene (Lelekou) (actress); Chiliomodian, Greece, 3/9/26

Papp, Joseph (Joseph Papirofsky) (stage producer, director); Brooklyn, N.Y. **(1921–1991)**

Paracelsus, Philippus (Aureolus Theophrastus Bombastus von Hohenheim) (physican); Einsiedeln, Switzerland **(1493–1541)**

Park, Chung Hee (ex-president of South Korea); Sangmo-ri, Korea **(1917–1979)**

Parker, Alan (director); London, 2/14/44

Parker, Charlie "Bird" (jazz musician); Kansas City, Kans. **(1920–1955)**

Parker, Dorothy (Dorothy Rothschild) (author); West End, N.J. **(1893–1967)**

Parker, Fess (actor); Fort Worth, Tex., 8/16/25

Parker, Sarah Jessica (actress); Nelsonville, Ohio, 3/25/65

Parker, Suzy (model, actress); San Antonio **(1933–2003)**

Parkinson, C(yril) Northcote (historian); Durham, England **(1909–1993)**

Parkman, Francis (historian); Boston **(1823–1893)**

Parks, Bert (Bert Jacobson) (entertainer); Atlanta **(1914–1992)**

Parks, Gordon (film director); Ft. Scott, Kans., 11/30/12

Parks, Rosa (civil rights activist); Tuskegee, Ala., 2/4/13

Parnell, Charles Stewart (statesman); Avondale, Ireland **(1846–1891)**

Parnis, Mollie (Mollie Parnis Livingston) (fashion designer); New York City **(1905?–1992)**

Parsons, Estelle (actress); Marblehead, Mass., 11/20/27

Parton, Dolly (singer); Locust Ridge, Tenn., 1/19/46

Pascal, Blaise (philosopher); Clermont, France **(1623–1662)**

Pasternak, Boris Leonidovich (author); Moscow **(1890–1960)**

Pasternak, Joseph (film producer); Szilagy-Somlyo, Hungary **(1901–1991)**

Pasteur, Louis (chemist); Dôle, France **(1822–1895)**

Pastor, Tony (Antonio) (actor, theater manager); New York City **(1837–1908)**

Pater, Walter (Horatio) (writer); London **(1839–1894)**

Patinkin, Mandy (Mandel) (actor, singer); Chicago, 11/30/52

Paton, Alan (author); Pietermaritzburg, South Africa **(1903–1988)**

Patric, Jason (actor); Queens, N.Y., 6/17/66

Patti, Adelina (soprano); Madrid **(1843–1919)**

Patton, George Smith, Jr. (general); San Gabriel, Calif. **(1885–1945)**

Paul, Alice (feminist, woman suffragist); Moorestown, N.J. **(1885–1977)**

Paul, Les (Lester William Polfus) (guitarist); Waukesha, Wis., 6/9/15

Paul VI (Giovanni Battista Montini) (Pope); Concesio, nr. Brescia, Italy **(1897–1978)**

Pauley, Jane (Margaret Jane Pauley) (TV newscaster); Indianapolis, 10/31/50

Pauling, Linus Carl (chemist, Nobel laureate); Portland, Ore. **(1901–1994)**

Pavarotti, Luciano (tenor); Modena, Italy, 10/12/35

Pavlov, Ivan Petrovich (physiologist); Ryazan district, Russia **(1849–1936)**

Pavlova, Anna (ballet dancer); St. Petersburg, Russia **(1885–1931)**

Paxton, Bill (actor); Fort Worth, Texas, 5/17/55

Peale, Norman Vincent (clergyman); Bowersville, Ohio **(1898–1993)**

Pearl, Minnie (Sarah Ophelia Colley Cannon) (comedienne, singer); Centerville, Tenn. **(1912–1996)**

Pears, Peter (tenor); Farnham, England **(1910–1986)**

Pearson, Drew (Andrew Russel Pearson) (columnist); Evanston, Ill. **(1897–1969)**

Pearson, Lester B. (statesman); Toronto **(1897–1972)**

Peary, Robert Edwin (explorer); Cresson, Pa. **(1856–1920)**

Peck, Gregory (Eldred Gregory Peck) (actor); La Jolla, Calif. **(1916–2003)**

Peckinpah, Sam (film director); Fresno, Calif. **(1925–1984)**

Peerce, Jan (tenor); New York City **(1904–1984)**

Pegler, (James) Westbrook (columnist); Minneapolis **(1894–1969)**

Pei, I(eoh) M(ing) (architect); Canton, China, 4/26/17

Penn, Arthur (director); Philadelphia, 9/27/22

Penn, Sean (actor, filmmaker); Los Angeles, 8/17/60

Penn, William (American colonist); London **(1644–1718)**

Penney, James C. (merchant); Hamilton, Mo. **(1875–1971)**

Peppard, George (actor); Detroit **(1928–1994)**

Pepys, Samuel (diarist); Bampton, England **(1633–1703)**

Perelman, S(idney) J(oseph) (writer); Brooklyn, N.Y. **(1904–1979)**

Perez, Rosie (actress, dancer, choreographer); Brooklyn, New York, 9/6/64

Pergolesi, Giovanni Battista (composer); Jesi, Italy **(1710–1736)**

Pericles (statesman); Athens died 429 b.c.

Perkins, Anthony (actor); New York City **(1932–1992)**

Perkins, Frances (social reformer); Boston **(1882–1965)**

Perlman, Itzhak (violinist); Tel Aviv, Israel, 8/31/45

Perlman, Rhea (actress); Brooklyn, N.Y., 3/31/48

Perón, Isabel (María Estela Martínez Cartas) (former chief of state); La Rioja, Argentina, 2/4/31

Perón, Juan D. (statesman); nr. Lobos, Argentina **(1895–1974)**

Perón, Maria Eva Duarte de (political leader); Los Toldos, Argentina **(1919–1952)**

Perot, H. Ross (business executive); Texarkana, Tex., 6/27/30

Perrine, Valerie (actress, dancer); Galveston, Tex., 9/3/43

Perry, Luke **(Coy Luther Perry III)** (actor); Fredericktown, Ohio, 10/11/66

Perry, Matthew (actor); Williamstown, Mass., 8/19/69

Pershing, John Joseph (general); Linn County, Mo. **(1860–1948)**

Pestalozzi, Johann (educator); Zurich, Switzerland **(1746–1827)**

Peters, Bernadette (Bernadette Lazzara) (actress); New York City, 2/28/48

Peters, Brock (actor, singer); New York City, 7/2/27

Peters, Jean (actress); Canton, Ohio **(1926–2000)**

Peters, Roberta (Roberta Peterman) (soprano); New York City, 5/4/30

Petit, Roland (choreographer, dancer); Villemombe, France, 1924

Petrarch (Francesco Petrarca) (poet); Arezzo, Italy **(1304–1374)**

Petty, Tom (folk/rock musician); Gainesville, Fla., 10/20/50

Pfeiffer, Michelle (actress); Santa Ana, Calif., 4/29/58

Philbin, Regis (talk show host); New York City, 8/25/33

Philip (Philip Mountbatten) (Duke of Edinburgh); Corfu, Greece, 6/10/21

Phillippe, Ryan (actor); New Castle, Del., 9/10/74

Phoenix, Joaquin (actor); San Juan, Puerto Rico, 10/28/74

Phoenix, River (actor); Madras, Ore. **(1970–1993)**

Piaf, Edith (Edith Gassion) (singer); Paris **(1916–1963)**

Piatigorsky, Gregor (cellist); Ekaterinoslav, Russia **(1903–1976)**

Piazza, Marguerite (soprano); New Orleans, 5/6/26

Picasso, Pablo (painter, sculptor); Málaga, Spain **(1881–1973)**

Pickett, Wilson (singer); Prattville, Ala., 3/18/41

Pickford, Mary (Gladys Mary Smith) (actress); Toronto **(1892–1979)**

Picon, Molly (actress); New York City **(1898–1992)**

Pidgeon, Walter (actor); East St. John, N.B., Canada **(1898–1984)**

Pierce, David Hyde (actor); Saratoga Springs, N.Y., 4/3/59

Pierce, Franklin (14th U.S. president); Hillsboro, N.H. **(1804–1869)**

Pileggi, Mitch (actor); Portland, Ore., 4/5/52

Pinkett-Smith, Jada (actress); Baltimore, 9/18/71

Pinsky, Robert (ex-poet laureate of the U.S.); Long Branch, N.J., 10/20/40

Pinochet (Ugarte), Augusto (former leader of Chile's military government); Valparaiso, Chile, 11/25/15

Pinter, Harold (playwright); London, 10/10/30

Pinza, Ezio (basso); Rome **(1892–1957)**

Pirandello, Luigi (dramatist, novelist); nr. Girgenti, Italy **(1867–1936)**

Piranesi, Giambattista (artist); Mestre, Italy **(1720–1778)**

Pissaro, Camille Jacob (painter); St. Thomas, U.S. Virgin Islands **(1830–1903)**

Piston, Walter (composer); Rockland, Maine **(1894–1976)**

Pitman, Sir [Isaac] James (educator, publisher); Bath, England **(1813–1897)**

Pitt, Brad (actor); Shawnee, Okla., 12/18/63

Pitt, William ("Younger Pitt") (statesman); nr. Bromley, England **(1759–1806)**

Pitts, ZaSu (actress); Parsons, Kans. **(1898–1963)**

Pius XII (Eugenio Pacelli) (Pope); Rome **(1876–1958)**

Pizarro, Francisco (explorer); Trujillo, Spain **(c. 1476–1541)**

Planck, Max (physicist); Kiel, Germany **(1858–1947)**

Plant, Robert (musician, singer, song writer); West Bromwich, Staffordshire, England , 8/20/48

Plath, Sylvia (poet); Boston **(1932–1963)**

Plato (Aristocles) (philosopher); Athens **(c. 427–347 b.c.)**

Pleasence, Donald (actor); Worksop, England **(1919–1995)**

Pleshette, Suzanne (actress); New York City, 1/31/37

Plimpton, George (author); New York City, 3/18/27

Plimpton, Martha (actress); New York City, 11/16/70

Plisetskaya, Maya (ballet dancer); Moscow, 11/20/25

Plowright, Joan (actress); Brigg, England, 10/28/29

Plummer, Christopher (actor); Toronto, 12/13/29 or 27

Plutarch (biographer); Chaeronea, Greece **(c. 46–c. 120)**

Pocahontas (Matoaka) (American Indian princess); Virginia **(c. 1595–1617)**

Podhoretz, Norman (author); Brooklyn, N.Y., 1/16/30

Poe, Edgar Allan (poet, story writer); Boston **(1809–1849)**

Poitier, Sidney (actor, director); Miami, Fla., 2/20/24

Polanski, Roman (director); Paris, 8/18/33

Polk, James Knox (11th U.S. president); Mecklenburg County, N.C. **(1795–1849)**

Pollack, Sydney (film director, producer, actor); Lafayette, Ind., 7/1/34

Pollard, Michael J. (actor); Passaic, N.J., 5/30/39

Pollock, Jackson (painter); Cody, Wyo. **(1912–1956)**

Polo, Marco (traveler); Venice **(c. 1254–1324)**

Pol Pot (Cambodian dictator); Kompong Thom, Cambodia **(1925–1998)**

Pompadour, Mme. de (Jeanne Antoinette Poisson) (courtesan); Versailles **(1721–1764)**

Pompey (Gnaeus Pompeius Magnus) (general); Rome **(106–48 b.c.)**

Ponce de León, Juan (explorer); Servas, Spain **(c. 1460–1521)**

Pons, Lily (coloratura soprano); Cannes, France **(1904–1976)**

Ponselle, Rosa (soprano); Meriden, Conn. **(1897–1981)**

Ponti, Carlo (director); Milan, Italy, 12/11/13

Pontormo, Jacopo da (painter); Pontormo, Italy **(1492–1557)**

Pope, Alexander (poet); London **(1688–1744)**

Porter, Cole (songwriter); Peru, Ind. **(1891–1964)**

Porter, Katherine Anne (novelist); Indian Creek, Tex. **(1891–1980)**

Portman, Natalie (actress); Jerusalem, 6/9/81

Posey, Parker (actress); Baltimore, 11/8/68

Post, Wiley (aviator); Grand Plain, Tex. **(1900–1935)**
Poston, Tom (actor); Columbus, Ohio, 10/17/27
Potëmkin, Grigori Aleksandrovich, Prince (statesman); Khizovo (Khizov), Belarus **(1739–1791)**
Potok, Chaim (author); New York City **(1929–2002)**
Potter, (Helen) Beatrix (author, illustrator); South Kensington, Middlesex, England **(1866–1943)**
Potts, Annie (actress); Nashville, Tenn., 10/28/52
Poulenc, Francis (composer); Paris **(1899–1963)**
Pound, Ezra (poet); Hailey, Idaho **(1885–1972)**
Poussin, Nicolas (painter); Villers, France **(1594–1665)**
Powell, Adam Clayton, Jr. (congressman); New Haven, Conn. **(1908–1972)**
Powell, Colin L. (secretary of state); New York City, 4/5/37
Powell, Dick (actor); Mt. View, Ark. **(1904–1963)**
Powell, Eleanor (actress, tap dancer); Springfield, Mass. **(1912–1982)**
Powell, Jane (Suzanne Burce) (actress, singer); Portland, Ore., 4/1/29
Powell, William (actor); Pittsburgh **(1892–1984)**
Power, Tyrone (actor); Cincinnati, Ohio **(1914–1958)**
Powers, Stefanie (Stefania Zofia Federkiewicz) (actress); Hollywood, Calif., 11/12/42
Praxiteles (sculptor); Athens **(c. 370–c. 330 B.C.)**
Preminger, Otto (director, producer); Vienna **(1906–1986)**
Prentiss, Paula (Paula Ragusa) (actress); San Antonio, 3/4/39
Presley, Elvis (singer, actor); Tupelo, Miss. **(1935–1977)**
Presley, Priscilla (actress); Brooklyn, N.Y., 5/24/45
Preston, Robert (Robert Preston Meservey) (actor); Newton Highlands, Mass. **(1918–1987)**
Previn, André (conductor); Berlin, 4/6/29
Price, Leontyne (Mary) (soprano); Laurel, Miss., 2/10/27
Price, Ray (country music artist); Perryville, Tex., 1/12/26
Price, Vincent (actor); St. Louis **(1911–1993)**
Pride, Charley (singer); Sledge, Miss., 3/18/38?
Priestley, Jason (actor, producer); Vancouver, B.C., Canada, 8/28/69
Priestley, J. B. (John B.) (author); Bradford, England **(1894–1984)**
Priestley, Joseph (chemist); nr. Leeds, England **(1733–1804)**
Primakov, Yevgeny (Russian political leader); Kiev, Ukraine, 10/29/29
Primrose, William (violist); Glasgow, Scotland **(1904–1982)**
Prince (Prince Rogers Nelson) (singer); Minneapolis, 6/7/58
Prince, Harold (stage producer); New York City, 1/30/28
Principal, Victoria (actress); Fukuoka, Japan, 1/3/45
Prinze, Freddie (actor); New York City **(1954–1977)**
Pritchett, V(ictor) S(awdon) (literary critic); Ipswich, England **(1900–1997)**
Procter, William (scientist); Cincinnati **(1872–1951)**
Prokofiev, Sergei Sergeevich (composer); St. Petersburg, Russia **(1891–1953)**
Proulx, E. Annie (novelist); Norwich, Conn., 8/22/35
Proust, Marcel (novelist); Paris **(1871–1922)**
Provine, Dorothy (actress); Deadwood, S.D., 1/20/37
Prowse, Juliet (actress, dancer); Bombay (Mumbai) **(1936–1996)**
Pryce, Jonathan (actor); Holywell, Wales, 6/1/47
Pryor, Richard (comedian); Peoria, Ill., 12/1/40
Ptolemy (Claudius Ptolemaeus) (astronomer, geographer); Ptolemais Hermii, Egypt, fl. 2nd cent.
Pucci, Emilio (Marchese di Barsento) (fashion designer); Naples, Italy **(1914–1992)**
Puccini, Giacomo (composer); Lucca, Italy **(1858–1924)**
Puente, Tito (band leader); New York City **(1923–2000)**
Pulaski, Casimir (military officer); Podolia, Poland **(1748–1779)**
Pulitzer, Joseph (publisher); Makó, Hungary **(1847–1911)**
Pullman, Bill (actor); Delphi, N.Y., 12/17/53
Pullman, George (inventor); Brockton, N.Y. **(1831–1897)**
Purcell, Henry (composer); London **(1658–1695)**
Pusey, Nathan M. (educator); Council Bluffs, Iowa **(1907–2001)**
Pushkin, Alexander Sergeevich (poet, dramatist); Moscow **(1799–1837)**
Putin, Vladimir (president of Russia); Leningrad, 1952
Puzo, Mario (novelist); New York City **(1920–1999)**
Pyle, Ernest Taylor (journalist); Dana, Ind. **(1900–1945)**
Pythagoras (mathematician, philosopher); Samos, Greece **(c. 582–c. 507A.D.)**

Q

Qaddafi, Muammar al- (Libyan leader); Libya, 1942
Quaid, Dennis (actor); Houston, 4/9/54
Quaid, Randy, (actor); Houston, 10/1/50
Quayle, Anthony (actor); Ainsdale, England **(1913–1989)**

Queen, Ellery: pen name of Frederic Dannay and Manfred B. Lee
Queen Latifah (Dana Owens) (rap musician, actress); Newark, New Jersey, 3/18/70
Queler, Eve (conductor); New York City, 1/1/36
Quennell, Sir Peter Courtney (biographer); Bromley, England **(1905–1993)**
Quindlen, Anna (writer); Philadelphia, 7/8/53
Quinn, Aidan (actor); Chicago, 3/8/59
Quinn, Anthony (Antonio Quiñones) (actor); Chihuahua, Mexico **(1915–2001)**

R

Rabe, David (playwright); Dubuque, Iowa, 3/10/40
Rabelais, François (satirist); nr. Chinon, France **(c. 1490–1553)**
Rabi, I(sidor) I(saac) (physicist); Rymanow, Poland **(1898–1988)**
Rabin, Yitzhak (former Israeli prime minister); Jerusalem **(1922–1995)**
Rachmaninoff, Sergei Wassilievitch (pianist, composer); Oneg Estate, Novgorod, Russia **(1873–1943)**
Racine, Jean Baptiste (dramatist); La Ferté-Milon, France **(1639–1699)**
Radner, Gilda (comedienne); Detroit **(1946–1989)**
Raft, George (actor); New York City **(1895–1980)**
Rainier III (Prince); Monaco, 5/31/23
Rains, Claude (actor); London **(1889–1967)**
Raitt, Bonnie (singer); Burbank, Calif., 11/8/49
Raitt, John (actor, singer); Santa Ana, Calif., 1/19/17
Raleigh, Sir Walter (courtier, navigator); London **(1552?–1618)**
Rambeau, Marjorie (actress); San Francisco **(1889–1970)**
Rameau, Jean-Philippe (composer); Dijon, France **(1683–1764)**
Rampal, Jean-Pierre (Louis) (flutist); Marseilles, France **(1922–2000)**
Rand, Ayn (novelist, philosopher); St. Petersburg, Russia **(1905–1982)**
Randall, Tony (Leonard Rosenberg) (actor); Tulsa, Okla. **(1920–2004)**
Randolph, A(sa) Philip (labor leader); Crescent City, Fla. **(1889–1979)**
Rankin, Jeannette (politician, pacifist); Missoula, Mont. **(1880–1973)**
Raphael (Raffaello Santi) (painter, architect); Urbino, Italy **(1483–1520)**
Rasputin, Grigori Efimovich (monk); Tobolsk Province, Russia **(1872–1916)**
Rathbone, Basil (Philip St. John Basil Rathbone) (actor); Johannesburg, South Africa **(1892–1967)**
Rather, Dan (TV newscaster); Wharton, Tex., 10/31/31
Rattigan, Terence (playwright); London **(1911–1977)**
Ratzenberger, John (actor); Bridgeport, Conn., 4/6/47
Rauschenberg, Robert (painter); Port Arthur, Tex., 10/22/25
Ravel, Maurice Joseph (composer); Ciboure, France **(1875–1937)**
Ray, Aldo (DaRe) (actor); Pen Argyl, Pa. **(1926–1991)**
Ray, Gene Anthony (actor, dancer); Harlem, N.Y., 5/24/63
Ray, Man (painter); Philadelphia **(1890–1976)**
Ray, Satyajit (film director); Calcutta **(1921–1992)**
Raye, Martha (Margie Yvonne Reed) (comedienne, actress); Butte, Mont. **(1916–1994)**
Rea, Stephen (actor); Belfast, Ireland, 10/31/43
Reagan, Ronald Wilson (40th U.S. president, actor); Tampico, Ill. **(1911–2004)**
Reasoner, Harry (TV commentator); Dakota City, Iowa **(1923–1991)**
Redding, Otis (singer); Dawson, Ga. **(1941–1967)**
Reddy, Helen (singer); Melbourne, Australia, 10/25/41
Redford, Robert (Charles Robert Redford, Jr.) (actor); Santa Monica, Calif., 8/18/37
Redgrave, Lynn (actress); London, 3/8/43
Redgrave, Sir Michael (actor); Bristol, England **(1908–1985)**
Redgrave, Vanessa (actress); London, 1/30/37
Redon, Odilon (artist); Bordeaux, France **(1840–1916)**
Reed, Donna (Donna Belle Mullenger) (actress); Denison, Iowa **(1921–1986)**
Reed, Lou (Lewis Allen Reed) (musician, guitarist, singer, song writer); Freeport, N.Y., 3/ 2/42
Reed, Rex (critic); Ft. Worth, 10/2/40
Reed, Walter (army surgeon); Belroi, Va. **(1851–1902)**
Reese, Della (Deloreese Patricia Early) (singer, actress); Detroit, 7/6/32
Reeve, Christopher (actor, activist); New York City, 9/25/52
Reeves, Jim (singer); Panola County, Tex. **(1923–1964)**
Reeves, Keanu (actor, musician); Beirut, Lebanon, 9/2/64
Reich, Robert (Clinton cabinet member); Scranton, Pa., 6/24/46
Reich, Steve (composer); New York City, 10/3/36
Reid, Wallace (actor); St. Louis **(1891–1923)**

Reiner, Carl (actor); New York City, 3/20/22

Reiner, Fritz (conductor); Budapest (1888–1963)

Reiner, Robert (actor, director, writer, producer); Bronx, N.Y., 3/6/45

Reinhardt, Max (Max Goldmann) (theater producer); nr. Vienna (1873–1943)

Reiser, Paul (actor, producer); New York City, 3/30/57

Remarque, Erich Maria (novelist); Osnabrük, Germany (1898–1970)

Rembrandt (Rembrandt Harmensz van Rijn) (painter); Leyden, Netherlands (1605–1669)

Remick, Lee (Ann) (actress); Boston (1935–1991)

Remnick, David (writer, editor); Hackensack, N.J., 10/29/58

Renfro, Brad (actor); Knoxville, Tenn., 7/25/82

Rennert, Günther (opera director, producer); Essen, Germany, 4/1/11

Rennie, Michael (actor); Bradford, England (1909–1971)

Reno, Janet (ex-U.S. attorney general); Miami, Fla., 7/21/38

Renoir, Jean (film director, writer); Paris (1894–1979)

Renoir, Pierre Auguste (painter); Limoges, France (1841–1919)

Resnais, Alain (film director); Vannes, France, 6/3/22

Resnik, Regina (mezzo-soprano); New York City, 8/30/22

Respighi, Ottorino (composer); Bologna, Italy (1879–1936)

Reston, James (journalist); Clydebank, Scotland (1909–1995)

Reuther, Walter (labor leader); Wheeling, W. Va. (1907–1970)

Revere, Paul (silversmith, hero of famous ride); Boston (1735–1818)

Revson, Charles (business executive); Boston (1906–1975)

Reynolds, Burt (actor, director, producer); Waycross, Ga., 2/11/36

Reynolds, Debbie (Marie Frances Reynolds) (actress); El Paso, Tex., 4/1/32

Reynolds, Sir Joshua (painter); nr. Plymouth, England (1723–1792)

Reynolds, Marjorie (Marjorie Goodspeed) (actress); Buhl, Idaho (1921–1997)

Reznor, Trent (musician); Mercer, Pa., 5/17/65

Rhodes, Cecil John (South African statesman); Bishop Stortford, England (1853–1902)

Ricci, Christina (actress); Santa Monica, Calif., 2/12/80

Rice, Anne (novelist); New Orleans, 10/14/41

Rice, Elmer (Elmer Leopold Reizenstein) (playwright); New York City (1892–1967)

Rice, Grantland (sports writer); Murfreesboro, Tenn. (1880–1954)

Rich, Buddy (Bernard) (drummer); Brooklyn, N.Y. (1917–1987)

Rich, Charlie (singer); Colt, Ark. (1932–1995)

Richard I the Lion-hearted (king of England); Oxford, England (1157–1199)

Richards, Ann (Dorothy Ann Willis) (ex-governor of Texas); Lakeview, Tex., 9/1/33

Richards, Keith (rock singer); Dartford, England, 12/18/43

Richards, Michael (actor); California, 7/21/48

Richardson, Elliot L. (ex-cabinet member); Boston (1920–1999)

Richardson, Sir Ralph (actor); Cheltenham, England (1902–1983)

Richardson, Tony (director); Shipley, England (1928–1991)

Richelieu, Duc de (Armand Jean du Plessis) (cardinal); Paris (1585–1642)

Richie, Lionel (singer, songwriter); Tuskegee, Ala., 6/20/49

Richter, Charles Francis (seismologist); Hamilton, Ohio (1900–1985)

Richter, Sviatoslav (pianist); Zhitomir, Ukraine (1914–1997)

Rickenbacker, Eddie (Edward V.) (aviator); Columbus, Ohio (1890–1973)

Rickles, Don (comedian); New York City, 5/8/26

Rickover, Vice Admiral Hyman G. (atomic energy expert); Russia (1900–1986)

Riddle, Nelson (composer); Hackensack, N.J. (1921–1985)

Ride, Sally K(risten) (astronaut, astrophysicist); Encino, Calif., 5/26/51

Ridgway, General Matthew B. (ex-Army chief of staff); Ft. Monroe, Va. (1895–1993)

Riemenschneider, Tilman (sculptor); Osterode, Germany (c. 1460–1531)

Rigg, Diana (actress); Doncaster, England, 7/20/38

Riley, James Whitcomb (poet); Greenfield, Ind. (1849–1916)

Rilke, Rainer Maria (poet); Prague (1875–1926)

Rimbaud, (Jean Nicolas) Arthur (poet); Charleville, France (1854–1891)

Rimes, LeAnn (singer); Jackson, Miss., 8/28/82

Rimsky-Korsakov, Nikolai Andreevich (composer); Tikhvin, Russia (1844–1908)

Rinehart, Mary (née Roberts) (novelist); Pittsburgh (1876–1958)

Ringwald, Molly (actress); Sacramento, Calif., 2/18/68

Ritchard, Cyril (actor, director); Sydney, Australia (1898–1977)

Ritter, John (Jonathan) (actor); Burbank, Calif. (1948–2003)

Ritter, Tex (Woodward Maurice Ritter) (singer); Panola County, Tex. (1905–1973)

Ritter, Thelma (actress); Brooklyn, N.Y. (1905–1969)

Rivera, Chita (Dolores Conchita Figuero del Rivero) (dancer, actress, singer); Washington, D.C., 1/23/33

Rivera, Diego (painter); Guanajuato, Mexico (1886–1957)

Rivera, Geraldo (Miguel Rivera) (TV host); New York City, 7/4/43

Rivers, Joan (comedienne); Brooklyn, N.Y., 6/8/33

Rivers, Larry (Yitzroch Loiza Grossberg) (painter); New York City (1923–2002)

Roach, Hal (film producer); Elmira, N.Y. (1892–1992)

Robards, Jason, Jr. (actor); Chicago (1922–2000)

Robards, Jason, Sr. (actor); Hillsdale, Mich. (1892–1963)

Robbins, Harold (Harold Rubin) (novelist); New York City (1916–1997)

Robbins, Jerome (Jerome Rabinowitz) (choreographer); New York City (1918–1998)

Robbins, Marty (singer); Glendale, Ariz. (1925–1982)

Robbins, Tim (Timothy Francis) (actor, director); West Covina, Calif., 10/16/58

Roberts, Cokie (Mary Martha Corinne Morrison Claiborne Boggs) (broadcast journalist); New Orleans, 12/27/43

Roberts, Eric (actor); Biloxi, Miss., 4/18/56

Roberts, Julia (actress); Smyrna, Ga., 10/28/67

Roberts, Oral (Granville) (evangelist, publisher); nr. Ada, Okla., 1/24/18

Robertson, Cliff (Clifford Parker Robertson III) (actor); La Jolla, Calif., 9/9/25

Robertson, Dale (Dayle) (actor); Oklahoma City, 7/14/23

Robeson, Paul (singer, actor); Princeton, N.J. (1898–1976)

Robespierre, Maximilien François Marie Isidore de (French Revolutionist); Arras, France (1758–1794)

Robinson, Bill "Bojangles" (Luther) (dancer); Richmond, Va. (1878–1949)

Robinson, Edward G. (Emanuel Goldenberg) (actor); Bucharest (1893–1973)

Robinson, Edwin Arlington (poet); Head Tide, Maine (1869–1935)

Robinson Peete, Holly (Holly Robinson) (actress); Philadelphia, 9/18/64

Robinson, Robert (chemist, Nobel laureate); Chesterfield, Derbyshire, England (1885–1975)

Robinson, Smokey (singer, songwriter); Detroit, 2/19/40

Rock, Chris (comedian, actor); Brooklyn, New York, 2/7/66

Rockefeller, David (banker); New York City, 6/12/15

Rockefeller, John Davison (business executive); Richford, N.Y. (1839–1937)

Rockefeller, John Davison, Jr. (industrialist); Cleveland (1874–1960)

Rockefeller, John D., 3rd (philanthropist); New York City (1906–1978)

Rockefeller, Laurance S. (conservationist); New York City (1910–2004)

Rockwell, Norman (painter, illustrator); New York City (1894–1978)

Roddenberry, Gene (creator of Star Trek); El Paso, Tex. (1921–1991)

Rodgers, Jimmie (singer); Meridian, Miss. (1897–1933)

Rodgers, Richard (composer); New York City (1902–1979)

Rodin, François Auguste René (sculptor); Paris (1840–1917)

Rodzinski, Artur (conductor); Spalato, Dalmatia (1894–1958)

Roeg, Nicolas (film director); London, 8/15/28

Roentgen, Wilhelm Konrad (physicist); Lennep, Prussia (1845–1923)

Roethke, Theodore (poet); Saginaw, Mich. (1908–1963)

Rogers, Buddy (Charles Rogers) (actor); Olathe, Kans. (1904–1999)

Rogers, Carl (psychologist); Oak Park, Ill. (1902–1987)

Rogers, Fred (TV producer, host); Latrobe, Pa. (1928–2003)

Rogers, Ginger (Virginia McMath) (dancer, actress); Independence, Mo. (1911–1995)

Rogers, Kenny (singer); Houston, 8/21/38

Rogers, Mimi (actress); Coral Gables, Fla., 1/27/56

Rogers, Roy (Leonard Frank Slye) (actor, singer); Cincinnati (1911–1998)

Rogers, Wayne (actor); Birmingham, Ala., 4/7/33

Rogers, Will (William Penn Adair Rogers) (humorist); Oologah, Okla. (1879–1935)

Rogers, William P. (ex-secretary of state); Norfolk, N.Y. (1913–2001)

Roland, Gilbert (Luis Antonio Damaso de Alonso) (actor); Juarez, Mexico (1905–1994)

Rolland, Romain (author); Clamecy, France (1866–1944)

Rollins, Sonny (saxophonist); New York City, 9/7/30

Romberg, Sigmund (composer); Szeged, Hungary (1887–1951)

Rome, Harold (composer); Hartford, Conn. (1908–1993)

Romero, Cesar (actor); New York City (1907–1994)

Romney, George W. (automobile executive, governor); Chihuahua, Mexico (1907–1995)

Romulo, Carlos P. (diplomat, educator); Manila (1899–1985)

Ronsard, Pierre de (poet); La Possonnière nr. Couture, France (1524–1585)
Ronstadt, Linda (singer); Tucson, Ariz., 7/15/46
Rooney, Andy (TV personality); Albany, N.Y., 1/14/19
Rooney, Mickey (Joe Yule, Jr.) (actor); Brooklyn, N.Y., 9/23/20
Roosevelt, (Anna) Eleanor (reformer, humanitarian); New York City (1884–1962)
Roosevelt, Franklin Delano (32nd U.S. president); Hyde Park, N.Y. (1882–1945)
Roosevelt, Theodore (26th U.S. president); New York City (1858–1919)
Rorem, Ned (composer); Richmond, Ind., 10/23/23
Rose, Billy (showman); New York City (1899–1966)
Rose, Leonard (concert cellist); Washington, D.C. (1918–1984)
Roseanne (Roseanne Barr) (actress); Salt Lake City, 11/3/52
Rosenberg, Ethel (spy); New York City (1915–1953)
Rosenberg, Julius (spy); New York City (1918–1953)
Ross, Betsy (Betsey Griscom) (flagmaker); Philadelphia (1752–1836)
Ross, Diana (singer); Detroit, 3/26/44
Ross, Katharine (actress); Hollywood, Calif., 1/29/42
Rossellini, Isabella (model, actress); Rome, Italy, 6/18/52
Rossellini, Roberto (film director); Rome (1906–1977)
Rossetti, Christina Georgina (poet); London (1830–1894)
Rossetti, Dante Gabriel (painter, poet); London (1828–1882)
Rossini, Gioacchino Antonio (composer); Pesaro, Italy (1792–1868)
Rosten, Leo (writer); Lódz, Poland (1908–1997)
Rostand, Edmond (dramatist); Marseilles, France (1868–1918)
Rostow, Walt Whitman (economist); New York City (1916–2003)
Rostropovich, Mstislav (cellist, conductor); Baku, Azerbaijan, 3/27/27
Roth, Henry (writer); Tysmenica, Ukraine (1906–1995)
Roth, Philip (novelist); Newark, N.J., 3/19/33
Roth, Tim (actor); London, 5/14/61
Rothko, Mark (Marcus Rothkovich) (painter); Russia (1903–1970)
Rouault, Georges (painter); Paris (1871–1958)
Roundtree, Richard (actor); New Rochelle, N.Y., 9/7/42
Rousseau, Henri (painter); Laval, France (1844–1910)
Rousseau, Jean Jacques (philosopher); Geneva (1712–1778)
Rovere, Richard H. (journalist); Jersey City, N.J., 5/5/15
Rowan, Carl Thomas (journalist); Ravenscroft, Tenn. (1925–2000)
Rowan, Dan (comedian); Beggs, Okla. (1922–1987)
Rowlands, Gena (actress); Cambria, Wis., 6/19/30
Rowling, J(oanne) K(athleen) (novelist); Chipping Sodbury, England, 7/31/65
Royko, Mike (columnist); Chicago (1932–1997)
Rubens, Sir Peter Paul (painter); Siegen, Germany (1577–1640)
Rubinstein, Arthur (concert pianist); Lódz, Poland (1887–1982)
Rubinstein, Helena (cosmetics executive); Kraków, Poland (1870–1965)
Rubinstein, John (actor, composer); Los Angeles, 12/8/46
Rucker, Darius (musician, singer, songwriter); Charleston, S.C., 5/13/66
Rudel, Julius (conductor); Vienna, 3/6/21
Ruffo, Titta (baritone); Italy (1878–1953)
Rumsfeld, Donald (sec. of defense); Chicago, 7/9/32
Runyon, (Alfred) Damon (journalist); Manhattan, Kans. (1884–1945)
Rush, Geoffrey (actor); Toowoomba, Australia, 7/6/51
Rushdie, (Ahmed) Salman (novelist); Bombay (Mumbai), 6/19/47
Rusk, Dean (ex-sec. of state); Cherokee County, Ga. (1909–1994)
Ruskin, John (art critic); London (1819–1900)
Russell, Keri (actress); Fountain Valley, Calif., 3/23/76
Russell, Lord Bertrand (Arthur William) (mathematician, philosopher); Trelleck, Wales (1872–1970)
Russell, Jane (actress); Bemidji, Minn., 6/21/21
Russell, Ken (film director); Southhampton, England, 7/3/27
Russell, Kurt (actor); Springfield, Mass., 3/17/51
Russell, Leon (pianist, singer); Lawton, Okla., 4/2/41
Russell, Lillian (Helen Louise Leonard) (soprano); Clinton, Iowa (1861–1922)
Russell, Mark (satirist); Buffalo, N.Y., 8/23/32
Russell, Nipsy (comedian); Atlanta, 10/13/24
Russell, Rosalind (actress); Waterbury, Conn. (1912–1976)
Russo, Rene (actress); Burbank, Calif., 2/17/54
Rustin, Bayard (civil rights leader); West Chester, Pa. (1910–1987)
Rutherford, Dame Margaret (actress); London (1892–1972)
Ryan, Meg (Margaret Mary Emily Anne Hyra) (actress); Fairfield, Conn., 11/19/61
Ryan, Robert (actor); Chicago (1909–1973)
Rydell, Bobby (Robert Ridarelli) (singer); Philadelphia, 4/26/42
Ryder, Winona (Winona Laura Horowitz) (actress); Winona, Minn., 10/29/71

Rysanek, Leonie (dramatic soprano); Vienna (1928–1998)

S

Saarinen, Eero (architect); Finland (1910–1961)
Sabin, Albert B. (polio researcher); Bialystok, Poland (1906–1993)
Sabu (Dastagir) (actor); Karapur, India (1924–1963)
Sacagawea (Shoshone Indian guide); Lemhi River valley (Idaho) (c. 1786–1812)
Sachs, Jeffrey D. (economist, educator); Michigan, 1954
Sadat, Anwar (former president); Egypt (1918–1981)
Sade, Marquis de (Donatien Alphonse François, Comte de Sade) (libertine, writer); Paris (1740–1814)
Safer, Morley (TV newscaster); Toronto, 11/8/31
Sagan, Carl (Edward) (astronomer, science writer); New York City (1934–1996)
Sagan, Françoise (novelist); Cajarc, France, 6/21/35
Sahl, Mort (Morton Lyon Sahl) (comedian); Montreal, 5/11/27
Saint, Eva Marie (actress); Newark, N.J., 7/4/24
St. Denis, Ruth (dancer, choreographer); Newark, N.J. (1878–1968)
St. James, Susan (Susan Miller) (actress); Los Angeles, 8/14/46
St. John, Jill (actress); Los Angeles, 8/19/40
St. Johns, Adela Rogers (journalist, author); Los Angeles (1894–1988)
Sainte-Marie, Buffy (Beverly) (folk singer); Craven, Sask., Canada, 2/20/41
Saint-Gaudens, Augustus (sculptor); Dublin (1848–1907)
Saint-Laurent, Yves (Henri Donat Mathieu) (fashion designer); Oran, Algeria, 8/1/36
Saint-Saens, Charles Camille (composer); Paris (1835–1921)
Sakharov, Andrei Dmitriyevich (nuclear physicist, peace activist); Russia (1921–1989)
Sales, Soupy (Milton Supman) (television entertainer); Franklinton, N.C., 1/6/26
Salinger, J(erome) D(avid) (novelist); New York City, 1/1/19
Salisbury, Harrison E. (journalist); Minneapolis (1908–1993)
Salk, Jonas (polio researcher); New York City (1914–1995)
Salk, Lee (psychologist); New York City (1926–1992)
Salomon, Haym (American Revolution financier); Leszno, Poland (1740–1785)
Sand, George (Amandine Lucille Aurore Dudevant, née Dupin) (novelist); Paris (1804–1876)
Sandburg, Carl (poet, biographer); Galesburg, Ill. (1878–1967)
Sanders, George (actor); St. Petersburg, Russia (1906–1972)
Sandler, Adam (comedian, musician, actor, screenwriter, singer); Brooklyn, N.Y., 9/9/66
Sands, Tommy (singer); Chicago, 8/27/37
Sanger, Margaret (birth-control advocate); Corning, N.Y. (1879–1966)
San Giacomo, Laura (actress); Hoboken, N.J., 11/14/62
Santayana, George (philosopher); Madrid (1863–1952)
Sappho (poet); Lesbos, Greece (610 B.C.–580 B.C.)
Sarandon, Susan (Susan Tomalin) (actress); New York City, 10/4/46
Sargent, John Singer (painter); Florence, Italy (1856–1925)
Sarnoff, David (radio executive); Minsk, Belarus (1891–1971)
Saroyan, William (novelist); Fresno, Calif. (1908–1981)
Sarto, Andrea del (Andrea Domenico d'Agnolo di Francesco) (painter); Florence, Italy (1486–1531)
Sartre, Jean-Paul (existentialist writer); Paris (1905–1980)
Sassoon, Vidal (hair stylist); London, 1/17/28
Satie, Erik (Alfred Leslie) (composer); Paris (1866–1925)
Saul (king of Israel) fl. 11th cent. B.C.
Savage, Fred (actor); Highland Park, Ill., 7/9/76
Savalas, Telly (Aristoteles) (actor); Garden City, N.Y. (1924–1994)
Savonarola, Girolamo (religious reformer); Ferrara, Italy (1452–1498)
Sawyer, Diane (broadcast journalist); Glasgow, Ky., 12/22/45
Sayão, Bidú (soprano); Rio de Janeiro (1904–1999)
Sayles, John (director, screenwriter, actor); Schenectady, N.Y., 9/28/50
Scarlatti, Alessandro (composer); Palermo, Italy (1659–1725)
Scarlatti, Domenico (composer); Naples, Italy (1685–1757)
Scavullo, Francesco (photographer); Staten Island, N.Y. (1929–2004)
Schama, Simon (historian); London, 2/13/45
Schapiro, Meyer (Meir) (art historian); Siauliai, Lithuania (1904–1996)
Schary, Dore (producer, writer); Newark, N.J. (1905–1980)
Schell, Maximilian (actor); Vienna, 12/8/30
Schiaparelli, Elsa (fashion designer); Rome (1890–1973)
Schiff, Dorothy (newspaper publisher); New York City (1903–1989)

Schiffer, Claudia (model, actress); Rheinberg/Dusseldorf, Germany, 8/25/70

Schiller, Johann Christoph Friedrich von (dramatist, poet); Marbach, Germany **(1759–1805)**

Schipa, Tito (tenor); Lecce, Italy **(1890–1965)**

Schippers, Thomas (conductor); Kalamazoo, Mich. **(1930–1977)**

Schlegel, Friedrich von (philosopher); Hanover, Germany **(1772–1829)**

Schlesinger, Arthur M., Jr. (historian); Columbus, Ohio, 10/15/17

Schnabel, Artur (pianist, composer); Lipnik, Austria **(1882–1951)**

Schneider, Romy (Rose-Marie Albach-Retty) (actress); Vienna **(1938–1982)**

Schoenberg, Arnold (composer); Vienna **(1874–1951)**

Schomberg, Arthur (bibliophile, antiquarian); San Juan, P.R. **(1874–1938)**

Schopenhauer, Arthur (philosopher); Danzig, Poland **(1788–1860)**

Schröder, Gerhard (chancellor of Germany); Mossenberg, Germany, 4/7/44

Schubert, Franz Peter (composer); Vienna **(1797–1828)**

Schulberg, Budd (novelist); New York City, 3/27/14

Schulz, Charles M. (cartoonist); Minneapolis **(1922–2000)**

Schumacher, Joel (film director, producer, screenwriter); New York City, 8/29/39

Schuman, Robert (statesman); Luxembourg **(1886–1963)**

Schuman, William (composer); New York City **(1910–1992)**

Schumann, Robert Alexander (composer); Zwickau, Germany **(1810–1856)**

Schwartz, Arthur (songwriter); Brooklyn, N.Y. **(1900–1984)**

Schwarzenegger, Arnold (bodybuilder, actor); Graz, Austria, 7/30/47

Schwarzkopf, Elisabeth (soprano); Poznán, Poland, 12/9/15

Schwarzkopf, H. Norman (retired general); Trenton, N.J., 8/22/34

Schweitzer, Albert (humanitarian, Nobel laureate); Kaysersburg, Upper Alsace **(1875–1965)**

Schwimmer, David (actor); New York City, 11/12/66

Scofield, Paul (actor); Hurstpierpoint, England, 1/21/22

Scorsese, Martin (actor, writer, director, producer); Flushing, N.Y., 11/17/42

Scott, George C. (actor); Wise, Va. **(1927–1999)**

Scott, Hazel (singer, pianist); Port of Spain, Trinidad **(1920–1981)**

Scott, Lizabeth (Emma Matzo) (actress); Scranton, Pa., 9/29/23

Scott, Randolph (Randolph Crane) (actor); Orange County, Va. **(1898–1987)**

Scott, Robert Falcon (explorer); Devonport, England **(1868–1912)**

Scott, Sir Walter (novelist); Edinburgh, Scotland **(1771–1832)**

Scott, Zachary (actor); Austin, Tex. **(1914–1965)**

Scotto, Renata (operatic soprano); Savona, Italy, 2/24/36

Scruggs, Earl Eugene (bluegrass musician); Cleveland County, N.C., 1/6/24

Seaborg, Glenn Theodore (chemist, Nobel laureate); Ishpeming, Mich. **(1912–1999)**

Seagal, Steven (actor); Lansing, Mich., 4/10/52

Seal (Sealhenry Olumide Samuel) (singer, songwriter); London, England, 2/19/63

Seattle (Chief Seattle) (Suquamish Indian leader); Blake Island (Wash.) **(c. 1786–1866)**

Sebastian, John (composer, singer); New York City, 3/17/44

Seberg, Jean (actress); Marshalltown, Iowa **(1938–1979)**

Sedaka, Neil (singer); Brooklyn, N.Y., 3/13/39

Sedgwick, Kyra (actress); New York City, 8/19/65

Seeger, Pete (folk singer); New York City, 5/3/19

Segal, Erich (novelist); Brooklyn, N.Y., 6/16/37

Segal, George (actor); New York City, 2/13/36

Segovia, Andrés (guitarist); Linares, Spain **(1893–1987)**

Seinfeld, Jerry (comedian); Brooklyn, N.Y., 4/29/54

Selena (Selena Quintanilla Perez) (singer); Lake Jackson, Tex. **(1971–1995)**

Selleck, Tom (actor); Detroit, 1/29/45

Sellars, Peter (theater director); Pittsburgh, 1958?

Sellers, Peter (actor); Southsea, England **(1925–1980)**

Selznick, David O. (producer); Pittsburgh **(1902–1965)**

Sendak, Maurice (Bernard) (children's book author, illustrator); Brooklyn, N.Y., 6/10/28

Sennett, Mack (Michael Sinnott) (film producer); Richmond, Que., Canada **(1880–1960)**

Sequoyah (Cherokee linguist); Taskigi, Tenn. **(c. 1770–1843)**

Serkin, Peter (pianist); New York City, 7/24/47

Serkin, Rudolf (pianist); Eger, Czech Republic **(1903–1991)**

Serling, Rod (writer, TV host); Syracuse, N.Y. **(1924–1975)**

Sessions, Roger (composer); Brooklyn, N.Y. **(1896–1985)**

Seurat, Georges (painter); Paris **(1859–1891)**

Seuss, Dr. (Theodor Seuss Geisel) (author, illustrator); Springfield, Mass. **(1904–1991)**

Sevareid, Eric (TV commentator); Velva, N.D. **(1912–1991)**

Severinsen, Doc (Carl) (band leader); Arlington, Ore., 7/7/27

Sevigny, Chlöe (actress); Darien, Conn., 1975

Sewell, Rufus (actor, musician); London, 10/29/67

Sexton, Anne (poet); Newton, Mass. **(1928–1974)**

Seymour, Jane (Joyce Penelope Wilhelmina Frankenburg) (actress); Wimbledon, England, 2/15/51

Shabazz, Betty (Betty Sanders) (civil rights activist); Detroit **(1936–1997)**

Shaffer, Peter (playwright); Liverpool, England, 5/15/26

Shaham, Gil (violinist); Urbana, Ill., 1971

Shahn, Ben(jamin) (painter); Kaunas, Lithuania **(1898–1969)**

Shakespeare, William (dramatist); Stratford on Avon, England **(1564–1616)**

Shakur, Tupac (Amaru Shakur) (singer, actor); Brooklyn, N.Y. **(1971–1996)**

Shandling, Garry (comedian, actor, producer); Chicago, 11/29/49

Shange, Ntozake (Paulette Williams) (poet, playwright); Trenton, N.J., 10/18/48

Shankar, Ravi (sitar player); Benares, India, 4/7/20

Sharif, Omar (Michael Shalhoub) (actor); Alexandria, Egypt, 4/10/32

Shatner, William (actor); Montreal, 3/22/31

Shaw, Artie (Arthur Arshawsky) (band leader); New York City, 5/23/10

Shaw, George Bernard (dramatist); Dublin **(1856–1950)**

Shaw, Irwin (novelist); Brooklyn, N.Y. **(1913–1984)**

Shaw, Robert (actor); Lancashire, England **(1927–1978)**

Shaw, Robert (chorale conductor); Red Bluff, Calif. **(1916–1999)**

Shawn, Ted (Edwin Myers Shawn) (dancer, choreographer); Kansas City, Mo. **(1891–1972)**

Shawn, Wallace (actor); New York City, 11/12/43

Shearer, Moira (ballet dancer); Dunfermline, Scotland, 1/17/26

Shearer, Norma (actress); Montreal **(1900–1983)**

Shearing, George (pianist); London, 8/13/20

Sheedy, Ally (Alexandra Sheedy) (actress, writer); New York City, 6/13/62

Sheen, Charlie (actor); Los Angeles, 9/3/65

Sheen, Fulton J. (Peter Sheen) (Roman Catholic bishop); El Paso, Ill. **(1895–1979)**

Sheen, Martin (Ramon Estevez) (actor); Dayton, Ohio, 8/3/40

Shelley, Mary Wollstonecraft Godwin (writer); London **(1797–1851)**

Shelley, Percy Bysshe (poet); nr. Horsham, England **(1792–1822)**

Shelton, Henry (chairman of the Joint Chiefs of Staff); Tarboro, N.C., 1/2/42

Shepard, Sam (Samuel Shepard Rogers) (playwright); Ft. Sheridan, Ill., 11/5/43

Shepherd, Cybill (actress); Memphis, Tenn., 2/18/50

Sheraton, Thomas (furniture designer); Stockton-on-Tees, England **(1751–1806)**

Sheridan, Ann (Clara Lou Sheridan) (actress); Denton, Tex. **(1915–1967)**

Sheridan, Philip (army officer); Albany, N.Y. **(1831–1888)**

Sheridan, Richard Brinsley (dramatist); Dublin **(1751–1816)**

Sherman, William Tecumseh (army officer); Lancaster, Ohio **(1820–1891)**

Sherwood, Robert Emmet (playwright); New Rochelle, N.Y. **(1896–1955)**

Shevardnadze, Eduard Amvrosiyevich (State Council chairman, Georgia); Mamati, Georgia, 1/25/28

Shields, Brooke (actress); New York City, 5/31/65

Shire, Talia (Coppola) (actress); Lake Success, N.Y., 4/25/46

Shirer, William L. (journalist, historian); Chicago **(1904–1993)**

Sholokhov, Mikhail (novelist); Veshenskaya, Russia **(1905–1984)**

Shore, Dinah (Frances Rose Shore) (singer); Winchester,Tenn. **(1917–1994)**

Short, Bobby (Robert Waltrip Short) (singer, pianist); Danville, Ill., 9/15/24

Short, Martin (actor); Hamilton, Ont., Canada, 3/26/50

Shostakovich, Dmitri (composer); St. Petersburg, Russia **(1906–1975)**

Shriner, Herb (humorist, host); Toledo, Ohio **(1918–1970)**

Shriver, Maria (TV co-host); Chicago, 11/6/55

Shriver, Sargent (Robert Sargent Shriver, Jr.) (business executive); Westminster, Md., 11/9/15

Shue, Andrew (actor, soccer player); South Orange, N.J., 2/20/67

Shue, Elisabeth (actress); Wilmington, Del., 6/10/63

Shulman, Max (novelist); St. Paul, Minn. **(1919–1988)**

Sibelius, Jean (Johann Julius Christian Sibelius) (composer); Tavastehus, Finland **(1865–1957)**

Sidney, Sir Philip (poet); Penshurst, England **(1554–1586)**

Sidney, Sylvia (Sophia Kosow) (actress); New York City **(1910–1999)**

Siegfried and Roy (illusionists) **Siegfried Fischbacher**; Rosenheim, Bavaria, Germany, 1939 **Roy Uwe Ludwig Horn**; Nordenham, nr. Bremen, Germany, 1944

Siepi, Cesare (basso); Milan, Italy, 2/10/23

Signoret, Simone (Simone Kaminker) (actress); Wiesbaden, Germany **(1921–1985)**

Sihanouk, Norodom (king of Cambodia); Cambodia, 10/31/22

Sikorsky, Igor I. (inventor); Kiev, Ukraine **(1889–1972)**

Sills, Beverly (Belle Silverman) (soprano, opera director); Brooklyn, N.Y., 5/25/29

Sills, Milton (actor); Chicago **(1882–1930)**

Silone, Ignazio (Secondo Tranquilli) (novelist); Pescina del Marsi, Italy **(1900–1978)**

Silver, Ron (Ron Zimelman) (actor); New York City, 7/2/46

Silverheels, Jay (Harold J. Smith) (actor); Brantford, Ont., Canada **(1919–1980)**

Silverman, Fred (broadcasting executive); New York City, 9/13/37

Silvers, Phil (Philip Silversmith) (comedian); Brooklyn, N.Y. **(1912–1985)**

Silverstein, Shel (writer, poet); Chicago **(1932–1999)**

Silverstone, Alicia (actress); San Francisco, 10/4/76

Simenon, Georges (Georges Sim) (mystery writer); Liège, Belgium **(1903–1989)**

Simmons, Jean (actress); Crouch Hill, London, 1/31/29

Simon, Carly (singer, songwriter); New York City, 6/25/45

Simon, Neil (playwright); Bronx, N.Y., 7/4/27

Simon, Norton (business executive); Portland, Ore. **(1907–1993)**

Simon, Paul (singer, songwriter); Newark, N.J., 10/13/1941

Simone, Nina (Eunice Kathleen Waymoa) (singer, pianist); Tryon, N.C. **(1933–2003)**

Sinatra, Frank (Francis Albert Sinatra) (singer, actor); Hoboken, N.J. **(1915–1998)**

Sinbad (David Adkins) (actor, comedian); Benton Harbor, Mich., 11/10/56

Sinclair, Upton Beall (novelist); Baltimore **(1878–1968)**

Singer, Isaac Bashevis (novelist); Radzymin, Poland **(1904–1991)**

Singleton, John (writer, director); Los Angeles, 1/6/68

Sinise, Gary (actor, director); Chicago, 3/17/55

Siqueiros, David (painter); Chihuahua, Mexico **(1896–1974)**

Sirtis, Marina (actress); London, 3/29/59

Siskel, Gene (film critic); Chicago **(1946–1999)**

Sisley, Alfred (painter); Paris **(1839–1899)**

Sitting Bull (Prairie Sioux Indian chief); on Grand River, S.D. **(c. 1835–1890)**

Skelton, Red (Richard) (comedian); Vincennes, Ind. **(1913–1997)**

Skerritt, Tom (actor); Detroit, 8/25/43

Skinner, B(urrhus) F(rederic) (psychologist); Susquehanna, Pa. **(1904–1990)**

Skinner, Otis (actor); Cambridge, Mass. **(1858–1942)**

Slater, Christian (Christopher Hawkins) (actor); New York City, 8/18/69

Slatkin, Leonard (conductor); Los Angeles, 9/1/44

Sloan, Alfred P., Jr. (industrialist); New Haven, Conn. **(1875–1965)**

Sloan, John (painter); Lock Haven, Pa. **(1871–1951)**

Smalley, Richard E. (chemist, Nobel laureate); Akron, Ohio, 6/6/43

Smetana, Bedrich (composer); Litomysl, Czech Republic **(1824–1884)**

Smith, Adam (economist); Kirkaldy, Scotland **(1723–1790)**

Smith, Alexis (actress); Penticton, Canada **(1921–1993)**

Smith, Alfred Emanuel (politician); New York City **(1873–1944)**

Smith, Bessie (blues singer); Chattanooga, Tenn. **(1894–1937)**

Smith, Sir C. Aubrey (actor); London **(1863–1948)**

Smith, David (sculptor); Decatur, Ind. **(1906–1965)**

Smith, Harry (TV co-anchor); Hammond, Ind., 8/21/51

Smith, Howard K. (TV commentator); Ferriday, La. **(1914–2002)**

Smith, Jaclyn (actress); Houston, 10/26/47

Smith, John (American colonist); Willoughby, Lincolnshire, England **(1580–1631)**

Smith, Joseph (religious leader); Sharon, Vt. **(1805–1844)**

Smith, Kate (Kathryn) (singer); Greenville, Va. **(1909–1986)**

Smith, Kevin (director, screenwriter); Red Bank, N.J., 8/2/70

Smith, Dame Maggie (actress); Ilford, England, 12/28/34

Smith, Patti Lee (singer, songwriter); Chicago, 12/30/46

Smith, Red (Walter) (sports columnist); Green Bay, Wis. **(1905–1982)**

Smith, Will (actor, rap singer); Philadelphia, 9/25/68

Smits, Jimmy (actor); New York City, 7/9/55

Smollett, Tobias (novelist); Dalquhurn, Scotland **(1721–1771)**

Smothers, Dick (Richard) (comedian); New York City, 11/20/39

Smothers, Tom (Thomas) (comedian); New York City, 2/2/37

Snipes, Wesley (actor); Orlando, Fla., 7/31/62

Snow, Lord (Charles Percy) (author); Leicester, England **(1905–1980)**

Snowdon, Earl of (Anthony Armstrong-Jones) (photographer); London, 3/7/30

Snyder, Tom (TV personality); Milwaukee, 5/12/36

Socrates (philosopher); Athens **(469–399 B.C.)**

Soderbergh, Steven (film director, screenwriter); Atlanta, Ga., 1/14/63

Solomon (king of Israel); Jerusalem, fl. 950 B.C.

Solon (lawgiver); Salamis, Greece **(c. 630–559 B.C.)**

Solti, Sir Georg (conductor); Budapest **(1912–1997)**

Solzhenitsyn, Aleksandr (novelist); Kislovodsk, Russia, 12/11/18

Somers, Suzanne (Suzanne Mahoney) (actress); San Bruno, Calif., 10/16/46

Somes, Michael (ballet dancer); Horsley, England **(1917–1994)**

Sommer, Elke (Elke Schletz) (actress); Berlin, 11/5/42

Sondheim, Stephen (composer); New York City, 3/22/30

Sonnenfeld, Barry (cinematographer, film director); New York City, 4/1/53

Sontag, Susan (author, film director); New York City, 1/28/33

Sophocles (dramatist); nr. Athens **(c. 496–406 B.C.)**

Sorbo, Kevin (actor); Mound, Minn., 9/24/58

Sorvino, Mira (actress); Tenafly, N.J., 9/28/67

Sorvino, Paul (actor); Brooklyn, N.Y., 4/13/39

Sothern, Ann (Harriette Lake) (actress); Valley City, N.D. **(1909–2001)**

Soul, David (David Solberg) (actor); Chicago, 8/28/43

Sousa, John Philip (composer); Washington, D.C. **(1854–1932)**

Soyer, Raphael (painter); Borisoglebsk, Russia **(1899–1987)**

Spaak, Paul-Henri (statesman); Brussels **(1899–1972)**

Spacek, Sissy (Mary Elizabeth Spacek) (actress); Quitman, Tex., 12/25/49

Spacey, Kevin (actor); South Orange, N.J., 7/26/59

Spade, David (actor, comedian); Birmingham, Mich., 7/22/65

Spader, James (actor); Boston, 2/7/60

Spark, Muriel (novelist); Edinburgh, Scotland, 2/1/18

Spears, Britney (pop singer); Kentwood, La., 12/1/81

Spector, Phil (rock producer); Bronx, N.Y., 12/25/40

Spelling, Aaron (producer); Dallas, 4/22/28

Spelling, Tori (Victoria) (actress); Los Angeles, 5/16/73

Spencer, Herbert (philosopher); Derby, England **(1820–1903)**

Spender, Stephen (poet); nr. London **(1909–1995)**

Spengler, Oswald (philosopher); Blankenburg, Germany **(1880–1936)**

Spenser, Edmund (poet); London **(1552?–1599)**

Spewack, Bella (playwright); Hungary **(1899–1990)**

Spiegel, Sam (producer); Jaroslaw, Poland **(1901–1985)**

Spielberg, Steven (director, producer, writer, actor); Cincinnati, 12/18/47

Spillane, Mickey (Frank Spillane) (mystery writer); Brooklyn, N.Y., 3/9/18

Spiner, Brent (actor); Houston, 2/2/49

Spinoza, Baruch (philosopher); Amsterdam, Netherlands **(1632–1677)**

Spitalny, Phil (orchestra leader) **(1890–1970)**

Spivak, Lawrence (TV producer); Brooklyn, N.Y. **(1900–1994)**

Spock, Benjamin (pediatrician, writer); New Haven, Conn. **(1903–1998)**

Springsteen, Bruce (singer, songwriter); Freehold, N.J., 9/23/49

Sproul, Robert G. (educator); San Francisco **(1891–1975)**

Squanto (Wampanoag Indian emissary); Patuxet (Plymouth Bay, Mass.) **(c. 1590–1622)**

Stack, Robert (Robert Modini) (actor); Los Angeles **(1919–2003)**

Stafford, Jo (singer); Coalinga, Calif., 11/12/18

Stahl, Lesley (broadcast journalist); Swampscott, Mass., 12/16/41

Stalin, Joseph Vissarionovich (Iosif V. Dzhugashvili) (Soviet leader); nr. Tiflis (Tbilisi), Georgia **(1879–1953)**

Stallone, Sylvester (actor, writer, director); New York City, 7/6/46

Stamp, Terence (actor); London, 1938

Stander, Lionel (actor); New York City **(1908–1994)**

Stanislavski (Konstantin Sergeevich Alekseev) (stage producer); Moscow **(1863–1938)**

Stanley, Sir Henry Morton (John Rowlands) (explorer); Denbigh, Wales **(1841–1904)**

Stanley, Kim (Patricia Reid) (actress); Tularosa, N.M. **(1925–2001)**

Stans, Maurice H. (ex-secretary of commerce); Shakope, Minn. **(1908–1998)**

Stanton, Elizabeth Cady (woman suffragist); Johnstown, N.Y. **(1815–1902)**

Stanton, Frank (broadcasting executive); Muskegon, Mich., 3/20/08

Stanwyck, Barbara (Ruby Stevens) (actress); Brooklyn, N.Y. **(1907–1990)**

Stapleton, Jean (Jeanne Murray) (actress); New York City, 1/19/23

Stapleton, Maureen (actress); Troy, N.Y., 6/21/25

Starker, János (cellist); Budapest, 7/5/24

Starr, Kenneth (independent counsel for Whitewater investigation); Vernon, Tex., 7/21/46

Starr, Ringo (Richard Starkey) (singer, songwriter); Liverpool, England, 7/7/40

Stassen, Harold E. (ex-government official); West St. Paul, Minn. (1907–2001)

Staudinger, Hermann (chemist, Nobel laureate); Worms, Germany (1881–1965)

Steegmuller, Francis (biographer); New Haven, Conn. (1906–1994)

Steel, Danielle (Danielle Fernande Schuelein-Steel) (novelist); New York City, 8/14/47

Steele, Tommy (singer); London, 12/17/36

Stefani, Gwen (singer); Orange County, Calif., 10/3/69

Stegner, Wallace (Earle) (novelist, critic); Lake Mills, Iowa (1909–1993)

Steichen, Edward Jean (photographer, artist); Luxembourg (1879–1973)

Steiger, Rod (Rodney) (actor); Westhampton, N.Y. (1925–2002)

Stein, Gertrude (author); Allegheny, Pa. (1874–1946)

Steinbeck, John Ernst (novelist); Salinas, Calif. (1902–1968)

Steinberg, David (comedian); Winnipeg, Man., Canada, 8/19/42

Steinberg, William (conductor); Cologne, Germany (1899–1978)

Steinem, Gloria (feminist, publisher); Toledo, Ohio, 3/25/34

Steinmetz, Charles (electrical engineer); Breslau, Poland (1865–1923)

Steenburgen, Mary (actress); Newport, Ark., 2/8/53

Stendhal (Marie Henri Beyle) (novelist); Grenoble, France (1783–1842)

Stern, Howard (radio personality); New York City, 1/2/54

Stern, Isaac (concert violinist); Kreminlecz, Russia (1920–2001)

Sterne, Laurence (novelist); Clonmel, Ireland (1713–1768)

Stevens, Cat (Steven Georgiou) (singer, songwriter); London, 7/21/47

Stevens, Connie (Concetta Ingolia) (singer); Brooklyn, N.Y., 8/8/38

Stevens, George (film director); Oakland, Calif. (1905–1975)

Stevens, Risë (mezzo-soprano); New York City, 6/11/13

Stevens, Wallace (poet); Reading, Pa. (1879–1955)

Stevenson, Adlai Ewing (statesman); Los Angeles (1900–1965)

Stevenson, McLean (actor); Bloomington, Ill. (1929–1996)

Stevenson, Parker (actor); Philadelphia, 6/4/52

Stevenson, Robert Louis Balfour (novelist, poet); Edinburgh, Scotland (1850–1894)

Stewart, James (actor); Indiana, Pa. (1908–1997)

Stewart, Jon (Jonathan Stewart Leibowitz) (comedian, actor); Trenton, N.J., 11/28/62

Stewart, Martha (entrepreneurial home stylist); Nutley, N.J., 8/3/41

Stewart, Patrick (actor); Mirfield, England, 7/13/40

Stewart, Rod (Roderick David) (singer); London, 1/10/45

Stieglitz, Alfred (photographer); Hoboken, N.J. (1864–1946)

Stiers, David Ogden (actor); Peoria, Ill., 10/31/42

Stiller, Ben (actor, director, comic); New York City, 11/30/65

Stiller, Jerry (actor); Brooklyn, N.Y., 6/8/29

Stills, Stephen (singer, songwriter); Dallas, 1/3/45

Stine, R. L. (Robert Lawrence Stine) (writer); Columbus, Ohio, 10/8/43

Sting (Gordon Matthew Sumner) (singer, composer); Wallsend, England, 10/2/51

Stipe, Michael (singer); Decatur, Ga., 1/4/60

Stockwell, Dean (actor); North Hollywood, Calif., 3/5/36

Stoker, Bram (novelist); Dublin (1847–1912)

Stokes, Carl (TV newscaster); Cleveland (1927–1996)

Stokowski, Leopold (conductor); London (1882–1977)

Stoltz, Eric (actor); Whittier, Calif., 9/30/61

Stone, Edward Durell (architect); Fayetteville, Ark. (1902–1978)

Stone, I(sidor) F(einstein) (journalist); Philadelphia (1907–1989)

Stone, Irving (Irving Tennenbaum) (novelist); San Francisco (1903–1989)

Stone, Lucy (woman suffragist); nr. West Brookfield, Mass. (1818–1893)

Stone, Oliver (director, writer, producer); New York City, 9/15/46

Stone, Robert (novelist); Brooklyn, N.Y., 8/21/37

Stone, Sharon (actress); Meadville, Pa., 3/10/58

Stone, Sly (Sylvester Stone) (rock musician) 1944

Stooges, The Three (comedy team) **Moe Howard** (Moses Horwitz); Brooklyn, N.Y. (1897–1975;) **Shemp Howard** (Samuel Horwitz); Brooklyn, N.Y. (1900–1955;) **Larry Fine** (Laurence Feinburg); Philadelphia (1911–1974;) **Curly Howard** (Jerome Horwitz); Brooklyn, N.Y. (1906 –1952)

Stoppard, Tom (Thomas Straussler) (playwright); Zlin, Slovakia, 7/3/37

Stout, Rex (mystery writer); Noblesville, Ind. (1886–1975)

Stowe, Harriet Elizabeth Beecher (novelist); Litchfield, Conn. (1811–1896)

Stowe, Madeleine (actress); Eagle Rock, Calif., 8/18/58

Strachey, (Giles) Lytton (biographer); London (1880–1932)

Stradivari, Antonio (violinmaker); Cremona, Italy (1644–1737)

Straight, Beatrice (actress); Old Westbury, N.Y. (1918–2001)

Strasberg, Lee (stage director); Budanov, Austria (1901–1982)

Strasberg, Susan (actress); New York City (1938–1999)

Stratas, Teresa (soprano); Toronto, 5/26/38

Straus, Oskar (composer); Vienna (1870–1954)

Strauss, Johann (composer); Vienna (1825–1899)

Strauss, Lewis L. (naval officer, scientist); Charleston, W. Va. (1896–1974)

Strauss, Peter (actor); New York City, 2/20/47

Strauss, Richard (composer); Munich, Germany (1864–1949)

Stravinsky, Igor (composer); Orlenbaum, Russia (1882–1971)

Streep, Meryl (Mary Louise) (actress); Summit, N.J., 6/22/49

Streisand, Barbra (singer, actress, director, producer, writer); Brooklyn, N.Y., 4/24/42

Strindberg, (Johan) August (dramatist); Stockholm (1849–1912)

Stritch, Elaine (actress); Detroit, 2/2/25

Stuart, Gilbert Charles (painter); Rhode Island (1755–1828)

Stuart, Gloria (film actress); Santa Monica, Calif., 7/4/10

Stuart, James Ewell Brown (known as Jeb) (Confederate army officer); Patrick County, Va. (1833–1864)

Sturges, Preston (Edmond P. Biden) (director, screenwriter, playwright); Chicago (1898–1959)

Stuyvesant, Peter (Governor of New Amsterdam); West Friesland, Netherlands (1592–1672)

Styne, Jule (Julius Kerwin Stein) (songwriter); London (1905–1994)

Styron, William (William Clark Styron, Jr.) (novelist); Newport News, Va., 6/11/25

Suharto (ex-president of Indonesia); Sedaju-Godean, Java, 2/20/21

Sukarno (Indonesian leader); Surabaja, Java (1901–1970)

Sullavan, Margaret Brooke (actress); Norfolk, Va. (1911–1960)

Sullivan, Sir Arthur Seymour (composer); London (1842–1900)

Sullivan, Ed (columnist, TV personality); New York City (1901–1974)

Sullivan, Frank (Francis John) (humorist); Saratoga Springs, N.Y. (1892–1976)

Sullivan, Louis Henry (architect); Boston (1856–1924)

Sulzberger, Arthur Ochs (newspaper publisher); New York City, 2/5/26

Sumac, Yma (singer); Ichocan, Peru, 9/10/27

Summer, Donna (La Donna Andrea Gaines) (singer); Boston, 12/31/48

Sun Ra (Herman "Sunny" Blount) (jazz composer); Birmingham, Ala. (1914?–1993)

Sun Tzu (writer, military strategist); China (fl. c. 500–320 B.C.)

Sun Yat-sen (statesman); nr. Macao (1866–1925)

Susann, Jacqueline (novelist); Philadelphia (1918–1974)

Susskind, David (TV producer); New York City (1920–1987)

Sutherland, Donald (actor); St. John, N.B., Canada, 7/17/34

Sutherland, Joan (soprano); Sydney, Australia, 11/7/26

Sutherland, Kiefer (actor); London, 12/18/66

Suzuki, Pat (actress); Cressey, Calif., 1931

Swados, Elizabeth (composer, playwright); Buffalo, N.Y., 2/5/51

Swank, Hilary (actress); Bellingham, Wash., 7/30/74

Swanson, Gloria (Gloria May Josephine Svensson) (actress); Chicago (1899–1983)

Swarthout, Gladys (soprano); Deepwater, Mo. (1904–1969)

Swayze, John Cameron (news commentator); Wichita, Kans. (1906–1995)

Swayze, Patrick (actor, dancer); Houston, 8/18/54

Swedenborg, Emanuel (scientist, philosopher, mystic); Stockholm (1688–1772)

Swift, Jonathan (satirist); Dublin (1667–1745)

Swinburne, Algernon Charles (poet); London (1837–1909)

Swit, Loretta (actress); Passaic, N.J., 11/4/37

Swope, Herbert Bayard (journalist); St. Louis (1882–1958)

Sydow, Max von (Carl Adolf von Sydow) (actor); Lund, Sweden, 4/10/29

Symons, Arthur (poet, critic); Milford Haven, Wales (1865–1945)

Synge, John Millington (dramatist); nr. Dublin (1871–1909)

Szilard, Leo (physicist); Budapest (1898–1964)

T

Taft, Robert Alphonso (legislator); Cincinnati (1889–1953)

Taft, William Howard (27th U.S. president); Cincinnati (1857–1930)

Tagore, Sir Rabindranath (poet); Calcutta (1861–1941)

Tallchief, Maria (ballet dancer); Fairfax, Okla., 1/24/25

Talleyrand-Pèrigord, Charles Maurice de (statesman); Paris (1754–1838)

Talmadge, Norma (actress); Niagara Falls, N.Y. (1897–1957)

Tamerlane (Timur) (Mongol conqueror); nr. Samarkand, Turkestan (c. 1336–1405)
Tamiroff, Akim (actor); Baku, Azerbaijan **(1899–1972)**
Tan, Amy (novelist); Oakland, Calif., 2/19/52
Tanaka, Tomoyuki (film producer); Osaka, Japan **(1910–1997)**
Tandy, Jessica (actress); London **(1909–1994)**
Tarbell, Ida Minerva (author, muckraker); Erie Co., Pa. **(1857–1944)**
Tarkington, (Newton) Booth (novelist); Indianapolis **(1869–1946)**
Tartikoff, Brandon (television executive); Freeport, N.Y. **(1949–1997)**
Tate, Allen (John Orley) (poet, critic); Winchester, Ky. **(1899–1979)**
Tate, Sharon (actress); Dallas **(1943–1969)**
Taylor, Deems (composer); New York City **(1885–1966)**
Taylor, Elizabeth (actress); London, 2/27/32
Taylor, Harold (educator); Toronto, 9/28/14
Taylor, James (singer, songwriter); Boston, 3/12/48
Taylor, Laurette (Laurette Cooney) (actress); New York City **(1884–1946)**
Taylor, Lili (actress); Glenco, Ill., 2/20/67
Taylor, Gen. Maxwell D. (former Army chief of staff); Keytesville, Mo. **(1901–1987)**
Taylor, Niki (model); Pembroke Pines, Fla., 3/5/75
Taylor, Paul (choreographer); Wilkinsburg, Pa., 7/29/30
Taylor, Rod (actor); Sydney, Australia, 1/11/30
Taylor, Zachary (12th U.S. president); Montebello, Orange County, Va. **(1784–1850)**
Tchaikovsky, Peter (Pëtr) Ilich (composer); Votkinsk, Russia **(1840–1893)**
Teasdale, Sara (poet); St. Louis **(1884–1933)**
Tebaldi, Renata (lyric soprano); Pesaro, Italy, 1/2/22
Tecumseh (Shawnee Indian chief); nr. Springfield, Ohio **(1768–1813)**
Te Kanawa, Kiri (soprano); Gisborne, New Zealand, 3/6/44
Telemann, Georg Philipp (composer); Magdeburg, Germany **(1681–1767)**
Teller, Edward (atomic physicist); Budapest **(1908–2003)**
Templeton, Alec Andrew (pianist, composer); Cardiff, Wales **(1910–1963)**
Tennille, Toni (singer); Montgomery, Ala., 5/8/43
Tennyson, Alfred (1st Baron Tennyson) (poet); Somersby, England **(1809–1892)**
Tenskwatawa (Shawnee prophet); Old Piqua, Ohio **(c. 1770– c. 1835)**
Terhune, Albert Payson (novelist, journalist); Newark, N.J. **(1872–1942)**
Terkel, Studs (writer, interviewer); New York City, 5/16/12
Terry, Ellen Alicia (actress); Coventry, England **(1848–1928)**
Terry-Thomas (Thomas Terry Hoar Stevens) (actor); London **(1911–1990)**
Tesla, Nikola (electrical engineer, inventor); Smiljan, Lika, Croatia **(1856–1943)**
Thackeray, William Makepeace (novelist); Calcutta **(1811–1863)**
Thalberg, Irving G. (producer); Brooklyn, N.Y. **(1899–1936)**
Thant, U (U.N. statesman); Pantanaw, Burma **(1909–1974)**
Tharp, Twyla (dancer, choreographer); Portland, Ind., 7/1/42
Thatcher, Margaret (former prime minister); Grantham, England, 10/13/25
Theodorakis, Mikis (composer); Chios, Greece, 7/29/25
Thicke, Alan (actor, composer); Kirland Lake, Ont., Canada, 3/1/47
Thieu, Nguyen Van (ex-president of South Vietnam); Trithuy, Vietnam, 4/5/23
Thomas, Danny (Amos Jacobs) (entertainer, TV producer); Deerfield, Mich. **(1912–1991)**
Thomas, Dylan Marials (poet); Carmarthenshire, Wales **(1914–1953)**
Thomas, JonathanTaylor (actor); Bethlehem, Pa., 9/8/81
Thomas, Kristen Scott (actress); Redruth, Cornwall, England, 1960
Thomas, Lowell (explorer, commentator); Woodington, Ohio **(1892–1981)**
Thomas, Marlo (actress); Detroit, 11/21/43
Thomas, Michael Tilson (conductor); Hollywood, Calif., 12/21/44
Thomas, Norman Mattoon (Socialist leader); Marion, Ohio **(1884–1968)**
Thomas, Philip Michael (actor); Columbus, Ohio, 5/26/49
Thomas, Richard (actor); New York City, 6/13/51
Thompson, Dorothy (writer); Lancaster, N.Y. **(1894–1961)**
Thompson, Emma (actress); London, 4/15/59
Thompson, Hunter (Stockton) (writer); Louisville, Ky., 7/18/39
Thompson, Lea (actress); Rochester, Minn., 5/31/61
Thomson, Virgil (Garnett) (composer); Kansas City, Mo. **(1896–1989)**
Thoreau, Henry David (naturalist, author); Concord, Mass. **(1817–1862)**
Thorndike, Dame Sybil (actress); Gainsborough, England **(1882–1976)**

Thorne-Smith, Courtney (actress); San Francisco, 11/8/67
Thornton, Billy Bob (actor, screenwriter); Hot Springs, Ark., 8/4/55
Thurber, James Grover (author, cartoonist); Columbus, Ohio **(1894–1961)**
Thurman, Robert A. F. (scholar, Indo-Tibetan Buddhist studies); New York City, 8/6/40
Thurman, Uma (actress); Boston, 4/29/70
Thurmond, (James) Strom (U.S. senator); Edgefield, S.C. **(1902–2003)**
Tibbett, Lawrence (baritone); Bakersfield, Calif. **(1896–1960)**
Tiberius Caesar Augustus (Roman emperor); Capri **(42 B.C.– A.D. 37)**
Tiegs, Cheryl (model, actress); Minnesota, 9/25/47
Tierney, Gene (actress); Brooklyn, N.Y. **(1920–1991)**
Tillich, Paul (philosopher, theologian); Starzeddel, Germany **(1886–1965)**
Tilly, Meg (Margaret Tilly) (actress); Texada Island, B.C., Canada, 2/14/60
Tintoretto, Il (Jacopo Robusti) (painter); Venice **(1518–1594)**
Tiny Tim (Herbert Khaury) (entertainer); New York City **(1932–1996)**
Tiomkin, Dmitri (composer); St. Petersburg, Russia **(1894–1979)**
Titian (Tiziano Vecelli) (painter); Pieve di Cadore, Italy **(1477–1576)**
Tito (Josip Broz or Brozovich) (president of Yugoslavia); Croatia (former Yugoslavia) **(1892–1980)**
Tocqueville, Alexis de (writer); Verneuil, France **(1805–1859)**
Todd, Michael (producer); Minneapolis **(1907–1958)**
Tolkien, J(ohn) R(onald) R(euel) (fantasy writer); Bloemfontein, South Africa **(1892–1973)**
Tolstoy, Count Leo (Lev) Nikolaevich (novelist); Tula Province, Russia **(1828–1910)**
Tomei, Marisa (actress); Brooklyn, N.Y., 12/4/64
Tomlin, Lily (actress, comedienne); Detroit, 9/1/36
Tone, Franchot (actor); Niagara Falls, N.Y. **(1905–1968)**
Tormé, Mel (Melvin) (singer); Chicago **(1925–1999)**
Torn, Rip (Elmore Torn, Jr.) (actor, director); Temple, Tex., 2/6/31
Torquemada, Tomásde (Spanish Inquisitor); Valladolid, Spain **(1420–1498)**
Toscanini, Arturo (orchestra conductor); Parma, Italy **(1867–1957)**
Totenberg, Nina (broadcast journalist); New York City, 1/14/44
Toulouse-Lautrec (Henri Marie Raymond de Toulouse-Lautrec Monfa) (painter); Albi, France **(1864–1901)**
Toynbee, Arnold J. (historian); London **(1889–1975)**
Tracy, Spencer (actor); Milwaukee **(1900–1967)**
Traubel, Helen (Wagnerian soprano); St. Louis **(1903–1972)**
Travanti, Daniel J. (actor); Kenosha, Wis., 3/7/40
Travolta, John (actor); Englewood, N.J., 2/18/54
Treacher, Arthur (actor); Brighton, England **(1894–1975)**
Tree, Sir Herbert Beerbohm (actor, manager); London **(1853–1917)**
Trevor, Claire (Wemlinger) (actress); New York City **(1909–2000)**
Trigère, Pauline (fashion designer); Paris **(1912–2002)**
Trilling, Diana (writer); New York City **(1905–1996)**
Trilling, Lionel (author, educator); New York City **(1905–1975)**
Trollope, Anthony (novelist); London **(1815–1882)**
Trotsky, Leon (Lev Davidovich Bronstein) (statesman); Elisavetgrad, Russia **(1879–1940)**
Trudeau, Garry (cartoonist); New York City, 1948
Trudeau, Pierre Elliott (former prime minister); Montreal **(1919–2000)**
Truffaut, François (film director); Paris **(1932–1984)**
Trujillo y Molina, Rafael Leonidas (dictator); San Cristóbal, Dominican Republic **(1891–1961)**
Truman, Harry S. (33rd U.S. president); near Lamar, Mo. **(1884–1972)**
Truman, Margaret (author); Independence, Mo., 2/17/24
Trump, Donald (business executive); New York City, 6/14/46
Truth, Sojourner (Isabella) (preacher, abolitionist); Ulster Co., N.Y. **(c. 1797–1883)**
Tryon, Thomas (actor, novelist); Hartford, Conn. **(1926–1991)**
Tsiolkovsky, Konstantin E. (father of cosmonautics); Izhevskoye, Russia **(1857–1935)**
Tsongas, Paul E. (politician); Lowell, Mass. **(1941–1997)**
Tubman, Harriet (Araminta) (abolitionist); Dorchester Co., Md. **(c. 1820–1913)**
Tuchman, Barbara (Wertheim) (historian, author); New York City **(1912–1989)**
Tucker, Forrest (actor); Plainfield, Ind. **(1919–1986)**
Tucker, Richard (tenor); New York City **(1913–1975)**
Tucker, Sophie (Sophia Kalish) (singer); Russia **(1884–1966)**
Tudor, Antony (choreographer); London **(1909–1987)**
Tune, Tommy (dancer, choreographer); Wichita Falls, Tex., 2/28/39
Turgenev, Ivan Sergeevich (novelist); Orel, Russia **(1818–1883)**
Turlington, Christy (model); San Francisco, 1/2/69
Turner, Frederick J. (historian); Portage, Wis. **(1861–1932)**

Turner, Ike (singer); Clarksdale, Miss., 11/5/31
Turner, Joseph M.W. (painter); London **(1775–1851)**
Turner, Kathleen (actress); Springfield, Mo., 6/19/54
Turner, Lana (Julia Jean Mildred Frances Turner) (actress); Wallace, Idaho **(1920–1995)**
Turner, Nat (civil rights leader); Southampton County, Va. **(1800–1831)**
Turner, Ted (business executive); Cincinnati, 11/19/38
Turner, Tina (Annie Mae Bullock) (singer); Nut Bush, Tenn., 11/26/39
Turpin, Ben (comedian); New Orleans **(1874–1940)**
Turturro, John (actor); Brooklyn, N.Y., 2/28/57
Twain, Mark (Samuel Langhorne Clemens) (author); Florida, Mo. **(1835–1910)**
Twain, Shania (Eileen Regina Twain) (country singer); Windsor, Ont., Canada, 8/28/65
Tweed, William Marcy (politician); New York City **(1823–1878)**
Twiggy (Leslie Hornby) (model); London, 9/19/49
Twining, Gen. Nathan F. (former Air Force chief of staff); Monroe, Wis. **(1897–1982)**
Twitty, Conway (Harold Lloyd Jenkins) (singer, guitarist); Friars Point, Miss. **(1933–1993)**
Tyler, John (10th U.S. president); Charles City County, Va. **(1790–1862)**
Tyler, Liv (actress, model); Portland, Maine, 7/1/77
Tyler, Steven (singer); New York City, 3/26/48
Tyson, Cicely (actress); New York City, 12/19/33

U

Uccello, Paolo (painter); Florence **(1397–1475)**
Udall, Stewart L. (ex-secretary of the interior); St. Johns, Ariz., 1/31/20
Uggams, Leslie (singer, actress); New York City, 5/25/43
Ulanova, Galina (ballet dancer); St. Petersburg, Russia **(1910–1998)**
Ullman, Tracey (actress, singer); Slough, England, 12/30/59
Ullmann, Liv (actress); Tokyo, 12/16/39
Ulrich, Skeet (actor, model); North Carolina, 1/20/70
Untermeyer, Louis (anthologist, poet); New York City **(1885–1977)**
Updike, John (novelist); Shillington, Pa., 3/18/32
Urey, Harold C. (chemist, Nobel laureate); Walkerton, Ind. **(1893–1981)**
Uris, Leon (novelist); Baltimore **(1924–2003)**
Ustinov, Peter (actor, producer); London, 4/16/21
Utrillo, Maurice (painter); Paris **(1883–1955)**

V

Vaccaro, Brenda (actress); Brooklyn, N.Y., 11/18/39
Vadim, Roger (Roger Vadim Plemiannikov) (film director); Paris **(1928–2000)**
Valentine, Karen (actress); Sabastopol, Calif., 5/25/47
Valentino, Rudolph (Rodolpho d'Antonguolla) (actor); Castellaneta, Italy **(1895–1926)**
Valentino (Valentino Garavani) (fashion designer); nr. Milan, Italy, 5/11/32
Valéry, Paul (Ambroise Toussaint Jules) (poet, critic); Sète, France **(1871–1945)**
Vallee, Rudy (Hubert Prior Rudy Vallée) (band leader, singer); Island Pond, Vt. **(1901–1986)**
Valli, Frankie (Frank Castellaccio) (singer); Newark, N.J., 5/3/37
Van Allen, James Alfred (space physicist); Mt. Pleasant, Iowa, 9/7/14
Van Buren, Abigail (Pauline Esther Friedman) (columnist); Sioux City, Iowa, 7/4/18
Van Buren, Martin (8th U.S. president); Kinderhook, N.Y. **(1782–1862)**
Vance, Vivian (Vivian Jones) (actress); Cherryvale, Kans. **(1909–1979)**
Van Der Beek, James (actor); Cheshire, Conn., 3/8/77
Vanderbilt, Alfred G. (sportsman); London **(1912–1999)**
Vanderbilt, Cornelius (financier); Port Richmond, N.Y. **(1794–1877)**
Vanderbilt, Gloria (fashion designer); New York City, 2/20/24
Van Doren, Carl (writer, educator); Hope, Ill. **(1885–1950)**
Van Doren, Mamie (actress); Rowena, S.D., 2/6/33
Vandross, Luther (R&B singer); New York City, 4/20/51
Van Dyke, Dick (actor); West Plains, Mo., 12/13/25
Vandyke (or Van Dyck), Sir Anthony (painter); Antwerp, Belgium **(1599–1641)**
Van Eyck, Jan (painter); Maeseyck, Belgium **(c. 1390–1441)**
Van Fleet, Jo (actress); Oakland, Calif. **(1915–1996)**

van Gogh, Vincent (painter); Groot Zundert, Brabant, The Netherlands **(1853–1890)**
van Hamel, Martine (ballet dancer); Brussels, 11/16/45
Van Heusen, Jimmy (Edward Chester Babcock) (songwriter); Syracuse, N.Y. **(1913–1990)**
Van Patten, Dick (actor); Richmond Hill, N.Y., 12/9/28
Van Peebles, Melvin (playwright); Chicago, 8/21/32
Vasari, Giorgio (art historian); Arezzo, Italy **(1511–1574)**
Vaughan, Sarah (singer); Newark, N.J. **(1924–1990)**
Vaughan Williams, Ralph (composer); Down Ampney, England **(1872–1958)**
Vaughn, Robert (actor); New York City, 11/22/32
Vaughn, Vince (actor); Minneapolis, 3/28/70
Veblen, Thorstein (economist, social critic); Cato Township, Wis. **(1857–1929)**
Veidt, Conrad (actor); Potsdam, Germany **(1893–1943)**
Velázquez, Diego Rodriguez de Silva y (painter); Seville, Spain **(1599–1660)**
Venturi, Robert (Charles) (architect); Philadelphia, 6/25/25
Verdi, Giuseppe (composer); Roncole, Italy **(1813–1901)**
Verdon, Gwen (actress); Culver City, Calif. **(1925–2000)**
Vereen, Ben (actor, singer); Miami, Fla., 10/10/46
Verlaine, Paul (poet); Metz, France **(1844–1896)**
Vermeer, Jan (or Jan van der Meer van Delft) (painter); Delft, Netherlands **(1632–1675)**
Verne, Jules (author); Nantes, France **(1828–1905)**
Veronese, Paolo (Paolo Cagliari) (painter); Verona, Italy **(1528–1588)**
Verrazano, Giovanni da (navigator); Florence, Italy **(c. 1485–1528)**
Verrett, Shirley (mezzo-soprano); New Orleans, 5/31/33
Versace, Gianni (fashion designer); Reggio di Calabria, Italy **(1946–1997)**
Vesalius, Andreas (anatomist); Brussels **(1515–1564)**
Vespucci, Amerigo (navigator); Florence, Italy **(1454–1512)**
Vico, Giovanni Battista (philosopher); Naples, Italy **(1668–1744)**
Victoria (queen of England); London **(1819–1901)**
Vidal, Gore (novelist); West Point, N.Y., 10/3/25
Vidor, King (film director, producer); Galveston, Tex. **(1895–1982)**
Vigoda, Abe (actor); New York City, 2/24/21
Villa, Pancho (Doroteo Arango) (revolutionary); Hacienda de Rio Grande, San Juan del Rio, Mexico **(1877–1923)**
Villella, Edward (ballet dancer); Bayside, Queens, N.Y., 10/1/36
Villon, François (François de Montcorbier) (poet); Paris **(1431–1463)**
Vinton, Bobby (singer); Canonsburg, Pa., 4/16/35
Virgil (or Vergil) (Publius Vergilius Maro) (poet); nr. Mantua, Italy **(70–19 B.C.)**
Vishnevskaya, Galina (soprano); St. Petersburg, Russia, 10/25/26
Vivaldi, Antonio (composer); Venice **(1678–1741)**
Vlaminck, Maurice de (painter); Paris **(1876–1958)**
Voight, Jon (actor); Yonkers, N.Y., 12/29/38
Volta, Alessandro (scientist); Como, Italy **(1745–1827)**
Voltaire (François Marie Arouet) (author); Paris **(1694–1778)**
von Braun, Wernher (rocket scientist); Wirsitz, Germany **(1912–1977)**
von Furstenberg, Betsy (Elizabeth Caroline Maria Agatha Felicitas Therese von Furstenberg-Hedringen) (actress); Nelheim-Heusen, Germany, 8/16/35
von Fürstenberg, Diane (Diane Simone Michelle Halfin) (fashion designer); Brussels, 12/31/46
von Hindenburg, Paul (statesman); Posen, Poland **(1847–1934)**
von Karajan, Herbert (conductor); Salzburg, Austria **(1908–1989)**
Vonnegut, Kurt, Jr. (novelist); Indianapolis, 11/11/22
Von Stade, Frederica (mezzo-soprano); Somerville, N.J., 6/1/45
Von Stroheim, Erich Oswald Hans Carl Maria von Nordenwall (actor, director); Vienna **(1885–1957)**
Von Zell, Harry (announcer); Indianapolis **(1906–1981)**
Vreeland, Diana (Diana Da Iziel) (fashion journalist, museum consultant); Paris **(1903?–1989)**

W

Wagner, Lindsay (actress); Los Angeles, 6/22/49
Wagner, Robert (actor); Detroit, 2/10/30
Wagner, Robert F. (ex-mayor of New York City); New York City **(1910–1991)**
Wagner, Wilhelm Richard (composer); Leipzig, Germany **(1813–1883)**
Wahlberg, Mark (actor, model, musician); Dorchester, Mass., 6/5/71
Waits, Tom (blues singer); Pomona, Calif., 12/7/49
Waldheim, Kurt (ex-UN secretary-general); St. Andrae-Wörden, Austria, 12/21/18

Walesa, Lech (Polish labor leader and ex-president); Popowo, Poland, 9/29/43

Walken, Christopher (actor); Queens, N.Y., 3/31/43

Walker, Alice (novelist, poet); Eatonon, Ga., 2/9/44

Walker, Nancy (Ann Myrtle Swoyer) (actress, comedienne); Philadelphia **(1922–1992)**

Walker, Robert (actor); Salt Lake City **(1918–1951)**

Walker, T-Bone (blues singer); Linden, Tex. **(1910–1975)**

Wallace, DeWitt (publisher); St. Paul, Minn. **(1889–1981)**

Wallace, George C. (ex-governor); Clio, Ala. **(1919–1998)**

Wallace, Irving (novelist); Chicago **(1916–1990)**

Wallace, Mike (Myron Wallace) (TV interviewer, commentator); Brookline, Mass., 5/9/18

Wallach, Eli (actor); Brooklyn, N.Y., 12/7/15

Wallenberg, Raoul (diplomat, humanitarian); Stockholm **(1912–1947)**

Wallenstein, Alfred (conductor); Chicago **(1898–1983)**

Waller, Thomas "Fats" (pianist); New York City **(1904–1943)**

Wallis, Hal (film producer); Chicago **(1899–1986)**

Walpole, Horace (statesman, novelist); London **(1717–1797)**

Walsh, J. T. (actor); San Francisco, Calif. **(1944–1998)**

Waltari, Mika (novelist); Helsinki **(1903–1979)**

Walter, Bruno (Bruno Walter Schlesinger) (orchestra conductor); Berlin **(1876–1962)**

Walters, Barbara (TV commentator); Boston, 9/25/31

Walton, Izaak (author); Stafford, England **(1593–1683)**

Wambaugh, Joseph (author, screenwriter); East Pittsburgh, 1/22/37

Wanamaker, John (merchant); Philadelphia **(1838–1922)**

Wanamaker, Sam (actor, director); Chicago **(1919–1993)**

Ward, Barbara (economist); York, England **(1914–1981)**

Ward, Rachel (actress); Cornwell Manor, England, 9/12/57

Warhol, Andy (Warhola) (artist); McKeesport, Pa. **(1928–1987)**

Waring, Fred (band leader); Tyrone, Pa. **(1900–1984)**

Warner, H. B. (Henry Bryan Warner Lickford) (actor); London **(1876–1958)**

Warren, Lesley Ann (actress); New York City, 8/16/46

Warren, Robert Penn (novelist); Guthrie, Ky. **(1905–1989)**

Warrick, Ruth (actress); St. Joseph, Mo., 6/29/15

Warwick, Dionne (singer); East Orange, N.J., 12/12/41

Washington, Booker T(aliaferro) (educator); Franklin County, Va. **(1856–1915)**

Washington, Denzel (actor); Mt. Vernon, N.Y., 12/28/54

Washington, George (1st U.S. president); Westmoreland County, Va. **(1732–1799)**

Washington, Harold (ex-mayor of Chicago); Chicago **(1922–1987)**

Waters, Ethel (actress, singer); Chester, Pa. **(1896–1977)**

Waters, Muddy (McKinley Morganfield) (singer, guitarist); Rolling Fork, Miss. **(1915–1983)**

Waterston, Sam (actor); Cambridge, Mass., 11/15/40

Watson, James Dewey (scientist, Nobel laureate); Chicago, 4/6/28

Watson, Thomas John (industrialist); Campbell, N.Y. **(1874–1956)**

Watt, James (inventor); Greenock, Scotland **(1736–1819)**

Watteau, Jean-Antoine (painter); Valanciennes, France **(1684–1721)**

Wattleton, Faye (family planning advocate); St. Louis, 7/8/43

Watts, André (concert pianist); Nuremberg, Germany, 6/20/46

Waugh, Alec (Alexander Raban Waugh) (novelist); London **(1898–1981)**

Waugh, Evelyn (novelist); London **(1903–1966)**

Wayans, Damon (actor, comedian, writer, producer); New York City, 9/4/60

Wayans, Keenan Ivory (actor, comedian, writer, director); New York City, 6/8/58

Wayne, Anthony (military officer); Waynesboro (family farm), nr. Paoli, Pa. **(1745–1796)**

Wayne, David (David McMeekan) (actor); Traverse City, Mich. **(1914–1995)**

Wayne, John (Marion Michael Morrison) (actor); Winterset, Iowa **(1907–1979)**

Weaver, Dennis (actor); Joplin, Mo., 6/4/25

Weaver, Fritz (actor); Pittsburgh, 1/19/26

Weaver, Sigourney (actress); New York City, 10/8/49

Webb, Clifton (Webb Parmelee Hollenbeck) (actor); Indianapolis **(1893–1966)**

Webb, Jack (actor, producer); Santa Monica, Calif. **(1920–1982)**

Weber, Karl Maria Friedrich Ernst von (composer); nr. Lübeck, Germany **(1786–1826)**

Webster, Daniel (statesman); Salisbury, N.H. **(1782–1852)**

Webster, Margaret (producer, director, actress); New York City **(1905–1973)**

Webster, Noah (lexicographer); West Hartford, Conn. **(1758–1843)**

Weill, Kurt (composer); Dessau, Germany **(1900–1950)**

Weir, Peter (director); Sydney, Australia, 8/21/44

Weissmuller, Johnny (Peter John Weissmuller) (actor, swimmer); Freidorf, Romania **(1904–1984)**

Weizmann, Chaim (statesman); Grodno Province, Russia **(1874–1952)**

Welch, Raquel (Raquel Tejada) (actress); Chicago, 9/5/40

Weld, Tuesday (Susan Ker Weld) (actress); New York City, 8/27/43

Welk, Lawrence (band leader); Strasburg, N.D. **(1903–1992)**

Welles, Orson (actor, director, producer); Kenosha, Wis. **(1915–1985)**

Wellington, Duke of (Arthur Wellesley) (statesman); Ireland **(1769–1852)**

Wells, H(erbert) G(eorge) (author); Bromley, England **(1866–1946)**

Wells-Barnett, Ida B. (journalist); Holly Springs, Miss. **(1862–1931)**

Welty, Eudora (novelist); Jackson, Miss. **(1909–2001)**

Wenner, Jann (publisher); New York City, 1/7/46

Werfel, Franz (novelist); Prague **(1890–1945)**

Werner, Oskar (Josef Schliessmayer) (actor, director); Vienna **(1922–1984)**

Wertheimer, Linda (radio journalist); Carlsbad, N.M., 3/19/43

Wertmueller, Lina (Arcanguela Felice Assunta W. von Elgg) (director); Rome, 8/14/28

Wesley, John (religious leader); Epworth Rectory, Lincolnshire, England **(1703–1791)**

West, Benjamin (painter); Springfield, Pa. **(1738–1820)**

West, Dame Rebecca (Cicily Fairfield) (novelist); County Kerry, Ireland **(1892–1983)**

West, Jessamyn (novelist); nr. North Vernon, Ind. **(1902–1984)**

West, Mae (actress); Brooklyn, N.Y. **(1893–1980)**

West, Nathanael (Nathan Weinstein) (novelist); New York City **(1902–1940)**

Westheimer, Dr.. Ruth (Karola Ruth Siegel) (human sexuality expert); Frankfurt, Germany, 1928

Westinghouse, George (inventor); Central Bridge, N.Y. **(1846–1914)**

Westmoreland, William Childs (ex-Army chief of staff); Saxon, S.C., 3/26/14

Weyden, Roger van der (painter); Tournai, Belgium **(c. 1400–1464)**

Wharton, Edith Newbold (née Jones) (novelist); New York City **(1862–1937)**

Wheatley, Phillis (poet); Senegal **(c. 1753–1784)**

Wheeler, Bert (Albert Jerome Wheeler) (comedian); Paterson, N.J. **(1895–1968)**

Whistler, James Abbott McNeill (painter, etcher); Lowell, Mass. **(1834–1903)**

Whitaker, Forest (actor); Longview, Tex., 7/15/61

White, Betty (actress); Oak Park, Ill., 1/17/22

White, Edmund (writer); Cincinnati, Ohio, 1/13/40

White, E(lwyn) B(rooks) (author); Mt. Vernon, N.Y. **(1899–1985)**

White, Pearl (actress); Green Ridge, Mo. **(1889–1938)**

White, Stanford (architect); New York City **(1853–1906)**

White, Theodore H. (historian); Boston **(1915–1986)**

White, Vanna (TV personality); Conway, S.C., 2/18/57

White, William Allen (journalist); Emporia, Kans. **(1868–1944)**

Whitehead, Alfred North (mathematician, philosopher); Isle of Thanet, England **(1861–1947)**

Whiteman, Paul (band leader); Denver **(1891–1967)**

Whiting, Margaret (singer, actress); Detroit, 7/22/24

Whitman, Walt (Walter) (poet); West Hills, N.Y. **(1819–1892)**

Whitmore, James (actor); White Plains, N.Y., 10/1/21

Whitney, Cornelius Vanderbilt (sportsman); New York City **(1899–1992)**

Whitney, Eli (inventor); Westboro, Mass. **(1765–1825)**

Whitney, John Hay (publisher); Ellsworth, Maine **(1904–1982)**

Whittier, John Greenleaf (poet); Haverhill, Mass. **(1807–1892)**

Wideman, John Edgar (writer); Washington, D.C., 6/14/41

Widmark, Richard (actor); Sunrise, Minn., 12/26/14

Wiesel, Elie (Eliezer) (author); Signet, Romania, 9/30/28

Wiesenthal, Simon (Nazi hunter); Buchach, Ukraine, 12/31/08

Wilde, Cornel (film actor, producer); New York City **(1915–1989)**

Wilde, Oscar Fingal O'Flahertie Wills (author); Dublin **(1854–1900)**

Wilder, Billy (Samuel Wilder) (film producer, director); Vienna **(1906–2002)**

Wilder, Gene (Jerome Silberman) (actor, writer, director, producer); Milwaukee, 6/11/35

Wilder, Thornton (author); Madison, Wis. **(1897–1975)**

Wilkins, Roy (civil rights leader); St. Louis **(1901–1981)**

William, Prince (heir to British throne); London, 6/21/82

Williams, Andy (singer); Wall Lake, Iowa, 12/3/30

Williams, Anson (actor, director); Los Angeles, 9/25/49

Williams, Billy Dee (actor); New York City, 4/6/37

Williams, Cindy (actress); Van Nuys, Calif., 8/22/47

Williams, Edward Bennett (lawyer); Hartford, Conn. **(1920–1988)**

Williams, Emlyn (actor, playwright); Mostyn, Wales **(1905–1987)**

Williams, Esther (actress, swimmer); Los Angeles, 8/8/23

Williams, Gluyas (cartoonist); San Francisco **(1888–1982)**

Williams, Hank, Sr. (Hiram King Williams) (singer); Georgiana, Ala. **(1923–1953)**

Williams, Joe (singer); Cordele, Ga. (1918–1999)
Williams, John T. (composer, conductor); Queens, N.Y., 2/8/32
Williams, Lucinda (singer, songwriter); Lake Charles, La., 1/26/53
Williams, Paul (singer, composer, actor); Omaha, Neb., 9/19/40
Williams, Robin (actor, producer); Chicago, 7/21/52
Williams, Roger (clergyman); London (1603?–1683)
Williams, Tennessee (Thomas L. Williams) (playwright); Columbus, Miss. (1911–1983)
Williams, Treat (Richard Williams) (actor); Rowayton, Conn., 12/1/51
Williams, Vanessa (actress, singer); Milwood, N.Y., 3/18/63
Williams, William Carlos (physician, poet); Rutherford, N.J. (1883–1963)
Williamson, Nicol (actor); Hamilton, Scotland, 9/14/38
Willkie, Wendell Lewis (lawyer); Elwood, Ind. (1892–1944)
Willis, Bruce (actor); Germany, 3/19/55
Willson, Meredith (composer); Mason City, Iowa (1902–1984)
Wilson, August (poet, writer, playwright); Pittsburgh, 4/27/45
Wilson, Brian (musician); Inglewood, Calif., 6/20/42
Wilson, Don (radio and TV announcer); Lincoln, Neb. (1900–1982)
Wilson, Dooley (actor, musician); Tyler, Tex. (1894–1953)
Wilson, Edmund (literary critic, author); Red Bank, N.J. (1895–1972)
Wilson, Flip (Clerow Wilson) (comedian); Jersey City, N.J. (1933–1998)
Wilson, Harold (ex-prime minister); Huddersfield, England (1916–1995)
Wilson, Nancy (singer); Chillicothe, Ohio, 2/20/37
Wilson, Sloan (novelist); Norwalk, Conn. (1920–2003)
Wilson, (Thomas) Woodrow (28th U.S. president); Staunton, Va. (1856–1924)
Winchell, Walter (columnist); New York City (1897–1972)
Windsor, Duchess of (Bessie Wallis Warfield) Blue Ridge Summit, Pa. (1896–1986)
Windsor, Duke of (formerly King Edward VIII of England); Richmond Park, England (1894–1972)
Winfrey, Oprah (TV host, producer); Kosciusko, Miss., 1/29/54
Winger, Debra (Mary Debra) (actress); Cleveland, 5/17/55
Winkler, Henry (actor, director, producer); New York City, 10/30/45
Winningham, Mare (actress); Phoenix, Ariz., 5/16/59
Winter, Johnny (guitarist); Leland, Miss., 2/23/44
Winters, Jonathan (comedian); Dayton, Ohio, 11/11/25
Winters, Shelley (Shirley Schrift) (actress); East St. Louis, Ill., 8/18/22
Winthrop, John (first governor, Massachusetts Bay Colony); Suffolk, England (1588–1649)
Wise, Stephen Samuel (rabbi); Budapest (1874–1949)
Withers, Jane (actress); Atlanta, 4/12/26
Witherspoon, Reese (actress); Nashville, 3/22/76
Wittig, Georg F. K. (chemist, Nobel laureate); Berlin, Germany (1897–1987)
Wittgenstein, Ludwig (Josef Johann) (philosopher); Vienna (1889–1951)
Wodehouse, P(elham) G(renville) (novelist); Guildford, England (1881–1975)
Wolf, Scott (actor); Boston, 6/4/68
Wolfe, Thomas Clayton (novelist); Asheville, N.C. (1900–1938)
Wolfe, Tom (journalist); Richmond, Va., 3/2/31
Wolff, Tobias (author); Birmingham, Ala., 6/19/45
Wolsey, Thomas (prelate, statesman); Ipswich, England (c. 1475–1530)
Wonder, Stevie (Steveland Judkins, later Steveland Morris) (singer, songwriter); Saginaw, Mich., 5/13/50
Wong, Anna May (Lu Tsong Wong) (actress); Los Angeles (1907–1961)
Woo, John (actor, film director, screenwriter); Guangzhou, Canton, China, 5/1/46
Wood, Elijah (actor); Cedar Rapids, Iowa, 1/28/81
Wood, Grant (painter); Anamosa, Iowa (1892–1942)
Wood, Natalie (Natasha Viparaeff) (actress); San Francisco (1938–1981)
Woods, James (actor); Vernal, Utah, 4/18/47
Woodhouse, Barbara (Blackburn) (dog trainer, author, TV personality); Rathfarnham, Ireland (1910–1988)
Woodruff, Judy (broadcast journalist); Tulsa, Okla., 11/20/46
Woodson, Carter G. (historian); New Canton, Va. (1875–1950)
Woodward, Edward (actor); Croydon, England, 6/1/30
Woodward, Joanne (actress); Thomasville, Ga., 2/27/30
Woodward, Robert Burns (chemist, Nobel laureate); Boston (1917–1979)
Woolf, (Adeline) Virginia (née Stephens) (novelist); London (1882–1941)
Woollcott, Alexander (author, critic); Phalanx, N.J. (1887–1943)

Woolley, Monty (Edgar Montillion Woolley) (actor); New York City (1888–1963)
Woolworth, Frank (merchant); Rodman, N.Y. (1852–1919)
Wopat, Tom (actor); Lodi, Wis., 9/9/50
Wordsworth, William (poet); Cockermouth, England (1770–1850)
Wouk, Herman (novelist); New York City, 5/27/15
Wovoka (Jack Wilson) (Paiute Indian religious leader); (western Nev.) (c. 1858–1932)
Wray, Fay (actress); nr. Cardston, Alb., Canada (19/07–2004)
Wren, Sir Christopher (architect); East Knoyle, England (1632–1723)
Wright, Frank Lloyd (architect); Richland Center, Wis. (1869–1959)
Wright, Martha (singer); Seattle, 3/23/26
Wright, Orville (inventor); Dayton, Ohio (1871–1948)
Wright, Richard (novelist); nr. Natchez, Miss. (1908–1960)
Wright, Wilbur (inventor); Millville, Ind. (1867–1912)
Wyatt, Jane (actress); Campgaw, N.J., 8/12/12
Wycliffe, John (church reformer); Hipswell, England (1320–1384)
Wyeth, Andrew (painter); Chadds Ford, Pa., 7/12/17
Wyle, Noah (actor); Hollywood, Calif., 6/4/71
Wyler, William (director); Mulhouse, France (1902–1981)
Wyman, Jane (Sarah Jane Fulks) (actress); St. Joseph, Mo., 1/4/14
Wynette, Tammy (Virginia Wynette Pugh) (singer); Tupelo, Miss. (1942–1998)
Wynn, Ed (Isaiah Edwin Leopold) (comedian); Philadelphia (1886–1966)
Wynn, Keenan (actor); New York City (1916–1986)

X

Xavier, St. Francis (Jesuit missionary); Pamplona, Navarre, Spain (1506–1552)
Xenophon (soldier, historian, essayist); Athens (c. 435–c. 355 B.C.)
Xerxes, the Great (king); Persian Empire (c. 519–465 B.C.)

Y

Yeats, William Butler (poet); nr. Dublin (1865–1939)
Yeltsin, Boris (Russian president); Yekaterinburg (then Sverdlovsk), Russia, 2/1/31
Yevtushenko, Yevgeny (poet); Zima, Russia, 7/18/33
York, Michael (actor); Fulmer, England, 3/27/42
York, Susannah (Fletcher) (actress); London, 1/9/42
Yorty, Samuel W. (ex-mayor of Los Angeles); Lincoln, Neb. (1909–1998)
Yothers, Tina (actress); Whittier, Calif., 5/5/73
Young, Alan (actor); North Shield, England, 11/19/19
Young, Andrew (civil rights leader); New Orleans, 3/12/32
Young, Brigham (religious leader); Whitingham, Vt. (1801–1877)
Young, Gig (Byron Barr) (actor); St. Cloud, Minn. (1917–1978)
Young, Loretta (Gretchen Young) (actress); Salt Lake City (1913–2000)
Young, Neil (singer, songwriter); Toronto, 11/12/45
Young, Robert (actor); Chicago (1907–1998)
Youngman, Henny (comedian); Whitechapel, London (1906–1998)

Z

Zane, Billy (William George Zane, Jr.) (actor); Chicago, 2/24/66
Zanuck, Darryl F. (producer); Wahoo, Neb. (1902–1979)
Zappa, Frank (Francis Vincent Zappa, Jr.) (singer, songwriter); Baltimore (1940–1993)
Zeffirelli, Franco (director); Florence, Italy, 2/12/23
Zellweger, Renee (actress); Katy, Texas, 4/25/69
Zemeckis, Robert (filmmaker); Chicago, 1952
Zhou Enlai (premier); Hualyin, China (1898–1976)
Ziegfeld, Florenz (theatrical producer); Chicago (1867–1932)
Ziegler, Karl (chemist, Nobel laureate); Helsa, Germany (1898–1973)
Zimbalist, Efrem (violinist); Rostov-on-Don, Russia (1889–1985)
Zimbalist, Efrem, Jr. (actor); New York City, 11/30/23
Zimbalist, Stephanie (actress); New York City, 10/8/56
Zinnemann, Fred (director); Vienna (1907–1997)
Zola, Emile (novelist); Paris (1840–1902)
Zoroaster (religious leader); Persian Empire (c. 628–c. 551 B.C.)
Zucker, Jerry (film producer, director); Milwaukee, 3/11/50
Zukerman, Pinchas (violinist); Tel Aviv, Israel, 7/16/48
Zukor, Adolph (movie executive); Risce, Hungary (1873–1976)
Zurbarán, Francisco de (painter); Fuentes de Cantos, Spain (1598–1664)
Zweig, Stefan (author); Vienna (1881–1942)
Zwingli, Huldrych (humanist); Wildaus, Switzerland (1484–1531)

U.S. Education

Highest Level of Educational Attainment of U.S. Population, 2002

Some high school	9.0%	Some college	17.0%	Bachelor's degree	17.7%	Doctoral degree	1.2%
High school graduate	32.1%	Associate's degree	8.3%	Master's degree	6.3%	Professional degree	1.5%

NOTE: Persons 25 years and older (182 million). *Source:* U.S. Dept. of Commerce, Bureau of the Census, *Current Population Survey.* From National Center for Educational Statistics, *Digest of Education Statistics, 2003.*

Educational Attainment by Race and Hispanic Origin, 1940–2002

(percent of population ages 25 and older, by years of school completed)

	White[1]			Black[1]			Hispanic		
Age and year	Less than 5 years of elementary school	High school completion or higher[2]	4 or more years of college[3]	Less than 5 years of elementary school	High school completion or higher[2]	4 or more years of college[3]	Less than 5 years of elementary school	High school completion or higher[2]	4 or more years of college[3]
April 1940	10.9%	26.1%	4.9%	41.8%	7.7%	1.3%	—	—	—
April 1950	8.9	36.4	6.6	32.6	13.7	2.2	—	—	—
April 1960	6.7	43.2	8.1	23.5	21.7	3.5	—	—	—
March 1970	4.2	57.4	11.6	14.7	36.1	6.1	—	—	—
March 1980	1.9	71.9	18.4	9.1	51.4	7.9	15.8%	44.5%	7.6%
March 1985	1.4	77.5	20.8	6.1	59.9	11.1	13.5	47.9	8.5
March 1990	1.1	81.4	23.1	5.1	66.2	11.3	12.3	50.8	9.2
March 1995	0.7	85.9	23.4	2.5	73.8	13.3	10.6	53.4	9.3
March 1997	0.6	86.3	26.2	2.0	75.3	13.3	9.4	54.7	10.3
March 1998	0.6	87.1	26.6	1.7	76.4	14.8	9.3	55.5	11.0
March 1999	0.6	87.7	27.7	1.8	77.4	15.5	9.0	56.1	10.9*
March 2000	0.5	88.4	28.1	1.6	78.9	16.6	8.7	57.0	10.6
March 2001	0.5	88.7	28.6	1.3	79.5	16.1	9.3	56.5	11.2
March 2002	0.5	88.7	29.4	1.6	79.2	17.2	8.7	57.0	11.1

NOTE: (—) = not available. 1. Includes persons of Hispanic origin for years prior to 1980. 2. Data for years prior to 1993 include all persons with at least 4 years of high school. 3. Data for 1993 and later years are for persons with a bachelor's or higher degree. *Source:* U.S. Department of Commerce, Bureau of the Census, U.S. Census of Population, 1960, Vol. 1, part 1; *Current Population Reports,* Series P-20 and unpublished data; and *1960 Census Monograph,* "Education of the American Population," by John K. Folger and Charles B. Nam. From U.S. Dept. of Education, National Center for Education Statistics, *Digest of Education Statistics 2003.*

Educational Attainment by Sex, 1910–2002

(percent of population ages 25 and older)

	Both sexes			Male			Female		
Year	Less than 5 years of elementary school	High school completion or higher[1]	4 or more years of college[2]	Less than 5 years of elementary school	High school completion or higher	4 or more years of college	Less than 5 years of elementary school	High school completion or higher	4 or more years of college
1910[3]	23.8%	13.5%	2.7%	—	—	—	—	—	—
1920[3]	22.0	16.4	3.3	—	—	—	—	—	—
1930[3]	17.5	19.1	3.9	—	—	—	—	—	—
April 1940	13.7	24.5	4.6	15.1%	22.7%	5.5%	12.4%	26.3%	3.8%
April 1950	11.1	34.3	6.2	12.2	32.6	7.3	10.0	36.0	5.2
April 1960	8.3	41.1	7.7	9.4	39.5	9.7	7.4	42.5	5.8
March 1970	5.3	55.2	11.0	5.9	55.0	14.1	4.7	55.4	8.2
March 1980	3.4	68.6	17.0	3.6	69.2	20.9	3.2	68.1	13.6
March 1990	2.5	77.6	21.3	2.7	77.7	24.4	2.2	77.5	18.4
March 1995	1.9	81.7	23.0	2.0	81.7	26.0	1.7	81.6	20.2
March 1997	1.7	82.1	23.9	1.8	82.0	26.2	1.6	82.2	21.7
March 1998	1.7	82.8	24.4	1.7	82.8	26.5	1.6	82.9	22.4
March 1999	1.6	83.4	25.2	1.6	83.5	27.5	1.6	83.4	23.1
March 2000	1.6	84.1	25.6	1.6	84.2	27.8	1.5	84.0	23.6
March 2001	1.6	84.3	26.1	1.6	84.4	28.0	1.5	84.2	24.3
March 2002	1.6	84.1	26.7	1.7	83.8	28.5	1.5	84.4	25.1

NOTE: (—) = not available. 1. Data for years prior to 1993 include all persons with at least 4 years of high school. 2. Data for 1993 and later years are for persons with a bachelor's degree or higher. 3. Estimates based on Bureau of the Census retrojection of 1940 Census data on education by age. *Source:* Based on data from the U.S. Department of Commerce, Bureau of the Census, *U.S Census of Population, 1960,* Vol. 1, part 1; *Current Population Reports,* Series P-20 and unpublished data; and *1960 Census Monograph,* "Education of the American Population," by John K. Folger and Charles B. Nam. From U.S. Dept. of Education, National Center for Education Statistics, *Digest of Education Statistics 2003.*

Enrollment in Educational Institutions, 1970–2002

(in thousands)

Year	Public elementary and secondary schools			Private elementary and secondary schools[1]			Degree-granting institutions[2]		
	Total	Pre-K through grade 8	Grades 9 through 12	Total	K through grade 8	Grades 9 through 12	Total	Public	Private
Fall 1970	45,894	32,558	13,336	5,363	4,052	1,311	8,581	6,428	2,153
Fall 1980	40,877	27,647	13,231	5,331	3,992	1,339	12,097	9,457	2,640
Fall 1990	41,217	29,878	11,338	5,234	4,084	1,150	13,819	10,845	2,974
Fall 1999	46,857	33,488	13,369	6,018	4,765	1,254	14,791	11,309	3,482
Fall 2000	47,204	33,688	13,515	6,162[3]	4,875[3]	1,287[3]	15,312	11,753	3,560
Fall 2001	47,688	33,952	13,736	6,202[3]	4,880[3]	1,322[3]	15,928	12,233	3,695
Fall 2002[3]	47,918	33,942	13,976	6,241	4,885	1,356	16,102	12,354	3,749

NOTE: Elementary and secondary enrollment excludes home-schooled children. Based on the National Household Education Survey, there were approximately 850,000 home-schooled children in spring 1999. 1. Beginning in fall 1980, data include estimates for an expanded universe of private schools. Therefore, direct comparisons with earlier years should be avoided. 2. Two- and four-year institutions eligible to participate in Title IV federal financial aid programs. 3. Projected. *Source:* U.S. Department of Education, National Center for Education Statistics, *Digest of Education Statistics 2003.*

High School Dropout Rates by Sex, 1960–2001

Year	Total	Male	Female
1960	27.2%	27.8%	26.7%
1970	15.0	14.2	15.7
1980	14.1	15.1	13.1
1985	12.6	13.4	11.8
1990	12.1	12.3	11.8
1995	12.0	12.2	11.7
1996	11.1	11.4	10.9
1997	11.0	11.9	10.1
1998	11.8	13.3	10.3
1999	11.2	11.9	10.5
2000	10.9	12.0	9.9
2001	10.7	12.2	9.3

High School Dropout Rates by Race/Ethnicity, 1960–2001

Year	White	Black	Hispanic
1960	—	—	—
1970	13.2%	27.9%	—
1980	11.4	19.1	35.2%
1985	10.4	15.2	27.6
1990	9.0	13.2	32.4
1995	8.6	12.1	30.0
1996	7.3	13.0	29.4
1997	7.6	13.4	25.3
1998	7.7	13.8	29.5
1999	7.3	12.6	28.6
2000	6.9	13.1	27.8
2001	7.3	10.9	27.0

NOTE: (—) = not available. Data apply to persons ages 16–24. Because of changes in data collection procedures, data for 1992–2000 may not be comparable with figures for earlier years. *Source:* U.S. Dept. of Education, National Center for Education Statistics, *Digest of Education Statistics 2002.*

Students with Disabilities

Type of disability	Percent of all students served by federally supported programs for students with disabilities[1]						
	1976–1977	1980–1981	1990–1991	1995–1996	1999–2000	2000–2001	2001–2002
All disabilities	8.32%	10.14%	11.55%	12.43%	13.21%	13.34%	13.34%
Specific learning disabilities	1.80	3.58	5.17	5.75	6.04	6.02	5.97
Speech or language impairments	2.94	2.86	2.39	2.28	2.30	2.30	2.27
Mental retardation	2.17	2.03	1.30	1.27	1.28	1.27	1.24
Emotional disturbance	0.64	0.85	0.95	0.98	1.00	1.00	1.00
Hearing impairments	0.20	0.19	0.14	0.15	0.15	0.15	0.15
Orthopedic impairments	0.20	0.14	0.12	0.14	0.15	0.15	0.15
Other health impairments	0.32	0.24	0.13	0.30	0.54	0.62	0.71
Visual impairments	0.09	0.08	0.06	0.06	0.06	0.05	0.05
Multiple disabilities	—	0.17	0.23	0.21	0.24	0.26	0.27
Deaf–blindness	—	(2)	(2)	(2)	(2)	(2)	(2)
Developmental delay	—	—	—	—	0.04	0.06	0.09
Autism and traumatic brain injury	—	—	—	0.09	0.17	0.20	0.25
Preschool disabled[3]	(4)	(4)	0.95	1.21	1.24	1.25	1.28

NOTE: Because of rounding, details may not add to totals. (—) = not available. 1. Based on the enrollment in public schools, kindergarten through 12th grade, including a relatively small number of prekindergarten students. Includes students ages 3 to 21. 2. Less than .05%. 3. Includes preschool children ages 3 to 5. 4. Included in count by specific disability. *Source:* U.S. Department of Education, Office of Special Education and Rehabilitative Services; National Center for Education Statistics. From *Digest of Education Statistics 2003.*

Expenditure per Pupil in Public Elementary and Secondary Schools

1959–60	1969–70	1979–80	1989–90	1994–95	1996–97	1997–98	1998–99	1999–2000	2000–01	2001–02[1]
$375	$816	$2,272	$4,980	$5,989	$6,393	$6,676	$7,013	$7,394	$7,898	$8,203

1. Estimated. *Source:* U.S. Dept. of Education, National Center for Education Statistics, *Digest of Education Statistics 2003.*

Funding for Public Elementary and Secondary Schools, 1919–1920 to 2000–2001

(in thousands, except percent)

School year	Total	Federal	State	Local	% Federal	% State	% Local
1919–1920	$ 970,121	$ 2,475	$ 160,085	$ 807,561	0.3%	16.5%	83.2%
1929–1930	2,088,557	7,334	353,670	1,727,553	0.4	16.9	82.7
1939–1940	2,260,527	39,810	684,354	1,536,363	1.8	30.3	68.0
1949–1950	5,437,044	155,848	2,165,689	3,115,507	2.9	39.8	57.3
1959–1960	14,746,618	651,639	5,768,047	8,326,932	4.4	39.1	56.5
1969–1970	40,266,923	3,219,557	16,062,776	20,984,589	8.0	39.9	52.1
1979–1980	96,881,165	9,503,537	45,348,814	42,028,813	9.8	46.8	43.4
1989–1990	208,547,573	12,700,784	98,238,633	97,608,157	6.1	47.1	46.8
1999–2000	372,943,802	27,097,866	184,613,352	161,232,584	7.3	49.5	43.2
2000–2001	400,919,024	29,086,413	199,146,586	172,686,024	7.3	49.7	43.1

Source: U.S. Department of Education, National Center for Education Statistics, *Digest of Education Statistics 2003.*

Public and Private Elementary and Secondary Pupil-Teacher Ratios, 1955–2002

Year	Total	Public	Private	Year	Total	Public	Private
1955	27.4	26.9	31.7[1]	1985	17.6	17.9	16.2
1960	26.4	25.8	30.7[1]	1990	16.9	17.2	14.7[1]
1965	25.1	24.7	28.3	1995	17.0	17.3	14.9
1970	22.4	22.3	23.0	2000	16.0	16.0	15.8[1]
1980	18.6	18.7	17.7	2002[2]	16.1	16.1	16.2

1. Estimated. 2. Projected. *Source:* U.S. Department of Education, National Center for Education Statistics; NCES Common Core of Data (CCD); Projections of Educational Statistics to 2013. From *Digest of Education Statistics 2003.*

General Educational Development (GED) Credentials Issued, 1971–2001

(in thousands)

Year	Number of credentials issued	Year	Number of credentials issued	Year	Number of credentials issued	Year	Number of credentials issued	Year	Number of credentials issued	Year	Number of credentials issued
1971	227	1976	333	1981	489	1986	428	1991	462	1997	460
1972	245	1977	332	1982	486	1987	444	1992	457	1998	481
1973	249	1978	381	1983	465	1988	410	1993	469	1999	498
1974	294	1979	426	1984	427	1989	357	1994	491	2000	487
1975	340	1980	479	1985	413	1990	410	1995	504	2001	648

Source: American Council on Education, General Educational Development Testing Service, *Who took the GED? Statistical Report,* various years.

Average SAT Scores[1]

	Verbal score					Mathematical score				
School year	Total	Male	Female	White	Black	Total	Male	Female	White	Black
1966–1967	543	540	545	n.a.	n.a.	516	535	495	n.a.	n.a.
1970–1971	532	531	534	n.a.	n.a.	513	529	494	n.a.	n.a.
1976–1977	507	509	505	n.a.	n.a.	496	520	474	n.a.	n.a.
1980–1981	502	508	496	n.a.	n.a.	492	516	473	n.a.	n.a.
1986–1987	507	512	502	524	428	501	523	481	514	411
1990–1991	499	503	495	518	427	500	520	482	513	419
1996–1997	505	507	503	526	434	511	530	494	526	423
1997–1998	505	509	502	n.a.	n.a.	512	531	496	n.a.	n.a.
1998–1999	505	509	502	527	434	511	531	495	528	422
1999–2000	505	507	504	528	434	514	533	498	530	426
2000–2001	506	509	502	529	433	514	533	498	531	426
2001–2002	504	507	502	527	430	516	534	500	533	427
2002–2003	507	512	503	529	431	519	537	503	534	426

NOTE: n.a. = not available. 1. Scholastic Assessment Test, formerly known as the Scholastic Aptitude Test. Minimum score 200; maximum score 800. Scores prior to 1986 have been converted to the recentered scale. *Source:* U.S. Dept. of Education, National Center for Education Statistics, *Digest of Education Statistics 2003.*

Cost of Higher Education, 1986–2002[1]

Year	All institutions	4-year institutions	2-year institutions	Year	All institutions	4-year institutions	2-year institutions
Public institutions				**Private institutions**			
1986–1987	$3,805	$4,138	$2,989	1986–1987	$ 9,676	$10,039	$ 6,384
1991–1992	5,138	5,693	3,623	1991–1992	13,892	14,258	9,632
1996–1997	6,530	7,334	4,404	1996–1997	18,039	18,442	11,954
1997–1998	6,813	7,673	4,509	1997–1998	18,516	19,070	12,921
1998–1999	7,107	8,027	4,604	1998–1999	19,368	19,929	13,319
1999–2000	7,310	8,275	4,720	1999–2000	20,186	20,706	13,965
2000–2001	7,586	8,653	4,839	2000–2001	21,368	21,856	14,788
2001–2002	8,022	9,196	5,137	2001–2002	22,413	22,896	15,825
2002–2003[2]	8,556	9,828	5,596	2002–2003[2]	23,503	23,940	17,760

1. Average undergraduate tuition, fees, and room and board. 2. Preliminary data based on fall 2001 enrollment weights. *Source:* U.S. Department of Education, National Center for Education Statistics, *Digest of Education Statistics 2003.*

Median Annual Income, by Level of Education, 1990–2001

Sex and year	Elementary/secondary			College					
	Less than 9th grade	9th to 12th grade, no completion[1]	High school completion (includes equivalency)[2]	Some college, no degree[3]	Associate degree[4]	Bachelor's[5]	Master's[4]	Professional[4]	Doctorate[4]
Men									
1990	$17,394	$20,902	$26,653	$31,734	—	$39,328	—	—	—
1992	17,294	21,274	27,280	32,103	$33,433	41,355	$49,973	$ 76,220	$57,418
1994	17,532	22,048	28,037	32,279	35,794	43,663	53,500	75,009	61,921
1996	17,962	22,717	30,709	34,845	37,131	45,846	60,508	85,963	71,227
1998	19,380	23,958	31,477	36,934	40,274	51,405	62,244	94,737	75,078
1999	20,429	25,035	33,184	39,221	41,638	52,985	66,243	100,000	81,687
2000	20,789	25,095	34,303	40,337	41,952	56,334	68,322	99,411	80,250
2001	21,361	26,209	34,723	41,045	42,776	55,929	70,899	100,000	86,965
Women									
1990	$12,251	$14,429	$18,319	$22,227	—	$28,017	—	—	—
1992	12,958	14,559	19,427	23,157	$25,624	30,326	$36,037	$ 46,257	$45,790
1994	12,430	15,133	20,373	23,514	25,940	31,741	39,457	50,615	51,119
1996	14,414	16,953	21,175	25,167	28,083	33,525	41,901	57,624	56,267
1998	14,467	16,482	22,780	27,420	29,924	36,559	45,283	57,565	57,796
1999	15,098	17,015	23,061	27,757	30,919	37,993	48,097	59,904	60,079
2000	15,978	17,919	24,970	28,697	31,071	40,415	50,139	58,957	57,081
2001	16,691	19,156	25,303	30,418	32,153	40,994	50,669	61,748	62,123

NOTE: Year-round, full-time workers 25 years and older. (—) = not available. 1. Includes 1 to 3 years high school for 1990. 2. Includes 4 years of high school for 1990, and equivalency certificates for the other years. 3. Includes 1 to 3 years of college and associate degrees for 1990. 4. Not reported separately for 1990. 5. Includes 4 years of college for 1990. *Source:* U.S. Dept. of Commerce, Bureau of the Census, Current Population Reports, Series P-60, "Money Income of Households, Families, and Persons in the United States," "Income, Poverty, and Valuation of Noncash Benefits," various years; and Series P-60, "Money Income in the United States," various years. From *Digest of Education Statistics 2003.*

College and University Endowments, 2003

Rank	Institution	Endowment[1]	Rank	Institution	Endowment[1]
1.	Harvard University (Cambridge, Mass.)	$19,294,735,000	10.	University of Pennsylvania (Philadelphia, Pa.)	3,547,473,030
2.	Yale University (New Haven, Conn.)	11,048,891,000	11.	University of Michigan (Ann Arbor, Mich.)	3,531,704,067
3.	Princeton University (Princeton, N.J.)	8,730,000,000	12.	Northwestern University (Evanston, Ill.)	3,370,776,878
4.	Leland Stanford Junior University (Stanford, Calif.)	8,613,805,000	13.	Texas A&M University (College Station, Tex.)	3,158,170,351
5.	Univ. of Texas System Administration (Austin, Tex.)	8,588,471,301	14.	University of Chicago (Chicago, Ill.)	3,079,097,000
6.	Massachusetts Institute of Technology (Cambridge, Mass.)	5,133,600,000	15.	Cornell University (Ithaca, N.Y.)	3,029,922,000
7.	Columbia University (New York, N.Y.)	4,343,151,000	16.	William Marsh Rice University (Houston, Tex.)	2,938,000,000
8.	Emory University (Atlanta, Ga.)	3,812,033,219	17.	University of Notre Dame (Notre Dame, Ind.)	2,609,000,000
9.	Washington University (St. Louis, Mo.)	3,569,344,000	18.	Duke University (Durham, N.C.)	2,565,162,568
			19.	Dartmouth College (Hanover, N.H.)	2,432,724,780

Rank	Institution	Endowment[1]
20.	University of Southern California (Los Angeles, Calif.)	2,113,666,000
21.	Vanderbilt University (Nashville, Tenn.)	1,987,810,494
22.	University of Virginia (Charlottesville, Va.)	1,832,866,000
23.	Univ of California, Berkeley (Berkeley, Calif.)	1,793,647,345
24.	Johns Hopkins University (Baltimore, Md.)	1,646,897,000
25.	Univ. of Texas at Austin (Austin, Tex.)	1,640,723,834
26.	University of Minnesota (Minneapolis, Minn.)	1,540,215,210
27.	Brown University (Providence, R.I.)	1,484,292,000
28.	Univ of California, Los Angeles (Los Angeles, Calif.)	1,332,254,149
29.	Rockefeller University (New York, N.Y.)	1,331,375,520
30.	New York University (New York, N.Y.)	1,318,785,000
31.	Case Western Reserve University (Cleveland, Ohio)	1,315,973,000
32.	California Institute of Technology (Pasadena, Calif.)	1,215,468,000
33.	Williams College (Williamstown, Mass.)	1,203,944,000
34.	University of Pittsburgh (Pittsburgh, Pa.)	1,170,831,000
35.	Grinnell College (Grinnell, Iowa)	1,111,615,000
36.	University of Rochester (Rochester, N.Y.)	1,090,121,030
37.	Univ of North Carolina at Chapel Hill (Chapel Hill, N.C.)	1,087,535,072
38.	Boston College (Chestnut Hill, Mass.)	1,072,699,000
39.	Purdue University (West Lafayette, Ind.)	1,046,665,493
40.	Wellesley College (Wellesley, Mass.)	1,043,937,529
41.	Georgia Institute of Technology (Atlanta, Ga.)	1,029,836,549
42.	University of Washington (Seattle, WA)	1,009,000,000
43.	University of Richmond (University of Richmond, Va.)	996,710,000
44.	Pomona College (Claremont, Calif.)	994,477,370
45.	Pennsylvania State University (University Park, Pa.)	965,500,000
46.	Ohio State University (Columbus, Ohio)	957,867,277
47.	Baylor College of Medicine (Houston, Tex.)	957,318,595
48.	Indiana University (Bloomington, Ind.)	941,068,074
49.	Swarthmore College (Swarthmore, Pa.)	930,372,000
50.	Amherst College (Amherst, Mass.)	877,151,048

NOTES: List includes only institutions that participated in the 2003 Voluntary Support of Education Survey. State systems that submitted combined endowments above the current cut-off are not included. 1. Endowment is market value at fiscal year-end 2003. *Source:* Council for Aid to Education, a subsidiary of RAND. Web: www.cae.org.

Top Fundraising Colleges and Universities, in Total Amount Raised, 2003

Rank	College or University	Amount raised
1.	Harvard University (Cambridge, Mass.)	$555,639,350
2.	Leland Stanford Junior University (Stanford, Calif.)	486,075,131
3.	University of Pennsylvania (Philadelphia, Pa.)	399,640,772
4.	University of Arkansas (Fayetteville, Ark.)	365,307,446
5.	Johns Hopkins University (Baltimore, Md.)	319,546,967
6.	Univ. of California, Los Angeles (Los Angeles, Calif.)	319,462,784
7.	Cornell University (Ithaca, N.Y.)	317,042,889
8.	University of Washington (Seattle, Wash.)	311,250,905
9.	Univ. of Texas at Austin (Austin, Tex.)	309,483,833
10.	University of Southern California (Los Angeles, Calif.)	305,981,845
11.	Duke University (Durham, N.C.)	296,827,299
12.	University of Wisconsin-Madison (Madison, Wis.)	286,914,546
13.	Columbia University (New York, N.Y.)	281,498,472
14.	University of Virginia (Charlottesville, Va.)	261,921,891
15.	Indiana University (Bloomington, Ind.)	249,988,250

Source: Council for Aid to Education, a subsidiary of RAND. Web: www.cae.org.

Top Fundraising Preparatory Schools, in Total Amount Raised, 2003

Rank	School	Amount raised
1.	The Culver Educational Foundation (Culver, Ind.)	$34,635,868
2.	Phillips Academy (Andover, Mass.)	27,032,111
3.	Phillips Exeter Academy (Exeter, N.H.)	24,388,939
4.	Choate Rosemary Hall (Wallingford, Conn.)	19,967,674
5.	St. Paul's School (Concord, N.H.)	15,892,704
6.	Lawrenceville School (Lawrenceville, N.J.)	15,383,324
7.	Peddie School (Hightstown, N.J.)	15,191,876
8.	Taft School (Watertown, Conn.)	15,055,301
9.	Deerfield Academy (Deerfield, Mass.)	14,756,768
10.	Hotchkiss School (Lakeville, Conn.)	14,399,068
11.	Harvard-Westlake School (North Hollywood, Calif.)	12,746,000
12.	Blake School (Hopkins, Minn.)	11,677,857
13.	Loomis Chaffee School (Windsor, Conn.)	10,680,673
14.	Groton School (Groton, Mass.)	10,416,855
15.	Norfolk Academy (Norfolk, Va.)	10,091,650

Source: Council for Aid to Education, a subsidiary of RAND. Web: www.cae.org.

Number of U.S. Colleges and Universities and Degrees Awarded

	Number[1]	Enrollment[2]		Number		Number
Public 4-year institutions	631	6,236,455	**Degrees awarded:[3]**			
Private 4-year institutions	1,835	3,440,953	Associate	595,133	Doctorate	44,160
Public 2-year institutions	1,081	5,996,701	Bachelor's	1,291,900	Professional	80,698
Private 2-year institutions	621	253,878	Master's	482,118		
Total	**4,168**	**15,927,987**				
Undergraduate		13,715,610	**Enrollment highlights:[2]**			
Graduate		1,903,730	Women	56.3%	Minority	28.8%
Professional		308,647	Full-time	59.3%	Foreign	3.5%

1. 2002–3 figures. 2. Fall 2001 figures. 3. 2001–2 figures. *Source: Chronicle of Higher Education.*

Accredited U.S. Senior Colleges and Universities

Criteria for inclusion: accredited four-year institutions offering at least a bachelor's degree. Because of space limitations, only schools with at least 800 students are included (a complete list, including smaller schools, can be found online at www.infoplease.com). "Percent women" refers to the percentage of women in the overall student body. "Percent students accepted" refers to the percentage of all applicants who are accepted. Schools are listed alphabetically within each state.
(Pr) = private; (Pu) = public.

Source: Peterson's Database, copyright 2004. Peterson's, a part of the Thomson Corporation. Web: http://petersons.com/.

		Percent		Tuition		
Institution name; city (Public/Private)	Students	Women	Students accepted	In-state	Out-of-state	Room and board
ALABAMA						
Alabama Agricultural and Mechanical University; Huntsville (Pu)	6,588	45%	22%	$ 3,540	$ 7,080	$3,300
Alabama State University; Montgomery (Pu)	6,024	37	22	3,600	7,200	3,700
American College of Computer & Information Sciences; Birmingham (Pr)	11,291					
Auburn University Montgomery; Montgomery (Pu)	5,298	99	21	3,900	11,700	4,890
Auburn University; Auburn University (Pu)	23,152	78	20	4,230	12,690	5,970
Birmingham-Southern College; Birmingham (Pr)	1,388	89	35	18,530	18,530	6,104
Columbia Southern University; Orange Beach (Pr)	2,200			3,750	3,750	
Concordia College; Selma (Pr)	851		8	6,000	6,000	3,600
Faulkner University; Montgomery (Pr)	2,585	55	26	9,750	9,750	4,800
Jacksonville State University; Jacksonville (Pu)	9,031	44	25	3,540	7,080	3,288
Miles College; Birmingham (Pr)	1,660	58	41	5,090	5,090	4,338
Oakwood College; Huntsville (Pr)	1,778	55	31	9,420	9,420	4,620
Samford University; Birmingham (Pr)	4,440	90	27	13,154	13,154	5,244
Spring Hill College; Mobile (Pr)	1,479	80	28	17,830	17,830	6,868
Stillman College; Tuscaloosa (Pr)	1,458	50		8,718	8,718	4,200
Troy State University Dothan; Dothan (Pu)	1,899	70	22	3,530	7,060	
Troy State University Montgomery; Montgomery (Pu)	3,758	99	11	3,530	7,060	
Troy State University; Troy (Pu)	8,031	67	17	3,530	7,060	4,580
Tuskegee University; Tuskegee (Pr)	3,176	81	41	11,060	11,060	5,940
University of Alabama at Birmingham; Birmingham (Pu)	16,357	81	19	3,480	8,700	
University of Alabama in Huntsville; Huntsville (Pu)	7,051	88	18	4,126	8,702	5,000
University of Alabama; Tuscaloosa (Pu)	20,291	87	25	4,134	11,294	4,906
University of Mobile; Mobile (Pr)	1,854	67	35	9,270	9,270	5,440
University of Montevallo; Montevallo (Pu)	3,121	79	34	4,500	9,000	3,638
University of North Alabama; Florence (Pu)	5,630	79	29	3,048	6,096	4,272
University of South Alabama; Mobile (Pu)	13,096	76	23	3,390	6,780	3,990
University of West Alabama; Livingston (Pu)	2,372	78	22	3,240	6,480	2,986
Virginia College at Birmingham; Birmingham (Pr)	2,407	86	53	8,820	8,820	
ALASKA						
University of Alaska Anchorage; Anchorage (Pu)	16,607	76	17	2,304	6,800	6,830
University of Alaska Fairbanks; Fairbanks (Pu)	8,724	84	11	2,700	8,430	5,310
University of Alaska Southeast; Juneau (Pu)	3,268	44	6	2,880	8,610	5,928
ARIZONA						
Arizona State University East; Mesa (Pu)	3,551	79	14	3,508	12,028	4,770
Arizona State University West; Phoenix (Pu)	7,105	62	29	3,508	12,028	
Arizona State University; Tempe (Pu)	48,901	88	24	3,508	12,028	6,453
Art Institute of Phoenix; Phoenix (Pr)	1,216		17	15,600	15,600	
Collins College: A School of Design and Technology; Tempe (Pr)	2,142	65				
DeVry University; Phoenix (Pr)	2,282		10	9,990	9,990	
Embry-Riddle Aeronautical University; Prescott (Pr)	1,669	80	10	20,700	20,700	5,808
Grand Canyon University; Phoenix (Pr)	4,113	69	15	14,500	14,500	7,130
Northcentral University; Prescott (Pr)	1,101		0			
Northern Arizona University; Flagstaff (Pu)	18,824			3,508	12,028	5,374
Prescott College; Prescott (Pr)	995	86	35	14,970	14,970	
University of Arizona; Tucson (Pu)	37,083	85	25	3,508	12,278	6,810

Institution name; city (Public/Private)	Students	Percent Women	Percent Students accepted	Tuition In-state	Tuition Out-of-state	Room and board
University of Phoenix Online Campus; Phoenix (Pr)	45,827		36%	$12,660	$12,660	
University of Phoenix–Phoenix Campus; Phoenix (Pr)	4,766		36	8,760	8,760	
University of Phoenix–Southern Arizona Campus; Tucson (Pr)	1,683		39	8,490	8,490	
Western International University; Phoenix (Pr)	3,751		41	9,180	9,180	
ARKANSAS						
Arkansas State University; State University (Pu)	10,573	66%	28	3,750	9,660	$ 3,640
Arkansas Tech University; Russellville (Pu)	6,249	56	24	3,540	7,080	3,725
Harding University; Searcy (Pr)	5,110	58	29	9,720	9,720	4,770
Henderson State University; Arkadelphia (Pu)	3,479	63	31	3,380	6,760	3,984
Hendrix College; Conway (Pr)	1,059	86	40	15,440	15,440	5,340
John Brown University; Siloam Springs (Pr)	1,834	82		13,716	13,716	5,040
Ouachita Baptist University; Arkadelphia (Pr)	1,530	80	38	13,870	13,870	4,800
Philander Smith College; Little Rock (Pr)	859	73	29	5,040	5,040	5,090
Southern Arkansas University–Magnolia; Magnolia (Pu)	3,008	81	29	3,250	4,940	3,460
University of Arkansas at Fort Smith; Fort Smith (Pu)	6,395	100	19	1,740	6,360	
University of Arkansas at Little Rock; Little Rock (Pu)	11,757	99	19	3,780	9,720	
University of Arkansas at Monticello; Monticello (Pu)	2,875	73	0	2,700	6,120	3,150
University of Arkansas at Pine Bluff; Pine Bluff (Pu)	3,251	68	29	2,820	6,570	5,180
University of Arkansas; Fayetteville (Pu)	16,405	85	23	3,810	10,560	5,087
University of Central Arkansas; Conway (Pu)	9,516	70	31	3,770	7,082	3,786
CALIFORNIA						
Academy of Art University; San Francisco (Pr)	6,702		16	13,200	13,200	12,000
Alliant International University; San Diego (Pr)	3,508	60	4	16,520	16,520	6,880
Art Center College of Design; Pasadena (Pr)	1,533	72	32	23,450	23,450	
Art Institute of California–San Diego; San Diego (Pr)	1,329			17,040	17,040	
Art Institute of California–San Francisco; San Francisco (Pr)	918			17,472	17,472	
Azusa Pacific University; Azusa (Pr)	8,191	83	25	18,790	18,790	5,696
Biola University; La Mirada (Pr)	4,666	78	28	19,564	19,564	5,967
Brooks Institute of Photography; Santa Barbara (Pr)	1,507		29	19,650	19,650	
California Baptist University; Riverside (Pr)	2,359	84	31	13,754	13,754	5,880
California College for Health Sciences; National City (Pr)	5,458			13,975	13,975	
California College of the Arts; San Francisco (Pr)	1,492	79	29	22,970	22,970	8,030
California Institute of Technology; Pasadena (Pr)	2,172	17	11	23,901	23,901	7,560
California Institute of the Arts; Valencia (Pr)	1,222	36	21	23,920	23,920	7,120
California Lutheran University; Thousand Oaks (Pr)	2,920	77	25	20,200	20,200	7,200
California Polytechnic State University, San Luis Obispo; San Luis Obispo (Pu)	18,303	38	31	-	6,768	7,619
California State Polytechnic University, Pomona; Pomona (Pu)	19,804	30	23	-	8,460	6,747
California State University, Bakersfield; Bakersfield (Pu)	7,924	63		-	5,640	4,900
California State University, Chico; Chico (Pu)	15,516	73	33	-	10,506	7,245
California State University, Dominguez Hills; Carson (Pu)	13,248	47	20	-	8,460	
California State University, Fresno; Fresno (Pu)	22,348	70	27	-	10,400	7,073
California State University, Fullerton; Fullerton (Pu)	32,592	66	25	-	8,460	
California State University, Hayward; Hayward (Pu)	13,455	47	28	-	8,460	
California State University, Long Beach; Long Beach (Pu)	34,715	49	28	-	8,460	6,000
California State University, Los Angeles; Los Angeles (Pu)	20,637	54		-	9,208	
California State University, Monterey Bay; Seaside (Pu)	3,020	83	36	-	9,024	6,190
California State University, Northridge; Northridge (Pu)	31,448	83	29	-	9,024	6,400
California State University, Sacramento; Sacramento (Pu)	28,375	52	27	-	8,927	6,523
California State University, San Bernardino; San Bernardino (Pu)	16,927	61	29	-	6,768	5,383
California State University, San Marcos; San Marcos (Pu)	7,723	73	24	-	6,768	
California State University, Stanislaus; Turlock (Pu)	8,072	64	25	-	8,460	7,242
Chapman University; Orange (Pr)	5,138	62	24	23,950	23,950	8,528
Claremont McKenna College; Claremont (Pr)	1,050	29	32	27,500	27,500	9,180
Concordia University; Irvine (Pr)	1,747	27	30	17,990	17,990	6,430
DeVry University; Fremont (Pr)	1,762		10	11,100	11,100	
DeVry University; Long Beach (Pr)	2,186		10	10,590	10,590	
DeVry University; Pomona (Pr)	2,565		9	10,590	10,590	
DeVry University; West Hills (Pr)	1,278		9	10,590	10,590	
Dominican University of California; San Rafael (Pr)	1,742	55	25	22,250	22,250	9,420
Fresno Pacific University; Fresno (Pr)	2,243	62	20	17,370	17,370	4,870
Golden Gate University; San Francisco (Pr)	4,299	100	2	9,984	9,984	
Holy Names University; Oakland (Pr)	943	62	25	19,970	19,970	7,800
Hope International University; Fullerton (Pr)	1,204	42	18	14,900	14,900	5,874
Humboldt State University; Arcata (Pu)	7,725	67	30	-	6,768	6,861
John F. Kennedy University; Pleasant Hill (Pr)	1,606			13,920	13,920	
La Sierra University; Riverside (Pr)	1,758	59	29	16,272	16,272	4,560
Loyola Marymount University; Los Angeles (Pr)	8,880	58	25	23,504	23,504	8,260
Master's College and Seminary; Santa Clarita (Pr)	1,426	54	25	17,000	17,000	6,050
Mills College; Oakland (Pr)	1,210	73	46	23,000	23,000	8,930
Mount St. Mary's College; Los Angeles (Pr)	2,127	86	40	19,722	19,722	8,224

Institution name; city (Public/Private)	Students	Percent Women	Percent Students accepted	Tuition In-state	Tuition Out-of-state	Room and board
Mt. Sierra College; Monrovia (Pr)	1,100	73%	23%	$10,000	$10,000	
National University; La Jolla (Pr)	17,064		7	8,550	8,550	
New College of California; San Francisco (Pr)	1,133		12	11,132	11,132	
Notre Dame de Namur University; Belmont (Pr)	1,798	89	17	20,050	20,050	$ 9,370
Occidental College; Los Angeles (Pr)	1,858	44	42	27,734	27,734	7,820
Otis College of Art and Design; Los Angeles (Pr)	1,066	63	45	22,820	22,820	
Pacific Union College; Angwin (Pr)	1,502	35	36	17,235	17,235	4,902
Pepperdine University; Malibu (Pr)	8,021	23	13	27,430	27,430	8,270
Pitzer College; Claremont (Pr)	942	50	38	26,640	26,640	7,796
Point Loma Nazarene University; San Diego (Pr)	3,170	64	31	18,000	18,000	6,380
Pomona College; Claremont (Pr)	1,555	21	37	26,890	26,890	9,980
Saint Mary's College of California; Moraga (Pr)	4,486	82	24	23,640	23,640	9,075
Samuel Merritt College; Oakland (Pr)	896	63	25	21,790	21,790	8,829
San Diego State University; San Diego (Pu)	33,676	50	31	-	8,460	8,787
San Francisco State University; San Francisco (Pu)	29,686	64	25	-	8,460	8,090
San Jose State University; San Jose (Pu)	28,932	52	24	-	6,768	8,465
Santa Clara University; Santa Clara (Pr)	7,794	66	22	25,365	25,365	9,336
Scripps College; Claremont (Pr)	834	54	68	26,964	26,964	8,600
Simpson College and Graduate School; Redding (Pr)	1,175	95	35	14,760	14,760	5,740
Sonoma State University; Rohnert Park (Pu)	8,371	84	31	-	8,460	7,411
Stanford University; Stanford (Pr)	17,823	13	13	28,563	28,563	9,073
University of California, Berkeley; Berkeley (Pu)	33,076	24	29	-	14,210	11,212
University of California, Davis; Davis (Pu)	30,229	60	30	-	14,210	9,143
University of California, Irvine; Irvine (Pu)	24,874	54	30	-	14,210	8,055
University of California, Los Angeles; Los Angeles (Pu)	38,598	24	29	-	14,210	10,452
University of California, Riverside; Riverside (Pu)	17,302	79	30	-	13,731	9,350
University of California, San Diego; La Jolla (Pu)	24,707	42	33	-	13,730	8,620
University of California, Santa Barbara; Santa Barbara (Pu)	20,847	50	34	-	13,731	9,236
University of California, Santa Cruz; Santa Cruz (Pu)	14,997	80	34	-	18,109	10,314
University of La Verne; La Verne (Pr)	3,604	56	17	20,500	20,500	7,750
University of Phoenix–Northern California Campus; Pleasanton (Pr)	4,765		45	12,150	12,150	
University of Phoenix–Sacramento Campus; Sacramento (Pr)	2,192		47	12,540	12,540	
University of Phoenix–San Diego Campus; San Diego (Pr)	2,453		40	11,760	11,760	
University of Phoenix–Southern California Campus; Fountain Valley (Pr)	7,757		46	12,660	12,660	
University of Redlands; Redlands (Pr)	2,311	71	40	23,796	23,796	8,478
University of San Diego; San Diego (Pr)	7,262	51	27	23,410	23,410	9,630
University of San Francisco; San Francisco (Pr)	8,159	82	23	23,220	23,220	9,350
University of Southern California; Los Angeles (Pr)	31,606	30	19	28,184	28,184	8,632
University of the Pacific; Stockton (Pr)	6,121	70	22	23,180	23,180	7,490
Vanguard University of Southern California; Costa Mesa (Pr)	1,673	80	35	15,928	15,928	5,510
Westmont College; Santa Barbara (Pr)	1,343	85	47	24,224	24,224	8,390
Whittier College; Whittier (Pr)	2,170	80	21	23,192	23,192	7,588
Woodbury University; Burbank (Pr)	1,404	79	25	20,070	20,070	7,183
COLORADO						
Adams State College; Alamosa (Pu)	8,370	75	6	1,798	7,428	5,730
Art Institute of Colorado; Denver (Pr)	2,226		22	18,752	18,752	5,760
Colorado Christian University; Lakewood (Pr)	1,583	76	28	15,040	15,040	5,320
Colorado College; Colorado Springs (Pr)	1,968	56	38	27,270	27,270	6,840
Colorado School of Mines; Golden (Pu)	3,398	79	13	5,640	18,830	6,100
Colorado State University; Fort Collins (Pu)	26,870	79	25	2,908	13,380	6,045
Colorado State University-Pueblo; Pueblo (Pu)	6,299	95	21	2,289	12,279	5,742
Colorado Technical University; Colorado Springs (Pr)	1,684	93	3	9,225	9,225	
Fort Lewis College; Durango (Pu)	4,182	78	33	2,020	10,560	5,564
Johnson & Wales University; Denver (Pr)	1,328	88		18,444	18,444	8,433
Jones International University; Englewood (Pr)	1,053			7,680	7,680	1,360
Mesa State College; Grand Junction (Pu)	5,560	92	32	1,856	7,508	6,266
Metropolitan State College of Denver; Denver (Pu)	20,261	79	20	2,130	8,737	
Naropa University; Boulder (Pr)	1,234	95	16	15,204	15,204	6,308
United States Air Force Academy; USAF Academy (Pu)	4,157	12	12			
University of Colorado at Boulder; Boulder (Pu)	32,041	80	23	3,192	19,508	6,754
University of Colorado at Colorado Springs; Colorado Springs (Pu)	7,620	74	30	4,378	19,210	6,729
University of Colorado at Denver; Denver (Pu)	15,596	70	13	3,028	14,656	
University of Denver; Denver (Pr)	9,521	79	15	24,264	24,264	7,275
University of Northern Colorado; Greeley (Pu)	13,204	71	28	2,520	11,646	5,782
University of Phoenix–Colorado Campus; Lone Tree (Pr)	2,905		31	8,610	8,610	
Western State College of Colorado; Gunnison (Pu)	2,385	79	22	1,783	8,965	5,680
CONNECTICUT						
Albertus Magnus College; New Haven (Pr)	2,216	79	38	16,668	16,668	7,330
Central Connecticut State University; New Britain (Pu)	12,131	55	21	2,648	8,570	6,706
Charter Oak State College; New Britain (Pu)	1,578			890	1,130	
Connecticut College; New London (Pr)	1,849	35	37			

Institution name; city (Public/Private)	Students	Percent Women	Percent Students accepted	Tuition In-state	Tuition Out-of-state	Room and board
Eastern Connecticut State University; Willimantic (Pu)	5,095	58%	27%	$ 2,648	$ 8,570	$ 6,614
Fairfield University; Fairfield (Pr)	5,053	49	29	26,100	26,100	8,920
Quinnipiac University; Hamden (Pr)	7,121	62	31	20,200	20,200	9,450
Sacred Heart University; Fairfield (Pr)	5,781	68	22	20,220	20,220	8,910
Saint Joseph College; West Hartford (Pr)	1,836	68	34	20,350	20,350	8,785
Southern Connecticut State University; New Haven (Pu)	12,143	61	21	2,648	8,570	7,100
Teikyo Post University; Waterbury (Pr)	1,325	66	17	16,950	16,950	7,375
Trinity College; Hartford (Pr)	2,371	36	31	28,740	28,740	7,810
United States Coast Guard Academy; New London (Pu)	1,016	7	20			
University of Bridgeport; Bridgeport (Pr)	3,165	84	7	17,008	17,008	8,000
University of Connecticut; Storrs (Pu)	22,053	53	25	5,260	16,044	6,888
University of Hartford; West Hartford (Pr)	7,245	64	20	21,330	21,330	8,610
University of New Haven; West Haven (Pr)	4,386	67	11	20,130	20,130	8,500
Wesleyan University; Middletown (Pr)	3,221	27	32	29,784	29,784	8,226
Western Connecticut State University; Danbury (Pu)	6,079	55	17	2,648	9,636	6,580
Yale University; New Haven (Pr)	11,471	11	17	28,400	28,400	8,600
DELAWARE						
Delaware State University; Dover (Pu)	3,178	50	28	3,996	8,976	6,344
Goldey-Beacom College; Wilmington (Pr)	1,324	78		11,025	11,025	
University of Delaware; Newark (Pu)	20,501	42	31	5,890	15,420	6,118
Wesley College; Dover (Pr)	2,167	68	28	13,000	13,000	6,200
Wilmington College; New Castle (Pr)	6,954		13	6,930	6,930	
DISTRICT OF COLUMBIA						
American University; Washington (Pr)	10,977	59	21	24,452	24,452	9,746
Gallaudet University; Washington (Pr)	1,573	71	22	9,000	9,000	8,030
Georgetown University; Washington (Pr)	13,164	23	19	27,864	27,864	10,033
Howard University; Washington (Pr)	10,658	56	29	10,130	10,130	5,570
Southeastern University; Washington (Pr)	994	72	8	8,640	8,640	
Strayer University; Washington (Pr)	20,138			9,841	9,841	
Catholic University of America; Washington (Pr)	5,740	82	16	22,200	22,200	9,002
George Washington University; Washington (Pr)	23,417	39	16	29,320	29,320	10,040
Trinity College; Washington (Pr)	1,637	78	21	16,220	16,220	7,170
University of the District of Columbia; Washington (Pu)	5,241	91	17	1,800	4,440	
FLORIDA						
Art Institute of Fort Lauderdale; Fort Lauderdale (Pr)	3,500	72		15,615	15,615	
Barry University; Miami Shores (Pr)	9,042	70	27	20,320	20,320	7,000
Bethune-Cookman College; Daytona Beach (Pr)	2,794	67	27	10,106	10,106	6,374
Carlos Albizu University, Miami Campus; Miami (Pr)	850	64	9	8,250	8,250	
DeVry University; Miramar (Pr)	844		4	10,590	10,590	
DeVry University; Orlando (Pr)	1,427		11	10,590	10,590	
Eckerd College; St. Petersburg (Pr)	1,631	77	36	22,538	22,538	5,970
Edward Waters College; Jacksonville (Pr)	1,320		13	7,567	7,567	5,469
Embry-Riddle Aeronautical University, Extended Campus; Daytona Beach (Pr)	10,416		0	20,700	20,700	6,370
Embry-Riddle Aeronautical University; Daytona Beach (Pr)	4,926	82	10	20,700	20,700	6,370
Flagler College; St. Augustine (Pr)	2,033	33	45	7,410	7,410	4,450
Florida Agricultural and Mechanical University; Tallahassee (Pu)	13,013	71	27	2,703	13,058	5,238
Florida Atlantic University; Boca Raton (Pu)	25,018	72	18	2,943	13,955	5,600
Florida Gulf Coast University; Fort Myers (Pu)	5,972	72	22	2,850	13,200	8,000
Florida Institute of Technology; Melbourne (Pr)	4,689	86	10	22,600	22,600	6,140
Florida International University; Miami (Pu)	33,228	43	23	2,668	13,696	8,822
Florida Memorial College; Miami-Dade (Pr)	1,771			8,947	8,947	4,547
Florida Metropolitan University–Brandon Campus; Tampa (Pr)	1,384	79	0	8,800	8,800	
Florida Metropolitan University–Fort Lauderdale Campus; Pompano Beach (Pr)	1,612			9,000	9,000	
Florida Metropolitan University–Jacksonville Campus; Jacksonville (Pr)	954			8,460	8,460	
Florida Metropolitan University–Melbourne Campus; Melbourne (Pr)	880	68		8,460	8,460	
Florida Metropolitan University–North Orlando Campus; Orlando (Pr)	1,444	68	33	8,460	8,460	
Florida Metropolitan University–Pinellas Campus; Clearwater (Pr)	1,201	70		8,460	8,460	
Florida Metropolitan University–South Orlando Campus; Orlando (Pr)	1,964	45	40	8,460	8,460	
Florida Metropolitan University–Tampa Campus; Tampa (Pr)	1,218	54	24	8,460	8,460	
Florida Southern College; Lakeland (Pr)	1,880	75	43	17,142	17,142	6,050
Florida State University; Tallahassee (Pu)	36,884	42	29	2,860	13,888	6,168
International Academy of Design & Technology; Tampa (Pr)	2,043	62		15,120	15,120	
International College; Naples (Pr)	1,500		25	8,160	8,160	
Jacksonville University; Jacksonville (Pr)	2,632	70	23	17,700	17,700	6,100
Johnson & Wales University; North Miami (Pr)	2,379	87		18,444	18,444	

Institution name; city (Public/Private)	Students	Percent Women	Percent Students accepted	Tuition In-state	Tuition Out-of-state	Room and board
Jones College; Miami (Pr)	837			$ 5,400	$ 5,400	
Lynn University; Boca Raton (Pr)	1,891	77%	22%	22,000	22,000	$ 8,000
Miami International University of Art & Design; Miami (Pr)	1,207	55	41	16,656	16,656	
Northwood University, Florida Campus; West Palm Beach (Pr)	959	61	19	13,485	13,485	6,840
Nova Southeastern University; Fort Lauderdale (Pr)	23,522	64	6	15,000	15,000	8,126
Palm Beach Atlantic University; West Palm Beach (Pr)	2,996	87	31	14,690	14,690	5,800
Ringling School of Art and Design; Sarasota (Pr)	989	67	33	18,860	18,860	8,470
Rollins College; Winter Park (Pr)	2,565	66	28	25,500	25,500	8,050
Saint Leo University; Saint Leo (Pr)	1,518	59	19	13,150	13,150	7,030
Southeastern College of the Assemblies of God; Lakeland (Pr)	1,675	85	32	9,000	9,000	5,329
St. Thomas University; Miami Gardens (Pr)	2,520	43	18	16,200	16,200	10,200
Stetson University; DeLand (Pr)	3,439	76	24	21,300	21,300	6,855
University of Central Florida; Orlando (Pu)	41,102	60	26	2,833	13,861	7,026
University of Florida; Gainesville (Pu)	47,858	52	26	2,780	13,808	5,800
University of Miami; Coral Gables (Pr)	15,235	44	26	26,280	26,280	8,323
University of North Florida; Jacksonville (Pu)	13,966	66	24	2,913	13,268	5,856
University of Phoenix–Fort Lauderdale Campus; Fort Lauderdale (Pr)	1,941			8,850	8,850	
University of Phoenix–Jacksonville Campus; Jacksonville (Pr)	1,589		40	8,850	8,850	
University of Phoenix–Orlando Campus; Maitland (Pr)	1,225		41	8,850	8,850	
University of Phoenix–Tampa Campus; Tampa (Pr)	1,434		35	8,850	8,850	
University of South Florida; Tampa (Pu)	40,945	62	23	2,909	13,937	6,508
University of Tampa; Tampa (Pr)	4,661	61	33	16,670	16,670	6,410
University of West Florida; Pensacola (Pu)	9,452	66	27	1,902	12,930	6,000
Warner Southern College; Lake Wales (Pr)	1,198	70	37	11,290	11,290	5,271
GEORGIA						
Agnes Scott College; Decatur (Pr)	923	66	65	20,310	20,310	7,760
Albany State University; Albany (Pu)	3,681	24	36	2,212	8,848	3,760
American InterContinental University; Atlanta (Pr)	1,277		16	14,805	14,805	
American InterContinental University; Atlanta (Pr)	1,248	44		22,400	22,400	
Armstrong Atlantic State University; Savannah (Pu)	6,653	65	26	2,212	8,848	
Art Institute of Atlanta; Atlanta (Pr)	2,699		31	16,560	16,560	
Augusta State University; Augusta (Pu)	6,116	65	28	2,212	8,846	
Berry College; Mount Berry (Pr)	2,045	83	42	15,220	15,220	6,190
Brewton-Parker College; Mt. Vernon (Pr)	1,109	96	39	9,600	9,600	4,300
Clark Atlanta University; Atlanta (Pr)	4,915	53	40	12,312	12,312	6,438
Clayton College & State University; Morrow (Pu)	5,661		20	2,244	8,848	
Columbus State University; Columbus (Pu)	6,937	70	24	2,212	8,848	5,270
Covenant College; Lookout Mountain (Pr)	1,266	61	42	17,750	17,750	5,600
Dalton State College; Dalton (Pu)	4,201	62	12	1,456	5,452	
DeVry University; Alpharetta (Pr)	1,532		13	9,990	9,990	
DeVry University; Decatur (Pr)	2,915		17	9,990	9,990	
Emory University; Atlanta (Pr)	11,362	42	22	27,600	27,600	8,920
Fort Valley State University; Fort Valley (Pu)	2,537	48	31	2,212	8,848	4,178
Georgia College & State University; Milledgeville (Pu)	5,695	62	28	3,002	12,008	6,282
Georgia Institute of Technology; Atlanta (Pu)	16,643	63	13	3,208	15,134	6,264
Georgia Southern University; Statesboro (Pu)	15,704	54	25	2,212	8,848	5,628
Georgia Southwestern State University; Americus (Pu)	2,410	74	25	2,212	8,848	4,204
Georgia State University; Atlanta (Pu)	28,042	56	25	3,208	12,832	
Kennesaw State University; Kennesaw (Pu)	17,477	70	26	2,778	9,414	
LaGrange College; LaGrange (Pr)	1,020	90	37	14,482	14,482	6,018
Life University; Marietta (Pr)	1,182	48	14	5,040	5,040	
Luther Rice Bible College and Seminary; Lithonia (Pr)	1,600	100	1	3,480	3,480	
Macon State College; Macon (Pu)	5,400			1,606	5,592	
Mercer University; Macon (Pr)	7,200	79	27	20,796	20,796	6,720
Morehouse College; Atlanta (Pr)	2,859	72	0	11,786	11,786	8,418
North Georgia College & State University; Dahlonega (Pu)	4,517	63	28	2,212	8,848	4,160
Oglethorpe University; Atlanta (Pr)	1,029	66	38	19,920	19,920	6,550
Paine College; Augusta (Pr)	972	7	37	8,448	8,448	3,940
Piedmont College; Demorest (Pr)	2,159	54	20	12,500	12,500	4,400
Reinhardt College; Waleska (Pr)	1,308	70	42	11,100	11,100	5,762
Savannah College of Art and Design; Savannah (Pr)	6,207	75	26	19,035	19,035	8,175
Savannah State University; Savannah (Pu)	2,752	37	33	2,830	9,466	4,498
Shorter College; Rome (Pr)	884	83	46	11,440	11,440	5,665
Southern Polytechnic State University; Marietta (Pu)	3,768	85	8	2,312	9,248	4,866
Spelman College; Atlanta (Pr)	2,063	39	68	11,950	11,950	7,625
State University of West Georgia; Carrollton (Pu)	10,255	62	29	2,212	8,848	4,406
Toccoa Falls College; Toccoa Falls (Pr)	847	75	36	10,850	10,850	4,300
University of Georgia; Athens (Pu)	33,878	75	28	3,208	13,984	5,756
University of Phoenix–Atlanta Campus; Atlanta (Pr)	1,096		38	9,420	9,420	
Valdosta State University; Valdosta (Pu)	10,547	68	30	2,212	8,848	5,002

Institution name; city (Public/Private)	Students	Percent Women	Students accepted	Tuition In-state	Out-of-state	Room and board
HAWAII						
Brigham Young University–Hawaii; Laie (Pr)	2,703	29%	37%	$ 2,580	$ 2,580	$4,660
Chaminade University of Honolulu; Honolulu (Pr)	1,742	96	25	13,380	13,380	7,930
Hawai'i Pacific University; Honolulu (Pr)	7,900	81	20	10,368	10,368	8,770
University of Hawaii at Hilo; Hilo (Pu)	3,300	66		2,376	7,944	5,081
University of Hawaii at Manoa; Honolulu (Pu)	19,863	59	26	3,408	9,888	5,675
University of Phoenix–Hawaii Campus; Honolulu (Pu)	1,273		39	11,070	11,070	
IDAHO						
Albertson College of Idaho; Caldwell (Pr)	830	79	39	13,900	13,900	5,050
Boise State University; Boise (Pu)	18,332	92	20	3,251	9,971	4,426
Idaho State University; Pocatello (Pu)	13,621	74	22	-	6,600	4,680
Lewis-Clark State College; Lewiston (Pu)	3,471	64	26	-	5,998	4,336
Northwest Nazarene University; Nampa (Pr)	1,565	70	28	15,330	15,330	4,440
University of Idaho; Moscow (Pu)	12,894	81	21	-	7,392	4,868
University of Phoenix–Idaho Campus; Meridian (Pr)				9,000	9,000	
ILLINOIS						
Augustana College; Rock Island (Pr)	2,309	68	40	20,397	20,397	5,781
Aurora University; Aurora (Pr)	3,450	56	19	14,250	14,250	5,514
Benedictine University; Lisle (Pr)	2,968		21	16,960	16,960	6,370
Bradley University; Peoria (Pr)	6,137	69	33	16,800	16,800	5,980
Chicago State University; Chicago (Pu)	7,040	42	23	4,382	9,034	5,700
Columbia College Chicago; Chicago (Pr)	9,915	90	26	14,880	14,880	7,340
Concordia University; River Forest (Pr)	1,706	21	27	17,900	17,900	5,400
DePaul University; Chicago (Pr)	23,610	73	18	18,750	18,750	8,790
DeVry University; Addison (Pr)	2,420		9	10,100	10,100	
DeVry University; Chicago (Pr)	3,000			10,100	10,100	
DeVry University; Tinley Park (Pr)	1,674		10	10,100	10,100	
Dominican University; River Forest (Pr)	2,900	82	17	17,850	17,850	5,660
Eastern Illinois University; Charleston (Pu)	11,522	78	30	3,563	10,688	6,210
East-West University; Chicago (Pr)	1,113	90	16	9,900	9,900	
Elmhurst College; Elmhurst (Pr)	2,593	73	39	18,600	18,600	6,030
Greenville College; Greenville (Pr)	1,342	95	33	15,666	15,666	5,566
Harrington College of Design; Chicago (Pr)	1,364	73	21	12,000	12,000	
Illinois College; Jacksonville (Pr)	1,016	72	36	13,300	13,300	5,800
Illinois Institute of Art; Chicago (Pr)	1,950	93		15,075	15,075	
Illinois Institute of Art-Schaumburg; Schaumburg (Pr)	1,107	75	20	15,075	15,075	
Illinois Institute of Technology; Chicago (Pr)	6,167	59	5	19,775	19,775	6,282
Illinois State University; Normal (Pu)	20,860	75	34	4,123	8,593	5,414
Illinois Wesleyan University; Bloomington (Pr)	2,106	43	41	24,390	24,390	5,840
International Academy of Design & Technology; Chicago (Pr)	2,769	54	23	17,200	17,200	
Judson College; Elgin (Pr)	1,166	79	33	15,800	15,800	6,000
Knox College; Galesburg (Pr)	1,127	73	38	24,105	24,105	5,925
Lake Forest College; Lake Forest (Pr)	1,348	68	39	24,096	24,096	5,764
Lewis University; Romeoville (Pr)	4,468	66	20	15,950	15,950	7,000
Loyola University Chicago; Chicago (Pr)	13,362	82	19	20,544	20,544	7,900
McKendree College; Lebanon (Pr)	2,115	73	33	15,200	15,200	5,920
Millikin University; Decatur (Pr)	2,633	74	41	18,834	18,834	6,123
Monmouth College; Monmouth (Pr)	1,162	76	34	18,600	18,600	5,000
Moody Bible Institute; Chicago (Pr)	1,732	50		-	-	6,340
National-Louis University; Chicago (Pr)	7,665		14	16,200	16,200	5,913
North Central College; Naperville (Pr)	2,458	71	32	19,041	19,041	6,375
North Park University; Chicago (Pr)	2,181	74	23	19,470	19,470	6,710
Northeastern Illinois University; Chicago (Pu)	11,825	71	17	3,300	6,600	
Northern Illinois University; De Kalb (Pu)	25,260	62	24	3,903	7,815	5,360
Northwestern University; Evanston (Pr)	16,266	33	19	28,404	28,404	8,967
Olivet Nazarene University; Bourbonnais (Pr)	4,314	78	19	14,160	14,160	5,500
Quincy University; Quincy (Pr)	1,269	94	30	16,400	16,400	6,735
Robert Morris College; Chicago (Pr)	5,139	76	27	13,500	13,500	
Rockford College; Rockford (Pr)	1,280	59	29	20,210	20,210	6,581
Roosevelt University; Chicago (Pr)	7,524	51	12	15,180	15,180	7,150
Saint Xavier University; Chicago (Pr)	5,566	68	22	16,500	16,500	6,464
School of the Art Institute of Chicago; Chicago (Pr)	2,728	83	32	24,000	24,000	
Southern Illinois University Carbondale; Carbondale (Pu)	21,387	77	23	4,245	8,490	4,903
Southern Illinois University Edwardsville; Edwardsville (Pu)	13,295	81	26	3,360	6,720	5,364
St. Augustine College; Chicago (Pr)	1,710		16	7,128	7,128	
Trinity Christian College; Palos Heights (Pr)	1,263	93	32	15,490	15,490	6,000
Trinity International University; Deerfield (Pr)	2,863	87	19	16,900	16,900	5,830
University of Chicago; Chicago (Pr)	13,887	40	11	28,689	28,689	9,315
University of Illinois at Chicago; Chicago (Pu)	25,763	61	21	4,898	14,594	6,620
University of Illinois at Urbana–Champaign; Champaign (Pu)	40,458	63	24	7,010	18,050	6,620
University of St. Francis; Joliet (Pr)	1,988	58	26	16,480	16,480	6,030
Western Illinois University; Macomb (Pu)	13,469	66	25	3,915	7,830	5,366
Wheaton College; Wheaton (Pr)	2,944	53	31	18,500	18,500	6,100

Institution name; city (Public/Private)	Students	Percent Women	Percent Students accepted	Tuition In-state	Tuition Out-of-state	Room and board
INDIANA						
Anderson University; Anderson (Pr)	2,506	72%	30%	$17,050	$17,050	$5,560
Ball State University; Muncie (Pu)	20,533	76	28	5,532	13,950	5,880
Bethel College; Mishawaka (Pr)	1,847	65	30	14,390	14,390	4,680
Butler University; Indianapolis (Pr)	4,424	77	36	20,990	20,990	7,040
Calumet College of Saint Joseph; Whiting (Pr)	1,332	73	15	9,000	9,000	
DePauw University; Greencastle (Pr)	2,365	63	40	24,000	24,000	7,050
Earlham College; Richmond (Pr)	1,262	77	33	23,920	23,920	5,416
Franklin College; Franklin (Pr)	1,038	86	40	16,750	16,750	5,270
Goshen College; Goshen (Pr)	920	61	38	16,320	16,320	5,800
Grace College; Winona Lake (Pr)	1,208	71	29	13,690	13,690	5,755
Hanover College; Hanover (Pr)	997	79	37	14,300	14,300	5,900
Huntington College; Huntington (Pr)	976	92	38	17,280	17,280	5,890
Indiana Institute of Technology; Fort Wayne (Pr)	3,390	92	19	15,590	15,590	6,030
Indiana State University; Terre Haute (Pu)	11,360	86	22	5,322	11,790	5,297
Indiana University Bloomington; Bloomington (Pu)	38,589	81	28	5,756	16,791	5,872
Indiana University East; Richmond (Pu)	2,568	79	19	4,118	10,068	
Indiana University Kokomo; Kokomo (Pu)	2,954	86	19	4,118	10,068	
Indiana University Northwest; Gary (Pu)	5,097	67	19	4,118	10,068	
Indiana University South Bend; South Bend (Pu)	7,280	83	20	4,181	10,773	
Indiana University Southeast; New Albany (Pu)	6,408	85	20	4,118	10,068	
Indiana University–Purdue University Fort Wayne; Fort Wayne (Pu)	11,806	97	16	4,535	10,983	
Indiana University–Purdue University Indianapolis; Indianapolis (Pu)	29,860	77	19	5,151	14,334	
Indiana Wesleyan University; Marion (Pr)	8,765	90	33	14,420	14,420	5,480
Manchester College; North Manchester (Pr)	1,170	79	35	16,940	16,940	6,340
Marian College; Indianapolis (Pr)	1,561	75	29	16,800	16,800	5,800
Oakland City University; Oakland City (Pr)	1,753	99	22	12,000	12,000	4,560
Purdue University Calumet; Hammond (Pu)	9,128	87	15	3,774	9,500	
Purdue University North Central; Westville (Pu)	3,467	83	13	4,344	10,503	
Purdue University; West Lafayette (Pu)	38,847	79	23	5,860	17,480	6,700
Rose-Hulman Institute of Technology; Terre Haute (Pr)	1,864	71	12	24,255	24,255	6,720
Saint Joseph's College; Rensselaer (Pr)	998	76	29	17,900	17,900	6,190
Saint Mary-of-the-Woods College; Saint Mary-of-the-Woods (Pr)	1,687	78	17	16,530	16,530	6,250
Saint Mary's College; Notre Dame (Pr)	1,475	82	69	21,624	21,624	7,289
Taylor University; Upland (Pr)	1,843	84	36	18,306	18,306	5,292
Tri-State University; Angola (Pr)	1,192	72	20	18,000	18,000	5,600
University of Evansville; Evansville (Pr)	2,650	86	33	18,900	18,900	5,510
University of Indianapolis; Indianapolis (Pr)	3,986	74	22	16,620	16,620	5,940
University of Notre Dame; Notre Dame (Pr)	11,415	29	26	27,170	27,170	6,930
University of Saint Francis; Fort Wayne (Pr)	1,834	73	33	14,900	14,900	5,450
University of Southern Indiana; Evansville (Pu)	9,899	93	24	3,825	9,128	5,140
Valparaiso University; Valparaiso (Pr)	3,850	82	28	20,000	20,000	5,480
Wabash College; Crawfordsville (Pr)	863	50	0	20,829	20,829	6,717
IOWA						
Briar Cliff University; Sioux City (Pr)	1,063	80	27	15,960	15,960	5,310
Buena Vista University; Storm Lake (Pr)	1,364	84	34	19,862	19,862	5,544
Central College; Pella (Pr)	1,698	83	37	17,609	17,609	6,145
Clarke College; Dubuque (Pr)	1,126	56	35	16,580	16,580	6,075
Coe College; Cedar Rapids (Pr)	1,317	71	33	21,280	21,280	5,780
Cornell College; Mount Vernon (Pr)	1,117	69	38	21,630	21,630	6,035
Dordt College; Sioux Center (Pr)	1,359	92	36	15,550	15,550	4,400
Drake University; Des Moines (Pr)	5,164	83	27	19,100	19,100	5,700
Graceland University; Lamoni (Pr)	2,359	58	27	14,650	14,650	4,750
Grand View College; Des Moines (Pr)	1,630	95	33	14,460	14,460	5,232
Grinnell College; Grinnell (Pr)	1,524	63	39	23,898	23,898	6,570
Iowa State University of Science and Technology; Ames (Pu)	27,380	90	25	4,342	13,684	5,740
Loras College; Dubuque (Pr)	1,764	96	32	17,370	17,370	5,895
Luther College; Decorah (Pr)	2,565	77	42	21,600	21,600	4,100
Morningside College; Sioux City (Pr)	1,176	74	27	15,450	15,450	5,260
Mount Mercy College; Cedar Rapids (Pr)	1,473	84	35	16,070	16,070	5,330
Northwestern College; Orange City (Pr)	1,285	83	43	15,290	15,290	4,350
Palmer College of Chiropractic; Davenport (Pr)	1,859		2	5,325	5,325	
Simpson College; Indianola (Pr)	1,937	86	30	17,908	17,908	6,062
St. Ambrose University; Davenport (Pr)	3,447	87	25	16,650	16,650	6,150
University of Dubuque; Dubuque (Pr)	1,253	82	19	16,000	16,000	5,420
University of Iowa; Iowa City (Pu)	29,744	82	24	4,342	14,634	5,930
University of Northern Iowa; Cedar Falls (Pu)	13,666	80	35	4,342	11,300	4,918
Upper Iowa University; Fayette (Pr)	840	56	21	15,056	15,056	5,020
Wartburg College; Waverly (Pr)	1,775	83	37	18,150	18,150	5,180
William Penn University; Oskaloosa (Pr)	1,499	65	41	13,820	13,820	4,610

Institution name; city (Public/Private)	Students	Percent Women	Students accepted	Tuition In-state	Out-of-state	Room and board
KANSAS						
Baker University; Baldwin City (Pr)	1,015	82%	42%	$14,210	$14,210	$5,300
Benedictine College; Atchison (Pr)	1,330	96	25	14,083	14,083	5,920
Emporia State University; Emporia (Pu)	6,278	74	25	2,200	8,338	4,222
Fort Hays State University; Hays (Pu)	7,373	94	19	2,032	8,165	4,843
Friends University; Wichita (Pr)	3,190	93		13,620	13,620	6,464
Haskell Indian Nations University; Lawrence (Pu)	1,028		6	-	-	70
Kansas State University; Manhattan (Pu)	23,050	60	24	3,510	11,400	5,080
Kansas Wesleyan University; Salina (Pr)	805	53	31	14,200	14,200	4,700
MidAmerica Nazarene University; Olathe (Pr)	1,952	41	28	11,910	11,910	5,828
Newman University; Wichita (Pr)	2,063			13,198	13,198	4,820
Pittsburg State University; Pittsburg (Pu)	6,731	54		2,962	8,784	4,166
Southwestern College; Winfield (Pr)	1,405	71	21	14,618	14,618	4,942
University of Kansas; Lawrence (Pu)	28,580	67	26	3,527	11,003	4,822
University of Saint Mary; Leavenworth (Pr)	881	47	15	13,574	13,574	5,294
Washburn University; Topeka (Pu)	7,002	100		4,050	9,150	4,972
Wichita State University; Wichita (Pu)	14,896	63	21	2,866	10,320	4,620
KENTUCKY						
Asbury College; Wilmore (Pr)	1,258	73	41	16,352	16,352	4,204
Bellarmine University; Louisville (Pr)	3,134	82	23	17,820	17,820	5,620
Berea College; Berea (Pr)	1,560	25	41	-	-	4,523
Campbellsville University; Campbellsville (Pr)	2,006	80	21	12,504	12,504	4,976
Centre College; Danville (Pr)	1,062	75	39	20,400	20,400	6,900
Cumberland College; Williamsburg (Pr)	1,727	72	26	11,098	11,098	4,926
Eastern Kentucky University; Richmond (Pu)	15,951	76	26	3,198	8,790	4,510
Georgetown College; Georgetown (Pr)	1,708	80	28	15,690	15,690	5,190
Kentucky State University; Frankfort (Pu)	2,306	52	24	2,828	8,472	5,394
Lindsey Wilson College; Columbia (Pr)	1,680	73	35	12,456	12,456	5,484
Midway College; Midway (Pr)	1,154	74	40	11,700	11,700	5,800
Morehead State University; Morehead (Pu)	9,509	71	25	3,364	8,948	4,100
Murray State University; Murray (Pu)	10,093	63	27	2,944	5,000	4,380
Northern Kentucky University; Highland Heights (Pu)	13,910	89	23	3,744	7,992	5,066
Pikeville College; Pikeville (Pr)	1,013	100	28	9,900	9,900	5,000
Spalding University; Louisville (Pr)	1,702	74	23	13,750	13,750	5,334
Sullivan University; Louisville (Pr)	4,928			11,735	11,735	
Thomas More College; Crestview Hills (Pr)	1,526	61		15,550	15,550	5,400
Transylvania University; Lexington (Pr)	1,134	88	39	17,010	17,010	6,120
Union College; Barbourville (Pr)	1,016	73	19	13,150	13,150	4,400
University of Kentucky; Lexington (Pu)	25,397	81	23	4,002	10,682	4,285
University of Louisville; Louisville (Pu)	20,825	79	18	4,344	11,856	4,312
Western Kentucky University; Bowling Green (Pu)	18,380	93	26	4,050	8,898	4,052
LOUISIANA						
Centenary College of Louisiana; Shreveport (Pr)	997	74	36	16,750	16,750	5,850
Dillard University; New Orleans (Pr)	2,312	64	42	10,600	10,600	6,440
Grambling State University; Grambling (Pu)	4,673	62		3,182	8,532	3,356
Grantham University; Slidell (Pr)	4,500			3,489	3,489	
Louisiana College; Pineville (Pr)	1,135	85	32	8,850	8,850	3,610
Louisiana State University and Agricultural and Mechanical College; Baton Rouge (Pu)	31,934	81	26	2,739	8,039	5,216
Louisiana State University Health Sciences Center; New Orleans (Pu)	2,888		19	3,214	5,714	
Louisiana State University in Shreveport; Shreveport (Pu)	4,377	68	24	2,194	6,524	
Louisiana Tech University; Ruston (Pu)	11,960	92	19	3,270	7,065	3,885
Loyola University New Orleans; New Orleans (Pr)	5,518	69	27	19,450	19,450	7,660
McNeese State University; Lake Charles (Pu)	8,447	88	24	2,050	8,116	3,788
New Orleans Baptist Theological Seminary; New Orleans (Pr)	2,712	82		3,600	3,600	
Nicholls State University; Thibodaux (Pu)	7,247	99	26	2,115	7,563	3,402
Northwestern State University of Louisiana; Natchitoches (Pu)	10,505	98	24	2,054	8,132	3,326
Our Lady of Holy Cross College; New Orleans (Pr)	1,432	97	37	5,400	5,400	
Our Lady of the Lake College; Baton Rouge (Pr)	1,807	91		6,150	6,150	
Southeastern Louisiana University; Hammond (Pu)	15,662	96	27	2,951	8,279	3,840
Southern University and Agricultural and Mechanical College; Baton Rouge (Pu)	8,884	57	32	3,066	8,858	4,306
Southern University at New Orleans; New Orleans (Pu)	5,000	100		2,678	6,416	
Tulane University; New Orleans (Pr)	12,443	56	17	29,810	29,810	7,641
University of Louisiana at Lafayette; Lafayette (Pu)	16,208	88	27	2,700	8,960	3,126
University of Louisiana at Monroe; Monroe (Pu)	8,571	99	26	2,040	7,992	1,645
University of New Orleans; New Orleans (Pu)	17,360	70	20	3,084	10,128	
University of Phoenix–Louisiana Campus; Metairie (Pr)	1,855			8,160	8,160	
Xavier University of Louisiana; New Orleans (Pr)	3,913	84	34	10,500	10,500	6,200

Institution name; city (Public/Private)	Students	Percent Women	Percent Students accepted	Tuition In-state	Tuition Out-of-state	Room and board
MAINE						
Bates College; Lewiston (Pr)	1,746	31%	37%			
Bowdoin College; Brunswick (Pr)	1,647	24	35	$29,470	$29,470	$ 7,670
Colby College; Waterville (Pr)	1,768	34	39			
Husson College; Bangor (Pr)	2,038	97	19	10,470	10,470	5,680
Maine Maritime Academy; Castine (Pu)	861	68	10	5,700	10,750	5,820
Saint Joseph's College of Maine; Standish (Pr)	953	79	47	17,430	17,430	7,530
Thomas College; Waterville (Pr)	829	73	17	14,300	14,300	6,340
University of Maine at Augusta; Augusta (Pu)	5,942		9	3,690	8,940	
University of Maine at Farmington; Farmington (Pu)	2,420	72	38	4,290	10,470	5,318
University of Maine at Fort Kent; Fort Kent (Pu)	924	91		3,690	8,940	4,880
University of Maine at Machias; Machias (Pu)	1,313	82	15	3,636	9,630	5,150
University of Maine at Presque Isle; Presque Isle (Pu)	1,546	87	25	3,690	9,240	4,965
University of Maine; Orono (Pu)	11,222	76	23	4,710	13,410	6,166
University of New England; Biddeford (Pr)	3,192	97	17	18,990	18,990	7,560
University of Southern Maine; Portland (Pu)	11,007	72	17	4,320	12,000	6,014
MARYLAND						
Bowie State University; Bowie (Pu)	5,454	48	22	3,551	10,894	6,020
Capitol College; Laurel (Pr)	801	90	6	16,500	16,500	
College of Notre Dame of Maryland; Baltimore (Pr)	3,030	73	16	18,700	18,700	7,600
Columbia Union College; Takoma Park (Pr)	1,183	54	30	14,698	14,698	5,295
Coppin State University; Baltimore (Pu)	4,003	47		3,142	8,964	5,952
Frostburg State University; Frostburg (Pu)	5,469	79	26	4,158	10,806	5,619
Goucher College; Baltimore (Pr)	2,311	65	27	24,150	24,150	8,350
Hood College; Frederick (Pr)	1,325	55	33	19,940	19,940	7,520
Johns Hopkins University; Baltimore (Pr)	6,229	30	21	28,730	28,730	9,142
Loyola College in Maryland; Baltimore (Pr)	6,033	71	23	26,010	26,010	8,630
Maryland Institute College of Art; Baltimore (Pr)	1,476	50	36	22,980	22,980	7,180
McDaniel College; Westminster (Pr)	3,294	83	21	22,860	22,860	5,280
Morgan State University; Baltimore (Pu)	6,621	34	30	5,078	12,076	6,570
Mount Saint Mary's University; Emmitsburg (Pr)	2,088	90	25	20,800	20,800	7,400
Salisbury University; Salisbury (Pu)	6,816	17	34	5,564	12,452	6,900
Sojourner-Douglass College; Baltimore (Pr)	1,124		32	5,400	5,400	
St. Mary's College of Maryland; St. Mary's City (Pu)	1,922	55	41	7,550	13,870	7,105
Towson University; Towson (Pu)	17,188	52	32	3,956	11,602	6,322
United States Naval Academy; Annapolis (Pu)	4,335	10	11			
University of Maryland Eastern Shore; Princess Anne (Pu)	3,762	58	28	3,563	8,898	5,630
University of Maryland University College; Adelphi (Pu)	25,857	100	5	5,208	9,576	
University of Maryland, Baltimore County; Baltimore (Pu)	11,872	58	24	7,388	14,240	7,007
University of Maryland, College Park; College Park (Pu)	35,262	43	24	5,568	16,242	7,608
University of Phoenix–Maryland Campus; Columbia (Pr)	1,704		35	10,200	10,200	
Villa Julie College; Stevenson (Pr)	2,710	63	34	12,816	12,816	
Washington College; Chestertown (Pr)	1,481	61	41	23,740	23,740	5,740
MASSACHUSETTS						
American International College; Springfield (Pr)	1,595	77	22	16,485	16,485	8,232
Amherst College; Amherst (Pr)	1,623	18	36	29,170	29,170	7,740
Anna Maria College; Paxton (Pr)	1,147	88	21	17,495	17,495	6,995
Assumption College; Worcester (Pr)	2,412	79	38	21,000	21,000	5,090
Babson College; Babson Park (Pr)	3,342	37	15	27,248	27,248	9,978
Bay Path College; Longmeadow (Pr)	1,314	82	52	16,890	16,890	8,020
Becker College; Worcester (Pr)	1,467	83	23	15,620	15,620	7,700
Bentley College; Waltham (Pr)	5,673	46	21	24,120	24,120	9,580
Berklee College of Music; Boston (Pr)	3,799	79	24	19,200	19,200	10,280
Boston College; Chestnut Hill (Pr)	13,611	31	28	27,080	27,080	9,300
Boston University; Boston (Pr)	29,048	52	24	28,512	28,512	9,288
Brandeis University; Waltham (Pr)	4,985	44	25	28,999	28,999	8,323
Bridgewater State College; Bridgewater (Pu)	9,626	72	28	910	7,050	5,922
Cambridge College; Cambridge (Pr)	2,700			9,000	9,000	
Clark University; Worcester (Pr)	3,084	63	28	26,700	26,700	5,150
College of the Holy Cross; Worcester (Pr)	2,773	42	39	27,560	27,560	8,440
Curry College; Milton (Pr)	2,599	69	19	19,870	19,870	8,150
Eastern Nazarene College; Quincy (Pr)	1,212	62	42	16,052	16,052	5,638
Elms College; Chicopee (Pr)	971	90	33	17,830	17,830	7,100
Emerson College; Boston (Pr)	4,385	48	28	22,144	22,144	9,828
Emmanuel College; Boston (Pr)	1,871	18	33	18,900	18,900	8,400
Endicott College; Beverly (Pr)	2,678	48	26	16,744	16,744	8,858
Fitchburg State College; Fitchburg (Pu)	4,948	61	21	970	7,050	5,506
Framingham State College; Framingham (Pu)	6,156	55	22	970	7,050	5,058
Gordon College; Wenham (Pr)	1,683	78	44	19,334	19,334	5,748
Hampshire College; Amherst (Pr)	1,332	55	40	28,832	28,832	7,689
Harvard University; Cambridge (Pr)	20,130	10	12	26,066	26,066	8,868
Lasell College; Newton (Pr)	1,099	68	47	16,600	16,600	8,500
Lesley University; Cambridge (Pr)	6,333	77	6	19,525	19,525	8,800

Institution name; city (Public/Private)	Students	Percent Women	Percent Students accepted	Tuition In-state	Tuition Out-of-state	Room and board
Massachusetts College of Art; Boston (Pu)	2,096	53%	29%	$ 1,030	$11,040	$ 9,800
Massachusetts College of Liberal Arts; North Adams (Pu)	1,811	67	25	1,030	9,975	5,620
Massachusetts College of Pharmacy and Health Sciences; Boston (Pr)	2,513	76	9	18,800	18,800	10,170
Massachusetts Institute of Technology; Cambridge (Pr)	10,340	16	12	29,400	29,400	8,710
Massachusetts Maritime Academy; Buzzards Bay (Pu)	948	60	9	1,030	11,510	5,809
Merrimack College; North Andover (Pr)	2,404	60	29	20,625	20,625	8,750
Mount Holyoke College; South Hadley (Pr)	2,152	52	72	29,170	29,170	8,580
Mount Ida College; Newton Center (Pr)	1,076	79		16,100	16,100	9,000
New England Institute of Art; Brookline (Pr)	1,045	57		16,140	16,140	9,000
Newbury College; Brookline (Pr)	1,167	88	18	14,050	14,050	7,500
Nichols College; Dudley (Pr)	1,672	83	11	19,223	19,223	7,810
Northeastern University; Boston (Pr)	18,760	47		25,600	25,600	9,810
Regis College; Weston (Pr)	1,083	87	39	19,910	19,910	9,090
Salem State College; Salem (Pu)	9,120	82	21	910	7,050	5,940
Simmons College; Boston (Pr)	4,121	68	22	22,860	22,860	9,450
Smith College; Northampton (Pr)	3,159	52	59	27,330	27,330	9,490
Springfield College; Springfield (Pr)	3,119	74	23	19,410	19,410	7,520
Stonehill College; Easton (Pr)	2,582	49	37	20,432	20,432	9,450
Suffolk University; Boston (Pr)	7,804	82	17	17,610	17,610	10,290
Tufts University; Medford (Pr)	9,509	26	20	28,859	28,859	8,640
University of Massachusetts Amherst; Amherst (Pu)	24,310	82	26	1,714	9,937	5,748
University of Massachusetts Boston; Boston (Pu)	12,394	55	20	6,977	17,637	
University of Massachusetts Dartmouth; North Dartmouth (Pu)	8,284	71	27	1,417	8,099	7,099
University of Massachusetts Lowell; Lowell (Pu)	11,706	62	14	1,454	8,567	5,724
Wellesley College; Wellesley (Pr)	2,312	41	70	27,134	27,134	8,612
Wentworth Institute of Technology; Boston (Pr)	3,273	70	8	15,000	15,000	8,200
Western New England College; Springfield (Pr)	4,448	76	15	19,460	19,460	8,100
Westfield State College; Westfield (Pu)	4,938	66	31	970	7,050	5,290
Wheaton College; Norton (Pr)	1,565	43	44	28,675	28,675	7,430
Wheelock College; Boston (Pr)	942	67	43	20,400	20,400	8,600
Williams College; Williamstown (Pr)	2,102	21	34	27,890	27,890	7,660
Worcester Polytechnic Institute; Worcester (Pr)	3,789	71	13	28,420	28,420	8,984
Worcester State College; Worcester (Pu)	5,470	56	20	970	7,050	5,500
MICHIGAN						
Adrian College; Adrian (Pr)	1,028	88	36	16,470	16,470	5,760
Albion College; Albion (Pr)	1,732	87	40	21,692	21,692	6,262
Alma College; Alma (Pr)	1,291	77	40	18,684	18,684	6,712
Andrews University; Berrien Springs (Pr)	2,995	58	19	14,200	14,200	4,980
Aquinas College; Grand Rapids (Pr)	2,338	79	32	16,400	16,400	5,494
Baker College of Auburn Hills; Auburn Hills (Pr)	3,177	100		5,940	5,940	
Baker College of Cadillac; Cadillac (Pr)	1,386	100		5,940	5,940	
Baker College of Clinton Township; Clinton Township (Pr)	4,510	100		5,940	5,940	
Baker College of Flint; Flint (Pr)	5,639	100		5,940	5,940	
Baker College of Jackson; Jackson (Pr)	1,593	100		5,940	5,940	
Baker College of Muskegon; Muskegon (Pr)	4,076	100		5,940	5,940	
Baker College of Owosso; Owosso (Pr)	2,538	100		5,940	5,940	
Baker College of Port Huron; Port Huron (Pr)	1,477	100		5,940	5,940	
Calvin College; Grand Rapids (Pr)	4,323	99	38	16,775	16,775	5,840
Central Michigan University; Mount Pleasant (Pu)	27,758	70	27	4,463	11,393	5,924
Cleary University; Ann Arbor (Pr)	968	97		11,040	11,040	
College for Creative Studies; Detroit (Pr)	1,218	74	30	18,720	18,720	
Cornerstone University; Grand Rapids (Pr)	2,353	76	32	14,420	14,420	5,426
Davenport University; Dearborn (Pr)	2,512	100	19	10,170	10,170	
Davenport University; Grand Rapids (Pr)	1,868	65	15	10,170	10,170	
Davenport University; Warren (Pr)	1,407	100	16	10,170	10,170	
Eastern Michigan University; Ypsilanti (Pu)	24,129	79	25	4,595	14,013	5,850
Ferris State University; Big Rapids (Pu)	11,821	73	24	6,044	12,088	6,326
Grand Valley State University; Allendale (Pu)	21,429	73	31	5,648	12,216	5,768
Hillsdale College; Hillsdale (Pr)	1,230	77	34	15,750	15,750	6,400
Hope College; Holland (Pr)	3,068	83	43	19,212	19,212	6,018
Kalamazoo College; Kalamazoo (Pr)	1,280	70	37	22,908	22,908	6,480
Kettering University; Flint (Pr)	3,126	71	11	21,184	21,184	4,924
Lake Superior State University; Sault Sainte Marie (Pu)	3,258	89	27	5,136	10,062	5,993
Lawrence Technological University; Southfield (Pr)	4,241	76	7	14,112	14,112	6,125
Madonna University; Livonia (Pr)	4,276	86	19	9,000	9,000	5,444
Marygrove College; Detroit (Pr)	5,584	60	4	11,500	11,500	5,800
Michigan State University; East Lansing (Pu)	44,542	71	27	5,925	15,885	5,230
Michigan Technological University; Houghton (Pu)	6,565	93	13	6,810	17,700	5,795
Northern Michigan University; Marquette (Pu)	9,326	84		4,632	7,920	5,724
Northwood University; Midland (Pr)	3,770	87	12	13,485	13,485	6,270
Oakland University; Rochester (Pu)	16,575	80	24	4,774	11,468	5,540

Institution name; city (Public/Private)	Students	Percent Women	Students accepted	Tuition In-state	Out-of-state	Room and board
Olivet College; Olivet (Pr)	1,070	59%	23%	$14,762	$14,762	$4,802
Rochester College; Rochester Hills (Pr)	1,001	42	19	10,272	10,272	5,624
Saginaw Valley State University; University Center (Pu)	9,168	90	29	4,799	10,398	5,645
Siena Heights University; Adrian (Pr)	2,153	64		14,130	14,130	5,220
Spring Arbor University; Spring Arbor (Pr)	3,531	86	33	14,700	14,700	5,290
University of Detroit Mercy; Detroit (Pr)	5,571	81	13	18,750	18,750	6,382
University of Michigan–Dearborn; Dearborn (Pu)	9,021	67	16	5,839	12,911	
University of Michigan–Flint; Flint (Pu)	6,152	81	28	5,274	10,274	
University of Michigan; Ann Arbor (Pu)	39,031	53	23	7,788	24,590	6,704
University of Phoenix–Metro Detroit Campus; Troy (Pr)	3,102		45	10,110	10,110	
Wayne State University; Detroit (Pu)	33,091	68		4,662	10,683	6,500
Western Michigan University; Kalamazoo (Pu)	29,178	86	26	4,934	12,446	6,496
MINNESOTA						
Argosy University/Twin Cities; Eagan (Pr)	1,334	86		10,867	10,867	
Augsburg College; Minneapolis (Pr)	3,172	82	30	18,900	18,900	5,900
Bemidji State University; Bemidji (Pu)	5,024	74	24	4,338	9,200	4,597
Bethel University; St. Paul (Pr)	3,303	91	35	18,700	18,700	6,380
Carleton College; Northfield (Pr)	1,943	30	39	28,362	28,362	5,868
College of Saint Benedict; Saint Joseph (Pr)	2,054	90	71	20,335	20,335	5,987
College of St. Catherine–Minneapolis; Minneapolis (Pr)	4,807	77	37	13,600	13,600	5,460
College of St. Catherine; St. Paul (Pr)	4,807	77	37	19,520	19,520	5,460
College of St. Scholastica; Duluth (Pr)	2,838	88	36	19,192	19,192	5,668
Concordia College; Moorhead (Pr)	2,856	86	43	16,420	16,420	4,540
Concordia University, St. Paul; St. Paul (Pr)	2,051	64	38	18,624	18,624	5,862
Crown College; St. Bonifacius (Pr)	1,031	82	29	13,168	13,168	5,552
Gustavus Adolphus College; St. Peter (Pr)	2,574	77	42	21,300	21,300	5,460
Hamline University; St. Paul (Pr)	4,469	75	18	20,582	20,582	6,220
Macalester College; St. Paul (Pr)	1,884	44	39	24,902	24,902	6,874
Martin Luther College; New Ulm (Pr)	1,020	98	36	6,020	6,020	2,290
Metropolitan State University; St. Paul (Pu)	6,467	67	14	3,600	7,980	
Minnesota State University Mankato; Mankato (Pu)	14,065	88	32	3,806	8,075	4,297
Minnesota State University Moorhead; Moorhead (Pu)	7,695	86	37	3,628	3,628	4,340
North Central University; Minneapolis (Pr)	1,227	55	39	9,840	9,840	4,680
Northwestern College; St. Paul (Pr)	2,592	94	35	17,400	17,400	5,620
Saint John's University; Collegeville (Pr)	2,067	89	0	20,335	20,335	5,788
Saint Mary's University of Minnesota; Winona (Pr)	4,996	75	10	15,890	15,890	5,220
Southwest Minnesota State University; Marshall (Pu)	5,636		19	3,945	3,945	4,491
St. Cloud State University; St. Cloud (Pu)	15,925	76	32	3,980	8,639	3,812
St. Olaf College; Northfield (Pr)	2,994	75	43	23,650	23,650	4,850
University of Minnesota, Crookston; Crookston (Pu)	2,320	89	11	5,471	5,471	4,684
University of Minnesota, Duluth; Duluth (Pu)	10,114	74	27	6,047	16,412	5,100
University of Minnesota, Morris; Morris (Pu)	1,861	83	38	6,908	6,908	4,800
University of Minnesota, Twin Cities Campus; Minneapolis (Pu)	49,474	76	21	5,962	17,592	6,044
University of St. Thomas; St. Paul (Pr)	11,037	87	16	18,975	18,975	6,484
Winona State University; Winona (Pu)	8,236	79	39	4,800	9,260	4,640
MISSISSIPPI						
Alcorn State University; Alcorn State (Pu)	3,309	22	28	3,459	7,965	3,821
Belhaven College; Jackson (Pr)	2,353	56	42	12,200	12,200	4,990
Delta State University; Cleveland (Pu)	3,785	26	29	3,348	7,965	3,270
Jackson State University; Jackson (Pu)	7,815	43	35	3,612	8,116	4,770
Millsaps College; Jackson (Pr)	1,200	84	35	17,346	17,346	6,768
Mississippi College; Clinton (Pr)	3,406	58	29	10,888	10,888	5,396
Mississippi State University; Mississippi State (Pu)	16,173	75	26	3,874	8,780	5,265
Mississippi University for Women; Columbus (Pu)	2,328	65		3,298	7,965	3,230
Mississippi Valley State University; Itta Bena (Pu)	4,009	99	44	3,411	7,965	3,544
Rust College; Holly Springs (Pr)	988	49	30	5,800	5,800	2,600
Tougaloo College; Tougaloo (Pr)	940	99	43	7,750	7,750	3,780
University of Mississippi; University (Pu)	13,804	80	24	3,916	8,826	5,300
University of Southern Mississippi; Hattiesburg (Pu)	14,894	49	32	3,874	8,752	4,785
William Carey College; Hattiesburg (Pr)	2,586	73	30	7,500	7,500	3,390
MISSOURI						
Avila University; Kansas City (Pr)	1,683	42	25	14,700	14,700	5,300
Central Bible College; Springfield (Pr)	817	71	27	6,942	6,942	3,942
Central Methodist College; Fayette (Pr)	932	73	31	13,160	13,160	4,920
Central Missouri State University; Warrensburg (Pu)	10,351	76	27	4,980	9,600	4,796
College of the Ozarks; Point Lookout (Pr)	1,348	14	41	-	-	3,250
Columbia College; Columbia (Pr)	1,068	59	28	11,362	11,362	4,770
Culver-Stockton College; Canton (Pr)	835	72	37	12,400	12,400	5,450
DeVry University; Kansas City (Pr)	1,931		11	9,990	9,990	
Drury University; Springfield (Pr)	1,933	77	29	12,995	12,995	4,885
Evangel University; Springfield (Pr)	1,852	81	41	10,610	10,610	4,130
Fontbonne University; St. Louis (Pr)	2,538	81	33	14,200	14,200	6,988

Institution name; city (Public/Private)	Students	Percent Women	Students accepted	Tuition In-state	Out-of-state	Room and board
Global University of the Assemblies of God; Springfield (Pr)	6,748			$ 2,160	$ 2,160	
Hannibal-LaGrange College; Hannibal (Pr)	1,133	94%		9,840	9,840	$3,780
Harris-Stowe State College; St. Louis (Pu)	1,911	47	15%	3,120	6,146	
Lincoln University; Jefferson City (Pu)	3,128	96	19	3,894	7,434	3,790
Lindenwood University; St. Charles (Pr)	7,838	46	21	11,200	11,200	5,400
Maryville University of Saint Louis; St. Louis (Pr)	3,301	73	26	15,200	15,200	6,650
Missouri Baptist University; St. Louis (Pr)	3,656	71	9	11,770	11,770	5,800
Missouri Southern State University; Joplin (Pu)	5,410	74	26	3,810	7,620	4,480
Missouri Valley College; Marshall (Pr)	1,623	67	23	12,600	12,600	5,200
Missouri Western State College; St. Joseph (Pu)	4,928	100	28	4,098	7,674	4,058
Northwest Missouri State University; Maryville (Pu)	6,514	87	29	4,845	8,355	5,042
Park University; Parkville (Pr)	11,868		6	5,600	5,600	5,180
Rockhurst University; Kansas City (Pr)	2,764	80	15	16,950	16,950	5,750
Saint Louis University; St. Louis (Pr)	11,217	70	21	22,050	22,050	7,740
Southeast Missouri State University; Cape Girardeau (Pu)	9,570	83	28	4,254	7,839	5,450
Southwest Baptist University; Bolivar (Pr)	3,563	86	24	11,200	11,200	3,700
Southwest Missouri State University; Springfield (Pu)	18,930	86	27	4,636	8,776	4,282
St. Louis College of Pharmacy; St. Louis (Pr)	927	44	12	16,200	16,200	6,500
Truman State University; Kirksville (Pu)	5,833	84	38	4,600	8,400	5,072
University of Missouri–Columbia; Columbia (Pu)	26,805	89	26	5,838	15,285	5,770
University of Missouri–Kansas City; Kansas City (Pu)	14,226	93	17	5,448	14,266	7,270
University of Missouri–Rolla; Rolla (Pu)	5,459	90	11	5,838	15,285	5,453
University of Missouri–St. Louis; St. Louis (Pu)	15,605	48	18	5,838	15,285	5,600
University of Phoenix–St. Louis Campus; St. Louis (Pr)	1,711		45	10,500	10,500	
Washington University in St. Louis; St. Louis (Pr)	13,020	20	17	28,300	28,300	9,240
Webster University; St. Louis (Pr)	7,250	58	17	15,480	15,480	6,368
Westminster College; Fulton (Pr)	821	75	27	12,300	12,300	5,430
William Jewell College; Liberty (Pr)	1,274	95	41	16,500	16,500	4,820
William Woods University; Fulton (Pr)	2,670		18	14,000	14,000	5,700
MONTANA						
Carroll College; Helena (Pr)	1,411	83	35	14,466	14,466	5,810
Montana State University–Billings; Billings (Pu)	4,670	96	22	4,180	11,540	4,430
Montana State University–Bozeman; Bozeman (Pu)	12,135	81	23	4,145	12,707	5,370
Montana State University–Northern; Havre (Pu)	1,589	82	27	4,100	11,220	5,600
Montana Tech of The University of Montana; Butte (Pu)	2,232		19	3,350	8,060	4,980
Rocky Mountain College; Billings (Pr)	938	85	35	13,950	13,950	4,900
University of Montana–Missoula; Missoula (Pu)	13,352	93	25	2,969	10,268	5,292
University of Montana–Western; Dillon (Pu)	1,160	100	28	2,875	10,380	4,500
University of Great Falls; Great Falls (Pr)	801	80	26	11,500	11,500	5,100
NEBRASKA						
Bellevue University; Bellevue (Pr)	5,110		22	4,350	4,350	
Chadron State College; Chadron (Pu)	2,711		28	2,610	5,220	3,862
College of Saint Mary; Omaha (Pr)	915	70	44	16,010	16,010	5,500
Concordia University; Seward (Pr)	1,317	89	37	16,000	16,000	4,480
Creighton University; Omaha (Pr)	6,537	88	22	19,202	19,202	6,826
Doane College; Crete (Pr)	2,273	84	27	15,400	15,400	4,600
Hastings College; Hastings (Pr)	1,113	80	32	14,782	14,782	4,530
Midland Lutheran College; Fremont (Pr)	946	86	41	16,310	16,310	4,420
Nebraska Wesleyan University; Lincoln (Pr)	1,840	93	31	16,140	16,140	4,530
Peru State College; Peru (Pu)	1,671	62	21	2,610	5,220	4,911
Union College; Lincoln (Pr)	903	49	37	12,750	12,750	3,630
University of Nebraska at Kearney; Kearney (Pu)	6,395	88	28	3,120	6,382	4,436
University of Nebraska at Omaha; Omaha (Pu)	13,997	85	22	3,518	10,358	3,998
University of Nebraska–Lincoln; Lincoln (Pu)	22,559	76	25	3,848	11,430	5,204
Wayne State College; Wayne (Pu)	3,317	100	33	2,610	5,220	3,920
NEVADA						
University of Nevada, Las Vegas; Las Vegas (Pu)	25,749	80	21	2,670	11,157	6,367
University of Nevada, Reno; Reno (Pu)	15,534	88	23	2,670	11,157	6,990
University of Phoenix–Nevada Campus; Las Vegas (Pr)	3,170		37	8,910	8,910	
NEW HAMPSHIRE						
Colby-Sawyer College; New London (Pr)	986	82	41	22,200	22,200	8,520
College for Lifelong Learning; Concord (Pu)	1,827			4,368	4,848	
Daniel Webster College; Nashua (Pr)	1,109	79	16	19,600	19,600	7,890
Dartmouth College; Hanover (Pr)	5,683	18	25	28,965	28,965	8,739
Franklin Pierce College; Rindge (Pr)	1,591	86	33	20,790	20,790	7,300
Keene State College; Keene (Pu)	4,920	71		5,400	10,800	5,682
New England College; Henniker (Pr)	1,136	97	21	20,480	20,480	7,740
Plymouth State College; Plymouth (Pu)	4,910	71	27	4,750	10,800	6,058
Rivier College; Nashua (Pr)	2,317	80	18	18,450	18,450	7,092
Saint Anselm College; Manchester (Pr)	2,008	71	38	21,410	21,410	8,090
Southern New Hampshire University; Manchester (Pr)	5,584	82	18	18,264	18,264	7,648
University of New Hampshire at Manchester; Manchester (Pu)	1,349	72	20	5,870	14,850	
University of New Hampshire; Durham (Pu)	14,431	69	30	6,770	17,130	6,234

Institution name; city (Public/Private)	Students	Percent Women	Students accepted	Tuition In-state	Out-of-state	Room and board
NEW JERSEY						
Bloomfield College; Bloomfield (Pr)	2,083	56%		$12,900	$12,900	$ 6,150
Caldwell College; Caldwell (Pr)	2,219	69	19%	16,960	16,960	7,000
Centenary College; Hackettstown (Pr)	2,182	73	31	17,000	17,000	7,150
College of New Jersey; Ewing (Pu)	6,912	48	39	6,131	10,706	7,744
College of Saint Elizabeth; Morristown (Pr)	1,848	81	26	16,450	16,450	8,130
DeVry University; North Brunswick (Pr)	2,547		7	10,100	10,100	
Drew University; Madison (Pr)	2,521	69	26	27,360	27,360	7,644
Fairleigh Dickinson University, College at Florham; Madison (Pr)	3,743	75	19	21,400	21,400	8,250
Fairleigh Dickinson University, Metropolitan Campus; Teaneck (Pr)	7,118	68	10	19,854	19,854	8,250
Felician College; Lodi (Pr)	1,526	72	0	14,500	14,500	7,200
Georgian Court University; Lakewood (Pr)	2,976	86	30	15,872	15,872	6,600
Kean University; Union (Pu)	12,978	64	24	4,448	6,810	7,755
Monmouth University; West Long Branch (Pr)	6,212	66	24	18,198	18,198	7,568
Montclair State University; Upper Montclair (Pu)	15,204	51	25	4,785	7,784	7,902
New Jersey City University; Jersey City (Pu)	9,361	52	20	4,560	8,868	6,586
New Jersey Institute of Technology; Newark (Pu)	8,770	68	8	7,332	12,700	8,076
Princeton University; Princeton (Pr)	6,849	10	25	28,540	28,540	8,109
Ramapo College of New Jersey; Mahwah (Pu)	5,631	43	31	5,270	9,525	7,792
Richard Stockton College of New Jersey; Pomona (Pu)	6,881	43	36	4,736	7,680	6,748
Rider University; Lawrenceville (Pr)	5,509	78	23	20,590	20,590	8,060
Rowan University; Glassboro (Pu)	9,667	51	31	5,396	10,792	7,394
Rutgers, The State University of New Jersey, Camden; Camden (Pu)	5,485	58	26	6,290	12,804	7,552
Rutgers, The State University of New Jersey, New Brunswick/Piscataway; New Brunswick (Pu)	35,318	54	28	6,290	12,804	7,711
Rutgers, The State University of New Jersey, Newark; Newark (Pu)	10,465	47	21	6,290	12,804	8,140
Saint Peter's College; Jersey City (Pr)	3,300	67		18,092	18,092	7,800
Seton Hall University; South Orange (Pr)	9,746	82	17	19,530	19,530	9,546
Stevens Institute of Technology; Hoboken (Pr)	4,548	51	7	26,000	26,000	8,500
Thomas Edison State College; Trenton (Pu)	10,233					
William Paterson University of New Jersey; Wayne (Pu)	11,210	61	29	7,120	11,510	7,630
NEW MEXICO						
College of Santa Fe; Santa Fe (Pr)	1,761	81	16	18,980	18,980	5,788
College of the Southwest; Hobbs (Pr)	894	16	28	6,720	6,720	5,400
Eastern New Mexico University; Portales (Pu)	3,706	74	26	1,776	7,332	4,290
New Mexico Highlands University; Las Vegas (Pu)	3,960	100	12	2,184	9,096	4,085
New Mexico Institute of Mining and Technology; Socorro (Pu)	1,798	98	11	2,156	8,677	4,200
New Mexico State University; Las Cruces (Pu)	16,174	84	26	2,418	10,296	4,560
University of New Mexico; Albuquerque (Pu)	25,686	75	22	3,313	11,954	5,910
University of Phoenix–New Mexico Campus; Albuquerque (Pr)	3,584		43	8,550	8,550	
Western New Mexico University; Silver City (Pu)	3,074			2,371	8,923	4,280
NEW YORK						
Adelphi University; Garden City (Pr)	7,355	71	21	16,800	16,800	8,500
Albany College of Pharmacy of Union University; Albany (Pr)	886	64	36	16,100	16,100	5,500
Alfred University; Alfred (Pr)	2,367	69	30	18,498	18,498	9,012
Bard College; Annandale-on-Hudson (Pr)	1,605	39	33	28,244	28,244	8,544
Barnard College; New York (Pr)	2,281	31	74	25,294	25,294	10,462
Bernard M. Baruch College of the City University of New York; New York (Pu)	15,126	36	25	4,000	8,640	
Boricua College; New York (Pr)	1,520	47		7,350	7,350	
Briarcliffe College; Bethpage (Pr)	2,911	80	29	12,720	12,720	
Brooklyn College of the City University of New York; Brooklyn (Pu)	15,513	36	20	4,000	8,640	
Buffalo State College, State University of New York; Buffalo (Pu)	11,157	53	29	4,350	10,300	5,866
Canisius College; Buffalo (Pr)	5,095	83	24	19,542	19,542	7,970
Cazenovia College; Cazenovia (Pr)	997	84	38	16,730	16,730	6,960
Central Yeshiva Tomchei Tmimim-Lubavitch; Brooklyn (Pr)	1,000			4,800	4,800	
City College of the City University of New York; New York (Pu)	12,400	35	18	4,080	8,640	
Clarkson University; Potsdam (Pr)	3,105	81	14	23,100	23,100	8,726
Colgate University; Hamilton (Pr)	2,800	31	37	29,740	29,740	7,155
College of Aeronautics; Flushing (Pr)	1,316	78	4	9,400	9,400	
College of Mount Saint Vincent; Riverdale (Pr)	1,626	75	32	18,600	18,600	7,800
College of New Rochelle; New Rochelle (Pr)	2,450	51	19	14,400	14,400	7,150
College of Saint Rose; Albany (Pr)	4,666	74	31	15,242	15,242	7,226

Institution name; city (Public/Private)	Students	Percent Women	Students accepted	Tuition In-state	Out-of-state	Room and board
College of Staten Island of the City University of New York; Staten Island (Pu)	12,422	100%	17%	$ 4,000	$ 8,640	
Columbia College; New York (Pr)	4,181	11	38	28,686	28,686	$ 8,802
Columbia University, School of General Studies; New York (Pr)	1,517	47		27,780	27,780	
Columbia University, The Fu Foundation School of Engineering and Applied Science; New York (Pr)	2,782	29	9	28,686	28,686	8,802
Cooper Union for the Advancement of Science and Art; New York (Pr)	955	12	24	-	-	12,500
Cornell University; Ithaca (Pr)	19,620	31	26	28,630	28,630	9,580
Culinary Institute of America; Hyde Park (Pr)	2,404	67	23	17,640	17,640	6,270
Daemen College; Amherst (Pr)	2,205	70	32	14,700	14,700	7,000
DeVry Institute of Technology; Long Island City (Pr)	1,927		10	11,100	11,100	
Dominican College; Orangeburg (Pr)	1,428	88	27	16,000	16,000	8,160
Dowling College; Oakdale (Pr)	6,247	97	16	13,890	13,890	
D'Youville College; Buffalo (Pr)	2,476	69	17	13,960	13,960	6,960
Elmira College; Elmira (Pr)	1,805	67	36	25,040	25,040	8,080
Excelsior College; Albany (Pr)	26,273					
Farmingdale State University of New York; Farmingdale (Pu)	5,949	55	16	4,350	10,300	7,680
Fashion Institute of Technology; New York (Pu)	10,765	47	36	4,350	10,300	6,549
Five Towns College; Dix Hills (Pr)	1,145	51	14	12,300	12,300	8,700
Fordham University; New York (Pr)	14,731	54	19	24,720	24,720	9,700
Globe Institute of Technology; New York (Pr)	844		12	8,950	8,950	10,533
Hamilton College; Clinton (Pr)	1,797	33	36	30,000	30,000	7,360
Hartwick College; Oneonta (Pr)	1,466	89	39	25,200	25,200	7,110
Hilbert College; Hamburg (Pr)	1,055	94	26	13,000	13,000	5,670
Hobart and William Smith Colleges; Geneva (Pr)	1,873	62	40	28,400	28,400	7,588
Hofstra University; Hempstead (Pr)	13,221	68	25	17,410	17,410	8,700
Houghton College; Houghton (Pr)	1,467	85	46	17,984	17,984	6,000
Hunter College of the City University of New York; New York (Pu)	20,797	30	26	4,000		
Iona College; New Rochelle (Pr)	4,388	64	24	17,750	17,750	9,698
Ithaca College; Ithaca (Pr)	6,496	63	38	22,264	22,264	9,466
John Jay College of Criminal Justice of the City University of New York; New York (Pu)	12,984	73		4,000	8,640	
Juilliard School; New York (Pr)	834	7	22	21,250	21,250	8,440
Keuka College; Keuka Park (Pr)	1,148	82	47	15,800	15,800	7,600
Le Moyne College; Syracuse (Pr)	3,403	72	31	18,440	18,440	7,450
Lehman College of the City University of New York; Bronx (Pu)	9,712	30	22	4,000	8,640	
Long Island University, Brooklyn Campus; Brooklyn (Pr)	8,008	69	24	17,052	17,052	6,480
Long Island University, C.W. Post Campus; Brookville (Pr)	8,425	77	20	19,510	19,510	7,730
Long Island University, Southampton College; Southampton (Pr)	1,453	63	36	19,510	19,510	8,810
Manhattan College; Riverdale (Pr)	3,233	53	30	17,800	17,800	8,100
Manhattan School of Music; New York (Pr)	855	32	16	23,300	23,300	
Manhattanville College; Purchase (Pr)	2,571	55	27	22,150	22,150	9,380
Marist College; Poughkeepsie (Pr)	5,616	71	32	18,432	18,432	8,634
Marymount College of Fordham University; Tarrytown (Pr)	1,083	82	53	17,850	17,850	9,260
Marymount Manhattan College; New York (Pr)	2,183	80	37	15,592	15,592	
Medaille College; Buffalo (Pr)	2,000	66	35	13,350	13,350	6,400
Medgar Evers College of the City University of New York; Brooklyn (Pu)	4,722	76	18	4,000	8,640	
Mercy College; Dobbs Ferry (Pr)	10,395		4	10,700	10,700	8,180
Metropolitan College of New York; New York (Pr)	1,592	71		16,380	16,380	
Molloy College; Rockville Centre (Pr)	3,007	67	34	14,430	14,430	
Mount Saint Mary College; Newburgh (Pr)	2,606	82	30	13,830	13,830	6,980
Nazareth College of Rochester; Rochester (Pr)	3,062	83	32	17,020	17,020	7,400
New York Institute of Technology; Old Westbury (Pr)	9,387	76	11	16,926	16,926	7,780
New York University; New York (Pr)	38,188	32	20	26,766	26,766	10,910
Niagara University; Niagara University (Pr)	3,548	80	33	16,700	16,700	7,670
Nyack College; Nyack (Pr)	2,814		27	13,500	13,500	7,000
Pace University; New York (Pr)	13,962	74	21	20,540	20,540	7,650
Parsons School of Design, New School University; New York (Pr)	2,958	42	39	25,330	25,330	10,810
Paul Smith's College of Arts and Sciences; Paul Smiths (Pr)	862	80		14,600	14,600	6,400
Polytechnic University, Brooklyn Campus; Brooklyn (Pr)	2,846	73	6	24,802	24,802	8,000
Pratt Institute; Brooklyn (Pr)	4,444	47	29	23,528	23,528	8,186
Purchase College, State University of New York; Purchase (Pu)	4,063	37	27	4,350	10,300	7,122
Queens College of the City University of New York; Flushing (Pu)	16,993	99	22	4,000	8,640	
Rensselaer Polytechnic Institute; Troy (Pr)	8,265	80	12	27,700	27,700	9,083

Institution name; city (Public/Private)	Students	Percent Women	Percent Students accepted	Tuition In-state	Tuition Out-of-state	Room and board
Roberts Wesleyan College; Rochester (Pr)	1,843	80%	30%	$16,134	$16,134	$ 6,200
Rochester Institute of Technology; Rochester (Pr)	14,685	70	18	21,027	21,027	7,833
Russell Sage College; Troy (Pr)	824	82	76	19,200	19,200	6,866
Sage College of Albany; Albany (Pr)	998	32	22	14,500	14,500	6,866
Sarah Lawrence College; Bronxville (Pr)	1,606	41	36	30,120	30,120	10,394
School of Visual Arts; New York (Pr)	3,365	68	31	18,200	18,200	10,000
Siena College; Loudonville (Pr)	3,379	63	37	17,555	17,555	7,215
Skidmore College; Saratoga Springs (Pr)	2,584	46	37	29,350	29,350	8,300
St. Bonaventure University; St. Bonaventure (Pr)	2,806	87	28	17,190	17,190	6,530
St. Francis College; Brooklyn Heights (Pr)	2,468	88	20	10,620	10,620	
St. John Fisher College; Rochester (Pr)	3,152	71	30	17,200	17,200	7,420
St. John's University; Jamaica (Pr)	19,777	68	23	19,600	19,600	10,100
St. Joseph's College, New York; Brooklyn (Pr)	1,226	66	28	10,955	10,955	
St. Joseph's College, Suffolk Campus; Patchogue (Pr)	3,831	77	41	10,955	10,955	
St. Lawrence University; Canton (Pr)	2,277	57	36	27,985	27,985	7,755
St. Thomas Aquinas College; Sparkill (Pr)	2,394	75	24	14,500	14,500	8,260
State University of New York at Binghamton; Binghamton (Pu)	13,385	45	30	4,350	10,300	7,100
State University of New York at New Paltz; New Paltz (Pu)	7,908	34	36	4,350	10,300	6,420
State University of New York at Oswego; Oswego (Pu)	8,465	57	33	4,350	10,300	7,540
State University of New York at Plattsburgh; Plattsburgh (Pu)	6,047	62	34	4,350	10,300	6,448
State University of New York College at Brockport; Brockport (Pu)	8,742	51	32	4,350	10,300	6,890
State University of New York College at Cortland; Cortland (Pu)	7,337	49	30	4,350	10,300	6,860
State University of New York College at Fredonia; Fredonia (Pu)	5,260	57	39	4,350	10,300	5,800
State University of New York College at Geneseo; Geneseo (Pu)	5,550	42	48	4,350	10,300	6,750
State University of New York College at Old Westbury; Old Westbury (Pu)	3,227	57	32	4,350	10,300	7,749
State University of New York College at Oneonta; Oneonta (Pu)	5,724	48	43	4,350	10,300	6,458
State University of New York College at Potsdam; Potsdam (Pu)	4,307	69	33	4,350	10,300	6,970
State University of New York College of Agriculture and Technology at Cobleskill; Cobleskill (Pu)	2,443	92	25	4,350	10,300	6,880
State University of New York College of Environmental Science and Forestry; Syracuse (Pu)	2,016	63	19	4,350	10,300	9,630
State University of New York Empire State College; Saratoga Springs (Pu)	10,252	62		4,350	10,300	
State University of New York Institute of Technology; Utica (Pu)	2,682	23	17	4,350	10,300	6,800
State University of New York Maritime College; Throggs Neck (Pu)	1,128	87	6	4,350	10,300	7,046
Stony Brook University, State University of New York; Stony Brook (Pu)	22,344	51	21	4,350	10,300	7,458
Syracuse University; Syracuse (Pr)	15,598	62	29	24,170	24,170	9,590
Touro College; New York (Pr)	11,447		21	10,400	10,400	5,000
Union College; Schenectady (Pr)	2,174	44	34	28,608	28,608	7,077
United States Merchant Marine Academy; Kings Point (Pu)	971	16	8			
United States Military Academy; West Point (Pu)	4,242	10	11			
United Talmudical Seminary; Brooklyn (Pr)	1,670			6,000	6,000	
University at Albany, State University of New York; Albany (Pu)	16,998	56	23	4,350	10,300	7,181
University at Buffalo, The State University of New York; Buffalo (Pu)	27,255	62	18	4,350	10,300	6,816
University of Rochester; Rochester (Pr)	8,543	49	17	26,900	26,900	8,770
Utica College; Utica (Pr)	2,465	77	31	19,980	19,980	8,070
Vassar College; Poughkeepsie (Pr)	2,444	29	43	29,095	29,095	7,490
Wagner College; Staten Island (Pr)	2,218	50	32	22,600	22,600	7,200
Yeshiva University; New York (Pr)	5,998	78	13	21,730	21,730	6,980
York College of the City University of New York; Jamaica (Pu)	5,672	31	35	4,000	8,640	
NORTH CAROLINA						
Appalachian State University; Boone (Pu)	14,343	66	30	1,596	10,963	4,435
Barton College; Wilson (Pr)	1,188	74	37	13,368	13,368	5,036
Belmont Abbey College; Belmont (Pr)	863	69	40	13,358	13,358	7,200
Campbell University; Buies Creek (Pr)	3,975	58	21	13,260	13,260	4,756
Catawba College; Salisbury (Pr)	1,471	64	35	16,400	16,400	5,600
Davidson College; Davidson (Pr)	1,712	32	36	24,987	24,987	7,371
Duke University; Durham (Pr)	12,398	23	17	28,475	28,475	8,210
East Carolina University; Greenville (Pu)	21,756	77	29	1,910	12,049	5,540
Elizabeth City State University; Elizabeth City (Pu)	2,308	76	32	1,118	8,989	4,608

Institution name; city (Public/Private)	Students	Percent Women	Percent Students accepted	Tuition In-state	Tuition Out-of-state	Room and board
Elon University; Elon (Pr)	4,584	45%	40%	$16,325	$16,325	$5,670
Fayetteville State University; Fayetteville (Pu)	5,329	85	25	1,321	10,682	3,820
Gardner-Webb University; Boiling Springs (Pr)	3,964	74	28	14,160	14,160	5,140
Greensboro College; Greensboro (Pr)	1,248	74	23	15,500	15,500	6,030
Guilford College; Greensboro (Pr)	2,101	69	41	18,700	18,700	5,940
High Point University; High Point (Pr)	2,918	87	41	13,370	13,370	6,610
Johnson C. Smith University; Charlotte (Pr)	1,474	48	32	10,992	10,992	5,046
Lenoir-Rhyne College; Hickory (Pr)	1,550	81	35	15,750	15,750	5,815
Livingstone College; Salisbury (Pr)	1,005	45	31	10,383	10,383	5,803
Mars Hill College; Mars Hill (Pr)	1,351	85		14,204	14,204	6,760
Meredith College; Raleigh (Pr)	2,152	87	51	18,065	18,065	5,000
Methodist College; Fayetteville (Pr)	2,255	76	21	15,650	15,650	5,840
Montreat College; Montreat (Pr)	1,035	78	39	14,121	14,121	4,442
Mount Olive College; Mount Olive (Pr)	2,289	74	34	10,400	10,400	4,450
North Carolina Agricultural and Technical State University; Greensboro (Pu)	8,319	81	25	1,544	10,911	4,968
North Carolina Central University; Durham (Pu)	7,191	89	26	1,653	11,022	4,311
North Carolina State University; Raleigh (Pu)	29,854	62	20	2,955	14,803	5,918
North Carolina Wesleyan College; Rocky Mount (Pr)	1,695	83	34	11,225	11,225	6,555
Pfeiffer University; Misenheimer (Pr)	2,027	72	21	13,550	13,550	5,430
Queens University of Charlotte; Charlotte (Pr)	1,964	74	22	15,650	15,650	6,190
Saint Augustine's College; Raleigh (Pr)	1,635	60	22	7,280	7,280	4,960
Salem College; Winston-Salem (Pr)	1,091	70	48	15,500	15,500	8,870
Shaw University; Raleigh (Pr)	2,616	44	32	7,800	7,800	5,654
Southeastern Baptist Theological Seminary; Wake Forest (Pr)	1,979		3			
University of North Carolina at Asheville; Asheville (Pu)	3,446	73	33	1,672	10,497	4,978
University of North Carolina at Chapel Hill; Chapel Hill (Pu)	26,359	37	26	2,955	14,803	6,045
University of North Carolina at Charlotte; Charlotte (Pu)	19,605	72	23	1,904	11,941	5,076
University of North Carolina at Greensboro; Greensboro (Pu)	14,328	47	30	1,717	12,091	4,760
University of North Carolina at Pembroke; Pembroke (Pu)	4,722	43	27	1,464	10,828	4,364
University of North Carolina at Wilmington; Wilmington (Pu)	10,929	54	37	1,703	11,278	5,578
Wake Forest University; Winston-Salem (Pr)	6,451	45	23	26,490	26,490	8,260
Warren Wilson College; Asheville (Pr)	851	79		16,424	16,424	5,120
Western Carolina University; Cullowhee (Pu)	7,561	74	23	1,426	10,787	3,826
Wingate University; Wingate (Pr)	1,495	82	32	14,200	14,200	6,000
Winston-Salem State University; Winston-Salem (Pu)	4,102	77	33	1,226	9,491	5,306
NORTH DAKOTA						
Dickinson State University; Dickinson (Pu)	2,461	99	26	3,139	7,406	3,350
Jamestown College; Jamestown (Pr)	1,152	98	35	8,750	8,750	3,850
Mayville State University; Mayville (Pu)	817		28	2,576	6,878	3,344
Minot State University; Minot (Pu)	3,825	86	31	2,730	7,289	3,274
North Dakota State University; Fargo (Pu)	11,623	61	23	3,600	9,009	4,471
University of Mary; Bismarck (Pr)	2,619	90	37	9,600	9,600	3,860
University of North Dakota; Grand Forks (Pu)	13,034	76	25	3,441	9,187	4,234
Valley City State University; Valley City (Pu)	998	91	28	2,652	7,080	3,254
OHIO						
Ashland University; Ashland (Pr)	6,835	86	14	17,518	17,518	6,632
Baldwin-Wallace College; Berea (Pr)	4,692	82	29	18,478	18,478	5,402
Bluffton College; Bluffton (Pr)	1,121	77	37	17,260	17,260	6,030
Bowling Green State University; Bowling Green (Pu)	18,534	90	29	5,940	12,900	5,892
Capital University; Columbus (Pr)	3,959	84	23	20,500	20,500	6,050
Case Western Reserve University; Cleveland (Pr)	9,186	75	10	24,100	24,100	7,660
Cedarville University; Cedarville (Pr)	2,997	81	35	14,944	14,944	5,010
Central State University; Wilberforce (Pu)	1,621	49	24	2,340	7,335	6,069
Cincinnati Bible College and Seminary; Cincinnati (Pr)	922	99	16	8,320	8,320	4,840
Cleveland State University; Cleveland (Pu)	16,014	78	15	6,072	11,940	7,805
College of Mount St. Joseph; Cincinnati (Pr)	2,110	76	29	16,000	16,000	5,845
College of Wooster; Wooster (Pr)	1,871	70	37	25,040	25,040	6,260
Columbus College of Art & Design; Columbus (Pr)	1,634	64	28	17,880	17,880	6,300
David N. Myers University; Cleveland (Pr)	1,177	65	28	11,160	11,160	
Defiance College; Defiance (Pr)	1,036	75	25	16,950	16,950	5,250
Denison University; Granville (Pr)	2,232	68	36	25,090	25,090	7,290
DeVry University; Columbus (Pr)	3,335		9	9,990	9,990	
Franciscan University of Steubenville; Steubenville (Pr)	2,281	84	32	14,670	14,670	5,250
Franklin University; Columbus (Pr)	6,286	100	14	6,720	6,720	
Heidelberg College; Tiffin (Pr)	1,243	98	27	13,500	13,500	6,276
Hiram College; Hiram (Pr)	1,110	88	33	20,440	20,440	7,100
John Carroll University; University Heights (Pr)	4,242	86		20,566	20,566	6,892
Kent State University; Kent (Pu)	23,536	89	27	6,882	13,314	7,920
Kenyon College; Gambier (Pr)	1,612	46	38	29,500	29,500	5,040
Lake Erie College; Painesville (Pr)	859	55	41	16,880	16,880	5,830
Lourdes College; Sylvania (Pr)	1,249	25	24	14,200	14,200	

Institution name; city (Public/Private)	Students	Percent Women	Percent Students accepted	Tuition In-state	Tuition Out-of-state	Room and board
Malone College; Canton (Pr)	2,206	85%	32%	$14,745	$14,745	$6,000
Marietta College; Marietta (Pr)	1,341	78	27	20,356	20,356	5,946
Miami University; Oxford (Pu)	16,795	71	36	7,019	16,789	6,680
Mount Union College; Alliance (Pr)	2,425	75	32	16,900	16,900	5,310
Mount Vernon Nazarene University; Mount Vernon (Pr)	2,392	86	36	13,794	13,794	4,653
Muskingum College; New Concord (Pr)	2,142	80	24	14,200	14,200	5,880
Notre Dame College; South Euclid (Pr)	943	47	20	16,990	16,990	6,200
Oberlin College; Oberlin (Pr)	2,898	36	38	29,500	29,500	7,250
Ohio Dominican University; Columbus (Pr)	2,566	76	35	17,200	17,200	5,500
Ohio Northern University; Ada (Pr)	3,451	80	19	24,435	24,435	6,030
Ohio State University at Lima; Lima (Pu)	1,338	99	23	4,443	14,430	
Ohio State University at Marion; Marion (Pu)	1,567	100	25	4,443	14,430	
Ohio State University–Mansfield Campus; Mansfield (Pu)	1,640	100	21	4,443	14,430	
Ohio State University–Newark Campus; Newark (Pu)	2,148	100	20	4,443	14,430	
Ohio State University; Columbus (Pu)	50,731	72	24	6,651	16,638	6,429
Ohio University–Chillicothe; Chillicothe (Pu)	2,000	52		4,008	10,146	
Ohio University–Eastern; St. Clairsville (Pu)	1,118		24	4,008	10,146	
Ohio University–Lancaster; Lancaster (Pu)	1,744	100	17	4,008	10,146	
Ohio University–Southern Campus; Ironton (Pu)	1,746	100	24	3,693	5,013	
Ohio University–Zanesville; Zanesville (Pu)	1,826	100	25	4,008	10,146	
Ohio University; Athens (Pu)	20,394	79	30	7,128	15,351	7,320
Ohio Wesleyan University; Delaware (Pr)	1,929	74	37	25,080	25,080	7,110
Otterbein College; Westerville (Pr)	3,031	84	30	20,133	20,133	5,952
Shawnee State University; Portsmouth (Pu)	3,693	100	27	4,212	7,497	6,297
Tiffin University; Tiffin (Pr)	1,407	91	24	13,590	13,590	5,900
Union Institute & University; Cincinnati (Pr)	2,910		21	7,776	7,776	
University of Akron; Akron (Pu)	24,335	87	17	5,846	13,335	6,326
University of Cincinnati; Cincinnati (Pu)	26,817	88	17	6,336	17,943	7,113
University of Dayton; Dayton (Pr)	10,284	97	21	18,390	18,390	5,890
University of Findlay; Findlay (Pr)	4,712	74	21	19,052	19,052	7,062
University of Rio Grande; Rio Grande (Pr)	2,076	100	19	9,718	10,532	5,768
University of Toledo; Toledo (Pu)	20,594	97	20	5,410	14,048	6,834
Urbana University; Urbana (Pr)	1,527	58	21	13,540	13,540	5,410
Ursuline College; Pepper Pike (Pr)	1,409	70	31	17,100	17,100	5,458
Walsh University; North Canton (Pr)	1,801	82	28	14,250	14,250	8,750
Wilberforce University; Wilberforce (Pr)	1,180	22	48	9,720	9,720	5,320
Wilmington College; Wilmington (Pr)	1,262	83	33	17,256	17,256	6,490
Wittenberg University; Springfield (Pr)	2,189	74	36	24,948	24,948	6,368
Wright State University; Dayton (Pu)	15,694	91	24	5,892	10,524	6,019
Xavier University; Cincinnati (Pr)	6,626	78	21	18,850	18,850	8,000
Youngstown State University; Youngstown (Pu)	12,850	99	23	5,328	10,536	5,700
OKLAHOMA						
Bacone College; Muskogee (Pr)	914	58	24	7,900	7,900	5,700
Cameron University; Lawton (Pu)	5,632	100	0	2,778	6,678	2,854
East Central University; Ada (Pu)	4,442		34	2,685	6,585	2,774
Langston University; Langston (Pu)	3,008	50	26	1,818	5,430	4,380
Northeastern State University; Tahlequah (Pu)	9,297	89	28	2,664	6,564	3,080
Northwestern Oklahoma State University; Alva (Pu)	2,126	99	23	2,697	6,597	2,720
Oklahoma Baptist University; Shawnee (Pr)	1,883	85	33	10,800	10,800	3,640
Oklahoma Christian University; Oklahoma City (Pr)	1,684	30		11,490	11,490	4,636
Oklahoma City University; Oklahoma City (Pr)	3,668	78	14	13,340	13,340	5,550
Oklahoma Panhandle State University; Goodwell (Pu)	1,226		31	1,800	3,292	2,810
Oklahoma State University; Stillwater (Pu)	23,577	89	25	2,513	8,459	5,468
Oral Roberts University; Tulsa (Pr)	4,117	64	33	13,550	13,550	5,900
Rogers State University; Claremore (Pu)	3,300	89	12	2,140	5,261	5,481
Southeastern Oklahoma State University; Durant (Pu)	4,203	80	23	1,950	5,850	3,200
Southern Nazarene University; Bethany (Pr)	2,199	41	35	11,310	11,310	4,958
Southwestern Oklahoma State University; Weatherford (Pu)	4,741	93	30	1,950	5,850	2,910
University of Central Oklahoma; Edmond (Pu)	15,246	88	28	1,950	5,850	3,670
University of Oklahoma; Norman (Pu)	24,483	82	25	2,541	9,054	5,485
University of Phoenix–Oklahoma City Campus; Oklahoma City (Pr)	855		39	8,550	8,550	
University of Science and Arts of Oklahoma; Chickasha (Pu)	1,449	86	23	2,100	6,000	3,530
University of Tulsa; Tulsa (Pr)	4,072	76	21	15,656	15,656	5,610
OREGON						
Art Institute of Portland; Portland (Pr)	1,327		24	15,750	15,750	7,695
Concordia University; Portland (Pr)	1,274	72	27	17,400	17,400	5,050
Eastern Oregon University; La Grande (Pu)	3,287	99	25	3,613	3,613	5,650
George Fox University; Newberg (Pr)	3,022	93	19	19,500	19,500	6,300
Lewis & Clark College; Portland (Pr)	3,071	68	24	23,886	23,886	7,030
Linfield College; McMinnville (Pr)	1,659	78	36	20,770	20,770	6,120
Marylhurst University; Marylhurst (Pr)	1,212	50	13	12,690	12,690	
Oregon Institute of Technology; Klamath Falls (Pu)	3,236	54	20	3,348	12,528	6,135

Institution name; city (Public/Private)	Students	Percent Women	Percent Students accepted	Tuition In-state	Tuition Out-of-state	Room and board
Oregon State University; Corvallis (Pu)	18,979	88%	24%	$ 3,642	$16,398	$6,336
Pacific University; Forest Grove (Pr)	2,420	84	19	19,330	19,330	5,540
Portland State University; Portland (Pu)	23,117	85	21	3,240	12,636	8,175
Reed College; Portland (Pr)	1,340	46	39	29,000	29,000	7,750
Southern Oregon University; Ashland (Pu)	5,506	90	26	3,138	11,808	6,039
University of Oregon; Eugene (Pu)	19,992	84	28	3,543	14,979	6,981
University of Phoenix–Oregon Campus; Portland (Pr)	1,514		35	9,540	9,540	
University of Portland; Portland (Pr)	3,263	72	32	21,800	21,800	6,670
Western Oregon University; Monmouth (Pu)	5,032	94	32	3,240	11,505	5,976
Willamette University; Salem (Pr)	2,590	74	26	25,300	25,300	6,600
PENNSYLVANIA						
Albright College; Reading (Pr)	2,127	72	40	22,880	22,880	7,149
Allegheny College; Meadville (Pr)	1,849	82	37	24,100	24,100	5,880
Alvernia College; Reading (Pr)	2,380	80	29	16,200	16,200	6,950
Arcadia University; Glenside (Pr)	3,417	75	21	20,990	20,990	8,620
Baptist Bible College of Pennsylvania; Clarks Summit (Pr)	837	87	29	10,800	10,800	4,982
Bloomsburg University of Pennsylvania; Bloomsburg (Pu)	8,282	70	35	4,598	11,496	5,000
Bryn Mawr College; Bryn Mawr (Pr)	1,781	51	51	26,830	26,830	9,370
Bucknell University; Lewisburg (Pr)	3,678	38	34	28,764	28,764	6,302
Cabrini College; Radnor (Pr)	2,203	83	28	19,670	19,670	8,550
California University of Pennsylvania; California (Pu)	6,428	75	25	4,598	6,948	5,378
Carlow College; Pittsburgh (Pr)	2,200			14,776	14,776	6,110
Carnegie Mellon University; Pittsburgh (Pr)	9,756	38	16	29,190	29,190	8,155
Cedar Crest College; Allentown (Pr)	1,777	73	35	20,596	20,596	7,274
Chatham College; Pittsburgh (Pr)	1,256	61	24	20,360	20,360	6,714
Chestnut Hill College; Philadelphia (Pr)	1,555	77	24	18,375	18,375	7,400
Cheyney University of Pennsylvania; Cheyney (Pu)	1,536	62	20	4,598	11,496	5,383
Clarion University of Pennsylvania; Clarion (Pu)	6,497	78	37	4,598	8,048	4,560
College Misericordia; Dallas (Pr)	2,360	77	33	17,060	17,060	7,500
Delaware Valley College; Doylestown (Pr)	2,037	82	24	18,654	18,654	7,372
DeSales University; Center Valley (Pr)	2,914	77	22	18,000	18,000	7,080
Dickinson College; Carlisle (Pr)	2,276	52	39	28,380	28,380	7,210
Drexel University; Philadelphia (Pr)	17,000	70	15	19,900	19,900	9,600
Duquesne University; Pittsburgh (Pr)	9,701	84	24	17,837	17,837	7,482
East Stroudsburg University of Pennsylvania; East Stroudsburg (Pu)	6,162	70	28	4,598	11,496	4,464
Eastern University; St. Davids (Pr)	3,253	78	30	16,780	16,780	7,200
Edinboro University of Pennsylvania; Edinboro (Pu)	8,045	69	29	4,598	6,898	5,086
Elizabethtown College; Elizabethtown (Pr)	1,988	70	40	22,500	22,500	6,300
Franklin and Marshall College; Lancaster (Pr)	1,923	58	33	28,810	28,810	7,070
Gannon University; Erie (Pr)	3,459	84	24	16,220	16,220	6,590
Geneva College; Beaver Falls (Pr)	2,121	60		14,980	14,980	6,370
Gettysburg College; Gettysburg (Pr)	2,597	46	37	28,424	28,424	6,972
Grove City College; Grove City (Pr)	2,314	41	37	9,376	9,376	4,852
Gwynedd-Mercy College; Gwynedd Valley (Pr)	2,615	58	22	16,200	16,200	7,300
Haverford College; Haverford (Pr)	1,163	30	38	28,612	28,612	9,020
Holy Family University; Philadelphia (Pr)	2,670	77	22	14,990	14,990	
Immaculata University; Immaculata (Pr)	3,381	85	11	17,200	17,200	8,000
Indiana University of Pennsylvania; Indiana (Pu)	13,868	60	28	4,598	11,496	4,704
Juniata College; Huntingdon (Pr)	1,396	75	38	22,240	22,240	6,290
King's College; Wilkes-Barre (Pr)	2,204	81	28	18,260	18,260	7,930
Kutztown University of Pennsylvania; Kutztown (Pu)	9,008	70	32	4,598	11,496	4,812
La Roche College; Pittsburgh (Pr)	1,771	69	30	15,220	15,220	6,474
La Salle University; Philadelphia (Pr)	5,949	68	23	22,760	22,760	8,770
Lafayette College; Easton (Pr)	2,285	36	34	25,946	25,946	8,069
Lancaster Bible College; Lancaster (Pr)	883	51	27	11,250	11,250	5,250
Lebanon Valley College; Annville (Pr)	1,906	73	31	21,860	21,860	6,360
Lehigh University; Bethlehem (Pr)	6,732	40	21	27,230	27,230	7,440
Lincoln University; Lincoln University (Pu)	1,938	40	24	4,840	8,238	6,368
Lock Haven University of Pennsylvania; Lock Haven (Pu)	4,908	81	33	4,598	9,496	5,224
Lycoming College; Williamsport (Pr)	1,417	80	39	21,088	21,088	5,866
Mansfield University of Pennsylvania; Mansfield (Pu)	3,520	77	33	4,598	11,496	5,248
Marywood University; Scranton (Pr)	3,136	79	26	18,560	18,560	8,134
Mercyhurst College; Erie (Pr)	3,795	77	35	15,780	15,780	6,414
Messiah College; Grantham (Pr)	2,952	79	45	18,880	18,880	6,340
Millersville University of Pennsylvania; Millersville (Pu)	7,861	61	31	4,598	11,496	5,450
Moravian College; Bethlehem (Pr)	2,107	68	35	21,663	21,663	7,095
Mount Aloysius College; Cresson (Pr)	1,473	74	40	14,940	14,940	5,700
Muhlenberg College; Allentown (Pr)	2,452	42	38	24,945	24,945	6,540
Neumann College; Aston (Pr)	2,589	96	27	15,820	15,820	7,480
Peirce College; Philadelphia (Pr)	1,765	78	17	10,800	10,800	
Pennsylvania State University Abington College; Abington (Pu)	3,202	78	21	8,620	13,250	

Institution name; city (Public/Private)	Students	Percent Women	Students accepted	Tuition In-state	Out-of-state	Room and board
Pennsylvania State University Altoona College; Altoona (Pu)	3,774	74%	24%	$ 8,896	$13,716	$5,940
Pennsylvania State University at Erie, The Behrend College; Erie (Pu)	3,683	79	20	8,896	15,466	5,940
Pennsylvania State University Berks Campus of the Berks–Lehigh Valley College; Reading (Pu)	2,428	74	17	8,896	13,716	6,490
Pennsylvania State University Harrisburg Campus of the Capital College; Middletown (Pu)	3,441	43	15	8,896	15,466	7,290
Pennsylvania State University Schuylkill Campus of the Capital College; Schuylkill Haven (Pu)	1,028	87	20	8,620	13,250	
Pennsylvania State University University Park Campus; University Park (Pu)	41,795	55	29	9,296	18,918	5,940
Philadelphia Biblical University; Langhorne (Pr)	1,397	76	28	12,445	12,445	5,650
Philadelphia University; Philadelphia (Pr)	3,093	70	33	19,962	19,962	7,370
Point Park University; Pittsburgh (Pr)	3,226	81	25	14,720	14,720	6,660
Robert Morris University; Moon Township (Pr)	4,816	91	18	13,484	13,484	6,954
Rosemont College; Rosemont (Pr)	1,069	70	29	17,650	17,650	8,000
Saint Francis University; Loretto (Pr)	1,945	87	23	18,292	18,292	7,346
Saint Joseph's University; Philadelphia (Pr)	7,565	48	19	24,095	24,095	9,400
Saint Vincent College; Latrobe (Pr)	1,508	75	28	19,000	19,000	6,060
Seton Hill University; Greensburg (Pr)	1,679	84	33	18,930	18,930	6,000
Shippensburg University of Pennsylvania; Shippensburg (Pu)	7,607	67	32	4,598	11,546	5,080
Slippery Rock University of Pennsylvania; Slippery Rock (Pu)	7,789	81	32	4,598	11,496	4,542
Susquehanna University; Selinsgrove (Pr)	2,009	70	40	23,170	23,170	6,510
Swarthmore College; Swarthmore (Pr)	1,500	24	38	28,500	28,500	8,914
Temple University; Philadelphia (Pu)	32,877	60	23	8,134	14,894	7,276
Thiel College; Greenville (Pr)	1,261	76	30	13,500	13,500	6,584
University of Pennsylvania; Philadelphia (Pr)	19,428	20	18	26,282	26,282	8,642
University of Phoenix–Philadelphia Campus; Wayne (Pr)	1,002		35	11,400	11,400	
University of Pittsburgh at Bradford; Bradford (Pu)	1,417	82	24	8,614	17,926	6,030
University of Pittsburgh at Greensburg; Greensburg (Pu)	1,918	89	26	8,614	17,926	6,770
University of Pittsburgh at Johnstown; Johnstown (Pu)	3,146	84	26	8,614	17,926	5,760
University of Pittsburgh; Pittsburgh (Pu)	26,795	48	21	8,614	17,926	6,800
University of Scranton; Scranton (Pr)	4,679	75	33	21,208	21,208	9,335
University of the Arts; Philadelphia (Pr)	2,142	51	34	20,860	20,860	
University of the Sciences in Philadelphia; Philadelphia (Pr)	2,687	68	42	19,934	19,934	8,352
Ursinus College; Collegeville (Pr)	1,485	74	37	27,500	27,500	6,900
Villanova University; Villanova (Pr)	10,619	53	23	25,673	25,673	8,827
Washington & Jefferson College; Washington (Pr)	1,233	40	34	22,860	22,860	6,310
Waynesburg College; Waynesburg (Pr)	1,887	78	27	13,520	13,520	5,520
West Chester University of Pennsylvania; West Chester (Pu)	12,695	46	33	4,598	11,496	5,642
Westminster College; New Wilmington (Pr)	1,577	77	38	19,370	19,370	5,990
Widener University; Chester (Pr)	5,821	74	11	21,400	21,400	8,795
Wilkes University; Wilkes-Barre (Pr)	4,390	81	13	18,680	18,680	8,430
York College of Pennsylvania; York (Pr)	5,515	74	30	8,000	8,000	5,950
PUERTO RICO						
American University of Puerto Rico; Bayamón (Pr)	4,060	100		3,360	3,360	
Bayamón Central University; Bayamón (Pr)	3,334	62		3,420	3,420	
Columbia College; Caguas (Pr)	898	60	18	3,380	3,380	
Inter American University of Puerto Rico, Aguadilla Campus; Aguadilla (Pr)	4,197		26	3,120	3,120	
Inter American University of Puerto Rico, Arecibo Campus; Arecibo (Pr)	3,926		33	3,120	3,120	
Inter American University of Puerto Rico, Barranquitas Campus; Barranquitas (Pr)	2,271	100		3,200	3,200	
Inter American University of Puerto Rico, Bayamón Campus; Bayamón (Pr)	5,264	65	27	3,522	3,522	
Inter American University of Puerto Rico, Fajardo Campus; Fajardo (Pr)	1,710	37		3,120	3,120	
Inter American University of Puerto Rico, Guayama Campus; Guayama (Pr)	1,246		3	1,682	1,682	
Inter American University of Puerto Rico, Metropolitan Campus; San Juan (Pr)	10,675	36		3,120	3,120	
Inter American University of Puerto Rico, Ponce Campus; Mercedita (Pr)	5,134	26	26	3,756	3,756	
Inter American University of Puerto Rico, San Germán Campus; San Germán (Pr)	6,210	95		3,900	3,900	2,400
Polytechnic University of Puerto Rico; Hato Rey (Pr)	5,702	92	9	5,040	5,040	
Pontifical Catholic University of Puerto Rico; Ponce (Pr)	7,468	89	28	4,160	4,160	2,840
Universidad Adventista de las Antillas; Mayagüez (Pr)	864	84	37	4,470	4,470	2,550
Universidad del Este; Carolina (Pr)	7,077	54	19	4,278	4,278	
Universidad del Turabo; Turabo (Pr)	8,065	66	18	4,278	4,278	
Universidad Metropolitana; Río Piedras (Pr)	5,857	57	18	4,278	4,278	

Institution name; city (Public/Private)	Students	Percent Women	Students accepted	Tuition In-state	Out-of-state	Room and board
University of Phoenix–Puerto Rico Campus; Guaynabo (Pr)	1,427		14%	$ 5,160	$ 5,160	
University of Puerto Rico at Humacao; Humacao (Pu)	4,507	48%	34	1,020		
University of Puerto Rico, Cayey University College; Cayey (Pu)	3,987	22	50			
University of Puerto Rico, Río Piedras; San Juan (Pu)	21,666	66	34	790	2,470	$4,940
University of the Sacred Heart; San Juan (Pr)	5,210	74	22	4,350	4,350	
RHODE ISLAND						
Brown University; Providence (Pr)	7,882	16	30	29,200	29,200	8,096
Bryant College; Smithfield (Pr)	3,459	59	20	22,458	22,458	8,546
Johnson & Wales University; Providence (Pr)	9,868	85	1	15,438	15,438	6,777
Providence College; Providence (Pr)	5,258	53	30	21,665	21,665	8,500
Rhode Island College; Providence (Pu)	8,923	73	24	3,300	9,500	6,340
Rhode Island School of Design; Providence (Pr)	2,294	35	43	26,200	26,200	7,370
Roger Williams University; Bristol (Pr)	4,918	80	22	19,920	19,920	9,456
Salve Regina University; Newport (Pr)	2,357	56	38	20,100	20,100	8,700
University of Rhode Island; Kingston (Pu)	14,791	70	22	4,136	14,268	7,518
SOUTH CAROLINA						
Anderson College; Anderson (Pr)	1,664	79	32	12,320	12,320	5,445
Benedict College; Columbia (Pr)	3,005	71	29	10,498	10,498	5,434
Charleston Southern University; Charleston (Pr)	2,990	80	25	14,426	14,426	5,544
Citadel, The Military College of South Carolina; Charleston (Pu)	3,695	31	2	4,999	13,410	4,778
Claflin University; Orangeburg (Pr)	1,546	51	33	7,970	7,970	5,184
Clemson University; Clemson (Pu)	17,016	52	25	6,934	14,532	5,038
Coastal Carolina University; Conway (Pu)	6,780	71	25	5,190	12,870	5,770
College of Charleston; Charleston (Pu)	11,536	60	36	5,770	13,032	6,117
Columbia College; Columbia (Pr)	1,515	86	46	16,930	16,930	5,245
Columbia International University; Columbia (Pr)	964	87	23	11,400	11,400	5,120
Converse College; Spartanburg (Pr)	1,124	69	35	18,915	18,915	5,795
Erskine College; Due West (Pr)	904	70	25	16,312	16,312	5,799
Francis Marion University; Florence (Pu)	3,590	76	36	4,947	9,894	4,282
Furman University; Greenville (Pr)	3,320	60	34	22,288	22,288	5,968
Lander University; Greenwood (Pu)	2,950	81	34	5,400	11,050	4,946
Morris College; Sumter (Pr)	1,007	94	41	7,190	7,190	3,564
North Greenville College; Tigerville (Pr)	1,615	95	33	9,100	9,100	5,280
Presbyterian College; Clinton (Pr)	1,175	78		18,360	18,360	5,811
South Carolina State University; Orangeburg (Pu)	4,466	80	27	5,570	10,850	4,672
Southern Wesleyan University; Central (Pr)	2,430	68	36	13,000	13,000	4,700
University of South Carolina Aiken; Aiken (Pu)	3,350	68	30	4,926	10,066	4,400
University of South Carolina Beaufort; Beaufort (Pu)	1,203	100		4,208	10,112	
University of South Carolina Spartanburg; Spartanburg (Pu)	4,507	49	31	5,310	10,936	4,310
University of South Carolina; Columbia (Pu)	25,288	64	22	5,548	14,886	5,327
Voorhees College; Denmark (Pr)	847	41	46	7,106	7,106	4,572
Winthrop University; Rock Hill (Pu)	6,558	66	36	6,652	12,258	4,630
Wofford College; Spartanburg (Pr)	1,132	80	35	19,815	19,815	6,100
SOUTH DAKOTA						
Augustana College; Sioux Falls (Pr)	1,848	79	42	16,766	16,766	5,026
Black Hills State University; Spearfish (Pu)	3,873	99	33	2,308	7,333	3,196
Colorado Technical University Sioux Falls Campus; Sioux Falls (Pr)	1,036		19	9,450	9,450	
Dakota State University; Madison (Pu)	2,291	93	16	4,378	9,090	3,089
Mount Marty College; Yankton (Pr)	1,185	80	30	12,506	12,506	4,670
Northern State University; Aberdeen (Pu)	3,083	92	19	2,163	6,875	3,306
Oglala Lakota College; Kyle (Pu)	1,000			1,560	1,560	
Sinte Gleska University; Rosebud (Pr)	1,200	100		2,700	2,700	
South Dakota School of Mines and Technology; Rapid City (Pu)	2,454	94	11	2,163	6,875	3,561
South Dakota State University; Brookings (Pu)	10,642	96	21	2,308	7,332	3,586
University of South Dakota; Vermillion (Pu)	8,093	83	18	2,163	6,875	3,504
University of Sioux Falls; Sioux Falls (Pr)	1,485	95	29	13,900	13,900	4,100
TENNESSEE						
Aquinas College; Nashville (Pr)	846	12	33	9,720	9,720	
Austin Peay State University; Clarksville (Pu)	7,623	94	30	3,132	11,064	4,096
Baptist College of Health Sciences; Memphis (Pr)	823					
Belmont University; Nashville (Pr)	3,629	75	32	15,164	15,164	6,032
Bethel College; McKenzie (Pr)	1,283	54	34	9,360	9,360	5,080
Carson-Newman College; Jefferson City (Pr)	2,115	88	33	12,900	12,900	4,800
Christian Brothers University; Memphis (Pr)	1,929	85	25	16,740	16,740	5,100
Crichton College; Memphis (Pr)	1,032	79	28	11,400	11,400	
Cumberland University; Lebanon (Pr)	1,420	66	22	12,130	12,130	4,480
East Tennessee State University; Johnson City (Pu)	11,624	82	27	3,132	11,064	4,658
Fisk University; Nashville (Pr)	880	66	46	10,900	10,900	5,770
Freed-Hardeman University; Henderson (Pr)	1,966	99	25	9,300	9,300	5,320
Johnson Bible College; Knoxville (Pr)	850	98	29	5,240	5,240	3,710

Institution name; city (Public/Private)	Students	Percent Women	Students accepted	Tuition In-state	Out-of-state	Room and board
Lambuth University; Jackson (Pr)	836	65%	36%	$11,290	$11,290	$5,178
Lane College; Jackson (Pr)	952	28	21	6,262	6,262	4,366
Lee University; Cleveland (Pr)	3,806	56	33	8,520	8,520	4,950
Lincoln Memorial University; Harrogate (Pr)	2,442	85	20	11,760	11,760	4,640
Lipscomb University; Nashville (Pr)	2,661	73	29	12,176	12,176	5,590
Maryville College; Maryville (Pr)	1,052	81	37	19,180	19,180	6,180
Middle Tennessee State University; Murfreesboro (Pu)	21,744	75	29	3,132	11,064	4,624
Milligan College; Milligan College (Pr)	838	76	38	14,750	14,750	4,600
Rhodes College; Memphis (Pr)	1,560	72	39	22,628	22,628	6,382
Southern Adventist University; Collegedale (Pr)	2,377	76	30	12,400	12,400	4,280
Tennessee State University; Nashville (Pu)	9,024	35	28	3,818	11,750	4,270
Tennessee Technological University; Cookeville (Pu)	9,107	81	21	3,778	11,710	5,092
Trevecca Nazarene University; Nashville (Pr)	1,911	67	19	11,960	11,960	5,408
Tusculum College; Greeneville (Pr)	2,132	76	36	14,110	14,110	5,880
Union University; Jackson (Pr)	2,774	61	28	13,750	13,750	4,640
University of Memphis; Memphis (Pu)	19,911	73		3,502	11,656	4,690
University of Tennessee at Chattanooga; Chattanooga (Pu)	8,528	52	28	3,852	11,504	
University of Tennessee at Martin; Martin (Pu)	5,810	51	29	3,846	11,496	3,800
University of Tennessee; Knoxville (Pu)	27,281	71	23	4,950	13,532	5,110
University of the South; Sewanee (Pr)	1,485	72	33	23,930	23,930	6,720
Vanderbilt University; Nashville (Pr)	11,092	40	21	27,720	27,720	9,457
TEXAS						
Abilene Christian University; Abilene (Pr)	4,648	53	35	12,750	12,750	5,080
Angelo State University; San Angelo (Pu)	6,043	99	27	2,064	7,728	4,646
Austin College; Sherman (Pr)	1,332	72	38	17,740	17,740	6,822
Baylor University; Waco (Pr)	13,937	82	35	16,750	16,750	5,434
College of Biblical Studies–Houston; Houston (Pr)	1,472		11	4,000	4,000	
Concordia University at Austin; Austin (Pr)	1,155	76	21	14,300	14,300	6,150
Dallas Baptist University; Dallas (Pr)	4,538	68	17	11,010	11,010	4,290
DeVry University; Irving (Pr)	2,730		9	9,960	9,960	
East Texas Baptist University; Marshall (Pr)	1,354	55	33	9,450	9,450	3,624
Hardin-Simmons University; Abilene (Pr)	2,361	53	25	11,400	11,400	3,699
Houston Baptist University; Houston (Pr)	2,340	62	34	11,100	11,100	4,680
Howard Payne University; Brownwood (Pr)	1,385	79	24	10,300	10,300	4,026
Lamar University; Beaumont (Pu)	10,379	68	21	2,520	10,530	5,760
LeTourneau University; Longview (Pr)	3,597	80	9	14,010	14,010	5,820
Lubbock Christian University; Lubbock (Pr)	1,933	72	28	10,662	10,662	4,380
McMurry University; Abilene (Pr)	1,376	61	28	12,930	12,930	5,046
Midwestern State University; Wichita Falls (Pu)	6,483	65	25	1,380	8,460	4,630
Northwood University, Texas Campus; Cedar Hill (Pr)	1,117	59	20	13,485	13,485	5,910
Our Lady of the Lake University of San Antonio; San Antonio (Pr)	3,245	65	24	14,650	14,650	5,082
Paul Quinn College; Dallas (Pr)	871	27	35	4,080	4,080	3,800
Prairie View A&M University; Prairie View (Pu)	7,808	98	23	1,380	8,460	5,826
Rice University; Houston (Pr)	4,959	24	19	18,850	18,850	7,880
Sam Houston State University; Huntsville (Pu)	13,460	76	29	2,550	9,630	4,160
Southern Methodist University; Dallas (Pr)	11,161	65	20	20,926	20,926	8,391
Southwestern Adventist University; Keene (Pr)	1,191	64	28	11,016	11,016	5,270
Southwestern Assemblies of God University; Waxahachie (Pr)	1,676	34		7,800	7,800	4,470
Southwestern University; Georgetown (Pr)	1,265	63	37	18,870	18,870	6,540
St. Edward's University; Austin (Pr)	4,443	70	22	14,710	14,710	6,018
St. Mary's University of San Antonio; San Antonio (Pr)	4,118	81	27	15,992	15,992	6,388
Stephen F. Austin State University; Nacogdoches (Pu)	11,408	73	29	2,639	8,307	4,766
Sul Ross State University; Alpine (Pu)	1,954	73	18	2,280	8,580	3,850
Tarleton State University; Stephenville (Pu)	8,845	90	24	2,670	9,750	4,804
Texas A&M International University; Laredo (Pu)	4,078	52	23	2,430	9,510	
Texas A&M University at Galveston; Galveston (Pu)	1,620	95	27	2,760	9,840	4,870
Texas A&M University–Commerce; Commerce (Pu)	8,359	56		3,624	10,704	5,004
Texas A&M University–Corpus Christi; Corpus Christi (Pu)	7,860	84	25	2,760	9,840	7,688
Texas A&M University–Kingsville; Kingsville (Pu)	6,840	99	20	1,380	8,460	3,966
Texas A&M University; College Station (Pu)	44,813	67	27	2,895	9,975	6,030
Texas Christian University; Fort Worth (Pr)	8,275	65	34	17,590	17,590	5,780
Texas Lutheran University; Seguin (Pr)	1,410	78	31	15,470	15,470	4,780
Texas Southern University; Houston (Pu)	10,891	44	19	1,104	6,768	5,824
Texas State University-San Marcos; San Marcos (Pu)	26,306	56	29	2,760	9,840	5,310
Texas Tech University; Lubbock (Pu)	28,549	67	24	2,760	9,840	6,023
Texas Wesleyan University; Fort Worth (Pr)	2,734	43	20	10,950	10,950	5,242
Texas Woman's University; Denton (Pu)	9,709	72	28	2,208	7,872	4,780
Trinity University; San Antonio (Pr)	2,633	64	34	18,402	18,402	7,290
University of Dallas; Irving (Pr)	3,157	89	12	17,612	17,612	6,494
University of Houston–Downtown; Houston (Pu)	10,528	100	17	3,164	10,244	
University of Houston; Houston (Pu)	35,066	78	21	1,380	8,460	5,870

Institution name; city (Public/Private)	Students	Percent Women	Students accepted	Tuition In-state	Out-of-state	Room and board
University of Mary Hardin-Baylor; Belton (Pr)	2,631	76%	36%	$10,650	$10,650	$4,000
University of North Texas; Denton (Pu)	31,065	68	23	2,292	7,958	4,885
University of Phoenix–Dallas Campus; Dallas (Pr)	1,711		43	9,360	9,360	
University of Phoenix–Houston Campus; Houston (Pr)	2,565		46	9,360	9,360	
University of St. Thomas; Houston (Pr)	4,875	89	12	15,000	15,000	6,840
University of Texas at Arlington; Arlington (Pu)	24,979	77	21	2,760	9,840	4,829
University of Texas at Austin; Austin (Pu)	51,426	47	27	3,120	10,240	6,082
University of Texas at Dallas; Richardson (Pu)	13,718	50	16	1,380	8,460	6,122
University of Texas at El Paso; El Paso (Pu)	18,542	98	21	3,030	10,110	
University of Texas at San Antonio; San Antonio (Pu)	24,665	99	27	2,760	9,840	7,898
University of Texas at Tyler; Tyler (Pu)	4,764	82	27	2,280	7,944	
University of Texas of the Permian Basin; Odessa (Pu)	2,695	88	29	2,580	9,660	4,176
University of Texas–Pan American; Edinburg (Pu)	15,914	64	24	3,456	11,232	3,488
University of the Incarnate Word; San Antonio (Pr)	4,434	87	21	14,000	14,000	5,510
Wayland Baptist University; Plainview (Pr)	1,034	98	29	8,100	8,100	3,354
West Texas A&M University; Canyon (Pu)	7,023	71	27	2,445	9,525	4,342
UTAH						
Brigham Young University; Provo (Pr)	33,008	78	29	3,150	3,150	5,354
Southern Utah University; Cedar City (Pu)	6,048	78	25	2,332	7,696	5,400
University of Phoenix–Utah Campus; Salt Lake City (Pr)	2,001		28	9,120	9,120	
University of Utah; Salt Lake City (Pu)	28,437	86	18	3,058	10,704	5,036
Utah State University; Logan (Pu)	16,460	94	24	2,615	8,420	3,930
Weber State University; Ogden (Pu)	18,821	100	20	2,632	7,958	5,313
Western Governors University; Salt Lake City (Pr)	1,128		5	4,780	4,780	
Westminster College; Salt Lake City (Pr)	2,498	82	27	16,704	16,704	5,300
VERMONT						
Castleton State College; Castleton (Pu)	1,879	79	26	5,646	12,200	6,014
Champlain College; Burlington (Pr)	2,584	63	22	12,925	12,925	8,955
Johnson State College; Johnson (Pu)	1,759	87	22	5,646	12,200	6,013
Lyndon State College; Lyndonville (Pu)	1,444	94	20	5,646	12,200	6,014
Middlebury College; Middlebury (Pr)	2,424	23	39			
Norwich University; Northfield (Pr)	2,707	91		17,630	17,630	6,722
Saint Michael's College; Colchester (Pr)	2,473	67	30	22,220	22,220	7,680
University of Vermont; Burlington (Pu)	10,967	75	28	8,696	21,748	6,680
Vermont Technical College; Randolph Center (Pu)	1,218	61	6	6,844	12,876	6,014
VIRGINIA						
Averett University; Danville (Pr)	2,849	89	19	16,600	16,600	6,020
Bridgewater College; Bridgewater (Pr)	1,403	88	37	16,990	16,990	8,160
Christopher Newport University; Newport News (Pu)	4,812	58	34	4,600	12,300	6,700
College of William and Mary; Williamsburg (Pu)	7,749	34	31	3,760	18,460	5,794
Eastern Mennonite University; Harrisonburg (Pr)	1,245	82	35	17,304	17,304	5,640
Emory & Henry College; Emory (Pr)	925	81	36	15,700	15,700	6,050
Ferrum College; Ferrum (Pr)	954	74	28	15,640	15,640	5,600
George Mason University; Fairfax (Pu)	28,246	66	18	3,630	13,470	6,040
Hampden-Sydney College; Hampden-Sydney (Pr)	1,039	71	0	20,446	20,446	7,020
Hampton University; Hampton (Pr)	5,790	62	32	12,864	12,864	6,118
Hollins University; Roanoke (Pr)	1,091	86	51	20,200	20,200	7,290
James Madison University; Harrisonburg (Pu)	16,203	62	38	5,058	13,280	5,966
Liberty University; Lynchburg (Pr)	9,050	96	23	11,520	11,520	5,200
Longwood University; Farmville (Pu)	4,252	70	41	3,046	8,972	5,298
Lynchburg College; Lynchburg (Pr)	2,013	76	31	21,270	21,270	4,800
Mary Baldwin College; Staunton (Pr)	1,731	76	40	19,234	19,234	5,525
Mary Washington College; Fredericksburg (Pu)	4,792	60	38	2,344	10,092	5,478
Marymount University; Arlington (Pr)	3,740	81	22	16,300	16,300	7,230
Norfolk State University; Norfolk (Pu)	6,846	71	26	1,920	11,340	5,882
Old Dominion University; Norfolk (Pu)	20,802	82	19	4,770	13,920	5,513
Radford University; Radford (Pu)	9,219	74	35	4,140	11,202	5,660
Randolph-Macon College; Ashland (Pr)	1,118	77	34	20,550	20,550	6,030
Roanoke College; Salem (Pr)	1,899	77	37	20,335	20,335	6,528
Shenandoah University; Winchester (Pr)	2,851	73	17	18,310	18,310	6,800
University of Richmond; University of Richmond (Pr)	3,626	42	28	24,940	24,940	5,160
University of Virginia; Charlottesville (Pu)	23,077	39	22	4,584	20,554	5,591
University of Virginia's College at Wise; Wise (Pu)	1,703	78	28	2,630	11,518	5,586
Virginia Commonwealth University; Richmond (Pu)	26,770	74	22	3,600	15,904	6,723
Virginia Intermont College; Bristol (Pr)	1,147	65	44	13,900	13,900	5,400
Virginia Military Institute; Lexington (Pu)	1,333	51	4	3,856	16,568	5,266
Virginia State University; Petersburg (Pu)	4,933	66	25	1,888	8,748	6,008
Virginia Union University; Richmond (Pu)	1,648	61	27	10,460	10,460	5,236
Virginia Wesleyan College; Norfolk (Pr)	1,429	80		19,200	19,200	6,150
Washington and Lee University; Lexington (Pr)	2,137	31	28	22,900	22,900	6,368
VIRGIN ISANDS						
University of the Virgin Islands; Charlotte Amalie (Pu)	2,788			2,730	8,190	5,830

Institution name; city (Public/Private)	Students	Percent Women	Students accepted	Tuition In-state	Out-of-state	Room and board
WASHINGTON						
Central Washington University; Ellensburg (Pu)	9,903	84%	31%	$ 3,654	$11,430	$5,745
City University; Bellevue (Pr)	7,124	100	2	7,960	7,960	
DeVry University; Federal Way (Pr)	1,124		9	11,100	11,100	
Eastern Washington University; Cheney (Pu)	10,337	81	31	3,582	12,438	5,200
Gonzaga University; Spokane (Pr)	5,778	77	25	20,510	20,510	5,960
Heritage College; Toppenish (Pr)	1,127	9	14	6,720	6,720	
Northwest College; Kirkland (Pr)	1,161	90	38	13,200	13,200	6,142
Pacific Lutheran University; Tacoma (Pr)	3,462	80	36	19,610	19,610	6,105
Saint Martin's College; Lacey (Pr)	1,489	76	26	17,600	17,600	5,355
Seattle Pacific University; Seattle (Pr)	3,728	92	32	18,822	18,822	7,017
Seattle University; Seattle (Pr)	6,659	78	22	20,070	20,070	6,858
Evergreen State College; Olympia (Pu)	4,380	93	38	3,651	13,332	5,772
University of Phoenix–Washington Campus; Seattle (Pr)	1,401		40	9,900	9,900	
University of Puget Sound; Tacoma (Pr)	2,760	71	39	25,190	25,190	6,400
University of Washington; Seattle (Pu)	39,246	68	23	4,968	16,124	6,726
Walla Walla College; College Place (Pr)	1,917	55	24	16,860	16,860	3,855
Washington State University; Pullman (Pu)	22,712	78	26	4,435	12,537	6,054
Western Washington University; Bellingham (Pu)	13,845	76	38	3,639	12,411	5,945
Whitman College; Walla Walla (Pr)	1,454	56	41	25,400	25,400	6,900
Whitworth College; Spokane (Pr)	2,298	75		19,810	19,810	6,350
WEST VIRGINIA						
American Public University System; Charles Town (Pr)	6,826			9,000	9,000	
Bethany College; Bethany (Pr)	900	73	34	12,760	12,760	6,300
Bluefield State College; Bluefield (Pu)	3,511	97	20	2,806	6,894	
Concord College; Athens (Pu)	3,026	63		3,198	7,278	4,938
Fairmont State University; Fairmont (Pu)	6,813	97	25	3,130	7,038	5,080
Glenville State College; Glenville (Pu)	1,377	100	32	2,952	7,306	4,860
Marshall University; Huntington (Pu)	13,960	88	24	2,746	8,430	5,856
Mountain State University; Beckley (Pr)	3,973	96	23	4,950	4,950	5,172
Shepherd University; Shepherdstown (Pu)	4,831	89	24	3,270	8,030	5,338
University of Charleston; Charleston (Pr)	1,018	63	40	17,400	17,400	6,390
West Liberty State College; West Liberty (Pu)	2,511	86	33	3,138	7,790	4,730
West Virginia State College; Institute (Pu)	4,992		29	2,754	6,334	4,400
West Virginia University Institute of Technology; Montgomery (Pu)	2,468	74	15	3,488	8,371	4,832
West Virginia University; Morgantown (Pu)	24,260	92	21	3,548	10,768	5,822
West Virginia Wesleyan College; Buckhannon (Pr)	1,621	79	35	18,200	18,200	5,200
Wheeling Jesuit University; Wheeling (Pr)	1,650	77	25	18,920	18,920	6,000
WISCONSIN						
Alverno College; Milwaukee (Pr)	2,160	56	35	13,488	13,488	5,260
Beloit College; Beloit (Pr)	1,332	69	39	24,166	24,166	5,478
Cardinal Stritch University; Milwaukee (Pr)	6,785	93	26	14,240	14,240	5,160
Carroll College; Waukesha (Pr)	2,953	78	33	17,020	17,020	5,360
Carthage College; Kenosha (Pr)	2,632	73	27	20,150	20,150	6,070
Concordia University Wisconsin; Mequon (Pr)	5,152	80	21	15,515	15,515	5,790
Edgewood College; Madison (Pr)	2,422	80	30	15,100	15,100	5,350
Lakeland College; Sheboygan (Pr)	3,829	68	17	13,715	13,715	5,441
Lawrence University; Appleton (Pr)	1,407	58	36	24,900	24,900	5,652
Maranatha Baptist Bible College; Watertown (Pr)	803	70	39	7,040	7,040	4,520
Marian College of Fond du Lac; Fond du Lac (Pr)	2,777	77	21	14,700	14,700	4,600
Marquette University; Milwaukee (Pr)	11,355	83	25	20,350	20,350	7,000
Milwaukee School of Engineering; Milwaukee (Pr)	2,383	65	8	23,034	23,034	5,445
Mount Mary College; Milwaukee (Pr)	1,600	78	26	15,100	15,100	5,100
Ripon College; Ripon (Pr)	998	84	35	19,700	19,700	5,055
Silver Lake College; Manitowoc (Pr)	1,104	77	13	14,350	14,350	
St. Norbert College; De Pere (Pr)	2,155	86	39	19,822	19,822	5,738
University of Wisconsin–Eau Claire; Eau Claire (Pu)	10,594	60	38	4,313	14,360	4,150
University of Wisconsin–Green Bay; Green Bay (Pu)	5,420	78	39	3,500	13,547	4,500
University of Wisconsin–La Crosse; La Crosse (Pu)	8,746	53	38	4,741	14,404	4,050
University of Wisconsin–Madison; Madison (Pu)	41,588	61		5,140	19,150	6,130
University of Wisconsin–Milwaukee; Milwaukee (Pu)	25,440	79	25	4,439	17,190	4,320
University of Wisconsin–Oshkosh; Oshkosh (Pu)	11,155	47	32	3,670	14,089	3,970
University of Wisconsin–Parkside; Kenosha (Pu)	5,072	60	26	4,074	14,121	5,760
University of Wisconsin–Platteville; Platteville (Pu)	6,077	80	21	3,500	13,546	4,196
University of Wisconsin–River Falls; River Falls (Pu)	5,893	76	39	4,450	14,496	3,968
University of Wisconsin–Stevens Point; Stevens Point (Pu)	9,029	75	34	3,500	13,547	3,964
University of Wisconsin–Stout; Menomonie (Pu)	7,708	66	29	5,024	15,360	4,038
University of Wisconsin–Superior; Superior (Pu)	2,874	77	28	4,276	14,322	4,246
University of Wisconsin–Whitewater; Whitewater (Pu)	10,817	68	32	4,278	14,324	3,742
Viterbo University; La Crosse (Pr)	2,549	88	29	14,900	14,900	5,110
WYOMING						
University of Wyoming; Laramie (Pu)	13,130	95	21	2,520	8,370	5,546

2005

January

S	M	T	W	T	F	S
						1
2	3	4	5	6	7	8
9	10	11	12	13	14	15
16	17	18	19	20	21	22
23	24	25	26	27	28	29
30	31					

1—New Year's Day
6—Epiphany
17—Martin Luther King, Jr.'s birthday observed
21—(Eid) al Adha*

February

S	M	T	W	T	F	S
		1	2	3	4	5
6	7	8	9	10	11	12
13	14	15	16	17	18	19
20	21	22	23	24	25	26
27	28					

2—Groundhog Day
8—Shrove Tuesday (Mardi Gras)
9—Ash Wednesday
9—Chinese New Year
10—1st Day of Muharram*
12—Lincoln's Birthday
14—Valentine's Day
21—Washington's Birthday (or Presidents' Day) observed
22—Washington's Birthday

March

S	M	T	W	T	F	S
		1	2	3	4	5
6	7	8	9	10	11	12
13	14	15	16	17	18	19
20	21	22	23	24	25	26
27	28	29	30	31		

17—St. Patrick's Day
20—Spring begins (EST)**
20—Palm Sunday
25—Good Friday
25—Purim*
27—Easter Sunday (Western)

April

S	M	T	W	T	F	S
					1	2
3	4	5	6	7	8	9
10	11	12	13	14	15	16
17	18	19	20	21	22	23
24	25	26	27	28	29	30

3—Daylight Saving Time begins
21—Mawlid an-Nabi*
24—1st Day of Passover*

May

S	M	T	W	T	F	S
1	2	3	4	5	6	7
8	9	10	11	12	13	14
15	16	17	18	19	20	21
22	23	24	25	26	27	28
29	30	31				

1—Orthodox Easter
5—Ascension Day
8—Mother's Day
15—Pentecost
30—Memorial Day observed

June

S	M	T	W	T	F	S
			1	2	3	4
5	6	7	8	9	10	11
12	13	14	15	16	17	18
19	20	21	22	23	24	25
26	27	28	29	30		

13—1st Day of Shavuot*
14—Flag Day
19—Father's Day
21—Summer begins (EDT)**

July

S	M	T	W	T	F	S
					1	2
3	4	5	6	7	8	9
10	11	12	13	14	15	16
17	18	19	20	21	22	23
24	25	26	27	28	29	30
31						

1—Canada Day
4—Independence Day

August

S	M	T	W	T	F	S
	1	2	3	4	5	6
7	8	9	10	11	12	13
14	15	16	17	18	19	20
21	22	23	24	25	26	27
28	29	30	31			

September

S	M	T	W	T	F	S
				1	2	3
4	5	6	7	8	9	10
11	12	13	14	15	16	17
18	19	20	21	22	23	24
25	26	27	28	29	30	

5—Labor Day
22—Autumn begins (EDT)**

October

S	M	T	W	T	F	S
						1
2	3	4	5	6	7	8
9	10	11	12	13	14	15
16	17	18	19	20	21	22
23	24	25	26	27	28	29
30	31					

2—Rosh Hashanah*
5—Ramadan begins*
10—Columbus Day observed
10—Thanksgiving Day (Canada)
13—Yom Kippur*
18—1st Day of Sukkot*
25—Shemini Atzeret*
30—Daylight Saving Time ends
31—Halloween

November

S	M	T	W	T	F	S
		1	2	3	4	5
6	7	8	9	10	11	12
13	14	15	16	17	18	19
20	21	22	23	24	25	26
27	28	29	30			

1—All Saints' Day
4—Ramadan ends (Eid al-Fitr)*
8—Election Day
11—Veterans Day
24—Thanksgiving Day (U.S.)
27—1st Sunday of Advent

December

S	M	T	W	T	F	S
				1	2	3
4	5	6	7	8	9	10
11	12	13	14	15	16	17
18	19	20	21	22	23	24
25	26	27	28	29	30	31

21—Winter begins (EST)**
25—Christmas Day
26—1st Day of Hanukkah*
26—1st Day of Kwanzaa

*All Jewish and Islamic holidays begin at sundown the day before they are listed here. The Islamic calendar is based on lunar observation; thus, given dates of holidays may vary by one or two days.
**See p. 325 for 2005 solstices and equinoxes.

2004

January
S	M	T	W	T	F	S
				1	2	3
4	5	6	7	8	9	10
11	12	13	14	15	16	17
18	19	20	21	22	23	24
25	26	27	28	29	30	31

February
S	M	T	W	T	F	S
1	2	3	4	5	6	7
8	9	10	11	12	13	14
15	16	17	18	19	20	21
22	23	24	25	26	27	28
29						

March
S	M	T	W	T	F	S
	1	2	3	4	5	6
7	8	9	10	11	12	13
14	15	16	17	18	19	20
21	22	23	24	25	26	27
28	29	30	31			

April
S	M	T	W	T	F	S
				1	2	3
4	5	6	7	8	9	10
11	12	13	14	15	16	17
18	19	20	21	22	23	24
25	26	27	28	29	30	

May
S	M	T	W	T	F	S
						1
2	3	4	5	6	7	8
9	10	11	12	13	14	15
16	17	18	19	20	21	22
23	24	25	26	27	28	29
30	31					

June
S	M	T	W	T	F	S
		1	2	3	4	5
6	7	8	9	10	11	12
13	14	15	16	17	18	19
20	21	22	23	24	25	26
27	28	29	30			

July
S	M	T	W	T	F	S
				1	2	3
4	5	6	7	8	9	10
11	12	13	14	15	16	17
18	19	20	21	22	23	24
25	26	27	28	29	30	31

August
S	M	T	W	T	F	S
1	2	3	4	5	6	7
8	9	10	11	12	13	14
15	16	17	18	19	20	21
22	23	24	25	26	27	28
29	30	31				

September
S	M	T	W	T	F	S
			1	2	3	4
5	6	7	8	9	10	11
12	13	14	15	16	17	18
19	20	21	22	23	24	25
26	27	28	29	30		

October
S	M	T	W	T	F	S
					1	2
3	4	5	6	7	8	9
10	11	12	13	14	15	16
17	18	19	20	21	22	23
24	25	26	27	28	29	30
31						

November
S	M	T	W	T	F	S
	1	2	3	4	5	6
7	8	9	10	11	12	13
14	15	16	17	18	19	20
21	22	23	24	25	26	27
28	29	30				

December
S	M	T	W	T	F	S
			1	2	3	4
5	6	7	8	9	10	11
12	13	14	15	16	17	18
19	20	21	22	23	24	25
26	27	28	29	30	31	

2006

January
S	M	T	W	T	F	S
1	2	3	4	5	6	7
8	9	10	11	12	13	14
15	16	17	18	19	20	21
22	23	24	25	26	27	28
29	30	31				

February
S	M	T	W	T	F	S
			1	2	3	4
5	6	7	8	9	10	11
12	13	14	15	16	17	18
19	20	21	22	23	24	25
26	27	28				

March
S	M	T	W	T	F	S
			1	2	3	4
5	6	7	8	9	10	11
12	13	14	15	16	17	18
19	20	21	22	23	24	25
26	27	28	29	30	31	

April
S	M	T	W	T	F	S
						1
2	3	4	5	6	7	8
9	10	11	12	13	14	15
16	17	18	19	20	21	22
23	24	25	26	27	28	29
30						

May
S	M	T	W	T	F	S
	1	2	3	4	5	6
7	8	9	10	11	12	13
14	15	16	17	18	19	20
21	22	23	24	25	26	27
28	29	30	31			

June
S	M	T	W	T	F	S
				1	2	3
4	5	6	7	8	9	10
11	12	13	14	15	16	17
18	19	20	21	22	23	24
25	26	27	28	29	30	

July
S	M	T	W	T	F	S
						1
2	3	4	5	6	7	8
9	10	11	12	13	14	15
16	17	18	19	20	21	22
23	24	25	26	27	28	29
30	31					

August
S	M	T	W	T	F	S
		1	2	3	4	5
6	7	8	9	10	11	12
13	14	15	16	17	18	19
20	21	22	23	24	25	26
27	28	29	30	31		

September
S	M	T	W	T	F	S
					1	2
3	4	5	6	7	8	9
10	11	12	13	14	15	16
17	18	19	20	21	22	23
24	25	26	27	28	29	30

October
S	M	T	W	T	F	S
1	2	3	4	5	6	7
8	9	10	11	12	13	14
15	16	17	18	19	20	21
22	23	24	25	26	27	28
29	30	31				

November
S	M	T	W	T	F	S
			1	2	3	4
5	6	7	8	9	10	11
12	13	14	15	16	17	18
19	20	21	22	23	24	25
26	27	28	29	30		

December
S	M	T	W	T	F	S
					1	2
3	4	5	6	7	8	9
10	11	12	13	14	15	16
17	18	19	20	21	22	23
24	25	26	27	28	29	30
31						

Astrological Signs

♈ **Aries (Ram):** March 21–April 19

♉ **Taurus (Bull):** April 20–May 20

♊ **Gemini (Twins):** May 21–June 20

♋ **Cancer (Crab):** June 21–July 22

♌ **Leo (Lion):** July 23–Aug. 22

♍ **Virgo (Virgin):** Aug. 23–Sept. 22

♎ **Libra (Scales):** Sept. 23–Oct. 22

♏ **Scorpio (Scorpion):** Oct. 23–Nov. 21

♐ **Sagittarius (Archer):** Nov. 22–Dec. 21

♑ **Capricorn (Goat):** Dec. 22–Jan. 19

♒ **Aquarius (Water Bearer):** Jan. 20–Feb. 18

♓ **Pisces (Fish):** Feb. 19–March 20

PERPETUAL CALENDAR

1800...4	1844...9	1888...8	1932.13	1976.12
1801...5	1845...4	1889...3	1933...1	1977...7
1802...6	1846...5	1890...4	1934...2	1978...1
1803...7	1847...6	1891...5	1935...3	1979...2
1804...8	1848.14	1892.13	1936.11	1980.10
1805...3	1849...2	1893...1	1937...6	1981...5
1806...4	1850...3	1894...2	1938...7	1982...6
1807...5	1851...4	1895...3	1939...1	1983...7
1808.13	1852.12	1896.11	1940...9	1984...8
1809...1	1853...7	1897...6	1941...4	1985...3
1810...2	1854...1	1898...7	1942...5	1986...4
1811...3	1855...2	1899...1	1943...6	1987...5
1812.11	1856.10	1900...2	1944.14	1988.13
1813...6	1857...5	1901...3	1945...2	1989...1
1814...7	1858...6	1902...4	1946...3	1990...2
1815...1	1859...7	1903...5	1947...4	1991...3
1816...9	1860...8	1904.13	1948.12	1992.11
1817...4	1861...3	1905...1	1949...7	1993...6
1818...5	1862...4	1906...2	1950...1	1994...7
1819...6	1863...5	1907...3	1951...2	1995...1
1820.14	1864.13	1908.11	1952.10	1996...9
1821...2	1865...1	1909...6	1953...5	1997...4
1822...3	1866...2	1910...7	1954...6	1998...5
1823...4	1867...3	1911...1	1955...7	1999...6
1824.12	1868.11	1912...9	1956...8	2000.14
1825...7	1869...6	1913...4	1957...3	2001...2
1826...1	1870...7	1914...5	1958...4	2002...3
1827...2	1871...1	1915...6	1959...5	2003...4
1828.10	1872...9	1916.14	1960.13	2004.12
1829...5	1873...4	1917...2	1961...1	2005...7
1830...6	1874...5	1918...3	1962...2	2006...1
1831...7	1875...6	1919...4	1963...3	2007...2
1832...8	1876.14	1920.12	1964.11	2008.10
1833...3	1877...2	1921...7	1965...6	2009...5
1834...4	1878...3	1922...1	1966...7	2010...6
1835...5	1879...4	1923...2	1967...1	2011...7
1836.13	1880.12	1924.10	1968...9	2012...8
1837...1	1881...7	1925...5	1969...4	2013...3
1838...2	1882...1	1926...6	1970...5	2014...4
1839...3	1883...2	1927...7	1971...6	2015...5
1840.11	1884.10	1928...8	1972.14	2016.13
1841...6	1885...5	1929...3	1973...2	2017...1
1842...7	1886...6	1930...4	1974...3	2018...2
1843...1	1887...7	1931...5	1975...4	2019...3

2020.11
2021...6
2022...7
2023...1
2024...9
2025...4
2026...5
2027...6
2028.14
2029...2
2030...3
2031...4
2032.12
2033...7
2034...1
2035...2
2036.10
2037...5
2038...6
2039...7
2040...8
2041...3
2042...4
2043...5
2044.13
2045...1
2046...2
2047...3
2048.11
2049...6
2050...7
2051...1
2052...9
2053...4
2054...5
2055...6
2056.14
2057...2
2058...3
2059...4
2060.12
2061...7
2062...1
2063...2

DIRECTIONS: The number given with each year in the key above is the number of the calendar to use for that year.

Calendars **1** through **6** (left column) and **3** through **6** (right column) are printed as monthly grids (January–December) for each numbered calendar type.

7

JANUARY	FEBRUARY	MARCH	APRIL
S M T W T F S	S M T W T F S	S M T W T F S	S M T W T F S
1	1 2 3 4 5	1 2 3 4 5	1 2
2 3 4 5 6 7 8	6 7 8 9 10 11 12	6 7 8 9 10 11 12	3 4 5 6 7 8 9
9 10 11 12 13 14 15	13 14 15 16 17 18 19	13 14 15 16 17 18 19	10 11 12 13 14 15 16
16 17 18 19 20 21 22	20 21 22 23 24 25 26	20 21 22 23 24 25 26	17 18 19 20 21 22 23
23 24 25 26 27 28 29	27 28	27 28 29 30 31	24 25 26 27 28 29 30
30 31			

MAY	JUNE	JULY	AUGUST
S M T W T F S	S M T W T F S	S M T W T F S	S M T W T F S
1 2 3 4 5 6 7	1 2 3 4	1 2	1 2 3 4 5 6
8 9 10 11 12 13 14	5 6 7 8 9 10 11	3 4 5 6 7 8 9	7 8 9 10 11 12 13
15 16 17 18 19 20 21	12 13 14 15 16 17 18	10 11 12 13 14 15 16	14 15 16 17 18 19 20
22 23 24 25 26 27 28	19 20 21 22 23 24 25	17 18 19 20 21 22 23	21 22 23 24 25 26 27
29 30 31	26 27 28 29 30	24 25 26 27 28 29 30	28 29 30 31
		31	

SEPTEMBER	OCTOBER	NOVEMBER	DECEMBER
S M T W T F S	S M T W T F S	S M T W T F S	S M T W T F S
1 2 3	1	1 2 3 4 5	1 2 3
4 5 6 7 8 9 10	2 3 4 5 6 7 8	6 7 8 9 10 11 12	4 5 6 7 8 9 10
11 12 13 14 15 16 17	9 10 11 12 13 14 15	13 14 15 16 17 18 19	11 12 13 14 15 16 17
18 19 20 21 22 23 24	16 17 18 19 20 21 22	20 21 22 23 24 25 26	18 19 20 21 22 23 24
25 26 27 28 29 30	23 24 25 26 27 28 29	27 28 29 30	25 26 27 28 29 30 31
	30 31		

8

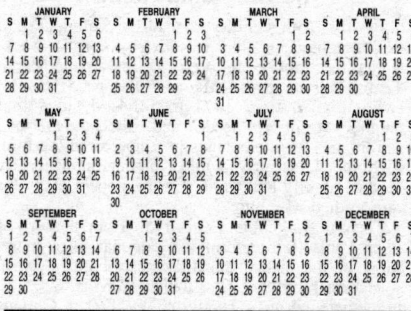

9

10

11

12

13

14

History of the Calendar

The purpose of the calendar is to reckon past or future time, to show how many days until a certain event takes place—the harvest or a religious festival—or how long since something important happened. The earliest calendars must have been strongly influenced by the geographical location of the people who made them. In colder countries, the concept of the year was determined by the seasons, specifically by the end of winter. But in warmer countries, where the seasons are less pronounced, the Moon became the basic unit for time reckoning; an old Jewish book says that "the Moon was created for the counting of the days."

Most of the oldest calendars were lunar calendars, based on the time interval from one new moon to the next—a so-called lunation. But even in a warm climate there are annual events that pay no attention to the phases of the Moon. In some areas it was a rainy season; in Egypt it was the annual flooding of the Nile River. The calendar had to account for these yearly events as well.

The Egyptian Calendar

The ancient Egyptians used a calendar with 12 months of 30 days each, for a total of 360 days per year. About 4000 B.C. they added five extra days at the end of every year to bring it more into line with the solar year.[1] These five days became a festival because it was thought to be unlucky to work during that time.

The Egyptians had calculated that the solar year was actually closer to 365¼ days, but instead of having a single leap day every four years to account for the fractional day (the way we do now), they let the one-quarter day accumulate. After 1,460 solar years, or four periods of 365 years, 1,461 Egyptian years had passed. This means that as the years passed, the Egyptian months fell out of sync with the seasons, so that the summer months eventually fell during winter. Only once every 1,460 years did their calendar year coincide precisely with the solar year.

In addition to the civic calendar, the Egyptians also had a religious calendar that was based on the 29½-day lunar cycle and was more closely linked with agricultural cycles and the movements of the stars.

Lunar Calendars

During antiquity the lunar calendar that best approximated a solar-year calendar was based on a 19-year period, with 7 of these 19 years having 13 months. In all, the period contained 235 months. Still using the lunation value of 29½ days, this made a total of 6,932½ days, while 19 solar years added up to 6,939.7 days, a difference of just one week per period and about five weeks per century.

Even the 19-year period required adjustment, but it became the basis of the calendars of the ancient Chinese, Babylonians, Greeks, and Jews. This same calendar was also used by the Arabs, but Muhammad later forbade shifting from 12 months to 13 months, so that the Islamic calendar, even today, has a lunar year of 354 days. As a result, the months of the Islamic calendar, as well as the Islamic religious festivals, migrate through all the seasons of the year.

The Roman Calendar

When Rome emerged as a world power, the difficulties of making a calendar were well known, but the Romans complicated their lives because of their superstition that even numbers were unlucky. Hence their months were 29 or 31 days long, with the exception of February, which had 28 days. However, four months of 31 days, seven months of 29 days, and one month of 28 days added up to only 355 days. Therefore the Romans invented an extra month called Mercedonius of 22 or 23 days. It was added every second year.

Even with Mercedonius, the Roman calendar eventually became so far off that **Julius Caesar,** advised by the astronomer Sosigenes, ordered a sweeping reform in 45 B.C. One year, made 445 days long by imperial decree, brought the calendar back in step with the seasons. Then the solar year (with the value of 365 days and 6 hours) was made the basis of the calendar. The months were 30 or 31 days in length, and to take care of the 6 hours, every fourth year was made a 366-day year. Moreover, Caesar decreed the year began with the first of January, not with the vernal equinox in late March.

This calendar was named the **Julian calendar,** after Julius Caesar, and it continues to be the calendar of the Eastern Orthodox churches to this day. However, despite the correction, the Julian calendar is still 11½ minutes longer than the actual solar year, and after a number of centuries, even 11½ minutes adds up.

The Gregorian Reform

By the 15th century the Julian calendar had drifted behind the solar calendar by about a week, so that the vernal equinox was falling around March 12 instead of around March 20. Pope Sixtus IV (who reigned from 1471 to 1484) decided that another reform was needed and called the German astronomer Regiomontanus to Rome to advise him. Regiomontanus arrived in 1475, but unfortunately he died shortly afterward, and the pope's plans for reform died with him.

Then in 1545, the Council of Trent authorized Pope Paul III to reform the calendar once more. Most of the mathematical and astronomical work was done by Father Christopher Clavius, S.J. The immediate correction, advised by Father Clavius and ordered by Pope Gregory XIII, was that Thursday, Oct. 4, 1582, was to be the last day of the Julian calendar. The next day would be Friday, Oct. 15. For long-range accuracy, a formula suggested by the Vatican librarian Aloysius Giglio was adopted: every fourth year is a leap year *unless* it is a century year like 1700 or 1800. Century years can be leap years *only* when they are divisible by 400 (e.g., 1600 and 2000). This rule eliminates three leap years in four centuries, making the calendar sufficiently accurate.

In spite of the revised leap year rule, an average calendar year is still about 26 seconds longer than the Earth's orbital period. But this discrepancy will need 3,323 years to build up to a single day.

---

1. The correct figures are lunation: 29 d, 12 h, 44 min, 2.8 sec (29.530585 d); solar year: 365 d, 5 h, 48 min, 46 sec (365.242216 d); 12 lunations: 354 d, 8 h, 48 min, 34 sec (354.3671 d).

Adoption of the Gregorian Calendar

Year	Country	Year	Country	Year	Country
1582	Catholic states of Italy, Portugal, Spain, Belgium, Holland, and Poland	1700	German, Swiss, and Dutch Protestant States, Denmark, and Norway	1873	Japan
1584	German and Swiss Catholic states	1752	Great Britain and its possessions (including the American colonies)	1875	Egypt
1587	Hungary			1918	Russia
				1924	Greece
				1926	Turkey
				1949	China

Reform Adopted Gradually

The Gregorian reform was not adopted throughout the West immediately. Most Catholic countries quickly changed to the Pope's new calendar in 1582. But Europe's Protestant princes chose to ignore the papal bull and continued with the Julian calendar. It was not until 1700 that the Protestant rulers of Germany and the Netherlands changed to the new calendar. In Great Britain (and its colonies) the shift did not take place until 1752, and in Russia a revolution was needed to introduce the Gregorian calendar in 1918. In Turkey, the Islamic calendar was used until 1926.

A Better Calendar?

Despite its widespread use, the Gregorian calendar has a number of weaknesses. It cannot be divided into equal halves or quarters; the number of days per month is haphazard; and months and years may begin on any day of the week. Holidays pegged to specific dates may also fall on any day of the week, and few Americans can predict when Thanksgiving will occur next year. Since Gregory XIII, many other proposals for calendar reform have been made, but none has been permanently adopted. In the meantime, the Gregorian calendar keeps the calendar dates in reasonable unison with astronomical events.   □

Time Measurement, Time Zones, and the International Date Line

The two natural cycles on which time measurements are based are the year and the day. The year is defined as the time required for Earth to complete one revolution around the Sun, while the day is the time required for Earth to complete one turn upon its axis. Earth needs 365 days plus about six hours to go around the Sun once, so a year does not consist of a round number of days; the fractional day has to be taken care of by an extra day every fourth year.

But because Earth, while turning upon its axis, also moves around the Sun, there are two kinds of days. A day may be defined as the interval between the highest point of the Sun in the sky on two successive days. This, averaged out over the year, produces the customary 24-hour day. But one might also define a day as the time interval between the moments when a certain point in the sky, say a conveniently located star, is directly overhead. This is called:

Sidereal time. A sidereal day is the time that it takes the Earth to complete one rotation on its axis so that a particular star can be observed twice at the meridian that runs directly overhead. Because the Earth is moving around the Sun as it rotates on its axis, the sidereal day is about four minutes shorter than the solar day, being equivalent to 23 hours, 56 minutes, and 4 seconds in mean solar time. As a result, a star will appear to rise about four minutes earlier every night, and different stars will be visible at different times of the year. Astronomers use a point that they call the "vernal equinox" to determine local sidereal time.

Apparent solar time is the time based directly on the Sun's position in the sky. In ordinary life the day runs from midnight to midnight. It begins when the Sun is invisible by being 12 hours from its zenith.

Mean solar time, rather than apparent solar time, is the basis for local civil and standard time. The mean solar time is based on the position of a fictitious "mean sun." The reason why this fictitious sun has to be introduced is the following: Earth turns on its axis regularly; it needs the same number of seconds regardless of the season. But the movement of Earth around the Sun is not regular because Earth's orbit is an ellipse. This has the result (as explained in the section on the seasons below) that Earth moves faster in January and slower in July. Though it is Earth that changes velocity, it looks to us as if the Sun does. In January, when Earth moves faster, the *apparent* movement of the Sun looks faster. The mean sun of time measurements, then, is a sun that moves regularly all year round; the real Sun will be either ahead of or behind the mean sun. The difference between the real Sun and the fictitious mean sun is called the *equation of time.*

Time zones. But if all clocks were actually set by mean solar time we would be plagued by a welter of time differences that would be "correct" but a major nuisance. A clock on Long Island, correctly showing mean solar time for its location (this would be *local civil time*), would be slightly ahead of a clock in Newark, N.J. The Newark clock would be slightly ahead of a clock in Trenton, N.J., which, in turn, would be ahead of a clock in Philadelphia. This condition prevailed until 1884, when a system of standard time was adopted by the International Meridian Conference. Earth's surface was divided into 24 zones. The standard time of each zone is the mean astronomical time of one of 24 meridians, 15 degrees apart, beginning at the Greenwich, England, meridian and extending east and west around the globe to the International Date Line. (This system was actually put into use a year earlier by the railroad companies of the U.S. and Canada who, until then, had to contend with some 100 conflicting local sun times observed in terminals across the land.)

For practical purposes, this convention is sometimes altered. For example, Alaska, for a time, consisted of four of the eight U.S. time zones: the Pacific standard time zone (east of Juneau) and the

6th (Juneau), 7th (Anchorage), and 8th (Nome) zones, encompassing the 135°, 150°, and 165° meridians, respectively. In 1983, by act of Congress, the entire state (except the westernmost Aleutians) was united into the 6th zone, Alaska standard time.

The eight U.S. standard time zones are: Atlantic (includes Puerto Rico and the Virgin Islands), eastern, central, mountain, Pacific, Alaska, Hawaii-Aleutian (includes all of Hawaii and those Aleutians west of the Fox Islands), and Samoa standard time.

The Date Line. While the time zones are based on the natural event of the Sun crossing a meridian, the date must be an arbitrary decision. The meridians are traditionally counted from the meridian of the observatory of Greenwich, in England, which is called the zero meridian. The logical place for changing the date

is 12 hours, or 180°, from Greenwich. Fortunately, the 180th meridian runs mostly through the open Pacific. The Date Line makes a zigzag in the north to incorporate the eastern tip of Siberia into the Siberian time system and then another one to incorporate a number of islands into the Hawaii-Aleutian time zone. In the south there is a similar zigzag for the purpose of tying a number of British-owned islands to the New Zealand time system. Otherwise, the Date Line is the same as 180° from Greenwich. At points to the east of the Date Line the calendar is one day earlier than at points to the west of it. A traveler going eastward across the Date Line from one island to another would not have to reset his watch because he would stay inside the time zone, but it would be the same time of the *previous* day.

For world and U.S. time zone map, *see* p. 523.

The Names of the Months

January: named after Janus, the god of doors and gates
February: named after Februalia, a time period when sacrifices were made to atone for sins
March: named after Mars, the god of war
April: from *aperire*, Latin for "to open" (buds)
May: named after Maia, the goddess of growth of plants
June: from *junius*, Latin for the goddess Juno

July: named after Julius Caesar in 44 B.C.
August: named after Augustus Caesar in 8 B.C.
September: from *septem*, Latin for "seven"
October: from *octo*, Latin for "eight"
November: from *novem*, Latin for "nine"
December: from *decem*, Latin for "ten"

NOTE: The earliest Latin calendar was a 10-month one, beginning with March; thus, September was the seventh month, October, the eighth, etc. July was originally called Quintilis, meaning fifth; August was originally called Sextilis, meaning sixth.

The Names of the Days of the Week

Latin	Old English	English	German	French	Italian	Spanish
Dies Solis	Sunnandaeg	Sunday	Sonntag	dimanche	domenica	domingo
Dies Lunae	Monandaeg	Monday	Montag	lundi	lunedì	lunes
Dies Martis	Tiwesdaeg	Tuesday	Dienstag	mardi	martedì	martes
Dies Mercurii	Wodnesdaeg	Wednesday	Mittwoch	mercredi	mercoledì	miércoles
Dies Jovis	Thunresdaeg	Thursday	Donnerstag	jeudi	giovedì	jueves
Dies Veneris	Frigedaeg	Friday	Freitag	vendredi	venerdì	viernes
Dies Saturni	Saeternesdaeg	Saturday	Samstag	samedi	sabato	sábado

NOTE: The seven-day week originated in ancient Mesopotamia and became part of the Roman calendar in A.D. 321. The names of the days are based on the seven celestial bodies (the Sun, the Moon, Mars, Mercury, Jupiter, Venus, and Saturn), believed at that time to revolve around Earth and influence its events. Most of Western Europe adopted the Roman nomenclature. The Germanic languages substituted Germanic equivalents for the names of four of the Roman gods: Tiw, the god of war, replaced Mars; Woden, the god of wisdom, replaced Mercury; Thor, the god of thunder, replaced Jupiter; and Frigg, the goddess of love, replaced Venus.

Daylight Saving Time

The United States. Daylight Saving Time, also called "summer time," is the practice of advancing clocks forward by one hour in the spring and setting them back by one hour in the fall in order to gain additional daylight during the early evening. The U.S. federal law that established "daylight time" in this country does not require its observance. Arizona, Hawaii, and the territories of Puerto Rico, Virgin Islands, and American Samoa do not use DST. These areas receive so much sun throughout the year that gaining another hour of sunlight in the summertime is not seen as a benefit.

Indiana. Indiana has a unique and complex time system. Not only is it split between two time zones (Eastern Standard and Central Standard), but parts

of the state observe Daylight Saving Time while others do not. Currently, 77 of the state's 92 counties are in the Eastern Time Zone but do not switch to daylight time in April. Instead they remain on standard time all year. That is, except for two counties near Cincinnati, Ohio, and Louisville, Ky., which do use daylight time. Indiana's system is rooted in its once farming-dominated economy. Farmers prefer early daylight to dry their fields and an early sunset to end their work at a reasonable hour. Further complicating Indiana timekeeping are the Indiana counties in the northwest corner of the state (near Chicago) and the southwestern tip (near Evansville), which fall in the Central Time Zone: these counties switch to daylight time each April.

So you can find yourself in quite a mess when you ask, "What time is it?" in Indiana in the warmer months. The Hoosier Daylight Coalition, a group made up of business leaders, parents, teachers, and police, is trying to organize legislation that would simplify things in Indiana. Its hope is that a change will bring new business to the area. But since polls show that half of Indiana residents like things the way they are, it won't be an easy sell.

Around the World. About 70 countries around the world observe Daylight Saving Time in some form. Here are some interesting facts:

• In Canada, every province except Saskatchewan observes DST. It remains on standard time.

• It wasn't until 1996 that Mexico adopted DST. Now all three Mexican time zones are on the same schedule as the United States.

• Also in 1996, members of the European Union agreed to observe a "summertime period" from the last Sunday in March to the last Sunday in October.

• In the winter months, Russia, which spans over 11 time zones, is always one hour ahead of standard time. In the summer, Russians turn their clocks ahead one more hour.

• Most countries near the equator don't deviate from standard time.

• In the Southern Hemisphere, where summer arrives in what we in the Northern Hemisphere consider the winter months, DST is observed from late October to late March.

• Three large regions in Australia do not participate in DST. Western Australia, the Northern Territory, and Queensland stay on standard time all year. The remaining south-central and southeastern sections of the continent (which is where Sydney and Melbourne are found) make the switch. This results in both vertical and horizontal time zones Down Under during the summer months

• China, which spans five time zones, uses only one. The entire country is always eight hours ahead of Universal Time and it does not observe DST.

• There is no DST period in Japan either.

U.S. Daylight Saving Time Schedule

Clocks are set forward one hour on the first Sunday in April at 2:00 a.m. local time and are set back one hour the last Sunday in October, also at 2:00 a.m.

2005	April 3	October 30
2006	April 2	October 29
2007	April 1	October 28
2008	April 6	October 26

The Seasons

The seasons are caused by the tilt of Earth's axis (23.4°) and not by the fact that Earth's orbit around the Sun is an ellipse. The average distance of Earth from the Sun is 93 million miles; the difference between aphelion (farthest away from the Sun) and perihelion (closest to the Sun) is 3 million miles, so that perihelion is about 91.4 million miles from the Sun. Earth goes through the perihelion point a few days after New Year's Day, just when the Northern Hemisphere has winter. Aphelion is passed during the first days of July. This by itself shows that the distance from the Sun is not important within these limits. What is important is that when Earth passes through perihelion, the northern end of Earth's axis happens to tilt away from the Sun, so that the areas beyond the Tropic of Cancer receive only slanting rays from a Sun low in the sky.

The tilt of Earth's axis is responsible for four lines you find on every globe. When, say, the North Pole is tilted away from the Sun as much as possible, the farthest points in the North which can still be reached by the Sun's rays are 23.5° from the pole. This is the Arctic Circle. The Antarctic Circle is the corresponding limit 23.4° from

the South Pole; the Sun's rays cannot reach beyond this point when we have midsummer in the North.

When the Sun is vertically above the equator, the day is of equal length all over Earth. This happens twice a year, and these are the "equinoxes" in March and in September. After having been over the equator in March, the Sun will seem to move northward. The northernmost point where the Sun can be straight overhead is 23.4° north of the equator. This is the Tropic of Cancer; the Sun can never be vertically overhead to the north of this line. Similarly the Sun cannot be vertically overhead to the south of a line 23.4° south of the equator—the Tropic of Capricorn.

This explains the climatic zones. In the belt (the Greek word *zone* means "belt") between the Tropic of Cancer and the Tropic of Capricorn, the Sun can be straight overhead; this is the tropical zone. The two zones where the Sun cannot be overhead but will be above the horizon every day of the year are the two temperate zones; the two areas where the Sun will not rise at all for varying lengths of time are the two polar areas, Arctic and Antarctic.   □

Seasons for the Northern Hemisphere, 2005

Spring Equinox: Mar. 20, 7:34 A.M. EST (12:33 UT[1]), Sun enters sign of Aries; spring begins.
Summer Solstice: June 21, 2:46 A.M. EDT (06:46 UT[1]), Sun enters sign of Cancer; summer begins.

Autumnal Equinox: Sept. 22, 6:23 P.M. EDT (22:23 UT[1]), Sun enters sign of Libra; fall begins.
Winter Solstice: Dec. 21, 1:35 P.M. EST (18:35 UT[1]), Sun enters sign of Capricorn; winter begins.

1. Universal Time (UT), also known as Greenwich Mean Time (GMT). *See* Astronomy for a conversion table of Universal Time.

The Islamic (Hijri) Calendar

The Islamic calendar is based on the lunar year of 354 days. The number of days each month is adjusted according to the lunar cycle, beginning about two days after the new moon. The months drift backward over the seasons, beginning again on the same day every 32½ years. The Islamic year begins on the first day of Muharram, and is counted from the year of the Hegira (*anno Hegirae*)—the year in which Muhammad emigrated from Mecca to Medina (A.D. 622). The year 2005 translates to A.H. 1425–1426.

Months	Number of days	Months	Number of days	Months	Number of days	Months	Number of days
Muharram	29 or 30	Rabi II	29 or 30	Rajab	29 or 30	Shawwal	29 or 30
Safar	29 or 30	Jumada I	29 or 30	Sha'ban	29 or 30	Dhu'l-Qa'dah	29 or 30
Rabi I	29 or 30	Jumada II	29 or 30	Ramadan	29 or 30	Dhu'l-Hijjah	29 or 30

The Jewish Calendar

The Jewish calendar is based on both solar and lunar years. The average lunar year of 354 days is adjusted to the solar year by the addition of a leap year and an intercalary month. Nisan is considered the first month, although the new year begins with Rosh Hashanah, on the first of Tishri, which is in fact the seventh month—the calendar has different starting points for different purposes. The year 2005 translates to the Jewish year 5765–5766.

Months	Number of days	Months	Number of days	Months	Number of days
Nisan (March–April)*	30	Tishri (Sept.–Oct.)	30	Shevat (Jan.–Feb.)	30
Iyar (April–May)	29	Heshvan (Oct.–Nov.)	29	Adar (Feb.–March)	29
Sivan (May–June)	30	in some years	30	in some years	30
Tammuz (June–July)	29	Kislev (Nov.–Dec.)	29	Adar Sheni	29
Av (July–Aug.)	30	in some years	30	(intercalary month	
Elul (Aug.–Sept.)	29	Tevet (Dec.–Jan.)	29	in leap year only)	

*The months correspond approximately to those of the Gregorian calendar.

The Hindu (Indian National) Calendar

The Indian National Calendar, often called the "Hindu Calendar," is based on both lunar and solar years. This calendar was introduced in 1957 in a government push for all of India to use the same calendar, but various traditional calendars are also used. The start of the Indian National Calendar year coincides with March 22, except in a leap year, when it coincides with March 21. The year is counted from the first year of the Saka era, in A.D. 78. The year 2005 translates to Saka era 1926–1927.

Month	Number of days	Month	Number of days	Month	Number of days	Month	Number of days
Caitra	30*	Asadha	31	Asvina	30	Pausa	30
Vaisakha	31	Sravana	31	Kartika	30	Magha	30
Jyaistha	31	Bhadra	31	Agrahayana	30	Phalguna	30

* In a leap year Caitra has 31 days.

The Chinese Calendar

The Chinese lunar year is divided into 12 months of 29 or 30 days. The calendar is adjusted to the length of the solar year by the addition of extra months at regular intervals. The years are arranged in major cycles of 60 years. Each successive year is named after one of 12 animals. These 12-year cycles are continuously repeated. The Chinese New Year is celebrated at the second new moon after the winter solstice and falls between January 21 and February 19 on the Gregorian calendar. The year 2005 translates to the Chinese year 4702–4703.

Rat	Ox	Tiger	Rabbit	Dragon	Snake	Horse	Sheep (Goat)	Monkey	Rooster	Dog	Pig
1900	1901	1902	1903	1904	1905	1906	1907	1908	1909	1910	1911
1912	1913	1914	1915	1916	1917	1918	1919	1920	1921	1922	1923
1924	1925	1926	1927	1928	1929	1930	1931	1932	1933	1934	1935
1936	1937	1938	1939	1940	1941	1942	1943	1944	1945	1946	1947
1948	1949	1950	1951	1952	1953	1954	1955	1956	1957	1958	1959
1960	1961	1962	1963	1964	1965	1966	1967	1968	1969	1970	1971
1972	1973	1974	1975	1976	1977	1978	1979	1980	1981	1982	1983
1984	1985	1986	1987	1988	1989	1990	1991	1992	1993	1994	1995
1996	1997	1998	1999	2000	2001	2002	2003	2004	2005	2006	2007
2008	2009	2010	2011	2012	2013	2014	2015	2016	2017	2018	2019

Holidays

Religious and Secular, 2005

In the United States, there are ten federal holidays set by law. Four are set by date (New Year's Day, Independence Day, Veterans Day, and Christmas Day). The other six are set by a day of the week and month: Martin Luther King, Jr.'s Birthday, Washington's Birthday, Memorial Day, Labor Day, Columbus Day, and Thanksgiving. All but the last are celebrated on Mondays to create three-day weekends for federal employees. All Jewish and Islamic holidays begin at sundown the day before they are listed here.

New Year's Day, Sat., Jan. 1. A federal holiday in the United States, New Year's Day has its origin in Roman times, when sacrifices were offered to Janus, the two-faced Roman deity who looked back on the past and forward to the future.

Epiphany (from Greek *epiphaneia*, "manifestation"), Thurs., Jan. 6. Falls on the 12th day after Christmas and commemorates the manifestation of Jesus Christ to the Gentiles, as represented by the Magi, the baptism of Jesus, and the miracle of the wine at the marriage feast at Cana. One of the three major Christian festivals, along with Christmas and Easter. Epiphany originally marked the beginning of the carnival season preceding Lent, and the evening preceding it is known as Twelfth Night.

Martin Luther King, Jr.'s Birthday, Mon., Jan. 17. (The actual date of his birthday is Jan. 15.) A federal holiday observed on the third Monday in January that honors the late civil rights leader. It became a federal holiday in 1986.

Eid al-Adha, Fri., Jan. 21. Eid al-Adha, or the Feast of Sacrifice, commemorates Abraham's willingness to obey God by sacrificing his son. Lasting for three days, it concludes the annual Hajj, or pilgrimage to Mecca. Muslims worldwide sacrifice a lamb or other animal and distribute the meat to relatives or the needy.

Groundhog Day, Weds., Feb. 2. Legend has it that if the groundhog sees his shadow, he'll return to his hole, and winter will last another six weeks.

Shrove Tuesday (Mardi Gras), Feb. 8. Falls the day before Ash Wednesday and marks the end of the carnival season, which once began on Epiphany but is now usually celebrated the last three days before Lent. In France, the day is known as Mardi Gras (Fat Tuesday), and celebrations are held in several American cities, particularly New Orleans.

Ash Wednesday, Feb. 9. The seventh Wednesday before Easter and the first day of Lent, which lasts 40 days. Having its origin sometime before A.D. 1000, it is a day of public penance and is marked in the Roman Catholic Church by the burning of the palms blessed on the previous year's Palm Sunday. With the ashes from the palms the priest then marks a cross with his thumb upon the forehead of each worshipper. The Anglican Church and a few Protestant groups in the United States also observe the day, but generally without the use of ashes.

Chinese New Year, Weds., Feb. 9, is the most important celebration in the Chinese calendar. Chinese months are reckoned by the lunar calendar, with each month beginning on the darkest day. New Year festivities traditionally start on the first day of the month and continue until the fifteenth, when the moon is brightest. In China, the New Year is a time for family reunions. In the United States, however, many early Chinese immigrants arrived without their families, and found a sense of community by celebrating the holiday through neighborhood associations.

Muharram, Thurs., Feb. 10. The month of Muharram marks the beginning of the Islamic liturgical year. On the tenth day of the month, many Muslims may observe a day of fasting, known as Ashurah.

Lincoln's Birthday, Sat., Feb. 12. A holiday in many states, this day was first formally observed in Washington, DC, in 1866, when both houses of Congress gathered for a memorial address in tribute to the assassinated president.

St. Valentine's Day, Mon., Feb. 14. The holiday's roots are in an ancient Roman fertility festival. Circa 496, Pope Gelasius I recast this pagan festival as a Christian feast day in honor of St. Valentine, but there are at least three different early saints by that name. How the day became associated with romance remains obscure, and is further clouded by various fanciful legends.

Washington's Birthday or Presidents' Day, Mon., Feb. 21. (The actual date of his birthday is Feb. 22.) A federal holiday observed the third Monday in February. It is a common misperception that the federal holiday was changed to "Presidents' Day" and now celebrates both Washington and Lincoln. Only Washington is commemorated by the federal holiday; 12 states, however, officially celebrate "Presidents' Day."

St. Patrick's Day, Thurs., March 17. St. Patrick, patron saint of Ireland, has been honored in America since the first days of the nation. Perhaps the most notable part of the observance is the annual St. Patrick's Day parade in New York City.

Palm Sunday, March 20. Observed the Sunday before Easter to commemorate the entry of Jesus into Jerusalem.

Purim (Feast of Lots), Fri., March 25. A day of joy and feasting celebrating the deliverance of the Jews from a massacre planned by the Persian minister Haman. The holiday is marked by the reading of the Book of Esther (the Megillah), by the exchange of gifts, and by donations to the poor.

Good Friday, March 25. The Friday before Easter, it commemorates the Crucifixion, which is retold during services from the Gospel according to St. John. A feature in Roman Catholic churches is the Liturgy of the Passion; there is no Consecration, the Host having been consecrated the previous day. The eating of hot-cross buns on this day is said to have started in England.

Easter Sunday, March 27. Observed in all Western Christian churches, Easter commemorates the Resurrection of Jesus. It is celebrated on the first Sunday after the full moon that occurs on or next after the vernal equinox (fixed at March 21) and is therefore celebrated between March 22 and April 25 inclusive. This date was fixed by the Council of Nicaea in A.D. 325.

Mawlid an-Nabi, Thurs., April 21. This holiday celebrates the birthday of Muhammad, the founder of Islam. It is fixed as the 12th day of the month of Rabi I in the Islamic calendar.

Passover (Pesach), Sun., April 24. The Feast of the Passover, also called the Feast of Unleavened Bread, commemorates the escape of the Jews from Egypt. As the Jews fled, they ate unleavened bread, and from that time the Jews have allowed no leavening in their houses during Passover, bread being replaced by matzoh.

Orthodox Easter (Pascha), Sun., May 1. The Orthodox church uses the same formula to calculate Easter as the Western church, but bases it on the traditional Julian calendar instead of the more contemporary Gregorian calendar. For this reason Orthodox Easter generally falls on a different date than the Western Christian Easter.

Ascension Day, Thurs., May 5. The Ascension of Jesus took place in the presence of His apostles 40 days after the Resurrection. It is traditionally thought to have occurred on Mount Olivet in Bethany.

Mother's Day, Sun., May 8. Observed the second Sunday in May, as proposed by Anna Jarvis of Philadelphia in 1907. West Virginia was the first state to recognize the holiday in 1910, and President Woodrow Wilson officially proclaimed Mother's Day a national holiday in 1914.

Pentecost (Whitsunday), May 15. This day commemorates the descent of the Holy Ghost upon the apostles 50 days after the Resurrection. "Whitsunday" is believed to have come from "white Sunday" when, among the English, white robes were worn by those baptized on the day.

Memorial Day, Mon., May 30. Memorial Day became a federal holiday in 1971 and is observed on the last Monday in May. It originated in 1868, when Union General John A. Logan designated a day in which the graves of Civil War soldiers would be decorated. Originally known as Decoration Day, the holiday was changed to Memorial Day within twenty years, becoming a holiday dedicated to the memory of all war dead.

Shavuot (Hebrew Pentecost), Mon., June 13. This festival, sometimes called the Feast of Weeks, or of Harvest, or of the First Fruits, falls 50 days after Passover and originally celebrated the end of the seven-week grain-harvesting season. In later tradition, it also celebrated the giving of the Law to Moses on Mount Sinai.

Flag Day, Tues., June 14. This day commemorates the adoption by the Continental Congress on June 14, 1777, of the Stars and Stripes as the U.S. flag.

Father's Day, Sun., June 19. Observed the third Sunday in June. The exact origin of the holiday is not clear, but it was first celebrated June 19, 1910, in Spokane, Wash. In 1966 President Lyndon Johnson signed a proclamation making Father's Day official.

Independence Day, Mon., July 4. The day of the adoption of the Declaration of Independence in 1776, celebrated in all states and territories. The observance began the next year in Philadelphia.

Labor Day, Mon., Sept. 5. A federal holiday observed the first Monday in September. Labor Day was first celebrated in New York in 1882 under the sponsorship of the Central Labor Union, following

the suggestion of Peter J. McGuire, of the Knights of Labor, that the day be set aside in honor of labor.

Rosh Hashanah (Jewish New Year), Tues., Oct. 4. This day marks the beginning of the Jewish year 5766 and opens the Ten Days of Penitence, which close with Yom Kippur.

First Day of Ramadan, Weds., Oct. 5. This day marks the beginning of a month-long fast that all Muslims must keep during the daylight hours. It commemorates the first revelation of the Qur'an. Following the last day of Ramadan, **Eid al-Fitr** is celebrated on Fri., Nov. 4.

Columbus Day, Mon., Oct. 10. A federal holiday, observed the second Monday in October, it commemorates Christopher Columbus's landing in the New World in 1492. Quite likely the first celebration of Columbus Day was that organized in 1792 by the Society of St. Tammany, or the Columbian Order, widely known as Tammany Hall.

Yom Kippur (Day of Atonement), Thurs., Oct. 13. This day marks the end of the Ten Days of Penitence that began with Rosh Hashanah. It is described in Leviticus as a "Sabbath of rest," and synagogue services begin the preceding sundown, resume the following morning, and continue to sundown.

Sukkot (Feast of Tabernacles), Tues., Oct. 18. This festival, also known as the Feast of the Ingathering, is both a harvest festival and a commemoration of the forty years of wandering after the Jews were freed from Egypt. The name refers to the small huts Jews live in during the festival, symbolic of the shelters used during their wandering. Some say that they also represent the huts used by workers during the annual fruit harvest.

Shemini Atzeret (Assembly of the Eighth Day), Tues., Oct. 25. This joyous holiday, encompassing Simchat Torah (Rejoicing in the Torah), falls immediately after the seven days of Sukkot. It marks the end of the year's weekly readings of the Torah (Five Books of Moses) in the synagogue, and the beginning of the new cycle of reading.

Halloween, Mon., Oct. 31. Eve of All Saints' Day, formerly called All Hallows and Hallowmass. Halloween is traditionally associated in some countries with customs such as bonfires, masquerading, and the telling of ghost stories. These are old Celtic practices marking the beginning of winter.

All Saints' Day, Tues., Nov. 1. A Roman Catholic and Anglican holiday celebrating all saints, known and unknown.

Election Day (legal holiday in certain states), Tues., Nov. 8. Since 1845, by act of Congress, the first Tuesday after the first Monday in November is the date for choosing presidential electors. State elections are also generally held on this day.

Veterans Day, Fri., Nov. 11. Armistice Day, a federal holiday, was established in 1926 to commemorate the signing in 1918 of the armistice ending World War I. On June 1, 1954, the name was changed to Veterans Day to honor all men and women who have served America in its armed forces.

Thanksgiving, Thurs., Nov. 24. A federal holiday observed the fourth Thursday in November by act of Congress (1941), it was the first such national proclamation issued by President Lincoln in 1863, on the urging of Mrs. Sarah J. Hale, editor of *Godey's*

Lady's Book. Most Americans believe that the holiday dates back to the day of thanks ordered by Governor Bradford of Plymouth Colony in New England in 1621, but scholars point out that days of thanks stem from ancient times.

Christmas (Feast of the Nativity), Sun., Dec. 25. The most widely celebrated holiday of the Christian year, Christmas is observed as the anniversary of the birth of Jesus. Christmas customs are centuries old. The mistletoe, for example, comes from the Druids, who, in hanging the mistletoe, hoped for peace and good fortune. Comparatively recent is the Christmas tree, first set up in Germany in the 17th century. Colonial Manhattan Islanders introduced the name Santa Claus, a corruption of the Dutch name St. Nicholas, who lived in fourth-century Asia Minor.

Hanukkah (Festival of Lights), Mon., Dec. 26. This festival was instituted by Judas Maccabaeus in 165 B.C. to celebrate the purification of the Temple of Jerusalem, which had been desecrated three years earlier by Antiochus Epiphanes, who set up a pagan altar and offered sacrifices to Zeus Olympius. In Jewish homes, a light is lighted on each night of the eight-day festival.

Kwanzaa, Mon., Dec. 26. This secular seven-day holiday was created by Black Studies professor Dr. Maulana Karenga in 1966, to reaffirm African values and serve as a communal celebration among African peoples in the diaspora. Modelled on first-fruits celebrations, it reflects seven principles, the *Nguzo Saba:* unity, self-determination, collective work and responsibility, cooperative economics, purpose, creativity, and faith.

Christian and Secular Holidays, 2004–2007

Year	Ash Wednesday	Easter	Pentecost	Labor Day	Election Day	Thanksgiving	1st Sun. Advent
2004	Feb. 25	April 11	May 30	Sept. 6	Nov. 2	Nov. 25	Nov. 28
2005	Feb. 9	March 27	May 15	Sept. 5	Nov. 8	Nov. 24	Nov. 27
2006	March 1	April 16	June 4	Sept. 4	Nov. 7	Nov. 23	Dec. 3
2007	Feb. 21	April 8	May 27	Sept. 3	Nov. 1	Nov. 22	Dec. 2

Shrove Tuesday: 1 day before Ash Wednesday. Palm Sunday: 7 days before Easter. Maundy Thursday: 3 days before Easter. Good Friday: 2 days before Easter. Holy Saturday: 1 day before Easter. Ascension Day: 10 days before Pentecost. Trinity Sunday: 7 days after Pentecost. Corpus Christi: 11 days after Pentecost.

Orthodox Holidays, 2004–2007

Year	Great Lent Begins	Pascha (Easter)	Ascension	Pentecost	Year	Great Lent Begins	Pascha (Easter)	Ascension	Pentecost
2004	Feb. 23	April 11	May 20	May 30	2006	March 6	April 23	June 1	June 11
2005	March 14	May 1	June 9	June 19	2007	Feb. 19	April 8	May 17	May 27

Jewish Holidays, 2004–2007

Year	Purim[1]	1st day Passover[2]	1st day Shavuot[3]	1st day Rosh Hashanah[4]	Yom Kippur[5]	1st day Sukkot[6]	Shemini Atzeret[7]	1st day Hanukkah[8]
2004	March 7	April 6	May 26	Sept. 16	Sept. 25	Sept. 30	Oct. 7	Dec. 8
2005	March 25	April 24	June 13	Oct. 4	Oct. 13	Oct. 18	Oct. 25	Dec. 26
2006	March 14	April 13	June 2	Sept. 23	Oct. 2	Oct. 7	Oct. 14	Dec. 16
2007	March 4	April 3	May 23	Sept. 13	Sept. 22	Sept. 27	Oct. 4	Dec. 5

1. Feast of Lots. 2. Feast of Unleavened Bread. 3. Hebrew Pentecost; or Feast of Weeks, or of Harvest, or of First Fruits. 4. Jewish New Year. 5. Day of Atonement. 6. Feast of Tabernacles, or of the Ingathering. 7. Assembly of the Eighth Day. 8. Festival of Lights.
NOTE: All holidays begin at sundown on the evening before the date given. Length of Jewish holidays: **Orthodox and Conservative:** *In Israel:* Purim: 1 day. Passover: 7 days; first and last are holy. Shavuot: 1 day. Rosh Hashanah: 2 days. Yom Kippur: 1 day. Sukkot: 7 days; first is holy. Shemini Atzeret: 1 day. Hanukkah: 8 days. *Outside Israel:* Purim: 1 day. Passover: 8 days; first 2 and last 2 are holy. Shavuot: 2 days. Rosh Hashanah: 2 days. Yom Kippur: 1 day. Sukkot: 7 days; first 2 are holy. Shemini Atzeret: 2 days (2nd called Simchat Torah). Hanukkah: 8 days. **Reform:** Purim: 1 day. Passover: 7 days; first and last are holy. Shavuot: 1 day. Rosh Hashanah: 1 day. Yom Kippur: 1 day. Sukkot: 7 days; first is holy. Shemini Atzeret: 1 day. Hanukkah: 8 days.

Islamic Holidays, 2004–2007 (A.H. 1424–1428)

In the Year of the Hegira	Muharram (Islamic New Year)	Mawlid an-Nabi (Muhammad's Birthday)	Ramadan begins	Eid al-Fitr (Ramadan ends)	Eid al-Adha (Festival of Sacrifice)
A.H. 1425	Feb. 22, 2004	May 2, 2004	Oct. 16, 2004	Nov. 14, 2004	Jan. 21, 2005
A.H. 1426	Feb. 10, 2005	April 21, 2005	Oct. 5, 2005	Nov. 4, 2005	Jan. 10, 2006
A.H. 1427	Jan. 31, 2006	April 11, 2006	Sept. 24, 2006	Oct. 24, 2006	Dec. 31, 2006
A.H. 1428	Jan. 20, 2007	March 31, 2007	Sept. 13, 2007	Oct. 13, 2007	Dec. 20, 2007

NOTE: All holidays begin at sundown on the evening before the date given. The Islamic calendar is based on lunar observation; thus, the above dates may vary by one or two days. Dates apply to North America.

Hindu Festival Dates, 2005

Source: Indian Calendars for the 21st Century, by Pal Singh Purewal

Jan. 13	Makar Sankranti	Aug. 19	Raksha Bandhan
Feb. 13	Vasant Panchami	Aug. 26	Sri Krishna Jayanti
March 8	Maha Shivaratri Vrat (fast)	Sept. 7	Ganesh Chaturathi
March 25	Holi (last day)	Sept. 18	Saradhas begin
April 9	Bikarami Samvat (2062 begins)	Oct. 4	Asuj Navratras begin
April 9	Chetra Navratras begin	Oct. 12	Dassehra
April 13	Vaisakhi (solar new year)	Oct. 20	Karva Chauth Vrat (fast)
April 17	Rama Navmi	Nov. 1	Diwali (Festival of Lights)

Sikh Festival Dates, 2005

Source: Indian Calendars for the 21st Century, by Pal Singh Purewal

Jan. 5	Birthday of Guru Gobind Singh Sahib	Sept. 1	First Parkash Guru Granth Sahib
Jan. 13	Maghi	Oct. 20	Installation of Holy Scriptures as Guru Granth
March 26	Hola Mohalla		Sahib
March 14	New Year's Day (Nanakshahi Era 537 begins)	Nov. 1	Bandi Chhor Divas (Diwali)
April 14	Vaisakhi (birth anniversary of Khalsa)	Nov. 15	Birthday of Guru Nanak Dev Sahib
June 16	Martyrdom of Guru Arjan Dev Sahib	Nov. 24	Martyrdom of Guru Tegh Bahadur Sahib

NOTE: Dates for Sikh and Hindu holidays are determined according to the date of their observance in India.

Jain Festival Dates, 2005

Source: Indian Calendars for the 21st Century, by Pal Singh Purewal

April 22	Sri Mahavir Jyanti	Oct. 17	Oli ends
May 11	Akshya Tritiya	Nov. 6	Jnana Panchami
Sept. 6	Samvatatsari	Nov.15	Rathayatra
Oct. 11	Oli begins		

Chinese New Year

2000	Feb. 5	**2003**	Feb. 1	**2006**	Jan. 29	**2009**	Jan. 26
2001	Jan. 24	**2004**	Jan. 22	**2007**	Feb. 18	**2010**	Feb. 14
2002	Feb. 12	**2005**	Feb. 9	**2008**	Feb. 7	**2011**	Feb. 3

State Holidays

Jan. 6, Three Kings' Day: P.R.
Jan. 8, Battle of New Orleans Day: La.
Jan. 11, De Hostos's Birthday: P.R.
Jan. 19, Robert E. Lee's Birthday: Ark., Fla., Ky., La., S.C.; (third Mon.): Ala., Miss.
Jan. 19, Confederate Heroes Day: Tex.
Jan. (third Mon.), Lee-Jackson-King Day: Va.
Jan. 30, F. D. Roosevelt's Birthday: Ky.
Feb. 15, Susan B. Anthony's Birthday: Fla., Minn.
March (first Tues.), Town Meeting Day: Vt.
March 2, Texas Independence Day: Tex.
March (first Mon.), Casimir Pulaski's Birthday: Ill.
March 17, Evacuation Day: Mass. (in Suffolk County)
March 20 (first day of spring), Youth Day: Okla.
March 22, Abolition Day: P.R.
March 25, Maryland Day: Md.
March 26, Prince Jonah Kuhio Kalanianaole Day: Hawaii
March (last Mon.), Seward's Day: Alaska
April 2, Pascua Florida Day: Fla.
April 13, Thomas Jefferson's Birthday: Ala., Okla.
April 16, De Diego's Birthday: P.R.
April (third Mon.), Patriots' Day: Maine, Mass.
April 21, San Jacinto Day: Tex.
April 22, Arbor Day: Nebr.
April 22, Oklahoma Day: Okla.
April 26, Confederate Memorial Day: Fla., Ga.
April (fourth Mon.), Fast Day: N.H.
April (last Mon.), Confederate Memorial Day: Ala., Miss.
May 1, Bird Day: Okla.
May 8, Truman Day: Mo.
May 11, Minnesota Day: Minn.
May 20, Mecklenburg Independence Day: N.C.

June (first Mon.), Jefferson Davis's Birthday: Ala., Miss.
June 3, Jefferson Davis's Birthday: Fla., S.C.
June 3, Confederate Memorial Day: Ky., La.
June 9, Senior Citizens Day: Okla.
June 11, King Kamehameha I Day: Hawaii
June 15, Separation Day: Del.
June 17, Bunker Hill Day: Mass. (in Suffolk County)
June 19, Emancipation Day: Tex.
June 20, West Virginia Day: W.Va.
July 17, Muñoz Rivera's Birthday: P.R.
July 24, Pioneer Day: Utah
July 25, Constitution Day: P.R.
July 27, Barbosa's Birthday: P.R.
Aug. (first Sun.), American Family Day: Ariz.
Aug. (first Mon.), Colorado Day: Colo.
Aug. (second Mon.), Victory Day: R.I.
Aug. 16, Bennington Battle Day: Vt.
Aug. (third Friday), Admission Day: Hawaii
Aug. 27, Lyndon B. Johnson's Birthday: Tex.
Aug. 30, Huey P. Long Day: La.
Sept. 9, Admission Day: Calif.
Sept. 12, Defenders' Day: Md.
Sept. 16, Cherokee Strip Day: Okla.
Sept. (first Sat. after full moon), Indian Day: Okla.
Oct. 10, Leif Eriksson Day: Minn.
Oct. 10, Oklahoma Historical Day: Okla.
Oct. 18, Alaska Day: Alaska
Oct. 31, Nevada Day: Nev.
Nov. 4, Will Rogers Day: Okla.
Nov. (week of the 16th), Oklahoma Heritage Week: Okla.
Nov. 19, Discovery Day: P.R.
Dec. 7, Delaware Day: Del.

Birthstones

Month	Stone	Month	Stone	Month	Stone
January	Garnet	June	Pearl, Alexandrite, or	October	Opal or Tourmaline
February	Amethyst		Moonstone	November	Topaz or Citrine
March	Aquamarine or Bloodstone	July	Ruby or Star Ruby	December	Turquoise, Lapis Lazuli,
April	Diamond	August	Peridot or Sardonyx		Blue Zircon, or Blue
May	Emerald	September	Sapphire or Star Sapphire		Topaz

Source: Jewelry Industry Council.

Traditional Wedding Anniversary Gift List

Anniv.	Gift	Anniv.	Gift	Anniv.	Gift	Anniv.	Gift
1st	Paper	7th	Copper, wool	13th	Lace	35th	Coral
2nd	Cotton	8th	Bronze, pottery	14th	Ivory	40th	Ruby
3rd	Leather	9th	Pottery, willow	15th	Crystal	45th	Sapphire
4th	Fruit, flowers	10th	Tin	20th	China	50th	Gold
5th	Wood	11th	Steel	25th	Silver	55th	Emerald
6th	Sugar	12th	Silk, linen	30th	Pearl	60th	Diamond

National Holidays Around the World

Afghanistan, Aug. 19
Albania, Nov. 28
Algeria, Nov. 1
Andorra, Sept. 8
Angola, Nov. 11
Antigua and Barbuda, Nov. 1
Argentina, May 25
Armenia, Sept. 21
Australia, Jan. 26
Austria, Oct. 26
Azerbaijan, May 28
Bahamas, July 10
Bahrain, Dec. 16
Bangladesh, March 26
Barbados, Nov. 30
Belarus, July 3
Belgium, July 21
Belize, Sept. 21
Benin, Aug. 1
Bhutan, Dec. 17
Bolivia, Aug. 6
Bosnia and Herzegovina, March 1
Botswana, Sept. 30
Brazil, Sept. 7
Brunei, Feb. 23
Bulgaria, March 3
Burkina Faso, Aug. 4
Burma, Jan. 4
Burundi, July 1
Cambodia, Nov. 9
Cameroon, May 20
Canada, July 1
Cape Verde, July 5
Central African Rep., Dec. 1
Chad, Aug. 11
Chile, Sept. 18
China, People's Rep. of, Oct. 1
Colombia, July 20
Comoros, July 6
Congo, Aug. 15
Congo, Dem. Rep. of, June 30
Costa Rica, Sept. 15
Côte d'Ivoire, Aug. 7
Croatia, June 25
Cuba, Jan. 1
Cyprus, Oct. 1
Czech Rep., May 8

Denmark, June 5
Djibouti, June 27
Dominica, Nov. 3
Dominican Rep., Feb. 27
East Timor, Nov. 28
Ecuador, Aug. 10
Egypt, July 23
El Salvador, Sept. 15
Equatorial Guinea, Oct. 12
Eritrea, May 24
Estonia, Feb. 24
Ethiopia, May 28
Fiji, Oct. 10
Finland, Dec. 6
France, July 14
Gabon, Aug. 17
Gambia, The, Feb. 18
Georgia, May 26
Germany, Oct. 3
Ghana, March 6
Greece, March 25
Grenada, Feb. 7
Guatemala, Sept. 15
Guinea, April 3
Guinea-Bissau, Sept. 10
Guyana, Feb. 23
Haiti, Jan. 1
Honduras, Sept. 15
Hungary, Aug. 20
Iceland, June 17
India, Jan. 26
Indonesia, Aug. 17
Iran, April 1
Ireland, March 17
Israel, April or May[1]
Italy, June 2
Jamaica, Aug.[1]
Japan, Dec. 23
Jordan, May 25
Kazakhstan, Oct. 25
Kenya, Dec. 12
Kiribati, July 12
Korea (North), Sept. 9
Korea (South), Aug. 15
Kuwait, Feb. 25
Kyrgyzstan, Aug. 31
Laos, Dec. 2
Latvia, Nov. 18
Lebanon, Nov. 22
Lesotho, Oct. 4

Liberia, July 26
Libya, Sept. 1
Liechtenstein, Aug. 15
Lithuania, Feb. 16
Luxembourg, June 23
Macedonia, Sept. 8
Madagascar, June 26
Malawi, July 6
Malaysia, Aug. 31
Maldives, July 26
Mali, Sept. 22
Malta, Sept. 21
Marshall Islands, May 1
Mauritania, Nov. 28
Mauritius, March 12
Mexico, Sept. 16
Micronesia, Federated States of, May 10
Moldova, Aug. 27
Monaco, Nov. 19
Mongolia, July 11
Morocco, March 3
Mozambique, June 25
Namibia, March 21
Nauru, Jan. 31
Nepal, Dec. 28
Netherlands, April 30
New Zealand, Feb. 6
Nicaragua, Sept. 15
Niger, Dec. 18
Nigeria, Oct. 1
Norway, May 17
Oman, Nov. 18
Pakistan, March 23
Palau, July 9
Panama, Nov. 3
Papua New Guinea, Sept. 16
Paraguay, May 14–15
Peru, July 28
Philippines, June 12
Poland, May 3
Portugal, June 10
Qatar, Sept. 3
Romania, Dec. 1
Russia, June 12
Rwanda, July 1
St. Kitts and Nevis, Sept. 19
St. Lucia, Feb. 22
St. Vincent and the Grenadines, Oct. 27

Samoa, June 1
San Marino, Sept. 3
São Tomé and Príncipe, July 12
Saudi Arabia, Sept. 23
Senegal, April 4
Serbia and Montenegro, April 27
Seychelles, June 18
Sierra Leone, April 27
Singapore, Aug. 9
Slovakia, Sept. 1
Slovenia, June 25
Solomon Islands, July 7
Somalia, July 1
South Africa, April 27
Spain, Oct. 12
Sri Lanka, Feb. 4
Sudan, Jan. 1
Suriname, Nov. 25
Swaziland, Sept. 6
Sweden, June 6
Switzerland, Aug. 1
Syria, April 17
Taiwan, Oct. 10
Tajikistan, Sept. 9
Tanzania, April 26
Thailand, Dec. 5
Togo, April 27
Tonga, June 4
Trinidad and Tobago, Aug. 31
Tunisia, March 20
Turkey, Oct. 29
Turkmenistan, Oct. 27
Tuvalu, Oct. 1
Uganda, Oct. 9
Ukraine, Aug. 24
United Arab Emirates, Dec. 2
United Kingdom, June[1]
United States, July 4
Uruguay, Aug. 25
Uzbekistan, Sept. 1
Vanuatu, July 30
Vatican, Oct. 22
Venezuela, July 5
Vietnam, Sept. 2
Yemen, May 22
Zambia, Oct. 24
Zimbabwe, April 18

1. Variable holidays, falling on a different date each year. *Source:* CIA World Factbook.

Roll Over, Martin Luther

Long the dominant faith affiliation in the U.S., Protestantism may not boast a majority in the future. What changes will that bring?

By David Van Biema TIME

Benchmark statistical moments are almost always anticlimactic. When the U.S. population shifted from rural to urban areas in 1920, there was no annunciatory thunderclap. And in about 2060, the year by which census figures suggest that non-Hispanic whites will become less than 50% of the population, the switch will have long been old news. Still, such dates have historical cachet, and 2004 soon may too. The University of Chicago's respected National Opinion Research Center (NORC) has reported that the proportion of adult Americans calling themselves Protestants, a steady 63% for decades, fell suddenly to 52% from 1993 to 2002. Not only that, the study's authors projected that "perhaps as early as this year the country will for the first time no longer have a Protestant majority." The heads-up provoked some spirited discussion about how important the eclipse might be, to whom, and why. Here are the key questions:

Is everything suddenly different? Hardly. As Boston College political scientist Alan Wolfe notes, "Even if Protestants dip below 50%, they're still twice as large as any other group. They're always going to be the largest group, ever, of anybody." But looking at the past, he admits this *is* a "big deal. John Jay wrote in the *Federalist* papers that we were united by a common religion. But based on this survey, you can't say that these days."

Are we losing Protestants or simply being flooded with non-Protestant immigrants? The latter has been suggested, disapprovingly, by Harvard political scientist Samuel Huntington. But NORC study co-author Tom W. Smith says, "immigration is a factor, but it's not the major thing." More important are a falling away of adult believers and a declining number of Protestant children who keep the faith. The Catholic proportion of the population has held steady at 23%. Neither Jews nor Muslims top 4%. The category that has really jumped (from 8% to 14%) in the past decade is people who say they don't subscribe to any religious identification. Most of this group aren't atheists, say scholars like Claude Fischer at the University of California, Berkeley. They still believe in basics like God, heaven, and the Bible as an inspired text, but prefer to think of themselves as spiritual rather than anything more specific.

Who is most affected by the Protestant swoon? Primarily the more liberal mainline denominations like United Methodists, the Presbyterian Church (USA), and the Episcopal Church. "We are losing our own children," says Kenneth Carder, Bishop of the Methodists' Mississippi Conference. But even some evangelical growth is tapering: the 16.3-million-member Southern Baptist Convention has conceded a drop-off in Sunday school enrollment.

Why is mainline Protestantism shrinking? Three explanations, proposed over decades, may each have some validity: Mainline churches did not require enough commitment, theologically or evangelistically, from congregants, whose enthusiasm waned accordingly; denominations that started out aggressively courting members turned to other tasks, such as social activism; and mainline birthrates lag behind the national average. Most mainline leaders claim their plight may hold hidden opportunities. The Rev. Dr. Bob Edgar, a Methodist minister and General Secretary of the National Council of Churches USA (whose membership historically has had a strong Protestant presence), notes, "the [Hebrew] prophets never had a majority, and yet they had important things to say. Maybe this is a positive wake-up call for us to worry less about numbers and more about faithfulness and relevancy. It's moral authority, not a function of size."

Although plausible, why does this sound a bit like rationalization? Because for centuries Protestantism's huge numbers had significant consequences: it bred most of America's founders and elite, and served as a template for its civil institutions and cultural assumptions. Huntington, a cheerleader, has credited it with our "core culture" of "individualism, the work ethic, and moralism." Protestant tropes of human perfectibility and the city on the hill continue to echo through political rhetoric. Comments Christian Smith, a sociologist at the University of North Carolina at Chapel Hill: "The mainline always thought, we *are* America. What's the big deal?"

If that's the case, should even non-Protestants mourn its decline? Not necessarily. By now, Protestantism's main nontheological message of radical individualism (or, as Berkeley sociologist Robert Bellah skeptically lampoons it, "You can be anything you want to be . . . and if you don't make it, you have no one to blame but yourself") is deeply encoded in our national self-understanding—and even upon other religions, once they have spent a few generations here. "Catholics for Choice?" snorts John Fonte, a senior fellow at the Hudson Institute. "That's Protestantism." Not quite, but it is proof that whatever its institutional trend, Protestantism's influence will live on. □

Major Religions of the World

There are twelve classical world religions—those religions most often included in history of world religion surveys and studied in world religions classes: Baha'i, Buddhism, Christianity, Confucianism, Hinduism, Islam, Jainism, Judaism, Shinto, Sikhism, Taoism, and Zoroastrianism. Here are overviews of the nine largest of these classical religions.

Judaism

Judaism is the oldest of the monotheistic faiths. It affirms the existence of one God, Yahweh, who entered into covenant with the descendants of Abraham, God's chosen people. Judaism's holy writings reveal how God has been present with them throughout their history. These writings are known as the Torah, specifically the five books of Moses, but most broadly conceived as the Hebrew Scriptures (traditionally called the Old Testament by Christians) and the compilation of oral tradition known as the Talmud (which includes the Mishnah, the oral law).

According to Scripture, the Hebrew patriarch Abraham (20th century? B.C.) founded the faith that would become known as Judaism. He obeyed the call of God to depart northern Mesopotamia and travel to Canaan. God promised to bless his descendants if they remained faithful in worship. Abraham's line descended through Isaac, then Jacob (also called Israel; his descendants came to be called Israelites). According to Scripture, 12 families that descended from Jacob migrated to Egypt, where they were enslaved. They were led out of bondage (13th century? B.C.) by Moses, who united them in the worship of Yahweh. The Hebrews returned to Canaan after a 40-year sojourn in the desert, conquering from the local peoples the "promised land" that God had provided for them.

The 12 tribes of Israel lived in a covenant association during the period of the judges (1200?–1000? B.C.), leaders known for wisdom and heroism. Saul first established a monarchy (r. 1025?–1005? B.C.); his successor, David (r. 1005?–965? B.C.), unified the land of Israel and made Jerusalem its religious and political center. Under his son, Solomon (r. 968?–928? B.C.), a golden era culminated in the building of a temple, replacing the portable sanctuary in use until that time. Following Solomon's death, the kingdom was split into Israel in the north and Judah in the south. Political conflicts resulted in the conquest of Israel by Assyria (721 B.C.) and the defeat of Judah by Babylon (586 B.C.). Jerusalem and its temple were destroyed, and many Judeans were exiled to Babylon.

During the era of the kings, the prophets were active in Israel and Judah. Their writings emphasize faith in Yahweh as God of Israel and of the entire universe, and they warn of the dangers of worshiping other gods. They also cry out for social justice.

The Judeans were permitted to return in 539 B.C. to Judea, where they were ruled as a Persian province. Though temple and cult were restored in Jerusalem, during the exile a new class of religious leaders had emerged—the scribes. They became rivals to the temple hierarchy and would eventually evolve into the party known as the Pharisees.

Persian rule ended when Alexander the Great conquered Palestine in 332 B.C. After his death, rule of Judea alternated between Egypt and Syria. When the Syrian ruler Antiochus IV Epiphanes tried to prevent the practice of Judaism, a revolt was led by the Maccabees (a Jewish family), winning Jewish independence in 128 B.C. The Romans conquered Jerusalem in 63 B.C.

During this period the Sadducees (temple priests) and the Pharisees (teachers of the law in the synagogues) offered different interpretations of Judaism. Smaller groups that emerged were the Essenes, a religious order; the Apocalyptists, who expected divine deliverance led by the Messiah; and the Zealots, who were prepared to fight for national independence. Hellenism also influenced Judaism at this time.

When the Zealots revolted, the Roman armies destroyed Jerusalem and its temple (A.D. 70). The Jews were scattered in the Diaspora (dispersion) and experienced much persecution. Rabbinic Judaism, developed according to Pharisaic practice and centered on Torah and synagogue, became the primary expression of faith. The Scriptures became codified, and the Talmud took shape. In the 12th century Maimonides formulated the influential 13 Articles of Faith, including belief in God, God's oneness and lack of physical or other form, the changelessness of Torah, restoration of the monarchy under the Messiah, and resurrection of the dead.

Two branches of European Judaism developed during the Middle Ages: the Sephardic, based in Spain and with an affinity to Babylonian Jews; and

Top Ten Organized Religions of the World

Statistics of the world's religions are only very rough approximations. Aside from Christianity, few religions, if any, attempt to keep statistical records; and even Protestants and Catholics employ different methods of counting members.

Religion	Members	Percentage	Religion	Members	Percentage
Christianity	1.9 billion	33.0%	Judaism	14 million	0.2
Islam	1.1 billion	20.0	Baha'ism	6.1 million	0.1
Hinduism	781 million	13.0	Confucianism	5.3 million	0.1
Buddhism	324 million	6.0	Jainism	4.9 million	0.1
Sikhism	19 million	0.4	Shintoism	2.8 million	0.0

NOTE: This list includes only organized religions and excludes more loosely defined groups such as Chinese or African traditional religions. *Sources:* Encyclopedia Britannica; www.adherents.com.

the Ashkenazic, based in Franco-German lands and affiliated with Rome and Palestine. Two forms of Jewish mysticism also arose at this time: medieval Hasidism and attention to the Kabbalah (a mystical interpretation of Scripture).

After a respite during the 18th-century Enlightenment, anti-Semitism again plagued European Jews in the 19th century, sparking the Zionist movement that culminated in the founding of the state of Israel in 1948. The Holocaust of World War II took the lives of more than 6 million Jews.

Jews today continue synagogue worship, which includes readings from the Law and the Prophets and prayers, such as the Shema (Hear, O Israel) and the Amidah (the 18 Benedictions). Religious life is guided by the commandments of the Torah, which include the practice of circumcision and Sabbath observance.

Present-day Judaism has three main expressions: Orthodox, Conservative, and Reform. Reform movements, resulting from the Haskala (Jewish Enlightenment) of the 18th century, began in western Europe but took root in North America. Reform Jews do not hold the oral law (Talmud) to be a divine revelation, and they emphasize ethical and moral teachings. Orthodox Jews follow the traditional faith and practice with great seriousness. They follow a strict kosher diet and keep the Sabbath with care. Conservative Judaism, which developed in the mid-18th century, holds the Talmud to be authoritative and follows most traditional practices, yet tries to make Judaism relevant for each generation, believing that change and tradition can complement each other. Because the Torah assumes belief in God but does not require it, a strong secular movement also exists within Judaism, including atheist and agnostic elements.

In general, Jews do not proselytize, but they do welcome newcomers to their faith.

Christianity

Christianity is a monotheistic religion founded by the followers of Jesus of Nazareth. Jesus, a Jew, was born in about 7 B.C. and assumed his public life, probably after his 30th year, in Galilee. The New Testament Gospels describe Jesus as a teacher and miracle worker. He proclaimed the kingdom of God, a future reality that is at the same time already present. Jesus set the requirements for participation in the kingdom of God as a change of heart and repentance for sins, love of God and neighbor, and concern for justice. Circa A.D. 30 he was executed on a cross in Jerusalem, a brutal form of punishment for those considered a political threat to the Roman Empire.

After his death his followers came to believe in him as the Christ, the Messiah. The Gospels report his resurrection and how the risen Jesus was witnessed by many of his followers. The apostle Paul helped spread the new faith in his missionary travels. Historically, Christianity arose out of Judaism and claims that Jesus fulfilled many of the promises of the Hebrew Scripture (often referred to as the Old Testament).

The new religion spread rapidly throughout the Roman Empire. In its first two centuries, Christianity began to take shape as an organization, developing distinctive doctrine, liturgy, and ministry. By the fourth century the Christian church had taken root in countries stretching from Spain in the West to Persia and India in the East. Christians had been subject to persecution by the Roman state, but gained tolerance under Constantine the Great (A.D. 313). The church became favored under his successors, and in 380 the emperor Theodosius proclaimed Christianity the state religion. Other religions were suppressed.

Because differences in doctrine threatened to divide the church, a standard Christian creed was formulated by bishops at successive ecumenical councils, the first of which was held in A.D. 325 (Nicaea). Important doctrines were defined concerning the Trinity—in other words, that there is one God in three persons: Father, Son, and Holy Spirit (Constantinople, A.D. 381), and the nature of Christ as both divine and human (Chalcedon, A.D. 541). Christians came to accept both Hebrew Scripture and the New Testament as authoritative. The New Testament comprises four Gospels (narratives of Jesus' life), 21 Epistles, The Acts of the Apostles, and Revelation.

Because of differences between Christians of the East and West, the unity of the church was broken in 1054. The religious center for the Eastern Orthodox Church was Constantinople, and the Roman Catholic Church defined doctrine and practice for Christians in the West. In 1517 the Reformation began, which ultimately caused a schism in the Western church. Reformers wished to correct certain practices within the Roman church, but they also came to view the Christian faith in a distinctly new way. The major Protestant denominations (Lutheran, Presbyterian, Reformed, and Anglican [Episcopalian]) thus came into being. Over the centuries, numerous denominations have broken with these major traditions, resulting in a spectrum of Christian expression.

In the 21st century, many Christians hope to regain a sense of unity through dialogue and cooperation among different traditions. The ecumenical movement led to the formation of the World Council of Churches in 1948 (Amsterdam), which has since been joined by many denominations.

Outlook of U.S. Adult Population: Religious or Secular

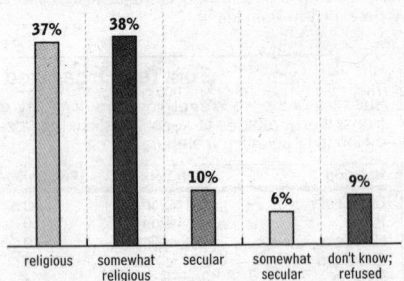

"When it comes to your outlook, do you regard yourself as..."

religious	somewhat religious	secular	somewhat secular	don't know; refused
37%	38%	10%	6%	9%

Source: Barry A. Kosmin, Egon Mayer, & Ariela Keysar
Copyright © American Religious Identification Survey, 2001

Through its missionary activity Christianity has spread to most parts of the globe.

Eastern Orthodoxy

Eastern Orthodoxy comprises the faith and practices stemming from ancient churches in the eastern part of the Roman Empire. It encompasses Orthodox churches in communion with the see of Constantinople.

The Orthodox, Catholic, Apostolic Church is the direct descendant of the Byzantine state church and consists of independent national churches that are united by doctrine, liturgy, and hierarchical organization (church leaders include deacons and priests, who may either be married or be monks before ordination, and bishops, who must be celibates). The heads of these churches are called patriarchs or metropolitans. Rivalry between the pope of Rome and the patriarch of Constantinople, as well as differences that existed for centuries between the eastern and western parts of the empire, led to a schism in 1054. The mutual excommunication pronounced in that year was lifted in 1965, however, and a climate of better understanding has ensued. Orthodox churches belong to the World Council of Churches.

Largest U.S. Churches, 2003

Denomination name	Members (thousands)
The Roman Catholic Church	65,270
Southern Baptist Convention	16,053
The United Methodist Church	8,298
The Church of God in Christ	5,500
The Church of Jesus Christ of Latter-day Saints	5,311
Evangelical Lutheran Church in America	5,100
National Baptist Convention, U.S.A., Inc.	5,000
National Baptist Convention of America, Inc.	3,500
Presbyterian Church (U.S.A.)	3,456
The Lutheran Church—Missouri Synod (LCMS)	2,540
African Methodist Episcopal Church	2,500
National Missionary Baptist Convention of America	2,500
Progressive National Baptist Convention, Inc.	2,500
Episcopal Church	2,333
Churches of Christ	1,500
Greek Orthodox Archdiocese of America	1,500
Pentecostal Assemblies of the World, Inc.	1,500
African Methodist Episcopal Zion Church	1,448
American Baptist Churches in the U.S.A	1,443
United Church of Christ	1,359
Baptist Bible Fellowship International	1,200
Christian Churches and Churches of Christ	1,072
The Orthodox Church in America	1,000
Jehovah's Witnesses	989
Church of God (Cleveland, Tennessee)	932
Seventh-Day Adventist Church	901
Christian Methodist Episcopal Church	850
Christian Church (Disciples of Christ) in the United States and Canada	805

NOTE: Includes the self-reported membership of religious bodies with 650,000 or more as reported to the Yearbook of American and Canadian Churches. Groups may be excluded if they do not supply information. The data are not standardized so comparisons between groups are difficult. The definition of "church member" is determined by the religious body. *Source: Yearbook of American & Canadian Churches,* 2003.

The Eastern Orthodox churches recognize only the canons of the seven ecumenical councils (325–787) as binding for faith, and they reject doctrines that have been added in the West.

The central worship service is called the Liturgy, which is understood as representing God's acts of salvation. Its center is the celebration of the Eucharist, or Lord's Supper. Icons (sacred pictures) have a special place in Orthodox worship. The mother of Christ, angels, and saints are venerated. The Orthodox Church and the Western Catholic Church recognize the same number of sacraments.

Orthodox churches are found in Greece, Turkey, Russia, the Balkans, and other parts of the former Soviet Union. In this century Orthodox faith has spread to western Europe and other parts of the world, particularly North America.

Eastern Rite Churches

These include the Uniate Churches that recognize the authority of the pope but keep their own traditional liturgies and those churches dating back to the fifth century that emancipated themselves from the Byzantine state church. They include the Melchites, Syrian Catholics, Maronites (Arab Christians in Lebanon), Catholic Copts and Ethiopians, the autonomous Nestorian Church, and others.

Roman Catholicism

Roman Catholicism comprises the beliefs and practices of the Roman Catholic Church. It stands under the authority of the bishop of Rome, the pope, and is led by him and bishops who are held to be, through ordination, successors of Peter and the apostles. Doctrine and sacraments are administered by the hierarchy of archbishops, bishops, priests, and deacons. As successor to Peter, the pope is considered the Vicar of Christ. Roman Catholics believe their church to be the one, holy, catholic, and apostolic church, possessing all the properties of the one, true church of Christ.

The faith of the church is understood to be identical with that taught by Christ and his apostles and contained in the Bible and tradition. New definitions of doctrines, such as the Immaculate Conception of Mary (1854) and the bodily

Roman Catholic Church Hierarchy

The Catholic clergy is organized in a strict, sometimes overlapping hierarchy:

Pope: Head of the church, he is based at the Vatican.

Cardinal: Appointed by the pope, there are 178 cardinals worldwide.

Archbishop: An archbishop is a bishop of a main or metropolitan diocese, also called an archdiocese.

Bishop: A bishop, like a priest, is ordained to this station.

Priest: An ordained minister who can administer most of the sacraments.

Deacon: A transitional deacon is a seminarian studying for the priesthood. A permanent deacon can be married and assists a priest by performing some of the sacraments.

Source: Time Magazine.

Assumption of Mary (1950), have been declared by popes, however. At Vatican Council I (1870) the pope was proclaimed "endowed with infallibility, *ex cathedra,* in other words, when exercising the office of pastor and teacher of all Christians."

The center of Roman Catholic worship is the celebration of the Mass, the Eucharist, which is the commemoration of Christ's sacrificial death and resurrection. Other sacraments are baptism, confirmation, penance, matrimony, anointing of the sick (formerly known as extreme unction), and holy orders. The Virgin Mary and the other saints, and their relics, are venerated, and prayers are made to them to intercede with God, in whose presence they are believed to dwell.

The Roman Catholic Church is the largest Christian organization in the world, found in most countries.

Vatican Council II (1962–1965) sought to "update" the church, bringing about changes in practice and more deeply involving the laity. The immensely popular Pope John Paul II (1978–) has taken a more conservative course and has reached out to Catholics worldwide through his extensive travels.

Protestantism

Protestantism encompasses the Christian churches that separated from Rome during the Reformation in the 16th century. This movement was initiated by an Augustinian monk, Martin Luther. The term *Protestant* was originally applied to followers of Luther, who protested at the Diet of Spires (1529) against the decree that prohibited all further ecclesiastical reforms. Other influential reformers included John Calvin, Ulrich Zwingli, and John Knox. Protestantism rejected attempts to tie God's revelation to earthly institutions and strictly adhered to the Word of God as sole authority in matters of faith and practice *(sola scriptura)*. Central in the reformers' understanding of the biblical message is the justification of the sinner by faith alone. The church is understood as a fellowship, and the priesthood of all believers is stressed.

The Augsburg Confession (1530) was the principal statement of Lutheran faith and practice. It became a model for other Protestant confessions of faith. Major Protestant denominations include the Lutheran, Reformed (Calvinist), Presbyterian, and Anglican (Episcopalian). Innumerable sects and

---

U.S. Protestant Groups

According to the Hartford Institute for Religious Research, U.S. Protestant groups are commonly divided into four broad categories:

Liberal Protestant: Episcopal, Presbyterian, Unitarian Universalist, United Church of Christ

Moderate Protestant: American Baptist, Disciples of Christ, Evangelical Lutheran, Mennonite, Reformed Church in America, United Methodist

Evangelical Protestant: Assemblies of God, Christian Reformed, Nazarene, Churches of Christ, Independent Christian Churches (Instrumental), Mega-churches, Nondenominational Protestant, Seventh-day Adventist, Southern Baptist

Historically Black Protestant denominations

---

denominations sprang from these roots, including Quakers, Baptists, Pentecostals, Congregationalists, Methodists, and nondenominational assemblies.

Since the latter part of the 19th century, national councils of churches have been established in many countries, for example, the Federal Council of Churches of Christ in America in 1908. Churches of a particular denomination have joined in federations and world alliances, beginning with the Anglican Lambeth Conference in 1867.

Protestant missionary activity, particularly strong in the 19th century, resulted in the founding of many churches in Asia and Africa. The ecumenical movement, which originated with Protestant missions, aims at unity among Christians and churches.

Islam

Islam, one of the three major monotheistic faiths, was founded in Arabia by Muhammad between 610 and 632. There are an estimated 5.5 million Muslims in North America and 1 billion Muslims worldwide.

Muhammad was born in A.D. 570 at Mecca and belonged to the Quraysh tribe, which was active in the caravan trade. At the age of 25 he joined the trade from Mecca to Syria in the employment of a rich widow, Khadija, whom he later married. Critical of the lax moral standards and polytheistic practices of the inhabitants of Mecca, he began to lead a contemplative life in the desert. In a dramatic religious vision, the angel Gabriel announced to Muhammad that he was to be a prophet. Encouraged by Khadija, he devoted himself to the reform of religion and society. Polytheism was to be abandoned. But leaders of the Quraysh generally rejected his teaching, and Muhammad gained only a small following and suffered persecution. He eventually fled Mecca.

The Hegira *(Hijra,* meaning "emigration") of Muhammad from Mecca to Medina, where he was not honored, to Medina, where he was well received, occurred in 622 and marks the beginning of the Muslim era. After a number of military conflicts with Mecca, in 630 he marched on Mecca and conquered it. Muhammad died at Medina in 632. His grave there has since been a place of pilgrimage.

Muhammad's followers, called Muslims, revered him as the prophet of Allah (God), the only God. Muslims consider Muhammad to be the last in the line of prophets that included Abraham and Jesus. Islam spread quickly, stretching from Spain in the west to India in the east within a century after the prophet's death. Sources of the Islamic faith are the Qur'an (Koran), regarded as the uncreated, eternal Word of God, and tradition *(hadith)* regarding sayings and deeds of the prophet.

Islam means "surrender to the will of Allah," the all-powerful, who determines humanity's fate. Good deeds will be rewarded at the Last Judgment in paradise, and evil deeds will be punished in hell.

The Five Pillars, or primary duties, of Islam are profession of faith; prayer, to be performed five times a day; almsgiving to the poor and the mosque (house of worship); fasting during daylight hours in the month of Ramadan; and pilgrimage to Mecca (the *hajj*) at least once in a Muslim's lifetime, if it is physically and financially possible. The pilgrimage includes homage to the ancient shrine of the Ka'aba, the most sacred site in Islam.

Countries with the Largest Muslim Populations

1. Indonesia	6. Iran
2. Pakistan	7. Egypt
3. India	8. Nigeria
4. Bangladesh	9. Algeria
5. Turkey	10. Morocco

Muslims gather for corporate worship on Fridays. Prayers and a sermon take place at the mosque, which is also a center for teaching of the Qur'an. The community leader, the *imam*, is considered a teacher and prayer leader.

Islam succeeded in uniting an Arab world of separate tribes and castes, but disagreements concerning the succession of the prophet caused a division in Islam between two groups, Sunnis and Shi'ites. The Shi'ites rejected the first three successors to Muhammad as usurpers, claiming the fourth, Muhammad's son-in-law Ali, as the rightful leader. The Sunnis (from the word *tradition*), the largest division of Islam (today more than 80%), believe in the legitimacy of the first three successors. Among these, other sects arose (such as the conservative Wahhabi of Saudi Arabia), as well as different schools of theology. Another development within Islam, beginning in the eighth and ninth centuries, was Sufism, a form of mysticism. This movement was influential for many centuries and was instrumental in the spread of Islam in Asia and Africa.

Islam has expanded greatly under Muhammad's successors. It is the principal religion of the Middle East, Asia, and the northern half of Africa.

Hinduism

Hinduism is the major religion of India, practiced by more than 80% of the population. In contrast to other religions, it has no founder. Considered the oldest religion in the world, it dates back, perhaps, to prehistoric times.

No single creed or doctrine binds Hindus together. Intellectually there is complete freedom of belief, and one can be monotheist, polytheist, or atheist. Hinduism is a syncretic religion, welcoming and incorporating a variety of outside influences.

The most ancient sacred texts of the Hindu religion are written in Sanskrit and called the *Vedas* (*vedah* means "knowledge"). There are four Vedic books, of which the Rig-Veda is the oldest. It discusses multiple gods, the universe, and creation. The dates of these works are unknown (1000 B.C.?). Present-day Hindus rarely refer to these texts but do venerate them.

The Upanishads (dated 1000–300 B.C.), commentaries on the Vedic texts, speculate on the origin of the universe and the nature of deity, and *atman* (the individual soul) and its relationship to *Brahman* (the universal soul). They introduce the doctrine of *karma* and recommend meditation and the practice of yoga.

Further important sacred writings include the Epics, which contain legendary stories about gods and humans. They are the Mahabharata (composed between 200 B.C. and A.D. 200) and the Ramayana. The former includes the Bhagavad-Gita (Song of the Lord), an influential text that describes the three paths to salvation. The Puranas (stories in verse, probably written between the 6th and 13th centuries) detail myths of Hindu gods and heroes and also comment on religious practice and cosmology.

According to Hindu beliefs, Brahman is the principle and source of the universe. This divine intelligence pervades all beings, including the individual soul. Thus the many Hindu deities are manifestations of the one Brahman. Hinduism is based on the concept of reincarnation, in which all living beings, from plants on earth to gods above, are caught in a cosmic cycle of becoming and perishing.

Life is determined by the law of karma—one is reborn to a higher level of existence based on moral behavior in a previous phase of existence. Life on earth is regarded as transient and a burden. The goal of existence is liberation from the cycle of rebirth and death and entrance into the indescribable state of *moksha* (liberation).

The practice of Hinduism consists of rites and ceremonies centering on birth, marriage, and death. There are many Hindu temples, which are considered to be dwelling places of the deities and to which people bring offerings. Places of pilgrimage include Benares on the Ganges, the most sacred river in India. Of the many Hindu deities, the most popular are the cults of Vishnu, Shiva, and Shakti, and their various incarnations. Also important is Brahma, the creator god. Hindus also venerate human saints.

Orthodox Hindu society in India was divided into four major hereditary classes: (1) the Brahmin (priestly and learned class); (2) the Kshatriya (military, professional, ruling, and governing occupations); (3) the Vaishya (landowners, merchants, and business occupations); and (4) the Sudra (artisans, laborers, and peasants). Below the Sudra was a fifth group, the Untouchables (lowest menial occupations and no social standing). The Indian government banned discrimination against the Untouchables in the constitution of India in 1950. Observance of class and caste distinctions varies throughout India.

In modern times work has been done to reform and revive Hinduism. One of the outstanding reformers was Ramakrishna (1836–1886), who inspired many followers, one of whom founded the Ramakrishna mission. The mission is active both in India and in other countries and is known for its scholarly and humanitarian works.

Buddhism

Buddhism was founded in the fourth or fifth century B.C. in northern India by a man known traditionally as Siddhartha (meaning "he who has reached the goal") Gautama, the son of a warrior prince. Some scholars believe that he lived from 563 to 483 B.C., though his exact life span is uncertain. Troubled by the inevitability of suffering in human life, he left home and a pampered life at the age of 29 to wander as an ascetic, seeking religious insight and a solution to the struggles of human existence. He passed through many trials and practiced extreme self-denial. Finally, while meditating under the bodhi tree ("tree of perfect knowledge"), he reached enlightenment and taught his followers about his new spiritual understanding.

Gautama's teachings differed from the Hindu faith prevalent in India at the time. Whereas in Hinduism the Brahmin caste alone performed religious functions and attained the highest spiritual understanding,

Gautama's beliefs were more egalitarian, accessible to all who wished to be enlightened. At the core of his understanding were the Four Noble Truths: (1) all living beings suffer; (2) the origin of this suffering is desire—for material possessions, power, and so on; (3) desire can be overcome; and (4) there is a path that leads to release from desire. This way is called the Noble Eightfold Path: right views, right intention, right speech, right action, right livelihood, right effort, right concentration, and right ecstasy.

Gautama promoted the concept of *anatman* (that a person has no actual self) and the idea that existence is characterized by impermanence. This realization helps one let go of desire for transient things. Still, Gautama did not recommend extreme self-denial but rather a disciplined life called the Middle Way. Like the Hindus, he believed that existence consisted of reincarnation, a cycle of birth and death. He held that it could be broken only by reaching complete detachment from worldly cares. Then the soul could be released into *nirvana* (literally "blowing out")—an indescribable state of total transcendence. Gautama traveled to preach the *dharma* (sacred truth) and was recognized as the Buddha (enlightened one). After his death his followers continued to develop doctrine and practice, which came to center on the Three Jewels: the *dharma* (the sacred teachings of Buddhism), the *sangha* (the community of followers, which now includes nuns, monks, and laity), and the Buddha. Under the patronage of the Mauryan emperor Ashoka (third century B.C.), Buddhism spread throughout India and to other parts of Asia. Monasteries were established, as well as temples dedicated to Buddha; at shrines his relics were venerated. Though by the fourth century A.D. Buddhist presence in India had dwindled, it flourished in other parts of Asia.

Numerous Buddhist sects have emerged. The oldest, called the Theravada (Way of the Elders) tradition, interprets Buddha as a great sage but not a deity. It emphasizes meditation and ritual practices that help the individual become an *arhat*, an enlightened being. Its followers emphasize the authority of the earliest Buddhist scriptures, the Tripitaka (Three Baskets), a compilation of sermons, rules for celibates, and doctrine. This sect is prevalent in Southeast Asia and Sri Lanka. It is sometimes called the Hinayana (Lesser Vehicle) tradition (once considered a pejorative term).

Between the second century B.C. and the second century A.D., the Mahayana (Greater Vehicle) tradition refocused Buddhism to concentrate less on individual attainment of enlightenment and more on concern for humanity. It promotes the ideal of the *bodhisattva* (enlightened being), who shuns entering nirvana until all sentient beings can do so as well, willingly remaining in the painful cycle of birth and death to perform works of compassion. Members of this tradition conceive of Buddha as an eternal being to whom prayers can be made; other Buddhas are revered as well, adding a polytheistic dimension to the religion. Numerous sects have developed from the Mahayana tradition, which has been influential in China, Korea, and Japan.

A third broad tradition, variously called Vajrayana (Diamond Vehicle), Mantrayana (Vehicle of the Mantra), or Tantric Buddhism, offers a quicker, more demanding way to achieve nirvana. Because of its level of challenge—enabling one to reach enlightenment in one lifetime—it requires the guidance of a spiritual leader. It is most prominent in Tibet and Mongolia.

Zen Buddhism encourages individuals to seek the Buddha nature within themselves and to practice a disciplined form of sitting meditation in order to reach *satori*—spiritual enlightenment.

Sikhism

A major religion of India and the fifth-largest faith in the world, Sikhism emerged in the Punjab under the guidance of the guru Nanak (1469–1539?). This region had been influenced by the Hindu *bhakti* movement, which promoted both the idea that God comprises one reality alone as well as the practice of devotional singing and prayer. The Muslim mystical tradition of Sufism, with its emphasis on meditation, also had some prominence there. Drawing on these resources, Nanak forged a new spiritual path.

In his youth, Nanak began to compose hymns. At the age of 29, he had a mystical experience that led him to proclaim "There is no Hindu; there is no Muslim." A strict monotheist, he rejected Hindu polytheism but accepted the Hindu concept of life as a cycle of birth, death, and rebirth; *moksha*, release from this cycle into unity with God, could be achieved only with the help of a guru, or spiritual teacher. Nanak believed that communion with God could be gained through devotional repetition of the divine name, singing of hymns and praises, and adherence to a demanding ethical code. He rejected idols and the Hindu caste system; it became a custom for Sikhs of all social ranks to take meals together. These beliefs are still central to modern Sikhism.

Nanak was first in a line of ten gurus who shaped and inspired Sikhism. The fifth, Arjun (1563–1606), compiled hymns and other writings by earlier Sikh gurus, as well as medieval Hindu and Muslim saints, in the *Adi Granth* (First Book), or *Guru Granth Sahib* (the Granth Personified). This book became the sacred scripture of Sikhism. In addition to his spiritual leadership, Arjun wielded considerable secular power as he grappled with leaders of the Mughal Empire.

The tenth guru, Gobind Singh (1666–1708), was both a scholar and a military hero. He established the Khalsa (community of pure ones), an order that combined spiritual devotion, personal discipline, and ideals of military valor. Baptism initiates new members into the Khalsa. The *Adi Granth* took its final form under the supervision of Gobind Singh, as did the *Dasam Granth* (Tenth Book), a collection of prayers, poetry, and narrative. After the deaths of his four sons, Gobind Singh declared the line of gurus at an end. The *Adi Granth* would instead be reverenced in houses of worship, taking the place of a living guru.

Today, Sikhs worship at *gurdwaras* (temples), where the *Adi Granth* is the object of devotion. This book is consulted regarding questions of faith and practice. On certain occasions, it is recited in its entirety (requiring more than a day) or carried in procession; offerings may be placed before it. Worshipful singing, meditation, and focus on the divine name remain essential to spiritual life. Some Sikhs undertake pilgrimages to historical *gurdwaras*, such as the Golden Temple of Amritsar, that are associated with the gurus. Some become disciples of living saints. There is no established Sikh priesthood.

Confucianism

Confucius (K'ung Fu-tzu), born in the state of Lu (northern China), lived from 551 to 479 B.C. He was a brilliant teacher, viewing education not merely as the accumulation of knowledge but as a means of self-transformation. His legacy was a system of thought emphasizing education, proper behavior, and loyalty. His effect on Chinese culture was immense.

The teachings of Confucius are contained in the *Analects*, a collection of his sayings as remembered by his students. They were further developed by philosophers such as Mencius (Meng Tse, fl. 400 B.C.). Confucianism is little concerned with metaphysical discussion of religion or with spiritual attainments. It instead emphasizes moral conduct and right relationships in the human sphere.

Cultivation of virtue is a central tenet of Confucianism. Two important virtues are *jen*, a benevolent and humanitarian attitude, and *li*, maintaining proper relationships and rituals that enhance the life of the individual, the family, and the state. The "five relations," between king and subject, father and son, man and wife, older and younger brother, and friend and friend, are of utmost importance. These relationships are reinforced by participation in rituals, including the formal procedures of court life and religious rituals such as ancestor worship.

Confucius revolutionized educational thought in China. He believed that learning was not to be focused only on attaining the skills for a particular profession, but for growth in moral judgment and self-realization. Confucius's standards for the proper conduct of government shaped the statecraft of China for centuries. Hundreds of temples in honor of Confucius testify to his stature as sage and teacher.

Confucianism was far less dominant in 20th-century China, at least on an official level. The state cult of Confucius was ended in 1911. Still, Confucian traditions and moral standards are part of the cultural essence of China and other East Asian countries.

Shinto

Shinto comprises the religious ideas and practices indigenous to Japan. Ancient Shinto focused on the worship of the *kami*, a host of supernatural beings that could be known through forms (objects of nature, remarkable people, abstract concepts such as justice) but were ultimately mysterious. Shinto has no formal dogma and no holy writ, though early collections of Japanese religious thought and practice (*Kojiki*, "Records of Ancient Matters," A.D. 712, and *Nihon shoki*, "Chronicles of Japan," A.D. 720) are highly regarded.

Shinto has been influenced by Confucianism and by Buddhism, which was introduced in Japan in the 6th century. Syncretic schools (such as Ryobu Shinto) emerged, as did other sects that rejected Buddhism (such as Ise Shinto).

Under the reign of the emperor Meiji (1868–1912), Shinto became the official state religion. State Shinto, the national cult, emphasized the divinity of the emperor, whose succession was traced back to the first emperor, Jimmu (660 B.C.), and beyond him to the sun goddess Amaterasu-o-mi-kami. State Shinto was disestablished after World War II.

Sect Shinto, deriving from sects that developed during the 19th and 20th centuries, continues to thrive in Japan. Shrines dedicated to particular *kami* are visited by parishioners for prayer and traditional ceremonies, such as presenting a newborn child to the *kami*. Traditional festivals celebrated at the shrines include purification rites, presentation of food offerings, prayer, sacred music and dance, and a feast.

No particular day of the week is set aside for prayer. A person may visit a shrine at will, entering through the *torii* (gateway). It is believed that the *kami* can respond to prayer and can offer protection and guidance.

A variety of Shinto sects and practices exist today. Ten-rikyo emphasizes faith healing. Folk Shinto is characterized by veneration of roadside shrines and rites related to agriculture. Buddhist priests serve at many Shinto shrines, and many families keep a small shrine, or god-shelf, at home. Veneration of ancestors and pilgrimage are also common practices.

Taoism

Taoism, one of the major religions of China, is based on ancient philosophical works, primarily the Tao Te Ching, "Classic of Tao and Its Virtue." Traditionally, this book was thought to be the work of Lao-tzu, a quasi-historical philosopher of the 6th century B.C.; scholars now believe that the book dates from about the 3rd century B.C. The philosopher Chuang Tzu (4th–3rd centuries B.C.) also contributed to the seminal ideas of Taoism.

Tao, "the Way," is the ultimate reality of the universe, according to Taoism. It is a creative process, and humans can live in harmony with it by clearing the self of obstacles. By cultivating *wu-wei*, a type of inaction characterized by humility and prudence, a person can participate in the simplicity and spontaneity of Tao. Striving to attain virtue or achievement is counterproductive and unnecessary. Taoism values mystical contemplation and balance. The human being is viewed as a microcosm of the universe, and the Chinese principle of *yin-yang*, complementary duality, is a model of harmony.

The religious practices of Taoism emerged from these ancient philosophies and from Chinese shamanistic tradition; by the 2nd century A.D., it constituted an organized religion. Longevity and immortality were sought through regulating the energies of the body through breathing exercises, meditation, and use of medicinal plants, talismans, and magical formulas. A cult of immortals, including the divinized Lao-tzu, also developed. Influenced by Buddhism, Taoists organized monastic orders. Temple worship and forms of divination, including the *I ching*, were practiced.

Since its beginnings, many sects have arisen within Taoism. All subscribe to the philosophical origins of the religion; some have emphasized faith healing, exorcism, the worship of the immortals, meditation, or alchemy. Buddhism and Confucianism influenced some sects; some operated as secret societies.

Though the present Chinese government has tried to suppress it, Taoism is still practiced in mainland China, Taiwan, and Hong Kong. It profoundly influenced Chinese art and literature, and Taoist ideas have become popular in the West.

Self-Described Religious Identification Among American Adults

Religious group	2001 Total (in thousands)	Percent of population	Religious group	2001 Total (in thousands)	Percent of population
Total Christian	**159,506**	**76.7%**	Fundamentalist	61	*
Catholic	50,873	24.5	Salvation Army	25	*
Baptist	33,830	16.3	Independent		
Protestant[1]	4,647	2.2	Christian Church	71	*
Methodist/Wesleyan	14,150	6.8	**Total other religions**	**7,740**	**3.7%**
Lutheran	9,580	4.6	Jewish[3]	2,831	1.4
Christian[1]	14,150	6.8	Muslim/Islamic	1,104	0.5
Presbyterian	5,596	2.7	Buddhist	1,082	0.5
Pentecostal/Charismatic	4,407	2.1	Unitarian/Universalist	629	0.3
Episcopalian/Anglican	3,451	1.7	Hindu	766	0.4
Mormon/Latter-day			Native American	103	*
Saints	2,787	1.3	Scientologist	55	*
Churches of Christ	2,593	1.2	Baha'i	84	*
Jehovah's Witness	1,331	0.6	Taoist	40	*
Seventh-Day Adventist	724	0.3	New Age	68	*
Assemblies of God	1,106	0.5	Eckankar	26	*
Holiness/Holy	569	0.3	Rastafarian	11	*
Congregational/United			Sikh	57	*
Church of Christ	1,378	0.7	Wiccan	134	0.1
Church of the Nazarene	544	0.3	Deity	49	*
Church of God	944	0.5	Druid	33	*
Orthodox (Eastern)	645	0.3	Santeria	22	*
Evangelical[2]	1,032	0.5	Pagan	140	0.1
Mennonite	346	0.2	Spiritualist	116	0.1
Christian Science	194	0.1	Ethical Culture	4	*
Church of the Brethren	358	0.2	Other unclassified	386	0.2
Born Again[2]	56	0.0	**No religion specified,**		
Nondenominational[2]	2,489	1.2	**total**	**29,481**	**14.2**
Disciples of Christ	492	0.2	Atheist	902	0.4
Reformed/Dutch Reform	289	0.1	Agnostic	991	0.5
Apostolic/New Apostolic	254	0.1	Humanist	49	*
Quaker	217	0.1	Secular	53	*
Full Gospel	168	0.1	No religion	27,486	13.2
Christian Reform	79	*	**Refused to reply**		
Foursquare Gospel	70	*	**to question**	**11,246**	**5.4**

NOTES: * Less than 0.05%. 1. No denomination supplied. 2. These categories are the most unstable as they do not refer to clearly identifiable denominations as much as underlying feelings about religion. Thus they may be the most subject to fluctuation over time. 3. Refers to Jews by religion only. The American Religious Identification Survey (ARIS) 2001 was based on a random telephone survey of 50,281 American residential households in the continental U.S.A. (48 states). Respondents were asked to describe themselves in terms of religion with an open-ended question. The self-description of respondents was not based on whether established religious bodies considered them to be members; rather, the survey sought to determine whether the respondents themselves regarded themselves as adherents of a religious community. These figures thus represent subjective, rather than objective, standards of religious identification. *Source:* Barry A. Kosmin and Ariela Keysar, American Religious Identification Survey, 2001 (copyright). From the forthcoming book *Religion in a Free Market* (Paramount Market Publishing, 2005)

Roman Catholic Pontiffs

Name	Birthplace	Reigned From	To	Name	Birthplace	Reigned From	To
St. Peter	Bethsaida	42?	67?	St. Callistus I	Rome	217	222
St. Linus	Tuscia	c. 67	76	St. Urban I	Rome	222	230
St. Anacletus (Cletus)	Rome	76	88	St. Pontian	Rome	230	235
				St. Anterus	Greece	235	236
St. Clement	Rome	88	97	St. Fabian	Rome	236	250
St. Evaristus	Greece	97	105	St. Cornelius	Rome	251	253
St. Alexander I	Rome	105	115	St. Lucius I	Rome	253	254
St. Sixtus I	Rome	115	125	St. Stephen I	Rome	254	257
St. Telesphorus	Greece	125	136	St. Sixtus II	Greece	257	258
St. Hyginus	Greece	136	140	St. Dionysius	Unknown	259	268
St. Pius I	Aquileia	140	155	St. Felix I	Rome	269	274
St. Anicetus	Syria	155	166	St. Eutychian	Luni	275	283
St. Soter	Campania	166	175	St. Caius	Dalmatia	283	296
St. Eleutherius	Epirus	175	189	St. Marcellinus	Rome	296	304
St. Victor I	Africa	189	199	St. Marcellus I	Rome	308	309
St. Zephyrinus	Rome	199	217				

Name	Birthplace	Reigned From	To	Name	Birthplace	Reigned From	To
St. Eusebius	Greece	309[1]	309[1]	Stephen III (IV)	Sicily	768	772
St. Meltiades	Africa	311	314	Adrian I	Rome	772	795
St. Sylvester I	Rome	314	335	St. Leo III	Rome	795	816
St. Marcus	Rome	336	336	Stephen IV (V)	Rome	816	817
St. Julius I	Rome	337	352	St. Paschal I	Rome	817	824
Liberius	Rome	352	366	Eugene II	Rome	824	827
St. Damasus I	Spain	366	384	Valentine	Rome	827	827
St. Siricius	Rome	384	399	Gregory IV	Rome	827	844
St. Anastasius I	Rome	399	401	Sergius II	Rome	844	847
St. Innocent I	Albano	401	417	St. Leo IV	Rome	847	855
St. Zozimus	Greece	417	418	Benedict III	Rome	855	858
St. Boniface I	Rome	418	422	St. Nicholas I (the Great)	Rome	858	867
St. Celestine I	Campania	422	432				
St. Sixtus III	Rome	432	440	Adrian II	Rome	867	872
St. Leo I (the Great)	Tuscany	440	461	John VIII	Rome	872	882
				Marinus I	Gallese	882	884
St. Hilary	Sardinia	461	468	St. Adrian III	Rome	884	885
St. Simplicius	Tivoli	468	483	Stephen V (VI)	Rome	885	891
St. Felix III (II)[2]	Rome	483	492	Formosus	Portus	891	896
St. Gelasius I	Africa	492	496	Boniface VI	Rome	896	896
Anastasius II	Rome	496	498	Stephen VI (VII)	Rome	896	897
St. Symmachus	Sardinia	498	514	Romanus	Gallese	897	897
St. Hormisdas	Frosinone	514	523	Theodore II	Rome	897	897
St. John I	Tuscany	523	526	John IX	Tivoli	898	900
St. Felix IV (III)	Samnium	526	530	Benedict IV	Rome	900	903
Boniface II	Rome	530	532	Leo V	Ardea	903	903
John II	Rome	533	535	Sergius III	Rome	904	911
St. Agapitus I	Rome	535	536	Anastasius III	Rome	911	913
St. Silverius	Campania	536	537	Landus	Sabina	913	914
Vigilius	Rome	537	555	John X	Tossignano	914	928
Pelagius I	Rome	556	561	Leo VI	Rome	928	928
John III	Rome	561	574	Stephen VII (VIII)	Rome	928	931
Benedict I	Rome	575	579	John XI	Rome	931	935
Pelagius II	Rome	579	590	Leo VII	Rome	936	939
St. Gregory I (the Great)	Rome	590	604	Stephen VIII (IX)	Rome	939	942
				Marinus II	Rome	942	946
Sabinianus	Tuscany	604	606	Agapitus II	Rome	946	955
Boniface III	Rome	607	607	John XII	Tusculum	955	964
St. Boniface IV	Marsi	608	615	Leo VIII[5]	Rome	963	965
St. Deusdedit (Adeodatus I)	Rome	615	618	Benedict V[5]	Rome	964	966
				John XIII	Rome	965	972
Boniface V	Naples	619	625	Benedict VI	Rome	973	974
Honorius I	Campania	625	638	Benedict VII	Rome	974	983
Severinus	Rome	640	640	John XIV	Pavia	983	984
John IV	Dalmatia	640	642	John XV	Rome	985	996
Theodore I	Greece	642	649	Gregory V	Saxony	996	999
St. Martin I	Todi	649	655	Sylvester II	Auvergne	999	1003
St. Eugene I[3]	Rome	654	657	John XVII	Rome	1003	1003
St. Vitalian	Segni	657	672	John XVIII	Rome	1004	1009
Adeodatus II	Rome	672	676	Sergius IV	Rome	1009	1012
Donus	Rome	676	678	Benedict VIII	Tusculum	1012	1024
St. Agatho	Sicily	678	681	John XIX	Tusculum	1024	1032
St. Leo II	Sicily	682	683	Benedict IX[6]	Tusculum	1032	1044
St. Benedict II	Rome	684	685	Sylvester III	Rome	1045	1045
John V	Syria	685	686	Benedict IX (2nd time)	Tusculum	1045	1045
Conon	Unknown	686	687				
St. Sergius I	Syria	687	701	Gregory VI	Rome	1045	1046
John VI	Greece	701	705	Clement II	Saxony	1046	1047
John VII	Greece	705	707	Benedict IX (3rd time)	Tusculum	1047	1048
Sisinnius	Syria	708	708				
Constantine	Syria	708	715	Damasus II	Bavaria	1048	1048
St. Gregory II	Rome	715	731	St. Leo IX	Alsace	1049	1054
St. Gregory III	Syria	731	741	Victor II	Germany	1055	1057
St. Zachary	Greece	741	752	Stephen IX (X)	Lorraine	1057	1058
Stephen II (III)[4]	Rome	752	757	Nicholas II	Burgundy	1059	1061
St. Paul I	Rome	757	767	Alexander II	Milan	1061	1073

Name	Birthplace	Reigned From	To	Name	Birthplace	Reigned From	To
St. Gregory VII	Tuscany	1073	1085	Paul II	Venice	1464	1471
Bl. Victor III	Benevento	1086	1087	Sixtus IV	Savona	1471	1484
Bl. Urban II	France	1088	1099	Innocent VIII	Genoa	1484	1492
Paschal II	Ravenna	1099	1118	Alexander VI	Jativa	1492	1503
Gelasius II	Gaeta	1118	1119	Pius III	Siena	1503	1503
Callistus II	Burgundy	1119	1124	Julius II	Savona	1503	1513
Honorius II	Flagnano	1124	1130	Leo X	Florence	1513	1521
Innocent II	Rome	1130	1143	Adrian VI	Utrecht	1522	1523
Celestine II	Città di Castello	1143	1144	Clement VII	Florence	1523	1534
Lucius II	Bologna	1144	1145	Paul III	Rome	1534	1549
Bl. Eugene III	Pisa	1145	1153	Julius III	Rome	1550	1555
Anastasius IV	Rome	1153	1154	Marcellus II	Montepulciano	1555	1555
Adrian IV	England	1154	1159	Paul IV	Naples	1555	1559
Alexander III	Siena	1159	1181	Pius IV	Milan	1559	1565
Lucius III	Lucca	1181	1185	St. Pius V	Bosco	1566	1572
Urban III	Milan	1185	1187	Gregory XIII	Bologna	1572	1585
Gregory VIII	Benevento	1187	1187	Sixtus V	Grottammare	1585	1590
Clement III	Rome	1187	1191	Urban VII	Rome	1590	1590
Celestine III	Rome	1191	1198	Gregory XIV	Cremona	1590	1591
Innocent III	Anagni	1198	1216	Innocent IX	Bologna	1591	1591
Honorius III	Rome	1216	1227	Clement VIII	Florence	1592	1605
Gregory IX	Anagni	1227	1241	Leo XI	Florence	1605	1605
Celestine IV	Milan	1241	1241	Paul V	Rome	1605	1621
Innocent IV	Genoa	1243	1254	Gregory XV	Bologna	1621	1623
Alexander IV	Anagni	1254	1261	Urban VIII	Florence	1623	1644
Urban IV	Troyes	1261	1264	Innocent X	Rome	1644	1655
Clement IV	France	1265	1268	Alexander VII	Siena	1655	1667
Bl. Gregory X	Piacenza	1271	1276	Clement IX	Pistoia	1667	1669
Bl. Innocent V	Savoy	1276	1276	Clement X	Rome	1670	1676
Adrian V	Genoa	1276	1276	Bl. Innocent XI	Como	1676	1689
John XXI[7]	Portugal	1276	1277	Alexander VIII	Venice	1689	1691
Nicholas III	Rome	1277	1280	Innocent XII	Spinazzola	1691	1700
Martin IV[8]	France	1281	1285	Clement XI	Urbino	1700	1721
Honorius IV	Rome	1285	1287	Innocent XIII	Rome	1721	1724
Nicholas IV	Ascoli	1288	1292	Benedict XIII	Gravina	1724	1730
St. Celestine V	Isernia	1294	1294	Clement XII	Florence	1730	1740
Boniface VIII	Anagni	1294	1303	Benedict XIV	Bologna	1740	1758
Bl. Benedict XI	Treviso	1303	1304	Clement XIII	Venice	1758	1769
Clement V	France	1305	1314	Clement XIV	Rimini	1769	1774
John XXII	Cahors	1316	1334	Pius VI	Cesena	1775	1799
Benedict XII	France	1334	1342	Pius VII	Cesena	1800	1823
Clement VI	France	1342	1352	Leo XII	Genga	1823	1829
Innocent VI	France	1352	1362	Pius VIII	Cingoli	1829	1830
Bl. Urban V	France	1362	1370	Gregory XVI	Belluno	1831	1846
Gregory XI	France	1370	1378	Pius IX	Senegallia	1846	1878
Urban VI	Naples	1378	1389	Leo XIII	Carpineto	1878	1903
Boniface IX	Naples	1389	1404	St. Pius X	Riese	1903	1914
Innocent VII	Sulmona	1404	1406	Benedict XV	Genoa	1914	1922
Gregory XII	Venice	1406	1415	Pius XI	Desio	1922	1939
Martin V	Rome	1417	1431	Pius XII	Rome	1939	1958
Eugene IV	Venice	1431	1447	John XXIII	Sotto il Monte	1958	1963
Nicholas V	Sarzana	1447	1455	Paul VI	Concesio	1963	1978
Callistus III	Jativa	1455	1458	John Paul I	Forno di Canale	1978	1978
Pius II	Siena	1458	1464	John Paul II	Wadowice, Poland	1978	

1. Or 310. 2. He should be called Felix II, and his successors of the same name should be numbered accordingly. The discrepancy was caused by the erroneous insertion in some lists of the name of St. Felix of Rome, Martyr. 3. He was elected during the exile of St. Martin I, who endorsed him as pope. 4. After St. Zachary died, a Roman priest named Stephen was elected but died before his consecration as bishop of Rome. His name is not included in all lists for this reason. In view of this historical confusion, the *National Catholic Almanac* lists the true Stephen II as Stephen II (III), the true Stephen III as Stephen III (IV), etc. 5. Confusion exists concerning the legitimacy of claims. If the deposition of John was invalid, Leo was an antipope until after the end of Benedict's reign. If the deposition of John was valid, Leo was the legitimate pope and Benedict an antipope. 6. If the triple removal of Benedict IX was not valid, Sylvester III, Gregory VI, and Clement II were antipopes. 7. Elimination was made of the name of John XX in an effort to rectify the numerical designation of popes named John. The error dates back to the time of John XV. 8. The names of Marinus I and Marinus II were construed as Martin. In view of these two pontificates and the earlier reign of St. Martin I, this pontiff was called Martin IV. *Source: National Catholic Almanac*, from *Annuarto Pontificio*.

The Books of the Bible

Below is the Protestant canon of the Bible (New Revised Standard Version). The Roman Catholic canon also includes the Deuterocanonical books as part of the Old Testament (these are considered apocryphal by most Protestants). The Hebrew Bible recognizes the books referred to as the Old Testament in the Protestant Bible, but not the Apocryphal/Deuterocanonical books or the New Testament.

The Old Testament with the Apocryphal/ Deuterocanonical Books
The Hebrew Scriptures
 Genesis
 Exodus
 Leviticus
 Numbers
 Deuteronomy
 Joshua
 Judges
 Ruth
 1 Samuel
 2 Samuel
 1 Kings
 2 Kings
 1 Chronicles
 2 Chronicles
 Ezra
 Nehemiah
 Esther
 Job
 Psalms

Proverbs
Ecclesiastes
Song of Solomon
Isaiah
Jeremiah
Lamentations
Ezekiel
Daniel
Hosea
Joel
Amos
Obadiah
Jonah
Micah
Nahum
Habakkuk
Zephaniah
Haggai
Zechariah
Malachi
The Apocryphal/ Deuterocanonical Books
 Tobit
 Judith

• Additions to the Book
   of Esther
 Wisdom of Solomon
 Ecclesiasticus, or the
   Wisdom of Jesus
   Son of Sirach
 Baruch
 The Letter of Jeremiah
 The Prayer of Azariah
   and the Song of the
   Three Jews
 Susanna
 Bel and the Dragon
 1 Maccabees
 2 Maccabees
 1 Esdras
 Prayer of Manasseh
 Psalm 151
 3 Maccabees
 2 Esdras
 4 Maccabees
The New Testament
 Matthew
 Mark
 Luke

John
Acts of the Apostles
Romans
1 Corinthians
2 Corinthians
Galatians
Ephesians
Philippians
Colossians
1 Thessalonians
2 Thessalonians
1 Timothy
2 Timothy
Titus
Philemon
Hebrews
James
1 Peter
2 Peter
1 John
2 John
3 John
Jude
Revelation

The Ten Commandments

The Ten Commandments, also called the Decalogue (Greek, "ten words"), were divine laws revealed to Moses by God on Mt. Sinai. Appearing in both Exodus (Ex. 20: 2–17) and Deuteronomy (Deut. 5:6–21), the commandments are numbered differently depending on whether they appear in a Catholic, Protestant, or Hebrew Bible. The following is the version given in the Revised Standard Version of the Bible.

You shall have no other gods before me.

You shall not make for yourself a graven image, or any likeness of anything that is in heaven above, or that is in the earth beneath, or that is in the water under the earth; you shall not bow down to them or serve them; for I the Lord your God am a jealous God, visiting the iniquity of the fathers upon the children to the third and the fourth generation of those who hate me, but showing steadfast love to thousands of those who love me and keep my commandments.

You shall not take the name of the Lord your God in vain; for the Lord will not hold him guiltless who takes his name in vain.

Remember the Sabbath day, to keep it holy. Six days you shall labor, and do all your work; but the seventh day is a Sabbath to the Lord your God; in it you shall not do any work, you, or your son, or your daughter, or your manservant, or your maidservant, or

your cattle, or the sojourner who is within your gates; for in six days the Lord made heaven and earth, the sea, and all that is in them, and rested the seventh day; therefore the Lord blessed the Sabbath day and hallowed it.

Honor your father and your mother, that your days may be long in the land which the Lord your God gives you.

You shall not kill.

You shall not commit adultery.

You shall not steal.

You shall not bear false witness against your neighbor.

You shall not covet your neighbor's wife, or his manservant, or his maidservant, or his ox, or his ass, or anything that is your neighbor's.

Source: Revised Standard Version of the Bible
(Ex. 20: 2–17)

The Seven Deadly Sins

In Christianity, the seven deadly sins are considered "deadly" because it is believed they can do terrible damage to the soul. The now-famous list does not appear in the Bible and may have been formulated by Gregory the Great (540–604). The deadly sins are sometimes known as "capital" or "cardinal" sins: pride, greed, lust, envy, gluttony, anger, and sloth.

Selected Worldwide Religious Sites

Amritsar, India: Site of the Golden Temple (Sikhism).

Axum, Ethiopia: Church of St. Mary of Zion (Ethiopian Orthodox), where the Ark of the Covenant is believed to be kept.

Bethlehem, Israel: Birthplace of Jesus.

Black Hills, South Dakota: Sacred to the Lakota Indian tribe, who traditionally go on vision quests in the hills.

Bodhi Gaya, India: Place where the Buddha reached enlightenment.

Canterbury, England: Seat of the archbishop of Canterbury (Anglican).

Czestochowa, Poland: Chapel of Our Lady of Czestochowa, the Black Madonna of Poland. This painting is said to have been made by St. Luke.

Dharamsala, India: Seat of the Dalai Lama in exile (Tibetan Buddhism).

Fatima, Portugal: Site of several visions of the Virgin Mary in 1917. A major pilgrimage site for Catholics.

Ganges River, India: Sacred to Hindus (Mother Ganges is a Hindu goddess); immersion in the Ganges symbolizes spiritual purification.

Haifa, Israel: Seat of the Baha'i faith.

Istanbul, Turkey: Seat of the patriarchate of Constantinople (Eastern Orthodox).

Jerusalem, Israel: Major holy site for Judaism, Christianity, and Islam. The Temple Mount compound is believed to be both the site of the First and Second Temples of Judaism and the place where redemption will occur when the Messiah arrives. The same area is also called Haram al-Sharif (The Noble Sanctuary) and is of significance to Muslims. Nearby is the Dome of the Rock, the spot from which Muhammad ascended into heaven. Just below Temple Mount is the Western Wall, a remnant of the Second Temple and the holiest site in Judaism, where Jews come to pray. The Wall is part of a larger wall that encloses the Dome of the Rock and the al-Aksa mosque. The al-Aksa mosque, one of the holiest mosques in Islam, was originally the site toward which Muslims bowed to pray. The Holy Sepulchre, in which Jesus was buried, and from which he returned from the dead, is in the northwest corner of the Old City.

Knock, Ireland: Pilgrimage site for Catholics where 15 people claimed to see a vision of the Virgin Mary, St. Joseph, and St. John the Evangelist in 1879. About 1½ million pilgrims visit the site annually.

Kusinara, India: Site of the Buddha's death.

Lhasa, Tibet: Potala Palace, historical abode of the Dalai Lama (Tibetan Buddhism).

Loch Derg, Ireland: Site of St. Patrick's purgatory, pilgrimage destination; pilgrims walk barefoot around the lake, praying, like St. Patrick did.

Lourdes, France: In 1858, the Virgin Mary is said to have appeared to St. Bernadette at Lourdes in seven visions. It is now a Catholic pilgrimage site with a spring that some believe has curative properties.

Lumbini, Nepal: Birthplace of the Buddha.

Mecca, Saudi Arabia: The center of Islam and the birthplace of Muhammad, Mecca is the place toward which Muslims bow to pray five times a day. Mecca is the destination of the *hajj*, the pilgrimage which all Muslims who are financially and physically able must make in their lifetime. An estimated one million Muslims make the *hajj* annually. The focus of their worship is the Great Mosque at the center of Mecca. It encloses the Ka'aba, a small building that, according to the Qu'ran, was erected by Abraham and his son Ishmael.

Medina, Saudi Arabia: Muhammad lived in Medina after escaping Mecca in A.D. 622; it is now a holy city that only Muslims may enter.

Medjugorje, Bosnia-Herzegovina: Catholic pilgrimage site where many have claimed visions of the Virgin Mary.

Mt. Athos, Greece: Pilgrimage site for Eastern Orthodox males; site of many monasteries.

Mt. Fuji, Japan: Sacred to Buddhists and Shintos.

Mt. Tai Shan, China: Sacred to Taoists and Buddhists, this mountain with many beautiful temples is thought to be a center of living energy.

Nazareth, Israel: Place where Jesus lived and began teaching.

Palitana, India: The most important pilgrimage site for Jains, Palitana boasts 863 temples on one mountain, Shatrunjaya Hill.

Salt Lake City, Utah: Seat of Church of Jesus Christ of Latter-day Saints.

Santiago de Compostela, Spain: One of the most important medieval pilgrimage sites; the pilgrimage route of Santiago de Compostela passes through France and Spain before ending up at the city's cathedral. Santiago is Saint James, who was martyred at Jerusalem c. A.D. 44.

Sarnath, India: Place where the Buddha preached his first sermon in the deer park.

Sea of Galilee, Israel: Place where Jesus performed the miracle of the loaves and the fishes and preached the Sermon on the Mount.

Sri Pada (Adam's Peak), Sri Lanka: Sacred to some Buddhists, Hindus, Muslims, and Christians, the temple on the top of Adam's Peak contains a large footprint believed to belong to either the Buddha, Shiva, Adam, or St. Thomas.

Tepeyac, Mexico City, Mexico: Site of the appearance of the Virgin of Guadalupe to Juan Diego in 1531; now home to the Basilica of the Virgin, one of the most-visited churches in the world.

Turin, Italy: Place where the Holy Shroud of Turin (linen cloth believed to bear the visage of Jesus Christ) is housed.

Uluru (Ayer's Rock), Australia: Sacred site of the aborigines of Australia. Now a major tourist attraction, though the aborigine people ask that tourists not climb the rock.

Varanasi, India: City on the banks of the Ganges River; those who die there reach instant enlightenment.

The Vatican: Seat of the papacy (Catholicism).

See Calendar and Holidays for listings of religious holidays.

A Primer on Same-Sex Marriage and Civil Unions

Definitions

"Same-sex marriage" means legal marriage between people of the same sex.

• Only Massachusetts issues marriage licenses to same-sex couples (since 2004).

"Civil union" is a new category of law that was created to extend rights to same-sex couples. These rights are recognized only in the state where the couple resides. Because civil union law is new, it is largely untested by the courts and is not widely understood.

• Only Vermont offers civil unions (since 2000). A civil union confers state-level spousal rights to same-sex couples while they reside in the state.

"Domestic partnership" is a new category of law that was created to extend rights to unmarried couples, including (but not necessarily limited to) same-sex couples. Laws vary among states, cities, and counties. Terminology also varies; for example, Hawaii has "reciprocal beneficiaries law." Any rights are recognized only on the state or local level.

• Statewide laws in California, Connecticut, Hawaii, Maine, and New Jersey and district-wide laws in the District of Columbia confer certain spousal rights to same-sex couples.

What's the Difference?

The most significant difference between marriage and civil unions (or domestic partnerships) is that only marriage offers federal benefits and protections.

According to the federal government's General Accounting Office (GAO), more than 1,100 rights and protections are conferred to U.S. citizens upon marriage. Areas affected include Social Security benefits, veterans' benefits, health insurance, Medicaid, hospital visitation, estate taxes, retirement savings, pensions, family leave, and immigration law.

Because civil unions and domestic partnerships are not federally recognized, any benefits available at the state or local level are subject to federal taxation. For example, a woman whose health insurance covers her female partner must pay federal taxes on the total employer cost for that insurance.

Federal Legislation: DOMA

In 1996, the Defense of Marriage Act (DOMA) was passed by Congress and signed into law by President Clinton. It allows each state to choose whether or not to recognize a same-sex union that is recognized in another state—thus allowing a choice of whether to enforce the U.S. Constitution's "full faith and credit" clause (which requires each state to recognize the laws and legal contracts of other states). It also creates a federal definition of marriage as a union of a man and a woman.

However, DOMA has yet to be fully tested in the courts. Because the U.S. Constitution does not give Congress the power to limit the scope of the "full faith and credit" clause—only to enforce its application—the constitutionality of DOMA has not been proven.

State Legislation

Since DOMA was passed in 1996, most of the states have passed similar legislation. But if same-sex marriage was not legal, why enact legislation against it?

State legislation against same-sex marriage serves two purposes. One, it writes into law a state's tradition of limiting marriage licenses to opposite-sex couples. Two, it may be used in efforts to overrule existing state or local rights and protections for same-sex couples and their children.

• Since 1996, the majority of states have passed laws that either define marriage as a union of one man and one woman or outlaw recognition of same-sex unions.

• Alaska, Louisiana, Missouri, Nebraska, and Nevada have amended their state constitution to define marriage as a union of one man and one woman. In addition, Hawaii amended its constitution to grant the state legislature "the power to reserve marriage to opposite-sex couples"

Federal Marriage Amendment

Because the constitutionality of DOMA and state legislation against same-sex marriage has yet to be fully tested by the courts, relying on legislation to settle the issue of same-sex marriage will take years. As a result, text for a proposed constitutional amendment known as the Federal Marriage Amendment (FMA) was introduced to Congress in 2003.

The amendment would define marriage as the union of a man and a woman and could be used to overrule state or local protections for same-sex couples and their children. To become part of the U.S. Constitution, the FMA would need to be approved by two thirds of Congress and then ratified by three fourths of state legislatures.

Around the World

Countries that issue marriage licenses to same-sex couples: Belgium (2003) and the Netherlands (since 2001); the Canadian provinces of Ontario and British Columbia since 2003, and Quebec, the Yukon, Manitoba, Nova Scotia, and Saskatchewan since 2004.

Countries that offer a legal status, sometimes known as registered partnership, that confers most or all spousal rights to same-sex couples: Denmark, Finland, Germany, Iceland, Norway, Sweden.

Countries that offer a legal status, sometimes known as unregistered cohabitation, that confers certain spousal rights to same-sex couples (and, in some of these countries, unmarried opposite-sex couples): Brazil, Canada, Croatia, France, Hungary, Israel, New Zealand, Portugal, South Africa, Spain, Switzerland.

—*Holly Hartman*

Same-Sex Partners Sharing Households in the U.S.

Nationwide, 594,391 same-sex partner households represented 1% of all coupled households, according to the 2000 Census. Of these, 301,026 were male partners and 293,365 were female partners.

Metropolitan Areas with the Highest Percentage of Same-Sex Households, 2000

Same-sex partner households by area	Number	Percent of all households in specified city	Same-sex partner households by area	Number	Percent of all households in specified city
San Francisco, Calif.	8,902	2.7%	Atlanta, Ga.	2,833	1.7%
Fort Lauderdale, Fla.	1,418	2.1	Minneapolis, Minn.	2,622	1.6
Seattle, Wash.	4,965	1.9	Washington, DC	3,678	1.5
Oakland, Calif.	2,650	1.8	Long Beach, Calif.	2,266	1.4
Berkeley, Calif.	788	1.8	Portland, Ore.	3,017	1.3

Source: Married-Couple and Unmarried-Partner Households: 2000, U.S. Census Bureau, Census 2000.

Gender of Sexual Partners in the United States

(sexually active only)

	Same gender		Both genders		Opposite gender	
	Men	Women	Men	Women	Men	Women
1988	2.3%	0.2%	0.3%	0.0%	97.4%	99.8%
1989	1.4	1.2	0.3	0.4	98.3	98.4
1990	1.1	0.5	0.9	0.0	98.0	99.5
1991	2.0	0.3	0.7	0.1	97.3	99.6
1993	1.8	1.8	0.3	0.4	97.9	97.8
1994	2.1	2.1	0.5	0.4	97.5	97.5
1996	3.5	2.1	0.6	0.9	96.0	97.0

Source: General Social Survey (GSS), National Opinion Research Center, University of Chicago, 1996.

Key Events in the Women's Rights Movement

1848 The first women's rights convention is held in Seneca Falls, New York. A Declaration of Sentiments, which outlines grievances and sets the agenda for the women's rights movement, is signed by 68 women and 32 men.

1850 The first National Women's Rights Convention takes place in Worcester, Mass., attracting more than 1,000 participants. National conventions are held yearly (except for 1857) through 1860.

1869 In May, Susan B. Anthony and Elizabeth Cady Stanton form the National Woman Suffrage Association. Its primary goal is to achieve voting rights for women by means of a congressional amendment to the Constitution.

In November Lucy Stone, Henry Blackwell, and others form the American Woman Suffrage Association, which focuses exclusively on gaining voting rights for women through amendments to individual state constitutions.

In December the territory of Wyoming passes the first women's suffrage law. In 1870, women begin serving on juries in the territory.

1890 The National Woman Suffrage Association and the American Woman Suffrage Association merge to form the National American Woman Suffrage Association (NAWSA). As the movement's mainstream organization, NAWSA wages state-by-state campaigns to obtain voting rights for women.

1893 Colorado is the first state to adopt an amendment granting women the right to vote. Utah and Idaho follow suit in 1896, Washington State in 1910, California in 1911, Oregon, Kansas, and Arizona in 1912, Alaska and Illinois in 1913, Montana and Nevada in 1914, New York in 1917, Michigan, South Dakota, and Oklahoma in 1918.

1896 The National Association of Colored Women is formed, bringing together more than 100 black women's clubs. Leaders in the black women's club movement include Josephine St. Pierre Ruffin, Mary Church Terrell, and Anna Julia Cooper.

1913 Alice Paul and Lucy Burns form the Congressional Union to work toward the passage of a federal amendment to give women the vote. The group is later renamed the National Women's Party. Members picket the White House and practice other forms of civil disobedience.

1919 The federal woman suffrage amendment, originally written by Susan B. Anthony and introduced in Congress in 1878, is passed by the House of Representatives and the Senate. It is then sent to the states for ratification.

1920 On Aug. 26, the 19th Amendment to the Constitution, granting women the right to vote, is signed into law.

1921 Margaret Sanger founds the American Birth Control League, which evolves into the Planned Parenthood Federation of America in 1942.

1936 The federal law prohibiting the dissemination of contraceptive information through the mail is modified, and birth control information is no longer classified as obscene. Throughout the 1940s and 1950s, birth control advocates are engaged in numerous legal suits.

1961 President John F. Kennedy establishes the President's Commission on the Status of Women and appoints Eleanor Roosevelt as chairwoman. The report issued by the commission in 1963 documents substantial discrimination against women in the workplace and urges reform, including fair hiring practices, paid maternity leave, and affordable child care.

1963 Betty Friedan publishes her highly influential book *The Feminine Mystique,* which becomes a best-seller and galvanizes the modern women's rights movement.

In June Congress passes the Equal Pay Act, making it illegal for employers to pay a woman less than what a man would receive for the same job.

1964 Title VII of the Civil Rights Act bars discrimination in employment on the basis of race and sex. At the same time it establishes the Equal Employment Opportunity Commission (EEOC) to investigate complaints and impose penalties.

1965 In *Griswold* v. *Connecticut,* the Supreme Court strikes down the one remaining state law prohibiting the use of contraceptives by married couples.

1966 The National Organization for Women (NOW) is founded. The largest women's rights group in the United States, NOW seeks to end sexual discrimination by means of legislative lobbying, litigation, and public demonstrations.

1967 Executive Order 11375 expands President Lyndon Johnson's affirmative action policy of 1965 to cover discrimination based on gender.

1968 The EEOC rules that sex-segregated help wanted ads in newspapers are illegal. This ruling is upheld in 1973 by the Supreme Court, opening the way for women to apply for higher-paying jobs hitherto open only to men.

1969 California becomes the first state to adopt a "no fault" divorce law, which allows couples to divorce by mutual consent. By 1985 every state has adopted a similar law. Laws are also passed regarding the equal division of common property.

1971 *Ms.* magazine is first published as a sample insert in *New York* magazine; 300,000 copies are sold out in 8 days. The first regular issue is published in July 1972. The magazine becomes the major forum for feminist voices and turns cofounder and editor Gloria Steinem into an icon of the modern feminist movement.

In *Eisenstadt* v. *Baird* the Supreme Court rules that the right to privacy includes an unmarried person's right to use contraceptives.

1972 The Equal Rights Amendment (ERA) is passed by Congress and sent to the states for ratification. Originally drafted by Alice Paul in 1923, the amendment reads: "Equality of rights under the law shall not be denied or abridged by the United States or by any State on account of sex." The amendment died in 1982 when it failed to achieve ratification by a minimum of 38 states.

Title IX of the Education Amendments bans sex discrimination in schools. As a result, the enrollment of women in athletics programs and professional schools increases dramatically.

1973 As a result of *Roe* v. *Wade,* the Supreme Court establishes a woman's legal right to abortion, overriding the antiabortion laws of many states.

1974 The Equal Credit Opportunity Act prohibits discrimination in consumer credit practices on the basis of sex, race, marital status, religion, national origin, age, or receipt of public assistance.

1978 The Pregnancy Discrimination Act bans employment discrimination against pregnant women.

1984 EMILY's List (Early Money Is Like Yeast) is established as a financial network for pro-choice Democratic women running for national political office. The organization makes a significant impact on the increasing number of women elected to Congress.

1986 In *Meritor Savings Bank* v. *Vinson,* the Supreme Court finds that sexual harassment is a form of illegal job discrimination.

1994 The Violence Against Women Act tightens federal penalties for sex offenders, funds services for victims of rape and domestic violence, and provides for special training of police officers.

The Wage Gap

Source: National Women's Law Center.

The wage gap is a statistical indicator often used as an index of the status of women's earnings relative to men's. It is also used to compare the earnings of other races and ethnicities to those of white males, a group generally not subject to race- or sex-based discrimination. The wage gap is expressed as a percentage (e.g., in 2003, women earned 76% as much as men) and is calculated by dividing the median annual earnings for women by the median annual earnings for men.

The Equal Pay Act was signed in 1963, making it illegal for employers to pay unequal wages to men and women who hold the same job and do the same work. At the time of the EPA's passage, women earned just 58 cents for every dollar earned by men. By 2003, 40 years later, that rate had only increased to 76 cents, an improvement of less than half a penny a year. Minority women fare the worst. African-American women earn just 65 cents to every dollar earned by white men, and for Hispanic women that figure drops to merely 54 cents per dollar.

The wage gap between women and men cuts across a wide spectrum of occupations. The Bureau of Labor Statistics reported in 1999 that female physicians earned 62.5% of the median weekly wages of male physicians, and women in sales occupations earned just 59.9% of men's wages in equivalent positions.

If working women earned the same as men (those who work the same number of hours; have the same education, age, and union status; and live in the same region of the country), their annual family incomes would rise by $4,000 and poverty rates would be cut in half.

2003 Median Annual Earnings by Race and Sex

Race/gender	Earnings	Wage ratio	Race/gender	Earnings	Wage ratio
White men	$41,211	100.0%	All men	$40,668	
Black men	$32,241	78.2	All women	$30,724	
White women	$31,169	75.6			
Black women	$26,965	65.4	Wage gap		75.5%
Hispanic men	$26,083	63.3			
Hispanic women	$22,363	54.3			

NOTE: Includes full-time, year-round workers ages 15 and above. "White" and "Black" exclude those who reported more than one race category. "Hispanic" includes all those who so identified, regardless of race. *Source:* U.S. Census Bureau, Current Population Survey, 2004 Annual Social and Economic Supplement.

Women's Earnings as a Percentage of Men's, 1951–2003

(for year-round, full-time work)

Year	Percent	Year	Percent	Year	Percent	Year	Percent	Year	Percent
1951	63.9%	1962	59.3%	1973	56.6%	1984	63.7%	1995	71.4%
1952	63.9	1963	58.9	1974	58.8	1985	64.6	1996	73.8
1953	63.9	1964	59.1	1975	58.8	1986	64.3	1997	74.2
1954	63.9	1965	59.9	1976	60.2	1987	65.2	1998	73.2
1955	63.9	1966	57.6	1977	58.9	1988	66.0	1999	72.2
1956	63.3	1967	57.8	1978	59.4	1989	68.7	2000	73.3
1957	63.8	1968	58.2	1979	59.7	1990	71.6	2001	76.3
1958	63.0	1969	58.9	1980	60.2	1991	69.9	2002	76.6
1959	61.3	1970	59.4	1981	59.2	1992	70.8	2003	75.5
1960	60.7	1971	59.5	1982	61.7	1993	71.5		
1961	59.2	1972	57.9	1983	63.6	1994	72.0		

Source: U.S. Women's Bureau and the National Committee on Pay Equity.

Wage Gap, Selected European Countries

Country	Women's wages as % of men's	Country	Women's wages as % of men's	Country	Women's wages as % of men's
Austria	79%	Germany	81%	Netherlands	79%
Belgium	89	Greece	87	Portugal	95
Denmark	86	Ireland	78	Spain	86[1]
Finland	81	Italy	91	Sweden	83
France	88	Luxembourg	82[2]	United Kingdom	78

NOTES: Figures are unadjusted, and reflect the average gross hourly earnings of all paid employees aged 16–64 who worked 15+ hours per week in 1999. 1. Estimated. 2. In 1996. *Source:* The Social Situation in the European Union: 2003

Gender Wage Gap by Selected Occupations, 2000

Occupation	Percent women	Earnings ratio (%)	Occupation	Percent women	Earnings ratio (%)
Occupations with estimated earnings[1] of under $20,000			**Occupations with estimated earnings[1] above $34,000**		
			Accountants and auditors	60%	72%
Waiter/waitress	69%	87%	Securities and financial serivces sales	33	57
Cleaning and building service occupations	40	80	Physicians	31	58
Cashiers	76	88	Teachers, college and university	38	79
Food preparation and service	50	90	Lawyers and judges	29	73
Maids and housemen	80	85	Economists	48	68
Occupations with estimated earnings[1] between $20,000 and $34,000			**Occupations in which the majority of workers are women**		
Bus driver	45%	79%	Registered nurse	91%	88%
Sales worker; retail and personal	56	64	Social worker	71	92
Mechanics and repairers	5	97	Admin. support, including clerical	77	80
Construction trades	2	79	Teachers, except college and universities	74	81
Truck drivers	4	71			

1. Approximate annual earnings were estimated by multiplying median weekly wages for men by 52 weeks. *Source:* National Committee on Pay Equity.

Ancestry of U.S. Population by Rank

2000 Rank	Ancestry group	Percent	2000 Rank	Ancestry group	Percent	2000 Rank	Ancestry group	Percent
1.	German	15.2%	30.	Korean	0.4%	59.	Iranian	0.1%
2.	Irish	10.8	31.	African[1]	0.4	60.	Hawaiian	0.1
3.	African American[1]	8.8	32.	Portuguese	0.4	61.	Yugoslavian	0.1
4.	English	8.7	33.	Greek	0.4	62.	Ecuadorian	0.1
5.	American[1]	7.2	34.	Japanese	0.4	63.	Spaniard	0.1
6.	Mexican	6.5	35.	Cuban	0.4	64.	Taiwanese	0.1
7.	Italian	5.6	36.	British	0.4	65.	Peruvian	0.1
8.	Polish	3.2	37.	Vietnamese	0.4	66.	Honduran	0.1
9.	French	3.0	38.	Swiss	0.3	67.	Pennsylvania German	0.1
10.	American Indian[1]	2.8	39.	Dominican	0.3	68.	Pakistani	0.1
11.	Scottish	1.7	40.	Ukrainian	0.3	69.	Latin American[1]	0.1
12.	Dutch	1.6	41.	Salvadoran	0.3	70.	Asian[1]	0.1
13.	Norwegian	1.6	42.	Slovak	0.3	71.	Nicaraguan	0.1
14.	Scotch-Irish	1.5	43.	Jamaican	0.3	72.	Arab[1]	0.1
15.	Swedish	1.4	44.	Austrian	0.3	73.	Cambodian	0.1
16.	White[1]	1.4	45.	Lithuanian	0.2	74.	Brazilian	0.1
17.	Puerto Rican	0.9	46.	Canadian	0.2	75.	Laotian	0.1
18.	Russian	0.9	47.	Finnish	0.2	76.	Slovene	0.1
19.	Hispanic[1]	0.9	48.	Colombian	0.2	77.	Trinidadian and	
20.	French Canadian	0.8	49.	Haitian	0.2		Tobagonian	0.1
21.	Chinese	0.8	50.	Guatemalan	0.2	78.	Nigerian	0.1
22.	Spanish	0.8	51.	Czechoslovakian	0.2	79.	Northern European[1]	0.1
23.	Filipino	0.8	52.	Lebanese	0.2	80.	Guyanese	0.1
24.	European[1]	0.7	53.	Scandinavian	0.2	81.	West Indian[1]	0.1
25.	Welsh	0.6	54.	United States[1]	0.1	82.	Thai	0.1
26.	Asian Indian	0.5	55.	Armenian	0.1	83.	Syrian	0.1
27.	Danish	0.5	56.	Croatian	0.1	84.	Egyptian	0.1
28.	Hungarian	0.5	57.	Romanian	0.1			
29.	Czech	0.4	58.	Belgian	0.1			

NOTES: Ancestry is a broad concept that can mean different things to different people. The ancestry groups listed on this table were self-identified. The Census Bureau defines ancestry as a person's ethnic origin, heritage, descent, or "roots," which may reflect their place of birth, place of birth of parents or ancestors, and ethnic identities that have evolved within the United States. Many respondents listed more than one area of ancestry; the sum of the persons reporting the ancestry is greater than the total. Ancestries making up at least 0.1% of the population are included in the table. Overall, about 500 different ancestries were reported during Census 2000. 1. Group may encompass several ancestries not listed separately. *Source:* U.S. Census Bureau, Ancestry: 2000, *issued June 2004.*

Persons Speaking a Language Other than English at Home, 2000

Language	Persons 5 years old and over who speak language	Language	Persons 5 years old and over who speak language
Population, 5 years and over	262,375,152	Persian	312,085
Speak only English	215,423,557	Gujarathi	235,988
Speak other language	46,951,595	Hindi	317,057
Spanish or Spanish Creole	28,101,052	Urdu	262,900
Other Indo-European languages	10,017,989	Other Indic languages	439,289
French (inc. Patois, Cajun)	1,643,838	Other Indo-European languages	327,946
French Creole	453,368	Asian and Pacific Island languages	6,960,065
Italian	1,008,370	Chinese	2,022,143
Portuguese or Portuguese Creole	564,630	Japanese	477,997
German	1,383,442	Korean	894,063
Yiddish	178,945	Mon-Khmer, Cambodian	181,889
Other West Germanic languages	251,135	Miao, Hmong	168,063
Scandinavian languages	162,252	Thai	120,464
Greek	365,436	Laotian	149,303
Russian	706,242	Vietnamese	1,009,627
Polish	667,414	Other Asian languages	398,434
Serbo-Croatian	233,865	Tagalog	1,224,241
Other Slavic languages	301,079	Other Pacific Island languages	313,841
Armenian	202,708	Other languages	1,872,489

Source: U.S. Census Bureau, Census 2000, Summary File 3, Table PCT 10, released Feb. 25, 2003.

Immigrants Admitted by Region and Top 20 Countries of Birth, 2002

Region and country of birth	Number	Percent	Region and country of birth	Number	Percent
All countries	1,063,732	100.0%	6. El Salvador	31,168	2.9
Africa	60,269	5.7	7. Cuba	28,272	2.7
Asia	342,099	32.2	8. Bosnia-Herzegovina	25,373	2.4
Europe	174,209	16.4	9. Dominican Republic	22,604	2.1
North America	404,437	38.0	10. Ukraine	21,217	2.0
Caribbean	96,489	9.1	11. Korea	21,021	2.0
Central America	68,979	6.5	12. Russia	20,833	2.0
Other North America	238,969	22.5	13. Haiti	20,268	1.9
Oceania	5,557	0.5	14. Canada	19,519	1.8
South America	74,506	7.0	15. Colombia	18,845	1.8
Unknown	2,655	0.2	16. Guatemala	16,229	1.5
Specific countries			17. United Kingdom	16,181	1.5
1. Mexico	219,380	20.6	18. Jamaica	14,898	1.4
2. India	71,105	6.7	19. Pakistan	13,743	1.3
3. China, People's Republic	61,282	5.8	20. Iran	13,029	1.2
4. Philippines	51,308	4.8	Subtotal	739,902	69.6
5. Vietnam	33,627	3.2	Other and unknown	323,830	30.4

Source: *2002 Yearbook of Immigration Statistics*, U.S. Citizenship and Immigration Services.

Countries of Birth of the Foreign-Born Population, 1850–2000

(resident population)

Ten leading countries by rank[1]	1850	1880	1900	1930	1960
1.	Ireland 962,000	Germany 1,967,000	Germany 2,663,000	Italy 1,790,000	Italy 1,257,000
2.	Germany 584,000	Ireland 1,855,000	Ireland 1,615,000	Germany 1,609,000	Germany 990,000
3.	Great Britain 379,000	Great Britain 918,000	Canada 1,180,000	United Kingdom 1,403,000	Canada 953,000
4.	Canada 148,000	Canada 717,000	Great Britain 1,168,000	Canada 1,310,000	United Kingdom 833,000
5.	France 54,000	Sweden 194,000	Sweden 582,000	Poland 1,269,000	Poland 748,000
6.	Switzerland 13,000	Norway 182,000	Italy 484,000	Soviet Union 1,154,000	Soviet Union 691,000
7.	Mexico 13,000	France 107,000	Russia 424,000	Ireland 745,000	Mexico 576,000
8.	Norway 13,000	China 104,000	Poland 383,000	Mexico 641,000	Ireland 339,000
9.	Holland 10,000	Switzerland 89,000	Norway 336,000	Sweden 595,000	Austria 305,000
10.	Italy 4,000	Bohemia 85,000	Austria 276,000	Czechoslovakia 492,000	Hungary 245,000

Ten leading countries by rank[1]	1970	1980	1990	2000
1.	Italy 1,009,000	Mexico 2,199,000	Mexico 4,298,000	Mexico 7,841,000
2.	Germany 833,000	Germany 849,000	China 921,000	China 1,391,000
3.	Canada 812,000	Canada 843,000	Philippines 913,000	Philippines 1,222,000
4.	Mexico 760,000	Italy 832,000	Canada 745,000	India 1,007,000
5.	United Kingdom 686,000	United Kingdom 669,000	Cuba 737,000	Cuba 952,000
6.	Poland 548,000	Cuba 608,000	Germany 712,000	Vietnam 863,000
7.	Soviet Union 463,000	Philippines 501,000	United Kingdom 640,000	El Salvador 765,000
8.	Cuba 439,000	Poland 418,000	Italy 581,000	Korea 701,000
9.	Ireland 251,000	Soviet Union 406,000	Korea 568,000	Dominican Republic 692,000
10.	Austria 214,000	Korea 290,000	Vietnam 543,000	Canada 678,000

1. In general, countries as reported at each census. Data are not totally comparable over time due to changes in boundaries for some countries. Great Britain excludes Ireland. United Kingdom includes Northern Ireland. China in 1990 includes Hong Kong and Taiwan. *Source: Profile of the Foreign-Born Population in the United States: 2000*, U.S. Census Bureau, 2001.

Population of the United States by Race and Hispanic/Latino Origin, Census 2000 and July 1, 2003

Race and Hispanic/Latino origin	July 1, 2003, population[1]	Percent of population	Census 2000, population	Percent of population
Total Population	290,809,777	100.0%	281,421,906	100.0%
Single race				
White	234,196,357	80.5	211,460,626	75.1
Black or African American	37,098,946	12.8	34,658,190	12.3
American Indian and Alaska Native	2,786,652	1.0	2,475,956	0.9
Asian	11,924,912	4.1	10,242,998	3.6
Native Hawaiian and other Pacific Islander	495,335	0.2	398,835	0.1
Two or more races	4,307,575	1.5	6,826,228	2.4
Some other race	n.a.[2]	n.a.	15,359,073	5.5
Hispanic or Latino	39,898,889	13.7	35,305,818	12.5

NOTE: Percentages do not add up to 100% due to rounding, and because Hispanics may be of any race and are therefore counted under more than one category. 1. June 14, 2004 estimate. 2. Those answering "other" have been allocated to one of the recognized race categories. Source: U.S. Census Bureau, Cenus 2000 Brief, March 2001, and National Population Estimates.

African-American Population

In 1790, when the first census was taken, African Americans numbered about 760,000—about 19% of the population. In 1860, at the start of the Civil War, the African-American population increased to 4.4 million, but the percentage rate dropped to 14% of the overall population of the country. The vast majority were slaves, with only 488,000 counted as "freemen." By 1900, the black population had doubled and reached 8.8 million. In 1910, about 90% of African Americans lived in the South, but large numbers began migrating north looking for better job opportunities and living conditions, and to escape Jim Crow and racial violence. The Great Migration, as it was called, spanned the 1890s to the 1970s. From 1916 through the 1960s, more than 6 million black people moved north. But in the 1970s and 1980s, that trend reversed, with more African Americans moving south to the Sunbelt than leaving it. By 1990, the African-American population reached about 30 million and represented 12% of the population, roughly the same proportion as in 1900.

Year	Population (millions)	Percent of population	Year	Population (millions)	Percent of population
1790	0.8	19.3%	1940	12.9	9.8
1800	1.0	18.9	1950	15.0	10.0
1850	3.6	15.7	1960	18.9	10.5
1900	8.8	11.6	1970	22.6	11.1
1910	9.8	10.7	1980	26.5	11.7
1920	10.5	9.9	1990	30.0	12.1
1930	11.9	9.7	2000	34.6	12.3

Source: Statistical Abstract of the United States: 2003, and We, The American Blacks, U.S. Census Bureau, 1993.

Black or African-American Population for the United States by Region, 2002

Area	Percent of black population	Percent of total population	Area	Percent of black population	Percent of total population
United States	100.0%	12.7%	Midwest	18.1%	10.2%
Region			South	55.3	19.8
Northeast	18.1	12.2	West	8.6	4.8

Source: U.S. Census Bureau, Current Population Survey, March 2002.

U.S. Hispanic/Latino Population, 2000

National origin	Population	Percent	National origin	Population	Percent
Total	35,305,818	100.0%	Other Central American	103,721	0.3
Mexican	20,640,711	58.5	South American	1,353,562	3.8%
Puerto Rican	3,406,178	9.6	Argentinean	100,864	0.3
Cuban	1,241,685	3.5	Bolivian	42,068	0.1
Dominican (Dominican Republic)	764,945	2.2	Chilean	68,849	0.2
Central American (excludes Mexican)	1,686,937	4.8	Colombian	470,684	1.3
			Ecuadorian	260,559	0.7
Costa Rican	68,588	0.2	Paraguayan	8,769	([1])
Guatemalan	372,487	1.1	Peruvian	233,926	0.7
Honduran	217,569	0.6	Uruguayan	18,804	0.1
Nicaraguan	177,684	0.5	Venezuelan	91,507	0.3
Panamanian	91,723	0.3	Other South American	57,532	0.2
Salvadoran	655,165	1.9	All other Hispanic or Latino	6,211,800	17.6

NOTE: Hispanics may be of any race. 1. Less than 0.1%. Source: U.S. Census Bureau, Census 2000.

U.S. Asian Population, 2000

National origin	Population[1]	Percent	National origin	Population[1]	Percent
Total[2]	**11,898,828**	**100.0%**	Korean	1,228,427	10.3%
Asian Indian	1,899,599	16.0	Laotian	198,203	1.7
Bangladeshi	57,412	0.5	Malaysian	18,566	0.2
Bhutanese	212	([3])	Maldivian	51	([3])
Burmese	16,720	0.1	Nepalese	9,399	0.1
Cambodian	206,052	1.7	Okinawan	10,599	0.1
Chinese, except Taiwanese	2,734,841	23.0	Pakistani	204,309	1.7
Filipino	2,364,815	19.9	Singaporean	2,394	([3])
Hmong	186,310	1.6	Sri Lankan	24,587	0.2
Indo-Chinese	199	([3])	Taiwanese	144,795	1.2
Indonesian	63,073	0.5	Thai	150,283	1.3
Iwo Jiman	78	([3])	Vietnamese	1,223,736	10.3
Japanese	1,148,932	9.7	Other Asian, not specified	369,430	3.1

1. The numbers by national origin do not add up to the total population figure because respondents may have put down more than one country. Respondents reporting several countries are counted several times. 2. Total includes Asians alone or in combination with one or more other races or other Asian groups. The Asian population alone in 2000 was 10,242,998. 3. Less than 0.1%. *Source:* U.S. Census Bureau, Census 2000.

Native Hawaiian and Other U.S. Pacific Islander Population, 2000

National origin	Population[1]	Percent	National origin	Population[1]	Percent
Total[2]	**874,414**	**100.0%**	Kosraean	226	([3])
Polynesian			Pohnpeian	700	0.1%
Native Hawaiian	401,162	45.9	Chuukese	654	0.1
Samoan	133,281	15.2	Yapese	368	([3])
Tongan	36,840	4.2	Marshallese	6,650	0.8
Tahitian	3,313	0.4	I-Kiribati	175	([3])
Tokelauan	574	0.1	Micronesian, not specified	9,940	1.1
Polynesian, not specified	8,796	1.0	**Melanesian**		
Micronesian			Fijian	13,581	1.6
Guamanian or Chamorro	92,611	10.6	Papua New Guinean	224	([3])
Mariana Islander	141	([3])	Solomon Islander	25	([3])
Saipanese	475	0.1	Ni-Vanuatu	18	([3])
Palauan	3,469	0.4	Melanesian, not specified	315	([3])
Carolinian	173	([3])	**Other Pacific Islander**	174,912	20.0

1. The numbers by national origin do not add up to the total population figure because respondents may have put down more than one country. Respondents reporting several countries are counted several times. 2. Total includes Native Hawaiian and other Pacific Islanders alone or in combination with other races or groups. Native Hawaiian and Pacific Islander population alone in 2000 was 398,835. 3. Less than 0.1%. *Source:* U.S. Census Bureau, Census 2000.

American Indian and Alaska Native Population by Selected Tribes, 2000

Tribe	Population[1]	Tribe	Population[1]
Total[2]	**4,119,301**	Pima	11,493
Apache	96,833	Potawatomi	25,595
Blackfeet	85,750	Pueblo	74,085
Cherokee	729,533	Puget Sound Salish	14,631
Cheyenne	18,204	Seminole	27,431
Chickasaw	38,351	Shoshone	12,026
Chippewa	149,669	Sioux	153,360
Choctaw	158,774	Tohono O'odham	20,087
Colville	9,393	Ute	10,385
Comanche	19,376	Yakama	10,851
Cree	7,734	Yaqui	22,412
Creek	71,310	Yuman	8,976
Crow	13,394	Other specified American	
Delaware	16,341	Indian tribes	357,658
Houma	8,713	American Indian tribe, not specified	195,902
Iroquois	80,822	Alaska Athabascan	18,838
Kiowa	12,242	Aleut	16,978
Latin American Indian	180,940	Eskimo	54,761
Lumbee	57,868	Tlingit-Haida	22,365
Menominee	9,840	Other specified Alaska Native tribes	3,973
Navajo	298,197	Alaska Native tribe, not specified	8,702
Osage	15,897	American Indian or Alaska Native	
Ottawa	10,677	tribe, not specified	1,056,457
Paiute	13,532		

1. The numbers by American Indian and Alaska Native tribe do not add up to the total population figure because respondents may have put down more than one tribe. Respondents reporting several tribes are counted several times. 2. Total includes American Indian and Alaska Natives alone or in combination with other tribal groups or races. Indian and Alaskan Native population alone in 2000 was 2,475,956. *Source:* U.S. Census Bureau, Census 2000.

Most Populous Indian Reservations, 2000

Reservation	Population[1]
Navajo Nation (Ariz.-N.M.-Utah)	175,228
Cherokee (Okla.)	104,482
Creek (Okla.)	77,253
Lumbee (N.C.)	62,327
Choctaw (Okla.)	39,984
Cook Inlet (Alaska)	35,972
Chickasaw (Okla.)	32,372
Calista (Alaska)	20,353
United Houma Nation (La.)	15,305
Sealaska (Alaska)	15,059
Pine Ridge (S.D.-Neb.)	14,484
Doyon (Alaska)	14,128
Kiowa-Comanche-Apache-Fort Sill Apache (Okla.)	13,045
Fort Apache (Ariz.)	11,854
Citizen Band Potawatomi Nation–Absentee Shawnee (Okla.)	10,617
Gila River (Ariz.)	10,578
Cheyenne/Arapaho (Okla.)	10,310
Tohono O'odham (Ariz.)	9,794
Osage (Okla.)	9,209
Rosebud (S.D.)	9,165
San Carlos (Ariz.)	9,065
Blackfeet (Mont.)	8,684
Yakama (Wash.)	8,193
Turtle Mountain (N.D.)	8,043
Flathead (Mont.)	7,883

1. Population listed includes only the American Indian and Alaska Native population alone or in combination with one or more races. Total population of reservation, which includes non-Indians, is not given. A reservation's total population is sometimes significantly larger than Indian population. Source: U.S. Census Bureau, 2000 Census of Population and Housing, Profiles of General Demographic Characteristics.

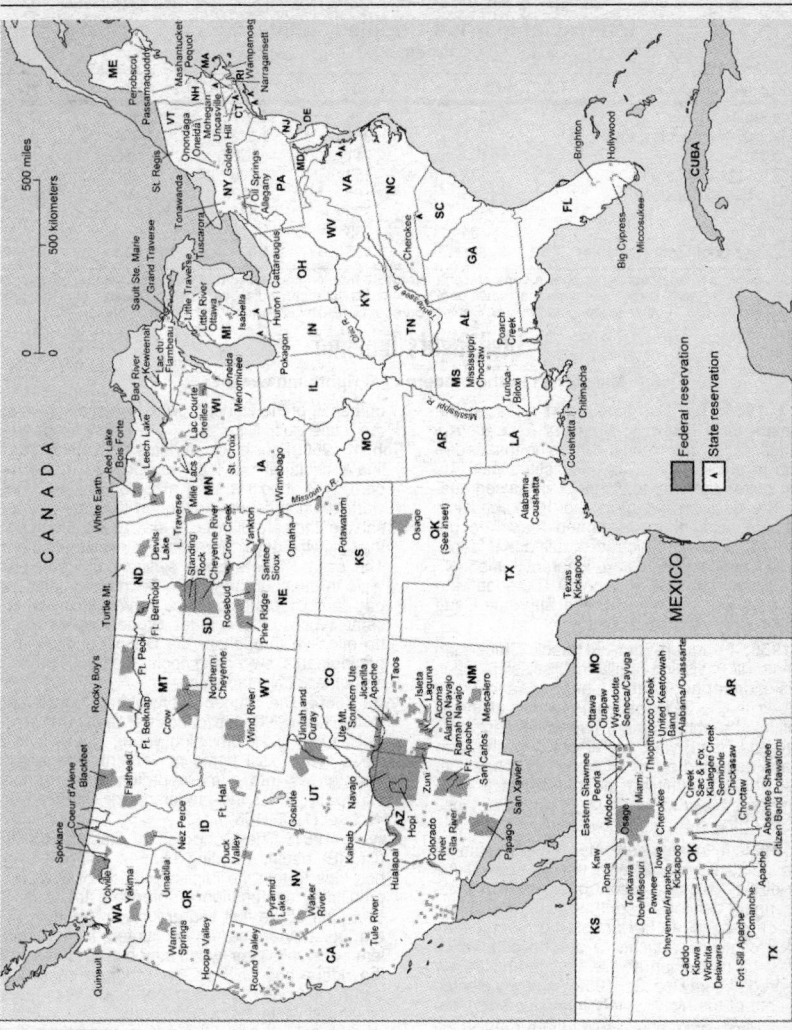

U.S. Federal and State Indian Reservations

Legend:
- Federal reservation
- ▲ State reservation

Interracial Married Couples, 1980–2000
(in thousands)

Race and origin of spouses	1980	1990	1995	2000	2002
Married couples, total[1]	49,714	53,256	54,937	56,497	57,919
Interracial married couples, total[2]	651	964	1,392	1,464	1,674
Black/White	167	211	328	363	395
Black husband/White wife	122	150	206	268	279
White husband/Black wife	45	61	122	95	116
White/other race[3]	450	720	988	1,051	1,222
Black/other race[3]	34	33	76	50	57
Hispanic/other origin (not Hispanic)	891	1,193	1,434	1,743	1,940

1. Includes other married couples not shown separately. 2. Interracial married couples with at least one spouse of white or black race. 3. "Other race" is any race other than white or black, such as American Indian, Japanese, Chinese, etc. This total excludes combinations of other races. *Source:* U.S. Census Bureau, *Statistical Abstract of the United States: 2003.*

Civil Rights Timeline
Milestones in the modern civil rights movement

May 17, 1954: The Supreme Court rules on the landmark case *Brown* v. *Board of Education of Topeka, Kans.,* unanimously agreeing that segregation in public schools is unconstitutional. The ruling paves the way for large-scale desegregation. The decision overturns the 1896 *Plessy* v. *Ferguson* ruling that sanctioned "separate but equal" segregation of the races, ruling that "separate educational facilities are inherently unequal." It is a victory for NAACP attorney Thurgood Marshall, who will later return to the Supreme Court as the nation's first black justice.

Aug. 1955: Fourteen-year-old black Chicagoan Emmett Till is visiting family in Mississippi when he is kidnapped, brutally beaten, shot, and dumped in the Tallahatchie River for allegedly whistling at a white woman. Two white men, J. W. Milam and Roy Bryant, are arrested for the murder and acquitted by an all-white jury. They later boast about committing the murder in a *Look* magazine interview. The case becomes a cause célèbre of the civil rights movement.

Dec. 1, 1955: In Montgomery, Ala., NAACP member Rosa Parks refuses to give up her seat at the front of the "colored section" of a bus to a white passenger, defying a southern custom of the time. In response to her arrest, the Montgomery black community launches a bus boycott, which will last for more than a year, until the buses are desegregated on Dec. 21, 1956. As newly elected president of the Montgomery Improvement Association (MIA), Reverend Martin Luther King, Jr., is instrumental in leading the boycott.

Jan.–Feb. 1957: Martin Luther King, Charles K. Steele, and Fred L. Shuttlesworth establish the Southern Christian Leadership Conference, of which King is made the first president. The SCLC becomes a major force in organizing the civil rights movement and bases its principles on nonviolence and civil disobedience. According to King, it is essential that the civil rights movement not sink to the level of the racists and hatemongers who oppose them: "We must forever conduct our struggle on the high plane of dignity and discipline," he urges.

Sept. 1957: In all-white Central High School in Little Rock, Ark., nine black students are blocked from entering the school on the orders of Governor Orval Faubus. President Eisenhower sends federal troops and the National Guard to intervene on behalf of the students, who become known as the "Little Rock Nine."

Feb. 1, 1960: Four black students from North Carolina Agricultural and Technical College in Greensboro, N.C., begin a sit-in at a segregated Woolworth's lunch counter. Although they are refused service, they are allowed to stay at the counter. In the following days, more black students join them. The event triggers many similar nonviolent protests throughout the South. Six months later the original four protesters are served lunch at the same Woolworth's counter. Student sit-ins would be effective throughout the Deep South in integrating parks, swimming pools, theaters, libraries, and other public facilities.

April 1960: The Student Nonviolent Coordinating Committee (SNCC) is founded at Shaw University in Raleigh, N.C., providing young blacks with a place in the civil rights movement. The SNCC later grows into a more radical organization, especially under the leadership of Stokely Carmichael (1966–1967).

May 4, 1961: The Congress of Racial Equality (CORE) begins sending student volunteers on bus trips to test the implementation of new laws prohibiting segregation in interstate travel facilities. One of the first two groups of "freedom riders," as they are called, encounters its first problem two weeks later, when a mob in Alabama sets the riders' bus on fire. The program continues, and by the end of the summer 1,000 volunteers, black and white, have participated.

Oct. 1, 1962: James Meredith becomes the first black student to enroll at the University of Mississippi. Violence and riots surrounding the incident cause President Kennedy to send 5,000 federal troops.

April 16, 1963: Martin Luther King is arrested and jailed during anti-segregation protests in Birmingham, Ala.; he writes his seminal "Letter From Birmingham City Jail," arguing that individuals have the moral duty to disobey unjust laws.

May 1963: During civil rights protests in Birmingham, Ala., Commissioner of Public Safety Eugene "Bull" Connor uses fire hoses and police dogs on black demonstrators. These images of brutality, which are televised and published widely, are instrumental in gaining sympathy for the civil rights movement around the world.

June 12, 1963: Mississippi's NAACP field secretary, 37-year-old Medgar Evers, is murdered outside his home in Jackson. Byron De La Beckwith is tried twice in 1964, both trials resulting in hung juries. Thirty years later he is convicted for murdering Evers.

Aug. 28, 1963: About 200,000 people join the March on Washington. Congregating at the Lincoln Memorial, in Washington, DC, participants listen as Martin Luther King delivers his famous "I Have a Dream" speech.

Sept. 15, 1963: Four young girls attending Sunday school in Birmingham, Ala., are killed when a bomb explodes at the Sixteenth Street Baptist Church, a popular location for civil rights meetings. Riots erupt in Birmingham, leading to the deaths of two more black youths.

Jan. 23, 1964: The 24th Amendment abolishes the poll tax, which originally had been instituted in 11 southern states after Reconstruction to make it difficult for poor blacks to vote.

Summer 1964: The Council of Federated Organizations (COFO), a network of civil rights groups that includes CORE and SNCC, launches a massive effort to register black voters during what becomes known as the Freedom Summer. It also sends delegates to the Democratic National Convention to protest—and attempt to unseat—the official all-white Mississippi contingent.

July 2, 1964: President Johnson signs the Civil Rights Act of 1964. The most sweeping civil rights legislation since Reconstruction, the Civil Rights Act prohibits discrimination of all kinds based on race, color, religion, or national origin. The law also provides the federal government with the powers to enforce desegregation.

Aug. 4, 1964: The bodies of three civil rights workers—two white, one black—are found in an earthen dam, six weeks into a federal investigation backed by President Johnson. James E. Chaney, 21; Andrew Goodman, 21; and Michael Schwerner, 24, had been working to register black voters in Mississippi, and, on June 21, had gone to investigate the burning of a black church. They were arrested by the police on speeding charges, incarcerated for several hours, and then released after dark into the hands of the Ku Klux Klan, who murdered them.

Feb. 21, 1965: Malcolm X, black nationalist and founder of the Organization of Afro-American Unity, is shot to death in Harlem. It is believed the assailants are members of the Black Muslim faith, which Malcolm had recently abandoned in favor of orthodox Islam.

March 7, 1965: Blacks begin a march from Selma, Ala., to Montgomery, Ala., in support of voting rights, but are stopped at the Pettus Bridge by a police blockade. Fifty marchers are hospitalized after police use tear gas, whips, and clubs against them. The incident is dubbed "Bloody Sunday" by the media.

Aug. 10, 1965: Congress passes the Voting Rights Act of 1965, making it easier for Southern blacks to register to vote. Literacy tests and other such requirements that were used to restrict black voting are made illegal.

Aug. 11–17, 1965: Race riots erupt in Watts, a black section of Los Angeles.

Sept. 24, 1965: Asserting that civil rights laws alone are not enough to remedy discrimination, President Johnson issues Executive Order 11246, which enforces affirmative action for the first time. It requires government contractors to "take affirmative action" toward prospective minority employees in all aspects of hiring and employment.

1966: The militant Black Panthers are founded in Oakland, Calif., by Huey Newton and Bobby Seale.

April 19, 1967: Stokely Carmichael, a leader of the Student Nonviolent Coordinating Committee (SNCC), coins the phrase "black power" in a speech in Seattle. He defines it as an assertion of black pride and "the coming together of black people to fight for their liberation by any means necessary." The term's radicalism alarms many who believe the civil rights movement's effectiveness and moral authority crucially depend on nonviolent civil disobedience.

June 12, 1967: In *Loving* v. *Virginia*, the Supreme Court rules that prohibiting interracial marriages is unconstitutional. Sixteen states that banned interracial marriage at the time are forced to revise their laws.

Summer 1967: Major race riots take place in Newark (July 12–16) and Detroit (July 23–30).

April 4, 1968: Martin Luther King, 39, is shot as he stands on the balcony outside his hotel room in Memphis, Tenn. Escaped convict and committed racist James Earl Ray is convicted of the crime.

April 11, 1968: President Johnson signs the Civil Rights Act of 1968, prohibiting discrimination in the sale, rental, and financing of housing.

April 20, 1971: The Supreme Court, in *Swann* v. *Charlotte-Mecklenburg Board of Education*, upholds busing as a legitimate means for achieving integration of public schools. Although largely unwelcome (and sometimes violently opposed) in local school districts, court-ordered busing plans in cities such as Charlotte, Boston, and Denver continue until the late 1990s.

June 28, 1978: In *Regents of the University of California* v. *Bakke*, the Supreme Court case imposed limitations on affirmative action, ruling that while race was a legitimate factor in school admissions, the use of inflexible quotas was not.

March 22, 1988: Overriding President Reagan's veto, Congress passes the Civil Rights Restoration Act, which expands the reach of nondiscrimination laws within private institutions receiving federal funds.

Nov. 22, 1991: After two years of debates, vetoes, and threatened vetoes, President Bush reverses himself and signs the Civil Rights Act of 1991, strengthening existing civil rights laws and providing for damages in cases of intentional employment discrimination.

April 29, 1992: The first race riots in decades erupt in south-central Los Angeles after a jury acquits four white police officers for the videotaped beating of African American Rodney King.

June 23, 2003: In the most important affirmative action decision since the 1978 *Bakke* case, the Supreme Court (5–4) upholds affirmative action in higher education, ruling that race can be one of many factors considered by colleges when selecting their students because it furthers "a compelling interest in obtaining the educational benefits that flow from a diverse student body."

Prisoners in the United States, 1990-2003

Year	Total inmates	Federal prisoners	State prisoners	Local jails
1990	1,148,702	58,838	684,544	405,320
1995	1,585,586	89,538	989,004	507,044
2000[1]	1,937,482	133,921	1,176,269	621,149
2003[1]	2,078,570	159,275	1,221,501	691,301

1. Total counts include federal inmates in non-secure privately operated facilities (6,143 in 2000 and 6,493 in 2003). *Source: Prison and Jail Inmates at Midyear 2003*, U.S. Bureau of Justice Statistics.

Federal Prison Inmates, by Most Serious Offense, 2001

Offense	Number of sentenced inmates in federal prisons	Offense	Number of sentenced inmates in federal prisons	Offense	Number of sentenced inmates in federal prisons
Total	**142,766**	Burglary	642	Immigration	15,012
Violent offenses	**16,117**	Fraud	7,617	Weapons	12,539
Homicide[1]	2,364	Other property	2,405	Other public-order	8,892
Robbery	10,218	**Drug offenses**	**78,501**	**Other/unknown[2]**	**1,041**
Other violent	3,535	**Public-order**			
Property offenses	**10,664**	**offenses**	**36,443**		

1. Includes murder, nonnegligent manslaughter, and negligent manslaughter. 2. Includes offenses not classifiable. *Source: Prisoners in 2002*, U.S. Bureau of Justice Statistics.

State Prison Inmates, by Offense, Gender, Race, and Hispanic Origin, 2001

Most serious offense	All	Male	Female	White	Black	Hispanic
Total	1,208,700	1,132,500	76,200	424,200	548,800	205,300
Violent offenses	596,100	571,700	24,400	208,100	267,800	102,600
Murder[1]	159,200	150,700	8,500	51,500	77,100	27,800
Manslaughter	16,900	15,000	1,900	6,300	6,300	3,500
Rape	30,900	30,600	300	15,100	11,700	2,700
Other sexual assault	87,600	86,600	1,000	50,700	21,300	12,600
Robbery	155,300	150,100	5,200	34,100	91,100	26,200
Assault	118,800	113,100	5,600	38,700	50,300	25,300
Other violent	27,400	25,500	1,900	11,700	10,000	4,700
Property offenses	233,000	213,100	20,000	101,800	92,300	32,500
Burglary	104,700	101,300	3,400	45,700	41,200	14,700
Larceny	45,500	39,600	5,800	17,400	20,300	6,100
Motor vehicle theft	18,000	17,300	700	6,900	6,700	4,200
Fraud	33,700	25,400	8,300	17,100	13,000	3,100
Other property	31,100	29,500	1,600	14,700	11,100	4,500
Drug offenses	246,100	222,900	23,200	57,300	139,700	47,000
Public-order offenses[2]	129,900	121,600	8,300	56,000	47,300	22,300
Other/unspecified[3]	3,600	3,200	400	900	1,700	800

NOTE: Data are for inmates with a sentence of more than one year under the jurisdiction of state correctional authorities. 1. Includes nonnegligent manslaughter. 2. Includes weapons, drunk driving, court offenses, commercialized vice, morals and decency charges, liquor law violations, and other public-order offenses. 3. Includes juvenile offenses and unspecified felonies. *Source: Prisoners in 2002*, U.S. Bureau of Justice Statistics.

Jail Inmates, by Offense, Gender, Race, and Hispanic Origin, 2002

Most serious offense	Total	Male	Female	White[1]	Black[1]	Hispanic
Number of jail inmates	**623,492**	**551,186**	**72,306**	**223,292**	**249,304**	**114,562**
Violent offenses	25.4%	26.5%	17.1%	21.8%	26.9%	27.1 %
Property offenses	24.4	23.3	32.4	28.1	24.0	17.5
Drug offenses	24.7	24.1	29.2	18.5	30.6	27.5
Public-order offenses	24.9	25.5	20.8	31.0	18.0	27.5
Other	0.5	0.5	0.6	0.7	0.4	n.a.
All offenses	**100.0**	**88.4**	**11.6**	**36.0**	**40.1**	**18.5**

NOTE: Excludes inmates whose offense was unknown. Racial statistics exclude 0.3% who did not specify a race. 1. Non-Hispanic. *Source: Profile of Jail Inmates, 2002*, U.S. Bureau of Justice Statistics.

Number of Persons Executed[1] by Jurisdiction, 1930–2003

State	Number executed since 1930	Number executed since 1977[2]	State	Number executed since 1930	Number executed since 1977[2]	State	Number executed since 1930	Number executed since 1977[2]
Texas	610	313	Oklahoma	129	69	Delaware	25	13
Georgia	400	34	Kentucky	105	2	Oregon	21	2
New York	329	0	Illinois	102	12	Connecticut	21	0
California	302	10	Tennessee	94	1	Utah	19	6
North Carolina	293	30	New Jersey	74	0	Iowa	18	0
Florida	227	57	Maryland	71	3	Kansas	15	0
South Carolina	190	28	Arizona	60	22	New Mexico	9	1
Virginia	181	89	Washington	51	4	Montana	8	2
Ohio	180	8	Indiana	52	11	Wyoming	8	1
Alabama	163	28	Colorado	48	1	Nebraska	7	3
Louisiana	160	27	District of Columbia	40	0	Idaho	4	1
Mississippi	160	6	West Virginia	40	0	Vermont	4	0
Pennsylvania	155	3	Nevada	39	9	New Hampshire	1	0
Arkansas	143	25	Federal system	36	3	South Dakota	1	0
Missouri	123	61	Massachusetts	27	0	**U.S. total**	**4,744**	**885**

NOTE: 65 people were executed in 2003. 1. Executed under civil authority; military authorities carried out an additional 160 executions, 1930–1997. 2. In 1972 the Supreme Court ruled that capital punishment, as it was then administered, was "cruel and unusual" and therefore unconstitutional. On July 1, 1976, however, the Court overturned the ruling by a 7–2 decision, and capital punishment was reinstated. *Source: Capital Punishment, 2003,* U.S. Bureau of Justice Statistics, and Death Penalty Information Center, www.deathpenaltyinfo.org.

Characteristics of Prisoners Under Sentence of Death

Characteristic	1980	1990	2000	Characteristic	1980	1990	2000
Race and age				**Marital status**			
White	418	1,368	1,990	Never married	268	998	1,749
Black and other	270	978	1,603	Married	229	632	739
Under 20 years	11	8	11	Divorced[1]	217	726	1,105
20 to 24 years	173	168	237	**Time elapsed since sentencing**			
25 to 34 years	334	1,110	1,103	Less than 12 months	185	231	208
35 to 54 years	186	1,006	2,019	12 to 47 months	389	753	786
55 years and over	10	64	223	48 to 71 months	102	438	507
Years of schooling completed				72 months and over	38	934	2,092
7 years or less	68	178	214	**Legal status at arrest**			
8 years	74	186	233	Not under sentence	384	1,345	2,202
9 to 11 years	204	775	1,157	Parole or probation[2]	115	578	921
12 years	162	729	1,184	Prison or escaped	45	128	126
More than 12 years	43	209	315	Unknown	170	305	344
Unknown	163	279	490	**Total**	**688**	**2,346**	**3,593**

NOTE: Excludes prisoners under sentence of death confined in local correctional systems pending appeal or who have not been committed to prison. 1. Includes persons married but separated, widows, widowers, and unknown. 2. Includes persons on mandatory conditional release, work release, leave, AWOL, or bail. *Source:* U.S. Bureau of Justice Statistics, *Capital Punishment,* annual, from *Statistical Abstract of the United States, 2003.*

Death Row Exonerations, 1973–2004[1]

Between 1973 and Feb. 2004, 113 inmates on death row have been exonerated and freed. The most common reasons for wrongful convictions are mistaken eyewitness testimony, the false testimony of informants and "incentivized witnesses," incompetent lawyers, defective or fraudulent scientific evidence, prosecutorial and police misconduct, and false confessions. In recent years, DNA played a role in overturning 12 of these wrongful death row convictions.

State	Number	State	Number	State	Number	State	Number
Florida	23	Pennsylvania	5	South Carolina	3	Nebraska	1
Illinois	17	New Mexico	4	Indiana	2	Nevada	1
Oklahoma	7	North Carolina	4	Massachusetts	2	Virginia	1
Texas	7	Ohio	4	Idaho	1	Washington	1
Arizona	6	Alabama	3	Kentucky	1	**Total**	**102**
Georgia	6	California	3	Maryland	1		
Louisiana	6	Missouri	3	Mississippi	1		

1. Latest release recorded, Alan Gell, Feb. 18, 2004. *Source:* The Death Penalty Information Center, www.deathpenaltyinfo.org.

Methods of Execution Used in Capital Punishment

State	Minimum age	Method	State	Minimum age	Method
Alabama	16	Lethal injection or electrocution	Nebraska	18	Electrocution
Alaska	—	No death penalty	Nevada	16	Lethal injection
Arizona[1, 2]	16	Lethal injection or gas	New Hampshire[8]	17	Lethal injection or hanging
Arkansas[3]	14	Lethal injection or electrocution	New Jersey	18	Lethal injection
California	18	Lethal injection or gas	New Mexico	18	Lethal injection
Colorado	18	Lethal injection	New York	18	Lethal injection
Connecticut	18	Lethal injection	North Carolina[9]	17	Lethal injection
Delaware[4]	16	Lethal injection or hanging	North Dakota	—	No death penalty
DC	—	No death penalty	Ohio	18	Lethal injection
Florida	17	Lethal injection or electrocution	Oklahoma[10]	16	Lethal injection, electrocution, or firing squad
Georgia	17	Lethal injection			
Hawaii	—	No death penalty	Oregon	18	Lethal injection
Idaho[2]	16	Lethal injection or firing squad	Pennsylvania[2]	16	Lethal injection
Illinois	18	Lethal injection	Rhode Island	—	No death penalty
Indiana	18	Lethal injection	South Carolina[2]	16	Lethal injection or electrocution
Iowa	—	No death penalty	South Dakota[2, 11]	16	Lethal injection
Kansas	18	Lethal injection	Tennessee[12]	18	Lethal injection or electrocution
Kentucky[5]	16	Lethal injection or electrocution	Texas	17	Lethal injection
Louisiana[2]	16	Lethal injection	Utah[6]	16	Lethal injection or firing squad
Maine	—	No death penalty	Vermont	—	No death penalty
Maryland	18	Lethal injection	Virginia[6]	16	Lethal injection or electrocution
Massachusetts	—	No death penalty	Washington	18	Lethal injection or hanging
Michigan	—	No death penalty	West Virginia	—	No death penalty
Minnesota	—	No death penalty	Wisconsin	—	No death penalty
Mississippi[6]	16	Lethal injection	Wyoming[13]	16	Lethal injection or gas
Missouri	16	Lethal injection or gas	Federal system[14]	18	Lethal injection
Montana[2, 7]	18	Lethal injection			

1. For those sentenced after 11/15/92, only lethal injection is authorized. 2. No minimum age by statute; 16 under U.S. Supreme Court ruling. 3. For those whose capital offense occurred on or after 7/4/83, only lethal injection is authorized. 4. For those whose capital offense occurred after 6/13/86, only lethal injection is authorized. 5. For those sentenced on or after 3/31/98, only lethal injection is authorized. 6. Minimum age defined by statute is 13 for Miss., and 14 for Utah and Va.; the effective age is 16 based on the states' interpretation of U.S. Supreme Court decisions. 7. Minimum age is 18 for capital sexual assault; age may be a mitigating factor for other capital crimes. 8. Hanging is authorized only if lethal injection cannot be given. 9. Minimum age is 14 if the person was already incarcerated for murder when the subsequent murder occurred. 10. Electrocution is authorized if lethal injection is ever held to be unconstitutional, and firing squad if both lethal injection and electrocution are held unconstitutional. 11. Juveniles may be transferred to adult court, but age can be a mitigating factor. 12. For those whose capital offense occurred after 12/31/98, only lethal injection is authorized. 13. Lethal gas is authorized if lethal injection is ever held to be unconstitutional. 14. For offenses under the Violent Crime Control and Law Enforcement Act of 1994, the method is that of the state in which the conviction took place. *Source: Capital Punishment, 2002,* U.S. Bureau of Justice Statistics, and the Death Penalty Information Center.

Federal Prosecutions of Public Corruption

Prosecution status	2001	2000	1999	1997	1996	1995	1994	1990	1985	1980
Total: Indicted	1,087	1,000	1,134	1,057	984	1,051	1,165	1,176	1,157	727
Convicted	920	938	1,065	853	902	878	969	1,084	997	602
Federal officials: Indicted	502	441	480	459	456	527	571	615	563	123
Convicted	414	422	460	392	459	438	488	583	470	131
State officials: Indicted	95	92	115	51	109	61	99	96	79	72
Convicted	61	91	80	49	83	61	97	79	66	51
Local officials: Indicted	224	211	237	255	219	236	248	257	248	247
Convicted	184	183	219	169	190	191	202	225	221	168

NOTE: Figures are latest available. *Source:* U.S. Department of Justice, *Federal Prosecutions of Corrupt Public Officials, 1970–1980,* and *Report to Congress on the Activities and Operations of the Public Integrity Section,* annual. From *Statistical Abstract of the United States, 2003.*

Law Enforcement Officers Killed or Assaulted[1]

	2001	2000	1999	1997	1996	1995	1994	1993	1990	1985	1980
Total officers killed	**220**	**135**	**107**	**132**	**112**	**133**	**141**	**129**	**133**	**145**	**164**
Officers assaulted											
Firearm	1,837	1,749	1,783	2,110	1,878	2,354	3,174	3,880	3,651	2,793	3,295
Knife or cutting instrument	1,176	1,015	990	971	871	1,356	1,510	1,486	1,647	1,715	1,653
Other dangerous weapon	8,190	8,132	7,392	5,800	5,069	6,414	7,197	7,155	7,423	5,263	5,415
Hands, fists, feet, etc.	45,463	47,502	44,861	43,268	38,790	47,638	53,086	50,412	59,370	51,953	47,484
Total assaulted	**56,666**	**58,398**	**55,026**	**52,149**	**46,608**	**57,762**	**64,967**	**62,933**	**72,091**	**61,724**	**57,847**

1. Covers officers killed feloniously and accidentally in line of duty; includes federal officers. NOTE: Data are latest available. *Source:* U.S. Federal Bureau of Investigation, *Law Enforcement Officers Killed and Assaulted,* annual. From *Statistical Abstract of the United States, 2003.*

Homicide Rate (per 100,000), 1950–2002

Year	Homicide rate	Year	Homicide rate	Year	Homicide rate	Year	Homicide rate	Year	Homicide rate
1950	4.6	1961	4.8	1972	9.0	1983	8.3	1994	9.0
1951	4.4	1962	4.6	1973	9.4	1984	7.9	1995	8.2
1952	4.6	1963	4.6	1974	9.8	1985	7.9	1996	7.4
1953	4.5	1964	4.9	1975	9.6	1986	8.6	1997	6.8
1954	4.2	1965	5.1	1976	8.8	1987	8.3	1998	6.3
1955	4.1	1966	5.6	1977	8.8	1988	8.4	1999	5.7
1956	4.1	1967	6.2	1978	9.0	1989	8.7	2000	5.5
1957	4.0	1968	6.9	1979	9.7	1990	9.4	2001	5.6
1958	4.8	1969	7.3	1980	10.2	1991	9.8	2002	5.6
1959	4.9	1970	7.9	1981	9.8	1992	9.3		
1960	5.1	1971	8.6	1982	9.1	1993	9.5		

Source: Crime in the United States, 2002, FBI, Uniform Crime Reports.

Murder Victims: by Race and Sex, 2002

Race and sex	Total no. victims	Percent distribution[1]	Race and sex	Total no. victims	Percent distribution[1]
Race			**Sex**		
White	6,757	48.1%	Male	10,779	76.7%
Black	6,730	47.9	Female	3,251	23.1
Other	377	2.7	Unknown	24	0.2
Unknown	190	1.4	**Total**	**14,054**	**100.0**

1. Because of rounding, percentages may not add up to 100. *Source: Crime in the United States, 2002*, FBI, Uniform Crime Reports.

Murder Victims: Types of Weapon Used, 2002

Type of weapon	Total no. victims	Percent distribution[1]	Type of weapon	Total no. victims	Percent distribution[1]
Firearms	9,369	66.7%	Explosives	11	0.1%
Knives or cutting instruments	1,767	12.6	Fire	104	0.7
Blunt objects (clubs, hammers, etc.)	666	4.7	Narcotics	48	0.3
			Strangulation	143	1.0
Personal weapons (hands, fists, feet, etc.)[2]	933	6.6	Asphyxiation	103	0.7
			Other weapon or not stated[3]	887	6.3
Poison	23	0.2	**Total**	**14,054**	**100.0**

1. Because of rounding, percentages may not add up to 100. 2. Pushed is included in personal weapons. 3. Includes drowning. *Source: Crime in the United States, 2002*, FBI, Uniform Crime Reports.

Murderers, by Sex and Race, 2002

Race and sex	Total no. murders	Percent distribution[1]	Race and sex	Total no. murders	Percent distribution[1]
Race			**Sex**		
White	5,356	33.9%	Male	10,285	65.0%
Black	5,579	35.3	Female	1,108	7.0
Other	274	1.7	Unknown	4,420	28.0
Unknown	4,604	29.1	**Total**	**15,813**	**100.0**

1. Because of rounding, percentages may not add up to 100. *Source: Crime in the United States, 2002*, FBI, Uniform Crime Reports.

Violent Crime Victimization Rates, 1993–2001

	Number of crime victims per 1,000 persons age 12 or older				Percent change, 1993–2001
	1993	1997	2000	2001	
Gender					
Male	59.8	45.8	32.9	27.3	−54.3%
Female	40.7	33.0	23.2	23.0	−43.5
Race and ethnicity					
White	47.9	38.3	27.1	24.5	−48.9
Black	67.4	49.0	35.3	31.2	−53.7
Hispanic	55.2	43.1	28.4	29.5	−46.6
Other	39.8	28.0	20.7	18.2	−54.3

NOTE: These rates are based on the collection year. Thus, the 1993, 1994, and 1995 rates differ from rates published in *Changes in Criminal Victimization, 1994–95* (March 1997, NCJ, 162032), which are based on data years. *Source: Criminal Victimization 2001*, U.S. Dept. of Justice.

Summary of Hate Crime Statistics, 2002

	Number of incidents	Number of offenses	Number of victims	Number of known offenders
Race	3,642	4,393	4,580	4,011
Anti-white	719	888	910	1,064
Anti-black	2,486	2,967	3,076	2,510
Anti-American Indian/Alaskan Native	62	68	72	52
Anti-Asian/Pacific Islander	217	268	280	242
Anti-multi-racial group	158	202	242	143
Ethnicity/national origin	1,102	1,345	1,409	1,247
Anti-Hispanic	480	601	639	656
Anti-other ethnicity/national origin	622	744	770	591
Religion	1,426	1,576	1,659	568
Anti-Jewish	931	1,039	1,084	317
Anti-Catholic	53	58	71	21
Anti-Protestant	55	57	58	34
Anti-Islamic	155	170	174	103
Anti-other religious group	198	217	237	73
Anti-multi-religious group	31	32	32	18
Anti-atheism/agnosticism/etc.	3	3	3	2
Sexual orientation	1,244	1,464	1,513	1,438
Anti-male homosexual	825	957	984	1,022
Anti-female homosexual	172	207	221	172
Anti-homosexual	222	259	267	225
Anti-heterosexual	10	26	26	6
Anti-bisexual	15	15	15	13
Disability	45	47	50	47
Anti-physical	20	20	20	21
Anti-mental	25	27	30	26
Multiple-bias incidents[1]	3	7	11	3
Total	7,642	8,832	9,222	7,314

1. A *multiple-bias incident* is a hate crime in which two or more offense types were committed as a result of two or more bias motivations. *Source: Crime in the United States, 2002,* FBI, Uniform Crime Reports.

Index of Crime, United States, 1979–2002

(rate per 100,000 inhabitants)

Year	Crime index total	Violent crime[1]	Prop- erty crime[2]	Murder and non- negligent man- slaughter	Forcible rape	Robbery	Aggra- vated assault	Burglary	Larceny- theft	Motor vehicle theft
1979	5,565.5	548.9	5,016.6	9.7	34.7	218.4	286.0	1,511.9	2,999.1	505.6
1980	5,950.0	596.6	5,353.3	10.2	36.8	251.1	298.5	1,684.1	3,167.0	502.2
1981	5,858.2	594.3	5,263.9	9.8	36.0	258.7	289.7	1,649.5	3,139.7	474.7
1982	5,603.6	571.1	5,032.5	9.1	34.0	238.9	289.2	1,488.8	3,084.8	458.8
1983	5,175.0	537.7	4,637.4	8.3	33.7	216.5	279.2	1,337.7	2,868.9	430.8
1984	5,031.3	539.2	4,492.1	7.9	35.7	205.4	290.2	1,263.7	2,791.3	437.1
1985	5,207.1	556.6	4,650.5	8.0	37.1	208.5	302.9	1,287.3	2,901.2	462.0
1986	5,480.4	617.7	4,862.6	8.6	37.9	225.1	346.1	1,344.6	3,010.3	507.8
1987	5,550.0	609.7	4,940.3	8.3	37.4	212.7	351.3	1,329.6	3,081.3	529.4
1988	5,664.2	637.2	5,027.1	8.4	37.6	220.9	370.2	1,309.2	3,134.9	582.9
1989	5,741.0	663.1	5,077.9	8.7	38.1	233.0	383.4	1,276.3	3,171.3	630.4
1990	5,820.3	731.8	5,088.5	9.4	41.2	257.0	424.1	1,235.9	3,194.8	657.8
1991	5,897.8	758.1	5,139.7	9.8	42.3	272.7	433.3	1,252.0	3,228.8	659.0
1992	5,660.2	757.5	4,902.7	9.3	42.8	263.6	441.8	1,168.2	3,103.0	631.5
1993	5,484.4	746.8	4,737.6	9.5	41.1	255.9	440.3	1,099.2	3,032.4	606.1
1994	5,373.5	713.6	4,660.0	9.0	39.3	237.7	427.6	1,042.0	3,026.7	591.3
1995	5,275.9	684.6	4,591.3	8.2	37.1	220.9	418.3	987.1	3,043.8	560.4
1996	5,086.6	636.5	4,450.1	7.4	36.3	201.9	390.9	944.8	2,797.7	525.6
1997	4,930.0	611.3	4,318.7	6.8	35.9	186.3	382.3	919.4	2,893.4	506.0
1998	4,619.3	567.5	4,051.8	6.3	34.5	165.4	361.3	863.0	2,729.0	459.8
1999	4,266.8	524.7	3,742.1	5.7	32.7	150.2	336.1	770.0	2,551.4	420.7
2000	4,124.0	506.1	3,617.9	5.5	32.0	144.9	323.6	728.4	2,475.3	414.2
2001	4,160.5	504.4	3,656.1	5.6	31.8	148.5	318.5	740.8	2,484.6	430.6
2002	4,118.8	494.6	3,624.1	5.6	33.0	145.9	310.1	746.2	2,445.8	432.1

1. Violent crimes are offenses of murder, forcible rape, robbery, and aggravated assault. 2. Property crimes are offenses of burglary, larceny-theft, and motor vehicle theft. Data are not included for the property crime of arson. *Source: Crime in the United States,* 2002, FBI, Uniform Crime Reports.

Arrests by Race, 2002

Offense charged	Percent distribution[1]				Offense charged	Percent distribution[1]			
	White	Black	American Indian or Alaskan Native	Asian or Pacific Islander		White	Black	American Indian or Alaskan Native	Asian or Pacific Islander
Total	71.5%	25.7%	1.3%	1.6%	Sex offenses, except forcible rape and prostitution	72.1%	26.0%	0.8%	1.2%
Murder[2]	45.9	50.1	2.4	1.6	Drug abuse violation	73.2	24.9	0.9	1.0
Forcible rape	62.0	36.0	1.1	1.0	Gambling	11.4	85.7		2.9
Robbery	38.6	58.9	0.5	2.0	Offenses against family and children	73.8	23.5	0.9	1.8
Aggravated assault	60.8	36.7	1.2	1.3	Driving under the influence	93.3	4.1	1.8	0.8
Burglary	72.4	25.2	1.1	1.3	Liquor laws	92.2	4.4	2.5	0.9
Larceny-theft	70.1	26.5	1.4	2.1	Drunkenness	90.0	7.4	1.9	0.7
Motor vehicle theft	58.3	38.3	1.4	2.0	Disorderly conduct	63.9	34.0	1.2	0.8
Arson	80.7	17.6	0.8	0.9	Vagrancy	75.6	22.8	0.9	0.7
Other assaults	62.9	34.7	1.2	1.2	All other offenses except traffic	74.9	22.3	1.2	1.6
Forgery and counterfeiting	78.1	19.5	0.9	1.5	Suspicion	69.7	28.2	0.6	1.5
Fraud	66.1	32.0	0.7	1.2	Curfew and loitering law violations	68.6	28.8	1.1	1.5
Embezzlement	69.3	28.6	0.1	2.0	Runaways	75.8	18.4	1.3	4.5
Stolen property—buying, receiving, possessing	56.5	41.4	0.7	1.4					
Vandalism	81.0	16.6	1.2	1.2					
Weapons possession	67.1	30.7	0.8	1.3					
Prostitution	43.8	54.6	0.5	1.1					

NOTE: For arrests 18 years and older. Total number of estimated arrests: 13.7 million. 1. Because of rounding, the percentages may not add up to total. 2. Includes nonnegligent manslaughter. *Source: Crime in the United States, 2002,* FBI, Uniform Crime Reports.

Crime Index by State, 2002

State	Crime index total		Violent crime	Property crime	Murder[1]	State	Crime index total		Violent crime	Property crime	Murder[1]
	Number	Rate per 100,000					Number	Rate per 100,000			
Ala.	200,331	4,465.2	19,931	180,400	303	Mont.	31,948	3,512.9	3,197	28,751	16
Alaska	27,745	4,309.7	3,627	24,118	33	Nebr.	73,606	4,256.7	5,248	68,178	48
Ariz.	348,467	6,386.3	30,171	318,296	387	Nev.	97,752	4,497.5	13,856	83,896	181
Ark.	112,672	4,157.5	11,501	101,171	142	N.H.	28,306	2,220.0	2,056	26,250	12
Calif.	1,384,872	3,943.7	208,388	1,176,484	2,395	N.J.	259,789	3,024.2	32,168	227,621	337
Colo.	195,936	4,347.8	15,882	180,054	179	N.M.	94,196	5,077.8	13,719	80,477	152
Conn.	103,719	2,997.2	10,767	92,952	80	N.Y.	537,121	2,803.7	95,030	442,091	909
Del.	31,803	3,939.0	4,836	26,967	26	N.C.	392,826	4,721.4	39,118	353,708	548
DC	45,799	8,022.3	9,322	36,477	264	N.D.	15,258	2,406.2	496	14,762	5
Fla.	905,957	5,420.6	128,721	777,236	911	Ohio	469,104	4,107.3	40,128	428,976	526
Ga.	385,830	4,507.2	39,271	346,559	606	Okla.	165,715	4,743.2	17,587	148,128	163
Hawaii	75,238	6,043.7	3,262	71,976	24	Ore.	171,443	4,868.4	10,298	161,145	72
Idaho	42,547	3,172.5	3,419	39,128	36	Pa.	350,446	2,841.0	49,578	300,868	624
Ill.[2]	506,086	4,016.4	78,214	427,872	949	P.R.	90,783	2,352.6	13,471	77,312	774
Ind.	230,966	3,750.0	22,001	208,965	362	R.I.	38,393	3,589.1	3,051	35,342	41
Iowa	101,265	3,448.2	8,388	92,877	44	S.C.	217,569	5,297.3	33,761	183,808	298
Kans.	110,997	4,087.0	10,229	100,768	78	S.D.	17,342	2,278.7	1,350	15,992	11
Ky.[2]	118,799	2,902.6	11,418	107,381	184	Tenn.	290,961	5,018.0	41,562	249,399	420
La.	228,528	5,098.1	29,690	198,838	593	Tex.	1,130,292	5,189.6	126,018	1,004,274	1,302
Maine	34,381	2,656.0	1,396	32,985	14	Utah	103,129	4,452.4	5,488	97,641	47
Md.	259,120	4,747.4	42,015	217,105	513	Vt.	15,600	2,530.0	658	14,942	13
Mass.	198,890	3,094.2	31,137	167,753	173	Va.	229,039	3,140.3	21,256	207,783	388
Mich.	389,366	3,874.1	54,306	335,060	678	Wash.	309,931	5,106.8	20,964	288,967	184
Minn.	177,454	3,535.1	13,428	164,026	112	W. Va.	45,320	2,515.2	4,221	41,099	57
Miss.	119,442	4,159.2	9,858	109,584	264	Wisc.	176,987	3,252.7	12,238	164,749	154
Mo.	261,077	4,602.4	30,557	230,520	331	Wyo.	17,858	3,580.9	1,364	16,494	15

NOTE: The Crime Index is composed of the violent and property crime categories. Violent crimes are murder, forcible rape, robbery, and aggravated assault. Property crimes are burglary, larceny-theft, and motor vehicle theft. Data are not included for the property crime of arson. 1. Includes nonnegligent manslaughter. 2. Limited data for 2002 were available for the states of Illinois and Kentucky; therefore, it was necessary that their crime counts be estimated. *Source: Crime in the United States, 2002,* FBI, Uniform Crime Reports.

Crime Rates for Selected Large Cities, 2001
(offenses known to the police per 100,000 inhabitants)

City ranked by population size, 2001[1]	Crime index, total	Violent crime				Property crime		
		Murder	Forcible rape	Robbery	Aggravated assault	Burglary	Larceny-theft	Motor vehicle theft
New York, N.Y.	3,286.7	8.2	19.1	351.5	471.3	393.4	1,669.4	373.8
Los Angeles, Calif.	5,029.3	15.6	37.4	456.1	879.0	682.7	2,113.0	845.5
Chicago, Ill.	(2)	22.9	(2)	633.3	877.2	892.1	3,349.6	951.5
Houston, Tex.	7,106.6	13.4	47.3	496.6	614.9	1,256.7	3,472.1	1,205.7
Philadelphia, Pa.	6,183.1	20.4	66.8	632.5	690.0	765.9	2,984.8	1,022.7
Phoenix, Ariz.	7,681.8	15.3	29.3	338.7	387.4	1,220.1	4,038.7	1,652.3
San Diego, Calif.	4,048.0	4.0	27.4	138.7	424.0	579.3	2,010.2	864.3
Dallas, Tex.	9,132.1	19.7	54.3	685.3	703.1	1,697.6	4,410.4	1,561.8
San Antonio, Tex.	8,243.3	8.5	42.0	183.3	581.6	1,197.5	5,697.3	533.0
Las Vegas, Nev.	4,524.2	11.9	40.0	328.1	295.4	902.1	2,003.5	943.3
Detroit, Mich.	9,431.6	41.3	68.2	742.0	1,338.9	1,578.6	3,096.7	2,565.9
San Jose, Calif.	2,754.5	2.4	36.0	77.9	492.7	321.7	1,485.1	338.6
Honolulu, Hawaii	5,469.9	2.3	33.1	112.8	128.8	828.8	3,732.1	632.0
Indianapolis, Ind.	5,143.5	14.0	55.4	349.1	512.0	1,132.9	2,283.0	797.1
San Francisco, Calif.	5,592.1	7.8	28.6	481.3	339.8	831.7	3,085.8	817.1
Jacksonville, Fla.	6,791.0	9.9	38.0	290.9	640.1	1,312.2	3,819.8	680.0
Columbus, Ohio	9,617.3	11.4	84.5	472.0	329.6	2,208.4	5,448.6	1,062.9
Austin, Tex.	6,470.8	3.9	40.8	176.2	252.9	1,112.6	4,384.8	499.7
Baltimore, Md.	9,607.4	38.7	44.8	869.7	1,286.3	1,649.3	4,481.5	1,237.1
Memphis, Tenn.	10,016.2	24.2	74.6	662.1	901.8	2,426.9	4,468.8	1,457.7
Charlotte-Mecklenburg, N.C.	7,817.8	10.4	46.0	470.7	694.5	1,616.0	4,287.9	692.3
Milwaukee, Wisc.	7,609.1	21.1	49.1	484.5	353.9	1,111.1	4,276.6	1,312.8
Boston, Mass.	6,315.6	11.0	61.0	426.2	745.3	713.2	2,974.6	1,384.3
El Paso, Tex.	5,345.4	3.5	35.2	134.4	587.7	442.9	3,823.2	318.5
Seattle, Wash.	8,053.0	4.4	28.7	278.5	413.6	1,167.8	4,630.4	1,529.7
Washington, DC	7,761.7	40.4	31.7	660.5	874.9	865.1	3,895.3	1,393.8
Denver, Colo.	5,314.1	7.9	55.6	219.4	256.6	990.4	2,566.7	1,217.4
Nashville, Tenn.	9,034.0	11.0	74.4	451.1	1,095.6	1,412.8	5,018.9	970.2
Fort Worth, Tex.	7,400.1	12.3	60.7	254.0	379.6	1,457.7	4,512.4	723.4
Portland, Ore.	8,040.3	3.9	56.8	235.9	551.7	1,041.2	5,280.0	870.8
Oklahoma City, Okla.	9,039.1	8.9	79.8	214.8	520.8	1,656.1	5,866.0	692.8
Tucson, Ariz.	9,883.0	8.3	63.8	337.3	548.6	1,301.6	6,200.5	1,423.0
New Orleans, La.	7,445.3	44.0	43.2	573.6	552.8	1,086.5	3,342.4	1,802.8
Cleveland, Ohio	6,899.1	16.1	130.2	688.1	506.0	1,656.1	2,696.8	1,205.8
Long Beach, Calif.	3,928.5	10.4	26.6	301.4	387.6	687.5	1,675.4	839.4
Albuquerque, N.M.	8,765.5	7.5	48.5	356.9	752.8	1,459.8	5,217.3	922.6
Kansas City, Mo.	11,245.3	23.2	71.8	532.8	966.1	1,677.8	6,105.8	1,867.8
Fresno, Calif.	7,961.2	9.2	46.4	312.7	572.1	1,194.4	4,223.6	1,603.3
Virginia Beach, Va.	3,749.0	2.8	25.7	84.8	80.8	530.1	2,808.6	216.3
Atlanta, Ga.	12,237.4	33.5	86.0	1,017.8	1,396.4	2,047.1	6,030.6	1,626.0
Sacramento, Calif.	7,402.9	9.6	40.8	347.3	400.4	1,222.4	3,853.8	1,528.5
Mesa, Ariz.	6,708.8	4.1	25.9	110.2	473.4	1,051.9	3,931.7	1,111.6
Oakland, Calif.	6,789.5	20.6	72.5	522.2	694.5	908.3	3,214.7	1,356.6
Tulsa, Okla.	7,447.9	8.6	65.0	196.9	883.2	1,487.6	3,884.0	922.5
Omaha, Neb.	7,557.1	6.4	40.2	223.3	424.6	795.7	4,963.9	1,103.8
Minneapolis, Minn.	6,935.1	11.1	103.2	502.4	443.7	1,058.1	3,761.8	1,054.8
Miami, Fla.	9,490.3	17.7	31.7	731.2	1,158.2	1,672.1	4,473.4	1,405.9
Colorado Springs, Colo.	5,034.8	3.8	61.5	117.6	302.7	809.4	3,378.6	361.2
St. Louis, Mo.	15,024.1	42.2	34.3	896.3	1,214.8	2,320.1	7,992.3	2,524.1
Wichita, Kans.	6,827.7	4.9	53.0	215.0	435.0	1,281.4	4,333.2	505.1
Santa Ana, Calif.	3,504.9	7.0	16.0	273.6	239.1	405.5	1,819.3	744.5
Pittsburgh, Pa.	5,772.5	16.1	39.2	405.4	407.4	950.8	3,153.4	800.2
Arlington, Tex.	7,209.7	4.4	42.6	201.7	376.5	1,043.1	4,799.9	741.5
Anaheim, Calif.	3,359.7	2.4	27.2	144.9	219.4	538.1	1,894.0	533.7
Cincinnati, Ohio	8,262.9	16.9	97.3	631.3	461.9	1,880.5	4,201.5	973.5
Toledo, Ohio	8,627.1	5.7	58.9	417.6	488.6	2,004.9	4,457.9	1,193.6
Tampa, Fla.	11,194.0	10.9	68.1	757.8	1,288.4	1,958.2	5,006.6	2,104.0
Buffalo, N.Y.	6,785.4	21.8	78.1	545.7	619.4	1,352.4	3,297.9	870.1
St. Paul, Minn.	6,562.3	3.1	76.1	234.3	456.9	1,036.7	3,947.5	807.6
Aurora, Colo.	5,953.7	6.0	68.7	166.3	326.6	642.5	3,698.4	1,045.2
Corpus Christi, Tex.	7,941.5	6.7	78.9	205.1	578.0	1,409.3	5,129.5	533.9
Raleigh, N.C.	6,618.8	3.6	32.4	286.3	456.6	1,418.5	3,948.5	472.9
Newark, N.J.	6,797.1	32.6	33.0	666.0	659.5	925.2	2,292.8	2,188.0
Anchorage, Alaska	5,013.1	3.8	79.7	145.7	434.0	609.3	3,280.9	459.8
Lexington, Ky.	4,973.2	9.2	45.8	275.1	274.0	960.1	3,112.1	296.9

1. Resident population estimated by the U.S. Census Bureau. 2. The rates for forcible rape and crime index are not shown because the forcible rape figures were not in accordance with national Uniform Crime Reporting guidelines. *Source:* U.S. FBI, *Crime in the United States,* annual. From *Statistical Abstract of the United States, 2003.*

Iraq War Timeline

Jan. 29, 2002: In his State of the Union address, President Bush calls Iraq part of an "axis of evil," and vows that the U.S. "will not permit the world's most dangerous regimes to threaten us with the world's most destructive weapons."

June 2: President Bush publicly introduces the new defense doctrine of preemption in a speech at West Point. Sometimes, he asserts, the U.S. must strike first against another state to prevent a potential threat from growing into an actual one.

Sept. 12: President Bush addresses the UN, challenging it to swiftly enforce its own resolutions against Iraq. If not, Bush contends, the U.S. must act on its own.

Oct. 11: Congress authorizes an attack on Iraq.

Nov. 8: The UN Security Council unanimously approves resolution 1441 imposing tough new arms inspections on Iraq.

Nov. 18: UN weapons inspectors return to Iraq for the first time in almost four years.

Jan. 28, 2003: In his State of the Union address, President Bush announces that he is ready to attack Iraq even without a UN mandate.

Feb. 14: An UN weapons inspections report on Iraq, chief inspector Hans Blix indicates that slight progress has been made in Iraq's cooperation with the weapons team.

Feb. 24–March 14: The U.S. and Britain's lobbying efforts among UN Security Council members to garner support for a strike on Iraq yield only two supporters (Spain and Bulgaria).

March 20: The war against Iraq begins 5:30 a.m. Baghdad time (9:30 p.m. EST, March 19), when the U.S. launches Operation Iraqi Freedom.

March 21: The major phase of the war begins with heavy aerial attacks on Baghdad and other cities. The campaign, publicized in advance by the Pentagon as an overwhelming barrage meant to instill "shock and awe," is actually more restrained.

March 24: Troops march within 50 miles of Baghdad. They encounter strong resistance from Iraqi soldiers and paramilitary fighters along the way.

March 26: About 1,000 paratroopers land in Kurdish-controlled Iraq to open a northern front.

March 30: U.S. Marines and Army troops launch first attack on Iraq's Republican Guard, about 65 miles outside Baghdad. Secretary of Defense Donald Rumsfeld deflects criticism that the U.S. has not deployed enough Army ground troops in Iraq.

April 2: Special operations forces rescue Pfc. Jessica Lynch from a hospital in Nasiriya. She was one of 12 soldiers captured by Iraqi troops on March 23.

April 5: U.S. tanks roll into the Iraqi capital and engage in firefights with Iraqi troops. Resistance weaker than anticipated. Heavy Iraqi casualties.

April 7: British forces take control of Basra, Iraq's second-largest city.

April 9: Baghdad falls to U.S. forces. Looters pillage government buildings, museums, hospitals, and stores. Statue of Saddam Hussein symbolically toppled.

April 11: Kirkuk falls to Kurdish fighters.

April 13: Marines rescue five U.S. soldiers captured by Iraqi troops on March 23 in Nasiriya, and two pilots shot down on March 24 near Karbala.

April 15: Gen. Jay Garner is appointed by the U.S. to run post-war Iraq.

May 1: President Bush declares an end to major combat operations.

May 12: Diplomat Paul Bremer replaces Jay Garner as Iraqi administrator.

June 15–29: About 1,300 troops launch Operation Desert Scorpion, combatting organized Iraqi resistance against American troops near Falluja.

July 13: Iraq's interim governing council, composed of 25 Iraqis appointed by American and British officials, is inaugurated. American administrator Paul Bremer, however, retains ultimate authority.

July 16: Gen. John Abizaid, commander of allied forces in Iraq, calls continued attacks on coalition troops a "guerrilla-type campaign" and says soldiers who will replace current troops may be deployed for year-long tours.

July 22: Saddam Hussein's sons, Uday and Qusay Hussein, die in firefight in a Mosul palace.

Aug. 19: Suicide bombing destroys UN headquarters in Baghdad, killing 24, including top envoy Sergio Vieira de Mello.

Aug. 29: A bomb kills one of Iraq's most important Shiite leaders, Ayatollah Muhammad Bakr al-Hakim, among about 80 others.

Sept. 7: President Bush announces that $87 billion is needed to cover additional military and reconstruction costs.

Oct. 23–24: The Madrid Conference, an international conference to raise funds for Iraq's reconstruction, yields $33 billion but falls short of the target of $56 billion.

Oct. 27: Four coordinated suicide attacks in Baghdad kill 43 and wound more than 200. Targets include the headquarters of the Red Crescent and three police stations. Insurgents increasingly victimize civilians, Iraqi security forces, and aid agencies, not simply U.S. troops.

Nov. 2: Iraqi guerrillas shoot down an American helicopter, killing 16 U.S. soldiers and injuring 21 others. Additional attacks this month make it the bloodiest since the war began: at least 75 U.S. soldiers die.

Nov. 14: The Bush administration reverses policy in a deal with the Iraqi Governing Council, agreeing to transfer power to an interim government much sooner, in 2004.

Dec. 9: Directive issued by Paul Wolfowitz, deputy secretary of defense, bars France, Germany, and Russia from bidding on lucrative contracts for rebuilding Iraq, creating a diplomatic furor.

Dec. 13: Saddam Hussein is captured by U.S. troops. He is found hiding in a hole near his hometown of Tikrit and surrenders without a fight.

Jan. 11, 2004: The Grand Ayatollah Ali al-Sistani, the most influential Shiite cleric in Iraq, says members of the country's interim government must be selected by direct vote. He opposes the U.S. plan to hold regional caucuses. The U.S. has argued that it would be impossible to ensure free and safe elections on such a tight timetable—the U.S. plans to hand control of the government to Iraqis on June 30.

Jan. 15: Thousands of Shiites hold a peaceful demonstration in Basra in support of direct elections.

Jan. 19: The U.S. asks the UN to intercede in the dispute over the elections process in Iraq.

Jan. 28: David Kay, the former head of the U.S. weapons inspection teams in Iraq, informs a senate committee that no WMD have been found in Iraq and that prewar intelligence was "almost all wrong" about Saddam Hussein's arsenal.

Feb. 2: Under pressure from both sides of the political aisle, President Bush calls for an independent commission to study intelligence failures.

Feb. 10: About 54 Iraqis are killed in a car bombing while applying for jobs at a police station. The next day an attack kills about 47 outside an army recruiting center. Iraqi security forces become a regular target of insurgents.

Feb. 23: UN envoy Lakhdar Brahimi issues a report concluding that the earliest that credible, direct elections could be held is early 2005.

March 2: Suicide attacks in Karbala on Shiite Islam's most holy feast day kill more than 85 and wound 233 others. It is believed that the perpetrators are attempting to foment unrest between Shiites and Sunnis.

March 8: The Iraqi Governing Council signs interim constitution.

March 31: Iraqi mob kills and mutilates four American civilian contract workers and drags them through the streets of Falluja.

April 4: U.S. troops begin assault on Falluja in response to March 31 killings. Coordinated attacks by Shiites are launched in the cities of Kufa, Karbala, Najaf, al-Kut, and Sadr City. The militias are led by Moktada al-Sadr.

April 9: U.S. contract worker Thomas Hamill is taken hostage. In all, more than 20 foreigners have been kidnapped in Iraq, and hostage-taking becomes a regular tactic of the insurgents.

April 15: The Bush administration agrees to a UN proposal to replace the Iraqi Governing Council with a caretaker government when the U.S. returns sovereignty to Iraqis on June 30.

April 22: U.S. announces that some Iraqi Baath Party officials who had been forced out of their jobs after the fall of Saddam Hussein will be allowed to resume their positions. About 400,000 lost their jobs, draining Iraq of skilled workers.

April 30: The appalling physical and sexual abuse of Iraqi prisoners at Abu Ghraib prison near Baghdad comes to light when photographs are released by the U.S. media. The images spark outrage around the world.

May 8: Nicholas Berg, an American contractor, is beheaded by Iraqi militants. Beheadings of foreign workers become a regular terrorist tactic.

May 17: A suicide bomber kills the head of the Governing Council, Izzedin Salim, and six others.

May 27: After seven weeks of fighting in Najaf, U.S. forces and militias loyal to al-Sadr reach a truce.

May 28: Iyad Allawi is designated prime minister of the Iraqi interim government. A Shiite neurologist, Allawi has close ties to the CIA.

June 1: Ghazi al-Yawar, a Sunni, is chosen president, a ceremonial post. The Governing Council decides to dissolve itself immediately rather than wait for the official handover of sovereignty.

June 16: The 9/11 Commission concludes in its report that there is "no credible evidence that Iraq and al-Qaeda cooperated on attacks against the United States." The link between al-Qaeda and Iraq was one of the justifications for the war.

June 28: In a surprise move, the United States transfers power back to Iraqis two days early. The ceremony was held in secret to thwart attacks by Iraqi insurgents.

July 7: Prime Minister Allawi signs a law permitting him to impose martial law.

July 9: The Senate Intelligence Committee releases a unanimous, bipartisan "Report on Pre-War Intelligence on Iraq," harshly criticizing the CIA and other American intelligence agencies for the "mischaracterization of intelligence." "Most of the major key judgments" on Iraq's weapons of mass destruction were "either overstated, or were not supported by, the underlying intelligence report." It also concluded that there was no "established formal relationship" between al-Qaeda and Saddam Hussein.

Aug. 24: The Pentagon-sponsored Schlesinger report's investigation into the Abu Ghraib scandal calls the prisoner abuse acts of "brutality and purposeless sadism," and rejects the idea that the abuse was simply the work of a few aberrant soldiers. It asserts that there were "fundamental failures throughout all levels of command, from the soldiers on the ground to Central Command and to the Pentagon."

Aug. 27: A bloody, three-week battle in Najaf between U.S. forces and militia of militant cleric al-Sadr ends in August when Shiite cleric Grand Ayatollah Ali al-Sistani negotiates a settlement.

Sept. 7: U.S. death toll in Iraq reaches 1,000; about 7,000 soldiers have been wounded. In August, attacks on American forces reached their highest level since the beginning of the war, an average of 87 per day. No official record of Iraqi civilian deaths is kept, but as of this date estimates range from 12,000 to 14,000 (Iraq Body Count).

Sept. 15: The Bush administration requests that the Senate divert $3.4 billion of the $18.4 billion Iraq reconstruction budget to improving security in the country. The worsening security situation—with pockets of Iraq essentially under the control of insurgents—threatens to disrupt national elections, scheduled for January. Republican and Democratic senators alike harshly criticize the request as a sign that the American campaign in Iraq has been poorly executed. Senators also denounce the slow progress in rebuilding Iraq: just 6% ($1 billion) of the reconstruction money approved by Congress has in fact been spent.

Sept. 15: In a BBC interview, UN Secretary General Kofi Annan says the war against Iraq was illegal and violated the UN Charter. The U.S., UK, and Australia vigorously reject his conclusion.

America's Wars: U.S. Casualties and Veterans

American Revolution (1775–1783)

Total servicemembers	217,000
Battle deaths	4,435
Nonmortal woundings	6,188

War of 1812 (1812–1815)

Total servicemembers	286,730
Battle deaths	2,260
Nonmortal woundings	4,505

Indian Wars (approx. 1817–1898)

Total servicemembers	106,000[1]
Battle deaths	1,000[1]

Mexican War (1846–1848)

Total servicemembers	78,718
Battle deaths	1,733
Other deaths in service (nontheater)	11,550
Nonmortal woundings	4,152

Civil War (1861–1865)

Total servicemembers (Union)	2,213,363
Battle deaths (Union)	140,414
Other deaths in service (nontheater) (Union)	224,097
Nonmortal woundings (Union)	281,881
Total servicemembers (Conf.)	1,050,000
Battle deaths (Conf.)	74,524
Other deaths in service (nontheater) (Conf.)	59,297[2]
Nonmortal woundings (Conf.)	unknown

Spanish-American War (1898–1902)

Total servicemembers	306,760
Battle deaths	385
Other deaths in service (nontheater)	2,061
Nonmortal woundings	1,662

World War I (1917–1918)

Total servicemembers	4,734,991
Battle deaths	53,402
Other deaths in service (nontheater)	63,114
Nonmortal woundings	204,002
Living veterans	fewer than 500

World War II (1940–1945)

Total servicemembers	16,112,566
Battle deaths	291,557
Other deaths in service (nontheater)	113,842
Nonmortal woundings	671,846
Living veterans	4,762,000[1]

Korean War (1950–1953)

Total servicemembers	5,720,000
Serving in-theater	1,789,000
Battle deaths	33,741
Other deaths in service (theater)	2,827
Other deaths in service (nontheater)	17,730
Nonmortal woundings	103,284
Living veterans	3,734,000[1]

Vietnam War (1964–1975)

Total servicemembers	8,744,000
Serving in-theater	3,403,000
Battle deaths	47,410
Other deaths in service (theater)	10,789
Other deaths in service (nontheater)	32,000
Nonmortal woundings	153,303
Living veterans	8,295,000[1]

Gulf War (1990–1991)

Total servicemembers	2,183,000
Serving in-theater	665,476
Battle deaths	147
Other deaths in service (theater)	382
Other deaths in service (nontheater)	1,565
Nonmortal woundings	467
Living veterans	1,852,000[1]

America's Wars Total

Military service during war	42,348,460
Battle deaths	651,008
Other deaths in service (theater)	13,998
Other deaths in service (nontheater)	525,256
Nonmortal woundings	1,431,290
Living war veterans	17,578,500[3]
Living veterans	25,038,459

1. Veterans Administration estimate as of Sept. 30, 2002. 2. Estimated figure. Does not include 26,000–31,000 who died in Union prisons. 3. Approximately 1,065,000 veterans had service in multiple conflicts. They are counted under each conflict, but only once in the total. *Source:* Department of Defense and Veterans Administration.

Post-Vietnam Combat Casualties[1]

Place	Dates	Casualties	Place	Dates	Casualties
Lebanon	Aug. 1982–Feb. 1984	254	Haiti	Sept. 1994–April 1996	4
Grenada	Oct.–Nov. 1983	18	Former	1992–2001	9
Libya	April 10–16, 1986	2	Yugoslavia		
Panama	Dec. 1989–Jan. 1990	23	Kosovo	March–June 1999	2
Persian Gulf	Jan. 16–April 6, 1991	147	Afghanistan	Oct. 2001–[2]	56
Somalia	Dec. 1992–May 1993	29	Iraq	March 20, 2003–[3]	789

1. Defined as battle deaths. Does not include deaths from accidents. 2. A total of 129 Americans have been killed, including 73 nonhostile attacks, as of June 26, 2004. "Operation Enduring Freedom" deaths cover other Asian regions as well as Afghanistan. 3. A total of 1,039 Americans have been killed, including 250 non-combat deaths. About 7,000 were wounded. Coalition deaths: UK, 65; Italy, 19; Poland, 13; Spain, 11; Ukraine, 8; Bulgaria, 6; Slovakia, 3; Thailand, 2; Netherlands, 2; and Denmark, El Salvador, Estonia, Hungary, and Latvia, 1 each (Sept. 23, 2004). *Source:* U.S. Dept. of Defense, AP, *Washington Post.*

American Prisoners of War

Congress defines a prisoner of war as a person who, while serving on active military, naval, or air service, is forcibly detained or interned in the line of duty by an enemy government or a hostile force.

	Total	WWI	WWII	Korea	Vietnam	Persian Gulf	Somalia	Iraq
Captured and interned	142,233	4,120	130,201	7,140	745	23	1	8
Returned to U.S. military control	125,208	3,973	116,129	4,418	661	23	1	8
Died while POW	17,004	147	14,072	2,701	84	0	0	0

NOTES: n.a. = not applicable. Not included are the more than 92,000 military personnel considered missing in action: WWI, 3,350; WWII, 78,773; Korea, 8,100; Vietnam, 1,912 (as of June 2002); and the Persian Gulf, 1. *Source:* U.S. Department of Veterans Affairs.

Highest-Ranking Officers in U.S. History

General and Commander-in-Chief[1]

George Washington (1732–1799), b. Westmoreland County, Va., unanimously voted by Congress on June 15, 1775, to the rank of general and commander-in-chief (of the Continental army).

General of the Armies[2]

John Joseph Pershing (1860–1948), b. Linn County, Mo., made permanent general of the armies, 1919.

General of the Army, General of the Air Force (Five-Stars)

George Catlett Marshall (1880–1959), b. Uniontown, Pa., promoted Dec. 1944.

Douglas MacArthur (1880–1964), b. Little Rock, Ark., promoted Dec. 1944.

Dwight David Eisenhower (1890–1969), b. Denison, Tex., promoted Dec. 1944.

Henry Harley Arnold (1886–1950), b. Gladwyne, Pa. Arnold had the unique distinction of being a five-star general twice—in 1944 as general of the army, and in June 1949 as general of the air force. He is the only air force general to have held the five-star rank.

Omar Nelson Bradley (1893–1981), b. Clark, Mo., promoted Sept. 1950.

Fleet Admiral (Five-Stars)

William Daniel Leahy (1875–1959), b. Hampton, Iowa, promoted Dec. 1944.

Ernest Joseph King (1878–1956), b. Lorain, Ohio, promoted Dec. 1944.

Chester William Nimitz (1885–1966), b. Fredericksburg, Tex., promoted Dec. 1944.

William Frederick Halsey (1882–1959), b. Elizabeth, N.J., promoted Dec. 1945.

1. On March 15, 1978, George Washington was promoted posthumously to the newly created rank of General of the Armies of the United States. Congress authorized this title to make it clear that Washington was the army's senior general. 2. General Pershing was given the option of five stars but he declined. *Source:* Department of Defense and U.S. Army Historian, Research and Analysis Center.

The Joint Chiefs of Staff (JCS)

The Joint Chiefs of Staff consist of the chairman, the vice chairman, the chief of staff of the army, the chief of naval operations, the chief of staff of the air force, and the commandant of the Marine Corps.

The collective body of the JCS is headed by the chairman (or vice chairman in the chairman's absence), who sets the agenda and presides over JCS meetings. Their responsibilities take precedence over their duties as the Chiefs of Military Services. The chairman is the principal military adviser to the president, the secretary of defense, and the National Security Council (NSC); however, all JCS members are by law military advisers, and they may respond to a request or voluntarily submit, through the chairman, advice or opinions to the president, the secretary of state, or the NSC. The Joint Chiefs of Staff have no executive authority to commit combatant forces.

In addition to their responsibilities on the JCS, the military service chiefs are responsible to the secretaries of their military departments for management of the services. The service chiefs serve for four years. By custom the vice chiefs of the services act for their chiefs in most matters having to do with day-to-day operation of the services.

Joint Chiefs of Staff, 2003

Chairman of the Joint Chiefs of Staff, General Richard B. Myers, U.S. Air Force; vice chairman of the Joint Chiefs of Staff, General Peter Pace, Marine Corps; General Peter J. Schoomaker, chief of staff of the U.S. Army; Admiral Vern Clark, chief of naval operations; General John P. Jumper, chief of staff of the U.S. Air Force; and General Michael W. Hagee, commandant of the Marine Corps.

Past Chairmen of the JCS

General of the Army, Omar N. Bradley, 1949–1953
Adm. Arthur W. Radford, U.S. Navy, 1953–1957
Gen. Nathan F. Twining, U.S. Air Force, 1957–1960
Gen. Lyman L. Lemnitzer, U.S. Army, 1960–1962
Gen. Maxwell D. Taylor, U.S. Army, 1962–1964
Gen. Earle G. Wheeler, U.S. Army, 1964–1970
Adm. Thomas H. Moorer, U.S. Navy, 1970–1974
Gen. George S. Brown, U.S. Air Force, 1974–1978
Gen. David C. Jones, U.S. Air Force, 1978–1982
Gen. John W. Vessey, Jr., U.S. Army, 1982–1985
Adm. William J. Crowe, U.S. Navy, 1985–1989
Gen. Colin L. Powell, U.S. Army, 1989–1993
Gen. John M. Shalikashvili, U.S. Army, 1993–1997
Gen. Henry H. Shelton, U.S. Army, 1997–2001

U.S. Military Spending, 1946–2004

(billions of 2002 dollars)

Year	Spending	Year	Spending	Year	Spending	Year	Spending	Year	Spending	Year	Spending
1946	$556.9	1956	$356.2	1966	$356.2	1976	$283.8	1986	$426.6	1996	$307.4
1947	52.4	1957	360.9	1967	412.0	1977	286.2	1987	427.9	1997	305.3
1948	103.9	1958	352.9	1968	449.3	1978	286.5	1988	426.4	1998	296.7
1949	144.2	1959	352.5	1969	438.1	1979	295.6	1989	427.7	1999	298.4
1950	141.2	1960	344.3	1970	406.3	1980	303.4	1990	409.7	2000	311.7
1951	224.3	1961	344.0	1971	370.6	1981	317.4	1991	358.1	2001	307.8
1952	402.1	1962	363.4	1972	343.8	1982	339.4	1992	379.5	2002	328.7
1953	442.3	1963	368.0	1973	313.3	1983	366.7	1993	358.6	2003	379.3[1]
1954	420.9	1964	364.4	1974	299.7	1984	381.7	1994	338.6	2004	379.9[1,2]
1955	376.9	1965	333.1	1975	293.3	1985	405.4	1995	321.6		

1. Figures based on requested defense budget, not actual spending. 2. In addition, Congress approved $87 billion to fund the war and reconstruction effort in Iraq. *Source:* Center for Defense Information.

U.S. Military Ranks

Source: U.S. Department of Defense.

Pay Grade	Army and Marine Corps	Navy and Coast Guard[1]	Air Force	Total number[2]
Commissioned Officers				
O-1	Second Lieutenant	Ensign	Second Lieutenant	24,351
O-2	First Lieutenant	Lieutenant Junior Grade	First Lieutenant	33,188
O-3	Captain	Lieutenant	Captain	69,337
O-4	Major	Lieutenant Commander	Major	44,172
O-5	Lieutenant Colonel	Commander	Lieutenant Colonel	28,884
O-6	Colonel	Captain	Colonel	11,797
O-7	Brigadier General	Rear Admiral	Brigadier General	432
O-8	Major General	Rear Admiral	Major General	276
O-9	Lieutenant General	Vice Admiral	Lieutenant General	126
O-10	General	Admiral	General	35
Special Grades[3]				
(5 stars)	General of the Army	Fleet Admiral	General of the Air Force	
Warrant Officers				
W-1	Warrant Officer	—	—	2,496
W-2–W-5	Chief Warrant Officer	Chief Warrant Officer[4]	—	13,459
TOTAL OFFICERS				**228,553**
Enlisted Personnel				
E-1	Private	Seaman Recruit	Recruit	47,180
E-2	Army Private/ Marine Private First Class	Seaman Apprentice	Airman	82,746
E-3	Army Private First Class/ Marine Lance Corporal	Seaman	Airman First Class	229,878
E-4	Corporal	Petty Officer, Third Class	Senior Airman	269,659
E-5	Sergeant	Petty Officer, Second Class	Staff Sergeant	249,707
E-6	Staff Sergeant	Petty Officer, First Class	Technical Sergeant	170,548
E-7	Army Sergeant First Class Marine Gunnery Sergeant	Chief Petty Officer	Master Sergeant	99,634
E-8	Master Sergeant	Senior Chief Petty Officer	Senior Master Sergeant	27,479
E-9	Sergeant Major	Master Chief Petty Officer	Chief Master Sergeant	10,891
Special Grades[5]				
	Sergeant Major	Master Chief Petty Officer	Chief Master Sergeant	
TOTAL ENLISTED				**1,187,722**
GRAND TOTAL				**1,416,275**

1. The United States Coast Guard operates within the Department of Homeland Security rather than the Department of Defense. 2. As of May 31, 2004. Excludes Coast Guard. 3. There are no living five-star commissioned officers. 4. Applies only to the Navy, not the Coast Guard. 5. Senior enlisted advisers. There is only one for each branch of service (Air Force, Army, Marine Corps, Navy). *Source:* Dept. of Defense and Center for Defense Information.

U.S. Military Personnel on Active Duty in Selected Regions/Countries,[1] 2004

Region/Country	Personnel[2]	Region/Country	Personnel[2]	Region/Country	Personnel[2]
United States and Territories	**1,168,195**	Russia	79	Israel	38
		Serbia (includes Kosovo)	128	Qatar	3,432
Continental U.S.	958,215			Saudi Arabia	291
Alaska	17,989	Spain*	1,968	**Sub-Saharan Africa**	**770**
Hawaii	35,810	Turkey*	1,863	Djibouti	539
Guam	3,315	United Kingdom*	11,801	**Western Hemisphere**	**2,201**
Puerto Rico	769	**East Asia and Pacific**	**97,724**	Brazil	37
Transients	31,397	Australia	205	Canada	147
Europe	**116,669**	China (includes Hong Kong)	60	Colombia	55
Belgium*	1,534	Japan	40,045	Cuba (Guantanamo)	700
Bosnia and Herzegovina	2,931	Korea, Rep. of	40,258	Ecuador	35
France*	82	Philippines	144	Haiti	455
Georgia	38	Singapore	196	Honduras	413
Germany*,[3]	75,603	Thailand	113	Peru	35
Greece*	562	**North Africa, Near East,**		**Undistributed[3]**	**33,421**
Greenland*	138	**and South Asia**	**6,907**	**Total foreign countries[6]**	**257,692**
Iceland*	1,754	Operation Iraqi Freedom[4]	211,028	Ashore	233,544
Italy*,[3]	13,354	Afghanistan[5]	c. 18,000	Afloat	24,148
Macedonia	104	Bahrain	1,496	NATO Countries	110,494
Netherlands*	722	Diego Garcia	491	**Total worldwide[6]**	**1,425,887**
Norway*	85	Egypt	350	Ashore	1,281,073
Portugal*	1,077			Afloat	144,814

NOTES: *NATO countries. 1. Only countries with 35 or more U.S. military personnel are listed. 2. As of March 31, 2004, unless otherwise noted. 3. Includes some service members deployed to Operation Iraqi Freedom. 4. In and around Iraq; data subject to change. 5. *Source: USA Today,* Sept. 22, 2004. 6. Includes all regions/countries, not simply those listed; excludes Operation Iraqi Freedom. *Source:* U.S. Department of Defense, *Selected Manpower Statistics, Annual.*

Active Duty Military Personnel, 1940–2002[1]

Year	Army	Air Force	Navy	Marine Corps	Total
1940	269,023		160,997	28,345	458,365
1945	8,266,373		3,319,586	469,925	12,055,884
1950	593,167	411,277	380,739	74,279	1,459,462
1955	1,109,296	959,946	660,695	205,170	2,935,107
1960	873,078	814,752	616,987	170,621	2,475,438
1965	969,066	824,662	669,985	190,213	2,653,926
1970	1,322,548	791,349	691,126	259,737	3,064,760
1975	784,333	612,751	535,085	195,951	2,128,120
1980	777,036	557,969	527,153	188,469	2,050,627
1985	780,787	601,515	570,705	198,025	2,151,032
1990	732,403	535,233	579,417	196,652	2,043,705
1991	710,821	510,432	570,262	194,040	1,985,555
1992	610,450	470,315	541,886	184,529	1,807,177
1993	572,423	444,351	509,950	178,379	1,705,103
1994	541,343	426,327	468,662	174,158	1,610,490
1995	508,559	400,409	434,617	174,639	1,518,224
1996	491,103	389,001	416,735	174,883	1,471,722
1997	491,707	377,385	395,564	173,906	1,438,562
1998	483,880	367,470	382,338	173,142	1,406,830
1999	479,426	360,590	373,046	172,641	1,385,703
2000	482,170	355,654	373,193	173,321	1,384,338
2001	480,801	353,571	377,810	172,934	1,385,116
2002	486,542	368,251	385,051	173,733	1,413,577

NOTE: Figures for 1998 through 2002 include cadets/midshipmen. 1. Military personnel on extended or continuous active duty. Excludes reserves on active duty for training. *Source:* Department of Defense.

The Medal of Honor

Often called the Congressional Medal of Honor, it is the nation's highest military award for "uncommon valor" by men and women in the armed forces. It is given for actions that are above and beyond the call of duty in combat against an armed enemy. The medal was first awarded by the army on March 25, 1863. More than 3,400 men have been awarded the medal, as well as one woman, Dr. Mary Walker, a surgeon in the Civil War.

Recipients of the medal are awarded $400 per month for life, a right to burial at Arlington National Cemetery, admission for them or their children to a service academy (if they qualify and quotas permit), and free travel on government aircraft to almost anywhere in the world, on a space-available basis. In 2004, there were 133 Medal of Honor recipients living.

Medal of Honor Recipients

	Total[1]	Army	Navy	Marines	Coast Guard	Air Force	Civilian
Civil War	1,522	1,196	305	17	—	—	4
Noncombat, 1865–1870	13	1	12	—	—	—	—
Indian Wars (1861–1898)	426	422	—	—	—	—	4
Korea (1871)	15	—	9	6	—	—	—
Noncombat, 1871–1899	106	—	104	2	—	—	—
Spanish-American War	110	31	64	15	—	—	—
Samoa	4	—	1	3	—	—	—
Philippines	80	69	5	6	—	—	—
China	59	4	22	33	—	—	—
Noncombat, 1901–1910	49	1	46	2	—	—	—
Philippines (1911)	6	1	5	—	—	—	—
Mexican Campaign (1914)	56	1	46	9	—	—	—
Haiti (1915)	6	—	—	6	—	—	—
Noncombat, 1915–1916	8	—	8	—	—	—	—
Dominican Republic	3	—	—	3	—	—	—
World War I	119	90	21	8	—	—	—
Haiti (1919–1920)	2	—	—	2	—	—	—
Nicaragua (1927–1933)	2	—	—	2	—	—	—
Noncombat, 1920–1940	17	1	15	1	—	—	—
World War II	464	324	57	82	1	—	—
Korean War	131	82	7	42	—	—	—
Vietnam War	245	159	16	57	—	13	—
Somalia (1993)	2	2	—	—	—	—	—
Unknown Soldiers	9	9	—	—	—	—	—
Total	**3,454**	**2,393**	**743**	**296**	**1**	**13**	**8**

1. These totals reflect the total number of Medals of Honor awarded through Aug. 2004. Nineteen men received a second award, and 5 of these double awardees received both the Army and Navy Medals of Honor for the same action. *Sources:* The Congressional Medal of Honor Society, Mt. Pleasant, S.C. Web: www.cmohs.org and Home of Heroes. Web: www.homeofheroes.com/moh/history/history_statistics.html.

U.S. Service Academies

U.S. Air Force Academy
Colorado Springs, Colo.
Established 1958
www.usafa.edu

U.S. Coast Guard Academy
New London, Conn.
Established 1876
www.cga.edu

U.S. Military Academy
West Point, N.Y.
Established 1802
www.usma.edu

U.S. Naval Academy
Annapolis, Md.
Established 1845
www.usna.edu

U.S. Merchant Marine Academy
Kings Point, N.Y.
Established 1943
www.usmma.edu

Last Civil War Widows

The last-known Union widow, Gertrude Janeway, died in Jan. 2003 in Tennessee. John Janeway joined the Union army in 1864 and was briefly a POW at Andersonville. The couple married in 1927, after waiting three years until Gertrude turned 18. John was 81.

The person thought to be the last-known Confederate widow, Alberta Martin, was born Dec, 4, 1906, and died at age 97 in Alabama on May 31, 2004. In 1927, at age 21, she married William Jasper Martin, then 81. Martin joined the Confederate army in May 1864. Upon her husband's death, she married his grandson from his first marriage.

The publicity surrounding Alberta Martin's death prompted relatives of Maudie Celia Hopkins of Arkansas to reveal that the 89-year-old was in fact the last civil war widow. Hopkins married 86-year-old William Cantrell on Feb. 2, 1934, when she was 19. She did so to escape poverty, but kept quiet about the unusual marriage, "I thought people would gossip about it." Cantrell, who served in the Virginia Infantry, supported her with his Confederate pension of "$25 every two or three months" until his death in 1937. Hopkins has outlived three other husbands.

Veterans of U.S. Wars and Their Dependents

Veterans' benefits have existed since the origins of the nation. As of Oct. 2002, 2,177,303 veterans, their dependents, and survivors of deceased veterans are receiving VA benefits and services.

	Veterans	Children[1]	Parents	Surviving spouses
Civil War	—	7	—	—
Indian Wars	—	1	—	—
Spanish-American War	—	198	—	262
Mexican Border	5	23	—	139
World War I	56	5,220	1	17,984
World War II	580,110	17,812	838	259,715
Korean Conflict	242,611	3,869	1,044	62,443
Vietnam Era	927,656	12,147	5,136	124,048
Gulf War[2]	426,865	9,332	366	7,663
Total wartime	**2,177,303**	**48,609**	**7,385**	**472,255**
Nonservice-connected	346,173	24,988	—	212,641
Service-connected	1,831,130	23,621	7,385	259,614
Total	**2,177,303**	**58,609**	**7,385**	**472,255**

1. Children connotes a minor or a dependent adult. 2. For VA benefits purposes, the Gulf War period of service remains open-ended and also includes those discharged from 1991 to date. *Source:* Department of Veterans Affairs and Department of Defense. Web: www.va.gov/pressrel/amwars01.htm.

Last Living Veterans of America's Wars

American Revolution (1775–1783)
- Last veteran, Daniel F. Bakeman, died 4/5/1869, age 109
- Last widow, Catherine S. Damon, died 11/11/06, age 92
- Last dependent, Phoebe M. Palmeter, died 4/25/11, age 90

War of 1812 (1812–1815)
- Last veteran, Hiram Cronk, died 5/13/05, age 105
- Last widow, Carolina King, died 6/28/36, age unknown
- Last dependent, Esther A. H. Morgan, died 3/12/46, age 89

Indian Wars (c. 1861–1898)
- Last veteran, Fredrak Fraske, died 6/18/73, age 101

Mexican War (1846–1848)
- Last veteran, Owen Thomas Edgar, died 9/3/29, age 98
- Last widow, Lena James Theobald, died 6/20/63, age 89
- Last dependent, Jesse G. Bivens, died 11/1/62, age 94

Civil War (1861–1865)
- Last Union veteran, Albert Woolson, died 8/2/56, age 109
- Last Confederate veteran, John Salling*, died 3/16/58, age 112

Spanish-American War (1898)
- Last veteran, Nathan E. Cook, died 9/10/92, age 106

*Disputed. *Source:* Department of Veterans Affairs and Department of Defense. Web: www.va.gov/pressrel/amwars01.htm.

For international military affairs, *see* p. 715.

The Blueberries of Mars

Was the Red Planet once a wet planet? A plucky Martian rover
finally delivers some hard evidence of a liquid past

By JEFFREY KLUGER TIME

Giovanni Schiaparelli could have told you there had been water on Mars. It was Schiaparelli who peered through his telescope one evening in 1877 and discovered what he took to be the Red Planet's famous canals. As it turned out, the canals were an optical illusion, but as more powerful telescopes and, later, spacecraft zoomed in for closer looks, there was no shortage of clues suggesting that Mars was once awash in water. Photographs shot from orbit show vast plains that resemble ancient sea floors, steep gorges that would dwarf the Grand Canyon, and sinuous surface scars that look an awful lot like dry riverbeds.

Given all that, why were NASA scientists so excited in March 2004 to announce that one of their Mars rovers, having crawled across the planet for five weeks, finally determined that Mars, at some point in its deep past, was indeed "drenched"—to use NASA's term—with liquid water?

Water Puzzle

Part of their excitement probably stems from sheer failure fatigue. NASA has had its share of setbacks in recent years—including a few disastrous missions to Mars. So it was with some relief that lead investigator Steve Squyres announced that the rover *Opportunity* had accomplished its primary mission. "The puzzle pieces have been falling into place," he told a crowded press conference, "and the last piece fell into place a few days ago."

But there was also, for the NASA team, the pleasure that comes from making a genuine contribution to space science. For despite all the signs pointing to Mars's watery past, until *Opportunity* poked its instruments into the Martian rocks, nobody was really sure how real that water was. At least some of the surface formations that look water-carved could have been formed by volcanism and wind. In 2002, University of Colorado researchers published a persuasive paper suggesting that any water on Mars was carried in by crashing comets and then quickly evaporated.

The experiments that put that theory to rest—and nailed down the presence of water for good—were largely conducted on one 10-inch-high, 65-foot-wide rock outcropping in the Meridiani Planum that mission scientists dubbed El Capitan. The surface of the formation is made up of fine layers—called parallel laminations—that are often laid down by minerals settling out of water. The rock is also randomly pitted with cavities called "vugs" that are created when salt crystals form in briny water and then fall out or dissolve away.

Chemical analyses of El Capitan, performed with two different spectrometers, support the visual evidence. They show that it is rich in sulfates known to form in the presence of water as well as a mineral called "jarosite," which not only forms in water but also actually contains a bit of water trapped in its matrix.

The most intriguing evidence comes in the form of the BB-size spherules—or "blueberries," as NASA calls them—scattered throughout the rock. Spheres like these can be formed either by volcanism or by minerals accreting under water, but the way the blueberries are mixed randomly through the rock—not layered on top, as they would have been after a volcanic eruption—strongly suggests the latter.

None of these findings are dispositive, but their combined weight persuaded NASA scientists to summarize their findings in unusually explicit language. "We have concluded that the rocks here were soaked with liquid water," said Squyres flatly. "The ground would have been suitable for life."

Life on Mars?

Does that mean that there was—or still is—life on Mars? The fossil record on Earth suggests that given enough time and H_2O, life will eventually emerge, but there's nothing in the current findings to prove that this happened on Mars. Without more knowledge of such variables as temperature, atmosphere, and the length of time Martian water existed, we can't simply assume that what happened on our planet would necessarily occur on another.

Opportunity and its twin robot *Spirit* are not equipped to search for life. Their mission is limited to looking for signs of water. But there's still a lot for them to do. Just knowing that rocks were wet doesn't tell you if the water was flowing or stationary, if it melted down from ice caps or seeped up through the ground. And if water was once there in such abundance, where did it go? *Opportunity*, which exceeded its planned 90-day mission, went looking for those answers, toddling off to investigate other rocks farther and farther from its landing site. *Spirit* conducted its own studies in Gusev Crater, on the opposite side of the planet.

The next step—the search for life—will have to wait until 2013 or so. That's when NASA has tentatively scheduled the first round trip to Mars—a mission that will pluck selected rocks off the Red Planet and bring them back home for closer study. Whether humans will ever follow those machines—President Bush's Jan. 2004 announcement of an ambitious space initiative notwithstanding—is impossible to say. ▫

Astronomical Terms

Aphelion: see **Orbit.**

Apogee: see **Orbit.**

Black hole: the theoretical end-product of the total gravitational collapse of a massive star or group of stars. Crushed even smaller than the incredibly dense neutron star, the black hole may become so dense that not even light can escape its gravitational field. In 1996, astronomers found strong evidence for a massive black hole at the center of the Milky Way. Recent evidence suggests that black holes are so common that they probably exist at the core of nearly all galaxies.

Conjunction: the alignment of two celestial objects at the same celestial longitude. Conjunction of the Moon and planets is often determined with reference to the Sun. For example, Saturn is said to be in conjunction with the Sun when Saturn and the Earth are aligned on opposite sides of the Sun.

Mercury and Venus, the two planets with orbits within Earth's orbit, have two positions of conjunction. Mercury, for example, is said to be in *inferior conjunction* when the Sun and the Earth are aligned on opposite sides of Mercury. Mercury is in *superior conjunction* when Mercury and the Earth are aligned on opposite sides of the Sun.

Elongation: the angular distance between two points in the sky as measured from a third point. The elongation of Mercury, for example, is the angular distance between Mercury and the Sun as measured from Earth. Planets whose orbits are outside the Earth's can have elongations between 0° and 180°. (When a planet's elongation is 0° it is at conjunction; when it is 180°, it is at opposition.) Because Mercury and Venus are within the Earth's orbit, their greatest elongations measured from the Earth are 28° and 47°, respectively.

Galaxy: gas and millions of stars held together by gravity. All that you can see in the sky (with a very few exceptions) belongs to our galaxy—a system of roughly 200 billion stars. The exceptions you can see are other galaxies. Our own galaxy, the rim of which we see as the "Milky Way," is about 100,000 light-years in diameter and about 10,000 light-years in thickness. Its shape is roughly that of a thick lens; more precisely, it is a *spiral nebula.* Astronomers have estimated that the universe could contain 40 to 50 billion galaxies. In 2002, a galaxy discovered by a team of astronomers led by Esther Hu of the University of Hawaii was determined to be the most distant object ever observed—13.6 billion light-years away.

Neutron star: an extremely dense star with a powerful gravitational pull. Some neutron stars

pulse radio waves into space as they spin; these are known as pulsars.

Occultation: the eclipse of one celestial object by another. For example, a star is occulted when the Moon passes between it and the Earth.

Opposition: the alignment of two celestial objects when their longitude differs by 180°. Opposition of the Moon and planets is often determined with reference to the Sun. For example, Saturn is said to be at opposition when Saturn and the Sun are aligned on opposite sides of the Earth. Only the planets whose orbits lie outside the Earth's can be in opposition to the Sun.

Orbit: the path traveled by an object in space. Theoretically, there are four mathematical figures, or models, of possible orbits: two are open (hyperbola and parabola) and two are closed (ellipse and circle), but in reality all closed orbits are ellipses. Ellipses can be nearly circular, as are the orbits of most planets, or very elongated, as are the orbits of most comets, but the orbit revolves around a fixed, or *focal*, point. In our solar system, the Sun's gravitational pull keeps the planets in their elliptical orbits; the planets hold their moons in place similarly. For planets, the point of the orbit closest to the Sun is the *perihelion,* and the point farthest from the Sun is the *aphelion.* For orbits around the Earth, the point of closest proximity is the *perigee;* the farthest point is the *apogee.* See also **Retrograde.**

Perigee: see **Orbit.**

Perihelion: see **Orbit.**

Planet: there is no set scientific definition for planet (from the Greek *planetes* "wanderers"), but as a rule of thumb, a planet: 1) must directly orbit a star or an object that has nuclear fusion; 2) must be small enough that it has not undergone internal nuclear fusion (i.e., it is not a star or starlike object); and 3) must be large enough that its self-gravity gives it the general shape of a sphere.

In 1994, Dr. Alexander Wolszcan, an astronomer at Pennsylvania State University, presented convincing evidence of the first known planets to exist outside our solar system. They circle a pulsar, or exploded star, in the constellation *Virgo.*

In 1995, several of these *extrasolar planets* were discovered orbiting stars similar to our Sun. Swiss astronomers found the first extrasolar planet (HD 209458b, nicknamed "Osiris") to circle a normal Sun-like star. As of Sept. 2004, 136 such planets have been discovered.

In Feb. 2004, using the Hubble Space Telescope, a team of scientists at the Institut d'Astrophysique de Paris announced that they had discovered oxygen and carbon in the atmosphere of "Osiris."

In Aug. 2004, NASA and the National Science Foundation announced the discovery of two new planets, the smallest yet found, about the size of Neptune. The discovery opens up the possibility of smaller, Earth-sized extrasolar planets.

Pulsar: a celestial object, believed to be a rapidly spinning neutron star, that emits intense bursts of radio waves at regular intervals.

Quasar: "quasi-stellar" object. Originally thought to be peculiar stars in our own galaxy, quasars are now believed to be the most remote objects in the universe.

Astronomy Websites

American Astronomical Society: www.aas.org

Asteroid and Comet Impact Hazards:
http://impact.arc.nasa.gov/index.html

Center for Earth and Planetary Studies:
www.nasm.si.edu/ceps

The International Astronomical Union: www.iau.org

NASA Home Page: www.nasa.gov

The Nine Planets: www.nineplanets.org

Planet Quest: http://planetquest.jpl.nasa.gov/

Space Telescope Science Institute (home of Hubble): www.stsci.edu/resources

U.S. Naval Observatory: www.usno.navy.mil

Quasars emit tremendous amounts of light and microwave radiation. Although they are not much bigger than Earth's solar system, quasars pour out 100 to 1,000 times as much light as an entire galaxy containing a hundred billion stars. It is believed that quasars are powered by massive black holes that suck up billions of stars.

Retrograde: describes the clockwise orbit or rotation of a planet or other celestial object, which is in the direction opposite to the Earth and most celestial bodies. As viewed from a position in space north of the solar system (from some great distance above the Earth's North Pole), all the planets revolve counterclockwise around the Sun, and all but Venus, Uranus, and Pluto rotate counterclockwise on their own axes. These three planets have retrograde motion.

Sometimes *retrograde* is also used to describe apparent backward motion as viewed from Earth. This motion happens when two objects rotate at different speeds around another fixed object. For example, the planet Mars appears to be retrograde when the Earth overtakes and passes by it as they both move around the Sun.

Satellite (or **moon**): an object in orbit around a planet. Until the discovery of Jupiter's four main moons by Galileo Galilei, celestial objects in orbit around a planet were called *moons*. However, upon Galilei's discovery, Johannes Kepler (in a letter to Galileo) suggested *satellite* (from the Latin *satelles,* which means "attendant") as a general term for such objects. The word *satellite* is used interchangeably with *moon,* and astronomers speak and write about the moons of Neptune, Saturn, etc. The term *satellite* is also used to describe man-made devices of any size that are launched into orbit.

Star: a celestial object consisting of intensely hot gases held together by gravity. Stars derive their energy from nuclear reactions going on in their interiors, generating heat and light. Stars are very large. Our Sun has a diameter of 865,400 mi—a comparatively small star.

A dwarf star is a small star that is of relatively low mass and average or below average luminosity. The Sun is a *yellow dwarf,* which is in its main sequence, or prime of life. This means that nuclear reactions of hydrogen maintain its size and temperature. By contrast, a *white dwarf* is a star at the end of its life, with low luminosity, small size, and very high density.

A *red giant* is a star nearing the end of its life. When a star begins to lose hydrogen and burn helium instead, it gradually collapses, and its outer region begins to expand and cool. The light we see from these stars is red because of their cooler temperature.

Supernova: a celestial phenomenon in which a star explodes, releasing a great burst of light. There are two basic types of supernova. Type Ia happens when a white dwarf star draws large amounts of matter from a nearby star until it can no longer support itself and collapses. The second more well-known kind of supernova, type IIa, is the result of the collapse of a massive star. (Massive is a classification for a star that is at least eight times the size of our Sun.) Once the star's nuclear fuel is exhausted, if its core is heavy enough, the star will collapse in on itself, releasing a huge amount of energy (the supernova), which may be brighter than the star's host galaxy.

The Milky Way, the galaxy containing our solar system, is about 100,000 light-years in diameter and about 10,000 light-years thick.

The Big Bang: Origin of the Universe

Before the universe as we now know it existed, there was no space or time. The Big Bang and its associated theories try to explain or describe the moment of change from nothingness and no time to the existence of the universe filled with space and marked by time. Many physicists describe this event as an explosion, or flash, hence the name *Big Bang.* The Big Bang is a process of expansion in our universe that is still active today.

The universe flashed into existence (according to the Big Bang theory) from a very small agglomeration of matter of extremely high density and temperatures. As a dense, hot globule of gas, containing nothing but hydrogen and a small amount of helium, it began expanding rapidly outward. There were no stars or planets. The first stars probably formed when the universe was about 200 million years old. Our Sun was formed 4.5 billion years ago, and through telescopes we can now see stars forming out of compressed pockets of hydrogen in outer space.

A 2003 study pinpointed the universe's age at 13.7 billion years, with just a 1% margin or error.

Birth and Death of a Star

Astronomers think that a star begins to form as a dense cloud of gas in the arms of spiral galaxies. Individual hydrogen atoms fall with increasing speed and energy toward the center of the cloud under the force of the star's gravity. The increase in energy heats the gas. When this process has continued for some millions of years, the temperature reaches about 20 million degrees Fahrenheit. At this temperature, the hydrogen within the star ignites and burns in a continuing series of nuclear reactions. The onset of these reactions marks the birth of a star.

When a star begins to exhaust its hydrogen supply, its life nears an end. The first sign of a star's old age is a swelling and reddening of its outer regions. Such an aging, swollen star is called a *red giant.* The Sun, a middle-aged star, will probably swell to a red giant in 5 billion years, vaporizing Earth and any creatures that may be on its surface. When all its fuel has been exhausted, a star cannot generate

Astronomical Constants

Light-year (distance traveled by light in one year)	5,880,000,000,000 mi
Parsec (parallax of one second, or stellar distances)	3.259 light-years
Velocity of light	c. 186,282.4 mi/sec
Astronomical unit (A.U.), or mean distance Earth to Sun	ca. 93,000,000 mi[1]
Mean distance, Earth to Moon	238,860 mi
General precession	50′.26
Obliquity of the ecliptic	23° 27′8′.26-0′.4684(t-1900)[2]
Equatorial radius of Earth	3963.34 statute mi
Polar radius of Earth	3949.99 statute mi
Earth's mean radius	3958.89 statute mi
Oblateness of Earth	1/297
Equatorial horizontal parallax of the moon	57′2′.70
Earth's mean velocity in orbit	18.5 mi/sec
Sidereal year	365d.2564
Tropical year	365d.2422
Sidereal month	27d.3217
Synodic month	29d.5306
Mean sidereal day	23h56m4s.091 of mean solar time
Mean solar day	24h3m56s.555 of sidereal time

1. Actual mean distance derived from radar bounces: 92,935,700 mi. The value of 92,897,400 mi (based on parallax of 8″.80) is used in calculations. 2. *t* refers to the year in question, for example, 2003.

sufficient pressure at its center to balance the crushing force of gravity. The star collapses under the force of its own weight; if it is a small star, it collapses gently and remains collapsed. Such a collapsed star, at its life's end, is called a *white dwarf.* The Sun will probably end its life in this way. A different fate awaits a large star. Its final collapse generates a violent explosion, blowing the innards of the star out into space. There, the materials of the exploded star mix with the primeval hydrogen of the universe. Later in the history of the galaxy, other stars are formed out of this mixture. The Sun is one of these stars. It contains the debris of countless other stars that exploded before the Sun was born.

Formation of the Solar System

Our solar system consists of one star (the Sun), nine planets and all their moons, several thousand minor planets called "asteroids" or "planetoids," and an equally large number of comets. The Sun's age was calculated in 1989 to be 4.5 billion years old, less than the 4.7 billion years previously believed. It was formed from a cloud of hydrogen mixed with small amounts of other substances that had been produced in the bodies of other stars before the Sun was born. This was the parent cloud of the solar system. The dense, hot gas at the center of the cloud gave rise to the Sun; the outer regions of the cloud—cooler and less dense—gave birth to the planets.

The Sun

All the stars, including our Sun, are gigantic balls of superheated gas, kept hot by atomic reactions in their centers. In our Sun, this atomic reaction is hydrogen fusion: four hydrogen atoms are combined to form one helium atom. The temperature at the core of our Sun is thought to be 36,000,000°F, or about 20,000,000°C, and the surface temperature averages 11,000°F, or about 6,000°C. The diameter of the Sun is 865,400 mi, and its surface area is approximately 12,000 times that of Earth. Compared with other stars, our Sun is just a bit below average in size and temperature, and is a yellow dwarf star. It is 4.5 billion years old, and its fuel supply (hydrogen) is estimated to be sufficient for another 5 billion years.

Our Sun is not motionless in space; in fact, it has two kinds of motion. One is a seemingly straight-line motion in the direction of the constellation Hercules at the rate of about 12 miles per second. But since the Sun is a part of the Milky Way system and since the whole system rotates slowly around its own center, the Sun also moves at the rate of 175 miles per second as part of the rotating Milky Way system.

In addition to this motion, the Sun rotates on its axis. Observations of the motion of sunspots (darkish areas that look like enormous whirling storms) and solar flares, which are usually associated with sunspots, have shown that the rotational period of the Sun is just short of 25 days. But this figure is valid for the Sun's equator only; the sections near the Sun's poles seem to have a rotational period of 34 days. Since the Sun generates its own heat and light, there is no temperature difference between poles and equator.

What we call the Sun's "surface" is scientifically known as the *photosphere.* Since the whole Sun is a ball of expanding hot gas, there is really no such thing as a surface; it is a question of visual impression. The layer outside the photosphere is known as the *chromosphere,* which extends several thousand miles beyond the photosphere. It is in steady motion, and often enormous prominences can be seen to burst from it, extending as much as 100,000 mi into space. Outside the chromosphere is the *corona.* The corona consists of very tenuous gases (essentially hydrogen) and makes a magnificent sight when the Sun is eclipsed.

In addition to heat and light, the Sun also generates solar wind, a stream of ionized particles that radiates outward through the solar system at high speeds. One of the effects of solar wind is that it forces the tails of comets to point away from the Sun. The solar wind also interacts with the Earth's magnetic field, causing the auroras and other phenomena. Solar flares—eruptions of hydrogen gas on the surface of the Sun—can also cause disturbances in the Earth's magnetic field.

As the Sun ages, it gradually expands and heats. It is estimated that the Sun's brilliancy will increase by 10% over the next 1.1 billion years or more, and, in about 6.5 billion years, our aging star will have

A Star's Magnitude

Magnitude is the degree of brightness of a star. In 1856, British astronomer Norman Pogson proposed a quantitative scale of stellar magnitudes, which was adopted by the astronomical community. He noted that we receive 100 times more light from a first magnitude star as from a sixth; thus with a difference of five magnitudes, there is a 100:1 ratio of incoming light energy, which is called *luminous flux*.

Because of the nature of human perception, equal intervals of brightness are actually equal ratios of luminous flux. Pogson's proposal was that one increment in magnitude be the fifth root

of 100. This means that each increment in magnitude corresponds to an increase in the amount of energy by 2.512, approximately. A fifth magnitude star is 2.512 times as bright as a sixth, and a fourth magnitude star is 6.310 times as bright as a sixth, and so on. The naked eye, upon optimum conditions, can see down to around the sixth magnitude, that is +6. Under Pogson's system, a few of the brighter stars now have negative magnitudes. For example, Sirius is –1.5. The lower the magnitude number, the brighter the object. The full moon has a magnitude of about –12.5, and the sun is a bright –26.51!

The Brightest Stars

Star	Constellation	Mag.	Dist (l.-y.)	Star	Constellation	Mag.	Dist (l.-y.)
Sirius	Canis Major	-1.6	8	Antares	Scorpius	1.2	170
Canopus	Carina	-0.9	650	Fomalhaut	Piscis Austrinus	1.3	27
Alpha Centauri	Centaurus	+0.1	4	Deneb	Cygnus	1.3	465
Vega	Lyra	0.1	23	Regulus	Leo	1.3	70
Capella	Auriga	0.2	42	Beta Crucis	Crux	1.5	465
Arcturus	Boötes	0.2	32	Eta Carinae	Carina	1–7	—
Rigel	Orion	0.3	545	Alpha-one Crucis	Crux	1.6	150
Procyon	Canis Minor	0.5	10	Castor	Gemini	1.6	44
Achernar	Eridanus	0.6	70	Gamma Crucis	Crux	1.6	—
Beta Centauri	Centaurus	0.9	130	Epsilon Canis Majoris	Canis Major	1.6	325
Altair	Aquila	0.9	18	Epsilon Ursae Majoris	Ursa Major	1.7	50
Betelgeuse	Orion	0.9	600	Bellatrix	Orion	1.7	215
Aldebaran	Taurus	1.1	54	Lambda Scorpii	Scorpius	1.7	205
Spica	Virgo	1.2	190	Epsilon Carinae	Carina	1.7	325
Pollux	Gemini	1.2	31	Mira	Cetus	2–10	250

doubled its present luminosity. The extreme heat generated will be catastrophic for Earth: the oceans will boil away and life as we know it will end. Eight billion years from now, the Sun's radius will extend beyond the present orbit of Venus, causing the total destruction of Earth.

The Moon

Mercury and Venus do not have any moons. The planet that comes after the Earth, Mars, has two very small moons. Jupiter has 4 major moons and at least 59 minor ones. Saturn, the ringed planet, has 31 known moons, of which 1 (Titan) is larger than the planet Mercury. Uranus has at least 27 moons (4 of them large) as well as rings, while Neptune has 1 large and 12 small moons. Pluto has one moon, discovered in 1978. Some astronomers still consider Pluto to be a "runaway moon" of Neptune.

Our Moon, with a diameter of 2,160 mi, is one of the larger moons in our solar system and is especially large when compared with the planet that it orbits. In fact, the common center of gravity of the Earth–Moon system is only about 1,000 mi below Earth's surface. The closest the Moon can come to us (its perigee) is 221,463 mi; the farthest it can go away (its apogee) is 252,710 mi. The period of rotation of the Moon is equal to its period of revolution around Earth, so from Earth we can see only one hemisphere of the Moon. Both periods are 27 days, 7 hours, 43 minutes, and 11.47 seconds. But while the rotation of the Moon is constant, its velocity in its orbit is not, since it moves more

slowly in apogee than in perigee. Consequently, some portions near the rim of the Moon that are not normally visible will appear briefly. This phenomenon is called *libration,* and by taking advantage of the librations, astronomers have succeeded in mapping approximately 59% of the lunar surface. The other 41% can never be seen from Earth but has been mapped by American and Russian Moon-orbiting spacecraft.

Though the Moon goes around Earth in the time mentioned, the interval from new moon to new moon is 29 days, 12 hours, 44 minutes, and 2.78 seconds. This delay of nearly two days is due to the fact that Earth is moving around the Sun, so that the Moon needs two extra days to reach a spot in its orbit where no part is illuminated by the Sun, as seen from Earth.

If the plane of Earth's orbit around the Sun (the ecliptic) and the plane of the Moon's orbit around Earth were the same, the Moon would be eclipsed by Earth every time it is full, and the Sun would be eclipsed by the Moon every time the Moon is "new" (it would be better to call it the "black moon" when it is in this position). But because the two orbits do not coincide, the Moon's shadow normally misses Earth and Earth's shadow misses the Moon. The inclination of the two orbital planes to each other is 5°.

The tides are caused by the Moon with the help of the Sun, but in the open ocean they are surprisingly low, amounting to about one yard. The very high tides that can be observed near the shore in some places are due to funneling effects of the shorelines.

At new moon and at full moon the tides raised by the Moon are reinforced by the Sun; these are the *spring tides*. If the Sun's tidal power acts at right angles to that of the Moon (quarter moons) we get the low *neap tides*.

The *Lunar Prospector* spacecraft, launched in Jan. 1998, found that as much as three billion metric tons of water ice is hidden in the permanently shaded craters at the poles. The water probably came from interstellar comets that crashed into the Moon. *Lunar Prospector* also confirmed that the Moon has a small core, supporting the theory that the Moon was ripped away from the early Earth when an object the size of Mars collided with the Earth. On July 31, 1999, the spacecraft was intentionally crashed to look for evidence of water ice—none was found.

Earth

Earth, circling the Sun at an average distance of 93 million miles, is the fifth-largest planet and the third from the Sun. It orbits the Sun at a speed of 67,000 mph, making one revolution in 365 days, 5 hours, 48 minutes, and 45.51 seconds. Earth completes one rotation on its axis every 23 hours, 56 minutes, and 4.09 seconds. Actually a bit pear-shaped rather than a true sphere, Earth has a diameter of 7,927 mi at the equator and a few miles less at the poles. It has an estimated mass of about 6.6 sextillion tons, with an average density of 5.52 grams per cubic centimeter. Earth's surface area encompasses 196,949,970 sq mi of which about three-fourths is water.

Origin of Earth

Earth, along with the other planets, is believed to have been born 4.5 billion years ago as a solidified cloud of dust and gases left over from the creation of the Sun. For perhaps 500 million years, the interior of Earth stayed solid and relatively cool, perhaps 2,000°F. The main ingredients, according to the best available evidence, were iron and silicates, with small amounts of other elements, some of them radioactive. As millions of years passed, energy released by radioactive decay—mostly of uranium, thorium, and potassium—gradually heated Earth, melting some of its constituents. The iron melted before the silicates, and, being heavier, sank toward the center. This forced up the silicates that it found there. After many years, the iron reached the center, almost 4,000 mi deep, and began to accumulate. No eyes were around at that time to view the turmoil that must have taken place on the face of Earth—gigantic heaves and bubblings on the surface, exploding volcanoes, and flowing lava covering everything in sight. Finally, the iron in the center accumulated as the core. Around it, a thin but fairly stable crust of solid rock formed as Earth cooled. Depressions in the crust were natural basins in which water, rising from the interior of the planet through volcanoes and fissures, collected to form the oceans. Slowly, Earth acquired its present appearance.

Earth Today

As a result of radioactive heating over millions of years, Earth's molten *core* is probably fairly hot today, around 11,000°F. By comparison, lead melts at around 800°F. Most of Earth's 2,100-mile-thick core is liquid, but the center of the core is mostly solid iron. The liquid outer portion, about 95% of the core, is constantly in motion. The interaction between the solid inner core and the fluid outer core creates a hydromagnetic dynamo that generates the magnetic field around Earth. The magnetic field protects the Earth from harmful cosmic radiation and makes navigation by compass possible. Scientists have observed a 10% decline in the dipolar magnetic field over the last 150 years. There is a point off the coast of Brazil where the field is 30% weaker, causing glitches in satellites and spacecraft flying through it. This weakening of the magnetic field has scientists speculating that it may eventually collapse in about 1,500–2,000 years and lead to a reversal of the South and North Poles. Polar reversals are a periodic occurrence.

Within the last decade, scientists have made some important discoveries about Earth's solid-iron core. In 1996, geophysicists discovered that the core rotates slightly faster than the rest of the planet and gains a quarter-turn every century. X-ray images of the inside of the Earth show that the core is not a perfect sphere—there are vast mountains 6 to 7 mi high and deep valleys. These features are in an inverse, or upside-down, relationship to similar features on the Earth's surface.

Outside the core is Earth's *mantle*, 1,800 mi thick and extending nearly to the surface. The mantle is composed of heavy silicate rock, similar to that brought up by volcanic eruptions. It is somewhere between liquid and solid, slightly yielding, and therefore contributing to an active, moving Earth. Most of Earth's radioactive material is in the thin *crust* that covers the mantle, but some is in the mantle and continues to give off heat. The crust's thickness ranges from 5 to 25 mi.

Continental Drift

A great deal of evidence confirms the theory that the continents of Earth, made mostly of relatively light granite, float in the slightly yielding mantle, like logs in a pond. For many years it had been noticed that if North and South America could be pushed toward western and southern Europe and western Africa, they would fit like pieces in a jigsaw puzzle. Today, there is little question—the continents have drifted widely and continue to do so.

In 10 million years, the world as we know it may be unrecognizable, with California drifting out to sea, Florida joining South America, and Africa moving farther away from Europe and Asia.

Earth's Atmosphere

The thin blanket of atmosphere that envelops Earth extends several hundred miles into space. From sea level—the very bottom of the ocean of air—to a height of about 60 mi, the air in the atmosphere is made up of the same gases in the same ratio: about 78% nitrogen, 21% oxygen, and the remaining 1% a mixture of argon, carbon dioxide, and tiny amounts of neon, helium, krypton, xenon, and other gases. The atmosphere becomes less dense with increasing altitude: more than three-fourths of Earth's huge envelope is concentrated in the first 5 to 10 mi above the surface. At sea level, a cubic foot of atmosphere weighs about an ounce and a quarter. The entire atmosphere weighs 5,700 trillion tons, and the force with which gravity holds it in place causes it to exert a pressure of nearly 15 psi. Going out from Earth's surface, the atmosphere is divided into five regions. The regions, and the heights to which they extend, are: *troposphere,* 0 to 7 mi (at middle latitudes);

stratosphere, 7 to 30 mi; mesosphere, 30 to 50 mi; thermosphere, 50 to 400 mi; and exosphere, above 400 mi. The boundaries between each of the regions are known respectively as the tropopause, stratopause, mesopause, and thermopause. Alternative terms often used for the layers above the troposphere are ozonosphere (for stratosphere) and ionosphere for the remaining upper layers.

The Seasons

Seasons are caused by the 23.4° tilt of Earth's axis, which alternately turns the North and South Poles toward the Sun. Times when the Sun's apparent path crosses the equator are known as equinoxes. Times when the Sun's apparent path is at the greatest distance from the equator are known as solstices. The lengths of the days are most extreme at each solstice. If Earth's axis were perpendicular to the plane of Earth's orbit around the Sun, there would be no seasons, and the days always would be equal in length. Since Earth's axis is at an angle, the Sun strikes Earth directly at the equator only twice a year: in March (vernal equinox) and September (autumnal equinox). In the Northern Hemisphere, spring begins at the vernal equinox, summer at the summer solstice, fall at the autumnal equinox, and winter at the winter solstice. The situation is reversed in the Southern Hemisphere.

Mercury

Mercury is the planet nearest the Sun. Appropriately named for the wing-footed Roman messenger of the gods, Mercury whizzes around the Sun at a speed of 30 miles per second, completing one circuit in 88 days. The days and nights are long on Mercury. It takes 59 Earth days for Mercury to make a single rotation. It spins at a rate of about 6 mph (about 10 km/h), measured at the equator, as compared to Earth's spin of about 1,000 mph (about 1,600 km/h) at the equator.

The photographs Mariner 10 (1974–1975) radioed back to Earth revealed an ancient, heavily cratered surface on Mercury, closely resembling our own Moon. The pictures showed huge cliffs, or scarps, crisscrossing the planet. These apparently were created when Mercury's interior cooled and shrank, compressing the planet's crust. The cliffs are as high as 1.2 mi (2 km) and as long as 932 mi (1,500 km). Another unique feature is the Caloris Basin, a large impact crater about 808 mi (1,300 km) in diameter.

Mercury, like Earth, appears to have a crust of light silicate rock. Scientists believe it has a heavy iron-rich core that makes up about half of its volume.

Instruments onboard Mariner 10 discovered that the planet has a weak magnetic field and a trace of atmosphere—a trillionth the density of Earth's and composed chiefly of argon, neon, and helium. The spacecraft reported temperatures ranging from 950°F (510°C) on Mercury's sunlit side to –346°F (–210°C) on the dark side. Mercury literally bakes in daylight and freezes at night.

Until the Mariner 10 probe, little was known about the planet. Even the best telescopic views from Earth showed Mercury as an indistinct object lacking any surface detail. The planet is so close to the Sun that it is usually lost in the Sun's glare.

Radar images taken by astronomers at Jet Propulsion Laboratories and California Institute of Technology during the summer of 1991 suggest that the polar regions of Mercury may be covered with patches of water ice. Although this seems impossible due to the planet's sizzling heat, the polar regions receive very little sunlight and may get as cold as –235°F (–148°C). The radar images showed bright patterns at the poles that are characteristic of ice reflecting radar signals. Other explanations may be offered for this unexpected discovery.

NASA's Messenger, the first Mercury mission in more than 30 years, was successfully launched on Aug. 3, 2004. Mercury will be almost completely mapped in color and images taken of areas missed by Mariner. Messenger will also measure the composition of the surface, atmosphere, and magnetosphere.

Mercury is visible to the naked eye at morning or evening twilight when it is at its greatest elongation.

Venus

Although Venus is Earth's closest neighbor, very little is known about the planet because it is permanently covered by thick clouds. In 1962, Soviet and American space probes, coupled with Earth-based radar and infrared spectroscopy, began slowly unraveling some of the mystery surrounding Venus. Twenty-eight years later, the Magellan spacecraft, sent by the United States, arrived at Venus in Aug. 1990 and began radar-mapping the planet's surface in greater detail.

According to the latest results, Venus's atmosphere exerts a pressure at the surface 94.5 times greater than Earth's. Walking on Venus would be as difficult as walking a half-mile beneath the ocean. Because of a thick blanket of carbon dioxide, a "greenhouse effect" exists on Venus. Venus intercepts twice as much of the Sun's light as does Earth. The light enters freely through the carbon dioxide gas and is changed to heat radiation in molecular collisions. But carbon dioxide prevents the heat from escaping. Consequently, the temperature of the surface of Venus is over 800°F (427°C), hot enough to melt lead.

The atmospheric composition of Venus is about 96% carbon dioxide, 4% nitrogen, and minor amounts of water, oxygen, and sulfur compounds. There are at least four distinct cloud and haze layers that exist at different altitudes above the planet's surface. The haze layers contain small aerosol particles, possibly droplets of sulfuric acid. A concentration of sulfur dioxide above the cloud tops has been observed to be decreasing since 1978. The source of sulfur dioxide at this altitude is unknown; it may be injected by volcanic explosions or atmospheric overturning.

Measurements of the Venusian atmosphere and its cloud patterns reveal nearly constant high-speed zonal winds, about 220 mph (100 meters per second) at the equator. The winds decrease toward the poles so that the atmosphere at cloud-top level rotates almost like a solid body. The wind speeds at the equator correspond to Venus's rotation period of four to five days at most latitudes. The circulation is always in the same direction—east to west—as Venus's slow retrograde motion. Earth's winds blow from west to east, the same direction as its rotation.

Venus is round, very different from the other planets and from the Moon. Venus has neither polar flattening nor an equatorial bulge. The diameter of Venus is 7,519 mi (12,100 km). Venus has a retrograde axial rotation period of 243.1 Earth days. The surface

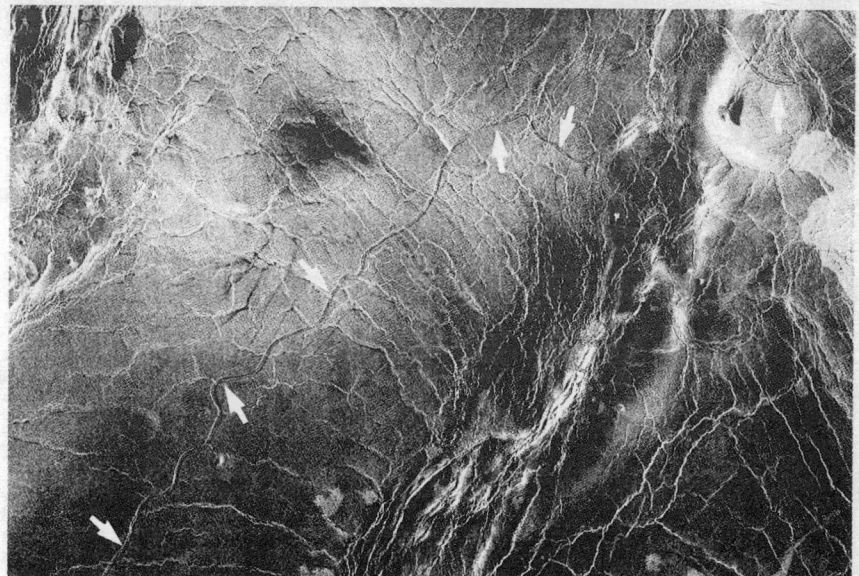

Longest Channel in the Solar System. *Magellan* took the above image of the channel on Venus and at 4,200 mi (6,800 km) long and an average of 1.1 mi (1.8 km) wide, it is longer than the Nile River, making it the longest known channel in the solar system. Parts of the channel were originally mapped by the Soviet *Venera 15* and *16* spacecraft orbiters, but the *Magellan* mission determined its length. *Source:* NASA.

atmospheric pressure is 1,396 psi (95 Earth atmospheres). The planet's mean distance from the Sun is 67.2 million miles (108.2 million kilometers). The period of its revolution around the Sun is 224.7 days.

The highest point on Venus is the summit of Maxwell Montes, 6.71 mi (10.8 km) above the mean level, more than a mile higher than Mount Everest. There is some evidence that this huge mountain is an active volcano. The lowest point is in the rift valley, Diana Chasma, 1.8 mi (2.9 km) below the mean level. This point is about one-fifth the greatest depth on Earth in the Marianas Trench.

Venus has an extreme lowland basin, Atalanta Planitia, which is about the size of Earth's North Atlantic Ocean basin. The smooth surface of the Atalanta Planitia resembles the mare basins of the Moon.

There are only two highland or continental masses on Venus: Ishtar Terra and Aphrodite Terra. Ishtar Terra is 6.8 mi (11 km) at its highest points (the highest peaks on Venus) and those of Aphrodite Terra rise to about 3.10 mi (5 km) above the planet. Ishtar Terra is about the size of the continental United States and Aphrodite Terra is about the size of Africa.

The unmanned NASA spacecraft *Magellan* was launched on May 4, 1989, from the shuttle *Atlantis* and arrived at Venus Aug. 10, 1990, to map most of the planet. Despite some problems with its radio transmissions, the results of the radar mapping delighted scientists and provided them with the sharpest images ever taken of the planet's surface. Images taken from *Magellan* show ten times more detail than ever seen before.

The radar images provided scientists with compelling evidence that the planet has been dominated by volcanism on a global scale. The photos also showed that the planet's second-highest mountain, Maat Mons, rising 5 mi (8 km) above the Venusian plains, appears to be covered with fresh lava and is possibly an active volcano.

Magellan discovered the longest known channel in the solar system on Venus. It is 4,200 mi (6,800 km) long and averages slightly over a mile (1.8 km) wide. Its origin is puzzling to scientists because high-temperature lava is unlikely to have caused such a long-distance flow on the surface, and there are no known substances that could remain liquid long enough under the planet's atmospheric pressure and temperature to have carved out this snakelike feature. The channel is slightly longer than the Nile River, the longest river on Earth.

Magellan ended its radar and emissions mapping in Sept. 1992 after covering 98% of the planet's surface. The spacecraft continued to gather data until Oct. 1994, when it was intentionally crashed into the planet's surface. The European Space Agency (ESA) plans a 2005 launch of the Venus Express to study the atmosphere and subsurface.

Venus is the brightest of all the planets and is often visible in the morning or evening, when it is frequently referred to as the Morning Star or Evening Star. At its brightest, it can sometimes be seen in full daylight with the naked eye, if one knows where to look.

A rare transit of Venus took place on June 8, 2004. This is when Venus crosses in front of the Sun and can be seen from the Earth. Transits occur in pairs eight years apart (June 6, 2012, is the date of the second transit in the current pair) and then the next duo of transits happens either 105½ or 121½ years later. Dec. 11, 2117, will see the next pair of transits begin.

Mars

Mars, on the other side of Earth from Venus, is Venus's direct opposite in terms of physical properties. Its atmosphere is cold, thin, and transparent, and readily permits observation of the planet's features. We know more about Mars than any other planet except Earth. Mars is a forbidding, rugged planet with huge volcanoes and deep chasms. The largest volcano, Olympus Mons (Olympic Mountain) rises 78,000 ft above the surface, higher than Mount Everest. The plains of Mars are pockmarked by the hits of thousands of meteors over the years.

Until the arrival of *Mars Pathfinder* and *Mars Global Surveyor* in 1997, most of our information about Mars came from the *Mariner* and *Viking* spacecrafts. *Mariner 9* orbited the planet in 1971 and photographed 100% of the planet, uncovering spectacular geological formations, including a Martian "Grand Canyon" that dwarfs the one on Earth. Called Valles Marineris (Mariner Valley), it stretches more than 3,000 mi along the equatorial region of Mars and is over 2.5 mi (4 km) deep in places and 50 to 62 mi (80 to 100 km) wide. The spacecraft's cameras also recorded what appeared to be dried riverbeds, suggesting the one-time presence of water on the planet. The latter idea gave encouragement to scientists looking for life on Mars, for where there is water, there may be life. However, to date, no evidence of life has been found. Temperatures range from 80°F at the equator during the day to –199°F at the poles at night.

Mars rotates upon its axis in nearly the same period as Earth—24 hours, 37 minutes—so that a Mars day is almost identical to an Earth day. Mars takes 687 days to make one trip around the Sun. Because of its eccentric orbit, Mars's distance from the Sun can vary by about 36 million miles. Its distance from Earth can vary by as much as 200 million miles. The atmosphere of Mars is much thinner than Earth's; atmospheric pressure is about 1% that of our planet. Its gravity is one-third of Earth's. Major constituents are carbon dioxide and nitrogen. Water vapor and oxygen are minor constituents. Mars's polar caps, composed mostly of frozen carbon dioxide (dry ice), recede and advance according to the Martian seasons.

Mars has four seasons like Earth, but they are much longer. For example, in the northern hemisphere, the Martian spring is 198 days, and the winter season lasts 158 days.

The *Mars Pathfinder* lander and its rover, *Sojourner*, set down on the edge of a boulder-strewn outflow channel known as *Ares Vallis* on July 4, 1997, and provided scientists with a wealth of information on the rocks, soils, and atmosphere of Mars. The lander sent back the first live pictures of the planet's topography, and its tiny rover explored a variety of rocks and analyzed their mineral composition with its cameras and on-board X-ray spectrometer.

In its three months of operation, the mission returned more than 16,000 images of the Martian landscape from the lander's camera and 550 images from the rover.

Scientists have inferred from the variety of rocks and sediments found in the *Ares* basin that the spacecraft landed in a channel that was once awash with torrential floods greater than any known on Earth.

The *Sojourner* rover traveled a total of about 328 ft (100 m), performed more than 16 chemical analyses of rocks and soil, and explored 820 sq ft (250 sq m) of the planet's surface. Communications were lost with the lander on Sept. 27, 1997, after 83 days of relaying data.

NASA launched the *Mars Global Surveyor* spacecraft on Nov. 7, 1996, to provide detailed maps of the planet's surface, its distribution of minerals, and to monitor its weather. The spacecraft entered Mars's orbit on Sept. 11, 1997, and began mapping operations in mid-March 1999.

Surveyor discovered the first clear evidence of an ancient hydrothermal system near the equator. This implies that water was stable at or near the surface and that a thicker atmosphere existed in Mars's early history.

Surveyor's three-dimensional views of the planet's northern polar ice cap showed often striking canyons and spiral troughs in the water and carbon dioxide ice that can reach depths as great as 3,600 ft below the surface. Its data also showed that large areas of the ice cap were extremely smooth, with elevations varying only a few feet over many miles.

NASA's Mars exploration program suffered a setback with the loss of the *Climate Orbiter* as it entered the Martian atmosphere in Sept. 1999. The following December scientists also failed to establish contact with the *Polar Lander* after it reached Mars.

In 2000, NASA announced that the *Mars Global Surveyor* had observed features that looked like gullies carved out by flowing water and deposits of soil and rocks that were transported by the flow. Because gullies had never been seen before on Mars, the *Surveyor* images suggested that there might be current sources of liquid water at or near the surface.

In the spring of 2002, NASA released exciting news that large quantities of water ice had been found just below the surface of Mars. The discovery was made by NASA's *Mars Odyssey* spacecraft, which was launched in April 2001 and has been collecting data since late 2001.

On June 10, 2003, NASA launched *Spirit*, the first of two Mars Exploration Rovers (MER), followed on July 7 by the takeoff of the second rover, *Opportunity*. *Spirit* landed on Mars in the Gusev Crater on Jan. 3, 2004, and within hours was transmitting the first panoramic images to Earth. *Opportunity* landed successfully on Jan. 25 in the Meridiani Planum region on the opposite side of the planet.

The main instruments on board the rovers are: a panoramic camera, a miniature thermal emission spectrometer for identifying rocks and soils and taking the temperature of the atmosphere, a Mossbauer spectrometer for studying the mineralogy of rocks and soil, an alpha particle x-ray spectrometer for chemical analysis of rocks and soil, magnets for collecting magnetic dust particles, a microscopic imager, and a rock abrasion tool to scrape rocks for a fresh surface to study.

Opportunity uncovered water evidence in the Meridiana Planum region in early March 2004. The rover discovered salts usually found in rocks either formed in water or subjected to long exposure to water. The physical characteristics of the rocks bolstered the water evidence with surfaces that appeared to have been pocked from salt deposits; round, BB-sized particles formed from mineral accumulation inside a porous, water-soaked rock;

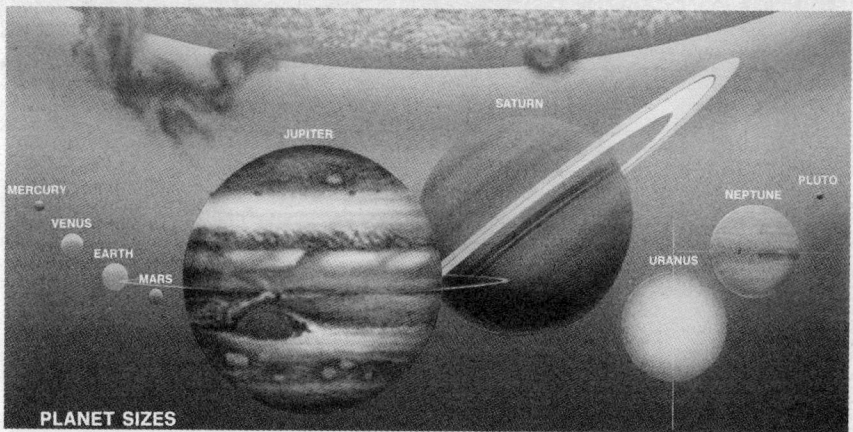

PLANET SIZES. Shown from left to right: Mercury, Venus, Earth, Mars, Jupiter, Saturn, Uranus, Neptune, and Pluto. *Copyright 1990 Hansen Planetarium, Salt Lake City, Utah. Reproduced with permission.*

and a pattern or layering usually associated with the action of water. A few days later on the other side of Mars, *Spirit* found water evidence in a rock that appeared to have minerals crystallized out of water.

The rovers were designed for a 90-day mission but were doing so well, NASA extended their duties until March 2005, or as long as they keep working.

Mars was named for the Roman god of war, because when seen from Earth its distinct red color reminded the ancient people of blood. We know now that the reddish hue reflects the oxidized (rusted) iron in the surface material.

The Martian Moons

Mars has two very small elliptical-shaped moons, Deimos and Phobos—the Greek names for the companions of the god Mars: Deimos (Terror) and Phobos (Fear). They were discovered in Aug. 1877 by the American astronomer Asaph Hall (1829–1907) of the U.S. Naval Observatory in Washington, DC.

The inner satellite, Phobos, is 16.78 mi (27 km) long, and it revolves around the planet in 7.6 hours. The short orbital period of Phobos means that the satellite travels around Mars three times in a Martian day. The outer moon, Deimos, is 9.32 mi (15 km) long, and it circles the planet in 30.35 hours.

Phobos orbits Mars at a distance of only 5,627 mi (9,378 km) and is closer to its planet than any other moon in the solar system. Observation of Phobos has revealed that the moon's orbit is actually decreasing downward; in about 40 million years it will crash into the planet's surface or break up into a ring.

Meteorites from Mars

Thirty meteorites, almost certainly from Mars, have been discovered as of March 2004. They are known as SNCs[1] (named for the towns where the original 12 meteorites were found: Shergotty, India, in 1865; Nakhla, Egypt, in 1911; and Chassigny, France, in 1815). This hypothesis was based largely on the composition of noble gases (particularly argon and xenon) trapped in the meteorites, and the shergottites in particular, which resemble measure-

[1. Pronounced "snick."]

ments of the Martian atmosphere made by the *Viking* spacecraft. Major element compositions of the SNCs are also similar to Martian soil analyses made by *Viking*.

The relatively young isotopic ages of the SNC meteorites (1.3 billion years or less) suggest that Mars has been volcanically active during its recent past.

A 40-pound meteorite that crashed to Earth in Nigeria in 1962 has been classified as coming from Mars. It was named Zagami for the region in which it was found. It is the largest single Martian meteorite ever found.

A 4-pound, 7-ounce (1.9-kilogram) meteorite, ALH 84001, found in the Allen Hills of Antarctica in 1984, was reclassified in 1993 as coming from the Red Planet, making it the tenth meteorite known to have originated from Mars. In 1996, NASA announced that meteorite ALH 84001 contained fossils of ancient Martian microbial life forms.

Two rock specimens weighing 8.6 oz (245.4 g) and 16 oz (452.6 g) that were found in the Mojave Desert about 20 years ago were classified in Feb. 2000 as the fourteenth Mars meteorite. The rocks are known as the Los Angeles meteorites.

The most recent finds in 2001, 2002, and 2003, were discovered in Antarctica and the deserts of northern Africa, which have become the favored hunting grounds for meteorite collectors, since there is little or no ground cover to hide the rocks.

In April 2004, the Mars Exploration Rover *Opportunity* analyzed "Bounce Rock," a rock it hit during its January landing. Bounce Rock's composition resembled the original Shergotty meteorite and matched even more closely a meteorite found in 1979 in Antarctica.

Jupiter

Jupiter is the largest planet in the solar system—a gaseous world as large as 1,300 Earths. Its equatorial diameter is 88,736 mi (142,800 km), while from pole to pole, Jupiter measures only 84,201 mi (133,500 km). For comparison, the diameter of Earth is 7,926.2 mi (12,756 km). The massive planet rotates at a dizzying speed—once every 9 hours and

Basic Planetary Data

	Mercury	Venus	Earth	Mars	Jupiter
Mean distance from Sun (millions of kilometers)	57.9	108.2	149.6	227.9	778.3
Mean distance from Sun (millions of miles)	36.0	67.24	92.9	141.71	483.88
Period of revolution	88 days	224.7 days	365.2 days	687 days	11.86 yrs
Rotation period	59 days	243 days retrograde	23 hr 56 min 4 sec	24 hr 37 min	9 hr 55 min 30 sec
Inclination of axis	Near 0°	3°	23°27'	25° 12'	3° 5'
Inclination of orbit to ecliptic	7°	3.4°	0°	1.9°	1.3°
Eccentricity of orbit	.206	.007	.017	.093	.048
Equatorial diameter (kilometers)	4,880	12,100	12,756	6,794	142,800
(miles)	3,032.4	7,519	7,926.2	4,194	88,736
Atmosphere (main components)	Virtually none	Carbon dioxide	Nitrogen oxygen	Carbon dioxide	Hydrogen helium
Satellites	0	0	1	2	63[1]
Rings	0	0	0	0	3

	Saturn	Uranus	Neptune	Pluto
Mean distance from Sun (millions of kilometers)	1,427	2,870	4,497	5,900
Mean distance from Sun (millions of miles)	887.14	1,783.98	2,796.46	3,666
Period of revolution	29.46 yrs	84 yrs	165 yrs	248 yrs
Rotation period	10 hr 40 min 24 sec	16.8 hr (?) retrograde	16 hr 11 min (?)	6 days 9 hr 18 mins retrograde
Inclination of axis	26°44'	97°55'	28°48'	60° (?)
Inclination of orbit to ecliptic	2.5°	0.8°	1.8°	17.2°
Eccentricity of orbit	.056	.047	.009	.254
Equatorial diameter (kilometers)	120,660	51,810	49,528	2,290 (?)
(miles)	74,978	32,193	30,775	1,423 (?)
Atmosphere (main components)	Hydrogen helium	Helium hydrogen methane	Hydrogen helium methane	None detected
Satellites	33[2]	27[3]	13[4]	1
Rings	1,000 (?)	11	4	?

1. Forty-five of these moons were discovered only recently, from 2000–2003. 2. Moons S/2000 S1 through S12 were discovered in late 2000, S/2003 S1 in early 2003, and Cassini-Huygens discovered S/2004 S1 and S2 in 2004. 3. S/2001 U2 and S/2003 U3 were announced in Fall 2003. 4. S/2003 N1 was announced in Fall 2003. *Source:* Basic NASA data and other sources.

55 minutes. It takes Jupiter almost 12 Earth years to complete a journey around the Sun.

The giant planet appears as a banded disk of turbulent clouds with all of its stripes running parallel to its bulging equator. Large dusky gray regions surround each pole. Darker gray or brown stripes called belts intermingle with lighter, yellow-white stripes called zones. The belts are regions of descending air masses and the zones are rising cloudy air masses. The strongest winds—up to 250 mph (400 km)—are found at boundaries between the belts and zones.

This uniquely colorful atmosphere is mainly 89% molecular hydrogen and 11% helium. It contains small amounts of methane, ammonia, ethane, and water.

Cloud-type lightning bolts similar to those on Earth have been found in the Jovian atmosphere. At the polar regions, auroras have been observed. A very thin ring of material less than 0.6 mi (1 km) in thickness and about 4,000 mi (6,000 km) in radial extent has been observed circling the planet about 35,000 mi (55,000 km) above the cloud tops.

The most prominent feature on Jupiter is its "Great Red Spot," an oval larger than the planet Earth. It is a tremendous atmospheric storm that rotates counter-clockwise with one revolution every six days at the outer edge, while at the center almost no motion can be seen. The spot is about 16,000 mi (25,000 km) on its long axis, and would cover three Earths. Along the outer rim the winds blow at speeds reaching 225 mph (360 km/h).

Jupiter is circled by faint rings. They are very tenuous and contain many microscopic-sized particles. The rings are formed by dust kicked up as interplanetary meteoroids smash into the planet's four small inner moons.

Jupiter emits 67% more heat than it absorbs from the Sun. This heat is thought to have been accumulated during the planet's formation several billion years ago.

Twenty-one fragments of comet Shoemaker-Levy 9 bombarded the cloud-covered surface of Jupiter, July 16–22, 1994. It was the most violent event in the recorded history of our solar system. The impact of the comet fragments caused towering plumes of debris and hot gas to rise from the planet's surface.

On Dec. 7, 1995, the *Galileo* spacecraft released a probe into Jupiter's atmosphere to study the planet's physical and chemical properties. The probe lasted 57 minutes and early results indicated a lower abundance of water than was expected. *Galileo* data has shown that Jupiter has both wet and dry regions, just as Earth has tropics and deserts. This could explain why the probe found less water than anticipated. These dry spots cover less than 1% of the Jovian atmosphere. The *Galileo* mission ended on Sept. 21, 2003, when the probe made a scheduled crash into the gas giant.

Jovian Moons

Jupiter has a total of 63 known satellites. The four great moons of Jupiter were discovered by Galileo Galilei (1564–1642) in Jan. 1610, and are called the Galilean satellites after their discoverer. Their names are Io, Europa, Ganymede, and Callisto. Like our Moon, the satellites always keep the same face turned toward the planet they circle. Jupiter's four largest moons all have thin atmospheres. A carbon dioxide atmosphere envelops Callisto; Europa and Ganymede each have thin oxygen atmospheres; and Io's contains sulfur dioxide.

Ganymede

Ganymede, 3,275 mi (5,270 km) in diameter, is Jupiter's largest moon, and it is also the largest satellite in the solar system. Ganymede is about one and one-half times the size of our Moon. It is heavily cratered and probably has the greatest variety of geologic process recorded on its surface. Ganymede is half water and half rock, resulting in a density about two-thirds that of Europa, an ice-coated satellite.

The first close-up photos of Ganymede, taken by the *Galileo* spacecraft during its June 1996 flyby, revealed a surface pockmarked with ancient craters and a landscape wrinkled and torn by the same forces that make mountains and move continents on Earth. *Galileo*'s findings also indicated that Ganymede is enveloped in its own magnetic field, possibly created by a molten iron core or even a thin layer of electricity-conducting salty water underneath its icy crust.

Ganymede is the first known moon with its own magnetosphere.

Europa

Europa, the brightest of Jupiter's satellites, is about 1,950 mi (3,160 km) in diameter or about the size of Earth's Moon. Its density is about three times that of water. The moon is covered with a thin ice crust and is crisscrossed with an amazingly complex network of ridges. Some of the fractures on its crust are more than 1,850 mi (3,000 km) long. Very few impact craters are visible on the surface. In fact, Europa is the smoothest object in the solar system. Its mostly flat surface doesn't exceed 0.62 mi (1 km) in height.

Galileo spacecraft photos taken at its closest flyby on Feb. 20, 1997, at a distance of 363 mi (586 km), showed the existence of ice flows on the surface that strongly suggest that the moon has a hidden subsurface ocean of water or ice-slush. The photos revealed chunky ice rafts that appear to be floating, comparable to icebergs on Earth. The presence of water and enough heat to keep water in a liquid state on Europa enhances the possibility that it could provide an environment for some form of extraterrestrial ocean life.

New evidence that a liquid ocean lies beneath Europa's crust was found when *Galileo* visited the moon in Jan. 2000. The spacecraft detected changes in Europa's magnetic field that are best explained by an electrically conducting (salty) body of water.

Callisto

Callisto, 2,400 mi (4,800 km) in diameter, is the outermost and, apparently, the least geologically active of Jupiter's four major satellites. Its density is less than twice that of water. Callisto has the oldest body and most cratered face of any body yet observed in the solar system. Like Ganymede, it seems to have a rocky core surrounded by ice. Unlike Ganymede, the surface of Callisto is completely covered with scars left by tens of thousands of meteoric impacts. Scientists estimate that it would take several billion years to accumulate the number of craters found there. So Callisto is believed to be inactive for at least that long. Although it is the darkest of the Galilean satellites, it is twice as bright as Earth's Moon.

Data from the *Galileo* spacecraft in 1998 suggest that Callisto has a salty ocean beneath its crust, similar to Europa's.

Io

Io, 2,262 mi (3,640 km) in diameter, is the most spectacular of the Galilean moons. Its brilliant colors of red, orange, and yellow set it apart from any other moon or planet. Active volcanoes have been detected on Io, with some plumes extending up to 200 mi (320 km) above the surface. The relative smoothness of Io's surface and its volcanic activity suggest that it has the youngest surface of Jupiter's moons. Its surface is composed of large amounts of sulfur and sulfur-dioxide frost, which account for the primarily yellow-orange surface color.

The volcanoes seem to eject a sufficient amount of sulfur dioxide to form a doughnut-shaped ring (torus) of ionized sulfur and oxygen atoms around Jupiter near Io's orbit. Close-up views taken in 1999 and 2000 showed that Io had more than 100 erupting volcanoes, gigantic lava flows and lava lakes, and towering, collapsing mountains. The eruptions of Loki, the most powerful volcano in the solar system, can be seen by Earth telescopes.

Observations by *Galileo* during 1998 revealed dozens of volcanic vents on Io where lava is hotter than any surface temperatures recorded on any planetary body in our solar system. At one such volcanic vent, known as Pillan Patera, two of the spacecraft's instruments indicated that the lava temperature may have been 3,140°F.

In 1996, the *Galileo* spacecraft detected a huge iron core within Io that occupies half the moon's diameter. *Galileo* also discovered evidence that Io has its own magnetic field.

Amalthea

Amalthea, Jupiter's innermost satellite, was discovered in 1892. It is so small—165 mi (265 km) long and 90 mi (150 km) wide—that it is extremely difficult to observe from Earth. Amalthea is an elongated, irregularly shaped satellite of reddish color. It orbits the planet every 12 hours and is in synchronous rotation, with its long axis always oriented toward Jupiter.

Originally thought to be heavily cratered, late 2002 data from the *Galileo* mission indicated that Amalthea may be a loosely-packed pile of rubble. It was discovered that the satellite had an unexpected low density, close to the density of ice. Amalthea

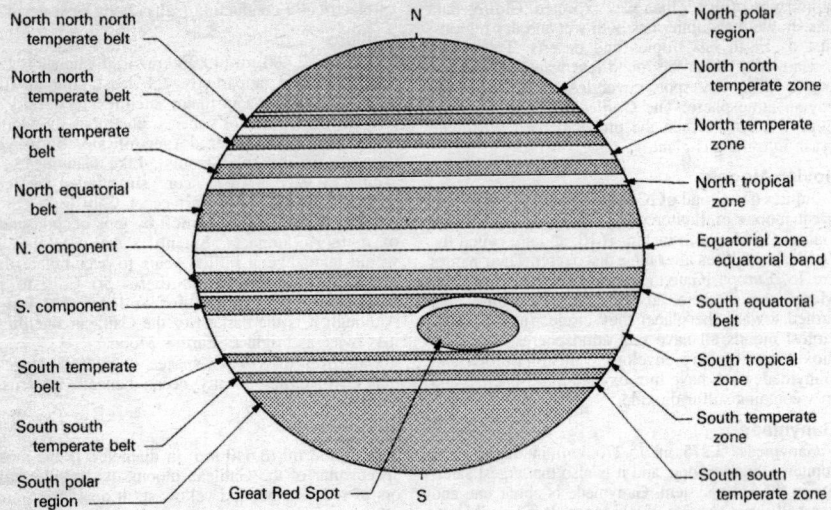

North north north temperate belt
North north temperate belt
North temperate belt
North equatorial belt
N. component
S. component
South temperate belt
South south temperate belt
South polar region
Great Red Spot
North polar region
North north temperate zone
North temperate zone
North tropical zone
Equatorial zone equatorial band
South equatorial belt
South tropical zone
South temperate zone
South south temperate zone

Schematic diagram of Jupiter's major features. *Source:* NASA.

may originally have been one piece that was bombarded and broken into chunks now held together by the gravity of the pieces. The gaps between the boulder-like pieces may make up more of the moon's volume than the actual rocks. Amalthea may be mostly rock with some ice, rather than the rock and iron it was previously held to be.

Jupiter's other named moons are Adrasta, Metis, Thebe, Leda, Himalia, Lysithea, Elara, Ananke, Carne, Pasiphae, Sinope; those discovered in 1999 and 2000 are Themisto, Iocaste, Harpalyke, Praxidike, Taygete, Chaldene, Kalyke, Callirrhoe, Megaclite, Isonoe, and Erinome. The 2001 moons are Euporie, Orthosie, Euanthe, Thyone, Hermippa, Pasithee, Kale, Aitne, Eurydome, Autonoe, and Sponde. The names come from members of Jupiter's (or Zeus's) entourage.

Between 2000 and 2003, 45 moons were found, bringing Jupiter's satellite total to 63, the greatest in the solar system. The new moons were generally small with distant retrograde orbits (orbital movement opposite to the planet's spin). Most of the new moons were sighted using Hawaii's Mauna Kea telescopes. Some astronomers believe that Jupiter's moon count could reach 100.

The Magnetosphere of Jupiter

Perhaps the largest structure in the solar system is the magnetosphere of Jupiter. This is the region of space that is filled with Jupiter's magnetic field and is bounded by the interaction of that magnetic field with the solar wind, which is the Sun's outward flow of charged particles. The plasma of electrically charged particles that exists in the magnetosphere is flattened into a large disk more than 3 million miles (4.8 million kilometers) in diameter, is coupled to the magnetic field, and rotates around Jupiter. The Galilean satellites are located in the inner regions of the magnetosphere and are subjected to intense radiation bombardment.

The intense radiation field that surrounds Jupiter is fatal to humans. If astronauts were able to approach the planet as close as the *Voyager 1* spacecraft did, they would receive a dose of 400,000 rads, or roughly 1,000 times the lethal dose for humans.

Even when nearest Earth, Jupiter is still almost 400 million miles away. However, because of its size, it may rival Venus in brilliance when near. Jupiter's four large moons may be seen through field glasses moving rapidly around Jupiter and changing their positions from night to night.

Saturn

Saturn, the second-largest planet in the solar system, is the least dense. Its mass is 95 times the mass of Earth and its density is 0.70 gram per cubic centimeter, so that it would float in an ocean if there were one big enough to hold it.

Saturn radiates about 80% more energy than it receives from the Sun. However, the excess thermal energy cannot be primarily attributed to Saturn's primordial heat loss, as is speculated for Jupiter.

Saturn's diameter is 74,978 mi (120,660 km) but 10% less at the poles, a consequence of its rapid rotation. Its axis of rotation is tilted by 27° and the length of its day is 10 hours, 39 minutes, and 24 seconds.

Saturn is composed primarily of liquid metallic hydrogen (about 80%) and the second most common element is believed to be helium.

Saturn's atmospheric appearance is very similar to Jupiter's with dark and light cloud markings and swirls, eddies, and curling ribbons; the belts and zones are more numerous and a thick haze mutes the markings. Temperatures recorded by *Voyager II* ranged from 82°K (−312°F) to 143°K (−202°F).

Winds blow at extremely high speeds on Saturn. Near the equator, the *Voyagers* measured winds of about 1,100 mph (500 meters per second). The winds blow primarily in an eastward direction.

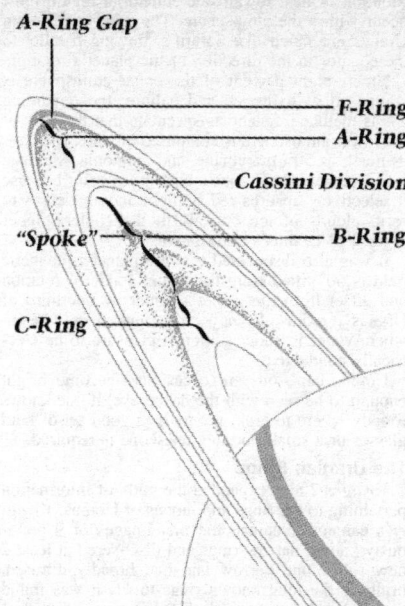

A-Ring Gap

F-Ring
A-Ring
Cassini Division
"Spoke"
B-Ring
C-Ring

NASA illustration of the divisions in Saturn's ring system.

Saturn's Rings

Saturn's spectacular ring system is unique in the solar system, with uncountable billions of tiny particles of water ice (with traces of other material) in orbit around the planet. The ring particles range in size from smaller than grains of sugar to as large as a house. The main rings stretch out from about 4,350 mi (7,000 km) to above the atmosphere of the planet out to the F ring, a total span of 45,984 mi (74,000 km). Saturn's rings can be likened to a phonograph, rings within rings numbering in the hundreds, and spokes in the B rings, and shepherding satellites controlling the F ring.

The main rings are called the A, B, and C rings moving from outside to inside. The gap between the A and B rings is called Cassini's Division and is named for the Italian-French astronomer Gian Domenico Cassini, who discovered four of Saturn's major moons and the dark, narrow gap, Cassini's Division, splitting the planet's rings.

Saturn's magnetic field has well-defined north and south magnetic poles, and is aligned with Saturn's axis of rotation to within one degree.

Saturn's Moons

Saturn has 33 known moons, 12 of which were discovered in late 2000 and are known by the temporary designations S/2000 S1 through S12. S/2003 S1 was discovered in Feb. 2003 and Cassini-Huygens discovered S/2004 S1 and S2 in 2004.. The five largest moons—Tethys, Dione, Rhea, Titan, and Iapetus—range from 650 to 3,200 mi (1,060 to 5,150 km) in diameter. The planet's outstanding satellite is Titan, first discovered by the Dutch astronomer Christiaan Huygens in 1656.

Titan

Titan is remarkable because it is the only known moon in the solar system that has a substantial atmosphere—largely nitrogen with a minor amount of methane and a rich variety of other hydrocarbons. Its surface is completely hidden from view (except at infrared and radio wavelengths) by a dense, hazy atmosphere.

The diameter of Titan is 3,200 mi (5,150 km), and it is the second-largest satellite in the solar system after Jupiter's Ganymede. Titan is larger than the planet Mercury.

Titan's surface temperature is about –280°F (–175°C), and its surface pressure is about 50% greater than the surface pressure of Earth. In 1990, radio telescope data showed that Titan reflects and scatters radio waves, suggesting that the satellite has a solid surface, possibly with small hydrocarbon lakes or ponds.

Infrared images of Titan taken in late 1999 by the W. M. Keck II telescope in Hawaii also revealed features that could be frozen land masses separated by frigid hydrocarbon seas and lakes. Other features might be highlands, and one dark area appeared to be a large impact crater or basin.

Cassini-Huygens

The Cassini-Huygens mission, launched in 1997 and a joint endeavor of NASA, the European Space Agency (ESA), and the Italian space agency, went into orbit around Saturn on June 30, 2004, and began sending images of Saturn's rings back to Earth the next day. Cassini will orbit Saturn 74 times and make 44 flybys of Titan. In Jan. 2005, the Huygens probe will descend through Titan's atmosphere, sending data back before landing on the surface. Scientists are hoping that the probe will survive the impact and continue to send data for a few minutes more.

Other Notable Saturnian Moons

The other four largest moons of Saturn are Tethys, Dione, Rhea, and Iapetus.

Tethys is 650 mi (1,060 km) in diameter. Its surface is heavily cratered, and it has a huge, globe-girdling canyon, Ithaca Chasma. Part of the canyon stretches over three-quarters of the satellite's surface. Ithaca Chasma is about 1,550 mi (2,500 km) long. It has an average width of about 62 mi (100 km) and a depth of 1.8 to 3.1 mi (3 to 5 km).

Tethys also has a huge impact crater named Odysseus that is 244 mi (4,400 km) in diameter, or more than one-third of the moon's diameter.

Dione is slightly larger than Tethys, 696 mi (1,120 km) in diameter, and is more than half composed of water ice. It has bright, wispy markings resembling thin veils covering its features.

Rhea, the largest of the inner satellites, is 951 mi (1,530 km) in diameter. It is composed mainly of water ice, causing its reflective surface to present an almost uniform white appearance.

Iapetus is the outermost of Saturn's icy satellites. Its appearance is unique because it has one dark and one bright hemisphere. The origin of the black coating of its dark face is unknown. Iapetus has a diameter of 907 mi (1,460 km).

Other notable moons of Saturn are Mimas, Enceladus, Hyperion, Phoebe, and Pan.

Mimas is small, only 244 mi (329 km) in diameter. It has a huge impact crater, Herschel, nearly one-third of its diameter. The crater is about 81 mi (130 km) wide and its icy peak rises almost 6.2 mi (10 km) above the floor.

Mimas is believed to be composed mainly of water and ice and to contain between 20% and 50% rock.

Enceladus is remarkable in that its surface shows signs of extensive and recent geological activity. There may be active water volcanism. The surface is extremely bright, reflecting more than 90% of incident sunlight. This suggests that its surface is composed of extremely pure ice without dust or rocks to contaminate it. Enceladus has a diameter of 310 mi (500 km).

Hyperion orbits between Iapetus and Titan. It is irregular in shape, measuring about 248 by 155 by 124 mi (400 by 250 by 200 km). It may be a remnant of a much larger object that was shattered by impact with another space body. It appears that Hyperion is composed primarily of water ice.

Hyperion orbits Saturn with an irregular motion ("chaotic tumbling").

Phoebe travels in a retrograde orbit at a distance of over 6.2 million miles (10 million kilometers) away from the planet. It is the darkest moon of Saturn and is the planet's only known satellite that does not keep the same face always turned to Saturn. It has been speculated that it is an asteroid that was captured by the planet. Phoebe rotates in about nine hours and orbits Saturn in 406 days. It has a diameter of 124 mi (200 km).

Pan was discovered in 1990 from *Voyager 2* photos taken in 1981. The satellite is estimated to be about 12.43 mi (20 km) in diameter, and it orbits within the Encke Gap, a 202-mile (325-kilometer) division in Saturn's A ring. It was identified by Johann Franz Encke (1791–1865) in 1837.

Saturn's other named moons are Atlas, Prometheus, Pandora, Epimetheus, Janus, Telesto, Calypso, and Helene. They are all nonspherical in shape and range from 15 to 120 mi (25 to 190 km) in diameter. 12 new moons were discovered in late 2000, one in 2003, and two more in 2004. Designated S/2000 S1 through S12, S/2003 S1, and S/2004 S1 and S2, these new moons are quite small—only about 3 to 30 mi (5 to 48 km) in diameter—and have weak elliptical orbits.

Saturn is the last of the planets visible to the naked eye. Saturn is never an object of overwhelming brilliance, but it looks like a bright star. The rings can be seen with a small telescope.

Uranus

Uranus, the first planet discovered in modern times by Sir William Herschel in 1781, is the seventh planet from the Sun, twice as far out as Saturn. Its mean distance from the Sun is 1,783 million miles (2,869 million kilometers). Uranus's equatorial diameter is 32,200 mi (51,810 km). The axis of Uranus is tilted at 97°, so it goes around the Sun nearly lying on its side.

Due to Uranus's unusual inclination, the polar regions receive more sunlight than its equatorial region during a Uranus year (equivalent to 84 Earth years). Scientists had thought that the temperature of its poles would be warmer than that at its equator, but *Voyager 2* discovered that the equatorial temperatures were similar to the temperatures at the poles, −344°F (−209°C), implying that some redistribution of heat toward the equatorial region must occur within the atmosphere. The wind patterns on Uranus are much like Saturn's, flowing parallel to the equator in the direction of the planet's rotation.

Ninety-eight percent of the upper atmosphere is composed of hydrogen and helium; the remaining 2% is methane. Scientists speculate that the bulk of the lower atmosphere is composed of water (perhaps as much as 50%), methane, and ammonia. Methane is responsible for Uranus's blue-green color because it selectively absorbs red sunlight and condenses to form clouds of ice crystals in the cooler, higher regions of Uranus's atmosphere.

It was also discovered that the planet's magnetic field is 60° tilted from the planet's axis of rotation and offset from the planet's center by one-third of Uranus's radius. It may be generated at a depth where water is under sufficient pressure to be electrically conductive.

Uranus can—on rare occasions—become bright enough to be seen with the naked eye, if one knows exactly where to look; normally, a good set of field glasses or a small portable telescope is required.

The Uranian Rings

Voyager 2 also expanded the body of information pertaining to the rings and moons of Uranus. *Voyager*'s cameras obtained the first images of 9 previously known narrow rings and discovered at least 2 new rings, one narrow and one broadly diffused, bringing the total known rings to 11. It was found that a highly structured distribution of fine dust exists throughout the ring system.

The outermost (epsilon) ring contains nothing smaller than fist-sized particles. It is flanked by two small moons discovered interior to the orbit of the Uranian moon Miranda. The moons exert a shepherding influence on the epsilon ring and on the outer edges of the gamma and delta rings.

All of the rings lie within one planetary radius[1] of Uranus's cloud tops. Most of Uranus's rings are narrow, ranging in width from 0.6 to 58 mi (1 to 93 km), and are only a few kilometers thick. The Uranian rings are colorless and extremely dark. The dark material may be either irradiated methane ice or organic-rich minerals mixed with water-impregnated, silicon-based compounds. There is evidence that incomplete rings, or "ring arcs," exist at Uranus.

The Uranian Moons

There are 27 known moons of Uranus. In order of decreasing distance from the planet, the moons are Setebos (1999 U1), Prospero (1999 U3), Sycorax, Stephano (1999 U2), Caliban, Oberon, Titania, Umbriel, Ariel, Miranda, Puck, 1986 U10, Belinda, Rosalind, Portia, Juliet, Desdemona, Cressida, Bianca, Ophelia, and Cordelia. Ten of the moons range in size from 16 to 67 mi (26 to 108 km) in diameter and, being closer to the planet, have faster periods of revolution (8–15 hours) than their more distant relatives.

Oberon and Titania

The two largest moons, Oberon, 942 mi (1,516 km) in diameter, and Titania, 982 mi (1,580 km) in diameter, are less than half the diameter of Earth's Moon. Titania, the reddest of Uranus's moons, may

---

1. The equatorial radius of Uranus is 15,880 mi (25,560 km) at a pressure of 1 bar.

have endured global tectonics as evidenced by complex valleys and fault lines etched into its surface. Smooth sections indicate that volcanic resurfacing has taken place.

Umbriel and Ariel

Umbriel and Ariel are roughly three-fourths the size of Oberon and Titania. Umbriel is the darkest of the large moons, with huge craters peppering its surface. Umbriel has a paucity of what are known as bright ray craters, which are formed on an older, darker surface when bright submerged ice is excavated and sprayed by meteoroid impacts.

In contrast, the surface of Ariel, the brightest of the Uranian moons, is relatively free of pockmarks due to volcanism that periodically erases the damage done by foreign projectiles. However, there are several extremely deep cuts on Ariel's surface.

Miranda

The smallest of Uranus's large moons, Miranda, 293 mi (472 km) in diameter, has been described as "the most bizarre body in the solar system," with the most geologically complex surface. Miranda's remarkable terrain consists of rolling, heavily cratered plains (the oldest known in the Uranian system) adjoined by three huge, 120- to 180-mile (200- to 300-kilometer) oval-to-trapezoidal regions known as coronae, which are characterized by networks of concentric canyons.

Puck

Puck was the first new moon discovered by *Voyager.* It is 96 mi (154 km) in diameter and makes a trip around Uranus every 18 hours. Puck is shaped somewhat like a potato, with a huge impact crater marring roughly one-fourth of its surface.

Caliban and Sycorax

In 1997, two new moons, the first with irregular, noncircular orbits, were discovered around Uranus. These far distant satellites were temporarily designated S/1997 U1 and S/1997 U2 and later named Caliban and Sycorax, respectively. Caliban has a diameter of 37 mi (60 km) and orbits Uranus at an average distance of 4.5 million miles (7.2 million kilometers). Sycorax has a diameter of 74.5 mi (120 km) and a much more elliptical orbit than Caliban, bringing it as close as 3.7 million miles (6 million km) to the planet.

New Uranian Moons Discovered

In Sept. 1999, Cornell University astronomers announced the discovery of three more satellites. The moons have been named Setebos, Stephano, and Prospero. The satellites are about 12 mi (20 km) in diameter and orbit in distant, elliptical paths. The moon Trinculo was announced in 2001. As of the spring of 2004, the Uranian moon count was up to 27.

Neptune

Little was known about Neptune until Aug. 1989, when NASA's *Voyager 2* became the first spacecraft to observe the planet. Passing about 3,000 mi (4,950 km) above Neptune's north pole, *Voyager 2* made its closest approach to any planet since leaving Earth 12 years prior. The spacecraft passed about 25,000 mi (40,000 km) from Neptune's largest moon, Triton, the last solid body that *Voyager 2* studied before continuing on to the outer boundary of the solar system.

Nearly 3 billion miles (4.5 billion kilometers) from the Sun, Neptune orbits the Sun once in 165

years, and therefore has made not quite a full circle around the Sun since it was discovered.[1]

With an equatorial diameter of 30,775 mi (49,528 km), Neptune is the smallest of our solar system's four gas giants, which also include Jupiter, Saturn, and Uranus.[2] Even so, its volume could hold nearly 60 Earths. Neptune is also denser than the other gas giants and about 64% heavier than if it were composed entirely of water.

Neptune has a blue color as a result of methane in its atmosphere. Methane preferentially absorbs the longer wavelengths of sunlight (those near the red end of the spectrum). What are left to be reflected are colors at the blue end of the spectrum. The atmosphere of Neptune is mainly composed of hydrogen, with helium and traces of methane and ammonia.

Neptune is a dynamic planet even though it receives only 3% as much sunlight as Jupiter does. *Voyager 2* discovered several large, dark spots that were prominent features on the planet. The largest spot was about the size of Earth and was designated the "Great Dark Spot" by its discoverers. It appeared to be an anticyclone similar to Jupiter's Great Red Spot. While Neptune's Great Dark Spot is comparable in size, relative to the planet, and at the same latitude (22°S latitude) as Jupiter's Great Red Spot, it was far more variable in size and shape than its Jovian counterpart. Bright, wispy "cirrus-type" clouds overlaid the Great Dark Spot at its southern and northeast boundaries.

At about 42°S latitude, a bright, irregularly shaped eastward-moving cloud circled much faster than did the Great Dark Spot, "scooting" around Neptune in about 16 hours. This "scooter" may have been a cloud plume rising between cloud decks.

Another spot, designated "D2," was located far to the south of the Great Dark Spot, at 55°S latitude. It is almond-shaped, with a bright central core, and moves eastward around the planet in about 16 hours.

In 1995, images taken by the Hubble Space Telescope showed that the Great Dark Spot has vanished. The great storm center has either dissipated or is obscured by other atmospheric conditions.

The atmosphere above Neptune's clouds is hotter near the equator, cooler in the mid-latitudes, and warm again at the south pole. Temperatures in the stratosphere were measured to be 750°K (900°F), while at the 100-millibar pressure level they were measured to be 55°K (−360°F).

Long, bright clouds, reminiscent of cirrus clouds on Earth, were seen high in Neptune's atmosphere. They appear to form above most of the methane, and consequently are not blue.

At northern low latitudes (27°N), *Voyager* captured images of cloud streaks casting their shadows on cloud decks estimated to be about 30 to 60 mi (50 to 100 km) below. The widths of these cloud streaks range from 30 to 125 mi (50 to 200 km).

1. Astronomers have studied Neptune since Sept. 23, 1846, when Johann Gottfried Galle, of the Berlin Observatory, and Louis d'Arrest, an astronomy student, discovered the eighth planet on the basis of mathematical predictions by Urbain Jean Joseph Le Verrier. Similar predictions were made independently by John Couch Adams. Galileo Galilei had seen Neptune during several nights of observing Jupiter, in Jan. 1613, but didn't realize he was seeing a new planet.
2. These four planets are about 4 to 12 times greater in diameter than Earth. They have no solid surfaces, but possess massive atmospheres that contain substantial amounts of hydrogen and helium with traces of other gases.

Cloud streaks were also seen in the southern polar regions (71°S) where the cloud heights were about 30 mi (50 km).

Most of the winds on Neptune blow in a westward direction, which is retrograde, or opposite to the rotation of the planet.

In Jan. 2000, astronomers announced taking the best Earth-based infrared images of Neptune, captured by the W. M. Keck II telescope in Hawaii. The images revealed giant 600-mph (966-km/hr) storms born of heat generated from the planet's still-contracting core. Storm features are pulled across the face of Neptune as it whirls through its 16-hour day.

The Magnetic Field of Neptune

Neptune's magnetic field is tilted 47° from the planet's rotation axis and is offset at least 0.55 radii, about 8,500 mi (13,500 km) from the physical center. The dynamo electric currents produced within the planet, therefore, must be relatively closer to the surface than for Earth, Jupiter, or Saturn. Because of its unusual orientation, and the tilt of the planet's rotation axis, Neptune's magnetic field goes through dramatic changes as the planet rotates in the solar wind.

Voyager's planetary radio astronomy instrument measured the periodic radio waves generated by the magnetic field and determined that the rotation rate of the interior of Neptune is 16 hours and 7 minutes.

Voyager also detected auroras, similar to the northern and southern lights on Earth, in Neptune's atmosphere. Unlike those on Earth, due to Neptune's complex magnetic field, the auroras are extremely complicated processes that occur over wide regions of the planet, not just near the planet's magnetic poles.

Neptune's Moons

Triton

The largest of Neptune's 13 known satellites, Triton was discovered in 1846 by British astronomer William Lassell. Triton circles Neptune in a tilted, circular, retrograde orbit, completing an orbit in 5.875 days at an average distance of 205,000 mi (330,000 km) above the planet's cloud tops.

Triton shows evidence of a remarkable geologic history, and *Voyager 2* images show active geyser-like eruptions spewing invisible nitrogen gas and dark dust particles 1 to 5 mi (2 to 8 km) into space.

Triton is about three-quarters the size of Earth's Moon and has a diameter of about 1,680 mi (2,705 km) and a mean density of about 2.066 grams per cubic centimeter. (The density of water is 1.0 grams per cubic centimeter.) This means that Triton contains more rock in its interior than the icy satellites of Saturn and Uranus.

The relatively high density and the retrograde orbit offer strong evidence that Triton did not originate near Neptune, but is a captured object.

An extremely thin atmosphere extends as much as 500 mi (800 km) above the satellite's surface. Tiny nitrogen ice particles may form thin clouds a few kilometers above the surface. Triton is very bright, reflecting 60% to 95% of the sunlight that strikes it. (By comparison, Earth's Moon reflects only 11%.)

The atmospheric pressure at Triton's surface is about 14 microbars, a mere 1/70,000th the surface pressure on Earth. Temperature at the surface is about 38°K (−391°F), making it the coldest surface of any body yet visited in the solar system.

Nereid

Nereid was discovered in 1949 through Earth-based telescopes. Little is known about Nereid, which is slightly smaller than Proteus, having a diameter of 211 mi (340 km). The satellite's surface reflects about 14% of the sunlight that strikes it. Nereid's orbit is the most eccentric in the solar system, ranging from about 841,100 mi (1,353,600 km) to 5,980,200 mi (9,623,700 km).

The Smaller Satellites

In addition to the previously known moons, Triton and Nereid, *Voyager 2* found 6 satellites in 1989. In 2003, astronomers announced that 5 new moons had been discovered, bringing the total to 13.

Proteus

Proteus is one of the darkest objects in the solar system—"as dark as soot" is a good description. It reflects only 6% of the sunlight that strikes it. Proteus is an ellipsoid about 258 mi (416 km) in diameter, larger than Nereid. It circles Neptune at a distance of about 57,700 mi (92,800 km) above the cloud tops, and completes one orbit in 26 hours and 54 minutes. Scientists say that it is about as large as a satellite can be without being pulled into a spherical shape by its own gravity.

Proteus and its tiny companions are cratered and irregularly shaped—they are not round—and show no signs of any geologic modifications. All circle the planet in the same direction as Neptune rotates and remain close to Neptune's equatorial plane.

Larissa

This object is only about 30,300 mi (48,800 km) from Neptune and circles the planet in 13 hours and 18 minutes. Its diameter is 120 mi (190 km).

Despina

The satellite is 17,200 mi (27,700 km) from Neptune's clouds and makes one orbit every 8 hours. Its diameter is about 90 mi (150 km).

Galatea

It lies 23,100 mi (37,200 km) from Neptune. Its diameter is 110 mi (180 km), and it completes an orbit in 10 hours and 18 minutes.

Thalassa

Thalassa appears to be about 50 mi (80 km) in diameter. It orbits Neptune in 7 hours and 30 minutes some 15,700 mi (25,200 km) above the cloud tops.

Naiad

Naiad is about 37 mi (60 km) in diameter and orbits Neptune about 14,400 mi (23,200 km) above the clouds in 7 hours and 6 minutes.

New Neptunian Moons

In Jan. 2003, astronomers from the Harvard-Smithsonian Center for Astrophysics and the National Research Council of Canada announced that three new moons had been discovered orbiting Neptune. Although S/2002 N1, S/2002 N2, and S2002 N3 are tiny, about 18–24 mi (30–40 km) in diameter, the astronomers made their discovery using ground-based telescopes in Chile and Hawaii. Two more moons were announced later in 2003, bringing the total to 13.

Neptune's Rings

Voyager found four rings and evidence of ring *arcs* or incomplete rings. The "Main Ring" orbits Neptune at about 23,812.5 mi (38,100 km) above the cloud tops.

The First Ten Minor Planets (Asteroids)

Name	Year of discovery	Mean distance from Sun (millions of mi)	Orbital period (years)	Diameter (mi)	Magnitude
1. Ceres	1801	257.0	4.60	485	7.4
2. Pallas	1802	257.4	4.61	304	8.0
3. Juno	1804	247.8	4.36	118	8.7
4. Vesta	1807	219.3	3.63	243	6.5
5. Astraea	1845	239.3	4.14	50	9.9
6. Hebe	1847	225.2	3.78	121	8.5
7. Iris	1847	221.4	3.68	121	8.4
8. Flora	1847	204.4	3.27	56	8.9
9. Metis	1848	221.7	3.69	78	8.9
10. Hygeia	1849	222.6	5.59	40(?)	9.5

The "Inner Ring" is about 17,750 mi (28,400 km) from Neptune's cloud tops. An "Inside Diffuse Ring"—a complete ring—is located about 10,687.5 mi (17,100 km) from the planet's cloud tops. Some scientists suspect that this ring may extend all the way down to Neptune's cloud tops. An area called "the Plateau" is a broad, diffuse sheet of fine material just outside the so-called Inner Ring. The fine material is approximately the size of smoke particles. All other rings contain a greater proportion of larger material.

Pluto

Pluto, the outermost and smallest planet in the solar system, is the only planet not visited by an exploring spacecraft. So little is known about it that it is difficult to classify. Its distance is so great that the Hubble Space Telescope cannot reveal its surface features. Appropriately named for the Roman god of the underworld, it must be frozen, dark, and dead. Pluto's mean distance from the Sun is 3,687.5 million miles (5,900 million kilometers).

In 1978, light-curve studies gave evidence of a moon revolving around Pluto within the same period as Pluto's rotation; therefore, it stays over the same point on Pluto's surface. In addition, it keeps the same face toward the planet. The satellite was later named Charon and is estimated to be about 789 mi (1,262.4 km) in diameter. Recent estimates indicate Pluto's diameter is about 1,441.6 mi (2,306.56 km), making the pair more like a double planet than any other in the solar system. Previously, the Earth–Moon system held this distinction. The density of Pluto is slightly greater than that of water.

There is evidence that Pluto has an atmosphere containing methane and polar ice caps that increase and decrease in size with the planet's seasons. It is not known to have water. The Hubble Space Telescope's faint-object camera revealed light and dark regions on Pluto indicating an ice cap at the planet's north pole. It is not known if there is an ice cap at Pluto's south pole.

Pluto was predicted by calculation when Percival Lowell (1855–1916) noticed irregularities in the orbits of Uranus and Neptune. Clyde Tombaugh (1906–1997) discovered the planet in 1930, precisely where Lowell predicted it would be. The name Pluto was chosen because the first two letters represent the initials of Percival Lowell.

Pluto has the most eccentric orbit in the solar system, bringing it at times closer to the Sun than Neptune. Pluto approached the perihelion of its orbit on Sept. 5, 1989, and until Feb. 1999 was closer to the Sun than Neptune. Even then, it could be seen only with a large telescope.

The *New Horizons* mission, scheduled to launch in 2006 and reach Pluto in 2015, would be the first to study Pluto, Charon, and the Kuiper Belt, a region beyond Neptune's orbit containing comets and what is believed to be detritus from the formation of the solar system.

Beyond Pluto: Sedna

NASA scientists reported in March 2004 that they have discovered a distant object in our solar system. They named the "planetoid" Sedna, after the Inuit goddess who created the sea creatures of the Arctic.

Sedna is the largest object discovered in the solar system since Clyde Tombaugh spotted Pluto in 1930. It's also the coldest, with its highest temperature a frigid –400°F. Eight billion miles from the Sun (that's three times farther away from the Sun than Pluto), Sedna is the most distant object in the solar system.

The Asteroids

Between the orbits of Mars and Jupiter are an estimated 30,000 pieces of rocky debris, known collectively as the asteroids, or planetoids. The first and, incidentally, the largest (Ceres), was discovered during the New Year's night of 1801 by the Italian astronomer Father Piazzi (1746–1826), and its orbit was calculated by the German mathematician Karl Friedrich Gauss (1777–1855). Gauss invented a new method of calculating orbits on that occasion. A few asteroids do not move in orbits beyond the orbit of Mars, but in orbits that cross the orbit of Mars. The first of them was named Eros because of this peculiar orbit. It had become the rule to bestow female names on the asteroids, but when it was found that Eros crossed the orbit of a major planet, it received a male name. These orbit-crossing asteroids are often referred to as the "male asteroids." A few of them—Albert, Adonis, Apollo, Amor, and Icarus— cross the orbit of Earth, and two of them may come closer than our Moon; but the crossing is like a bridge crossing a highway, not like two highways intersecting. Hence there is very little danger of collision from these bodies. They are all small, 3 to 5 mi (4.8 to 8.0 km) in diameter, and therefore very difficult objects to identify, even when quite close. Some scientists believe the asteroids represent the remains of an exploded planet.

On Oct. 29, 1991, the *Galileo* spacecraft took a historic photograph of asteroid 951 Gaspra from a distance of 10,000 mi (16,000 km) away. It was the first close-up photo ever taken of· an asteroid in space. Gaspra is an irregular, potato-shaped object about 12.5 mi (20 km) by 7.5 mi (12 km) by 7 mi (11.2 km) in size. Its surface is covered with a layer of loose rubble and its terrain is marked by several dozen craters.

NASA's *Near-Earth Asteroid Rendezvous* spacecraft was launched on Feb. 17, 1996. (Near-Earth asteroids come within 121 million miles [195 million kilometers] of the Sun. Their orbits come close enough that one could eventually hit Earth.) It flew within 750 mi (1,200 km) of minor planet 253 Mathilde on June 27, 1997, and took spectacular images of the dark, crater-battered world. The asteroid's mean diameter was found to be 33 mi (52.8 km). The *NEAR* spacecraft discovered that the carbon-rich Mathilde is one of the darkest objects in the solar system, only reflecting about 3% of the Sun's light, making it twice as dark as a chunk of charcoal. The asteroid is almost completely cratered, and at least five of its craters just on the lighted side are larger than 12 mi (19.2 km).

On Feb. 14, 2000, *NEAR* successfully entered into orbit around Eros and remained in orbit for one year, taking photographs of the asteroid and gathering information about its composition, structure, size, and shape. The spacecraft landed safely on the surface of Eros in a controlled crash on Feb. 12, 2001. Against tremendous odds, it continued to relay information for another two weeks before being shut down.

NEAR measured Eros to be 21 mi (33.6 km) long by 8 mi (12.8 km) wide and 8 mi (12.8 km) deep. It rotates once every 5.27 hours and has no visible moons. *NEAR* data also showed that the asteroid's ancient surface is covered with craters, ridges, boulders, and other complex features.

NEAR was the first spacecraft to orbit an asteroid and the first craft to operate on solar power so far from the Sun. *NEAR* gathered about 160,000 images of Eros, about 10 times more than was planned. The spacecraft was renamed *NEAR-Shoemaker* in honor of geologist Dr. Eugene M. Shoemaker (1928–1997), who researched the influence of asteroids and comets in shaping planets.

In March 2004, a 98-foot (30-meter) diameter asteroid made the closest-ever asteroid flyby of Earth, coming within 26,500 mi (43,000 km) of our planet. Scientists believed that had the asteroid (named 2004 FH) entered the Earth's atmosphere, it would have broken up with no damage to the planet.

Comets

Comets, according to the noted astronomer Fred L. Whipple (1906–2004), are enormous "snowballs" of frozen gases (mostly carbon dioxide, methane, and water vapor) and contain very little solid material. The whole behavior of comets can then be explained as the behavior of frozen gas being heated by the Sun. When the comet Kohoutek made its first appearance to human observers in 1973, its behavior seemed to confirm this theory, and later the international study by five spacecraft that encountered Halley's comet in March 1986 confirmed Whipple's idea of the make-up of comets.

Up until the middle of the 16th century, comets were believed to be phenomena of the upper atmosphere; they were usually explained as "burning vapors" which had risen from "distant swamps." That nobody had ever actually seen burning vapors rise from a swamp did not matter.

But a large comet that appeared in 1577 was carefully observed by Tycho Brahe (1546–1601), a Danish astronomer who insisted on precise measurements for everything. It was Tycho Brahe's accumulation of literally thousands of precise measurements that later enabled his younger collaborator, Johannes Kepler (1571–1630), to discover the laws of planetary motion. Measuring the motion of the comet of 1577, Brahe could show that it had been far beyond the atmosphere, even though he could not give figures for the distance. Brahe's work proved that comets were astronomical and not meteorological phenomena.

In 1682, the second Astronomer Royal of Great Britain, Dr. Edmond Halley (1656–1742), checked the orbit of a bright comet that was in the sky and then compared it with earlier comet orbits that were known in part. Halley found that the comet of 1682 was the third to move through what appeared to be the same orbit, and that the three appearances were roughly 76 years apart. Halley concluded that this was the same comet, moving around the Sun in a closed orbit, like the planets. He predicted that it would reappear in 1758 or 1759. Halley himself died in 1742, but a large comet appeared 16 years after his death as predicted and was immediately referred to as "Halley's comet."

Halley's comet appeared again in 1986, sparking a worldwide effort to study it up close. Five satellites in all took readings from the comet at various distances. Two Soviet craft, *Vega 1* and *Vega 2*, went in close to provide detailed pictures of the comet, including the first of the comet's core. The European Space Agency's craft, *Giotto*, entered the comet itself, coming to within 450 mi of the comet's center and successfully passing through its tail. In addition, two Japanese craft, the *Suisei* and the *Sakigake*, passed at a farther distance and analyzed the cloud and tail of the comet and the effect of solar radiation upon it.

Astronomers refer to comets as *periodic* or *nonperiodic*, but the latter term does not mean that these comets have no period; it merely means that their period is not known. The actual periods of comets run from 3.3 years (the shortest known) to many thousands of years. Their orbits are elliptical, like those of the planets, but they are very eccentric, long, and narrow ellipses. Only comet Schwassmann-Wachmann has an orbit that has such a low eccentricity (for a cometary orbit) that it could be the orbit of a minor planet.

When a comet coming from deep space approaches the Sun, it is at first indistinguishable from a minor planet. Somewhere between the orbits of Mars and Jupiter, its outline becomes fuzzy; it is said to develop a *coma* (the word used here is the Latin word *coma*, which means "hair," not the phonetically identical Greek word that means "deep sleep"). Then, near the orbit of Mars, the comet develops its tail, which at first trails behind. This grows steadily as the comet comes closer and closer to the Sun. As it rounds the Sun (as first noticed by Girolamo Fracastoro, 1483–1553), the tail always points away from the Sun so that the comet, when moving away from the Sun, points its tail ahead like the landing lights of an airplane.

The reason for this behavior is that the tail is pushed in these directions by the radiation pressure of the Sun. It sometimes happens that a comet loses its tail at perihelion; it then grows another one. Although the tail is clearly visible against the black of the sky, it is very tenuous. It has been said that if the tail of Halley's comet could be compressed to the density of iron, it would fit into a small suitcase.

Although very low in mass, comets are among the largest members of the solar system. The nucleus of a comet may be up to 10,000 mi in diameter; its coma between 10,000 and 50,000 mi in diameter; and its tail as long as 28 million miles.

Comet Shoemaker-Levy 9 broke up into 21 fragments in July 1992 and crashed into the surface of Jupiter, July 16–22, 1994, in the most violent event in the recorded history of the solar system.

In 1951, Dutch astronomer Gerard Kuiper first suggested the existence of a disk-shaped swarm of short-period comets that begin beyond the orbit of Neptune and extend past Pluto. In 1995, the Hubble Space Telescope detected the long-sought Kuiper Belt and an estimated 200 million comets were discovered orbiting it.

In Sept. 2001, the *Deep Space 1* craft flew just 1,300 mi (2,200 km) from the Comet Borrelly and sent images and data about the comet's core. Scientists determined that the comet's nucleus and coma are more complex than previously thought. The *Stardust* mission, launched in 1999, collected space dust, gathered particles from Comet Wild 2, and in Jan. 2004, took pictures of the comet's nucleus. *Stardust* will return to Earth with the samples in 2006.

Meteors and Meteorites

The term *meteor* for what is usually called a *shooting star* bears an unfortunate resemblance to the term *meteorology,* the science of weather and weather forecasting. This resemblance is due to an ancient misunderstanding that wrongly considered meteors an atmospheric phenomenon. Actually, the streak of light in the sky that scientists call a meteor is essentially an astronomical phenomenon: the entry of a small piece of cosmic matter into our atmosphere.

The distinction between *meteors* and *fireballs* (formerly also called *bolides*) is merely one of convenience; a fireball is an unusually bright meteor. Incidentally, it also means that a fireball is larger than a faint meteor.

Objects that enter our atmosphere become visible when they are about 60 mi above the ground. The fact that they grow hot enough to emit light is not due to the "friction" of the atmosphere, as one often reads. The phenomenon responsible for the heating is one of compression. Unconfined air cannot move faster than the speed of sound. Since the entering meteorite moves with 30 to 60 times the speed of sound, the air simply cannot get out of the way. Therefore, it is compressed like the air in the cylinder of a diesel engine and is heated by compression. This heat—or part of it—is transferred to the moving object. The details of this process are now fairly well understood as a result of reentry tests with ballistic-missile nose cones.

The average weight of an object producing a faint *shooting star* is only a small fraction of an ounce. Even a bright fireball may not weigh more than 2 or 3 lb. Naturally, the smaller objects are worn to dust by the passage through the atmosphere; only rather

large ones reach the ground. Those that are found are called meteorites. (The *meteor,* to repeat, is the term for the light streak in the sky.) Thousands of meteorites fall to Earth each year.

The largest meteorite known is still embedded in the ground near Grootfontein in southwest Africa and is estimated to weigh 70 tons. The second-largest known is the 34-ton Anighito (on exhibit in the Hayden Planetarium, New York), which was found by Admiral Peary in 1892 at Cape York in Greenland. The largest meteorite found in the United States is the Willamette meteorite (found in Oregon, weight ca. 15 tons), but large portions of this meteorite weathered away before it was found. Its weight as it struck the ground may have been 20 tons.

All these are iron meteorites (an iron meteorite normally contains about 7% nickel), which form one class of meteorites. The other class consists of the stony meteorites, and between them there are the so-called stony irons. Tektites consist of silica-rich glass similar to our volcanic glass obsidian, and because of the similarity, there is doubt in a number of cases whether the glass is of terrestrial or of extraterrestrial origin.

Though no meteorite larger than the Grootfontein is actually known, we do know that Earth has, on occasion, been struck by much larger bodies. Evidence for such hits are the meteorite craters, of which an especially good example is located near the Cañon Diablo in Arizona. Another meteor crater in the United States is a rather old crater near Odessa, Tex. Some scientists theorize that the mass extermination of dinosaurs from the face of Earth 65 million years ago was due to a large meteor that struck our planet at that time.

Meteor showers are caused by multitudes of very small bodies traveling in swarms. Earth travels in its orbit through these swarms like a car driving through falling snow. The point from which the meteors seem to emanate is called the *radiant* and is named for the constellation in that area. The Perseid meteor shower in August is the most spectacular of the year, boasting, at peak, roughly 60 meteors per hour under good atmospheric conditions.

The Constellations

Constellations are groupings of stars that form easily recognized and remembered patterns, such as Orion and the Big Dipper. The Big Dipper is actually an asterism, not a constellation, because it is only part of the constellation Ursa Major (the Big Bear). Actually, the stars in the majority of all constellations do not "belong together." Usually they are at greatly varying distances from Earth and just happen to lie more or less in the same line of sight as seen from our solar system. But in a few cases, the stars of a constellation are actually associated; most of the bright stars of the Big Dipper travel together and form what astronomers call an *open cluster.*

If you observe a planet, say Mars, for one complete revolution, you will see that it passes successively through 12 constellations. All planets (except Pluto at certain times) can be observed only in these 12 constellations, which form the so-called zodiac, and the Sun also moves through the zodiacal signs, though the Sun's apparent movement is actually caused by the movement of Earth.

Although the constellations are due mainly to the optical accident of line of sight and have no real

The 88 Recognized Constellations

In astronomical works, the Latin names of the constellations are used. The letter N or S following the Latin name indicates whether the constellation is located to the north or south of the Zodiac. The letter Z indicates that the constellation is within the Zodiac.

Latin name	Letter	English version	Latin name	Letter	English version	Latin name	Letter	English version
Andromeda	N	Andromeda	Delphinus	N	Dolphin	Pegasus	N	Pegasus
Antlia	S	Airpump	Dorado	S	Swordfish (Gold-fish)	Perseus	N	Perseus
Apus	S	Bird of Paradise				Phoenix	S	Phoenix
Aquarius	Z	Water Bearer	Draco	N	Dragon	Pictor	S	Painter (or his Easel)
Aquila	N	Eagle	Equuleus	N	Filly			
Ara	S	Altar	Eridanus	S	Eridanus (river)	Pisces	Z	Fishes
Aries	Z	Ram	Fornax	S	Furnace	Piscis Austrinus	S	Southern Fish
Auriga	N	Charioteer	Gemini	Z	Twins	Puppis	S	Poop (of Argo)[1]
Boötes	N	Herdsmen	Grus	S	Crane	Pyxis	S	Mariner's Compass
Caelum	S	Sculptor's Tool	Hercules	N	Hercules			
Camelopardalis	N	Giraffe	Horologium	S	Clock	Reticulum	S	Net
Cancer	Z	Crab	Hydra	N	Sea Serpent	Sagitta	N	Arrow
Canes Venatici	N	Hunting Dogs	Hydrus	S	Water Snake	Sagittarius	Z	Archer
Canis Major	S	Great Dog	Indus	S	Indian	Scorpius	Z	Scorpion
Canis Minor	S	Little Dog	Lacerta	N	Lizard	Sculptor	S	Sculptor
Capricornus	Z	Goat (or Sea-Goat)	Leo	Z	Lion	Scutum	N	Shield
			Leo Minor	N	Little Lion	Serpens	N	Serpent
Carina	S	Keel (of Argo)[1]	Lepus	S	Hare	Sextans	S	Sextant
Cassiopeia	N	Cassiopeia	Libra	Z	Scales	Taurus	Z	Bull
Centaurus	S	Centaur	Lupus	S	Wolf	Telescopium	S	Telescope
Cepheus	N	Cepheus	Lynx	N	Lynx	Triangulum	N	Triangle
Cetus	S	Whale	Lyra	N	Lyre (Harp)	Triangulum Australe	S	Southern Triangle
Chameleon	S	Chameleon	Mensa	S	Table (mountain)			
Circinus	S	Compasses	Microscopium	S	Microscope	Tucana	S	Toucan
Columba	S	Dove	Monoceros	S	Unicorn	Ursa Major	N	Big Dipper[2]
Coma Berenices	N	Berenice's Hair	Musca	S	Southern Fly	Ursa Minor	N	Little Dipper[3]
Corona Australis	S	Southern Crown	Norma	S	Rule (straight-edge)	Vela	S	Sail (of Argo)[1]
Corona Borealis	N	Northern Crown				Virgo	Z	Virgin
Corvus	S	Crow (Raven)	Octans	S	Octant	Volans	S	Flying Fish
Crater	S	Cup	Ophiuchus	N	Serpent-Bearer	Vulpecula	N	Fox
Crux	S	Southern Cross	Orion	N	Orion			
Cygnus	N	Swan	Pavo	S	Peacock			

1. The original constellation Argo Navis (the Ship Argo) has been divided into Carina, Puppis, and Vela. Normally the brightest star in each constellation is designated by alpha, the first letter of the Greek alphabet, the second brightest by beta, the second letter of the Greek alphabet, and so forth. But the Greek letters run through Carina, Puppis, and Vela as if it were still one constellation. 2. The Big Dipper is only a part of the constellation Ursa Major (Great Bear) and is not a constellation by itself. 3. The Little Dipper is called Ursa Minor (Little Bear).

significance, astronomers have retained them as reference areas. It is much easier to speak of a star in Orion than to give its geometrical position in the sky. During the Astronomical Congress of 1928, it was decided to recognize 88 constellations. A description of their agreed-upon boundaries was published at Cambridge, England, in 1930, under the title *Atlas Céleste*.

The Auroras

The "northern lights" (*Aurora borealis*) as well as the "southern lights" (*Aurora australis*) are upper-atmosphere phenomena of astronomical origin. The auroras center around the magnetic (not the geographical) poles of Earth, which explains why, in the Western Hemisphere, they have been seen as far to the south as New Orleans and Florida, while the equivalent latitude in the Eastern Hemisphere never sees an aurora. The northern magnetic pole happens to be in the Western Hemisphere.

The lower limit of an aurora is at about 50 mi (80 km). Upper limits have been estimated to be as high as 400 mi (640 km). Since about 1880, a connection between the auroras on Earth and sunspots has been suspected and has gradually come to be accepted. It was said that the sunspots probably eject "particles" (later the word *electrons* was substituted), which on striking Earth's atmosphere cause the auroras. But this explanation suffered from certain difficulties. Sometimes a very large sunspot group on the Sun, with individual spots bigger than Earth itself, would not cause an aurora. Moreover, even if a sunspot caused an aurora, the time that passed between the appearance of the one and the occurrence of the other was highly unpredictable.

This problem of the time lag is, in all probability, solved by the discovery of the Van Allen belt[1], a double layer of charged subatomic particles around Earth. The inner layer, with its center some 1,500 mi (2,400 km) from the ground, reaches from about 40°N to about 40°S and does not touch the atmosphere. The outer layer, much larger and with its center several thousand miles from the ground, does touch the atmosphere in the vicinity of the magnetic poles.

It seems probable that the "leakage" of electrons from the outer Van Allen layer causes the auroras. A new burst of electrons from the Sun seems to be caught in the outer layer first. Under the assumption that all electrons are first caught in the outer layer, the time lag can be understood. There has to be an "overflow" from the outer layer to produce an aurora.

1. Named after the American physicist, James Alfred Van Allen (1914–), who discovered the broad bands of intense radiation surrounding Earth in 1958.

Phenomena, 2005

Configurations of Sun, Moon, and Planets

NOTE: The hour listings are in Universal Time. For conversion to U.S. time zones, *see* Conversion of Universal Time to Civil Time, p. 420. Terms in boldface can be found on pp. 397–398.

JANUARY

Day	Phenomenon	Hour
2	Earth is at **perihelion**.	0100
3	LAST QUARTER	1800
4	Jupiter is 0° 4′ north of the Moon. **Occultation** of Jupiter by the Moon.	0200
6	Saturn is 7° south of Pollux, the brightest star in the constellation Gemini.	1000
7	Mars is 3° north of the Moon.	1900
7	Antares, the brightest star in the constellation Scorpius, is 1° 3′ south of the Moon. **Occultation** of Antares by the Moon.	2000
7	Mars is 5° north of Antares, the brightest star in the constellation Scorpius.	2100
9	Mercury is 5° north of the Moon.	0200
9	Venus is 5° north of the Moon.	0300
10	The Moon is at **perigee**.	1000
10	NEW MOON	1200
11	Neptune is 5° north of the Moon.	2300
13	Uranus is 4° north of the Moon.	0800
13	Saturn is at **opposition**.	2300
14	Mercury is 0° 3′ south of Venus.	0100
17	FIRST QUARTER	0700
23	The Moon is at **apogee**.	1900
24	Saturn is 5° south of the Moon.	0800
25	FULL MOON	1100
31	Jupiter is 0° 9′ north of the Moon. **Occultation** of Jupiter by the Moon.	1100

FEBRUARY

Day	Phenomenon	Hour
2	LAST QUARTER	0700
2	Jupiter appears to be motionless in the sky as it goes from direct motion to **retrograde** motion.	1600
3	Neptune is in **conjunction** with the Sun.	1900
4	Antares, the brightest star in the constellation Scorpius, is 1° 1′ south of the Moon. **Occultation** of Antares by the Moon.	0500
7	Mars is 4° north of the Moon.	1300
7	The Moon is at **perigee**.	2200
8	NEW MOON	2200
14	Pallas, the second-largest asteroid, appears to be motionless in the sky as it goes from direct motion to **retrograde** motion.	0700
14	Mercury is in superior **conjunction**.	1100
14	Venus is 1° 0′ south Neptune.	1900
16	FIRST QUARTER	0000
20	The Moon is at **apogee**.	0500
20	Saturn is 5° south of the Moon.	1100
24	FULL MOON	0500
24	The asteroid Juno is in **conjunction** with the Sun.	1700
25	Uranus is in **conjunction** with the Sun.	0700
27	Jupiter is 1° 2′ north of the Moon. **Occultation** of Jupiter by the Moon.	1500

MARCH

Day	Phenomenon	Hour
3	Antares, the brightest star in the constellation Scorpius, is 0° 8′ south of the Moon. **Occultation** of Jupiter by the Moon.	1100
3	LAST QUARTER	1800
6	Mars is 5° north of the Moon.	0600
8	Neptune is 5° north of the Moon.	0000
8	The Moon is at **perigee**.	0400
10	NEW MOON	0900
11	Mercury is 3° north of the Moon.	1600

Day	Phenomenon	Hour
12	Mercury is at its greatest **elongation**, at 18° east of the Sun.	1800
17	FIRST QUARTER	1900
19	Mercury appears to be motionless in the sky as it moves from its greatest **elongation** east of the Sun back toward a position west of the Sun as viewed from the Earth.	1600
19	Saturn is 5° south of the Moon.	1600
19	The Moon is at **apogee**.	2300
20	Equinox	1300
21	Ceres, the largest asteroid, appears to be motionless in the sky as it goes from direct motion to **retrograde** motion.	2000
22	Saturn appears to be motionless in the sky as it goes from **retrograde** to direct motion.	0000
23	Pallas, the second-largest asteroid, is at **opposition**.	0700
25	FULL MOON	2100
26	Jupiter is 1° 0′ north of the Moon. **Occultation** of Jupiter by the Moon.	1600
27	Pluto appears to be motionless in the sky as it goes from direct motion to **retrograde** motion.	0800
29	Mercury is in inferior **conjunction**.	1600
30	Antares, the brightest star in the constellation Scorpius, is 0° 7′ south of the Moon. **Occultation** of Antares by the Moon.	1700
31	Venus is in superior **conjunction**.	0300

APRIL

Day	Phenomenon	Hour
2	LAST QUARTER	0100
3	Jupiter is at **opposition**.	1600
3	Mars is 4° north of the Moon.	2200
4	Neptune is 5° north of the Moon.	0900
4	The Moon is at **perigee**.	1100
5	Uranus is 3° north of the Moon.	2200
7	Mercury is 3° north of the Moon.	1400
8	NEW MOON. Annular-total eclipse of the Sun.	2100
11	Mercury appears to be motionless in the sky as it moves toward its greatest **elongation** west of the Sun from a position east of the Sun as viewed from Earth.	0200
13	Mars is 1° 2′ south of Neptune.	0000
16	Saturn is 5° south of the Moon.	0100
16	FIRST QUARTER	1500
16	The Moon is at **apogee**.	1900
22	Jupiter is 0° 6′ north of the Moon. **Occultation** of Jupiter by the Moon.	1800
24	FULL MOON. Penumbral eclipse of the Moon.	1000
26	Mercury is at its greatest **elongation**, at 27° west of the Sun.	1700
26	Antares, the brightest star in the constellation Scorpius, is 0° 7′ south of the Moon. **Occulation** of Antares by the Moon.	2300
29	The Moon is at **perigee**.	1000

MAY

Day	Phenomenon	Hour
1	LAST QUARTER	0600
1	Neptune is 5° north of the Moon.	1500
2	Mars is 3° north of the Moon.	1500
3	Uranus is 3° north of the Moon.	0600
5	The asteroid Juno is 0° 08′ north of the Moon. **Occultation** of Juno by the Moon.	1400

Day	Phenomenon	Hour
6	Mercury is 3° south of the Moon.	1000
7	Pallas, the second-largest asteroid, appears to be motionless in the sky as it goes from **retrograde** to direct motion.	0100
8	NEW MOON	0900
8	Ceres, the largest asteroid, is at **opposition**.	1800
11	Vesta, the third-largest asteroid, is in **conjunction** with the Sun.	0300
13	Saturn is 5° south of the Moon.	1300
14	The Moon is at **apogee**.	1400
14	Mars is 1° 2′ south of Uranus.	2000
16	FIRST QUARTER	0900
18	Venus is 6° north of Aldebaran, the brightest star in the constellation Taurus.	2100
19	Jupiter is 0° 4′ north of the Moon. **Occultation** of Jupiter by the Moon.	2200
20	Neptune appears to be motionless in the sky as it goes from direct motion to **retrograde** motion.	0300
23	FULL MOON	2000
24	Antares, the brightest star in the constellation Scorpius, is 0° 8′ south of the Moon. **Occultation** of Antares by the Moon.	0800
26	The Moon is at **perigee.**	1100
28	Neptune is 5° north of the Moon.	2100
30	LAST QUARTER	1200
30	Uranus is 3° north of the Moon.	1200
31	Saturn is 7° south of Pollux, the brightest star in the constellation Gemini.	0500
31	Mars is 0° 5′ north of the Moon. **Occultation** of Mars by the Moon.	0900

JUNE

Day	Phenomenon	Hour
3	Mercury is in superior **conjunction**.	0900
5	Jupiter appears to be motionless in the sky as it goes from **retrograde** to direct motion.	2200
6	NEW MOON	2200
8	Venus is 4° south of the Moon.	1200
10	Saturn is 5° south of the Moon.	0200
11	The Moon is at **apogee**.	0600
14	Pluto is at **opposition**.	0300
15	FIRST QUARTER	0100
15	Uranus appears to be motionless in the sky as it goes from direct motion to **retrograde** motion.	0700
16	Jupiter is 0° 4′ north of the Moon. **Occultation** of Jupiter by the Moon.	0700
20	Antares, the brightest star in the constellation Scorpius, is 0° 7′ south of the Moon. **Occultation** of Antares by the Moon.	1800
21	Solstice	0700
22	FULL MOON	0400
23	The Moon is at **perigee**.	1200
23	Venus is 5° south of Pollux, the brightest star in the constellation Gemini.	1200
24	Mercury is 5° south of Pollux, the brightest star in the constellation Gemini.	0800
25	Neptune is 5° north of the Moon.	0400
25	Venus is 1° 3′ north of Saturn.	2100
26	Mercury is 1° 4′ north of Saturn.	0600
26	Uranus is 3° north of the Moon.	1900
27	Mercury is 0° 08′ south of Venus.	2100
28	LAST QUARTER	1800
29	Mars is 2° south of the Moon.	0400
30	Ceres, the largest asteroid, appears to be motionless in the sky as it goes from **retrograde** to direct motion.	1300

JULY

Day	Phenomenon	Hour
5	Earth is at **aphelion**.	0500
6	NEW MOON	1200
7	Mercury is 1° 6′ south of Venus.	0800
8	Mercury is 5° south of the Moon.	1800
8	The Moon is at **apogee**.	1800
8	Venus is 3° south of the Moon.	1900
9	Mercury is at its greatest **elongation**, at 26° east of the Sun.	0300
13	Jupiter is 0° 8′ north of the Moon. **Occultation** of Jupiter by the Moon.	1800
14	FIRST QUARTER	1500
18	Antares, the brightest star in the constellation Scorpius, is 0° 6′ south of the Moon. **Occultation** of Antares by the Moon.	0400
21	FULL MOON	1100
21	The moon is at **perigee**.	2000
22	Mercury appears to be motionless in the sky as it moves from its greatest **elongation** east of the Sun back toward a position west of the Sun as viewed from Earth.	0500
22	Neptune is 4° north of the Moon.	1300
22	Venus is 1° 2′ north of Regulus, the brightest star in the constellation Leo.	1500
23	Saturn is in **conjunction** with the Sun.	1700
24	Uranus is 2° north of the Moon.	0300
27	Mars is 4° south of the Moon.	2000
28	LAST QUARTER	0300

AUGUST

Day	Phenomenon	Hour
4	The Moon is at **apogee**.	2200
5	NEW MOON	0300
6	Mercury is in inferior **conjunction**.	0000
8	Venus is 1° 2′ south of the Moon. **Occultation** of Venus by the Moon.	0400
8	Neptune is at **opposition**.	1600
10	Jupiter is 1° 3′ north of the Moon. **Occultation** of Jupiter by the Moon.	0800
13	FIRST QUARTER	0300
14	Antares, the brightest star in the constellation Scorpius, is 0° 4′ south of the Moon. **Occultation** of Antares by the Moon.	1300
15	Mercury appears to be motionless in the sky as it moves toward its greatest **elongation** west of the Sun from a position east of the Sun as viewed from Earth.	1300
18	Neptune is 5° north of the Moon.	2300
19	The Moon is at **perigee.**	0600
19	FULL MOON	1800
20	Uranus is 2° north of the Moon.	1200
23	Mercury is at its greatest **elongation**, at 18° west of the Sun.	2300
25	Mars is 6° south of the Moon.	0700
26	LAST QUARTER	1500
31	Saturn is 5° south of the Moon.	1700

SEPTEMBER

Day	Phenomenon	Hour
1	The Moon is at **apogee**.	0300
1	Uranus is at **opposition**.	0300
2	Venus is 1° 4′ south of Jupiter.	1200
3	Pluto appears to be motionless in the sky as it goes from **retrograde** to direct motion.	0300
3	NEW MOON	1900
4	Mercury is 1° 1′ north of Regulus, the brightest star in the constellation Leo.	1100
5	Venus is 1° 8′ north of Spica, the brightest star in the constellation Virgo.	2100
7	Jupiter is 1° 8′ north of the Moon.	0000
7	Spica, the brightest star in the constellation Virgo, is 1° 3′ south of the Moon. **Occultation** of Spica by the Moon.	0600
7	Venus is 0° 6′ north of the Moon. **Occultation** of Venus by the Moon.	0900

Day	Phenomenon	Hour
10	Antares, the brightest star in the constellation Scorpius, is 0° 2′ south of the Moon. **Occultation** of Antares by the Moon.	2000
11	FIRST QUARTER	1200
15	Neptune is 5° north of the Moon.	0800
16	The Moon is at **perigee**.	1400
16	Uranus is 2° north of the Moon.	2100
18	FULL MOON	0200
18	Mercury is in superior **conjunction**.	0300
21	Jupiter is 3° north of Spica, the brightest star in the constellation Virgo.	2200
22	Mars is 6° south of the Moon.	0700
22	Equinox	2200
25	LAST QUARTER	0700
28	Saturn is 5° south of the Moon.	0500
28	The moon is at **apogee**.	1500

OCTOBER

Day	Phenomenon	Hour
1	Mars appears to be motionless in the sky as it goes from direct motion to **retrograde** motion.	1000
3	NEW MOON. Annular eclipse of the Sun.	1000
4	Mercury is 2° north of Spica, the brightest star in the constellation Virgo.	0800
6	Mercury is 1° 5′ south of Jupiter.	0700
7	Venus is 1° 4′ north of the Moon.	0600
8	Antares, the brightest star in the constellation Scorpius, is 0° 2′ south of the Moon. **Occultation** of Antares by the Moon.	0100
10	FIRST QUARTER	1900
12	Neptune is 5° north of the Moon.	1500
14	Uranus is 3° north of the Moon.	0500
14	The Moon is at **perigee**.	1400
16	Venus is 1° 6′ north of Antares, the brightest star in the constellation Scorpius.	1800
17	FULL MOON. Partial eclipse of the Moon.	1200
19	Mars is 5° south of the Moon.	1300
22	Jupiter is in **conjunction** with the Sun.	1300
25	LAST QUARTER	0100
25	Saturn is 4° south of the Moon.	1700
26	The Moon is at **apogee**.	1000
26	Neptune appears to be motionless in the sky as it goes from **retrograde** to direct motion.	2200
30	Mars makes its closest approach to Earth since 2003.	0300
31	Spica, the brightest star in the constellation Virgo, is 1° 2′ south of the Moon. **Occultation** of Spica by the Moon.	1900

NOVEMBER

Day	Phenomenon	Hour
2	NEW MOON	0100
2	The asteroid Juno appears to be motionless in the sky as it goes from direct motion to **retrograde** motion.	2000
3	Mercury is at its greatest **elongation**, at 24° east of the Sun.	1600
3	Venus is at its greatest **elongation**, at 47° east of the Sun.	1900
3	Mercury is 1° 3′ north of the Moon.	2300
4	Antares, the brightest star in the constellation Scorpius, is 0° 2′ south of the Moon. **Occultation** of Antares by the Moon.	0700
5	Venus is 1° 4′ north of the Moon.	1900
7	Mars is at **opposition**.	0800
8	Neptune is 5° north of the Moon.	2000
9	FIRST QUARTER	0200
9	Mercury is 1° 9′ north of Antares, the brightest star in the constellation Scorpius.	1600
10	The Moon is at **perigee**.	0000
10	Uranus is 3° north of the Moon.	1000

Day	Phenomenon	Hour
14	Mercury appears to be motionless in the sky as it moves from its greatest **elongation** east of the Sun back toward a position west of the Sun as viewed from the Earth.	0900
15	Mars is 3° south of the Moon.	0600
16	FULL MOON	0100
16	Uranus appears to be motionless in the sky as it goes from **retrograde** to direct motion.	0700
18	Pallas, the second-largest asteroid, is in **conjunction** with the Sun.	0200
18	Mercury is 3° north of Antares, the brightest star in the constellation Scorpius.	1600
19	Vesta, the third-largest asteroid, appears to be motionless in the sky as it goes from direct motion to **retrograde** motion.	1600
22	Saturn is 4° south of the Moon.	0300
22	Saturn appears to be motionless in the sky as it goes from direct motion to **retrograde** motion.	1800
23	The Moon is at **apogee**.	0600
23	LAST QUARTER	2200
24	Mercury is in inferior **conjunction**.	1600
28	Spica, the brightest star in the constellation Virgo, is 1° 1′ south of the Moon. **Occultation** of Spica by the Moon.	0400
29	Jupiter is 3° north of the Moon.	0800

DECEMBER

Day	Phenomenon	Hour
1	NEW MOON	1500
4	Mercury appears to be motionless in the sky as it moves toward its greatest **elongation** west of the Sun to a position east of the Sun as viewed from Earth.	0100
4	Venus is 2° north of the Moon.	1800
5	The Moon is at **perigee**.	0500
6	Neptune is 4° north of the Moon.	0300
7	Uranus is 2° north of the Moon.	1600
8	FIRST QUARTER	1000
9	The asteroid Juno is at **opposition**.	0800
9	Venus is at its greatest brilliancy.	1300
10	Mars appears to be motionless in the sky as it goes from **retrograde** motion to direct motion.	2300
12	Mars is 1° 3′ south of the Moon. Occultation of Mars by the Moon.	0500
12	Mercury is at its greatest **elongation**, at 21° west of the Sun.	1300
15	FULL MOON	1600
16	Pluto is in **conjunction** with the Sun.	0400
19	Saturn is 4° south of the Moon.	0900
20	Mercury is 6° north of Antares, the brightest star in the constellation Scorpius.	0700
21	The Moon is at **apogee**.	0300
21	Solstice	1900
23	Venus appears to be motionless in the sky as it moves from its greatest **elongation** east of the Sun back toward a position west of the Sun as viewed from Earth.	0500
23	LAST QUARTER	2000
25	Spica, the brightest star in the constellation Virgo, is 0° 9′ south of the Moon. **Occultation** of Spica by the Moon.	1400
27	Jupiter is 4° north of the Moon.	0400
28	Ceres, the largest asteroid, is in **conjunction** with the Sun.	1200
29	Antares, the brightest star in the constellation Scorpius, is 0° 2′ south of the Moon. **Occultation** of Antares by the Moon.	0200
30	Mercury is 5° north of the Moon.	0000
31	NEW MOON	0300

Conversion of Universal Time (UT) to Civil Time

UT	EDT[1]	EST[2]	CST[3]	MST[4]	PST[5]
00	*8P	*7P	*6P	*5P	*4P
01	*9P	*8P	*7P	*6P	*5P
02	*10P	*9P	*8P	*7P	*6P
03	*11P	*10P	*9P	*8P	*7P
04	M	*11P	*10P	*9P	*8P
05	1A	M	*11P	*10P	*9P
06	2A	1A	M	*11P	*10P
07	3A	2A	1A	M	*11P
08	4A	3A	2A	1A	M
09	5A	4A	3A	2A	1A
10	6A	5A	4A	3A	2A
11	7A	6A	5A	4A	3A
12	8A	7A	6A	5A	4A
13	9A	8A	7A	6A	5A
14	10A	9A	8A	7A	6A
15	11A	10A	9A	8A	7A
16	N	11A	10A	9A	8A
17	1P	N	11A	10A	9A
18	2P	1P	N	11A	10A
19	3P	2P	1P	N	11A
20	4P	3P	2P	1P	N
21	5P	4P	3P	2P	1P
22	6P	5P	4P	3P	2P
23	7P	6P	5P	4P	3P

NOTES: * denotes previous day. N = noon. M = midnight. 1. Eastern Daylight Time. 2. Eastern Standard Time, same as Central Daylight Time. 3. Central Standard Time, same as Mountain Daylight Time. 4. Mountain Standard Time, same as Pacific Daylight Time. 5. Pacific Standard Time.

Eclipses of the Sun and Moon, 2005

Note: The day of an eclipse is given in Universal Time (U.T.) and may start a day earlier or later depending on your time zone.

Apr. 8. Annular-total eclipse of the Sun. Visible in New Zealand, part of Antarctica, southern United States, Central America, the Caribbean, and South America except eastern and southern parts.

Apr. 24. Penumbral eclipse of the Moon. The beginning of the penumbral phase visible in North America, Central America, South America, New Zealand, eastern Australia, eastern Indonesia, most of Antarctica, the North Pacific Ocean except the extreme western part, the South Pacific Ocean, the Bering Sea, the western Atlantic Ocean; the end visible in western North America, most of Mexico, the extreme southern tip of South America, Indonesia, eastern Asia, New Zealand, Australia, Antarctica except coastal Queen Maud Land, the Pacific Ocean, and the eastern Indian Ocean.

Oct. 3. Annular eclipse of the Sun. Visible in eastern Greenland, Iceland, Europe (including the British Isles), Africa except southern tip, western Asia including India.

Oct. 17. Partial eclipse of the Moon. The beginning of the umbral phase visible in central and western North America, northern Central America, northern Greenland, the Arctic region, eastern Asia, Indonesia, Australia, New Zealand, Wilkes Land and coastal Marie Byrd Land of Antarctica, the North Pacific Ocean, the South Pacific Ocean except eastern part, and the eastern Indian Ocean; the end visible in western North America, northern Greenland, the Arctic region, Asia except the extreme western part, Indonesia, Australia, New Zealand, part of Wilkes Land in Antarctica, the North Pacific Ocean, the South Pacific Ocean except eastern part, and the eastern Indian Ocean.

Visibility of Planets in Morning and Evening Twilight, 2005

	Morning		Evening
Venus	January 1–February 19	Venus	May 9–December 31
Mars	January 1–November 7	Mars	November 7–December 31
Jupiter	January 1–April 3	Jupiter	April 3–October 9
	November 5–December 31	Saturn	January 13–July 5
Saturn	January 1–January 13		
	August 11–December 31		

Secrets of the Rings

What the planetary probe Cassini-Huygens discovered when it got to Saturn—and the wonders it may uncover in the mission to come

By JEFFREY KLUGER TIME

In July 2004, the Cassini-Huygens mission began an extended tour of the glittering Saturnian system with its seven rings, 33 moons, and untold cosmic secrets. By any measure, this is the most sophisticated planetary probe NASA has ever flown. About the size of a small bus, the *Cassini* orbiter is more than 22 ft tall and weighs more than 6 tons when fueled. An engineering marvel, it is packed with a dozen scientific instruments and powered by a miniature nuclear generator. Carried on its side like a high-tech papoose is the *Huygens* lander, a 9-foot, 700-pound wok-shaped probe that will explore Saturn's mysterious moon Titan.

The payoff—for space scientists and curious civilians—could be staggering. Three other planets in the solar system—Jupiter, Uranus, and Neptune—have rings, but they are faint and thready things, nothing like the magnificently complex cosmic jewelry that decorates Saturn. Seven of the other nine planets have moons, but none that perform the gravitational dances among themselves and within the rings that Saturn's do. And no planet has a moon anything like Titan, a world with much of the preorganic chemistry that Earth had 4.5 billion years ago—offering scientists a one-of-a-kind window into our vanished past.

Saturn as Microcosm

The Saturnian system is, in a very real sense, the solar system writ small. And while other spacecraft have glimpsed it before—*Pioneer 11* in 1979, *Voyager 1* and 2 in 1980 and 1981—they were mere flybys, quick hits by ships snapping a few pictures before whizzing off into deeper space. Cassini-Huygens—named after 17th-century astronomers Jean Dominique Cassini and Christiaan Huygens—is there to stay.

The centerpiece of the Saturnian system is, of course, the planet itself, and plans call for it to get a going-over that it has never had before. The second largest of the solar system's four gas giants, Saturn—like its big brother Jupiter—is sometimes described as a starlike body with a chemistry of hydrogen and helium but without sufficient mass to light a nuclear furnace. That doesn't mean, however, that Saturn isn't roaring with activity.

By far the planet's most dramatic feature is its hellish weather. Winds blow around the Saturnian equator at 1,100 mph—five to ten times the speed of the most powerful winds on Earth. Giant hurricanes tear through the planet's atmosphere, often two or more storms at a time, which then meet up before dying out. Displays of light similar to Earth's aurora borealis illuminate Saturn's skies, thanks to charged particles falling in from its moons. And where the auroras aren't flashing, lightning may be striking.

Cassini will use an elaborate suite of instruments to determine why all this meteorological hubbub is taking place on a planet that is so cold—with cloud-top temperatures of –218°F—that it shouldn't be able to cook up much weather. The best guess is that internal heat left over from the gravitational collapse that formed the planet in the first place is keeping things warm. *Cassini* will deploy its cameras, infra-red sensors, chemical spectrographs, and more to deconstruct the planet's atmosphere and find out for sure. Other instruments will map the planet's magnetosphere and gravitational field, perhaps confirming the theory that even so massive a ball of gas as Saturn has a solid core.

The Rings of Saturn

But it is by its rings that Saturn is known, and it was close-up pictures of those rings that stole the show. Within minutes of *Cassini*'s arrival, the ship's camera had fired off 61 shots of the rings, and by ten o'clock the next morning, wide-eyed *Cassini* scientists were showing them to the press.

Scientists have known since *Voyager* that the seven broad bands that make up the ring system are not undifferentiated masses of material but rather are made up of hundreds of individual strands, like the grooves in a record album. The strands are made up of billions of bits of rubble and ice, some of them crystals smaller than a grain of sand, some of them boulders bigger than a house.

As the pictures from *Cassini* reveal, the interaction of this orbiting material can create bizarre effects. The edge of one ring shows elegant scalloping, presumably caused by the gravitational wake of a moon cruising alongside it.

Other images show that the moving moons cause equally graceful formations within the rings by tugging on particles and causing them to pile up and thin out, pile up and thin out, rippling outward in what ring scientists call a "density wave." Another kind of wave known as a "bending wave" is caused by a moon that orbits at an angle inclined to the ring plane, warping or corrugating the ring's edge.

Although *Cassini* will never again be as close to the rings as it was in July 2004, it took only black-and-white pictures on the way into orbit. In orbit it will shoot between 100 and 200 images a day, most of them in color.

Though no one is sure how the rings formed, some of the material is almost certainly the remains of small pulverized moons that were destroyed either by a cataclysmic meteor hit or when they wandered too close to a gravitational danger zone known as the "Roche limit," the altitude above a planet at which the difference in gravity between the end of an object closest to the planet and the end farthest from the planet is great enough to pull the object apart while not pulling the remains out of orbit. Instead, the rubble disperses around the planet. Photographs of the debris could help confirm this phenomenon and could even turn up smaller, still undiscovered moons hiding within the rings.

More Discoveries to Come

If Cassini-Huygens traveled all the way to Saturn and returned nothing but data on the planet and its rings, the mission would probably still be judged a success. Yet the true scientific goods will come when the spacecraft trains its instruments on the swirl of Saturnian moons. It would be nearly impossible for one ship to visit all 33 known satellites in Saturn's litter, so NASA has selected nine of them, both for their scientific promise and their comparatively convenient locations. The exotic names of the chosen moons—Phoebe, Titan, Iapetus, Enceladus, Mimas, Tethys, Hyperion, Dione and Rhea—hint at the exotic science that awaits.

Iapetus, for example, is a two-toned world, its leading edge dark, its trailing edge white. There are many theories advanced for this—including the possibility that there are hemisphere-wide volcanoes or that the moon is picking up dust as it moves through its orbit, staining its face and leaving the other side clean.

Enceladus holds mysteries of its own. A bright white world with a relatively smooth face, it appears to have been repeatedly resurfaced by some kind of underground slurry or perhaps by ice volcanoes. In some places, once-deep crevasses have been largely filled in and craters have been cut neatly in half, leaving one side deep and raw and the other covered, as if by snowdrifts. The area of the Saturnian ring that follows in the wake of Enceladus is slightly thicker than the rest, as if the moon were pumping out some kind of frozen exhaust, leaving a plume in its wake like the smoke from a steamship.

Other questions should be answered when Cassini flies by Hyperion, a tumbling moon that appears to have been knocked off its pins by a collision eons ago and has never regained its footing; and Tethys, a moon that bears such a massive impact scar that only the barest geological margin keeps it from shattering altogether.

It is Titan, however, that will be the main attraction. One of the largest moons in the solar system—larger than Mercury or Pluto—Titan would be a perfectly good planet if it were orbiting the Sun under its own steam. NASA scientists were keenly disappointed when the Voyager 1 spacecraft flew by Titan in 1980. The moon's dense, orange atmosphere completely concealed its surface from view, revealing not a clue about what was happening on the ground.

Scientists speculate that there may be quite a bit happening. Rich in nitrogen as well as ethane, methane, and other carbon-based gases, the Titanian air contains the raw chemical material believed to be needed to give rise to life—and just the kind that probably existed on the primordial Earth. Titan's frigid temperature—about −280°F—would surely have prevented life from emerging. Nonetheless,

over time the candlelike heat of the distant Sun may have slow-cooked some of the organic materials, forming more complex molecules. What's more, if there is lightning in Titan's atmosphere, the random jolts could have shocked even bigger molecules into existence.

The Cassini-Huygens mission will investigate Titan from many angles. Of the 59 flybys of the nine selected moons, 45 will be devoted to Titan—most at a distance of just 590 mi. Preliminary images revealed a bright cloud pattern about the size of Arizona near the south pole and what appeared to be a massive impact crater.

But there will be much more. Radar will pierce the Titanian cloud cover, mapping plains, mountains and perhaps even lakes of liquid ethane and methane—though early observations cast new doubt on the existence of the lakes. Spectrometers and other instruments will take the chemical measure of the moon's air, and cameras will again try to photograph Titan from outside in.

Cassini's best shot at the moon will come on Christmas Eve 2004, when the Huygens probe is fired toward Titan, heading for a Jan. 14, 2005, rendezvous. On arrival, it will make a 2½-hour descent through the atmosphere by parachute. If it isn't destroyed by the landing, the probe could survive on the surface for an extra 30 minutes or so.

The brief three hours that Huygens lasts will be busy. The probe carries six instruments, including radar, an aerosol collector, a camera, and wind instruments. The hardware will switch on by an altitude of 93 mi and will record data all the way down. When Huygens lands, sensors will continue to take readings—assuming it doesn't smack against a mountain or capsize in a methane lake. Even if it does, the landing—NASA's first splashdown since the return of the last Apollo spacecraft in 1975—will make space history.

End of an Era

Barring breakdowns or accidents, Cassini should send back data at least until 2008. If it exceeds its nominal life span it could survive for nearly a decade. When it finally does wink out, it could mark an end in more ways than one.

Cassini-Huygens is widely thought to be the last of NASA's great Cadillac probes—multibillion-dollar ships stuffed with instruments and complex backup systems. In the planning stage for 19 years, the craft cost $1.4 billion to design and build and nearly $2 billion to fly. When NASA adopted its "faster, better, cheaper" philosophy in the 1990s, it drove the cost of its unmanned ships down to the range of a couple of hundred million dollars—mostly by relying on off-the-shelf parts and eliminating redundant systems.

If Cassini really does represent the end of an era, it's a glorious end. Space scientists can justly take pride in the ship they have built and launched. They ought to be humbled too by the enormousness of the frontier they are mapping. "We have always tended to underestimate the splendor that the solar system has to offer," says Cassini physicist Larry Soderblum. Knowing that this may be the last time—at least in our lives—that we get such a good look at Saturn makes the wonder of what we're seeing all the sweeter. □

Hubble Space Telescope

The $2 billion Edwin P. Hubble Space Telescope (HST) was lifted into orbit by the space shuttle *Discovery* on April 25, 1990. Weighing approximately 25,500 lb (11,000 kg) and measuring 43 ft (13 m) long by 14 ft (4 m) wide, or roughly the size of a school bus, HST is the most complex and sensitive space observatory ever constructed, and it has become astronomers' principal tool for exploring the universe.

During its lifetime, the space telescope has required intermittent servicing. In June 1990, just two months after HST was launched into orbit, astronomers discovered that there was a spherical aberration in one of the telescope's mirrors. In 1991, two of the craft's six gyroscopes failed, and a third failed on Nov. 18, 1993, causing additional problems. NASA successfully repaired the space telescope during the Dec. 2–13, 1993, mission of the *Endeavour*. Three more repair and upgrade missions were made to HST through 2002.

A fifth servicing mission, scheduled for July 2003, was canceled after the *Columbia* space shuttle disaster. Without servicing, Hubble is expected to be out of commission by 2008.

After NASA announced that the telescope would not be repaired due to the risks to a human crew, outcry from scientists, politicians, and the public forced the agency to consider sending a robotic repair mission. In July 2004, a panel from the National Academy of Sciences urged NASA to save the Hubble, voicing a preference for a staffed mission and citing the complexity and uncertainty of a first-time robotic attempt. The agency hoped to make a decision about the rescue by Oct. 2004 in order to prepare for a Dec. 2007 launch deadline.

Hubble is slated to be decommissioned in 2010 and replaced by the next-generation James Webb Space Telescope, scheduled to be launched in 2011. The new observatory will have a primary mirror that is 20 ft in diameter, compared to the Hubble's 8-foot reflector.

Major Space Explorations

Ongoing Missions

Voyager (U.S.)
Destination: Jupiter and Saturn. **Launched:** Aug. 20 *(Voyager 2)* and Sept. 5 *(Voyager 1)*, 1977. **Mission:** To explore Jupiter and the other outer planets. Launched in 1977, *Voyager 1* and *Voyager 2* passed Jupiter in 1979 and sent back surprising color TV images of that planet and its moons. *Voyager 1* passed Saturn in Nov. 1980. *Voyager 2* passed Saturn in Aug. 1981 and Uranus in Jan. 1986. *Voyager 2* encountered Neptune on Aug. 29, 1989, and made many discoveries. It found four rings around the planet, six new moons, a giant spot, and evidence of volcanic-like activity on its largest moon, Triton. The spacecraft sent back over 9,000 pictures of the planet and its system. *Voyager 2* remains the only spacecraft ever to have visited the worlds of Neptune and Uranus. On Feb. 13, 1990, at a distance of 3.7 billion miles, *Voyager 1* took its final pictures of the Sun and six of its planets as seen from deep space. NASA released the extraordinary images to the public on June 6, 1990. Only Mercury, Mars, and Pluto were not seen.

In its quarter-century of exploration, the *Voyager* project has returned immense amounts of information. *Voyager I*, at 9 billion miles from the Sun, is currently the most distant human-made object in the universe, and *Voyager 2* is 7 billion miles from the Sun. Both spacecraft currently constitute the Voyager Interstellar Mission (VIM), the study of the region of space beyond the Sun's influence (the heliopause), at the outer boundary of the solar system. Both spacecraft continue to relay news of their surroundings through the Deep Space Network (DSN).

Ulysses (U.S. and European Space Agency)
Destination: The Sun. **Launched:** Oct. 6, 1990. **Mission:** An international project to study the Sun and map the interstellar space above and below its poles. The spacecraft was put into orbit at right angles to the solar system's ecliptic plane. This spe- cial orbit enabled *Ulysses* to examine for the first time the Sun's north and south polar regions. Besides investigating the Sun, the spacecraft is also studying phenomena from the Milky Way and beyond. The spacecraft completed its first full orbit around the Sun on April 17, 1998, and continues to orbit the Sun. *Ulysses* made its closest approach to Jupiter in Feb. 2004.

Mars Global Surveyor (U.S.)
Destination: Mars. **Launched:** Nov. 7, 1996. **Arrival:** Sept. 11, 1997. **Mission:** An orbiting spacecraft designed to provide detailed maps of the planet's surface and distribution of minerals, and to monitor the Martian weather. Six instruments are studying Martian surface, atmosphere, and gravitational and magnetic fields. *Surveyor*'s cameras are able to distinguish features as small as 10 ft across.

The primary mapping mission was delayed until March 1999, due to problems with the craft's solar panels. *MGS* completed its primary mission in Jan. 2001, and is currently in an extended mission phase. Having studied the planet's entire surface, atmosphere, and interior, *MGS* has returned more Mars data than all other Martian missions combined. Its most significant results include photographs of gullies and debris flow that suggest the presence of water at or near the planet's surface. *MGS* is collecting and transmitting data from the Mars Exploration Rovers.

Cassini-Huygens (U.S., the European Space Agency, and the Italian Space Agency)
Destination: Saturn. **Launched:** Oct. 15, 1997. **Arrival:** July 1, 2004. **Mission:** Will orbit Saturn for four years. The Cassini-Huygens mission is named for the Italian-French astronomer Jean Dominique Cassini, who discovered four of Saturn's major moons, and the Dutch scientist Christiaan Huygens, the first to find Saturn's rings and its largest moon, Titan. *Cassini-Huygens* encountered Jupiter on Dec. 30, 2000, and flew down the giant planet's magnetotail (the elongated tail of a planet's

magnetic field facing away from the Sun), performing studies complementing the *Galileo* mission until March 31, 2001. On July 1, 2004, *Cassini* reached Saturn's rings and went into the first of 74 orbits of the planet and began sending back images of the rings and the moons. On Dec. 25, 2004, the *Huygens* probe will separate from the *Cassini* spacecraft and in Jan. 2005 will descend to Titan, transmitting information for up to three hours. The *Cassini* craft is slated to continue its mission until July 1, 2008. See "Secrets of the Rings," p. 421.

Stardust (U.S.)

Destination: Comet Wild 2. **Launched:** Feb. 7, 1999. **Mission:** To fly through the coma of Comet Wild 2, capture particles spewing out of the comet, take pictures of the comet, and return comet dust samples to Earth. *Stardust* will be the first mission to return with comet samples. Additionally, the *Stardust* spacecraft will bring back samples of interstellar dust, which is believed to include remnants from the formation of the solar system. On April 18, 2002, *Stardust* reached the farthest distance from the Sun ever traveled by a solar-powered spacecraft, 2.72 AU (253 million miles or 407 million kilometers). In Jan. 2004, *Stardust* reached the comet, sent back the best images of a comet ever taken, and collected comet particles destined to return to Earth Jan. 16, 2006.

2001 Mars Odyssey (U.S.)

Destination: Mars. **Launched:** April 7, 2001. **Arrival:** Oct. 24, 2001. **Mission:** To conduct mineralogical mapping of the planet and study the radiation risk to humans over the course of three years. A goal of the program is to determine if Mars's atmosphere could support life.

Mars Odyssey's primary mission will continue through Aug. 2004, mapping the amount and distribution of chemical elements and minerals that form the Martian surface and searching especially for evidence of hydrogen in the subsurface. In addition to its scientific mission, *Mars Odyssey* provides support to the Mars Exploration Rovers program (MER), serving as the communications relay for MER's rovers. About 75% of MER's *Spirit* rover's pictures have been relayed to Earth via *Odyssey*.

Wilkinson Microwave Anisotropy Probe (WMAP) (U.S.)

Destination: Solar orbit. **Launched:** June 30, 2001. **Arrival:** Oct. 1, 2001. **Mission:** To reveal conditions as they existed in the early universe by measuring the properties of cosmic microwave background radiation (CMB), the radiant heat left over from the Big Bang, over the full sky. Each sky scan takes approximately six months, and in April 2002, *WMAP* completed its first. The full sky map will be updated as more data is received and analyzed. Data from *WMAP*'s first full sky scan was released in Feb. 2003, revealing a map of the oldest light in the universe, 13.7 billion years old. The mission is slated to continue mapping until 2006.

Genesis (U.S.)

Destination: The Sun. **Launched:** Aug. 8, 2001. **Return:** Sept. 8, 2004. **Mission:** To gather samples of charged particles of the solar wind and return them to Earth. The drogue parachute of the return capsule failed to deploy, sending the craft plunging into the Utah desert at 193 miles per hour (311 kilometers per hour). Scientists are analyzing the contents of the science canister to determine if any samples can be salvaged.

Mars Express (European Space Agency)

Destination: Mars. **Launched:** June 2, 2003. **Arrival:** Dec. 26, 2003. **Mission:** To search for subsurface water from orbit and drop a lander on the Martian surface. Instruments on the orbiting spacecraft will study the atmosphere and the planet's structure and geology. The lander, *Beagle 2* (named after the ship on which Charles Darwin sailed), was scheduled to take photographs, gather soil samples, and examine rocks and soil microscopically—all in the search for signs of past life on Mars. *Beagle 2* separated from the orbiter on Dec. 19, 2003, but contact was lost. The orbiter continued its mission, imaging the planet's entire surface, mapping the composition of the surface and atmosphere, determining the structure of the subsurface, and studying the atmosphere.

Mars Exploration Rovers (MER) (U.S.)

Destination: Mars. **Launched:** June 10, 2003 (*Spirit*) and July 7 (*Opportunity*). **Arrival:** Jan. 2004. **Mission:** To deploy, in two different locations, *Spirit* and *Opportunity*, two identical long-range rovers (larger than *Pathfinder*'s *Sojourner*) that can trek up to 300 yards (100 m) across the surface in a Martian day. The rovers' sophisticated instruments enable them to act as mobile field geologists, taking color pictures, analyzing soil and rocks, and searching for past and present evidence of water. The rovers were designed to operate for 90 days but were performing so well the mission was extended. *Spirit* made a successful landing on Jan. 3, 2004, and started beaming 3-D images of the planet the next day. On Jan. 6, *Spirit* began to send sharp color pictures of the planet back to Earth. *Opportunity* landed on Jan. 24, 2004, on the opposite side of Mars from *Spirit* and began sending images the next day. Both rovers, on opposite sides of the planet, found evidence that water was present, and even flowed, in the planet's past. See "The Blueberries of Mars," p. 396.

MESSENGER (MErcury Surface, Space ENvironment, GEochemistry, and Ranging mission) (U.S.)

Destination: Mercury. **Launched:** Aug. 3, 2004. **Arrival:** 2011. **Mission:** The first mission to study Mercury from orbit. *MESSENGER* is intended to spend at least a year in orbit photographing the planet, studying its makeup, and charting Mercury's magnetic field.

Future Missions
(Note: Dates are tentative.)

Selene SELenological and ENgineering Explorer (Japan)

Destination: The Moon. **Launch:** 2005. **Mission:** A spacecraft that will study the origin and evolution of the Moon, orbiting it for one year. It will map the entire surface and gather data on chemical and mineralogical composition, magnetic fields, and interior structure. After a year, the propulsion module of the orbiter will separate from the spacecraft and soft-land on the lunar surface to continue the mission for two more months.

Space Technology 5 (U.S.)
Destination: Earth's magnetosphere. **Launch:** 2005. **Mission:** Fourth deep-space mission of NASA's New Millennium program. The Nanosat Constellation Trailblazer, known as Space Technology 5 or ST5, will test methods for operating three miniature spacecraft as a single system. Each of the spacecraft is about 17 in. (42 cm) across by 8 in. (20 cm) high and weighs about 47 lb.

AIM (U.S.)
Destination: Earth orbit. **Launch:** 2006. **Mission:** *AIM*, the Aeronomy of Ice in the Mesosphere mission, will be employed to help scientists investigate the causes of the recent rise in noctilucent (glow-in-the-dark) clouds, wispy swirls that form about 50 mi (80 km) above the surface of the earth. The presence of the clouds over the polar regions has increased markedly in recent decades, and is thought by many scientists to be related to higher concentrations of greenhouse gases in Earth's atmosphere.

New Horizons (U.S.)
Destination: Pluto-Kuiper Belt. **Launch:** Jan. 2006. **Arrival:** Summer 2015. **Mission:** To study the worlds at the edge of our solar system. *New Horizons* will be the first mission specifically designed to study Pluto and its moon Charon. This mission plans to map Pluto's and Charon's surface appearances, study surface compositions, and probe their atmospheres. *New Horizons* then will go to the Kuiper Belt, located beyond Neptune's orbit, and examine Kuiper Belt objects, thought to be similar to the composition of the cores of the giant planets.

Herschel Space Observatory (European Space Agency)
Destination: Earth's magnetosphere. **Launch:** 2007. **Mission:** To study how the first stars and galaxies were formed and to search for water in space. Formerly called the Far Infrared and Submillimetre Telescope (FIRST), Herschel will be equipped with an infrared telescope, a high-resolution spectrograph, and two infrared cameras. Construction of the observatory began in the spring of 2002.

U.S. Unstaffed Planetary and Lunar Programs

Lunar Orbiter. Series of spacecraft designed to orbit the Moon, taking pictures and obtaining data in support of the subsequent staffed *Apollo* landings.

The U.S. launched five *Lunar Orbiter*s between Aug. 10, 1966, and Aug. 2, 1967.

Mariner. Designation for a series of spacecraft designed to fly past or orbit the planets, particularly Mercury, Venus, and Mars. *Mariner*s provided the early information on Venus and Mars. *Mariner 9*, orbiting Mars in 1971, returned the most revealing photographs of that planet and helped pave the way for a *Viking* landing in 1976. *Mariner 10* explored Venus and Mercury in 1973 and was the first probe to use a planet's gravity to propel it toward another.

Pioneer. Designation for the United States' first series of sophisticated interplanetary spacecraft. *Pioneer*s *10* and *11* reached Jupiter in 1973 and 1974 and continued on to explore Saturn and the other outer planets. *Pioneer 11*, renamed *Pioneer Saturn*, examined the Saturn system in Sept. 1979. Significant discoveries were the finding of a small new moon and a narrow new ring. In 1986, *Pioneer 10* was the first man-made object to escape the solar system. *Pioneer Venus 1* and *2* reached Venus in 1978 and provided detailed information about that planet's surface and atmosphere.

Ranger. NASA's earliest Moon-exploration program. Spacecraft were designed for a crash landing on the Moon, taking pictures and returning scientific data up to the moment of impact. Provided the first close-up views of the lunar surface. The *Ranger*s provided more than 17,000 close-up pictures, giving us more information about the Moon in a few years than in all the time that had gone before.

Surveyor. Series of unstaffed spacecraft designed to land gently on the Moon and provide information on the surface in preparation for the staffed lunar landings. *Surveyor*'s legs were instrumented to return data on the surface hardness of the Moon. *Surveyor* dispelled the fear that *Apollo* spacecraft might sink several feet or more into the lunar dust.

Viking. Designation for two spacecraft designed to conduct detailed scientific examination of the planet Mars, including a search for life. *Viking 1* landed on July 20, 1976; *Viking 2*, Sept. 3, 1976. More was learned about the red planet in a few short months than in all previous missions, but the question of whether there is life on Mars remains unresolved.

Notable Unstaffed Lunar and Interplanetary Probes

Spacecraft	Launch date	Destination	Remarks
Pioneer 3 (U.S.)	Dec. 6, 1958	Moon	Max. alt.: 66,654 mi. Discovered outer Van Allen layer.
Luna 2 (USSR)	Sept. 12, 1959	Moon	Impacted on Sept. 14. First space vehicle to reach Moon.
Luna 3 (USSR)	Oct. 4, 1959	Moon	Flew around Moon and transmitted first pictures of lunar far side, Oct. 7.
Mariner 2 (U.S.)	Aug. 27, 1962	Venus	Venus probe. Successful mid-course correction. Passed 21,648 mi from Venus Dec. 14, 1962. Reported 800°F surface temp. Contact lost Jan. 3, 1963, at 54 million mi.
Ranger 7 (U.S.)	July 28, 1964	Moon	Impacted near Crater Guericke 68.5 hr after launch. Sent 4,316 pictures during last 15 min of flight as close as 1,000 ft above lunar surface.
Mariner 4 (U.S.)	Nov. 28, 1964	Mars	Transmitted first close-up pictures on June 14, 1965, from altitude of 6,000 mi.
Luna 9 (USSR)	Jan. 31, 1966	Moon	220 lb instrument capsule soft-landed Feb. 3, 1966. Sent back about 30 pictures.

Spacecraft	Launch date	Destination	Remarks
Surveyor 1 (U.S.)	May 30, 1966	Moon	Landed June 2, 1966. Sent almost 10,400 pictures, a number after surviving the 14-day lunar night.
Lunar Orbiter 1 (U.S.)	Aug. 10, 1966	Moon	Orbited Moon Aug. 14. 21 pictures sent.
Surveyor 3 (U.S.)	April 17, 1967	Moon	Soft-landed on Oceanus Procellarum 65 hr after launch. Scooped and tested lunar soil.
Venera 4 (USSR)	June 12, 1967	Venus	Arrived Oct. 17. Instrument capsule sent temperature and chemical data.
Surveyor 5 (U.S.)	Sept. 8, 1967	Moon	Landed near lunar equator Sept. 10. Radiological analysis of lunar soil. Mechanical claw for digging soil.
Surveyor 7 (U.S.)	Jan. 6, 1968	Moon	Landed near Crater Tycho Jan. 10. Soil analysis. Sent 3,343 pictures.
Pioneer 9 (U.S.)	Nov. 8, 1968	Sun	Achieved orbit. Six experiments returned solar radiation data.
Venera 5 (USSR)	Jan. 5, 1969	Venus	Landed May 16, 1969. Returned atmospheric data.
Mariner 6 (U.S.)	Feb. 24, 1969	Mars	Came within 2,000 mi of Mars July 31, 1969. Sent back data and TV pictures.
Luna 16 (USSR)	Sept. 12, 1970	Moon	Soft-landed Sept. 20, scooped up rock, returned to Earth Sept. 24.
Luna 17 (USSR)	Nov. 10, 1970	Moon	Soft-landed on Sea of Rains Nov. 17. Lunokhod 1, self-propelled vehicle, used for first time. Sent TV photos, made soil analysis, etc.
Mariner 9 (U.S.)	May 30, 1971	Mars	First craft to orbit Mars, Nov. 13. 7,300 pictures, 1st close-ups of one of Mars's moons. Transmission ended Oct. 27, 1972.
Luna 20 (USSR)	Feb. 14, 1972	Moon	Soft-landed Feb. 21 in Sea of Fertility. Returned Feb. 25 with rock samples.
Pioneer 10 (U.S.)	March 3, 1972	Jupiter	620-million-mi flight path through asteroid belt past Jupiter Dec. 3, 1973, to give man first close-up of planet. In 1986, it became first man-made object to escape solar system.
Luna 21 (USSR)	Jan. 8, 1973	Moon	Soft-landed Jan. 16. Lunokhod 2 (moon-car) scooped up soil samples, returned them to Earth Jan. 27.
Mariner 10 (U.S.)	Nov. 3, 1973	Venus, Mercury	Passed Venus Feb. 5, 1974. Arrived Mercury March 29, 1974, for man's first close-up look at planet. First time gravity of one planet (Venus) used to propel spacecraft toward another (Mercury).
Viking 1 (U.S.)	Aug. 20, 1975	Mars	Carrying life-detection labs. Landed July 20, 1976, for detailed scientific research, including pictures. Designed to work for only 90 days, it operated for almost 6½ years before it went silent in Nov. 1982.
Viking 2 (U.S.)	Sept. 9, 1975	Mars	Like Viking 1. Landed Sept. 3, 1976. Functioned 3½ years.
Luna 24 (USSR)	Aug. 9, 1976	Moon	Soft-landed Aug. 18, 1976. Returned soil samples Aug. 22, 1976.
Voyager 2 (U.S.)	Aug. 20, 1977	Jupiter, Saturn, Uranus	Launched before Voyager 1. Encountered Jupiter in July 1979; flew by Saturn Aug. 1981; passed Uranus Jan. 1986; and passed Neptune in Aug. 1989.
Voyager 1 (U.S.)	Sept. 5, 1977	Jupiter, Saturn	Flyby mission. Reached Jupiter in March 1979; passed Saturn Nov. 1980; passed Uranus 1986.
Pioneer Venus 1 (U.S.)	May 20, 1978	Venus	Arrived Dec. 4 and orbited Venus, photographing surface and atmosphere. Crashed into planet's surface mid-Oct. 1992 after circling Venus for 14 years.
Pioneer Venus 2 (U.S.)	Aug. 8, 1978	Venus	Four-part multiprobe, landed Dec. 9.
Venera 13 (USSR)	Oct. 30, 1981	Venus	Landed March 1, 1982. Took first X-ray fluorescence analysis of the planet's surface. Transmitted data 2 hours, 7 minutes.
VEGA 1 (USSR)	Deployed on Venus, June 10, 1985	Halley's Comet	In flyby over Venus while en route to encounter Halley's Comet, VEGA 1 and 2 dropped scientific capsules onto Venus to study atmosphere and surface material. Encountered Halley's Comet on March 6 and March 9, 1986. Took TV pictures and studied comet's dust particles.
VEGA 2 (USSR)	Deployed on Venus, June 14, 1985	Halley's Comet	See VEGA 1 above.
Suisei (Japan)	Aug. 18, 1985	Halley's Comet	Spacecraft made flyby of comet and studied atmosphere with ultraviolet camera; observed rotation nucleus (March 8, 1986).
Sakigake (Japan)	Jan. 8, 1985	Halley's Comet	Spacecraft made flyby to study solar wind and magnetic fields; detected plasma waves (March 11, 1986).
Giotto (E.S.A.)	July 2, 1985	Halley's Comet	European Space Agency spacecraft made closest approach to comet (March 13, 1986). Studied atmosphere and magnetic fields. Sent back best pictures of nucleus. Flew by comet Grigg-Skjellerup July 10, 1992. Unable to send pictures.

Spacecraft	Launch date	Destination	Remarks
Phobos Mission (USSR)	July 7 and July 12, 1988	Mars and Phobos	Two spacecraft to probe Martian moon Phobos starting April 1989. Were to study orbit and soil chemistry, and send TV pictures and data of planet. Contact was lost with *Phobos 1* in Aug. 1988 and with *Phobos 2* in March 1989 after it reached the Martian moon.
Magellan (U.S.)	May 4, 1989	Venus	Arrived at Venus on Aug. 10, 1990, and made a geologic map of planet with a powerful radar. Crashed into Venus Oct. 12, 1994.
Galileo (U.S.)	Oct. 18, 1989	Jupiter	To study Jupiter's atmosphere and its moons during 22-month mission.
Ulysses (U.S., E.S.A.)	Oct. 6, 1990	Sun	To study the poles of the Sun and interstellar space above and below the poles. First solar encounter was in 1994, second encounter in 1995.
Gamma-Ray Observatory (U.S.)	April 7, 1991	Earth orbit	To make first survey of gamma-ray sources across the whole sky, studying explosive energy sources such as supernovae, quasars, neutron stars, pulsars, and black holes. Mission ended, it was deorbited and crashed into Pacific Ocean, June 4, 2000.
Clementine (U.S.)	Jan. 25, 1994	Moon and asteroid 1620 Geographos	Entered lunar orbit Feb. 21 and took close-up photos of lunar surface for two months. Computer malfunction prevented planned rendezvous with *Geographos*.
Near-Earth Asteroid Rendezvous (NEAR) (U.S.)	Feb. 17, 1996	Asteroid 433 Eros	Photographed asteroid 253 Mathilde June 27, 1997. Entered into orbit around Eros Feb. 14, 2000, and landed on surface in controlled crash Feb. 12, 2001. Took detailed measurements and generated about 160,000 images of Eros. Renamed NEAR-Shoemaker in honor of geologist Eugene M. Shoemaker. First craft to orbit an asteroid.
Mars Pathfinder (U.S.)	Dec. 5, 1996	Ares Vallis, Mars	Landed July 4, 1997. The spacecraft lander and its rover, *Sojourner*, provided a wealth of information on the Martian rocks, soil, and atmosphere. Sent back the first live pictures. All *Pathfinder*'s objectives were fulfilled and communications failed on Sept. 27, 1997.
Lunar Prospector (U.S.)	Jan. 6, 1998	Moon	Orbited Moon for one year, mapped chemical composition of lunar surface. Found frozen water at north and south poles. At end of its mission on July 31, 1999, it was intentionally crashed into south polar crater in hope of detecting plume of water ice, but no cloud of molecular water vapor was observed by powerful Earth telescopes.
Deep Space 1 (U.S.)	Oct. 24, 1998	Deep space	The first launch of NASA's New Millennium Program, a series of missions to test new technologies. Famous for its July 1999 photos of the near-Earth Braille asteroid and the first-ever photos of a comet nucleus when it staged a risky flyby of the comet Borelly in Sept. 2001. The second phase of New Millennium, *Deep Space 2*, was launched in 1999, but NASA lost contact with it in Dec. 1999.
Space Infrared Telescope Facility (SIRTF) (U.S.)	Aug. 25, 2003	Earth-trailing solar orbit	Final mission in NASA's Great Observatories Program which has four observatories studying the universe in different kinds of light—visible (Hubble Space Telescope), gamma rays (Compton Gamma-Ray Observatory), x-rays (Chandra X-Ray Observatory), and infrared (SIRTF).
Mars Exploration Rovers (U.S.)	June 10, 2003 *(Spirit)*; July 7, 2003 *(Opportunity)*	Mars	Both rovers landed safely on Mars in Jan. 2004 and sent images back to Earth. Evidence of water was found by both rovers.

U.S. Staffed Space Flight Programs

Mercury. *Project Mercury*, initiated in 1958 and completed in 1963, was the United States' first human-in-space program. It was designed to further knowledge about humanity's capabilities in space.

In April 1959, seven military-jet test pilots were introduced to the public as America's first astronauts. They were: Lt. M. Scott Carpenter, USN; Capt. L. Gordon Cooper, Jr., USAF; Lt. Col. John H. Glenn, Jr., USMC; Cap. Virgil I. Grissom, USAF; Lt. Cdr. Walter M. Schirra, Jr., USN; Lt. Cdr. Alan B. Shepard, Jr., USN; and Capt. Donald K. Slayton, USAF. Six of the original seven would make a Mercury flight. Slayton was grounded for medical reasons but remained a director of NASA's astronaut office. He returned to flight status in 1975 as Docking Module Pilot on the *Apollo-Soyuz* flight.

Flight Summary

Each astronaut named his capsule and added the numeral 7 to denote the teamwork of the original astronauts.

May 5, 1961. Alan B. Shepard, Jr., made a suborbital flight in *Freedom 7* and became the first American in space. Time: 15 minutes, 22 seconds.

July 21, 1961. Virgil I. Grissom made the second successful suborbital flight in *Liberty Bell 7*, but spacecraft sank shortly after splashdown. Time: 15 minutes, 37 seconds. Grissom was later killed in *Apollo 1* fire, Jan. 27, 1967.

Feb. 20, 1962. John H. Glenn, Jr., made a three-orbit flight in *Friendship 7* and became the first American in orbit. Time: 4 hours, 55 minutes.

May 24, 1962. M. Scott Carpenter duplicated Glenn's flight in *Aurora 7.* Time: 4 hours, 56 minutes.

Oct. 3, 1962. Walter M. Schirra, Jr., made a six-orbit engineering test flight in *Sigma 7.* Time: 9 hours, 13 minutes.

May 15–16, 1963. L. Gordon Cooper, Jr., performed the last *Mercury* mission and completed 22 orbits in *Faith 7* to evaluate effects of one day in space. Time: 34 hours, 19 minutes.

The Women in Space Program

In 1960, NASA also tested the first female trainees for astronaut duty in the *Mercury* program. Thirteen out of America's 25 top female civilian pilots (women weren't allowed to be military pilots then) passed the same rigorous testing that male candidates underwent in the *Mercury 7* space program. Although all the pilots proved fit to become *Mercury* astronauts, NASA suddenly canceled its testing of qualified women in July 1961, claiming that they required jet test-pilot training at Edwards Air Force Base. Unfortunately, instruction at Edwards was closed to women. This new requirement ended America's chance to put the first women in space.

It is ironic that unlike her skilled American counterparts, Valentina Tereshkova, the first woman to fly in space, was a textile factory worker when she entered the Soviet space program. She had no experience as a pilot and her only qualification was that of an amateur parachute jumper before being trained as a cosmonaut in 1962.

These outstanding "Mercury 13" candidates deserve much credit for preparing the way for American women in space. They were: Jerrie Cobb, Rhea Allison, Jane Hart, Mary Wallace Funk, Jean Hixson, Myrtle Cagle, Irene Leverton, Sarah Gorelick, twins Jan and Marion Dietrich, Gene Stumbough, Bernice Steadman, and Gerry Sloan Truhill.

Gemini. *Gemini* was an extension of *Project Mercury,* to determine the effects of prolonged space flight on humans for two weeks or longer—the time it would take to reach the Moon and return. "Walks in space" provided invaluable information for astronauts' later walks on the Moon. The *Gemini* spacecraft, twice as large as the *Mercury* capsule, accommodated two astronauts. Its crew named the project *Gemini* for the third constellation of the Zodiac and its twin stars, Castor and Pollux. The capsule differed from the *Mercury* spacecrafts in that it had hatches above the capsules so that the astronauts could leave the spacecraft and perform spacewalks or extra-vehicular activities (EVAs).

There were 10 staffed flights in the *Gemini* program, starting with *Gemini 3* on March 23, 1965, and ending with the *Gemini 12* mission on Nov. 15, 1966. *Gemini 1* and *2* were unstaffed test flights of the equipment.

Apollo. *Apollo* was the designation for the United States' effort to land a person on the Moon and return him safely to Earth. The goal was successfully accomplished with *Apollo 11* on July 20, 1969, culminating eight years of rehearsal and centuries of dreaming. Astronauts Neil A. Armstrong and Col. Edwin E. Aldrin, Jr., scooped up and brought back the first lunar rocks ever seen on Earth—about 47 pounds.

Tragedy struck Jan. 27, 1967, on the launch pad during a preflight test of what would have become *Apollo 1,* the first staffed mission. Astronauts Lt. Col. Virgil "Gus" Grissom, Lt. Col. Edward H. White, and Lt. Cdr. Roger Chafee lost their lives when a fire swept through the command module.

Six *Apollo* flights followed, ending with *Apollo 17* in December 1972. The last three *Apollos* carried mechanized vehicles called lunar rovers for wide-ranging surface exploration of the Moon by astronauts. The rendezvous and docking of an *Apollo* spacecraft with a Russian *Soyuz* craft in Earth orbit on July 18, 1975, closed out the *Apollo* program.

During the Apollo project, the following 12 astronauts explored the lunar terrain: Col. Edwin E. "Buzz" Aldrin, Jr., and Neil A. Armstrong, *Apollo 11;* Cdr. Alan L. Bean and Cdr. Charles "Pete" Conrad, Jr., *Apollo 12;* Edgar D. Mitchell and Alan B. Shepard, *Apollo 14;* Lt. Col. James B. Irwin and Col. David R. Scott, *Apollo 15;* Col. Charles M. Duke, Jr., and Capt. John W. Young, *Apollo 16;* and Capt. Eugene A. Cernan and Dr. Harrison H. Schmitt, *Apollo 17.*

Apollo was a three-part spacecraft: the command module (CM), the crew's quarters and flight control section; the service modules (SM) for the propulsion and spacecraft support systems (when together, the two modules were called CSM); and the lunar module (LM) that took two of the crew to the lunar surface, supported them on the Moon, and returned them to the CSM in orbit.

The third lunar attempt, *Apollo 13,* April 11–17, 1970, 5 days, 22.9 hours, was aborted after the service module oxygen tank ruptured. The *Apollo 13* crew members were James A. Lovell, Jr., John L. Swigert, Jr., and Fred W. Haise, Jr. The mission was classified as a "successful failure" because the crew was rescued.

Skylab. America's first Earth-orbiting space station was launched May 14, 1973. *Project Skylab* was designed to demonstrate that men can work and live in space for prolonged periods without ill effects. Originally the spent third stage of a *Saturn 5* Moon rocket, *Skylab* measured 118 ft from stem to stern, and carried the most varied assortment of experimental equipment ever assembled in a single spacecraft. Three three-man crews visited the space stations, spending more than 740 hours observing the Sun and bringing home more than 175,000 solar pictures. These were the first recordings of solar activity above Earth's obscuring atmosphere. *Skylab* also evaluated systems designed to gather information on Earth's resources and environmental conditions. *Skylab*'s biomedical findings indicated that humans adapt well to space for at least a period of three months, provided they have a proper diet and adequately programmed exercise, sleep, work, and recreation periods. *Skylab* orbited Earth at a distance of about 300 mi. Five years after the last *Skylab* mission, the 77-ton space station's orbit began to deteriorate faster than expected, owing to unexpectedly high sunspot activity. On July 11, 1979, the parts of *Skylab* that did not burn up in the atmosphere came crashing down on parts of Australia and the Indian Ocean. No one was hurt.

Space Shuttle. The space shuttle *Columbia* was successfully launched on April 12, 1981. The second shuttle, *Challenger,* made its maiden flight on April 4, 1983. The third shuttle, *Discovery,* made its first flight on Aug. 30, 1984. The fourth space shuttle, *Atlantis,* made its maiden flight on Oct. 3, 1985.

A tragedy occurred on Jan. 28, 1986, when the shuttle *Challenger* exploded, killing the crew of seven 73 seconds after takeoff.

The crew members who were killed were: Francis R. Scobee, shuttle commander; Cdr. Michael J. Smith, pilot; mission specialists Judith A. Resnik, Lt. Col. Ellison S. Onizuka, and Ronald E. McNair; and payload specialists Gregory B. Jarvis and Christa McAuliffe (who was to be the first civilian schoolteacher in space).

The cause of the explosion was a rupture in a seal on one of the booster rockets, which let a jet of flame escape, igniting the fuel. The weakness in the seal was caused by the cold air temperature when the shuttle was launched.

The fifth orbiter, *Endeavour,* was built as a replacement for *Challenger.* It was named after the 16th-century British explorer James Cook's first ship. *Endeavour* was launched on its maiden voyage on May 7, 1992, with a crew of seven astronauts. During the mission, Dr. Kathryn Thornton became the second American woman to walk in space (Kathy Sullivan was the first in 1984).

The crew of the 50th shuttle mission, aboard the *Endeavour,* launched Sept. 12, 1992, included the first black woman astronaut, Dr. Mae C. Jemison, and the first married couple to fly together in space, Air Force Lt. Col. Mark C. Lee and Dr. N. Jan Davis.

Lt. Col. Eileen M. Collins became the first woman to pilot a shuttle, *Discovery,* during the spacecraft's historic rendezvous with the Russian space station *Mir* on Feb. 6, 1995. The shuttle *Atlantis* made the first link-up with the *Mir* on June 29, 1995.

The shuttle *Columbia* spent a record 17 days, 15 hours in space, Nov. 19–Dec. 7, 1996.

Lt. Col. Collins became the first woman to command a space shuttle when *Columbia* was launched in July 1999 on a mission to deploy the Chandra X-ray Observatory (formerly called AXAF).

Senator John Glenn, 76, the first American to orbit the Earth, flew as a payload specialist on the Oct. 1998 *Discovery* mission. He studied the effects of aging and microgravity on the human body.

In recent years, many of NASA's human space-flight expeditions have involved improvement of the International Space Station. On May 27, 1999, the space shuttle *Discovery* began Flight STS-96, the first shuttle docking to the International Space Station. Crewmembers brought new equipment to better operations between the Unity and Zarya modules, including nearly 1,360 kg of equipment for use by future ISS astronauts. In 2000, work on the ISS continued; two successive *Atlantis* missions spent several days making improvements. On Nov. 2, 2001, the ISS celebrated its first full year of continuous international human presence in space. On June 19, 2002, Capt. Daniel Bursch and Col. Carl Walz broke the U.S. record for space flight endurance, having spent 196 days aboard the International Space Station.

The shuttle program's second tragedy occurred on Feb. 1, 2003, when the shuttle *Columbia* broke up upon reentry into the Earth's atmosphere.

All crew members were killed: Rick Husband, shuttle commander; William McCool, pilot; payload commander Michael Anderson; payload specialist Ilan Ramon, also the first Israeli astronaut; mission specialists David M. Brown, Laurel Blair Salton Clark, and Kalpana Chawla, the first Indian-American woman in space.

The shuttle was returning after a 16-day scientific mission and was only minutes away from landing. The Columbia Accident Investigation Board subsequently ascertained that a chunk of fuel-tank foam insulation slammed into the wing edge during liftoff, creating a hole that allowed hot gases to enter the shuttle on reentry into the atmosphere.

Soviet Staffed Space Flight Programs

Vostok. The Soviets's first staffed capsule, roughly spherical, used to place the first six cosmonauts in Earth orbit (1961–1965).

Voskhod. Adaptation of the *Vostok* capsule to accommodate two and three cosmonauts. *Voskhod 1* orbited three persons, and *Voskhod 2* orbited two persons, performing the world's first staffed extra-vehicular activity.

Soyuz. Late-model staffed spacecraft with provisions for three cosmonauts and a "working compartment" accessible through a hatch. Soyuz is the Russian word for "union." The *Soyuz* spacecraft routinely brought cosmonauts and their foreign "guests" to the *Mir* space station. *Soyuz 19,* launched July 15, 1975, docked with the American *Apollo* spacecraft.

Salyut. Earth-orbiting space stations intended for prolonged occupancy and revisitation by cosmonauts. They were usually launched by Soviet Proton rockets. *Salyut 1* was launched April 19, 1971. *Salyut 2,* launched April 3, 1973, malfunctioned in orbit and was never occupied. *Salyut 3* was launched June 25, 1974. *Salyut 4* was launched Dec. 26, 1974. *Salyut 5* was launched June 22, 1976. *Salyut 6* was launched on Sept. 29, 1977. *Salyut 7* was launched on April 19, 1982. A record-breaking Russian endurance flight was set (Feb. 8, 1984–Oct. 2, 1985) when Soviet astronauts spent 237 days in orbit aboard *Salyut 7. Salyut 7* reentered the atmosphere and crashed into the Atlantic Ocean on Feb. 6, 1991.

Mir. Soviet space station, launched into orbit on Feb. 20, 1986. The Russian government had planned to deorbit the abandoned *Mir* in early 2000 due to lack of funds, but the space station got a new lease on life when private investors provided the cash to keep the craft in orbit. The new Russian partners, MirCorp, a Netherlands-based company, funded cosmonauts Sergei Zaloytin and Alexander Kaleri's return mission to reopen and repair the *Mir,* April 4 to June 15, 2000. However, *Mir* was deorbited on March 23, 2001.

Since the deorbiting of *Mir,* Russia's space program has revolved around projects at the International Space Station. Financial problems continue to curb cosmonaut capabilities, forcing the Russian Space Agency to seek funds elsewhere: in 2001, American businessman Dennis Tito paid a reported $20 million to become the world's first space tourist aboard a Russian spacecraft.

Notable Staffed Space Flights

Designation and country	Date	Astronauts	Flight time	Remarks
Vostok 1 (USSR)	April 12, 1961	Yuri A. Gagarin	1hr, 48 min	First person in space.
MR III (U.S.)	May 5, 1961	Alan B. Shepard, Jr.	15 min	Range 486 km (302 mi), peak 187 km (116.5 mi); capsule recovered. First American in space.
Vostok 2 (USSR)	Aug. 6–7, 1961	Gherman S. Titov	25 hr, 18 min	First long-duration flight.
MA VI (U.S.)	Feb. 20, 1962	John H. Glenn, Jr.	4 hr, 55 min	First American in orbit.
MA IX (U.S.)	May 15–16, 1963	L. Gordon Cooper, Jr.	34 hr, 20 min	Longest *Mercury* flight.
Vostok 6 (USSR)	June 16–19, 1963	Valentina V. Tereshkova	2 days, 22 hr, 50 min	First woman in space.
Voskhod 1 (USSR)	Oct. 12, 1964	Vladimir M. Komarov, Konstantin P. Feoktistov, Boris G. Yegorov	24 hr, 17 min	First 3-person orbital flight; also first flight without space suits.
Voskhod 2 (USSR)	March 18, 1965	Alexei A. Leonov, Pavel I. Belyayev	26 hr, 2 min	First "space walk" (by Leonov), 10 min.
GT III (U.S.)	March 23, 1965	Virgil I. Grissom, John W. Young	4hr, 53 min	First American 2-person crew.
GT IV (U.S.)	June 3–7, 1965	James A. McDivitt, Edward H. White, II	4 days, 1 hr, 48 min	First American "space walk" (by White), lasting slightly over 20 min.
GT VIII (U.S.)	March 16–17, 1966	Neil A. Armstrong, David R. Scott	10 hr, 42 min	First docking between staffed spacecraft and an unstaffed space vehicle (an orbiting *Agena* rocket).
Apollo 7 (U.S.)	Oct. 11–22, 1968	Walter M. Schirra, Jr., Donn F. Eisele, R. Walter Cunningham	10 days, 19 hr, 9 min	First staffed test of *Apollo* command module; first live TV transmissions from orbit.
Soyuz 3 (USSR)	Oct. 26–30, 1968	Georgi T. Bergeovoi	3 days, 22 hr, 51 min	First rendezvous and possible docking by Soviet cosmonaut.
Apollo 8 (U.S.)	Dec. 21–27, 1968	Frank Borman, James A. Lovell, Jr., William A. Anders	6 days, 3 hr	First spacecraft in circumlunar orbit; TV transmissions from this orbit. The three astronauts were also the first astronauts to view the whole Earth.
Apollo 9 (U.S.)	Mar. 3–13, 1969	James A. McDivitt, David R. Scott, Russell L. Schweikart	10 days, 1 hr, 1 min	First staffed flight of Lunar Module.
Apollo 10 (U.S.)	May 18–26, 1969	Thomas P. Stafford, Eugene A. Cernan, John W. Young	8 days, 3 min	First descent to within nine miles of Moon's surface by staffed craft.
Apollo 11 (U.S.)	July 16–24, 1969	Neil A. Armstrong, Edwin E. Aldrin, Jr., Michael Collins	8 days, 3 hr, 18 min	First staffed landing and EVA on Moon; soil and rock samples collected; experiments left on lunar surface.
Soyuz 6 (USSR)	Oct. 11–16, 1969	Gorgiy Shonin, Valriy Kabasov	4 days, 22 hr, 42 min	Three spacecraft and seven men put into Earth's orbit simultaneously for first time.
Apollo 12 (U.S.)	Nov. 14–24, 1969	Charles Conrad, Jr., Richard F. Gordon, Jr., Alan Bean	10 days, 4 hr, 36 min	Staffed lunar landing mission; investigated *Surveyor 3* spacecraft; collected lunar samples. EVA time: 15 hr, 30 min.
Apollo 13 (U.S.)	April 11–17, 1970	James A. Lovell, Jr., Fred W. Haise, Jr., John L. Swigert, Jr.	5 days, 22 hr, 54 min	Third staffed lunar landing attempt; aborted due to pressure loss in liquid oxygen in service module and failure of fuel cells.
Apollo 14 (U.S.)	Jan. 31–Feb. 9, 1971	Alan B. Shepard, Stuart A. Roosa, Edgar D. Mitchell	9 days, 42 min	Third staffed lunar landing: returned largest amount of lunar material.
Soyuz 11 (USSR)	June 6–30, 1971	Georgiy Tomofeyevich Dobrovolskiy, Vladislav Nikolayevich Volkov, Viktor Ivanovich Patsyev	23 days, 17 hrs, 40 min	Longest stay in space. Linked up with first space station, *Salyut 1*. Astronauts died just before reentry due to loss of pressurization in spacecraft.
Apollo 15 (U.S.)	July 26–Aug. 7, 1971	David R. Scott, James B. Irwin, Alfred M. Worden	12 days, 7 hr, 12 min	Fourth staffed lunar landing; first use of lunar rover propelled by Scott and Irwin; first live pictures of LM lift-off from Moon; exploration time: 18 hr.
Apollo 16 (U.S.)	April 16–27, 1972	John W. Young, Thomas K. Mattingly, Charles M. Duke, Jr.	11 days, 1 hr, 51 min	Fifth staffed lunar landing; second use of lunar rover vehicle, propelled by Young and Duke. Exploration time: 20 hr, 14 min. Mattingly's in-flight "walk in space" was 1 hr, 23 min. Approximately 213 lb of lunar rock returned.
Apollo 17 (U.S.)	Dec. 7–19, 1972	Eugene A. Cernan, Ronald E. Evans, Harrison H. Schmitt	12 days, 13 hr, 51 min	Sixth and last staffed lunar landing; third to carry lunar rover. Exploration time: 22 hr, 05 min, 3 sec. 250 lbs of lunar samples returned to Earth.
Skylab SL-2 (U.S.)	May 25–June 22, 1973	Charles Conrad, Jr., Joseph P. Kerwin, Paul J. Weitz	28 days, 50 min	First staffed *Skylab* launch. Established Skylab Orbital Assembly and conducted scientific and medical experiments.

Designation and country	Date	Astronauts	Flight time	Remarks
Skylab SL-3 (U.S.)	July 28–Sept. 25, 1973	Alan L. Bean, Jr., Jack R. Lousma, Owen K. Garriott	59 days, 11 hr, 9 min	Second staffed Skylab launch. New crew remained in space for 59 days, continuing scientific and medical experiments and Earth observations from orbit.
Skylab SL-4 (U.S.)	Nov. 16, 1973– Feb. 8, 1974	Gerald Carr, Edward Gibson, William Pogue	84 days, 1 hr, 16 min	Third staffed Skylab launch; obtained medical data on crew for use in extending the duration of staffed space flight; crews "walked in space" 4 times, totaling 44 hr, 40 min. Splashdown in Pacific, Feb. 9, 1974.
Apollo/Soyuz Test Project (U.S. and USSR)	July 15–24, 1975 (U.S.)	U.S.: Brig. Gen. Thomas P. Stafford, Vance D. Brand, Donald K. Slayton	9 days, 5 min	World's first international staffed rendezvous and docking in space; aimed at developing a space rescue capability.
Apollo/Soyuz Test Project (U.S. and USSR)	July 15–21, 1975 (USSR)	USSR: Col. A. A. Leonov, V. N. Kubasov	9 days, 7 hr, 35 min	Apollo and Soyuz docked and crewmen exchanged visits on July 17, 1975. Mission duration for Soyuz: 142 hr, 31 min. For Apollo: 217 hr, 28 min.
Columbia (U.S.)	April 12–14, 1981	Capt. Robert L. Crippen, John W. Young	2 days, 5 hr, 20 min	Maiden voyage of space shuttle.
Challenger (U.S.)	Jan. 28, 1986	Francis R. Scobee, Gregory Jarvis, Christa McAuliffe, Ronald McNair, Ellison Onizuka, Judith Resnik, Michael Smith	73 sec	Exploded upon takeoff from Kennedy Space Center, killing all 7 crew members. A booster lock ignited the fuel, causing the explosion.
Mir (USSR)	Dec. 21, 1987– Dec. 21, 1988	Col. Vladimir Titov, Musa Manarov	366 days	Set current record for Soviet team endurance flight in orbiting space station.
Endeavour (U.S.)	May 7–16, 1992	Richard J. Hieb, Maj. Thomas D. Akers, Cdr. Pierre J. Thugt	8 days, 23 hr, 17 min	The three mission specialists remained free of the Endeavour for 8 hr, 20 min on May 13 during the repair of communications satellite, setting an absolute record for extravehicular duration in space. First capture of a satellite using hands only.
Endeavour (U.S.)	Dec. 2–13, 1993	Col. Richard O. Covey, Cdr. Kenneth D. Bowersox, Lt. Col. Tom Akers, Dr. Jeffrey A. Hoffman, Dr. Story Musgrave, Claude Nicollier, Dr. Kathryn C. Thornton	10 days, 19 hr, 59 min	Repaired Hubble Space Telescope. Replaced gyroscopes, solar arrays, camera, electronics, and hardware. Installed COSTAR corrective optics to compensate for flaw in Hubble's primary mirror. Record five space walks in a single mission.
Mir-17 (Russia)	Jan. 8, 1994– Mar. 22, 1995	Dr. Valery Polyakov	439[1] days	Record single endurance flight in orbiting space station. Returned to Earth with crewmates, cosmonaut Helena Kondakova and commander Alexander Viktorenko, who spent 169 days each in Mir.
Discovery (U.S.)	Feb. 3–11, 1995	Cdr. James D. Wetherbee, Lt. Col. Eileen M. Collins, Dr. Janice Voss, Dr. Bernard A. Harris, Jr., Dr. C. Michael Foale, Russian cosmonaut Co. Vladimir G. Titov	8 days, 6 hr, 29 min	First rendezvous of U.S. spacecraft with a Russian space station (Mir), Feb. 6. Lt. Col. Collins was first female shuttle pilot. Deployed and retrieved solar observatory satellite. Extravehicular activity to test new space suit modifications and practice space station assembly techniques. EVA time: 4 hr, 35 min.
Soyuz TM-21 (Russia)	March 14–22, 1995	Russian cosmonauts Lt. Col. Vladimir N. Dezhurov and Gennady M. Strekalov, and U.S. astronaut Dr. Norman E. Thagard		Dr. Thagard became the first American astronaut to fly aboard a Soyuz spacecraft with a Russian crew launched from Baikonur Space Center in Kazakhstan. He also became the first American to enter the Mir space station on March 16.
Atlantis (U.S.)	June 27–July 7, 1995	Lt. Col. Charles J. Prescourt, Capt. Robert L. (Hoot) Gibson, Dr. Eileen S. Baker, Gregory J. Harbaugh, Dr. Bonnie Dunbar; Russian cosmonauts: Mir-19 commander Anatoly Y. Solovyev, Nikolai M. Budarin	10 days	Marked 100th human mission in U.S. space program and first shuttle link-up with Mir: docked June 29, undocked July 4. Joined spacecraft held a record 10 people: 6 Americans and 4 Russians. Three Mir crew (Mir-18 commander Lt. Col. Vladimir N. Dezhurov, cosmonaut Grennady M. Strekalov, and U.S. astronaut Dr. Norman E. Thagard) returned to Earth aboard the Atlantis. Cosmonauts Solovyev and Budarin remained aboard Mir.

Designation and country	Date	Astronauts	Flight time	Remarks
Atlantis (U.S.)	Nov. 12–20, 1995	Col. Kenneth D. Cameron, Lt. Col. James D. Halsell, Jr., Col. Jerry L. Ross, Lt. Col. William S. McArthur, Jr., Canadian Major Chris A. Hadfield, who operated the robot arm	8 days, 4 hr, 31 min	Second docking with *Mir*. Carried 15-foot-long, Russian-made docking module and attached it to *Mir*. Brought 2 new solar-powered panels for *Mir* and also supplies and scientific equipment. U.S. and Russian astronauts spent 3 days together on *Mir* conducting experiments.
Endeavour (U.S.)	Jan. 11–20, 1996	Col. Brian Duffy, Brent Jett, Dr. Leroy Chiao, Capt. Winston E. Scott, Dr. Daniel T. Berry, and Japanese astronaut Koichi Wakata, who operated the robot arm	8 days, 22 hr, 1 min	Deployed and retrieved NASA satellite, retrieved Japanese satellite. Two spacewalks performed to test spacesuit components and practice space station construction, tools, and techniques. Total EVA time: 13 hr.
Atlantis (U.S.)	March 22–31, 1996	Col. Kevin P. Chilton, Lt. Col. Richard A. Searfoss, Dr. Ronald M. Sega, Dr. Linda M. Goodwin, Lt. Col. Michael R. Clifford, Shannon W. Lucid	9 days, 5 hr, 15 min	Third link-up with *Mir* (March 22–27). Clifford and Goodwin conducted 6-hour spacewalk in shuttle cargo bay while docked with *Mir*. Lucid remained on board *Mir* for scheduled 140-day tour to conduct biomedical and material science experiments. Booster problems delayed her return until mid-September. Lucid was first American woman to live on *Mir*. On July 15, 1996, she broke the previous record for the longest U.S. manned space flight.
Endeavour (U.S.)	May 19–29, 1996	Col. John H. Casper, Lt. Col. Curtis L. Brown, Jr., Cdr. Daniel W. Bursch, Mario Runco, Jr., Dr. Andrew S. W. Thomas, Canadian astronaut Dr. Marc Garneau	10 days, 0 hr, 40 min	Made record of four satellite rendezvous, including three with small PAMS satellite to test the concept of a self-stabilizing satellite in orbit. Deployed and retrieved a Spartan satellite that carried an experimental inflatable antenna.
Columbia (U.S.)	June 20–July 7, 1996	Col. Terence T. Henricks, Kevin R. Kregel, Lt. Col. Susan J. Helms, Richard M. Linnehan, Cdr. Charles E. Brady, Jr., Dr. Jean-Jacques Favier (France), Dr. Robert Brent Thirsk (Canada)	16 days, 21 hr, 48 min	Studied the effects of weightlessness on people, plants, and animals, and material manufacturing in near-zero gravity.
Atlantis (U.S.)	Sept. 16–26, 1996	William F. Readdy, Terrence W. Wilcutt, Thomas D. Akers, John E. Blaha, Jerome Apt, Carl E. Walz. Download: Shannon W. Lucid	10 days, 3hr, 19 min	Fourth *Mir* docking. Carried a Spacelab module. Transferred supplies and equipment to *Mir*. After breaking all American and women's space endurance records (188 days, 5 hr, 0 min), Lucid returned with *Atlantis* crew. John E. Blaha remained on *Mir* for a four-month stay.
Columbia (U.S.)	Nov. 19–Dec. 7, 1996	Kenneth D. Cockrell, Cdr. Kent V. Rominger, Tamara E. Jernigan, Thomas D. Jones, Dr. F. Story Musgrave	17 days, 15 hr, 53 min	Deployed and recovered two free-flying satellites: an ultraviolet telescope and Wake Shield (semiconductor processing) Facility. Dr. Musgrave, 61, became first person to fly on all five space shuttles.
Atlantis (U.S.)	Jan. 12–22, 1997	Capt. Michael A. Baker, Cdr. Brent W. Jett, Jr., John M. Grunsfeld, Marsha S. Ivins, Peter J.K. Wiscoff, Dr. Jerry L. Linenger. Download: John E. Blaha	10 days, 4 hr, 6 min	Fifth *Mir* docking (Jan.14–19). Carried Spacehab double module. Transferred supplies to *Mir*. Conducted experiments in Spacehab and *Mir*. John E. Blaha returned with *Atlantis* crew after 128 days in space, 118 aboard *Mir*. Jerry Linenger remained aboard *Mir* for 4.5-month stay.
Discovery (U.S.)	Feb. 11–21, 1997	Cdr. Kenneth Bowersox, Lt. Col. Scott J. Harowitz, Col. Mark C. Lee, Steven A. Hawley, Gregory J. Harbaugh, Steven L. Smith, Joseph R. Tanner	9 days, 23 hr, 38 min	Second space telescope servicing mission. Installed new imaging spectrograph and infrared camera. Also patched torn telescope insulating cover. Deployed telescope at higher altitude: 335 x 321 nautical mile orbit. Mission required five spacewalks totaling 33 hr, 11 min.
Atlantis (U.S.)	May 15–24, 1997	Col. Charles J. Precourt, Lt. Col. Eileen M. Collins, Edward T. Lu, Maj. Carlos I. Noriega, Jean-François Clervoy (France), Elena V. Kondakova (Russia), C. Michael Foale. Download: Dr. Jerry M. Linenger	9 days, 5 hr, 20 min	Sixth *Mir* docking (May 16–21). Carried a Spacehab double module. Transferred supplies and equipment. Jerry M. Linenger returned with *Atlantis* after 132 days in space. Michael Foale remained on *Mir* for a 4.5-month stay.

Designation and country	Date	Astronauts	Flight time	Remarks
Atlantis (U.S.)	Sept. 25–Oct. 6, 1997	James T. Wetherbee, Michael J. Boomfield, Col. Vladimir G Titov, Scott E. Parazynski, Jean-Loup J. M. Chretien (France), Wendy B. Lawrence. Up: Dr. David Wolf. Down: C. Michael Foale	10 days, 19 hr, 22 min	Seventh *Mir* docking (Sept. 27–Oct. 3). 5-hr spacewalks (Oct.1) retrieved U.S. experimental packages from *Mir* for return to Earth. Transferred supplies. Tested emergency jet packs for space station workers. Dr. David Wolf replaced Michael Foale on *Mir* for 4-month stay.
Endeavour (U.S.)	Jan. 22–31, 1998	Lt. Col. Terrence W. Wilcutt, Joe F. Edwards, Bonnie J. Dunbar, Maj. Michael P. Anderson, James F. Reilly, II, Salizhan S. Sharipov (Kyrgyzstan). Up: Andrew S. W. Thomas. Down: Dr. David Wol	8 days, 19 hr, 48 min	Eighth *Mir* docking (Jan. 24–29). Thomas replaced David Wolf after 128 days in orbit. Thomas is the seventh and last American to live aboard *Mir*.
Discovery (U.S.)	June 2–12, 1998	Col. Charles J. Precourt, Cmdr. Dominic L. Gorie, Cmdr. Wendy B. Lawrence, Franklin R. Chang-Diaz, Janet Kavandi, Valeriy Ruymin (Russia). Down: Andrew S. W. Thomas	9 days, 19 hr, 54 min	Ninth and final *Mir* docking mission concluded the joint U.S.–Russian program as a precursor to the International Space Station partnership. Thomas returned to Earth after a 4.5-month stay.
Discovery (U.S.)	Oct. 29–Nov.7, 1998	Lt. Col. Curtis L. Brown, Maj. Steven W. Lindsey, Stephen K. Robinson, Dr. Scott E. Parazynski, Pedro Duque (Spain), Dr. Chiaki Mukai (Japan), Sen. John H. Glenn, Jr.	8 days, 21 hr, 56 min	Deployed and retrieved *Spartan* solar observing satellite. Did research with Hubble Telescope Optical Systems Test Platform (HOST). Studied the effects of aging and microgravity in space.
Endeavour (U.S.)	Dec. 4–15, 1998	Col. Robert D. Cabana, Capt. Frederick W. Sturckow, Lt. Col. Nancy Currie, Col. Jerry L. Ross, James H. Newman, Sergei K. Krikalev (Russia)	11 days, 19 hr, 18 min	International Space Station assembly mission. Connected Node 1, "Unity," to Functional Cargo Block, "Zarya." Ross and Newman made three spacewalks, total EVA: 21 hr, 22 min.
Discovery (U.S.)	May 27–June 6, 1999	Cmdr. Ken V. Rominger, Rick D. Husband, Ellen Ochoa, Tamara E. Jernigan, Daniel T. Barry, Julie Payette (Canada), Valery Tokarev (Russia)	9 days, 19 hr, 13 min	Docked 5 days, 18 hr with uninhabited International Space Station. Readied it for arrival of first resident crew. Jernigan and Barry conducted space walks (7 hr, 55 min) for assembly work.
Columbia (U.S.)	July 22–27, 1999	Lt. Col. Eileen M. Collins, Capt. Jeffrey S. Ashby, Steven A. Hawley, Lt. Col. Catherine G. Coleman, Col. Michel Tognini (France)	4 days, 22 hr, 50 min	Deployed Chandra X-ray Observatory (formerly AXAF). Eileen Collins became the first female shuttle commander.
Discovery (U.S.)	Dec. 19–27, 1999	Col. Curtis L. Brown Jr., Lt. Cmdr. Scott J. Kelly, Steven L. Smith, C. Michael Foale, John M. Grunsfeld, Claude Nicollier (Switzerland), Jean-François Clervoy (France)	7 days, 23 hr, 10 min	Third Hubble Space Telescope servicing mission. Three EVAs totaled 24 hr, 33 min: Dec. 22, Smith and Grunsfeld, 8 hr, 15 min; Dec. 23, Foale and Nicollier, 8 hr, 10 min; Dec. 24, Smith and Grunsfeld, 8 hr, 8 min.
Endeavour (U.S.)	Feb.11–22, 2000	Cmdr. Dominic L. Pudwill Gorie, Janet Lynn Kavandi, Janet Voss, Kevin R. Kregel, Mamoru Mohri (Japan), Gerhard P. J. Thiele (Germany)	11 days, 5 hr, 38 min	Radar mapping obtained most detailed topographical map of Earth to date.
Atlantis (U.S.)	Sept. 8–18, 2000	Lt. Col. Terance Wilcutt, Lt. Cmdr. Scott Altman, Edward Tsang Lu, Richard Mastracchio, Lt. Cmdr. Dan Burbank, Col. Yuri I. Malenchenko (Russia), Boris Morukov (Russia)	10 days, 18 hr, 41 min	Prepared International Space Station for arrival of first resident crew. Outfitted *Zvezda* module.

Designation and country	Date	Astronauts	Flight time	Remarks
Discovery (U.S.)	Oct. 11–22, 2000	Col. Brian Duffy, Lt. Col. Pamela A. Melroy, Koichi Wakata (Japan), Peter J. K. Wisoff, Cmdr. Michael E. Lopez-Alegria, Col. William S. McArthur, Jr.	10 days, 19 hr, 28 min	Assembled Integrated Truss Structure on space station to allow solar arrays to be installed. 100th space shuttle flight.
Soyuz (Russia)	Oct. 31, 2000–March 18, 2001	William M. Shepherd, Yuri Gidzenko (Russia), Sergei Krikalev (Russia)	138 days, 18 hr, 39 min	Expedition One, first crew aboard International Space Station.
Discovery (U.S.)	March 8–21, 2001	Capt. James D. Wetherbee, Lt. Col. James M. Kelly, Andrew S. W. Thomas, Paul W. Richards, Yury Usachev (Russia), Jim Voss, Susan Helms	12 days, 19 hr, 49 min	Delivered Expedition Two crew (Usachev, Voss, Helms) to space station and returned Expedition One crew (Shepherd, Krikalev, Gidzenko) to Earth.
Discovery (U.S.)	Aug. 10–Aug. 22, 2001	Col. Scott J. Horowitz, Lt. Col. Frederick W. Sturckow, Col. Patrick G. Forrester, Daniel T. Barry, Frank Culbertson, Lt. Col. Vladimir Dezhurov (Russia), Mikhail Tyurin (Russia)	11 days, 21 hr, 13 min	Delivered Expedition Three crew (Culbertson, Dezhurov, Tyurin) to space station and returned Expedition Two crew (Usachev, Voss, Helms) to Earth.
Endeavour (U.S.)	Dec. 5–17, 2001	Capt. Dominic Gorie, Lt. Cmdr. Mark E. Kelly, Linda M. Godwin, Daniel M. Tani, Col. Yuri Onufrienko (Russia), Col. Carl E. Walz, Capt. Daniel W. Bursch	11 days, 19 hr, 36 min	Delivered Expedition Four crew (Onufrienko, Walz, Bursch) to space station and returned Expedition Three crew (Culbertson, Tyurin, Dezhurov) to Earth.
Columbia (U.S.)	March 1–12, 2002	Cmdr. Scott Altman, Lt. Col. Duane Carey, Nancy Currie, John Grunsfield, Richard Linnehan, Michael Massimino, James Newman	10 days, 22 hr, 10 min	Fourth Hubble Space Telescope servicing mission. The latest upgrades leave Hubble with a new power unit, camera, and solar arrays. Five EVAs lasted a total of 35 hr 55 min.
Atlantis (U.S.)	April 8–19, 2002	Lt. Col. Michael Bloomfield, Stephen Frick, Rex Walheim, Ellen Ochoa, Lee Morin, Jerry Ross, Steven Smith.	10 days, 19 hr, 42 min	Installed S0 (S-Zero) Truss, the backbone for future expansion, onto International Space Station. Prepared Mobile Transporter, first railroad in space. Jerry Ross made two space walks, retaining U.S. record for most space walks (nine) and total space-walking time (58 hr, 18 min).
Endeavour (U.S.)	June 5–19, 2002	Kenneth D. Cockrell, Lt. Col. Paul Lockhart, Philippe Perrin (France), Franklin Chang-Diaz, Col. Valery Korzun (Russia), Peggy Whitson, Sergei Treschev (Russia).	13 days, 20 hr, 35 min	Delivered Expedition Five crew (Korzun, Whitson, Treschev) to space station and returned Expedition Four crew (Onufrienko, Walz, Bursch) to Earth. On June 19, Walz and Bursch broke the U.S. space flight endurance record (previously held by Shannon Lucid, who spent 188 days in space in 1996). The two spent a total of 196 days in space.
Columbia (U.S.)	Jan. 16–Feb. 1, 2003	Rick Husband, William McCool, Michael Anderson, Kalpana Chawla, David Brown, Laurel B. Clark, Ilan Ramon	16 days	Exploded upon reentry into Earth's atmosphere, killing all 7 crew members.
Soyuz TMA-2 (Russia)	Apr. 26–Oct. 28, 2003	Yuri Malenchenko (Russia), Ed Lu, Ken Bowersox, Don Pettit, Nikolai Budarin (Russia)	185 days	With shuttle flights grounded, *Soyuz TMA-2* delivered Expedition Seven crew (Malenchenko, Lu) to space station. Expedition Six crew (Bowersox, Pettit, Budarin) returned to Earth via *Soyuz TMA-1*, docked at space station since Dec. 1, 2002([2]). On Aug. 10, Malenchenko became the first man to get married from space.
Shenzhou V (China)	Oct. 15–16, 2003	Lt. Col. Yang Liwei	21 hr	With the launch of *Shenzhou V*, China became the third country, after the former Soviet Union and the United States, to have a space program.
SpaceShipOne (U.S., private)	June 21, 2004	Mike Melvill	4.5 hr	The first private staffed ship to leave the atmosphere. It achieved an altitude of 328,491 ft.

NOTES: EVA = Extravehicular Activity. The letters MR stand for Mercury (capsule) and Redstone (rocket); MA, for Mercury and Atlas (rocket); GT, for Gemini (capsule) and Titan-II (rocket). The first astronaut listed in the Gemini and Apollo flights is the command pilot. The Mercury capsules had names: MR-III was *Freedom 7*, MR-IV was *Liberty Bell 7*, MA-VI was *Friend-ship 7*, MA-VII was *Aurora 7*, MA-VIII was *Sigma 7*, and MA-IX was *Faith 7*. The figure 7 referred to the fact that the first group of U.S. astronauts numbered seven men. Only one Gemini capsule had a name: GT-III was called *Molly Brown* (after the Broadway musical *The Unsinkable Molly Brown*); thereafter the practice of naming the capsules was discontinued. 1. From launch to landing. 2. *Soyuz TMA-1* returned May 3, 2003.

Famous Firsts in Aviation

1783 **First balloon flight.** Jacques and Joseph Montgolfier of Annonay, France, sent up a small smoke-filled balloon about mid-November.

First hydrogen-filled balloon flight. Jacques A. C. Charles, Paris physicist, supervised construction by A. J. and M. N. Robert of a 13-foot-diameter balloon that was filled with hydrogen. It got up to about 3,000 ft and traveled about 16 mi in a 45-minute flight (Aug. 27).

First human balloon flights. A Frenchman, Jean Pilâtre de Rozier, made the first captive-balloon ascension (Oct. 15). With the Marquis d'Arlandes, Pilâtre de Rozier made the first free flight, reaching a peak altitude of about 500 ft, and traveling about 5½ mi in 20 min. (Nov. 21).

1784 **First powered balloon.** Gen. Jean Baptiste Marie Meusnier developed the first propeller-driven and elliptically shaped balloon—the crew cranking three propellers on a common shaft to give the craft a speed of about 3 mph.

First balloon flight by a woman. Mme. Thible, a French opera singer (June 4).

1793 **First balloon flight in America.** Jean Pierre Blanchard, a French pilot, made it from Philadelphia to near Woodbury, N.J., in just over 45 min. (Jan. 9).

1794 **First military use of the balloon.** Jean Marie Coutelle, using a balloon built for the French Army, made two 4-hour observation ascents. The military purpose of the ascents seems to have been to damage the enemy's morale.

1797 **First parachute jump.** André-Jacques Garnerin dropped from about 6,500 ft over Monceau Park in Paris in a 23-foot-diameter parachute made of white canvas with a basket attached (Oct. 22).

1843 **First air transport company.** In London, William S. Henson and John Stringfellow filed articles of incorporation for the Aerial Transit Company (March 24). It failed.

1852 **First dirigible.** Henri Giffard, a French engineer, flew in a controllable (more or less) steam-engine-powered balloon, 144 ft long and 39 ft in diameter, inflated with 88,000 cu ft of coal gas. It reached 6.7 mph on a flight from Paris to Trappe (Sept. 24).

1860 **First aerial photographers.** Samuel Archer King and William Black made two photos of Boston, which are still in existence.

1872 **First gas-engine-powered dirigible.** Paul Haenlein, a German engineer, flew in a semi-rigid-frame dirigible, powered by a 4-cylinder internal-combustion engine running on coal gas drawn from the supporting bag.

1873 **First transatlantic attempt.** *The New York Daily Graphic* sponsored the attempt with a 400,000-cubic-foot balloon carrying a lifeboat. A rip in the bag during inflation brought the collapse of the balloon and the project.

1897 **First successful metal dirigible.** An all-metal dirigible, designed by David Schwarz, a Hungarian, took off from Berlin's Tempelhof Field and, powered by a 16-horsepower Daimler engine, got several miles before leaking gas caused it to crash (Nov. 13).

1900 **First zeppelin flight.** Germany's Count Ferdinand von Zeppelin flew the first of his long series of rigid-frame airships. It attained a speed of 18 mph and got 3½ mi before its steering gear failed (July 2).

1903 **First successful heavier-than-air machine flight.** Aviation was really born on the sand dunes at Kitty Hawk, N.C., when Orville Wright crawled to his prone position between the wings of the biplane he and his brother Wilbur had built, opened the throttle of their home-made 12-horsepower engine, and took to the air. He covered 120 ft in 12 sec. Later that day, in one of four flights, Wilbur stayed up 59 sec. and covered 852 ft (Dec. 17).

Wilbur and Orville Wright with their second powered machine; Huffman prairie, Dayton, Ohio. *Source:* Library of Congress.

1904 **First airplane maneuvers.** Orville Wright made the first turn with an airplane (Sept. 15); five days later his brother Wilbur made the first complete circle.

1905 **First airplane flight over half an hour.** Orville Wright kept his craft up 33 min., 17 sec. (Oct. 4).

1906 **First European airplane flight.** Alberto Santos-Dumont, a Brazilian, flew a heavier-than-air machine at Bagatelle Field, Paris (Sept. 13).

1908 **First airplane fatality.** Lt. Thomas E. Selfridge, U.S. Army Signal Corps, was in a group evaluating the Wright plane at Fort Myer, Va. He was up 75 ft with Orville Wright when the propeller hit a bracing wire and was broken, throwing the plane out of control, killing Selfridge and seriously injuring Wright (Sept. 17).

1909 **First cross-Channel flight.** Louis Blériot flew in a 25-horsepower Blériot VI monoplane from Les Baraques near Calais, France, to Dover Castle, England, in a 26.61-mi (38-kilometer) 37-min. flight across the English Channel (July 25).

First International Aviation Competition Meeting. American Glenn Curtiss narrowly beat France's Louis Blériot in the main event and won the Gordon Bennett Cup. Meet held at Rheims, France (Aug. 22–28).

1910 **First licensed woman pilot.** Baroness Raymonde de la Roche of France, who learned to fly in 1909, received ticket No. 36 on March 8.

First flight from shipboard. Lt. Eugene Ely, USN, took a Curtiss plane off from the deck of the cruiser *Birmingham* at Hampton Roads, Va., and flew to Norfolk (Nov. 14). The following January he reversed the process, flying from Camp Selfridge to the deck of the armored cruiser *Pennsylvania* in San Francisco Bay (Jan. 18).

First aircraft to take off from water. Henri Fabre in a Gnome-powered floatplane, at Martigues, France (March 28).

1911 **First U.S. woman pilot.** Harriet Quimby, a magazine writer, got ticket No. 37, making her the first licensed American female pilot.

1912 **First woman's cross-Channel flight.** Harriet Quimby flew from Dover, England, across the English Channel and landed at Hardelot, France, in a Blériot monoplane loaned to her by Louis Blériot (April 16). She was later killed in a flying accident over Dorchester Bay during a Harvard-Boston aviation meet on July 1, 1912.

First parachute jump from a powered airplane. Albert Berry jumped in a test over Jefferson Barracks military post, St. Louis (March 1). Some sources credit Grant Morton as making first jump in 1911.

1913 **First multi-engined aircraft.** Built and flown by Igor Ivan Sikorsky while still in his native Russia.

1914 **First aerial combat.** In Aug., Allied and German pilots and observers started shooting at each other with pistols and rifles—with negligible results.

1915 **First air raids on England.** German zeppelins dropped bombs on four English communities (Jan. 19).

1918 **First U.S. air squadron.** The U.S. Army Air Corps made its first independent raids over enemy lines, in DH-4 planes (British-designed) powered with 400-hp American-designed Liberty engines (April 8).

First regular airmail service. Operated for the Post Office Department by the Army, the first regular service was inaugurated with one round trip a day (except Sunday) between Washington, DC, and New York City (May 15).

1919 **First transatlantic flight.** The NC-4, one of four Curtiss flying boats commanded by Lt. Comdr. Albert C. Read, reached Lisbon, Portugal (May 27), after hops from Trepassy Bay, Newfoundland, to Horta, Azores (May 16–17), to Ponta Delgada (May 20). The Liberty-powered craft was piloted by Walter Hinton.

First nonstop transatlantic flight. Capt. John Alcock and Lt. Arthur Whitten Brown, British World War I flyers, made the 1,900-mile trip from St. John's, Newfoundland, to Clifden, Ireland, in 16 hr., 12 min. in a Vickers-Vimy bomber with two 350-horsepower Rolls-Royce engines (June 15–16).

First lighter-than-air transatlantic flight. The British dirigible R-34, commanded by Maj. George H. Scott, left Firth of Forth, Scotland (July 2), and touched down at Mineola, L.I., 108 hr. later. The eastbound trip was made in 75 hr. (completed July 13).

First scheduled London–Paris passenger service (using airplanes). Aircraft Travel and Transport inaugurated London–Paris service (Aug. 25). Later the company started the first trans-Channel mail service on the same route (Nov. 10).

First free-fall parachute jump. Leslie Irvin jumped over McCook Field, Dayton, Ohio, to prove that one won't lose consciousness during a delayed free-fall using a manually operated parachute (April 28).

1921 **First U.S. black female pilot.** Bessie Coleman received license June 15. Was killed April 30, 1926, in flying accident.

First naval vessel sunk by aircraft. Two battleships being scrapped by treaty were sunk by bombs dropped from Army planes in demonstration put on by Brig. Gen. William S. Mitchell (July 21).

First helium balloon. The C-7, nonrigid Navy dirigible was first to use noninflammable helium as lifting gas, making a flight from Hampton Roads, Va., to Washington, D.C. (Dec. 1).

1922 **First member of Caterpillar Club.** Lt. (later Maj. Gen.) Harold Harris bailed out of a crippled plane he was testing at McCook Field, Dayton, Ohio (Oct. 20), and became the first man to join the Caterpillar Club—those whose lives have been saved by parachutes.

1923 **First nonstop transcontinental flight.** Lts. John A. Macready and Oakley Kelly flew a single-engine Fokker T-2 nonstop from New York to San Diego, a distance of just over 2,500 mi in 26 hr., 50 min. (May 2–3).

First autogyro flight. Juan de la Cierva, a brilliant Spanish mathematician, made the first successful flight in a rotary wing aircraft in Madrid (June 9).

1924 **First round-the-world flight.** Four Douglas Cruiser biplanes of the U.S. Army Air Corps took off from Seattle under command of Maj. Frederick Martin (April 6). 175 days later, two of the planes (Lt. Lowell Smith's and Lt. Erik Nelson's) landed in Seattle after a circuitous route—one source saying 26,345 mi, another saying 27,553 mi.

1926 **First polar flight.** Then–Lt. Cmdr. Richard E. Byrd, acting as navigator, and Floyd Bennett as pilot, flew a Trimotor Fokker from Kings Bay, Spitsbergen, over the North Pole and back in 15½ hr. (May 8–9).

1927 **First solo nonstop transatlantic flight.** Charles Augustus Lindbergh lifted his Wright-powered Ryan monoplane, *Spirit of St. Louis,* from Roosevelt Field, N.Y., to stay aloft 33 hr. 39 min. and travel 3,600 mi to Le Bourget Field outside Paris (May 20–21). Although 91 persons in 13 separate flights crossed the Atlantic before him, he flew directly between two great world cities and did it alone.

Orville Wright, Major John F. Curry, and Colonel Charles Lindbergh, who came to pay Orville a personal call at Wright field, Dayton, Ohio, June 22, 1927. *Source:* Library of Congress.

First transatlantic passenger. Charles A. Levine was piloted by Clarence D. Chamberlin from Roosevelt Field, N.Y., to Eisleben, Germany, in a Wright-powered Bellanca (June 4–5).

1928 **First east–west transatlantic crossing.** Baron Guenther von Huenefeld, piloted by German Capt. Hermann Koehl and Irish Capt. James Fitzmaurice, left Dublin for New York City (April 12) in a single-engine all-metal Junkers-monoplane. Some 37 hr. later, they crashed on Greely Island, Labrador. Rescued.

First U.S.–Australia flight. Sir Charles Kingsford-Smith and Capt. Charles T. P. Ulm, Australians, and two American navigators, Harry W. Lyon and James Warner, crossed the Pacific from Oakland to Brisbane. They went via Hawaii and the Fiji Islands in a trimotor Fokker (May 31–June 8).

First transarctic flight. Sir Hubert Wilkins, an Australian explorer, and Carl Ben Eielson, who served as pilot, flew from Point Barrow, Alaska, to Spitsbergen (mid-April).

1929 **First of the endurance records.** With Air Corps Maj. Carl Spaatz in command and Capt. Ira Eaker as chief pilot, an Army Fokker, aided by refueling in the air, remained aloft 150 hr. 40 min. at Los Angeles (Jan. 1–7).

First round-the-world airship flight. The LZ-127, known as the *Graf Zeppelin*, flew 21,300 mi in 20 days and 4 hr. Also set distance record (Aug.).

First blind flight. James H. Doolittle proved the feasibility of instrument-guided flying when he took off and landed entirely on instruments (Sept. 24).

First rocket-engine flight. Fritz von Opel, a German auto maker, stayed aloft in his small rocket-powered craft for 75 sec., covering nearly 2 mi (Sept. 30).

First South Pole flight. Comdr. Richard E. Byrd, with Bernt Balchen as pilot, Harold I. June, radio operator, and Capt. A. C. McKinley, photographer, flew a trimotor Fokker from the Bay of Whales, Little America, over the South Pole and back (Nov. 28–29).

1930 **First Paris–New York nonstop flight.** Dieudonné Costes and Maurice Bellonte, French pilots, flew a Hispano-powered Breguet biplane from Le Bourget Field to Valley Stream, L.I., in 37 hr., 18 min. (Sept. 2–3).

1931 **First flight into the stratosphere.** Auguste Piccard, a Swiss physicist, and Charles Knipfer ascended in a balloon from Augsburg, Germany, and reached a height of 51,793 ft in a 17-hr. flight that terminated on a glacier near Innsbruck, Austria (May 27).

First nonstop transpacific flight. Hugh Herndon and Clyde Pangborn took off from Sabishiro Beach, Japan, dropped their landing gear, and flew 4,860 mi to near Wenatchee, Wash., in 41 hr. 13 min. (Oct. 4–5).

1932 **First woman's transatlantic solo.** Amelia Earhart, flying a Pratt & Whitney Wasp-powered Lockheed Vega, flew alone from Harbor Grace, Newfoundland, to Ireland in approximately 15 hr. (May 20–21).

First westbound transatlantic solo. James A. Mollison, a British pilot, took a de Havilland Puss Moth from Portmarnock, Ireland, to Pennfield, New Brunswick (Aug. 18).

First woman airline pilot. Ruth Rowland Nichols, first woman to hold three international records at the same time—speed, distance, and altitude—was employed by N.Y.–New England Airways.

1933 **First round-the-world solo.** Wiley Post took a Lockheed Vega, *Winnie Mae*, 15,596 mi around the world in 7 days, 18 hr., 49½ min. (July 15–22).

1937 **First successful helicopter flight.** Hanna Reitsch, a German pilot, flew Dr. Heinrich Focke's FW-61 in free, fully controlled flight at Bremen (July 4). Ms. Reitsch was also the first woman civil and military aviation test pilot.

Amelia Earhart, 1897–1937.
Source: Library of Congress.

First woman known to fly combat. Sabiha Gokcen, Turkish female army pilot, bombed and strafed Kurdish tribesmen during a rebellion.

1939 **First turbojet flight.** Just before their invasion of Poland, the Germans flew a Heinkel He-178 plane powered by a Heinkel S3B turbojet (Aug. 27).

1940 **First wartime use of military gliders.** German commandos made a successful glider assault on Belgium's Fort Eben-Emael during WWII (May 10).

1941–1945 **Most combat missions flown by a pilot in any war.** Captain Hans-Ulrich Rudel of Germany flew 2,530 combat missions during WWII while flying a JU-87 Stuka dive bomber. He survived the war.

1942–1945 **Top-scoring fighter pilot of any war.** German Luftwaffe ace Maj. Erich Hartmann scored 352 victories all while flying a Messerschmitt BF 109 during WWII. He was involved in 800 dogfights, and flew 1,425 missions. Maj. Hartmann survived the war.

1942 **First enemy bombing of U.S. mainland.** During WWII, a floatplane launched from a Japanese submarine off Cape Blanco, Ore., dropped incendiary bombs on the Oregon forest in two attempts to start forest fires and terrorize American civilians, but the bombs did little damage (Sept. 9 and 29).

First American jet plane flight. Robert Stanley, chief pilot for Bell Aircraft Corp., flew the Bell XP-59 *Airacomet* at Muroc Army Base, Calif. (Oct. 1).

First woman fighter pilot to shoot down an enemy aircraft. Soviet Lieutenant Lilya Litvyak, flying a Yak-1 fighter of the women's 586th Fighter Aviation Regiment, shot down two German planes over Stalingrad (Sept. 13).

1944 **First production stage rocket-engine fighter plane.** The German Messerschmitt Me 163B *Komet* (test flown 1941) became operational in June 1944. Some 350 of these delta-wing fighters were built before WWII in Europe ended.

1947 **First piloted supersonic flight in an airplane.** Capt. Charles E. Yeager, U.S. Air Force, flew the X-1 rocket-powered research plane built by Bell

Aircraft Corp., faster than the speed of sound at Muroc Air Force Base, Calif. (Oct. 14).

1949   First round-the-world nonstop flight. Capt. James Gallagher and USAF crew of 13 flew a Boeing B-50A Superfortress around the world nonstop from Ft. Worth, returning to same point: 23,452 mi in 94 hr., 1 min., with four aerial refuelings en route (Feb. 27–March 2).

1950   First nonstop transatlantic jet flight. Col. David C. Schilling (USAF) flew 3,300 mi from England to Limestone, Maine, in 10 hr., 1 min. (Sept. 22).

1951   First solo across North Pole. Charles F. Blair, Jr., flew a converted P-51 (May 29).

1952   First jetliner service. The De Havilland Comet flight was inaugurated by BOAC between London and Johannesburg, South Africa. Flight, including stops, took 23 hr., 38 min. (May 2).
First transatlantic helicopter flight. Capt. Vincent H. McGovern and 1st Lt. Harold W. Moore piloted two Sikorsky H-19s from Westover, Mass., to Prestwick, Scotland (3,410 mi). Trip was made in five stops, with a flying time of 42 hr., 25 min. (July 15–31).
First transatlantic round trip in same day. A British Canberra twin-jet bomber flew from Aldergrove, Northern Ireland, to Gander, Newfoundland, and back in 7 hr., 59 min. flying time (Aug. 26).

1955   First transcontinental round trip in same day. Lt. John M. Conroy piloted an F-86 Sabrejet across U.S. (Los Angeles–New York) and back—5,085 mi—in 11 hr., 33 min., 27 sec. (May 21).

1957   First round-the-world nonstop jet plane flight. Maj. Gen. Archie J. Old, Jr., USAF, led a flight of three Boeing B-52 bombers, powered with eight 10,000-pound-thrust Pratt & Whitney Aircraft J57 engines around the world in 45 hr., 19 min; distance 24,325 mi; average speed 525 mph (completed Jan. 18).

1958   First transatlantic jet passenger service. BOAC, New York to London (Oct. 4). Pan American started daily service, New York to Paris (Oct. 26).
First domestic jet passenger service. National Airlines inaugurated service between New York and Miami (Dec. 10).

1968   Prototype of world's first supersonic airliner. The Soviet-designed Tupolev Tu-144 made its first flight, Dec. 31. It first achieved supersonic speed on June 5, 1969.

1973   First female pilot of a major U.S. scheduled airline. Emily H. Warner became employed by Frontier Airlines on Jan. 29 as second officer on a Boeing 737.

1976   First regularly scheduled commercial supersonic transport (SST) flights begin. Air France and British Airways inaugurated service (Jan. 21). Air France flew the Paris–Rio de Janeiro route; B.A., the London–Bahrain. Both airlines began SST service to Washington, D.C. (May 24).

1977   First successful human-powered aircraft. Paul MacCready, an aeronautical engineer from Pasadena, Calif., was awarded the Kremer Prize for creating the world's first successful human-powered aircraft. The *Gossamer Condor* was flown by Bryan Allen over the required 3-mile course on Aug. 23.

1978   First successful transatlantic balloon flight. Three Albuquerque, N.M., men, Ben Abruzzo, Larry Newman, and Maxie Anderson, completed the crossing (Aug. 16.; landed, Aug. 17) in their helium-filled balloon, *Double Eagle II.*

1979   First man-powered aircraft to fly across the English Channel. The Kremer Prize for the Channel crossing was won by Bryan Allen, who flew the *Gossamer Albatross* from Folkestone, England, to Cap Gris-Nez, France, in 2 hr., 55 min. (June 12).

1980   First successful balloon flight over the North Pole. Sidney Conn and his wife, Eleanor, in hot-air balloon *Joy of Sound* (April 11).
First transcontinental balloon flight, and also record for longest overland voyage in a balloon. Maxie Anderson and his son, Kris, completed four-day flight from Fort Baker, Calif., to successful landing outside Matane, Quebec, in their helium-filled balloon, *Kitty Hawk* (May 12).
First long-distance solar-powered flight. Janice Brown, a 98-pound former teacher, flew a tiny experimental solar-powered aircraft, *Solar Challenger*, 6 mi in 22 min. near Marana, Ariz. (Dec. 3). The craft was powered by a 2.75-horsepower engine.
First solar-powered aircraft to fly across the English Channel. Stephen R. Ptacek flew the 210-pound *Solar Challenger* at an average speed of 30 mph from Corneilles-en-Vexin near Paris to the Royal Manston Air Force Base in southeast England in 5 hr., 30 min. (July 7).

1984   First solo transatlantic balloon flight. Joe W. Kittinger landed Sept. 18 near Savona, Italy, in his helium-filled balloon, *Rosie O'Grady's Balloon of Peace,* after a flight of 3,535 mi from Caribou, Maine.

1986   First nonstop flight around the world without refueling. From Edwards AFB, Calif., Dick Rutan and Jeana Yeager flew in *Voyager* around the world (24,986.727 mi), returning to Edwards in 216 hr., 3 min., 44 sec. (Dec. 14–23).

1987   First transatlantic hot-air balloon flight. Richard Branson and Per Lindstrand flew 2,789.6 mi from Sugarloaf Mt., Maine, to Ireland in the hot-air balloon *Virgin Atlantic Flyer* (July 2–4).

1991   First transpacific hot-air balloon flight. Richard Branson and Per Lindstrand flew about 6,700 mi from Miyakonyo, Japan, to 150 mi west of Yellowknife, Northwest Territories, Canada (Jan. 15–17).

1993   First woman to copilot a commercial supersonic plane. Barbara Harmer, British Airways, flew as first officer on the Concorde from London to New York City (March 25).

1995   First solo transpacific balloon flight. Steve Fossett made a flight of more than 5,430 mi from Seoul, South Korea, to Leader, Saskatchewan, Canada, in a helium-filled balloon. Also set record for distance (Feb. 18–21, 1995).

1999   First nonstop round-the-world balloon flight. Bertrand Piccard (Switzerland) and Brian Jones (UK) flew 28,431 mi (45,755 km) from Chateaux d'Oex, Switzerland, to Dakhla, Egypt, in 19 days, 21 hr., and 55 min. (March 1–21).

2001   First solar-powered flight to shatter altitude records. NASA's solar-powered propeller-driven plane *Helios* reached an altitude of 96,500 ft during a flight over Hawaii, breaking not only the 80,200-foot record for propeller-driven aircraft, but the 85,068-foot record for all nonrocket aircraft as well (Aug. 13–14).

2002   First solo nonstop round-the-world balloon flight. Steve Fossett (U.S.) flew from Northam, West Australia, to Lake Yamma Yamma, Queensland, Australia, landing after 14 days, 19 hrs. He broke three balloon records along the way: fastest time around the world, measured by crossing 117° East longitude (13 days, 3 min.), longest distance flown solo (20,483.25 mi; 32,963.35 km), and longest time flown solo (355 hrs, 50 min.) (June 19–July 3).

2004   **First non-stop 10,000-mile-plus passenger airline flight.** Singapore Airlines launched a nonstop 18 1/2 hour, 10,335-mile flight on the longrange Airbus 340-500 between Singapore to Newark, New Jersey (June 28–29).

Absolute World Records

(maximum performance in any class)

Source: National Aeronautic Association

Speed Around the World, Nonstop, Nonrefueled

Speed (mph)	Date	Plane	Pilots	Place
115.65	Dec. 14–23, 1986	*Voyager*	Dick Rutan & Jeana Yeager (U.S.)	Edwards AFB, Calif.—Edwards AFB, Calif.

Distance, Great Circle Without Landing, also Distance, Closed Circuit Without Landing

Distance (mi)	Date	Plane	Pilots	Place
24,986.727	Dec. 14–23, 1986	*Voyager*	Dick Rutan & Jeana Yeager (U.S.)	Edwards AFB, Calif.—Edwards AFB, Calif.

Speed over a Straight Course

Speed (mph)	Date	Plane type	Pilot	Place
2,193.16	July 28, 1976	Lockheed SR-71A	Capt. Eldon W. Joersz (USAF)	Beale AFB, Calif.

Speed over a Closed Circuit

Speed (mph)	Date	Plane type	Pilot	Place
2,092.294	July 27, 1976	Lockheed SR-71A	Maj. Adolphus H. Bledsoe, Jr. (USAF)	Beale AFB, Calif.

Altitude

Height (ft)	Date	Plane type	Pilot	Place
123,523.58	Aug. 31, 1977	MIG-25, E-266M	Alexander Fedotov (USSR)	USSR

Altitude in Horizontal Flight

Height (ft)	Date	Pilot	Place
85,068.997	July 28, 1976	Capt. Robert C. Helt (USAF)	Beale AFB, Calif.

Altitude, Aircraft Launched from a Carrier Airplane

Height (ft)	Date	Plane type	Pilot	Place
314,750.00	July 17, 1962	N. American X-15-1	Maj. Robert White (USAF)	Edwards AFB, Calif.

World-Class Helicopter Records

Selected records. *Source:* National Aeronautic Association

Great Circle Distance Without Landing
International: 2,213.04 mi; 3,561.55 km.
Robert G. Ferry (U.S.) in Hughes YOH-6A helicopter powered by Allison T-63-A-5 engine; from Culver City, Calif., to Ormond Beach, Fla., April 6–7, 1966.

Distance, Closed Circuit Without Landing
International: 1,739.96 mi; 2,800.20 km.
Jack Schweibold (U.S.) in Hughes YOH-6A helicopter powered by Allison T-63-A-5 engine; Edwards Air Force Base, Calif., March 26, 1966.

Altitude without Payload
International: 40,820 ft; 12,442 m.
Jean Boulet (France) in Alouette SA 315-001 *Lama* powered by Artouste IIIB 735 KW engine; Istres, France, June 21, 1972.

Speed around the World, Eastbound
40.99 mph; 65.97 kph.
Joe Ronald Bower (U.S.) pilot, in Bell JetRanger III, powered by one Allison 250-C20J (317 shp), covered 23,800 mi in 24 days, 4 hr., 36 min. June 28–July 22, 1994.

Speed around the World, Westbound
57.01 mph; 91.75 kph.

Joe Ronald Bower (U.S.) pilot, John W. Williams (U.S.), co-pilot in Bell 430 powered by 2 Allison 250–C40, (811 shp), Aug. 17–Sept. 3, 1996.

Absolute World Records, Balloons

Selected records. *Source:* National Aeronautic Association
Altitude
113,739.9 ft; 34,668 m.
Cmdr. M.D. Ross (U.S.) and Lt. Cmdr. V.A. Prather, *Lee Lewis Memorial*, Gulf of Mexico, May 4, 1961.
Distance
25,360 mi; 40,814 km.
Bertrand Piccard (Switzerland) and Brian Jones (UK), *Cameron Balloons R-650*, Château d'Oex, Switzerland, to Dakhla, Egypt, March 1–21, 1999.
Duration
477 hr., 47 min.
Bertrand Piccard (Switzerland) and Brian Jones (UK), *Cameron Balloons R-650*, Château d'Oex, Switzerland, to Dakhla, Egypt, March 1–21, 1999.
Fastest time around the world
312 hr., 3 min.
Steve Fossett (U.S.), Spirit of Freedom, Northam, Western Australia to Lake Yamma Yamma, Queensland, Australia. Flight, June 19–July 3; record broken on July 2, 2002.

U.S. Postal Rates and Fees

Domestic Rates, last revised by the U.S. Postal Service on June 30, 2002

First-Class Mail

First-Class Mail includes all personal correspondence, all bills and statements of accounts, all matter sealed or otherwise closed against inspection, and matter wholly or partly in writing or typewriting. Any mailable items may be sent as First-Class Mail. Each piece must weigh 13 oz or less. Pieces over 13 oz can be sent as Priority Mail.

Single-Piece Letter/Flat Rates

1st oz	$0.37
Each additional oz	0.23

Weight not over (oz)	Rate	Weight not over (oz)	Rate
1*	$0.37	9	$2.21
2	0.60	10	2.44
3	0.83	11	2.67
4	1.06	12	2.90
5	1.29	13	3.13
6	1.52	Over 13 oz, see	
7	1.75	Priority Mail.	
8	1.98		

*Nonstandard surcharge may apply to pieces weighing 1 oz or less based on size.

Card Rates

Single postcard (commercial)	$0.23
Single postal card sold by United States Postal Service	0.25

Postcard Dimensions: Not larger than 4¼ by 6 in. by 0.016 in. thick. Not smaller than 3½ by 5 in. by 0.007 in. thick.

Express Mail

Express Mail is the fastest service, with next day delivery by 12 noon to most destinations. Express Mail is delivered 365 days a year—with no extra charge for Saturday, Sunday, or holiday delivery. Items must weigh 70 lbs or less and measure 108 in. or less in combined length and girth.

Customer Service—1-800-222-1811. Order Express Mail supplies and labels, arrange pickup service, obtain delivery information between ZIP Codes, and determine delivery status.

Post Office to Addressee Service

Up to 8 oz	$13.65
Up to 2 lbs	17.85
Up to 3 lbs	21.05
Up to 4 lbs	24.20
Up to 5 lbs	27.30
Up to 6 lbs	30.40
Up to 7 lbs	33.45
Over 7 lbs, see postmaster.	

Express Mail Flat-Rate Envelope

$13.65, regardless of weight or destination, for matter sent in a flat-rate envelope provided by the Postal Service.

Priority Mail

Priority Mail offers 2-day service to most domestic destinations. Items must weigh 70 lbs or less and measure 108 in. or less in combined length and girth. Items that weigh less than 15 lbs but measure more than 84 in. (combined length and girth) are charged the 15 lb rate ($11.05)*.

Single-Piece Rates*

Up to 1 lb	$3.85
Up to 2 lbs	3.95
Up to 3 lbs	4.75
Up to 4 lbs	5.30
Up to 5 lbs	5.85
Over 5 pounds, see postmaster.	

*Rates are given for zones local through 3.

Priority Mail Flat-Rate Envelope

$3.85, regardless of weight or destination, for matter sent in a flat-rate envelope provided by the Postal Service.

Media Mail (Book Rate)

Generally used for books (at least eight pages), film (16 mm or narrower), printed music, printed test materials, sound recordings, play scripts, printed educational charts, loose-leaf pages and binders consisting of medical information, and computer-readable media. Advertising restrictions apply. Packages must measure 108 in. or less in combined length and girth.

Weight not over (lbs)	Rate	Weight not over (lbs)	Rate
1	$1.42	9	$4.54
2	1.84	10	4.84
3	2.26	11	5.14
4	2.68	12	5.44
5	3.10	13	5.74
6	3.52	14	6.04
7	3.94	15	6.34
8	4.24	16	6.64

Special Services (Domestic Mail)

Certificate of Mailing

Provides evidence of mailing only. Certificate of mailing does not provide a record of delivery. Must be purchased at time of mailing. Available for First-Class Mail, Priority Mail, Parcel Post, Bound Printed Matter, and Media Mail.
Fee, in addition to postage—$0.90

Certified Mail

Provides the sender with a mailing receipt. A delivery record is maintained by the USPS. No insurance provided. Available with First-Class Mail and Priority Mail. For an additional fee, certified mail may be combined with restricted delivery or return receipt.
Fee, in addition to postage—$2.30

Insurance

Provides coverage against loss or damage. Coverage up to $5,000 for Parcel Post, Bound Printed Matter, and Media Mail matter as well as merchandise mailed at Priority Mail or First-Class Mail rates. Items must not be insured for more than their value. Insured mail must be presented to a retail employee at a post office or a rural carrier.

Liability	Fee, in addition to postage
$.01 to $50.00	$1.30
$50.01 to $100.00	2.20
$100.01 to $200.00	3.20
$200.01 to $300.00	4.20
$300.01 to $400.00	5.20
$400.01 to $500.00	6.20
$500.01 to $600.00	7.20
$600.01 to $5,000	*

*$7.00 plus $1.00 for each $100 or fraction over $600 in declared value.

Money Orders

Provides safe transmission of money. Available in amounts up to $1,000.
Fee up to $500, in addition to postage—$0.90
Fee up to $1,000, in addition to postage—$1.25

Registered Mail

Provides maximum protection and security for valuables. Provides sender with mailing receipt and a delivery record is maintained by the USPS. A record of mailing is maintained at the mailing post office. Available only for items paid at Priority Mail and First-Class Mail rates.

	Declared Value	Fee, in addition to postage
Without Insurance	$0.00	$ 7.50
With Insurance	$0.01 to $100	8.00
	$100.01 to $500.00	8.85
	$500.01 to $1,000.00	9.70
	$1,000.01 to $2,000.00	10.55

For higher values, consult your postmaster.

Restricted Delivery

Permits a mailer to direct delivery only to the addressee or addressee's authorized agent. The addressee must be an individual specified by name. Available for First-Class Mail, Priority Mail, Parcel Post, Bound Printed Matter, and Media Mail that is sent certified mail, COD, mail insured for more than $50, or registered mail.
Fee, in addition to postage—$3.50

Return Receipt

Available only for Express Mail, Certified Mail, COD, Insured Mail for more than $50.00, or Registered Mail.

Requested at time of mailing:
Showing to whom (signature), date, and addressee's address (in conjunction with another service) $1.75
Requested after mailing:
Showing to whom (signature) and date delivered $3.25

Special Handling

Provides preferential handling, but not preferential delivery, to extent practicable in dispatch and transportation. Available for First-Class Mail, Priority Mail, Parcel Post, Bound Printed Matter, and Media Mail.

Fee, in addition to postage:
Pieces weighing not more than 10 pounds—$5.95
Pieces weighing more than 10 pounds—$8.25

Collect on Delivery (COD)

Allows mailers to collect the price of goods and/or postage on merchandise ordered by addressee when it is delivered. Fees include insurance. Maximum amount $1,000; see postmaster for details.

Sizes for Domestic Mail

Mail must meet these standards:
• Thickness—No less than 0.007 in. thick. Pieces that are ¼ in. thick or less must be at least 3½ in. high, 5 in. long, and rectangular in shape.
• Combined length and girth—No more than 108 in.
• Weight—No more than 70 lbs.
Postcards must be:
• Minimum 3½ in. high, 5 in. long by .007 in. thick.
• Maximum 4¼ in. high, 6 in. long by .016 in. thick.

The Mail-Order Merchandise Rule

The mail-order rule adopted by the Federal Trade Commission in October 1975 provides that when you order by mail:
• You must receive the merchandise when the seller says you will.
• If you are not promised delivery within a certain time period, the seller must ship the merchandise to you no later than 30 days after your order comes in.
• If you don't receive it shortly after that 30-day period, you can cancel your order and get your money back.

ZIP Codes

The ZIP Code was instituted in 1963 and allows for electronic processing and delivery of mail. An envelope that does not include a ZIP Code in the delivery address must be manually sorted, which increases the cost of sorting the mail and causes mail to be delayed en route to the delivery address. ZIP Code directories are available for use or sale at your local post office, or you can look up ZIP Codes on-line: www.usps.gov/ncsc/.

In 1983, the Postal Service began to use an expanded ZIP Code called ZIP+4. It is composed of the original five-digit code plus a four-digit add-on. The four-digit add-on number identifies a geographic segment within the five-digit delivery area such as a city block, an office building, an individual high-volume receiver of mail, or any other unit that would aid efficient mail sorting and delivery.

Postal Information Websites

United States Postal Service: http://www.usps.gov/
ZIP Code Lookup: http://www.usps.gov/zip4/
U.S. Postal Service Rate Calculators:
  domestic: http://postcalc.usps.gov/
  international: http://ircalc.usps.gov/
  business: http://dbcalc.usps.gov/

International Postal Rates

Single Piece Letter-Post

Weight not over (oz)	Canada	Mexico	Western Europe and Israel	Australia, Japan, New Zealand	Other countries
1	$ 0.60	$ 0.60	$ 0.80	$ 0.80	$ 0.80
2	0.85	0.85	1.60	1.70	1.55
3	1.10	1.25	2.40	2.60	2.30
4	1.35	1.65	3.20	3.50	3.05
5	1.60	2.05	4.00	4.40	3.80
6	1.85	2.45	4.80	5.30	4.55
7	2.10	2.85	5.60	6.20	5.30
8	2.35	3.25	6.40	7.10	6.05
12	3.10	4.00	7.55	8.40	7.65
16	3.75	5.15	8.70	9.70	9.25
20	4.40	6.30	9.85	11.00	10.85
24	5.05	7.45	11.00	12.30	12.45
28	5.70	8.60	12.15	13.60	14.05
32	6.35	9.75	13.30	14.90	15.65
36	7.00	10.95	14.50	16.25	17.35
40	7.65	12.15	15.70	17.60	19.05
44	8.30	13.35	16.90	18.95	20.75
48	8.95	14.55	18.10	20.30	22.45
52	9.65	15.80	19.35	21.70	24.20
56	10.35	17.05	20.60	23.10	25.95
60	11.05	18.30	21.85	24.50	27.70
64	11.75	19.55	23.10	25.90	29.45

NOTE: Last revised by the U.S. Postal Service on June 30, 2002. Maximum weight: 64 oz. **Postcards and Postal Rates:** Canada and Mexico—$0.50; all others—$0.70.

U.S. Letter Rates Since the Civil War

The first U.S. postage stamps were issued on July 1, 1847. At that time, postal rates varied by distance traveled—under 300 miles, letters cost 5 cents per ½ oz; over 300 miles, letters cost 10 cents per ½ oz. (These rates fluctuated in the decade that followed.) Until prepayment became mandatory on April 1, 1855, Americans had the option to pay collect, which could entail higher rates. Since July 1, 1863, letters sent to all parts of the United States have been charged at the same rate.

July 1, 1863	3 cents per ½ oz.	Dec. 31, 1975	13 cents for 1st oz.
Oct. 1, 1883	2 cents per ½ oz.	May 29, 1978	15 cents for 1st oz.
July 1, 1885	2 cents per 1 oz.	March 22, 1981	18 cents for 1st oz.
Nov. 2, 1917	3 cents per 1 oz.	Nov. 1, 1981	20 cents for 1st oz.
July 1, 1919	2 cents per 1 oz.	Feb. 17, 1985	22 cents for 1st oz.
July 6, 1932	3 cents per 1 oz.	April 3, 1988	25 cents for 1st oz.
Aug. 1, 1958	4 cents per 1 oz.	Feb. 3, 1991	29 cents for 1st oz.
Jan. 7, 1963	5 cents per 1 oz.	Jan. 1, 1995	32 cents for 1st oz.
Jan. 7, 1968	6 cents per 1 oz.	Jan. 10, 1999	33 cents for 1st oz.
May 16, 1971	8 cents per 1 oz.	Jan. 7, 2001	34 cents for 1st oz.
March 2, 1974	10 cents per 1 oz.	June 30, 2002	37 cents for 1st oz.

State Abbreviations and State Postal Codes

State	Abbreviation	Postal code	State	Abbreviation	Postal code	State	Abbreviation	Postal code
Alabama	Ala.	AL	Kentucky	Ky.	KY	Ohio	Ohio	OH
Alaska	Alaska	AK	Louisiana	La.	LA	Oklahoma	Okla.	OK
Arizona	Ariz.	AZ	Maine	Maine	ME	Oregon	Ore.	OR
Arkansas	Ark.	AR	Maryland	Md.	MD	Pennsylvania	Pa.	PA
California	Calif.	CA	Massachusetts	Mass.	MA	Puerto Rico	P.R.	PR
Colorado	Colo.	CO	Michigan	Mich.	MI	Rhode Island	R.I.	RI
Connecticut	Conn.	CT	Minnesota	Minn.	MN	South Carolina	S.C.	SC
Delaware	Del.	DE	Mississippi	Miss.	MS	South Dakota	S.D.	SD
Dist. of Columbia	D.C.	DC	Missouri	Mo.	MO	Tennessee	Tenn.	TN
Florida	Fla.	FL	Montana	Mont.	MT	Texas	Tex.	TX
Georgia	Ga.	GA	Nebraska	Nebr.	NE	Utah	Utah	UT
Guam	Guam	GU	Nevada	Nev.	NV	Vermont	Vt.	VT
Hawaii	Hawaii	HI	New Hampshire	N.H.	NH	Virginia	Va.	VA
Idaho	Idaho	ID	New Jersey	N.J.	NJ	Virgin Islands	V.I.	VI
Illinois	Ill.	IL	New Mexico	N.M.	NM	Washington	Wash.	WA
Indiana	Ind.	IN	New York	N.Y.	NY	West Virginia	W.Va.	WV
Iowa	Iowa	IA	North Carolina	N.C.	NC	Wisconsin	Wis.	WI
Kansas	Kans.	KS	North Dakota	N.D.	ND	Wyoming	Wyo.	WY

The Seven Wonders of the World

Since ancient times, people have put together many "seven wonders" lists. The content of these lists tends to vary, and none is definitive. The seven wonders that are most widely agreed upon as being in the original list are the **Seven Wonders of the Ancient World**. (* indicates photo can be found in the Headline History section.)

The **Pyramids of Egypt*** are three pyramids at Giza, outside modern Cairo. The largest pyramid, built by Khufu (Cheops), a king of the fourth dynasty, had an original estimated height of 482 ft (now approximately 450 ft). The base has sides 755 ft long. It contains 2,300,000 blocks; the average weight of each is 2.5 tons. Estimated date of completion is 2680 B.C. Of all the Ancient Wonders, the pyramids alone survive.

The **Hanging Gardens of Babylon** were supposedly built by Nebuchadnezzar around 600 B.C. to please his queen, Amuhia. They are also associated with the mythical Assyrian queen, Semiramis. Archeologists surmise that the gardens were laid out atop a vaulted building, with provisions for raising water. The terraces were said to rise from 75 to 300 ft.

The **Statue of Zeus (Jupiter) at Olympia** was made of gold and ivory by the Greek sculptor Phidias (5th century B.C.). Reputed to be 40 ft high, the statue has been lost without a trace, except for reproductions on coins.

The **Temple of Artemis (Diana) at Ephesus** was begun about 350 B.C., in honor of a non-Hellenic goddess who later became identified with the Greek goddess of the same name. The temple, with Ionic columns 60 ft high, was destroyed by invading Goths in A.D. 262.

The **Mausoleum at Halicarnassus** was erected by Queen Artemisia in memory of her husband, King Mausolus of Caria in Asia Minor, who died in 353 B.C. Some remains of the structure are in the British Museum. This shrine is the source of the modern word "mausoleum."

The **Colossus at Rhodes** was a bronze statue of Helios (Apollo), about 105 ft high. The work of the sculptor Chares, who reputedly labored for 12 years before completing it in 280 B.C., it was destroyed during an earthquake in 224 B.C.

The **Pharos (Lighthouse) of Alexandria** was built by Sostratus of Cnidus during the 3rd century B.C. on the island of Pharos off the coast of Egypt. It was destroyed by an earthquake in the 13th century.

(Some lists include the Walls of Babylon in place of the second or seventh wonder.)

Famous Structures

Ancient

The **Great Sphinx** of Egypt, one of the wonders of ancient Egyptian architecture, adjoins the pyramids of Giza and has a length of 240 ft. Built in the fourth dynasty, it is approximately 4,500 years old. A 10-year $2.5 million restoration project was completed in 1998. Other Egyptian buildings of note include the *Temples of Karnak, Edfu,* and *Abu Simbel* and the *Tombs at Beni Hassan.*

The **Parthenon*** of Greece, built on the Acropolis in Athens, was the chief temple to the goddess Athena. It was believed to have been completed by 438 B.C. The present temple remained intact until the 5th century A.D. Today, though the Parthenon is in ruins, its majestic proportions are still discernible.

Other great structures of the ancient Greek world were the *Temples* at Paestum (c. 540 and 420 B.C.); the famous *Erechtheum* (c. 421–405 B.C.), the *Temple of Athena Niké* (c. 426 B.C.), and the *Olympieum* (begun in the 6th century B.C.) in Athens; the *Athenian Treasury* at Delphi (c. 515 B.C.); and the *Theater* at Epidaurus (c. 325 B.C.).

The **Colosseum** (Flavian Amphitheater) of Rome, the largest and most famous of the Roman amphitheaters, was opened for use A.D. 80. Elliptical in shape, it consisted of three stories and an upper gallery, rebuilt in stone in its present form in the third century A.D. It was principally used for gladiatorial combat and could seat between 40,000 and 50,000 spectators.

The **Pantheon** at Rome, begun by Agrippa in 27 B.C. as a temple, was rebuilt in its present circular form by Hadrian (A.D. 118–128). Literally the Pantheon was intended as a temple of "all the gods." It is remarkable for its perfect preservation today, and has served continuously for 20 centuries as a place of worship.

Famous Roman triumphal arches, built to commemorate major military victories, include the **Arch of Titus** (c. A.D. 80) and the **Arch of Constantine** (c. A.D. 315).

Teotihuacán, located in central Mexico, was the largest city in the Americas at its height between A.D. 300 and 900. Built on a grid plan with a central avenue known as the Street of the Dead, it is the site of two enormous pyramid temples and the temple of the plumed serpent god Quetzalcoatl.

Later European

St. Mark's Cathedral in Venice (1063–1071), one of the great examples of Byzantine architecture, was begun in the 9th century. Partly destroyed by fire in 976, it was later rebuilt as a Byzantine edifice.

Other famous examples of Byzantine architecture are *St. Sophia* in Istanbul (532–537); *San Vitale* in Ravenna (542); and *Assumption Cathedral* in the Kremlin, Moscow (begun in 1475).

The cathedral group at Pisa (1067–1173), one of the most celebrated groups of structures built in Romanesque style, consists of the cathedral, the cathedral's baptistery, and the campanile (**Leaning Tower***). The campanile, a form of bell tower, is 180 ft high and now leans 13.5 ft out of the perpendicular.

Other examples of Romanesque architecture include the *Vézelay Abbey* in France (1130) and *Durham Cathedral* in England.

The **Alhambra** (1248–1354), located in Granada, Spain, is universally esteemed as one of the greatest masterpieces of Muslim architecture. Designed as a palace and fortress for the Moorish monarchs of Granada, it is surrounded by a heavily fortified wall more than a mile in perimeter.

The **Tower of London** is a group of buildings and towers covering 13 acres along the north bank of the Thames. The central *White Tower,* begun in 1078 during the reign of William the Conqueror, was originally a fortress and royal residence, but was later used as a prison. The *Bloody Tower* is associated with Anne Boleyn and other notables.

Westminster Abbey, in London, was begun in 1050 and completed in 1065. It was rebuilt and enlarged in several phases, beginning in 1245. With only two exceptions (Edward V and Edward VIII), every British monarch since William the Conqueror has been crowned in the abbey.

Notre-Dame de Paris (begun in 1163), one of the great examples of Gothic architecture, is a twin-towered church with a steeple over the crossing and immense flying buttresses supporting the masonry at the rear of the church.

Other famous Gothic structures are *Chartres Cathedral* (France; 12th century); *Sainte-Chapelle* (Paris, France; 1246–1248); *Reims Cathedral* (France; 13th–14th centuries; rebuilt after its almost complete destruction in World War I); *Rouen Cathedral* (France; 13th–16th centuries); *Salisbury Cathedral* (England; 1220–1260); *York Minster* or the *Cathedral of St. Peter* (England; 1220–1472); *Milan Cathedral* (Italy; begun in 1386); and *Cologne Cathedral* (Germany; 13th–19th centuries; damaged in World War II but completely restored).

The **Duomo*** (cathedral) in Florence, with its pink, white, and green marble façade, has become a symbol of the city and the Renaissance. Construction began in 1296, and was completed nearly 200 years later, with the addition of Brunelleschi's massive dome. The adjacent baptistery is famous for its gilded bronze doors by Ghiberti.

The **Vatican** is a group of buildings in Rome comprising the official residence of the pope. The *Basilica of St. Peter,* the largest church in the Christian world, was begun in 1452, and it was rebuilt between 1506 and 1626. The *Sistine Chapel,* begun in 1473, is noted for frescoes by Michelangelo.

Other examples of Renaissance architecture are the *Palazzo Riccardi,* the *Palazzo Pitti,* and the *Palazzo Strozzi* in Florence; the *Palazzo Farnese* in Rome; the *Palazzo Grimani* (completed c. 1550) in Venice; the *Escorial* (1563–93) near Madrid; the *Town Hall* of Seville (1527–32); the *Louvre,* Paris; the *Château* at Blois, France; *St. Paul's Cathedral,* London (1675–1710; badly damaged in World War II); the *École Militaire,* Paris (1752); the *Pazzi Chapel,* Florence, designed by Brunelleschi (1429); and the *Palace of Fontainebleau* and the *Château de Chambord* in France.

The **Palace of Versailles** in France, containing the famous Hall of Mirrors, was built during the reign of Louis XIV in the 17th century and served as the royal palace until 1793. Built on the colossal scale typical of many works of baroque architec-

ture, the palace is also noted for its gardens, which include some 1,400 fountains.

The **Eiffel Tower,** in Paris, was built for the Exposition of 1889 by Alexandre Gustave Eiffel. It is 984 ft high (1,056 ft including the television tower).

The **Guggenheim Bilbao Museum** (1993–97) in Bilbao, Spain, was designed by Frank Gehry. The undulating form of this riverfront building, clad in glass and gleaming sheets of titanium, has been compared to a fish, a boat, and water itself.

Asian, African, and American

The **Taj Mahal*** (1632–1650), at Agra, India, built by Shah Jahan as a tomb for his wife, is considered by some as the most perfect example of the Mogul style and by others as the most beautiful building in the world. Four slim white minarets flank the building, which is topped by a white dome; the entire structure is made of marble.

The **Dome of the Rock** (687–691) in Jerusalem is considered the first great work of Muslim architecture. It is noted for its beautiful mosaics of scrolling vines and flowers, and for its dome, which was originally covered in pure gold.

Another well-known Muslim edifice is the **Citadel,** located on an outcrop of limestone overlooking Cairo. Begun in 810, it was fortified (1176–1183) by Saladin during the Crusades.

Other famed Muslim edifices are the *Tombs of the Mamelukes* (15th century) in Cairo, the *Tomb of Humayun* in Delhi, the *Blue Mosque* (1468) at Tabriz, and the *Tamerlane Mausoleum* at Samarkand.

Angkor Wat, outside the city of Angkor Thom, Cambodia, is one of the most beautiful examples of Cambodian or Khmer architecture. The sanctuary was built during the 12th century.

The **Great Wall of China** (begun c. 214 B.C.), designed specifically as a defense against nomadic tribes, has large watch towers that could be called buildings. It was erected by Emperor Ch'in Shih Huang Ti and is 1,400 mi long. Built mainly of earth and stone, it varies in height between 18 and 30 ft.

The **Forbidden City** (1407–1420) in Beijing served as the seat of imperial power during the Ming and Qing dynasties (1368–1911). It is the world's largest palace complex, covering about 183 acres and including 9,999 buildings.

Typical of Chinese architecture are the pagodas or temple towers. Among some of the better-known pagodas are the *Great Pagoda of the Wild Geese* at Sian (founded in 652) and *Nan t'a* (11th century) at Fang Shan.

The painted wooden **Torii,** or Gateway, at Miyajima Island, Japan, stands in the tidal flats opposite the historic Itsukushima Shrine. Built in the traditional Shinto style, with two columns supporting a concave crosspiece on top, the gate serves to welcome the spirits of the dead as they come from across the Inland Sea.

Other famous Japanese buildings include the Buddhist temples of **Horyuji** (7th century) and **Todaiji** (8th century) at Nara.

Machu Picchu is an ancient Inca fortress in the Andes Mountains of Peru. Thought to have been built and occupied from the mid–15th century, it is surrounded on three sides by stepped agricultural terraces, which are connected to the main plazas and buildings by thousands of stone steps.

United States

The **Chrysler Building** (1928–30) in New York City is one of the finest examples of Art Deco–style architecture. Built for automotive magnate Walter P. Chrysler, the building uses decorative elements borrowed from automobiles. At 1,046 ft it was briefly the world's tallest building.

The **Empire State Building** (1930–31) is one of the most popular tourist attractions in Manhattan. Features include a tiered structure that recalls ancient pyramids and a mast at the top for mooring dirigibles. Rising to 1,250 ft (not including the mast), it remained the tallest building in the world until the 1970s.

The elegant **Seagram Building,** (1954–58) by Ludwig Mies van der Rohe, soars above an open plaza in Manhattan. Its slim steel frame is covered in amber-gray glass and costly bronze. It has been called the world's most imitated office building.

The **Cathedral of St. John the Divine,** in New York City, was begun in 1892 and is now two-thirds completed. When completed, it will be the largest cathedral in the world: 601 ft long, 146 ft wide at the nave, 320 ft wide at the transept. The east end is Romanesque-Byzantine style, and the nave and west end are Gothic.

The **Brooklyn Bridge** (1869–83) was the remarkable achievement of engineer John Roebling. The first steel-wire suspension bridge in the world, it has a main span of 1,596 ft.

The smooth, circular form of the **Guggenheim New York Museum** (1943–59), designed by Frank Lloyd Wright, is a Manhattan landmark. The main gallery space features a six-story concrete ramp that spirals up a glass-topped atrium.

The **Sears Tower** in Chicago is, at 1,450 ft, the tallest building in the United States. Constructed between 1974 and 1976 for Sears, Roebuck and Company, the structure is composed of 75-foot square tubes that rise to varying levels.

San Francisco's **Golden Gate Bridge,** completed in 1937, is one of the most recognizable structures in the United States. Designed by Joseph B. Strauss, this elegant suspension bridge has a main span of 4,200 ft.

The Seattle **Space Needle** was the futuristic centerpiece of the 1962 Seattle World's Fair. The 605-ft-tall Needle is topped by an observation deck and a revolving restaurant.

* Photos of these structures can be found in the Headline History section.

World's Tallest Buildings[1]

Rank	Building, city	Year	Stories	Height m	Height ft
1.	Taipei 101, Taipei, Taiwan	2004	101	509	1,670
2.	Petronas Tower 1, Kuala Lumpur, Malaysia	1998	88	452	1,483
3.	Petronas Tower 2, Kuala Lumpur, Malaysia	1998	88	452	1,483
4.	Sears Tower, Chicago	1974	110	442	1,450
5.	Jin Mao Building, Shanghai	1999	88	421	1,381
6.	Two International Finance Centre, Hong Kong	2003	88	415	1,362
7.	CITIC Plaza, Guangzhou, China	1996	80	391	1,283
8.	Shun Hing Square, Shenzhen, China	1996	69	384	1,260
9.	Empire State Building, New York	1931	102	381	1,250
10.	Central Plaza, Hong Kong	1992	78	374	1,227
11.	Bank of China, Hong Kong	1989	72	369	1,209
12.	Emirates Tower One, Dubai	1999	54	355	1,165
13.	Turntex Sky Tower, Kaohsiung, Taiwan	1997	85	348	1,140
14.	Aon Centre, Chicago	1973	80	346	1,136
15.	The Center, Hong Kong	1998	73	346	1,135
16.	John Hancock Center, Chicago	1969	100	344	1,127
17.	Ryugyong Hotel, Pyongyang, N. Korea	1995	105	330	1,083
18.	Burj al Arab Hotel, Dubai	1999	60	321	1,053
19.	Chrysler Building, New York	1930	77	319	1,046
20.	Bank of America Plaza, Atlanta	1993	55	310	1,023
21.	U.S. Bank Tower, Los Angeles	1990	73	310	1,018
22.	Menara Telekom Headquarters, Kuala Lumpur	1999	55	310	1,017
23.	Emirates Tower Two, Dubai	2000	56	309	1,014
24.	AT&T Corporate Center, Chicago	1989	60	307	1,007
25.	JP Morgan Chase Tower, Houston	1982	75	305	1,002
26.	Baiyoke Tower II, Bangkok	1997	85	304	997
27.	Two Prudential Plaza, Chicago	1990	64	303	995
28.	Kingdom Centre, Riyadh	2002	41	302	992
29.	First Canadian Place, Toronto	1975	72	298	978
30.	Wells Fargo Plaza, Houston	1983	71	296	972
31.	Landmark Tower, Yokohama, Japan	1993	70	296	971
32.	311 South Wacker Drive, Chicago	1990	65	293	961
33.	SEG Plaza, Shenzhen	2000	71	292	957
34.	American International Building, New York	1932	67	290	952
35.	Cheung Kong Center, Hong Kong	1999	63	290	951
36.	Key Tower, Cleveland	1991	57	289	947
37.	Plaza 66, Shanghai	2001	66	288	945
38.	One Liberty Place, Philadelphia	1987	61	288	945
39.	Sunjoy Tomorrow Square, Shanghai	2003	55	285	934
40.	Bank of America Center, Seattle	1984	76	284	933
41.	Chongqing World Trade Center, Chongqing	UC05	60	283	929
42.	The Trump Building, New York	1930	71	283	927
43.	Bank of America Plaza, Dallas	1985	72	281	921
44.	United Overseas Bank Plaza, Singapore	1992	66	280	919
45.	Republic Plaza, Singapore	1995	66	280	919
46.	Overseas Union Bank Centre, Singapore	1986	63	280	919
47.	Citigroup Center, New York	1977	59	279	915
48.	Hong Kong New World Building, Shanghai	2002	61	278	913

Rank	Building, city	Year	Sto-ries	Height m	ft	Rank	Building, city	Year	Sto-ries	Height m	ft
49.	Scotia Plaza, Toronto	1989	68	275	902	75.	Sorrento 1, Hong Kong	2003	75	256	841
50.	Williams Tower, Houston	1983	64	275	901	76.	U.S. Steel Tower, Pittsburgh	1970	64	256	841
51.	Wuhan World Trade Tower, Wuhan	1998	60	273	896	77.	Mokdong Hyperion Tower A, Seoul	2003	69	256	840
52.	Renaissance Tower, Dallas	1975	56	270	886	78.	Rinku Gate Tower, Izumisano	1996	56	256	840
53.	Dapeng International Plaza, Guangzhou	UC04	56	269	883	79.	The Harbourside, Hong Kong	2003	74	255	837
54.	21st Century Tower, Dubai	2003	55	269	883	80.	Langham Place Office Tower, Hong Kong	UC04	59	255	837
55.	Al Faisaliah Center, Riyadh	2000	30	267	876	81.	Capital Tower, Singapore	2000	52	254	833
56.	900 North Michigan Ave., Chicago	1989	66	265	871	82.	Highcliff, Hong Kong	2003	73	253	831
57.	Bank of America Corporate Center, Charlotte	1992	60	265	871	83.	Osaka World Trade Center, Osaka	1995	55	252	827
58.	SunTrust Plaza, Atlanta	1992	60	265	871	84.	Jiali Plaza, Wuhan	1997	61	251	824
59.	Triumph Palace, Moscow	UC04	61	264	866	85.	Rialto Tower, Melbourne	1985	63	251	823
60.	Shenzhen Special Zone Daily Tower, Shenzhen	1998	42	264	866	86.	One Atlantic Center, Atlanta	1987	50	250	820
61.	Tower Palace Three, Tower G, Seoul	2004	73	264	865	87.	Wisma 46, Jakarta	1995	46	250	820
62.	Trump World Tower, New York	2001	72	262	861	88.	Korea Life Insurance Company, Seoul	1985	60	249	817
63.	Water Tower Place, Chicago	1976	74	262	859	89.	CitySpire, New York	1989	75	248	814
64.	Aon Center, Los Angeles	1974	62	262	858	90.	One Chase Manhattan Plaza, New York	1961	60	248	813
65.	BCE Place–Canada Trust Tower, Toronto	1990	53	261	856	91.	State Tower, Bangkok	2001	68	247	811
66.	Post & Telecommunication Hub, Guangzhou	2002	66	260	853	92.	Bank One Tower, Indianapolis	1989	48	247	811
67.	Transamerica Pyramid, San Francisco	1972	48	260	853	93.	Conde Nast Building, New York	1999	48	247	809
68.	G.E. Building, New York	1933	70	259	850	94.	MetLife, New York	1963	59	246	808
69.	Bank One Plaza, Chicago	1969	60	259	850	95.	Bloomberg Tower, New York	UC04	55	246	806
70.	Commerzbank Zentrale, Frankfurt	1997	56	259	850	96.	JR Central Towers, Nagoya	2000	51	245	804
71.	Two Liberty Place, Philadelphia	1990	58	258	848	97.	City Gate Tower, Ramat-Gan	2001	67	244	801
72.	Philippine Bank of Communications, Makati	2000	55	258	848	98.	Shin Kong Life Tower, Taipei, Taiwan	1993	51	244	801
73.	Park Tower, Chicago	2000	67	257	844	99.	Chifley Tower, Sydney	1992	50	244	801
74.	Messeturm, Frankfurt	1990	64	257	843	100.	Menara Maybank, Kuala Lumpur	1988	50	244	799

NOTES: Height is measured from sidewalk level of main entrance to structural top of building. This includes spires, but does not include antennas or flag poles. UC = under construction, number indicates year of expected completion. 1. World Trade Center twin towers of New York City ranked fifth and sixth (at 1,368 ft and 1,362 ft) on this list until their destruction on Sept. 11, 2001. *Source:* Council on Tall Buildings and Urban Habitat, Lehigh University, 2004. Web: www.ctbuh.org.

World's Tallest Towers

Tower, city	Year	Height (m)	Height (ft)	Tower, city	Year	Height (m)	Height (ft)
Canadian National (CN) Tower, Toronto, Canada	1975	553	1,815	Tianjin TV Tower, Tianjin, China	1991	415	1,362
Ostankino Tower, Moscow, Russia	1967	537	1,762	Kiev TV Tower, Kiev, Ukraine	1973	385	1,263
Oriental Pearl Tower, Shanghai, China	1995	468	1,535	Tashkent Tower, Tashkent, Uzbekistan	1985	375	1,230
Menara Kuala Lumpur, Kuala Lumpur, Malaysia	1996	421	1,403	Liberation Tower, Kuwait City, Kuwait	1996	372	1,221
Central Radio & TV Tower, Beijing, China	1992	405	1,329	Alma-Ata Tower, Almaty, Kazakhstan	1983	371	1,217

NOTES: Height is from top to bottom, antennas included. A tower differs from a building in that the latter has floors, and is designed for residential, business, or manufacturing use. The structures listed here are principally telecommunications towers, and while they may have observation decks or restaurants, they do not have floors all the way up. Towers and buildings are free-standing structures; this list does not include masts supported by guy wires. The tallest mast currently standing is the KVLY-TV Mast in North Dakota, built in 1963; it is 629 m (2,063 ft) tall. The tallest mast of all time was the Warszawa Radio Mast near Konstantynów, Poland, built in 1974; it was 646 m (2,120 ft) tall before collapsing during renovation work in 1991. (Note that the name of a building or mast may include the word "tower," but that does not affect its status.) This list also does not include the Petronius Platform, built in 2000 in the Gulf of Mexico, which is 610 m (2,001 ft) tall without its spire, or 640 m (2,100 ft) with it. While it is the world's tallest freestanding structure, 535 m (1,754 ft) of it is underwater and it is partly supported by buoyancy. *Sources:* Structurae, Emporis, Wikipedia, and other sources.

Notable Modern Bridges

Name	Location	Length of main span		Year completed
		ft	m	
Suspension	**United States**			
Verrazano-Narrows	Lower New York Bay	4,260	1,298	1964
Golden Gate	San Francisco Bay	4,200	1,280	1937
Mackinac	Mackinac Straits, Mich.	3,800	1,158	1957
George Washington	Hudson River at New York City	3,500	1,067	1931
Tacoma Narrows II	Puget Sound at Tacoma, Wash.	2,800	853	1950
San Francisco–Oakland Bay[1]	San Francisco Bay	2,310	704	1936
Bronx-Whitestone	East River, New York City	2,300	701	1939
Delaware Memorial[1]	Delaware River near Wilmington, Del.	2,150	655	1951, 1968
Seaway Skyway	St. Lawrence River at Ogdensburg, N.Y.	2,150	655	1960
Walt Whitman	Delaware River at Philadelphia	2,000	610	1957
Ambassador International	Detroit River at Detroit	1,850	564	1929
Throgs Neck	East River, New York City	1,800	549	1961
Benjamin Franklin	Delaware River at Philadelphia	1,750	533	1926
Bear Mountain	Hudson River at Peekskill, N.Y.	1,632	497	1924
William Preston Lane, Jr.[1]	Chesapeake Bay, Md.	1,600	488	1952, 1973
Williamsburg	East River, New York City	1,600	488	1903
Newport	Narragansett Bay at Newport, R.I.	1,600	488	1969
Brooklyn	East River, New York City	1,596	486	1883
Mid-Hudson	Poughkeepsie, N.Y.	1,495	457	1930
	International			
Akashi Kaikyo	Hyogo, Japan	6,529	1,990	1998
Izmit Bay	Marmara Sea, Turkey	5,472	1,668	UC
Storebælt	Denmark	5,328	1,624	1998
Humber	Humberside, England	4,626	1,410	1981
Jiangyin	Yangtze River, China	4,543	1,385	1999
Tsing Ma	Hong Kong	4,518	1,377	1997
Höga Kusten (High Coast)	Västernorrland, Sweden	3,969	1,210	1997
Minami Bisan-Seto	Japan	3,609	1,100	1988
Second Bosporus	Istanbul, Turkey	3,576	1,090	1988
First Bosporus	Istanbul, Turkey	3,524	1,074	1973
Third Kurushima	Japan	3,379	1,030	1999
Second Kurushima	Japan	3,346	1,020	1999
Ponte 25 de Abril	Tagus River at Lisbon, Portugal	3,323	1,013	1966
Forth Road	Queensferry, Scotland	3,300	1,006	1964
Kita Bisan-Seto	Japan	3,248	990	1988
Severn	Severn River at Beachley, England	3,240	988	1966
Yichang	Yangtze River, Hubei Province, China	3,150	960	2001
Shimotsui Straits	Japan	3,084	940	1988
Xiling Yangtze	Three Gorges Dam, China	2,952	900	1996
Cantilever	**United States**			
Commodore John Barry	Chester, Pa.	1,644	501	1974
Crescent City Connection[1]	Mississippi River, New Orleans, La.	1,576	480	1958, 1985
Transbay Bridge	San Francisco Bay	1,400	427	1936
Baton Rouge	Mississippi River, La.	1,235	376	1968
Tappan Zee	Hudson River at Tarrytown, N.Y.	1,212	369	1955
	International			
Quebec Railway	Quebec, Canada	1,800	549	1917
Forth Railway[1]	Queensferry, Scotland	1,710	521	1890
Minato Ohashi	Osaka, Japan	1,673	510	1974
Howrah	Hooghly River at Calcutta, India	1,500	457	1943
Steel Arch	**United States**			
New River Gorge	Fayetteville, W. Va.	1,700	518	1977
Bayonne	Kill Van Kull at Bayonne, N.J.	1,675	510	1931
Fremont	Portland, Ore.	1,255	383	1973
Roosevelt Lake	Roosevelt, Ariz.	1,080	329	1990
Glen Canyon	Page, Ariz.	1,028	313	1959
	International			
Lupu Bridge	Shanghai, China	1,800	550	2003
Sydney Harbor	Sydney, Australia	1,670	509	1932
Port Mann	Fraser River at Vancouver, British Columbia	1,200	366	1964
Yanjisha[2]	Guangzhou, China	1,181	360	2000
Thatcher Ferry	Panama Canal, Panama	1,128	344	1962

Name	Location	Length of main span		Year completed
		ft	m	
Cable-stayed	**United States**			
Clark	Alton, Ill.	1,360	415	1994
Dames Point	Jacksonville, Fla.	1,300	396	1988
Fred Hartman	Baytown, Tex.	1,250	381	1995
Sidney Lanier	Brunswick River, Ga.	1,250	381	2003
Hale Boggs Memorial	Luling, La.	1,222	373	1983
Sunshine Skyway	Tampa, Fla.	1,200	366	1987
	International			
Tatara	Honshu-Shikoku, Japan	2,920	890	1999
Pont de Normandie	Le Havre, France	2,808	856	1995
Second Nanjing	Yangtze River, Nanjing, China	2,060	628	2001
Wuhan Third Yangtze	Wuhan, Hubei Province, China	2,028	618	2000
Qingzhou Minjiang	Fuzhou, China	1,985	605	1996
Yang Pu	Shanghai, China	1,975	602	1993
Xupu	Shanghai, China	1,936	590	1997
Meiko Chuo	Aichi, Japan	1,936	590	1997
Rion-Antirion	Greece	1,837	560	2004
Skarnsundet	near Trondheim, Norway	1,739	530	1991
Queshi	Guangdong Province, China	1,700	518	1999
Tsurumi Tsubasa	Kanagawa, Japan	1,673	510	1995
Jingzhou	Yangtze River, Hubei Province, China	1,640	500	2002
Oresund	Denmark/Sweden	1,614	492	2000
Ikuchi	Honshu-Shikoku, Japan	1,608	490	1991
Higashi Kobe	Hyogo, Japan	1,591	485	1994
Zhanjiang Bay	Guangdong Province, China	1,575	480	1998
Ting Kau	Hong Kong	1,558	475	1997
Seohae Grand	South Korea	1,542	470	2000
Continuous Truss	**United States**			
Astoria	Columbia River, Ore.	1,232	376	1966
Croton Reservoir	Croton, N.Y.	1,052	321	1970
Ravenswood	Ohio River, Ravenswood, W. Va.	902	275	1981
Central	Ohio River, Newport, Ky.	850	259	1995
Braga Memorial	Taunton River at Somerset, Mass.	840	256	1965
Kingston-Rhinecliff	Kingston, N.Y.	800	244	1957
Mark Clark Expressway I-526	Cooper River at Charleston, S.C.	800	244	1992
	International			
Oshima	Oshima Island, Japan	1,066	325	1976
Tenmon	Kumamoto, Japan	984	300	1966
Kuronoseto	Nagashima-Kyushu, Japan	984	300	1974
Graf Spee	Germany	839	256	1936
Concrete Arch	**United States**			
Natchez Trace Pkwy.	Franklin, Tenn.	582	177	1994
Westinghouse	Pittsburgh, Pa.	460	140	1931
Jack's Run	Pittsburgh, Pa.	400	120	1930
Cappelen	Minneapolis, Minn.	400	120	1923
	International			
Wanxian	Wanxian, Sichuan Province, China	1,378	420	1997
Krk (I)	Krk, Croatia	1,280	390	1980
Jiangjiehe	Guizhou Province, China	1,083	330	1995
Gladesville	Parramatta River at Sydney, Australia	1,000	305	1964
Amizade	Paraná River at Foz do Iguassu, Brazil	951	290	1964
Bloukrans	Bloukrans River, South Africa	892	272	1983
Arrábida	Porto, Portugal	886	270	1963
Sandö	Angerman River at Kramfors, Sweden	866	264	1943
Confederation	Northumberland Strait, Canada	820	250	1997
Sibenik	Sibenik, Croatia	808	246	1966
Krk (II)	Krk, Croatia	800	244	1979
Fiumarella	Catanzaro, Italy	758	231	1961
Zaporozhe	Old Dnepr River, Ukraine	748	228	1952
Esla	Esla River at Zamora, Spain	645	197	1940
Segmental Construction	**United States**			
Jesse H. Jones Memorial	Houston Ship Channel, Tex.	750	228	1982

NOTES: UC = under construction in 2004. 1. Twin span. 2. Concrete-filled steel tubes. *Sources:* National Steel Bridge Alliance, Swedish Institute of Steel Construction, Structurae, Federal Highway Administration.

World's Highest Dams

Name	River, location	Structural height		Gross reservoir capacity		Year completed
		ft	m	Thousands of ac ft	Millions of cu m	
Rogun	Vakhsh, Tajikistan	1099	335	9,404	11,600	1985
Nurek	Vakhsh, Tajikistan	984	300	8,512	10,500	1980
Grande Dixence	Dixence, Switzerland	935	285	324	400	1962
Inguri	Inguri, Georgia	892	272	801	1,100	1984
Vaiont	Vaiont, Italy	859	262	137	169	1961
Manuel M. Torres	Grijalva, Mexico	856	261	1,346	1,660	1981
Tehri	Bhagirathi, India	856	261	2,869	3,540	UC
Alvaro Obregon	Mextiquic, Mexico	853	260	n.a.	n.a.	1926
Mauvoisin	Drance de Bagnes, Switzerland	820	250	146	180	1957
Alberto Lleras	Orinoco, Colombia	797	243	811	1,000	1989
Mica	Columbia, Canada	797	243	20,000	24,670	1972
Sayano-Shushenskaya	Yenisei, Russia	794	242	25,353	31,300	1980
Ertan	Yangtze/Yalong, China	787	240	4,702	5,800	1999
La Esmeralda	Batá, Colombia	778	237	661	815	1975
Kishau	Tons, India	774	236	1,946	2,400	1985
Oroville	Feather, Calif., U.S.	770	235	3,538	4,299	1968
El Cajón	Humuya, Honduras	768	234	4,580	5,650	1984
Chirkey	Sulak, Russia	764	233	2,252	2,780	1977
Bhakra	Sutlej, India	741	226	8,002	9,870	1963
Luzzone	Brenno di Luzzone, Switzerland	738	225	71	87	1963
Hoover	Colorado, Ariz.-Nev., U.S.	732	223	28,500	35,154	1936
Contra	Verzasca, Switzerland	722	220	70	86	1965
Mratinje	Piva, Herzegovina	722	220	713	880	1973
Dworshak	North Fork Clearwater, Idaho, U.S.	717	219	3,453	4,259	1974
Glen Canyon	Colorado, Ariz., U.S.	710	216	27,000	33,304	1964

NOTES: UC = under construction in 2004. n.a. = not available. China's Three Gorges dam on the Yangtze River, begun in 1993 and expected to be completed in 2009, will be the world's largest and highest dam. *Sources:* International Commission on Large Dams, *World Register of Dams 1998,* and other sources.

World's Largest Dams

Dam	Location	Volume (thousands)		Year completed
		cu m	cu yds	
Syncrude Tailings	Canada	540,000	706,320	UC
Chapetón	Argentina	296,200	387,410	UC
Pati	Argentina	238,180	274,026	UC
New Cornelia Tailings	United States	209,500	274,026	1973
Tarbela	Pakistan	121,720	159,210	1976
Kambaratinsk	Kyrgyzstan	112,200	146,758	UC
Fort Peck	Montana	96,049	125,628	1940
Lower Usuma	Nigeria	93,000	121,644	1990
Cipasang	Indonesia	90,000	117,720	UC
Atatürk	Turkey	84,500	110,522	1990
Yacyretá-Apipe	Paraguay/Argentina	81,000	105,944	1998
Guri (Raul Leoni)	Venezuela	78,000	102,014	1986
Rogun	Tajikistan	75,500	98,750	1985
Oahe	South Dakota	70,339	92,000	1963
Mangla	Pakistan	65,651	85,872	1967
Gardiner	Canada	65,440	85,592	1968
Afsluitdijk	Netherlands	63,400	82,927	1932
Oroville	California	59,639	78,008	1968
San Luis	California	59,405	77,700	1967
Nurek	Tajikistan	58,000	75,861	1980
Garrison	North Dakota	50,843	66,500	1956
Cochiti	New Mexico	48,052	62,850	1975
Tabka (Thawra)	Syria	46,000	60,168	1976
Bennett W.A.C.	Canada	43,733	57,201	1967
Tucuruí	Brazil	43,000	56,242	1984

NOTE: UC = under construction in 2004. China's Three Gorges dam on the Yangtze River, begun in 1993 and expected to be completed in 2009, will be the world's largest and highest dam. *Source:* Department of the Interior, Bureau of Reclamation and *International Water Power and Dam Construction.*

Famous Ship Canals

Name	Location	Length (mi)[1]	Width (ft)	Depth (ft)	Locks	Year opened
Albert	Belgium	80.0	53.0	16.5	6	1939
Amsterdam-Rhine	Netherlands	45.0	164.0	41.0	3	1952
Beaumont–Port Arthur	United States	40.0	200.0	34.0	—	1916
Canal du Midi	France	149.0	n.a.	n.a.	100	1692
Chesapeake and Delaware	United States	14.0	450.0	35.0	—	1829
Erie Canal	United States	363.0	70.0	7.0	82	1825
Grand Canal	China	1,085.0	n.a.	n.a.	n.a.	7th cent.
Göta Canal	Sweden	240.0	n.a.	n.a.	58	1832
Houston	United States	50.0	([2])	40.0	—	1914
Kiel (Nord-Ostsee Kanal)	Germany	61.3	144.0	36.0	4	1895
Panama	Panama	50.7	110.0	41.0	12	1914
St. Lawrence Seaway	U.S. and Canada	2,400.0[3]	([4])	—	—	1959
Montreal to Prescott	U.S. and Canada	11.5	80.0	30.0	7	1959
Welland	Canada	27.5	80.0	27.0	8	1931
Sault Ste. Marie	Canada	1.2	60.0	16.8	1	1895
Sault Ste. Marie	United States	1.6	80.0	25.0	4	1915
Suez	Egypt	119.9[5]	1197.5	68.9	—	1869

1. Statute miles. 2. 300–400 ft. 3. From Montreal to Duluth. 4. 442–550 ft; there are 11.5 mi of locks, 80 ft wide and 30 ft deep. 5. From Port Said lighthouse to entrance channel in Suez roads. *Source:* American Society of Civil Engineers.

Notable Tunnels

Name	Location	Length		Year completed
		mi	km	
Railroad, excluding subways				
Seikan	Tsugaru Strait, Japan	33.5	53.9	1988
Channel Tunnel[1]	English Channel, England-France	31.1	50.0	1994
Iwate Ichinohe	Tanigawa Mountains, Japan	16.0	25.8	2002
Daishimizu	Mikuni Mountain Range, Japan	13.8	22.2	1982
Simplon (I and II)	Alps, Switzerland-Italy	12.3	19.8	1906, 1922
Vereina	Klosters-Sagliains, Switzerland	11.8	19.1	1999
Shin Kanmon	Kanmon Strait, Japan	11.6	18.7	1975
Apennine	Bologna-Florence, Italy	11.5	18.5	1934
Qinling I-II	Qinling Mountains, China	11.5	18.5	2002
Rokkô	Rokkô Mountain, Japan	10.1	16.3	1972
Furka Base	Andermatt-Brig, Switzerland	9.6	15.4	1982
Haruna	Gunma Prefecture, Japan	9.5	15.4	1982
Severomuyskiy	Baikal-Amur, Russia	9.5	15.3	2001
Gorigamine	Takasaki-Nagano, Japan	9.4	15.2	1997
Monte Santomarco	Paola-Cosenza, Italy	9.3	15.0	1987
St. Gotthard	Swiss Alps	9.3	15.0	1882
Nakayama	Nakayama Pass, Hokkaido, Japan	9.2	14.9	1982
Lötschberg	Swiss Alps	9.1	14.6	1913
Mount MacDonald	Rogers Pass, Glacier Nat'l Park, Canada	9.1	14.6	1989
Romeriksporten	Oslo-Gardermoen airport, Norway	9.1	14.6	1999
Vehicular				
Laerdal	Laerdal–Aurland, Norway	15.2	24.5	2000
St. Gotthard	Alps, Switzerland	10.2	16.4	1980
Arlberg	Austrian Alps	8.7	14.0	1979
Fréjus	French Alps	8.0	12.9	1980
Mt. Blanc	Alps, France-Italy	7.0	11.3	1965
Gudvanga	Bergen-Oslo, Norway	7.1	11.4	1991
Folgefonn	Odda-Gjerde, Norway	6.9	11.2	2001
Kanetsu (southbound)	Tokyo-Niigata, Japan	6.9	11.0	1991
Kanetsu (northbound)	Tokyo-Niigata, Japan	6.8	10.9	1985
Gran Sasso d'Italia (E and W)	Abruzzo, Italy	6.3	10.2	1984, 1995
Aqualine Expressway	Tokyo Bay, Japan	5.9	9.5	1997
Mt. Ena	Japan Alps, Japan	5.3	8.5	1976[2]
Westerschelde	Zeeuwsch-Vlaanderen–Zuid-Beveland, Netherlands	4.1	6.6	2003
Great St. Bernard	Alps, Switzerland-Italy	3.4	5.5	1964

1. Three-tunnel system including two rail tunnels (one carries passengers from England to France, the other from France to England) and a central service tunnel. 2. Parallel tunnel begun in 1976. *Sources:* American Society of Civil Engineers and International Bridge, Tunnel & Turnpike Association, and The World's Longest Tunnel Page, Web: home.no.net/lotsberg/.

See also World's Largest Subway Systems, p. 612.

Conversion Factors

To change	To	Multiply by	To change	To	Multiply by
acres	square feet	43,560	liters	quarts (liquid)	1.0567
acres	square miles	.001562	meters	feet	3.2808
atmospheres	cms. of mercury	76	meters	miles	.0006214
Btu	kilowatt-hour	.0002931	meters	yards	1.0936
Btu/hour	watts	.2931	metric tons	tons (long)	.9842
bushels	cubic inches	2150.4	metric tons	tons (short)	1.1023
centimeters	inches	.3937	miles	kilometers	1.6093
centimeters	feet	.03281	miles	feet	5280
cubic feet	cubic meters	.0283	miles (nautical)	miles (statute)	1.1516
cubic meters	cubic feet	35.3145	miles (statute)	miles (nautical)	.8684
cubic meters	cubic yards	1.3079	miles/hour	feet/minute	88
cubic yards	cubic meters	.7646	millimeters	inches	.0394
fathoms	feet	6.0	ounces (avdp)	grams	28.3495
feet	meters	.3048	ounces	pounds	.0625
feet	miles (nautical)	.0001645	ounces (troy)	ounces (avdp)	1.09714
feet	miles (statute)	.0001894	pecks	liters	8.8096
feet/second	miles/hour	.6818	pints (dry)	liters	.5506
furlongs	feet	660.0	pints (liquid)	liters	.4732
furlongs	miles	.125	pounds (ap or troy)	kilograms	.3732
gallons (U.S.)	liters	3.7853	pounds (avdp)	kilograms	.4536
grains	grams	.0648	pounds	ounces	16
grams	ounces (avdp)	.0353	quarts (dry)	liters	1.1012
grams	pounds	.002205	quarts (liquid)	liters	.9463
hectares	acres	2.4710	radians	degrees	57.30
hectoliters	bushels (U.S.)	2.8378	rods	meters	5.029
horsepower	watts	745.7	rods	feet	16.5
horsepower	Btu/hour	2,547	square feet	square meters	.0929
hours	days	.04167	square kilometers	square miles	.3861
inches	millimeters	25.4000	square meters	square feet	10.7639
inches	centimeters	2.5400	square miles	square kilometers	2.5900
kilograms	pounds (avdp or troy)	2.2046	square yards	square meters	.8361
kilometers	miles	.6214	tons (long)	metric tons	1.016
kilowatt-hour	Btu	3412	tons (short)	metric tons	.9072
knots	nautical miles/hour	1.0	tons (long)	pounds	2240
knots	statute miles/hour	1.151	tons (short)	pounds	2000
liters	gallons (U.S.)	.2642	watts	Btu/hour	3.4121
liters	pints (dry)	1.8162	watts	horsepower	.001341
liters	pints (liquid)	2.1134	yards	meters	.9144
liters	quarts (dry)	.9081	yards	miles	.0005682

NOTE: avdp = avoirdupois weight, ap = apothecaries' weight. *See also* p.539.

Fahrenheit and Celsius (Centigrade) Scales

°Celsius	°Fahrenheit	°Celsius	°Fahrenheit
−273.15	−459.67	30	86
−250	−418	35	95
−200	−328	40	104
−150	−238	45	113
−100	−148	50	122
−50	−58	55	131
−40	−40	60	140
−30	−22	65	149
−20	−4	70	158
−10	14	75	167
0	32	80	176
5	41	85	185
10	50	90	194
15	59	95	203
20	68	100	212
25	77		

Zero on the Fahrenheit scale represents the temperature produced by the mixing of equal weights of snow and common salt.

	°Fahrenheit	°Celsius
Boiling point of water	212°	100°
Freezing point of water	32°	0°
Absolute zero	−459.6°	−273.1°

Absolute zero is theoretically the lowest possible temperature, the point at which all molecular motion would cease.

To convert Fahrenheit to Celsius (Centigrade), subtract 32 and divide by 1.8.

To convert Celsius (Centigrade) to Fahrenheit, multiply by 1.8 and add 32.

Cardinal, Ordinal, and Nominal Numbers

Cardinal numbers, known as the "counting numbers," indicate quantity. **Ordinal numbers** indicate the order or rank of things in a set (e.g., sixth in line; fourth place). **Nominal numbers** name or identify something (e.g., a zip code or a player on a team.) They do not show quantity or rank.

Roman Numerals

Roman numerals are expressed by letters of the alphabet and are rarely used today except for formality or variety. There are four basic principles for reading Roman numerals:

1. A letter repeated once or twice repeats its value that many times (XXX = 30, CC = 200, etc.).
2. One or more letters placed after another letter of greater value increases the greater value by the amount of the smaller (VI = 6, LXX = 70, MCC = 1200, etc.).
3. A letter placed before another letter of greater value decreases the greater value by the amount

of the smaller (IV = 4, XC = 90, CM = 900, etc.). Several rules apply for subtraction: (a) only subtract powers of ten (I, X, or C, but not V or L); (b) only subtract one number from another; (c) do not subtract a number from one that is more than 10 times greater (that is, you can subtract 1 from 10 [IX] but not from 20—there is no such number as IXX).

4. A bar placed on top of a letter or string of letters increases the numeral's value by 1,000 times (XV = 15, $\overline{XV}$ = 15,000).

Letter	Value	Letter	Value	Letter	Value	Letter	Value	Letter	Value
I	1	VII	7	XL	40	C	100	$\overline{C}$	100,000
II	2	VIII	8	L	50	D	500	$\overline{D}$	500,000
III	3	IX	9	LX	60	M	1,000	$\overline{M}$	1,000,000
IV	4	X	10	LXX	70	$\overline{V}$	5,000		
V	5	XX	20	LXXX	80	$\overline{X}$	10,000		
VI	6	XXX	30	XC	90	$\overline{L}$	50,000		

Mean and Median

The arithmetic mean, also called the average, of a series of quantities is obtained by finding the sum of the quantities and dividing it by the number of quantities. In the series 1, 3, 5, 18, 19, 20, 25, the mean or average is 13—in other words, 91 divided by 7.

The median of a series is that point which so divides it that half the quantities are on one side, half on the other. In the above series, the median is 18.

The median often better expresses the common-run, since it is not, as is the mean, affected by an excessively high or low figure. In the series 1, 3, 4, 7, 55, the median of 4 is a truer expression of the common-run than is the mean of 14.

Prime Numbers between 1 and 1,000

2	3	5	7	11	13	17	19	23
29	31	37	41	43	47	53	59	61	67
71	73	79	83	89	97	101	103	107	109
113	127	131	137	139	149	151	157	163	167
173	179	181	191	193	197	199	211	223	227
229	233	239	241	251	257	263	269	271	277
281	283	293	307	311	313	317	331	337	347
349	353	359	367	373	379	383	389	397	401
409	419	421	431	433	439	443	449	457	461
463	467	479	487	491	499	503	509	521	523
541	547	557	563	569	571	577	587	593	599
601	607	613	617	619	631	641	643	647	653
659	661	673	677	683	691	701	709	719	727
733	739	743	751	757	761	769	773	787	797
809	811	821	823	827	829	839	853	857	859
863	877	881	883	887	907	911	919	929	937
941	947	953	967	971	977	983	991	997	(1009)

World's Largest Known Prime Number

The largest currently known prime, $2^{24036583} - 1$, was found by Josh Findley through the Great Internet Mersenne Prime Search (GIMPS) project on May 15, 2004. It is 7,235,733 digits long, almost one million digits more than the previous record

holder. The Electronic Frontier Foundation is offering a $100,000 award to whomever is the first to find a prime number with at least ten million digits; it seems likely that this will be claimed within the next few years.

Portraits and Designs of U.S. Paper Currency

Currency[1]	Portrait	Design on back	Currency[1]	Portrait	Design on back
$1	Washington	ONE between obverse and reverse of Great Seal of U.S.	$50[6]	Grant	U.S. Capitol
$2[2]	Jefferson	Monticello	$100[7]	Franklin	Independence Hall
$2[3]	Jefferson	"The Signing of the Declaration of Independence"	$500	McKinley	Ornate FIVE HUNDRED
			$1,000	Cleveland	Ornate ONE THOUSAND
$5[4]	Lincoln	Lincoln Memorial	$5,000	Madison	Ornate FIVE THOUSAND
$10[4]	Hamilton	U.S. Treasury Building	$10,000	Chase	Ornate TEN THOUSAND
$20[5]	Jackson	White House	$100,000[8]	Wilson	Ornate ONE HUNDRED THOUSAND

1. Denominations of $500 and higher were discontinued in 1969. 2. Discontinued in 1966. 3. New issue, April 1976. 4. New issue, May 2000. 5. New issue, fall 2003. 6. New issue, spring 2004. 7. New issue, March 1996. 8. For use only in transactions between Federal Reserve System and Treasury Department.

A Facelift for the $50 and Two New Nickels

In 2004, the U.S. Treasury unveiled its latest redesigned bill: the $50. The bill incorporates security features introduced in the 1990s, including a watermark and a security thread—both visible when the bill is held up to the light—and color-shifting ink.

Two new nickels were also introduced in 2004, the first new designs for the nickel since 1938. The new nickels commemorate the 200th anniversary of the Louisiana Purchase and the Lewis and Clark expedition.

New Quarters and Dollar Coin

The 50 State Quarters Program Act began in 1999 and is expected to run until 2008, with five new quarters released every year over ten years. The quarters are being released in the order that the states joined the union. 700 million copies of each quarter will be produced. Each quarter will feature a different state design on the back

In 2000, a new dollar coin, featuring the Shoshone guide Sacagawea, replaced the Susan B. Anthony coin, whose reserves are running low.

State	Date of statehood	Issued	Design
Delaware	Dec. 7, 1787	1999	Caesar Rodney's horseback ride
Pennsylvania	Dec. 12, 1787	1999	Commonwealth statue, keystone, and outline of state
New Jersey	Dec. 18, 1787	1999	Washington crossing the Delaware River
Georgia	Jan. 2, 1788	1999	Peach, Live Oak, and outline of state
Connecticut	Jan. 9, 1788	1999	The Charter Oak
Massachusetts	Feb. 6, 1788	2000	Minuteman statue and outline of state
Maryland	April 28, 1788	2000	Maryland Statehouse and White Oak
South Carolina	May 23, 1788	2000	Palmetto tree, Carolina wren, and Yellow Jessamine
New Hampshire	June 21, 1788	2000	Old Man of the Mountain rock formation
Virginia	June 25, 1788	2000	First three ships to Jamestown
New York	July 26, 1788	2001	Statue of Liberty, state outline, the words, "Gateway to Freedom," 11 stars
North Carolina	Nov. 21, 1789	2001	First flight at Kitty Hawk
Rhode Island	May 29, 1790	2001	A sailboat on the open sea, commemorating the "Ocean State"
Vermont	March 4, 1791	2001	Camel's Hump Mountain, maple trees with sap buckets
Kentucky	June 1, 1792	2001	Federal Hill, or "My Old Kentucky Home," race horse behind a fence
Tennessee	June 1, 1796	2002	Fiddle, trumpet, guitar, and musical score
Ohio	March 1, 1803	2002	Early airplane, astronaut, and state outline
Louisiana	April 30, 1812	2002	Pelican, horn with musical notes, and outline of Louisiana Purchase
Indiana	Dec. 11, 1816	2002	Race car and state outline
Mississippi	Dec. 10, 1817	2002	Blossoms and leaves of two magnolias
Illinois	Dec. 3, 1818	2003	Abraham Lincoln and state outline
Alabama	Dec. 14, 1819	2003	Helen Keller, with name in English and Braille
Maine	March 15, 1820	2003	The Pemaquid Point Light House and a schooner
Missouri	Aug. 10, 1821	2003	Lewis and Clark travelling down the Missouri River
Arkansas	June 15, 1836	2003	Rice stalks, a diamond, and a mallard, representing the "Natural State"
Michigan	Jan. 26, 1837	2004	Outline of state and Great Lakes
Florida	March 3, 1845	2004	Galleon, space shuttle, strip of land with palm trees, "Gateway to Discovery"
Texas	Dec. 29, 1845	2004	State outline and star encircled by lariat, representing the "Lone Star State"
Iowa	Dec. 28, 1846	2004	One-room schoolhouse, based on a Grant Wood painting
Wisconsin	May 29, 1848	2004	Cow's head, cheese, corn, and "Forward" motto

Customary U.S. Weights and Measures

Linear Measure

12 inches (in.) = 1 foot (ft.)
3 feet = 1 yard (yd)
5½ yards = 1 rod (rd), pole, or perch (16½ ft.)
40 rods = 1 furlong (fur) = 220 yds = 660 ft.
8 furlongs = 1 statute mile (mi.) = 1,760 yds
= 5,280 ft.
3 land miles = 1 league
5,280 feet = 1 statute or land mile
6,076.11549 feet = 1 international nautical mile

Area Measure

144 square inches = 1 sq ft.
9 square feet = 1 sq yd = 1,296 sq in.
30¼ square yards = 1 sq rd = 272¼ sq ft.
160 square rods = 1 acre = 4,840 sq yds
= 43,560 sq ft.
640 acres = 1 sq mi.
1 mile square = 1 section (of land)
6 miles square = 1 township = 36 sections
= 36 sq mi.

Cubic Measure

1,728 cubic inches = 1 cu ft.
27 cubic feet = 1 cu yd

Liquid Measure

When necessary to distinguish the liquid pint or quart from the dry pint or quart, the word "liquid" or the abbreviation "liq" should be used in combination with the name or abbreviation of the liquid unit.

4 gills (gi) = 1 pint (pt) (= 28.875 cu in.)
2 pints = 1 quart (qt) (= 57.75 cu in.)
4 quarts = 1 gallon (gal) (= 231 cu in.)
= 8 pts = 32 gills

Apothecaries' Fluid Measure

60 minims (min.) = 1 fluid dram (fl dr) (= 0.2256 cu in.)
8 fluid drams = 1 fluid ounce (fl oz) (= 1.8047 cu in.)
16 fluid ounces = 1 pt (= 28.875 cu in.) = 128 fl drs
2 pints = 1 qt (= 57.75 cu in.) = 32 fl oz
= 256 fl drs
4 quarts = 1 gal (= 231 cu in.) = 128 fl oz
= 1,024 fl drs

Avoirdupois Weight

When necessary to distinguish the avoirdupois dram from the apothecaries' dram, or to distinguish the avoirdupois dram or ounce from the fluid dram or ounce, or to distinguish the avoirdupois ounce or pound from the troy or apothecaries' ounce or pound, the word "avoirdupois" or the abbreviation "avdp" should be used in combination with the name or abbreviation of the avoirdupois unit. (The "grain" is the same in avoirdupois, troy, and apothecaries' weights.)

$27\frac{11}{32}$ grains = 1 dram (dr)
16 drams = 1 oz = $437\frac{1}{2}$ grains
16 ounces = 1 lb = 256 drams = 7,000 grains
100 pounds = 1 hundredweight (cwt)[1]
20 hundredweights = 1 ton (tn) = 2,000 lbs[1]

In "gross" or "long" measure, the following values are recognized:

112 pounds = 1 gross or long cwt[1]
20 gross or long hundredweights = 1 gross or long ton = 2,240 lbs[1]

1. When the terms "hundredweight" and "ton" are used unmodified, they are commonly understood to mean the 100-pound hundredweight and the 2,000-pound ton, respectively; these units may be designated "net" or "short" when necessary to distinguish them from the corresponding units in gross or long measure.

Dry Measure

When necessary to distinguish the dry pint or quart from the liquid pint or quart, the word "dry" should be used in combination with the name or abbreviation of the dry unit.

2 pints = 1 qt (= 67.2006 cu in.)
8 quarts = 1 peck (pk) (= 537.605 cu in.) = 16 pts
4 pecks = 1 bushel (bu) (= 2,150.42 cu in.) = 32 qts

Apothecaries' Weight

20 grains = 1 scruple (s ap)
3 scruples = 1 dram apothecaries' (dr ap) = 60 grains
8 drams apothecaries' = 1 ounce apothecaries' (oz ap) = 24 scruples = 480 grains
12 ounces apothecaries' = 1 pound apothecaries' (lb ap) = 96 drams apothecaries' = 288 scruples = 5,760 grains

Units of Circular Measure

Second (") = —
Minute (') = 60 seconds
Degree (°) = 60 minutes
Right angle = 90 degrees
Straight angle = 180 degrees
Circle = 360 degrees

Troy Weight

24 grains = 1 pennyweight (dwt)
20 pennyweights = 1 ounce troy (oz t) = 480 grains
12 ounces troy = 1 pound troy (lb t) = 240 pennyweights = 5,760 grains

Gunter's or Surveyor's Chain Measure

7.92 inches = 1 link (li)
100 links = 1 chain (ch) = 4 rods = 66 ft.
80 chains = 1 statute mile = 320 rods = 5,280 ft.

The International System (Metric)

Source: Department of Commerce, National Bureau of Standards.

The International System of Units is a modernized version of the metric system, established by international agreement, that provides a logical and interconnected framework for all measurements in science, industry, and commerce. The system is built on a foundation of seven basic units, and all other units are derived from them. (Use of metric weights and measures was legalized in the United States in 1866, and our customary units of weights and measures are defined in terms of the meter and kilogram.)

Length. Meter. Up until 1983, the meter was defined as 1,650,763.73 wavelengths in a vacuum of the orange-red line of the spectrum of krypton-86. Since then, it is equal to the distance traveled by light in a vacuum in 1/299,792,45 of a second.

Time. Second. The second is defined as the duration of 9,192,631,770 cycles of the radiation associated with a specified transition of the cesium-133 atom.

Mass. Kilogram. The standard for the kilogram is a cylinder of platinum-iridium alloy kept by the International Bureau of Weights and Measures at Paris. A duplicate at the National Bureau of Standards serves as the mass standard for the United States. The kilogram is the only base unit still defined by a physical object.

Temperature. Kelvin. The kelvin is defined as the fraction 1/273.16 of the thermodynamic temperature of the triple point of water; that is, the point at which water forms an interface of solid, liquid, and vapor. This is defined as 0.01°C on the Centigrade or Celsius scale and 32.02°F on the Fahrenheit scale. The temperature 0 K is called "absolute zero."

Electric Current. Ampere. The ampere is defined as that current that, if maintained in each of two long parallel wires separated by one meter in free space, would produce a force between the two wires (due to their magnetic fields) of 2×10^{-7} newton for each meter of length. (A newton is the unit of force that when applied to one kilogram mass would experience an acceleration of one meter per second per second.)

Luminous Intensity. Candela. The candela is defined as the luminous intensity of 1/600,000 of a square meter of a cavity at the temperature of freezing platinum (2,042°K).

Amount of Substance. Mole. The mole is the amount of substance of a system that contains as many elementary entities as there are atoms in 0.012 kilogram of carbon-12.

Tables of Metric Weights and Measures

Linear Measure

10 millimeters (mm) = 1 centimeter (cm)
10 centimeters = 1 decimeter (dm) = 100 millimeters
10 decimeters = 1 meter (m) = 1,000 millimeters
10 meters = 1 dekameter (dam)
10 dekameters = 1 hectometer (hm) = 100 meters
10 hectometers = 1 kilometer (km) = 1,000 meters

Volume Measure

10 milliliters (ml) = 1 centiliter (cl)
10 centiliters = 1 deciliter (dl) = 100 milliliters
10 deciliters = 1 liter (l) = 1,000 milliliters
10 liters = 1 dekaliter (dal)
10 dekaliters = 1 hectoliter (hl) = 100 liters
10 hectoliters = 1 kiloliter (kl) = 1,000 liters

Area Measure

100 square millimeters (mm^2) = 1 sq centimeter (cm^2)
10,000 square centimeters = 1 sq meter (m^2) = 1,000,000 sq millimeters
100 square meters = 1 are (a)
100 ares = 1 hectare (ha) = 10,000 sq meters
100 hectares = 1 sq kilometer (km^2) = 1,000,000 sq meters

Cubic Measure

1,000 cubic millimeters (mm^3) = 1 cu centimeter (cm^3)
1,000 cubic centimeters = 1 cu decimeter (dm^3) = 1,000,000 cu millimeters
1,000 cubic decimeters = 1 cu meter (m^3) = 1 stere = 1,000,000 cu centimeters = 1,000,000,000 cu millimeters

Weight

10 milligrams (mg) = 1 centigram (cg)
10 centigrams = 1 decigram (dg) = 100 milligrams
10 decigrams = 1 gram (g) = 1,000 milligrams
10 grams = 1 dekagram (dag)

10 dekagrams = 1 hectogram (hg) = 100 grams
10 hectograms = 1 kilogram (kg) = 1,000 grams
1,000 kilograms = 1 metric ton (t)

Metric and U.S. Equivalents

1 angstrom[1] (light wave measurement)	0.1 nanometer 0.000 000 1 millimeter 0.000 000 004 inch
1 cable's length	120 fathoms 720 feet 219.456 meters
1 centimeter	0.3937 inch
1 decimeter	3.937 inches
1 dekameter	32.808 feet
1 fathom	6 feet 1.8288 meters
1 foot	0.3048 meter
1 furlong	10 chains (surveyor's) 660 feet 220 yards ⅛ statute mile 201.168 meters
1 inch	2.54 centimeters
1 kilometer	0.621 mile
1 league (land)	3 statute miles 4.828 kilometers
1 meter	39.37 inches 1.094 yards
1 micrometer	0.001 millimeter 0.000 039 37 inch
1 mil	0.001 inch 0.025 4 millimeter
1 mile (statute or land)	5,280 feet 1.609 kilometers
1 mile (nautical international)	1.852 kilometers 1.151 statute miles 0.999 U.S. nautical miles
1 millimeter	0.03937 inch
1 nanometer	0.001 micrometer or 0.000 000 039 37 inch
1 point (typography)	0.013 837 inch ¹⁄₇₂ inch (approximately) 0.351 millimeter
1 rod, pole, or perch	16½ feet 5.0292 meters
1 yard	0.9144 meter

Areas or Surfaces

1 acre	43,560 square feet 4,840 square yards 0.405 hectare
1 are	119.599 square yards 0.025 acre
1 hectare	2.471 acres
1 square centimeter	0.155 square inch
1 square decimeter	15.5 square inches
1 square foot	929.030 square centimeters
1 square inch	6.4516 square centimeters
1 square kilometer	0.386 square mile 247.105 acres
1 square meter	1.196 square yards 10.764 square feet
1 square mile	258.999 hectares
1 square millimeter	0.002 square inch
1 square rod, square pole or square perch	25.293 square meters
1 square yard	0.836 square meters

Capacities or Volumes

1 barrel, liquid	31 to 42 gallons[2]	1 quart, liquid (U.S.)	57.75 cubic inches
			0.946 liter
1 bushel (U.S.) struck	2,150.42 cubic inches		0.833 British quart
measure[3]	35.238 liters	1 quart (British)	69.354 cubic inches
1 bushel, heaped	2,747.715 cubic inches		1.032 U.S. dry quarts
(U.S.)	1.278 bushels, struck measure[4]		1.201 U.S. liquid quarts
1 cord (firewood)	128 cubic feet	1 tablespoon,	3 teaspoons
1 cubic centimeter	0.061 cubic inch	measuring	4 fluid drams
1 cubic decimeter	61.024 cubic inches		½ fluid ounce
1 cubic foot	7.481 gallons	1 teaspoon,	⅓ tablespoon
	28.316 cubic decimeters	measuring	1⅓ fluid drams
1 cubic inch	0.554 fluid ounce	1 carat	200 milligrams
	4.433 fluid drams		3.086 grains
	16.387 cubic centimeters	1 dram, apothecaries'	60 grains
1 cubic meter	1.308 cubic yards		3.888 grams
1 cubic yard	0.765 cubic meter	1 dram, avoirdupois	27 11⁄32 (=27.344) grains
1 cup, measuring	8 fluid ounces		1.772 grams
	½ liquid pint	1 grain	64.798 91 milligrams
1 dram, fluid or liquid	⅛ fluid ounces	1 gram	15.432 grains
(U.S.)	0.226 cubic inch		0.035 avoirdupois ounce
	3.697 milliliters	1 kilogram	2.205 pounds
	1.041 British fluid drachms	1 microgram (µg—	0.000 001 gram
1 dekaliter	2.642 gallons	the Greek letter mu	
	1.135 pecks	in combination with	
1 gallon (U.S.)	231 cubic inches	the letter g)	
	3.785 liters	1 milligram	0.015 grain
	0.833 British gallon	1 ounce, avoirdupois	437.5 grains
	128 U.S. fluid ounces		0.911 troy or apothecaries' ounce
1 gallon (British	277.42 cubic inches		28.350 grams
Imperial)	1.201 U.S. gallons	1 ounce, troy or	480 grains
	4.546 liters	apothecaries'	1.097 avoirdupois ounces
	160 British fluid ounces		31.103 grams
1 hectoliter	26.418 gallons	1 pennyweight	1.555 grams
	2.838 bushels	1 point	0.01 carat
1 liter	1.057 liquid quarts		2 milligrams
	0.908 dry quart	1 pound, avoirdupois	7,000 grains
	61.024 cubic inches		1.215 troy or apothecaries'
1 milliliter	0.271 fluid dram		pounds
	16.231 minims		453.592 37 grams
	0.061 cubic inch	1 pound, troy or	5,760 grains
1 ounce, fluid or liquid	1.805 cubic inch	apothecaries'	0.823 avoirdupois pound
(U.S.)	29.574 milliliters		373.242 grams
	1.041 British fluid ounces	1 ton, gross or long[5]	2,240 pounds
1 peck	8.810 liters		1.12 net tons
1 pint, dry	33.600 cubic inches		1.016 metric tons
	0.551 liter	1 ton, metric	2,204.623 pounds
1 pint, liquid	28.875 cubic inches		0.984 gross ton
	0.473 liter		1.102 net tons
1 quart, dry (U.S.)	67.201 cubic inches	1 ton, net or short	2,000 pounds
	1.101 liters		0.893 gross ton
	0.969 British quart		0.907 metric ton

1. The angstrom is basically defined as 10^{-10} meter. 2. There is a variety of "barrels" established by law or usage. For example, federal taxes on fermented liquors are based on a barrel of 31 gallons; many state laws fix the "barrel for liquids" at 31½ gallons; one state fixes a 36-gallon barrel for cistern measurement; federal law recognizes a 40-gallon barrel for "proof spirits"; by custom, 42 gallons compose a barrel of crude oil or petroleum products for statistical purposes, and this equivalent is recognized "for liquids" by four states. 3. "Struck measure" refers to a struck, or level, bushel. It is the only official bushel measure in the UK. 4. Frequently recognized as 1¼ bushels, struck measure. 5. The gross or long ton is used commercially in the United States to only a limited extent, usually in restricted industrial fields. These units are the same as the British "ton."

Definitions of Gold Terminology

The term "fineness" defines a gold content in parts per thousand. For example, a gold nugget containing 885 parts of pure gold, 100 parts of silver, and 15 parts of copper would be considered 885-fine.

The word "karat" indicates the proportion of solid gold in an alloy based on a total of 24 parts. Thus, 14-karat (14K) gold indicates a composition of 14 parts of gold and 10 parts of other metals.

The term "gold-filled" is used to describe articles of jewelry made of base metal that are covered on one or more surfaces with a layer of gold alloy. No article having a gold alloy portion of less than one twentieth by weight may be marked "gold-filled." Articles may be marked "rolled gold plate" provided the proportional fraction and fineness designations are also shown.

Electroplated jewelry items carrying at least 7 millionths of an inch of gold on significant surfaces may be labeled "electroplate." Plate thicknesses less than this may be marked "gold-flashed" or "gold-washed."

Bolts and Screws: Conversion from Fractions of an Inch to Millimeters

Inch	mm	Inch	mm	Inch	mm	Inch	mm
1/64	0.40	17/64	6.75	33/64	13.10	49/64	19.45
1/32	0.79	9/32	7.14	17/32	13.50	25/32	19.84
3/64	1.19	19/64	7.54	35/64	13.90	51/64	20.24
1/16	1.59	5/16	7.94	9/16	14.29	13/16	20.64
5/64	1.98	21/64	8.33	37/64	14.69	53/64	21.03
3/32	2.38	11/32	8.73	19/32	15.08	27/32	21.43
7/64	2.78	23/64	9.13	39/64	15.48	55/64	21.83
1/8	3.18	3/8	9.53	5/8	15.88	7/8	22.23
9/64	3.57	25/64	9.92	41/64	16.27	57/64	22.62
5/32	3.97	13/32	10.32	21/32	16.67	29/32	23.02
11/64	4.37	27/64	10.72	43/64	17.06	59/64	23.42
3/16	4.76	7/16	11.11	11/16	17.46	15/16	23.81
13/64	5.16	29/64	11.51	45/64	17.86	61/64	24.21
7/32	5.56	15/32	11.91	23/32	18.26	31/32	24.61
15/64	5.95	31/64	12.30	47/64	18.65	63/64	25.00
1/4	6.35	1/2	12.70	3/4	19.05	1	25.40

Cooking Measurement Equivalents

1 tablespoon (tbsp) = 3 teaspoons (tsp)
1/16 cup = 1 tablespoon
1/8 cup = 2 tablespoons
1/6 cup = 2 tablespoons + 2 teaspoons
1/4 cup = 4 tablespoons
1/3 cup = 5 tablespoons + 1 teaspoon
3/8 cup = 6 tablespoons
1/2 cup = 8 tablespoons
2/3 cup = 10 tablespoons + 2 teaspoons
3/4 cup = 12 tablespoons

1 cup = 48 teaspoons
1 cup = 16 tablespoons
8 fluid ounces (fl oz) = 1 cup
1 pint (pt) = 2 cups
1 quart (qt) = 2 pints
4 cups = 1 quart
1 gallon (gal) = 4 quarts
16 ounces (oz) = 1 pound (lb)
1 milliliter (ml) = 1 cubic centimeter (cc)
1 inch (in) = 2.54 centimeters (cm)

Source: United States Dept. of Agriculture (USDA).

U.S.–Metric Cooking Conversions

U.S. to Metric

Capacity		Weight	
1/5 teaspoon	1 milliliter	1 oz	28 grams
1 teaspoon	5 ml	1 pound	454 grams
1 tablespoon	15 ml		
1 fluid oz	30 ml		
1/5 cup	47 ml		
1 cup	237 ml		
2 cups (1 pint)	473 ml		
4 cups (1 quart)	.95 liter		
4 quarts (1 gal.)	3.8 liters		

Metric to U.S.

Capacity		Weight	
1 milliliter	1/5 teaspoon	1 gram	.035 ounce
5 ml	1 teaspoon	100 grams	3.5 ounces
15 ml	1 tablespoon	500 grams	1.10 pounds
100 ml	3.4 fluid oz	1 kilogram	2.205 pounds
240 ml	1 cup		35 oz
1 liter	34 fluid oz		
	4.2 cups		
	2.1 pints		
	1.06 quarts		
	0.26 gallon		

Prefixes and Multiples

Prefix	Symbol	Equivalent	Multiple/submultiple	Prefix	Symbol	Equivalent	Multiple/submultiple
yocto	y	septillionth part	10^{-24}	deka	da	tenfold	10
zepto	z	sextillionth part	10^{-21}	hecto	h	hundredfold	10^2
atto	a	quintillionth part	10^{-18}	kilo	k	thousandfold	10^3
femto	f	quadrillionth part	10^{-15}	mega	M	millionfold	10^6
pico	p	trillionth part	10^{-12}	giga	G	billionfold	10^9
nano	n	billionth part	10^{-9}	tera	T	trillionfold	10^{12}
micro	µ	millionth part	10^{-6}	peta	P	quadrillionfold	10^{15}
milli	m	thousandth part	10^{-3}	exa	E	quintillionfold	10^{18}
centi	c	hundredth part	10^{-2}	zetta	Z	sextillionfold	10^{21}
deci	d	tenth part	10^{-1}	yotta	Y	septillionfold	10^{24}

Common Formulas

CIRCUMFERENCE
Circle: $C = \pi d$, in which π is 3.1416 and d the diameter.

AREA
Triangle: $A = \dfrac{ab}{2}$, in which a is the base and b the height.

Square: $A = a^2$, in which a is one of the sides.

Rectangle: $A = ab$, in which a is the base and b the height.

Trapezoid: $A = \dfrac{h(a+b)}{2}$, in which h is the height, a the longer parallel side, and b the shorter.

Regular pentagon: $A = 1.720a^2$, in which a is one of the sides.

Regular hexagon: $A = 2.598a^2$, in which a is one of the sides.

Regular octagon: $A = 4.828a^2$, in which a is one of the sides.

Circle: $A = \pi r^2$, in which π is 3.1416 and r the radius.

VOLUME
Cube: $V = a^3$, in which a is one of the edges.

Rectangular prism: $V = abc$, in which a is the length, b is the width, and c the depth.

Pyramid: $V = \dfrac{Ah}{3}$, in which A is the area of the base and h the height.

Cylinder: $V = \pi r^2 h$, in which π is 3.1416, r the radius of the base, and h the height.

Cone: $V = \dfrac{\pi r^2 h}{3}$, in which π is 3.1416, r the radius of the base, and h the height.

Sphere: $V = \dfrac{4 \pi r^3}{3}$, in which π is 3.1416 and r the radius.

TEMPERATURE SCALES
Degrees Fahrenheit to Degrees Celsius:
$$T_C = \frac{5}{9}(T_F - 32)$$

Degrees Celsius to Degrees Fahrenheit:
$$T_F = \frac{9}{5} T_C + 32$$

Degrees Celsius to Kelvin:
$$T_K = T_C + 273.15$$

MISCELLANEOUS
Distance in feet traveled by falling body:
$d = 16t^2$, in which t is the time in seconds.

Speed of sound in feet per second through any given temperature of air:
$$V = \frac{1087 \sqrt{273 + t}}{16.52}$$, in which t is the temperature Celsius.

Cost in cents of operation of electrical device:
$$C = \frac{Wtc}{1000}$$, in which W is the number of watts, t the time in hours, and c the cost in cents per kilowatt-hour.

Conversion of matter into energy (Einstein's Theorem): $E = mc^2$, in which E is the energy in ergs, m the mass of the matter in grams, and c the speed of light in centimeters per second:
$$(c^2 = 9 \times 10^{20})$$

Decimal Equivalents of Common Fractions

1/2	.5000	1/10	.1000	2/7	.2857	3/11	.2727	5/9	.5556	7/11	.6364
1/3	.3333	1/11	.0909	2/9	.2222	4/5	.8000	5/11	.4545	7/12	.5833
1/4	.2500	1/12	.0833	2/11	.1818	4/7	.5714	5/12	.4167	8/9	.8889
1/5	.2000	1/16	.0625	3/4	.7500	4/9	.4444	6/7	.8571	8/11	.7273
1/6	.1667	1/32	.0313	3/5	.6000	4/11	.3636	6/11	.5455	9/10	.9000
1/7	.1429	1/64	.0156	3/7	.4286	5/6	.8333	7/8	.8750	9/11	.8182
1/8	.1250	2/3	.6667	3/8	.3750	5/7	.7143	7/9	.7778	10/11	.9091
1/9	.1111	2/5	.4000	3/10	.3000	5/8	.6250	7/10	.7000	11/12	.9167

First Aid for Crossword Puzzlers

We cannot begin to list all the odd words you might encounter in your daily and Sunday crossword puzzles, for such words run into the thousands. But we have tried to include those that turn up most frequently, as well as many others that should be of help to you when you are unable to go any further.

We do not guarantee that the definitions in your puzzle will be exactly the same as ours, although we have checked every word with a standard dictionary and have followed its definition.

In nearly every case, we have used as the key word the principal noun of the definition, rather than any adjective, adjective phrase, or noun used as an adjective. And, to simplify your searching, we have grouped the words according to the number of spaces you have to fill.

Words of Two Letters

Ambary, DA
And (French, Latin), ET
Article (Arabic), AL
  (French), LA, LE, UN
  (Spanish), EL, LA, UN
At the (French), AU
  (Spanish), AL
Behold, LO
Bird: Hawaiian, OO
Birthplace: Abraham's, UR
Bone, OS
Buddha, FO
Butterfly: Peacock, IO
Champagne, AY
Chaos, NU
Chief: Burmese, BO
Coin: Roman, AS
  Siamese, AT
Concerning, RE
Dialect: Chinese, WU
Double (Egy. relig.), KA
Drama: Japanese, NO
Egg (comb. form), OO
Esker, OS

Eye (Scottish), EE
Factor: Amplification, MU
Fifty (Greek), NU
Fish: Carplike, ID
Force, OD
Forty (Greek), MU
From (French, Latin, Spanish), DE
  (Latin prefix), AB
From the (French), DU
God: Babylonian, EA, ZU
  Egyptian sun, RA
  Hindu unknown, KA
  Semitic, EL
Goddess: Babylonian, AI
  Greek Earth, GE
Gold (heraldry), OR
Gulf: Arctic, OB
Heart (Egy. relig.), AB
Indian: South American, GE
King: Of Bashan, OG
Language: Artificial, RO
  Assamese, AO
Lava: Hawaiian, AA

Letter: Greek, MU, NU, PI, XI
  Hebrew, HE, PE
Lily: Palm, TI
Measure: Chinese, HO, HU, KO, LI, MU, PU, TO, TU
  Japanese, GO, JO, MO, RI, SE, TO
  Netherlands, EL
  Portuguese, PE
  Siamese, WA
  Swedish, AM
  Type, EM, EN
  Vietnamese, LY
Monk: Buddhist, BO
Month: Jewish, AB
Mouth, OS
Mulberry: Indian, AL
Native: Burmese, WA
Note: Of scale, DO, FA, MI, LA, RE, TI
Of (French, Latin, Spanish), DE
Of the (French), DU

One (Scottish), AE
Pagoda: Chinese, TA
Plant: East Indian fiber, DA
Ridge: Sandy, AS, OS
River: Russian, OB
Sloth: Three-toed, AI
Soul (Egy. relig.), BA
Sound: Hindu mystic, OM
Suffix: Comparative, ER
To the: French, AU
  Spanish, AL
Tree: Buddhist sacred, BO
Tribe: Assamese, AO
Type: Jumbled, PI
Weight: Chinese, LI
  Danish, ES
  Japanese, MO
  Roman, AS
  Vietnamese, TA
Whirlwind: Faeroe Is., OE
Yes (German), JA
  (Italian, Spanish), SI
  (Russian), DA

Words of Three Letters

Adherent, IST
Again, BIS
Age, ERA
Antelope: African, GNU, KOB
Apricot: Japanese, UME
Article (German), DAS, DEM, DEN, DER, DES, DIE, EIN
  (French), LES, UNE
  (Spanish), LAS, LOS, UNA
Banana: Polynesian, FEI
Barge, HOY
Bass: African, IYO
Beak, NEB, NIB
Beard: Grain, AWN
Beetle: June, DOR
Being, ENS
Berry: Hawthorn, HAW
Beverage: Hawaiian, AVA
Bird: Australian, EMU
  Crowlike, JAY
  Extinct, MOA
  Fabulous, ROC
  Frigate, IWA
  Parson, POE, TUE, TUI
  Sea, AUK
Blackbird, ANI, ANO
Born, NEE
Bronze: Roman, AES
Bugle: Yellow, IVA
By way of, VIA
Canton: Swiss, URI
Cap: Turkish, FEZ
Catnip, NEP
Character: In "Faerie Queene," UNA
Coin (Money of account):
  Afghan, PUL
  Albanian, LEK
  Bulgarian, LEV, LEW

French, ECU, SOU
Guyanese, BIT
Indian, PIE
Japanese, SEN, YEN
Korean, WON
Lithuanian, LIT
Macao, Timor, AVO
Palestinian, MIL
Persian, PUL
Peruvian, SOL
Rumanian, BAN, LEU, LEY
Scandinavian, ORE
Siamese, ATT
Collection: Facts, ANA
Commune: Belgian, ANS, ATH
  Netherlands, EDE, EPE
Community: Russian, MIR
Constellation: Southern, ARA
Contraction: Poetic, EEN, EER, OER
Covering: Apex of roof, EPI
Crab: Fiddler, UCA
Crag: Rocky, TOR
Cry: Crow, rook, raven, CAW
Cup: Wine, AMA
Cymbal, Oriental, TAL, ZEL
Disease: Silkworm, UJI
Division: Danish territorial, AMT
  Geologic, EON
Doctrine, ISM
Dowry, DOT
Dry (French), SEC
Dynasty: Chinese, CHI, HAN, SUI, WEI, YIN
Eagle: Sea, ERN
Earth (comb. form), GEO
Egg: Louse, NIT
Eggs: Fish, ROE
Emmet, ANT

Enzyme, ASE
Equal (comb. form), ISO
Extension: building, ELL
Far (comb. form), TEL
Farewell, AVE
Fiber: Palm, TAL
Finial, EPI
Fish: Carplike, IDE
  Pikelike, GAR
Flatfish, DAB
Fleur-de-lis, LIS, LYS
Food: Hawaiian, POI
Formerly, NEE
Friend (French), AMI
Game: Card, LOO
Garment: Camel-hair, ABA
Gateway, DAR
Gazelle: Tibetan, GOA
Genus: Ducks, AIX
  Grasses, POA
  Grasses (maize), ZEA
  Herbs or shrubs, IVA
  Lizards, UTA
  Rodents (incl. house mice), MUS
  Ruminants (incl. cattle), BOS
  Swine, SUS
Gibbon: Malay, LAR
God: Assyrian, SIN
  Babylonian, ABU, ANU, BEL, HEA, SIN, UTU
  Irish sea, LER
  Phrygian, MEN
  Polynesian, ORO
Goddess: Babylonian, AYA
  Etruscan, UNI
  Hindu, SRI, UMA, VAC
  Teutonic, RAN

Governor: Algerian, DEY
  Turkish, BEY
Grampus, ORC
Grape, UVA
Grass: Meadow, POA
Gypsy, ROM
Hail, AVE
Hare: Female, DOE
Hawthorn, HAW
Hay: Spread for drying, TED
Herb: Japanese, UDO
  Perennial, PIA
  Used for blue dye, WAD
Herd: Whales, GAM, POD
Hero: Spanish, CID
High (music), ALT
Honey (pharm.), MEL
Humorist: American, ADE
I (Latin), EGO
I love (Latin), AMO
Indian: Algonquin, FOX, SAC, WEA
  Chimakuan, HOH
  Keresan, SIA
  Mayan, MAM
  Shoshonean, UTE
  Siouan, KAW, OTO
  South American, ITE, ONA, URO, YAO
  Tierra del Fuego, ONA
  Wakashan, AHT
Ingot, PIG
Inlet: Narrow, RIA
Island: Cyclades, IOS
  Dodecanese, COS, KOS
  (French), ILE
  River, AIT
Jackdaw, DAW

John (Gaelic), IAN
Keelbill, ANI, ANO
Kiln, OST
King: British legendary, LUD
Kobold, NIS
Lace: To make, TAT
Lamprey, EEL
Language: Artificial, IDO
  Bantu, ILA
  Siamese, LAO, TAI
Leaf: Palm, OLA, OLE
Leaving, ORT
Left: Cause to turn, HAW
Letter: Greek, CHI, ETA, PHI,
  PSI, RHO, TAU
  Hebrew, MEM, NUN, SIN,
  TAV, VAU
Lettuce, COS
Life (comb. form), BIO
Lily: Palm, TOI
Lizard, EFT
Louse: Young, NIT
Love (Anglo-Irish), GRA
Lute: Oriental, TAR
Macaw: Brazilian, ARA
Marble, TAW
Match: Shooting (French), TIR
Meadow, LEA
Measure: Abyssinian, TAT
  Algerian, PIK
  Arabian, DEN, SAA
  Belgian, VAT
  Bulgarian, OKA, OKE
  Chinese, FEN, TOU, YIN
  Cloth, ELL
  Cyprus, OKA, OKE, PIK
  Czech, LAN, SAH
  Danish, FOD, MIL, POT
  Dominican Republic, ONA
  Dutch, old, AAM
  East Indian, KIT
  Egyptian, APT, HEN, PIK,
  ROB
  Electric, MHO, OHM
  Energy, ERG
  English, PIN
  Estonian, TUN
  French, POT
  German, AAM
  Greek, PIK
  Hebrew, CAB, HIN, KOR,
  LOG
  Hungarian, AKO
  Icelandic, FET
  Indian, GAZ, GUZ, JOW,
  KOS
  Japanese, BOO, CHO, KEN,
  RIN, SHO, SUN, TAN
  Malabar, ADY
  Metric (land), ARE
  Netherlands, KAN, KOP,
  MUD, VAT, ZAK
  Norwegian, FOT, POT
  Persian, GAZ, GUZ, MOU,
  ZAR, ZER
  Polish, CAL
  Rangoon, DHA, LAN
  Roman, PES, URN
  Russian, FUT, LOF
  Scottish, COP

Siamese, KEN, NIU, RAI,
  SAT, SEN, SOK, WAH, YOT
  Somaliland, TOP
  Spanish, PIE
  Straits Settlements, PAU,
  TUN
  Swedish, ALN, FOT, MIL,
  REF, TUM
  Swiss, POT
  Tunisian, SAA
  Turkish, OKA, OKE, PIK
  Vietnamese, GON, MAU,
  NGU, VUO, SAO, TAO, TAT
  Wire, MIL
  Württemberg, IMI
  Yarn, LEA
  Yugoslav, OKA, RIF
Milk, LAC
Milkfish, AWA
Moccasin, PAC
Money: Yap stone, FEI
Money of Account (also Coin):
  Anglo-Saxon, ORA, ORE
  French, SOU
  Indian, LAC
  Japanese, RIN
  Virgin Islands, BIT
Monkey: Capuchin, SAI
Morsel, ORT
Mother: Peer Gynt's, ASE
Mountain: Asia Minor, IDA
Mulberry: Indian, AAL, ACH,
  AWL
Muttonbird: New Zealand, OII
Nahoor, SNA
Native: Mindanao, ATA
Neckpiece, BOA
Newt, EFT
No (Scottish), NAE
Note: Guido's highest, ELA
  Of scale, SOL
Nursemaid: Oriental, AMA, IYA
Ocher: Yellow, SIL
One (Scottish), YIN
Ornament: Pagoda, TEE
Oven: Polynesian, UMU
Ox: Tibetan, YAK
Pagoda: Chinese, TAA
Parrot: Hawk, HIA
  New Zealand, KEA
Part: Footlike, PES
Particle: Electrified, ION
Pasha, DEY
Pass: Mountain, COL
Paste: Rice, AME
Pea: Indian split, DAL
Peasant: Philippine, TAO
Penpoint, NEB, NIB
Piece out, EKE
Pigeon, NUN
Pine: Textile screw, ARA
Pistol (slang), GAT
Pit: Baking, IMU
Plant: Pepper, AVA
Play: By Capek, RUR
Poem: Old French, DIT
Porgy: Japanese, TAI
Priest: Biblical high, ELI
Prince: Ethiopian, RAS

Pseudonym: Dickens', BOZ
Queen: Fairy, MAB
Quince: Bengal, BEL
Record: Ship's, LOG
Refuse: Flax (Scottish), PAB,
  POB
Resin, LAC
Resort, SPA
Revolver (slang), GAT
Right: Cause to turn, GEE
River: Scottish or English, DEE
  (Spanish), RIO
  Swiss, AAR
Room: Harem, ODA
Rootstock: Fern, ROI
Rose (Persian), GUL
Ruff: Female, REE
Rule: Indian, RAJ
Sailor, GOB, TAR
Saint: Female (abbr.), STE
  Islamic, PIR
Salt, SAL
Sash: Japanese, OBI
Scrap, ORT
Seed: Poppy, MAW
  Small, PIP
Self, EGO
Serpent: Vedic sky, AHI
Sesame, TIL
Sheep: Female, EWE
  Indian, SHA
  Male, RAM
Sheepfold (Scottish), REE
Shelter, LEE
Shield, ECU
Shooting match (French), TIR
Shrew: European, ERD
Shrub: Evergreen, YEW
Silkworm, ERI
Snake, ASP, BOA
Soak, RET
Son-in-law: Mohammed's, ALI
Sorrel: Wood, OCA
Spade: Long, narrow, LOY
Spirit: Malignant, KER
Spot: Playing-card, PIP
Spread for drying, TED
Spring: Mineral, SPA
Sprite: Water, NIX
Statesman: Japanese, ITO
Stern: Toward, AFT
Stomach: Bird's, MAW
Street (French), RUE
Summer (French), ETE
Sun, SOL
Swamp, BOG, FEN
Swan: Male, COB
Tea: Chinese, CHA
Temple: Shinto, SHA
Thing (law), RES
Title: Etruscan, LAR
  Monk's, FRA
  Portuguese, DOM
  Spanish, DON
  Turkish, AGA, BEY
Tool: Cutting, ADZ, AXE
  Mining, GAD
  Piercing, AWL
Tree: Candlenut, AMA
  Central American, EBO

East Indian, SAJ, SAL
Evergreen, YEW
Hawaiian, KOA, KOU
Indian, BEL, DAR
Linden, LIN
New Zealand, AKE
Philippine, DAO, TUA, TUI
Rubber, ULE
South American, APA
Tribe: New Zealand, ATI
Turmeric, REA
Twice, BIS
Twin: Siamese, ENG
Uncle (dialect), EAM, EME
Veil: Chalice, AER, AIR
Vessel: Wine, AMA
Vestment: Ecclesiastical, ALB
Vetch: Bitter, ERS
Victorfish, AKU
Vine: New Zealand, AKA
  Philippine, IYO
Wallaba, APA
Wapiti, ELK
Water (French), EAU
Waterfall, LIN
Watering place: Prussian, EMS
Weave: Designating plain,
  UNI
Weight: Bulgarian, OKA, OKE
  Burmese, MOO, VIS
  Chinese, FEN, HAO, KIN,
  SSU, TAN, YIN
  Cyprus, OKA, OKE
  Danish, LOD, ORT, VOG
  East Indian, TJI
  Egyptian, KAT, OKA, OKE
  English, for wool, TOD
  German, LOT
  Greek, MNA, OKA, OKE
  Indian, SER
  Japanese, FUN, KIN, RIN,
  SHI
  Korean, KON
  Malacca, KIP
  Mongolian, LAN
  Netherlands, ONS
  Norwegian, LOD
  Polish, LUT
  Rangoon, PAI
  Roman, BES
  Russian, LOT
  Siamese, BAT, HAP, PAI
  Swedish, ASS, ORT
  Turkish, OKA, OKE
  Vietnamese, CAN
  Yugoslav, OKA, OKE
Whales: Herd, GAM, POD
Wildebeest, GNU
Wing, ALA
Witticism, MOT
Wolframite, CAL
Worm: African, LOA
Wreath: Hawaiian, LEI
Yale, ELI
Yam: Hawaiian, HOI
Yes (French), OUI
Young: Bring forth, EAN
Z (letter), ZED

Words of Four Letters

Aborigine: Borneo, DYAK
Agave, ALOE
Animal: Footless, APOD
Ant: White, ANAI, ANAY
Antelope: African, ASSE, BISA, GUIB,
  KOBA, KUDU, ORYX, POKU, PUKU,
  TOPI, TORA
Apoplexy: Plant, ESCA
Apple, POME
Apricot, ANSU
Ardor, ELAN
Armadillo, APAR, PEBA, PEVA, TATU
Ascetic: Islamic, SUFI
Association: Chinese, TONG

Astronomer: Persian, OMAR
Avatar: Of Vishnu, RAMA
Axillary, ALAR
Band: Horizontal (heraldry), FESS
Barracuda, SPET
Bark: Mulberry, TAPA
Base: Column, DADO
Bearing (heraldry), ORLE
Beer: Russian, KVAS
Beige, ECRU
Being, ESSE
Beverage: Japanese rice, SAKE
Bird: Asian, MINA, MYNA
  Egyptian sacred, IBIS

Extinct, DODO, MAMO
Flightless, KIWI
Gull-like, TERN
Hawaiian, IIWI, MAMO
Parson, KOKO
Unfledged, EYAS
Birds: As class, AVES
Black, EBON
  (French), NOIR
Blackbird: European, MERL
Boat: Flat-bottomed, DORY
Bone: Forearm, ULNA
Bones, OSSA
Box, Japanese, INRO

Bravo (rare), EUGE
Buffalo: Indian wild, ARNA
Bull (Spanish), TORO
Burden, ONUS
Cabbage: Sliced, SLAW
Caliph: Islamic, OMAR
Canoe: Malay, PRAU, PROA
Cap: Military, KEPI
Cape, NESS
Capital: Ancient Irish, TARA
Case: Article, ETUI
Cat: Wild, BALU, EYRA
Chalcedony, SARD
Chamber: Indian ceremonial, KIVA
Channel: Brain, ITER
Cheese: Dutch, EDAM
Chest: Sepulchral stone, CIST
Chieftain: Arab, EMIR
Church: Part of, APSE, NAVE
    (Scottish), KIRK
Claim (law), LIEN
Cluster: Flower, CYME
Coin: Chinese, TAEL, YUAN
    German, MARK
    Indian, ANNA
    Iranian, RIAL
    Italian, LIRA
    Moroccan, OKIA
    Siamese, BAHT
    South American, PESO
    Spanish, DURO, PESO
    Turkish, PARA
Commune: Belgian, AATH
Composition: Musical, OPUS
Compound: Chemical, DIOL
Constellation: Southern, PAVO
Council: Russian, DUMA
Counsel, REDE
Covering: Seed, ARIL
Cross: Egyptian, ANKH
Cry: Bacchanalian, EVOE
Cup (Scottish), TASS
Cupbearer, SAKI
Dagger, DIRK
    Malay, KRIS
Dam: River, WEIR
Dash, ELAN
Date: Roman, IDES
Dawn: Pertaining to, EOAN
Dean: English, INGE
Decay: In fruit, BLET
Deer: Sambar, MAHA
Disease: Skin, ACNE
Disk: Solar, ATEN
Dog: Hunting, ALAN
Drink: Hindu intoxicating, SOMA
Duck, SMEE, SMEW, TEAL
Dynasty: Chinese, CHEN, CHIN, CHOU,
    CHOW, HSIA, MING, SUNG, TANG,
    TSIN
    Mongol, YUAN
Eagle: Biblical, GIER
    Sea, ERNE
Ear: Pertaining to, OTIC
Egyptian: Christian, COPT
Entrance: Mine, ADIT
Esau, EDOM
Escutcheon: Voided, ORLE
Eskers, OSAR
Evergreen: New Zealand, TAWA
Fairy: Persian, PERI
Family: Italian, ESTE
Far (comb. form), TELE
Farewell, VALE
Father (French), PERE
Fennel: Philippine, ANIS
Fever: Malarial, AGUE
Fiber: East Indian, JUTE
Firn, NEVE
Fish: Carplike, DACE
    Hawaiian, ULUA
    Herringlike, SHAD
    Mackerellike, CERO
    Marine, HAKE
    Sea, LING, MERO, OPAH
    Spiny-finned, GOBY

Food: Tropical, TARO
Foot: Metric, IAMB
Formerly, ERST
Founder: Of Carthage, DIDO
France: Southern, MIDI
Furze, ULEX
Gaelic, ERSE
Gaiter, SPAT
Game: Card, FARO, SKAT
Garlic: European wild, MOLY
Garment: Hindu, SARI
    Roman, TOGA
Gazelle, CORA
Gem, JADE, ONYX, OPAL, RUBY
Genus: Amphibians (incl. frogs), RANA
    Amphibians (incl. tree toads), HYLA
    Antelopes, ORYX
    Auks, ALCA, URIA
    Bees, APIS
    Birds (American ostriches), RHEA
    Birds (cranes), CRUS
    Birds (magpies), PICA
    Birds (peacocks), PAVO
    Cetaceans, INIA
    Ducks (incl. mallards), ANAS
    Fishes (burbots), LOTA
    Fishes (incl. bowfins), AMIA
    Geese (snow geese), CHEN
    Gulls, XEMA
    Herbs, ARUM, GEUM
    Insects (water scorpions), NEPA
    Lilies, ALOE
    Mammals (humans), HOMO
    Orchids, DISA
    Owls, ASIO, BUBO, OTUS
    Palms, NIPA
    Sea birds, SULA
    Sheep, OVIS
    Shrubs, Eurasian, ULEX
    Shrubs (hollies), ILEX
    Shrubs (incl. Virginia Willow), ITEA
    Shrubs, tropical, EVEA
    Snakes (sand snakes), ERYX
    Swans, OLOR
    Trees, chocolate, COLA
    Trees (ebony family), MABA
    Trees (incl. maples), ACER
    Trees (olives), OLEA
    Trees, tropical, EVEA
    Turtles, EMYS
Goat: Wild, IBEX, KRAS, TAHR, TAIR,
    THAR
God: Assyrian, ASUR
    Babylonian, ADAD, ADDU, ENKI,
    ENZU, IRRA, NABU, NEBO, UTUG
    Celtic, LLEU, LLEW
    Hindu, AGNI, CIVA, DEVA, DEWA,
    KAMA, RAMA, SIVA, VAYU
    Phrygian, ATYS
    Semitic, BAAL
    Teutonic, HLER
Goddess: Babylonian, ERUA, GULA
    Hawaiian, PELE
    Hindu, DEVI, KALI, SHRI, VACH
Gooseberry: Hawaiian, POHA
Gourd, PEPO
Grafted (heraldry), ENTE
Grandfather (obsolete), AIEL
Grandparents: Pertaining to, AVAL
Grass: Hawaiian, HILO
Gray (French), GRIS
Green (heraldry), VERT
Groom: Indian, SYCE
Half (prefix), DEMI, HEMI, SEMI
Hamlet, DORP
Hammerhead: Part of, PEEN
Handle, ANSA
Harp: Japanese, KOTO
Hartebeest, ASSE, TORA
Hautboy, OBOE
Hawk: Taken from nest (falconry), EYAS
Hearing (law), OYER
Heater: For liquids, ETNA
Herb: Aromatic, ANET, DILL
    Fabulous, MOLY
    Perennial, GEUM, SEGO

Pot, WORT
    Used for blue dye, WADE, WOAD
Hill: Flat-topped, MESA
    Sand, DENE, DUNE
Hoarfrost, RIME
Hog: Immature female, GILT
Holly, ILEX
House: Cow, BYRE
    (Spanish), CASA
Ice: Floating, FLOE
Image, ICON, IKON
Incarnation: Of Vishnu, RAMA
Indian: Algonquin, CREE, SAUK
    Central American, MAYA
    Iroquoian, ERIE
    Mexican, CORA
    Peruvian, CANA, INCA, MORO
    Shoshonean, HOPI
    Siouan, OTOE
    Southwestern, HOPI, PIMA, YUMA,
    ZUNI
Insect: Immature, PUPA
Instrument: Stringed, LUTE, LYRE
Ireland, EIRE, ERIN
Jacket: English, ETON
Jail (British), GAOL
Jar, OLLA
Judge: Islamic, CADI
Juniper: European, CADE
Kiln, OAST, OVEN
King: British legendary, LUDD, NUDD
Kiss, BUSS
Knife: Philippine, BOLO
Koran: Section of, SURA
Laborer: Spanish American, PEON
Lake: Mountain, TARN
    (Scottish), LOCH
Lamp: Miner's, DAVY
Landing place: Indian, GHAT
Language: Buddhist, PALI
    Japanese, AINU
Latvian, LETT
Layer: Of iris, UVEA
Leaf: Palm, OLAY, OLLA
Legislature: Ukrainian, RADA
Lemur, LORI
Leopard, PARD
Let it stand, STET
Letter: Greek, BETA, IOTA, ZETA
    Hebrew, AYIN, BETH, CAPH, KOPH,
    RESH, SHIN, TETH, YODH
    Papal, BULL
Lily, ALOE
Literature: Hindu sacred, VEDA
Lizard, GILA
    Monitor, URAN
Loquat, BIWA
Magistrate: Genoese or Venetian, DOGE
Man (Latin), HOMO
Mark: Omission, DELE
Marmoset: South American, MICO
Meadow: Fertile, VEGA
Measure: Electric, VOLT, WATT
    Force, DYNE
    Hebrew, OMER
    Printing, PICA
    Spanish or Portuguese, VARA
    Swiss land, IMMI
Medley, OLIO
Merganser, SMEW
Milk (French), LAIT
Molding, GULA
    Curved, OGEE
Mongoose: Crab-eating, URVA
Monk: Tibetan, LAMA
Monkey: African, MONA, WAAG
    Ceylonese, MAHA
    Cochin-China, DOUC
    South American, SAKI, TITI
Monkshood, ATIS
Month: Jewish, ADAR, ELUL, IYAR
Mother (French), MERE
Mountain: Thessaly, OSSA
Mouse: Meadow, VOLE
Mythology: Norse, EDDA
Nail (French), CLOU

Native: Philippine, MORO
Nest: Of pheasants, NIDE
Network, RETE
No (German), NEIN
Noble: Islamic, AMIR
Notice: Death, OBIT
Novel: By Zola, NANA
Nursemaid: Oriental AMAH, AYAH, EYAH
Nut: Philippine, PILI
Oak: Holm, ILEX
Oil (comb. form), OLEO
Ostrich: American, RHEA
Oven, KILN, OAST
Owl: Barn, LULU
Ox: Celebes wild, ANOE
 Extinct wild, URUS
Palm, ATAP, NIPA, SAGO
Parliament, DIET
Parrot: New Zealand, KAKA
Pass: Indian mountain, GHAT
Passage: Closing (music), CODA
Peach: Clingstone, PAVY
Peasant: Indian, RYOT
 Old English, CARL
Pepper: Australasian, KAVA
Perfume, ATAR
Persia, IRAN
Person: Extraordinary, ONER
Pickerel or pike, ESOX
Pitcher, EWER
Plant: Aromatic, NARD
 Century, ALOE
 Indigo, ANIL
 Pepper, KAVA
Platform: Raised, DAIS
Plum: Wild, SLOE
Pods: Vegetable, OKRA, OKRO
Poem: Epic, EPOS
Poet: Persian, OMAR
 Roman, OVID
Poison, BANE
 Arrow, INEE
Porkfish, SISI
Portico: Greek, STOA
Premium, AGIO
Priest: Islamic, IMAM
Prima donna, DIVA
Prong: Fork, TINE
Pseudonym: Lamb's, ELIA
Queen: Carthaginian, DIDO
 Hindu, RANI
Rabbit, CONY
Race: Of Japan, AINU
Rail: Ducklike, COOT
 North American, SORA
Redshank, CLEE
Refuse: After pressing, MARC
Regiment: Turkish, ALAI
Reliquary, ARCA
Resort: Italian, LIDO
Ridges: Sandy, ASAR, OSAR
River: German, ELBE, ODER
 Italian, ADDA
 Siberian, LENA
Road: Roman, ITER

Rockfish: California, RENA
Rodent: Mouselike, VOLE
 South American, PACA
Rootstock, TARO
Salamander, NEWT
Salmon: Silver, COHO
 Young, PARR
Same (Greek), HOMO
 (Latin), IDEM
Sauce: Fish, ALEC
School: English, ETON
Seaweed: AGAR, ALGA, KELP
Secular, LAIC
Sediment, SILT
Seed: Dill, ANET
 Of vetch, TARE
Serf, ILOT
Sesame, TEEL
Settlement: Eskimo, ETAH
Shark: Atlantic, GATA
 European, TOPE
Sheep: Wild, UDAD
Sheltered, ALEE
Shield, EGIS
Ship: Jason's, ARGO
 Left side of, PORT
 Two-masted, BRIG
Shrine: Buddhist, TOPE
Shrub: New Zealand, TUTU
Sign: Magic, RUNE
Silkworm, ERIA
Skin: Beaver, PLEW
Skink: Egyptian, ADDA
Slave, ESNE
Sloth: Two-toed, UNAU
Smooth, LENE
Snow: Glacial, NEVE
Soapstone, TALC
Society: African secret, EGBO, PORO
Son: Of Seth, ENOS
Song (German), LIED
 Unaccompanied, GLEE
Sound: Lung, RALE
Sour, ACID
Sow: Young, GILT
Spike: Brad-shaped, BROB
Spirit: Buddhist evil, MARA
Stake: Poker, ANTE
Star: Temporary, NOVA
Starch: East Indian, SAGO
Stone: Precious, OPAL
Strap: Bridle, REIN
Strewn (heraldry), SEME
Sweetsop, ATES, ATTA
Sword: Fencing, EPEE, FOIL
Tambourine: African, TAAR
Tapir: Brazilian, ANTA
Tax, CESS
Tea: South American, MATE
Therefore (Latin), ERGO
Thing: Extraordinary, ONER
Three (dice, cards, etc.), TREY
Thrush: Hawaiian, OMAO
Tide, NEAP

Tipster: Racing, TOUT
Tissue, TELA
Title: Etruscan, LARS
 Hindu, BABU
 Indian, RAJA
 Islamic, EMIR, IMAM
 Persian, BABA
 Spanish, DONA
 Turkish, AGHA, BABA
Toad: Largest-known, AGUA
 Tree, HYLA
Tool: Cutting, ADZE
Track: Deer, SLOT
Tract: Sandy, DENE
Tree: Apple, SORB
 Central American, EBOE
 East Indian, TEAK
 Eucalyptus, YATE
 Guyanese and Trinidadian, MORA
 Javanese, UPAS
 Linden, LIME, LINN, TEIL, TILL
 Sandarac, ARAR
 Sassafras, AGUE
 Tamarisk salt, ATLE
Tribe: Moro, SULU
Trout, CHAR
Vessel: Arab, DHOW
Vestment: Ecclesiastical, COPE
Vetch, TARE
Vine: East Indian, SOMA
Violinist: Famous, AUER
Vortex, EDDY
Wampum, PEAG
Wapiti, STAG
Waste: Allowance for, TRET
Watchman: Indian, MINA
Water (Spanish), AGUA
Waterfall, LINN
Wavy (heraldry), ONDE, UNDE
Wax, CERE
 Chinese, PELA
Weed: Biblical, TARE
Weight: Ancient, MINA
 Danish (pl.), ESER
 East Asian, TAEL
 Greek, MINA
 Siamese, BAHT
Well done (rare), EUGE
Whale, CETE
 Killer, ORCA
 White, HUSE, HUSO
Whirlpool, EDDY
Wife: Of Geraint, ENID
Willow: Virginia, ITEA
Wine, PORT
Winged, ALAR
 (Heraldry), AILE
Wings, ALAE
Withered, SERE
Without (French), SANS
Wool: To comb, CARD
Work, OPUS
Wrong: Civil, TORT
Young: Bring forth, YEAN

Words of Five Letters

Abode of dead: Babylonian, ARALU
Aborigine: Borneo, DAYAK
Aftersong, EPODE
Aloe, AGAVE
Animal: Footless, APODE
Ant, EMMET
Antelope: African, ADDAX, BEISA,
 CAAMA, ELAND, GUIBA, ORIBI,
 TIANG
 Goat, GORAL, SEROW
 Indian, SASIN
 Siberian, SAIGA
Arch: Pointed, OGIVE
Armadillo, APARA, POYOU, TATOU
Arrowroot, ARARU
Artery: Trunk, AORTA
Association: Russian, ARTEL
 Secret, CABAL
Author: English, READE

Automaton, GOLEM, ROBOT
Award: Motion-picture, OSCAR
Basket: Fishing, CREEL
Beer: Russian, KVASS
Bible: Islamic, KORAN, QUR'AN
Bird: Asian, MINAH, MYNAH
 Indian, SHAMA
 Larklike, PIPIT
 Loonlike, GREBE
 Oscine, VIREO
 South American, AGAMI
 Swimming, GREBE
Black: (French), NOIRE
 (Heraldry), SABLE
Blackbird: European, MERLE, OUSEL,
 OUZEL
Block: Glacial, SERAC
Blue (heraldry), AZURE
Boat: Eskimo, BIDAR, UMIAK

Bobwhite, COLIN, QUAIL
Bone (comb. form), OSTEO
 Leg, TIBIA
 Thigh, FEMUR
Broom: Twig, BESOM
Brother (French), FRERE
 Moses, AARON
Canoe: Eskimo, BIDAR, KAYAK
Cape: Papal, FANON, ORALE
Card: Old playing, TAROT
Caravansary, SERAI
Caterpillar: New Zealand, AWETO
Catkin, AMENT
Cavity: Stone, GEODE
Cephalopod, SQUID
Cetacean, WHALE
Chariot, ESSED
Cheek: Pertaining to, MALAR
Chieftain: Arab, EMEER

Child (Scottish), BAIRN
Cigar, CLARO
Coating: Seed, TESTA
Cockatoo: Palm, ARARA
Coin: Costa Rican, COLON
 Danish, KRONE
 Ecuadorian, SUCRE
 English, GROAT, PENCE
 French, FRANC
 German, KRONE, TALER
 Hungarian, PENGO
 Icelandic, KRONA
 Indian, RUPEE
 Iraqi, DINAR
 Norwegian, KRONE
 Polish, ZLOTY
 Russian, COPEC, KOPEK, RUBLE
 Swedish, KRONA
 Turkish, ASPER
 Yugoslav, DINAR
Collar: Papal, FANON, ORALE
 Roman, RABAT
Commune: Italian, TREIA
Composition: Choral, MOTET
Compound: Chemical, ESTER
Conceal (law), ELOIN
Council: Ecclesiastical, SYNOD
Court: Anglo-Saxon, GEMOT
 Inner, PATIO
Crest: Mountain, ARETE
Crown: Papal, TIARA
Cuttlefish, SEPIA
Date: Roman, NONES
Decree: Islamic, IRADE
 Russian, UKASE
Deposit: Loam, LOESS
Desert: Gobi, SHAMO
Devilfish, MANTA
Disease: Cereals, ERGOT
Disk, PATEN
Dog: Wild, DHOLE, DINGO
Dormouse, LEROT
Drum, TABOR
Duck: Sea, EIDER
Dynasty: Chinese, CHING, LIANG,
 SHANG
Earthquake, SEISM
Eel, ELVER, MORAY
Ermine: European, STOAT
Ether: Crystalline, APIOL
Fabric: Velvetlike, PANNE
Fabulist, AESOP
Family: Italian, CENCI
Fiber: West Indian, SISAL
Fig: Smyrna, ELEME, ELEMI
Figure: Of speech, TROPE
Finch: European, SERIN
Fish: American small, KILLY
Flower: Garden, ASTER
Friend (Spanish), AMIGO
Fruit: Tropical, MANGO
Fungus: Rye, ERGOT
Furze, GORSE
Gateway, TORAN, TORII
Gem, AGATE, BERYL, PEARL, TOPAZ
Genus: Barnacles, LEPAS
 Bears, URSUS
 Birds (loons), GAVIA
 Birds (nuthatches), SITTA
 Cats, FELIS
 Dogs, CANIS
 Fishes (chiros), ELOPS
 Fishes (perch), PERCA
 Geese, ANSER
 Grasses, STIPA
 Grasses (incl. oats), AVENA
 Gulls, LARUS
 Hares, rabbits, LEPUS
 Hawks, BUTEO
 Herbs, old world, INULA
 Herbs, trailing or climbing, APIOS
 Herbs, tropical, TACCA, URENA
 Horses, EQUUS
 Insects (olive flies), DACUS
 Lice, plant, APHIS
 Lichens, USNEA

Lizards, AGAMA
Moles, TALPA
Mollusks, OLIVA
Monkeys, CEBUS
Palms, ARECA
Pigeons, GOURA
Plants (amaryllis family), AGAVE
Ruminants (goats), CAPRA
Shrubs, Asiatic, SABIA
Shrubs (heath), ERICA
Shrubs (incl. raspberry), RUBUS
Shrubs, tropical, IXORA, TREMA,
 URENA
Ticks, ARGAS
Trees (of elm family), TREMA, ULMUS
Trees, tropical, IXORA, TREMA
Goat: Bezoar, PASAN
God: Assyrian, ASHIR, ASHUR, ASSUR
 Babylonian, DAGAN, SIRIS
 Gaelic, DAGDA
 Hindu, BHAGA, INDRA, SHIVA
 Japanese, EBISU
 Philistine, DAGON
 Phrygian, ATTIS
 Teutonic, AEGIR, GYMIR
 Welsh, DYLAN
Goddess: Babylonian, ISTAR, NANAI
 Hindu, DURGA, GAURI, SHREE
Group: Of six, HEXAD
Grove: Sacred to Diana, NEMUS
Growing out, ENATE
Guitar: Hindu, SITAR
Gull: PEWEE, PEWIT
Hartebeest, CAAMA
Headdress: Jewish or Persian, TIARA
 Liturgical, MITER, MITRE
Heath, ERICA
Herb: Grasslike marsh, SEDGE
Heron, EGRET
Hog: Young, SHOAT, SHOTE
Image, EIKON
Indian: Cariban, ARARA
 Iroquoian, HURON
 Mexican, AZTEC, OPATA, OTOMI
 Muskhogean, CREEK
 Siouan, OSAGE, TETON
 Spanish American, ARARA, CARIB
Inflorescence: Racemose, AMENT
Insect: Immature, LARVA
Intrigue, CABAL
Iris: Yellow, SEDGE
Juniper, GORSE, RETEM
Kidneys: Pertaining to, RENAL
King: British legendary, LLUDD
Kite: European, GLEDE
Kobold, NISSE
Land: Cultivated, ARADA, ARADO
Landholder (Scottish), LAIRD, THANE
Language: Dravidian, TAMIL
Lariat, LASSO, REATA
Laughing, RIANT
Lawgiver: Athenian, DRACO, SOLON
Leaf: Calyx, SEPAL
 Fern, FROND
Lemur, LORIS
Letter: English, AITCH
 Greek, ALPHA, DELTA, GAMMA,
  KAPPA, OMEGA, SIGMA, THETA
 Hebrew, ALEPH, CHETH, GIMEL,
  SADHE, ZAYIN
Lichen, USNEA
Lighthouse, PHARE
Lizard: Old World, AGAMA
Loincloth, DHOTI
Louse: Plant, APHID
Macaw: Brazilian, ARARA
Mahogany: Philippine, ALMON
Mammal: Badgerlike, RATEL
 Civetlike, GENET
 Giraffelike, OKAPI
 Raccoonlike, COATI
Man (French), HOMME
Marble, AGATE
Mark: Insertion, CARET
Market place: Greek, AGORA
Marsupial: Australian, KOALA

Measure: Electric, FARAD, HENRY
 Energy, JOULE
 Metric, LITER, STERE
 Printing, AGATE
 Russian, VERST
Mixture: Smelting, MATTE
Mohicans: Last of, UNCAS
Molding: Convex, OVOLO, TORUS
Mole, TALPA
Monkey: African, PATAS
 Capuchin, SAJOU
 Howling, ARABA
Monkshood, ATEES
Month: Jewish, NISAN, SIVAN, TEBET
Museum (French), MUSEE
Musketeer, ATHOS
Native: Aleutian, ALEUT
 New Zealand, MAORI
Neckpiece: Ecclesiastical, AMICE
Nerve (comb. form), NEURO
Nest: Eagle's or hawk's, AERIE
 Insect's, NIDUS
Net: Fishing, SEINE
Newsstand, KIOSK
Nitrogen, AZOTE
Noble: Islamic, AMEER
Nodule: Stone, GEODE
Nostrils, NARES
Notched irregularly, EROSE
Nymph: Islamic, HOURI
Official: Roman, EDILE
Oleoresin, ELEMI
Opening: Mouthlike, STOMA
Oration: Funeral, ELOGE
Ostiole, STOMA
Page: Left-hand, VERSO
 Right-hand, RECTO
Palm, ARECA, BETEL
Park: Colorado, ESTES
Perfume, ATTAR
Philosopher: Greek, PLATO
Pillar: Stone, STELA, STELE
Pinnacle: Glacial, SERAC
Plain, LLANO
Plant: Century, AGAVE
 Climbing, LIANA
 Dwarf, CUMIN
 East Asian perennial, RAMIE
 Medicinal, SENNA
 Mustard family, CRESS
Plate: Communion, PATEN
Poem: Lyric, EPODE
Point: Lowest, NADIR
Poplar, ABELE, ALAMO, ASPEN
Porridge: Spanish American, ATOLE
Post: Stair, NEWEL
Priest: Islamic, IMAUM
Protozoan, AMEBA
Queen: (French), REINE
 Hindu, RANEE
Rabbit, CONEY
Rail, CRAKE
Red (heraldry), GULES
Religion: Moslem, Muslim, ISLAM
Resin, ELEMI
Revoke (law), ADEEM
Rich man, MIDAS, NABOB
Ridge: Sandy, ESKAR, ESKER
River: French, LOIRE, SEINE
Rockfish: California, REINA
Rootstock: Fragrant, ORRIS
Ruff: Female, REEVE
Sack: Pack, KYACK
Salt: Ethereal, ESTER
Saltpeter, NITER, NITRE
Salutation: Eastern, SALAM
Sandpiper: Old World, TEREK
Scented, OLENT
School: Fish, SHOAL
 French public, LYCEE
Scriptures: Islamic, KORAN
Seaweeds, ALGAE
Seed: Aromatic, ANISE
Seraglio, HAREM, SERAI
Serf, HELOT
Sheep: Wild, AUDAD

Sheeplike, OVINE
Shield, AEGIS
Shoe: Wooden, SABOT
Shoots: Pickled bamboo, ACHAR
Shot: Billiard, CAROM, MASSE
Shrine: Buddhist, STUPA
Shrub: Burning bush, WAHOO
  Ornamental evergreen, TOYON
  Used in tanning, SUMAC
Silk: Watered, MOIRE
Sister (French), SOEUR
  (Latin), SOROR
Six: Group of, HEXAD
Skeleton: Marine, CORAL
Slave, HELOT
Snake, ABOMA, ADDER, COBRA, RACER
Soldier: French, POILU
  Indian, SEPOY
Sour, ACERB
Spirit: Air, ARIEL
Staff: Shepherd's, CROOK
Starwort, ASTER
Steel (German), STAHL
Stockade: Russian, ETAPE

Stop (nautical), AVAST
Storehouse, ETAPE
Subway: Parisian, METRO
Tapestry, ARRAS
Tea: Paraguayan, YERBA
Temple: Hawaiian, HEIAU
Terminal: Positive, ANODE
Theater: Greek, ODEON, ODEUM
Then (French), ALORS
Thread: Surgical, SETON
Thrush: Wilson's, VEERY
Title: Hindu, BABOO
  Indian, RAJAH, SAHEB, SAHIB
  Islamic, EMEER, IMAUM
Tree: Buddhist sacred, PIPAL
  East Indian cotton, SIMAL
  Hickory, PECAN
  Light-wooded, BALSA
  Malayan, TERAP
  Mediterranean, CAROB
  Mexican, ABETO
  Mexican pine, OCOTE
  New Zealand, MAIRE
  Philippine, ALMON
  Rain, SAMAN

South American, UMBRA
Tamarack, LARCH
Tamarisk salt, ATLEE
West Indian, ACANA
Trout, CHARR
Troy, ILION, ILIUM
Twin: Siamese, CHANG
Vestment: Ecclesiastical, STOLE
Violin: Famous, AMATI, STRAD
Volcano: Mud, SALSE
Wampum, PEAGE
War cry: Greek, ALALA
Wavy (heraldry), UNDEE
Weight: Jewish, GERAH
Wen, TALPA
Wheat, SPELT
Wheel: Persian water, NORIA
Whitefish, CISCO
Willow, OSIER
Window: Bay, ORIEL
Wine, MEDOC, RHINE, TINTA, TOKAY
Winged, ALATE
Woman (French), FEMME
Year: Excess of solar over lunar, EPACT
Zoroastrian, PARSI

Words of Six or More Letters

Agave, MAGUEY
Alkaloid: Crystalline, ESERIN, ESERINE
Alligator, CAYMAN
Amphibole, EDENITE, URALITE
Ant: White, TERMITE
Antelope: African, DIKDIK, DUIKER,
  GEMSBOK, IMPALA, KOODOO
  European, CHAMOIS
  Indian, NILGAI, NILGAU, NILGHAI,
  NILGHAU
Ape: Asian or East Indian, GIBBON
Appendage: Leaf, STIPEL, STIPULE
Armadillo, PELUDO, TATOUAY
Arrowroot, ARARAO
Ascetic: Jewish, ESSENE
Ass: Asian wild, ONAGER
Avatar: Of Vishnu, KRISHNA
Babylonian, ELAMITE
Badge: Shoulder, EPAULET
Baldness, ALOPECIA
Barracuda, SENNET
Bark: Aromatic, SINTOC
Bearlike, URSINE
Beetle, ELATER
Bible: Zoroastrian, AVESTA
Bird: Sea, PETREL
  South American, SERIEMA
  Wading, AVOCET, AVOSET
Bone: Leg, FIBULA
Branched, RAMATE
Brother (Latin), FRATER
Bunting: European, ORTOLAN
Call: Trumpet, SENNET
Canoe: Eskimo, BAIDAR, OOMIAK
Caravansary, IMARET
Cat: Asian or African, CHEETAH
  Leopardlike, OCELOT
Cenobite: Jewish, ESSENE
Centerpiece: Table, EPERGNE
Cetacean, DOLPHIN, PORPOISE
Chariot, ESSEDA, ESSEDE
Chief: Seminole, OSCEOLA
Claim: Release as (law), REMISE
Clock: Water, CLEPSYDRA
Cloud, CUMULUS, NIMBUS
Coach: French hackney, FIACRE
Coin: Czech, KORUNA
  Dutch, GUILDER
  Ethiopian, TALARI
  Finnish, MARKKA
  German, THALER
  Greek, DRACHMA
  Haitian, GOURDE
  Honduran, LEMPIRA
  Hungarian, FORINT
  Indo-Chinese, PIASTER
  Panamanian, BALBOA
  Paraguayan, GUARANI
  Portuguese, ESCUDO

  Russian, COPECK, KOPECK, ROUBLE
  Spanish, PESETA
  Venezuelan, BOLIVAR
Communion: Last holy, VIATICUM
Conceal (law), ELOIGN
Confection, PRALINE
Construction: Sentence, SYNTAX
Convexity: Shaft of column, ENTASIS
Court: Anglo-Saxon, GEMOTE
Cow: Sea, DUGONG, MANATEE
Cylindrical, TERETE
Dagger, STILETTO
  Malay, CREESE, KREESE
Date: Roman, CALENDS, KALENDS
Deer, CARIBOU, WAPITI
Disease: Plant, ERINOSE
Doorkeeper, OSTIARY
Dragonflies: Order of, ODANATA
Drink: Of gods, NECTAR
Drum: TABOUR
  Moorish, ATABAL, ATTABAL
Duck: Fish-eating, MERGANSER
  Sea, SCOTER
Dynasty: Chinese, MANCHU
Eel, CONGER
Edit, REDACT
Envelope: Flower, PERIANTH
Eskimo, AMERIND
Ether: Crystalline, APIOLE
Excuse (law), ESSOIN
Eyespots, OCELLI
Fabric, ESTAMENE, ESTAMIN, ETAMINE
Falcon: European, KESTREL
Figure: Used as column, CARYATID, TELAMON
Fine: For punishment, AMERCE
Fish: Asian fresh-water, GOURAMI
  Pikelike, BARRACUDA
Five: Group of, PENTAD
Fly: African, TSETSE
Foot: Metric, ANAPEST, IAMBUS
Foxlike, VULPINE
Frying pan, SPIDER
Fur, KARAKUL
Galley: Greek or Roman, BIREME, TRIREME
Game: Card, ECARTE
Garment: Greek, CHLAMYS
Gateway, GOPURA, TORANA
Genus: Birds (ravens, crows), CORVUS
  Eels, CONGER
  Fishes, ANABAS
  Foxes, VULPES
  Herbs, ANEMONE
  Insects, CICADA
  Lemurs, GALAGO
  Mints (incl. catnip), NEPETA

Mollusks, ANOMIA, ASTARTE, TEREDO
Mollusks (incl. oysters), OSTREA
Monkeys (spider monkeys), ATELES
Thrushes (incl. robins), TURDUS
Trees (of elm family), CELTIS
Trees (inc. dogwood), CORNUS
Trees, tropical American, SAPOTA
Wrens, NANNUS
Gibbon, SIAMANG, WOUWOU
Gland: Salivary, RACEMOSE
Goat: Bezoar, PASANG
Goatlike, CAPRINE
God: Assyrian, ASHSHUR, ASSHUR
  Babylonian, BABBAR, MARDUK,
  MERODACH, NANNAR, NERGAL,
  SHAMASH
  Hindu, BRAHMA, KRISHNA, VISHNU
  Tahitian, TAAROA
Goddess: Babylonian, ISHTAR
  Hindu, CHANDI, HAIMAVATI,
  LAKSHMI, PARVATI, SARASVATI,
  SARASWATI
Government, POLITY
Governor: Persian, SATRAP
Grandson (Scottish), NEPOTE
Group: Of five, PENTAD
  Of nine, ENNEAD
  Of seven, HEPTAD
Hare: in first year, LEVERET
Harpsichord, SPINET
Herb: Alpine, EDELWEISS
  Chinese, GINSENG
  South African, FREESIA
Hermit, EREMITE
Hero: Legendary, PALADIN
Heron, BITTERN
Horselike, EQUINE
Hound: Short-legged, BEAGLE
House (French), MAISON
Idiot, CRETIN
Implement: Stone, NEOLITH
Incarnation: Hindu, AVATAR
Indian, APACHE, COMANCHE, PAIUTE, SENECA
Inn: Turkish, IMARET
Insects: Order of, DIPTERA
Instrument: Japanese banjolike, SAMISEN
  Musical, CLAVIER, SPINET
Interstice, AREOLA
Ironwood, COLIMA
Juniper: Old Testament, RAETAM
Kettledrum, ATABAL
King: Fairy, OBERON
Kneecap, PATELLA
Knife, MACHETE
Langur: Sumatran, SIMPAI
Legislature: Spanish, CORTES

Lemur: African, GALAGO
  Madagascar, AYEAYE
Letter: Greek, EPSILON, LAMBDA,
  OMICRON, UPSILON
  Hebrew, DALETH, LAMEDH, SAMEKH
Lighthouse, PHAROS
Lizard, IGUANA
Llama, ALPACA
Lockjaw, TETANUS
Locust, CICADA, CICALA
Macaw: Brazilian, MARACAN
Maid: Of Astolat, ELAINE
Mammal: Madagascar, TENDRAC,
  TENREC
Man (Spanish), HOMBRE
Marmoset: South American, TAMARIN
Marsupial, BANDICOOT, WOMBAT
Massacre, POGROM
Mayor: Spanish, ALCALDE
Measure: Electric, AMPERE, COULOMB,
  KILOWATT
Medicine: Quack, NOSTRUM
Member: Religious order, CENOBITE
Molasses, TREACLE
Monkey: African, GRIVET, NISNAS
  Asian, LANGUR
  Philippine, MACHIN
  South American, PINCHE, SAIMIRI,
  SAMIRI, SAPAJOU
Monster, CHIMERA, GORGON
  (Comb. form), TERATO
  Cretan, MINOTAUR
Month: Jewish, HESHVAN, KISLEV,
  SHEBAT, TAMMUZ, TISHRI, VEADAR
Mountain: Asia Minor, ARARAT
Mulct, AMERCE
Musketeer, ARAMIS, PORTHOS
Nearsighted, MYOPIC
Net, TRAMMEL
New York City, GOTHAM
Nine: Group of, ENNEAD
Nobleman: Spanish, GRANDEE
Official: Roman, AEDILE
Onyx: Mexican, TECALI
Order: Dragonflies, ODANATA
  Insects, DIPTERA
Organ: Plant, PISTIL

Ornament: Shoulder, EPAULET
Overcoat: Military, CAPOTE
Ox: Wild, BANTENG
Oxidation: Bronze or copper, PATINA
Paralysis: Incomplete, PARESIS
Pear: Alligator, AVOCADO
Persimmon: Mexican, CHAPOTE
Pipe: Peace, CALUMET
Plaid (Scottish), TARTAN
Plain, PAMPAS, STEPPE, TUNDRA
Plant: Buttercup family, ANEMONE
  Century, MAGUEY
  On rocks, LICHEN
Plowing: Fit for, ARABLE
Poem: Heroic, EPOPEE
  Six-lined, SESTET
Point: Highest, ZENITH
Potion: Love, PHILTER, PHILTRE
Protozoan, AMOEBA
Punish, AMERCE
Purple (heraldry), PURPURE
Queen: Fairy, TITANIA
Race: Skiing, SLALOM
Rat, BANDICOOT, LEMMING
Retort, RIPOST, RIPOSTE
Ring: Harness, TERRET
  Little, ANNULET
Rodent: Jumping, JERBOA
  Spanish American, AGOUTI, AGOUTY
Sailor: East Indian, LASCAR
Salmon: Young, GRILSE
Salutation: Eastern, SALAAM
Sandpiper, PLOVER
Sandy, ARENOSE
Sapodilla, SAPOTA, SAPOTE
Saw: Surgical, TREPAN
Seven: Group of, HEPTAD
Sexes: Common to both, EPICENE
Shawl: Mexican, SERAPE
Sheathing: Flower, SPATHE
Sheep: Wild, AOUDAD, ARGALI
Shipworm, TEREDO
Shoes: Mercury's winged, TALARIA
Shortening: Syllable, SYSTOLE
Shrub, SPIRAEA
Sickle-shaped, FALCATE

Silver (heraldry), ARGENT
Snake, ANACONDA
Speech: Loss of, APHASIA
Spiral, HELICAL
Staff: Bishop's, CROSIER, CROZIER
Stalk: Plant, PETIOLE
State: Swiss, CANTON
Studio, ATELIER
Swan: Young, CYGNET
Swimming, NATANT
Sword-shaped, ENSATE
Terminal: Negative, CATHODE
Third (music), TIERCE
Thrust: Fencing, RIPOST, RIPOSTE
Tile: Pertaining to, TEGULAR
Tomb: Empty, CENOTAPH
Tooth (comb. form), ODONTO
Tower: Islamic, MINARET
Tree: African timber, BAOBAB
  Black gum, TUPELO
  East Indian, MARGOSA
  Locust, ACACIA
  Malayan, SINTOC
  Marmalade, SAPOTE
Urn: Tea, SAMOVAR
Vehicle, LANDAU, TROIKA
Verbose, PROLIX
Viceroy: Egyptian, KHEDIVE
Vulture: American, CONDOR
Warehouse (French), ENTREPOT
Whale: White, BELUGA
Whirlpool, VORTEX
Will: Addition to, CODICIL
  Having left, TESTATE
Wind, CHINOOK, MONSOON, SIMOOM,
  SIMOON, SIROCCO
Window: In roof, DORMER
Wine, BARBERA, BURGUNDY,
  CABERNET, CHABLIS, CHIANTI,
  CLARET, MUSCATEL, RIESLING,
  SAUTERNE, SHERRY, ZINFANDEL
Wolfish, LUPINE
Woman: Boisterous, TERMAGANT
Woolly, LANATE
Workshop, ATELIER
Zoroastrian, PARSEE

Old Testament Names

We do not pretend that this list is all-inclusive. We list only those names that occur most often in crossword puzzles.

Aaron: First high priest of Jews; son of Amram; brother of Miriam and Moses; father of Abihu, Eleazer, Ithamar, and Nadab.
Abel: Son of Adam and Eve; slain by Cain.
Abigail: Wife of Nabal; later, wife of David.
Abihu: Son of Aaron.
Abimelech: King of Gerar.
Abner: Commander of army of Saul and Ishbosheth; slain by Joab.
Abraham (or Abram): Patriarch; forefather of the Jews; son of Terah; husband of Sarah; father of Isaac and Ishmael.
Absalom: Son of David and Maacah; revolted against David; slain by Joab.
Achish: King of Gath; gave refuge to David.
Achsa (or Achsah): Daughter of Caleb; wife of Othniel.
Adah: Wife of Lamech.
Adam: First man; husband of Eve; father of Cain, Abel, and Seth.
Adonijah: Son of David and Haggith.
Agag: King of Amalek; spared by Saul; slain by Samuel.
Ahasuerus: King of Persia; husband of Vashti and, later, Esther; sometimes identified with Xerxes the Great.
Ahijah: Prophet; foretold accession of Jeroboam.
Ahinoam: Wife of David.
Amasa: Commander of army of David; slain by Joab.
Amnon: Son of David and Ahinoam; raped Tamar; slain by Absalom.
Amram: Husband of Jochebed; father of Aaron, Miriam and Moses.
Asenath: Wife of Joseph.
Asher: Son of Jacob and Zilpah.

Balaam: Prophet; rebuked by his donkey for cursing God.
Barak: Jewish captain; associated with Deborah.
Baruch: Secretary to Jeremiah.
Bathsheba: Wife of Uriah; later, wife of David.
Belshazzar: Crown prince of Babylon.
Benaiah: Warrior of David; proclaimed Solomon King.
Ben-Hadad: Name of several kings of Damascus.
Benjamin: Son of Jacob and Rachel.
Bezaleel: Chief architect of Tabernacle.
Bilhah: Servant of Rachel; mistress of Jacob.
Bildad: Comforter of Job.
Boaz: Husband of Ruth; father of Obed.
Cain: Son of Adam and Eve; slayer of Abel; father of Enoch.
Cainan: Son of Enos.
Caleb: Spy sent out by Moses to visit Canaan; father of Achsa.
Canaan: Son of Ham.
Chilion: Son of Elimelech; husband of Orpah.
Cush: Son of Ham; father of Nimrod.
Dan: Son of Jacob and Bilhah.
Daniel: Prophet; saved from lions by God.
Deborah: Hebrew prophetess and judge; helped Israelites conquer Canaanites.
Delilah: Mistress and betrayer of Samson.
Elam: Son of Shem.
Eleazar: Son of Aaron; succeeded him as high priest.
Eli: High priest and judge; teacher of Samuel; father of Hophni and Phinehas.
Eliakim: Chief minister of Hezekiah.
Eliezer: Servant of Abraham.
Elihu: Comforter of Job.
Elijah (or Elias): Prophet; went to heaven in chariot of fire.

Elimelech: Husband of Naomi; father of Chilion and Mahlon.
Eliphaz: Comforter of Job.
Elisha (or Eliseus): Prophet; successor of Elijah.
Elkanah: Husband of Hannah; father of Samuel.
Enoch: Son of Cain.
Enoch: Father of Methuselah.
Enos: Son of Seth; father of Cainan.
Ephraim: Son of Joseph.
Esau: Son of Isaac and Rebecca; sold his birthright to his twin brother Jacob.
Esther: Jewish wife of Ahasuerus; saved Jews from Haman's plotting.
Eve: First woman; wife of Adam.
Ezra (or Esdras): Hebrew scribe and priest.
Gad: Son of Jacob and Zilpah.
Gehazi: Servant of Elisha.
Gideon: Israelite hero; defeated Midianites.
Goliath: Philistine giant; slain by David.
Hagar: Handmaid of Sarah; concubine of Abraham; mother of Ishmael.
Haggith: Mother of Adonijah.
Ham: Son of Noah; father of Cush, Mizraim, Phut, and Canaan.
Haman: Chief minister of Ahasuerus; hanged on gallows prepared for Mordecai.
Hannah: Wife of Elkanah; mother of Samuel.
Hanun: King of Ammonites.
Haran: Brother of Abraham; father of Lot.
Hazael: King of Damascus.
Hephzi-Bah: Wife of Hezekiah; mother of Mannaseh.
Hiram: King of Tyre.
Holofernes: General of Nebuchadnezzar; slain by Judith.
Hophni: Son of Eli.
Isaac: Hebrew patriarch; son of Abraham and Sarah; half brother of Ishmael; husband of Rebecca; father of Esau and Jacob.
Ishmael: Son of Abraham and Hagar; half brother of Isaac.
Issachar: Son of Jacob and Leah.
Ithamar: Son of Aaron.
Jabal: Son of Lamech and Adah.
Jabin: King of Hazor.
Jacob: Hebrew patriarch; founder of Israel; son of Isaac and Rebecca; husband of Leah and Rachel; father of sons Asher, Benjamin, Dan, Gad, Issachar, Joseph, Judah, Levi, Naphtali, Reuben, Simeon, and Zebulun, and daughter Dinah.
Jael: Slayer of Sisera.
Japheth: Son of Noah.
Jehoiada: High priest; husband of Jehoshabeath; revolted against Athaliah and made Joash King of Judah.
Jehoshabeath (or Jehosheba): Daughter of Jehoram of Judah; wife of Jehoiada.
Jephthah: Judge in Israel; sacrificed his only daughter because of vow.
Jesse: Son of Obed; father of David.
Jethro: Midianite priest; father of Zipporah.
Jezebel: Phoenician princess; wife of Ahab; mother of Ahaziah, Athaliah, and Jehoram.
Joab: Commander in chief under David; slayer of Abner, Absalom, and Amasa.
Job: Patriarch; underwent many afflictions; comforted by Bildad, Elihu, Eliphaz and Zophar.
Jochebed: Wife of Amram.
Jonah: Prophet; cast into sea and swallowed by great fish.
Jonathan: Son of Saul; friend of David.
Joseph: Son of Jacob and Rachel; sold into slavery by his brothers; husband of Asenath; father of Ephraim and Manassah.
Joshua: Successor of Moses; son of Nun.
Jubal: Son of Lamech and Adah.
Judah: Son of Jacob and Leah.
Judith: Slayer of Holofernes.
Kish: Father of Saul.

Laban: Father of Leah and Rachel.
Lamech: Son of Methuselah; father of Noah.
Lamech: Husband of Adah and Zillah; father of Jabal, Jubal, and Tubal-Cain.
Leah: Daughter of Laban; wife of Jacob; sister of Rachel.
Levi: Son of Jacob and Leah.
Lot: Son of Haran; escaped destruction of Sodom.
Maacah: Mother of Absalom and Tamar.
Mahlon: Son of Elimelech; first husband of Ruth.
Manasseh: Son of Joseph.
Melchizedek: King of Salem.
Methuselah: Patriarch; son of Enoch; father of Lamech.
Michal: Daughter of Saul; wife of David.
Miriam: Prophetess; daughter of Amram; sister of Aaron and Moses.
Mizraim: Son of Ham.
Mordecai: Uncle of Esther; with her aid, saved Jews from Haman's plotting.
Moses: Prophet and lawgiver; son of Amram; brother of Aaron and Miriam; husband of Zipporah.
Naaman: Syrian captain; cured of leprosy by Elisha.
Nabal: Husband of Abigail.
Naboth: Owner of vineyard; stoned to death because he would not sell it to Ahab.
Nadab: Son of Aaron.
Nahor: Father of Terah.
Naomi: Wife of Elimelech; mother-in-law of Ruth.
Naphtali: Son of Jacob and Bilhah.
Nathan: Prophet; reproved David for causing Uriah's death.
Nebuchadnezzar (or Nebuchadrezzar): King of Babylon; destroyer of Jerusalem.
Nehemiah: Jewish leader; empowered by Artaxerxes to rebuild Jerusalem.
Nimrod: Mighty hunter; son of Cush.
Noah: Patriarch; son of Lamech; escaped Deluge by building Ark; father of Ham, Japheth and Shem.
Nun (or Non): Father of Joshua.
Obed: Son of Boaz; father of Jesse.
Og: King of Bashan.
Orpah: Wife of Chilion.
Othniel: Kenezite; judge of Israel; husband of Achsa.
Phinehas: Son of Eleazer.
Phinehas: Son of Eli.
Phut (or Put): Son of Ham.
Potiphar: Egyptian official; bought Joseph.
Rachel: Wife of Jacob; mother of Joseph; sister of Leah.
Rebecca (or Rebekah): Wife of Isaac; mother of Esau and Jacob.
Reuben: Son of Jacob and Leah.
Ruth: Wife of Mahlon, later of Boaz; daughter-in-law of Naomi.
Samson: Judge of Israel; famed for strength; betrayed by Delilah.
Samuel: Hebrew judge and prophet; son of Elkanah.
Sarah (or Sara, Sarai): Wife of Abraham; mother of Isaac.
Sennacherib: King of Assyria.
Seth: Son of Adam; father of Enos.
Shem: Son of Noah; father of Elam.
Simeon: Son of Jacob and Leah.
Sisera: Canaanite captain; slain by Jael.
Tamar: Daughter of David and Maachah; raped by Amnon.
Terah: Son of Nahor; father of Abraham.
Tubal-Cain: Son of Lamech and Zillah.
Uriah: Husband of Bathsheba; sent to death in battle by David.
Vashti: Wife of Ahasuerus; set aside by him.
Zadok: High priest during David's reign.
Zebulun (or Zabulon): Son of Jacob and Leah.
Zillah: Wife of Lamech.
Zilpah: Servant of Leah; mistress of Jacob.
Zipporah: Daughter of Jethro; wife of Moses.
Zophar: Comforter of Job.

Kings of Judah and Israel

Kings Before Division of Kingdom
Saul: First King of Israel; son of Kish; father of Ish-Bosheth, Jonathan and Michal.
Ish-Bosheth (or Eshbaal): King of Israel; son of Saul.
David: King of Judah; later of Israel; son of Jesse; husband of Abigail, Ahinoam, Bathsheba, Michal, etc.; father of Absalom, Adonijah, Amnon, Solomon, Tamar, etc.
Solomon: King of Israel and Judah; son of David; father of Rehoboam.
Rehoboam: Son of Solomon; during his reign the kingdom was divided into Judah and Israel.

Kings of Judah (Southern Kingdom)
Rehoboam: First King.
Abijah (or Abijam or Abia): Son of Rehoboam.
Asa: Probably son of Abijah.
Jehoshaphat: Son of Asa.
Jehoram (or Joram): Son of Jehoshaphat; husband of Athaliah.
Ahaziah: Son of Jehoram and Athaliah.
Athaliah: Daughter of King Ahab of Israel and Jezebel; wife of Jehoram; only queen to occupy the throne of Judah.
Joash (or Jehoash): Son of Ahaziah.

Amaziah: Son of Joash.
Uzziah (or Azariah): Son of Amaziah.
Jotham: Regent, later King; son of Uzziah.
Ahaz: Son of Jotham.
Hezekiah: Son of Ahaz; husband of Hephzi-Bah.
Manasseh: Son of Hezekiah and Hephzi-Bah.
Amon: Son of Manasseh.
Josiah (or Josias): Son of Amon.
Jehoahaz (or Joahaz): Son of Josiah.
Jehoiakim: Son of Josiah.
Jehoiachin: Son of Jehoiakim.
Zedekiah: Son of Josiah; kingdom overthrown by Babylonians under Nebuchadnezzar.

Kings of Israel (Northern Kingdom)
Jeroboam I: Led secession of Israel.
Nadab: Son of Jeroboam I.
Baasha: Overthrew Nadab.
Elah: Son of Baasha.
Zimri: Overthrew Elah.
Omri: Overthrew Zimri.

Ahab: Son of Omri; husband of Jezebel.
Ahaziah: Son of Ahab.
Jehoram (or Joram): Son of Ahab.
Jehu: Overthrew Jehoram.
Jehoahaz (or Joahaz): Son of Jehu.
Jehoash (or Joash): Son of Jehoahaz.
Jeroboam II: Son of Jehoash.
Zechariah: Son of Jeroboam II.
Shallum: Overthrew Zechariah.
Menahem: Overthrew Shallum.
Pekahiah: Son of Menahem.
Pekah: Overthrew Pekahiah.
Hoshea: Overthrew Pekah; kingdom overthrown by Assyrians under Sargon II.

Prophets
Major. Isaiah, Jeremiah, Ezekiel, Daniel.
Minor. Hosea, Obadiah, Nahum, Haggai, Joel, Jonah, Habakkuk, Zechariah, Amos, Micah, Zephaniah, Malachi.

Greek and Roman Mythology

Most of the Greek deities were adopted by the Romans, although in many cases there was a change of name. In the list below, information is given under the Greek name; the name in parentheses is the Roman equivalent. However, all Latin names are listed with cross-references to the Greek ones. In addition, there are several deities that are exclusively Roman. **Bold** words within entries indicate cross references.

Achelous: River god; son of Oceanus and Tethys and said to be the father of the Sirens.
Acheron: One of several **Rivers of Underworld.**
Achilles: Greek warrior; slew Hector at Troy; slain by Paris, who wounded him in his vulnerable heel.
Actaeon: Hunter; surprised Artemis bathing; changed by her to stag; and killed by his dogs.
Admetus: King of Thessaly; his wife, Alcestis, offered to die in his place.
Adonis: Beautiful youth loved by Aphrodite.
Aeacus: One of three judges of dead in Hades; son of Zeus.
Aeëtes: King of Colchis; father of Medea; keeper of Golden Fleece.
Aegeus: Father of Theseus; believing Theseus killed in Crete, he drowned himself; Aegean Sea named for him.
Aegisthus: Son of Thyestes; slew Atreus; with Clytemnestra, his paramour, slew Agamemnon; slain by Orestes.
Aegyptus: Brother of Danaus; his sons, except Lynceus, slain by Danaides.
Aeneas: Trojan; son of Anchises and Aphrodite; after fall of Troy, led his followers eventually to Italy; loved and deserted Dido.
Aeolus: One of several **Winds.**
Aesculapius: See Asclepius.
Aeson: King of Ioclus; father of Jason; overthrown by his brother Pelias; restored to youth by Medea.
Aether: Personification of sky.
Aethra: Mother of Theseus.
Agamemnon: King of Mycenae; son of Atreus; brother of Menelaus; leader of Greeks against Troy; slain on his return home by Clytemnestra and Aegisthus.
Aglaia: One of several **Graces.**
Ajax: Greek warrior; killed himself at Troy because Achilles's armor was awarded to Odysseus.
Alcestis: Wife of Admetus; offered to die in his place but saved from death by Hercules.
Alcmene: Wife of Amphitryon; mother by Zeus of Hercules.
Alcyone: One of several **Pleiades.**
Alecto: One of several **Furies.**
Alectryon: Youth changed by Ares into cock.
Althaea: Wife of Oeneus; mother of Meleager.
Amazons: Female warriors in Asia Minor; supported Troy against Greeks.
Amor: See Eros.
Amphion: Musician; husband of Niobe; charmed stones to build fortifications for Thebes.
Amphitrite: Sea goddess; wife of Poseidon.
Amphitryon: Husband of Alcmene.
Anchises: Father of Aeneas.
Ancile: Sacred shield that fell from heavens; palladium of Rome.
Andraemon: Husband of Dryope.
Andromache: Wife of Hector.
Andromeda: Daughter of Cepheus; chained to cliff for monster to devour; rescued by Perseus.
Anteia: Wife of Proetus; tried to induce Bellerophon to elope with her.

Anteros: God who avenged unrequited love.
Antigone: Daughter of Oedipus; accompanied him to Colonus; performed burial rite for Polynices and hanged herself.
Antinoüs: Leader of suitors of Penelope; slain by Odysseus.
Aphrodite (Venus): Goddess of love and beauty; daughter of Zeus and Dione; mother of Eros.
Apollo: God of beauty, poetry, music; later identified with Helios as Phoebus Apollo; son of Zeus and Leto.
Aquilo: One of several **Winds.**
Arachne: Maiden who challenged Athena to weaving contest; changed to spider.
Ares (Mars): God of war; son of Zeus and Hera.
Argo: Ship in which Jason and followers sailed to Colchis for Golden Fleece.
Argus: Monster with hundred eyes; slain by Hermes; his eyes placed by Hera into peacock's tail.
Ariadne: Daughter of Minos; aided Theseus in slaying Minotaur; deserted by him on island of Naxos and married to Dionysus.
Arion: Musician; thrown overboard by pirates but saved by dolphin.
Artemis (Diana): Goddess of moon; huntress; twin sister of Apollo.
Asclepius (Aesculapius): Mortal son of Apollo; slain by Zeus for raising dead; later deified as god of medicine. Also known as Asklepios.
Astarte: Phoenician goddess of love; variously identified with Aphrodite, Selene, and Artemis.
Asterope: See Sterope.
Astraea: Goddess of Justice; daughter of Zeus and Themis.
Atalanta: Princess who challenged her suitors to a foot race; Hippomenes won race and married her.
Athena (Minerva): Goddess of wisdom; known poetically as Pallas Athene; sprang fully armed from head of Zeus.
Atlas: Titan; held world on his shoulders as punishment for warring against Zeus; son of Iapetus.
Atreus: King of Mycenae; father of Menelaus and Agamemnon; brother of Thyestes, three of whose sons he slew and served to him at banquet; slain by Aegisthus.
Atropos: One of several **Fates.**
Aurora: See Eos.
Auster: One of several **Winds.**
Avernus: Infernal regions; name derived from small vaporous lake near Vesuvius which was fabled to kill birds and vegetation.
Bacchus: See Dionysus.
Bellerophon: Corinthian hero; killed Chimera with aid of Pegasus; tried to reach Olympus on Pegasus and was thrown to his death.
Bellona: Roman goddess of war.
Boreas: One of several **Winds.**
Briareus: Monster of hundred hands; son of Uranus and Gaea.
Briseis: Captive maiden given to Achilles; taken by Agamemnon in exchange for loss of Chryseis, which caused Achilles to cease fighting, until death of Patroclus.
Cadmus: Brother of Europa; planter of dragon seeds from which first Thebans sprang.

Calliope: One of several **Muses.**

Calypso: Sea nymph; kept Odysseus on her island Ogygia for seven years.

Cassandra: Daughter of Priam; prophetess who was never believed; slain with Agamemnon.

Castor: One of **Dioscuri.**

Celaeno: One of several **Pleiades.**

Centaurs: Beings half man and half horse; lived in mountains of Thessaly.

Cephalus: Hunter; accidentally killed his wife Procris with his spear.

Cepheus: King of Ethiopia; father of Andromeda.

Cerberus: Three-headed dog guarding entrance to Hades.

Ceres: See Demeter.

Chaos: Formless void; personified as first of gods.

Charon: Boatman on Styx who carried souls of dead to Hades; son of Erebus.

Charybdis: Female monster; personification of whirlpool.

Chimera: Female monster with head of lion, body of goat, tail of serpent; killed by Bellerophon.

Chiron: Most famous of centaurs.

Chronos: Personification of time.

Chryseis: Captive maiden given to Agamemnon; his refusal to accept ransom from her father Chryses caused Apollo to send plague on Greeks besieging Troy.

Circe: Sorceress; daughter of Helios; changed Odysseus's men into swine.

Clio: One of several **Muses.**

Clotho: One of several **Fates.**

Clytemnestra: Wife of Agamemnon, whom she slew with aid of her paramour, Aegisthus; slain by her son Orestes.

Cocytus: One of several **Rivers of Underworld.**

Creon: Father of Jocasta; forbade burial of Polynices; ordered burial alive of Antigone.

Creüsa: Princess of Corinth, for whom Jason deserted Medea; slain by Medea, who sent her poisoned robe; also known as Glaüke.

Creusa: Wife of Aeneas; died fleeing Troy.

Cronus (Saturn): Titan; god of harvests; son of Uranus and Gaea; dethroned by his son Zeus.

Cupid: See Eros.

Cybele: Anatolian nature goddess; adopted by Greeks and identified with Rhea.

Cyclopes: Race of one-eyed giants (singular: Cyclops).

Daedalus: Athenian artificer; father of Icarus; builder of Labyrinth in Crete; devised wings attached with wax for him and Icarus to escape Crete.

Danae: Princess of Argos; mother of Perseus by Zeus, who appeared to her in form of golden shower.

Danaïdes: Daughters of Danaüs; at his command, all except Hypermnestra slew their husbands, the sons of Aegyptus.

Danaüs: Brother of Aegyptus; father of Danaïdes; slain by Lynceus.

Daphne: Nymph; pursued by Apollo; changed to laurel tree.

Decuma: One of several **Fates.**

Deino: One of several **Graeae.**

Demeter (Ceres): Goddess of agriculture; mother of Persephone.

Diana: See Artemis.

Dido: Founder and queen of Carthage; stabbed herself when deserted by Aeneas.

Diomedes: Greek hero; with Odysseus, entered Troy and carried off Palladium, sacred statue of Athena.

Diomedes: Owner of man-eating horses, which Hercules, as ninth labor, carried off.

Dione: Titan goddess; mother by Zeus of Aphrodite.

Dionysus (Bacchus): God of wine; son of Zeus and Semele.

Dioscuri: Twins Castor and Pollux; sons of Leda by Zeus.

Dis: See Pluto, Hades.

Dryads: Wood nymphs.

Dryope: Maiden changed to Hamadryad.

Echo: Nymph who fell hopelessly in love with Narcissus; faded away except for her voice.

Electra: Daughter of Agamemnon and Clytemnestra; sister of Orestes; urged Orestes to slay Clytemnestra and Aegisthus.

Electra: One of several **Pleiades.**

Elysium: Abode of blessed dead.

Endymion: Mortal loved by Selene.

Enyo: One of several **Graeae.**

Eos (Aurora): Goddess of dawn.

Epimetheus: Brother of Prometheus; husband of Pandora.

Erato: One of several **Muses.**

Erebus: Spirit of darkness; son of Chaos.

Erinyes: One of several **Furies.**

Eris: Goddess of discord.

Eros (Amor or Cupid): God of love; son of Aphrodite.

Eteocles: Son of Oedipus, whom he succeeded to rule alternately with Polynices; refused to give up throne at end of year; he and Polynices slew each other.

Eumenides: One of several **Furies.**

Euphrosyne: One of several **Graces.**

Europa: Mortal loved by Zeus, who, in form of white bull, carried her off to Crete.

Eurus: One of several **Winds.**

Euryale: One of several **Gorgons.**

Eurydice: Nymph; wife of Orpheus.

Eurystheus: King of Argos; imposed twelve labors on Hercules.

Euterpe: One of several **Muses.**

Fates: Goddesses of destiny; Clotho (Spinner of thread of life), Lachesis (Determiner of length), and Atropos (Cutter of thread); also called Moirae. Identified by Romans with their goddesses of fate; Nona, Decuma, and Morta; called Parcae.

Fauns: Roman deities of woods and groves.

Faunus: See Pan.

Favonius: One of several **Winds.**

Flora: Roman goddess of flowers.

Fortuna: Roman goddess of fortune.

Furies: Avenging spirits; Alecto, Megaera, and Tisiphone; known also as Erinyes or Eumenides.

Gaea: Goddess of earth; daughter of Chaos; mother of Titans; known also as Ge, Gea, Gaia, etc.

Galatea: Statue of maiden carved from ivory by Pygmalion; given life by Aphrodite.

Galatea: Sea nymph; loved by Polyphemus.

Ganymede: Beautiful boy; successor to Hebe as cupbearer of gods.

Glaucus: Mortal who became sea divinity by eating magic grass.

Golden Fleece: Fleece from ram that flew Phrixos to Colchis; Aeëtes placed it under guard of dragon; carried off by Jason.

Gorgons: Female monsters; Euryale, Medusa, and Stheno; had snakes for hair; their glances turned mortals to stone.

Graces: Beautiful goddesses; Aglaia (Brilliance), Euphrosyne (Joy), and Thalia (Bloom); daughters of Zeus.

Graeae: Sentinels for Gorgons.; Deino, Enyo, and Pephredo; had one eye among them, which passed from one to another.

Hades (Dis): Name sometimes given Pluto; also, abode of dead, ruled by Pluto.

Haemon: Son of Creon; promised husband of Antigone; killed himself in her tomb.

Hamadryads: Tree nymphs.

Harpies: Monsters with heads of women and bodies of birds.

Hebe (Juventas): Goddess of youth; cupbearer of gods before Ganymede; daughter of Zeus and Hera.

Hecate: Goddess of sorcery and witchcraft.

Hector: Son of Priam; slayer of Patroclus; slain by Achilles.

Hecuba: Wife of Priam.

Helen: Fairest woman in world; daughter of Zeus and Leda; wife of Menelaus; carried to Troy by Paris, causing Trojan War.

Heliades: Daughters of Helios; mourned for Phaëthon and were changed to poplar trees.

Helios (Sol): God of sun; later identified with Apollo.

Helle: Sister of Phrixos; fell from ram of Golden Fleece; water where she fell named Hellespont.

Hephaestus (Vulcan): God of fire; celestial blacksmith; son of Zeus and Hera; husband of Aphrodite.

Hera (Juno): Queen of heaven; wife of Zeus.

Hercules: Hero and strong man; son of Zeus and Alcmene; performed twelve labors or deeds to free from bondage under Eurystheus; after death, his mortal share was destroyed, and he became immortal. Also known as Herakles or Heracles. Labors: (1) killing Nemean lion; (2) killing Lernaean Hydra; (3) capturing Erymanthian boar; (4) capturing Ceryneian hind; (5) killing man-eating Stymphalian birds; (6) procuring girdle of Hippolyte; (7) cleaning Augean stables; (8) capturing Cretan bull; (9) capturing man-eating horses of Diomedes; (10) capturing cattle of Geryon; (11) procuring golden apples of Hesperides; (12) bringing Cerberus up from Hades.

Hermes (Mercury): God of physicians and thieves; messenger of gods; son of Zeus and Maia.

Hero: Priestess of Aphrodite; Leander swam Hellespont nightly to see her; drowned herself at his death.

Hesperus: Evening star.

Hestia (Vesta): Goddess of hearth; sister of Zeus.

Hippolyte: Queen of Amazons; wife of Theseus.

Hippolytus: Son of Theseus and Hippolyte; falsely accused by Phaedra of trying to kidnap her; slain by Poseidon at request of Theseus.

Hippomenes: Husband of Atalanta, whom he beat in race by dropping golden apples, which she stopped to pick up.

Hyacinthus: Beautiful youth accidentally killed by Apollo, who caused flower to spring up from his blood.

Hydra: Nine-headed monster in marsh of Lerna; slain by Hercules.

Hygeia: Personification of health.

Hyman: God of marriage.

Hyperion: Titan; early sun god; father of Helios.

Hypermnestra: Daughter of Danaüs; refused to kill her husband Lynceus.

Hypnos (Somnus): God of sleep.

Iapetus: Titan; father of Atlas, Epimetheus, and Prometheus.

Icarus: Son of Daedalus; flew too near sun with wax-attached wings and fell into sea and was drowned.

Io: Mortal maiden loved by Zeus; changed by Hera into heifer.

Iobates: King of Lycia; sent Bellerophon to slay Chimera.

Iphigenia: Daughter of Agamemnon; offered as sacrifice to Artemis at Aulis; carried by Artemis to Tauris where she became priestess; escaped from there with Orestes.

Iris: Goddess of rainbow; messenger of Zeus and Hera.

Ismene: Daughter of Oedipus; sister of Antigone.

Iulus: Son of Aeneas.

Ixion: King of Lapithae; for making love to Hera he was bound to endlessly revolving wheel in Tartarus.

Janus: Roman god of gates and doors; represented with two opposite faces.

Jason: Son of Aeson; to gain throne of Ioclus from Pelias, went to Colchis and brought back Golden Fleece; married Medea; deserted her for Creüsa.

Jocasta: Wife of Laius; mother of Oedipus; unwittingly became wife of Oedipus; hanged herself when relationship was discovered.

Juno: *See* Hera.

Jupiter: *See* Zeus.

Juventas: *See* Hebe.

Lachesis: One of several **Fates.**

Laius: Father of Oedipus, by whom he was slain.

Laocoön: Priest of Apollo at Troy; warned against bringing wooden horse into Troy; destroyed with his two sons by serpents sent by Athena.

Lares: Roman ancestral spirits protecting descendants and homes.

Latona: *See* Leto.

Lavinia: Wife of Aeneas after defeat of Turnus.

Leander: Swam Hellespont nightly to see Hero; drowned in storm.

Leda: Mortal loved by Zeus in form of swan; mother of Helen, Clytemnestra, Dioscuri.

Lethe: One of several **Rivers of Underworld.**

Leto (Latona): Mother by Zeus of Artemis and Apollo.

Lucina: Roman goddess of childbirth; identified with Juno.

Lynceus: Son of Aegyptus; husband of Hypermnestra; slew Danaüs.

Maia: Daughter of Atlas; mother of Hermes.

Maia: One of several **Pleiades.**

Manes: Souls of dead Romans, particularly of ancestors.

Mars: *See* Ares.

Marsyas: Shepherd; challenged Apollo to music contest and lost; flayed alive by Apollo.

Medea: Sorceress; daughter of Aeëtes; helped Jason obtain Golden Fleece; when deserted by him for Creüsa, killed her children and Creüsa.

Medusa: One of several **Gorgons.** slain by Perseus, who cut off her head.

Megaera: One of several **Furies.**

Meleager: Son of Althaea; his life would last as long as brand burning at his birth; Althaea quenched and saved it but destroyed it when Meleager slew his uncles.

Melpomene: One of several **Muses.**

Memnon: Ethiopian king; made immortal by Zeus; son of Tithonus and Eos.

Menelaus: King of Sparta; son of Atreus; brother of Agamemnon; husband of Helen.

Mentor: Tutor of Telemachus and friend of Odysseus. In the *Odyssey*, on several occasions, Athena assumes form of Mentor to give advice to Telemachus or Odysseus

Mercury: *See* Hermes.

Merope: One of several **Pleiades.** Merope is said to have hidden in shame for loving a mortal.

Mezentius: Cruel Etruscan king; ally of Turnus against Aeneas; slain by Aeneas.

Midas: King of Phrygia; given gift of turning to gold all he touched.

Minerva: *See* Athena.

Minos: King of Crete; after death, one of three judges of dead in Hades; son of Zeus and Europa.

Minotaur: Monster, half man and half beast, kept in Labyrinth in Crete; slain by Theseus.

Mnemosyne: Goddess of memory; mother by Zeus of Muses.

Moirae: One of several **Fates.**

Momus: God of ridicule.

Morpheus: God of dreams.

Mors: *See* Thanatos.

Morta: One of several **Fates.**

Muses: Goddesses presiding over arts and sciences: Calliope (epic poetry), Clio (history), Erato (lyric and love poetry), Euterpe (music), Melpomene (tragedy), Polymnia or Polyhymnia (sacred poetry), Terpsichore (choral dance and song), Thalia (comedy and bucolic poetry), Urania (astronomy); daughters of Zeus and Mnemosyne.

Naiads: Nymphs of waters, streams, and fountains.

Napaeae: Wood nymphs.

Narcissus: Beautiful youth loved by Echo; in punishment for not returning her love, he was made to fall in love with his image reflected in pool; pined away and became flower.

Nemesis: Goddess of retribution.

Neoptolemus: Son of Achilles; slew Priam; also known as Pyrrhus.

Neptune: *See* Poseidon.

Nereids: Sea nymphs; attendants on Poseidon.

Nestor: King of Pylos; noted for wise counsel in expedition against Troy.

Nike: Goddess of victory.

Niobe: Daughter of Tantalus; wife of Amphion; her children slain by Apollo and Artemis; changed to stone but continued to weep her loss.

Nona: One of several **Fates.**

Notus: One of several **Winds.**

Nox: *See* Nyx.

Nymphs: Beautiful maidens; minor deities of nature.

Nyx (Nox): Goddess of night.

Oceanids: Ocean nymphs; daughters of Oceanus.

Oceanus: Eldest of Titans; god of waters.

Odysseus (Ulysses): King of Ithaca; husband of Penelope; wandered ten years after fall of Troy before arriving home.

Oedipus: King of Thebes; son of Laius and Jocasta; unwittingly murdered Laius and married Jocasta; tore his eyes out when relationship was discovered.

Oenone: Nymph of Mount Ida; wife of Paris, who abandoned her; refused to cure him when he was poisoned by arrow of Philoctetes at Troy.

Ops: *See* Rhea.

Oreades: Mountain nymphs.

Orestes: Son of Agamemnon and Clytemnestra; brother of Electra; slew Clytemnestra and Aegisthus; pursued by Furies until his purification by Apollo.

Orion: Hunter; slain by Artemis and made heavenly constellation.

Orpheus: Famed musician; son of Apollo and Muse Calliope; husband of Eurydice.

Pales: Roman goddess of shepherds and herdsmen.

Palinurus: Aeneas' pilot; fell overboard in his sleep and was drowned.

Pan (Faunus): God of woods and fields; part goat; son of Hermes.

Pandora: Opener of box containing human ills; mortal wife of Epimetheus.

Parcae: One of several **Fates.**

Paris: Son of Priam; gave apple of discord to Aphrodite, for which she enabled him to carry off Helen; slew Achilles at Troy; slain by Philoctetes.

Patroclus: Great friend of Achilles; wore Achilles' armor and was slain by Hector.

Pegasus: Winged horse that sprang from Medusa's body at her death; ridden by Bellerophon when he slew Chimera.

Pelias: King of Ioclus; seized throne from his brother Aeson; sent Jason for Golden Fleece; slain unwittingly by his daughters at instigation of Medea.

Pelops: Son of Tantalus; his father cooked and served him to gods; restored to life; Peloponnesus named for him.

Penates: Roman household gods.

Penelope: Wife of Odysseus; waited faithfully for him for many years while putting off numerous suitors.

Pephredo: One of several **Graeae.**

Periphetes: Giant; son of Hephaestus; slain by Theseus.

Persephone (Proserpine): Queen of infernal regions; daughter of Zeus and Demeter; wife of Pluto.

Perseus: Son of Zeus and Danaë; slew Medusa; rescued Andromeda from monster and married her.

Phaedra: Daughter of Minos; wife of Theseus; caused the death of her stepson, Hippolytus.

Phaethon: Son of Helios; drove his father's sun chariot and was struck down by Zeus before he set world on fire.

Philoctetes: Greek warrior who possessed Hercules' bow and arrows; slew Paris at Troy with poisoned arrow.

Phineus: Betrothed of Andromeda; tried to slay Perseus but turned to stone by Medusa's head.

Phlegethon: One of several **Rivers of Underworld.**

Phosphor: Morning star.

Phrixus: Brother of Helle; carried by ram of Golden Fleece to Colchis.

Pirithous: Son of Ixion; friend of Theseus; tried to carry off Persephone from Hades; bound to enchanted rock by Pluto.

Pleiades: Alcyone, Celaeno, Electra, Maia, Merope, Sterope or Asterope, Taygeta; seven daughters of Atlas; transformed into heavenly constellation, of which six stars are visible (Merope is said to have hidden in shame for loving a mortal).

Pluto (Dis): God of Hades; brother of Zeus.

Plutus: God of wealth.

Pollux: One of **Dioscuri.**

Polyhymnia: *See* Polymnia.

Polymnia (Polyhymnia): One of several **Muses.**

Polynices: Son of Oedipus; he and his brother Eteocles killed each other; burial rite, forbidden by Creon, performed by his sister Antigone.

Polyphemus: Cyclops; devoured six of Odysseus's men; blinded by Odysseus.

Polyxena: Daughter of Priam; betrothed to Achilles, whom Paris slew at their betrothal; sacrificed to shade of Achilles.

Pomona: Roman goddess of fruits.

Pontus: Sea god; son of Gaea.

Poseidon (Neptune): God of sea; brother of Zeus.

Priam: King of Troy; husband of Hecuba; ransomed Hector's body from Achilles; slain by Neoptolemus.

Priapus: God of regeneration.

Procris: Wife of Cephalus, who accidentally slew her.

Procrustes: Giant; stretched or cut off legs of victims to make them fit iron bed; slain by Theseus.

Proetus: Husband of Anteia; sent Bellerophon to Iobates to be put to death.

Prometheus: Titan; stole fire from heaven for man. Zeus punished him by chaining him to rock in Caucasus where vultures devoured his liver daily.

Proserpine: *See* Persephone.

Proteus: Sea god; assumed various shapes when called on to prophesy.

Psyche: Beloved of Eros; punished by jealous Aphrodite; made immortal and united with Eros.

Pygmalion: King of Cyprus; carved ivory statue of maiden which Aphrodite gave life as Galatea.

Pyramus: Babylonian youth; made love to Thisbe through hole in wall; thinking Thisbe slain by lion, killed himself.

Python: Serpent born from slime left by Deluge; slain by Apollo.

Quirinus: Roman war god.

Remus: Brother of Romulus; slain by him.

Rhadamanthus: One of three judges of dead in Hades; son of Zeus and Europa.

Rhea (Ops): Daughter of Uranus and Gaea; wife of Cronus; mother of Zeus; identified with Cybele.

Rivers of Underworld. Acheron (woe), Cocytus (wailing), Lethe (forgetfulness), Phlegethon (fire), Styx (across which souls of dead were ferried by Charon).

Romulus: Founder of Rome; he and Remus suckled in infancy by she-wolf; slew Remus; deified by Romans.

Sarpedon: King of Lycia; son of Zeus and Europa; slain by Patroclus at Troy.

Saturn: *See* Cronus.

Satyrs: Hoofed demigods of woods and fields; companions of Dionysus.

Sciron: Robber; forced strangers to wash his feet, then hurled them into sea where tortoise devoured them; slain by Theseus.

Scylla: Female monster inhabiting rock opposite Charybdis; menaced passing sailors.

Selene: Goddess of moon.

Semele: Daughter of Cadmus; mother by Zeus of Dionysus; demanded Zeus appear before her in all his splendor and was destroyed by his lightning bolts.

Sibyis: Various prophetesses; most famous, Cumaean sibyl, accompanied Aeneas into Hades.

Sileni: Minor woodland deities similar to satyrs (singular: silenus). Sometimes Silenus refers to eldest of satyrs, son of Hermes or of Pan.

Silvanus: Roman god of woods and fields.

Sinis: Giant; bent pines, with which he hurled victims against side of mountain; slain by Theseus.

Sirens: Minor deities who lured sailors to destruction with their singing.

Sisyphus: King of Corinth; condemned in Tartarus to roll huge stone to top of hill; it always rolled back down again.

Sol: *See* Helios.

Somnus: *See* Hypnos.

Sphinx: Monster of Thebes; killed those who could not answer her riddle; slain by Oedipus. Name also refers to other monsters having body of lion, wings, and head and bust of woman.

Sterope (Asterope): One of several **Pleiades.**

Stheno: One of several **Gorgons.**

Styx: One of several **Rivers of Underworld.** The souls of the dead were ferried across the Styx by Charon.

Symplegades: Clashing rocks at entrance to Black Sea; Argo passed through, causing them to become forever fixed.

Syrinx: Nymph pursued by Pan; changed to reeds, from which he made his pipes.

Tantalus: Cruel king; father of Pelops and Niobe; condemned in Tartarus to stand chin-deep in lake surrounded by fruit branches; as he tried to eat or drink, water or fruit always receded.

Tartarus: Underworld below Hades; often refers to Hades.

Taygeta: One of several **Pleiades.**

Telemachus: Son of Odysseus; made unsuccessful journey to find his father.

Tellus: Roman goddess of earth.

Terminus: Roman god of boundaries and landmarks.

Terpsichore: One of several **Muses.**

Terra: Roman earth goddess.

Thalia: One of several **Graces.** Also one of several **Muses.**

Thanatos (Mors): God of death.

Themis: Titan goddess of laws of physical phenomena; daughter of Uranus; mother of Prometheus.

Theseus: Son of Aegeus; slew Minotaur; married and deserted Ariadne; later married Phaedra.

Thisbe: Beloved of Pyramus; killed herself at his death.

Thyestes: Brother of Atreus; Atreus killed three of his sons and served them to him at banquet.

Tiresias: Blind soothsayer of Thebes.

Tisiphone: One of several **Furies.**

Titans: Early gods from which Olympian gods were derived; children of Uranus and Gaea.

Tithonus: Mortal loved by Eos; changed into grasshopper.

Triton: Demigod of sea; son of Poseidon.

Turnus: King of Rutuli in Italy; betrothed to Lavinia; slain by Aeneas.

Ulysses: *See* Odysseus.

Urania: One of several **Muses.**

Uranus: Personification of Heaven; husband of Gaea; father of Titans; dethroned by his son Cronus.

Venus: *See* Aphrodite.

Vertumnus: Roman god of fruits and vegetables; husband of Pomona.

Vesta: *See* Hestia.

Vulcan: *See* Hephaestus.

Winds: Aeolus (keeper of winds), Boreas (Aquilo) (north wind), Eurus (east wind), Notus (Auster) (south wind), Zephyrus (Favonius) (west wind).

Zephyrus: One of several **Winds.**

Zeus (Jupiter): Chief of Olympian gods; son of Cronus and Rhea; husband of Hera.

Norse Mythology

Aesir: Chief gods of Asgard.

Andvari: Dwarf; robbed of gold and magic ring by Loki.

Angerbotha (Angrbotha): Giantess; mother by Loki of Fenrir, Hel, and Midgard serpent.

Asgard (Asgarth): Abode of gods.

Ask (Aske, Askr): First man; created by Odin, Hoenir, and Lothur.

Asynjur: Goddesses of Asgard.

Atli: Second husband of Gudrun; invited Gunnar and Hogni to his court, where they were slain; slain by Gudrun.

Audhumla (Audhumbla): Cow that nourished Ymir; created Buri by licking ice cliff.

Balder (Baldr, Baldur): God of light, spring, peace, joy; son of Odin; slain by Hoth at instigation of Loki.

Bifrost: Rainbow bridge connecting Midgard and Asgard.

Bragi (Brage): God of poetry; husband of Ithunn.

Branstock: Great oak in hall of Volsungs; into it, Odin thrust Gram, which only Sigmund could draw forth.

Brynhild: Valkyrie; wakened from magic sleep by Sigurd; married Gunnar; instigated death of Sigurd; killed herself and was burned on pyre beside Sigurd.

Bur (Bor): Son of Buri; father of Odin, Hoenir, and Lothur.

Buri (Bori): Progenitor of gods; father of Bur; created by Audhumla.

Embla: First woman; created by Odin, Hoenir, and Lothur.

Fafnir: Son of Rodmar, whom he slew for gold in Otter's skin; in form of dragon, guarded gold; slain by Sigurd.

Fenrir: Wolf; offspring of Loki; swallows Odin at Ragnarok and is slain by Vitharr.

Forseti: Son of Balder.

Frey (Freyr): God of fertility and crops; son of Njorth; originally one of **Vanir.**

Freya (Freyja): Goddess of love and beauty; sister of Frey; originally one of **Vanir.**

Frigg (Frigga): Goddess of sky; wife of Odin.

Garm: Watchdog of Hel; slays, and is slain by, Tyr at Ragnarok.

Gimle: Home of blessed after Ragnarok.

Giuki: King of Nibelungs; father of Gunnar, Hogni, Guttorm, and Gudrun.

Glathsehim (Gladsheim): Hall of gods in Asgard.

Gram (meaning "Angry"): Sigmund's sword; rewelded by Regin; used by Sigurd to slay Fafnir.

Greyfell: Sigmund's horse; descended from Sleipnir.

Grimhild: Mother of Gudrun; administered magic potion to Sigurd which made him forget Brynhild.

Gudrun: Daughter of Giuki; wife of Sigurd; later wife of Atli and Jonakr.

Gunnar: Son of Giuki; in his semblance Sigurd won Brynhild for him; slain at hall of Atli.

Guttorm: Son of Giuki; slew Sigurd at Brynhild's request.

Heimdall (Heimdallr): Guardian of Asgard.

Hel: Goddess of dead and queen of underworld; daughter of Loki.

Hiordis: Wife of Sigmund; mother of Sigurd.

Hoenir: One of creators of Ask and Embla; son of Bur.

Hogni: Son of Giuki; slain at hall of Atli.

Hoth (Hoder, Hodur): Blind god of night and darkness; slayer of Balder at instigation of Loki.

Ithunn (Ithun, Iduna): Keeper of golden apples of youth; wife of Bragi.

Jonakr: Third husband of Gudrun.

Jormunrek: Slayer of Swanhild; slain by sons of Gudrun.

Jotunnheim (Jotunheim): Abode of giants.

Lif and Lifthrasir: First man and woman after Ragnarok.

Loki: God of evil and mischief; instigator of Balder's death.

Lothur (Lodur): One of creators of Ask and Embla.

Midgard (Midgarth): Abode of mankind; the earth.

Midgard Serpent: Sea monster; offspring of Loki; slays, and is slain by, Thor at Ragnarok.

Mimir: Giant; guardian of well in Jotunnheim at root of Yggdrasill; knower of past and future.

Mjolnir: Magic hammer of Thor.

Nagifar: Ship to be used by giants in attacking Asgard at Ragnarok; built from nails of dead men.

Nanna: Wife of Balder.

Nibelungs: Dwellers in northern kingdom ruled by Giuki.

Niflheim (Nifelheim): Outer region of cold and darkness; abode of Hel.

Njorth: Father of Frey and Freya; originally one of **Vanir.**

Norns: Demigoddesses of fate: Urth (Urdur) (past), Verthandi (Verdandi) (present), Skuld (future).

Odin (Othin): Head of **Aesir;** creator of world with Vili and Ve; equivalent to Woden (Wodan, Wotan) in Teutonic mythology.

Otter: Son of Rodmar; slain by Loki; his skin filled with gold hoard of Andvari to appease Rodmar.

Ragnarok: Final destruction of present world in battle between gods and giants; some minor gods will survive, and Lif and Lifthrasir will repeople world.

Regin: Blacksmith; son of Rodmar; foster-father of Sigurd.

Rerir: King of Huns; son of Sigi.

Rodmar: Father of Regin, Otter, and Fafnir; demanded Otter's skin be filled with gold; slain by Fafnir, who stole gold.

Sif: Wife of Thor.

Siggeir: King of Goths; husband of Signy; he and his sons slew Volsung and his sons, except Sigmund; slain by Sigmund and Sinflotli.

Sigi: King of Huns; son of Odin.

Sigmund: Son of Volsung; brother of Signy, who bore him Sinflotli; husband of Hiordis, who bore him Sigurd.

Signy: Daughter of Volsung; sister of Sigmund; wife of Siggeir; mother by Sigmund of Sinflotli.

Sigurd: Son of Sigmund and Hiordis; wakened Brynhild from magic sleep; married Gudrun; slain by Guttorm at instigation of Brynhild.

Sigyn: Wife of Loki.

Sinflotli: Son of Sigmund and Signy.

Skuld: One of several **Norns.**

Sleipnir (Sleipner): Eight-legged horse of Odin.

Surt (Surtr): Fire demon; slays Frey at Ragnarok.

Svartalfaheim: Abode of dwarfs.

Swanhild: Daughter of Sigurd and Gudrun; slain by Jormunrek.

Thor: God of thunder; oldest son of Odin; equivalent to Germanic deity Donar.

Tyr: God of war; son of Odin; equivalent to Tiu in Teutonic mythology.

Ull (Ullr): Son of Sif; stepson of Thor.

Urth: One of several **Norns.**

Valhalla (Valhall): Great hall in Asgard where Odin received souls of heroes killed in battle.

Vali: Odin's son; Ragnarok survivor.

Valkyries: Virgins, messengers of Odin, who selected heroes to die in battle and took them to Valhalla; generally considered as nine in number.

Vanir: Early race of gods; three survivors, Njorth, Frey, and Freya, are associated with **Aesir.**

Ve: Brother of Odin; one of creators of world.

Verthandi: One of several **Norns.**

Vili: Brother of Odin; one of creators of world.

Vingolf: Abode of goddesses in Asgard.

Vitharr (Vithar): Son of Odin; survivor of Ragnarok.

Volsung: Descendant of Odin, and father of Signy, Sigmund; his descendants were called Volsungs.

Yggdrasill: Giant ash tree springing from body of Ymir and supporting universe; its roots extended to Asgard, Jotunnheim, and Niffheim.

Ymir (Ymer): Primeval frost giant killed by Odin, Vili, and Ve; world created from his body; also, from his body sprang Yggdrasill.

Egyptian Mythology

Aaru: Abode of the blessed dead.

Amen (Amon, Ammdn): One of chief Theban deities; united with sun god under form of Amen-Ra; husband of Mut.

Amenti: Region of dead where souls were judged by Osiris.

Anubis: Guide of souls to Amenti; son of Osiris; jackal-headed.

Apis: Sacred bull, an embodiment of Ptah; identified with Osiris as Osiris-Apis or Serapis.

Geb (Keb, Seb): Earth god; father of Osiris; represented with goose on head.

Hathor (Athor): Goddess of love and mirth; cow-headed.

Horus: God of day; son of Osiris and Isis; hawk-headed.

Isis: Goddess of motherhood and fertility; sister and wife of Osiris.

Khepera: God of morning sun.

Khnemu (Khnum, Chnuphis, Chnemu, Chnum): Ram-headed god.

Khonsu (Khensu, Khuns): Son of Amen and Mut.

Mentu (Ment): Solar deity, sometimes considered god of war; falcon-headed.

Min (Khem, Chem): Principle of physical life.

Mut (Maut): Wife of Amen.

Nephthys: Goddess of the dead; sister and wife of Set.

Nu: Chaos from which world was created, personified as a god.

Nut: Goddess of heavens; consort of Geb.

Osiris: God of underworld and judge of dead; son of Geb and Nut; brother and husband of Isis.

Ptah (Phtha): Chief deity of Memphis.

Ra: God of the Sun, the supreme god; son of Nut; Pharaohs claimed descent from him; represented as lion, cat, or falcon.

Serapis: God uniting attributes of Osiris and Apis.

Set (Seth): God of darkness or evil; brother and enemy of Osiris; brother and husband of Nephthys.

Shu: Solar deity; son of Ra and Hathor.

Tem (Atmu, Atum, Tum): Solar deity.

Thoth (Dhouti): God of wisdom and magic; scribe of gods; ibis-headed.

A Concise Guide to Grammar and Style

This section discusses and illustrates the basic conventions of American capitalization, italicization, and punctuation.

Capitalization

Capitalize the following:

- **Proper nouns and adjectives derived from proper nouns:**

Marie Curie	China, Chinese
Smokey Robinson	Darwin, Darwinian

  But vocabulary words derived from proper nouns are generally lowercase:

china cups	plaster of paris
french fries	vienna sausage

- **The names of geographic divisions, regions, and localities and topographical features such as rivers, lakes, and mountains:**

North Pole	Gulf States
Middle East	Atlantic Ocean
Southern Hemisphere	Rocky Mountains
the North	Lake Tahoe
Lower East Side	Erie Canal

  Do not capitalize directions: She lives 10 miles north of Boston.

- **The names of nationalities, ethnic groups, tribes, and languages:**

Spanish	Bantu
Asian American	Creole

- **Titles when preceding a name:**

President Lincoln	Aunt Mary
Queen Victoria	Doctor Johnson
Senator Kennedy	Professor Davies

  Do not capitalize such terms elsewhere: a biography of the queen; the senator's speech; my aunt, Mary Wilson; the president's fundraising efforts; the residence of the vice president.

- **Epithets:** Ivan the Terrible; Lincoln is known as the Great Emancipator.

- **The names of political and judicial bodies, social organizations, councils, and departments:**

U.S. Senate	Rotary Club
Democratic Party	United Negro College Fund
State Department	U.S. Supreme Court

- **The names for periods, events, and documents of historical importance:**

Middle Ages	Constitution
Renaissance	Treaty of Versailles
Battle of Waterloo	Magna Carta

- **The names for streets, buildings, and monuments:**

Fifth Avenue	World Trade Center
Broadway	Statue of Liberty

- **The names for the supreme deity and sacred works:**

God, the Father Almighty	Bible
Yahweh	Talmud
Allah	Qu'ran

- **The names for religious denominations and their members:**

  Buddhism, Buddhists
  Catholicism, Catholics
  Judaism, Jews
  Methodist Church, Methodists
  Society of Friends, Quakers

- **The days of the week, months of the year, holidays, and holy days:**

Thursday	Labor Day
December	Passover

- **The pronoun I:**

  I told her I didn't want to go.

- **The first word in the salutation and complimentary close of a letter:**

  My dear Carol . . .
  Very truly yours . . .

- **The first word of a sentence:**

  Are you hungry? Lunch will be served soon.

- **The first word of a direct quotation, except when the quotation is split:**

  I asked, "Do you really like bats?"
  "Yes," said Holly, "they're so cute."

- **The first word and all the key words in the title of a literary or other artistic work:**

  The Bluest Eye (novel)
  A Streetcar Named Desire (play)
  "The Road Not Taken" (poem)
  Starry Night (painting)
  "Only the Lonely" (song)

- **The names of ships, aircraft, and space vehicles:**

  USS *Maine*
  The Spirit of St. Louis
  space shuttle *Challenger*

- **The names of constellations, planets, and stars:**

Milky Way	Saturn
the asteroid Juno	Little Dipper

- **The names of geologic eras, periods, epochs, and names of prehistoric divisions:**

Paleozoic Era	*Pleistocene*
Quaternary Period	*Stone Age*

- **The genus but not the species name in binomial nomenclature:**

  Canis familiaris (dog)
  Malus pumila (apple tree)

Italicization

Italicize the following (or underline if writing by hand or using a typewriter):

- **The titles of books, plays, book-length poems, magazines, and newspapers:**

War and Peace	*TIME* magazine
Twelfth Night	*National Geographic*
Beowulf	*Miami Herald*

- **The titles of movies and radio and television programs:**

Finding Nemo	*Law & Order*
Car Talk	*Masterpiece Theater*

- **The titles of works of art, including paintings, sculptures, and major musical compositions:**

  Mona Lisa (painting)
  The Thinker (sculpture)
  Swan Lake (ballet)
  Porgy and Bess (opera)

  Do not italicize musical compositions named by number or key: Symphony No. 4; Quartet in E minor.

- **Words, letters, and numbers used as such:**

  How do you spell *ache*?
  Does your name end with a *c* or a *k*?
  The *6* looked like a *0*.

- **Foreign words and phrases that have not been assimilated into English:**

  Alex's *Weltanschauung* was gloomy.
  Ed made a *tarte au citron* for dessert.

- **Words and phrases that are being emphasized:**

  Paris was *the* place to be in the '20s.

- **The names of the plaintiff and defendant in legal citations:** *Johnson* v. *Smith*.

- **The names of ships, aircraft, and space vehicles:**

  USS *Maine*
  The Spirit of St. Louis
  space shuttle *Challenger*

- **The New Latin names of genera, species, subspecies, and varieties in botanical and zoological nomenclature:** *Quercus alba; Homo sapiens.*

Punctuation

End Marks

- **Use a period after a declarative or imperative statement:**

  I went to the library.
  Sign your name here.

- **Use a question mark after a direct question or to indicate uncertainty:**

  What is your name?
  Chaucer's dates are 1340?–1400.

  Do not use a question mark after an indirect question: I asked them what time they were leaving.

- **Use an exclamation point after an exclamatory or emphatic sentence or an interjection:**

  Give me a break!
  Hey! Ouch! Wow!

Comma

Use a comma:

- **To separate words in a list or series:**

  The baby likes grapes, bananas, and cantaloupe.

- **To separate two or more adjectives that come before a noun when *and* can be substituted without changing the meaning:**

  He had a kind, generous nature.
  The dog had thick, soft, shiny fur.

  Do not use the comma if the adjectives together express a single idea or the noun is a compound made up of an adjective and a noun:

  The kitchen had bright yellow curtains.
  A majestic bald eagle soared overhead.

- **To set off words or phrases in apposition to a noun:**

  George Eliot, the great 19th-century novelist, was born in 1819.

  Do not use commas when the appositive word or phrase is essential to the meaning of the sentence:

  The novelist George Eliot was born in 1819.

- **To set off nonessential phrases and clauses:**

  My French professor, who has an odd sense of humor, has been teaching for some 30 years.

  Do not use commas when the phrase or clause is essential to the meaning of the sentence:

  The professor who teaches my French class has an odd sense of humor.

- **To separate the independent clauses joined by a coordinating conjunction in a compound sentence:**

  He lives in New York, and she lives in London.
  Some people like golf, but others prefer tennis.

- **To set off interrupters such as *of course, however, I think,* and *by the way* from the rest of the sentence:**

  She knew, of course, that he was lying.
  By the way, I'll be away next week.

- **To set off an introductory word, phrase, or clause at the beginning of a sentence:**

  Yes, I'd like to go with you.
  After some years, we met again.
  Being tall, she often gets teased.

- **To set off a word in direct address:**

  Thanks, guys, for all your help.
  How was your trip, Kathy?

- **To set off a tag question:**

  You won't do that again, will you?

- **To introduce a short quotation:**

  The queen said, "Let them eat cake!"

- **To close the salutation in a personal letter and the complimentary close in a business or personal letter:**

  Dear Mary, ... Sincerely, Fred

- **To set off titles and degrees:**

  Sarah Little, Ph.D.   Robert Johnson, Jr.

- **To separate sentence elements that might be read incorrectly without the comma:**

  As they entered, in the shadows you could see a figure lurking.

- **To set off the month and day from the year in full dates:**

  The conference will be held on August 6, 2001.

  Do not use a comma when only the month and year appear:

  The conference will be held in August 2001.

- **To set off the city and state in an address:**

  Sam Green
  10 Joy Street
  Boston, MA 02116

  If the address is inserted into text, add a second comma after the state:

  Cincinnati, Ohio, is their home.

Colon

Use a colon:

- **To introduce a list, or words, phrases, and clauses that explain, enlarge upon, or summarize what has gone before:**

  Please provide the following: your name, address, and phone number.

  "No honest poet can ever feel quite sure of the permanent value of what he has written: He may have wasted his time and messed up his life for nothing."—T. S. Eliot

- **To introduce a long quotation:**

  In 1780 John Adams wrote: "English is destined to be in the next and succeeding centuries more generally the language of the world than Latin was in the last or French is in the present age . . ."

- **To separate hour and minute(s) in standard time notation:**

  The train arrives at 9:30.

- **To close the salutation in a business letter:**

  Dear Sir or Madam:

Semicolon

Use a semicolon:

- **To separate the independent clauses in a compound sentence not joined by a conjunction:**

  Only two seats were left; we needed three.

  The situation is hopeful; the storm may lift soon.

- **To separate two independent clauses, the second of which begins with an adverb such as *however, consequently, moreover,* and *therefore*:**

  We waited an hour; however, we couldn't hang around indefinitely.

- **To separate elements already punctuated with commas:**

  Invitations were mailed to the various professors, associate professors, and assistant professors; the secretary of the department; and some of the grad students.

Dashes & Hyphens

- **Use a dash to indicate a sudden break in continuity or to set off an explanatory, a defining, or an emphatic phrase:**

  The sky grew dark—where were the kids?

  Dairy foods—milk, cheese, yogurt—are a good source of calcium.

- **Use a hyphen to join the elements of a compound word or to join the elements of a compound modifier before a noun:**

  well-wisher   ice-skating rink
  fifty-three   college-age students

- **Use a hyphen to divide a word at the end of a line:**

  Rasputin is one of history's most enigmatic and intriguing figures.

Brackets & Parentheses

- **Use brackets to set off words or letters in quoted matter that have been added by someone other than the author:**

  "She [Willa Cather] is certainly one of the great American writers of the 20th century."

- **Use parentheses to set off nonessential information:**

  We spent an hour (more or less) cleaning up.

Apostrophe

Use an apostrophe to indicate:

- **The possessive case of singular and plural nouns, indefinite pronouns, and proper nouns:**

  my sister's son   somebody's lunch
  my two sisters' sons   Charles's house
  the children's toys   the Rosses' friends

- **The plural of letters, numbers, symbols, and words used as such:**

  too many *thus*'s   ten 5's in a row
  spelled with two *e*'s   delete some &'s

- **Missing letters in contractions and missing numbers in dates:**

  I'm (I am)   class of '95
  ma'am (madam)   winter of '97–'98

Quotation Marks

Use quotation marks:

- **To set off direct quotations:**

  "Let's go to the beach," she suggested.

- **To set off titles of short stories, articles, chapters, essays, songs, poems, and individual radio and television programs:**

  Chapter 9, "The New Englishes"
  sang the "Star-Spangled Banner"
  "The Apparent Trap" episode of *Frasier*

- **To set off words and phrases that are being used in an unusual or questionable way or might be preceded by *so-called*:**

  Mari's "fine" was a day's volunteer work.

  According to the article, bees appear to "remember" landmarks.

Commonly Mispronounced Words

aegis: *ee-jis,* not *ay-jis*
asterisk: *as-ter-isk,* not *as-ter-ik*
alumnae: *a-lum-nee,* not *a-lum-nay*
archipelago: *ar-ki-PEL-a-go,* not *arch-i-pel-a-go*
athlete: *ath-leet,* not *ath-a-leet*
candidate: *kan-di-dayt,* not *kan-i-dayt*
chimera: *kiy-MEER-a,* not *CHIM-er-a*
disastrous: *di-zas-tres,* not *di-zas-ter-es*
electoral: *e-LEK-tor-al,* not *e-lek-TOR-al*
etcetera: *et-set-er-a,* not *ek-set-er-a*
lambaste: *lam-bayst,* not *lam-bast*
larvae: *lar-vee,* not *lar-vay*
library: *li-brar-y,* not *li-bar-y*
mischievous: *MIS-che-vus,* not *mis-CHEE-vee-us*
mispronunciation: *mis-pro-nun-see-ay-shun,* not *mis-pro-nown-see-ay-shun*

nuclear: *noo-klee-ur,* not *noo-kyu-lur*
nuptial: *nup-shul,* not *nup-shoo-al*
primer: (schoolbook) *prim-mer,* not *pry-mer*
picture: *pik-cher,* not *pit-cher*
prescription: *prih-skrip-shun,* not *per-skrip-shun*
prerogative: *pre-rog-a-tive,* not *per-rog-a-tive*
peremptory: *per-emp-tuh-ree,* not *pre-emp-tuh-ree*
probably: *prob-a-blee,* not *pra-lee* or *prob-lee*
Realtor: *reel-ter,* not *ree-la-ter*
supposedly: *su-pos-ed-lee,* not *su-pos-ab-lee*
spurious: *spyoor-ee-us,* not *spur-ee-us*
ticklish: *tik-lish,* not *tik-i-lish*
triathlon: *try-ath-lon,* not *try-ath-a-lon*

National Spelling Bee

The National Spelling Bee was launched by the Louisville, Kentucky, *Courier-Journal* in 1925. With competitions, cash prizes, and a trip to the nation's capital, it was hoped the Bee would stimulate "general interest among pupils in a dull subject." The Scripps Howard News Service took over the Bee in 1941. Over the years the national finals have grown from a mere 9 contestants to about 250. In 2004, 14-year-old South Bend, Ind., eighth-grader David Scott Tidmarsh took home $12,000 cash, among other prizes, for correctly spelling *autochthonous*. Here are the winning words that made past spellers into national champions.

1925	gladiolus	1945	NO BEE	1965	eczema	1985	milieu
1926	abrogate	1946	semaphore	1966	ratoon	1986	odontalgia
1927	luxuriance	1947	chlorophyll	1967	chihuahua	1987	staphylococci
1928	albumen	1948	psychiatry	1968	abalone	1988	elegiacal
1929	asceticism	1949	dulcimer	1969	interlocutory	1989	spoliator
1930	fracas	1950	haruspex	1970	croissant	1990	fibranne
1931	foulard	1951	insouciant	1971	shalloon	1991	antipyretic
1932	knack	1952	vignette	1972	macerate	1992	lyceum
1933	propitiatory	1953	soubrette	1973	vouchsafe	1993	kamikaze
1934	deteriorating	1954	transept	1974	hydrophyte	1994	antediluvian
1935	intelligible	1955	custaceology	1975	incisor	1995	xanthosis
1936	interning	1956	condominium	1976	narcolepsy	1996	vivisepulture
1937	promiscuous	1957	schappe	1977	cambist	1997	euonym
1938	sanitarium	1958	syllepsis	1978	deification	1998	chiaroscurist
1939	canonical	1959	cacolet	1979	maculature	1999	logorrhea
1940	therapy	1960	troche	1980	elucubrate	2000	demarche
1941	initials	1961	smaragdine	1981	sarcophagus	2001	succedaneum
1942	sacrilegious	1962	esquamulose	1982	psoriasis	2002	prospicience
1943	NO BEE	1963	equipage	1983	Purim	2003	pococurante
1944	NO BEE	1964	sycophant	1984	luge	2004	autochthonous

Most Widely Spoken Languages in the World

Language	Approx. number of speakers
1. Chinese (Mandarin)	1,075,000,000
2. English	514,000,000
3. Hindustani	496,000,000
4. Spanish	425,000,000
5. Russian	275,000,000
6. Arabic	256,000,000
7. Bengali	215,000,000
8. Portuguese	194,000,000
9. Malay-Indonesian	176,000,000
10. French	129,000,000

Source: Ethnologue, 13th Edition, and other sources.

Most Studied Foreign Languages in the U.S.[1]

Language	Fall 2002 enrollments	% change from 1998
1. Spanish	746,267	13.7 %
2. French	201,979	1.5
3. German	91,100	2.3
4. Italian	63,899	29.6
5. American Sign Language	60,781	432.2[2]
6. Japanese	52,238	21.1
7. Chinese	34,153	20.0
8. Latin	29,841	14.1
9. Russian	23,921	0.5
10. Ancient Greek[3]	20,376	24.2

1. By number of foreign language enrollments in U.S. institutions of higher education. 2. This is larger than the actual growth rate; it reflects past underreporting. 3. If combined, Biblical Hebrew and Modern Hebrew claim 10th place, with 22,802 enrolled and a 44% change. *Source:* Association of Departments of Foreign Languages at the Modern Language Association, *Foreign Language Enrollments in United States Institutions of Higher Education, Fall 2002.*

Easily Confused or Misused Words

affect / effect *Effect* is usually a noun that means a result or the power to produce a result: "The sound of the falling rain had a calming effect, nearly putting me to sleep." *Affect* is usually a verb that means to have an influence on: "His loud humming was affecting my ability to concentrate." Note that *effect* can also be a verb meaning to bring about or execute: "The speaker's somber tone effected a dampening in the general mood of the audience."

all right / alright Although *alright* is widely used, it is considered nonstandard English. As the *American Heritage Dictionary* notes, it's not "all right to use alright."

allusion / illusion *Allusion* is a noun that means an indirect reference: "The speech made allusions to the final report." *Illusion* is a noun that means a misconception: "The policy is designed to give an illusion of reform."

alternately / alternatively *Alternately* is an adverb that means in turn; one after the other: "We alternately spun the wheel in the game." *Alternatively* is an adverb that means on the other hand; one or the other: "You can choose a large bookcase or, alternatively, you can buy two small ones."

beside / besides *Beside* is a preposition that means next to: "Stand here beside me." *Besides* is an adverb that means also: "Besides, I need to tell you about the new products my company offers."

bimonthly / semimonthly *Bimonthly* is an adjective that means every two months: "I brought the cake for the bimonthly office party." *Bimonthly* is also a noun that means a publication issued every two months: "The company publishes several popular bimonthlies." *Semimonthly* is an adjective that means happening twice a month: "We have semimonthly meetings on the 1st and the 15th."

capital / capitol The city or town that is the seat of government is called the *capital*; the building in which the legislative assembly meets is the *capitol*. The term *capital* can also refer to an accumulation of wealth or to a capital letter.

cite / site *Cite* is a verb that means to quote as an authority or example: "I cited several eminent scholars in my study of water resources." It also means to recognize formally: "The public official was cited for service to the city." It can also mean to summon before a court of law: "Last year the company was cited for pollution violations." *Site* is a noun meaning location: "They chose a new site for the factory just outside town."

complement / compliment *Complement* is a noun or verb that means something that completes or makes up a whole: "The red sweater is a perfect complement to the outfit." *Compliment* is a noun or verb that means an expression of praise or admiration: "I received compliments about my new outfit."

comprise / compose According to the traditional rule, the whole comprises the parts, and the parts compose the whole. Thus, the board comprises five members, whereas five members compose (or make up) the board. It is also correct to say that the board is composed (not comprised) of five members.

connote / denote *Connote* is a verb that means to imply or suggest: "The word 'espionage' connotes mystery and intrigue." *Denote* is a verb that means

to indicate or refer to specifically: "The symbol for 'pi' denotes the number 3.14159."

discreet / discrete *Discreet* is an adjective that means prudent, circumspect, or modest: "Her discreet handling of the touchy situation put him at ease." *Discrete* is an adjective that means separate or individually distinct: "Each company in the conglomerate operates as a discrete entity."

disinterested / uninterested *Disinterested* is an adjective that means unbiased or impartial: "We appealed to the disinterested mediator to facilitate the negotiations." *Uninterested* is an adjective that means not interested or indifferent: "They seemed uninterested in our offer."

emigrant / immigrant *Emigrant* is a noun that means one who leaves one's native country to settle in another: "The emigrants spent four weeks aboard ship before landing in Los Angeles." *Immigrant* is a noun that means one who enters and settles in a new country: "Most of the immigrants easily found jobs." One emigrates *from* a place; one immigrates *to* another.

farther / further *Farther* is an adjective and adverb that means to or at a more distant point: "We drove 50 miles today; tomorrow, we will travel 100 miles farther." *Further* is an adjective and adverb that means to or at a greater extent or degree: "We won't be able to suggest a solution until we are further along in our evaluation of the problem." It can also mean in addition or moreover: "They stated further that they would not change the policy."

few / less *Few* is an adjective that means small in number. It is used with countable objects: "This department has few employees." *Less* is an adjective that means small in amount or degree. It is used with objects of indivisible mass: "Which jar holds less water?"

figuratively / literally *Figuratively* is an adverb that means metaphorically or symbolically: "Happening upon the shadowy figure, they figuratively jumped out of their shoes." *Literally* is an adverb that means actually: "I'm not exaggerating when I say I literally fell off my chair." It also means according to the exact meaning of the words: "I translated the Latin passage literally."

foreword / forward *Foreword* is a noun that means an introductory note or preface: "In my foreword I explained my reasons for writing the book." *Forward* is an adjective or adverb that means toward the front: "I sat in the forward section of the bus." "Please step forward when your name is called." *Forward* is also a verb that means to send on: "Forward the letter to the customer's new address."

founder / flounder In its primary sense *founder* means to sink below the surface of the water: "The ship foundered after colliding with an iceberg." By extension, *founder* means to fail utterly. *Flounder* means to move about clumsily, or to act with confusion. A good synonym for *flounder* is blunder: "After floundering through the first half of the course, Amy finally passed with the help of a tutor."

hanged / hung *Hanged* is the past tense and past participle of hang when the meaning is to execute by suspending by the neck: "They hanged the prisoner for treason." "The convicted killer was hanged at dawn." *Hung* is the past tense and participle of hang when the meaning is to suspend from above with no support from below: "I hung the painting on the wall." "The painting was hung at a crooked angle."

historic / historical In general usage, *historic* refers to what is important in history, while *historical* applies more broadly to whatever existed in the past whether it was important or not: "a historic summit meeting between the prime ministers;" "historical buildings torn down in the redevelopment."

i.e. / e.g. The abbreviation *e.g.* means for example (from Latin *exempli gratia*): "Her talents were legion and varied (e.g., deep sea diving, speed reading, bridge, and tango dancing)." The abbreviation *i.e.* means that is or in other words (from Latin *id est*): "The joy of my existence (i.e., my stamp collection) imbues my life with meaning."

it's / its *It's* is a contraction for it is, whereas *its* is the possessive form of it: "It's a shame that we cannot talk about its size."

laid / lain / lay *Laid* is the past tense and the past participle of the verb lay and not the past tense of lie. *Lay* is the past tense of the verb lie and *lain* is the past participle: "He laid his books down and lay down on the couch, where he has lain for an hour."

lend / loan Although some people feel *loan* should only be used as a noun, *lend* and *loan* are both acceptable as verbs in standard English: "Can you lend (loan) me a dollar?" However, only *lend* should be used in figurative senses: "Will you lend me a hand?"

nonplussed Meaning perplexed or bewildered, *nonplussed* is very often thought to mean just the opposite—calm, unruffled, cool-as-a-cucumber. A common mistake is to think the word means not "plussed," but no such word exists. *Nonplussed* originates from the Latin *non* (no) and *plus* (more, further), and means a state in which no more can be

done—one is so perplexed that further action is impossible. "The lexicographer grew increasingly agitated and nonplussed by the frequency with which she noted the misuse of *nonplussed*."

passed / past *Passed* is the past tense and past participle of *pass*. *Past* refers to time gone by; it is also a preposition meaning beyond. "In the past decade, I passed over countless opportunities; I was determined not to let them get past me again."

penultimate Meaning "next to last," *penultimate* is often mistakenly used to mean "the very last," or the ultimate: "The perfectionist was crestfallen when he was awarded the penultimate prize; the grand prize went to another."

principal / principle *Principal* is a noun that means a person who holds a high position or plays an important role: "The school principal has 20 years of teaching experience." *Principal* is also an adjective that means chief or leading: "The necessity of moving to another city was the principal reason I turned down the job offer." *Principle* is a noun that means a rule or standard: "They refused to compromise their principles."

stationary / stationery *Stationary* is an adjective that means fixed or unmoving: "They maneuvered around the stationary barrier in the road." *Stationery* is a noun that means writing materials: "We printed the letters on company stationery."

their/there/they're *Their* is the possessive form of they; *there* refers to place; and *they're* is the contraction of *they are*. "They're going there because their mother insisted they become proficient in Serbo-Croatian."

who's / whose *Who's* is the contraction of *who is*. *Whose* is the possessive form of *who*. "Who's going to figure out whose job it is to clean the stables?"

Some Basic Phrases in Other Languages

	The language itself	hello	good bye	please	thank you	English	yes	no	traditional toast
German	Deutsch	hallo	auf Wiedersehen	bitte	danke	Englisch	ja	nein	prosit
Dutch	Nederlands	hallo	tot ziens	alstublieft	dankjewel	engels	ja	nee	proost
Danish	dansk	hej	farvel	(¹)	tak	engelsk	ja	nej	skål
Swedish	svenska	hej	hejdå	tack	tack	engelska	ja	nej	skål
French	français	bonjour	au revoir	s'il vous plaît	merci	anglais	oui	non	santé
Spanish	español	hola	adiós	por favor	gracias	inglés	sí	no	salud
Italian	italiano	ciao	arrivederci	per favore	grazie	inglese	si	no	salute
Hebrew	ivrit	shalom	lehitraot	bevakasha	toda	anglit	ken	lo	le-chaim
Irish	Gaeilge	fáilte	slán	le do thoil	go raibh maith agat	Béarla	sea²	ní ha³	slainte
Swahili	Kiswahili	(⁴)	kwa heri	tafadhali	asante	Kingereza	ndiyo	siyo	—
Japanese	nihongo	konnichiwa	sayonara	kudasai	arigatou	eigo	hai	iie	kanpai
Finnish	suomi	päivää	näkemiin	ole hyvä	kiitos	englanti	kyllä	ei	kippis
Indonesian	bahasa Indonesia	selamat pagi	selamat tinggal⁵	tolong	terima kasih	bahasa Inggris	ya	tidak	—

1. There is no single word or expression that directly corresponds to "please." Polite requests are made in different ways. 2. Literally, "it is." This can only be used in answering a question with the verb "to be." In Irish there is no word for "yes" or "no." Instead, the speaker repeats the verb from the question in the affirmative or the negative: Did you sleep well? I did. Are you coming? I am not. 3. Literally, "it is not." See above. 4. There is no single word for "hello." Which greeting is used will depend on the relative ages, number (singular or plural), and/or race of the speakers. For example, "hujambo," reply "sijambo," would be used by two people of similar age and race, whereas "jambo," reply "jambo," would be used by a white person and a black person. 5. Said by the person leaving; "selamat jalan" is said by the person staying.

Foreign Words and Phrases[1]

The English meanings given below are not necessarily literal translations.

ad absurdum (ad ab-sir′dum) [Lat.]: to the point of absurdity. "He tediously repeated his argument *ad absurdum.*"

ad infinitum (ad in-fun-eye′tum) [Lat.]: to infinity. "The lecture seemed to drone on *ad infinitum.*"

ad nauseam (ad noz′ee-um) [Lat.]: to a sickening degree. "The politician uttered one platitude after another *ad nauseam.*"

aficionado (uh-fish′ya-nah′doh) [Span.]: an ardent devotee. "I was surprised at what a baseball *aficionado* she had become."

angst (angkst) [Ger.]: dread and anxiety. "Sylvia's teenage *angst* was nothing compared to the parental *angst* experienced by the two individuals whose duty it was to raise her."

annus mirabilis (an′us muh-ra′buh-lis) [Lat.]: wonderful year. "Last year was the *annus mirabilis* for my company."

a priori (ah pree-or′ee) [Lat.]: based on theory rather than observation. "The fact that their house is in such disrepair suggests *a priori* that they are having financial difficulties."

au courant (oh′ koo-rahn′) [Fr.]: up-to-date. "The shoes, the hair, the clothes—every last detail of her dress, in fact—was utterly *au courant.*"

beau geste (boh zhest′) [Fr.]: a fine or noble gesture, often futile. "My fellow writers supported me by writing letters of protest to the publisher, but their *beau geste* could not prevent the inevitable."

beau monde (boh′ mond′) [Fr.]: high society. "Such elegant decor would impress even the *beau monde.*"

bête noire (bet nwahr′) [Fr.]: something or someone particularly disliked. "Talk of the good old college days way back when had become his *bête noire,* and he began to avoid his school friends."

bon mot (bon moe′) [Fr.]: a witty remark or comment. "One *bon mot* after another flew out of his mouth, charming the audience."

bon vivant (bon vee-vahnt′) [Fr.]: a person who lives luxuriously and enjoys good food and drink. "It's true he's quite the *bon vivant,* but when he gets down to business he conducts himself like a Spartan."

carpe diem (kar′pay dee′um) [Lat.]: seize the day. "So what if you have an 8:00 a.m. meeting tomorrow and various appointments? *Carpe diem!*"

carte blanche (kart blonsh′) [Fr.]: unrestricted power to act on one's own. "I may have *carte blanche* around the office, but at home I'm a slave to my family's demands."

casus belli (kay′sus bel′eye) [Lat.]: an act justifying war. "The general felt that the banana republic's insolent remarks about our national honor were enough of a *casus belli* to launch an attack."

cause célèbre (koz suh-leb′ruh) [Fr.]: a widely known controversial case or issue. "The Sacco and Vanzetti trial became an international *cause célèbre* during the 1920s."

caveat emptor (kav′ee-ot emp′tor) [Lat.]: let the buyer beware. "Before you leap at that real estate deal, *caveat emptor!*"

comme ci comme ça (kom see′ kom sah′) [Fr.]: so-so. "The plans for the party strike me as *comme ci comme ça.*"

comme il faut (kom eel foe′) [Fr.]: as it should be; fitting. "His end was truly *comme il faut.*"

coup de grâce (koo de grahss′) [Fr.]: finishing blow. "After an already wildly successful day, the *coup de grâce* came when she won best all-around athlete."

cri de coeur (kree′ de kur′) [Fr.]: heartfelt appeal. "About to leave the podium, he made a final *cri de coeur* to his people to end the bloodshed."

de rigueur (duh ree-gur′) [Fr.]: strictly required, as by etiquette, usage, or fashion. "Loudly proclaiming one's support for radical causes had become *de rigueur* among her crowd."

deus ex machina (day′us ex mahk′uh-nuh) [Lat.]: a contrived device to resolve a situation. "Stretching plausibility, the movie concluded with a *deus ex machina* ending in which everyone was rescued at the last minute."

dolce vita (dole′chay vee′tuh) [Ital.]: sweet life; the good life perceived as one of physical pleasure and self-indulgence. "My vacation this year is going to be two uninterrupted weeks of *dolce vita.*"

doppelgänger (dop′pul-gang-ur) [Ger.]: a ghostly double or counterpart of a living person. "I could not shake the sense that some shadowy *doppelgänger* echoed my every move."

enfant terrible (ahn-fahn′ tay-reeb′luh) [Fr.]: an incorrigible child; an outrageously outspoken or bold person. "He played the role of *enfant terrible,* jolting us with his blunt assessment."

entre nous (ahn′truh noo′) [Fr.]: between ourselves; confidentially. "*Entre nous,* their marriage is on the rocks."

ex cathedra (ex kuh-thee′druh) [Lat.]: with authority; used especially of those pronouncements of the pope that are considered infallible. "I resigned myself to obeying; my father's opinions were *ex cathedra* in our household."

ex post facto (ex′ post fak′toh) [Lat.]: retroactively. "I certainly hope that the change in policy will be honored *ex post facto.*"

fait accompli (fate ah-kom-plee′) [Fr.]: an accomplished fact, presumably irreversible. "There's no use protesting—it's a *fait accompli.*"

faux pas (foh pah′) [Fr.]: a social blunder. "Suddenly, she realized she had unwittingly committed yet another *faux pas.*"

flagrante delicto (fla-grahn′tee di-lik′toh) [Lat.]: in the act. "The detective realized that without hard evidence he had no case; he would have to catch the culprit *flagrante delicto.*"

glasnost (glaz′nohst) [Rus.]: open and frank discussion: initiated by Mikhail Gorbachev in 1985 in the Soviet Union. "Once the old chairman retired, the spirit of *glasnost* pervaded the department."

hoi polloi (hoy′ puh-loy′) [Gk.]: the common people. "Marie Antoinette recommended cake to the *hoi polloi.*"

in loco parentis (in loh'koh pa-ren'tiss) [Lat.]: in the place of a parent. "The court appointed a guardian for the children, to serve *in loco parentis.*"

in medias res (in me'-dee-as rays) [Lat.]: in the middle of a sequence of occurences. "The film begin *in medias res,* with a panting, terrified man running through the night."

in situ (in sit'too) [Lat.]: situated in the original or natural position. "I prefer seeing statues *in situ* rather than in the confines of a museum."

in vino veritas (in vee'no vare'i-toss) [Lat.]: in wine there is truth. "By the end of the party, several of the guests had made a good deal of their private lives public, prompting the host to murmur to his wife, '*in vino veritas.*'"

ipso facto (ip'soh fak'toh) [Lat.]: by the fact itself. "An extremist, *ipso facto,* cannot become part of a coalition."

je ne sais quoi (zheh neh say kwah') [Fr.]: I know not what; an elusive quality. "She couldn't explain it, but there was something *je ne sais quoi* about him that she found devastatingly attractive."

mano a mano (mah'no ah mah'no) [Span.]: directly or face-to-face in a confrontation or conflict. "'Stay out of it,' he admonished his friends, 'I want to handle this guy *mano a mano.*'"

mea culpa (may'uh kul'puh) [Lat.]: I am to blame. "His *mea culpa* was so offhand that I hardly think he meant it."

memento mori (muh-men'toh more'ee) [Lat.]: a reminder that you must die. "The skull rested on the mantlepiece as a *memento mori.*"

mise en scene (mee' zahn sen) [Fr.]: the stage setting; surroundings. "The *mise en scene* for the sci-fi movie was molded, futuristic furniture and blinding klieg lights."

mot juste (moh zhoost') [Fr.]: the exact, appropriate word. "'Rats!' screamed the defiant three-year-old, immensely proud of his *mot juste.*"

ne plus ultra (nee' plus ul'truh) [Lat.]: the most intense degree of a quality or state. "Pulling it from the box, he realized he was face to face with the *ne plus ultra* of computers."

nom de plume (nom duh ploom') [Fr.]: pen name. "Deciding it was time to sit down and begin a novel, the would-be writer spent the first several hours deciding upon a suitable *nom de plume.*"

persona non grata (per-soh'nuh non grah'tuh) [Lat.]: unacceptable or unwelcome person. "Once I was cut out of the will, I became *persona non grata* among my relatives."

prima facie (pry'ma fay'she) [Lat.]: at first sight, clear and evident. "Although her husband implored, 'I can explain!' the sight of another woman wrapped in his arms was *prima facie* evidence that he was a deceitful lout."

pro bono (pro boh'noh) [Lat.]: done or donated without charge; free. "The lawyer's *pro bono* work gave him a sense of value that his work on behalf of the corporation could not."

quid pro quo (kwid' pro kwoh') [Lat.]: something for something; an equal exchange. "She vowed that when she had the means, she would return his favors *quid pro quo.*"

sans souci (sahn soo-see') [Fr.]: carefree. "After serveral glasses of champagne, their mood turned distinctly *sans souci.*"

savoir-faire (sav'wahr fair') [Fr.]: the ability to say and do the correct thing. "She presided over the gathering with impressive *savoir-faire.*"

schadenfreude (shah den froy'deh) [Ger.]: pleasure at someone else's misfortunes. "*Schadenfreude* suffused the classroom after the insufferably supercilious class pet was caught cheating by the teacher."

sic transit gloria mundi (sick tran'sit glor'ee-uh mun'dee) [Lat.]: thus passes away the glory of the world. "Watching the aging former football quarterback lumber down the street, potbellied and dissipated, his friend shook his head in disbelief and muttered, '*sic transit gloria mundi.*'"

sine qua non (sin'ay kwah nohn') [Lat.]: indispensable element or condition. "Lemon is the *sine qua non* of this recipe."

sotto voce (suh'tow voh'chee) [Ital.]: in a quiet voice, attempting not to be overheard. "While the others were distracted, he filled me in *sotto voce* on all the deliciously sordid details of the scandal."

sui generis (su'ee jen'e-ris) [Lat.]: unique. "Adjusting her pirate's hat and fringed hula skirt, Zelda sashayed into the party, knowing her fashion statement was *sui generis.*"

terra incognita (tare'uh in-kog-nee'tuh) [Lat.]: unknown territory. "When the conversation suddenly switched from contemporary fiction to medieval Albanian playwrights, he felt himself entering *terra incognita.*"

veni, vidi, vici (ven'ee vee'dee vee'chee) [Lat.]: I came, I saw, I conquered. "After the takeover the business mogul gloated, '*veni, vidi, vici.*'"

vox populi (voks pop'yoo-lie) [Lat.]: the voice of the people. "My sentiments echo those of the *vox populi.*"

Wanderjahr[2] (vahn'der-yahr) [Ger.]: a year or period of travel, especially following one's schooling. "The trio took off on their *Wanderjahr,* intent on visiting every museum between Edinburgh and Rome."

Weltanschauung[2] (velt'an-shou'ung) [Ger.]: a world view or philosophy of life. "His *Weltanschauung* gradually metamorphized from a grim and pessimistic one to a sunny, but no less complex, view."

Weltschmerz[2] (velt'shmerts) [Ger.]: sorrow over the evils of the world. "His poetry expressed a certain *Weltschmerz,* or world-weariness."

Zeitgeist[2] (zite'guyst) [Ger.]: the thought or sensibility characteristic of a particular period of time. "She blamed it on the *Zeitgeist,* which encouraged hedonistic excess."

---

1. Foreign words and phrases should be set in italics (or underlined if written in longhand) if their meanings are likely to be unknown to the reader. Whether the expression is familiar or unfamiliar, however, is a matter of judgment. In this list, all foreign words have been italicized for the sake of emphasis. 2. German nouns are capitalized. A familiar German expression that is not italicized, however, should be lowercased, following the English conventions of not capitalizing common nouns. "His proclivities leaned more to the occult than to the philosophical: a poltergeist he could understand; the *Zeitgeist* he could not."

Latin and Greek Word Elements

English is a living language, and it is growing all the time. One way that new words come into the language is when words are borrowed from other languages. New words are also created when words or word elements, such as roots, prefixes, and suffixes, are combined in new ways.

Many English words and word elements can be traced back to Latin and Greek. Often you can guess the meaning of an unfamiliar word if you know the meaning.

A **word root** is a part of a word. It contains the core meaning of the word, but it cannot stand alone. A **prefix** is also a word part that cannot stand alone. It is placed at the beginning of a word to change its meaning. A **suffix** is a word part that is placed at the end of a word to change its meaning. Often you can guess the meaning of an unfamiliar word if you know the meaning of its parts; that is, the root and any prefixes or suffixes that are attached to it.

Latin Roots, Prefixes, and Suffixes

Latin was the language spoken by the ancient Romans. As the Romans conquered most of Europe, the Latin language spread throughout the region. Over time, the Latin spoken in different areas developed into separate languages, including Italian, French, Spanish, and Portuguese. These languages are considered "sisters," as they all descended from Latin, their "mother" language.

In 1066 England was conquered by William, duke of Normandy, which is in northern France. For several hundred years after the Norman invasion, French was the language of court and polite society in England. It was during this period that many French words were borrowed into English. Linguists estimate that some 60% of our common everyday vocabulary today comes from French. Thus many Latin words came into English indirectly through French.

Many Latin words came into English directly, though, too. Monks from Rome brought religious vocabulary as well as Christianity to England beginning in the 6th century. From the Middle Ages onward many scientific, scholarly, and legal terms were borrowed from Latin.

During the 17th and 18th centuries, dictionary writers and grammarians generally felt that English was an imperfect language whereas Latin was perfect. In order to improve the language, they deliberately made up a lot of English words from Latin words. For example, fraternity, from Latin fraternitas, was thought to be better than the native English word brotherhood.

Many English words and word parts can be traced back to Latin and Greek. The following table lists some common Latin roots.

Latin root	Basic meaning	Example words
-dict-	to say	contradict, dictate, diction, edict, predict
-duc-	to lead, bring, take	deduce, produce, reduce
-gress-	to walk	digress, progress, transgress
-ject-	to throw	eject, inject, interject, project, reject, subject
-pel-	to drive	compel, dispel, impel, repel
-pend-	to hang	append, depend, impend, pendant, pendulum
-port-	to carry	comport, deport, export, import, report, support
-scrib-, -script-	to write	describe, description, prescribe, prescription, subscribe, subscription, transcribe, transcription
-tract-	to pull, drag, draw	attract, contract, detract, extract, protract, retract, traction
-vert-	to turn	convert, divert, invert, revert

From the example words in the above table, it is easy to see how roots combine with prefixes to form new words. For example, the root -tract-, meaning "to pull," can combine with a number of prefixes, including de- and re-. Detract means literally "to pull away" (de-, "away, off") and retract means literally "to pull back" (re-, "again, back"). The following table gives a list of Latin prefixes and their basic meanings.

Latin prefix	Basic meaning	Example words
co-	together	coauthor, coedit, coheir
de-	away, off; generally indicates reversal or removal in English	deactivate, debone, defrost, decompress, deplane
dis-	not, not any	disbelief, discomfort, discredit, disrepair, disrespect
inter-	between, among	international, interfaith, intertwine, intercellular, interject
non-	not	nonessential, nonmetallic, nonresident, nonviolence, nonskid, nonstop
post-	after	postdate, postwar, postnasal, postnatal
pre-	before	preconceive, preexist, premeditate, predispose, prepossess, prepay
re-	again; back, backward	rearrange, rebuild, recall, remake, rerun, rewrite
sub-	under	submarine, subsoil, subway, subhuman, substandard
trans-	across, beyond, through	transatlantic, transpolar

Words and word roots may also combine with suffixes. Here are examples of some important English suffixes that come from Latin:

Latin suffix	Basic meaning	Example words
-able, -ible	forms adjectives and means "capable or worthy of"	likable, flexible
-ation	forms nouns from verbs	create, creation; civilize, civilization
-fy, -ify	forms verbs and means "to make or cause to become"	purify, acidify, humidify
-ment	forms nouns from verbs	entertain, entertainment; amaze, amazement
-ty, -ity	forms nouns from adjectives	subtlety, certainty, cruelty, frailty, loyalty, royalty; eccentricity, electricity, peculiarity, similarity, technicality

Greek Roots, Prefixes, and Suffixes

The following table lists some common Greek roots.

Greek root	Basic meaning	Example words
-anthrop-	human	misanthrope, philanthropy, anthropomorphic
-chron-	time	anachronism, chronic, chronicle, synchronize, chronometer
-dem-	people	democracy, demography, demagogue, endemic, pandemic
-morph-	form	amorphous, metamorphic, morphology
-path-	feeling, suffering	empathy, sympathy, apathy, apathetic, psychopathic
-pedo-, -ped-	child, children	pediatrician, pedagogue
-philo-, -phil-	having a strong affinity or love for	philanthropy, philharmonic, philosophy
-phon-	sound	polyphonic, cacophony, phonetics

The following table gives a list of Greek prefixes and their basic meanings.

Greek prefix	Basic meaning	Example words
a-, an-	without	achromatic, amoral, atypical, anaerobic
anti-, ant-	opposite; opposing	anticrime, antipollution, antacid
auto-	self, same	autobiography, automatic, autopilot
bio-, bi-	life, living organism; biology, biological	biology, biophysics, biotechnology, biopsy
geo-	Earth; geography	geography, geomagnetism, geophysics, geopolitics
hyper-	excessive, excessively	hyperactive, hypercritical, hypersensitive
micro-	small	microcosm, micronucleus, microscope
mono-	one, single, alone	monochrome, monosyllable, monoxide
neo-	new, recent	neonatal, neophyte, neoconservatism, neofascism, neodymium
pan-	all	panorama, panchromatic, pandemic, pantheism
thermo-, therm-	heat	thermal, thermometer, thermostat

Words and word roots may also combine with suffixes. Here are examples of some important English suffixes that come from Greek:

Greek suffix	Basic meaning	Example words
-ism	forms nouns and means "the act, state, or theory of"	criticism, optimism, capitalism
-ist	forms agent nouns from verbs ending in -ize or nouns ending in -ism and is used like -er	conformist, copyist, cyclist
-ize	forms verbs from nouns and adjectives	formalize, jeopardize, legalize, modernize, emphasize, hospitalize, industrialize, computerize
-gram	something written or drawn, a record	cardiogram, telegram
-graph	something written or drawn; an instrument for writing, drawing, or recording	monograph; phonograph, seismograph
-logue, -log	speech, discourse; to speak	monologue, dialogue, travelogue
-logy	discourse, expression; science, theory, study	phraseology, biology, dermatology
-meter, -metry	measuring device; measure	geometry, kilometer, parameter, perimeter
-oid	forms adjectives and nouns and means "like, resembling" or "shape, form"	humanoid, spheroid, trapezoid
-phile	one that loves or has a strong affinity for; loving	audiophile, Francophile
-phobe, -phobia	one that fears a specified thing; an intense fear of a specified thing	agoraphobe, agoraphobia, xenophobe, xenophobia
-phone	sound; device that receives or emits sound; speaker of a language	homophone, geophone, telephone, Francophone

American Sign Language

Sign language for the deaf was first systematized in France during the 18th century by Abbot Charles-Michel l'Epée. French Sign Language (FSL) was brought to the United States in 1816 by Thomas Gallaudet, founder of the American School for the Deaf in Hartford, Conn. He developed American Sign Language (ASL), a language of gestures and hand symbols that express words and concepts.

In many respects, sign language is just like any spoken language, with a rich vocabulary and a highly organized, rule-governed grammar. But in sign language, information is processed through the eyes rather than the ears. Thus, facial expression and body movement play an important part in conveying information.

In spoken language, the relationship between most words and the objects and concepts they represent is arbitrary—there is nothing about the word "tree" that actually suggests a tree, either in the way it is spelled or pronounced. In the same way, in sign language most signs do not suggest, or imitate, the thing or idea they represent, and must be learned. Sign language may be acquired naturally as a child's first language, or it may be learned through study and practice.

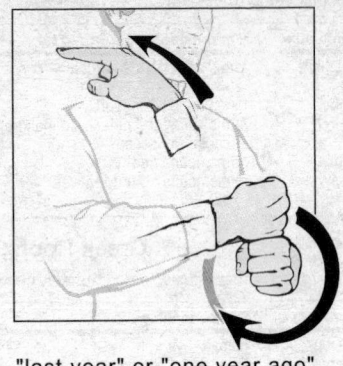

"last year" or "one year ago"

Sign language shares other similarities with spoken languages. Like any living language, ASL grows and changes over time to accommodate native users' needs. ASL also has regional varieties, equivalent to spoken accents, with different signs being used in different parts of the country.

American Manual Alphabet

Along with sign language and lip reading, many deaf people also communicate with the manual alphabet, which uses finger positions that correspond to the letters of the alphabet to spell out words and names.

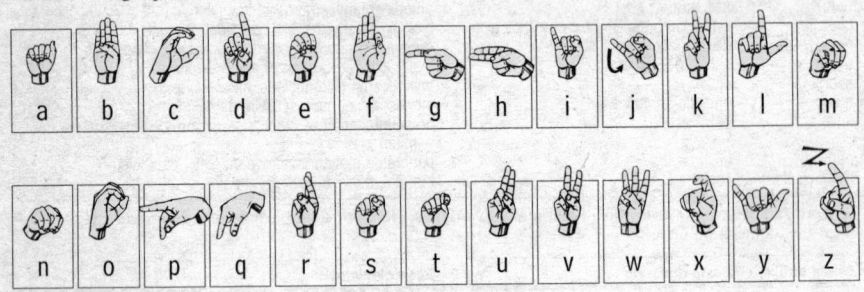

Braille Alphabet

Braille is a system of printing and writing for the blind created in 1824 by Louis Braille (1809–1852), a French inventor who went blind from an accident when he was three. Each character in Braille is made up of an arrangement of one-to-six raised points used in 63 possible combinations. Braille is read by passing the fingers over the raised characters. A universal Braille code for English-speaking countries was adopted in 1932.

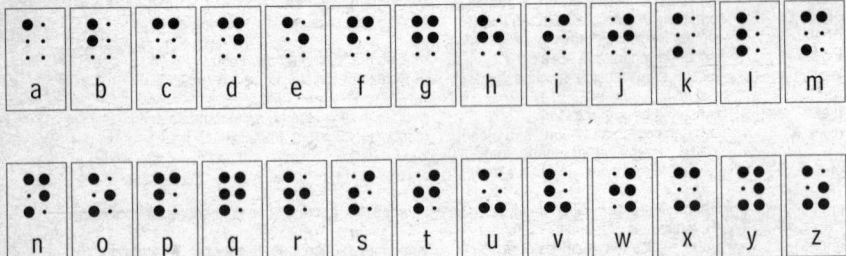

The Race to the North Pole

Robert E. Peary claimed he got there first. But so did Frederick A. Cook. Which of the two explorers really seized the Arctic Grail?

Special to the TIME Almanac. From LIFE's "The Greatest Adventures of All Time."

Ninety-two years after two Americans, Robert Edwin Peary and Frederick Albert Cook, both claimed to have been the first to reach the North Pole, experts are still arguing over which of them—if either—turned the trick. Certainty remains elusive.

Cook's Checkered Past

Cook's case is weaker, not least because Cook is such a lousy character witness for himself. A physician, he was, to be sure, also an accomplished outdoorsman. He had served as surgeon on Peary's first Arctic expedition in 1891 and had done some serious mountaineering in the years prior to his North Pole assault. But consider the mountaineering as Exhibit A against the man: In 1906, Cook stated that he had made the first successful ascent of Alaska's Mount McKinley. Later, his summit photographs were revealed as fakes, and Cook's climbing partner recanted his corroboration. Exhibit B could be Cook's conviction for mail fraud, a smear erased—sort of—by a presidential pardon in 1940, the year of Cook's death. So that's Frederick A. Cook.

Peary the Misanthrope

Peary was no sweetheart either. The U.S. Navy commander was unlikable, arrogant, and extraordinarily self-involved. A married man with a son and a daughter, he fathered two Eskimo children during his Arctic adventures. (Though he associated with Eskimos during his entire career, Peary proved to be no friend to the northern people: As detailed in Kenn Harper's *Give Me My Father's Body: The Life of Minik, The New York Eskimo,* in 1897 Peary presented six Eskimos as "specimens" to the American Museum of Natural History in New York City. Four of the group died almost immediately of influenza.) Peary once said of Matthew Henson, his African-American assistant of 22 years, "Henson must go all the way. I can't make it without him." Throughout the Arctic, Henson cooked, built igloos, tended the dogs and walked every cold and painful step, while his boss was hauled on a sledge by Eskimos. But when evidence indicated that Henson had quite possibly reached the Pole before him, Peary never spoke to the man again. So that's Robert E. Peary.

Charlatan or Hero?

Cook and Peary were right for the task, as the goal they had in sight could be reached only by a driven man of considerable ego. The North Pole was the single greatest target for adventurers at the turn of the century. In the 1890s the Norwegian Fridtjof Nansen sailed his ship to Spitsbergen but ultimately failed to reach the Pole; the Swede Salomon Andrée tried to reach the Pole by balloon but failed; Peary tried for the Pole on dogsled but failed. The North Pole, floating on a sea 13,410 feet deep, its surface ice perpetually shifting and drifting, cracking and freezing again, was a cruel siren: By the early 20th century it had already claimed the lives of hundreds of adventurers.

Peary, 52, felt certain that his 1908 expedition would be his last. His six previous trips to the Arctic had earned him considerable renown—in 1891–92 he had proved Greenland to be an island by exploring its northern coast, and his 1905 polar trek had established a farthest-north record—but he would remain unfulfilled if he did not reach 90 degrees north.

He either did or did not do so on April 6, 1909, after an over-the-ice journey of 37 days, accompanied on the last stretch by Henson and four Eskimos. Before Peary could even cable the news, his old colleague Cook blindsided him by announcing from the Shetland Islands that he had stood atop the world a full year earlier. It seemed, initially, that he might have, but the journals he presented as proof were said by experts to have been doctored, and the Eskimo guides that Cook trotted out as witnesses proved as worthy as his McKinley corroborator. The Eskimos finally admitted that Cook had, in fact, never left sight of land—land that ends hundreds of miles south of the Pole.

In recent years, Peary's claim has also come under a cloud: Did he get there? Were his measurements accurate? The truth may never be known. In 1989 the National Geographic Society, after commissioning the Navigation Foundation to spend more than a year investigating 225 cubic feet of documents, announced that Peary, who had been made a rear admiral before his death in 1920, had very likely come within five miles of the North Pole—and perhaps had stood upon the spot itself. Whatever the truth is, favor does seem to rest much more comfortably with Peary than with Cook. As Peter Freuchen, the noted Danish explorer and writer who knew both men, once put it: "Cook was a liar and a gentleman; Peary was neither." □

Explorations

Country or place	Event	Explorer	Date
AFRICA			
Sierra Leone	Explored	Hanno, Carthaginian seaman	c. 520 B.C.
Zaire River (Congo)	Mouth visited[1]	Diogo Cão, Portuguese explorer	c. 1484
Cape of Good Hope	Rounded	Bartolomeu Diaz, Portuguese explorer	1488
Gambia River	Explored	Mungo Park, Scottish explorer	1795
Sahara	Crossed	Dixon Denham and Hugh Clapperton, English explorers	1822–1823
Zambezi River	Explored[1]	David Livingstone, Scottish explorer	1851
Sudan	Explored	Heinrich Barth, German explorer	1852–1855
Victoria Falls	Explored[1]	David Livingstone, Scottish explorer	1855
Lake Tanganyika	Explored[1]	Richard Burton and John Speke, British explorers	1858
Lake Victoria, identified as the source of the Nile	Explored	John Speke, British explorer	1858
Zaire River (Congo)	Traced	Sir Henry M. Stanley, British explorer	1877
ASIA			
Punjab (India)	Invaded	Alexander the Great, king of Macedonia	327 B.C.
China	Explored	Marco Polo, Italian traveler	c. 1272
Tibet	Visited	Odoric of Pordenone, Italian monk	c. 1325
Southern China	Explored	Niccolò dei Conti, Venetian traveler	c. 1440
India	Explored (Cape route)	Vasco da Gama, Portuguese navigator	1498
Japan	Visited	St. Francis Xavier of Spain, missionary	1549
Arabia	Explored	Carsten Niebuhr, German explorer	1762
China	Explored	Ferdinand Richthofen, German scientist	1868
Mongolia	Explored	Nikolai M. Przhevalsky, Russian explorer	1870–1873
Central Asia	Explored	Sven Hedin, Swedish scientist	1890–1908
EUROPE			
Shetland Islands	Visited	Pytheas of Massilia (Marseille), Greek navigator and geographer	c. 325 B.C.
North Cape	Rounded	Ottar, Norwegian explorer	c. 870
Iceland	Colonized	Norwegian noblemen	c. 890–900
NORTH AMERICA			
Greenland	Colonized	Eric the Red, Norwegian	c. 985
Labrador, Newfoundland, Nova Scotia (?)	Explored[1]	Leif Ericsson, Norse explorer	1000
West Indies	Explored[1]	Christopher Columbus, Italian	1492
North America	Coast explored[1]	Giovanni Caboto (John Cabot), for British	1497
Pacific Ocean	Sighted[1]	Vasco Núñez de Balboa, Spanish explorer	1513
Florida	Explored	Ponce de León, Spanish explorer	1513
Mexico	Conquered	Hernando Cortés, Spanish adventurer	1519–1521
St. Lawrence River	Explored[1]	Jacques Cartier, French navigator	1534
Southwest United States	Explored	Francisco Coronado, Spanish explorer	1540–1542
Colorado River	Explored[1]	Hernando de Alarcón, Spanish explorer	1540
Mississippi River	Explored[1]	Hernando de Soto, Spanish explorer	1541
Frobisher Bay	Explored[1]	Martin Frobisher, English seaman	1576
Maine Coast	Explored	Samuel de Champlain, French explorer	1604
Jamestown, Va.	Settled	John Smith, English colonist	1607
Hudson River	Explored	Henry Hudson, English navigator	1609
Hudson Bay (Canada)	Explored[1]	Henry Hudson	1610
Baffin Bay	Explored[1]	William Baffin, English navigator	1616
Lake Michigan	Navigated	Jean Nicolet, French explorer	1634
Arkansas River	Explored[1]	Jacques Marquette and Louis Jolliet, French explorers	1673
Mississippi River	Explored	Sieur de La Salle, French explorer	1682
Bering Strait	Explored[1]	Vitus Bering, Danish explorer	1728
Alaska	Explored[1]	Vitus Bering	1741
Mackenzie River (Canada)	Explored[1]	Sir Alexander Mackenzie, Scottish-Canadian explorer	1789
Northwest United States	Explored	Meriwether Lewis and William Clark, American explorers	1804–1806
Northeast Passage (Arctic Ocean)	Navigated	Nils Nordenskjöld, Swedish explorer	1879
Greenland	Explored	Robert E. Peary, American explorer	1892
Northwest Passage	Navigated	Roald Amundsen, Norwegian explorer	1906

Country or place	Event	Explorer	Date
SOUTH AMERICA			
Continent	Explored	Christopher Columbus, Italian	1498
Brazil	Explored[1]	Pedro Alvarez Cabral, Portuguese	1500
Peru	Conquered	Francisco Pizarro, Spanish explorer	1532–1533
Amazon River	Explored	Francisco Orellana, Spanish explorer	1541
Cape Horn	Explored[1]	Willem C. Schouten, Dutch navigator	1615
OCEANIA			
Papua New Guinea	Explored	Jorge de Menezes, Portuguese explorer	1526
Australia	Explored	Abel Janszoon Tasman, Dutch navigator	1642
Tasmania	Explored[1]	Abel Janszoon Tasman	1642
Australia	Crossed	John McDouall Stuart, English explorer	1862
Australia	Explored	Robert Burke and William Wills, Australian explorers	1861
New Zealand	Sighted (and named)	Abel Janszoon Tasman, Dutch navigator	1642
New Zealand	Explored	James Cook, English navigator	1769
ARCTIC, ANTARCTIC, AND MISCELLANEOUS			
Africa, Middle East, Asia, and Europe	Explored	Ibn Batuta, greatest Arab traveler	1325–1349
Ocean exploration	Expedition	Ferdinand Magellan's ships circled globe for Spain	1519–1522
Galápagos Islands	Explored	Diego de Rivadeneira, Spanish captain	1535
Spitsbergen	Explored	Willem Barents, Dutch navigator	1596
Antarctic Circle	Crossed	James Cook, English navigator	1773
Antarctica	Explored[1]	Nathaniel Palmer, American whaler (archipelago), and Fabian Gottlieb von Bellingshausen, Russian admiral (mainland)	1820–1821
Antarctica	Explored	Charles Wilkes, American explorer	1840
North Pole	Reached[2]	Robert E. Peary, American explorer	1909
South Pole	Reached	Roald Amundsen, Norwegian explorer	1911

1. First European to reach the area. 2. Admiral Peary's claim to have reached the Pole has been disputed from the beginning—as was the claim made by his former colleague, Dr. Frederick Cook, who has been generally dismissed as a charlatan. The credit ultimately went to Peary, a claim officially backed by the U.S. Congress. But recent scholarship, including evidence culled from the journals and diaries of both Cook and Peary, has cast doubt on both explorers' veracity. If it is the case that neither reached the Pole, then the credit goes to Joseph Fletcher, who landed a U.S. Air Force C-47 plane there in 1952.

Geography Glossary

latitude lines Imaginary lines running horizontally around the globe. Also called parallels, latitude lines are equidistant from each other. Each degree of latitude is about 69 miles (110 km) apart. Zero degrees (0°) latitude is the equator, the widest circumference of the globe. Latitude is measured from 0° to 90° north and 0° to 90° south—90° north is the North Pole and 90° south is the South Pole.

longitude lines Imaginary lines, also called meridians, running vertically around the globe. Unlike latitude lines, longitude lines are not parallel. Meridians meet at the poles and are widest apart at the equator. Zero degrees longitude (0°) is called the prime meridian. The degrees of longitude run 180° east and 180° west from the prime meridian.

geographic coordinates Latitude and longitude lines form an imaginary grid over the Earth's surface. By combining longitude and latitude measurements, any location on earth can be determined. The units of measurement for geographic coordinates are degrees (°), minutes ('), and seconds ("). Like a circle, the Earth has 360 degrees. Each degree is divided into 60 minutes, which in turn is divided into 60 seconds. Latitude and longitude coordinates also include cardinal directions: north or south of the equator for latitude, and east or west of the prime meridian for longitude. The geographic coordinates of New York City, for example, are 40° N, 74° W, meaning that it is located 40 degrees north

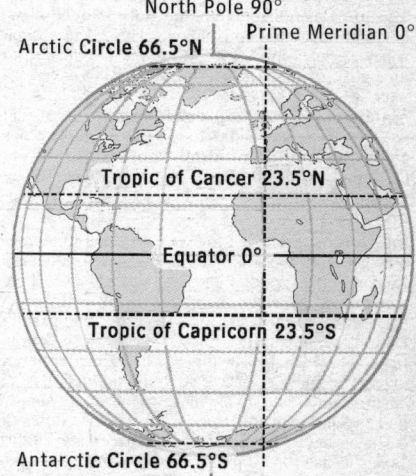

latitude and 74 degrees west longitude. Using minutes and seconds as well as degrees, the coordinates for New York would be 40°42'51" N, 74°0'23" W.

Mercator Projection	Robinson Projection
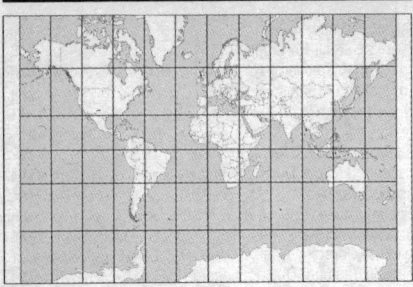	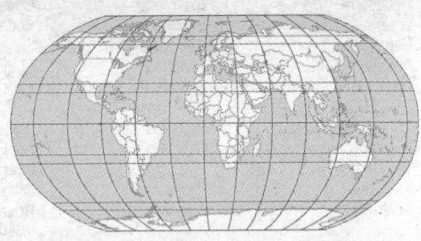

(Latitude is always listed first.) A less common format for listing coordinates is in decimal degrees. The Tropic of Cancer, for example, can be expressed in degrees and minutes (23°30′ N) or in decimal degrees (23.5° N).

hemisphere A hemisphere is half the Earth's surface. The four hemispheres are the Northern and Southern hemispheres, divided by the equator (0° latitude), and the Eastern and Western hemispheres, divided by the prime meridian (0° longitude) and the International Date Line (180°).

equator Zero degrees latitude. The Sun is directly overhead the equator at noon on the two equinoxes (March and Sept. 20 or 21). The equator divides the globe into the Northern and Southern hemispheres. The equator appears halfway between the North and South poles, at the widest circumference of the globe. It is 24,901.55 miles (40,075.16 km) long.

prime meridian Zero degrees longitude (0°). The prime meridian runs through the Royal Greenwich Observatory in Greenwich, England (the location was established in 1884 by international agreement). The prime meridian divides the globe into the Western and Eastern hemispheres. The Earth's time zones are measured from the prime meridian. The time at 0° is called Universal Time (UT) or Greenwich Mean Time (GMT). With the Greenwich meridian as the starting point, each 15° east and west marks a new time zone. The 24 time zones extend east and west around the globe for 180° to the International Date Line. When it is noon along the prime meridian, it is midnight along the International Date Line.

International Date Line Located at 180° longitude (180° E and 180° W are the same meridian). Regions to the east of the International Date Line are counted as being one calendar day earlier than the regions to the west. Although the International Date Line generally follows the 180° meridian (most of which lies in the Pacific Ocean), it does diverge in places. Since 180° runs through several countries, it would divide those countries not simply into two different time zones, but into two different calendar days. To avoid such unnecessary confusion, the date line dips and bends around countries to permit them to share the same time.

Tropic of Cancer A line of latitude located at 23°30' north of the equator. The Sun is directly overhead the Tropic of Cancer on the summer solstice in the Northern Hemisphere (June 20 or 21). It

marks the northernmost point of the tropics, which falls between the Tropic of Cancer and the Tropic of Capricorn.

Tropic of Capricorn A line of latitude located at 23°30' south. The Sun is directly overhead the Tropic of Capricorn on the summer solstice in the Southern Hemisphere (Dec. 20 or 21). It marks the southernmost point of the tropics.

Arctic Circle A line of latitude located at 66°30' north, delineating the Northern Frigid Zone of the Earth.

Antarctic Circle A line of latitude located at 66°30' south, delineating the Southern Frigid Zone of the Earth.

globe The most accurate map of the Earth, duplicating its spherical shape and relative size.

map projections Two-dimensional representations of the three-dimensional Earth. Because projections attempt to present the spherical Earth on a flat plane, they inevitably produce distortions. Map projections are numerous and complex (e.g., there are a variety of cylindrical, conic, or azimuthal projections). Each projection has advantages and serves different purposes, and each produces different types of distortions in direction, distance, shape, and relative size of areas. One of the most famous projections is the Mercator, created by Geradus Mercator in 1569. It is a rectangular-shaped map in which all longitude and latitude lines are parallel and intersect at right angles (on a globe, meridians are not parallel, but grow narrower, eventually converging at the poles). Near the equator, the scale of the Mercator is accurate, but the farther one moves toward the poles, the greater the distortion—Antarctica in the far south and Greenland in the far north, for example, appear gigantic. The Mercator projection was used well into the 20th century, but has now been superseded by others, including the widely used Robinson projection. The Robinson projection is an elliptical-shaped map with a flat top and bottom. Developed in 1963 by Arthur H. Robinson, it is an orthophanic ("right appearing") projection, which attempts to reflect the spherical appearance of the Earth. The meridians, for example, are curved arcs, which gives the flat map a three-dimensional appearance. But to convey the likeness of a curved, three-dimensional globe, the Robinson projection must in fact distort shape, area, scale, and distance. The Albers, Lambert, Mollweide, and Winkel Tripel are some of the other commonly used map projections.

The Continents

A continent is defined as a large unbroken land mass completely surrounded by water, although in some cases continents are (or were in part) connected by land bridges. The seven continents are North America, South America, Europe, Asia, Africa, Australia, and Antarctica. The island groups in the Pacific are often called Oceania but this name does *not* imply that scientists consider them the remains of a continent.

Political considerations have often overridden geographical facts when it came to naming continents. Geographically, Europe, including the British Isles, is a large western peninsula of the continent of Asia; and many geographers, when referring to Europe and

Asia, speak of the Eurasian continent. But traditionally, Europe is counted as a separate continent, with the Ural and the Caucasus mountains forming the line of demarcation between Europe and Asia. To the south of Europe, Asia has an odd-shaped peninsula jutting westward, which has a large number of political subdivisions. The northern section is taken up by Turkey; to the south of Turkey there are Syria, Iraq, Israel, Jordan, Saudi Arabia, and a number of smaller Arab countries. All these are part of Asia. Traditionally, the island of Cyprus in the Mediterranean is also considered to be part of Asia. The Caribbean islands, Central America, and Greenland are considered part of North America.

Continental Drift and Plate-Tectonics Theory

Source: U.S. Dept. of the Interior, Geological Survey

According to the theory of continental drift, the world was made up of a single continent through most of geologic time. That continent eventually separated and drifted apart, forming into the seven continents we have today. The first comprehensive theory of continental drift was suggested by the German meteorologist Alfred Wegener in 1912. The hypothesis asserts that the continents consist of lighter rocks that rest on heavier crustal material—similar to the manner in which icebergs float on water. Wegener contended that the relative positions

of the continents are not rigidly fixed but are slowly moving—at a rate of about one yard per century.

According to the generally accepted plate-tectonics theory, scientists believe that Earth's surface is broken into a number of shifting slabs or plates, which average about 50 miles in thickness. These plates move relative to one another above a hotter, deeper, more mobile zone at average rates as great as a few inches per year. Most of the world's active volcanoes are located along or near the boundaries between shifting plates and are called plate-boundary volcanoes.

World Land Areas and Elevations

Area	Approximate land area sq. km	Approximate land area sq. mi.	Percentage of total land area	Elevation, feet and meters	
				Highest	Lowest
WORLD	148,647,000	57,393,000	100.0%	Mt. Everest, Tibet-Nepal, 29,035 ft. (8,850 m)[1]	Dead Sea, Israel-Jordan, 1,349 ft. below sea level (−411 m)
AFRICA	30,065,000	11,608,000	20.2	Mt. Kilimanjaro, Tanzania, 19,340 ft. (5,895 m)	Lake Assal, Djibouti, 512 ft. below sea level (−156 m)
ANTARCTICA	13,209,000	5,100,000	8.9	Vinson Massif, Ellsworth Mts., 16,066 ft. (4,897 m)	Lowest land point hidden within Bentley Subglacial Trench[2]
ASIA (includes the Middle East)	44,579,000	17,212,000	30.0	Mt. Everest, Tibet-Nepal, 29,035 ft. (8,850 m)	Dead Sea, Israel-Jordan, 1,349 ft. below sea level (−411 m)
AUSTRALIA (includes Oceania)	8,112,000	3,132,000	5.3	Mt. Kosciusko, Australia, 7,310 ft. (2,228 m)	Lake Eyre, Australia, 52 ft. below sea level (−12 m)
EUROPE (the Ural Mountains in Russia form the boundary between Europe and Asia)	9,938,000	3,837,000	6.7	Mt. Elbrus, Russia/Georgia, 18,510 ft. (5,642 m)	Caspian Sea, Russia/Kazakhstan 92 ft. below sea level (−28 m)
NORTH AMERICA (includes Central America and the Caribbean)	24,474,000	9,449,000	16.5	Mt. McKinley, Alaska, 20,320 ft. (6,194 m)	Death Valley, Calif., 282 ft. below sea level (−86 m)
SOUTH AMERICA	17,819,000	6,879,000	12.0	Mt. Aconcagua, Argentina, 22,834 ft. (6,960 m)	Valdes Peninsula, Argentina 131 ft. below sea level (−40 m)

1. The 1954 elevation of Everest, 29,028 ft. (8,848 m) was revised on Nov. 11, 1999, and now stands at 29,035 ft. (8,850 m).
2. Bentley Subglacial Trench itself (ice, not land) is −8,327 ft. below sea level (−2,538 m). *Source:* WorldAtlas.com.

Volcanoes of the World

Source: U.S. Dept. of the Interior, Geological Survey

About 550 volcanoes have erupted on Earth's surface since recorded history; about 60 are active each year. Far more have erupted unobserved on the ocean floor. Most volcanoes exist at the boundaries of Earth's crustal plates, such as the famous Ring of Fire that surrounds the Pacific Ocean plate. Fifty volcanoes have erupted in the United States since recorded history, and the United States ranks third, behind Indonesia and Japan, in the number of historically active volcanoes.

Volcanoes are built by the accumulation of their own eruptive products—lava, bombs (crusted over ash flows), and tephra (airborne ash and dust). A volcano is most commonly a conical hill or mountain built around a vent that connects with reservoirs of molten rock below the surface of Earth. The term *volcano* also refers to the opening or vent through which molten rock and gases are expelled.

Driven by buoyancy and gas pressure, the molten rock, which is lighter than the surrounding solid rock, forces its way upward and may ultimately break though zones of weaknesses in Earth's crust. If so, an eruption begins, and the molten rock may pour from the vent as nonexplosive lava flows, or it may shoot violently into the air as dense clouds of lava fragments. Larger fragments fall back around the vent, and accumulations of fall-back fragments may move downslope as ash flows under the force of gravity. Some of the finer ejected materials may be carried by the wind and fall to the ground many miles away. The finest ash particles may be injected miles into the atmosphere and carried many times around the world by stratospheric winds before settling out.

Molten rock below the surface of Earth that rises in volcanic vents is known as **magma,** but after it erupts from a volcano it is called lava. Originating many

tens of miles beneath the ground, the ascending magma commonly contains some crystals, fragments of surrounding (unmelted) rocks, and dissolved gases, but it is primarily a liquid composed of oxygen, silicon, aluminum, iron, magnesium, calcium, sodium, potassium, titanium, and manganese. Magmas also contain many other chemical elements in trace quantities. Upon cooling, the liquid magma may precipitate crystals of various minerals until solidification is complete to form an igneous or magmatic rock.

Lava is red-hot when it pours or blasts out of a vent but soon changes to dark red, gray, black, or some other color as it cools and solidifies. Very hot, gas-rich lava containing abundant iron and magnesium is fluid and flows like hot tar, whereas cooler, gas-poor lava high in silicon, sodium, and potassium flows sluggishly, like thick honey, or in other cases, like pasty, blocky masses.

All magmas contain dissolved gases, and as they rise to the surface to erupt, the confining pressures are reduced and the dissolved gases are liberated either quietly or explosively. If the lava is a thin fluid (not viscous), the gases may escape easily. But if the lava is thick and pasty (highly viscous), the gases will not move freely but will build up tremendous pressure and ultimately escape with explosive violence, throwing out great masses of solid rock as well as lava, dust, and ashes.

The violent separation of gas from lava may produce rock froth called **pumice.** Some of this froth is so light—because of the many gas bubbles—that it floats on water. In many eruptions the froth is shattered explosively into small fragments that are hurled high into the air in the form of volcanic cinders (red or black), volcanic ash (commonly tan or gray), and volcanic dust. ☐

Recent Volcanic Activity

(**Bold** indicates activity in 2004)

Volcano	Date of last eruption or activity	Volcano	Date of last eruption or activity
Adatara, Honshu, Japan	Sept. 15, 1997	Eastern Gemini Seamount, Vanuatu	Feb. 23, 1996
Akutan, Alaska	March 10, 1996		
Ambrym Island, Vanuatu	**ongoing**	**Egoni, Indonesia**	**Jan. 29, 2004**
Amukta, Alaska	Sept. 17, 1996	Erta Ale, Ethiopia	Jan. 14, 2003
Anatahan, Mariana Islands	**April 26, 2004**	Etna, Sicily, Italy	Nov. 9, 2003
Arenal, Costa Rica	Sept. 5, 2003	Fernandina, Galápagos	Jan. 25, 1995
Asama, Honshu, Japan	April 18, 2003	Fogo, Cape Verde	April 2, 1995
Aso, Kyushu, Japan	**Jan. 14, 2004**	**Fuego, Guatemala**	**ongoing**
Axial Seamount	Jan. 25–28, 1998	Gamalama, Indonesia	Oct. 13, 2003
Bandai, Honshu, Japan	Aug. 16, 2000	Grimsvotn, Iceland	Dec. 18–28, 1998
Barren Island, Indian Ocean	March 18, 2003	Guagua Pichincha, Ecuador	April 17, 2003
Bezymianny, Kamchatka, Russia	**Jan. 22, 2004**	Hachijo-Jima, Izu Islands, Japan	Sept. 10, 2002
Bromo, Java, Indonesia	Nov. 30, 2000	Hakkoda, Japan	July 12, 1997
Mount Cameroon, Cameroon	June 7, 2000	Hekla, Iceland	Feb. 26, 2000
Canlaon, Philippines	July 11, 2003	Mount Hili Aludo, Indonesia	May 13, 1997
Cerro Azul, Galápagos Islands, Ecuador	Oct. 5, 1998	Hosho, Kyushu, Japan	Oct. 12, 1995
		Ijen, Java, Indonesia	Feb. 5, 2001
Cerro Negro, Nicaragua	Aug. 6, 1999	Iwate-san, Honshu, Japan	July 10, 1998
Chiginagak, Alaska	Nov. 7, 1997	Jackson Segment, N. Gorda Ridge (nr. Oregon)	April 3, 2001
Chikurachki, Kuril Islands, Russia	June 2003		
Mt. Cleveland, Chuginadak, Alaska	March 20, 2001	Kaba, Sumatra, Indonesia	Aug. 17, 2000
Colima, Mexico	Dec. 30, 2003	Mount Karangetang, Indonesia	Sept. 28, 2003
Copahue, Argentina and Chile	July 16, 2000	**Karymsky, Kamchatka, Russia**	**ongoing**
Dukono, Indonesia	**ongoing**	**Kavachi Seamount, Solomon Islands**	**March 15, 2004**
East Epi, Vanuatu	**recently renewed**		

Volcano	Date of last eruption or activity
Kelut, Java, Indonesia	Jan. 29, 2001
Kick-'em-Jenny (nr. Grenada)	March 15, 2003
Kikai, Japan	**March 24, 2004**
Kilauea, Hawaii	**ongoing**
Kliuchevskoi, Kamchatka, Russia	**ongoing**
Komagatake, Hokkaido, Japan	Nov. 8, 2000
Korovin, Alaska	June 30, 1998
Krakatau, Indonesia	March 27, 2001
Langila, New Britain	July 11, 2002
Lamongan, Indonesia	Sept. 24, 2003
Lascar, Chile	Dec. 9, 2003
Leroboleng, Indonesia	July 29, 2003
Mount Lewotobi, Indonesia	May 30, 2003
Llaima, Chile	April 11, 2003
Loihi Seamount, Hawaii	July 26, 1996
Lokon, Sulawesi, Indonesia	Sept. 12, 2003
Long Valley caldera, California	April 2, 1996
Lopevi, Central Islands, Vanuatu	June 14, 2003
La Madera, Nicaragua	Sept. 27, 1996
Manam, Papua New Guinea	**March 28, 2004**
Maroa, New Zealand	March 30, 2001
Masaya, Nicaragua	Oct. 4, 2003
Mauna Loa, Hawaii	March 18, 2003
Mayon, Philippines	Oct. 13, 2003
McDonald Island, Australia	Dec. 1996
Merapi, Indonesia	March 3, 2002
Metis Shoal, Tonga	June 6, 1995
Momotombo, Nicaragua	April 4, 1996
Monowai Seamount, Kermadec Islands	Dec. 5, 1997
Nyamuragira, Congo (Dem. Rep.)	Feb. 6, 2001
Nyiragongo, Congo (Dem. Rep.)	Feb. 2003
Okmok, Alaska	May 2, 1997
Mount Oyama, Japan	April 2, 2002
Pacaya, Guatemala	July 5, 2003
Pago, Papua New Guinea	**March 17, 2004**
Papandayan, Java, Indonesia	Nov. 11, 2002
Pavlof, Alaska	June 3, 1997

Volcano	Date of last eruption or activity
Peuet Sague, Indonesia	April 27, 1998
Piparo, Trinidad	Feb. 22, 1997
Piton de la Fournaise, Réunion	**Jan. 9, 2004**
Popocatepetl, Mexico	Sept. 21, 2003
Rabaul, Papua New Guinea	Feb. 17, 2003
Reventador, Ecuador	**Feb. 21, 2004**
Rincon de la Vieja, Costa Rica	Feb. 16, 1998
Rotorua, New Zealand	Jan. 26, 2001
Ruapehu, New Zealand	Sept. 13, 1999
Ruby Seamount, Mariana Islands	Oct. 25, 1995
Mount St. Helens, Washington	July 1, 1998
Sakura-Jima, Japan	**April 24, 2004**
San Cristobal, Nicaragua	May 10, 2001
Santa Maria, Guatemala	**ongoing**
Semeru, Java, Indonesia	**April 21, 2004**
Sheveluch, Kamchatka, Russia	**ongoing**
Shin-dake, Kuchinoerabujima Island, Japan	Aug. 26, 1999
Shishaldin, Unimak Island, Alaska	May 15, 2000
Soufriere Hills, Montserrat, West Indies	**March 29, 2004**
South Sister, Oregon	May 8, 2001
Stromboli, Italy	Nov. 2002
Soputan, Indonesia	Sept. 4, 2003
Tavurvur, Papua New Guinea	Sept. 6, 2000
Taal, Philippines	Sept. 30, 1999
Telica, Nicaragua	Aug. 11, 1999
Terceira, Azores	Jan. 8, 1999
Tonga (unnamed volcano)	Jan. 18, 1999
Tungurahua, Ecuador	**ongoing**
Ulawun, Papua New Guinea	**April 14, 2004**
Usu, Japan	April 17, 2000
Veniaminof, Alaska	**April 13, 2004**
Villarrica, Chile	May 30, 2000
White Island, New Zealand	**ongoing**
Yasur, Tanna Island, Vanuatu	**ongoing**
Yellowstone, Wyoming	Jan. 9, 1998
Zacatecas, Mexico	June 1997

Source: Volcano World. Web: www.volcanoworld.org.

The Deadliest Volcanic Eruptions

Volcano	Year	Deaths	Major cause of deaths
Tambora, Indonesia	1815	92,000	Starvation
Krakatau, Indonesia	1883	36,417	Tsunami
Mount Pelee, Martinique	1902	29,025	Ash flows
Ruiz, Colombia	1985	25,000	Mudflows
Unzen, Japan	1792	14,300	Volcano collapse, tsunami
Laki, Iceland	1783	9,350	Starvation
Kelut, Indonesia	1919	5,110	Mudflows
Galunggung, Indonesia	1882	4,011	Mudflows
Vesuvius, Italy	1631	3,500	Mudflows, lava flows
Vesuvius, Italy	79	3,360	Ash flows, falls
Papandayan, Indonesia	1772	2,957	Ash flows
Lamington, Papua New Guinea	1951	2,942	Ash flows
El Chichon, Mexico	1982	2,000	Ash flows
Soufriere, St. Vincent	1902	1,680	Ash flows
Oshima, Japan	1741	1,475	Tsunami
Asama, Japan	1783	1,377	Ash flows, mudflows
Taal, Philippines	1911	1,335	Ash flows
Mayon, Philippines	1814	1,200	Mudflows
Agung, Indonesia	1963	1,184	Ash flows
Cotopaxi, Ecuador	1877	1,000	Mudflows
Pinatubo, Philippines	1991	800	Disease
Komagatake, Japan	1640	700	Tsunami
Ruiz, Colombia	1845	700	Mudflows
Hibok-Hibok, Philippines	1951	500	Ash flows

NOTE: All eruptions with more than 500 known human fatalities. Based on data in *Volcanic Hazards: A Sourcebook on the Effects of Eruptions* by Russell J. Blong (Academic Press, 1984). *Source:* Volcano World. Web: www.volcanoworld.org.

Deadliest Earthquakes on Record

(50,000 deaths or more)

Date	Location	Deaths	Magnitude	Date	Location	Deaths	Magnitude
Jan. 23, 1556	Shansi, China	830,000	n.a.	Sept. 1290	Chihli, China	100,000	n.a.
July 27, 1976	Tangshan, China	255,000[1]	8.0	Nov. 1667	Shemakha, Caucasia	80,000	n.a.
Aug. 9, 1138	Aleppo, Syria	230,000	n.a.	Nov. 18, 1727	Tabriz, Iran	77,000	n.a.
May 22, 1927	near Xining, China	200,000	8.3	Nov. 1, 1755	Lisbon, Portugal	70,000	8.7
Dec. 22, 856[2]	Damghan, Iran	200,000	n.a.	Dec. 25, 1932	Gansu, China	70,000	7.6
Dec. 16, 1920	Gansu, China	200,000	8.6	May 31, 1970	Peru	66,000	7.8
March 23, 893[2]	Ardabil, Iran	150,000	n.a.	1268[4]	Silicia, Asia Minor	60,000	n.a.
Sept. 1, 1923	Kwanto, Japan	143,000	8.3	Jan. 11, 1693	Sicily, Italy	60,000	n.a.
Oct. 5, 1948	Ashgabat, Turkmenistan, USSR	110,000	7.3	May 30, 1935	Quetta, Pakistan	30,000–60,000	7.5
Dec. 28, 1908	Messina, Italy	70,000–100,000[3]	7.5	Feb. 4, 1783	Calabria, Italy	50,000	n.a.
				June 20, 1990	Iran	50,000	7.7

1. Official. Estimated death toll as high as 655,000. 2. Note that these dates are prior to A.D. 1000. No digit is missing. 3. Estimated. 4. No date available. *Source:* National Earthquake Information Center, U.S. Geological Survey. Data compiled from several sources.

The Ten Largest[1] Earthquakes of the 20th Century

Location	Date	Magnitude[2]	Location	Date	Magnitude[2]
1. Chile	May 22, 1960	9.5	6. Rat Islands, Aleutian Islands	Feb. 4, 1965	8.7
2. Prince William Sound, Alaska	March 28, 1964[3]	9.2	7. India-China border	Aug. 15, 1950	8.6
3. Andreanof Islands, Aleutian Islands	March 9, 1957	9.1	8. Kamchatka	Feb. 3, 1923	8.5
4. Kamchatka	Nov. 4, 1952	9.0	9. Banda Sea, Indonesia	Feb. 1, 1938	8.5
5. Off the coast of Ecuador	Jan. 31, 1906	8.8	10. Kuril Islands	Oct. 13, 1963	8.5

1. In terms of magnitude. 2. Moment magnitude. 3. March 28, 03:36:14 UT (March 27, 5:36 P.M. local time) *Source:* National Earthquake Information Center, U.S. Geological Survey.

The Severity of an Earthquake

Source: National Earthquake Information Center, U.S. Geological Survey

Earthquakes are the result of forces deep within Earth's interior that continuously affect its surface. The energy from these forces is stored in a variety of ways within the rocks. When this energy is released suddenly—by shearing movements along faults in the crust of Earth, for example—an earthquake results. The area of the fault where the sudden rupture takes place is called the focus or hypocenter of the earthquake. The point on Earth's surface directly above the focus is called the epicenter of the earthquake.

The severity of an earthquake can be expressed in terms of both intensity and magnitude. The two terms are quite different, however, and they are often confused. Intensity is based on the observed effects of ground shaking on people, buildings, and natural features. It varies from place to place within the disturbed region depending on the location of the observer with respect to the earthquake epicenter. Magnitude is related to the amount of seismic energy released at the hypocenter of the earthquake. It is based on the amplitude of the earthquake waves recorded on instruments, which have a common calibration. Magnitude is thus represented by a single, instrumentally determined value.

The Richter Magnitude Scale

Seismic waves are the vibrations from earthquakes that travel through Earth; they are recorded on instruments called seismographs. Seismographs record a zigzag trace that shows the varying amplitude of ground oscillations beneath the instrument. Sensitive seismographs, which greatly magnify these ground motions, can detect strong earthquakes from sources anywhere in the world. The time, location, and magnitude of an earthquake can be determined from the data recorded by seismograph stations.

The Richter magnitude scale was developed in 1935 by Charles F. Richter of the California Institute of Technology as a mathematical device to compare the size of earthquakes. The magnitude of an earthquake is determined from the logarithm of the amplitude of waves recorded by seismographs. Adjustments are included in the magnitude formula to compensate for the variation in the distance between the various seismographs and the epicenter of the earthquakes. On the Richter Scale, magnitude is expressed in whole numbers and decimal fractions. For example, a magnitude of 5.3 might be computed for a moderate earthquake, and a strong earthquake might be rated as magnitude 6.3. Because of the logarithmic basis of the scale, each whole number increase in magnitude represents a tenfold increase in measured amplitude; as an estimate of energy, each whole number step in the magnitude scale corresponds to the release of about 31 times more energy than the amount associated with the preceding whole number value. Although the Richter Scale has no upper limit, the largest known shocks have had magnitudes in the 8.8 to 8.9 range.

Why Are There So Many Earthquake Magnitude Scales?

Earthquake size, as measured by the Richter Scale, is a well-known, but not well understood, concept. What is even less well understood is the proliferation of magnitude scales and their relation to Richter's original magnitude scale. Richter's magnitude scale was first created for measuring the size of earthquakes occurring in southern California, using relatively high-frequency data from nearby seismograph stations. This magnitude scale was referred to as ML, with the L standing for local.

As more seismograph stations were installed around the world, it became apparent that the method developed by Richter was strictly valid only for certain frequency and distance ranges. In order to take advantage of the growing number of globally distributed seismograph stations, new magnitude scales that are an extension of Richter's original idea were developed. These include body-wave magnitude, "mb," and surface-wave magnitude, "MS." Each is valid for a particular frequency range and type of seismic signal. In its range of validity each is equivalent to the Richter magnitude.

Because of the limitations of all three magnitude scales—ML, mb, and MS—a new, more uniformly applicable extension of the magnitude scale, known as moment magnitude, or "MW," was developed. In particular, for very large earthquakes moment magnitude gives the most reliable estimate of earthquake size. New techniques that take advantage of modern telecommunications have recently been implemented, allowing reporting agencies to obtain rapid estimates of moment magnitude for significant earthquakes. So nowadays, when most seismologists announce a magnitude number, they are rarely referring to the Richter Scale.

The Modified Mercalli Intensity Scale

The effect of an earthquake on Earth's surface is called the intensity. The intensity scale consists of a series of certain key responses, such as people awakening, movement of furniture, damage to chimneys, and finally—total destruction. Although numerous intensity scales have been developed over the past several hundred years to evaluate the effects of earthquakes, the one currently used in the United States is the Modified Mercalli (MM) Intensity Scale. It was developed in 1931 by the American seismologists Harry Wood and Frank Neumann. This scale, composed of 12 increasing levels of intensity that range from imperceptible shaking to catastrophic destruction, is designated by Roman numerals. It does not have a mathematical basis; instead it is an arbitrary ranking based on observed effects. The Modified Mercalli Intensity value assigned to a specific site after an earthquake has a more meaningful measure of severity to the nonscientist than the magnitude because intensity refers to the effects actually experienced at that place.

Frequency of Earthquakes Worldwide

Descriptor	Magnitude	Annual average	Descriptor	Magnitude	Annual average
Great	8 or higher	1[1]	Light	4–4.9	c. 13,000
Major	7–7.9	17[2]	Minor	3–3.9	c. 130,000
Strong	6–6.9	134[2]	Very minor	2–2.9	c. 1,300,000
Moderate	5–5.9	1,319[2]			

1. Based on observations since 1900. 2. Based on observations since 1990. Source: National Earthquake Information Center, U.S. Geological Survey.

Number of Earthquakes Worldwide, 1990–2004, and Mortality Figures

Magnitude	1990	1994	1995	1996	1997	1998	1999	2000	2001	2002	2003	2004
8.0–9.9	0	2	3	1	0	2	0	1	1	0	1	0
7.0–7.9	12	13	22	21	20	14	23	14	15	13	14	5
6.0–6.9	115	161	185	160	125	113	123	158	126	130	140	76
5.0–5.9	1,635	1,542	1,327	1,223	1,118	979	1,106	1,345	1,243	1,218	1,194	712
4.0–4.9	4,493	4,544	8,140	8,794	7,938	7,303	7,042	8,045	8,084	8,584	8,466	5,734
3.0–3.9	2,457	5,000	5,002	4,869	4,467	5,945	5,521	4,784	6,151	7,005	7,626	3,973
2.0–2.9	2,364	5,369	3,838	2,388	2,397	4,091	4,201	3,758	4,162	6,419	7,726	4,297
1.0–1.9	474	779	645	295	388	805	715	1,026	944	1,137	2,491	1,333
0.1–0.9	0	17	19	1	4	10	5	5	1	10	134	103
No magnitude	5,062	1,944	1,826	2,186	3,415	2,426	2,096	3,120	2,938	2,937	3,610	3,100
Total	16,612	19,371	21,007	19,938	19,872	21,688	20,832	22,256	23,534	27,454	31,402[1]	19,333[1]
Estimated deaths	51,916	1,038	7,949	419	2,907	8,928	22,711	231	21,357	1,685	29,019	785

1. As of Sept., 2004. Source: National Earthquake Information Center, U.S. Geological Survey. Web: neic.usgs.gov/neis/eqlists/eqstats.html

Major Earthquakes around the World, 2004

Date	Location	Magnitude[1]	Date	Location	Magnitude[1]
Jan. 3	Southeast of the Loyalty Islands, New Caledonia	7.1	July 25	Southern Sumatra, Indonesia	7.3
Feb. 5	Papua, Indonesia	7.0	Sept. 5	Near the south coast of western Honshu, Japan	7.2
Feb. 7	Near the south coast of Papua, Indonesia	7.3	Sept. 5	Near the south coast of Honshu, Japan	7.4
July 15	Fiji Region	7.1			

NOTE: A major earthquake is defined here as having a magnitude of 7.0 or more. 1. Unless otherwise indicated, magnitudes listed are moment magnitudes, the newest, most uniformly applicable magnitude scale. Source: National Earthquake Information Center, U.S. Geological Survey. Web: neic.usgs.gov/neis/bulletin/mag7.html

Estimated Deaths from Earthquakes, 2004[1]

Date	Region	Magnitude	Number killed[2]	Date	Region	Magnitude	Number killed[2]
Jan. 1	Bali Region, Indonesia	5.8	1	May 8	Pakistan	4.4	1
				May 28	Northern Iran	6.3	35
Feb. 5	Papua, Indonesia	7.0	37	July 1	Eastern Turkey	5.4	18
Feb. 14	Pakistan	5.5	24	July 12	Slovenia	5.0	1
Feb. 16	Southern Sumatra, Indonesia	5.2	5	July 18	North Island of New Zealand	5.6	1
Feb. 24	Burundi	4.7	3	July 18	Central Afghanistan	5.1	2
Feb. 24	Near north coast of Morocco	6.4	628	July 30	Eastern Turkey	4.8	1
				Aug. 10	Hindu Kush region, Afghanistan	6.0	2
March 1	Eastern Turkey	3.8	6				
March 25	Eastern Turkey	5.6	10	Aug. 10	Sichuan-Yunnan-Guizhou region, China	5.1	4
April 5	Hindu Kush region, Afghanistan	6.6	3				
				Aug. 11	Eastern Turkey	5.5	1
May 1	Taiwan	5.2	2	**Total**			**785**

1. As of August 2004. 2. Includes "missing and presumed dead." *Source:* National Earthquake Information Center, U.S. Geological Survey. Web: neic.usgs.gov/neis/bulletin/mag7.html

The World's 14 Highest Mountain Peaks (above 8,000 meters)

All 14 of the world's 8,000-meter peaks are located in the Himalaya or the Karakoram ranges in Asia. According to Everestnews.com, only 11 climbers have reached the summits of all 14: Reinhold Messner (Italy) was first, followed by Jerzy Kukuczka (Poland), Ehardt Loretan (Switzerland), Carlos Carsolio (Mexico), Krzysztof Wielicki (Poland), Juan Oiarzabal (Spain), Sergio Martini (Italy), Park Young Seok (Korea), Hang-Gil Um (Korea), Alberto Inurrategui (Spain), and Han Wang Yong (Korea).

Mountain	Location	Height Meters	Feet	First to summit (nationality)	Date
1. Everest[1]	Nepal/Tibet	8,850	29,035	Edmund Hillary (New Zealander, UK), Tenzing Norgay (Nepalese)	May 29, 1953
2. K2 (Godwin Austen)	Pakistan/China	8,611	28,250	A. Compagnoni, L. Lacedelli (Italian)	July 31, 1954
3. Kangchenjunga	Nepal/India	8,586	28,169	G. Band, J. Brown, N. Hardie, S. Streather (UK)	May 25, 1955
4. Lhotse	Nepal/Tibet	8,516	27,940	F. Luchsinger, E. Reiss (Swiss)	May 18, 1956
5. Makalu	Nepal/Tibet	8,463	27,766	J. Couzy, L. Terray, J. Franco, G. Magnone-Gialtsen, J. Bouier, S. Coupé, P. Leroux, A. Vialatte (French)	May 15, 1955
6. Cho Oyu	Nepal/Tibet	8,201	26,906	H. Tichy, S. Jöchler (Austrian), Pasang Dawa Lama (Nepalese)	Oct. 19, 1954
7. Dhaulagiri	Nepal	8,167	26,795	A. Schelbert, E. Forrer, K. Diemberger, P. Diener (Swiss), Nyima Dorji, Nawang Dorji (Nepalese)	May 13, 1960
8. Manaslu	Nepal	8,163	26,781	T. Imamishi, K. Kato, M. Higeta, (Japanese) G. Norbu (Nepalese)	May 9, 1956
9. Nanga Parbat	Pakistan	8,125	26,660	Hermann Buhl (Austrian)	July 3, 1953
10. Annapurna	Nepal	8,091	26,545	M. Herzog, L. Lachenal (French)	June 3, 1950
11. Gasherbrum I	Pakistan/China	8,068	26,470	P. K. Schoeing, A. J. Kauffman	July 4, 1958
12. Broad Peak	Pakistan/China	8,047	26,400	M. Schmuck, F. Wintersteller, K. Diemberger, H. Buhl (Austrian)	June 9, 1957
13. Gasherbrum II	Pakistan/China	8,035	26,360	F. Moravec, S. Larch, H. Willenpart (Austrian)	July 7, 1956
14. Shisha Pangma	Tibet	8,013	26,289	Hsu Ching and team of 9 (Chinese)	May 2, 1964

1. The 1955 elevation of Everest, 29,028 ft. (8,848 m), was revised on Nov. 11, 1999, and now stands at 29,035 ft. (8,850 m).

Highest Mountain Peaks of the World

(*See* p. 502 for U.S. peaks.)

Mountain peak	Range	Location	Height ft.	m	Mountain peak	Range	Location	Height ft.	m
Annapurna II	Himalayas	Nepal	26,041	7,937	Nanda Devi	Himalayas	India	25,663	7,824
Gyachung Kang	Himalayas	Nepal	25,910	7,897	Masherbrum	Karakoram	Kashmir[1]	25,660	7,821
					Rakaposhi	Karakoram	Pakistan	25,551	7,788
Disteghil Sar	Karakoram	Pakistan	25,858	7,882	Kanjut Sar	Karakoram	Pakistan	25,461	7,761
Himalchuli	Himalayas	Nepal	25,801	7,864	Kamet	Himalayas	India/Tibet	25,446	7,756
Nuptse	Himalayas	Nepal	25,726	7,841					

Mountain peak	Range	Location	Height ft.	m
Namcha Barwa	Himalayas	Tibet	25,445	7,756
Gurla Mandhata	Himalayas	Tibet	25,355	7,728
Ulugh Muztagh	Kunlun	Tibet	25,340	7,723
Kungur	Muztagh Ata	China	25,325	7,719
Tirich Mir	Hindu Kush	Pakistan	25,230	7,690
Saser Kangri	Karakoram	India	25,172	7,672
Makalu II	Himalayas	Nepal	25,120	7,657
Minya Konka (Gongga Shan)	Daxue Shan	China	24,900	7,590
Kula Kangri	Himalayas	Bhutan	24,783	7,554
Chang-tzu	Himalayas	Tibet	24,780	7,553
Muztagh Ata	Muztagh Ata	China	24,757	7,546
Skyang Kangri	Himalayas	Kashmir	24,750	7,544
Ismail Samani Peak (formerly Communism Peak)	Pamirs	Tajikistan	24,590	7,495
Jongsong Peak	Himalayas	Nepal	24,472	7,459
Pobeda Peak	Tien Shan	Kyrgyzstan	24,406	7,439
Sia Kangri	Himalayas	Kashmir	24,350	7,422
Haramosh Peak	Karakoram	Pakistan	24,270	7,397
Istoro Nal	Hindu Kush	Pakistan	24,240	7,388
Tent Peak	Himalayas	Nepal	24,165	7,365
Chomo Lhari	Himalayas	Tibet/Bhutan	24,040	7,327
Chamlang	Himalayas	Nepal	24,012	7,319
Kabru	Himalayas	Nepal	24,002	7,316
Alung Gangri	Himalayas	Tibet	24,000	7,315
Baltoro Kangri	Himalayas	Kashmir	23,990	7,312
Muztagh Ata (K-5)	Kunlun	China	23,890	7,282
Mana	Himalayas	India	23,860	7,273
Baruntse	Himalayas	Nepal	23,688	7,220
Nepal Peak	Himalayas	Nepal	23,500	7,163
Amne Machin	Kunlun	China	23,490	7,160
Gauri Sankar	Himalayas	Nepal/Tibet	23,440	7,145
Badrinath	Himalayas	India	23,420	7,138
Nunkun	Himalayas	Kashmir	23,410	7,135
Lenin Peak	Pamirs	Tajikistan/Kyrgyzstan	23,405	7,134
Pyramid	Himalayas	Nepal	23,400	7,132
Api	Himalayas	Nepal	23,399	7,132
Pauhunri	Himalayas	India/China	23,385	7,128
Trisul	Himalayas	India	23,360	7,120
Korzhenevski Peak	Pamirs	Tajikistan	23,310	7,105
Kangto	Himalayas	Tibet	23,260	7,090
Nyainqentanglha	Nyainqentanglha Shan	China	23,255	7,088
Trisuli	Himalayas	India	23,210	7,074
Dunagiri	Himalayas	India	23,184	7,066
Revolution Peak	Pamirs	Tajikistan	22,880	6,974
Aconcagua	Andes	Argentina	22,834	6,960
Ojos del Salado	Andes	Argentina/Chile	22,664	6,908
Bonete	Andes	Argentina/Chile	22,546	6,872
Ama Dablam	Himalayas	Nepal	22,494	6,856
Tupungato	Andes	Argentina/Chile	22,310	6,800
Moscow Peak	Pamirs	Tajikistan	22,260	6,785
Pissis	Andes	Argentina	22,241	6,779
Mercedario	Andes	Argentina/Chile	22,211	6,770
Huascarán	Andes	Peru	22,205	6,768
Llullaillaco	Andes	Argentina/Chile	22,057	6,723
El Libertador	Andes	Argentina	22,047	6,720
Cachi	Andes	Argentina	22,047	6,720
Kailas	Himalayas	Tibet	22,027	6,714
Incahuasi	Andes	Argentina/Chile	21,720	6,620
Yerupaja	Andes	Peru	21,709	6,617
Kurumda	Pamirs	Tajikistan	21,686	6,610
Galan	Andes	Argentina	21,654	6,600
El Muerto	Andes	Argentina/Chile	21,463	6,542
Sajama	Andes	Bolivia	21,391	6,520
Nacimiento	Andes	Argentina	21,302	6,493
Illampu	Andes	Bolivia	21,276	6,485
Illimani	Andes	Bolivia	21,201	6,462
Coropuna	Andes	Peru	21,083	6,426
Laudo	Andes	Argentina	20,997	6,400
Ancohuma	Andes	Bolivia	20,958	6,388
Cuzco (Ausangate)	Andes	Peru	20,945	6,384

1. Kashmir is divided between India, Pakistan, and China, and the three countries dispute the boundaries. *Source:* National Geographic Society.

Climbing the Seven Summits

About 80 mountaineers have climbed all "Seven Summits"—the highest peak on each of the seven continents. The first was Dick Bass, an American businessman, on April 30, 1985. The seven summits are Mt. Everest (Asia) 29,035 ft., Mt. Aconcagua (South America) 22,834 ft., Mt. McKinley (North America) 20,320 ft., Mt. Kilimanjaro (Africa) 19,340 ft., Mt. Elbrus (Europe) 18,510 ft., Vinson Massif (Antarctica) 16,066 ft., and Kosciusko (Australia) 7,310 ft. Some climbers believe that the true Seven Summits should include Carstensz Pyramid (16,023 ft.) in Irian Jaya, Indonesia, rather than Australia's Kosciusko. Carstensz is the highest summit in Australia/Oceania, but strictly speaking, Oceania is not a continent.

Oceans and Seas

Name	Area sq. mi.	Area sq. km	Average depth ft.	Average depth m	Greatest known depth ft.	Greatest known depth m	Place of greatest known depth
Pacific Ocean	60,060,700	155,557,000	13,215	4,028	36,198	11,033	Mariana Trench
Atlantic Ocean	29,637,900	76,762,000	12,880	3,926	30,246	9,219	Puerto Rico Trench
Indian Ocean	26,469,500	68,556,000	13,002	3,963	24,460	7,455	Sunda Trench
Southern Ocean[1]	7,848,300	20,327,000	13,100–16,400	4,000–5,000	23,736	7,235	South Sandwich Trench
Arctic Ocean	5,427,000	14,056,000	3,953	1,205	18,456	5,625	77°45′N; 175°W
Mediterranean Sea[2]	1,144,800	2,965,800	4,688	1,429	15,197	4,632	Off Cape Matapan, Greece
Caribbean Sea	1,049,500	2,718,200	8,685	2,647	22,788	6,946	Off Cayman Islands
South China Sea	895,400	2,319,000	5,419	1,652	16,456	5,016	West of Luzon
Bering Sea	884,900	2,291,900	5,075	1,547	15,659	4,773	Off Buldir Island
Gulf of Mexico	615,000	1,592,800	4,874	1,486	12,425	3,787	Sigsbee Deep
Okhotsk Sea	613,800	1,589,700	2,749	838	12,001	3,658	146°10′E; 46°50′N
East China Sea	482,300	1,249,200	617	188	9,126	2,782	25°16′N; 125°E
Hudson Bay	475,800	1,232,300	420	128	600	183	Near entrance
Japan Sea	389,100	1,007,800	4,429	1,350	12,276	3,742	Central Basin
Andaman Sea	308,000	797,700	2,854	870	12,392	3,777	Off Car Nicobar Island
North Sea	222,100	575,200	308	94	2,165	660	Skagerrak
Red Sea	169,100	438,000	1,611	491	7,254	2,211	Off Port Sudan
Baltic Sea	163,000	422,200	180	55	1,380	421	Off Gotland

NOTE: For Caspian Sea, *see* Large Lakes of the World. 1. A decision by the International Hydrographic Organization in spring 2000 delimited a fifth world ocean. 2. Includes Black Sea and Sea of Azov.

Large Lakes of the World

Name and location	Area sq. mi.	Area km	Length mi.	Length km	Maximum depth ft.	Maximum depth m
Caspian Sea, Azerbaijan-Russia-Kazakhstan-Turkmenistan-Iran[1]	152,239	394,299	745	1,199	3,104	946
Superior, U.S.-Canada	31,820	82,414	383	616	1,333	406
Victoria, Tanzania-Uganda	26,828	69,485	200	322	270	82
Huron, U.S.-Canada	23,010	59,596	247	397	750	229
Michigan, U.S.	22,400	58,016	321	517	923	281
Aral, Kazakhstan-Uzbekistan	13,000	33,800	266	428	223	68
Tanganyika, Tanzania-Congo	12,700	32,893	420	676	4,708	1,435
Baikal, Russia	12,162	31,500	395	636	5,712	1,741
Great Bear, Canada	12,000	31,080	232	373	270	82
Nyasa, Malawi-Mozambique-Tanzania	11,600	30,044	360	579	2,316	706
Great Slave, Canada	11,170	28,930	298	480	2,015	614
Chad,[2] Chad-Niger-Nigeria	9,946	25,760	—	—	23	7
Erie, U.S.-Canada	9,930	25,719	241	388	210	64
Winnipeg, Canada	9,094	23,553	264	425	204	62
Ontario, U.S.-Canada	7,520	19,477	193	311	778	237
Balkhash, Kazakhstan	7,115	18,428	376	605	87	27
Ladoga, Russia	7,000	18,130	124	200	738	225
Onega, Russia	3,819	9,891	154	248	361	110
Titicaca, Bolivia-Peru	3,141	8,135	110	177	1,214	370
Nicaragua, Nicaragua	3,089	8,001	110	177	230	70
Athabaska, Canada	3,058	7,920	208	335	407	124
Rudolf, Kenya	2,473	6,405	154	248	—	—
Reindeer, Canada	2,444	6,330	152	245	—	—
Eyre, South Australia	2,400[3]	6,216	130	209	varies	varies
Issyk-Kul, Kyrgyzstan	2,394	6,200	113	182	2,297	700
Urmia,[2] Iran	2,317	6,001	81	130	49	15
Torrens, South Australia	2,200	5,698	130	209	—	—
Vänern, Sweden	2,141	5,545	87	140	322	98
Winnipegosis, Canada	2,086	5,403	152	245	59	18
Mobutu Sese Seko, Uganda	2,046	5,299	100	161	180	55
Nettilling, Baffin Island, Canada	1,950	5,051	70	113	—	—
Nipigon, Canada	1,870	4,843	72	116	—	—
Manitoba, Canada	1,817	4,706	140	225	22	7
Great Salt, U.S.	1,800	4,662	75	121	15–25	5–8
Kioga, Uganda	1,700	4,403	50	80	about 30	9

NOTE: Area more than 1,700 sq. mi. 1. The Caspian Sea is called "sea" because the Romans, finding it salty, named it *Mare Caspium.* Many geographers, however, consider it a lake because it is land-locked. 2. Figures represent high-water data. 3. Varies with the rainfall of the wet season. It has been reported to dry up almost completely on occasion.

Principal Rivers of the World

(*See* pp. 500–501 for other U.S. rivers.)

River	Source	Outflow	Approx. length mi.	km
Nile	Tributaries of Lake Victoria, Africa	Mediterranean Sea	4,180	6,690
Amazon	Glacier-fed lakes, Peru	Atlantic Ocean	3,912	6,296
Mississippi-Missouri-Red Rock	Source of Red Rock, Montana	Gulf of Mexico	3,710	5,970
Chang Jiang (Yangtze)	Tibetan plateau, China	China Sea	3,602	5,797
Ob	Altai Mts., Russia	Gulf of Ob	3,459	5,567
Huang Ho (Yellow)	Eastern part of Kunlan Mts., West China	Gulf of Chihli	2,900	4,667
Yenisei	Tannu-Ola Mts., western Tuva, Russia	Arctic Ocean	2,800	4,506
Paraná	Confluence of Paranaiba and Grande rivers	Río de la Plata	2,795	4,498
Irtish	Altai Mts., Russia	Ob River	2,758	4,438
Zaire (Congo)	Confluence of Lualab and Luapula rivers, Congo	Atlantic Ocean	2,716	4,371
Heilong (Amur)	Confluence of Shilka (Russia) and Argun (Manchuria) rivers	Tatar Strait	2,704	4,352
Lena	Baikal Mts., Russia	Arctic Ocean	2,652	4,268
Mackenzie	Head of Finlay River, British Columbia, Canada	Beaufort Sea (Arctic Ocean)	2,635	4,241
Niger	Guinea	Gulf of Guinea	2,600	4,184
Mekong	Tibetan highlands	South China Sea	2,500	4,023
Mississippi	Lake Itasca, Minnesota	Gulf of Mexico	2,348	3,779
Missouri	Confluence of Jefferson, Gallatin, and Madison rivers, Montana	Mississippi River	2,315	3,726
Volga	Valdai plateau, Russia	Caspian Sea	2,291	3,687
Madeira	Confluence of Beni and Maumoré rivers, Bolivia–Brazil boundary	Amazon River	2,012	3,238
Purus	Peruvian Andes	Amazon River	1,993	3,207
São Francisco	Southwest Minas Gerais, Brazil	Atlantic Ocean	1,987	3,198
Yukon	Junction of Lewes and Pelly rivers, Yukon Territory, Canada	Bering Sea	1,979	3,185
St. Lawrence	Lake Ontario	Gulf of St. Lawrence	1,900	3,058
Rio Grande	San Juan Mts., Colorado	Gulf of Mexico	1,885	3,034
Brahmaputra	Himalayas	Ganges River	1,800	2,897
Indus	Himalayas	Arabian Sea	1,800	2,897
Danube	Black Forest, Germany	Black Sea	1,766	2,842
Euphrates	Confluence of Murat Nehri and Kara Su rivers, Turkey	Shatt-al-Arab	1,739	2,799
Darling	Central part of Eastern Highlands, Australia	Murray River	1,702	2,739
Zambezi	11°21'S, 24°22'E, Zambia	Mozambique Channel	1,700	2,736
Tocantins	Goiás, Brazil	Pará River	1,677	2,699
Murray	Australian Alps, New South Wales	Indian Ocean	1,609	2,589
Nelson	Head of Bow River, western Alberta, Canada	Hudson Bay	1,600	2,575
Paraguay	Mato Grosso, Brazil	Paraná River	1,584	2,549
Ural	Southern Ural Mts., Russia	Caspian Sea	1,574	2,533
Ganges	Himalayas	Bay of Bengal	1,557	2,506
Amu Darya (Oxus)	Nicholas Range, Pamir Mts., Turkmenistan	Aral Sea	1,500	2,414
Japurá	Andes, Colombia	Amazon River	1,500	2,414
Salween	Tibet, south of Kunlun Mts.	Gulf of Martaban	1,500	2,414
Arkansas	Central Colorado	Mississippi River	1,459	2,348
Colorado	Grand County, Colorado	Gulf of California	1,450	2,333
Dnieper	Valdai Hills, Russia	Black Sea	1,419	2,284
Ohio-Allegheny	Potter County, Pennsylvania	Mississippi River	1,306	2,102
Irrawaddy	Confluence of Nmai and Mali rivers, northeast Burma	Bay of Bengal	1,300	2,092
Orange	Lesotho	Atlantic Ocean	1,300	2,092
Orinoco	Serra Parima Mts., Venezuela	Atlantic Ocean	1,281	2,062
Pilcomayo	Andes Mts., Bolivia	Paraguay River	1,242	1,999
Xi Jiang (Si Kiang)	Eastern Yunnan Province, China	China Sea	1,236	1,989
Columbia	Columbia Lake, British Columbia, Canada	Pacific Ocean	1,232	1,983
Don	Tula, Russia	Sea of Azov	1,223	1,968
Sungari	China–North Korea boundary	Amur River	1,215	1,955
Saskatchewan	Canadian Rocky Mts.	Lake Winnipeg	1,205	1,939
Peace	Stikine Mts., British Columbia, Canada	Great Slave River	1,195	1,923
Tigris	Taurus Mts., Turkey	Shatt-al-Arab	1,180	1,899

Large Islands of the World

Island	Location and political affiliation	Area sq. mi.	Area sq. km
Greenland	North Atlantic (Danish)	839,999	2,175,597
New Guinea	Southwest Pacific (West Papua [Irian Jaya], Indonesia, western part; Papua New Guinea, eastern part)	309,000	800,311
Borneo	West mid-Pacific (Indonesian, south part; Brunei and Malaysian, north part)	287,300	744,108
Madagascar	Indian Ocean (Malagasy Republic)	227,000	587,931
Baffin	North Atlantic (Canadian)	195,926	507,451
Sumatra	Northeast Indian Ocean (Indonesian)	182,859	473,605
Honshu	Sea of Japan–Pacific (Japanese)	89,176	230,966
Great Britain	Off coast of NW Europe (England, Scotland, and Wales)	88,795	229,979
Victoria	Arctic Ocean (Canadian)	83,896	217,291
Ellesmere	Arctic Ocean (Canadian)	75,767	196,236
Sulawesi (Celebes)	West mid-Pacific (Indonesian)	73,057	189,218
South Island	South Pacific (New Zealand)	58,384	151,215
Java	Indian Ocean (Indonesian)	51,038	132,189
North Island	South Pacific (New Zealand)	44,702	115,778
Cuba	Caribbean Sea (republic)	42,803	110,860
Newfoundland	North Atlantic (Canadian)	42,031	108,860
Luzon	West mid-Pacific (Philippines)	40,420	104,688
Iceland	North Atlantic (republic)	39,800	103,082
Mindanao	West mid-Pacific (Philippines)	36,537	94,631
Ireland	West of Great Britain (republic, south part; United Kingdom, north part)	32,597	84,426
Hokkaido	Sea of Japan–Pacific (Japanese)	32,245	83,515
Sakhalin (Karafuto)	North of Japan (Russian)	29,500	76,405
Hispaniola	Caribbean Sea (Dominican Republic, east part; Haiti, west part)	29,300	75,887
Banks	Arctic Ocean (Canadian)	27,038	70,028
Tasmania	South of Australia (Australian)	26,200	67,858
Sri Lanka (Ceylon)	Indian Ocean (republic)	24,900	64,491
Devon	Arctic Ocean (Canadian)	21,331	55,247

NOTE: Australia is not included in this list because it is defined as a continent rather than an island.

Highest Waterfalls of the World

Name(s) (foreign)	Location	Height Feet	Height Meters
Angel (Salto Angel)	Canaima Nat'l Park, Venezuela	3,212	979
Tugela	Natal Nat'l Park, South Africa	2,800	850
Utigord (Utigordsfoss)	Norway	2,625	800
Monge (Mongefoss)	Marstein, Norway	2,540	774
Mutarazi (Mtarazi)	Nyanga Nat'l Park, Zimbabwe	2,499	762
Yosemite	Yosemite Nat'l Park, California, U.S.	2,425	739
Pieman	Alpine Nat'l Park, Victoria, Australia	2,346	715
Espelands (Espelandsfoss)	Hardanger Fjord, Norway	2,307	703[1]
Lower Mar Valley (Østra Mardolafoss)	Eikesdal, Norway	2,151	655[2]
Tyssestrengene	Odda, Norway	2,123	647[2]
Cuquenan (Salto Kukenan)	Kukenan Tepuy, Venezuela	2,000	610
Sentinel	Yosemite Nat'l Park, California, U.S.	2,000	610
Dudhsagar	Goa/Karnataka, India	1,969	600
Sutherland	Milford Sound, New Zealand	1,904	580
Kjell (Kjellfossen)	Gudvanger, Norway	1,841	561
Kahiwa	Molokai, Hawaii, U.S.	1,750	533
Takkakaw	Yoho Nat'l Park, B.C., Canada	1,650	503
Ribbon	Yosemite Nat'l Park, California, U.S.	1,612	491
King George VI	Guyana	1,600	488
Upper Mar Valley (Mardalsfossen)	nr. Eikesdal, Norway	1,536	468
Kaliuwaa (Sacred)	Pahu, Hawaii, U.S.	1,520	463
Della	Strathcona Provincial Park, B.C., Canada	1,444	440
Gavarnie	nr. Lourdes, France	1,384	422
Cachoeira da Fumaça (Glass or Smoke)	Chapada Diamantia Nat'l Park, Brazil	1,378	420
Giessbach	Bern, Switzerland	1,312	400
Krimmler	Hohe Tauern Nat'l Park, Austria	1,250	381
Vettis (Vettisfoss)	Jotunheimen, Norway	1,215	370
Papalaua	Molokai, Hawaii, U.S.	1,200	366
Tin Mine	Kosciusko Nat'l Park, Australia	1,182	360

1. Unofficial (estimated) height. Subject to revision. 2. Incorporated in hydroelectric scheme. Greatly diminished flow.
Sources: Merriam Webster's Geographical Dictionary, Third Edition (1997), www.britannica.com, www.waterfallsnorthwest. com, www.americanparknetwork.com, www.ga.gov.au/education/facts/landforms/waterfal.htm/, www.atlas.gc.ca/site/english/facts/waterfalls.html, The State of Hawaii Data Book 2001.

Polar Regions

Antarctica

The second smallest continent, mostly south of the Antarctic Circle.

Area: 14.2 million sq. km (5.5 million sq. mi.).

Geographic South Pole: Earth's southernmost point, at latitude 90°S, where all lines of longitude meet.

Magnetic South Pole: The magnetic South Pole shifts about 5 miles (km) a year and is now located at about 66°S and 139°E on the Adélie Coast of Antarctica.

Terrain: About 98% thick ice sheet and 2% barren rock; glaciers form ice shelves along about half of the coastline, and floating ice shelves constitute 11% of the area of the continent. **Ice sheet:** The continental ice sheet contains approximately 7 million cubic miles (30 million cu km) of ice, representing about 90% of the world's total. **Major ice shelves:** Amery, Filchner, Larsen, Ronne, Ross. Ice shelves make up about 10% of Antarctica's ice, and are floating sheets of ice attached to land that project out into coastal waters.

Climate: The coldest, windiest, driest continent.

Regions: East Antarctica (c. 3,000,000 sq. mi./ 7,770,000 sq. km), the largest portion of the continent, is a high, ice-covered plateau. West Antarctica (c. 2,500,000 sq. mi./6,475,000 sq. km), is an archipelago of mountainous islands connected by ice. A mountain range divides them.

Elevation extremes: *Lowest point:* Bentley Subglacial Trench –8,327 ft. below sea level (–2,538 m)—the lowest land elevation is hidden within the trench. *Highest point:* Vinson Massif 16,066 ft. (4,897 m), Ellsworth Mountains.

The Arctic

Region, primarily made up of the frozen Arctic Ocean, that surrounds the North Pole. Land masses include islands and the northern parts of the European, Asian, and North American continents.

Area: 14.056 million sq. km (5.4 million sq. mi.), largely frozen ocean.

Geographic North Pole: Northern end of Earth's axis, located at about latitude 90°N.

Magnetic North Pole: Continues to shift and is located at about 78°N and 104°W in the Queen Elizabeth Islands of northern Canada.

Terrain: Central surface covered by a perennial drifting polar icepack that averages about 3 meters in thickness; the icepack is surrounded by open seas during the summer, but more than doubles in size during the winter and extends to the encircling landmasses.

Climate: Polar climate characterized by persistent cold and relatively narrow annual temperature ranges; winters characterized by continuous darkness, cold and stable weather conditions, and clear skies; summers characterized by continuous daylight, damp and foggy weather, and weak cyclones with rain or snow.

Regions: The Arctic is divided by the summer isotherm, a climatic boundary between regions with summer temperatures averaging 50°F (or 10°C)—the subarctic—and colder regions (the true Arctic).

Elevation extremes: *Lowest point:* Fram Basin –4,665 m. *Highest point:* sea level 0 m.

Interesting Caves and Caverns of the World

Aggtelek. In village of same name, northern Hungary. Large stalactitic cavern about 5 mi. long.

Altamira Cave. Near Santander, Spain. Contains Stone Age animal paintings on roof and walls.

Antiparos. On island of same name in the Grecian Archipelago. Some stalactites are 20 ft. long. Brilliant colors and fantastic shapes.

Blue Grotto. On island of Capri, Italy. Sea cavern hollowed out in limestone by constant wave action. Now half filled with water because of sinking coast. Name derived from unusual blue light permeating the cave. Source of light is a submerged opening allowing light to pass through the water.

Carlsbad Caverns. Southeast New Mexico. Contains some of the largest and most impressive stalactites and stalagmites, particularly in the Lechuguilla Cave.

Fingal's Cave. On island of Staffa off coast of western Scotland. Penetrates about 200 ft. inland. Contains basaltic columns almost 40 ft. high.

Jenolan Caves. In Blue Mountain plateau, New South Wales, Australia. Beautiful stalactitic formations.

Kent's Cavern. Near Torquay, England. Source of much information on Paleolithic humans.

Lascaux Cave. Southwestern France. Features prehistoric cave paintings estimated to be tens of thousands of years old. Closed to the public.

Lubang Nasib Bagus. Sarawak, Malaysia. World's largest cave chamber: 2,300 ft. long, 1,480 ft. wide, and everywhere at least 230 ft. high.

Luray Caverns. Near Luray, Va. Has large stalactitic and stalagmitic columns of many colors.

Mogao Caves. Located along the old Silk Route in China, Mogao is composed of 492 cells and cave sanctuaries that are famous for their statues and wall paintings, spanning a thousand years of Buddhist art.

Mammoth Cave. This limestone cavern in central Kentucky is the longest cave system in the world. Cave area is about 10 mi. in diameter but has 345 mi. of irregular subterranean passageways at various levels, plus underground lakes and rivers.

Peak Cavern or Devil's Hole. Derbyshire, England. About 2,250 ft. into a mountain. Lowest part is about 600 ft. below the surface.

Postojna Grotto. Postojna, Slovenia. Largest cavern in Europe; numerous beautiful stalactites. Famous example of a karst cave—grooved and irregularly eroded limestone formations carved out by underground streams. Pivka River flows through part of it.

Singing Cave. Iceland. A lava cave; name derived from echoes of people singing in it.

Waitomo Cave. North Island, New Zealand. Glowworms on cave ceiling look like thousands of stars in the night sky.

Wind Cave. In Black Hills of South Dakota. Limestone caverns with stalactites and stalagmites almost entirely missing. Variety of crystal formations called "boxwork."

Wyandotte Cave. In Crawford County, southern Indiana. A limestone cavern with five levels of passages; one of the largest in North America. "Monumental Mountain," approximately 135 ft. high, is believed to be one of the world's largest underground "mountains."

Principal Deserts of the World

Deserts are arid regions, generally receiving less than ten inches of precipitation a year, or regions where the potential evaporation rate is twice as great as the precipitation.

The world's deserts are divided into four categories. **Subtropical deserts** are the hottest, with parched terrain and rapid evaporation. Although **cool coastal deserts** are located within the same latitudes as subtropical deserts, the average temperature is much cooler because of frigid offshore ocean currents. **Cold winter deserts** are marked by stark temperature differences from season to season, ranging from 100° F (38° C) in the summer to 10° F (−12° C) in the winter. **Polar regions** are also considered to be deserts because nearly all moisture in these areas is locked up in the form of ice.

Desert	Location	Size	Topography
SUBTROPICAL DESERTS			
Sahara	Morocco, Western Sahara, Algeria, Tunisia, Libya, Egypt, Mauritania, Mali, Niger, Chad, Ethiopia, Eritrea, Somalia	3.5 million sq. mi.	70% gravel plains, sand, and dunes. Contrary to popular belief, the desert is only 30% sand. The world's largest nonpolar desert gets its name from the Arabic word *Sahra'*, meaning desert
Arabian	Saudi Arabia, Kuwait, Qatar, United Arab Emirates, Oman, Yemen	1 million sq. mi.	Gravel plains, rocky highlands; one-fourth is the Rub al-Khali ("Empty Quarter"), the world's largest expanse of unbroken sand
Kalahari	Botswana, South Africa, Namibia	220,000 sq. mi.	Sand sheets, longitudinal dunes
Australian Desert			
Gibson	Australia (southern portion of the Western Desert)	120,000 sq. mi.	Sandhills, gravel, grass. These three regions of desert are collectively referred to as the Great Western Desert— otherwise known as "the Outback." Contains Ayers Rock, or Uluru, one of the world's largest monoliths
Great Sandy	Australia (northern portion of the Western Desert)	150,000 sq. mi.	
Great Victoria	Australia (southernmost portion of the Western Desert)	250,000 sq. mi.	
Simpson and Sturt Stony	Australia (eastern half of the continent)	56,000 sq. mi.	Simpson's straight, parallel sand dunes are the longest in the world—up to 125 mi. Encompasses the Stewart Stony Desert, named for the Australian explorer
Mojave	U.S.: Arizona, Colorado, Nevada, Utah, California	54,000 sq. mi.	Mountain chains, dry alkaline lake beds, calcium carbonate dunes
Sonoran	U.S.: Arizona, California; Mexico	120,000 sq. mi.	Basins and plains bordered by mountain ridges; home to the Saguaro cactus
Chihuahuan	Mexico; southwestern U.S.	175,000 sq. mi.	Shrub desert; largest in North America
Thar	India, Pakistan	175,000 sq. mi.	Rocky sand and sand dunes
COOL COASTAL DESERTS			
Namib	Angola, Namibia, South Africa	13,000 sq. mi.	Gravel plains
Atacama	Chile	54,000 sq. mi.	Salt basins, sand, lava; world's driest desert
COLD WINTER DESERTS			
Great Basin	U.S.: Nevada, Oregon, Utah	190,000 sq. mi.	Mountain ridges, valleys, 1% sand dunes
Colorado Plateau	U.S.: Arizona, Colorado, New Mexico, Utah, Wyoming	130,000 sq. mi.	Sedimentary rock, mesas, and plateaus— includes the Grand Canyon and is also called the "Painted Desert" because of the spectacular colors in its rocks and canyons
Patagonian	Argentina	260,000 sq. mi.	Gravel plains, plateaus, basalt sheets
Kara-Kum	Uzbekistan, Turkmenistan	135,000 sq. mi.	90% gray layered sand—name means "black sand"
Kyzyl-Kum	Uzbekistan, Turkmenistan, Kazakhstan	115,000 sq. mi.	Sands, rock—name means "red sand"
Iranian	Iran	100,000 sq. mi.	Salt, gravel, rock
Taklamakan	China	105,000 sq. mi.	Sand, dunes, gravel
Gobi	China, Mongolia	500,000 sq. mi.	Stony, sandy soil, steppes (dry grasslands)
POLAR			
Arctic	U.S., Canada, Greenland, Iceland, Norway, Sweden, Finland, Russia		Snow, glaciers, tundra
Antarctic	Antarctica	5.4 million sq. mi.	Ice, snow, bedrock

Latitude and Longitude of World Cities
(and time corresponding to 12:00 noon, Eastern Standard Time)

City	Latitude °	'	Longitude °	'	Time
Aberdeen, Scotland	57	9 N	2	9 W	5:00 p.m.
Adelaide, Australia	34	55 S	138	36 E	2:30 a.m.[1]
Algiers, Algeria	36	50 N	3	0 E	6:00 p.m.
Amsterdam, Netherlands	52	22 N	4	53 E	6:00 p.m.
Ankara, Turkey	39	55 N	32	55 E	7:00 p.m.
Asunción, Paraguay	25	15 S	57	40 W	1:00 p.m.
Athens, Greece	37	58 N	23	43 E	7:00 p.m.
Auckland, New Zealand	36	52 S	174	45 E	5:00 a.m.[1]
Bangkok, Thailand	13	45 N	100	30 E	midnight
Barcelona, Spain	41	23 N	2	9 E	6:00 p.m.
Beijing, China	39	55 N	116	25 E	1:00 a.m.[1]
Belém, Brazil	1	28 S	48	29 W	2:00 p.m.
Belfast, Northern Ireland	54	37 N	5	56 W	5:00 p.m.
Belgrade, Yugoslavia	44	52 N	20	32 E	6:00 p.m.
Berlin, Germany	52	30 N	13	25 E	6:00 p.m.
Birmingham, England	52	25 N	1	55 W	5:00 p.m.
Bogotá, Colombia	4	32 N	74	15 W	12:00 noon
Bombay, India	19	0 N	72	48 E	10:30 p.m.
Bordeaux, France	44	50 N	0	31 W	6:00 p.m.
Bremen, Germany	53	5 N	8	49 E	6:00 p.m.
Brisbane, Australia	27	29 S	153	8 E	3:00 a.m.[1]
Brussels, Belgium	50	52 N	4	22 E	6:00 p.m.
Bucharest, Romania	44	25 N	26	7 E	7:00 p.m.
Budapest, Hungary	47	30 N	19	5 E	6:00 p.m.
Buenos Aires, Argentina	34	35 S	58	22 W	2:00 p.m.
Cairo, Egypt	30	2 N	31	21 E	7:00 p.m.
Calcutta, India	22	34 N	88	24 E	10:30 p.m.
Canton, China	23	7 N	113	15 E	1:00 a.m.[1]
Cape Town, South Africa	33	55 S	18	22 E	7:00 p.m.
Caracas, Venezuela	10	28 N	67	2 W	1:00 p.m.
Cayenne, French Guiana	4	49 N	52	18 W	2:00 p.m.
Chihuahua, Mexico	28	37 N	106	5 W	10:00 a.m.
Chongqing, China	29	46 N	106	34 E	1:00 a.m.[1]
Copenhagen, Denmark	55	40 N	12	34 E	6:00 p.m.
Córdoba, Argentina	31	28 S	64	10 W	2:00 p.m.
Dakar, Senegal	14	40 N	17	28 W	5:00 p.m.
Darwin, Australia	12	28 S	130	51 E	2:30 a.m.[1]
Djibouti, Djibouti	11	30 N	43	3 E	8:00 p.m.
Dublin, Ireland	53	20 N	6	15 W	5:00 p.m.
Durban, South Africa	29	53 S	30	53 E	7:00 p.m.
Edinburgh, Scotland	55	55 N	3	10 W	5:00 p.m.
Frankfurt, Germany	50	7 N	8	41 E	6:00 p.m.
Georgetown, Guyana	6	45 N	58	15 W	1:00 p.m.
Glasgow, Scotland	55	50 N	4	15 W	5:00 p.m.
Guatemala City, Guatemala	14	37 N	90	31 W	11:00 a.m.
Guayaquil, Ecuador	2	10 S	79	56 W	12:00 noon
Hamburg, Germany	53	33 N	10	2 E	6:00 p.m.
Hammerfest, Norway	70	38 N	23	38 E	6:00 p.m.
Havana, Cuba	23	8 N	82	23 W	12:00 noon
Helsinki, Finland	60	10 N	25	0 E	7:00 p.m.
Hobart, Tasmania	42	52 S	147	19 E	3:00 a.m.[1]
Hong Kong, China	22	20 N	114	11 E	1:00 a.m.[1]
Iquique, Chile	20	10 S	70	7 W	1:00 p.m.
Irkutsk, Russia	52	30 N	104	20 E	1:00 a.m.
Jakarta, Indonesia	6	16 S	106	48 E	midnight
Johannesburg, South Africa	26	12 S	28	4 E	7:00 p.m.
Kingston, Jamaica	17	59 N	76	49 W	12:00 noon
Kinshasa, Congo	4	18 S	15	17 E	6:00 p.m.
Kuala Lumpur, Malaysia	3	8 N	101	42 E	1:00 a.m.[1]
La Paz, Bolivia	16	27 S	68	22 W	1:00 p.m.
Lima, Peru	12	0 S	77	2 W	12:00 noon
Lisbon, Portugal	38	44 N	9	9 W	5:00 p.m.
Liverpool, England	53	25 N	3	0 W	5:00 p.m.
London, England	51	32 N	0	5 W	5:00 p.m.
Madrid, Spain	40	26 N	3	42 W	6:00 p.m.
Manchester, England	53	30 N	2	15 W	5:00 p.m.
Manila, Philippines	14	35 N	120	57 E	1:00 a.m.[1]
Marseilles, France	43	20 N	5	20 E	6:00 p.m.
Mazatlán, Mexico	23	12 N	106	25 W	10:00 a.m.
Mecca, Saudi Arabia	21	29 N	39	45 E	8:00 p.m.
Melbourne, Australia	37	47 S	144	58 E	3:00 a.m.[1]
Mexico City, Mexico	19	26 N	99	7 W	11:00 a.m.
Milan, Italy	45	27 N	9	10 E	6:00 p.m.
Montevideo, Uruguay	34	53 S	56	10 W	2:00 p.m.
Moscow, Russia	55	45 N	37	36 E	8:00 p.m.
Munich, Germany	48	8 N	11	35 E	6:00 p.m.
Nagasaki, Japan	32	48 N	129	57 E	2:00 a.m.[1]
Nagoya, Japan	35	7 N	136	56 E	2:00 a.m.[1]
Nairobi, Kenya	1	25 S	36	55 E	8:00 p.m.
Nanjing (Nanking), China	32	3 N	118	53 E	1:00 a.m.[1]
Naples, Italy	40	50 N	14	15 E	6:00 p.m.
New Delhi, India	28	35 N	77	12 E	10:30 p.m.
Newcastle-on-Tyne, England	54	58 N	1	37 W	5:00 p.m.
Odessa, Ukraine	46	27 N	30	48 E	7:00 p.m.
Osaka, Japan	34	32 N	135	30 E	2:00 a.m.[1]
Oslo, Norway	59	57 N	10	42 E	6:00 p.m.
Panama City, Panama	8	58 N	79	32 W	12:00 noon
Paramaribo, Suriname	5	45 N	55	15 W	2:00 p.m.
Paris, France	48	48 N	2	20 E	6:00 p.m.
Perth, Australia	31	57 S	115	52 E	1:00 a.m.[1]
Plymouth, England	50	25 N	4	5 W	5:00 p.m.
Port Moresby, Papua New Guinea	9	25 S	147	8 E	3:00 a.m.[1]
Prague, Czech Republic	50	5 N	14	26 E	6:00 p.m.
Rangoon, Myanmar	16	50 N	96	0 E	11:30 p.m.
Reykjavík, Iceland	64	4 N	21	58 W	5:00 p.m.
Rio de Janeiro, Brazil	22	57 S	43	12 W	2:00 p.m.
Rome, Italy	41	54 N	12	27 E	6:00 p.m.
Salvador, Brazil	12	56 S	38	27 W	2:00 p.m.
Santiago, Chile	33	28 S	70	45 W	1:00 p.m.
St. Petersburg, Russia	59	56 N	30	18 E	8:00 p.m.
São Paulo, Brazil	23	31 S	46	31 W	2:00 p.m.
Shanghai, China	31	10 N	121	28 E	1:00 a.m.[1]
Singapore, Singapore	1	14 N	103	55 E	1:00 a.m.[1]
Sofia, Bulgaria	42	40 N	23	20 E	7:00 p.m.
Stockholm, Sweden	59	17 N	18	3 E	6:00 p.m.
Sydney, Australia	34	0 S	151	0 E	3:00 a.m.[1]
Tananarive, Madagascar	18	50 S	47	33 E	8:00 p.m.
Teheran, Iran	35	45 N	51	45 E	8:30 p.m.
Tokyo, Japan	35	40 N	139	45 E	2:00 a.m.[1]
Tripoli, Libya	32	57 N	13	12 E	7:00 p.m.
Venice, Italy	45	26 N	12	20 E	6:00 p.m.
Veracruz, Mexico	19	10 N	96	10 W	11:00 a.m.
Vienna, Austria	48	14 N	16	20 E	6:00 p.m.
Vladivostok, Russia	43	10 N	132	0 E	3:00 a.m.[1]
Warsaw, Poland	52	14 N	21	0 E	6:00 p.m.
Wellington, New Zealand	41	17 S	174	47 E	5:00 a.m.[1]
Zürich, Switzerland	47	21 N	8	31 E	6:00 p.m.

1. On the following day.

Miscellaneous Data for the United States

Highest point: Mount McKinley, Alaska   20,320 ft. (6,198 m)
Lowest point: Death Valley, Calif.   282 ft. (86 m) below sea level
Approximate mean elevation   2,500 ft. (763 m)
Points farthest apart (50 states): Log Point, Elliot Key, Fla.,   5,859 mi. (9,429 km)
  and Kure Island, Hawaii
Geographic center (50 states): in Butte County, S.D. (west of Castle Rock)   44°58′N lat.103°46′W long.
Geographic center (48 conterminous states): in Smith County, Kan. (near   39°50′N lat. 98°35′W long.
Lebanon)
Boundaries:
  Between Alaska and Canada   1,538 mi. (2,475 km)
  Between the 48 conterminous states and Canada (incl. the Great Lakes)   3,987 mi. (6,416 km)
  Between the United States and Mexico   1,933 mi. (3,111 km)

Source: U.S. Geological Survey.

Extreme Points of the United States (50 States)

Extreme point	Latitude	Longitude	Distance[1] mi.	km
Northernmost point: Point Barrow, Alaska	71°23′ N	156°29′ W	2,507	4,034
Easternmost point: West Quoddy Head, Maine	44°49′ N	66°57′ W	1,788	2,997
Southernmost point: Ka Lae (South Cape), Hawaii	18°55′ N	155°41′ W	3,463	5,573
Westernmost point: Cape Wrangell, Alaska (Attu Island)	52°55′ N	172°27′ E	3,625	5,833

1. From geographic center of United States (incl. Alaska and Hawaii), west of Castle Rock, S.D., 44°58′ lat., 103°46′ W long. If measured from the prime meridian in Greenwich, England, Cape Wrangell, Attu Island, Alaska, would be the easternmost point.

The Continental Divide

The Continental Divide is a ridge of high ground that runs irregularly north and south through the Rocky Mountains and separates eastward-flowing from westward-flowing streams. The waters that flow eastward empty into the Atlantic Ocean, chiefly by way of the Gulf of Mexico; those that flow westward empty into the Pacific. Every continent with the exception of Antarctica has a continental divide.

Rivers of the United States
(350 or more miles long)

Alabama-Coosa (600 mi.; 966 km): From junction of Oostanula and Etowah R. in Georgia to Mobile R.

Altamaha-Ocmulgee (392 mi.; 631 km): From junction of Yellow R. and South R., Newton Co. in Georgia to Atlantic Ocean.

Apalachicola-Chattahoochee (524 mi.; 843 km): From Towns Co. in Georgia to Gulf of Mexico in Florida.

Arkansas (1,459 mi.; 2,348 km): From Lake Co. in Colorado to Mississippi R. in Arkansas.

Brazos (923 mi.; 1,490 km): From junction of Salt Fork and Double Mountain Fork in Texas to Gulf of Mexico.

Canadian (906 mi.; 1,458 km): From Las Animas Co. in Colorado to Arkansas R. in Oklahoma.

Cimarron (600 mi.; 966 km): From Colfax Co. in New Mexico to Arkansas R. in Oklahoma.

Colorado (1,450 mi.; 2,333 km): From Rocky Mountain National Park in Colorado to Gulf of California in Mexico.

Colorado (862 mi.; 1,387 km): From Dawson Co. in Texas to Matagorda Bay.

Columbia (1,243 mi.; 2,000 km): From Columbia Lake in British Columbia to Pacific Ocean (entering between Oregon and Washington).

Colville (350 mi.; 563 km): From Brooks Range in Alaska to Beaufort Sea.

Connecticut (407 mi.; 655 km): From Third Connecticut Lake in New Hampshire to Long Island Sound in Connecticut.

Cumberland (720 mi.; 1,159 km): From junction of Poor and Clover Forks in Harlan Co. in Kentucky to Ohio R.

Delaware (390 mi.; 628 km): From Schoharie Co. in New York to Liston Point, Delaware Bay.

Gila (649 mi.; 1,044 km): From Catron Co. in New Mexico to Colorado R. in Arizona.

Green (360 mi.; 579 km): From Lincoln Co. in Kentucky to Ohio R. in Kentucky.

Green (730 mi.; 1,175 km): From Sublette Co. in Wyoming to Colorado R. in Utah.

Illinois (420 mi.; 676 km): From St. Joseph Co. in Indiana to Mississippi R. at Grafton in Illinois.

James (sometimes called *Dakota*) (710 mi.; 1,143 km): From Wells Co. in North Dakota to Missouri R. in South Dakota.

Kanawha-New (352 mi.; 566 km): From junction of North and South Forks of New R. in North Carolina, through Virginia and West Virginia (New R. becoming Kanawha R.), to Ohio R.

Kansas (743 mi.; 1,196 km): From source of Arikaree R. in Elbert Co., Colorado, to Missouri R. at Kansas City, Kansas.

Koyukuk (470 mi.; 756 km): From Brooks Range in Alaska to Yukon R.

Kuskokwim (724 mi.; 1,165 km): From Alaska Range in Alaska to Kuskokwim Bay.

Licking (350 mi.; 563 km): From Magoffin Co. in Kentucky to Ohio R. at Cincinnati in Ohio.

Little Missouri (560 mi.; 901 km): From Crook Co. in Wyoming to Missouri R. in North Dakota.

Milk (625 mi.; 1,006 km): From junction of forks in Alberta Province to Missouri R.

Mississippi (2,348 mi.; 3,779 km): From Lake Itasca in Minnesota to mouth of Southwest Pass in Louisiana.

Mississippi-Missouri-Red Rock (3,710 mi.; 5,970 km): From source of Red Rock R. in Montana to mouth of Southwest Pass in Louisiana.

Missouri (2,315 mi.; 3,726 km): From junction of Jefferson R., Gallatin R., and Madison R. in Montana to Mississippi R. near St. Louis.

Missouri-Red Rock (2,540 mi.; 4,090 km): From source of Red Rock R. in Montana to Mississippi R. near St. Louis.

Mobile-Alabama-Coosa (645 mi.; 1,040 km): From junction of Etowah R. and Oostanula R. in Georgia to Mobile Bay.

Neosho (460 mi.; 740 km): From Morris Co. in Kansas to Arkansas R. in Oklahoma.

Niobrara (431 mi.; 694 km): From Niobrara Co. in Wyoming to Missouri R. in Nebraska.

Noatak (350 mi.; 563 km): From Brooks Range in Alaska to Kotzebue Sound.

North Canadian (800 mi.; 1,290 km): From Union Co. in New Mexico to Canadian R. in Oklahoma.

North Platte (618 mi.; 995 km): From Jackson Co. in Colorado to junction with South Platte R. in Nebraska to form Platte R.

Ohio (981 mi.; 1,579 km): From junction of Allegheny R. and Monongahela R. at Pittsburgh to Mississippi R. between Illinois and Kentucky.

Ohio-Allegheny (1,306 mi.; 2,102 km): From Potter Co. in Pennsylvania to Mississippi R. at Cairo in Illinois.

Osage (500 mi.; 805 km): From east-central Kansas to Missouri R. near Jefferson City in Missouri.

Ouachita (605 mi.; 974 km): From Polk Co. in Arkansas to Red R. in Louisiana.

Pearl (411 mi.; 661 km): From Neshoba County in Mississippi to Gulf of Mexico (Mississippi-Louisiana).

Pecos (926 mi.; 1,490 km): From Mora Co. in New Mexico to Rio Grande in Texas.

Pee Dee-Yadkin (435 mi.; 700 km): From Watauga Co. in North Carolina to Winyah Bay in South Carolina.

Pend Oreille–Clark Fork (531 mi.; 855 km): Near Butte in Montana to Columbia R. on Washington-Canada border.

Platte (990 mi.; 1593 km): From source of Grizzly Creek in Jackson Co., Colorado, to Missouri R. south of Omaha, Nebraska.

Porcupine (569 mi.; 916 km): From Yukon Territory, Canada, to Yukon R. in Alaska.

Potomac (383 mi.; 616 km): From Garrett Co. in Maryland to Chesapeake Bay at Point Lookout in Maryland.

Powder (375 mi.; 603 km): From junction of forks in Johnson Co. in Wyoming to Yellowstone R. in Montana.

Red (1,290 mi.; 2,080 km): From source of Tierra Blanca Creek in Curry County, New Mexico, to Mississippi R. in Louisiana.

Red (also called *Red River of the North*) (545 mi.; 877 km): From junction of Otter Tail R. and Bois de Sioux R. in Minnesota to Lake Winnipeg in Manitoba, Canada.

Republican (445 mi.; 716 km): From junction of North Fork and Arikaree R. in Nebraska to junction with Smoky Hill R. in Kansas to form the Kansas R.

Rio Grande (1,900 mi.; 3,060 km): From San Juan Co. in Colorado to Gulf of Mexico.

Roanoke (380 mi.; 612 km): From junction of forks in Montgomery Co. in Virginia to Albemarle Sound in North Carolina.

Sabine (380 mi.; 612 km): From junction of forks in Hunt Co. in Texas to Sabine Lake between Texas and Louisiana.

Sacramento (377 mi.; 607 km): From Siskiyou Co. in California to Suisun Bay.

Saint Francis (425 mi.; 684 km): From Iron Co. in Missouri to Mississippi R. in Arkansas.

Salmon (420 mi.; 676 km): From Custer Co. in Idaho to Snake R.

San Joaquin (350 mi.; 563 km): From junction of forks in Madera Co. in California to Suisun Bay.

San Juan (360 mi.; 579 km): From Archuleta Co. in Colorado to Colorado R. in Utah.

Santee-Wateree-Catawba (538 mi.; 866 km): From McDowell Co. in North Carolina to Atlantic Ocean in South Carolina.

Smoky Hill (540 mi.; 869 km): From Cheyenne Co. in Colorado to junction with Republican R. in Kansas to form Kansas R.

Snake (1,038 mi.; 1,670 km): From Ocean Plateau in Wyoming to Columbia R. in Washington.

South Platte (424 mi.; 682 km): From Park Co. in Colorado to junction with North Platte R. in Nebraska to form Platte R.

Stikine (379 mi.; 610 km): From British Columbia in Canada to Stikine Strait near Wrangell, Alaska.

Susquehanna (444 mi.; 715 km): From Otsego Lake in New York to Chesapeake Bay in Maryland.

Tanana (659 mi.; 1,060 km): From Wrangell Mts. in Yukon Territory, Canada, to Yukon R. in Alaska.

Tennessee (652 mi.; 1,049 km): From junction of Holston R. and French Broad R. in Tennessee to Ohio R. in Kentucky.

Tennessee–French Broad (886 mi.; 1,417 km): From Transylvania Co. in North Carolina to Ohio R. at Paducah in Kentucky.

Tombigbee (525 mi.; 845 km): From junction of forks in Itawamba Co. in Mississippi to Mobile R. in Alabama.

Trinity (360 mi.; 579 km): From junction of forks in Dallas Co. in Texas to Galveston Bay.

Wabash (512 mi.; 824 km): From Darke Co. in Ohio to Ohio R. between Illinois and Indiana.

Washita (500 mi.; 805 km): From Hemphill Co. in Texas to Red R. in Oklahoma.

White (722 mi.; 1,160 km): From Madison Co. in Arkansas to Mississippi R.

Wisconsin (430 mi.; 692 km): From Vilas Co. in Wisconsin to Mississippi R.

Yellowstone (692 mi.; 1,110 km): From Park Co. in Wyoming to Missouri R. in North Dakota.

Yukon (1,979 mi.; 3,185 km): From source of McNeil R. in Yukon Territory, Canada, to Bering Sea in Alaska.

Coastline of the United States

State	Lengths, statute miles		State	Lengths, statute miles	
	General coastline[1]	Tidal shoreline[2]		General coastline[1]	Tidal shoreline[2]
Atlantic Coast:			**Gulf Coast:**		
Maine	228	3,478	Florida (Gulf)	770	5,095
New Hampshire	13	131	Alabama	53	607
Massachusetts	192	1,519	Mississippi	44	359
Rhode Island	40	384	Louisiana	397	7,721
Connecticut	—	618	Texas	367	3,359
New York	127	1,850	Total Gulf Coast	1,631	17,141
New Jersey	130	1,792	**Pacific Coast:**		
Pennsylvania	—	89	California	840	3,427
Delaware	28	381	Oregon	296	1,410
Maryland	31	3,190	Washington	157	3,026
Virginia	112	3,315	Hawaii	750	1,052
North Carolina	301	3,375	Alaska (Pacific)	5,580	31,383
South Carolina	187	2,876	Total Pacific Coast	7,623	40,298
Georgia	100	2,344	**Arctic Coast:**		
Florida (Atlantic)	580	3,331	Alaska (Arctic)	1,060	2,521
Total Atlantic Coast	2,069	28,673	Total Arctic Coast	1,060	2,521
			States Total	**12,383**	**88,633**

1. Figures are lengths of general outline of seacoast. Measurements are made with unit measure of 30 minutes of latitude on charts as near scale of 1:1,200,000 as possible. Coastline of bays and sounds is included to point where they narrow to width of unit measure, and distance across at such point is included. 2. Figures were obtained in 1939–1940 with recording instrument on the largest-scale maps and charts then available. Shoreline of outer coast, offshore islands, sounds, bays, rivers, and creeks is included to head of tidewater, or to point where tidal waters narrow to width of 100 feet. *Source:* Department of Commerce, National Oceanic and Atmospheric Administration, National Ocean Service.

Mountain Peaks in the United States Higher Than 14,000 Feet

Name	State	Height (ft.)	Name	State	Height (ft.)	Name	State	Height (ft.)
Mt. McKinley	Alaska	20,320	Castle Peak	Colo.	14,265	Windom Peak	Colo.	14,082
Mt. St. Elias	Alaska	18,008	Quandary Peak	Colo.	14,265	Mt. Columbia	Colo.	14,073
Mt. Foraker	Alaska	17,400	Mt. Evans	Colo.	14,264	Mt. Augusta	Alaska	14,070
Mt. Bona	Alaska	16,500	Longs Peak	Colo.	14,255	Missouri Mtn.	Colo.	14,067
Mt. Blackburn	Alaska	16,390	Mt. Wilson	Colo.	14,246	Humboldt Peak	Colo.	14,064
Mt. Sanford	Alaska	16,237	White Mtn.	Calif.	14,246	Mt. Bierstadt	Colo.	14,060
Mt. Vancouver	Alaska	15,979	North Palisade	Calif.	14,242	Sunlight Peak	Colo.	14,059
South Buttress	Alaska	15,885	Mt. Cameron	Colo.	14,238	Split Mtn.	Calif.	14,058
Mt. Churchill	Alaska	15,638	Mt. Shavano	Colo.	14,229	Handies Peak	Colo.	14,048
Mt. Fairweather	Alaska	15,300	Crestone Needle	Colo.	14,197	Culebra Peak	Colo.	14,047
Mt. Hubbard	Alaska	14,950	Mt. Belford	Colo.	14,197	Mt. Lindsey	Colo.	14,042
Mt. Bear	Alaska	14,831	Mt. Princeton	Colo.	14,197	Ellingwood Point	Colo.	14,042
East Buttress	Alaska	14,730	Mt. Yale	Colo.	14,196	Middle Palisade	Calif.	14,040
Mt. Hunter	Alaska	14,573	Mt. Bross	Colo.	14,172	Little Bear Peak	Colo.	14,037
Browne Tower	Alaska	14,530	Kit Carson Mtn.	Colo.	14,165	Mt. Sherman	Colo.	14,036
Mt. Alverstone	Alaska	14,500	Mt. Wrangell	Alaska	14,163	Redcloud Peak	Colo.	14,034
Mt. Whitney	Calif.	14,494[1]	Mt. Sill	Calif.	14,162	Mt. Langley	Calif.	14,027
University Peak	Alaska	14,470	Mt. Shasta	Calif.	14,162	Conundrum Peak	Colo.	14,022
Mt. Elbert	Colo.	14,433	El Diente Peak	Colo.	14,159	Mt. Tyndall	Calif.	14,019
Mt. Massive	Colo.	14,421	Point Success	Wash.	14,158	Pyramid Peak	Colo.	14,018
Mt. Harvard	Colo.	14,420	Maroon Peak	Colo.	14,156	Wilson Peak	Colo.	14,017
Mt. Rainier	Wash.	14,410	Tabeguache Mtn.	Colo.	14,155	Wetterhorn Peak	Colo.	14,015
Mt. Williamson	Calif.	14,370	Mt. Oxford	Colo.	14,153	North Maroon Peak	Colo.	14,014
La Plata Peak	Colo.	14,361	Mt. Sneffels	Colo.	14,150	San Luis Peak	Colo.	14,014
Blanca Peak	Colo.	14,345	Mt. Democrat	Colo.	14,148	Middle Palisade	Calif.	14,012
Uncompahgre Peak	Colo.	14,309	Capitol Peak	Colo.	14,130	Mt. Muir	Calif.	14,012
Crestone Peak	Colo.	14,294	Liberty Cap	Wash.	14,112	Mt. of the Holy Cross	Colo.	14,005
Mt. Lincoln	Colo.	14,286	Pikes Peak	Colo.	14,110	Huron Peak	Colo.	14,003
Grays Peak	Colo.	14,270	Snowmass Mtn.	Colo.	14,092	Thunderbolt Peak	Calif.	14,003
Mt. Antero	Colo.	14,269	Mt. Russell	Calif.	14,088	Sunshine Peak	Colo.	14,001
Torreys Peak	Colo.	14,267	Mt. Eolus	Colo.	14,083			

1. National Geodetic Survey. *Source:* U.S. Dept. of the Interior, Geological Survey.

Highest, Lowest, and Mean Elevations in the United States

State	Elevation (ft.)[1]	Highest point	Elevation (ft.)	Lowest point	Elevation (ft.)
Alabama	500	Cheaha Mountain	2,405	Gulf of Mexico	Sea level
Alaska	1,900	Mt. McKinley	20,320	Pacific Ocean	Sea level
Arizona	4,100	Humphreys Peak	12,633	Colorado River	70
Arkansas	650	Magazine Mountain	2,753	Ouachita River	55
California	2,900	Mt. Whitney	14,494	Death Valley	−282[2]
Colorado	6,800	Mt. Elbert	14,433	Arkansas River	3,350
Connecticut	500	Mt. Frissell, on south slope	2,380	Long Island Sound	Sea level
Delaware	60	Ebright Road, Del.–Pa. state line	448	Atlantic Ocean	Sea level
D.C.	150	Tenleytown, at Reno Reservoir	410	Potomac River	1
Florida	100	Sec. 30, T6N, R20W, Walton County	345	Atlantic Ocean	Sea level
Georgia	600	Brasstown Bald	4,784	Atlantic Ocean	Sea level
Hawaii	3,030	Puu Wekiu, Mauna Kea	13,796	Pacific Ocean	Sea level
Idaho	5,000	Borah Peak	12,662	Snake River	710
Illinois	600	Charles Mound	1,235	Mississippi River	279
Indiana	700	Franklin Township, Wayne County	1,257	Ohio River	320
Iowa	1,100	Sec. 29, T100N, R41W, Osceola County	1,670	Mississippi River	480
Kansas	2,000	Mt. Sunflower	4,039	Verdigris River	679
Kentucky	750	Black Mountain	4,139	Mississippi River	257
Louisiana	100	Driskill Mountain	535	New Orleans	−8[2]
Maine	600	Mt. Katahdin	5,267	Atlantic Ocean	Sea level
Maryland	350	Backbone Mountain	3,360	Atlantic Ocean	Sea level
Massachusetts	500	Mt. Greylock	3,487	Atlantic Ocean	Sea level
Michigan	900	Mt. Arvon	1,979	Lake Erie	572
Minnesota	1,200	Eagle Mountain	2,301	Lake Superior	600
Mississippi	300	Woodall Mountain	806	Gulf of Mexico	Sea level
Missouri	800	Taum Sauk Mountain	1,772	St. Francis River	230
Montana	3,400	Granite Peak	12,799	Kootenai River	1,800
Nebraska	2,600	Johnson Township, Kimball County	5,424	Missouri River	840
Nevada	5,500	Boundary Peak	13,140	Colorado River	479
New Hampshire	1,000	Mt. Washington	6,288	Atlantic Ocean	Sea level
New Jersey	250	High Point	1,803	Atlantic Ocean	Sea level
New Mexico	5,700	Wheeler Peak	13,161	Red Bluff Reservoir	2,842
New York	1,000	Mt. Marcy	5,344	Atlantic Ocean	Sea level
North Carolina	700	Mt. Mitchell	6,684	Atlantic Ocean	Sea level
North Dakota	1,900	White Butte	3,506	Red River	750
Ohio	850	Campbell Hill	1,549	Ohio River	455
Oklahoma	1,300	Black Mesa	4,973	Little River	289
Oregon	3,300	Mt. Hood	11,239	Pacific Ocean	Sea level
Pennsylvania	1,100	Mt. Davis	3,213	Delaware River	Sea level
Rhode Island	200	Jerimoth Hill	812	Atlantic Ocean	Sea level
South Carolina	350	Sassafras Mountain	3,560	Atlantic Ocean	Sea level
South Dakota	2,200	Harney Peak	7,242	Big Stone Lake	966
Tennessee	900	Clingmans Dome	6,643	Mississippi River	178
Texas	1,700	Guadalupe Peak	8,749	Gulf of Mexico	Sea level
Utah	6,100	Kings Peak	13,528	Beaverdam Wash	2,000
Vermont	1,000	Mt. Mansfield	4,393	Lake Champlain	95
Virginia	950	Mt. Rogers	5,729	Atlantic Ocean	Sea level
Washington	1,700	Mt. Rainier	14,410	Pacific Ocean	Sea level
West Virginia	1,500	Spruce Knob	4,861	Potomac River	240
Wisconsin	1,050	Timms Hill	1,951	Lake Michigan	579
Wyoming	6,700	Gannett Peak	13,804	Belle Fourche River	3,099
United States	**2,500**	**Mt. McKinley (Alaska)**	**20,320**	**Death Valley (California)**	**−282[2]**

1. Approximate mean elevation. 2. Below sea level. *Source:* U.S. Geological Survey.

Latitude and Longitude of U.S. and Canadian Cities
(and time corresponding to 12:00 noon, Eastern Standard Time)

City	Lat. °	Lat. ′	Long. °	Long. ′	Time	City	Lat. °	Lat. ′	Long. °	Long. ′	Time
Albany, N.Y.	42	40	73	45	12:00 noon	Memphis, Tenn.	35	9	90	3	11:00 a.m.
Albuquerque, N.M.	35	05	106	39	10:00 a.m.	Miami, Fla.	25	46	80	12	12:00 noon
Amarillo, Tex.	35	11	101	50	11:00 a.m.	Milwaukee, Wis.	43	2	87	55	11:00 a.m.
Anchorage, Alaska	61	13	149	54	8:00 a.m.	Minneapolis, Minn.	44	59	93	14	11:00 a.m.
Atlanta, Ga.	33	45	84	23	12:00 noon	Mobile, Ala.	30	42	88	3	11:00 a.m.
Austin, Tex.	30	16	97	44	11:00 a.m.	Montgomery, Ala.	32	21	86	18	11:00 a.m.
Baker, Ore.	44	47	117	50	9:00 a.m.	Montpelier, Vt.	44	15	72	32	12:00 noon
Baltimore, Md.	39	18	76	38	12:00 noon	Montreal, Que., Can.	45	30	73	35	12:00 noon
Bangor, Maine	44	48	68	47	12:00 noon	Moose Jaw, Sask., Can.	50	37	105	31	11:00 a.m.
Birmingham, Ala.	33	30	86	50	11:00 a.m.	Nashville, Tenn.	36	10	86	47	11:00 a.m.
Bismarck, N.D.	46	48	100	47	11:00 a.m.	Nelson, B.C., Can.	49	30	117	17	9:00 a.m.
Boise, Idaho	43	36	116	13	10:00 a.m.	Newark, N.J.	40	44	74	10	12:00 noon
Boston, Mass.	42	21	71	5	12:00 noon	New Haven, Conn.	41	19	72	55	12:00 noon
Buffalo, N.Y.	42	55	78	50	12:00 noon	New Orleans, La.	29	57	90	4	11:00 a.m.
Calgary, Alba., Can.	51	1	114	1	10:00 a.m.	New York, N.Y.	40	47	73	58	12:00 noon
Carlsbad, N.M.	32	26	104	15	10:00 a.m.	Nome, Alaska	64	25	165	30	8:00 a.m.
Charleston, S.C.	32	47	79	56	12:00 noon	Oakland, Calif.	37	48	122	16	9:00 a.m.
Charleston, W. Va.	38	21	81	38	12:00 noon	Oklahoma City, Okla.	35	26	97	28	11:00 a.m.
Charlotte, N.C.	35	14	80	50	12:00 noon	Omaha, Neb.	41	15	95	56	11:00 a.m.
Cheyenne, Wyo.	41	9	104	52	10:00 a.m.	Ottawa, Ont., Can.	45	24	75	43	12:00 noon
Chicago, Ill.	41	50	87	37	11:00 a.m.	Philadelphia, Pa.	39	57	75	10	12:00 noon
Cincinnati, Ohio	39	8	84	30	12:00 noon	Phoenix, Ariz.	33	29	112	4	10:00 a.m.
Cleveland, Ohio	41	28	81	37	12:00 noon	Pierre, S.D.	44	22	100	21	11:00 a.m.
Columbia, S.C.	34	0	81	2	12:00 noon	Pittsburgh, Pa.	40	27	79	57	12:00 noon
Columbus, Ohio	40	0	83	1	12:00 noon	Portland, Maine	43	40	70	15	12:00 noon
Dallas, Tex.	32	46	96	46	11:00 a.m.	Portland, Ore.	45	31	122	41	9:00 a.m.
Denver, Colo.	39	45	105	0	10:00 a.m.	Providence, R.I.	41	50	71	24	12:00 noon
Des Moines, Iowa	41	35	93	37	11:00 a.m.	Quebec, Que., Can.	46	49	71	11	12:00 noon
Detroit, Mich.	42	20	83	3	12:00 noon	Raleigh, N.C.	35	46	78	39	12:00 noon
Dubuque, Iowa	42	31	90	40	11:00 a.m.	Reno, Nev.	39	30	119	49	9:00 a.m.
Duluth, Minn.	46	49	92	5	11:00 a.m.	Richfield, Utah	38	46	112	5	10:00 a.m.
Eastport, Maine	44	54	67	0	12:00 noon	Richmond, Va.	37	33	77	29	12:00 noon
Edmonton, Alb., Can.	53	34	113	28	10:00 a.m.	Roanoke, Va.	37	17	79	57	12:00 noon
El Centro, Calif.	32	38	115	33	9:00 a.m.	Sacramento, Calif.	38	35	121	30	9:00 a.m.
El Paso, Tex.	31	46	106	29	10:00 a.m.	St. John, N.B., Can.	45	18	66	10	1:00 p.m.
Eugene, Ore.	44	3	123	5	9:00 a.m.	St. Louis, Mo.	38	35	90	12	11:00 a.m.
Fargo, N.D.	46	52	96	48	11:00 a.m.	Salt Lake City, Utah	40	46	111	54	10:00 a.m.
Flagstaff, Ariz.	35	13	111	41	10:00 a.m.	San Antonio, Tex.	29	23	98	33	11:00 a.m.
Fort Worth, Tex.	32	43	97	19	11:00 a.m.	San Diego, Calif.	32	42	117	10	9:00 a.m.
Fresno, Calif.	36	44	119	48	9:00 a.m.	San Francisco, Calif.	37	47	122	26	9:00 a.m.
Grand Junction, Colo.	39	5	108	33	10:00 a.m.	San Jose, Calif.	37	20	121	53	9:00 a.m.
Grand Rapids, Mich.	42	58	85	40	12:00 noon	San Juan, P.R.	18	30	66	10	1:00 p.m.
Havre, Mont.	48	33	109	43	10:00 a.m.	Santa Fe, N.M.	35	41	105	57	10:00 a.m.
Helena, Mont.	46	35	112	2	10:00 a.m.	Savannah, Ga.	32	5	81	5	12:00 noon
Honolulu, Hawaii	21	18	157	50	7:00 a.m.	Seattle, Wash.	47	37	122	20	9:00 a.m.
Hot Springs, Ark.	34	31	93	3	11:00 a.m.	Shreveport, La.	32	28	93	42	11:00 a.m.
Houston, Tex.	29	45	95	21	11:00 a.m.	Sioux Falls, S.D.	43	33	96	44	11:00 a.m.
Idaho Falls, Idaho	43	30	112	1	10:00 a.m.	Sitka, Alaska	57	10	135	15	8:00 a.m.
Indianapolis, Ind.	39	46	86	10	12:00 noon	Spokane, Wash.	47	40	117	26	9:00 a.m.
Jackson, Miss.	32	20	90	12	11:00 a.m.	Springfield, Ill.	39	48	89	38	11:00 a.m.
Jacksonville, Fla.	30	22	81	40	12:00 noon	Springfield, Mass.	42	6	72	34	12:00 noon
Juneau, Alaska	58	18	134	24	8:00 a.m.	Springfield, Mo.	37	13	93	17	11:00 a.m.
Kansas City, Mo.	39	6	94	35	11:00 a.m.	Syracuse, N.Y.	43	2	76	8	12:00 noon
Key West, Fla.	24	33	81	48	12:00 noon	Tampa, Fla.	27	57	82	27	12:00 noon
Kingston, Ont., Can.	44	15	76	30	12:00 noon	Toledo, Ohio	41	39	83	33	12:00 noon
Klamath Falls, Ore.	42	10	121	44	9:00 a.m.	Toronto, Ont., Can.	43	40	79	24	12:00 noon
Knoxville, Tenn.	35	57	83	56	12:00 noon	Tulsa, Okla.	36	09	95	59	11:00 a.m.
Las Vegas, Nev.	36	10	115	12	9:00 a.m.	Vancouver, B.C., Can.	49	13	123	06	9:00 a.m.
Lewiston, Idaho	46	24	117	2	9:00 a.m.	Victoria, B.C., Can.	48	25	123	21	9:00 a.m.
Lincoln, Neb.	40	50	96	40	11:00 a.m.	Virginia Beach, Va.	36	51	75	58	12:00 noon
London, Ont., Can.	43	2	81	34	12:00 noon	Washington, D.C.	38	53	77	02	12:00 noon
Long Beach, Calif.	33	46	118	11	9:00 a.m.	Wichita, Kan.	37	43	97	17	11:00 a.m.
Los Angeles, Calif.	34	3	118	15	9:00 a.m.	Wilmington, N.C.	34	14	77	57	12:00 noon
Louisville, Ky.	38	15	85	46	12:00 noon	Winnipeg, Man., Can.	49	54	97	7	11:00 a.m.
Manchester, N.H.	43	0	71	30	12:00 noon						

For more on U.S. geography, *see* National Parks, pp. 592–596.

2004 In an uneasy time, Americans were divided by a presidential race and battles over gay rights, while triumphs in space and the Athens Games were overshadowed by turmoil in Iraq and bombs in Madrid

ALL PICTURES: AP/WIDE WORLD PHOTOS, UNLESS OTHERWISE CREDITED

ON PATROL: A U.S. soldier assumes a protective stance in the Talbiyah district of Baghdad on April 15, 2004, during a weapons-search operation. Despite the formal transfer of power to an interim Iraqi government in late June, some 140,000 American troops remained in Iraq and faced a strong insurgency movement more than a year after a U.S.-led coalition toppled the government of strongman Saddam Hussein.

NATION Saddam Hussein faced a judge in Iraq, and the U.S. handed over power to an interim government, but insurgents kept fighting

ATROCITIES: Fallujah, Najaf, and several other cities in Iraq remained hotbeds of insurgency. Above, rebels burn U.S. humvees in Fallujah on March 25. Six days later four foreign contractors were killed; their bodies were dragged through the city's streets, burned, and hanged from a bridge.

SHAME: In April 2004, the world was shocked by photographs of Iraqi detainees being abused by U.S. soldiers and independent contractors in the Abu Ghraib prison in Baghdad. The photos led to courts-martial and recriminations, as critics charged that the Bush Administration was sanctioning torture.

IN THE DOCK: Former Iraqi President Saddam Hussein was captured by American troops as he hid in a tiny underground "spider hole" outside Tikrit on Dec. 13, 2003. He was arraigned before an Iraqi judge in a court near Baghdad on July 1, 2004. Hussein, whose two sons were killed after his regime was toppled in the 2003 war, will be tried for crimes against the Iraqi people.

HAND-OFF: Paul Bremer, U.S. administrator of Iraq, transferred power to interim Iraqi leaders on June 28, two days ahead of time, in order to thwart any attempts by rebel forces to disrupt the process. Here, Bremer presents the official documents to Iraq's Chief Justice. Third from left is Iraqi Prime Minister Iyad Allawi; at right is Iraqi President Ghazi al-Yawar.

DEMOCRATS: Ten major candidates vied for the party's presidential nomination, with Massachusetts Senator John F. Kerry, a decorated Vietnam veteran, emerging as the nominee after a number of victories in key primaries. Kerry picked primary rival John Edwards, a first-term Senator from North Carolina and successful trial lawyer, as his running mate. The party convention was held in July in Boston.

REPUBLICANS: Incumbent George W. Bush hit the campaign trail early to seek re-election, as polls showed the 2004 race might be just as close as the stalemated 2000 election. At the G.O.P. convention in New York City in late August, Bush kept Dick Cheney as his running mate, despite polls showing the Vice President to be far less popular than the President. A soft economy and ongoing woes in Iraq bedeviled the incumbents.

BATTERED: Hurricane Charley devastated a broad swath of Florida, striking on the Gulf Coast and cutting across the state's center on Aug. 13. The region's biggest storm since Andrew in '92, it left 25 dead, thousands homeless, and a cleanup bill in the billions.

HE'S OUT: "I am a gay American," said New Jersey Governor James McGreevey. The father of two resigned after a former sex partner threatened to expose him.

9/11 COMMISSION: A bipartisan panel explored the 2001 terrorist attacks and recommended broad changes, including a single chief for all U.S. intelligence efforts.

WORLD Genocide stalked Sudan, while Israel built a wall to protect itself. But deadly bombings in Madrid showed terrorism's long reach

SPAIN'S WOE: Bombs struck trains in Madrid on March 11, killing 202 people and wounding 1,400. An al-Qaeda group based in Morocco is believed to be responsible. Days later an antiwar government was elected; it withdrew Spain's troops from Iraq.

TURNABOUT: After renouncing terrorism, Libya's Muammar Qaddafi shed his pariah status and attended several meetings of the European Community.

GREAT WALL: Palestinians gather in February to protest the 25-ft.-high barrier built by Israel to divide Palestinian-occupied areas of the West Bank from Israeli-occupied areas. In July the World Court at the Hague ordered Israel to tear down the wall, to no avail.

MISERY IN SUDAN: Displaced women seek shelter at the Zam Zam refugee camp in the Darfur region of Sudan in July 2004. The African nation was the scene of a vicious ongoing ethnic war, in which as many as 50,000 black Africans have been killed, many raped, and 1 million driven into exile by pro-Arab militias backed by Sudan's government.

COUP IN HAITI: Victorious rebel leader Guy Philippe enters Port au Prince on March 1 after his troops deposed President Jean-Baptiste Aristide, who fled to Africa and blamed the U.S. for planning his downfall.

INDIA'S LEADER: Manmohan Singh became Prime Minister of India in May 2004 after the Congress Party upset the ruling Hindu-nationalist B.J.P. party led by A.B. Vajpayee. Singh is the first Sikh to serve as India's PM.

BUSINESS The U.S. economy struggled and corporate executives went on trial, while dizzy dotcom values returned with Google's IPO

CHARGED: Kenneth Lay, former CEO of fallen energy giant Enron, was arraigned in July and charged with securities fraud.

GUILTY: Lifestyle doyen Martha Stewart was convicted of obstructing justice and sentenced to serve five months in prison.

INTERNET MILLIONAIRES: Sergey Brin, left, and Larry Page founded the Internet-search engine company Google in 1998. In the fall of 2004 they sold shares in the firm in an initial public offering on the stock market that made each of them millions.

SOCIETY Fanned by the presidential race, America's culture wars raged hotter than ever, with gay marriage at the center of controversy

DOUBLE VISION: Americans debated gay marriage after the Massachusetts Supreme Court struck down a law forbidding it in November 2003. In San Francisco, Mayor Gavin Newsom, above, defied state law and began issuing marriage licenses to gay couples in February 2004. The weddings were voided by the state Supreme Court in August.

RIDICULE: Critics of President Bush cheered director Michael Moore's attack on the Administration's war in Iraq, *Fahrenheit 9/11,* making it a major hit.

PASSION: Christian moviegoers made director Mel Gibson's low-budget *The Passion of the Christ* a $370 million U.S. box-office hit, stunning Hollywood.

SCIENCE Our eyes turned to the solar system as NASA planetary probes sent startling new visions of Mars and Saturn back to Earth

MARS DUO: Two NASA roving vehicles, *Spirit* and *Opportunity,* rambled over the rocky terrain of Mars, sending back a wealth of data about the geography and geology of the Red Planet. The photo at left, taken by *Opportunity* on March 2, 2004, shows a detail of the rock NASA scientists named "El Capitan." Readings sent by both craft supported theories that the surface of Mars once held substantial amounts of water. The rovers worked well past their scheduled three-month mission.

SATURN VISIT: After a journey of nearly seven years, NASA's Cassini-Huygens probe went into orbit around Saturn, giving us our best views yet of the giant ringed planet and its moons. The probe recorded storms and lightning on Saturn's surface and discovered a new radiation belt inside the rings. Most of the rings are water ice, which is white, if pure. The colors visible at right in a probe photo taken on July 21 are believed to reflect other materials present in the rings, such as rock or carbon compounds.

SPORT Cycling's ironman pedaled to a sixth title, a beloved golfer won his first major, and a band of underdogs stole the Lakers' crown

ENCORE! Clearly outpacing his competitors, U.S. cycling veteran Lance Armstrong took the lead in the mountains to become the first six-time winner of the Tour de France.

WHO'S NO. 1? Chauncey Billups, above, led Detroit's gritty Pistons to the NBA title, ending the reign of the Los Angeles Lakers.

AT LAST! Fan favorite Phil Mickelson, a left-hander, exults after sinking a final putt to win his first major tourney, the Masters.

BACK TO THE SOURCE: Concerns over tardy preparations vanished when the Summer Olympics opened in Athens with ceremonies evoking the Games' ancient heritage.

CHAMPS! Retiring U.S. stars Mia Hamm, left, Julie Foudy, Brandi Chastain, Kristine Lilly, and Joy Fawcett won gold in soccer.

BIG SPLASH: American swimmer Michael Phelps, 19, lived up to advance ballyhoo. He won eight medals, including six golds.

MILESTONES We mourned a beloved President, a singer whose soulful sounds broke new ground, a film rebel, and a queen of cuisine

ICON: Ronald Reagan died on June 5 after a lengthy battle with Alzheimer's. His body lay in state in the U.S. Capitol rotunda, right. Fellow presidents joined mourners at his funeral in the National Cathedral.

TIME LIFE PICTURES

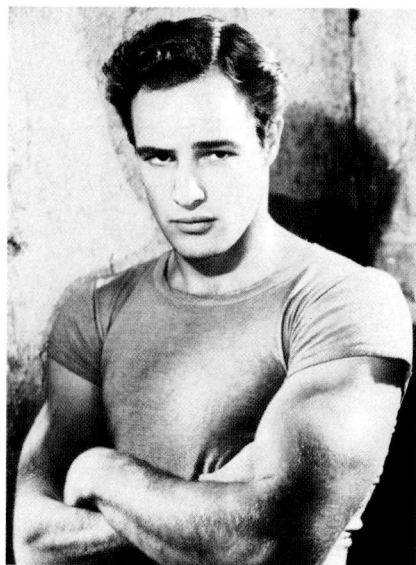

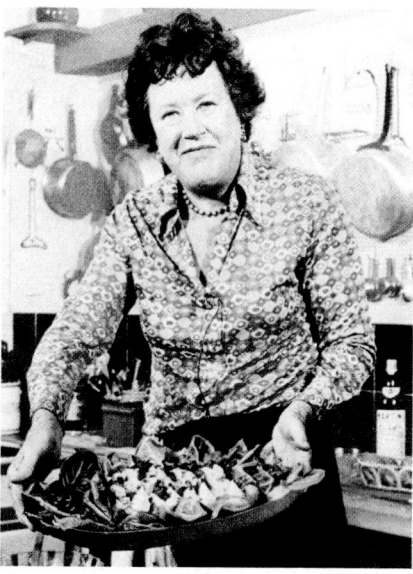

MARLON BRANDO, 80: The great Method actor rocketed to fame on Broadway, then became Hollywood's iconic rebel male star.

JULIA CHILD, 91: The beloved TV chef introduced Americans to classic cooking with gusto, know-how, and a dash of spice.

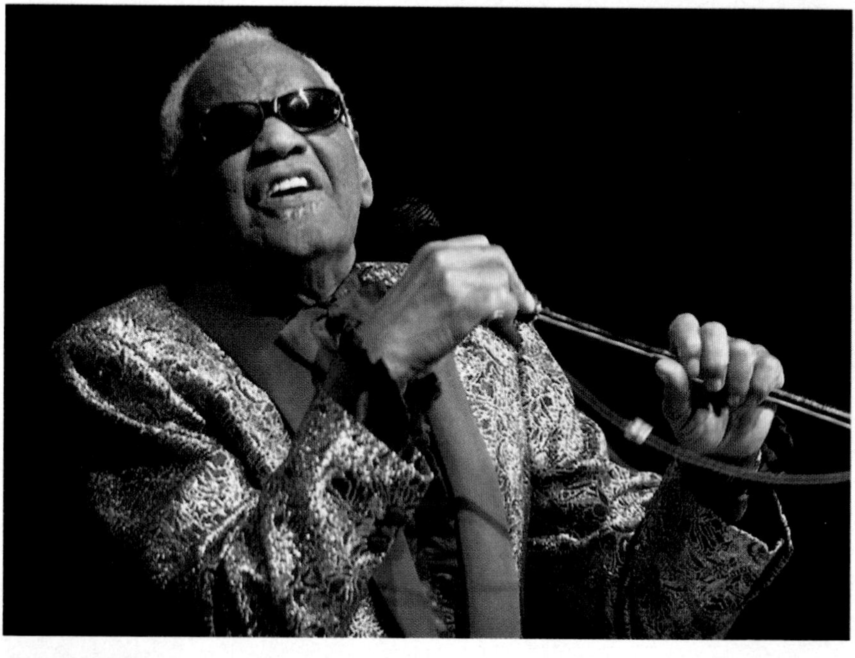

RAY CHARLES, 73: The stirring, soulful vocalist was a central figure in 20th century American music; his art crossed all boundaries, and his appeal straddled generations.

Afghanistan

Albania

Algeria

Andorra

Angola

Antigua &
Barbuda

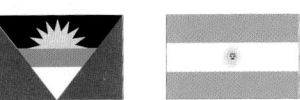
Argentina

Armenia

Australia

Austria

Azerbaijan

Bahamas

Bahrain

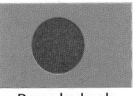
Bangladesh

Barbados

Belarus

Belgium

Belize

Benin

Bhutan

Bolivia

Bosnia-
Herzegovina

Botswana

Brazil

Brunei

Bulgaria

Burkina Faso

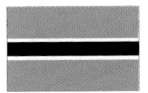
Burundi

Cambodia

Cameroon

Canada

Cape Verde

Central African
Republic

Chad

Chile

China

Colombia

Comoros

Congo, Dem.
Republic of the

Congo, Rep. of

Costa Rica

Côte d'Ivoire

Croatia

Cuba

Cyprus

Czech Republic

Denmark

Djibouti

Dominica

Dominican Rep.

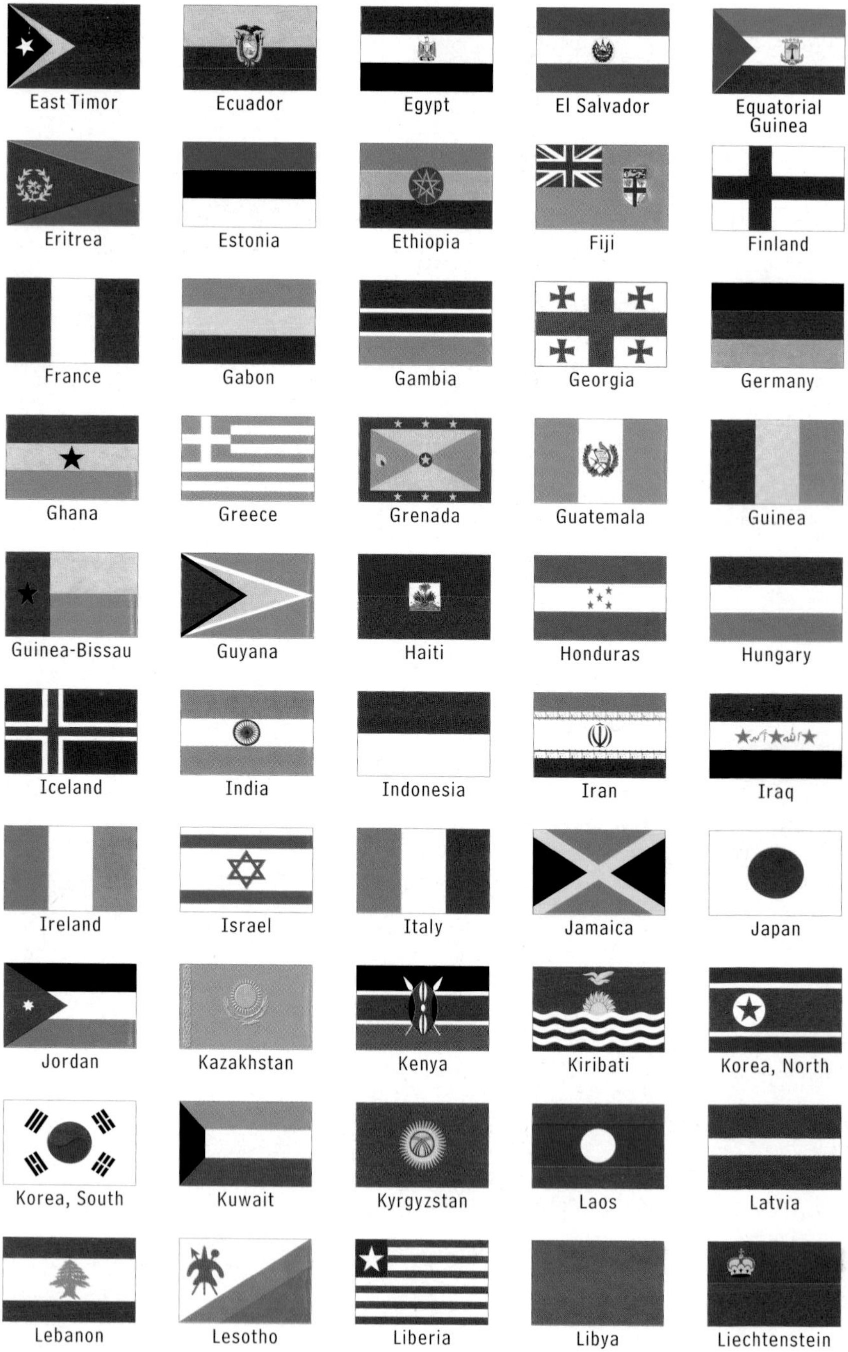

East Timor	Ecuador	Egypt	El Salvador	Equatorial Guinea
Eritrea	Estonia	Ethiopia	Fiji	Finland
France	Gabon	Gambia	Georgia	Germany
Ghana	Greece	Grenada	Guatemala	Guinea
Guinea-Bissau	Guyana	Haiti	Honduras	Hungary
Iceland	India	Indonesia	Iran	Iraq
Ireland	Israel	Italy	Jamaica	Japan
Jordan	Kazakhstan	Kenya	Kiribati	Korea, North
Korea, South	Kuwait	Kyrgyzstan	Laos	Latvia
Lebanon	Lesotho	Liberia	Libya	Liechtenstein

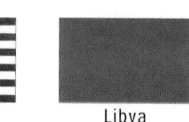

Lithuania Luxembourg Macedonia Madagascar Malawi

Malaysia Maldives Mali Malta Marshall Islands

Mauritania Mauritius Mexico Micronesia Moldova

Monaco Mongolia Morocco Mozambique Myanmar

Namibia Nauru Nepal Netherlands New Zealand

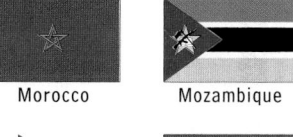

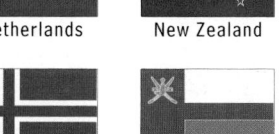

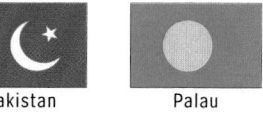

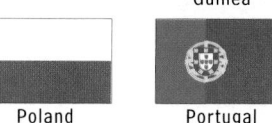

Nicaragua Niger Nigeria Norway Oman

Pakistan Palau Panama Papua New Guinea Paraguay

Peru Philippines Poland Portugal Qatar

Romania Russia Rwanda St. Kitts & Nevis St. Lucia

St. Vincent & The Grenadines Samoa San Marino São Tomé & Príncipe Saudi Arabia

Senegal

Serbia &
Montenegro

Seychelles

Sierra Leone

Singapore

Slovakia

Slovenia

Solomon Islands

Somalia

South Africa

Spain

Sri Lanka

Sudan

Suriname

Swaziland

Sweden

Switzerland

Syria

Taiwan

Tajikistan

Tanzania

Thailand

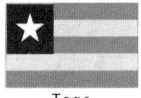
Togo

Tonga

Trinidad &
Tobago

Tunisia

Turkey

Turkmenistan

Tuvalu

Uganda

Ukraine

United Arab
Emirates

United Kingdom

United States

Uruguay

Uzbekistan

Vanuatu

Vatican City

Venezuela

Vietnam

Yemen

Zambia

Zimbabwe

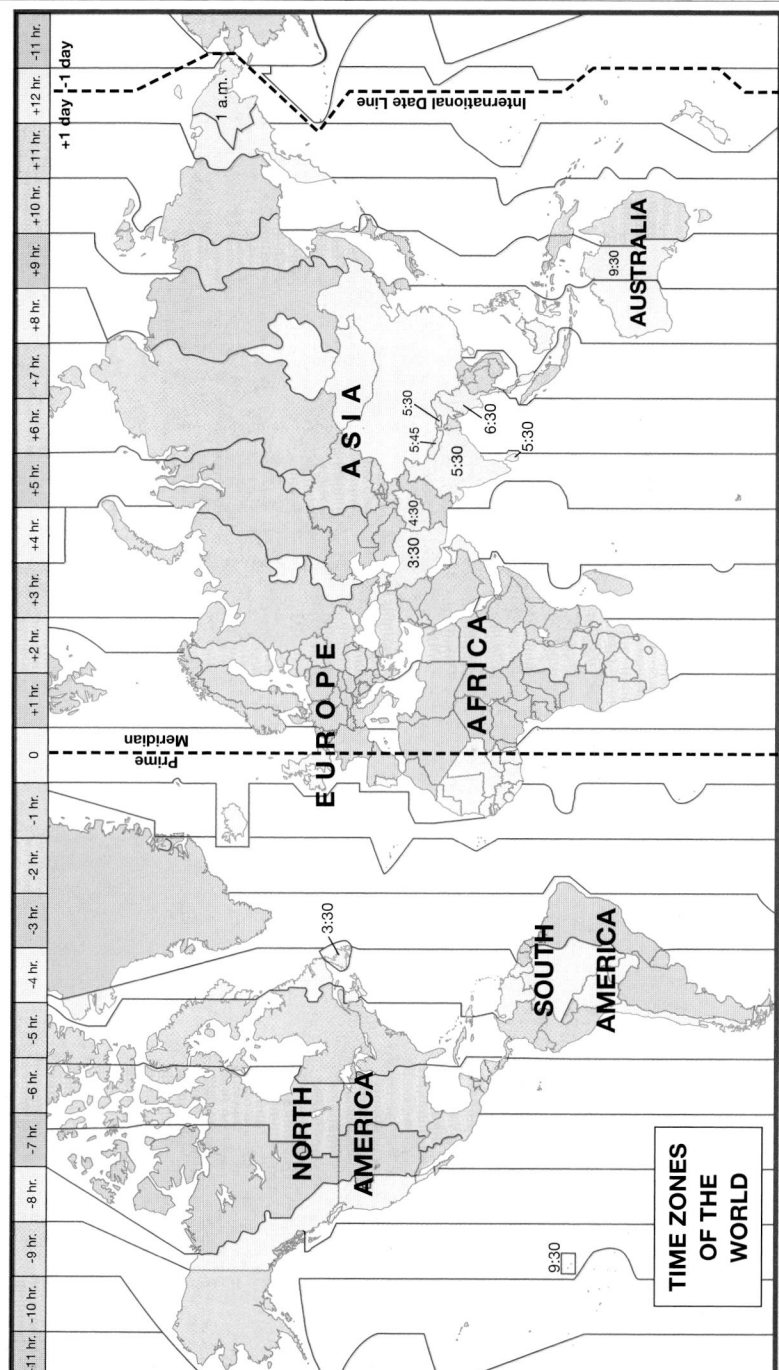

TIME ZONES OF THE WORLD

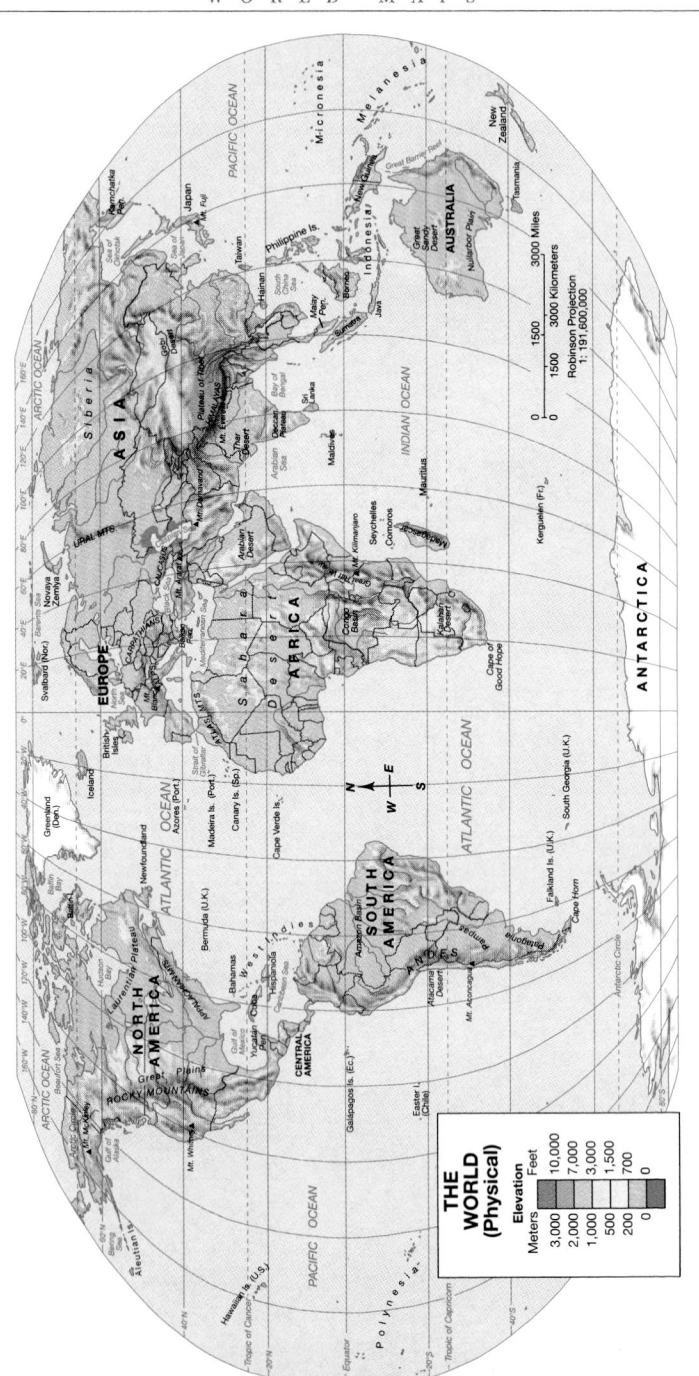

THE
WORLD
(Physical)

Elevation

Meters	Feet
3,000	10,000
2,000	7,000
1,000	3,000
500	1,500
200	700
0	0

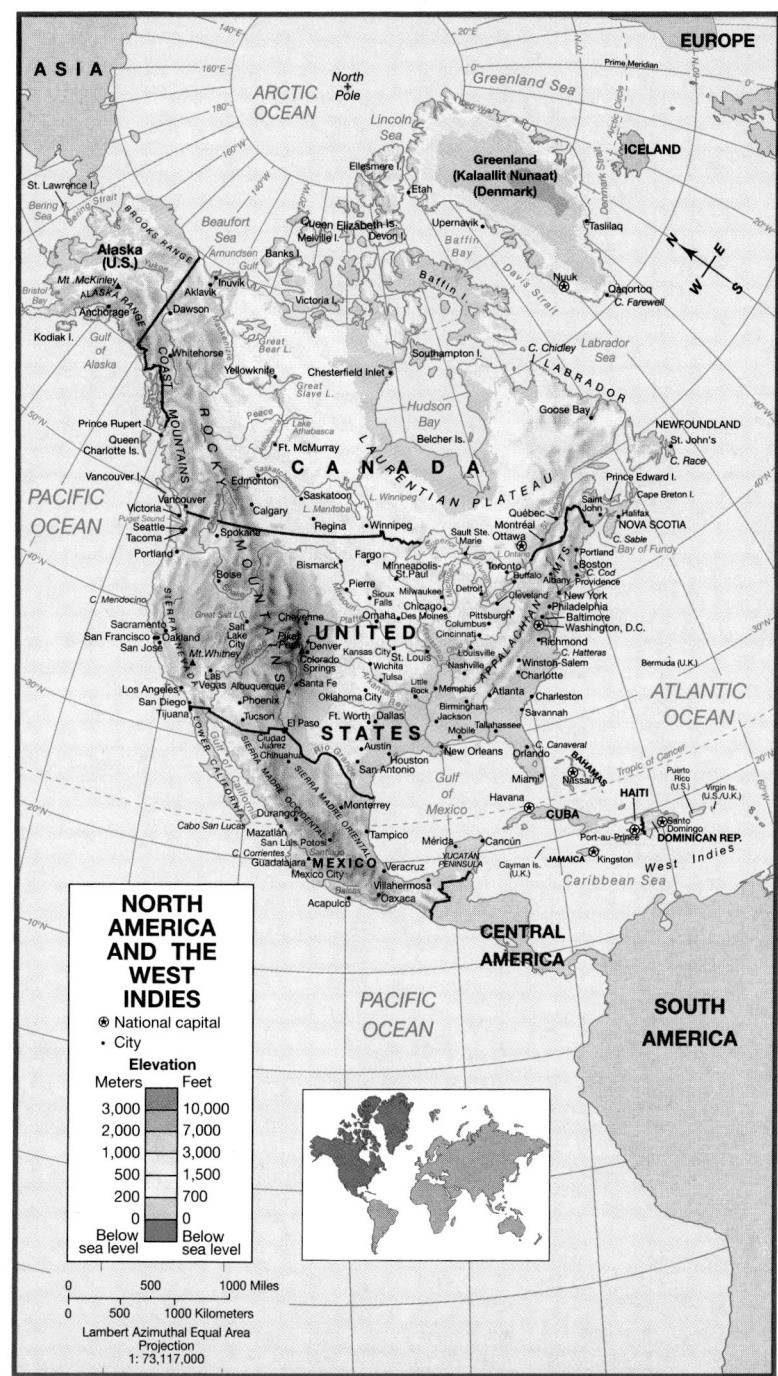

NORTH AMERICA AND THE WEST INDIES

⊛ National capital
• City

Elevation

Meters	Feet
3,000	10,000
2,000	7,000
1,000	3,000
500	1,500
200	700
0	0
Below sea level	Below sea level

0   500   1000 Miles

0   500   1000 Kilometers

Lambert Azimuthal Equal Area
Projection
1: 73,117,000

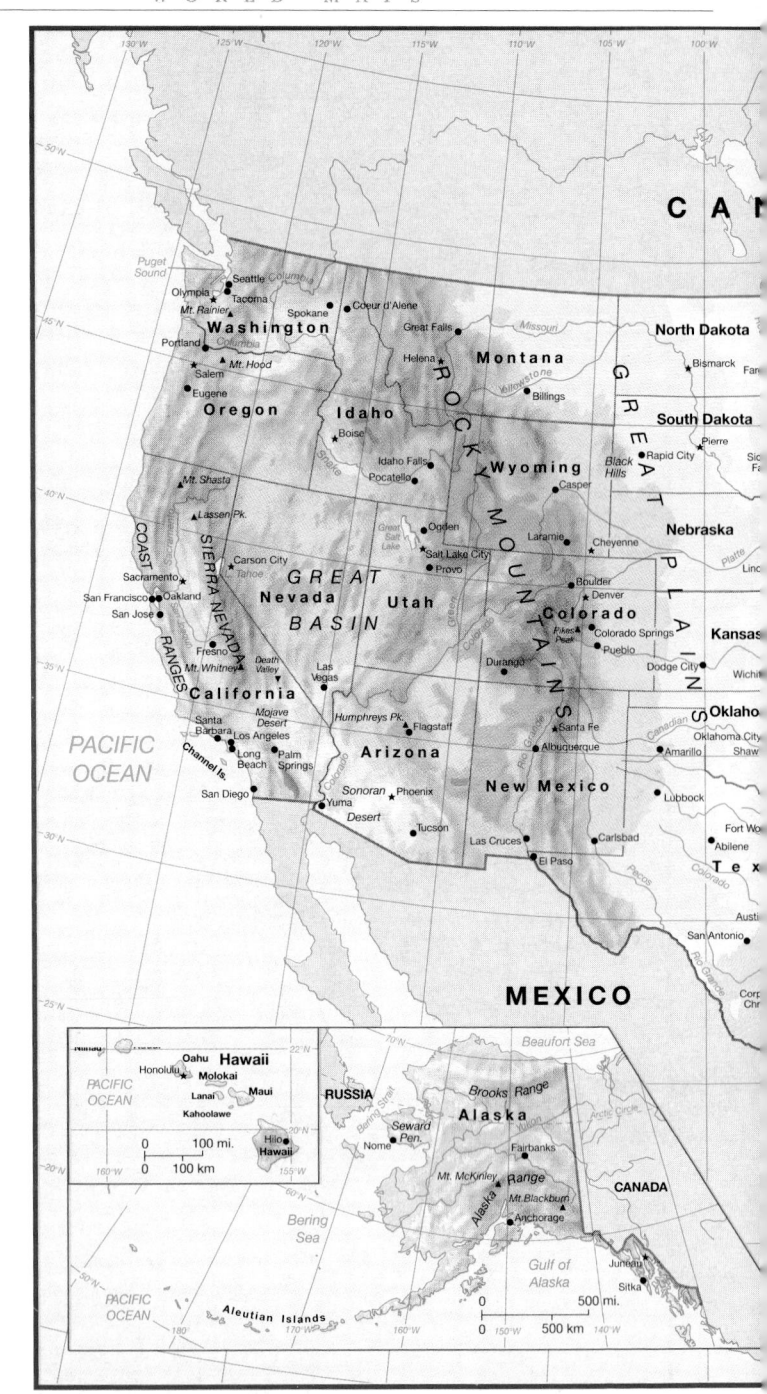

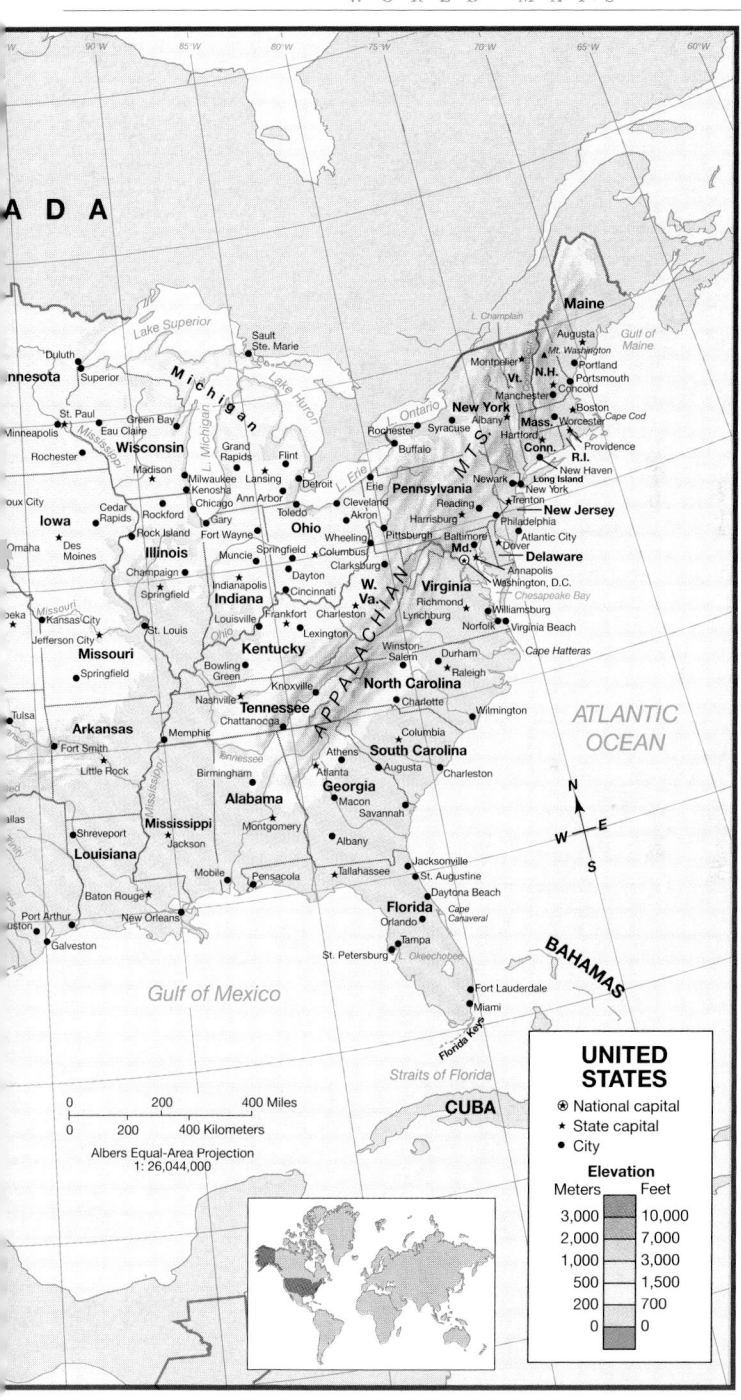

UNITED STATES
- ⊛ National capital
- ★ State capital
- ● City

Elevation

Meters	Feet
3,000	10,000
2,000	7,000
1,000	3,000
500	1,500
200	700
0	0

0   200   400 Miles
0   200   400 Kilometers
Albers Equal-Area Projection
1: 26,044,000

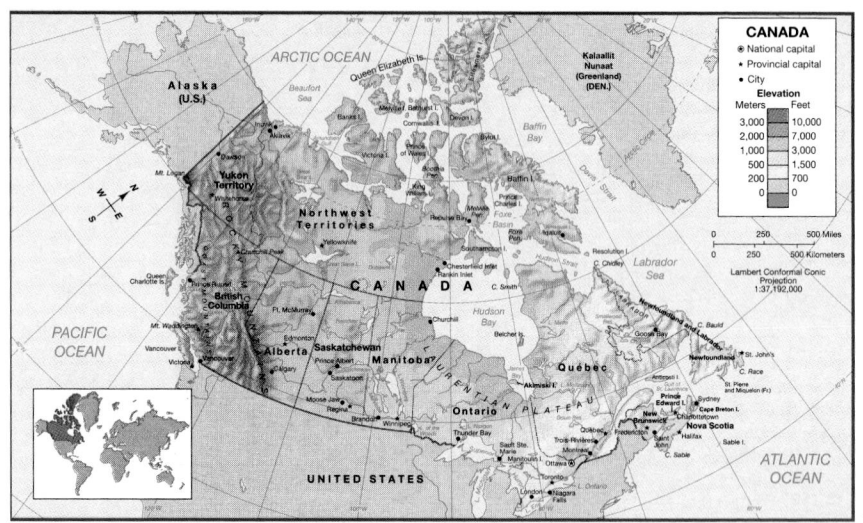

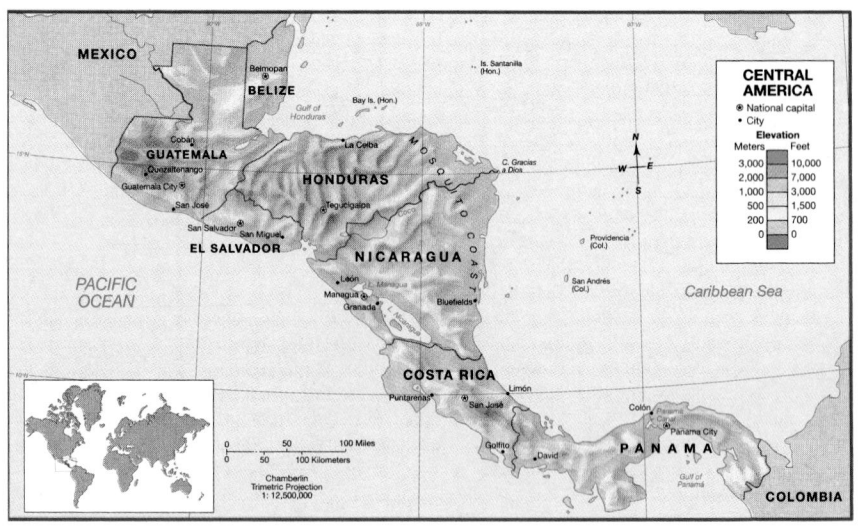

Galápagos Is. (Ecuador)

I. Marchena
I. San Salvador
I. Santa Cruz
I. Fernandina
I. San Cristóbal
I. Sta. María
I. Española

CENTRAL AMERICA

Caribbean Sea

WEST INDIES

Tropic of Cancer

Neth. Antilles (Neth.)
I. de Margarita
Curaçao
Gulf of Venezuela
Gulf of Paria

Barranquilla
Cartagena
Maracaibo
Caracas
Morawhanna
Georgetown
New Amsterdam
Paramaribo

Montería
Medellín
Cúcuta
San Cristóbal
Ciudad Bolívar
Bucaramanga
Bogotá
Devil's I.
Cayenne

VENEZUELA

GUYANA
SURINAME
French Guiana (Fr.)

ATLANTIC OCEAN

Gulf of Panama
Gulf of Urabá
C. Corrientes
Buenaventura
Cali
Mt. Huila

I. de Maracá
I. Caviana

COLOMBIA

I. Malpelo (Colombia)

ECUADOR
Mt. Cotopaxi
Mt. Chimborazo
Quito
Ambato
Cuenca
Guayaquil
Gulf of Guayaquil
Iquitos
Manaus
Belém
Equator
I. São Luis
Fortaleza

Piura
C. São Roque

PERU
Trujillo
Mt. Huascarán
Recife

Callao
Lima
Cuzco
BRAZIL
Salvador

El Misti
Arequipa
La Paz
BOLIVIA
Trinidad
Santa Cruz
Brasília
Cochabamba
Potosí
Sucre
R. São Francisco

PACIFIC OCEAN

Iquique
Belo Horizonte

Antofagasta
C. São Tomé
Rio de Janeiro

PARAGUAY
Asunción
São Paulo
Santos

San Miguel de Tucumán
Tropic of Capricorn

San Felix (Chile)
San Ambrosio (Chile)
Curitiba
I. de Santa Catarina

CHILE
Mt. Ojos del Salado
Córdoba
Pôrto Alegre
Rivera

Viña del Mar
Mt. Aconcagua
Salto
Paysandú
URUGUAY
I. de Santa Catarina

Juan Fernández Is. (Chile)
Valparaíso
Santiago
Mendoza
Rosario
Montevideo
L. Miní

I. Alejandro Selkirk
I. Robinson Crusoe
Vol. Maipo
Buenos Aires
La Plata
Río de la Plata

Concepción
ARGENTINA
C. San Antonio
Mar del Plata

I. de Chiloé
Bahía Blanca
Negro

Gulf of San Matías
Pen. Valdés

ATLANTIC OCEAN

Archipiélago de los Chonos
Gulf of Corcovado
Pen. Taitao
C. Tres Montes
Gulf of San Jorge

Gulf of Penas
Falkland Islands
(U.K.; claimed by Arg.)
Stanley

Strait of Magellan
Tierra del Fuego
I. de los Estados
I. Sta. Inés
Cape Horn
South Georgia (U.K.)

Antarctic Circle

SOUTH AMERICA
⊗ National capital
• City

Elevation

Meters	Feet
3,000	10,000
2,000	7,000
1,000	3,000
500	1,500
200	700
0	0

0   300   600 Miles
0   300   600 Kilometers

Lambert Azimuthal Equal-Area Projection
1: 43,697,000

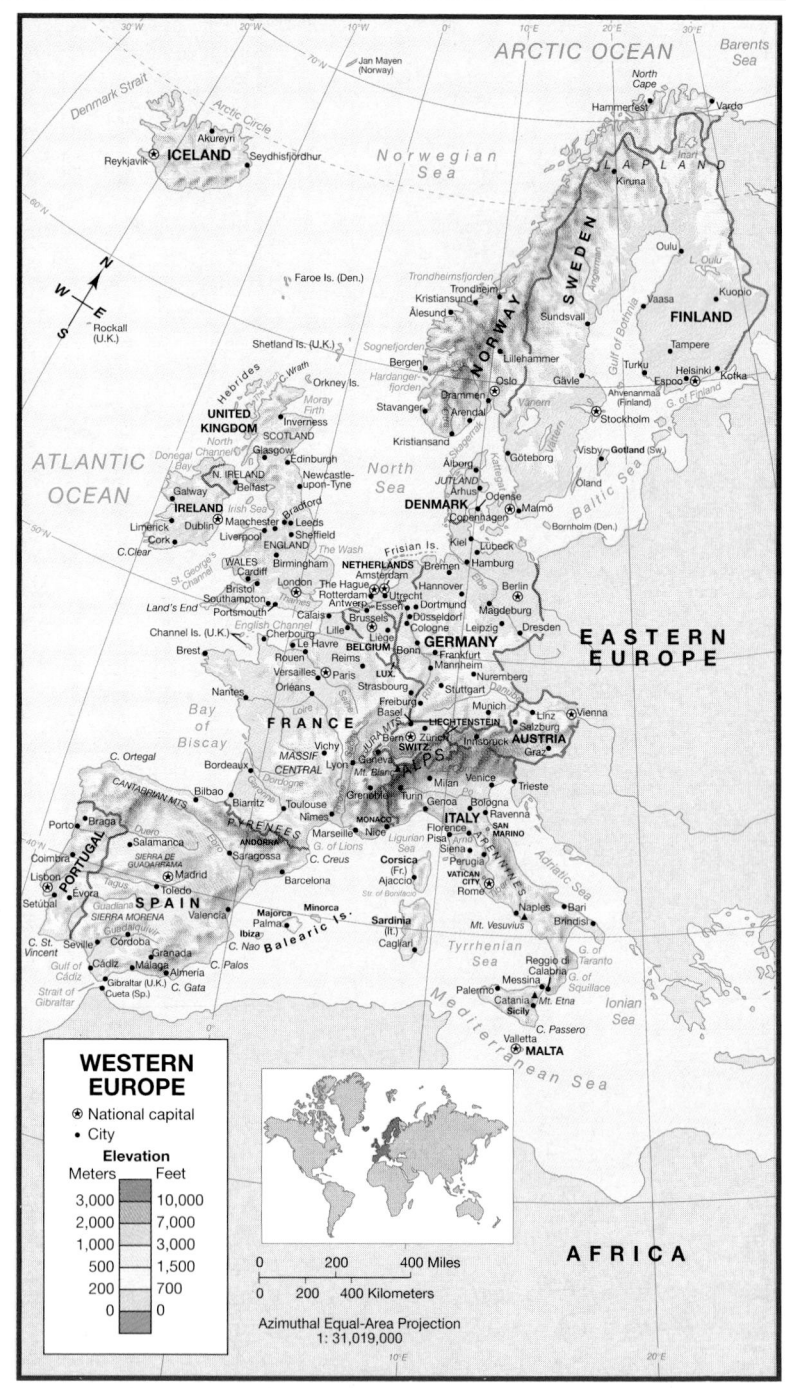

WESTERN EUROPE

⊛ National capital
• City

Elevation

Meters	Feet
3,000	10,000
2,000	7,000
1,000	3,000
500	1,500
200	700
0	0

0   200   400 Miles

0   200   400 Kilometers

Azimuthal Equal-Area Projection
1: 31,019,000

A F R I C A

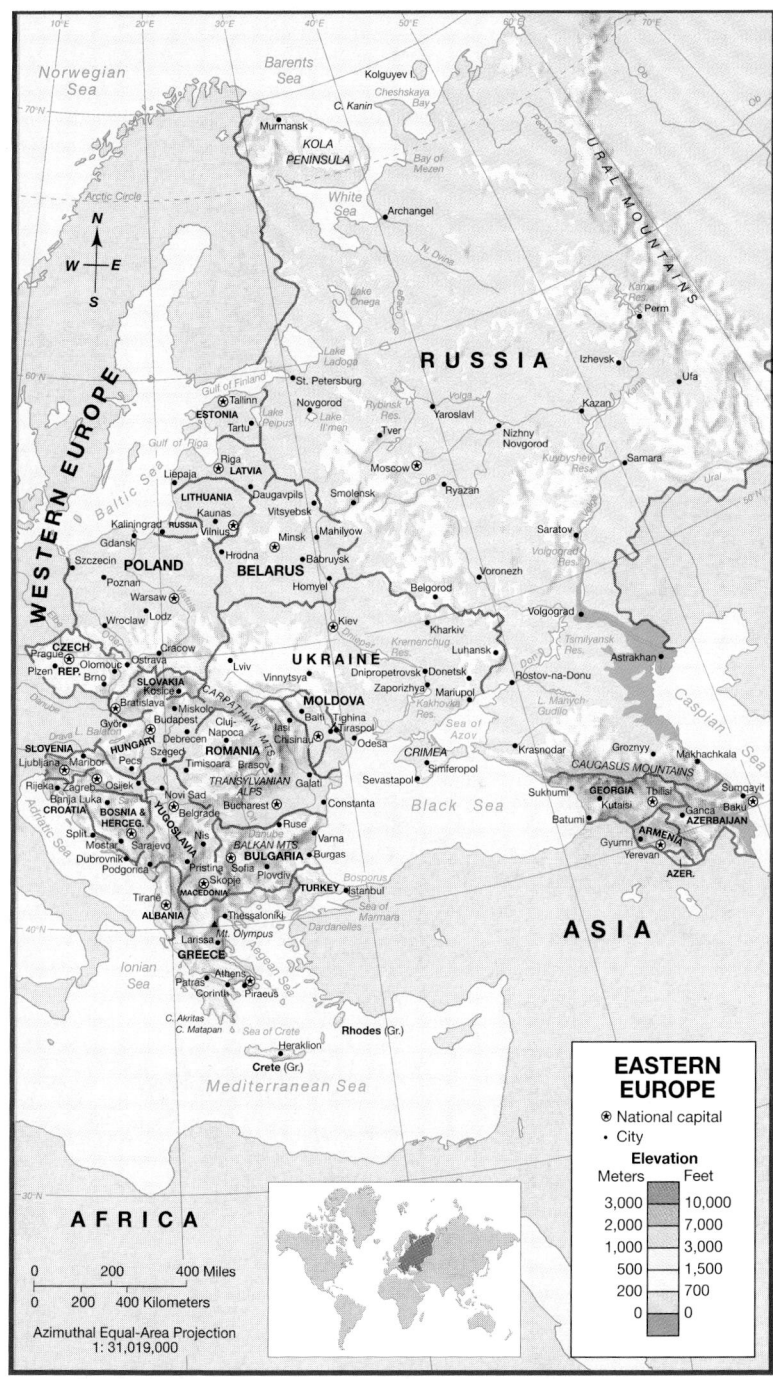

Norwegian Sea

Barents Sea

Kolguyev I.

Cheshskaya Bay

C. Kanin

Murmansk

KOLA PENINSULA

Bay of Mezen

White Sea

Archangel

N. Dvina

URAL MOUNTAINS

Arctic Circle

N

W — E

S

Lake Onega

Kama Res.

Perm

Lake Ladoga

RUSSIA

Izhevsk

Ufa

St. Petersburg

Tallinn

ESTONIA

Novgorod

Rybinsk R.

Yaroslavl

Nizhny Novgorod

Kazan

Kama

Lake Peipus

Tartu

Lake Il'men

Tver

WESTERN EUROPE

Gulf of Finland

Riga

LATVIA

Liepaja

Gulf of Riga

Moscow

Oka

Ryazan

Volga

Samara

Kuybyshev Res.

Smolensk

LITHUANIA

Daugavpils

Vitsyebsk

Saratov

Kaliningrad

Kaunas

RUSSIA

Vilnius

Minsk

Mahilyow

Voronezh

Volgograd Res.

Gdansk

Hrodna

Babruysk

BELARUS

Homyel

Belgorod

Ural

Szczecin

POLAND

Kiev

Volgograd

Poznan

Warsaw

Kharkiv

Astrakhan

Wroclaw

Lodz

Kremenchug Res.

Luhansk

Don

Tsimlyansk Res.

Caspian Sea

CZECH

Prague

Cracow

UKRAINE

Dnipropetrovsk

Donetsk

Rostov-na-Donu

Plzen

REP.

Olomouc

Ostrava

Lviv

Vinnytsya

Zaporizhya

Brno

SLOVAKIA

Kosice

CARPATHIAN MTS

Kakhovka Res.

L. Manych-Gudilo

Groznyy

Makhachkala

Bratislava

Miskolc

MOLDOVA

Balti

Tighina

Odesa

Sea of Azov

Krasnodar

Gyor

Budapest

Cluj-Napoca

Iasi

Chisinau

Tiraspol

CAUCASUS MOUNTAINS

Sumqayit

SLOVENIA

Debrecen

ROMANIA

CRIMEA

Sukhumi

GEORGIA

Baku

Ljubljana

HUNGARY

Pecs

Szeged

Timisoara

Brasov

Galati

Simferopol

Tbilisi

Maribor

TRANSYLVANIAN

Sevastopol

Kutaisi

Ganca

AZERBAIJAN

Rijeka

Zagreb

Osijek

Novi Sad

ALPS

Bucharest

Constanta

Black Sea

Batumi

ARMENIA

Banja Luka

Belgrade

Ruse

Gyumri

AZER.

CROATIA

BOSNIA &

YUGOSLAVIA

Nis

Danube

Varna

Yerevan

Split

HERCEG.

BALKAN MTS.

BULGARIA

Burgas

Mostar

Sarajevo

Pristina

Sofia

Plovdiv

Dubrovnik

Podgorica

Skopje

TURKEY

Istanbul

Bosporus

Tirane

MACEDONIA

Thessaloniki

Sea of Marmara

ALBANIA

Mt. Olympus

GREECE

Larissa

Dardanelles

ASIA

Ionian Sea

Patras

Athens

Aegean Sea

Corinth

Piraeus

C. Akritas

C. Matapan

Sea of Crete

Rhodes (Gr.)

Heraklion

Crete (Gr.)

Mediterranean Sea

AFRICA

0   200   400 Miles

0   200   400 Kilometers

Azimuthal Equal-Area Projection
1: 31,019,000

EASTERN EUROPE

⊛ National capital

• City

Elevation

Meters		Feet
3,000		10,000
2,000		7,000
1,000		3,000
500		1,500
200		700
0		0

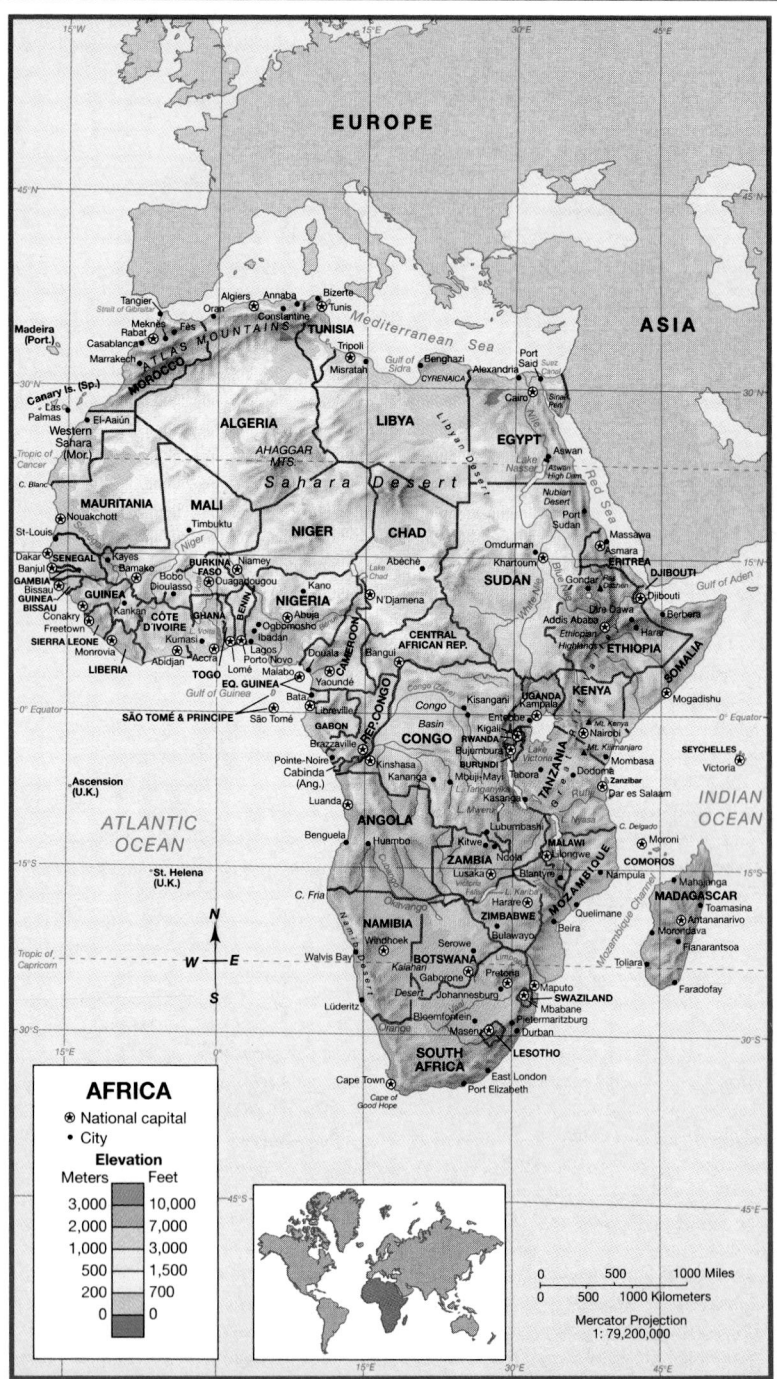

AFRICA

⊛ National capital
• City

Elevation

Meters		Feet
3,000		10,000
2,000		7,000
1,000		3,000
500		1,500
200		700
0		0

Mercator Projection
1: 79,200,000

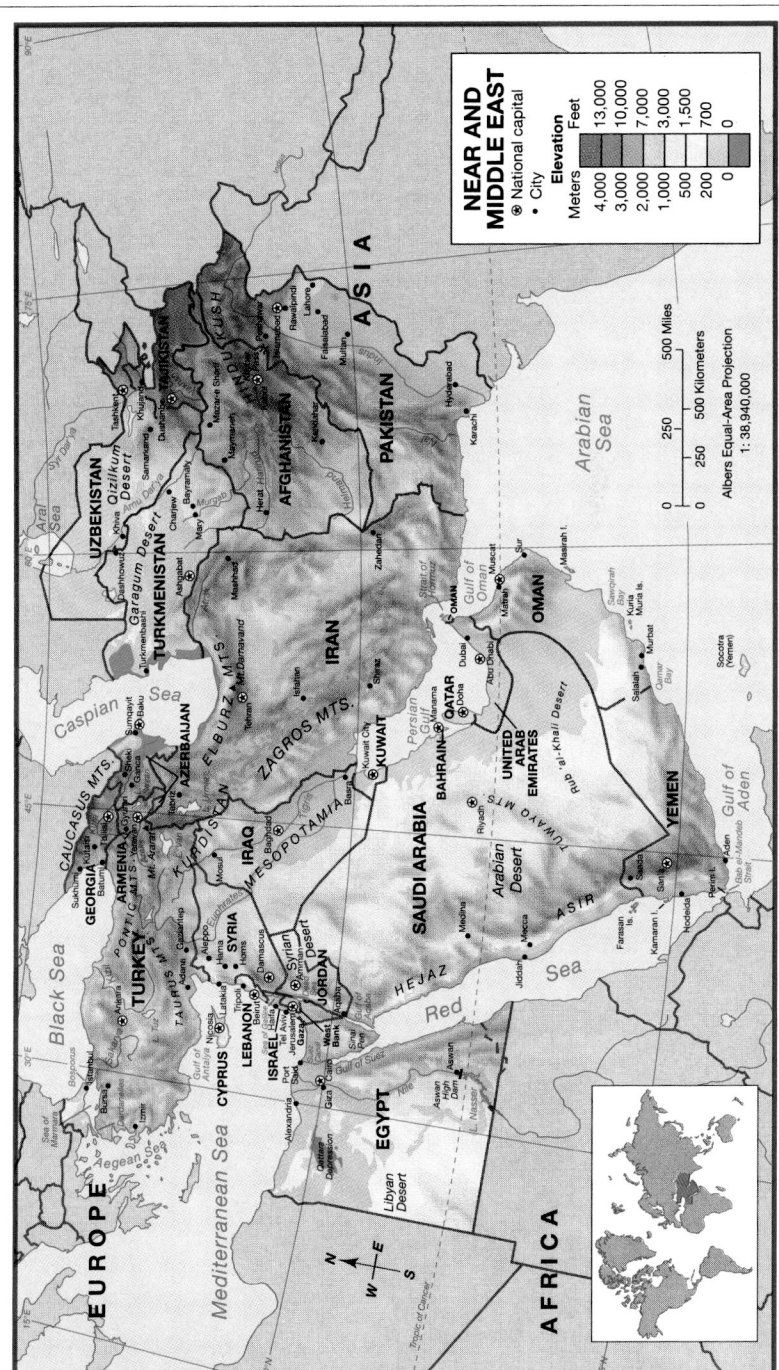

NEAR AND MIDDLE EAST

⊛ National capital
• City

Elevation

Meters	Feet
4,000	13,000
3,000	10,000
2,000	7,000
1,000	3,000
500	1,500
200	700
0	0

Albers Equal-Area Projection
1: 38,940,000

0   250   500 Miles
0   250   500 Kilometers

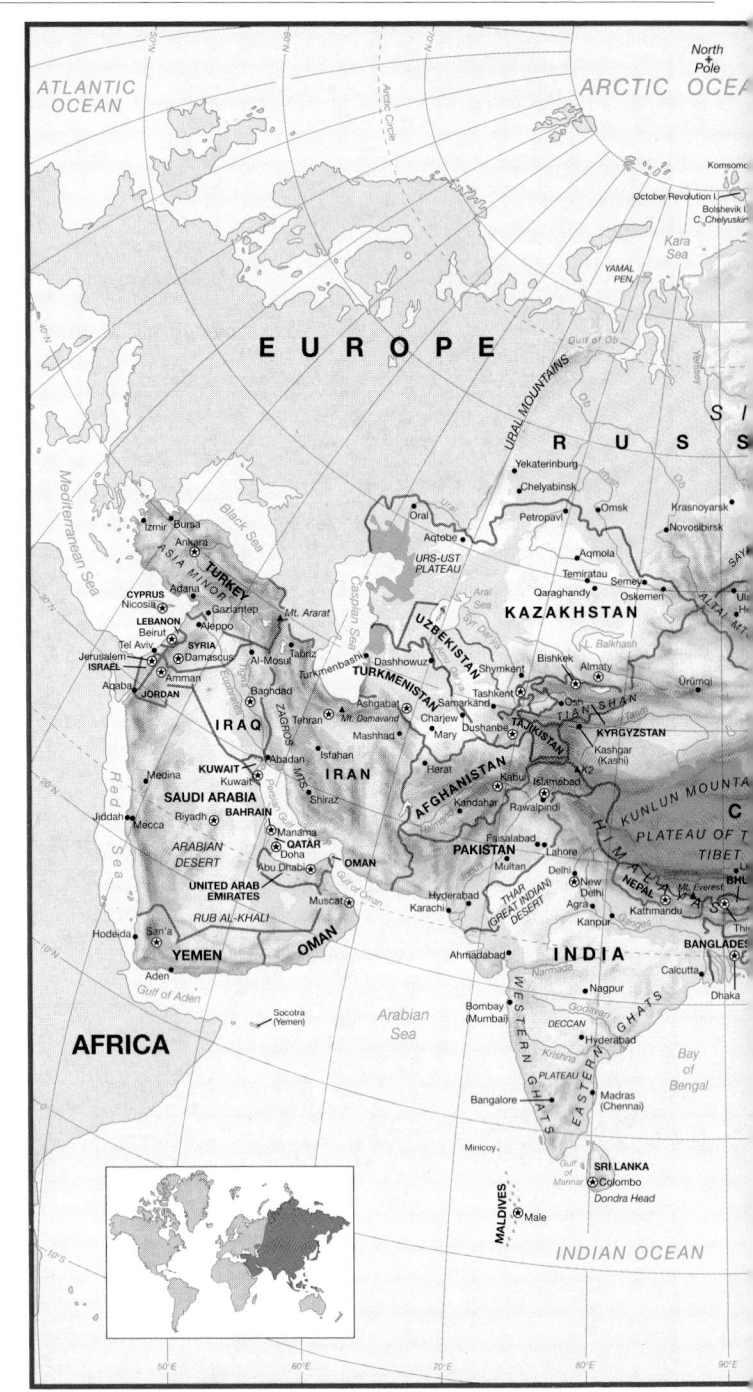

ASIA

⊛ National capital
• City
∿ Great Wall of China

Elevation

Meters	Feet
6,000	19,000
3,000	10,000
2,000	7,000
1,000	3,000
500	1,500
200	700
0	0

0 ___ 500 ___ 1000 Miles
0 ___ 500 ___ 1000 Kilometers

Lambert Azimuthal Equal-Area
Projection
1:61,016,000

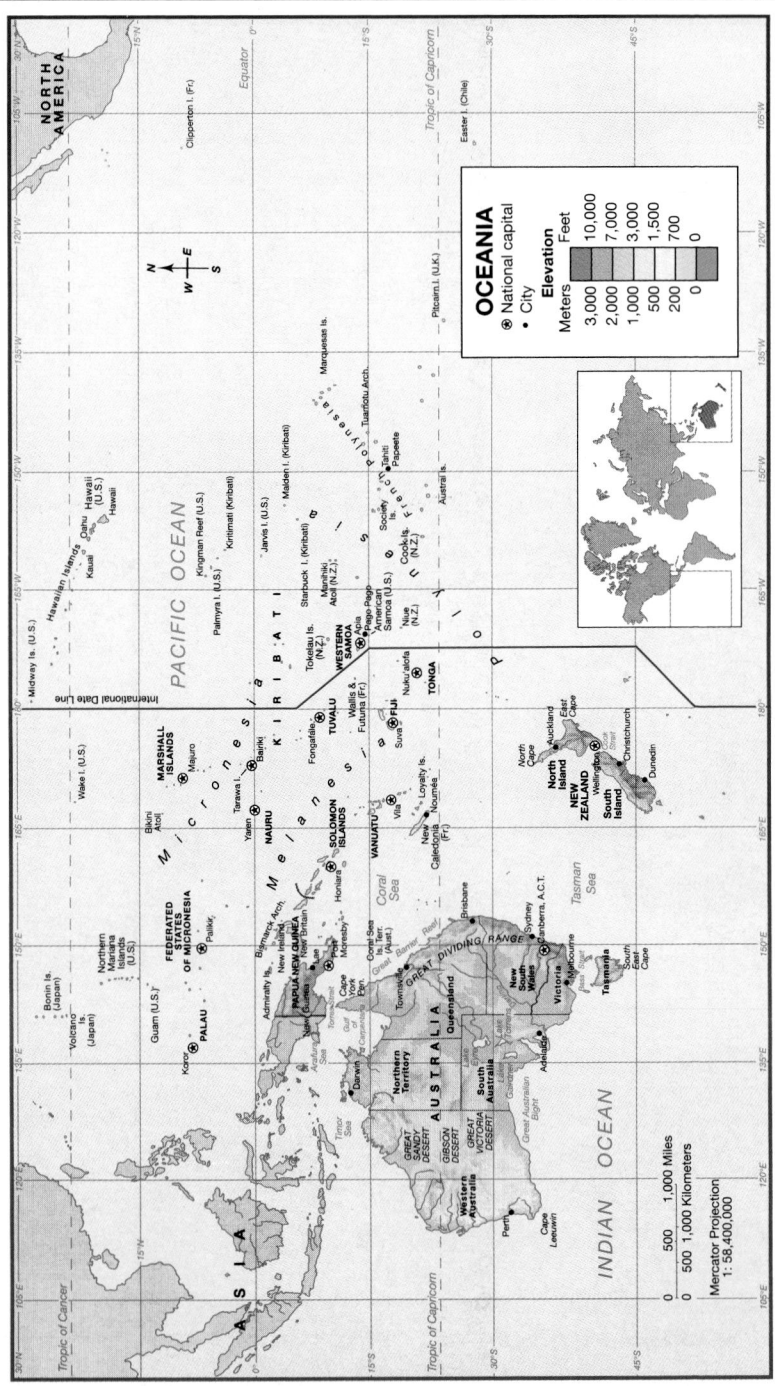

OCEANIA

⊛ National capital
• City

Elevation

Meters	Feet
3,000	10,000
2,000	7,000
1,000	3,000
500	1,500
200	700
0	0

NORTH AMERICA

Clipperton I. (Fr.)

Equator

Tropic of Capricorn

Easter I. (Chile)

Pitcairn I. (U.K.)

PACIFIC OCEAN

Marquesas Is.

Tuamotu Arch.

Papeete
Tahiti

Society Is.
Cook Is. (N.Z.)

French Polynesia

Hawaiian Islands
Oahu
Hawaii (U.S.)
Kauai
Hawaii

Kingman Reef (U.S.)
Kiritimati (Kiribati)

Jarvis I. (U.S.)
Malden I. (Kiribati)

Starbuck I. (Kiribati)
Manihiki
Atoll (N.Z.)

Niue (N.Z.)

Australia I.

Midway Is. (U.S.)

Palmyra I. (U.S.)

K I R I B A T I

Tokelau Is. (N.Z.)
WESTERN SAMOA
Apia
American Samoa (U.S.)
Pago Pago

Nuku'alofa
TONGA

International Date Line

Wake I. (U.S.)

M i c r o n e s i a

MARSHALL ISLANDS
Majuro
Bikini Atoll
Tarawa I.
NAURU
Yaren
Bairiki

Funafuti
TUVALU
Wallis & Futuna (Fr.)
FIJI
Suva

New Caledonia (Fr.)
Noumea
Loyalty Is.
Vila
VANUATU

North Cape
East Cape
Auckland
North Island
NEW ZEALAND
Wellington
South Island
Christchurch
Cook Strait
Dunedin

Bonin Is. (Japan)
Volcano Is. (Japan)
Guam (U.S.)
Northern Mariana Islands (U.S.)
PALAU
Koror
FEDERATED STATES OF MICRONESIA
Palikir

M e l a n e s i a

Admiralty Is.
Bismarck Arch.
New Ireland
New Britain
PAPUA NEW GUINEA
Port Moresby
SOLOMON ISLANDS
Honiara
Cape York Pen.

Coral Sea
Coral Sea Is. Terr. (Aust.)

Brisbane
New South Wales
Sydney
Canberra, A.C.T.
Victoria
Melbourne
Tasmania
South East Cape

Tasman Sea

GREAT DIVIDING RANGE

Townsville
Queensland
Great Barrier Reef

A S I A

Timor Sea

Darwin
Northern Territory

AUSTRALIA

GREAT SANDY DESERT
GIBSON DESERT
GREAT VICTORIA DESERT
South Australia
Western Australia
Adelaide
Great Australian Bight

Perth
Cape Leeuwin

INDIAN OCEAN

N
W ← → E
S

Tropic of Cancer

Tropic of Capricorn

0   500   1,000 Miles
0   500   1,000 Kilometers

Mercator Projection
1:58,400,000

The Secrets of Eating Smarter

Want to live a longer, healthier life? The best way to start is by eating foods that keep weight off and disease away

By Christine Gorman TIME

It's 6:45 P.M. After a bruising day at the office and a hair-raising commute on the freeway, you are standing in the kitchen about to prepare a healthy, satisfying dinner for your spouse, your two school-age children, and yourself. As usual, all they want to know is, "What's for dinner?" and "When do we eat?" You dump a box of thin spaghetti into a pot of boiling water, zap 3 cups of green beans in the microwave, pop a loaf of frozen garlic bread into the toaster oven, and pour a medium-size jar of marinara sauce into a saucepan to simmer. While all that's bubbling, you chop up half a head of iceberg lettuce and a couple of tomatoes for the salad, which you'll sprinkle with a light dressing. Dessert will be two scoops of frozen yogurt per person and a plate of assorted low-fat cookies for the family to share.

Sounds pretty healthy, right? Wrong. While this meal may be better than what most Americans eat for dinner, it's enough food for a family twice the size of yours. In addition, it contains some nutritional traps that in the best-case scenario will make you fat, and in the worst will increase your chances of developing diabetes, heart disease, and certain types of cancer. Think you know the pitfalls? Read on. You may be surprised.

Here are a few of the problems:

• Most light salad dressings are too heavy on sugar and salt and too light on nutrition. A better choice is a simple oil-and-vinegar dressing, which—although packed with calories—contains lots of heart-healthy monounsaturated fatty acids and no saturated fat.

• You're serving your family too many highly processed foods. The latest research shows that such foods won't keep them satisfied for very long and may make them hungrier in the long run.

• Having different kinds of cookies to choose from makes it more likely that your family will eat more cookies than they should. The fewer our choices, the less we eat.

• Your portion sizes are far too generous. According to the U.S. Food Guide Pyramid, you're giving each member of your family 4 servings of spaghetti, 1½ servings of marinara sauce and 2 servings of frozen yogurt. The whole meal contains 1,500 calories per person, or 80% of the daily requirement for a sedentary office worker.

• Let's not even get started on whether the tomatoes should be cooked or raw, how much salt and trans fats there are in the garlic bread, or how many calories are packed into that marinara sauce.

It just goes to show that it's hard to eat healthy even when we try. We've all heard that fruits and vegetables are good for us, that restaurant portions are too big, that we should exercise more. But even a casual glance at public-health statistics suggests that Americans don't know how to put that information into practice. Two out of three Americans are overweight or obese. The incidence of Type 2 diabetes among children is climbing. And any gains we've made against heart disease by quitting smoking may be . . . up in smoke.

A Glut of Information?

Alarmed by the worsening trends, health experts have unleashed a flood of nutritional advice for consumers—much of it contradictory. One expert says red meat is bad. Another says bacon keeps you trim. Someone says skip the potatoes, and someone else says eat the skin. And let's face it, controversy sells. Diet books and magazine articles try to grab our attention by telling us everything we thought we knew was wrong. (It's not.)

Even the government-approved labels on our food can lead us astray. Serving sizes bear no relationship to the helpings we usually eat. Low-fat products are not necessarily low in calories. And now the Food and Drug Administration (FDA) says we should be on the lookout for trans fats—a lesser-known type of fat that is every bit as bad for the heart as saturated fat—although we won't learn which products are the worst offenders until 2006.

Meanwhile, the food pyramid, which serves as the basis for all meals prepared in the federal school-lunch program, is about to be changed. The next revision, however, won't be out until 2005. Not that we necessarily mind the data smog: being perplexed can ease our conscience. As long as we can point to a general state of nutritional confusion, we don't have to take responsibility for our ever expanding waistlines.

The truth is that nutritionists have a fairly good idea about what constitutes a healthy diet as well as plenty of solid evidence to back that up. As a rule, they tell us, we should eat lots of fruits and vegetables, favor whole grains over highly processed cereals, and make red meat an occasional treat rather than the daily centerpiece of our evening meal. And we shouldn't eat any more than our body needs.

Small Changes, Big Rewards

The problem is that no matter how much we think we know about what goes into a healthy meal, we often misjudge the results. Some vegetable dishes, it turns out, are healthier than others, some grain products are less processed than others, some fish are safer than others. You may think you are eating right, but by making subtle changes in what you eat and how you eat it, you could start eating considerably healthier.

The rewards are worth the effort. Studies show that as much as 80% of heart disease and 90% of diabetes can be tied to unhealthy eating and lifestyle habits. Doctors have proved that a diet emphasizing fruits and vegetables as well as small amounts of nuts and dairy products can lower blood pressure and "bad" cholesterol as effectively as many medications. Evidence is growing that adding fiber to your diet and avoiding highly refined foods can help prevent or delay the onset of Type 2 diabetes.

You don't have to sacrifice flavor. You don't have to go hungry. You do need to put in some effort—much of it in the kitchen—and accept that there really is no free lunch. But with a little planning and a better understanding of some of the basic food traps, we can all eat better and smarter.

Begin by Eating Less

"Everything in Moderation" is a great motto—until you realize that moderation means different things to different people. Better to nail down some specifics and measure them using a tough-to-fudge yardstick—the much dreaded but ultimately very helpful concept of the calorie.

At its heart, the rule for losing weight is simple: eat fewer calories than you burn. As anyone who

---

What You Need to Know About Grains and Cereals

Brain Food

Thousands of years ago, our forebears learned how to domesticate staples such as rice, wheat, and millet (as well as such less well known grains as amaranth and quinoa), which led in turn to cities, civilization, and telemarketing. Packed with complex carbohydrates and essential vitamins such as B and E, grains still account for most of the calories consumed in the world.

Physics Lesson

But the more we grind, mill, refine, and strip grains of their constituent parts, such as bran, the fiber-rich outer layer, the more quickly our bodies are able to digest them—and the sooner

we're hungry again. In ascending order of processing:

Whole Grain Only outer husk removed

Cracked or steel cut Grains are cut into pieces

Flaked or rolled Kernels are flattened by rollers

Flour Whole or polished grains ground into a powder

Cereal Solution

You should replace as many refined carbs as you can with whole grains such as brown or wild rice, bulgur, barley, and whole-grain flours. A seven-grain dinner roll isn't as scary as it sounds. And if you don't relish a side dish of buckwheat groats, add some to soups and salads. If you

don't like whole-wheat pasta (and who does?), eat your favorite but less of it.

Beyond Rice and Pasta

Amaranth More protein than most grains

Wild rice A marsh grass, native to North America

Millet Ancient grain used as birdseed in the United States

What You Need to Know About Fruits and Vegetables

Botanical Bounty

The latest scientific research has shown—and the evidence continues to mount—that the plant kingdom is filled with gifts that can help fight off the ravages of chronic disease. A large group of compounds called phytochemicals (see below), found in plants ranging from garlic to cabbage to tea leaves, has been shown to help fight disease by preventing the cellular damage caused by chemicals called free radicals. A diet rich in fiber also has been shown to help reduce the risk of heart disease, stroke, high blood pressure, obesity, diabetes, and cancer. Fiber and phytochemicals are a one-two punch that should be reason enough to eat your peas and broccoli.

An Apple a Day

Fruit is a natural energy source, and there's nothing wrong with eating an apple a day. But why stop there? As always, variety is key, and there's a whole world of fruit to be savored and enjoyed. Look for new ways to add fruit to your daily routine. Begin your day with a fruit smoothie or throw a handful of banana slices and mixed berries on your cereal. Add peaches, pears, or melons to your lunch, and make fresh or dried fruit a sweet, satisfying snack. Try fish and meat with tropical-fruit salsa. Be adventurous. Find out—finally—what a loquat or a persimmon tastes like.

Spud Trouble

Americans love their potatoes—but too much for their own good. We eat 140 pounds per capita yearly. And while an unadorned potato is low in fat and a good source of nutrients, it is also primarily a carbohydrate that is almost immediately turned into sugar in the body. Besides, who eats plain potatoes? We love to dress them up—mashed with butter or gravy, baked with sour cream, deep-fried, scalloped, or au gratin. You don't have to stop eating potatoes—just don't eat them to the exclusion of other vegetables.

The Juice Trap

Starting each day with a glass of juice is a healthy morning ritual. But we need to remember that the juice has more calories—sometimes even added sugar—and less fiber than the fruit.

Fiber

Soluble fiber, which dissolves and becomes gummy in water, slows digestion, promoting a sense of fullness. It is found in apples, citrus fruits, and carrots.

Insoluble fiber, also known as roughage, speeds the passage of food through the intestines. It is found in wheat bran, veggies, and whole grains.

Phytochemicals

You may have seen these compounds touted as supplements. Flavonoids, one kind of phytochemical, grow naturally in citrus fruits, onions, apples, and grapes. Researchers think flavonoids may protect against cancer. Indoles, another kind of phytochemical, are found in cruciferous vegetables (such as broccoli and Brussels sprouts) and may offer protection against a host of chronic diseases. Other phytochemicals include:

CAROTENOIDS Beta-carotene, the best-known carotenoid, gives color to carrots and other orange, red, and yellow produce and is converted to vitamin A in our bodies. Lutein and zeaxanthin (from green vegetables) and lycopene (from tomatoes) may protect against coronary-artery disease, cataracts, macular degeneration, and cancer. All the more reason to eat colorful meals.

ISOFLAVINS Plant estrogens—soy foods are a particularly rich source—seem to have some of the same effects as estrogen. Benefits may include lower blood-lipid levels; decreased risk of hormone-related cancers of the breast, ovaries, endometrium, and prostate; and relief from menopausal symptoms.

AND DON'T FORGET: Don't like tofu? Soybeans—when roasted—make a good snack. Or try cooking some green soybeans (edamame) like lima beans. Soy milk also makes a delicious milk shake.

has ever tried to shed a couple of pounds knows all too well, that's often harder than it sounds. Eat too little, and your body ratchets down its metabolism so that it doesn't need as much energy, and you regain weight more easily. One way to counteract that is to boost your level of physical activity to increase the number of calories you burn. But when it comes to weight control, exercise—though necessary—can take you only so far.

Think about it, and you'll understand why. Food is so plentiful and so readily available that you're always going to be able to eat more than you can sweat off. The average American consumes 530 calories more per day now than he or she did in 1970. That's roughly what you'd get from eating 2½ cups of cooked pasta. You would have to walk an extra two hours a day to burn that off.

That doesn't mean you should forget about exercising—the benefits to your heart, bones, and peace of mind are just too great. It does mean you have to pay more attention to the "calories in" side of the equation. Even if you're happy when you step on the scales, you can't eat the way you did when you were a teenager. As you grow older, your body needs fewer calories to keep going. Certain exercises—like yoga and weight training—help counteract the trend because they build muscle, which burns more calories than fat. But to avoid gaining weight, you will have to eat less.

What You Need to Know About Dairy and Snacks

Good News, Bad News

Milk, cheese, and other dairy products are terrific sources of protein and calcium—the latter a crucial building block of bones and teeth. That's why kids especially, but adults too, should eat plenty. Yet dairy foods are also full of saturated fat, which is bad for your heart. Here's how to resolve the conflict:

Comfort-Food Follies

A nightly bowl of Häagen-Dazs may help smooth out the day's frustrations, but it also gives you 12 grams of saturated fat, 330 calories, and 85 mg of cholesterol in a 4 ounce serving. You can satisfy your craving almost as well with low-fat frozen yogurt. The dairy case is also packed with low- and nonfat milk, yogurt, and cheeses. Aim for two to

three servings a day, says the USDA, and remember that serving sizes may be a lot smaller than you think.

Snack Smarter

The way many of us pig out between meals, you would think snacks were a vital food group that included such high-calorie staples as potato chips, cheese curls, buttered popcorn, cookies, and soda. No wonder we're obese. But between-meal cravings can be tamed without loading up on the fat and processed sugar that most of these foods contain. Fruits and vegetables are far less fattening, and as a bonus they are actually good for you. Even nuts are fine in moderate portions.

Secret Formula

The basic ingredients in a lot of sweet snacks are sugar, trans fats,

and refined starch, all fattening and low in nutrition—but also so cheap that it costs almost nothing to double the size of a product. You may think that getting 12 more ounces for only half the price is a real steal, but it is sure no dietary bargain. Don't mistake supersizing for economizing.

Secrets of Portion Control

So, what are some smart ways of cutting back? Start by fooling both your eyes and your stomach. As you reduce the amount of food you eat, use smaller plates to keep your meals from looking skimpy. Begin a couple of meals each week with an apple or a cup of soup. Either will help curb your appetite.

Watch out for the portion-size trap. For reasons known only to bureaucrats, the portion sizes provided in the U.S. government's food pyramid can differ dramatically from those indicated on a product's food label. (One set of figures is regulated by the U.S. Department of Agriculture (USDA), and the other, which appears on product labels, is regulated by the FDA.) A single serving of pasta is ½ cup (cooked) according to the USDA, 1 cup according to the FDA, and at least 2 cups according to most families.

Eat a variety of fruits and vegetables, but limit your choices of everything else, particularly snacks. Giving folks a wide choice of foods in a single meal, scientists have shown, encourages them to eat more. "It works for every species ever tested—humans, rats, fish, cats," says Susan Roberts, professor of nutrition at Tufts University near Boston. If there are two types of cookies on a plate, the temptation is to eat one of each.

Eventually, you will have to become familiar with the calorie count of your foods. Just a couple of days of measuring or weighing what you eat and calculating the calories you consume can be a real eye opener. You don't have to do this for the rest of your life, just long enough to get a feel for it. Many nutritionists recommend eating healthy frozen dinners, whose calorie counts are printed on the package, as a good way to make the transition to smaller

portion sizes. How many calories you should eat in a day depends on whether you want to lose or maintain weight. The American Heart Association's rule of thumb is to multiply your weight in pounds by 13 (15 if you're active). If you want to lose weight, subtract 250 calories.

All Fats Are Not Created Equal

For more than 30 years, most researchers agreed that the healthiest diets were those that were low in the percentage of calories attributable to fat. Now they realize that just as there are good and bad types of cholesterol, there are good and bad types of fat. The good fats—found in foods like fish, olive oil, avocados, and walnuts—actually improve cholesterol levels in the blood and significantly reduce the risk that the heart will suddenly stop.

As for the bad fats, there are now two villains instead of just one. Saturated fats—typically found in red meat, butter, and ice cream—are still champion artery cloggers. But trans fats—found primarily in processed foods, such as margarines and many commercially baked or fried foods, but also in whole milk—may be even worse.

Good fats do more than help protect the heart. They also seem to delay hunger pangs. "People on these high-starch, low-fat diets are often hungry soon after they eat. They would be more satisfied eating nuts or a salad with a full-fat dressing," says Dr. Walter Willett, chairman of the department of nutrition at the Harvard School of Public Health and author of *Eat, Drink, and Be Healthy* (Fireside; 2001). "And longer-term studies are showing that people tend to be able to control their weight better over the long run on a moderate or higher-fat diet than on a low-fat diet."

Fats have more flavor—just remember that there's a smart way to include fat in your diet and lots of unhealthy ones. Good fats contain double the calories (9 calories per gram) of either proteins or carbohydrates (4 calories per gram). So there's little room for error. If you eat nuts, you're going to have to eat less of something else.

What about the Mediterranean diet? you ask. Researchers have long been fascinated by the traditional Greek and Italian diets of the 1960s, which contained as much as 40% fat but didn't trigger a lot of heart attacks. Don't assume that what worked for Greeks and Italians 40 years ago will work for you.

After all, they typically ate a pound of fruit a day (equal to four medium apples) and little red meat, and many of them got lots of exercise tilling fields and tending livestock.

Moreover, you can go overboard trying to avoid trans fats. Yes, there is a small amount of trans fat in whole milk, but whole milk is what most pediatricians recommend for children from age 1 to 2. Their brains need all kinds of fats to develop properly. After they reach age 2, you've got to be on the lookout for saturated fats as well.

What You Need To Know About Meat, Fish, and Eggs

Many cuts of meat—red meat in particular—are high in the saturated fats that have been linked to heart disease.

Brain Food

Meat has been a precious food commodity and a great complete source of protein, vitamins and other nutrients since prehistoric times. In fact, many anthropologists think that man's transition from a diet heavy on vegetables to a diet emphasizing meat may have played a key role in the evolution of our species. And although vegetarianism has become increasingly popular in recent years, meat of some variety is still the centerpiece of the lunch and dinner menus in most American homes and restaurants.

Pumping Iron

Red meat in particular is a rich source of iron, which plays an important part in building muscles and healthy blood. Studies of vegetarians have discovered that they risk becoming iron deficient, which can lead to anemia. The B vitamins found in ample quantities in meat are critical for proper energy production.

Overproteined

Our ancient ancestors hunted for their meat and expended a lot of energy chasing it down.

Today our animal protein is raised on feedlots and in cages, and delivered in great abundance nearly to our door. We eat roughly twice as much protein as we need, according to some estimates, risking injury to our kidneys and livers.

Tame Your Inner Carnivore

Go ahead, enjoy your bacon cheeseburger. But make it a once- or twice-a-month extravaganza. Go lean if you can, but above all, go easy. Remember that meat doesn't have to be an all-or-nothing proposition. Many dishes, such as stir fries and salads, can incorporate small quantities of meat but still satisfy. A pasta sauce can be 25% meat and 75% vegetables.

And watch those portion sizes. The USDA considers 3 ounces of meat to be one serving. When was the last time you ordered a 3-ounce hamburger or rib-eye steak?

Fruits of the Sea

For a low-fat alternative to red meat, it's hard to beat seafood. Fish and shellfish with high levels of omega-3 fatty acids have been shown to lower the risk of heart disease and may reduce men's risk of prostate cancer.

Seafood, however, is not perfect. Among the problems it presents is that fish, particularly oily fish, can concentrate toxins in their flesh. The metal mercury is a particular concern. Among fish with the highest levels of mercury are: swordfish, shark, tilefish, and king mackerel.

More bad news: salmon (both farmed and, to a lesser extent, caught) can contain worrisome levels of PCBs.

Stinkers in the Bait Bucket

Freshwater anglers are advised that their catch can contain various toxins, depending on the waters it comes from. In some cases, the Environmental Protection Agency advises anglers to limit their intake to one fish a week. And some species from particularly polluted waters should never be eaten under any circumstances.

Guidelines

The jury is still out on some of these recommendations, but to play it safe, children and pregnant or nursing women should eat no more than 12 ounces of fish a week and completely avoid swordfish, shark, mackerel, and tilefish. (The rest of us can eat these once or twice a month.) It's uncertain whether tuna is a concern for children and pregnant women, but the FDA gives it safe marks for the rest of us.

Go Fish

The news is not all cautionary. You can catch—and eat—your limit with shellfish, flounder, cod, tilapia, and a host of other catches-of-the-day. And don't forget the small fry: herring and sardines are high in omega-3s and low in toxins.

Incredible Edible

Yes, it's safe to go back to the henhouse. Eggs are a complete protein and are loaded with nutrients and vitamins A, B_{12}, folic acid, and riboflavin—probably the best bargain in the grocery store. But eggs have twice the cholesterol of beef, so three or four a week are plenty.

Finally, no matter how much McDonald's reduces the amount of trans fat in its French fries, they are never, alas, going to be a health food.

The Color Factor

Make sure the vegetables you eat are as colorful as possible—in order to get a wide variety of nutrients and those ever important antioxidants. Using spinach instead of iceberg lettuce in a salad, for example, will double the dietary fiber consumed, more than quadruple the calcium and potassium, more than triple the folate, and provide seven times as much vitamin C. Your goal should be to eat at least five ½-cup servings of fruits and vegetables a day—and preferably more. (Nine is divine, according to the latest nutritional research.)

Don't assume that fresh is the only game in town. Because frozen fruits and vegetables are chilled immediately after being picked, they often contain more nutrients than produce that has been sitting on the shelf for a few days.

The basic rules for eating smarter couldn't be simpler. Watch your total intake of calories. Burn off as many calories as you take in. And be choosy about the foods you eat—not just for a couple of weeks or months but for the rest of your life. "It takes work," says Dr. John Swartzberg, who chairs the editorial board of the U.C. Berkeley Wellness Letter. "We live in a fast-food world." The sooner we accept that that is not the healthiest of environments for us, the better off we'll be.

So, what's for dinner?   □

What You Need to Know About Nuts, Beans, and Oils

Magic Foods

In other cultures, nuts, seeds, and beans make up a major part of the diet, supplying all sorts of key nutrients that are hard to replace. If Americans could incorporate more of them into meals, much as we have embraced olive oil to replace less healthy sources of fat, our collective health would improve, and the average waistline would shrink. Here's why:

Seal of Approval

Although we tend to think of them as snack foods, nuts and seeds are actually terrific sources of protein, healthy oils, and other nutrients, especially vitamin E. For that reason, the American Heart Association has allowed packages of nuts to carry the qualified health claim that they "may reduce the risk of heart disease."

Restraining Order

But, yes, you can have too much of a good thing. For all their benefits, nuts and seeds are high-calorie foods because of the oils they contain. Beyond that, they often come heavily dosed with salt, sugar, or both. Tossing back bagfuls of salted, sugared beer nuts while watching the ball game on TV is not the same as going to the gym.

Sometimes You Feel Like a Nut

As a healthier alternative to chips or pretzels, try reaching for almonds, walnuts, pecans, or plain old goobers. But, again, use moderation. Once you start eating nuts, it's hard to stop. Think handfuls, not bowlfuls. Eat like a bird: add seeds such as sunflower, pumpkin, and sesame to your diet in trail mix, granola, muffins, bread, and occasionally even cookies.

Follow the Path of the Bean

No restraint is necessary with kidney beans, lentils, chickpeas, and their brother beans. They're low in fat and calories and packed with fiber, protein, and minerals—and they fill you up to boot. There's a big, beautiful world of legumes, and they play an important role in many ethnic cuisines. Use them dried, fresh, canned, or frozen in soups, stews, chilies, curries, pilafs, and falafel.

Lesser of Two Evils?

When all fat became bad, anything nonfat became good. Unfortunately, "low-fat" or "fat-free" products are often high in sugar, making them caloric catastrophes.

Battle of the Food Pyramids

The USDA's Food Guide Pyramid has turned into a battleground over how much fat is good for you. On one side are those like Dr. Dean Ornish of U.C. San Francisco, who want you to slash fat intake to 10% of daily calories. On the other is Harvard's Dr. Walter

Willett, who favors the Mediterranean diet, which permits as much as 40% of calories to come from fat as long as they are from a healthy source of fat, like olive oil.

Fat Stats

Sure, we know there are saturated fats in red meat and butter. But here's a bunch of other usual suspects, showing what percentage of total fat is saturated.

Coconut oil	92%
Butterfat	64%
Beef fat	52%
Palm oil	51%
Lard	41%
Chicken fat	31%
Peanut oil	18%
Soybean oil	15%
Olive oil	14%
Corn oil	13%
Sunflower oil	9%
Safflower oil	9%
Canola oil	6%

OUT: Breads and pastas are high in carbs

IN: Steak and other protein-rich foods are low in carbs

Welcome to America, a Low-Carb Nation

Millions of Americans embrace a new dietary regimen. Is the low-carb craze good science—or just good marketing?

By Daniel Kadlec TIME

Welcome to Low-Carb America! The nation's latest diet fad promises two things Americans just can't resist—pounds to drop and profits to crop—so it seems as if everyone is giving the low-carb culture a whirl. Whoopi Goldberg does it. So do Jennifer Aniston and Bill Clinton. What's good enough for the famed is, of course, appealing to the rest of us. Some 26 million Americans were on a hard-core low-carb diet in 2004. And 70 million more were limiting their carb intake without formally dieting, according to a poll by Opinion Dynamics Corp.

Counting carbs has become as powerful a fixture in the economy as it has in society. Some 586 distinct new low-carb foods and beverages hit the grocery shelves in the first quarter of 2004, up from 633 in all of 2003 and 339 in 2002, bringing the total over just two years to 1,558 new entries. Low-carb-related sales from such consumables as Michelob Ultra beer and books like *Dr. Atkins' New Diet Revolution* are expected to hit $30 billion in 2004, reported *LowCarbiz*, a trade publication that owes its existence to carbophobia.

A Brief Weight Loss

Still, not everyone is convinced: critics of the carb counters' revolution claim that Atkins, South Beach, Zone, and other protein-packed eating regimens are part of a fad that will soon run its course, like low-fat diets in the 1980s. But they can't deny that hundreds of thousands of Americans have dropped 20 or 50 or 100 lbs after cutting carbs from their meals.

Both sides found support for their arguments in recent studies. New research showed that the low-carb Atkins diet really does melt the pounds away—at least in the short run. Subjects in two trials ate either a low-carb diet or a conventional low-calorie, high-carb menu. At the end of six months, the carb cutters lost twice as many pounds as the calorie counters. The pounds, however, quickly reappeared after the first part of the study was completed. By the end of the next six months, the two test groups showed no difference in the amount of weight they'd lost. The studies also found that those who ate the low-carb way enjoyed higher levels of HDL, or "good" cholesterol, but it's not yet clear whether this boost offers enough benefit to the heart to compensate for the extra fat consumed in protein-rich diets.

Exactly why all those pounds melt away when we give up potatoes and bread remains something of a mystery to the dieting public. Is it mostly the temporary loss of water weight? Do low-carb fanatics lose weight while consuming more calories, as a Harvard study suggests, or do they end up eating less because they simply get bored with the high-protein life? Or is there some sort of metabolic magic when steak, eggs, and cheese replace the starches in our diet?

Dr. Robert Atkins, who got the ball rolling in 1972, controversially ascribed the weight loss to ketosis, the fat-burning state a body reaches when deprived of carbs. His critics have bordered on fanatic, their stridency growing in proportion to the diet's increase in popularity.

Yet there are signs that carb counting may be working. One market-research firm, NPD, found in 2003 that after six consecutive years of weight gain, the number of overweight adult Americans fell 1 percentage point, to 55%. Was it carb counting? No one really knows. But at fast-food restaurants, salad orders (low in carbs) rose 12%, while French-fry (carb mountain) consumption fell 10%.

The Nutritionists Speak

The more carb-counting becomes ingrained in our lives, the more worried many nutritionists grow. They argue that low-carb weight loss, while real, will not last for many folks, who once they stop dieting will obey their taste buds and return to the junk foods they love.

What if they stay off carbs indefinitely? This is where the jury is out. A growing body of medical evidence supports the notion that low-carb dieting can work for weight loss in the short term, and that getting slimmer is beneficial in fighting heart disease and diabetes. The study of long-term effects is only now getting under way, and one worry is the higher cholesterol counts that can accompany a diet rich in fatty meats. Without question, high cholesterol levels contribute to heart disease.

Good Carbs, Bad Carbs

How does carb counting work? In simple terms, carbs are digested or broken down into sugars, which then circulate in the bloodstream. As sugar levels in the blood rise, so does insulin. Peaks of insulin push the body to store excess sugar as fat. By cutting carbs, you effectively cut sugar surges, and thus not only store less fat but also start to burn off more of the fat you have.

If this were the whole story, of course, there would be little controversy and none of the colossal food frenzy being waged among companies desperate to get on the right side of the carb culture.

But there is a second front in the carb wars: good carbs vs. bad carbs. The good ones are found in whole-grain breads, beans, fruits, and vegetables. They contain fiber and break down slowly when digested, avoiding those damaging sugar and insulin spikes. The bad ones are found in white rice, potatoes, most commercial breads, and all manner of processed crackers, cookies, chips, soda, and candy bars. Bad carbs break down more quickly and cause sugar overload.

As you might imagine, those in the carb business are trying to claim that their carbs are the benevolent ones. All this spin can make the low-carb universe difficult to navigate. But there are a few simple things to keep in mind:

• First, watch out for bald-faced low-carb claims—they might be "carbage." That's because the Food and Drug Administration (FDA) has yet to define what constitutes a low- or light- or reduced-carb anything. Hence the proliferation of fuzzier labeling terms like "carb smart," "carb conscious," "carb aware," and "carb fit." Russell Stover, for example, received a warning letter from the agency about the name of its Low Carb line of chocolates. The company has offered to change the name but hopes it won't have to since the FDA announced in March 2004 that the agency will come up with a definition for "low carb."

• Second, there is the confusing notion of net carbs. Some manufacturers subtract the good carbs from the bad ones and advertise the difference. This is a slippery slope because the FDA insists that a carb is a carb is a carb. Just remember: net carbs are not the same as fewer carbs.

• Third, some low-carb products are so loaded with extra calories that they pose an unnecessary hurdle to weight loss. Take Subway's traditional 280-calorie 6-inch sandwich, the one that helped Jared slim down and find a gig as Subway's pitchman. That's about half the calories of the Atkins-friendly Subway chicken-bacon-ranch wrap. Want real results? Order the traditional sandwich on the tortilla wrap for fewer carbs and fewer calories.

• Finally, some low-carb products never had many carbs to begin with. Wish-Bone Carb Options ranch dressing has zero carbs, but the regular version has just 1 g per 2-tablespoon serving. Unless you're knocking the stuff back like beer at a frat party, the difference is a joke.

Low-Carb, Big Business

Food brands are reinventing themselves as carb awareness builds. When baseball opened for business in April 2004, many ballparks were promoting low-carb concessions, from bison burgers on low-carb buns at Cleveland's Jacobs Field to braised pork "wings" at St. Louis' Busch Stadium. Krispy Kreme says it will have a low-sugar—and therefore lower-carb—doughnut by the end of 2004.

In grocery stores, niche firms like Atkins Nutritionals, founded by the late Dr. Atkins, and Ketogenics have so far produced most of the low-carb breakfast bars and other packaged foods to hit the grocery aisles. But now the big boys are crowding into the act. Frito-Lay has unveiled Tostitos and Doritos Edge, in which soy protein is used in place of starch to lower the chips' carb count. Unilever has a Carb Options line of 32 products that includes reformulated Ragú sauce, Wish-Bone salad dressing, and Lipton tea with fewer carbs.

The diet craze has made waves throughout the food industry: pasta companies are screaming, while butchers are beaming. Even the late-2003 mad-cow scare failed to put a dent in beef consumption. Pork bellies, which give us bacon, are trading at record high prices. Egg prices have hit a 20-year high. Some economists go so far as to credit the low-carb culture as a chief force in revitalizing America's Farm Belt economy.

What's Next?

Can anything stop the low-carb culture? That's not likely in the short run. It will be years before we have conclusive long-term research on the diet's potential health risks. The arrival of big food companies in this fray means big money is at play and low-carb living will be marketed with a vengeance. The undisputed benefit of low-carb products to diabetics means a durable customer base.

So the fast results and pure simplicity of cutting carbs promise lasting appeal. That is, until we get sick of it. In the end, the biggest risk to the culture may be the inevitable false or misleading low-carb claims and influx of products that ladle on heapings of calories in exchange for carbs. If enough people are seduced by these foods and fail to lose weight, low carbs will go the way of low fat: a strategy that works when you stick to the rules but finally fails when marketers rush in with promises no one can keep. □

The Skinny on Carbs

From Dr. Atkins to the caveman diet, here's the rundown on the low-carb industry and its most popular diets

You Do the Math

Until the Food and Drug Administration rules on the legal definition of "low carb" or "carb lite," companies can get in trouble explicitly marketing their products as such. Nutrition labels can be used, however, to break down a food's carbohydrate content, enabling dieters to subtract so-called nonimpact carbs. Those include fiber and artificial sweeteners such as sugar alcohols, which don't raise blood-sugar levels.

Industry Jargon

Foodmakers created the idea of "net carbs" or "impact carbs" to zero in on the amount of carbohydrates that affect insulin levels.

The Miracle Worker

The proliferation of low-carb treats is largely due to Splenda, a zero-calorie sugar derivative that handles heat better than Equal or Sweet'N Low, and some think it tastes better, too.

The Fine Print

Some low-carb sweets rely on sugar alcohols, which are slowly digested carbs that have no impact on insulin levels but sugar alcohols, if consumed in excess, can wreak havoc on your digestive tract.

Low-Carb Diets: How They Differ

Dr. Atkins' New Diet Revolution

The pioneering low-carb regimen created by the late Dr. Robert Atkins begins with a two-week induction period that limits dieters to 20 grams of net carbs a day, ideally via 2 cups of salad and 1 cup of non-starchy vegetables. Atkins claims the low-carb intake leads to **ketosis,** in which the body burns fat for energy. Successive phases of the meaty diet gradually add more carbs—nuts, berries, and veggies—as weight loss slows.

The South Beach Diet

Instead of counting carbs, Dr. Arthur Agatson focuses on the **glycemic index,** or how much a particular food raises your blood sugar. Rapid spikes can make you hungrier faster and therefore lead to overeating. South Beach's induction phase is similar to Atkins's, but then it allows more fruits and veggies as well as whole-grain breads and pastas.

Protein Power

Drs. Michael and Mary Eades have devised an insulin-management plan that resembles *The Zone* in some ways and bases protein minimums and carbohydrate maximums on your body composition and activity level.

The Schwarzbein Principle

Because stress hormones play an important role in controlling food cravings, Dr. Diana Schwarzbein emphasizes the need for **stress management** as well as metabolic healing. As in *Protein Power,* her diet plan tailors carb intake to body type and activity level, and also includes options for vegetarians.

The Fat Flush Plan

Nutritionist Ann Louise Gittleman zeroes in on **"false fat,"** water retention triggered either by dehydration or by common allergies or sensitivities to a trio of sin foods (wheat, dairy, and sugar). Her "fat-flushing," "liver-loving" low-carb diet calls for drinking eight glasses of cranberry water a day to deter water retention and help "clean up" cellulite, plus a glass of hot water with fresh lemon juice to aid fat metabolism and stall carbohydrate digestion.

Neanderthin

Ray Audette's *Caveman Diet* doesn't involve carb or calorie counting or any peculiar formulas but instead urges wannabe Paleolithic dieters to ask one simple question: Could I eat this if I were naked with a sharp stick on the savanna? That guiding principle rules out grains, beans, potatoes, dairy, sugar, and virtually all processed foods.

America's Obesity Crisis

Why are we losing the war with weight? The villains include
ourselves, but the urge to gorge may be a relic of man's past

By Michael D. Lemonick TIME

It's hardly news anymore that Americans are just too fat. If the endless parade of articles, TV specials, and fad diet books weren't proof enough, a quick look around the mall, the beach, or the crowd at any baseball game will leave no room for doubt: our individual weight problems have become a national crisis.

Even so, the actual numbers are shocking. Fully two thirds of U.S. adults are officially overweight, and about half of those have graduated to full-blown obesity. The rates for African Americans and Latinos are even higher. Among kids between 6 and 19 years old, 15%, or 1 in 6, are overweight.

And things haven't been moving in a promising direction. Just two decades ago, the incidence of overweight in adults was well under 50%, while the rate for kids was only a third what it is today. From 1996 to 2001, 2 million teenagers and young adults joined the ranks of the clinically obese. People are clearly worried. A TIME/ABC News poll released in May 2004 showed that 58% of Americans would like to lose weight, nearly twice the percentage who felt that way in 1951.

It wouldn't be such a big deal if the problem were simply aesthetic. But excess poundage takes a terrible toll on the human body, significantly increasing the risk of heart disease, high blood pressure, stroke, diabetes, infertility, gall-bladder disease, osteoarthritis, and many forms of cancer. The *Journal of the American Medical Association* reported in March 2004 that poor diet and physical inactivity could soon overtake tobacco as the leading cause of preventable death in the United States.

Origins of Obesity

So why is it happening? The obvious answer is that we eat too much high-calorie food and don't burn it off with enough exercise. It's natural to try to find villains to blame—fast-food joints or food companies or even ourselves for having too little willpower. But the ultimate reason for obesity may be rooted deep within our genes.

Although our physiology has stayed pretty much the same for the past 50,000 years or so, we humans have utterly transformed our environment. Technology has almost completely removed physical exercise from the day-to-day lives of most Americans. At the same time, it has filled supermarket shelves with cheap, mass-produced, good-tasting food that is packed with calories. And technology delivers constant, inviting messages that say "Eat this now" to everyone old enough to watch TV.

Our first ancestors probably ate much as their cousins the apes did, foraging for fruits, shoots, nuts, tubers, and other vegetation in the forests and savannas of Africa. Because most wild plants are relatively low in calories, it took constant work just to stay alive. Fruits, full of natural sugars like fructose and glucose, were an unusually concentrated source of energy, and the instinct to seek out and consume them evolved in many mammals long before humans ever arose. But humanity's appetite for animal fat and protein is probably more recent.

It was some 2.5 million years ago that our hominid ancestors developed a taste for meat. The fossil record shows that the human brain became markedly bigger and more complex about the same time. Meat provided a concentrated source of protein, vitamins, minerals, and fatty acids that helped our human ancestors grow taller.

The appetite for meat and sweets was essential to human survival, but it didn't lead to obesity for several reasons. The wild game our ancestors ate was high in protein but very low in fat—only about 4%, compared with as much as 36% in grain-fed supermarket beef. Beyond that, hunting and gathering took enormous physical work. In essence, early humans ate what amounted to the best of the high-protein Atkins diet and the low-fat Ornish diet and worked out almost nonstop.

It's really only in the past 100 years that cars and other machinery have dramatically reduced the need for physical labor. And as exercise has vanished from everyday life, the technology of food production has become much more sophisticated. And thanks to mass production, all that food is relatively cheap. It's also absurdly convenient.

Evolving during a time of scarcity, humans developed an instinctive desire for basic tastes—sweet, fat, salt—that they could never fully satisfy. As a result, says Rutgers University anthropologist Lionel Tiger, "we don't have a cut-off mechanism for eating. Our bodies tell us, 'Fat is good to eat but hard to get.'" The second half of that equation is no longer true, but the first remains a powerful drive.

The Good News

Is there reason for hope? Yes. Scientists are hard at work trying to understand the basic biochemistry of hunger and fat metabolism; policymakers are pushing for better labels and nutritional information; school boards are giving their cafeteria menus a closer look; urban planners are rethinking our cities and towns to get us out of the car and onto our feet; Americans in record numbers are putting themselves on low-carb and low-calorie diets; and more and more foodmakers are beginning to see increased awareness of the obesity epidemic not as a threat but as a business opportunity.

How can Americans begin to wage war on this epidemic? Campaigns against smoking and drunk driving have raised the national consciousness about these public-health issues dramatically. There's no reason to think an anti-obesity campaign can't do so as well—as long as everyone involved acknowledges that the problem is real and that solving it will be a long, difficult haul. After all, it's not easy to fight millions of years of evolution. □

A–Z Guide to Health and Medicine News

This just in, from AIDS to Zoonosis

By **DAVID BJERKLIE, ALICE PARK, and SORA SONG** TIME

A

AIDS AIDS is still a death sentence in much of world, so President Bush pledged $15 billion over five years for the relief of the disease in the most severely affected nations of Africa and the Caribbean. At least $10 billion a year is needed, according to UN estimates, but the world's richest countries spend a total of about $2.8 billion annually.

In the United States, experts reported that for the first time since the mid-1990s, the number of HIV infections rose, by 1%. They believe some of the climb can be traced to the fact that more and more HIV patients are living longer, thanks to a potent combination of drugs that can control the virus. Unfortunately, if survivors fail to follow prevention guidelines, they may pass HIV along to others.

There were disappointing results on the research front as well. Scientists found that some anti-AIDS therapies seem to increase the risk of heart attack 25%, at least in the first few years of treatment. In addition, studies showed that taking a break—or "drug holiday"—from the grueling pill-popping schedule does not improve the body's ability to overcome drug-resistant forms of HIV.

The first vaccine to be widely tested in humans failed to protect test subjects from HIV. But the information gained should help in the development of future vaccines.

ALZHEIMER'S New estimates show that by 2050, a record 13.2 million older Americans will be affected by this progressive brain disease, 3 million more than previous projections. Although the illness is still definitively diagnosed only at autopsy, advances are being made in finding it earlier. Doctors can improve the accuracy of detection 30% by combining various cognitive tests with positron-emission tomography (PET). PET is an imaging technique that shows the brain's metabolism at work. Preliminary research suggests that it may also be possible for physicians to detect certain telltale signs of Alzheimer's disease—the so-called amyloid and tau proteins—in the spinal fluid.

Of course, knowing you have early Alzheimer's doesn't help much if it can't be treated. Fortunately, therapies are improving. Exelon and memantine, drugs usually used to treat the symptoms of dementia in moderate cases of Alzheimer's, may be even more useful in delaying the progression of early disease.

Neuroscientists were disappointed in 2002 when a potential vaccine for Alzheimer's disease ended up causing severe inflammation of the brain. (One woman died several months after being vaccinated. Further study confirmed that her brain was inflamed, though some of her brain plaques, a symptom of Alzheimer's, seem to have shrunk.) Doctors are making progress toward finding ways to avoid the inflammation.

ANTIBIOTICS Babies who are six months old or younger face a risk when given antibiotics for the first time. A Detroit study found that such infants were 1½ times as likely to develop allergies and twice as likely to develop asthma as babies who didn't take the drugs. But exposure to dander from two or more household pets seems to reduce these risks.

McDonald's, the world's largest fast-food chain, said that by the end of 2004 it would stop using meat from animals that had been excessively treated with antibiotics. The decision may help curtail the practice of dosing healthy animals with antibiotics to plump them up for slaughter. Doctors hope this will reduce the opportunity for disease-causing bacteria, present in meat, to become resistant to drugs.

B

BERRIES Better aim your grocery cart toward the fruit aisle. Studies in animals hint that berries are bursting with benefits. For one thing, they are chock-full of antioxidants, which help absorb some of the toxic molecules called free radicals that the body pro-

duces during metabolism. Cranberries may pack a one-two punch. They seem to boost levels of HDL, the so-called good cholesterol, which soaks up artery-clogging fat. They may also reduce the amount of damage to the brain that occurs after a stroke. Blueberries appear to lower the risk of heart disease by keeping arteries elastic and making them less prone to wear and tear when the body is under stress.

BIRTH CONTROL Women in the United States are a step closer to getting emergency contraception without the need for a doctor's prescription. An advisory panel of the Food and Drug Administration (FDA) recommended that the morning-after pill become available over the counter. If approved, Plan B, as the two-pill regimen would be called, would enable women to end pregnancies within 72 hours of unprotected intercourse.

BLOOD PRESSURE The National Heart, Lung and Blood Institute changed its guidelines in 2003. What it used to call a "high normal" level—from

120/80 mm Hg to 139/89 mm Hg—is now considered prehypertensive. The move should prompt more people to lower their salt intake and to exercise, both ways to avoid high blood pressure.

C

CANCER:

• **Breast** A group of drugs called aromatase inhibitors that were once used to treat metastatic breast cancer is helpful in less advanced cases as well. They target tumors that need estrogen by lowering the amount of estrogen in the body. Women who took aromatase inhibitors for five years after taking tamoxifen (which also shrinks estrogen-sensitive tumors) reduced their risk of recurrence by almost half.

• **Colon** There's a good alternative to the dreaded colonoscopy. Tests showed that virtual colonoscopy, which images the colon by combining C.T. scans, can be as reliable at detecting tumors—provided the right 3-D software is used. And in the first trial of its kind, Avastin, a drug designed to starve a tumor by cutting off its blood supply, showed promise against colon cancer when used in conjunction with chemotherapy. Doctors are exploring its use against other solid tumors.

• **Lung** Most cases of lung cancer are too advanced for treatment by the time they are detected, but researchers at Duke University are working on a blood test that could detect the disease in its earliest stages, when the cancer may still be treatable. Their aim is to detect traces of a protein, called serum amyloid A, that is elevated in cancer patients but not in healthy people.

• **Prostate** About 75% of U.S. men over 50 have been screened for prostate cancer with the prostate-specific antigen (PSA) test, but the threshold level that doctors use to biopsy suspicious growths misses up to 82% of cancers. Harvard researchers reported that lowering the PSA level at which doctors recommend biopsies could double the rate at which they detect cancers.

CHOCOLATE Sweet news: besides tasting great, chocolate can do you some good. It's rich in flavonoids, which can raise levels of good cholesterol, and antioxidants, which limit cell damage. Heating chocolate seems to release antioxidants, so go for the hot cocoa.

Not all chocolate is created equal, however. Dark chocolate is more potent than its paler cousin in raising antioxidant levels, possibly because the milk in milk chocolate binds to antioxidants. In addition, German research found that the dark stuff can lower blood pressure.

D

DIABETES Expanding waistlines continue to feed the epidemic. Doctors hope that by shifting their attention to prediabetes—a condition that significantly increases the risk of Type 2 diabetes, the most common form of the illness—they can reduce the number of folks who develop full-blown diabetes and such devastating complications as heart and kidney trouble, strokes, and blindness.

The American Diabetes Association broadened the definition of prediabetes to include those with fasting blood-sugar levels of 100 mg/dL (it had been 110 mg/dL).

Because diabetics face fewer complications if they avoid hypertension, the American College of Physicians now recommends that diabetics keep their blood pressure below 135/80 mm Hg.

DIET Another scattering of studies showed that the low-carb Atkins diet really does melt the pounds away—at least in the short run. Subjects in two trials ate either a low-carb diet or a conventional low-calorie, high-carb menu. At the end of six months, the carb cutters lost twice as many pounds as the calorie counters.

The pounds, however, quickly reappeared after the first part of the study was completed. By the end of the next six months, the two test groups showed no difference in the amount of weight they had lost. The studies also found that those who ate the low-carb way enjoyed higher levels of HDL, but it's not yet clear whether this boost provides enough of a benefit to the heart to compensate for the extra fat consumed in the Atkins-style diets.

E

ELECTRON-BEAM COMPUTED TOMOGRAPHY Much as heart doctors know about the risk factors that contribute to heart disease—high cholesterol, high blood pressure, stress, and lack of physical activity—they still have no reliable way to predict who will and who won't suffer a heart attack.

Until now. It turns out that excess deposits of calcium in the lining of the arteries, which can be measured using electron-beam computed tomography (EBCT), are a good indication that potentially dangerous fatty plaques exist. The correlation is strong enough that the American Heart Association is weighing a recommendation of EBCT screening for

healthy adults who have a greater than average risk of heart disease, including smokers and those with a strong family history. As an added benefit, patients can take home their EBCT image, complete with gummed-up arteries, and use it as a reminder to stick with that exercise program and low-fat diet.

EPHEDRA Since 1997 the FDA has been keeping track of ephedra, an herb used in dietary supplements for weight loss and energy boosts. In 2004 the agency finally amassed enough data on the herb's side effects—from high blood pressure to stroke and sudden death—to justify a proposed ban of the supplement. The move comes too late for the Baltimore Orioles' Steve Bechler, who died during spring training after taking the supplement. But health officials expect that a ban will save other lives.

F

FLU The flu season of 2003–2004 was one to remember, but not because it was a historically bad one. Rather, it was because the annual ordeal started earlier than usual, took the lives of nearly 100 youngsters, and raised concerns that the supply of vaccine couldn't meet demand and might not be effective against this strain of virus. At the same time, health officials urged that all healthy babies between the ages of 6 months and 23 months be vaccinated. Thankfully, the worries proved to be overblown, but as experts at the Centers for Disease Control and Prevention (CDC) pointed out, when it comes to the flu, it's far better to be safe than sorry.

G

GREEN TEA How healthful is a cup of green tea? Let us count the ways. Recent studies suggest that chemically active compounds in the soothing drink may help lower cholesterol, aid the immune system in fighting off infections, assist in weight loss, and protect against cancers of the lung, colon, breast, liver, prostate, pancreas, bladder, and skin. Tea may also help us prevent diabetes and bad breath. Keep

in mind, though, that the studies are preliminary and sometimes even contradictory. Enjoy your cup of tea, but don't expect it to be a cure-all.

H

HEART The news reports dubbed it "Drano for the heart," and if the results are confirmed in larger trials, they may signal an exciting new approach in fighting cardiovascular disease, America's leading cause of death. "It" is a genetically rare type of HDL, or "good" cholesterol, dubbed ApoA-1 Milano. First identified 30 years ago in a small group of people living in northern Italy, this super HDL is even more protective against heart disease than regular HDL. In a study released in fall 2003, researchers injected a synthetic version of ApoA-1 Milano into 47 patients and found that unlike drugs that merely slow the dangerous buildup of plaque in the arteries, super HDL reduced the size of the plaques—and did so in the dramatically short period of five weeks. The experimental drug also stabilized the plaques that remained and reduced their level of inflammation, making them less likely to burst. Though the study was too small to be definitive, it certainly stirred a lot of interest at the American Heart Association's meeting in November 2003. After years of being preoccupied with lowering levels of LDL, the "bad" cholesterol, doctors and patients may soon be focusing on how to pump up vessel-cleansing HDL.

HORMONE REPLACEMENT THERAPY Information released in 2003 put a few more nails in the coffin of long-term hormone-replacement therapy (HRT). Further examination of the data from the Women's Health Initiative, a study that involved more than 16,000 women, showed that the combination of estrogen and progestin not only raised a postmenopausal woman's risk of heart disease and breast cancer but also increased her risk of stroke and doubled her chances of developing dementia if she was 65 or older. The grim research results, on top of those released in 2002, have translated into plummeting prescriptions for Wyeth Pharmaceuticals, manufacturer of Prempro (the company also helped fund the critical studies): the tally of 2003 sales of the hormone combo is expected to be down 50% from 2002 sales, which were down 25% from 2001 sales.

I

INSOMNIA The value of a good night's sleep is hard to overstate. And researchers are increasingly finding that sleep doesn't just improve the quality of life—it actually prolongs life as well. An analysis of eight sleep studies showed that healthy adults age 60 and older who experienced poor sleep—characterized by long stretches of wakefulness during the night—had double the normal risk of early death. Other studies link poor sleep to lower immune-system function as well as an increased risk for certain types of cancer. But to what lengths should you go to make sure you get enough sleep? Today's sleeping pills can help, but are they safe to take in the long term? The drug company Sepracor has been testing a new pill, Estorra, that appears to be both safe and effective when taken for six months. The drug is under review for approval by the FDA. No doubt competitors will be looking at their own sleep drugs to see if they can pass the six-month test.

K

KNEE SURGERY Arthroscopic knee surgery has been a popular treatment for people whose knees are racked by osteoarthritis. Minimally invasive, it flushes out debris in the joint and smooths bone surfaces without major surgery. But a surprising study showed that the operation is no more effective than a placebo. One in three patients reported improvement, whether having had real surgery or a sham operation with all the same pre- and post-op procedures but no actual treatment. Even if the placebo benefit is ignored, the study still casts doubt on surgery that succeeds only one third of the time. Patients may be better off doing strengthening exercises and taking off a few pounds to ease the burden on their aching knees.

L

LEAD Lead poisoning doesn't seem like much of a problem these days, but new research gives fresh cause for concern. It seems that blood levels of lead previously thought to be safe can actually cause intellectual impairment. Not only that, but quite a bit of damage seems to occur at low levels of exposure. A five-year study found that kids with a blood-lead level at the acceptable threshold of 10 micrograms per deciliter (mcg/dl) scored seven points lower on an IQ test than kids with a level of only 1 mcg/dl. The guidelines for safe lead levels have been revised repeatedly over the years, from 60 mcg/dl before 1970 to 25 mcg/dl in 1985 to 10 mcg/dl. They may have to change again. The CDC estimates that 1 in 10 children under age 6 has a blood level of 5 mcg/dl or higher.

LONGEVITY Various studies have shown that identical twins live longer than fraternal twins. Researchers think they know why: communication. Identical twins appear to keep in touch by phone or mail more often; such social support is known to improve health. The extra bit of close contact translated into a median life-span of 82 years vs. 80.5 years for fraternal twins.

M

MAD COW Word came just two days before Christmas 2003 that the dreaded disease, formally known as bovine spongiform encephalopathy (BSE), had arrived in the United States. Tests confirmed that a 6-year-old dairy cow, which had been ground into hamburger two weeks earlier, was a carrier. Although the cow had entered the United States from Canada in 2001, more than 30 countries quickly banned U.S. beef imports. The U.S. Department of Agriculture in turn recalled 10,000 lbs of ground beef and instituted a series of measures to reassure consumers, including a ban on the slaughter of cattle too sick or injured to walk. The cow in question was born a few months before a ban on feeding cattle the pulverized remains of their kin,

the most likely path of infection, went into effect in Canada and the United States. Only 20,000 of the 35 million cattle slaughtered in the United States each year are tested for BSE.

O

OBESITY What will it take to get our attention? Obesity accounts for 280,000 deaths in the United States each year. If current trends continue, the battle of the bulge will overtake smoking as the primary cause of preventable death. Some researchers believe that today's wide-bodied kids will have shorter life-spans than their parents.

The number of overweight kids has tripled in the past 20 years, and some two thirds of American adults are either overweight or obese. Sure, stomach stapling is all the rage—100,000 operations in 2003—but the costly, risky procedure is no answer for the massive masses.

Meanwhile, the search is on for a magic pill. One study found that a natural compound called PYY reduces appetite and food intake when given to test subjects intravenously. Another study found that a natural fatty acid, OEA (oleylethanolamide), also seems to regulate hunger and metabolism—at least in mice. Research on both compounds is still in the early stages, but they could be the basis for new treatments targeting obesity. What to do until these wonder drugs arrive at the local pharmacy? Yep. Eat less, and exercise more.

P

PARKINSON'S The quaking, shaking symptoms of this degenerative disease, which afflicts 1.5 million Americans, have been notoriously tough to treat. For 40 years, efforts have focused on drugs that regulate the function of a key neurotransmitter called dopamine. Now attention is shifting. Doctors have begun implanting electrodes on both sides of the brain to stimulate its inner regions—an approach that has shown some success in treating intractable epilepsy.

And a drug unrelated to dopamine, istradefylline, seems to reduce tremors and slowness in Parkinson's patients with advanced disease.

Given that the condition can only be slowed, not cured, prevention may be the best bet. A long-term study of 140,000 adults suggests that regular use of nonaspirin painkillers such as Motrin or Aleve may offer some protection. Another prevention strategy is to avoid head injuries. Studies have shown that individuals who have experienced a head injury serious enough to require hospitalization have an eightfold higher risk of suffering from Parkinson's disease later in life.

PAXIL A group of antidepressants called SSRIs may be doing wonders to lift moods in adults, but concern is growing over their use in teens and kids. First, researchers in Britain found that youngsters taking Paxil were more likely to have suicidal thoughts. Regulators there decided the drug should not be given to children. In the United States, the FDA quickly followed suit. Six months later, the British regulators warned against the use of five other antidepressants in young people. Doctors on both sides of the pond still think that Prozac is OK, but expect the United States to take a closer look at all other SSRIs.

S

SARS The first reports of an unusual and severe form of pneumonia came in February 2003, from doctors in Hong Kong. In March 2003, the brand-new disease SARS—severe acute respiratory syndrome—claimed its first victim in the island city. Soon SARS was suspected to have infected more than 7,600 people in 30 countries, including Taiwan, Canada, and the United States. Travel was restricted, schools were shut down, and panicked residents of hard-hit countries wore masks outside their homes, if they went out at all. But by April 2003, with a swiftness the World Health Organization called stunning, scientists had identified the novel virus at the root of SARS—a member of the coronavirus family, which usually causes nothing more than a bad cold—and sequenced the new pathogen's genome. Chinese health officials were roundly criticized when it became clear that the bug had actually made its first appearance late in 2002 in the southern Chinese province of Guangdong; a more timely alert might have helped stem its spread. By year's end, U.S. researchers had successfully tested an experimental SARS vaccine in monkeys.

SMALLPOX Although smallpox was declared eradicated in 1980, the U.S. government remains concerned that stocks of the virus might fall into terrorist hands and be unleashed on the public. To counter that scenario, federal scientists are testing a new generation of safer vaccines (the old one is the most lethal vaccine around, killing an estimated one or two of every million who take it) and helping to fund a multimillion-dollar effort to create a pill to treat and possibly prevent infection. In 2003 the Bush administration offered a version of the old vaccine, on a voluntary basis, to key civilian health-care workers. The initiative ground to a halt in June 2003 after just 38,000 of the 500,000 intended subjects were inoculated. There just weren't enough doctors and nurses willing to risk a potentially fatal reaction.

SMOKING Cigarettes are still bad for you, and it's still as hard as ever to quit. But researchers have found two more good reasons—particularly for women—to tough it out. A study of 3,000 smokers, age 40 and older, showed that female smokers had twice the risk of lung cancer as their male counter-

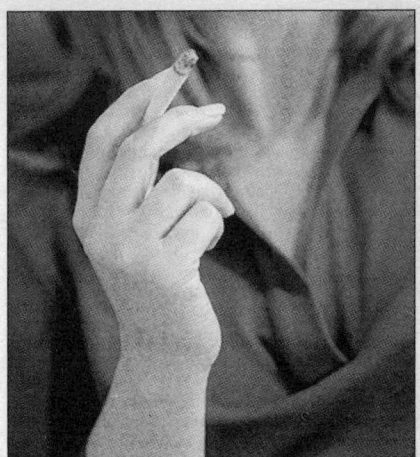

parts, independent of age or the amount they smoked. Further, in a separate study of 5,300 smokers, scientists found that giving up cigarettes benefits women more than men. In the first year after quitting, the women's lung function improved more than twice as much as the men's, and it stayed better throughout the five-year study.

T

TRANS FATS There's fat, and then there's trans fat (e.g., "hydrogenated" oils)—also known as trans-fatty acids. Food manufacturers began using them in place of saturated fats in the 1980s. Trans fats extended the shelf life of certain products, and foodmakers thought they made edibles safer. Turns out trans fats, like saturated fats, raise bad cholesterol (LDL) and may lower good cholesterol (HDL). As if that weren't bad enough, they may also increase the risk of diabetes. Current labeling guidelines don't require manufacturers to state how many grams of trans fats are in a product, but the FDA has called for food labels to come clean. Look for trans-fat grams on all labels beginning Jan. 1, 2006.

Ironically, many nutrition experts advised us to stop eating butter in favor of margarine in the 1980s, in order to reduce our intake of fats. Today, nutritionists recommend using margarine specifically labeled as not including trans fats.

V

VACCINES The threat of bioterrorism jump-started dormant plans to create reliable vaccines against some of the world's deadliest agents. In October 2003, U.S.-government scientists began their first human trial of an experimental vaccine against Ebola, a lethal African virus that triggers severe internal bleeding and kills up to 90% of its victims. Experts have long feared that Ebola could be turned into a devastating bioweapon. Meanwhile, at Harvard, researchers created an anthrax vaccine that, unlike older vaccines, targets both the toxins created by the bacterium and the bug itself.

VISION There's a new Lasik in town. You remember the old Lasik, the eye operation that improves vision by reshaping the cornea with lasers. The new version is called wavefront-guided Lasik and depends on technology developed by astronomers to correct problems in high-powered telescopes. Wavefront Lasik uses 200 little lenses to map the cornea, taking into account all its bumps and abnormalities to produce a highly accurate, individualized prescription. Conventional Lasik, by contrast, applies one standard formula to each eye. If the old Lasik is off the rack, wavefront is a custom-fit procedure. Studies show that the new method reduces the occurrence of common postsurgical side effects, such as halos, glare, and bad night vision. But the risks of eye surgery still apply. Cost: up to $3,000 per eye.

VITAMINS News continued to trickle in on the pros and cons of taking vitamins. Here's a look at the latest discoveries.

• **Beta-Carotene** Found in carrots and other colorful produce, this antioxidant and vitamin A precursor may help fight cancer—but not necessarily for everyone. A Dartmouth study showed that beta-carotene supplements were associated with a 44% reduction in the risk of precancerous colon tumors in subjects who neither drink nor smoke. But they appeared to double the risk of tumors in smokers who drink at least once a day.

• **Vitamin B** Finnish researchers concluded that B_{12} (found in meat, milk, and fortified cereal) may beat the blues. Depressed patients with the highest levels of vitamin B_{12} in their blood responded best to treatment.

Researchers in Boston found that high blood levels of vitamins B_6 and B_{12}, along with folate, are linked to a reduced risk of breast cancer in some women. And another study, at Georgetown, suggested that B_{12} and B_6 may slow the progression of Alzheimer's disease by lowering blood levels of the amino acid homocysteine.

• **Vitamins C and E** Could strawberries and nuts prevent a stroke? Maybe. People who smoke have an increased risk of stroke, but diets high in vitamins C and E were found to cut the risk by 70% and 20%, respectively. In a separate study, the same vitamins, given to children with abnormally high cholesterol, led to improved blood-vessel function. A third study, of more than 6,700 people, showed that the higher the level of vitamin C in the blood, the less likely a person would be infected by Helicobacter pylori, a microbe that can cause peptic ulcers and stomach cancer.

• **Vitamin D** A comprehensive study of more than 3,000 U.S. veterans found that fiber-rich diets that contain lots of vitamin D—the so-called sun vitamin, which is also plentiful in mackerel, salmon, and fortified milk—significantly reduce the incidence of precancerous growths in the colon. British researchers linked an abundance of vitamin D to fewer fractures in people 65 years and older.

W

WINE Score two more points for red wine. Researchers have long believed that the antioxidants in wine promote heart health. Now they have nosed out a couple more beneficial compounds. The waxy skins of grapes contain chemicals called saponins,

also found in olive oil and soybeans, that researchers believe may lower cholesterol. Grapes, especially those grown in cooler climates, also contain resveratrol, which may play a role in longevity. The chemical has been shown in the lab to prolong the life of yeast by 70%, and it mimics the effects of a low-calorie diet, which can extend life span, at least in rodents, 30% to 50%. Scientists don't know whether resveratrol will turn out to be the fountain of youth for humans, but in the meantime, what better excuse to raise a glass or two of Bordeaux a day?

WRINKLES Move over, Botox. Hyaluronan is the new rejuvenator. Found in the umbilical cord, some bacteria, and the red combs of roosters, hyaluronan reduces inflammation in arthritic knees and prevents scar tissue after surgery. It's also what makes up the gel Restylane, a Medicis product recently approved by the FDA to plump wrinkles around the nose and mouth. (Botox is used to erase crow's-feet, furrowed brows, and other frown lines.) Europeans and Canadians have been using Restylane for years. Another wrinkle buster, Hylaform, manufactured by Genzyme, is awaiting FDA approval.

Z

ZOONOSIS Some infectious diseases, called zoonoses (singular *zoonosis*), routinely leap from animals to humans, often with devastating effects. AIDS and Ebola originated in apes, Creutzfeldt-Jakob in cattle, West Nile in birds, and SARS in a little-known animal called the palm civet. In 2003, the exotic-pet trade took a 3-pound Gambian rat from Africa to Wisconsin, where it infected a prairie dog with monkeypox—the first occurrence in North America. From the prairie dog, it jumped to a human and ultimately to 87 people in six Midwestern states. Increased globalization means these alien diseases are borne around the world with appalling speed. Makes you wonder, What next?

Understanding AIDS

Acquired Immune Deficiency Syndrome, or AIDS, was first reported in mid-1981 in the United States; it is believed to have originated in Sub-Saharan Africa. The human immunodeficiency virus (HIV) that causes AIDS was identified in 1983, and by 1985 tests to detect the virus were available. The credit for discovering the AIDS virus is jointly shared by Dr. Robert Gallo, a researcher at the National Cancer Institute, and Luc Montagnier of the Pasteur Institute, France.

Destruction of Immune System

A fatal and incurable disease caused by HIV, AIDS attacks and destroys the immune system, gradually leaving the individual defenseless against illnesses that lead to death. These illnesses are referred to as "opportunistic" infections or diseases: in AIDS patients the most common are Pneumocystis carinii pneumonia (PCP), a parasitic infection of the lungs, and a type of cancer known as Kaposi's sarcoma (KS). Other opportunistic infections include unusually severe infections with yeast, cytomegalovirus, herpes virus, and parasites such as Toxoplasma or Cryptosporidia. Milder infections with these organisms do not suggest immune deficiencies. Symptoms of full-blown AIDS include a persistent cough, fever, and difficulty in breathing. Multiple purplish blotches and bumps on the skin may indicate Kaposi's sarcoma. The virus can also cause brain damage.

People infected with the virus can have a wide range of symptoms—from none to mild to severe. At least a fourth to a half of those infected with HIV will develop AIDS within four to ten years. Many experts think the percentage will grow much higher.

Transmission

Although the first reported cases involved homosexual men in Los Angeles who were infected through sexual contact, the principal mode of transmission throughout the world is through the exchange of bodily fluids during heterosexual intercourse. According to the World Health Organization, extensive spread of HIV appears to have begun in the late 1970s and early 1980s. It spread in men and women with multiple sexual partners in East and Central Africa and among homosexual and bisexual men in certain urban areas of the Americas, Australasia, and Western Europe.

In addition to sexual contact, AIDS has been spread by intravenous drug users sharing infected hypodermic needles. The virus can also be passed on through transfused blood or its components. It may also be transmitted from infected mother to infant before, during, or shortly after birth.

Two major types of HIV have been recognized, HIV-l and HIV-2. HIV-l is the dominant type worldwide. HIV-2 is found principally in West Africa but cases have been reported in East Africa, Europe, Asia, and Latin America. There are at least ten different genetic subtypes of HIV-l, but their biological and epidemiological significance is unclear at present. Both HIV-l and HIV-2 are transmitted in the same ways.

Pandemic

With no cure at present, prudence could save thousands of people who have yet to be exposed to the virus. Use of condoms lessens the possibility of transmission as does the elimination of sharing hypodermic needles. The fate of many will depend less on science than on the ability of large numbers of human beings to change their behavior in the face of growing danger.

The introduction of highly active antiretroviral therapy in 1996 was a turning point for those with access to sophisticated health-care systems. Although they can't cure HIV/AIDS, antiretrovirals (ARVs) and their use in combination, "cocktails," have dramatically reduced mortality and morbidity and prolonged and improved the lives of sufferers.

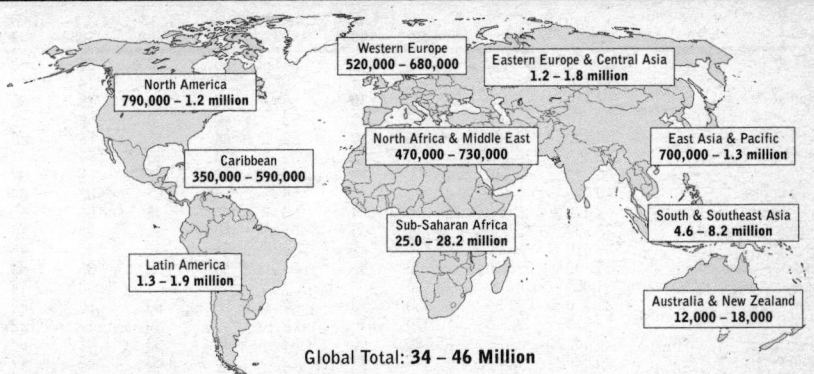

Global Estimates[1] of the HIV/AIDS Epidemic as of End 2003

Western Europe
520,000 – 680,000

Eastern Europe & Central Asia
1.2 – 1.8 million

North America
790,000 – 1.2 million

North Africa & Middle East
470,000 – 730,000

East Asia & Pacific
700,000 – 1.3 million

Caribbean
350,000 – 590,000

Sub-Saharan Africa
25.0 – 28.2 million

South & Southeast Asia
4.6 – 8.2 million

Latin America
1.3 – 1.9 million

Australia & New Zealand
12,000 – 18,000

Global Total: 34 – 46 Million

Note: 1. Number of people currently infected with HIV/AIDS. *Source:* World Health Organization, UNAIDS.

However, 95% of people with HIV/AIDS live in developing countries, where access to these medicines remains unacceptably limited and the costs prohibitively expensive. Progress has recently been made in India, however, as Indian pharmaceutical companies are producing generic versions of ARVs and selling them for less than $1 a day. Officials estimate that about 12,000 Indians are currently taking such medications. Another obstacle is that not everyone can tolerate the potent medications and their side effects. Doctors are also reporting a significant increase of patients with drug-resistant HIV strains. Some 100 separate drugs are either in use or being tested for use against AIDS. Meanwhile, HIV has been spreading, with rising rates of infection in Eastern Europe, Russia, China, and Southeast Asia, prompting some scientists to grimly warn that the epidemic has only just begun.

Status of the World AIDS Epidemic, End of 2003

	Total	Adults	Children under 15 years
People newly infected with HIV in 2003	5 million	4.2 million	700,000
Number of people living with HIV/AIDS	40 million	37 million	2.5 million
AIDS deaths in 2003	3 million	2.5 million	500,000

Source: World Health Organization, UNAIDS. Web: www.unaids.org.

HIV/AIDS Statistics and Features by World Region

World region	Epidemic started	Adults & children living with HIV/AIDS	Adults & children newly infected with HIV	Adult prevalence rate[1]	Adult & child deaths due to AIDS
Sub-Saharan Africa	late '70s– early '80s	25.0–28.2 million	3.0–3.4 million	7.5–8.5%	2.2–2.4 million
North Africa & Middle East	late '80s	470,000–730,000	43,000–67,000	0.2–0.4	35,000–50,000
South & Southeast Asia	late '80s	4.6–8.2 million	610,000–1.1 million	0.4–0.8	330,000–590,000
East Asia & Pacific	late '80s	700,000–1.3 million	150,000–270,000	0.1–0.1	32,000–58,000
Latin America	late '70s– early '80s	1.3–1.9 million	120,000–180,000	0.5–0.7	49,000–70,000
Caribbean	late '70s– early '80s	350,000–590,000	45,000–80,000	1.9–3.1	30,000–50,000
Eastern Europe & Central Asia	early '90s	1.2–1.8 million	180,000–280,000	0.5–0.9	23,000–37,000
Western Europe	late '70s– early '80s	520,000–680,000	30,000–40,000	0.3–0.3	2,600–3,400
North America	late '70s– early '80s	790,000–1.2 million	36,000–54,000	0.5–0.7	12,000–18,000
Australia & New Zealand	late '70s– early '80s	12,000–18,000	700–1,000	0.1–0.1	<100
Total		**34–46 million**	**4.2–5.8 million**	**0.9–1.3%**	**2.5–3.5 million**

As of Dec. 2003. 1. The proportion of adults (15 to 49 years of age) living with HIV/AIDS in 2003, using 2003 population numbers. *Source:* World Health Organization, UNAIDS. Web: www.unaids.org.

Cancer: Estimated New Cases (2004) and Survival Rates in the U.S.

	Estimated new cases, 2004			Five-year relative survival rates[1] (percent)					
				White		Black		All races	
Site	Total	Male	Female	1983– 1985	1992– 1998	1983– 1985	1992– 1998	1983– 1985	1992– 1998
All sites[2]	1,368,030	699,560	668,470	54%	64%	40%	53%	52%	62%
Lung	173,770	93,110	80,660	14	15	11	12	14	15
Breast[3]	217,440	1,450	215,990	79	88	63	73	78	86
Colon	106,370	50,400	55,970	58	63	49	53	58	62
Rectum	40,570	23,220	17,350	56	62	44	53	55	62
Prostate	230,110	230,110	n.a.	76	98	64	93	75	97
Bladder	60,240	44,640	15,600	78	82	60	65	78	82
Uterine corpus	40,320	n.a.	40,320	85	86	54	61	83	84
Non-Hodgkins lymphoma[4]	54,370	28,850	25,520	54	56	45	46	54	55
Oral cavity and pharynx	28,260	18,550	9,710	55	59	35	35	53	56
Leukemia[4]	33,440	19,020	14,420	42	47	34	38	41	46
Melanoma—skin	55,100	29,900	25,200	85	89	74	66	85	89
Pancreas	31,860	15,740	16,120	3	4	5	4	3	4
Kidney	35,710	22,080	13,630	56	62	55	60	56	62
Stomach	22,710	13,640	9,070	16	21	19	20	17	22
Ovary	25,580	n.a.	25,580	40	53	42	53	41	53
Uterine cervix	10,520	n.a.	10,520	71	72	60	60	69	71

NOTE: n.a. = not applicable. 1. The 5-year relative survival rate indicates that a person will not die from causes directly related to their cancer within 5 years. 2. Includes other sites not shown separately. 3. Survival rates for females only. 4. All types combined. *Source:* U.S. National Institutes of Health, National Cancer Institute.

What Is Cancer?

Source: National Cancer Institute.

Cancer is a group of many different diseases that have some important things in common. Cancer affects our cells, the body's basic unit of life.

To understand cancer, it is helpful to know what happens when normal cells become cancerous. Usually, cells grow, divide, and produce more cells as they are needed to keep the body healthy. Sometimes, however, the process goes astray—cells keep dividing when new cells are not needed. The mass of extra cells forms a growth or tumor.

Benign tumors are not cancer. They often can be removed and, in most cases, they do not come back. Cells in benign tumors do not spread to other parts of the body. Most important, benign tumors are rarely a threat to life.

Malignant tumors are cancer. Cells in malignant tumors are abnormal and divide without control or order. These cancer cells can invade and destroy the tissue around them. Cancer cells can also break away from a malignant tumor and enter the bloodstream or lymphatic system (these two networks of vessels carry blood and lymph throughout the body). The process by which cancer spreads from the original tumor to form new tumors in other parts of the body is called metastasis.

America's Best Hospitals, 2004

The annual *U.S. News & World Report* list of the United States' best hospitals is prepared by the National Opinion Research Center at the University of Chicago. The list recognizes hospitals that excel in many specialties.

1. Johns Hopkins Hospital, Baltimore, Md.
2. Mayo Clinic, Rochester, Minn.
3. Massachusetts General Hospital, Boston, Mass.
4. Cleveland Clinic, Cleveland, Ohio
5. UCLA Medical Center, Los Angeles, Calif.
6. Duke University Medical Center, Durham, N.C. (tie)
6. University of California, San Francisco Medical Center, San Francisco, Calif. (tie)
8. Barnes-Jewish Hospital, St. Louis, Mo.
9. New York Presbyterian Hospital, New York, N.Y. (tie)
9. University of Washington Medical Center, Seattle, Wash. (tie)

National Transplant Data

Registered U.S. Patients Waiting for Transplants

Kidney	58,517	Lung	3,940	Heart/Lung	194
Liver	17,458	Kidney/Pancreas	2,447	Intestine	194
Heart	3,498	Pancreas	1,609	**Total patients**	85,788[1]

NOTE: As of June 18, 2004. Patients can be listed with more than one transplant center, thus the number of registrations is greater than the actual number of patients. 1. Some patients are waiting for more than one organ; therefore the total number of patients is less than the sum of patients waiting for each organ. *Source:* United Network for Organ Sharing.

Number of U.S. Transplants Per Year, 1988–2003

	1988	1990	1995	2000	2003		1988	1990	1995	2000	2003
Heart	1,676	2,107	2,355	2,194	2,057	Liver	1,713	2,690	3,931	4,961	5,671
Heart/Lung	74	52	69	48	29	Lung	33	203	872	956	1,085
Intestine	—	5	46	79	116	Pancreas	79	69	107	436	502
Kidney	8,873	9,416	11,054	13,402	15,120	**Total:**					
Kidney/Pancreas	170	459	919	913	871	**All organs**	**12,618**	**15,001**	**19,353**	**22,989**	**25,451**

NOTE: Kidney-pancreas transplants are counted apart from kidney transplants and pancreas transplants and do not show up in the totals for the individual organs. Double kidney, double lung, and heart-lung transplants are each counted as one transplant. All other multi-organ transplants are included in the total for each individual organ. *Source:* National Organ Procurement and Transplantation Network.

Americans Without Health Insurance[1] by Characteristic, 2003

Characteristic	Percent	Characteristic	Percent
Total	**15.6%**	$75,000 or more	8.2%
Race and ethnicity		**Age**	
White	14.6	Under 18 years	11.4
Non-Hispanic	11.1	18 to 24 years	30.2
Black	19.6	25 to 34 years	26.4
Asian and Pacific Islander	18.8	35 to 44 years	18.1
Hispanic[2]	32.7	45 to 64 years	13.9
Household income		65 years and over	0.8
Less than $25,000	24.2	**Nativity**	
$25,000 to $49,999	19.9	Native	13.0
$50,000 to $74,999	12.5	Foreign born	34.5

1. For the entire year. 2. Hispanics may be of any race. *Source:* U.S. Census Bureau, *Current Population Reports, 2002.*

Percent of Americans Without Health Insurance by State, 2002

State	Percent	State	Percent	State	Percent
Alabama	12.7%	Louisiana	18.4%	Oklahoma	17.3%
Alaska	18.7	Maine	11.3	Oregon	14.6
Arizona	16.8	Maryland	13.4	Pennsylvania	11.3
Arkansas	16.3	Massachusetts	9.9	Rhode Island	9.8
California	18.2	Michigan	11.7	South Carolina	12.5
Colorado	16.1	Minnesota	7.9	South Dakota	11.5
Connecticut	10.5	Mississippi	16.7	Tennessee	10.8
Delaware	9.9	Missouri	11.6	Texas	25.8
DC	13.0	Montana	15.3	Utah	13.4
Florida	17.3	Nebraska	10.2	Vermont	10.7
Georgia	16.1	Nevada	19.7	Virginia	13.5
Hawaii	10.0	New Hampshire	9.9	Washington	14.2
Idaho	17.9	New Jersey	13.9	West Virginia	14.6
Illinois	14.1	New Mexico	21.1	Wisconsin	9.8
Indiana	13.1	New York	15.8	Wyoming	17.7
Iowa	9.5	North Carolina	16.8		
Kansas	10.4	North Dakota	10.9	**Total U.S.**	**15.2**
Kentucky	13.6	Ohio	11.9		

NOTE: These estimates should not be used to rank the states. Results from different samplings could easily show different estimates and rankings because of small sampling sizes. *Source:* U.S. Census Bureau, *March 2003, Current Population Survey.*

Sexually Transmitted Diseases (STDs)

More than 25 diseases are spread primarily through sexual activity. The latest estimates indicate that there are 15 million new sexually transmitted disease cases in the United States each year. Approximately one-fourth of these new infections are in teenagers. Nearly two-thirds of all STD cases occur in people younger than 25 years.

Reported Cases of Sexually Transmitted Disease in the U.S., 2002

Disease	Total			Disease	Total		
	Male	Female	Total		Male	Female	Total
Chlamydia	179,585	652,858	834,555	Granuloma Inguinale	7	2	9
Gonorrhea	171,504	179,648	351,852	Lymphogranuloma venereum	17	2	19
Syphilis	20,534	12,271	32,871				
Chancroid	24	42	67				

Source: U.S. Centers for Disease Control and Prevention.

U.S. Abortion Statistics, 1972–2000

	1972	1980	1985	1990	1995	1997	2000
Reported no. legal abortions	586,760	1,297,606	1,328,570	1,429,247	1,210,883	1,186,039	857,475
Abortion ratio[1]	180	359	354	344	311	306	245
Abortion rate[2]	13	25	24	24	20	20	16
Percentage distribution							
Age group (yrs)							
≤19	32.6%	29.2%	26.3%	22.4%	20.1%	20.1%	18.8%
20–24	32.5	35.5	34.7	33.2	32.5	31.7	32.8
≥25	34.9	35.3	39.0	44.4	47.4	48.2	48.4
Marital status							
Married	29.7	23.1	19.3	21.7	19.7	19.0	18.7
Unmarried	70.3	76.9	80.7	78.3	80.3	81.0	81.3

NOTE: The number of areas reporting a given characteristic varied. 1. Number of legal induced abortions per 1,000 live births. 2. Number of legal induced abortions per 1,000 women aged 15–44 years. *Source:* U.S. Centers for Disease Control and Prevention. *Abortion Surveillance: Preliminary Analysis—United States, 2000.*

Abortion Rates in Western Industrialized Countries

Country	Rate per 1,000	Country	Rate per 1,000
United States	21.3	Canada	16.4
Australia	22.2	England & Wales	15.6
Sweden	18.7	Germany	7.6
Denmark	16.5	Holland	6.5

NOTE: 1996 data, except the U.S. (2000 data). *Source:* The Alan Guttmacher Institute and Physicians for Reproductive Choice and Health.

Leading Causes of Mortality Throughout the World, 2002

Rank	Cause	All countries Total deaths (in thousands)	% of total	Rank	Cause	All countries Total deaths (in thousands)	% of total
1.	Ischemic heart disease	7,181	12.6%	10.	Road traffic accidents	1,192	2.1%
2.	Cerebrovascular disease	5,509	9.7	11.	Childhood diseases	1,124	2.0
3.	Lower respiratory infections	3,884	6.8	12.	Other unintentional injuries	923	1.6
4.	HIV/AIDS	2,777	4.9	13.	Hypertensive heart disease	911	1.6
5.	Chronic obstructive pulmonary disease	2,748	4.8	14.	Self-inflicted	873	1.5
6.	Diarrheal diseases	1,798	3.2	15.	Stomach cancer	850	1.5
7.	Tuberculosis	1,566	2.7	16.	Cirrhosis of the liver	786	1.4
8.	Malaria	1,272	2.2	17.	Nephritis/nephrosis	677	1.2
9.	Cancer of trachea/bronchus/ lung	1,243	2.2	18.	Colon/rectum cancer	622	1.1
				19.	Liver cancer	618	1.1
				20.	Measles	611	1.1

Source: The World Health Report, 2003, The World Health Organization (WHO).

Overview of Drug Use in the United States

Source: Substance Abuse and Mental Health Services Administration.

The *National Survey on Drug Use and Health,* an annual survey conducted by the Substance Abuse and Mental Health Services Administration (SAMHSA), estimates the prevalence of illicit drug use in the United States. Some of the more notable statistics from the 2002 study follow.

• An estimated 19.5 million Americans age 12 years or older were current users of illicit drugs in 2002, meaning they used an illicit drug at least once during the 30 days prior to being interviewed. This represents 8.3% of the population 12 years or older. By comparison, in 2001 the survey found that 7.1% of this population were current illicit drug users.

• Marijuana is the most commonly used illicit drug, with 14.6 million users (a rate of 6.2 %). An estimated 2.0 million persons (0.9%) were current cocaine users, 567,000 of whom used crack. Hallucinogens were used by 1.2 million persons, including 676,000 users of Ecstasy. There were an estimated 166,000 current heroin users. An estimated 6.2 million persons, or 2.6% of the population age 12 or older, were current users of psychotherapeutic drugs taken nonmedically. In 2002, approximately 1.9 million persons aged 12 or older had used Oxy-Contin nonmedically at least once in their lifetime.

• Among youths aged 12 to 17, 11.6% were current illicit drug users. The rate of use was highest among young adults (18 to 25 years) at 20.2%. Among adults aged 26 or older, 5.8% reported current illicit drug use.

• The rates of current illicit drug use were highest among American Indians/Alaska Natives (10.1%) and persons reporting two or more races (11.4%). Rates were 9.7% for blacks, 8.5% for whites, and 7.2% for Hispanics. Asians had the lowest rate at 3.5%.

• An estimated 17.4% of unemployed adults aged 18 or older were current illicit drug users in 2002 compared with 8.2% of those employed full time and 10.5% of those employed part time. However, most drug users were employed. Of the 16.6 million illicit drug users aged 18 or older in 2002, 12.4 million (74.6%) were employed either full or part time.

• In 2002, an estimated 11.0 million persons reported driving under the influence of an illicit drug during the past year. This corresponds to 4.7% of the population aged 12 or older. The rate was 10% or greater for each age from 17 to 25, with 21 year olds reporting the highest rate of any age (18.0%). Among adults aged 26 or older, the rate was 3.0%.

Drug Use by Americans, 12 Years and Older

Type of drug	Ever used 1979	1990	2000	2002	Current user 1979	1990	2000	2002
Any illicit drug[1]	n.a.	n.a.	38.9%	46.0%	n.a.	n.a.	6.3 %	8.3%
Marijuana and hashish	27.9 %	30.5 %	34.2	40.4	13.2 %	5.4%	4.8	6.2
Cocaine	8.6	11.2	11.2	14.4	2.6	0.9	0.5	0.9
Crack	n.a.	n.a.	2.4	3.6	n.a.	n.a.	0.1	0.2
Hallucinogens	8.9	7.9	11.7	14.6	1.9	0.4	0.4	0.5
LSD	n.a.	n.a.	8.8	10.4	n.a.	n.a.	0.2	0.0
PCP	n.a.	n.a.	2.6	3.2	n.a.	n.a.	0.0	0.0
Ecstasy	n.a.	n.a.	2.9	4.3	n.a.	n.a.	n.a.	0.3
Heroin	1.3	0.8	1.2	1.6	0.1	n.a.	0.1	0.1
Stimulants[2]	n.a.	5.5	6.6	9.0	n.a.	0.6	0.4	0.5
Methamphetamine	n.a.	n.a.	4.0	5.3	n.a.	n.a.	0.2	0.3
Sedatives[2]	n.a.	2.8	3.2	4.2	n.a.	0.2	0.1	0.2
Tranquilizers[2]	n.a.	4.0	5.8	8.2	n.a.	0.6	0.4	0.8

NOTE: Current users are those who used drugs at least once within month prior to this study. n.a. = not available. 1. Any illicit drug indicates use at least once of marijuana/hashish, cocaine (including crack), heroin, hallucinogens (including LSD and PCP), inhalants, or any prescription-type psychotherapeutic used nonmedically. 2. Nonmedical use; does not include over-the-counter drugs. *Source:* U.S. Substance Abuse and Mental Health Services Administration (SAMHSA), Office of Applied Studies, *National Survey on Drug Use and Health, 2002.*

Alcohol Use, Binge Alcohol Use, and Heavy Alcohol Use in the Past Month, by Demographic Characteristics, 2002

Characteristic	Type of alcohol use			Characteristic	Type of alcohol use		
	Any alcohol use	Binge alcohol use	Heavy alcohol use		Any alcohol use	Binge alcohol use	Heavy alcohol use
Age				Black or African American	39.9%	21.0%	4.4%
12–17	17.6%	10.7%	2.5%	American Indian or Alaska Native	44.7	27.9	8.7
18–25	60.5	40.9	14.9	Native Hawaiian or other Pacific Islander	—	25.2	8.3
26 or older	53.9	21.4	5.9				
Gender				Asian	37.1	12.4	2.6
Male	57.4	31.2	10.8	Two or more races	49.9	19.8	7.5
Female	44.9	15.1	3.0	Hispanic or Latino	42.8	24.8	5.9
Hispanic origin and race				**Total**	**51.0**	**22.9**	**6.7**
Not Hispanic or Latino	52.1	22.6	6.9				
White	55.0	23.4	7.5				

Source: SAMHSA, Office of Applied Studies, *National Survey on Drug Use and Health, 2002.*

Smoking Prevalence Among U.S. Adults, 1965–2000
(as a percent of population, 18 years of age and older)

Year	Overall population	Males	Females	White male	Black male	White female	Black female
1965	41.9%	51.2%	33.7%	50.4%	58.8%	33.9%	31.8%
1985	29.9	32.2	27.9	31.3	40.2	27.9	30.9
1990	25.3	28.0	22.9	27.6	32.8	23.5	20.8
1995	24.6	26.5	22.7	26.2	29.4	23.4	23.5
2000	23.1	25.2	21.1	25.5	25.7	22.0	20.7

Source: *Health, United States, 2002*, U.S. Centers for Disease Control and Prevention.

Cigarette Use Among Americans by Characteristics, 2002

Characteristic	Time Period			Characteristic	Time Period		
	Lifetime	Past year	Past month		Lifetime	Past year	Past month
Age				American Indian or Alaska Native	79.9%	45.1%	37.1%
12–17	33.3%	20.3%	13.0%	Native Hawaiian or other Pacific Islander	—	—	—
18–25	71.2	49.0	40.8				
26 or older	73.7	28.5	25.2	Asian	46.4	21.6	17.7
Gender				Two or more races	74.5	38.8	35.0
Male	73.8	33.3	28.7	Hispanic or Latino	57.1	28.5	23.0
Female	64.8	27.6	23.4	**Total**	**69.1**	**30.3**	**26.0**
Hispanic origin and race							
Not Hispanic or Latino	70.8	30.6	26.4				
White	74.0	31.0	26.9				
Black or African American	58.7	29.4	25.3				

Source: SAMHSA, Office of Applied Studies, *National Survey on Drug Use and Health, 2002.*

Blood Pressure Explained

Blood pressure is the force of blood against the walls of arteries. Blood pressure is recorded as two numbers—the systolic pressure (as the heart beats) over the diastolic pressure (as the heart relaxes between beats). The measurement is written with one above or before the other, with the systolic number on top and the diastolic number on the bottom. For example, a blood pressure measurement of 120/80 mm Hg (millimeters of mercury) is expressed verbally as "120 over 80."

Normal blood pressure is less than 120 mm Hg systolic and less than 80 mm Hg diastolic.

When systolic and diastolic blood pressures fall into different categories, the higher category should be used to classify blood pressure level. For example, 160/80 mm Hg would be stage 2 hypertension (high blood pressure).

Category	Blood pressure level (mm Hg)	
	Systolic	Diastolic
Normal	< 120	< 80
Prehypertension	120–139	80–89
High Blood Pressure		
Stage 1 hypertension	140–159	90–99
Stage 2 hypertension	≥160	≥100

NOTE: < means less than; ≥ means greater than or equal to. Source: National Heart, Lung, and Blood Institute.

Blood Types

Human blood is grouped into four types: A, B, AB, and O. Each letter refers to a kind of antigen, or protein, on the surface of red blood cells. For example, the surface of red blood cells in Type A blood has antigens known as A-antigens.

Each blood type is also grouped by its Rhesus factor, or Rh factor. Blood is either Rh positive (Rh+) or Rh negative (Rh-). About 85% of Americans have Rh+ blood.

Rhesus refers to another type of antigen, or protein, on the surface of red blood cells. The name Rhesus comes from Rhesus monkeys, in which the protein was discovered.

Blood types become very important when a blood transfusion is necessary. In a blood transfusion, a patient must receive a blood type that is compatible with his or her own blood type—that is, the donated blood must be accepted by the patient's own blood. If the blood types are not compatible, red blood cells will clump together, making clots that can block blood vessels and cause death.

Type O- blood is considered the "universal donor" because it can be donated to people of any blood type. Type AB+ blood is considered the "universal recipient" because people with this type can receive any blood type.

Blood type	Percent of Americans with this type	Who can receive this type
O+	37%	O+, A+, B+, AB+
O-	6	All blood types
A+	34	A+, AB+
A-	6	A+, A-, AB+, AB-
B+	10	B+, AB+
B-	2	B+, B-, AB+, AB-
AB+	4	AB+
AB-	1	AB+, AB-

Percentage of U.S. Adults Engaging in Leisure Time Physical Activity, 2001

Characteristic	Persons who meet recommended activity[1]	Persons with insufficient activity[2]	Characteristic	Persons who meet recommended activity[1]	Persons with insufficient activity[2]
Total	45.4%	54.6%	30 to 44 years old	46.5%	53.5%
Male	47.9	52.1	45 to 64 years old	40.7	59.3
Female	43.0	57.0	65 to 74 years old	36.1	63.9
White, non-Hispanic	48.2	51.8	75 years old and over	26.9	73.1
Black, non-Hispanic	35.3	64.7	**School years completed**		
Hispanic	38.3	61.7	Less than 12 years	34.5	65.5
Other	42.2	57.8	12 years	43.0	57.0
Males			Some college	47.0	53.0
18 to 29 years old	57.8	42.2	College	50.9	49.1
30 to 44 years old	48.3	51.7	**Household income**		
45 to 64 years old	43.4	56.6	Less than $10,000	35.4	64.6
65 to 74 years old	45.7	54.3	$10,000 to $19,999	36.8	63.2
75 years old and over	38.4	61.6	$20,000 to $34,999	42.7	57.3
Females			$35,000 to $49,999	47.7	52.3
18 to 29 years old	49.8	50.2	$50,000 and over	52.0	48.0

NOTE: Covers persons 18 years old and over. 1. Recommended activity is physical activity at least 5 times a week for 30 minutes at a time or vigorous physical activity for 20 minutes at a time at least 3 times a week. 2. Persons whose reported physical activity does not meet recommended level. *Source:* U.S. National Center for Chronic Disease Prevention and Health Promotion, "Nutrition and Physical Activity," and unpublished data. From *Statistical Abstract of the United States, 2003.*

Physical Activity Levels Among American Children Ages 9–13, 2002

Characteristic	Percent participated in organized physical activity	Percent participated in free-time physical activity	Characteristic	Percent participated in organized physical activity	Percent participated in free-time physical activity
Total	38.5%	77.4%	Race/ethnicity		
Sex			Black, non-Hispanic	24.1%	74.7%
Female	38.6	74.1	Hispanic	25.9	74.6
Male	38.3	80.5	White, non-Hispanic	46.6	79.3
Age			Parental education		
9	36.1	75.8	<High school	19.4	75.3
10	37.5	77.0	High school	28.3	75.4
11	43.1	78.9	>High school	46.8	78.7
12	37.7	77.5	Parental income		
13	38.1	78.0	≤$25,000	23.5	74.1
			$25,001–$50,000	32.8	78.6
			>$50,000	49.1	78.3

Source: U.S. Centers for Disease Control and Prevention.

Measuring Body Mass

Body mass index (BMI) is measure of body fat based on height and weight that applies to both adult men and adult women. To determine BMI, weight in kilograms is divided by height in meters, squared. To calculate your body mass index from the table below, locate your height in inches in the left-hand column, then follow it across until you locate your weight; the number at the very top is your body mass index. A BMI of less than 18.5 is considered underweight, 18.5 to 24.9 is considered normal weight, 25 to 29.9 is considered overweight, and one of 30 or above is considered obese.

Body Mass Index Chart

Height (inches)	19	20	21	22	23	24	25	26	27	28	29	30	31	32	33	34	35
	\<--							Body weight (pounds)								-->	
58	91	96	100	105	110	115	119	124	129	134	138	143	148	153	158	162	167
59	94	99	104	109	114	119	124	128	133	138	143	148	153	158	163	168	173
60	97	102	107	112	118	123	128	133	138	143	148	153	158	163	168	174	179
61	100	106	111	116	122	127	132	137	143	148	153	158	164	169	174	180	185
62	104	109	115	120	126	131	136	142	147	153	158	164	169	175	180	186	191
63	107	113	118	124	130	135	141	146	152	158	163	169	175	180	186	191	197
64	110	116	122	128	134	140	145	151	157	163	169	174	180	186	192	197	204
65	114	120	126	132	138	144	150	156	162	168	174	180	186	192	198	204	210
66	118	124	130	136	142	148	155	161	167	173	179	186	192	198	204	210	216
67	121	127	134	140	146	153	159	166	172	178	185	191	198	204	211	217	223
68	125	131	138	144	151	158	164	171	177	184	190	197	203	210	216	223	230
69	128	135	142	149	155	162	169	176	182	189	196	203	209	216	223	230	236
70	132	139	146	153	160	167	174	181	188	195	202	209	216	222	229	236	243
71	136	143	150	157	165	172	179	186	193	200	208	215	222	229	236	243	250
72	140	147	154	162	169	177	184	191	199	206	213	221	228	235	242	250	258
73	144	151	159	166	174	182	189	197	204	212	219	227	235	242	250	257	265
74	148	155	163	171	179	186	194	202	210	218	225	233	241	249	256	264	272
75	152	160	168	176	184	192	200	208	216	224	232	240	248	256	264	272	279
76	156	164	172	180	189	197	205	213	221	230	238	246	254	263	271	279	287

Source: National Heart, Lung, and Blood Institute.

Recommended Daily Fat Intake

Total calories per day	Saturated fat in grams	Total fat in grams	Total calories per day	Saturated fat in grams	Total fat in grams
1,600	18 or less	53	2,500[1]	25 or less	80
2,000[1]	20 or less	65	2,800	31 or less	93
2,200	24 or less	73			

1. Percent daily values on nutrition facts labels are based on a 2,000 calorie diet. Values for 2,000 and 2,500 calories are rounded to the nearest 5 grams to be consistent with the nutrition facts label. Source: Dietary Guidelines for Americans, 2000.

National Health Expenditures According to Type of Expenditure, 1960–2001

Type of expenditure	1960	1970	1980	1990	2000	2001
National health expenditures	$26.7	$73.1	$245.8	$696.0	$1,310.0	$1,424.5
Health services and supplies	25.0	67.3	233.5	669.6	1,262.3	1,372.6
Personal health care	23.4	63.2	214.6	609.4	1,137.6	1,236.4
Hospital care	9.2	27.6	101.5	253.9	416.5	451.2
Professional services	8.3	20.7	67.3	216.9	425.0	462.4
Physician and clinical services	5.4	14.0	47.1	157.5	288.8	313.6
Other professional services	0.4	0.7	3.6	18.2	38.8	42.3
Dental services	2.0	4.7	13.3	31.5	60.7	65.6
Other personal health care	0.6	1.3	3.3	9.6	36.7	40.9
Nursing home and home health	0.9	4.4	20.1	65.3	125.5	132.1
Home health care	0.1	0.2	2.4	12.6	31.7	33.2
Nursing home care	0.8	4.2	17.7	52.7	93.8	98.9
Retail outlet sales of medical products	5.0	10.5	25.7	73.3	170.5	190.7
Prescription drugs	2.7	5.5	12.0	40.3	121.5	140.6
Other medical products	2.3	5.0	13.7	33.1	48.9	50.1
Government administration and net cost of private health insurance	1.2	2.8	12.1	40.0	80.7	89.7
Government public health activities	0.4	1.4	6.7	20.2	44.1	46.4
Investment	1.7	5.7	12.3	26.4	47.7	52.0
Research	0.7	2.0	5.5	12.7	29.1	32.8
Construction	1.0	3.8	6.8	13.7	18.6	19.2

Source: Health, United States, 2003, U.S. Centers for Disease Control and Prevention.

Life-Saving Skills Summary

Skill	Adult (9 years and older)	Child (1 to 8 years)	Infant (birth to 1 year)
Rescue breathing (used when victim is not breathing)	Give 1 slow breath about every 5 seconds; about 1½ seconds per breath; 1 minute = about 10 to 12 breaths	Give 1 slow breath about every 3 seconds; about 1½ seconds per breath; 1 minute = about 20 breaths	Give 1 slow breath about every 3 seconds; about 1½ seconds per breath; 1 minute = about 20 breaths
CPR (used if victim is not breathing *and* does not have a heartbeat)	Depth of compression is about 2 inches; compressions are performed with both hands; complete 15 compressions in about 10 seconds; do cycles of 15 compressions and 2 breaths	Depth of compression is about 1½ inches; compressions are performed with 1 hand; complete 5 compressions in about 3 seconds; do cycles of 5 compressions and 1 breath	Depth of compression is about 1 inch; compressions are performed with 2 fingers; complete 5 compressions in about 3 seconds; do cycles of 5 compressions and 1 breath
Choking (conscious)	Determine if person is choking; stand behind person and deliver abdominal thrusts; repeat until object is expelled or victim loses consciousness	Determine if child is choking; stand or kneel behind child and deliver abdominal thrusts; repeat until object is expelled or child loses consciousness	Determine if infant is choking; give 5 back blows; give 5 chest thrusts; repeat until object is expelled or infant loses consciousness
Choking (unconscious)	Give 2 slow breaths; retilt head and give 2 slow breaths; give up to 5 abdominal thrusts; do finger sweep; give 2 slow breaths; repeat abdominal thrusts, finger sweep, and 2 slow breaths	Give 2 slow breaths; retilt head and give 2 slow breaths; give up to 5 abdominal thrusts; check for object in throat; do finger sweep if object is visible; give 2 slow breaths; repeat abdominal thrusts, foreign-body check/finger sweep, and 2 slow breaths	Give 2 slow breaths; retilt head and give 2 slow breaths; give 5 back blows; give 5 chest thrusts; check for object in throat; do finger sweep if object is visible; repeat back blows, chest thrusts, foreign-body check/finger sweep, and 2 slow breaths

Rescue Breathing

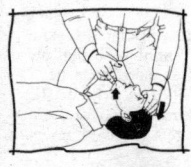

1. With head tilted back, pinch nose shut.

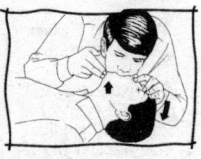

2. ADULT: Give 1 slow breath about every 5 seconds.

CHILD/INFANT: Give 1 slow breath about every 3 seconds.

CPR (Adult)

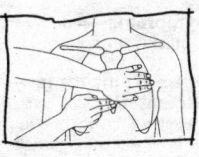

1. Find hand position.

2. Position shoulders over hands. Compress chest 15 times.

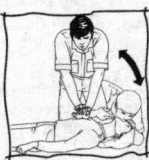

3. Give 2 slow breaths. Recheck pulse and breathing. If no pulse, continue sets of 15 compressions and 2 breaths.

Choking

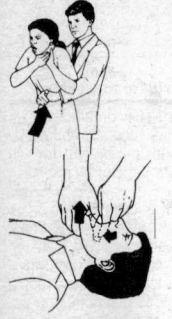

If conscious but choking, give abdominal thrusts until object comes out.

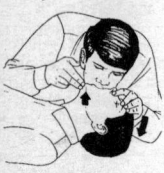

If a person becomes unconscious:

Step 1. Clear any object from mouth.

Step 2. Give 2 slow breaths.

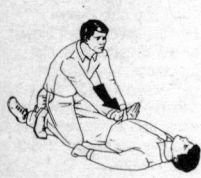

If air won't go in, give up to 5 abdominal thrusts.

Other Emergencies

Burns

First Degree: Signs/Symptoms—reddened skin. **Treatment**—Immerse quickly in cold water or apply ice until pain stops.

Second Degree: Signs/Symptoms—reddened skin, blisters. **Treatment**—(1) Cut away loose clothing. (2) Cover with several layers of cold moist dressings or, if limb is involved, immerse in cold water for relief of pain. (3) Treat for shock.

Third Degree: Signs/Symptoms—skin destroyed, tissues damaged, charring. **Treatment**—(1) Cut away loose clothing (do not remove clothing adhered to skin). (2) Cover with several layers of sterile, cold, moist dressings for relief of pain and to stop burning action. (3) Treat for shock.

Poisons

Treatment—(1) Dilute by drinking large quantities of water. (2) Induce vomiting except when poison is corrosive or a petroleum product. (3) Call the poison-control center or a doctor.

Shock

Shock may accompany any serious injury: blood loss, breathing impairment, heart failure, burns. Shock can kill—treat as soon as possible and continue until medical aid is available.

Signs/Symptoms—(1) Shallow breathing. (2) Rapid and weak pulse. (3) Nausea, collapse, vomiting. (4) Shivering. (5) Pale, moist skin. (6) Mental confusion. (7) Drooping eyelids, dilated pupils.

Treatment—(1) Establish and maintain an open airway. (2) Control bleeding. (3) Keep victim lying down. Exception: Head and chest injuries, heart attack, stroke, sun stroke. If no spine injury, victim may be more comfortable and breathe better in a semi-reclining position. If in doubt, keep the victim flat. Elevate the feet unless injury would be aggravated. Maintain normal body temperature. Place blankets under and over victim.

Frostbite

Most frequently frostbitten: toes, fingers, nose, and ears. It is caused by exposure to cold.

Signs/Symptoms—(1) Skin becomes pale or a grayish-yellow color. (2) Parts feel cold and numb. (3) Frozen parts feel doughy.

Treatment—(1) Victim should be wrapped in woolen cloth and kept dry. (2) Do not rub, chafe, or manipulate frostbitten parts. (3) Bring victim indoors. (4) Place affected parts in warm water (102°F to 105°F) and make sure water remains warm. Never thaw if the victim has to go back out into the cold, which may cause the affected area to be refrozen. (5) Do not use hot water bottles or a heat lamp, and do not place victim near a hot stove. (6) For serious frostbite, seek medical aid for thawing because pain will be intense and tissue damage extensive.

Heat Cramps

Affects people who work or do strenuous exercises in a hot environment. To prevent it, such people should drink large amounts of cool water and add a pinch of salt to each glass of water.

Signs/Symptoms—(1) Painful muscle cramps in legs and abdomen. (2) Faintness. (3) Profuse perspiration.

Treatment—(1) Move victim to a cool place. (2) Give victim sips of salted drinking water (one teaspoon of salt to one quart of water). (3) Apply manual pressure to the cramped muscle.

Heat Exhaustion

Signs/Symptoms—(1) Pale and clammy skin. (2) Profuse perspiration. (3) Rapid and shallow breathing. (4) Weakness, dizziness, and headache.

Treatment—(1) Care for victim as if he or she were in shock. (2) Remove victim to a cool area, do not allow chilling. (3) If body gets too cold, cover victim.

Heat Stroke

Signs/Symptoms—(1) Face is red and flushed. (2) Victim becomes rapidly unconscious. (3) Skin is hot and dry with no perspiration.

Treatment—(1) Lay victim down with head and shoulders raised. (2) Reduce the high body temperature as quickly as possible. (3) Apply cold applications to the body and head. (4) Use ice and fan if available. (5) Watch for signs of shock and treat accordingly. (6) Get medical aid as soon as possible.

The Revolution in Radio

Don't touch that dial! Online and satellite stations are finally starting to chip away at the dominance of AM/FM broadcast "McRadio"

By DAREN FONDA TIME

Bill and Rebecca Goldsmith are making a living from an idea that would probably get you laughed out of business school: running an Internet radio station commercial free. From their home in Paradise, Calif., in the foothills of the Sierra Nevada, they operate Radioparadise.com, a format-busting station that spins a tasteful mix of music ranging from the Beatles to Norah Jones to the Strokes. Fewer than 5,000 listeners tune in during peak times, but fans like it so much, they sent the couple $120,000 in contributions in 2003, covering the cost of bandwidth, song royalties, and other expenses and leaving enough to support a "comfortable lifestyle," says Bill Goldsmith, who quit a 30-year career in FM radio to run and DJ his homegrown version.

Tuning Out Broadcast Radio

If you can't bear another spin of Britney Spears, you're one of the reasons that stations like Radioparadise are beginning to prosper. After years of unmet promise, online stations are building audiences even as regular radio struggles through a decade-long slump (time spent listening is down 14% since 1994, according to the ratings firm Arbitron). Critics say industry consolidation has turned AM/FM stations into McRadio: nationally uniform, repetitive, and clogged with ads and promos. But scores of high-quality alternatives are now competing for your ears (and dollars).

Just a few years ago, online radio heads were mainly tech geeks willing to put up with patchy, low-quality sound. These days about 19 million people listen to online radio at least once a week, up from 7 million in 2000, according to Arbitron. Online listenership is growing at an average 43% a year as more people get broadband connections at home and tune in for content that's unavailable or in short supply on commercial stations, from blues to folk to Al Franken's new liberal Air America network, which is broadcast in just a few markets on the AM/FM dial but was streamed 2 million times in its first week, according to its exclusive webcaster, RealNetworks. "People are fed up with terrestrial radio," says Dave Goldberg, who oversees Yahoo's music site and radio network, Launchcast, which draws 1 million listeners a week.

So far, digital radio's growth isn't hurting big radio empires such as Clear Channel. With 1,213 stations and roughly a 30% ratings share in markets such as Phoenix, Ariz., and Milwaukee, Wis., Clear Channel had a record 2003: revenues of $8.9 billion and a net income of $1.1 billion. But listeners are

clearly spending less time with terrestrial radio. One cause may simply be more media competition, from DVDs to video games to an expanding universe of digital TV. But critics of the radio industry say consolidation is partly to blame too. They claim Clear Channel and other big groups have ruined the airwaves by homogenizing song lists, politicizing the dial with conservative talk, and sucking out local flavor with voice-tracking technology, which enables DJs to sound like local talent even if they're a thousand miles away. Clear Channel contends that its cost-cutting measures have saved hundreds of stations from bankruptcy and that it's the programming's popularity, reflected in ratings, that ultimately drives the business.

Seeking New Music

Nonetheless, teenagers and young adults are increasingly going online to find new music (not just file-sharing networks), particularly alternative content that rarely gets airplay on the commercial FM dial. About 13% of Americans ages 12 to 24 now listen to online radio on a weekly basis, up from 6% of that age group in 2001, according to Edison Media Research/Arbitron. With 185 stations, AOL's radio network, which, like TIME, is part of Time Warner, draws a weekly listenership of 1.5 million (by that measure, Arbitron notes, it's the nation's largest online network). Advertising remains tiny, but that may change. Ronning Lipset, an upstart Internet-radio ad firm in New York City, recently started packaging AOL, Live365.com, MSN, and Yahoo into a kind of national network, which has a combined audience of at least 250,000 listeners in a quarter hour, the minimum needed to appeal to national-media planners.

For now the AM/FM industry doesn't seem too concerned. Arbitron estimates that 228 million Americans ages 12 and up still listen to broadcast radio weekly, and radio remains the top broadcast medium after TV for advertisers who want to reach a mass market. Radio ad sales in Arbitron markets are forecast to rise 5.5% in 2004, to $14 billion, according to BIA Financial Network, a media consultancy in Chantilly, Va. Yet as more consumers tune to stations like Radioparadise, those numbers could slip. Goldsmith's thoughtful playlists are organized by musical theme, moving from, say, a bluesy Tracy Chapman tune to a Latin-blues Carlos Santana track to a rock-blues number by the Hellecasters. He heeds listener feedback and says the only thing he really cares about is "playing good music," regardless of whether it's a hot single being pitched by a promoter or a classic. That's why his fans are pulling out their wallets to support him. □

Composition of Home Broadband Market

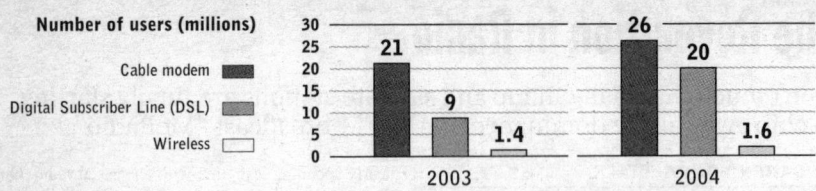

Source: Pew Internet & American Life Project. http://www.pewinternet.org/reports/pdfs/PIP_Broadband04.DataMemo.pdf.

Internet Access and Usage in the U.S.

	Total adults	Any online/ Internet usage[1]	Have Internet access			Used the Internet in past 30 days		
			Home/ work/ other	Home	Work	Home/ work/ other	Home	Work
Total adults (thousands)	211,845	133,673	168,448	130,617	73,805	130,228	109,755	61,752
Percent	100.0%	100.0%	100.0%	100.0%	100.0%	100.0%	100.0%	100.0%
Men	48.0%	48.3%	48.3%	49.4%	50.7%	48.3%	48.9%	50.5%
Women	52.0	51.7	51.7	50.6	49.3	51.7	51.1	49.5
Education								
Graduated college plus	24.5	35.3	29.6	34.3	46.1	35.9	38.2	50.2
Attended college	27.0	33.4	30.7	31.8	31.8	33.6	33.2	31.5
Did not attend college	48.5	31.3	39.7	33.9	22.2	30.5	28.6	18.3
Age								
Age 18–34	31.4	36.9	34.0	32.1	33.2	37.1	34.4	33.4
Age 35–54	39.8	45.5	42.8	46.1	53.6	45.7	47.2	54.1
Age 55+	28.7	17.6	23.2	21.8	13.2	17.2	18.3	12.4
Employment								
Employed full time	52.9	63.6	58.8	61.0	87.8	63.9	62.9	89.4
Employed part-time	10.9	12.5	12.0	12.3	11.7	12.5	13.0	10.2
Occupation								
Professional	10.4	15.6	13.0	15.0	24.5	15.9	16.8	25.4
Exec./manager/administrator	9.8	14.2	11.9	13.5	23.1	14.4	14.7	25.7
Clerical/sales/technical	18.2	24.0	21.3	21.9	33.2	24.3	23.2	34.1
Precision/crafts/repair	6.8	6.3	6.8	6.7	6.5	6.2	6.2	5.4
Household income								
$150,000 or more	6.7	9.5	8.2	10.1	12.7	9.7	10.7	14.0
$75,000–149,999	24.1	33.0	28.9	33.8	41.0	33.3	35.8	42.9
$50,000–74,999	20.3	24.1	22.9	24.3	24.4	24.2	24.2	24.0
Less than $50,000	49.0	33.4	40.0	31.8	22.0	32.8	29.3	19.2

1. Any online/Internet usage is a net of those who looked at or used the Internet or any online service at home, work, or another place in the last 30 days. *Source:* MRI CyberStats, spring 2004.

Where Americans Use the Internet

Home only	36%	Work only	7%
Home and work	34%	Another place only	3%
Home and another place other than work	10%	Work and another place other than home	2%
Home and work and another place	8%		

Margin of error is ±2%. *Source:* Pew Internet & American Life Project tracking survey, May–October 2002.

Top Email Services (U.S.)

Brand or channel	Unique audience (thousands)	Active reach (percent)	Brand or channel	Unique audience (thousands)	Active reach (percent)
Yahoo! Mail	39,841	25.98%	IncrediMail	2,175	1.42%
MSN Hotmail	34,646	22.59	Netscape Web Mail	2,111	1.38
AOL Email	29,548	19.27			

Source: Nielsen//NetRatings, April 2004.

Top Domains/Websites

	Unique visitors[1] (thousands)		Unique visitors[1] (thousands)
Total Internet audience	155,130	The Weather Channel	23,907
Yahoo! sites	113,190	Walt Disney Internet Group (WDIG)	23,542
Time Warner Network	111,750	Real.com Network	22,713
MSN-Microsoft sites	110,121	Symantec	21,422
Google sites	65,996	Monster	20,107
eBay	60,106	Shopping.com sites	19,643
Amazon sites	39,083	Expedia Travel	17,696
Terra Lycos	38,390	SBC Communications	17,366
About/Primedia	38,263	Gorilla Nation Media	17,255
Excite Network	29,047	Ask Jeeves	17,247
Viacom Online	28,020	iVillage.com	17,082
Verizon Communications Corporation	24,135	AT&T Properties	16,929
CNET Networks	24,041	EA Online	16,618

NOTE: Audience: All persons at U.S. home/work/college/university locations. 1. Unique visitors over one-month period, April 2004. *Source:* comScore Media Metrix (comScore Media Metrix is a division of comScore Networks, Inc.).

Top General News Sites

	Unique visitors[1] (thousands)		Unique visitors[1] (thousands)
Total Internet audience	155,130	BBC sites	7,251
General News category	85,316	IBS Network	6,757
Yahoo! News	22,272	Discovery.com sites	5,994
AOL News	21,876	Tribune Newspapers	5,928
CNN	20,458	Google News	5,238
MSNBC	19,162	ABCNews Digital	4,868
New York Times Digital	9,451	FoxNews.com	3,425
Knight Ridder Digital	7,823	Advance Publications, Inc	3,220
USAToday sites	7,260		

NOTE: Audience: All persons at U.S. home/work/college/university locations. 1. Unique visitors over one-month period, April 2004. *Source:* comScore Media Metrix (comScore Media Metrix is a division of comScore Networks, Inc.).

Top Travel Sites

	Unique visitors[1] (thousands)		Unique visitors[1] (thousands)
Total Internet audience	155,130	Priceline.com	6,924
Travel category	63,104	Hotwire.com	6,452
Expedia Travel	17,696	TripAdvisor.com	5,487
Orbitz.com	13,768	Yahoo! Travel	5,345
Trip Network, Inc.	12,027	Delta Airlines	4,597
Travelocity	11,739	American Airlines	4,399
Southwest.com	7,308	NWA.com	3,279
AOL Travel	7,183	Travelzoo sites	3,261
Hotels.com sites	7,085		

NOTE: Audience: All persons at U.S. home/work/college/university locations. 1. Unique visitors over one-month period, April 2004. *Source:* comScore Media Metrix (comScore Media Metrix is a division of comScore Networks, Inc.).

Top Entertainment Sites

	Unique visitors[1] (thousands)		Unique visitors[1] (thousands)
Total Internet audience	155,130	MSN Entertainment	12,896
Entertainment category	121,300	Disney Online	12,071
Viacom Online	28,020	LAUNCH	10,897
WindowsMedia	23,952	Ticketmaster	10,098
Real.com Network	22,713	IMDB.com	9,438
AOL Entertainment	19,917	UGO Networks	9,207
Gorilla Nation Media	17,255	Yahoo! Movies	8,360
Sony Online	13,993	IGN/Gamespy	7,799
eUniverse Network	13,569		

NOTE: Audience: All persons at U.S. home/work/college/university locations. 1. Unique visitors over one-month period, April 2004. *Source:* comScore Media Metrix (comScore Media Metrix is a division of comScore Networks, Inc.).

Top 10 U.S. Internet Advertisers

Advertisers	Impressions[1,2] (thousands)	Advertisers	Impressions[1,2] (thousands)
1. AT&T Wireless Services, Inc.	3,579,859	6. YourGiftCards.com	1,526,920
2. Netflix, Inc.	2,309,323	7. Classmates Online, Inc.	1,350,187
3. InterActiveCorp	1,981,797	8. LowerMyBills.com, Inc.	1,341,842
4. Fun Web Products	1,719,080	9. Ameritrade Holding Corporation	1,185,234
5. Dell Computer Corporation	1,615,837	10. Scottrade, Inc.	1,174,168

1. Impressions reported exclude house ads, which are ads that run on an advertiser's own Web property. 2. Unique visitors over one-month period, April 2004. *Source:* Nielsen//NetRatings AdRelevance, April 2004.

Top Search Engines

		Unique audience[1] (thousands)	Active reach (percent)			Unique audience[1] (thousands)	Active reach (percent)
1.	Google	65,379	42.63%	4.	AOL Search	21,204	13.83%
2.	Yahoo! Search[2]	46,292	30.18	5.	Ask Jeeves	12,943	8.44
3.	MSN Search[2]	43,983	28.68				

1. Unique visitors over one-month period, April 2004. 2. Domain AutoSearch error pages have been removed from the rankings for MSN Search and Yahoo! Search. The sites in the above table that do not exclude Domain AutoSearch error pages consequently reflect higher audience traffic. *Source:* Nielsen//Net Ratings NetView, April 2004.

How Internet Access Has Changed

	2000	2002		2000	2002
Men	51%	60%	**Household income**		
Women	46	56	< $30,000	31%	38%
			$30,000–$50,000	52	65
Race/Ethnicity[1]			$50,000–$75,000	67	74
Whites	50%	60%	$75,000+	78	86
Blacks	34	45	**Education**		
Hispanics	43	54	Did not graduate from high school	17%	23%
			High school grad	34	45
Age			Some college	63	72
18–29	69%	74%	College plus	75	82
30–49	60	67	**Community type**		
50–64	45	52	Rural	43%	49%
65+	14	18	Suburban	54	63
			Urban	53	58

Margin of error is ±2.5% for 2000 and ±2% for 2002. *Source:* Pew Internet & American Life Project tracking survey, April 2000 and March–May 2002. 1. The 2000 numbers for the race category are based on the March, April, and May–June 2000 data sets. Margin of error is ±1%.

Internet Activities

	Activity	Percent of those with Internet access
1.	Send email	91%
2.	Use a search engine to find information	88
3.	Search for a map or driving directions	84
4.	Do an Internet search to answer a specific question	80
5.	Research a product or service before buying it	78
6.	Look for information on a hobby or interest	76
7.	Check the weather	75
8.	Get news	70
9.	Surf the Web for fun	67
10.	Get travel information	66
10.	Look for health/medical information	66
10.	Look for information from a government website	66

Source: Pew Internet & American Life Project Tracking surveys (March 2000–present). Last updated: April 23, 2004.

How Many Online Worldwide?

World total	**605.6 million**	Middle East	5.12 million
Africa	6.31 million	Canada & U.S.	182.67 million
Asia/Pacific	187.24 million	Latin America	33.35 million
Europe	190.91 million		

NOTE: These are estimated figures, as of Sept. 2002, based on several surveys. *Source:* Nua Internet Surveys.

Top 15 Countries in Internet Usage, 2002

	Internet users (thousands)	Share %		Internet users (thousands)	Share %
1. U.S.	160,700	24.13%	10. India	16,580	2.49%
2. Japan	64,800	9.73	11. Brazil	15,840	2.38
3. China	54,500	6.71	12. Russia	13,500	2.03
4. Germany	30,350	8.18	13. Australia	10,450	1.57
5. UK	27,150	4.08	14. Spain	10,390	1.56
6. South Korea	26,900	4.04	15. Taiwan	9,510	1.43
7. Italy	20,850	3.13	**Top 15 Total**	**496,000**	**74.48**
8. Canada	17,830	2.68	**Worldwide**		
9. France	16,650	2.50	**Total**	**665,910**	**100.00**

Source: Computer Industry Almanac, Inc. Web: www.c-i-a.com. Reprinted with permission.

Online Consumer Spending by Product, 2001–2003

Category	Online retail spending (billions of dollars)			Category	Online retail spending (billions of dollars)		
	2001	2002	2003		2001	2002	2003
Total	**$31.0**	**$40.4**	**$51.7**	Jewelry	0.9	1.1	1.3
PCs	6.9	7.5	8.8	Grocery	0.7	1.0	1.6
Peripherals	2.1	2.3	2.5	Pets	0.1	0.2	0.3
Software	2.0	2.6	2.9	Toys	1.0	1.2	1.3
Consumer electronics	1.5	2.0	2.5	Sporting goods	0.7	0.9	1.2
Books	2.3	2.8	3.1	Flowers	0.6	0.8	1.0
Music	0.8	0.9	1.3	Specialty gifts	0.6	0.8	1.0
Videos	0.6	0.9	1.1	Furniture	0.1	0.3	0.4
Movie tickets	0.2	0.3	0.4	Large appliances	0.3	0.5	0.7
Event tickets	1.6	2.1	2.7	Housewares/small			
Over-the-counter drugs	0.1	0.1	0.2	appliances	0.6	1.1	1.9
Nutraceuticals	0.1	0.1	0.3	Art and collectibles	0.3	0.5	0.6
Medical supplies and				Home improvement	0.3	0.6	1.0
contact lenses	0.1	0.2	0.3	Garden supplies	0.1	0.2	0.3
Personal care	0.1	0.2	0.5	Office products	0.6	1.1	1.7
Apparel	3.3	4.7	6.1	Auto parts	—	0.1	0.3
Footwear	0.5	0.8	1.0	Other	1.8	2.6	3.3

NOTE: (—) represents or rounds to zero. *Source:* Jupiter Media Metrix, Inc. From *Statistical Abstract of the United States: 2003.*

Computer Usage in the U.S.

(percent of U.S. adults in each group who use computers)

Men	73%	**Household income**	
Women	72	< $30,000	55%
Generation		$30,000–$49,999	82
Gen Y (ages 18–27)	85	$50,000–$74,999	92
Gen X (ages 28–39)	87	$75,000+	93
Trailing Boomers (ages 40–49)	84	**Community type**	
Leading Boomers (ages 50–58)	76	Urban	75
Matures (ages 59–68)	57	Suburban	76
After work (ages 69+)	24	Rural	61
Race and ethnicity		**Educational attainment**	
Whites	73	Less than high school	39
Blacks	62	High school graduate	67
Hispanics (English speaking)	75	Some college courses	84
		College graduate/graduate degree	91

Margin of error is ±2% *Source:* Pew Internet & American Life Project Tracking Survey, Feb. 3–March 1, 2004.

Ratings of Games on the Internet

ECI	EI	TI	MI	AOI
Early Childhood Interactive	Everyone Interactive	Teen Interactive	Mature Interactive	Adults Only Interactive
Content suitable for children age 3 and older.	Content suitable for children age 6 and older.	Content suitable for those age 13 and older.	Content suitable for those age 17 and older.	Content suitable for adults only.

Video Game Ratings

EC	E	T	M	AO
Early Childhood	Everyone	Teen	Mature	Adults Only
Content suitable for children age 3 and older.	Content suitable for children age 6 and older; game may contain minimal violence, some comic mischief, and some crude language.	Content suitable for those age 13 and older. Game may contain violent content, mild or strong language, and suggestive themes.	Content suitable for those age 17 and older. Game may include more intense violence or language than products rated T and may include mature sexual themes.	Content suitable for adults only. Game may include graphic depictions of sex and/or violence. Products rated AO are not intended to be sold or rented to anyone under the age of 18.

Top-Selling Software, 2003

Rank	Title	Publisher	Average price	Rank	Title	Publisher	Average price
1.	TurboTax 2002 Deluxe	Intuit	$40	6.	Taxcut 2002 Deluxe	Block Financial	$ 25
2.	Norton Antivirus 2003	Symantec	44	7.	MS Windows XP Home Ed Upgr	Microsoft	99
3.	TurboTax 2002	Intuit	20	8.	MS Office XP Student & Teacher Ed Acad	Microsoft	136
4.	Norton Antivirus 2004	Symantec	42	9.	Taxcut 2002 State	Block Financial	25
5.	TurboTax 2002 Multi State 45	Intuit	29	10.	Norton Internet Security 2003	Symantec	65

Source: NPD Group/NPDTechworld. Web: www.npd.com.

Top-Selling Education Software, 2003

Rank	Title	Publisher	Average price	Rank	Title	Publisher	Average price
1.	Instant Immersion Spanish JC	Topics Entertainment	$10	6.	Instant Immersion Spanish	Topics Entertainment	$18
2.	Adventure Workshop 1st–3rd Grade	Riverdeep Interactive	19	7.	Adventure Workshop Preschool–1st Grade	Riverdeep Interactive	18
3.	Mavis Beacon Teaches Typing 15.0	Riverdeep Interactive	20	8.	Dora the Explorer Lost City Adventure	Atari	19
4.	Dora the Explorer Backpack Adventure	Atari	18	9.	Jumpstart Kindergarten JC	Vivendi Universal	10
5.	Adventure Workshop 4th–6th Grade	Riverdeep Interactive	19	10.	Blue's ABC Time Activities JC	Atari	10

Source: NPD Group/NPDTechworld. Web: www.npd.com.

Top-Selling Business Software, 2003

Rank	Title	Publisher	Average price	Rank	Title	Publisher	Average price
1.	MS Office XP Student & Teacher Ed Acad	Microsoft	$136	6.	Pop-up Stopper Companion 3.0	Panicware	$ 29
2.	MS Office 2003 Student/Teacher Ed	Microsoft	147	7.	Act! 6.0	Interact Commerce	196
3.	Ad Subtract	Valusoft (THQ)	19	8.	MS Office XP Pro	Microsoft	484
4.	McAfee SpamKiller 4.0	Network Associates	29	9.	Winfax Pro 10.0	Symantec	97
5.	MS Office XP	Microsoft	407	10.	MS Office XP Pro Upgr	Microsoft	296

Source: NPD Group/NPDTechworld. Web: www.npd.com.

Top-Selling Game Software, 2003

Rank	Title	Publisher	Average price	Rank	Title	Publisher	Average price
1.	The Sims: Superstar Expansion Pack	Electronic Arts	$29	5.	Warcraft III: Frozen Throne Expansion Pack	Vivendi Universal	$33
2.	The Sims Deluxe	Electronic Arts	38	6.	The Sims: Unleashed Expansion Pack	Electronic Arts	28
3.	Command & Conquer: Generals	Electronic Arts	45	7.	Sim City 4	Electronic Arts	46
4.	The Sims: Makin' Magic Expansion Pack	Electronic Arts	31	8.	Call of Duty	Activision	45
				9.	MS Age of Mythology	Microsoft	38
				10.	Battlefield 1942	Electronic Arts	45

Source: NPD Group/NPDTechworld. Web: www.npd.com.

Stem Cells: The Promise and the Paradox

These basic building blocks of human development offer potential cures for a host of diseases, but their use poses ethical questions

By the Editors of TIME

Stem cells are sometimes called "magic seeds" for their ability to replicate indefinitely and morph into any kind of tissue. Stem cells are the first to develop in embryos; they are nature's blank slates, capable of becoming any of nearly 220 cell types that make up the human body. Stem cells are also present in adults in bone marrow and fat cells, among others. In recent years, scientists have come to believe these building-block cells, from embryos or adults, will lead to cures for diseases we've long thought untreatable.

There are four potential sources for embryonic human stem cells: fertility clinics (which routinely fertilize more eggs than they use, creating a stockpile of thousands of unwanted human embryos stored in freezers), fetuses from terminated pregnancies (usually obtained from abortion clinics), cloning (specifically, so-called therapeutic cloning, in which researchers stimulate an unfertilized human egg to develop into a blastocyst—a rounded cavity bounded by a single layer of cells), and custom-fertilization (embryos created specifically to harvest stem cells). However, abortion opponents (and quite a few others) find all of these sources—each of which involves the death of an embryo—disturbing and unethical.

Federal, State, and Private Funding

In a closely watched 2001 decision, President Bush green-lighted federal funding for stem-cell research, but only on 78 already existing specimens (or "lines") of the tissue. (In fact, by 2004, fewer than two dozen of those lines had turned out to be usable.) The White House subsequently announced that the Bush administration opposed all forms of human cloning, and President Bush reaffirmed his policy in 2004, after former first lady Nancy Reagan and 58 senators asked Bush to relax the stem-cell funding restrictions—and despite polls showing 3 out of 5 Americans favor stem-cell research.

In Feb. 2003 the House of Representatives passed a ban on human cloning research (this blanket prohibition would include therapeutic cloning to obtain stem cells, even though this method is distinct from "reproductive cloning" in that it does not lead to the birth of a human being). A similar measure has stalled in the Senate. With no federal legislation to restrict or ban the technology, several states are moving forcefully into the vacuum. California and New Jersey have passed laws specifically authorizing the cloning of human eggs to create stem cells, and several other states are considering similar bills—even as other states are aiming to put restrictions in place that go beyond those favored by the Bush Administration. Meanwhile, universities are expanding their research programs, fearing that they could lose their brightest scientists to programs overseas, which have more liberal stem-cell policies.

Nonembryonic Sources

One way around the ethical and political logjam would be to find a source for stem cells other than human embryos. Recently, there have been tantalizing hints that this possibility may be inching closer to reality. In a scientific first, researchers reported in March 2002 that adult stem cells for blood, which normally circulate in the bloodstream to replenish dying blood cells, can also morph into skin, liver, and intestinal tissue; other experts strongly questioned the report. If true, the finding suggests that the body may have a stash of universal repair cells, capable of being dispatched to wherever they are needed, and that this stock of adult stem cells could someday be used to treat disease without having to rely on human embryos.

In March 2003 a National Institutes of Health (NIH) researcher found that pulp from baby teeth also contains a number of stem cells. But unlike the stem cells found in embryos, which can grow into any of the body's tissues, the stem cells in baby teeth seem to transform themselves only into bone, nerve and fat cells, limiting their usefulness. It's too early to tell whether either of these discoveries will translate into a practical new source for stem cells, but the prospect is promising.

A matched set of articles published by the British science journal Nature in June 2002 seemed calculated to provide succor to both sides in the simmering stem-cell debate. In one study, a University of Minnesota team isolated bone-marrow cells from adult mice, grew them in dishes, and injected them into mouse embryos, where they developed into nerve, liver, and other types of cells. In the other study, scientists from the NIH did similar work with stem cells from mouse embryos, which developed into brain cells that produce dopamine and could be used to treat Parkinson's disease. Proponents of human therapeutic cloning hailed the NIH study as proof that scientists need to work with stem cells taken from embryos. Foes cited the Minnesota work as proof that the same results can be achieved without using embryos.

Overseas Research

While stem-cell research in the U.S. is held back by moral and political debates, the outlook overseas is very different. The governments of Britain, Singapore, China, Australia, Japan, South Korea, and Israel all provide stem-cell funding. In Feb. 2004, South Korean scientists announced they had in fact cloned an embryo and extracted stem cells from it. If foreign countries are investing in stem-cell science, the research will ultimately get done. But, says a stem-cell research pioneer, "the U.S. is the 800-pound gorilla when it comes to resources for science. If we continue to limit funding, things will proceed much more slowly."

Another concern: foreign governments and companies can patent their stem-cell lines and then reap big rewards by licensing them to others. Some scientists inside the U.S. government, however, are determined to make the best of the limited funding. "Remember," says one NIH researcher, "that before the president made his decision, there was zero federal support for embryonic-stem-cell research." The bottom line: this area of research is so promising that it will continue to be pursued, by both commercial and government-backed scientists.   □

Major Discoveries About Human Ancestors

Living and extinct human beings and their near-human ancestors are called "hominids" and belong to the *Hominidae* family of primates. They should not be confused with "hominoids," which belong to the *Hominoidea* superfamily of primates and include apes and humans. Scientists theorize that the human and ape lines branched off from a common ancestor 8 million to 6 million years ago.

Years ago	Species	Discovered	Remarks
5.8–5.2 million	*Ardipithecus ramidus kadabba*	1997–1998 in Alayla, Ethiopia	May be oldest known human ancestor. About the size of modern chimpanzees, or 4 ft tall standing. May have walked upright
c. 4.4 million	*Ardipithecus ramidus ramidus*	1994 in Aramis, Ethiopia	Similar to *A. ramidus kadabba*
c. 4.2 million	*Australopithecus anamensis*	1995, two sites at Lake Turkana in Kenya: Kanapoi and Allia Bay	Possible ancestor of *A. afarensis* (Lucy). Walked upright
c. 3.2 million	*Australopithecus afarensis*	1974 at Hadar in the Afar triangle of eastern Ethiopia; Laetoli, Tanzania	Nicknamed "Lucy." Her skeleton was 3.5 ft (100 cm) tall. Had apelike skull. Walked fully upright. Lived in family groups throughout eastern Africa
c. 2.5 million	*Australopithecus africanus*	1924 at Taung, northern Cape Province, South Africa	Descendant of "Lucy." Lived in social groups
c. 2 million	*Australopithecus robustus*	1938 in Kromdraai, South Africa	Was related to *A. africanus*
c. 2 million	*Homo habilis* ("skillful" or "handy man")	1960 in Olduvai Gorge, Tanzania	First brain enlargement; is believed to have used stone tools
c. 1.8 million	*Homo erectus* ("upright man")	1891 at Trinil, Java, Indonesia	Brain size twice that of *australopithecine* species. "Java Man" may have been a direct ancestor of *Homo sapiens* or instead developed on a separate evolutionary track. He is the first hominid to use fire and the hand ax, and to live in caves
c. 160,000(?)	*Homo sapiens idaltu* ("knowing or wise elder man")	1997, Herto, Middle Awash region, Ethiopia	Anatomically modern humans
c. 100,000(?)	*Homo sapiens sapiens* ("knowing or wise man")	1868, Cro-Magnon, France	Anatomically modern humans

Scientific Classification

Classification, or taxonomy, is a system of categorizing living things. There are seven divisions in the system: (1) Kingdom; (2) Phylum or Division; (3) Class; (4) Order; (5) Family; (6) Genus; (7) Species.

Kingdom is the broadest division. While scientists currently disagree as to how many kingdoms there are, most support a five-kingdom (Animalia, Plantae, Protista, Monera, and Fungi) system. The lowest division is species, which consists of organisms that are capable of interbreeding to produce fertile offspring. Species are identified by two names (binomial nomenclature). The first name is the genus, the second is the species.

For example, a lion is *Panthera leo,* a tiger is *Panthera tigris.* The first word is always capitalized, the second is not, and both should be italicized. Humans, of course, are *Homo sapiens.* The full classification for a lion would be: Kingdom, Animalia (animals); Phylum, Chordata (vertebrate animals); Class, Mammalia (mammals); Order, Carnivora (meat eaters); Family, Felidae (all cats); Genus, Panthera (great cats); Species, leo (lions).

The Periodic Table

Although some elements, such as gold and iron, have been known to humans since prehistoric times, it wasn't until the 17th century that the first scientific discovery of an element (phosphorus) was made. Only 12 elements were known prior to 1700, but as more and more elements were discovered—by 1900 there were more than 80—scientists tried to find a way to organize them systematically, according to their physical and chemical properties.

Today, the periodic table (*see* next page) organizes the elements in horizontal rows, or periods, by order of increasing atomic number, which equals the number of protons in the atomic nucleus of each element. The elements are also organized in vertical columns, or groups, based on similar physical characteristics and chemical behavior. This arrangement developed side by side with atomic theory over about 200 years, and it continues to evolve as new elements are discovered.

Early Attempts

One of the earliest attempts to organize the elements based on their chemical and physical properties was made by German chemist Johann Dobereiner. In 1817 Dobereiner noticed that certain elements that were chemically similar could be grouped together in threes, for example, calcium, strontium, and barium; lithium, sodium, and potassium; chlorine, bromine, and iodine. In each group of three, the atomic weight of one element fell halfway between the atomic weights of the other two elements. The pattern seemed too remarkable to be a coincidence. Based on his findings, Dobereiner proposed the Law of Triads in 1829. His work soon prompted other scientists to find patterns among even larger groups of elements.

Another attempt to systematically organize the elements based on their properties was made by the French geologist Alexandre-Émile Beguyer de Chancourtois in 1862. He devised a kind of spiral graph that was arranged on a cylinder, with the elements ordered by increasing atomic weight and with similar elements lined up vertically. De Chancourtois was the first to notice the periodicity of the elements, that is, when the elements were arranged according to their atomic weights, similar elements seemed to occur at regular intervals.

A year later, the English chemist John Newlands also attempted to classify the known elements of his day based on their atomic weight. Like de Chancourtois, he noticed a repeating pattern—every eighth element had similar properties. Newlands called this the Law of Octaves. Although the tables worked out by both de Chancourtois and Newlands were important precursors to the periodic table, neither received much attention at the time.

Mendeleev

The next milestone in the development of the periodic table was set by the Russian chemist Dmitri Mendeleev, who is generally acknowledged as the "father" of the modern periodic table. Mendeleev wrote out the names of the elements, along with their atomic weights and other properties, on cards, which he then laid out in rows and columns much like a game of solitaire. When the elements were ordered according to atomic weight, Mendeleev, like de Chancourtois and Newlands, could see that certain chemical properties were repeated periodically; however, not all the elements fit this pattern neatly. Mendeleev's solution was to move certain elements to new positions, despite their accepted weight, in order to group them with other elements sharing similar properties. (Nearly half a century later, after the periodic table was revised according to atomic number rather than atomic weight, these elements fell into place.)

Mendeleev's work on periodic law—which states that the properties of elements recur periodically as their atomic weights increase—was announced in 1869. At about the same time, a German chemist named Julius Lothar Meyer independently arrived at a periodic table that was remarkably similar to Mendeleev's. Unfortunately for Meyer, Mendeleev presented his work to the scientific community first. However, Mendeleev's table was also superior to Meyer's because he left a number of empty spaces to account for elements that were yet to be discovered.

20th-Century Revisions

The first major change to the periodic table occurred following the discovery of an entirely new group of elements, the noble gases, between 1895 and 1901. They were called the noble gases because they were believed to be inert—incapable of reacting with other elements to form compounds. (Today it is known that they do enter into chemical combinations, only reluctantly.) These elements were simply added on in a separate column under helium.

The first major revision of the entire periodic table was carried out by Henry Gwyn-Jeffries Moseley, an English physicist who began his research under Ernest Rutherford. In 1914, Moseley showed that each atomic nucleus could be assigned a number that was equal to the number of units of positive charge (later identified as "protons") associated with it. Once the periodic table was reorganized according to this atomic number instead of atomic weight, the few discrepancies in Mendeleev's system disappeared.

Over the years other revisions of the table have been made, including the incorporation of the rare-earth elements (lanthanide series) and the synthetic elements (technetium, promethium, and all the elements with atomic number 93 or higher). The actinides, which are radioactive and mainly synthetic, and the lanthanides do not fit into the same pattern of repeated properties as the other elements, so they are generally shown below the periodic table in separate rows. Most of these changes were the work of American chemist Glenn Seaborg, who codiscovered elements 94 (plutonium) through 102 (nobelium) between 1940 and 1958. Seaborg also suggested a superactinide series of elements, with atomic numbers 122 through 153, but so far none of these has been synthesized or detected. □

Periodic Table of Elements

Legend:

Number ——— 1		
Period ——— 1	**H** ——— Symbol	
Weight ——— 1.00794	Hydrogen ——— Name	

Group ——— 1

Number	Symbol	Name	Weight
1	H	Hydrogen	1.00794
2	He	Helium	4.002602
3	Li	Lithium	6.941
4	Be	Beryllium	9.012182
5	B	Boron	10.811
6	C	Carbon	12.0107
7	N	Nitrogen	14.0067
8	O	Oxygen	15.9994
9	F	Flourine	18.9984032
10	Ne	Neon	20.1797
11	Na	Sodium	22.98977
12	Mg	Magnesium	24.305
13	Al	Aluminum	26.981538
14	Si	Silicon	28.0855
15	P	Phosphorus	30.973761
16	S	Sulfur	32.065
17	Cl	Chlorine	35.453
18	Ar	Argon	39.948
19	K	Potassium	39.0983
20	Ca	Calcium	40.078
21	Sc	Scandium	44.95591
22	Ti	Titanium	47.867
23	V	Vanadium	50.9415
24	Cr	Chromium	51.9961
25	Mn	Manganese	54.938049
26	Fe	Iron	55.845
27	Co	Cobalt	58.9332
28	Ni	Nickel	58.6934
29	Cu	Copper	63.546
30	Zn	Zinc	65.39
31	Ga	Gallium	69.723
32	Ge	Germanium	72.64
33	As	Arsenic	74.9216
34	Se	Selenium	78.96
35	Br	Bromine	79.904
36	Kr	Krypton	83.8
37	Rb	Rubidium	85.4678
38	Sr	Strontium	87.62
39	Y	Yttrium	88.90585
40	Zr	Zirconium	91.224
41	Nb	Niobium	92.90638
42	Mo	Molybdenum	95.94
43	Tc	Technetium	98[1]
44	Ru	Ruthenium	101.07
45	Rh	Rhodium	102.9055
46	Pd	Palladium	106.42
47	Ag	Silver	107.8682
48	Cd	Cadmium	112.411
49	In	Indium	114.818
50	Sn	Tin	118.71
51	Sb	Antimony	121.76
52	Te	Tellurium	127.60
53	I	Iodine	126.90447
54	Xe	Xenon	131.293
55	Cs	Cesium	132.90545
56	Ba	Barium	137.327
72	Hf	Hafnium	178.49
73	Ta	Tantalum	180.9479
74	W	Tungsten	183.84
75	Re	Rhenium	186.207
76	Os	Osmium	190.23
77	Ir	Iridium	192.217
78	Pt	Platinum	195.078
79	Au	Gold	196.96655
80	Hg	Mercury	200.59
81	Tl	Thallium	204.3833
82	Pb	Lead	207.2
83	Bi	Bismuth	208.98038
84	Po	Polonium	209[1]
85	At	Astatine	210[1]
86	Rn	Radon	222
87	Fr	Francium	223[1]
88	Ra	Radium	226
104	Rf	Rutherfordium	261[1]
105	Db	Dubnium	262[1]
106	Sg	Seaborgium	266
107	Bh	Bohrium	264[1]
108	Hs	Hassium	277[1]
109	Mt	Meitnerium	268[1]
110	Ds	Darmstadtium	269[1]
111	Uuu	Unununium	272
112	Uub	Ununbium	285[1]
113	—		(—)
114	Uuq	Ununquadium	289
115	—		(—)
116	—		(—)
117	—		(—)
118	—		(—)

Lanthanide Series (Period 6)

Number	Symbol	Name	Weight
57	La	Lanthanum	138.9055
58	Ce	Cerium	140.116
59	Pr	Praseodymium	140.90765
60	Nd	Neodymium	144.24
61	Pm	Promethium	145
62	Sm	Samarium	150.36
63	Eu	Europium	151.964
64	Gd	Gadolinium	157.25
65	Tb	Terbium	158.92534
66	Dy	Dysprosium	162.5
67	Ho	Holmium	164.93032
68	Er	Erbium	167.259
69	Tm	Thulium	168.93421
70	Yb	Ytterbium	173.04
71	Lu	Lutetium	174.967

Actinide Series (Period 7)

Number	Symbol	Name	Weight
89	Ac	Actinium	227[1]
90	Th	Thorium	232.0381
91	Pa	Protactinium	231.03588
92	U	Uranium	238.02891
93	Np	Neptunium	237[1]
94	Pu	Plutonium	244[1]
95	Am	Americium	243
96	Cm	Curium	247[1]
97	Bk	Berkelium	247[1]
98	Cf	Californium	251[1]
99	Es	Einsteinium	252[1]
100	Fm	Fermium	257[1]
101	Md	Mendelevium	258[1]
102	No	Nobelium	259
103	Lr	Lawrencium	262

Category legend:

- Alkali Metals ☐
- Alkaline Earth Metals
- Transition Metals
- Other Metals
- Non-Metals
- Noble Gases

Notes: Elements 111, 112, and 114 are under review. A temporary system of naming recommended by J. Chatt has been used above. 1. Mass number of the longest-lived isotope that is known. Source: International Union of Pure and Applied Chemistry (IUPAC). Web: http://www.chem.qmw.ac.uk/iupac/AtWt/

The Elements

Elements are the building blocks of nature. Water, for example, is a compound consisting of the elements hydrogen and oxygen. Each element is a pure substance that cannot be split up into any simpler pure substance.

The smallest particle of an element that can exist is an atom. An atom consists of subatomic particles. The most important of these are protons, which have positive electrical charges; electrons, which have negative electrical charges; and neutrons, which are electrically neutral.

The atomic number of an element is the number of protons in one atom of the element. Each element has a different atomic number. For example, the atomic numbers of hydrogen and oxygen are 1 and 8, respectively.

Elements with atomic numbers 1 (hydrogen) to 94 (plutonium) occur naturally on Earth. The remaining artificial elements have been created since 1940 by using nuclear reactors and particle accelerators. Element 100 is named fermium. Elements with atomic numbers 101 onward are known as the transfermium elements. They are also known as heavy elements because their atoms have very large masses compared with atoms of hydrogen, the lightest of all elements.

Chemical Elements

Element	Symbol	Atomic no.	Atomic wt.	Specific gravity	Melting point °C	Boiling point °C	No. of isotopes[1]	Discoverer	Year
Actinium	Ac	89	227[2]	10.07[3]	1051	3198	11	Debierne/Giesel	1899/1902
Aluminum	Al	13	26.981538	2.6989	660.32	2519	8	Wöhler	1827
Americium	Am	95	243[2]	13.67	1176	2011	13[4]	Seaborg et al.	1944
Antimony	Sb	51	121.76	6.61	630.63	1587	29	Early historic times	—
Argon	Ar	18	39.948	1.7837[5]	−189.35	−185.85	8	Rayleigh and Ramsay	1894
Arsenic (gray)	As	33	74.9216	5.73	817	603	14	Albertus Magnus	1250
Astatine	At	85	210[2]	—	302	—	21	Corson et al.	1940
Barium	Ba	56	137.327	3.5	727	1897	25	Davy	1808
Berkelium	Bk	97	247[2]	14.00[6]	1050 (α form)	—	8[4]	Seaborg et al.	1949
Beryllium	Be	4	9.012182	1.848	1287	2471	6	Vauquelin	1798
Bismuth	Bi	83	208.98038	9.747	271.40	1564	19	Geoffroy the Younger	1753
Bohrium	Bh	107	264[2]	—	—	—	—	Armbruster and Münzenberg	1981
Boron	B	5	10.811	2.37[7]	2075	4000	6	Gay-Lussac and Thénard; Davy	1808
Bromine	Br	35	79.904	3.12[5]	−7.2	58.8	19	Balard	1826
Cadmium	Cd	48	112.411	8.65	321.07	767	22	Stromeyer	1817
Calcium	Ca	20	40.078	1.55	842	1484	14	Davy	1808
Californium	Cf	98	251[2]	—	900	—	12[4]	Seaborg et al.	1950
Carbon	C	6	12.0107	1.8–3.5[8]	4492 (graphite)	3825	7	Prehistoric	—
Cerium	Ce	58	140.116	6.771	798	3443	19	Berzelius and Hisinger; Klaproth	1803
Cesium	Cs	55	132.90545	1.873	28.5	671	22	Bunsen and Kirchoff	1860
Chlorine	Cl	17	35.453	1.56[5]	−101.5	−34.04	11	Scheele	1774
Chromium	Cr	24	51.9961	7.18-7.20	1907	2671	9	Vauquelin	1797
Cobalt	Co	27	58.9332	8.9	1495	2927	14	Brandt	c.1735
Copper	Cu	29	63.546	8.96	1084.62	2562	11	Prehistoric	—
Curium	Cm	96	247[2]	13.51[3]	1345	3100	13[4]	Seaborg et al.	1944
Darmstadtium[9]	Ds	110	281[2]	—	—	—	—	S. Hofmann et al.	1994
Dubnium	Db	105	262[2]	—	—	—	—	Ghiorso et al.	1970
Dysprosium	Dy	66	162.5	8.540	1412	2567	21	de Boisbaudran	1886
Einsteinium	Es	99	252[2]	—	860	—	12[4]	Ghiorso et al.	1952
Erbium	Er	68	167.259	9.045	1529	2868	16	Mosander	1843
Europium	Eu	63	151.964	5.283	822	1529	21	Demarcay	1901
Fermium	Fm	100	257[2]	—	1527	—	10[4]	Ghiorso et al.	1953
Fluorine	F	9	18.9984032	1.108[5]	−219.67	−188.12	6	Moissan	1886
Francium	Fr	87	223[2]	—	27	—	21	Perey	1939
Gadolinium	Gd	64	157.25	7.898	1313	3273	17	de Marignac	1880
Gallium	Ga	31	69.723	5.904	29.76	2204	14	de Boisbaudran	1875
Germanium	Ge	32	72.64	5.323	938.25	2833	17	Winkler	1886
Gold	Au	79	196.96655	19.32	1064.18	2856	21	Prehistoric	—
Hafnium	Hf	72	178.49	13.31	2233	4603	17	Coster and von Hevesy	1923
Hassium	Hs	108	277[2]	—	—	—	—	Armbruster and Münzenberg	1983
Helium	He	2	4.002602	0.1785[5]	−272.2	−268.934	5	Janssen	1868
Holmium	Ho	67	164.93032	8.781	1474	2700	29	Delafontaine and Soret	1878
Hydrogen	H	1	1.00794	0.070[5]	−259.34	−252.87	3	Cavendish	1766
Indium	In	49	114.818	7.31	156.60	2072	34	Reich and Richter	1863
Iodine	I	53	126.90447	4.93	113.7	184.4	24	Courtois	1811
Iridium	Ir	77	192.217	22.42	2446	4428	25	Tennant	1804
Iron	Fe	26	55.845	7.894	1538	2861	10	Prehistoric	—
Krypton	Kr	36	83.8	3.733[5]	−157.38	−153.22	23	Ramsay and Travers	1898
Lanthanum	La	57	138.9055	6.166	918	3464	19	Mosander	1839
Lawrencium	Lr	103	262[2]	—	1627	—	20[4]	Ghiorso et al.	1961

Element	Symbol	Atomic no.	Atomic wt.	Specific gravity	Melting point °C	Boiling point °C	No. of isotopes[1]	Discoverer	Year
Lead	Pb	82	207.2	11.35	327.46	1749	29	Prehistoric	—
Lithium	Li	3	6.941	0.534	180.50	1342	5	Arfvedson	1817
Lutetium	Lu	71	174.967	9.835	1663	3402	22	Urbain/ von Welsbach	1907
Magnesium	Mg	12	24.305	1.738	650	1090	8	Black	1755
Manganese	Mn	25	54.938049	7.21–7.44[10]	1246	2061	11	Gahn, Scheele, and Bergman	1774
Meitnerium	Mt	109	268[2]	—	—	—	—	GSI, Darmstadt, West Germany	1982
Mendelevium	Md	101	258[2]	—	827	—	3[4]	Ghiorso et al.	1955
Mercury	Hg	80	200.59	13.546	-38.83	356.73	26	Prehistoric	—
Molybdenum	Mo	42	95.94	10.22	2623	4639	20	Scheele	1778
Neodymium	Nd	60	144.24	6.80 & 7.004[10]	1021	3074	16	von Welsbach	1885
Neon	Ne	10	20.1797	0.89990 (g/10°C/1 atm)	-248.59	-246.08	8	Ramsay and Travers	1898
Neptunium	Np	93	237[2]	20.25	644	—	15[4]	McMillan and Abelson	1940
Nickel	Ni	28	58.6934	8.902	1455	2913	11	Cronstedt	1751
Niobium (Columbium)	Nb	41	92.90638	8.57	2477	4744	24	Hatchett	1801
Nitrogen	N	7	14.0067	0.808[5]	-210.00	-195.79	8	Rutherford	1772
Nobelium	No	102	259[2]	—	827	—	7[4]	Ghiorso et al.	1958
Osmium	Os	76	190.23	22.57	3033	5012	19	Tennant	1803
Oxygen	O	8	15.9994	1.14[5]	-218.79	-182.95	8	Priestley/Scheele	1774
Palladium	Pd	46	106.42	12.02	1554.9	2963	21	Wollaston	1803
Phosphorus (white)	P	15	30.973761	1.82	44.15	280.5	7	Brand	1669
Platinum	Pt	78	195.078	21.45	1768.4	3825	32	Ulloa/Wood	1735/1741
Plutonium	Pu	94	244[2]	19.84	640	3228	16[4]	Seaborg et al.	1940
Polonium	Po	84	209[2]	9.32	254	962	34	Curie	1898
Potassium	K	19	39.0983	0.862	63.5	759	10	Davy	1807
Praseodymium	Pr	59	140.90765	6.772	931	3520	15	von Welsbach	1885
Promethium	Pm	61	145[2]	—	1042	3000	14	Marinsky et al.	1945
Protactinium	Pa	91	231.03588	15.37[3]	1572	—	14	Hahn and Meitner	1917
Radium	Ra	88	226[2]	5.0?	700	—	15	Pierre and Marie Curie	1898
Radon	Rn	86	222[2]	4.4[5]	-71	-61.7	20	Dorn	1900
Rhenium	Re	75	186.207	21.02	3186	5596	21	Noddack, Berg, and Tacke	1925
Rhodium	Rh	45	102.9055	12.41	1964	3695	20	Wollaston	1803
Rubidium	Rb	37	85.4678	1.532	39.30	688	20	Bunsen and Kirchoff	1861
Ruthenium	Ru	44	101.07	12.44	2334	4150	16	Klaus	1844
Rutherfordium	Rf	104	261[2]	—	—	—	—	Ghiorso et al.	1969
Samarium	Sm	62	150.36	7.536	1074	1794	17	Boisbaudran	1879
Scandium	Sc	21	44.95591	2.989	1541	2836	15	Nilson	1878
Seaborgium	Sg	106	266[2]	—	—	—	—	Ghiorso et al.	1974
Selenium (gray)	Se	34	78.96	4.79	220.5	685	20	Berzelius	1817
Silicon	Si	14	28.0855	2.33	1414	3265	8	Berzelius	1824
Silver	Ag	47	107.8682	10.5	961.78	2162	27	Prehistoric	—
Sodium	Na	11	22.98977	0.971	97.80	883	7	Davy	1807
Strontium	Sr	38	87.62	2.54	777	1382	18	Davy	1808
Sulfur	S	16	32.065	2.07[10]	95.3 (rhombic)	444.60	10	Prehistoric	—
Tantalum	Ta	73	180.9479	16.654	3017	5458	19	Ekeberg	1801
Technetium	Tc	43	98[2]	11.50[3]	2157	4265	23	Perrier and Segré	1937
Tellurium	Te	52	127.60	6.24	449.51	988	29	von Reichenstein	1782
Terbium	Tb	65	158.92534	8.234	1356	3230	24	Mosander	1843
Thallium	Tl	81	204.3833	11.85	304	1473	28	Crookes	1861
Thorium	Th	90	232.0381	11.72	1750	4788	12	Berzelius	1828
Thulium	Tm	69	168.93421	9.314	1545	1950	18	Cleve	1879
Tin (white)	Sn	50	118.71	7.31	231.93	2602	28	Prehistoric	—
Titanium	Ti	22	47.867	4.55	1668	3287	9	Gregor	1791
Tungsten	W	74	183.84	19.3	3422	5555	22	J. and F. d'Elhuyar	1783
Uranium	U	92	238.02891	19.05	1135	4131	15	Peligot	1841
Vanadium	V	23	50.9415	6.11	1910	3407	9	del Rio	1801
Xenon	Xe	54	131.293	3.52[5]	-111.79	-108.12	31	Ramsay and Travers	1898
Ytterbium	Yb	70	173.04	6.972	819	1196	16	Marignac	1878
Yttrium	Y	39	88.90585	4.457	1522	3345	21	Gadolin	1794
Zinc	Zn	30	65.39	7.133	419.5	907	15	Prehistoric	—
Zirconium	Zr	40	91.224	6.506[3]	1855	4409	20	Klaproth	1789

NOTES: Elements 111, 112, and 114 are under review and are thus not included. ≈ means "approximately." < means "less than." 1. Isotopes are different forms of the same element having the same atomic number but different atomic weights. 2. Mass number of the longest-lived isotope that is known. 3. Calculated figure. 4. Artificially produced. 5. Liquid. 6. Estimated. 7. Amorphous. 8. Depending on whether amorphous, graphite, or diamond. 9. In 2003, the International Union of Pure and Applied Chemistry named element 110 Darmstadtium after Darmstadt, Germany, its place of discovery. 10. Depending on allotropic form.

Table of Geological Periods

It is generally assumed that planets are formed by the accretion of gas and dust in a cosmic cloud, but there is no way of estimating the length of this process. Our Earth acquired its present size, more or less, between 4 billion and 5 billion years ago. Life on Earth originated about 2 billion years ago, but there are no good fossil remains from periods earlier than the Cambrian, which began about 490 million years ago.

The known geological history of Earth since the Precambrian Time is subdivided into three eras, each of which includes a number of periods. They, in turn, are subdivided into epochs and stage ages.

In an epoch, a certain section may be especially well known because of rich fossil finds.

New Geological Period

In March 2004, geologists added a new time period to Earth's chronology—the Ediacaran Period. The Ediacaran Period lasted about 50 million years, from 600 million years ago to about 542 million years ago. It was the last period of the Precambrian's Neoproterozoic Era. Multicelled organisms first appeared during this time. This period is the first new one added in 120 years.

Precambrian Time

The Precambrian's lower limit is not defined, but ended about 542 million years ago. The Precambrian encompasses about 90% of the Earth's history.

Eonothem eon	Duration[1]	Eras	Events
Archaean (Greek *archaios* = ancient)	2,500?	Eoarchean (Greek *eos* = dawn + *archaios* = ancient) Paleoarchean (Greek *palaios* = old) Mesoarchean (Greek *mesos* = middle) Neoarchean (Greek *neo* = new)	Formation of oceans, atmosphere, and continents; bacteria
Proterozoic (Greek *proteros* = earlier + *zoön* = animal)	c. 2,000	Paleoproterozoic (Greek *palaios* = old) Mesoproterozoic (Greek *mesos* = middle) Neoproterozoic (Greek *neo* = new)	Oxygen build-up; multicelled organisms

1. In millions of years.

Paleozoic Era

This era began 542 million years ago and lasted about 291 million years. The name was compounded from Greek *palaios* (old) and *zoön* (animal).

Period	Duration[1]	Epochs	Events
Cambrian (*Cambria*, Latin name for Wales)	54	Lower Cambrian Middle Cambrian Upper Cambrian	Invertebrate sea life proliferating during this and the following period
Ordovician (Latin *Ordovices*, people of early Britain)	45	Lower Ordovician Upper Ordovician	Diverse marine life, including vertebrates; vascular plants
Silurian (Latin *Silures*, people of early Wales)	28	Lower Silurian Upper Silurian	Coral reefs; giant scorpions; first jawed fish
Devonian (Devonshire in England)	57	Lower Devonian Upper Devonian	Numerous fishes, other sea life; many plants, first trees; wingless insects
Carboniferous (Latin *carbo* = coal + *fero* = to bear)	60	Upper, Middle, and Lower Mississippian[2] Upper, Middle, and Lower Pennsylvanian[2]	Maximum coal formation in swampy forests; insects, amphibians, reptiles; fishes, clams, crustaceans
Permian (district of Perm in Russia)	48	Lower Permian Upper Permian	Large reptiles, amphibians; most species become extinct

1. In millions of years. 2. Mississippian and Pennsylvanian names are used only in the U.S.

Mesozoic Era

This era began 251 million years ago and lasted about 186 million years. The name was compounded from Greek *mesos* (middle) and *zoön* (animal). Popular name: Age of Reptiles.

Period	Duration[1]	Epochs	Events
Triassic (*trias* = triad)	51	Lower Triassic Middle Triassic Upper Triassic	Early dinosaurs, crocodiles, turtles; first mammals
Jurassic (Jura Mountains)	54	Lower Jurassic Middle Jurassic Upper Jurassic	Many seagoing reptiles; early large dinosaurs; later, flying reptiles (pterosaurs), earliest known birds
Cretaceous (Latin *creta* = chalk)	80	Lower Cretaceous Upper Cretaceous	Dinosaurs and other reptiles dominate; seed-bearing plants appear

1. In millions of years.

Cenozoic Era[1]

This era began 66 million years ago and includes the geological present. The name was compounded from Greek *kainos* (new) and *zoön* (animal). Popular name: Age of Mammals.

Period	Duration[2]	Epochs	Events
Paleogene (Greek *palaios* = old + *genes* = born)	42	Paleocene (Greek *palaios* = old + *kainos* = new). Eocene (Greek *eos* = dawn). Oligocene (Greek *oligos* = few).	Rich insect fauna, early bats, increasingly diverse varieties of mammals and birds
Neogene (Greek *neo* = new + *genes* = born)	23	Miocene (Greek *meios* = less + *kainos* = new). Pliocene (Greek *pleios* = more). Pleistocene (Greek *pleistos* = most) (popular name: Ice Age). Holocene (Greek *holos* = entire), the last 10,000 years to the present.	Further development of mammals and birds. Various forms of humans, including *Homo sapiens*

1. This table reflects the divisions used by the International Commission on Stratigraphy. The U.S. Geological Survey divides the Cenozoic Era into the Tertiary Period (with the Paleocene, Eocene, Oligocene, Miocene, and Pliocene Epochs) and the Quaternary Period (with the Pleistocene and Holocene Epochs). 2. In millions of years.

Branches of Science

Science describes an area of knowledge, typically about something in the physical world, that can be explained in terms of scientific observation or the scientific method. The scientific method is a discovery process that has evolved over several hundred years and can be summarized as follows:

- a phenomenon in the physical world is observed
- an explanation, or hypothesis, for the phenomenon is formed
- the hypothesis is tested by means of objective, reproducible experiments

If the results of the experiments support the hypothesis, it becomes accepted as scientific theory. Later, if new information is found to contradict the hypothesis, it may be revised or abandoned in favor of a new hypothesis, which is then subjected to additional experiments.

The sciences that describe the physical universe are categorized in different ways. The largest distinction in science is whether a science is pure, or theoretical, or whether it is applied, or practical. Pure science explains a phenomenon, while applied science determines how a particular phenomenon may be put to use. In general, pure science is divided into the following categories:

- Physical sciences, which deal with matter and energy and allow us to describe the material universe in terms of weight, mass, volume, and other standard, objective measures.
- Earth sciences, which explain the phenomena of the Earth, its atmosphere, and the solar system to which it belongs.
- Life sciences, which describe living organisms, their internal processes, and their relationship to each other and the environment.

However, these three categories of pure science have areas of overlap, where one type of phenomenon may be associated with another. For example, light (studied in physics) is the energy source behind the (chemical) process of photosynthesis, or food production, in plants (studied in biology). For this reason, distinctions between pure sciences, and even between pure and applied sciences, can blur, and a new compound science can develop. An example of this is biochemistry, in which the chemical processes of living things (such as photosynthesis) are observed and explained.

Physical sciences	Life sciences	Earth sciences

Physics
  Kinetics
  Mechanics
  Electromagnetics
  Thermodynamics
	Biology
	Botany
	Zoology
		Geology
		Meteorology
		Astronomy

Chemistry
  Inorganic Chemistry
  Electrochemistry
  Analytical Chemistry		

Examples of Overlapping Sciences		
Physics + Chemistry = Physical Chemistry	Biology + Chemistry = Biochemistry Organic Chemistry	Geology + Chemistry = Geochemistry
Astronomy + Physics = Astrophysics	Biology + Geology = Paleontology	Geology + Astronomy = Astrogeology
	Biology + Astronomy + Physics = Astronautics	

Roundup of Recent Science Discoveries

By Borgna Brunner

Sedna Debuts, Rattling Poor Pluto

On March 15, 2004, astronomers confirmed the discovery of the most distant object ever identified in our solar system. Twice as far from the Sun as any known object, this red mass has an unusually elliptical orbit that takes a staggering 10,500 years to complete. Officially called 2003 VB12, its discoverers claim that it is the first known object from the long-hypothesized Oort Cloud, believed to be home to billions of frozen comets. The object's surface temperature is about minus 400°F (minus 240°C). Its frigid celestial homeland inspired its informal name, Sedna, the Inuit goddess of the icy northern oceans. In addition to its unparalleled coldness and distance, Sedna also distinguishes itself as the largest object identified since Pluto's discovery in 1930. About three-quarters of the size of Pluto, it is considered a planetoid (a minor planet or asteroid). Thought to be composed of rock and ice, it has a reddish hue similar to that of Mars.

In the process of defining Sedna, poor Pluto's fragile standing as a planet has once again come under attack—you may recall that unpleasant business back in 1999 when rumors circulated in the press darkly hinting that Pluto was in danger of a demotion. The International Astronomical Union (IAU) even found it necessary to issue a press release reassuring a distraught public that "no proposal to change the status of Pluto as the ninth planet" was in the works. But while the IAU continues to stand by Pluto, plenty of astronomers would like to wrest it from the company of its eight planetary brethren, pointing out that Pluto has less family resemblance to sublime Saturn than to brassy little Sedna. One of Sedna's discoverers, Mike Brown of the California Institute of Technology, makes a compelling case against Pluto, though coming from a partisan of the new planetoid, it's not nearly as cold-blooded as you might expect:

> Either Pluto is not a planet, or many other things are planets. Which is a better choice? I want my planets to be more special, not less special, so I favor Pluto not being a planet. Emotionally, though, I have to admit that I have grown up thinking Pluto is this special odd-ball planet at the edge of the solar system. While I now know scientifically that Pluto is less special, it's still hard to let go.

What with quasars, red giants, and brown dwarfs presumably taking up their time, why are astronomers still arguing about something as fundamental as whether Pluto deserves to be called a planet? Astonishingly, there's no official scientific definition of a planet, beyond a few principles: it must orbit a star and be spherical, and it cannot have been subject to internal nuclear fusion, which would make it a star. Astronomer Gibor Basri of the University of California, Berkeley, admits, "It's something of an embarrassment that we currently have no definition of what a planet is. People like to classify things. We live on a planet; it would be nice to know what that was."

Back when astronomers first welcomed Pluto into the solar system, it was thought to be the fifth largest planet, 12% larger than our own. Not only has sophisticated astronomical measurement reduced it to ninth place, but given that astronomers have only scratched the surface of the sky—surveying just 15% so far—there are sure to be even bigger, more brazen Sednas in Pluto's future.

Grand Old Galaxy

It's not news among scientists that our galaxy is one of the very oldest in the universe, but until now researchers were unable to determine just how old—estimates ranged from 10.4 billion to 16 billion years. Now astronomers have been able to narrow down their calculations to within 800 million years of the Milky Way's birth. Give or take a few million, the Milky Way has reached the grand old age of 13.6 billion years.

The age of the Milky Way is in part gauged by calculating the age of two of its oldest stars (called A0228 and A2111, part of the globular cluster NGC 6397). Once astronomers determined these stars were 13.4 billion years old, they knew that the Milky Way was at least as old as these galactic inhabitants. But while these are the oldest stars that have been discovered in our galaxy, they are in fact members of a second generation of stars. Were scientists to locate stars from the very first generation, they would have a far more accurate benchmark with which to measure the age of the Milky Way.

How do scientists know that stars A0228 and A2111 are old, but not among the oldest? A first-generation star is made up almost exclusively of hydrogen, and has a relatively short, violent life. When it explodes as a supernova, its death generates the creation of heavier elements. Second-generation stars, such as A0228 and A2111, are built from those heavier elements.

These two second-generation stars actually reveal a lot more than their own age. One of the elements they contain is beryllium. Because beryllium is known to increase over time, it works as a kind of "cosmic clock." It permits astronomers to calculate the interval of time between when the first generation of stars exploded and synthesized beryllium, and when this second generation of stars containing beryllium was formed. That interval has been measured to be about 200 million years. An international team of astronomers used the European Southern Observatory's Very Large Telescope (VLT), located in Chile, to make these highly complex measurements. "Just a few years ago," team leader Luca Pasquini remarked, "Any observation like this would have been impossible and just remained an astronomer's dream!"

By adding that interval of 200 million years to the age of the two stars (13.4 billion years), astronomers were able to estimate the age of the first generation of stars in our galaxy—13.6 billion years—and thus at the age of the Milky Way itself. Given that scientists now fix the age of the universe at 13.7 billion years, that makes us the proud denizens of one of the most established and venerable of galaxies.

Gone Fishing

A partial inventory of the latest expedition of the Census of Marine Life (CoML), which in the summer of 2004 ventured into one of the least explored regions of our oceans, revealed 180 species of midwater fish, 87 near-bottom fish, 5 never-before-seen squid and angler fish, and one astoundingly massive ring of plankton. CoML is a highly ambitious undertaking whose mission is to record the life within our oceans. The billion-dollar project involves more than 300 scientists from 53 countries and will take a decade to complete. Hundreds of thousands of animals and plants are to be inventoried, adding tremendously to the 210,000 marine life forms known to science. Census scientists estimate that perhaps only one-tenth of the life in our oceans is currently accounted for. "We haven't spent enough time exploring our own planet," says Barbara A. Block, a Johns Hopkins professor involved in the census, "We don't like to tell anyone we're ignorant about the oceans, but we are."

The most recent expedition of the census was the Norway-led MAR-ECO voyage that explored the Mid-Atlantic Ocean Ridge over two months in the summer of 2004. The 3,728-mile-long Mid-Atlantic Ocean Ridge stretches from Iceland to the Azores, a range of volcanic undersea mountains whose height and length rival anything on dry land. It is one of the least explored areas on the planet. Scientists were surprised to find it so densely populated and diverse. Among the most exotic of their discoveries was an *Aphyonus gelatinosus,* a fish covered with a pink and blue gelatinous layer; and a deep-sea angler fish, from whose head protrudes something resembling a glowing fishing rod, which is used to lure its prey conveniently close to its mouth. Another unusual find was a tremendously wide ring of plankton that spanned 6.2 miles. And census scientists are still puzzling over one pair of ragged claws scuttling across the floors of silent seas. After discovering a series of mysterious, evenly spaced, 5-cm-wide holes that looked as though some creature had "used a sewing machine to create this landscape," scientists eventually collared an unlikely culprit—a blind, deep-sea lobster.

A Leg Up on Lucy

What first separated us from the apes on the evolutionary tree was bipedalism, our ability to walk upright (bigger brains developed much later). The most famous of all early bipeds was of course Lucy, *Australopithecus afarensis,* estimated to be 3.2 million years old. As Donald Johanson, Lucy's discoverer, puts it, "bipedalism is the most distinctive, apparently earliest, defining characteristic of humans." Since Lucy's discovery in 1974, however, at least one older human ancestor has been confirmed: *Australopithecus anamensis,* uncovered in 1995, was on his feet about a million years before Lucy.

In the years since this last discovery, several finds have challenged the age of our earliest ancestors. None, however, has yet found wide acceptance among paleoanthropologists. One of the most dramatic—and blisteringly controversial—was the discovery in 2000 of *Orrorin tugenensis,* uncovered in Kenya by French paleoanthropologists Brigitte Senut and Martin Pickford. These fossil fragments from five chimp-sized creatures date back an astounding 6 million years. But *Orrorin's* credentials as a hominid, to put it diplomatically, were sharply called into question by the scientific community. As a London *Telegraph* article at the time described *Orrorin's* reception, it "provoked an unseemly outbreak of name-calling, litigation, and academic feuding between some of the world's finest anthropological minds." While *Orrorin* is indeed 6 million years old, no definitive proof confirmed that it was anything other than our nearest relative, the chimpanzee.

But powerful evidence that *Orrorin* walked upright has now been offered by Robert Eckhardt, professor of developmental genetics and evolutionary morphology at Pennsylvania State University. After performing a CT scan on *Orrorin's* fossilized thighbone, Eckhard concluded that it contained the properties of a human thighbone rather than those of a chimp or ape. "Now, for the first time, we have solid evidence dated to six million years ago of an intermediate creature between humans and the apes that demonstrated upright posture and bipedalism," Eckhard maintained, "And the dating of this fossil is unusually secure." If these assertions gain acceptance in the contentious world of paleoanthropology, then the evolutionary split between apes and hominids occurred at least 2 million years earlier than previously thought—*Orrorin,* our newest oldest ancestor, would have walked the Earth an amazing 6 million years ago.

Betting on Black Holes

In July 2004, celebrated physicist Stephen Hawking announced that for the past 30 years he had been wrong about black holes. What's more, his error cost him a long-standing bet, obliging him to present a baseball encyclopedia to John Preskill of the California Institute of Technology. On the bright side, Hawking's black hole recantation had a rather exciting side-effect: "I think," he ventured, "I have solved a major problem in theoretical physics."

Formed from a collapsed star, a black hole is a "cosmic vacuum cleaner," whose gravitational pull is so strong that it sucks up everything in its way. In 1976, Hawking theorized that black holes emit random radiation (later named "Hawking radiation") and lose mass until they eventually evaporate without a trace. All the matter sucked into a black hole, and all "information" about it (its quantum mechanical properties), would then be lost forever.

But Hawking's theory contradicts an essential principle of quantum physics: no information can ever be truly destroyed. Black holes, if Hawking was right, defy the laws of the universe as we know it. This radical theory, according to Preskill, "precipitated a genuine crisis in fundamental physics." Preskill resisted accepting what became known as the black hole "information paradox," and in 1997 Hawking (along with another colleague) bet him that "information swallowed by a black hole is forever hidden from the outside universe and can never be revealed, even as the black hole evaporates and completely disappears."

Seven years later, Hawking claims to have solved the very paradox he created. According to his revised theory, black holes eventually open up, revealing information about what went into them—"the information remains firmly in our universe," Hawking asserted. Preskill was pleased enough at having won the bet, but acknowledged, "I'll be honest, I didn't understand the talk." Neither did most others in the audience of the 17th International Conference on General Relativity and Gravitation in Dublin, leaving a stunned group of 800 scientists not sure what had hit them. Hawking's published proof of his revolutionary findings will follow, but in the meantime, he has paid off his bet to Preskill. The bettors had agreed upon an encyclopedia, which, unlike a black hole, is something "from which information can be recovered at will."

See also new medical discoveries, pp. 547–551; stem-cell research, 569–570; Saturn exploration, 421–422; and Mars discoveries, 369.

Inventions & Discoveries

See also Famous Firsts in Aviation, Nobel Prizes.

Adrenaline: (isolation of) John Jacob Abel, U.S., 1897.
Aerosol can: Erik Rotheim, Norway, 1926.
Air brake: George Westinghouse, U.S., 1868.
Air conditioning: Willis Carrier, U.S., 1911.
Airship: (non-rigid) Henri Giffard, France, 1852; (rigid) Ferdinand von Zeppelin, Germany, 1900.
Aluminum manufacture: (by electrolytic action) Charles M. Hall, U.S., 1866.
Anatomy, human: (*De fabrica corporis humani*, an illustrated systematic study of the human body) Andreas Vesalius, Belgium, 1543; (comparative: parts of an organism are correlated to the functioning whole) Georges Cuvier, France, 1799–1805.
Anesthetic: (first use of anesthetic—ether—on humans) Crawford W. Long, U.S., 1842.
Antibiotics: (first demonstration of antibiotic effect) Louis Pasteur, Jules-François Joubert, France, 1887; (discovery of penicillin, first modern antibiotic) Alexander Fleming, Scotland, 1928; (penicillin's infection-fighting properties) Howard Florey, Ernst Chain, England, 1940.
Antiseptic: (surgery) Joseph Lister, England, 1867.
Antitoxin, diphtheria: Emil von Behring, Germany, 1890.
Appliances, electric: (fan) Schuyler Wheeler, U.S., 1882; (flatiron) Henry W. Seely, U.S., 1882; (stove) Hadaway, U.S., 1896; (washing machine) Alva Fisher, U.S., 1906.
Aqualung: Jacques-Yves Cousteau, Emile Gagnan, France, 1943.
Aspirin: Dr. Felix Hoffman, Germany, 1899.
Astronomical calculator: The Antikythera device, Greece, first century B.C.. Found off island of Antikythera in 1900.
Atom: (nuclear model of) Ernest Rutherford, England, 1911.
Atomic structure: (formulated nuclear model of atom, Rutherford model) Ernest Rutherford, England, 1911; (proposed current concept of atomic structure, the Bohr model) Niels Bohr, Denmark, 1913.
Atomic theory: (ancient) Leucippus, Democritus, Greece, c. 500 B.C.; Lucretius, Rome c.100 B.C.; (modern) John Dalton, England, 1808.
Automobile: (first with internal combustion engine, 250 rpm) Karl Benz, Germany, 1885; (first with practical high-speed internal combustion engine, 900 rpm) Gottlieb Daimler, Germany, 1885; (first true automobile, not carriage with motor) René Panhard, Emile Lavassor, France, 1891; (carburetor, spray) Charles E. Duryea, U.S., 1892.
Autopilot: (for aircraft) Elmer A. Sperry, U.S., c.1910, first successful test, 1912, in a Curtiss flying boat.
Avogadro's law: (equal volumes of all gases at the same temperature and pressure contain equal number of molecules) Amedeo Avogadro, Italy, 1811.
Bacteria: Anton van Leeuwenhoek, The Netherlands, 1683.
Balloon, hot-air: Joseph and Jacques Montgolfier, France, 1783.

Science Websites

National Science Foundation: www.nsf.gov
National Academy of Sciences: www.nas.edu
Science News Online: www.sciencenews.org
Popular Science: www.popsci.com
Periodic Table of Elements:
    www.infoplease.com/periodictable.php
Dinosauria Online: www.dinosauria.com
Discovery Channel Online: www.discovery.com
Cosmology 101: http://map.gsfc.nasa.gov/m_uni.html
American Museum of Natural History:
    www.amnh.org
Newton (for K–12 teachers and students):
    www.newton.dep.anl.gov
Science Blog: www.scienceblog.com/
The Smithsonian Web: www.si.edu
Scientific American: www.sciam.com

Barbed wire: (most popular) Joseph E. Glidden, U.S., 1873.
Bar codes (computer-scanned binary signal code): (retail trade use) Monarch Marking, U.S. 1970; (industrial use) Plessey Telecommunications, England, 1970.
Barometer: Evangelista Torricelli, Italy, 1643.
Bicycle: Karl D. von Sauerbronn, Germany, 1816; (first modern model) James Starley, England, 1884.
Big Bang theory: (the universe originated with a huge explosion) George LeMaitre, Belgium, 1927; (modified LeMaitre theory labeled "Big Bang") George A. Gamow, U.S., 1948; (cosmic microwave background radiation discovered, confirms theory) Arno A. Penzias and Robert W. Wilson, U.S., 1965.
Blood, circulation of: William Harvey, England, 1628.
Boyle's law: (relation between pressure and volume in gases) Robert Boyle, Ireland, 1662.
Braille: Louis Braille, France, 1829.
Bridges: (suspension, iron chains) James Finley, Pa., 1800; (wire suspension) Marc Seguin, Lyons, 1825; (truss) Ithiel Town, U.S., 1820.
Bullet: (conical) Claude Minié, France, 1849.
Calculating machine: (logarithms: made multiplying easier and thus calculators practical) John Napier, Scotland, 1614; (slide rule) William Oughtred, England, 1632; (digital calculator) Blaise Pascal, 1642; (multiplication machine) Gottfried Leibniz, Germany, 1671; (important 19th-century contributors to modern machine) Frank S. Baldwin, Jay R. Monroe, Dorr E. Felt, W. T. Ohdner, William Burroughs, all U.S.; ("analytical engine" design, included concepts of programming, taping) Charles Babbage, England, 1835.
Calculus: Isaac Newton, England, 1669; (differential calculus) Gottfried Leibniz, Germany, 1684.

Camera: (hand-held) George Eastman, U.S., 1888; (Polaroid Land) Edwin Land, U.S., 1948.

"Canals" of Mars: Giovanni Schiaparelli, Italy, 1877.

Carpet sweeper: Melville R. Bissell, U.S., 1876.

Car radio: William Lear, Elmer Wavering, U.S., 1929, manufactured by Galvin Manufacturing Co., "Motorola."

Cells: (word used to describe microscopic examination of cork) Robert Hooke, England, 1665; (theory: cells are common structural and functional unit of all living organisms) Theodor Schwann, Matthias Schleiden, 1838–1839.

Cement, Portland: Joseph Aspdin, England, 1824.

Chewing gum: (spruce-based) John Curtis, U.S., 1848; (chicle-based) Thomas Adams, U.S., 1870.

Cholera bacterium: Robert Koch, Germany, 1883.

Circuit, integrated: (theoretical) G.W.A. Dummer, England, 1952; (phase-shift oscillator) Jack S. Kilby, Texas Instruments, U.S., 1959.

Classification of plants: (first modern, based on comparative study of forms) Andrea Cesalpino, Italy, 1583; (classification of plants and animals by genera and species) Carolus Linnaeus, Sweden, 1737–1753.

Clock, pendulum: Christian Huygens, The Netherlands, 1656.

Coca-Cola: John Pemberton, U.S., 1886.

Combustion: (nature of) Antoine Lavoisier, France, 1777.

Compact disk: RCA, U.S., 1972.

Computers: (first design of analytical engine) Charles Babbage, 1830s; (ENIAC, Electronic Numerical Integrator and Calculator, first all-electronic, completed) John Presper Eckert, Jr., John Mauchly, U.S., 1945; (dedicated at University of Pennsylvania) 1946; (UNIVAC, Universal Automatic Computer, handled both numeric and alphabetic data) 1951; (personal computer) Steve Wozniak, U.S., 1976.

Concrete: (reinforced) Joseph Monier, France, 1877.

Condensed milk: Gail Borden, U.S., 1853.

Conditioned reflex: Ivan Pavlov, Russia, c.1910.

Conservation of electric charge: (the total electric charge of the universe or any closed system is constant) Benjamin Franklin, U.S., 1751–1754.

Contagion theory: (infectious diseases caused by living agent transmitted from person to person) Girolamo Fracastoro, Italy, 1546.

Continental drift theory: (geographer who pieced together continents into a single landmass on maps) Antonio Snider-Pellegrini, France, 1858; (first proposed in lecture) Frank Taylor, U.S., 1912; (first comprehensive detailed theory) Alfred Wegener, Germany, 1912.

Contraceptive, oral: Gregory Pincus, Min Chuch Chang, John Rock, Carl Djerassi, U.S., 1951.

Converter, Bessemer: William Kelly, U.S., 1851.

Cosmetics: Egypt, c. 4000 B.C.

Cosmic string theory: (first postulated) Thomas Kibble, UK, 1976.

Cotton gin: Eli Whitney, U.S., 1793.

Crossbow: China, c. 300 B.C.

Cyclotron: Ernest O. Lawrence, U.S., 1931.

Defibrillator: Dr. William Bennett Kouwenhoven, U.S., 1932; (implantable) M. Stephen Heilman, MD, Dr. Alois Langer, Morton Mower, MD, Michel Mirowski, MD, 1980.

Deuterium: (heavy hydrogen) Harold Urey, U.S., 1931.

Disease: (chemicals in treatment of) crusaded by Philippus Paracelsus, 1527–1541; (germ theory) Louis Pasteur, France, 1862–1877.

DNA: (deoxyribonucleic acid) Friedrich Meischer, Germany, 1869; (determination of double-helical structure) F. H. Crick, England and James D. Watson, U.S., 1953.

Dye: (aniline, start of synthetic dye industry) William H. Perkin, England, 1856.

Dynamite: Alfred Nobel, Sweden, 1867.

Electric cooking utensil: (first) patented by St. George Lane-Fox, England, 1874.

Electric generator (dynamo): (laboratory model) Michael Faraday, England, 1832; Joseph Henry, U.S., c.1832; (hand-driven model) Hippolyte Pixii, France, 1833; (alternating-current generator) Nikola Tesla, U.S., 1892.

Thomas Alva Edison
(1847–1931) *Library of Congress*

Electric lamp: (arc lamp) Sir Humphrey Davy, England, 1801; (fluorescent lamp) A.E. Becquerel, France, 1867; (incandescent lamp) Sir Joseph Swann, England, Thomas A. Edison, U.S., contemporaneously, 1870s; (carbon arc street lamp) Charles F. Brush, U.S., 1879; (first widely marketed incandescent lamp) Thomas A. Edison, U.S., 1879; (mercury vapor lamp) Peter Cooper Hewitt, U.S., 1903; (neon lamp) Georges Claude, France, 1911; (tungsten filament) Irving Langmuir, U.S., 1915.

Electrocardiography: Demonstrated by Augustus Waller, Switzerland, 1887; (first practical device for recording activity of heart) Willem Einthoven, 1903, Netherlands.

Electromagnet: William Sturgeon, England, 1823.

Electron: Sir Joseph J. Thompson, England, 1897.

Electronic mail: Ray Tomlinson, U.S., 1972.

Elevator, passenger: (safety device permitting use by passengers) Elisha G. Otis, U.S., 1852; (elevator utilizing safety device) 1857.

E = mc²: (equivalence of mass and energy) Albert Einstein, Switzerland, 1907.

Engine, internal combustion: No single inventor. Fundamental theory established by Sadi Carnot, France, 1824; (two-stroke) Etienne Lenoir, France, 1860; (ideal operating cycle for four-stroke) Alphonse Beau de Roche, France, 1862; (operating four-stroke) Nikolaus Otto, Germany, 1876; (diesel) Rudolf Diesel, Germany, 1892; (rotary) Felix Wankel, Germany, 1956.

Evolution: (organic) Jean-Baptiste Lamarck, France, 1809; (by natural selection) Charles Darwin, England, 1859.

Exclusion principle: (no two electrons in an atom can occupy the same energy level) Wolfgang Pauli, Germany, 1925.

Expanding universe theory: (first proposed) George LeMaitre, Belgium, 1927; (discovered first direct evidence that the universe is expanding) Edwin P. Hubble, U.S., 1929; (Hubble constant: a measure of the rate at which the universe is expanding) Edwin P. Hubble, U.S., 1929.

Falling bodies, law of: Galileo Galilei, Italy, 1590.

Fermentation: (microorganisms as cause of) Louis Pasteur, France, c.1860.

Fiber optics: Narinder Kapany, England, 1955.

Fibers, man-made: (nitrocellulose fibers treated to change flammable nitrocellulose to harmless cellulose, precursor of rayon) Sir Joseph Swann, England, 1883; (rayon) Count Hilaire de Chardonnet, France, 1889; (Celanese) Henry and Camille Dreyfuss, U.S., England, 1921; (research on polyesters and polyamides, basis for modern man-made fibers) U.S., England, Germany, 1930s; (nylon) Wallace H. Carothers, U.S., 1935.

Frozen food: Clarence Birdseye, U.S., 1924.

Gene transfer: (recombinant DNA organism) Herbert Boyer, Stanley Cohen, U.S., 1973; (human) Steven Rosenberg, R. Michael Blaese, W. French Anderson, U.S., 1989.

Geometry, elements of: Euclid, Alexandria, Egypt, c. 300 B.C.; (analytic) René Descartes, France; and Pierre de Fermat, Switzerland, 1637.

Gravitation, law of: Sir Isaac Newton, England, c.1665 (published 1687).

Gunpowder: China, c.700.

Gyrocompass: Elmer A. Sperry, U.S., 1905.

Gyroscope: Jean Léon Foucault, France, 1852.

Halley's Comet: Edmund Halley, England, 1705.

Heart implanted in human, permanent artificial: Dr. Robert Jarvik, U.S., 1982.

Heart, temporary artificial: Willem Kolff, Netherlands, U.S., 1957.

Helicopter: (double rotor) Heinrich Focke, Germany, 1936; (single rotor) Igor Sikorsky, U.S., 1939.

Helium first observed on sun: Sir Joseph Lockyer, England, 1868.

Heredity, laws of: Gregor Mendel, Austria, 1865.

Holograph: Dennis Gabor, England, 1947.

Home videotape systems (VCR): (Betamax) Sony, Japan, 1975; (VHS) Matsushita, Japan, 1975.

Ice age theory: Louis Agassiz, Swiss-American, 1840.

Induction, electric: Joseph Henry, U.S., 1828.

Insulin: (first isolated) Sir Frederick G. Banting and Charles H. Best, Canada, 1921; (discovery first published) Banting and Best, 1922; (Nobel Prize awarded for purification for use in humans) John Macleod and Banting, 1923; (first synthesized) China, 1966.

Intelligence testing: Alfred Binet, Theodore Simon, France, 1905.

Interferon: Alick Isaacs, England, Jean Lindemann, Switzerland, 1957.

Isotopes: (concept of) Frederick Soddy, England, 1912; (stable isotopes) J. J. Thompson, England, 1913; (existence demonstrated by mass spectrography) Francis W. Aston, England, 1919.

Jet propulsion: (engine) Sir Frank Whittle, England, Hans von Ohain, Germany, 1936; (aircraft) *Heinkel He 178,* 1939.

Kinetic theory of gases: (molecules of a gas are in a state of rapid motion) Daniel Bernoulli, Switzerland, 1738.

Laser: (theoretical work on) Charles H. Townes, Arthur L. Schawlow, U.S., N. Basov, A. Prokhorov, U.S.S.R., 1958; (first working model) T. H. Maiman, U.S., 1960.

Lawn mower: Edwin Budding, John Ferrabee, England, 1830–1831.

LCD (liquid crystal display): Hoffmann-La Roche, Switzerland, 1970.

Lens, bifocal: Benjamin Franklin, U.S., c.1760.

Leyden jar: (prototype electrical condenser) Canon E. G. von Kleist of Kamin, Pomerania, 1745; independently evolved by Cunaeus and P. van Musschenbroek, University of Leyden, Holland, 1746, from where name originated.

Light, nature of: (wave theory) Christian Huygens, The Netherlands, 1678; (electromagnetic theory) James Clerk Maxwell, England, 1873.

Light, speed of: (theory that light has finite velocity) Olaus Roemer, Denmark, 1675.

Lightning rod: Benjamin Franklin, U.S., 1752.

Lock, cylinder: Linus Yale, U.S., 1851.

Locomotive: (steam powered) Richard Trevithick, England, 1804; (first practical, due to multiple-fire-tube boiler) George Stephenson, England, 1829; (largest steam-powered) Union Pacific's "Big Boy," U.S., 1941.

Loom: (horizontal, two-beamed) Egypt, c. 4400 B.C.; (Jacquard drawloom, pattern controlled by punch cards) Jacques de Vaucanson, France, 1745, Joseph-Marie Jacquard, 1801; (flying shuttle) John Kay, England, 1733; (power-driven loom) Edmund Cartwright, England, 1785.

Machine gun: (hand-cranked multibarrel) Richard J. Gatling, U.S., 1862; (practical single barrel, belt-fed) Hiram S. Maxim, Anglo-American, 1884.

Magnet, Earth is: William Gilbert, England, 1600.

Match: (phosphorus) François Derosne, France, 1816; (friction) Charles Sauria, France, 1831; (safety) J. E. Lundstrom, Sweden, 1855.

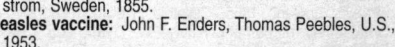

Benjamin Franklin (1706–1790)

Measles vaccine: John F. Enders, Thomas Peebles, U.S., 1953.

Metric system: revolutionary government of France, 1790–1801.

Microphone: Charles Wheatstone, England, 1827.

Microscope: (compound) Zacharias Janssen, The Netherlands, 1590; (electron) Vladimir Zworykin et al., U.S., Canada, Germany, 1932–1939.

Microwave oven: Percy Spencer, U.S., 1947.

Motion, laws of: Isaac Newton, England, 1687.

Motion pictures: Thomas A. Edison, U.S., 1893.

Motion pictures, sound: Product of various inventions. First picture with synchronized musical score: *Don Juan,* 1926; with spoken dialogue: *The Jazz Singer,* 1927; both Warner Bros.

Motor, electric: Michael Faraday, England, 1822; (alternating-current) Nikola Tesla, U.S., 1892.

Motorcycle: (motor tricycle) Edward Butler, England, 1884; (gasoline-engine motorcycle) Gottlieb Daimler, Germany, 1885.

Moving assembly line: Henry Ford, U.S., 1913.

Neptune: (discovery of) Johann Galle, Germany, 1846.

Neptunium: (first transuranic element, synthesis of) Edward M. McMillan, Philip H. Abelson, U.S., 1940.

Neutron: James Chadwick, England, 1932.

Neutron-induced radiation: Enrico Fermi et al., Italy, 1934.

Nitroglycerin: Ascanio Sobrero, Italy, 1846.

Nuclear fission: Otto Hahn, Fritz Strassmann, Germany, 1938.

Nuclear reactor: Enrico Fermi, Italy, et al., 1942.

Ohm's law: (relationship between strength of electric current, electromotive force, and circuit resistance) Georg S. Ohm, Germany, 1827.

Oil well: Edwin L. Drake, U.S., 1859.

Oxygen: (isolation of) Joseph Priestley, England, 1774; Karl Scheele, Sweden, 1773.

Ozone: Christian Schönbein, Germany, 1839.

Pacemaker: (internal) Clarence W. Lillehie, Earl Bakk, U.S., 1957.

Paper: China, c.100 A.D.

Parachute: Louis S. Lenormand, France, 1783.

Pen: (fountain)Lewis E. Waterman, U.S., 1884; (ball-point, for marking on rough surfaces) John H. Loud, U.S., 1888; (ball-point, for handwriting) Lazlo Biro, Argentina, 1944.

Periodic law: (that properties of elements are functions of their atomic weights) Dmitri Mendeleev, Russia, 1869.

Periodic table: (arrangement of chemical elements based on periodic law) Dmitri Mendeleev, Russia, 1869.

Phonograph: Thomas A. Edison, U.S., 1877.

Photography: (first paper negative, first photograph, on metal) Joseph Nicéphore Niepce, France, 1816–1827; (discovery of fixative powers of hyposulfite of soda) Sir John Herschel, England, 1819; (first direct positive image on silver plate, the daguerreotype) Louis Daguerre, based on work with Niepce, France, 1839; (first paper negative from which a number of positive prints could be made) William Talbot, England, 1841. Work of these four men, taken together, forms basis for all modern photography. (First color images) Alexandre Becquerel, Claude Niepce de Saint-Victor, France, 1848–1860; (commercial color film with three emulsion layers, Kodachrome) U.S., 1935.

Photovoltaic effect: (light falling on certain materials can produce electricity) Edmund Becquerel, France, 1839.

Piano: (Hammerklavier) Bartolommeo Cristofori, Italy, 1709; (pianoforte with sustaining and damper pedals) John Broadwood, England, 1873.

Planetary motion, laws of: Johannes Kepler, Germany, 1609, 1619.

Plant respiration and photosynthesis: Jan Ingenhousz, Holland, 1779.

Plastics: (first material, nitrocellulose softened by vegetable oil, camphor, precursor to Celluloid) Alexander Parkes, England, 1855; (Celluloid, involving recognition of vital effect of camphor) John W. Hyatt, U.S., 1869; (Bakelite, first completely synthetic plastic) Leo H. Baekeland, U.S., 1910; (theoretical background of macromolecules and process of polymerization on which modern plastics industry rests) Hermann Staudinger, Germany, 1922; (polypropylene and low-pressure method for producing high-density polyethylene) Robert Banks, Paul Hogan, U.S., 1958.

Plate tectonics: Alfred Wegener, Germany, 1912–1915.

Plow, forked: Mesopotamia, before 3000 B.C.

Plutonium, synthesis of: Glenn T. Seaborg, Edwin M. McMillan, Arthur C. Wahl, Joseph W. Kennedy, U.S., 1941.

Polio, vaccine: (experimentally safe dead-virus vaccine) Jonas E. Salk, U.S., 1952; (effective large-scale field trials) 1954; (officially approved) 1955; (safe oral live-virus vaccine developed) Albert B. Sabin, U.S., 1954; (available in the U.S.) 1960.

**Johann Gutenberg
(c. 1400–1468)**

Positron: Carl D. Anderson, U.S., 1932.

Pressure cooker: (early version) Denis Papin, France, 1679.

Printing: (block) Japan, c.700; (movable type) Korea, c.1400, Johann Gutenberg, Germany, c.1450; (lithography, offset) Aloys Senefelder, Germany, 1796; (rotary press) Richard Hoe, U.S., 1844; (linotype) Ottmar Mergenthaler, U.S., 1884.

Probability theory: René Descartes, France, and Pierre de Fermat, Switzerland, 1654.

Proton: Ernest Rutherford, England, 1919.

Prozac: (antidepressant fluoxetine) Bryan B. Malloy, Scotland, and Klaus K. Schmiegel, U.S., 1972; (released for use in U.S.) Eli Lilly & Company, 1987.

Psychoanalysis: Sigmund Freud, Austria, c.1904.

Pulsars: Antony Hewish and Jocelyn Bell Burnel, England, 1967.

Quantum theory: (general) Max Planck, Germany, 1900; (sub-atomic) Niels Bohr, Denmark, 1913; (quantum mechanics) Werner Heisenberg, Erwin Schrödinger, Germany, 1925.

Quarks: Jerome Friedman, Henry Kendall, Richard Taylor, U.S., 1967.

Quasars: Marten Schmidt, U.S., 1963.

Rabies immunization: Louis Pasteur, France, 1885.

Radar: (limited to one-mile range) Christian Hulsmeyer, Germany, 1904; (pulse modulation, used for measuring height of ionosphere) Gregory Breit, Merle Tuve, U.S., 1925; (first practical radar—radio detection and ranging) Sir Robert Watson-Watt, England, 1934–1935.

Radio: (electromagnetism, theory of) James Clerk Maxwell, England, 1873; (spark coil, generator of electromagnetic waves) Heinrich Hertz, Germany, 1886; (first practical system of wireless telegraphy) Guglielmo Marconi, Italy, 1895; (first long-distance telegraphic radio signal sent across the Atlantic) Marconi, 1901; (vacuum electron tube, basis for radio telephony) Sir John Fleming, England, 1904; (triode amplifying tube) Lee de Forest, U.S., 1906; (regenerative circuit, allowing long-distance sound reception) Edwin H. Armstrong, U.S., 1912; (frequency modulation—FM) Edwin H. Armstrong, U.S., 1933.

Radioactivity: (X-rays) Wilhelm K. Roentgen, Germany, 1895; (radioactivity of uranium) Henri Becquerel, France, 1896; (radioactive elements, radium and polonium in uranium ore) Marie Sklodowska-Curie, Pierre Curie, France, 1898; (classification of alpha and beta particle radiation) Pierre Curie, France, 1900; (gamma radiation) Paul-Ulrich Villard, France, 1900.

Radiocarbon dating, carbon-14 method: (discovered) Willard F. Libby, U.S., 1947; (first demonstrated) U.S., 1950.

Radio signals, extraterrestrial: first known radio noise signals were received by U.S. engineer, Karl Jansky, originating from the Galactic Center, 1931.

Radio waves: (cosmic sources, led to radio astronomy) Karl Jansky, U.S., 1932.

Razor: (safety, successfully marketed) King Gillette, U.S., 1901; (electric) Jacob Schick, U.S., 1928, 1931.

Reaper: Cyrus McCormick, U.S., 1834.

Refrigerator: Alexander Twining, U.S., James Harrison, Australia, 1850; (first with a compressor device) the Domelse, Chicago, U.S., 1913.

Refrigerator ship: (first) the *Frigorifique,* cooling unit designed by Charles Teller, France, 1877.

Relativity: (special and general theories of) Albert Einstein, Switzerland, Germany, U.S., 1905–1953.

Revolver: Samuel Colt, U.S., 1835.

Richter scale: Charles F. Richter, U.S., 1935.

Rifle: (muzzle-loaded) Italy, Germany, c.1475; (breech-loaded) England, France, Germany, U.S., c.1866; (bolt-action) Paul von Mauser, Germany, 1889; (automatic) John Browning, U.S., 1918.

Rocket: (liquid-fueled) Robert Goddard, U.S., 1926.

Roller bearing: (wooden for cartwheel) Germany or France, c.100 B.C.

Rotation of Earth: Jean Bernard Foucault, France, 1851.

Royal Observatory, Greenwich: established in 1675 by Charles II of England; John Flamsteed first Astronomer Royal.

Rubber: (vulcanization process) Charles Goodyear, U.S., 1839.

Saccharin: Constantine Fuhlberg, Ira Remsen, U.S., 1879.

Safety pin: Walter Hunt, U.S., 1849.

Saturn, ring around: Christian Huygens, The Netherlands, 1659.

"Scotch" tape: Richard Drew, U.S., 1929.

Screw propeller: Sir Francis P. Smith, England, 1836; John Ericsson, England, worked independently of and simultaneously with Smith, 1837.

Seat belt: (three point) Nils Bohlin, Sweden, 1962.

Seismograph: (first accurate) John Milne, England, 1880.

Sewing machine: Elias Howe, U.S., 1846; (continuous stitch) Isaac Singer, U.S., 1851.

Solar energy: First realistic application of solar energy using parabolic solar reflector to drive caloric engine on steam boiler, John Ericsson, U.S., 1860s.

Solar system, universe: (Sun-centered universe) Nicolaus Copernicus, Warsaw, 1543; (establishment of planetary orbits as elliptical) Johannes Kepler, Germany, 1609; (infinity of universe) Giordano Bruno, Italian monk, 1584.

Spectrum: (heterogeneity of light) Sir Isaac Newton, England, 1665–1666.

Spectrum analysis: Gustav Kirchhoff, Robert Bunsen, Germany, 1859.

Spermatozoa: Anton van Leeuwenhoek, The Netherlands, 1683.

Spinning: (spinning wheel) India, introduced to Europe in Middle Ages; (Saxony wheel, continuous spinning of wool or cotton yarn) England, c.1500–1600; (spinning jenny) James Hargreaves, England, 1764; (spinning frame) Sir Richard Arkwright, England, 1769; (spinning mule, completed mechanization of spinning, permitting production of yarn to keep up with demands of modern looms) Samuel Crompton, England, 1779.

Star catalog: (first modern) Tycho Brahe, Denmark, 1572.

Steam engine: (first commercial version based on principles of French physicist Denis Papin) Thomas Savery, England, 1639; (atmospheric steam engine) Thomas Newcomen, England, 1705; (steam engine for pumping water from collieries) Savery, Newcomen, 1725; (modern condensing, double acting) James Watt, England, 1782; (high-pressure) Oliver Evans, U.S., 1804.

Steamship: Claude de Jouffroy d'Abbans, France, 1783; James Rumsey, U.S., 1787; John Fitch, U.S., 1790; (high-pressure) Oliver Evans, U.S., 1804. All preceded Robert Fulton, U.S., 1807, credited with launching first commercially successful steamship.

Stethoscope: René Laënnec, France, 1819.

Sulfa drugs: (parent compound, para-aminobenzene-sulfanomide) Paul Gelmo, Austria, 1908; (antibacterial activity) Gerhard Domagk, Germany, 1935.

Superconductivity: (theory) John Bardeen, Leon Cooper, John Scheiffer, U.S., 1957.

Symbolic logic: George Boule, 1854; (modern) Bertrand Russell, Alfred North Whitehead, England, 1910–1913.

Tank, military: Sir Ernest Swinton, England, 1914.

Tape recorder: (magnetic steel tape) Valdemar Poulsen, Denmark, 1899.

Teflon: DuPont, U.S., 1943.

Telegraph: Samuel F. B. Morse, U.S., 1837.

Telephone: Alexander Graham Bell, U.S., 1876.

Telescope: Hans Lippershey, The Netherlands, 1608; (astronomical) Galileo Galilei, Italy, 1609; (reflecting) Isaac Newton, England, 1668.

Television: (Iconoscope–T.V. camera table) Vladimir Zworykin, U.S., 1923, and also kinescope (cathode ray tube) 1928; (mechanical disk-scanning method) successfully demonstrated by J.L. Baird, Scotland, C.F. Jenkins, U.S., 1926; (first all-electric television image) Philo T. Farnsworth, U.S., 1927; (color, mechanical disk) Baird, 1928; (color, compatible with black and white) George Valensi, France, 1938; (color, sequential rotating filter) Peter Goldmark, U.S., first introduced, 1951; (color, compatible with black and white) commercially introduced in U.S., National Television Systems Committee, 1953.

Thermodynamics: (first law: energy cannot be created or destroyed, only converted from one form to another) Julius von Mayer, Germany, 1842; James Joule, England, 1843; (second law: heat cannot of itself pass from a colder to a warmer body) Rudolph Clausius, Germany, 1850; (third law: the entropy of ordered solids reaches zero at the absolute zero of temperature) Walter Nernst, Germany, 1918.

Thermometer: (open-column) Galileo Galilei, c.1593; (clinical) Santorio Santorio, Padua, c.1615; (mercury, also Fahrenheit scale) Gabriel D. Fahrenheit, Germany, 1714; (centigrade scale) Anders Celsius, Sweden, 1742; (absolute-temperature, or Kelvin, scale) William Thompson, Lord Kelvin, England, 1848.

Tire, pneumatic: Robert W. Thompson, England, 1845; (bicycle tire) John B. Dunlop, Northern Ireland, 1888.

Toilet, flush: Product of Minoan civilization, Crete, c. 2000 B.C. Alleged invention by "Thomas Crapper" is untrue.

Tractor: Benjamin Holt, U.S., 1900.

Transformer, electric: William Stanley, U.S., 1885.

Transistor: John Bardeen, Walter H. Brattain, William B. Shockley, U.S., 1947.

Tuberculosis bacterium: Robert Koch, Germany, 1882.

Typewriter: Christopher Sholes, Carlos Glidden, U.S., 1867.

Uncertainty principle: (that position and velocity of an object cannot both be measured exactly, at the same time) Werner Heisenberg, Germany, 1927.

Uranus: (first planet discovered in recorded history) William Herschel, England, 1781.

Vaccination: Edward Jenner, England, 1796.

Vacuum cleaner: (manually operated) Ives W. McGaffey, U.S., 1869; (electric) Hubert C. Booth, England, 1901; (upright) J. Murray Spangler, U.S., 1907.

Van Allen (radiation) Belt: (around Earth) James Van Allen, U.S., 1958.

Video disk: Philips Co., The Netherlands, 1972.

Vitamins: (hypothesis of disease deficiency) Sir F. G. Hopkins, Casimir Funk, England, 1912; (vitamin A) Elmer V. McCollum, M. Davis, U.S., 1912–1914; (vitamin B) McCollum, U.S., 1915–1916; (thiamin, B_1) Casimir Funk, England, 1912; (riboflavin, B_2) D. T. Smith, E. G. Hendrick, U.S., 1926; (niacin) Conrad Elvehjem, U.S., 1937; (B_6) Paul Gyorgy, U.S., 1934; (vitamin C) C. A. Hoist, T. Froelich, Norway, 1912; (vitamin D) McCollum, U.S., 1922; (folic acid) Lucy Wills, England, 1933.

Voltaic pile: (forerunner of modern battery, first source of continuous electric current) Alessandro Volta, Italy, 1800.

Wallpaper: Europe, 16th and 17th century.

Wassermann test: (for syphilis) August von Wassermann, Germany, 1906.

Wheel: (cart, solid wood) Mesopotamia, c.3800–3600 B.C.

Windmill: Persia, c.600.

World Wide Web: (developed while working at CERN) Tim Berners-Lee, England, 1989; (development of Mosaic browser makes WWW available for general use) Marc Andreeson, U.S., 1993.

Xerography: Chester Carlson, U.S., 1938.

Yellow Fever: (transmission of)Walter Reed, U.S., 1900.

Zero: India, c. 600; (absolute zero temperature, cessation of all molecular energy) William Thompson, Lord Kelvin, England, 1848.

Zipper: W. L. Judson, U.S., 1891.

Samuel F. B. Morse (1791–1872)
Library of Congress

The National Inventors Hall of Fame

The National Inventors Hall of Fame,™ established in 1973 and located in Akron, Ohio, honors the women and men responsible for the great technological advances that make human, social, and economic progress possible. The Class of 2004 inductees have made accomplishments in medicine, engineering, computing, and more.

Frederick Banting, 1891–1941, **Charles Best,** 1899–1978, **James Collip,** 1892–1965, *Purified Insulin.* Canadian scientists Banting, Best, and Collip determined that insulin injections would help keep diabetics alive and developed techniques for extracting, isolating, and injecting it. Although not a cure, insulin remains the most effective means for treating the disease.

Vannevar Bush, 1890–1974, *Differential Analyzer.* During WWII, Bush headed the Office of Scientific Research and Development, overseeing the work of 6,000 scientists developing over 200 military weapons and instruments. His most significant invention was the differential analyzer, an analog computer that solved differential equations with as many as 18 independent variables.

Harry Coover, 1919–, *Superglue.* Coover's invention of a new class of adhesives has influenced medicine, industry, and consumers. At Eastman Chemical, Coover discovered cyanoacrylate adhesives (CA), soon known as superglue. Early use of CA during the Vietnam War allowed for the quick closure of wounds.

Wallace Coulter, 1913–1998, *Coulter Principle.* A common diagnostic medical tool, the complete blood count would not be possible without Coulter's invention of the Coulter Counter. Coulter received numerous honors and was awarded 74 patents for his work in hematology.

Ray Dolby, 1933–, *Dolby Noise Reduction.* During the 1960s, Dolby discovered a way to dramatically reduce the "hiss" from analog tape sound recording and reproduction, revolutionizing the audio industry. As a result, the cassette became the most popular form of recorded music in the 1970s, and cinema audiences were able to enjoy surround sound from almost all movies.

Edith Flanigen, 1929–, *Molecular Sieves.* A pioneer in silicate and molecular sieve chemistry, Flanigen invented or co-invented over 200 synthetic materials. Her work with zeolite Y made oil refining more efficient, cleaner, and safer, and she also invented an emerald synthesizing process.

Robert Gallo, 1937–, **Luc Montagnier,** 1932–, *HIV Isolation and Identification.* Robert Gallo and Luc Montagnier both discovered HIV, determining that the virus was the cause of AIDS, and making it more possible to control the disease. Formerly a cancer researcher at the National Cancer Institute, Gallo now heads the Institute of Human Virology in Baltimore. Montagnier is the former director of the Centre National de la Recherché Scientifique (CNRS), and he is the co-founder of the World Foundation for AIDS Research and Prevention.

Ivan Getting, 1912–2003, **Bradford Parkinson,** 1935–, *Global Positioning System—GPS.* During the 1950s, Getting advanced the concept of using a system of satellites to allow the calculation of precise positioning data for rapidly moving vehicles. Parkinson created and ran the NAVSTAR GPS Joint Program Office from 1972–78. GPS is now routinely used for air traffic control systems, ships, trucks and cars, mechanized farming, search and rescue, tracking environmental changes, and more.

John Gibbon, 1903–1973, *Heart-Lung Machine.* Gibbon's development of the heart-lung machine made possible the first successful open-heart operation in 1953. Improved versions allow surgeons today to perform bypass surgery and heart transplants. A renowned surgeon and teacher, Gibbon authored the textbook *Surgery of the Chest.*

Lloyd Hall, 1894–1971, *Food Preservatives.* Hall made great strides in keeping food fresh and making it more flavorful. He created food preservatives, meat-curing products, seasonings, emulsions, bakery products, antioxidants, protein hydrolysates, and numerous other products. He also discovered and developed novel techniques for sterilizing spices, cereals, and other foods and pharmaceuticals.

Elias Howe, 1819–1867, *Sewing Machine.* Howe invented the first practical sewing machine after watching his wife sew. His machine's locked-stitch technique is still used today.

Charles D. Kelman, 1930–, *Cataract Surgery.* In 1963, Kelman designed the ultrasonic phacoemulsifier, which liquefies cataracts so they can be removed by suction. The pioneering procedure reduced the risk of complications and transformed a 10-day hospital stay to an outpatient procedure.

Bernard Oliver, 1916–1995, **Claude Shannon,** 1916–2001, *Pulse Code Modulation.* Oliver and Shannon developed the first high-speed digital transmission system based on coded electronic pulses, making digital telephone systems and compact discs possible. Oliver had a respected career at Bell Laboratories and also at Hewlett-Packard, where he was pivotal in developing the first hand-held calculator. Shannon, who also had a long and prolific Bell Labs career, is considered the father of information theory, which is considered the foundation of today's computer technology.

Norbert Rillieux, 1806–1894, *Automated Sugar Refining.* Rillieux automated modern sugar production and made it dramatically more efficient, while producing a much higher quality of sugar. It transformed the lives of slaves who were previously forced to endure the dangerous and backbreaking task of boiling sugar cane in open cauldrons. His process elevated the U.S. from a minor role in the sugar industry to a major producer.

John Roebling, 1806–1869, *Suspension Bridge.* The age of the suspension bridge was ushered in by engineer and inventor Roebling. Roebling saw the potential of steel wire as a bridge building component and invented machinery to twist the wire into cables. He oversaw the construction of many bridges but died before his most famous bridge, the Brooklyn Bridge, was completed in 1883.

The Tragedy of Tar Creek

Superfund was created to ensure that America's toxic-waste dumps got cleaned up. Here's an inside look at one of its failures

By **MARGOT ROOSEVELT** TIME

To get a better view of the situation, John Sparkman guns his flame-red truck up a massive pile of gravel. From the summit, a lifeless brown wasteland stretches to the horizon, like a scene from a science-fiction movie. Mountains of mine tailings, some as tall as 13-story buildings, others as wide as four football fields, loom over streets, homes, churches, and schools. Dust, laced with lead, cadmium, and other poisonous metals, blows off the man-made hills and 800 acres of dry settling ponds. "It gets in your teeth," says Sparkman, head of a local citizens' group. "It cakes in your ears and hair. It's like we've been environmentally raped."

Poisoned Wasteland

Hyperbole? Drive through the desolate towns around Picher, Okla., and you might think differently. This is eco-assault on an epic scale. The prairie here in the northeast corner of the state is punctured with 480 open mine shafts and 30,000 drill holes. Little League fields have been built over an immense underground cavity that could collapse at any time. Acid mine waste flushes into drinking wells. When the water rises in Tar Creek, which runs through the site, a neon-orange scum oozes onto the roadside.

But the grimmest legacy of a century of intensive lead and zinc mining are the "lead heads" or "chat rats," as the kids who grew up around here are known. As toddlers, they played in sandboxes of chat—the powdery output of mills after ore is extracted from rock. As preteens, they rode their bikes across the gravel mounds and swam in lime-green sinkholes. Their parents used mine tailings to make driveways and foundations, never thinking that contaminated dust might blow through the heating ducts of their ranch houses. In the past decade, studies have shown that up to 38% of local children have had high levels of lead in their blood—an exposure that can cause permanent neurological damage and learning disabilities. "Our kids hit a brick wall," says Kim Pace, principal of the Picher-Cardin Elementary School. "Their eyes skip and jump. It takes them 100 repetitions to learn a sound."

The Hot Spots

Sixty-five million Americans live within four miles of a Superfund site. The top ten states:

New Jersey	113	Florida	51
California	96	Washington	47
Pennsylvania	92	Texas	43
New York	90	Illinois	40
Michigan	67	Wisconsin	39

Superfund by the Numbers

Number of sites on the priority list since 1980	1,518
Number of Superfund sites listed today	1,240
Number of sites cleaned up and deleted from the list	278
Number of sites currently being cleaned up	622
Number of highly toxic sites eligible for listing	2,500
Number of years, on average, it takes to decontaminate a site	11
Decline in Superfund appropriations since 1993, adjusted for inflation	35%
Number of cleanups completed in the 2003 fiscal year under President Bush	40
Average number of annual cleanups under President Clinton	76

It wasn't supposed to be like this. In 1980, Congress passed the Comprehensive Environmental Response, Compensation and Liability Act—commonly known as the Superfund law—one of the boldest environmental statutes in U.S. history. It was a law designed to fit all circumstances. It covered existing plants whose owners could be forced to clean up their dumps. It covered polluted sites long since abandoned by their owners: defunct factories, refineries, and mines. Even when companies followed the standard, if dubious, practices of the day—dumping toxic waste in rivers, burying it in leaky drums, or just leaving it, as in Oklahoma, to blow in the wind—they would be held accountable. And if they refused to clean up their messes, the Environmental Protection Agency (EPA) would do so for them and charge triple damages for its trouble. In the event that the perpetrators had disappeared or gone out of business, a general tax on polluting industries—a "Superfund"—would pay to fix the damage.

Superfund Under Siege

But today Superfund is a program under siege, plagued by partisan politics, industry stonewalling, and bureaucratic inertia. The U.S. government has spent $27 billion on the effort and forced individual polluters to spend an additional $21 billion. Love Canal, the deadly dump in New York State that spurred the law's passage, has been capped with a layer of clay, and the EPA proposed last month to take it off the list. So far, 278 sites have been delisted. But there are thousands more out there. According to the General Accounting Office (GAO), 1 out of 4 Americans still lives within four miles of a Superfund site—many of these sites killing fields saturated with cancer-causing chemicals and other toxins.

The GAO reports that the program's budget fell 35% in inflation-adjusted dollars over the past decade. And environmentalists say that Bush appointees are slowing the pace of cleanups and failing to list potential new sites. According to the EPA's inspector general, 29 projects in 17 states were underfunded last year. The administration, charges New Jersey senator Frank Lautenberg, a Democrat, has "allowed—deliberately—these sites to rot where they are."

Tar Creek Debacle

Tar Creek is a case in point. Two decades after it was targeted on the very first Superfund priority list, the 40-sq.-mi. site is worse off than ever. Early on, the government confined its effort to the polluted creek, without looking at chat piles, soil, air quality, or the danger of subsidence. Was it a lack of knowledge of the danger, as the EPA claims? Or industry influence, as environmentalists charge? Whatever the reason, federal attorneys settled with mining companies for pennies on the dollar. Now, after fruitless efforts to contain 28 billion gallons of acid mine water, contamination is spreading across a vast watershed. And although the EPA trucked out toxic dirt from about 2,000 homes and schools, Tar Creek's children still show elevated lead levels at six times the national average.

Administration officials say they are cleaning up the nation's 1,240 highest-priority sites as fast as they can. But that will be harder, since the multibillion-dollar industry-paid trust fund, set aside for abandoned sites such as Tar Creek, ran dry in October 2003. The fund was supplied by taxes on the purchase of toxic chemicals and petroleum and on corporate profits above $2 million. But the Republican-led Congress allowed the fees to expire in 1995. Bush is the first president to oppose the levies, and in March 2004 Lautenberg and other Senate Democrats lost a narrow vote to reinstate them. In protest, the Sierra Club aired "Make Polluters Pay" TV ads in Pennsylvania, Florida, and Michigan—all swing states. And on April 15, tax day, activists in 25 states picketed post offices to object. "We went from polluters paying to citizens paying," says Oklahoma environmentalist Earl Hatley. "Now EPA doesn't have the money for megasites like Tar Creek."

With the EPA's clout slackening, private attorneys are moving in. At Tar Creek, lawyers are suing seven mining companies on behalf of scores of lead-exposed children. A separate suit demanding a cleanup was filed by the Quapaw Indians, whose land was leased for the mines. And environmentalist Robert F. Kennedy, Jr., has joined a class-action suit to force companies to relocate the population of two polluted Oklahoma towns, Picher and Cardin. Court papers suggest that mining executives knew as early as the 1930s that the contaminated dust was dangerous but sought to, in their words, "dissuade" the government from intervening. A mining-company lawyer says the charge is based on "out-of-context reading" of historical documents.

Just how dangerous that dust might be is still a matter of dispute. Doctors at the Harvard School of Public Health have begun extensive studies in Tar Creek, not just of lead exposure but also of the cocktail mix of lead, manganese, cadmium, and other metals that interact in unknown ways. "We're looking at four generations of poisoning," says Rebecca Jim of the L.E.A.D. agency, a local group.

Tar Creek is an extreme case. But like Tolstoy's unhappy families, every Superfund site is tragic and contentious in its own way. In Libby, Mont., a massive mine blanketed the town with asbestos dust, killing at least 215 people and sickening 1,100 more with cancer and lung disease—yet cleanup funds have been cut so sharply that it could take 10 to 15 years to finish the job. In Coeur d'Alene, Idaho, miners dumped 60 million tons of toxic metals into waterways, but state officials are fighting a Superfund cleanup, fearing a stigma that might hurt tourism. In New York, General Electric, which contaminated 40 miles of the Hudson River with cancer-causing PCBs, has hired high-profile attorney Laurence Tribe to convince federal courts that the Superfund law is unconstitutional. And in New Jersey, where the rabbits frolicking around the Chemical Insecticide Corp. plant once grew green-tinged fur, cleanup funds were restored only after locals sent green plush bunnies to members of Congress.

Losing Hope

At Tar Creek, many residents have given up hope. Even the EPA, which has spent $107 million at the site, isn't sure if it can ever be repaired. "We don't have an off-the-shelf remedy," says EPA Superfund official Randy Deitz. "What do you do with the enormous chat piles? When does cleanup become impracticable? We have limited resources." In a show of no-confidence, the Oklahoma legislature passed a $5 million buyout for all families with children under six in April 2004. John Sparkman, who heads the Tar Creek Steering Committee, a group of buyout supporters, veers between cynicism and despair. "They think we're poor white trash," he says bitterly, driving past Picher's boarded-up storefronts. "The votes here don't affect any federal election—so why bother? We've agitated till we can't agitate anymore." Meanwhile, at Tar Creek, the toxic dust keeps blowing in the wind. □

Forbidden Fruit

Fruits and vegetables highest in pesticides			Fruits and vegetables lowest in pesticides		
Apples	Nectarines	Potatoes	Asparagus	Cauliflower	Onions
Celery	Peaches	Raspberries (red)	Avocados	Corn	Papayas
Cherries	Pears	Spinach	Bananas	Kiwi	Pineapples
Grapes (imported)	Peppers	Strawberries	Broccoli	Mangoes	Sweet peas

Source: Environmental Working Group (www.ewg.org). The research is based on more than 100,000 laboratory tests conducted by the Dept. of Agriculture and the Food and Drug Administration. Their "dirty dozen" list has remained the same since 1993.

World Energy Consumption and Carbon Dioxide Emissions, 1990–2025

Region	Energy consumption (quadrillion btu)				Carbon dioxide emissions (million metric tons)			
	1990	2001	2010	2025	1990	2001	2010	2025
Industrialized nations	182.8	211.5	236.3	281.4	10,462	11,634	12,938	15,643
Eastern Europe/Former Soviet Union	76.3	53.3	59.0	75.6	4,902	3,148	3,397	4,313
Developing nations								
Asia	52.5	85.0	110.6	173.4	3,994	6,012	7,647	11,801
Middle East	13.1	20.8	25.0	34.1	846	1,299	1,566	2,110
Africa	9.3	12.4	14.6	21.5	656	843	971	1,413
Central and South America	14.4	20.9	25.4	36.9	703	964	1,194	1,845
Total developing	89.3	139.2	175.5	265.9	6,200	9,118	11,379	17,168
Total world	348.4	403.9	470.8	622.9	21,563	23,899	27,715	37,124

Sources: 1990 and 2001: Energy Information Administration (EIA), International Energy Annual 2001, DOE/EIA=0219 (2001) (Washington, DC, Feb. 2003). 2010, and 2025: EIA, System for the Analysis of Global Energy Markets (2004). Web: www.eia.doe.gov/iea/.

Top World Oil Producers, Exporters, Consumers, and Importers, 2003

(millions of barrels per day)

Producers[1]	Total oil production	Exporters[2]	Net oil exports	Consumers[3]	Total oil consumption	Importers[4]	Net oil imports
1. Saudi Arabia	9.95	1. Saudi Arabia	8.38	1. United States	20.0	1. United States	11.1
2. United States	8.84	2. Russia	5.81	2. China	5.6	2. Japan	5.3
3. Russia	8.44	3. Norway	3.02	3. Japan	5.4	3. Germany	2.5
4. Iran	3.87	4. Iran	2.48	4. Germany	2.6	4. South Korea	2.2
5. Mexico	3.79	5. United Arab		5. Russia	2.6	5. China	2.0
6. China	3.54	Emirates	2.29	6. India	2.2	6. France	2.0
7. Norway	3.27	6. Venezuela	2.23	7. South Korea	2.2	7. Italy	1.7
8. Canada	3.11	7. Kuwait	2.00	8. Canada	2.2	8. Spain	1.5
9. United Arab		8. Nigeria	1.93	9. Brazil	2.1	9. India	1.4
Emirates	2.66	9. Mexico	1.74	10. France	2.1		
10. Venezuela	2.58	10. Algeria	1.64	10. Mexico	2.1		
11. United Kingdom	2.39	11. Libya	1.25				
12. Kuwait	2.32						
13. Nigeria	2.25						

NOTE: OPEC members in italics. 1. Table includes all countries with total oil production exceeding 2 million barrels per day in 2002. Includes crude oil, natural gas liquids, condensate, refinery gain, and other liquids. 2. Includes all countries with net exports exceeding 1 million barrels per day in 2002. 3. Includes all countries that consumed more than 2 million barrels per day in 2002. 4. Includes all countries that imported more than 1 million barrels per day in 2002. Source: Energy Information Administration (EIA). www.eia.doe.gov/emev/topworldtables1_2.html.

Greatest Oil Reserves by Country, 2003

2002 rank	Country	2003 proved reserves (billion barrels)	2002 rank	Country	2003 proved reserves (billion barrels)
1.	Saudi Arabia	261.7	6.	Russia	58.8
2.	Iraq	115.0	7.	Venezuela	53.1
3.	Iran	100.1	8.	Nigeria	32.0
4.	Kuwait	98.9	9.	Libya	30.0
5.	United Arab Emirates	63.0	10.	China	23.7

NOTES: Figures for Russia are "explored reserves," which are understood to be proved plus some probable. All other figures are proved reserves recoverable with present technology and prices. Source: World Oil, Vol. 224, No. 8 (Aug. 2003). From: U.S. Energy Information Administration, International Energy Annual 2002 (March–June 2004).

Greatest Natural Gas Reserves by Country, 2003

2002 rank	Country	2003 proved reserves (trillion cu ft)	2002 rank	Country	2003 proved reserves (trillion cu ft)
1.	Russia	1,700.0	6.	United Arab Emirates	204.1
2.	Qatar	916.0	7.	United States	186.9
3.	Iran	913.6	8.	Nigeria	178.5
4.	Other former USSR	332.1	9.	Algeria	170.0
5.	Saudi Arabia	234.6	10.	Venezuela	149.2

NOTES: Figures for Russia are "explored reserves," which are understood to be proved plus some probable. All other figures are proved reserves recoverable with present technology and prices. Source: World Oil, Vol. 224, No. 8 (Aug. 2003). From: U.S. Energy Information Administration, International Energy Annual 2002 (March-June 2004).

World Net Electricity Consumption by Selected Regions, 1990–2025
(billion kilowatt-hours)

Region	2001	Projections				Average annual percent change, 2001–2025
		2010	2015	2020	2025	
United States	3,386	4,055	4,429	4,811	5,207	1.8%
Japan	788	870	920	965	1,012	1.0
Eastern Europe/ former Soviet Union	1,815	2,181	2,447	2,706	2,941	2.0
China	1,237	1,856	2,322	2,825	3,410	4.3
India	554	751	896	1,053	1,216	3.3
Africa	384	499	602	716	808	3.1
Central and South America	668	864	1,000	1,196	1,425	3.2
Total industralized countries	7,296	8,456	9,173	9,910	10,697	1.6
Total developing countries	4,179	5,721	6,833	8,072	9,434	3.5
Total world	13,290	16,358	18,453	20,688	23,072	2.3

Sources: Energy Information Administration (EIA): *International Energy Outlook 2004.*

America's 25 Most Ozone-Polluted Metropolitan Areas, 2004

Rank 2004	Metropolitan area	Rank 2004	Metropolitan area
1.	Los Angeles–Riverside–Orange County, Calif.	13.	New York–Newark–Bridgeport, N.Y.-N.J.-Conn.-Pa.
2.	Fresno, Calif.	14.	Charlotte-Gastonia-Salisbury, N.C.-S.C.
3.	Bakersfield, Calif.	15.	Cleveland-Akron-Elyria, Ohio
4.	Visalia-Porterville, Calif.	16.	Greensboro–Winston-Salem–High Point, N.C.
5.	Houston-Baytown-Huntsville, Tex.	17.	Pittsburgh–New Castle, Pa.
6.	Merced, Calif.	18.	Phoenix-Mesa-Scottsdale, Ariz.
7.	Sacramento-Arden-Arcade-Truckee, Calif.-Nev.	19.	San Diego–Carlsbad–San Marcos, Calif.
8.	Hanford-Corcoran, Ga.	20.	Modesto, Calif.
9.	Knoxville-Sevierville–La Follette, Tenn.	21.	Atlanta–Sandy Springs–Gainsville, Ga.
10.	Dallas–Fort Worth, Tex.	22.	Morristown-Newport, Tenn.
11.	Washington-Baltimore–Northern Va. DC-Md.-Va.-W. Va.	23.	Raleigh-Durham-Cary, N.C.
12.	Philadelphia-Wilmington–Atlantic City, Pa.-N.J.-Del.-Md.	24.	Lancaster, Pa.
		25.	Sheboygan, Wis.

Source: State of the Air: 2004, American Lung Association.

Major Air Pollutants

Pollutant	Sources	Effects
Ozone. A gas that can be found in two places. Near the ground (the troposphere), it is a major part of smog. Higher in the air (the stratosphere), it helps block radiation from the sun.	Ozone is not created directly, but is formed when nitrogen oxides and volatile organic compounds mix in sunlight. That is why ozone is mostly found in the summer. Nitrogen oxides come from burning gasoline, coal, or other fossil fuels. There are many types of volatile organic compounds, and they come from sources ranging from factories to trees.	Ozone near the ground can cause a number of health problems. Ozone can lead to more frequent asthma attacks in people who have asthma and can cause sore throats, coughs, and breathing difficulty. It may even lead to premature death. Ozone can also hurt plants and crops.
Carbon monoxide. A gas that comes from the burning of fossil fuels, mostly in cars. It cannot be seen or smelled.	Carbon monoxide is released when engines burn fossil fuels. Emissions are higher when engines are not tuned properly, and when fuel is not completely burned. Cars emit a lot of the carbon monoxide found outdoors.	Carbon monoxide makes it hard for body parts to get the oxygen they need to run correctly. Exposure to carbon monoxide makes people feel dizzy and tired and gives them headaches.

Pollutant	Sources	Effects
Nitrogen dioxide. A reddish-brown gas that comes from the burning of fossil fuels. It has a strong smell at high levels.	Nitrogen dioxide mostly comes from power plants and cars. Nitrogen dioxide is formed in two ways—when nitrogen in the fuel is burned, or when nitrogen in the air reacts with oxygen at very high temperatures.	People who are exposed to nitrogen dioxide for a long time have a higher chance of getting respiratory infections. Nitrogen dioxide reacts in the atmosphere to form acid rain, which can harm plants and animals.
Particulate matter. Solid or liquid matter that is suspended in the air. To remain in the air, particles usually must be less than 0.1-mm wide and can be as small as 0.00005 mm.	Particulate matter can be divided into two types—coarse particles and fine particles. Coarse particles are formed from sources like road dust, sea spray, and construction. Fine particles are formed when fuel is burned in automobiles and power plants.	Particulate matter that is small enough can enter the lungs and cause health problems. Some of these problems include more frequent asthma attacks, respiratory problems, and premature death.
Sulfur dioxide. A corrosive gas that cannot be seen or smelled at low levels but can have a "rotten egg" smell at high levels.	Sulfur dioxide mostly comes from the burning of coal or oil in power plants. It also comes from factories that make chemicals, paper, or fuel. Like nitrogen dioxide, sulfur dioxide reacts in the atmosphere to form acid rain and particles.	Sulfur dioxide exposure can affect people who have asthma or emphysema by making it more difficult for them to breathe. It can also irritate people's eyes, noses, and throats. Sulfur dioxide can harm trees and crops, damage buildings, and make it harder for people to see long distances.
Lead. A blue-gray metal that is very toxic and is found in a number of forms and locations.	Outside, lead comes from cars in areas where unleaded gasoline is not used. Lead can also come from power plants and other industrial sources. Inside, lead paint is an important source of lead, especially in houses where paint is peeling.	High amounts of lead can be dangerous for small children and can lead to lower IQs and kidney problems. For adults, exposure to lead can increase the chance of having heart attacks or strokes.
Toxic air pollutants. A large number of chemicals that are known or suspected to cause cancer. Some important pollutants in this category include arsenic, asbestos, benzene, and dioxin.	Each toxic air pollutant comes from a slightly different source, but many are created in chemical plants or are emitted when fossil fuels are burned. Some toxic air pollutants, like asbestos and formaldehyde, can be found in building materials and can lead to indoor air problems. Many toxic air pollutants can also enter the food and water supply.	Toxic air pollutants can cause cancer. Some toxic air pollutants can also cause birth defects. Other effects depend on the pollutant, but can include skin and eye irritation and breathing problems.
Stratospheric ozone depleters. Chemicals that can destroy the ozone in the stratosphere. These chemicals include chlorofluorocarbons (CFCs), halons, and other compounds that include chlorine or bromine.	CFCs are used in air conditioners and refrigerators, since they work well as coolants. They can also be found in aerosol cans and fire extinguishers. Other stratospheric ozone depleters are used as solvents in industry.	If the ozone in the stratosphere is destroyed, people are exposed to more radiation from the sun (ultraviolet radiation). This can lead to skin cancer and eye problems. Higher ultraviolet radiation can also harm plants and animals.
Greenhouse gases. Gases that stay in the air for a long time and warm up the planet by trapping sunlight. This is called the "greenhouse effect" because the gases act like the glass in a greenhouse. Some of the important greenhouse gases are carbon dioxide, methane, and nitrous oxide.	Carbon dioxide is the most important greenhouse gas. It comes from the burning of fossil fuels in cars, power plants, houses, and industry. Methane is released during the processing of fossil fuels, and also comes from natural sources like cows and rice paddies. Nitrous oxide comes from industrial sources and decaying plants.	The greenhouse effect can lead to changes in the climate of the planet. Some of these changes might include more temperature extremes, higher sea levels, changes in forest composition, and damage to land near the coast. Human health might be affected by diseases that are related to temperature or by damage to land and water.

Source: Jonathan Levy, Harvard School of Public Health. Based on information provided by the Environmental Protection Agency.

U.S. Emissions of Greenhouse Gases, 1990–2002

(million metric tons of gas for carbon dioxide and methane; thousand metric tons for nitrous oxide)

Gas	1990	1995	1996	1997	1998	1999	2000	2001	2002
Carbon dioxide	4,969.4	5,273.5	5,454.8	5,533.0	5,540.0	5,630.7	5,805.5	5,789.0	5,795.6
Methane	31.7	31.1	29.9	29.6	28.9	28.7	28.2	28.0	26.6
Nitrous oxide	1.2	1.3	1.2	1.2	1.2	1.2	1.2	1.2	1.1

Source: Compiled by the U.S. Energy Information Administration. Web: www.eia.doe.gov.

Animals and Nature

Animal Names: Male, Female, and Young

Animal	Male	Female	Young	Animal	Male	Female	Young	Animal	Male	Female	Young
Ass	Jack	Jenny	Foal	Duck	Drake	Duck	Duckling	Sheep	Ram	Ewe	Lamb
Bear	Boar	Sow	Cub	Elephant	Bull	Cow	Calf	Swan	Cob	Pen	Cygnet
Cat	Tom	Queen	Kitten	Fox	Dog	Vixen	Cub	Swine	Boar	Sow	Piglet
Cattle	Bull	Cow	Calf	Goose	Gander	Goose	Gosling	Tiger	Tiger	Tigress	Cub
Chicken	Rooster	Hen	Chick	Horse	Stallion	Mare	Foal	Whale	Bull	Cow	Calf
Deer	Buck	Doe	Fawn	Lion	Lion	Lioness	Cub	Wolf	Dog	Bitch	Pup
Dog	Dog	Bitch	Pup	Rabbit	Buck	Doe	Bunny				

Source: James G. Doherty, general curator, The Wildlife Conservation Society.

Gestation, Incubation, and Longevity of Selected Animals

Animal	Gestation or incubation, in days (average)	Longevity, in years (record exceptions)	Animal	Gestation or incubation, in days (average)	Longevity, in years (record exceptions)
Ass	365	18–20 (63)	Horse	329–345 (336)	20–25 (50+)
Bear	180–240[1]	15–30 (47)	Human	253–303	([2])
Cat	52–69 (63)	10–12 (26+)	Kangaroo	32–39[1]	4–6 (23)
Chicken	22	7–8 (14)	Lion	105–113 (108)	10 (29)
Cow	280	9–12 (39)	Monkey	139–270[1]	12–15[1] (29)
Deer	197–300[1]	10–15 (26)	Mouse	19–31[1]	1–3 (4)
Dog	53–71 (63)	10–12 (24)	Parakeet (Budgerigar)	17–20 (18)	8 (12+)
Duck	21–35[1] (28)	10 (15)	Pig	101–130 (115)	10 (22)
Elephant	510–730[1] (624)	30–40 (71)	Pigeon	11–19	10–12 (39)
Fox	51–63[1]	8–10 (14)	Rabbit	30–35 (31)	6–8 (15)
Goat	136–160 (151)	12 (17)	Rat	21	3 (5)
Groundhog	31–32	4–9	Sheep	144–152[1] (151)	12 (16)
Guinea pig	58–75 (68)	3 (6)	Squirrel	44	8–9 (15)
Hamster, golden	15–17	2 (8)	Whale	365–547[1]	n.a.
Hippopotamus	220–255 (240)	30 (49+)	Wolf	60–63	10–12 (16)

1. Depending on kind. 2. For human life expectancy charts, *see* Life Expectancy at Birth by Race and Sex, p. 192. *Source:* James G. Doherty, general curator, The Wildlife Conservation Society.

Speed of Animals

Most of the following measurements are for maximum speeds over approximate quarter-mile distances. Exceptions—which are included to give a wide range of animals—are the lion and elephant, whose speeds were clocked in the act of charging; the whippet, which was timed over a 200-yard course; the cheetah over a 100-yard distance; humans for a 15-yard segment of a 100-yard run; and the black mamba snake, six-lined race runner, spider, giant tortoise, three-toed sloth, and garden snail, which were measured over various small distances.

Animal	Speed (mph)	Animal	Speed (mph)	Animal	Speed (mph)
Peregrine falcon	200.00+	Zebra	40.00	White-tailed deer	30.00
Cheetah	70.00	Mongolian wild ass	40.00	Human	27.89
Pronghorn antelope	61.00	Greyhound	39.35	Elephant	25.00
Lion	50.00	Whippet	35.50	Black mamba snake	20.00
Thomson's gazelle	50.00	Jackal	35.00	Six-lined race runner	18.00
Wildebeest	50.00	Mule deer	35.00	Squirrel	12.00
Quarter horse	47.50	Rabbit (domestic)	35.00	Pig (domestic)	11.00
Cape hunting dog	45.00	Giraffe	32.00	Chicken	9.00
Elk	45.00	Reindeer	32.00	House mouse	8.00
Coyote	43.00	Cat (domestic)	30.00	Spider (*Tegenearia atrica*)	1.17
Gray fox	42.00	Kangaroo	30.00	Giant tortoise	0.17
Hyena	40.00	Grizzly bear	30.00	Three-toed sloth	0.15
Ostrich	40.00	Wart hog	30.00	Garden snail	0.03

Source: Natural History Magazine, March 1974, copyright 1974; The American Museum of Natural History; and James G. Doherty, general curator, The Wildlife Conservation Society.

Animal Group Terminology

Source: James G. Doherty, general curator, The Wildlife Conservation Society.

ants: colony
bears: sleuth, sloth
bees: grist, hive, swarm
birds: flight, volery
cats: clutter, clowder
cattle: drove
chicks: brood, clutch
clams: bed
cranes: sedge, seige
crows: murder
doves: dule
ducks: brace, team
elephants: herd
elks: gang
finches: charm

fish: school, shoal, draught
foxes: leash, skulk
geese: flock, gaggle, skein
gnats: cloud, horde
goats: trip
gorillas: band
hares: down, husk
hawks: cast
hens: brood
hogs: drift
horses: pair, team
hounds: cry, mute, pack
kangaroos: troop
kittens: kindle, litter
larks: exaltation

lions: pride
locusts: plague
magpies: tiding
mules: span
nightingales: watch
oxen: yoke
oysters: bed
parrots: company
partridges: covey
peacocks: muster, ostentation
pheasants: nest, bouquet
pigs: litter
ponies: string
quail: bevy, covey

rabbits: nest
seals: pod
sheep: drove, flock
sparrows: host
storks: mustering
swans: bevy, wedge
swine: sounder
toads: knot
turkeys: rafter
turtles: bale
vipers: nest
whales: gam, pod
wolves: pack, route
woodcocks: fall

Endangered and Threatened Species

Group	Endangered[1]		Threatened[2]		Total species	Species with recovery plans
	U.S.	Foreign	U.S.	Foreign		
Mammals	65	251	9	17	342	54
Birds	78	175	14	6	273	77
Reptiles	14	64	22	15	115	32
Amphibians	12	8	9	1	30	14
Fishes	71	11	44	0	126	96
Clams	62	2	8	0	72	57
Snails	21	1	11	0	33	22
Insects	35	4	9	0	48	29
Arachnids	12	0	0	0	12	5
Crustaceans	18	0	3	0	21	13
Animal subtotal	**388**	**516**	**129**	**39**	**1,072**	**399**
Flowering plants	571	1	144	0	716	574
Conifers and cycads	2	0	1	2	5	2
Ferns and allies	24	0	2	0	26	26
Lichens	2	0	0	0	2	2
Plant subtotal	**599**	**1**	**147**	**2**	**749**	**604**
Total	**987**	**517**	**276**	**41**	**1,821**[3]	**1,003**

NOTE: As of Sept. 1, 2004. 1. *Endangered species* are those in danger of extinction. 2. *Threatened species* are those likely to become an endangered species within the foreseeable future. 3. Nine U.S. species have dual status. *Source:* U.S. Fish and Wildlife Service. Web: http://ecos.fws.gov/tess_public/html/boxscore.html.

Water Supply of the World

The Antarctic Icecap is the largest supply of fresh water, representing nearly 2% of the world's total of fresh and salt water. As can be seen from the table below, the amount of water in our atmosphere is over 10 times as much as the water in all the rivers taken together. The fresh water actually available for human use in lakes and rivers and the accessible ground water amounts to only about one-third of 1% of the world's total water supply.

	Surface area (sq mi)	Volume (cu mi)	Percentage of total[1]
Salt water			
The oceans	139,500,000	317,000,000	97.2%
Inland seas and saline lakes	270,000	25,000	0.008
Fresh water			
Freshwater lakes	330,000	30,000	0.009
All rivers (average level)	—	300	0.0001
Antarctic Icecap	6,000,000	6,300,000	1.9
Arctic Icecap and glaciers	900,000	680,000	0.21
Water in the atmosphere	197,000,000	3,100	0.001
Ground water within half a mile from surface	—	1,000,000	0.31
Deep-lying ground water	—	1,000,000	0.31
Total (rounded)	**—**	**326,000,000**	**100.00**

1. All figures are estimated. *Source:* Department of the Interior, Geological Survey.

The National Park System

Source: Department of the Interior, National Park Service.

The National Park System of the United States is administered by the National Park Service, a bureau of the Department of the Interior. Started with the establishment of Yellowstone National Park on March 1, 1872, the system includes not only the most extraordinary and spectacular scenic exhibits in the United States, but also a large number of sites distinguished for their historic or prehistoric importance, scientific interest, or superior recreational assets. The National Park System is made up of 388 areas covering more than 84 million acres in every state except Delaware. It also includes areas in the District of Columbia, American Samoa, Guam, Puerto Rico, and the Virgin Islands. A list of the areas follows, exluding those without "national" status. See also the excellent website of the Park Service: www.nps.gov.

NATIONAL PARKS

Name, location, and year authorized	Acreage	Outstanding characteristics
Acadia (Maine), 1919	47,548.94	Rugged seashore on Mt. Desert Island and adjacent mainland
Arches (Utah), 1971	76,518.98	Unusual stone arches, windows, pedestals caused by erosion
Badlands (S.D.), 1978	242,755.94	Arid land of fossils, prairie, bison, deer, bighorn sheep, antelope
Big Bend (Tex.), 1935	801,163.21	Mountains and desert bordering the Rio Grande
Biscayne (Fla.), 1980	172,924.07	Aquatic, coral reef park south of Miami
Black Canyon of the Gunnison (Colo.), 1999	30,243.53	Canyon with narrow opening, sheer walls, and startling depths
Bryce Canyon (Utah), 1924	35,835.08	Area of brilliantly colored, grotesque eroded rocks
Canyonlands (Utah), 1964	337,597.83	Colorful wilderness with impressive red-rock canyons, spires, arches
Capitol Reef (Utah), 1971	241,904.26	Highly colored sedimentary rock formations in high, narrow gorges
Carlsbad Caverns (N.M.), 1930	46,766.45	One of the world's largest known caves
Channel Islands (Calif.), 1980	249,561.00	Area is rich in marine mammals, sea birds, endangered species, and archeology
Congaree (S.C.), 2003	21,743.58	Contains the largest contiguous tract of old-growth bottomland hardwood forest remaining in the U.S.
Crater Lake (Ore.), 1902	183,224.05	Deep blue lake in heart of inactive volcano
Cuyahoga Valley (Ohio), 2000	32,860.73	Wilderness area offering recreational, historic, and cultural attractions, including scenic rail journeys
Death Valley (Calif.-Nev.), 1994	3,340,409.65	Largest desert, surrounded by high mountains, containing the lowest point in the Western Hemisphere
Denali (Alaska), 1917	4,740,911.72	Contains Mt. McKinley, N. America's highest mountain (20,320 ft)
Dry Tortugas (Fla.), 1992	64,701.22	Located 70 mi off Key West. Features an underwater nature trail
Everglades (Fla.), 1934	1,508,491.84	Subtropical area with abundant bird and animal life
Gates of the Arctic (Alaska), 1980	7,523,897.74	Diverse north central wilderness contains part of Brooks Range
Glacier (Mont.), 1910	1,013,572.41	Rocky Mountain scenery with many glaciers and lakes
Glacier Bay (Alaska), 1980	3,224,840.31	Popular for wildlife, whale-watching, glacier-calving, scenery
Grand Canyon (Ariz.), 1919	1,217,403.32	Mile-deep gorge, 4 to 18 mi wide, 217 mi long
Grand Teton (Wyo.), 1929	309,994.66	Picturesque range of high mountain peaks
Great Basin (Nev.), 1986	77,180.00	Exceptional scenic, biologic, geologic attractions
Great Smoky Mts. (N.C.-Tenn.), 1926	521,495.36	Highest mountain range east of Black Hills; luxuriant plant life
Guadalupe Mountains (Tex.), 1966	86,415.97	Contains highest point in Texas: Guadalupe Peak (8,751 ft)
Haleakala (Hawaii), 1916	29,830.15	World-famous 10,023-ft Haleakala volcano (dormant)
Hawaii Volcanoes (Hawaii), 1916	209,695.38	Spectacular volcanic area; luxuriant vegetation at lower levels
Hot Springs (Ark.), 1921	5,550.25	47 mineral hot springs said to have therapeutic value
Isle Royale (Mich.), 1931	571,790.11	Largest wilderness island in Lake Superior; moose, wolves, lakes
Joshua Tree (Calif.), 1994	784,162.05	Desert region featuring Joshua trees and a great variety of plants and animals
Katmai (Alaska), 1980	3,674,529.68	Expansion may assure brown bear's preservation. Park is known for fishing, 1912 eruption of Novarupta, bears
Kenai Fjords (Alaska), 1980	669,982.99	Mountain goats, marine mammals, birdlife are features at this seacoast park near Seward
Kings Canyon (Calif.), 1890	461,901.20	Huge canyons; high mountains; giant sequoias
Kobuk Valley (Alaska), 1980	1,750,736.82	Native culture and anthropology center around the broad Kobuk River in northwest Alaska
Lake Clark (Alaska), 1980	2,619,733.21	Park provides scenic and wilderness recreation across Cook Inlet from Anchorage
Lassen Volcanic (Calif.), 1916	106,372.36	Exhibits of impressive volcanic phenomena
Mammoth Cave (Ky.), 1926	52,830.19	Vast limestone labyrinth with underground river

Name, location, and year authorized	Acreage	Outstanding characteristics
Mesa Verde (Colo.), 1906	52,121.93	Best-preserved prehistoric cliff dwellings in United States
Mount Rainier (Wash.), 1899	235,625.00	Single-peak glacial system; dense forests, flowered meadows
North Cascades (Wash.), 1968	504,780.94	Roadless Alpine landscape; jagged peaks; mountain lakes; glaciers
Olympic (Wash.), 1938	922,650.94	Finest Pacific Northwest rain forest; scenic mountain park
Petrified Forest (Ariz.), 1962	93,532.57	Extensive natural exhibit of petrified wood
Redwood (Calif.), 1968	112,512.97	Coastal redwood forests; contains world's tallest-known tree (369.2 ft)
Rocky Mountain (Colo.), 1915	265,765.03	Section of the Rocky Mountains; 107 named peaks over 10,000 ft
Saguaro (Ariz.), 1994	91,445.16	Giant saguaro cacti, unique to the Sonoran Desert, sometimes reach a height of 50 ft in this cactus forest
Sequoia (Calif.), 1890	404,051.17	Giant sequoias; magnificent High Sierra scenery, including Mt. Whitney
Shenandoah (Va.), 1926	199,038.07	Tree-covered mountains; scenic Skyline Drive
Theodore Roosevelt (N.D.), 1978	70,446.89	Scenic valley of Little Missouri River; T.R. Ranch; wildlife
Virgin Islands (U.S. V.I.), 1956	14,688.87	Beaches; lush hills; prehistoric Carib Indian relics
Voyageurs (Minn.), 1971	218,200.17	Wildlife, canoeing, fishing, hiking
Wind Cave (S.D.), 1903	28,295.03	Limestone caverns in Black Hills; bison herd
Wolf Trap Farm (Va.), 2003	130.28	The nation's first National Park for the Performing Arts
Wrangell–St. Elias (Alaska), 1980	8,323,147.59	Largest park system area has abundant wildlife, second highest peak in U.S. (Mt. St. Elias); adjoins Canadian park
Yellowstone (Wyo.-Mont.-Idaho), 1872	2,219,790.71	World's greatest geyser area; abundant falls, wildlife, canyons
Yosemite (Calif.), 1890	761,266.28	Mountains; inspiring gorges and waterfalls; giant sequoias
Zion (Utah), 1919	146,597.64	Multicolored gorge in heart of southern Utah desert

Name and location	Total acreage
National Historical Parks	
Adams (Mass.)	23.82
Appomattox Court House (Va.)	1,772.36
Boston (Mass.)	43.32
Cane River Creole (La.)	207.38
Cedar Creek and Belle Grove (Va.)	3,566.61
Chaco Culture (N.M.)	33,960,19
Chesapeake and Ohio Canal (Md.-W.Va.-DC)	19,575.25
Colonial (Va.)	9,452.41
Cumberland Gap (Ky.-Tenn.-Va.)	20,463.15
Dayton Aviation Heritage (Ohio)	86.46
George Rogers Clark (Ind.)	26.17
Harpers Ferry (W.Va.-Md.)	2,501.67
Hopewell Culture (Ohio)	1,169.96
Independence (Pa.)	44.80
Jean Lafitte (La.)	20,004.90
Kalaupapa (Hawaii)	10,778.88
Kaloko-Honokohau (Hawaii)	1,160.91
Keweenaw (Mich.)	1,869.40
Klondike Gold Rush (Alaska-Wash.)	13,191.35
Lowell (Mass.)	141.34
Lyndon B. Johnson (Tex.)	1,570.15
Marsh-Billings-Rockefeller (Vt.)	643.07
Minute Man (Mass.)	970.83
Morristown (N.J.)	1,711.36
Natchez (Miss.)	105.31
New Bedford Whaling (Mass.)	34.00
New Orleans Jazz (La.)	5.13
Nez Perce (Idaho)	2,494.59
Pecos (N.M.)	6,670.08
Pu'uhonua o Honaunau (Hawaii)	181.80
Rosie the Riveter/WWII Home Front (Calif.)	145.19
Salt River Bay (U.S. V.I.)	947.75
San Antonio Missions (Tex.)	825.92
San Francisco Maritime (Calif.)	49.86
San Juan Island (Wash.)	1,751.99
Saratoga (N.Y.)	3,392.42

Name and location	Total acreage
Sitka (Alaska)	113.17
Tumacácori (Ariz.)	46.28
Valley Forge (Pa.)	3,464.26
War in the Pacific (Guam)	2,036.98
Women's Rights (N.Y.)	7.44
National Monuments	
Agate Fossil Beds (Neb.)	3,055.22
Alibates Flint Quarries (Tex.)	1,370.97
Aniakchak (Alaska)	137,176.00
Aztec Ruins (N.M.)	317.80
Bandelier (N.M.)	33,676.67
Booker T. Washington (Va.)	223.92
Buck Island Reef (U.S. V.I.)	19,015.47
Cabrillo (Calif.)	159.94
Canyon de Chelly (Ariz.)	83,840.00
Cape Krusenstern (Alaska)	649,085.04
Capulin Volcano (N.M.)	792.84
Casa Grande Ruins (Ariz.)	472.50
Castillo de San Marcos (Fla.)	20.21
Castle Clinton (N.Y.)	1.00
Cedar Breaks (Utah)	6,154.60
Chiricahua (Ariz.)	11,984.73
Colorado (Colo.)	20,533.93
Craters of the Moon (Idaho)	304,727.05
Devils Postpile (Calif.)	798.46
Devils Tower (Wyo.)	1,346.91
Dinosaur (Utah-Colo.)	210,277.55
Effigy Mounds (Iowa)	2,526.39
Ellis Island (N.J.-N.Y.)	27.50
El Malpais (N.M.)	114,276.95
El Morro (N.M.)	1,278.72
Florissant Fossil Beds (Colo.)	5,998.09
Fort Frederica (Ga.)	241.42
Fort Matanzas (Fla.)	300.11
Fort McHenry (National Monument and Historic Shrine) (Md.)	43.26
Fort Pulaski (Ga.)	5,623.10
Fort Stanwix (N.Y.)	15.52

Name and location	Total acreage
Fort Sumter (S.C.)	199.57
Fort Union (N.M.)	720.60
Fossil Butte (Wyo.)	8,198.00
George Washington Birthplace (Va.)	550.23
George Washington Carver (Mo.)	210.00
Gila Cliff Dwellings (N.M.)	533.13
Governor's Island (N.Y.)	22.78
Grand Portage (Minn.)	709.97
Great Sand Dunes (Colo.)	42,272.18
Hagerman Fossil Beds (Idaho)	4,351.15
Hohokam Pima (Ariz.)	1,690.00
Homestead (Neb.)	195.11
Hovenweep (Utah-Colo.)	784.93
Jewel Cave (S.D.)	1,273.51
John Day Fossil Beds (Ore.)	14,056.73
Lava Beds (Calif.)	46,559.87
Little Bighorn Battlefield (Mont.)	765.34
Minidoka Internment (Idaho)	72.75
Montezuma Castle (Ariz.)	857.69
Muir Woods (Calif.)	553.55
Natural Bridges (Utah)	7,636.49
Navajo (Ariz.)	360.00
Ocmulgee (Ga.)	701.54
Oregon Caves (Ore.)	487.98
Organ Pipe Cactus (Ariz.)	330,688.86
Parashant (Ariz.)	n.a.
Petroglyph (N.M.)	7,231.63
Pinnacles (Calif.)	17,614.05
Pipe Spring (Ariz.)	40.00
Pipestone (Minn.)	281.78
Poverty Point (La.)	910.85
Rainbow Bridge (Utah)	160.00
Russell Cave (Ala.)	310.45
Salinas Pueblo Missions (N.M.)	1,071.42
Scotts Bluff (Neb.)	3,004.81
Statue of Liberty (N.Y.-N.J.)	58.38
Sunset Crater Volcano (Ariz.)	3,040.00
Timpanogos Cave (Utah)	250.00
Tonto (Ariz.)	1,120.00
Tuzigoot (Ariz.)	800.62
Virgin Islands Coral Reef (V.I.)	13,892.78
Walnut Canyon (Ariz.)	3,579.46
White Sands (N.M.)	143,732.92
Wupatki (Ariz.)	35,422.13
Yucca House (Colo.)	33.87

National Preserves

Aniakchak (Alaska)	465,603.00
Bering Land Bridge (Alaska)	2,697,393.11
Big Cypress (Fla.)	720,565.67
Big Thicket (Tex.)	97,168.03
Craters of the Moon (Idaho)	410,000.00
Denali (Alaska)	1,334,117.99
Gates of the Arctic (Alaska)	948,607.96
Glacier Bay (Alaska)	58,406.00
Great Sand Dunes (Colo.)	41,686.00
Jean Lafitte (La.)	20,004.90
Katmai (Alaska)	418,699.22
Lake Clark (Alaska)	1,410,291.99
Little River Canyon (Ala.)	13,632.96
Mojave (Calif.)	1,531,831.60
Noatak (Alaska)	6,569,904.43
Tallgrass Prairie (Kans.)	10,894.00
Wrangell-St. Elias (Alaska)	4,852,753.10
Yukon-Charley Rivers (Alaska)	2,526,512.31

Name and location	Total acreage

National Reserves

City of Rocks (Idaho)	14,107.19
Ebey's Landing (Nat'l Historical Reserve) (Wash.)	19,323.99
New Jersey Pinelands (N.J.)	1,100,000

National Military Parks

Chickamauga and Chattanooga (Ga.-Tenn.)	8,266.34
Fredericksburg and Spotsylvania (Va.)	8,361.92
Gettysburg (Pa.)	5,990.31
Guilford Courthouse (N.C.)	228.59
Horseshoe Bend (Ala.)	2,040.00
Kings Mountain (S.C.)	3,945.29
Pea Ridge (Ark.)	4,300.35
Shiloh (Tenn.)	4,024.88
Vicksburg (Miss.)	1,753.16

National Battlefields

Antietam (Md.)	3,244.37
Big Hole (Mont.)	1,010.61
Cowpens (S.C.)	841.56
Fort Donelson (Tenn.)	551.69
Fort Necessity (Pa.)	902.80
Monocacy (Md.)	1,647.01
Moores Creek (N.C.)	87.75
Petersburg (Va.)	2,659.19
Stones River (Tenn.)	709.36
Tupelo (Miss.)	1.00
Wilson's Creek (Mo.)	1,749.91

National Battlefield Parks

Kennesaw Mountain (Ga.)	2,884.14
Manassas (Va.)	5,067.92
Richmond (Va.)	2,151.94

National Battlefield Site

Brices Cross Roads (Miss.)	1.00

National Historic Sites

Abraham Lincoln Birthplace (Ky.)	344.50
Allegheny Portage Railroad (Pa.)	1,249.20
Andersonville (Ga.)	494.61
Andrew Johnson (Tenn.)	16.68
Bent's Old Fort (Colo.)	798.80
Boston African-American (Mass.)	0.59
Brown v. Board of Education (Kans.)	1.85
Carl Sandburg Home (N.C.)	263.65
Charles Pinckney (S.C.)	28.45
Chimney Rock (Nebr.)	83.36
Christiansted (U.S. V.I.)	27.15
Clara Barton (Md.)	8.59
Edgar Allan Poe (Pa.)	0.52
Edison (N.J.)	21.25
Eisenhower (Pa.)	690.46
Eleanor Roosevelt (N.Y.)	180.50
Eugene O'Neill (Calif.)	13.19
First Ladies (Ohio)	0.33
Ford's Theatre (Lincoln Museum) (DC)	0.29
Fort Bowie (Ariz.)	999.45
Fort Davis (Tex.)	473.87
Fort Laramie (Wyo.)	832.85
Fort Larned (Kan.)	718.39
Fort Point (Calif.)	29.00
Fort Raleigh (N.C.)	512.93
Fort Scott (Kan.)	16.69

Name and location	Total acreage
Fort Smith (Ark.-Okla.)	75.05
Fort Union Trading Post (N.D.-Mont.)	443.81
Fort Vancouver (Wash.)	208.89
Frederick Douglass (DC)	8.53
Frederick Law Olmsted (Mass.)	7.21
Friendship Hill (Pa.)	674.56
Gloria Dei Church (Pa.)	3.71
Golden Spike (Utah)	2,735.28
Grant-Kohrs Ranch (Mont.)	1,618.38
Hampton (Md.)	62.04
Harry S. Truman (Mo.)	6.67
Herbert Hoover (Iowa)	186.80
Home of F. D. Roosevelt (N.Y.)	799.98
Hopewell Furnace (Pa.)	848.06
Hubbell Trading Post (Ariz.)	160.09
James A. Garfield (Ohio)	7.82
Jamestown (Va.)	22.5
Jimmy Carter (Ga.)	70.86
John F. Kennedy (Mass.)	0.09
John Muir (Calif.)	344.73
Knife River Indian Villages (N.D.)	1,758.35
Lincoln Home (Ill.)	12.24
Little Rock Central High School (Ark.)	27.28
Longfellow (Mass.)	1.98
Lower East Side Tenement Museum (N.Y.)	n.a.
Maggie L. Walker (Va.)	1.29
Manzanar (Calif.)	813.81
Martin Luther King, Jr. (Ga.)	38.66
Martin Van Buren (N.Y.)	39.55
Mary McLeod Bethune Council House (DC)	0.07
Minuteman Missile (S.D.)	15.00
Nicodemus (Kans.)	161.35
Ninety Six (S.C.)	989.14
Palo Alto Battlefield (Tex.)	3,407.46
Pennsylvania Avenue (DC)	0.00
Puukohola Heiau (Hawaii)	86.24
Ronald Reagan Boyhood Home (Ill.)	1.01
Sagamore Hill (N.Y.)	83.02
Saint-Gaudens (N.H.)	148.15
Saint Paul's Church (N.Y.)	6.13
Salem Maritime (Mass.)	9.02
Sand Creek Massacre (Colo.)	12,583.34
San Juan (P.R.)	75.13
Saugus Iron Works (Mass.)	8.51
Sewall-Belmont House (DC)	0.35
Springfield Armory (Mass.)	54.93
Steamtown (Pa.)	62.48
Theodore Roosevelt Birthplace (N.Y.)	0.11
Theodore Roosevelt Inaugural (N.Y.)	1.03
Thomas Stone (Md.)	328.25
Touro Synagogue (R.I.)	0.23
Tuskegee Airmen (Ala.)	86.69
Tuskegee Institute (Ala.)	57.92
Ulysses S. Grant (Mo.)	9.60
Vanderbilt Mansion (N.Y.)	211.65
Washita Battlefield (Okla.)	315.20
Weir Farm (Conn.)	74.20
Whitman Mission (Wash.)	99.93
William Howard Taft (Ohio)	3.10

Name and location	Total acreage
National Memorials	
Arkansas Post (Ark.)	746.88
Arlington House, the Robert E. Lee Memorial (Va.)	27.91
Chamizal (Tex.)	54.90
Coronado (Ariz.)	4,750.22
David Berger (Ohio)	n.a.
De Soto (Fla.)	26.84
Father Marquette (Mich.)	52.00
Federal Hall (N.Y.)	0.45
Fort Caroline (Fla.)	138.39
Fort Clatsop (Ore.)	125.20
Franklin Delano Roosevelt (DC)	7.50
General Grant (N.Y.)	0.76
Hamilton Grange (N.Y.)	1.04
Jefferson National Expansion (Mo.)	192.83
John Ericsson (DC)	0.41
Johnstown Flood (Pa.)	164.12
Korean War Veterans (DC)	2.20
Lincoln Boyhood (Ind.)	199.65
Lincoln (DC)	107.43
Lyndon Baines Johnson Memorial Grove on the Potomac (DC)	17.00
Mount Rushmore (S.D.)	1,278.45
Oklahoma City (Okla.)	6.24
Perry's Victory and International Peace (Ohio)	25.39
Port Chicago Naval Magazine (Calif.)	n.a.
Roger Williams (R.I.)	4.56
Thaddeus Kosciuszko (Pa.)	0.02
Theodore Roosevelt Island (DC)	88.50
Thomas Jefferson (DC)	18.36
USS *Arizona* (Hawaii)	10.50
Vietnam Veterans (DC)	2.00
Washington Monument (DC)	106.01
Wright Brothers (N.C.)	428.44

National Seashores	
Assateague Island (Md.-Va.)	39,733.43
Canaveral (Fla.)	57,661.69
Cape Cod (Mass.)	43,604.94
Cape Hatteras (N.C.)	30,321.46
Cape Lookout (N.C.)	28,243.36
Cumberland Island (Ga.)	36,415.13
Fire Island (N.Y.)	19,579.47
Gulf Islands (Fla.-Miss.)	137,792.89
Padre Island (Tex.)	130,434.27
Point Reyes (Calif.)	71,067.66

National Lakeshores	
Apostle Islands (Wis.)	69,371.89
Indiana Dunes (Ind.)	15,044.47
Pictured Rocks (Mich.)	73,235.53
Sleeping Bear Dunes (Mich.)	71,194.71

National Park System Rivers	
Alagnak Wild River (Alaska)	30,665.45
Big South Fork National River (Ky.-Tenn.)	125,310.34
Bluestone National Scenic River (W.Va.)	4,309.51
Buffalo National River (Ark.)	94,293.31
Delaware National Scenic River (Pa.)	1,973.33
Great Egg Harbor Scenic and Recreational River (N.J.-Pa.)	43,311.42
Mississippi National River (Minn.)	53,775.00
Missouri National Recreational River (Neb.)	45,350.00
New River Gorge National River (W.Va.)	70,465.89

Name and location	Total acreage
Niobrara National Scenic River (Neb.)	5,992.96
Obed Wild and Scenic River (Tenn.)	5,173.69
Ozark National Scenic Riverways (Mo.)	80,785.04
Rio Grande Wild and Scenic River (Tex.)	9,600.00
St. Croix National Scenic Riverway (Minn.-Wis.)	67,460.31
Upper Delaware Scenic and Recreational River (Pa.)	74,999.56

National Historic Area

Aleutian WWII (Alaska)	81.00

National Heritage Areas

Cane River (La.)	116,000
Essex (Mass.)	352,000

National Recreation Areas

Amistad (Tex.)	58,500.00
Bighorn Canyon (Wyo.-Mont.)	120,296.22
Big South Fork (Ky.-Tenn.)	125,310.34
Boston Harbor Islands (Mass.)	1,482.25
Chattahoochee River (Ga.)	9,164.53
Chickasaw (Okla.)	9,888.83
Curecanti (Colo.)	41,972.42
Delaware Water Gap (Pa.-N.J.)	66,740.46
Gateway (N.Y.-N.J.)	26,606.63
Gauley River (W.Va.)	11,505.59
Glen Canyon (Ariz.-Utah)	1,254,306.19
Golden Gate (Calif.)	74,815.56
Lake Chelan (Wash.)	61,946.72
Lake Mead (Ariz.-Nev.)	1,495,664.00
Lake Meredith (Tex.)	44,977.63
Lake Roosevelt (Wash.)	100,390.31
Mississippi (Minn.)	53,775.00
Ross Lake (Wash.)	117,574.59
Santa Monica Mountains (Calif.)	153,672.77
Whiskeytown-Shasta-Trinity (Calif.)	42,503.46

National Heritage Corridors

Blackstone River Valley (Mass.-R.I.)	400,000
Delaware and Lehigh (Pa.)	n.a.
Erie Canalway (N.Y.)	3,087,360
Illinois and Michigan Canal (Ill.)	n.a.
Quinebaug and Shetucket Rivers Valley (Conn.)	694,000

Name and location	Total acreage
National Historic Trails[1]	
Ala Kahakai	175
California	5,500
El Camino Real de Tierra Adentro	404
Juan Bautista de Anza	1,210
Lewis and Clark	3,700
Mormon Pioneer	1,300
Old Spanish	2,700
Oregon	2,170
Overmountain Victory	330
Pony Express	1,800
Santa Fe	900
Selma to Montgomery	54
Trail of Tears	2,200

1. Approx. length in miles, not area, is provided for trails. The actual length of publically accessible trails is often substantially less than that given.

National Scenic Trails[1]

Appalachian	2,174
Ice Age	1,000
Natchez Trace	444
North Country	4,000
Potomac Heritage	421.5

1. Approx. length in miles, not area, is provided for trails.

National Cemeteries[1]

Antietam (Md.)	11.36
Battleground (DC)	1.03
Chalmette Cemetery (La.)	17.5
Fort Donelson (Tenn.)	15.30
Fredericksburg (Va.)	12.00
Gettysburg (Pa.)	20.58
Poplar Grove (Va.)	8.72
Shiloh (Tenn.)	10.05
Stones River (Tenn.)	719.81
Vicksburg (Miss.)	116.28
Yorktown (Va.)	2.91

1. The National Cemeteries are not independent areas of the National Park System; each is part of a military park, battlefield, etc., except Battleground. Their acreage is kept separately. Arlington National Cemetery is under the Department of the Army.

Ten Most Visited National Parks, 2003

Rank	Name and location	Number of visitors	Rank	Name and location	Number of visitors
1.	Great Smoky Mountains National Park, Tenn.	9,366,845	6.	Yellowstone National Park, Wyo.-Mont.-Idaho	3,019,375
2.	Grand Canyon National Park, Ariz.	4,124,900	7.	Cuyahoga Valley National Park, Ohio	2,879,591
3.	Yosemite National Park, Calif.	3,378,664	8.	Zion National Park, Utah	2,458,792
4.	Olympic National Park, Wash.	3,225,327	9.	Acadia National Park, Maine	2,431,062
5.	Rocky Mountain National Park, Colo.	3,067,256	10.	Grand Teton National Park, Wyo.	2,355,693

Source: Based on data from the National Park Service. Web: www.nps.gov.

Lightning: It's More Common Than You Think

Lightning kills more people in the U.S. in an average year than hurricanes or tornadoes, with an annual average of 67 documented deaths and about 300 documented injuries in the United States. It is believed that many cases go unreported, and that the true totals are around 100 deaths and 1,000 injuries per year. However, because it usually strikes only one or two people at a time, lightning gets less attention than other deadly weather phenomena.

Lightning Safety

The safest place to be during a thunderstorm is in a sturdy enclosed building, one that has electrical wiring and plumbing, or metal gutters, a lightning rod, or some other way of conducting electricity from the roof to the ground. Buildings that lack any of the above—such as small sheds, open garages, and bus shelters—should be avoided.

Another safe option is an enclosed car with a hard metal top and metal sides. If lightning strikes, the car's metal body will conduct the charge down to the ground—contrary to popular belief, the rubber of the wheels offers no protection. Close the windows, lean away from the door, and don't touch the steering wheel, ignition, or radio.

If you're caught outdoors, avoid open areas, trees, light poles, water, open vehicles, metal fences, and metal bleachers. A cave is a good shelter, but move as far as possible from the cave entrance.

More information on lightning safety can be found at http://www.lightningsafety.noaa.gov/.

States with the Most Reported Deaths by Lightning, 1959–2003

Rank	State	1959–2003	1990–2003	Rank	State	1959–2003	1990–2003
1.	Florida	425	126	11.	Arkansas	117	13
2.	Texas	195	52	12.	Alabama	101	24
3.	North Carolina	181	29	12.	Michigan	101	13
4.	Ohio	136	31	14.	Oklahoma	98	17
5.	New York	134	15	15.	Illinois	97	24
6.	Tennessee	133	16	15.	Mississippi	97	14
7.	Louisiana	132	23	17.	Georgia	95	23
8.	Colorado	123	39	18.	South Carolina	89	19
8.	Maryland	123	12	19.	New Mexico	88	14
10.	Pennsylvania	121	25	20.	Kentucky	87	12

Source: National Severe Storms Laboratory, National Oceanic and Atmospheric Administration (NOAA).

Costliest Hurricanes in the United States[1]
(U.S. Mainland)

Rank	Hurricane	Location	Year	Category[2]	Damage (in billions)	Rank	Hurricane	Location	Year	Category[2]	Damage (in billions)
1.	Andrew	Fla./La.	1992	5[3]	$26.5	6.	Georges	Fla./Miss./Ala.	1998	2	$2.31
2.	Hugo	S.C.	1989	4	7.0	7.	Frederic	Ala./Miss.	1979	3	2.3
3.	Floyd	Mid Atlantic/NE U.S.	1999	2	4.5	8.	Agnes	Fla./NE U.S.	1972	1	2.1
4.	Fran	N.C.	1996	3	3.2	9.	Alicia	Tex.	1983	3	2.0
5.	Opal	Fla./Ala.	1995	3	3.0	10.	Bob	N.C./NE U.S.	1991	2	1.5
						10.	Juan	La.	1985	1	1.5

NOTE: Damages are listed in U.S. dollars and are not adjusted for inflation. 1. 1900–2000. 2. Saffir-Simpson Hurricane scale: Cat. 1 = weak; Cat. 5 = devastating. 3. Hurricane Andrew was upgraded in Aug. 2002 from Cat. 4 to 5. Source: National Oceanic and Atmospheric Administration (NOAA).

Deadliest Hurricanes in the United States[1]
(U.S. Mainland)

Rank	Hurricane	Year	Category[2]	Deaths	Rank	Hurricane	Year	Category[2]	Deaths
1.	Galveston, Tex.	1900	4	8,000[3]	6.	Audrey (SW La./N. Tex.)	1957	4	390
2.	Lake Okeechobee, Fla.	1928	4	1,836	7.	NE U.S.	1944	3	390[5]
3.	Florida Keys/S. Tex.	1919	4	600[4]	8.	Grand Isle, La.	1909	4	350
4.	New England	1938	3	600	9.	New Orleans, La.	1915	4	275
5.	Florida Keys	1935	5	408	10.	Galveston, Tex.	1915	4	275

1. 1900–2000. 2. Saffir-Simpson Hurricane scale: Cat. 1 = weak; Cat. 5 = devastating. 3. May actually have been as high as 10,000 to 12,000. 4. Over 500 of these lost on ships at sea; 600–900 estimated deaths. 5. Some 344 of these lost on ships at sea. Source: National Oceanic and Atmospheric Administration (NOAA).

Most Intense[1] Hurricanes in the United States[2]
(U.S. Mainland)

Rank	Hurricane	Year	Category[3]	Rank	Hurricane	Year	Category[3]
1.	Florida Keys	1935	5	6.	Donna (Fla./Eastern U.S.)	1960	4
2.	Camille (Miss./La./Va.)	1969	5	7.	Galveston, Tex.	1900	4
3.	Andrew (Fla./La.)	1992	5[4]	8.	Grand Isle, La.	1909	4
4.	Florida Keys/Tex.	1919	4	9.	New Orleans, La.	1915	4
5.	Lake Okeechobee, Fla.	1928	4	10.	Carla (Tex.)	1961	4

1. Intensity is for time of landfall. May have been stronger at other times. 2. 1900–2000. 3. Saffir-Simpson Hurricane scale: Cat. 1 = weak; Cat. 5 = devastating. 4. Hurricane Andrew was upgraded in Aug. 2002 from Cat. 4 to 5. *Source:* National Oceanic and Atmospheric Administration (NOAA).

Atlantic Hurricane Names

Because hurricanes often occur at the same time, officials assign short, distinctive names to the storms to avoid confusion among weather stations, coastal bases, and ships at sea. Since 1953, Atlantic tropical storms have been named from lists created by the National Hurricane Center and now maintained and updated by the World Meteorological Organization. The lists featured only women's names until 1979, when men's and women's names were alternated. Six lists are used in rotation. Thus, the 2004 list will be used again in 2010. A storm is given a name once its winds reach an intensity of 40 mph. In addition to the Atlantic list of names, there are ten other lists corresponding to other storm-prone regions of the world.

2004	2005	2006	2007	2008	2009
Alex	Arlene	Alberto	Andrea	Arthur	Ana
Bonnie	Bret	Beryl	Barry	Bertha	Bill
Charley	Cindy	Chris	Chantal	Cristobal	Claudette
Danielle	Dennis	Debby	Dean	Dolly	Danny
Earl	Emily	Ernesto	Erin	Edouard	Erika
Frances	Franklin	Florence	Felix	Fay	Fred
Gaston	Gert	Gordon	Gabrielle	Gustav	Grace
Hermine	Harvey	Helene	Humberto	Hanna	Henri
Ivan	Irene	Isaac	Ingrid	Ike	Ida
Jeanne	Jose	Joyce	Jerry	Josephine	Joaquin
Karl	Katrina	Kirk	Karen	Kyle	Kate
Lisa	Lee	Leslie	Lorenzo	Laura	Larry
Matthew	Maria	Michael	Melissa	Marco	Mindy
Nicole	Nate	Nadine	Noel	Nana	Nicholas
Otto	Ophelia	Oscar	Olga	Omar	Odette
Paula	Philippe	Patty	Pablo	Paloma	Peter
Richard	Rita	Rafael	Rebekah	Rene	Rose
Shary	Stan	Sandy	Sebastien	Sally	Sam
Tomas	Tammy	Tony	Tanya	Teddy	Teresa
Virginie	Vince	Valerie	Van	Vicky	Victor
Walter	Wilma	William	Wendy	Wilfred	Wanda

Source: National Hurricane Center, National Oceanic and Atmospheric Administration (NOAA).

Retired Hurricane Names

When hurricanes are particularly destructive, their names are retired from the list of usable names. Any country affected by a particularly terrible storm can request that the name be retired by petitioning the World Meteorological Organization. Below is a list of infamous hurricanes that have been sent into retirement.

Name	Year	Location(s) affected	Name	Year	Location(s) affected
Agnes	1972	Florida, Northeast U.S.	David	1979	Lesser Antilles, Hispanola, Florida, and Eastern U.S.
Alicia	1983	North Texas			
Allen	1980	Antilles, Mexico, South Texas	Diana	1990	Mexico
Allison[1]	2001	Texas	Diane	1955	Mid-Atlantic U.S. and Northeast U.S.
Andrew	1992	Bahamas, South Florida, and Louisiana	Donna	1960	Bahamas, Florida, and Eastern U.S.
Anita	1977	Mexico	Dora	1964	Northeast Florida
Audrey	1957	Louisiana, North Texas	Elena	1985	Mississippi, Alabama, Western Florida
Betsy	1965	Bahamas, Southeast Florida, Southeast Louisiana	Ekiuse	1975	Antilles, Northwest Florida, Alabama
			Fabian	2003	Bermuda
Beulah	1967	Antilles, Mexico, South Texas	Flora	1963	Haiti, Cuba
Bob	1991	North Carolina, Northeast U.S.	Floyd	1999	North Carolina, eastern seaboard
Camille	1969	Louisiana, Mississippi, and Alabama	Frederic	1979	Alabama and Mississippi
Carla	1961	Texas	Gilbert	1988	Lesser Antilles, Jamaica, Yucatan Peninsula, Mexico
Carmen	1974	Mexico			
Carol	1954	Northeast U.S.	Gloria	1985	North Carolina, Northeast U.S.
Celia	1970	South Texas	Hattie	1961	Belize, Guatemala
Cleo	1964	Lesser Antilles, Haiti, Cuba, Florida	Hazel	1954	Antilles, North and South Carolina
Connie	1955	North Carolina	Hilda	1964	Louisiana

Name	Year	Location(s) affected		Name	Year	Location(s) affected
Hugo	1989	Antilles, South Carolina		Keith	2000	Belize, Nicaragua, Mexico
Ione	1955	North Carolina		Klaus	1990	Martinique
Inez	1966	Lesser Antilles, Hispanola, Cuba, Florida Keys, Mexico		Lenny	1999	Antilles
				Lili	2002	Lesser Antilles, Haiti, Jamaica, Cuba, Louisiana
Iris	2001	Belize				
Isabel	2003	North Carolina, Northeast U.S.		Luis	1995	Lesser Antilles
Isidore	2002	Western Cuba, Yucatan, Louisiana		Marilyn	1995	Lesser Antilles, Puerto Rico
Janet	1955	Lesser Antilles, Belize, Mexico		Michelle	2001	Honduras, Nicaragua, Jamaica, Cayman Islands, Cuba
Joan	1988	Curacao, Venezuela, Colombia, Nicaragua (crossed into Pacific and became Miriam)		Mitch	1998	Central America, Nicaragua, Honduras
				Opal	1995	Central America, Mexico, Florida
Juan	2003	Nova Scotia		Roxanne	1995	Mexico

1. Tropical storm. *Source:* National Hurricane Center, National Oceanic and Atmospheric Administration (NOAA).

The 20 Deadliest Tornadoes in the United States

Date	Location(s)	Deaths	Date	Location(s)	Deaths
1. March 18, 1925	Tri-State (Mo., Ill., Ind.)	689	10. May 18, 1902	Goliad, Tex.	114
2. May 6, 1840	Natchez, Miss.	317	12. March 23, 1913	Omaha, Neb.	103
3. May 27, 1896	St. Louis, Mo.	255	13. May 26, 1917	Mattoon, Ill.	101
4. April 5, 1936	Tupelo, Miss.	216	14. June 23, 1944	Shinnston, W. Va.	100
5. April 6, 1936	Gainesville, Ga.	203	15. April 18, 1880	Marshfield, Mo.	99
6. April 9, 1947	Woodward, Okla.	181	16. June 1, 1903	Gainesville, Holland, Ga.	98
7. April 24, 1908	Amite La.; Purvis, Miss.	143	16. May 9, 1927	Poplar Bluff, Mo.	98
8. June 12, 1899	New Richmond, Wis.	117	18. May 10, 1905	Snyder, Okla.	97
9. June 8, 1953	Flint, Mich.	115	19. April 24, 1908	Natchez, Miss.	91
10. May 11, 1953	Waco, Tex.	114	20. June 9, 1953	Worcester, Mass.	90

Source: Storm Prediction Center at the National Weather Service, National Oceanic and Atmospheric Administration (NOAA). Web: www.spc.noaa.gov/archive/tornadoes/t-deadly.html.

2003 Tornado Fatality Information

Tornado Fatalities by State

State	Deadly tornadoes	Fatalities
Missouri	8	19
Tennessee	2	12
Kansas	3	8
Georgia	2	6
Kentucky	2	3
Illinois	2	2
Nebraska	2	2
Florida	1	1
New Jersey	1	1
Total	23	54

Circumstances

Circumstance	Fatalities
Mobile home	25
Permanent home	24
Business	1
Outside/Open	3
Other/Unknown	1
Total	54

Source: Storm Prediction Center at the National Weather Service, National Oceanic and Atmospheric Administration (NOAA). Web: www.spc.noaa.gov/climo/torn/2003deadlytorn.html.

Greatest Snowfalls in North America

	Place	Date	Inches	Centimeters
24 hours	Silver Lake, Colo.	April 14–15, 1921	76	195.6
1 month	Tamarack, Calif.	Jan. 1911	390	991
1 storm	Mt. Shasta Ski Bowl, Calif.	Feb. 13–19, 1959	189	480
1 season	Mount Baker, Wash.	1998–1999	1,140	2,895.6

Source: U.S. Army Corps of Engineers, Engineer Topographic Laboratories.

Recorded Weather Extremes

Highest average annual mean temperature (world): Dallol, Ethiopia (Oct. 1960–Dec. 1966), 94° F (34.4° C). **(U.S.):** Key West, Fla. (30-year normal), 78.2° F (25.7° C).

Lowest average annual mean temperature (world): Plateau Station, Antarctica, –70° F (–56.7° C). **(U.S.):** Barrow, Alaska (30-year normal), 9.3° F (–12.6° C).

Greatest average yearly rainfall (world): Cherrapunji, India (74-year avg), 450 in. (1,143 cm). **(U.S.):** Mt. Waialeale, Kauai, Hawaii (32-year avg), 460 in. (1,168 cm).

Minimum average yearly rainfall (world): Arica, Chile (59-year avg), 0.03 in. (0.08 cm) (no rainfall for 14 consecutive years). **(U.S.):** Death Valley, Calif. (42-year avg), 1.63 in. (4.14 cm). Bagdad, Calif., holds the U.S. record for the longest period with no measurable rain, 767 days, from Oct. 3, 1912 to Nov. 8, 1914.

Hottest summer average in Western Hemisphere (U.S.): Death Valley, Calif., 98° F (36.7° C).

Longest hot spell (world): Marble Bar, W. Australia, 100° F (37.8° C) (or above) for 162 consecutive days, Oct. 30, 1923 to Apr. 7, 1924.

Largest hailstone (U.S.): Aurora, Neb., 7 in. (17.8 cm) in diameter, 18.75 in. (47.6 cm) in circumference, June 22, 2003.

World and U.S. Extremes of Climate

Highest Recorded Temperatures

	Place	Date	Degrees Fahrenheit	Degrees Celsius
World (Africa)	El Azizia, Libya	Sept. 13, 1922	136	58
North America (U.S.)	Death Valley, Calif.	July 10, 1913	134	57
Asia	Tirat Tsvi, Israel	June 21, 1942	129	54
Australia	Cloncurry, Queensland	Jan. 16, 1889	128	53
Europe	Seville, Spain	Aug. 4, 1881	122	50
South America	Rivadavia, Argentina	Dec. 11, 1905	120	49
Canada	Midale and Yellow Grass, Saskatchewan, Canada	July 5, 1937	113	45
Oceania	Tuguegarao, Philippines	April 29, 1912	108	42
Persian Gulf (sea-surface)		Aug. 5, 1924	96	36
Antarctica	Vanda Station, Scott Coast	Jan. 5, 1974	59	15
South Pole		Dec. 27, 1978	7.5	−14

Lowest Recorded Temperatures

	Place	Date	Degrees Fahrenheit	Degrees Celsius
World (Antarctica)	Vostok	July 21, 1983	−129	−89
Asia	Oimekon, Russia	Feb. 6, 1933	−90	−68
	Verkhoyansk, Russia	Feb. 7, 1892	−90	−68
Greenland	Northice	Jan. 9, 1954	−87	−66
North America (excl. Greenland)	Snag, Yukon, Canada	Feb. 3, 1947	−81	−63
United States	Prospect Creek, Alaska	Jan. 23, 1971	−80	−62
U.S. (excl. Alaska)	Rogers Pass, Mont.	Jan. 20, 1954	−70	−56.5
Europe	Ust 'Shchugor, Russia	Jan.[1]	−67	−55
South America	Sarmiento, Argentina	June 1, 1907	−27	−33
Africa	Ifrane, Morocco	Feb. 11, 1935	−11	−24
Australia	Charlotte Pass, N.S.W.	June 29, 1994	−9	−22
Oceania	Mauna Kea, Hawaii	May 17, 1979	12	−11

1. Exact date unknown; lowest in 15-year period.

Greatest Rainfalls

	Place	Date	Inches	Centimeters
1 minute (World)	Unionville, Md.	July 4, 1956	1.23	3.1
20 minutes (World)	Curtea-de-Arges, Romania	July 7, 1889	8.1	20.5
42 minutes (World)	Holt, Mo.	June 22, 1947	12	30.5
12 hours (World)	Grand Ilet, La Réunion	Jan. 26, 1980	46	114
24 hours (World)	Foc-Foc, La Réunion	Jan. 7–8, 1966	72	182.5
24 hours (N. Hemisphere)	Paishih, Taiwan	Sept. 10–11, 1963	49	125
24 hours (Australia)	Bellenden Ker, Queensland	Jan. 4, 1979	44	114
24 hours (U.S.)	Alvin, Tex.	July 25–26, 1979	43	109
24 hours (Canada)	Ucluelet Brynnor Mines, British Columbia	Oct. 6, 1967	19	49
5 days (World)	Commerson, La Réunion	Jan. 23–28, 1980	156	395
1 month (World)	Cherrapunji, India	July 1861	366	930
12 months (World)	Cherrapunji, India	Aug. 1860–Aug. 1861	1,042	2,647
12 months (U.S.)	Kukui, Maui, Hawaii	Dec. 1981–Dec. 1982	739	1878

Lowest Average Annual Precipitation Extremes

Continent	Place	Lowest avg. (in.)	Elevation (ft)	Years of record
World (South America)	Arica, Chile	0.03	95	59
Africa	Wadi Halfa, Sudan	<0.10	410	39
Antarctica	Amundsen-Scott South Pole Station	0.80[1]	9,186	10
North America	Batagues, Mexico	1.20	16	14
Asia	Aden, Yemen	1.80	22	50
Australia	Mulka (Troudaninna), South Australia	4.05	160[2]	42
Europe	Astrakhan, Russia	6.40	45	25
Oceania	Puako, Hawaii, Hawaii	8.93	5	13

1. The value given is the average amount of solid snow accumulating in one year as indicated by snow markers. The liquid content of the snow is undetermined. 2. Approximate elevation. *Source:* U.S. Army Corps of Engineers, Engineer Topographic Laboratories.

Record Highest Temperatures by State

State	Temp. °F	Temp. °C	Date	Station	Elevation in feet
Alabama	112	44	Sept. 5, 1925	Centerville	345
Alaska	100	38	June 27, 1915	Fort Yukon	est. 420
Arizona	128	53	June 29, 1994	Lake Havasu City	505
Arkansas	120	49	Aug. 10, 1936	Ozark	396
California	134	57	July 10, 1913	Greenland Ranch	-178
Colorado	118	48	July 11, 1888	Bennett	5,484
Connecticut	106	41	July 15, 1995	Danbury	450
Delaware	110	43	July 21, 1930	Millsboro	20
D.C.	106	41	July 20, 1930	Washington	410
Florida	109	43	June 29, 1931	Monticello	207
Georgia	112	44	Aug. 20, 1983	Greenville	860
Hawaii	100	38	Apr. 27, 1931	Pahala	850
Idaho	118	48	July 28, 1934	Orofino	1,027
Illinois	117	47	July 14, 1954	E. St. Louis	410
Indiana	116	47	July 14, 1936	Collegeville	672
Iowa	118	48	July 20, 1934	Keokuk	614
Kansas	121	49	July 24, 1936[1]	Alton (near)	1,651
Kentucky	114	46	July 28, 1930	Greensburg	581
Louisiana	114	46	Aug. 10, 1936[1]	Plain Dealing	268
Maine	105	41	July 10, 1911[1]	North Bridgton	450
Maryland	109	43	July 10, 1936[1]	Cumberland & Frederick	623; 325
Massachusetts	107	42	Aug. 2, 1975	New Bedford & Chester	120; 640
Michigan	112	44	July 13, 1936	Mio	963
Minnesota	114	46	July 6, 1936[1]	Moorhead	904
Mississippi	115	46	July 29, 1930	Holly Springs	600
Missouri	118	48	July 14, 1954[1]	Warsaw & Union	705; 560
Montana	117	47	July 5, 1937	Medicine Lake	1,950
Nebraska	118	48	July 24, 1936[1]	Minden	2,169
Nevada	125	52	June 29, 1994	Laughlin	605
New Hampshire	106	41	July 4, 1911	Nashua	125
New Jersey	110	43	July 10, 1936	Runyon	18
New Mexico	122	50	June 27, 1994	Waste Isolat. Pilot Pit	3,418
New York	108	42	July 22, 1926	Troy	35
North Carolina	110	43	Aug. 21, 1983	Fayetteville	213
North Dakota	121	49	July 6, 1936	Steele	1,857
Ohio	113	45	July 21, 1934[1]	Gallipolis (near)	673
Oklahoma	120	49	June 27, 1994[1]	Tipton	1,350
Oregon	119	48	Aug. 10, 1898	Pendleton	1,074
Pennsylvania	111	44	July 10, 1936[1]	Phoenixville	100
Rhode Island	104	40	Aug. 2, 1975	Providence	51
South Carolina	111	44	June 28, 1954[1]	Camden	170
South Dakota	120	49	July 5, 1936	Gannvalley	1,750
Tennessee	113	45	Aug. 9, 1930[1]	Perryville	377
Texas	120	49	Aug. 12, 1936	Seymour	1,291
Utah	117	47	July 5, 1895	Saint George	2,880
Vermont	105	41	July 4, 1911	Vernon	310
Virginia	110	43	July 15, 1954	Balcony Falls	725
Washington	118	48	Aug. 5, 1961[1]	Ice Harbor Dam	475
West Virginia	112	44	July 10, 1936[1]	Martinsburg	435
Wisconsin	114	46	July 13, 1936	Wisconsin Dells	900
Wyoming	114	46	July 12, 1900	Basin	3,500

1. Also on earlier dates at the same or other places. *Source:* National Climatic Data Center, Asheville, N.C., and Storm Phillips, STORMFAX, INC.

Record Lowest Temperatures by State

State	Temp. °F	Temp. °C	Date	Station	Elevation in feet
Alabama	–27	–33	Jan. 30, 1966	New Market	760
Alaska	–80	–62	Jan. 23, 1971	Prospect Creek Camp	1,100
Arizona	–40	–40	Jan. 7, 1971	Hawley Lake	8,180
Arkansas	–29	–34	Feb. 13, 1905	Pond	1,250
California	–45	–43	Jan. 20, 1937	Boca	5,532
Colorado	–61	–52	Feb. 1, 1985	Maybell	5,920
Connecticut	–32	–36	Feb. 16, 1943	Falls Village	585
Delaware	–17	–27	Jan. 17, 1893	Millsboro	20
D.C.	–15	–26	Feb. 11, 1899	Washington	410
Florida	–2	–19	Feb. 13, 1899	Tallahassee	193
Georgia	–17	–27	Jan. 27, 1940	CCC Camp F-16	est. 1,000
Hawaii	12	–11	May 17, 1979	Mauna Kea	13,770
Idaho	–60	–51	Jan. 18, 1943	Island Park Dam	6,285
Illinois	–36	–38	Jan. 5, 1999	Congerville	635
Indiana	–36	–38	Jan. 19, 1994	New Whiteland	785
Iowa	–47	–44	Feb. 3, 1996	Elkader	770
Kansas	–40	–40	Feb. 13, 1905	Lebanon	1,812
Kentucky	–37	–38	Jan. 19, 1994	Shelbyville	730
Louisiana	–16	–27	Feb. 13, 1899	Minden	194
Maine	–48	–44	Jan. 19, 1925	Van Buren	510
Maryland	–40	–40	Jan. 13, 1912	Oakland	2,461
Massachusetts	–35	–37	Jan. 12, 1981	Chester	640
Michigan	–51	–46	Feb. 9, 1934	Vanderbilt	785
Minnesota	–60	–51	Feb. 2, 1996	Tower	1,460
Mississippi	–19	–28	Jan. 30, 1966	Corinth	420
Missouri	–40	–40	Feb. 13, 1905	Warsaw	700
Montana	–70	–57	Jan. 20, 1954	Rogers Pass	5,470
Nebraska	–47	–44	Feb. 12, 1899	Camp Clarke	3,700
Nevada	–50	–46	Jan. 8, 1937	San Jacinto	5,200
New Hampshire	–47	–44	Jan. 29, 1934	Mt. Washington	6,262
New Jersey	–34	–37	Jan. 5, 1904	River Vale	70
New Mexico	–50	–46	Feb. 1, 1951	Gavilan	7,350
New York	–52	–47	Feb. 18, 1979[1]	Old Forge	1,720
North Carolina	–34	–37	Jan. 21, 1985	Mt. Mitchell	6,525
North Dakota	–60	–51	Feb. 15, 1936	Parshall	1,929
Ohio	–39	–39	Feb. 10, 1899	Milligan	800
Oklahoma	–27	–33	Jan. 18, 1930	Watts	958
Oregon	–54	–48	Feb. 10, 1933[1]	Seneca	4,700
Pennsylvania	–42	–41	Jan. 5, 1904	Smethport	est. 1,500
Rhode Island	–23	–31	Jan. 11, 1942	Kingston	100
South Carolina	–19	–28	Jan. 21, 1985	Caesars Head	3,115
South Dakota	–58	–50	Feb. 17, 1936	McIntosh	2,277
Tennessee	–32	–36	Dec. 30, 1917	Mountain City	2,471
Texas	–23	–31	Feb. 8, 1933[1]	Seminole	3,275
Utah	–69	–56	Feb. 1, 1985	Peter's Sink	8,092
Vermont	–50	–46	Dec. 30, 1933	Bloomfield	915
Virginia	–30	–34	Jan. 22, 1985	Mountain Lake	3,870
Washington	–48	–44	Dec. 30, 1968	Mazama & Winthrop	2,120; 1,765
West Virginia	–37	–38	Dec. 30, 1917	Lewisburg	2,200
Wisconsin	–55	–48	Feb. 4, 1996	Couderay	1,300
Wyoming	–66	–54	Feb. 9, 1933	Riverside R.S.	6,500

1. Also on earlier dates at the same or other places. *Source:* National Climatic Data Center, Asheville, N.C., and Storm Phillips, STORMFAX, INC.

Record Monthly High and Low Temperatures in the United States

Source: National Climatic Data Center, Asheville, N.C., and Storm Phillips, STORMFAX, Inc.

January

The highest temperature ever recorded for the month of January occurred on January 17, 1936, and again in 1954, in Laredo, Tex. (elevation 421 ft), where the temperature reached 98°F.

The lowest temperature ever recorded for the month of January occurred on January 20, 1954, in Rogers Pass, Mont. (elevation 5,470 ft), where the temperature fell to –70°F.

February

The highest temperature ever recorded for the month of February occurred on February 3, 1963, in Montezuma, Ariz. (elevation 735 ft), where the temperature reached 105°F.

The lowest temperature ever recorded for the month of February occurred on February 1, 1985, at the Peters Sink station in Utah (elevation 8,095 ft), where the temperature fell to –69°F.

March

The highest temperature ever recorded for the month of March occurred on March 31, 1954, in Rio Grande City, Tex. (elevation 168 ft), where the temperature reached 108°F.

The lowest temperature ever recorded for the month of March occurred on March 17, 1906, in Snake River, Wyo. (elevation 6,862 ft), where the temperature dropped to –50°F.

April

The highest temperature ever recorded for the month of April occurred on April 25, 1898, at Volcano Springs, Calif. (elevation –220 ft), where the temperature reached 118°F.

The lowest temperature ever recorded for the month of April occurred on April 5, 1945, in Eagle Nest, N.M. (elevation 8,250 ft), where the temperature dropped to –36°F.

May

The highest temperature ever recorded for the month of May occurred on May 27, 1896, in Salton, Calif. (elevation –263 ft), where the temperature reached 124°F.

The lowest temperature ever recorded for the month of May occurred on May 7, 1964, in White Mountain 2, Calif. (elevation 12,470 ft), where the temperature dropped to –15°F.

June

The highest temperature ever recorded for the month of June occurred on June 23, 1902, at Volcano Springs, Calif. (elevation –220 ft), where the temperature reached 129°F.

The lowest temperature ever recorded for the month of June occurred on June 13, 1907, in Tamarack, Calif. (elevation 8,000 ft), where the temperature dropped to 2°F.

July

The highest temperature ever recorded for the month of July occurred on July 10, 1913, at Greenland Ranch, Calif. (elevation –178 ft), where the temperature reached 134°F.

The lowest temperature ever recorded for the month of July occurred on July 21, 1911, at Painter, Wyo. (elevation 6,800 ft), where the temperature fell to 10°F.

August

The highest temperature ever recorded for the month of August occurred on August 12, 1933, at Greenland Ranch, Calif. (elevation –178 ft), where the temperature reached 127°F.

The lowest temperature ever recorded for the month of August occurred on August 25, 1910, in Bowen, Mont. (elevation 6,080 ft), where the temperature fell to 5°F.

September

The highest temperature ever recorded for the month of September occurred on September 2, 1950, in Mecca, Calif. (elevation –175 ft), where temperature reached 126°F.

The lowest temperature ever recorded for the month of September occurred on September 24, 1926, at Riverside Ranger Station, Mont. (elevation 6,700 ft), where the temperature fell to –9°F.

October

The highest temperature ever recorded for the month of October occurred on October 5, 1917, in Sentinel, Ariz. (elevation 685 ft), where the temperature reached 116°F.

The lowest temperature ever recorded for the month of October occurred on October 29, 1917, in Soda Butte, Wyo. (elevation 6,600 ft), where the temperature fell to –33°F.

November

The highest temperature ever recorded for the month of November occurred on November 12, 1906, in Craftonville, Calif. (elevation 1,759 ft), where the temperature reached 105°F.

The lowest temperature ever recorded for the month of November occurred on November 16, 1959, at Lincoln, Mont. (elevation 5,130 ft), where the temperature fell to –53°F.

December

The highest temperature ever recorded for the month of December occurred on December 8, 1938, in La Mesa, Calif. (elevation 539 ft), where the temperature reached 100°F.

The lowest temperature ever recorded for the month of December occurred on December 19, 1924, at Riverside Ranger Station, Mont. (elevation 6,700 ft), where the temperature fell to –59°F.

Climate of 100 Selected U.S. Cities

(For world cities, *see* p. 271)

| City | Average monthly temperature (°F)[1] | | | | Precipitation | | Snowfall[2] | |
| | Jan. | April | July | Oct. | Average annual | | Average annual | Number of years |
					(in.)[1]	(days)[3]	(in.)[3]	observed[4]
Albany, N.Y.	22.2	46.6	71.1	49.3	38.60	136	64.4	57
Albuquerque, N.M.	35.7	55.6	78.5	57.3	9.47	60	11.0	64
Anchorage, Alaska	15.8	36.3	58.4	34.1	16.08	115	70.8	39 / 60
Asheville, N.C.	35.8	54.1	73.0	55.2	47.07	126	15.3	39
Atlanta, Ga.	42.7	61.6	80.0	62.8	50.20	115	2.1	69 / 65
Atlantic City, N.J.	32.1	50.6	75.3	55.1	40.59	113	16.2	60 / 54
Austin, Texas	50.2	68.3	84.2	70.6	33.65	85	0.9	62 / 58
Baltimore, Md.	32.3	53.2	76.5	55.4	41.94	115	21.5	53
Baton Rouge, La.	50.1	66.6	81.7	68.1	63.08	110	0.2	52 / 46
Billings, Mont.	24.0	46.1	72.0	48.1	14.77	96	56.9	69
Birmingham, Ala.	21.7	44.1	68.7	48.1	38.65	161	84.8	52
Bismarck, N.D.	10.2	43.3	70.4	45.2	16.84	96	44.3	64
Boise, Idaho	30.2	50.6	74.7	52.8	12.19	89	20.6	64
Boston, Mass.	29.3	48.3	73.9	54.1	42.53	127	42.8	52 / 66
Bridgeport, Conn.	29.9	48.9	74.0	54.7	44.15	119	26.2	55 / 49
Buffalo, N.Y.	24.5	45.3	70.8	50.7	40.54	169	93.6	60
Burlington, Vt.	18.0	43.5	70.6	47.7	36.05	154	79.3	60
Caribou, Maine	9.5	38.1	65.6	42.8	37.44	161	112.1	64 / 63
Casper, Wyo.	22.3	42.7	70.0	45.7	13.03	94	77.8	53
Charleston, S.C.	47.9	64.2	81.7	66.2	51.53	114	0.7	61 / 57
Charleston, W.Va.	33.4	54.3	73.9	55.1	44.05	151	34.0	56 / 49
Charlotte, N.C.	41.7	60.9	80.3	61.7	43.51	112	5.6	64
Cheyenne, Wyo.	25.9	41.6	67.7	45.4	15.45	100	55.8	68
Chicago, Ill.	22.0	47.8	73.3	52.1	36.27	125	38.0	45 / 44
Cleveland, Ohio	25.7	47.6	71.9	52.2	38.71	155	57.6	62
Columbia, S.C.	44.6	63.2	82.0	63.7	48.27	109	1.9	56 / 55
Columbus, Ohio	28.3	52.0	75.1	54.7	38.52	137	28.2	64 / 56
Concord, N.H.	20.1	44.6	70.0	47.8	37.60	127	64.5	62
Dallas-Ft. Worth, Texas	44.1	65.0	85.0	67.2	34.73	79	2.6	50 / 45
Denver, Colo.	29.2	47.6	73.4	51.0	15.81	89	60.3	61
Des Moines, Iowa	20.4	50.6	76.1	52.8	34.72	108	33.3	64 / 60
Detroit, Mich.	24.5	48.1	73.5	51.9	32.89	135	41.3	45
Dodge City, Kan.	30.1	53.9	79.8	57.1	22.35	78	20.3	61
Duluth, Minn.	8.4	39.0	65.5	43.5	31.00	134	80.6	62 / 60
El Paso, Texas	45.1	64.6	83.3	64.9	9.43	49	5.3	64 / 57
Fairbanks, Alaska	-9.7	31.7	62.4	23.5	10.34	106	67.7	52
Fargo, N.D.	6.8	43.5	70.6	45.3	21.19	101	40.8	61
Grand Junction, Colo.	26.1	50.9	76.8	52.7	8.99	72	23.6	57
Grand Rapids, Mich.	22.4	46.3	71.4	49.9	37.13	144	73.3	40
Hartford, Conn.	25.7	48.9	73.7	51.9	46.16	128	49.6	49 / 44
Helena, Mont.	20.2	44.1	67.8	44.8	11.32	95	46.9	63 / 58
Honolulu, Hawaii	73.0	75.6	80.8	80.2	18.29	96	0.0	54 / 52
Houston, Texas	51.8	68.5	83.6	70.4	47.84	105	0.4	34 / 69
Indianapolis, Ind.	26.5	52.0	75.4	54.6	40.95	126	23.9	64 / 72
Jackson, Miss.	45.0	63.4	81.4	64.4	55.95	110	1.0	40 / 38
Jacksonville, Fla.	53.1	66.6	81.6	69.4	52.34	116	trace	62 / 60
Juneau, Alaska	25.7	40.8	56.8	42.3	58.33	223	97.0	59
Kansas City, Mo.	26.9	54.4	78.5	56.8	37.98	104	19.9	31 / 69
Knoxville, Tenn.	37.6	57.8	77.7	58.8	48.22	127	11.5	61 / 58
Las Vegas, Nev.	47.0	66.0	91.2	68.7	4.49	26	1.2	55 / 48
Lexington, Ky.	32.0	54.6	76.1	56.6	45.91	130	16.1	59 / 53
Little Rock, Ark.	40.1	61.4	82.4	63.3	50.93	104	5.2	61 / 56
Long Beach, Calif.	57.0	63.0	73.8	68.6	12.94	31	trace	59 / 52
Los Angeles, Calif.	57.1	60.8	69.3	66.9	13.15	35	trace	68 / 62
Louisville, Ky.	33.0	56.4	78.4	58.5	44.54	124	16.4	56
Madison, Wisc.	17.3	45.9	71.6	49.3	32.95	120	43.8	55
Memphis, Tenn.	39.9	62.1	82.5	63.8	54.65	107	5.1	53 / 49
Miami, Fla.	68.1	75.7	83.7	78.8	58.53	131	trace	61 / 59
Milwaukee, Wisc.	20.7	45.2	72.0	51.4	34.81	125	47.0	63
Minneapolis–St. Paul, Minn.	13.1	46.6	73.2	48.7	29.41	115	49.9	65 / 62
Mobile, Ala.	50.1	66.1	81.5	67.7	66.29	121	0.4	62 / 61
Montgomery, Ala.	46.6	64.3	81.8	65.4	54.77	108	0.4	59 / 52
Mt. Washington, N.H.	5.2	22.9	48.7	30.2	101.91	209	259.9	71
Nashville, Tenn.	36.8	58.5	79.1	59.9	48.11	119	10.1	62 / 58
Newark, N.J.	31.3	52.3	77.2	56.4	46.25	122	28.3	62
New Orleans, La.	52.6	68.2	82.7	70.0	64.16	114	0.2	55 / 51
New York, N.Y.	32.1	52.5	76.5	56.6	49.69	121	28.6	134 / 135
Norfolk, Va.	40.1	57.4	79.1	61.1	45.74	116	7.8	55 / 53

City	Average monthly temperature (°F)[1]				Precipitation		Snowfall[2]	
					Average annual		Average annual	Number of years
	Jan.	April	July	Oct.	(in.)[1]	(days)[3]	(in.)[3]	observed[4]
Oklahoma City, Okla.	36.7	59.7	82.0	62.0	35.85	83	9.5	64
Olympia, Wash.	38.1	47.4	62.8	49.7	50.79	163	16.7	62 / 55
Omaha, Neb.	21.7	51.4	76.7	53.2	30.22	99	30.1	67 / 68
Philadelphia, Pa.	32.3	53.1	77.6	57.2	42.05	117	20.8	63 / 61
Phoenix, Ariz.	54.2	70.2	92.8	74.6	8.29	36	trace	64 / 62
Pittsburgh, Pa.	27.5	49.9	72.6	52.5	37.85	152	43.6	51
Portland, Maine	21.7	43.7	68.7	47.7	45.83	129	70.4	63
Portland, Ore.	39.9	51.2	68.1	54.3	37.07	153	6.5	63 / 55
Providence, R.I.	28.7	48.6	73.3	53.0	46.45	124	36.0	50
Raleigh, N.C.	39.7	59.1	78.8	60.0	43.05	113	7.5	59
Reno, Nev.	33.6	48.6	71.3	52.0	7.48	51	24.3	61 / 54
Richmond, Va.	36.4	57.1	77.9	58.3	43.91	114	13.8	66 / 64
Roswell, N.M.	40.0	60.5	80.8	61.4	13.34	54	11.7	31 / 51
Sacramento, Calif.	46.3	58.9	75.4	64.4	17.93	58	trace	64 / 50
Salt Lake City, Utah	29.2	50.0	77.0	52.5	16.50	91	58.7	75
San Antonio, Texas	50.3	68.6	84.3	70.7	32.92	82	0.7	61 / 58
San Diego, Calif.	57.8	62.6	70.9	67.6	10.77	41	trace	63 / 60
San Francisco, Calif.	49.4	56.2	62.8	61.0	20.11	63	trace	76 / 69
Savannah, Ga.	49.2	65.3	82.1	67.1	49.58	111	0.4	53 / 48
Seattle-Tacoma, Wash.	40.9	50.2	65.3	52.7	37.07	155	11.4	59 / 52
Sioux Falls, S.D.	14.0	45.7	73.0	48.0	24.69	98	41.2	58
Spokane, Wash.	27.3	46.5	68.6	47.2	16.67	112	48.6	56
Springfield, Ill.	25.1	52.8	76.3	55.5	35.56	113	23.2	56
St. Louis, Mo.	29.6	56.6	80.2	58.3	38.75	111	19.6	46 / 67
Tampa, Fla.	61.3	71.5	82.5	75.8	44.77	106	trace	57
Toledo, Ohio	23.9	48.3	73.0	51.8	33.21	134	37.1	48 / 43
Tucson, Ariz.	51.7	66.0	86.5	70.5	12.17	53	1.2	63
Tulsa, Okla.	36.4	60.8	83.5	62.6	42.42	91	10.2	64
Vero Beach, Fla.	63.0	71.5	81.7	76.4	51.93	126	trace	20 / 18
Washington, D.C.	34.9	56.1	79.2	58.8	39.35	113	17.1	62 / 60
Wichita, Kan.	30.2	55.3	81.0	58.6	30.38	85	15.9	50
Wilmington, Del.	31.5	52.4	76.6	55.8	42.81	117	21.1	56 / 53

1. Based on 30-year period 1971–2000. 2. Includes ice pellets and sleet; data since April 1988 also include hail. 3. Based on years observed, indicated in final column. 4. Through 2003. Where two figures are shown, the first figure is for precipitation data, the second for snowfall data. *Source:* National Oceanic and Atmospheric Administration (NOAA).

Revised Wind Chill Index

Source: The National Weather Service

The wind chill temperature index measures how cold people feel when outside. Wind chill is based on the rate of heat loss from exposed skin caused by wind and cold. As the wind increases, it draws heat from the body, driving down skin temperature and eventually the internal body temperature. The wind therefore makes it feel much colder. If the temperature is 0°F and the wind is blowing at 15 mph, the wind chill is –19°F. At this wind chill temperature, exposed skin can freeze in 30 minutes.

A revised wind chill table was introduced by the National Weather Service on Nov. 1, 2001. The new index was tested on human subjects and is based on heat loss from exposed skin. The old index, formulated in 1945 by Antarctic explorers, measured the cooling rate of water.

Wind speed (mph)	Temperature (°F)																	
	40	35	30	25	20	15	10	5	0	–5	–10	–15	–20	–25	–30	–35	–40	–45
5	36	31	25	19	13	7	1	–5	–11	–16	–22	–28	–34	–40	–46	–52	–57	–63
10	34	27	21	15	9	3	–4	–10	–16	–22	–28	–35	–41	–47	–53	–59	–66	–72
15	32	25	19	13	6	0	–7	–13	–19	–26	–32	–39	–45	–51	–58	–64	–71	–77
20	30	24	17	11	4	–2	–9	–15	–22	–29	–35	–42	–48	–55	–61	–68	–74	–81
25	29	23	16	9	3	–4	–11	–17	–24	–31	–37	–44	–51	–58	–64	–71	–78	–84
30	28	22	15	8	1	–5	–12	–19	–26	–33	–39	–46	–53	–60	–67	–73	–80	–87
35	28	21	14	7	0	–7	–14	–21	–27	–34	–41	–48	–55	–62	–69	–76	–82	–89
40	27	20	13	6	–1	–8	–15	–22	–29	–36	–43	–50	–57	–64	–71	–78	–84	–91
45	26	19	12	5	–2	–9	–16	–23	–30	–37	–44	–51	–58	–65	–72	–79	–86	–93
50	26	19	12	4	–3	–10	–17	–24	–31	–38	–45	–52	–60	–67	–74	–81	–88	–95
55	25	18	11	4	–3	–11	–18	–25	–32	–39	–46	–54	–61	–68	–75	–82	–89	–97
60	25	17	10	3	–4	–11	–19	–26	–33	–40	–48	–55	–62	–69	–76	–84	–91	–98

Frostbite Times: **Bold = 30 minutes** *Italic = 10 Minutes* ***Bold italic = 5 minutes***

Formula: Wind Chill (°F) = $35.74 + 0.6215T - 35.75(V^{0.16}) + 0.4275T(V^{0.16})$

Where, T = Air Temperature (°F) V = Wind Speed (mph)

See Weights and Measures, p. 451, for Fahrenheit and Celsius scales.

Flying the Friendlier Skies

It's not just the low fares that's attracting us to discount airlines.
They're beating the major airlines on cabin comforts too

By **SALLY B. DONNELLY** TIME

Stephen Kulakowski sat in the boarding area at Boston's Logan International Airport, waiting for his JetBlue flight to Orlando and looking apprehensive. It was only the fourth airplane trip for the 19-year-old college freshman. But what really worried him was the suspiciously low one-way ticket—priced at $92.60—on an airline he had barely heard of. By the time he landed in Florida, the experience on board had left him wanting to fly again. "The flight attendants greeted everyone, the leather seats made it feel like first class, and the satellite TVs were great," said Kulakowski.

Challenging the Big Six

That's just the kind of glowing report that has major airlines fighting for their lives. Low-fare carriers are no longer simply competing on ticket price, they are also raising the bar with the services they offer. While the Big Six airlines (American, Delta, Continental, Northwest, United, and US Airways) struggle with high costs and dissatisfied passengers, small, low-cost airlines like JetBlue, AirTran, Frontier, and Spirit have learned to please customers, make money, and grab market share, all at the same time. They have become major players in the industry. Low-fare carriers, including pioneer Southwest Airlines and the improved America West, account for 30% of the market, compared with just 5% a decade ago.

The Big Six are desperately trying to adapt to the new rules of the marketplace. They are striving to match the smaller airlines' fares, and American and Delta started giving away tickets to counter Jet-Blue's recent expansion. But the most dramatic escalation of the air war was the creation of two totally new airlines. In 2004, United, which has been in bankruptcy since Dec. 2002, has started flying its own knock-off low-fare airline called "Ted." Ted is aimed squarely at Frontier, the low-cost airline that has eaten away at United's dominance in flights out of Denver. Frontier accounts for 16% of that airport's passengers, up from 8% five years ago. In 2003, Delta created Song, a brightly colored, all-coach carrier, with a sassy marketing style, that flies lots of leisure routes to cities like West Palm Beach, Fla., and Las Vegas. Song is targeted at JetBlue, which has most of its flights on the East Coast. But even as United and Delta try to reach down to compete in the low-fare arena, that market has been changing radically.

Cheap, but with Class

Though Southwest actually created the no-frills, low-fare business model 30 years ago, the new-generation carriers have transformed the perception of cheap airlines. Price clearly still matters: airfares are on average 50% lower than they were 25 years ago, allowing for inflation, according to AirlineForecasts, an industry research firm. But passengers also expect better service—even if they do have to bring their own food. JetBlue, which started flying in 2000 from its New York base, was the game changer. Its spanking new Airbus jets, live satellite TV, and consumer-friendly policy of never bumping a passenger have significantly raised customer expectations of low-fare carriers. Its clever marketing campaign drew passengers who in the past might have shunned off-brand airlines. Indeed, the densest concentration of JetBlue passengers can be found in Manhattan's affluent Upper East Side.

Low Fare, High Quality

Just because an airline doesn't have a first-class section doesn't mean it isn't first-rate. In the 14th annual Airline Quality Rating study, JetBlue and two other budget carriers, Southwest and America West, took three of the four top slots. Fourteen airlines were evaluated on services like on-time arrivals, based on data from the U.S. Department of Transportation. "In the late '90s, the big airlines said to their customers, 'You have to be a premier traveler or we're not going to care about you much,'" says Wichita State marketing professor Dean Headley, who co-authored this year's report with Brent Bowen of the University of Nebraska. "[No-frills carriers] told passengers, 'We're going to get you from here to there—with your bags—and we're going to make it as pleasant as possible.'"

Airline Quality Rating*

1. JetBlue	4. America West	7. Continental	10. ATA
2. Alaska	5. US Airways	8. AirTran	11. American
3. Southwest	6. Northwest	9. United	12. Delta

*The Airline Quality Rating is based on an evaluation of data covering on-time arrivals, involuntary denied boardings (overbookings), mishandled baggage, and consumer complaint rates. All data used in the analysis are based on month-to-month-findings provided by the U.S. Department of Transportation for calendar year 2003.

The new entrants from United and Delta face a difficult battle against this latest generation of low-cost carriers. Major airlines have tried many times in the past to start an airline within an airline to compete against low-cost competitors. All such attempts have failed. United and Delta are trying again, a sign that they realize their financial problems will not be solved simply by getting over the post-9/11 travel slump and the recent recession. "We know which way the industry is going—towards quality, low-cost carriers," says John Selvaggio, the head of Song. "We had to play both defense and offense." Song's fares are competitive, the TV and music offerings that the company is installing on board are enticing, and the flight attendants have apparently been encouraged to shed the stoic professionalism of mainline Delta Air Lines and put on an irreverent face. On a recent Song trip, a flight attendant asked over the p.a. system, "Can I have your attention?" As travelers looked up from their video screens and newspapers, she proceeded to ask for a man by name and told him to stand in the aisle. "Mike is single, 26, and looking for a good woman," she chirped, leaving passengers to wonder if they were on an airplane flight or in a bar at spring break. More disconcerting are Song's plane interiors, which are blue accented with orange and a green that appears to be of Soviet vintage. And while the food is tasty—Asian chicken salad, turkey focaccia—you have to pay for it.

Nor is it clear how Ted and Song can make money. The staff at both airlines work at the same high-wage rates as their mainline colleagues, yet the fares are much cheaper. One airport executive is skeptical: "Ted calls itself a low-cost operation, but it will also be a low-revenue producer."

The clear victor in this battle is the airline passenger. "There has never been a better time to be looking for a cheap ticket," says Frontier's CFO Paul Tate. Stephen Kulakowski couldn't agree more—he happily flew home from Florida on JetBlue. □

Distinctive Destinations from the National Trust for Historic Preservation: 2004

Source: National Trust for Historic Preservation.

From a Spanish settlement to a historic resort community nestled in a beautiful Rocky Mountain valley, America offers alternative vacation destinations that symbolize an increasing dedication to historic preservation. The National Trust for Historic Preservation, the country's largest private, nonprofit preservation organization, offers an annual list of unique and lovingly preserved communities that make interesting alternatives to the homogenization of many other vacation spots.

Astoria, Ore. (pop. 9,800): The oldest U.S. settlement west of the Rockies, Astoria has long been revered by residents and visitors alike for its picture-perfect setting on the Columbia River. This port city provides a bounty of historic sites, natural beauty, and great seafood.

Galena, Ill. (pop. 3,600): Rich deposits of lead ore near Galena were the source of many fortunes in the 19th century. Today, spectacular architecture and reminders of eras past are the real treasures in this hilly riverside town that touts down-home charm and plenty to keep visitors busy.

Glenwood Springs, Colo. (pop. 7,700): Snugly nestled in a beautiful valley, this historic resort community serves up a restorative dose of natural hot springs, exciting outdoor activities, eclectic dining and shopping, and evocative links with the Rocky Mountain frontier past.

Guthrie, Okla. (pop. 10,000): Literally born overnight in the epic Oklahoma Land Rush of 1889, Guthrie was Oklahoma's first territorial capitol. Today, this unique and thriving community offers many opportunities for visitors to experience the rough-and-ready spirit of the Wild West.

Lewisburg, W.Va. (pop. 3,600): Civil War history, arts, folklore, and natural splendor are plentiful in historic Lewisburg, where visitors can soak up small-town charm while enjoying interesting architecture, sophisticated shops and galleries, and a wide range of outdoor adventures.

Macon, Ga. (pop. 97,000): Shaped by diverse cultures spanning 12,000 years of history, this friendly city boasts thousands of historic buildings and charming neighborhoods, plus museums that celebrate everything from ancient civilizations to sports and rock-and-roll.

Marshall, Mich. (pop. 7,460): Famed as an open-air textbook of 19th-century American architecture, Marshall's expansive historic district boasts tree-lined streets, interesting shops and restaurants, and an inviting atmosphere that entices visitors to linger and enjoy themselves.

Napa, Calif. (pop. 70,000): The hub of the famed Napa Valley wine region, this charming city was a staging site for the Gold Rush of the late 1850's. Today its historic neighborhoods showcase great architecture and enjoyable attractions—plus an inviting year-round climate.

New Paltz, N.Y. (pop. 6,000): A hip college town with a proud history, New Paltz combines the vibrancy of a campus environment with the traditions of its French Huguenot past—all displayed in a setting that offers great natural beauty and glimpses of centuries gone by.

Newport, R.I. (pop. 25,000): Calling itself "America's First Resort," this compact, walkable community is a treasure-trove of museums, historic buildings, and rocky shoreline—all reminders of the city's past as a bustling colonial port and a 19th-century millionaires' playground.

Oberlin, Ohio (pop. 8,200): Often called "the most cosmopolitan small town in America," Oberlin nurtured many of the major reform movements of the 19th and early 20th centuries. Today it nurtures visitors with interesting historic sites, varied cultural offerings, and easy-going charm.

Old San Juan, Puerto Rico (pop. 443,000): Founded in 1521 as a military stronghold and base for Spanish explorers, this picturesque urban center offers something for everyone: colorful colonial architecture, lush patios and plazas, historic sites, shops and restaurants for every taste, hopping nightlife, and great nearby beaches.

The World's Top Tourism Destinations
(international tourist arrivals)

2001 rank	Country	Arrivals (million) 2001	2002	Percent change 2001/2002	2002 market share	2001 rank	Country	Arrivals (million) 2001	2002	Percent change 2001/2002	2002 market share
1.	France	76.5	77.0	2.4%	11.0%	6.	United Kingdom	22.8	24.2	5.9%	3.4%
2.	Spain	49.5	51.7	3.3	7.4	7.	Canada	19.7	20.1	1.9	2.9
3.	United States	45.5	41.9	−6.7	6.0	8.	Mexico	19.8	19.7	−0.7	2.8
4.	Italy	39.1	39.8	0.6	5.7	9.	Austria	18.2	18.6	2.4	2.6
5.	China	33.2	36.8	11.0	5.2	10.	Germany	17.9	18.0	0.6	2.6

Source: World Tourism Organization (WTO). Web: www.world-tourism.org.

International Destinations of American Tourists, 2002

	All U.S. travelers	For leisure and visiting friends/ relatives	For business and conventions		All U.S. travelers	For leisure and visiting friends/ relatives	For business and conventions
Total number of travelers	23,397,000	18,624,000	7,487,000	**Leisure/recreational activities**[1]			
International destinations visited				Dining in restaurants	86%	85%	90%
Europe	43%	43%	48%	Shopping	76	80	67
Western Europe	41	41	46	Visit historical places	50	56	38
United Kingdom	14	13	19	Sightseeing in cities	43	48	33
France	10	10	9	Visit small towns/villages	42	48	25
Italy	7	8	6	Touring the countryside	35	41	21
Germany	7	6	10	Cultural sites	31	35	21
Spain	4	4	3	Art gallery, museum	28	32	22
Netherlands	4	4	4	Nightclub/dancing	24	26	18
Ireland	2	3	2	Water sports/ sunbathing	22	25	10
Switzerland	2	2	3	Guided tours	15	17	8
Eastern Europe	3	3	3	Concert, play, musical	15	16	11
Caribbean	18	20	9	Ethnic heritage sites	12	13	7
Dominican Republic	5	5	3	Amusement/ theme parks	9	11	5
Jamaica	4	5	2	Visit national parks	9	10	5
Bahamas	3	4	1	Casinos/gambling	7	8	3
South America	8	7	7	Golf/tennis	6	7	6
Brazil	2	2	3	Camping/hiking	5	6	3
Central America	7	7	5	Environmental sights	5	5	3
Costa Rica	2	2	1	Cruises	5	6	2
Africa	2	2	3	Sporting events	4	4	4
Middle East	4	3	4	Hunting/fishing	3	3	1
Asia	19	17	27	Snow skiing	2	2	1
Japan	6	5	9				
Hong Kong	3	3	5				
China	3	2	5				
Taiwan	3	3	4				
South Korea	3	2	4				
India	2	2	2				
Thailand	2	2	2				
Singapore	2	1	3				
Oceania	4	4	4				
Australia	2	3	3				

1. Multiple response. *Source:* U.S. Dept. of Commerce, ITA, Office of Travel & Tourism Industries.

World's Top Five Tourism Earners, 2002

	$ in billions
1. United States	$80.7
2. Spain	36.7
3. France	33.5
4. Italy	29.0
5. China	19.9

Source: World Tourism Organization (WTO).

Top States Visited by U.S. Tourists, 2002

1.	California	6.	North Carolina
2.	Florida	7.	Virginia
3.	Texas	8.	Ohio
4.	Pennsylvania	9.	Georgia
5.	New York	10.	Illinois

Source: Travel Industry Association of America; Travelscope®.

Top U.S. States and Cities Visited by Overseas Travelers, 2003[1]

State/territory	Number of arrivals	U.S. city	Number of arrivals
1. New York	4.1 million	1. New York	4.0 million
2. Florida	4.1 million	2. Los Angeles	2.2 million
3. California	4.0 million	3. Miami	2.2 million
4. Hawaii	2.0 million	4. Orlando	1.8 million
5. Nevada	1.4 million	5. San Francisco	1.6 million
6. Guam	901,000	6. Oahu/Honolulu	1.6 million
7. Illinois	901,000	7. Las Vegas	1.3 million
8. Massachusetts	901,000	8. Metro DC area	901,000
9. Texas	901,000	9. Chicago	721,000
10. New Jersey	721,000	10. Boston	721,000
Top 10 state/territory total	**19.9 million**	**Top 10 city total**	**17.0 million**

NOTE: Includes travelers for business and pleasure, international travelers in transit through the United States, and students; excludes travel by international personnel and international businessmen employed in the United States. 1. Excludes visitors from Canada and Mexico. *Source:* U.S. Dept. of Commerce, Office of Travel and Tourism Industries/International Trade Administration.

Overseas Travelers to the U.S., 2003

Residence of travelers to the U.S.[1]	Arrivals[2]	Percent of total overseas arrivals	Residence of travelers to the U.S.[1]	Arrivals[2]	Percent of total overseas arrivals
Total overseas	**18,026,213**	**100.0%**	Venezuela	284,423	1.6%
Western Europe	8,294,083	46.0	Colombia	280,259	1.6
United Kingdom	3,936,112	21.8	Peru	154,324	0.9
Germany	1,180,212	6.5	Argentina	150,719	0.8
France	688,887	3.8	Central America	655,841	3.6
Italy	408,633	2.3	El Salvador	177,240	1.0
Netherlands	373,690	2.1	Guatemala	151,891	0.8
Spain	284,031	1.6	Asia (Far East)	5,003,261	27.8
Ireland	254,320	1.4	Japan	3,169,682	17.6
Switzerland	230,042	1.3	South Korea	617,573	3.4
Sweden	211,386	1.2	India	272,161	1.5
Belgium	151,069	0.8	China/Hong Kong	271,438	1.5
Eastern Europe	344,594	1.9	Taiwan	238,999	1.3
Caribbean	998,266	5.5	Oceania	524,599	2.9
Bahamas	253,229	1.4	Australia	405,698	2.3
Jamaica	159,484	0.9	Middle East	447,112	2.5
Dominican Republic	153,019	0.8	Israel	249,034	1.4
South America	1,522,191	8.4	Africa	236,266	1.3
Brazil	348,945	1.9			

1. All numbers are rounded to the nearest thousand. Country estimates are only listed if they generated at least 150,000 overseas visitors. 2. The arrivals data reported above are the total arrival figures reported in the 2003 Summary of International Travel to the U.S. *Source:* U.S. Dept. of Commerce, ITA, Office of Travel & Tourism Industries, 2004.

Current Travel Warnings for U.S. Citizens[1]

Travel warnings are issued when the State Department recommends that Americans avoid a certain country. The countries listed below are currently on that list. In addition to this list, the State Department issues Consular Information Sheets for every country of the world with information on such matters as the health conditions, crime, unusual currency or entry requirements, or any areas of instability.

Country	Most recent warning issued	Country	Most recent warning issued
Afghanistan	2/4/04	Iraq	3/23/04
Algeria	3/8/04	Israel	4/28/04
Angola	10/2/03	Kenya	9/25/03
Bahrain	7/3/04	Lebanon	12/4/03
Bosnia and Herzegovina	11/12/03	Liberia	1/7/04
Burundi	8/12/03	Libya	3/5/04
Central African Republic	4/15/04	Nepal	4/7/04
Colombia	3/3/04	Nigeria	12/29/04
Côte d'Ivoire	2/4/04	Pakistan	1/29/04
Dem. Rep. of the Congo (formerly Zaire)	1/22/04	Somalia	10/31/03
Haiti	3/11/04	Sudan	11/14/03
Indonesia	3/19/04	Yemen	8/20/03
Iran	5/12/03	Zimbabwe	1/22/04

NOTE: In the wake of the terrorist attacks on the World Trade Center and the Pentagon on Sept. 11, 2001, the State Department issued a worldwide caution for U.S. citizens traveling abroad. 1. As of July 2004. *Source:* U.S. Department of State. Web: http://travel.state.gov.

Average Number of Vacation Days Around the World Per Year

Italy	42 days	Brazil	34 days	Korea	25 days
France	37 days	United Kingdom	28 days	Japan	25 days
Germany	35 days	Canada	26 days	U.S.	13 days

Source: World Tourism Organization (WTO).

Average Daily Temperatures (°F) in Tourist Cities

(For U.S. cities, *see* Climate of Selected U.S. Cities, pp. 599–600)

Location	January High	January Low	April High	April Low	July High	July Low	October High	October Low
Acapulco (Mexico)	87	72	87	73	89	77	89	77
Amsterdam (Netherlands)	41	34	53	40	69	55	57	46
Athens (Greece)	54	42	67	52	90	72	74	60
Auckland (New Zealand)	73	60	67	56	56	46	63	52
Bangkok (Thailand)	89	69	94	78	91	77	89	76
Beijing (China)	35	15	68	44	87	71	67	44
Belgrade (Yugoslavia)	38	28	62	43	81	60	64	46
Berlin (Germany)	35	26	55	38	74	55	55	41
Bombay (India)	83	67	89	76	85	77	89	76
Cairo (Egypt)	65	47	83	57	96	70	86	65
Calcutta (India)	80	55	97	75	89	79	89	74
Cape Town (South Africa)	69	56	66	54	60	50	65	53
Caracas (Venezuela)	75	56	81	60	78	61	79	61
Copenhagen (Denmark)	36	29	50	37	72	55	53	42
Dublin (Ireland)	47	35	54	38	67	51	57	43
Glasgow (Scotland)	43	34	53	38	66	52	54	43
Hamilton (Bermuda)	68	58	71	59	85	73	79	69
Helsinki (Finland)	27	17	43	31	71	57	45	37
Hong Kong (China)	67	51	79	67	90	78	84	70
Istanbul (Turkey)	48	36	59	45	78	64	66	53
Jerusalem (Israel)	55	41	73	50	87	63	81	59
Kingston (Jamaica)	86	67	87	70	90	73	88	73
Lagos (Nigeria)	88	74	89	77	82	74	85	74
Lisbon (Portugal)	56	46	64	52	79	63	69	57
London (United Kingdom)	44	35	56	40	73	55	58	44
Madrid (Spain)	50	34	63	43	89	61	67	48
Mexico City (Mexico)	66	42	77	51	73	53	70	50
Montreal (Canada)	22	6	51	33	79	60	56	39
Moscow (Russia)	21	9	47	31	76	55	46	34
Nairobi (Kenya)	77	53	75	57	69	51	77	54
Nassau (Bahamas)	77	65	81	69	88	75	85	73
Oslo (Norway)	30	20	50	34	73	56	49	37
Paris (France)	42	32	60	41	76	55	59	44
Prague (Czech Republic)	34	25	55	40	74	58	54	44
Quebec (Canada)	19	3	45	30	77	58	51	37
Rio de Janeiro (Brazil)	84	73	80	69	75	63	77	66
Rome (Italy)	54	39	68	46	88	64	73	53
San José (Costa Rica)	75	58	79	62	77	62	77	60
San Juan (Puerto Rico)	81	70	83	72	86	76	86	75
Seoul (Korea)	33	17	62	42	84	70	67	47
Singapore	86	73	89	75	87	75	88	74
Stockholm (Sweden)	31	23	45	32	70	55	48	39
Sydney (Australia)	79	65	73	57	62	44	72	55
Taipei (Taiwan)	66	54	77	63	92	76	81	67
Tokyo (Japan)	48	31	64	48	84	71	70	56
Toronto (Canada)	30	17	51	35	79	60	57	42
Vancouver (Canada)	42	32	55	41	71	55	57	44
Vienna (Austria)	34	26	57	41	75	59	55	44
Zurich (Switzerland)	36	26	60	41	77	56	57	43

U.S. Passport Information

With a few exceptions, a passport is required for all U.S. citizens to depart and enter the United States and to enter most foreign countries.

Application for a passport may be made at a passport agency, many federal and state courts, probate courts, some county and municipal offices, and some post offices. The thirteen major cities with U.S. passport agencies are Boston, Chicago, Honolulu, Houston, Los Angeles, Miami, New Orleans, New York, Norwalk, Conn., Philadelphia, San Francisco, Seattle, and Washington, DC.

If you would like more information about obtaining or renewing a passport, visit the State Dept. website (travel.state.gov) or call the National Passport Information Center, 1-888-362-8668.

World's 25 Busiest Airports by Passengers and Cargo, 2003

Airport	Total passengers[1]	2002–2003 percent change	Airport	Total cargo[1]	2002–2003 percent change
1. Atlanta, Hartsfield (ATL)	76,086,792	2.9%	Memphis (MEM)	3,390,515	0.0
2. Chicago, O'Hare (ORD)	69,354,154	4.2	Hong Kong (HKG)	2,668,624	6.5
3. London, Heathrow (LHR)	63,468,620	0.2	Tokyo, Narita (NRT)	2,147,212	7.3
4. Tokyo, Haneda (HND)	63,172,925	3.4	Anchorage (ANC)[2]	2,097,488	2.7
5. Los Angeles (LAX)	54,969,053	−2.2	Seoul (ICN)	1,843,054	8.0
6. Dallas/Ft. Worth (DFW)	53,243,061	0.8	Los Angeles (LAX)	1,806,164	2.7
7. Frankfurt-Main (FRA)	48,351,664	−0.2	Frankfurt-Main (FRA)	1,650,599	1.2
8. Paris, Charles de Gaulle (CDG)	48,122,038	−0.4	Miami (MIA)	1,637,278	0.8
9. Amsterdam, Schiphol (AMS)	39,959,161	−1.9	New York (JFK)	1,633,026	2.9
10. Denver (DEN)	37,462,428	5.1	Singapore (SIN)	1,632,409	−1.7
11. Phoenix, Sky Harbor (PHX)	37,409,388	5.2	Louisville (SDF)	1,617,907	6.2
12. Las Vegas (LAS)	36,265,705	3.6	Chicago, O'Hare (ORD)	1,604,755	23.7
13. Madrid (MAD)	35,694,331	5.2	Taipei (TPE)	1,500,071	8.6
14. Houston (IAH)	34,119,680	0.6	Paris, Charles de Gaulle (CDG)	1,481,200	5.9
15. Minneapolis/St. Paul (MSP)	33,195,873	2.0	Amsterdam, Schiphol (AMS)	1,353,729	5.1
16. Detroit (DTW)	32,679,350	0.2	London, Heathrow (LHR)	1,300,420	−0.8
17. New York (JFK)	31,712,728	5.0	Shanghai (PUG)	1,189,303	87.3
18. Bangkok (BKK)	30,175,379	−6.2	Dubai (DXB)	956,845	21.9
19. London, Gatwick (LGW)	30,007,209	1.3	Bangkok (BKK)	950,487	−0.7
20. Miami (MIA)	29,595,618	−1.5	Indianapolis (IND)	890,615	2.8
21. Newark (EWR)	29,584,600	1.2	Newark (EWR)	868,164	1.0
22. San Francisco (SFO)	29,296,681	−6.8	Atlanta, Hartsfield (ATL)	797,419	8.6
23. Orlando (MCO)	27,316,221	2.5	Osaka (KIX)	793,476	−1.5
24. Hong Kong (HKG)	26,774,000	−21.0	Tokyo, Haneda (HND)	722,533	2.2
25. Seattle/Tacoma (SEA)	26,752,768	0.2	Dallas/Ft. Worth (DFW)	667,527	−0.3

NOTES: Total passengers enplaned and deplaned, passengers in transit counted once. Total cargo loaded and unloaded, freight and mail (in metric tons). 1. Results are preliminary. 2. Includes transit freight. *Source:* Airports Council International World Headquarters, Geneva, Switzerland. Web: www.airports.org.

Consumer Complaints[1] Against Major U.S. Airlines by Airline,[2] 2003

Rank	Airline	Complaints	System-wide passenger boardings	Complaints per 100,000 passenger boardings
1.	Southwest Airlines	106	74,788,501	0.14
2.	ExpressJet Airlines	24	11,376,605	0.21
3.	SkyWest Airlines	34	11,421,158	0.30
4.	JetBlue Airways	28	8,973,449	0.31
5.	American Eagle Airlines	61	11,925,053	0.51
6.	Alaska Airlines	78	15,047,033	0.52
7.	Atlantic Southeast Airlines	55	9,293,833	0.59
8.	ATA Airlines	65	9,847,846	0.66
9.	Atlantic Coast Airlines	65	8,598,599	0.76
10.	Delta Air Lines	656	84,250,319	0.78
11.	United Airlines	548	66,153,078	0.83
12.	AirTran Airways	97	11,654,706	0.83
13.	America West Airlines	168	20,050,292	0.84
14.	American Airlines	781	88,798,446	0.88
15.	US Airways	373	41,264,286	0.90
16.	Northwest Airlines	492	51,975,656	0.95
17.	Continental Airlines	371	38,936,200	0.95

1. Consumer complaints filed with the U.S. Department of Transportation. Complaints range from flight problems and over-sales to baggage and customer service. 2. Includes U.S. airlines with at least 1% of total domestic scheduled-service passenger revenues. *Source:* Office of Aviation Enforcement and Proceedings, U.S. Dept. of Transportation, *Air Travel Consumer Report.*

Consumer Complaints[1] Against Foreign Airlines, 2003

Foreign airlines	Total complaints	Foreign airlines	Total complaints	Foreign airlines	Total complaints
Aer Lingus	12	Air Jamaica	40	KLM	24
Aerocalifornia	21	Alitalia Airlines	65	Lan Chile Airlines	11
Aeroflot	10	Allegro Airlines	10	Lot Polish Airlines	11
Aeromar	53	Austrian Airlines	14	Lufthansa	47
Aeromexico	10	British Airways	110	Mexicana	29
Air Canada	36	Cathay Pacific Airways	17	TACA Airlines	31
Air France	102	EVA Airways	10	Virgin Atlantic	27
Air India	33	Iberia Airlines	22	Other foreign airlines	243

1. Consumer complaints filed with the U.S. Department of Transportation. The complaints range from flight problems and oversales to baggage and customer service. The validity of the complaints has not been determined. *Source:* Office of Aviation Enforcement and Proceedings, U.S. Dept. of Transportation, *Air Travel Consumer Report.*

Getting to Work in the City
Commuting characteristics for the 15 largest U.S. cities by population, 2000

2000 rank	City of residence	Total workers 16 years and over	Means of transportation (%)						Average travel time to work (min.)
			Drove alone	Carpool	Public transit	Walked	Other means	Worked at home	
1.	New York, N.Y.	3,332,698	24.1%	6.4%	56.3%	9.3%	1.4%	2.5%	39.0
2.	Los Angeles, Calif.	1,592,463	67.1	14.9	9.5	2.9	1.6	4.0	28.1
3.	Chicago, Ill.	1,252,949	50.5	12.8	27.6	5.6	0.9	2.5	33.1
4.	Houston, Tex.	919,762	72.9	14.7	6.0	2.6	1.2	2.6	25.9
5.	Philadelphia, Pa.	587,156	47.6	10.4	28.0	10.4	1.7	1.9	29.2
6.	Phoenix, Ariz.	589,860	71.9	17.0	3.6	1.9	2.5	3.2	24.7
7.	San Diego, Calif.	579,615	78.5	10.4	4.6	2.3	1.2	2.9	22.6
8.	Dallas, Tex.	560,913	73.4	14.5	5.1	2.2	2.3	2.5	25.2
9.	San Antonio, Tex.	490,076	78.7	13.9	3.6	1.6	0.9	1.4	21.5
10.	Detroit, Mich.	317,179	76.4	12.8	6.2	2.3	1.2	1.0	24.2
11.	San Jose, Calif.	450,093	73.0	16.9	4.9	1.7	0.8	2.7	26.4
12.	Indianapolis, Ind.	407,377	81.9	10.2	2.2	2.5	1.5	1.7	21.6
13.	San Francisco, Calif.	419,601	41.1	9.3	32.1	8.8	3.9	4.8	29.6
14.	Jacksonville, Fla.	350,797	81.9	11.4	1.9	1.5	1.5	1.8	22.6
15.	Columbus, Ohio	353,192	82.5	9.3	3.0	2.0	0.7	2.5	20.7
	Total for U.S.	**127,448,586**	**76.3**	**11.2**	**5.2**	**2.7**	**1.4**	**3.2**	**24.3**

NOTES: Percentages may not add up to 100%, due to rounding. *Source:* U.S. Bureau of the Census. Web: www.census.gov/.

Traffic Congestion in U.S. Cities, 2002

Rank	Urban area	Annual delay per person in hours	Rank	Urban area	Annual delay per person in hours
1.	Los Angeles, Calif.	136	26.	Albuquerque, N.M.	45
2.	San Francisco-Oakland, Calif.	92	28.	Nashville, Tenn.	44
3.	Washington, DC-Md.-Va.	84	29.	Cincinnati, Ohio-Ky.	43
4.	Seattle-Everett, Wash.	82	29.	W. Palm Beach-Boca Raton-Delray Beach, Fla.	43
5.	Houston, Tex.	75	29.	Indianapolis, Ind.	43
6.	San Jose, Calif.	74	29.	San Antonio, Tex.	43
6.	Dallas-Fort Worth, Tex.	74	29.	St. Louis, Mo.-Ill.	43
8.	New York, N.Y.-Northeastern N.J.	73	34.	Sacramento, Calif.	42
9.	Atlanta, Ga.	70	34.	Philadelphia, Pa.-N.J.	42
10.	Miami-Hialeah, Fla.	69	36.	Providence-Pawtucket, R.I.-Mass.	41
11.	Chicago, Ill.-Northwestern Ind.	67	37.	Las Vegas, Nev.	38
11.	Boston, Mass.	67	38.	Columbus, Ohio	36
11.	Denver, Colo.	67	39.	Tacoma, Wash.	34
14.	Orlando, Fla.	66	39.	Memphis, Tenn.-Ark.-Miss.	34
15.	San Bernardino-Riverside, Calif.	64	41.	Milwaukee, Wis.	32
16.	Ft. Lauderdale-Hollywood-Pompano Beach, Fla.	61	41.	Jacksonville, Fla.	32
16.	Austin, Tex.	61	43.	Birmingham, Ala.	31
18.	Phoenix, Ariz.	59	44.	Colorado Springs, Colo.	27
19.	Detroit, Mich.	55	45.	Charleston, S.C.	26
20.	Minneapolis-St. Paul, Minn.	54	46.	Tucson, Ariz.	25
21.	San Diego, Calif.	51	46.	Norfolk-Newport News-Virginia Beach, Va.	25
22.	Baltimore, Md.	50	46.	Omaha, Neb.-Iowa	25
23.	Portland-Vancouver, Ore.-Wash.	47	49.	Fresno, Calif.	24
23.	Charlotte, N.C.	47	49.	Honolulu, Hawaii	24
25.	Louisville, Ky.-Ind.	46	49.	Pensacola, Fla.	24
26.	Tampa-St. Petersburg-Clearwater, Fla.	45			

NOTE: Study conducted in 75 urbanized areas. *Source:* Texas Transportation Institute, the Texas A&M University System. *The 2002 Urban Mobility Report,* David Schrank and Tim Lomax. Web: http://mobility.tamu.edu.

World's Largest Subway Systems
(by ridership)

City	Date system completed	Number of riders (year)	Length (km)	City	Date system completed	Number of riders (year)	Length (km)
Moscow	1935	3.2 bil (1997)	340	Paris	1900	1.2 bil (1998)	211
Tokyo	1927	2.6 bil (1997/98)	281+	Osaka	1933	957 mil (1997)	114
Seoul	1974	1.4 bil (1993)	278+	London	1863	866 mil (1999)	415
Mexico City	1969	1.4 bil (1996)	202	Hong Kong	1979	790 mil (1999)	82
New York City	1904	1.3 bil (2001)	371	St. Petersburg	1955	721 mil (1996)	110

Sources: Jane's Urban Transport Systems, 2002–2003 edition, and individual subway websites.

Fatalities by Transportation Mode, 1970–2002

Mode	1970	1980	1990	2000	2002	Mode	1970	1980	1990	2000	2002
Air						Pedalcyclists	760	965	859	693	662
U.S. air carrier[1]	146	1	39	92	0[P]	Other[6]	40,637	669	584	591	774
Commuter carrier[2]	n.a.	37	6	5	0[P]	**Railroad**					
On-demand air taxi[3]	n.a.	105	51	71	33	Highway-rail grade crossing	1,440	833	698	425	355[P]
General aviation[4]	1,310	1,239	767	595[R]	576[P]	Railroad	785	584	599	512	596[P]
Highway						Transit	n.a.	n.a.	339	295	n.a.
Passenger car occupants	n.a.	27,449	24,092	20,699	20,416	**Waterborne[7]**					
Motorcyclists	2,280	5,144	3,244	2,897	3,244	Vessel-related	178	206	85	49[R]	28[P]
Truck occupants[5]						Not related to vessel casualties	420	281	101	88[R]	48[P]
Light	n.a.	7,486	8,601	11,526	12,182	Recreational boating	1,418	1,360	865	701	n.a.
Large	n.a.	1,262	705	754	684						
Bus occupants	n.a.	46	32	22	45						
Pedestrians	8,950	8,070	6,482	4,763	4,808						

NOTES: n.a. = not available; P = preliminary data; R = revised data. 1. Carriers with 10 or more seats. 2. Carriers with fewer than 10 seats. 3. Nonscheduled service. 4. All other operations. 5. Large trucks are defined as trucks over 10,000 pounds gross vehicle weight. Light trucks are defined as trucks of 10,000 pounds gross vehicle weight rating or less, including pickups, vans, truck-based station wagons, and utility vehicles. 6. Includes occupants of other vehicle types and other nonmotorists. For 1960–1970, the U.S. Department of Transportation, National Highway Traffic Safety Administration did not break out fatality data to the same level of detail as in later years, so fatalities for those years also include occupants of passenger cars, trucks, and buses. 7. Vessel-related casualties include those involving damage to vessels such as collisions or groundings. Fatalities not related to vessel casualties include deaths from falling overboard or from accidents involving onboard equipment. *Source:* U.S. Dept. of Transportation, Bureau of Transportation Statistics, *National Transportation Statistics, 2003.*

U.S. Driving Fatalities, Total and Alcohol-Related

Year	Total	Alcohol-related	Percent	Year	Total	Alcohol-related	Percent
	Fatalities				**Fatalities**		
1982	43,945	26,173	60%	1993	40,150	17,908	45%
1983	42,589	24,635	58	1994	40,716	17,308	43
1984	44,257	24,762	56	1995	41,817	17,732	42
1985	43,825	23,167	53	1996	42,065	17,749	42
1986	46,087	25,017	54	1997	42,013	16,711	40
1987	46,390	24,094	52	1998	41,501	16,673	40
1988	47,087	23,833	51	1999	41,717	16,572	40
1989	45,582	22,424	49	2000	41,945	17,380	41
1990	44,599	22,587	51	2001	42,196	17,400	41
1991	41,508	20,159	49	2002	42,815	17,419	41
1992	39,250	18,290	47				

Source: 1982–2001 (Final) FARS Files and 2002 FARS Annual Report File, FHWA's Highway Statistics Annual Series, from the National Center for Statistics and Analysis.

Alcohol-Related Traffic Fatalities on Holidays, 2002

Holiday 2002	Total traffic fatalities	Total fatalities alcohol-related	Percent fatalities alcohol-related	Time period monitored
New Year's Eve (2001)	118	45	38.1%	12/31/01
New Year's Day	165	94	57.0	1/1/02
New Year's Holiday	575	301	52.3	6:00 p.m. 12/29/01–5:59 a.m. 1/2/02
Super Bowl Sunday	147	86	58.5	2/3/02–5:59 a.m. 2/4/02
St. Patrick's Day	158	72	45.6	3/17/02–5:59 a.m. 3/18/02
Memorial Day	491	237	48.2	6 p.m. 5/24/02–5:59 a.m. 5/28/02
Fourth of July	683	330	48.3	6 p.m. 7/3/02–5:59 a.m. 7/5/02
Labor Day weekend	541	300	55.5	6 p.m. 8/30/02–5:59 a.m. 9/3/02
Halloween	268	109	40.7	10/31/21–11/1/02
Thanksgiving	543	255	47.0	6 p.m. 11/27/02–5:59 a.m. 12/02/02
Thanksgiving–New Year's	4,019	1,561	38.8	11/27/02–12/31/02
Christmas	130	68	52.3	6 p.m. 12/24/02–5:59 a.m. 12/26/02
New Year's Eve (2002)	123	57	46.3	12/31/02

Source: Mothers Against Drunk Driving (MADD). Web: www.madd.org.

Most Dangerous Mode of Transportation

According to the National Safety Council, buses, trains, and airlines have much lower death rates than automobiles when the risk is expressed as passenger deaths per mile of travel.

In 2000, the passenger death rate in automobiles was 0.80 per 100 million passenger-miles. The rates for buses, trains, and airlines were 0.05, 0.03, and 0.02, respectively.

Driving Laws, 2004

Currently all states plus DC have child safety seat laws and enforce a drinking age of 21. As of May 2004, 47 states had blood alcohol concentration (bac) limits of 0.08—there have been concerted state and national efforts to lower the rate from 0.10. A national speed limit of 55 mph was imposed in 1974, and in 1987 it was modified to allow 65-mile-per-hour speeds on some rural freeways. The federal law was entirely repealed in 1995, giving states the right to set their own limits. As of May 2004, graduated licensing laws were in effect in 40 states plus DC, 37 of which prohibit young drivers from driving during high-risk nighttime and early morning hours.

State	Minimum age for driver's license[1]	Blood alcohol concentration limit[2]	Administrative license suspension[3]	Alcohol ignition interlock device[4]	Mandatory belt-use law seating positions	Motorcycle helmet law[5]	Maximum allowable speed limit 1995	2003
Alabama	17	0.08	90 days	no	front	yes	65	70
Alaska	16	0.08	90 days	yes	all	18[6]	—	65
Arizona	16	0.08	90 days	yes	front[7]	18	55	75
Arkansas	16	0.08	120 days	yes	front	21	65	70
California	17	0.08	4 months	yes	all	yes	55	70
Colorado	17	0.10	3 months	yes	front	no	65	75
Connecticut	16 + 10 mo.	0.08	90 days	no	front	18	55	65
Delaware	16 + 10 mo.	0.10	3 months	yes	all	19[8]	—	65
DC	18	0.08	2–90 days	no	all	yes	55	55
Florida	18	0.08	6 months	yes	front[7]	21[9]	65	70
Georgia	18	0.08	1 year	yes	front[7]	yes	55	70
Hawaii	16	0.08	3 months	yes	front[7]	18	—	60
Idaho	16	0.08	90 days	yes	all	18	65	75
Illinois	17	0.08	3 months	yes	front	no	65	65
Indiana	18	0.08	180 days	yes	front	18	65	65
Iowa	17	0.08	180 days	yes	front	no	65	65
Kansas	16	0.08	30 days	yes	front	18	65	70
Kentucky	16 + 6 mo.	0.08	—	yes	all	21[10]	65	65
Louisiana	17	0.08	90 days	yes	front	18[9]	65	70
Maine	16 + 6 mo.	0.08	90 days	yes	all	15[10]	65	65
Maryland	17 + 7 mo.	0.08	45 days	yes	front	yes	55	65
Massachusetts	18	0.08	90 days	no	all	yes	55	65
Michigan	17	0.08	—	yes	front[7]	yes	65	70
Minnesota	16	0.10	90 days	no	front[7]	18[10]	65	70
Mississippi	16	0.08	90 days	yes	front[7]	yes	65	70
Missouri	18	0.08	30 days	yes	front[7]	yes	70	70
Montana	15	0.08	—	yes	all	18	65	75
Nebraska	17	0.08	90 days	yes	front	yes	65	75
Nevada	16	0.08	90 days	yes	all	yes	55	75
New Hampshire	17 + 1 mo.	0.08	6 months	yes	—	no	65	65
New Jersey	18	0.08	—	yes	front[7]	yes	—	65
New Mexico	16 + 6 mo.	0.08	90 days	yes	all	18	65	75
New York	17	0.08	variable	yes	all	yes	55	65
North Carolina	16 + 6 mo.	0.08	30 days	yes	front	yes	65	70
North Dakota	16	0.08	91 days	yes	front	18	65	75
Ohio	17	0.08	90 days	yes	front	18[11]	65	65
Oklahoma	16	0.08	180 days	yes	front	18	65	75
Oregon	17	0.08	90 days	yes	all	yes	65	65
Pennsylvania	17	0.08	—	yes	front[7]	21[11]	55	65
Rhode Island	17 + 6 mo.	0.08	—	yes	all	21[6, 11]	55	65
South Carolina	16 + 6 mo.	0.08	—	yes	all	21	65	70
South Dakota	16	0.08	—	no	front	18	65	75
Tennessee	17	0.08	—	yes	front	yes	65	70
Texas	16 + 6 mo.	0.08	90 days	yes	front[7]	21[9]	65	75
Utah	17	0.08	90 days	yes	all	18	55	75
Vermont	16 + 6 mo.	0.08	90 days	no	all	yes	65	65
Virginia	18	0.08	7 days	yes	front	yes	65	65
Washington	17	0.08	90 days	yes	all	yes	55	70
West Virginia	17	0.08	6 months	yes	front[7]	yes	65	65
Wisconsin	16 + 9 mo.	0.08	6 months	yes	front[7]	18[10]	65	65
Wyoming	16	0.08	90 days	no	all	19	65	75

1. Refers to minimum age for driver's license with no restrictions on unsupervised nighttime driving or carrying passengers. Driver education may be a prerequisite, and one may be limited to carrying only seat-belted passengers. 2. Blood alcohol concentration that constitutes the threshold of legal intoxication. 3. How long (or if) licenses can be suspended before conviction, if drivers fail or refuse to take a chemical test. 4. Legislation for instruments designed to prevent drivers from starting their cars when breath alcohol content is at or above a set point. 5. Presence of law, or age below which riders are required to wear helmet. 6. All passengers required to wear helmet. 7. Required for certain ages at all seating positions. 8. Helmet must also be carried on the motorcycle, whether or not it is worn, for persons 19 and older. 9. Helmet optional for those over listed age if they have proper insurance. (In Texas, they may instead complete a training and safety course.) 10. Helmets must be worn by cyclists holding learners' permits. 11. First-year novices required to wear helmet. (In Penn., first two years, unless driver completes a safety course.) *Source:* Insurance Institute for Highway Safety; Web: www.hwysafety.org.

Car and Driver, "10Best Cars," 2004

Car and Driver's 22nd annual list of the 10 best cars sold in America

- Acura TSX (1)
- Honda Accord (18)
- Audi S4 Quattro (1)
- Honda S2000 (4)
- BMW 3-Series/M3 (13)
- Infiniti G35 (2)
- Chevrolet Corvette (10)
- Mazda RX8 (1)
- Ford Focus (5)
- Toyota Prius (1)

NOTE: Cars are not numerically ranked on the list. Numbers in parenthesis indicate number of times a car has made the 10Best list. Source: *Car and Driver*, Jan. 2004.

Car and Driver, "5Best Trucks," 2004

Car and Driver's fourth annual list of the five best trucks in five categories

Category	Truck	Category	Truck
Pickup	Ford F-150 (1)	Luxury Sport-Utility Vehicle	Cadillac SRX (1)
Small Sport-Utility Vehicle	Subaru Forester 2.5XT (1)	Van	Toyota Sienna (1)
Large Sport-Utility Vehicle	Honda Pilot (3)		

NOTE: Cars are not numerically ranked on the list. Numbers in parenthesis indicate number of times a truck has made the 5Best list. Source: *Car and Driver*, March 2004.

Most Popular Car Colors, 2002–2003

(Percentage of vehicles manufactured during 2002 and 2003 model years in North America)

Luxury	2002	2003	Sport/Compact	2002	2003
1. Med./Dk. Gray	7.2%	23.3%	1. Silver	24.6%	20.1%
2. Silver	32.1	18.8	2. Black	14.3	13.6
3. White Met.	17.7	17.8	3. Med./Dk. Gray	6.7	11.9
4. White	11.8	12.6	4. Med./Dk. Blue	12.9	11.1
5. Black	8.5	10.9	5. Med. Red	5.5	9.2
6. Med. Red	6.0	3.9	6. White	8.8	9.0
7. Med./Dk. Blue	8.6	3.8	7. Lt. Brown	4.3	8.1
8. Gold	3.0	3.6	8. Bright Red	6.9	6.3
9. Lt. Blue	n.a.	3.1	9. Bright Blue	n.a.	3.0
10. Lt. Brown	1.7	0.9	10. Yellow	n.a.	2.6

Full/Intermediate	2002	2003	SUV/Truck/Van	2002	2003
1. Silver	28.1%	27.9%	1. White	19.3%	22.3%
2. Lt. Brown	11.6	17.4	2. Silver	18.0	17.0
3. Med./Dk. Gray	6.2	13.8	3. Black	12.4	11.6
4. White	11.8	13.5	4. Med./Dk. Blue	11.4	9.3
5. Black	11.2	10.2	5. Med/Dk. Gray	7.5	8.8
6. Med. Red	7.6	7.4	6. Med./Dk. Green	6.7	7.0
7. Med./Dk. Green	5.3	7.1	7. Lt. Brown	5.1	6.3
8. Med./Dk. Blue	9.5	6.1	8. Med. Red	7.1	6.2
9. Bright Red	n.a.	2.2	9. Bright Red	4.5	4.1
10. Gold	3.4	1.7	10. Dark Red	n.a.	1.8

Source: DuPont Herberts Automotive Systems, Troy, Mich. 2003 DuPont Automotive Color Popularity Survey Results. Web: www.dupont.com.

Most Stolen Cars, 2003

Rank	Year, make, model	Rank	Year, make, model	Rank	Year, make, model
1.	1995 Saturn SL	5.	1995 Acura Integra	9.	2002 Mitsubishi Montero
2.	1998 Acura Integra	6.	1997 Acura Integra	10.	2000 Honda Civic
3.	1994 Saturn SL	7.	1996 Acura Integra	11.	1991 Acura Legend
4.	1999 Acura Integra	8.	1994 Acura Integra	12.	1999 Honda Civic

NOTE: The most stolen vehicle report is based on total losses identified as stolen and not recovered. CCC does not include temporary auto-related thefts such as "joy-rides" or theft of car items such as stereos. *Source:* CCC Information Services, Inc.

Most Expensive Cars, 2004

Rank	Make, model		Rank	Make, model	
1.	Ferrari Enzo Ferrari	$652,000	6.	Lamborghini Murciélago	$282,000
2.	Porsche Carrera GT	440,000	7.	Bentley Arnage RL	256,990
3.	Saleen S7	440,000	8.	Aston Martin V12 Vanquish	236,000
4.	Maybach 62	357,000	9.	Ferrari 575M Maranello	228,339
5.	Rolls-Royce Phantom	320,000	10.	Ferrari 360 Modena Spider	193,150

NOTE: All base prices are for 2004 models. Includes only vehicles currently sold in the U.S. *Source:* Forbes.com.

Top-Selling Light Trucks in the U.S., 1999–2001

Rank	1999	Number	2000	Number	2001	Number
1.	Ford F Series	806,579	Ford F Series	820,248	Ford F Series	1,330,230
2.	Chevy Silverado	533,177	Chevy Silverado	634,118	Ford Explorer	611,766
3.	Dodge Ram Pickup	428,930	Ford Explorer	445,157	Dodge Ram Pickup	539,877
4.	Ford Explorer	428,772	Dodge Ram Pickup	380,874	Ford Ranger	386,274
5.	Ford Ranger	348,358	Ford Ranger	330,125	Dodge Caravan	386,174
6.	Jeep Grand Cherokee	300,031	Dodge Caravan	285,739	Jeep Grand Cherokee	326,910
7.	Dodge Caravan	293,100	Jeep Grand Cherokee	271,723	GMC Sierra	306,580
8.	Chevrolet S10 Pickup	233,669	Chevrolet S Blazer	225,948	Chevy Tahoe	301,777
9.	Ford Expedition	233,125	Ford Windstar	222,298	Ford Windstar	257,247
10.	Chevrolet S Blazer	232,140	Ford Expedition	213,483	Ford Expedition	253,200

Source: Ward's AutoInfoBank. Web: www.wardsauto.com.

Top-Selling Passenger Cars in the U.S., 1999–2001

Rank	1999	Number	2000	Number	2001	Number
1.	Toyota Camry	448,162	Toyota Camry	422,961	Toyota Camry	616,054
2.	Honda Accord	404,192	Honda Accord	404,515	Honda Accord	596,321
3.	Ford Taurus	368,327	Ford Taurus	382,035	Ford Taurus	517,523
4.	Honda Civic	318,308	Honda Civic	324,528	Honda Civic	487,336
5.	Chevrolet Cavalier	272,122	Ford Focus	286,166	Ford Focus	381,748
6.	Ford Escort	260,486	Chevrolet Cavalier	236,803	Chevy Cavalier	372,909
7.	Toyota Corolla	249,128	Toyota Corolla	230,156	Toyota Corolla	338,534
8.	Pontiac Grand Am	234,936	Pontiac Grand Am	214,923	Chevy Impala	302,953
9.	Chevrolet Malibu	218,540	Chevrolet Malibu	207,376	Pontiac Grand Am	267,070
10.	Saturn S	207,977	Saturn S	177,355	Chevy Malibu	264,841

Source: Ward's AutoInfoBank. Web: www.wardsauto.com.

Least and Most Polluting Cars, 2004

The *ACEEE's Green Book®*, a buyer's guide to environmentally friendly passenger vehicles, rates cars according to their emissions and fuel consumption, and publishes an annual list of the "greenest" and "meanest" (i.e., most polluting).

The Greenest Vehicles of 2004

Make, model	MPG: city	MPG: hwy.	Green[1] score
1. Honda Civic GX	30	34	57
2. Honda Insight	57	56	56
3. Toyota Prius	60	51	53
4. Honda Civic Hybrid	47	48	51
5. Toyota Echo	35	43	43
6. Nissan Sentra	28	35	42
7. Honda Civic HX	36	44	42
8. Mazda 3	28	35	41
9. Toyota Corolla	32	40	40
10. Hyundai Elantra	27	34	40
11. Scion xA	32	38	40
12. Honda Civic	32	38	40

The Meanest Vehicles of 2004

Make, model	MPG: city	MPG: hwy.	Green[1] score
1. Volkswagen Touareg	17	23	9
2. Land Rover Range Rover	12	16	12
3. Ford Excursion	12	16	12
4. Dodge Ram Pickup 1500	9	15	12
5. Lexus LX 470	13	17	13
6. Toyota Land Cruiser	13	17	13
7. Hummer H2	13	16	13
8. GMC Yukon XL K2500	13	17	13
9. Chevrolet Suburban K2500	13	17	13
10. Toyota Sequoia	14	17	14
11. Lamborghini Murcielago	9	13	14
12. Land Rover Discovery Series II	12	16	14

MPG = miles per gallon. 1. The green score runs on a scale from 0 to 100. The top vehicles this year score a 57, the average is 27, and the worst gas-guzzlers score around 10. The score is based on automakers' test results for fuel economy and emissions as reported to the EPA, as well as an estimate of pollution from vehicle manufacturing, from the production and distribution of fuel, and from vehicle tailpipes. It also factors in air pollution. *Source:* American Council for an Energy-Efficient Economy (ACEEE). Web: www.greencar.com.

Parents Magazine and AAA Best Cars for Families, 2004

Economy
• Honda Civic
• Scion xB
• Volkswagen Jetta

Sedans
• Honda Accord
• Chevrolet Malibu
• Toyota Camry

Station Wagons
• Chrysler Pacifica
• Volvo V70
• Pontiac Vibe

Sport Utility Vehicles (SUVs)
• Ford Explorer
• Volkswagen Touareg
• Nissan Murano

Minivans
• Toyota Sienna
• Nissan Quest
• Honda Odyssey

Source: AAA and *Parents Magazine*, April 2004.

Age and Gender Distribution of U.S. Licensed Drivers, 2002

Age	Male drivers		Female drivers		Total drivers	
	Number	Percent of total drivers	Number	Percent of total drivers	Number	Percent of total drivers
Under 16	14,515	0.0%	13,717	0.0%	28,232	0.0%
19 and under	4,772,152	4.9	4,526,106	4.7	9,298,258	4.8
20–24	8,424,540	8.6	8,115,247	8.4	16,539,787	8.5
25–29	8,727,305	9.0	8,372,379	8.6	17,099,684	8.8
30–34	9,737,052	10.0	9,378,312	9.7	19,115,364	9.8
35–39	10,189,184	10.5	9,936,933	10.3	20,126,117	10.4
40–44	10,614,344	10.9	10,584,498	10.9	21,198,842	10.9
45–49	9,941,582	10.2	9,997,864	10.3	19,939,446	10.3
50–54	8,735,627	9.0	8,788,501	9.1	17,524,128	9.0
55–59	7,148,429	7.3	7,141,534	7.4	14,289,963	7.4
60–64	5,371,340	5.5	5,377,859	5.6	10,749,199	5.5
65–69	4,253,857	4.4	4,284,304	4.4	8,538,161	4.4
70–74	3,647,137	3.7	3,788,721	3.9	7,435,858	3.8
75–79	2,936,969	3.0	3,173,171	3.3	6,110,140	3.1
80–84	1,849,298	1.9	2,079,929	2.1	3,929,227	2.0
85 and over	1,112,647	1.1	1,288,812	1.3	2,401,459	1.2
Total	97,461,463	100.0	96,834,170	100.0	194,295,633	100.0

Source: U.S. Department of Transportation, Federal Highway Administration, *Highway Statistics 2002.*

Licensed Drivers and Vehicle Registrations

Year	Resident population (millions)	Drivers (millions)	Motor vehicles (millions)	Year	Resident population (millions)	Drivers (millions)	Motor vehicles (millions)
1960	180	87	74	1982	232	150	160
1961	183	89	76	1983	234	154	164
1962	186	91	79	1984	236	155	166
1963	188	94	83	1985	239	157	172
1964	191	95	86	1986	241	159	176
1965	194	99	90	1987	243	161	179
1966	196	101	94	1988	246	163	184
1967	197	103	97	1989	248	166	187
1968	199	105	101	1990	248	167	189
1969	201	108	105	1991	252	169	188
1970	204	112	108	1992	255	173	190
1971	207	114	113	1993	258	173	194
1972	209	118	119	1994	260	175	198
1973	211	122	126	1995	263	177	202
1974	213	125	130	1996	265	180	206
1975	215	130	133	1997	268	183	208
1976	218	134	139	1998	270	185	208
1977	220	138	142	1999	273	187	212
1978	222	141	148	2000	281	191	218
1979	225	143	152	2001	281	191	226
1980	227	145	156	2002	288	191	230
1981	230	147	158				

Source: U.S. Department of Transportation, Federal Highway Administration, *Highway Statistics 2002.*

U.S. Railroad Ridership, 1988–2003

(millions)

	1988	1989	1990	1993	1994	1995	1996	1997	1998	1999	2000	2001	2002	2003
Amtrak system	21.5	21.4	22.2	22.1	21.2	20.7	19.7	20.2	21.1	21.5	22.5	23.5	23.4	24.0
Northeast Corridor	11.2	11.1	11.2	10.3	11.7	11.6	11.0	11.1	11.9	12.3	12.9	13.5	13.8	13.6
Intercity + West	10.3	10.3	11.0	11.8	9.4	9.1	8.7	9.1	9.2	9.2	9.6	10.0	9.6	10.5
Commuter trains[1]	15.4	17.4	18.0	32.9	39.5	42.2	45.9	48.5	54.0	58.3	61.6	n.a.	n.a.	n.a.
Total	36.9	38.8	40.2	55.0	60.7	62.9	65.6	68.7	75.1	79.8	84.1	n.a.	n.a.	n.a.

NOTE: n.a. = not available. 1. Includes only commuter trains run by Amtrak under contract. *Source:* National Assoc. of Railroad Passengers. Based on Amtrak annual reports. Web: www.narprail.org.

Is Your Job Going Abroad?

Why short-term pain might translate into long-term gain

By Jyoti Thottam   TIME

Rosen Sharma is sure about one thing. His nine-month-old company, Solidcore, a start-up that makes backup security systems for computers, could not survive without outsourcing. By lowering his development costs, the 18 engineers who work for him in India for as little as one-fourth the salary of their American counterparts allow him to spend money on 13 senior managers, engineers, and marketing people in Silicon Valley. If he doesn't outsource, in fact, the venture capitalists who fund start-ups like his won't give him a nickel. Sharma's Indian-American team, tethered by a broadband connection, gets his product in front of customers faster and cheaper.

But Sharma's sharp analysis loses its edge when he thinks about what decisions like his will mean for future generations. He believes that companies like his will always need senior people in the U.S. "But if you're graduating from college today, where are the entry-level jobs?" Sharma asks quietly. How do you get to that secure, skilled job when the path that leads you there has disappeared?

Homeland Insecurity

That's an issue that economists, politicians, and workers are struggling with as the U.S. finds itself in the middle of a structural shift in the economy that no one quite expected. There must be a mix-up here. We ordered a recovery, heavy on the jobs, please.

What we're getting is a new kind of homeland insecurity powered by the rise of outsourcing, a bland yet ominous piece of business jargon that seems to imply that every call center, insurance-claims processor, programming department, and Wall Street back office is being moved to India, Ireland, or some other place thousands of miles away.

To be sure, public anxiety has blurred some important distinctions. To set them straight: most of the jobs that have shifted to places like Mexico and China in the past several decades have been in manufacturing. Some have also blamed trade-liberalization deals like the North American Free Trade Agreement (NAFTA), which the Labor Department estimates was responsible for the loss of more than 500,000 U.S. jobs between 1994 and 2002. That's a significant number but modest in comparison with the millions of jobs that are created and lost annually in the constant churn of the U.S. economy.

Outsourcing accounts for less than 10% of the 2.3 million jobs lost in the U.S. over the past three years. But the trend is speeding up.

How Did We Get Here?

Before acquiring its current incendiary meaning, "outsourcing" referred to the practice of turning over noncritical parts of a business to a company that specialized in that activity. At first it was ancillary functions like running the cafeteria or cleaning

---

What's Going Overseas

Wages in many foreign countries are **substantially lower** than in the U.S. for comparable work. Some examples:

Typical salaries of programmers

Philippines, Malaysia, Russia, Poland, China, India — Up to $11,000, Canada, Ireland, Israel — Up to $80,000, U.S.

Annual pay, in thousands (0, 20, 40, 60, 80)

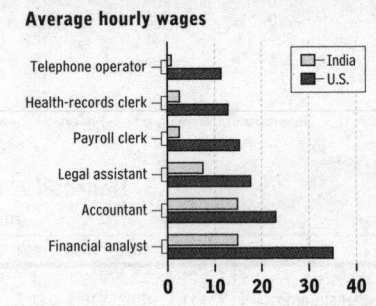

Average hourly wages

India / U.S.

Telephone operator, Health-records clerk, Payroll clerk, Legal assistant, Accountant, Financial analyst

(0, 10, 20, 30, 40)

Types of jobs at risk:

Telephone call center • Computer operator, data entry • Business and financial support • Paralegal and legal assistant • Diagnostic support services • Accounting, bookkeeping, payroll

Source: Forrester Research; McKinsey & Co.; Fisher Center for Real Estate and Urban Economics, University of California, Berkeley.

---

the offices. Then it started moving up to corporate-service functions. But as the price of information technology (IT) fell and the Internet exploded, fiber-optic capacity began popping up around the world. Which meant that all you needed to run a call center, or a customer-service center, was IT and employees who spoke English. Hello, India.

From there, multinational companies began moving up the food chain. Silicon Valley, which for years had been importing highly educated Indian code writers—driving up wage and real estate costs—discovered it was a lot cheaper to export the work to the same highly educated folks over there. So did Wall Street, which employs an army of accountants, analysts, and bankers to pore over documents, do deal analysis, and maintain databases.

"There is no safety net for $80,000-a-year programmers," says Jared Bernstein, senior economist at the Economic Policy Institute. Their education is supposed to provide that. Bernstein says that after the factory closings of the 1980s and the emergence of the "knowledge economy," many liberals and conservatives alike had reached a consensus that manufacturing jobs could not be saved but the "lab coat" jobs would always stay here. But now the white-collar middle class is feeling the sting of insecurity that manufacturing workers know so well.

Why haven't companies that started outsourcing reversed course and brought the jobs back home now that the economy is improving? To some extent, companies are gun-shy about committing to full-time workers and the attendant fringe benefits. Instead of rushing to expand their computer systems and hiring people to maintain them, firms are keeping their outsourcing companies on speed dial.

That's why outsourcing to India has exploded during the recovery. It jumped 60% in 2003 compared with 2002, according to the research magazine *Dataquest*, as corporations used some of their profits (not to mention tax breaks) to expand overseas hiring. That translates to 140,000 jobs outsourced to India in 2003.

John McCarthy, author of the Forrester Research landmark study that predicted 3.3 million jobs would move overseas by 2015 (there are about 130 million jobs in the U.S. today), says the gains in outsourcing didn't come from new companies jumping on the bandwagon. The most dramatic changes came from outsourcing dabblers who finally made a commitment and now allocate as much as 30% of their IT budgets offshore.

Left Behind

Vince Kosmac of Orlando, Fla., has lived both sad chapters of outsourcing—the blue-collar and white-collar versions. He was a trucker in the 1970s and '80s, delivering steel to plants in Johnstown, Pa. When steel melted down to lower-cost competitors in Brazil and China, he used the G.I. Bill to get a degree in computer science. "The conventional wisdom was, 'Nobody can take your education away from you,'" he says bitterly. "Guess what? They took my education away." For nearly 20 years, he worked as a programmer and saved enough for a comfortable life. But programming jobs went missing two years ago, and he is impatient with anyone who suggests that he "retrain" again.

Thanks to technology, more kinds of work can now be spun off into contracts rather than tied to employees. Once a person's labor can be reduced to a contract, it matters little whether the contract is filled in India or Indiana; the only relevant issue is cost. And the speed of technological change accelerates the process. As soon as a job becomes routine enough to describe in a spec sheet, it becomes vulnerable to outsourcing. Jobs like data entry, which are routine by nature, were the first among obvious candidates for outsourcing. But with today's advanced engineering, design and financial-analysis skills can, with time, become well-enough understood to be spelled out in a contract and signed away.

While it's small consolation to workers who lose their jobs, outsourcing has become an essential element of corporate strategy, even for small companies. "Any start-up today, particularly a software company, that does not have an outsourcing strategy is at a competitive disadvantage," says Robin Vasan, managing director of Mayfield, a venture-capital firm based in Menlo Park, Calif.

The move to outsourcing forces a company to use its resources where they count most, like product development. "For some of them, it's almost a question of survival. If they don't develop new products, they'll fail," says Laxmi Narayanan, CEO of Cognizant, an outsourcing firm based in Teaneck, N.J. Nielsen Media Research, which rates television shows, used Cognizant's programmers in India to develop NetRatings for websites. That new line of business allowed the company to hire sales staff and analysts in the U.S. to interpret the ratings for clients and eventually to start selling the product in Asia.

Should Outsourcing Be Controlled?

During the presidential campaign there was talk that there ought to be a law against outsourcing—or at least something to slow it down. Various schemes have been proposed, such as tax initiatives or trade barriers to keep jobs from moving. Some companies may feel political pressure. Dell has moved some call-center support for business-enterprise customers back to the U.S., but the company cited poor service as the reason.

Analysts doubt that any protectionist strategy will slow what appears to be a permanent shift in the way the U.S. does business. Structural change like this is inevitable and recurring. It's just that the transition can be ugly. New England was a textile center until that business went south, to the Carolinas, then east, to China. Software supplanted steel in Pittsburgh, Pa. In both places, high-tech companies later occupied some of the old mill buildings. Now some of those companies' programmers have gone the way of loom operators and steel rollers.

As demand for Indian workers increases, their prices are rising, just like anything else. But at some point in the future, the trend that is pulling jobs out of America will catch up with India. Somewhere a lower-wage alternative will develop—Central Asia, the Philippines, or Thailand—and Indian politicians and workers will be clamoring about foreigners taking their jobs. It's not pretty wherever it happens, but it's just the way the business world turns.   □

Occupations with the Largest Job Growth, 2000–2012

(by number of new jobs; numbers in thousands of jobs)

Occupation	Employment		Change	
	2000	2012	Number	Percent
Medical assistants	365	579	215	59%
Home health aides	580	859	279	48
Computer software engineers, applications	394	573	179	46
Personal and home care aides	608	854	246	40
Computer systems analysts	468	653	184	39
Postsecondary teachers	1,581	2,184	603	38
Security guards	995	1,313	317	32
Management analysts	577	753	176	30
Receptionists and information clerks	1,100	1,425	325	29
Registered nurses	2,284	2,908	623	27

Source: U.S. Department of Labor, Bureau of Labor Statistics, *Monthly Labor Review*, Feb. 2004. Web: www.bls.gov.

Occupations with the Largest Job Decline, 2000–2012

(numbers in thousands of jobs)

Occupation	Employment		Change	
	2000	2012	Number	Percent
Telephone operators	50	22	–28	–56%
Word processors and typists	241	148	–93	–39
Textile knitting and weaving machine setters, operators, and tenders	53	33	–20	–39
Sewing machine operators	315	216	–99	–31
Textile winding, twisting, and drawing out machine setters, operators, and tenders	66	46	–20	–30
Textile bleaching and dyeing machine operators and tenders	27	19	–8	–29
Fishers and related fishing workers	36	27	–10	–27
Textile cutting machine setters, operators, and tenders	34	26	–8	–23
Farmers and ranchers	1,158	920	–238	–21
Sewers, hand	36	29	–8	–21

Source: U.S. Department of Labor, Bureau of Labor Statistics, *Monthly Labor Review*, Feb. 2004. Web: www.bls.gov.

Median Weekly Earnings of Selected Occupations, 2003

Occupation	Both sexes		Men		Women	
	Number of workers (in thousands)	Median weekly earnings	Number of workers (in thousands)	Median weekly earnings	Number of workers (in thousands)	Median weekly earnings
Total, 16 years and over	100,302	$ 620	56,227	$ 695	44,076	$552
Management occupations	10,115	1,023	6,143	1,172	3,973	849
Business and financial operations occupations	4,378	842	1,904	1,014	2,474	744
Professional and related occupations	21,186	845	9,671	1,005	11,516	739
Architecture and engineering occupations	2,487	1,053	2,142	1,094	345	827
Legal occupations	1,024	1,051	491	1,480	533	796
Education, training, and library occupations	5,884	754	1,625	904	4,258	708
Healthcare practitioner and technical occupations	4,630	816	1,176	1,002	3,454	770
Healthcare support occupations	2,023	400	221	469	1,802	396
Protective service occupations	2,405	630	1,964	666	441	505
Food preparation and serving related occupations	3,819	349	1,933	373	1,886	326
Building and grounds cleaning and maintenance occupations	3,280	390	2,123	421	1,157	329
Sales and related occupations	9,924	598	5,557	731	4,367	452
Office and administrative support occupations	15,184	523	3,899	584	11,286	513
Farming, fishing, and forestry occupations	778	369	626	384	152	318
Construction and extraction occupations	5,973	599	5,831	602	141	497
Installation, maintenance, and repair occupations	4,331	673	4,155	675	176	629
Production occupations	8,599	519	6,069	583	2,530	406
Transportation and material moving occupations	6,501	520	5,664	547	837	410

Source: U.S. Department of Labor, Bureau of Labor Statistics. Web: stats.bls.gov.

Occupations with the Highest Fatality Rates, 2002

(average fatality rate for all occupations: 4.0 per 100,000)

Occupation	Fatality rate (per 100,000 employed)	Number of fatalities	Occupation	Fatality rate (per 100,000 employed)	Number of fatalities
Timber cutters	117.8	86	Roofers	37.0	87
Fishers	71.1	33	Electric power installers	32.5	41
Pilots and navigators	69.8	90	Farm occupations	28.0	519
Structural metal workers	58.2	39	Construction laborers	27.7	302
Drivers/sales workers	37.9	58	Truck drivers	25.0	808

Source: U.S. Department of Labor, Bureau of Labor Statistics, Census of Fatal Occupational Injuries, 2002.

10 Leading Occupations of Employed Women Full-time Wage and Salary Workers, 2003 Annual Averages

(employment in thousands)

Occupation	Total employed women	Total employed (both sexes)	Percent women	Women's median weekly earnings
Total, 16 years and older (all employed women full-time wage and salary workers)	44,076	100,302	43.9%	$552
Secretaries and administrative assistants	2,692	2,794	96.3	531
Elementary and middle-school teachers	1,780	2,208	80.6	757
Registered nurses	1,650	1,829	90.2	887
Nursing, psychiatric, and home health aides	1,144	1,285	89.0	372
Cashiers	1,040	1,378	75.5	315
Customer service representatives	1,038	1,503	69.1	503
First-line supervisors/managers of office and administrative support	984	1,450	67.9	609
First-line supervisors/managers of retail sales workers	938	2,259	41.5	496
Bookkeeping, accounting, and auditing clerks	894	978	91.4	512
Receptionists and information clerks	831	892	93.2	446

Source: U.S. Department of Labor, Bureau of Labor Statistics, Annual Averages 2003. For gender wage gap, *see* pp. 373–374.

10 Occupations with the Highest Median Earnings

Rank	Occupation
1.	Physicians and surgeons
2.	Dentists
3.	Chief executives
4.	Podiatrists
5.	Lawyers
6.	Engineering managers
7.	Optometrists
8.	Petroleum engineers
9.	Natural sciences managers
10.	Actuaries

Source: U.S. Census Bureau, 1999.

10 Occupations with the Lowest Median Earnings

Rank	Occupation
1.	Dishwashers
2.	Counter attendants, food concession
3.	Child-care workers
4.	Maids and housekeeping cleaners
5.	Dining room, cafeteria attendants, bartender helpers
6.	Food preparation workers
7.	Teacher assistants
8.	Restaurant hosts, hostesses
9.	Food prep and serving workers
10.	Waiters and waitresses

Economic Outlook Through 2012

Source: Bureau of Labor Statistics, *Monthly Labor Review,* Feb. 2004, www.bls.gov/opub/mlr/2001/11/art1abs.htm.

Every two years the Bureau of Labor Statistics (BLS) publishes its latest projections on the structure of the economy, labor force demographics, and future job growth. The following is a summary of the most recent BLS projections, which were released in Feb. 2004.

Recovery Predicted

After the boom of the 1990s, the U.S. economy suffered a number of serious setbacks, including: the bursting of the technology bubble; the Sept. 11, 2001, terrorist attacks; significant losses of stock market wealth; a stagnant job market; corporate accounting scandals; and uncertainties related to the war in Iraq.

Although the economy has had difficulty shaking off a stubborn slowdown, recent statistical data suggest that we are now poised for a more sustained recovery. The BLS expects the gross domestic product (GDP) to reach $12.6 trillion in chained 1996 dollars by 2012, an increase of $3.2 trillion during the 2002–12 decade. This translates to an average annual rate of growth for real GDP of 3.0% over the period, 0.2% lower than the historical rate of 3.2% from 1992 to 2002.

A slower growth of civilian household employment, from 1.3% a year during the 1992–2002 period to 1.2% from 2002 to 2012, is expected to result in an increase of 17.3 million employees over the latter period, still greater than the increase of 15.8 million employees over the preceding 10-year period.

Consumer Spending to Grow

Personal consumption spending, which makes up two-thirds of economic activity, is expected to grow at an average annual rate of 2.8% from 2002 to 2012, sliding down from the historical high of 3.7% rate posted during the preceding 10-year period.

Consumer spending on durable goods, especially for cars and light trucks, was most notable during the past three years. Sales of autos roared to a peak of 17.2 million units in 2000, as the value of sales incentives reached a new high and buyers responded eagerly to the incentives.

Among consumer purchases of services, a major contributor to growth is health care expenditures. The growing number of elderly in the population, as well as advances in medical technology, has resulted in a greater demand for health services. Spending on medical services increased 2.5% per year during the 1992–2002 period. Over the coming 10 years, due to the importance of the demographic factors, spending on medical services is expected to continue to post solid gains at a growth rate of 3.0% annually.

Continued Trade Deficit

Globalization and international competition have played an important role in U.S. economic activity. With the world assumed to become more open to trade, the share of GDP accounted for by both exports and imports is expected to grow apace. A continued decline in the exchange rate will stimulate U.S. exports abroad and increase international competitiveness. Real exports are expected to grow at a 5.7% annual rate between 2002 and 2012. Both exports of goods and services also are expected to grow at the same rate of 5.7% annually per year during the projection period.

Imports are projected to grow at a rate of 5.2% annually over the 2002–12 projection period, much lower than the 8.7% annual rate of growth for imports over the 1992–2002 span. Imports of goods are expected to grow at 5.6% per year, and a 3.6% annual rate of growth is projected for imports of services during the 2002–12 period. As a result, net exports (exports minus imports) are projected to continue to make a negative contribution to the aggregate demand, reaching $734.6 billion in real terms by 2012. Although the Bureau projects a continued increase in the trade surplus in services, the surplus in services still cannot offset the even larger deficit in goods.

Disposable Income on the Rise

On a per capita basis, nominal disposable income is projected to increase at an average annual rate of 4.3% from 2002 to 2012, reaching a level of $41,459 in the latter year; a gain of more than $14,200 over the projection span. In real terms— that is, chained 1996 dollars—per capita income is projected to grow 1.7% per year from 2002 to 2012. Accordingly, real standard of living would rise over the projection period, at least measured on the basis of growth of disposable personal income.

Employment Outlook

Overall, civilian household employment is projected to increase by 1.2% per year from 2002 to 2012. The result is that about 17.3 million employed persons will be added to the economy over the 10-year projection period. Total employment measured on a nonfarm establishment basis is projected to grow at a rate of 1.6% between 2002 to 2012, from 130.4 million to 152.1 million, an increase of 21.7 million jobs.

Characteristics of the Civilian Labor Force, 1990–2010

(in thousands)

Group	Level			Percent change			Percent distribution		
	1990	2000	2010*	1980–1990	1990–2000	2000–2010*	1990	2000	2010*
Total	125,840	140,863	157,721	17.7%	11.9%	12.0%	100.0%	100.0%	100.0%
Age									
16 to 24	22,492	22,715	26,081	−11.1	1.0	14.8	17.9	16.1	16.5
25 to 54	88,322	99,974	104,994	32.6	13.2	5.0	70.2	71.0	66.6
55 and older	15,026	18,175	26,646	−0.1	21.0	46.6	11.9	12.9	16.9
Sex									
Men	69,011	75,247	82,221	12.3	9.0	9.3	54.8	53.4	52.1
Women	56,829	65,616	75,500	24.9	15.5	15.1	45.2	46.6	47.9
Race									
White	107,447	117,574	128,043	14.8	9.4	8.9	85.4	83.5	81.2
Black	13,740	16,603	20,041	26.5	20.8	20.7	10.9	11.8	12.7
Asian and other[1]	4,653	6,687	9,636	87.9	43.7	44.1	3.7	4.7	6.1
Hispanic origin	10,720	15,368	20,947	74.4	43.4	36.3	8.5	10.9	13.3
Other than Hispanic origin	115,120	125,495	136,774	14.2	9.0	9.0	91.5	89.1	86.7
White non-Hispanic	97,818	102,963	109,118	11.6	5.3	6.0	77.0	73.1	69.2

NOTE: Data apply to workers age 16 and older. * Projected. 1. The "Asian and other" group includes (1) Asians and Pacific Islanders and (2) American Indians and Alaska Natives. The historical data are derived by subtracting "black" and "white" from the total; projections are made directly, not by subtraction. Source: Monthly Labor Review, Nov. 2001.

Employment Status by Race, 1975–2003

Year	Employment rate	Unemployment rate	Year	Employment rate	Unemployment rate
White			1995	57.1%	10.4%
1975	56.7%	7.8%	2000	60.8	7.6
1980	60.0	6.3	2001	59.7	8.7
1985	61.0	6.2	2002	58.1	10.3
1990	63.7	4.8	2003	57.4	10.8
1995	63.8	4.9	**Hispanic[1]**		
2000	65.1	3.5	1975	53.4	12.2
2001	64.4	4.2	1980	57.6	10.1
2002	63.4	5.1	1985	57.8	10.5
2003	63.0	5.2	1990	61.9	8.2
			1995	59.7	9.3
Black			2000	64.7	5.7
1975	50.1	14.8	2001	64.9	6.6
1980	52.3	14.3	2002	63.9	7.5
1985	53.4	15.1	2003	63.1	7.7
1990	56.7	11.4			

NOTE: Data apply to workers age 16 and older. 1. Hispanic persons may be of any race. *Source:* U.S. Department of Labor, Bureau of Labor Statistics. Web: data.bls.gov.

Persons in the Labor Force, 1840–2003

Year	Labor force[1] Number (thousands)	Labor force[1] Percent of working-age population	Year	Labor force[1] Number (thousands)	Labor force[1] Percent of working-age population
1840	5,420	46.6%	1940	52,789	52.2%
1850	7,697	46.8	1950	60,054	53.5
1860	10,533	47.0	1960	69,877	55.3
1870	12,925	45.8	1970	82,049	58.2
1880	17,392	47.3	1980	106,085	62.0
1890	23,318	49.2	1990	125,182	65.3
1900	29,073	50.2	2000	140,863	67.2
1910	37,371	52.2	2001	141,815	66.9
1920	42,434	51.3	2002	144,863	66.6
1930	48,830	49.5	2003	146,510	66.2

1. For 1840 to 1930, the data relate to the population and gainful workers at age 10 and over; for 1940 to 1960, the data relate to the population and labor force at age 14 and over; for 1970 and 1980, the data relate to the population and labor force at age 16 and over. For 1940 to 1980, the data include the Armed Forces. *Source:* U.S. Department of Labor, Bureau of Labor Statistics. Web: data.bls.gov.

Employed and Unemployed Persons by Occupation
(in thousands; 16 years and over)

Occupations	Employed 2002	Employed 2003	Unemployed 2002 (number)	Unemployed 2002 (percent)	Unemployed 2003 (number)	Unemployed 2003 (percent)
Total	136,485	137,736	8,378	5.8%	8,774	6.0%
Management, professional, and related occupations	47,180	47,929	1,482	3.0	1,556	3.1
Management, business, and financial operations	19,823	19,934	622	3.0	627	3.1
Professional and related occupations	27,358	27,995	859	3.0	929	3.2
Service	21,766	22,086	1,544	6.6	1,681	7.1
Sales and office	35,408	35,496	2,110	5.6	2,070	5.5
Office and administrative support	19,580	19,536	1,112	5.4	1,076	5.2
Natural resources, construction, and maintenance	13,562	14,205	1,155	7.8	1,244	8.1
Farming, fishing, and forestry	1,040	1,050	142	12.0	136	11.4
Construction and extraction	7,898	8,114	788	9.1	814	9.1
Installation, maintenance, and repair	4,623	5,041	225	4.6	295	5.5
Production, transportation, and material moving	18,569	18,020	1,530	7.6	1,555	7.9
Production	10,081	9,700	848	7.8	807	7.7
Transportation and material moving	8,488	8,320	682	7.4	748	8.2

Source: U.S. Department of Labor, Bureau of Labor Statistics. Web: data.bls.gov.

Employment Status by Sex, 1970–2003

| | | Civilian labor force | | | |
| | | Employed | | Unemployed | |
Year	Civilian noninstitutional population (in thousands)	Total (in thousands)	Percent of population	Total (in thousands)	Percent of labor force
Total both sexes					
1970	137,085	78,678	57.5%	4,093	4.9%
1975	153,153	85,846	56.1	7,929	8.5
1980	167,745	99,303	59.2	7,637	7.1
1985	178,206	107,150	60.1	8,312	7.2
1990	189,164	118,793	62.8	7,047	5.6
1995	198,584	124,900	62.9	7,404	5.6
2000	212,577	136,891	64.4	5,692	4.0
2003	221,168	137,736	62.3	8,774	6.0
Women					
1970	72,782	29,688	40.8	1,855	5.9
1975	80,860	33,989	42.0	3,486	9.3
1980	88,348	42,117	47.7	3,370	7.4
1985	93,736	47,259	50.4	3,791	7.4
1990	98,787	53,689	54.3	3,140	5.5
1995	103,406	57,523	55.6	3,421	5.6
2000	110,613	63,586	57.5	2,717	4.1
2003	114,733	64,404	56.1	3,868	5.7
Men					
1970	64,304	48,990	76.2	2,238	4.4
1975	72,291	51,857	71.7	4,442	7.9
1980	79,398	57,186	72.0	4,267	6.9
1985	84,469	59,891	70.9	4,521	7.0
1990	90,377	65,104	72.0	3,906	5.7
1995	95,178	67,377	70.8	3,983	5.6
2000	101,964	73,305	71.9	2,975	3.9
2003	106,435	73,332	68.9	4,906	6.3

Source: Current Population Survey, U.S. Department of Labor, Bureau of Labor Statistics. Web: www.bls.gov/cps/wlf-tables2.pdf.

Farm and Non-Farm Labor Force, 1940–2003
(number in thousands)

| | Civilian labor force employed | | | | Civilian labor force employed | | |
Year	Total	Agriculture	Nonagricultural industries	Year	Total	Agriculture	Nonagricultural industries
1940[1]	47,520	9,540	37,980	1980	99,302	3,364	95,938
1945[1]	52,820	8,580	44,240	1985	107,150	3,179	103,971
1950	58,918	7,160	51,758	1990[2]	118,793	3,223	115,570
1955	62,170	6,450	55,722	1995	124,900	3,440	121,460
1960[2]	65,778	5,458	60,318	2000[3]	136,891	2,464	134,427
1965	71,088	4,361	66,726	2001	136,933	2,299	134,635
1970	78,678	3,463	75,215	2002	136,485	2,311	134,174
1975	85,846	3,408	82,438	2003	137,736	2,275	135,461

1. Data for persons age 14 and over. Beginning 1950, data relate to persons age 16 and over. 2. Not strictly comparable with data for prior years. 3. Beginning in Jan. 2000, data are not strictly comparable with data for 1999 and earlier years because of the revisions in the population controls used in the household survey. *Source:* U.S. Department of Labor, Bureau of Labor Statistics. Web: www.bls.gov/cps/cpsaat1.pdf.

Unemployment Rate by Race, Age, and Sex, 2001–2003

	2001	2002	2003		2001	2002	2003
White				Men, 20 years and over	8.0%	9.5%	10.3%
Total, 16 years and over	4.2%	5.1%	5.2%	Women, 20 years and over	7.0	8.8	9.2
Total, 16–19 years	12.7	14.5	15.2				
Men, 20 years and over	3.7	4.7	5.0	**Hispanic or Latino**			
Women, 20 years and over	3.6	4.4	4.4	Total, 16 years and over	6.6	7.5	7.7
				Total, 16–19 years	17.7	20.1	20.0
Black				Men, 20 years and over	5.2	6.4	6.4
Total, 16 years and over	8.6	10.2	10.8	Women, 20 years and over	6.6	7.2	7.8
Total, 16–19 years	29.0	29.8	33.0				

Source: U.S. Department of Labor, Bureau of Labor Statistics. Web: data.bls.gov.

Overall Unemployment Rate in the Civilian Labor Force, 1920–2004

Year	Rate	Year	Rate	Year	Rate	Year	Rate	Year	Rate	Year	Rate
1920	5.2%	1946	3.9%	1966	3.8%	1986	7.0%	1996	5.4%	2004	
1928	4.2	1948	3.8	1968	3.6	1987	6.2	1997	4.9	Jan.	5.6%
1930	8.7	1950	5.3	1970	4.9	1988	5.5	1998	4.5	Feb.	5.6
1932	23.6	1952	3.0	1972	5.6	1989	5.3	1999	4.2	March	5.7
1934	21.7	1954	5.5	1974	5.6	1990	5.6	2000	4.0	April	5.6
1936	16.9	1956	4.1	1976	7.7	1991	6.8	2001	4.8	May	5.6
1938	19.0	1958	6.8	1978	6.1	1992	7.5	2002	5.8	June	5.6
1940	14.6	1960	5.5	1980	7.1	1993	6.9	2003	6.0	July	5.5
1942	4.7	1962	5.5	1982	9.7	1994	6.1			August	5.4
1944	1.2	1964	5.2	1984	7.5	1995	5.6				

NOTES: Estimates prior to 1940 are based on sources other than direct enumeration. Data prior to 1948 are for persons age 14 and over. Data beginning in 1948 are for persons age 16 and over. *Source:* U.S. Department of Labor, Bureau of Labor Statistics. Web: stats.bls.gov.

Mothers in the Labor Force, 1955–2002

	Percentage of mothers with children		
Year	Under 18 years	6 to 17 years	Under 6 years[1]
1955	27.0%	38.4%	18.2%
1965	35.0	45.7	25.3
1975	47.4	54.9	39.0
1980	56.6	64.3	46.8
1985	62.1	69.9	53.5
1990	66.7	74.7	58.2
1991	66.6	74.4	58.4
1992	67.2	75.9	58.0
1993	67.0	75.4	57.9
1994	68.4	76.0	60.3
1995	69.7	76.4	62.3
1996	70.2	77.2	62.3
1997	72.1	78.1	65.0
1998	72.3	78.4	65.2
1999	72.1	78.5	64.4
2000	72.9	79.0	65.3
2001	72.7	79.4	64.4
2002	72.2	78.6	64.1

1. May also have older children. NOTE: 1955 data are for April; 1965 and 1975–1994 data are for March. Data for 1994 and subsequent years are not directly comparable to previous years because of major revisions to the survey. *Source:* U.S. Department of Labor, Bureau of Labor Statistics. Web: data.bls.gov.

Women in the Labor Force, 1900–2003

Year	Number[1] (thousands)	% female population aged 16 and over[1]	% of labor force population aged 16 and over[1]
1900	5,319	18.8%	18.3%
1910	7,445	21.5	19.9
1920	8,637	21.4	20.4
1930	10,752	22.0	22.0
1940	12,845	25.4	24.3
1950	18,389	33.9	29.6
1960	23,240	37.7	33.4
1970	31,543	43.3	38.1
1980	45,487	51.5	42.5
1990[2]	56,829	57.5	45.2
1995[3]	60,944	58.9	46.1
2000	66,303	60.2	46.6
2001	66,848	60.1	46.5
2002	67,363	59.8	46.5
2003	68,272	59.5	47.0

1. For 1900–1930, data relate to population and labor force age 10 and over; for 1940, to population and labor force age 14 and over; beginning 1950, to civilian population and labor force age 16 and over. 2. Data beginning in 1990 are not strictly comparable with data for prior years because population controls were adjusted. 3. Data beginning 1994 are not strictly comparable with data for prior years because of a major revision to survey methodology. *Source:* U.S. Department of Labor, Women's Bureau. Web: www.dol.gov.

Work Stoppages (Strikes) Involving 1,000 Workers or More

Year	Work stoppages	Workers involved (thousands)	Days idle (thousands)	Year	Work stoppages	Workers involved (thousands)	Days idle (thousands)
1950	424	1,698	30,390	1991	40	392	4,584
1960	222	896	13,260	1992	35	364	3,989
1970	381	2,468	52,761	1993	35	182	3,981
1975	235	965	17,563	1994	45	322	5,020
1980	187	795	20,844	1995	31	192	5,771
1983	81	909	17,461	1996	37	273	4,889
1984	62	376	8,499	1997	29	339	4,497
1985	54	324	7,079	1998	34	387	5,116
1986	69	533	11,861	1999	17	73	1,996
1987	46	174	4,481	2000	39	394	20,419
1988	40	118	4,381	2001	29	99	1,151
1989	51	452	16,996	2002	19	46	660
1990	44	185	5,926	2003	14	129	4,091

NOTE: Refers to stoppages that began in the year. Days idle is total for all stoppages in effect. Workers are counted more than once if they were involved in more than one stoppage during the year. *Source:* U.S. Department of Labor, Bureau of Labor Statistics. Web: data.bls.gov.

National Labor Organizations with Membership over 100,000

Members	Union[1]
2,679,396	National Education Association of the United States[2]
1,602,882	Service Employees International Union
1,358,723	United Food and Commercial Workers International Union
1,350,000	American Federation of State, County, and Municipal Employees
1,328,000	International Brotherhood of Teamsters
770,090	American Federation of Teachers
743,957	Laborers' International Union of North America
700,548	International Brotherhood of Electrical Workers
627,408	International Association of Machinists and Aerospace Workers
624,585	International Union, United Automobile, Aerospace, and Agricultural Implement Workers of America
557,136	Communications Workers of America
523,271	United Brotherhood of Carpenters and Joiners of America[2]
512,312	United Steelworkers of America
390,902	International Union of Operating Engineers
388,480	National Postal Mail Handlers Union
325,914	United Association of Journeymen and Apprentices of the Plumbing and Pipe-Fitting Industry of the U.S. and Canada
294,315	National Association of Letter Carriers
262,786	Paper, Allied-Industrial, and Chemical International Union
261,551	International Association of Fire Fighters
249,151	Hotel Employees and Restaurant Employees International Union

Members	Union[1]
239,147	American Postal Workers Union
209,876	Union of Needletrades, Industrial, and Textile Employees
204,282	American Federation of Government Employees
182,597	Amalgamated Transit Union
150,882	Office and Professional Employees International Union
149,808	American Nurses Association[2]
140,641	Sheet Metal Workers International Association
130,928	International Association of Bridge, Structural, Ornamental, and Reinforcing Iron Workers
115,511	International Brotherhood of Painters and Allied Trades
110,000	Transport Workers Union of America
109,917	Bakery, Confectionery, Tobacco Workers, and Grain Millers International Union
109,188	American Association of Classified School Employees[2]
108,205	International Union of Electronic, Electrical, Salaried, Machine, and Furniture Workers
104,102	International Alliance of Theatrical Stage Employees, Moving Picture Technicians, Artists, and Allied Crafts of the U.S. and Canada
101,810	The National Rural Letter Carriers' Association[2]
101,745	United Mine Workers of America
100,427	International Union of Bricklayers and Allied Craftworkers

1. Unless otherwise noted, unions are AFL-CIO affiliated. 2. Not AFL-CIO affiliated. *Source:* U.S. Department of Labor.

Union Affiliation of Employed Wage and Salary Workers, 1983–2003

Year	Total employed (in thousands)	Percent of employed represented by unions	Year	Total employed (in thousands)	Percent of employed represented by unions
1983	88,290	23.3%	1995	110,038	16.7%
1985	94,521	20.5	2000	120,786	14.9
1990	104,876	18.2	2002	121,826	14.5
1993	106,101	17.6	2003	122,358	14.3

Source: U.S. Department of Labor, Bureau of Labor Statistics. Web: www.bls.gov.

Employed Wage and Salary Workers Represented by Unions, 2003

Occupation	Percent of workers	Industry	Percent of workers
Professional and related occupations	20.6%	Public sector	41.5%
Natural resources, construction, and maintenance occupations	20.3	Transportation and utilities	27.3
		Manufacturing	14.3
Production, transportaiton, and material moving occupations	19.8	Information	9.4
Management, professional, and related occupations	15.0	Education and health services	9.4
		Private Sector	9.0
Service occupations	12.7		
Sales and office occupations	9.2		

Source: U.S. Bureau of Labor Statistics. Web: stats.bls.gov/cps/unionmem.pdf

Union Membership, by States

Source: Monthly Labor Review Online, Bureau of Labor Statistics. Web: http://www.bls.gov.

In 2003, 12.9% of wage and salary workers were union members, down from 13.3% in 2002. The number of persons belonging to a union fell by 369,000 over the year to 15.8 million in 2003. The union membership rate has steadily declined from a high of 20.1% in 1983. Union membership among wage and salary workers shows a distinct geographic pattern, according to the Current Population Survey. Union membership is highest in the Northeast, Midwest, and Pacific regions, and lowest in the South.

Four states had union membership rates over 20% in 2003: New York (24.6%), Hawaii (23.8%), Alaska (22.3%), and Michigan (21.9%). This is the same rank order as in both 2001 and 2002. These states, along with New Jersey, have been among the most unionized since at least 1995. North Carolina and South Carolina continued to report the lowest union membership rates, 3.1% and 4.2%, respectively.

The largest numbers of union members lived in California (2.4 million), New York (1.9 million), and Illinois (1.0 million). About half (7.9 million) of the 15.8 million union members in the U.S. lived in six states (California, New York, Illinois, Michigan, Ohio, and Pennsylvania), although these states accounted for just over one-third of wage and salary employment nationally.

Union Membership Rates by State, 2003 Annual Average

(U.S. Rate = 12.9%)

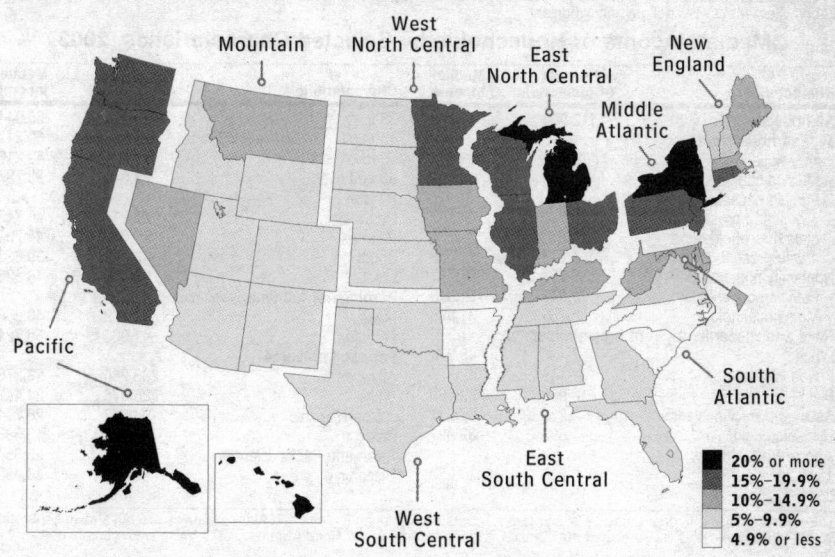

■	20% or more
■	15%–19.9%
■	10%–14.9%
■	5%–9.9%
□	4.9% or less

Source: Current Population Survey, Bureau of Labor Statistics. Web: www.bls.gov/cps/unionmem.pdf.

Median Four-Person Family Income
(in current dollars)

Year	Income	Percent change	Year	Income	Percent change	Year	Income	Percent change
2002	$62,732	–0.9%	1992	$44,251	2.8%	1982	$27,619	5.1%
2001	63,278	1.7	1991	43,056	4.6	1981	26,274	8.0
2000	62,228	3.7	1990	41,151	1.0	1980	24,332	8.6
1999	59,981	7.0	1989	40,763	4.4	1979	22,395	9.6
1998	56,061	5.1	1988	39,051	6.1	1978	20,428	9.1
1997	53,350	3.6	1987	36,812	6.0	1977	18,723	8.1
1996	51,518	3.7	1986	34,716	5.9	1976	17,315	9.3
1995	49,687	5.7	1985	32,777	5.4	1975	15,848	7.5
1994	47,012	4.1	1984	31,097	6.6			
1993	45,161	2.1	1983	29,184	5.7			

Source: Income Statistics Branch/HHES Division, U.S. Bureau of the Census. Web: www.census.gov.

Federal Minimum Wage Rates, 1955–2004

Year	Current dollars	Constant (1996) dollars[1]	Year	Current dollars	Constant (1996) dollars[1]	Year	Current dollars	Constant (1996) dollars[1]	Year	Current dollars	Constant (1996) dollars[1]
	Value of the minimum wage			**Value of the minimum wage**			**Value of the minimum wage**			**Value of the minimum wage**	
1955	$0.75	$4.39	1968	$1.60	$7.21	1981	$3.35	$5.78	1994	$4.25	$4.50
1956	1.00	5.77	1969	1.60	6.84	1982	3.35	5.45	1995	4.25	4.38
1957	1.00	5.58	1970	1.60	6.47	1983	3.35	5.28	1996	4.75	4.75
1958	1.00	5.43	1971	1.60	6.20	1984	3.35	5.06	1997	5.15	5.03
1959	1.00	5.39	1972	1.60	6.01	1985	3.35	4.88	1998	5.15	4.96
1960	1.00	5.30	1973	1.60	5.65	1986	3.35	4.80	1999	5.15	4.85
1961	1.15	6.03	1974	2.00	6.37	1987	3.35	4.63	2000	5.15	4.69
1962	1.15	5.97	1975	2.10	6.12	1988	3.35	4.44	2001	5.15	4.56
1963	1.25	6.41	1976	2.30	6.34	1989	3.35	4.24	2002	5.15	4.49
1964	1.25	6.33	1977	2.30	5.95	1990	3.80	4.56	2003	5.15	4.39
1965	1.25	6.23	1978	2.65	6.38	1991	4.25	4.90	2004	5.15	4.42
1966	1.25	6.05	1979	2.90	6.27	1992	4.25	4.75			
1967	1.40	6.58	1980	3.10	5.90	1993	4.25	4.61			

1. Adjusted for inflation using the CPI-U (Consumer Price Index for All Urban Consumers). *Source:* U.S. Department of Labor. Web: http://www.dol.gov/esa/whd/flsa/.

Median Income of Households by Selected Characteristics, 2003

Characteristic	Number (thousands)	Median income	Characteristic	Number (thousands)	Median income
All households	**112,000**	**$43,318**	35 to 44	23,222	55,044
Type of household			45 to 54	23,137	60,242
Family households	76,217	53,991	55 to 64	16,824	49,215
Married-couple families	57,719	62,405	65 and over	23,048	23,787
Female householder, no husband present	13,781	29,307	**Region**		
Male householder, no wife present	4,717	41,959	Northeast	21,017	46,742
Nonfamily households	35,783	25,741	Midwest	25,643	44,732
Female householder	19,647	21,313	South	40,742	39,823
Male householder	16,136	31,928	West	24,598	46,820
Race and Hispanic origin of householder			**Earnings of full-time, year-round workers**		
White	93,196	45,572	Male	58,772	40,668
Non-Hispanic	81,148	47,777	Female	41,908	30,724
Black	13,969	29,689	**Per capita income**		
Asian and Pacific Islander	4,235	55,262	All races[2]	288,280	23,276
Hispanic origin[1]	11,693	32,997	White	236,875	24,442
Age of householder			Non-Hispanic	194,877	26,774
15 to 24	6,610	27,053	Black	37,651	15,583
25 to 34	19,159	44,779	Asian and Pacific Islander	12,905	23,654
			Hispanic origin[1]	40,425	13,492

1. Persons of Hispanic origin may be of any race. 2. Data for American Indians and Alaska Natives are not shown separately in this table. *Source:* U.S. Bureau of the Census, *Money Income in the United States: 2003.* Web: www.census.gov.

Distribution of Household Income by Race

Income range	White			Black			Hispanic origin[1]		
	1972	1985	2003	1972	1985	2003	1972	1985	2003
Number of households (thousands)	60,618	76,576	91,962	6,809	9,797	13,629	2,655	5,213	11,693
Percent distribution									
Under $5,000	3.6%	2.9%	2.8%	8.3%	7.7%	6.9%	3.8%	4.9%	4.5%
$5,000 to $9,999	7.9	7.4	4.8	15.4	17.0	10.8	8.6	11.8	6.3
$10,000 to $14,999	7.5	7.3	6.6	13.0	11.2	9.7	12.1	11.4	8.1
$15,000 to $24,999	14.1	14.7	12.8	20.0	18.7	16.0	20.7	18.8	17.6
$25,000 to $34,999	15.0	13.8	11.8	15.6	13.4	13.3	20.5	15.4	15.8
$35,000 to $49,999	20.9	18.2	15.0	13.7	14.1	15.0	18.9	16.8	16.7
$50,000 to $74,999	19.7	19.2	18.5	10.9	11.4	14.6	11.4	13.1	15.9
$75,000 to $99,999	6.8	9.2	11.5	2.2	4.5	7.0	2.6	5.3	7.7
$100,000 and over	4.6	7.4	16.1	1.0	1.9	6.7	1.5	2.5	7.5
Median income	$36,510	$38,226	$45,631	$21,311	$22,742	$29,645	$27,552	$26,803	$32,997

1. Persons of Hispanic origin may be of any race. *Source:* U.S. Bureau of the Census: *Income, Poverty, and Health Insurance Coverage in the United States, 2003.*

Per Capita Personal Income

Year	Amount	Year	Amount	Year	Amount	Year	Amount	Year	Amount	Year	Amount
1935	$ 474	1970	$ 3,893	1983	$12,352	1989	$18,176	1995	$23,562	2001	$30,413
1945	1,223	1975	5,851	1984	13,585	1990	19,188	1996	24,651	2002	30,906
1950	1,501	1979	8,638	1985	14,427	1991	19,652	1997	25,924	2003	31,632
1955	1,881	1980	9,910	1986	15,122	1992	20,576	1998	27,203		
1960	2,219	1981	10,949	1987	15,968	1993	21,231	1999	28,546		
1965	2,773	1982	11,731	1988	17,052	1994	22,086	2000	29,469		

Source: U.S. Department of Commerce, Bureau of Economic Analysis, Survey of Current Business. Web: www.bea.doc.gov/bea/regional/spi/.

Consumer Credit Outstanding[1]
(in billions of dollars)

	Total	Commercial banks	Finance companies	Credit unions	Savings institutions	Nonfinancial business	Pools of securitized assets[2]
1975	$ 168.7	$ 82.9	$ 32.7	$ 25.7	n.a.	n.a.	n.a.
1980	302.1	147.0	62.3	44.0	n.a.	n.a.	n.a.
1985	526.3	245.1	111.7	72.7	n.a.	n.a.	n.a.
1990	751.9	347.1	133.3	93.1	n.a.	n.a.	n.a.
1995	1,122.8	502.0	152.1	131.9	$40.1	$85.1	$211.6
1999	1,426.2	499.8	181.6	167.9	61.5	80.3	435.1
2000	1,566.5	541.5	193.2	184.4	64.6	82.7	500.1
2001	1,702.8	558.0	236.5	189.6	69.1	67.9	581.7
2002	1,762.3	587.4	232.3	195.7	68.6	56.9	621.4
2003	2,025.5	636.4	295.4	205.9	77.9	70.3	625.0

1. Covers most short- and intermediate-term credit extended to individuals, excluding loans secured by real estate. 2. Outstanding balances of pools upon which securities have been issued; these balances are no longer carried on the balance sheets of the loan originators. n.a. = not available. Source: Federal Reserve Board. Web http://www.federalreserve.gov/default.htm.

Per Capita Personal Income by State

State	1980	1990	2000	2003	State	1980	1990	2000	2003
Alabama	$ 7,465	$14,899	$23,521	$26,338	Montana	$ 8,342	$14,743	$22,518	25,920
Alaska	13,007	20,887	29,642	33,568	Nebraska	8,895	17,379	27,630	30,758
Arizona	8,854	16,262	24,988	26,838	Nevada	10,848	20,248	29,506	31,266
Arkansas	7,113	13,779	21,995	24,289	New Hampshire	9,150	20,231	33,169	34,702
California	11,021	20,656	32,149	33,749	New Jersey	10,966	24,182	37,118	40,427
Colorado	10,143	18,818	32,434	34,283	New Mexico	7,940	14,213	21,931	25,541
Connecticut	11,532	25,426	40,702	43,173	New York	10,179	22,322	34,689	36,574
Delaware	10,059	19,719	31,012	32,810	North Carolina	7,780	16,284	26,882	28,235
DC	12,251	24,643	38,838	48,342	North Dakota	8,642	15,320	24,708	29,204
Florida	9,246	18,785	27,764	30,446	Ohio	9,399	17,547	27,977	29,944
Georgia	8,021	17,121	27,794	29,442	Oklahoma	9,018	15,117	23,650	26,656
Hawaii	10,129	20,905	27,851	30,913	Oregon	9,309	17,201	27,660	29,340
Idaho	8,105	15,304	23,727	25,911	Pennsylvania	9,353	18,884	29,504	31,998
Illinois	10,454	20,159	31,856	33,690	Rhode Island	9,227	19,035	29,113	31,916
Indiana	8,914	16,815	26,933	28,783	South Carolina	7,392	15,101	24,000	26,132
Iowa	9,226	16,683	26,431	29,043	South Dakota	7,800	15,628	25,958	29,234
Kansas	9,880	17,639	27,374	29,935	Tennessee	7,711	15,903	25,946	28,455
Kentucky	7,679	14,751	24,085	26,252	Texas	9,439	16,747	27,752	29,372
Louisiana	8,412	14,279	23,090	26,100	Utah	7,671	14,063	23,436	24,977
Maine	7,760	17,041	25,380	28,831	Vermont	7,957	17,444	26,848	30,740
Maryland	10,394	22,088	33,482	37,331	Virginia	9,413	19,543	31,120	33,671
Massachusetts	10,103	22,248	37,704	39,815	Washington	10,256	19,268	31,230	33,332
Michigan	9,801	18,239	29,127	30,439	West Virginia	7,764	13,964	21,738	24,379
Minnesota	9,673	18,784	31,935	34,443	Wisconsin	9,364	17,399	28,100	30,898
Mississippi	6,573	12,578	20,900	23,448	Wyoming	11,018	16,905	27,372	32,808
Missouri	8,812	17,407	27,206	29,252	**United States**	**9,494**	**18,667**	**29,469**	**31,632**

NOTE: Per capita personal income was computed using midyear population estimates of the Bureau of the Census. Source: U.S. Department of Commerce, Bureau of Economic Analysis, Survey of Current Business. Web: www.bea.doc.gov/bea/regional/spi/.

Poverty in the United States

Source: U.S. Bureau of the Census, Aug. 2004 supplement to the Current Population Survey (CPS). Web: www.census.gov.

The poverty rate in 2003 rose to 12.5%, up from 12.1% in 2002. About 35.9 million people were poor in 2003, 1.3 million more than in 2002. Both the number and rate have risen for three consecutive years, from 31.6 million and 11.3% in 2000, to 35.9 million and 12.5% in 2003.

For children under 18 years old, both the poverty rate and the number in poverty rose between 2002 and 2003, from 16.7% to 17.6%, and from 12.1 million to 12.9 million, respectively. The poverty rate of children under 18 remained higher than that of 18-to-64-year olds and that of seniors aged 65 and over (10.8% and 10.2%, respectively, both unchanged from 2002). In addition, children represented 35.9% of the people in poverty, compared with 25.4% of the total population.

The poverty rate for people reporting white as their only race was 10.5% in 2003, up from 10.2% in 2002. For blacks, neither the poverty rate nor the number in poverty changed significantly between 2002 and 2003. People who reported black as their only race, for example, had a poverty rate of 24.4% in 2003 and 24.1% in 2002. Among people who indicated Asian as their only race, 11.8% were in

poverty in 2003, higher than the 10.1% in 2002. The number in poverty also increased (from 1.2 million to 1.4 million).

The poverty rate and number of families in poverty increased to 10.0% and 7.6 million in 2003, up from 9.6% and 7.2 million in 2002. Married-couple families showed no change in either their poverty rate or their number in poverty (5.4% and 3.1 million in 2003). In contrast, the poverty rates and numbers in poverty increased for both female householders with no husband present (to 28.0% and 3.9 million in 2003, up from 26.5% and 3.6 million in 2002) and male householders with no wife present (to 13.5% and 640,000 in 2003, up from 12.1% and 560,000 in 2002).

In 2003, the poverty rates for the Northeast (11.3%), Midwest (10.7%), South (14.1%), and West (12.6%) all were unchanged from 2002, leaving the South with the highest rate. Two of the four regions showed increases in the number of people in poverty from 2002 to 2003: the number in the Midwest rose from 6.6 million to 6.9 million and the number in the South rose from 14.0 million to 14.5 million.

Weighted Average Poverty Thresholds[1] for Families, 1960–2003

Calendar year	Individual[2]	Families of 2 persons or more					
		2 persons[2]	3 persons	4 persons	5 persons	6 persons	7 persons
1960	$1,490	$ 1,924	$ 2,359	$ 3,022	$ 3,560	$ 4,002	$ 4,921[3]
1965	1,582	2,048	2,514	3,223	3,797	4,264	5,248[3]
1970	1,954	2,525	3,099	3,968	4,680	5,260	6,468[3]
1975	2,724	3,506	4,293	5,500	6,499	7,316	9,022[3]
1980	4,190	5,363	6,565	8,414	9,966	11,269	12,761
1985	5,469	6,998	8,573	10,989	13,007	14,696	16,656
1990	6,652	8,509	10,419	13,359	15,792	17,839	20,241
1995	7,763	9,933	12,158	15,569	18,408	20,804	23,552
1996	7,995	10,223	12,516	16,036	18,952	21,389	24,268
1997	8,183	10,473	12,802	16,400	19,380	21,886	24,802
1998	8,316	10,634	13,003	16,660	19,680	22,228	25,257
1999	8,501	10,869	13,290	17,029	20,127	22,727	25,912
2000	8,959	11,531	13,470	17,761	21,419	24,636	28,347
2001	9,214	11,859	13,853	18,267	22,029	25,337	29,154
2002	9,359	12,047	14,480	18,244	21,469	24,038	26,924
2003	9,573	12,321	14,810	18,660	21,959	24,586	27,538

1. Annual income. 2. Householder under 65 years. 3. For years before 1980, data are for families with seven persons or more. *Source:* U.S. Bureau of the Census. Web: www.census.gov.

Persons Below Poverty Level, 1975–2003

(in thousands)

Year	All persons	Percent	White	Percent	Black	Percent	Hispanic origin[1]	Percent	Asian and Pac. Isl.	Percent
1975	25,877	12.3%	17,770	9.7%	7,545	31.3%	2,991	26.9%	n.a.	n.a.
1980	29,272	13.0	19,699	10.2	8,579	31.3	3,491	25.7	n.a.	n.a.
1985	33,064	14.0	22,860	11.4	8,926	31.3	5,236	29.0	n.a.	n.a.
1990	33,585	13.5	22,326	10.7	9,837	31.9	6,006	28.1	858	12.2%
1995	36,425	13.8	24,423	11.2	9,872	29.3	8,574	30.3	1,411	14.6
2000	31,139	11.3	21,291	9.4	7,901	22.1	7,155	21.2	1,226	10.8
2001	32,907	11.7	22,739	9.9	8,136	22.7	7,997	21.4	1,275	10.2
2002	34,570	12.1	23,466	10.2	8,602	24.1	8,555	21.8	1,161[2]	10.1
2003	35,861	12.5	24,272	10.5	8,781	24.4	9,051	22.5	1,401	11.8

n.a. = not available. 1. Persons of Hispanic origin may be of any race. 2. For years 2002 and 2003, figures refer to people who reported Asian and did not report any other race category. *Source:* U.S. Bureau of the Census. Web: www.census.gov.

People and Families in Poverty by Selected Characteristics, 2002 and 2003

Characteristic	2003		2002	
	Number (thousands)	Percent[1]	Number (thousands)	Percent[1]
INDIVIDUALS				
Total	35,861	12.5%	34,570	12.1%
In families	25,684	10.8	24,534	10.4
Householder	7,607	10.0	7,229	9.6
Related children under 18	12,340	17.2	11,646	16.3
Related children under 6	4,654	19.8	4,296	18.5
In unrelated subfamilies	464	38.6	417	33.7
Reference person	191	37.6	167	31.7
Children under 18	271	41.7	241	35.4
Unrelated individual	9,713	20.4	9,618	20.4
Male	4,154	18.0	4,023	17.7
Female	5,559	22.6	5,595	22.9
Race[2] and Hispanic origin				
White	24,272	10.5	23,466	10.2
Non-Hispanic	15,902	8.2	15,567	8.0
Black	8,781	24.4	8,602	24.1
Asian	1,401	11.8	1,161	10.1
Hispanic[3]	9,051	22.5	8,555	21.8
Age				
Under 18	12,866	17.6	12,133	16.7
18 to 64	19,443	10.8	18,861	10.6
65 and over	3,552	10.2	3,576	10.4
Nativity				
Native	29,965	11.8	29,012	11.5
Foreign born	5,897	17.2	5,558	16.6
Naturalized citizen	1,309	10.0	1,285	10.0
Not a citizen	4,588	21.7	4,273	20.7
Region				
Northeast	6,052	11.3	5,871	10.9
Midwest	6,932	10.7	6,616	10.3
South	14,548	14.1	14,019	13.8
West	8,329	12.6	8,064	12.4
Residence				
Inside metropolitan areas	28,367	12.1	27,096	11.6
Inside central cities	14,551	17.5	13,784	16.7
Outside central cities	13,816	9.1	13,311	8.9
Outside metropolitan areas	7,495	14.2	7,474	14.2
FAMILIES				
Total	7,607	10.0	7,229	9.6
Type of Family				
Married-couple	3,115	5.4	3,052	5.3
Female householder, no husband present	3,856	28.0	3,613	26.5
Male householder, no wife present	636	135	564	12.1

1. Percentage of total population. 2. Data for American Indians and Alaska Natives are not shown separately. 3. Hispanics may be of any race. *Source:* U.S. Census Bureau, *Current Population Survey,* 2003 and 2004 Annual Demographic Supplements.

Weekly Household Food Spending per Person, 2002

Category	Number of households[1]	Per person	Category	Number of households[1]	Per person
All households	**101,987**	**$37.50**	Women living alone	14,957	$45.00
Household composition:			Men living alone	11,395	52.00
With children < 18	36,919	30.00	With elderly	22,405	36.67
At least one child < 6	16,407	26.67	Elderly, living alone	9,003	40.00
Married-couple families	24,973	30.00	**Race/ethnicity of households:**		
Female head, no spouse	9,062	26.67	White non-Hispanic	75,439	40.00
Male head, no spouse	2,203	30.00	Black non-Hispanic	12,525	30.00
Other household with child[2]	682	30.00	Hispanic[3]	9,881	30.00
With no children < 18	65,068	44.00	Other non-Hispanic	4,142	35.00
More than one adult	38,716	40.00			

1. Totals exclude households that did not answer questions about spending on food. These represented 6.0% of all households. 2. Households with children in complex living arrangements, e.g., children of other relatives or unrelated roommate or border. 3. Hispanics may be of any race. *Source:* Economic Research Service, U.S. Department of Agriculture, *Household Food Security in the United States, 2002.* Web: www.ers.usda.gov

Percent of People in Poverty by State, 2001–2003

State	3-year average 2001–2003	2-year average 2001–2002	2-year average 2002–2003	State	3-year average 2001–2003	2-year average 2001–2002	2-year average 2002–2003
United States	12.1%	11.9%	12.3%	Missouri	10.1%	9.8%	10.3%
Alabama	15.1	15.2	14.7	Montana	14.0	13.4	14.3
Alaska	9.0	8.7	9.2	Nebraska	9.9	10.0	10.2
Arizona	13.9	14.1	13.5	Nevada	9.0	8.0	9.9
Arkansas	18.5	18.8	18.8	New Hampshire	6.0	6.1	5.8
California	12.9	12.8	13.1	New Jersey	8.2	8.0	8.3
Colorado	9.4	9.2	9.7	New Mexico	18.0	17.9	18.0
Connecticut	7.9	7.8	8.2	New York	14.2	14.1	14.2
Delaware	7.7	7.9	8.2	North Carolina	14.2	13.4	15.0
DC	17.3	17.6	16.9	North Dakota	11.7	12.7	10.6
Florida	12.7	12.6	12.6	Ohio	10.4	10.1	10.3
Georgia	12.0	12.1	11.5	Oklahoma	14.0	14.6	13.5
Hawaii	10.7	11.4	10.3	Oregon	11.7	11.3	11.7
Idaho	11.0	11.4	10.8	Pennsylvania	9.9	9.5	10.0
Illinois	11.8	11.5	12.7	Rhode Island	10.7	10.3	11.3
Indiana	9.2	8.8	9.5	South Carolina	14.0	14.7	13.5
Iowa	8.5	8.3	9.1	South Dakota	10.9	10.0	12.1
Kansas	10.3	10.1	10.4	Tennessee	14.3	14.5	14.4
Kentucky	13.7	13.4	14.3	Texas	15.8	15.3	16.3
Louisiana	16.9	16.9	17.2	Utah	9.8	10.2	9.5
Maine	11.8	11.9	12.5	Vermont	9.4	9.8	9.2
Maryland	7.7	7.3	8.0	Virginia	9.3	8.9	10.0
Massachusetts	9.7	9.5	10.1	Washington	11.4	10.8	11.8
Michigan	10.8	10.5	11.5	West Virginia	16.9	16.6	17.1
Minnesota	7.1	6.9	6.9	Wisconsin	8.8	8.2	9.2
Mississippi	17.9	18.9	17.2	Wyoming	9.1	8.8	9.4

Source: U.S. Census Bureau, Current Population Survey, 2002, 2003, and 2004 Annual Demographic Supplements. Web: www.census.gov.

Social Welfare Expenditures Under Public Programs
(in millions of dollars)

Item	1965	1970	1975	1980	1985	1990	1995
Amount							
Gross domestic product	$701,000	$1,023,100	$1,590,800	$2,718,900	$4,108,000	$5,682,900	$7,186,900
Total social welfare expenditures[1]	77,084	145,979	288,967	492,213	731,840	1,048,951	1,505,136
Social insurance	28,123	54,691	123,013	229,754	369,595	513,822	705,483
Public aid	6,283	16,488	41,447	72,703	98,362	146,811	253,530
Health and medical programs	6,155	10,030	16,535	26,762	38,643	61,684	85,507
Veterans' programs	6,031	9,078	17,019	21,466	27,042	30,916	39,072
Education	28,108	50,846	80,834	121,050	172,048	258,332	365,625
Housing	318	701	3,172	6,879	12,598	19,468	29,361
Other social welfare	2,066	4,145	6,947	13,599	13,552	17,918	26,558
All health and medical care[2]	9,302	24,801	51,022	99,145	170,665	274,472	435,075
As percent of gross domestic product							
Gross domestic product	100.0%	100.0%	100.0%	100.0%	100.0%	100.0%	100.0%
Total social welfare expenditures	11.0	14.3	18.2	18.1	17.8	18.5	20.9
Social insurance	4.0	5.3	7.7	8.5	9.0	9.0	9.8
Public aid	.9	1.6	2.6	2.7	2.4	2.6	3.5
Health and medical programs	.9	1.0	1.0	1.0	.9	1.1	1.2
Veterans' programs	.9	.9	1.1	.8	.7	.5	.5
Education	4.0	5.0	5.1	4.5	4.2	4.5	5.1
Housing	(3)	.1	.2	.3	.3	.3	.4
Other social welfare	.3	.4	.4	.5	.3	.3	.4
All health and medical care	1.3	2.4	3.2	3.6	4.2	4.8	6.1

NOTES: Through 1976, fiscal year ended June 30 for federal government, most states, and some localities. Beginning in 1977, federal fiscal year ended Sept. 30. 1. Represents program and administrative expenditures from federal, state, and local public revenues and trust funds under public law. Includes workers' compensation and temporary disability insurance payments made through private carriers and self-insurers. Includes capital outlay and some expenditures abroad. 2. Combines "health and medical programs" with medical services provided in connection with social insurance, public aid, veterans', and "other social welfare" categories. 3. Less than 0.05%. *Source:* Social Security Administration. Web: www.ssa.gov/statistics/Supplement/1999/tables/index.html.

Food Stamp Households, 2001

Household type	Households Number (in thousands)	Percent	Sex, race, and Hispanic origin	Participants Number (in thousands)	Percent
Total	**7,450**	**100.0%**	**Total**	**17,297**	**100.0%**
With children	3,992	53.6	Male	6,949	40.2
Single-parent households	2,690	36.1	Female	10,347	59.8
Married-couple households	572	7.7	White, non-Hispanic	7,088	41.0
Other	730	9.8	Black, non-Hispanic	6,097	35.2
With elderly	1,520	20.4	Hispanic	3,171	18.3
Living alone	1,220	16.4	Asian	563	3.3
Not living alone	300	4.0	Native American	275	1.6
Disabled	2,063	27.7	Other	103	0.6
Living alone	1,190	16.0			
Not living alone	873	11.7			

Source: U.S. Dept. of Agriculture, Food and Nutrition Service, *Characteristics of Food Stamp Households: Fiscal Year 2001*, Jan. 2003. From *Statistical Abstract of the United States, 2003.*

Food Insecurity and Hunger, 2002

(numbers in thousands)

Category	Total number[1]	Food secure Number	Percent	Food insecure Total Number	Percent	Without hunger Number	Percent	With hunger Number	Percent
All households	**108,601**	**96,543**	**88.9%**	**12,058**	**11.1%**	**8,259**	**7.6%**	**3,799**	**3.5%**
Household composition:									
With children < 18	38,647	32,268	83.5	6,379	16.5	4,899	12.7	1,480	3.8
Married couple families	26,069	23,357	89.6	2,712	10.4	2,204	8.5	508	1.9
Female head, no spouse	9,496	6,456	68.0	3,040	32.0	2,212	23.3	828	8.7
Male head, no spouse	2,375	1,855	78.1	520	21.9	381	16.0	139	5.9
Other household with child[2]	707	599	84.7	108	15.3	102	14.4	6	.8
With no children < 18	69,954	64,276	91.9	5,678	8.1	3,360	4.8	2,318	3.3
More than one adult	41,538	38,929	93.7	2,609	6.3	1,651	4.0	958	2.3
Women living alone	16,174	14,472	89.5	1,702	10.5	985	6.1	717	4.4
Men living alone	12,242	10,875	88.8	1,367	11.2	724	5.9	643	5.3
Households with elderly	24,791	23,229	93.7	1,562	6.3	1,099	4.4	463	1.9
Elderly living alone	10,072	9,327	92.6	745	7.4	490	4.9	255	2.5
Race/ethnicity of households:									
White non-Hispanic	80,266	73,859	92.0	6,407	8.0	4,294	5.3	2,113	2.6
Black non-Hispanic	13,515	10,546	78.0	2,969	22.0	1,999	14.8	970	7.2
Hispanic[3]	10,344	8,099	78.3	2,245	21.7	1,654	16.0	591	5.7
Other non-Hispanic	4,475	4,038	90.2	437	9.8	313	7.0	124	2.8

1. Total households in each category exclude households whose food security status is unknown. 2. Households with children in complex living arrangements, e.g., children of other relatives or unrelated roommate or boarder. 3. Hispanics may be of any race. *Source:* Economic Research Service, U.S. Dept. of Agriculture, *Household Food Security in the United States, 2002.* Web: http://www.ers.usda.gov/publications/fanrr29/fanrr29b.pdf.

Social Security

Source: Social Security Administration.

The original Social Security Act was passed in 1935 and is administered by the Social Security Administration and other agencies within the Department of Health and Human Services.

What Does Social Security Offer?

The Social Security contribution you pay gives you four different kinds of protection: (1) retirement benefits, (2) survivors' benefits, (3) disability benefits, and (4) Medicare hospital insurance benefits.

Retirement Benefits

Currently, as a worker you become eligible for the full amount of your retirement benefits at age 65. You may retire at age 62 and get 80% of your full benefit. The closer you are to age 65 when you start collecting your benefit, the larger the fraction of your full benefit you will get.

The amount of the retirement benefit you are entitled to at age 65 is the key to all other benefits under the program. The retirement benefit is based on covered earnings, which will be updated (indexed) to reflect the increases in average wages that have occurred since the earnings were paid. Your largest 35 years of adjusted earnings are averaged together and a formula is applied to the adjusted average to figure the benefit rate.

Survivor Benefits

This feature of the Social Security program gives your family valuable life-insurance protection. The amount of protection is again geared to what the worker would be entitled to if he had been age 65 when he died. Your survivors could get:

1. A one-time cash payment of $255 for your spouse or minor children if you have enough work credits.
2. A benefit for each child until he or she reaches 18 (or 19, if the child is in full-time attendance at an elementary or secondary school), or at any age if disabled before 22.
3. A benefit for your widow(er), at any age, if she/he has your entitled children under 16 or disabled in care.
4. Your spouse or divorced spouse can get a widow's, widower's, or surviving divorced spouse's benefit starting at age 60. A widow, or widower, who first becomes entitled at 65 or later will get 100% of his or her deceased spouse's basic amount (or the amount of the deceased spouse's reduced benefits).
5. Dependent parents can sometimes collect survivors' benefits. They are usually eligible if: (a) they were getting at least half their support from the deceased worker; (b) they have reached 62; (c) they are not eligible for a greater retirement benefit based on their own earnings; and (d) they have not married since the worker's death.

Disability Benefits

Disability benefits can be paid to several groups of people:
• Disabled workers under age 65 and their families.
• Persons disabled before age 22 who continue to be disabled. These benefits are payable as early as age 18 when a parent (or step-parent or grandparent under certain circumstances) receives Social Security retirement or disability benefits or when an insured parent dies.
• Disabled widows and widowers and (under certain conditions) disabled, surviving, and divorced spouses of workers who were insured at death. These benefits are payable as early as 50.

The SSA determines whether or not you qualify for disability benefits based on criteria including the severity of your condition and the earnings you continue to receive after you become disabled. To be considered for disability benefits, you should file a claim with a Social Security office as soon as you become disabled.

Medicare Program

Medicare is the nation's largest health insurance program. Generally, you are eligible for Medicare if you or your spouse worked for at least ten years in Medicare-covered employment and you are 65 years old and a citizen or permanent resident of the United States. You might also qualify for coverage if you are a younger person with a disability or with chronic kidney disease.

Medicare-covered services include:
• **Hospital insurance.** Financial assistance is available for necessary medical care and services furnished by Medicare-certified hospitals, skilled nursing facilities, home health agencies, and hospices.
• **Inpatient hospital care.** Medicare helps pay for up to 90 days of inpatient hospital care in each benefit period. Covered services include your semiprivate room and meals, general nursing services, operating and recovery room costs, intensive care, drugs, laboratory tests, X rays, and all other necessary medical services and supplies.
• **Skilled nursing facility care.** If you meet certain conditions, Medicare will help pay for up to 100 days in a participating skilled nursing facility in each benefit period.
• **Home health care.** If you meet certain conditions, Medicare pays the full approved cost of covered home health care services. This includes part-time or intermittent skilled nursing services prescribed by a physician for treatment or rehabilitation of homebound patients.
• **Hospice care.** Medicare helps pay for hospice care for terminally ill beneficiaries who select the hospice care benefit.
• **Medical insurance (Part B).** Medicare Part B helps pay for doctor's services, outpatient hospital services (including emergency room visits), ambulance transportation, diagnostic tests, laboratory services, some preventive care like mammography and Pap smear screening, outpatient therapy services, durable medical equipment and supplies, and a variety of other health services.

Average Monthly Social Security Benefits, 1940–2002

Year	Retired workers			Disabled workers			Non-disabled widow(er)s
	Total	Men	Women	Total	Men	Women	
1940	$ 22.71	$ 23.26	$ 18.38	—	—	—	$ 20.36
1945	25.11	25.71	19.99	—	—	—	20.17
1950[1]	29.03	30.16	22.98	—	—	—	21.65
1955	69.74	75.86	56.05	—	—	—	49.68
1960	81.73	92.03	63.26	$ 91.16	$ 94.02	$ 78.91	62.12
1965[1]	82.69	90.89	68.78	93.26	97.89	80.27	73.81
1970	123.82	136.80	103.67	139.79	148.39	115.74	106.95
1975[2]	196.42	220.35	160.50	220.60	241.48	175.27	185.34
1980[2]	321.10	374.00	244.90	352.10	388.80	269.70	277.50
1985[3]	432.00	509.60	322.20	459.20	514.00	345.00	431.10
1990[3]	550.50	654.60	403.30	566.90	637.80	438.90	541.10
1995[3]	671.70	794.30	505.80	675.70	767.30	546.00	662.50
1999	757.71	904.62	697.50	754.12	846.48	629.63	776.07
2000	844.60	951.50	729.60	787.00	883.00	661.10	811.80
2001	874.50	984.90	755.90	814.90	913.80	688.70	840.80
2002	895.00	1,007.81	774.90	834.32	935.60	708.63	861.09

1. Jan.–Aug. 2. Jan.–May. 3. Jan.–Nov. *Source:* Social Security Administration, *Social Security Bulletin: Annual Statistical Supplement, 2003.*

Gross Domestic Product or Expenditure, 1930–2003

(in billions of dollars)

Item	1930	1940	1950	1960	1970	1980	1990	2000	2003
Gross domestic product	$91.2	$101.4	$293.8	$526.4	$1,038.5	$2,789.5	$5,803.1	$9,817.0	$10,987.9
Personal consumption expenditures	70.1	71.3	192.2	331.7	648.5	1,757.1	3,839.9	6,739.4	7,757.4
Gross private domestic investment	10.8	13.6	54.1	78.9	152.4	479.3	861.0	1,735.5	1,670.6
Exports of goods and services	4.4	4.9	12.4	27.0	59.7	280.8	552.4	1,096.3	1,048.9
Imports of goods and services	4.1	3.4	11.6	22.8	55.8	293.8	630.3	1,475.8	1,543.8
Government[1]	10.0	15.0	46.8	111.6	233.8	566.2	1,180.2	1,721.6	2,054.8

1. Government consumption expenditures and gross investment. *Source:* U.S. Bureau of Economic Analysis, April 30, 2004. Web: www.bea.gov.

The Public Debt

Year	Gross debt amount	Year	Gross debt amount	Year	Gross debt amount	Year	Gross debt amount
1800	$82,976,294	1855	$ 35,586,957	1910	$ 2,652,665,838	1965	$ 320,904,110,042
1805	82,312,151	1860	64,842,288	1915	3,058,136,873	1970	389,158,403,690
1810	53,173,218	1865	2,680,647,870	1920	25,952,456,406	1975	576,649,000,000[1]
1815	99,833,660	1870	2,480,672,428	1925	20,516,193,888	1980	930,210,000,000[1]
1820	91,015,566	1875	2,232,284,532	1930	16,185,309,831	1985	1,945,941,616,460
1825	83,788,433	1880	2,120,415,371	1935	28,700,892,625	1990	3,233,313,451,777
1830	48,565,407	1885	1,863,964,873	1940	42,967,531,038	1995	4,973,982,900,709
1835	33,733	1890	1,552,140,205	1945	258,682,187,410	2000	5,674,178,209,887
1840	3,573,344	1895	1,676,120,983	1950	257,357,352,351	2001	5,807,463,412,200
1845	15,925,303	1900	2,136,961,092	1955	280,768,553,189	2002	6,228,235,965,597
1850	63,452,774	1905	2,274,615,064	1960	290,216,815,242	2003	6,783,231,062,744

NOTE: Figures as of Jan. 1 for years 1800–1840; as of July 1 for years 1845–1920; as of June 30 for years 1925–1950; as of Dec. 31 for years 1955–1985; as of Sept. 30 for years 1990–present. 1. Rounded to millions. *Source:* U.S. Department of the Treasury, The Public Debt Online. Web: www.publicdebt.treas.gov/opd/opdpdodt.htm.

Federal Outlays by Agency, 2002–2004

(in millions of dollars)

Department or agency	2002	2003	2004 (estimate)
Legislative Branch	$ 3,218	$ 3,427	$ 4,269
The Judiciary	4,823	5,123	5,306
Agriculture	68,731	72,390	77,739
Commerce	5,314	5,676	6,194
Defense—Military	331,951	388,870	435,674
Education	46,282	57,400	62,815
Energy	17,681	19,385	20,623
Health and Human Services	465,812	505,345	547,898
Homeland Security	17,557	31,967	30,663
Housing and Urban Development	31,885	37,474	46,177
Interior	9,739	9,210	9,965
Justice	21,112	21,539	23,488
Labor	64,704	69,593	59,949
State	9,453	9,261	11,301
Transportation	56,024	50,807	58,010
Treasury	370,558	366,987	368,981
Veterans Affairs	50,884	56,887	60,318
Corps of Engineers	4,797	4,751	4,308
Other Defense— Civil Programs	35,157	39,883	41,881
Environmental Protection Agency	7,450	8,061	8,129
Executive Office of the President	451	387	6,612

Department or agency	2002	2003	2004 (estimate)
General Services Administration	$ −677	$ 573	$ 778
International Assistance Programs	13,336	13,462	17,365
National Aeronautics and Space Administration	14,430	14,552	14,604
National Science Foundation	4,188	4,736	5,346
Office of Personnel Management	52,512	54,136	57,568
Small Business Administration	493	1,558	3,978
Social Security Administration:			
On-budget	45,816	46,333	48,620
Off-budget	442,011	461,401	481,875
Other Independent Agencies:			
On-budget	16,636	12,158	16,351
Off-budget	−651	−5,245	−4,956
Undistributed offsetting receipts:			
On-budget	−115,009	−117,303	−116,055
Off-budget	−85,698	−93,147	−96,940
Total outlays	**$2,010,970**	**$2,157,637**	**$2,318,834**

Source: Budget of the United States Government, Fiscal Year 2005.

Receipts and Outlays of the Federal Government, 1789–2005
(in millions of dollars)

Year	Total Receipts	Total Outlays	Total Surplus or deficit (–)	On-budget[1] Receipts	On-budget[1] Outlays	On-budget[1] Surplus or deficit (–)
1789–1849	$ 1,160	$ 1,090	$ 70	$ 1,160	$ 1,090	$ 70
1850–1900	14,462	15,453	–991	14,462	15,453	–991
1905	544	567	–23	544	567	–23
1910	676	694	–18	676	694	–18
1915	683	746	–63	683	746	–63
1920	6,649	6,358	291	6,649	6,358	291
1925	3,641	2,924	717	3,641	2,924	717
1930	4,058	3,320	738	4,058	3,320	738
1935	3,609	6,412	–2,803	3,609	6,412	–2,803
1940	6,548	9,468	–2,920	5,998	9,482	–3,484
1945	45,159	92,712	–47,553	43,849	92,569	–48,720
1950	39,443	42,562	–3,119	37,336	42,038	–4,702
1955	65,451	68,444	–2,933	60,370	64,461	–4,091
1960	92,492	92,191	301	81,851	81,341	510
1965	116,817	118,228	–1,411	100,094	101,699	–1,605
1970	192,807	195,649	–2,842	159,348	168,042	–8,694
1975	279,090	332,332	–53,242	216,633	271,892	–55,260
1980	517,112	590,947	–73,835	403,903	476,618	–72,715
1985	734,088	946,423	–212,334	547,918	769,615	–221,698
1990	1,031,969	1,253,198	–221,229	750,314	1,028,133	–277,819
1995	1,351,830	1,515,837	–164,007	1,000,751	1,227,173	–226,422
2000	2,025,218	1,788,826	236,392	1,544,634	1,458,061	86,573
2002	1,853,173	2,010,975	–157,802	1,337,852	1,655,313	–317,461
2003	1,782,342	2,157,637	–375,295	1,258,500	1,794,628	–536,128
2004[2]	1,798,093	2,318,834	–520,741	1,264,089	1,938,855	–674,766
2005[2]	2,036,273	2,399,843	–363,570	1,461,172	2,004,104	–542,932

NOTES: 1789–1842: federal fiscal year ended Dec. 31; 1844–1976: June 30; 1977–present: Sept. 30. 1. Excludes the Social Security surplus. For years prior to 1933, on-budget surplus was not calculated separately. 2. Estimated. Source: The Budget for Fiscal Year 2005.

The Federal Budget, 2002–2007
(in billions of dollars)

Description	Actual 2002	Actual 2003	Estimates 2004	Estimates 2005	Estimates 2006	Estimates 2007
Receipts by source						
Individual income taxes	$ 858.3	$ 793.7	$ 765.4	$ 873.8	$ 956.5	$1,049.3
Corporate income taxes	148.0	131.8	168.7	230.2	250.0	251.0
Social insurance and retirement receipts	700.8	713.0	732.4	793.9	834.0	878.7
Excise taxes	67.0	67.5	70.8	73.2	75.8	77.9
Estate and gift taxes	26.5	22.0	23.9	21.4	23.9	21.5
Customs duties and fees	18.6	19.9	22.6	22.1	24.4	26.2
Miscellaneous receipts:	33.9	34.5	34.3	36.5	41.2	46.2
Adjustment for revenue uncertainty	—	—	–20.0	–15.0	—	—
Total receipts	**$1,853.2**	**$1,782.3**	**$1,798.1**	**$2,036.3**	**$2,205.7**	**$2,350.8**
Outlays by function						
National defense	348.6	404.9	453.7	450.6	436.1	447.1
International affairs	22.4	21.2	34.2	37.8	32.5	31.9
General science, space, and technology	20.8	20.9	22.3	24.4	24.7	25.7
Energy	0.5	–0.8	1.0	1.8	1.9	1.7
Natural resources and environment	29.5	29.7	31.7	30.9	30.4	30.8
Agriculture	22.0	22.6	20.1	22.3	20.9	20.6
Commerce and housing credit	–0.4	–1.6	7.7	2.7	–1.2	–0.4
Transportation	61.8	67.1	68.1	69.9	70.3	70.4
Community and regional development	13.0	18.9	18.8	17.0	15.1	15.2
Education, training, employment, and social services	70.5	82.6	87.2	89.0	88.9	87.8
Health	196.5	219.6	243.5	252.6	267.7	285.3
Medicare	230.9	249.4	270.5	294.2	341.0	376.6
Income security	312.5	334.4	339.5	348.1	353.2	357.4
Social security	456.0	474.7	496.2	515.0	533.5	556.2
Veterans' benefits and services	51.0	57.0	60.5	67.5	66.8	66.0
Administration of justice	35.2	35.4	41.6	42.8	42.3	41.2
General government	17.0	23.0	25.4	19.1	19.4	18.4
Net interest	171.0	153.1	156.3	177.9	213.4	246.2
Allowances	—	—	—	–0.8	–6.0	–7.1
Undistributed offsetting receipts	–47.4	–54.4	–59.3	–63.1	–77.4	–78.9
Total outlays	**$2,011.0**	**$2,157.6**	**$2,318.8**	**$2,399.8**	**$2,473.3**	**$2,592.1**

Source: Department of the Treasury and Office of Management and Budget.

Summary of Federal Government Expenditure, by State and Territory, Fiscal Year 2002
(in millions of dollars)

State and outlying area	Total	Retirement and disability	Other direct payments	Grants	Procurement	Salaries and wages
United States total	$1,917,637	$612,996	$422,239	$412,371	$270,965	$199,066
Alabama	34,291	11,717	7,086	6,344	6,035	3,109
Alaska	7,562	981	560	3,127	1,396	1,499
Arizona	34,761	11,471	6,193	6,664	7,291	3,142
Arkansas	18,372	6,777	5,202	4,047	1,095	1,251
California	206,401	59,256	45,166	48,084	34,753	19,143
Colorado	26,229	8,073	4,753	4,740	4,526	4,138
Connecticut	25,387	7,348	5,088	5,279	6,216	1,456
Delaware	4,766	1,851	1,121	1,121	207	465
District of Columbia	33,533	1,876	2,130	4,832	10,875	13,821
Florida	104,814	43,709	25,961	16,350	9,757	9,038
Georgia	51,336	15,945	10,160	10,500	7,364	7,366
Hawaii	10,474	2,899	1,435	1,835	1,621	2,684
Idaho	8,378	2,713	1,690	1,837	1,357	781
Illinois	70,275	24,068	20,223	14,975	4,664	6,344
Indiana	34,200	12,877	9,345	6,969	2,802	2,208
Iowa	18,839	6,570	6,169	4,060	955	1,084
Kansas	17,496	5,973	4,614	3,272	1,653	1,984
Kentucky	28,880	9,795	5,906	6,346	3,978	2,854
Louisiana	29,988	9,225	8,092	7,437	2,773	2,461
Maine	9,205	3,267	1,580	2,270	1,240	848
Maryland	49,537	12,789	7,285	6,312	13,488	9,664
Massachusetts	47,480	13,436	11,537	12,339	6,793	3,376
Michigan	55,909	21,241	14,564	13,279	3,539	3,286
Minnesota	27,056	9,225	7,089	6,492	2,228	2,022
Mississippi	21,308	6,688	5,000	5,046	2,734	1,840
Missouri	42,347	13,051	9,916	8,429	7,313	3,637
Montana	6,974	2,199	1,752	1,912	350	760
Nebraska	11,583	3,774	3,767	2,342	591	1,109
Nevada	10,737	4,425	2,126	1,840	1,250	1,096
New Hampshire	6,937	2,726	1,216	1,632	788	574
New Jersey	50,673	17,906	13,131	10,822	4,840	3,974
New Mexico	17,478	4,174	2,154	3,954	5,393	1,802
New York	128,994	39,201	31,389	42,461	7,417	8,526
North Carolina	48,180	17,971	10,369	10,939	2,923	5,978
North Dakota	6,437	1,384	2,643	1,425	329	655
Ohio	65,976	24,599	16,181	14,844	5,243	5,109
Oklahoma	24,355	8,393	5,187	5,108	2,515	3,152
Oregon	19,839	7,687	4,652	4,814	994	1,692
Pennsylvania	85,601	31,194	22,917	18,017	7,415	6,058
Rhode Island	7,503	2,479	1,650	2,094	495	786
South Carolina	26,103	9,708	5,063	5,592	3,105	2,636
South Dakota	6,315	1,702	2,099	1,506	378	631
Tennessee	39,276	13,196	8,309	8,658	5,912	3,200
Texas	123,431	37,324	27,648	24,858	20,581	13,019
Utah	12,302	3,723	1,869	2,697	2,084	1,929
Vermont	4,111	1,304	736	1,281	431	359
Virginia	74,537	18,634	8,515	7,714	26,170	13,504
Washington	40,218	13,063	7,994	8,296	5,586	5,278
West Virginia	13,361	5,460	2,780	3,298	602	1,221
Wisconsin	28,844	11,158	6,830	7,255	1,888	1,713
Wyoming	3,666	1,095	553	1,234	319	465
American Samoa	154	39	2	93	13	6
Micronesia	140	—	13	126	1	—
Guam	1,114	198	78	251	308	279
Marshall Islands	203	1	—	58	144	—
Northern Marianas	102	21	3	66	9	3
Palau	42	—	—	41	1	—
Puerto Rico	14,062	5,282	2,658	4,828	365	930
Virgin Islands	573	138	90	266	29	50
Undistributed	18,996	17	—	65	15,844	3,071

NOTE: Detail may not add to total due to rounding. *Source: U.S. Census Bureau, Consolidated Federal Funds Report for Fiscal Year 2002.* Web: www.census.gov.

U.S. Direct Investment in Other Countries, 2003
(in millions of dollars)

	All industries	Mining	Utilities	Manufacturing	Whole-sale trade	Infor-mation	Banks	Finance, insurance	Services	Other industries
All countries	$151,884	$9,816	$–213	$28,370	$12,802	$5,578	$693	$30,149	$4,497	$60,191
Canada	13,826	1,594	363	6,374	512	230	151	2,656	168	1,780
Europe	99,191	1,913	–1,506	16,237	10,162	5,064	1,011	17,185	1,591	47,534
Austria	316	(*)	0	423	–579	59	(D)	–10	25	(D)
Belgium	759	2	0	628	424	15	53	–292	–36	–36
Czech Republic	144	(*)	–15	154	25	(D)	(D)	44	–1	–2
Denmark	63	(D)	0	–102	(D)	(D)	0	(D)	(D)	(D)
Finland	329	0	0	–2	205	–10	0	(D)	43	(D)
France	1,504	8	(D)	–332	626	114	189	656	–74	(D)
Germany	8,676	43	13	285	2,038	207	504	276	154	5,157
Greece	63	–1	0	36	(D)	8	(D)	(D)	2	–58
Hungary	249	(*)	(D)	150	44	3	(D)	–2	3	(D)
Ireland	9,093	(D)	(*)	2,548	351	3,605	299	777	118	(D)
Italy	3,485	–31	–20	2,065	41	387	–109	177	151	823
Luxembourg	5,241	0	0	(D)	(D)	(D)	(D)	–572	(D)	6,033
Netherlands	14,968	228	(D)	2,093	2,169	320	7	2,602	–91	(D)
Norway	1,680	1,575	(*)	198	–148	–8	10	(D)	12	(D)
Poland	451	–2	5	495	–27	55	–177	27	14	61
Portugal	109	1	0	42	125	17	(*)	–13	–10	–52
Russia	237	75	0	55	8	(D)	13	3	–9	(D)
Spain	3,375	–49	2	1,173	(D)	188	53	–642	12	(D)
Sweden	3,000	0	0	(D)	227	–105	(D)	–166	24	(D)
Switzerland	14,444	3	0	5,087	2,081	–307	545	–290	34	7,291
Turkey	41	(*)	25	–105	56	–2	39	10	10	7
United Kingdom	30,455	139	743	2,115	981	499	–798	14,106	1,114	11,556
Other	508	–295	(D)	201	27	(D)	(D)	(D)	27	351
Latin America and Other Western Hemisphere	13,171	2,197	363	2,053	427	–630	–1	4,896	–100	3,967
South America	997	1,072	479	–660	112	–887	–98	–205	26	1,158
Argentina	207	–28	(D)	–421	(D)	–70	–182	185	–2	807
Brazil	–266	267	179	–742	–14	–518	67	–602	163	932
Chile	–246	156	(D)	85	37	–449	60	113	69	(D)
Colombia	195	1	1	69	27	(D)	(D)	47	–12	(D)
Ecuador	267	146	2	–31	(D)	(D)	(D)	(D)	(*)	12
Peru	463	421	(D)	10	24	(D)	(D)	6	–4	–10
Venezuela	440	175	117	321	70	(D)	(D)	69	–197	–126
Other	–63	–67	(D)	48	–6	18	–57	(D)	8	–10
Central America	6,545	174	128	1,888	–97	34	2,519	1,716	–16	199
Costa Rica	34	(*)	0	(D)	(D)	4	0	6	–1	15
Honduras	53	0	(*)	35	8	(*)	(D)	1	0	(D)
Mexico	5,667	120	84	1,717	–88	8	2,327	1,640	–19	–122
Panama	686	55	(D)	(D)	61	(D)	(D)	71	3	296
Other	104	(*)	(D)	93	(D)	(D)	(D)	–3	1	(D)
Other Western Hemisphere	5,630	951	–244	825	412	222	–2,422	3,386	–110	2,610
Barbados	379	0	(D)	(D)	124	(D)	(D)	124	–7	82
Bermuda	1,832	30	17	(D)	547	68	0	2,242	(D)	–775
Dominican Republic	–56	0	(D)	–9	–7	(D)	(D)	–2	(*)	5
United Kingdom Islands, Caribbean	3,057	472	–264	442	–311	94	(D)	1,009	–59	(D)
Other	417	449	(D)	620	58	(D)	(D)	12	(D)	(D)
Africa	2,211	1,647	–5	–17	–96	60	–170	–29	34	787
Egypt	183	270	0	–106	–1	1	(D)	(D)	(*)	(D)
Nigeria	340	–145	0	16	–21	0	(D)	0	(D)	(D)
South Africa	89	–10	0	21	–79	124	(D)	–10	–20	(D)
Other	1,598	1,532	–5	52	5	–64	–61	(D)	(D)	(D)
Middle East	2,093	724	124	338	167	–188	60	189	70	609
Israel	517	(*)	(D)	205	115	(D)	(D)	(D)	106	(D)
Saudi Arabia	400	(D)	(D)	21	40	(D)	4	2	–12	(D)
United Arab Emirates	108	(D)	(D)	(D)	14	13	(D)	(D)	–2	(D)
Other	1,068	503	(D)	(D)	–2	1	(D)	(D)	–22	(D)
Asia and Pacific	21,392	1,742	449	3,385	1,631	1,043	–359	5,252	2,733	5,514
Australia	3,881	113	179	1,415	–16	–169	317	868	526	648
China	1,540	147	(D)	761	497	4	87	(D)	(D)	(D)
Hong Kong	1,725	0	(D)	477	298	51	–98	–485	163	(D)
India	243	11	54	53	128	–54	9	46	138	–143
Indonesia	72	970	141	–4	(D)	–64	–172	(D)	19	–800
Japan	5,800	(D)	0	–984	(*)	876	–430	3,820	(D)	(D)

	All indus-tries	Mining	Util-ities	Manu-facturing	Whole-sale trade	Infor-mation	Banks	Finance, insur-ance	Services	Other indus-tries
Korea, Republic of	954	(*)	0	438	−17	37	−38	448	41	45
Malaysia	763	173	0	369	40	76	(D)	11	(D)	(D)
New Zealand	291	4	(*)	105	(D)	−30	(D)	82	31	(D)
Philippines	−325	−42	−1	−445	61	−24	(D)	36	15	(D)
Singapore	5,699	−25	2	804	(D)	307	−256	293	(D)	(D)
Taiwan	936	(*)	0	273	222	30	−13	331	−5	98
Thailand	−560	134	−32	86	(D)	3	11	(D)	(D)	(D)
Other	372	(D)	−22	35	(D)	(*)	−9	(D)	(*)	106

* Less than $500,000 (+/−). (D) Suppressed to avoid disclosure of data of individual companies. *Source:* U.S. Department of Commerce, Bureau of Economic Analysis. Web: http://www.bea.doc.gov/bea/di/di1usdbal.htm.

U.S. Contributions to International Organizations
(in millions of dollars)

Organization	2003	2004 (est.)	2005 (est.)
UN and affiliated agencies:			
Food and Agriculture Org.	$72	$72	$83
Int'l Atomic Energy Agency	58	63	70
Int'l Civil Aviation Org.	12	13	13
Int'l Labor Organization	57	63	65
Int'l Maritime Organization	1	1	1
Int'l Telecommunications Union	7	7	7
UN—Regular	240	317	362
UN—War Crimes Tribunals	26	30	31
UN—Capital Master Plan	6	—	—
Universal Postal Union	2	2	2
World Health Org.	93	94	96
World Intellectual Property Org.	1	1	1
World Meteorological Org.	9	10	10
UNESCO	—	82	72
UN—Capital Master Plan Loan Subsidy	—	—	6
Subtotal	*584*	*755*	*819*
Inter-American organizations:			
Inter-American Institute for Cooperation on Agriculture	17	17	17
Organization of American States	54	55	56
Pan American Health Org.	56	57	57
Subtotal	*127*	*129*	*130*
Regional organizations:			
Asia-Pacific Economic Cooperation	1	1	1
North Atlantic Assembly	1	1	1
North Atlantic Treaty Organization	55	56	44
Org. for Economic Cooper-ation and Development	69	82	67
South Pacific Commission	1	1	1
Subtotal	*127*	*141*	*114*
Other international organizations:			
Org. for the Prohibition of Chemical Weapons	16	19	18

Organization	2003	2004 (est.)	2005 (est.)
OPCW—Title IV & V	$5	$7	$6
World Trade Org./GATT	15	19	19
Other Int'l Organizations	10	9	10
Subtotal	*46*	*54*	*53*
UN Buydown	17	—	—
Exchange Rate Changes	—	−79	79
Subtotal	*17*	*−79*	*79*
Total Int'l Organizations	**901**	**1,000**	**1,195**
International peacekeeping activities:			
UN Disengagement Observer Force	10	11	11
UN Interim Force in Lebanon	22	25	25
UN Iraq-Kuwait Observer Mission	4	—	—
UN Mission for the Referendum in Western Sahara	5	12	11
UN Mission in Kosovo	71	89	74
UN Mission in Cyprus	6	7	6
UN Observer Mission in Georgia	8	9	8
War Crimes Tribunal—Yugoslavia	17	19	19
War Crimes Tribunal—Rwanda	14	17	17
UN Mission in Sierra Leone	148	69	33
UN Transitional Administra-tion in East Timor	50	12	—
UN Organization Mission in the Democratic Republic of the Congo	170	213	187
UN Mission in Ethiopia and Eritria	49	53	44
Strategic Deployment Stocks	25	—	—
Liberia Operations	—	209	215
New Peacekeeping Mission	—	50	—
Total Peacekeeping Activities	**599**	**795**	**650**

NOTE: All years are fiscal years. *Source:* Budget of the United States Government Fiscal Year 2005.

Consumer Price Index for All Urban Consumers

Group	2003	2002	2001	2000	1995	1990	1985	1980	1975	1970	1965	1960	1950
All items	184.0	179.9	177.1	172.2	152.4	130.7	107.6	82.4	53.8	38.8	31.5	29.6	24.1
Food and beverages	180.5	176.8	173.6	168.4	148.9	132.1	105.6	86.7	60.2	40.1	n.a.	n.a.	n.a.
Housing	184.8	180.3	176.4	169.6	148.5	128.5	107.7	81.1	50.7	36.4	n.a.	n.a.	n.a.
Apparel	120.9	124.0	127.3	129.6	132.0	124.1	105.0	90.9	72.5	59.2	47.8	45.7	40.3
Transportation	157.6	152.9	154.3	153.3	139.1	120.5	106.4	83.1	50.1	37.5	31.9	29.8	22.7
Medical care	297.1	285.6	272.8	260.8	220.5	162.8	113.5	74.9	47.5	34.0	25.2	22.3	15.1

NOTES: 1982–1984 = 100. n.a. = not available. *Source:* U.S. Department of Labor, Bureau of Labor Statistics. Web: data.bls.gov.

Producer Price Indexes by Major Commodity Groups

Commodity	2003	2002	2000	1995	1990	1985	1980	1975	1970
All commodities	**138.1**	**131.1**	**132.7**	**124.7**	**116.3**	**103.2**	**89.8**	**58.4**	**38.1**
Farm products	111.5	99.0	99.5	107.4	112.2	95.1	102.9	77.0	45.8
Processed foods and feeds	143.4	136.2	133.1	127.0	121.9	103.5	95.9	72.6	44.6
Textile products and apparel	119.8	119.9	121.4	120.8	114.9	102.9	89.7	67.4	52.4
Hides, skins, and leather products	162.3	157.6	151.5	153.7	141.7	108.9	94.7	56.5	42.0
Fuels and related products and power	112.9	93.2	103.5	78.0	82.2	91.4	82.8	35.4	15.3
Chemicals and allied products	161.8	151.9	151.0	142.5	123.6	103.7	89.0	62.0	35.0
Rubber and plastic products	130.1	126.8	125.5	124.3	113.6	101.9	90.1	62.2	44.9
Lumber and wood products	177.4	173.3	178.2	178.1	129.7	106.6	101.5	62.1	39.9
Pulp, paper, and allied products	190.0	185.9	183.7	172.2	141.3	113.3	86.3	59.0	37.5
Metals and metal products	129.2	125.9	128.1	134.5	123.0	104.4	95.0	61.5	38.7
Machinery and equipment	121.9	122.9	124.0	126.6	120.7	107.2	86.0	57.9	40.0
Furniture and household durables	133.9	133.5	132.6	128.2	119.1	107.1	90.7	67.5	51.9
Nonmetallic mineral products	148.2	146.2	142.5	129.0	114.7	108.6	88.4	54.4	35.3
Transportation equipment	145.7	144.6	143.8	139.7	121.5	107.9	82.9	56.7	41.9

NOTES: 1982 = 100. *Source:* U.S. Department of Labor, Bureau of Labor Statistics, Division of Industrial Prices and Price Indexes. Web: data.bls.gov.

Exports and Imports of Goods and Services, 1980–2010

Category	Billions of chained 1996 dollars				Average annual rate of change		
	1980	1990	2000	2010[1]	1980–1990	1990–2000	2000–2010[1]
Exports of goods and services	**$333.4**	**$575.7**	**$1,133.2**	**$2,393.7**	**5.6%**	**7.0%**	**7.8%**
Goods	238.9	393.2	836.1	1,821.2	5.1	7.8	8.1
Foods, feeds, and beverages	44.7	44.4	60.0	91.4	–0.1	3.1	4.3
Industrial supplies and materials	86.9	111.7	168.2	228.4	2.5	4.2	3.1
Capital goods, except autos	56.0	124.8	394.9	1,123.1	8.3	12.2	11.0
Computers	1.0	12.3	85.6	406.0	28.5	21.4	16.8
Civilian aircraft and parts	26.9	40.9	43.1	78.2	4.3	0.5	6.1
Other	48.5	79.1	271.5	740.4	5.0	13.1	10.6
Autos and parts	28.3	39.8	78.3	154.5	3.5	7.0	7.0
Consumer goods	25.1	48.1	89.8	182.7	6.7	6.4	7.4
Other merchandise exports	14.8	32.4	45.9	103.3	8.1	3.6	8.4
Services	89.0	183.4	299.3	591.7	7.5	5.0	7.1
Residual[2]	–31.8	–16.5	–8.6	–182.9	—	—	—
Imports of goods and services	**$326.3**	**$632.2**	**$1,532.3**	**$3,282.7**	**6.8%**	**9.3%**	**7.9%**
Goods	260.6	497.9	1,315.6	2,954.5	6.7	10.2	8.4
Foods, feeds, and beverages	20.9	30.4	49.4	61.9	3.8	5.0	2.3
Industrial supplies and materials	118.1	142.4	254.5	331.6	1.9	6.0	2.7
Petroleum and products	51.5	59.5	86.0	96.6	1.4	3.8	1.2
Other	55.0	83.6	167.9	234.8	4.3	7.2	3.4
Capital goods, except autos	18.5	88.8	451.7	1,428.6	17.0	17.7	12.2
Computers	0.2	11.6	152.6	670.2	50.1	29.4	15.9
Civilian aircraft and parts	6.0	13.5	23.9	36.7	8.5	5.8	4.4
Other	19.1	68.9	279.3	824.0	13.7	15.0	11.4
Autos and parts	52.5	101.6	192.5	322.8	6.8	6.6	5.3
Consumer goods	49.8	112.8	293.5	858.9	8.5	10.0	11.3
Other merchandise imports	12.4	35.2	80.9	148.0	11.0	8.7	6.2
Services	65.6	136.6	218.7	352.8	7.6	4.8	4.9
Residual[3]	–6.7	–21.5	–12.6	–323.9	—	—	—
Trade Deficit	**$ 7.1**	**$–56.5**	**$ –399.1**	**$ –889.1**	**—**	**21.6%**	**8.3%**

1. Projected. 2. The residual following the detailed categories for exports is the difference between the aggregate of "exports of goods and services" and the sum of the figures for those separate categories for exports of goods and services. 3. The residual following the detailed categories for imports is the difference between the aggregate of "imports of goods and services" and the sum of the figures for those separate categories for imports of goods and services. *Source:* Bureau of Labor Statistics, *Monthly Labor Review,* Nov. 2001.

The Shrinking Value of the Dollar

Year	Amount it took to equal $1 in 1913	Year	Amount it took to equal $1 in 1913	Year	Amount it took to equal $1 in 1913	Year	Amount it took to equal $1 in 1913
1913	$1.00	1945	$1.82	1975	$ 5.43	2001	$17.89
1920	2.02	1950	2.43	1980	8.32	2002	18.17
1925	1.77	1955	2.71	1985	10.87	2003	18.59
1930	1.69	1960	2.99	1990	13.20	2004	19.10
1935	1.38	1965	3.18	1995	15.39		
1940	1.41	1970	3.92	2000	17.39		

Source: Bureau of Labor Statistics. Web: http://stats.bls.gov/.

Imports and Exports of Leading Commodities
by Principal SITC Groupings (in millions of dollars)

Item	2003 Cumulative Exports	2003 Cumulative Imports	Item	2003 Cumulative Exports	2003 Cumulative Imports
Total balance of payment basis	$349,212	$608,175	Live animals	184	885
Net adjustments	−5,800	1,792	Meat and preparations	3,376	2,147
Selected commodities:			Metal manufactures, n.e.s.	5,711	8,894
ADP equipment; office machines	14,029	37,599	Metal ores; scrap	2,597	1,405
Airplane parts	7,201	2,325	Metalworking machinery	2,008	2,639
Airplanes	11,731	5,748	Mineral fuels, other	1,199	850
Alcoholic bev.,distilled	242	1,666	Natural gas	797	9,691
Aluminum	1,457	3,707	Nickel	205	589
Animal feeds	1,917	298	Oils/fats, vegetable	620	620
Basketware, etc.	2,256	3,736	Optical goods	1,112	1,508
Cereal flour	806	1,099	Paper and paperboard	4,873	7,348
Chemicals—medicinal	9,296	15,428	Petroleum preparations	3,916	14,119
Chemicals—organic	9,886	16,719	Photographic equipment	1,628	2,438
Chemicals—plastics	10,318	6,025	Platinum	236	1,286
Cigarettes	753	155	Pottery	37	834
Clothing	2,596	31,701	Power generating machinery	15,643	16,234
Coal	784	558	Printed materials	2,173	1,853
Coffee	2	824	Pulp and waste paper	1,972	1,306
Copper	569	1,499	Records/magnetic media	2,014	2,490
Cork, wood, lumber	1,721	3,390	Rice	519	104
Corn	2,264	130	Rubber tires and tubes	1,070	2,622
Cotton, raw and linters	1,719	16	Scientific instruments	13,760	11,134
Crude oil	103	49,534	Ships, boats	608	1,180
Electrical machinery	33,799	39,476	Silver and bullion	93	358
Fish and preparations	1,358	4,880	Soybeans	3,404	22
Footwear	249	7,954	Specialized ind. mach.	11,865	10,428
Furniture and bedding	1,724	11,977	Sugar	2	266
Gem diamonds	142	6,153	Television, VCR, etc.	8,045	30,350
General industrial machinery	15,035	19,622	Textile yarn, fabric	5,305	8,395
Glass	1,293	1,116	Tobacco, unmanufactured	569	326
Glassware	320	907	Toys/games/sporting goods	1,526	8,010
Gold, nonmonetary	2,297	1,271	Vegetables and fruits	3,807	6,213
Hides and skins	804	38	Vehicles	31,682	85,617
Iron and steel mill products	3,274	5,672	Watches/clocks/parts	109	1,569
Jewelry	919	3,142	Wheat	1,513	47
Lighting, plumbing	621	2,831	Wood manufactures	768	4,090
Liquefied propane/butane	322	1,110			

NOTES: SITC = Standard International Trade Classification. Details may not equal totals due to rounding. Data not season-ally adjusted. *Source:* U.S. Census Bureau, Foreign Trade Division. Web: http://www.census.gov/foreign-trade/Press-Release/current_press_release/exh15.txt.

Retail Prices of Selected Foods in U.S. Cities, 1890–1970

(in cents per unit indicated)

Year	Flour (5 lbs)	Bread (lb)	Round steak (lb)	Bacon (lb)	Butter (lb)	Eggs (doz.)	Milk (½ gal.)	Oranges (doz.)	Potatoes (10 lbs)	Coffee (lb)	Sugar (5 lbs)
1970	58.9¢	24.3¢	130.2¢	94.9¢	86.6¢	61.4¢	65.9¢	86.4¢	89.7¢	91.1¢	64.8¢
1965	58.1	20.9	108.4	81.3	75.4	52.7	52.6	77.8	93.7	83.3	59.0
1960	55.4	20.3	105.5	65.5	74.9	57.3	52.0	74.8	71.8	75.3	58.2
1955	53.8	17.7	90.3	65.9	70.9	60.6	46.2	52.8	56.4	93.0	52.1
1950	49.1	14.3	93.6	63.7	72.9	60.4	41.2	49.3	46.1	79.4	48.7
1945	32.1	8.8	40.6	41.1	50.7	58.1	31.2	48.5	49.3	30.5	33.4
1940	21.5	8.0	36.4	27.3	36.0	33.1	25.6	29.1	23.9	21.2	26.0
1935	25.3	8.3	36.0	41.3	36.0	37.6	23.4	22.0	19.1	25.7	28.2
1930	23.0	8.6	42.6	42.5	46.4	44.5	28.2	57.1	36.0	39.5	30.5
1925	30.5	9.3	36.2	47.1	55.2	55.4	27.8	57.1	36.0	50.4	35.0
1920	40.5	11.5	39.5	52.3	70.1	68.1	33.4	63.2	63.0	47.0	97.0
1915	21.0	7.0	23.0	26.9	35.8	34.1	17.6	n.a.	15.0	30.0	33.0
1910	18.0	n.a.	17.4	25.5	35.9	33.7	16.8	n.a.	17.0	n.a.	30.0
1905	16.0	n.a.	14.0	18.1	29.0	27.2	14.4	n.a.	17.0	n.a.	30.0
1900	12.5	n.a.	13.2	14.3	26.1	20.7	13.6	n.a.	14.0	n.a.	30.5
1895	12.0	n.a.	12.3	13.0	24.9	20.6	13.6	n.a.	14.0	n.a.	26.5
1890	14.5	n.a.	12.3	12.5	25.5	20.8	13.6	n.a.	16.0	n.a.	34.5

NOTE: n.a. = not available. *Source:* U.S. Bureau of the Census, *Historical Statistics of the United States, Colonial Times to 1970, Bicentennial Edition, Part 2.*

Per Capita Consumption of Principal Foods[1]

(in pounds unless otherwise noted)

Food	1990	1995	1999	2000	2002	Food	1990	1995	1999	2000	2002
Red meats[2,3,4]	112.3	115.1	117.7	113.5	114.0	Butter and margarine (product weight)	15.3	13.7	12.9	12.8	n.a.
Beef	63.9	64.4	65.8	64.4	64.5	Shortening	22.2	22.5	21.6	23.1	n.a.
Veal	0.9	0.8	0.6	0.5	0.5	Lard and beef tallow	2.2	4.3	5.7	6.0	n.a.
Lamb & mutton	1.0	0.9	0.9	0.8	0.9	Salad and cooking oils	25.3	26.9	29.4	35.2	n.a.
Pork	46.4	49.0	50.5	47.7	48.2	Fruits and vegetables	656.0	694.3	719.0	707.7	683.6
Poultry[2,3,4]	56.3	62.9	68.3	66.5	70.7	Fruit	272.6	284.9	297.9	279.4	271.7
Chicken	42.4	48.8	54.2	52.9	56.8	Vegetables	383.5	409.4	421.2	428.3	412.0
Turkey	13.8	14.1	14.1	13.6	14.0	Peanuts (shelled)	6.0	5.7	6.4	5.8	5.8
Fish and shellfish	15.0	14.9	15.2	15.2	15.6	Tree nuts (shelled)	2.4	1.9	2.7	2.3	3.0
Eggs[4,5]	234.1	232.3	249.7	251.0	254.5	Flour and cereal products[8]	181.0	192.8	201.9	199.9	191.3
Cheese	24.6	27.3	29.8	29.8	30.5	Wheat flour	136.0	141.8	148.4	146.3	136.7
Cottage cheese	3.4	2.7	2.7	2.6	2.6	Rice (milled basis)	15.8	18.9	19.4	19.7	19.2
Beverage milks	221.8	209.8	203.8	200.9	188.8	Caloric sweeteners[9]	136.9	149.8	158.4	152.4	146.1
Yogurt (excluding frozen)	4.2	6.2	6.2	6.7	7.4	Coffee (green bean equiv.)	10.3	8.0	10.0	10.3	9.2
Ice cream	15.8	15.7	16.8	16.5	16.7	Cocoa (chocolate liquor equiv.)	4.3	3.6	4.6	4.7	3.9
Lowfat ice cream[6]	7.7	7.5	7.9	7.3	6.5						
All dairy products, milk equivalent, milkfat basis[7]	568.3	583.8	597.9	593.0	585.3						
Fats and oils	63.0	66.3	68.5	74.5	n.a.						

1. In pounds, retail weight unless otherwise stated. Consumption normally represents total supply minus exports, nonfood use, and ending stocks. Calendar-year data, except fresh citrus fruits, peanuts, tree nuts, and rice, which are on crop-year basis. 2. Totals may not add up due to rounding. 3. Boneless, trimmed weight. Chicken series revised to exclude amount of ready-to-cook chicken going to pet food as well as some water leakage that occurs when chicken is cut up before packaging. 4. Excludes shipments to the U.S. territories. 5. Number per capita. 6. Formerly known as ice milk. 7. Includes condensed and evaporated milk and dry milk products. 8. Includes rye, corn, oats, and barley products. Excludes quantities used in alcoholic beverages, corn sweeteners, and fuel. 9. Dry weight equivalent. *Source:* U.S. Department of Agriculture, Economic Research Service. Web: www.usda.gov.

Credit Card Use, 1992–2001

General-purpose credit cards include Mastercard, Visa, Optima, and Discover. All dollar figures are given in constant 1998 dollars based on consumer price index data as published by the U.S. Bureau of Labor Statistics.

				Percent of cardholding families who:		
Age of family head and family income[1]	Percent having a general-purpose credit card	Percent having a balance after last month's bills	Median balance[2]	Almost always pay off the balance	Sometimes pay off the balance	Hardly ever pay off the balance
1992 total	62.4%	52.6%	$1,200	53.0%	19.6%	27.4%
1995 total	66.5	52.6	1,700	52.4	20.1	27.5
1998 total	67.5	54.7	2,000	53.8	19.3	26.9
2001 total	72.7	53.7	1,800	55.3	19.0	25.6
Under 35 years old	64.2	68.2	1,800	40.6	24.1	35.4
35 to 44 years old	76.9	62.9	2,000	47.0	22.8	30.2
45 to 54 years old	80.0	57.3	2,000	54.3	19.3	26.4
55 to 64 years old	76.0	48.2	2,000	59.8	17.8	22.3
65 to 74 years old	76.5	30.0	1,100	75.8	11.0	13.2
75 years old and over	59.7	24.2	700	81.2	9.3	9.4
Less than $10,000	28.5	67.4	1,000	45.3	23.0	31.7
$10,000 to $24,999	56.1	57.0	1,000	49.5	19.9	30.6
$25,000 to $49,999	76.1	61.3	1,700	46.7	19.7	33.6
$50,000 to $99,999	87.9	53.9	2,000	55.2	20.8	24.0
$100,000 and more	95.8	36.1	3,000	75.2	13.9	10.9

1. Families include one-person units. 2. Among families having a balance. *Source:* Board of Governors of the Federal Reserve System, unpublished data. From *Statistical Abstract of the United States, 2003.*

Personal Consumption Expenditures

Category	Billions of chained 1996 dollars				Average annual rate of change (percent)		
	1980	1990	2000	2010 (projected)	1980–90	1990–2000	2000–2010 (projected)
Gross domestic product	$4,900.9	$6,707.9	$9,224.0	$12,835.6	3.2%	3.2%	3.4%
Personal consumption expenditures	3,193.0	4,474.5	6,257.8	8,786.5	3.4	3.4	3.5
Durable goods	279.8	487.1	895.5	1,455.4	5.7	6.3	5.0
New light vehicles	88.3	159.9	218.6	307.3	6.1	3.2	3.5
Other motor vehicles and parts	54.1	86.2	129.3	176.2	4.8	4.1	3.1
Personal computers	.0	1.6	108.8	802.4	(1)	52.1	22.1
Software	.0	.5	17.8	36.3	(1)	43.7	7.4
Furniture	95.5	160.4	294.6	483.2	5.3	6.3	5.1
Ophthalmic products	6.2	16.1	20.4	27.7	10.1	2.4	3.1
Other durable goods	53.5	80.8	152.9	256.1	4.2	6.6	5.3
Nondurable goods	1,065.8	1,369.6	1,849.9	2,635.5	2.5	3.1	3.6
Food and beverages	585.4	722.4	881.3	1,102.8	2.1	2.0	2.3
Clothing and shoes	124.0	197.2	335.3	511.0	4.7	5.5	4.3
Gasoline and motor oil	94.8	113.1	136.6	169.8	1.8	1.9	2.2
Fuel oil and coal	17.7	13.1	13.8	15.5	–3.0	.6	1.1
Tobacco products	65.6	52.0	42.8	46.5	–2.3	–1.9	.8
Drugs and medicines	54.5	80.3	139.9	316.6	4.0	5.7	8.5
Other nondurable goods	138.9	194.3	305.7	497.5	3.4	4.6	5.0
Services	1,858.4	2,616.2	3,527.7	4,784.5	3.5	3.0	3.1
Housing	541.5	696.2	850.1	1,070.2	2.5	2.0	2.3
Household operation	202.9	259.8	377.6	579.2	2.5	3.8	4.4
Electricity	66.7	83.2	103.9	137.7	2.2	2.2	2.9
Natural gas	31.1	29.5	32.8	30.8	–0.5	1.1	–0.6
Telephone	40.0	62.6	141.8	296.2	4.6	8.5	7.6
Other	66.2	85.9	100.8	142.5	2.6	1.6	3.5
Transportation services	124.7	173.4	251.3	318.5	3.4	3.8	2.4
Motor vehicle leases	—	5.5	37.6	49.1	(2)	21.2	2.7
Other	—	168.1	213.6	269.2	(2)	2.4	2.3
Medical services	487.6	710.9	903.9	1,174.9	3.8	2.4	2.7
Recreation services	79.7	145.0	227.0	408.1	6.2	4.6	6.0
Personal business services	242.8	363.2	554.8	759.0	4.1	4.3	3.2
Financial services	94.4	154.2	222.7	292.5	5.0	3.7	2.8
Other	147.4	209.0	332.4	467.4	3.6	4.7	3.5
Other services	170.8	267.0	362.3	488.3	4.6	3.1	3.0
Residual[3]	–35.6	–20.5	–68.7	–789.4			
Personal consumption expenditures + GDP	65.2	66.7	67.8	68.5			

NOTE: (—) Indicates data not available. 1. Undefined because of denominator with value zero. 2. Not applicable. 3. The residual is the difference between the first line and the sum of the most detailed lines. *Source:* Historical data, Bureau of Economic Analsysis; projected data, Bureau of Labor Statistics. *Monthly Labor Review,* Nov. 2002.

Average Prices of Selected Fuels and Electricity, 1980–2001

**(In dollars per unit, except electricity, in cents per kWh.
Represents price to end-users, except as noted.)**

Type	1980	1990	1994	1995	1996	1997	1998	1999	2000	2001
Crude oil, composite (bbl)[1]	28.07	22.22	15.59	17.23	20.71	19.04	12.52	17.51	28.26	22.96
Motor gasoline (gal.):[2]										
Unleaded regular	1.25	1.16	1.11	1.15	1.23	1.23	1.06	1.17	1.51	1.46
Unleaded premium	n.a.	1.35	1.31	1.34	1.41	1.42	1.25	1.36	1.69	1.66
No. 2 heating oil (gal.)	0.97	1.06	0.88	0.87	0.99	0.98	0.85	0.88	1.31	1.25
No. 2 diesel fuel (gal.)	0.82	0.73	0.55	0.56	0.68	0.64	0.49	0.58	0.94	0.84
Residual fuel oil (gal.)	0.61	0.44	0.35	0.39	0.46	0.42	0.31	0.37	0.60	0.53
Natural gas, residential (1,000 cu/ft)	3.68	5.80	6.41	6.06	6.34	6.94	6.82	6.69	7.76	n.a.
Electricity, residential (kWh)	5.36	7.83	8.38	8.40	8.36	8.43	8.26	8.16	8.22	8.48

NOTE: n.a. = not available. 1. Refiner acquisition cost. 2. Average, all service. *Source:* U.S. Energy Information Administration, *Monthly Energy Review.* From *Statistical Abstract of the United States, 2002.*

Farm Indexes

(1990–1992 = 100)

Year	Prices paid by farmers[1]	Prices rec'd by farmers[2]	Ratio[3]	Year	Prices paid by farmers[1]	Prices rec'd by farmers[2]	Ratio[3]
1975	47	73	155	1996	115	112	98
1980	75	98	131	1997	118	107	91
1985	86	91	106	1998	115	102	89
1990	99	104	105	1999	115	96	83
1991	100	100	99	2000	120	96	80
1992	101	98	97	2001	123	102	83
1993	103	101	98	2002	124	98	79
1994	106	100	94	2003	128	106	83
1995	109	102	93	2004	133	122	92

1. Commodities and services, interest, taxes, and wage rates. 2. All farm products. 3. Ratio of index of prices received by farmers to index of prices paid by farmers. May not compute directly due to rounding. *Source:* U.S. Department of Agriculture, National Agricultural Statistics Service. Web: www.usda.gov.

Number of Farms by State, 2001–2003

State	2001	2002	2003	State	2001	2002	2003
Alabama	46,000	45,000	45,000	Nebraska	50,000	49,400	48,500
Alaska	600	610	610	Nevada	3,050	3,000	3,000
Arizona	10,400	10,300	10,300	New Hampshire	3,300	3,400	3,400
Arkansas	48,000	47,500	47,500	New Jersey	9,800	9,900	9,900
California	81,000	79,700	78,500	New Mexico	17,800	17,700	17,500
Colorado	30,900	31,400	31,400	New York	37,500	37,000	37,000
Connecticut	4,200	4,200	4,200	North Carolina	55,000	54,200	53,500
Delaware	2,500	2,400	2,300	North Dakota	30,600	30,500	30,300
Florida	44,000	44,000	44,000	Ohio	78,000	77,800	77,600
Georgia	49,200	49,300	49,300	Oklahoma	84,000	83,500	83,500
Hawaii	5,500	5,500	5,500	Oregon	40,000	40,000	40,000
Idaho	24,500	25,000	25,000	Pennsylvania	58,500	58,200	58,200
Illinois	75,000	73,000	73,000	Rhode Island	830	850	850
Indiana	62,100	60,300	59,500	South Carolina	24,400	24,500	24,400
Iowa	92,000	90,660	90,000	South Dakota	32,000	31,800	31,600
Kansas	64,500	64,500	64,500	Tennessee	88,000	87,500	87,000
Kentucky	88,000	87,000	87,000	Texas	228,600	229,000	229,000
Louisiana	28,000	27,500	27,200	Utah	15,500	15,300	15,300
Maine	7,150	7,200	7,200	Vermont	6,600	6,600	6,500
Maryland	12,300	12,200	12,100	Virginia	47,900	47,600	47,500
Massachusetts	6,100	6,100	6,100	Washington	36,500	36,000	35,500
Michigan	53,000	53,300	53,300	West Virginia	20,800	20,800	20,800
Minnesota	81,000	80,900	80,000	Wisconsin	77,000	77,000	76,500
Mississippi	42,000	42,200	42,800	Wyoming	9,200	9,200	9,200
Missouri	108,000	107,000	106,000	**U.S. total**	**2,148,630**	**2,135,360**	**2,126,860**
Montana	27,800	27,900	28,000				

NOTE: A farm is any establishment from which $1,000 or more of agricultural products were sold or would normally be sold during the year. *Source:* U.S. Department of Agriculture. Web: www.usda.gov.

Number of Farms, Land in Farms, and Average-Size Farm: United States, 1990–2003

Year	Number of farms	Land in farms (1,000 acres)	Average farm size (acres)	Year	Number of farms	Land in farms (1,000 acres)	Average farm size (acres)
1990	2,145,820	986,850	460	1997	2,190,510	956,010	436
1991	2,116,760	981,736	464	1998	2,191,360	953,500	435
1992	2,107,840	978,503	464	1999	2,192,070	947,440	432
1993	2,201,590	968,845	440	2000	2,172,280	943,090	434
1994	2,197,690	965,935	440	2001	2,155,680	941,310	437
1995	2,196,400	962,515	438	2002	2,158,090	941,480	436
1996	2,190,500	958,675	438	2003	2,126,860	938,750	441

NOTE: A farm is any establishment from which $1,000 or more of agricultural products were sold or would normally be sold during the year. *Source:* U.S. Department of Agriculture. Web: www.usda.gov.

Agricultural Output by State, 2003 Crops

State	Corn (1,000 bu)	Wheat (1,000 bu)	Cotton, ginned (1,000 ba)	Potatoes (1,000 cwt)	Rice (1,000 cwt)	Cattle (1,000 head)	Hogs and pigs[1] (1,000 head)
Alabama	23,180	3,150	820.0	389		1,440	165
Alaska						12.5	1.5
Arizona	4,180	11,912	566.0	2,090		840	127
Arkansas	49,000	28,500	1,800.0		95,860	1,850	310
California	27,200	34,070	1,870.0	17,319	38,624	5,250	135
Colorado	120,150	78,160		26,198		2,650	770
Connecticut						56	3.8
Delaware	19,926	1,927		864		21	18.0
Florida	3,198	492	130.0	9,400		1,750	30.0
Georgia	36,765	10,580	2,100.0			1,290	295
Hawaii						151	23.0
Idaho	7,000	87,300		123,180		2,000	26.0
Illinois	1,812,200	52,650		2,196		1,360	3,950
Indiana	786,940	29,670		925		860	3,100
Iowa	1,884,000	1,159				3,550	15,800
Kansas	300,000	480,000	100.0	1,026		6,350	1,630
Kentucky	147,960	20,460				2,430	380
Louisiana	67,000	5,740	1,015.0		26,397	860	20.0
Maine				17,030		93	6.5
Maryland	50,430	5,365		1,104		240	40.0
Massachusetts				770		50	14.5
Michigan	263,340	44,880		15,015		990	950
Minnesota	970,900	105,482		22,330		2,450	6,400
Mississippi	71,550	6,125	2,100.0		15,912	1,070	305
Missouri	302,400	53,070	710.0	1,882	10,484	4,500	2,950
Montana	2,380	137,530		3,339		2,450	170
Nebraska	1,124,200	83,720		9,860		6,200	2,900
Nevada		549		3,320		510	5.0
New Hampshire						40	2.9
New Jersey	6,893	1,092		702		46	12.0
New Mexico	8,640	4,200	86.0	2,132		1,550	2.5
New York	53,240	6,360		6,510		1,450	73.0
North Carolina	72,080	14,760	1,100.0	2,975		900	9,900
North Dakota	131,040	317,090		27,440		1,880	150
Ohio	478,920	68,000		1,290		1,220	1,520
Oklahoma	23,750	179,400	210.0			5,400	2,340
Oregon	5,100	53,540		20,991		1,360	27.0
Pennsylvania	102,350	7,095		3,915		1,630	1,100
Rhode Island				150		5.5	2.6
South Carolina	22,575	7,215	330.0			435	300
South Dakota	427,350	116,241		340		3,700	1,260
Tennessee	82,530	13,500	875.0			2,270	215
Texas	194,700	96,600	4,292.0	6,528	11,880	14,000	930
Utah	2,015	5,585		335		880	660
Vermont						285	2.1
Virginia	37,950	7,360	120.0	1,550		1,630	370
Washington	13,650	139,345		93,150		1,100	24.0
West Virginia	3,105	287				405	10.0
Wisconsin	367,650	12,300		32,800		3,350	490
Wyoming	6,450	4,065				1,290	124
Total U.S.	10,113,887	2,336,526	18,224.0	459,045	199,157	96,100.0	60,040

1. Preliminary. *Source:* U.S. Department of Agriculture, National Agricultural Statistics Service. Web: www.usda.gov.

Largest Bankruptcies, 1980–Present

Company	Bankruptcy date	Total assets pre-bankruptcy (in millions)	Company	Bankruptcy date	Total assets pre-bankruptcy (in millions)
Worldcom, Inc.[1]	7/21/2002	$103,914	Kmart Corp.	1/22/2002	14,600
Enron Corp.[2]	12/2/2001	63,392	FINOVA Group, Inc. (The)	3/7/2001	14,050
Conseco, Inc	12/18/2002	61,392	HomeFed Corp.	10/22/1992	13,885
Texaco, Inc.	4/12/1987	35,892	Southeast Banking Corp.	9/20/1991	13,390
Financial Corp. of America	9/9/1988	33,864	NTL, Inc.	5/8/2002	13,003
Global Crossing Ltd.	1/28/2002	30,185	Reliance Group Holdings, Inc.	6/12/2001	12,598
Pacific Gas and Electric Co.	4/6/2001	29,770	Imperial Corp. of America	2/28/1990	12,263
UAL Corp.	12/9/2002	25,197	Federal-Mogul Corp.	10/1/2001	10,150
Adelphia Communications	6/25/2002	21,499	First City Bancorp. of Texas	10/31/1992	9,943
MCorp	3/31/1989	20,228	First Capital Holdings	5/30/1991	9,675
Mirant Corporation	7/14/2003	19,415	Baldwin-United	9/26/1983	9,383
First Executive Corp.	5/13/1991	15,193			
Gibraltar Financial Corp.	2/8/1990	15,011			

1. Worldcom, Inc. assets taken from the audited annual report dated 12/31/2001. 2. The Enron assets were taken from the tax documents filed on 11/19/2001. The company has announced that the financials were under review at the time of filing for Chapter 11. *Source:* New Generation Research, Inc. Web: www.bankruptcydata.com.

Leading National Advertisers
(in millions; ranked by total U.S. advertising spending)

Rank	Advertiser	2003 ad dollars	Rank	Advertiser	2003 ad dollars
1.	General Motors Corp.	$3,429.9	14.	GlaxoSmithKline	1,553.7
2.	Procter & Gamble Co.	3,322.7	15.	SBC Communications	1,511.0
3.	Time Warner	3,097.3	16.	McDonald's Corp.	1,368.3
4.	Pfizer	2,838.5	17.	Unilever	1,332.1
5.	DaimlerChrysler	2,317.5	18.	Altria Group	1,311.0
6.	Ford Motor Co.	2,233.8	19.	Nissan Motor Co.	1,300.7
7.	Walt Disney Co.	2,129.3	20.	Merck & Co.	1,264.4
8.	Johnson & Johnson	1,995.7	21.	Viacom	1,248.8
9.	Sony Corp.	1,814.8	22.	L'Oreal	1,239.4
10.	Toyota Motor Corp.	1,682.7	23.	PepsiCo	1,212.2
11.	Verizon Communications	1,674.2	24.	Home Depot	1,149.9
12.	Sears, Roebuck & Co.	1,633.6	25.	Microsoft Corp.	1,147.2
13.	General Electric Co.	1,575.7			

Source: AdAge. Web: adage.com.

World Port Ranking, 2002

	Total cargo volume, metric tons (1,000s)				Container traffic (TEUs) (1,000s)[1]		
Rank	Port	Country	Tons	Rank	Port	Country	TEUs
1.	Singapore	Singapore	335,156	1.	Hong Kong	China	19,144
2.	Rotterdam	Netherlands	321,851	2.	Singapore	Singapore	16,941
3.	Shanghai	China	238,606	3.	Busan	South Korea	9,436
4.	South Louisiana	United States	196,445	4.	Shanghai	China	8,620
5.	Hong Kong	China	192,510	5.	Kaohsiung	Taiwan	8,493
6.	Houston	United States	161,190	6.	Shenzhen	China	7,614
7.	Chiba	Japan	158,929	7.	Rotterdam	Netherlands	6,515
8.	Nagoya	Japan	158,020	8.	Los Angeles	United States	6,106
9.	Kwangyang	South Korea	153,447	9.	Hamburg	Germany	5,374
10.	Ningbo	China	150,000	10.	Antwerp	Belgium	4,777
11.	Ulsan	South Korea	148,412	11.	Port Kelang	Malaysia	4,533
12.	Inchon	South Korea	146,181	12.	Long Beach	United States	4,524
13.	Busan	South Korea	143,772	13.	Dubai	U.A.E.	4,194
14.	Guangzhou	China	140,395	14.	Yantian	China	4,181
15.	Antwerp	Belgium	131,629	15.	New York/New Jersey	United States	3,749
16.	Kaohsiung	Taiwan	129,414	16.	Quingdao	China	3,410
17.	Tianjin	China	129,000	17.	Bremen/Bremerhafen	Germany	3,032
18.	New York/New Jersey	United States	122,103	18.	Gioia Tauro	Italy	2,954
19.	Qinhuangdao	China	121,152	19.	Felixstowe	United Kingdom	2,750
20.	Qingdao	China	120,000	20.	Tokyo	Japan	2,712
21.	Yokohama	Japan	118,072	21.	Tanjung Priok	Indonesia	2,680
22.	Dalian	China	107,538	22.	Tanjung Pelepas	Indonesia	2,660
23.	Hamburg	Germany	98,272	23.	Laem Chabang	Thailand	2,657
24.	Marseilles	France	92,261	24.	Manila	Philippines	2,462
25.	Dampier	Australia	92,228	25.	Tianjin	China	2,410

1. TEU denotes twenty-foot equivalent units. *Source:* American Association of Port Authorities. Web: www.aapa-ports.org.

United States' Largest Banks
(in millions of U.S. dollars)

Rank	Name (city, state)	Consolidated assets	Rank	Name (city, state)	Consolidated assets
1.	J. P. Morgan Chase & Company (New York, N.Y.)	$628,662	17.	ABN Amro North America Holding Company (Chicago, Ill.)	61,259
2.	Bank of America Corp. (Charlotte, N.C.)	617,962	18.	Fifth Third Bancorp (Cincinnati, Ohio)	57,373
3.	Citigroup (New York, N.Y.)	582,123	19.	Citigroup (Sioux Falls, S.D.)	56,550
4.	Wachovia Corp. (Charlotte, N.C.)	353,541	20.	MBNA Corp. (Wilmington, Del.)	56,496
5.	Bank One Corp. (Chicago, Ill.)	256,787	21.	Comerica (Detroit, Mich.)	52,684
6.	Wells Fargo & Company (San Francisco, Calif.)	250,474	22.	Southtrust Corp. (Birmingham, Ala.)	51,885
7.	FleetBoston Financial Corp. (Providence, R.I.)	192,265	23.	M&T Bank Corp. (Buffalo, N.Y.)	49,202
8.	U.S. BC (Cincinnati, Ohio)	189,159	24.	Wells Fargo & Company (Minneapolis, Minn.)	48,802
9.	Suntrust Banks, Inc. (Atlanta, Ga.)	124,454	25.	National City Corp. (Cleveland, Ohio)	46,276
10.	HSBC North America Inc. (Buffalo, N.Y.)	92,958	26.	ABN Amro North America Holding Company (Troy, Mich.)	45,670
11.	Bank of New York Company, Inc. (New York, N.Y.)	89,258	27.	Amsouth Bancorporation (Birmingham, Ala.)	45,629
12.	State Street Corp. (Boston, Mass.)	80,435	28.	Regions Financial Corp. (Birmingham, Ala.)	45,248
13.	Keycorp (Cleveland, Ohio)	74,321	29.	Charter One Financial, Inc. (Cleveland, Ohio)	42,699
14.	BB&T Corp. (Winston-Salem, N.C.)	67,584	30.	National City Corp. (Indianapolis, Ind.)	42,549
15.	Bank One Corp. (Columbus, Ohio)	65,194			
16.	PNC Financial Services Group, Inc. (Pittsburgh, Pa.)	62,037			

NOTE: As of Dec. 31, 2003. *Source:* Federal Reserve System, National Information Center.

Largest U.S. Businesses

2003 rank	Company	Revenues ($ millions)	2003 rank	Company	Revenues ($ millions)
1.	Wal-Mart Stores	$258,681.0	40.	AT&T	$34,529.0
2.	Exxon Mobil	213,199.0	41.	Medco Health Solutions	34,264.5
3.	General Motors	195,645.2	42.	United Parcel Service	33,485.0
4.	Ford Motor	164,496.0	43.	J.C. Penney	32,923.0
5.	General Electric	134,187.0	44.	Dow Chemical	32,632.0
6.	ChevronTexaco	112,937.0	45.	Walgreen	32,505.4
7.	ConocoPhillips	99,468.0	46.	Microsoft	32,187.0
8.	Citigroup	94,713.0	47.	Allstate	32,149.0
	International Business		48.	Lockheed Martin	31,844.0
9.	Machines	89,131.0	49.	Wells Fargo	31,800.0
10.	American Intl. Group	81,300.0	50.	Lowe's	31,263.0
11.	Hewlett-Packard	73,061.0	51.	United Technologies	31,034.0
12.	Verizon Communications	67,752.0	52.	Archer Daniels Midland	30,708.0
13.	Home Depot	64,816.0	53.	Intel	30,141.0
14.	Berkshire Hathaway	63,859.0	54.	UnitedHealth Group	28,823.0
15.	Altria Group	60,704.0	55.	Northrop Grumman	28,686.0
16.	McKesson	57,129.2	56.	Delphi	28,096.0
17.	Cardinal Health	56,829.5	57.	Prudential Financial	27,907.0
18.	State Farm Insurance	56,064.6	58.	Merrill Lynch	27,745.0
19.	Kroger	53,790.8	59.	DuPont	27,730.0
20.	Fannie Mae	53,766.9	60.	Walt Disney	27,061.0
21.	Boeing	50,485.0	61.	Motorola	27,058.0
22.	Amerisourcebergen	49,657.3	62.	PepsiCo	26,971.0
23.	Target	48,163.0	63.	CVS	26,588.0
24.	Bank of America Corp.	48,065.0	64.	Viacom	25,585.3
25.	Pfizer	49,950.0	65.	Sprint	26,202.0
26.	J.P. Morgan Chase	44,363.0	66.	Sysco	26,140.3
27.	Time Warner	43,877.0	67.	Kmart Holding	26,032.0
28.	Procter & Gamble	43,377.0	68.	TIAA-CREF	26,016.2
29.	Costco Wholesale	42,545.6	69.	American Express	25,866.0
30.	Johnson & Johnson	41,862.0	70.	New York Life Insurance	25,699.7
31.	Dell Computer	41,444.0	71.	International Paper	25,200.0
32.	Sears Roebuck	41,124.0	72.	Tyson Foods	24,549.0
33.	SBC Communications	40,843.0	73.	Wachovia Corp.	24,474.0
34.	Valero Energy	37,968.6	74.	Goldman Sachs Group	23,623.0
35.	Marathon Oil	37,137.0	75.	Duke Energy	23,483.0
36.	MetLife	36,261.0	76.	Honeywell Intl.	23,103.0
37.	Safeway	35,552.7	77.	Caterpillar	22,763.0
38.	Albertson's	35,436.0	78.	Best Buy	22,673.0
39.	Morgan Stanley	34,933.0	79.	Johnson Controls	22,646.0

2003 rank	Company	Revenues ($ millions)	2003 rank	Company	Revenues ($ millions)
80.	BellSouth	22,635.0	91.	Coca-Cola	21,044.0
81.	Ingram Micro	22,613.0	92.	Bristol-Myers Squibb	20,671.0
82.	FedEx	22,487.0	93.	Wellpoint Health Networks	20,359.7
83.	Merck	22,485.9	94.	Georgia-Pacific	20,255.0
84.	ConAgra Foods	22,052.5	95.	Weyerhaeuser	19,873.0
85.	HCA	21,808.0	96.	Abbott Laboratories	19,680.6
86.	Alcoa	21,728.0	97.	Autonation	19,381.1
87.	Electronic Data Systems	21,596.0	98.	Williams	19,245.7
88.	Bank One Corp.	21,454.0	99.	Supervalu	19,160.4
89.	Comcast	21,263.0	100.	Cisco Systems	18,878.0
90.	Mass. Mutual Life Insurance	21,075.8			

Source: Fortune 500, © 2004 Time, Inc. All rights reserved. For more detailed information, visit *Fortune* on the Web, www.fortune.com/.

Most and Least Fuel Efficient Vehicles, 2003

Most fuel efficient	MPG City	MPG Hwy.	Least fuel efficient	MPG City	MPG Hwy.
Overall: Honda Insight	61	68	**Two seater:** Ferrari Enzo Ferrari	8	12
Two seater: Honda Insight	61	68	**Compact car:** Bentley Continental R	11	16
Compact car: Toyota Prius	52	45	**Midsize car:** Bentley Arnage	10	14
Midsize car: Honda Accord	26	34	**Large car:** Bentlley Arnage LWB	10	14
Large car: Chevrolet Impala	21	32	**Small station wagon:** BMW 540i Sport Wagon	17	21
Small station wagon: Volkswagen Jetta Wagon (diesel)	42	50	**Midsize station wagon:** Audi S6 Avant	15	21
Midsize station wagon: Ford Focus station wagon	27	36	**Small pickup truck (tie):** Chevrolet S10 Pickup 2WD and GMC Sonoma 2WD	16	22
Small pickup truck: Chevrolet S10 Pickup (Flex-Fuel) 2WD	22	28	**Standard pickup truck:** Dodge Ram 1500 Pickup 4WD	11	15
Standard pickup truck (tie): Ford Ranger Pickup 2WD and Mazda B2300 2WD	24	28	**Sport utility vehicle:** Mercedes-Benz G500 AWD	12	14
Sport utility vehicle: Toyota Rav4 2WD	25	31	**Minivan:** Kia Sedona	15	20
Minivan (tie): Chrysler Voyager/ Town & Country 2WD and Dodge Caravan 2WD	19	27	**Passenger van:** Dodge Ram Wagon 2500 2WD	12	17
Passenger van (tie): Chevrolet Astro 2WD and GMC Safari 2WD	15	20			

Source: www.Fueleconomy.gov.

Life Insurance in Force

(in millions of dollars)

As of Dec. 31	Ordinary	Group	Industrial	Credit	Total
1900	$ 6,124	—	$ 1,449	—	$ 7,573
1915	16,650	$ 100	4,279	—	21,029
1930	78,576	9,801	17,963	$ 73	106,413
1945	101,550	22,172	27,675	365	151,762
1950	149,116	47,793	33,415	3,844	234,168
1955	216,812	101,345	39,682	14,493	372,332
1960	341,881	175,903	39,563	29,101	586,448
1965	499,638	308,078	39,818	53,020	900,554
1970	734,730	551,357	38,644	77,392	1,402,123
1975	1,083,421	904,695	39,423	112,032	2,139,571
1980	1,760,474	1,579,355	35,994	165,215	3,541,038
1985	3,247,289	2,561,595	28,250	215,973	6,053,107
1990	5,366,982	3,753,506	24,071	248,038	9,392,597
1995	6,872,252	4,604,856	18,134	201,083	11,696,325
1998	8,505,894	5,735,273	17,365	212,917	14,471,449
1999	(1)	6,110,218	(1)	213,453	15,496,069
2000	(1)	6,376,127	(1)	200,770	15,953,267
2001	(1)	6,765,074	(1)	178,851	16,289,648
2002	(1)	6,876,075	(1)	158,534	16,346,338

1. Starting in 1999, the figures for Ordinary and Industrial have been combined as Individual, for a total of $9,172,397 in 1999, $9,376,370 in 2000, $9,345,723 in 2001, and $9,311,729 in 2002. *Source:* American Council of Life Insurers.

Top NYSE Stocks by Dollar Value

2003 Rank	Issue (symbol)	2003 dollar volume (in millions)	2003 Rank	Issue (symbol)	2003 dollar volume (in millions)
1.	Pfizer Inc (PFE)	$121,742.4	26.	Kohl's Corporation (KSS)	48,775.0
2.	International Business Machines (IBM)	118,537.3	27.	Hewlett Packard Company (HPQ)	$48,345.2
3.	Citigroup Inc. (C)	113,211.7	28.	Eli Lilly and Company (LLY)	48,109.8
4.	General Electric Company (GE)	105,729.4	29.	Wyeth (WYE)	47,452.2
5.	Bank of America Corporation (BAC)	97,217.3	30.	Coca-Cola Company (KO)	47,317.8
6.	Wal-Mart Stores (WMT)	90,488.3	31.	SBC Communications (SBC)	46,278.6
7.	Exxon Mobil Corporation (XOM)	85,419.5	32.	ChevronTexaco Corporation (CVX)	43,342.8
8.	Johnson & Johnson (JNJ)	85,185.4	33.	TYCO Int'l, Ltd. (TYC)	40,569.0
9.	American Int'l Group, Inc. (AIG)	75,530.9	34.	Lowe's Companies, Inc. (LOW)	40,464.8
10.	Merck & Co. (MRK)	74,763.8	35.	General Motors Corporation (GM)	40,101.6
11.	Goldman Sachs Group (GS)	69,957.8	36.	First Data Corporation (FDC)	40,076.7
12.	Philip Morris Companies (MO)	69,179.6	37.	American Express Company (AXP)	39,934.9
13.	Procter & Gamble Company (PG)	62,984.5	38.	Genentech, Inc. (DNA)	39,006.7
14.	Fannie Mae (FNM)	61,951.5	39.	Nokia Corporation (NOK)	38,251.5
15.	Home Depot, Inc. (HD)	58,144.1	40.	Lehman Brothers Holdings, Inc. (LEH)	38,245.3
16.	3M Company (MMM)	57,937.5	41.	Medtronic, Inc. (MDT)	38,180.7
17.	J.P. Morgan Chase & Co. (JPM)	56,934.3	42.	Pepsico, Inc. (PEP)	37,750.0
18.	Merrill Lynch & Co. (MER)	54,812.4	43.	Boston Scientific Corporation (BSX)	37,089.9
19.	Verizon Communications (VZ)	54,079.6	44.	UnitedHealth Group, Inc. (UNH)	36,824.4
20.	Viacom Inc. (VIA.B)	51,797.7	45.	Cardinal Health, Inc. (CAH)	36,023.1
21.	Freddie Mac (FRE)	51,454.2	46.	United Technologies Corporation (UTX)	35,039.2
22.	Texas Instruments Incorporated (TXN)	50,818.5	47.	Abbott Laboratories (ABT)	34,011.2
23.	Morgan Stanley (MWD)	50,731.9	48.	Best Buy Company (BBY)	33,885.7
24.	Time Warner Inc. (TWX)	50,716.7	49.	United Parcel Service, Inc. (UPS)	33,861.0
25.	Wells Fargo & Company (WFC)	50,430.9	50.	Sears Roebuck & Company (S)	$33,143.9

Source: New York Stock Exchange.

Most Active Stocks on NYSE

2003 rank	Company name (symbol)	2003 share volume (in millions)	2003 rank	Company name (symbol)	2003 share volume (in millions)
1.	Lucent Technologies Inc.(LU)	6,147.8	26.	Johnson & Johnson (JNJ)	1,623.6
2.	Nortel Networks Corporation (NT)	3,943.0	27.	Taiwan Semiconductor (TSM)	1,517.2
3.	Pfizer Inc (PFE)	3,816.8	28.	Verizon Communications (VZ)	1,513.8
4.	General Electric Company (GE)	3,789.1	29.	Schering–Plough Corporation (SGP)	1,437.5
5.	Time Warner Inc. (TWX)	3,537.9	30.	Merck & Co. (MRK)	1,430.1
6.	EMC Corporation (EMC)	2,807.4	31.	Advanced Micro Devices, Inc. (AMD)	1,410.3
7.	Citigroup Inc. (C)	2,742.5	32.	Int'l Business Machines (IBM)	1,398.6
8.	Motorola, Inc. (MOT)	2,607.1	33.	McDonald's Corporation (MCD)	1,389.1
9.	Hewlett-Packard Company (HPQ)	2,471.8	34.	Agere Systems Inc.(AGRA)	1,354.8
10.	Texas Instruments Inc. (TXN)	2,423.6	35.	El Paso Corporation (EP)	1,336.3
11.	AT&T Wireless Services, Inc. (AWE)	2,423.5	36.	American Int'l Group, Inc. (AIG)	1,334.2
12.	Nokia Corporation (NOK)	2,394.9	37.	Bank of America Corporation (BAC)	1,294.1
13.	Exxon Mobil Corporation (XOM)	2,372.0	38.	Viacom Inc. (VIA.B)	1,261.5
14.	Tyco International (TYC)	2,264.7	39.	AT&T Corporation (T)	1,237.6
15.	Micron Technology, Inc. (MU)	2,026.3	40.	Bristol-Myers Squibb (BMY)	1,205.8
16.	Home Depot, Inc. (HD)	1,999.3	41.	MBNA Corporation (KRB)	1,198.7
17.	SBC Communications (SBC)	1,967.9	42.	Merrill Lynch & Co. (MER)	1,188.7
18.	Ford Motor Company (F)	1,867.1	43.	Gap, Inc. (GPS)	1,149.4
19.	J.P. Morgan Chase & Co. (JPM)	1,855.7	44.	Wyeth (WYE)	1,145.1
20.	Corning Incorporated (GLW)	1,754.1	45.	Calpine Corporation (CPN)	1,144.6
21.	Sprint Corporation (PCS Grp.) (PCS)	1,745.7	46.	Morgan Stanley (MWD)	1,104.4
22.	Philip Morris Companies (MO)	1,745.1	47.	Coca-Cola Company (KO)	1,083.3
23.	Liberty Media Corporation (L)	1,702.5	48.	Cendant Corporation (CD)	1,078.3
24.	Wal-Mart Stores (WMT)	1,674.2	49.	First Data Corporation (FDC)	1,051.4
25.	Walt Disney Company (DIS)	1,665.8	50.	General Motors (GM)	1,048.6

Source: New York Stock Exchange.

Top NASDAQ Stocks by Market Value, 2003

Rank	Name	Symbol	Market value (in thousands)	Rank	Name	Symbol	Market value (in thousands)
1.	Microsoft Corporation	MSFT	$295,937,277	26.	Starbucks Corporation	SBUX	$13,054,827
2.	Intel Corporation	INTC	209,350,600	27.	Bed Bath & Beyond Inc.	BBBY	12,836,455
3.	Cisco Systems, Inc.	CSCO	167,267,880	28.	Biogen, Inc.	BGEN	12,784,959
4.	Dell Computer Corporation	DELL	87,114,832	29.	Apollo Group, Inc.	APOL	11,926,694
5.	Amgen Inc.	AMGN	79,705,949	30.	Gilead Sciences, Inc.	GILD	11,801,991
6.	Oracle Corporation	ORCL	69,148,527	31.	KLA-Tencor Corporation	KLAC	11,398,382
7.	Comcast Corporation	CMCSA	44,484,652	32.	Genzyme Corporation	GENZ	11,048,008
8.	QUALCOMM Incorporated	QCOM	43,147,829	33.	SouthTrust Corporation	SOTR	10,863,623
9.	eBay Inc.	EBAY	41,737,155	34.	Chiron Corporation	CHIR	10,696,115
10.	Applied Materials, Inc.	AMAT	37,320,929	35.	Teva Pharmaceutical Industries Limited	TEVA	10,669,022
11.	Fifth Third Bancorp	FITB	33,628,905	36.	Symantec Corporation	SYMC	10,628,208
12.	Nextel Communications, Inc.	NXTL	29,852,108	37.	Intuit Inc.	INTU	10,492,393
13.	Yahoo! Inc.	YHOO	29,633,838	38.	Northern Trust Corporation	NTRS	10,197,983
14.	Comcast Corporation	CMCSK	27,686,487	39.	PACCAR Inc.	PCAR	9,931,972
15.	Interactive Corp.	IACI	21,952,676	40.	Biomet, Inc.	BMET	9,260,295
16.	Amazon.com, Inc.	AMZN	21,104,567	41.	Adobe Systems Incorporated	ADBE	9,145,189
17.	Costco Wholesale Corporation	COST	17,019,257	42.	Altera Corporation	ALTR	8,578,688
18.	Maxim Integrated Products, Inc.	MXIM	16,291,938	43.	Cintas Corporation	CTAS	8,555,828
19.	VERITAS Software Corporation	VRTS	15,828,864	44.	PeopleSoft, Inc.	PSFT	8,544,837
20.	Sun Microsystems, Inc.	SUNW	14,602,435	45.	EchoStar Communications Corporation	DISH	8,366,605
21.	Electronic Arts Inc.	ERTS	14,207,019	46.	Broadcom Corporation	BRCM	8,001,232
22.	Paychex, Inc.	PAYX	14,025,739	47.	Apple Computer, Inc.	AAPL	7,836,956
23.	Staples, Inc.	SPLS	13,517,513	48.	Flextronics International Ltd.	FLEX	7,807,340
24.	Xilinx, Inc.	XLNX	13,224,517	49.	Fiserv, Inc.	FISV	7,663,485
25.	Linear Technology Corporation	LLTC	13,142,878	50.	Hudson City Bancorp, Inc.	HCBK	7,284,515

Source: The NASDAQ Stock Market, Inc.

Most Active NASDAQ Stocks, 2003

Rank	Name	Symbol	Total volume (in thousands)	Rank	Name	Symbol	Total volume (in thousands)
1.	Microsoft Corporation	MSFT	16,782,267	27.	Xilinx, Inc.	XLNX	2,294,826
2.	Intel Corporation	INTC	14,711,830	28.	Applied Digital Solutions, Inc.	ADSX	2,258,953
3.	Cisco Systems, Inc.	CSCO	14,664,944	29.	Internet Capital Group, Inc.	ICGE	2,230,339
4.	Sun Microsystems, Inc.	SUNW	13,230,334	30.	Altera Corporation	ALTR	2,225,381
5.	Sirius Satellite Radio Inc.	SIRI	12,530,653	31.	PeopleSoft, Inc.	PSFT	2,192,929
6.	Oracle Corporation	ORCL	10,820,706	32.	Symantec Corporation	SYMC	2,172,999
7.	Applied Materials, Inc.	AMAT	7,518,967	33.	Novellus Systems, Inc.	NVLS	2,148,532
8.	JDS Uniphase Corporation	JDSU	7,375,780	34.	InterActiveCorp	IACI	2,142,063
9.	Nextel Communications, Inc.	NXTL	4,924,617	35.	Comcast Corporation	CMCS	2,110,022
10.	Dell Computer Corporation	DELL	4,912,910	36.	Atmel Corporation	ATML	2,082,965
11.	Redback Networks Inc.	RBAK	4,275,847	37.	NVIDIA Corporation	NVDA	2,073,373
12.	ADC Telecommunications, Inc.	ADCT	3,597,397	38.	Charter Communications, Inc.	CHTR	2,000,344
13.	Brocade Communications Systems, Inc.	BRCD	3,220,080	39.	VERITAS Software Corporation	VRTS	1,942,689
14.	Yahoo! Inc.	YHOO	3,137,893	40.	Maxim Integrated Products, Inc.	MXIM	1,874,174
15.	QUALCOMM Incorporated	QCOM	3,132,440	41.	Corvis Corporation	CORV	1,804,418
16.	eBay Inc.	EBAY	3,038,350	42.	Electronic Arts Inc.	ERTS	1,746,313
17.	Broadcom Corporation	BRCM	2,983,360	43.	Network Appliance, Inc.	NTAP	1,678,197
18.	CIENA Corporation	CIEN	2,961,037	44.	Sanmina-SCI Corporation	SANM	1,674,183
19.	Juniper Networks, Inc.	JNPR	2,955,244	45.	Conexant Systems, Inc.	CNXT	1,595,196
20.	Siebel Systems, Inc.	SEBL	2,894,006	46.	Sina Corporation	SINA	1,548,380
21.	RF Micro Devices, Inc.	RFMD	2,715,592	47.	QLogic Corporation	QLGC	1,538,863
22.	Amgen Inc.	AMGN	2,599,561	48.	Linear Technology Corporation	LLTC	1,529,165
23.	KLA-Tencor Corporation	KLAC	2,558,168	49.	Ivanhoe Energy, Inc.	IVAN	1,479,501
24.	BEA Systems, Inc.	BEAS	2,477,965	50.	PMC–Sierra, Inc.	PMCS	1,378,064
25.	Flextronics International Ltd.	FLEX	2,322,974				
26.	Amazon.com, Inc.	AMZN	2,307,225				

Source: The NASDAQ Stock Market, Inc.

Plastic That Pays Back

The latest wrinkle in credit is the reward card that encourages you spend more at your favorite store. Should you bite?

Barbara Kiviat TIME

Credit card issuers know that you, as a consumer, are more loyal to brands like Avon, Barnes & Noble, and Amazon than you'll ever be to them. The first time an offer of a lower interest rate lands in your mailbox, you're likely to be off—which is why card companies are increasingly hitching their stars to other brands. To win your favor, they're offering to help you buy more of your favorite products. Is there a downside to these deals?

Buying Points

The specifics of co-branded cards vary quite a bit, but generally, for each dollar you charge, you receive a point. Points can be redeemed at affiliated companies—for lattes at Starbucks, chinos at the Gap, flights on Delta. The number of accounts offering rewards jumped from 35 million to 56 million in 2003, according to the industry-tracking Nilson Report. And the offers keep rolling in. Bank One and Visa recently launched a card with Sony; American Express added to its program a company called Space Adventures, which sells "space flight experiences," including airplane rides that simulate weightlessness. According to Synovate, a market-research firm, U.S. households received 263 million pitches for co-branded credit cards in the last quarter of 2003, up 35% from the same period the year before. Many of these cards not only give you redeemable points every time you charge, but also give you bonus points when you spend at affiliated companies.

It may sound like a win-win situation, but watch out for the terms of the deal. "It can be fun and occasionally lucrative to get rewards," says Gail Hillebrand, an attorney with Consumers Union. "But don't allow the marketing to distract you from the true cost." Some factors to consider:

• **ANNUAL FEE.** Many co-branded cards, especially those affiliated with airlines, charge $40 to $90 a year just to belong to the program.

• **ANNUAL PERCENTAGE RATE AND GRACE PERIOD.** Interest rates for these cards average 1 percentage point higher than for nonaffiliated cards, according to Bankrate.com. "The interest charges can easily outweigh the benefit," says Greg McBride, an analyst at Bankrate.com. If you carry a balance, your first priority should be finding the lowest possible ongoing interest rate (not the teaser rate). If you don't carry a balance, make sure the card has a grace period of at least 25 days, or else you might incur charges anyway.

• **RESTRICTIONS.** Read that fine-print pamphlet for any caveats about how rewards can be earned or spent. For example, points on the Southwest Airlines Rapid Rewards card expire after 12 months, so you have to rack up 19,200 points (or $19,200 in everyday purchases) in one year to qualify for a free ticket. □

How to Right a Wrong

Source: Federal Trade Commission (FTC).

Most companies want to make you happy so you'll come back and recommend them to your friends. But when you find a company that's not making the grade, how do you resolve the problem?

Mail and Telephone Order Sales

Shopping by phone or mail can be a convenient alternative to shopping at a store. But if your merchandise arrives late or not at all, you have some rights. By law, a company should ship your order within the time stated in its ads. If no time is promised, the company should ship your order within 30 days after receiving it. If the company is unable to ship within the promised time, they must give you an "option notice." This notice gives you the choice of agreeing to the delay or canceling your order and receiving a prompt refund. There is one exception to the 30-day rule. If a company doesn't promise a shipping time, and you're applying for credit to pay for your purchase, the company has 50 days to ship after receiving your order.

You're protected by the Fair Credit Billing Act (FCBA) when you use your credit card to pay for purchases.

Billing Errors

If you find an error on your credit or charge card statement, you can dispute the charge and withhold payment on the challenged amount while the charge is in dispute. The error might be a charge for the wrong amount, for something you did not accept, or for an item that was not delivered as agreed. Of course, you still must pay any part of the bill that isn't in dispute, including the finance charges on the undisputed amount. If you decide to dispute a charge:

• Write to the creditor at the address indicated on the monthly statement for "billing inquiries."

Include your name, address, credit card number, and a description of the billing error.

• Send your letter in a timely fashion. It must reach the creditor within 60 days after the first bill containing the error was mailed to you.

• The creditor must acknowledge your complaint in writing within 30 days after receiving it, unless the problem has been resolved. The creditor must resolve the dispute within two billing cycles (and not more than 90 days) after receiving the letter.

Unsatisfactory Goods or Services

You also may dispute charges for unsatisfactory goods or services. To take advantage of this protection, you must:

• have made the purchase in your home state or within 100 miles of your current billing address. The charge must be for more than $50.

• make a good-faith effort first to resolve the dispute with the seller. However, you are not required to use any special procedure to do so.

Door-to-Door Sales

Shopping at home can be convenient and enjoyable. But there may be times when you change your mind about an in-home purchase. The FTC's Cooling-Off Rule gives you three days to cancel purchases of $25 or more made at your home, workplace, or dormitory, or at facilities rented by the seller on a temporary short-term basis, such as hotel or motel rooms, convention centers, fairgrounds, and restaurants.

Some types of sales can't be canceled even if they occur in locations normally covered by the rule. The rule does not cover sales that:

• are under $25.

• are for goods or services not primarily intended for personal, family, or household use. The rule applies to courses of instruction or training.

• are made entirely by mail or telephone.

• are the result of prior negotiations at the seller's permanent location where the goods are sold regularly.

• are made as part of your request for the seller to do repairs or maintenance on your personal property (purchases made beyond the maintenance or repair request are covered).

• are of arts and crafts sold at fairs or locations such as shopping malls, civic centers, and schools.

• are of automobiles, vans, trucks, or other motor vehicles sold at temporary locations, provided the seller has at least one permanent place of business.

Under the rule, the salesperson must tell you about your cancellation rights at the time of sale. The salesperson also must give you two copies of a cancellation form (one to keep and one to send back) and a copy of your contract or receipt. The contract or receipt should be dated, show the name and address of the seller, and explain your right to cancel. The contract or receipt must be in the same language that's used in the sales presentation.

How to Cancel a Door-to-Door Sale

To cancel a sale, sign and date one copy of the cancellation form. You don't have to give a reason for canceling the purchase. Mail it to the address given for cancellations, making sure the envelope is postmarked before midnight of the third business day after the contract date. (Saturday is considered a business day; Sundays and federal holidays are not.) Because proof of the mailing date and receipt are important, consider sending the cancellation form by certified mail so you can get a return receipt. Keep the other copy of the cancellation form for your records. If the seller did not provide cancellation forms, write your own cancellation letter.

If you cancel your purchase, the seller has 10 days to cancel and return any promissory notes or other negotiable instruments you signed; refund all your money and tell you whether any product left with you will be picked up; and return any trade-in.

Within 20 days, the seller either must pick up the items left with you, or reimburse you for mailing expenses, if you agreed to send back the items. If you received any goods from the seller, you must make them available to the seller in as good condition as when you received them. If you don't make the items available—or if you agree to return the items but don't—you remain obligated under the contract.

Stolen Identity: A Consumer Nightmare

Source: Federal Trade Commission (FTC).

A new type of criminal has emerged—one who can wreak havoc with your finances and credit and destroy your good reputation. It's relatively easy for a determined thief to steal your name, your Social Security number, your credit card number, or some other bit of personal information without your knowledge and commit fraud in your name.

Unfortunately, you may not find out that your identity has been stolen until you receive bills for credit card accounts that you never opened, debts that you never incurred, or charges on your bills that you didn't sign for, authorize, or know anything about.

How Can This Happen?

When you make everyday transactions like writing a check at a store, charging purchases, renting a car, mailing your tax return, calling home on your cell phone, ordering new checks, or applying for a credit card, chances are that you don't give this a second thought. But crooks known as "identity thieves" may be paying attention. Each transaction requires you to share your personal information such as your bank and credit card account numbers, your Social Security number, name, address, and phone numbers. Despite your best efforts to control your personal information, skilled thieves can use a variety of methods, low- and high-tech, to gain access to your data.

How Your Identity Is Stolen

The Federal Trade Commission (FTC) has listed the following ways that imposters can get your personal information and take over your identity:

• They steal your wallet and purse containing your identification and credit and bank cards.

• They steal your mail, including your bank and credit card statements, pre-approved credit offers, telephone calling cards, and tax information.

• They complete a "change of address" form to divert your mail to another location.

• They rummage through your trash, or the trash of businesses, for personal data in a practice known as "dumpster diving."

• They fraudulently obtain your credit card report by posing as a landlord, employer, or someone else who may have a legitimate need for and a legal right to the information.

• They get your business or personnel records at work.

• They find personal information in your home.

• They use personal information you share on the Internet.

• They buy your personal information from "inside" sources. For example, an identity thief may pay a store employee for information about you that appears on an application for goods, services, or credit.

How Your Stolen Identity Is Used

The crooks call your credit card company and, pretending to be you, ask to change the mailing address on your credit card account. The imposter then runs up charges on your account. Because your bills are being sent to the new address, it may take some time before you realize that there is a problem.

Thieves can also open a new credit card account using your name, date of birth, and Social Security number. When they use the credit card and don't pay the bills, the delinquent account is reported on your credit report.

Other scenarios include establishing a phone or wireless service in your name, opening a bank account in your name and writing bad checks on it, and buying cars by taking out auto loans in your name.

Minimize Risk

Sign your credit cards upon receipt. Only carry cards that you need. Do not carry your Social Security card. Never write your PIN or Social Security number on anything you are going to throw away. Shred documents containing your Social Security number.

Do not release personal information such as your Social Security or bank account number over the phone unless you made the phone call and understand why the information is necessary.

Obtain an annual copy of your credit report from the three main credit bureaus and ensure the material is correct.

Be aware of credit card billing cycles. If you do not receive a bill on time, contact the company. A thief charging purchases to your account would likely change your billing address, so that it would take you longer to discover the fraud.

To thwart an identity thief who may pick through your trash or recycling bins to capture your personal information, tear or shred your charge receipts, copies of credit applications, insurance forms, physician statements, checks and bank statements, expired charge cards that you're discarding, and credit offers you get in the mail.

Try not to store financial information on your laptop unless absolutely necessary. If you do, use a strong password—a combination of letters (upper and lower case), numbers, and symbols. Don't use an automatic log-in feature that saves your user name and password so you don't have to enter them each time you log into or enter a site. And always log off when you're finished. That way, if your laptop gets stolen, it's harder for the thief to access your personal information.

Use a secure browser—software that encrypts or scrambles information you send over the Internet—to guard the security of your online transactions. Be sure your browser has the most up-to-date encryption capabilities by using the latest version available from the manufacturer. You also can download some browsers for free over the Internet. When submitting information, look for the "lock" icon on the browser's status bar to be sure your information is secure during transmission.

Before you dispose of a computer, delete personal information. Deleting files using the keyboard or mouse commands may not be enough because the files may stay on the computer's hard drive, where they may be easily retrieved. Use a "wipe" utility program to overwrite the entire hard drive. It makes the files unrecoverable.

If You're a Victim

Do these three things immediately:

1) Contact the fraud departments of each of the three major credit bureaus and report that your identity has been stolen. Ask that a "fraud alert" be placed on your file and that no new credit be granted without your approval.

Main Credit Reporting Bureaus:

Equifax, P.O. Box 740241, Atlanta, GA 30374-0241, 888-766-0008

Experian, P.O. Box 9532, Allen, TX 75013, 888-397-3742

Trans Union, P.O. Box 6790, Fullerton, CA, 92834, 800-680-7289

2) For any accounts that have been fraudulently accessed or opened, contact the security departments of the appropriate creditors or financial institutions. Close these accounts. Put passwords (not your mother's maiden name) on any new accounts you open. If your checks have been stolen or misused, close the account and ask your bank to notify the appropriate check verification service. You can also contact these major check verification companies. Ask that retailers who use their databases not accept your checks.

Major Check Verification Companies:

TeleCheck, 800-710-9898
Certegy, Inc., 800-437-5120
International Check Services, 800-631-9656

3) File a report with your local police or the police where the identity theft took place. Get a copy of the report in case the bank, credit card company, or others need proof of the crime later on.

4) File a complaint with the FTC. To file a complaint, visit www.consumer.gov/idtheft, call the FTC's Identity Theft Hotline: toll-free 1-877-IDTHEFT (438-4338), or write: Identity Theft Clearinghouse, Federal Trade Commission, 600 Pennsylvania Avenue, NW, Washington, DC 20580.

National Consumer Organizations

NOTE: For other organizations, *see* Societies & Associations, pp. 658–667.

AARP: Consumer Affairs Section, 601 E St. NW, Washington, DC 20049; 888-687-2277; Web: www.aarp.org.

Offers information on housing, insurance, funeral practices, eligibility for public benefits, financial security, transportation, and consumer protection issues on behalf of mid-life and older consumers.

Alliance Against Fraud in Telemarketing & Electronic Commerce (AAFTEC): c/o National Consumers League, 1701 K St. NW, Suite 1200, Washington, DC 20006; 202-835-3323; 202-835-0747 (fax); Web: www.fraud.org/aaft/aaftset.htm.

Combats telemarketing and Internet fraud through consumer education.

American Council on Consumer Interests (ACCI): 415 South Duff, Suite C., Ames, IA 50010-6600; 515-956-4666; 515-233-3101 (fax); Web: consumerinterests.org.

Provides research-based information on topics of consumer interest. Provides information about consumer publications, policies, and resources.

American Council on Science and Health (ACSH): 1995 Broadway, 2nd Fl., New York, NY 10023-5860; 212-362-7044; 212-362-4919 (fax); Web: www.acsh.org.

A consumer education consortium concerned with issues related to food, nutrition, chemicals, pharmaceuticals, lifestyle, the environment, and health.

American Savings Education Council (ASEC): 2121 K St. NW, Suite 600, Washington, DC 20037-1896; 202-659-0670; 202-775-6360 (fax); Web: www.asec.org.

Raises public awareness about what is needed to ensure long-term personal financial independence.

Better Business Bureau (BBB): 4200 Wilson Blvd., Suite 800, Arlington, VA 22203-1838; 703-276-0100; Web: www.bbb.org.

Offers a variety of consumer services including educational materials, information on charities and other organizations seeking public donations, and mediation and arbitration services.

Center for Auto Safety (CAS): 1825 Connecticut Ave. NW, Suite 330, Washington, DC 20009-5708; 202-328-7700; Web: www.autosafety.org.

Founded by Consumers Union and Ralph Nader in 1970 to advocate for auto safety and quality.

Center for Science in the Public Interest (CSPI): 1875 Connecticut Ave. NW, Suite 300, Washington, DC 20009; 202-332-9110; 202-265-4954 (fax); Web: www.cspinet.org.

Provides research, education, and advocacy on nutrition, health, food safety, and related issues.

Center for the Study of Services/Consumers' Checkbook: Consumers' Checkbook Headquarters, 733 15th St. NW, Suite 820, Washington, DC 20005; 800-213-7283; Web: www.checkbook.org.

Aids consumers in selecting doctors, hospitals, health plans, cars, and finding bargains.

Coalition Against Insurance Fraud: 1012 14th St. NW, Suite 200, Washington, DC 20005; 202-393-7330; 202-393-7329 (fax); Web: www.insurancefraud.org.

Organization of consumers, government agencies, and insurers dedicated to combating all forms of insurance fraud.

Congress Watch: 215 Pennsylvania Ave., SE, Washington, DC 20003; 202-546-4996; 202-547-7392 (fax); Web: www.citizen.org.

An arm of Public Citizen, Congress Watch works for consumer-related legislation, regulation, and policies in such areas as campaign financing and health and safety.

Consumer Action (CA): 717 Market St., Suite 310, San Francisco, CA 94103-2109; 415-777-9635 (multilingual consumer complaint hotline); 415-777-9456 (voice/ttd); Web: www.consumer-action.org.

Advocates for credit, finance, HMO, and telecommunications issues.

Consumer Federation of America (CFA): 1424 16th St. NW, Suite 604, Washington, DC 20036; 202-387-6121; Web: www.consumerfed.org.

Composed of more than 260 organizations, CFA is a consumer advocacy and education organization. CFA focuses much of its advocacy in the areas of financial service, utilities, product safety, transportation, health care, and food safety.

Consumers Union of U.S., Inc. (CU): 101 Truman Ave., Yonkers, NY 10703-1057; 914-378-2000; Web: www.consumersunion.org.

Publisher of *Consumer Reports.* Researches and tests consumer goods and services.

Families USA Foundation: 1334 G St. NW, Washington, DC 20005; 202-628-3030; 202-347-2417 (fax); Web: www.familiesusa.org.

Advocates for high-quality, affordable healthcare.

Federal Communications Commission (FCC): 445 12th St. SW, Washington, DC 20554; 888-CALL-FCC or 888-225-5322; 866–418–0232 (fax); Web: www.fcc.gov.

Offers information to help consumers avoid unwanted telephone solicitations and to report other abusive techniques.

Federal Trade Commission (FTC): CRC-240, Washington, DC 20580; 1-877-FTC-HELP or 202-326-2222; Web: www.ftc.gov.

Enforces a variety of federal antitrust and consumer protection laws.

HALT: An Organization of Americans for Legal Reform: 1612 K St. NW, Suite 510, Washington, DC 20006; 202-887-8255, toll-free: 888-367-4258; 202-887-9699 (fax); Web: www.halt.org.

Helps consumers handle their legal affairs.

Housing and Urban Development (HUD): 451 7th St. SW, Washington, DC 20410; 202-708-1112; 800-347-3735 (fraud, waste, abuse complaints); Web: www.hud.gov/consumer/index.cfm.

Enforces federal laws and regulations that protect you from discrimination, fraud, and unscrupulous practices in buying and renting a home.

Internet Fraud Complaint Center (IFCC): Web: www.ifccfbi.gov.

Provides victims of Internet fraud a convenient, easy-to-use reporting mechanism that alerts authorities of a suspected criminal or civil violation. The IFCC is a partnership between the FBI and the National White Collar Crime Center.

Military Sentinel: Web: www.consumer.gov/military.

Allows members of the U.S. Armed Forces to enter consumer complaints directly into a database that is immediately accessible by over 500 law enforcement organizations throughout the United States, Canada, and Australia.

National Association of Consumer Agency Administrators (NACAA): Two Brentwood Commons, Suite 150, 750 Old Hickory Boulevard, Brentwood, Tennessee 37207; 1-866-SAY-NACAA or 615-371-6125; Web: www.nacaanet.org.

A nonprofit association for administrators of government consumer-protection agencies. NACAA members work directly with consumers to solve problems, advance relevant legislation, and support consumer outreach and education.

National Community Reinvestment Coalition (NCRC): 733 15th St. NW, Suite 540, Washington, DC 20005; 202-628-8866; 202-628-9800 (fax); Web: www.ncrc.org.

Works toward ending discriminatory banking practices and increasing the flow of private capital and credit into underserved communities.

National Consumer Law Center (NCLC): 77 Summer St., 10th Fl., Boston, MA 02110-1006; 617-542-8010; 617-542-8028 (fax); Web: www.consumerlaw.org.

Focuses on the interests of low-income consumers in court, before administrative agencies, and before legislatures.

National Consumers League (NCL): 1701 K St. NW, Suite 1200, Washington, DC 20006; 202-835-3323; 202-835-0747 (fax); Web: nclnet.org.

Founded in 1899, NCL is America's pioneer consumer advocacy organization. It focuses on consumer health and safety protection as well as fairness in the marketplace and workplace.

National Council on Aging (NCOA): 300 D St. SW, Suite 801, Washington, DC 20024; 202-479-1200; 202-479-0735 (fax); Web: www.ncoa.org.

Advocates for public policies and provides programs and services that serve older persons.

National Foundation for Credit Counseling (NFCC): 801 Roeder Rd., Suite 900, Silver Spring, MD 20910; 301-589-5600; 301-495-5623 (fax); Web: www.nfcc.org.

Provides assistance with stressful financial situations.

National Fraud Information Center/Internet Fraud Watch (NFIC/IFW): c/o National Consumers League, 1701 K St. NW, Suite 1200, Washington, DC 20006; 800-876-7060; Web: www.fraud.org.

Helps to prevent telemarketing fraud and online and Internet fraud, and assists in filing complaints.

National Senior Citizens Law Center: 1101 14th St. NW, Suite 400, Washington, DC 20005; 202-289-6976; 202-289-7224 (fax); Web: www.nsclc.org.

Helps low-income and older Americans with legal services.

Public Citizen: 1600 20th St. NW, Washington, DC 20009; 202-588-1000; Web: www.citizen.org.

Represents consumer interests in Congress, the courts, government agencies, and the media. Its divisions include Auto Safety, Congress Watch, Critical Mass (Energy & Environment Program), Global Trade Watch, Health Research Group, and the Litigation Group.

U.S. Public Interest Research Group (U.S. PIRG): 218 D St. SE, Washington, DC 20003; 202-546-9707; 202-546-2461 (fax); Web: www.uspirg.org.

Advocates on issues such as the environment, product safety, financial privacy, and identity theft.

Women's Bureau, Dept. of Labor: 200 Constitution Ave. NW, Room S-3002, Washington, DC 20210; 800-827-5335, 202-693-6710; 202-693-6725 (fax); Web: www.dol.gov/wb.

Advocates for work issues such as sexual harassment, pregnancy discrimination, and child care.

Recalls

Several federal agencies enforce product-safety regulations and provide recall information. The central website providing access to recall information is www.recall.gov. Recalls are also posted regularly at www.pueblo.gsa.gov.

Appliances, children's products, clothing, electronics, furniture, household items, lighting, outdoor products, sports and exercise equipment: U.S. Consumer Product Safety Commission (CPSC); **Phone:** 800-638-2772; **Web:** www.cpsc.gov

Cars, child safety seats, motor vehicles and related equipment, tires: National Highway Traffic Safety Administration (NHTSA); **Phone:** 888-DASH-2-DOT; **Web:** www.nhtsa.dot.gov

Cosmetics, drugs, food, medical devices, pet and farm-animal feed, plasma and blood products, vaccines, veterinary products: Food and Drug Administration (FDA); **Phone:** 888-INFO-FDA; **Web:** www.fda.gov

Eggs, meat, poultry products: Food Safety and Inspection Service (FSIS); **Phone:** 888-674-6854; **Web:** www.fsis.usda.gov

Fungicides, pesticides, rodenticides, vehicle emissions: Environmental Protection Agency (EPA); **Phone:** 800-858-7378; **Web:** www.epa.gov

Recreational boats and boating equipment: U.S. Coast Guard (USCG); **Phone:** 800-368-5674; **Web:** www.uscgboating.org

Complaint Resources

Source: The Federal Citizen Information Center.

Here's a list of federal agencies where you can file a complaint against a company. The topic areas are arranged alphabetically.

Airline Baggage and Service: Aviation Consumer Protection Division, U.S. Department of Transportation, Room 4107, C-75, Washington, DC 20590; 202-366-2220; Email: airconsumer@ost.dot.gov.

Alcohol, Tobacco and Firearms: Bureau of Alcohol, Tobacco and Firearms, Office of Liaison and Public Information, 650 Massachusetts Ave. NW, Room 8290, Washington, DC 20226; Email: atffmail@atfhq.atf.treas.gov.

Auto Dealers: Federal Trade Commission, CRC-240, Washington, DC 20580; 877-FTC-HELP (382-4357).

Automobile—Vehicles and Equipment: U.S. Department of Transportation, National Highway Traffic Safety Administration, Office of Defects Investigation, NSA-10.01, 400 7th St. SW, Washington, DC 20590; 888-DASH-2-DOT (327-4236); 202-366-7882 (fax).

Banking—Federal Savings & Loan and Federal Savings Banks: Office of Thrift Supervision, 1700 G St. NW, Washington, DC 20552; 800-613-6743; 800-613-6743 (fax); Email: Customer.Assistance@occ.treas.gov.

Banking—Institutions with National or "NA" in the name: Customer Assistance Group, 1301 McKinney St., Suite 3710, Houston, TX 77010; 713-336-4301; 800-613-6743 (fax); Email: Customer.Assistance@occ.treas.gov.

Banking—State Chartered Banks: Federal Deposit Insurance Corporation, Compliance and Consumer Affairs, 550 17th St. NW, Washington, DC 20429; 800-934-3342.

Banking—All others in the Federal Reserve System: Alabama, Florida, Georgia, Louisiana, Mississippi, Tennessee: Consumer Complaints Supervision and Regulation Department, Federal Reserve Bank of Atlanta, 104 Marietta St. NW, Atlanta, GA 30303-2713; 404-589-7239. **Delaware, New Jersey, Pennsylvania:** Online complaint form: www.phil.frb.org/forms/consumercomplaint.htm. **All others:** Board of Governors of the Federal Reserve, Division of Consumer and Community Affairs, 20 & C Streets NW, Stop 801, Washington, DC 20551; 202-452-3693.

Cable Television Complaints: Federal Communications Commission, Cable Services Bureau, Consumer Protection and Competition Division, 445 12th St. SW, Washington, DC 20554; 888-CALL-FCC (225-5322).

Cell Phones, Pagers, Wireless: Federal Communications Commission, Wireless Telecommunications Bureau, Enforcement and Consumer Information Division, Informal Complaints and Public Inquiry Branch, 1270 Fairfield Rd., Gettysburg, PA 17325; 888-CALL-FCC or 888-TELL-FCC (TTY); 717-338-2694 (fax).

Consumer Products (except cars, food, drugs, cosmetics, and medicine): 800-638-2772.

Charities: Federal Trade Commission, CRC-240, Washington, DC 20580; 877-FTC-HELP (382-4357).

Cosmetics: Complaints Coordinator, Office of Cosmetics and Colors, 200 C St. SW (HFS-106), Washington, DC 20204; 800-270-8869 (automated phone system); 202-205-5098 (fax).

Companies (including finance, mortgage, credit card, and credit bureau): Federal Trade Commission, CRC-240, Washington, DC 20580; 877-FTC-HELP (382-4357).

Credit Unions: National Credit Union Administration, Office of Public & Congressional Affairs, 1775 Duke St., Alexandria, VA 22314-3428; 703-518-6330.

Food (except meat and poultry): Center for Food Safety and Applied Nutrition, Food and Drug Administration, 200 C St. SW, HFS-555, Washington, DC 20204; 301-443-1240 (emergency only).

Health Clubs and Exercise Equipment: Federal Trade Commission, CRC-240, Washington, DC 20580; 877-FTC-HELP (382-4357).

Home Improvement: Federal Trade Commission, CRC-240, Washington, DC 20580; 877-FTC-HELP (382-4357).

Investments: Securities and Exchange Commission, Office of Investor Education and Assistance, 450 5th St. NW, Washington, DC 20549-0213; 202-942-7040; 202-942-9634 (fax).

Meat and Poultry: Food Safety and Inspection Service, United States Department of Agriculture, Washington, DC 20250-3700; 800-535-4555 (voice), 202-720-3333 (Washington, DC area), 800-256-7072 (TDD/TTY).

Medicines, Drugs, Medical Devices, Medical Drugs, and Products Sold Online: MedWatch, The FDA Medical Products Reporting Program, Food and Drug Administration, 5600 Fishers La., Rockville, MD 20852-9787; 301-443-1240 (emergency only); 800-FDA-1088 (332-1088) to request a complaint form; 800-FDA-0178 (332-0178) to fax a complaint form.

Online Service, Auctions, Websites, E-commerce: Federal Trade Commission, CRC-240, Washington, DC 20580; 877-FTC-HELP (382-4357).

Retail Stores: Federal Trade Commission, CRC-240, Washington, DC 20580; 877-FTC-HELP (382-4357).

Spam or Junk Email: Federal Trade Commission, CRC-240, Washington, DC 20580; 877-FTC-HELP (382-4357); Forward spam or junk email: uce@ftc.gov.

Securities and Stocks: Securities and Exchange Commission, Office of Investor Education and Assistance, 450 5th St. NW, Washington, DC 20549-0213; 202-942-7040; 202-942-9634 (fax).

Telephone Service (Billing, Access, Service, Long Distance): Federal Communications Commission, Consumer Information Bureau, Consumer Complaints—Telephone, Washington, DC 20554; 888-CALL-FCC or 888-TELL-FCC (TTY).

Vaccines: 800-822-7967 or 301-217-9660.

Patents

Source: Department of Commerce, Patent and Trademark Office.

A patent, in the most general sense, is a document issued by a government, conferring some special right or privilege. The term is now restricted mainly to patents for inventions and, occasionally, land patents.

The grant of a patent for an invention gives the inventor the privilege, for a limited period of time, of excluding others from making, using, or selling a certain article.

In the United States, the law provides that a patent may be granted, for a term of 20 years from the date of application, to any person who has invented or discovered any new and useful art, machine, manufacture, or composition of matter, as well as any new and useful improvements thereof. A patent may also be granted to a person who has invented or discovered and asexually reproduced a new and distinct variety of plant (other than a tuber-propagated one) or has invented a new, original, and

ornamental design for an article of manufacture, for a term of 20 years and 14 years, respectively.

A patent is granted only upon receipt of a complete, regularly filed application and the appropriate fees, and upon determination that the invention is new, useful, and, in view of the prior art, unobvious to one skilled in the art. The disclosure must be of such nature as to enable others to reproduce the invention.

Patents are not granted for printed matter, for methods of doing business, or for devices for which claims contrary to natural laws are made. Applications for a perpetual-motion machine have been made from time to time, but until a working model is presented that actually fulfills the claim, no patent will be issued.

A complete application, which must be addressed to the Commissioner of Patents and Trademarks, Washington, DC 20231, consists of a specification with one or more claims; oath or declaration; drawing (whenever the nature of the case admits of it); and a basic filing fee of $380. The filing fee is not returned to the applicant if the patent is refused. If the patent is allowed, other fees are required. Phone 1-800-786-9199 for the latest fees.

Trademarks

Source: Department of Commerce, Patent and Trademark Office.

A trademark may be defined as a word, letter, device, or symbol, as well as any combination of these, that is used in connection with merchandise and that points distinctly to the origin of the goods.

Certificates of registration of trademarks are issued under the seal of the Patent and Trademark Office and may be registered by the owner if he or she is engaged in interstate or foreign commerce. Federal jurisdiction over trademarks arises under the commerce clause of the Constitution. Effective Nov. 16, 1989, applications to register may also be based on a "bona fide intention to use the mark in commerce." Trademarks may be registered by foreign owners who comply with U.S. law, as well as by citizens of foreign countries with which the United States has treaties relating to trademarks. U.S. citizens may register trademarks in foreign countries by complying with the laws of those countries. The right to registration and protection of trademarks in many foreign countries is guaranteed by treaties.

General jurisdiction in trademark cases involving federal registrations is given to federal courts. Adverse decisions of examiners on applications for registration are appealable to the Trademark Trial and Appeal Board, whose affirmances and decisions in *inter partes* proceedings are subject to court review. Before adopting a trademark, a person should make a search of prior marks to avoid unwittingly infringing upon them.

The duration of a trademark registration is ten years, but it may be renewed indefinitely for 10-year periods, provided the trademark is still in use at the time of expiration.

The application fee for registering is $325 per class.

Copyrights

Source: Excerpted from *Copyright Basics (Circular 1),* U.S. Copyright Office.

Copyright is a form of protection provided by the laws of the United States to the creators of "original works of authorship," including literary, dramatic, musical, artistic, and certain other intellectual works. This protection is available to both published and unpublished works. The 1976 Copyright Act generally gives the owner of a copyright the exclusive right to do and to authorize others to do the following:

• to reproduce the copyrighted work in copies or phonorecords;

• to prepare derivative works based upon the copyrighted work;

• to distribute copies or phonorecords of the copyrighted work to the public by sale or other transfer of ownership, or by rental, lease, or lending;

• to perform and/or display the copyrighted work publicly; and

• in the case of sound recordings, to perform the work publicly by means of a digital audio transmission.

It is illegal for anyone to violate these rights. However, these rights are not unlimited in scope. In some cases they are limited by the doctrine of "fair use," or by a "compulsory license" under which certain limited uses of copyrighted works are permitted in exchange for payment.

What Works Are Protected

Copyright protects "original works of authorship" that are fixed in a tangible form of expression. The fixation need not be directly perceptible so long as it may be communicated with the aid of a machine or device. Categories include:

• literary works;

• musical works, including any accompanying words;

• dramatic works, including any accompanying music;

• pantomimes and choreographic works;

• pictorial, graphic, and sculptural works;

• motion pictures and other audiovisual works;

• sound recordings; and

• architectural works.

These categories should be viewed quite broadly. For example, computer programs and most "compilations" are registrable as "literary works." Maps and architectural plans are registrable as "pictorial, graphic, and sculptural works."

What Is Not Protected

Several categories of material are generally not eligible for federal copyright protection. These include, among others:

• works that have not been fixed in a tangible form of expression—for example, choreographic works that have not been notated or recorded, or improvisational speeches or performances that have not been written or recorded;

• titles, names, short phrases, and slogans; familiar symbols or designs; mere variations of typographic ornamentation, lettering, or coloring; mere listings of ingredients or contents;

• ideas, procedures, methods, systems, processes, concepts, principles, discoveries, or devices, as distinguished from descriptions, explanations, or illustrations;

• works consisting entirely of information that is common property and containing no original authorship—for example, standard calendars, height and weight charts, tape measures and rulers, and lists or tables taken from public documents or other common sources.

U.S. Societies and Associations

Names are listed alphabetically according to key word in title; figure in parentheses is year of founding; other figure is membership.

The following is a partial list selected for general readership interest. A comprehensive listing of approximately 23,000 national and international organizations can be found in the *Encyclopedia of Associations*, 39th ed., 2002, published by Gale Research Company, 835 Penobscot Building, 645 Griswold St., Detroit, Mich. 48226-4049, available in most public libraries.

AARP (American Association of Retired Persons) (1958): 601 E. St. N.W., Washington, D.C. 20049. 33,000,000. Phone: (888) 687-2277. www.aarp.org.

Abortion Federation, National (1977): 1755 Mass. Ave., Ste. 600, Washington, D.C. 20036. Phone: (202) 667-5881www.prochoice.org.

Accountants, American Institute of Certified Public (1887): 1211 Avenue of the Americas, New York, N.Y. 10036-8775. 330,000. Phone: (212) 596-6200. www.aicpa.org.

ACSM: American Congress on Surveying and Mapping (1941): 6 Montgomery Village Ave., Ste. 403, Gaithersburg, Md. 20879. 8,000. Phone: (240) 632-9716. www.acsm.net.

Actors' Equity Association (1913): 165 W. 46th St., New York, N.Y. 10036. 40,000. Phone: (212) 869-8530. www.actorsequity.org.

Actuaries, Society of (1949): 475 N. Martingale Rd., Ste. 800, Schaumburg, Ill. 60173-2226. 16,500. Phone: (847) 706-3500. www.soa.org.

Adirondack Mountain Club (1922): 814 Goggins Rd., Lake George, N.Y. 12845-4117. 22,000. Phone: (518) 668-4447. www.adk.org.

Aeronautic Association, National (1905): 1815 N. Fort Myer Dr., Ste. 500, Arlington, Va. 22209. 300,000. Phone: (703) 527-0226. www.naa-usa.org.

Africa-American Institute, The (1953): 420 Lexington Ave., Ste. 1706, New York, N.Y. 10170-0002. Phone: (212) 949-5666. www.aaionline.org.

AFS Intercultural Programs—USA (American Field Service) (1947): 71 W. 23rd St., 17th Fl., New York, N.Y. 10010. 100,000. Phone: (212) 807-8686. www.afs.org.

Agricultural History Society (1919): University of Arkansas at Little Rock/Department of History, 2801 S. University Ave., Little Rock, Ark. 72204-1099. 1,400. Phone: (501) 569-8782. http://agriculturalhistory.ualr.edu/.

Agronomy, American Society of (1907): 677 S. Segoe Rd., Madison, Wis. 53711-1086. 11,400. Phone: (608) 273-8080; fax: (608) 273-2021. www.agronomy.org.

Air & Waste Management Association (1907): One Gateway Center, 3rd Flr., Pittsburgh, Pa. 15222. 14,000. Phone: (412) 232-3444. www.awma.org.

Aircraft Association, Experimental (1953): EAA Aviation Center, P.O. Box 3086, Oshkosh, Wis. 54903-3086. 170,000. Phone: (920) 426-4800. www.eaa.org.

Aircraft Owners and Pilots Association (1939): 421 Aviation Way, Frederick, Md. 21701-4798. 350,000. Phone: (301) 695-2000; fax: (301) 695-2375. www.aopa.org.

Air Force Association (1946): 1501 Lee Highway, Arlington, Va. 22209-1198. 150,000. Phone: (703) 247-5800. www.afa.org.

Air Line Pilots Association (1931): 535 Herndon Pkwy., Herndon, Va. 20170. 50,000. Phone: (703) 689-2270. www.alpa.org.

Al-Anon Family Group Headquarters, Inc. For families and friends of alcoholics. (1951): 1600 Corporate Landing Pkwy., Virginia Beach, Va. 23454-5617. 33,000 groups worldwide. Phone: (757) 563-1600. www.al-anon.org.

Alcoholics Anonymous (1935): A.A. World Services, Inc., P.O. Box 459, New York, N.Y. 10163. 2,160,013. Phone: (212) 870-3400. www.aa.org.

Alexander Graham Bell Association for the Deaf (1890): 3417 Volta Place N.W., Washington, D.C. 20007-2778. 6,200. Phone: (202) 337-5220 V, 337-5221 TTY; fax: (202) 337-8314. www.agbell.org.

Alzheimer's Association (1980): 225 N. Michigan Ave., Ste. 1700, Chicago, Ill. 60601-7633. 200 chapters. Phone: (312) 335-8700; (800) 272-3900. www.alz.org.

American Academy of Allergy, Asthma and Immunology (1943): 611 E. Wells St., Milwaukee, Wis. 53202. 5,000. Phone: (414) 272-6071. www.aaaai.org.

American Alliance for Health, Physical Education, Recreation and Dance (1885): 1900 Association Dr., Reston, Va. 20191. 26,000. Phone: (800) 213-7193. www.aahperd.org.

American Automobile Association (1902): 1000 AAA Dr., Heathrow, Fla. 32746-5063. Phone: (407) 444-7000. www.aaa.com.

American Civil Liberties Union (1920): 125 Broad St., 18th Flr., New York, N.Y. 10004-2400. 275,000. Phone: (212) 549-2500. www.aclu.org.

American Contract Bridge League (1927): 2990 Airways Blvd., Memphis, Tenn. 38116-3847. Phone: (901) 332-5586; fax: (901) 398-7754. www.acbl.org.

American Federation of Labor and Congress of Industrial Organizations (AFL-CIO) (1955): 815 16th St. N.W., Washington, D.C. 20006. 13,000,000. Phone: (202) 637-5000. www.aflcio.org.

American Federation of Musicians of the United States and Canada (1896): 1501 Broadway, Ste. 600, New York, N.Y. 10036. Phone: (212) 869-1330. www.afm.org.

American Forests (1875): P.O. Box 2000, Washington, D.C. 20013. 115,000. Phone: (202) 737-2457. www.americanforests.org.

American Foundrymen's Society, Inc. (1896): 505 State St., Des Plaines, Ill. 60016-8399. 13,000. Phone: (847) 824-0181; (800) 537-4237. www.afsinc.org.

American Friends Service Committee (1917): 1501 Cherry St., Philadelphia, Pa. 19102-1479. Phone: (215) 241-7000. www.afsc.org.

American Geographical Society, The (1851): 120 Wall St., Ste. 100, New York, N.Y. 10005-3904. 1,500. Phone: (212) 422-5456; fax: (212) 422-5480. email: amgeosoc@earthlink.net. www.amergeog.org.

American Geriatrics Society (1942): 350 Fifth Ave., Ste. 801, New York, N.Y. 10118. 6,000. Phone: (212) 308-1414; fax: (212) 832-8646. www.americangeriatrics.org.

American Heart Association (1924): 7272 Greenville Ave., Dallas, Tex. 75231-4596. 4,200,000 volunteers. Phone: (800) AHA-USA1. www.americanheart.org.

American Historical Association (1884): 400 A St. S.E., Washington, D.C. 20003-3889. 15,000. Phone: (202) 544-2422. www.historians.org.

American Indian Affairs, Association on (1923): Box 268, Sisseton, S.D. 57262. 40,000. Phone: (605) 698-3998. www.indian-affairs.org.

American Jewish Committee (1906): P.O. Box 705, New York, N.Y. 10105. 100,000. Phone: (212) 751-4000. www.ajc.org.

American Kennel Club (1884): 260 Madison Ave., New York, N.Y. 10016. 500+ member clubs. Phone: (212) 696-8200; (919) 233-9767 (customer service). www.akc.org.

American Legion, The (1919): 700 N. Pennsylvania St., Indianapolis, Ind. 46206. 3,000,000. Phone: (317) 630-1200. www.legion.org.

American Legion Auxiliary (1919): 777 N. Meridian St., 3rd Flr., Indianapolis, Ind. 46204. 1,000,000. Phone: (317) 955-3845. www.legion-aux.org.

American Mensa, Ltd. (1960): 1229 Corporate Drive West, Arlington, Tex. 76006–6103. 50,000. Phone: (817) 607-0060. www.us.mensa.org.

American Montessori Society (1960): 281 Park Avenue South, 6th Flr., New York, N.Y. 10010-6102. Phone: (212) 358-1250; fax: (212) 358-1256. www.amshq.org.

American Museum of Natural History (1869): Central Park West at 79th St., New York, N.Y. 10024-5192. 500,000. Phone: (212) 769-5606. www.amnh.org.

American Planning Association (1917) and American Institute of Certified Planners: Administrative Offices: 122 S. Michigan Ave., Chicago, Ill. 60603. 30,000. Phone: (312) 431-9100. www.planning.org.

Americans for Democratic Action, Inc. (1947): 1625 K St. N.W., Ste. 210, Washington, D.C. 20006. 70,000. Phone: (202) 785-5980. www.adaction.org.

American Society for Nutritional Sciences (1928): 9650 Rockville Pike, Ste. 4500, Bethesda, Md. 20814-3990. 3,600. Phone: (301) 530-7050. www.asns.org.

American Society for Public Administration (ASPA) (1939): 1120 G St. N.W., Ste. 700, Washington, D.C. 20005. 12,000. Phone: (202) 393-7878. www.aspanet.org.

American Universities, Association of (1900): 1200 New York Avenue NW, Ste. 550, Washington, D.C. 20005. Phone: (202) 408-7500. www.aau.edu.

American Water Resources Association (1964): 4 W. Federal St., P.O. Box 1626, Middleburg, Va. 20118-1626. Phone: (540) 687-8390. www.awra.org.

Amnesty International USA (1961): 322 Eighth Ave., New York, N.Y. 10001. 300,000. Phone: (212) 807-8400. www.amnestyusa.org.

AMVETS (American Veterans of World War II, Korea, and Vietnam) (1943): 4647 Forbes Blvd., Lanham, Md. 20706-4380. 250,000. Phone: (877) 7AMVETS. www.amvets.org.

Animals, The American Society for the Prevention of Cruelty to (ASPCA) (1866): 424 E. 92nd St., New York, N.Y. 10128-6804. 400,000+. Phone: (212) 876-7700. www.aspca.org.

Animals, The Fund For, Inc. (1967): 200 W. 57th St., New York, N.Y. 10019. 175,000. Phone: (212) 246-2096. www.fund.org.

Anthropological Association, American (1902): 2200 Wilson Blvd., Ste. 600, Arlington, Va. 22201. 11,500. Phone: (703) 528-1902. www.aaanet.org.

Anti-Defamation League (1913): 823 United Nations Plaza, New York, N.Y. 10017-3560. Phone: (212) 885-7700. www.adl.org.

Anti-Vivisection Society, The American (1883): 801 Old York Rd., #204, Jenkintown, Pa. 19046-1685. 15,000. Phone: (215) 887-0816; fax: (215) 887-2088. www.aavs.org.

Appraisers, American Society of (1936): 555 Herndon Parkway, Ste. 125, Herndon, Va. 20170. 6,500. Phone: (703) 478-2228. www.appraisers.org.

Arboriculture, International Society of (1924): P.O. Box 3129, Champaign, Ill. 61826-3129. 8,000.

Phone: (217) 355-9411; fax (217) 355-9516. email: isa@isa-arbor.com. www.isa-arbor.com/.

Archaeological Institute of America (1879): 656 Beacon St., Boston, Mass. 02215-2006. 11,000. Phone: (617) 353-9361. email: aia@aai.bu.edu. www.archaeological.org.

Architects, The American Institute of (1857): 1735 New York Ave. N.W., Washington, D.C. 20006-5292. 59,000. Phone: (202) 626-7300. www.aia.org.

Architectural Historians, Society of (1940): 1365 N. Astor St., Chicago, Ill. 60610-2144. 4,000. Phone: (312) 573-1365; fax: (312) 573-1141. www.sah.org.

Army, Association of the United States (1950): 2425 Wilson Blvd., Arlington, Va. 22201-3385. 100,000+. Phone: (800) 336-4570. www.ausa.org.

Arthritis Foundation (1948): P.O. Box 7669, Atlanta, Ga. 30357-0669. Over 150 local offices. Phone: (800) 283-7800. www.arthritis.org.

Arts, National Endowment for the (1965): 1100 Pennsylvania Ave. N.W., Washington, D.C. 20506. Phone: (202) 682-5400. arts.endow.gov.

ASM International ® (formerly the American Society for Metals) (1913): 9639 Kinsman Rd., Materials Park, Ohio 44073-0002. 44,000. Phone: (440) 338-5151; fax: (440) 338-4634. www.asm-intl.org.

Association for Investment Management and Research (1990): 560 Ray C. Hunt Dr., Charlottesville, Va. 22903-0668. 36,000. Phone: (800) 247-8132. www.aimr.com.

Astronomical Society, American (1899): 2000 Florida Ave., Ste. 400, Washington, D.C. 20009. 6,300. Phone: (202) 328-2010. www.aas.org.

Atheists, American (1963): P.O. Box 5733, Parsippany, N.J. 07054-6733. 40,000 families. Phone: (908) 276-7300. www.atheists.org.

Audubon Society, National (1905): 700 Broadway, New York, N.Y. 10003-9562. 550,000. Phone: (212) 979-3000. www.audubon.org.

Authors League of America (1912): 330 W. 42nd St., 29th Flr., New York, N.Y. 10036-6902. 14,000. Phone: (212) 268-1208.

Autism Society of America (1965): 7910 Woodmont Ave., Ste. 300, Bethesda, Md. 20814-3067. 18,000+. Phone: (301) 657-0881; (800) 3AUTISM. www.autism-society.org.

Automobile Club, National (1924): 1151 East Hillsdale Blvd., Foster City, Calif. 94404. 200,000. Phone: (650) 294-7000. www.nationalautoclub.com.

Bar Association, American (1878): 321 North Clark Street, Chicago, Ill. 60610. 371,000. Phone: (312) 988-5000. www.abanet.org.

Barber Shop Quartet Singing in America, Society for the Preservation and Encouragement of (SPEBSQSA, Inc.) (1938): 7930 Sheridan Rd., Kenosha, Wis. 53143. 34,000. Phone: (800) 876-SING. www.spebsqsa.org.

Better Business Bureaus, Council of (1912): 4200 Wilson Blvd., Ste. 800, Arlington, Va. 22203-1838. Phone: (703) 276-0100; fax: (703) 525-8277. www.bbb.org.

Bible Society, American (1816): 1865 Broadway, New York, N.Y. 10023-7505. Phone: (800) 32-BIBLE; (212) 408-1200. www.americanbible.org.

Biblical Literature, Society of (1880): 825 Houston Mill Road, Ste. 350, Atlanta, Ga. 30329. 7,000 members, 1,200 subscribers. Phone: (404) 727-3100; fax: (404) 727-3101. www.sbl-site.org.

Big Brothers Big Sisters of America (1977): 230 N. 13th St., Philadelphia, Pa. 19107. Phone: (215) 567-7000. www.bbbsa.org.

Biochemistry and Molecular Biology, American Society for (1906): 9650 Rockville Pike, Bethesda, Md. 20814. 10,000. Phone: (301) 530-7145. www.asbmb.org.

Biological Sciences, American Institute of (1947): 1444 I St. N.W., Ste. 200, Washington, D.C. 20005. 6,000. Phone: (202) 628-1500. www.aibs.org.

Blind, American Council of the (1961): 1155 15th St. N.W., Ste. 1004, Washington, D.C. 20005. 40,000. Phone: (202) 467-5081. www.acb.org.

Blind, National Federation of the (1940): 1800 Johnson St., Baltimore, Md. 21230. 50,000. Phone: (410) 659-9314. www.nfb.org.

B'nai B'rith International (1843): 2020 K St. N.W., Washington, D.C. 20006. 500,000. Phone: (202) 857-6600. www.bnaibrith.org.

Booksellers Association, American (1900): 828 So. Broadway, Tarrytown, N.Y. 10591. 4,500. Phone: (914) 591-2665, (800) 637-0037. www.bookweb.org.

Boys & Girls Clubs of America (1906): 1230 West Peachtree St. N.W., Atlanta, Ga., 30309. 2,800,000 youth served. Phone: (404) 487-5700. www.bgca.org.

Boy Scouts of America (1910): 1325 W. Walnut Hill Lane, P.O. Box 152079, Irving, Tex. 75015-2079. 4.8 mil. www.scouting.org.

Brady Campaign, The (1974) (formerly Handgun Control, Inc.): 1225 Eye St. N.W., Ste. 1100, Washington, D.C. 20005. 380,000. Phone: (202) 898-0792. www.bradycampaign.org.

Broadcasters, National Association of (1922): 1771 N St. N.W., Washington, D.C. 20036-2891. Phone: (202) 429-5300. www.nab.org.

Brookings Institution, The (1916): 1775 Massachusetts Ave. N.W., Washington, D.C. 20036-2188. Phone: (202) 797-6000. www.brookings.org.

Business Education Association, National (1946): 1914 Association Dr., Reston, Va. 20191-1596. 16,000. Phone: (703) 860-8300; fax: (703) 620-4483. email: nbea@nbea.org; www.nbea.org.

Business Women's Association, American (1949): 9100 Ward Parkway, P.O. Box 8728, Kansas City, Mo. 64114-0728. 80,000. Phone: (800) 228-0007. fax: (816) 361-4991. email: abwa@abwahq.org. www.abwahq.org.

Camp Fire USA (1910): 4601 Madison Ave., Kansas City, Mo. 64112-1278. 629,000. Phone: (816) 756-1950. www.campfire.org.

Camping Association, The American (1910): 5000 State Rd. 67 N., Martinsville, Ind. 46151-7902. 5,500, 2,000+ camps. Phone: (765) 342-8456. www.acacamps.org.

Cancer Society, American (1913): 1599 Clifton Rd. N.E., Atlanta, Ga. 30329. Over 2 million volunteers. Phone: (800) ACS-2345 or check local listings. www.cancer.org.

CARE, Inc. (1945): 151 Ellis St. NE, Atlanta, Ga. 30303-2439. Programs in 62 developing countries. Phone: (404) 681-2552. www.care.org.

Carnegie Endowment for International Peace (1910): 1779 Massachusetts Ave., N.W., Washington, D.C. 20036–2103. Phone: (202) 483-7600; fax: (202) 483-1840. www.ceip.org.

Catholic Charities USA (1910): 1731 King St., Ste. 200, Alexandria, Va. 22314. 1,400 agencies and institutions. Phone: (703) 549-1390. www.catholiccharitiesusa.org.

Catholic Daughters of the Americas (1903): 10 W. 71st St., New York, N.Y. 10023. 115,000. Phone: (212) 877-3041. www.catholicdaughters.org.

Catholic War Veterans of the U.S.A. Inc. (1935): 441 N. Lee St., Alexandria, Va. 22314. 35,000. Phone: (703) 549-3622. www.cwv.org.

Cerebral Palsy Associations, Inc., United (1949): 1660 L St. N.W., Ste. 700, Washington, D.C. 20036. 153 affiliates. Phone: (800) USA-5-UCP, (202) 776-0406, TTY (202) 973-7197. www.ucp.org.

Chamber of Commerce of the U.S. (1912): 1615 H St. N.W., Washington, D.C. 20062. 220,000. Phone: (202) 659-6000. www.uschamber.com.

Chemical Engineers, American Institute of (1908): 3 Park Ave., New York, N.Y. 10016-5991. 52,000. Phone: (212) 591-8100; (800) 242-4363. www.aiche.org.

Chemical Society, American (1876): 1155 16th St. N.W., Washington, D.C. 20036. 151,024. Phone: (800) 227-5558. www.chemistry.org.

Chess Federation, United States (1939): 3054 NYS Rte. 9W, New Windsor, N.Y. 12553. 50,000+. Phone: (845) 562-8350. www.uschess.org.

Child Labor Committee, National (1904): 1501 Broadway, Ste. 403, New York, N.Y. 10036. Phone: (212) 840-1801. www.kapow.org.

Children's Book Council (1945): 12 W. 37th St., 2nd Fl., New York, N.Y. 10018-7480. Phone: (212) 966-1990; fax: (212) 966-2073. email: staff@cbcbooks.org. www.cbcbooks.org.

Child Welfare League of America (1920): 440 First St. N.W., 3rd Fl., Washington, D.C. 20001-2085. 1,000 agencies. Phone: (202) 638-2952. www.cwla.org.

Chiropractic Association, American (1963): 1701 Clarendon Blvd., Arlington, Va. 22209. 22,000. Phone: (800) 986-4636; fax: (703) 243-2593. www.amerchiro.org.

Cities, National League of (1924): 1301 Pennsylvania Ave. N.W., Washington, D.C. 20004-1763. 18,000 cities and towns. Phone: (202) 626-3000. www.nlc.org.

Civil Air Patrol, National Headquarters (1941): 105 S. Hansell St., Bldg. 714, Maxwell AFB, Ala. 36112-6332. 53,000. Phone: (334) 953-4287. www.cap.gov.

Civil Engineers, American Society of (1852): 1801 Alexander Bell Dr., Reston, Va. 20191-4400. 123,000. Phone: (800) 548–ASCE (2723); (703) 295-6300. www.asce.org.

Clinical Pathologists, American Society of (1922): 2100 W. Harrison St., Chicago, Ill. 60612. 77,200. Phone: (312) 738-1336. www.ascp.org.

College Fund, United Negro (UNCF) (1944): 8260 Willow Oaks Corporate Dr., P.O. Box 10444, Fairfax, Va. 22031. 39 member institutions. Phone: (703) 205-3400, (800) 331-2244; fax: (703) 205-3576. www.uncf.org.

Colleges and Employers, National Association of (formerly College Placement Council) (1956): 62 Highland Ave., Bethlehem, Pa. 18017. 3,200. Phone: (800) 544-5272. www.naceweb.org.

Common Cause (1970): 1250 Connecticut Ave. N.W., Washington, D.C. 20036. 250,000. Phone: (202) 833-1200. www.commoncause.org.

Composers/USA, National Association of (1933): P.O. Box 49256, Barrington Station, Los Angeles, Calif. 90049. 600. Phone: (310) 541-8213. www.music-usa.org/nacusa/.

Congress of Racial Equality (CORE) (1942): 817 Broadway, 3rd Flr., New York, N.Y. 10003. Nationwide network of chapters. Phone: (212) 598-4000; fax: (212) 598-4141. www.core-online.org.

Conscientious Objectors, Central Committee for (1948): 1515 Cherry St., Philadelphia, Pa. 19102. Phone: (215) 563-8787. 405 14th St., #205, Oakland, Calif. 94612. Phone: (510) 465-1617. www.objector.org.

Conservation Engineers, Association of (1961): John Bruner, 125 W. 25th St., Cheyenne, Wyo. 82002. Phone: (307) 777-6325. www.conservation.state.mo.us/engineering/ace.

Consumer Federation of America (1968): 1424 16th St. N.W., Ste. 604, Washington, D.C. 20036. 260 member organizations. Phone: (202) 387-6121. www.consumerfed.org.

Consumers League, National (1899): 1701 K St. N.W., Ste. 1200, Washington, D.C. 20006. Phone: (202) 835-3323. www.natlconsumersleague.org.

Consumers Union (1936): 101 Truman Ave., Yonkers, N.Y. 10703-1057. 4.6 million subscribers to *Consumer Reports Magazine.* Phone: (914) 378-2000. www.consumersunion.org.

Country Music Association (1958): One Music Circle South, Nashville, Tenn. 37203. 6,000. Phone: (615) 244-2840. www.cmaworld.com.

Credit Management, National Association of (1896): 8840 Columbia 100 Parkway, Columbia, Md. 21045-2158. 30,000+ members. Phone: (410) 740-5560. www.nacm.org.

Credit Union National Association (1934): P.O. Box 431, Madison, Wis. 53701-0431. 51 state leagues representing 12,400 credit unions. Phone: (800) 356-9655. www.cuna.org.

Crime and Delinquency, National Council on (1907): 1970 Broadway, Ste. 500, Oakland, Calif. 94612. Phone: (510) 208-0500. www.nccd-crc.org.

CSA/USA, Celiac Sprue Association/United States of America, Inc., (1978): P.O. Box 31700, Omaha, Neb. 68131-0700. 6 regions in U.S., 74 chapters, 36 active resource units. Phone: (877) CSA-4CSA; fax: (402) 558-1347. www.csaceliacs.org.

Dairy Council, National (1915): 10255 W. Higgins Rd. Ste. 900, Rosemont, Ill. 60018. www.nationaldairycouncil.org.

Daughters of the American Revolution, National Society (1896): 1776 D St. N.W., Washington, D.C. 20006-5303. 172,000. Phone: (202) 628-1776. www.dar.org.

Deaf, National Association of the (1880): 814 Thayer Ave., Silver Spring, Md. 20910-4500. 51 state association affiliates. Phone: (301) 587-1788 V; (301) 587-1789 TTY. www.nad.org.

Defenders of Wildlife (1947): 1130 17th St. N.W., Washington, D.C. 20030. 200,000 members and supporters. Phone: (202) 682-9400. www.defenders.org.

Dental Association, American (1859): 211 E. Chicago Ave., Chicago, Ill. 60611. 141,000. Phone: (312) 440-2500. www.ada.org.

Diabetes Association, American (1940): 1701 N. Beauregard St., Alexandria, Va. 22311. Phone: (703) 549-1500; (800) 342-2383. www.diabetes.org/.

Dignity (1969): 1500 Massachusetts Ave. N.W., Ste. 11, Washington, D.C. 20005. 5,000. Phone: (202) 861-0017 and (800) 877-8797. www.dignityusa.org.

Disabled American Veterans (1920): 3725 Alexandria Pike, Cold Spring, Ky. 41076. 1,400,000. Phone: (859) 441-7300. www.dav.org.

Dowsers, Inc., The American Society of (1961): P.O. Box 24, Danville, Vt. 05828. 5,000. Phone: (800) 711-9530. email: ASD@dowsers.org. www.dowsers.org.

Ducks Unlimited, Inc. (1937): One Waterfowl Way, Memphis, Tenn. 38120. 600,000. Phone: (800) 45DUCKS. www.ducks.org.

Earthwatch (1971): 3 Clock Tower Place, Ste. 100, Box 75, Maynard, Mass. 01754. 75,000. Phone: (978) 461-0081. www.earthwatch.org.

Eastern Star, Order of, General Grand Chapter (1876): 1618 New Hampshire Ave. N.W., Washington, D.C. 20009-2549. 1,207,301. Phone: (202) 667-4737. www.easternstar.org.

Easter Seal Society, The National (1919): 230 W. Monroe, Ste. 1800, Chicago, Ill. 60606. 109 state and local affiliate societies operating 500 service sites. Phone: (312) 726-6200; (312) 726-4258 TTY. www.easter-seals.org.

Economic Association, American (1885): 2014 Broadway, Ste. 305, Nashville, Tenn. 37203. 22,000. 5,500 inst. subscribers. Phone: (615) 322-2595. www.vanderbilt.edu/AEA.

Edison Electric Institute (1933): 701 Pennsylvania Ave. N.W., Washington, D.C. 20004-2696. Phone: (202) 508-5000. www.eei.org.

Education, American Council on (ACE), (1918): One Dupont Circle N.W., Washington, D.C. 20036-1193. 1,600+ colleges and universities and 200+ higher education associations. Phone: (202) 939-9300. www.acenet.edu.

Educational Exchange, Council on International (1947): 7 Custom House St., 3rd Fl., Portland, Maine 04101. Phone: (800) 40-STUDY. www.ciee.org.

Educational Research Association, American (1916): 1230 17th St. N.W., Washington, D.C. 20036-3078. 22,000. Phone: (202) 223-9485. www.aera.net.

Education Association, National (1857): 1201 16th St. N.W., Washington, D.C. 20036-3290. 2.3 million. Phone: (202) 833-4000. www.nea.org.

Electrochemical Society, The (1902): 65 S. Main St., Pennington, N.J. 08534-2839. 7,000. Phone: (609) 737-1902; fax: (609) 737-2743. email: ecs@electrochem.org. www.electrochem.org.

Elks of the U.S.A., Benevolent and Protective Order of the (1868): 2750 N. Lakeview Ave., Chicago, Ill. 60614-1889. 1,300,000. Phone: (773) 755-4700. www.elks.org/default.cfm.

Energy Engineers, Association of (1977): 4025 Pleasantdale Rd., Ste. 420, Atlanta, Ga. 30340. 8,500. Phone: (770) 447-5083; fax: (770) 446-3969. email: info@aeecenter.org. www.aeecenter.org.

English-Speaking Union of the United States (1920): 144 E. 39th St., New York, N.Y. 10016. 18,000. Phone: (212) 877-1200. www.english-speakingunion.org.

Entomological Society of America (1889): 10001 Derekwood Lane, Ste. 100, Lanham, Md. 20706-4876. 7,400+. Phone: (301) 731-4535; fax: (301) 731-4538. email: esa@entsoc.org. www.entsoc.org.

Esperanto League for North America, The (1952): P.O. Box 1129, El Cerrito, Calif. 94530. Over 1,000. Phone: (800) 377-3726. www.esperanto-usa.org.

Exceptional Children, The Council for (1922): 1110 N. Glebe Rd., Ste. 300, Arlington, Va. 22201-5704. 54,000. Phone: (703) 620-3660 V; (703) 264-9446 TTY; fax: (703) 264-9494. email: cec@cec.sped.org. www.cec.sped.org.

Exploration Geophysicists, Society of (1930): 8801 South Yale, Tulsa, Okla. 74137-3575. 16,536. Phone: (918) 497-5500. www.seg.org.

Family and Consumer Sciences, American Association of (1909): 1555 King St., Alexandria, Va. 22314. 14,500. Phone: (703) 706-4600. www.aafcs.org.

Family Campers & RVers (1949): 176 Tyler Ave., Englewood, Fla. 34223-3651. 42,000 families. www.fcrv.org.

Family, Career, and Community Leaders of America [evolved from Future Homemakers of America, Inc. (1945)]: 1910 Association Dr., Reston, Va. 20191-1584. 230,000. Phone: (703) 476-4900. www.fcclainc.org.

Family Physicians, American Academy of (1947): 11400 Tomahawk Creek Pkwy., Leawood, Kans. 66211-2672. 88,000. Phone: (913) 906-6000. www.aafp.org.

Family Relations, National Council on (1938): 3989 Central Ave. N.E., #550, Minneapolis, Minn. 55421. 42,000 families. Phone: (888) 781-9331. www.ncfr.com.

Farm Bureau Federation, American (1919): 600 Maryland Ave., S.W., Ste. 800, Washington, D.C. 20024. 4.7 million member families. Phone: (202) 406-3600. www.fb.com.

Federal Bar Association (1920): 2215 M St. N.W., Washington, D.C. 20037. 15,000. Phone: (202) 785-1614; fax: (202) 785-1568. www.fedbar.org.

Federal Employees, National Federation of (1917): 1016 16th St. N.W., Washington, D.C. 20036. 150,000. Phone: (202) 862-4400. www.nffe.org.

Fellowship of Reconciliation (1915): 521 N. Broadway, Nyack, N.Y. 10960. 20,000. Phone: (845) 358-4601. www.forusa.org.

Female Executives, National Association for (1972): P.O. Box 156, Congers, N.Y. 10920. 150,000+. Phone: (800) 927-NAFE. www.nafe.com.

FFA Organization, National (1928): P.O. Box 68960, 6060 FFA Dr., Indianapolis, Ind. 46268. 457,278. Phone: (317) 802-6060. www.ffa.org.

Fire Protection Association, National (1896): One Batterymarch Park, Quincy, Mass. 02169-7471. 65,000+. Phone: (617) 770-3000. www.nfpa.org.

Flag Foundation, National (1968): Flag Plaza, 1275 Bedford Ave, Pittsburgh, Pa. 15219. 3,000+. Phone: (412) 261-1776. www.americanflags.org.

Fleet Reserve Association (1924): 125 N. West St., Alexandria, Va. 22314-2754. 162,000. Phone: (703) 683-1400. www.fra.org.

Foreign Policy Association (1918): 470 Park Ave. So., New York, N.Y. 10016-6819. Phone: (212) 481-8100. www.fpa.org.

Foreign Relations, Council on (1921): 58 E. 68th St., New York, N.Y. 10021. 3,400. Phone: (212) 434-9400. www.cfr.org.

Foreign Study, American Institute for (1964): River Plaza, 9 W. Broad St., Stamford, Conn. 06902-3788. Phone: (800) 727-2437. www.aifs.org.

Forensic Sciences, American Academy of (1948): 410 N. 21st St., Ste. 203., P.O. Box 669, Colorado Springs, Colo. 80901-0669. 4,315. Phone: (719) 636-1100; fax: (719) 636-1993. www.aafs.org.

Foresters, Society of American (1900): 5400 Grosvenor Lane, Bethesda, Md. 20814. 18,000. Phone: (301) 897-8720. www.safnet.org.

4-H Program (early 1900s): 1400 Independence Ave., S.W., Washington, D.C. 20250. 5.6 million. Phone: (202) 720-2908. www.4-h.org/.

Freedom of Information Center (1958): 133 Neff Annex, Univ. of Missouri, Columbia, Mo. 65211. Phone: (573) 882-4856. www.missouri.edu/~foiwww/

French Institute/Alliance Française (1898): 22 E. 60th St., New York, N.Y. 10022. 9,000. Phone: (212) 355-6100. www.fiaf.org.

Friends of Animals Inc. (1957): 777 Post Rd., Darien, Conn. 06820. 120,000. Phone: (203) 656-1522. www.friendsofanimals.org/.

Friends of the Earth (1969): 1717 Massachusetts Avenue, N.W., Ste. 600, Washington, D.C. 20036-2002. 35,000. Phone: (877) 843-8687. www.foe.org.

Gamblers Anonymous: Box 17173, Los Angeles, Calif. 90017. Phone: (213) 386-8789. www.gamblersanonymous.org.

Gay and Lesbian Task Force, National (1973): 1325 Massachusetts Ave. N.W., Ste. 600, Washington, D.C. 20005. 35,000 members. Phone: (202) 393-5177. www.thetaskforce.org.

Genealogical Society, National (1903): 4527 17th St. N., Arlington, Va. 22207-2399. 17,000+. Phone: (703) 525-0050; fax: (703) 525-0052. www.ngsgenealogy.org.

Geographers, Association of American (1904): 1710 16th St. N.W., Washington, D.C. 20009-3198. 7,000. Phone: (202) 234-1450; fax: (202) 234-2744. email: gaia@aag.org. www.aag.org.

Geographic Education, National Council for (1915): 206A Martin Hall, Jacksonville State University, Jacksonville, Ala. 36265-1602. 3,700. Phone: (256) 782-5293. www.ncge.org.

Geographic Society, National (1888): 1145 17th St. N.W., Washington, D.C. 20036-4688. 9,200,000. Phone: (800) 647-5463. www.nationalgeographic.com.

Geological Institute, American (1948): 4220 King St., Alexandria, Va. 22302-1502. 34 geoscience societies representing 100,000 geoscientists. Phone: (703) 379-2480. www.agiweb.org/.

Geological Society of America, Inc. (1888): P.O. Box 9140, Boulder, Colo. 80301-9140. 15,000. Phone: (303) 447-2020. www.geosociety.org.

German American National Congress, The (Deutsch-Amerikanischer National Kongress— D.A.N.K.) (1958): 4740 N. Western Ave., Executive Office, Chicago, Ill. 60625-2097. Phone: (773) 275-1100. www.dank.org.

Gideons International, The (1889): P.O. Box 140800, Nashville, Tenn. 37214-0800. 130,000. Phone: (615) 883-8533. www.gideons.org.

Gifted, The Association for the (1958): 26 Cedar Hill Place, N.E., Albuquerque, N.M. 87122. Phone: (505) 828-1001. www.cectag.org

Girl Scouts of the U.S.A. (1912): 420 Fifth Ave., New York, N.Y. 10018-2798. 2,500,000. Phone: (212) 852-8000. www.girlscouts.org.

Girls Incorporated (1945): 120 Wall St., 3rd. Flr., New York, N.Y. 10005. 350,000. Phone: (800) 374-4475. www.girlsinc.org.

Graphoanalysis Society, International (1929): 842 Fifth Ave., New Kensington, Pa. 15068. 10,000. Phone: (724) 472-9701. www.igas.com.

Gray Panthers (1970): 733 15th St. N.W., Ste. 437, Washington, D.C. 20005. Over 50 chapters (networks). Phone: (202) 737-1160. www.graypanthers.org.

Greenpeace (1971): 702 H St. N.W., Washington, D.C. 20001. 2.5 million. Phone: (800) 326-0959. www.greenpeaceusa.org.

Guide Dog Foundation for the Blind, Inc.® (1946): 371 E. Jericho Turnpike, Smithtown, N.Y. 11787-2976. 100,000. Phone: (631) 265-2121; (800) 548-4337; fax: (631) 361-5192. www.guidedog.org.

Hadassah, The Women's Zionist Organization of America (1912): PO Box 5507, New York, N.Y. 10087-5507. 385,000. Phone: (800) 664-5646. www.hadassah.org.

Heating, Refrigerating and Air-Conditioning Engineers, Inc., American Society of (1959): 1791 Tullie Circle N.E., Atlanta, Ga. 30329. 50,000. Phone: (404) 636-8400. www.ashrae.org.

Helicopter Association International (1948): 1635 Prince St., Alexandria, Va. 22314. Phone: (703) 683-4646. www.rotor.com.

Historians, The Organization of American (1907): 112 N. Bryan St., Bloomington, Ind. 47408-4199. 12,000. Phone: (812) 855-7311. www.oah.org.

Historic Preservation, National Trust for (1949): 1785 Massachusetts Ave. N.W., Washington, D.C. 20036. 275,000. Phone: (202) 588–6000. www.nationaltrust.org.

Horse Council, Inc., American (1969): 1616 H St. N.W., 7th Fl., Washington, D.C. 20006. More than 190 organizations and 2,400 individuals. Phone: (202) 296-4030. www.horsecouncil.org.

Horse Shows Association, Inc., American (1917): 4047 Iron Works Parkway, Lexington, Ky. 40511. 70,000+. Phone: (859) 258-2472. www.ahsa.org.

Horticultural Association, National Junior (1935): 15 Railroad Ave., Homer City, Pa. 15748. Phone: (724) 479-3254. www.njha.org.

Horticultural Society, American (1922): 7931 East Boulevard Dr., Alexandria, Va. 22308. 22,000. Phone: (703) 768-5700 or (800) 777-7931; fax: (703) 768-8700. www.ahs.org.

Hostelling International—American Youth Hostels (1934): 8401 Colesville Rd., Ste. 600, Silver Spring, Md. 20910. 120,000. Phone: (301) 495-1240 for membership and reservations. www.hiayh.org.

Humane Association, American (1877): 63 Inverness Drive East, Englewood, Colo. 80112-5117. Phone: (866) 242-1877. www.americanhumane.org.

Humane Society of the United States (1954): 2100 L St. N.W., Washington, D.C. 20037. 5,000,000. Phone: (202) 452-1100. www.hsus.org.

Humanities, National Endowment for the (1965): 1100 Pennsylvania Ave. N.W., Washington, D.C. 20506. Phone: (202) 606-8400. www.neh.fed.us.

Hydrogen Energy, International Association for (1975): P.O. Box 248266, Coral Gables, Fla. 33124. 2,500. Phone: (305) 284-4666. www.iahe.org.

Industrial Engineers, Institute of (1948): 3577 Parkway Lane, Ste. 200, Norcross, Ga. 30092. 17,000+. Phone: (800) 494-0460. www.iienet.org.

Insurance and Financial Advisors, National Association of (1890): 2901 Telestar Court, Falls Church, Va. 22042–1205. 108,000. Phone: (877) TO-NAIFA. www.naifa.org..

Izaak Walton League of America (1922): 707 Conservation Lane, Gaithersburg, Md. 20878-2983. 50,000+. Phone: (800) 453-5463. www.iwla.org.

Jewish Community Centers Association (JCC) of North America (1917): 15 E. 26th St., New York, N.Y. 10010-1579. 275+ affiliated Jewish Community Centers, YM-YWHAs, and camps serving 1 million+ members. Phone: (212) 532-4958; fax: (212) 481-4174. email: info@jcca.org. www.jcca.org.

Jewish Congress, American (1918): Stephen Wise Congress House,15 East 84th St., New York, N.Y. 10028. 50,000. Phone: (212) 879-4500. www.ajcongress.org.

Jewish Historical Society, American (1892): 15 W. 16th St., New York, N.Y. 10011. 3,500. Phone: (212) 294-6160; fax: (212) 294-6161. email: ajhs@ajhs.org. www.ajhs.org.

Jewish War Veterans of the U.S.A. (1896): 1811 R St. N.W., Washington, D.C. 20009-1659. Phone: (202) 265-6280. www.jwv.org.

Jewish Women, National Council of (1893): 53 W. 23rd St., New York, N.Y. 10010. 90,000. Phone: (800) 829–NCJW. www.ncjw.org.

John Birch Society (1958): P.O. Box 8040, Appleton, Wis. 54912. Under 100,000. Phone: (920) 749-3780; fax: (920) 749-5062. www.jbs.org.

Journalists, Society of Professional (1909): 3909 N. Meridian St., Indianapolis, Ind. 46208. 13,500. Phone: (317) 927-8000. www.spj.org.

Judaism, American Council for (1943): P.O. Box 9009, Alexandria, Va. 22304. Phone: (703) 836-2546. www.acjna.org

Junior Achievement Inc. (1919): One Education Way, Colorado Springs, Colo. 80906. 5.2 million. Phone: (719) 540-8000; fax: (719) 540-6299. www.ja.org.

Junior Chamber of Commerce, The United States, Jaycees (1920): P.O. Box 7, Tulsa, Okla. 74102-0007. 113,000. Phone: (918) 584-2481; fax: (918) 584-4422. www.usjaycees.org.

Junior Leagues International, Inc., Association of (1921): 132 W. 31st St., 11th flr.; New York, N.Y. 10001-3406. 295 Leagues, 193,000+ members. Phone: (212) 951-8300. www.ajli.org.

Junior State of America (1934): 400 South El Camino Real, Ste. 300, San Mateo, Calif. 94402. 15,000. Phone: (650) 347-1600. www.jsa.org.

Kiwanis International (1915): 3636 Woodview Trace, Indianapolis, Ind. 46268. 316,000. Phone: (317) 875-8755. email: kiwanismail@kiwanis.org. www.kiwanis.org.

Knights of Columbus (1852): One Columbus Plaza, New Haven, Conn. 06510. 1,600,000. Phone: (203) 752-4000. www.kofc.org.

Knights Templar, Grand Encampment of (1816): 5097 N. Elston Ave., Ste. 101, Chicago, Ill. 60630-2460. 220,000. Phone: (773) 777-3300. www.knightstemplar.org.

La Leche League International (1956): 1400 N. Meacham Rd., Schaumburg, Ill. 60173-4808. 50,000. Phone: (847) 519-7730. www.lalecheleague.org.

Law, American Society of International (1906): 2223 Massachusetts Ave. N.W., Washington, D.C. 20008. 4,300. Phone: (202) 939-6000. www.asil.org.

League of Women Voters of the U.S. (1920): 1730 M St. N.W., Washington, D.C. 20036-4508. Phone: (202) 429-1965; fax: (202) 429-0854. www.lwv.org.

Legal Aid and Defender Association, National (1911): 1140 Connecticut Ave. N.W., Washington, D.C. 20036. 2,400. Phone: (202) 452-0620. www.nlada.org.

Legal Professionals, National Association of (1949): 314 East 3rd St., Ste. 210, Tulsa, Okla. 74120-2409. 6,000. Phone: (918) 582-5188. www.nals.org.

Leukemia & Lymphoma Society (1949): 1311 Mamaroneck Ave., White Plains, N.Y. 10605. Phone: (914) 949-5213. www.leukemia-lymphoma.org.

Library Association, American (1876): 50 E. Huron St., Chicago, Ill. 60611. 57,000. Phone: (800) 545-2433. www.ala.org.

Lions Clubs International (1917): 300 22nd St., Oak Brook, Ill. 60523-8842. 1,419,408. Phone: (630) 571-5466. www.lionsclubs.org.

Lung Association, American (1904): 61 Broadway, New York, N.Y. 10006. 99 constituent and affiliate associations. Phone: (212) 315-8700. www.lungusa.org.

Magazine Editors, American Society of (1963): 810 Seventh Ave., 24th Fl., New York, N.Y. 10019. 900. Phone: (212) 872-3737. www.magazine.org.

Management Accountants, Institute of (1919): 10 Paragon Dr., Montvale, N.J. 07645-1759. 80,000. Phone: (800) 638-4427. www.imanet.org.

Management Association, American (1923): 1601 Broadway, New York, N.Y. 10019. 700,000. Phone: (212) 586-8100. www.amanet.org.

Management Consultants, Institute of (1968): 2025 M St. N.W., Ste. 800, Washington, D.C. 20036–2557. 25 chapters. Phone: (202) 367-1134. www.imcusa.org.

Manufacturers, National Association of (1895): 1331 Pennsylvania Ave. N.W., Washington, D.C. 20004-1790. Approx. 14,000. Phone: (202) 637-3000. www.nam.org.

Manufacturing Engineers, Society of: One SME Drive, Dearborn, Mich. 48121. Phone: (313) 271–1500 x 1078; fax: (313) 240–8251. www.sme.org.

March of Dimes Birth Defects Foundation (1938): 1275 Mamaroneck Ave., White Plains, N.Y. 10605. 104 chapters. Phone: (888) 663-4637. www.modimes.org.

Marine Corps Association (1913): 715 Broadway, Quantico, Va. 22134. 100,723. Phone: (703) 640-6161; (800) 336-0291. www.mca-marines.org.

Marine Technology Society (1963): 5565 Sterrett Place, Ste. 108, Columbia, Md. 21044. 2,000+. Phone: (410) 884-5330; fax: (202) 429-9417. www.mtsociety.org.

Masons, Ancient and Accepted Scottish Rite, Northern Masonic Jurisdiction, Supreme Council 33 (1813): P.O. Box 519, Lexington, Mass. 02420-0519. 330,000. Phone: (781) 862-4410. www.supremecouncil.org/

Masons, Ancient and Accepted Scottish Rite, Southern Jurisdiction, Supreme Council (1801): 1733 16th St. N.W., Washington, D.C. 20009. 500,000. Phone: (202) 232-3579. www.srmason-sj.org/web

Mathematical Association of America (1915): P.O. Box 91112, Washington, D.C. 20090-1112. Phone: (800) 331-1622. www.maa.org.

Mathematical Society, American (1888): 201 Charles St., Providence, R.I. 02940-6248. Phone: (401) 455-4000. email: ams@ams.org. www.ams.org.

Mayflower Descendants, General Society of (1897): P.O. Box 3297, Plymouth, Mass. 02361. 24,500+. Phone: (508) 746-3188. www.mayflower.org.

Mechanical Engineers, American Society of (1880): 3 Park Ave., New York, N.Y. 10016-5990. 125,000. Phone: (800) 843-2763. www.asme.org.

Medical Association, American (1847): 515 N. State St., Chicago, Ill. 60610. 300,000 physicians. Phone: (312) 464-5000. www.ama-assn.org.

Mental Health Association, National (1909): 2001 N. Beauregard St., 12th Fl., Alexandria, Va., 22311. 340 affiliates. Phone: (703) 684-7722; (800) 969-NMHA; TTY (800) 433-5959; fax: (703) 684-5968. email: nmhainfo@aol.com. www.nmha.org

Meteorological Society, American (1919): 45 Beacon St., Boston, Mass. 02108-3693. 11,000+. Phone: (617) 227-2425. www.ametsoc.org/ams.

Military Chaplains Association of the U.S.A. (1925): P.O. Box 7056, Arlington, Va. 22207-7056. 1,500. Phone: (703) 276-2189. www.mca-usa.org.

Mining, Metallurgical, and Petroleum Engineers, The American Institute of (1871): 8307 Shaffer Parkway, Littleton, Colo. 80127-4012. 4 Member Societies: Society for Mining, Metallurgy and Exploration; The Minerals, Metals & Materials Society; Iron & Steel Society; Society of Petroleum Engineers. Phone: (303) 948-4255; fax: (303) 948-4260. email: aime@aimehq.org. www.aimehq.org.

Model Aeronautics, Academy of (1936): 5161 East Memorial Dr., Muncie, Ind. 47302. 150,000. Phone: (765) 287-1256. www.modelaircraft.org/templates/ama/.

Modern Language Association of America (1883): 26 Broadway, 3rd Fl., New York, N.Y. 10004-1789. 30,000+. Phone: (646) 576-5000. www.mla.org.

Moose International, Inc. (1888): Rte. 31, Mooseheart, Ill. 60539. 1,600,000+. Phone: (630) 859-2000. www.mooseintl.org.

Mothers Against Drunk Driving (MADD) (1980): 511 E. John Carpenter Frwy., Ste. 700, Irving, Tex. 75062. 3 million members and supporters. Victim hotline: (800) GET-MADD. www.madd.org.

Motion Picture Arts & Sciences, Academy of (1927): 8949 Wilshire Blvd., Beverly Hills, Calif. 90211-1972. Phone: (310) 247-3000. www.oscars.org.

Multiple Sclerosis Society, National (1946): 733 Third Ave., New York, N.Y. 10017. 350,000. Phone: (800) FIGHT-MS (344-4867). www.nationalmssociety.org.

Muscular Dystrophy Association (1950): 3300 East Sunrise Dr., Tucson, Ariz. 85718. 2,300,000 volunteers. Phone: (800) 572-1717. www.mdausa.org.

Museums, American Association of (1906): 1575 Eye St. N.W., Ste. 400, Washington, D.C. 20005. 16,000+. Phone: (202) 289-1818; fax: (202) 289-6578, TTY (202) 289-8439. www.aam-us.org.

Muzzle Loading Rifle Association, National (1933): P.O. Box 67, Friendship, Ind. 47021-0067. 25,000. Phone: (812) 667-5131. www.nmlra.org.

NAFSA: Association of International Educators (1948): 1307 New York Ave. N.W., 8th Flr., Washington, D.C. 20005-4701. 8,000+. Phone: (202) 737-3699. www.nafsa.org.

National Abortion and Reproductive Rights Action League (NARAL) (1969): 1156 15th St. N.W., Washington, D.C. 20005. 500,000. Phone: (202) 973-3000. www.naral.org.

National Association for the Advancement of Colored People (1909): 4805 Mt. Hope Dr., Baltimore, Md. 21215. 500,000+. Phone: (877) NAACP-98. www.naacp.org.

National Association of Insurance and Financial Advisors (1890): 2901 Telestar Court, Falls Church, Va. 22042-1205. 80,000. Phone: (703) 770-8100. www.naifa.org/index.html.

National Conference for Community and Justice, The (founded as The Natl. Conf. of Christians & Jews) (1927): 475 Park Avenue South, 19th Flr., New York, N.Y. 10016-6901. Phone: (212) 545-1300. www.nccj.org.

National Cooperative Business Association (formerly Cooperative League of the U.S.A.)

(1916): 1401 New York Ave. N.W., Ste. 1100, Washington, D.C. 20005. Phone: (202) 638-6222. www.ncba.org.

National Council of La Raza (1968): 1111 19th St. N.W., Ste. 1000, Washington, D.C. 20036. 20,000+. Phone: (202) 785-1670. www.nclr.org.

National Council of the Churches of Christ in the USA (1950): 475 Riverside Drive, Rm. 850, New York, N.Y. 10115. 35 Protestant and Orthodox communions. Phone: (212) 870-2227. www.ncccusa.org.

National Grange of the Order of Patrons of Husbandry (1867): 1616 H St. N.W., Washington, D.C. 20006-4999. 300,000. Phone: (202) 628-3507; fax: (202) 347-1091. www.nationalgrange.org.

National Press Club (1908): National Press Bldg., 529 14th St. N.W., 13th Flr., Washington, D.C. 20045. 4,500+. Phone: (202) 662-7500. npc.press.org.

National PTA (National Congress of Parents and Teachers) (1897): 330 N. Wabash Ave., Ste. 2100, Chicago, Ill. 60611. 6.5 million. Phone: (800) 307-4782. email: info@pta.org. www.pta.org.

National Rifle Association of America (1871): 11250 Waples Mill Rd., Fairfax, Va. 22030. 3,300,000. Phone: (703) 267-1000. www.nra.org.

National Urban League, Inc. (1910): 120 Wall St., New York, N.Y. 10005. 115 affiliates in 34 states and D.C. Phone: (212) 558-5300. www.nul.org.

National Wildlife Federation (1936): 11100 Wildlife Center Dr., Reston, Va. 20190. 4,000,000+. Phone: (703) 438-6000. www.nwf.org.

Nature Conservancy, The (1951): 4245 N. Fairfax Dr., Ste. 100, Arlington, Va. 22203-1606. 900,000. Phone: (800) 628-6860. http://nature.org.

Naturopathic Physicians, American Association of (1986): 3201 New Mexico Ave. N.W., Ste. 350, Washington, D.C. 20016. 1,700. Phone: (866) 538-2267. www.naturopathic.org.

Naval Architects and Marine Engineers, The Society of (1893): 601 Pavonia Ave., Jersey City, N.J. 07306. 10,000+. Phone: (800) 798-2188; fax: (201) 798-4975. www.sname.org.

Naval Engineers, American Society of (1888): 1452 Duke St., Alexandria, Va. 22314. 6,800. Phone: (703) 836-6727; fax: (703) 836-7491. www.navalengineers.org.

Naval Institute, United States (1873): 291 Wood Rd., Annapolis, Md. 21402. 80,000+. Phone: (410) 268-6110. www.usni.org.

Navigation, The Institute of (1945): 3975 University Dr., Ste. 390, Fairfax, Va. 22030. 3,800. Phone: (703) 383-9688; fax: (703) 383-9689. email: membership@ion.org. www.ion.org.

Navy League of the United States (1902): 2300 Wilson Blvd., Arlington, Va. 22201-3308. 71,500. Phone: (703) 528-1775. www.navyleague.org.

NDIA (National Defense Industrial Association) (1997): 2111 Wilson Blvd., Ste. 400, Arlington, Va. 22201. 28,000 individual, 900 companies. Phone: (703) 522-1820. www.ndia.org.

Neurofibromatosis Foundation, Inc., The National (1978): 95 Pine St., 16th Flr., New York, N.Y. 10005. 38,000. Phone: (800) 323-7938; in N.Y. State (212) 344-NNFF; fax: (212) 747-0004. email: nnff@aol.com. www.nf.org.

Newspaper Association of America (1992): 1921 Gallows Rd., Ste. 600, Vienna, Va. 22182–3900. 70,000+ newspaper executives. Phone (703) 902-1600. www.naa.org.

Nondestructive Testing, Inc., The American Society for (1941): 1711 Arlingate Lane, P.O. Box 28518, Columbus, Ohio 43228-0518. 10,240. Phone: (800) 222-ASNT. www.asnt.org.

Nuclear Society, American (1954): 555 N. Kensington Ave., La Grange Park, Ill. 60526. 13,000. Phone: (708) 352-6611. www.ans.org.

Numismatic Association, American (1891): 818 N. Cascade Ave., Colorado Springs, Colo. 80903-3279. 28,000. Phone: (719) 632-2646. email: ana@money.org. www.money.org.

Nurses Association, American (1897): 600 Maryland Ave. S.W., Ste. 100, Washington, D.C. 20024. 180,000. Phone: (800) 274-4ANA. www.ana.org.

Ocean Conservancy, The (formerly Center for Marine Conservation) (1972): 1725 De Sales St. N.W., Ste. 600, Washington, D.C. 20036. 120,000. Phone: (202) 429-5609. www.oceanconservancy.org/

Odd Fellows, Sovereign Grand Lodge, Independent Order of (1819): 422 Trade St., Winston-Salem, N.C. 27101. 460,000. Phone: (336) 725-5955. www.ioof.org.

Olympic Committee, United States (1921): One Olympic Plaza, Colorado Springs, Colo. 80909-5760. Phone: (719) 866-4500. www.olympic-usa.org.

Optimist International (1919): 4494 Lindell Blvd., St. Louis, Mo. 63108. 130,000+. Phone: (314) 371-6000. www.optimist.org.

Optometric Association, American (1898): 243 N. Lindbergh Blvd., St. Louis, Mo. 63141. 32,000. Phone: (314) 991-4100. www.aoanet.org.

Ornithologists' Union, American (1883): 1313 Dolley Madison Blvd., Ste. 402, McLean, Va. 22101. 4,000. Phone: (202) 357-2051. www.aou.org.

Overeaters Anonymous, Inc. (1960): World Service Office, P.O. Box 44020, Rio Rancho, N.M. 87174–4020. 150,000. Phone: (505) 891-2664. www.overeatersanonymous.org.

Parents, Families and Friends of Lesbians and Gays (1981): 1726 M St. N.W., Ste. 400, Washington, D.C. 20036. 77,000 households. Phone: (202) 467-8180. www.pflag.org.

Parents Without Partners (1957): 1650 South Dixie Hwy., Ste. 510, Boca Raton, Fla. 33432. 50,000+. Phone: (561) 391-8833. www.parentswithoutpartners.org.

Peace Action (a merger of SANE and the Nuclear Weapons Freeze Campaign) (1957): 1100 Wayne Ave., Ste. 1020, Silver Spring, Md. 20910. 55,000. Phone: (301) 565-4050. www.webcom.com/peaceact.

People For the American Way (1980): 2000 M St. N.W., Ste. 400, Washington, D.C. 20036. 300,000. Phone: (202) 467-4999. www.pfaw.org.

Petroleum Geologists, American Association of (1917): 1444 South Boulder Ave., Tulsa, Okla. 74119. 31,500. Phone: (918) 584-2555. www.aapg.org.

Pharmaceutical Association, American (1852): 2215 Constitution Ave. N.W., Washington, D.C. 20037-2985. 50,000+. Phone: (202) 628-4410. www.aphanet.org.

Philatelic Society, American (1886): 100 Match Factory Place, Bellefonte, Pa. 16823. 55,000+. Phone: (814) 933-3803. www.stamps.org.

Photogrammetry and Remote Sensing, American Society for (1934): 5410 Grosvenor Lane, Ste. 210, Bethesda, Md. 20814-2160. 7,000+. Phone: (301) 493-0290; fax: (301) 493-0208. email: asprs@asprs.org. www.asprs.org.

Photographic Society of America (1934): 3000 United Founders Blvd., Ste. 103, Oklahoma City, Okla. 73112-3940. Phone: (405) 843-1437. www.psa-photo.org.

Physical Society, The American (1899): One Physics Ellipse, College Park, Md. 20740-3844. 41,000. Phone: (301) 209-3200. www.aps.org.

Physical Therapy Association, American (APTA) (1921): 1111 N. Fairfax St., Alexandria, Va. 22314-1488. 66,000+. Phone: (703) 684-2782. www.apta.org.

Physics, American Institute of (1931): One Physics Ellipse, College Park, Md. 20740-3843. 125,000. Phone: (301) 209-3100. www.aip.org.

Pilot International (1921): Pilot International Headquarters, 244 College St., P.O. Box 4844, Macon, Ga. 31208-4844. 25,000. Phone: (478) 743-7403. www.pilotinternational.org.

Planetary Society, The (1980): 65 N. Catalina Ave., Pasadena, Calif. 91106-2301. 100,000. Phone: (626) 793-5100. www.planetary.org.

Planned Parenthood® Federation of America, Inc., (1916): 434 West 33rd St. New York, N.Y. 10001. 150 affiliates. Phone: (212) 541-7800; fax: (212) 245-1845. www.plannedparenthood.org.

Plastics Engineers, Society of (1942): P.O. Box 403, 14 Fairfield Dr., Brookfield, Conn. 06804-0403. 32,000+. Phone: (203) 775-0471. www.4spe.org.

Police and Concerned Citizens, American Federation of (1966): American Police Hall of Fame, 6350 Horizon Dr., Titusville, Fla. 32780. 100,000. Phone: (321) 264-0911. www.aphf.org/p14_afop.html.

Police, International Association of Chiefs of (1893): 515 N. Washington St., Alexandria, Va. 22314-2357. 19,000+. Phone: (703) 836-6767. www.theiacp.org.

Political and Social Science, American Academy of (1889): 3814 Walnut St., Philadelphia, Pa. 19104-6197. Phone: (215) 746-6500. www.aapss.org/.

Political Science, Academy of (1880): 475 Riverside Dr., Ste. 1274, New York, N.Y. 10115-1274. 8,500. Phone: (212) 870-2500. www.psqonline.org.

Population Connection (formerly Zero Population Growth) (1968): 1400 Sixteenth St. N.W., Ste. 320, Washington, D.C. 20036. 55,000. Phone: (202) 332-2200. http://www.populationconnection.org/.

Prevent Blindness America (1908): 500 E. Remington Rd., Schaumburg, Ill. 60173. 21 affiliates and divisions. Phone: (800) 331-2020. www.preventblindness.org.

Professional Engineers, National Society of (1934): 1420 King St., Alexandria, Va. 22314-2794. 60,000. Phone: (703) 684-2800; fax: (703) 836-4875. www.nspe.org.

Professional Photographers of America, Inc. (1880): 229 Peachtree St. N.W., #2200, Atlanta, Ga. 30303-2206. 14,000. Phone: (404) 522-8600. www.ppa.com.

Psychiatric Association, American (1844): 1000 Wilson Blvd., Ste. 1825, Arlington, Va. 22209-3901. 40,537. Phone: (703) 907-7300. www.psych.org.

Psychoanalytic Association, The American (1911): 309 E. 49th St., New York, N.Y. 10017. 3,000+ psychoanalysts. Phone: (212) 752-0450; fax: (212) 593-0571. www.apsa.org.

Psychological Association, American (1892): 750 First St. N.E., Washington, D.C. 20002–4242. 159,000. Phone: (202) 336 5500; (202) 336-6123 TTY. www.apa.org.

Public Health Association, American (1872): 800 I St. N.W., Washington, D.C. 20001-3710. 50,000+. Phone: (202) 777-2742. www.apha.org.

Puppeteers of America (1937): P.O. Box 29417, Parma, Ohio 44129-0417. Phone: (888) 568-6235. www.puppeteers.org

Quality, The American Society for (1946): 600 N. Plankinton Ave., Milwaukee, Wis. 53203. 135,000+. Phone: (414) 272-8575. www.asq.org.

Railroads, Association of American (1934): 50 F St. N.W., Washington, D.C. 20001-1564. Phone: (202) 639-2100. www.aar.org.

Recording Arts & Sciences, Inc., National Academy of (1957): 3402 Pico Blvd., Santa Monica, Calif. 90405. 13,000. Phone: (310) 392-3777. www.grammy.com.

Red Cross, American (1881): 2025 E Street N.W., Washington, D.C. 20006. Approx. 1,650 chapters. Phone: (202) 303-4498. www.redcross.org.

Rehabilitation Association, National (1925): 633 S. Washington St., Alexandria, Va. 22314. 12,000.

Phone: (703) 836-0850; TDD: (703) 836-0849.
www.nationalrehab.org.

Reserve Officers Association of the United States (1922): 1 Constitution Ave. N.E., Washington, D.C. 20002-5655. 93,000. Phone: (800) 809-9448. www.roa.org.

Retired Federal Employees, National Association (1921): 606 N. Washington St., Alexandria, Va. 22314. 400,000+. Phone: (703) 838-7760. www.narfe.org.

Reye's Syndrome Foundation, National (1974): P.O. Box 829, Bryan, Ohio 43506-0829. Phone: (800) 233-7393; fax: (419) 636-9897. email: nsrf@reyessyndrome.org. www.reyessyndrome.org.

RID-USA (Remove Intoxicated Drivers) (1978): Box 520, Schenectady, N.Y. 12301. Phone: (518) 372-0034/(518) 393-HELP; fax: (518) 370-4917. www.crisny.org/not-for-profit/ridusa/.

Right to Life, Committee, Inc., National (1973): 512 10th St. N.W., Washington, D.C. 20004. Phone: (202) 626-8800. www.nrlc.org

Rotary International (1905): One Rotary Center, 1560 Sherman Ave., Evanston, Ill. 60201. 1.2 million in 161 countries and 35 geographical regions. Phone: (847) 866-3000. www.rotary.org.

SAE (Society of Automotive Engineers) (1905): 400 Commonwealth Dr., Warrendale, Pa. 15096-0001. 80,000. Phone: (724) 776-4847. www.sae.org.

Safety Council, National (1913): 1121 Spring Lake Dr., Itasca, Ill. 60143-3201. Phone: (630) 285-1121. www.nsc.org.

Salvation Army, The (1865): National Headquarters, P.O. Box 269, Alexandria, Va. 22313. 453,150. Phone: (703) 684-5500. www.salvationarmy.org.

Save-the-Redwoods League (1918): 114 Sansome St., Rm 1200, San Francisco, Calif. 94104-3823. 45,000. Phone: (415) 362-2352. www.savetheredwoods.org.

Science, American Association for the Advancement of (1848): 1200 New York Ave. N.W., Washington, D.C. 20005. 143,000. Phone: (202) 326-6400. www.aaas.org.

Science and Health, American Council on (1978): 1995 Broadway, 2nd Flr., New York, N.Y. 10023-5860. Phone: (212) 362-7044; fax: (212) 362-4919. email: acsh@acsh.org. www.acsh.org.

Science Fiction Society, World (1939): P.O. Box 426159, Kendall Square Station, Cambridge, Mass. 02142. email: mpc@wsfs.org www.wsfs.org.

Scientists, Federation of American (FAS) (1945): 1717 K St. N.W., Ste. 209, Washington, D.C. 20036. 4,000. Phone: (202) 546-3300. www.fas.org.

SCRABBLE® Association, National (1978): P.O. Box 700, 403 Front Street Garden, Greenport, N.Y. 11944. 10,000. Phone: (631) 477-0033. www.scrabble-assoc.org

Screen Actors Guild (1933): 5757 Wilshire Blvd., Los Angeles, Calif. 90036-3600. 96,000. Phone: (323) 954-1600. www.sag.com.

Sculpture Society, National (1893): 237 Park Ave., New York, N.Y. 10017. 4,000. Phone: (212) 764-5645. www.nationalsculpture.org

Seeing Eye Inc., The (1929): P.O. Box 375, Morristown, N.J. 07963-0375. Phone: (973) 539-4425. www.seeingeye.org.

Senior Citizens, National Alliance of (1974): 2525 Wilson Blvd., Arlington, Va. 22201. 117,000. Fax: (703) 528-4380.

Shrine of North America and Shriners Hospitals for Children, The (1872 and 1922): 2900 Rocky Point Drive, Tampa, Fla. 33607-1460. 525,000. Phone: (813) 281-0300. www.shrinershq.org.

Sierra Club (1892): 85 2nd Street, San Francisco, Calif. 94105-3441. 700,000+. Phone: (415) 977-5500. www.sierraclub.org.

SIETAR INTERNATIONAL (The International Society for Intercultural Education, Training and Research) (1974): 8835 S.W. Canyon Lane, Ste.

238, Portland, Ore. 97225. 12,500. Phone: (503) 297-4622. www.sietarinternational.org.

Simon Wiesenthal Center (1977): 1399 South Roxbury, Los Angeles, Calif. 90035. 400,000 member families. Phone: (800) 900-9036. www.wiesenthal.org.

Small Business United, National (1937): 1156 15th St. N.W., Washington, D.C. 20005. 65,000+. Phone: (202) 293-8830; fax: (202) 872-8543. email: nsbu@nsbu.org.

Social Work Education, Council on (1952): 1725 Duke St., Ste. 500, Alexandria, Va. 22314. Phone: (703) 683-8080; fax: (703) 683-8099. www.cswe.org.

Social Workers, National Association of (1955): 750 First St. N.E., Ste. 700, Washington, D.C. 20002-4241. Phone: (202) 408-8600. www.naswdc.org.

Society for Integrative and Comparative Biology (formerly the American Society of Zoologists) (1890): 1313 Dolley Madison Blvd. #402, McLean, Va. 22101. 2,100. Phone: (703) 790-1745; (800) 955-1236. email: SICB@BurkInc.com www.sicb.org.

Soil and Water Conservation Society (1945): 945 S.W. Ankeny Rd., Ankeny, Iowa 50021. 10,000. Phone: (515) 289-2331; fax: (515) 289-1227. www.swcs.org.

Songwriters Guild of America, The (1931): 1500 Harbor Blvd., Weehawken, N.J. 07087-6732. Phone: (201) 867-7603. www.songwriters.org.

Sons of Italy in America, Order (1905): 219 E St. N.E., Washington, D.C. 20002. 500,000. Phone: (202) 547-2900. www.osia.org.

Sons of the American Revolution, National Society of the (1889): 1000 S. 4th St., Louisville, Ky. 40203. 26,000. Phone: (502) 589-1776. www.sar.org.

Soroptimist International of the Americas (1921): 1709 Spruce St., Philadelphia, Pa. 19103-6103. 100,000. Phone: (215) 893-9000. www.soroptimist.org/

Southern Early Childhood Association (formerly SACUS) (1948): P.O. Box 55930, Little Rock, Ark. 72215-5930. 21,000. Phone: (800) 305-7322; fax: (501) 227-5297. email: seca@aristotle.net. www.southernearlychildhood.org.

Space Society, National (1974): 1620 I (Eye) St. N.W., Ste. 615, Washington, D.C. 20006. Phone: (202) 429-1600; fax: (202) 463-8497. www.nss.org/.

Special Olympics International, Inc. (1968): 1325 G St. N.W., Ste. 500, Washington, D.C., 20005. 1,000,000. Phone: (202) 628-3630. www.specialolympics.org.

Speech-Language-Hearing Association, American (1925): 10801 Rockville Pike, Rockville, Md. 20852. 99,000+. Phone & TTY: (800) 638-8255. www.asha.org.

Sports Car Club of America Inc. (1944): P.O. Box 19400, Topeka, Kans. 66619-0400. 55,000. Phone: (800) 770-2055. www.scca.org.

Statistical Association, American (1839): 1429 Duke St., Alexandria, Va. 22314-3415. 19,000. Phone: (888) 231-3473. www.amstat.org.

Student Association, United States (1947): 1413 K Street N.W., 9th Flr., Washington, D.C. 20005. 350 schools (3.5 million students). Phone: (202) 347-8772. www.usstudents.org.

Surgeons, American College of (1913): 633 North Saint Clair, Chicago, Ill. 60611-3211. 56,000+. Phone: (312) 202-5000. www.facs.org.

Symphony Orchestra League, American (1942): 33 W. 60th St., 5th Fl., New York, N.Y. 10023-7905. 5,500. Phone: (212) 262-5161. www.symphony.org.

TASH: The Association for Persons with Severe Handicaps (1974): 29 W. Susquehanna Ave., Ste. 210, Baltimore, Md. 21204. 8,500. Phone: (410) 828-8274. www.tash.org.

Tax Foundation (1937): 1900 M St. N.W., Ste. 550, Washington, D.C. 20036. Phone: (202) 464-6200; fax: (202) 464-6201. email: taxfnd@intr.net. www.taxfoundation.org

Teachers, American Federation of (1916): 555 New Jersey Ave. N.W., Washington, D.C., 20001. 900,000+. Phone: (202) 879-4400. www.aft.org.

Testing & Materials, American Society for (1898): 100 Barr Harbor Dr., W. Conshohocken, Pa. 19428-2959. 35,000. Phone: (610) 832-9585. www.astm.org.

The Arc (1950): 1010 Wayne Ave., Ste. 650, Silver Spring, Md. 20910. A national organization on mental retardation. 140,000 members, 1,200 state and local chapters. Phone: (301) 565-3842. www.thearc.org.

Theosophical Society in America, The (1875): P.O. Box 270, Wheaton, Ill. 60189-0270. 4,400. Phone: (630) 668-1571. www.theosophical.org.

Tin Can Sailors, Inc. (1976): P.O. Box 100, Somerset, Mass. 02726. 20,900. Phone: (800) 223-5535. www.destroyers.org.

Toastmasters International (1924): P.O. Box 9052, Mission Viejo, Calif. 92690-7052. 170,000. Phone: (949) 858-8255; fax: (949) 858-1207. www.toastmasters.org.

TOUGHLOVE International (1977): P.O. Box 1069, Doylestown, Pa. 18901. 500 registered groups. Phone: (215) 348-7090. www.toughlove.org.

TransAfrica Forum (1981): 1426 21st St. N.W., Washington, D.C. 20036. Phone: (202) 223-1960; fax: (202) 223-1966. www.transafricaforum.org.

Travel Agents, American Society of (ASTA) (1931): 1101 King St., Alexandria, Va. 22314. 26,000. Phone: (703) 739-2782. www.astanet.com.

Travelers Aid International (1851): 1612 K St. N.W., Ste. 506, Washington, D.C. 20006. 45 agencies, 500+ corporate representatives. Phone: (202) 546-1127; fax: (202) 546-9112. www.travelersaid.org.

Tuberous Sclerosis Association, Inc., National (1974): 801 Roeder Rd., Ste. 750, Silver Spring, Md. 20910. 5,000. Phone: (800) 225-6872; fax: (301) 562-9870. www.tsalliance.org.

UFOs, National Investigations Committee on (1967): 21601 Devonshire St. #217, Chatsworth, Calif. 91311-8415. Phone: (818) 882-0052. www.nicufo.org.

UNICEF, U.S. Committee for (1947): 333 E. 38th St., New York, N.Y. 10016. 20,000 volunteers. Phone: (800) 4UNICEF. www.unicefusa.org.

Union of Concerned Scientists (1969): 2 Brattle Square, Cambridge, Mass. 02238. 70,000. Phone: (617) 547-5552. www.ucsusa.org.

United Daughters of the Confederacy® (1894): 328 N. Boulevard, Richmond, Va. 23220-4057. 24,000. Phone: (804) 355-1636. www.hqudc.org.

United Jewish Communities (formerly United Jewish Appeal) (1939): P.O. Box 30, Old Chelsea Station, New York, N.Y. 10113. Phone: (212) 284-6500. www.ujc.org.

United Way of America (1918): 701 N. Fairfax St., Alexandria, Va. 22314-2045. 1,400 local United Ways. Phone: (703) 836-7100; fax: (703) 683-7840. http://nationalunitedway.org

University Women, American Association of (1881): 1111 16th St. N.W., Washington, D.C. 20036. 150,000. Phone: (800) 326-AAUW (2289); TDD: (202) 785-7777. www.aauw.org.

USO (United Service Organizations) (1941): World Headquarters, 2111 Wilson Boulevard, Ste. 1200, Arlington, Va. 22201. 121 centers worldwide. Phone: (703) 908-6400. www.uso.org.

Veterans Committee, American (AVC) (1944): Bethesda, Md. 20817. 15,000. Phone & fax: (301) 320-6490. www.usmm.net/avc-mast45.html

Veterans of Foreign Wars of the U.S. (1899): 406 W. 34th St., Kansas City, Mo. 64111. VFW and Auxiliary, 2.1 million. Phone: (816) 756-3390. www.vfw.org.

Veterinary Medical Association, American (1863): 1931 N. Meacham Rd., Ste. 100, Schaumburg, Ill. 60173. 62,000. Phone: (847) 925-8070. www.avma.org.

Volunteers of America (1896): 1660 Duke St., Alexandria, Va. 22314-3421. 40,000+ volunteers. Phone: (703) 341-5000; (800) 899-0089. www.voa.org.

War Resisters League (1923): 339 Lafayette St., New York, N.Y. 10012. 12,000. Phone: (212) 228-0450; fax: (212) 228-6193. www.warresisters.org.

Washington Legal Foundation (1977): 2009 Massachusetts Ave. N.W., Washington, D.C. 20036. 100,000. Phone: (202) 588-0302. www.wlf.org.

Water Quality Association (1974): 4151 Naperville Rd., Lisle, Ill. 60532. 2,200. Phone: (630) 505-0160. www.wqa.org.

Welding Society, American (1919): 550 N.W. LeJeune Rd., Miami, Fla. 33126. 50,000. Phone: (305) 443-9353; (800) 443-9353. www.aws.org.

Wildlife Fund (U.S.), World (1961): 1250 24th St. N.W., Washington, D.C. 20037. 1.2 million. Phone: (202) 293-4800. www.wwf.org.

Woman's Christian Temperance Union, National (1874): 1730 Chicago Ave., Evanston, Ill. 60201-4585. Under 20,000. Phone: (847) 864-1397. www.wctu.org.

Women, National Organization for (NOW) (1966): 733 15th St. N.W., 2nd fl., Washington, D.C. 20005. 500,000. Phone: (202) 628-8669. www.now.org.

Women Police, The International Association of (1915): P.O. Box 2710 Phoenix, Ariz. 85002. 3,000. Phone: (602) 382-8781. www.iawp.org.

Women's American ORT (1927): 250 Park Ave. South, New York, N.Y. 10003. Chapters throughout the U.S. Phone: (800) 51–WAORT. www.waort.org.

Women's Educational and Industrial Union (1877): 356 Boylston St., Boston, Mass. 02116. 1,500. Phone: (617) 536-5651; fax: (617) 247-8826. www.weiu.org.

Women's International League for Peace and Freedom (1915): 1213 Race St., Philadelphia, Pa. 19107–1691. 10,000. Phone: (215) 563-7110. www.wilpf.org.

World Future Society (1966): 7910 Woodmont Ave., Ste. 450, Bethesda, Md. 20814. 30,000. Phone: (301) 656-8274; fax: (301) 951-0394. www.wfs.org.

World Health, American Association for (1953): 1825 K St. N.W., Washington, D.C. 20006. Phone: (202) 466-5883; fax: (202) 466-5896. email: AAWHstaff@aol.com. www.thebody.com/aawh/aawhpage.html.

World Peace, International Association of Educators for (1967): P.O. Box 3282, Mastin Lake Station, Huntsville, Ala. 35810-0282. 102 countries. Phone: (256) 534-5501. www.iaewp.com.

World Peace Foundation (1910): 79 John F. Kennedy St., Cambridge, Mass. 02138. Phone: (617) 496-2258; fax: (617) 491-8588. www.worldpeacefoundation.org

Worldwatch Institute (1974): 1776 Massachusetts Ave. N.W., Washington, D.C. 20036-1904. Global environmental research organization. Phone: (202) 452-1999; fax: (202) 296-7365. email: worldwatch@worldwatch.org. www.worldwatch.org.

Writers Union, National (1981): 113 University Place, 6th Flr., New York, N.Y. 10003. 6,500. Phone: (212) 254-0279. www.nwu.org.

YMCA of the USA (1844): 101 N. Wacker Dr., Chicago, Ill. 60606. 16.9 million. Phone: (312) 977-0031. www.ymca.net.

Young Women's Christian Association of the U.S.A. (1858 in U.S.A., 1855 in England): 1015 18th St., N.W., Ste. 110, Washington, D.C 20036. 2,000,000. Phone: (202) 467 0801. www.ywca.org.

Zionist Organization of America (1897): 4 E. 34th St., New York, N.Y. 10016. 50,000. Phone: (212) 481-1500; fax: (212) 481-1515. www.zoa.org.

In any broad overview of history, arbitrary compartmentalization of facts is self-defeating (and makes locating interrelated people, places, and things that much harder). Therefore, Headline History is designed as a "timeline"—a chronology that highlights both the march of time and interesting, sometimes surprising, juxtapositions.

See also related sections of the almanac, particularly Inventions and Discoveries, U.S. Government and History, and Countries of the World.

B.C.

Before Christ (B.C.) or Before the Common Era (B.C.E.)

**Ra, Egyptian
Sun God
(3000–2000 B.C.)**

4.5 billion B.C. Planet Earth formed.

3 billion B.C. First signs of primeval life (bacteria and blue-green algae) appear in oceans.

600 million B.C. Earliest date to which fossils can be traced.

4.4 million B.C. Earliest known hominid fossils (*Ardipithecus ramidus*) found in Aramis, Ethiopia, 1994.

4.2 million B.C. *Australopithecus anamensis* found in Lake Turkana, Kenya, 1995.

3.2 million B.C. *Australopithecus afarensis* (nicknamed "Lucy") found in Ethiopia, 1974.

2.5 million B.C. *Homo habilis* ("Skillful Man"). First brain expansion; is believed to have used stone tools.

1.8 million B.C. *Homo erectus* ("Upright Man"). Brain size twice that of *Australopithecine* species.

1.7 million B.C. *Homo erectus* leaves Africa.

100,000 B.C. First modern *Homo sapiens* in South Africa.

70,000 B.C. Neanderthal man (use of fire and advanced tools).

35,000 B.C. Neanderthal man replaced by later groups of *Homo sapiens* (i.e., Cro-Magnon man, etc.).

18,000 B.C. Cro-Magnons replaced by later cultures.

15,000 B.C. Migrations across Bering Straits into the Americas.

10,000 B.C. Semi-permanent agricultural settlements in Old World.

10,000–4,000 B.C. Development of settlements into cities and development of skills such as the wheel, pottery, and improved methods of cultivation in Mesopotamia and elsewhere.

5500–3000 B.C. Predynastic Egyptian cultures develop (5500–3100 B.C.); begin using agriculture (c. 5000 B.C.). Earliest known civilization arises in Sumer (4500–4000 B.C.). Earliest recorded date in Egyptian calendar (4241 B.C.). First year of Jewish calendar (3760 B.C.). First phonetic writing appears (c. 3500 B.C.). Sumerians develop a city-state civilization (c. 3000 B.C.). Copper used by Egyptians and Sumerians. Western Europe is neolithic, without metals or written records.

**The Great Pyramid
at Giza
(c. 2680 B.C.)**

3000–2000 B.C. Pharaonic rule begins in Egypt. King Khufu (Cheops), 4th dynasty (2700–2675 B.C.), completes construction of the Great Pyramid at Giza (c. 2680 B.C.). The Great Sphinx of Giza (c. 2540 B.C.) is built by King Khafre. Earliest Egyptian mummies. Papyrus. Phoenician settlements on coast of what is now Syria and Lebanon. Semitic tribes settle in Assyria. Sargon, first Akkadian king, builds Mesopotamian empire. The Gilgamesh epic (c. 3000 B.C.). Abraham leaves Ur (c. 2000 B.C.). Systematic astronomy in Egypt, Babylon, India, China.

3000–1500 B.C. The most ancient civilization on the Indian subcontinent, the sophisticated and extensive Indus Valley civilization, flourishes in what is today Pakistan. In Britain, Stonehenge erected according to some unknown astronomical rationale. Its three main phases of construction are thought to span c. 3000–1500 B.C.

**Stonehenge
(c. 3000–1500 B.C.)**

2000–1500 B.C. Hyksos invaders drive Egyptians from Lower Egypt (17th century B.C.). Amosis I frees Egypt from Hyksos (c. 1600 B.C.). Assyrians rise to power—cities of Ashur and Nineveh. Twenty-four-character alphabet in Egypt. Israelites enslaved in Egypt. Cuneiform inscriptions used by Hittites. Peak of Minoan culture on Isle of Crete—earliest form of written Greek. Hammurabi, king of Babylon, develops oldest existing code of laws (18th century B.C.).

1500–1000 B.C. Ikhnaton develops monotheistic religion in Egypt (c. 1375 B.C.). His successor, Tutankhamen, returns to earlier gods. Moses leads Israelites out of Egypt into Canaan—Ten Commandments. Greeks destroy Troy (c. 1193 B.C.). End of Greek civilization in Mycenae with invasion of Dorians. Chinese civilization develops under Shang Dynasty. Olmec civilization in Mexico—stone monuments; picture writing.

1000–900 B.C. Solomon succeeds King David, builds Jerusalem temple. After Solomon's death, kingdom divided into Israel and Judah. Hebrew elders begin to write Old Testament books of Bible. Phoenicians colonize Spain with settlement at Cadiz.

900–800 B.C. Phoenicians establish Carthage (c. 810 B.C.). The *Iliad* and the *Odyssey*, perhaps composed by Greek poet Homer.

**Pythagoras
(582?–507? B.C.)**

800–700 B.C. Prophets Amos, Hosea, Isaiah. First recorded Olympic games (776 B.C.). Legendary founding of Rome by Romulus (753 B.C.). Assyrian king Sargon II conquers Hittites, Chaldeans, Samaria (end of Kingdom of Israel). Earliest written music. Chariots introduced into Italy by Etruscans.

700–600 B.C. End of Assyrian Empire (616 B.C.)—Nineveh destroyed by Chaldeans (Neo-Babylonians) and Medes (612 B.C.). Founding of Byzantium by Greeks (c. 660 B.C.). Building of the Acropolis in Athens. Solon, Greek lawgiver (640–560 B.C.). Sappho of Lesbos, Greek poet (fl. c. 610–580 B.C.). Lao-tse, Chinese philosopher and founder of Taoism (born c. 604 B.C.).

**Buddha
(563?–483? B.C.)**

600–500 B.C. Babylonian King Nebuchadnezzar builds empire, destroys Jerusalem (586 B.C.). Babylonian Captivity of the Jews (starting 587 B.C.). Hanging Gardens of Babylon. Cyrus the Great of Persia creates great empire, conquers Babylon (539 B.C.), frees the Jews. Athenian democracy develops. Aeschylus, Greek dramatist (525–465 B.C.). Pythagoras, Greek philosopher and mathematician (582?–507? B.C.). Confucius (551–479 B.C.) develops ethical and social philosophy in China. The *Analects* or Lun-yü ("collected sayings") are compiled by the second generation of Confucian disciples. Buddha (563?–483? B.C.) founds Buddhism in India.

SOME ANCIENT CIVILIZATIONS

Name	Approximate dates	Location	Major cities
Akkadian	2350–2230 B.C.	Mesopotamia, parts of Syria, Asia Minor, Iran	Akkad, Ur, Erich
Assyrian	1800–889 B.C.	Mesopotamia, Syria	Assur, Nineveh, Calah
Babylonian	1728–1686 B.C. (old) 625–539 B.C. (new)	Mesopotamia, Syria, Palestine	Babylon
Cimmerian	750–500 B.C.	Caucasus, northern Asia Minor	—
Egyptian	2850–715 B.C.	Nile valley	Thebes, Memphis, Tanis
Etruscan	900–396 B.C.	Northern Italy	—
Greek	900–200 B.C.	Greece	Athens, Sparta, Thebes, Mycenae, Corinth
Hittite	1640–1200 B.C.	Asia Minor, Syria	Hattusas, Nesa
Indus Valley	3000–1500 B.C.	Pakistan, Northwestern India	—
Lydian	700–547 B.C.	Western Asia Minor	Sardis, Miletus
Mede	835–550 B.C.	Iran	Media
Minoan	3000–1100 B.C.	Crete	Knossos
Persian	559–330 B.C.	Iran, Asia Minor, Syria	Persepolis, Pasargadae
Phoenician	1100–332 B.C.	Palestine (colonies: Gibraltar, Carthage, Sardinia)	Tyre, Sidon, Byblos
Phrygian	1000–547 B.C.	Central Asia Minor	Gordion
Roman	500 B.C.–A.D. 300	Italy, Mediterranean region, Asia Minor, western Europe	Rome, Byzantium
Scythian	800–300 B.C.	Caucasus	—
Sumerian	3200–2360 B.C.	Mesopotamia	Ur, Nippur

**Confucius
(551–479 B.C.)**

**Parthenon
(447–432 B.C.)**

**Plato
(427?–348 or 347 B.C.)**

**Augustus Caesar
(63 B.C.–A.D. 14)**

**Roman Aqueduct
Montpellier, France**

500–400 B.C. Greeks defeat Persians: battles of Marathon (490 B.C.), Thermopylae (480 B.C.), Salamis (480 B.C.). Peloponnesian Wars between Athens and Sparta (431–404 B.C.)—Sparta victorious. Pericles comes to power in Athens (462 B.C.). Flowering of Greek culture during the Age of Pericles (450–400 B.C.). The Parthenon is built in Athens as a temple of the goddess Athena (447–432 B.C.). Ictinus and Callicrates are the architects and Phidias is responsible for the sculpture. Sophocles, Greek dramatist (496?–406 B.C.). Hippocrates, Greek "Father of Medicine" (born 460 B.C.). Xerxes I, king of Persia (rules 485–465 B.C.).

400–300 B.C. Pentateuch—first five books of the Old Testament evolve in final form. Philip of Macedon, who believed himself to be a descendant of the Greek people, assassinated (336 B.C.) after subduing the Greek city-states; succeeded by son, Alexander the Great (356–323 B.C.), who destroys Thebes (335 B.C.), conquers Tyre and Jerusalem (332 B.C.), occupies Babylon (330 B.C.), invades India, and dies in Babylon. His empire is divided among his generals; one of them, Seleucis I, establishes Middle East empire with capitals at Antioch (Syria) and Seleucia (in Iraq). Trial and execution of Greek philosopher Socrates (399 B.C.). Dialogues recorded by his student, Plato (c. 427–348 or 347 B.C.). Euclid's work on geometry (323 B.C.). Aristotle, Greek philosopher (384–322 B.C.). Demosthenes, Greek orator (384–322 B.C.). Praxiteles, Greek sculptor (400–330 B.C.).

300–251 B.C. First Punic War (264–241 B.C.): Rome defeats the Carthaginians and begins its domination of the Mediterranean. Temple of the Sun at Teotihuacán, Mexico (c. 300 B.C.). Invention of Mayan calendar in Yucatán—more exact than older calendars. First Roman gladiatorial games (264 B.C.). Archimedes, Greek mathematician (287–212 B.C.).

250–201 B.C. Second Punic War (219–201 B.C.): Hannibal, Carthaginian general (246–142 B.C.), crosses the Alps (218 B.C.), reaches gates of Rome (211 B.C.), retreats, and is defeated by Scipio Africanus at Zama (202 B.C.). Great Wall of China built (c. 215 B.C.).

200–151 B.C. Romans defeat Seleucid King Antiochus III at Thermopylae (191 B.C.)—beginning of Roman world domination. Maccabean revolt against Seleucids (167 B.C.).

150–101 B.C. Third Punic War (149–146 B.C.): Rome destroys Carthage, killing 450,000 and enslaving the remaining 50,000 inhabitants. Roman armies conquer Macedonia, Greece, Anatolia, Balearic Islands, and southern France. Venus de Milo (c. 140 B.C.). Cicero, Roman orator (106–43 B.C.).

100–51 B.C. Julius Caesar (100–44 B.C.) invades Britain (55 B.C.) and conquers Gaul (France) (c. 50 B.C.). Spartacus leads slave revolt against Rome (71 B.C.). Romans conquer Seleucid empire. Roman general Pompey conquers Jerusalem (63 B.C.). Cleopatra on Egyptian throne (51–31 B.C.). Chinese develop use of paper (c. 100 B.C.). Virgil, Roman poet (70–19 B.C.). Horace, Roman poet (65–8 B.C.).

50–1 B.C. Caesar crosses Rubicon to fight Pompey (50 B.C.). Herod made Roman governor of Judea (37 B.C.). Caesar murdered (44 B.C.). Caesar's nephew, Octavian, defeats Mark Antony and Cleopatra at Battle of Actium (31 B.C.), and establishes Roman empire as Emperor Augustus; rules 27 B.C.–A.D. 14. Pantheon built for the first time under Agrippa, 27 B.C. Ovid, Roman poet (43 B.C.–A.D. 18).

A.D.

Christian Era (A.D.) or the Common Era (C.E.)

1–49 Birth of Jesus Christ (variously given from 4 B.C. to A.D. 7). After Augustus, Tiberius becomes emperor (dies, A.D. 37), succeeded by Caligula (assassinated, A.D. 41), who is followed by Claudius. Crucifixion of Jesus (probably A.D. 30). Han dynasty in China founded by Emperor Kuang Wu Ti. Buddhism introduced to China.

50–99 Claudius poisoned (A.D. 54), succeeded by Nero (commits suicide, A.D. 68). Missionary journeys of Paul the Apostle (A.D. 34–60). Jews revolt against Rome; Jerusalem destroyed (A.D. 70). Roman persecutions of Christians begin (A.D. 64). Colosseum built in Rome (A.D. 71–80). Trajan (rules A.D. 98–116); Roman empire extends to Mesopotamia, Arabia, Balkans. First Gospels of St. Mark, St. John, St. Matthew.

100–149 Hadrian rules Rome (A.D. 117–138); codifies Roman law, rebuilds Pantheon, establishes postal system, builds wall between England and Scotland. Jews revolt under Bar Kokhba (A.D. 122–135); final Diaspora (dispersion) of Jews begins.

150–199 Marcus Aurelius rules Rome (A.D. 161–180). Oldest Mayan temples in Central America (c. A.D. 200).

200–249 Goths invade Asia Minor (c. A.D. 220). Roman persecutions of Christians increase. Persian (Sassanid) empire re-established. End of Chinese Han dynasty.

Mayan Pyramid at Chichén Itzá

250–299 Increasing invasions of the Roman empire by Franks and Goths. Buddhism spreads in China. Classic period of Mayan civilization (A.D. 250–900); develop hieroglyphic writing, advances in art, architecture, science.

300–349 Constantine the Great (rules A.D. 312–337) reunites eastern and western Roman empires, with new capital (Constantinople) on site of Byzantium (A.D. 330); issues Edict of Milan legalizing Christianity (A.D. 313); becomes a Christian on his deathbed (A.D. 337). Council of Nicaea (A.D. 325) defines orthodox Christian doctrine. First Gupta dynasty in India (c. A.D. 320).

350–399 Huns (Mongols) invade Europe (c. A.D. 360). Theodosius the Great (rules A.D. 392–395)—last emperor of a united Roman empire. Roman empire permanently divided in A.D. 395: western empire ruled from Rome; eastern empire ruled from Constantinople.

400–449 Western Roman empire disintegrates under weak emperors. Alaric, king of the Visigoths, sacks Rome (A.D. 410). Attila, Hun chieftain, attacks Roman provinces (A.D. 433). St. Patrick returns to Ireland (A.D. 432) and brings Christianity to the island. St. Augustine's *City of God* (A.D. 411).

Celtic Cross

450–499 Vandals destroy Rome (A.D. 455). Western Roman empire ends as Odoacer, German chieftain, overthrows last Roman emperor, Romulus Augustulus, and becomes king of Italy (A.D. 476). Ostrogothic kingdom of Italy established by Theodoric the Great (A.D. 493). Clovis, ruler of the Franks, is converted to Christianity (A.D. 496). First schism between western and eastern churches (A.D. 484).

500–549 Eastern and western churches reconciled (519). Justinian I, the Great (483–565), becomes Byzantine emperor (527), issues his first code of civil laws (529), conquers North Africa, Italy, and part of Spain. Plague spreads through Europe (542 *et seq.*). Arthur, semi-legendary king of the Britons (killed, c. 537). Boëthius, Roman scholar (executed, 524).

550–599 Beginnings of European silk industry after Justinian's missionaries smuggle silkworms out of China (553). Mohammed, Muhammad founder of Islam (570–632). Buddhism in Japan (c. 560). St. Augustine of Canterbury brings Christianity to Britain (597). After killing about half the population, plague in Europe subsides (594).

Japanese Pagoda

600–649 Mohammed flees from Mecca to Medina (the *Hegira*); first year of the Muslim calendar (622). Muslim empire grows (634). Arabs conquer Jerusalem (637), destroy Alexandrian library (641), conquer Persians (641). Fatima, Mohammed's daughter (606–632).

650–699 Arabs attack North Africa (670), destroy Carthage (697). Venerable Bede, English monk (672–735).

700–749 Arab empire extends from Lisbon to China (by 716). Charles Martel, Frankish leader, defeats Arabs at Tours/Poitiers, halting Arab advance in Europe (732). Charlemagne (742–814). Introduction of pagodas in Japan from China.

750–799 Charlemagne becomes king of the Franks (771). Caliph Harun al-Rashid rules Arab empire (786–809); the "golden age" of Arab culture. Vikings begin attacks on Britain (790), land in Ireland (795). City of Machu Picchu flourishes in Peru.

Viking Ship (c. 900)

800–849 Charlemagne crowned first Holy Roman Emperor in Rome (800). Charlemagne dies (814), succeeded by his son, Louis the Pious, who divides France among his sons (817). Arabs conquer Crete, Sicily, and Sardinia (826–827).

850–899 Norsemen attack as far south as the Mediterranean but are thwarted (859), discover Iceland (861). Alfred the Great becomes king of Britain (871), defeats Danish invaders (878). Russian nation founded by Vikings under Prince Rurik, establishing capital at Novgorod (855–879).

900–949 Beginning of Mayan Post-Classical period (900–1519). Vikings discover Greenland (c. 900). Arab Spain under Abd ar-Rahman III becomes center of learning (912–961). Otto I becomes King of Germany (936).

950–999 Mieczyslaw I becomes first ruler of Poland (960). Eric the Red establishes first Viking colony in Greenland (982). Hugh Capet elected King of France in 987; Capetian dynasty to rule until 1328. Musical notation systematized (c.

**Mesa Verde
Cliff Dwellings
(c. 1000–1300)**

**Cathedral and Tower
at Pisa**

Chartres Cathedral

**King John
(1167–1216)**

990). Vikings and Danes attack Britain (988–999). Otto I crowned Holy Roman Emperor by Pope John XII (962).

1000–1099 (A.D.)

c. 1000–1300 Classic Pueblo period of Anasazi culture; cliff dwellings.

c. 1000 Hungary and Scandinavia converted to Christianity. Viking raider Leif Eriksson discovers North America, calls it Vinland. *Beowulf*, Old English epic.

c. 1008 Murasaki Shikibu finishes *The Tale of Genji*, the world's first novel.

1009 Muslims destroy Holy Sepulchre in Jerusalem.

1013 Danes control England. Canute takes throne (1016), conquers Norway (1028), dies (1035); kingdom divided among his sons: Harold Harefoot (England), Sweyn (Norway), Hardecanute (Denmark).

1040 Macbeth murders Duncan, king of Scotland.

1053 Robert Guiscard, Norman invader, establishes kingdom in Italy, conquers Sicily (1072).

1054 Final separation between Eastern (Orthodox) and Western (Roman) churches.

1055 Seljuk Turks, Asian nomads, move west, capture Baghdad, Armenia (1064), Syria, and Palestine (1075).

1066 William of Normandy invades England, defeats last Saxon king, Harold II, at Battle of Hastings, crowned William I of England ("the Conqueror").

1068 Construction on the cathedral in Pisa, Italy, begins.

1073 Emergence of strong papacy when Gregory VII is elected. Conflict with English and French kings and German emperors will continue throughout medieval period.

1095 At Council of Clermont, Pope Urban II calls for a holy war to wrest control of Jerusalem from Muslims, which launches the First Crusade (1096), one of at least 8 European military campaigns between 1095 and 1291 to regain the Holy Land.

1100–1199 (A.D.)

1100–1300 Construction of Cathedral at Chartres, France.

1144 Second Crusade begins.

c. 1150 Angkor Wat is completed.

1150–1167 Universities of Paris and Oxford founded in France and England.

1162 Thomas á Becket named Archbishop of Canterbury, murdered by Henry II's men (1170). Troubadours (wandering minstrels) glorify romantic concepts of feudalism.

1169 Ibn-Rushd begins translating Aristotle's works.

1189 Richard I ("the Lionhearted") succeeds Henry II in England, killed in France (1199), succeeded by King John. Third Crusade.

1200–1299 (A.D.)

1200–1204 Fourth Crusade.

1211 Genghis Khan invades China, captures Peking (1214), conquers Persia (1218), invades Russia (1223), dies (1227).

1212 Children's Crusade.

1215 King John forced by barons to sign Magna Carta at Runneymede, limiting royal power.

1217 Fifth Crusade.

1228 Sixth Crusade.

THE CRUSADES (1096–1291)

In 1095 at Council of Clermont, Pope Urban II calls for war to rescue Holy Land from Muslim infidels. The *First Crusade* (1096) is assembled in response to Emperor Alexius I. The Christians capture Antioch (1098) and Jerusalem (1099). They establish the Crusader States, ruled by Europeans. It is the only successful crusade. The *Second Crusade* begins after the Seljuk Turks recapture Edessa, one of the Crusader States, in 1144. It is led by King Louis VIII of France and Holy Roman Emperor Conrad III. Crusaders perish in Asia Minor (1147).

Saladin controls Egypt (1171), unites Islam in holy war *(jihad)* against Christians, recaptures Jerusalem

(1187). *Third Crusade* (1189) under kings of France, England, and Germany fails to reduce Saladin's power. *Fourth Crusade* (1200–1204)—French knights sack Greek Christian Constantinople, establish Latin empire in Byzantium. Greeks reestablish Orthodox faith (1262).

Children's Crusade (1212)—only one of 30,000 French children and about 200 of 20,000 German children survive to return home. Other Crusades—*Fifth*, against Egypt (1217), *Sixth* (1228), *Seventh* (1248), *Eighth* (1270). Mamelukes conquer Acre; end of the Crusades (1291).

1231 The Inquisition begins as Pope Gregory IX assigns Dominicans responsibility for combating heresy. Torture used (1252). Ferdinand and Isabella establish Spanish Inquisition (1478). Tourquemada, Grand Inquisitor, forces conversion or expulsion of Spanish Jews (1492). Forced conversion of Moors (1499). Inquisition in Portugal (1531). First Protestants burned at the stake in Spain (1543). Spanish Inquisition abolished (1834).

1241 Mongols defeat Germans in Silesia, invade Poland and Hungary, withdraw from Europe after Ughetai, Mongol leader, dies.

1248 Seventh Crusade.

1251 Kublai Khan governs China, becomes ruler of Mongols (1259), establishes Yuan dynasty in China (1280), invades Burma (1287), dies (1294).

1260 Chartres cathedral consecrated.

1270 Eighth Crusade.

1271 Marco Polo of Venice travels to China, in court of Kublai Khan (1275–1292), returns to Genoa (1295) and writes *Travels*.

1273 Thomas Aquinas stops work on *Summa Theologica*, the basis of all Catholic theological teaching; never completes it.

1295 English King Edward I summons the Model Parliament.

Thomas Aquinas
(1225–1274)

1300–1399 (A.D.)

1312–1337 Mali Empire reaches its height in Africa under King Mansa Musa.

c. 1325 The beginning of the Renaissance in Italy: writers Dante, Petrarch, Boccaccio; painter Giotto. Development of *Noh* drama in Japan. Aztecs establish Tenochtitlán on site of modern Mexico City. Peak of Muslim culture in Spain. Small cannon in use.

1337–1453 Hundred Years' War—English and French kings fight for control of France.

1347–1351 At least 25 million people die in Europe's "Black Death" (bubonic plague).

1368 Ming Dynasty begins in China.

1376–1382 John Wycliffe, pre-Reformation religious reformer, and followers translate Latin Bible into English.

1378 The Great Schism (to 1417)—rival popes in Rome and Avignon, France, fight for control of Roman Catholic Church.

c. 1387 Chaucer's *Canterbury Tales*.

1399 Tamerlane begins last great conquest.

The Duomo in
Florence

1400–1499 (A.D.)

1407 Casa di San Giorgio, one of the first public banks, founded in Genoa.

1415 Henry V defeats French at Agincourt. Jan Hus, Bohemian preacher and follower of Wycliffe, burned at stake in Constance as heretic.

1418–1460 Portugal's Prince Henry the Navigator sponsors exploration of Africa's coast.

1420 Brunelleschi begins work on the Duomo in Florence.

1428 Joan of Arc leads French against English, captured by Burgundians (1430) and turned over to the English, burned at the stake as a witch after ecclesiastical trial (1431).

1438 Incas rule in Peru.

1450 Florence becomes center of Renaissance arts and learning under the Medicis.

1453 Turks conquer Constantinople, end of the Byzantine empire, beginning of the Ottoman empire.

1455 The Wars of the Roses, civil wars between rival noble factions, begin in England (to 1485). Having invented printing with movable type at Mainz, Germany, Johann Gutenberg completes first Bible.

1462 Ivan the Great rules Russia until 1505 as first czar; ends payment of tribute to Mongols.

1492 Moors conquered in Spain by troops of Ferdinand and Isabella. Columbus becomes first European to encounter Caribbean islands, returns to Spain (1493). Second voyage to Dominica, Jamaica, Puerto Rico (1493–1496). Third voyage to Orinoco (1498). Fourth voyage to Honduras and Panama (1502–1504).

1497 Vasco da Gama sails around Africa and discovers sea route to India (1498). Establishes Portuguese colony in India (1502). John Cabot, employed by England, reaches and explores Canadian coast. Michelangelo's *Bacchus* sculpture.

Joan of Arc
(1412–1431)

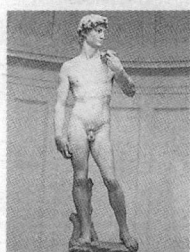

Michelangelo's David
(1504)

1500–1599 (A.D.)

1501 First black slaves in America brought to Spanish colony of Santo Domingo.

c. 1503 Leonardo da Vinci paints the *Mona Lisa*. Michelangelo sculpts the *David* (1504).

Balboa
(1475–1517)

**Martin Luther
(1483–1546)**

**Henry VIII
(1491–1547)**

**Queen Elizabeth I
(1533–1603)**

**William Shakespeare
(1564–1616)**

**Rembrandt van Rijn
(1606–1669)**

1506 St. Peter's Church started in Rome; designed and decorated by such artists and architects as Bramante, Michelangelo, da Vinci, Raphael, and Bernini before its completion in 1626.

1509 Henry VIII ascends English throne. Michelangelo paints the ceiling of the Sistine Chapel.

1513 Balboa becomes the first European to encounter the Pacific Ocean. Machiavelli's *The Prince.*

1517 Turks conquer Egypt, control Arabia. Martin Luther posts his 95 theses denouncing church abuses on church door in Wittenberg—start of the Reformation in Germany.

1519 Ulrich Zwingli begins Reformation in Switzerland. Hernando Cortes conquers Mexico for Spain. Charles I of Spain is chosen Holy Roman Emperor Charles V. Portuguese explorer Ferdinand Magellan sets out to circumnavigate the globe.

1520 Luther excommunicated by Pope Leo X. Suleiman I ("the Magnificent") becomes Sultan of Turkey, invades Hungary (1521), Rhodes (1522), attacks Austria (1529), annexes Hungary (1541), Tripoli (1551), makes peace with Persia (1553), destroys Spanish fleet (1560), dies (1566). Magellan reaches the Pacific, is killed by Philippine natives (1521). One of his ships under Juan Sebastián del Cano continues around the world, reaches Spain (1522).

1524 Verrazano, sailing under the French flag, explores the New England coast and New York Bay.

1527 Troops of the Holy Roman Empire attack Rome, imprison Pope Clement VII—the end of the Italian Renaissance. Castiglione writes *The Courtier.* The Medici family expelled from Florence.

1532 Pizarro marches from Panama to Peru, kills the Inca chieftain, Atahualpa, of Peru (1533). Machiavelli's *The Prince* published posthumously.

1535 Reformation begins as Henry VIII makes himself head of English Church after being excommunicated by Pope. Sir Thomas More executed as traitor for refusal to acknowledge king's religious authority. Jacques Cartier sails up the St. Lawrence River, basis of French claims to Canada.

1536 Henry VIII executes second wife, Anne Boleyn. John Calvin establishes Reformed and Presbyterian form of Protestantism in Switzerland, writes *Institutes of the Christian Religion.* Danish and Norwegian Reformations. Michelangelo's *Last Judgment.*

1541 John Knox leads Reformation in Scotland, establishes Presbyterian church there (1560).

1543 Publication of *On the Revolution of Heavenly Bodies* by Polish scholar Nicolaus Copernicus—giving his theory that the earth revolves around the sun.

1545 Council of Trent to meet intermittently until 1563 to define Catholic dogma and doctrine, reiterate papal authority.

1547 Ivan IV ("the Terrible") crowned as czar of Russia, begins conquest of Astrakhan and Kazan (1552), battles nobles (boyars) for power (1564), kills his son (1580), dies, and is succeeded by his weak and feeble-minded son, Fyodor I.

1553 Roman Catholicism restored in England by Queen Mary I.

1556 Akbar the Great becomes Mogul emperor of India, conquers Afghanistan (1581), continues wars of conquest (until 1605).

1558 Queen Elizabeth I ascends the throne (rules to 1603). Restores Protestantism, establishes state Church of England (Anglicanism). Renaissance will reach height in England—Shakespeare, Marlowe, Spenser.

1561 Persecution of Huguenots in France stopped by Edict of Orleans. French religious wars begin again with massacre of Huguenots at Vassy. St. Bartholomew's Day Massacre—thousands of Huguenots murdered (1572). Amnesty granted (1573). Persecution continues periodically until Edict of Nantes (1598) gives Huguenots religious freedom (until 1685).

1568 Protestant Netherlands revolts against Catholic Spain; independence will be acknowledged by Spain in 1648. High point of Dutch Renaissance—painters Rubens, Van Dyck, Hals, and Rembrandt.

1570 Japan permits visits of foreign ships. Queen Elizabeth I excommunicated by Pope. Turks attack Cyprus and war on Venice. Turkish fleet defeated at Battle of Lepanto by Spanish and Italian fleets (1571). Peace of Constantinople (1572) ends Turkish attacks on Europe.

1580 Francis Drake returns to England after circumnavigating the globe; knighted by Queen Elizabeth I (1581). Montaigne's *Essays* published.

1582 Pope Gregory XIII implements the Gregorian calendar.

1583 William of Orange rules the Netherlands; assassinated on orders of Philip II of Spain (1584).

1587 Mary, Queen of Scots, executed for treason by order of Queen Elizabeth I. Monteverdi's *First Book of Madrigals.*

1588 Defeat of the Spanish Armada by English. Henry, King of Navarre and Protestant leader, recognized as Henry IV, first Bourbon king of France. Converts to Roman Catholicism in 1593 in attempt to end religious wars.

1590 Henry IV enters Paris, wars on Spain (1595), marries Marie de Medici (1600), assassinated (1610). Spenser's *The Faerie Queen.* El Greco's *St. Jerome.* Galileo's experiments with falling objects.

1598 Boris Godunov becomes Russian czar. Tycho Brahe describes his astronomical experiments.

Catherine de Medici
(1519–1589)

1600–1699 (A.D.)

1600 Giordano Bruno burned as a heretic. English East India Company established.

1603 Ieyasu rules Japan, moves capital to Edo (Tokyo). Shakespeare's *Hamlet.*

1605 Cervantes's *Don Quixote de la Mancha,* the first modern novel.

1607 Jamestown, Virginia, established—first permanent English colony on American mainland. Pocahontas, daughter of Chief Powhatan, saves life of John Smith.

1609 Samuel de Champlain establishes French colony of Quebec. The *Relation,* the first newspaper, debuts in Germany.

1610 Galileo sees the moons of Jupiter through his telescope.

1611 Gustavus Adolphus elected King of Sweden. King James Version of the Bible published in England. Rubens paints his *Descent from the Cross.*

1614 John Napier discovers logarithms.

1618 Start of the Thirty Years' War—Protestants revolt against Catholic oppression; Denmark, Sweden, and France will invade Germany in later phases of war. Kepler proposes last of three laws of planetary motion.

1619 A Dutch ship brings the first African slaves to British North America.

1620 Pilgrims, after three-month voyage in *Mayflower,* land at Plymouth Rock. Francis Bacon's *Novum Organum.*

1623 New Netherland founded by Dutch West India Company.

1630 Massachusetts Bay Colony.

1632 Maryland founded by Lord Baltimore.

1633 Inquisition forces Galileo (astronomer) to recant his belief in Copernican theory.

1642 English Civil War. Cavaliers, supporters of Charles I, against Roundheads, parliamentary forces. Oliver Cromwell defeats Royalists (1646). Parliament demands reforms. Charles I offers concessions, brought to trial (1648), beheaded (1649). Cromwell becomes Lord Protector (1653). Rembrandt paints his *Night Watch.*

1643 Taj Mahal completed.

1644 End of Ming Dynasty in China—Manchus come to power. Descartes's *Principles of Philosophy.*

1648 End of the Thirty Years' War. German population about half of what it was in 1618 because of war and pestilence.

1658 Cromwell dies; son Richard resigns and Puritan government collapses.

1660 English Parliament calls for the restoration of the monarchy; invites Charles II to return from France.

1661 Charles II is crowned King of England. Louis XIV begins personal rule as absolute monarch; starts to build Versailles.

1664 British take New Amsterdam from the Dutch. English limit "Nonconformity" with reestablished Anglican Church. Isaac Newton's experiments with gravity.

1665 Great Plague in London kills 75,000.

1666 Great Fire of London. Molière's *Misanthrope.*

1667 Milton's *Paradise Lost,* widely considered the greatest epic poem in English.

1682 Pennsylvania founded by William Penn.

1683 War of European powers against the Turks (to 1699). Vienna withstands three-month Turkish siege; high point of Turkish advance in Europe.

1684 Gottfried Wilhelm Leibniz's calculus published.

1685 James II succeeds Charles II in England, calls for freedom of conscience (1687). Protestants fear restoration of Catholicism and demand "Glorious Revolution." William of Orange invited to England and James II escapes

Galileo
(1564–1642)

Pocahontas
(c. 1595–1617)

Taj Mahal

John Milton
(1608–1674)

to France (1688). William III and his wife, Mary, crowned. In France, Edict of Nantes of 1598, granting freedom of worship to Huguenots, is revoked by Louis XIV; thousands of Protestants flee.

1689 Peter the Great becomes Czar of Russia—attempts to westernize nation and build Russia as a military power. Defeats Charles XII of Sweden at Poltava (1709). Beginning of the French and Indian Wars (to 1763), campaigns in America linked to a series of wars between France and England for domination of Europe.

1690 William III of England defeats former king James II and Irish rebels at Battle of the Boyne in Ireland. John Locke's *Human Understanding*.

Sir Isaac Newton
(1642–1727)

1700–1799 (A.D.)

1701 War of the Spanish Succession begins—the last of Louis XIV's wars for domination of the continent. The Peace of Utrecht (1714) will end the conflict and mark the rise of the British Empire. Called Queen Anne's War in America, it ends with the British taking New Foundland, Acadia, and Hudson's Bay Territory from France, and Gibraltar and Minorca from Spain.

1704 Deerfield (Mass.) Massacre of English colonists by French and Indians. Bach's first cantata. Jonathan Swift's *Tale of a Tub*. *Boston News Letter*—first newspaper in America.

1707 United Kingdom of Great Britain formed—England, Wales, and Scotland joined by parliamentary Act of Union.

1729 Bach's *St. Matthew Passion*. Isaac Newton's *Principia* translated from Latin into English.

1732 Benjamin Franklin begins publishing *Poor Richard's Almanack*. James Oglethorpe and others found Georgia.

Frederick the Great
(1712–1786)

1735 John Peter Zenger, New York editor, acquitted of libel in New York, establishing press freedom.

1740 Capt. Vitus Bering, Dane employed by Russia, discovers Alaska. Frederick II "the Great" crowned king of Prussia.

1746 British defeat Scots under Stuart Pretender Prince Charles at Culloden Moor. Last battle fought on British soil.

1751 Publication of the *Encyclopédie* begins in France, the "bible" of the Enlightenment.

1755 Samuel Johnson's *Dictionary* first published. Great earthquake in Lisbon, Portugal—over 60,000 die. U.S. postal service established.

Samuel Johnson
(1709–1784)

1756 Seven Years' War (French and Indian Wars in America) (to 1763), in which Britain and Prussia defeat France, Spain, Austria, and Russia. France loses North American colonies; Spain cedes Florida to Britain in exchange for Cuba. In India, over 100 British prisoners die in "Black Hole of Calcutta."

1757 Beginning of British Empire in India as Robert Clive, British commander, defeats Nawab of Bengal at Plassey.

1759 British capture Quebec from French. Voltaire's *Candide*. Haydn's *Symphony No. 1*.

THE REVOLUTIONARY WAR

Conflicts increase between colonists and Britain on western frontier because of royal edict limiting western expansion (1763) and regulation of colonial trade and increased taxation of colonies (Writs of Assistance allow search for illegal shipments, 1761; Sugar Act, 1764; Currency Act, 1764; Stamp Act, 1765; Quartering Act, 1765; Duty Act, 1767). Boston Massacre (1770). Lord North attempts conciliation (1770). Boston Tea Party (1773), followed by punitive measures passed by Parliament—the "Intolerable Acts."

First Continental Congress (1774) sends "Declaration of Rights and Grievances" to King George III, urges colonies to form Continental Association. Paul Revere's ride and Lexington and Concord battle between Massachusetts Minutemen and British (1775).

Second Continental Congress (1775), while sending "olive branch" to the king, begins to raise army, appoints Washington commander-in-chief, and seeks alliance with France. Some colonial legislatures urge their delegates to vote for independence. Declaration of Independence **(July 4, 1776).**

Major Battles of the Revolutionary War: *Long Island:* Howe defeats Putnam's division of Washington's Army in Brooklyn Heights, but Americans escape across East River (1776). *Trenton and Princeton:* Washington defeats Hessians at Trenton, British at Princeton. Winters at Morristown (1776–1777). Howe winters in Philadelphia; Washington at Valley Forge (1777–1778). Burgoyne surrenders British army to General Gates at *Saratoga* (1777).

France recognizes American independence (1778). The War moves south: Savannah captured by British (1778); Charleston occupied (1780); Americans fight successful guerrilla actions under Marion, Pickens, and Sumter. In the West, George Rogers Clark attacks Forts Kaskaskia and Vincennes (1778–1779), defeating British in the region. Cornwallis surrenders at *Yorktown,* Virginia **(Oct. 19, 1781).** By 1782, Britain is eager for peace because of conflicts with European nations. *Peace of Paris* (1783): Britain recognizes American independence.

1762 Catherine II ("the Great") becomes czarina of Russia. Jean Jacques Rousseau's *Social Contract.* Mozart tours Europe as six-year-old prodigy.

1765 James Watt invents the steam engine. Britain imposes the Stamp Act on the American colonists.

1769 Sir William Arkwright patents a spinning machine—an early step in the Industrial Revolution.

1770 The Boston Massacre.

1772 Joseph Priestley and Daniel Rutherford independently discover nitrogen. Partition of Poland—in 1772, 1793, and 1795, Austria, Prussia, and Russia divide land and people of Poland, end its independence.

1773 The Boston Tea Party.

1774 First Continental Congress drafts "Declaration of Rights and Grievances."

1775 The American Revolution begins with battle of Lexington and Concord. Second Continental Congress. Priestley discovers hydrochloric and sulfuric acids.

**Benjamin Franklin
(1706–1790)**

1776 Declaration of Independence. Gen. George Washington crosses the Delaware Christmas night. Adam Smith's *Wealth of Nations.* Edward Gibbon's *Decline and Fall of the Roman Empire.* Thomas Paine's *Common Sense.* Fragonard's *Washerwoman.* Mozart's *Haffner Serenade.*

1778 Capt. James Cook discovers Hawaii. Franz Mesmer uses hypnotism.

1781 Immanuel Kant's *Critique of Pure Reason.* Herschel discovers Uranus.

1783 Revolutionary War ends with Treaty of Paris. William Blake's poems. Beethoven's first printed works.

1784 Crimea annexed by Russia. John Wesley's *Deed of Declaration,* the basic work of Methodism.

1785 Russians settle Aleutian Islands.

1787 The Constitution of the United States signed. Lavoisier's work on chemical nomenclature. Mozart's *Don Giovanni.*

**George Washington
(1732–1799)**

1788 French *Parlement* presents grievances to Louis XVI who agrees to convening of Estates-General in 1789—not called since 1613. Goethe's *Egmont.* Laplace's *Laws of the Planetary System.*

1789 French Revolution begins with the storming of the Bastille. In U.S., Washington elected president with all 69 votes of the Electoral College, takes oath of office in New York City. Vice President: John Adams. Secretary of State: Thomas Jefferson. Secretary of Treasury: Alexander Hamilton.

1790 H.M.S. *Bounty* mutineers settle on Pitcairn Island. Aloisio Galvani experiments on electrical stimulation of the muscles. Philadelphia temporary capital of U.S. as Congress votes to establish new capital on Potomac. U.S. population about 3,929,000, including 698,000 slaves. Lavoisier formulates *Table of 31 chemical elements.*

**Alexander Hamilton
(1755–1804)**

1791 U.S. Bill of Rights ratified. Boswell's *Life of Johnson.*

1792 Mary Wollstonecraft's *Vindication of the Rights of Woman.*

1793 Louis XVI and Marie Antoinette executed. Reign of Terror begins in France. Eli Whitney invents the cotton gin, spurring the growth of the cotton industry and helping to institutionalize slavery in the U.S. South.

1794 Kosciusko's uprising in Poland quelled by the Russians. In U.S., Whiskey Rebellion in Pennsylvania as farmers object to liquor taxes. Reign of Terror ends with execution of Robespierre.

1796 Napoléon Bonaparte, French general, defeats Austrians. In the U.S., Washington's Farewell Address (**Sept. 17**); John Adams elected president; Thomas Jefferson, vice president. Edward Jenner introduces smallpox vaccination.

1798 Napoleon extends French conquests to Rome and Egypt. U.S. Navy Department established.

**Ludwig van Beethoven
(1770–1827)**

FRENCH REVOLUTION (1789–1799)

Revolution begins when Third Estate (Commons) delegates swear not to disband until France has a constitution. Paris mob storms Bastille, symbol of royal power (**July 14, 1789**). National Assembly votes for Constitution, Declaration of the Rights of Man, a limited monarchy, and other reforms (1789–1790). Legislative Assembly elected, Revolutionary Commune formed, and French Republic proclaimed (1792). War of the First Coalition—Austria, Prussia, Britain, Netherlands, and Spain fight to restore French nobility (1792–

1797). Start of series of wars between France and European powers that will last, almost without interruption, for 23 years. Louis XVI and Marie Antoinette executed. Committee of Public Safety begins Reign of Terror as political control measure. Interfactional rivalry leads to mass killings. Danton and Robespierre executed. Third French Constitution sets up Directory government (1795). Napoleon abolishes the Directory, establishes the Consulate, becomes the First Consul of France (1799).

Napoléon Bonaparte
(1769–1821)

Edgar Allan Poe
(1809–1849)

Richard Wagner
(1813–1883)

Harriet Beecher
Stowe
(1811–1896)

Walt Whitman
(1819–1892)

1799 Rosetta Stone discovered in Egypt. Napoleon leads coup that overthrows Directory, establishes the Consulate, becomes First Consul—one of three who rule France together.

1800–1899 (A.D.)

1800 Napoleon conquers Italy, firmly establishes himself as First Consul in France. In the U.S., federal government moves to Washington, D.C. Robert Owen's social reforms in England. William Herschel discovers infrared rays. Alessandro Volta produces electricity.

1801 Austria makes temporary peace with France. United Kingdom of Great Britain and Ireland established with one monarch and one parliament; Catholics excluded from voting.

1803 U.S. negotiates Louisiana Purchase from France: for $15 million, U.S. doubles its domain, increasing its territory by 827,000 sq. mi. (2,144,500 sq km), from Mississippi River to Rockies and from Gulf of Mexico to British North America.

1804 Haiti declares independence from France; first black nation to gain freedom from European colonial rule. Napoleon transforms the Consulate of France into an empire, proclaims himself emperor of France, systematizes French law under *Code Napoleon.* In the U.S., Alexander Hamilton is mortally wounded in duel with Aaron Burr. Lewis and Clark expedition begins exploration of what is now northwest U.S.

1805 Lord Nelson defeats the French-Spanish fleets in the Battle of Trafalgar. Napoleon victorious over Austrian and Russian forces at the Battle of Austerlitz.

1807 Robert Fulton makes first successful steamboat trip on *Clermont* between New York City and Albany.

1808 French armies occupy Rome and Spain, extending Napoleon's empire. Britain begins aiding Spanish guerrillas against Napoleon in Peninsular War. In the U.S., Congress bars importation of slaves. Beethoven's *Fifth* and *Sixth Symphonies* performed.

1812 Napoleon's Grand Army invades Russia in June. Forced to retreat in winter, most of Napoleon's 600,000 men are lost. In the U.S., war with Britain declared over freedom of the seas for U.S. vessels (War of 1812). USS *Constitution* sinks British frigate.

1814 French defeated by allies (Britain, Austria, Russia, Prussia, Sweden, and Portugal) in War of Liberation. Napoleon exiled to Elba, off Italian coast. Bourbon king Louis XVIII takes French throne. George Stephenson builds first practical steam locomotive.

1815 Napoleon returns: "Hundred Days" begin. Napoleon defeated by Wellington at Waterloo, banished again to St. Helena in South Atlantic. Congress of Vienna: victorious allies change the map of Europe. War of 1812 ends with Treaty of Ghent.

1819 Simón Bolívar liberates New Granada (now Colombia, Venezuela, and Ecuador) as Spain loses hold on South American countries; named president of Colombia.

1820 Missouri Compromise—Missouri admitted as slave state but slavery barred in rest of Louisiana Purchase north of 36°30′ N.

1821 Guatemala, Panama, and Santo Domingo proclaim independence from Spain.

1822 Greeks proclaim a republic and independence from Turkey. Turks invade Greece. Russia declares war on Turkey (1828). Greece also aided by France and Britain. War ends and Turks recognize Greek independence (1829). Brazil becomes independent of Portugal. Schubert's *Eighth Symphony* ("The Unfinished").

1823 U.S. Monroe Doctrine warns European nations not to interfere in Western Hemisphere.

1824 Mexico becomes a republic, three years after declaring independence from Spain. Bolívar liberates Peru, becomes its president. Beethoven's *Ninth Symphony.*

1825 First passenger-carrying railroad in England.

1826 Joseph-Nicéphore Niepce takes the world's first photograph.

WAR OF 1812

British interference with American trade, impressment of American seamen, and "War Hawks" drive for western expansion lead to war. American attacks on Canada foiled; U.S. Commodore Perry wins battle of Lake Erie (1813). British capture and burn Washington (1814) but fail to take Fort McHenry at Baltimore. Andrew Jackson repulses assault on New Orleans but Treaty of Ghent ends war (1815). War settles little but strengthens U.S. as independent nation.

1830 French invade Algeria. Louis Philippe becomes "Citizen King" as revolution forces Charles X to abdicate. Mormon church formed in U.S. by Joseph Smith.

1831 Polish revolt against Russia fails. Belgium separates from the Netherlands. In U.S., Nat Turner leads unsuccessful slave rebellion.

1833 Slavery abolished in British Empire.

1834 Charles Babbage invents "analytical engine," precursor of computer. McCormick patents reaper.

1836 Boer farmers start "Great Trek"—Natal, Transvaal, and Orange Free State founded in South Africa. Mexican army besieges Texans in Alamo. Entire garrison, including Davy Crockett and Jim Bowie, wiped out. Texans gain independence from Mexico after winning Battle of San Jacinto. Dickens's *Pickwick Papers.*

**Dred Scott
(1795?–1858)**

1837 Victoria becomes queen of Great Britain. Mob kills Elijah P. Lovejoy, Illinois abolitionist publisher.

1839 First Opium War (to 1842) between Britain and China, over importation of drug into China.

1840 Lower and Upper Canada united.

1841 U.S. President Harrison dies (**April 4**) one month after inauguration; John Tyler becomes first vice president to succeed to presidency.

1842 Crawford Long uses first anesthetic (ether).

1843 Wagner's opera *The Flying Dutchman.*

1844 Democratic convention calls for annexation of Texas and acquisition of Oregon ("Fifty-four-forty-or-fight"). Five Chinese ports opened to U.S. ships. Samuel F. B. Morse patents telegraph.

**Charles Darwin
(1809–1882)**

1845 Congress adopts joint resolution for annexation of Texas. Edgar Allan Poe publishes *The Raven and Other Poems.*

1846 U.S. declares war on Mexico. California and New Mexico annexed by U.S. Brigham Young leads Mormons to Great Salt Lake. W. T. Morton uses ether as anesthetic. Sewing machine patented by Elias Howe. Frederick Douglass launches abolitionist newspaper *The North Star.* Failure of potato crop causes famine in Ireland.

1848 Revolt in Paris: Louis Philippe abdicates; Louis Napoleon elected president of French Republic. Revolutions in Vienna, Venice, Berlin, Milan, Rome, and Warsaw. Put down by royal troops in 1848–1849. U.S.-Mexico War ends; Mexico cedes claims to Texas, California, Arizona, New Mexico, Utah, Nevada. U.S. treaty with Britain sets Oregon Territory boundary at 49th parallel. Karl Marx and Friedrich Engels's *Communist Manifesto.* Harriet Tubman escapes from slavery and joins the Underground Railroad. Women's Rights Convention in Seneca Falls, N.Y.

**Frederick Douglass
(1817–1895)**

1849 California gold rush begins.

1850 Henry Clay opens great debate on slavery, warns South against secession.

1851 Herman Melville's *Moby-Dick.*

1852 South African Republic established. Louis Napoleon proclaims himself Napoleon III ("Second Empire"). Harriet Beecher Stowe's *Uncle Tom's Cabin.*

1853 Crimean War begins as Turkey declares war on Russia. Commodore Perry reaches Tokyo.

**Harriet Tubman
(c. 1820–1913)**

1854 Britain and France join Turkey in war on Russia. In U.S., Kansas-Nebraska Act permits local option on slavery; rioting and bloodshed. Japanese allow American trade. Antislavery men in Michigan form Republican Party. Tennyson's *Charge of the Light Brigade.* Thoreau's *Walden.*

1855 Armed clashes in Kansas between pro- and anti-slavery forces. Florence Nightingale nurses wounded in Crimea. Walt Whitman's *Leaves of Grass.*

1856 Flaubert's *Madame Bovary.*

1857 Supreme Court, in Dred Scott decision, rules that a slave is not a citizen. Financial crisis in Europe and U.S. Great Mutiny (Sepoy Rebellion) begins in India. India placed under crown rule as a result.

1858 Pro-slavery constitution rejected in Kansas. Abraham Lincoln makes strong antislavery speech in Springfield, Ill.: "This Government cannot endure permanently half slave and half free." Lincoln-Douglas debates. First trans-Atlantic telegraph cable completed by Cyrus W. Field.

**Samuel Clemens
(Mark Twain)
(1835–1910)**

1859 John Brown raids Harpers Ferry; is captured and hanged. Work begins on Suez Canal. Unification of Italy starts under leadership of Count Cavour, Sardinian premier. Joined by France in war against Austria. Jean-Joseph-Étienne Lenoir builds first practical internal-combustion engine. Edward Fitzgerald's translation of *The Rubaiyat of Omar Khayyam.* Charles Darwin's *Origin of Species.* J. S. Mill's *On Liberty.*

**Abraham Lincoln
(1809–1865)**

**Robert E. Lee
(1807–1870)**

**William Tecumseh
Sherman
(1820–1891)**

1860 South Carolina secedes from the Union.

1861 U.S. Civil War begins as attempts at compromise fail. Mississippi, Florida, Alabama, Georgia, Louisiana, and Texas secede; with South Carolina, they form the Confederate States of America, with Jefferson Davis as president. Virginia, Arkansas, Tennessee, North Carolina secede and join Confederacy. First Battle of Bull Run (Manassas). Congress creates Colorado, Dakota, and Nevada territories; adopts income tax; Lincoln inaugurated. Serfs emancipated in Russia. Pasteur's theory of germs. Independent Kingdom of Italy proclaimed under Sardinian king Victor Emmanuel II.

1862 Several major Civil War battles: Battle of Shiloh, Second Battle of Bull Run (Manassas), Battle of Antietam. Salon des Refusés introduces impressionism.

1863 French capture Mexico City; proclaim Archduke Maximilian of Austria emperor. Battle of Gettysburg.

1864 Gen. Sherman's Atlanta campaign and "march to the sea."

1865 Gen. Lee surrenders to Grant at Appomattox; the Civil War is over. Lincoln fatally shot at Ford's Theater by John Wilkes Booth. Vice President Johnson sworn as successor. Booth caught and dies of gunshot wounds; four conspirators are hanged. Joseph Lister begins antiseptic surgery. Gregor Mendel's *Law of Heredity*. Lewis Carroll's *Alice's Adventures in Wonderland*.

1866 Alfred Nobel invents dynamite (patented in Britain, 1867). Seven Weeks' War: Austria defeated by Prussia and Italy.

1867 Austria-Hungary Dual Monarchy established. French leave Mexico; Maximilian executed. Dominion of Canada established. U.S. buys Alaska from Russia for $7,200,000. South African diamond field discovered. Japan ends 675-year shogun rule. Volume I of Marx's *Das Kapital*. Strauss's *Blue Danube*.

1868 Revolution in Spain; Queen Isabella deposed, flees to France. In U.S., Fourteenth Amendment giving civil rights to blacks is ratified. Georgia under military government after legislature expels blacks.

1869 First U.S. transcontinental rail route completed. James Fisk and Jay Gould's attempt to control gold market causes Black Friday panic. Suez Canal opens. Mendeleev's periodic table of elements.

1870 Franco-Prussian War (to 1871): Napoleon III capitulates at Sedan. Revolt in Paris; Third Republic proclaimed.

1871 France surrenders Alsace-Lorraine to Germany; war ends. German Empire proclaimed with Prussian King as Kaiser Wilhelm I. Fighting with Apaches begins in American West. Boss Tweed corruption exposed in New York. The Chicago Fire, with 250 deaths and $196-million damage. Stanley meets Livingstone in Africa.

1872 Congress gives amnesty to most Confederates. Jules Verne's *Around the World in 80 Days*.

THE CIVIL WAR

Apart from the matter of slavery, the Civil War arose out of both the economic and political rivalry between an agrarian South and an industrial North and the issue of the right of states to secede from the Union.

1861 After South Carolina secedes **(Dec. 20, 1860)**, Mississippi, Florida, Alabama, Georgia, Louisiana, and Texas follow, forming the Confederate States of America, with Jefferson Davis as president **(Jan.–March)**. War begins as Confederates fire on Fort Sumter **(April 12)**. Lincoln calls for 75,000 volunteers. Southern ports blockaded by superior Union naval forces. Virginia, Arkansas, Tennessee, and North Carolina secede to complete 11-state Confederacy. Union army advancing on Richmond repulsed at first Battle of Bull Run (Manassas) **(July)**.

1862 Edwin M. Stanton named secretary of war **(Jan.)**. Grant wins first important Union victory in West, at Fort Donelson; Nashville falls **(Feb.)**. Ironclads, Union's *Monitor* and Confederate's *Virginia (Merrimac)* duel at Hampton Roads **(March)**. New Orleans falls to Union fleet under Farragut; city occupied **(April)**. Grant's army escapes defeat at Shiloh. Memphis falls as Union gunboats control upper Mississippi **(June)**. Confederate general Robert E. Lee victorious at second Battle of Bull Run (Manassas) **(Aug.)**. Union army under McClellan halts Lee's attack on Washington in the Battle of Antietam **(Sept.)**. Lincoln removes McClellan

for lack of aggressiveness. Burnside's drive on Richmond fails at Fredericksburg **(Dec.)**. Union forces under Rosecrans chase Bragg through Tennessee; battle of Murfreesboro **(Oct.–Jan. 1863)**.

1863 Lee defeats Hooker at Chancellorsville; "Stonewall" Jackson, Confederate general, dies **(May)**. Confederate invasion of Pennsylvania stopped at Gettysburg by George Meade—Lee loses 20,000 men—the greatest battle of the war **(July)**. That and the Union victory at Vicksburg mark the war's turning point. Union general George H. Thomas, the "Rock of Chickamauga," holds Bragg's forces on Georgia-Tennessee border **(Sept.)**. Sherman, Hooker, and Thomas drive Bragg back to Georgia. Tennessee restored to the Union **(Nov.)**.

1864 Ulysses S. Grant named commander-in-chief of Union forces **(March)**. In the Wilderness campaign, Grant forces Lee's Army of Northern Virginia back toward Richmond **(May–June)**. Sherman's Atlanta campaign and "march to the sea" **(May–Sept.)**. Farragut's victory at Mobile Bay **(Aug.)**. Hood's Confederate army defeated at Nashville. Sherman takes Savannah **(Dec.)**.

1865 Sheridan defeats Confederates at Five Forks; Confederates evacuate Richmond **(April)**. On **April 9**, Lee surrenders to Grant at Appomattox.

1873 Economic crisis in Europe. U.S. establishes gold standard.

1875 First Kentucky Derby.

1876 Sioux kill Gen. George A. Custer and 264 troopers at Little Big Horn River. Alexander Graham Bell patents the telephone.

1877 After presidential election of 1876, electoral commission gives disputed electoral college votes to Rutherford B. Hayes despite Tilden's popular majority. Russo-Turkish war (ends in 1878 with power of Turkey in Europe broken). Reconstruction ends in the American South. Thomas Edison patents phonograph. The Nez Perce leader Chief Joseph is forced to surrender. Tchaikovsky's *Swan Lake.*

1878 Congress of Berlin revises Treaty of San Stefano, ending Russo-Turkish War; makes extensive redivision of southeast Europe. First commercial telephone exchange opened in New Haven, Conn.

**Johannes Brahms
(1833–1897)**

1879 Thomas A. Edison invents electric light.

1880 U.S.-China treaty allows U.S. to restrict immigration of Chinese labor.

1881 President Garfield fatally shot by assassin; Vice President Arthur succeeds him. Charles J. Guiteau convicted and executed (1882).

1882 Terrorism in Ireland after land evictions. Britain invades and conquers Egypt. Germany, Austria, and Italy form Triple Alliance. In U.S., Congress adopts Chinese Exclusion Act. Rockefeller's Standard Oil Trust is first industrial monopoly. In Berlin, Robert Koch announces discovery of tuberculosis germ.

1883 Congress creates Civil Service Commission. Brooklyn Bridge and Metropolitan Opera House completed.

1884 Berlin West Africa Conference held in Berlin (lasting until **Feb. 1885**), at which the major European nations discuss expansion in Africa.

**Chief Joseph
(c. 1840–1904)**

1885 British general Charles G. "Chinese" Gordon killed at Khartoum in Egyptian Sudan. World's first skyscraper built in Chicago.

1886 Bombing at Haymarket Square, Chicago, kills seven policemen and injures many others. Eight alleged anarchists accused—three imprisoned, one commits suicide, four hanged. (In 1893, Illinois governor Altgeld, critical of trial, pardons three survivors.) Statue of Liberty dedicated. Geronimo, Apache Indian chief, surrenders.

1887 Queen Victoria's Golden Jubilee. Sir Arthur Conan Doyle's first Sherlock Holmes story, *A Study in Scarlet.*

1888 Historic March blizzard in northeast U.S.—many perish, property damage exceeds $25 million. George Eastman's box camera (the Kodak). J. B. Dunlop invents pneumatic tire. Jack the Ripper murders in London.

1889 Second (Socialist) International founded in Paris. Indian Territory in Oklahoma opened to settlement. Thousands die in Johnstown, Pa. flood. Eiffel Tower built for the Paris exposition. Mark Twain's *A Connecticut Yankee in King Arthur's Court.*

Statue of Liberty

1890 Congress votes to pass Sherman Antitrust Act. Sioux chief Sitting Bull arrested and killed by police on Pine Ridge reservation; two weeks later, U.S. troops kill over 200 Sioux at Battle of Wounded Knee.

1892 Battle between steel strikers and Pinkerton guards at Homestead, Pa.; union defeated after militia intervenes. Silver mine strikers in Idaho fight non-union workers; U.S. troops dispatched. Diesel engine patented.

1893 New Zealand becomes first country in the world to grant women the vote.

1894 Sino-Japanese War begins (ends in 1895 with China's defeat). In France, Capt. Alfred Dreyfus convicted on false treason charge (pardoned in 1906). In U.S., Jacob S. Coxey of Ohio leads "Coxey's Army" of unemployed on Washington. Eugene V. Debs calls general strike of rail workers to support Pullman Company strikers; strike broken, Debs jailed for six months. Edison's kinetoscope given first public showing in New York City.

**Marie Curie
(1867–1934)**

1895 X-rays discovered by German physicist Wilhelm Roentgen. Auguste and Louis Lumière premiere motion pictures at a café in Paris.

SPANISH-AMERICAN WAR (1898–1899)

War fires stoked by "jingo journalism" as American people support Cuban rebels against Spain. American business sees economic gain in Cuban trade and resources and American power zones in Latin America. Outstanding events: Submarine mine sinks U.S. battleship *Maine* in Havana Harbor **(Feb. 15)**; 260 killed; responsibility never fixed. Congress declares independence of Cuba **(April 19).** Spain declares war on U.S. **(April 24);** Congress **(April 25)** formally declares nation has been at war with Spain since April 21. Commodore George Dewey wins seven-hour battle of Manila Bay **(May 1).** Spanish fleet destroyed off Santiago, Cuba **(July 3);** city surrenders **(July 17).** Treaty of Paris (ratified by Senate 1899) ends war. U.S. given Guam and Puerto Rico and agrees to pay Spain $20 million for Philippines. Cuba independent of Spain; under U.S. military control for three years until **May 20, 1902.** Yellow fever is eradicated and political reforms achieved.

**Sigmund Freud
(1856–1939)**

**Carrie Chapman Catt
(1859–1947)**

**Albert Einstein
(1879–1955)**

**Vladimir Lenin
(1870–1924)**

**Robert Peary
(1856–1920)**

1896 Supreme Court's *Plessy* v. *Ferguson* decision—"separate but equal" doctrine. Alfred Nobel's will establishes prizes for peace, science, and literature. Marconi receives first wireless patent in Britain. William Jennings Bryan delivers "Cross of Gold" speech at Democratic Convention in Chicago. First modern Olympic games held in Athens, Greece.

1897 Theodor Herzl launches Zionist movement.

1898 Chinese "Boxers," anti-foreign organization, established. They stage uprisings against Europeans in 1900; U.S. and other Western troops relieve Peking legations. U.S. Battleship *Maine* is sunk in Havana Harbor. Spanish-American War begins. U.S. destroys Spanish fleet near Santiago, Cuba. Pierre and Marie Curie discover radium and polonium.

1899 Boer War (or South African War): conflict between British and Boers (descendants of Dutch settlers of South Africa). Causes rooted in longstanding territorial disputes and in friction over political rights for English and other "uitlanders" following 1886 discovery of vast gold deposits in Transvaal. (British victorious as war ends in 1902.) Casualties: 5,774 British dead, about 4,000 Boers. Union of South Africa established in 1908 as confederation of colonies; becomes British dominion in 1910.

1900–2003 (A.D.)

1900 Hurricane ravages Galveston, Tex.; 6,000–8,000 dead. Fauvist movement in painting begins, led by Henri Matisse. Sigmund Freud's *The Interpretation of Dreams.* Carrie Chapman Catt succeeds Susan B. Anthony as president of National Woman Suffrage Association.

1901 Queen Victoria dies, and is succeeded by her son, Edward VII. As President McKinley begins second term, he is shot fatally by anarchist Leon Czolgosz. Theodore Roosevelt sworn in as successor.

1902 Enrico Caruso's first gramophone recording. Aswan Dam completed.

1903 Wright brothers, Orville and Wilbur, fly first powered, controlled, heavier-than-air plane at Kitty Hawk, N.C. Henry Ford organizes Ford Motor Company. The Boston Red Sox win the first World Series against the Pittsburgh Pirates. W.E.B. Du Bois publishes *The Souls of Black Folk.*

1904 Russo-Japanese War begins—competition for Korea and Manchuria. *Entente Cordiale:* Britain and France settle their international differences. General theory of radioactivity by Rutherford and Soddy. New York City subway opens.

1905 In Russo-Japanese War, Port Arthur surrenders to Japanese; Russia suffers other defeats. President Roosevelt mediates Treaty of Portsmouth, N.H., which recognizes Japan's control of Korea and restores southern Manchuria to China. The Russian Revolution of 1905 begins on "Bloody Sunday" when troops fire onto a defenseless group of demonstrators in St. Petersburg. Strikes and riots follow. Sailors on battleship *Potemkin* mutiny; reforms, including first Duma (parliament), established by Czar Nicholas II's "October Manifesto." Albert Einstein's special theory of relativity and other key theories in physics. Franz Lehar's *Merry Widow.*

1906 San Francisco earthquake and three-day fire; more than 500 dead. Roald Amundsen, Norwegian explorer, fixes magnetic North Pole.

1907 Second Hague Peace Conference, of 46 nations, adopts 10 conventions on rules of war. Financial panic of 1907 in U.S. Mahler begins work on "Song of the Earth." Oklahoma becomes 46th state. Picasso's *Les Demoiselles d'Avignon* introduces cubism.

1908 Earthquake kills 150,000 in southern Italy and Sicily. U.S. Supreme Court, in Danbury Hatters' case, outlaws secondary union boycotts. Model T produced by Ford Motor Company.

1909 North Pole reportedly reached by American explorers Robert E. Peary and Matthew Henson. The National Association for the Advancement of Colored People is founded in New York by prominent black and white intellectuals and led by W.E.B. Du Bois.

1910 Boy Scouts of America incorporated. Angel Island, in San Francisco Bay, becomes immigration center for Asians entering U.S.

1911 First use of aircraft as offensive weapon in Turkish-Italian War. Italy defeats Turks and annexes Tripoli and Libya. Chinese Republic proclaimed after revolution overthrows Manchu dynasty. Sun Yat-sen named president. Mexican Revolution: Porfirio Diaz, president since 1877, replaced by Francisco Madero. Triangle Shirtwaist Company fire in New York; 146 killed. Amundsen reaches South Pole. Ernest Rutherford discovers the structure of the atom. Richard Strauss's *Der Rosenkavalier.* Irving Berlin's *Alexander's Ragtime Band.*

1912 Balkan Wars (1912–1913) resulting from territorial disputes: Turkey defeated by alliance of Bulgaria, Serbia, Greece, and Montenegro; London peace treaty (1913) partitions most of European Turkey among the victors. In second war (1913), Bulgaria attacks Serbia and Greece and is defeated after Romania intervenes and Turks recapture Adrianople. *Titanic* sinks on maiden voyage; over 1,500 drown. New Mexico and Arizona admitted as states.

1913 Suffragists demonstrate in London. Garment workers strike in New York and Boston; win pay raise and shorter hours. Henry Ford develops first moving assembly line. 16th Amendment (income tax) and 17th (popular election of U.S. senators) adopted. Bill creating U.S. Federal Reserve System becomes law. Stravinsky's *The Rite of Spring*. Woodrow Wilson becomes 28th U.S. president. Armory Show introduces modern art to U.S.; Duchamp's *Nude Descending a Staircase* shocks public.

W.E.B. Du Bois
(1868–1963)

1914 World War I begins: Austrian Archduke Francis Ferdinand and wife Sophie are assassinated; Austria declares war on Serbia, Germany on Russia and France, Britain on Germany. Panama Canal officially opens. Congress sets up Federal Trade Commission, passes Clayton Antitrust Act. U.S. Marines occupy Veracruz, Mexico, intervening in civil war to protect American interests.

1915 *Lusitania* sunk by German submarine. Second Battle of Ypres. U.S. banks lend $500 million to France and Britain. Genocide of estimated 600,000 to 1 million Armenians by Turkish soldiers. D. W. Griffith's film *Birth of a Nation*. Albert Einstein's *General Theory of Relativity*.

1916 Congress expands armed forces. Battle of Verdun. Battle of the Somme. Tom Mooney arrested for San Francisco bombing (pardoned in 1939). Pershing fails in raid into Mexico in quest of rebel Pancho Villa. U.S. buys Virgin Islands from Denmark for $25 million. President Wilson re-elected with "he kept us out of war" slogan. "Black Tom" explosion at munitions dock in Jersey City, N.J., $40,000,000 damages; traced to German saboteurs. Margaret Sanger opens first birth control clinic. Easter Rebellion in Ireland put down by British troops. Jeannette Rankin becomes first woman elected to Congress.

Woodrow Wilson
(1856–1924)

1917 First U.S. combat troops in France as U.S. declares war on Germany (**April 6**). Third Battle of Ypres. Russian Revolution of 1917—climax of long unrest under czars. February Revolution—Nicholas II forced to abdicate, liberal government created. Kerensky becomes prime minister and forms provisional government (**July**). In October Revolution, Bolsheviks seize power in armed coup d'état led by Lenin and Trotsky. Kerensky flees. Balfour Declaration promises Jewish homeland in Palestine. U.S. declares war on Austria-Hungary (**Dec. 7**). Armistice between

Bessie Smith
(1894–1937)

WORLD WAR I (1914–1918)

Imperial, territorial, and economic rivalries led to the "Great War" between the Central Powers (Austria-Hungary, Germany, Bulgaria, and Turkey) and the Allies (U.S., Britain, France, Russia, Belgium, Serbia, Greece, Romania, Montenegro, Portugal, Italy, and Japan). About 10 million combatants killed, 20 million wounded.

1914 Austrian Archduke Francis Ferdinand and wife assassinated in Sarajevo by Serbian nationalist, Gavrilo Princip (**June 28**). Austria declares war on Serbia (**July 28**). Germany declares war on Russia (**Aug. 1**), on France (**Aug. 3**), invades Belgium (**Aug. 4**). Britain declares war on Germany (**Aug. 4**). Germans defeat Russians in Battle of Tannenberg on Eastern Front (**Aug.**). First Battle of the Marne (**Sept.**). German drive stopped 25 miles from Paris. By end of year, war on the Western Front is "positional" in the trenches.

1915 German submarine blockade of Great Britain begins (**Feb.**). Dardanelles Campaign—British land in Turkey (**April**), withdraw from Gallipoli (**Dec.–Jan. 1916**). Germans use gas at second Battle of Ypres (**April–May**). *Lusitania* sunk by German submarine—1,198 lost, including 128 Americans (**May 7**). On Eastern Front, German and Austrian "great offensive" conquers all of Poland and Lithuania; Russians lose 1 million men (by **Sept. 6**). "Great Fall Offensive" by Allies results in little change from 1914 (**Sept.–Oct.**). Britain and France declare war on Bulgaria (**Oct. 14**).

1916 Battle of Verdun—Germans and French each lose about 350,000 men (**Feb.**). Extended submarine warfare begins (**March**). British-German sea battle of Jutland (**May**); British lose more ships, but German fleet never ventures forth again. On Eastern Front, Brusilov offensive demoralizes Russians, costs them 1 million men (**June–Sept.**). Battle of the Somme—British lose over 400,000; French, 200,000; Germans, about 450,000; all with no strategic results (**July–Nov.**). Romania declares war on Austria-Hungary (**Aug. 27**). Bucharest captured (**Dec.**).

1917 U.S. declares war on Germany (**April 6**). Submarine warfare at peak (**April**). On Italian Front, Battle of Caporetto—Italians retreat, losing 600,000 prisoners and deserters (**Oct.–Dec.**). On Western Front, Battles of Arras, Champagne, Ypres (third battle), etc. First large British tank attack (**Nov.**). U.S. declares war on Austria-Hungary (**Dec. 7**). Armistice between new Russian Bolshevik government and Germans (**Dec. 15**).

1918 Great offensive by Germans (**March–June**). Americans' first important battle role at Château-Thierry—as they and French stop German advance (**June**). Second Battle of the Marne (**July–Aug.**)—start of Allied offensive at Amiens, St. Mihiel, etc. Battles of the Argonne and Ypres panic German leadership (**Sept.–Oct.**). British offensive in Palestine (**Sept.**). Germans ask for armistice (**Oct. 4**). British armistice with Turkey (**Oct.**). German Kaiser abdicates (**Nov.**). Hostilities cease on Western Front (**Nov. 11**).

Mahatma Gandhi
(1869–1948)

William Butler Yeats
(1865–1939)

Robert Frost
(1874–1963)

Pablo Picasso
(1881–1973)

Babe Ruth
(George Herman Ruth)
(1895–1948)

new Russian Bolshevik government and Germans (**Dec. 15**). Sigmund Freud's *Introduction to Psychoanalysis.*

1918 Russian revolutionaries execute the former czar and his family. Russian Civil War between Reds (Bolsheviks) and Whites (anti-Bolsheviks); Reds win in 1920. Allied troops (U.S., British, French) intervene (**March**); leave in 1919. Second Battle of the Marne (**July–Aug.**) German Kaiser abdicates (**Nov.**); hostilities cease on the Western Front. Japanese hold Vladivostok until 1922. Worldwide influenza epidemic strikes; by 1920, nearly 20 million are dead. In U.S. alone, 500,000 perish.

1919 Third International (Comintern) establishes Soviet control over international Communist movements. Paris peace conference. Versailles Treaty, incorporating Woodrow Wilson's draft Covenant of League of Nations, signed by Allies and Germany; rejected by U.S. Senate. Congress formally ends war in 1921. 18th (Prohibition) Amendment adopted. Alcock and Brown make first trans-Atlantic nonstop flight. Mahatma Gandhi initiates satyagraha ("truth force") campaigns, beginning his nonviolent resistance movement against British rule in India.

1920 League of Nations holds first meeting at Geneva, Switzerland. U.S. Dept. of Justice "red hunt" nets thousands of radicals; aliens deported. Women's suffrage (19th) amendment ratified. Treaty of Sèvres dissolves Ottoman Empire. First Agatha Christie mystery. Sinclair Lewis's *Main Street.*

1921 Reparations Commission fixes German liability at 132 billion gold marks. German inflation begins. Major treaties signed at Washington Disarmament Conference limit naval tonnage and pledge to respect territorial integrity of China. In U.S., Nicola Sacco and Bartolomeo Vanzetti, Italian-born anarchists, convicted of armed robbery murder; case stirs worldwide protests; they are executed in 1927.

1922 Mussolini marches on Rome; forms Fascist government. Irish Free State, a self-governing dominion of British Empire, officially proclaimed. Kemal Atatürk, founder of modern Turkey, overthrows last sultan. James Joyce's *Ulysses.*

1923 Adolf Hitler's "Beer Hall Putsch" in Munich fails; in 1924 he is sentenced to five years in prison where he writes *Mein Kampf;* released after eight months. Occupation of Ruhr by French and Belgian troops to enforce reparations payments. Widespread Ku Klux Klan violence in U.S. Earthquake destroys third of Tokyo. George Gershwin's *Rhapsody in Blue.* Bessie Smith, known as "the Empress of the Blues," makes her first record. Irish poet William Butler Yeats wins Nobel Prize in Literature.

1924 Death of Lenin; Stalin wins power struggle, rules as Soviet dictator until death in 1953. Italian Fascists murder Socialist leader Giacomo Matteotti. Interior Secretary Albert B. Fall and oilmen Harry Sinclair and Edward L. Doheny are charged with conspiracy and bribery in the Teapot Dome scandal, involving fraudulent leases of naval oil reserves. In 1931, Fall is sentenced to year in prison; Doheny and Sinclair acquitted of bribery. Nathan Leopold and Richard Loeb convicted in "thrill killing" of Bobby Franks in Chicago; defended by Clarence Darrow; sentenced to life imprisonment. (Loeb killed by fellow convict in 1936; Leopold paroled in 1958, dies in 1971.) Robert Frost wins first of four Pulitzers.

1925 Nellie Tayloe Ross elected governor of Wyoming; first woman governor elected in U.S. Locarno conferences seek to secure European peace by mutual guarantees. John T. Scopes convicted and fined for teaching evolution in a public school in Tennessee "Monkey Trial"; sentence set aside. John Logie Baird, Scottish inventor, transmits human features by television. Hitler publishes Volume I of *Mein Kampf.*

1926 General strike in Britain brings nation's activities to standstill. U.S. marines dispatched to Nicaragua during revolt; they remain until 1933. Gertrude Ederle of U.S. is first woman to swim English Channel. Ernest Hemingway's *The Sun Also Rises.*

1927 German economy collapses. Socialists riot in Vienna; general strike follows acquittal of Nazis for political murder. Trotsky expelled from Russian Communist Party. Charles A. Lindbergh flies first successful solo nonstop flight from New York to Paris. Ruth Snyder and Judd Gray convicted of murder of Albert Snyder; they are executed at Sing Sing prison in 1928. Philo T. Farnsworth demonstrates working television model. Georges Lemaître proposes Big Bang Theory. Babe Ruth hits 60 home runs in the season; record stands for next 34 years. *The Jazz Singer,* with Al Jolson, first part-talking motion picture.

1928 Kellogg-Briand Pact, outlawing war, signed in Paris by 65 nations. Alexander Fleming discovers penicillin. Richard E. Byrd starts expedition to Antarctic; returns in 1930. Anthropologist Margaret Mead publishes *Coming of Age in Samoa. Oxford English Dictionary* published after 44 years of research.

1929 Trotsky expelled from USSR Lateran Treaty establishes independent Vatican City. In U.S., stock market prices collapse, with U.S. securities losing $26 billion—first phase of Depression and world economic crisis. St. Valentine's Day gangland massacre in Chicago. Edwin Powell Hubble proposes theory of expanding universe.

1930 Britain, U.S., Japan, France, and Italy sign naval disarmament treaty. Nazis gain in German elections. Cyclotron developed by Ernest O. Lawrence, U.S. physicist. Pluto discovered by astronomers.

1931 Spain becomes a republic with overthrow of King Alfonso XIII. German industrialists finance 800,000-strong Nazi party. British parliament enacts statute of Westminster, legalizing dominion equality with Britain. Mukden Incident begins Japanese occupation of Manchuria. In U.S., Hoover proposes one-year moratorium on war debts. Harold C. Urey discovers heavy hydrogen. Gangster Al Capone sentenced to 11 years in prison for tax evasion (freed in 1939; dies in 1947). Notorious Scottsboro trial begins, exposing depth of Southern racism. "The Star Spangled Banner" officially becomes national anthem.

1932 Nazis lead in German elections with 230 Reichstag seats. Famine in USSR. In U.S., Congress sets up Reconstruction Finance Corporation to stimulate economy. Veterans march on Washington—most leave after Senate rejects payment of cash bonuses; others removed by troops under Douglas MacArthur. U.S. protests Japanese aggression in Manchuria. Amelia Earhart is first woman to fly Atlantic solo. Charles A. Lindbergh's baby son kidnapped, killed. (Bruno Richard Hauptmann arrested in 1934, convicted in 1935, executed in 1936.)

1933 Hitler appointed German chancellor, gets dictatorial powers. Reichstag fire in Berlin; Nazi terror begins. Germany and Japan withdraw from League of Nations. Giuseppe Zangara executed for attempted assassination of president-elect Roosevelt in which Chicago mayor Cermak is fatally shot. Roosevelt inaugurated ("the only thing we have to fear is fear itself"); launches New Deal. Prohibition repealed. USSR recognized by U.S.

1934 Chancellor Dollfuss of Austria assassinated by Nazis. Hitler becomes führer. USSR admitted to League of Nations. Dionne sisters, first quintuplets to survive beyond infancy, born in Canada. Mao Zedong begins the Long March north with 100,000 soldiers.

1935 Saar incorporated into Germany after plebiscite. Nazis repudiate Versailles Treaty, introduce compulsory military service. Mussolini invades Ethiopia; League of Nations invokes sanctions. Roosevelt opens second phase of

Benito Mussolini
(1883–1945)

Joseph Stalin
(1879–1953)

Adolf Hitler
(1889–1945)

THE HOLOCAUST (1933-1945)

"Holocaust" is the term describing the Nazi annihilation of about 6 million Jews (two thirds of the pre-World War II European Jewish population), including 4,500,000 from Russia, Poland, and the Baltic; 750,000 from Hungary and Romania; 290,000 from Germany and Austria; 105,000 from The Netherlands; 90,000 from France; 54,000 from Greece.

The Holocaust was unique in its being *genocide*—the systematic destruction of a people solely because of religion, race, ethnicity, nationality, or sexual preference—on an unmatched scale. Along with the Jews, another 9 to 10 million people—Gypsies, Slavs (Poles, Ukrainians, and Belarussians), homosexuals, and the disabled—were exterminated.

1933 Hitler named German Chancellor **(Jan.).** Dachau, first concentration camp, established **(March).** Boycotts against Jews begin **(April).**

1935 Anti-Semitic Nuremberg Laws passed by Reichstag; Jews lose citizenship and civil rights **(Sept.).**

1937 Buchenwald concentration camp opens **(July).**

1938 Extension of anti-Semitic laws to Austria after annexation **(March).** *Kristallnacht* (Night of Broken Glass)—anti-Semitic riots and destruction of Jewish institutions in Germany and Austria **(Nov. 9).** 26,000 Jews sent to concentration camps; Jewish children expelled from schools **(Nov. 9–10).** Expropriation of Jewish property and businesses **(Dec.).**

1940 As war continues, Einsatzgruppen (mobile killing squads) follow German army into conquered lands, rounding up and massacring Jews and other "undesirables."

1941 Goering instructs Heydrich to carry out the "final solution to the Jewish question" **(July 31).** Deportation of German Jews begins; massacres of Jews in Odessa and Kiev **(Nov.);** and in Riga and Vilna **(Dec.).**

1942 Mass killings using Zyklon-B begin at Auschwitz-Birkenau **(Jan.).** Nazi leaders attend Wannsee Conference to coordinate the "final solution" **(Jan. 20).** 100,000 Jews from Warsaw Ghetto deported to Treblinka death camp **(July).**

1943 Warsaw Ghetto uprisings **(Jan.** and **April);** Ghetto exterminated **(May).**

1944 476,000 Hungarian Jews sent to Auschwitz **(May–June).** D-day **(June 6).** Soviet Army liberates Maidanek death camp **(July).** Nazis try to hide evidence of death camps **(Nov.).**

1945 As Allies advance, Nazis force concentration camp inmates on death marches. Americans liberate Buchenwald and British liberate Bergen-Belsen camps **(April).** Nuremberg War Crimes Trial **(Nov. 1945–Oct. 1946).**

Dorothea Lange's photo "Migrant Mother" (1936) documented the Great Depression (1929–1940)

New Deal in U.S., calling for social security, better housing, equitable taxation, and farm assistance. Huey Long assassinated in Louisiana.

1936 Germans occupy Rhineland. Italy annexes Ethiopia. Rome-Berlin Axis proclaimed (Japan to join in 1940). Trotsky exiled to Mexico. King George V dies; succeeded by son, Edward VIII, who soon abdicates to marry an American-born divorcée, and is succeeded by brother, George VI. Spanish civil war begins. Hundreds of Americans join the "Lincoln Brigades." (Franco's fascist forces defeat Loyalist forces by 1939, when Madrid falls.) War between China and Japan begins, to continue through World War II. Japan and Germany sign anti-Comintern pact; joined by Italy in 1937.

1937 Hitler repudiates war guilt clause of Versailles Treaty; continues to build German power. Italy withdraws from League of Nations. U.S. gunboat *Panay* sunk by Japanese in Yangtze River. Japan invades China, conquers most of coastal area. Amelia Earhart lost somewhere in Pacific on round-the-world flight. Picasso's *Guernica* mural.

1938 Hitler marches into Austria; political and geographical union of Germany and Austria proclaimed. Munich Pact—Britain, France, and Italy agree to let Germany partition Czechoslovakia. Douglas "Wrong-Way" Corrigan flies from New York to Dublin. Fair Labor Standards Act establishes minimum wage. Orson Welles's radio broadcast *War of the Worlds*.

1939 Germany invades Poland; occupies Bohemia and Moravia; renounces pact with England and concludes 10-year non-aggression pact with USSR. Russo-Finnish War begins; Finns to lose one-tenth of territory in 1940 peace treaty. World War II begins. In U.S., Roosevelt submits $1,319-million defense budget, proclaims U.S. neutrality, and declares limited emergency. Einstein writes FDR about feasibility of atomic bomb. New York World's Fair opens. DAR refuses to allow Marian Anderson to perform. *Gone with the Wind* premieres.

Amelia Earhart (1897–1937)

WORLD WAR II (1939–1945)

Axis powers (Germany, Italy, Japan, Hungary, Romania, Bulgaria) *versus* Allies (U.S., Britain, France, USSR, Australia, Belgium, Brazil, Canada, China, Denmark, Greece, Netherlands, New Zealand, Norway, Poland, South Africa, Yugoslavia).

1939 Germany invades Poland and annexes Danzig; Britain and France give Hitler ultimatum (**Sept. 1**), declare war (**Sept. 3**). Disabled German pocket battleship *Admiral Graf Spee* blown up off Montevideo, Uruguay, on Hitler's orders (**Dec. 17**). Limited activity ("Sitzkrieg") on Western Front.

1940 Nazis invade Netherlands, Belgium, and Luxembourg (**May 10**). Chamberlain resigns as Britain's prime minister; Churchill takes over (**May 10**). Germans cross French frontier (**May 12**) using air/tank/infantry "Blitzkrieg" tactics. Dunkerque evacuation—about 335,000 out of 400,000 Allied soldiers rescued from Belgium by British civilian and naval craft (**May 26–June 3**). Italy declares war on France and Britain; invades France (**June 10**). Germans enter Paris; city undefended (**June 14**). France and Germany sign armistice at Compiègne (**June 22**). Nazis bomb Coventry, England (**Nov. 14**).

1941 Germans launch attacks in Balkans. Yugoslavia surrenders—General Mihajlovic continues guerrilla warfare; Tito leads left-wing guerrillas (**April 17**). Nazi tanks enter Athens; remnants of British Army quit Greece (**April 27**). Hitler attacks Russia (**June 22**). Atlantic Charter—FDR and Churchill agree on war aims (**Aug. 14**). Japanese attacks on Pearl Harbor, Philippines, Guam force U.S. into war; U.S. Pacific fleet crippled (**Dec. 7**). U.S. and Britain declare war on Japan. Germany and Italy declare war on U.S.; Congress declares war on those countries (**Dec. 11**).

1942 British surrender Singapore to Japanese (**Feb. 15**). Roosevelt orders Japanese and Japanese Americans in western U.S. to be exiled to "relocation centers," many for the remainder of the war (**Feb. 19**). U.S. forces on Bataan peninsula in Philippines surrender (**April 9**). U.S. and Filipino troops on Corregidor island in Manila Bay surrender to Japanese (**May 6**). Village

of Lidice in Czechoslovakia razed by Nazis (**June 10**). U.S. and Britain land in French North Africa (**Nov. 8**).

1943 Casablanca Conference—Churchill and FDR agree on unconditional surrender goal (**Jan. 14–24**). German 6th Army surrenders at Stalingrad—turning point of war in Russia (**Feb. 1–2**). Remnants of Nazis trapped on Cape Bon, ending war in Africa (**May 12**). Mussolini deposed; Badoglio named premier (**July 25**). Allied troops land on Italian mainland after conquest of Sicily (**Sept. 3**). Italy surrenders (**Sept. 8**). Nazis seize Rome (**Sept. 10**). Cairo Conference: FDR, Churchill, Chiang Kai-shek pledge defeat of Japan, free Korea (**Nov. 22–26**). Teheran Conference: FDR, Churchill, Stalin agree on invasion plans (**Nov. 28–Dec. 1**).

1944 U.S. and British troops land at Anzio on west Italian coast and hold beachhead (**Jan. 22**). U.S. and British troops enter Rome (**June 4**). D-Day—Allies launch Normandy invasion (**June 6**). Hitler wounded in bomb plot (**July 20**). Paris liberated (**Aug. 25**). Athens freed by Allies (**Oct. 13**). Americans invade Philippines (**Oct. 20**). Germans launch counteroffensive in Belgium—Battle of the Bulge (**Dec. 16**).

1945 Yalta Agreement signed by FDR, Churchill, Stalin—establishes basis for occupation of Germany, returns to Soviet Union lands taken by Germany and Japan; USSR agrees to friendship pact with China (**Feb. 11**). Mussolini killed at Lake Como (**April 28**). Admiral Doenitz takes command in Germany; suicide of Hitler announced (**May 1**). Berlin falls (**May 2**). Germany signs unconditional surrender terms at Rheims (**May 7**). Allies declare V-E Day (**May 8**). Potsdam Conference—Truman, Churchill, Atlee (after **July 28**), Stalin establish council of foreign ministers to prepare peace treaties; plan German postwar government and reparations (**July 17–Aug. 2**). A-bomb dropped on Hiroshima by U.S. (**Aug. 6**). USSR declares war on Japan (**Aug. 8**). Nagasaki hit by A-bomb (**Aug. 9**). Japan agrees to surrender (**Aug. 14**). V-J Day—Japanese sign surrender terms aboard battleship *Missouri* (**Sept. 2**).

1940 Hitler invades Norway, Denmark **(April 9)**, the Netherlands, Belgium, Luxembourg **(May 10)**, and France **(May 12)**. Churchill becomes Britain's prime minister. Trotsky assassinated in Mexico **(Aug. 20)**. Estonia, Latvia, and Lithuania annexed by USSR. U.S. trades 50 destroyers for leases on British bases in Western Hemisphere. Selective Service Act signed. The first official network television broadcast is put out by NBC.

1941 Germany attacks the Balkans and Russia. Japanese surprise attack on U.S. fleet at Pearl Harbor brings U.S. into World War II; U.S. and Britain declare war on Japan. Manhattan Project (atomic bomb research) begins. Roosevelt enunciates "four freedoms," signs Lend-Lease Act, declares national emergency, promises aid to USSR. Orson Welles's *Citizen Kane.*

Franklin Delano Roosevelt (1882–1945)

1942 Declaration of United Nations signed in Washington **(Jan. 1)**. Nazi leaders attend Wannsee Conference to coordinate the "final solution to the Jewish question," the systematic genocide of Jews known as the Holocaust. Women's military services established. Enrico Fermi achieves nuclear chain reaction. More than 120,000 Japanese and persons of Japanese ancestry living in western U.S. moved to "relocation centers," some for the duration of the war (Executive Order 9066). Coconut Grove nightclub fire in Boston kills 492 **(Nov. 28)**.

1943 Churchill and Roosevelt hold Casablanca Conference **(Jan. 14–23)**. Mussolini deposed. President freezes prices, salaries, and wages to prevent inflation. Income tax withholding introduced.

1944 Allies invade Normandy on D-Day **(June 6)**. G.I. Bill of Rights enacted. Bretton Woods Conference creates International Monetary Fund and World Bank **(July 1–22)**. Dumbarton Oaks Conference—U.S., British Commonwealth, and USSR propose establishment of United Nations **(Aug. 21–Oct. 7)**. Battle of the Bulge **(Dec. 16)**. Gunnar Myrdal's *An American Dilemma.*

Winston Churchill (1874–1965)

1945 Yalta Conference (Roosevelt, Churchill, Stalin) plans final defeat of Germany **(Feb. 4–11)**. FDR dies **(April 12)**. Hitler commits suicide **(April 30)**; Germany surrenders **(May 7)**; **May 8** is declared V-E Day. Potsdam Conference (Truman, Churchill, Stalin) establishes basis of German reconstruction **(July–Aug.)**. U.S. drops atomic bombs on Japanese cities of Hiroshima **(Aug. 6)** and Nagasaki **(Aug. 9)**. Japan signs official surrender on V-J Day **(Sept. 2)**. United Nations established **(Oct. 24)**. First electronic computer, ENIAC, built.

1946 First meeting of UN General Assembly opens in London **(Jan. 10)**. Winston Churchill's "Iron Curtain" speech warns of Soviet expansion **(March 5)**. League of Nations dissolved **(April)**. Italy abolishes monarchy **(June)**. Verdict in Nuremberg war trial: 12 Nazi leaders (including 1 tried in absentia) sentenced to hang; 7 imprisoned; 3 acquitted **(Oct. 1)**. Goering commits suicide a few hours before 10 other Nazis are executed **(Oct. 15)**. Juan Perón becomes president of Argentina. Benjamin Spock's childcare classic published.

Harry S. Truman (1884–1972)

1947 Britain nationalizes coal mines **(Jan. 1)**. Peace treaties for Italy, Romania, Bulgaria, Hungary, Finland signed in Paris **(Feb. 10)**. Soviet Union rejects U.S. plan for UN atomic-energy control **(March 4)**. Truman proposes Truman Doctrine, which was to aid Greece and Turkey in resisting communist expansion **(March 12)**. Marshall Plan for European recovery proposed—a coordinated program to help European nations recover from ravages of war **(June)**. (By the time it ended in 1951, this "European Recovery Program" had cost $13 billion.) India and Pakistan gain independence from Britain **(Aug. 15)**. U.S. Air Force pilot Chuck Yeager becomes first person to break the sound barrier **(Oct. 14)**. Jackie Robinson joins the Brooklyn Dodgers. Anne Frank's *The Diary of a Young Girl* published.

Atomic Bomb

1948 Gandhi assassinated in New Delhi by Hindu fanatic **(Jan. 30)**. Burma **(Jan. 4)** and Ceylon **(Feb. 4)** granted independence by Britain. Communists seize power in Czechoslovakia **(Feb. 23–25)**. Organization of American States (OAS) Charter signed at Bogotá, Colombia **(April 30)**. Nation of Israel proclaimed; British end mandate at midnight; Arab armies attack **(May 14)**. Berlin blockade begins **(June 24)**, prompting Allied airlift **(June 26)**. (Blockade ends **May 12, 1949;** airlift continues until **Sept. 30, 1949.**) Stalin and Tito break **(June 28)**. Independent Republic of Korea is proclaimed, following election supervised by UN **(Aug. 15)**. Verdict in Japanese war trial: 18 imprisoned **(Nov. 12)**; Tojo and six others hanged **(Dec. 23)**. United States of Indonesia established as Dutch and Indonesians settle conflict **(Dec. 27)**. Alger Hiss, former

Anne Frank (1929–1945)

Tennessee Williams
(1911–1983)

Woody Guthrie
(1912–1967)

Dwight D. Eisenhower
(1890–1969)

Dag Hammarskjöld
(1905–1961)

U.S. State Department official, indicted on perjury charges after denying passing secret documents to communist spy ring; convicted in second trial (1950) and sentenced to five-year prison term. Truman ends racial segregation in military. Alfred Kinsey publishes *Sexual Behavior in the American Male.* Tennessee Williams's *A Streetcar Named Desire* wins Pulitzer.

1949 Cease-fire in Palestine **(Jan. 7)**. Truman proposes Point Four Program to help world's less developed areas **(Jan. 20)**. Israel signs armistice with Egypt **(Feb. 24)**. Start of North Atlantic Treaty Organization (NATO)—treaty signed by 12 nations **(April 4)**. Federal Republic of Germany (West Germany) established **(May 23)**. First successful Soviet atomic test **(July 14)**. Communist People's Republic of China formally proclaimed by Chairman Mao Zedong **(Oct. 1)**. German Democratic Republic (East Germany) established under Soviet rule **(Oct. 7)**. South Africa institutionalizes apartheid.

1950 Brink's robbery in Boston; almost $3 million stolen **(Jan. 17)**. Truman orders development of hydrogen bomb **(Jan. 31)**. Robert Schuman proposes Schuman Plan to pool European coal and steel **(May 9)**. Korean War begins when North Korean Communist forces invade South Korea **(June 25)**. Assassination attempt on President Truman by Puerto Rican nationalists **(Nov. 1)**. McCarthyism begins.

1951 Julius and Ethel Rosenberg sentenced to death for passing atomic secrets to Russians **(March)**. Spurred by Schuman Plan, six nations form European Coal and Steel Community **(April)**; effective 1952. Japanese peace treaty signed in San Francisco by 49 nations **(Sept. 8)**. Color television introduced in U.S. Libya gains independence **(Dec. 24)**.

1952 George VI dies; his daughter becomes Elizabeth II **(Feb. 6)**. AEC announces "satisfactory" experiments in hydrogen-weapons research; eyewitnesses tell of blasts near Enewetak **(Nov.)**. Ralph Ellison's *The Invisible Man.*

1953 Gen. Dwight D. Eisenhower inaugurated president of United States **(Jan. 20)**. Stalin dies **(March 5)**. Malenkov becomes Soviet premier; Beria, minister of interior; Molotov, foreign minister **(March 6)**. Dag Hammarskjöld begins term as UN secretary-general **(April 10)**. James Watson and Francis Crick publish their discovery of the molecular model of DNA **(April–May)**. Edmund Hillary of New Zealand and Tenzing Norgay of Nepal reach top of Mt. Everest **(May 29)**. East Berliners rise against Communist rule; quelled by tanks **(June 17)**. Egypt becomes republic ruled by military junta **(June 18)**. Julius and Ethel Rosenberg executed in Sing Sing prison **(June 19)**. Korean armistice signed **(July 27)**. Moscow announces explosion of hydrogen bomb **(Aug. 20)**. Tito becomes president of Yugoslavia. James Watson, Francis Crick, and Rosalind Franklin discover structure of DNA. Ernest Hemingway wins Pulitzer for *The Old Man and the Sea.*

1954 First atomic submarine *Nautilus* launched **(Jan. 21)**. Five U.S. congressmen shot on floor of House as Puerto Rican nationalists fire from spectators' gallery; all five recover **(March 1)**. Soviet Union grants sovereignty to East Germany **(March 23)**. *Army* v. *McCarthy* inquiry—Senate subcommittee report blames both sides **(April 22–June 17)**. Dien Bien Phu, French military outpost in Vietnam, falls to Vietminh army **(May 7)**. U.S. Supreme Court (in *Brown* v. *Board of Education of Topeka*) unanimously bans racial segregation in public schools **(May 17)**. Eisenhower launches world atomic pool without Soviet Union **(Sept. 6)**. Eight-nation Southeast Asia defense treaty (SEATO) signed at Manila **(Sept. 8)**. Dr. Jonas Salk starts inoculating children against polio. Algerian War of Independence against France begins **(Nov.)**; France struggles to maintain colonial rule until 1962 when it agrees to Algeria's independence. William Faulkner's *A Fable* wins Pulitzer.

KOREAN WAR (1950–1953)

1950 North Korean Communist forces invade South Korea **(June 25)**. UN calls for cease-fire and asks UN members to assist South Korea **(June 27)**. Truman orders U.S. forces into Korea **(June 27)**. North Koreans capture Seoul **(June 28)**. Gen. Douglas MacArthur designated commander of unified UN forces **(July 8)**. Pusan Beachhead—UN forces counterattack and capture Seoul **(Aug.–Sept.)**, capture Pyongyang, North Korean capital **(Oct.)**. Chinese Communists enter war **(Oct. 26)**, force UN retreat toward 39th parallel **(Dec.)**.

1951 Gen. Matthew B. Ridgway replaces MacArthur after he threatens Chinese with massive retaliation **(April 11)**. Armistice negotiations **(July)** continue with interruptions until June 1953.

1953 Armistice signed **(July 27)**. Chinese troops withdraw from North Korea **(Oct. 26, 1958)**, but over 200 violations of armistice noted in **1959**.

1955 Nikolai A. Bulganin becomes Soviet premier, replacing Malenkov (**Feb. 8**). Churchill resigns; Anthony Eden succeeds him (**April 6**). West Germany becomes a sovereign state (**May 5**). Western European Union (WEU) comes into being (**May 6**). Warsaw Pact, east European mutual defense agreement, signed (**May 14**). Argentina ousts Perón (**Sept. 19**). President Eisenhower suffers coronary thrombosis in Denver (**Sept. 24**). Rosa Parks refuses to sit at the back of the bus. Martin Luther King, Jr., leads black boycott of Montgomery, Ala., bus system (**Dec. 1**); desegregated service begins **Dec. 21, 1956**. AFL and CIO become one organization—AFL-CIO (**Dec. 5**). Tennessee Williams's *Cat on a Hot Tin Roof* wins Pulitzer.

Fidel Castro
(1926–)

1956 Nikita Khrushchev, First Secretary of USSR Communist Party, denounces Stalin's excesses (**Feb. 24**). First aerial H-bomb tested over Namu islet, Bikini Atoll—10 million tons TNT equivalent (**May 21**). Workers' uprising against Communist rule in Poznan, Poland, is crushed (**June 28–30**); rebellion inspires Hungarian students to stage a protest against Communism in Budapest (**Oct. 23**). Egypt takes control of Suez Canal (**July 26**). Hungarian rebellion forces Soviet troops to withdraw from Budapest (**Oct.**). Israel launches attack on Egypt's Sinai peninsula and drives toward Suez Canal (**Oct. 29**). Imre Nagy announces Hungary's withdrawal from Warsaw Pact (**Nov. 1**); Soviet troops enter and reclaim Budapest (**Nov. 4**). British and French invade Port Said on the Suez Canal (**Nov. 5**). Cease-fire forced by U.S. pressure stops British, French, and Israeli advance (**Nov. 6**). Morocco gains independence. Ingmar Bergman's *The Seventh Seal*. Woody Guthrie composes "This Land is Your Land." Allen Ginsberg's *Howl*.

John H. Glenn, Jr.
(1921–)

1957 Eisenhower Doctrine calls for aid to Mideast countries which resist armed aggression from Communist-controlled nations (**Jan. 5**). The "Little Rock Nine" integrate Arkansas high school. Eisenhower sends troops to quell mob and protect school integration (**Sept. 24**). Russians launch *Sputnik I,* first Earth-orbiting satellite—the Space Age begins (**Oct. 4**).

1958 European Economic Community (Common Market) becomes effective (**Jan. 1**). Army's Jupiter-C rocket fires first U.S. Earth satellite, *Explorer I,* into orbit (**Jan. 31**). Egypt and Syria merge into United Arab Republic (**Feb. 1**). Khrushchev becomes premier of Soviet Union as Bulganin resigns (**Mar. 27**). Gen. Charles de Gaulle becomes French premier (**June 1**), remaining in power until 1969. Eisenhower orders U.S. Marines into Lebanon at request of President Chamoun, who fears overthrow (**July 15**). New French constitution adopted (**Sept. 28**), de Gaulle elected president of 5th Republic (**Dec. 21**).

Martin Luther King, Jr.
(1929–1968)

1959 Cuban President Batista resigns and flees—Castro takes over (**Jan. 1**). Tibet's Dalai Lama escapes to India (**Mar. 31**). St. Lawrence Seaway opens, allowing ocean ships to reach Midwest (**April 25**). Alaska and Hawaii become states. Leakeys discover hominid fossils.

1960 American U-2 spy plane, piloted by Francis Gary Powers, shot down over Russia (**May 1**). Khrushchev kills Paris summit conference because of U-2 (**May 16**). Top Nazi murderer of Jews, Adolf Eichmann, captured by Israelis in Argentina (**May 23**)—executed in Israel in 1962. Powers sentenced to prison for 10 years (**Aug. 19**)—freed in **February 1962** in exchange for Soviet spy. Communist China and Soviet Union split in conflict over Communist ideology. Senegal, Ghana, Nigeria, Madagascar, and Zaire (Belgian Congo) gain independence. Cuba begins confiscation of $770 million of U.S. property (**Aug. 7**). There are 900 U.S. military advisers in South Vietnam.

John F. Kennedy
(1917–1963)

1961 U.S. breaks diplomatic relations with Cuba (**Jan. 3**). Robert Frost recites "The Gift Outright" at John F. Kennedy's inauguration as president of U.S. (**Jan. 20**). Moscow announces putting first man in orbit around Earth, Maj. Yuri A. Gagarin (**April 12**). Cuba invaded at Bay of Pigs by an estimated 1,200 anti-Castro exiles aided by U.S.; invasion crushed (**April 17**). First U.S. spaceman, Navy Cmdr. Alan B. Shepard, Jr., rockets 116.5 miles up in 302-mile trip (**May 5**). Virgil Grissom becomes second American astronaut, making 118-mile-high, 303-mile-long rocket flight over Atlantic (**July 21**). Gherman Stepanovich Titov is launched in Soviet spaceship *Vostok II:* makes 17½ orbits in 25 hours, covering 434,960 miles before landing safely (**Aug. 6**). East Germans erect Berlin Wall between East and West Berlin to halt flood of refugees (**Aug. 13**). USSR fires 50-megaton hydrogen bomb, biggest explosion in history (**Oct. 29**). There are 2,000 U.S. military advisers in South Vietnam.

**James H. Meredith
(1933–)**

**Betty Friedan
(1921–)**

1962 Lt. Col. John H. Glenn, Jr., is first American to orbit Earth—three times in 4 hr 55 min (**Feb. 20**). France transfers sovereignty to new republic of Algeria (**July 3**). Cuban missile crisis—USSR to build missile bases in Cuba; Kennedy orders Cuban blockade, lifts blockade after Russians back down (**Aug.–Nov.**). James H. Meredith, escorted by federal marshals, registers at University of Mississippi (**Oct. 1**). Pope John XXIII opens Second Vatican Council (**Oct. 11**)—Council holds four sessions, finally closing **Dec. 8, 1965**. Cuba releases 1,113 prisoners of 1961 invasion attempt (**Dec. 24**). Burundi, Jamaica, Western Samoa, Uganda, and Trinidad and Tobago become independent. William Faulkner wins Pulitzer for *The Reivers*. Rachel Carson's *Silent Spring*.

1963 France and West Germany sign treaty of cooperation ending four centuries of conflict (**Jan. 22**). Michael E. De Bakey implants artificial heart in human for first time at Houston hospital; plastic device functions and patient lives for four days (**April 21**). Pope John XXIII dies (**June 3**)—succeeded **June 21** by Cardinal Montini, who becomes Paul VI. U.S. Supreme Court rules no locality may require recitation of Lord's Prayer or Bible verses in public schools (**June 17**). U.K.'s Profumo scandal (**June**). Civil rights rally held by 200,000 blacks and whites in Washington, D.C.; Martin Luther King delivers "I have a dream" speech (**Aug. 28**). Washington-to-Moscow "hot line" communications link opens, designed to reduce risk of accidental war (**Aug. 30**). President Kennedy shot and killed by sniper in Dallas, Tex. Lyndon B. Johnson becomes president same day (**Nov. 22**). Lee Harvey Oswald, accused assassin of President Kennedy, is shot and killed by Jack Ruby, Dallas nightclub owner (**Nov. 24**). Kenya achieves independence. Betty Friedan publishes *The Feminine Mystique*. There are 15,000 U.S. military advisers in South Vietnam.

VIETNAM WAR (1950–1975)

U.S., South Vietnam, and Allies versus North Vietnam and National Liberation Front (Viet Cong).

1950 President Truman sends 35-man military advisory group to aid French fighting to maintain colonial power in Vietnam.

1954 After defeat of French at Dien Bien Phu, Geneva Agreements (**July**) provide for withdrawal of French and Vietminh to either side of demarcation zone (DMZ) pending reunification elections, which are never held. Presidents Eisenhower and Kennedy (from 1954 onward) send civilian advisers and, later, military personnel to train South Vietnamese.

1960 Communists form National Liberation Front in South.

1960–1963 U.S. military advisers in South Vietnam rise from 900 to 15,000.

1963 Ngo Dinh Diem, South Vietnam's premier, slain in coup (**Nov. 1**).

1964 North Vietnamese torpedo boats reportedly attack U.S. destroyers in Gulf of Tonkin (**Aug. 2**). President Johnson orders retaliatory air strikes. Congress approves Gulf of Tonkin resolution (**Aug. 7**) authorizing president to take "all necessary measures" to win in Vietnam, allowing for the war's expansion.

1965 U.S. planes begin combat missions over South Vietnam. In **June**, 23,000 American advisers committed to combat. By end of year over 184,000 U.S. troops in area.

1966 B-52s bomb DMZ, reportedly used by North Vietnam for entry into South (**July 31**).

1967 South Vietnam National Assembly approves election of Nguyen Van Thieu as president (**Oct. 21**).

1968 U.S. has almost 525,000 men in Vietnam. In Tet offensive (**Jan.–Feb.**), Viet Cong guerrillas attack Saigon, Hue, and some provincial capitals. In My Lai massacre, American soldiers kill 300 Vietnamese villagers (**March 16**). President Johnson orders halt to U.S. bombardment of North Vietnam (**Oct. 31**). Saigon and N.L.F. join U.S. and North Vietnam in Paris peace talks.

1969 President Nixon announces Vietnam peace offer (**May 14**)—begins troop withdrawals (**June**). Viet Cong forms Provisional Revolutionary Government. U.S. Senate calls for curb on commitments (**June 25**). Ho Chi Minh, 79, North Vietnam president, dies (**Sept. 3**); collective leadership chosen. Some 6,000 U.S. troops pulled back from Thailand and 1,000 marines from Vietnam (announced **Sept. 30**). Massive demonstrations in U.S. protest and support war policies (**Oct. 15**).

1970 U.S. troops invade Cambodia in order to destroy North Vietnamese sanctuaries (**May 1**).

1971 Congress bars use of combat troops, but not air power, in Laos and Cambodia (**Jan. 1**). South Vietnamese troops, with U.S. air cover, fail in Laos thrust. Many American ground forces withdrawn from Vietnam combat. *New York Times* publishes Pentagon papers, classified material on expansion of war (**June**).

1972 Nixon responds to North Vietnamese drive across DMZ by ordering mining of North Vietnam ports and heavy bombing of Hanoi-Haiphong area (**April 1**). Nixon orders "Christmas bombing" of North to get North Vietnamese back to conference table (**Dec.**).

1973 President orders halt to offensive operations in North Vietnam (**Jan. 15**). Representatives of North and South Vietnam, U.S., and N.L.F. sign peace pacts in Paris, ending longest war in U.S. history (**Jan. 27**). Last American troops departed in their entirety (**March 29**).

1974 Both sides accuse each other of frequent violations of cease-fire agreement.

1975 Full-scale warfare resumes. South Vietnam premier Nguyen Van Thieu resigns (**April 21**). South Vietnamese government surrenders to North Vietnam; U.S. Marine embassy guards and U.S. civilians and dependents evacuated (**April 30**). More than 140,000 Vietnamese refugees leave by air and sea, many to settle in U.S. Provisional Revolutionary Government takes control (**June 6**).

1976 Election of National Assembly paves way for reunification of North and South.

1964 U.S. Supreme Court rules that congressional districts should be roughly equal in population (**Feb. 17**). Jack Ruby convicted of murder in slaying of Lee Harvey Oswald; sentenced to death by Dallas jury (**March 14**)—conviction reversed **Oct. 5, 1966;** Ruby dies **Jan. 3, 1967,** before second trial can be held. Three civil rights workers—Schwerner, Goodman, and Cheney—murdered in Mississippi (**June**). Twenty-one arrests result in trial and conviction of seven by federal jury. Nelson Mandela sentenced to life imprisonment (**June 11**). Congress approves Gulf of Tonkin resolution (**Aug. 7**). President's Commission on the Assassination of President Kennedy issues Warren Report concluding that Lee Harvey Oswald acted alone. The Beatles appear on *The Ed Sullivan Show.*

The Beatles

1965 Rev. Dr. Martin Luther King, Jr., and more than 2,600 other blacks arrested in Selma, Ala., during three-day demonstrations against voter-registration rules (**Feb. 1**). Malcolm X, black-nationalist leader, shot to death at Harlem rally in New York City (**Feb. 21**). U.S. Marines land in Dominican Republic as fighting persists between rebels and Dominican army (**April 28**). Medicare, senior citizens' government medical assistance program, begins (**July 1**). Blacks riot for six days in Watts section of Los Angeles: 34 dead, over 1,000 injured, nearly 4,000 arrested, fire damage put at $175 million (**Aug. 11–16**). Power failure in Ontario plant blacks out parts of eight states of northeast U.S. and two provinces of southeast Canada (**Nov. 9**). Ralph Nader's *Unsafe at Any Speed.*

Malcolm X
(1925–1965)

1966 Black teenagers riot in Watts, Los Angeles; two men killed and at least 25 injured (**March 15**). Supreme Court decides *Miranda* v. *Arizona.*

1967 Three Apollo astronauts—Col. Virgil I. Grissom, Col. Edward White II, and Lt. Cmdr. Roger B. Chaffee—killed in spacecraft fire during simulated launch (**Jan. 27**). Biafra secedes from Nigeria (**May 30**). Israeli and Arab forces battle; six-day war ends with Israel occupying Sinai Peninsula, Golan Heights, Gaza Strip, and east bank of Suez Canal (**June 5**). Red China announces explosion of its first hydrogen bomb (**June 17**). Racial violence in Detroit; 7,000 National Guardsmen aid police after night of rioting. Similar outbreaks occur in New York City's Spanish Harlem, Rochester, N.Y., Birmingham, Ala., and New Britain, Conn. (**July 23**). Thurgood Marshall sworn in as first black U.S. Supreme Court justice (**Oct. 2**). Dr. Christiaan N. Barnard and team of South African surgeons perform world's first successful human heart transplant (**Dec. 3**)—patient dies 18 days later.

Thurgood Marshall
(1908–1993)

1968 North Korea seizes U.S. Navy ship *Pueblo;* holds 83 on board as spies (**Jan. 23**). Tet offensive, turning point in Vietnam war (**Jan.–Feb.**). My Lai massacre (**March 16**). President Johnson announces he will not seek or accept presidential renomination (**March 31**). Martin Luther King, Jr., civil rights leader, is slain in Memphis (**April 4**)—James Earl Ray, indicted in murder, captured in London on **June 8**. In 1969 Ray pleads guilty and is sentenced to 99 years. Sen. Robert F. Kennedy is shot and critically wounded in Los Angeles hotel after winning California primary (**June 5**)—dies **June 6**. Sirhan B. Sirhan convicted 1969. Czechoslovakia is invaded by Russians and Warsaw Pact forces to crush liberal regime (**Aug. 20**).

Lyndon B. Johnson
(1908–1973)

1969 Richard M. Nixon is inaugurated 37th president of the U.S. (**Jan. 20**). Stonewall riot in New York City marks beginning of gay rights movement (**June 28**). *Apollo 11* astronauts—Neil A. Armstrong, Edwin E. Aldrin, Jr., and Michael Collins—take man's first walk on moon (**July 20**). Sen. Edward M. Kennedy pleads guilty to leaving scene of fatal accident at Chappaquiddick, Mass. (**July 18**), in which Mary Jo Kopechne was drowned—gets two-month suspended sentence (**July 25**). Woodstock Festival (**Aug. 15–17**). *Sesame Street* debuts. Internet (ARPA) goes online.

Richard Nixon
(1913–1994)

1970 Biafra surrenders after 32-month fight for independence from Nigeria (**Jan. 15**). Rhodesia severs last tie with British crown and declares itself a racially segregated republic (**March 1**). U.S. troops invade Cambodia (**May 1**). Four students at Kent State University in Ohio slain by National Guardsmen at demonstration protesting incursion into Cambodia (**May 4**). Senate repeals Gulf of Tonkin resolution (**June 24**).

1971 Supreme Court rules unanimously that busing of students may be ordered to achieve racial desegregation (**April 20**). Anti-war militants attempt to disrupt government business in Washington (**May 3**)—police and military units arrest as many as 12,000; most are later released. *Pentagon Papers* published (**June**). Twenty-sixth Amendment to U.S. Constitution lowers voting age to 18. UN seats Communist China and expels Nationalist China (**Oct. 25**).

**Mao Zedong
(1893–1976)**

**Duke Ellington
(1899–1974)**

**Gerald R. Ford
(1913–)**

**Jimmy Carter
(1924–)**

1972 President Nixon makes unprecedented eight-day visit to Communist China and meets with Mao Zedong (**Feb. 21–27**). Britain takes over direct rule of Northern Ireland in bid for peace (**March 24**). Gov. George C. Wallace of Alabama is shot by Arthur H. Bremer at Laurel, Md., political rally (**May 15**). Five men are apprehended by police in attempt to bug Democratic National Committee headquarters in Washington, D.C.'s Watergate complex—start of the Watergate scandal (**June 17**). Supreme Court rules that death penalty is unconstitutional (**June 29**). Eleven Israeli athletes at Olympic Games in Munich are killed after eight members of an Arab terrorist group invade Olympic Village; five guerrillas and one policeman are also killed (**Sept. 5**). "Christmas bombing" of North Vietnam (**Dec. 25**).

1973 Great Britain, Ireland, and Denmark enter European Economic Community (**Jan. 1**). Supreme Court rules on *Roe* v. *Wade* (**Jan. 22**). Vietnam War ends with signing of peace pacts (**Jan. 27**). Nixon, on national TV, accepts responsibility, but not blame, for Watergate; accepts resignations of advisers H. R. Haldeman and John D. Ehrlichman, fires John W. Dean III as counsel (**April 30**). Greek military junta abolishes monarchy and proclaims republic (**June 1**). U.S. bombing of Cambodia ends, marking official halt to 12 years of combat activity in Southeast Asia (**Aug. 15**). Chile's Marxist president, Salvadore Allende, is overthrown (**Sept. 11**). Fourth and biggest Arab-Israeli conflict begins as Egyptian and Syrian forces attack Israel as Jews mark Yom Kippur, holiest day in their calendar (**Oct. 6**). Spiro T. Agnew resigns as vice president and then, in federal court in Baltimore, pleads no contest to charges of evasion of income taxes on $29,500 he received in 1967, while governor of Maryland. He is fined $10,000 and put on three years' probation (**Oct. 10**). In the "Saturday Night Massacre," Nixon fires special Watergate prosecutor Archibald Cox and Deputy Attorney General William D. Ruckelshaus; Attorney General Elliot L. Richardson resigns (**Oct. 20**). Egypt and Israel sign U.S.-sponsored cease-fire accord (**Nov. 11**). Duke Ellington's autobiography, *Music Is My Mistress,* is published.

1974 Patricia Hearst, 19-year-old daughter of publisher Randolph Hearst, kidnapped by Symbionese Liberation Army (**Feb. 5**). House Judiciary Committee adopts three articles of impeachment charging President Nixon with obstruction of justice, failure to uphold laws, and refusal to produce material subpoenaed by the committee (**July 30**). Richard M. Nixon announces he will resign the next day, the first president to do so (**Aug. 8**). Vice President Gerald R. Ford of Michigan is sworn in as 38th president of the U.S. (**Aug. 9**). Ford grants "full, free, and absolute pardon" to ex-president Nixon (**Sept. 8**).

1975 John N. Mitchell, H. R. Haldeman, John D. Ehrlichman found guilty of Watergate cover-up (**Jan. 1**); sentenced to 30 months to 8 years in jail (**Feb. 21**). Pol Pot and Khmer Rouge take over Cambodia (**April**). American merchant ship *Mayaguez,* seized by Cambodian forces, is rescued in operation by U.S. Navy and Marines, 38 of whom are killed (**May 15**). *Apollo* and *Soyuz* spacecraft take off for U.S.-Soviet link-up in space (**July 15**). President Ford escapes assassination attempt in Sacramento, Calif. (**Sept. 5**). President Ford escapes second assassination attempt in 17 days (**Sept. 22**).

1976 Supreme Court rules that blacks and other minorities are entitled to retroactive job seniority (**March 24**). Ford signs Federal Election Campaign Act (**May 11**). Supreme Court rules that death penalty is not inherently cruel or unusual and is a constitutionally acceptable form of punishment (**July 3**). Nation celebrates bicentennial (**July 4**). Israeli airborne commandos attack Uganda's Entebbe Airport and free 103 hostages held by pro-Palestinian hijackers of Air France plane; one Israeli and several Ugandan soldiers killed in raid (**July 4**). Mysterious disease that eventually claims 29 lives strikes American Legion convention in Philadelphia (**Aug. 4**). Jimmy Carter elected U.S. president (**Nov. 2**).

1977 First woman Episcopal priest ordained (**Jan. 1**). Scientists identify previously unknown bacterium as cause of mysterious "legionnaire's disease" (**Jan. 18**). Carter pardons Vietnam draft evaders (**Jan. 21**). Scientists report using bacteria in lab to make insulin (**May 23**). Supreme Court rules that states are not required to spend Medicaid funds on elective abortions (**June 20**). Deng Xiaoping, purged Chinese leader, restored to power as "Gang of Four" is expelled from Communist Party (**July 22**). South African activist Stephen Biko dies in police custody

(Sept. 12). Nuclear-proliferation pact, curbing spread of nuclear weapons, signed by 15 countries, including U.S. and USSR **(Sept. 21).**

1978 President chooses Federal Appeals Court Judge William H. Webster as F.B.I. Director **(Jan. 19).** Rhodesia's prime minister Ian D. Smith and three black leaders agree on transfer to black majority rule **(Feb. 15).** U.S. Senate approves Panama Canal neutrality treaty **(March 16);** votes treaty to turn canal over to Panama by year 2000 **(April 18).** Former Italian premier Aldo Moro kidnapped by left wing terrorists, who kill five bodyguards **(March 16);** he is found slain **(May 9).** Californians in referendum approve Proposition 13 for nearly 60% slash in property tax revenues **(June 6).** Supreme Court, in Bakke case, bars quota systems in college admissions but affirms constitutionality of programs giving advantage to minorities **(June 28).** Pope Paul VI, dead at 80, mourned **(Aug. 6);** new Pope, John Paul I, 65, dies unexpectedly after 34 days in office **(Sept. 28);** succeeded by Karol Cardinal Wojtyla of Poland as John Paul II **(Oct. 16).** "Framework for Peace" in Middle East signed by Egypt's president Anwar Sadat and Israeli premier Menachem Begin after 13-day conference at Camp David led by President Carter **(Sept. 17).** Jim Jones's followers commit mass suicide in Jonestown, Guyana **(Nov. 18).**

Pope John Paul II
(1920–)

1979 Oil spills pollute ocean waters in Atlantic and Gulf of Mexico **(Jan. 1, June 8, July 21).** Ohio agrees to pay $675,000 to families of dead and injured in Kent State University shootings **(Jan. 4).** Vietnam and Vietnam-backed Cambodian insurgents announce fall of Phnom Penh, Cambodian capital, and collapse of Pol Pot regime **(Jan. 7).** Shah leaves Iran after year of turmoil **(Jan. 16);** revolutionary forces under Muslim leader, Ayatollah Ruhollah Khomeini, take over **(Feb. 1** *et seq.***).** Nuclear power plant accident at Three Mile Island, Pa., releases radiation **(March 28).** Conservatives win British election; Margaret Thatcher new prime minister **(May 3).** Carter and Brezhnev sign SALT II agreement **(June 14).** Nicaraguan president Gen. Anastasio Somoza Debayle resigns and flees to Miami **(July 17);** Sandinistas form government **(July 19).** Earl Mountbatten of Burma, 79, British World War II hero, and three others killed by blast on fishing boat off Irish coast **(Aug. 27);** two I.R.A. members accused **(Aug. 30).** Iranian militants seize U.S. embassy in Teheran and hold hostages **(Nov. 4).** Soviet invasion of Afghanistan stirs world protests **(Dec. 27).**

Anwar Sadat
(1918–1981)

1980 Six U.S. embassy aides escape from Iran with Canadian help **(Jan. 29).** F.B.I.'s undercover operation "Abscam" (for Arab scam) implicates public officials **(Feb. 2).** U.S. breaks diplomatic ties with Iran **(April 7).** Eight U.S. servicemen are killed and five are injured as helicopter and cargo plane collide in abortive desert raid to rescue American hostages in Teheran **(April 25).** Supreme Court upholds limits on federal aid for abortions **(June 30).** Shah of Iran dies at 60 **(July 27).** Anastasio Somoza Debayle, ousted Nicaraguan ruler, and two aides assassinated in Asunción, Paraguay capital **(Sept. 17).** Iraq troops hold 90 square miles of Iran after invasion; 8-year Iran-Iraq war begins **(Sept. 19).** Ronald Reagan elected president in Republican sweep **(Nov. 4).** Three U.S. nuns and lay worker found shot in El Salvador **(Dec. 4).** John Lennon of the Beatles shot dead in New York City **(Dec. 8).** Smallpox eradicated.

Ayatollah Ruhollah
Khomeini
(1900–1989)

1981 Ronald Reagan takes oath as 40th president **(Jan. 20).** U.S.-Iran agreement frees 52 hostages held in Teheran since 1979 **(Jan. 20);** hostages welcomed back in U.S. **(Jan. 25).** President Reagan wounded by gunman, with press secretary and two law-enforcement officers **(March 30).** Pope John Paul II wounded by gunman **(May 14).** Supreme Court rules, 4–4, that former president Nixon and three top aides may be required to pay monetary damages for unconstitutional wiretap of home telephone of former national security aide **(June 22).** Reagan nominates Judge Sandra Day O'Connor, 51, of Arizona, as first woman on Supreme Court **(July 7).** More than 110 die in collapse of aerial walkways in lobby of Hyatt Regency Hotel in Kansas City; 188 injured **(July 18).** Air controllers strike, disrupting flights **(Aug. 3);** government dismisses strikers **(Aug. 11).** AIDS is first identified.

Ronald Reagan
(1911–2004)

1982 British overcome Argentina in Falklands war **(April 2–June 15).** Israel invades Lebanon in attack on P.L.O. **(June 4).** John W. Hinckley, Jr., found not guilty because of insanity in shooting of President Reagan **(June 21).** Alexander M. Haig, Jr., resigns as secretary of state **(June 25).** Equal Rights Amendment fails ratification **(June 30).** Princess

Sandra Day O'Connor
(1930–)

**Indira Gandhi
(1917–1984)**

**Corazon Aquino
(1933–)**

**Mikhail S. Gorbachev
(1931–)**

**Margaret Thatcher
(1925–)**

**Sally K. Ride
(1951–)**

Grace, 52, dies of injuries when car plunges off mountain road; daughter Stephanie, 17, suffers serious injuries **(Sept. 14).** Lebanese Christian Phalangists kill hundreds of people in two Palestinian refugee camps in West Beirut **(Sept. 15).** Leonid Brezhnev, Soviet leader, dies at 75 **(Nov. 10).** Yuri V. Andropov, 68, chosen as successor **(Nov. 15).** Permanent artificial heart implanted in human for first time in Dr. Barney B. Clark, 61, at University of Utah Medical Center in Salt Lake City **(Dec. 2).**

1983 Pope John Paul II signs new Roman Catholic code incorporating changes brought about by Second Vatican Council **(Jan. 25).** Second space shuttle, *Challenger,* makes successful maiden voyage, which includes the first U.S. space walk in nine years **(April 4).** U.S. Supreme Court declares many local abortion restrictions unconstitutional **(June 15).** Sally K. Ride, 32, first U.S. woman astronaut in space as a crew member aboard space shuttle *Challenger* **(June 18).** U.S. admits shielding former Nazi Gestapo chief Klaus Barbie, 69, the "butcher of Lyon," wanted in France for war crimes **(Aug. 15).** Benigno S. Aquino, Jr., 50, political rival of Philippines president Marcos, slain in Manila **(Aug. 21).** South Korean Boeing 747 jetliner bound for Seoul apparently strays into Soviet airspace and is shot down by a Soviet SU-15 fighter after it had tracked the airliner for two hours; all 269 aboard are killed, including 61 Americans **(Aug. 30).** Terrorist explosion kills 237 U.S. Marines in Beirut **(Oct. 23).** U.S. and Caribbean allies invade Grenada **(Oct. 25).**

1984 Bell System broken up **(Jan. 1).** France gets first deliveries of Soviet natural gas **(Jan. 1).** Syria frees captured U.S. Navy pilot, Lieut. Robert C. Goodman, Jr. **(Jan. 3).** U.S. and Vatican exchange diplomats after 116-year hiatus **(Jan. 10).** Reagan orders U.S. Marines withdrawn from Beirut international peacekeeping force **(Feb. 7).** Yuri V. Andropov dies at 69; Konstantin U. Chernenko, 72, named Soviet Union leader **(Feb. 9).** Italy and Vatican agree to end Roman Catholicism as state religion **(Feb. 18).** Reagan ends U.S. role in Beirut by relieving Sixth Fleet from peacekeeping force **(March 30).** Congress rebukes President Reagan on use of federal funds for mining Nicaraguan harbors **(April 10).** Soviet Union withdraws from summer Olympic games in U.S., and other bloc nations follow **(May 7** *et seq.***).** José Napoleón Duarte, moderate, elected president of El Salvador **(May 11).** Three hundred slain as Indian Army occupies Sikh Golden Temple in Amritsar **(June 6).** Thirty-ninth Democratic National Convention, in San Francisco, nominates Walter F. Mondale and Geraldine A. Ferraro **(July 16–19).** Thirty-third Republican National Convention, at Dallas, renominates President Reagan and Vice President Bush **(Aug. 20–25).** Brian Mulroney and Conservative party win Canadian election in landslide **(Sept. 4).** Indian prime minister Indira Gandhi assassinated by two Sikh bodyguards; 1,000 killed in anti-Sikh riots; son Rajiv succeeds her **(Oct. 31).** President Reagan re-elected in landslide with 59% of vote **(Nov. 6).** Toxic gas leaks from Union Carbide plant in Bhopal, India, killing 2,000 and injuring 150,000 **(Dec. 3).**

1985 Ronald Reagan, 73, takes oath for second term as 40th president **(Jan. 20).** General Westmoreland settles libel action against CBS **(Feb. 18).** Prime Minister Margaret Thatcher addresses Congress, endorsing Reagan's policies **(Feb. 20).** USSR leader Chernenko dies at 73 and is replaced by Mikhail Gorbachev, 54 **(March 11).** Two Shi'ite Muslim gunmen capture TWA airliner with 133 aboard, 104 of them Americans **(June 14);** 39 remaining hostages freed in Beirut **(June 30).** Supreme Court, 5–4, bars public school teachers from parochial schools **(July 1).** Arthur James Walker, 50, retired naval officer, convicted by federal judge of participating in Soviet spy ring operated by his brother, John Walker **(Aug. 9).** P.L.O. terrorists hijack *Achille Lauro,* Italian cruise ship, with 80 passengers, plus crew **(Oct. 7);** American, Leon Klinghoffer, killed **(Oct. 8);** Italian government toppled by political crisis over hijacking **(Oct. 16).** John A. Walker and son, Michael I. Walker, 22, sentenced in Navy espionage case **(Oct. 28).** Reagan and Gorbachev meet at summit **(Nov. 19);** agree to step up arms control talks and renew cultural contacts **(Nov. 21).** Terrorists seize Egyptian Boeing 737 airliner after takeoff from Athens **(Nov. 23);** 59 dead as Egyptian forces storm plane on Malta **(Nov. 24).** U.S. budget-balancing bill enacted **(Dec. 12).**

1986 Spain and Portugal join European Economic Community **(Jan. 1).** President freezes Libyan assets in U.S. **(Jan. 8).** Supreme Court bars racial bias in trial jury selection **(Jan. 14).** *Voyager 2* spacecraft reports secrets of Uranus **(Jan. 26).** Space shuttle *Challenger* explodes after launch at Cape Canaveral, Fla., killing all seven aboard **(Jan. 28).** Haiti president

Jean-Claude Duvalier flees to France **(Feb. 7).** President Marcos flees Philippines after ruling 20 years, as newly elected Corazon Aquino succeeds him **(Feb. 26).** Prime Minister Olof Palme of Sweden shot dead **(Feb. 28).** Austrian president Kurt Waldheim's service as Nazi army officer revealed **(March 3).** Union Carbide agrees to settlement with victims of Bhopal gas leak in India **(March 22).** Halley's comet yields information on return visit **(April 10).** U.S. planes attack Libyan "terrorist centers" **(April 14).** Desmond Tutu elected archbishop in South Africa **(April 14).** Major nuclear accident at Soviet Union's Chernobyl power station alarms world **(April 26** *et seq.*). Ex-Navy analyst, Jonathan Jay Pollard, 31, guilty as spy for Israel **(June 4).** Supreme Court reaffirms abortion rights **(June 11).** World Court rules U.S. broke international law in mining Nicaraguan waters **(June 27).** Supreme Court voids automatic provisions of budget-balancing law **(July 7).** Jerry A. Whitworth, ex-Navy radioman, convicted as spy **(July 24);** he is also part of Walker family spy ring. Muslim captors release Rev. Lawrence Martin Jenco **(July 26).** Senate Judiciary Committee approves William H. Rehnquist as chief justice of U.S. **(Aug. 14).** House votes arms appropriations bill rejecting administration's "star wars" policy **(Aug. 15).** Three Lutheran church groups in U.S. set to merge **(Aug. 29).** Congress overrides Reagan veto of stiff sanctions against South Africa **(Sept. 29 and Oct. 2).** Congress approves immigration bill barring hiring of illegal aliens, with amnesty provision **(Oct. 17).** Reagan signs $11.7-billion budget reduction measure **(Oct. 21).** He approves sweeping revision of U.S. tax code **(Oct. 22).** Democrats triumph in elections, gaining eight seats to win Senate majority **(Nov. 4).** Secret initiative to send arms to Iran revealed **(Nov. 6** *et seq.*); Reagan denies exchanging arms for hostages and halts arms sales **(Nov. 19);** diversion of funds from arms sales to Nicaraguan Contras revealed **(Nov. 25).**

William Rehnquist
(1924–)

1987 William Buckley, U.S. hostage in Lebanon, reported slain **(Jan. 20).** Supreme Court rules Rotary Clubs must admit women **(May 4).** Iraqi missiles kill 37 in attack on U.S. frigate *Stark* in Persian Gulf **(May 17);** Iraqi president apologizes **(May 18).** Prime Minister Thatcher wins rare third term in Britain **(June 11).** Supreme Court justice Lewis F. Powell, Jr., retires **(June 26).** Klaus Barbie, 73, Gestapo wartime chief in Lyon, sentenced to life by French court for war crimes **(July 4).** Oliver North, Jr., tells congressional inquiry higher officials approved his secret Iran-Contra operations **(July 7–10).** Admiral John M. Poindexter, former National Security Adviser, testifies he authorized use of Iran arms sale profits to aid Contras **(July 15–22).** Secretary of State George P. Shultz testifies he was deceived repeatedly on Iran-Contra affair **(July 23–24).** Defense Secretary Caspar W. Weinberger tells inquiry of official deception and intrigue **(July 31, Aug. 3).** Reagan says Iran arms-Contra policy went astray and accepts responsibility **(Aug. 12).** Severe earthquake strikes Los Angeles, leaving 100 injured and six dead **(Oct. 1).** Senate, 58–42, rejects Robert H. Bork as Supreme Court justice **(Oct. 23).**

George Bush
(1924–)

1988 U.S. and Canada reach free trade agreement **(Jan. 2).** Robert C. McFarlane, former National Security Adviser, pleads guilty in Iran-Contra case **(March 11).** U.S. Navy ship shoots down Iranian airliner in Persian Gulf, mistaking it for jet fighter; 290 killed **(July 3).** Terrorists kill nine tourists on Aegean cruise **(July 11).** Democratic convention nominates Gov. Michael Dukakis of Massachusetts for president and Texas senator Lloyd Bentsen for vice president **(July 17** *et seq.*). Republicans nominate George Bush for president and Indiana senator Dan Quayle for vice president **(Aug. 15** *et seq.*). Plane blast kills Pakistani president Mohammad Zia ul-Haq **(Aug. 17).** Republicans sweep 40 states in election. Bush beats Dukakis **(Nov. 8).** Benazir Bhutto, first Islamic woman prime minister, chosen to lead Pakistan **(Dec. 1).** Pan-Am 747 explodes from terrorist bomb and crashes in Lockerbie, Scotland, killing all 259 aboard and 11 on ground **(Dec. 21).**

Benazir Bhutto
(1953–)

1989 U.S. planes shoot down two Libyan fighters over international waters in Mediterranean **(Jan. 4).** Emperor Hirohito of Japan dead at 87 **(Jan. 7).** George Herbert Walker Bush inaugurated as 41st U.S. president **(Jan. 20).** Iran's Ayatollah Khomeini declares author Salman Rushdie's book *The Satanic Verses* offensive and sentences him to death **(Feb. 14).** Ruptured tanker *Exxon Valdez* sends 11 million gallons of crude oil into Alaska's Prince William Sound **(March 24).** Tens of thousands of Chinese students take over Beijing's Tiananmen Square in rally for democracy **(April 19** *et seq.*). U.S. jury convicts Oliver North in Iran-Contra

François Mitterrand
(1916–1996)

General Colin Powell
(1937–)

affair (**May 4**). More than one million in Beijing demonstrate for democracy; chaos spreads across nation (**mid-May** *et seq.*). Mikhail S. Gorbachev named Soviet president (**May 25**). Thousands killed in Tiananmen Square as Chinese leaders take hard line toward demonstrators (**June 4** *et seq.*). Army general Colin R. Powell is first black chairman of Joint Chiefs of Staff (**Aug. 9**). P. W. Botha quits as South Africa's president (**Aug. 14**). *Voyager 2* spacecraft speeds by Neptune after making startling discoveries about the planet and its moons (**Aug. 29**). Deng Xiaoping resigns from China's leadership (**Nov. 9**). After 28 years, Berlin Wall is open to West (**Nov. 11**). Czech Parliament ends Communists' dominant role (**Nov. 30**). Romanian uprising overthrows Communist government (**Dec. 15** *et seq.*); President Ceausescu and wife executed (**Dec. 25**). U.S. troops invade Panama, seeking capture of Gen. Manuel Noriega (**Dec. 20**); resistance to U.S. collapses (**Dec. 24**). Dalai Lama wins Nobel Peace Prize.

1990 World Wide Web debuts, popularizes Internet. Gen. Manuel Noriega surrenders in Panama (**Jan. 3**). Yugoslav Communists end 45-year monopoly of power (**Jan. 22**). Soviet Communists relinquish sole power (**Feb. 7**). South Africa frees Nelson Mandela, imprisoned 27½ years (**Feb. 11**). Violeta Barrios de Chamorro inaugurated as Nicaraguan president. Hubble Space Telescope launched (**April 25**). U.S.-Soviet summit reaches accord on armaments (**June 1**). Western Alliance ends cold war and proposes joint action with Soviet Union and Eastern Europe (**July 6**). U.S. Appeals Court overturns Oliver North's Iran-Contra conviction (**July 20**). Iraqi troops invade Kuwait and seize petroleum reserves, setting off Persian Gulf War (**Aug. 2** *et seq.*). East and West Germany reunited (**Oct. 3**). Republicans set back in midterm elections (**Nov. 8**). Gorbachev assumes emergency powers (**Nov. 17**). Leaders of 34 nations in Europe and North America proclaim a united Europe (**Nov. 21**). Margaret Thatcher resigns as British prime minister (**Nov. 22**); John Major succeeds her (**Nov. 28**). Lech Walesa wins Poland's runoff presidential election (**Dec. 9**). Haiti elects leftist priest as president in first democratic election (**Dec. 17**).

1991 U.S. and Allies at war with Iraq (**Jan. 15**). Warsaw Pact dissolves military alliance (**Feb. 25**). Cease-fire ends Persian Gulf War; UN forces are victorious (**April 3**). Europeans end sanctions on South Africa (**April 15**). Supreme Court limits death row appeals (**April 16**). Winnie Mandela sentenced in kidnapping (**May 13**). William H. Webster retires as director of CIA; Robert H. Gates succeeds him (**May 14**). France agrees to sign 1968 treaty banning spread of atomic weapons (**June 3**). Communist government of Albania resigns (**June 4**). Jiang Qing, widow of Mao, commits suicide (**June 4**). South African Parliament repeals apartheid laws (**June 5**). Warsaw Pact dissolved (**July 1**). Boris N. Yeltsin inaugurated as first freely elected president of Russian Republic (**July 10**). Bush-Gorbachev summit negotiates strategic arms reduction treaty (**July 31**). China accepts nuclear nonproliferation treaty (**Aug. 10**). Lithuania, Estonia, and Latvia win independence (**Aug. 25**); Bush recognizes them (**Sept. 2**). Haitian

---

THE PERSIAN GULF WAR (Jan. 16, 1991–April 6, 1991)

1990 Iraq invades its tiny neighbor, Kuwait, after talks break down over oil production and debt repayment. Iraqi president Saddam Hussein later annexes Kuwait and declares it a 19th province of Iraq (**Aug. 2**). President Bush believes that Iraq intends to invade Saudi Arabia and take control of the region's oil supplies. He begins organizing a multinational coalition to seek Kuwait's freedom and restoration of its legitimate government. The UN Security Council authorizes economic sanctions against Iraq. Bush orders U.S. troops to protect Saudi Arabia at the Saudis' request and "Operation Desert Shield" begins (**Aug. 6**). 230,000 American troops arrive in Saudi Arabia to take defensive action, but when Iraq continues a huge military buildup in Kuwait, the President orders an additional 200,000 troops deployed to prepare for a possible offensive action by the U.S.-led coalition forces. He subsequently obtains a UN Security Council resolution setting a **Jan. 15, 1991** deadline for Iraq to withdraw unconditionally from Kuwait (**Nov. 8**).

1991 Bush wins congressional approval for his position with the most devastating air assault in history against military targets in Iraq and Kuwait (**Jan. 16**). He rejects a Soviet-Iraq peace plan for a gradual withdrawal that does not comply with all the UN resolutions and gives Iraq an ultimatum to withdraw from Kuwait by noon **Feb. 23** (**Feb. 22**). The president orders the ground war to begin (**Feb. 24**). In a brilliant and lightning-fast campaign, U.S. and coalition forces smash through Iraq's defenses and defeat Saddam Hussein's troops in only four days of combat. Allies enter Kuwait City (**Feb. 26**). Iraqi army sets fire to over 500 of Kuwait's oil wells as final act of destruction to Kuwait's infrastructure. Bush orders a unilateral cease-fire 100 hours after the ground offensive started (**Feb. 27**). Allied and Iraqi military leaders meet on battlefield to discuss terms for a formal cease-fire to end the Gulf War. Iraq agrees to abide by all of the UN resolutions (**Mar. 3**). The first Allied prisoners of war are released (**Mar. 4**). Official cease-fire accepted and signed (**April 6**). 532,000 U.S. forces served in Operation Desert Storm. There were a total of 147 U.S. battle deaths during the Gulf War, 145 nonbattle deaths, and 467 wounded in action.

troops seize president in uprising (**Sept. 30**). U.S. suspends assistance to Haiti (**Oct. 1**). Professor Anita Hill accuses Judge Clarence Thomas of sexual harassment (**Oct. 6**); Senate, 52–48, confirms Thomas for Supreme Court after stormy hearings (**Oct. 15**). Israel and Soviet Union resume relations after 24 years (**Oct. 18**). U.S. indicts two Libyans in 1988 bombing of Pan Am Flight 103 over Lockerbie, Scotland (**Nov. 15**). Anglican envoy Terry Waite and U.S. Prof. Thomas M. Sutherland freed by Lebanese (**Nov. 18**). Last three U.S. hostages freed in Lebanon (**Dec. 2–4**). Soviet Union breaks up after President Gorbachev's resignation; constituent republics form Commonwealth of Independent States (**Dec. 25**).

Hubble Space Telescope

1992 Yugoslav Federation broken up (**Jan. 15**). Bush and Yeltsin proclaim formal end to cold war (**Feb. 1**). U.S. lifts trade sanctions against China (**Feb. 21**). U.S. recognizes three former Yugoslav republics (**April 7**). Gen. Noriega, former Panama leader, convicted in U.S. court (**April 9**). Four police officers acquitted in Los Angeles beating of Rodney King; rioting erupts in South-Central Los Angeles (**April 29** *et seq.*). Caspar W. Weinberger indicted in Iran-Contra affair (**June 16**). Last Western hostages freed in Lebanon (**June 17**). Supreme Court reaffirms right to abortion (**June 29**). Democrats nominate Bill Clinton and Al Gore (**July 1**). Gen. Noriega sentenced to 40 years on drug charges (**July 10**). Court clears *Exxon Valdez* skipper (**July 10**). Israeli Parliament approves Yitzhak Rabin's coalition government, dominated by Labor Party (**July 13**). Police officers acquitted in April on criminal charges in Rodney King beating are indicted on federal civil rights charges (**Aug. 5**). North American trade compact announced (**Aug. 12**). Republicans renominate Bush and Quayle (**Aug. 20**). UN expels Serbian-dominated Yugoslavia (**Sept. 22**). Senate ratifies second Strategic Arms Limitation Treaty (**Oct. 1**). Top Japanese leader, Shin Kanemaru, resigns in scandal (**Oct. 14**). Bill Clinton elected president, Al Gore vice president; Democrats keep control of Congress (**Nov. 3**). Russian Parliament approves START treaty (**Nov. 4**). U.S. forces leave Philippines, ending nearly a century of American military presence (**Nov. 24**). Czechoslovak Parliament approves separation into two nations (**Nov. 25**). UN approves U.S.-led force to guard food for Somalia (**Dec. 3**). Prince and Princess of Wales agree to separate (**Dec. 9**). Bush pardons former Reagan administration officials involved in Iran-Contra affair (**Dec. 24**).

Lech Walesa
(1943–)

1993 Vaclav Havel elected as Czech president (**Jan. 26**). Clinton agrees to compromise on military's ban on homosexuals (**Jan. 29**). U.S. begins airlift of supplies to besieged Bosnia towns (**Feb. 28**). Federal agents besiege Texas Branch Davidian religious cult after six are killed in raid (**March 1** *et seq.*). Five arrested, sixth sought in bombing of World Trade Center in New York (**March 29**). Two police officers convicted on federal civil rights charges in Rodney King beating (**April 17**); sentenced (**Aug. 4**). Fire kills 72 as cult standoff in Texas ends with federal assault (**April 19**). President of Sri Lanka assassinated (**May 1**). British Commons approves European unity pact (**May 20**). Twenty-two UN troops killed in Somalia (**June 5**). Ruth Bader Ginsburg appointed to Supreme Court (**June 14**). Iraq accepts UN weapons monitoring (**July 19**). Vincent W. Foster, Jr., senior White House lawyer, commits suicide (**July 22**). Midwest flood damage expected to exceed $10 billion (**July 24**). Israeli-Palestinian accord reached (**Aug. 28**). U.S. agents blamed in Waco, Tex., siege (**Oct. 1**). Yeltsin's forces crush revolt in Russian Parliament (**Oct. 4** *et seq.*). China breaks nuclear test moratorium (**Oct. 5**). Canada's opposition Liberal Party regains power in landslide (**Oct. 25**). Europe's Maastricht Treaty takes effect, creating European Union (**Nov. 1**). Jean Chretien sworn in as Canada's 20th prime minister (**Nov. 4**). House of Representatives approves North American Free Trade Agreement (**Nov. 17**); Senate follows (**Nov. 21**). South Africa adopts majority rule constitution (**Nov. 18**). Clinton signs Brady bill regulating firearms purchases (**Nov. 30**). Toni Morrison wins Nobel prize for literature.

Toni Morrison
(1931–)

Ruth Bader Ginsburg
(1933–)

1994 Serbs' heavy weapons pound Sarajevo (**Jan. 5–6**). Olympic figure skater Nancy Kerrigan attacked (**Jan. 6**); three arrested in attack (**Jan. 13**). Major earthquake jolts Los Angeles; 51 dead (**Jan. 17** *et seq.*). Clinton ends trade embargo on Vietnam (**Feb. 9**). Aldrich Ames, high C.I.A. official, charged with spying for Soviets (**Feb. 22**). Four convicted in World Trade Center bombing (**March 4**). Mexican presidential candidate assassinated (**March 23**). Rwandan genocide of Tutsis by Hutus begins; estimated 800,000 slaughtered in c. 100 days (**April 6**). South Africa holds first interracial national election (**April 29**);

Boris Yeltsin
(1931–)

Nelson Mandela
(1918–)

Jean-Bertrand Aristide
(1953–)

Dalai Lama
(1935–)

Yitzhak Rabin
(1922–1995)

Seamus Heaney
(1939–)

Nelson Mandela elected president. Israel and Palestinians sign accord **(May 4).** Clinton accused of sexual harassment while governor of Arkansas **(May 6).** Congress votes protection for women's health clinics **(May 12).** O. J. Simpson arrested in killings of wife, Nicole Brown Simpson, and friend, Ronald Goldman **(June 18).** Supreme Court approves limit on abortion protests **(June 30).** Senate confirms Stephen G. Breyer for Supreme Court **(July 29).** Women's health clinic doctor shot dead outside Florida clinic **(July 29).** Major league baseball players strike **(Aug. 13).** "Carlos the Jackal," international terrorist, captured **(Aug. 15).** IRA declares cease-fire in Northern Ireland **(Aug. 31).** Small plane crashes into White House **(Sept. 12).** Baseball owners end season and cancel World Series **(Sept. 14).** Powerful earthquake strikes Japan **(Oct. 4).** Aristide returns to joyous Haiti **(Oct. 4).** U.S. sends forces to Persian Gulf **(Oct. 7).** Ulster Protestants declare cease-fire **(Oct. 13).** Israel and Jordan sign peace treaty **(Oct. 17).** Reagan, 83, reveals he has Alzheimer's disease **(Nov. 6).** G.O.P. wins control of House and Senate **(Nov. 8).** Aristide forms Haitian government with prime minister and full cabinet **(Nov. 9).** Clinton orders Bosnian arms embargo ended **(Nov. 10).** Newt Gingrich named House Speaker **(Dec. 5).** Bentsen resigns as Treasury Secretary **(Dec. 6).** Russians attack secessionist Republic of Chechnya **(Dec. 11** *et seq.*). John Salvi kills two at Massachusetts Planned Parenthood clinic **(Dec. 30).**

1995 Republicans take control of Congress **(Jan. 4).** More than 5,000 dead in Japanese earthquake **(Jan. 17** *et seq.*). Criminal trial of O. J. Simpson opens in California **(Jan. 24).** U.S. rescues Mexico's economy with $20-billion aid program **(Feb. 21).** Senate rejects balanced-budget amendment **(March 2).** Nerve gas attack in Tokyo subway kills eight and injures thousands. The Aum Shinrikyo ("Supreme Truth") cult is to blame **(March 20).** Major League Baseball strike ends **(April 2).** Appeals court upholds woman's plea to enter Citadel military academy **(April 13).** UN Council votes easier sanctions for Iraq **(April 14).** Scores killed as terrorist's car bomb blows up block-long Oklahoma City federal building **(April 19);** Timothy McVeigh, 27, Army veteran, arrested as suspect **(April 21);** authorities seek second suspect, link right-wing paramilitary groups to bombing **(April 22).** Death toll 2,000 in Rwanda massacre **(April 22).** Fighting escalates in Bosnia and Croatia **(May 1).** U.S. shuttle docks with Russian space station **(June 27).** F.B.I. suspends four in Idaho siege inquiry **(Aug. 11).** France explodes nuclear device in Pacific; wide protests ensue **(Sept. 5).** Senator Bob Packwood of Oregon resigns under pressure for sexual and official misconduct **(Sept. 6).** Israelis and Palestinians agree on transferring West Bank to Arabs **(Sept. 24).** Los Angeles jury finds O. J. Simpson not guilty of murder charges **(Oct. 3).** Pope John Paul II visits U.S. on whirlwind tour **(Oct. 4–8).** Warring parties agree on cease-fire in Bosnia **(Oct. 5).** Million Man March draws hundreds of thousands of black men to capital **(Oct. 16).** Quebec narrowly rejects independence from Canada **(Oct. 30).** Israeli prime minister Yitzhak Rabin slain by Jewish extremist at peace rally **(Nov. 4).** U.S. servicemen admit rape of Japanese schoolgirl in Okinawa **(Nov. 7).** Nigeria hangs writer Ken Saro-Wiwa and eight other minority rights advocates **(Nov. 10).** Irish voters approve end to constitutional ban on divorce **(Nov. 24).** Combatants sign Bosnia peace treaty **(Dec. 14).** House move stalls Congress–White House negotiations to avert government shutdown **(Dec. 20).** Seamus Heaney wins Nobel prize for literature.

1996 U.S. budget crisis in fourth month **(Jan 3).** Clinton approves resumption of many government operations **(Jan. 6).** Senate ratifies major arms reduction treaty **(Jan. 26).** France announces end to nuclear tests **(Jan. 29).** At least 73 dead in Sri Lankan suicide bombing **(Feb. 1).** Suicide bombers kill 59 in Israel **(March 4).** Bob Dole sweeps Republican primaries **(March 5).** Britain alarmed by deadly cow disease **(March 20** *et seq.*). UN tribunal charges war crimes by Bosnian Muslims and Croats **(March 22).** Commerce Secretary Ronald H. Brown killed in plane crash **(April 3).** FBI arrests suspected Unabomber **(April 3).** Clinton signs line-item veto bill **(April 9).** President blocks ban on late-term abortions **(April 10).** ValuJet crashes in Everglades; all 110 aboard killed **(May 11).** Chechnya peace treaty signed **(May 27).** Israel elects Benjamin Netanyahu as prime minister **(May 31).** China agrees to world ban on atomic testing (**June 6**). Leaders in Balkans sign accord on arms limits (**June 14**). Jazz great Ella Fitzgerald dies (**June 15**). Truck bomb kills 19 at U.S. base in Saudi Arabia (**June 25**). Boris Yeltsin is reelected in Russian election (**July 3**). Prince Charles and Princess Diana agree on divorce (**July 12**). 747 airliner crashes in Atlantic off Long Island; all 230 aboard perish (**July 17**). Bomb mars Summer Olympic games in Atlanta (**July 25**). Clinton signs bill to raise minimum wage (**Aug. 2**). Congress passes welfare reform bill (**Aug. 2**); approved by Clinton (**Aug. 22**). Republican convention opens in San Diego (**Aug. 12**); Bob Dole and Jack Kemp nominated (**Aug. 14**). Democrats convene in Chicago (**Aug. 26**). Iraqis strike at Kurdish enclave (**Aug. 31**); after warning, U.S. attacks Iraq's southern air defenses (**Sept. 2–3**); Iraq halts attacks on U.S. planes enforcing flight exclusion zones in north and south (**Sept. 13**). Violence flares in Jerusalem over Israel opening tourist tunnel (**Sept. 24**). Taliban Muslim fundamentalists capture Afghan capital (**Sept. 27**). Ethnic violence breaks out in Zairian refugee camps (**Oct. 13**); thousands of refugees from Rwanda and Burundi abandon camps (**Oct. 21**). Clinton-Gore ticket wins national election; Republicans retain control of Congress (**Nov. 5**). Mid-air collision in India kills 342 (**Nov. 12**). Texaco settles racial bias suit (**Nov. 15**). Hundreds of thousands of Hutu refugees return to Rwanda (**Nov. 15–18**). Clinton appoints Madeleine Albright as first female U.S. secretary of state (**Dec. 5**). Kofi Annan named UN secretary-general (**Dec. 13**). FBI agent charged with spying for Moscow (**Dec. 18**). Thousands march in Belgrade in continuing protest against president's annulment of election results (**Dec. 26**).

Ella Fitzgerald
(1918–1996)

Madeleine Albright
(1937–)

1997 Two Hutu sentenced to death in Rwandan genocide (**Jan. 3**). Floods cause wide damage in U.S. West (**Jan. 5**). Newt Gingrich reelected as House Speaker (**Jan. 7**). Hebron agreement signed; Israel gives up large part of West Bank city of Hebron (**Jan. 16**). U.S. shuttle joins Russian space station (**Jan. 17**). Gingrich found guilty of ethics violations (**Jan. 17**). President Clinton starts second term (**Jan. 20**). U.S., U.K., and France agree to freeze Nazis' gold loot (**Feb. 3**). O. J. Simpson found liable in civil suit (**Feb. 5**). Deng Xiaoping, Chinese leader, dead at 92 (**Feb. 19**). Israeli government approves establishment of Jewish settlement in East Jerusalem, a setback in Middle East peace process (**Feb. 26**). Tornadoes wreak havoc in Arkansas, Ohio, and Kentucky (**March 3**). State of anarchy in Albania when third of population loses savings because of pyramid schemes (**March 13**). Hale-Bopp comet is the closest it will be to Earth until 4397 (**March 22**). Heaven's Gate cult members commit mass suicide in California (**March 27**). U.S. Appeals Court upholds California ban on affirmative action (**April 8**). U.S. judge upholds California marijuana law (**April 11**). Tiger Woods breaks multiple records in Masters golf tournament (**April 13**). Fire kills 300 pilgrims outside Mecca (**April 15**). Senate, 74–26, approves chemical-weapons treaty (**April 24**). Thousands flee North Dakota flood (**April 27**). Sergeant Major of the Army, Gene C. McKinney, charged in sex cases (**May 7**). Russian president Yeltsin signs Chechnya peace treaty (**May 12**). U.S.-Russian spaceship linkup in orbit ends (**May 21**). U.S. jobless rate for May reported 4.8%, lowest since 1973 (**June 6**). European Union bolsters currency merger (**June 16**). Congress votes major tax cuts (**June 26**). Hong Kong returns to Chinese rule (**June 30**). U.S. spacecraft begins exploration of Mars (**July 4**). Andrew Cunanan murders fashion designer Gianni Versace (**July 15**). Khmer Rouge hold trial of longtime leader Pol Pot (**July 25**). White House and GOP agree on measure to balance budget (**July 28**). U.S. spacecraft transmits thousands of pictures from Mars (**Aug. 8**). Clinton exercises new line-item veto (**Aug. 11**). Timothy J. McVeigh sentenced to death for Oklahoma City bombing (**Aug. 14**). Princess Diana, 36, killed with two others in Paris car crash (**Aug. 31**). Three Islamic suicide bombers kill four persons in Jerusalem (**Sept. 4**). Mother Teresa dead at 87 (**Sept. 5**). Swiss plan first payment to Holocaust victims (**Sept. 17**). Militant Taliban leaders seize Kabul (**Sept. 27**). Iraq expels all U.S. members of UN arms-inspection team (**Oct. 29**). GOP victorious in off-year elections (**Nov. 4**). Pakistani convicted in 1993 CIA killings (**Nov. 10**). Two convicted in New York World Trade Center bombing (**Nov. 12**). Egyptian Islamic militants kill 62 at Luxor tourist site (**Nov. 17**). FBI ends 16-month investigation of crash of Flight 800 off Long Island; denies sabotage (**Nov. 18**). European Union plans to admit six nations (**Dec. 13**). U.S. company launches first commercial spy satellite (**Dec. 24**). Paris court convicts "Carlos the Jackal" of murder (**Dec. 24**).

Kofi Annan
(1938–)

Hale-Bopp Comet

Princess Diana
(1961–1997)

Mother Teresa (1910–1997)

100

Euro 100

Mars Sojourner Rover

William J. Clinton (1946–)

Gerhard Schröder (1944–)

1998 Ramzi Ahmed Yousef sentenced to life for 1993 World Trade Center bombing (**Jan. 9**). Pope John Paul II visits Cuba (**Jan. 21–25**). President accused in White House sex scandal; denies allegations of affair with White House intern, Monica Lewinsky (**Jan. 21** *et seq.*). President outlines first balanced budget in 30 years (**Feb. 3**). U.S. plane cuts ski cable in Italy and sends car plunging; 20 killed (**Feb. 3**). Thousands dead in Afghanistan quake (**Feb. 4** *et seq.*). U.S. court rules line-item veto unconstitutional (**Feb. 12**). Serbs battle ethnic Albanians in Kosovo (**March 5** *et seq.*). U.S. drops condemnation of China's human rights record (**March 13**). Hindu nationalist Vajpayee becomes India's prime minister (**March 19**). FDA approves Viagra, male impotence drug (**March 27**). Federal judge in Arkansas throws out Paula Jones case (**April 1**). Landmark peace settlement, the Good Friday Accord, reached in Northern Ireland (**April 10**). U.S. trade deficit biggest in decade (**April 17**). Europeans agree on single currency, the euro (**May 3**). Unabomber, Theodore Kaczynski, sentenced to four life terms (**May 4**). India conducts three atomic tests despite worldwide disapproval (**May 11, 13**). Indonesian dictator Suharto steps down after 32 years in power (**May 21**). Pakistan stages five nuclear tests in response to India's (**May 29, 30**). Serbs renew attack on Kosovo rebels (**June 1**). Life sentence meted out to Terry Nichols, convicted in Oklahoma City bombing fatal to 168 (**June 4**). Nigerian dictator Sani Abacha dies (**June 8**). Congress votes to overhaul IRS (**July 9**). Iraq ends cooperation with UN arms inspectors (**Aug. 5**). U.S. embassies in Kenya and Tanzania bombed (**Aug. 7**). Clinton admits to affair with White House intern in televised address to nation (**Aug. 17**). Russia fights to avert financial collapse (**Aug. 17**). U.S. cruise missiles hit suspected terrorist bases in Sudan and Afghanistan (**Aug. 20**). North Korea fires missile across Japan (**Aug. 31**). Swissair jet crashes; kills 229 (**Sept. 2**). Starr Report by independent counsel outlines case for impeachment proceedings against president (**Sept. 11**). Senate sustains veto of bill to outlaw late-term abortions (**Sept. 18**). Iran lifts death threat against Salman Rushdie (**Sept. 24**). German chancellor Helmut Kohl defeated by Gerhard Schröder (**Sept. 27**). U.S. budget surplus largest in three decades (**Oct. 5**). Matthew Shepard, gay Wyoming student, fatally beaten in hate crime (**Oct. 6**). NATO, on verge of air strikes, reaches settlement with Milosevic on Kosovo (**Oct. 12**). Former Chilean dictator Pinochet arrested in London (**Oct. 16**). Wye Mills Agreement between Netanyahu and Arafat moves Middle East peace talks forward (**Oct. 23**). More than 10,000 die in Central American hurricane, Mitch (**Nov. 1**). Democrats unexpectedly gain five House seats in national election; Republicans keep control of House and Senate (**Nov. 3**). House Speaker Gingrich to step down (**Nov. 9**). House panel drafts impeachment charges; votes along party lines to approve four articles (**Dec. 11–12**). Clinton orders air strikes on Iraq (**Dec. 16–19**). House impeaches President Clinton along party lines on two charges, perjury and obstruction of justice (**Dec. 19**).

1999 U.S. agrees to ease restrictions on Cuba (**Jan. 4**). Dennis Hastert elected to replace Newt Gingrich as Speaker of the House (**Jan. 6**). NBA ends 191-day labor dispute (**Jan. 6**). International Olympic Committee expels six members as bribery scandal widens (**Jan. 24**). King Hussein of Jordan dies (**Feb. 7**). Senate acquits President Clinton of impeachment charges (**Feb. 12**). Gen. Olusegun Obasanjo elected president of Nigeria (**Feb. 28**). First nonstop balloon flight around world completed in 20 days by Bertrand Piccard (Switzerland) and Brian Jones (UK) (**March 1–20**). Marine pilot acquitted in killing of 20 in 1998 Italian ski gondola accident; Italians outraged (**March 4**). U.S. accuses China of stealing nuclear secrets (**March 5**). Joe DiMaggio dies at age 84 (**March 8**). Czech Republic, Poland, and Hungary join NATO (**March 12**). NATO launches air strikes on Serbia to end attacks against ethnic Albanians in Kosovo (**March 24**). Dr. Jack Kevorkian convicted of second-degree murder in assisted-suicide case (**March 26**). "Melissa" computer virus spreads through the Internet (**March 27**). Libya hands over two suspects in 1988 Pan Am jet bombing (**April 5**). Two Colo. students go on shooting spree in Columbine High School, killing 15, including themselves (**April 20**). NATO bombs mistakenly hit Chinese embassy in Belgrade (**May 7**). Citadel graduates its first woman (**May 8**). Crime rate in U.S. falls for seventh consecutive year (**May 16**). Ehud Barak defeats Benjamin Netanyahu in Israeli prime minister election (**May 17**). U.S. inspects suspected nuclear weapons site in North Korea, finds nothing (**May 20–24**). Serbs sign agreement to pull troops out of Kosovo after 11 weeks of NATO air attacks (**June 9**). Nelson Mandela retires as president of South Africa; succeeded by Thabo Mbeki (**June 16**). Britain's Prince Edward marries Sophie Rhys-Jones (**June 19**). Kurd leader Abdullah Ocalan sentenced to death for treason in Turkey (**June 29**). White supremacist goes on shooting spree in Midwest, killing three including self and wounding eight (**July 2–5**). U.S. soccer team tops China for women's World Cup (**July 10**). Taiwanese leader Lee Teng-hui challenges "One China" policy (**July 11**). Serial killer Rafael Reséndez-Ramirez surrenders himself to U.S. authorities (**July 13**). John F. Kennedy, Jr., wife Carolyn Bessette Kennedy, and sister-in-law Lauren Bessette killed in plane crash off coast of Martha's Vineyard (**July 16**). Col. Eileen Collins becomes first female to head a space shuttle mission (**July 16**). Falun Gong meditation sect banned by Chinese government (**July 22**). Day-trader kills 9 and wounds 13 in two Atlanta brokerage offices before committing suicide (**July 29**). Yeltsin replaces Prime Minister Stepashin with Vladimir Putin in fourth government shakeup in 17 months (**Aug. 9**). Islamic militants declare independence for Dagestan and announce holy war against Russia (**Aug. 10**). White supremacist opens fire at Jewish community center in LA, wounding five and killing one as he flees (**Aug. 10**). More than 17,000 people die in 7.4 earthquake in Turkey (**Aug. 17**). Attorney General Janet Reno reopens investigation of 1993 Waco, Tex., stand-off (**Aug. 25**). People of East Timor vote for independence from Indonesia (**Aug. 31**). Israeli prime minister Ehud Barak and PLO leader Yasir Arafat announce peace accord (**Sept. 4**). Larry Gene Ashbrook goes on rampage in Tex. church, killing seven and himself (**Sept. 15**). NASA accidentally loses $125 million spacecraft as it orbits Mars (**Sept. 23**). Dozens of people exposed to radiation in Japan's worst nuclear accident (**Sept. 30**). Russia sends ground troops to Chechnya as conflict with Islamic militants intensifies (**Oct. 1**). World population reaches six billion milestone (**Oct. 11**). Military coup led by Gen. Pervez Musharraf overthrows Pakistani government (**Oct. 12**). Tobacco companies admit to harm caused by cigarette smoking (**Oct. 13**). Senate rejects 1996 nuclear test-ban treaty; international leaders upset by U.S. stand (**Oct. 13**). Indonesia elects Muslim leader Abdurrahman Wahid president (**Oct. 20**). Pro golfer Payne Stewart and five others killed in plane crash (**Oct. 25**). EgyptAir flight crashes over Atlantic, killing all 217 on board (**Oct. 31**). Judge finds Microsoft to be a monopoly (**Nov. 5**). U.S. and China reach landmark trade agreement (**Nov. 15**). China launches first spacecraft (**Nov. 21**). Five-year-old Cuban refugee Elián González gets caught in politically charged custody battle (**Nov. 25**). World Trade Organization conference disrupted by violent protests in Seattle (**Nov. 29** *et seq.*). New Northern Ireland government begins self-rule for first time in 25 years (**Dec. 2**). Muslim terrorists hijack Indian Airlines jet with 189 on board (**Dec. 24**).

2000 Socialist president, Ricardo Lagos, elected in Chile (**Jan. 16**). George W. Bush and Al Gore take Iowa caucuses in U.S. presidential race (**Jan. 22**). Austria at center of European dispute after conservative People's Party forms coalition with the far-right Freedom Party, headed by xenophobe Jörg Haider (**Feb. 3**). First Lady Hillary Clinton officially enters N.Y. Senate race (**Feb. 6**). Hijackers seize Afghan plane; release hostages in Stansted, England (**Feb. 6–12**). Britain ends self-rule in Northern Ireland after Irish Republican Army misses disarmament deadline (**Feb. 11**). NEAR spacecraft becomes first to orbit an asteroid (**Feb. 14**). Wary investors cause stock plunge; beginning of the end of the Internet stock boom (**Feb. 25**). Reformists win control of Iranian parliament for first time since 1979 Islamic revolution (**Feb. 26**). Gun maker Smith & Wesson limits the manufacture and distribution of handguns in light of lawsuits (**March 17**). Mass murder or suicide of hundreds in Ugandan doomsday cult (**March 18**). Acting Russian president Vladimir V. Putin formally chosen for post (**March 25**). Microsoft loses antitrust suit; appeal expected (**April 3**). Controversial Osprey plane crash kills 19 marines (**April 8**). Cuban boy Elián González reunited with father after federal raid of Miami relatives' home (**April 22**). Vermont approves same-sex unions (**April 25**). "I love you" virus disrupts computers worldwide (**May 4**). South Carolina removes Confederate battle flag from capitol dome (**May 18**). Chile ends Augusto Pinochet's immunity, clearing way for trial on murder and torture charges during years as dictator (**May 24**). Israeli troops withdraw from Lebanese security zone after 22 years of occupation (**May 24**). Former Indonesian president Suharto under house arrest,

Thabo Mbeki
(1942–)

Eileen Collins
(1956–)

Hillary Clinton
(1947–)

Vladimir Putin
(1952–)

Vicente Fox Quesada
(1942–)

Vojislav Kostunica
(1944–)

Yasir Arafat
(1929–)

Ariel Sharon
(1928–)

charged with corruption and abuse of power **(May 29)**. Britain restores parliamentary powers to Northern Ireland after Sinn Fein agrees to disarm **(June 4)**. Presidents of North and South Korea sign peace accord, ending half-century of antagonism **(June 15)**. British find 58 bodies of illegal Asian immigrants suffocated in Dutch truck that transported them **(June 20)**. Elián González returns to Cuba with father **(June 23)**. U.S. navy resumes shelling exercises of Puerto Rico's Vieques Island, used as a training site **(June 25)**. Human genome deciphered; expected to revolutionize the practice of medicine **(June 26)**. Iraq believed to resume missile program **(June 30)**. Vicente Fox Quesada elected president of Mexico **(July 2)**. Bashar al-Assad succeeds late father, Hafez al-Assad, as Syrian president **(July 10)**. Concorde crash kills 113 near Paris **(July 25)**. Republican convention picks Texas governor George W. Bush as presidential candidate; Dick Cheney for vice presidential spot **(Aug. 2)**. Democratic convention selects Vice President Al Gore and Sen. Joseph I. Lieberman to head ticket **(Aug. 14)**. Los Alamos scientist Wen Ho Lee, accused of stealing sensitive nuclear weapons data, freed after serving nine months in prison **(Sept. 13)**. Olympic Games open in Australia **(Sept. 15)**. Six-year Whitewater investigation of the Clintons ends without indictments **(Sept. 20)**. Yugoslav opposition claims victory; incumbent Slobodan Milosevic denies results **(Sept. 25)**. Danish voters reject euro **(Sept. 26)**. Abortion pill, RU-486, wins U.S. approval **(Sept. 28)**. Palestinians and Israelis clash, spurred by visit of right-wing Israeli leader Ariel Sharon to a joint Jewish/Muslim holy site; "Al Aksa intifada" continues unabated **(Sept. 30** *et seq.***)**. Nationwide uprising overthrows Yugoslavian president Milosevic **(Oct. 5)**. Vojislav Kostunica sworn in as Yugoslav president **(Oct. 7)**. 17 U.S. sailors on navy destroyer *Cole* die in Yemen terrorist explosion **(Oct. 12)**. U.S. presidential election closest in decades; Bush's slim lead in Florida leads to automatic recount in that state **(Nov. 7–8)**. Republicans file federal suit to block manual recount of Florida presidential election ballots sought by Democrats **(Nov. 11)**. Philippine president Joseph Estrada impeached after receiving gambling payoffs **(Nov. 13)**. Florida Supreme Court rules hand count of presidential ballots may continue **(Nov. 21)**. Global warming talks collapse at Hague conference **(Nov. 25)**. Florida Secretary of State Katherine Harris certifies Bush as winner by 537 votes **(Nov. 26)**. Mad Cow disease alarms Europe **(Nov. 30** *et seq.***)**. Israeli prime minister Ehud Barak resigns **(Dec. 9)**. U.S. Supreme Court orders halt to manual recount of presidential votes in Florida **(Dec. 9)**. Supreme Court seals Bush victory by 5–4; rules there can be no further recounting **(Dec. 12)**.

2001 Congo president Laurent Kabila assassinated by bodyguard **(Jan. 16)**. In final days of presidency, Bill Clinton issues controversial pardons, including one for Marc Rich, billionaire fugitive financier **(Jan. 20)**. George W. Bush is sworn in as 43rd president **(Jan. 20)**. Earthquake kills thousands in India **(Jan. 26** *et seq.***)**. Libyan convicted in Flight 103 bombing over Lockerbie, Scotland **(Jan. 31)**. Right-winger Ariel Sharon wins election in Israel **(Feb. 6)**. U.S. submarine *Greeneville* sinks Japanese fishing boat, killing 9 **(Feb. 9)**. FBI agent Robert Hanssen is charged with spying for Russia for 15 years **(Feb. 20)**. The long-simmering resentment of Macedonia's ethnic Albanians erupts into violence **(March 15** *et seq.***)**. British livestock epidemic, foot-and-mouth disease, reaches crisis levels **(March 23)**. Bush abandons global-warming treaty (Kyoto Protocol), angering European leaders **(March 30)**. U.S. spy plane and Chinese jet collide. The 24 crew members of the U.S. plane are detained for 11 days; U.S. issues a formal statement of regret **(April 2** *et seq.***)**. Race riots in Cincinnati continue for several days following a shooting of an unarmed black man by a white police officer **(April 7** *et seq.***)**. U.S. millionaire Dennis Tito becomes first space tourist, visiting the International Space Station aboard a Russian booster **(April 28)**. Former Klansman Thomas E. Blanton convicted of 1963 murder of four black girls in Birmingham, Ala. **(May 1)**. After a Palestinian suicide bomber kills 5 and wounds more than 100 in a Netanya shopping mall, Israeli warplanes retaliate by bombing West Bank and Gaza strip **(May 18)**. Four are declared guilty in 1998 terrorist bombings of U.S. embassies in Kenya and Tanzania **(May 29)**. Balance of the Senate shifts after Jim Jeffords of Vermont changes his party affiliation from Republican to Independent. The move strips Republicans of control of the Senate and gives Democrats the narrowest of majorities (50–49–1) **(June 5)**. Bush signs new tax-cut law, cutting taxes by $1.35 trillion over

11 years, the largest tax cut in 2 decades (**June 7**). Mohammad Khatami, Iran's moderate president, is reelected in a landslide (**June 9**). Oklahoma City bomber Timothy McVeigh executed (**June 11**). Syrian forces evacuate Beirut area after decades of occupation (**June 19**). Former Yugoslav president Slobodan Milosevic is delivered to UN tribunal in The Hague to await war-crimes trial (**June 29**). Without U.S., 178 nations reach agreement on climate accord, which rescues, though dilutes, 1997 Kyoto Protocol (**July 23**). Bush allows stem cell research, approving federal funds for studies using existing strains of stem cells (**Aug. 9**). After six months of fighting, a peace agreement is signed between rebels and the Macedonian government (**Aug. 13**). Budget surplus dwindles; some blame the slowing economy and the Bush tax cut (**Aug. 22**). Terrorists attack United States. Hijackers ram jetliners into twin towers of New York City's World Trade Center and the Pentagon. A fourth hijacked plane crashes 80 mi outside of Pittsburgh. Toll of dead is more than 3,000. Within days, Islamic militant Osama bin Laden and the al-Qaeda terrorist network are identified as the parties behind the attacks (**Sept. 11**). Anthrax scare rivets nation, as anthrax-laced letters are sent to various media and government officials. Several die after handling the letters (**October 5** *et seq.*). In response to Sept. 11 terrorist attacks, U.S. and British forces launch bombing campaign against Taliban government and al-Qaeda terrorist camps in Afghanistan. Bombings continue on a daily basis (**Oct. 7** *et seq.*). Irish Republican Army announces that it has begun to dismantle its weapons arsenal, marking a dramatic leap forward in Northern Ireland peace process (**Oct. 23**). Plane crash kills 260 in Queens, N.Y. (**Nov. 12**). Afghani factions create a post-Taliban government (**Nov. 27**). Enron Corp., one of world's largest energy companies, files for bankruptcy (**Dec. 2**). Israel condemns the Palestinian Authority as a "terror-supporting entity" and severs ties with leader Yasir Arafat following mounting violence against Israelis. The Israeli Army begins bombing Palestinian areas (**Dec. 4** *et seq.*). Taliban regime in Afghanistan collapses after two months of bombing by American warplanes and fighting by Northern Alliance ground troops (**Dec. 9**). Hamid Karzai, new interim Afghan leader, is sworn in (**Dec. 22**).

2002 The euro currency debuts in 12 European countries (**Jan. 2**). U.S. takes Taliban and al-Qaeda prisoners to Guantanamo Bay (**Jan. 10**). Defrocked priest John Geoghan convicted of child molestation; church's role in cover-up sparks national outrage (**Jan. 18**). U.S. reporter Daniel Pearl kidnapped in Pakistan (**Jan. 23**). Kenneth L. Lay, chairman of bankrupt energy trader Enron, resigns; company under federal investigation for hiding debt and misrepresenting earnings (**Jan. 24**). President Bush's first State of Union address labels Iran, Iraq, and North Korea "an axis of evil" (**Jan. 29**). Queen Elizabeth II of England marks 50 years as monarch (**Feb 6**). The trial of Slobodan Milosevic on charges of crimes against humanity opens at The Hague (**Feb. 12**). American Taliban soldier John Walker Lindh charged with supporting terrorism (**Feb. 13**). Reporter Pearl confirmed dead in Pakistan (**Feb. 21**). Angolan UNITA rebel leader Jonas Savimbi killed in battle (**Feb. 22**). Tamil Tigers and Sri Lankan government sign a cease-fire agreement (**Feb. 22**). Hundreds in India die in Hindu-Muslim clashes (**March 2**). U.S. and Afghan troops launch Operation Anaconda against remaining al-Qaeda and Taliban fighters in Afghanistan (**March 2**). Saudi peace proposal—offering Israel normal relations with all Arab nations in return for withdrawal from occupied territories—approved at Arab League summit (**March 28**). Israeli tanks and warplanes attack West Bank towns of Nablus, Jenin, Bethlehem, and others in response to string of Palestinian suicide attacks. In the first three months of 2002, 14 suicide bombers killed dozens of Israeli civilians and wounded hundreds (**March 29–April 21**). Israeli prime minister Sharon calls for exile of Palestinian leader Yasir Arafat (**April 2**). UNITA Rebels and Angolan government sign a cease-fire ending 30 years of civil war (**April 4**). International Criminal Court wins UN ratification, but U.S. refuses to ratify (**April 11**). Venezuelan president Hugo Chavez ousted in coup, then reinstated (**April 12, 14**). U.S. and Russia reach landmark arms agreement to cut both countries' nuclear arsenals by up to two-thirds over the next ten years (**May 13**). East Timor becomes a new nation (**May 20**). In letter to Director, FBI lawyer Coleen Rowley criticizes FBI for thwarting terrorist efforts (**May 21**). Dirty bomb plot foiled with arrest of Jose Padilla (**June 10**). U.S. abandons 31-year-old Antiballistic Missile treaty (**June**

Mohammad Khatami (1943–)

World Trade Center

Hamid Karzai (1957–)

Jacques Chirac (1932–)

Tony Blair
(1953–)

Hu Jintao
(1942–)

13). At national conference, U.S. bishops recommend zero tolerance policy for priests who abuse children (**June 14**). Arthur Andersen firm convicted of destroying documents relating to former client Enron Corp. (**June 15**). Bush announces U.S. will not recognize an independent Palestinian state until Yasir Arafat is replaced (**June 24**). WorldCom, after admitting to misstating profits, files for bankruptcy—largest claim in U.S. history (**July 21**). Pennsylvania miners rescued after spending 77 hours in a dark, flooded mine shaft (**July 28**). Bush signs corporate reform bill in response to spate of corporate scandals (**July 30**). Bush addresses United Nations, calls for a "regime change" in Iraq (**Sept. 12**). Tyco executives L. Dennis Kozlowski and Mark Swartz indicted in stock-fraud scheme (**Sept. 12**). Five al-Qaeda terrorist suspects arrested in New York (**Sept. 13**). Terrorist bomb in Bali kills hundreds (**Oct. 12**). Government suspended in Northern Ireland in protest of suspected IRA spy ring (**Oct. 14**). Former ImClone Executive Sam Waksal pleads guilty to charges including fraud and perjury (**Oct. 15**). North Korea admits to developing nuclear arms in defiance of treaty (**Oct. 16**). Vatican calls for softening of U.S. bishops' abuse policy (**Oct. 18**). Chechen rebels take 763 hostages in Moscow theater; Russian authorities release a gas into theater, killing 116 hostages and freeing remaining survivors (**Oct. 23–26**). Snipers prey upon DC suburbs, killing ten and wounding others (**Oct. 2–24**). Police arrest two sniper suspects, John Allen Muhammad and John Lee Malvo (**Oct. 24**). CIA kills six al-Qaeda members in Yemen (**Nov. 4**). Republicans retake the Senate in midterm elections; gain additional House seats (**Nov. 5**). UN Security Council passes unanimous resolution calling on Iraq to disarm or else face "serious consequences" (**Nov. 8**). China's Jiang Zemin officially retires as general secretary; Hu Jintao named as his successor (**Nov. 14**). UN arms inspectors return to Iraq (**Nov. 18**). EPA relaxes Clean Air Act (**Nov. 22**). Bush signs legislation creating cabinet-level Department of Homeland Security (**Nov. 25**). Boston archbishop Cardinal Bernard Law resigns over growing child sexual abuse scandal in the Catholic Church (**Dec. 13**). Trent Lott steps down as Republican leader after furor over pro-segregationist remark (**Dec. 20**). Sen. Bill Frist unanimously elected Republican leader of the Senate (**Dec. 23**).

2003 North Korea withdraws from treaty on the nonproliferation of nuclear weapons (**Jan. 10**). Illinois governor George Ryan commutes 167 death row sentences, calling capital punishment flawed (**Jan. 11**). White House announces huge deficits expected to top $200 billion in 2003 (**Jan. 15**). The UN's report on Iraqi weapons inspections is highly critical, but not damning (**Jan. 27**). In State of the Union address, Bush announces that he is ready to attack Iraq even without a UN mandate (**Jan. 28**). Ariel Sharon elected Israeli prime minister (**Jan. 29**). Space shuttle *Columbia* explodes, killing all seven astronauts (**Feb. 1**). Nine-week general strike in Venezuela calling for President Chavez's resignation ends in defeat (**Feb. 2**). U.S. Secretary of State Powell presents Iraq war rationale to UN, citing Iraqi weapons as imminent threat to world security (**Feb. 5**). Massive peace demonstrations take place around the world, protesting potential invasion of Iraq (**Feb. 15**). UN Security Council members France, Germany, and Russia insist that "the military option should only be a last resort" concerning Iraq (**Feb. 24**). Serbian prime minister Zoran Djindjic assassinated (**March 12**). Hu Jintao succeeds Chinese president Jiang Zemin (**March 15**). The United States and Britain launch war against Iraq (**March 19**). Baghdad falls to U.S. troops (**April 9**). European Union expands by ten nations (**April 16**). First Palestinian prime minister, Mahmoud Abbas, sworn in (**April 29**). U.S.-backed "road map" for peace proposed for Middle East (**April 30**). The United States declares official end to combat operations in Iraq (**May 1**). U.S. diplomat Paul Bremer becomes civil administrator of occupied Iraq (**May 12**). Bush signs ten-year, $350-billion tax-cut package, the third-largest tax cut in U.S. history (**May 28**). Terrorists strike in Saudi Arabia, killing 34 at Western compound; Al-Qaeda suspected (**May 12**). Burmese opposition leader Aung San Suu Kyi again placed under house arrest by military regime (**May 30**). Eric Rudolph, Olympic bombing suspect, arrested (**May 31**). International Atomic Energy Agency (IAEA) discovers Iran's concealed nuclear activities and calls for intensified inspections (**June 18**). In one of the most important rulings on the issue of affirmative action in 25 years, the U.S. Supreme Court decisively upholds the use of affirmative action in higher education (**June 23**). Palestinian militant groups announce cease-fire toward Israel (**June 29**). Secretary of Defense Donald Rumsfeld announces price of Iraq war is about $3.9 billion a month, nearly double the April estimate (**July 9**). Iraq's interim governing council is inaugurated (**July 13**). Saddam Hussein's sons killed in firefight (**July 22**). Mutinous troops attempt unsuccessful coup in Philippines (**July 27**). Terrorist bombing at Indonesian hotel kills ten (**Aug. 6**). Liberia's autocratic president Charles Taylor forced to leave civil war–ravaged country (**Aug. 11**). NATO assumes control of peacekeeping force in Afghanistan (**Aug. 11**). Libya accepts blame for 1988 bombing of flight over Lockerbie, Scotland; agrees to pay $2.7 billion to the families of the 270 victims (**Aug. 15**). Suicide bombing destroys UN headquarters in Baghdad, killing 24, including top envoy Sergio Vieira de Mello (**Aug. 19**). Palestinian suicide bombing in Jerusalem kills 20 Israelis, including 6 children (**Aug. 19**). Venezuelan opposition files petition for referendum to recall President Hugo Chavez (**Aug. 20**). After Israel retaliates for suicide bombing by killing top member of Hamas, militant Palestinian groups formally withdraw from cease-fire in effect since June 29 (**Aug. 24**). Investigation into the loss of space shuttle *Columbia* cites egregious organizational problems at NASA (**Aug. 25**). Congressional Budget Office predicts federal deficit of $480 billion in 2004 and $5.8 trillion by 2013 (**Aug. 26**). Palestinian prime minister Mahmoud Abbas resigns; "road map" to peace effectively collapses (**Sept. 6**). California governor Gray Davis ousted in recall vote; actor Arnold Schwarzenegger elected in his place (**Oct. 7**). UN votes in favor of a resolution ordering Israel to end construction of security barrier dividing Israeli and Palestinian areas (**Oct. 24**). Bush signs bill banning so-called partial-birth abortion procedure (**Nov. 5**). President Bush signs $87.5 billion emergency package for post-war Iraq reconstruction; this supplements $79 billion approved in April (**Nov. 5**). New Palestinian prime minister Ahmed Qurei takes office (**Nov. 12**). Alabama chief justice Roy S. Moore forced from office after his refusal to remove monument of the Ten Commandments (**Nov. 13**). The Bush Administration reverses policy, agrees to transfer power to an interim Iraqi government sooner than originally planned (**Nov 14**). Suicide bombers attack two synagogues in Istanbul, Turkey, killing 25 (**Nov. 15**). Massachusetts Supreme Court rules in favor of gay marriage (**Nov. 18**). Another terrorist attack in Istanbul kills 26; Al-Qaeda suspected in both (**Nov. 20**). Georgian president Eduard Shevardnadze resigns after weeks of protests (**Nov. 23**). John A. Muhammad, convicted in the 2002 Washington, DC, area shootings, receives death sentence (**Nov. 24**). President Bush eliminates steel tariffs after WTO says U.S. violated trade laws (**Dec. 4**). Saddam Hussein is captured by American troops (**Dec. 13**). Paul Martin succeeds Jean Chretien as Canadian prime minister (**Dec. 12**). Libyan leader Muammar Qaddafi announces he will give up weapons program (**Dec. 19**).

George W. Bush
(1946–)

Saddam Hussein
(1937–)

For 2004 chronology, *see* Current Events pp. 32–42.

A Profile of the World

Source: The World Factbook, 2004.

Geography

Total area: 510.072 million sq km (196.940 million sq mi). **Land area:** 148.94 million sq km (57.506 million sq mi). **Water area:** 361.132 million sq km (139.434 million sq mi). **Coastline:** 356,000 km (221,208 mi). **Note:** 70.8% of the world is water, 29.2% is land.

Terrain: Highest elevation is Mt. Everest at 8,850 m (29,035 ft) and lowest land depression is the Dead Sea at –411 m (–1,349 ft) below sea level. The greatest ocean depth is the Mariana Trench at –10,924 m (–35,840 ft) in the Pacific Ocean.

Land use: *Arable land:* 10.58%. *Permanent crops:* 1%. *Other:* 88.42% (1998 est.). *Irrigated land:* 2,714,320 sq km (1,048,005 sq mi).

People

Population: 6,394,491,485 (Sept. 2004 est.).

Growth rate: 1.14% (2004 est.).

Birth rate: 20.24 births/1,000 population (2004 est.).

Death rate: 8.86 deaths/1,000 population (2004 est.).

Sex ratio (at birth): 1.06 males/female (2004 est.).

Infant mortality rate: 50.31 deaths/1,000 live births (2004 est.).

Life expectancy at birth: *Total population:* 64.05 years. *Male:* 62.48 years. *Female:* 65.7 years (2004 est.).

Total fertility rate: 2.62 children born/woman (2004 est.).

Literacy: Age 15 and over who can read and write (1995 est.). *Total population:* 77%. *Male:* 83%. *Female:* 71%.

Government and Economy

Political divisions: 193 sovereign nations, 61 dependent areas, and 6 disputed territories.

Economy: Global output (GWP) rose by 3.7% in 2003, led by China (9.1%), India (7.6%), and Russia (7.3%). Growth results in the major industrial countries varied from a loss by Germany (–0.1%) to a strong gain by the United States (3.1%). The nation-state, as a bedrock economic-political institution, is steadily losing control over international flows of people, goods, funds, and technology. Internally, the central government often finds its control over resources slipping as separatist regional movements gain momentum. The addition of 80 million people each year exacerbates the problems of pollution, desertification, underemployment, epidemics, and famine. Terrorism is a further growing risk to global prosperity.

GWP: (gross world product/purchasing power parity)—$51.4 trillion (2003 est.).

GWP—real growth rate: 3.7% (2003 est.).

GWP/PPP—per capita: $8,200 (2003 est.).

GWP composition: agriculture 4%, industry 32%, services 64% (2002 est.).

Inflation rate (consumer price index): developed countries 1% to 4% typically; developing countries 5% to 60% typically (2003 est.).

Unemployment rate: 30% combined unemployment and underemployment in many non-industrialized countries; developed countries typically 4%–12% unemployment.

Exports: $7.24 trillion (f.o.b., 2003 est.).

Imports: $7.24 trillion (f.o.b., 2003 est.).

External debt: $2 trillion for less developed nations (2002 est.).

Military expenditures: roughly 2% of GWP (1999 est.).

Territories, Colonies, and Dependencies

Source: The World Factbook, 2004

The following is a list of dependencies—territories under the jurisdiction of another country.

Under Australian Jurisdiction (6)
Ashmore and Cartier Islands
Christmas Island
Cocos (Keeling) Islands
Coral Sea Islands
Heard Island and McDonald Islands
Norfolk Island

Under Danish Jurisdiction (2)
Faeroe Islands
Greenland

Under Dutch Jurisdiction (2)
Aruba
Netherlands Antilles

Under French Jurisdiction (16)
Bassas da India
Clipperton Island
Europa Island
French Guiana
French Polynesia
French Southern and Antarctic Lands
Glorioso Islands
Guadeloupe
Juan de Nova Island

Martinique
Mayotte
New Caledonia
Réunion
Saint Pierre and Miquelon
Tromelin Island
Wallis and Futuna

Under New Zealand Jurisdiction (3)
Cook Islands
Niue
Tokelau

Under Norwegian Jurisdiction (3)
Bouvet Island
Jan Mayen
Svalbard

Under UK Jurisdiction (15)
Anguilla
Bermuda
British Indian Ocean Territory
British Virgin Islands
Cayman Islands
Falkland Islands

Gibraltar
Guernsey
Jersey
Isle of Man
Montserrat
Pitcairn Islands
Saint Helena
South Georgia and the South Sandwich Islands
Turks and Caicos Islands

Under U.S. Jurisdiction (14)
American Samoa
Baker Island
Guam
Howland Island
Jarvis Island
Johnston Atoll
Kingman Reef
Midway Islands
Navassa Island
Northern Mariana Islands
Palmyra Atoll
Puerto Rico
Virgin Islands
Wake Island

Disputed Territories (6): Antarctica, Gaza Strip, Paracel Islands, Spratly Islands, West Bank, Western Sahara

Country Statistics at a Glance

Country rankings of the type presented below cannot pretend to be definitive; instead they aspire only to provide the reader with an approximation of the high and low ends on a particular scale. Country data vary enormously depending on the sources, and the absence of reliable data on some countries requires their omission, which further skews the results.

	LARGEST COUNTRIES[1] (in sq mi)*: 2004	
1.	Russia	6,592,735
2.	Canada	3,855,081
3.	United States	3,717,792
4.	China	3,705,386
5.	Brazil	3,286,470
6.	Australia	2,967,893
7.	India	1,269,338
8.	Argentina	1,068,296
9.	Kazakhstan	1,049,150
10.	Sudan	967,493

	SMALLEST COUNTRIES[1] (in sq mi)*: 2004	
1.	Vatican City	0.17
2.	Monaco	0.75
3.	Nauru	8.11
4.	Tuvalu	10.0
5.	San Marino	23.6
6.	Liechtenstein	62.0
7.	Marshall Islands	70.0
8.	Saint Kitts and Nevis	101.0
9.	Maldives	116.0
10.	Malta	122.0

	HIGHEST POPULATION DENSITY[2] (per sq mi): 2004	
1.	Monaco	42,861
2.	Singapore	16,279
3.	Vatican City	5,362
4.	Malta	3,253
5.	Maldives	2,930
6.	Bahrain	2,640
7.	Bangladesh	2,542
8.	Barbados	1,672
9.	Taiwan	1,638
10.	Nauru	1,580

	LOWEST POPULATION DENSITY[2] (per sq mi): 2004	
1.	Western Sahara	2.6
2.	Mongolia	4.6
3.	Namibia	6.1
4.	Australia	6.7
	Botswana	6.7
6.	Suriname	6.9
7.	Iceland	7.4
8.	Mauritania	7.5
9.	Libya	8.3
10.	Canada	8.4

	HIGHEST GDP PER CAPITA[3] (PPP in U.S. dollars): 2003	
1.	Luxembourg	$55,100
2.	United States	37,800
3.	Norway	37,700
4.	San Marino	34,600
5.	Switzerland	32,800
6.	Denmark	31,200
7.	Iceland	30,900
8.	Austria	30,000
9.	Ireland	29,800
10.	Canada	29,700

	LOWEST GDP PER CAPITA[3] (PPP in U.S. dollars): 2003	
1.	Somalia	$500
	Sierra Leone	500
	East Timor	500
4.	Tanzania	600
	Malawi	600
	Congo, Dem. Rep. of	600
	Burundi	600
8.	Ethiopia	700
	Eritrea	700
	Congo, Rep. of	700
	Comoros	700
	Afghanistan	700

	HIGHEST INFLATION[3]: 2003	
1.	Zimbabwe	383.4%
2.	Angola	106.0
3.	Myanmar	52.8
4.	Haiti	37.3
5.	Venezuela	31.1
6.	Belarus	30.0
7.	Iraq	27.5
8.	Malawi	27.4
9.	Ghana	26.4
10.	Uzbekistan	21.9

	LOWEST INFLATION[3]: 2003	
1.	Nauru	−3.6%
2.	Brunei	−2.0
3.	Lithuania	−1.0
4.	Barbados	−0.5
5.	St. Vincent and the Grenadines	−0.4
6.	Japan	−0.3
7.	Taiwan	−0.2
8.	Czech Republic	0.0
9.	Uganda	0.1
10.	Oman	0.3

	HIGHEST INFANT MORTALITY RATE[2] (deaths per 1,000 births): 2004	
1.	Angola	192.5
2.	Afghanistan	166.0
3.	Sierra Leone	145.2
4.	Mozambique	137.1
5.	Western Sahara	133.6
6.	Liberia	130.5
7.	Niger	122.7
8.	Somalia	118.5
9.	Mali	118.0
10.	Tajikistan	112.1

	LOWEST INFANT MORTALITY RATE[2] (deaths per 1,000 births): 2004	
1.	Singapore	2.3
2.	Sweden	2.8
3.	Japan	3.3
	Iceland	3.3
5.	Finland	3.6
6.	Norway	3.7
7.	Malta	3.9
8.	Czech Republic	4.0
9.	Andorra	4.1
10.	Germany	4.2

	HIGHEST LIFE EXPECTANCY[2] (in years): 2004	
1.	Andorra	83.5
2.	Singapore	81.5
	San Marino	81.5
4.	Japan	81.0
5.	Switzerland	80.3
	Sweden	80.3
	Australia	80.3
8.	Iceland	80.2
9.	Canada	80.0
10.	Italy	79.5

	LOWEST LIFE EXPECTANCY[2] (in years): 2004	
1.	Botswana	30.8
2.	Zambia	35.2
3.	Angola	36.8
	Lesotho	36.8
5.	Mozambique	37.1
6.	Malawi	37.5
	Swaziland	37.5
8.	Zimbabwe	37.8
9.	Rwanda	39.2
10.	Namibia	40.5

NOTE: Only countries for which statistics were available in sources 1, 2, or 3 figure in these lists. *Size refers to the total area of a country, which includes the land area plus bodies of water. *Sources:* 1. Information Please Database. 2. U.S. Census Bureau, International Database. 3. *The World Factbook, 2004.*

Total Population of the World by Decade, 1950–2040

(historical and projected)

Year	Total world population (mid-year figures)	Ten-year growth rate (%)	Year	Total world population (mid-year figures)	Ten-year growth rate (%)
1950	2,556,000,053	18.9%	2000	6,082,966,429	12.6%
1960	3,039,451,023	22.0	2010[1]	6,848,932,929	10.7
1970	3,706,618,163	20.2	2020[1]	7,584,821,144	8.7
1980	4,453,831,714	18.5	2030[1]	8,246,619,341	7.3
1990	5,278,639,789	15.2	2040[1]	8,850,045,889	5.6

1. Projected. *Source:* U.S. Census Bureau, International Database.

World's 50 Most Populous Countries: 2004

Rank	Country	Population	Rank	Country	Population	Rank	Country	Population
1.	China	1,298,847,624	19.	Thailand	64,865,523	35.	Morocco	32,209,101
2.	India	1,065,070,607	20.	France	60,424,213	36.	Algeria	32,129,324
3.	United States	293,027,571	21.	United Kingdom	60,270,708	37.	Kenya	32,021,856
4.	Indonesia	238,452,952	22.	Congo, Dem. Rep. of	58,317,930	38.	Afghanistan	28,513,677
5.	Brazil	184,101,109	23.	Italy	58,057,477	39.	Peru	27,544,305
6.	Pakistan	159,196,336	24.	Korea, South	48,598,175	40.	Nepal	27,070,666
7.	Russia	143,782,338	25.	Ukraine	47,732,079	41.	Uzbekistan	26,410,416
8.	Bangladesh	141,340,476	26.	Myanmar (Burma)	42,720,196	42.	Uganda	26,404,543
9.	Nigeria	137,253,133	27.	South Africa	42,718,530	43.	Saudi Arabia	25,795,938
10.	Japan	127,333,002	28.	Colombia	42,310,775	44.	Iraq	25,374,691
11.	Mexico	104,959,594	29.	Spain	40,280,780	45.	Venezuela	25,017,387
12.	Philippines	86,241,697	30.	Sudan	39,148,162	46.	Malaysia	23,522,482
13.	Vietnam	82,689,518	31.	Argentina	39,144,753	47.	Taiwan	22,749,838
14.	Germany	82,424,609	32.	Poland	38,626,349	48.	Korea, North	22,697,553
15.	Egypt	76,117,421	33.	Tanzania	36,588,225	49.	Romania	22,355,551
16.	Turkey	68,893,918	34.	Canada	32,507,874	50.	Ghana	20,757,032
17.	Ethiopia	67,851,281						
18.	Iran	67,503,205						

Source: U.S. Census Bureau, International Database.

Most Populous Cities of the World: 2004

Rank	City[1]	Population	Rank	City[1]	Population
1.	Shanghai, China	13,278,500	11.	Jakarta, Indonesia	8,987,800
2.	Mumbai (Bombay), India	12,622,500	12.	Mexico City, Mexico	8,705,100
3.	Buenos Aires, Argentina	11,928,400	13.	Lagos, Nigeria	8,682,200
4.	Moscow, Russia	11,273,400	14.	Lima, Peru	8,380,600
5.	Karachi, Pakistan	10,889,100	15.	Tokyo, Japan	8,294,200
6.	Delhi, India	10,400,900	16.	New York City, U.S.	8,091,700
7.	Manila, Philippines	10,330,100	17.	Cairo, Egypt	7,609,700
8.	São Paulo, Brazil	10,260,100	18.	London, UK	7,593,300
9.	Seoul, South Korea	10,165,400	19.	Teheran, Iran	7,317,200
10.	Istanbul, Turkey	9,631,700	20.	Beijing, China	7,209,900

1. Refers to the city proper, as opposed to an urban agglomeration, which would also count the surrounding urban areas in the total. *Source:* © Stefan Helders, World Gazetteer, 2004. Reprinted with permission. Web: www.world-gazetteer.com.

World's Most Populous Urban Agglomerations[1]: 2004

Rank	Name	Est. population	Rank	Name	Est. population
1.	Tokyo, Japan	31,224,700	11.	Cairo, Egypt	15,863,300
2.	New York–Philadelphia, U.S.	30,107,600	12.	Calcutta, India	14,362,500
			13.	Manila, Philippines	14,083,300
3.	Mexico City, Mexico	21,503,700	14.	Shanghai, China	13,972,300
4.	Seoul, South Korea	20,156,000	15.	Buenos Aires, Argentina	13,238,600
5.	São Paulo, Brazil	19,090,200	16.	Moscow, Russia	12,219,500
6.	Jakarta, Indonesia	18,206,700	17.	Rio de Janeiro, Brazil	11,566,700
7.	Osaka–Kobe–Kyoto, Japan	17,608,500	18.	Teheran, Iran	11,474,200
8.	Delhi, India	17,367,300	19.	Paris, France	11,419,400
9.	Mumbai (Bombay), India	17,340,900	20.	Rhein–Ruhr, Germany	11,291,100
10.	Los Angeles, U.S.	16,710,400			

NOTE: The definitions of agglomerations vary significantly from city to city, hence the difficulty of compiling an accurate, comparative list of the world's most populous urban areas. 1. Includes metropolitan areas and surrounding urban agglomerations. Agglomerations include a central city and bordering urban areas. Some agglomerations have more than one central city (e.g., Tokyo includes Yokohama and Kawasaki; New York includes Newark and Paterson, N.J.). *Sources:* © Stefan Helders, *World Gazetteer, 2004.* Reprinted with permission. Web: www.world-gazetteer.com.

Area and Population of Countries

(mid-2004 estimates)

Country	Area (in sq km)	Population	Country	Area (in sq km)	Population
Afghanistan	647,500	28,513,677	Grenada	344	89,357
Albania	28,748	3,544,808	Guatemala	108,890	14,280,596
Algeria	2,381,740	32,129,324	Guinea	245,857	9,246,462
Andorra	468	69,865	Guinea-Bissau	36,120	1,388,363
Angola	1,246,700	10,978,552	Guyana	214,970	705,803
Antigua and Barbuda	443	68,320	Haiti	27,750	7,656,166
Argentina	2,766,890	39,144,753	Honduras	112,090	6,823,568
Armenia	29,800	2,991,360	Hungary	93,030	10,032,375
Australia	7,686,850	19,913,144	Iceland	103,000	293,966
Austria	83,858	8,174,762	India	3,287,590	1,065,070,607
Azerbaijan	86,600	7,868,385	Indonesia	1,919,440	238,452,952
Bahamas, The	13,940	299,697	Iran	1,648,000	67,503,205
Bahrain	665	677,886	Iraq	437,072	25,374,691
Bangladesh	144,000	141,340,476	Ireland	70,280	3,969,558
Barbados	431	278,289	Israel	20,770	6,199,008
Belarus	207,600	10,310,520	Italy	301,230	58,057,477
Belgium	30,510	10,348,276	Jamaica	10,991	2,713,130
Belize	22,966	272,945	Japan	377,835	127,333,002
Benin	112,620	7,250,033	Jordan	92,300	5,611,202
Bhutan	47,000	2,185,569	Kazakhstan	2,717,300	15,143,704
Bolivia	1,098,580	8,724,156	Kenya	582,650	32,021,856
Bosnia and Herzegovina	51,129	4,007,608	Kiribati	811	100,798
Botswana	600,370	1,561,973	Korea, North	120,540	22,697,553
Brazil	8,511,965	184,101,109	Korea, South	98,480	48,598,175
Brunei	5,770	365,251	Kuwait	17,820	2,257,549
Bulgaria	110,910	7,517,973	Kyrgyzstan	198,500	5,081,429
Burkina Faso	274,200	13,574,820	Laos	236,800	6,068,117
Burundi	27,830	6,231,221	Latvia	64,589	2,306,306
Cambodia	181,040	13,363,421	Lebanon	10,400	3,777,218
Cameroon	475,440	16,063,678	Lesotho	30,355	1,865,040
Canada	9,984,670	32,507,874	Liberia	111,370	3,390,635
Cape Verde	4,033	415,294	Libya	1,759,540	5,631,585
Central African Republic	622,984	3,742,482	Liechtenstein	160	33,436
Chad	1,284,000	9,538,544	Lithuania	65,200	3,607,899
Chile	756,950	15,823,957	Luxembourg	2,586	462,690
China	9,596,960	1,298,847,624	Macedonia	25,333	2,071,210
Colombia	1,138,910	42,310,775	Madagascar	587,040	17,501,871
Comoros	2,170	651,901	Malawi	118,480	11,906,855
Congo, Democratic Republic			Malaysia	329,750	23,522,482
of the (formerly Zaire)	2,345,410	58,317,930	Maldives	300	339,330
Congo, Republic of the	342,000	2,998,040	Mali	1,240,000	11,956,788
Costa Rica	51,100	3,956,507	Malta	316	396,851
Côte d'Ivoire	322,460	17,327,724	Marshall Islands	181.3	57,738
Croatia	56,542	4,496,869	Mauritania	1,030,700	2,998,563
Cuba	110,860	11,308,764	Mauritius	2,040	1,220,481
Cyprus	9,250	775,927	Mexico	1,972,550	104,959,594
Czech Republic	78,866	10,246,178	Micronesia,		
Denmark	43,094	5,413,392	Federated States of	702	108,155
Djibouti	23,000	466,900	Moldova	33,843	4,446,455
Dominica	754	69,278	Monaco	1.95	32,270
Dominican Republic	48,730	8,833,634	Mongolia	1,565,000	2,751,314
East Timor	15,007	1,019,252	Morocco	446,550	32,209,101
Ecuador	283,560	13,212,742	Mozambique	801,590	18,811,731
Egypt	1,001,450	76,117,421	Myanmar (Burma)	678,500	42,720,196
El Salvador	21,040	6,587,541	Namibia	825,418	1,954,033
Equatorial Guinea	28,051	523,051	Nauru	21	12,809
Eritrea	121,320	4,447,307	Nepal	140,800	27,070,666
Estonia	45,226	1,341,664	Netherlands	41,526	16,318,199
Ethiopia	1,127,127	67,851,281	New Zealand	268,680	3,993,817
Fiji	18,270	880,874	Nicaragua	129,494	5,359,759
Finland	337,030	5,214,512	Niger	1,267,000	11,360,538
France	547,030	60,424,213	Nigeria	923,768	137,253,133
Gabon	267,667	1,355,246	Norway	324,220	4,574,560
Gambia, The	11,300	1,546,848	Oman	212,460	2,903,165
Georgia	69,700	4,693,892	Pakistan	803,940	159,196,336
Germany	357,021	82,424,609	Palau	458	20,016
Ghana	239,460	20,757,032	Panama	78,200	3,000,463
Greece	131,940	10,647,529	Papua New Guinea	462,840	5,420,280

Country	Area (in sq km)	Population	Country	Area (in sq km)	Population
Paraguay	406,750	6,191,368	Swaziland	17,363	1,169,241
Peru	1,285,220	27,544,305	Sweden	449,964	8,986,400
Philippines	300,000	86,241,697	Switzerland	41,290	7,450,867
Poland	312,685	38,626,349	Syria	185,180	18,016,874
Portugal	92,391	10,524,145	Taiwan	35,980	22,749,838
Qatar	11,437	840,290	Tajikistan	143,100	7,011,556
Romania	237,500	22,355,551	Tanzania	945,087	36,588,225
Russia	17,075,200	143,782,338	Thailand	514,000	64,865,523
Rwanda	26,338	7,954,013	Togo	56,785	5,556,812
Saint Kitts and Nevis	261	38,836	Tonga	748	110,237
Saint Lucia	616	164,213	Trinidad and Tobago	5,128	1,096,585
Saint Vincent and the Grenadines	389	117,193	Tunisia	163,610	9,974,722
Samoa	2,944	177,714	Turkey	780,580	68,893,918
San Marino	61.2	28,503	Turkmenistan	488,100	4,863,169
São Tomé and Príncipe	1,001	181,565	Tuvalu	26	11,468
Saudi Arabia	1,960,582	25,795,938	Uganda	236,040	26,404,543
Senegal	196,190	10,852,147	Ukraine	603,700	47,732,079
Serbia and Montenegro	102,350	10,825,900	United Arab Emirates	82,880	2,523,915
Seychelles	455	80,832	United Kingdom	244,820	60,270,708
Sierra Leone	71,740	5,883,889	United States	9,629,091	293,027,571
Singapore	692.7	4,353,893	Uruguay	176,220	3,399,237
Slovakia	48,845	5,423,567	Uzbekistan	447,400	26,410,416
Slovenia	20,273	2,011,473	Vanuatu	12,200	202,609
Solomon Islands	28,450	523,617	Vatican City	0.44	911
Somalia	637,657	8,304,601	Venezuela	912,050	25,017,387
South Africa	1,219,912	42,718,530	Vietnam	329,560	82,689,518
Spain	504,782	40,280,780	Western Sahara	266,000	267,405
Sri Lanka	65,610	19,905,165	Yemen	527,970	20,024,867
Sudan	2,505,810	39,148,162	Zambia	752,614	10,462,436
Suriname	163,270	436,935	Zimbabwe	390,580	12,671,860

Source: U.S. Census Bureau, International Database, and *The World Factbook, 2004.*

The Death Penalty Worldwide

According to Amnesty International, during 2003 more than 1,146 people were executed in 28 countries, and more than 2,756 people were sentenced to death in 63 countries. For U.S. figures, *see* p. 383.

Death Penalty Outlawed (year)[1]
Andorra (1990)
Angola (1992)
Australia (1984)
Austria (1950)
Azerbaijan (1998)
Belgium (1996)
Bermuda (1999)
Bosnia-Herzegovina (1997)
Bulgaria (1998)
Cambodia (1989)
Canada (1976)
Cape Verde (1981)
Colombia (1910)
Costa Rica (1877)
Côte d'Ivoire (2000)
Croatia (1990)
Cyprus (1983)
Czech Republic (1990)
Denmark (1933)
Djibouti (1995)
Dominican Republic (1966)
East Timor (1999)
Ecuador (1906)
Estonia (1998)
Finland (1949)
France (1981)
Georgia (1997)
Germany (1987)
Guinea-Bissau (1993)

Haiti (1987)
Honduras (1956)
Hungary (1990)
Iceland (1928)
Ireland (1990)
Italy (1947)
Kiribati (1979)
Liechtenstein (1987)
Lithuania (1998)
Luxembourg (1979)
Macedonia (1991)
Malta (1971)
Marshall Islands (1986)
Mauritius (1995)
Micronesia (1986)
Moldova (1995)
Monaco (1962)
Mozambique (1990)
Namibia (1990)
Nepal (1990)
Netherlands (1870)
New Zealand (1961)
Nicaragua (1979)
Norway (1905)
Palau (n.a.)
Panama (1903)
Paraguay (1992)
Poland (1997)
Portugal (1867)
Romania (1989)
Samoa (2004)
San Marino (1848)
São Tomé and Príncipe (1990)

Serbia and Montenegro (2002)
Seychelles (1993)
Slovak Republic (1990)
Slovenia (1989)
Solomon Islands (1966)
South Africa (1995)
Spain (1978)
Sweden (1921)
Switzerland (1942)
Turkmenistan (1999)
Tuvalu (1978)
Ukraine (1999)
United Kingdom (1973)
Uruguay (1907)
Vanuatu (1980)
Vatican City State (1969)
Venezuela (1863)

Death Penalty Permitted in Exceptional Cases[2]
Albania (2000)
Argentina (1984)
Armenia (2003)
Bolivia (1997)
Brazil (1979)
Chile (2001)
Cook Islands (n.a.)
El Salvador (1983)

Fiji (1979)
Greece (1993)
Israel (1954)
Latvia (1999)
Mexico (n.a.)
Peru (1979)
Turkey (2004)

De Facto Ban on Death Penalty[3] (year)[4]
Algeria (1993)
Benin (1987)
Bhutan (1964)
Brunei Darussalam (1957)
Burkina Faso (1988)
Central African Republic (1981)
Congo (Republic) (1982)
Gambia (1981)
Grenada (1978)
Kenya (n.a.)
Madagascar (1958)
Maldives (1952)
Mali (1980)
Mauritania (1987)
Nauru (1968)
Niger (1976)
Papua New Guinea (1950)
Russian Federation (1999)
Senegal (1967)
Sri Lanka (1976)

Suriname (1982)
Togo (n.a.)
Tonga (1982)
Tunisia (1990)

Death Penalty Permitted
Afghanistan
Antigua and Barbuda
Bahamas
Bahrain
Bangladesh
Barbados
Belarus
Belize
Botswana
Burundi
Cameroon
Chad
China (People's Republic)
Comoros
Congo (Democratic Republic)
Cuba
Dominica
Egypt
Equatorial Guinea
Eritrea
Ethiopia
Gabon
Ghana
Guatemala
Guinea
Guyana

India	Kyrgyzstan	Nigeria	Saudi Arabia	Trinidad and Tobago
Indonesia	Laos	Oman	Sierra Leone	Uganda
Iran	Lebanon	Pakistan	Singapore	United Arab
Iraq	Lesotho	Palestinian Authority	Somalia	Emirates
Jamaica	Liberia	Philippines	Sudan	United States of
Japan	Libya	Qatar	Swaziland	America
Jordan	Malawi	Rwanda	Syria	Uzbekistan
Kazakhstan	Malaysia	St. Kitts and Nevis	Taiwan	Vietnam
Korea, North	Mongolia	St. Lucia	Tajikistan	Yemen
Korea, South	Morocco	St. Vincent and the	Tanzania	Zambia
Kuwait	Myanmar	Grenadines	Thailand	Zimbabwe

NOTE: n.a. = date not available. 1. Year death penalty abolished for most, though not necessarily all crimes. 2. Exceptional crimes include some committed under military law or crimes committed in wartime. 3. Death penalty is sanctioned by law but has not been the practice for ten or more years. 4. Year of last execution. *Source:* Amnesty International.

Infant Mortality and Life Expectancy for Selected Countries, 2004

Country	Infant mortality[1]	Life expectancy[2]	Country	Infant mortality[1]	Life expectancy[2]	Country	Infant mortality[1]	Life expectancy[2]
Albania	22.3	77.1	Germany	4.2	78.5	Pakistan	74.4	62.6
Angola	192.5	36.8	Greece	5.6	78.9	Panama	20.9	72.1
Australia	4.8	80.3	Guatemala	36.9	65.2	Peru	33.0	69.2
Austria	4.7	78.9	Hungary	8.7	72.2	Poland	8.7	74.2
Bangladesh	64.3	61.7	India	57.9	64.0	Portugal	5.1	77.3
Brazil	30.7	71.4	Iran	42.9	69.7	Russia	17.0	66.4
Canada	4.8	80.0	Ireland	5.5	77.4	Slovakia	7.6	74.2
Chile	9.1	76.4	Israel	7.2	79.2	South Africa	62.2	44.2
China	25.3	72.0	Italy	6.1	79.5	Spain	4.5	79.4
Costa Rica	10.3	76.6	Japan	3.3	81.0	Sri Lanka	14.8	72.9
Cyprus	7.4	77.5	Kenya	62.6	44.9	Sweden	2.8	80.3
Czech Republic	4.0	75.8	Korea, South	7.2	75.6	Switzerland	4.4	80.3
Denmark	4.6	77.4	Mexico	21.7	74.9	Syria	30.6	69.7
Ecuador	24.5	76.0	Mozambique	137.1	37.1	United Kingdom	5.2	78.3
Egypt	33.9	70.7	New Zealand	6.0	78.5	United States	6.6	77.4
Finland	3.6	78.2	Nigeria	70.5	50.5	Venezuela	23.0	74.1
France	4.3	79.4	Norway	3.7	79.2	Zimbabwe	67.1	37.8

1. Infant deaths per 1,000 live births. 2. Life expectancy at birth, in years, both sexes. *Source:* U.S. Census Bureau, International Database.

Crude Birth and Death Rates for Selected Countries
(per 1,000 population)

Country	Birth rate 2004	2003	2002	1990	1985	1980	1975	Death rate 2004	2003	2002	1990	1985	1980	1975
Australia	12.4	12.6	12.71	15.4	15.7	15.3	16.9	7.4	7.3	7.25	7.0	7.5	7.4	7.9
Austria	8.9	9.4	9.58	11.6	11.6	12.0	12.5	9.6	9.7	9.73	10.6	11.9	12.2	12.8
Belgium	10.6	10.4	10.58	12.6	11.5	12.7	12.2	10.2	10.1	10.08	10.6	11.2	11.6	12.2
Czech Republic[1]	9.1	9.0	9.08	13.4	14.5	16.4	19.6	10.5	10.7	10.76	11.7	11.8	12.1	11.5
France	12.3	12.5	11.94	13.5	13.9	14.8	14.1	9.1	9.1	9.04	9.3	10.1	10.2	10.6
Germany[2]	8.4	8.6	8.99	11.4	9.6	10.0	9.7	10.4	10.3	10.36	11.2	11.5	11.6	12.1
Greece	9.7	9.8	9.82	10.2	11.7	15.4	15.7	10.1	9.9	9.79	9.3	9.4	9.1	8.9
Ireland	14.5	14.6	14.62	15.1	17.6	21.9	21.5	7.9	7.9	8.01	9.1	9.4	9.7	10.6
Israel	18.4	18.7	18.91	22.2	23.5	24.1	28.2	6.2	6.2	6.21	6.2	6.6	6.7	7.1
Italy	9.1	9.2	8.93	9.8	10.1	11.2	14.8	10.2	10.1	10.13	9.4	9.5	9.7	9.9
Japan	9.6	9.6	10.03	9.9	11.9	13.7	17.2	8.8	8.6	8.53	6.7	6.2	6.2	6.4
Mauritius	15.8	16.1	16.34	21.0	18.8	27.0	25.1	6.8	6.8	6.81	6.5	6.8	7.2	8.1
Netherlands	11.4	11.3	11.58	13.3	12.3	12.8	13.0	8.7	8.7	8.67	8.6	8.5	8.1	8.3
New Zealand	14.0	14.1	14.23	18.0	15.6	—	18.4	7.5	7.5	7.55	7.9	8.4	—	8.1
Norway	11.9	12.2	12.39	14.3	12.3	12.5	14.1	9.5	9.7	9.78	10.7	10.7	10.1	9.9
Panama	20.4	20.8	18.60	23.9	26.6	26.8	32.3	6.4	6.2	4.96	—	—	—	—
Poland	10.6	10.5	10.29	14.3	18.2	19.5	18.9	10.0	10.0	9.97	10.2	10.3	9.8	8.7
Portugal	10.9	11.4	11.50	11.8	12.8	16.4	19.1	10.4	10.2	10.21	10.4	9.6	9.9	10.4
Romania	10.7	10.8	10.81	13.6	15.8	—	—	11.7	12.2	12.27	10.6	10.9	—	—
Switzerland	9.8	9.6	9.84	12.5	11.6	11.3	12.3	8.4	8.8	8.79	9.5	9.2	9.2	8.7
Tunisia	15.7	16.5	16.83	25.8	31.3	35.2	36.6	5.0	5.0	5.00	—	—	—	—
United Kingdom	10.9	11.0	11.34	13.9	13.3	13.5	12.5	10.2	10.2	10.30	11.2	11.8	11.8	11.9
United States	14.1	14.1	14.10	16.7	15.7	16.2	14.0	8.3	8.4	8.70	8.6	8.7	8.9	8.9

1. Data prior to 1994 pertain to the former Czechoslovakia. 2. All data pertaining to Germany prior to 1990 are for West Germany. NOTE: (—) = not available. *Source:* United Nations, *Monthly Bulletin of Statistics, June 1997.* Data for 2002, 2003, 2004 from the U.S. Census Bureau, International Database.

The 2003 Transparency International Corruption Perceptions Index

According to the annual survey by the Berlin-based organization Transparency International, the world's least corrupt country is Finland and its most corrupt is Bangladesh. The index defines corruption as the abuse of public office for private gain, and measures the degree to which corruption is perceived to exist among a country's public officials and politicians. It is a composite index, drawing on 17 surveys from 13 independent institutions, which gathered the opinions of business people and country analysts. Because of the absence of reliable data, only 133 of the world's countries are included in the survey. The scores range from 10 (squeaky clean) to zero (highly corrupt). A score of 5.0 is the number Transparency International considers the borderline figure distinguishing countries that do and do not have a serious corruption problem. Countries that have improved their rating since the 2002 index were Austria, Belgium, Colombia, France, Germany, Ireland, Malaysia, Norway, and Tunisia. Countries that have a worse rating since 2002 include Argentina, Belarus, Chile, Canada, Israel, Luxembourg, Poland, the U.S., and Zimbabwe.

Country rank	Country	2003 CPI Score	Country rank	Country	2003 CPI Score	Country rank	Country	2003 CPI Score
1.	Finland	9.7	46.	Belize	4.5		Yemen	2.6
2.	Iceland	9.6		Saudi Arabia	4.5	92.	Albania	2.5
3.	Denmark	9.5	48.	Mauritius	4.4		Argentina	2.5
	New Zealand	9.5		South Africa	4.4		Ethiopia	2.5
5.	Singapore	9.4	50.	Costa Rica	4.3		Gambia	2.5
6.	Sweden	9.3		Greece	4.3		Pakistan	2.5
7.	Netherlands	8.9		South Korea	4.3		Philippines	2.5
8.	Australia	8.8	53.	Belarus	4.2		Tanzania	2.5
	Norway	8.8	54.	Brazil	3.9		Zambia	2.5
	Switzerland	8.8		Bulgaria	3.9	100.	Guatemala	2.4
11.	Canada	8.7		Czech Republic	3.9		Kazakhstan	2.4
	Luxembourg	8.7	57.	Jamaica	3.8		Moldova	2.4
	United Kingdom	8.7		Latvia	3.8		Uzbekistan	2.4
14.	Austria	8.0	59.	Colombia	3.7		Venezuela	2.4
	Hong Kong	8.0		Croatia	3.7		Vietnam	2.4
16.	Germany	7.7		El Salvador	3.7	106.	Bolivia	2.3
17.	Belgium	7.6		Peru	3.7		Honduras	2.3
18.	Ireland	7.5		Slovakia	3.7		Macedonia	2.3
	United States	7.5	64.	Mexico	3.6		Serbia and Montenegro	2.3
20.	Chile	7.4		Poland	3.6		Sudan	2.3
21.	Israel	7.0	66.	China	3.4		Ukraine	2.3
	Japan	7.0		Panama	3.4		Zimbabwe	2.3
23.	France	6.9		Sri Lanka	3.4	113.	Congo, Republic of the	2.2
	Spain	6.9		Syria	3.4		Ecuador	2.2
25.	Portugal	6.6	70.	Bosnia and Herzegovina	3.3		Iraq	2.2
26.	Oman	6.3		Dominican Republic	3.3		Sierra Leone	2.2
27.	Bahrain	6.1		Egypt	3.3		Uganda	2.2
	Cyprus	6.1		Ghana	3.3	118.	Côte d'Ivoire	2.1
29.	Slovenia	5.9		Morocco	3.3		Kyrgyzstan	2.1
30.	Botswana	5.7		Thailand	3.3		Libya	2.1
	Taiwan	5.7	76.	Senegal	3.2		Papua New Guinea	2.1
32.	Qatar	5.6	77.	Turkey	3.1	122.	Indonesia	1.9
33.	Estonia	5.5	78.	Armenia	3.0		Kenya	1.9
	Uruguay	5.5		Iran	3.0	124.	Angola	1.8
35.	Italy	5.3		Lebanon	3.0		Azerbaijan	1.8
	Kuwait	5.3		Mali	3.0		Cameroon	1.8
37.	Malaysia	5.2		Palestine	3.0		Georgia	1.8
	United Arab Emirates	5.2	83.	India	2.8		Tajikistan	1.8
39.	Tunisia	4.9		Malawi	2.8	129.	Myanmar	1.6
40.	Hungary	4.8		Romania	2.8		Paraguay	1.6
41.	Lithuania	4.7	86.	Mozambique	2.7	131.	Haiti	1.5
	Namibia	4.7		Russia	2.7	132.	Nigeria	1.4
43.	Cuba	4.6	88.	Algeria	2.6	133.	Bangladesh	1.3
	Jordan	4.6		Madagascar	2.6			
	Trinidad and Tobago	4.6		Nicaragua	2.6			

Source: Transparency International, 2003. Web: www.transparency.org.

The Bribe Payers' Index

The Bribe Payers' Index ranks the 21 leading exporting countries according to the degree to which their companies are perceived to be paying bribes abroad to senior public officials. According to the latest survey, published by Transparency International in 2002, the countries most likely to offer bribes are Russia, China, Taiwan, and South Korea. All of these countries have laws criminalizing corrupt payments to foreign officials.

World's Ten Most Corrupt Leaders[1]

Name	Position	Estimates of funds allegedly embezzled[1] (in U.S. $)
1. Mohamed Suharto	President of Indonesia (1967–1998)	$15 to 35 billion
2. Ferdinand Marcos	President of the Philippines (1972–1986)	5 to 10 billion
3. Mobutu Sese Seko	President of Zaire (1965–1997)	5 billion
4. Sani Abacha	President of Nigeria (1993–1998)	2 to 5 billion
5. Slobodan Milosevic	President of Serbia/Yugoslavia (1989–2000)	1 billion
6. Jean-Claude Duvalier	President of Haiti (1971–1986)	300 to 800 million
7. Alberto Fujimori	President of Peru (1990–2000)	600 million
8. Pavlo Lazarenko	Prime Minister of Ukraine (1996–1997)	114 to 200 million
9. Arnoldo Alemán	President of Nicaragua (1997–2002)	100 million
10. Joseph Estrada	President of the Philippines (1998–2001)	78 to 80 million

1. Defined as former political leaders who have been accused of embezzling the most funds from their countries over the past two decades. 2. All sums are estimates of alleged embezzlement. *Source:* Transparency International Global Corruption Report 2004. Web: www.transparency.org/pressreleases_archive/2004/2004.03.25.gcr_relaunch.html.

Most and Least Livable Countries: UN Human Development Index, 2004

The Human Development Index (HDI), published annually by the UN, ranks nations according to their citizens' quality of life rather than strictly by a nation's traditional economic figures. The criteria for calculating rankings include life expectancy, educational attainment, and adjusted real income.

"Most Livable" Countries, 2004		"Least Livable" Countries, 2004	
1. Norway	16. France	1. Sierra Leone	16. Tanzania
2. Sweden	17. Denmark	2. Niger	17. Benin
3. Australia	18. New Zealand	3. Burkina Faso	18. Guinea
4. Canada	19. Germany	4. Mali	19. Rwanda
5. Netherlands	20. Spain	5. Burundi	20. East Timor
6. Belgium	21. Italy	6. Guinea-Bissau	21. Senegal
7. Iceland	22. Israel	7. Mozambique	22. Eritrea
8. United States	23. Greece	8. Ethiopia	23. Gambia
9. Japan	24. Singapore	9. Central African Republic	24. Djibouti
10. Ireland	25. Portugal	10. Congo, Dem. Rep. of the	25. Haiti
11. Switzerland	26. Slovenia	11. Chad	26. Mauritania
12. United Kingdom	27. Korea, South	12. Angola	27. Nigeria
13. Finland	28. Barbados	13. Malawi	28. Madagascar
14. Austria	29. Cyprus	14. Zambia	29. Yemen
15. Luxembourg	30. Malta	15. Côte d'Ivoire	30. Kenya

Source: Human Development Report, 2004, United Nations. Web: hdr.undp.org.

Kingdoms and Monarchs of the World

Country	Monarch	Type of monarchy	Country	Monarch	Type of monarchy
Bahrain	King Hamad bin Isa al-Khalifa	Constitutional	Monaco	Prince Rainier III	Constitutional
			Morocco	King Muhammad VI	Constitutional
Belgium	King Albert II	Constitutional	Nepal	King Gyandendra	Constitutional
Bhutan	King Jigme Singye Wangchuck	Constitutional	Netherlands	Queen Beatrix	Constitutional
			Norway	King Harald V	Constitutional
Brunei	Sultan Haji Hassanal Bolkiah	Constitutional	Oman	Sultan Qabus ibn Sa'id	Absolute
			Qatar	Emir Sheik Hamad ibn Khalifa al-Thani	Traditional
Cambodia	King Norodom Sihanouk	Constitutional			
Denmark	Queen Margrethe II	Constitutional	Samoa	Malietoa Tanumafili II	Constitutional
Japan	Emperor Akihito	Constitutional	Saudi Arabia	King Fahd bin 'Abdulaziz	Absolute
Jordan	King Abdullah II	Constitutional	Spain	King Juan Carlos I	Parliamentary
Kuwait	Sheik Jaber al-Ahmad al-Sabah	Constitutional	Swaziland	King Mswati III	Absolute
			Sweden	King Carl XVI Gustaf	Constitutional
Lesotho	King Letsie III	Constitutional	Thailand	King Bhumibol Adulyadej	Constitutional
Liechtenstein	Prince Hans Adam II	Constitutional	Tonga	King Taufa'ahau Tupou IV	Constitutional
Luxembourg	Grand Duke Henri	Constitutional	United Kingdom	Queen Elizabeth II[1]	Constitutional[2]
Malaysia	King Syed Sirajuddin	Constitutional			

1. Queen Elizabeth II is also the Sovereign of 15 countries in the Commonwealth of Nations: Antigua and Barbuda, Australia, the Bahamas, Barbados, Belize, Canada, Grenada, Jamaica, New Zealand, Papua New Guinea, St. Kitts and Nevis, St. Lucia, St. Vincent and the Grenadines, the Solomon Islands, and Tuvalu. 2. Also parliamentary democracy.

World's 50 Poorest Countries, 2004

UN list of least developed countries[1]

Afghanistan, Angola, Bangladesh, Benin, Bhutan, Burkina Faso, Burundi, Cambodia, Cape Verde, Central African Republic, Chad, Comoros, Democratic Republic of Congo, Djibouti, Equatorial Guinea, Eritrea, Ethiopia, Gambia, Guinea, Guinea-Bissau, Haiti, Kiribati, Lao People's Democratic Republic, Lesotho, Liberia, Madagascar, Malawi, Maldives, Mali, Mauritania, Mozambique, Myanmar, Nepal, Niger, Rwanda, Samoa, São Tomé and Príncipe, Senegal, Sierra Leone, Solomon Islands, Somalia, Sudan, East Timor, Togo, Tuvalu, Uganda, Tanzania, Vanuatu, Yemen, Zambia.

Trends among the world's poorest countries

In the second half of the 1990s the average per capita income in the world's poorest countries, when measured in terms of current prices and official exchange rates, was $0.72 a day and the average per capita consumption was $0.57 a day. This implies that on average there was only $0.15 a day per person to spend on private capital formation, public investment in infrastructure, and the running of vital public services, including health, education, administration, and law and order.

In 2001, 34% of the population aged between 15 and 24 was illiterate in the poorest countries.

About 60% of the poorest countries experienced civil conflict of varying intensity and duration in the period 1990–2001 that, in most cases, erupted after a period of economic stagnation and regression. In Rwanda, for example, average private consumption per capita fell by more than 12% between 1980 and 1993, the year before the genocide occurred.

1. The UN classifies countries as "least developed" based on three criteria: (1) annual gross domestic product (GDP) below $900 per capita; (2) quality of life, based on life expectancy at birth, per capita calorie intake, primary and secondary school enrollment rates, and adult literacy; and (3) economic vulnerability, based on instability of agricultural productions and exports, inadequate diversification, and economic smallness. Half or more of the population in the 50 least developed countries listed above are estimated to live at or below the absolute poverty line of U.S. $1 dollar per day.

Gap Between Rich and Poor: World Income Inequality

Percentage share of income (poorest and richest 20% of population)

Countries with greatest inequality	Gini index	Lowest 20%	Highest 20%	Countries with greatest equality	Gini Index	Lowest 20%	Highest 20%
1. Sierra Leone	62.9	1.1	63.4	1. Slovak Republic	19.5	11.9	31.4
2. Central African Republic	61.3	2.0	65.0	2. Belarus	21.7	11.4	33.3
3. Swaziland	60.9	2.7	64.4	3. Hungary	24.4	10.0	34.4
4. Brazil	60.7	2.2	64.1	4. Denmark	24.7	9.6	34.5
5. Nicaragua	60.3	2.3	63.6	5. Japan	24.9	10.6	35.7
6. South Africa	59.3	2.9	64.8	6. Sweden	25.0	9.6	34.5
7. Paraguay	57.7	1.9	60.7	7. Czech Republic	25.4	10.3	35.9
8. Colombia	57.1	3.0	60.9	8. Finland	25.6	10.0	35.8
9. Chile	56.7	3.3	61.0	9. Norway	25.8	9.7	35.8
10. Honduras	56.3	2.2	59.4	10. Bulgaria	26.4	10.1	36.8
11. Guinea-Bissau	56.2	2.1	58.9	11. Luxembourg	26.9	9.4	36.5
12. Lesotho	56.0	2.8	60.1	12. Italy	27.3	8.7	36.3
13. Guatemala	55.8	3.8	60.6	13. Slovenia	28.4	9.1	37.7
14. Burkina Faso	55.1	4.6	60.4	14. Belgium	28.7	8.3	37.3
15. Mexico	53.1	3.5	57.4	15. Egypt	28.9	9.8	39.0
16. Zambia	52.6	3.3	56.6	15. Rwanda	28.9	9.7	39.1
17. Hong Kong, China	52.2	4.4	57.1	17. Croatia	29.0	8.8	38.0
17. El Salvador	52.2	3.3	56.4	17. Ukraine	29.0	8.8	37.8
19. Papua New Guinea	50.9	4.5	56.5	19. Germany	30.0	8.2	38.5
20. Nigeria	50.6	4.4	55.7	20. Austria	31.0	6.9	38.0
21. Mali	50.5	4.6	56.2	21. Romania	31.1	8.0	39.5
21. Niger	50.5	2.6	53.3	22. Pakistan	31.2	9.5	41.1
23. Gambia, The	50.2	4.0	55.3	23. Canada	31.5	7.5	39.3
24. Zimbabwe	50.1	4.7	55.7	24. Korea, South	31.6	7.5	39.3
25. Venezuela	49.5	3.0	53.2	24. Poland	31.6	7.8	39.7
26. Malaysia	49.2	4.4	54.3	26. Indonesia	31.7	9.0	41.1
27. Russian Federation	48.7	4.4	53.7	27. Latvia	32.4	7.6	40.3
28. Panama	48.5	3.6	52.8	27. Lithuania	32.4	7.8	40.3
29. Cameroon	47.7	4.6	53.1	29. Spain	32.5	7.5	40.3
30. Dominican Republic	47.4	5.1	53.3	30. Netherlands	32.6	7.3	40.1

NOTE: Countries are ranked according to the Gini index (or coefficient), a measure of income inequality within a country. A country's Gini rating is between 0 and 100, with 0 indicating perfect equality and 100 indicating absolute inequality. (The U.S. rates 40.8 on the Gini index—the poorest 20% of its population receive 5.2% of income; the richest 20% receive 46.4%.)
Source: World Development Index 2002, The World Bank.

Largest Military Expenditures, 2003

(Military expenditure: in MER[1] dollar terms)

Rank	Country	Level [2] ($ billions)	Per capita ($)	World share (%)	Rank	Country	Level [2] ($ billions)	Per capita ($)	World share (%)
1.	United States	$417.4	$1,419	47%	10.	South Korea	$ 13.9	$ 292	2%
2.	Japan	46.9	367	5	11.	Russia	13.0[3]	91	1
3.	United Kingdom	37.1	627	4	12.	India	12.4	12	1
4.	France	35.0	583	4	13.	Israel	10.0	1,551	1
5.	China	32.8[3]	25	4	14.	Turkey	9.9	139	1
6.	Germany	27.2	329	3	15.	Brazil	9.2	51	1
7.	Italy	20.8	362	2		Subtotal top			
8.	Iran[4]	19.2	279	2		15	723.8		82
9.	Saudi Arabia	19.1	789	2[3]		World	879.0		100

1. MER = market exchange rate. 2. Figures are in U.S. $ billions, at constant (2000) prices and exchange rates. 3. Stockholm International Peace Research Institute (SIPRI) estimates. 4. Data for Iran includes expenditure for public order and safety and is a slight overestimate. *Source: SIPRI Yearbook 2004*, Stockholm International Peace Research Institute.

Significant Ongoing Armed Conflicts, 2004

Main warring parties	Year began[1]	Main warring parties	Year began[1]
Middle East		**Africa**	
U.S. and UK vs. Iraq	2003	Algeria vs. Armed Islamic Group (GIA)	1991
Israel vs. Palestinian Authority/Hamas/Hezbollah/ Palestinian separatists	1948	Burundi: Tutsi vs. Hutu	1988
		Democratic Republic of Congo and allies vs. Rwanda, Uganda, and indigenous rebels[3]	1997
Asia		Somalia vs. rival clans	1991
Afghanistan: U.S., UK, and Coalition Forces vs. al-Qaeda and Taliban	2001	Sudan vs. Dafur rebel groups	2003
India vs. Kashmiri separatist groups/Pakistan	1948	Uganda vs. Lord's Resistance Army (LRA)	1986
India vs. Assam insurgents (various)	1979	**Europe**	
Indonesia vs. Aceh separatists[2]	1976	Russia vs. Chechen separatists	1994
Indonesia vs. Christians and Muslims in Molucca Islands	1977	**Latin America**	
		Colombia vs. National Liberation Army (ELN)	1978
Indonesia vs. Irian Jaya separatists	1969	Colombia vs. Revolutionary Armed Forces of Colombia (FARC)	1978
Nepal vs. Maoist rebels	1995		
Philippines vs. Mindanaoan separatists (MILF/ASG)	1971	Colombia vs. Autodefensas Unidas de Colombia (AUC)	1990

NOTE: As of Aug. 2004. 1. Where multiple parties and long-standing but sporadic conflict are concerned, date of first combat deaths is given. 2. 2002 ceasefire abandoned; fighting resumed in May 2003. 3. Ceasefire agreements signed in 2002, but violence continues. *Source:* Center for Defense Information, www.cdi.org and Project Ploughshares, www.ploughshares.ca.

Recently Suspended Armed Conflicts

Main warring parties	Year began– year ceasefire occurred	Main warring parties	Year began– year ceasefire occurred
Sudan vs. Sudanese People's Liberation Army[1]	1983–2004	Sierra Leone vs. RUF	1991–2002
		Chad vs. Muslim separatists (MDJT)	1998–2002
Solomon Islands vs. Malaitan Eagle Force and Isatabu Freedom Movement	1998–2003	Taliban vs. Northern Alliance	1995–2001
		Indonesia vs. East Timor	1975–2000
Liberia vs. LURD rebels	2000–2003	Tajikistan vs. United Tajik Opposition (UTO)	1992–2000
Côte d'Ivoire vs. rebels[2]	2002–2003		
Angola vs. UNITA	1975–2002	Ethiopia vs. Eritrea	1998–2000
Sri Lanka vs. Tamil Eelan	1978–2002	Fiji vs. insurgents	2000

1. Peace agreement signed May 26, 2004. 2. In 2004, Côte d'Ivoire again seemed close to civil war. *Sources:* Center for Defense Information, www.cdi.org, Project Ploughshares, www.ploughshares.ca, and news sources.

Countries with Nuclear Weapons Capability

Acknowledged: Britain, China, France, India, Pakistan, Russia, United States
Unacknowledged: Israel
Seeking: Iran, North Korea[1]

Abandoned: South Africa—Constructed but then voluntarily dismantled six uranium bombs. Belarus, Kazakhstan, Ukraine—When Soviet Union broke up, these former states possessed nuclear warheads that they have since given up.

1. In Dec. 2002, North Korea revealed that it had violated its 1994 agreement to freeze its nuclear weapons program and has been developing a nuclear bomb. On April 24, 2003, North Korea announced it possessed a nuclear bomb but this claim has not been verified. *Source:* U.S. State Department and *Time* magazine.

See also UN peacekeeping missions, p. 906

Worldwide Refugees and Asylum Seekers, 2003

Originating country	Number	Originating country	Number	Originating country	Number
Former Palestine	3,000,000[1]	Bosnia and Herzegovina	142,200	Cuba	28,200[1]
Afghanistan	2,500,000[1]	Bhutan	128,700	Uganda	28,000
Sudan	600,000	Sri Lanka	105,700	Haiti	25,800
Myanmar (Burma)	586,000[1]	North Korea	101,700[1]	Georgia	25,000
Congo, Dem. Rep. of	440,000	Serbia and Montenegro	70,100	Indonesia	23,600
Liberia	384,000[1]	Sierra Leone	68,000	Mauritania	23,000
Burundi	355,000	Tajikistan	59,800	Pakistan	21,000
Angola	323,000[1]	Philippines	58,500	Mexico	20,700
Vietnam	307,200	Côte d'Ivoire	55,000	Congo, Rep. of	20,000
Iraq	280,600[1]	Russia	49,000	Ethiopia	19,000
Eritrea	280,000[1]	Rwanda	46,000[1]	Cambodia	16,100
Somalia	277,000	Central African Republic	41,000	Laos	15,000
Colombia	233,600	Turkey	40,000	Senegal	13,000
Croatia	209,100	Nigeria	39,000	Ghana	12,000
Western Sahara	190,000[1]	India	35,800	Guatemala	11,600
China	157,500	Iran	35,000	Ukraine	11,200

NOTE: Countries from which at least 11,200 civilians have fled to become refugees or asylum seekers or in which that many have been internally displaced. Estimates of the numbers of uprooted persons are often fragmentary. 1. Sources vary significantly. *Source: World Refugee Survey 2004,* U.S. Committee on Refugees.

Countries Receiving Refugees and Asylum Seekers

Country	Number	Country	Number	Country	Number
Iran	1,335,000[1]	Saudi Arabia	240,900	Congo, Rep. of	91,000
Pakistan	1,219,000[1]	Uganda	231,500[1]	Germany	90,800
Gaza Strip	923,000	Guinea	223,000[1]	Malaysia	75,700
West Bank	665,000	Kenya	219,000[1]	Yemen	75,000[1]
Syria	497,000[1]	Venezuela	182,300	Côte D'Ivoire	74,000[1]
Tanzania	480,000[1]	Algeria	170,000[1]	Canada	70,200
Thailand	421,500	Jordan	163,700[1]	Sierra Lione	70,000[1]
China	396,000[1]	Russia	161,300[1]	Egypt	69,000[1]
India	316,900	Chad	156,000	Kuwait	65,000
Serbia and Montenegro	291,100	Nepal	134,600	Liberia	60,000[1]
Sudan	280,000[1]	Iraq	131,500[1]	United Kingdom	55,700
Lebanon	256,000[1]	Bangladesh	119,900[1]	Central African Republic	51,000
United States	244,200	Ethiopia	112,000[1]		
Congo, Dem. Rep. of	241,000[1]	South Africa	104,000		

NOTE: Countries to which at least 50,000 civilians have fled to become refugees or asylum seekers, or in which that many have been internally displaced, as of Dec. 31, 2003. 1. Sources vary significantly. *Source: World Refugee Survey 2004,* U.S. Committee on Refugees.

U.S.-Designated Foreign Terrorist Organizations[1]

Name and base of operations	Goals and targets	Est. strength	Year founded	Activities
Abu Nidal Organization (ANO) a.k.a. Fatah; Iraq	Targets U.S., UK, France, Israel, moderate Palestinians, the PLO, Arab countries	400	1974	Attacks in 20 countries, killing or injuring 900. Leader Abu Nidal died in 2002
Abu Sayyaf Group; Philippines, Malaysia	Aims to create Islamic state in Philippines; profit-driven terror	200-500	1991	Kidnappings, bombings, assassinations, and extortion
Al-Aqsa Martyrs Brigade; West Bank, Gaza Strip, Israel	Aims to drive out Israelis and to establish a Palestinian state	Unknown	2000	Shootings, suicide operations (first female suicide bombing)
Ansar al-Islam (AI); Iraqi Kurds and Arabs	Aims to create an Islamic state in Iraq; allied with al-Qaeda	700–1,000	2001	Ambushes and attacks
Armed Islamic Group (GIA); Algeria	Aims to replace Algerian regime with an Islamic state	Less than 100	1992	Massacred thousands of civilians, targeted foreigners
Asbat al-Ansar; Lebanon	Aims to create Islamic state, opposes peace with Israel	300	1990s	Assassinations, bombings of Western targets, failed coup
Aum Shinrikyo (Aum); Japan, Russia	Claims U.S. will start WWIII with Japan, beginning Armageddon	Less than 1,000	1987	Chemical attacks on Tokyo subways, no recent activity
Basque Fatherland and Liberty (ETA); Spain, France	Targets Spanish and French government interests, tourists	Unknown	1959	Since 1960, more than 850 killed, hundreds injured

Name and base of operations	Goals and targets	Est. strength	Year founded	Activities
Communist Party of the Philippines/New People's Army (CPP/NPA); Philippines	Targets Philippine security forces, politicians, judges, government informers, NPA rebels	More than 10,000	1969	Assassinations, murders, attacks on U.S. personnel and interests
Gama'a al-Islamiyya (Islamic Group); Egypt	Aims to replace Egypt's government with an Islamic state	Unknown	1973	1993 World Trade Center bombings, attacks on tourists
HAMAS (Islamic Resistance Movement); West Bank, Gaza Strip, Israel	Aims to replace Israel with Palestinian Islamic state using political and violent means	Unknown	1987	Large-scale suicide bombings and attacks against Israelis and Palestinian collaborators
Harakat ul-Mujahidin (HUM); Pakistan	Targets Indian troops, Kashmiri civilians, and Western interests	Several hundred	1985	Linked to al-Qaeda, hijacked Indian airliner in 1999
Hezbollah (Party of God); Lebanon, worldwide cells	Dedicated to eliminating Israel, is anti-U.S. and anti-Israel	A few hundred	1982	Suicide bombings of U.S. Marine barracks (241 killed), hijacked 1985 TWA Flight 847
Islamic Movement of Uzbekistan (IMU); South Asia, Tajikistan, Iran	Aims to remove Karimov, establish an Islamic state, and to fight anti-Islamic opponents	Less than 700	1991	Car bombs, taking foreign hostages, most active in Kyrgyzstan and Tajikistan
Jaish-e-Mohammed (JEM) (Army of Mohammed); Pakistan	Aims to unite Kashmir with Pakistan, targets Indian government and political leaders	Several hundred	2000	Murder of U.S. journalist, Indian Parliament bombing, anti-Christian attacks
Jemaah Islamiya organization (JI); cells span Southeast Asia	Plotted against tourist spots, U.S., Israeli, British, and Australian diplomatic buildings	Unknown	1990s	Bombings in Indonesia and Philippines, 2002 Bali bombings (202 killed, 300 wounded)
Al-Jihad; Cairo, Egypt, Yemen, Afghanistan, Pakistan, Lebanon, UK	Aims to replace the Egyptian government with Islamic state, attack U.S., Israeli interests	Several hundred	1970s	Attacks on Egyptian government personnel, assassinated Anwar Sadat
Kahane Chai (Kach); Israel, West Bank	Organizes protests against the Israeli Government	Unknown	1994	Threats made to Arabs, Palestinians and Israeli officials
Kurdistan Workers' Party (PKK) a.k.a. KADEK; Turkey, Europe, Middle East	Targets Turkish security forces, officials, and villagers who oppose organization	4,000–5,000	1974	Attacked diplomatic and commercial facilities, bombed tourist sites
Lashkar-e- Tayyiba (LT) (Army of the Righteous); Pakistan	Targets Indian troops and civilians in Kashmir	several hundred	1989	Attacks on border security forces and Indian Parliament
Lashkar i Jhangvi; Pakistan, Afghanistan	Anti-Shi'ite group aims to create a Muslim state in Pakistan.	less than 100	1996	Armed attacks, bombings, attempted assassinations
Liberation Tigers of Tamil Eelam (LTTE); Sri Lanka	Targets key personnel, senior political and military leaders	8,000–10,000	1976	Assassinations, suicide bombers: "The Black Tigers"
Mujahedin-e Khalq Organization (MEK); Iraq	Largest armed Iranian opposition to the present government, advocates a secular Iranian regime	3,800	1960s	Assassinations, terrorist bombings, foreign military-aided assaults, large-scale overseas attacks
National Liberation Army (ELN); Colombia, Venezuela	Targets foreign employees from large corporations	3,000	1965	Kidnapping, hijacking, bombing, and extortion
Palestine Islamic Jihad (PIJ); Israel, West Bank, Gaza Strip	Targets Israeli military and civilians, opposes secularism	Unknown	1970s	Suicide bombings, attacks on Israeli interests
Palestine Liberation Front (PLF); Iraq	Known for aerial attacks against Israel	Unknown	1970s	Attacked Italian ship Achille Lauro, murdered a U.S. citizen
Popular Front for the Liberation of Palestine (PFLP); Syria, Lebanon, Israel, West Bank, Gaza Strip	Targets Israel's "illegal occupation" of Palestine and opposes negotiations with Israel	Unknown	1967	International terrorist acts in the 1970s, attacks against Israel and moderate Arab targets since 1978
Popular Front for the Liberation of Palestine–General Command (PFLP-GC); Syria	Attacks in Europe and the Middle East. Targets Israel, West Bank, and Gaza Strip	several hundred	1968	Unusual attacks: hot air balloons, hang gliders, Lebanese guerrilla operations
Al-Qaeda; Afghanistan until 2001, Southeast Asia, Middle East, worldwide cells	Targets "non-Islamic" regimes and U.S. citizens	several thousand	1980s	Bombings of embassies and USS Cole; September 11, 2001, U.S. attacks

Name and base of operations	Goals and targets	Est. strength	Year founded	Activities
Real IRA; Northern Ireland, UK, Irish Republic	Targets civilians, military, police, and Protestant communities	100–200 activists	1998	Ignores cease-fire, Omagh bombing, more than 80 attacks since 1999
Revolutionary Armed Forces of Colombia (FARC); Colombia	Targets Colombian political, military, and economic interests, also foreign citizens	9,000–12,000	1964	Bombings, mortar attacks, kidnappings, extortion, guerrilla warfare, and drug trafficking
Revolutionary Nuclei (formerly ELA); Athens, Greece	Targets U.S. and European interests and government buildings in Greece	Believed small	1995	Arson attacks, low-level bombings, usually striking in early-morning hours
Revolutionary Organization 17 November; Athens, Greece	Seeks removal of U.S. bases, Turkish military, and the severing of NATO and EU ties	Believed small	1975	Assassinations, bombings, improvised rocket attacks, supported by bank robberies
Revolutionary People's Liberation Army/Front (DHKP-C); Turkey	Anti-U.S., anti-NATO, and anti-Turkish establishment group	Unknown	1978	Attacks on U.S. interests, suicide bombings
Salafist Group for Call and Combat (GSPC); Algeria	Military and government targets, pledges to avoid civilians	Several hundred	1992	Attacks military, police, and government convoys
Shining Path (Sendero Luminoso, SL); Peru	Aims to build communist regime, targets political enemies	400–500 militants	1960s	30,000 dead, assassinations, bombings, villiage raids
United Self-Defense Forces of Colombia (AUC); Colombia	Targets "insurgents" from FARC and ELN	8,000–11,000	1997	Assassinations, guerrilla warfare, and drug trafficking

1. On April 22, 2004, the U.S. State Department designated these 37 groups as Foreign Terrorist Organizations (FTOs). *Source:* U.S. Department of State, Office of Counterterrorism, Center for Defense Information, Terrorism Project.

Telephones and Computers by Country, 2001

(rates per 1,000 persons)

Country	Telephone main lines	Cellular phone subscribers	Personal computers[1]	Country	Telephone main lines	Cellular phone subscribers	Personal computers[1]
Algeria	61	3	7	Japan	586	588	349
Argentina	224	193	91	Korea, South	486	621	481
Australia	519	576	516	Kuwait	208	386	120
Austria	468	817	335	Lebanon	221	239	60
Belgium	498	746	233	Malaysia	198	314	126
Brazil	218	167	63	Mexico	137	217	69
Bulgaria	359	191	n.a.	Morocco	41	164	14
Canada	676	362	460	Netherlands	621	767	428
Chile	233	342	107	New Zealand	477	599	393
China[2]	137	110	19	Norway	720	815	508
Colombia	171	76	42	Pakistan	23	6	4
Cuba	51	1	20	Panama	130	164	38
Czech Republic	378	680	146	Peru	78	59	48
Denmark	720	738	540	Philippines	42	150	22
Dominican Republic	110	147	n.a.	Poland	295	260	85
Ecuador	104	67	23	Portugal	427	774	117
Egypt	104	43	16	Puerto Rico	346	316	n.a.
Finland	548	804	424	Romania	184	172	36
France	574	605	337	Russia	243	38	50
Germany	634	682	382	Saudi Arabia	145	113	63
Ghana	12	9	3	Singapore	471	724	508
Greece	529	751	81	South Africa	111	242	70
Guatemala	65	97	13	Spain	434	734	168
Honduras	47	36	12	Sweden	739	790	561
Hungary	375	498	100	Switzerland	743	728	538
India	38	6	6	Syria	103	12	16
Indonesia	35	31	11	Taiwan	573	969	253
Iran	169	32	70	Thailand	99	123	28
Iraq	29	—	n.a.	Turkey	285	295	41
Ireland	485	774	391	United Kingdom	588	770	366
Israel	466	907	246	**United States**	667	451	625
Italy	472	883	195	Uruguay	283	155	110
Jamaica	205	244	50	Venezuela	109	264	53

— Represents or rounds to zero. n.a. = Not available. 1. In many countries mainframe computers are used extensively, and thousands of users can be connected to a single mainframe computer; thus the number of PCs understates the total use of computers. *Source:* International Telecommunications Union, Geneva, Switzerland, *World Telecommunication Indicators*, (copyright). From *Statistical Abstract of the United States: 2003.*

Tax Burden by Country, 2002

Country	Single person without children	One-earner family with two children	Country	Single person without children	One-earner family with two children
Australia	23.6%	14.7%	Korea	8.7%	8.1%
Austria	28.6	9.0	Luxembourg	22.1	–3.6
Belgium	41.4	21.6	Mexico	3.6	3.6
Canada	25.7	15.1	Netherlands	28.7	17.2
Czech Republic	23.7	3.7	Norway	28.8	17.9
Denmark	43.1	30.5	Poland	31.0	25.0
Finland	31.7	23.2	Portugal	16.5	5.2
France	26.5	14.2	Slovak Republic	19.3	3.1
Germany	41.2	18.6	Spain	19.2	10.4
Greece	16.5	17.0	Sweden	30.4	21.0
Hungary	29.1	7.8	Switzerland	21.5	8.6
Ireland	16.4	–0.8	Turkey	30.0	30.0
Italy	28.1	12.2	United Kingdom	23.3	10.8
Japan	16.2	11.9	United States	24.3	11.3

Source: Organization for Economic Cooperation and Development, Paris, France, *Taxing Wages, 2001–2002* (copyright). From *Statistical Abstract of the United States: 2003.*

Economic Statistics by Country, 2003

Country	GDP/PPP	GDP/PPP per capita	Real growth rate (%)	Inflation (%)	Country	GDP/PPP	GDP/PPP per capita	Real growth rate (%)	Inflation (%)
Afghanistan	$20 billion	$ 700	29.0%	5.2%	Côte d'Ivoire	24.5 billion	$ 1,400	–1.9%	4.1%
Albania	16.1 billion	4,500	7.0	3.3	Croatia	47.1 billion	10,700	4.5	1.5
Algeria	194.3 billion	5,900	7.3	3.1	Cuba	31.6 billion	2,800	1.3	5.0
Andorra	1.3 billion[1]	19,000[1]	3.8[1]	4.3[1]	Cyprus*	8.9 billion	16,000	1.6	4.0
Angola	20.6 billion	1,900	7.1	106.0[2]		1.2 billion	5,600	2.6	12.6
Antigua and Barbuda	750 million[2]	11,000[2]	3.0[2]	0.4[1]	Czech Republic	160.5 billion	15,700	2.5	0.0
Argentina	432.7 billion	11,200	8.0	3.7	Denmark	167.7 billion	31,200	0.3	2.1
Armenia	11.8 billion	3,900	9.9	4.3	Djibouti	619 million[2]	1,300[2]	3.5[2]	2.0[2]
Australia	570.3 billion	28,900	2.8	2.7	Dominica	380 million[2]	5,400[2]	–1.0	1.0[3]
Austria	245.5 billion	30,000	0.8	1.2	Dominican Republic	52.2 billion	6,000	–1.8	21.2
Azerbaijan	26.3 billion	3,400	9.9	2.9	East Timor	440 million[3]	500[3]	–3.0	8.0
Bahamas, The	5.1 billion	16,800	1.0	1.7[2]	Ecuador	45.5 billion	3,300	2.6	6.1
Bahrain	11.4 billion	17,100	3.6	0.4	Egypt	294.3 billion	3,900	2.8	4.5
Bangladesh	258.8 billion	1,900	5.3	5.3	El Salvador	31 billion	4,800	1.4	2.1
Barbados	4.5 billion	16,200	–0.6	–0.5	Equatorial Guinea	1.3 billion[2]	2,700[2]	20.0[2]	6.0[2]
Belarus	61.9 billion	6,000	6.1	30.0	Eritrea	3.3 billion[2]	700[2]	2.0[2]	15.0[3]
Belgium	298.2 billion	29,000	0.8	1.4	Estonia	17.4 billion	12,300	4.8	1.5
Belize	1.3 billion[2]	4,900[2]	3.7[2]	1.9[2]	Ethiopia	48.5 billion	700	–2.0	12.6
Benin	7.7 billion	1,100	5.5	3.3[2]	Fiji	5 billion	5,800	4.8	1.6[2]
Bhutan	2.7 billion[2]	1,300[2]	7.7[2]	3.0[2]	Finland	141.7 billion	27,300	1.5	1.1
Bolivia	20.9 billion	2,400	2.1	2.0[3]	France	1.65 trillion	27,500	0.1	2.0
Bosnia and Herzegovina	24.4 billion	6,100	3.8	3.5[2]	Gabon	7.3 billion	5,500	1.2	2.3[2]
Botswana	13.9 billion	8,800	7.6	8.1[2]	Gambia, The	2.6 billion	1,700	0.5	5.5[2]
Brazil	1.4 trillion	7,600	0.1	9.3	Georgia	12.2 billion	2,500	5.5	5.0
Brunei	6.5 billion[2]	18,600[2]	3.0[2]	–2.0[2]	Germany	2.3 trillion	27,600	–0.1	0.9
Bulgaria	57.1 billion	7,600	4.4	5.6	Ghana	44.5billion	2,200	4.8	26.4
Burkina Faso	14.3 billion	1,100	4.6	4.5	Greece	212.2 billion	19,900	4.0	3.3
Burundi	3.8 billion	600	0.0	11.0	Grenada	440 million[2]	5,000[2]	2.5[2]	2.8[3]
Cambodia	22.8 billion	1,700	5.5	3.0	Guatemala	56.5 billion	4,100	2.2	5.6
Cameroon	27.6 billion	1,800	3.6	4.5[2]	Guinea	18.9 billion	2,100	2.2	8.0
Canada	957.7 billion	29,700	1.6	2.8	Guinea-Bissau	1.2 billion	900	1.8	4.0[2]
Cape Verde	600 million[2]	1,400[2]	4.0[2]	3.0[2]	Guyana	2.8 billion	4,000	0.3	4.7[2]
Central African Rep.	4.6 billion	1,200	1.0	3.6[3]	Haiti	12.2 billion	1,600	–1.0	37.3
Chad	10.9 billion	1,200	15.0	6.0[2]	Honduras	17.5 billion	2,600	2.5	7.7
Chile	154.6 billion	9,900	3.2	1.1	Hungary	139.7 billion	13,900	2.8	4.7
China	6.5 trillion	5,000	9.1	1.2	Iceland	8.7 billion	30,900	2.6	2.0
Colombia	262.5 billion	6,300	3.4	7.2	India	3.0 trillion	2,900	7.6	4.6
Comoros	441 million[2]	700[2]	2.0[2]	3.5[3]	Indonesia	758.1 billion	3,200	4.0	6.9
Congo, Dem. Rep. of	35.6 billion	600	6.0	14.0	Iran	477.8 billion	7,000	6.0	18.0
Congo, Rep. of	2.2 billion	700	2.0	4.0[2]	Iraq	38.79 billion	1,600	–20.0	27.5
Costa Rica	35.2 billion	9,000	5.2	9.4	Ireland	117 billion	29,800	2.1	3.7
					Israel	120.6 billion	19,700	1.0	1.1

Country	GDP/PPP	GDP/PPP per capita	Real growth rate (%)	Inflation (%)
Italy	1.6 trillion	$26,800	0.5%	2.3%
Jamaica	10.2 billion	3,800	1.9	14.1
Japan	3.6 trillion	28,000	2.3	−0.3
Jordan	23.6 billion	4,300	3.1	3.5
Kazakhstan	105.3 billion	7,000	9.0	6.2
Kenya	33.1 billion	1,000	1.7	9.6
Kiribati	79 million[3]	800[3]	1.5[3]	2.5[3]
Korea, North	22.6 billion	1,000	1.0	n.a.
Korea, South	855.3 billion	17,700	2.8	3.5
Kuwait	39.5 billion	18,100	4.4	1.2
Kyrgyzstan	7.7 billion	1,600	6.0	4.0
Laos	10.3 billion	1,700	5.7	7.8[3]
Latvia	23.8 billion	10,100	6.8	2.8
Lebanon	17.8 billion	4,800	3.0	2.5
Lesotho	5.6 billion	3,000	4.2	10.0[2]
Liberia	3.3 billion	1,000	3.0	15.0
Libya	35 billion	6,400	3.2	2.8
Liechtenstein	825 million[4]	25,000[4]	11.0[4]	1.0[3]
Lithuania	40.2 billion	11,200	7.1	−1.0
Luxembourg	25 billion	55,100	1.2	2.0
Macedonia, The Former Yugoslav Republic of	13.8 billion	6,700	2.8	1.2
Madagascar	13 billion	800	6.0	3.5
Malawi	6.8 billion	600	1.7	27.4[3]
Malaysia	207.2 billion	9,000	4.9	1.2
Maldives	1.3 billion[2]	3,900[2]	2.3[2]	1.0[2]
Mali	10.5 billion	900	0.5	4.5[2]
Malta	7.1 billion	17,700	0.8	0.8
Marshall Is.	115 million[3]	1,600[3]	1.0[3]	2.0[3]
Mauritania	5.2 billion	1,800	4.5	7.0
Mauritius	13.8 billion	11,400	4.1	6.4[2]
Mexico	942.2 billion	9,000	1.2	4.0
Micronesia	277 million	2,000[2]	1.0[2]	1.0[2]
Moldova	7.8 billion	1,800	6.3	11.7
Monaco	870 million[4]	27,000[4]	n.a.	n.a.
Mongolia	4.9 billion	1,800	5.0	1.5[2]
Morocco	128.3 billion	4,000	6.0	3.6[2]
Mozambique	21.2 billion	1,200	7.0	15.2[2]
Myanmar	78.8 billion	1,900	5.2	52.8
Namibia	13.7 billion	7,100	3.3	8.0
Nauru	60 million[3]	5,000[3]	n.a.	−3.6[5]
Nepal	38 billion	1,400	2.4	2.9[2]
Netherlands	461.4 billion	28,600	−0.7	2.0
New Zealand	85.3 billion	21,600	3.4	1.8
Nicaragua	11.5 billion	2,200	1.4	5.3
Niger	9.1 billion	800	3.8	3.0[2]
Nigeria	110.8 billion	800	3.4	11.7[2]
Norway	171.6 billion	37,700	0.5	2.6
Oman	37.5 billion	13,400	3.3	0.3
Pakistan	317.7 billion	2,100	5.4	3.1[6]
Palau	174 million	9,000[3]	1.0[3]	3.4[1]
Panama	18.6 billion	6,300	3.2	1.3
Papua New Guinea	11.4 billion	2,200	0.7	17.2
Paraguay	28 billion	4,600	1.3	10.5[2]
Peru	146.9 billion	5,200	4.0	2.2
Philippines	390.7 billion	4,600	4.5	3.1
Poland	426.7 billion	11,000	3.6	0.7
Portugal	182.3 billion	$18,000	−1.0%	3.1%
Qatar	17.5 billion	21,500	8.5	2.0
Romania	154.4 billion	6,900	4.5	14.3
Russia	1.3 trillion	8,900	7.3	12.0
Rwanda	10.1 billion	1,300	3.5	5.5[2]
Saint Kitts and Nevis	339 million[2]	8,800[2]	−1.9[2]	1.7[3]
Saint Lucia	866 million[2]	5,400[2]	3.3[2]	3.0[3]
Saint Vincent and the Grenadines	339 million[2]	2,900[2]	−0.5[2]	−0.4[3]
Samoa	1 billion[2]	5,600[2]	5.0[2]	4.0[3]
San Marino	940 million[3]	34,600[3]	7.5[3]	3.3[3]
São Tomé and Príncipe	200 million[2]	1,200[2]	4.0[2]	9.0[2]
Saudi Arabia	286.2 billion	11,800	4.7	1.0
Senegal	16.9 billion	1,600	4.5	3.0[2]
Serbia and Montenegro	24 billion	2,300	2.0	11.6
Seychelles	626 million[2]	7,800[2]	1.5[2]	0.5[2]
Sierra Leone	3.1 billion	500	6.5	1.0[2]
Singapore	109.1 billion	23,700	0.8	0.7
Slovakia	72.3 billion	13,300	3.9	8.6
Slovenia	36.9 billion	18,300	2.5	5.6
Solomon Is.	800 million[3]	1,700[3]	−10.0[3]	9.0[2]
Somalia	4.4 billion	500	2.1	n.a.
South Africa	456.7 billion	10,700	1.9	9.9[2]
Spain	885.5 billion	22,000	2.4	2.6
Sri Lanka	73.5 billion	3,700	5.2	9.0
Sudan	70.8 billion	1,900	6.1	8.8
Suriname	1.5 billion	3,500	1.5	17.0[2]
Swaziland	5.7 billion	4,900	2.2	11.8[2]
Sweden	238.1 billion	26,800	1.6	2.3
Switzerland	239.8 billion	32,800	−0.3	0.5
Syria	58 billion	3,300	0.9	1.5
Taiwan	528.6 billion	23,400	3.2	−0.2[2]
Tajikistan	7 billion	1,000	9.9	16.0
Tanzania	21.6 billion	600	5.2	4.6
Thailand	475.7 billion	7,400	6.3	1.8
Togo	8.2 billion	1,500	3.2	4.0[2]
Tonga	236 million[3]	2,200[3]	3.0[3]	10.3[2]
Trinidad and Tobago	10.6 billion	9,600	4.5	3.7
Tunisia	68.8 billion	6,900	6.0	2.7
Turkey	455.3 billion	6,700	5.0	18.4
Turkmenistan	27.1 billion	5,700	20.0	11.0
Tuvalu	n.a.	1,100[1]	3.0[1]	5.0[1]
Uganda	36.1 billion	1,400	4.4	0.1[2]
Ukraine	256.5 billion	5,300	8.2	8.2
UAE	57.7 billion	23,200	5.2	3.2
UK	1.7 trillion	27,700	2.1	3.0
U.S.	11 trillion	37,800	3.1	2.1
Uruguay	43 billion	12,600	0.3	10.2
Uzbekistan	44.1 billion	1,700	3.4	21.9
Vanuatu	563 million[2]	2,900[2]	−0.3[2]	2.0[2]
Venezuela	117.9 billion	4,800	−9.2	31.1
Vietnam	203.9 billion	2,500	7.3	3.9[2]
Yemen	15.2 billion	800	3.1	12.3
Zambia	8.6 billion	800	4.0	21.5[3]
Zimbabwe	24 billion	1,900	−13.6	383.4

NOTES: Definitions: Gross domestic product (GDP): The value of all goods and services produced domestically. Purchasing power parity (PPP): The PPP method involves the use of standardized international dollar price weights, which are applied to the GDP produced in a given economy. The data derived from the 1998 method provide a better comparison of economic well-being between countries than conversions at official currency exchange rates. n.a. = not available. *First line of figures for Greek Cyprus, second for Turkish Cyprus. 1. 2000 est. 2. 2002 est. 3. 2001 est. 4. 1999 est. 5. 1993 est. 6. 1997 est. *Source: The World Factbook, 2004.*

Major sources: The World Factbook 2004; Center for International Research, U.S. Bureau of the Census; The Columbia Encyclopedia; The World Book Encyclopedia; Encyclopædia Britannica; U.S. State Dept.; and various newspapers.
(Information as of Sept. 2004; for updated country information, see www.infoplease.com/countries.html.)

Definitions: Gross domestic product (GDP): The value of all goods and services produced domestically; purchasing power parity (PPP): The PPP method involves the use of standardized international dollar price weights, which are applied to the GDP produced in a given economy. The data derived from the PPP method provide a better comparison of economic well-being between countries than conversions at official currency exchange rates. Literacy rates and population figures are supplied by the U.S. Census Bureau.

Afghanistan

ISLAMIC EMIRATE OF AFGHANISTAN
National name: Dowlat-e Eslami-ye Afghanestan
President: Hamid Karzai (2002)
Area: 250,000 sq mi (647,500 sq km)
Population (2004 est.): 28,513,677 (growth rate: 4.9%); birth rate: 47.3/1000; infant mortality rate: 166.0/1000; life expectancy: 42.5; density per sq mi: 114
Capital and largest city (2003 est.): Kabul, 2,206,300.
Other large cities: Kandahar, 349,300; Mazar-i-Sharif, 246,900; Charikar, 202,600; Herat, 171,500. **Monetary unit:** Afghani. **Languages:** Pashtu, Dari Persian, other Turkic and minor languages. **Ethnicity/race:** Pashtun 42%, Tajik 27%, Hazara 9%, Uzbek 9%, minor ethnic groups (Chahar Aimaks, Turkmen, Baloch, and others). **Religion:** Islam (Sunni 80%, Shiite 19%), other 1%. **Literacy rate:** 36% (1999 est.)
Economic summary: GDP/PPP (2003 est.): $20 billion; per capita $700. **Real growth rate:** 29%. **Inflation:** 5.2%. **Unemployment:** n.a. **Arable land:** 12%. **Agriculture:** opium, wheat, fruits, nuts, wool, mutton, sheepskins, lambskins. **Labor force** (2001 est): 11.8 million; agriculture 80%, industry 10%, services 10% (1990 est.). **Natural resources:** natural gas, petroleum, coal, copper, chromite, talc, barites, sulfur, lead, zinc, iron ore, salt, precious and semiprecious stones. **Industries:** small-scale production of textiles, soap, furniture, shoes, fertilizer, cement; handwoven carpets; natural gas, coal, copper. **Exports:** $98 million (2002 est.): opium, fruits and nuts, handwoven carpets, wool, cotton, hides and pelts, precious and semi-precious gems. **Imports:** $1.007 billion (2002 est.): capital goods, food, textiles, petroleum products. **Major trading partners:** Pakistan, India, Germany, UAE, Belgium, Russia, South Korea, Japan, Kenya (2002).

Geography Afghanistan, approximately the size of Texas, is bordered on the north by Turkmenistan, Uzbekistan, and Tajikistan, on the extreme northeast by China, on the east and south by Pakistan, and by Iran on the west. The country is split east to west by the Hindu Kush mountain range, rising in the east to heights of 24,000 ft (7,315 m). With the exception of the southwest, most of the country is covered by high snowcapped mountains and is traversed by deep valleys.

Government In June 2002 a multiparty republic replaced an interim government that had been established in Dec. 2001, following the fall of the Islamic Taliban government.

History Darius I and Alexander the Great were the first to use Afghanistan as the gateway to India. Islamic conquerors arrived in the 7th century, and Genghis Khan and Tamerlane followed in the 13th and 14th centuries.

In the 19th century, Afghanistan became a battleground in the rivalry between imperial Britain and czarist Russia for control of Central Asia. Three Anglo-Afghan wars (1839–1842, 1878–1880, and 1919) ended inconclusively. In 1893 Britain established an unofficial border, the Durand Line, separating Afghanistan from British India, and London granted full independence in 1919. Emir Amanullah founded an Afghan monarchy in 1926.

During the cold war, King Mohammed Zahir Shah developed close ties with the Soviet Union, accepting extensive economic assistance from Moscow. He was deposed in 1973 by his cousin Mohammed Daoud, who proclaimed a republic. Daoud was killed in a 1978 coup, and Noor Taraki took power, setting up a Marxist regime. He, in turn, was executed in Sept. 1979, and Hafizullah Amin became president. Amin was killed in Dec. 1979, as the Soviets launched a full-scale invasion of Afghanistan and installed Babrak Karmal as president.

The Soviets, and the Soviet-backed Afghan government, were met with fierce popular resistance. Guerrilla forces, calling themselves *mujahideen,* pledged a jihad, or holy war, to expel the invaders. Initially armed with outdated weapons, the mujahideen became a focus of U.S. cold war strategy against the Soviet Union, and with Pakistan's help, Washington began funneling sophisticated arms to the resistance. Moscow's troops were soon bogged down in a no-win conflict with determined Afghan fighters. In 1986 Karmal resigned, and was replaced by Mohammad Najibullah. In April 1988 the USSR, U.S., Afghanistan, and Pakistan signed accords calling for an end to outside aid to the warring factions. In return, a Soviet withdrawal took place in Feb. 1989, but the pro-Soviet government of President Najibullah was left in the capital, Kabul.

By mid-April 1992 Najibullah was ousted as Islamic rebels advanced on the capital. Almost immediately, the various rebel groups began fighting one another for control. Amid the chaos of competing factions, a group calling itself the Taliban—consisting of Islamic students—seized control of Kabul in Sept. 1996. It imposed harsh fundamentalist laws, including stoning for adultery and severing hands for theft. Women were prohibited from work and school, and they were required to cover themselves from head to foot in public. By fall 1998 the Taliban controlled about 90% of the country and, with its scorched-earth tactics and human rights abuses, had turned itself into an international pariah. Only three countries, Pakistan, Saudi Arabia, and the UAR, recognized the Taliban as Afghanistan's legitimate government

On Aug. 20, 1998, U.S. cruise missiles struck a terrorist training complex in Afghanistan believed to have been financed by Osama bin Laden, a wealthy Islamic radical sheltered by the Taliban. The U.S. asked for the deportation of Bin Laden, whom they believed was involved in the bombing of the U.S. embassies in Kenya and Tanzania on Aug. 7, 1998. The UN also demanded the Taliban hand over Bin Laden for trial.

In Sept. 2001, legendary guerrilla leader Ahmed Shah Masoud was killed by suicide bombers, a seeming death knell for the anti-Taliban forces, a loosely connected group referred to as the Northern Alliance. Days later, terrorists attacked New York's World Trade Center towers and the Pentagon, and Bin Laden emerged as the primary suspect in the tragedy.

On Oct. 7, after the Taliban repeatedly and defiantly refused to turn over Bin Laden, the U.S. and its allies began daily air strikes against Afghan military installations and terrorist training camps. Five weeks later, with the help of U.S. air support, the Northern Alliance managed with breathtaking speed to take the key cities of Mazar-i-Sharif and Kabul, the capital. On Dec. 7, the Taliban regime collapsed entirely when its troops fled their last stronghold, Kandahar. However, al-Qaeda members and other mujahideen from various parts of the Islamic world who had earlier fought alongside the Taliban persisted in pockets of fierce resistance, forcing U.S. and allied troops to maintain a presence in Afghanistan. Osama bin Laden and Taliban leader Mullah Muhammad Omar remained at large.

In Dec. 2001, Hamid Karzai, a Pashtun (the dominant ethnic group in the country) and the leader of the powerful 500,000-strong Populzai clan, was named head of Afghanistan's interim government; in June 2002, he formally became president. The U.S. maintained about 12,000 troops to combat the remnants of the Taliban and al-Qaeda, and about 31 nations have also contributed NATO-led peacekeeping forces. But attacks on American-led forces have intensified since the war, and warlords continue to maintain tight regional control. In a highly aggressive and uncharacteristic move, Karzai attempted to rein in one of the most powerful warlords, Ismail Khan, by removing him from the governorship of Herat, a western province, in Sept. 2004. Violent protests followed Khan's ouster.

Afghanistan's *loya jirga,* or grand assembly, ratified a new constitution on Jan. 4, 2004. Low voter registration and the ongoing threat posed by insurgents prompted President Karzai to postpone elections scheduled for June 2004. The presidential vote was put off until Oct. 2004 and parliamentary elections until April 2005.

Albania

THE REPUBLIC OF ALBANIA

National name: Republika E Shqiperise
President: Alfred Moisiu (2002)
Prime Minister: Fatos Nano (2002)
Area: 11,100 sq mi (28,748 sq km)
Population (2004 est.): 3,544,808 (growth rate: 0.5%); birth rate: 15.1/1000; infant mortality rate: 22.3/1000; life expectancy: 77.1; density per sq mi: 319
Capital and largest city (2003 est.): Tirana, 353,400.
  Other large cities: Durres, 113,900; Elbasan, 97,000.
Monetary unit: Lek. **Languages:** Albanian (Tosk is the official dialect), Greek. **Ethnicity/race:** Albanian 95%, Greeks 3%, other 2%: Vlachs, Gypsies, Serbs, and Bulgarians (1989 est.). **Religions:** Islam 70%, Albanian Orthodox 20%, Roman Catholic 10% (est.).
  Literacy rate: 87% (2003 est.)
Economic summary: GDP/PPP (2003 est.): $16.13 billion; per capita $4,500. **Real growth rate:** 7%. **Inflation:** 3.3%. **Unemployment:** 15.8% officially; may be as high as 30% (2003 est.). **Arable land:** 21%. **Agriculture:** wheat, corn, potatoes, vegetables, fruits, sugar beets, grapes; meat, dairy products. **Labor force:** 1.35 million (not including 352,000 emigrant workers and 261,000 domestically unemployed);

agriculture 50%, industry and services 50%. **Industries:** food processing, textiles and clothing; lumber, oil, cement, chemicals, mining, basic metals, hydropower. **Natural resources:** petroleum, natural gas, coal, chromium, copper, timber, nickel, hydropower. **Exports:** $425 million (f.o.b., 2003 est.): textiles and footwear; asphalt, metals and metallic ores, crude oil; vegetables, fruits, tobacco. **Imports:** $1.76 billion (f.o.b., 2003 est.): machinery and equipment, foodstuffs, textiles, chemicals. **Major trading partners:** Italy, Germany, Greece, Turkey, Yugoslavia, Bulgaria.

Geography Albania is situated on the eastern shore of the Adriatic Sea, with Montenegro and Serbia to the north, Macedonia to the east, and Greece to the south. Slightly larger than Maryland, Albania may be divided into two major regions: a mountainous highland region (north, east, and south) constituting 70% of the land area, and a western coastal lowland region that contains nearly all of the country's agricultural lands and is the most densely populated part of Albania.

Government Emerging democracy.

History A part of Illyria in ancient times and later of the Roman Empire, Albania was ruled by the Byzantine Empire from 535 to 1204. An alliance (1444–1466) of Albanian chiefs failed to halt the advance of the Ottoman Turks, and the country remained under at least nominal Turkish rule for more than four centuries, until it proclaimed its independence on Nov. 28, 1912.

Largely agricultural, Albania is one of the poorest countries in Europe. A battlefield in World War I, after the war it became a republic in which a conservative Muslim landlord, Ahmed Zogu, proclaimed himself president in 1925 and king (Zog I) in 1928. He ruled until Italy annexed Albania in 1939. Communist guerrillas under Enver Hoxha seized power in 1944, near the end of World War II. Hoxha was a devotee of Stalin, emulating the Soviet leader's repressive tactics, imprisoning or executing landowners and others who did not conform to the socialist ideal. Hoxha eventually broke with Soviet communism in 1961 because of differences with Khrushchev and then aligned himself with Chinese communism, which he also abandoned in 1978 after the death of Mao. From then on Albania went its own way to forge its individual version of the socialist state and became one of the most isolated—and economically underdeveloped—countries in the world. Hoxha was succeeded by Ramiz Alia in 1982.

Elections in March 1991 gave the Communists a decisive majority. But a general strike and street demonstrations soon forced the all-Communist cabinet to resign. In June 1991 the Communist Party of Labor renamed itself the Socialist Party and renounced its past ideology. The opposition Democratic Party won a landslide victory in the 1992 elections, and Sali Berisha, a former cardiologist, became Albania's first elected president. The following year, ex-Communists, including Ramiz Alia and former prime minister Fatos Nano, were imprisoned on corruption charges.

But Albania's experiment with democratic reform and a free-market economy went disastrously awry in March 1997, when large numbers of its citizens invested in shady get-rich-quick pyramid schemes. When five of these schemes collapsed in the beginning of the year, robbing Albanians of an estimated $1.2 billion in savings, their rage turned against the government, which appeared to have sanctioned the nationwide swindle. Rioting broke out, the country's fragile infrastructure collapsed, and gangsters and rebels overran the country, plunging it into virtual anarchy. A multinational protection force eventually restored order and set up the elections that formally ousted President Sali Berisha.

In spring 1999, Albania was heavily involved in the affairs of its fellow ethnic Albanians to the north, in Kosovo. Albania served as an outpost for NATO troops and took in approximately 440,000 Kosovar refugees, about half the total number of ethnic Albanians who were driven from their homes in Kosovo.

Ilir Meta, elected prime minister in 1999, rapidly moved forward in his first years to modernize the economy, privatize business, fight crime, and reform the judiciary and tax systems. He resigned in Jan. 2002, frustrated by political infighting. In June 2002, former general Alfred Moisiu was elected president, endorsed by both the Socialists (headed by Fatos Nano) and the Democrats (led by Sali Berisha) in an effort to end the unproductive political fractiousness that has stalemated the government. The political duel between Nano and Berisha, however, continued into 2003 and 2004, and little improvement was evident in the standard of living for Albanians.

Algeria

DEMOCRATIC AND POPULAR REPUBLIC OF ALGERIA

National name: Al Jumhuriyah al Jaza'iriyah ad Dimuqratiyah ash Shabiyah
President: Abdel-Aziz Bouteflika (1999)
Prime Minister: Ahmed Ouyahia (2003)
Area: 919,590 sq mi (2,381,740 sq km)
Population (2004 est.): 32,129,324 (growth rate: 1.3%); birth rate: 17.8/1000; infant mortality rate: 32.2/1000; life expectancy: 72.7; density per sq mi: 35
Capital and largest city (2003 est.): Algiers, 3,917,000 (metro. area), 1,742,800 (city proper). **Other large cities:** Oran, 752,200; Constantine, 530,100; Batna, 278,100; Annaba, 246,700. **Monetary unit:** Dinar.
Languages: Arabic (official), French, Berber dialects.
Ethnicity/race: Arab-Berber 99%, European less than 1%. **Religion:** Islam (Sunni) 99% (state religion), Christian and Jewish 1%. **Literacy rate:** 70%
Economic summary: GDP/PPP (2003 est.): $194.3 billion; per capita $5,900 . **Real growth rate:** 7.3%. **Inflation:** 3.1%. **Unemployment:** 28.4%. **Arable land:** 3%. **Agriculture:** wheat, barley, oats, grapes, olives, citrus, fruits; sheep, cattle. **Labor force:** 9.5 million; government 29%, agriculture 25%, construction and public works 15%, industry 11%, other 20% (1996 est.). **Industries:** petroleum, natural gas, light industries, mining, electrical, petrochemical, food processing. **Natural resources:** petroleum, natural gas, iron ore, phosphates, uranium, lead, zinc. **Exports:** $24.96 billion (f.o.b., 2003 est.): petroleum, natural gas, and petroleum products 97%. **Imports:** $12.42 billion (f.o.b., 2003 est): capital goods, foodstuffs, consumer goods. **Major trading partners:** Italy, Spain, France, U.S., Brazil, Germany

Geography Nearly four times the size of Texas, Algeria is bordered on the west by Morocco and Western Sahara and on the east by Tunisia and Libya. The Mediterranean Sea is to the north, and to the south are Mauritania, Mali, and Niger. The Saharan region, which is 85% of the country, is almost completely uninhabited. The highest point is Mount Tahat in the Sahara, which rises 9,850 ft (3,000 m).

Government Parliamentary republic.

History Excavations in Algeria have indicated that *Homo erectus* resided there between 500,000 and 700,000 years ago. Phoenician traders settled on the Mediterranean coast in the 1st millennium B.C. As ancient Numidia, Algeria became a Roman colony, part of what was called Mauretania Caesariensis, at the close of the Punic Wars (145 B.C.). Conquered by the Vandals about A.D. 440, it fell from a high state of civilization to virtual barbarism, from which it partly recovered after an invasion by Arabs about 650. Christian during its Roman period, the indigenous Berbers were then converted to Islam. Falling under the control of the Ottoman Empire by 1536, Algiers served for three centuries as the headquarters of the Barbary pirates. Ostensibly to rid the region of the pirates, the French occupied Algeria in 1830 and made it a part of France in 1848.

Algerian independence movements led to the uprisings of 1954–1955, which developed into full-scale war. In 1962, French president Charles de Gaulle began the peace negotiations, and on July 5, 1962, Algeria was proclaimed independent. In Oct. 1963, Ahmed Ben Bella was elected president, and the country became socialist. He began to nationalize foreign holdings and aroused opposition. He was overthrown in a military coup on June 19, 1965, by Col. Houari Boumediène, who suspended the constitution and sought to restore economic stability. Boumedienne was succeeded by Col. Chadli Bendjedid after his death in 1978. Berbers rioted in 1980 when Arabic was made the country's only official language. Algeria entered a major recession. when world oil prices plummeted in the 1980s.

The fundamentalist Islamic Salvation Front (Front Islamique du Salut; FIS) won the largest number of votes in the country's first-ever parliamentary elections in Dec. 1991. To thwart the electoral results, the army cancelled the general election, which plunged the country into a bloody civil war. An estimated 100,000 people have been massacred by Islamic terrorists since war began in Jan. 1992. The undeclared civil war escalated in its brutality and senselessness in 1997–1998. Islamic extremists, who had originally focused their attacks on government officials and then shifted to intellectuals and journalists, abandoned political motivations entirely and targeted defenseless villagers. The mass slaughters were as savage as they were random, and the government was markedly ineffectual in stemming the violence.

Abdel-Aziz Bouteflika's ascension to the presidency in April 1999 was initially expected to bring peace and some economic improvement to this desperate war-torn country. Bouteflika, however, remains locked in power struggles with the military, whose support is crucial. Despite the appearance of democracy, Algeria remains in essence a military dictatorship. In 2001 violence by Islamic militants was again on the rise, and the long-disaffected Berber minority engaged in several large-scale protests.

Algeria's most destructive earthquake in two decades struck near the capital on May 21, 2003, killing more than 2,000 people and injuring many thousands more.

In April 2004 presidential elections, praised by international monitors for their fairness, incumbent Bouteflika won 85% of the vote. Bouteflika stated that his second term would be devoted to solving the three-year-old crisis in the Berber region of Kabylia, freeing women from restrictive family codes, and bringing about "true national reconciliation" from the civil war. The country's dire economic situation has improved slightly, but Algeria still faces a high unemployment problem—nearly 30%.

Andorra

PRINCIPALITY OF ANDORRA

National name: Valls d'Andorra
Head of Government: Marc Forné Molné (1994)
Chiefs of State (Coprinces): Frederic de Saint-Sernin for France and Nemesi Marques Oste for Spain
Area: 181 sq mi (468 sq km)
Population (2004 est.): 69,865 (growth rate: 1.0%); birth rate: 9.3/1000; infant mortality rate: 4.1/1000; life expectancy: 83.5; density per sq mi: 387
Capital and largest city (2003 est.): Andorra la Vella, 23,000. **Monetary units:** Euro. **Languages:** Catalán (official), French, Castilian, Portuguese. **Ethnicity/race:** Spanish 43%, Andorran 33%, Portuguese 11%, French 7%, other 6% (1998). **Religion:** Roman Catholic (predominant). **Literacy rate:** 100%
Economic summary: GDP/PPP (2000 est.): $1.3 billion; per capita $19,000. **Real growth rate:** 3.8%. **Inflation:** 4.3%. **Unemployment:** 0% (1996 est.). **Arable land:** 2%. **Agriculture:** small quantities of tobacco, rye, wheat, barley, oats, vegetables; sheep. **Labor force:** 33,000 (2001 est.); agriculture 1%, industry 21%, services 78% (2000 est.). **Industries:** tourism (particularly skiing), cattle raising, timber, tobacco, banking. **Natural resources:** hydropower, mineral water, timber, iron ore, lead. **Exports:** $58 million (f.o.b., 1998): tobacco products, furniture. **Imports:** $1.077 billion (1998): consumer goods, food, electricity. **Major trading partners:** France, Spain, U.S.

Geography Andorra is nestled high in the Pyrénées Mountains on the French-Spanish border.

Government A parliamentary coprincipality composed of the bishop of Urgel (Spain) and the president of France. Their representatives are listed above. The principality was internationally recognized as a sovereign state in 1993.

History An autonomous and semi-independent coprincipality, Andorra has been under the joint suzerainty of the French state and the Spanish bishops of Urgel since 1278. It maintains closer ties to Spain, however, and Catalán is its official language. In the late 20th century, Andorra became a popular tourist and winter sports destination and a wealthy international commercial center because of its banking facilities, low taxes, and lack of customs duties. In 1990 Andorra approved a customs union treaty with the EU permitting free movement of industrial goods between the two, but with Andorra applying the EU's external tariffs to third countries. Andorra became a member of the UN in 1993 and a member of the Council of Europe in 1994.

Angola

REPUBLIC OF ANGOLA

President: José Eduardo dos Santos (1979)
Prime Minister: Fernando da Piedade Dias dos Santos (2003)
Area: 481,351 sq mi (1,246,700 sq km)
Population (2004 est.): 10,978,552 (growth rate: 1.9%); birth rate: 45.1/1000; infant mortality rate: 192.5/1000; life expectancy: 36.8; density per sq mi: 23
Capital and largest city (2003 est.): Luanda, 2,297,200. **Other large cities:** Huambo, 171,000; Lubango, 136,000. **Monetary unit:** New Kwanza. **Languages:** Portuguese (official), Bantu and other African languages. **Ethnicity/race:** Ovimbundu 37%, Kimbundu 25%, Bakongo 13%, mestico (mixed European and Native African) 2%, European 1%, other 22%. **Religions:** Indigenous 47%, Roman Catholic 38%, Protestant 15% (1998 est.). **Literacy rate:** 42% (1998 est.)

Economic summary: GDP/PPP (2003 est.): $20.59 billion; per capita $1,900. **Real growth rate:** 7.14%. **Inflation:** 106% (2002 est.). **Unemployment:** extensive unemployment and underemployment affecting more than half the population. **Arable land:** 2%. **Agriculture:** bananas, sugarcane, coffee, sisal, corn, cotton, manioc (tapioca), tobacco, vegetables, plantains; livestock; forest products; fish. **Labor force:** 6.23 million (2001 est); agriculture 85%, industry and services 15%. **Industries:** petroleum; diamonds, iron ore, phosphates, feldspar, bauxite, uranium, and gold; cement; basic metal products; fish processing; food processing; brewing; tobacco products; sugar; textiles. **Natural resources:** petroleum, diamonds, iron ore, phosphates, copper, feldspar, gold, bauxite, uranium. **Exports:** $9.669 billion (f.o.b., 2003 est.): crude oil, diamonds, refined petroleum products, gas, coffee, sisal, fish and fish products, timber, cotton. **Imports:** $4.08 billion (f.o.b., 2003 est.): machinery and electrical equipment, vehicles and spare parts; medicines, food, textiles, military goods. **Major trading partners:** U.S., EU, China, South Korea, South Africa, Brazil.

Geography Angola, more than three times the size of California, extends for more than 1,000 mi (1,609 km) along the South Atlantic in southwest Africa. The Democratic Republic of the Congo and the Republic of Congo are to the north and east, Zambia is to the east, and Namibia is to the south. A plateau averaging 6,000 ft (1,829 m) above sea level rises abruptly from the coastal lowlands. Nearly all the land is desert or savanna, with hardwood forests in the northeast.

Government Angola underwent a transition from a one-party socialist state to a nominally multiparty democracy in 1992.

History The original inhabitants of Angola are thought to have been Khoisan speakers. After 1000, large numbers of Bantu speakers migrated to the region and became the dominant group. Angola derives its name from the Bantu kingdom of Ndongo, whose name for its king is *ngola*.

Explored by the Portuguese navigator Diego Cão in 1482, Angola became a link in trade with India and Southeast Asia. Later it was a major source of slaves for Portugal's New World colony of Brazil. Development of the interior began after the Berlin Conference in 1885 fixed the colony's borders, and British and Portuguese investment fostered mining, railways, and agriculture.

Following World War II, independence movements began but were sternly suppressed by Portuguese military force. The major nationalist organizations were the Popular Movement for the Liberation of Angola (MPLA), a Marxist party; National Front for the Liberation of Angola (FNLA); and the National Union for the Total Independence of Angola (UNITA). After 14 years of war, Portugal finally granted independence to Angola in 1975. The MPLA, which had led the independence movement, has controlled the government ever since. But no period of peace followed Angola's long war for independence. UNITA disputed the MPLA's ascendancy, and civil war broke out almost immediately. With the Soviet Union and Cuba supporting the Marxist MPLA, and the United States and South Africa supporting the anticommunist UNITA, the country became a cold war battleground.

With the waning of the cold war and the withdrawal of Cuban troops in 1989, the MPLA began to make the transition to a multiparty democracy. Despite shifting ideologies, the civil war continued, with UNITA's charismatic rebel leader, Jonas Savimbi, armed and sustained by his control of approximately 80% of the country's diamond trade. Free elections took place in

1992, with incumbent president José Eduardo dos Santos and the MPLA winning the UN-certified election over Savimbi and UNITA. Savimbi then withdrew, charging election fraud, and the civil war resumed.

Four years of relative peace took place between 1994 and 1998, when the UN, at a cost of $1.6 billion, oversaw the 1994 Lusaka peace accord. In 1997 it was agreed that a coalition government with UNITA would be implemented. But Savimbi violated the accord repeatedly by refusing to give up his strongholds, failing to demobilize his army, and retaking territory. As a result, the government suspended coalition rule in Sept. 1998, and the country again plunged into civil war. Angola's citizens continued to suffer. The hostilities affected an estimated 4 million people, about a third of the total population, and there were almost 2 million refugees.

On Feb. 22, 2002, government troops killed Jonas Savimbi, and his exhausted troops were ready to lay down their arms. Six weeks later, on April 4, rebel leaders signed a cease-fire deal with the government, signalling the end of 30 years of civil war. Within another five weeks, 80% of the rebels had been disarmed. While peace finally seemed secure, more than a half-million Angolans were faced with starvation. Thousands of Angolan refugees returned to their country in 2003, where their prospects are bleak.

Angola is the second-largest oil producer in sub-Saharan Africa, yet its people are among the continent's poorest. The corruption of the dos Santos government bears much of the blame. According to the International Monetary Fund, more than $4 billion in oil receipts have disappeared from Angola's treasury in the last six years.

Antigua and Barbuda

Sovereign: Queen Elizabeth II (1952)
Governor-General: James Beethoven Carlisle (1993)
Prime Minister: Baldwin Spencer (2004)
Land area: 171 sq mi (443 sq km)
Population (2004 est.): 68,320 (growth rate: 0.6%); birth rate: 17.7/1000; infant mortality rate: 20.2/1000; life expectancy: 71.6; density per sq mi: 399
Capital and largest city (2003 est.): St. John's, 23,500.
  Other large cities: English Harbour, 2,900; Codrington (capital of Barbuda), est. pop. 870.
Monetary unit: East Caribbean dollar. **Language:** English (official), local dialects. **Ethnicity/race:** black, British, Portuguese, Lebanese, Syrian. **Religions:** Christian (predominantly Anglican and other Protestant; some Roman Catholic). **Literacy rate:** 89% (1960 est.)
Economic summary: GDP/PPP (2002 est.): $750 million; per capita $11,000. **Real growth rate:** 3%. **Inflation:** 0.4% (2000 est.). **Unemployment:** 11% (2001 est.). **Arable land:** 18%. **Agriculture:** cotton, fruits, vegetables, bananas, coconuts, cucumbers, mangoes, sugarcane; livestock. **Labor force:** 30,000; commerce and services 82%, agriculture 11%, industry 7% (1983). **Industries:** tourism, construction, light manufacturing (clothing, alcohol, household appliances). **Natural resources:** negl; pleasant climate fosters tourism. **Exports:** $689 million (2002): petroleum products, manufactures, machinery and transport equipment, food and live animals. **Imports:** $692 million (2002 est.): food and live animals, machinery and transport equipment, manufactures, chemicals, oil. **Major trading partners:** OECS, Barbados, Guyana, Trinidad and Tobago, U.S., UK, Canada. **Member of Commonwealth of Nations**

Geography Antigua, the larger of the two main islands, is 108 sq mi (280 sq km). The island dependencies of Redonda (an uninhabited rocky islet) and Barbuda (a coral island formerly known as Dulcina) are 0.5 sq mi (1.30 sq km) and 62 sq mi (161 sq km), respectively.

Government Constitutional monarchy.

History Antigua was explored by Christopher Columbus in 1493 and named for the Church of Santa Maria de la Antigua in Seville. Antigua was colonized by Britain in 1632; Barbuda was first colonized in 1678. The country joined the West Indies Federation in 1958. With the breakup of the federation, it became one of the West Indies Associated States in 1967, self-governing its internal affairs. Full independence was granted Nov. 1, 1981.

The Bird family has controlled the islands since Vere C. Bird founded the Antigua Labor Party in the mid-1940s. While tourism and financial services have turned the country into one of the more prosperous in the Caribbean, law enforcement officials have charged that Antigua and Barbuda is a major center of money laundering, drug trafficking, and arms smuggling. Several scandals have tainted the Bird family, especially the 1995 conviction of Prime Minister Lester Bird's brother, Ivor, for cocaine smuggling. In 2000, Antigua and 35 other offshore banking centers agreed to reforms meant to prevent money laundering.

In March 2004, the Bird political dynasty came to an end when labor activist Baldwin Spencer defeated Lester Bird, who had been prime minister since 1994.

Argentina

ARGENTINE REPUBLIC

National name: República Argentina.
President: Néstor Kirchner (2003)
Area: 1,068,296 sq mi (2,766,890 sq km)
Population (2004 est.): 39,144,753 (growth rate: 1.0%); birth rate: 17.2/1000; infant mortality rate: 15.7/1000; life expectancy: 75.7; density per sq mi: 37
Capital and largest city (2003 est.): Buenos Aires, 13,076,300 (metro. area), 12,116,400 (city proper).
  Other large cities: Córdoba, 1,486,200; Rosario, 1,276,900; Mendoza, 988,600; Mar del Plata, 683,700.
Monetary unit: Peso. **Languages:** Spanish (official), English, Italian, German, French. **Ethnicity/race:** white (mostly Spanish and Italian) 97%; mestizo, Amerindian, other 3%. **Religions:** Roman Catholic 92%, Protestant 2%, Jewish 2%, other 4%. **Literacy rate:** 96.2% (1995 est.)
Economic summary: GDP/PPP (2003 est.): $432.7 billion; per capita $11,200. **Real growth rate:** 8%. **Inflation:** 3.7%. **Unemployment:** 16.3% (Sept. 2003). **Arable land:** 9%. **Agriculture:** sunflower seeds, lemons, soybeans, grapes, corn, tobacco, peanuts, tea, wheat; livestock. **Labor force:** 15 million (1999); agriculture n.a., industry n.a., services n.a. **Industries:** food processing, motor vehicles, consumer durables, textiles, chemicals and petrochemicals, printing, metallurgy, steel. **Natural resources:** fertile plains of the pampas, lead, zinc, tin, copper, iron ore, manganese, petroleum, uranium. **Exports:** $29.57 billion (f.o.b., 2003 est.): edible oils, fuels and energy, cereals, feed, motor vehicles. **Imports:** $13.27 billion (f.o.b., 2003 est.): machinery and equipment, motor vehicles, chemicals, metal manufactures, plastics. **Major trading partners:** Brazil, U.S., Chile, Spain, Germany, China.

Geography Second in South America only to Brazil in size and population, Argentina is a plain, rising from the Atlantic to the Chilean border and the towering Andes peaks. Aconcagua (22,834 ft., 6,960 m) is the highest peak in the world outside Asia. Argentina is also bordered by Bolivia and Paraguay on the north, and by Uruguay and Brazil on the east.

Government Republic.

History First explored in 1516 by Juan Díaz de Solis, Argentina developed slowly under Spanish colonial rule. Buenos Aires was settled in 1580; the cattle industry was thriving as early as 1600. Invading British forces were expelled in 1806–1807, and after Napoléon conquered Spain (1808), the Argentinians set up their own government in 1810. On July 9, 1816, independence was formally declared.

As it had in World War I, Argentina proclaimed neutrality at the outbreak of World War II, but in the closing phase declared war on the Axis powers on March 27, 1945. Juan D. Perón, an army colonel, emerged as the strongman of the postwar era, winning the presidential elections of 1946 and 1951. Perón's political strength was reinforced by his second wife—Eva Duarte de Perón (Evita)—and her popularity with the working classes. Although she never held a government post, Evita acted as de facto minister of health and labor, establishing a national charitable organization, and awarding generous wage increases to the unions, who responded with political support for Perón. Opposition to Perón's increasing authoritarianism led to a coup by the armed forces, which sent Perón into exile in 1955, three years after Evita's death. Argentina entered a long period of military dictatorships with brief intervals of constitutional government.

The former dictator returned to power in 1973 and his third wife, Isabel Martínez de Perón, was elected vice president. After Perón's death in 1974, she became the hemisphere's first woman chief of state, assuming control of a nation teetering on economic and political collapse. In 1975, terrorist acts by left- and right-wing groups killed some 700 people. The cost of living rose 355%, while strikes and demonstrations were constant. On March 24, 1976, a military junta led by army commander Lt. Gen. Jorge Rafael Videla seized power and imposed martial law.

The military began the "dirty war" to restore order and eradicate its opponents. The Argentine Commission for Human Rights, in Geneva, has charged the junta with 2,300 political murders, over 10,000 political arrests, and the disappearances of 20,000 to 30,000 people. While violence declined, the economy remained in chaos. In March 1981 Videla was deposed by Field Marshal Roberto Viola, who in turn was succeeded by Lt. Gen. Leopoldo Galtieri.

On April 2, 1982, Galtieri invaded the British-held Falkland Islands, known as Las Islas Malvinas (Malvinas Islands) in Spanish, in what was seen as an attempt to increase his popularity. Great Britain, however, won a decisive victory, and Galtieri resigned in disgrace three days after Argentina's surrender. Maj. Gen. Reynaldo Bignone took over June 14, amid increasing pro-democratic public sentiment. As the 1983 elections approached, inflation hit 900% and Argentina's crippling foreign debt reached unprecedented levels.

In the presidential election of Oct. 1983, Raúl Alfonsín, leader of the Radical Civic Union, handed the Peronist Party its first defeat since its founding. Growing unemployment and quadruple-digit inflation, however, led to a Peronist victory in the elections of May 1989. Alfonsín resigned a month later in the wake of riots over high food prices, in favor of the new Peronist president, Carlos Menem. In 1991, Menem promoted economic austerity measures that deregulated businesses and privatized state-owned industries. But beginning in Sept. 1998, eight years into Menem's two-term presidency, Argentina entered its worst recession in a decade. Menem's economic policies, tolerance of corruption, and pardoning of military leaders involved in the dirty war eventually lost him the support of the poor and the working class who had elected him.

In Dec. 1999 Fernando de la Rua became president. Despite the introduction of several tough economic austerity plans, by 2001 the recession slid into its third year. The IMF gave Argentina $13.7 billion in emergency aid in Jan. 2001 and $8 billion in Aug. 2001. The international help was not enough, however, and by the end of 2001, Argentina verged on economic collapse. Rioters protesting government austerity measures forced de la Rua to resign in Dec. 2001. Argentina then defaulted on its $155 billion foreign debt payments, the largest such default in history.

After more instability, Congress named Eduardo Duhalde president on Jan. 1, 2002. Duhalde soon announced an economic plan devaluing the Argentine peso, which had been pegged to the dollar for a decade. The devaluation plunged the banking industry into crisis and wiped out much of the savings of the middle class, plunging millions of Argentinians into poverty.

In July 2002, former junta leader Galtieri and 42 other military officers were arrested and charged with the torture and execution of 22 leftist guerrillas during Argentina's 7-year military dictatorship. In recent years, judges have found legal loopholes allowing them to circumvent the blanket amnesty laws passed in 1986 and 1987, which have allowed many accused of atrocities during the dirty war to walk free.

Peronist Néstor Kirchner, the former governor of Santa Cruz, became Argentina's president in May 2003, after former president Carlos Menem abandoned the race. Kirchner has vowed to aggressively reform the courts, police, and armed services, and to repeal amnesty laws for perpetrators of the dirty war. Argentina's economy has been rebounding since its near collapse in 2001, with an impressive growth rate of about 8% since President Kirchner took office. But doubts have been raised about efforts at repaying its record public debt default.

Armenia

President: Robert Kocharian (1998)
Prime Minister: Andranik Markarian (2000)
Area: 11,506 sq mi (29,800 sq km)
Population (2004 est.): 2,991,360 (growth rate: –0.3%); (Armenian, 93%; others, Kurds, Ukrainians, and Russians); birth rate: 11.4/1000; infant mortality rate: 24.2/1000; life expectancy: 71.2; density per sq mi: 260
Capital and largest city (2003 est.): Yerevan, 1,462,700 (metro. area), 1,267,600 (city proper). **Other large cities:** Vanadzor, 147,400; Gyumri (Leninakan), 125,300; Abovian, 59,300. **Monetary unit:** Dram. **Language:** Armenian 96%, Russian 2%, other 2%. **Ethnicity/race:** Armenian 93%, Russian 2%, Azeri 1%, other (mostly Yezidi Kurds) 4% (2002). Note: as of the end of 1993, virtually all Azeris had emigrated from Armenia. **Religion:** Armenian Apostolic 94%, other Christian 4%, Yezidi 2%. **Literacy rate:** 99% (1989 est.)
Economic summary: GDP/PPP (2003 est.): $11.79 billion; per capita $3,900. **Real growth rate:** 9.9%. **Inflation:** 4.3%. **Unemployment:** 20% (2001 est.). Note: official rate is 10.9% for 2000. **Arable land:** 18%. **Agriculture:** fruit (especially grapes), vegetables; livestock. **Labor force:** 1.4 million (2001); agriculture 44%, services 14%, industry 42% (2000 est.). **Industries:** metal-cutting machine tools, forging-pressing machines, electric motors, tires, knitted wear, hosiery, shoes, silk fabric, chemicals, trucks, instruments, microelectronics, gem cutting, jewelry manufacturing, software development, food processing, brandy. **Natural resources:** small deposits

of gold, copper, molybdenum, zinc, alumina. **Exports:** $735 million (f.o.b., 2003 est.): diamonds, scrap metal, machinery and equipment, brandy, copper ore. **Imports:** $1.8 billion (f.o.b., 2003 est.): natural gas, petroleum, tobacco products, foodstuffs, diamonds. **Major trading partners:** Belgium, Russia, U.S., Iran.

Geography Armenia is located in the southern Caucasus and is the smallest of the former Soviet republics. It is bounded by Georgia on the north, Azerbaijan on the east, Iran on the south, and Turkey on the west. Contemporary Armenia is a fraction of the size of ancient Armenia. A land of rugged mountains and extinct volcanoes, its highest point is Mount Aragats, 13,435 ft (4,095 m).

Government Republic.

History One of the world's oldest civilizations, Armenia once included Mount Ararat, which biblical tradition identifies as the mountain that Noah's ark rested on after the flood. It was the first country in the world to officially embrace Christianity as its religion (c. A.D. 300).

In the 6th century B.C., Armenians settled in the kingdom of Urartu (the Assyrian name for Ararat), which was in decline. Under Tigrane the Great (fl. 95–55 B.C.) the Armenian empire reached its height and became one of the most powerful in Asia, stretching from the Caspian to the Mediterranean Seas. Throughout most of its long history, however, Armenia has been invaded by a succession of empires. Under constant threat of domination by foreign forces, Armenians became both cosmopolitan as well as fierce protectors of their culture and tradition.

Over the centuries Armenia was conquered by Greeks, Romans, Persians, Byzantines, Mongols, Arabs, Ottoman Turks, and Russians. From the 16th century through World War I major portions of Armenia were controlled by their most brutal invader, the Ottoman Turks, under whom the Armenians experienced discrimination, religious persecution, heavy taxation, and armed attacks. In response to Armenian nationalist stirrings, the Turks massacred thousands of Armenians in 1894 and 1896. The most horrific massacre took place in April 1915 during World War I, when the Turks ordered the deportation of the Armenian population to the deserts of Syria and Mesopotamia. According to the majority of historians, between 600,000 and 1.5 million Armenians were murdered or died of starvation. The Armenian massacre is considered the first genocide in the 20th century. Turkey denies that a genocide took place, and claims that a much smaller number died in a civil war.

After the Turkish defeat in World War I, the independent Republic of Armenia was established on May 28, 1918, but survived only until Nov. 29, 1920, when it was annexed by the Soviet Army. On March 12, 1922, the Soviets joined Georgia, Armenia, and Azerbaijan to form the Transcaucasian Soviet Socialist Republic, which became part of the USSR. In 1936, after a reorganization, Armenia became a separate constituent republic of the USSR. Since 1988, Armenia has been involved in a territorial dispute with Azerbaijan over the enclave of Nagorno-Karabakh, to which both lay claim. Also in 1988, a devastating earthquake killed thousands and wreaked economic havoc.

Armenia declared its independence from the collapsing Soviet Union on Sept. 23, 1991. In 1992–1994, Armenia successfully fought Azerbaijan for control of Nagorno-Karabakh. The majority of the enclave are Armenian Christians who want to secede from Azerbaijan and either become part of Armenia or gain full independence. Enormous casualties were involved.

An Armenian diaspora has existed throughout the nation's history, and Armenian emigration has been particularly heavy since independence from the Soviet Union. An estimated 60% of the total 8 million Armenians worldwide live outside the country, with 1 million each in the U.S. and Russia. Other significant Armenian communities are located in Georgia, France, Iran, Lebanon, Syria, Argentina, and Canada.

Australia

COMMONWEALTH OF AUSTRALIA

Sovereign: Queen Elizabeth II (1952)
Governor-General: Michael Jeffery (2003)
Prime Minister: John Howard (1996)
Area: 2,967,893 sq mi (7,686,850 sq km)
Population (2004 est.): 19,913,144 (growth rate: 0.9%); birth rate: 12.4/1000; infant mortality rate: 4.8/1000; life expectancy: 80.3; density per sq mi: 7
Capital (2003 est.): Canberra, 327,700. **Largest cities:** Sydney, 4,250,100; Melbourne, 3,610,800; Brisbane, 1,545,700; Perth, 1,375,200; Adelaide, 1,087,600.
Monetary unit: Australian dollar. **Language:** English, native languages. **Ethnicity/race:** Caucasian 92%, Asian 7%, aboriginal (353,000) and other 1%.
Religions: Anglican 26.1%, Roman Catholic 26%, other Christian 24.3%. **Literacy rate:** 100% (1980 est.)
Economic summary: GDP/PPP (2003 est.): $570.3 billion; per capita $28,900. **Real growth rate:** 2.8%. **Inflation:** 2.7%. **Unemployment:** 6.1%. **Arable land:** 7%. **Agriculture:** wheat, barley, sugarcane, fruits; cattle, sheep, poultry. **Labor force:** 9.2 million; services 73%, industry 22%, agriculture 5% (1997 est.). **Industries:** mining, industrial and transportation equipment, food processing, chemicals, steel. **Natural resources:** bauxite, coal, iron ore, copper, tin, silver, uranium, nickel, tungsten, mineral sands, lead, zinc, diamonds, natural gas, petroleum. **Exports:** $68.67 billion (2003 est.): coal, gold, meat, wool, alumina, iron ore, wheat, machinery and transport equipment. **Imports:** $82.91 billion (2003 est.): machinery and transport equipment, computers and office machines, telecommunication equipment and parts; crude oil and petroleum products. **Major trading partners:** Japan, U.S., South Korea, China, New Zealand, Singapore, UK, Germany, Malaysia. **Member of Commonwealth of Nations**

Geography The continent of Australia, with the island state of Tasmania, is approximately equal in area to the United States (excluding Alaska and Hawaii). Mountain ranges run from north to south along the east coast, reaching their highest point in Mount Kosciusko (7,308 ft; 2,228 m). The western half of the continent is occupied by a desert plateau that rises into barren, rolling hills near the west coast. The Great Barrier Reef, extending about 1,245 mi (2,000 km), lies along the northeast coast. The island of Tasmania (26,178 sq mi; 67,800 sq km) is off the southeast coast.

Government Democracy. Symbolic executive power is vested in the British monarch, who is represented throughout Australia by the governor-general.

History The first inhabitants of Australia were the Aborigines, who migrated there at least 40,000 years ago from Southeast Asia. There may have been between a half million to a full million Aborigines at the time of European settlement; today there are about 350,000. Dutch, Portuguese, and Spanish ships sighted Australia in the 17th century; the Dutch landed at the Gulf of Carpentaria in 1606. In 1616 the territory became known as New Holland. The British arrived in 1688, but it was not until Captain James Cook's voyage in 1770 that Great Britain claimed possession of the vast island, calling it New South Wales. A British penal colony was set up at Port Jackson (what is now Sydney) in 1788, and about 161,000 transported English convicts were settled there until the system was suspended in 1839.

Free settlers and former prisoners established six colonies: New South Wales (1786), Tasmania (then Van Diemen's Land) (1825), Western Australia (1829), South Australia (1834), Victoria (1851), and Queensland (1859). Various gold rushes attracted settlers, as did the mining of other minerals. Sheep farming and grain soon became important economic enterprises. The six colonies became states and in 1901 federated into the Commonwealth of Australia with a constitution that incorporated British parliamentary and U.S. federal traditions. Australia became known for its liberal legislation: free compulsory education, protected trade unionism with industrial conciliation and arbitration, the secret ballot, women's suffrage, maternity allowances, and sickness and old-age pensions.

Australia fought alongside Britain in World War I, notably with the Australia and New Zealand Army Corps (ANZAC) in the Dardanelles campaign (1915). Participation in World War II brought Australia closer to the United States. Parliamentary power in the second half of the 20th century shifted between three political parties: the Australian Labour Party, the Liberal Party, and the National Party. Australia relaxed its discriminatory immigration laws in the 1960s and 1970s, which favored Northern Europeans. Thereafter, about 40% of its immigrants came from Asia, diversifying a population that was predominantly of English and Irish heritage.

In March 1996 the opposition Liberal Party–National Party coalition easily won the national elections, removing the Labour Party after 13 years in power. Pressure from the new, conservative One Nation Party threatened to reduce the gains made by Aborigines and to limit immigration. An Aboriginal movement had grown in the 1960s that gained full citizenship and improved education for the country's poorest socioeconomic group.

In Sept. 1999, Australia led the international peacekeeping force sent to restore order in East Timor after pro-Indonesian militias begun massacring civilians to thwart East Timor's referendum on independence. Australia's relations with East Timor have soured since then over a dispute over oil reserves claimed by both countries.

In Nov. 1999, Australia's 11.6 million voters rejected a referendum that would have ended Australia's formal allegiance to the British Crown. The referendum would have replaced the British governor-general with an Australian president chosen by Parliament. Although the vast majority of Australians do not consider themselves monarchists, they rejected the referendum because it did not provide for direct, popular elections but gave Parliament the power to select the president.

In 2000, Prime Minister Howard instituted a new tax system, lowering income and corporate taxes, and adding sales taxes on goods and services.

John Howard won a third term in Nov. 2001, primarily as the result of his tough policy against illegal immigration. It has also brought him considerable criticism: refugees attempting to enter Australia—most of them from Afghanistan, Iran, and Iraq, and numbering about 5,000 annually—have been imprisoned in bleak detention camps and subjected to a lengthy immigration process. Asylum-seekers have staged riots and hunger strikes. Howard has also dealt with refugees

with the "Pacific solution," which re-routes boat people from Australian shores to camps in Papua New Guinea and Nauru. In 2004, however, the government began easing its policies on immigration.

Prime Minister Howard sent 2,000 Australian troops to fight alongside American and British troops in the 2003 Iraq war, despite strong opposition among Australians. There were no Australian casualties. Australia released the Flood report in 2004, an assessment of pre-war intelligence on Iraq, which described the evidence supporting Iraq's possession of WMD as "thin, ambiguous, and incomplete." But like similar U.S. and UK intelligence reports, it cleared the government of manipulating the intelligence.

In July 2003, Australia successfully restored order to the Solomon Islands, which had descended into lawlessness during a brutal civil war.

Australia has been the victim of two significant terrorist attacks in recent years: the 2002 Bali, Indonesia, bombings by a group with ties to al-Qaeda in which 202 died, many of whom were Australian, and the 2004 attack on the Australian embassy in Indonesia, which killed ten.

Australian External Territories

Norfolk Island (13.36 sq mi; 34.6 sq km) was placed under Australian administration in 1914. Population 1,853 (July 2003 est.). Formerly a notorious penal colony, Norfolk Island became home to the entire population of Pitcairn Island in 1856. The 194 residents of tiny Pitcairn—all of whom were the descendants of the mutineers from the HMS *Bounty* and their Tahitian wives—embarked on the 3,700-mile journey to Norfolk because of overpopulation. Many Norfolk residents can trace their genealogy directly to the adventurers from *Bounty*.

The Ashmore and Cartier Islands (1.93 sq mi), situated in the Indian Ocean off the northwest coast of Australia, came under Australian administration in 1934.

Heard Island and the McDonald Islands (159 sq mi; 412 sq km), lying in the sub-Antarctic, were placed under Australian administration in 1947. The islands are uninhabited.

Christmas Island (52 sq mi; 135 sq km) is situated in the Indian Ocean. It came under Australian administration in 1958. Most of the island's residents are phosphate miners. The population is 1,508 (2001 census).

Coral Sea Islands (400,000 sq mi; 1,036,000 sq km, but only a few sq mi of land) became a territory of Australia in 1969. There is no permanent population on the islands.

Cocos (Keeling) Islands are made up of a group of 27 small coral islands in two separate atolls in the Indian Ocean, 1,721 mi (2,768 km) northwest of Perth. West Island is the largest, about 6.2 mi (10 km) long. The islands became an Australian territory in 1955. In April 1984 the residents voted to merge with Australia. The population of the Cocos is 630 (July 2003 est.).

Austria

REPUBLIC OF AUSTRIA

National name: Republik Österreich

President: Heinz Fischer (2004)

Chancellor: Wolfgang Schüssel (2000)

Area: 32,378 sq mi (83,858 sq km)

Population (2004 est.): 8,174,762 (growth rate: 0.1%); birth rate 8.9/1000; infant mortality rate: 4.7/1000; life expectancy: 78.9; density per sq mi: 252

Capital and largest city (2003 est.): Vienna, 2,041,300 (metro area), 1,523,600 (city proper). **Other large**

cities: Graz, 219,500; Linz, 185,300; Salzburg, 145,500; Innsbruck, 115,600. **Monetary units:** Euro (formerly schilling). **Languages:** German 98% (official nationwide); Slovene, Croatian, Hungarian (each official in one region). **Ethnicity/race:** German 88.5%, recent immigrant groups 10% (includes Turks, Bosnians, Serbians, Croatians), indigenous minorities 1.5% (includes Croatians, Slovenes, Hungarians, Czechs, Slovaks, Roma)(2001). **Religions:** Roman Catholic 74%, Protestant 5%, Islam 4%, other 17%. **Literacy rate:** 98%

Economic summary: GDP/PPP (2003 est.): $245.5 billion; per capita $30,000. **Real growth rate:** 0.8%. **Inflation:** 1.2%. **Unemployment:** 4.3%. **Arable land:** 17%. **Agriculture:** grains, potatoes, sugar beets, wine, fruit; dairy products, cattle, pigs, poultry; lumber. **Labor force:** 4.3 million (2001); services 67%, industry and crafts 29%, agriculture and forestry 4%. **Industries:** construction, machinery, vehicles and parts, food, chemicals, lumber and wood processing, paper and paperboard, communications equipment, tourism. **Natural resources:** iron ore, oil, timber, magnesite, lead, coal, lignite, copper, hydropower. **Exports:** $83.45 billion (f.o.b., 2003): machinery and equipment, motor vehicles and parts, paper and paperboard, metal goods, chemicals, iron and steel; textiles, foodstuffs. **Imports:** $81.59 billion (f.o.b., 2003 est.): machinery and equipment, motor vehicles, chemicals, metal goods, oil and oil products; foodstuffs. **Major trading partners:** EU, Switzerland, U.S., Hungary.

Geography Slightly smaller than Maine, Austria includes much of the mountainous territory of the eastern Alps (about 75% of the area). The country contains many snowfields, glaciers, and snowcapped peaks, the highest being the Grossglockner (12,530 ft; 3,819 m). The Danube is the principal river. Forests and woodlands cover about 40% of the land.

Government Federal republic.

History Settled in prehistoric times, the central European land that is now Austria was overrun in pre-Roman times by various tribes, including the Celts. After the fall of the Roman Empire, of which Austria was part, the area was invaded by Bavarians and Slavic Avars. Charlemagne conquered the area in 788 and encouraged colonization and Christianity. In 1252, Ottokar, king of Bohemia, gained possession, only to lose the territories to Rudolf of Hapsburg in 1278. Thereafter, until World War I, Austria's history was largely that of its ruling house, the Hapsburgs. Austria emerged from the Congress of Vienna in 1815 as the continent's dominant power. The *Ausgleich* of 1867 provided for a dual sovereignty, the empire of Austria and the kingdom of Hungary, under Franz Joseph I, who ruled until his death on Nov. 21, 1916. The Austrian-Hungarian minority rule of this immensely diverse empire, which included German, Czech, Romanian, Serbian, and many other lands, became increasingly difficult in an age of emerging nationalist movements. When Archduke Francis Ferdinand was assassinated by a Serbian nationalist in Sarajevo in 1914, World War I, as well as the destruction of the Austro-Hungarian Empire, began.

During World War I, Austria-Hungary was one of the Central powers with Germany, Bulgaria, and Turkey, and the conflict left the country in political chaos and economic ruin. Austria, shorn of Hungary, was proclaimed a republic in 1918, and the monarchy was dissolved in 1919. A parliamentary democracy was set up by the constitution of Nov. 10, 1920. To check the power of Nazis advocating union with Germany, Chancellor Engelbert Dolfuss in 1933 established a dictatorship, but he was assassinated by the Nazis on July 25, 1934. Kurt von Schuschnigg, his successor, struggled to keep Austria independent, but on March 12, 1938, German troops occupied the country, and Hitler proclaimed its *Anschluss* (union) with Germany, annexing it to the Third Reich.

After World War II, the U.S. and Britain declared the Austrians a "liberated" people. But the Russians prolonged the occupation. Finally Austria concluded a state treaty with the USSR and the other occupying powers and regained its independence on May 15, 1955. The second Austrian republic, established Dec. 19, 1945, on the basis of the 1920 constitution (amended in 1929), was declared by the federal Parliament to be permanently neutral.

On June 8, 1986, former UN secretary-general Kurt Waldheim was elected to the ceremonial office of president in a campaign marked by controversy over his alleged links to Nazi war crimes in Yugoslavia. Austria became a member of the European Union in 1995, but it retained its strict constitutional neutrality and forbade the stationing of foreign troops on its soil.

In Feb. 2000 the conservative People's Party formed a coalition with the far-right Freedom Party, headed by Jörg Haider. A nationalist against immigration, Haider had made several controversial remarks praising some Nazi policies, which he has since recanted. His gradual rise to power was credited to voters weary of decades of stasis under the rule of the Social Democrats. The European Union condemned Austria's new coalition, froze diplomatic contacts, and imposed sanctions, accusing Haider of being a racist, xenophobe, and Nazi-sympathizer. Given the controversy, Haider chose not to join the government, but he continued to wield influence from the sidelines.

In Sept. 2002, the coalition between the People's Party and the Freedom Party dissolved after a shake-up in the Freedom Party, instigated by Haider. In Nov. 2002, the People's Party made large gains in general elections. After failed coalition talks with other parties, the People's Party again formed a government with the Freedom Party in Feb. 2003. A government plan to overhaul the country's pension program led to widespread strikes in May and June 2003—the first national strikes in decades.

In 2004, Heinz Fischer, known as the "left conscience" of the Social Democrat party, was elected to the largely ceremonial role of president.

Azerbaijan

REPUBLIC OF AZERBAIJAN

President: Ilham Aliyev (2003)
Prime Minister: Artur Rasizade (2003)
Area: 33,436 sq mi (86,600 sq km)
Population (2003 est.): 7,868,385 (growth rate: 0.5%); birth rate: 19.8/1000; infant mortality rate: 82.1/1000; life expectancy: 63.3; density per sq mi: 235
Capital and largest city (2003 est.): Baku, 2,118,600 (metro area), 1,235,400 (city proper), a port on the Caspian Sea. **Other large cities (2004 est.):** Ganja, 303,000; Sumgait, 280,500. **Monetary unit:** Manat.
Languages: Azerbaijani Turkic 89%, Russian 3%, Armenian 2%, other 6% (1995 est.). **Ethnicity/race:** Azeri 90%, Dagestani 3.2%, Russian 2.5%, Armenian 2%, other 2.3% (1998 est.). Note: almost all Armenians live in the separatist Nagorno-Karabakh region. **Religions:** Islam 93.4%, Russian Orthodox 2.5%, Armenian Orthodox 2.3%, other 1.8% (1995 est.). **Literacy rate:** 97% (1989 est.)
Economic summary: GDP/PPP (2003 est.): $26.34 billion; per capita $3,400. **Real growth rate:** 9.9%. **Inflation:** 2.9%. **Unemployment:** 16% (official rate is

1.2%). **Arable land:** 19%. **Agriculture:** cotton, grain, rice, grapes, fruit, vegetables, tea, tobacco; cattle, pigs, sheep, goats. **Labor force:** 3.7 million (2001); agriculture and forestry 32%, industry and construction 15%, services 53% (1997). **Industries:** petroleum and natural gas, petroleum products, oilfield equipment; steel, iron ore, cement; chemicals and petrochemicals; textiles. **Natural resources:** petroleum, natural gas, iron ore, nonferrous metals, alumina. **Exports:** $2.605 billion (f.o.b., 2003 est.): oil and gas 90%, machinery, cotton, foodstuffs. **Imports:** $2.498 billion (f.o.b., 2003 est.): machinery and equipment, foodstuffs, metals, chemicals. **Major trading partners:** Italy, France, Israel, Turkey, Russia, U.S., Iran, Germany.

Geography Azerbaijan is located on the western shore of the Caspian Sea at the southeast extremity of the Caucasus. The region is a mountainous country. About 7% of it is arable land. The Kura River Valley is the area's major agricultural zone.

Government Constitutional republic.

History Northern Azerbaijan was known as Caucasian Albania in ancient times. The area was the site of many conflicts involving Arabs, Kazars, and Turks. After the 11th century, the territory became dominated by Turks and eventually a stronghold of the Shiite Muslim religion and Islamic culture. The territory of Soviet Azerbaijan was acquired by Russia from Persia through the Treaty of Gulistan in 1813 and the Treaty of Turkamanchai in 1828.

After the Bolshevik Revolution, Azerbaijan declared its independence from Russia in May 1918. The republic was reconquered by the Red Army in 1920, and was annexed into the Transcaucasian Soviet Socialist Republic in 1922. It was later reestablished as a separate Soviet Republic on Dec. 5, 1936. Azerbaijan declared independence from the collapsing Soviet Union on Aug. 30, 1991.

Since 1988, Azerbaijan and Armenia have been feuding over the enclave of Nagorno-Karabakh. The majority of the enclave's inhabitants are Armenian Christians agitating to secede from the predominantly Muslim Azerbaijan and join with Armenia. War broke out in 1988 when Nagorno-Karabakh tried to break away and annex itself to Armenia, and 30,000 died before a cease-fire agreement was reached in 1994, with Armenia regaining its hold over the disputed enclave. Final plans on the status of Nagorno-Karabakh have yet to be determined.

The country's economic troubles are expected to be transformed through Western investment in Azerbaijan's oil resources, an untapped reserve whose estimated worth is trillions of dollars. Since 1994, the Azerbaijan state oil company (SOCAR) has signed several billion-dollar agreements with international oil companies. Azerbaijan's pro-Western stance and its careful economic management have made it the most attractive of the oil-rich Caspian countries for foreign investment. In the years since its independence, the country has undergone rapid privatization and the IMF gave it high marks as one of the most successful economic overhauls ever. In Sept. 2002, construction of the 1,100-mile Baku-Tblisi-Ceyhan pipeline (a route through Georgia and Turkey) began. Major investors are Britain's BP (33%), Azerbaijan's SOCAR (25%), the U.S.'s Unocal (8.9%), and Norway's Statoil (8.7%).

In 2003, President Heydar Aliyev, who was seriously ill, chose his son as the new prime minister, paving the way for his eventual succession. The opposition protested strenuously. In October elections, the president's son, Ilham Aliyev, was elected president. Heydar Aliyev died in December.

Bahamas

COMMONWEALTH OF THE BAHAMAS

Sovereign: Queen Elizabeth II (1952)
Governor-General: Ivy Dumont (2001)
Prime Minister: Perry Christie (2002)
Area: 5,382 sq mi (13,940 sq km)
Population (2004 est.): 299,697 (growth rate: 0.7%); birth rate: 18.2/1000; infant mortality rate: 25.7/1000; life expectancy: 65.6; density per sq mi: 56
Capital and largest city (2003 est.): Nassau, 222,200.
Monetary unit: Bahamian dollar. **Language:** English (official), Creole (among Haitian immigrants).
Ethnicity/race: black 85%, white 12%, Asian and Hispanic 3%. **Religions:** Baptist 32%, Anglican 20%, Roman Catholic 19%, Methodist 6%, Church of God 6%, other Protestant 12%. **Literacy rate:** 98.2% (1995 est.)
Economic summary: GDP/PPP (2003 est.): $5.099 billion; per capita $16,800 (2000 est.). **Real growth rate:** 1%. **Inflation:** 1.7%. **Unemployment:** 6.9% (2001 est.). **Arable land:** 1%. **Agriculture:** citrus, vegetables; poultry. **Labor force:** 156,000 (1999); tourism 40%, other services 50%, industry 5%, agriculture 5% (1995 est.). **Industries:** tourism, banking, cement, oil refining and transshipment, salt, rum, aragonite, pharmaceuticals, spiral-welded steel pipe. **Natural resources:** salt, aragonite, timber, arable land. **Exports:** $617 million (2002 est.): fish and crawfish; rum, salt, chemicals; fruit and vegetables (1999). **Imports:** $1.614 billion (2002 est.): machinery and transport equipment, manufactures, chemicals, mineral fuels; food and live animals (1999). **Major trading partners:** U.S., France, Germany, UK, South Korea, Italy, Japan. **Member of Commonwealth of Nations**

Geography The Bahamas are an archipelago of about 700 islands and 2,400 uninhabited islets and cays lying 50 mi off the east coast of Florida. They extend for about 760 mi (1,223 km). Only about 30 of the islands are inhabited; the most important is New Providence (80 sq mi; 207 sq km), on which the capital, Nassau, is situated. Other islands include Grand Bahama, Abaco, Eleuthera, Andros, Cat Island, and San Salvador (or Watling's Island).

Government Parliamentary democracy.

History The Arawak Indians were the first inhabitants of the Bahamas. Columbus's first encounter with the New World was on Oct. 12, 1492, when he landed on the Bahamian island of San Salvador. The British first built settlements on the islands in the 17th century. In the early 18th century, the Bahamas were a favorite pirate haunt.

The Bahamas were a crown colony from 1717 until they were granted internal self-government in 1964. The islands moved toward greater autonomy in 1968 after the overwhelming victory in general elections of the Progressive Liberal Party, led by Prime Minister Lynden O. Pindling, over the predominantly white United Bahamians Party. With its new mandate from the 85% black population, Pindling's government negotiated a new constitution with Britain under which the colony became the Commonwealth of the Bahama Islands in 1969. On July 10, 1973, the Bahamas became an independent nation.

Once heavily reliant on agriculture and fishing, the Bahamas has diversified its economy into tourism, financial services, and international shipping. While it enjoys a per capita income that is among the top 30 in the world, there is a big gap between the urban middle class and poor farmers. In addition, the nation is vulnerable to hurricanes, which regularly inflict serious damage.

Bahrain

STATE OF BAHRAIN

King: Hamad ibn Isa al-Khalifah (1999)
Prime Minister: Khalifah ibn Sulman al-Khalifah (1970)
Area: 257 sq mi (665 sq km)
Population (2004 est.): 677,886 (growth rate: 1.6%);
birth rate: 18.5/1000; infant mortality rate: 17.9/1000;
life expectancy: 74.0; density per sq mi: 2,640
Capital and largest city (2003 est.): Al-Manámah,
527,000 (metro area), 149,900 (city proper). **Monetary
unit:** Bahrain dinar. **Languages:** Arabic, English,
Farsi, Urdu. **Ethnicity/race:** Bahraini 63%, Asian 19%,
other Arab 10%, Iranian 8%. **Religion:** Islam (Shiite
70%, Sunni 30%). **Literacy rate:** 89% (2003 est.)
Economic summary: GDP/PPP (2003 est) $11.38
billion; per capita $17,100. **Real growth rate:** 3.6%.
Inflation: 0.4%. **Unemployment:** 15% (1998 est.).
Arable land: 4.35%. **Agriculture:** fruit, vegetables;
poultry, dairy products; shrimp, fish. **Labor force:**
295,000 (1998 est.) note: 44% of the population in the
15-64 age group is non-national; industry, commerce,
and service 79%, government 20%, agriculture 1%
(1997 est.). **Industries:** petroleum processing and
refining, aluminum smelting, offshore banking, ship
repairing; tourism. **Natural resources:** oil, associated
and nonassociated natural gas, fish, pearls. **Exports:**
$6.492 billion (2003 est.): petroleum and petroleum
products, aluminum, textiles. **Imports:** $5.126 billion
(2003 est.): crude oil, machinery, chemicals. **Major
trading partners:** U.S., India, Saudi Arabia, Japan,
Germany, UK.

Geography Bahrain, which means "two seas,"is an
archipelago in the Persian Gulf off the coast of Saudi
Arabia. The islands for the most part are level
expanses of sand and rock. A causeway connects
Bahrain to Saudi Arabia.

Government Constitutional monarchy.

History Known in ancient times as Dilmun, Bahrain was an important center of trade by the 3rd millennium B.C. The islands were ruled by the Persians in
the 4th century A.D., and then by Arabs until 1541,
when the Portuguese invaded them. Persia again
claimed Bahrain in 1602. In 1783 Ahmad ibn
al-Khalifah took over, and the al-Khalifahs remain the
ruling family today. Bahrain became a British protectorate in 1820. It did not gain full independence until
Aug. 14, 1971.

Although oil was discovered in Bahrain in the
1930s, it was relatively little compared to other Gulf
states, and the wells are expected to be the first in the
region to dry up. Sheik Isa ibn-Sulman al-Khalifah,
who became emir in 1961, was determined to diversify
his country's economy, and set about establishing Bahrain as a major financial center. The country provides
its people with free medical care, education, and old-
age pensions.

Conflicts between the Shiites and Sunnis are a continuing problem in Bahrain. The Sunni minority, to
which the ruling al-Khalifah family belongs, controls
nearly all the power and wealth in the country. Shiite
Muslims have continued to agitate for more representation in government, and minor violent clashes have
led to about two dozen deaths since 1994.

Bahrain has been an important Western ally, serving
as a Western air base during the Persian Gulf War in
1991 and the Iraq war in 2003. It continues to serve as
the base of the United States' Fifth Fleet, which patrols
the Gulf.

The emir, Sheik Isa ibn Sulman al-Khalifah, died in
1999 after four decades of rule. He was succeeded by
his son, Sheik Hamad ibn Isa al-Khalifah, who gave
himself the title of king but also began a sweeping
democratization of the country: censorship has been
relaxed and draconian laws repealed, exiles have been
repatriated, and the stateless Bidoons have been granted
citizenship. In a Feb. 2001 referendum, which permitted
women to vote for the first time, Bahrainis overwhelmingly supported the transformation of the traditional
monarchy into a constitutional one. In Oct. 2002, Bahrain had its first parliamentary election since 1973.

Bangladesh

PEOPLE'S REPUBLIC OF BANGLADESH

President: Iajuddin Ahmed (2002)
Prime Minister: Khaleda Zia (2001)
Area: 55,598 sq mi (144,000 sq km)
Population (2004 est.): 141,340,476 (growth rate: 2.1%);
birth rate: 30.0/1000; infant mortality rate: 64.3/1000; life
expectancy: 61.7; density per sq mi: 2,542
Capital and largest city (2003 est.): Dhaka, 10,356,500
(metro.area), 8,942,300 (city proper). **Other large
cities:** Chittagong, 2,592,400; Khulna, 1,211,500.
Monetary unit: Taka. **Principal Languages:** Bangla
(official), English. **Ethnicity/race:** Bengali 98%, tribal
groups, non-Bengali Muslims (1998). **Religions:** Islam
83%, Hindu 16%, other 1%. **Literacy rate:** 43% (2003
est.)
Economic summary: GDP/PPP (2003 est.): $258.8
billion; per capita $1,900. **Real growth rate:** 5.3%.
Inflation: 5.3%. **Unemployment:** 40% (includes
underemployment) (2002 est.). **Arable land:** 60.7%.
Agriculture: rice, jute, tea, wheat, sugarcane,
potatoes, tobacco, pulses, oilseeds, spices, fruit; beef,
milk, poultry. **Labor force:** 64.1 million (1998); note:
extensive export of labor to Saudi Arabia, Kuwait,
UAE, Oman, Qatar, and Malaysia; agriculture 63%,
services 26%, industry 11% (FY95/96). **Industries:**
cotton textiles, jute, garments, tea processing, paper
newsprint, cement, chemical fertilizer, light
engineering, sugar. **Natural resources:** natural gas,
arable land, timber, coal. **Exports:** $6.713 billion (2003
est.): garments, jute and jute goods, leather, frozen
fish and seafood (2001). **Imports:** $9.459 billion (2003
est.): machinery and equipment, chemicals, iron and
steel, textiles, foodstuffs, petroleum products, cement
(2000). **Major trading partners:** U.S., Germany, UK,
France, Italy, India, China, Singapore, Japan, Hong
Kong, South Korea. **Member of Commonwealth of
Nations**

Geography Bangladesh, on the northern coast of
the Bay of Bengal, is surrounded by India, with a
small common border with Myanmar in the southeast.
The country is low-lying riverine land traversed by
the many branches and tributaries of the Ganges and
Brahmaputra Rivers. Tropical monsoons and frequent
floods and cyclones inflict heavy damage in the delta
region.

Government Parliamentary democracy.

History What is now called Bangladesh is part of
the historic region of Bengal, the northeast portion of
the Indian subcontinent. Bangladesh consists primarily of East Bengal (West Bengal is part of India and
its people are primarily Hindu) plus the Sylhet district of the Indian state of Assam.

The earliest reference to the region was to a kingdom called Vanga, or Banga (c. 1000 B.C.). Buddhists
ruled for centuries, but by the 10th century Bengal was
primarily Hindu. In 1576, Bengal became part of the
Mogul Empire, and the majority of East Bengalis converted to Islam. Bengal was ruled by British India from
1757 until Britain withdrew in 1947, and Pakistan was

founded out of the two predominantly Muslim regions of the Indian subcontinent. For almost 25 years after independence from Britain, its history was part of Pakistan's (see Pakistan).

West Pakistan and East Pakistan were united by religion (Islam), but their peoples were separated by culture, physical features, and 1,000 miles of Indian territory.

Tension between East and West Pakistan developed from the outset because of their vast geographic, economic, and cultural differences. East Pakistan's Awami League, a political party founded by the Bengali nationalist Sheik Mujibur Rahman in 1949, sought independence from West Pakistan. Although 56% of the population resided in East Pakistan, the West held the lion's share of political and economic power. In 1970 East Pakistanis secured a majority of the seats in the National Assembly. President Yahya Khan postponed the opening of the National Assembly in an attempt to circumvent East Pakistan's demand for greater autonomy. As a consequence East Pakistan seceded, and the independent state of Bangladesh, or Bengali nation, was proclaimed on March 26, 1971. Civil war broke out, and with the help of Indian troops in the last few weeks of the war, East Pakistan defeated West Pakistan on Dec. 16, 1971. An estimated 1 million Bengalis were killed in the fighting or later slaughtered. Ten million more took refuge in India. In Feb. 1974, Pakistan agreed to recognize the independent state of Bangladesh.

Founding president Sheikh Mujibur was assassinated in 1975, as was the next president, Zia ur-Rahman. On March 24, 1982, Gen. Hossain Mohammad Ershad, army chief of staff, took control in a bloodless coup but was forced to resign on Dec. 6, 1990, amid violent protests and numerous allegations of corruption. A succession of prime ministers governed in the 1990s, including Khaleda Zia, wife of the assassinated president Zia ur-Rahman, and Sheikh Hasina Wazed, the daughter of Sheik Mujibur.

Prime Minister Sheikh Hasina completed her five-year term as prime minister in July 2000—the first leader to do so since the country gained independence from Pakistan in 1974. In Oct. 2001 elections, Khaleda Zia again won the prime ministership.

Parliament amended the constitution in May 2004 to set aside 45 seats for women. The new women MPs will not be directly elected, however. They will be selected by party, in proportion to how each party fared in the most recent election.

Severe flooding in July and August 2004 killed about 600 people and left up to 30 million homeless.

About 20 people were killed and hundreds injured in Dhaka in August when several bombs exploded at an antigovernment rally organized by the opposition Awami League.

Barbados

Sovereign: Queen Elizabeth II (1952)
Governor-General: Sir Clifford Husbands (1996)
Prime Minister: Owen Arthur (1994)
Area: 166 sq mi (431 sq km)
Population (2004 est.): 278,289 (growth rate: 0.4%); birth rate: 13.0/1000; infant mortality rate: 12.6/1000; life expectancy: 71.6; density per sq mi: 1,672
Capital and largest city (2003 est.): Bridgetown, 98,900. **Monetary unit:** Barbados dollar. **Language:** English. **Ethnicity/race:** black 90%, white 4%, Asian and mixed 6%. **Religions:** Protestant 67% (Anglican 40%, Pentecostal 8%, Methodist 7%, other 12%), Roman Catholic 4%, none 17%, other 12%. **Literacy rate:** 97% (1995 est.)

Economic summary: GDP/PPP (2003 est.): $4.496 billion; per capita: $16,200. **Real growth rate:** –0.6%. **Inflation:** –0.5%. **Unemployment:** 10.7%. **Arable land:** 37%. **Agriculture:** sugarcane, vegetables, cotton. **Labor force:** 128,500 (2001 est.); services 75%, industry 15%, agriculture 10% (1996 est.). **Industries:** tourism, sugar, light manufacturing, component assembly for export. **Natural resources:** petroleum, fish, natural gas. **Exports:** $206 million (2002): sugar and molasses, rum, other foods and beverages, chemicals, electrical components. **Imports:** $1.039 billion (2002): consumer goods, machinery, foodstuffs, construction materials, chemicals, fuel, electrical components. **Major trading partners:** U.S., Trinigad and Tobago, UK, Jamaica, Saint Lucia, Japan. **Member of Commonwealth of Nations**

Geography An island in the Atlantic about 300 mi (483 km) north of Venezuela, Barbados is only 21 mi long (34 km) and 14 mi across (23 km) at its widest point. It is circled by fine beaches and narrow coastal plains. The highest point is Mount Hillaby (1,105 ft; 337 m) in the north-central area.

Government Parliamentary democracy.

History Barbados is thought to have been originally inhabited by Arawak Indians. By the time Europeans explored the island, however, it was uninhabited. The Portuguese were the first Europeans to set foot on the island, but it was the British who first established a colony there in 1627. Colonists first cultivated tobacco and cotton, but by the 1640s they had switched to sugar, which was enormously profitable. Slaves were brought in from Africa to work sugar plantations, and eventually the population was about 90% black. A slave revolt took place in 1816; slavery was abolished in the British Empire in 1834.

Barbados was the administrative headquarters of the Windward Islands until it became a separate colony in 1885. Barbados was a member of the Federation of the West Indies from 1958 to 1962. Britain granted the colony independence on Nov. 30, 1966, and it became a parliamentary democracy within the Commonwealth. Since independence, Barbados has been politically stable. However, local anger over rulings by the final appeals court, appointed by Queen Elizabeth, led to the creation in 1997 of a constitutional commission to consider abandoning all ties to Great Britain. In May 2003, Prime Minister Arthur won a third term.

Belarus

REPUBLIC OF BELARUS

President: Alyaksandr Lukashenka (1994)
Prime Minister: Syarhey Sidorski (2003)
Area: 80,154 sq mi (207,600 sq km)
Population (2004 est.): 10,310,520 (growth rate: –0.1%); birth rate: 10.5/1000; infant mortality rate: 13.6/1000; life expectancy: 68.6; density per sq mi: 129
Capital and largest city (2003 est.): Mensk (Minsk), 1,769,500. **Other large cities:** Gomel, 502,200; Mogilyov, 374,000; Vitebsk, 355,800; Grodno, 314,100; Brest, 306,300; Bobruysk, 228,100. **Monetary unit:** Belorussian ruble. **Language:** Belorussian (White Russian), Russian, other. **Ethnicity/race:** Belorussian 81.2%, Russian 11.4%, Polish, Ukrainian, and other 7.4%. **Religion:** Eastern Orthodox 80%, other (including Roman Catholic, Protestant, Jewish, and Muslim) 20% (1997 est.). **Literacy rate:** 100% (2003 est.)
Economic summary: GDP/PPP (2003 est.): $61.91 billion; per capita $6,000. **Real growth rate:** 6.1%.

Inflation: 30%. **Unemployment:** 2.1% officially registered unemployed (Dec. 2000); large number of underemployed workers. **Arable land:** 30%. **Agriculture:** grain, potatoes, vegetables, sugar beets, flax; beef, milk. **Labor force:** 4.8 million (2000 est.); industry and construction n.a., agriculture and forestry n.a., services n.a. **Industries:** metal-cutting machine tools, tractors, trucks, earthmovers, motorcycles, television sets, chemical fibers, fertilizer, textiles, radios, refrigerators. **Natural resources:** forests, peat deposits, small quantities of oil and natural gas, granite, dolomitic limestone, marl, chalk, sand, gravel, clay. **Exports:** $9.413 billion (f.o.b., 2003 est.): machinery and equipment, mineral products, chemicals, metals; textiles, foodstuffs. **Imports:** $11.09 billion (f.o.b., 2003 est.): mineral products, machinery and equipment, chemicals, foodstuffs, metals. **Major trading partners:** Russia, Latvia, Ukraine, Lithuania, Germany.

Geography Much of Belarus (formerly the Belorussian Soviet Socialist Republic of the USSR, and then Byelorussia) is a hilly lowland with forests, swamps, and numerous rivers and lakes. There are wide rivers emptying into the Baltic and Black Seas. Its forests cover over one-third of the land and its peat marshes are a valuable natural resource. The largest lake is Narach, 31 sq mi (79.6 sq km).

Government Republic.

History In the 5th century A.D., Belarus (also known as White Russia) was colonized by east Slavic tribes. Kiev dominated it from the 9th to 12th centuries. After the destruction of Kiev by the Mongols in the 13th century, the territory was conquered by the dukes of Lithuania, although it retained a degree of autonomy. Belarus became part of the Grand Duchy of Lithuania, which merged with Poland in 1569. Following the partitions of Poland in 1772, 1793, and 1795, in which Poland was divided among Russia, Prussia, and Austria, Belarus became part of the Russian empire.

Following World War I, Belarus proclaimed itself a republic, only to find itself occupied by the Red Army soon after its March 1918 announcement. The Polish-Soviet War of 1918–1921 was fought to decide the fate of Belarus. West Belarus was ceded to Poland; the larger eastern part formed the Belorussian SSR, and was then joined to the USSR in 1922. In 1939, the Soviet Union took back West Belarus from Poland under the secret protocol of the Nazi-Soviet Nonaggression Pact and incorporated it into the Belorussian Soviet Socialist Republic. Occupied by the Nazis in World War II, Belarus was one of the most devastated battlefields.

When the Chernobyl nuclear power plant in Ukraine exploded in 1986, 70% of its radioactivity fell on the Belorussian SSR. Cancer and other illnesses have multiplied as a result.

Belarus declared its sovereignty in July 1990 and its independence in Aug. 1991. It became a cofounder of the Commonwealth of Independent States (CIS) in Dec. 1991. In Jan. 1994, the country's Parliament ousted its reform-minded leader, Stanislav Shushkevich, in protest against his support for market economics. He was replaced by Alyaksandr Lukashenka, who over the next two years greatly expanded the powers of the presidency. Lukashenka sought to renew ties with Russia, and, with much fanfare, Belarus and Russia signed a treaty in April 1997 aimed at significantly increasing cooperation between the two states, stopping just short of union. The Russian financial crisis that began in fall 1998 severely affected Belarus's Soviet-style planned economy.

The EU and the U.S. have denounced the increasingly oppressive political atmosphere and human rights violations in Belarus under the Soviet-style authoritarianism of President Lukashenka. In 1999, the year Lukashenka was to step down, he rigged a national referendum allowing him to cancel the elections and remain president. Lukashenka's government has been accused of running a death squad that has killed dozens, including opposition party members and underworld figures. After harassing the opposition and curtailing their campaign activities, Lukashenka won reelection in the Sept. 9, 2001, presidential race. In 2004, the Council of Europe strongly criticized the Belarus government for blocking investigations into the disappearances of four dissidents in 1999 and 2000.

Belgium

KINGDOM OF BELGIUM

National name: Royaume de Belgique—Koninkrijk België
Sovereign: King Albert II (1993)
Prime Minister: Guy Verhofstadt (1999)
Area: 11,780 sq mi (30,510 sq km)
Population (2004 est.): 10,348,276 (growth rate: 0.2%); birth rate: 10.6/1000; infant mortality rate: 4.8/1000; life expectancy: 78.4; density per sq mi: 878
Capital and largest city (2003 est.): Brussels, 1,750,600 (metro area), 981,200 (city proper). **Other large cities:** Antwerp, 952,600 (metro area), 450,000 (city proper); Ghent, 226,900; Charleroi, 201,200; Liège, 185,700; Bruges, 117,200. **Monetary units:** Euro (formerly Belgian franc). **Languages:** Dutch (Flemish) 60%, French 40%, German less than 1% (all official); legally bilingual (Dutch and French). **Ethnicity/race:** Fleming 58%, Walloon 31%, mixed or other 11%. **Religion:** Roman Catholic 75%, Protestant or other 25%. **Literacy rate:** 98% (2003 est.)
Economic summary: GDP/PPP (2003 est.): $298.2 billion; per capita $29,000. **Real growth rate:** 0.8%. **Inflation:** 1.4%. **Unemployment:** 8.1%. **Arable land:** 25%. **Agriculture:** sugar beets, fresh vegetables, fruits, grain, tobacco; beef, veal, pork, milk. **Labor force:** 4.44 million (2001); services 73%, industry 25%, agriculture 2% (1999 est.). **Industries:** engineering and metal products, motor vehicle assembly, processed food and beverages, chemicals, basic metals, textiles, glass, petroleum, coal. **Natural resources:** coal, natural gas. **Exports:** $182.9 billion (f.o.b., 2003 est.): machinery and equipment, chemicals, diamonds, metals and metal products, foodstuffs. **Imports:** $173 billion (f.o.b., 2003 est.): machinery and equipment, chemicals, metals and metal products, foodstuffs. **Major trading partners:** Germany, France, Netherlands, UK, U.S., Italy, Ireland.

Geography Located in western Europe, Belgium has about 40 mi of seacoast on the North Sea, at the Strait of Dover, and is approximately the size of Maryland. The Meuse and the Schelde, Belgium's principal rivers, are important commercial arteries.

Government Parliamentary democracy under a constitutional monarch. Under the 1994 constitution, autonomy was granted to the Walloon region (Wallonia), the Flemish region (Flanders), and the bilingual Brussels-Capital region; autonomy was also guaranteed for the Flemish-, French-, and German-speaking "communities." The central government retains responsibility for foreign policy, defense, taxation, and social security.

History Belgium occupied part of the Roman province of Belgica, named after the Belgae, a people of ancient Gaul. The area was conquered by Julius Caesar in

57–50 B.C., then was overrun by the Franks in the 5th century A.D. It was part of Charlemagne's empire in the 8th century, then in the next century was absorbed into Lotharingia and later into the duchy of Lower Lorraine. In the 12th century it was partitioned into the duchies of Brabant and Luxembourg, the bishopric of Liège, and the domain of the count of Hainaut, which included Flanders. In the 16th century, Belgium, with most of the area of the low countries, passed to the duchy of Burgundy and was inherited by Charles V, who incorporated it into his Holy Roman Empire. Then, in 1555, the low countries were united with Spain. By the Treaty of Utrecht in 1713, the country's sovereignty passed to Austria. During the wars that followed the French Revolution, Belgium was occupied and later annexed to France. But with the downfall of Napoléon, the Congress of Vienna in 1815 gave the country to the Netherlands. The Belgians revolted in 1830 and declared their independence.

Germany's invasion of Belgium in 1914 set off World War I. The Treaty of Versailles (1919) gave the areas of Eupen, Malmédy, and Moresnet to Belgium. Leopold III succeeded Albert, king during World War I, in 1934. In World War II, Belgium was overwhelmed by Nazi Germany, and Leopold III was held prisoner. When he attempted to return in 1950, socialists and liberals revolted. He abdicated July 16, 1951, and his son, Baudouin, became king. Because of growing opposition to Belgian rule in its African colonies, Belgium granted independence to the Congo (now Democratic Republic of the Congo) in 1960 and to Ruanda-Urundi (now the nations of Rwanda and Burundi) in 1962.

Divisions between Flemings and Walloons grew, and linguistic regionalization increased, culminating in the revised constitution of 1994, which granted more autonomy to Belgium's three regions and language "communities."

In the 1990s the Belgian government was involved in numerous scandals that tainted it with a reputation for incompetence and corruption. In 1991, a deputy prime minister was murdered in a contract killing that remained unsolved. In 1998, Belgian statesman and former NATO secretary-general Willy Claes was convicted of bribery. International relations fared no better. Belgian peacekeeping troops abandoned Rwanda, a former colony, at the height of the 1994 genocide against the Tutsis. The discovery of the Dutroux child-sex-and-murder ring in 1996 led to further national outrage that was compounded by disclosures that official negligence and corruption had resulted in even more children's deaths. As the scandal continued into 1997, it fueled pressure for reform of the political, judicial, and police systems. In 1999, a public health scandal and cover-up involving Dioxin, a cancer-causing chemical, resulted in the resignation of Prime Minister Jean-Luc Dehaene. Dehaene was credited with a significant upturn in the economy during his tenure.

The new prime minister, Guy Verhofstadt of the Liberal Party, cobbled together a coalition of six political parties in June 1999. He promised a series of reforms aimed at the legal system and the civil service.

Under its controversial "universal jurisdiction" law, Belgian prosecutors were able to try anyone accused of war crimes, whatever their nationality and wherever the crimes took place. In 2001, Belgian courts convicted four Rwandans, including two nuns, for their role in the massacre of the Tutsi people in Rwanda. In 2003, however, Belgium amended the law, severely limiting its scope—the country found itself overwhelmed with quixotic lawsuits against at least 30 world leaders, including George W. Bush, Fidel Castro, Ariel Sharon, and Yasir Arafat.

In May 2003, Prime Minister Verhofstadt's coalition of Liberals and Socialists won a large victory in national elections. Verhofstadt has passed extremely liberal social policies, including the legalization of gay marriage, euthanasia, and marijuana.

Belize

Sovereign: Queen Elizabeth II (1952)
Governor-General: Sir Colville Young (1993)
Prime Minister: Said Musa (1998)
Area: 8,867 sq mi (22,966 sq km)
Population (2004 est.): 272,945 (growth rate: 2.4%); birth rate: 29.9/1000; infant mortality rate: 26.4/1000; life expectancy: 67.4; density per sq mi: 31
Capital (2003 est.): Belmopan, 8,700. **Largest city:** Belize City, 52,600. **Monetary unit:** Belize dollar.
Languages: English (official), Spanish, Mayan, Garifuna (Carib), Creole. **Ethnicity/race:** mestizo 48.7%, Creole 24.9%, Maya 10.6%, Garifuna 6.1%, other 9.7%.
Religions: Roman Catholic 49.6%, Protestant 27% (Anglican 5.3%, Methodist 3.5%, Mennonite 4.1%, Seventh-Day Adventist 5.2%, Pentecostal 7.4%, Jehovah's Witnesses 1.5%), none 9.4%, other 14%.
Literacy rate: 94% (2003 est.)
Economic summary: GDP/PPP (2002 est.): $1.28 billion; per capita $4,900. **Real growth rate:** 3.7%. **Inflation:** 1.9%. **Unemployment:** 9.1%. **Arable land:** 2.81%. **Agriculture:** bananas, coca, citrus, sugar; fish, cultured shrimp; lumber; garments. **Labor force:** 90,000; note: shortage of skilled labor and all types of technical personnel; agriculture 27%, industry 18%, services 55% (2001 est.). **Industries:** garment production, food processing, tourism, construction. **Natural resources:** arable land potential, timber, fish, hydropower. **Exports:** $207.8 million (f.o.b., 2003 est.): sugar, bananas, citrus, clothing, fish products, molasses, wood. **Imports:** $500.6 million (f.o.b., 2003 est.): machinery and transport equipment, manufactured goods; fuels, chemicals, pharmaceuticals; food, beverages, tobacco. **Major trading partners:** U.S., UK, Peru, Mexico, Netherlands Antilles, Japan, Cuba. **Member of Commonwealth of Nations**

Geography Belize is situated on the Caribbean Sea, south of Mexico and east and north of Guatemala in Central America. In area, it is about the size of New Hampshire. Most of the country is heavily forested with various hardwoods. Mangrove swamps and cays along the coast give way to hills and mountains in the interior. The highest point is Victoria Peak, 3,681 ft (1,122 m).

Government Parliamentary democracy within the British Commonwealth.

History The Mayan civilization spread into the area of Belize between 1500 B.C. and A.D. 300 and flourished until about 1200. Several major archeological sites—notably Caracol, Lamanai, Lubaantun, Altun Ha, and Xunantunich—reflect the advanced civilization and much denser population of that period. European contact began in 1502 when Columbus sailed along the coast. The first recorded European settlement was begun by shipwrecked English seamen in 1638. Over the next 150 years, more English settlements were established. This period was also marked by piracy, indiscriminate logging, and sporadic attacks by Indians and neighboring Spanish settlements. Both Spain and Britain lay claim to the land until Britain defeated the Spanish in the battle of St. George's Cay (1798). It became a colony of Great Britain in 1840, known as British Honduras, and a Crown colony in

1862. Full internal self-government was granted in Jan. 1964. In 1973, the country changed its name to Belize.

Belize became independent on Sept. 21, 1981. But Guatemala, which had made claims on the territory since the 1800s, refused to recognize it. British troops remained in the country to defend it. Although the dispute between Guatemala and Great Britain remained unresolved, Guatemala recognized Belize's sovereignty in Sept. 1991. Guatemala, however, still claims more than half of Belize's territory.

Benin

REPUBLIC OF BENIN

National name: Republique du Benin
President: Mathieu Kérékou (1996)
Area: 43,483 sq mi (112,620 sq km)
Population (2004 est.): 7,250,033 (growth rate: 2.9%); birth rate: 42.6/1000; infant mortality rate: 85.9/1000; life expectancy: 50.8; density per sq mi: 167
Capital (2003 est.): Porto-Novo (official), 231,600.
Largest cities: Cotonou (de facto capital) 734,600; Parakou 205,300; Djougou, 184,200. **Monetary unit:** CFA Franc. **Languages:** French (official), Fon, Yoruba, tribal languages. **Ethnicity/race:** African 99% (42 ethnic groups, most important being Fon, Adja, Yoruba, Bariba), Europeans 5,500. **Religions:** indigenous 50%, Christian 30%, Islam 20%. **Literacy rate:** 41% (2000)
Economic summary: GDP/PPP (2003 est.): $7.742 billion; per capita $1,100. **Real growth rate:** 5.5%. **Inflation:** 3.3%. **Unemployment:** n.a. **Arable land:** 15%. **Agriculture:** cotton, corn, cassava (tapioca), yams, beans, palm oil, peanuts, livestock (2001). **Labor force:** n.a. **Industries:** textiles, food processing, chemical production, construction materials (2001). **Natural resources:** small offshore oil deposits, limestone, marble, timber. **Exports:** $485 million (f.o.b., 2003 est.): cotton, crude oil, palm products, cocoa. **Imports:** $726 million (f.o.b., 2003 est.): foodstuffs, capital goods, petroleum products. **Major trading partners:** India, Italy, Indonesia, China, Thailand, Brazil, UK, Niger, France.

Geography This West African nation on the Gulf of Guinea, between Togo on the west and Nigeria on the east, is about the size of Tennessee. It is bounded also by Burkina Faso and Niger on the north. The land consists of a narrow coastal strip that rises to a swampy, forested plateau and then to highlands in the north. A hot and humid climate blankets the entire country.

Government Republic under a multiparty democratic rule.

History The Abomey kingdom of the Dahomey, or Fon, peoples was established in 1625. A rich cultural life flourished, and Dahomey's wooden masks, bronze statues, tapestries, and pottery are world renowned. One of the smallest and most densely populated regions in Africa, Dahomey was annexed by the French in 1893 and incorporated into French West Africa in 1904. It became an autonomous republic within the French Community in 1958, and on Aug. 1, 1960, Dahomey was granted its independence within the Community.

Gen. Christophe Soglo deposed the first president, Hubert Maga, in an army coup in 1963. He dismissed the civilian government in 1965, proclaiming himself chief of state. A group of young army officers seized power in Dec. 1967, deposing Soglo. In Dec. 1969, Benin had its fifth coup of the decade, with the army again taking power. In May 1970, a three-man presidential commission with a six-year term was created to take over the government. In May 1972, yet another army coup ousted the triumvirate and installed Lt. Col. Mathieu Kérékou as president. Between 1974 and 1989 Dahomey embraced socialism, and changed its name to the People's Republic of Benin. The name *Benin* commemorates an African kingdom that flourished from the 15th to the 17th century in what is now southwest Nigeria. In 1990, Benin abandoned Marxist ideology, began moving toward multiparty democracy, and changed its name again, to the Republic of Benin.

By the end of the 1980s, Benin's economy was near collapse. As its oil boom ended, Nigeria expelled 100,000 Beninese migrant workers and closed the border with Benin. Kérékou's socialist collectivization of Benin's agriculture and the ballooning bureaucracy further damaged the economy. By 1988, international financial institutions feared Benin would default on its loans and pressured Kérékou to make financial reforms.

Kérékou subsequently embarked on a major privatization campaign, cut the government payroll, and reduced social services, prompting student and labor union unrest. Fearing a revolution, Kérékou agreed to a new constitution and free elections. In 1991, Nicéphore Soglo, an economist and former director of the International Bank for Reconstruction and Development, was elected president. Although he enjoyed widespread support at first, Soglo gradually became unpopular as austerity measures reduced living standards and a 50% currency devaluation in 1994 caused inflation. Kérékou defeated Soglo in the 1996 elections, and was easily reelected in March 2001.

Bhutan

KINGDOM OF BHUTAN

National name: Druk-yul
Ruler: King Jigme Singye Wangchuck (1972)
Prime Minister: Lyonpo Yeshey Zimba (2004)
Area: 18,147 sq mi (47,000 sq km)
Population (2004 est.): 2,185,569 (growth rate: 2.1%); birth rate: 34.4/1000; infant mortality rate: 102.6/1000; life expectancy: 54.0; density per sq mi: 120
Capital and largest city (2003 est.): Thimphu (official), 60,200. **Monetary unit:** Ngultrum. **Language:** Dzongkha (official), Tibetan dialects (among Bhotes), Nepalese dialects (among Nepalese). **Ethnicity/race:** Bhote 50%, ethnic Nepalese 35%, indigenous or migrant tribes 15%. **Religions:** Lamaistic Buddhist 75%, Indian- and Nepalese-influenced Hinduism 25%. **Literacy rate:** 42% (1995 est.)
Economic summary: GDP/PPP (2002 est.): $2.7 billion; per capita $1,300. **Real growth rate:** 7.7%. **Inflation:** 3%. **Unemployment:** n.a. **Arable land:** 3%. **Agriculture:** rice, corn, root crops, citrus, foodgrains; dairy products, eggs. **Labor force:** n.a.; note: massive lack of skilled labor (1997 est.); agriculture 93%, services 5%, industry and commerce 2%. **Industries:** cement, wood products, processed fruits, alcoholic beverages, calcium carbide. **Natural resources:** timber, hydropower, gypsum, calcium carbide. **Exports:** $154 million (f.o.b., 2000 est.): electricity (to India), cardamom, gypsum, timber, handicrafts, cement, fruit, precious stones, spices. **Imports:** $196 million (c.i.f., 2000 est.): fuel and lubricants, grain, machinery and parts, vehicles, fabrics, rice. **Major trading partners:** U.S., UK, Pakistan, France, Japan, Germany, Singapore, South Korea (2002).

Geography Mountainous Bhutan, half the size of Indiana, is situated on the southeast slope of the Himalayas, bordered on the north and east by Tibet and on the south and west and east by India. The landscape consists of a succession of lofty and rugged mountains and deep valleys. In the north, towering peaks reach a height of 24,000 ft (7,315 m).

Government In the 1990s, the king gradually gave up absolute rule, transforming his kingdom into a constitutional monarchy.

History Although archeological exploration of Bhutan has been limited, evidence of civilization in the region dates back to at least 2000 B.C. Aboriginal Bhutanese, known as Monpa, are believed to have migrated from Tibet. The traditional name of the country since the 17th century has been Drukyul, Land of the Drokpa (Dragon People), a reference to the dominant branch of Tibetan Buddhism that is still practiced in the Himalayan kingdom.

British troops invaded the region in 1865 and negotiated an agreement under which Britain agreed to pay an annual allowance to the Bhutanese monarchy on condition of good behavior. A treaty between India and the seat of government, Thimphu, in 1949 increased this subsidy and placed Bhutan's foreign affairs under Indian control. Until the 1960s Bhutan was largely isolated from the rest of the world, and its people carried on a tranquil, traditional way of life, farming and trading, which had remained intact for centuries. After China invaded Tibet, however, Bhutan strengthened its ties and contact with India in an effort to avoid Tibet's fate. New roads and other connections to India began to end its isolation. In the 1960s Bhutan also undertook social modernization, abolishing slavery and the caste system, emancipating women, and enacting land reform. In 1985, Bhutan made its first diplomatic links with non-Asian countries.

A pro-democracy campaign emerged in 1991, which the government claimed was composed largely of Nepali immigrants. As a result, some 100,000 Nepali civil servants were either evicted or encouraged to emigrate. Most of them crossed the border back into Nepal, where they were housed in UN-administered refugee camps. Several rounds of talks aimed at deciding which country should claim the refugees have yielded few results, and the refugees have continued to languish in the camps for more than a decade.

In 1998, King Jigme Singye Wangchuck voluntarily curtailed his powerful monarchy by yielding to the formerly rubber-stamp legislature, giving it the right to remove him from leadership and appoint his cabinet. The move was the largest step to date in a gradual program to dilute the monarchy after nearly a century of absolute rule. Bhutan edged closer to becoming a parliamentary democracy in Dec. 2002, with the release of a draft constitution.

In a weeklong offensive in Dec. 2003, thousands of Bhutanese troops attacked several Indian separatist groups and destroyed their camps in southern part of the country. The groups—the United Liberation Front of Assam (ULFA), the National Democratic Front of Bodoland (NDFB), and the Kamtapur Liberation Organization (KLO), have maintained camps in Bhutan for about 10 years.

Bolivia

REPUBLIC OF BOLIVIA

National name: República de Bolivia
President: Carlos Mesa (2003)
Area: 424,162 sq mi (1,098,580 sq km)
Population (2004 est.): 8,724,156 (growth rate: 1.6%); birth rate: 24.7/1000; infant mortality rate: 54.6/1000; life expectancy: 65.1; density per sq mi: 21
Historic and judicial capital (2003 est.): Sucre,

204,200; **Administrative capital:** La Paz, 1,576,100 (metro. area), 830,500 (city proper). **Other large cities:** Santa Cruz, 1,168,700; Cochabamba, 815,800; El Alto, 728,500; Oruro, 211,700. **Monetary unit:** Boliviano. **Languages:** Spanish, Quechua, Aymara (all official). **Ethnicity/race:** Quechua 30%, mestizo 30%, Aymara 25%, white 15%. **Religion:** Roman Catholic 95%, Protestant (Evangelical Methodist) 5%. **Literacy rate:** 87% (2003 est.)
Economic summary: GDP/PPP (2003 est.): $20.88 billion; per capita $2,400. **Real growth rate:** 2.1%. **Inflation:** 2% (2001 est.). **Unemployment:** 7.6% (2000) with widespread underemployment. **Arable land:** 2%. **Agriculture:** soybeans, coffee, coca, cotton, corn, sugarcane, rice, potatoes; timber. **Labor force:** 2.5 million (2001); agriculture n.a., industry n.a., services n.a. **Industries:** mining, smelting, petroleum, food and beverages, tobacco, handicrafts, clothing. **Natural resources:** tin, natural gas, petroleum, zinc, tungsten, antimony, silver, iron, lead, gold, timber, hydropower. **Exports:** $1.495 billion (f.o.b., 2003 est.): soybeans, natural gas, zinc, gold, wood (2000). **Imports:** $1.505 billion (f.o.b., 2003 est.): capital goods, raw materials and semi-manufactures, chemicals, petroleum, food. **Major trading partners:** Brazil, Switzerland, U.S., Venezuela, Colombia, Peru, Argentina, Chile, Japan, China.

Geography Landlocked Bolivia is equal in size to California and Texas combined. Brazil forms its eastern border; its other neighbors are Peru and Chile on the west and Argentina and Paraguay on the south. The western part, enclosed by two chains of the Andes, is a great plateau—the Altiplano, with an average altitude of 12,000 ft (3,658 m). Almost half the population lives on the plateau, which contains Oruro, Potosí, and La Paz. At an altitude of 11,910 ft (3,630 m), La Paz is the highest administrative capital city in the world. The Oriente, a lowland region ranging from rain forests to grasslands, comprises the northern and eastern two-thirds of the country. Lake Titicaca, at an altitude of 12,507 ft (3,812 m), is the highest commercially navigable body of water in the world.

Government Republic.

History Famous since Spanish colonial days for its mineral wealth, modern Bolivia was once a part of the ancient Incan empire. After the Spaniards defeated the Incas in the 16th century, Bolivia's predominantly Indian population was reduced to slavery. The remoteness of the Andes helped protect the Bolivian Indians from the European diseases that decimated other South American Indians. But the existence of a large indigenous group forced to live under the thumb of their colonizers created a stratified society of haves and have-nots that continues to this day.

By the end of the 17th century the mineral wealth had begun to dry up. The country won its independence in 1825 and was named after Simón Bolívar, the famous liberator. Hampered by internal strife, Bolivia lost great slices of territory to three neighboring nations. Several thousand square miles and its outlet to the Pacific were taken by Chile after the War of the Pacific (1879–1884). In 1903, a piece of Bolivia's Acre Province, rich in rubber, was ceded to Brazil. And in 1938, after losing the Chaco War of 1932–1935 to Paraguay, Bolivia gave up its claim to nearly 100,000 square mi of the Gran Chaco. Political instability ensued.

In 1965, a guerrilla movement mounted from Cuba and headed by Maj. Ernesto (Ché) Guevara began a revolutionary war. With the aid of U.S. military advisers, the Bolivian army smashed the guerrilla movement, capturing and killing Guevara on Oct. 8, 1967. A string of military coups followed before the military returned the government to civilian rule in 1982, when Hernán Siles Zuazo became president. At that point, Bolivia was regularly shut down by work stoppages and had the lowest per capita income in South America.

In June 1993, free-market advocate Gonzalo Sánchez de Lozada was elected president. He was succeeded by former general Hugo Bánzer, an ex-dictator turned democrat who became president for the second time in Aug. 1997. Bánzer made significant progress in wiping out illicit coca production and drug trafficking, which has pleased the United States. However, the eradication of coca, a major crop in Bolivia since Incan times, has plunged many Bolivian farmers into abject poverty.

In Aug. 2002, Gonzalo Sánchez de Lozada again became president, pledging to continue economic reforms and to create jobs. In Feb. 2003, rioting took place in protest against a proposed income tax, which the government then withdrew. In October Sánchez resigned after two months of rioting and strikes over a gas exporting project that protesters believed would benefit foreign companies more than Bolivians. His vice president, Carlos Mesa, best known as a journalist and historian with little experience in government, replaced him.

The new president has managed to remain popular despite continued social unrest. In a July 2004 referendum on the future of the country's significant natural gas reserves—the second largest in South America—Bolivians overwhelmingly supported Mesa's plan to exert more control over foreign gas companies. The referendum skirted the issue of nationalizing gas companies and ridding the country of foreign oil investment, which is what many leftist groups have called for. Mesa thereby managed to satisfy the strong anti-privitization sentiment among Bolivians without shutting the door on some limited form of privatization in the future.

Bosnia and Herzegovina

THE FEDERATION OF BOSNIA AND HERZEGOVINA

Presidency, Chairman of the (rotating): Sulejman Tihic (2004)
Prime Minister: Adnan Terzic (2002)
Area: 19,741 sq mi (51,129 sq km)
Population (2004 est.): 4,007,608 (all data dealing with population is subject to considerable error because of the dislocations caused by military action and ethnic cleansing) (growth rate: 0.5%); birth rate: 12.6/1000; infant mortality rate: 21.9/1000; life expectancy: 72.6; density per sq mi: 203
Capital and largest city (2003 est.): Sarajevo, 581,500 (unofficial). **Other large cities:** Banja Luka, 189,700; Tuzla 119,200; Mostar, 90,800. **Monetary unit:** Marka.
Language: Bosnian, Croatian, Serbian (all official).
Ethnicity/race: Bosniak 48%, Serb 37.1%, Croat 14.3%, other 0.6% (2000) . **Religions:** Muslim 40%, Orthodox 31%, Roman Catholic 15%, other 14%.
Literacy rate: n.a.
Economic summary: GDP/PPP (2003 est.): $24.39 billion; per capita $6,100. **Real growth rate:** 3.8%. **Inflation:** 3.5%. **Unemployment:** 40% (2002 est.). **Arable land:** 10%. **Agriculture:** wheat, corn, fruits, vegetables; livestock. **Labor force:** 1.026 million (2001); agriculture n.a., industry n.a., services n.a. **Industries:** steel, coal, iron ore, lead, zinc, manganese, bauxite, vehicle assembly, textiles, tobacco products, wooden furniture, tank and aircraft assembly, domestic appliances, oil refining (2001). **Natural resources:** coal, iron, bauxite, manganese, forests, copper, chromium, lead, zinc, hydropower. **Exports:** $1.28 billion (f.o.b., 2003 est.): metals, clothing, wood products. **Imports:** $4.7 billion (f.o.b., 2003 est.): machinery and equipment, chemicals, fuels, foodstuffs. **Major trading partners:** Italy, Croatia, Germany, Austria, Slovenia, Greece, Hungary.

Geography Bosnia and Herzegovina make up a triangular-shaped republic, about half the size of Kentucky, on the Balkan peninsula. The Bosnian region in the north is mountainous and covered with thick forests. The Herzegovina region in the south is largely rugged, flat farmland. It has a narrow coastline without natural harbors stretching 13 mi (20 km) along the Adriatic Sea.

Government Emerging democracy, with a rotating, tripartite presidency divided between predominantly Serb, Croatian, and Bosniak political parties.

History Since the time of the Roman Empire, the Balkans has been a crossroads of religions and civilizations. The ethnic groups now known as Bosnians, Croats, and Serbs are largely the result of different religious and cultural identities created by contact with neighboring empires that expanded and contracted in the Balkans over centuries. With minor differences, they speak the same language, called Serbo-Croatian or sometimes Bosnian.

Called Illyricum in ancient times, the area now called Bosnia and Herzegovina was conquered by the Romans in the 2nd and 1st centuries B.C. and folded into the Roman province of Dalmatia. In the 4th and 5th centuries A.D. Goths overran that portion of the declining Roman Empire and occupied the area until the 6th century, when the Byzantine Empire claimed it. Slavs began settling the region during the 7th century. Around 1200, Bosnia won independence from Hungary and endured as an independent Christian state for some 260 years.

The expansion of the Ottoman Empire into the Balkans introduced another cultural, political, and religious framework. The Turks defeated the Serbs at the famous battle of Kosovo in 1389. They conquered Bosnia in 1463. During the roughly 450 years Bosnia and Herzegovina were under Ottoman rule, many Christian Slavs became Muslim. A Bosnian Islamic elite gradually developed and ruled the country on behalf of the Turkish overlords. As the borders of the Ottoman Empire began to shrink in the 19th century, Muslims from elsewhere in the Balkans migrated to Bosnia. Bosnia also developed a sizable Jewish population, with many Jews settling in Sarajevo after their expulsion from Spain in 1492. However, through the 19th century the term *Bosnian* commonly included residents of all faiths. A relatively secular society, intermarriage among religious groups was not unknown.

Neighboring Serbia and Montenegro fought against the Ottoman Empire in 1876, and were aided by the Russians, their fellow Slavs. At the Congress of Berlin in 1878, following the end of the Russo-Turkish War (1877–1878), Austria-Hungary was given a mandate to occupy and govern Bosnia and Herzegovina, in an effort by Europe to ensure that Russia did not dominate the Balkans. Although the provinces were still officially part of the Ottoman Empire, they were annexed by the Austro-Hungarian Empire on Oct. 7, 1908. As a result, relations with Serbia, which had claims on Bosnia and Herzegovina, became embittered. The hostility between the two countries climaxed in the assassination of Austrian Archduke Franz Ferdinand in Sarajevo on June 28, 1914, by a Serbian nationalist. This event precipitated the start of World War I (1914–1918). Bosnia and Herzegovina were annexed to Serbia as part of the newly formed Kingdom of Serbs, Croats, and Slovenes on Oct. 26, 1918. The name was later changed to Yugoslavia in 1929.

When Germany invaded Yugoslavia in 1941, Bosnia and Herzegovina were made part of Nazi-controlled Croatia. During the German and Italian occupation, Bosnian and Herzegovinian resistance fighters fought a fierce guerrilla war against the Ustachi, the Croatian Fascist troops. At the end of World War II, Bosnia and Herzegovina were reunited into a single state as one of the six republics of the newly reestablished Communist Yugoslavia under Marshall Tito. His authoritarian control kept the ethnic enmities of his patchwork nation in check. Tito died in 1980, and with growing economic dissatisfaction and the fall of the iron curtain over the next decade, Yugoslavia began to splinter.

In Dec. 1991, Bosnia and Herzegovina declared independence from Yugoslavia and asked for recognition by the European Union (EU). In a March 1992 referendum, Bosnian voters chose independence, and President Izetbegovic declared the nation an independent state. Unlike the other former Yugoslav states, which were generally composed of a dominant ethnic group, Bosnia was an ethnic tangle of Muslims (44%), Serbs (31%), and Croats (17%), and this mix contributed to the duration and savagery of its fight for independence.

Both the Croatian and Serbian presidents had planned to partition Bosnia between themselves. Attempting to carve out their own enclaves, the Serbian minority, with the help of the Serbian Yugoslav army, took the offensive and laid siege, particularly to Sarajevo, and began its ruthless campaigns of ethnic cleansing, which involved the expulsion or massacre of Muslims. Croats also began carving out their own communities. By the end of Aug. 1992, rebel Bosnian Serbs had conquered over 60% of Bosnia. The war did not begin to wane until NATO stepped in, bombing Serb positions in Bosnia in Aug. and Sept. 1995. Serbs entered the UN safe havens of Tuzla, Zepa, and Srebrenica, where they murdered thousands. About 250,000 died in the war between 1992 and 1995.

U.S.-sponsored peace talks in Dayton, Ohio, led to an agreement in 1995 that called for a Muslim-Croat federation and a Serb entity within the larger federation of Bosnia. Sixty thousand NATO troops were to supervise its implementation. Fighting abated and orderly elections were held in Sept. 1996. President Alija Izetbegovic, a Bosnian Muslim, or Bosniak, won the majority of votes to become the leader of the three-member presidency, each representing one of the three ethnic groups.

But this alliance of unreconstructed enemies had little success in creating a working government or keeping violent clashes in check. The terms of the Dec. 1995 Dayton Peace Accord were largely ignored by Bosnian Serbs, with its former president, archnationalist Radovan Karadzic, still in de facto control of the Serbian enclave. Many indicted war criminals, including Karadzic, remain at large. NATO proved to be a largely ineffective peacekeeping force.

The crucial priorities facing postwar Bosnian leaders were rebuilding the economy, resettling the estimated 1 million refugees still displaced, and establishing a working government. Progress on these goals has been minimal, and a massive corruption scandal uncovered in 1999 severely tested the goodwill of the international community.

In 1994, the UN's International Criminal Tribunal for the former Yugoslavia opened in The Hague, Netherlands. In Aug. 2001, Radislav Drstic, a Bosnian Serb general, was found guilty of genocide in the killing of up to 8,000 Bosnian Muslims in Srebrenica in 1995. It was the first genocide conviction in Europe since the UN genocide treaty was drawn up in 1951. In 2001, the trial of former Serbian president Slobodan Milosevic began (and continues today). He was charged with crimes against humanity.

Under pressure from Paddy Ashdown, the international administrator of Bosnia, Bosnian Serb leaders finally admitted in June 2004 that Serbian troops were responsible for the massacre of up to 8,000 Bosnian Muslims in Srebrenica in 1995. Until then, Serb leaders had refused to acknowledge guilt in the worst civilian massacre since World War II. Thus far, only 13 individuals have been indicted by the UN International Criminal Tribunal for their role in the killings, and Bosnian Serb Army commander Ratko Mladic, who orchestrated the massacre, continues to remain at large. In August, a small, largely symbolic step was taken toward unifying the country when a world-famous 14th-century Ottoman bridge in Mostar was rebuilt—destroyed during the war, it now once again spans the Croatian and Bosnian sections of the city.

Botswana

REPUBLIC OF BOTSWANA

President: Festus Mogae (1998)
Area: 231,803 sq mi (600,370 sq km)
Population (2004 est.): 1,561,973 (growth rate: –0.9%); birth rate: 24.7/1000; infant mortality rate: 70.0/1000; life expectancy: 30.8; density per sq mi: 7
Capital and largest city (2003 est.): Gaborone, 195,000. **Monetary unit:** Pula. **Languages:** English (official), Setswana. **Ethnicity/race:** Tswana (or Setswana) 79%, Kalanga 11%, Basarwa 3%, other (including Kgalagadi and white) 7%. **Religions:** indigenous beliefs 85%, Christian 15%. **Literacy rate:** 80% (2003 est.)
Economic summary: GDP/PPP (2003 est.): $13.9 billion; per capita $8,800. **Real growth rate:** 7.6%. **Inflation:** 8.1%. **Unemployment:** 40% (official rate is 21%) (2001 est.). **Arable land:** 1%. **Agriculture:** livestock, sorghum, maize, millet, beans, sunflowers, groundnuts. **Labor force:** 264,000 formal sector employees (2000). **Industries:** diamonds, copper, nickel, salt, soda ash, potash; livestock processing; textiles. **Natural resources:** diamonds, copper, nickel, salt, soda ash, potash, coal, iron ore, silver. **Exports:** $2.544 billion (f.o.b, 2003 est.): diamonds 90%, copper, nickel, soda ash, meat, textiles. **Imports:** $1.753 billion (f.o.b, 2003 est.): foodstuffs, machinery, electrical goods, transport equipment, textiles, fuel and petroleum products, wood and paper products, metal and metal products. **Major trading partners:** European Free Trade Association (EFTA), Southern African Customs Union (SACU), Zimbabwe. **Member of Commonwealth of Nations**

Geography Twice the size of Arizona, Botswana is in south-central Africa, bounded by Namibia, Zambia, Zimbabwe, and South Africa. Most of the country is near-desert, with the Kalahari occupying the western part of the country. The eastern part is hilly, with salt lakes in the north.

Government Parliamentary republic.

History The earliest inhabitants of the region were the San, who were followed by the Tswana. About half the country today is ethnic Tswana. The term for the country's people, *Batswana*, refers to national rather than ethnic origin.

Encroachment by the Zulu in the 1820s and by Boers from Transvaal in the 1870s and 1880s threatened the peace of the region. In 1885, Britain established the area as a protectorate, then known as

Bechuanaland. In 1961, Britain granted a constitution to the country. Self-government began in 1965, and on Sept. 30, 1966, the country became independent. Botswana is Africa's oldest democracy.

The new country maintained good relations with its white-ruled neighbors, but gradually changed its policies, harboring rebel groups from South Rhodesia as well as some from South Africa.

Although Botswana is rich in diamonds, it has high unemployment and stratified socioeconomic classes. In 1999 it suffered its first budget deficit in 16 years because of a slump in the international diamond market. Yet it remains one of the wealthiest as well as most stable countries on the continent.

After 17 years in power, President Ketumile Masire retired in 1997, and Festus Mogae, an Oxford-educated economist, became the new president. Mogae has won high marks from the international financial community for continuing to privatize Botswana's mining and industrial operations.

Although Botswana's economic outlook remains strong, the devastation that AIDS has caused threatens to destroy the country's future. In 2001, Botswana had the highest rate of HIV infection in the world: 350,000 of its 1.6 million people were infected, and half the population between 25 and 29 were dying of the disease. In 2002, however, Botswana, with the help of international donors, launched an ambitious national campaign that provided free anti-viral drugs to anyone who needed them. By March 2004, Botswana no longer had the world's highest HIV infection rate. But with 37.5% of the population infected, the country remains on the brink of catastrophe.

Brazil

FEDERATIVE REPUBLIC OF BRAZIL

National name: República Federativa do Brasil
President: Luiz Inácio Lula da Silva (2003)
Area: 3,286,470 sq mi (8,511,965 sq km)
Population (2004 est.): 184,101,109 (growth rate: 1.1%); birth rate: 17.3/1000; infant mortality rate: 30.7/1000; life expectancy: 71.4; density per sq mi: 56
Capital (2003 est.): Brasília, 2,160,100. **Largest cities:** São Paulo, 18,847,400 (metro. area), 10,195,000 (city proper); Rio de Janeiro, 11,437,100 (metro. area), 6,119,800 (city proper); Salvador, 2,590,400; Belo Horizonte, 2,347,500; Recife, 1,485,500; Porto Alegre, 1,372,700. **Monetary unit:** Real. **Language:** Portuguese (official), Spanish, English, French. **Ethnicity/race:** white (includes Portuguese, German, Italian, Spanish, Polish) 55%, mixed white and black 38%, black 6%, other (includes Japanese, Arab, Amerindian) 1%. **Religion:** Roman Catholic 80%. **Literacy rate:** 80% (2003 est.)
Economic summary: GDP/PPP (2003 est.): $1.379 trillion; per capita $7,600. **Real growth rate:** 0.1%. **Inflation:** 9.3%. **Unemployment:** 12.2%. **Arable land:** 6%. **Agriculture:** coffee, soybeans, wheat, rice, corn, sugarcane, cocoa, citrus; beef. **Labor force:** 79 million (1999 est.); services 53%, agriculture 23%, industry 24%. **Industries:** textiles, shoes, chemicals, cement, lumber, iron ore, tin, steel, aircraft, motor vehicles and parts, other machinery and equipment. **Natural resources:** bauxite, gold, iron ore, manganese, nickel, phosphates, platinum, tin, uranium, petroleum, hydropower, timber. **Exports:** $73.28 billion (f.o.b., 2003 est.): transport equipment, iron ore, soybeans, footwear, coffee, autos. **Imports:** $48.25 billion (f.o.b., 2003 est.): machinery, electrical, and transport equipment, chemical products, oil. **Major trading partners:** U.S., Argentina, Germany, China, Netherlands, France.

Geography Brazil covers nearly half of South America and is the continent's largest nation. It extends 2,965 mi (4,772 km) north-south, 2,691 mi (4,331 km) east-west, and borders every nation on the continent except Chile and Ecuador. Brazil may be divided into the Brazilian Highlands, or plateau, in the south and the Amazon River Basin in the north. More than a third of Brazil is drained by the Amazon and its more than 200 tributaries. The Amazon is navigable for ocean steamers to Iquitos, Peru, 2,300 mi (3,700 km) upstream. Southern Brazil is drained by the Plata system—the Paraguay, Uruguay, and Paraná Rivers.

Government Federal republic.

History Brazil is the only Latin American nation that derives its language and culture from Portugal. The native inhabitants mostly consisted of the nomadic Tupí-Guaraní Indians. Adm. Pedro Alvares Cabral claimed the territory for Portugal in 1500. The early explorers brought back a wood that produced a red dye, *pau-brasil*, from which the land received its name. Portugal began colonization in 1532 and made the area a royal colony in 1549.

During the Napoleonic Wars, King João VI, fearing the advancing French armies, fled Portugal in 1808 and set up his court in Rio de Janeiro. João was drawn home in 1820 by a revolution, leaving his son as regent. When Portugal tried to reimpose colonial rule, the prince declared Brazil's independence on Sept. 7, 1822, becoming Pedro I, emperor of Brazil. Harassed by his Parliament, Pedro I abdicated in 1831 in favor of his five-year-old son, who became emperor in 1840 (Pedro II). The son was a popular monarch, but discontent built up, and in 1889, following a military revolt, he abdicated. Although a republic was proclaimed, Brazil was ruled by military dictatorships until a revolt permitted a gradual return to stability under civilian presidents.

President Wenceslau Braz cooperated with the Allies and declared war on Germany during World War I. In World War II, Brazil again cooperated with the Allies, welcoming Allied air bases, patrolling the South Atlantic, and joining the invasion of Italy after declaring war on the Axis powers.

After a military coup in 1964, Brazil had a series of military governments. Gen. João Baptista de Oliveira Figueiredo became president in 1979 and pledged a return to democracy in 1985. The election of Tancredo Neves on Jan. 15, 1985, the first civilian president since 1964, brought a nationwide wave of optimism, but when Neves died several months later, Vice President José Sarney became president. Collor de Mello won the election of late 1989, pledging to lower hyperinflation with free-market economics. When Collor faced impeachment by Congress because of a corruption scandal in Dec. 1992 and resigned, Vice President Itamar Franco assumed the presidency.

A former finance minister, Fernando Cardoso, won the presidency in the Oct. 1994 election with 54% of the vote. Cardoso sold off inefficient government-owned monopolies in the telecommunication, electrical power, port, mining, railway, and banking industries.

In Jan. 1999, the Asian economic crisis spread to Brazil. Rather than prop up the currency through financial markets, Brazil opted to let the currency float, which sent the real plummeting—at one time as much as 40%. Cardoso was highly praised by the international community for quickly turning around his country's economic crisis. Despite his efforts, however, the economy continued to slow throughout 2001, and the country also faced an energy crisis. The IMF offered Brazil an additional aid package in Aug. 2001. And in Aug. 2002, to ensure that Brazil would not be dragged down by neighboring Argentina's catastrophic economic problems, the IMF agreed to lend Brazil a phenomenal $30 billion over fifteen months.

In Jan. 2003, Luiz Inácio Lula da Silva, a former trade union leader and factory worker widely known by the name Lula, became Brazil's first working-class president. As leader of Brazil's only socialist party, the Workers' Party, Lula pledged to increase social services and improve the lot of the poor. But he also recognized that a distinctly non-socialist program of fiscal austerity was needed to rescue the economy. The president's first major legislative success was a plan to reform the country's debt-ridden pension system, which operated under an annual $20 billion deficit. Civil servants staged massive strikes opposing this and other reforms, and Lula's popularity temporarily slid. But while public debt and inflation remain a problem in 2004, Brazil's economy showed signs of growth and unemployment was down. Polls in Aug. 2004 demonstrated that the majority of Brazilians supported Lula's tough economic reform efforts.

Brunei Darussalam

STATE OF BRUNEI DARUSSALAM

Sultan: Haji Hassanal Bolkiah (1967)
Area: 2,228 sq mi (5,770 sq km)
Population (2004 est.): 365,251 (growth rate: 2.0%); birth rate: 19.3/1000; infant mortality rate: 13.1/1000; life expectancy: 74.5; density per sq mi: 164
Capital and largest city (2003 est.): Bandar Seri Begawan, 78,000. **Other large cities:** Kuala Belait 27,800, Seria 23,400. **Monetary unit:** Brunei dollar. **Languages:** Malay (official), English, Chinese. **Ethnicity/race:** Malay 67%, Chinese 15%, indigenous 6%, other 12%. **Religions:** Islam (official religion) 67%, Buddhist 13%, Christian 10%, indigenous beliefs and other 10%. **Literacy rate:** 92% (2003 est.)
Economic summary: GDP/PPP (2002 est.): $6.5 billion; per capita $18,600. **Real growth rate:** 3%. **Inflation:** –2%. **Unemployment:** 10% (2001 est.). **Arable land:** 1%. **Agriculture:** rice, vegetables, fruits, chickens, water buffalo. **Labor force:** 143,400; note: includes foreign workers and military personnel; temporary residents make up 40% of labor force (1999 est.); government 48%, production of oil, natural gas, services, and construction 42%, agriculture, forestry, and fishing 10% (1999 est.). **Industries:** petroleum, petroleum refining, liquefied natural gas, construction. **Natural resources:** petroleum, natural gas, timber. **Exports:** $3.439 billion (f.o.b., 2003 est.): crude oil, natural gas, refined products. **Imports:** $1.63 billion (c.i.f., 2003 est.): machinery and transport equipment, manufactured goods, food, chemicals. **Major trading partners:** Japan, South Korea, Thailand, Australia, U.S., China, Singapore, Malaysia, UK, Hong Kong.

Geography About the size of Delaware, Brunei is an independent sultanate on the northwest coast of the island of Borneo in the South China Sea, wedged between the Malaysian states of Sabah and Sarawak.

Government Constitutional sultanate.

History Brunei was trading with China during the 6th century, and, through allegiance to the Javanese Majapahit kingdom (13th to 15th century), it came under Hindu influence. In the early 15th century, with the decline of the Majapahit kingdom and widespread conversion to Islam, Brunei became an independent sultanate. It was a powerful state from the 16th to the 19th century, ruling over the northern part of Borneo and adjacent island chains. But it fell into decay and lost Sarawak in 1841, becoming a British protectorate in 1888 and a British dependency in 1905. Japan occupied Brunei during World War II; it was liberated by Australia in 1945.

The sultan regained control over internal affairs in 1959, but Britain retained responsibility for the state's defense and foreign affairs until 1984, when the sultanate became fully independent. Sultan Bolkiah was crowned in 1967 at the age of 22, succeeding his father, Sir Omar Ali Saifuddin, who had abdicated. During his reign, exploitation of the rich Seria oilfield had made the sultanate wealthy. Brunei has one of the highest per capita incomes in Asia, and the sultan is believed to be one of the richest men in the world. In Aug. 1998, Oxford-educated Prince Al-Muhtadee Billah was inaugurated as heir to the 500-year-old monarchy. The crown prince married a 17-year-old commoner, Sarah Salleh, in an extravagant ceremony in Sept. 2004.

The sultan has had to punish his wayward younger brother, Prince Jefri, for squandering billions of dollars on pet projects and lavish personal items during his tenure as finance minister and head of the Brunei Investment Agency. In Feb. 2000, Prince Jefri was charged with misappropriation of state funds.

Bulgaria

REPUBLIC OF BULGARIA

National name: Republika Bulgariya
President: Georgi Purvanov (2002)
Prime Minister: Simeon Saxe-Coburg Gotha (2001)
Area: 42,822 sq mi (110,910 sq km)
Population (2004 est.): 7,517,973 (growth rate: –0.9%); birth rate: 9.7/1000; infant mortality rate: 21.3/1000; life expectancy: 71.8; density per sq mi: 176
Capital and largest city (2003 est.): Sofia, 1,088,700. **Other large cities:** Plovdiv, 338,200; Varna, 312,300; Burgas, 192,000; Ruse, 161,000. **Monetary unit:** Lev. **Language:** Bulgarian; secondary languages strongly correspond to ethnic breakdown. **Ethnicity/race:** Bulgarian 83.9%, Turk 9.4%, Roma 4.7%, other (including Macedonian, Armenian, Tatar, Circassian) 2%. **Religions:** Bulgarian Orthodox 82.6%, Islam 12.2%, Roman Catholic 1.7%, Jewish 0.1%, Protestant, Gregorian-Armenian, and other 3.4% (1998). **Literacy rate:** 99% (2003 est.)
Economic summary: GDP/PPP (2003 est.): $57.13 billion; per capita $7,600. **Real growth rate:** 4.4%. **Inflation:** 5.6%. **Unemployment:** 13.5%. **Arable land:** 39%. **Agriculture:** vegetables, fruits, tobacco, livestock, wine, wheat, barley, sunflowers, sugar beets. **Labor force:** 3.83 million (2000 est.); agriculture 26%, industry 31%, services 43% (1998 est.). **Industries:** electricity, gas and water; food, beverages and tobacco; machinery and equipment, base metals, chemical products, coke, refined petroleum, nuclear fuel. **Natural resources:** bauxite, copper, lead, zinc, coal, timber, arable land. **Exports:** $7.337 billion (f.o.b., 2003 est.): clothing, footwear, iron and steel, machinery and equipment, fuels. **Imports:** $9.723 billion (f.o.b., 2003 est.): fuels, minerals, and raw materials; machinery and equipment; metals and ores; chemicals and plastics; food, textiles. **Major trading partners:** Italy, Germany, Turkey, Greece, France, U.S., Russia

Geography Bulgaria shares borders with Serbia, Macedonia, Romania, Greece, and Turkey. Two mountain ranges and two great valleys mark the topography of Bulgaria, a country the size of Tennessee and situated on the Black Sea. The Maritsa is Bulgaria's principal river, and the Danube also flows through the country.

Government Parliamentary democracy.

History The Thracians lived in what is now known as Bulgaria from about 3500 B.C. They were incorporated into the Roman Empire by the first century A.D. At the decline of the empire, the Goths, Huns, Bulgars, and Avars invaded. The Bulgars, who crossed the Danube from the north in 679, took control of the region. Although the country bears the name of the Bulgars, the Bulgar language and culture died out, replaced by a Slavic language, writing, and religion. In 865, Boris I adopted Orthodox Christianity. The Bulgars twice conquered most of the Balkan peninsula between 893 and 1280. But in 1396 they were invaded by the Ottoman Empire, which made Bulgaria a Turkish province until 1878. Ottoman rule was harsh and inescapable, given Bulgaria's proximity to its oppressor. In 1878, Russia forced Turkey to give Bulgaria its independence after the Russo-Turkish War (1877–1878), but the European powers, fearing Russia's and Bulgaria's dominance in the Balkans, intervened at the Congress of Berlin (1878), limited Bulgaria's territory, and fashioned it into a small principality ruled by Alexander of Battenburg, the nephew of the Russian czar.

Alexander was succeeded in 1887 by Prince Ferdinand of Saxe-Coburg-Gotha, who declared a kingdom independent of the Ottoman empire on Oct. 5, 1908. In the First Balkan War (1912–1913), Bulgaria and the other members of the Balkan League fought against Turkey to regain Balkan territory. Angered by the small portion of Macedonia it received after the battle—it considered Macedonia an integral part of Bulgaria—the country instigated the Second Balkan War (June–Aug. 1913) against Turkey as well as its former allies. Bulgaria lost the war and all the territory it had gained in the First Balkan War. Bulgaria joined Germany in World War I in the hope of again gaining Macedonia. After this second failure, Ferdinand abdicated in favor of his son in 1918. Boris III squandered Bulgaria's resources and assumed dictatorial powers in 1934–1935. Bulgaria fought on the side of the Nazis in World War II, but after Russia declared war on Bulgaria on Sept. 5, 1944, Bulgaria switched sides. Three days later, on Sept. 9, 1944, a Communist coalition took control of the country and set up a government under Kimon Georgiev.

A Soviet-style People's Republic was established in 1947 and Bulgaria acquired the reputation of being the most slavishly loyal to Moscow of all the East European Communist countries. The general secretary of the Bulgarian Communist Party, Todor Zhikov, resigned in 1989 after 35 years in power. His successor, Peter Mladenov, purged the Politburo, ended the Communist monopoly on power, and held free elections in May 1990 that led to a surprising victory for the Communist Party, renamed the Bulgarian Socialist Party (BSP). Mladenov was forced to resign in July 1990.

In Oct. 1991, the Union of Democratic Forces won, forming Bulgaria's first non-Communist government since 1946. Power shifted back and forth between the pro-Western Union of Democratic Forces (UDF) and the BSP during the 1990s. The economy continued to deteriorate amid growing concern over the spread of organized crime. A new UDF government, led by Prime Minister Ivan Kostov, was elected in 1997 to overhaul the economic system and institute reforms aimed at stemming corruption. Progress on both fronts remained slow. As a result, the UDF lost the July 2001 election to the former king of Bulgaria, leader of the Simeon II National Movement (SNM). The new prime minister, Simeon Saxe-Coburg-Gotha (Simeon II), had been dethroned 55 years earlier (at age nine) during the Communist take-over of the country.

Bulgaria was one of just four UN Security Council members to support the war in Iraq, and in July 2003 it sent a security force of 500 to help police the country. Bulgaria became a member of NATO in 2004.

Burkina Faso

National name: Burkina Faso
President: Blaise Compaoré (1987)
Prime Minister: Paramanga Ernest Yonli (2000)
Area: 105,869 sq mi (274,200 sq km)
Population (2004 est.): 13,574,820 (growth rate: 2.6%); birth rate: 44.5/1000; infant mortality rate: 98.7/1000; life expectancy: 44.2; density per sq mi: 128
Capital and largest city (2003 est.): Ouagadougou, 962,100. **Monetary unit:** CFA Franc. **Languages:** French (official); native African (Sudanic) languages 90%. **Ethnicity/race:** Mossi (over 40%), Gurunsi, Senufo, Lobi, Bobo, Mande, Fulani. **Religions:** Islam 50%, indigenous beliefs 40%, Christian (mainly Roman Catholic) 10%. **Literacy rate:** 27% (2003 est.)
Economic summary: GDP/PPP (2003 est.): $14.33 billion; per capita $1,100. **Real growth rate:** 4.6%. **Inflation:** 4.5%. **Unemployment:** n.a. **Arable land:** 12%. **Agriculture:** cotton, peanuts, shea nuts, sesame, sorghum, millet, corn, rice; livestock. **Labor force:** 5 million; note: a large part of the male labor force migrates annually to neighboring countries for seasonal employment (2003). **Industries:** cotton lint, beverages, agricultural processing, soap, cigarettes, textiles, gold. **Natural resources:** manganese, limestone, marble; small deposits of gold, antimony, copper, nickel, bauxite, lead, phosphates, zinc, silver. **Exports:** $293 million (f.o.b., 2003 est.): cotton, livestock, gold. **Imports:** $633.6 million (f.o.b., 2003 est.): capital goods, food products, petroleum. **Major trading partners:** Singapore, Italy, Colombia, France, India, Ghana, Japan, Thailand, Côte d'Ivoire, Togo.

Geography Slightly larger than Colorado, Burkina Faso, formerly known as Upper Volta, is a landlocked country in West Africa. Its neighbors are Côte d'Ivoire, Mali, Niger, Benin, Togo, and Ghana. The country consists of extensive plains, low hills, high savannas, and a desert area in the north.

Government Parliamentary.

History Burkina Faso was originally inhabited by the Bobo, Lobi, and Gurunsi peoples, with the Mossi and Gurma peoples immigrating to the region in the 14th century. The lands of the Mossi empire became a French protectorate in 1897, and by 1903 France had subjugated the other ethnic groups. Called Upper Volta by the French, it became a separate colony in 1919, was partitioned among Niger, the Sudan, and Côte d'Ivoire in 1932, and was reconstituted in 1947. An autonomous republic within the French Community, Upper Volta became independent on Aug. 5, 1960.

President Maurice Yameogo was deposed on Jan. 3, 1966, by a military coup led by Col. Sangoulé Lamizana, who dissolved the National Assembly and suspended the constitution. Constitutional rule returned in 1978 with the election of an Assembly and a presidential vote in June in which Gen. Lamizana won by a narrow margin over three other candidates.

On Nov. 25, 1980, Col. Sayé Zerbo led a bloodless coup that toppled Lamizana. In turn, Maj. Jean-Baptiste Ouedraogo ousted Zerbo on Nov. 7, 1982. But the real revolutionary change occurred the following year when a 33-year-old flight commander, Thomas Sankara, took control. A Marxist-Leninist, he challenged the traditional Mossi chiefs, advocated women's liberation, and allied the country with North Korea, Libya, and Cuba. To sever ties to the colonial past, Sankara changed the name of the country in 1984 to Burkina Faso, which combines two of the nation's languages and means "the land of upright men."

While Sankara's investments in schools, food production, and clinics brought some improvement in living standards, foreign investment declined, many businesses left the country, and unhappy labor unions began strikes. On Oct. 15, 1987, formerly loyal soldiers assassinated Sankara. His best friend and ally Blaise Compaoré became president. Compaoré immediately set about "rectifying" Sankara's revolution. In 1991 he agreed to economic reforms proposed by the World Bank. A new constitution paved the way for elections in 1991, which Compaoré won easily, although opposition parties boycotted. In 1998, he was reelected by a landslide.

Burma (Myanmar)

SEE MYANMAR.

Burundi

REPUBLIC OF BURUNDI

National name: Republika Y'Uburundi
President: Domitien Ndayizeye (2003)
Area: 10,745 sq mi (27,830 sq km)
Population (2004 est.): 6,231,221 (growth rate: 2.2%); birth rate: 39.7/1000; infant mortality rate: 70.4/1000; life expectancy: 43.4; density per sq mi: 580
Capital and largest city (2003 est.): Bujumbura, 331,700. **Other large city:** Gitega, 45,700. **Monetary unit:** Burundi franc. **Languages:** Kirundi and French (official), Swahili. **Ethnicity/race:** Hutu (Bantu) 85%, Tutsi (Hamitic) 14%, Twa (Pygmy) 1%. **Religions:** Roman Catholic 62%, indigenous 23%, Islam 10%, Protestant 5%. **Literacy rate:** 52% (2003 est.)
Economic summary: GDP/PPP (2003 est.): $3.83 billion; per capita $600. **Real growth rate:** 0%. **Inflation:** 11%. **Unemployment:** n.a. **Arable land:** 30%. **Agriculture:** coffee, cotton, tea, corn, sorghum, sweet potatoes, bananas, manioc (tapioca); beef, milk, hides. **Labor force:** 2.99 million (2002). **Industries:** light consumer goods such as blankets, shoes, soap; assembly of imported components; public works construction; food processing. **Natural resources:** nickel, uranium, rare earth oxides, peat, cobalt, copper, platinum (not yet exploited), vanadium, arable land, hydropower. **Exports:** $40 million (f.o.b., 2003 est.): coffee, tea, sugar, cotton, hides. **Imports:** $128 million (f.o.b., 2003 est.): capital goods, petroleum products, foodstuffs. **Major trading partners:** Switzerland, Germany, Belgium, Kenya, Rwanda, Netherlands, Saudi Arabia, Tanzania, France, India.

Geography Wedged between Tanzania, the Democratic Republic of the Congo, and Rwanda in east-central Africa, Burundi occupies a high plateau divided by several deep valleys. It is equal in size to Maryland.

Government Republic.

History The original inhabitants of Burundi were the Twa, a Pygmy people who now make up only 1% of the population. Today the population is divided between the Hutu (approximately 85%) and the Tutsi, approximately 14%. While the Hutu and Tutsi are considered to be two separate ethnic groups, scholars point out that they speak the same language, have a history of intermarriage, and share many cultural characteristics. Traditionally, the differences between the two groups were occupational rather than ethnic. Agricultural people were considered Hutu, while the cattle-owning elite were identified as Tutsi. Supposedly Tutsi were tall and thin, while Hutu were short and square, but in fact it is often impossible to tell one from the other. The 1933 requirement by the Belgians that everyone carry an identity card indicating tribal ethnicity as Tutsi or Hutu increased the distinction. Since independence, the land-owning Tutsi aristocracy has dominated Burundi.

Burundi was once part of German East Africa. Belgium won a League of Nations mandate in 1923, and subsequently Burundi, with Rwanda, was transferred to the status of a United Nations trust territory. In 1962, Burundi gained independence and became a kingdom under Mwami Mwambutsa IV, a Tutsi. A Hutu rebellion took place in 1965, leading to brutal Tutsi retaliations. Mwambutsa was deposed by his son, Ntaré V, in 1966. Ntaré in turn was overthrown the same year in a military coup by Premier Michel Micombero, also a Tutsi. In 1970–1971, a civil war erupted, leaving more than 100,000 Hutu dead.

On Nov. 1, 1976, Lt. Col. Jean-Baptiste Bagaza led a coup and assumed the presidency. He suspended the constitution and announced that a 30-member Supreme Revolutionary Council would be the governing body. In Sept. 1987 Bagaza was overthrown by Maj. Pierre Buyoya, who became president. Ethnic hatred again flared in Aug. 1988, and about 20,000 Hutu were slaughtered. Buyoya, however, began reforms to heal the country's ethnic rift. The Burundi Democracy Front's candidate, Melchior Ndadaye, won the country's first democratic presidential elections, held on June 2, 1993. Ndadaye, the first Hutu to assume power in Burundi, was killed within months during a coup. The second Hutu president, Cyprien Ntaryamira, was killed on April 6, 1994, when a plane carrying him and the Rwandan president was shot down. As a result, Hutu youth gangs began massacring Tutsi; the Tutsi-controlled army retaliated by killing Hutus.

The frequency of ethnic clashes increased, developing into a low-intensity civil war. A six-nation regional proposal to send troops into Burundi to maintain peace and order was devised in July 1996. Distrustful of the scheme, the Tutsi-dominated army led a coup deposing the Hutu president and installed Maj. Pierre Buyoya that month. More than 300,000 people have been killed in the civil war since 1993, with the Tutsi-dominated army and the Hutu rebel forces responsible for the slaughter. After several aborted ceasefires, a 2001 peace plan included a power-sharing agreement that has been relatively successful: Buyoya, a Tutsi, governed the new transitional government for the first 18 months; then, in April 2003, a Hutu president, Domitien Ndayizeye, assumed power until scheduled elections in Oct. 2004. With a new interim government in place, the ceasefire continuing to hold, and elections forthcoming, Burundi's eleven-year civil war may be finally ending.

In Aug. 2004, 160 Congolese Tutsis in a Burundian refugee camp were massacred by Burundian Hutus, once again threatening the stability of the country.

Cambodia

King: Norodom Sihanouk (1993)
Prime Minister: Hun Sen (1998)
Area: 69,900 sq mi (181,040 sq km)
Population (2004 est.): 13,363,421 (growth rate: 1.8%); birth rate: 27.1/1000; infant mortality rate: 73.7/1000; life expectancy: 58.4; density per sq mi: 191
Capital and largest city (2003 est.): Phnom Penh, 1,169,800. **Monetary unit:** Riel. **Languages:** Khmer (official), French, English. **Ethnicity/race:** Khmer 90%,

Vietnamese 5%, Chinese 1%, other 4%. **Religions:** Theravada Buddhist 95%, others 5%. **Literacy rate:** 70% (2003 est.)

Economic summary: GDP/PPP (2003 est.): $22.76 billion; per capita $1,700. **Real growth rate:** 5.5%. **Inflation:** 3%. **Unemployment:** 2.5% (2000 est.). **Arable land:** 21%. **Agriculture:** rice, rubber, corn, vegetables. **Labor force:** 7 million; agriculture 80% (2001 est.). **Industries:** tourism, garments, rice milling, fishing, wood and wood products, rubber, cement, gem mining, textiles. **Natural resources:** timber, gemstones, some iron ore, manganese, phosphates, hydropower potential. **Exports:** $1.616 billion (f.o.b., 2003 est.): timber, garments, rubber, rice, fish. **Imports:** $2.124 billion (f.o.b., 2003 est.): petroleum products, cigarettes, gold, construction materials, machinery, motor vehicles. **Major trading partners:** U.S., Germany, UK, Singapore, Thailand, China, Hong Kong, South Korea, Vietnam.

Geography Situated on the Indochinese peninsula, Cambodia is bordered by Thailand and Laos on the north and Vietnam on the east and south. The Gulf of Thailand is off the western coast. The size of Missouri, the country consists chiefly of a large alluvial plain ringed by mountains, and on the east is the Mekong River. The plain is centered around Lake Tonle Sap, which is a natural storage basin of the Mekong.

Government Multiparty liberal democracy under a constitutional monarchy.

History The area that is present-day Cambodia came under Khmer rule about 600, when the region was at the center of a vast empire that stretched over most of Southeast Asia. Under the Khmers, who were Hindus, a magnificent temple complex was constructed at Angkor. Buddhism was introduced in the 12th century during the rule of Jayavaram VII. However, the kingdom, then known as Kambuja, fell into decline after Jayavaram's reign and was nearly annihilated by Thai and Vietnamese invaders. Its power steadily diminished until 1863, when France colonized the region, joining Cambodia, Laos, and Vietnam into a single protectorate known as French Indochina.

The French quickly usurped all but ceremonial powers from the monarch, Norodom. When he died in 1904, the French passed over his sons and handed the throne to his brother, Sisowath. Sisowath and his son ruled until 1941, when Norodom Sihanouk was elevated to power. Sihanouk's coronation, along with the Japanese occupation during the war, worked to reinforce a sentiment among Cambodians that the region should be free from outside control. After World War II, Cambodians sought independence, but France was reluctant to part with its colony. Cambodia was granted independence within the French Union in 1949. But the French-Indochinese War provided an opportunity for Sihanouk to gain full military control of the country. He abdicated in 1955 in favor of his parents, remaining head of the government, and when his father died in 1960, became chief of state without returning to the throne. In 1963, he sought a guarantee of Cambodia's neutrality from all parties to the Vietnam War.

However, North Vietnamese and Vietcong troops had begun using eastern Cambodia as a safe haven from which to launch attacks into South Vietnam, making it increasingly difficult to stay out of the war. An indigenous Communist guerrilla movement known as the Khmer Rouge also began to put pressure on the government in Phnom Penh. On March 18, 1970, while Sihanouk was abroad, anti-Vietnamese riots broke out and Sihanouk was overthrown by Gen. Lon Nol. The Vietnam peace agreement of 1973 stipulated withdrawal of foreign forces from Cambodia, but fighting continued between Hanoi-backed insurgents and U.S.-supplied government troops.

Combat climaxed in April 1975 when the Lon Nol regime was overthrown by Pol Pot, leader of the Khmer Rouge forces. The four years of nightmarish Khmer Rouge rule led to the state-sponsored extermination of citizens by its own government. Between 1 million and 2 million people were massacred on the "killing fields" of Cambodia or worked to death through forced labor. Pol Pot's radical vision of transforming the country into a Marxist agrarian society led to the virtual extermination of the country's professional and technical class.

Pol Pot was ousted by Vietnamese forces on Jan. 8, 1979, and a new pro-Hanoi government led by Heng Samrin was installed. Pol Pot and 35,000 Khmer Rouge fighters fled into the hills of western Cambodia, where they were joined by forces loyal to the ousted Sihanouk in a guerrilla movement aimed at overthrowing the Heng Samrin government. The Vietnamese plan originally called for a withdrawal by early 1990 and a negotiated political settlement. The talks became protracted, however, and a UN agreement was not signed until 1992, when Sihanouk was appointed leader of an interim Supreme National Council convened to run the country until elections could be held in 1993.

Free elections in May 1993 saw the defeat of Heng Samrin's successor, Hun Sen, who refused to accept the outcome of the vote and insisted instead on a power-sharing agreement. Under the arrangement, Hun Sen and Sihanouk's son, Prince Norodom Ranariddh, would act as co-prime ministers. The Khmer Rouge stronghold in the western jungles splintered in 1997, with factions either battling each other or defecting. Ranariddh and Hun Sen both courted Khmer Rouge factions in an effort to shore up their power. In early July, Hun Sen took advantage of the charged political atmosphere to depose Ranariddh, the country's only popularly elected leader. Hun Sen later launched a brutal purge, executing more than 40 political opponents. Shortly after the July coup, the Khmer Rouge organized a show trial of their notorious leader, Pol Pot, who had not been seen by the West in more than two decades. He was sentenced to house arrest for his crimes against humanity. He died on April 15, 1998. In the July 1998 election, Hun Sen defeated opposition leaders Sam Rainsy and Prince Ranariddh, but the opposition parties accused him of voter fraud. Cambodia was able to regain its UN seat, lost nearly a year earlier as a result of Hun Sen's coup.

Elections in July 2003 resulted in a stalemate—none of the parties won the two-thirds majority required to govern alone. Ranariddh refused to form a coalition with Hun Sen, calling him an autocrat and accusing him of corruption. After months of negotiations, Ranariddh and Hun Sen agreed in June 2004 to form a coalition, with Hun Sen remaining prime minister. In August, Cambodia's parliament ratified the country's entry into the World Trade Organization.

Cameroon

REPUBLIC OF CAMEROON

National name: République du Cameroun
President: Paul Biya (1982)
Prime Minister: Peter Mafany Musonge (1996)
Area: 183,567 sq mi (475,440 sq km)
Population (2004 est.): 16,063,678 (growth rate: 2.0%); birth rate: 35.1/1000; infant mortality rate: 69.2/1000; life expectancy: 48.0; density per sq mi: 88
Capital: Yaoundé, 1,395,200 (metro. area), 1,154,400

(city proper). **Largest city:** Douala, 1,490,500 (metro.area), 1,274.300 (city proper) . **Monetary unit:** CFA Franc. **Languages:** French, English (both official); 24 major African language groups. **Ethnicity/ race:** Cameroon Highlanders 31%, Equatorial Bantu 19%, Kirdi 11%, Fulani 10%, Northwest Bantu 8%, Eastern Nigritic 7%, other African 13%, non-African less than 1%. **Religions:** indigenous beliefs 40%, Christian 40%, Islam 20%. **Literacy rate:** 79% (2003 est.)

Economic summary: GDP/PPP (2003 est.): $27.59 billion; per capita $1,800. **Real growth rate:** 3.6%. **Inflation:** 4.5% (2002 est.). **Unemployment:** 30% (2001 est.). **Arable land:** 13%. **Agriculture:** coffee, cocoa, cotton, rubber, bananas, oilseed, grains, root starches; livestock; timber. **Labor force:** n.a.; agriculture 70%, industry and commerce 13%, other 17%. **Industries:** petroleum production and refining, food processing, light consumer goods, textiles, lumber. **Natural resources:** petroleum, bauxite, iron ore, timber, hydropower. **Exports:** $1.873 billion (f.o.b., 2003 est.): crude oil and petroleum products, lumber, cocoa beans, aluminum, coffee, cotton. **Imports:** $1.959 billion (f.o.b., 2003 est.): machinery, electrical equipment, transport equipment, fuel, food. **Major trading partners:** Italy, Spain, France, U.S., Netherlands, Taiwan, China, UK, Nigeria, Belgium, Germany.

Geography Cameroon is a Central African nation on the Gulf of Guinea, bordered by Nigeria, Chad, the Central African Republic, the Republic of Congo, Equatorial Guinea, and Gabon. It is nearly twice the size of Oregon. Mount Cameroon (13,350 ft; 4,069 m), near the coast, is the highest elevation in the country. The main rivers are the Benue, Nyong, and Sanaga.

Government After a 1972 plebiscite, a unitary republic was formed out of East and West Cameroon to replace the former federal republic.

History Bantu speakers were among the first groups to settle Cameroon, followed by the Muslim Fulani in the 18th and 19th centuries. The land escaped colonial rule until 1884, when treaties with tribal chiefs brought the area under German domination. After World War I, the League of Nations gave the French a mandate over 80% of the area, and the British 20% adjacent to Nigeria. After World War II, when the country came under a UN trusteeship in 1946, self-government was granted, and the Cameroon People's Union emerged as the dominant party by campaigning for reunification of French and British Cameroon and for independence. Accused of being under Communist control, the party waged a campaign of revolutionary terror from 1955 to 1958, when it was crushed. In British Cameroon, unification was also promoted by the leading party, the Kamerun National Democratic Party, led by John Foncha.

France set up Cameroon as an autonomous state in 1957, and the next year its legislative assembly voted for independence by 1960. In 1959 a fully autonomous government of Cameroon was formed under Ahmadou Ahidjo. Cameroon became an independent republic on Jan. 1, 1960. In 1961 the southern part of the British territory joined the new Federal Republic of Cameroon and the northern section voted for unification with Nigeria. The president of Cameroon since independence, Ahmadou Ahidjo was replaced in 1982 by the prime minister, Paul Biya. Both administrations have been authoritarian.

With the expansion of oil, timber, and coffee exports, the economy has continued to improve, although corruption is prevalent, and environmental degradation remains a concern. In June 2000 the World Bank agreed to provide more than $200 million to build a $3.7 billion pipeline connecting the oil fields in neighboring Chad with the Cameroon coast.

Canada

Sovereign: Queen Elizabeth II (1952)
Governor-General: Adrienne Clarkson (1999)
Prime Minister: Paul Martin (2003)
Area: 3,855,081 sq mi (9,984,670 sq km)
Population (2004 est.): 32,507,874 (growth rate: 0.9%); birth rate: 10.9/1000; infant mortality rate: 4.8/1000; life expectancy: 80.0; density per sq mi: 8
Capital (2003 est.): Ottawa, Ontario, 1,089,100 (metro. area), 852,100 (city proper). **Largest cities (metropolitan areas):** Toronto, 5,508,000, 4,494,200 (city proper); Montreal, 3,248,000; Vancouver, 1,865,300; Calgary, 1,089,100; Edmonton, 966,200; Quebec, 689,400; Winnipeg, 675,800; Hamilton, 636,900 (part of Toronto metro. area); London, 439,400; Kitchener, 426,200 . **Monetary unit:** Canadian dollar. **Languages:** English 59.3%, French 23.2% (both official); other 17.5%. **Ethnicity/race:** British Isles origin 28%, French origin 23%, other European 15%, indigenous Indian and Inuit 2%, other, mostly Asian, African, Arab 6%, mixed background 26%. **Religions:** Roman Catholic 46%, Protestant 36%, other 18% (based on 1991 census). **Literacy rate:** 97% (1986 est.)
Economic summary: GDP/PPP (2003 est.): $957.7 billion; per capita $29,700. **Real growth rate:** 1.6%. **Inflation:** 2.8%. **Unemployment:** 7.7%. **Arable land:** 5%. **Agriculture:** wheat, barley, oilseed, tobacco, fruits, vegetables; dairy products; forest products; fish. **Labor force:** 16.4 million (2001 est.); services 74%, manufacturing 15%, construction 5%, agriculture 3%, other 3% (2000). **Industries:** transportation equipment, chemicals, processed and unprocessed minerals, food products; wood and paper products; fish products, petroleum and natural gas. **Natural resources:** iron ore, nickel, zinc, copper, gold, lead, molybdenum, potash, diamonds, silver, fish, timber, wildlife, coal, petroleum, natural gas, hydropower. **Exports:** $279.3 billion (f.o.b., 2003 est.): motor vehicles and parts, industrial machinery, aircraft, telecommunications equipment; chemicals, plastics, fertilizers; wood pulp, timber, crude petroleum, natural gas, electricity, aluminum. **Imports:** $240.4 billion (f.o.b., 2003 est.): machinery and equipment, motor vehicles and parts, crude oil, chemicals, electricity, durable consumer goods. **Major trading partners:** U.S., Japan, UK, China.

Geography Covering most of the northern part of the North American continent and with an area larger than that of the United States, Canada has an extremely varied topography. In the east the mountainous maritime provinces have an irregular coastline on the Gulf of St. Lawrence and the Atlantic. The St. Lawrence plain, covering most of southern Quebec and Ontario, and the interior continental plain, covering southern Manitoba and Saskatchewan and most of Alberta, are the principal cultivable areas. They are separated by a forested plateau rising from Lakes Superior and Huron.

Westward toward the Pacific, most of British Columbia, Yukon, and part of western Alberta are covered by parallel mountain ranges, including the Rockies. The Pacific border of the coast range is ragged with fjords and channels. The highest point in Canada is Mount Logan (19,850 ft; 6,050 m), which is in the Yukon. The two principal river systems are the Mackenzie and the St. Lawrence. The St. Lawrence, with its tributaries, is navigable for over 1,900 mi (3,058 km).

Canadian Prime Ministers Since 1867

Term	Prime Minister	Party	Term	Prime Minister	Party
1867–1873	Sir John A. Macdonald	Conservative	1930–1935	Richard B. Bennett	Conservative
1873–1878	Alexander Mackenzie	Liberal	1935–1948	W. L. Mackenzie King	Liberal
1878–1891	Sir John A. Macdonald	Conservative	1948–1957	Louis S. St. Laurent	Liberal
1891–1892	Sir John J. C. Abbott	Conservative	1957–1963	John G. Diefenbaker	Conservative
1892–1894	Sir John S. D. Thompson	Conservative	1963–1968	Lester B. Pearson	Liberal
1894–1896	Sir Mackenzie Bowell	Conservative	1968–1979	Pierre Elliott Trudeau	Liberal
1896	Sir Charles Tupper	Conservative	1979–1980	Charles Joseph Clark	Conservative
1896–1911	Sir Wilfrid Laurier	Liberal	1980–1984	Pierre Elliott Trudeau	Liberal
1911–1917	Sir Robert L. Borden	Conservative	1984	John Turner	Liberal
1917–1920	Sir Robert L. Borden	Unionist	1984–1993	Brian Mulroney	Conservative
1920–1921	Arthur Meighen	Unionist	1993	Kim Campbell	Conservative
1921–1926	W. L. Mackenzie King	Liberal	1993–2003	Jean Chrétien	Liberal
1926	Arthur Meighen	Conservative	2003–	Paul Martin	Liberal
1926–1930	W. L. Mackenzie King	Liberal			

Government Canada is a federation of ten provinces (Alberta, British Columbia, Manitoba, New Brunswick, Newfoundland and Labrador, Nova Scotia, Ontario, Prince Edward Island, Quebec, and Saskatchewan) and three territories (Northwest Territories, Yukon, and as of April 1, 1999, Nunavut). Formally considered a constitutional monarchy, Canada is governed by its own House of Commons. While the governor-general is officially the representative of Queen Elizabeth II, in reality the governor-general acts only upon the advice of the Canadian prime minister.

History The first inhabitants of Canada were native Indian peoples, primarily the Inuit (Eskimo). The Norse explorer Leif Eriksson probably reached the shores of Canada (Labrador or Nova Scotia) in 1000, but the history of the white man in the country actually began in 1497, when John Cabot, an Italian in the service of Henry VII of England, reached Newfoundland or Nova Scotia. Canada was taken for France in 1534 by Jacques Cartier. The actual settlement of New France, as it was then called, began in 1604 at Port Royal in what is now Nova Scotia; in 1608, Quebec was founded. France's colonization efforts were not very successful, but French explorers by the end of the 17th century had penetrated beyond the Great Lakes to the western prairies and south along the Mississippi to the Gulf of Mexico. Meanwhile, the English Hudson's Bay Company had been established in 1670. Because of the valuable fisheries and fur trade, a conflict developed between the French and English; in 1713, Newfoundland, Hudson Bay, and Nova Scotia (Acadia) were lost to England. During the Seven Years' War (1756–1763), England extended its conquest, and the British general James Wolfe won his famous victory over Gen. Louis Montcalm outside Quebec on Sept. 13, 1759. The Treaty of Paris in 1763 gave England control.

At that time the population of Canada was almost entirely French, but in the next few decades, thousands of British colonists emigrated to Canada from the British Isles and from the American colonies. In 1849, the right of Canada to self-government was recognized. By the British North America Act of 1867, the dominion of Canada was created through the confederation of Upper and Lower Canada, Nova Scotia, and New Brunswick. In 1869, Canada purchased from the Hudson's Bay Company the vast middle west (Rupert's Land) from which the provinces of Manitoba (1870), Alberta (1905), and Saskatchewan (1905) were later formed. In 1871, British Columbia joined the dominion, and in 1873, Prince Edward Island followed. The country was linked from coast to coast in 1885 by the Canadian Pacific Railway.

During the formative years between 1866 and 1896, the Conservative Party, led by Sir John A. Macdonald, governed the country, except during the years 1873–1878. In 1896 the Liberal Party took over and, under Sir Wilfrid Laurier, an eminent French Canadian, ruled until 1911. By the Statute of Westminster in 1931 the British dominions, including Canada, were formally declared to be partner nations with Britain, "equal in status, in no way subordinate to each other," and bound together only by allegiance to a common Crown.

Newfoundland became Canada's tenth province on March 31, 1949, following a plebiscite. Canada also includes three territories—the Yukon Territory, the Northwest Territories, and the newest territory, Nunavut. This new territory includes all of the Arctic north of the mainland, Norway having recognized Canadian sovereignty over the Sverdrup Islands in the Arctic in 1931.

The Liberal Party, led by William Lyon Mackenzie King, dominated Canadian politics from 1921 until 1957, when it was succeeded by the Progressive Conservatives. The Liberals, under the leadership of Lester B. Pearson, returned to power in 1963. Pearson remained prime minister until 1968, when he retired and was replaced by a former law professor, Pierre Elliott Trudeau. Trudeau maintained Canada's defensive alliance with the United States but began moving toward a more independent policy in world affairs.

Faced with an increasingly violent separatist movement in the predominantly French province of Quebec, Trudeau introduced the Official Languages Bill, which

Population by Provinces and Territories

Province	2003	2004
	(in thousands)	
Alberta	3,142.1	3,183.3
British Columbia	4,135.8	4,177.4
Manitoba	1,159.9	1,168.3
New Brunswick	750.5	750.5
Newfoundland and Labrador	519.4	519.0'
Nova Scotia	835.4	936.5
Ontario	12,193.3	12,332.6
Prince Edward Island	137.5	138.4
Quebec	7,472.9	7,520.9
Saskatchewan	994.8	995.1
Northwest Territories	41.7	42.3
Yukon Territory	30.8	31.5
Nunavut	29.2	29.6

NOTE: As of April 1, 2004. *Source: Statistics Canada.*

encouraged bilingualism in the federal government; he also gave an economic portfolio to a French-speaking minister, Jean Chrétien. Both measures increased the power of French-speaking politicians in the federal government.

In 1976, the Parti Québécois (PQ) won the provincial Quebec elections, and René Lévesque became premier. The Quebec government passed Bill 101 in 1977, which established numerous rules promoting the French-speaking culture; for example, only French was to be used for commercial signs and for most public school instruction. Many of Bill 101's provisions have since been amended, striking more of a compromise; commercial signs, for example, may now be in French and English, provided that the French lettering is twice the size of the English. Quebec held a referendum in May 1980 on whether it should seek independence from Canada; it was defeated by 60% of the voters.

Resolving a dispute that had occupied Trudeau since the beginning of his tenure, Queen Elizabeth II signed the Constitution Act (also called the Canada Act) in Ottawa on April 17, 1982, thereby cutting the last legal tie between Canada and Britain. The constitution retains Queen Elizabeth as queen of Canada and keeps Canada's membership in the Commonwealth. This constitution was accepted by every province except Quebec.

In the national election on Sept. 4, 1984, the Progressive Conservative Party scored an overwhelming victory, fundamentally changing the country's political landscape. The Conservatives, led by Brian Mulroney, won the highest political majority in Canadian history. The dominant foreign issue was a free-trade pact with the U.S., a treaty bitterly opposed by the Liberal and New Democratic Parties. The conflict led to elections in Nov. 1988 that solidly reelected Mulroney and gave him a mandate to proceed with the agreement.

The issue of separatist sentiments in French-speaking Quebec flared up again in 1990 with the failure of the Meech Lake Accord. The accord was designed to bring Quebec into the constitution while easing its residents' fear of losing their identity within the English-speaking majority by giving it status as a "distinct society."

The economy continued to be mired in a long recession that many blamed on the free-trade agreement. Brian Mulroney's popularity continued to decline, causing him to resign before the next election. In June 1993 the governing Progressive Conservative Party chose Defense Minister Kim Campbell as its leader, making her the first female prime minister in Canadian history. The national election in Oct. 1993 resulted in the reemergence of the Liberal Party and the installation of Jean Chrétien as prime minister.

The Quebec referendum on secession in Oct. 1995 yielded a narrow rejection of the proposal, and separatists vowed to try again. Since then, however, the Quebec Liberal Party has replaced the Bloc Québécois as the ruling party.

On April 1, 1999, the Northwest Territories were officially divided to create a new territory in the east that would be governed by Canada's Inuits, who make up 85% of the area's population.

In July 2000, Stockwell Day of the new right-wing Canadian Alliance Party unexpectedly emerged as the leader of Canada's opposition. In Nov. 2000 elections, however, Prime Minister Jean Chrétien won a landslide victory for a third five-year term. After the election, the conservatives rapidly lost steam.

In recent years, Canada has introduced some of the world's most liberal social policies. Medical marijuana for the terminally or chronically ill was legalized in 2001; it began legally dispensing marijuana by prescription in July 2003. In 2003, Ontario and British Columbia legalized same-sex marriage; Quebec, the Yukon, and Manitoba followed suit in 2004. Same-sex marriage is now legal in provinces and territories representing 80% of Canada's population.

Canada-U.S. relations were strained in 2003 when Canada refused to join Washington's coalition supporting the war in Iraq. In December, Canada was incensed when the U.S. included the country on its list of countries banned from bidding on future reconstruction contracts in Iraq. Despite Canada's opposition to the war in Iraq, it had contributed $240 million to reconstruction efforts in Iraq and sent 2,000 soldiers to Afghanistan. Relations with the United States improved in Jan. 2004 after President Bush reversed the policy.

In Dec. 2003, Chrétien stepped down and handed the prime ministership to the new leader of Canada's Liberal Party, former finance minister Paul Martin. Chrétien had announced in 2002 that he would not seek a fourth term—conflict between Chrétien and Martin had divided and weakened the Liberal Party in recent years. A financial scandal uncovered in Feb. 2004 under Chretien's rule further diminished the party's standing. In June 2004, Martin was reelected prime minister, but the Liberal Party lost its majority in Parliament, which it had dominated for 11 years.

Cape Verde

REPUBLIC OF CAPE VERDE

National name: República de Cabo Verde
President: Pedro Pires (2001)
Prime Minister: José Maria Neves (2001)
Area: 1,557 sq mi (4,033 sq km)
Population (2004 est.): 415,294 (growth rate: 0.7%); birth rate: 26.1/1000; infant mortality rate: 49.1/1000; life expectancy: 70.1; density per sq mi: 267
Capital and largest city (2003 est.): Praia, 99,400.
Other large city: Mindelo, 66,100. **Monetary unit:** Cape Verdean escudo. **Languages:** Portuguese, Criuolo. **Ethnicity/race:** Creole (mulatto) 71%, African 28%, European 1%. **Religion:** Roman Catholic (infused with indigenous beliefs), Protestant (mostly Church of the Nazarene). **Literacy rate:** 77% (2003 est.)
Economic summary: GDP/PPP (2002 est.): $600 million; per capita $1,400. **Real growth rate:** 4%. **Inflation:** 3%. **Unemployment:** 21% (2000 est.). **Arable land:** 10%. **Agriculture:** bananas, corn, beans, sweet potatoes, sugarcane, coffee, peanuts; fish. **Labor force:** n.a. **Industries:** food and beverages, fish processing, shoes and garments, salt mining, ship repair. **Natural resources:** salt, basalt rock, limestone, kaolin, fish. **Exports:** $50.68 million (f.o.b., 2003 est.): fuel, shoes, garments, fish, hides. **Imports:** $315.5 million (f.o.b., 2003 est.): foodstuffs, industrial products, transport equipment, fuels. **Major trading partners:** Portugal, UK, France, U.S., Netherlands, Germany.

Geography Cape Verde, only slightly larger than Rhode Island, is an archipelago in the Atlantic 385 mi (500 km) west of Senegal.

The islands are divided into two groups: Barlavento in the north, composed of Santo Antão (291 sq mi; 754 sq km), Boa Vista (240 sq mi; 622 sq km), São Nicolau (132 sq mi; 342 sq km), São Vicente (88 sq mi; 246 sq km), Sal (83 sq mi; 298 sq km), and Santa Luzia (13 sq mi; 34 sq km); and Sotavento in the south, consisting of São Tiago (383 sq mi; 992 sq km), Fogo (184 sq mi; 477 sq km), Maio (103 sq mi; 267 sq km), and Brava (25 sq mi; 65 sq km). The islands are mostly mountainous, with the land deeply scarred by erosion. There is an active volcano on Fogo.

Government Republic.

History Uninhabited upon their discovery in 1456, the Cape Verde islands became part of the Portuguese empire in 1495. A majority of today's inhabitants are of mixed Portuguese and African ancestry.

Positioned on the great trade routes between Africa, Europe, and the New World, the islands became a prosperous center for the slave trade but suffered economic decline after the slave trade was abolished in 1876. In the 20th century, Cape Verde served as a shipping port.

In 1951, Cape Verde's status changed from a Portuguese colony to an overseas province, and in 1961 the inhabitants became full Portuguese citizens. An independence movement led by the African Party for the Independence of Guinea-Bissau (another former Portuguese colony) and Cape Verde (PAIGC) was founded in 1956. Following the 1974 coup in Portugal, after which Portugal began abandoning its colonial empire, the islands became independent (July 5, 1975).

On Jan. 13, 1991, the first multiparty elections since independence resulted in the ruling African Party for the Independence of Cape Verde (PAICV) losing its majority to the Movement for Democracy Party (MPD). The MPD candidate, Antonio Monteiro, won the subsequent presidential election, and was easily reelected in 1996.

In an effort to take advantage of its proximity to cross-Atlantic sea and air lanes, the government has embarked on a major expansion of its port and airport capacities. It is also modernizing the fishing fleet and enhancing its fish processing industry. These projects are being partly paid for by the EU and the World Bank, making Cape Verde one of the largest per capita aid recipients in the world. Disenchantment with the government's privatization program, continued high unemployment, and widespread poverty helped defeat the MPD in elections held in Jan. 2001. The PAICV swept back into power and José Maria Neves became prime minister.

Central African Republic

National name: République Centrafricaine
President: Gen. François Bozizé (2003)
Prime Minister: Célestin Gaombalet (2003)
Area: 240,534 sq mi (622,984 sq km)
Population (2004 est.): 3,742,482 (growth rate: 1.6%); birth rate: 35.6/1000; infant mortality rate: 92.2/1000; life expectancy: 41.4; density per sq mi: 16
Capital and largest city (2003 est.): Bangui, 810,000 (metro.area), 669,800 (city proper). **Monetary unit:** CFA Franc. **Languages:** French (official); Sangho (lingua franca, national), tribal languages. **Ethnicity/race:** Baya 33%, Banda 27%, Mandjia 13%, Sara 10%, Mboum 7%, M'Baka 4%, Yakoma 4%, other 2%. **Religions:** indigenous beliefs 35%, Protestant and Roman Catholic (both with animist influence) 25% each, Islam 15%. **Literacy rate:** 51% (2003 est.)
Economic summary: GDP/PPP (2003 est.): $4.584 billion; per capita $1,200. **Real growth rate:** 1%. **Inflation:** 3.6% (2001 est.). **Unemployment:** 8% (23% for Bangui) (2001 est.). **Arable land:** 3%. **Agriculture:** cotton, coffee, tobacco, manioc (tapioca), yams, millet, corn, bananas; timber. **Labor force:** n.a. **Industries:** diamond mining, logging, brewing, textiles, footwear, assembly of bicycles and motorcycles. **Natural resources:** diamonds, uranium, timber, gold, oil, hydropower. **Exports:** $172 million (f.o.b., 2003 est.): diamonds, timber, cotton, coffee, tobacco. **Imports:** $136 million (f.o.b., 2003 est.): food, textiles, petroleum products, machinery, electrical equipment, motor vehicles, chemicals, pharmaceuticals. **Major trading partners:** Benelux, Spain, Kazakhstan, France, U.S., Cameroon, Germany.

Geography Situated about 500 mi (805 km) north of the equator, the Central African Republic is a landlocked nation bordered by Cameroon, Chad, the Sudan, the Democratic Republic of the Congo, and the Republic of Congo. The Ubangi and the Shari are the largest of many rivers.

Government Multiparty republic since 1991.

History From the 16th to 19th century, the people of this region were ravaged by slave traders. The Banda, Baya, Ngbandi, and Azande make up the largest ethnic groups.

The French occupied the region in 1894. As the colony of Ubangi-Shari, what is now the Central African Republic was united with Chad in 1905. In 1910 it was joined with Gabon and the Middle Congo to become French Equatorial Africa. After World War II a rebellion in 1946 forced the French to grant self-government. In 1958 the territory voted to become an autonomous republic within the French Community, and on Aug. 13, 1960, President David Dacko proclaimed the republic's independence from France. Dacko moved the country into Beijing's orbit, but was overthrown in a coup on Dec. 31, 1965, by Col. Jean-Bédel Bokassa, army chief of staff.

On Dec. 4, 1976, the Central African Republic became the Central African Empire. Marshal Jean-Bédel Bokassa, who had ruled the republic since he took power in 1965, was declared Emperor Bokassa I. Brutality and excess characterized his regime. He was overthrown in a coup on Sept. 20, 1979. Former president David Dacko returned to power and changed the country's name back to the Central African Republic. An army coup on Sept. 1, 1981, deposed President Dacko again.

In 1991, President André Kolingba, under pressure, announced a move toward parliamentary democracy. In elections held in Aug. 1993, Prime Minister Ange-Félix Patassé defeated Kolingba. Part of Patassé's popularity rested on his pledge to pay the back salaries of the military and civil servants.

A 1994 economic upturn was too small to effectively improve the catastrophic financial condition of the nation. Patassé was unable to pay the salaries due government workers, and the military revolted in 1996. At Patassé's request, French troops suppressed the uprising. In 1998 the United Nations sent an all-African peacekeeping force to the country. In elections held in Sept. 1999, amid widespread charges of massive fraud, Patassé easily defeated Kolingba. Patassé survived a coup attempt in May 2001, but two years later, in March 2003, he was overthrown by Gen. François Bozizé. In the last two years, thousands of people fled the country's turmoil, creating a humanitarian crisis in neighboring Chad.

Chad

REPUBLIC OF CHAD

National name: République du Tchad
President: Idriss Déby (1990)
Prime Minister: Moussa Faki (2003)
Area: 495,752 sq mi (1,284,000 sq km)
Population (2004 est.): 9,538,544 (growth rate: 3.0%); birth rate: 46.5/1000; infant mortality rate: 94.8/1000; life expectancy: 48.2; density per sq mi: 19
Capital and largest city (2003 est.): N'Djamena, 609,600. **Monetary unit:** CFA Franc. **Languages:**

French, Arabic (both official); Sara; more than 120 languages and dialects. **Ethnicity/race:** 200 distinct groups. North and center, mostly Muslim: Arabs, Gorane (Toubou, Daza, Kreda), Zaghawa, Kanembou, Ouaddai, Baguirmi, Hadjerai, Fulbe, Kotoko, Hausa, Boulala, and Maba. South, mostly Christian or animist: Sara (Ngambaye, Mbaye, Goulaye), Moundang, Moussei, Massa.. **Religions:** Islam 51%, Christian 35%, animist 7%, other 7%. **Literacy rate:** 48% (2003 est.)

Economic summary: GDP/PPP (2003 est.): $10.86 billion; per capita $1,200. **Real growth rate:** 15%. **Inflation:** 6% (2002 est.). **Unemployment:** n.a. **Arable land:** 3%. **Agriculture:** cotton, sorghum, millet, peanuts, rice, potatoes, manioc (tapioca); cattle, sheep, goats, camels. **Labor force:** n.a.; agriculture more than 85% (subsistence farming, herding, and fishing). **Industries:** oil, cotton textiles, meatpacking, beer brewing, natron (sodium carbonate), soap, cigarettes, construction materials. **Natural resources:** petroleum (unexploited but exploration under way), uranium, natron, kaolin, fish (Lake Chad). **Exports:** $365 million (f.o.b., 2003 est.): cotton, cattle, gum arabic. **Imports:** $760 million (f.o.b., 2003 est.): machinery and transportation equipment, industrial goods, petroleum products, foodstuffs, textiles. **Major trading partners:** Portugal, Germany, U.S., Czech Republic, France, Nigeria, Poland, Spain, Morocco.

Geography A landlocked country in north-central Africa, Chad is about 85% the size of Alaska. Its neighbors are Niger, Libya, the Sudan, the Central African Republic, Cameroon, and Nigeria. Lake Chad, from which the country gets its name, lies on the western border with Niger and Nigeria. In the north is a desert that runs into the Sahara.

Government Republic.

History The area around Lake Chad has been inhabited since at least 500 B.C. In the 8th century A.D. Berbers began migrating to the area. Islam arrived in 1085, and by the 16th century a trio of rival kingdoms flourished: the Kanem-Bornu, the Baguirmi, and Ouaddaï. In 1883–1893, all three kingdoms came under the rule of the Sudanese conqueror Rabih al-Zubayr. In 1900, Rabih was overthrown by the French, who absorbed these kingdoms into the colony of French Equatorial Africa, as part of Ubangi-Shari (now the Central African Republic), in 1913. In 1946, the territory, now known as Chad, became an autonomous republic within the French Community. An independence movement led by the first premier and president, François (later Ngarta) Tombalbaye, achieved complete independence on Aug. 11, 1960. Tombalbaye was killed in the 1975 coup and succeeded by Gen. Félix Malloum, who faced a Libyan-financed civil war throughout his tenure in office. In 1977, Libya seized a strip of Chadian land and launched an invasion two years later.

Nine rival groups meeting in Lagos, Nigeria, in March 1979 agreed to form a provisional government headed by Goukouni Oueddei, a former rebel leader. Fighting broke out again in Chad in March 1980, when Defense Minister Hissen Habré challenged Goukouni and seized the capital. Libyan president Muammar al-Qaddafi, in Jan. 1981, proposed a merger of Chad with Libya. The Libyan proposal was rejected and Libyan troops withdrew from Chad that year, but in 1983 they poured back into the northern part of the country in support of Goukouni. France, in turn, sent troops to southern Chad in support of Habré. Government troops then launched an offensive in early 1987 that drove the Libyans out of most of the country.

In 1990, Idriss Déby, a former defense minister and head of the Patriotic Salvation Movement, overthrew Habré, suspended the constitution, and dissolved the legislature. In 1994 a new constitution was drafted and an amnesty for political prisoners was declared. Déby won multiparty elections in 1996 and was reelected in 2001. His rule has been marked by repression and corruption.

The Movement for Democracy and Justice in Chad (MDJC), led by Déby's former defense minister, Youssouf Togoimi, began fighting against the government in 1998. In Jan. 2002 a ceasefire was declared, but clashes persisted. In Jan. 2003, Chad's southeast-based rebels, the National Resistance Army, also signed a ceasefire with the government. The insurgency began in 1998, one of a half-dozen rebellions Déby has faced during his rule.

In June 2000 the World Bank agreed to provide more than $200 million to build a $3.7 billion pipeline connecting the oil fields in Chad to those in Cameroon. Oil revenues are estimated to earn $2.5 billion over the next 30 years. Human rights groups are concerned it will only benefit the oil companies and the political elite in Cameroon and Chad. The World Bank, however, has forced Chad to agree to spend 80% of the resulting oil revenues on education, health, infrastructure, and other social welfare projects desperately needed by this impoverished country. In Nov. 2004, Chad received its first oil check. In the next 25 years Chad is expected to make $80 million per year, increasing the government treasury by 50%.

In 2004, hundreds of thousands of refugees fled the fighting in Sudan's Darfur region for Chad, where they face hunger and disease in desperately undersupplied refugee camps.

Chile

REPUBLIC OF CHILE

National name: República de Chile
President: Ricardo Lagos (2000)
Area: 292,258 sq mi (756,950 sq km)
Population (2004 est.): 15,823,957 (growth rate: 1.0%); birth rate: 15.8/1000; infant mortality rate: 9.1/1000; life expectancy: 76.4; density per sq mi: 54
Capital and largest city (2003 est.): Santiago, 5,333,100 (metro.area), 4,372,800 (city proper). **Other large cities:** Viña del Mar, 303,100; Valparaíso, 274,100; Talcahuano, 252,800; Temuco, 247,200; Concepción, 217,600. **Monetary unit:** Chilean Peso. **Language:** Spanish. **Ethnicity/race:** white and white-Amerindian 95%, Amerindian 3%, other 2%. **Religions:** Roman Catholic 89%, Protestant 11%, small Jewish and Muslim populations. **Literacy rate:** 96% (2003 est.)
Economic summary: GDP/PPP (2003 est.): $154.6 billion; per capita $9,900. **Real growth rate:** 3.2%. **Inflation:** 1.1%. **Unemployment:** 8.5%. **Arable land:** 3%. **Agriculture:** wheat, corn, grapes, beans, sugar beets, potatoes, fruit; beef, poultry, wool; fish; timber. **Labor force:** 5.68 million (2000 est.); agriculture 14%, industry 27%, services 59% (1997 est.). **Industries:** copper, other minerals, foodstuffs, fish processing, iron and steel, wood and wood products, transport equipment, cement, textiles. **Natural resources:** copper, timber, iron ore, nitrates, precious metals, molybdenum, hydropower. **Exports:** $20.44 billion (f.o.b., 2003 est.): copper, fish, fruits, paper and pulp, chemicals. **Imports:** $17.4 billion (f.o.b., 2003 est.): consumer goods, chemicals, motor vehicles, fuels, electrical machinery, heavy industrial machinery, food. **Major trading partners:** U.S., Japan, China, Mexico, Italy, UK, Argentina, Brazil, Germany.

Geography Situated south of Peru and west of Bolivia and Argentina, Chile fills a narrow 1,800-mile (2,897 km) strip between the Andes and the Pacific. One-third of Chile is covered by the towering ranges of the Andes. In the north is the driest place on Earth, the Atacama Desert, and in the center is a 700-mile-long (1,127 km), thickly populated valley with most of Chile's arable land. At the southern tip of Chile's mainland is Punta Arenas, the southernmost city in the world, and beyond that lies the Strait of Magellan and Tierra del Fuego, an island divided between Chile and Argentina. The southernmost point of South America is Cape Horn, a 1,390-foot (424 m) rock on Horn Island in the Wollaston group, which belongs to Chile. Chile also claims sovereignty over 482,628 sq mi (1,250,000 sq km) of Antarctic territory; the Juan Fernández Islands, about 400 mi (644 km) west of the mainland; and Easter Island, about 2,000 mi (3,219 km) west.

Government Republic.

History Chile was originally under the control of the Incas in the north and the nomadic Araucanos in the south. In 1541, a Spaniard, Pedro de Valdivia, founded Santiago. Chile won its independence from Spain in 1818 under Bernardo O'Higgins and an Argentinian, José de San Martin. O'Higgins, dictator until 1823, laid the foundations of the modern state with a two-party system and a centralized government.

The dictator from 1830 to 1837, Diego Portales, fought a war with Peru in 1836–1839 that expanded Chilean territory. Chile fought the War of the Pacific with Peru and Bolivia from 1879 to 1883, winning Antofagasta, Bolivia's only outlet to the sea, and extensive areas from Peru. Pedro Montt led a revolt that overthrew José Balmaceda in 1891 and established a parliamentary dictatorship lasting until a new constitution was adopted in 1925. Industrialization began before World War I and led to the formation of Marxist groups. Juan Antonio Ríos, president during World War II, was originally pro-Nazi but in 1944 led his country into the war on the side of the Allies.

In 1970, Salvador Allende became the first president in a non-Communist country freely elected on a Marxist program. Allende quickly established relations with Cuba and the People's Republic of China, introduced Marxist economic and social reforms, and nationalized many private companies, including U.S.-owned ones. In Sept. 1973, Allende was overthrown and killed in a military coup covertly sponsored by the CIA, ending a 46-year era of constitutional government in Chile.

The coup was led by a four-man junta headed by Army Chief of Staff Augusto Pinochet, who eventually assumed the office of president. Committed to "exterminat[ing] Marxism," the junta suspended Parliament, banned political activity, and severely curbed civil liberties. Pinochet's brutal dictatorship led to the imprisonment, torture, execution, and expulsion of thousands of Chileans. The economy, in tatters under Allende's socialist revolution, gradually improved after Chile's return to privatization under Pinochet. In 1989, Pinochet lost a plebiscite on whether he should remain in power. He stepped down in Jan. 1990 in favor of Patricio Aylwin, who was elected in Dec. 1989 as the head of a 17-party coalition. In Dec. 1993, Eduardo Frei Ruiz-Tagle, the candidate of a center-left coalition and son of a previous president, was elected president.

Pinochet, who had retained his post as army commander in chief after the 1989 plebiscite, retired in March 1998. In Oct. 1998, he was arrested and detained in England on an extradition request issued by a Spanish judge who sought Pinochet in connection with the disappearance of Spanish citizens during his rule. British courts ultimately denied his extradition, and Pinochet returned to Chile in March 2000, where the courts eventually ruled that he was mentally unfit to stand trial. In 2004, however, Chile's Supreme Court stripped him of immunity, and he is expected to face trial for at least some of the abuses that occurred during his 17-year rule.

Ricardo Lagos became president in March 2000, the first socialist to run the country since Allende. Chile's economic growth slowed to 3% for 2001, partly the result of a drop in international copper prices and the economic turmoil in neighboring Argentina. In 2003 there were several minor financial scandals involving insider information and bribery. In response, Lagos introduced new reforms promising greater transparency. In 2004, Chile passed a law permitting divorce for the first time.

China

PEOPLE'S REPUBLIC OF CHINA

National name: Zhonghua Renmin Gongheguo
President: Hu Jintao (2003)
Prime Minister: Wen Jiabao (2003)
Area: 3,705,386 sq mi (9,596,960 sq km)[1]
Population (2004 est.): 1,298,847,624 (growth rate: 0.6%); birth rate: 13.0/1000; infant mortality rate: 25.3/1000; life expectancy: 72.0; density per sq mi: 351
Capital (2003 est.): Beijing, 9,376,200 (metro. area), 6,619,000 (city proper). **Largest cities:** Shanghai, 12,039,900 (metro. area), 9,005,600 (city proper); Tianjin (Tientsin), 4,333,900; Wuhan, 3,959,700; Shenyang (Mukden), 3,574,100; Guangzhou, 3,473,800; Haerbin, 2,904,900; Xian, 2,642,100; Chungking (Chongqing) 2,370,100; Chengdu, 2,011,000; Hong Kong (Xianggang), 1,361,200.
Monetary unit: Yuan/Renminbi. **Languages:** Standard Chinese (Mandarin/Putonghua), Yue (Cantonese), Wu (Shanghaiese), Minbei (Fuzhou), Minnan (Hokkien-Taiwanese), Xiang, Gan, Hakka dialects, minority languages. **Ethnicity/race:** Han Chinese 91.9%, Zhuang, Uygur, Hui, Yi, Tibetan, Miao, Manchu, Mongol, Buyi, Korean, and other nationalities 8.1%.. **Religions:** Christian 3%-4%; Daoist (Taoist), Buddhist, Muslim 1%-2%. Officially atheist (2002 est.). **Literacy rate:** 86% (2003 est.)
Economic summary: GDP/PPP (2003 est.): $6.449 trillion; per capita $5,000. **Real growth rate:** 9.1% (official data). **Inflation:** 1.2%. **Unemployment:** urban unemployment roughly 10%; substantial unemployment and underemployment in rural areas. **Arable land:** 13%. **Agriculture:** rice, wheat, potatoes, sorghum, peanuts, tea, millet, barley, cotton, oilseed; pork; fish. **Labor force:** 753.6 million (2002 est.); agriculture 50%, industry 22%, services 28% (2001 est.). **Industries:** iron and steel, coal, machine building, armaments, textiles and apparel, petroleum, cement, chemical fertilizers, footwear, toys, food processing, automobiles, consumer electronics, telecommunications. **Natural resources:** coal, iron ore, petroleum, natural gas, mercury, tin, tungsten, antimony, manganese, molybdenum, vanadium, magnetite, aluminum, lead, zinc, uranium, hydropower potential (world's largest). **Exports:** $436.1 billion (f.o.b., 2003 est.): machinery and equipment; textiles and clothing, footwear, toys and sporting goods; mineral fuels. **Imports:** $397.4 billion (f.o.b., 2003 est.): machinery and equipment, mineral fuels, plastics, iron and steel, chemicals. **Major trading partners:** U.S., Hong Kong, Japan, South Korea, Taiwan, Germany.

---

1. Including Manchuria and Tibet.

Geography The greater part of the country is mountainous. Its principal ranges are the Tien Shan, the Kunlun chain, and the Trans-Himalaya. In the southwest is Tibet, which China annexed in 1950. The Gobi Desert lies to the north. China proper consists of three great river systems: the Yellow River (Huang He), 2,109 mi (5,464 km) long; the Yangtze River (Chang Jiang), the third-longest river in the world at 2,432 mi (6,300 km); and the Pearl River (Zhu Jiang), 848 mi (2,197 km) long.

Government Communist state.

History The earliest recorded human settlements in what is today called China were discovered in the Huang He basin and date from about 5000 B.C. During the Shang dynasty (1500–1000 B.C.), the precursor of modern China's ideographic writing system developed, allowing the emerging feudal states of the era to achieve an advanced stage of civilization, rivaling in sophistication anything found at the time in Europe, the Middle East, or the Americas. It was following this initial flourishing of civilization, in a period known as the Chou dynasty (1122–249 B.C.), that Lao-tse, Confucius, Mo Ti, and Mencius laid the foundation of Chinese philosophical thought.

The feudal states, often at war with one another, were first united under Emperor Ch'in Shih Huang Ti, during whose reign (246–210 B.C.) work was begun on the Great Wall of China, a monumental bulwark against invasion from the West. Although the Great Wall symbolized China's desire to protect itself from the outside world, under the Han dynasty (206 B.C.–A.D. 220), the civilization conducted extensive commercial trading with the West.

In the T'ang dynasty (618–907)—often called the golden age of Chinese history—painting, sculpture, and poetry flourished, and woodblock printing, which enabled the mass production of books, made its earliest known appearance. The Mings, last of the native rulers (1368–1644), overthrew the Mongol, or Yuan, dynasty (1271–1368) established by Kublai Khan. The Mings in turn were overthrown in 1644 by invaders from the north, the Manchus.

China remained largely isolated from the rest of the world's civilizations, closely restricting foreign activities. By the end of the 18th century only Canton (location of modern-day Hong Kong) and the Portuguese port of Macao were open to European merchants. But with the first Anglo-Chinese War in 1839–1842, a long period of instability and concessions to Western colonial powers began. Following the war, several ports were opened up for trading, and Hong Kong was ceded to Britain. Treaties signed after further hostilities (1856–1860) weakened Chinese sovereignty and gave foreigners immunity from Chinese jurisdiction. European powers took advantage of the disastrous Sino-Japanese War of 1894–1895 to gain further trading concessions from China. Peking's response, the Boxer Rebellion (1900), was suppressed by an international force.

The death of Empress Dowager Tzu Hsi in 1908 and the accession of the infant emperor Hsüan T'ung (Pu-Yi) were followed by a nationwide rebellion led by Dr. Sun Yat-sen, who overthrew the Manchus and became the first president of the Provisional Chinese Republic in 1911. Dr. Sun resigned in favor of Yuan Shih-k'ai, who suppressed the Republicans in a bid to consolidate his power. Yuan's death in June 1916 was followed by years of civil war between rival militarists and Dr. Sun's Republicans. Nationalist forces, led by General Chiang Kai-shek and with the advice of Communist experts, soon occupied most of China, setting up a Kuomintang regime in 1928. Internal strife continued, however, and Chiang eventually broke with the Communists.

On Sept. 18, 1931, Japan launched an invasion of Manchuria, capturing the province. Tokyo set up a puppet state dubbed Manchukuo and installed the last Manchu emperor, Henry Pu-Yi (Hsüan T'ung), as its nominal leader. Japanese troops moved to seize China's northern provinces in July 1937 but were resisted by Chiang, who had been able to use the Japanese invasion to unite most of China behind him. Within two years, however, Japan had seized most of the nation's eastern ports and railways. The Kuomintang government retreated first to Hankow and then to Chungking, while the Japanese set up a puppet government at Nanking, headed by Wang Jingwei.

Japan's surrender to the Western Allies in 1945 touched off civil war between the Kuomintang forces under Chiang and Communists led by Mao Zedong, who had been battling since the 1930s for control of China. Despite U.S. aid, the Kuomintang were overcome by the Soviet-supported Communists, and Chiang and his followers were forced to flee the mainland, establishing a government-in-exile on the island of Formosa (Taiwan). The Mao regime proclaimed the People's Republic of China on Oct. 1, 1949, with Beijing as the new capital and Zhou Enlai as premier.

After the Korean War began in June 1950, China led the Communist bloc in supporting North Korea, and on Nov. 26, 1950, the Mao regime sent troops to assist the North in its efforts to capture the South.

In an attempt to restructure China's primarily agrarian economy, Mao undertook the "Great Leap Forward" campaign in 1958, a disastrous program that aimed to combine the establishment of rural communes with a crash program of village industrialization. The Great Leap forced the abandonment of farming activities, leading to widespread famine in which more than 20 million people died of malnutrition.

In 1959, a failed uprising against China's invasion and occupation of Tibet forced Tibetan Buddhism's spiritual leader, the Dalai Lama, and 100,000 of his followers to flee to India. The invasion of Tibet and a perceived rivalry for the leadership of the world Communist movement caused a serious souring of relations between China and the USSR, former allies. In 1965 Tibet was formally made an autonomous region of China. China's harsh religious and cultural persecution of Tibetans, which continues to this day, has spawned growing international protest.

The failure of the Great Leap Forward touched off a power struggle within the Chinese Communist Party between Mao and his supporters and a reformist faction including future premier Deng Xiaoping. Mao moved to Shanghai, and from that base he and his supporters waged what they called the Cultural Revolution. Beginning in the spring of 1966, Mao ordered the closing of schools and the formation of ideologically pure Red Guard units, dominated by youths and students. The Red Guards campaigned against "old ideas, old culture, old habits, and old customs." Millions died as a series of violent purges were carried out. By early 1967, the Cultural Revolution had succeeded in bolstering Mao's position as China's paramount leader.

Anxious to exploit the Sino-Soviet rift, the Nixon administration made a dramatic announcement in July 1971 that National Security Adviser Henry Kissinger had secretly visited Beijing and reached an agreement whereby Nixon would visit China. The movement toward reconciliation, which signaled the end of the U.S. containment policy toward

China, provided momentum for China's admission to the UN. Despite U.S. opposition to expelling Taiwan (Nationalist China), the world body overwhelmingly voted to oust Taiwan in favor of Beijing's Communist government.

President Nixon went to Beijing for a week early in 1972, meeting Mao as well as Zhou. The summit ended with a historic communiqué on Feb. 28, in which both nations promised to work toward improved relations. Full diplomatic relations were barred by China as long as the U.S. continued to recognize the legitimacy of Nationalist China.

Following Zhou's death on Jan. 8, 1976, his successor, Vice Premier Deng Xiaoping, was supplanted within a month by Hua Guofeng, former minister of public security. Hua became permanent premier in April. In Oct. he was named successor to Mao as chairman of the Communist Party. But Mao's death on Sept. 10 unleashed the bitter intraparty rivalries that had been suppressed since the Cultural Revolution. Old opponents of Mao launched a campaign against his widow, Jiang Qing, and three of her "radical" colleagues. The so-called Gang of Four was denounced for having undermined the party, the government, and the economy. They were tried and convicted in 1981. Meanwhile, in 1977, Deng Xiaoping was reinstated as deputy premier, chief of staff of the army, and member of the Central Committee of the Politburo.

Beijing and Washington announced full diplomatic relations on Jan. 1, 1979, and the Carter administration abrogated the Taiwan defense treaty. Deputy Premier Deng sealed the agreement with a visit to the U.S. that coincided with the opening of embassies in both capitals on March 1. On Deng's return from the U.S., Chinese troops invaded and briefly occupied an area along Vietnam's northern border. The action was seen as a response to Vietnam's invasion of Cambodia and ouster of the Khmer Rouge government, which China had supported.

In 1981, Deng protégé Hu Yaobang replaced Hua Guofeng as party chairman. Deng became chairman of the committee's military commission, giving him control over the army. The body's 215 members concluded the session with a statement holding Mao Zedong responsible for the "grave blunder" of the Cultural Revolution.

Under Deng Xiaoping's leadership, meanwhile, China's Communist ideology went through a massive reinterpretation, and sweeping economic changes were set in motion in the early 1980s. The Chinese scrapped the personality cult that idolized Mao Zedong, muted Mao's old call for class struggle and exportation of the Communist revolution, and imported Western technology and management techniques to replace the Marxist tenets that had slowed modernization. Deng concluded an agreement for the return of Hong Kong following the expiration of Britain's 99-year lease on the territory on July 1, 1997.

The removal of Hu Yaobang as party chairman in Jan. 1987 signaled a hard-line resurgence within the party. Hu—who had become a hero to many reform-minded Chinese—was replaced by former premier Zhao Ziyang. With the death of Hu in April 1989, the ideological struggle spilled into the streets of the capital, as student demonstrators occupied Beijing's Tiananmen Square in May, calling for democratic reforms. Less than a month later, the demonstrations were crushed in a bloody crackdown as troops and tanks moved into the square and fired on protesters, killing several hundred.

In annual sessions of the rubber-stamp National People's Congress in 1992 and 1993, the government called for accelerating the drive for economic reform, but the sessions were widely seen as an effort to maintain China's moves toward a market economy while retaining political authoritarianism. At the session in 1993, Communist Party leader Jiang Zemin was elected president, while hard-liner Li Peng was reelected to another five-year term as prime minister. Since 1993, the Chinese economy has continued to grow rapidly.

Deng Xiaoping's death in Feb. 1997 left a younger generation in charge of managing the enormous country. In 1998, Prime Minister Zhu Rongji introduced a sweeping program to privatize state-run businesses and further liberalize the nation's economy, a move lauded by Western economists.

On July 1, 1997, when Britain's lease on the New Territories expired, Hong Kong returned to Chinese sovereignty, and in 1999, the Portuguese colony of Macao also was returned to Chinese rule.

In Aug. 1999, China rounded up thousands of members of the Falun Gong sect, a highly popular religious movement that combines elements of Buddhism, Taoism, and martial arts. China, which has now outlawed the sect, was thought to consider the apolitical spiritual group threatening because its numbers exceeded the membership of the Chinese Communist Party.

China was admitted to the World Trade Organization in Nov. 2001. Its entry ended a 15-year debate over whether China is entitled to the full trading rights of capitalist countries.

In Nov. 2002, Vice President Hu Jintao became general secretary of the Communist Party at the 16th Party Congress, succeeding President Jiang. But Jiang retained various positions of power, including head of the Central Military Commission, and filled the Politburo Standing Committee with his protégés. Jiang thus positioned himself to rule as éminence grise for the next several years. Hu Jintao assumed the presidency in March 2003.

The World Health Organization labeled severe acute respiratory syndrome (SARS) a "worldwide health threat" in March 2003. Officials believe the potentially deadly virus originated in Guangdong Province. After coming under fire by the WHO for underreporting the number of its SARS cases, China finally revealed the alarming extent of its epidemic.

China became the third country (after Russia and the U.S.) to launch a person into space in Oct. 2003, when Yang Liwei orbited the Earth 14 times aboard the *Shenzhou V* spacecraft.

On Sept. 24, 2004, former president Jiang Zemin stepped down as China's military chief, thus completing the transfer of power to President Hu that had begun nearly two years earlier.

Hong Kong

Status: Special Administrative Region of China
Chief Executive: Tung Chee Hwa (1997)
Area: 422 sq mi (1,092 sq km)
Population (2004 est.): 6,855,125 (growth rate: 0.6%); birth rate: 7.2/1000; infant mortality rate: 3.0/1000; life expectancy: 81.4; density per sq mi: 16,259

Hong Kong consists of the island of Hong Kong (32 sq mi; 83 sq km), Stonecutters' Island, Kowloon Peninsula, and the New Territories on the adjoining mainland. The island of Hong Kong was ceded to Britain in 1841. Stonecutters' Island and Kowloon were annexed in 1860, and the New Territories, which are mainly agricultural lands, were leased from China in 1898 for 99 years. On July 1, 1997, Hong Kong was returned to

China. The vibrant capitalist enclave retains its status as a free port, with its laws to remain unchanged for 50 years. Chief Executive Tung Chee Hwa formulated a policy agenda based upon the concept of "one country, two systems," thus preserving Hong Kong's economic independence.

In a series of massive demonstrations in July 2003, more than 500,000 people took to the streets of Hong Kong to protest proposed anti-subversion laws that curtailed civil rights. Surprisingly, Tung Chee-hwa scrapped the law in September. After pro-democracy parties handed pro-China parties a stunning defeat in November elections, China quickly moved to stifle the democracy movement. In April 2004, Beijing officials banned popular elections for Hong Kong's chief executive, scheduled for 2007, and also postponed indefinitely the expansion of the number of popularly elected legislators. Hundreds of thousands of protesters took to the streets again in July, this time boldly calling for democracy and criticizing the Chinese government. Pro-democracy candidates took about 60% of the popular vote in Sept. 2004 elections, but Beijing's legislative system granted them only 40% of the seats in the legislature.

Macao

Status: Special Administrative Region of China
Chief Executive: Edmund Ho (1999)
Area: 10 sq mi (25.4 sq km)
Population (2004 est.): 445,286 (average annual growth rate: 0.9%); birth rate: 8.0/1000; infant mortality rate: 4.4/1000; life expectancy: 82.0; density per sq mi: 45,405

Colonized by the Portuguese in 1557, Macao was the oldest European outpost in China. In 1987, Portugal and China reached an agreement to return Macao to Chinese rule on Dec. 20, 1999. They agreed upon provisions to insure the autonomy of Macao, including its right to elect local leaders, the right of its residents to travel freely, and the right to maintain its way of life for 50 years after the start of Chinese rule.

Colombia

REPUBLIC OF COLOMBIA

National name: República de Colombia
President: Alvaro Uribe (2002)
Area: 439,733 sq mi (1,138,910 sq km)
Population (2004 est.): 42,310,775 (growth rate: 1.5%); birth rate: 21.2/1000; infant mortality rate: 21.7/1000; life expectancy: 71.4; density per sq mi: 96
Capital and largest city (2003 est.): Santafé de Bogotá, 6,837,800. **Other large cities:** Cali, 2,283,200; Medellín, 1,957,800; Barranquilla, 1,330,400; Cartagena, 901,500. **Monetary unit:** Colombian Peso. **Language:** Spanish. **Ethnicity/race:** mestizo 58%, white 20%, mulatto 14%, black 4%, mixed black-Amerindian 3%, Amerindian 1%. **Religion:** Roman Catholic 90%. **Literacy rate:** 93% (2003 est.)
Economic summary: GDP/PPP (2003 est.): $262.5 billion; per capita $6,300. **Real growth rate:** 3.4%. **Inflation:** 7.2%. **Unemployment:** 13.6%. **Arable land:** 2%. **Agriculture:** coffee, cut flowers, bananas, rice, tobacco, corn, sugarcane, cocoa beans, oilseed, vegetables; forest products; shrimp. **Labor force:** 18.3 million (1999 est.); services 46%, agriculture 30%, industry 24% (1990). **Industries:** textiles, food processing, oil, clothing and footwear, beverages, chemicals, cement; gold, coal, emeralds. **Natural resources:** petroleum, natural gas, coal, iron ore, nickel, gold, copper, emeralds, hydropower. **Exports:**

$12.96 billion (f.o.b., 2003 est.): petroleum, coffee, coal, apparel, bananas, cut flowers. **Imports:** $13.06 billion (f.o.b., 2003 est.): industrial equipment, transportation equipment, consumer goods, chemicals, paper products, fuels, electricity. **Major trading partners:** U.S., Venezuela, Ecuador, Mexico, Japan, Brazil, Germany.

Geography Colombia is bordered on the northwest by Panama, on the east by Venezuela and Brazil, and on the southwest by Peru and Ecuador. Through the western half of the country, three Andean ranges run north and south. The eastern half is a low, jungle-covered plain, drained by spurs of the Amazon and Orinoco Rivers, inhabited mostly by isolated tropical-forest Indian tribes. The fertile plateau and valley of the eastern range are the most densely populated parts of the country.

Government Republic.

History Little is known about the various Indian tribes who inhabited Colombia before the Spanish arrived. In 1510 Spaniards founded Darien, the first permanent European settlement on the American mainland. In 1538 they established the colony of New Granada, the area's name until 1861.

After a 14-year struggle, during which time Simón Bolívar's Venezuelan troops won the battle of Boyacá in Colombia on Aug. 7, 1819, independence was attained in 1824. Bolívar united Colombia, Venezuela, Panama, and Ecuador in the Republic of Greater Colombia (1819–1830), but lost Venezuela and Ecuador to separatists. Two political parties dominated the region: the Conservatives believed in a strong central government and a powerful church; the Liberals believed in a decentralized government, strong regional power, and a less influential role for the church. Bolívar was himself a Conservative, while his vice president, Francisco de Paula Santander, was the founder of the Liberal Party.

Santander served as president between 1832 and 1836, a period of relative stability, but by 1840 civil war erupted. Other periods of Liberal dominance (1849–1857 and 1861–1880), which sought to disestablish the Roman Catholic Church, were marked by insurrection. Nine different governments followed, each rewriting the constitution. In 1861 the country was called the United States of New Granada; in 1863 it became the United States of Colombia; and in 1885, it became the Republic of Colombia.

In 1899 a brutal civil war broke out, the War of a Thousand Days, that lasted until 1902. The following year, Colombia lost its claims to Panama because it refused to ratify the lease to the U.S. of the Canal Zone. Panama declared its independence in 1903.

The Conservatives held power until 1930, when revolutionary pressure put the Liberals back in power. The Liberal administrations of Enrique Olaya Herrera and Alfonso López (1930–1938) were marked by social reforms that failed to solve the country's problems, and in 1946, a period of insurrection and banditry broke out, referred to as La Violencia, which claimed hundreds of thousands of lives by 1958. Laureano Gómez (1950–1953); the army chief of staff, Gen. Gustavo Rojas Pinilla (1953–1956); and a military junta (1956–1957) sought to curb disorder by repression.

Marxist guerrilla groups organized in the 1960s and 1970s, most notably the May 19th Movement (M-19), the National Liberation Army (ELN), and the Revolutionary Armed Forces of Colombia (FARC), plunging the country into violence and instability. In the 1970s and 1980s, Colombia became one of the international centers for illegal drug production and trafficking, and at times the drug cartels (the Medillin and Cali cartels were the most notorious) virtually controlled the country. In the 1990s, numerous right-wing paramilitary groups also formed, made up of drug traffickers and landowners. The umbrella group for these paramilitaries is the United Self-Defense Forces of Colombia (AUC).

Belisario Betancur Cuartas, a Conservative who assumed the presidency in 1982, unsuccessfully attempted to stem the guerrilla violence. In an official war against drug trafficking, Colombia became a public battleground with bombs, killings, and kidnappings. By 1989, homicide had become the leading cause of death in the nation. Elected president in 1990, César Gaviria Trujillo proposed lenient punishment in exchange for surrender by the leading drug dealers. Ernesto Samper of the Liberal Party became president in 1994. In 1996 he was accused of accepting campaign contributions from drug traffickers, but the House of Representatives absolved him of the charges.

Andrés Pastrana Arango was elected president in 1998, pledging to clean up corruption. In Dec. 1999 the Colombian military reported that 2,787 people were kidnapped that year—the largest number in the world—and blamed rebels. The murder rate soared in 1999, with some 23,000 people reported killed by leftist guerrillas, right-wing paramilitaries, drug traffickers, and common criminals. The violence has created more than 100,000 refugees, while 2 million Colombians have fled the country in recent years.

In Aug. 2000, the U.S. government approved "Plan Colombia," pledging $1.3 billion to fight drug trafficking. Pastrana used the plan to undercut drug production and prevent guerrilla groups from benefiting from drug sales. In Aug. 2001, Pastrana signed "war legislation," which expanded the rights of the military in dealing with rebels.

Alvaro Uribe of the Liberal party easily won the presidential election in May 2002. He took office in August, pledging to get tough on the rebels and drug traffickers by increasing military spending and seeking U.S. military cooperation. An upsurge in violence accompanied his inauguration, and Uribe declared a state of emergency within a week. In his first year, Uribe beefed up Colombia's security forces with the help of U.S. special forces, launched an aggressive campaign against the drug trade, and passed several economic reform bills.

In May 2004, the UN announced that Colombia's 39-year-long drug war had created the worst humanitarian crisis in the Western Hemisphere. More than 2 million people have been forced to leave their homes and several Indian tribes are close to extinction. It now has the third largest displaced population in the world, with only Sudan and the Congo having more. Uribe has produced some impressive results in fixing his country's ills, however. According to his defense minister, during 2003 more than 16,000 suspected leftist guerrillas and right-wing paramilitary vigilantes either surrendered, were apprehended, or were killed. The U.S. Office of National Drug Control Policy has announced that coca production has declined by 30% in the last two years—Colombia produces 75% of the world's cocaine.

Comoros

UNION OF COMOROS ISLANDS

President: Azali Assoumani (2002)
Area: 838 sq mi (2,170 sq km)
Population (2004 est.): 651,901 (growth rate: 1.4%); birth rate: 28.7/1000; infant mortality rate: 93.9/1000; life expectancy: 49.5; density per sq mi: 778

Capital and largest city (2003 est.): Moroni (on Grande Comoro), 60,200. **Monetary unit:** Franc. **Languages:** Arabic and French (both official), Shikomoro (Swahili/Arabic blend). **Ethnicity/race:** Antalote, Cafre, Makoa, Oimatsaha, Sakalava. **Religions:** Sunni Muslim 98%, Roman Catholic 2%. **Literacy rate:** 57% (2003 est.)
Economic summary: GDP/PPP: (2002 est.) $441 million; per capita $700. **Real growth rate:** 2%. **Inflation:** 3.5% (2001 est.). **Unemployment:** 20% (1996 est.). **Arable land:** 35%. **Agriculture:** vanilla, cloves, perfume essences, copra, coconuts, bananas, cassava (tapioca). **Labor force:** 144,500 (1996 est.): agriculture 80%. **Industries:** tourism, perfume distillation. **Natural resources:** negl. **Exports:** $28 million (f.o.b., 2002 est.): vanilla, ylang-ylang, cloves, perfume oil, copra. **Imports:** $88 million (f.o.b., 2002 est.): rice and other foodstuffs, consumer goods; petroleum products, cement, transport equipment. **Major trading partners:** France, Germany, U.S., Singapore, Netherlands, South Africa, Japan, Kenya, UAE, Mauritius, Thailand (2002).

Geography The Comoros Islands—Grande Comoro (Ngazidja), Anjouan, Mohéli, and Mayotte (which is not part of the country and retains ties to France)—are an archipelago of volcanic origin in the Indian Ocean, 190 mi off the coast of Mozambique.

Government Emerging republic.

History Comoros was frequented by travelers from Africa, Madagascar, Indonesia, and Arabia before the first Europeans encountered the islands. Arabic influence has been the strongest.

France colonized Mayotte in 1843 and by 1904 had annexed the remainder of the archipelago. In a 1974 referendum, 95% of the population voted for independence. The exception was Mayotte, which, with its Christian majority, voted against joining the other mainly Islamic islands in independence. Today it remains a French overseas territory.

The remaining Comoros islands declared themselves independent on July 6, 1975, with Ahmed Abdallah as president. A month after independence, he was overthrown by Justice Minister Ali Soilih. This was only the beginning of Comoros's chronic instability: the country has gone through more than 20 coups since independence and has experienced several attempts at secession. Orchestrating at least four of these coups was a group of white mercenaries known as Les Affreux (The Terrible Ones), and their notorious leader, Frenchman "Colonel" Bob Denard. Denard fled Comoros in 1989, when 3,000 French soldiers were sent after him.

The island of Anjouan declared independence on Aug. 3, 1997, after months of protests and clashes with security forces. The secessionists wanted a return to French rule, contending that independence from France has brought economic disaster and political chaos. Mohéli, the smallest island, also seceded. But France refused to support the secession of either island. In Sept. 1997, President Mohamed Taki's forces attempted to retake Anjouan but failed.

In 1999, Col. Azali Assoumani led a coup, overthrowing interim president Tadjidine. He promised interim military rule would end in a year, a pledge the Organization of African Unity would continue to remind him of. After years of aborted peace talks, a new constitution was approved in March 2002, and the three islands were reunited. Each island elected its own president, and in May a federal president was elected from Grande Comoro, former military coup leader Assoumani. In Feb. 2003, a coup against Assoumani was thwarted.

Congo, Republic of

REPUBLIC OF CONGO

National name: République Populaire du Congo
President: Denis Sassou-Nguesso (1997)
Area: 132,046 sq mi (342,000 sq km)
Population (2004 est.): 2,998,040 (growth rate: 3.0%);
birth rate: 44.7/1000; infant mortality rate: 94.7/1000;
life expectancy: 49.1; density per sq mi: 23
Capital and largest city (2003 est.): Brazzaville,
1,169,900. **Other large city:** Pointe-Noire, 544,200.
Monetary unit: CFA Franc. **Languages:** French
(official), Lingala, Monokutuba, Kikongo, many local
languages and dialects. **Ethnicity/race:** Kongo 48%,
Sangha 20%, M'Bochi 12%, Teke 17%, Europeans
(mostly French) and other 3% . **Religions:** Christian
50%, animist 48%, Islam 2%. **Literacy rate:** 84%
(2003 est.)
Economic summary: GDP/PPP (2003 est.): $2.186
billion; per capita $700. **Real growth rate:** 2%.
Inflation: 4% (2002 est.). **Unemployment:** n.a.
Arable land: 1%. **Agriculture:** cassava (tapioca),
sugar, rice, corn, peanuts, vegetables, coffee, cocoa;
forest products. **Labor force:** n.a. **Industries:**
petroleum extraction, cement, lumber, brewing, sugar,
palm oil, soap, flour, cigarettes. **Natural resources:**
petroleum, timber, potash, lead, zinc, uranium, copper,
phosphates, natural gas, hydropower. **Exports:** $2.293
billion (f.o.b., 2003): petroleum, lumber, plywood,
sugar, cocoa, coffee, diamonds. **Imports:** $666.9
million (f.o.b., 2003 est.): capital equipment,
construction materials, foodstuffs. **Major trading
partners:** Taiwan, South Korea, China, U.S.,
Germany, France, Italy, Belgium, India.

Geography The Congo is situated in west-central
Africa astride the equator. It borders Gabon, Cam-
eroon, the Central African Republic, the Democratic
Republic of the Congo, and the Angola exclave of
Cabinda, with a short stretch of coast on the South
Atlantic. Its area is nearly three times that of Pennsyl-
vania. Most of the inland is tropical rain forest,
drained by tributaries of the Congo River.

Government Dictatorship.

History In precolonial times, the region now called
the Republic of Congo was dominated by three kingdoms: Kongo (originating about 1000), the Loango
(flourishing in the 17th century), and Tio. After the
Portuguese located the Congo River in 1482, commerce was carried on with the tribes, especially the
slave trade.

The Frenchman Pierre Savorgnan de Brazza signed a
treaty with Makoko, ruler of the Bateke people, in
1880, thus establishing French control. It was first
called French Congo, and after 1905 Middle Congo.
With Gabon and Ubangi-Shari, it became the colony of
French Equatorial Africa in 1910. Abuse of laborers led
to public outcry against the French colonialists as well
as rebellions among the Congolese, but the exploitation
of the native workers continued until 1930. During
World War II the colony joined Chad in supporting the
Free French cause against the Vichy government. The
Congo proclaimed its independence without leaving
the French Community in 1960, calling itself the
Republic of Congo.

Congo's second president, Alphonse Massemba-
Débat, instituted a Marxist-Leninist government. In
1968, Maj. Marien Ngouabi overthrew him but kept
Congo on a socialist course. He was sworn in for a
second five-year term in 1975. A four-man commando
squad assassinated Ngouabi on March 18, 1977. Col.
Joachim Yhombi-Opango, army chief of staff, assumed

the presidency on April 4. Yhombi-Opango resigned on
Feb. 4, 1979, and was replaced by Col. Denis Sassou-
Nguesso.

In July 1990 the leaders of the ruling party voted
to end the one-party system. A national political
conference, hailed as a model for sub-Saharan
Africa, renounced Marxism in 1991, and scheduled
the country's first free elections for 1992. Pascal
Lissouba became the country's first democratically
elected president.

Political and ethnic tensions intensified in 1993 after
legislative elections, when the opposition's rejection of
the results developed into violence. A peace agreement
was signed between the government and the opposition
in Aug. 1994. A four-month civil war (June 5–Oct. 15,
1997) devastated Brazzaville, the capital. Buttressed by
military aid from Angola, former Marxist dictator
Denis Sassou-Nguesso overthrew President Lissouba.
In late 1999 a peace agreement was signed between
Sassou-Nguesso, who comes from the north, and the
rebels representing the populous south. The postwar
period has been traumatic for the desperately poor
country.

In March 2002, President Sassou-Nguesso was
reelected with 89.4% of the vote. His opponents were
either barred from the country or withdrew from the
election.

The so-called Ninja rebels continued to battle government forces, each attempting to gain or maintain
control of the country's rich oil reserves and each
seemingly unconcerned about the toll this new outbreak of violence is taking on civilians. In May 2003,
the government and Ninja rebels signed an agreement
to end hostilities.

Congo, Democratic Republic of the

DEMOCRATIC REPUBLIC OF THE CONGO

President: Joseph Kabila (2001)
Area: 905,563 sq mi (2,345,410 sq km)
Population (2004 est.): 58,317,930 (growth rate: 2.9%);
birth rate: 45.1/1000; infant mortality rate: 96.6/1000;
life expectancy: 48.9; density per sq mi: 64
Capital and largest city (2003 est.): Kinshasa,
6,541,300. **Other large cities:** Lubumbashi,
1,105,900; Mbuji-Mayi, 938,000; Kolwezi, 832,400;
Kisangani, 523,000 . **Monetary unit:** Congolese franc.
Languages: French (official), Lingala, Kingwana,
Kikongo, Tshiluba. **Ethnicity/race:** over 200 African
ethnic groups, the majority are Bantu; the four largest
tribes—Mongo, Luba, Kongo (all Bantu), and the
Mangbetu-Azande (Hamitic)—make up about 45% of
the population. **Religions:** Roman Catholic 50%,
Protestant 20%, Kimbanguist 10%, Islam 10%; other
syncretic and indigenous, 10%. **Literacy rate:** 66%
(2003 est.)
Economic summary: GDP/PPP (2003 est.): $35.62
billion; per capita $600. **Real growth rate:** 6%.
Inflation: 14%. **Unemployment:** n.a. **Arable land:**
3%. **Agriculture:** coffee, sugar, palm oil, rubber, tea,
quinine, cassava (tapioca), palm oil, bananas, root
crops, corn, fruits; wood products. **Labor force:** 14.51
million (1993 est.). **Industries:** mining (diamonds,
copper, zinc), mineral processing, consumer products
(including textiles, footwear, cigarettes, processed
foods and beverages), cement. **Natural resources:**
cobalt, copper, cadmium, petroleum, industrial and
gem diamonds, gold, silver, zinc, manganese, tin,
germanium, uranium, radium, bauxite, iron ore, coal,
hydropower, timber. **Exports:** $1.417 billion (f.o.b.,
2003 est.): diamonds, copper, crude oil, coffee, cobalt.
Imports: $933 million (f.o.b., 2003 est.): foodstuffs,

mining and other machinery, transport equipment, fuels. **Major trading partners:** Belgium, U.S., Zimbabwe, Finland, South Africa, Nigeria, France, Germany, Netherlands, Kenya.

Geography The Congo, in west-central Africa, is bordered by the Congo Republic, the Central African Republic, the Sudan, Uganda, Rwanda, Burundi, Tanzania, Zambia, Angola, and the Atlantic Ocean. It is one-quarter the size of the U.S. The principal rivers are the Ubangi and Bomu in the north and the Congo in the west, which flows into the Atlantic. The entire length of Lake Tanganyika lies along the eastern border with Tanzania and Burundi.

Government Dictatorship.

History Formerly the Belgian Congo, this territory was inhabited by ancient Negrito peoples (Pygmies), who were pushed into the mountains by Bantu and Nilotic invaders. The American correspondent Henry M. Stanley navigated the Congo River in 1877 and opened the interior to exploration. Commissioned by King Leopold II of the Belgians, Stanley made treaties with native chiefs that enabled the king to obtain personal title to the territory at the Berlin Conference of 1885.

Leopold accumulated a vast personal fortune from ivory and rubber through Congolese slave labor; 10 million people are estimated to have died from forced labor, starvation, and outright extermination during Leopold's colonial rule. His brutal exploitation of the Congo eventually became an international cause célèbre, prompting Belgium to take over administration of the Congo, which remained a colony until agitation for independence forced Brussels to grant freedom on June 30, 1960. In elections that month, two prominent nationalists won: Patrice Lumumba of the leftist Mouvement National Congolais became prime minister and Joseph Kasavubu of the ABAKO party became head of state. But within weeks of independence, the Katanga Province, led by Moise Tshombe, seceded from the new republic, and another mining province, South Kasai, followed. Belgium sent paratroopers to quell the civil war, and with Kasavubu and Lumumba of the national government in conflict, the United Nations flew in a peacekeeping force.

Kasavubu staged an army coup in 1960 and handed Lumumba over to the Katangan forces. A UN investigating commission found that Lumumba had been killed by a Belgian mercenary in the presence of Tshombe, who was then the president of Katanga. U.S. and Belgian involvement in the assassination have been alleged. Dag Hammarskjold, UN secretary-general, died in a plane crash en route to a peace conference with Tshombe on Sept. 17, 1961.

Tshombe rejected a national reconciliation plan submitted by the UN in 1962. Tshombe's troops fired on the UN force in December, and in the ensuing conflict Tshombe capitulated on Jan. 14, 1963. The peacekeeping force withdrew, and, in a complete about-face, Kasavubu named Tshombe premier in order to fight a spreading rebellion. Tshombe used foreign mercenaries, and with the help of Belgian paratroops airlifted by U.S. planes, defeated the most serious opposition, a Communist-backed regime in the northeast.

Kasavubu abruptly dismissed Tshombe in 1965, but was then himself ousted by Gen. Joseph-Desiré Mobutu, army chief of staff. The new president nationalized the Union Minière, the Belgian copper mining enterprise that had been a dominant force in the Congo since colonial days. Mobutu eliminated opposition to win the election in 1970. In 1975, he nationalized

much of the economy, barred religious instruction in schools, and decreed the adoption of African names. He changed the country's name to Zaire and his own to Mobuto Sese Seko, which means "the all-powerful warrior who, because of his endurance and inflexible will to win, will go from conquest to conquest leaving fire in his wake." In 1977, invaders from Angola calling themselves the Congolese National Liberation Front pushed into Shaba and threatened the important mining center of Kolwezi. France and Belgium provided military aid to defeat the rebels.

Laurent Kabila and his long-standing but little-known guerrilla movement launched a seven-month campaign that ousted Mobutu in May 1997, ending one of the world's most corrupt and megalomaniacal regimes. The last of the CIA-nurtured cold war despots, Mobutu deftly courted France and the U.S., which used Zaire as a launching pad for covert operations against bordering countries, particularly Marxist Angola. Mobutu's disastrous policies drove his country to economic collapse while he siphoned off millions of dollars for himself.

The country was renamed the Democratic Republic of the Congo, its name before Mobutu changed it to Zaire in 1971. But elation over Mobutu's downfall faded as Kabila's own autocratic style emerged, and he seemed devoid of a clear plan for reconstructing the country. He stymied UN human rights investigations and continued to depend on foreign troops for border skirmishes rather than establish a strong national army. Many Congolese dismissed him as a puppet ruler who allowed his country to be overrun by outsiders, particularly the Rwandans. At the same time, he alienated many of his former supporters who helped him establish power, including Rwanda and Uganda.

In Aug. 1998, Congolese rebel forces, backed by Kabila's former allies, Rwanda and Uganda, gained control of a large portion of the country until Angolan, Namibian, and Zimbabwean troops came to Kabila's aid. In 1999, the Lusaka Accord was signed by all six of the countries involved, as well as by most, but not all, of the various rebel groups.

In Jan. 2001, Kabila was assassinated, allegedly by one of his bodyguards. His young and inexperienced son Joseph became the new president, and demonstrated a willingness to engage in talks to end the civil war. In April 2002, the government agreed to a power-sharing arrangement with Ugandan-supported rebels, and in July, the presidents of the Congo and Rwanda signed an accord: Rwanda promised to withdraw its 35,000 troops from the eastern Congolese border; the Congo would in turn disarm the thousands of Hutu militiamen in its territory, who threatened Rwandan security. In Sept. 2002, Uganda also signed a peace accord with the nation. But the warring parties were slow to depart; most had been looting the Congo of its natural resources and had little incentive to end the war. More than 2.5 million people are estimated to have died in the Congo's complex four-year civil war, which has involved seven foreign armies and numerous rebel groups that often fought among themselves.

Despite the peace agreement and power-sharing plan signed between the main parties in the Congolese war, the fighting and killing continued. In April 2003, hundreds of civilians were massacred in the eastern province of Ituri in an ethnic conflict. In June a French force with a UN mandate was deployed to defend the population from further tribal fighting. Joseph Kabila signed a new constitution in April, and on July 17, 2003, Congo's new power-sharing government was inaugurated. The new government includes 4 vice presidents and 36 ministers, 16 of which are former rebels. But in 2004, peace was dangerously insecure. In May, an insurgency in Bukavu erupted, other areas of Congo grew restive, and Rwanda continued to support various rebel groups fighting the government.

Costa Rica

REPUBLIC OF COSTA RICA

National name: República de Costa Rica
President: Abel Pacheco (2002)
Area: 19,730 sq mi (51,100 sq km)
Population (2004 est.): 3,956,507 (growth rate: 1.5%); birth rate: 19.0/1000; infant mortality rate: 10.3/1000; life expectancy: 76.6; density per sq mi: 201
Capital and largest city (2003 est.): San José, 1,527,300 (metro. area), 337,200 (city proper).
Monetary unit: Colón. **Language:** Spanish (official), English. **Ethnicity/race:** white (including mestizo) 94%, black 3%, Amerindian 1%, Chinese 1%, other 1%. **Religion:** Roman Catholic 76.3%, Evangelical 13.7%, Jehovah's Witnesses 1.3%, other Protestant 0.7%, other 4.8%, none 3.2%. **Literacy rate:** 96% (2003 est.)
Economic summary: GDP/PPP (2003 est.): $35.16 billion; per capita $9,000. **Real growth rate:** 5.2%. **Inflation:** 9.4%. **Unemployment:** 6.7%. **Arable land:** 4%. **Agriculture:** coffee, pineapples, bananas, sugar, corn, rice, beans, potatoes; beef; timber. **Labor force:** 1.8 million (July 2003); agriculture 20%, industry 22%, services 58% (1999 est.). **Industries:** microprocessors, food processing, textiles and clothing, construction materials, fertilizer, plastic products. **Natural resources:** hydropower. **Exports:** $6.176 billion (2003 est.): coffee, bananas, sugar; pineapples; textiles, electronic components, medical equipment. **Imports:** $7.057 billion (2003 est.): raw materials, consumer goods, capital equipment, petroleum. **Major trading partners:** U.S., Netherlands, UK, Japan, Mexico.

Geography This Central American country lies between Nicaragua to the north and Panama to the south. Its area slightly exceeds that of Vermont and New Hampshire combined. It has a narrow Pacific coastal region. Cocos Island (10 sq mi; 26 sq km), about 300 mi (483 km) off the Pacific Coast, is under Costa Rican sovereignty.

Government Democratic republic.

History Costa Rica was inhabited by an estimated 25,000 Indians when Columbus explored it in 1502. Few of the Indians survived the Spanish conquest, which began in 1563. The region grew slowly and was administered as a Spanish province. Costa Rica achieved independence in 1821 but was absorbed for two years by Agustín de Iturbide in his Mexican empire. It became a republic in 1848. Except for the military dictatorship of Tomás Guardia from 1870 to 1882, Costa Rica has enjoyed one of the most democratic governments in Latin America.

In the 1970s, rising oil prices, falling international commodity prices, and inflation hurt the economy. Efforts have since been made to reduce reliance on coffee, banana, and beef exports. Tourism is now a major business. Oscar Arias Sanchez, who became president in 1986, was awarded the Nobel Peace Prize in 1987 for his role in negotiating settlements to both the Nicaraguan and the Salvadoran civil wars.

José Maria Figueres Olsen of the National Liberation Party became president in 1994. He opposed economic suggestions made by the International Monetary Fund, instead favoring greater government intervention in the economy. The World Bank subsequently withheld $100 million of financing. In 1998, Miguel Angel Rodríguez of the Social Christian Unity Party became president, pledging economic reforms, such as privatization. In 2000, Costa Rica and Nicaragua resolved a long-standing dispute over navigation of the San Juan River, which forms their border. A psychiatrist, Abel Pacheco, also of the Social Christian Unity Party, won the presidency in elections held in April 2002. In May 2003, several national strikes took place, by energy and telecommunications workers over privatization, and by teachers over their salaries.

Côte d'Ivoire

REPUBLIC OF CÔTE D'IVOIRE

National name: République de la Côte d'Ivoire
President: Laurent Gbagbo (2000)
Prime Minister: Seydou Diarra (2003)
Area: 124,502 sq mi (322,460 sq km)
Population (2004 est.): 17,327,724 (growth rate: 2.1%); birth rate: 39.6/1000; infant mortality rate: 97.1/1000; life expectancy: 42.5; density per sq mi: 139
Capital (2003 est.): Yamoussoukro (official), 185,600 . **Largest city:** Abidjan, (administrative capital) 4,113,600 (metro. area), 3,427,500 (city proper). **Monetary unit:** CFA Franc. **Languages:** French (official) and African languages (Diaula esp.). **Ethnicity/race:** Akan 42.1%, Voltaiques (Gur) 17.6%, Northern Mandes 16.5%, Krous 11%, Southern Mandes 10%, other 2.8% (includes 130,000 Lebanese and 14,000 French) (1998). **Religions:** indigenous 25%-40%, Islam 35%-40%, Christian 20%-30% (2001). **Literacy rate:** 51% (2003 est.)
Economic summary: GDP/PPP (2003 est.): $24.51 billion; per capita $1,400. **Real growth rate:** –1.9%. **Inflation:** 4.1%. **Unemployment:** 13% in urban areas (1998). **Arable land:** 9%. **Agriculture:** coffee, cocoa beans, bananas, palm kernels, corn, rice, manioc (tapioca), sweet potatoes, sugar, cotton, rubber; timber. **Labor force:** 68% agricultural (1996 est.). **Industries:** foodstuffs, beverages; wood products, oil refining, truck and bus assembly, textiles, fertilizer, building materials, electricity. **Natural resources:** petroleum, natural gas, diamonds, manganese, iron ore, cobalt, bauxite, copper, hydropower. **Exports:** $5.299 billion (f.o.b., 2003 est.): cocoa, coffee, timber, petroleum, cotton, bananas, pineapples, palm oil, fish. **Imports:** $2.781 billion (f.o.b., 2003 est.): fuel, capital equipment, foodstuffs. **Major trading partners:** France, Netherlands, U.S., Germany, Mali, Belgium, Spain, Nigeria, China, Italy.

Geography Côte d'Ivoire (also known as the Ivory Coast), in western Africa on the Gulf of Guinea, is a little larger than New Mexico. Its neighbors are Liberia, Guinea, Mali, Burkina Faso, and Ghana. The country consists of a coastal strip in the south, dense forests in the interior, and savannas in the north.

Government Presidential/parliamentary democracy until Dec. 1999, when a coup installed a military dictatorship.

History Côte d'Ivoire was originally made up of numerous isolated settlements; today it represents more than sixty distinct tribes, including the Baoule, Bete, Senoufou, Agni, Malinke, Dan, and Lobi. Côte d'Ivoire attracted both French and Portuguese merchants in the 15th century who were in search of ivory and slaves. French traders set up establishments early in the 19th century, and in 1842, the French obtained territorial concessions from local tribes, gradually extending their influence along the coast and inland. The area was organized as a territory in 1893, became an autonomous republic in the French Union after

World War II, and achieved independence on Aug. 7, 1960. Côte d'Ivoire formed a customs union in 1959 with Dahomey (Benin), Niger, and Burkina Faso. The nation's economy is one of the most developed in sub-Saharan Africa. It is the world's largest exporter of cocoa and one of the largest exporters of coffee.

From independence until his death in 1993, Felix Houphouët-Boigny served as president. Massive protests by students, farmers, and professionals forced the president to legalize opposition parties and hold the first contested presidential election in Oct. 1990, which Houphouët-Boigny won with 81% of the vote.

Beginning in Sept. 1998, thousands of demonstrators protested a constitutional revision that granted President Henri Konan Bédié greatly enhanced powers. Bédié also promoted the concept of *ivoirité*, which, roughly translated, means "pure Ivoirian pride." Although its defenders describe *ivoirité* as a term of positive national pride, it has led to a dangerous xenophobia, with numerous ethnic Malians and Burkinans being driven out of the country in 1999.

President Bédié was overthrown in the country's first military coup in Dec. 1999, and Gen. Robert Guei assumed control of the country. As a result, the majority of foreign aid to the country ceased.

In what were seen as the first steps toward reasserting democracy, voters overwhelmingly approved a draft constitution in July 2000. However, the document permitted only those of "pure Ivoirian" stock to run for president, thereby excluding nearly 40% of the population. Guei, who had promised to stay in power only to "sweep the house clean," instead decided to run for president in Oct. 2000 elections. Gen. Guei ran against a civilian opposition candidate, Laurent Gbagbo. Each declared victory in an election most believe to have been rife with fraud. Popular outcry against Guei soon turned violent, forcing him to leave the country, and Gbagbo assumed the presidency. Many observers questioned his mandate, however, since the popular opposition leader Alassane Ouattara had been excluded from the election on the specious grounds that he was not a pure-blooded Ivoirian. It was not until June 2002 that Ouattara was finally granted full Ivoirian citizenship, which will allow him to run in the next presidential election in 2005. Hundreds have died in violence sparked by the dispute.

Mutineering soldiers attempted a coup on Sept. 19, 2002. Guei and Interior Minister Doudou were killed in fighting between government soldiers and the rebels. President Gbagbo accused Guei of staging the coup. Fighting continued, even after a French-brokered peace accord was signed on Jan. 25, 2003, calling for the government to share power with the rebels. President Gbagbo's supporters found such a plan unacceptable, and there was rioting in the capital. The war was finally declared officially over in July. The peace, supported by 4,000 UN-sponsored French peacekeeping troops, is fragile, however. Pro-government and rebel militias remain armed, and in 2004, Northern and Muslim rebels still controlled half the country.

Croatia

REPUBLIC OF CROATIA

President: Stipe Mesic (2000)
Prime Minister: Ivo Sanader (2003)
Area: 21,831 sq mi (56,542 sq km)
Population (2004 est.): 4,496,869 (growth rate: 0.0%); birth rate: 9.5/1000; infant mortality rate: 7.0/1000; life expectancy: 74.1; density per sq mi: 206
Capital and largest city (2003 est.): Zagreb, 685,500. **Other large cities:** Split, 173,600; Rijeka, 142,500; Osijek, 89,600. **Monetary unit:** Kuna. **Language:**

Croatian 96% (official), other 4% (including Italian, Hungarian, Czech, Slovak, German). **Ethnicity/race:** Croat 89.6%, Serb 4.5%, Bosniak 0.5%, Hungarian 0.4%, Slovene 0.3%, Czech 0.2%, Roma 0.2%, Albanian 0.1%, Montenegrin 0.1%, others 4.1% (2001). **Religions:** Roman Catholic 87.8%, Orthodox 4.4%, Muslim 1.3%, Protestant 0.3%, others and unknown 6.2% (2001) . **Literacy rate:** 99% (2003 est.)
Economic summary: GDP/PPP (2003 est.): $47.14 billion; per capita $10,700. **Real growth rate:** 4.5%. **Inflation:** 1.5%. **Unemployment:** 18.9%. **Arable land:** 24%. **Agriculture:** wheat, corn, sugar beets, sunflower seed, barley, alfalfa, clover, olives, citrus, grapes, soybeans, potatoes; livestock, dairy products. **Labor force:** 1.79 million; agriculture 13.2%, industry 25.4%, services 46.4% (2002). **Industries:** chemicals and plastics, machine tools, fabricated metal, electronics, pig iron and rolled steel products, aluminum, paper, wood products, construction materials, textiles, shipbuilding, petroleum and petroleum refining, food and beverages; tourism. **Natural resources:** oil, some coal, bauxite, low-grade iron ore, calcium, natural asphalt, silica, mica, clays, salt, hydropower. **Exports:** $6.355 billion (f.o.b., 2003 est.): transport equipment, textiles, chemicals, foodstuffs, fuels. **Imports:** $12.86 billion (f.o.b., 2003 est.): machinery, transport and electrical equipment, chemicals, fuels and lubricants, foodstuffs. **Major trading partners:** Italy, Bosnia and Herzegovina, Germany, Slovenia, Austria, Russia, France.

Geography Croatia is a former Yugoslav republic on the Adriatic Sea. It is about the size of West Virginia. Part of Croatia is a barren, rocky region lying in the Dinaric Alps. The Zagorje region north of the capital, Zagreb, is a land of rolling hills, and the fertile agricultural region of the Pannonian Plain is bordered by the Drava, Danube, and Sava rivers in the east. Over one-third of Croatia is forested.

Government Presidential/parliamentary democracy.

History Croatia, at one time the Roman province of Pannonia, was settled in the 7th century by the Croats. They converted to Christianity between the 7th and 9th centuries and adopted the Roman alphabet under the suzerainty of Charlemagne. In 925, the Croats defeated Byzantine and Frankish invaders and established their own independent kingdom, which reached its peak during the 11th century. A civil war ensued in 1089, which later led to the country being conquered by the Hungarians in 1091. The signing of the *Pacta Conventa* by Croatian tribal chiefs and the Hungarian king in 1102 united the two nations politically under the Hungarian monarch, but Croatia retained its autonomy.

Following the defeat of the Hungarians by the Turks at the battle of Mohács in 1526, Croatia (along with Hungary) elected Austrian Archduke Ferdinand of Hapsburg as their king. After the establishment of the Austro-Hungarian kingdom in 1867, Croatia became part of Hungary until the collapse of Austria-Hungary in 1918 following its defeat in World War I. On Oct. 29, 1918, Croatia proclaimed its independence and joined in union with Montenegro, Serbia, and Slovenia to form the Kingdom of Serbs, Croats, and Slovenes. The name was changed to Yugoslavia in 1929.

When Germany invaded Yugoslavia in 1941, Croatia became a Nazi puppet state. Croatian Fascists, the Ustachi, slaughtered countless Serbs and Jews during the war. After Germany was defeated in 1945, Croatia was made into a republic of the newly reestablished communist nation of Yugoslavia; however, Croatian nationalism persisted. After Yugoslavian leader Tito's death in 1980, Croatia's demands for independence began multiplying.

In 1990, free elections were held, and the communists were defeated by a nationalist party led by Franjo Tudjman. In June 1991, the Croatian Parliament passed a declaration of independence from Yugoslavia. Six months of intensive fighting with the Serbian-dominated Yugoslavian army followed, claiming thousands of lives and wreaking mass destruction.

A UN cease-fire was arranged on Jan. 2, 1992. The Security Council in February approved sending a 14,000-member peacekeeping force to monitor the cease-fire and protect the minority Serbs in Croatia. In a 1993 referendum the Serb-occupied portion of Croatia (Krajina) resoundingly voted for integration with Serbs in Bosnia and Serbia proper. Although the Zagreb government and representatives of Krajina signed a cease-fire in March 1994, further negotiations broke down. In a lightning-quick operation, the Croatian army retook western Slavonia in May 1995. Similarly, in August, the central Croatian region of Krajina, held by Serbs, was returned to Zagreb's control.

Announcing on television in 1999 that "national issues are more important than democracy," President Tudjman continued to alienate Croatians with his authoritarian rule, out-of-touch nationalism, and disastrous handling of the war-shattered economy. In Dec. 1999, Tudjman died. Less than a month later, his Croatian Democratic Union (HDZ) party was defeated by a reformist center-left coalition headed by Ivica Racan. But in Nov. 2003 elections, a right-wing coalition led by the nationalist HDZ once again assumed power. The new prime minister, Ivo Sanader, claims that his party is now far less nationalist and far more moderate than in its earlier incarnation under Tudjman. In 2003, Croatia formally submitted its application to join the EU.

Cuba

REPUBLIC OF CUBA

National name: República de Cuba
President: Fidel Castro (1976)
Area: 42,803 sq mi (110,860 sq km)
Population (2004 est.): 11,308,764 (growth rate: 0.3%); birth rate: 12.2/1000; infant mortality rate: 6.5/1000; life expectancy: 77.0; density per sq mi: 264
Capital and largest city (2003 est.): Havana, 2,686,000 (metro. area), 2,343,700 (city proper). **Other large cities:** Santiago de Cuba, 554,400; Camagüey, 354,400; Holguin, 319,300; Guantánamo, 274,300; Santa Clara, 251,800. **Monetary unit:** Cuban Peso.
Language: Spanish. **Ethnicity/race:** mulatto 51%, white 37%, black 11%, Chinese 1%. **Religion:** nominally 85% Roman Catholic before Castro assumed power. **Literacy rate:** 97% (2003 est.)
Economic summary: GDP/PPP (2003 est.): $31.59 billion; per capita $2,800. **Real growth rate:** 1.3%. **Inflation:** 5%. **Unemployment:** 3.2%. **Arable land:** 33%. **Agriculture:** sugar, tobacco, citrus, coffee, rice, potatoes, beans; livestock. **Labor force:** 4.3 million (2000 est.); agriculture 24%, industry 25%, services 51% (1999). **Industries:** sugar, petroleum, tobacco, chemicals, construction, services, nickel, steel, cement, agricultural machinery, biotechnology. **Natural resources:** cobalt, nickel, iron ore, copper, manganese, salt, timber, silica, petroleum, arable land. **Exports:** $1.467 billion (f.o.b, 2003 est.): sugar, nickel, tobacco, fish, medical products, citrus, coffee. **Imports:** $4.531 billion (f.o.b, 2003 est.): petroleum, food, machinery and equipment, chemicals. **Major trading partners:** Netherlands, Russia, Canada, Spain, China, Italy, France, Mexico, U.S., Brazil.
Geography The largest island of the West Indies group (equal in area to Pennsylvania), Cuba is also the westernmost—just west of Hispaniola (Haiti and the Dominican Republic), and 90 mi (145 km) south of Key West, Fla., at the entrance to the Gulf of Mexico. The island is mountainous in the southeast and south-central area (Sierra Maestra). It is flat or rolling elsewhere. Cuba also includes numerous smaller islands, islets, and cays.

Government Communist state.

History Arawak (or Taino) Indians inhabiting Cuba when Columbus landed on the island in 1492 died from diseases brought by sailors and settlers. By 1511, Spaniards under Diego Velásquez had established settlements. Havana's superb harbor made it a common transit point to and from Spain.

In the early 1800s, Cuba's sugarcane industry boomed, requiring massive numbers of black slaves. A simmering independence movement turned into open warfare from 1867 to 1878. Slavery was abolished in 1886. In 1895, the poet José Marti led the struggle that finally ended Spanish rule, thanks largely to U.S. intervention in 1898 after the sinking of the battleship *Maine* in Havana harbor.

An 1899 treaty made Cuba an independent republic under U.S. protection. The U.S. occupation, which ended in 1902, suppressed yellow fever and brought large American investments. The 1901 Platt Amendment allowed the U.S. to intervene in Cuba's affairs, which it did four times from 1906 to 1920. Cuba terminated the amendment in 1934.

In 1933 a group of army officers, including army sergeant Fulgencio Batista, overthrew President Gerardo Machado. Batista became president in 1940, running a corrupt police state.

In 1956, Fidel Castro Ruz launched a revolution from his camp in the Sierra Maestra mountains. Castro's brother Raul, and Ernesto (Ché) Guevara, an Argentine physician, were his top lieutenants. Many anti-Batista landowners supported the rebels. The U.S. ended military aid to Cuba in 1958, and on New Year's Day 1959, Batista fled into exile and Castro took over the government.

The U.S. initially welcomed what looked like a democratic Cuba, but a rude awakening came within a few months when Castro established military tribunals for political opponents and jailed hundreds. Castro disavowed Cuba's 1952 military pact with the U.S., confiscated U.S. assets, and established Soviet-style collective farms. The U.S. broke relations with Cuba on Jan. 3, 1961, and Castro formalized his alliance with the Soviet Union. Thousands of Cubans fled the country.

In 1961 a U.S.-backed group of Cuban exiles invaded Cuba. Planned during the Eisenhower administration, the invasion was given the go-ahead by President John Kennedy, although he refused to give U.S. air support. The landing at the Bay of Pigs on April 17, 1961, was a fiasco. The invaders did not receive popular Cuban support and were easily repulsed by the Cuban military.

A Soviet attempt to install medium-range missiles in Cuba—capable of striking targets in the United States with nuclear warheads—provoked a crisis in 1962. Denouncing the Soviets for "deliberate deception," on Oct. 22 Kennedy said that the U.S. would blockade Cuba so the missiles could not be delivered. Six days later Soviet premier Nikita Khrushchev ordered the missile sites dismantled and returned to the USSR, in return for a U.S. pledge not to attack Cuba.

The U.S. established limited diplomatic ties with Cuba on Sept. 1, 1977, making it easier for Cuban Americans to visit the island. Contact with the more affluent Cuban Americans prompted a wave of discontent in Cuba, producing a flood of asylum seekers. In response, Castro opened the port of Mariel to a "freedom flotilla" of boats from the U.S., allowing 125,000 to flee to Miami. After the refugees arrived, it was discovered their ranks were swelled with prisoners, mental patients, homosexuals, and others unwanted by the Cuban government.

Cuba fomented communist revolution around the world, especially in Angola, where thousands of Cuban troops were sent in the 1980s.

Russian aid, which had long supported Cuba's failing economy, ended when communism collapsed in eastern Europe in 1990. Cuba's foreign trade also plummeted, producing a severe economic crisis. In 1993, Castro permitted limited private enterprise, allowed Cubans to possess convertible currencies, and encouraged foreign investment in its tourist industry. In March 1996, the U.S. tightened its embargo with the Helms-Burton Act.

Christmas became an official holiday in 1997, for the first time since the revolution, in response to Pope John Paul II's 1998 visit to Cuba, which raised hopes for greater religious freedom.

In June 2000, Castro won a publicity bonanza when the Clinton administration sent Elian Gonzalez, a young Cuban boy found clinging to an inner tube near Miami, back to Cuba. The U.S. Cuban community had demanded that the boy remain in Miami rather than be returned to his father in Cuba. By many accounts, the influential Cuban Americans lost public sympathy by pitting political ideology against familial bonds.

In March and April 2003, Castro sent nearly 80 dissidents to prison with long sentences, prompting an international condemnation of Cuba's harsh crackdown on human rights.

The Bush administration tightened its embargo in June 2004, allowing Cuban Americans to return to the island only once every three years (instead of every year), and restricting the amount of U.S. cash that can be spent there to $50 per day.

Cyprus

REPUBLIC OF CYPRUS

National name: Kypriaki Dimokratia—Kibris Cumhuriyeti
President: Tassos Papadopoulos (2003)
Area: 3,571 sq mi (9,250 sq km)
Population (2004 est.): 775,927 (growth rate: 0.5%); birth rate: 12.7/1000; infant mortality rate: 7.4/1000; life expectancy: 77.5; density per sq mi: 217
Capital and largest city (2003 est.): Lefkosia (Nicosia) (in government-controlled area), 197,600. **Monetary unit:** Cyprus pound. **Languages:** Greek, Turkish (both official); English. **Ethnicity/race:** Current: Greek 77%, Turkish 18% (each concentrated almost exclusively in separate areas); other 5% (2001). **Religions:** Greek Orthodox 78%, Islam 18%, Maronite, Armenian Apostolic, and other 4%. **Literacy rate:** 98% (2003 est.)
Economic summary: GDP/PPP: Greek Cypriot area (2003 est.): $8.9 billion; $16,000 per capita; Turkish Cypriot area (2003 est.): $1.217 billion; $5,600 per capita. **Real growth rate:** Greek Cypriot area: 1.6%; Turkish Cypriot area: 2.6%. **Inflation:** Greek Cypriot area: 4%; Turkish Cypriot area: 12.6%.
Unemployment: Greek Cypriot area: 3.4% (2002 est.); Turkish Cypriot area: 5.6%. **Arable land:** 11%. **Agriculture:** potatoes, citrus, vegetables, barley, grapes, olives, vegetables. **Labor force** (2000): Greek Cypriot area: 306,000; Turkish Cypriot area: 95,025 (2000); Greek Cypriot area: services 73%, industry 22%, agriculture 5% (2000); Turkish Cypriot area:

services 56.4%, industry 22.8%, agriculture 20.8% (1998). **Industries:** food, beverages, textiles, chemicals, metal products, tourism, wood products. **Natural resources:** copper, pyrites, asbestos, gypsum, timber, salt, marble, clay earth pigment. **Exports:** Greek Cypriot area: $1.054 billion (f.o.b., 2003 est.): citrus, potatoes, pharmaceuticals, cement, clothing and cigarettes; Turkish Cypriot area: $46 million (f.o.b., 2003 est.): citrus, potatoes, textiles. **Imports:** Greek Cypriot area: $4.637 billion (f.o.b., 2003 est.): consumer goods, petroleum and lubricants, intermediate goods, machinery, transport equipment; Turkish Cypriot area: $301 million (f.o.b., 2003 est.): food, minerals, chemicals, machinery. **Major trading partners:** UK, Greece, UAE, France, Russia, Germany, Italy, South Korea, Japan. **Member of Commonwealth of Nations**

Geography The third-largest island in the Mediterranean (one and one-half times the size of Delaware), Cyprus lies off the southern coast of Turkey and the western shore of Syria. The highest peak is Mount Olympus at 6,406 ft (1,953 m).

Government Republic. Mediation efforts by the UN seek to achieve reunification of the island under one federated system of government.

History Cyprus was the site of early Phoenician and Greek colonies. For centuries its rule passed through many hands. It fell to the Turks in 1571, and a large Turkish colony settled on the island.

In World War I, at the outbreak of hostilities with Turkey, Britain annexed the island. It was declared a Crown colony in 1925. For centuries the Greek population, regarding Greece as its mother country, has sought self-determination and reunion with Greece *(enosis)*. The resulting quarrel with Turkey threatened NATO. Cyprus became an independent nation on Aug. 16, 1960, with Britain, Greece, and Turkey as guarantor powers.

Archbishop Makarios, president since 1959, was overthrown on July 15, 1974, by a military coup led by the Cypriot National Guard. The new regime named Nikos Giorgiades Sampson as president and Bishop Gennadios as head of the Cypriot Church to replace Makarios. Diplomacy failed to resolve the crisis. Turkey invaded Cyprus by sea and air on July 20, 1974, asserting its right to protect the Turkish Cypriot minority. Geneva talks involving Greece, Turkey, Britain, and the two Cypriot factions failed in mid-August, and the Turks subsequently gained control of 40% of the island. Some 180,000 Greek Cypriots were uprooted by the Turkish troops. Greece made no armed response to the superior Turkish force but bitterly suspended military participation in the NATO alliance. The tension continued after Makarios returned to become president on Dec. 7, 1974. He offered self-government to the Turkish minority, but rejected any solution "involving transfer of populations and amounting to partition of Cyprus."

Turkish Cypriots proclaimed a separate state under Rauf Denktash in the northern part of the island on Nov. 15, 1983, naming it the "Turkish Republic of Northern Cyprus." The UN Security Council, in its Resolution 541 of Nov. 18, 1983, declared this action illegal and called for withdrawal. No country except Turkey has recognized this illegal entity.

In 1988, George Vassiliou, a conservative and critic of UN proposals to reunify Cyprus, became president. The purchase of missiles capable of reaching the Turkish coast evoked threats of retaliation from Turkey in 1997, and Cyprus's plans to deploy more missiles in Aug. 1999 again raised Turkey's ire.

The continued strife between Greek Cypriots and Turkish Cypriots threatened Cyprus's potential EU membership—it had met all the economic standards—and provided a great incentive to both sides to resolve their differences. UN-sponsored talks between the Greek and Turkish leaders, Kleridas and Denktash, continued intensively in 2002, but without resolution. In Dec. 2002, the EU invited Cyprus to join in 2004, provided the UN plan was accepted by February 2003. Without reunification, only Greek Cyprus was to be welcomed into the EU. But just weeks before the UN deadline, Kleridas was defeated by right-wing candidate Tassos Papadopoulos in presidential elections. Papadopoulos had a reputation as a hard-liner on reunification and had rejected all previous UN attempts to reunify Cyprus. The UN deadline passed, and by mid-March, the UN declared that the talks had failed. In April 2004, dual referendums were held, with the Greek side overwhelmingly rejecting the most recent UN reunification plan, and the Turkish side voting in favor. In May, Greek Cyprus alone became a part of the EU.

Czech Republic

President: Vaclav Klaus (2003)
Prime Minister: Stanislav Gross (2004)
Area: 30,450 sq mi (78,866 sq km)
Population (2004 est.): 10,246,178 (growth rate: 0%); birth rate: 9.1/1000; infant mortality rate: 4.0/1000; life expectancy: 75.8; density per sq mi: 336
Capital and largest city (2003 est.): Prague, 1,378,700 (metro. area), 1,169,800 (city proper). **Other large cities:** Brno, 376,400; Ostrava, 317,700; Plzen, 164,900; Olomouc, 102,900. **Monetary unit:** Koruna. **Languages:** Czech. **Ethnicity/race:** Czech 81.2%, Moravian 13.2%, Slovak 3.1%, Polish 0.6%, German 0.5%, Silesian 0.4%, Roma (Gypsy) 0.3%, Hungarian 0.2%, other 0.5% (1991). **Religions:** atheist 39.8%, Roman Catholic 39.2%, Protestant 4.6%, Orthodox 3%, other 13.4%. **Literacy rate:** 100% (1999 est.)
Economic summary: GDP/PPP (2003 est.): $160.5 billion; per capita $15,700. **Real growth rate:** 2.5%. **Inflation:** 0%. **Unemployment:** 10.5%. **Arable land:** 40%. **Agriculture:** wheat, potatoes, sugar beets, hops, fruit; pigs, poultry. **Labor force:** 5.203 million (1999 est.); agriculture 5%, industry 35%, services 60% (2001 est.). **Industries:** metallurgy, machinery and equipment, motor vehicles, glass, armaments. **Natural resources:** hard coal, soft coal, kaolin, clay, graphite, timber. **Exports:** $46.77 billion (f.o.b., 2003 est.): machinery and transport equipment 44%, intermediate manufactures 25%, chemicals 7%, raw materials and fuel 7% (2000). **Imports:** $50.4 billion (f.o.b., 2003 est.): machinery and transport equipment 40%, intermediate manufactures 21%, raw materials and fuels 13%, chemicals 11% (2000). **Major trading partners:** Germany, Slovakia, Austria, UK, Poland, France, Italy, Russia.

Geography The Czech Republic's central European landscape is dominated by the Bohemian Massif, which rises to heights of 3,000 ft (900 m) above sea level. This ring of mountains encircles a large elevated basin, the Bohemian Plateau. The principal rivers are the Elbe and the Vltava.

Government Parliamentary democracy.

History Probably about the 5th century A.D., Slavic tribes from the Vistula basin settled in the region of Bohemia, Moravia, and Silesia. The Czechs founded the kingdom of Bohemia and the Premyslide dynasty, which ruled Bohemia and Moravia from the 10th to the 16th century. One of the Bohemian kings, Charles IV, Holy Roman emperor, made Prague an imperial capital and a center of Latin scholarship. The Hussite movement founded by Jan Hus (1369?–1415) linked the Slavs to the Reformation and revived Czech nationalism, previously under German domination. A Hapsburg, Ferdinand I, ascended the throne in 1526. The Czechs rebelled in 1618, precipitating the Thirty Years' War (1618–1648). Defeated in 1620, they were ruled for the next 300 years as part of the Austrian empire. Full independence from the Hapsburgs was not achieved until the end of World War I, following the collapse of the Austrian-Hungarian Empire.

A union of the Czech lands and Slovakia was proclaimed in Prague on Nov. 14, 1918, and the Czech nation became one of the two component parts of the newly formed Czechoslovakian state. In March 1939, German troops occupied Czechoslovakia, and Czech Bohemia and Moravia became German protectorates for the duration of World War II. The former government returned in April 1945 when the war ended and the country's pre-1938 boundaries were restored. When elections were held in 1946, Communists became the dominant political party and gained control of the Czechoslovakian government in 1948. Thereafter, the former democracy was turned into a Soviet-style state.

Nearly 42 years of Communist rule ended with the nearly bloodless "velvet revolution" in 1989. Václav Havel, a leading playwright and dissident, was elected president of Czechoslovakia in 1989. Havel, imprisoned twice by the Communist regime and his plays banned, became an international symbol for human rights, democracy, and peaceful dissent. The return of democratic political reform saw a strong Slovak nationalist movement emerge by the end of 1991, which sought independence for Slovakia. When the general elections of June 1992 failed to resolve the continuing coexistence of the two republics within the federation, Czech and Slovak political leaders agreed to separate their states into two fully independent nations. On Jan. 1, 1993, the Czechoslovakian federation was dissolved and two separate independent countries were established—the Czech Republic and Slovakia. The Czech Republic joined NATO in March 1999.

In Aug. 2002, severe flooding caused 70,000 people in Prague and 200,000 nationwide to be evacuated.

President Václav Havel left office in Feb. 2003, after 13 years as president. Over the years, Havel lost some of his immense popularity with Czechs, who became disenchanted with his failings as a political leader. But internationally, Havel has remained a towering figure of moral authority and courage. In March, Vaclav Klaus became the Czech Republic's second president. A conservative economist, he and Havel often clashed. In May 2004, the Czech Republic joined the EU.

Denmark

KINGDOM OF DENMARK

National name: Kongeriget Danmark
Sovereign: Queen Margrethe II (1972)
Prime Minister: Anders Fogh Rasmussen (2001)
Area: 16,639 sq mi (43,094 sq km)[1]
Population (2004 est.): 5,413,392 (growth rate: 0.4%); birth rate: 11.6/1000; infant mortality rate: 4.6/1000; life expectancy: 77.4; density per sq mi: 325
Capital and largest city (2003 est.): Copenhagen, 1,094,400. **Other large cities:** Århus, 220,700; Odense, 144,600; Ålborg, 120,600. **Monetary unit:** Krone. **Languages:** Danish, Faeroese, Greenlandic (Inuit dialect), German; English is the predominant second language. **Ethnicity/race:** Scandinavian, Inuit, Faroese, German, Turkish, Iranian, Somali. **Religions:** Evangelical Lutheran 95%, other Protestant and Roman Catholic 3%, Muslim 2%. **Literacy rate:** 100%

Economic summary: GDP/PPP (2003 est.): $167.7 billion; per capita $31,200. **Real growth rate:** 0.3%. **Inflation:** 2.1%. **Unemployment:** 6%. **Arable land:** 56%. **Agriculture:** barley, wheat, potatoes, sugar beets; pork, dairy products; fish. **Labor force:** 2.856 million (2000 est.); services 79%, industry 17%, agriculture 4% (2002 est.). **Industries:** food processing, machinery and equipment, textiles and clothing, chemical products, electronics, construction, furniture and other wood products, shipbuilding, windmills. **Natural resources:** petroleum, natural gas, fish, salt, limestone, stone, gravel and sand. **Exports:** $64.16 billion (f.o.b., 2003 est.): machinery and instruments, meat and meat products, dairy products, fish, chemicals, furniture, ships, windmills. **Imports:** $54.47 billion (f.o.b., 2003 est.): machinery and equipment, raw materials and semimanufactures for industry, chemicals, grain and foodstuffs, consumer goods. **Major trading partners:** Germany, Sweden, UK, U.S., France, Norway, Japan, Netherlands, Italy.

1. Excluding Faeroe Islands and Greenland.

Geography Smallest of the Scandinavian countries (half the size of Maine), Denmark occupies the Jutland peninsula, a lowland area. The country also consists of several islands in the Baltic Sea; the two largest are Sjælland, the site of Copenhagen, and Fyn.

Government Constitutional monarchy.

History From 10,000 to 1500 B.C., the population of present-day Denmark evolved from a society of hunters and fishers into an agricultural one. Called Jutland by the end of the 8th century, its mariners were among the Vikings, or Norsemen, who raided western Europe and the British Isles from the 9th to 11th century.

The country was Christianized by Saint Ansgar and Harald Blaatand (Bluetooth)—the first Christian king—in the 10th century. Harald's son, Sweyn, conquered England in 1013. Sweyn's son, Canute the Great, who reigned from 1014 to 1035, united Denmark, England, and Norway under his rule; the southern tip of Sweden was part of Denmark until the 17th century. On Canute's death, civil war tore apart the country until Waldemar I (1157–1182) reestablished Danish hegemony over the north.

In 1282, the nobles won the Great Charter, and Eric V was forced to share power with Parliament and a Council of Nobles. Waldemar IV (1340–1375) restored Danish power, checked only by the Hanseatic League of north German cities allied with ports from Holland to Poland. Denmark, Norway, and Sweden united under the rule of his daughter Margrethe in 1397. But Sweden later achieved autonomy and in 1523, under Gustavus I, independence.

Denmark supported Napoléon, for which it was punished at the Congress of Vienna in 1815 by the loss of Norway to Sweden. In 1864, the Prussians under Bismarck and the Austrians made war on Denmark as an initial step in the formation of Germany. Denmark was neutral in World War I.

In 1940, Denmark was invaded by the Nazis. King Christian X reluctantly cautioned his fellow Danes to accept the occupation, but there was widespread resistance against the Nazis. Denmark was the only occupied country in World War II to save all its Jews from extermination, by smuggling them out of the country.

Beginning in 1944, Denmark's relationship with its territories changed substantially. In that year, Iceland declared its independence from Denmark, ending a union that had existed since 1380. In 1948, the Faeroe Islands, which had also belonged to Denmark since 1380, were granted home rule, and in 1953, Greenland officially became a territory of Denmark.

In 2001 elections, the dominant Social-Democrat Party lost to Anders Fogh Rasmussen of the center-right Liberal Party, which formed a coalition with the Conservative Party. Prime Minister Fogh Rasmussen, author of *From Socialist to Minimalist State*, is a strong proponent of privitization, deregulation, and limited government.

Immigration to Denmark fell dramatically in 2002, after Fogh Rasmussen instituted Europe's most restrictive laws for asylum-seekers. Because of Denmark's social welfare benefits, it had become a much sought-after haven for refugees.

Denmark was a strong ally to the U.S. during the Iraq war, one of five countries to contribute combat troops (the others were the U.S., UK, Australia, and Poland).

Outlying Territories of Denmark

Faeroe Islands

Status: Autonomous part of Denmark
Chief of State: Queen Margrethe II (1972)
High Commissioner: Birgit Kleis (2001)
Prime Minister: Jóannes Eidesgaard (2004)
Area: 540 sq mi (1,399 sq km)
Population (2004 est.): 46,662 (average annual growth rate: 0.7%); birth rate: 13.9/1000; infant mortality rate: 6.4/1000; life expectancy: 79.1; density per sq mi: 86
Capital and largest city (2003 est.): Tórshavn, 17,300.
Monetary unit: Faeroese krone. **Languages:** Faeroese, Danish (both official). **Ethnicity/race:** Scandinavian. **Religions:** Evangelical Lutheran. **Literacy rate:** n.a.

This group of 18 islands, of which 17 are inhabited, is located in the North Atlantic about 200 mi (322 km) northwest of the Shetland Islands. They were settled by the Vikings, the ancestors of the modern-day Faeroese, in the 8th century. The Faeroese language is derived from Old Norse. The islands joined Denmark in 1386 and have been part of the Danish kingdom ever since. The Faeroes have had home rule, under Danish authority, since 1948.

Greenland

Status: Autonomous part of Denmark
Chief of State: Queen Margrethe II (1972)
High Commissioner: Gunnar Martens (1995)
Premier: Jonathan Motzfeldt (1997)
Area: 836,326 sq mi (incl. 677,851 sq mi covered by icecap) (2,166,086 sq km)
Population (2004 est.): 56,384 (average annual growth rate: 0%); birth rate: 16.0/1000; infant mortality rate: 16.3/1000; life expectancy: 69.3; density per sq mi: 0.07
Capital and largest city (2003 est.): Godthaab, 14,100.
Monetary unit: Krone. **Languages:** Greenlandic (East Inuit), Danish, English. **Ethnicity/race:** Greenlander 88% (Eskimos and Greenland-born whites), Danish and other 12% (2000). **Religions:** Evangelical Lutheran. **Literacy rate:** n.a.

The Inuit are believed to have crossed from North America to northwest Greenland, the world's largest island, between 4000 B.C. and A.D. 1000. Greenland was colonized in 985–986 by Eric the Red. The Norse settlements declined in the 14th century, however, mainly as a result of a cooling in Greenland's climate, and in the 15th century they became extinct. In 1721, Greenland was recolonized by the Royal Greenland Trading Company of Denmark.

Greenland was under U.S. protection during World War II, but maintained Danish sovereignty. A definitive agreement for the joint defense of Greenland within the framework of NATO was signed in 1951. A large U.S.

air base at Thule in the far north was completed in 1953. Under 1953 amendments to the Danish constitution, Greenland became part of Denmark, with two representatives in the Danish Folketing. On May 1, 1979, Greenland gained home rule, with its own local Parliament (Landsting).

Djibouti

REPUBLIC OF DJIBOUTI

National name: Jumhouriyya Djibouti
President: Ismail Omar Guelleh (1999)
Prime Minister: Dileita Mohamed Dileita (2001)
Area: 8,880 sq mi (23,000 sq km)
Population (2004 est.): 466,900 (growth rate: 2.1%); birth rate: 40.4/1000; infant mortality rate: 105.5/1000; life expectancy: 43.1; density per sq mi: 53
Capital (1995 est.): Djibouti, 383,000. **Monetary unit:** Djibouti franc. **Languages:** French and Arabic (both official), Somali, Afar. **Ethnicity/race:** Somali 60%, Afar 35%, French, Arab, Ethiopian, and Italian 5%. **Religions:** Islam 94%, Christian 6%. **Literacy rate:** 68% (2003 est.)
Economic summary: GDP/PPP (2002 est.): $619 million; per capita $1,300. **Real growth rate:** 3.5%. **Inflation:** 2%. **Unemployment:** 50% (2000 est.). **Arable land:** 0%. **Agriculture:** fruits, vegetables; goats, sheep, camels. **Labor:** 282,000 (2000). **Industries:** construction, agricultural processing. **Natural resources:** geothermal areas. **Exports:** $155 million (f.o.b., 2002 est.): reexports, hides and skins, coffee (in transit). **Imports:** $665 million (f.o.b., 2002 est.): foods, beverages, transport equipment, chemicals, petroleum products. **Major trading partners:** Somalia, Yemen, Pakistan, Ethiopia, UAE, Saudi Arabia, U.S., France, China, Netherlands.

Geography Djibouti lies in northeast Africa on the Gulf of Aden at the southern entrance to the Red Sea. It borders on Ethiopia, Eritrea, and Somalia. The country, the size of Massachusetts, is mainly a stony desert, with scattered plateaus and highlands.

Government Republic with a unicameral legislature.

History Ablé immigrants from Arabia migrated to what is now Djibouti in about the 3rd century B.C. Their descendants are the Afars, one of the two main ethnic groups that make up Djibouti today. Somali Issas arrived thereafter. Islam came to the region in 825.

Djibouti was acquired by France between 1843 and 1886 by treaties with the Somali sultans. Small, arid, and sparsely populated, it is important chiefly because of the capital city's port, the terminal of the Djibouti–Addis Ababa railway that carries 60% of Ethiopia's foreign trade. Originally known as French Somaliland, the colony voted in 1958 and 1967 to remain under French rule. It was renamed the Territory of the Afars and Issas in 1967 and took the name of its capital city on June 27, 1977, when France transferred sovereignty to the new independent nation of Djibouti. On Sept. 4, 1992, voters approved in referendum a new multiparty constitution. In 1991, conflict between the Afars and the Issa-dominated government erupted and the continued warfare has ravaged the country.

The dictatorial president, Hassan Gouled Aptidon, who had run the country since its independence, finally stepped aside in 1999, and Ismail Omar Guelleh was elected president. In March 2000, the main Afars rebel group signed a peace accord with the government. The fighting, severe drought, and the presence of tens of thousands of refugees from its war-torn neighbors, Ethiopia and Somalia, have severely strained Djibouti's agricultural capacity.

In April 2000 experts estimated some 150,000 people, or more than one-quarter of the population, needed food aid. The United Nations agreed to spend $2.7 million to increase the city of Djibouti's port facilities since it is a crucial regional grain terminus. In 2002, Djibouti became a key U.S. military base used to combat terrorism.

Dominica

COMMONWEALTH OF DOMINICA

President: Nicholas Liverpool (2003)
Prime Minister: Roosevelt Skerrit (2004)
Area: 291 sq mi (754 sq km)
Population (2004 est.): 69,278 (growth rate: –0.5%); birth rate: 16.3/1000; infant mortality rate: 14.8/1000; life expectancy: 74.4; density per sq mi: 238
Capital and largest city (2003 est.): Roseau, 20,000.
Monetary unit: East Caribbean dollar. **Languages:** English (official) and French patois. **Ethnicity/race:** black, mixed black and European, European, Syrian, Carib Amerindian. **Religions:** Roman Catholic 77%, Protestant 15% (Methodist 5%, Pentecostal 3%, Seventh-Day Adventist 3%, Baptist 2%, other 2%), none 2%, other 6%. **Literacy rate:** 94% (2003 est.)
Economic summary: GDP/PPP (2002 est.): $380 million; per capita $5,400. **Real growth rate:** –1%. **Inflation:** 1% (2001 est.). **Unemployment:** 23% (2000 est.). **Arable land:** 4%. **Labor force:** 25,000 (1999 est); agriculture 40%, industry and commerce 32%, services 28%. **Agriculture:** bananas, citrus, mangoes, root crops, coconuts, cocoa; forest and fishery potential not exploited. **Industries:** soap, coconut oil, tourism, copra, furniture, cement blocks, shoes. **Natural resources:** timber, hydropower, arable land. **Exports:** $39 million (f.o.b., 2003 est.): bananas, soap, bay oil, vegetables, grapefruit, oranges. **Imports:** $98.2 million (f.o.b., 2003 est.): manufactured goods, machinery and equipment, food, chemicals. **Major trading partners:** UK, Jamaica, U.S., Antigua and Barbuda, Guyana, Trinidad and Tobago, China, South Korea, Japan. **Member of Commonwealth of Nations**

Geography Dominica (pronounced Dom-in-EEK-a) is a mountainous island of volcanic origin in the Lesser Antilles in the Caribbean, south of Guadeloupe and north of Martinique.

Government Parliamentary democracy.

History Explored by Columbus in 1493, Dominica was claimed by Britain and France until 1763, when it was formally ceded to Britain. Along with other Windward Isles, it became a self-governing member of the West Indies Associated States in free association with Britain in 1967.

Dissatisfaction over the slow pace of reconstruction after Hurricane David devastated the island in Sept. 1979 brought a landslide victory to Mary Eugenia Charles of the Freedom Party in July 1980. The Freedom Party won again in 1985 and 1990, and the government sold state enterprises. The opposition United Workers' Party won in June 1995. In 1997 Dominica became the first Caribbean country to participate in the work of Green Globe, aiming to make Dominica a model ecotourism destination. Although the island is poorer than some of its Caribbean neighbors, Dominica has a relatively low crime rate and does not have the extremes of wealth and poverty evident on other islands. Economic austerity measures, including higher taxes, were introduced in 2002. Massive protests followed.

In 2004, Dominica agreed to cut diplomatic ties with Taiwan after mainland China promised to give it $100 million in aid.

Dominican Republic

National name: República Dominicana
President: Leonel Fernández (2004)
Area: 18,815 sq mi (48,730 sq km)
Population (2004 est.): 8,833,634 (growth rate: 1.3%);
birth rate: 23.6/1000; infant mortality rate: 33.3/1000;
life expectancy: 67.6; density per sq mi: 470
Capital and largest city (2003 est.): Santo Domingo,
2,851,300 (metro.area), 2,252,400 (city proper). **Other
large city:** Santiago de los Caballeros, 501,800.
Monetary unit: Dominican Peso. **Languages:**
Spanish. **Ethnicity/race:** white 16%, black 11%,
mixed 73%. **Religion:** Roman Catholic 95%. **Literacy
rate:** 85% (2003 est.)
Economic summary: GDP/PPP (2003 est.): $52.16
billion; per capita $6,000. **Real growth rate:** −1.8%.
Inflation: 21.2%. **Unemployment:** 15.5%. **Arable
land:** 21%. **Agriculture:** sugarcane, coffee, cotton,
cocoa, tobacco, rice, beans, potatoes, corn, bananas;
cattle, pigs, dairy products, beef, eggs. **Labor force:**
2.3 million to 2.6 million (2000 est); services and
government 58.7%, industry 24.3%, agriculture 17%
(1998 est.). **Industries:** tourism, sugar processing,
ferronickel and gold mining, textiles, cement, tobacco.
Natural resources: nickel, bauxite, gold, silver.
Exports: $5.524 billion (f.o.b., 2003 est.): ferronickel,
sugar, gold, silver, coffee, cocoa, tobacco, meats,
consumer goods. **Imports:** $7.911 billion (f.o.b., 2003
est.): foodstuffs, petroleum, cotton and fabrics,
chemicals and pharmaceuticals. **Major trading
partners:** U.S., Canada, UK, Venezuela, Mexico,
Spain.

Geography The Dominican Republic in the West
Indies occupies the eastern two-thirds of the island of
Hispaniola, which it shares with Haiti. Its area equals
that of Vermont and New Hampshire combined.
Duarte Peak, at 10,417 ft (3,175 m), is the highest
point in the West Indies.

Government Representative democracy.

History The Dominican Republic was explored by
Columbus on his first voyage in 1492. He named it La
Española, and his son, Diego, was its first viceroy. The
capital, Santo Domingo, founded in 1496, is the oldest
European settlement in the Western Hemisphere.

Spain ceded the colony to France in 1795, and Haitian blacks under Toussaint L'Ouverture conquered it
in 1801. In 1808 the people revolted and captured
Santo Domingo the next year, setting up the first republic. Spain regained title to the colony in 1814. In 1821
Spanish rule was overthrown, but in 1822 the colony
was reconquered by the Haitians. In 1844 the Haitians
were thrown out, and the Dominican Republic was
established, headed by Pedro Santana. Uprisings and
Haitian attacks led Santana to make the country a province of Spain from 1861 to 1865.

President Buenaventura Báez, faced with an
economy in shambles, attempted to have the country
annexed to the U.S. in 1870, but the U.S. Senate
refused to ratify a treaty of annexation. Disorder continued until the dictatorship of Ulíses Heureaux; in
1916, when chaos broke out again, the U.S. sent in a
contingent of marines, who remained until 1934.

A sergeant in the Dominican army trained by the
marines, Rafaél Leonides Trujillo Molina, overthrew
Horacio Vásquez in 1930 and established a dictatorship
that lasted until his assassination in 1961, 31 years
later. In 1962, Juan Bosch of the leftist Dominican
Revolutionary Party, became the first democratically
elected president in four decades.

In 1963, a military coup ousted Bosch, and installed
a military-backed civilian triumvirate. Leftists rebelled

against the new regime in April 1965, and U.S. president Lyndon Johnson sent in marines and troops. After
a cease-fire in May, a compromise installed Hector
Garcia-Godoy as provisional president. In 1966, right-
wing candidate Joaquin Balaguer won in free elections
against Bosch, and U.S. and other foreign troops withdrew.

In 1978 the army suspended the counting of ballots
when Balaguer trailed in a fourth-term bid. After a
warning from President Jimmy Carter, however, Balaguer accepted the victory of Antonio Guzmán of the
Dominican Revolutionary Party. In 1982 elections, Salvador Jorge Blanco of the Dominican Revolutionary
Party defeated Balaguer and Bosch. Balaguer was
again elected president in May 1986 and remained in
office for the next ten years.

In 1996, U.S.-raised Leonel Fernández secured more
than 51% of the vote through an alliance with Balaguer. The first item on the president's agenda was the
partial sale of some state-owned enterprises. Fernández
was praised for ending decades of isolationism and
improving ties with other Caribbean countries, but he
was criticized for not fighting corruption and alleviat-
ing the poverty that affects 60% of the population.

In Aug. 2000 the center-left Hipólito Mejía was
elected president amid popular discontent over power
outages in the recently privatized electric industry. In
2001 the army was deployed in major cities to fight
rising crime. In May 2004 presidential elections, the
previous president, Leonel Fernández (1996–2000),
won 57% of the vote, defeating incumbent Hipólito
Mejía. He vowed to institute austerity measures to rescue the country from its current economic crisis.

East Timor

EAST TIMOR

President: José Alexandre (Xanana) Gusmão (2002)
Prime Minister: Mari Alkatiri (2002)
Area: 5,794 sq mi (15,007 sq km)
Population (2004 est.): 1,019,252 (growth rate: 2.1%);
birth rate: 27.5/1000; infant mortality rate: 48.9/1000;
life expectancy: 65.6; density per sq mi: 176
Capital and largest city (2003 est.): Dili, 50,800.
Monetary unit: U.S. dollar. **Languages:** Tetum,
Portuguese (official); Bahasa Indonesia, English; other
indigenous languages, including Tetum, Galole,
Mambae, and Kemak. **Ethnicity/race:** Austronesian
(Malayo-Polynesian), Papuan, small Chinese minority.
Religions: Roman Catholic 90%, Islam 4%, Protestant
3%, Hindu 0.5%, Buddhist, animist (1992 est.).
Literary rate: 48% (2001)
Economic summary: GDP/PPP (2001 est.): $440
billion; per capita $500. **Real growth rate:** −3%.
Inflation: 8% (2003 est.. **Unemployment:** 50%
(including underemployment) (1992 est.). **Arable land:**
n.a. **Agriculture:** coffee, rice, maize, cassava, sweet
potatoes, soybeans, cabbage, mangoes, bananas,
vanilla. **Labor force:** n.a. **Industries:** printing, soap
manufacturing, handicrafts, woven cloth. **Natural
resources:** gold, petroleum, natural gas, manganese,
marble. **Exports:** $8 million (2001 est.): coffee,
sandalwood, marble; note—the potential for oil and
vanilla exports. **Imports:** $237 million (2001 est.):
mainly food. **Major trading partners:** n.a.

Geography East Timor is located in the eastern part
of Timor, an island in the Indonesian archipelago that
lies between the South China Sea and the Indian
Ocean. East Timor includes the enclave of Oecussi,
which is located within West Timor (Indonesia). After
Indonesia, East Timor's closest neighbor is Australia,
400 mi to the south. It is semi-arid and mountainous.

Government Republic.

History Timor was first colonized by the Portuguese in 1520. The Dutch, who claimed many of the surrounding islands, took control of the western portion of the island in 1613. Portugal and the Netherlands fought over the island until an 1860 treaty divided Timor, granting Portugal the eastern half of the island as well as the western enclave of Oecussi (the first Portuguese settlement on the island). Australia and Japan fought each other on the island during World War II; nearly 50,000 East Timorese died during the subsequent Japanese occupation.

In 1949, the Netherlands gave up its colonies in the Dutch West Indies, including West Timor, and the nation of Indonesia was born. East Timor remained under Portuguese control until 1975, when the Portuguese abruptly pulled out after 455 years of colonization. The sudden Portuguese withdrawal left the island vulnerable. On July 16, 1976, 9 days after the Democratic Republic of East Timor was declared an independent nation, Indonesia invaded and annexed it. Although no country except Australia officially recognized the annexation, Indonesia's invasion was sanctioned by the United States and other western countries, who had cultivated Indonesia as a trading partner and cold-war ally (Fretilin, the East Timorese political party spearheading independence, was Marxist at the time).

Indonesia's invasion and its brutal occupation of East Timor—small, remote, and desperately poor—largely escaped international attention. East Timor's resistance movement was violently suppressed by Indonesian military forces, and more than 200,000 Timorese were reported to have died from famine, disease, and fighting since the annexation. Indonesia's human rights abuses finally began receiving international notice in the 1990s, and in 1996 two East Timorese activists, Bishop Carlos Filipe Ximenes Belo and José Ramos-Horta, received the Nobel Peace Prize for their efforts to gain freedom peacefully.

After Indonesia's hard-line president Suharto left office in 1998, his successor, B. J. Habibie, unexpectedly announced his willingness to hold a referendum on East Timorese independence, reversing 25 years of Indonesian intransigence. As the referendum on self-rule drew closer, fighting between separatist guerrillas and pro-Indonesian paramilitary forces in East Timor intensified. The UN-sponsored referendum had to be rescheduled twice because of violence. On Aug. 30, 1999, 78.5% of the population voted to secede from Indonesia. But in the days following the referendum, pro-Indonesian militias and Indonesian soldiers retaliated by razing towns, slaughtering civilians, and forcing a third of the population out of the province. After enormous international pressure, Indonesia finally agreed to allow UN forces into East Timor on Sept. 12. Led by Australia, an international peacekeeping force began restoring order to the ravaged region.

The UN Transitional Authority in East Timor (UNTAET) then governed the territory for nearly three years. On May 20, 2002, nationhood was declared. Charismatic rebel leader José Alexandre Gusmão, who was imprisoned by Indonesia from 1992 to 1999, was overwhelmingly elected the nation's first president on April 14, 2002. The president has a largely symbolic role; real power rests with the parliament and Prime Minister Mari Alkatiri, also a former guerrilla leader.

The first new country of the millennium, East Timor is also one of the world's poorest. Its meager infrastructure was destroyed by the Indonesian militias in 1999 and the economy, primarily made up of subsistence farming and fishing, is in shambles. East Timor's off-shore gas and oil reserves promised the only real hope for lifting it out of poverty, but a dispute with Australia over the rights to the oil reserves in the East Timor Sea has currently thwarted those efforts. The oil and gas fields lie much closer to East Timor than to Australia, but a 1989 deal between Indonesia and Australia set the maritime boundary along Australia's continental shelf, which gives it control of 85% of the sea and most of the oil. East Timor wants the border redrawn halfway between the two countries, and estimates that this would allow it to earn $12 billion over the next 30 years, as opposed to $4.4 billion. The two countries reached a temporary agreement in August 2004, which granted East Timor a larger share of the oil and gas revenues. In exchange, it would no longer request that the maritime border be redrawn.

Ecuador

REPUBLIC OF ECUADOR

National name: República del Ecuador
President: Lucio Gutiérrez (2003)
Area: 109,483 sq mi (283,560 sq km)
Population (2004 est.): 13,212,742 (growth rate: 1.0%); birth rate: 23.2/1000; infant mortality rate: 24.5/1000; life expectancy: 76.0; density per sq mi: 121
Capital (2003 est.): Quito, 1,780,700 (metro. area), 1,443,900 (city proper). **Largest cities:** Guayaquil, 2,597,600 (metro. area), 2,013,500 (city proper); Cuenca, 285,700. **Monetary unit:** U.S. dollar.
Languages: Spanish (official), Quechua, other Amerindian languages. **Ethnicity/race:** mestizo (mixed Amerindian and white) 65%, Amerindian 25%, Spanish 7%, black 3%. **Religion:** Roman Catholic 95%.
Literacy rate: 93% (2003 est.)
Economic summary: GDP/PPP (2003 est.): $45.46 billion; per capita $3,300. **Real growth rate:** 2.6%. **Inflation:** 6.1%. **Unemployment:** 9.8% underemployment 47%. **Arable land:** 6%. **Agriculture:** bananas, coffee, cocoa, rice, potatoes, manioc (tapioca), plantains, sugarcane; cattle, sheep, pigs, beef, pork, dairy products; balsa wood; fish, shrimp . **Labor force:** 3.8 million (urban) (2002); agriculture 30%, industry 25%, services 45% (2001 est.). **Industries:** petroleum, food processing, textiles, metal work, paper products, wood products, chemicals, plastics, fishing, lumber. **Natural resources:** petroleum, fish, timber, hydropower. **Exports:** $6.073 billion (2003 est.): petroleum, bananas, shrimp, coffee, cocoa, cut flowers, fish. **Imports:** $6.22 billion (2003 est.): machinery and equipment, chemicals, raw materials, fuels; consumer goods. **Major trading partners:** U.S., Colombia, South Korea, Germany, Italy, Japan, Chile, Brazil.

Geography Ecuador, about equal in area to Nevada, is in the northwest part of South America fronting on the Pacific. To the north is Colombia and to the east and south is Peru. Two high and parallel ranges of the Andes, traversing the country from north to south, are topped by tall volcanic peaks. The highest is Chimborazo at 20,577 ft (6,272 m). The Galápagos Islands (or Colón Archipelago; 3,029 sq mi; 7,845 sq km), in the Pacific Ocean about 600 mi (966 km) west of the South American mainland, became part of Ecuador in 1832.

Government Republic.

History The tribes in the northern highlands of Ecuador formed the Kingdom of Quito around 1000. It was absorbed, by conquest and marriage, into the Inca empire. Spanish conquistador Francisco Pizarro conquered the land in 1532, and through the 17th century a Spanish colony thrived by exploitation of the Indians. The first revolt against Spain occurred in 1809. In

1819, Ecuador joined Venezuela, Colombia, and Panama in a confederacy known as Greater Colombia.

When Greater Colombia collapsed in 1830, Ecuador became independent. Revolts and dictatorships followed; it had 48 presidents during the first 131 years of the republic. Conservatives ruled until the revolution of 1895 ushered in nearly a half century of Radical Liberal rule, during which the church was disestablished and freedom of worship, speech, and press was introduced. Although it was under military rule in the 1970s, the country did not experience the violence and repression characteristic of other Latin American military regimes. Its last 30 years of democracy, however, have been largely ineffectual because of a weak executive branch and a strong, fractious Congress.

Peru invaded Ecuador in 1941 and seized a large tract of Ecuadorian territory in the disputed Amazon. In 1981 and 1995 war broke out again. In May 1999, Ecuador and Peru signed a treaty ending a nearly 60-year border dispute involving the stretch of Amazon jungle.

In 1998, Ecuador experienced one of its worst economic crises. El Niño caused $3 billion in damage; the price of its principal export, oil, plunged; and its inflation rate, 43%, was the highest in Latin America. In 1999, the government was near bankruptcy, the currency lost 40% of its value against the dollar, and the poverty rate soared to 70%, doubling in five years. The president's economic austerity plan was protested with massive strikes in March 1999.

President Jamil Mahuad was overthrown in Jan. 2000, in the first military coup in Latin America in a decade. The junta gave power to the vice president, Gustavo Noboa. Faced with the worst economic crisis in Ecuador's history, Noboa restructured Ecuador's foreign debt, adopted the U.S. dollar as the national currency, and continued privatization of state-owned industries, generating enormous opposition. In Feb. 2001, the government cut fuel prices after violent protests by Indians, who are among Ecuador's most disadvantaged people.

Within two years, Ecuador's economy had rebounded from the brink of collapse. The economy grew by 5.4% for 2001, the highest rate in Latin America. Inflation was 22%, down from 91% in 2000, and the budget was balanced. But chronic corruption among senior government officials, as well as among the courts and the judiciary, has continued.

Lucio Gutiérrez, a leftist colonel best known for orchestrating the 2000 coup against President Jamil Mahuad, was elected to the presidency in 2003 on an anti-corruption platform. He became Ecuador's sixth president in seven years. His attempts to introduce austere fiscal reforms, however, quickly alienated his political base, and numerous national strikes took place over 2003. But some economic improvements were seen in 2003: the GDP grew by an estimated 2.7%, and inflation dropped to a remarkable 6%.

Egypt

ARAB REPUBLIC OF EGYPT

President: Hosni Mubarak (1981)
Prime Minister: Ahmed Nazif (2004)
Area: 386,660 sq mi (1,001,450 sq km)
Population (2004 est.): 76,117,421 (growth rate: 1.8%); birth rate: 23.8/1000; infant mortality rate: 33.9/1000; life expectancy: 70.7; density per sq mi: 197
Capital and largest city (2003 est.): Cairo, 15,892,400 (metro. area), 7,937,700 (city proper). **Other large cities:** Alexandria, 3,891,000; Giza, 2,597,600 (part of Cairo metro. area); Shubra el Khema, 1,018,000 (part of Cairo metro. area); El Mahalla el Kubra, 462,300.

Monetary unit: Egyptian pound. **Language:** Arabic (official), English and French widely understood by educated classes. **Ethnicity/race:** Eastern Hamitic stock (Egyptians, Bedouins, and Berbers) 99%, Greek, Nubian, Armenian, other European (primarily Italian and French) 1%. **Religions:** Islam (mostly Sunni) 94%, Coptic Christian and other 6%. **Literacy rate:** 58% (2003 est.)
Economic summary: GDP/PPP (2003 est.): $294.3 billion; per capita $3,900. **Real growth rate:** 2.8%. **Inflation:** 4.5%. **Unemployment:** 9.9%. **Arable land:** 3%. **Agriculture:** cotton, rice, corn, wheat, beans, fruits, vegetables; cattle, water buffalo, sheep, goats. **Labor force:** 20.1 million; agriculture 29%, industry 22%, services 49% (2000 est.). **Industries:** textiles, food processing, tourism, chemicals, hydrocarbons, construction, cement, metals. **Natural resources:** petroleum, natural gas, iron ore, phosphates, manganese, limestone, gypsum, talc, asbestos, lead, zinc. **Exports:** $8.759 billion (f.o.b., 2003 est.): crude oil and petroleum products, cotton, textiles, metal products, chemicals. **Imports:** $14.75 billion (f.o.b., 2003 est.): machinery and equipment, foodstuffs, chemicals, wood products, fuels. **Major trading partners:** U.S., Italy, UK, Germany, France, China.

Geography Egypt, at the northeast corner of Africa on the Mediterranean Sea, is bordered on the west by Libya, on the south by the Sudan, and on the east by the Red Sea and Israel. It is nearly one and one-half times the size of Texas. Egypt is divided into two unequal, extremely arid regions by the landscape's dominant feature, the northward-flowing Nile River. The Nile starts 100 mi (161 km) south of the Mediterranean and fans out to a sea front of 155 mi between the cities of Alexandria and Port Said.

Government Republic.

History Egyptian history dates back to about 4000 B.C., when the kingdoms of upper and lower Egypt, already highly sophisticated, were united. Egypt's golden age coincided with the 18th and 19th dynasties (16th to 13th centuries B.C.), during which the empire was established. Persia conquered Egypt in 525 B.C., Alexander the Great subdued it in 332 B.C., and then the dynasty of the Ptolemies ruled the land until 30 B.C., when Cleopatra, last of the line, committed suicide and Egypt became a Roman, then Byzantine, province. Arab caliphs ruled Egypt from 641 until 1517, when the Turks took it for their Ottoman Empire.

Napoléon's armies occupied the country from 1798 to 1801. In 1805, Mohammed Ali, leader of a band of Albanian soldiers, became pasha of Egypt. After completion of the Suez Canal in 1869, the French and British took increasing interest in Egypt. British troops occupied Egypt in 1882, and British resident agents became its actual administrators, though it remained under nominal Turkish sovereignty. In 1914, this fiction was ended, and Egypt became a protectorate of Britain.

Egyptian nationalism forced Britain to declare Egypt an independent sovereign state on Feb. 28, 1922, although the British reserved rights for the protection of the Suez Canal and the defense of Egypt. In 1936, by an Anglo-Egyptian treaty of alliance, all British troops and officials were to be withdrawn, except from the Suez Canal Zone. When World War II started, Egypt remained neutral. British imperial troops finally ended the Nazi threat to Suez in 1942 in the battle of El Alamein, west of Alexandria. In 1951, Egypt abrogated the 1936 treaty and the 1899 Anglo-Egyptian condominium of the Sudan. Rioting and attacks on

British troops in the Suez Canal Zone followed, reaching a climax in Jan. 1952. The army, led by Gen. Mohammed Naguib, seized power on July 23, 1952. Three days later, King Farouk abdicated in favor of his infant son. The monarchy was abolished and a republic proclaimed on June 18, 1953, with Naguib holding the posts of provisional president and premier. He relinquished the latter in 1954 to Gamal Abdel Nasser, leader of the ruling military junta, who was confirmed as president in a referendum on June 23, 1956.

Nasser's policies embroiled his country in continual conflict. In 1956, the U.S. and Britain withdrew their pledges of financial aid for the building of the Aswan High Dam. In response, Nasser nationalized the Suez Canal and expelled British oil and embassy officials. Israel, barred from the canal and exasperated by terrorist raids, invaded the Gaza Strip and the Sinai Peninsula. Britain and France, after demanding Egyptian evacuation of the canal zone, attacked Egypt on Oct. 31, 1956. Worldwide pressure forced Britain, France, and Israel to halt the hostilities. A UN emergency force occupied the canal zone, and all troops were evacuated in the spring of 1957.

From 1956 to 1961, Egypt and Syria united to form a single country called the United Arab Republic (UAR). Syria ended this relationship in 1961 after a military coup, but Egypt continued to call itself the UAR until 1971.

On June 5, 1967, Israel invaded the Sinai Peninsula, the East Bank of the Jordan River, and the zone around the Gulf of Aqaba. A UN cease-fire on June 10 saved the Arabs from complete rout. Nasser declared the 1967 cease-fire void along the canal in April 1969 and began a war of attrition. The U.S. peace plan of June 19, 1970, resulted in Egypt's agreement to reinstate the cease-fire for at least three months (from Aug.) and to accept Israel's existence within "recognized and secure" frontiers that might emerge from UN-mediated talks. In return, Israel accepted the principle of withdrawing from occupied territories. On Sept. 28, 1970, Nasser died of a heart attack. Anwar el-Sadat, an associate of Nasser and a former newspaper editor, became the next president.

In July 1972, Sadat ordered the expulsion of Soviet "advisers and experts" from Egypt because the Russians had not provided the sophisticated weapons he felt were needed to retake territory lost to Israel in 1967. The fourth Arab-Israeli War broke out on Oct. 6, 1973, during the Jewish holiday of Yom Kippur. Egypt swept deep into the Sinai, while Syria strove to throw Israel off the Golan Heights. A UN-sponsored truce was accepted on Oct. 22. In Jan. 1974, both sides agreed to a settlement negotiated by U.S. secretary of state Henry A. Kissinger that gave Egypt a narrow strip along the entire Sinai bank of the Suez Canal. In June, President Nixon made the first visit by a U.S. president to Egypt and full diplomatic relations were established. The Suez Canal was cleared and reopened on June 5, 1975.

In the most audacious act of his career, Sadat flew to Jerusalem at the invitation of Prime Minister Menachem Begin and pleaded before Israel's Knesset on Nov. 20, 1977, for a permanent peace settlement. The Arab world reacted with fury—only Morocco, Tunisia, Sudan, and Oman approved. Egypt and Israel signed a formal peace treaty on March 26, 1979. The pact ended 30 years of war and established diplomatic and commercial relations.

Egyptian and Israeli officials met in the Sinai desert on April 26, 1979, to implement the peace treaty calling for the phased withdrawal of occupation forces from the peninsula. By mid-1980, two-thirds of the Sinai was transferred, but progress was not matched elsewhere—the negotiation of Arab autonomy in the Gaza Strip and the West Bank remained stymied. Sadat halted further talks in Aug. 1980 because of continued Israeli settlement of the West Bank. On Oct. 6, 1981, Sadat was assassinated by extremist Muslim soldiers at a parade in Cairo. Vice President Hosni Mubarak, a former air force chief of staff, succeeded him. Israel completed the return of the Sinai to Egyptian control on April 25, 1982. Israel's invasion of Lebanon in June brought a marked cooling in Egyptian-Israeli relations, but not a disavowal of the peace treaty.

The government has concentrated much of its time and attention in recent years on combating Islamic extremists, who have in particular targeted Copts (Egyptian Christians). In 1997, a terrorist attack on foreign tourists killed 70. During the 1990s, about 26,000 Islamic militants were imprisoned and dozens were executed.

In 2004, Mubarak replaced his prime minister, as well as half his cabinet and half of Egypt's 26 regional governors.

El Salvador

REPUBLIC OF EL SALVADOR

National name: República de El Salvador
President: Antonio Saca (2004)
Area: 8,124 sq mi (21,040 sq km)
Population (2004 est.): 6,587,541 (growth rate: 1.8%); birth rate: 27.5/1000; infant mortality rate: 25.9/1000; life expectancy: 70.9; density per sq mi: 811
Capital and largest city (2003 est.): San Salvador, 1,791,700 (metro. area), 504,700 (city proper). **Other large cities:** Santa Ana, 167,200; San Miguel, 145,100; Zacatecoluca, 36,700. **Monetary unit:** Colón; U.S. dollar. **Language:** Spanish, Nahua (among some Amerindians). **Ethnicity/race:** mestizo 90%, white 9%, Amerindian 1%. **Religion:** Catholics 83%; growing population of evangelical Protestants (1992). **Literacy rate:** 80% (2003 est.)
Economic summary: GDP/PPP (2003 est.): $30.99 billion; per capita $4,800. **Real growth rate:** 1.4%. **Inflation:** 2.1%. **Unemployment:** 6.5%—but the economy has much underemployment. **Arable land:** 27%. **Agriculture:** coffee, sugar, corn, rice, beans, oilseed, cotton, sorghum; shrimp; beef, dairy products. **Labor force:** 2.35 million (1999); agriculture 30%, industry 15%, services 55% (1999 est.). **Industries:** food processing, beverages, petroleum, chemicals, fertilizer, textiles, furniture, light metals. **Natural resources:** hydropower, geothermal power, petroleum, arable land. **Exports:** $3.162 billion (2003 est.): offshore assembly exports, coffee, sugar, shrimp, textiles, chemicals, electricity. **Imports:** $5.466 billion (2003 est.): raw materials, consumer goods, capital goods, fuels, foodstuffs, petroleum, electricity. **Major trading partners:** U.S., Guatemala, Honduras, Nicaragua, Mexico, France.

Geography Situated on the Pacific coast of Central America, El Salvador has Guatemala to the west and Honduras to the north and east. It is the smallest of the Central American countries, its area equal to that of Massachusetts, and the only one without an Atlantic coastline. Most of the country is on a fertile volcanic plateau about 2,000 ft (607 m) high.

Government Republic.

History The Pipil Indians, descendants of the Aztecs, likely migrated to the region in the 11th century. In 1525, Pedro de Alvarado, a lieutenant of Cortés, conquered El Salvador.

El Salvador, with the other countries of Central America, declared its independence from Spain on

Sept. 15, 1821, and was part of a federation of Central American states until that union dissolved in 1838. For decades after its independence, El Salvador experienced numerous revolutions and wars against other Central American republics. From 1931 to 1979 El Salvador was ruled by a series of military dictatorships.

In 1969, El Salvador invaded Honduras after Honduran landowners deported several thousand Salvadorans. The four-day war became known as the "football war" because it broke out during a soccer game between the two countries.

In the 1970s discontent with societal inequalities, a poor economy, and the repressive measures of dictatorship led to civil war between the government, controlled by the right-wing Nationalist Republican Alliance (ARENA), and leftist antigovernment guerrilla units, whose leading group was the Farabundo Martí National Liberation Front (FMLN). The U.S. intervened on the side of the military, despite its scores of human rights violations. Between 1979 and 1981, about 30,000 people were killed by right-wing death squads backed by the military. The presidency of José Napoleón Duarte, a moderate civilian, from 1984–1989, offered an alternative to the political extremes of right and left, but Duarte was unable to end the war and in 1989, Alfredo Cristiani of ARENA was elected. On Jan. 16, 1992, the government signed a peace treaty with the guerrilla forces, formally ending the 12-year civil war that had killed 75,000.

In 1998, Hurricane Mitch devastated the country, leaving 200 dead and over 30,000 homeless. In Jan. and Feb. 2001, major earthquakes struck El Salvador, damaging about 20% of the nation's housing. An even worse disaster beset the country in the summer when a severe drought destroyed 80% of the country's crops, causing famine in the countryside.

In 2004, Antonio Saca of ARENA was elected president.

Equatorial Guinea

REPUBLIC OF EQUATORIAL GUINEA

National name: República de Guinea Ecuatorial
President: Col. Teodoro Obiang Nguema Mbasogo (1979)
Prime Minister: Miguel Abia Biteo Borico (2004)
Area: 10,830 sq mi (28,051 sq km)
Population (2004 est.): 523,051 (growth rate: 2.4%); birth rate: 36.6/1000; infant mortality rate: 87.1/1000; life expectancy: 55.2; density per sq mi: 48
Capital and largest city (2003 est.): Malabo, 92,900.
Monetary unit: CFA Franc. **Languages:** Spanish, French (both official); pidgin English, Fang, Bubi, Ibo.
Ethnicity/race: Bioko (primarily Bubi, some Fernandinos), Río Muni (primarily Fang), Europeans less than 1,000, mostly Spanish. **Religions:** nominally Christian and predominantly Roman Catholic, pagan practices. **Literacy rate:** 86% (2003 est.)
Economic summary: GDP/PPP (2002 est.): $1.27 billion; per capita $2,700. **Real growth rate:** 20%. **Inflation:** 6%. **Unemployment:** 30% (1998 est.). **Arable land:** 5%. **Agriculture:** coffee, cocoa, rice, yams, cassava (tapioca), bananas, palm oil nuts; livestock; timber. **Labor force:** n.a. **Industries:** petroleum, fishing, sawmilling, natural gas. **Natural resources:** oil, petroleum, timber, small unexploited deposits of gold, manganese, uranium, titanium, iron ore. **Exports:** $2.1 billion (f.o.b, 2003 est.): petroleum, methanol, timber, cocoa. **Imports:** $1.371 billion (f.o.b. 2003 est.): petroleum sector equipment, other equipment. **Major trading partners:** U.S., Spain, China, Canada, France, UK, Norway, Netherlands, Italy.

Geography Equatorial Guinea, formerly Spanish Guinea, consists of Río Muni (10,045 sq mi; 26,117 sq km), on the western coast of Africa, and several islands in the Gulf of Guinea, the largest of which is Bioko (formerly Fernando Po) (785 sq mi; 2,033 sq km). The other islands are Annobón, Corisco, Elobey Grande, and Elobey Chico. The total area is twice that of Connecticut.

Government Dictatorship.

History The mainland was originally inhabited by Pygmies. The Fang and Bubi migrated there in the 17th century and to the main island of Fernando Po (now called Bioko) in the 19th century. In the 18th century, the Portuguese ceded land to the Spanish that included Equatorial Guinea. From 1827 to 1844, Britain administered Fernando Po, but it was then reclaimed by Spain. Río Muni, the mainland, was not occupied by the Spanish until 1926. Spanish Guinea, as it was then called, gained independence from Spain on Oct. 12, 1968. It is Africa's only Spanish-speaking country.

From the outset, President Francisco Macías Nguema, considered the father of independence, began a brutal reign, destroying the economy of the fledgling country and abusing human rights. Calling himself the "Unique Miracle," Nguema is considered one of the worst despots in African history. In 1971, the U.S. State Department reported that his regime was "characterized by abandonment of all government functions except internal security, which was accomplished by terror; this led to the death or exile of up to one-third of the population." In 1979, Nguema was overthrown and executed by his nephew, Lieut. Col. Teodoro Obiang Nguema Mbasogo. Obiang has been gradually modernizing the country but has retained many of his uncle's dictatorial practices, including the amassing of personal wealth by siphoning it from the public coffers. In 2003, state radio compared him to God.

A recent off-shore oil boom resulted in the economy's growth by 71.2% in 1997, the first year of the petroleum bonanza, and it has sustained this phenomenal rate of growth. It is unlikely, however, that the country's new wealth will benefit the average citizen—the president's family and cronies control the industry.

In 2004, a plot by about 60 foreign white mercenaries to overthrow the government was thwarted when their plane made a stop in Zimbabwe.

Eritrea

President: Isaias Afwerki (1993)
Area: 46,842 sq mi (121,320 sq km)
Population (2004 est.): 4,447,307 (growth rate: 2.6%); birth rate: 39.0/1000; infant mortality rate: 75.6/1000; life expectancy: 52.7; density per sq mi: 95
Capital and largest city (2003 est.): Asmara, 899,000 (metro. area), 400,000 (city proper). **Other large cities:** the ports of Massawa, 30,700; and Assab, 56,300. **Monetary unit:** Nakfa. **Languages:** Afar, Arabic, Tigre and Kunama, Tigrinya, other Cushitic languages. **Ethnicity/race:** ethnic Tigrinya 50%, Tigre and Kunama 40%, Afar 4%, Saho (Red Sea coast dwellers) 3%. **Religions:** Islam, Eritrean Orthodox Christianity, Roman Catholic, Protestant. **Literacy rate:** 59% (2003 est.)
Economic summary: GDP/PPP (2002 est.): $3.3 billion; per capita $700. **Real growth rate:** 2%. **Inflation:** 15% (2001). **Unemployment:** n.a. **Arable land:** 4%. **Agriculture:** sorghum, lentils, vegetables, corn, cotton, tobacco, coffee, sisal; livestock, goats; fish. **Labor force:** n.a.; agriculture 80%, industry and services 20%. **Industries:** food processing, beverages, clothing and textiles. **Natural resources:** gold, potash, zinc, copper, salt, possibly oil and natural gas, fish.

Exports: $56 million (f.o.b., 2003 est.): livestock, sorghum, textiles, food, small manufactures (2000). **Imports:** $600 million (f.o.b., 2003 est.): machinery, petroleum products, food, manufactured goods (2000). **Major trading partners:** Italy, Germany, France, U.S., Netherlands, Ukraine, Turkey (2002).

Geography Eritrea was formerly the northernmost province of Ethiopia and is about the size of Indiana. Much of the country is mountainous. Its narrow Red Sea coastal plain is one of the hottest and driest places in Africa. The cooler central highlands have fertile valleys that support agriculture. Eritrea is bordered by the Sudan on the north and west, the Red Sea on the north and east, and Ethiopia and Djibouti on the south.

Government A transitional government committed to a democratic system.

History Eritrea was part of the first Ethiopian kingdom of Aksum until its decline in the 8th century. It came under the control of the Ottoman Empire in the 16th century, and later of the Egyptians. The Italians captured the coastal areas in 1885, and the Treaty of Uccialli (May 2, 1889) gave Italy sovereignty over part of Eritrea. The Italians named their colony after the Roman name for the Red Sea, *Mare Erythraeum*, and ruled it up until World War II. The British captured Eritrea in 1941 and later administered it as a UN Trust Territory until it became federated with Ethiopia on Sept. 15, 1952. It was made an Ethiopian province on Nov. 14, 1962. A civil war broke out against the Ethiopian government, led by rebel groups who opposed the union and wanted independence for Eritrea. Fighting continued over the next 32 years.

In 1991, the Ethiopian People's Revolutionary Democratic Front deposed the country's hardline communist dictator Mengistu. Without Mengistu's troops to battle, the Eritrean People's Liberation Front was able to gain control of Asmara, the Eritrean capital, and form a provisional government. In 1993, a referendum on Eritrean independence was held, supported by the UN and the new Ethiopian government. Eritrean voters almost unanimously opted for an independent republic. Ethiopia recognized Eritrea's sovereignty on May 3, 1993, and sought a new era of cooperation between the two countries.

The cooperation did not last long. Following Eritrea's independence, Eritrea and Ethiopia disagreed about the exact demarcation of their borders, and in May 1998 border clashes broke out. After an eight-month lull that both sides used to reinforce their 600-mile common border, war broke out in earnest. Both impoverished countries spent millions of dollars on warplanes and weapons, about 80,000 people were killed, and refugees were legion. The war essentially ended in a stalemate, and a formal peace agreement was signed in Dec. 2000. The United Nations has supplied more than 4,000 troops to continue patrolling the buffer zone between the two nations. An international boundary commission ruled on the disputed border between the two countries on April 13, 2002. Ethiopia disputed the new border, escalating tensions once again. In 2003, resolution of the border question was postponed indefinitely.

Estonia

REPUBLIC OF ESTONIA

National name: Eesti
President: Arnold Rüütel (2001)
Prime Minister: Juhan Parts (2003)
Area: 17,462 sq mi (45,226 sq km)

Population (2004 est.): 1,341,664 (growth rate: –0.7%); birth rate: 9.8/1000; infant mortality rate: 8.1/1000; life expectancy: 71.4; density per sq mi: 77
Capital and largest city (2003 est.): Tallinn, 379,000. **Other large city:** Tartu, 100,100. **Monetary unit:** Kroon. **Languages:** Estonian (official), Russian, Ukrainian, Finnish, other. **Ethnicity/race:** Estonian 65.3%, Russian 28.1%, Ukrainian 2.5%, Belorussian 1.5%, Finn 1%, other 1.6% (1998). **Religions:** Evangelical Lutheran, Russian Orthodox, Estonian Orthodox, Baptist, Methodist, Seventh-Day Adventist, Roman Catholic, Pentecostal, Word of Life, Jewish. **Literacy:** 100% (2003 est.)
Economic summary: GDP/PPP (2003 est.): $17.37 billion; per capita $12,300. **Real growth rate:** 4.8%. **Inflation:** 1.5%. **Unemployment:** 5.5%. **Arable land:** 27%. **Agriculture:** potatoes, vegetables; livestock and dairy products; fish. **Labor force:** 608,600 (2001 est.); industry 20%, agriculture 11%, services 69% (1999 est.). **Industries:** engineering, electronics, wood and wood products, textile; information technology, telecommunications. **Natural resources:** oil shale, peat, phosphorite, clay, limestone, sand, dolomite, arable land, sea mud. **Exports:** $4.075 billion (f.o.b., 2003 est.): machinery and equipment 33%, wood and paper 15%, textiles 14%, food products 8%, furniture 7%, metals, chemical products (2001). **Imports:** $5.535 billion (f.o.b., 2003 est.): machinery and equipment 33.5%, chemical products 11.6%, textiles 10.3%, foodstuffs 9.4%, transportation equipment 8.9% (2001). **Major trading partners:** Finland, Sweden, UK, Latvia, Germany, Russia.

Geography Estonia is mainly a lowland country that is bordered by the Baltic Sea, Latvia, and Russia. It has numerous lakes and forests and many rivers, most draining northward into the Gulf of Finland or eastward into Lake Peipus, its largest lake.

Government Parliamentary democracy.

History Estonians resisted the assaults of Vikings, Danes, Swedes, and Russians before the 13th century. In 1346, the Danes, who possessed northern Estonia, sold the land to the Teutonic Knights of Germany, who already possessed Livonia (southern Estonia and Latvia). The Teutonic Knights reduced the Estonians to serfdom. In 1526, the Swedes took over, and the power of the German (Balt) landowning class was reduced. But after 1721, when Russia succeeded Sweden as the ruling power under the Peace of Nystad, the Estonians were subject to a double bondage—the Balts and the czarist officials. The oppression lasted until the closing months of World War I, when Estonia finally achieved independence after a victorious war (1918–1920). But shortly after the start of World War II, the nation was occupied by Russian troops and incorporated as the 16th republic of the USSR in 1940. Germany occupied the nation from 1941 to 1944, when it was retaken by the Soviets.

Estonia declared independence from the Soviet Union in March 1990. Soviet resistance ensued, but after recognition by European and other countries, the Soviet Union acknowledged Estonian nationhood on Sept. 6, 1991. UN membership followed on Sept. 17, 1991. The newly independent nation embraced free-market reforms. Fueled by foreign investments, economic advances continue. At the end of 1998, Estonia relaxed the strict citizenship requirements that kept the country's Russian speakers—about one-third of the population—from gaining citizenship. This reform eased the way for Estonia's entry into the European Union, which took place in 2004, the year it also joined NATO.

Ethiopia

FEDERAL DEMOCRATIC REPUBLIC OF ETHIOPIA

President: Girma Woldegiorgis (2001)
Prime Minister: Meles Zenawi (1995)
Area: 435,184 sq mi (1,127,127 sq km)
Population (2004 est.): 67,851,281 (growth rate: 1.9%); birth rate: 39.2/1000; infant mortality rate: 102.1/1000; life expectancy: 40.9; density per sq mi: 156
Capital and largest city (2003 est.): Addis Ababa, 2,716,200. **Monetary unit:** Birr. **Languages:** Amharic (official), Tigrigna, Orominga, Guaragigna, Somali, Arabic, English, over 70 others. **Ethnicity/race:** Oromo 40%, Amhara and Tigrean 32%, Sidamo 9%, Shankella 6%, Somali 6%, Afar 4%, Gurage 2%, other 1%. **Religions:** Islam 45%–50%, Ethiopian Orthodox 35%–40%, animist 12%, other 3%–8%. **Literacy rate:** 43% (2003 est.)
Economic summary: GDP/PPP (2003 est.): $48.47 billion; per capita $700. **Real growth rate:** –2%. **Inflation:** 12.6%. **Unemployment:** n.a. **Arable land:** 10%. **Agriculture:** cereals, pulses, coffee, oilseed, sugarcane, potatoes, qat; hides, cattle, sheep, goats. **Labor force:** n.a; agriculture and animal husbandry 80%, government and services 12%, industry and construction 8% (1985). **Industries:** food processing, beverages, textiles, chemicals, metals processing, cement. **Natural resources:** small reserves of gold, platinum, copper, potash, natural gas, hydropower. **Exports:** $537 million (f.o.b., 2003 est.): coffee, qat, gold, leather products, live animals, oilseeds. **Imports:** $1.964 billion (f.o.b., 2003 est.): food and live animals, petroleum and petroleum products, chemicals, machinery, motor vehicles, cereals, textiles. **Major trading partners:** UK, Djibouti, Germany, Italy, Japan, Saudi Arabia, U.S., China, India.

Geography Ethiopia is in east-central Africa, bordered on the west by the Sudan, the east by Somalia and Djibouti, the south by Kenya, and the northeast by Eritrea. It has several high mountains, the highest of which is Ras Dashan at 15,158 ft (4,620 m). The Blue Nile, or Abbai, rises in the northwest and flows in a great semicircle before entering the Sudan. Its chief reservoir, Lake Tana, lies in the northwest.

Government Federal republic.

History Archeologists have found the oldest known human ancestors in Ethiopia, including *Ardipithecus ramidus kadabba* (c. 5.8–5.2 million years old) and *Australopithecus anamensis* (c. 4.2 million years old). Originally called Abyssinia, Ethiopia is sub-Saharan Africa's oldest state, and its Solomonic dynasty claims descent from King Menelik I, traditionally believed to have been the son of the queen of Sheba and King Solomon. The current nation is a consolidation of smaller kingdoms that owed feudal allegiance to the Ethiopian emperor.

Hamitic peoples migrated to Ethiopia from Asia Minor in prehistoric times. Semitic traders from Arabia penetrated the region in the 7th century B.C. Its Red Sea ports were important to the Roman and Byzantine Empires. Coptic Christianity was brought to the region in A.D. 341, and a variant of it became Ethiopia's state religion. Ancient Ethiopia reached its peak in the 5th century, then was isolated by the rise of Islam and weakened by feudal wars.

Modern Ethiopia emerged under Emperor Menelik II, who established its independence by routing an Italian invasion in 1896. He expanded Ethiopia by conquest. Disorders that followed Menelik's death brought his daughter to the throne in 1917, with his cousin, Tafari Makonnen, as regent and heir apparent. When the empress died in 1930, Tafari was crowned Emperor Haile Selassie I.

Haile Selassie, called the "Lion of Judah," outlawed slavery and tried to centralize his scattered realm, in which 70 languages were spoken. In 1931, he created a constitution, revised in 1955, that called for a Parliament with an appointed senate and an elected chamber of deputies, and a system of courts. But basic power remained with the emperor.

Fascist Italy invaded Ethiopia on Oct. 3, 1935, forcing Haile Selassie into exile in May 1936. Ethiopia was annexed to Eritrea, then an Italian colony, and to Italian Somaliland, forming Italian East Africa. In 1941, British troops routed the Italians, and Haile Selassie returned to Addis Ababa. In 1952, Eritrea was incorporated into Ethiopia.

On Sept. 12, 1974, Haile Selassie was deposed, the constitution suspended, and Ethiopia proclaimed a socialist state under a collective military dictatorship called the Provisional Military Administrative Council (PMAC), also known as the Derg. U.S. aid stopped, and Cuban and Soviet aid began. Lt. Col. Mengistu Haile Mariam became head of state in 1977. During this period Ethiopia fought against Eritrean secessionists as well as Somali rebels, and the government fought against its own people in a campaign called the "red terror." Thousands of political opponents were killed. Mengistu remained leader until 1991, when his greatest supporter, the Soviet Union, dismantled itself.

A group called the Ethiopian People's Revolutionary Democratic Front seized the capital in 1991, and in May a separatist guerrilla organization, the Eritrean People's Liberation Front, took control of the province of Eritrea. The two groups agreed that Eritrea would have an internationally supervised referendum on independence. This election took place in April 1993 with almost unanimous support for Eritrean independence. Ethiopia accepted and recognized Eritrea as an independent state within a few days. Sixty-eight leaders of the former military government were put on trial in April 1996 on charges that included genocide and crimes against humanity.

Since Eritrea's independence, Eritrea and Ethiopia had disagreed about the exact demarcation of their borders, and in May 1998 Eritrea initiated border clashes that developed into a full-scale war that left more than 80,000 dead and further destroyed both countries' ailing economies. After a costly and bloody two-year war, a permanent cease-fire was reached in June 2000—Ethiopia had the upper hand when the fighting ceased—and a formal peace agreement was signed in Dec. 2000. The United Nations has provided more than 4,000 peacekeeping forces to patrol the buffer zone between the two nations. An international commission defined a new border between the two countries in April 2002. Ethiopia disputed the new border, escalating tensions between the two countries once again. In 2003, the border question was put on hold indefinitely.

In 2003, in an effort to solve its chronic shortage of food, and to lessen its dependence upon international aid, Ethiopia began relocating 2 million farmers from their parched highland homes to areas with more fertile soil in the western part of the country. The largest relocation program in African history, however, has turned into a disaster. The majority of those resettled are still unable to support themselves, and, most alarmingly, much of the fertile regions where the farmers have been resettled are rife with malaria.

Fiji

REPUBLIC OF THE FIJI ISLANDS

President: Ratu Josefa Iloilo (2000)
Prime Minister: Laisenia Qarase (2001)
Area: 7,054 sq mi (18,270 sq km)
Population (2004 est.): 880,874 (growth rate: 1.4%);
birth rate: 22.9/1000; infant mortality rate: 13.0/1000;
life expectancy: 69.2; density per sq mi: 125
Capital and largest city (2003 est.): Suva (on Viti
Levu), 177,300. **Monetary unit:** Fiji dollar.
Languages: English (official), Fijian, Hindustani.
Ethnicity/race: Fijian 51%, Indian 44%, European,
other Pacific Islanders, overseas Chinese, and other
5% (1998). **Religions:** Christian 52% (Methodist 37%,
Roman Catholic 9%), Hindu 38%, Islam 8%, other 2%.
Literacy rate: 94% (2003 est.)
Economic summary: GDP/PPP (2003 est.): $5.007
billion; per capita $5,800. **Real growth rate:** 4.8%.
Inflation: 1.6% (2002 est.). **Unemployment:** 7.6%
(1999). **Arable land:** 11%. **Agriculture:** sugarcane,
coconuts, cassava (tapioca), rice, sweet potatoes,
bananas; cattle, pigs, horses, goats; fish. **Labor force:**
137,000 (1999); agriculture, including subsistence
agriculture 70% (2001 est.). **Industries:** tourism, sugar,
clothing, copra, gold, silver, lumber, small cottage
industries. **Natural resources:** timber, fish, gold, copper,
offshore oil potential, hydropower. **Exports:** $609 million
(f.o.b., 2002): sugar, garments, gold, timber, fish,
molasses, coconut oil. **Imports:** $835 million (c.i.f.,
2002): manufactured goods, machinery and transport
equipment, petroleum products, food, chemicals. **Major
trading partners:** U.S., Australia, UK, Japan, Samoa,
Singapore, China.

Geography Fiji consists of 332 islands in the southwest Pacific Ocean about 1,960 mi (3,152 km) from
Sydney, Australia. About 110 of these islands are
inhabited. The two largest are Viti Levu (4,109 sq mi;
10,642 sq km) and Vanua Levu (2,242 sq mi; 5,807 sq
km).

Government Republic.

History Fiji, which had been inhabited since the second millennium B.C., was explored by the Dutch and
the British in the 17th and 18th centuries. In 1874, an
offer of cession by the Fijian chiefs was accepted, and
Fiji was proclaimed a possession and dependency of
the British Crown. In the 1880s large-scale cultivation
of sugarcane began. Over the next 40 years, more than
60,000 indentured laborers from India were brought to
the island to work the plantations. By 1920, all indentured servitude had ended. Racial conflict between
Indians and the indigenous Fijians has been central to
the small island's history.

Fiji became independent on Oct. 10, 1970. In Oct.
1987, Brig. Gen. Sitiveni Rabuka staged a coup to prevent an Indian-dominated coalition party from taking
power. The military coup caused an exodus of thousands of Fijians of Indian origin who suffered ethnic
discrimination at the hands of the government.

A new constitution, which took effect in July 1998,
provided for a multiracial cabinet and raised the prospect of a coalition government. The previous constitution had guaranteed dominance to ethnic Fijians. In
1999, Fiji's first ethnic Indian prime minister, Mahendra Chaudhry, took office.

Continuing ethnic tensions, partly fueled by economic problems, plunged Fiji into a national nightmare
in 2000. On May 19, a group of armed soldiers entered
the Parliament and took three dozen people hostage,
including President Chaudhry. George Speight, a part-
Fijian businessman, led the insurrection, and demanded

that the 1998 constitution be rewritten to allow dominance of ethnic Fijians. The standoff lasted two
months. In July 2000, Speight and other coup leaders
were taken into custody and charged with treason. In
Feb. 2002, Speight was sentenced to death, but his
sentence was commuted.

Although the coup was eventually foiled, deposed
prime minister Chaudhry and his democratically
elected government were not restored to power.
Instead, the military and the Great Council of Chiefs, a
group of 50 traditional Fijian leaders, appointed an
interim government dominated by ethnic Fijians. Elections were held in 2001, but no party achieved a majority. Interim prime minister Laisenia Qarase's Fijian
United Party won 31 of 71 seats, and Qarase was
sworn in as prime minister in September. His cabinet
consisted entirely of ethnic Fijians, but a court ruled in
2002 that ethnic Indians must be included. In July
2003, Fiji's Supreme Court unanimously upheld that
decision, declaring Qarase's government unconstitutional. In 2004, political infighting stalled the implementation of a new multi-ethnic cabinet.

Much to Prime Minister Qarase's displeasure, Vice
President Ratu Jope Seniloli and four other prominent
figures were convicted for their part in the 2000 coup
and imprisoned in Aug. 2004.

Finland

REPUBLIC OF FINLAND

National name: Suomen Tasavalta—Republiken Finland
President: Tarja Halonen (2000)
Prime Minister: Matti Vanhanen (2003)
Area: 130,127 sq mi (337,030 sq km)
Population (2004 est.): 5,214,512 (growth rate: 0.2%);
birth rate: 10.6/1000; infant mortality rate: 3.6/1000; life
expectancy: 78.2; density per sq mi: 40
Capital and largest city (2003 est.): Helsinki, 1,162,900
(metro. area), 582,600 (city proper). **Other large
cities:** Espoo, 229,500; Tampere, 201,200; Vantaa,
189,200; Turku, 178,100. **Monetary units:** Euro
(formerly markka). **Languages:** Finnish 93.4%,
Swedish 5.9% (both official); small Sami- (Lapp) and
Russian-speaking minorities. **Ethnicity/race:** Finn
93%, Swede 6%, Sami (Lapp) 0.11%, Romany
(Gypsy) 0.12%, Tatar 0.02%. **Religions:** Evangelical
Lutheran 89%, Greek Orthodox 1%, none 9%, other
1%. **Literacy rate:** 100% (1980 est.)
Economic summary: GDP/PPP (2003 est.): $141.7
billion; per capita $27,300. **Real growth rate:** 1.5%.
Inflation: 1.1%. **Unemployment:** 9.2%. **Arable land:**
7%. **Agriculture:** barley, wheat, sugar beets, potatoes;
dairy cattle; fish. **Labor force:** 2.6 million (2000 est.);
public services 32%, industry 22%, commerce 14%,
finance, insurance, and business services 10%,
agriculture and forestry 8%, transport and
communications 8%, construction 6%. **Industries:**
metal products, electronics, shipbuilding, pulp and
paper, copper refining, foodstuffs, chemicals, textiles,
clothing. **Natural resources:** timber, copper, zinc, iron
ore, silver. **Exports:** $54.28 billion (f.o.b., 2003 est.):
machinery and equipment, chemicals, metals; timber,
paper, pulp (1999). **Imports:** $37.35 billion (f.o.b.,
2003 est.): foodstuffs, petroleum and petroleum
products, chemicals, transport equipment, iron and
steel, machinery, textile yarn and fabrics, grains
(1999). **Major trading partners:** Germany, UK, U.S.,
Sweden, Russia, Netherlands, France, Denmark.

Geography Finland is three times the size of Ohio.
It is heavily forested and contains thousands of lakes,
numerous rivers, and extensive areas of marshland.
Except for a small highland region in the extreme
northwest, the country is a lowland less than 600 ft

(180 m) above sea level. Off the southwest coast are the Swedish-populated Åland Islands (581 sq mi; 1,505 sq km), which have had an autonomous status since 1921.

Government Republic.

History The first inhabitants of Finland were the Sami (Lapp) people. When Finnish speakers migrated to Finland in the first millennium B.C., the Sami were forced to move northward to the arctic regions, with which they are traditionally associated. The Finns' repeated raids on the Scandinavian coast impelled Eric IX, the Swedish king, to conquer the country in 1157. It was made a part of the Swedish kingdom and converted to Christianity.

By 1809 the whole of Finland was conquered by Alexander I of Russia, who set up Finland as a grand duchy. The period of Russification (1809–1914) sapped Finnish political power and made Russian the country's official language. When Russia became engulfed by the March Revolution of 1917, Finland seized the opportunity to declare independence on Dec. 6, 1917.

The USSR attacked Finland on Nov. 30, 1939, after Finland refused to give into Soviet territorial demands. The Finns staged a strong defense for three months before being forced to cede the Soviets 16,000 sq mi (41,440 sq km). Under German pressure, the Finns joined the Nazis against Russia in 1941, but were defeated again and forced to cede the Petsamo area to the USSR. In 1948, a treaty of friendship and mutual assistance was signed by the two nations. Finland continued to pursue a foreign policy of nonalignment throughout the cold war era.

Running on a platform to revitalize the economy, Ahtisaari, a Social Democrat, won the country's first direct presidential election in a runoff in Feb. 1994. Previously, presidents had been chosen by electors. Finland became a member of the European Union in Jan. 1995. On Jan. 1, 1999, Finland, along with ten other European countries, adopted the euro as its currency. In 2000, Tarja Halonen, who had been Finland's foreign minister, became its first woman president.

Since 1998, Finland has been judged to be the world's least corrupt country, according to the annual corruption survey by the Berlin-based organization Transparency International. In April 2003, Finland appointed its first female prime minister, making it the only country in Europe with both a female president and prime minister. But Prime Minister Jaatteenmaki resigned after only two months in office when it was revealed that she had used leaked classified information against her rival in the election. In June, Defense Minister Matti Vanhanen was selected by Parliament to replace her.

France

FRENCH REPUBLIC

National name: République Française
President: Jacques Chirac (1995)
Prime Minister: Jean-Pierre Raffarin (2002)
Area: 211,208 sq mi (547,030 sq km)
Population (2004 est.): 60,424,213 (growth rate: 0.4%); birth rate: 12.3/1000; infant mortality rate: 4.3/1000; life expectancy: 79.4; density per sq mi: 286
Capital and largest city (2003 est.): Paris, 11,330,700 (metro. area), 2,110,400 (city proper). **Other large cities:** Marseille, 820,700; Lyon, 443,900; Toulouse, 411,800; Nice, 332,000; Nantes, 282,300; Strasbourg, 272,600; Bordeaux, 217,000. **Monetary units:** Euro (formerly French franc). **Languages:** French 100%, rapidly declining regional dialects (Provençal, Breton, Alsatian, Corsican, Catalan, Basque, Flemish).

Ethnicity/race: Celtic and Latin with Teutonic, Slavic, North African, Southeast Asian, and Basque minorities. **Religions:** Roman Catholic 83%-88%, Protestant 2%, Islam 5%-10%, Jewish 1%. **Literacy rate:** 99% (1980 est.)

Economic summary: GDP/PPP (2003 est.): $1.654 trillion; per capita $27,500. **Real growth rate:** 0.1%. **Inflation:** 2%. **Unemployment:** 9.6%. **Arable land:** 33%. **Agriculture:** wheat, cereals, sugar beets, potatoes, wine grapes; beef, dairy products; fish. **Labor force:** 27.1 million; services 71%, industry 25%, agriculture 4% (1997). **Industries:** machinery, chemicals, automobiles, metallurgy, aircraft, electronics; textiles, food processing; tourism. **Natural resources:** coal, iron ore, bauxite, zinc, potash, timber, fish. **Exports:** $346.5 billion (f.o.b., 2003 est.): machinery and transportation equipment, aircraft, plastics, chemicals, pharmaceutical products, iron and steel, beverages. **Imports:** $339.9 billion (f.o.b., 2003 est.): machinery and equipment, vehicles, crude oil, aircraft, plastics, chemicals. **Major trading partners:** Germany, UK, Spain, Italy, U.S., Belgium, Netherlands.

Geography France is about 80% the size of Texas. In the Alps near the Italian and Swiss borders is western Europe's highest point—Mont Blanc (15,781 ft; 4,810 m). The forest-covered Vosges Mountains are in the northeast, and the Pyrénées are along the Spanish border. Except for extreme northern France, the country may be described as four river basins and a plateau. Three of the streams flow west—the Seine into the English Channel, the Loire into the Atlantic, and the Garonne into the Bay of Biscay. The Rhône flows south into the Mediterranean. For about 100 mi (161 km), the Rhine is France's eastern border. In the Mediterranean, about 115 mi (185 km) east-southeast of Nice, is the island of Corsica (3,367 sq mi; 8,721 sq km).

Government Fifth republic.

History Archeological excavations indicate that France has been continuously settled since Paleolithic times. The Celts, who were later called *Gauls* by the Romans, migrated from the Rhine valley into what is now France. In about 600 B.C. Greeks and Phoenicians established settlements along the Mediterranean, most notably at Marseille. Julius Caesar conquered part of Gaul in 57–52 B.C., and it remained Roman until Franks invaded in the 5th century A.D.

The Treaty of Verdun (843) divided the territories corresponding roughly to France, Germany, and Italy among the three grandsons of Charlemagne. Charles the Bald inherited *Francia Occidentalis,* which became an increasingly feudalized kingdom. By 987, the crown passed to Hugh Capet, a princeling who controlled only the Ile-de-France, the region surrounding Paris. For 350 years, an unbroken Capetian line added to its domain and consolidated royal authority until the accession in 1328 of Philip VI, first of the Valois line. France was then the most powerful nation in Europe, with a population of 15 million.

The missing pieces in Philip Valois's domain were the French provinces still held by the Plantagenet kings of England, who also claimed the French crown. Beginning in 1338, the Hundred Years' War eventually settled the contest. After France's victory in the final battle, Castillon (1453), the Valois were the ruling family, and the English had no French possessions left except Calais. Once Burgundy and Brittany were added, the Valois dynasty's holdings resembled modern France. Protestantism spread throughout France in the 16th century and led to civil wars. Henry IV, of the Bourbon dynasty, issued the Edict of Nantes (1598), granting religious tolerance to the Huguenots (French

Protestants). Absolute monarchy reached its apogee in the reign of Louis XIV (1643–1715), the Sun King, whose brilliant court was the center of the Western world.

After a series of costly foreign wars that weakened the government, the French Revolution plunged France into a bloodbath beginning in 1789 with the establishment of the First Republic and ending with a new

authoritarianism under Napoléon Bonaparte, who had successfully defended the infant republic from foreign attack and then made himself first consul in 1799 and emperor in 1804. The Congress of Vienna (1815) sought to restore the pre-Napoléonic order in the person of Louis XVIII, but industrialization and the middle class, both fostered under Napoléon, built pressure for change, and a revolution in 1848 drove Louis

Rulers of France

Name	Born	Ruled[1]
Carolingian Dynasty		
Pepin the Short	c. 714	751–768
Charlemagne[2]	742	768–814
Louis I the Pious[3]	778	814–840
Charles I the Bald[4]	823	840–877
Louis II the Stammerer	846	877–879
Louis III[5]	c. 863	879–882
Carloman[5]	?	879–884
Charles II the Fat[6]	839	884–887[7]
Eudes (Odo), count of Paris	?	888–898
Charles III the Simple[8]	879	893–923[9]
Robert I[10]	c. 865	922–923
Rudolf (Raoul), duke of Burgundy	?	923–936
Louis IV d'Outremer	c. 921	936–954
Lothair	941	954–986
Louis V the Sluggard	c. 967	986–987
Capetian Dynasty		
Hugh Capet	c. 940	987–996
Robert II the Pious[11]	c. 970	996–1031
Henry I	1008	1031–1060
Philip I	1052	1060–1108
Louis VI the Fat	1081	1108–1137
Louis VII the Young	c.1121	1137–1180
Philip II (Philip Augustus)	1165	1180–1223
Louis VIII the Lion	1187	1223–1226
Louis IX (St. Louis)	1214	1226–1270
Philip III the Bold	1245	1270–1285
Philip IV the Fair	1268	1285–1314
Louis X the Quarreler	1289	1314–1316
John I[12]	1316	1316
Philip V the Tall	1294	1316–1322
Charles IV the Fair	1294	1322–1328
House of Valois		
Philip VI	1293	1328–1350
John II the Good	1319	1350–1364
Charles V the Wise	1337	1364–1380
Charles VI the Well-Beloved	1368	1380–1422
Charles VII	1403	1422–1461
Louis XI	1423	1461–1483
Charles VIII	1470	1483–1498
Louis XII the Father of the People	1462	1498–1515
Francis I	1494	1515–1547
Henry II	1519	1547–1559
Francis II	1544	1559–1560
Charles IX	1550	1560–1574
Henry III	1551	1574–1589
House of Bourbon		
Henry IV of Navarre	1553	1589–1610
Louis XIII	1601	1610–1643
Louis XIV the Great	1638	1643–1715

Name	Born	Ruled[1]
Louis XV the Well-Beloved	1710	1715–1774
Louis XVI	1754	1774–1792[13]
Louis XVII (Louis Charles de France)[14]	1785	1793–1795
First Republic		
National Convention	—	1792–1795
Directory (Directoire)	—	1795–1799
Consulate		
Napoléon Bonaparte[15]	1769	1799–1804
First Empire		
Napoléon I	1769	1804–1815[16]
Restoration of House of Bourbon		
Louis XVIII le Désiré	1755	1814–1824
Charles X	1757	1824–1830[17]
Bourbon-Orleans Line		
Louis Philippe ("Citizen King")	1773	1830–1848[18]
Second Republic		
Louis Napoléon[19]	1808	1848–1852
Second Empire		
Napoléon III (Louis Napoléon)	1808	1852–1870[20]
Third Republic (Presidents)		
Louis Adolphe Thiers	1797	1871–1873
Marie E. P. M. de MacMahon	1808	1873–1879
François P. J. Grévy	1807	1879–1887
Sadi Carnot	1837	1887–1894
Jean Casimir-Périer	1847	1894–1895
François Félix Faure	1841	1895–1899
Émile Loubet	1838	1899–1906
Clement Armand Fallières	1841	1906–1913
Raymond Poincaré	1860	1913–1920
Paul E. L. Deschanel	1856	1920–1920
Alexandre Millerand	1859	1920–1924
Gaston Doumergue	1863	1924–1931
Paul Doumer	1857	1931–1932
Albert Lebrun	1871	1932–1940
Vichy Government (Chief of State)		
Henri Philippe Pétain	1856	1940–1944
Provisional Government (Presidents)		
Charles de Gaulle	1890	1944–1946
Félix Gouin	1884	1946–1946
Georges Bidault	1899	1946–1947
Fourth Republic (Presidents)		
Vincent Auriol	1884	1947–1954
René Coty	1882	1954–1959
Fifth Republic (Presidents)		
Charles de Gaulle	1890	1959–1969
Georges Pompidou	1911	1969–1974
Valéry Giscard d'Estaing	1926	1974–1981
François Mitterrand	1916	1981–1995
Jacques Chirac	1932	1995–

1. For kings and emperors through the Second Empire, year of end of rule is also that of death, unless otherwise indicated. 2. Crowned Emperor of the West in 800. His brother, Carloman, ruled as king of the Eastern Franks from 768 until his death in 771. 3. Holy Roman Emperor, 814–840. 4. Holy Roman Emperor, 875–877 as Charles II. 5. Ruled jointly, 879–882. 6. Holy Roman Emperor, 881–887, as Charles III. 7. Died 888. 8. King, 893–898, in opposition to Eudes. 9. Died 929. 10. Not counted in regular line of kings of France by some authorities. Elected by nobles killed in Battle of Soissons. 11. Sometimes called Robert I. 12. Posthumous son of Louis X; lived for only five days. 13. Executed 1793. 14. Titular king only. He died in prison according to official reports, but many pretenders appeared during the Bourbon restoration. 15. As first consul, Napoléon held the power of government. In 1804, he became emperor. 16. Abdicated first time, June 1814. Reentered Paris, March 1815, after escape from Elba; Louis XVIII fled to Ghent. Abdicated second time, June 1815. He named as his successor his son, Napoléon II, who was not acceptable to the Allies. He died 1821. 17. Died 1836. 18. Died 1850. 19. President; became emperor in 1852. 20. Died 1873.

Philippe, last of the Bourbons, into exile. Prince Louis Napoléon, a nephew of Napoléon I, declared the Second Empire in 1852 and took the throne as Napoléon III. His opposition to the rising power of Prussia ignited the Franco-Prussian War (1870–1871), which ended in his defeat, his abdication, and the creation of the Third Republic.

A new France emerged from World War I as the continent's dominant power. But four years of hostile occupation had reduced northeast France to ruins. Beginning in 1919, French foreign policy aimed at keeping Germany weak through a system of alliances, but it failed to halt the rise of Adolf Hitler and the Nazi war machine. On May 10, 1940, Nazi troops attacked, and, as they approached Paris, Italy joined with Germany. The Germans marched into an undefended Paris and Marshal Henri Philippe Pétain signed an armistice on June 22. France was split into an occupied north and an unoccupied south, Vichy France, which became a totalitarian German puppet state with Pétain as its chief. Allied armies liberated France in Aug. 1944, and a provisional government in Paris headed by Gen. Charles de Gaulle was established. The Fourth Republic was born on Dec. 24, 1946. The empire became the French Union; the National Assembly was strengthened and the presidency weakened; and France joined NATO. A war against communist insurgents in French Indochina, now Vietnam, was abandoned after the defeat of French forces at Dien Bien Phu in 1954. A new rebellion in Algeria threatened a military coup, and on June 1, 1958, the Assembly invited de Gaulle to return as premier with extraordinary powers. He drafted a new constitution for a Fifth Republic, adopted on Sept. 28, which strengthened the presidency and reduced legislative power. He was elected president on Dec. 21, 1958.

France next turned its attention to decolonialization in Africa; the French protectorates of Morocco and Tunisia had received independence in 1956. French West Africa was partitioned and the new nations were granted independence in 1960. Algeria, after a long civil war, finally became independent in 1962. Relations with most of the former colonies remained amicable. De Gaulle took France out of the NATO military command in 1967 and expelled all foreign-controlled troops from the country. De Gaulle's government was weakened by massive protests in May 1968 when student rallies became violent and millions of factory workers engaged in wildcat strikes across France. After normalcy was reestablished in 1969, de Gaulle's successor, Georges Pompidou, modified Gaullist policies to include a classical laissez-faire attitude toward domestic economic affairs. The conservative, pro-business climate contributed to the election of Valéry Giscard d'Estaing as president in 1974.

Socialist François Mitterrand attained a stunning victory in the May 10, 1981, presidential election. The victors immediately moved to carry out campaign pledges to nationalize major industries, halt nuclear testing, suspend nuclear power plant construction, and impose new taxes on the rich. The Socialists' policies during Mitterrand's first two years created a 12% inflation rate, a huge trade deficit, and devaluations of the franc. In March 1986, a center-right coalition led by Jacques Chirac won a slim majority in legislative elections. Chirac became prime minister, initiating a period of "cohabitation" between him and the Socialist president, Mitterrand. Mitterrand's decisive reelection in 1988 led to Chirac being replaced as premier by Michel Rocard, a Socialist. Relations, however, cooled with Rocard, and in May 1991 he was replaced with Edith Cresson, France's

first female prime minister and, like Mitterrand, a Socialist. But Cresson's unpopularity forced Mitterrand to replace Cresson with a more well-liked Socialist, Pierre Bérégovoy, who eventually was embroiled in a scandal and committed suicide. Mitterrand did succeed in helping draft the Maastricht Treaty and, after winning a slim victory in a referendum, confirming close economic and security ties between France and the European Union (EU).

On his third try Chirac won the presidency in May 1995, campaigning vigorously on a platform to reduce unemployment. Elections for the National Assembly in 1997 gave the Socialist coalition a majority. Shortly after becoming president, Chirac resumed France's nuclear testing in the South Pacific, despite widespread international protests as well as rioting in the countries affected by it. Socialist leader Lionel Jospin became prime minister in 1997. In the spring of 1999, the country took part in the NATO airstrikes in Kosovo, despite some internal opposition.

Jean-Marie Le Pen, leader of the right-wing, anti-immigrant National Front party, shocked France in April 2002 with his second-place finish in the first round of France's presidential election. He took 17% of the vote, eliminating Lionel Jospin, the Socialist prime minister, who tallied 16%. Jospin, stunned by the result, announced that he was retiring from politics and threw his support behind incumbent President Jacques Chirac, who won with an overwhelming 82.2% of the vote in the run-off election. Chirac's center-right coalition won an absolute majority in Parliament. In July 2002, Chirac survived an assassination attempt by a right-wing extremist.

During the fall 2002 and winter 2003 diplomatic wrangling at the United Nations over Iraq, France repeatedly defied the U.S. and Britain by calling for more weapons inspections and diplomacy before resorting to war. Relations between the U.S. and France have remained severely strained over Iraq.

France sent peacekeeping forces to assist two African countries in 2002 and 2003, Côte d'Ivoire and the Democratic Republic of the Congo.

Prime Minister Raffarin's plan to overhaul the national pension system sparked numerous strikes across France in May and June 2003, involving tens of thousands of sanitation workers, teachers, transportation workers, and air traffic controllers. In August, a deadly heat wave killed an estimated 10,000 people, mostly elderly. The catastrophe occurred during two weeks of 104°F (40°C) temperatures.

In 2004, the French government passed a law banning the wearing of Muslim headscarves and other religious symbols in schools. The government maintained that the wearing of conspicuous religious symbols threatened the country's secular identity; others contended it curtailed religious freedom.

In March 2004 regional elections, the Socialist Party made enormous gains over Chirac's Union for a Popular Movement (UMP) party. Unpopular economic reforms are credited for the UMP's defeat.

Overseas Departments

Overseas Departments elect representatives to the National Assembly, and the same administrative organization as that of continental France applies to them.

French Guiana (including Inini)

Status: Overseas Department
Prefect: Henri Masse (1999)
Area: 35,135 sq mi (91,000 sq km)
Population (2004 est.): 191,309 (growth rate: 2.2%);
 birth rate 21.0/1000; infant mortality rate 12.5/1000; life

expectancy: 76.9; density per sq mi: 5
Capital and largest city (2003 est.): Cayenne, 60,500.
Monetary unit: Franc. **Language:** French. **Ethnicity/
race:** black or mulatto 66%, white 12%, East Indian,
Chinese, Amerindian 12%, other 10%. **Religion:**
Roman Catholic. **Literacy rate:** 83% (1982 est.)
Economic summary: GDP/PPP (2003 est.): $1.551
billion; per capita $8,300. **Real growth rate:** n.a.
Inflation: 1.5% (2002 est.). **Unemployment:** 22%
(2001). **Arable land:** negl. **Agriculture:** corn, rice,
manioc (tapioca), sugar, cocoa, vegetables, bananas;
cattle, pigs, poultry. **Labor force:** 58,800 (1997);
services, government, and commerce 60.6%, industry
21.2%, agriculture 18.2% (1980). **Industries:**
construction, shrimp processing, forestry products,
rum, gold mining. **Natural resources:** bauxite, timber,
gold (widely scattered), cinnabar, kaolin, fish. **Exports:**
$155 million (f.o.b., 2002 est.): shrimp, timber, gold,
rum, rosewood essence, clothing. **Imports:** $625
million (c.i.f., 2002 est.): food (grains, processed
meat), machinery and transport equipment, fuels and
chemicals. **Major trading partners:** France,
Switzerland, U.S., Trinidad and Tobago, Italy.

French Guiana, lying north of Brazil and east of
Suriname on the northeast coast of South America, was
variously settled by the Spanish, Dutch, and French.
The Treaty of Breda awarded France the territory in
1667. The French used it as a penal colony between
1852 and 1939, which included the infamous Devil's
Island. In 1947 it became an overseas department of
France. Since then, many indigenous French Guianians
have called for increased autonomy, although only
around 5% favor independence from France, partly due
to the vast subsidies from the French government. The
European Space Center at Kourou has brought a corner
of French Guiana into the modern world and attracted
a sizable expatriate workforce.

Guadeloupe

Status: Overseas Department
Prefect: Paul Girot de Langlade (2004)
Area: 687 sq mi (1,780 sq km)
Population (2004 est.): 444,515 (growth rate: 1.0%);
birth rate: 15.8/1000; infant mortality rate: 8.8/1000; life
expectancy: 77.7; density per sq mi: 647
Capital (2003 est.): Basse-Terre, 12,900. **Largest city:**
Abymes, 65,700. **Monetary unit:** Franc. **Languages:**
French 99% (official), Creole patois. **Ethnicity/race:**
black or mulatto 90%, white 5%, East Indian,
Lebanese, Chinese less than 5%. **Religion:** Roman
Catholic 95%, Hindu and pagan African 4%, Protestant
1%. **Literacy rate:** 98% (1977 est.)
Economic summary: GDP/PPP (2003 est.): $3.513
billion; per capita $8,000. **Real growth rate:** n.a.
Inflation: n.a. **Unemployment:** 27.8% (1998). **Arable
land:** 11%. **Agriculture:** bananas, sugarcane, tropical
fruits and vegetables; cattle, pigs, goats. **Labor force:**
125,900 (1997). **Industries:** construction, cement,
rum, sugar, tourism. **Natural resources:** cultivable
land, beaches and climate that foster tourism.
Exports: $140 million (f.o.b., 1997): bananas, sugar,
rum. **Imports:** $1.7 billion (c.i.f., 1997): foodstuffs,
fuels, vehicles, clothing and other consumer goods,
construction materials. **Major trading partners:**
France, Martinique, U.S., Germany, Japan,
Netherlands Antilles.

Guadeloupe, in the West Indies about 300 mi (483
km) southeast of Puerto Rico, was explored by Columbus in 1493. It consists of the twin islands of Basse-
Terre and Grande-Terre and five dependencies—Marie-
Galante, Les Saintes, La Désirade, St. Barthélemy, and
the northern three-fifths of St. Martin. The volcano

Soufrière (4,813 ft; 1,467 m), also called La Grande
Soufrière, is the highest point on Guadeloupe.

French colonization began in 1635, and in 1674
Guadeloupe became part of the domain of France. In
1946, it became an overseas department of France.

Martinique

Status: Overseas Department
Prefect: Michel Cadot (2000)
Area: 425 sq mi (1,100 sq km)
Population (2004 est.): 429,510 (growth rate: 0.8%);
birth rate: 14.6/1000; infant mortality rate: 7.3/1000; life
expectancy: 78.9; density per sq mi: 1,011
Capital and largest city (2003 est.): Fort-de-France,
170,300 (metro. area), 96,400 (city proper). **Other
large cities:** Le Lamentin, 36,400; Schoelcher,
21,400; Sainte-Marie, 20,600. **Monetary unit:** Franc.
Languages: French, Creole patois. **Ethnicity/race:**
African and African-white-Indian mixture 90%, white
5%, East Indian, Lebanese, Chinese less than 5%.
Religion: Roman Catholic 85%, Protestant 10.5%,
Muslim 0.5%, Hindu 0.5%, other 3.5% (1997).
Literacy rate: 97.7% (2003 est.)
Economic summary: GDP/PPP (2003 est.): $6.117
billion; per capita $14,400. **Real growth rate:** n.a.
Inflation: 3.9% (1990). **Unemployment:** 27.2%
(1998). **Arable land:** 9%. **Agriculture:** pineapples,
avocados, bananas, flowers, vegetables, sugarcane.
Labor force: 165,900 (1998); agriculture 10%,
industry 17%, services 73% (1997). **Industries:**
construction, rum, cement, oil refining, sugar, tourism.
Natural resources: coastal scenery and beaches,
cultivable land. **Exports:** $250 million (f.o.b., 1997):
refined petroleum products, bananas, rum, pineapples
(2001 est.). **Imports:** $2 billion (c.i.f., 1997): petroleum
products, crude oil, foodstuffs, construction materials,
vehicles, clothing and other consumer goods. **Major
trading partners:** France, Guadeloupe, Venezuela,
Germany, Italy, U.S.

Martinique, a mountainous island lying in the
Lesser Antilles about 300 mi (483 km) northeast of
Venezuela, was probably explored by Columbus in
1502 and was taken for France in 1635. Martinique
became a domain of the French crown in 1674. It
became an overseas department of France in 1946.

Réunion

Status: Overseas Department
Prefect: Jean Doubigny (1998)
Area: 972 sq mi (2,517 sq km)
Population (2004 est.): 766,153 (growth rate: 1.4%);
birth rate: 19.7/1000; infant mortality rate: 8.0/1000; life
expectancy: 73.7; density per sq mi: 788
Capital and largest city (2003 est.): Saint-Denis,
142,600. **Other large cities:** Saint-Paul, 95,100;
Saint-Pierre, 74,700; Le Tampon, 65,400. **Monetary
unit:** Franc. **Languages:** French (official), Creole.
Ethnicity/race: French, African, Malagasy, Chinese,
Pakistani, Indian. **Religion:** Roman Catholic 86%,
Hindu, Muslim, Buddhist (1995). **Literacy rate:** 89%
(2003 est.)
Economic summary: GDP/PPP (2003 est.): $9.387
billion; per capita $12,400. **Real growth rate:** 2.5%
(2002 est.). **Inflation:** n.a. **Unemployment:** 36% (1999
est.). **Arable land:** 13%. **Agriculture:** sugarcane,
vanilla, tobacco, tropical fruits, vegetables, corn. **Labor
force:** 309,900 (2000); agriculture 13%, industry 12%,
services 75% (2000). **Industries:** sugar, rum,
cigarettes, handicraft items, flower oil extraction.
Natural resources: fish, arable land, hydropower.
Exports: $214 million (f.o.b., 1997): sugar, rum and
molasses, perfume essences, lobster. **Imports:** $2.5
billion (c.i.f., 1997): manufactured goods, food,

beverages, tobacco, machinery and transportation equipment, raw materials, and petroleum products. **Major trading partners:** France, Japan, Comoros, Bahrain, Germany, Italy.

Of volcanic origin, Réunion consists mostly of rugged mountains and short torrential rivers. It is located about 450 mi (724 km) east of Madagascar, in the Indian Ocean. First explored by Portuguese navigators in the 16th century, the island of Réunion, then uninhabited, was taken as a French possession in 1642. African slaves were imported first to work coffee and then sugar plantations; with the abolition of slavery in 1848, indentured laborers from Indochina, India, and East Africa were brought in. In 1947, Réunion became an overseas department of France.

Overseas Territories

Overseas Territories are comparable to Departments except that their administrative organization includes a locally elected government.

French Polynesia

Status: Overseas Territory
High Commissioner: Jean Aribaud (1999)
President: Oscar Temaru (2004)
Area: 1,609 sq mi (4,167 sq km)
Population (2004 est.): 266,339 (growth rate: 1.6%); birth rate: 17.3/1000; infant mortality rate: 8.6/1000; life expectancy: 75.7; density per sq mi: 166
Capital (2003 est.): Papeete (on Tahiti), 111,400 (metro. area), 30,200 (city proper). **Monetary unit:** Pacific financial community franc. **Languages:** French, Tahitian (both official). **Ethnicity/race:** Polynesian 78%, Chinese 12%, local French 6%, metropolitan French 4%. **Religions:** Protestant 54%, Roman Catholic 30%, other 10%, no religion 6%. **Literacy rate:** 98% (1977)
Economic summary: GDP/PPP (2001 est.): $4.58 billion; per capita $17,500 . **Real growth rate:** 4%. **Inflation:** 1.5% (2002 est.). **Unemployment:** 11.8% (1994). **Arable land:** 2%. **Agriculture:** coconuts, vanilla, vegetables, fruits; poultry, beef, dairy products, coffee. **Labor force:** 70,000 (1996); agriculture 13%, industry 19%, services 68% (1997). **Industries:** tourism, pearls, agricultural processing, handicrafts, phosphates. **Natural resources:** timber, fish, cobalt, hydropower. **Exports:** $244 million (f.o.b.): cultured pearls, coconut products, mother-of-pearl, vanilla, shark meat (1997). **Imports:** $1.341 billion (f.o.b., 2002): fuels, foodstuffs, machinery and equipment. **Major trading partners:** France, Japan, U.S., Australia, New Zealand.

The term *French Polynesia* is applied to the scattered French possessions in the South Pacific—Mangareva (Gambier), Makatea, the Marquesas Islands, Rapa, Rurutu, Rimatara, the Society Islands, the Tuamotu Archipelago, Tubuai, Raivavae, and the island of Clipperton—which were organized into a single colony in 1903. There are 120 islands, of which 25 are uninhabited. The principal and most populous island—Tahiti, in the Society group—was claimed by the French in 1768. The indigenous people are mostly Maoris.

The Pacific Nuclear Test Center on the atoll of Mururoa, 744 mi (1,200 km) from Tahiti, was completed in 1966. In 1975 worldwide opposition forced the French to move the testing underground on Fangataufa. To compensate the residents for the nuclear weapons tests in 1995–1996, France offered a 10-year $194-million annual compensation package. An independence movement continues to flourish in French Polynesia.

New Caledonia and Dependencies

Status: Overseas Territory
President: Marie-Noëlle Thémereau (2004)
High Commissioner: Thierry Lataste (1998)
Area: 7,359 sq mi (19,060 sq km)
Population (2004 est.): 213,679 (growth rate: 1.3%); birth rate: 19.0/1000; infant mortality rate: 7.9/1000; life expectancy: 73.8; density per sq mi: 29
Capital (2003 est.): Nouméa, 134,500 (metro. area), 86,400 (city proper). **Monetary unit:** Pacific financial community franc. **Languages:** French (official), 33 Melanesian and Polynesian dialects. **Ethnicity/race:** Kanak (Melanesian) 42.5%, European 37.1%, Wallisian 8.4%, Polynesian 3.8%, Indonesian 3.6%, Vietnamese 1.6%, other 3%. **Religions:** Roman Catholic 60%, Protestant 30%. **Literacy rate:** 91% (1976 est.)
Economic summary: GDP/PPP (2003 est.): $3.158 billion; per capita $15,000 (2002 est.). **Real growth rate:** n.a. **Inflation:** −0.6% (2000 est.). **Unemployment:** 19% (1996). **Arable land:** 0.4%. **Agriculture:** vegetables; beef, deer, other livestock products. **Labor force:** 79,395 (including 15,018 unemployed, 1996); agriculture 7%, industry 23%, services 70% (1999 est.). **Industries:** nickel mining and smelting. **Natural resources:** nickel, chrome, iron, cobalt, manganese, silver, gold, lead, copper. **Exports:** $448 million (f.o.b., 2002): ferronickels, nickel ore, fish. **Imports:** $1.007 billion (f.o.b., 2002): machinery and equipment, fuels, chemicals, foodstuffs. **Major trading partners:** Japan, France, Taiwan, South Africa, Spain, Australia, Italy, Singapore.

New Caledonia (6,466 sq mi; 16,747 sq km), about 1,070 mi (1,722 km) northeast of Sydney, Australia, was explored by Capt. James Cook in 1774 and annexed by France in 1853. The government also administers the Isle of Pines, the Loyalty Islands (Uvéa, Lifu, and Maré), the Belep Islands, the Huon Island group, and Chesterfield Islands. The native people are Melanesians called the Kanak. In 1984, the French National Assembly passed a law that granted internal autonomy to New Caledonia. In 1998 the Nouméa Accords postponed discussions about independence for the territory until at least 2013.

Southern and Antarctic Lands

Status: Overseas Territory
Administrator: François Garde (2000)
Area: 3,023 sq mi (7,829 sq km, excluding Adélie Land)
Capital: Port-au-Français

This territory is uninhabited except for the personnel of scientific bases. It consists of Adélie Land (166,752 sq mi; 431,888 sq km) on the Antarctic mainland (which the U.S. does not recognize) and the following islands in the southern Indian Ocean: the Kerguelen and Crozet archipelagos and the islands of Saint-Paul and New Amsterdam.

Wallis and Futuna Islands

Status: Overseas Territory
Administrator: Christian Job (2002)
Area: 106 sq mi (274 sq km)
Population (2004 est.): 15,880 (growth rate: 1.0); birth rate: 21.7/1000; infant mortality rate: 18.3/1000; life expectancy: 74.9; density per sq mi: 150
Capital (2003 est.): Mata-Utu, 1,300. **Languages:** French, Wallisian. **Ethnicity/race:** Polynesian. **Religion:** Roman Catholic. **Literacy rate:** 50% (1969 est.)
Economic summary: GDP/PPP (2003 est.): $57.6 million; per capita $3,700 (2001 est.). **Real growth rate:** n.a. **Inflation:** n.a. **Unemployment:** n.a. **Arable land:** 5%.

Agriculture: breadfruit, yams, taro, bananas; pigs, goats. **Labor force:** n.a.; agriculture, livestock, and fishing 80%, government 4% (2001 est.). **Industries:** copra, handicrafts, fishing, lumber. **Natural resources:** negl. **Exports:** $250,000 (f.o.b., 1999): copra, chemicals, construction materials. **Imports:** $300,000 (f.o.b., 1999): chemicals, machinery, passenger ships, consumer goods. **Major trading partners:** Italy, Croatia, U.S., Denmark, France, Australia, New Zealand.

The two island groups in the South Pacific between Fiji and Samoa were settled by French missionaries at the beginning of the 19th century. A protectorate was established in the 1880s. There is a French-appointed high administrator, a 20-member Territorial Assembly, and a deputy and a senator to the French national Parliament. The three traditional Polynesian kings also help decide internal policy matters. Following a referendum by the Polynesian inhabitants, the status was changed to that of an Overseas Territory in 1961.

Territorial Collectivities

The Territorial Collectivity status was created in 1976 for Mayotte; it was conceived as being midway between an Overseas Territory and an Overseas Department.

Saint Pierre and Miquelon
Status: Territorial Collectivity
Prefect: Claude Valleix (2002)
Area: 93 sq mi (242 sq km)
Population (2004 est.): 6,995 (growth rate: 0.3%); birth rate: 14.2/1000; infant mortality rate: 7.8/1000; life expectancy: 78.3; density per sq mi: 75
Capital (2003 est.): Saint Pierre, 5,900. **Language:** French (official). **Ethnicity/race:** Basques and Bretons (French fishermen). **Religion:** Roman Catholic 99%. **Literacy rate:** 99% (1982 est.)
Economic summary: GDP/PPP (2003 est.): $48.3 million, supplemented by annual payments from France of about $60 million; per capita $6,900 (2001 est.). **Real growth rate:** n.a. **Inflation:** 2.1% (1991–96 average). **Unemployment:** 9.8% (1997). **Arable land:** 13%. **Agriculture:** vegetables; poultry, cattle, sheep, pigs; fish. **Labor force:** 3,261 (1999); fishing 18%, industry (mainly fish processing) 41%, services 41% (1996 est.). **Industries:** fish processing and supply base for fishing fleets; tourism. **Natural resources:** fish, deepwater ports. **Exports:** $12 million (f.o.b., 1999): fish and fish products, soybeans, animal feed, mollusks and crustaceans, fox and mink pelts. **Imports:** $55 million (f.o.b., 1999): meat, clothing, fuel, electrical equipment, machinery, building materials. **Major trading partners:** U.S., Zambia, Ecuador, France, Canada, Spain (2002).

The sole remnant of the French colonial empire in North America, these islands were first occupied by the French in 1604. Their importance arises from their proximity to the Grand Banks, located 10 mi south of Newfoundland, making them the center of the French Atlantic cod fisheries.

Mayotte
Status: Territorial Collectivity
Prefect: Pierre Bayle (1998)
Area: 144 sq mi (374 sq km)
Population (2004 est.): 186,026 (growth rate: 4.1%); birth rate: 42.2/1000; infant mortality rate: 64.2/1000; life expectancy: 61.0; density per sq mi: 1,288
Capital (2003 est.): Dzaoudzi 15,100. **Largest City:** Mamoudzou, 45,700. **Languages:** Mahorian (a Swahili dialect), French (official language) spoken by 35% of the population. **Religions:** Islam 97%, Christian (mostly Roman Catholic)
Economic summary: GDP/PPP (1998 est.): $85 million; per capita $2,600. **Real growth rate:** n.a. **Inflation:** n.a. **Unemployment:** 38% (1999). **Arable land:** n.a. **Agriculture:**vanilla, ylang-ylang (perfume essence), coffee, copra. **Labor force:** 48,800 (2000). **Industries:** newly created lobster and shrimp industry, construction. **Natural resources:** negl. **Exports:** $3.44 million (f.o.b., 1997): ylang-ylang (perfume essence), vanilla, copra, coconuts, coffee, cinnamon. **Imports:** $141.3 million (f.o.b., 1997): food, machinery and equipment, transportation equipment, metals, chemicals. **Major trading partners:** France, Comoros, Réunion, Africa, Southeast Asia.

France gained colonial control over Mayotte in 1843. It is the most populous of the four Comoros Islands in the Indian Ocean off Mozambique in Africa. Mayotte chose to remain a French dependency rather than join the other Comoran islands in declaring independence in 1975. Comoros laid claim to Mayotte shortly after independence and continues to do so. In July 2000, 70% of voters opted to accept greater autonomy but remain a part of France.

Gabon
GABONESE REPUBLIC

National name: République Gabonaise
President: Omar Bongo (1967)
Premier: Jean-François Ntoutoume (1999)
Area: 103,346 sq mi (267,667 sq km)
Population (2004 est.): 1,355,246 (growth rate: 2.5%); birth rate: 36.4/1000; infant mortality rate: 54.3/1000; life expectancy: 56.5; density per sq mi: 13
Capital and largest city (2003 est.): Libreville, 661,600. **Other large cities:** Port-Gentil, 116,200; Franceville, 41,300. **Monetary unit:** CFA Franc. **Languages:** French (official), Fang, Myene, Bateke, Bapounou/ Eschira, Bandjabi. **Ethnicity/race:** Bantu tribes, including four major tribal groupings: Fang, Punu, Nzeiby, Mbede (Obamba/Bateke); other Africans and Europeans 11.3%, including 0.8% French and 0.8% persons of dual nationality. **Religions:** Christian 55%-75%, Animist, Islam less than 1%. **Literacy rate:** 63% (1995 est.)
Economic summary: GDP/PPP (2003 est.): $7.301 billion; per capita $5,500. **Real growth rate:** 1.2%. **Inflation:** 2.3% (2002 est.). **Unemployment:** 21% (1997 est.). **Arable land:** 1%. **Agriculture:** cocoa, coffee, sugar, palm oil, rubber; cattle; okoume (a tropical softwood); fish. **Labor force:** 600,000 (1999 est); agriculture 60%, services 25%, industry 15%. **Industries:** petroleum extraction and refining; manganese, and gold mining; chemicals; ship repair; food and beverage; textile; lumbering and plywood; cement. **Natural resources:** petroleum, manganese, uranium, gold, timber, iron ore, hydropower. **Exports:** $2.891 billion (f.o.b., 2003 est.): crude oil 77%, timber, manganese, uranium (2001). **Imports:** $1.079 billion (f.o.b., 2003 est.): machinery and equipment, foodstuffs, chemicals, construction materials. **Major trading partners:** U.S., France, China, Netherlands Antilles, Netherlands. **Member of French Community**

Geography This West African country with the Atlantic as its western border is also bounded by Equatorial Guinea, Cameroon, and the Congo. Its area is slightly less than Colorado's. Most of the country is covered by a dense tropical forest.

Government Republic.

History The earliest humans in Gabon were believed to be the Babinga, or Pygmies, dating back to 7000 B.C., who were later followed by Bantu groups from southern and eastern Africa. Now there are many tribal groups in the country, the largest being the Fang peoples, who constitute 25% of the population.

Gabon was first explored by the Portuguese navigator Diego Cam in the 15th century. In 1472, the Portuguese explorers encountered the mouth of the Como River, and named it "Rio de Gabao," river of Gabon, which later became the name of the country. The Dutch began arriving in 1593, and the French in 1630. In 1839, the French founded their first settlement on the left bank of the Gabon estuary and gradually occupied the hinterland during the second half of the 19th century. The land became a French territory in 1888, an autonomous republic within the French Union after World War II, and an independent republic on Aug. 17, 1960.

After his conversion to Islam in 1973, President Bongo changed his given name, Albert Bernard, to Omar. He was reelected every five years since he took office in 1967. Strikes and riots led to a transitional constitution in May 1990 legalizing political parties and calling for free elections. In its first multiparty election in Dec. 1993, the incumbent president received just over 51% of the vote, while the opposition candidate refused to accept defeat; he alleged fraud and tried to establish a rival government.

In Dec. 1998, President Bongo, who had ruled the country for 31 years, was elected for an additional seven. Gabon lacks roads, schools, and adequate health care, yet the oil-rich country has lined the pockets of its ruler, who, according to the French weekly *L'Autre Afrique*, is said to own more real estate in Paris than any other foreign leader. Despite his reputation for corruption and authoritarianism, Bongo has a strong national following. In July 2003, the country's constitution was changed, allowing Bongo to remain in power indefinitely.

Gambia, The

REPUBLIC OF THE GAMBIA

President: Yahya Jammeh (1994)
Area: 4,363 sq mi (11,300 sq km)
Population (2004 est.): 1,546,848 (growth rate: 3.0%); birth rate: 40.3/1000; infant mortality rate: 73.5/1000; life expectancy: 54.8; density per sq mi: 355
Capital (2003 est.): Banjul, 46,700. **Largest city:** Serekunda, 344,100. **Monetary unit:** Dalasi. **Languages:** English (official), Mandinka, Wolof, Fula, other indigenous. **Ethnicity/race:** African 99% (Mandinka 42%, Fula 18%, Wolof 16%, Jola 10%, Serahuli 9%, other 4%), non-African 1%. **Religions:** Islam 90%, Christian 9%, indigenous 1%. **Literacy rate:** 40% (2003 est.)
Economic summary: GDP/PPP (2003 est.): $2.597 billion; per capita $1,700. **Real growth rate:** 0.5% (2001 est.). **Inflation:** 5.5% (2002 est.). **Unemployment:** n.a. **Arable land:** 20%. **Agriculture:** rice, millet, sorghum, peanuts, corn, sesame, cassava (tapioca), palm kernels; cattle, sheep, goats. **Labor force:** 400,000; agriculture 75%, industry, commerce, and services 19%, government 6%. **Industries:** processing peanuts, fish, and hides; tourism; beverages; agricultural machinery assembly, woodworking, metalworking; clothing. **Natural resources:** fish. **Exports:** $156 million (f.o.b., 2003 est.): peanut products, fish, cotton lint, palm kernels, re-exports. **Imports:** $271 million (f.o.b., 2003 est.): foodstuffs, manufactures, fuel, machinery and transport equipment. **Major trading partners:** France, UK, Malaysia, Italy, Germany, Belgium, South Africa, China, Senegal, Brazil, Netherlands, India, Hong Kong.
Member of Commonwealth of Nations

Geography Situated on the Atlantic coast in westernmost Africa and surrounded on three sides by Sene-

gal, Gambia is twice the size of Delaware. The Gambia River flows for 200 mi (322 km) through Gambia on its way to the Atlantic. The country, the smallest on the continent, averages only 20 mi (32 km) in width.

Government Republic.

History Since the 13th century, the Wolof, Malinke, and Fulani peoples settled in what is now The Gambia. The Portuguese were the first European explorers, encountering the Gambia River in 1455, and in 1681 the French founded an enclave at Albredabut. During the 17th century, Gambia was settled by various companies of English merchants. Slavery was the chief source of revenue before it was abolished in 1807. Gambia became a Crown colony in 1843 and an independent nation within the Commonwealth of Nations on Feb. 18, 1965. Full independence was approved in a 1970 referendum, and on April 24 of that year Gambia proclaimed itself a republic.

Dauda Kairaba Jawara served as Gambia's president from 1970–1994. A military coup led by Capt. Yahya Jammeh deposed the president in July 1994, suspended the constitution, and banned existing political parties. Jammeh promised new elections, which were held in Sept. 1996, and he won 55% of the vote against his nearest rival, Ousseynou Darboe. In April 1997, he completed the promised return to civilian rule. Censorship of the press and other repressive measures continue to mar the country's transition to democracy.

Unrest plagued Gambia throughout much of 2000. In January Jammeh crushed a coup attempt staged by some of his own bodyguards, and in April violent student protests rocked the country. The peanut export system collapsed in the same year from mismanagement, leaving farmers unpaid and unable to sell a bumper crop of the country's main commodity. In 2001, Jammeh lifted the ban against various opposition parties he had outlawed after his 1994 coup. He was reelected in Oct. 2001 with 53% of the vote.

Georgia

GEORGIA

National Name: Sakartvelo
President: Mikhail Saakashvili (2004)
Prime Minister: Zurab Zhvania (2004)
Minister of State: Avtandil Jorbenadze (2001)
Area: 26,911 sq mi (69,700 sq km)
Population (2004 est.): 4,693,892 (growth rate: –0.4%); birth rate: 10.1/1000; infant mortality rate: 19.3/1000; life expectancy: 75.6; density per sq mi: 174
Capital and largest city (2003 est.): Tbilisi, 1,440,000 (metro. area), 1,240,200 (city proper). **Other large cities:** Kutaisi, 268,800; Batoumi, 145,400; and Sokhumi, 110,300. **Monetary unit:** Lari. **Languages:** Georgian 71% (official), Russian 9%, Armenian 7%, Azerbaijani 6%, other 7% (Abkhaz is the official language in Abkhazia). **Ethnicity/race:** Georgian 70.1%, Armenian 8.1%, Russian 6.3%, Azeri 5.7%, Ossetian 3%, Abkhaz 1.8%, other 5%. **Religions:** Georgian Orthodox 65%, Islam 11%, Russian Orthodox 10%, Armenian Orthodox 8%, unknown 6%. **Literacy rate:** 99% (1999 est.)
Economic summary: GDP/PPP (2003 est.): $12.18 billion; per capita $2,500. **Real growth rate:** 5.5%. **Inflation:** 5%. **Unemployment:** 17% (2001 est.). **Arable land:** 11%. **Agriculture:** citrus, grapes, tea, hazelnuts, vegetables; livestock. **Labor force:** 2.1 million (2001 est.); industry 20%, agriculture 40%, services 40% (1999 est.). **Industries:** steel, aircraft, machine tools, electrical appliances, mining (manganese and copper), chemicals, wood products,

wine. **Natural resources:** forests, hydropower, manganese deposits, iron ore, copper, minor coal and oil deposits; coastal climate and soils allow for important tea and citrus growth. **Exports:** $615 million (2003 est.): scrap metal, machinery, chemicals; fuel reexports; citrus fruits, tea, wine. **Imports:** $1.25 billion (2003 est.): fuels, machinery and parts, transport equipment, grain and other foods, pharmaceuticals. **Major trading partners:** Turkey, Italy, Russia, Greece, Netherlands, Spain, Turkmenistan, Ukraine, Azerbaijan, U.S., Germany, Bulgaria, Romania, France.

Geography Georgia is bordered by the Black Sea in the west, by Turkey and Armenia in the south, by Azerbaijan in the east, and Russia in the north. The republic also includes the Abkhazia and Ajara autonomous republics and South Ossetia.

Government Republic.

History Georgia became a kingdom about 4 B.C. and Christianity was introduced in A.D. 337. During the reign of Queen Tamara (1184–1213), its territory included the whole of Transcaucasia. During the 13th century, Tamerlane and the Mongols decimated its population. From the 16th century on, the country was the scene of a struggle between Persia and Turkey. In the 18th century it became a vassal to Russia in exchange for protection from the Turks and Persians.

Georgia joined Azerbaijan and Armenia in 1917 to establish the anti-Bolshevik Transcaucasian Federation, and upon its dissolution, proclaimed its independence in 1918. In 1922, Georgia, Armenia, and Azerbaijan were annexed by the USSR and formed the Transcaucasian Soviet Socialist Republic. In 1936, it became a separate Soviet republic. Under Soviet rule Georgia was transformed from an agrarian country to a largely industrial, urban society.

Georgia proclaimed its independence from the USSR on April 6, 1991. In Jan. 1992, its leader, Zviad Gamsakhurdia, was sacked and later accused of dictatorial policies, the jailing of opposition leaders, human rights abuses, and clamping down on the media. A ruling military council was established by the opposition until a civilian authority could be restored. In 1992, Eduard Shevardnadze, the Soviet Union's foreign minister under Gorbachev, became president.

In 1992–1993, the government engaged in armed conflict with separatists in the breakaway province of Abkhazia. In 1994, Russia and Georgia signed a cooperation treaty that authorized Russia to keep three military bases in Georgia and allowed Russians to train and equip the Georgian army. In 1996, Georgia and its breakaway region of South Ossetia agreed to a cessation of hostilities in their six-year conflict. With little progress in resolving the Abkhazia situation, however, Parliament in April 1997 voted overwhelmingly to threaten Russia with loss of its military bases should it fail to extend Russian military control over the separatist region. In 1998, the U.S. and Britain began an operation to remove nuclear material from Georgia, dangerous remains from its Soviet years. A darling of the West since his days as the Soviet Union's foreign minister, Shevardnadze was viewed far less favorably by his own people, who were frustrated by unemployment, poverty, cronyism, and rampant corruption. In the 2000 presidential elections, Shevardnadze was reelected with 80% of the vote, though international observers determined the election was marred by irregularities.

In 2002, U.S. troops trained Georgia's military in antiterrorism measures in the hopes that Georgian troops would subdue Muslim rebels fighting in the country. Tensions between Georgia and Russia were strained over the Pankisi Gorge, a lawless region of Georgia that Russia said had become a haven for Islamic militants and Chechen rebels.

In May 2003, work began on the Georgian section of the enormously ambitious Baku-Tbilisi-Ceyhan oil pipeline, which runs from Azerbaijan through Georgia to Turkey.

Massive demonstrations began after the preliminary results of the Nov. 2, 2003, parliamentary elections. The opposition party (and international monitors) claimed that the elections were rigged in favor of Shevardnadze and the political parties who support him. After more than three weeks of massive protests, Shevardnadze resigned on Nov. 30. Georgians compared the turn of events to Czechoslovakia's velvet revolution. In Jan. 2004 presidential elections, Mikhail Saakashvili, the key opposition leader, won in a landslide. The 36-year-old lawyer built his reputation as a reformer committed to ending corruption.

Saakashvili's first major challenge was asserting control over the breakaway region of Ajaria. Its leader, Aslan Abashidze, refused to recognize the new Georgian president, but after several months of confrontations, he was forced to resign in May 2004 and leave the country. Efforts to reintegrate the two other breakaway regions he inherited, South Ossetia and Abkhazia, have proven more difficult. Critics feel Saakashvili has approached the matter too aggressively, aggravating the secessionist impulses of these regions and raising the ire of Russia, which lends support to both breakaway areas.

Germany
FEDERAL REPUBLIC OF GERMANY

National name: Bundesrepublik Deutschland
President: Horst Köhler (2004)
Chancellor: Gerhard Schröder (1998)
Area: 137,846 sq mi (357,021 sq km)
Population (2004 est.): 82,424,609 (growth rate: 0%); birth rate: 8.5/1000; infant mortality rate: 4.2/1000; life expectancy: 78.5; density per sq mi: 598
Capital and largest city (2003 est.): Berlin (capital since Oct. 3, 1990), 3,933,300 (metro. area), 3,274,500 (city proper). **Other large cities:** Hamburg, 1,686,100; Munich, 1,185,400; Cologne, 965,300; Frankfurt, 648,000; Essen, 588,800; Dortmund, 587,600; Stuttgart, 581,100; Düsseldorf, 568,900; Bremen, 527,900; Hanover, 516,300; Duisburg, 513,400. **Monetary units:** Euro (formerly Deutsche mark). **Language:** German. **Ethnicity/race:** German 91.5%, Turkish 2.4%, Italian 0.7%, Greek 0.4%, Polish 0.4%, other 4.6%. **Religions:** Protestant 34%, Roman Catholic 34%, Islam 3.7%, Unaffiliated or other 28.3%. **Literacy rate:** 99% (1977 est.)
Economic summary GDP/PPP (2003 est.): $2.271 trillion; per capita $27,600. **Real growth rate:** –0.1%. **Inflation:** 0.9%. **Unemployment:** 10.7%. **Arable land:** 34%. **Agriculture:** potatoes, wheat, barley, sugar beets, fruit, cabbages; cattle, pigs, poultry. **Labor force:** 41.9 million (2001); industry 33.4%, agriculture 2.8%, services 63.8% (1999). **Industries:** among the world's largest and most technologically advanced producers of iron, steel, coal, cement, chemicals, machinery, vehicles, machine tools, electronics, food and beverages; shipbuilding; textiles. **Natural resources:** iron ore, coal, potash, timber, lignite, uranium, copper, natural gas, salt, nickel, arable land. **Exports:** $696.9 billion (f.o.b., 2003 est.): machinery, vehicles, chemicals, metals and manufactures, foodstuffs, textiles. **Imports:** $585 billion (f.o.b., 2003 est.): machinery, vehicles, chemicals, foodstuffs,

textiles, metals. **Major trading partners:** France, U.S., UK, Italy, Netherlands, Austria, Belgium, Spain, Switzerland, China.

Geography Located in central Europe, Germany is made up of the North German Plain, the Central German Uplands (Mittelgebirge), and the Southern German Highlands. The Bavarian plateau in the southwest averages 1,600 ft (488 m) above sea level, but it reaches 9,721 ft (2,962 m) in the Zugspitze Mountains, the highest point in the country. Germany's major rivers are the Danube, the Elbe, the Oder, the Weser, and the Rhine. Germany is about the size of Montana.

Government Federal republic.

History The Celts are believed to have been the first inhabitants of Germany. They were followed by German tribes at the end of the 2nd century B.C. German invasions destroyed the declining Roman Empire in the 4th and 5th centuries A.D. One of the tribes, the Franks, attained supremacy in western Europe under Charlemagne, who was crowned Holy Roman Emperor in 800. By the Treaty of Verdun (843), Charlemagne's lands east of the Rhine were ceded to the German Prince Louis. Additional territory acquired by the Treaty of Mersen (870) gave Germany approximately the area it maintained throughout the Middle Ages. For several centuries after Otto the Great was crowned king in 936, German rulers were also usually heads of the Holy Roman Empire.

By the 14th century, the Holy Roman Empire was little more than a loose federation of the German princes who elected the Holy Roman emperor. In 1438, Albert of Hapsburg became emperor, and for the next several centuries the Hapsburg line ruled the Holy Roman Empire until its decline in 1806. Relations between state and church were changed by the Reformation, which began with Martin Luther's 95 theses, and came to a head in 1547, when Charles V scattered the forces of the Protestant League at Mühlberg. The Counter Reformation followed. A dispute over the succession to the Bohemian throne brought on the Thirty Years' War (1618–1648), which devastated Germany and left the empire divided into hundreds of small principalities virtually independent of the emperor.

Meanwhile, Prussia was developing into a state of considerable strength. Frederick the Great (1740–1786) reorganized the Prussian army and defeated Maria Theresa of Austria in a struggle over Silesia. After the defeat of Napoléon at Waterloo (1815), the struggle between Austria and Prussia for supremacy in Germany continued, reaching its climax in the defeat of Austria in the Seven Weeks' War (1866) and the formation of the Prussian-dominated North German Confederation (1867). The architect of this new German unity was Otto von Bismarck, a conservative, monarchist, and militaristic Prussian prime minister. He unified all of Germany in a series of three wars against Denmark (1864), Austria (1866), and France (1870–1871). On Jan. 18, 1871, King Wilhelm I of Prussia was proclaimed German emperor in the Hall of Mirrors at Versailles. The North German Confederation, created in 1867, was abolished, and the Second German Reich, consisting of the North and South German states, was born. With a powerful army, an efficient bureaucracy, and a loyal bourgeoisie, Chancellor Bismarck consolidated a powerful centralized state.

Wilhelm II dismissed Bismarck in 1890 and embarked upon a "New Course," stressing an intensified colonialism and a powerful navy. His chaotic foreign policy culminated in the diplomatic isolation of Germany and the disastrous defeat in World War I (1914–1918). The Second German Empire collapsed following the defeat of the German armies in 1918, the naval mutiny at Kiel, and the flight of the kaiser to the Netherlands. The Social Democrats, led by Friedrich Ebert and Philipp Scheidemann, crushed the communists and established a moderate state, known as the Weimar Republic, with Ebert as president. President Ebert died on Feb. 28, 1925, and on April 26, Field Marshal Paul von Hindenburg was elected president. The mass of Germans regarded the Weimar Republic as a child of defeat, imposed upon a Germany whose legitimate aspirations to world leadership had been thwarted by a world conspiracy. Added to this were a crippling currency debacle, a tremendous burden of reparations, and acute economic distress.

Adolf Hitler, an Austrian war veteran and a fanatical nationalist, fanned discontent by promising a Greater Germany, abrogation of the Treaty of Versailles, restoration of Germany's lost colonies, and the destruction of the Jews, whom he scapegoated as the reason for Germany's downfall and depressed economy. When the Social Democrats and the Communists refused to combine against the Nazi threat, President von Hindenburg made Hitler the chancellor on Jan. 30, 1933. With the death of von Hindenburg on Aug. 2, 1934, Hitler repudiated the Treaty of Versailles and began full-scale rearmament. In 1935, he withdrew Germany from the League of Nations, and the next year he reoccupied the Rhineland and signed the Anti-Comintern pact with Japan, at the same time strengthening relations with Italy. Austria was annexed in March 1938. By the Munich agreement in Sept. 1938, he gained the Czech Sudetenland, and in violation of this agreement he completed the dismemberment of Czechoslovakia in March 1939. His invasion of Poland on Sept. 1, 1939, precipitated World War II.

Hitler established death camps to carry out "the final solution to the Jewish question." By the end of the war, Hitler's Holocaust had killed 6 million Jews, as well as Gypsies, homosexuals, Communists, the handicapped, and others not fitting the Aryan ideal. After some dazzling initial successes in 1939–1942, Germany surrendered unconditionally to Allied and Soviet military commanders on May 8, 1945. On June 5 the four-nation Allied Control Council became the de facto government of Germany.

(For details of World War II and of the Holocaust, *see* Headline History, World War II.)

At the Berlin (or Potsdam) Conference (July 17–Aug. 2, 1945) President Truman, Premier Stalin, and Prime Minister Clement Attlee of Britain set forth the guiding principles of the Allied Control Council: Germany's complete disarmament and demilitarization, destruction of its war potential, rigid control of industry, and decentralization of the political and economic structure. Pending final determination of territorial questions at a peace conference, the three victors agreed to the ultimate transfer of the city of Königsberg (now Kaliningrad) and its adjacent area to the USSR and to the administration by Poland of former German territories lying generally east of the Oder-Neisse Line. For purposes of control, Germany was divided into four national occupation zones.

The Western powers were unable to agree with the USSR on any fundamental issues. Work of the Allied Control Council was hamstrung by repeated Soviet vetoes; and finally, on March 20, 1948, Russia walked out of the Council. Meanwhile, the U.S. and Britain had taken steps to merge their zones economically (Bizone); on May 31, 1948, the U.S., Britain, France, and the Benelux countries agreed to set up a German state comprising the three Western zones. The USSR reacted by clamping a blockade on all ground communications between the Western zones and West Berlin, an enclave in the Soviet zone. The Western Allies countered by organizing a gigantic airlift to fly supplies into the beleaguered city. The USSR was finally forced to lift the blockade on May 12, 1949.

The Federal Republic of Germany was proclaimed on May 23, 1949, with its capital at Bonn. In free elections, West German voters gave a majority in the Constituent Assembly to the Christian Democrats, with the Social Democrats largely making up the opposition. Konrad Adenauer became chancellor, and Theodor Heuss of the Free Democrats was elected first president.

The East German states adopted a more centralized constitution for the Democratic Republic of Germany, put into effect on Oct. 7, 1949. The USSR thereupon dissolved its occupation zone but Soviet troops remained. The Western Allies declared that the East German Republic was a Soviet creation undertaken without self-determination and refused to recognize it. Soviet forces created a state controlled by the secret police with a single party, the Socialist Unity (Communist) Party.

Agreements in Paris in 1954 giving the Federal Republic full independence and complete sovereignty came into force on May 5, 1955. Under the agreement, West Germany and Italy became members of the Brussels treaty organization created in 1948 and renamed the Western European Union. West Germany also became a member of NATO. In 1955, the USSR recognized the Federal Republic. The Saar territory, under an agreement between France and West Germany, held a plebiscite and despite economic links to France, elected to rejoin West Germany on Jan. 1, 1957.

The division between West Germany and East Germany was intensified when the Communists erected the Berlin Wall in 1961. In 1968, the East German Communist leader, Walter Ulbricht, imposed restrictions on West German movements into West Berlin. The Soviet-bloc invasion of Czechoslovakia in Aug. 1968 added to the tension. West Germany signed a treaty with Poland in 1970, renouncing force and setting Poland's western border as the Oder-Neisse Line. It subsequently resumed formal relations with Czechoslovakia in a pact that "voided" the Munich treaty that gave Nazi Germany the Sudetenland. By 1973, normal relations were established between East and West Germany and the two states entered the United Nations.

West German chancellor Willy Brandt, winner of a Nobel Peace Prize for his foreign policies, was forced to resign in 1974 when an East German spy was discovered to be one of his top staff members. Succeeding him was a moderate Social Democrat, Helmut Schmidt. Schmidt staunchly backed U.S. military strategy in Europe, staking his political fate on placing U.S. nuclear missiles in Germany unless the Soviet Union reduced its arsenal of intermediate missiles. He also strongly opposed nuclear freeze proposals.

Helmut Kohl of the Christian Democrat Party became chancellor in 1982. An economic upswing in 1986 led to Kohl's reelection. The fall of the Communist government in East Germany left only Soviet objections to German reunification to be dealt with. On the night of Nov. 9, 1989, the Berlin Wall came down, making reunification all but inevitable. In July 1990, Kohl asked Soviet leader Gorbachev to drop his objections in exchange for financial aid from (West) Germany. Gorbachev agreed, and on Oct. 3, 1990, the German Democratic Republic acceded to the Federal Republic and Germany became a united and sovereign state for the first time since 1945.

A reunited Berlin serves as the official capital of unified Germany, although the government would continue to have administrative functions in Bonn during the 12-year transition period. The issues of the cost of reunification and the modernization of the former East Germany were serious considerations facing the reunified nation.

In its most important election in decades, on Sept. 27, 1998, Germans chose Social Democrat Gerhard Schröder as chancellor over Christian Democrat incumbent Helmut Kohl, ending a 16-year-long rule that oversaw the reunification of Germany and symbolized the end of the cold war in Europe. A centrist, Schröder campaigned for "the new middle" and promised to rectify Germany's high unemployment rate of 10.6%.

Tension between the old-style left-wing and the more probusiness pragmatists within Schröder's government came to a head with the abrupt resignation of Finance Minister Oskar Lafontaine in March 1999, who was also chairman of the ruling Social Democratic Party. Lafontaine's plans to raise taxes on industry and raise German wages—already nearly the highest in the world—went against the more centrist policies of Schröder. Hans Eichel was chosen to become the next finance minister.

Germany joined the other NATO allies in the military conflict in Kosovo in 1999. Before the Kosovo crisis, Germans had not participated in an armed conflict since World War II. Germany agreed to take 40,000 Kosovar refugees, the most of any NATO country.

In Dec. 1999, former chancellor Helmut Kohl and other high officials in the Christian Democrat Party (CDU) admitted accepting tens of millions of dollars in illegal donations during the 1980s and 1990s. The enormity of the scandal led to the virtual dismemberment of the CDU in early 2000, a party that had long been a stable conservative force in German politics.

In July 2000, Schröder managed to pass significant tax reforms that would lower the top income-tax rate from 51% to 42% by 2005. He also eliminated the capital gains tax on companies selling shares in other companies, a measure that was expected to spur mergers. In May 2001, the German Parliament authorized the payment of $4.4 billion in compensation to 1.2 million surviving Nazi-era slave laborers.

Schröder was narrowly reelected in Sept. 2002, defeating conservative businessman Edmund Stoiber. Schröder's Social Democrats and coalition partner, the Greens, won a razor-thin majority in Parliament. Schröder's deft handling of Germany's catastrophic floods in August and his tough stance against U.S. plans for a preemptive attack on Iraq buoyed him in the weeks leading up to the election. Germany's continued reluctance to support the U.S.'s call for military action against Iraq severely strained its relations with Washington.

Germany's recession continued in 2003—for the previous three years Europe's biggest economy had the lowest growth rate among EU countries. In Aug. 2003, Schröder unfurled an ambitious fiscal reform package, and called his proposal "the most significant set of structural reforms in the social history of Germany." The reforms reduced some of the benefits of Germany's generous social welfare system, including national health insurance and unemployment compensation.

Ghana

REPUBLIC OF GHANA

President: John Agyekum Kufuor (2001)
Area: 92,456 sq mi (239,460 sq km)
Population (2004 est.): 20,757,032 (growth rate: 1.4%); birth rate: 24.9/1000; infant mortality rate: 52.2/1000;

life expectancy: 56.3; density per sq mi: 225
Capital and Largest City (2003 est.): Accra, 2,825,800 (metro. area), 1,661,400 (city proper). **Other large cities:** Kumasi, 645,100; Tamale, 279,600. **Monetary unit:** Cedi. **Languages:** English (official), African languages (including Akan, Moshi-Dagomba, Ewe, and Ga). **Ethnicity/race:** black African 98.5% (major tribes: Akan 44%, Moshi-Dagomba 16%, Ewe 13%, Ga 8%, Gurma 3%, Yoruba 1%), European and other 1.5% (1998). **Religions:** Christian 63%, indigenous beliefs 21%, Islam 16%. **Literacy rate:** 75% (2003 est.)
Economic summary: GDP/PPP (2003 est.): $44.49 billion; per capita $2,200. **Real growth rate:** 4.8%. **Inflation:** 26.4%. **Unemployment:** 20% (1997 est.). **Arable land:** 16%. **Agriculture:** cocoa, rice, coffee, cassava (tapioca), peanuts, corn, shea nuts, bananas; timber. **Labor force:** 9 million (2000 est.); agriculture 60%, industry 15%, services 25% (1999 est.). **Industries:** mining, lumbering, light manufacturing, aluminum smelting, food processing. **Natural resources:** gold, timber, industrial diamonds, bauxite, manganese, fish, rubber, hydropower. **Exports:** $2.642 billion (f.o.b., 2003 est.): gold, cocoa, timber, tuna, bauxite, aluminum, manganese ore, diamonds. **Imports:** $3.24 billion (f.o.b., 2003 est.): capital equipment, petroleum, foodstuffs. **Major trading partners:** Netherlands, UK, U.S., Germany, France, Nigeria, Belgium, Italy, China, Côte d'Ivoire. **Member of Commonwealth of Nations**

Geography A West African country bordering on the Gulf of Guinea, Ghana is bounded by Côte d'Ivoire to the west, Burkina Faso to the north, Togo to the east, and the Atlantic Ocean to the south. It compares in size to Oregon, and its largest river is the Volta.

Government Constitutional democracy.

History Several major civilizations flourished in the general region of what is now Ghana. The ancient empire of Ghana (located 500 mi northwest of the contemporary state) reigned until the 13th century. The Akan peoples established the next major civilization, beginning in the 13th century, and then the Ashanti empire flourished in the 18th and 19th centuries.

Called the Gold Coast, the area was first seen by Portuguese traders in 1470. They were followed by the English (1553), the Dutch (1595), and the Swedes (1640). British rule over the Gold Coast began in 1820, but it was not until after quelling the severe resistance of the Ashanti in 1901 that it was firmly established. British Togoland, formerly a colony of Germany, was incorporated into Ghana by referendum in 1956. Created as an independent country on March 6, 1957, Ghana, as the result of a plebiscite, became a republic on July 1, 1960.

Premier Kwame Nkrumah attempted to take leadership of the Pan-African Movement, holding the All-African People's Congress in his capital, Accra, in 1958 and organizing the Union of African States with Guinea and Mali in 1961. But he oriented his country toward the Soviet Union and China and built an autocratic rule over all aspects of Ghanaian life. In Feb. 1966, while Nkrumah was visiting Beijing and Hanoi, he was deposed by a military coup led by Gen. Emmanuel K. Kotoka.

A series of military coups followed and on June 4, 1979, Flight Lt. Jerry Rawlings overthrew Lt. Gen. Frederick Akuffo's military rule. Rawlings permitted the election of a civilian president to go ahead as scheduled the following month, and Hilla Limann, candidate of the People's National Party, took office. Rawlings's three-month rule was one of Ghana's bloodiest periods, with executions of numerous government officials and business leaders. Two years later Rawlings staged another coup, charging the civilian government with corruption. As chairman of the Provisional National Defense Council, Rawlings scrapped the constitution, instituted an austerity program, and reduced budget deficits over the next decade. He then returned the country to civilian rule, and won the presidency in multiparty elections in 1992 and again in 1996.

A major cocoa producer, Ghana has been hurt by slumps in cocoa prices. In July 2000, Ghana and neighboring countries began destroying massive amounts of cocoa to drive up the price. Together they produce 70% of the world's cocoa. Since gold is Ghana's largest source of foreign exchange, fluctuating prices have hammered the economy, and mining companies cut 10,000 jobs in 1999. Saudi Arabian investors rescued Ashanti Goldfields, the largest company in sub-Saharan Africa, from near collapse in Feb. 2000.

In Jan. 2001, John Agyekum Kufuor was elected president. In 2002, he set up a National Reconciliation Commission to review human rights abuses during of the country's period of military rule.

Greece

HELLENIC REPUBLIC

National name: Elliniki Dimokratia
President: Kostis Stephanopoulos (1995)
Prime Minister: Kostas Karamanlis (2004)
Area: 50,942 sq mi (131,940 sq km)
Population (2004 est.): 10,647,529 (growth rate: 0.2%); birth rate: 9.7/1000; infant mortality rate: 5.6/1000; life expectancy: 78.9; density per sq mi: 209
Capital (2003 est.): Athens, 3,247,000 (metro. area), 747,300 (city proper). **Other large cities:** Thessaloníki, 361,200; Piraeus, 179,300; Patras, 167,000. **Monetary unit:** Euro (formerly drachma). **Language:** Greek 99% (official), English, French. **Ethnicity/race:** Greek 98%, other 2%; note: the Greek government states there are no ethnic divisions in Greece. **Religions:** Greek Orthodox 98%, Islam 1.3%, other 0.7%. **Literacy rate:** 98% (2003 est.)
Economic summary: GDP/PPP (2003 est.): $212.2 billion; per capita $19,900. **Real growth rate:** 4%. **Inflation:** 3.3%. **Unemployment:** 9.8%. **Arable land:** 22%. **Agriculture:** wheat, corn, barley, sugar beets, olives, tomatoes, wine, tobacco, potatoes; beef, dairy products. **Labor force:** 4,406,700; industry 20%, agriculture 20%, services 59% (2000 est.). **Industries:** tourism; food and tobacco processing, textiles; chemicals, metal products; mining, petroleum. **Natural resources:** bauxite, lignite, magnesite, petroleum, marble, hydropower potential. **Exports:** $5.899 billion (f.o.b., 2003 est.): food and beverages, manufactured goods, petroleum products, chemicals, textiles. **Imports:** $33.27 billion (f.o.b., 2003 est.): machinery, transport equipment, fuels, chemicals. **Major trading partners:** Germany, Italy, UK, Bulgaria, U.S., Cyprus, Russia, South Korea, France, Netherlands, Belgium.

Geography Located in southern Europe, Greece forms an irregular-shaped peninsula in the Mediterranean with two additional large peninsulas projecting from it: the Chalcidice and the Peloponnese. The Greek Islands are generally subdivided into two groups, according to location: the Ionian Islands (including Corfu, Cephalonia, and Leucas) west of the mainland and the Aegean Islands (including Euboea, Samos, Chios, Lesbos, and Crete) to the east and south. North-central Greece, Epirus, and western Macedonia are all mountainous. The main chain of the Pindus Mountains extends from northwest Greece to the Peloponnese. Mount Olympus, rising to 9,570 ft (2,909 m), is the highest point in the country.

Government Parliamentary republic.

History Indo-European peoples, including the Mycenaeans, began entering Greece about 2000 B.C. and set up sophisticated civilizations. About 1200 B.C., the Dorians, another Indo-European people, invaded Greece, and a dark age followed, known mostly through the Homeric epics. At the end of this time, classical Greece began to emerge (c. 750 B.C.) as a loose composite of city-states with a heavy involvement in maritime trade and a devotion to art, literature, politics, and philosophy. Greece reached the peak of its glory in the 5th century B.C., but the Peloponnesian War (431–404 B.C.) weakened the nation, and it was conquered by Philip II and his son Alexander the Great of Macedonia, who considered themselves Greek. By the middle of the 2nd century B.C., Greece had declined to the status of a Roman province. It remained within the eastern Roman Empire until Constantinople fell to the Crusaders in 1204. In 1453, the Turks took Constantinople and by 1460, Greece was a province in the Ottoman empire. The Greek war of independence (immortalized by the poet Byron) began in 1821, and by 1827 Greece won independence with sovereignty guaranteed by Britain, France, and Russia.

The protecting powers chose Prince Otto of Bavaria as the first king of modern Greece in 1832 to reign over an area only slightly larger than the Peloponnese peninsula. Chiefly under the next king, George I, chosen by the protecting powers in 1863, Greece acquired much of its present territory. During his 57-year reign, a period in which he encouraged parliamentary democracy, Thessaly, Epirus, Macedonia, Crete, and most of the Aegean islands were added from the disintegrating Turkish empire. Unfavorable economic conditions forced about one-sixth of the entire Greek population to emigrate (mostly to the U.S.) in the late 19th and early 20th centuries. An unsuccessful war against Turkey after World War I brought down the monarchy, which was replaced by a republic in 1923.

Two military dictatorships and a financial crisis brought back the exiled king, George II, but only until 1941, when Italian and German invaders defeated tough Greek resistance. After British and Greek troops liberated the country in Oct. 1944, Communist guerrillas staged a long military campaign against the government; the Greek civil war, infamous for its brutality, began in Dec. 1944 and continued until Oct. 16, 1949, when the Communist guerrillas conceded defeat. The Greek government received U.S. aid under the Truman Doctrine, the predecessor of the Marshall Plan, to fight against the Communists.

Greece was a charter member of the UN, and became a member of the North Atlantic Treaty Organization (NATO) in 1951. A military junta seized power in April 1967, sending young King Constantine II into exile. Col. George Papadopoulos, a leader of the junta, gradually attempted to modify his hardline, right-wing image. A coup ousted Papadopoulos in Nov. 1973.

A referendum in Dec. 1974, five months after the demise of the military dictatorship, ended the Greek monarchy and established a republic. Former premier Karamanlis returned from exile to become premier of Greece's first civilian government since 1967. Greece has continued to be ruled by freely elected civilian governments ever since. On Jan. 1, 1981, Greece became the 10th member of the European Union. Andreas Papandreou, son of former premier George Papandreou, founded the Panhellenic Socialist Movement (PASOK) and became Greece's first socialist premier (1981–1989).

Greece continued to experience tensions with Turkey over a disputed, unpopulated 10-acre island and over Cyprus, which is divided into Greek and Turkish sectors.

The pro-Western socialist prime minister Kostas Simitis (1996–2004) was credited with reviving the Greek economy. Still, *The Economist* magazine estimated in 2001 that it would be at least another 15 years before the per capita GDP in Greece comes close to the current EU average.

In the summer of 2002, the government was finally able to crack down on the 17 November (17N) terrorist organization, which had eluded the Greek authorities for the previous 27 years. The radical leftist group was responsible for more than 20 assassinations of American, British, and Greek diplomats, military personnel, and businessmen. Greece was criticized for decades by the international community for being soft on terrorism, and confidence in its ability to provide adequate security during the 2004 Olympics was weak. In parliamentary elections in March 2004, the conservative New Democracy party swept to power, defeating Pasok, the ruling socialist party. The new prime minister, Kostas Karamanlis, vowed to deliver a safe and successful Olympics, and in spite of last-minute construction, the Athens Olympics were widely hailed as a triumph. It cost Greece $10 billion to hold the games.

Grenada

STATE OF GRENADA

Sovereign: Queen Elizabeth II (1952)
Governor-General: Sir Daniel Williams (1996)
Prime Minister: Keith C. Mitchell (1995)
Area: 133 sq mi (344 sq km)
Population (2004 est.): 89,357 (growth rate 0.1%); birth rate: 22.6/1000; infant mortality rate: 14.6/1000; life expectancy: 64.5; density per sq mi: 673
Capital and largest city (2003 est.): St. George's, 4,300. **Monetary unit:** East Caribbean dollar.
Language: English (official), French patois. **Ethnicity/race:** black 82%, mixed black and European 13%, European and East Indian 5%, and trace of Arawak/Carib Amerindian. **Religions:** Roman Catholic 53%, Anglican 13.8%, other Protestant 33.2%. **Literacy rate:** 90% (1970 est.)
Economic summary: GDP/PPP (2002 est.): $440 million; per capita $5,000. **Real growth rate:** 2.5%. **Inflation:** 2.8% (2001 est.). **Unemployment:** 12.5% (2000). **Arable land:** 6%. **Agriculture:** bananas, cocoa, nutmeg, mace, citrus, avocados, root crops, sugarcane, corn, vegetables. **Labor force:** 42,300 (1996); services 62%, agriculture 24%, industry 14% (1999 est.). **Industries:** food and beverages, textiles, light assembly operations, tourism, construction. **Natural resources:** timber, tropical fruit, deepwater harbors. **Exports:** $46 million (2002 est.): bananas, cocoa, nutmeg, fruit and vegetables, clothing, mace. **Imports:** $208 million (2002 est.): food, manufactured goods, machinery, chemicals, fuel. **Major trading partners:** Germany, U.S., Bangladesh, Netherlands, Saint Lucia, Antigua and Barbuda, France, Trinidad and Tobago, UK. **Member of Commonwealth of Nations**

Geography Grenada (the first "a" is a long vowel) is the most southerly of the Windward Islands, about 100 mi (161 km) from the Venezuelan coast. It is a volcanic island traversed by a mountain range, the highest peak of which is Mount St. Catherine (2,756 ft; 840 m).

Government Constitutional monarchy. A governor-general represents the sovereign, Elizabeth II.

History The Arawak Indians were the first to inhabit Grenada, but they were all eventually massacred by the Carib Indians. When Columbus arrived in 1498 he encountered the Caribs, who continued to rule over the island for another 150 years. The French gained control of the island in 1672 and held on to it until 1762, when the British invaded. Black slaves were granted freedom in 1833. After more than 200 years of British rule, most recently as part of the West Indies Associated States, Grenada became independent on Feb. 7, 1974, with Eric M. Gairy as prime minister.

In 1979, the Marxist New Jewel Movement staged a coup, and its leader, Maurice Bishop, became prime minister. Bishop, a protégé of Cuba's President Castro, was killed in a military coup on Oct. 19, 1983.

In an effort to establish order on the island and eliminate the Cuban military presence, U.S. president Ronald Reagan ordered an invasion of Grenada on Oct. 25, 1983, involving over 1,900 U.S. troops and a small military force from Barbados, Dominica, Jamaica, St. Lucia, and St. Vincent. The troops met strong resistance from Cuban military personnel on the island but soon occupied it. After a gradual withdrawal of peacekeeping forces, a centrist coalition led by Herbert A. Blaize won a parliamentary majority in 1984. The New National Party (NNP), led by Keith C. Mitchell, won a majority in the 1995 parliamentary elections. He won reelection again in 1999 and 2003.

In Sept. 2004, Grenada suffered the most damage of any country from Hurricane Ivan, which killed 39 and left thousands homeless.

Guatemala

REPUBLIC OF GUATEMALA

National name: República de Guatemala
President: Oscar Berger (2004)
Area: 42,042 sq mi (108,890 sq km)
Population (2004 est.): 14,280,596 (growth rate: 2.6%); birth rate: 34.6/1000; infant mortality rate: 36.9/1000; life expectancy: 65.2; density per sq mi: 340
Capital and largest city (2003 est.): Guatemala City, 2,655,900 (metro. area), 1,128,800 (city proper).
Other large cities: Mixco, 287,600; Villa Nueva, 138,900. **Monetary unit:** Quetzal. **Languages:** Spanish 60%, Amerindian languages 40% (23 officially recognized Amerindian languages, including Quiche, Cakchiquel, Kekchi, Mam, Garifuna, and Xinca).
Ethnicity/race: Mestizo (Ladino)—mixed Amerindian-Spanish ancestry—55%, Amerindian (Mayan) or predominantly Amerindian 43%, whites and others 2%. **Religions:** Roman Catholic, Protestant, indigenous Mayan beliefs. **Literacy rate:** 71% (2003 est.)
Economic summary: GDP/PPP (2003 est.): $56.53 billion; per capita $4,100. **Real growth rate:** 2.2%. **Inflation:** 5.6%. **Unemployment:** 7.5% (1999 est.). **Arable land:** 13%. **Agriculture:** sugarcane, corn, bananas, coffee, beans, cardamom; cattle, sheep, pigs, chickens. **Labor force:** 4.2 million (1999 est.); agriculture 50%, industry 15%, services 35% (1999 est.). **Industries:** sugar, textiles and clothing, furniture, chemicals, petroleum, metals, rubber, tourism. **Natural resources:** petroleum, nickel, rare woods, fish, chicle, hydropower. **Exports:** $2.763 billion (f.o.b., 2003 est.): coffee, sugar, bananas, fruits and vegetables, cardamom, meat, apparel, petroleum, electricity. **Imports:** $5.749 billion (f.o.b., 2003 est.): fuels, machinery and transport equipment, construction materials, grain, fertilizers, electricity. **Major trading partners:** U.S., El Salvador, Nicaragua, Mexico, South Korea, China.

Geography The northernmost of the Central American nations, Guatemala is the size of Tennessee. Its neighbors are Mexico on the north and west, and Belize, Honduras, and El Salvador on the east. The country consists of three main regions—the cool highlands with the heaviest population, the tropical area along the Pacific and Caribbean coasts, and the tropical jungle in the northern lowlands (known as the Petén).

Government Constitutional democratic republic.

History Once the site of the impressive ancient Mayan civilization, Guatemala was conquered by Spanish conquistador Pedro de Alvarado in 1524 and became a republic in 1839 after the United Provinces of Central America collapsed. From 1898 to 1920, dictator Manuel Estrada Cabrera ran the country, and from 1931 to 1944, Gen. Jorge Ubico Castaneda served as strongman.

After Ubico's overthrow in 1944 by the "October Revolutionaries," a group of left-leaning students and professionals, liberal-democratic coalitions led by Juan José Arévalo (1945–1951) and Jacobo Arbenz Guzmán (1951–1954) instituted social and political reforms that strengthened the peasantry and urban workers at the expense of the military and big landowners like the U.S.-owned United Fruit Company. With covert U.S. backing, Col. Carlos Castillo Armas led a coup in 1954, and Arbenz took refuge in Mexico. A series of repressive regimes followed, and by 1960 the country was plunged into a civil war between military governments, right-wing vigilante groups, and leftist rebels that would last 36 years, the longest civil war in Latin American history. Death squads murdered an estimated 50,000 leftists and political opponents during the 1970s. In 1977, the U.S. cut off military aid to the country because of its egregious human rights abuses. The indigenous Mayan indians were singled out for special brutality by the right-wing death squads. By the end of the war, 200,000 citizens were dead.

A succession of military juntas dominated during the civil war, until a new constitution was passed and civilian Marco Vinicio Cerezo Arévalo was elected and took office in 1986. He was followed by Jorge Serrano Elías in 1991. In 1993, Serrano moved to dissolve Congress and the Supreme Court and suspend constitutional rights, but the military deposed Serrano and allowed the inauguration of Ramiro de Leon Carpio, the former attorney general for human rights. A peace agreement was finally signed in Dec. 1996 by President Álvaro Arzú Irigoyen.

In 1999, a Guatemalan truth commission blamed the army for 93% of the atrocities and the rebels (the Guatemalan National Revolutionary Unit) for 3%. The former guerrillas apologized for their crimes, and President Clinton apologized for U.S. support of the right-wing military governments. The army has not acknowledged its guilt. Alfonso Portillo Cabrera, closely associated with the former dictatorship of Efrain Rios Montt (1982–1983), became president in Jan. 2000. In Aug. 2000, Portillo apologized for the former government's human rights abuses and pledged to prosecute those responsible and compensate victims.

In July 2003, the country's highest court ruled that former coup leader and military dictator Efrain Rios Montt, responsible for a massacre of tens of thousands of civilians during the civil war, was eligible to run for president in November. The ruling conflicted with the constitution, which bans anyone who seized power in a coup from running for the presidency. But in November, Rios Montt was soundly defeated by two candidates, conservative Oscar Berger and center-leftist Alvaro Colom. In the run-off election in December, Berger was elected president.

In 2004, Guatemala experienced an alarmingly violent crime wave. More than 2,000 murders took place, and were blamed on crime gangs and bands of teenagers.

Guinea

REPUBLIC OF GUINEA

National name: République de Guinée
President: Lansana Conté (1984)
Premier: vacant (2004)
Area: 94,925 sq mi (245,857 sq km)
Population (2004 est.): 9,246,462 (growth rate: 2.4%); birth rate: 42.3/1000; infant mortality rate: 91.8/1000; life expectancy: 49.7; density per sq mi: 97
Capital and largest city (2003 est.): Conakry, 1,767,200. **Monetary unit:** Guinean franc.
Languages: French (official), native tongues (Malinké, Susu, Fulani). **Ethnicity/race:** Peuhl 40%, Malinke 30%, Susu 20%, smaller tribes 10%. **Religions:** Islam 85%, Christian 8%, indigenous 7%. **Literacy rate:** 36% (1995 est.).
Economic summary: GDP/PPP (2003 est.): $18.87 billion; per capita $2,100. **Real growth rate:** 2.2%. **Inflation:** 8%. **Unemployment:** n.a. **Arable land:** 4%. **Agriculture:** rice, coffee, pineapples, palm kernels, cassava (tapioca), bananas, sweet potatoes; cattle, sheep, goats; timber. **Labor force:** 3 million (1999); agriculture 80%, industry and services 20% (2000 est.). **Industries:** bauxite, gold, diamonds; alumina refining; light manufacturing and agricultural processing industries. **Natural resources:** bauxite, iron ore, diamonds, gold, uranium, hydropower, fish. **Exports:** $726 million (f.o.b., 2003 est.): bauxite, alumina, gold, diamonds, coffee, fish, agricultural products. **Imports:** $646 million (f.o.b., 2003 est.): petroleum products, metals, machinery, transport equipment, textiles, grain and other foodstuffs. **Major trading partners:** South Korea, Spain, Cameroon, Belgium, U.S., Ireland, France, Russia, Germany, Côte d'Ivoire, Italy, China.

Geography Guinea, in West Africa on the Atlantic, is also bordered by Guinea-Bissau, Senegal, Mali, Côte d'Ivoire, Liberia, and Sierra Leone. Slightly smaller than Oregon, the country consists of a coastal plain, a mountainous region, a savanna interior, and a forest area in the Guinea Highlands. The highest peak is Mount Nimba at 5,748 ft (1,752 m).

Government Republic.

History Beginning in 900, the Susu migrated from the north and began settling in the area that is now Guinea. The Susu civilization reached its height in the 13th century. Today the Susu make up about 20% of Guinea's population. From the 16th to the 19th century, the Fulani empire dominated the region. In 1849, the French claimed it as a protectorate. First called Rivières du Sud, the protectorate was rechristened French Guinea, and finally, in 1895, it became part of French West Africa.

Guinea achieved independence on Oct. 2, 1958, and became an independent state with Sékou Touré as president. Under Touré, the country became the first avowedly Marxist state in Africa. Diplomatic relations with France were suspended in 1965, with the Soviet Union replacing France as the country's chief source of economic and technical assistance.

Prosperity came in 1960 after the start of exploitation of bauxite deposits. Touré was reelected to a seven-year term in 1974 and again in 1981. Touré died after 26 years as president in March 1984. A week later, a military regime headed by Col. Lansana Conté took power.

In 1989, President Conté announced that Guinea would move to a multiparty democracy, and in 1991, voters approved a new constitution. In Dec. 1993 elections, the president's Unity and Progress Party took almost 51% of the vote. In 2001, a government referendum was passed that eliminated presidential limits, thus allowing Conté to run for a third term in 2003. Despite the trappings of multiparty rule, Conté has ruled the country with an iron fist.

Guinea has had ongoing difficulties with its neighbor Liberia, which was embroiled in a long civil war during the 1990s and again in 2000–2003. Guinea had taken sides against rebel leader Charles Taylor in Liberia's civil war and was part of the Nigerian-led ECOMOG forces that intervened in the crisis. As a consequence, President Conté's relations with Taylor remained sour after Taylor became Liberia's president in 1997. The fighting in Liberia spilled over the border into Guinea on several occasions. Sierra Leone's recent civil war also caused problems for neighboring Guinea. Already burdened by an inadequate infrastructure and a weak economy, an influx of nearly 300,000 refugees from Sierra Leone has overwhelmed the country.

In Dec. 2003 President Conté was reelected to a third term. In April 2004, after two months on the job, Prime Minister Lonseny Fall resigned and went into exile, claiming that the president would not allow him to govern effectively.

Guinea-Bissau

REPUBLIC OF GUINEA-BISSAU

National name: República da Guiné-Bissau
President: Henrique Rosa (interim) (2003)
Prime Minister: Carlos Gomes Júnior (2004)
Area: 13,946 sq mi (36,120 sq km)
Population (2004 est.): 1,388,363 (growth rate: 2.0%); birth rate: 38.0/1000; infant mortality rate: 108.7/1000; life expectancy: 47.0; density per sq mi: 100
Capital and largest city (2003 est.): Bissau, 296,900.
Monetary unit: CFA Franc. **Languages:** Portuguese (official), Criolo, African languages. **Ethnicity/race:** African 99% (Balanta 30%, Fula 20%, Manjaca 14%, Mandinga 13%, Papel 7%), European and mulatto less than 1%. **Religions:** indigenous beliefs 50%, Islam 45%, Christian 5%. **Literacy rate:** 42% (2002 est.)
Economic summary: GDP/PPP (2003 est.): $1.164 billion; per capita $900. **Real growth rate:** 1.8%. **Inflation:** 4% (2002 est.). **Unemployment:** n.a. **Arable land:** 11%. **Agriculture:** rice, corn, beans, cassava (tapioca), cashew nuts, peanuts, palm kernels, cotton; timber; fish. **Labor force:** 480,000 (l999); agriculture 82% (2000 est.). **Industries:** agricultural products processing, beer, soft drinks. **Natural resources:** fish, timber, phosphates, bauxite, unexploited deposits of petroleum. **Exports:** $54 million (f.o.b., 2002 est.): cashew nuts, shrimp, peanuts, palm kernels, sawn lumber. **Imports:** $104 million (f.o.b., 2002 est.): foodstuffs, machinery and transport equipment, petroleum products. **Major trading partners:** India, Uruguay, Thailand, Senegal, Portugal, Taiwan.

Geography A neighbor of Senegal and Guinea in West Africa, on the Atlantic coast, Guinea-Bissau is about half the size of South Carolina. The country is a low-lying coastal region of swamps, rain forests, and mangrove-covered wetlands, with about 25 islands off the coast.

Government Republic.

History The land now known as Guinea-Bissau was once the kingdom of Gabú, which was part of the larger Mali empire. After 1546 Gabú became more autonomous, and at least portions of the kingdom existed until 1867. The first European to encounter Guinea-Bissau was the Portuguese explorer Nuño Tristão in 1446; colonists in the Cape Verde Islands obtained trading rights in the territory, and it became a center of the Portuguese slave trade. In 1879, the connection with the islands was broken.

The African Party for the Independence of Guinea-Bissau and Cape Verde (another Portuguese colony) was founded in 1956, and guerrilla warfare by nationalists grew increasingly effective. By 1974 the rebels controlled most of the countryside, where they formed a government that was soon recognized by scores of countries. The military coup in Portugal in April 1974 brightened the prospects for freedom, and in August the Lisbon government signed an agreement granting independence to the province. The new republic took the name Guinea-Bissau.

In Nov. 1980, Premier João Bernardo Vieira headed a military coup that deposed Luis Cabral, president since 1974. In his 19 years of rule, Vieira was criticized for crony capitalism and corruption and for failing to alleviate the poverty of Guinea-Bissau, one of the world's poorest countries. Vieira also brought in troops from Senegal and the Republic of Guinea to help fight against an insurgency movement, a highly unpopular move. In May 1999 rebels deposed Vieira.

Following a period of military rule, Kumba Yalá, a former teacher and popular leader of Guinea-Bissau's independence movement, was elected president in 2000. In Sept. 2003 he was deposed in a military coup by Gen. Verissimo Correia Seabra, who then appointed an interim president and a prime minister. Yalá's increasingly repressive measures and refusal to hold elections were cited as the cause. In March 2004 general elections, Carlos Gomes Júnior became prime minister.

Guyana

COOPERATIVE REPUBLIC OF GUYANA

President: Bharrat Jagdeo (1999)
Prime Minister: Samuel Hinds (1999)
Area: 83,000 sq mi (214,970 sq km)
Population (2004 est.): 705,803 (growth rate: 0.6%); birth rate: 17.9/1000; infant mortality rate: 37.2/1000; life expectancy: 62.4; density per sq mi: 9
Capital and largest city (2003 est.): Georgetown, 227,700. **Monetary unit:** Guyanese dollar.
Languages: English (official), Amerindian dialects, Creole, Hindi, Urdu. **Ethnicity/race:** East Indian 50%; black 36%; Amerindian 7%; white, Chinese, and mixed 7%. **Religions:** Christian 50%, Hindu 35%, Islam 10%, other 5%. **Literacy rate:** 99% (2003 est.)
Economic summary: GDP/PPP (2003 est.): $2.792 billion; per capita $4,000. **Real growth rate:** 0.3%. **Inflation:** 4.7% (2002 est.). **Unemployment:** 9.1% (2000) (understated). **Arable land:** 2%. **Labor force:** 418,000 (2001 est.); agriculture n.a., industry n.a., services n.a. **Agriculture:** sugar, rice, wheat, vegetable oils; beef, pork, poultry, dairy products; fish (shrimp). **Industries:** bauxite, sugar, rice milling, timber, textiles, gold mining. **Natural resources:** bauxite, gold, diamonds, hardwood timber, shrimp, fish. **Exports:** $512 million (f.o.b., 2003 est.): sugar, gold, bauxite/alumina, rice, shrimp, molasses, rum, timber. **Imports:** $612 million (f.o.b., 2003 est.): manufactures, machinery, petroleum, food. **Major trading partners:** Canada, U.S., Netherlands Antilles, UK, Jamaica, Portugal, Trinidad and Tobago, Italy, Cuba. **Member of Commonwealth of Nations**

Geography Guyana is the size of Idaho and is situated on the northern coast of South America east of Venezuela, west of Suriname, and north of Brazil. A tropical forest covers more than 80% of the country.

Government Republic.

History The Warrou people were the indigenous inhabitants of Guyana. The Dutch, English, and French established colonies in what is now known as Guyana, but by the early 17th century the majority of the settlements were Dutch. During the Napoleonic wars Britain took over the Dutch colonies of Berbice, Demerara, and Essequibo, which became British Guiana in 1831.

Slavery was outlawed in 1834, and the great need for plantation workers led to a large wave of immigration, primarily of East Indians. Today, about half of the population is of East Indian descent and about 36% are of African descent.

In 1889, Venezuela voiced its claim to a large swathe of Guyanese territory, but ten years later an international tribunal ruled the land belonged to British Guiana.

British Guiana became a Crown colony in 1928, and in 1953 it was granted home rule. In 1950, Cheddi Jagan, who was Indian-Guyanese, and Forbes Burnham, who was Afro-Guyanese, created the colony's first political party, the Progressive People's Party (PPP), which was dedicated to gaining the colony's independence. In the 1953 elections, Cheddi Jagan was elected chief minister. The British, however, alarmed by Jagan's Marxist views, suspended the constitution and government within months and installed an interim government. In 1955, the PPP split, with Burnham breaking off to create the People's National Congress (PNC). The leftist Jagan of the PPP and the more moderate Burnham of the PNC were to dominate Guyanese politics for decades to come. In 1961, Britain granted the colony autonomy, and Jagan became prime minister (1961–1964). Strikes and rioting weakened Jagan's rule, much of it believed to be the result of covert CIA operations. In 1964, Burnham succeeded Jagan as prime minister, a position he retained after the country gained full independence on May 26, 1966. With independence, the country returned to its traditional name, Guyana.

In 1978, the country gained worldwide attention when American religious cult leader Jim Jones and 900 of his followers committed mass suicide in Jonestown, Guyana.

Burnham ruled Guyana until his death in 1985 (from 1980 to 1985, after a change in the constitution, he served as president). Guyana's first independent decades were marked by continued racial unrest between Indian-Guyanese and Afro-Guyanese as well as economic malaise.

Desmond Hoyte of the PNC became president in 1985, but in 1992 the PPP reemerged, winning a majority in the general election. Jagan became president, and the former Marxist succeeded in reviving the economy. After his death in 1997, his wife, Janet Jagan, was elected president. Former finance minister Bharrat Jagdeo assumed the presidency in 1999.

Guyana's potential economic development was hurt in 2000 as border disputes with both Venezuela to the west and Suriname to the east heated up. Suriname and Guyana have been unable to resolve the border dispute in an oil-rich coastal area. Venezuela's president Hugo Chavez has revived the 19th-century claim to more than half of Guyana's territory.

In March 2001, Bharrat Jagdeo won a second term in elections that underscored Guyana's bitter racial tensions. The reelection of Jagdeo, an ethnic East Indian, caused rioting among Afro-Guyanese, who claimed widespread election fraud.

Haiti

REPUBLIC OF HAITI

National name: République d'Haïti
President: Boniface Alexandre (interim) (2004)
Prime Minister: Gérard Latortue (interim) (2004)
Area: 10,714 sq mi (27,750 sq km)
Population (2004 est.): 7,656,166 (growth rate: 1.7%); birth rate: 33.8/1000; infant mortality rate: 74.4/1000; life expectancy: 51.8; density per sq mi: 715
Capital and largest city (2003 est.): Port-au-Prince, 1,764,000 (metro. area), 1,119,000 (city proper).
Monetary unit: Gourde. **Languages:** Creole and French (both official). **Ethnicity/race:** black 95%, mulatto and white 5%. **Religions:** Roman Catholic 80%, Protestant 16% (Baptist 10%, Pentecostal 4%, Adventist 1%, other 1%), other 3%, none 1%. Note: roughly half the population practices Vaudou.. **Literacy rate:** 53% (2003 est.)
Economic summary: GDP/PPP (2003 est.): $12.18 billion; per capita $1,600. **Real growth rate:** –1%. **Inflation:** 37.3%. **Unemployment:** widespread unemployment and underemployment; more than two-thirds of the labor force do not have formal jobs (2002 est.). **Arable land:** 20%. **Agriculture:** coffee, mangoes, sugarcane, rice, corn, sorghum; wood. **Labor force:** 3.6 million; note: shortage of skilled labor, unskilled labor abundant; agriculture 66%, services 25%, industry 9%. **Industries:** sugar refining, flour milling, textiles, cement, light assembly industries based on imported parts. **Natural resources:** bauxite, copper, calcium carbonate, gold, marble, hydropower. **Exports:** $321 million (f.o.b., 2003 est.): manufactures, coffee, oils, cocoa. **Imports:** $1.028 million (f.o.b., 2003 est.): food, manufactured goods, machinery and transport equipment, fuels, raw materials. **Major trading partners:** U.S., Dominican Republic, Canada, Colombia.

Geography Haiti, in the West Indies, occupies the western third of the island of Hispaniola, which it shares with the Dominican Republic. About the size of Maryland, Haiti is two-thirds mountainous, with the rest of the country marked by great valleys, extensive plateaus, and small plains.

Government Republic with an elected government.

History Explored by Columbus on Dec. 6, 1492, Haiti's native Arawaks fell victim to Spanish rule. In 1697, Haiti became the French colony of Saint-Dominique, which became a leading sugarcane producer dependent on slaves. In 1791, an insurrection erupted among the slave population of 480,000, resulting in a declaration of independence by Pierre-Dominique Toussaint l'Ouverture in 1801. Napoléon Bonaparte suppressed the independence movement, but it eventually triumphed in 1804 under Jean-Jacques Dessalines, who gave the new nation the Arawak name *Haiti*. It was the world's first independent black republic.

The revolution wrecked Haiti's economy. Years of strife between the light-skinned mulattos who dominated the economy and the majority black population, plus disputes with neighboring Santo Domingo, continued to hurt the nation's development. After a succession of dictatorships a bankrupt Haiti accepted a U.S. customs receivership from 1905 to 1941. Occupation by U.S. Marines from 1915 to 1934 brought stability. Haiti's high population growth made it the most densely populated nation in the hemisphere.

In 1949, after four years of democratic rule by President Dumarsais Estimé, dictatorship returned under Gen. Paul Magloire, who was succeeded by François Duvalier, nicknamed "Papa Doc," in 1957. Duvalier's secret police, the "Tontons Macoutes," ensured political stability with brutal efficiency. Duvalier's son, Jean-Claude, or "Baby Doc," succeeded his father when he died in 1971 as ruler of the poorest nation in the Western Hemisphere. In the early 1980s, Haiti became one of the first countries to face an AIDS epidemic. Fear of the disease caused tourists to stay away, and the tourist industry collapsed, causing rising unemployment. Unrest generated by the economic crisis forced Baby Doc to flee the country in 1986.

Throughout the 1990s the international community tried to establish democracy in Haiti. The country's first elected chief executive, Jean-Bertrand Aristide, a leftist Roman Catholic priest who seemed to promise a new era in Haiti, took office in Feb. 1991. The military, however, took control in a coup nine months later. A UN peacekeeping force, led by the U.S.—Operation Uphold Democracy—arrived in 1994. Aristide was restored to office and René Preval became his successor in 1996 elections. U.S. soldiers and UN peacekeepers left in 2000. Haiti's government, however, remained ineffectual and its economy was in ruins. With widespread unemployment, Haiti produces a steady flow of refugees to the U.S.

In 2000, former president Aristide was reelected president in elections boycotted by the opposition and questioned by many foreign observers. The U.S. and other countries threatened Haiti, already one of the Western hemisphere's poorest countries, with sanctions unless democratic procedures are strengthened. Haiti has the highest rates of AIDS, malnutrition, and infant mortality in the region. Aristide, once a charismatic champion of democracy, grew more authoritarian and seemed incapable of improving the lot of his people. Violent protests rocked the country in Jan. 2004, the month of Haiti's bicentennial, with protestors demanding Aristide resign. By February, a full-blown armed revolt was underway, and Aristide's hold on power continued to slip. The protests, groups of armed rebels, and French and American pressure led to the ousting of Aristide on Feb. 29. Thereafter a U.S.-led international force of 2,300 entered the chaos-engulfed country to restore order, and an interim government took over. In July, the international community pledged $1 billion in aid. In September, Hurricane Jeanne ravaged Haiti, killing more than 2,400 people.

Honduras

REPUBLIC OF HONDURAS

National name: República de Honduras
President: Ricardo Maduro (2002)
Area: 43,277 sq mi (112,090 sq km)
Population (2004 est.): 6,823,568 (growth rate: 2.2%); birth rate: 31.0/1000; infant mortality rate: 29.6/1000; life expectancy: 66.2; density per sq mi: 158
Capital and largest city (2003 est.): Tegucigalpa, 1,436,000 (metro. area), 1,248,300 (city proper).
Monetary unit: Lempira. **Languages:** Spanish (official), Amerindian dialects; English widely spoken in business. **Ethnicity/race:** mestizo 90%, Amerindian 7%, black 2%, white 1%. **Religions:** Roman Catholic 97%, growing population of evangelical Protestants. **Literacy rate:** 76% (2003 est.)
Economic summary: GDP/PPP (2003 est.): $17.46 billion; per capita $2,600. **Real growth rate:** 2.5%. **Inflation:** 7.7%. **Unemployment:** 27.5%. **Arable land:** 15%. **Agriculture:** bananas, coffee, citrus; beef; timber; shrimp. **Labor force:** 2.3 million (1997 est.); agriculture 34%, industry 21%, services 45% (2001 est.). **Industries:** sugar, coffee, textiles, clothing, wood products. **Natural resources:** timber, gold, silver,

copper, lead, zinc, iron ore, antimony, coal, fish, hydropower. **Exports:** $1.37 billion (f.o.b., 2003 est.): coffee, bananas, shrimp, lobster, meat; zinc, lumber (2000). **Imports:** $3.11 billion (f.o.b., 2003 est.): machinery and transport equipment, industrial raw materials, chemical products, fuels, foodstuffs (2000). **Major trading partners:** U.S., El Salvador, Guatemala, Mexico.

Geography Honduras, in the north-central part of Central America, has a Caribbean as well as a Pacific coastline. Guatemala is to the west, El Salvador to the south, and Nicaragua to the east. The second-largest country in Central America, Honduras is slightly larger than Tennessee. Generally mountainous, the country is marked by fertile plateaus, river valleys, and narrow coastal plains.

Government Democratic constitutional republic.

History During the first millennium, Honduras was inhabited by the Maya. Columbus explored the country in 1502. Honduras, with four other Central American nations, declared its independence from Spain in 1821 to form a federation of Central American states. In 1838, Honduras left the federation and became independent. Political unrest rocked Honduras in the early 1900s, resulting in an occupation by U.S. Marines. Dictator Gen. Tiburcio Carias Andino established a strong government in 1932.

In 1969, El Salvador invaded Honduras after Honduran landowners deported several thousand Salvadorans. Five thousand people ultimately died in what is called "the football war," because it broke out during a soccer game between the two countries. By threatening economic sanctions and military intervention, the Organization of American States (OAS) induced El Salvador to withdraw. After a decade of military rule, parliamentary democracy returned with the election of Roberto Suazo Córdova as president in 1982. However, Honduras faced severe economic problems and tensions along its border with Nicaragua. "Contra" rebels, waging a guerrilla war against the Sandinista regime in Nicaragua, used Honduras as a training and staging area. The U.S. also used Honduras for military exercises and built bases to train Honduran and Salvadoran troops.

In 1997, Carlos Flores Facussé of the Liberal Party was elected president. He began to reform the economy and modernize the government. In recent years, Honduras has faced high unemployment, inflation, and economic over-dependence on coffee and bananas. In Oct. 1998, Hurricane Mitch killed some 13,000 Hondurans, left 2 million homeless, and caused more than $5 billion in damage.

In 2002, Ricardo Maduro became president, promising to lessen crime and corruption, but his hardline efforts, growing increasingly more repressive, have not improved these problems.

Hungary

REPUBLIC OF HUNGARY

National name: Magyar Köztársaság
President: Ferenc Mádl (2000)
Prime Minister: Ferenc Gyurcsány (2004)
Area: 35,919 sq mi (93,030 sq km)
Population (2004 est.): 10,032,375 (growth rate: –0.3%); birth rate: 9.8/1000; infant mortality rate: 8.7/1000; life expectancy: 72.3; density per sq mi: 279
Capital and largest city (2003 est.): Budapest, 2,597,000 (metro. area), 1,769,500 (city proper). **Other large cities:** Debrecen, 210,500; Miskolc, 182,600; Szeged, 173,200; Pécs, 163,900. **Monetary unit:** Forint.

Languages: Magyar (Hungarian), 98.2%; other, 1.8%.
Ethnicity/race: Hungarian 89.9%, Roma 4%, German 2.6%, Serb 2%, Slovak 0.8%, Romanian 0.7%.
Religions: Roman Catholic 67.5%, Calvinist 20%, Lutheran 5%, atheist and others 7.5%. **Literacy rate:** 99% (2003 est.)
Economic summary: GDP/PPP (2003 est.): $139.7 billion; per capita $13,900. **Real growth rate:** 2.8%. **Inflation:** 4.7%. **Unemployment:** 6.1%. **Arable land:** 52%. **Agriculture:** wheat, corn, sunflower seed, potatoes, sugar beets; pigs, cattle, poultry, dairy products. **Labor force:** 4.2 million (1997); services 65%, industry 27%, agriculture 8% (1996). **Industries:** mining, metallurgy, construction materials, processed foods, textiles, chemicals (especially pharmaceuticals), motor vehicles. **Natural resources:** bauxite, coal, natural gas, fertile soils, arable land. **Exports:** $42.03 billion (f.o.b., 2003 est.): machinery and equipment, other manufactures, food products, raw materials, fuels and electricity (2001). **Imports:** $46.19 billion (f.o.b., 2003 est.): machinery and equipment, other manufactures, fuels and electricity, food products, raw materials (2001). **Major trading partners:** Germany, Austria, Italy, France, U.S., UK, Russia, China.

Geography This central European country is the size of Indiana. Most of Hungary is a fertile, rolling plain lying east of the Danube River and drained by the Danube and Tisza Rivers. In the extreme northwest is the Little Hungarian Plain. South of that area is Lake Balaton (250 sq mi; 648 sq km).

Government Parliamentary democracy.

History By 14 B.C., western Hungary was part of the Roman Empire's provinces of Pannonia and Dacia. The area east of the Danube was never a part of the Roman Empire and was largely occupied by various Germanic and Asiatic peoples. In 896 all of Hungary was invaded by the Magyars, who founded a kingdom. Christianity was accepted during the reign of Stephen I (Saint Stephen), 977–1038. A devastating invasion by the Mongols killed half of Hungary's population in 1241. The peak of Hungary's great period of medieval power came during the reign of Louis I the Great (1342–1382), whose dominions touched the Baltic, Black, and Mediterranean seas. War with the Turks broke out in 1389, and for more than 100 years the Turks advanced through the Balkans. When the Turks smashed a Hungarian army in 1526, western and northern Hungary accepted Hapsburg rule to escape Turkish occupation. Transylvania became independent under Hungarian princes. Intermittent war with the Turks was waged until a peace treaty was signed in 1699.

After the suppression of the 1848 revolt, led by Louis Kossuth, against Hapsburg rule, the dual monarchy of Austria-Hungary was set up in 1867. The dual monarchy was defeated with the other Central Powers in World War I. After a short-lived republic in 1918, the chaotic Communist rule of 1919 under Béla Kun ended with the Romanians occupying Budapest on Aug. 4, 1919. When the Romanians left, Adm. Nicholas Horthy entered the capital with a national army. The Treaty of Trianon of June 4, 1920, by which the Allies parceled out Hungarian territories, cost Hungary 68% of its land and 58% of its population.

In World War II, Hungary allied with Germany, which aided the country in recovering lost territories. Following the German invasion of Russia on June 22, 1941, Hungary joined the attack against the Soviet Union, but withdrew in defeat from the eastern front by May 1943. Germany occupied the country for the remainder of the war and set up a puppet government.

Hungarian Jews and gypsies were sent to death camps. The German regime was driven out by the Soviets in 1944–1945.

By the Treaty of Paris (1947), Hungary had to give up all territory it had acquired since 1937 and to pay $300 million reparations to the USSR, Czechoslovakia, and Yugoslavia. In 1948, the Communist Party, with the support of Soviet troops, seized control. Hungary was proclaimed a People's Republic and one-party state in 1949. Industry was nationalized, the land collectivized into state farms, and the opposition terrorized by the secret police. The terror, modeled after that of the USSR, reached its height with the trial and life imprisonment of József Cardinal Mindszenty, the leader of Hungary's Roman Catholics, in 1948. On Oct. 23, 1956, an anti-Communist revolution broke out in Budapest. To cope with it, the Communists set up a coalition government and called former premier Imre Nagy back to head the government. But he and most of his ministers sympathized with the anti-Communist opposition, and he declared Hungary a neutral power, withdrawing from the Warsaw Treaty and appealing to the United Nations for help. One of his ministers, János Kádár, established a counterregime and asked the USSR to send in military power. Soviet troops and tanks suppressed the revolution in bloody fighting after 190,000 people had fled the country. Under Kádár (1956–1988), Communist Hungary maintained more liberal policies in the economic and cultural spheres, and Hungary became the most liberal of the Soviet-bloc nations of eastern Europe. Continuing his program of national reconciliation, Kádár emptied prisons, reformed the secret police, and eased travel restrictions.

In 1989, Hungary's Communists abandoned their monopoly on power voluntarily, and the constitution was amended in Oct. 1989 to allow for a multiparty state. The last Soviet troops left Hungary in June 1991, thereby ending almost 47 years of military presence. The transition to a market economy proved difficult. In April 1999, Hungary became part of NATO, and in May 2004, it joined the EU.

Iceland

REPUBLIC OF ICELAND

National name: Lydveldid Island
President: Ólafur Ragnar Grímsson (2004)
Prime Minister: Halldór Ásgrímsson (2004)
Area: 39,768 sq mi (103,000 sq km)[1]
Population (2004 est.): 293,966 (growth rate: 1.0%); birth rate: 13.8/1000; infant mortality rate: 3.3/1000; life expectancy: 80.2; density per sq mi: 7
Capital and largest city (2003 est.): Reykjavik, 184,200 (metro. area), 114,800 (city proper). **Monetary unit:** Icelandic króna. **Language:** Icelandic, English, Nordic languages, German widely spoken. **Ethnicity/race:** homogeneous mixture of Norse/Celtic descendants 94%, population of foreign origin 6%. **Religions:** Church of Iceland (Evangelical Lutheran) 87.1%, other Protestant 4.1%, Roman Catholic 1.7%, other 7.1% (2002). **Literacy rate:** 100% (1997 est.)
Economic summary: GDP/PPP (2003 est.): $8.678 billion; per capita $30,900. **Real growth rate:** 2.6%. **Inflation:** 2%. **Unemployment:** 3.5%. **Arable land:** 1%. **Agriculture:** potatoes, green vegetables, chicken, pork, mutton; fish. **Labor force:** 159,000 (2000); agriculture 5.1%, fishing and fish processing 11.8%, manufacturing 12.9%, construction 10.7%, other services 59.5% (1999). **Industries:** fish processing; aluminum smelting, ferrosilicon production, geothermal power; tourism. **Natural resources:** fish, hydropower, geothermal power, diatomite. **Exports:** $2.379 billion (f.o.b., 2003 est.): fish and fish products 70%, animal

products, aluminum, diatomite and ferrosilicon.
Imports: $2.59 billion (2003 est.): machinery and equipment, petroleum products; foodstuffs, textiles.
Major trading partners: Germany, UK, Netherlands, U.S., Spain, Denmark, Portugal, Norway, Sweden.

1. Including some offshore islands.

Geography Iceland, an island about the size of Kentucky, lies in the north Atlantic Ocean east of Greenland and just touches the Arctic Circle. It is one of the most volcanic regions in the world. More than 13% is covered by snowfields and glaciers, and most of the people live in the 7% of the island that is made up of fertile coastland. The Gulf Stream keeps Iceland's climate milder than one would expect from an island near the Arctic Circle.

Government Constitutional republic.

History The earliest inhabitants of Iceland were Irish hermits, who left the island upon the arrival of the pagan Norse people in the late 9th century. A constitution drawn up c. 930 created a form of democracy and provided for an *Althing*, the world's oldest practicing legislative assembly. The island's early history was preserved in the Icelandic sagas of the 13th century.

In 1262–1264, Iceland came under Norwegian rule and passed to ultimate Danish control through the unification of the kingdoms of Norway, Sweden, and Denmark (the Kalmar Union) in 1397.

In 1874, Icelanders obtained their own constitution, and in 1918, Denmark recognized Iceland, via the Act of Union, as a separate state with unlimited sovereignty. It remained, however, nominally under the Danish monarchy.

During the German occupation of Denmark in World War II, British, then American, troops occupied Iceland and used it for a strategic air base. While officially neutral, Iceland cooperated with the Allies throughout the conflict. On June 17, 1944, after a popular referendum, the Althing proclaimed Iceland an independent republic.

The country joined the North Atlantic Treaty Organization in 1949, and subsequently received an American air force base in 1951. In 1970, it was admitted to the European Free Trade Association. Iceland unilaterally extended its territorial fishing limit from 3 to 200 nautical mi in 1972, precipitating a dispute with the UK known as the "cod wars," which ended in 1976, when the UK recognized the new limits. In 1980, the Icelanders elected a woman to the office of the presidency, the first elected female chief of state (i.e., president as distinct from prime minister) in the world. After the recession of the early 1990s, Iceland's economy rebounded.

At the International Whaling Commission meeting in July 2001, Iceland refused to agree to the continuation of the moratorium on commercial whaling that has been in effect since 1986. In 2003, after a 14-year lull, it began hunting whales for scientific research.

In May 2003, David Oddsson was reelected, making him the longest-serving prime minister in Europe. In 2004, in a pre-arranged agreement made between the two parties of the coalition government, Oddsson and Foreign Minister Halldór Ásgrímsson switched positions.

India

REPUBLIC OF INDIA

National name: Bharat
President: A.P.J. Abdul Kalam (2002)
Prime Minister: Manmohan Singh (2004)
Area: 1,269,338 sq mi (3,287,590 sq km)

Population (2004 est.): 1,065,070,607 (growth rate: 1.4%); birth rate: 22.8/1000; infant mortality rate: 57.9/1000; life expectancy: 64.0; density per sq mi: 839
Capital (2003 est.): New Delhi, 17,037,900 (metro. area), 10,203,700 (city proper). **Largest cities:** Bombay (Mumbai), 17,012,100 (metro.area), 12,383,100 (city proper); Calcutta (Kolkata), 14,090,200 (metro.area), 4,760,800 (city proper); Bangalore, 4,461,100; Madras (Chennai), 4,382,100; Ahmedabad, 3,653,700; Hyderabad, 3,585,600; Kanpur, 2,631,800.
Monetary unit: Rupee. **Principal languages:** Hindi (official), English (official), Bengali, Gujarati, Kashmiri, Malayalam, Marathi, Oriya, Punjabi, Tamil, Telugu, Urdu, Kannada, Assamese, Sanskrit, Sindhi (all recognized by the constitution). Dialects, 1,600+.
Ethnicity/race: Indo-Aryan 72%, Dravidian 25%, Mongoloid and other 3% (2000). **Religions:** Hindu 81.3%, Islam 12%, Christian 2.3%, Sikh 1.9%, other (including Buddhists, Jains, and Parsis) 2.5%. **Literacy rate:** 60% (2003 est.)
Economic summary: GDP/PPP (2003 est.): $3.022 trillion; per capita $2,900. **Real growth rate:** 7.6%. **Inflation:** 4.6%. **Unemployment:** 9.1%. **Arable land:** 54%. **Agriculture:** rice, wheat, oilseed, cotton, jute, tea, sugarcane, potatoes; cattle, water buffalo, sheep, goats, poultry; fish. **Labor force:** 406 million (1999); agriculture 60%, services 23%, industry 17% (1999). **Industries:** textiles, chemicals, food processing, steel, transportation equipment, cement, mining, petroleum, machinery, software. **Natural resources:** coal (fourth-largest reserves in the world), iron ore, manganese, mica, bauxite, titanium ore, chromite, natural gas, diamonds, petroleum, limestone, arable land. **Exports:** $57.24 billion (f.o.b., 2003 est.): textile goods, gems and jewelry, engineering goods, chemicals, leather manufactures. **Imports:** $74.15 billion (f.o.b., 2003 est.): crude oil, machinery, gems, fertilizer, chemicals. **Major trading partners:** U.S., UK, UAE, Hong Kong, Germany, China, Belgium, Singapore. **Member of Commonwealth of Nations**

Geography One-third the area of the United States, the Republic of India occupies most of the subcontinent of India in southern Asia. It borders on China in the northeast. Other neighbors are Pakistan on the west, Nepal and Bhutan on the north, and Burma and Bangladesh on the east.

The country can be divided into three distinct geographic regions: the Himalayan region in the north, which contains some of the highest mountains in the world, the Gangetic Plain, and the plateau region in the south and central part. Its three great river systems have extensive deltas and all rise in the Himalayas: the Ganges, the Indus, and the Brahmaputra.

Government Federal republic.

History One of the earliest civilizations, the Indus Valley civilization flourished on the Indian subcontinent from c. 2600 B.C. to c. 2000 B.C. It is generally accepted that the Aryans entered India c. 1500 B.C. from the northwest, finding a land that was already home to an advanced civilization. They introduced Sanskrit and the Vedic religion, a forerunner of Hinduism. Buddhism was founded in the 6th century B.C. and was spread throughout northern India, most notably by one of the great ancient kings of the Mauryan dynasty, Asoka (c. 269–232 B.C.), who also unified most of the Indian subcontinent for the first time.

In 1526, Muslim invaders founded the great Mogul empire, centered on Delhi, which lasted, at least in name, until 1857. Akbar the Great (1542–1605) strengthened and consolidated this empire. The long reign of his great-grandson, Aurangzeb (1618–1707),

represents both the greatest extent of the Mogul empire and the beginning of its decay.

Vasco da Gama, the Portuguese explorer, landed in India in 1498, and for the next 100 years the Portuguese had a virtual monopoly on trade with the subcontinent. Meanwhile, the English founded the East India Company, which set up its first factory at Surat in 1612 and began expanding its influence, fighting the Indian rulers and the French, Dutch, and Portuguese traders simultaneously.

Bombay, taken from the Portuguese, became the seat of English rule in 1687. The defeat of French and Mogul armies by Lord Clive in 1757 laid the foundation of the British Empire in India. The East India Company continued to suppress native uprisings and extend British rule until 1858, when the administration of India was formally transferred to the British Crown following the Sepoy Mutiny of native troops in 1857–1858.

After World War I, in which the Indian states sent more than 6 million troops to fight beside the Allies, Indian nationalist unrest rose to new heights under the leadership of a Hindu lawyer, Mohandas K. Gandhi, called Mahatma Gandhi. His philosophy of civil disobedience called for nonviolent noncooperation against British authority. He soon became the leading spirit of the Indian National Congress Party, which was the spearhead of revolt. In 1919, the British gave added responsibility to Indian officials, and in 1935, India was given a federal form of government and a measure of self-rule.

In 1942, with the Japanese pressing hard on the eastern borders of India, the British War Cabinet tried and failed to reach a political settlement with nationalist leaders. The Congress Party took the position that the British must quit India. Fearing mass civil disobedience, the government of India carried out widespread arrests of Congress leaders, including Gandhi.

Gandhi was released in 1944 and negotiations for a settlement were resumed. Finally, in Aug. 1947, India gained full independence. The victory was soured, however, by the partitioning of the predominantly Muslim regions of the north into the separate nation of Pakistan. The Muslim League, led by Mohammed Ali Jinnah, demanded a separate nation for the Muslim minority to prevent Hindu political and social domination. Indian Hindus, however, had hoped for a unified rather than balkanized Indian subcontinent. Lord Mountbatten as viceroy partitioned India along religious lines and split the provinces of Bengal and the Punjab, which both nations claimed. The partition of Pakistan and India led to the largest migration in human history, with 17 million people fleeing across the borders in both directions to escape the bloody riots occurring among sectarian groups. Armed conflict also broke out over rival claims to the princely states of Jammu and Kashmir.

Jawaharlal Nehru, nationalist leader and head of the Congress Party, was made prime minister. In 1949, a constitution was approved, making India a sovereign republic. Under a federal structure the states were organized on linguistic lines. The dominance of the Congress Party contributed to stability. In 1956, the republic absorbed former French settlements. Five years later, the republic forcibly annexed the Portuguese enclaves of Goa, Damao, and Diu.

Nehru died in 1964. His successor, Lal Bahadur Shastri, died on Jan. 10, 1966. Nehru's daughter, Indira Gandhi, became prime minister, and she continued his policy of nonalignment.

In 1971, the Pakistani army moved in to quash the independence movement in East Pakistan that was supported by India, and some 10 million Bengali refugees poured across the border into India, creating social, economic, and health problems. After numerous border incidents, India invaded East Pakistan and in two weeks forced the surrender of the Pakistani army. East Pakistan was established as an independent state and renamed Bangladesh.

In May 1975, the 300-year-old kingdom of Sikkim became a full-fledged Indian state. Situated in the Himalayas, Sikkim was a virtual dependency of Tibet until the early 19th century. Under an 1890 treaty between China and Great Britain, it became a British protectorate, and was made an Indian protectorate after Britain quit the subcontinent.

In the summer of 1975, the world's largest democracy veered suddenly toward authoritarianism when a judge in Allahabad, Indira Gandhi's home constituency, found Gandhi's landslide victory in the 1971 elections invalid because civil servants had illegally aided her campaign. Amid demands for her resignation, Gandhi decreed a state of emergency on June 26 and ordered mass arrests of her critics, including all opposition party leaders except the Communists.

Despite strong opposition to her repressive measures, particularly resentment against compulsory birth control programs, Gandhi, in 1977, announced parliamentary elections for March. At the same time, she freed most political prisoners. The landslide victory of Morarji R. Desai unseated Gandhi, but she staged a spectacular comeback in the elections of Jan. 1980.

In 1984, Gandhi ordered the Indian army to root out a band of Sikh holy men and gunmen who were using the most sacred shrine of the Sikh religion, the Golden Temple in Amritsar, as a base for terrorist raids in a violent campaign for greater political autonomy in the strategic Punjab border state. The perceived sacrilege to the Golden Temple kindled outrage among many of India's 14 million Sikhs and brought a spasm of mutinies and desertions by Sikh officers and soldiers in the army.

On Oct. 31, 1984, Indira Gandhi was assassinated by two men identified by police as Sikh members of her bodyguard. The ruling Congress Party chose her older son, Rajiv Gandhi, to succeed her as prime minister for four years. While running for reelection, former prime minister Rajiv Gandhi was assassinated on May 22, 1991, by Tamil militants who objected to India's mediation of the civil war in Sri Lanka.

The ruling Congress Party lost the parliamentary elections of May 1996, and its waning resulted in a period of political instability. The Hindu nationalist Bharatiya Janata Party (BJP) then became the dominant force in politics, with Atal Bihari Vajpayee becoming prime minister twice in two years.

In May 1998, India set off five nuclear tests, surprising the international community, which widely condemned India's pronuclear stance. Despite international urging for restraint, Pakistan responded by conducting several nuclear tests of its own two weeks later. India has resisted signing the Comprehensive Test Ban Treaty for nuclear weapons and has been slapped with sanctions by the U.S. and other countries. Less than a year later, in April 1999, both India and Pakistan tested nuclear-capable ballistic missiles.

India and Pakistan have held various talks about the disputed territory of Kashmir, which is the issue at the base of their chronic antagonism and their displays of nuclear strength. India controls two-thirds of this Himalayan region, which is the only Indian state that is predominantly Muslim.

The Indian Air Force launched air strikes on May 26, 1999, and later sent in ground troops against Islamic guerrilla forces in Kashmir. India blamed Pakistan for orchestrating violence in Kashmir by sending soldiers and mercenaries across the so-called Line of Control that divides Kashmir between India and Pakistan. Pakistan countered that the guerrillas are independent Kashmiri freedom fighters struggling for India's ouster from the region. Most international sources agreed with India's assumption that Pakistan was arming the soldiers. In Aug. 1999, Pakistan was forced to withdraw, but fighting continued sporadically during the coming year.

In Oct. 2001, violence again broke out in the region when a suicide bombing by a Pakistan-based militant organization killed 38 in India-controlled Kashmir. India retaliated with heavy shelling across the Line of Control. India, angered by Washington's sudden coziness to Pakistan following Sept. 11, took the opportunity to point out that while Pakistan might be helping the U.S. fight terrorism on the Afghan front, it was simultaneously supporting terrorism on its own borders with India. On Dec. 13, 2001, suicide bombers attacked the Indian parliament, killing 14 people. Indian officials blamed the deadly attack on Islamic militants supported by Pakistan.

Hope for a peaceful solution to the conflict in Kashmir was raised Nov. 2002, when a newly elected coalition government in India-controlled Jammu and Kashmir vowed to reach out to separatists and to improve conditions in the state. But hopes were dashed in March 2003, following the slaughter of 24 Hindus in Indian-controlled Kashmir. Officials blamed the massacre on Islamic militants. Days after the violence, both India and Pakistan test-fired short-range missiles capable of carrying nuclear warheads. Two bombs exploded in Bombay in August, killing more than 50 people and injuring about 150. Indian officials blamed Lashkar-e-Taiba, a Pakistan-based militant Islamic group. But in Nov. 2003, India and Pakistan declared their first formal cease-fire in 14 years. The cease-fire applies to the entire Line of Control dividing Kashmir. Relations have continued to thaw between the two countries. Three rounds of bilateral talks have taken place in 2004. While no real progress on the stalemate was made, both governments have agreed to implement confidence-building measures.

In one of the most dramatic political upsets in modern Indian history, the Indian National Congress Party, led by Sonia Gandhi, prevailed in parliamentary elections, prompting prime minister Atal Bihari Vajpayee to resign in May 2004. Although the country prospered economically under Vajpayee's rule, a substantial number of India's poor felt they had not benefitted from India's economic growth. Sonia Gandhi, the Italian-born widow of former Prime Minister Rajiv Gandhi, dealt a further shock to the country when she refused to become prime minister. The BJP had vociferously protested Gandhi's expected elevation to prime minister because of her foreign birth. The Congress Party instead chose former finance minister Manmohan Singh, who became India's first Sikh prime minister.

Indonesia

REPUBLIC OF INDONESIA

National name: Republik Indonesia
President: Susilo Bambang Yudhoyono (2004)
Area: 741,096 sq mi (1,919,440 sq km)
Population (2004 est.): 238,452,952 (growth rate: 1.5%); birth rate: 21.1/1000; infant mortality rate: 36.8/1000; life expectancy: 69.3; density per sq mi: 322
Capital and largest city (2003 est.): Jakarta, 17,891,000 (metro. area), 8,827,900 (city proper). **Other large cities:** Surabaya, 3,038,800; Bandung, 2,733,500; Medan, 2,204,300; Semarang, 1,267,100.

Monetary unit: Rupiah. **Languages:** Bahasa Indonesia (official), English, Dutch, Javanese, and more than 580 other languages and dialects. **Ethnicity/race:** Javanese 45%, Sundanese 14%, Madurese 7.5%, coastal Malays 7.5%, other 26%. **Religions:** Islam 88%, Protestant 5%, Roman Catholic 3%, Hindu 2%, Buddhist 1%, other 1%. **Literacy rate:** 89% (2003 est.)

Economic summary: GDP/PPP (2003 est.): $758.1 billion; per capita $3,200. **Real growth rate:** 4%. **Inflation:** 6.9%. **Unemployment:** 10.5%. **Arable land:** 10%. **Agriculture:** rice, cassava (tapioca), peanuts, rubber, cocoa, coffee, palm oil, copra; poultry, beef, pork, eggs. **Labor force:** 100.5 million (2002); agriculture 45%, industry 16%, services 39% (1999 est.) **Industries:** petroleum and natural gas; textiles, apparel, and footwear; mining, cement, chemical fertilizers, plywood; rubber; food; tourism. **Natural resources:** petroleum, tin, natural gas, nickel, timber, bauxite, copper, fertile soils, coal, gold, silver. **Exports:** $63.89 billion (f.o.b., 2003 est.): oil and gas, electrical appliances, plywood, textiles, rubber. **Imports:** $40.22 billion (f.o.b., 2003 est.): machinery and equipment; chemicals, fuels, foodstuffs. **Major trading partners:** Japan, U.S., Singapore, South Korea, China, Taiwan, Australia.

Geography Indonesia is an archipelago in Southeast Asia consisting of 17,000 islands (6,000 inhabited) and straddling the equator. The largest islands are Sumatra, Java (the most populous), Bali, Kalimantan (Indonesia's part of Borneo), Sulawesi (Celebes), the Nusa Tenggara islands, the Moluccas Islands, and Irian Jaya (also called West Papua), the western part of New Guinea. Its neighbor to the north is Malaysia and to the east is Papua New Guinea.

Indonesia, part of the "ring of fire," has the largest number of active volcanoes in the world. Earthquakes are frequent. The "Wallace Line," a zoological demarcation between Asian and Australian flora and fauna, divides Indonesia.

Government Republic.

History The 17,000 islands that make up Indonesia were home to a diversity of cultures and indigenous beliefs when the islands came under the influence of Hindu priests and traders in the first and second centuries A.D. Muslim invasions began in the 13th century, and most of the archipelago had converted to Islam by the 15th century Portuguese traders arrived early in the next century but were ousted by the Dutch around 1595. The Dutch United East India Company established posts on the island of Java, in an effort to control the spice trade.

After Napoleon subjugated the Netherlands in 1811, the British seized the islands but returned them to the Dutch in 1816. In 1922, Indonesia was made an integral part of the Dutch kingdom. During World War II, Japan seized the islands. Tokyo was primarily interested in Indonesia's oil, which was vital to the war effort, and tolerated fledgling nationalists such as Sukarno and Mohammed Hatta. After Japan's surrender, Sukarno and Hatta proclaimed Indonesian independence on Aug. 17, 1945. Allied troops, mostly British Indian forces, fought nationalist militias to reassert the prewar status quo until the arrival of Dutch troops.

In Nov. 1946, a draft agreement on forming a Netherlands-Indonesian Union was reached, but differences in interpretation resulted in more fighting between Dutch and nationalist forces. Following a bitter war for independence, leaders on both sides agreed to terms of a union on Nov. 2, 1949. The transfer of sovereignty took place in Amsterdam on Dec. 27, 1949. In Feb. 1956, Indonesia abrogated the union, and began seizing Dutch property in the islands.

In 1963, Netherlands New Guinea (the Dutch portion of the island of New Guinea) was transferred to Indonesia and renamed West Irian, which became Irian Jaya in 1973 and West Papua in 2000. Hatta and Sukarno, the cofathers of Indonesian independence, split over Sukarno's concept of "guided democracy," and under Sukarno's rule the Indonesian Communist Party (PKI) steadily increased its influence.

Sukarno was named president for life in 1966. Sukarno enjoyed mass support for his policies, but a growing power struggle between the military and the PKI loomed over his government. After an attempted military coup was put down by army chief of staff General Suharto and officers loyal to him, Suharto's forces killed hundreds of thousands of suspected communists in a massive purge aimed at undermining Sukarno's rule.

Suharto took over the reins of government and gradually eased Sukarno out of office, completing his consolidation of power in 1967. Under Suharto the military assumed an overarching role in national affairs, and relations with the West were enhanced. Indonesia's economy improved dramatically and national elections were permitted, although the opposition was so tightly controlled as to virtually choke off dissent.

In 1975, Indonesia invaded the former Portuguese half of the island of Timor; it seized the territory in 1976. A separatist movement developed at once. Unlike the rest of Indonesia, which had been a Dutch colony, East Timor was governed by the Portuguese for 400 years, and while 90% of Indonesians are Muslim, the East Timorese are primarily Catholic. More than 200,000 Timorese are reported to have died from famine, disease, and fighting since the annexation. In 1996, two East Timorese resistance activists, Bishop Carlos Filipe Ximenes Belo and José Ramos-Horta, received the Nobel Peace Prize.

In the summer of 1997, Indonesia suffered a major economic setback, along with most other Asian economies. Banks failed and the value of Indonesia's currency, the rupiah, plummeted. Antigovernment demonstrations and riots broke out, directed mainly at the country's prosperous ethnic Chinese. As the economic crisis deepened, student demonstrators occupied the national Parliament, demanding Suharto's ouster. On May 21, 1998, Suharto stepped down, ending 32 years of rule, and handed over power to Vice President B. J. Habibie.

June 7, 1999, marked Indonesia's first free parliamentary election since 1955. The ruling Golkar Party took a backseat to the Indonesian Democratic Party-Struggle (PDI-P), led by Megawati Sukarnoputri, the daughter of Sukarno, Indonesia's first president.

The ethnic, religious, and political tensions kept in check during Suharto's 32 years of authoritarian rule erupted in the months following his downfall. Rioting and violence shook the provinces of Aceh, Ambon (in the Moluccas), Borneo, and Irian Jaya. But nowhere was the violence more brutal and unjust than in East Timor. Habibie unexpectedly ended 25 years of Indonesian intransigence by announcing in Feb. 1999 that he was willing to hold a referendum on East Timorese independence. Twice rescheduled because of violence, a UN-organized referendum took place on Aug. 30, 1999, with 78.5% of the population voting to secede from Indonesia. In the days following the election, pro-Indonesian militias and Indonesian soldiers massacred civilians and forced a third of the population out of the region. After enormous international pressure, the government, which was either unwilling or unable to stop the violent rampage, finally agreed to allow UN forces into East Timor on Sept. 12, 1999. East Timor achieved independence on May 20, 2002.

On Oct. 20, 1999, in a surprising upset, the Indonesian parliament elected Abdurrahman Wahid as the new president of Indonesia, defeating Megawati Sukarnoputri, the popular leader of the Indonesian Democratic Party-Struggle. Wahid was a Sufi cleric as well as an adept politician with a reputation for honesty and moderation.

In the fall of 2000 and winter of 2001, President Wahid came under increasing criticism for corruption and incompetence. He was blamed for not stopping ethnic clashes and killings in Aceh, Irian Jaya, the Moluccas Islands, and especially in Borneo, where the Dayak people turned against Madurese immigrants, slaughtering hundreds. Wahid was forced from power in July 2001, and Vice President Megawati Sukarnoputri assumed the helm. Popular among the poor, Megawati's retiring nature and lack of political experience led some to question her ability to govern this fledgling democracy beleaguered by separatist movements and continuous violence.

A terrorist bombing on Oct. 12, 2002, at a night club in Bali killed more than 200 people, mostly tourists. In Aug.–Sept. 2003, Amrozi bin Nurhasyim and Imam Samudra, members of Jemaah Islamiyah, an Islamic terrorist group linked with al-Qaeda, were sentenced to death for their roles in the bombing. But the radical Muslim cleric Abu Bakar Bashir, believed to be the head of Jemaah Islamiyah, was only given a light three-year sentence on lesser charges, causing parts of the international community to question Indonesia's commitment to fighting terrorism. Authorities arrested Bashir in April 2004—on the same day he was set to be released from prison—claiming they had new evidence that proved he is in fact the leader of Jemaah Islamiyah and that he approved the Bali bombing.

In May 2003, President Megawati declared military rule in Aceh and launched an offensive intended to destroy the Free Aceh Movement. The invasion marked the end of a cease-fire that was signed in Dec. 2002 between the Indonesian government and Aceh separatists. Megawati replaced military rule in Aceh with a state of emergency in May 2004. Some 12,000 have been killed in the conflict since 1976.

Megawati's PDI-P party fared poorly in April 2004 elections, placing second behind the Golkar Party of former President Suharto. In July, retired general Susilo Bambang Yudhoyono placed first in the country's first direct presidential elections, but did not garner enough votes to win outright. However, he soundly defeated Megawati in the September run-off. Yudhoyono promised to crack down on crime, the separatist movements in Aceh and Papua, and corruption. He also said he would track down the terrorists who attacked Jakarta's Marriott Hotel in Aug. 2003 and the Australian Embassy in Sept. 2004.

Iran

ISLAMIC REPUBLIC OF IRAN

Chief of State: Ayatollah Ruhollah Khamenei (1989)
President: Mohammad Khatami (1997)
Area: 636,293 sq mi (1,648,000 sq km)
Population (2004 est.): 67,503,205 (growth rate: 0.7%); birth rate: 17.1/1000; infant mortality rate: 42.9/1000; life expectancy: 69.7; density per sq mi: 106
Capital and largest city (2003 est.): Teheran, 11,224,800 (metro. area), 7,893,700 (city proper).

Other large cities: Mashad, 2,061,100; Isfahan, 1,378,600; Tabriz, 1,213,400. **Monetary unit:** Rial.
Languages: Persian and Persian dialects 58%, Turkic and Turkic dialects 26%, Kurdish 9%, Luri 2%, Balochi 1%, Arabic 1%, Turkish 1%, other 2%. **Ethnicity/race:** Persian 51%, Azerbaijani 24%, Gilaki and Mazandarani 8%, Kurd 7%, Arab 3%, Lur 2%, Baloch 2%, Turkmen 2%, other 1%. **Religions:** Islam 98% (Shi'a 89%, Sunni 9%); Zoroastrian, Jewish, Christian, and Baha'i 2%. Literacy rate: 79% (2003 est.)
Economic summary: GDP/PPP (2003 est.): $477.8 billion; per capita $7,000. **Real growth rate:** 6%. **Inflation:** 18%. **Unemployment:** 15.7% (2002 est.). **Arable land:** 10%. **Agriculture:** wheat, rice, other grains, sugar beets, fruits, nuts, cotton; dairy products, wool; caviar. **Labor force:** 20 million; note: shortage of skilled labor (2002 est) agriculture 30%, industry 25%, services 45% (2001 est.). **Industries:** petroleum, petrochemicals, textiles, cement and other construction materials, food processing (particularly sugar refining and vegetable oil production), metal fabricating, armaments. **Natural resources:** petroleum, natural gas, coal, chromium, copper, iron ore, lead, manganese, zinc, sulfur. **Exports:** $29.88 billion (f.o.b., 2003 est.): petroleum 85%, carpets, fruits and nuts, iron and steel, chemicals. **Imports:** $25.26 billion (f.o.b., 2003 est.): industrial raw materials and intermediate goods, capital goods, foodstuffs and other consumer goods, technical services, military supplies. **Major trading partners:** Japan, China, UAE, Italy, South Korea, South Africa, Germany, France, Russia.

Geography   Iran, a Middle Eastern country south of the Caspian Sea and north of the Persian Gulf, is three times the size of Arizona. It shares borders with Iraq, Turkey, Azerbaijan, Turkmenistan, Armenia, Afghanistan, and Pakistan.

The Elburz Mountains in the north rise to 18,603 ft (5,670 m) at Mount Damavend. From northwest to southeast, the country is crossed by a desert 800 mi (1,287 km) long.

Government   Iran has been an Islamic theocracy since the Pahlavi monarchy regime was overthrown on Feb. 11, 1979.

History   The region now called Iran was occupied by the Medes and the Persians in the 1500s B.C., until the Persian king Cyrus the Great overthrew the Medes and became ruler of the Achaemenid (Persian) Empire, which reached from the Indus to the Nile at its zenith in 525 B.C. Persia fell to Alexander in 331–330 B.C., and a succession of other rulers: the Seleucids (312–302 B.C.), the Greek-speaking Parthians (247 B.C.–A.D. 226), the Sasanians (224–c. 640), and the Arab Muslims (in 641). By the mid-800s Persia had become an international scientific and cultural center. In the 12th century it was invaded by the Mongols. The Safavid dynasty (1501–1722), under whom the dominant religion became Shiite Islam, followed, and was then replaced by the Qajar dynasty (1794–1925).

During the Qajar dynasty, the Russians and the British fought for economic control of the area, and during World War I, Iran's neutrality did not stop it from becoming a battlefield for Russian and British troops. A coup in 1921 brought Reza Kahn to power. In 1925, he became shah and changed his name to Reza Shah Pahlavi. He subsequently did much to modernize the country and abolished all foreign extraterritorial rights.

The country's pro-Axis allegiance in World War II led to Anglo-Russian occupation of Iran in 1941 and deposition of the shah in favor of his son, Mohammed Reza Pahlavi. Pahlavi's Westernization programs alienated the clergy, and his authoritarian rule led to massive demonstrations during the 1970s, to which the shah responded with the imposition of martial law in Sept. 1978. The shah and his family fled Iran on Jan. 16, 1979, and the exiled cleric Ayatollah Ruhollah Khomeini returned to establish an Islamic theocracy. Khomeini proceeded with his plans for revitalizing Islamic traditions. He urged women to return to the veil; banned alcohol, Western music, and mixed bathing; shut down the media; closed universities; and eliminated political parties.

Revolutionary militants invaded the U.S. embassy in Teheran on Nov. 4, 1979, seized staff members as hostages, and precipitated an international crisis. Khomeini refused all appeals, even a unanimous vote by the UN Security Council demanding immediate release of the hostages. Iranian hostility toward Washington was reinforced by the Carter administration's economic boycott and deportation order against Iranian students in the U.S., the break in diplomatic relations, and ultimately an aborted U.S. raid in April 1980 aimed at rescuing the hostages.

As the first anniversary of the embassy seizure neared, Khomeini and his followers insisted on their original conditions: guarantee by the U.S. not to interfere in Iran's affairs, cancellation of U.S. damage claims against Iran, release of $8 billion in frozen Iranian assets, an apology, and the return of the assets held by the former imperial family. These conditions were largely met and the 52 American hostages were released on Jan. 20, 1981, ending 444 days in captivity.

The sporadic war with Iraq regained momentum in 1982, as Iran launched an offensive in March and regained much of the border area occupied by Iraq in late 1980. The stalemated war with Iraq dragged on well into 1988. Although Iraq expressed its willingness to cease fighting, Iran stated that it would not stop the war until Iraq agreed to pay for war damages and to punish the Iraqi government leaders involved in the conflict. On July 20, 1988, Khomeini, after a series of Iranian military reverses, agreed to cease-fire negotiations with Iraq. A cease-fire went into effect on Aug. 20, 1988. Khomeini died in June 1989 and Ayatollah Ruhollah Khamenei succeeded him as the supreme leader.

By early 1991 the Islamic revolution appeared to have lost much of its militancy. Attempting to revive a stagnant economy, President Rafsanjani took measures to decentralize the command system and introduce free-market mechanisms.

Mohammad Khatami, a little-known moderate cleric, former newspaperman, and national librarian, won the presidential election with 70% of the vote on May 23, 1997, a stunning victory over the conservative ruling elite. Khatami has supported greater social and political freedoms, and has made overtures for friendlier relations with the West. But his steps toward liberalizing the strict clerical rule governing the country have put him at odds with the supreme leader, Ayatollah Khamenei.

Signaling a seismic change in Iran's political environment, reform candidates won the overwhelming majority of seats in Feb. 2000 parliamentary elections, thereby wresting control from hard-liners, who had dominated the Parliament since the 1979 Islamic revolution. The Parliament's reformist transformation greatly buttressed the efforts of Khatami in constructing a nation of "lasting pluralism and Islamic democracy." Khatami has walked a jittery tightrope between student groups and other liberals pressuring him to introduce bolder freedoms, and Iran's military and conservative clerical elite (including Khamenei), who have expressed growing impatience with the president's liberalizing measures.

In June 2001 elections, Khatami demonstrated the overwhelming popularity of his reforms by winning reelection with 77% of the vote. Khatami's new cabinet, composed of 20 moderates, disappointed liberals who hoped he would step up the pace of reform. Friction between Iran's reformers and conservatives increased in 2002.

Iran cooperated in the fight against global terrorism after the Sept. 11 bombings, assisting its war-torn neighbor Afghanistan in restoring peace. Yet U.S. President Bush announced in Jan. 2002 that Iran was part of an "axis of evil," considering it one of the most active state sponsors of international terrorism. After the U.S.-led war in Iraq, the U.S. accused Iran of pursuing an illegal nuclear program and harboring suspected al-Qaeda terrorists.

By 2003, Iran was fanning much of the world's suspicions that it had illegal nuclear ambitions. In June 2003, the International Atomic Energy Agency (IAEA) criticized Iran's concealment of much of its nuclear facilities and called on the country to permit more rigorous inspections of its nuclear sites. In Aug. 2003, the IAEA found traces of highly enriched uranium in a nuclear facility; in the face of this evidence and intense international pressure, Iran reluctantly agreed in December to suspend its uranium enrichment program and allow for thorough IAEA inspections.

On Dec. 26, the most destructive earthquake of 2003 devastated the historic city of Bam, killing an estimated 28,000 to 30,000 of its 80,000 residents.

The latest struggle between reformists and conservatives in Iran's Islamic government erupted in Jan. 2004 when the hard-line Guardian Council disqualified more than 3,500 people who had registered to run for parliament in February elections. Among those rejected were more than 80 current members of the 290-seat parliament. The Guardian Council gave no explanation concerning the disqualified candidates. Vociferous protests by reformists followed, and senior reformist politicians threatened to resign if the rejected reformists were not allowed to run. Hard-liners reinstated a few reformist candidates, but when elections went forward, 2,500 reformist candidates were excluded. On Feb. 20, conservatives won a landslide victory, a devastating setback for Iran's reformist movement.

Despite Iran's promises at the end of 2003, the IAEA again censured the country in June 2004 for failing to fully cooperate with nuclear inspections. Neither U.S. threats nor Europe's coaxing managed to halt Iran's alarming defiance.

Iraq

REPUBLIC OF IRAQ

National name: Jumhouriyat Al Iraq
President: Ghazi al-Yawar (interim) (2004)
Prime Minister: Iyad Allawi (interim) (2004)
Area: 168,753 sq mi (437,072 sq km)
Population (2004 est.): 25,374,691 (growth rate: 2.7%); birth rate: 33.1/1000; infant mortality rate: 52.7/1000; life expectancy: 68.3; density per sq mi: 150
Capital and largest city (2003 est.): Baghdad, 6,777,300 (metro. area), 5,772,000 (city proper).
Largest cities: Mosul, 1,791,600; Basra, 1,377,000; Irbil, 864,900; Kirkuk, 755,700. **Monetary unit:** U.S. dollar . **Languages:** Arabic (official), Kurdish (official in Kurdish regions), Assyrian, Armenian. **Ethnicity/race:** Arab 75%–80%, Kurdish 15%–20%, Turkoman, Assyrian, or other 5%. **Religions:** Islam 97% (Shiite 60%–65%, Sunni 32%–37%), Christian or other 3%.

Literacy rate: 40% (2003 est.)
Economic summary: GDP/PPP (2003 est.): $38.79 billion; per capita $1,600. **Real growth rate:** –20%. **Inflation:** 27.5%. **Unemployment:** n.a. **Arable land:** 12%. **Agriculture:** wheat, barley, rice, vegetables, dates, cotton; cattle, sheep. **Labor force:** 7.8 million (2004 est); agriculture n.a., industry n.a., services n.a. **Industries:** petroleum, chemicals, textiles, construction materials, food processing. **Natural resources:** petroleum, natural gas, phosphates, sulfur. **Exports:** $7.542 billion (f.o.b., 2003, est.): crude oil. **Imports:** $6.521 billion (f.o.b., 2003, est.): food, medicine, manufactures. **Major trading partners:** U.S., Canada, France, Jordan, Netherlands, Italy, Morocco, Spain, China, Germany, Russia, Australia, Vietnam, Japan.

Geography   Iraq, a triangle of mountains, desert, and fertile river valley, is bounded on the east by Iran, on the north by Turkey, on the west by Syria and Jordan, and on the south by Saudi Arabia and Kuwait. It is twice the size of Idaho. The country has arid desert land west of the Euphrates, a broad central valley between the Euphrates and the Tigris, and mountains in the northeast.

Government   The dictatorship of Saddam Hussein collapsed on April 9, 2003, after U.S. and British forces invaded the country. An interim Iraqi government officially took over from the U.S. occupation authority on June 28, 2004. National elections are planned for January 2005.

History   From earliest times Iraq was known as Mesopotamia—the land between the rivers—for it embraces a large part of the alluvial plains of the Tigris and Euphrates rivers.

An advanced civilization existed by 4000 B.C. Sometime after 2000 B.C. the land became the center of the ancient Babylonian and Assyrian empires. Mesopotamia was conquered by Cyrus the Great of Persia in 538 B.C., and by Alexander in 331 B.C. After an Arab conquest in 637–640, Baghdad became the capital of the ruling caliphate. The country was cruelly pillaged by the Mongols in 1258, and during the 16th, 17th, and 18th centuries was the object of repeated Turkish-Persian competition.

Nominal Turkish suzerainty imposed in 1638 was replaced by direct Turkish rule in 1831. In World War I, Britain occupied most of Mesopotamia and was given a mandate over the area in 1920. The British renamed the area Iraq and recognized it as a kingdom in 1922. In 1932, the monarchy achieved full independence. Britain again occupied Iraq during World War II because of its pro-Axis stance in the initial years of the war.

Iraq became a charter member of the Arab League in 1945, and Iraqi troops took part in the Arab invasion of Palestine in 1948.

At age 3, King Faisal II succeeded his father, Ghazi I, who was killed in an automobile accident in 1939. Faisal and his uncle, Crown Prince Abdul-Illah, were assassinated in July 1958 in a swift revolutionary coup that ended the monarchy and brought to power a military junta headed by Abdul Karem Kassim. Kassim reversed the monarchy's pro-Western policies, attempted to rectify the economic disparities between rich and poor, and began to form alliances with Communist countries.

Kassim was overthrown and killed in a coup staged on March 8, 1963, by the military and the Baath Socialist Party. The Baath Party advocated secularism, pan-Arabism, and socialism. The following year, the new leader, Abdel Salam Arif, consolidated his power by driving out the Baath Party. He adopted a new constitution in 1964. In 1966, he died in a helicopter crash. His brother, Gen. Abdel Rahman Arif, assumed the presidency, crushed the opposition, and won an indefinite extension of his term in 1967.

Arif's regime was ousted in July 1968 by a junta led by Maj. Gen. Ahmed Hassan al-Bakr of the Baath Party. Bakr and his second-in-command, Saddam Hussein, imposed authoritarian rule in an effort to end the decades of political instability that followed World War II. One of the world's leading producers of oil, Iraq's oil revenues were used to develop one of the strongest military forces in the region.

On July 16, 1979, President Bakr was succeeded by Saddam Hussein, whose regime steadily developed an international reputation for repression, human rights abuses, and terrorism.

A long-standing territorial dispute over control of the Shatt-al-Arab waterway between Iraq and Iran broke into full-scale war on Sept. 20, 1980, when Iraq invaded western Iran. The eight-year war cost the lives of an estimated 1.5 million people, and finally ended in a UN-brokered cease-fire in 1988. Poison gas was used by both Iran and Iraq.

In July 1990, President Hussein asserted spurious territorial claims on Kuwaiti land. A mediation attempt by Arab leaders failed, and on Aug. 2, 1990, Iraqi troops invaded Kuwait and set up a puppet government. The UN unsuccessfully imposed trade sanctions against Iraq to pressure it to withdraw. On Jan. 18, 1991, UN forces, under the leadership of U.S. general Norman Schwarzkopf, launched the Gulf War (Operation Desert Storm), liberating Kuwait in less than a week.

The war did little to dwarf Iraq's resilient dictator. Rebellions by both Shiites and Kurds, encouraged by the U.S., were brutally crushed. In 1991, the UN set up a northern no-fly zone to protect Iraq's Kurdish population; in 1992 a southern no-fly zone was established as a buffer between Iraq and Kuwait and to protect Shiites.

The UN Security Council imposed sanctions beginning in 1990 that barred Iraq from selling oil except in exchange for food and medicine. The sanctions against Iraq failed to crush its leader but caused catastrophic suffering among its people—the country's infrastructure was in ruins, and disease, malnutrition, and the infant mortality rate skyrocketed.

The UN weapons inspections team mandated to ascertain that Iraq had destroyed all its nuclear, chemical, biological, and ballistic arms after the war was continually thwarted by Saddam Hussein. In Nov. 1997, he expelled the American members of the UN inspections team, a standoff that stretched on until Feb. 1998. But in Aug. 1998, Hussein again put a halt to the inspections. On Dec. 16, the United States and Britain began Operation Desert Fox, four days of intensive air strikes. From then on, the U.S. and Britain conducted hundreds of air strikes on Iraqi targets within the no-fly zones. The sustained, low-level warfare continued unabated into 2003.

After the Sept. 11, 2001, terrorist attacks, President Bush began calling for a "regime change" in Iraq, describing the nation as part of an "axis of evil." The alleged existence of weapons of mass destruction, the thwarting of UN weapons inspections, Iraq's alleged links to terrorism, and Saddam Hussein's despotism and human rights abuses were the major reasons cited for necessitating a preemptive strike against the country. The Arab world and much of Europe condemned the hawkish and unilateral U.S. stance. The UK, however, declared its intention to support the U.S. in military action. On Sept. 12, 2002, Bush addressed the UN, challenging the organization to swiftly enforce its own resolutions against Iraq, or else the U.S. would act on its own. On Nov. 8, the UN Security Council unanimously approved a resolution imposing tough new arms inspections on Iraq. On Nov. 26, new inspections of Iraq's military holdings began.

The UN's formal report at the end of Jan. 2003 was not promising, with chief weapons inspector Hans Blix lamenting that "Iraq appears not to have come to a genuine acceptance, not even today, of the disarmament that was demanded of it." While the Bush administration felt the report cemented its claim that a military solution was imperative, several permanent members of the UN Security Council—France, Russia, and China—urged that the UN inspectors be given more time to complete their task. The U.S. and Britain's intense lobbying efforts among the other UN Security Council members yielded only two other supporters, Spain and Bulgaria. Bush and Blair continued to call for war, insisting that they would go ahead with a "coalition of the willing" if not with UN support. All diplomatic efforts ceased by March 17, when President Bush delivered an ultimatum to Saddam Hussein to leave the country within 48 hours or face war.

On March 20, the war against Iraq began with the launch of Operation Iraqi Freedom. In the coming days, the U.S. and Britain met greater-than-expected resistance as they attempted to march on Baghdad. But by April 9, U.S. forces took control of the capital, signalling the collapse of Saddam Hussein's regime. Numerous high-ranking Baathists, including Hussein's two sons, Qusay and Uday, were killed or captured in the first months of the war. Finally, after eight months of searching, the U.S. military captured Saddam Hussein on Dec. 13. The deposed leader was found hiding in a hole near his hometown of Tikrit and surrendered without a fight.

Although the war had been officially declared over on May 1, 2003, the country remained enveloped in violence and chaos, and coalition forces continued to meet Iraqi resistance and fighting. Many essential services, such as electricity and water, were lacking. Iraqis began protesting almost immediately against the delay in self-rule and the absence of a timetable to end the U.S. occupation. In July, the U.S. administrator for Iraq, Paul Bremer, appointed an Iraqi governing council.

Months of searching for Iraq's weapons of mass destruction—one of the prime reasons the Bush and Blair administrations cited for launching the war—yielded no hard evidence, and both administrations and their intelligence agencies came under fire. There were also mounting allegations that the existence of these weapons was exaggerated or distorted as a pretext to justify the war.

Continued instability kept 140,000 American and 11,000 British troops in Iraq, as well as about 10,000 coalition troops. The Pentagon estimated that the war was costing the U.S. $4 billion a month. The U.S. launched several tough military campaigns to subdue Iraqi resistance, which also had the effect of further alienating the populace.

In fall 2003, President Bush asked Congress for $87 billion in additional military and construction spending for Iraq. He also recast the rationale for war, no longer citing the danger of weapons of mass destruction, but instead describing Iraq as "the central front" in the war against terrorism—a free and democratic Iraq would serve as a model for the rest of the Middle East.

In Nov. 2003, 75 U.S. soldiers were killed, making it the bloodiest month since the war began. The rising death toll prompted a reversal in the Bush administration's Iraq policy. In a deal with the Iraqi Governing Council, the U.S. agreed to transfer power to an interim government in July 2004, much earlier than originally planned. But the U.S. plan to hold caucuses to select a transitional national assembly by the end of May was opposed by Grand Ayatollah Ali al-Sistani, the country's most powerful Shiite leader. Al-Sistani called for direct elections, and thousands of Shiites held a series of massive but peaceful protests throughout the country in support. The U.S. turned to the UN to help resolve the issue—until now it had sidelined the UN's participation in Iraq's reconstruction.

In Jan. 2004, the CIA's chief weapons inspector, David Kay, resigned his post and aired his conclusion that U.S. intelligence about Iraq's weapons of mass destruction "was almost all wrong." His report set off a fire storm of allegations: Did the U.S. receive bad intelligence, or did the Bush administration manipulate the intelligence to build the case for war, or both? The public outcry led President Bush in February to appoint a commission to investigate the intelligence failures.

Violence increased against ordinary Iraqis; those cooperating with the U.S.-led government, particularly Iraqi police and security forces, were especially targeted. In April, an uprising by separate factions of Sunnis and Shiites in at least eight Iraqi cities against the American occupation led to the worst violence of the war. Radical Shiite cleric Moktada al-Sadr launched an uprising in the holy city of Najaf. In Falluja, after four U.S. contractors were killed and mutilated, U.S. troops went after Sunni guerrillas. A spate of kidnapping, targeting foreign civilian workers, rattled many of the nations supplying peacekeeping forces.

On April 16, the U.S. and Britain accepted a plan offered by the UN to turn over power to an interim Iraqi government on June 30, and hold national elections by Jan. 31, 2005. The U.S. also reversed its policy of banning Baath party officials from positions of responsibility in Iraq—the U.S. had fired all high-ranking members and disbanded the Iraqi army, affecting about 400,000 positions, depleting Iraq of its skilled workforce.

In late April, the appalling physical and sexual abuse and humiliation of Iraqi prisoners at Abu Ghraib prison near Baghdad came to light when photographs were released by the U.S. media. The images sparked outrage around the world.

In a surprise move, the United States transferred power back to Iraqis two days early, on June 28. Former exile and Iraqi Government Council member Iyad Allawi became prime minister of the Iraqi interim government, and Ghazi al-Yawar, a Sunni Muslim, was chosen president, a largely ceremonial post.

On July 9, the Senate Intelligence Committee released a unanimous, bipartisan "Report on Pre-War Intelligence on Iraq," evaluating the intelligence assessments that formed the basis for the Bush administration's justifications for the war. It harshly criticized the CIA and other intelligence agencies: "most of the major key judgments" on Iraq's weapons of mass destruction were "either overstated, or were not supported by, the underlying intelligence report." It disputed the CIA's assertions that Iraq was reconstituting its nuclear program, that it had chemical and biological weapons, and that it was developing an unmanned aerial vehicle for use in delivering biological warfare agents. It also concluded that there was no "established formal relationship" between al-Qaeda and Saddam Hussein. The following week, Britain's Butler report on pre-Iraq intelligence echoed the American findings (though in a much milder tone) that pre-war intelligence exaggerated Saddam Hussein's threat. Australia's intelligence report, released a week later, judged its own pre-war intelligence to be "thin, ambiguous, and incomplete." Like the U.S. and UK intelligence reports, however, it cleared its government of manipulating the intelligence.

In August, the Pentagon-sponsored Schlesinger report's investigation into Abu Ghraib called the prisoner abuse at the hand of the American military acts of "brutality and purposeless sadism," rejected the idea that the abuse was simply the work of a few aberrant soldiers, and asserted that there were "fundamental failures throughout all levels of command, from the soldiers on the ground to Central Command and to the Pentagon."

A bloody, three-week battle in Najaf between the U.S. forces and the militia of militant cleric al-Sadr ended in August when Shiite cleric Grand Ayatollah Ali al-Sistani negotiated a settlement. That month, attacks on American forces reached their highest level since the beginning of the war, an average of 87 per day. The American death toll in Iraq reached 1,000 in early September; about 7,000 soldiers had been wounded. No official record of Iraqi civilian deaths is kept, but as of Sept. 2004, estimates ranged from 12,000 to 14,000 (Iraq Body Count). The worsening security situation was criticized by Democrats and Republicans alike. Not only were pockets of Iraq essentially under the control of insurgents, but the progress on rebuilding Iraq has been slow: just 6% ($1 billion) of the reconstruction money approved by Congress in 2003 had in fact been used on reconstruction projects.

See also Iraq War Timeline, pp. 389–390.

Ireland

National name: Ireland, or Eire in the Irish language
President: Mary McAleese (1997)
Taoiseach (Prime Minister): Bertie Ahern (1997)
Area: 27,135 sq mi (70,280 sq km)
Population (2004 est.): 3,969,558 (growth rate: 1.2%); birth rate: 14.5/1000; infant mortality rate: 5.5/1000; life expectancy: 77.4; density per sq mi: 146
Capital (2003 est.): Dublin, 1,018,500. **Other large cities:** Cork, 193,400; Limerick, 84,900; Galway, 67,200. **Monetary units:** Euro (formerly Irish pound [punt]). **Languages:** English, Irish (Gaelic). **Ethnicity/race:** Celtic, English. **Religions:** Roman Catholic 91.6%, Anglican 2.5%, other 5.9%. **Literacy rate:** 98% (1981 est.)
Economic summary: GDP/PPP (2003 est.): $117 billion; per capita $29,800. **Real growth rate:** 2.1%. **Inflation:** 3.7%. **Unemployment:** 5%. **Arable land:** 19%. **Agriculture:** turnips, barley, potatoes, sugar beets, wheat; beef, dairy products. **Labor force:** 1.8 million (2001); agriculture 8%, industry 29%, services 64% (2002 est.). **Industries:** food products, brewing, textiles, clothing; chemicals, pharmaceuticals, machinery, transportation equipment, glass and crystal; software. **Natural resources:** zinc, lead, natural gas, barite, copper, gypsum, limestone, dolomite, peat, silver. **Exports:** $98.31 billion (f.o.b., 2003 est.): machinery and equipment, computers, chemicals, pharmaceuticals; live animals, animal products (1999). **Imports:** $57.54 billion (f.o.b., 2003 est.): data processing equipment, other machinery and equipment, chemicals; petroleum and petroleum products, textiles, clothing. **Major trading partners:** UK, U.S., Belgium, Germany, France.

Geography Ireland is situated in the Atlantic Ocean and separated from Great Britain by the Irish Sea. Half the size of Arkansas, it occupies the entire island except for the six counties that make up Northern Ireland. Ireland resembles a basin—a central plain rimmed with mountains, except in the Dublin region. The mountains are low, with the highest peak, Carrantuohill in County Kerry, rising to 3,415 ft (1,041 m). The principal river is the Shannon, which begins in the north-central area, flows south and southwest for about 240 mi (386 km), and empties into the Atlantic.

Government Republic.

History In the Stone and Bronze Ages, Ireland was inhabited by Picts in the north and a people called the Erainn in the south, the same stock, apparently, as in all the isles before the Anglo-Saxon invasion of Britain. About the 4th century B.C., tall, red-haired Celts arrived from Gaul or Galicia. They subdued and assimilated the inhabitants and established a Gaelic civilization. By the beginning of the Christian Era, Ireland was divided into five kingdoms—Ulster, Connacht, Leinster, Meath, and Munster. Saint Patrick introduced Christianity in 432, and the country developed into a center of Gaelic and Latin learning. Irish monasteries, the equivalent of universities, attracted intellectuals as well as the pious and sent out missionaries to many parts of Europe and, some believe, to North America.

Norse depredations along the coasts, starting in 795, ended in 1014 with Norse defeat at the Battle of Clontarf by forces under Brian Boru. In the 12th century, the pope gave all of Ireland to the English Crown as a papal fief. In 1171, Henry II of England was acknowledged "Lord of Ireland," but local sectional rule continued for centuries, and English control over the whole island was not reasonably absolute until the 17th century. In the Battle of the Boyne (1690), the Catholic King James II and his French supporters were defeated by the Protestant King William III (of Orange). An era of Protestant political and economic supremacy began.

By the Act of Union (1801), Great Britain and Ireland became the "United Kingdom of Great Britain and Ireland." A steady decline in the Irish economy followed in the next decades. The population had reached 8.25 million when the great potato famine of 1846–1848 took many lives and drove more than 2 million people to immigrate to North America.

In the meantime, anti-British agitation continued along with demands for Irish home rule. The advent of World War I delayed the institution of home rule and resulted in the Easter Rebellion in Dublin (April 24–29, 1916), in which Irish nationalists unsuccessfully attempted to throw off British rule. Guerrilla warfare against British forces followed proclamation of a republic by the rebels in 1919. The Irish Free State was established as a dominion on Dec. 6, 1922, with six northern counties remaining as part of the United Kingdom. A civil war ensued between those supporting the Anglo-Irish Treaty that established the Irish Free State and those repudiating it because it led to the partitioning of the island. The Irish Republican Army (IRA), led by Eamon de Valera, fought against the partition but lost. De Valera joined the government in 1927 and became prime minister in 1932. In 1937 a new constitution changed the nation's name to Éire. Ireland remained neutral in World War II.

In 1948, De Valera was defeated by John A. Costello, who demanded final independence from Britain. The Republic of Ireland was proclaimed on April 18, 1949, and withdrew from the Commonwealth. From the 1960s onwards, two antagonistic currents dominated Irish politics. One sought to bind the wounds of the rebellion and civil war. The other was the effort of the outlawed Irish Republican Army and more moderate groups to bring Northern Ireland into the republic. The "troubles"—the violence and terrorist acts between Republicans and Unionists in both the Republic of Ireland and Northern Ireland—would plague the island for the remainder of the century and beyond.

Under the First Programme for Economic Expansion (1958–1963), economic protection was dismantled and foreign investment encouraged. This prosperity brought profound social and cultural changes to what had been one of the poorest and least technologically advanced countries in Europe. Ireland joined the European Economic Community (now the EU) in 1973. In the 1990 presidential election, Mary Robinson was elected the republic's first woman president. The election of a candidate with socialist and feminist sympathies was regarded as a watershed in Irish political life, reflecting the changes taking place in Irish society. Irish voters approved the Maastricht Treaty, which paved the way for the establishment of the EU, by a large majority in a referendum held in 1992. In 1993, the Irish and British governments signed a joint peace initiative (the Downing Street Declaration), in which they pledged to seek mutually agreeable political structures in Northern Ireland and between the two islands. A referendum on allowing divorce under certain conditions—hitherto constitutionally forbidden—was narrowly passed in Nov. 1995.

In 1998 hope for a solution to the troubles in Northern Ireland seemed palpable. A landmark settlement, the Good Friday Agreement of April 10, 1998, called for Protestants to share political power with the minority Catholics, and gave the Republic of Ireland a voice in Northern Irish affairs. The resounding commitment to the settlement was demonstrated in a dual referendum on May 22: the North approved the accord by a vote of 71% to 29%, and in the Irish Republic 94% favored it. After numerous stops and starts, the new government in Northern Ireland was formed on Dec. 2, 2000, but it has been suspended four times since then (and has remained suspended since Oct. 2002) primarily because of Sinn Fein's reluctance to disarm its military wing, the IRA, a key stipulation of the Good Friday Accord. Ireland has continued to call for Sinn Fein to comply.

In June 2001, Ireland voted against expansion of the EU to include other countries, which came as a shock to the 14 other EU members. To the relief of the EU, in Oct. 2002 Ireland endorsed the expansion (the Nice Treaty).

Despite a number of recent corruption and bribery scandals, most of which involved the centrist Fianna Fáil party of Prime Minister Bertie Ahern, the party won 81 of 166 seats in May 2002. Ahern became the first Irish prime minister in 33 years to be elected to a second successive term.

In Aug. 2003, Michael McKevitt, leader of the Real IRA, was sentenced to 20 years in prison. The Real IRA split from the IRA because it opposed the Northern Irish peace process.

See also Northern Ireland, under United Kingdom.

Israel

STATE OF ISRAEL

National name: Medinat Yisra'el
President: Moshe Katsav (2000)
Prime Minister: Ariel Sharon (2001)
Area: 8,019 sq mi (20,770 sq km)
Population (2004 est.): 6,199,008 (growth rate: 1.3%); birth rate: 18.5/1000; infant mortality rate: 7.2/1000; life expectancy: 79.2; density per sq mi: 773

Capital and largest city (2003 est.): Jerusalem, 695,500. **Other large cities:** Tel Aviv, 365,300; Haifa, 280,200. **Monetary unit:** Shekel. **Languages:** Hebrew (official), Arabic, English. **Ethnicity/race:** Jewish 80.1% (Europe/Americas/Oceania-born 32.1%, Israel-born 20.8%, Africa-born 14.6%, Asia-born 12.6%), non-Jewish 19.9% (mostly Arab) (1996 est.). **Religions:** Judaism 80.1%, Islam 14.6% (mostly Sunni), Christian 2.1%, others 3.2% (1996 est.). **Literacy rate:** 95% (2003 est.)
Economic summary: GDP/PPP (2003 est.): $120.6 billion; per capita $19,700. **Real growth rate:** 1%. **Inflation:** 1.1%. **Unemployment:** 10.7%. **Arable land:** 17%. **Agriculture:** citrus, vegetables, cotton; beef, poultry, dairy products. **Labor force:** 2.6 million; public services 31.2%, manufacturing 20.2%, finance and business 13.1%, commerce 12.8%, construction 7.5%, personal and other services 6.4%, transport, storage, and communications 6.2%, agriculture, forestry, and fishing 2.6% (1996). **Industries:** high-technology projects (including aviation, communications, computer-aided design and manufactures, medical electronics), wood and paper products, potash and phosphates, food, beverages, and tobacco, caustic soda, cement, diamond cutting. **Natural resources:** timber, potash, copper ore, natural gas, phosphate rock, magnesium bromide, clays, sand. **Exports:** $29.32 billion (f.o.b., 2003 est.): machinery and equipment, software, cut diamonds, agricultural products, chemicals, textiles and apparel. **Imports:** $32.27 billion (f.o.b., 2003 est.): raw materials, military equipment, investment goods, rough diamonds, fuels, grain, consumer goods. **Major trading partners:** U.S., Belgium, Germany, UK, Switzerland, Italy.

1. Israel proclaimed Jerusalem as its capital in 1950, but the U.S., like nearly all other countries, maintains its embassy in Tel Aviv.

Geography Israel, slightly larger than Massachusetts, lies at the eastern end of the Mediterranean Sea. It is bordered by Egypt on the west, Syria and Jordan on the east, and Lebanon on the north. Its maritime plain is extremely fertile. The southern Negev region, which comprises almost half the total area, is largely a desert. The Jordan, the only important river, flows from the north through Lake Hule (Waters of Merom) and Lake Kinneret (Sea of Galilee or Sea of Tiberias), finally entering the Dead Sea, 1,349 ft (411 m) below sea level—the world's lowest land elevation.

Government Parliamentary democracy.

History Palestine, considered a holy land by Jews, Muslims, and Christians, and homeland of the modern state of Israel, was known as Canaan to the ancient Hebrews. Palestine's name derives from the Philistines, a people who occupied the southern coastal part of the country in the 12th century B.C.

A Hebrew kingdom established in 1000 B.C. was later split into the kingdoms of Judah and Israel; they were subsequently invaded by Assyrians, Babylonians, Egyptians, Persians, Romans, and Alexander the Great of Macedonia. By A.D. 135, few Jews were left in Palestine; most lived in the scattered and tenacious communities of the Diaspora. Palestine became a center of Christian pilgrimage after the emperor Constantine converted to that faith. The Arabs took Palestine from the Byzantine empire in 634–640. Interrupted only by Christian Crusaders, Muslims ruled Palestine until the 20th century. During World War I, British forces defeated the Turks in Palestine and governed the area under a League of Nations mandate from 1923.

As part of the 19th-century Zionist movement, Jews had begun settling in Palestine as early as 1820. This effort to establish a Jewish homeland received British approval in the Balfour Declaration of 1917. During the 1930s, Jews persecuted by the Hitler regime poured into Palestine. The postwar acknowledgment of the Holocaust—Hitler's genocide of 6 million Jews—increased international interest in and sympathy for the cause of Zionism. However, Arabs in Palestine and surrounding countries bitterly opposed prewar and postwar proposals to partition Palestine into Arab and Jewish sectors. The British mandate to govern Palestine ended after the war, and, in 1947, the UN voted to partition Palestine. When the British officially withdrew on May 14, 1948, the Jewish National Council proclaimed the State of Israel.

U.S. recognition came within hours. The next day, Arab forces from Egypt, Jordan, Syria, Lebanon, and Iraq invaded the new nation. By the cease-fire on Jan. 7, 1949, Israel had increased its original territory by 50%, taking western Galilee, a broad corridor through central Palestine to Jerusalem, and part of modern Jerusalem. Chaim Weizmann and David Ben-Gurion became Israel's first president and prime minister. The new government was admitted to the UN on May 11, 1949.

The next clash with Arab neighbors came when Egypt nationalized the Suez Canal in 1956 and barred Israeli shipping. Coordinating with an Anglo-French force, Israeli troops seized the Gaza Strip and drove through the Sinai to the east bank of the Suez Canal, but withdrew under U.S. and UN pressure. In the Six-Day War of 1967, Israel made simultaneous air attacks against Syrian, Jordanian, and Egyptian air bases, totally defeating the Arabs. Expanding its territory by 200%, Israel at the cease-fire held the Golan Heights, the West Bank of the Jordan River, Jerusalem's Old City, and all of the Sinai and the east bank of the Suez Canal.

In the face of Israeli reluctance even to discuss the return of occupied territories, the fourth Arab-Israeli War erupted on Oct. 6, 1973, with a surprise Egyptian and Syrian assault on the Jewish high holy day of Yom Kippur. Initial Arab gains were reversed when a cease-fire took effect two weeks later, but Israel suffered heavy losses.

A dramatic breakthrough in the tortuous history of Mideast peace efforts occurred on Nov. 9, 1977, when Egypt's president Anwar Sadat declared his willingness to talk peace. Prime Minister Menachem Begin, on Nov. 15, extended an invitation to the Egyptian leader to address the Knesset in Jerusalem. Sadat's arrival in Israel four days later raised worldwide hopes, but a peace agreement between Egypt and Israel was long in coming. On March 14, 1979, the Knesset approved a final peace treaty, and 12 days later, Begin and Sadat signed the document, together with President Jimmy Carter, in a White House ceremony. Israel began its withdrawal from the Sinai, which it had annexed from Egypt, on May 25.

Although Israel withdrew its last settlers from the Sinai in April 1982, the fragile Mideast peace was shattered on June 9, 1982, by a massive Israeli assault on southern Lebanon, where the Palestinian Liberation Organization was entrenched. The PLO had long plagued Israelis with terrorist actions. Israel destroyed PLO strongholds in Tyre and Sidon and reached the suburbs of Beirut on June 10. A U.S.-mediated accord between Lebanon and Israel, signed on May 17, 1983, provided for Israeli withdrawal from Lebanon. Israel eventually withdrew its troops from the Beirut area but kept them in southern Lebanon, where occasional skirmishes would continue. Lebanon, under pressure from Syria, canceled the accord in March 1984.

A continual source of tension has been the relationship between the Jews and the Palestinians living within Israeli territories. Most Arabs fled the region when the state of Israel was declared, but those who remain now make up almost one-fifth of the population of Israel. They are about two-thirds Muslim, as well as Christian and Druze. Palestinians living on the West Bank and the Gaza Strip fomented the riots begun in 1987, known as the *intifada*. Violence heightened as Israeli police cracked down and Palestinians retaliated. Continuing Jewish settlement of lands designated for Palestinians has added to the unrest.

In 1988, the leader of the PLO, Yasir Arafat, reversed decades of PLO polemic by acknowledging Israel's right to exist. He stated his willingness to enter negotiations to create a Palestinian political entity that would coexist with the Israeli state.

In 1991, Israel was struck by Iraqi missiles during the Persian Gulf War. The Israelis did not retaliate in order to preserve the international coalition against Iraq. In 1992, Yitzhak Rabin became prime minister. He halted the disputed Israeli settlement of the occupied territories.

Highly secretive talks in Norway resulted in the landmark Oslo Accord between the PLO and the Israeli government in 1993. The accord stipulated a five-year plan in which Palestinians of the West Bank and the Gaza Strip would gradually become self-governing. Arafat became president of the new Palestinian Authority. In 1994, Israel signed a peace treaty with Jordan; Israel still has no formal peace agreement with Syria or Lebanon.

On Nov. 4, 1995, Prime Minister Rabin was slain by a Jewish extremist, jeopardizing the tenuous progress toward peace. Shimon Peres succeeded him until May 1996 elections for the Knesset gave Israel a new hardline prime minister, Benjamin Netanyahu, by a razor-thin margin. Netanyahu reversed or stymied much of the Oslo Agreement, contending that it offered too many concessions too fast and jeopardized Israelis' safety.

Israeli-Palestinian peace negotiations in 1997 were repeatedly undermined by both sides. Although the Hebron Accord was signed in January, calling for the withdrawal of Israeli troops from the city, the construction of new Jewish settlements on the West Bank in March profoundly upset progress toward peace. Terrorism erupted again in 1997 when radical Hamas suicide bombers claimed the lives of more than 20 Israeli civilians. Netanyahu, accusing Palestinian Authority president Arafat of lax security, retaliated with draconian sanctions against Palestinians working in Israel, including the withholding of millions of dollars in tax revenue, a blatant violation of the Oslo Agreement. Netanyahu also persisted in authorizing right-wing Israelis to build new settlements in mostly Arab East Jerusalem. Arafat, meanwhile, seemed unwilling or unable to curb the violence of extremist Arabs.

An Oct. 1998 summit at Wye Mills, Md., generated the first real progress in the stymied Middle East peace talks in 19 months, with Netanyahu and Arafat settling several important interim issues called for by the 1993 Oslo Peace Agreement. The peace accord, however, began unraveling almost immediately. By the end of April 1999, Israel had made 41 air raids on Hezbollah guerrillas in Lebanon. The guerrillas were fighting against Israeli troops and their allies, the South Lebanon Army militia, who occupied a security zone set up in 1985 to guard Israel's borders. Public pressure in Israel to withdraw the troops grew.

Labor party leader Ehud Barak won the 1999 election and announced that he planned not only to pursue peace with the Palestinians, but to establish relations with Syria and end the low-grade war in Southern Lebanon with the Iranian-armed Hezbollah guerrillas. In Dec. 1999, Israeli-Syrian talks resumed after a nearly four-year hiatus. By Jan. 2000, however, talks had broken down when Syria demanded a detailed discussion of the return of all of the Golan Heights. In Feb., new Hezbollah attacks on Israeli troops in southern Lebanon led to Israel's retaliatory bombing as well as Barak's decision to pull out of Lebanon. Israeli troops pulled out of Lebanon on May 24, 2000, after 18 consecutive years of occupation.

Peace talks in July 2000 at Camp David between Barak and Arafat ended unsuccessfully, despite President Clinton's strongest efforts—the status of Jerusalem was the primary sticking point. In September, Likud leader Ariel Sharon visited the compound called Temple Mount by Jews and Haram al-Sharif by Muslims, a fiercely contested site that is sacred to both Jews and Muslims. The visit set off the worst violence in years, killing around 400 people, mostly Palestinians. The violence (dubbed the Al-Aksa intifada) and the stalled peace process fueled growing concerns about Israeli security, paving the way for hard-liner Sharon's stunning landslide victory over Barak in Feb. 2001. Violence on both sides continued at an alarming rate. Palestinians carried out some of the most horrific suicide bombings and terrorist attacks in years (Hamas and the Al-Aksa Martyr Brigade claimed responsibility for the majority of them), killing Israeli civilians at cafés, bus stops, and supermarkets. In retaliation, Israel unleashed bombing raids on Palestinian territory and sent troops and tanks to occupy West Bank and Gaza cities.

In 2003, in an attempt to restart the stalled Israeli-Palestinian peace process, Israel and the United States resolved to circumvent Arafat, whom Sharon called "irrelevant" and an obstacle. Under U.S. pressure, Arafat reluctantly appointed a prime minister in April, who was to replace him in negotiating the peace process, Mahmoud Abbas, formerly Arafat's second-in-command. On May 1, the "Quartet" (the U.S., UN, EU, and Russia) unfurled the "road map" for peace, which envisioned the creation of a Palestinian state by 2005. Although Sharon publicly acknowledged the need for a Palestinian state and Abbas committed himself to ending Palestinian violence, the road map quickly led nowhere, with neither side honoring their obligations: Abbas, with little real political power, did not disable terrorist organizations, and Sharon did not dismantle settlements, much less prevent new ones from cropping up. Sharon also persisted in building the highly controversial security barrier dividing Israeli and Palestinian areas (in October, a UN resolution condemning the barrier passed 144–4, with only the U.S., Israel, Micronesia, and the Marshall Islands supporting it).

Hopes for the road map were shattered in Aug. 2003 with the suicide bombing of an Israeli bus that killed 20, including 6 children, and with Israel's assassination of senior Hamas leader Abu Shanab. As Israel stepped up its "targeted killings" and Palestinian attacks on Israeli civilians continued, Abbas resigned, and was replaced by Ahmed Qurei. In September, further exacerbating tensions and alarming much of the world, Israel announced that it was prepared to "remove" Arafat.

On March 22, 2004, Israel assassinated Sheik Ahmed Yassin, the founder and spiritual leader of the militant group Hamas. Protests throughout the Arab world followed. Less than a month later, on April 17, Israel assassinated Hamas's new leader, Abdel Aziz Rantisi.

On April 14, President Bush endorsed Sharon's unilateral withdrawal plan: Israel stated it would withdraw from the Gaza Strip, but would hold on to large blocks of land in the West Bank and reject the "right of return" for Palestinian refugees. Bush's support of the plan was seen throughout the Arab world as the United States siding with Israel against the Palestinians. Sharon's Likud party, however, rejected his Gaza withdrawal plan in a May vote. The prime minister then attempted to form a coalition with the Labor party in order to pursue the Gaza withdrawal, but the Likud party rejected his coalition plan in August. While endorsing withdrawal from Gaza, Sharon was firming up Israel's hold on the West Bank by approving construction of new houses with settlements, which critics consider a violation of the all-but-moribund "road map."

In May, the UN Security Council condemned Israel's attack on the Rafah refugee camp in the Gaza strip, the largest Israeli military operation in Gaza in decades. About 40 Palestinians, half of whom were civilians, were killed while participating in a protest march, and more than 1,000 Palestinians were left homeless after bulldozers razed their homes. The Israeli military claimed the razing was necessary to secure the border between Egypt and the Gaza strip.

On July 9, the International Court of Justice at The Hague ruled that the Israel West Bank barrier was illegal. In response to a ruling by Israel's Supreme Court, and not the ICJ's ruling, Israel revised the route of its barrier so that it did not cut into Palestinian land—the UN estimated that the original route would have taken almost 15% of West Bank territory for Israel. The new route will attempt to insure that Palestinians aren't subject to undue hardships—separating villagers from their farmland, for example. Thus far, about 120 miles of the barrier have been completed; the entire length is expected to stretch 437 miles.

Italy

ITALIAN REPUBLIC

National name: Repubblica Italiana
President: Carlo Azeglio Ciampi (1999)
Prime Minister: Silvio Berlusconi (2001)
Area: 116,305 sq mi (301,230 sq km)
Population (2004 est.): 58,057,477 (growth rate: 0.1%); birth rate: 9.1/1000; infant mortality rate: 6.1/1000; life expectancy: 79.5; density per sq mi: 499
Capital and largest city (2003 est.): Rome, 3,550,900 (metro. area), 2,455,600 (city proper). **Other large cities:** Milan, 1,180,700; Naples, 991,700; Turin, 856,000; Palermo, 651,500; Genoa, 602,500; Bologna, 369,300; Florence, 351,600; Bari, 311,900; Catania, 305,900; Venice, 265,700. **Monetary units:** Euro (formerly lira). **Languages:** Italian (official); German-, French-, and Slovene-speaking minorities. **Ethnicity/race:** Italian (includes small clusters of German-, French-, and Slovene-Italians in the north and Albanian- and Greek-Italians in the south). **Religions:** Roman Catholic (predominant), Protestant, Jewish, Islamic. **Literacy rate:** 99% (2003 est.)
Economic summary: GDP/PPP (2003 est.): $1.552 trillion; per capita $26,800. **Real growth rate:** 0.5%. **Inflation:** 2.3%. **Unemployment:** 9.2%. **Arable land:** 28.%. **Agriculture:** fruits, vegetables, grapes, potatoes, sugar beets, soybeans, grain, olives; beef, dairy products; fish. **Labor force:** 23.6 million (2001 est.); services 63%, industry 32%, agriculture 5% (2001). **Industries:** tourism, machinery, iron and steel, chemicals, food processing, textiles, motor vehicles, clothing, footwear, ceramics. **Natural resources:** mercury, potash, marble, sulfur, natural gas and crude oil reserves, fish, coal, arable land. **Exports:** $278.1

billion (f.o.b., 2003 est.): engineering products, textiles and clothing, production machinery, motor vehicles, transport equipment, chemicals; food, beverages and tobacco; minerals and nonferrous metals. **Imports:** $271.1 billion (f.o.b., 2003 est.): engineering products, chemicals, transport equipment, energy products, minerals and nonferrous metals, textiles and clothing; food, beverages and tobacco. **Major trading partners:** Germany, France, U.S., UK, Spain, Netherlands, Belgium.

Geography Italy, slightly larger than Arizona, is a long peninsula shaped like a boot, surrounded on the west by the Tyrrhenian Sea and on the east by the Adriatic. It is bounded by France, Switzerland, Austria, and Slovenia to the north. The Apennine Mountains form the peninsula's backbone; the Alps form its northern boundary. The largest of its many northern lakes is Garda (143 sq mi; 370 sq km); the Po, its principal river, flows from the Alps on Italy's western border and crosses the Lombard plain to the Adriatic Sea. Several islands form part of Italy; the largest are Sicily (9,926 sq mi; 25,708 sq km) and Sardinia (9,301 sq mi; 24,090 sq km).

Government Republic.

History The migrations of Indo-European peoples into Italy probably began about 2000 B.C. and continued down to 1000 B.C. From about the 9th century B.C. until it was overthrown by the Romans in the 3rd century B.C., the Etruscan civilization dominated the area. By 264 B.C. all Italy south of Cisalpine Gaul was under the leadership of Rome. For the next seven centuries, until the barbarian invasions destroyed the western Roman Empire in the 4th and 5th centuries A.D., the history of Italy is largely the history of Rome. From 800 on, the Holy Roman Emperors, Roman Catholic popes, Normans, and Saracens all vied for control over various segments of the Italian peninsula. Numerous city-states, such as Venice and Genoa, whose political and commercial rivalries were intense, and many small principalities flourished in the late Middle Ages. Although Italy remained politically fragmented for centuries, it became the cultural center of the Western world from the 13th to the 16th centuries.

In 1713, after the War of the Spanish Succession, Milan, Naples, and Sardinia were handed over to the Hapsburgs of Austria, which lost some of its Italian territories in 1735. After 1800, Italy was unified by Napoléon, who crowned himself king of Italy in 1805; but with the Congress of Vienna in 1815, Austria once again became the dominant power in a disunited Italy. Austrian armies crushed Italian uprisings in 1820–1821 and 1831. In the 1830s, Giuseppe Mazzini, a brilliant liberal nationalist, organized the Risorgimento (Resurrection), which laid the foundation for Italian unity. Disappointed Italian patriots looked to the House of Savoy for leadership. Count Camille di Cavour (1810–1861), premier of Sardinia in 1852 and the architect of a united Italy, joined England and France in the Crimean War (1853–1856), and in 1859 helped France in a war against Austria, thereby obtaining Lombardy. By plebiscite in 1860, Modena, Parma, Tuscany, and the Romagna voted to join Sardinia. In 1860, Giuseppe Garibaldi conquered Sicily and Naples and turned them over to Sardinia. Victor Emmanuel II, king of Sardinia, was proclaimed king of Italy in 1861. The annexation of Venetia in 1866 and of papal Rome in 1870 marked the complete unification of peninsular Italy into one nation under a constitutional monarchy.

Italy declared its neutrality upon the outbreak of World War I on the ground that Germany had embarked upon an offensive war. In 1915, Italy entered the war on the side of the Allies but obtained less territory than it expected in the postwar settlement. Benito ("Il Duce") Mussolini, a former socialist, organized discontented Italians in 1919 into the Fascist Party to "rescue Italy from Bolshevism." He led his Black Shirts in a march on Rome and, on Oct. 28, 1922, became premier. He transformed Italy into a dictatorship, embarking on an expansionist foreign policy with the invasion and annexation of Ethiopia in 1935 and allying himself with Adolf Hitler in the Rome-Berlin Axis in 1936. When the Allies invaded Italy in 1943, Mussolini's dictatorship collapsed; he was executed by Partisans on April 28, 1945, at Dongo on Lake Como. Following the armistice with the Allies (Sept. 3, 1943), Italy joined the war against Germany as a cobelligerent. A June 1946 plebiscite rejected monarchy and a republic was proclaimed. The peace treaty of Sept. 15, 1947, required Italian renunciation of all claims in Ethiopia and Greece and the cession of the Dodecanese islands to Greece and of five small Alpine areas to France. The Trieste area west of the new Yugoslav territory was made a free territory (until 1954, when the city and a 90-square-mile zone were transferred to Italy and the rest to Yugoslavia).

Italy became an integral member of NATO and the European Economic Community (later the EU) as it successfully rebuilt its postwar economy. A prolonged outbreak of terrorist activities by the left-wing Red Brigades threatened domestic stability in the 1970s, but by the early 1980s the terrorist groups had been suppressed. "Revolving door" governments, political instability, scandal, and corruption characterized Italian politics in the 1980s and 1990s.

Italy adopted the euro as its currency in Jan. 1999. Treasury Secretary Carlo Ciampi, who is credited with the economic reforms that permitted Italy to enter the European Monetary Union, was elected president in May 1999. Italy joined its NATO partners in the Kosovo crisis. Aviano Air Base in northern Italy was a crucial base for launching air strikes into Kosovo and Yugoslavia.

In June 2001, Silvio Berlusconi, a conservative billionaire, was sworn in as prime minister. He pledged to reduce unemployment, cut taxes, revamp the educational system, and reform the bureaucracy. His critics are alarmed by the apparent massive conflict of interest of a prime minister who also owns 90% of Italy's media. He has also been accused of Mafia connections and was under indictment for tax fraud and bribery. Found guilty in three out of four of his trials, he was acquitted in all of them on appeal. Several other cases are pending.

In Nov. 2002, Giulio Andreotti, who served as Italy's prime minister numerous times between 1972 and 1992, was sentenced to 24 years for ordering the Mafia to murder a journalist in 1979. At 84, however, he was deemed too old for prison.

In 2003, Parliament passed an immunity law for top government officials that meant the latest corruption trial involving Berlusconi—he is accused of bribing judges in 1985—would be suspended while he remained in office.

At the end of 2003, Italian food giant Parmalat was accused of a massive accounting fraud scheme—$5 billion the company claimed was in fact nonexistent.

Jamaica

Sovereign: Queen Elizabeth II (1952)
Governor-General: Sir Howard Cooke (1991)
Prime Minister: Percival J. Patterson (1992)
Area: 4,244 sq mi (10,991 sq km)
Population (2004 est.): 2,713,130 (growth rate: 0.7%);

birth rate: 16.9/1000; infant mortality rate: 12.8/1000; life expectancy: 76.1; density per sq mi: 639
Capital and largest city (2003 est.): Kingston, 937,700 (metro. area), 590,500 (city proper). **Monetary unit:** Jamaican dollar. **Languages:** English, Jamaican Creole. **Ethnicity/race:** black 90.9%, East Indian 1.3%, white 0.2%, Chinese 0.2%, mixed 7.3%, other 0.1%. **Religions:** Protestant 61.3% (Church of God 21.2%, Baptist 8.8%, Anglican 5.5%, Seventh-Day Adventist 9%, Pentecostal 7.6%, Methodist 2.7%, United Church 2.7%, Brethren 1.1%, Jehovah's Witness 1.6%, Moravian 1.1%), Roman Catholic 4%, other including some spiritual cults 34.7%. **Literacy rate:** 88% (2003 est.)

Economic summary: GDP/PPP (2003 est.): $10.21 billion; per capita $3,800. **Real growth rate:** 1.9%. **Inflation:** 14.1%. **Unemployment:** 15.9%. **Arable land:** 16%. **Agriculture:** sugarcane, bananas, coffee, citrus, potatoes, vegetables; poultry, goats, milk. **Labor force:** 1.12 million (1998); services 60%, agriculture 21%, industry 19% (1998). **Industries:** tourism, bauxite, textiles, food processing, light manufactures, rum, cement, metal, paper, chemical products. **Natural resources:** bauxite, gypsum, limestone. **Exports:** $1.355 billion (f.o.b., 2003 est.): alumina, bauxite; sugar, bananas, rum. **Imports:** $3.265 billion (f.o.b., 2003 est.): machinery and transport equipment, construction materials, fuel, food, chemicals, fertilizers. **Major trading partners:** U.S., Canada, Norway, UK, Germany, Netherlands, Trinidad and Tobago, Japan. **Member of Commonwealth of Nations**

Geography Jamaica is an island in the West Indies, 90 mi (145 km) south of Cuba and 100 mi (161 km) west of Haiti. It is a little smaller than Connecticut. The island is made up of coastal lowlands, a limestone plateau, and the Blue Mountains, a group of volcanic hills, in the east.

Government Constitutional parliamentary democracy.

History Jamaica was inhabited by Arawak Indians when Columbus explored it in 1494 and named it St. Iago. It remained under Spanish rule until 1655, when it became a British possession. Buccaneers operated from Port Royal, also the capital, until it fell into the sea in an earthquake in 1692. Disease decimated the Arawaks, so black slaves were imported to work on the sugar plantations. During the 17th and 18th centuries the British were consistently harassed by the Maroons, armed bands of freed slaves roaming the countryside. Abolition of the slave trade (1807), emancipation of the slaves (1833), and a drop in sugar prices eventually led to a depression that resulted in an uprising in 1865. The following year Jamaica became a Crown colony, and conditions improved considerably. Introduction of bananas reduced dependence on sugar.

On May 5, 1953, Jamaica gained internal autonomy, and, in 1958, it led in organizing the West Indies Federation. A nationalist labor leader, Sir Alexander Bustamente, later campaigned to withdraw from the federation. After a referendum, Jamaica became independent on Aug. 6, 1962. Michael Manley, of the socialist People's National Party, became prime minister in 1972.

The Labour Party defeated Manley in 1980 and its capitalist-oriented leader, Edward P. G. Seaga, became prime minister. He encouraged private investment and began an austerity program. Like other Caribbean countries, Jamaica was hard-hit by the 1981–1982 recession. Devaluation of the Jamaican dollar made Jamaican products more competitive on the world market and the country achieved record growth in tourism and agriculture. While manufacturing also grew, food prices rose as much as 75% and thousands of Jamaicans fell deeper into poverty.

In 1989, Manley was reelected, but he resigned in 1992 and was replaced by P. J. Patterson. In May 1997, the government signed a "Ship-Rider Agreement," allowing U.S. authorities to enter Jamaican waters and search vessels with the Jamaican government's permission, to fight drug trafficking. In 2001, violence between politically connected gangs escalated in Kingston, promoting fears that the tourist industry could suffer. In Oct. 2002, Patterson won his third term in office.

Japan

National name: Nippon
Emperor: Akihito (1989)
Prime Minister: Junichiro Koizumi (2001)
Area: 145,882 sq mi (377,835 sq km)
Population (2004 est.): 127,333,002 (growth rate: 0.1%); birth rate: 9.6/1000; infant mortality rate: 3.3/1000; life expectancy: 81.0; density per sq mi: 873
Capital and largest city (2003 est.): Tokyo, 31,139,900 (metro. area), 8,240,100 (city proper). **Other large cities:** Yokohama, 3,494,900 (part of Tokyo metro. area); Osaka, 2,597,000; Nagoya, 2,189,700; Sapporo, 1,848,000; Kobe, 1,529,900 (part of Osaka metro. area); Kyoto, 1,470,600 (part of Osaka metro. area); Fukuoka, 1,368,900; Kawasaki, 1,276,200 (part of Tokyo metro. area); Hiroshima, 1,132,700. **Monetary unit:** Yen. **Language:** Japanese. **Ethnicity/race:** Japanese 99%, other 1% (mostly Korean). **Religions:** Shintoist and Buddhist 84%, other 16% (including Christian 0.7%). **Literacy rate:** 99% (1995 est.)

Economic summary: GDP/PPP (2003 est.): $3.567 trillion; per capita $28,000. **Real growth rate:** 2.3%. **Inflation:** −0.3%. **Unemployment:** 5.3%. **Arable land:** 12%. **Agriculture:** rice, sugar beets, vegetables, fruit; pork, poultry, dairy products, eggs; fish. **Labor force:** 66.66 million; services 70%, industry 25%, agriculture 5% (2002 est.). **Industries:** among world's largest and technologically advanced producers of motor vehicles, electronic equipment, machine tools, steel and nonferrous metals, ships, chemicals; textiles, processed foods. **Natural resources:** negligible mineral resources, fish. **Exports:** $447.1 billion (f.o.b., 2003 est.): motor vehicles, semiconductors, office machinery, chemicals. **Imports:** $346.6 billion (f.o.b., 2003 est.): machinery and equipment, fuels, foodstuffs, chemicals, textiles, raw materials (2001). **Major trading partners:** U.S., China, South Korea, Taiwan, Hong Kong, Indonesia, Australia.

Geography An archipelago in the Pacific, Japan is separated from the east coast of Asia by the Sea of Japan. It is approximately the size of Montana. Japan's four main islands are Honshu, Hokkaido, Kyushu, and Shikoku. The Ryukyu chain to the southwest was U.S.-occupied from 1945 to 1972, when it reverted to Japanese control, and the Kurils to the northeast are Russian-occupied.

Government Constitutional monarchy with a parliamentary government.

History Legend attributes creation of Japan to the sun goddess, from whom the emperors were descended. The first of them was Jimmu, supposed to have ascended the throne in 660 B.C., a tradition that constituted official doctrine until 1945.

Recorded Japanese history begins in approximately A.D. 400, when the Yamato clan, eventually based in Kyoto, managed to gain control of other family groups in central and western Japan. Contact with Korea introduced Buddhism to Japan at about this time. Through the 700s Japan was much influenced by China, and the Yamato clan set up an imperial court similar to that of China. In the ensuing centuries, the authority of the imperial court was undermined as powerful gentry families vied for control.

At the same time, warrior clans were rising to prominence as a distinct class known as samurai. In 1192, the Minamoto clan set up a military government under their leader, Yoritomo. He was designated shogun (military dictator). For the following 700 years, shoguns from a succession of clans ruled in Japan, while the imperial court existed in relative obscurity.

First contact with the West came in about 1542, when a Portuguese ship off course arrived in Japanese waters. Portuguese traders, Jesuit missionaries, and Spanish, Dutch, and English traders followed. Suspicious of Christianity and of Portuguese support of a local Japanese revolt, the shoguns of the Tokugawa period (1603–1867) prohibited all trade with foreign countries; only a Dutch trading post at Nagasaki was permitted. Western attempts to renew trading relations failed until 1853, when Commodore Matthew Perry sailed an American fleet into Tokyo Bay. Trade with the West was forced upon Japan under terms less than favorable to the Japanese. Strife caused by these actions brought down the feudal world of the shoguns. In 1868, the emperor Meiji came to the throne, and the shogun system was abolished.

Japan quickly made the transition from a medieval to a modern power. An imperial army was established with conscription, and parliamentary government was formed in 1889. The Japanese began to take steps to extend their empire. After a brief war with China in 1894–1895, Japan acquired Formosa (Taiwan), the Pescadores Islands, and part of southern Manchuria. China also recognized the independence of Korea (Chosen), which Japan later annexed (1910).

In 1904–1905, Japan defeated Russia in the Russo-Japanese War, gaining the territory of southern Sakhalin (Karafuto) and Russia's port and rail rights in Manchuria. In World War I, Japan seized Germany's Pacific islands and leased areas in China. The Treaty of Versailles then awarded Japan a mandate over the islands. At the Washington Conference of 1921–1922, Japan agreed to respect Chinese national integrity, but, in 1931, invaded Manchuria. The following year, Japan set up this area as a puppet state, "Manchukuo," under Emperor Henry Pu-Yi, the last of China's Manchu dynasty. On Nov. 25, 1936, Japan joined the Axis. The invasion of China came the next year, followed by the Pearl Harbor attack on the U.S. on Dec. 7, 1941. Japan won its first military engagements during the war, extending its power over a vast area of the Pacific. Yet, after 1942, the Japanese were forced to retreat, island by island, to their own country. The dropping of atomic bombs on the cities of Hiroshima and Nagasaki in 1945 by the United States finally brought the government to admit defeat. Japan surrendered formally on Sept. 2, 1945, aboard the battleship *Missouri* in Tokyo Bay. Southern Sakhalin and the Kuril Islands reverted to the USSR, and Formosa (Taiwan) and Manchuria to China. The Pacific islands remained under U.S. occupation.

Gen. Douglas MacArthur was appointed supreme commander of the U.S. occupation of postwar Japan (1945–1952). In 1947, a new constitution took effect. The emperor became largely a symbolic head of state. The U.S. and Japan signed a security treaty in 1951, allowing for U.S. troops to be stationed in Japan. In 1952, Japan regained full sovereignty, and, in 1972, the U.S. returned to Japan the Ryuku Islands, including Okinawa.

Japan's postwar economic recovery was nothing short of remarkable. New technologies and manufacturing were undertaken with great success. A shrewd trade policy gave Japan larger shares in many Western markets, an imbalance that caused some tensions with the U.S. The close involvement of Japanese government in the country's banking and industry produced accusations of protectionism. Yet economic growth continued through the 1970s and 1980s, eventually making Japan the world's second-largest economy (after the U.S.).

During the 1990s, Japan suffered an economic downturn prompted by scandals involving government officials, bankers, and leaders of industry. Japan succumbed to the Asian economic crisis in 1998, experiencing its worst recession since World War II. These setbacks led to the resignation of Prime Minister Ryutaro Hashimoto in July 1998. He was replaced by Keizo Obuchi. In 1999, Japan seemed to make slight progress in an economic recovery. Prime Minister Obuchi died of a stroke in May 2000 and was succeeded by Yoshiro Mori, whose administration was dogged by scandal and blunders from the outset.

Despite attempts to revive the economy, fears that Japan would slide back into recession increased in early 2001. The embattled Mori resigned in April 2001 and was replaced by Liberal Democrat Junichiro Koizumi—the country's 11th prime minister in 13 years. Koizumi's plans to revitalize the country's tattered economy with painful reforms were buoyed in July elections, when his coalition dominated parliamentary elections. Koizumi's popularity was fleeting, however, and after two years in office the economy remained in a slump and his attempts at reform were thwarted.

At an unprecedented summit meeting in North Korea in Sept. 2002, President Kim Jong Il apologized to Koizumi for North Korea's kidnapping of Japanese citizens during the 1970s and 1980s, and Koizumi pledged a generous aid package—both significant steps toward normalizing relations. Koizumi met again with Kim in May 2004 and agreed to give North Korea $10 million and 250,000 tons of food in exchange for five of the children of the kidnapped Japanese citizens who had returned to Japan in 2002.

Koizumi was overwhelmingly reelected in Sept. 2003 and promised to push ahead with tough economic reforms.

Two Japanese aid workers and a journalist were kidnapped in Iraq in April 2004. They were released unharmed after being held hostage for a week. There are 550 Japanese troops in Iraq participating in the reconstruction of that nation. Japanese soldiers have not been deployed to a combat region since World War II.

Jordan

THE HASHEMITE KINGDOM OF JORDAN

National name: Al-Mamlaka al-Urduniya al-Hashemiyah
Ruler: King Abdullah II (1999)
Prime Minister: Faisal al-Fayez (2003)
Area: 35,637 sq mi (92,300 sq km) excludes West Bank
Population (2004 est.): 5,611,202 (growth rate: 2.7%); birth rate: 22.7/1000; infant mortality rate: 18.1/1000; life expectancy: 78.1; density per sq mi: 153
Capital and largest city (2003 est.): Amman, 2,677,500 (metro. area), 1,293,200. **Other large cities:** Zarka, 512,200; Irbid, 267,200; As-Salt, 200,400. **Monetary unit:** Jordanian dinar. **Languages:** Arabic (official),

English. **Ethnicity/race:** Arab 98%, Circassian 1%, Armenian 1%. **Religions:** Islam (Sunni) 92%, Christian 6% (mostly Greek Orthodox), other 2%. **Literacy rate:** 91% (2003 est.)
Economic summary: GDP/PPP (2003 est.): $23.64 billion; per capita $4,300. **Real growth rate:** 3.1%. **Inflation:** 3.5%. **Unemployment:** 16% official rate; actual rate is 25%–30% (2001 est.). **Arable land:** 3%. **Agriculture:** wheat, barley, citrus, tomatoes, melons, olives; sheep, goats, poultry. **Labor force:** 1.36 million (2002); services 82.5%, industry 12.5%, agriculture 5% (2001 est.). **Industries:** phosphate mining, pharmaceuticals, petroleum refining, cement, potash, light manufacturing, pharmaceuticals, tourism. **Natural resources:** phosphates, potash, shale oil. **Exports:** $2.908 billion (f.o.b. 2003 est.): phosphates, fertilizers, potash, agricultural products, manufactures, pharmaceuticals. **Imports:** $4.946 billion (f.o.b. 2003 est.): commodities: crude oil, machinery, transport equipment, food, live animals, manufactured goods. **Major trading partners:** Iraq, U.S., India, Saudi Arabia, Israel, Germany, China, France, UK, Italy.

Geography The Middle East kingdom of Jordan is bordered on the west by Israel and the Dead Sea, on the north by Syria, on the east by Iraq, and on the south by Saudi Arabia. It is comparable in size to Indiana. Arid hills and mountains make up most of the country. The southern section of the Jordan River flows through the country.

Government Constitutional hereditary monarchy.

History In biblical times, the country that is now Jordan contained the lands of Edom, Moab, Ammon, and Bashan. Together with other Middle Eastern territories, Jordan passed in turn to the Assyrians, the Babylonians, the Persians, and, about 330 B.C., the Seleucids. Conflict between the Seleucids and the Ptolemies enabled the Arabic-speaking Nabataeans to create a kingdom in southeast Jordan. In A.D. 106 it became part of the Roman province of Arabia and in 633–636 was conquered by the Arabs. In the 16th century, Jordan submitted to Ottoman Turkish rule and was administered from Damascus. Taken from the Turks by the British in World War I, Jordan (formerly known as Transjordan) was separated from the Palestine mandate in 1920, and in 1921, placed under the rule of Abdullah ibn Hussein.

In 1923, Britain recognized Jordan's independence, subject to the mandate. In 1946, grateful for Jordan's loyalty in World War II, Britain abolished the mandate. That part of Palestine occupied by Jordanian troops was formally incorporated by action of the Jordanian Parliament in 1950. King Abdullah was assassinated in 1951. His son Talal, who was mentally ill, was deposed the next year. Talal's son Hussein, born on Nov. 14, 1935, succeeded him.

From the beginning of his reign, Hussein had to steer a careful course between his powerful neighbor to the west, Israel, and rising Arab nationalism, frequently a direct threat to his throne. Riots erupted when he joined the Central Treaty Organization (the Baghdad Pact) in 1955, and he incurred further unpopularity when Britain, France, and Israel attacked the Suez Canal in 1956, forcing him to place his army under nominal command of the United Arab Republic of Egypt and Syria. The 1961 breakup of the UAR eased Arab national pressure on Hussein, who was the first to recognize Syria after it reclaimed its independence. Jordan was swept into the 1967 Arab-Israeli War, however, and lost the old city of Jerusalem and all of its territory west of the Jordan River, the West Bank. Embittered Palestinian guerrilla forces virtually took over sections of Jordan in the aftermath of defeat, and open warfare broke out between the Palestinians and government forces in 1970.

Despite intervention of Syrian tanks, Hussein's Bedouin army defeated the Palestinians. The Jordanians drove out the Syrians and 12,000 Iraqi troops who had been in the country since the 1967 war. Ignoring protests from other Arab states, Hussein, by mid-1971, crushed Palestinian strength in Jordan and shifted the problem to Lebanon, where many of the guerrillas had fled. As Egypt and Israel neared final agreement on a peace treaty early in 1979, Hussein met with Yasir Arafat, the PLO leader, on March 17, and issued a joint statement of opposition. Although the U.S. pressed Jordan to break Arab ranks on the issue, Hussein elected to side with the great majority, cutting ties with Cairo and joining the boycott against Egypt.

Jordan's stance during the Persian Gulf War strained relations with the U.S. and led to the termination of U.S. aid. The signing of a national charter by King Hussein and leaders of all the main political groups in June 1991 meant political parties were permitted in exchange for acceptance of the constitution and the monarchy. King Hussein's decision to join the Middle East peace talks in mid-1991 helped restore his country's relations with the U.S.

In July 1994, King Hussein and the Israeli prime minister Yitzhak Rabin signed a declaration ending the state of belligerency between the two countries. A peace agreement between the two countries was signed on Oct. 26, 1994, although a clause in it calling the king the "custodian" of Islamic holy shrines in Jerusalem angered the PLO. In the wake of the agreement Jordan's relations with the U.S. and with the moderate Arab states, including Saudi Arabia, warmed. In 1997, Jordan, determined to attract foreign investment, began negotiating with the United States about membership in the World Trade Organization. In Jan. 1999, King Hussein unexpectedly deposed his brother, Prince Hassan, who had been heir apparent for 34 years, and named his eldest son as the new crown prince. A month later, King Hussein died of cancer, and Abdullah, 37, a popular military leader with little political experience, became king.

In 2002–2003, Jordan found itself caught in the middle of the mounting hostility between the U.S. and Iraq—many of Jordan's 5 million Palestinians were supporters of Hussein's Iraq. But at the same time, Jordan could not anger its superpower benefactor—the U.S. is its largest aid donor.

Kazakhstan

REPUBLIC OF KAZAKHSTAN

President: Nursultan A. Nazarbayev (1990)
Prime Minister: Daniyal Akhmetov (2003)
Area: 1,049,150 sq mi (2,717,300 sq km)
Population (2004 est.): 15,143,704 (growth rate: 0.3%); birth rate: 15.5/1000; infant mortality rate: 30.5/1000; life expectancy: 66.1; density per sq mi: 14
Capital (2003 est.): Astana, 288,200 (formerly Aqmola; capital since 1997). **Largest cities:** Almaty (former capital), 1,045,900; Karaganda, 404,600; Shymkent, 333,500; Taraz, 305,700; Pavlodar, 299,500; Ust-Kamenogorsk, 288,000; Aqtöbe, 234,400.
Monetary unit: Tenge. **Languages:** Kazak (Qazaq, state language) 64.4%; Russian (official, used in everyday business) 95% (2001 est.). **Ethnicity/race:** Kazak (Qazaq) 53.4%, Russian 30%, Ukrainian 3.7%, Uzbek 2.5%, German 2.4%, Tatar 1.4%, other 6.6% (1999). **Religions:** Islam 47%, Russian Orthodox 44%, Protestant 2%, other 7%. **Literacy rate:** 98% (1999 est.)

Economic summary: GDP/PPP (2003 est.): $105.3 billion; per capita $7,000. **Real growth rate:** 9%. **Inflation:** 6.2%. **Unemployment:** 8.6%. **Arable land:** 11%. **Agriculture:** grain (mostly spring wheat), cotton; livestock. **Labor force:** 8.4 million (1999); industry 30%, agriculture 20%, services 50% (2002 est.). **Industries:** oil, coal, iron ore, manganese, chromite, lead, zinc, copper, titanium, bauxite, gold, silver, phosphates, sulfur, iron and steel; tractors and other agricultural machinery, electric motors, construction materials. **Natural resources:** major deposits of petroleum, natural gas, coal, iron ore, manganese, chrome ore, nickel, cobalt, copper, molybdenum, lead, zinc, bauxite, gold, uranium. **Exports:** $12.72 billion (f.o.b., 2003 est.): oil and oil products 58%, ferrous metals 24%, chemicals 5%, machinery 3%, grain, wool, meat, coal (2001). **Imports:** $8.621 billion (f.o.b., 2003 est.): machinery and equipment 41%, metal products 28%, foodstuffs 8% (2001). **Major trading partners:** Russia, Bermuda, China, Germany, Italy, Ukraine, France, U.S.

Geography Kazakhstan lies in the north of the central Asian republics and is bounded by Russia in the north, China in the east, Kyrgyzstan and Uzbekistan in the south, and the Caspian Sea and part of Turkmenistan in the west. It has almost 1,177 mi (1,894 km) of coastline on the Caspian Sea. Kazakhstan is slightly more than twice the size of Texas. The territory is mostly steppe land with hilly plains and plateaus.

Government Republic.

History The indigenous Kazakhs were a nomadic Turkic people who belonged to several divisions of Kazakh hordes. They grouped together in settlements and lived in dome-shaped tents made of felt called "yurts." Their tribes migrated seasonally to find pastures for their herds of sheep, horses, and goats. Although they had chiefs, the Kazakhs were rarely united as a single nation under one great leader. Their tribes fell under Mongol rule in the 13th century and they were dominated by Tartar khanates until the area was conquered by Russia in the 18th century.

The area became part of the Kirgiz Autonomous Republic formed by the Soviet authorities in 1920, and in 1925 this entity's name was changed to the Kazakh Autonomous Soviet Socialist Republic (Kazakh ASSR). After 1927, the Soviet government began forcing the nomadic Kazakhs to settle on collective and state farms, and the Soviets continued the czarist policy of encouraging large numbers of Russians and other Slavs to settle in the region.

Owing to the region's intensive agricultural development and its use as a testing ground for nuclear weapons by the Soviet government, serious environmental problems developed by the late 20th century. Along with the other central Asian republics, Kazakhstan obtained its independence from the collapsing Soviet Union in 1991. Kazakhstan proclaimed its membership in the Commonwealth of Independent States on Dec. 21, 1991, along with ten other former Soviet republics. In 1993, the country overwhelmingly approved the Nuclear Non-Proliferation Treaty. President Nursultan Nazarbayev restructured and consolidated many operations of the government in 1997, eliminating a third of the government ministries and agencies. In 1997, the national capital was changed from Almaty, the largest city, to Astana (formerly Aqmola).

In Jan. 1999, Nazarbayev was sworn into office for another seven years, although the election was widely criticized when an opposition leader was disqualified on a technicality. Despite his authoritarianism, Nazarbayev, who has ruled Kazakhstan since 1989, when it was still part of the Soviet Union, is a widely popular leader. Kazakhstan has the potential for becoming one of central Asia's richest countries because of its huge mineral and oil resources and its liberalized economy, which encourages Western investment. In 2000, oil was discovered in Kazakhstan's portion of the Caspian Sea—it is believed to be the largest oil find in 30 years. In March 2001, a pipeline opened to transport oil from the Tengiz fields to the Russian Black Sea port of Novorossiysk. In 2004, Kazakhstan signed a deal allowing China to build an oil pipeline to the Chinese border.

But as its economic outlook blossoms, Kazakhstan's scarce democratic principles continue to wither. In the past several years, the president has harassed the independent media, arrested opposition leaders, and passed a law making it virtually impossible for new political parties to form.

Kenya

REPUBLIC OF KENYA

National name: Jamhuri ya Kenya
President: Mwai Kibaki (2002)
Area: 224,961 sq mi (582,650 sq km)
Population (2004 est.): 32,021,856 (growth rate: 1.1%); birth rate: 27.8/1000; infant mortality rate: 62.6/1000; life expectancy: 44.9; density per sq mi: 142
Capital and largest city (2003 est.): Nairobi, 3,064,800 (metro. area), 2,411,900 (city proper). **Other large city:** Mombasa, 712,600. **Monetary unit:** Kenya shilling.
Languages: English (official), Swahili (national), and several other languages spoken by 25 ethnic groups.
Ethnicity/race: Kikuyu 22%; Luhya 14%; Luo 13%; Kalenjin 12%; Kamba 11%; Kisii 6%; Meru 6%; other African 15%; Asian, European, and Arab 1%. **Religions:** Protestant 45%, Roman Catholic 33%, indigenous beliefs 10%, Islam 10%, others 2% (note: estimates vary widely). **Literacy rate:** 85% (2003 est.)
Economic summary: GDP/PPP (2003 est.): $33.09 billion; per capita $1,000. **Real growth rate:** 1.7%. **Inflation:** 9.6%. **Unemployment:** 40% (2001 est.). **Arable land:** 7%. **Agriculture:** tea, coffee, corn, wheat, sugarcane, fruit, vegetables; dairy products, beef, pork, poultry, eggs. **Labor force:** 12.95 million (2001 est.); agriculture 75%–80%. **Industries:** small-scale consumer goods (plastic, furniture, batteries, textiles, soap, cigarettes, flour), agricultural products processing; oil refining, cement; tourism. **Natural resources:** gold, limestone, soda ash, salt, rubies, fluorspar, garnets, wildlife, hydropower. **Exports:** $2.514 billion (f.o.b., 2003 est.): tea, horticultural products, coffee, petroleum products, fish, cement. **Imports:** $3.705 billion (f.o.b., 2003 est.): machinery and transportation equipment, petroleum products, motor vehicles, iron and steel, resins and plastics. **Major trading partners:** Uganda, UK, U.S., Netherlands, Pakistan, Tanzania, Egypt, UAE, Saudi Arabia, South Africa, France, China, Japan, India.
Member of Commonwealth of Nations

Geography Kenya lies across the equator in east-central Africa, on the coast of the Indian Ocean. It is twice the size of Nevada. Kenya borders Somalia to the east, Ethiopia to the north, Tanzania to the south, Uganda to the west, and Sudan to the northwest. In the north, the land is arid; the southwest corner is in the fertile Lake Victoria Basin; and a length of the eastern depression of the Great Rift Valley separates western highlands from those that rise from the lowland coastal strip.

Government Republic.

History Paleontologists believe people may first have inhabited Kenya about 2 million years ago. In the 700s, Arab seafarers established settlements along the coast, and the Portuguese took control of the area in the early 1500s. More than 40 ethnic groups reside in Kenya. Its largest group, the Kikuyu, migrated to the region at the beginning of the 18th century.

The land became a British protectorate in 1890 and a Crown colony in 1920, when it went by the name British East Africa. Nationalist stirrings began in the 1940s, and in 1952 the Mau Mau movement, made up of Kikuyu militants, rebelled against the government. The fighting lasted until 1956.

On Dec. 12, 1963, Kenya became fully independent. Jomo Kenyatta, a nationalist leader during the independence struggle who had been jailed by the British, became its first president.

From 1964 to 1992, the country was ruled as a one-party state by the Kenya African National Union (KANU), first under Kenyatta and then under Daniel arap Moi. Demonstrations and riots pressured Moi to allow for multiparty elections in 1992.

The economy did not flourish under Daniel arap Moi's rule. In the 1990s, Kenya's infrastructure began disintegrating and official graft was rampant, contributing to the withdrawal of much foreign aid. In early 1995, President Moi moved against the opposition and ordered the arrest of anyone who insulted him.

A series of disasters plagued Kenya in 1997 and 1998: severe flooding destroyed roads, bridges, and crops; epidemics of malaria and cholera overwhelmed the ineffectual health care system; and ethnic clashes erupted between the Kikuyu and Kalenjin ethnic groups in the Rift Valley.

On Aug. 7, 1998, the U.S. embassy in Nairobi was bombed by terrorists, killing 243 and injuring more than 1,000. The embassy in neighboring Tanzania was bombed the same day, killing ten.

In a successful effort to win back IMF and World Bank funding, which had been suspended because of Kenya's corruption and poor economic practices, President Moi appointed his high-profile critic and political opponent, Richard Leakey, as head of the civil service in 1999. A third-generation white Kenyan, son of paleontologists Louis and Mary Leakey, he had been a highly effective reformer as head of the Kenya Wildlife Service. But after 20 months during which he made a promising start at cleaning up Kenya's corrupt bureaucracy, Leakey was sacked by Moi. Kenya is regularly ranked among the ten most corrupt countries in the world, according to the watchdog group Transparency International.

An anticorruption law, sponsored by the ruling party, failed to pass in Parliament in Aug. 2001, and imperiled Kenya's chances for international aid. Opposition leaders called the law a cynical ploy meant to give the appearance of reform—the proposed law, they contended, was in fact too weak and full of loopholes to make a dent in corruption.

Opposition leader Mwai Kibaki won the Dec. 2002 presidential election, defeating Moi's protégé, Uhuru Kenyatta (term limits prevented Moi, in power for 24 years, from running again). Kibaki promised to put an end to the country's rampant corruption. In his first few months, Kibaki did initiate a number of reforms—ordering a crackdown on corrupt judges and police and instituting free primary school education—and international donors opened their coffers again.

But by 2004, disappointment in Kibaki set in when little further progress was evident, and a long-awaited new constitution, meant to limit the president's power, still had not been delivered.

Kiribati

REPUBLIC OF KIRIBATI

President: Anote Tong (2003)
Area: 313 sq mi (811 sq km)
Population (2004 est.): 100,798 (growth rate: 2.3%); birth rate: 31.0/1000; infant mortality rate: 49.9/1000; life expectancy: 61.3; density per sq mi: 322
Capital and largest city (2003 est.): Tarawa, 26,600.
Monetary unit: Australian dollar. **Languages:** English (official), I-Kiribati (Gilbertese). **Ethnicity/race:** predominantly Micronesian, some Polynesian.
Religions: Roman Catholic 52%, Protestant (Congregational) 40%, some Seventh-Day Adventist, Muslim, Baha'i, Latter-day Saints, and Church of God (1999). **Literacy rate:** n.a.
Economic summary: GDP/PPP (2001 est.): $79 million, supplemented by a nearly equal amount from external sources; per capita $800. **Real growth rate:** 1.5%. **Inflation:** 2.5%. **Unemployment:** 2%; underemployment 70% (1992 est.). **Arable land:** 0%. **Agriculture:** copra, taro, breadfruit, sweet potatoes, vegetables; fish. **Labor force:** 7,870 economically active, not including subsistence farmers (2001 est.). **Industries:** fishing, handicrafts. **Natural resources:** phosphate (production discontinued in 1979). **Exports:** $35 million (f.o.b., 2002): copra 62%, seaweed, fish. **Imports:** $83 million (c.i.f., 2002): foodstuffs, machinery and equipment, miscellaneous manufactured goods, fuel. **Major trading partners:** Japan, Thailand, South Korea, France, Australia, Fiji, Japan, Latvia, U.S., New Zealand. **Member of Commonwealth of Nations**

Geography Kiribati, formerly the Gilbert Islands, consists of three widely separated main groups of southwest Pacific islands: the Gilberts on the equator, the Phoenix Islands to the east, and the Line Islands farther east. Ocean Island, producer of phosphates until it was mined out in 1981, is also included in the 2 million square miles of ocean. Most of the islands of Kiribati are low-lying coral atolls built on a submerged volcanic chain and encircled by reefs.

Government Republic.

History Kiribati was first settled by early Austronesian-speaking peoples long before the 1st century A.D. Fijians and Tongans arrived about the 14th century and subsequently merged with the older groups to form the traditional I-Kiribati Micronesian society and culture. The islands were first sighted by British and American ships in the late 18th and early 19th centuries, and the first British settlers arrived in 1837. A British protectorate since 1892, the Gilbert and Ellice Islands became a Crown colony in 1915–1916. Kiritimati (Christmas) Atoll became a part of the colony in 1919; the Phoenix Islands were added in 1937.

Tarawa and others of the Gilbert group were occupied by Japan during World War II. Tarawa was the site of one of the bloodiest battles in U.S. Marine Corps history when Marines landed in Nov. 1943 to dislodge the Japanese defenders. The Gilbert Islands and Ellice Islands (now Tuvalu) were separated in 1975 and granted internal self-government by Britain. Kiribati became independent on July 12, 1979.

Kiribati's 1995 act of moving the international date line far to the east, so that it encompassed Kiribati's Line Islands group, courted controversy. The move, which fulfilled one of President Tito's campaign promises, was intended to enable Kiribati to become the first country to see the dawn on Jan. 1, 2000, and welcome the new millennium—an event of significance for tourism. In 1999, Kiribati gained UN membership.

In 2002, Kiribati passed a controversial law enabling it to shut down newspapers. The legislation followed the launching of Kiribati's first successful nongovernment-run newspaper. Anote Tong of the opposition party Boutokaan Te Koaua was elected president in 2003.

Korea, North

DEMOCRATIC PEOPLE'S REPUBLIC OF KOREA

National name: Choson Minjujuui Inmin Konghwaguk
Head of State: Kim Jong Il (1994)
Premier: Hong Song Nam (1997)
Area: 46,540 sq mi (120,540 sq km)
Population (2004 est.): 22,697,553 (growth rate: 1.0%); birth rate: 16.8/1000; infant mortality rate: 24.8/1000; life expectancy: 71.1; density per sq mi: 488
Capital and largest city (2003): Pyongyang, 3,222,000 (metro. area), 2,767,900. **Monetary unit:** Won.
Language: Korean. **Ethnicity/race:** racially homogeneous; small Chinese community, a few ethnic Japanese. **Religions:** Buddhism and Confucianism; religious activities almost nonexistent. **Literacy rate:** 99% (1990 est.)
Economic summary: GDP/PPP (2003 est.): $22.85 billion; per capita $1,000. **Real growth rate:** 1%. **Inflation:** n.a. **Unemployment:** n.a. **Arable land:** 14%. **Agriculture:** rice, corn, potatoes, soybeans, pulses; cattle, pigs, pork, eggs. **Labor force:** 9.6 million; agricultural 36%, nonagricultural 64%. **Industries:** military products; machine building, electric power, chemicals; mining (coal, iron ore, magnesite, graphite, copper, zinc, lead, and precious metals), metallurgy; textiles, food processing; tourism. **Natural resources:** coal, lead, tungsten, zinc, graphite, magnesite, iron ore, copper, gold, pyrites, salt, fluorspar, hydropower. **Exports:** $1.044 million (f.o.b., 2002 est.): minerals, metallurgical products, manufactures (including armaments); textiles and fishery products. **Imports:** $2.042 billion (c.i.f., 2002 est.): petroleum, coking coal, machinery and equipment; textiles, grain. **Major trading partners:** China, Japan, Costa Rica, Brazil, India, Thailand, Germany, Singapore, Qatar.

Geography Korea is a 600-mile (966 km) peninsula jutting out from Manchuria and China (and a small portion of the USSR). North Korea occupies an area slightly smaller than Pennsylvania north of the 38th parallel.

The country is almost completely covered by a series of north-south mountain ranges separated by narrow valleys. The Yalu River forms part of the northern border with Manchuria.

Government Authoritarian socialist; one-man dictatorship.

History The ancient history of the Korean peninsula can be traced to the Neolithic Age, when Turkic-Manchurian-Mongol peoples migrated into the region from China. The first agriculturally based settlements appeared around 6000 B.C. Some of the larger communities of this era were established along the Han-gang River near modern-day Seoul, others near Pyongyang and Pusan. According to ancient lore, Korea's earliest civilization, known as Choson, was founded in 2333 B.C. by Tan-gun.

In the 17th century, Korea became a vassal state of China and was cut off from outside contact until the Sino-Japanese War of 1894–1895. Following Japan's victory, Korea was granted independence. By 1910, Korea had been annexed by Japan, which developed the country but never won over the Korean nationalists, who continued to agitate for independence.

After Japan's surrender at the conclusion of World War II, the Korean peninsula was partitioned into two occupation zones, divided at the 38th parallel. The USSR controlled the north, with the U.S. taking charge of the south. In 1948, the division was made permanent with the establishment of the separate regimes of North and South Korea. The Democratic People's Republic of Korea (North Korea) was established on May 1, 1948, with Kim Il Sung as president.

Hoping to unify the Koreas under a single Communist government, the North launched a surprise invasion of South Korea on June 25, 1950. In the following days, the UN Security Council condemned the attack and demanded an immediate withdrawal.

President Harry S. Truman ordered U.S. air and naval units into action to enforce the UN order. The British government followed suit, and soon a UN multinational command was set up to aid the South Koreans.

The North Korean invaders swiftly seized Seoul and surrounded the allied forces in the peninsula's southeast corner near Pusan. In a desperate bid to reverse the military situation, UN Commander Gen. Douglas MacArthur ordered an amphibious landing at Inchon on Sept. 15 and routed the North Korean army. MacArthur's forces pushed north across the 38th parallel, approaching the Yalu River.

Prompted by this successful counteroffensive, Communist China entered the war, forcing the UN troops into a headlong retreat. Seoul was lost again, then regained. Ultimately, the war stabilized near the 38th parallel, but dragged on for two years while negotiations took place. An armistice was agreed to on July 27, 1953.

Kim Il Sung's death on July 8, 1994, introduced a period of uncertainty, as his son, Kim Jong Il, assumed the leadership mantle. Negotiations over the country's suspected atomic weapons dragged on, but an agreement was reached in June 1995 that included a provision for providing the North with a South Korean nuclear reactor.

The nuclear crises that characterized the mid-1990s were overshadowed when famine struck the nation's 24 million inhabitants in 1998 and 1999. Two years of floods had been followed by severe droughts in 1997 and 1998, causing devastating crop failures. Because of a lack of fuel and machinery parts, and weather conditions that encouraged parasites, only 10% of North Korea's rice fields could be worked. The staggering food crisis necessitated foreign aid. In the fall of 1999, the severe famine, which claimed an estimated 2 million to 3 million lives, had begun to wane.

In Sept. 1998, North Korea launched a test missile over Japan, claiming it was simply a scientific satellite. This launch alarmed Japan, and much of the rest of the world, about North Korea's intentions regarding reentry into the nuclear arms race. In 1999, North Korea agreed to allow the United States to conduct ongoing inspections of a suspected nuclear development site, Kumchangri, which North Korea admitted had been devised for "a sensitive military purpose." In exchange, the U.S. would increase food aid and initiate a program for bringing potato production to the country.

Antagonism between North and South Korea erupted into open aggression twice within six months in late 1998 and 1999, with South Korea hitting one North Korean vessel and sinking two others that were discovered trespassing in South Korean waters. Tension with South Korea eased dramatically in June 2000, when South Korea's president, Kim Dae Jung, met with North Korea's President Kim Jong Il in Pyongyang. The summit marked the first-ever meeting of the two countries' leaders. But efforts toward reconciliation fizzled thereafter, and various minor military skirmishes followed.

In Jan. 2002, President Bush described North Korea as part of an "axis of evil." Such open hostility marked a dramatic shift in U.S. policy toward North Korea from the Clinton administration's policy of engagement.

In July 2002, North Korea began a series of radical economic initiatives aimed at reforming the devastated economy and introducing free-market policies. The country devalued its currency, raised food prices by as much as 50%, and increased wages.

The reclusive and secretive North Korea stunned the world in late 2002 with two shocking admissions. In September, the government acknowledged that it had kidnapped about a dozen Japanese in the 1970s and 1980s for the purposes of training North Korean spies. In October, confronted with U.S. intelligence, North Korea admitted that it had violated a 1994 agreement freezing its nuclear-weapons program and had in fact been developing nuclear bombs.

In late December, North Korea expelled UN weapons inspectors from the country and announced it could no longer agree to the terms of the nuclear Non-Proliferation Treaty (NPT), officially withdrawing from it in January 2003. During talks with China and the U.S. in April, North Korea announced that it had already produced nuclear weapons and threatened to test or export them. In July North Korean officials reported that the country had reprocessed enough plutonium to build six nuclear bombs. Kim has regularly used threats and hostile acts to try to wring aid from the international community, but it was difficult to decipher how he expected to accomplish his aims—economic aid and a safeguard against U.S. attack—through such reckless brinkmanship. Refusing to bow to North Korea's demands, the United States informed the nation's diplomats that it would not begin to negotiate until North Korea first dismantled its nuclear program. China took on the role of mediator between North Korea and the U.S., urging less inflexibility on both sides. A modest breakthrough occurred when officials from the U.S., North Korea, China, Russia, South Korea, and Japan met in August in Beijing, although nothing substantive resulted. Another round of six-nation negotiations in Feb. 2004 were also inconclusive.

A massive explosion rocked Ryongchon, a city northwest of the capital, Pyongyang, in April 2004. Initial reports indicated the explosion was caused by the collision of two trains carrying fuel, but officials later said the blast was set off when a train car carrying explosives touched a live power cable. Hundreds were feared dead. The normally insular North Korean government asked the UN for help in dealing with the aftermath of the tragedy.

The International Atomic Energy Agency announced in May 2004 that is has strong evidence that North Korea supplied Libya with about two tons of uranium. If true, this would indicate that North Korea has moved beyond selling missile technology.

At a third round of negotiations on North Korea's nuclear weapons program in June 2004, the U.S. offered North Korea the delivery of heavy fuel oil and a "provisional security guarantee" if it agrees to disclose details of its weapons program, allow inspections, and begin to dismantle its nuclear program within three months. North Korea did not respond to the offer. Instead, the country's negotiator threatened to test one of its nuclear weapons.

Korea, South

REPUBLIC OF KOREA

National name: Taehan Min'guk
President: Roh Moo Hyun (2003)
Prime Minister: Lee Hae-chan (2004)
Area: 38,023 sq mi (98,480 sq km)
Population (2004 est.): 48,598,175 (growth rate: 0.6%); birth rate: 12.3/1000; infant mortality rate: 7.2/1000; life expectancy: 75.6; density per sq mi: 1,278
Capital and largest city (2003 est.): Seoul, 19,969,100 (metro. area), 9,630,600 (city proper). **Other large cities:** Pusan, 3,504,900; Inchon, 2,479,600 (part of Seoul metro. area); Taegu, 2,369,800. **Monetary unit:** Won. **Language:** Korean, English widely taught. **Ethnicity/race:** homogeneous (except for about 20,000 Chinese). **Religions:** no affiliation 46%, Christian 26%, Buddhist 26%, Confucianist 1%, other 1%. **Literacy rate:** 98% (2003 est.)
Economic summary: GDP/PPP (2003 est.): $855.3 billion; per capita $17,700. **Real growth rate:** 2.8%. **Inflation:** 3.5%. **Unemployment:** 3.4%. **Arable land:** 17%. **Agriculture:** rice, root crops, barley, vegetables, fruit; cattle, pigs, chickens, milk, eggs; fish. **Labor force:** 23 million; services 69%, industry 21.5%, agriculture 9.5% (2001). **Industries:** electronics, automobile production, chemicals, shipbuilding, steel, textiles, clothing, footwear, food processing. **Natural resources:** coal, tungsten, graphite, molybdenum, lead, hydropower potential. **Exports:** $201.3 billion (f.o.b., 2003 est.): electronic products, machinery and equipment, motor vehicles, steel, ships; textiles, clothing, footwear; fish. **Imports:** $175.6 billion (f.o.b., 2003 est.): macmachinery, electronics and electronic equipment, oil, steel, transport equipment, textiles, organic chemicals, grains. **Major trading partners:** U.S., China, Japan, Hong Kong, Saudi Arabia.

Geography Slightly larger than Indiana, South Korea lies below the 38th parallel on the Korean peninsula. It is mountainous in the east; in the west and south are many harbors on the mainland and offshore islands.

Government Republic.

History South Korea came into being after World War II, the result of a 1945 agreement reached by the Allies at the Potsdam Conference, making the 38th parallel the boundary between a northern zone of the Korean peninsula to be occupied by the USSR and southern zone to be controlled by U.S. forces. (For details, see Korea, North.)

Elections were held in the U.S. zone in 1948 for a national assembly, which adopted a republican constitution and elected Syngman Rhee as the nation's president. The new republic was proclaimed on Aug. 15 and was recognized as the legal government of Korea by the UN on Dec. 12, 1948.

On June 25, 1950, North Korean Communist forces launched a massive surprise attack on South Korea, quickly overrunning the capital, Seoul. U.S. armed intervention was ordered on June 27 by President Harry S. Truman, and on the same day the UN invoked military sanctions against North Korea. Gen. Douglas MacArthur was named commander of the UN forces. U.S. and South Korean troops fought a heroic holding action, but by the first week of August were forced back to a 4,000-square-mile beachhead in southeast Korea. There they stood off superior North Korean forces until Sept. 15, when a major UN amphibious assault was launched deep behind Communist lines at Inchon, the port of Seoul.

By Sept. 30, UN forces were in complete control of South Korea. They then crossed the 38th parallel and pursued retreating Communist forces into North Korea. In late October, as UN forces neared the Sino-Korean border, several hundred thousand Chinese Communist troops entered the conflict, pushing MacArthur's forces back to the border between North and South Korea. By the time truce talks began on July 10, 1951, UN forces had crossed over the parallel again and were driving back into North Korea. Cease-fire negotiations dragged on for two years before an armistice was finally signed at Panmunjom on July 27, 1953, leaving a devastated Korea in need of large-scale rehabilitation. No official peace treaty has ever been signed between the former combatants.

President Syngman Rhee, after 12 years in office, was forced to resign in 1960 amid rising discontent with his autocratic leadership. Po Sun Yun was elected to succeed him, but political instability continued. In 1961, Gen. Park Chung Hee seized power and subsequently began a program of economic reforms designed to stimulate the nation's economy. The U.S. stepped up military aid, strengthening South Korea's armed forces to 600,000 men. Park's assassination on Oct. 26, 1979, by Kim Jae Kyu, head of the Korean Central Intelligence Agency, brought a liberalizing trend as new president Choi Kyu Hah freed imprisoned dissidents.

The release of opposition leader Kim Dae Jung in Feb. 1980 sparked antigovernment demonstrations that turned into riots, which were brutally suppressed by authorities. Kim, the most visible leader of the opposition, was imprisoned again. Choi resigned on Aug. 16. Chun Doo Hwan, head of a military Special Committee for National Security Measures, was the sole candidate as the electoral college confirmed him as president on Aug. 27. In 1986–1987, South Korea's opposition demanded the president be selected by direct popular vote. After weeks of protest and rioting, Chun agreed to the demand. A split in the opposition led to Roh Tae Woo's election on Dec. 16, 1987.

In Aug. 1996 Roh was convicted on bribery charges, and Chun was convicted for bribery as well as his role in the 1979 coup and the 1980 crackdown on rioters. In 1997, an accumulation of corrupt business practices and bad loans led to a series of bankruptcies and a massive devaluation of South Korea's currency. The political instability that followed helped former dissident Kim Dae Jung become the first South Korean president ever to be elected from the political opposition.

In 1998 the Asian economic crisis bottomed out in South Korea. The nation began rebounding in 1999—the only sizable Asian economy to do so.

Antagonism between North and South Korea erupted into open aggression in 1998 and in 1999. Tensions eased dramatically in June 2000, when President Kim Dae Jung met with the North's president, Kim Jong Il, in Pyongyang. The summit marked the first-ever meeting of the countries' leaders. President Kim Dae Jung won the Nobel Peace Prize in Oct. 2000 for his Sunshine Policy, which included initiating peace and reconciliation with North Korea.

Roh Moo Hyun of the ruling Millennium Democratic Party became president in February 2003 and promptly faced daunting problems. His vow to pursue his predecessor's Sunshine Policy toward North Korea was put to the test as the North continued to taunt the world with boasts about its nuclear capabilities. In addition, many South Koreans had begun to resent U.S. influence over their country. In March 2004, the conservative National Assembly voted overwhelmingly to impeach Roh, claiming he had violated election laws. More than 70% of the public, however, condemned the move, and thousands of his supporters took to the streets to protest. South Koreans showed their disapproval of Roh's impeachment at the polls in April, when they gave the liberal pro-Roh Uri Party a majority in the National Assembly. The Constitutional Court dismissed the impeachment in May, and Roh was reinstated as president.

Iraqi insurgents linked to Jordanian militant Abu Musab al-Zarqawi kidnapped and beheaded a South Korean interpreter in June, after the government refused to give in to the group's demand that it abandon plans to deploy 3,000 troops to Iraq.

In September, officials told the International Atomic Energy Agency that in 2000, a group of rogue scientists had produced a small amount of weapons-grade uranium, a violation of several treaties.

Kuwait

STATE OF KUWAIT

National name: Dawlat al-Kuwayt
Emir: Sheik Jaber al-Ahmad al-Sabah (1977)
Prime Minister: Sheik Sabah al-Ahmad al-Sabah (2003)
Area: 6,880 sq mi (17,820 sq km)
Population (2004 est.): 2,257,549 (growth rate: 3.4%); birth rate: 21.9/1000; infant mortality rate: 10.3/1000; life expectancy: 76.8; density per sq mi: 328
Capital (2003 est.): Kuwait, 1,709,800 (metro.area), 32,600 (city proper). **Largest city:** as-Salimiyah, 146,900. **Monetary unit:** Kuwaiti dinar. **Languages:** Arabic (official), English. **Ethnicity/race:** Kuwaiti 45%, other Arab 35%, South Asian 9%, Iranian 4%, other 7%. **Religions:** Islam 85% (Sunni 70%, Shiite 30%); Christian, Hindu, Parsi, and other 15%. **Literacy rate:** 84% (2003 est.)
Economic summary: GDP/PPP (2003 est.): $39.54 billion; per capita $18,100. **Real growth rate:** 4.4%. **Inflation:** 1.2%. **Unemployment:** 7% (2002 est.). **Arable land:** 0.34%. **Agriculture:** practically no crops; fish. **Labor force:** 1.3 million (1998 est.); note: non-Kuwaitis represent about 80% of the labor force; agriculture n.a., industry n.a., services n.a. **Industries:** petroleum, petrochemicals, desalination, food processing, construction materials. **Natural resources:** petroleum, fish, shrimp, natural gas. **Exports:** $22.29 billion (f.o.b., 2003 est.): oil and refined products, fertilizers. **Imports:** $9.606 billion (f.o.b., 2003 est.): food, construction materials, vehicles and parts, clothing. **Major trading partners:** Japan, South Korea, U.S., Singapore, Taiwan, Netherlands, Pakistan, Saudi Arabia, UK, Italy, France.

Geography Kuwait is situated northeast of Saudi Arabia at the northern end of the Persian Gulf, south of Iraq. It is slightly larger than Hawaii. The low-lying desert land is mainly sandy and barren.

Government Kuwait is a constitutional monarchy, governed by the al-Sabah family.

History Kuwait is believed to have been part of an early civilization in the 3rd millennium B.C. and to have traded with Mesopotamian cities. Archeological and historical traces disappeared around the first millennium B.C. At the beginning of the 18th century A.D., the 'Anizah tribe of central Arabia founded Kuwait City, which became an autonomous sheikdom by 1756. 'Abd Rahim of the al-Sabah became the first sheik, and his descendants continue to rule Kuwait today. In the late 18th and early 19th centuries, the sheikdom belonged to the fringes of the Ottoman Empire. Kuwait obtained British protection in 1897 when the sheik feared that the Turks would expand their hold over the area. In 1961, Britain ended the protectorate, giving Kuwait independence, but agreed to give military aid on request. Iraq immediately threatened to occupy the area, and the British sent troops to defend Kuwait. Soon afterward the Arab League sent in troops, replacing the British. Iraq's claim was dropped when the Arab League recognized Kuwait's independence on July 20, 1961. Kuwait typically followed a neutral and mediatory policy among Arab states.

Oil was discovered there in the 1930s, and Kuwait proved to have 20% of the world's known oil resources. Since 1946 it has been the world's second-largest oil exporter. The sheik, who receives half the profits, devotes most of them to the education, welfare, and modernization of his kingdom. In 1966, Sheik Sabah designated a relative, Jaber al-Ahmad al-Sabah, as his successor. By 1968, the sheikdom had established a model welfare state, and it sought to establish dominance among the sheikdoms and emirates of the Persian Gulf.

In July 1990, Iraqi president Saddam Hussein blamed Kuwait for falling oil prices. After a failed Arab mediation attempt to solve the dispute peacefully, Iraq invaded Kuwait on Aug. 2, 1990, set up a pro-Iraqi provisional government, and drained Kuwait of its economic resources. A coalition of Arab and Western military forces drove Iraqi troops from Kuwait in a mere four days, from Feb. 23–27, 1991, ending the Persian Gulf War. The emir returned to his country from Saudi Arabia in mid-March. Martial law, in effect since the end of the Gulf War, ended in late June. The U.S. sent 2,400 troops to the country in Aug. 1992, ostensibly as part of a training exercise, though it was widely interpreted as a show of strength to Saddam Hussein.

The general election of Oct. 1992 was a success for supporters of a return to Islamic law. A political independent was named speaker of the Parliament, and the opposition held 31 of the 50 seats. Iraqi "training" maneuvers near the Kuwaiti border in Oct. 1994 renewed fears of aggression in the country. A Kuwaiti appeal brought the quick deployment of U.S. and British troops and equipment. In 1999, the emir gave women the right to vote and run for Parliament. Later in 1999, however, Parliament defeated the ruler's decree. Kuwaiti society has grown increasingly conservative under the influence of Islamic fundamentalists. In 2003, traditionalists won a sweeping victory in parliamentary elections. The emir and crown prince (who served as prime minister) are elderly and ailing; in July 2003, the country's de facto leader, foreign minister Sabah al-Ahmad al-Sabah, replaced the crown prince as prime minister.

Kyrgyzstan

THE KYRGYZ REPUBLIC

President: Askar Akayev (1990)
Prime Minister: Nikolay Tanayev (2002)
Area: 76,641 sq mi (198,500 sq km)
Population (2004 est.): 5,081,429; (Kyrgyz, 52.4%; Russian, 18%; Uzbek, 12.9%; Ukrainian, 2.5%; German, 2.4%; other, 11.8%) (growth rate: 1.2%); birth rate: 22.1/1000; infant mortality rate: 36.8/1000; life expectancy: 67.8; density per sq mi: 66
Capital and largest city (2003 est.): Bishkek (formerly Frunze), 824,900. **Other large city:** Osh 225,600.
Monetary unit: Som. **Languages:** Kyrgyz, Russian (both official). **Ethnicity/race:** Kyrgyz 64.9%, Uzbek 13.8%, Russian 12.5%, Dungan 1.1%, Ukrainian 1%, Uygur 1%, other 5.7% (1999). **Religions:** Islam, 75%; Russian Orthodox, 20%; other, 5%. **Literacy rate:** 97% (1989 est.)
Economic summary: GDP/PPP (2003 est.): $7.725

billion; per capita $1,600. **Real growth rate:** 6%. **Inflation:** 4%. **Unemployment:** 7.2% (1999 est.). **Arable land:** 7%. **Agriculture:** tobacco, cotton, potatoes, vegetables, grapes, fruits and berries; sheep, goats, cattle, wool. **Labor force:** 2.7 million (2000); agriculture 55%, industry 15%, services 30% (2000 est.). **Industries:** small machinery, textiles, food processing, cement, shoes, sawn logs, refrigerators, furniture, electric motors, gold, rare earth metals. **Natural resources:** abundant hydropower; significant deposits of gold and rare earth metals; locally exploitable coal, oil, and natural gas; other deposits of nepheline, mercury, bismuth, lead, and zinc. **Exports:** $548 million (f.o.b., 2003 est.): cotton, wool, meat, tobacco; gold, mercury, uranium, natural gas, hydropower; machinery; shoes. **Imports:** $601 million (f.o.b., 2003 est.): oil and gas, machinery and equipment, chemicals, foodstuffs. **Major trading partners:** Switzerland, Russia, UAE, China, Kazakhstan, U.S., Uzbekistan.

Geography Kyrgyzstan (formerly Kirghizia) is a rugged country with the Tien Shan mountain range covering approximately 95% of the whole territory. The mountaintops are perennially covered with snow and glaciers. Kyrgyzstan borders Kazakhstan on the north and northwest, Uzbekistan in the southwest, Tajikistan in the south, and China in the southeast. The republic is the same size in area as the state of Nebraska.

Government Constitutional republic.

History The native Kyrgyz are a Turkic people who in ancient times first settled in the Tien Shan mountains. They were traditionally pastoral nomads. There was extensive Russian colonization in the 1900s and Russian settlers were given much of the best agricultural land. This led to an unsuccessful and disastrous revolt by the Kyrgyz people in 1916. Kyrgyzstan became part of the Soviet Federated Socialist Republic in 1924, and was made an autonomous republic in 1926. It became a constituent republic of the USSR in 1936. The Soviets forced the Kyrgyz to abandon their nomadic culture and brought modern farming and industrial production techniques into their society. It has greatly changed their traditional way of life.

Kyrgyzstan proclaimed its independence from the Soviet Union on Aug. 31, 1991. On Dec. 21, 1991, Kyrgyzstan joined the Commonwealth of Independent States. The country joined the UN and the IMF in 1992 and adopted a shock-therapy economic program. Voters endorsed market reforms in a referendum held in Jan. 1994, and in 1996, referendum voters overwhelmingly endorsed proposed constitutional changes that enhanced the power of the president. Representatives of the country along with those of Russia, China, Kazakhstan, and Tajikistan signed a nonaggression agreement in April 1996. In March 1997, Russian border control was extended until the end of the year as authorities in Kyrgyzstan grew increasingly concerned about the growth of the illegal narcotics trade in the country.

Since 1999, several groups of radical Islamic gunmen, believed to be from Uzbekistan or Tajikistan, have led raids and kidnappings from camps in Kyrgyzstan's mountains.

In elections held Oct. 30, 2000, President Askar Akayev easily won reelection with nearly 75% of the vote. The election, however, was marred by allegations of fraud, diminishing Kyrgyzstan's claim to be the centerpiece of Central Asian democracy.

In 2001, Kyrgyzstan permitted troops from the U.S. and seven other nations to be stationed in the country in support of efforts to fight against the Taliban and al-Qaeda in neighboring Afghanistan. In 2002, construction of a large U.S. airbase began outside of Bishkek. In Feb. 2003, a controversial referendum expanded Akayev's powers, and in June Parliament granted him lifelong immunity from prosecution.

Laos

LAO PEOPLE'S DEMOCRATIC REPUBLIC

President: Khamtai Siphandon (2001)
Prime Minister: Boungnang Vorachith (2001)
Area: 91,428 sq mi (236,800 sq km)
Population (2004 est.): 6,068,117 (growth rate: 2.4%); birth rate: 36.5/1000; infant mortality rate: 87.1/1000; life expectancy: 54.7; density per sq mi: 66
Capital and largest city (2003 est.): Vientiane, 194,200. **Monetary unit:** New Kip. **Languages:** Lao (official), French, English, various ethnic languages. **Ethnicity/race:** Lao Loum (lowland) 68%, Lao Theung (upland) 22%, Lao Soung (highland) including the Hmong ("Meo") and the Yao (Mien) 9%, ethnic Vietnamese/Chinese 1%. **Religions:** Buddhist 60%, animist and other 40% (including Christian 1.5%). **Literacy rate:** 53% (2003 est.)
Economic summary: GDP/PPP (2003 est.): $10.34 billion; per capita $1,700. **Real growth rate:** 5.7%. **Inflation:** 7.8% (2001 est.). **Unemployment:** 5.7% (1997 est.). **Arable land:** 3%. **Agriculture:** sweet potatoes, vegetables, corn, coffee, sugarcane, tobacco, cotton; tea, peanuts, rice; water buffalo, pigs, cattle, poultry. **Labor force:** 2.6 million (2001 est); agriculture 80% (1997 est.). **Industries:** tin and gypsum mining, timber, electric power, agricultural processing, construction, garments, tourism. **Natural resources:** timber, hydropower, gypsum, tin, gold, gemstones. **Exports:** $332 million (2003 est.): wood products, garments, electricity, coffee, tin. **Imports:** $492 million (f.o.b., 2003 est.): machinery and equipment, vehicles, fuel, consumer goods. **Major trading partners:** Vietnam, Thailand, France, Germany, China.

Geography A landlocked nation in Southeast Asia occupying the northwest portion of the Indochinese peninsula, Laos is surrounded by China, Vietnam, Cambodia, Thailand, and Burma. It is twice the size of Pennsylvania. Laos is a mountainous country, especially in the north, where peaks rise above 9,000 ft (2,800 m). Dense forests cover the northern and eastern areas. The Mekong River, which forms the boundary with Burma and Thailand, flows through the country for 932 mi (1,500 km) of its course.

Government Communist state.

History The Lao people migrated into Laos from southern China from the 8th century onward. In the 14th century, the first Laotian state was founded, the Lan Xang kingdom, which ruled Laos until it split into three separate kingdoms in 1713. During the 18th century the three kingdoms came under Siamese (Thai) rule, and, in 1893, became a French protectorate. Its territory was incorporated into the union of Indochina. A strong nationalist movement developed during World War II, but France reestablished control in 1946 and made the king of Luang Prabang constitutional monarch of all Laos. France granted semiautonomy in 1949 and then, spurred by the Viet Minh rebellion in Vietnam, full independence within the French Union in 1950.

In 1951, Prince Souphanouvong organized the Pathet Lao, a Communist independence movement, in North Vietnam. Viet Minh and Pathet Lao forces invaded central Laos, and civil war resulted. By the Geneva agreements of 1954 and an armistice of 1955, two northern provinces were given to the Pathet Lao: the rest went to the royal regime. Full sovereignty was given to the kingdom by the Paris agreements of Dec. 29, 1954. In 1957, Prince Souvanna Phouma, the royal premier, and Pathet Lao leader Prince Souphanouvong, the premier's half-brother, agreed to reestablishment of a unified government, with Pathet Lao participation and integration of Pathet Lao forces into the royal army. The agreement broke down in 1959, and armed conflict began anew.

In 1960, the struggle became three-way as Gen. Phoumi Nosavan, controlling the bulk of the royal army, set up in the south a pro-Western revolutionary government headed by Prince Boun Oum. General Phoumi took Vientiane in December, driving Souvanna Phouma into exile in Cambodia. The Soviet bloc supported Souvanna Phouma. In 1961, a ceasefire was arranged and the three princes agreed to a coalition government headed by Souvanna Phouma.

But North Vietnam, the U.S. (in the form of CIA personnel), and China remained active in Laos after the settlement. North Vietnam used a supply line (Ho Chi Minh Trail) running down the mountain valleys of eastern Laos into Cambodia and South Vietnam, particularly after the 1970 U.S.–South Vietnamese incursion into Cambodia stopped supplies via Cambodian seaports.

An agreement reached in 1973 revived the coalition government. The Communist Pathet Lao seized complete power in 1975, installing Souphanouvong as president and Kaysone Phomvihane as premier. Since then other parties and political groups have been moribund and most of their leaders have fled the country. The monarchy was abolished on Dec. 2, 1975, when the Pathet Lao ousted a coalition government and King Sisavang Vatthana abdicated.

The Supreme People's Assembly in Aug. 1991 adopted a new constitution that dropped all references to socialism but retained the one-party state. In addition to implementing market-oriented policies, the country has passed laws governing property, inheritance, and contracts.

During the 1990s, the country began making more diplomatic overtures toward its neighbors. In 1995, the U.S. announced a lifting of its ban on aid to the nation. By most international estimates, Laos is one of the 10 poorest countries in the world. The subsistence farmers who make up more than 80% of the population have been plagued with bad agricultural conditions—alternately floods and drought—since 1993.

Since March 2000, Vientiane has been rocked by a series of unexplained blasts. The activity has been widely attributed to a group of Hmong tribesmen based in the north. The anti-Communist rebel group has been protesting the government's reluctance to embrace democratic reforms. Others attribute the bombs to rival factions in the government or military.

Latvia

THE REPUBLIC OF LATVIA

National name: Latvija
President: Vaira Vike-Freiberga (1999)
Prime Minister: Indulis Emsis (2004)
Area: 24,938 sq mi (64,589 sq km)
Population (2004 est.): 2,306,306 (growth rate: –0.7%); birth rate: 8.9/1000; infant mortality rate: 9.7/1000; life expectancy: 70.9; density per sq mi: 92
Capital and largest city (2003 est.): Riga, 867,700 (metro. area), 706,200 (city proper). **Other large cities:** Daugavpils, 111,700; Liepaja, 82,300.
Monetary unit: Lats. **Language:** Latvian (official),

Lithuanian, Russian, other. **Ethnicity/race:** Latvian 57.7%, Russian 29.6%, Belorussian 4.1%, Ukrainian 2.7%, Polish 2.5%, Lithuanian 1.4%, other 2% (2002). **Religions:** Lutheran, Roman Catholic, Russian Orthodox. **Literacy:** 100% (2003 est.)
Economic summary: GDP/PPP (2003 est.): $23.77 billion; per capita $10,100. **Real growth rate:** 6.8%. **Inflation:** 2.8%. **Unemployment:** 8.7%. **Arable land:** 29%. **Agriculture:** grain, sugar beets, potatoes, vegetables; beef, pork, milk, eggs; fish. **Labor force:** 1.1 million (2001 est.); agriculture 15%, industry 25%, services 60% (2000 est.). **Industries:** buses, vans, street and railroad cars, synthetic fibers, agricultural machinery, fertilizers, washing machines, radios, electronics, pharmaceuticals, processed foods, textiles; note—dependent on imports for energy and raw materials. **Natural resources:** peat, limestone, dolomite, amber, hydropower, wood, arable land. **Exports:** $3 billion (f.o.b., 2003 est.): wood and wood products, machinery and equipment, metals, textiles, foodstuffs. **Imports:** $4.921 billion (f.o.b., 2003 est.): machinery and equipment, chemicals, fuels, vehicles. **Major trading partners:** UK, Sweden, Germany, U.S., Lithuania, Russia, Estonia, Denmark, Finland, Italy.

Geography Latvia borders Estonia on the north, Lithuania in the south, the Baltic Sea with the Gulf of Riga in the west, Russia in the east, and Belarus in the southeast. Latvia is largely a fertile lowland with numerous lakes and hills to the east.

Government Parliamentary democracy.

History Baltic tribespeople settled along the Baltic Sea and, lacking a centralized government, fell prey to more powerful peoples. In the 13th century they were overcome by the Livonian Brothers of the Sword, a German order of knights whose mission was to conquer and Christianize the Baltic region. The land became part of the state of Livonia until 1561. Germans made up the ruling class of Livonia and Baltic tribes made up the peasantry. German became the official language of the region.

Poland conquered the territory in 1562, and occupied it until Sweden took over the land in 1629, and ruled over it until 1721. Then the land passed to Russia. From 1721 until 1918, the Latvians remained Russian subjects, although they preserved their language, customs, and folklore.

The Russian Revolution of 1917 gave them their opportunity for freedom, and the Latvian republic was proclaimed on Nov. 18, 1918. The republic lasted little more than 20 years. Plagued by political instability, Latvia essentially became a dictatorship under President Karlis Ulmanis. It was occupied by Russian troops in 1939 and incorporated into the Soviet Union in 1940. Latvia allied itself with Germany in World War II, and German armies occupied the nation from 1941 to 1944. Of the 70,000 Jews living in Latvia during the war, 95% were massacred. In 1944, Russia again took control of Latvia.

Latvia was one of the most economically well-off and industrialized parts of the Soviet Union. When a coup against Soviet president Mikhail Gorbachev failed in 1991, the Baltic nations saw an opportunity to free themselves from Soviet domination and, following the actions of Lithuania and Estonia, Latvia declared its independence on Aug. 21, 1991. European and most other nations quickly recognized their independence, and on Sept. 2, 1991, President Bush announced full diplomatic recognition for Latvia, Estonia, and Lithuania. The Soviet Union recognized Latvia's independence on Sept. 6, and UN membership followed on Sept. 17, 1991.

Because Latvians' ethnic identity had been quashed throughout its history by foreign rulers, the new Latvian republic set up strict citizenship laws, limiting citizenship to ethnic Latvians and to those who had lived in the region before Soviet rule in 1940. This denied about 452,000 of the country's 740,000 ethnic Russians of citizenship.

Latvia's bid to join the European Union required that it speed up naturalization of minorities, in particular its large number of Russians. In 1998, a referendum passed easing the citizenship rules, although it was still necessary to be competent in the Latvian language, which many believe is unreasonable to expect of older or poorly educated ethnic Russians. To aid in admission to NATO, Parliament in 2002 passed a law no longer requiring parliamentary candidates to speak Latvian. In June 2003, Prime Minister Vike-Freiberga easily won reelection, but by the following year his coalition had unravelled. In March 2004, Green Party leader Indulis Emsis took over as prime minister—it was the eleventh government formed since Latvia's independence from Russia. Latvia became a member of both the EU and NATO in 2004.

Lebanon

REPUBLIC OF LEBANON

National name: Al-Joumhouriya al-Lubnaniya
President: Émile Lahoud (1998)
Premier: Rafiq al-Hariri (2000)
Area: 4,015 sq mi (10,400 sq km)
Population (2004 est.): 3,777,218 (growth rate: 1.3%); birth rate: 19.3/1000; infant mortality rate: 25.5/1000; life expectancy: 72.4; density per sq mi: 941
Capital and largest city (2003 est.): Beirut, 1,916,100 (metro. area), 1,171,000 (city proper). **Other large cities:** Tripoli, 212,900; Sidon, 149,000. **Monetary unit:** Lebanese pound. **Languages:** Arabic (official), French, English, Armenian. **Ethnicity/race:** Arab 95%, Armenian 4%, other 1%. **Religions:** Islam 70% (including Shi'a, Sunni, Druze, Isma'ilite, Alawite, Nusayri), Christian 30% (including Orthodox Christian, Catholic, Protestant), Jewish negl.. **Literacy rate:** 87% (2003 est.)
Economic summary: GDP/PPP (2003 est.): $17.82 billion; per capita $4,800. **Real growth rate:** 3%. **Inflation:** 2.5%. **Unemployment:** 18% (1997 est.). **Arable land:** 18%. **Agriculture:** citrus, grapes, tomatoes, apples, vegetables, potatoes, olives, tobacco; sheep, goats. **Labor force:** 1.5 million; note: in addition, there are as many as 1 million foreign workers (2001 est.); services n.a., industry n.a., agriculture n.a. **Industries:** banking; food processing; jewelry; cement; textiles; mineral and chemical products; wood and furniture products; oil refining; metal fabricating. **Natural resources:** limestone, iron ore, salt, water-surplus state in a water-deficit region, arable land. **Exports:** $1.359 billion (f.o.b., 2003 est.): foodstuffs and tobacco, textiles, chemicals, precious stones, metal products, electrical products, jewelry, paper products. **Imports:** $6.073 billion (f.o.b., 2003): foodstuffs, electrical products, vehicles, minerals, chemicals, textiles, fuels. **Major trading partners:** Switzerland, Saudi Arabia, UAE, U.S., Jordan, Turkey, Italy, France, Germany, Syria, China, Belgium, UK.

Geography Lebanon lies at the eastern end of the Mediterranean Sea north of Israel and west of Syria. It is four-fifths the size of Connecticut. The Lebanon Mountains, which parallel the coast on the west, cover most of the country, while on the eastern border is the Anti-Lebanon range. Between the two lies the Bekaa Valley, the principal agricultural area.

Government Republic.

History After World War I, France was given a League of Nations mandate over Lebanon and its neighbor Syria, which together had previously been a single political unit in the Ottoman Empire. France divided them in 1920 into separate colonial administrations, drawing a border that separated predominantly Muslim Syria from the kaleidoscope of religious communities in Lebanon, where Maronite Christians were then dominant. After 20 years of the French mandate regime, Lebanon's independence was proclaimed on Nov. 26, 1941, but full independence came in stages. Under an agreement between representatives of Lebanon and the French National Committee of Liberation, most of the powers exercised by France were transferred to the Lebanese government on Jan. 1, 1944. The evacuation of French troops was completed in 1946.

According to the National Pact, different religious communities are represented in the government by having a Maronite Christian president, a Sunni Muslim prime minister, and a Shiite National Assembly speaker. The arrangement worked for two decades.

Civil war broke out in 1958, with Muslim factions led by Kamal Jumblat and Saeb Salam rising in insurrection against the Lebanese government headed by President Camille Chamoun, a Maronite Christian favoring close ties to the West. At Chamoun's request, President Eisenhower, on July 15, sent U.S. troops to reestablish the government's authority.

Clan warfare between various religious factions in Lebanon goes back centuries. The hodgepodge includes Maronite Christians, who since independence have dominated the government; Sunni Muslims, who have prospered in business and shared political power; the Druze, who hold a faith incorporating aspects of Islam and Gnosticism; and Shiite Muslims.

A new—and bloodier—Lebanese civil war that broke out in 1975 resulted in the addition of still another ingredient in the brew—the Syrians. In the fighting between Lebanese factions, 40,000 Lebanese were estimated to have been killed and 100,000 wounded between March 1975 and Nov. 1976. At that point, a Syrian-dominated Arab Deterrent Force intervened at the request of the Lebanese and brought large-scale fighting to a halt.

Palestinian guerrillas staging raids on Israel from Lebanese territory drew punitive Israeli raids on Lebanon and two large-scale Israeli invasions, in 1978 and again in 1982. In the first invasion, the Israelis entered the country in March 1978 and withdrew that June, after the UN Security Council created a 6,000-man peacekeeping force for the area, called UNIFIL. As they departed, the Israelis turned their strongholds over to a Christian militia that they had organized, instead of to the UN force.

The second Israeli invasion came on June 6, 1982, after an assassination attempt by Palestinian terrorists on the Israeli ambassador in London. As a base of the PLO, Lebanon became the Israelis' target. Nearly 7,000 Palestinians were dispersed to other Arab nations. The violence seemed to have come to an end when, on Sept. 14, Bashir Gemayel, the 34-year-old president-elect, was killed by a bomb that destroyed the headquarters of his Christian Phalangist Party. Following his assassination, Christian militiamen massacred about 1,000 Palestinians in the Israeli-controlled Sabra and Shatila refugee camps, but Israel denied responsibility.

The massacre in the refugee camps prompted the return of a multinational peacekeeping force. Its mandate was to support the central Lebanese government, but it soon found itself drawn into the struggle for power between different Lebanese factions. The country was engulfed in chaos and instability. During their stay in Lebanon, 241 U.S. Marines and about 60 French soldiers were killed, most of them in suicide bombings of the Marine and French army compounds on Oct. 23, 1983. The multinational force withdrew in the spring of 1984. In 1985, the majority of Israeli troops withdrew from the country, but Israel left some troops along a buffer zone on the southern Lebanese border, where they engaged in ongoing skirmishes with Palestinian groups. The Palestinian terrorist group Hezbollah or "Party of God," was formed in the 1980s during Israel's second invasion of Lebanon. With financial backing from Iran, it has launched attacks against Israel for more than 20 years.

In July 1986, Syrian observers took a position in Beirut to monitor a peacekeeping agreement. The agreement broke down and fighting between Shiite and Druze militia in West Beirut became so intense that Syrian troops mobilized in Feb. 1987, suppressing militia resistance. In 1991 a treaty of friendship was signed with Syria, which in effect gave Syria control over Lebanon's foreign relations. In early 1991, the Lebanese government, backed by Syria, regained control over the south and disbanded various militias, thereby ending the 16-year civil war, which had destroyed much of the infrastructure and industry of Lebanon.

In June 1999, just before Israeli prime minister Benjamin Netanyahu left office, Israel bombed Southern Lebanon, its most severe attack on the country since 1996. In May 2000, Israel's new prime minister, Ehud Barak, withdrew Israeli troops after 18 consecutive years of occupation.

In the summer of 2001, Syria withdrew nearly all of its 25,000 troops from Beirut and surrounding areas. About 15,000 troops, however, remained in the countryside. With the continuation of Israeli-Palestinian violence in 2002, Hezbollah began again building up forces along the Lebanese-Israeli border.

In Aug. 2004, in a stark reminder of Syria's continuing iron grip in Lebanon, Syria insisted that Lebanon's pro-Syrian president, Émile Lahoud, remain in office beyond the constitutional limit of one six-year term. Despite outrage in the country, the Lebanese parliament did Syria's bidding, permitting Lahoud to serve for three more years.

A UN Security Council resolution in Sept. 2004 demanded Syria remove the troops it had stationed in Lebanon for past 28 years. Syria responded by moving about 3,000 troops from the vicinity of Beirut to eastern Lebanon, a gesture that was viewed by many as merely cosmetic.

Lesotho

KINGDOM OF LESOTHO

Sovereign: King Letsie III (1996)
Prime Minister: Pakalitha Mosisili (1998)
Area: 11,720 sq mi (30,355 sq km)
Population (2004 est.): 1,865,040 (growth rate: 0.1%); birth rate: 26.9/1000; infant mortality rate: 85.2/1000; life expectancy: 36.8; density per sq mi: 159
Capital and largest city (2003 est.): Maseru 173,700.
Monetary unit: Maluti. **Languages:** English, Sesotho (both official); Zulu, Xhosa. **Ethnicity/race:** Sotho 99.7%, Europeans, Asians, and other 0.3%.
Religions: Christian 80%, indigenous beliefs 20%.
Literacy rate: 85% (2003 est.)
Economic summary: GDP/PPP (2003 est.): $5.594 billion; per capita $3,000. **Real growth rate:** 4.2%. **Inflation:** 10% (2002 est.). **Unemployment:** 45%

(2002). **Arable land:** 11%. **Agriculture:** corn, wheat, pulses, sorghum, barley; livestock. **Labor force:** 838,000 (2000); 86% of resident population engaged in subsistence agriculture; roughly 35% of the active male wage earners work in South Africa. **Industries:** food, beverages, textiles, apparel assembly, handicrafts; construction; tourism. **Natural resources:** water, agricultural and grazing land, some diamonds and other minerals. **Exports:** $450 million (f.o.b., 2003 est.): manufactures 75% (clothing, footwear, road vehicles), wool and mohair, food and live animals (2000). **Imports:** $661 million (f.o.b., 2003 est.): food; building materials, vehicles, machinery, medicines, petroleum products (2000). **Major trading partners:** U.S., Canada, France, Hong Kong, China. **Member of Commonwealth of Nations**

Geography Mountainous Lesotho, the size of Maryland, is surrounded by the Republic of South Africa.

Government Parliamentary constitutional monarchy.

History Lesotho (formerly Basutoland) was constituted a native state under British protection by a treaty signed with the native chief Moshoeshoe in 1843. It was annexed to Cape Colony in 1871, but in 1884 it was restored to direct control by the Crown. The colony of Basutoland became the independent nation of Lesotho on Oct. 4, 1966, with King Moshoeshoe II as sovereign.

In the 1970 elections, Ntsu Mokhehle, head of the Basutoland Congress Party, claimed a victory, but Prime Minister Leabua Jonathan declared a state of emergency, suspended the constitution, and arrested Mokhehle. King Moshoeshoe II returned after a compromise with Jonathan in which the new constitution would name him head of state but forbid his participation in politics.

After the king refused to approve the replacement in Feb. 1990 of individuals dismissed by Justin Metsino Lekhanya, the chairman of the Military Council, the latter stripped the king of his executive power. Then in early March, Lekhanya sent the king into exile. In November, the king was dethroned, and his son was sworn in as King Letsie III.

Lekhanya was himself forced to resign in April 1991, and Col. Ramaema became the new chairman in May. In Jan. 1995, the crown reverted to the father of Letsie III, Moshoeshoe II. Letsie again became crown prince. In 1996, however, King Moshoeshoe died in an automobile accident, and Letsie again assumed the throne.

In fall 1998, hundreds of demonstrators protested for weeks in front of the king's palace, claiming voting fraud in the May elections that put Prime Minister Pakalitha Mosisili in power. They demanded that the government step down and hold new elections. Troops from South Africa and Botswana entered the country to stop the riots and put down an army mutiny.

Lesotho faces one of the highest rates of HIV infection in the world, leading some demographers to predict that the country's population could begin declining in several years if current trends continue.

Liberia

REPUBLIC OF LIBERIA

President: Gyude Bryant (2003)
Area: 43,000 sq mi (111,370 sq km)
Population (2004 est.): 3,390,635 (growth rate: 2.7%); birth rate: 44.8/1000; infant mortality rate: 130.5/1000; life expectancy: 47.9; density per sq mi: 79
Capital and largest city (2003 est.): Monrovia, 1,348,900 (metro. area), 550,200 (city proper).
Monetary unit: Liberian dollar. **Languages:** English

20% (official), some 20 ethnic-group languages. **Ethnicity/race:** indigenous African tribes 95% (including Kpelle, Bassa, Gio, Kru, Grebo, Mano, Krahn, Gola, Gbandi, Loma, Kissi, Vai, Bella, Mandingo, and Mende), Americo-Liberians 2.5% (descendants of former U.S. slaves), Congo People 2.5% (descendants of former Caribbean slaves). **Religions:** traditional 40%, Christian 40%, Islam 20%. **Literacy rate:** 58% (2003 est.)
Economic summary: GDP/PPP (2003 est.): $3.261 billion; per capita $1,000. **Real growth rate:** 3%. **Inflation:** 15%. **Unemployment:** 85%. **Arable land:** 2%. **Agriculture:** rubber, coffee, cocoa, rice, cassava (tapioca), palm oil, sugarcane, bananas; sheep, goats; timber. **Labor force:** agriculture 70%, industry 8%, services 22% (2000 est.). **Industries:** rubber processing, palm oil processing, timber, diamonds. **Natural resources:** iron ore, timber, diamonds, gold, hydropower. **Exports:** $1.079 billion (f.o.b., 2003 est.): rubber, timber, iron, diamonds, cocoa, coffee. **Imports:** $5.051 billion (f.o.b., 2003 est.): fuels, chemicals, machinery, transportation equipment, manufactured goods; foodstuffs. **Major trading partners:** Germany, Poland, France, China, Italy, U.S., South Korea, Japan, Singapore.

Geography Lying on the Atlantic in the southern part of West Africa, Liberia is bordered by Sierra Leone, Guinea, and Côte d'Ivoire. It is comparable in size to Tennessee. Most of the country is a plateau covered by dense tropical forests, which thrive under an annual rainfall of about 160 in. a year.

Government Republic.

History Africa's first republic, Liberia was founded in 1822 as a result of the efforts of the American Colonization Society to settle freed American slaves in West Africa. The society contended that the immigration of blacks to Africa was an answer to the problem of slavery as well as to what it felt was the incompatibility of the races. Over the course of forty years, about 12,000 slaves were voluntarily relocated. Originally called Monrovia, the colony became the Free and Independent Republic of Liberia in 1847.

The English-speaking Americo-Liberians, descendants of former American slaves, make up only 5% of the population, but have historically dominated the intellectual and ruling class. Liberia's indigenous population is composed of 16 different ethnic groups.

The government of Africa's first republic was modeled after that of the United States, and Joseph Jenkins Roberts of Virginia was elected the first president. Ironically, Liberia's constitution denied indigenous Liberians equal rights with the lighter-skinned American emigrants and their descendants.

After 1920, considerable progress was made toward opening up the interior, a process that was speeded in 1951 by the establishment of a 43-mile (69-km) railroad to the Bomi Hills from Monrovia. In July 1971, while serving his sixth term as president, William V. S. Tubman died following surgery and was succeeded by his long-time associate, Vice President William R. Tolbert, Jr.

Tolbert was ousted in a military coup on April 12, 1980, by Master Sgt. Samuel K. Doe, backed by the U.S. government. Doe's rule was characterized by corruption and brutality. A rebellion led by Charles Taylor, a former Doe aide, and the National Patriotic Front of Liberia (NPFL), started in Dec. 1989; the following year, Doe was assassinated. The Economic Community of West African States (ECOWAS) negotiated with the government and the rebel factions and attempted to restore order, but the civil war raged on.

By April 1996, factional fighting by the country's warlords had destroyed any last vestige of normalcy and civil society. The civil war finally ended in 1997.

In what was considered by international observers to be a free election, Charles Taylor won 75% of the presidential vote in July 1997. The country had next to no health care system, and the capital was without electricity and running water. Taylor supported Sierra Leone's brutal Revolutionary United Front (RUF) in the hopes of toppling his neighbor's government, and in exchange for diamonds, which enriched his personal coffers. As a consequence, the UN issued sanctions.

In 2002, rebels—Liberians United for Reconciliation and Democracy (LURD)—intensified their attacks on Taylor's government. By June 2003, LURD and other rebel groups controlled two-thirds of the country. Finally, on Aug. 11, Taylor stepped down and went into exile in Nigeria. Gyude Bryant, a businessman seen as a coalition-builder, was selected by the various factions as the new president. By the time he was exiled, Taylor had bankrupted his own country, siphoning off $100 million. According to the *New York Times,* Taylor left Liberia the world's poorest nation. In 2004, international donors promised more that $500 million in aid.

Libya

SOCIALIST PEOPLE'S LIBYAN ARAB JAMAHIRIYA

Chief of State: Col. Muammar al-Qaddafi (1969)
Prime Minister: Mubarak Abdallah al-Shamikh (2000)
Area: 679,358 sq mi (1,759,540 sq km)
Population (2004 est.): 5,631,585 (growth rate: 2.4%); birth rate: 27.2/1000; infant mortality rate: 25.7/1000; life expectancy: 76.3; density per sq mi: 8
Capital and largest city (2003 est.): Tripoli, 2,357,800 (metro. area), 1,269,700 (city proper). **Other large city:**Benghazi, 734,900. **Monetary unit:** Libyan dinar.
Languages: Arabic, Italian and English widely understood in major cities. **Ethnicity/race:** Berber and Arab 97%, Greeks, Maltese, Italians, Egyptians, Pakistanis, Turks, Indians, Tunisians. **Religion:** Islam (Sunni) 97%. **Literacy rate:** 83% (2003 est.)
Economic summary: GDP/PPP (2003 est.): $35 billion; per capita $6,400. **Real growth rate:** 3.2%. **Inflation:** 2.8%. **Unemployment:** 30% (2001). **Arable land:** 1%. **Agriculture:** wheat, barley, olives, dates, citrus, vegetables, peanuts, soybeans; cattle. **Labor force:** 1.6 million (2001 est.); services and government 54%, industry 29%, agriculture 17% (1997 est.). **Industries:** petroleum, food processing, textiles, handicrafts, cement. **Natural resources:** petroleum, natural gas, gypsum. **Exports:** $14.32 billion (f.o.b., 2003 est.): crude oil, refined petroleum products. **Imports:** $6.282 billion (f.o.b., 2003 est.): machinery, transport equipment, food, manufactured goods. **Major trading partners:** Italy, Germany, Spain, Turkey, Switzerland, South Korea, UK, Tunisia, Japan, France.

Geography Libya stretches along the northeast coast of Africa between Tunisia and Algeria on the west and Egypt on the east; to the south are the Sudan, Chad, and Niger. It is one-sixth larger than Alaska. A greater part of the country lies within the Sahara. Along the Mediterranean coast and farther inland is arable plateau land.

Government Military dictatorship.

History The first inhabitants of Libya were Berber tribes. In the 7th century B.C., Phoenicians colonized the eastern section of Libya, called Cyrenaica, and Greeks colonized the western portion, called Tripolitania. Tripolitania was for a time under Carthaginian control. It became part of the Roman Empire from 46 B.C. to A.D. 436, after which it was sacked by the Vandals. Cyrenaica belonged to the Roman Empire from the 1st century B.C. until its decline, after which it was invaded by Arab forces in 642. Beginning in the 16th century, both Tripolitania and Cyrenaica nominally became part of the Ottoman Empire.

Tripolitania was one of the outposts for the Barbary pirates who raided Mediterranean merchant ships or required them to pay tribute. In 1801, the pasha of Tripoli raised the price of tribute, which led to the Tripolitan war with the United States. When the peace treaty was signed on June 4, 1805, U.S. ships no longer had to pay tribute to Tripoli.

Following the outbreak of hostilities between Italy and Turkey in 1911, Italian troops occupied Tripoli. Italian sovereignty was recognized in 1912. Libyans continued to fight the Italians until 1914, by which time Italy controlled most of the land. Italy formally united Tripolitania and Cyrenaica in 1934 as the colony of Libya.

Libya was the scene of much desert fighting during World War II. After the fall of Tripoli on Jan. 23, 1943, it came under Allied administration. In 1949, the UN voted that Libya should become independent, and in 1951 it became the United Kingdom of Libya. Oil was discovered in the impoverished country in 1958, and eventually transformed its economy.

On Sept. 1, 1969, 27-year-old Col. Muammar al-Qaddafi deposed the king and revolutionized the country, making it a pro-Arabic, anti-Western, Islamic republic with socialist leanings. It was also rabidly anti-Israeli. A notorious firebrand, Qaddafi aligned himself with dictators, such as Uganda's Idi Amin, and fostered anti-Western terrorism.

On Aug. 19, 1981, two U.S. Navy F-14s shot down two Soviet-made SU-22s of the Libyan air force that had attacked them in air space above the Gulf of Sidra. On March 24, 1986, U.S. and Libyan forces skirmished in the Gulf of Sidra, and two Libyan patrol boats were sunk. Qaddafi's troops also supported rebels in Chad but suffered major military reverses in 1987. A two-year-old U.S. covert policy to destabilize the Libyan government ended in failure in Dec. 1990.

On Dec. 21, 1988, a Boeing 747 exploded in flight over Lockerbie, Scotland, the result of a terrorist bomb, killing all 259 people aboard and 11 on the ground. This and other acts of terrorism, including the bombing of a Berlin discoteque in 1986, and the downing of a French UTA airliner in 1989 that killed 170, turned Libya into a pariah in the eyes of the west. Two Libyan intelligence agents were indicted in the Lockerbie bombing, but Qaddafi refused to hand them over, leading to UN-approved trade and air traffic embargoes in 1992. In 1999, Libya finally surrendered the two men, who were tried in the Netherlands in 2000–2001. One was found guilty of mass murder; the other defendant was found innocent. Libya had hoped its faint-hearted cooperation would lead to suspended sanctions, which had severely affected the Libyan economy. The UN did suspend its sanctions, but they were not formally removed for another four years, until Sept. 2003, when Libya finally admitted its guilt in the Lockerbie bombing and agreed to pay $2.7 billion to the families. In 2004, Libya also agreed to compensate the families of the victims of the UTA airliner bombing ($170 million) and the Berlin disco bombing ($35 million).

After months of secret talks with the U.S. and Britain, Qaddafi surprised the world in Dec. 2003 by announcing he would give up the pursuit of weapons of mass destruction and submit to full UN weapons inspections. After inspections at four secret sites, the International Atomic Energy Agency concluded that

Libya's progress on a nuclear bomb had been in the very nascent stages. In June 2004, the U.S. and Libya restored diplomatic relations after a 24-year hiatus.

Liechtenstein

PRINCIPALITY OF LIECHTENSTEIN

Ruler: Prince Hans Adam II (1989)
Head of Government: Otmar Hasler (2001)
Area: 62 sq mi (160 sq km)
Population (2004 est.): 33,436 (growth rate: –0.3%); birth rate: 8.5/1000; infant mortality rate: 4.8/1000; life expectancy: 79.4; density per sq mi: 541
Capital and largest city (2003 est.): Vaduz, 5,300.
Monetary unit: Swiss franc. **Languages:** German (official), Alemannic dialect. **Ethnicity/race:** Alemannic 86%; Italian, Turkish, and other 14%. **Religions:** Roman Catholic, 76.2%, Protestant, 7%; unknown, 10.6%; other, 6.2% (2002). **Literacy rate:** 100% (1981 est.)
Economic summary: GDP/PPP (1999 est.): $825 million; per capita $25,000. **Real growth rate:** 11%. **Inflation:** 1% (2001). **Unemployment:** 1.3% (Sept. 2002). **Arable land:** 25%. **Agriculture:** wheat, barley, corn, potatoes; livestock, dairy products. **Labor force:** 29,000 of whom 19,000 are foreigners; 13,000 commute from Austria, Switzerland, and Germany to work each day (Dec. 2001); industry 47.4%, services 51.3%, agriculture 1.3%. **Industries:** electronics, metal manufacturing, dental products, ceramics, pharmaceuticals, food products, precision instruments, tourism, optical instruments. **Natural resources:** hydroelectric potential, arable land. **Exports:** $2.47 billion (1996): small specialty machinery, connectors for audio and video, parts for motor vehicles, dental products, hardware, prepared foodstuffs, electronic equipment, optical products. **Imports:** $917.3 million (1996): agricultural products, raw materials, machinery, metal goods, textiles, foodstuffs, motor vehicles. **Major trading partners:** EU, U.S., Switzerland.

Geography Tiny Liechtenstein, not quite as large as Washington, DC, lies on the east bank of the Rhine River south of Lake Constance between Austria and Switzerland. It consists of low valley land and Alpine peaks. Falknis (8,401 ft; 2,561 m) and Naafkopf (8,432 ft; 2,570 m) are the tallest.

Government Hereditary constitutional monarchy.

History The Liechtensteiners are descended from the Alemanni tribe that came into the region after A.D. 500. Founded in 1719, Liechtenstein was a member of the German Confederation from 1815 to 1866, when it became an independent principality. It abolished its army in 1868 and has managed to stay neutral and undamaged in all European wars since then. Liechtenstein still claims 1,600 sq km of Czech territory (the royal family's ancestral home) confiscated in 1918; the Czech Republic insists that restitution does not go back before Feb. 1948, when the Communists seized power. In a referendum on July 1, 1984, male voters granted women the right to vote in national (but not local) elections. A treaty negotiated between EFTA (European Free Trade Association) and the EU linking the two as the European Economic Area was ratified by Liechtenstein in a Dec. 1993 vote, but Switzerland rejected it. After renegotiation the treaty was again subjected to a referendum in April 1995 and approved. Liechtenstein won a special concession limiting immigration.

Blacklisted in 2000 as a center for money laundering, Liechtenstein toughened its laws and made major efforts to clean up its financial practices. In 2002, the country was removed from the OECD's (Organization of Economic Cooperation and Development's) money-laundering blacklist.

In March 2003, Liechtenstein's people overwhelmingly voted to give its prince more powers, including the right to dismiss governments and approve judicial nominees. Prince Hans Adam II had threatened to leave the country if his demands for more authority were not met. Before the vote, he had already possessed more power than any other European monarch.

In Aug. 2003 he announced that he would give up the day-to-day ruling of the country in one year's time. In Aug. 2004, his son, Prince Alois, 36, was handed the reins, while Hans Adam II remained the official head of state. The move is a precursor to succession.

Lithuania

REPUBLIC OF LITHUANIA

National name: Lietuva
President: Valdas Adamkus (2004)
Prime Minister: Algirdas Brazauskas (2001)
Area: 25,174 sq mi (65,200 sq km)
Population (2004 est.): 3,607,899 (growth rate: –0.2%); birth rate: 10.8/1000; infant mortality rate: 7.1/1000; life expectancy: 73.5; density per sq mi: 143
Capital and largest city (2003 est.): Vilnius, 543,500.
Other large cities: Kaunas, 379,800; Klaipėda, 193,400. **Monetary unit:** Litas. **Languages:** Lithuanian (official), Polish, Russian. **Ethnicity/race:** Lithuanian 80.6%, Russian 8.7%, Polish 7%, Belorussian 1.6%, other 2.1%. **Religions:** Roman Catholic (primarily); others include Lutheran, Russian Orthodox, Protestant, evangelical Christian Baptist, Islam, Judaism. **Literacy:** 100% (2003 est.)
Economic summary: GDP/PPP (2003 est.): $40.17 billion; per capita $11,200. **Real growth rate:** 7.1%. **Inflation:** –1%. **Unemployment:** 10.7%. **Arable land:** 45%. **Agriculture:** grain, potatoes, sugar beets, flax, vegetables; beef, milk, eggs; fish. **Labor force:** 1.5 million (2001 est); industry 30%, agriculture 20%, services 50% (1997 est.). **Industries:** metal-cutting machine tools, electric motors, television sets, refrigerators and freezers, petroleum refining, shipbuilding (small ships), furniture making, textiles, food processing, fertilizers, agricultural machinery, optical equipment, electronic components, computers, amber. **Natural resources:** peat, arable land. **Exports:** $7.89 billion (f.o.b., 2003 est.): mineral products 23%, textiles and clothing 16%, machinery and equipment 11%, chemicals 6%, wood and wood products 5%, foodstuffs 5%. **Imports:** $9.2 billion (f.o.b., 2003 est.): mineral products 21%, machinery and equipment 17%, transport equipment 11%, chemicals 9%, textiles and clothing 9%, metals 5% (2001). **Major trading partners:** Latvia, Germany, UK, Poland, U.S., France, Russia, Sweden, Denmark, Italy.

Geography Lithuania is situated on the eastern shore of the Baltic Sea and borders Latvia on the north, Belarus on the east and south, and Poland and the Kaliningrad region of Russia on the southwest. It is a country of gently rolling hills, many forests, rivers and streams, and lakes. Its principal natural resource is agricultural land.

Government Parliamentary democracy.

History The Liths, or Lithuanians, united in the 12th century under the rule of Mindaugas, who became king in 1251. Through marriage, one of the later Lithuanian rulers became the king of Poland (Ladislaus II) in 1386, uniting the countries. In 1410, the Poles and Lithuanians defeated the powerful Teutonic Knights at Tannenberg. From the 14th to the 16th century, Poland and Lithuania made up one of medieval

Europe's largest empires, stretching from the Black Sea almost to Moscow. The two countries formed a confederation for almost 200 years, and in 1569 they formally united. Russia, Prussia, and Austria partitioned Poland in 1772, 1792, and 1795. As a consequence, Lithuania came under Russian rule after the last partition. Russia attempted to immerse Lithuania in Russian culture and language, but anti-Russian sentiment continued to grow. Following World War I and the collapse of Russia, Lithuania declared independence (1918), under German protection.

The republic was then annexed by the Soviet Union in 1940. From June 1941 to 1944, it was occupied by German troops, with whom Lithuania served in World War II. Some 240,000 Jews were massacred in Lithuania during the Nazi years. In 1944, the Soviets again annexed Lithuania.

The Lithuanian independence movement reemerged in 1988. In 1990, Vytautas Landsbergis, the non-Communist head of the largest Lithuanian popular movement (Sajudis), was elected president. On the same day, the Supreme Council rejected Soviet rule and declared the restoration of Lithuania's independence, the first Baltic republic to take this action. Confrontation with the Soviet Union ensued along with economic sanctions, but they were lifted after both sides agreed to a face-saving compromise.

Lithuania's independence was quickly recognized by major European and other nations, including the United States. The Soviet Union finally recognized the independence of the Baltic states on Sept. 6, 1991. UN admittance followed on Sept. 17, 1991. Successful implementation of structural and legislative reforms in Lithuania attracted greater foreign direct investments by the mid-1990s.

In late 2002, Lithuania was accepted for membership in the EU and NATO, and it joined both in 2004. In Jan. 2003 Rolandas Paksas defeated the incumbent, Valdas Adamkus, in the presidential election. It was a surprising upset, given that Adamkus had helped bring about his country's entry into NATO and the European Union. In April 2004, President Paksas was removed from office after his conviction for dealings with Russian mobsters. It was Lithuania's worst political crisis since independence from the Soviet Union. In July 2004, Valdas Adamkus was again elected president.

Luxembourg

GRAND DUCHY OF LUXEMBOURG

National name: Grand-Duché de Luxembourg
Ruler: Grand Duke Henri (2000)
Premier: Jean-Claude Juncker (1995)
Area: 998 sq mi (2,586 sq km)
Population (2004 est.): 462,690 (growth rate: 1.3%); birth rate: 12.2/1000; infant mortality rate: 4.9/1000; life expectancy: 78.6; density per sq mi: 463
Capital and largest city (2003 est.): Luxembourg, 78,800. **Monetary units:** Euro (formerly Luxembourg franc). **Languages:** Luxermbourgish (national) French, German (both administrative). **Ethnicity/race:** Celtic base (with French and German blend), Portuguese, Italian, Slavs (from Montenegro, Albania, and Kosovo), and European (guest and worker residents).
Religions: Roman Catholic 87%; Protestant, Jewish, Islamic 13% (2000). **Literacy rate:** 100% (2003 est.)
Economic summary: GDP/PPP (2003 est.): $25.01 billion; per capita $55,100. **Real growth rate:** 1.2%. **Inflation:** 2%. **Unemployment:** 3%. **Arable land:** 25%. **Agriculture:** barley, oats, potatoes, wheat, fruits, wine grapes; livestock products. **Labor force:** 262,300 (of whom 87,400 are foreign cross-border workers primarily from France, Belgium, and Germany) (2000);

services 90.1%, industry 8%, agriculture 1.9% (1999 est.). **Industries:** banking, iron and steel, food processing, chemicals, metal products, engineering, tires, glass, aluminum. **Natural resources:** iron ore (no longer exploited), arable land. **Exports:** $8.571 billion (f.o.b., 2002): machinery and equipment, steel products, chemicals, rubber products, glass. **Imports:** $11.61 billion (c.i.f., 2002): minerals, metals, foodstuffs, quality consumer goods. **Major trading partners:** Germany, France, Belgium, UK, Italy, Spain, Netherlands, Taiwan.

Geography Luxembourg is about half the size of Delaware. The Ardennes Mountains extend from Belgium into the northern section of Luxembourg. The rolling plateau of the fertile Bon Pays is in the south.

Government Constitutional monarchy.

History Luxembourg, once part of Charlemagne's empire, became an independent state in 963, when Siegfried, count of Ardennes, became sovereign of Lucilinburhuc ("Little Fortress"). In 1060, Conrad, a descendant of Siegfried, took the title count of Luxembourg. From the 15th to the 18th century, Spain, France, and Austria held the duchy in turn. The Congress of Vienna in 1815 made it a Grand Duchy and gave it to William I, king of the Netherlands. In 1839, the Treaty of London ceded the western part of Luxembourg to Belgium. The eastern part, continuing in personal union with the Netherlands and a member of the German Confederation, became autonomous in 1848 and a neutral territory by decision of the London Conference of 1867, governed by its grand duke. Germany occupied the duchy in World Wars I and II. Allied troops liberated the enclave in 1944.

Luxembourg joined NATO in 1949, the Benelux Economic Union (with Belgium and the Netherlands) in 1948, and the European Economic Community (later the EU) in 1957. In 1961, Prince Jean, son and heir of Grand Duchess Charlotte, was made head of state, acting for his mother. She abdicated in 1964, and Prince Jean became grand duke. Grand Duchess Charlotte died in 1985. Luxembourg's Parliament approved the Maastricht Accord, paving the way for the economic unity of the EU in July 1992. Crown Prince Henri was sworn in as grand duke in Oct. 2000, replacing his father, Jean, who had been head of state for 26 years. In 2002, the euro became the country's new currency.

Macedonia

REPUBLIC OF MACEDONIA[1]

National Name: Republika Makedonija
President: Branko Crvenkovski (2004)
Prime Minister: Hari Kostov (2004)
Area: 9,928 sq mi (25,713 sq km)
Population (2004 est.): 2,071,210 (growth rate: 0.4%); birth rate: 13.1/1000; infant mortality rate: 11.7/1000; life expectancy: 74.7; density per sq mi: 212
Capital and largest city (2003 est.): Skopje, 587,300 (metro. area), 452,500 (city proper). **Other large cities:** Bitola, 84,400; Kumanovo, 78,900; Prilep, 56,900. **Monetary unit:** Denar. **Languages:** Macedonian 68%, Albanian 25% (both official); Turkish 3%, Serbo-Croatian 2%, other 2%. **Ethnicity/race:** Macedonian 64.2%, Albanian 25.2%, Turkish 3.8%, Roma (Gypsy) 2.7%, Serb 1.8%, other 2.3% (2002). **Religions:** Macedonian Orthodox 70%, Islam 29%, other 1% (1994)
Economic summary: GDP/PPP (2003 est.): $13.81 billion; per capita $6,700. **Real growth rate:** 2.8%. **Inflation:** –2.6%. **Unemployment:** 36.7%. **Arable**

land: 24%. **Agriculture:** rice, tobacco, wheat, corn, millet, cotton, sesame, mulberry leaves, citrus, vegetables; beef, pork, poultry, mutton. **Labor force:** 860,000; agriculture n.a., industry n.a., services n.a. **Industries:** coal, metallic chromium, lead, zinc, ferronickel, textiles, wood products, tobacco, food processing, buses. **Natural resources:** chromium, lead, zinc, manganese, tungsten, nickel, low-grade iron ore, asbestos, sulfur, timber, arable land. **Exports:** $1.346 billion (f.o.b., 2003 est.): food, beverages, tobacco; miscellaneous manufactures, iron and steel. **Imports:** $2.184 billion (f.o.b., 2003 est.): machinery and equipment, chemicals, fuels; food products. **Major trading partners:** Germany, Italy, U.S., Croatia, Greece, Bulgaria, Slovenia, Turkey, Ukraine, Austria.

1. The UN recognized the Republic of Macedonia on April 8, 1993, under the temporary name the Former Yugoslav Republic of Macedonia. The U.S. recognized Macedonia as a state in Feb. 1994.

Geography Macedonia is a landlocked state in the heart of the Balkans and is slightly smaller than the state of Vermont. It is a mountainous country with small basins of agricultural land. The Vardar is the largest and most important river.

Government Parliamentary democracy.

History The Republic of Macedonia occupies the western half of the ancient Kingdom of Macedonia. Historic Macedonia was defeated by Rome and became a Roman province in 148 B.C. After the Roman Empire was divided in A.D. 395, Macedonia was intermittently ruled by the Byzantine Empire until Turkey took possession of the land in 1371. The Ottoman Turks dominated Macedonia for the next five centuries, until 1913. During the 19th and 20th centuries, there was a constant struggle by the Balkan powers to possess Macedonia for its economic wealth and its strategic military corridors. The Treaty of San Stefano in 1878, ending the Russo-Turkish War, gave the largest part of Macedonia to Bulgaria. Bulgaria lost much of its Macedonian territory when it was defeated by the Greeks and Serbs in the Second Balkan War of 1913. Most of Macedonia went to Serbia and the remainder was divided among Greece and Bulgaria.

In 1918, Serbia, which included much of Macedonia, joined in union with Croatia, Slovenia, and Montenegro to form the Kingdom of Serbs, Croats, and Slovenes, which was renamed Yugoslavia in 1929. Bulgaria joined the Axis powers in World War II and occupied parts of Yugoslavia, including Macedonia, in 1941. During the occupation of their country, Macedonian resistance fighters fought a guerrilla war against the invading troops. The Yugoslavian federation was reestablished after the defeat of Germany in 1945, and in 1946, the government removed the Vardar territory of Macedonia from Serbian control and made it an autonomous Yugoslavian republic. Later, when President Tito recognized the Macedonian people as a separate nation, Macedonia's distinct culture and language were able to flourish, no longer suppressed by outside rule.

On Sept. 8, 1991, Macedonia declared its independence from Yugoslavia and asked for recognition from the European Union nations. It became a member of the UN in 1993 under the provisional name of the Former Yugoslav Republic of Macedonia (FYROM) because Greece vociferously protested Macedonia's right to the name, which is also the name of a large northern province of Greece. To Greece, the use of the name implies Macedonia's interest in territorial expansion into the Greek province. Greece has imposed two trade embargoes against the country as a result.

Tensions between ethnic Albanians and Macedonians continued to rise during the Kosovo crisis, during which more than 140,000 refugees streamed into the country from neighboring Kosovo. Most of the refugees returned to Kosovo in 2000.

The long-simmering resentment of Macedonia's ethnic Albanians erupted into violence in March 2001, prompting the government to send troops into the heavily Albanian western section of the country. The rebels sought greater autonomy within Macedonia. In Aug. 2001, after six months of fighting, the rebels and the Macedonian government signed a peace agreement that allowed a British-led NATO force to enter the country and disarm the guerrillas. In Nov. 2001, Macedonia's Parliament agreed to constitutional amendments giving broader rights to its Albanian minority. Albanian became one of the country's two official languages.

In Sept. 2002 elections, a center-left coalition ousted the governing coalition, which had been embroiled in previous years' guerrilla insurgency. Branko Crvenkovski of the Together for Macedonia coalition became the new prime minister. In Feb. 2004, President Boris Trajkovski was killed in a plane crash. Prime Minister Crvenkovski was then elected president, and former Interior Minister Hari Kostov became prime minister.

Madagascar

REPUBLIC OF MADAGASCAR

National name: Repoblikan'i Madagasikara
President: Marc Ravalomanana (2002)
Prime Minister: Jacques Sylla (2002)
Area: 226,656 sq mi (587,040 sq km)
Population (2004 est.): 17,501,871 (growth rate: 3.0%); birth rate: 41.9/1000; infant mortality rate: 78.5/1000; life expectancy: 56.5; density per sq mi: 77
Capital and largest city (2003 est.): Antananarivo, 1,390,800. **Monetary unit:** Malagasy franc.
  Languages: Malagasy and French (both official).
Ethnicity/race: Malayo-Indonesian (Merina and related Betsileo), Cotiers (mixed African, Malayo-Indonesian, and Arab ancestry— Betsimisaraka, Tsimihety, Antaisaka, Sakalava), French, Indian, Creole, Comoran. **Religions:** indigenous beliefs 52%, Christian 41%, Islam 7%. **Literacy rate:** 69% (2003 est.)
Economic summary: GDP/PPP (2003 est.): $13.02 billion; per capita $800. **Real growth rate:** 6%. **Inflation:** 3.5%. **Unemployment:** 5.9% (1998). **Arable land:** 4%. **Agriculture:** coffee, vanilla, sugarcane, cloves, cocoa, rice, cassava (tapioca), beans, bananas, peanuts; livestock products. **Labor force:** 7.3 million (2000). **Industries:** meat processing, soap, breweries, tanneries, sugar, textiles, glassware, cement, automobile assembly plant, paper, petroleum, tourism. **Natural resources:** graphite, chromite, coal, bauxite, salt, quartz, tar sands, semiprecious stones, mica, fish, hydropower. **Exports:** $700 million (f.o.b., 2003 est.): coffee, vanilla, shellfish, sugar; cotton cloth, chromite, petroleum products. **Imports:** $920 million (f.o.b., 2003 est.): capital goods, petroleum, consumer goods, food. **Major trading partners:** France, U.S., Netherlands, Germany, Mauritius, Iran, Bahrain, Hong Kong, South Africa, China.

Geography Madagascar lies in the Indian Ocean off the southeast coast of Africa opposite Mozambique. The world's fourth-largest island, it is twice the size of Arizona. The country's low-lying coastal area gives way to a central plateau. The once densely wooded interior has largely been cut down.

Government Multiparty republic.

History The Malagasy are of mixed Malayo-Indonesian and African-Arab ancestry. Indonesians are believed to have migrated to the island about 700. King Andrianampoinimerina (1787–1810), ruled the major kingdom on the island, and his son, Radama I (1810–1828), unified much of the island. The French made the island a protectorate in 1885, and then, in 1894–1895, ended the monarchy, exiling Queen Rànavàlona III to Algiers. A colonial administration was set up, to which the Comoro Islands were attached in 1908, and other territories later. In World War II, the British occupied Madagascar, which retained ties to Vichy France.

An autonomous republic within the French Community since 1958, Madagascar became an independent member of the community in 1960. In May 1973, an army coup led by Maj. Gen. Gabriel Ramanantsoa ousted Philibert Tsiranana, president since 1959. Comdr. Didier Ratsiraka, named president on June 15, 1975, announced that he would follow a socialist course and, after nationalizing banks and insurance companies, declared all mineral resources nationalized. Repression and censorship characterized his regime. Ratsiraka was reelected in 1989 in a suspicious election that led to riots as well as the formation of a multiparty system in 1990. In 1991, Ratsiraka agreed to share power with the democratically minded opposition leader, Albert Zafy, who then overwhelmingly won the presidential elections in Feb. 1993. But Zafy was impeached by Parliament for abusing his constitutional powers during an economic crisis and lost the 1996 presidential election to Ratsiraka, who became president in Feb. 1997.

The Dec. 2001 presidential election between incumbent president Didier Ratsiraka and Marc Ravalomanana, the mayor of Antananarivo, proved inconclusive and a run-off vote was scheduled. But Ravalomanana claimed the election was rigged, and on Feb. 22, 2002, declared himself president. In response, Ratsiraka declared martial law and set up a rival capital in Toamasina, and Madagascar in effect found itself with two presidents and two capitals. After a recount in April, the High Constitutional Court declared Ravalomanana was the winner with 51.5% of the vote. Ratsiraka, however, refused to accept the outcome, but eventually fled to France in July, and Madagascar's six-month civil war ended.

In early 2004, tropical cyclones devastated parts of the island; thousands were left homeless.

Malawi

REPUBLIC OF MALAWI

President: Bingu wa Mutharika (2004)
Area: 45,745 sq mi (118,480 sq km)
Population (2004 est.): 11,906,855 (growth rate: 2.1%); birth rate: 44.4/1000; infant mortality rate: 104.2/1000; life expectancy: 37.5; density per sq mi: 260
Capital (2003 est.): Lilongwe, 499,200. **Largest city:** Blantyre, 547,500. **Monetary unit:** Kwacha.
Languages: English and Chichewa (both official), others important regionally. **Ethnicity/race:** Chewa, Nyanja, Tumbuko, Yao, Lomwe, Sena, Tonga, Ngoni, Ngonde, Asian, European. **Religions:** Protestant 55%, Roman Catholic 20%, Islam 20%, indigenous beliefs 3%, other 2%. **Literacy rate:** 63% (2003 est.)
Economic summary: GDP/PPP (2003 est.): $6.845 billion; per capita $600. **Real growth rate:** 1.7%. **Inflation:** 27.4% (2001 est.). **Unemployment:** n.a. **Arable land:** 20%. **Agriculture:** tobacco, sugarcane, cotton, tea, corn, potatoes, cassava (tapioca), sorghum, pulses; groundnuts, Macadamia nuts; cattle, goats. **Labor force:** 4.5 million (2001 est.); agriculture

86% (1997 est.). **Industries:** tobacco, tea, sugar, sawmill products, cement, consumer goods. **Natural resources:** limestone, arable land, hydropower, unexploited deposits of uranium, coal, and bauxite.
Exports: $455 million (f.o.b., 2003 est.): tobacco, tea, sugar, cotton, coffee, peanuts, wood products, apparel.
Imports: $505 million (f.o.b., 2003 est.): food, petroleum products, semimanufactures, consumer goods, transportation equipment. **Major trading partners:** U.S., Germany, South AFrica, Egypt, Japan, Netherlands, Russia, UK, Zambia, India. **Member of Commonwealth of Nations**

Geography Malawi is a landlocked country about the size of Pennsylvania. Located in southeast Africa, it is surrounded by Mozambique, Zambia, and Tanzania. Lake Malawi, formerly Lake Nyasa, occupies most of the country's eastern border. The north-south Rift Valley is flanked by mountain ranges and high plateau areas.

Government Multiparty democracy.

History Early human inhabitants of what is now Malawi date to 8000–2000 B.C. Bantu-speaking peoples migrated there between the 1st and 4th centuries A.D. A large slave trade took place in the 18th and 19th centuries and brought Islam to the region. At the same time, missionaries introduced Christianity. Several major kingdoms were established in the precolonial period: the Maravi in 1480, the Ngonde in 1600, and the Chikulamayembe in the 18th century.

The first European to make extensive explorations in the area was David Livingstone in the 1850s and 1860s. In 1884, Cecil Rhodes's British South African Company received a charter to develop the country. The company came into conflict with the Arab slavers in 1887–1889. Britain annexed what was then called the Nyasaland territory in 1891 and made it a protectorate in 1892. Sir Harry Johnstone, the first high commissioner, used Royal Navy gunboats to wipe out the slavers.

Between 1951 and 1953, Britain combined Nyasaland with the colonies of Northern and Southern Rhodesia to form a federation, a move protested by black Africans who were wary of alignment with the ultra conservative white-minority rule in South Rhodesia. On July 6, 1964, Nyasaland became the independent nation of Malawi. Two years later, it became a republic within the Commonwealth of Nations. Dr. Hastings K. Banda became Malawi's first prime minister (a title later changed to president). In his first month as ruler, he declared, "one party, one leader, one government, and no nonsense about it." In 1971, he became president for life, further consolidating his authoritarian rule. In addition to allowing former colonialists to retain considerable power in the country, he maintained warm relations with the white-minority government of South Africa. These policies drew heavy criticism from citizens of Malawi and other African nations. In 1992, Banda faced violent protests.

Bakili Muluzi of the United Democratic Front (UDF) won the country's first free election in May 1994, ending Banda's 30-year rule. In 1999, Muluzi was reelected. While Malawi was no longer the repressive society it was under Banda, Muluzi's government was tainted by corruption scandals. Senior officials are believed to have sold off 160,000 tons of reserve maize in 2000, despite the signs of a coming famine. In 2002 and 2003, the country faced severe food shortages, with more than 3 million people close to starvation.

In May 2004, Bingu wa Mutharika, an economist and crony of Muluzi, was elected president in elections that were widely considered irregular.

Malaysia

Head of State: King Syed Sirajuddin Syed Putra Jamalullail
Prime Minister: Abdullah Badawi (2003)
Area: 127,316 sq mi (329,750 sq km)
Population (2004 est.): 23,522,482 (growth rate: 1.8%); birth rate: 23.4/1000; infant mortality rate: 18.4/1000; life expectancy: 72.0; density per sq mi: 185
Capital and largest city (2003 est.): Kuala Lumpur, 3,688,200 (metro. area), 1,403,400. **Other large cities:** Kelang, 683,200; Johor Bharu, 682,100.
Monetary unit: Ringgit. **Languages:** Bahasa Melayu (Malay, official), English, Chinese dialects (Cantonese, Mandarin, Hokkien, Hakka, Hainan, Foochow), Tamil, Telugu, Malayalam, Panjabi, Thai; several indigenous languages (including Iban, Kadazan) in East Malaysia.
Ethnicity/race: Malay and other indigenous 58%, Chinese 24%, Indian 8%, others 10% (2000).
Religions: Muslim, Buddhist, Daoist, Hindu, Christian, Sikh; Shamanism (East Malaysia). **Literacy rate:** 89% (2003 est.)
Economic summary: GDP/PPP (2003 est.): $207.2 billion; per capita $9,000. **Real growth rate:** 4.9%. **Inflation:** 1.2%. **Unemployment:** 3.4%. **Arable land:** 6%. **Agriculture:** Peninsular Malaysia—rubber, palm oil, cocoa, rice; Sabah—subsistence crops, rubber, timber, coconuts, rice; Sarawak—rubber, pepper; timber. **Labor force:** 10.4 million; local trade and tourism 28%, manufacturing 27%, agriculture, forestry, and fisheries 16%, services 10%, government 10%, construction 9% (2000 est.). **Industries:** Peninsular Malaysia—rubber and oil palm processing and manufacturing, light manufacturing industry, electronics, tin mining and smelting, logging and processing timber; Sabah—logging, petroleum production; Sarawak—agriculture processing, petroleum production and refining, logging. **Natural resources:** tin, petroleum, timber, copper, iron ore, natural gas, bauxite. **Exports:** $98.4 billion (f.o.b., 2003 est.): electronic equipment, petroleum and liquefied natural gas, wood and wood products, palm oil, rubber, textiles, chemicals. **Imports:** $74.4 billion (f.o.b., 2003 est.): electronics, machinery, petroleum products, plastics, vehicles, iron and steel products, chemicals. **Major trading partners:** U.S., Singapore, Japan, China, Hong Kong, Thailand, South Korea, Taiwan. **Member of Commonwealth of Nations**

Geography Malaysia is on the Malay Peninsula in southeast Asia. The nation also includes Sabah and Sarawak on the island of Borneo to the east. Its area slightly exceeds that of New Mexico.

Most of Malaysia is covered by forest, with a mountain range running the length of the peninsula. Extensive forests provide ebony, sandalwood, teak, and other woods.

Government Constitutional monarchy.

History The ancestors of the people that now inhabit the Malaysian peninsula first migrated to the area between 2500 and 1500 B.C. Those living in the coastal regions had early contact with Chinese and Indians; seafaring traders from India brought with them Hinduism, which was blended with the local animist beliefs. As Muslims conquered India, they spread the religion of Islam to Malaysia. In the 15th century A.D., Islam acquired a firm hold on the region when the Hindu ruler of the powerful city-state of Malacca, Parameswara Dewa Shah, converted to Islam.

British and Dutch interest in the region grew in the 1800s, with the British East India Company estab-

lishing a trading settlement on the island of Singapore. Trade soared, with Singapore's population growing from only 5,000 in 1820 to nearly 100,000 in just 50 years. In the 1880s, Britain formally established protectorates in Malaysia. At about the same time, rubber trees were introduced from Brazil. With the mass production of automobiles, rubber became a valuable export, and laborers were brought in from India to work the rubber plantations.

Following the Japanese occupation of Malaysia during World War II, a growing nationalist movement prompted the British to establish the semi-autonomous Federation of Malaya in 1948. But Communist guerrillas took to the jungles to begin a war of national liberation against the British, who declared a state of emergency to quell the insurgency, which lasted until 1960.

The independent state of Malaysia came into existence on Sept. 16, 1963, as a federation of Malaya, Singapore, Sabah (North Borneo), and Sarawak. In 1965, Singapore withdrew from the federation to become a separate nation. Since 1966, the 11 states of former Malaya have been known as West Malaysia, and Sabah and Sarawak have been known as East Malaysia.

By the late 1960s Malaysia was torn by communal rioting directed against Chinese and Indians, who controlled a disproportionate share of the country's wealth. Beginning in 1968, the government moved to achieve greater economic balance through a national economic policy.

In the 1980s, Dr. Mohamad Mahathir succeeded Datuk Hussein as prime minister. Mahathir instituted economic reforms that would transform Malaysia into one of the so-called Asian Tigers. Throughout the 1990s, Mahathir embarked on a massive project to build a new capital from scratch in an attempt to bypass congested Kuala Lumpur.

Beginning in 1997 and continuing through the next year, Malaysia suffered from the Asian currency crisis. Instead of following the economic prescriptions of the International Monetary Fund and World Bank, the prime minister opted for fixed exchange rates and capital controls. In late 1999, Malaysia was on the road to economic recovery, and it appeared Mahathir's measures were working.

Mahathir sacked his heir apparent, Anwar Ibrahim, from his posts as deputy prime minister and finance minister in Sept. 1998, after a disagreement over how to deal with the country's economic problems. In defiance, Anwar launched a reform movement attacking the government. The prime minister then jailed Anwar, who was beaten and convicted on trumped-up charges of corruption and sodomy.

In Oct. 2003, Mahathir retired after 22 years in office. His rule led to his country's enormous economic growth but was also characterized by repression and human rights abuses.

Malaysia's new prime minister, Abdullah Badawi, has a more statesman-like reputation, and in his first year in office made headway on reducing corruption and instituting reforms. In March 2004, the ruling National Front coalition won an astonishing 90% of parliamentary seats, and Abdullah was reelected on his own merits.

Malaysia's high court overturned Anwar's sodomy conviction in Sept. 2004, and the former deputy prime minister was released after serving six years in prison. The international community praised Abdullah for not interfering with the court's ruling.

Maldives

REPUBLIC OF MALDIVES

President: Maumoon Abdul Gayoom (1978)
Area: 116 sq mi (300 sq km)
Population (2004 est.): 339,330 (growth rate: 2.9%);
birth rate: 36.1/1000; infant mortality rate: 58.3/1000;
life expectancy: 63.7; density per sq mi: 2,930
Capital and largest city (2003 est.): Malé, 81,600.
Monetary unit: Rufiya. **Languages:** Maldivian Dhivehi
(official); English spoken by most government officials.
Ethnicity/race: South Indians, Sinhalese, Arabs.
Religion: Islam (Sunni). **Literacy rate:** 97% (2003
est.)
Economic summary: GDP/PPP (2002 est.): $1.25
billion; per capita $3,900. **Real growth rate:** 2.3%.
Inflation: 1%. **Unemployment:** negl. **Arable land:**
3%. **Agriculture:** coconuts, corn, sweet potatoes; fish.
Labor force: 88,000 (2000); agriculture 22%, industry
18%, services 60% (1995). **Industries:** fish
processing, tourism, shipping, boat building, coconut
processing, garments, woven mats, rope, handicrafts,
coral and sand mining. **Natural resources:** fish.
Exports: $90 million (f.o.b., 2002 est.): fish, clothing.
Imports: $392 million (f.o.b., 2002 est.): consumer
goods, intermediate and capital goods, petroleum
products. **Major trading partners:** U.S., Sri Lanka,
Thailand, Japan, UK, Singapore, UAE, India, Malaysia.

Geography The Republic of Maldives is a group of
atolls in the Indian Ocean about 417 mi (671 km)
southwest of Sri Lanka. Its 1,190 coral islets stretch
over an area of 35,200 square mi (90,000 sq km). With
concerns over global warming and the shrinking of the
polar ice caps, Maldives is directly threatened, as none
of its islands rises more than six feet above sea level.

Government Republic.

History The Maldives (formerly called the Maldive
Islands) were first settled in the 5th century B.C. by
Buddhist seafarers from India and Sri Lanka.
According to tradition, Islam was adopted in A.D.
1153. Originally the islands were under the suzerainty of Ceylon (now Sri Lanka). They came under British protection in 1887 and were a dependency of the
then-colony of Ceylon until 1948. An independence
agreement with Britain was signed July 26, 1965.
For centuries a sultanate, the islands adopted a
republican form of government in 1952, but the sultanate was restored in 1954. In 1968, however, as the
result of a referendum, a republic was again established in the recently independent country. Ibrahim
Nasir, the authoritarian president since 1968, was
removed from office and replaced by the more progressive Maumoon Abdul Gayoom in 1978. Gayoom
was elected to a sixth five-year term in 2003.

Mali

REPUBLIC OF MALI

National name: République de Mali
President: Amadou Toumani Touré (2002)
Prime Minister: Ousmane Issoufi Maïga (2004)
Area: 478,764 sq mi (1,240,000 sq km)
Population (2004 est.): 11,956,788 (growth rate: 2.8%);
birth rate: 47.3/1000; infant mortality rate: 118.0/1000;
life expectancy: 45.3; density per sq mi: 25
Capital and largest city (2003 est.): Bamako,
1,323,200 (metro. area), 935,400. **Monetary unit:**
CFA Franc. **Languages:** French (official), Bambara
80%, numerous African languages. **Ethnicity/race:**
Mande 50% (Bambara, Malinke, Sarakole), Peul 17%,
Voltaic 12%, Tuareg and Moor 10%, Songhai 6%,
other 5%. **Religions:** Islam 90%, indigenous beliefs
9%, Christian 1%. **Literacy rate:** 46% (2003 est.)
Economic summary: GDP/PPP (2003 est.): $10.53
billion; per capita $900. **Real growth rate:** 0.5%.
Inflation: 4.5% (2002 est.). **Unemployment:** 14.6%
urban areas; 5.3% rural areas (2001 est.). **Arable
land:** 4%. **Agriculture:** cotton, millet, rice, corn,
vegetables, peanuts; cattle, sheep, goats. **Labor
force:** 3.93 million (2001 est); agriculture and fishing
80% (2001 est.). **Industries:** food processing;
construction; phosphate and gold mining. **Natural
resources:** gold, phosphates, kaolin, salt, limestone,
uranium, hydropower note: bauxite, iron ore,
manganese, tin, and copper deposits are known but
not exploited. **Exports:** $915 million (f.o.b., 2002 est.):
cotton, gold, livestock. **Imports:** $927 million (f.o.b.,
2002 est.): petroleum, machinery and equipment,
construction materials, foodstuffs, textiles. **Major
trading partners:** Thailand, Italy, India, Brazil,
Germany, Spain, Portugal, Taiwan, Côte d'Ivoire,
France, Senegal.

Geography Most of Mali, in West Africa, lies in the
Sahara. A landlocked country four-fifths the size of
Alaska, it is bordered by Guinea, Senegal, Mauritania,
Algeria, Niger, Burkina Faso, and the Côte d'Ivoire.
The only fertile area is in the south, where the Niger
and Senegal rivers provide irrigation.

Government Republic.

History Caravan routes have passed through Mali
since A.D. 300. The Malinke empire ruled regions of
Mali from the 12th to 16th centuries, and the Songhai
empire reigned over the Timbuktu-Gao region in the
15th century. Morocco conquered Timbuktu in 1591,
and ruled over it for two centuries. Subjugated by
France by the end of the 19th century, the land
became a colony in 1904 (named French Sudan in
1920) and in 1946 became part of the French Union.
On June 20, 1960, it became independent and, under
the name of Sudanese Republic, was federated with
the Republic of Senegal in the Mali federation. However, Senegal seceded from the federation on Aug. 20,
1960, and the Sudanese Republic then changed its
name to the Republic of Mali on Sept. 22.

In the 1960s, Mali concentrated on economic development, continuing to accept aid from both Soviet bloc
and Western nations, as well as international agencies.
In the late 1960s, it began retreating from close ties
with China. But a purge of conservative opponents
brought greater power to President Modibo Keita, and
in 1968, the influence of the Chinese and their Malian
sympathizers increased. The army overthrew the government on Nov. 19, 1968, and brought Mali under
military rule for the next 20 years. Mali and Burkina
Faso fought a brief border war from Dec. 25th to 29th,
1985. In 1991, dictator Moussa Traoré was overthrown,
and Mali made a peaceful transition to democracy. In
1992, Alpha Konaré became Mali's first democratically
elected president.

Mali's second multiparty national elections took
place in May 1997, with President Konaré winning
reelection.

Konaré won international praise for his efforts to
revive Mali's faltering economy. His adherence to International Monetary Fund guidelines increased foreign
investment and helped make Mali the second-largest
cotton producer in Africa. Konaré was also the chairman of the 15-nation ECOWAS (the Economic Community of West African States), which in recent years
has concentrated on brokering peace in Sierra Leone,
Liberia, and Guinea. Konaré retired after serving the
two five-year terms permitted by the constitution.

In June 2002, Amadou Toumani Touré was elected
president. A highly popular and respected public figure,

he engineered the 1991 coup that freed the country from military rule. In 2004, he appointed Ousmane Issoufi Maïga as the new prime minister.

Malta

MALTA

President: Eddie Fenech Adami (2004)
Prime Minister: Lawrence Gonzi (2004)
Area: 122 sq mi (316 sq km)
Population (2004 est.): 396,851 (growth rate: 0.4%); birth rate: 10.1/1000; infant mortality rate: 3.9/1000; life expectancy: 78.7 density per sq mi: 3,253
Capital (2003 est.): Valletta, 194,200 (metro. area) 6,900 (city proper). **Largest city:** Birkirkara, 21,600.
Monetary unit: Maltese lira. **Languages:** Maltese and English (both official). **Ethnicity/race:** Maltese (descendants of ancient Carthaginians and Phoenicians, with strong elements of Italian and other Mediterranean stock). **Religion:** Roman Catholic 98%. **Literacy rate:** 93% (2003 census)
Economic summary: GDP/PPP (2003 est.): $7.082 billion; per capita $17,700. **Real growth rate:** 0.8%. **Inflation:** 0.8%. **Unemployment:** 7%. **Arable land:** 31%. **Agriculture:** potatoes, cauliflower, grapes, wheat, barley, tomatoes, citrus, cut flowers, green peppers; pork, milk, poultry, eggs. **Labor force:** 160,000 (2002 est) industry 24%, services 71%, agriculture 5% (1999 est.). **Industries:** tourism; electronics, ship building and repair, construction; food and beverages, textiles, footwear, clothing, tobacco. **Natural resources:** limestone, salt, arable land. **Exports:** $2.175 billion (f.o.b., 2003 est.): machinery and transport equipment, manufactures. **Imports:** $2.761 billion (f.o.b., 2003 est.): machinery and transport equipment, manufactured and semi-manufactured goods; food, drink, and tobacco. **Major trading partners:** Singapore, U.S., UK, Germany, France, China, Italy, South Korea, Japan, Spain. **Member of Commonwealth of Nations**

Geography The five Maltese islands—Malta, Gozo, Comino, Comminotto, and Filflawith—have a combined land area smaller than Philadelphia. Malta is located in the Mediterranean Sea, about 60 mi (97 km) south of the southeast tip of Sicily.

Government Republic.

History The strategic importance of Malta was recognized by the Phoenicians, who occupied it, as did, in turn, the Greeks, Carthaginians, and Romans. The apostle Paul was shipwrecked there in A.D. 60. With the division of the Roman Empire in A.D. 395, Malta was assigned to the eastern portion dominated by Constantinople. Between 870 and 1090, it came under Arab rule. In 1091, the Norman noble Roger I, then ruler of Sicily, came to Malta with a small retinue and defeated the Arabs. The Knights of St. John (Malta), who obtained the three habitable Maltese islands of Malta, Gozo, and Comino from Charles V in 1530, reached their highest fame when they withstood an attack by superior Turkish forces in 1565. Napoléon seized Malta in 1798, but the French forces were ousted by British troops the next year, and British rule was confirmed by the Treaty of Paris in 1814.

Malta was heavily attacked by German and Italian aircraft during World War II but was never invaded by the Axis powers. It became an independent nation on Sept. 21, 1964, and a republic on Dec. 13, 1974, but remained in the British Commonwealth. In 1979, when its alliance with Great Britain ended, Malta sought to guarantee its neutrality through agreements with other countries. Although Malta applied for membership in the European Union, when the Labour Party won the election in Oct. 1996, it froze Malta's EU application and withdrew from the NATO Partnership for Peace program in an effort to maintain its neutrality. When the Nationalist Party won the Sept. 1998 elections, however, it revived the EU accession bid, and in May 2004 Malta joined the EU.

Marshall Islands

REPUBLIC OF THE MARSHALL ISLANDS

President: Kessai H. Note (2000)
Total land area: 70 sq mi (181.3 sq km), includes the atolls of Bikini, Eniwetok, and Kwajalein
Population (2004 est.): 57,738 (growth rate: 2.3%); birth rate: 33.9/1000; infant mortality rate: 30.5/1000; life expectancy: 69.7; density per sq mi: 825
Capital and largest city (2003 est.): Majuro, 20,500. **Languages:** Marshallese (two major dialects from the Malayo-Polynesian family), English (both official); Japanese. **Ethnicity/race:** Micronesian. **Religions:** Christian (mostly Protestant). **Literacy rate:** 94% (1999)
Economic summary: GDP/PPP (2001 est.): $115 million; per capita $1,600. **Real growth rate:** 1%. **Inflation:** 2%. **Unemployment:** 30.9% (1999 est.). **Arable land:** 17%. **Agriculture:** coconuts, tomatoes, melons, taro, breadfruit, fruits; pigs, chickens. **Labor force:** 28,698 (1996 est); agriculture 21.4%, industry 20.9%, services 57.7%. **Industries:** copra, fish, tourism, craft items from shell, wood, and pearls. **Natural resources:** coconut products, marine products, deep seabed minerals. **Exports:** $9 million (f.o.b., 2000): copra cake, coconut oil, handicrafts, fish. **Imports:** $54 million (f.o.b., 2000): foodstuffs, machinery and equipment, fuels, beverages and tobacco. **Major trading partners:** U.S., Japan, Australia, China, New Zealand, Singapore, Fiji, Philippines.

Geography The Marshall Islands, east of the Carolines, are divided into two chains: the western, or Ralik, group, including the atolls Jaluit, Kwajalein, Wotho, Bikini, and Eniwetok; and the eastern, or Ratak, group, including the atolls Mili, Majuro, Maloelap, Wotje, and Likiep. The islands are of the coral-reef type and rise only a few feet above sea level. The Marshall Islands comprise an area slightly larger than Washington, DC.

Government Constitutional government in free association with the U.S.

History Micronesian peoples were the first inhabitants of the archipelago. The islands were explored by the Spanish in the 16th century and were named for a British captain in 1788. Germany unsuccessfully attempted to colonize the islands in 1885. Japan claimed them in 1914, but after several battles during World War II, the U.S. seized them from the Japanese. In 1947, the UN made the island group, along with the Mariana and Caroline archipelagos, a U.S. trust territory.

U.S. nuclear testing took place between 1946 and 1958 on the islands of Bikini and Eniwetok. The people of Bikini were removed to another island, and a total of 23 U.S. atomic and hydrogen bomb tests were conducted. Despite clean-up attempts, the islands remain uninhabited today because of nuclear contamination. The U.S. paid the islands $183.7 million in damages in 1983, and in 1999, the U.S. approved a one-time $3.8-million payment to the relocated people of Bikini atoll.

The United States and the Marshall Islands signed a Compact of Free Association in 1986, which meant the islands became self-governing but would receive U.S. military and economic aid, roughly $65 million a year. The Marshall Islands were admitted to the UN on Sept. 17, 1991.

Kwajalein atoll is the site of an American military base, and has been used for missile defense testing since the 1960s.

In 2000, Kessai Note became the first commoner to become president—his predecessors had been island chiefs. He ran on an anticorruption ticket and is attempting to make his small nation more self-sufficient. In 2003, the U.S. and the Marshall Islands agreed on a new Compact of Free Association, an extension of the lease to use the Kwajalein military base in exchange for economic aid. In Jan. 2004, Parliament reelected President Note.

Mauritania

ISLAMIC REPUBLIC OF MAURITANIA

National name: République Islamique de Mauritanie
President: Col. Maaouye Ould Sidi Ahmed Taya (1992)
Prime Minister: Sghair Ould M'Bareck (2003)
Area: 397,953 sq mi (1,030,700 sq km)
Population (2004 est.): 2,998,563 (growth rate: 2.9%); birth rate: 41.8/1000; infant mortality rate: 72.4/1000; life expectancy: 52.3; density per sq mi: 8
Capital and largest city (2003 est.): Nouakchott, 661,400. **Monetary unit:** Ouguiya. **Languages:** Hassaniya Arabic, Wolof (both official); Pulaar, Soninke, French. **Ethnicity/race:** mixed Maur/black 40%, Maur 30%, black 30%. **Religion:** Islam 100%. **Literacy rate:** 42% (2003 est.)
Economic summary: GDP/PPP (2003 est.): $5.195 billion; per capita $1,800. **Real growth rate:** 4.5%. **Inflation:** 7%. **Unemployment:** 21% (1999 est.). **Arable land:** 0.5%. **Agriculture:** dates, millet, sorghum, rice, corn, dates; cattle, sheep. **Labor force:** 786,000 (2001); agriculture 50%, services 40%, industry 10% (2001 est.). **Industries:** fish processing, mining of iron ore and gypsum. **Natural resources:** iron ore, gypsum, copper, phosphate, diamonds, gold, oil, fish. **Exports:** $541 million (f.o.b., 2002): iron ore, fish and fish products, gold. **Imports:** $860 million (f.o.b., 2002): machinery and equipment, petroleum products, capital goods, foodstuffs, consumer goods. **Major trading partners:** Italy, France, Spain, Germany, Belgium, Japan, China.

Geography Mauritania, three times the size of Arizona, is situated in northwest Africa with about 350 mi (592 km) of coastline on the Atlantic Ocean. It is bordered by Morocco on the north, Algeria and Mali on the east, and Senegal on the south. The country is mostly desert, with the exception of the fertile Senegal River valley in the south and grazing land in the north.

Government Republic under military government. The legal system is based on Islam.

History Mauritania was first inhabited by blacks and Berbers, and it became a center for the Berber Almoravid movement in the 11th century, which sought to spread Islam through western Africa. It was first explored by the Portuguese in the 15th century, but by the 19th century the French gained control. They organized the area into a territory in 1904, and in 1920 it became one of the colonies that comprised French West Africa. In 1946, it became a French Overseas territory.

Mauritania became an independent nation on Nov. 28, 1960, and was admitted to the United Nations in 1961 over the strenuous opposition of Morocco, which claimed the territory. In the late 1960s, the government sought to make Arab culture dominant. Racial and ethnic tensions between Moors, Arabs, Berbers, and blacks were frequent.

Mauritania and Morocco divided the territory of Spanish Sahara (later called Western Sahara) between them after the Spanish departed in 1975, with Mauritania controlling the southern third. The Polisario Front, indigenous Saharawi rebels, fought for the territory against both Mauritania and Morocco. Increased military spending and rising casualties in the region helped bring down the civilian government of Ould Daddah in 1978. A succession of military rulers followed. In 1979, Mauritania withdrew from Western Sahara.

In 1984, Col. Maaouye Ould Sidi Ahmed Taya took control of the government. He relaxed Islamic law, fought corruption, instituted economic reforms urged by the International Monetary Fund, and held the country's first multiparty parliamentary elections in 1986. Although the 1991 constitution set up a multiparty democracy, politics remains based on ethnic and racial lines. The primary conflict is between blacks who dominate southern regions, and the Moorish-Arabic north, which runs the country. Racial tensions reached a peak in 1989 when Mauritania went to war with Senegal in a dispute over the border. As each country repatriated citizens of the other, critics accused Mauritania of taking the opportunity to expel thousands of blacks.

Although Mauritania officially abolished slavery in 1980, the nation continues to tolerate the enslavement of blacks by North African Arabs. In 1993, the U.S. State Department estimated that there were more than 90,000 chattel slaves in the country.

In 1992, Taya won the nation's first multiparty presidential election, which opponents charged was rigged. Taya's attempts to restructure the economy provoke periodic protests, the most serious of which were the bread riots in Nouakchott in 1995.

In 2002, the government banned a political party, Action for Change (AC), which had campaigned for greater rights for blacks, calling it racist and violent. Two other opposition parties have been banned in the past few years. The IMF granted Mauritania debt relief in June 2002, wiping out $1.1 billion, half of Mauritania's overall debt.

Coup attempts in June 2003 and Aug. 2004 were thwarted. President Taya's crackdown on Islamists, and his support for Israel and the U.S., are believed to have sparked the attempts to overthrow him.

Mauritius

President: Karl Offman (2002)
Prime Minister: Paul Berenger (2003)
Area: 788 sq mi (2,040 sq km)
Population (2004 est.): 1,220,481 (growth rate: 0.8%); birth rate: 15.9/1000; infant mortality rate: 15.6/1000; life expectancy: 72.1; density per sq mi: 1,550
Capital and largest city (2003 est.): Port Louis, 577,200 (metro. area), 143,800 (city proper).
Monetary unit: Mauritian rupee. **Languages:** English, French (both official); Creole, Hindi, Urdu, Hakka, Bojpoori. **Ethnicity/race:** Indo-Mauritian 68%, Creole 27%, Sino-Mauritian 3%, Franco-Mauritian 2%. **Religions:** Hindu 52%, Christian 28.3% (Roman Catholic 26%, Protestant 2.3%), Islam 16.6%, other 3.1%. **Literacy rate:** 86% (2003 est.)
Economic summary: GDP/PPP (2003 est.): $13.85 billion; per capita $11,400. **Real growth rate:** 4.1%. **Inflation:** 6.4% (2002 est.). **Unemployment:** 8.8% (2002 est.). **Arable land:** 49%. **Agriculture:**

sugarcane, tea, corn, potatoes, bananas, pulses; cattle, goats; fish. **Labor force:** 514,000 (1995); construction and industry 36%, services 24%, agriculture and fishing 14%, trade, restaurants, hotels 16%, transportation and communication 7%, finance 3% (1995). **Industries:** food processing (largely sugar milling), textiles, clothing; chemicals, metal products, transport equipment, nonelectrical machinery; tourism. **Natural resources:** arable land, fish. **Exports:** $1.965 billion (f.o.b., 2003 est.): clothing and textiles, sugar, cut flowers, molasses. **Imports:** $2.136 billion (f.o.b., 2003 est.): manufactured goods, capital equipment, foodstuffs, petroleum products, chemicals. **Major trading partners:** UK, France, U.S., Madagascar, Belgium, South Africa, India, China. **Member of Commonwealth of Nations**

Geography Mauritius is a mountainous island in the Indian Ocean east of Madagascar.

Government Parliamentary democracy within the British Commonwealth.

History After a brief Dutch settlement, French immigrants who came in 1715 named the island Île de France and established the first road and harbor infrastructure, as well as the sugar industry, under the leadership of Gov. Mahe de Labourdonnais. Blacks from Africa and Madagascar came as slaves to work in the sugarcane fields. In 1810, the British captured the island and in 1814, by the Treaty of Paris, it was ceded to Great Britain along with its dependencies.

Indian immigration, which followed the abolition of slavery in 1835, rapidly changed the fabric of Mauritian society, and the country flourished with the increased cultivation of sugarcane. The opening of the Suez Canal in 1869 heralded the decline of Mauritius as a port of call for ships rounding the southern tip of Africa, bound for South and East Asia. The economic instability of the price of sugar, the main crop, in the first half of the 20th century brought civil unrest, then economic, administrative, and political reforms. Mauritius became independent on March 12, 1968.

The effects of Cyclone Claudette in 1979, and of falling world sugar prices in the early 1980s, led the government to initiate a vigorous program of agricultural diversification and to develop the processing of imported goods for the export market. The country formally broke ties with the British Crown in March 1992, becoming a republic within the Commonwealth.

In addition to sugarcane, textile production and tourism are the leading industries. Primary education is free, and Mauritius boasts one of the highest literacy rates in sub-Saharan Africa.

With a complicated ethnic mix—about 30% of the population is of African descent, the remainder is mostly of Indian descent, both Hindu and Muslim—political allegiances are organized according to class and ethnicity.

In Feb. 2002, Mauritius went through four successive presidents. Two resigned within days of each other, each after refusing to sign a controversial anti-terrorism law that severely curtails the rights of suspects. The law, supported by the prime minister, was ultimately signed by a third, interim president. At the end of February, a fourth president, Karl Offman, was elected by Parliament.

In Oct. 2003, Paul Berenger, a white Mauritian of French ancestry, became the first non-Hindu prime minister in the history of Mauritius. Berenger and the previous prime minister, Anerood Jugnauth, formed a coalition during Sept. 2000 elections. Under their agreement, Jugnauth served as prime minister for three years and Berenger assumed the presidency for the remaining two years of the term.

Mexico

UNITED MEXICAN STATES

Official name: Estados Unidos Mexicanos **President:** Vicente Fox Quesada (2000) **Area:** 761,602 sq mi (1,972,550 sq km) **Population (2004 est.):** 104,959,594 (growth rate: 1.2%); birth rate: 21.4/1000; infant mortality rate: 21.7/1000; life expectancy: 74.9; density per sq mi: 138 **Capital and largest city (2003 est.):** Mexico City, 21,233,900 (metro. area), 8,681,400 (city proper). **Other large cities:** Ecatepec, 1,731,900 (part of Mexico City metro. area); Guadalajara, 1,665,800; Puebla, 1,345,500; Nezahualcóyotl, 1,250,700 (part of Mexico City metro. area); Monterrey, 1,135,000. **Monetary unit:** Mexican peso. **Languages:** Spanish, various Mayan, Nahuatl, and other regional indigenous languages. **Ethnicity/race:** mestizo (Amerindian-Spanish) 60%, Amerindian or predominantly Amerindian 30%, white 9%, other 1%. **Religions:** nominally Roman Catholic 89%, Protestant 6%, other 5%. **Literacy rate:** 92% (2003 est.) **Economic summary:** GDP/PPP (2003 est.): $942.2 billion; per capita $9,000. **Real growth rate:** 1.2%. **Inflation:** 4%. **Unemployment:** urban—3.3% plus underemployment of perhaps 25%. **Arable land:** 13%. **Agriculture:** corn, wheat, soybeans, rice, beans, cotton, coffee, fruit, tomatoes; beef, poultry, dairy products; wood products. **Labor force:** 41.5 million; agriculture 20%, industry 24%, services 56% (1998). **Industries:** food and beverages, tobacco, chemicals, iron and steel, petroleum, mining, textiles, clothing, motor vehicles, consumer durables, tourism. **Natural resources:** petroleum, silver, copper, gold, lead, zinc, natural gas, timber. **Exports:** $164.8 billion (f.o.b., 2003 est.): manufactured goods, oil and oil products, silver, fruits, vegetables, coffee, cotton. **Imports:** $168.9 billion (f.o.b., 2003 est.): metalworking machines, steel mill products, agricultural machinery, electrical equipment, car parts for assembly, repair parts for motor vehicles, aircraft, and aircraft parts. **Major trading partners:** U.S., Canada, Japan.

Geography Mexico is bordered by the United States to the north, and Belize and Guatemala to the southeast. Mexico is about one-fifth the size of the United States. Baja California in the west is an 800-mile (1,287-km) peninsula and forms the Gulf of California. In the east are the Gulf of Mexico and the Bay of Campeche, which is formed by Mexico's other peninsula, the Yucatán. The center of Mexico is a great, high plateau, open to the north, with mountain chains on the east and west and with ocean-front lowlands lying outside of them.

Government Federal republic.

History At least three great civilizations—the Mayas, the Olmecs, and later the Toltecs—preceded the wealthy Aztec empire, conquered in 1519–1521 by the Spanish under Hernando Cortés. Spain ruled Mexico as part of the viceroyalty of New Spain for the next 300 years until Sept. 16, 1810, when the Mexicans first revolted. They won independence in 1821.

From 1821 to 1877, there were two emperors, several dictators, and enough presidents and provisional executives to make a new government on the average of every nine months. Mexico lost Texas (1836), and after defeat in the war with the U.S. (1846–1848) it lost the area that is now California, Nevada, and Utah, most of Arizona and New Mexico, and parts of Wyoming and Colorado under the Treaty of Guadalupe Hidalgo. In 1855, the Indian patriot Benito Juárez began a series of reforms, including the disestablishment of the

Catholic Church, which owned vast property. The subsequent civil war was interrupted by the French invasion of Mexico (1861) and the crowning of Maximilian of Austria as emperor (1864). He was overthrown and executed by forces under Juárez, who again became president in 1867.

The years after the fall of the dictator Porfirio Diaz (1877–1880 and 1884–1911) were marked by bloody political-military strife and trouble with the U.S., culminating in the punitive U.S. expedition into northern Mexico (1916–1917) in unsuccessful pursuit of the revolutionary Pancho Villa. Since a brief civil war in 1920, Mexico has enjoyed a period of gradual agricultural, political, and social reforms. The Partido Nacional Revolucionario (PNR; National Revolutionary Party), dominated by revolutionary and reformist politicians from northern Mexico, was established in 1929; it continued to control Mexico throughout the 20th century and was renamed the Partido Revolucionario Institucional (PRI; Institutional Revolutionary Party) in 1946. Relations with the U.S. were disturbed in 1938 when all foreign oil wells were expropriated, but a compensation agreement was reached in 1941.

Following World War II, the government emphasized economic growth. During the mid-1970s, under the leadership of President José López Portillo, Mexico became a major petroleum-producer. By the end of Portillo's term, however, Mexico had accumulated a huge external debt because of the government's unrestrained borrowing on the strength of its petroleum revenues. The collapse of oil prices in 1986 cut Mexico's export earnings. In Jan. 1994, Mexico joined Canada and the United States in the North American Free Trade Agreement (NAFTA), which will phase out all tariffs over a 15-year period, and in Jan. 1996, it became a founding member of the World Trade Organization (WTO).

In 1995, the U.S. agreed to prevent the collapse of Mexico's private banks. In return, the U.S. won virtual veto power over much of Mexico's economic policy. In 1997, in what observers called the freest elections in Mexico's history, the PRI lost control of the lower legislative house and the mayoralty of Mexico City in a stunning upset. To increase democracy, President Ernesto Zedillo said in 1999 that he would break precedent and not personally choose the next PRI presidential nominee. Several months later, Mexico held its first presidential primary, which was won by former interior secretary Francisco Labastida, Zedillo's closest ally among the candidates.

In elections held July 2, 2000, the PRI lost the presidency, ending 71 years of one-party rule. Vicente Fox Quesada, of the conservative National Action Party (PAN), took 43% of the vote to Labastida's 36%. Fox vowed tax reform, an overhaul of the legal system, and a reduction in power of the central government. By 2002, however, Fox had made little headway on his ambitious reform agenda. Disfavor with Fox was evident in 2003 parliamentary elections, when the PRI rebounded, winning 224 of the 500 seats in the lower house. After the elections, Fox admitted publicly that many Mexicans were disappointed with his government thus far.

In 2004, a two-year investigation into the "dirty war," which Mexico's authoritarian government waged against its opponents in the 1960s and 1970s, led to an indictment—later dropped—against former president Luis Echeverria for ordering the 1971 shooting of student protesters.

Micronesia

FEDERATED STATES OF MICRONESIA

President: Joseph J. Urusemal (2003)
Total area: 271 sq mi (702 sq km). Land area, same (includes islands of Pohnpei, Yap, Chuuk, and Kosrae)
Population (2004 est.): 108,155 (growth rate: 0); birth rate: 25.8/1000; infant mortality rate: 31.3/1000; life expectancy: 69.4; density per sq mi: 399
Capital: (2003 est.) Palikir 11,600. **Languages:** English (official, common), Chukese, Pohnpeian, Yapase, Kosrean, Ulithian, Woleaian, Nukuoro, Kapingamarangi. **Ethnicity/race:** nine ethnic Micronesian and Polynesian groups. **Religions:** Roman Catholic 50%, Protestant 47%. **Literacy rate:** 89% (1980 est.)
Economic summary: GDP/PPP (2002 est.): $277 million; note: GDP is supplemented by grant aid, averaging perhaps $100 million annually; per capita $2,000. **Real growth rate:** 1%. **Inflation:** 1%. **Unemployment:** 16% (1999 est.). **Arable land:** 6%. **Agriculture:** black pepper, tropical fruits and vegetables, coconuts, cassava (tapioca), betel nuts, sweet potatoes; pigs, chickens. **Labor force:** n.a.; two-thirds are government employees. **Industries:** tourism, construction, fish processing, specialized aquaculture, craft items from shell, wood, and pearls. **Natural resources:** forests, marine products, deep-seabed minerals. **Exports:** $22 million (f.o.b., FY99/00 est.): fish, garments, bananas, black pepper. **Imports:** $149 million (f.o.b., FY99/00 est.): food, manufactured goods, machinery and equipment, beverages. **Major trading partners:** Japan, U.S., Guam, Australia.

Geography The Federated States of Micronesia is composed of the island states of Yap, Chuuk (Truk), Pohnpei (Ponape), and Kosrae, all in the Caroline Islands. The islands vary geologically from high mountainous islands to low coral atolls, with volcanic outcroppings on Pohnpei, Kosrae, and Chuuk. They are located 3,200 mi (5,150 km) west-southwest of Hawaii, in the north Pacific Ocean.

Government Constitutional government in free association with the United States since Nov. 1986.

History The islands, inhabited by Micronesian and Polynesian peoples, were colonized by Spain in the 17th century. Germany purchased them from Spain in 1898. They were occupied by the Japanese in 1914, but American forces seized them from the Japanese during World War II. On April 2, 1947, the United Nations Security Council created the Trust Territory of the Pacific Islands. The trust placed the Northern Mariana, Caroline, and Marshall Islands under the administration of the United States.

The Micronesian Federation (FMA) became self-governing in 1979. In 1983, the FMA voted to accept a Compact of Free Association with the U.S., and in Nov. 1986, the U.S. government declared the Trust Territory agreements no longer in effect—thereby granting the Federated States of Micronesia full independence. In Nov. 2002, the Compact was renewed for another 20 years.

The FMA was admitted to the United Nations on Sept. 17, 1991. In July 1993, the country became a member of the International Monetary Fund. Micronesia, as well as many other South Pacific countries, is alarmed by the effect continued global warming will have on its islands—the consequent rise in the level of the oceans threatens low-lying islands with flooding and, eventually, with submergence.

Moldova

REPUBLIC OF MOLDOVA

President: Vladimir Voronin (2001)
Prime Minister: Vasile Tarlev (2001)
Area: 13,067 sq mi (33,843 sq km)
Population (2004 est.): 4,446,455 (growth rate: 0.2%);
birth rate: 14.8/1000; infant mortality rate: 41.0/1000;
life expectancy: 65.0; density per sq mi: 340
Capital and largest city (2003 est.): Chisinau, 772,500
(metro. area), 709,900 (city proper). **Other large
cities:** Tiraspol, 209,800; Beltsy, 175,400; Bendery
(Tighina), 144,900. **Monetary unit:** Leu. **Languages:**
Moldovan (official; virtually the same as Romanian),
Russian, Gagauz (a Turkish dialect). **Ethnicity/race:**
Moldavian/Romanian 64.5%, Ukrainian 13.8%,
Russian 13%, Gagauz 3.5%, Jewish 1.5%, Bulgarian
2%, other 1.7% (1989 est.). **Religions:** Eastern
Orthodox 98%, Jewish 1.5%, Baptist and other 0.5%
(2000). **Literacy rate:** 99% (2003 est.).
Economic summary: GDP/PPP (2003 est.): $7.792
billion; per capita $1,800. **Real growth rate:** 6.3%.
Inflation: 11.7%. **Unemployment:** 8% (roughly 25% of
working age Moldovans are employed abroad) (2002
est.). **Arable land:** 54%. **Agriculture:** vegetables,
fruits, wine, grain, sugar beets, sunflower seed,
tobacco; beef, milk. **Labor force:** 1.7 million (1998);
agriculture 40%, industry 14%, services 46% (1998).
Industries: food processing, agricultural machinery,
foundry equipment, refrigerators and freezers, washing
machines, hosiery, sugar, vegetable oil, shoes, textiles.
Natural resources: lignite, phosphorites, gypsum,
arable land, limestone. **Exports:** $790 million (f.o.b.,
2003 est.): foodstuffs, textiles, machinery. **Imports:**
$1.34 billion (f.o.b., 2003 est.): mineral products and
fuel 32%, machinery and equipment, chemicals,
textiles (2000). **Major trading partners:** Russia, Italy,
Germany, Ukraine, Romania, U.S., Belarus, Spain.

Geography Moldova (formerly Moldavia) is a landlocked republic of hilly plains lying west of the Carpathian Mountains between the Prut and Dniester
(Dnestr) Rivers. The country is sandwiched between
Romania and Ukraine. The area is a very fertile region
with rich black soil (chernozem) covering three-
quarters of the territory.

Government Democratic republic.

History Most of what is now Moldova was the independent principality of Moldavia in the 14th century.
In the 16th century it came under Ottoman Turkish
rule. Russia acquired Moldavian territory in 1791,
and again in 1812 (the Treaty of Bucharest) when
Turkey gave up the province of Bessarabia[1] to Russia. Turkey held the rest of Moldavia but it was
passed to Romania in 1918. Russia did not recognize
the cession of this territory.

In 1924, the USSR established Moldavia as an
Autonomous Soviet Socialist Republic. As a result of
the Nazi-Soviet Nonaggression Pact of 1939, Romania
was forced to cede all of Bessarabia to the Soviet
Union in 1940. The Soviets merged the Moldavia
ASSR with the Romanian-speaking districts of Bessarabia to form the Moldavian Soviet Socialist Republic.
During World War II, Romania joined Germany in the
attack on the Soviet Union and reconquered Bessarabia. But Soviet troops retook the territory in 1944 and
reestablished the Moldavian SSR.

For many years, Romania and the USSR disputed
each other's territorial claims over Bessarabia. Following the aborted coup against Soviet president Mikhail
Gorbachev, Moldavia proclaimed its independence in
Sept. 1991, and changed its name to the Romanian
spelling, Moldova.

Conflict between ethnic Romanians and the Russian-
Ukrainian majority in Trans-Dniester erupted upon
independence. Trans-Dniester separatists (primarily
ethnic Russians and Ukrainians) fought for independence from Moldova in 1992; about 1,500 died in the
conflict. Unrest continues in Trans-Dniester. In the
south, Gagauz, which is composed mostly of Turkic
Christians, has also attempted secession.

The Russian financial crisis in fall 1998 severely
affected Moldova, which relied on Russia for 60% of
its foreign trade. Economic disaster caused an exodus
of an estimated 600,000 Moldovans since then—
Moldova is considered the poorest country in Europe.
In Feb. 2001, the Communist Party won an overwhelming victory in parliamentary elections, and their
leader, Vladimir Voronin, became prime minister. Voronin has attempted to forge closer relations with Moscow, thus sparking protests among those who advocate
for closer cultural and ethnic ties to Romania.

In July 2004, Trans-Dniester closed down several
Romanian-language schools; Moldova retaliated by
imposing trade sanctions.

1. The area between the Prut and Dniester rivers.

Monaco

PRINCIPALITY OF MONACO

National name: Principauté de Monaco
Ruler: Prince Rainier III (1949)
Minister of State: Patrick Leclercq (2000)
Area: 0.75 sq mi (465 acres) (1.95 sq km)
Population (2004 est.): 32,270 (growth rate: 0.4%); birth
rate: 9.4/1000; infant mortality rate: 5.5/1000; life
expectancy: 79.4; density per sq mi: 42,861
Capital (2003 est.): Monaco, 1,400. **Largest city:** Monte
Carlo, 15,400. **Monetary unit:** Euro. **Languages:**
French (official), English, Italian, Monégasque.
Ethnicity/race: French 47%, Monegasque 16%, Italian
16%, other 21%. **Religion:** Roman Catholic 90%.
Literacy rate: 99% (2003 est.)
Economic summary: GDP/PPP (1999 est.): $870 million;
$27,000 per capita. **Real growth rate:** n.a. **Inflation:**
n.a. **Unemployment:** 3.1% (1998). **Arable land:** 0%.
Agriculture: none. **Labor force:** 30,540 (Jan. 1994).
Natural resources: none. **Industries:** tourism,
construction, small-scale industrial and consumer
products. **Exports:** n.a. **Imports:** n.a. Full customs
integration with France, which collects and rebates
Monegasque trade duties; also participates in EU.

Geography Monaco is a tiny, hilly wedge driven
into the French Mediterranean coast; it is 9 mi east of
Nice, France.

Government Constitutional monarchy.

History The Phoenicians, and after them the Greeks,
had a temple on the Monacan headland honoring Hercules. From *Monoikos,* the Greek surname for this
mythological strong man, the principality took its
name. After being independent for 800 years, Monaco
was annexed to France in 1793 and was placed under
Sardinia's protection in 1815. By the Franco-
Monegasque treaty of 1861, Monaco went under
French guardianship but continued to be independent.
A treaty made with France in 1918 contained a clause
providing that, in the event that the male Grimaldi
dynasty should die out, Monaco would become an
autonomous state under French protection.

Monaco has a tourist business that runs as high as
1.5 million visitors a year and is famous for its beaches
and casinos, expecially world famous Monte Carlo. It
had gaming tables as early as 1856.

Prince Rainier III, born on May 31, 1923, succeeded his grandfather, Louis II, on the latter's death, May 9, 1949. Rainier was married, in 1956, to U.S. actress Grace Kelly and they subsequently had three children. Their son, Prince Albert Louis Pierre (b. 1958) is heir to the throne. Immensely popular, Princess Grace died on Sept. 14, 1982, of injuries received in a car accident near Monte Carlo. She was 52.

Monaco's practice of providing a tax shelter for French businessmen resulted in a 1962 dispute between the countries. A compromise was reached by which French citizens with less than five years' residence in Monaco were taxed at French rates, and taxes were imposed on Monegasque companies doing more than 25% of their business outside the principality.The country was admitted to the UN in May 1993, making it the smallest country represented there. It celebrated the 700th anniversary of the Grimaldi reign during 1997. In 2002, the constitution was revised to ensure that the Grimaldis retain the throne even if Crown Prince Albert has no heir.

Mongolia

MONGOLIA

President: Natsagiyn Bagabandi (1997)
Prime Minister: Tsakhiagiyn Elbegdorj (2004)
Area: 604,247 sq mi (1,565,000 sq km)
Population (2004 est.): 2,751,314 (growth rate: 1.4%); birth rate: 21.4/1000; infant mortality rate: 55.5/1000; life expectancy: 64.2; density per sq mi: 5
Capital and largest city (2003 est.): Ulaan Baatar, 804,200. **Monetary unit:** Tugrik. **Languages:** Mongolian, 90%; also Turkic and Russian (1999). **Ethnicity/race:** Mongol (predominantly Khalkha) 85%, Turkic (of which Kazak is the largest group) 7%, Tungusic 4.6%, other (including Chinese and Russian) 3.4% (1998). **Religions:** Tibetan Buddhist Lamaism 96%, Islam (primarily in the southwest), Shamanism, and Christian 4% (1998). **Literacy rate:** 99% (2003 est.)
Economic summary: GDP/PPP (2003 est.): $4.877 billion; per capita $1,800. **Real growth rate:** 5%. **Inflation:** 1.5% (2002 est.). **Unemployment:** 4.6% (2002). **Arable land:** 1%. **Agriculture:** wheat, barley, potatoes, forage crops; sheep, goats, cattle, camels, horses. **Labor force:** 1.4 million (2001); primarily herding/agricultural. **Industries:** construction materials, mining (coal, copper, molybdenum, fluorspar, and gold); oil; food and beverages, processing of animal products. **Natural resources:** oil, coal, copper, molybdenum, tungsten, phosphates, tin, nickel, zinc, wolfram, fluorspar, gold, silver, iron, phosphate. **Exports:** $524 million (f.o.b., 2002 est.): copper, livestock, animal products, cashmere, wool, hides, fluorspar, other nonferrous metals. **Imports:** $691 million (c.i.f., 2002 est.): machinery and equipment, fuels, food products, industrial consumer goods, chemicals, building materials, sugar, tea. **Major trading partners:** China, U.S., Russia, South Korea, Germany, Japan.

Geography Mongolia lies in central Asia between Siberia on the north and China on the south. It is slightly larger than Alaska.

The productive regions of Mongolia—a tableland ranging from 3,000 to 5,000 ft (914 to 1,524 m) in elevation—are in the north, which is well drained by numerous rivers, including the Hovd, Onon, Selenga, and Tula. Much of the Gobi Desert falls within Mongolia.

Government Parliamentary republic now in transition from Communism.

History Nomadic tribes that periodically plundered agriculturally based China from the west are recorded in Chinese history dating back more than 2,000 years. It was to protect China from these marauding peoples that the Great Wall was constructed around 200 B.C. The name *Mongol* comes from a small tribe whose leader, Ghengis Khan, began a conquest that would eventually encompass an enormous empire stretching from Asia to Europe, as far west as the Black Sea and as far south as India and the Himalayas. But by the 14th century, the kingdom was in serious decline, with invasions from a resurgent China and internecine warfare.

The State of Mongolia was formerly known as Outer Mongolia. It contains the original homeland of the historic Mongols, whose power reached its zenith during the 13th century under Kublai Khan. The area accepted Manchu rule in 1689, but after the Chinese Revolution of 1911 and the fall of the Manchus in 1912, the northern Mongol princes expelled the Chinese officials and declared independence under the Khutukhtu, or "Living Buddha."

In 1921, Soviet troops entered the country, and facilitated the establishment of a republic by Mongolian revolutionaries in 1924. China also made a claim to the region, but was too weak to assert it. Under the 1945 Chinese-Russian Treaty, China agreed to give up Outer Mongolia, which, after a plebiscite, became a nominally independent country.

Allied with the USSR in its dispute with China, Mongolia began mobilizing troops along its borders in 1968 when the two powers became involved in border clashes on the Kazakh-Sinkiang frontier to the west and at the Amur and Ussuri Rivers. A 20-year treaty of friendship and cooperation, signed in 1966, entitled Mongolia to call upon the USSR for military aid in the event of invasion.

In 1989, the Mongolian democratic revolution began, led by Sanjaasurengiyn Zorig. Free elections held in Aug. 1990 produced a multiparty government, though it was still largely Communist. As a result, Mongolia has moved only gradually toward a market economy. With the collapse of the USSR, however, Mongolia was deprived of Soviet aid. Primarily in reaction to the economic turmoil, the Communist Mongolian People's Revolutionary Party (MPRP) won a significant majority in parliamentary elections in 1992. In 1996, however, the Democratic Alliance, an electoral coalition, defeated the MPRP, breaking with Communist rule for the first time since 1921. But in 1997, a former Communist and chairman of the People's Revolutionary Party, Natsagiyn Bagabandi, was elected president, further strengthening the hand of the anti-reformers.

Disagreement within Mongolia's ruling coalition over the pace and direction of market reforms in April 1998 caused a shakeup that thrust Tsakhiagiyn Elbegdorj, a pro-reform politician, into the prime minister's position. But parliamentary cross-purposes led to his resignation, and a succession of prime ministers followed.

Former Communist Natsagiyn Bagabandi was reelected president in 2001. In 2004 elections, however, the MPRP was dealt a stunning blow, reducing its number of seats in parliament from 72 to 36. The opposition Motherland Democratic Coalition took 34 seats, and in August, its leader, Tsakhiagiyn Elbegdorj, was appointed prime minister to lead a coalition government.

Morocco

KINGDOM OF MOROCCO

National name: al-Mamlaka al-Maghrebia
Ruler: King Muhammad VI (1999)
Prime Minister: Driss Jettou (2002)
Area: 172,413 sq mi (446,550 sq km)
Population (2004 est.): 32,209,101 (growth rate: 1.6%); birth rate: 22.8/1000; infant mortality rate: 43.3/1000; life expectancy: 70.4; density per sq mi: 187
Capital (2003 est.): Rabat, 1,636,600. **Largest cities:** Casablanca, 3,397,000; Fez, 941,800; Marrakech, 755,200. **Monetary unit:** Dirham. **Languages:** Arabic (official), Berber dialects, French often used for business, government, and diplomacy. **Ethnicity/race:** Arab-Berber 99.1%, Jewish 0.2%, other 0.7%. **Religions:** Islam 98.7%, Christian 1.1%, Jewish 0.2%. **Literacy rate:** 52% (2003 est.)
Economic summary: GDP/PPP (2003 est.): $128.3 billion; per capita $4,000. **Real growth rate:** 6%. **Inflation:** 3.6% (2002 est.). **Unemployment:** 19%. **Arable land:** 20%. **Agriculture:** barley, wheat, citrus, wine, vegetables, olives; livestock. **Labor force:** 11 million (1999); agriculture 50%, services 35%, industry 15% (1999 est.). **Industries:** phosphate rock mining and processing, food processing, leather goods, textiles, construction, tourism. **Natural resources:** phosphates, iron ore, manganese, lead, zinc, fish, salt. **Exports:** $8.466 billion (f.o.b., 2003 est.): clothing, fish, inorganic chemicals, transistors, crude minerals, fertilizers (including phosphates), petroleum products, fruits, vegetables. **Imports:** $12.75 billion (f.o.b., 2003 est.): crude petroleum, textile fabric, telecommunications equipment, wheat, gas and electricity, transistors, plastics. **Major trading partners:** France, Spain, UK, Germany, Italy, U.S., Saudi Arabia.

Geography Morocco, about one-tenth larger than California, lies across the Strait of Gibraltar on the Mediterranean and looks out on the Atlantic from the northwest shoulder of Africa. Algeria is to the east and Mauritania to the south. On the Atlantic coast there is a fertile plain. The Mediterranean coast is mountainous. The Atlas Mountains, running northeastward from the south to the Algerian frontier, average 11,000 ft (3,353 m) in elevation.

Government Constitutional monarchy.

History Morocco has been the home of the Berbers since the second millennium B.C. In A.D. 46, Morocco was annexed by Rome as part of the province of Mauritania until the Vandals overran this portion of the declining empire in the 5th century. The Arabs invaded circa 685, bringing Islam. The Berbers joined them in invading Spain in 711, but then revolted against the Arabs, resenting their secondary status. In 1086, Berbers took control of large areas of Moorish Spain until they were expelled in the 13th century.

The land was rarely unified and was usually ruled by small tribal states. Conflicts between Berbers and Arabs were chronic. Portugal and Spain began invading Morocco, which helped to unify the land in defense. In 1660, Morocco came under the control of the Alawite dynasty. It is a sherif dynasty—descended from the prophet Muhammad—and rules Morocco to this day.

During the 17th and 18th centuries Morocco was one of the Barbary states, the headquarters of pirates who pillaged Mediterranean traders. European powers became interested in colonizing the country beginning in 1840, and there were frequent clashes with the French and Spanish. Finally, in 1904, France and Spain concluded a secret agreement that divided Morocco into zones of French and Spanish influence, with France controlling almost all of Morocco and Spain controlling the small southwest portion, which became known as Spanish Sahara. Morocco became an even greater object of European rivalry by the turn of the century, leading almost to a European war in 1905 when Germany attempted to gain a foothold in the mineral-rich country. By the terms of the Algeciras Conference (1906), the sultan of Morocco maintained control of his lands and France's privileges were curtailed. The conference was a telling indication of what was to come in World War I, with Germany and Austria-Hungary lining up on one side of the territorial dispute, and France, Britain, and the United States on the other.

In 1912, the sultan of Morocco, Moulay Abd al-Hafid, permitted the French protectorate status. Nationalism began to grow during World War II. Sultan Mohammed V was deposed by the French in 1953 and replaced by his uncle, but nationalist agitation forced his return in 1955. In 1956, France and Spain recognized the independence and sovereignty of Morocco. On his death on Feb. 26, 1961, Mohammed V's son succeeded him as King Hassan II. In the 1990s, King Hassan promulgated "Hassanian democracy," which allowed for significant political freedom while at the same time retaining ultimate power for the monarch. In Aug. 1999, King Hassan II died after 38 years on the throne and his son, Prince Sidi Muhammad, was crowned King Muhammad VI. Since then Muhammad VI has pledged to make the political system more open, to allow freedom of expression, and to support economic reform. He has also advocated giving more rights to women, which has been opposed by Islamic fundamentalists. The entrenched political elite and the military have also been leery of some reform proposals. With about 20% of the population living in dire poverty, economic expansion is a prime goal.

Morocco's occupation of Western Sahara (formerly Spanish Sahara) has been repeatedly criticized by the international community. In the 1970s, tens of thousands of Moroccans crossed the border into Spanish Sahara to back their government's contention that the northern part of the territory was historically part of Morocco. Spain, which had controlled the territory since 1912, withdrew in 1976, creating a power vacuum that was filled by Morocco in the north and Mauritania in the south. When Mauritania withdrew in Aug. 1979, Morocco overran the remainder of the territory. A rebel group, the Polisario Front, has fought against Morocco since 1976 for the independence of Western Sahara on behalf of the indigenous Saharawis. The Polisario and Morocco agreed in Sept. 1991 to a UN-negotiated cease-fire, which was contingent on a referendum regarding independence. For the past decade, however, Morocco has opposed the referendum. In 2002, King Mohammed VI reasserted that he "will not renounce an inch of" Western Sahara.

On May 16, 2003, terrorists, believed to be associated with al-Qaeda, killed 33 people in several simultaneous attacks. Four bombs targeted Jewish, Spanish, and Belgian buildings in Casablanca. In the 2004 terrorist bombings in Madrid, Spain, numerous Moroccans were implicated.

Mozambique

REPUBLIC OF MOZAMBIQUE

National name: República de Moçambique
President: Joaquim Chissanó (1986)
Prime Minister: Luisa Diogo (2004)
Area: 309,494 sq mi (801,590 sq km)
Population (2004 est.): 18,811,731 (growth rate: 1.2%);

birth rate: 36.1/1000; infant mortality rate: 137.1/1000; life expectancy: 37.1; density per sq mi: 61
Capital and largest city (2003 est.): Maputo, 1,691,000 (metro. area), 1,114,000 (city proper). **Monetary unit:** Metical. **Languages:** Portuguese (official), Bantu languages. **Ethnicity/race:** indigenous tribal groups 99.66% (Shangaan, Chokwe, Manyika, Sena, Makua, and others), Europeans 0.06%, Euro-Africans 0.2%, Indians 0.08%. **Religions:** indigenous beliefs 50%, Christian 30%, Islam 20%. **Literacy rate:** 48% (2003 est.)
Economic summary: GDP/PPP (2003 est.): $21.23 billion; per capita $1,200. **Real growth rate:** 7%. **Inflation:** 15.2% (2002 est.). **Unemployment:** 21% (1997 est.). **Arable land:** 4%. **Agriculture:** cotton, cashew nuts, sugarcane, tea, cassava (tapioca), corn, coconuts, sisal, citrus and tropical fruits, potatoes, sunflowers; beef, poultry. **Labor force:** 9.2 million (2000 est.); agriculture 81%, industry 6%, services 13% (1997 est.). **Industries:** food, beverages, chemicals (fertilizer, soap, paints), aluminum, petroleum products, textiles, cement, glass, asbestos, tobacco. **Natural resources:** coal, titanium, natural gas, hydropower, tantalum, graphite. **Exports:** $795 million (f.o.b., 2003 est.): aluminum, prawns, cashews, cotton, sugar, citrus, timber; bulk electricity. **Imports:** $1.142 billion (f.o.b., 2003 est.): machinery and equipment, vehicles, fuel, chemicals, metal products, foodstuffs, textiles. **Major trading partners:** Belgium, South Africa, Germany, France, U.S., Australia, Japan, Malaysia.

Geography Mozambique stretches for 1,535 mi (2,470 km) along Africa's southeast coast. It is nearly twice the size of California. Tanzania is to the north; Malawi, Zambia, and Zimbabwe to the west; and South Africa and Swaziland to the south. The country is generally a low-lying plateau broken up by 25 sizable rivers that flow into the Indian Ocean. The largest is the Zambezi, which provides access to central Africa.

Government Multiparty republic.

History Bantu-speakers migrated to Mozambique in the first millennium, and Arab and Swahili traders settled the region thereafter. It was explored by Vasco da Gama in 1498, and first colonized by Portugal in 1505. By 1510, the Portuguese had control of all the former Arab sultanates on the east African coast. Portuguese colonial rule was repressive.

Guerrilla activity began in 1963 and became so effective by 1973 that Portugal was forced to dispatch 40,000 troops to fight the rebels. A cease-fire was signed in Sept. 1974, and after having been under Portuguese colonial rule for 470 years, Mozambique became independent on June 25, 1975. The first president, Samora Moises Machel, had been the head of the National Front for the Liberation of Mozambique (FRELIMO) in its ten-year guerrilla war for independence. He died in a plane crash in 1986 and was succeeded by his foreign minister, Joaquim Chissanó.

On Jan. 25, 1985, after a decade of independence, the government was locked in a paralyzing war with antigovernment guerrillas, the Mozambique National Resistance (MNR or Renamo), who were backed by the white minority government in South Africa. The guerrilla movement weakened President Chissanó's attempts to institute socialism, which he then decided to abandon in 1989. A new constitution was drafted calling for three branches of government and granting civil liberties. A cease-fire agreement was signed in Oct. 1992 between the government and the MNR, ending 16 years of civil war.

In multiparty elections in 1994 President Chissanó won. In Nov. 1995 the country was the first non-former British colony to become a member of the British Commonwealth. The president's disciplined economic plan was highly successful, winning the country foreign confidence and aid. While Mozambique posted some of the world's largest economic growth rates in the late 1990s, it has suffered enormous setbacks because of natural disaster—the enormous damage caused by severe flooding in the winters of 2000 and 2001. Hundreds have died and thousands were displaced.

In 2002 Chissanó announced he would not seek a third term in the 2004 presidential election. FRELIMO selected independence hero Armando Guebuza as their new candidate.

Myanmar

UNION OF MYANMAR

National name: Pyidaungsu Myanmar Naingngandau
Head of State: Senior Gen. Than Shwe (1992)
Prime Minister: Gen. Khin Nyunt (2003)
Area: 261,969 sq mi (678,500 sq km)
Population (2004 est.): 42,720,196 (growth rate: 0.5%); birth rate: 18.6/1000; infant mortality rate: 68.8/1000; life expectancy: 56.0; density per sq mi: 163
Capital and largest city (2003 est.): Rangoon (Yangon), 4,344,100. **Other large city:** Mandalay, 1,147,400. **Monetary unit:** Kyat. **Languages:** Burmese, minority languages. **Ethnicity/race:** Burman 68%, Shan 9%, Karen 7%, Rakhine 4%, Chinese 3%, Mon 2%, Indian 2%, other 5%. **Religions:** Buddhist 89%, Christian 4% (Baptist 3%, Roman Catholic 1%), Islam 4%, Animist 1%, other 2%. **Literacy rate:** 83% (1995 est.)
Economic summary: GDP/PPP (2003 est.): $78.8 billion; per capita $1,900. **Real growth rate:** 5.2%. **Inflation:** 52.8%. **Unemployment:** 5.1% (2001 est.). **Arable land:** 15%. **Agriculture:** rice, pulses, beans, sesame, groundnuts, sugarcane; hardwood; fish and fish products. **Labor force:** 23.7 million (1999 est.); agriculture 70%, industry 7%, services 23% (2001 est.). **Industries:** agricultural processing; knit and woven apparel; wood and wood products; copper, tin, tungsten, iron; construction materials; pharmaceuticals; fertilizer. **Natural resources:** petroleum, timber, tin, antimony, zinc, copper, tungsten, lead, coal, some marble, limestone, precious stones, natural gas, hydropower. **Exports:** $2.434 billion (f.o.b., 2003 est.): gas, wood products, pulses, beans, fish, rice. **Imports:** $2.071 billion (f.o.b., 2003 est.): machinery, transport equipment, construction materials, crude oil; food products. **Major trading partners:** Thailand, U.S., India, China, Singapore, Malaysia, Taiwan, South Korea, Japan.

Geography Slightly smaller than Texas, Myanmar occupies the Thailand/Cambodia portion of the Indochinese peninsula. India lies to the northwest and China to the northeast. Bangladesh, Laos, and Thailand are also neighbors. The Bay of Bengal touches the southwest coast. The fertile delta of the Irrawaddy River in the south contains a network of intercommunicating canals and nine principal river mouths.

Government Military regime. In 1989, the military government changed the name of Burma to Myanmar. The U.S. State Department does not recognize the name Myanmar or the military regime that represents it.

History The ethnic origins of modern Myanmar (known historically as Burma) are a mixture of Indo-Aryans, who began pushing into the area around 700

B.C., and the Mongolian invaders under Kublai Khan who penetrated the region in the 13th century. Anawrahta (1044–1077) was the first great unifier of Myanmar.

In 1612, the British East India Company sent agents to Burma, but the Burmese doggedly resisted efforts of British, Dutch, and Portuguese traders to establish posts along the Bay of Bengal. Through the Anglo-Burmese War in 1824–1826 and two subsequent wars, the British East India Company expanded to the whole of Burma. By 1886, Myanmar was annexed to India, then became a separate colony in 1937.

During World War II, Burma was a key battle-ground; the 800-mile Burma Road was the Allies' vital supply line to China. The Japanese invaded the country in Dec. 1941, and by May 1942 had occupied most of it, cutting off the Burma Road. After one of the most difficult campaigns of the war, Allied forces liberated most of Burma prior to the Japanese surrender in Aug. 1945.

Burma became independent on Jan. 4, 1948. In 1962, left-wing general Ne Win staged a coup, banned political opposition, suspended the constitution, and introduced the "Burmese way of socialism." After 25 years of economic hardship and repression, the Burmese people held massive demonstrations in 1987 and 1988. These were brutally quashed by the State Law and Order Council (SLORC). In 1989, the military government officially changed the name of the country to Myanmar.

In May 1990 elections, the opposition National League for Democracy (NLD) won in a landslide. But the military, or SLORC, refused to recognize the election results. The leader of the opposition, Aung San Suu Kyi, was awarded the Nobel Peace Prize in 1991, which focused world attention on SLORC's repressive policies. Daughter of the assassinated general Aung San, who was revered as the father of Burmese independence, Suu Kyi remained under house arrest from 1989 until 1995. A new constitution was drafted in 1994 that called for an elected executive branch but appeared designed specifically to forbid Suu Kyi from becoming president. Suu Kyi continued to protest against the government, but almost every move she made was answered with a counterblow from SLORC.

Although the ruling junta has maintained a tight grip on Myanmar since 1988, it has not been able to subdue an insurgency in the country's south that has gone on for decades. The ethnic Karen movement has sought an independent homeland along Myanmar's southern border with Thailand. In Jan. 2004, the military government and the insurgents from the Karen National Union agreed to end the fighting, but they stopped short of signing a cease-fire.

From 2000 to 2002, Suu Kyi was again placed under house arrest. In spring 2003, the government cracked down once again on the democracy movement, detaining Suu Kyi and shuttering NLD headquarters. The regime opened a constitutional convention in May 2004, but many observers doubted its legitimacy.

Namibia

REPUBLIC OF NAMIBIA

President: Sam Nujoma (1990)
Prime Minister: Theo-Ben Gurirab (2002)
Area: 318,694 sq mi (825,418 sq km)
Population (2004 est.): 1,954,033 (growth rate: 1.2%); birth rate: 33.5/1000; infant mortality rate: 69.6/1000; life expectancy: 40.5; density per sq mi: 6
Capital and largest city (2003 est.): Windhoek, 221,000. **Summer capital:** Swakopmund, 26,200.
Monetary unit: Namibian dollar. **Languages:** English

7% (official), Afrikaans common language of most of the population and about 60% of the white population, German 32%, indigenous languages: Oshivambo, Herero, Nama. **Ethnicity/race:** black 87.5%, white 6%, mixed 6.5%. Note: about 50% of the population belong to the Ovambo tribe and 9% to the Kavangos tribe; other ethnic groups are: Herero 7%, Damara 7%, Nama 5%, Caprivian 4%, Bushmen 3%, Baster 2%, Tswana 0.5%. **Religion:** Christian 80%–90% (Lutheran at least 50%), indigenous beliefs 10%–20%. **Literacy rate:** 84% (2003 est.)

Economic summary: GDP/PPP (2003 est.): $13.72 billion; per capita $7,100. **Real growth rate:** 3.3%. **Inflation:** 8%. **Unemployment:** 35% (1998). **Arable land:** 1%. **Agriculture:** millet, sorghum, peanuts; livestock; fish. **Labor force:** 725,000 (2000); agriculture 47%, industry 25%, services, 28% (1999 est.). **Industries:** meatpacking, fish processing, dairy products; mining (diamond, lead, zinc, tin, silver, tungsten, uranium, copper). **Natural resources:** diamonds, copper, uranium, gold, lead, tin, lithium, cadmium, zinc, salt, vanadium, natural gas, hydropower, fish; note: suspected deposits of oil, coal, and iron ore. **Exports:** $1.09 billion (f.o.b., 2003 est.): diamonds, copper, gold, zinc, lead, uranium; cattle, processed fish, karakul skins. **Imports:** $1.371 billion (f.o.b., 2003 est.): foodstuffs; petroleum products and fuel, machinery and equipment, chemicals. **Major trading partners:** EU, U.S.

Geography Namibia is bounded on the north by Angola and Zambia, on the east by Botswana, and on the east and south by South Africa. It is for the most part a portion of the high plateau of southern Africa, with a general elevation of from 3,000 to 4,000 ft.

Government Republic.

History The San peoples may have inhabited what is now Namibia more than 2,000 years ago. The Bantu-speaking Herero migrated there in the 1600s. The Ovambo, the largest ethnic group today, migrated there in the 1800s.

In the late 15th century, the Portuguese explorer Bartolomeu Dias became the first European to visit Namibia. Formerly called South-West Africa, the territory became a German colony in 1884. Between 1904 and 1908, German troops massacred tens of thousands of Hereros, who had revolted against colonial domination. In 1915, during World War I, Namibian territory was taken over by South African forces, and became a South African mandate by the terms of the Treaty of Versailles in 1920.

South Africa's intention to incorporate the territory was rejected by the UN in 1946, but in 1949, the territory was brought into much closer association with South Africa. A black Marxist separatist group, the South West African People's Organization (SWAPO), formed in 1960, and began small-scale guerrilla attacks aimed at achieving independence. In 1968, the UN called for South Africa's withdrawal from the territory, which was officially renamed Namibia. South Africa refused. Under a 1974 Security Council resolution, South Africa was required to begin the transfer of power or face UN action. Prime Minister Balthazar J. Vorster rejected UN supervision, claiming that his government was prepared to negotiate Namibian independence, but not with SWAPO. The UN had recognized SWAPO as the "sole legitimate representative" of the Namibian people.

South Africa handed over limited powers to a new, multiracial administration in 1985 (the previous government had enforced South Africa's apartheid laws). Installation of the new government ended South Africa's direct rule, but South Africa retained an effective veto over the new government's decisions. Finally, in 1988 South Africa agreed to Namibian independence. SWAPO leader Sam Nujoma was elected president, and on March 21, 1990, Namibia achieved independence.

Nujoma was reelected in 1994, and again in 1999, after the constitution was amended to allow him to seek a third term. Nujoma announced in Nov. 2001 that he would not seek reelection when his term expires in 2004.

In 2004, Germany issued a formal apology for the massacre of Hereros by German colonial troops between 1904 and 1908.

Nauru
REPUBLIC OF NAURU

President: Ludwig Scotty (2004)
Area: 8.11 sq mi (21 sq km)
Population (2004 est.): 12,809 (growth rate: 1.9%); birth rate: 25.6/1000; infant mortality rate: 10.1/1000; life expectancy: 62.3; density per sq mi: 1,580
Capital and largest city (2003 est.): Yaren, 4,900.
Monetary unit: Australian dollar. **Languages:** Nauruan (official), English. **Ethnicity/race:** Nauruan 58%, other Pacific Islander 26%, Chinese 8%, European 8%. **Religions:** Christian (two-thirds Protestant, one-third Roman Catholic). **Literacy rate:** n.a
Economic summary: GDP/PPP (2001 est.): $60 million; per capita $5,000. **Real growth rate:** n.a. **Inflation:** −3.6% (1993). **Unemployment:** 0% (2002 est.). **Arable land:** 0%. **Agriculture:** coconuts. **Labor force:** employed in mining phosphates, public administration, education, and transportation. **Industries:** phosphate mining, offshore banking, coconut products. **Natural resources:** phosphates, fish. **Exports:** $18 million (f.o.b., 2002): phosphates. **Imports:** $31 million (c.i.f., 2002): food, fuel, manufactures, building materials, machinery. **Major trading partners:** India, South Korea, Australia, New Zealand, Netherlands, U.S., Ireland, Malaysia. **Special relationship within the Commonwealth of Nations**

Geography Nauru (pronounced NAH-oo-roo) is an island in the Pacific just south of the equator, about 2,500 mi (4,023 km) southwest of Honolulu. Phosphate mining has virtually destroyed the tiny nation's ecology, turning its tropical vegetation into a barren, rocky wasteland.

Government Republic.

History In 1798, a British navigator became the first European to visit the island. Germany annexed it in 1888, and by the turn of the century, phosphate, a lucrative fertilizer, began to be mined. The island was placed under joint Australian, New Zealand, and British mandate after World War I. The Japanese occupied the island during World War II, and forced 1,200 Nauruans—roughly two-thirds of the population—to relocate. In 1947, it became a UN trusteeship administered by Australia. By 1967, the phosphate mining industry finally came under control of the islanders, and on Jan. 31, 1968, Nauru became one of the world's smallest independent republics. For a period of time, Nauru's phosphate made the tiny country's per capita income the highest in the world, after Saudi Arabia.

As its phosphate stores began to run out (by 2006, its reserves will be exhausted), the island was reduced to an environmental wasteland. Nauru appealed to the International Court of Justice to compensate for the damage from almost a century of phosphate strip-mining by foreign companies. In 1993, Australia

offered Nauru an out-of-court settlement of $2.5 million Australian dollars annually for 20 years. New Zealand and the UK additionally agreed to pay a one-time settlement of $12 million each. Declining phosphate prices, the high cost of maintaining an international airline, and the government's financial mismanagement combined to make the economy collapse in the late 1990s. By the millennium Nauru was virtually bankrupt.

In 2000, the G7 nations put pressure on the country to review its banking system, which is used by Russian criminals for money laundering.

Since Sept. 2001, Nauru has accepted three boatloads of Asian refugees destined for Australia. Australia compensated the island with $20 million and other financial incentives for taking this refugee problem off its hands. The detention camps, which held more than 400 asylum seekers in 2003, are said to be extremely bleak and lack medical care.

Bernard Dowiyogo, elected in 2003 as president for the seventh time (nonsequentially), died in March 2003 following emergency heart surgery. Ludwig Scotty, a senior cabinet minister, was elected in May 2003 elections. But in August, Scotty was sacked in a no-confidence vote, and René Harris, who has twice served as president, was elected to the post. But, given Nauru's tumultuous politics, by June 2004 Scotty had again regained the presidency.

Nepal
KINGDOM OF NEPAL

Ruler: King Gyanendra Bir Bikram Shah Deva (2001)
Prime Minister: Sher Bahadur Deuba (2004)
Area: 54,363 sq mi (140,800 sq km)
Population (2004 est.): 27,070,666 (growth rate: 2.2%); birth rate: 32.0/1000; infant mortality rate: 68.8/1000; life expectancy: 59.4; density per sq mi: 498
Capital and largest city (2003 est.): Kathmandu, 1,203,100 (metro. area), 729,000 (city proper). **Other large cities:** Biratnagar, 174,600; Lalitpur, 169,100.
Monetary unit: Nepalese rupee. **Languages:** Nepali 90% (official), over 40 other languages and major dialects, English (1995). **Ethnicity/race:** Brahmin, Chetri, Newar, Gurung, Magar, Tamang, Rai, Limbu, Sherpa, Tharu, and others (1995). **Religions:** Hindu 86.2%, Buddhist 7.8%, Islam 3.8%, other 2.2% (1995). **Literacy rate:** 45% (2003 est.)
Economic summary: GDP/PPP (2003 est.): $38.07 billion; per capita $1,400. **Real growth rate:** 2.4%. **Inflation:** 2.9% (2002 est.). **Unemployment:** 47% (2001 est.). **Arable land:** 20%. **Agriculture:** rice, corn, wheat, sugarcane, root crops; milk, water buffalo meat. **Labor force:** 10 million (1996 est.); note: severe lack of skilled labor; agriculture 81%, services 16%, industry 3%. **Industries:** tourism, carpet, textile; small rice, jute, sugar, and oilseed mills; cigarette; cement and brick production. **Natural resources:** quartz, water, timber, hydropower, scenic beauty, small deposits of lignite, copper, cobalt, iron ore. **Exports:** $568 million (f.o.b., 2002 est.), but does not include unrecorded border trade with India: carpets, clothing, leather goods, jute goods, grain. **Imports:** $1.419 billion (f.o.b., 2002 est.): gold, machinery and equipment, petroleum products, fertilizer. **Major trading partners:** India, U.S., Germany, China, UAE, Singapore, Hong Kong, Saudi Arabia, Kuwait.

Geography A landlocked country the size of Arkansas, lying between India and the Tibetan Autonomous Region of China, Nepal contains Mount Everest (29,035 ft; 8,850 m), the tallest mountain in the world. Along its southern border, Nepal has a strip of level land that is partly forested, partly cultivated. North of that is the slope of the main section of the Himalayan range, including Everest and many other peaks higher than 8,000 m.

Government In Nov. 1990, King Birendra promulgated a new constitution and introduced a multiparty parliamentary democracy in Nepal.

History The first civilizations in Nepal, which flourished around the 6th century B.C., were confined to the fertile Kathmandu Valley where the present-day capital of the same name is located. It was in this region that Prince Siddhartha Gautama was born circa 563 B.C. Gautama achieved enlightenment as Buddha, and spawned Buddhist belief.

Nepali rulers' early patronage of Buddhism largely gave way to Hinduism, reflecting the increased influence of India, around the 12th century. Though the successive dynasties of the Gopalas, the Kiratis, and the Licchavis expanded their rule, it was not until the reign of the Malla kings from 1200–1769 that Nepal assumed the approximate dimensions of the modern state.

The kingdom of Nepal was unified in 1768 by King Prithvi Narayan Shah, who had fled India following the Moghul conquests of the subcontinent. Under Shah and his successors Nepal's borders expanded as far west as Kashmir and as far east as Sikkim (now part of India). A commercial treaty was signed with Britain in 1792, and again in 1816 after more than a year of hostilities with the British East India Company.

In 1923, Britain recognized the absolute independence of Nepal. Between 1846 and 1951, the country was ruled by the Rana family, which always held the office of prime minister. In 1951, however, the king took over all power and proclaimed a constitutional monarchy. Mahendra Bir Bikram Shah became king in 1955. After Mahendra died of a heart attack in 1972, Prince Birendra, at 26, succeeded to the throne.

In 1990, a prodemocracy movement forced King Birendra to lift the ban on political parties. The first free election in three decades provided a victory for the liberal Nepali Congress Party in 1991, although the Communists made a strong showing. A small but growing Maoist guerrilla movement, seeking to overthrow the constitutional monarchy and install a Communist government, began operating in the countryside in 1996.

On June 1, 2001, King Birendra was shot and killed by his son, Crown Prince Dipendra. Angered by his family's disapproval of his choice of a bride, he also killed his mother and several other members of the royal family before shooting himself. Prince Gyanendra, the younger brother of King Birendra, was then crowned king.

The Maoist guerrillas significantly stepped up their insurgency in 2001, and King Gyanendra declared a state of emergency in November and ordered the army to crack down on the group. The rebels intensified their campaign in 2002, and the government responded with equal intensity, killing hundreds of Maoists, the largest toll since the insurgency began in 1996. In Aug. 2003, the Maoist rebels withdrew from peace talks with the government and ended a cease-fire that had been signed in Jan. 2003. The following August, the rebels blockaded Kathmandu for a week, cutting off shipments of food and fuel to the capital.

In Aug. 2004, 12 Nepalese laborers were taken hostage and executed in Iraq by a group of insurgents called the Army of Ansar al-Sunna. Violent protest against Muslims erupted in Kathmandu.

The Netherlands

KINGDOM OF THE NETHERLANDS

National name: Koninkrijk der Nederlanden
Sovereign: Queen Beatrix (1980)
Prime Minister: Jan Peter Balkenende (2002)
Area: 16,033 sq mi (41,526 sq km)
Population (2004 est.): 16,318,199 (growth rate: 0.6%); birth rate: 11.4/1000; infant mortality rate: 5.1/1000; life expectancy: 78.7; density per sq mi: 1,018
Capital and largest city (2003 est.): Amsterdam (official), 737,900; The Hague (administrative capital), 465,900. **Other large cities:** Rotterdam, 600,700; Utrecht, 263,900; Eindhoven, 206,900. **Monetary units:** Euro (formerly guilder). **Language:** Dutch, Frisian (both official). **Ethnicity/race:** Dutch 83%, other 17% (9% of non-Western origin, mainly Turks, Moroccans, Antilleans, Surinamese, and Indonesians) (1999 est.). **Religions:** Roman Catholic 31%, Protestant 21%, Islam 4.4%, other 3.6%, unaffiliated 40% (1998). **Literacy rate:** 99% (2000 est.)
Economic summary: GDP/PPP (2003 est.): $461.4 billion; per capita $28,600. **Real growth rate:** –0.7%. **Inflation:** 2%. **Unemployment:** 4.2%. **Arable land:** 27%. **Agriculture:** grains, potatoes, sugar beets, fruits, vegetables; livestock. **Labor force:** 7.2 million (2000); services 73%, industry 23%, agriculture 4% (1998 est.). **Industries:** agroindustries, metal and engineering products, electrical machinery and equipment, chemicals, petroleum, construction, microelectronics, fishing. **Natural resources:** natural gas, petroleum, arable land. **Exports:** $253.2 billion (f.o.b., 2003 est.): machinery and equipment, chemicals, fuels; foodstuffs. **Imports:** $217.7 billion (f.o.b., 2003 est.): machinery and transport equipment, chemicals, fuels; foodstuffs, clothing. **Major trading partners:** Germany, Belgium, UK, France, Italy, U.S., China, Japan.

Geography The Netherlands, on the coast of the North Sea, is twice the size of New Jersey. Part of the great plain of north and west Europe, the Netherlands has maximum dimensions of 190 by 160 mi (360 by 257 km) and is low and flat except in Limburg in the southeast, where some hills rise up to 322 m (1056 ft). About half the country's area is below sea level, making the famous Dutch dikes a requisite for the use of much land. Reclamation of land from the sea through dikes has continued through recent times. All drainage reaches the North Sea, and the principal rivers—Rhine, Maas (Meuse), and Schelde—have their sources outside the country.

Government Constitutional monarchy.

History Julius Caesar found the low-lying Netherlands inhabited by Germanic tribes—the Nervii, Frisii, and Batavi. The Batavi on the Roman frontier did not submit to Rome's rule until 13 B.C., and then only as allies.

The Franks controlled the region from the 4th to the 8th century, and it became part of Charlemagne's empire in the 8th and 9th centuries. The area later passed into the hands of Burgundy and the Austrian Hapsburgs, and finally in the 16th century came under Spanish rule.

When Philip II of Spain suppressed political liberties and the growing Protestant movement in the Netherlands, a revolt led by William of Orange broke out in 1568. Under the Union of Utrecht (1579), the seven northern provinces became the United Provinces of the Netherlands. War between the United Provinces and Spain continued into the 17th century, but in 1648 Spain finally recognized Dutch independence.

The Dutch East India Company was established in 1602, and by the end of the 17th century Holland was one of the great sea and colonial powers of Europe.

The nation's independence was not completely established until after the Thirty Years' War (1618–1648), when the country's rise as a commercial and maritime power began. In 1688, the English Parliament invited William of Orange, stadtholder, and his wife, Mary Stuart, to rule England as William III and Mary II. William then used the combined resources of England and the Netherlands to wage war on Louis XIV's France. In 1814, all the provinces of Holland and Belgium were merged into one kingdom, but in 1830 the southern provinces broke away to form the kingdom of Belgium. A liberal constitution was adopted by the Netherlands in 1848. The country remained neutral during World War I.

In spite of its neutrality in World War II, the Netherlands was invaded by the Nazis in May 1940, and the Dutch East Indies were later taken by the Japanese. The nation was liberated in May 1945. In 1948, after a reign of 50 years, Queen Wilhelmina abdicated and was succeeded by her daughter Juliana.

In 1949, after a four-year war, the Netherlands granted independence to the Dutch East Indies, which became the Republic of Indonesia. The Netherlands also joined NATO that year. The Netherlands joined the European Economic Community (later, the EU) in 1958. In 1999, it adopted the single European currency, the euro.

In 1963, it turned over the western half of New Guinea to Indonesia, ending 300 years of Dutch presence in Asia. Attainment of independence by Suriname on Nov. 25, 1975, left the Netherlands Antilles and Aruba as the country's only overseas territories.

The Netherlands has extremely liberal social policies: prostitution is legal, and it became the first nation in the world to legalize same-sex marriages (2000) and euthanasia (2002).

Wim Kok's government resigned in April 2002 after a report concluded that Dutch UN troops failed to prevent a massacre of Bosnian Muslims by Bosnian Serbs in a UN safe haven near Srebrenica in 1995. Explaining his action, the popular prime minister said, "The international community is big and anonymous. We are taking the consequences of the international community's failure in Srebrenica."

The country's normally bland political scene was further rocked with the May 2002 assassination of Pim Fortuyn, a right-wing, anti-immigrant politician. Days later, his party, Lijst Pim Fortuyn, placed second in national elections, behind Jan Peter Balkenende's Christian Democrats. Leading the country into a marked shift to the right, Balkenende formed a three-way center-right coalition government with his Christian Democrats, Lijst Pim Fortuyn, and the People's Party for Freedom and Democracy. Balkenende became prime minister in July 2002.

In 2003, the Netherlands sent 1,100 troops to Iraq to support the U.S. troops stationed there.

Netherlands Autonomous Countries

Netherlands Antilles
Status: Part of the Kingdom of the Netherlands
Governor: Frits Goedgedrag (2002)
Prime Minister: Etienne Ys (2004)
Area: 371 sq mi (960 sq km)
Population (2004 est.): 218,126 (growth rate: 0.9%); birth rate: 15.4/1000; infant mortality rate: 10.4/1000; life expectancy: 75.6; density per sq mi: 588
Capital and largest city (2003 est.): Willemstad,

60,100. **Languages:** Dutch (official), Papiamento predominates, English widely spoken, Spanish. **Ethnicity/race:** mixed black 85%, Carib Amerindian, white, East Asian. **Religions:** Roman Catholic, Protestant, Jewish, Seventh-Day Adventist. **Literacy rate:** 97% (2003 est.)
Economic summary: GDP/PPP (2003 est.): $2.45 billion; per capita $11,400. **Real growth rate:** 0.5%. **Inflation:** 2.1%. **Unemployment:** 15.6% (2002 est.). **Arable land:** 10%. **Agriculture:** aloes, sorghum, peanuts, vegetables, tropical fruit. **Labor force:** 89,000 (2000); agriculture 1%, industry 13%, services 86% (2000 est.). **Industries:** tourism (Curacao, Sint Maarten, and Bonaire), petroleum refining (Curacao), petroleum transshipment facilities (Curacao and Bonaire), light manufacturing (Curacao). **Natural resources:** phosphates (Curacao only), salt (Bonaire only). **Exports:** $1.579 billion (f.o.b., 2002): petroleum products. **Imports:** $2.233 billion (f.o.b., 2002): crude petroleum, food, manufactures. **Major trading partners:** U.S., Guatemala, Venezuela, Guyana, Singapore, Cuba, Mexico.

The Netherlands Antilles are composed of two groups of Caribbean islands 500 mi (805 km) apart: the first group, composed of Curaçao (173 sq mi; 448 sq km) and Bonaire (95 sq mi; 246 sq km), is located about 40 mi (64 km) off the Venezuelan coast. Oiginally inhabited by Arawak Indians, these two islands as well as Aruba were claimed by Spain in 1527, and then by the Dutch in 1643. The Dutch Lesser Antilles to the north—Saint Eustatius, the southern part of Saint Martin (Dutch: Sint Maarten), and Saba—make up the remainder of the island federation. First inhabited by the Carib Indians, Saint Martin was explored by Columbus in 1493. In 1845, the six islands (then including Aruba) officially formed the Netherlands Antilles. In 1994, the islands voted to preserve their federation with the Netherlands.

Aruba
Status: Part of the Kingdom of the Netherlands
Governor: Fredis Refunjol (2004)
Prime Minister: Nelson O. Oduber (2001)
Area: 75 sq mi (193 sq km)
Population (2004 est.): 71,218 (growth rate: 0.5%); birth rate: 11.5/1000; infant mortality rate: 6.0/1000; life expectancy: 79.0; density per sq mi: 956
Capital and largest city (2003 est.): Oranjestad, 20,700. **Languages:** Dutch (official), Papiamento, English, Spanish. **Ethnicity/race:** mixed European/Caribbean Indian 80%. **Religions:** Roman Catholic 82%, Protestant 8%, Hindu, Muslim, Confucian, Jewish. **Literacy rate:** 97% (2003 est.)
Economic summary: GDP/PPP (2002 est.): $1.94 billion; per capita $28,000. **Real growth rate:** –1.5%. **Inflation:** 3.2%. **Unemployment:** 0.6% (2003 est.). **Arable land:** 11% aloe plantations included (0.01%). **Agriculture:** aloes; livestock; fish. **Labor force:** 41,501 (1997 est.); most employment is in wholesale and retail trade and repair, followed by hotels and restaurants; oil refining. **Industries:** tourism, transshipment facilities, oil refining. **Natural resources:** negl.; white sandy beaches. **Exports:** $128 million (including oil reexports) (f.o.b., 2002): live animals and animal products, art and collectibles, machinery and electrical equipment, transport equipment. **Imports:** $841 million (f.o.b., 2002 est.): machinery and electrical equipment, crude oil for refining and reexport, chemicals; foodstuffs. **Major trading partners:** Netherlands, Colombia, Panama, U.S., Netherlands Antilles, Venezuela, UK.

Aruba, an island slightly larger than Washington, DC, lies 18 mi (28.9 km) off the coast of Venezuela in the southern Caribbean.

The Arawak Indians were the first inhabitants of Aruba. Spain explored the island in 1499, and more than a century later the Netherlands (1636) claimed the island. After a brief rule by the British, the Dutch again took control of the island in 1816, and it officially became part of the Netherlands Antilles in 1845.

On Jan. 1, 1986, Aruba seceded from the federation, but decided in 1994 to indefinitely postpone the transition to full independence. The Netherlands controls Aruba's defense and foreign affairs, but all internal affairs are handled by an island government directing its own civil service, judiciary, revenue, and currency.

New Zealand

Sovereign: Queen Elizabeth II (1952)
Governor-General: Dame Silvia Cartwright (2001)
Prime Minister: Helen Clark (1999)
Area: 103,737 sq mi (268,680 sq km) (excluding dependencies)
Population (2004 est.): 3,993,817 (growth rate: 1.1%); birth rate: 14.0/1000; infant mortality rate: 6.0/1000; life expectancy: 78.5; density per sq mi: 38
Capital (2003 est.): Wellington, 342,500 (metro. area), 165,100 (city proper). **Largest cities:** Auckland, 369,300 (metro. area), 359,500 (city proper); Christchurch, 334,100. **Monetary unit:** New Zealand dollar. **Languages:** English, Maori (both official) . **Ethnicity/race:** New Zealand European 74.5%, Maori 9.7%, other European 4.6%, Pacific Islander 3.8%, Asian and others 7.4%. **Religions:** Anglican 24%, Presbyterian 18%, Roman Catholic 15%, Methodist 5%, Baptist 2%, other Protestant 3%, unspecified or none 33% (1986). **Literacy rate:** 99% (1980 est.)
Economic summary: GDP/PPP (2003 est.): $85.26 billion; per capita $21,600. **Real growth rate:** 3.4%. **Inflation:** 1.8%. **Unemployment:** 5.1%. **Arable land:** 6%. **Agriculture:** wheat, barley, potatoes, pulses, fruits, vegetables; wool, beef, dairy products; fish. **Labor force:** 1.92 million (2001 est.): services 65%, industry 25%, agriculture 10% (1995). **Industries:** food processing, wood and paper products, textiles, machinery, transportation equipment, banking and insurance, tourism, mining. **Natural resources:** natural gas, iron ore, sand, coal, timber, hydropower, gold, limestone. **Exports:** $15.86 billion (2003 est.): dairy products, meat, wood and wood products, fish, machinery. **Imports:** $16.06 billion (2003 est.): machinery and equipment, vehicles and aircraft, petroleum, electronics, textiles, plastics. **Major trading partners:** Australia, U.S., Japan, UK, China, South Korea, Germany. **Member of Commonwealth of Nations**

Geography New Zealand, about 1,250 mi (2,012 km) southeast of Australia, consists of two main islands and a number of smaller, outlying islands so scattered that they range from the tropical to the antarctic. The country is the size of Colorado. New Zealand's two main components are the North Island and the South Island, separated by Cook Strait. The North Island (44,281 sq mi; 115,777 sq km) is 515 mi (829 km) long and volcanic in its south-central part. This area contains many hot springs and beautiful geysers. South Island (58,093 sq mi; 151,215 sq km) has the Southern Alps along its west coast, with Mount Cook (12,316 ft; 3754 m) the highest point. Other inhabited islands include Stewart Island, the Chatham Islands, and Great Barrier Island.

Government Parliamentary democracy.

History Maoris were the first inhabitants of New Zealand, arriving on the islands in about 1000. Maori oral history maintains the Maoris came to the island in seven canoes from other parts of Polynesia. In 1642, New Zealand was explored by Abel Tasman, a Dutch navigator. British captain James Cook made three voyages to the islands, beginning in 1769. Britain formally annexed the islands in 1840.

The Treaty of Waitangi (Feb. 6, 1840) between the British and several Maori tribes promised to protect Maori land if the Maoris recognized British rule. Encroachment upon the land by British settlers was relentless, however, and skirmishes between the two groups intensified.

From the outset, the country has been in the forefront in instituting social welfare legislation. New Zealand was the world's first country to give women the right to vote (1893). It adopted old-age pensions (1898); a national child welfare program (1907); social security for the aged, widows, and orphans, along with family benefit payments; minimum wages; a 40-hour workweek and unemployment and health insurance (1938); and socialized medicine (1941).

New Zealand fought with the Allies in both world wars as well as in Korea. In 1999, it became part of the UN peacekeeping force sent to East Timor. In June 2002, Prime Minister Helen Clark apologized to the Samoans for the unfair treatment they received during colonial rule. The Labour Party's Clark was elected to a second term as prime minister in July 2002. In June 2003, Parliament legalized prostitution 60–59.

Cook Islands and Overseas Territories

The Cook Islands (93 sq mi; 241 sq km) were placed under New Zealand administration in 1901. They achieved self-governing status in association with New Zealand in 1965. **Population (July 2004 est.):** 21,200.

Niue (100 sq mi; 259 sq km) was formerly administered as part of the Cook Islands. It was placed under separate New Zealand administration in 1901 and achieved self-governing status in association with New Zealand in 1974. The capital is Alofi. **Population (2003 est.):** 2,145.

Tokelau (3.86 sq mi; 10 sq km) was formerly administered as part of the Gilbert and Ellice Islands colony. It was placed under New Zealand administration in 1925. **Population (2003 est.):** 1,418.

Nicaragua

REPUBLIC OF NICARAGUA

National name: República de Nicaragua
President: Enrique Bolaños (2002)
Area: 49,998 sq mi (129,494 sq km)
Population (2004 est.): 5,359,759 (growth rate: 2.0%); birth rate: 25.5/1000; infant mortality rate: 30.2/1000; life expectancy: 70.0; density per sq mi: 107
Capital and largest city (2003 est.): Managua, 1,390,500 (metro. area), 1,146,000 (city proper). **Monetary unit:** Gold cordoba. **Language:** Spanish (official); English and indigenous languages on Atlantic coast. **Ethnicity/race:** mestizo 69%, white 17%, black 9%, Amerindian 5%. **Religions:** Roman Catholic 85%, Protestant. **Literacy rate:** 68% (2003 est.)
Economic summary: GDP/PPP (2003 est.): $11.49 billion; per capita $2,200. **Real growth rate:** 1.4%. **Inflation:** 5.3%. **Unemployment:** 22% plus considerable underemployment. **Arable land:** 20%. **Agriculture:** coffee, bananas, sugarcane, cotton, rice, corn, tobacco, sesame, soya, beans; beef, veal, pork, poultry, dairy products. **Labor force:** 1.7 million (1999); services 43%, agriculture 42%, industry 15%

(1999 est.). **Industries:** food processing, chemicals, machinery and metal products, textiles, clothing, petroleum refining and distribution, beverages, footwear, wood. **Natural resources:** gold, silver, copper, tungsten, lead, zinc, timber, fish. **Exports:** $632 million (f.o.b., 2003 est.): coffee, bananas, sugarcane, cotton, rice, corn, tobacco, sesame, soya, beans; beef, veal, pork, poultry, dairy products. **Imports:** $1.658 billion (f.o.b., 2003 est.): machinery and equipment, raw materials, petroleum products, consumer goods. **Major trading partners:** U.S., El Salvador, Honduras, Costa Rica, Venezuela, Guatemala, Mexico, South Korea.

Geography Largest but most sparsely populated of the Central American nations, Nicaragua borders on Honduras to the north and Costa Rica to the south. It is slightly larger than New York State. Nicaragua is mountainous in the west, with fertile valleys. Two big lakes, Nicaragua and Managua, are connected by the Tipitapa River. The Pacific coast is volcanic and very fertile. The Caribbean coast, swampy and indented, is aptly called the "Mosquito Coast."

Government Republic.

History Nicaragua, which derives its name from the chief of the area's leading Indian tribe at the time of the Spanish Conquest, was first settled by the Spanish in 1522. The country won independence in 1838. For the next century, Nicaragua's politics were dominated by the competition for power between the Liberals, who were centered in the city of León, and the Conservatives, centered in Granada.

To back up its support of the new Conservative government in 1909, the U.S. sent a small detachment of Marines to Nicaragua from 1912 to 1925. The Bryan-Chamorro Treaty of 1916 (terminated in 1970) gave the U.S. an option on a canal route through Nicaragua and naval bases. U.S. Marines were sent again to quell disorder after the 1924 elections. A guerrilla leader, Gen. César Augusto Sandino, fought the U.S. troops from 1927 until their withdrawal in 1933.

After ordering Sandino's assassination, Gen. Anastasio Somoza García was dictator from 1936 until his own assassination in 1956. He was succeeded by his son Luis, who alternated with trusted family friends in the presidency until his death in 1967. He was succeeded by his brother, Maj. Gen. Anastasio Somoza Debayle. The Somozas ruled Nicaragua with an iron fist, reducing its dependence on banana exports, exiling political foes, and amassing a family fortune.

Sandinista guerrillas, leftists who took their name from Sandino, launched an offensive in 1979. After seven weeks of fighting, Somoza fled the country on July 17, 1979. The Sandinistas assumed power two days later. On Jan. 23, 1981, the Reagan administration suspended U.S. aid, charging that Nicaragua, with the aid of Cuba and the Soviet Union, was supplying arms to rebels in El Salvador. The Sandinistas denied the charges. Later that year, Nicaraguan guerrillas known as "Contras" began a war to overthrow the Sandinistas. Elections were finally held on Nov. 4, 1984, with Daniel Ortega, the Sandinista junta coordinator, winning the presidency. The war intensified in 1986–1987. Negotiations sponsored by the Contadora (neutral Latin American) nations foundered, but Costa Rican president Oscar Arias promoted a treaty signed by Central American leaders in Aug. 1987.

Violetta Barrios de Chamorro, owner of the opposition paper *La Prensa*, led a broad anti-Sandinista coalition to victory in the 1990 elections, ending 11 years of Sandinista rule. Enthusiasm for Chamorro gradually faded. Business groups were dissatisfied with the pace of reforms; Sandinistas, upset with what they regarded as the dismantling of their earlier achievements, threatened to take up arms again; and many people were disillusioned over governmental corruption.

Former Managua mayor and Conservative candidate Arnoldo Alemán won the 1996 election. Former Sandinista leader Daniel Ortega was his closest rival.

In 1998, Hurricane Mitch killed more than 9,000 people, left 2 million people homeless, and caused $10 billion in damages. Many people fled to the U.S., which offered Nicaraguans an immigration amnesty program until July 1999. Nicaragua remains one of the poorest countries in the Western Hemisphere.

In Nov. 2001 presidential elections, Enrique Bolaños, the ruling Liberal party leader, defeated Ortega, who was attempting a comeback.

In Aug. 2002, former president Arnoldo Alemán was charged with fraud and embezzlement, and in 2003 he was sent to prison for 20 years. Current president Bolaños triumphantly called it the "frying of the Big Fish." The anti-corruption watchdog, Transparency International, ranks Alemán among the ten most corrupt leaders of the past two decades.

The country received an enormous show of support from the international community in 2004 when the IMF and World Bank forgave $4.5 billion of Nicaragua's debt.

Niger

REPUBLIC OF NIGER

National name: République du Niger
President: Tandja Mamadou (1999)
Prime Minister: Hama Amadou (1999)
Area: 489,189 sq mi (1,267,000 sq km)
Population (2004 est.): 11,360,538 (growth rate: 2.7%); birth rate: 48.9/1000; infant mortality rate: 122.7/1000; life expectancy: 42.2; density per sq mi: 23
Capital and largest city (2003 est.): Niamey, 748,600. **Other large cities:** Zinder, 202,300; Maradi, 189,000. **Monetary unit:** CFA Franc. **Languages:** French (official), Hausa, Djerma. **Ethnicity/race:** Hausa 56%, Djerma 22%, Fula 8.5%, Tuareg 8%, Beri Beri (Kanouri) 4.3%, Arab, Toubou, and Gourmantche 1.2%, about 1,200 French expatriates. **Religions:** Islam 80%, indigenous beliefs and Christian 20%. **Literacy rate:** 18% (2003 est.)
Economic summary: GDP/PPP (2003 est.): $9.062 billion; per capita $800. **Real growth rate:** 3.8%. **Inflation:** 3% (2002 est.). **Unemployment:** n.a. **Arable land:** 4%. **Agriculture:** cowpeas, cotton, peanuts, millet, sorghum, cassava (tapioca); rice; cattle, sheep, goats, camels, donkeys, horses, poultry. **Labor force:** 70,000 receive regular wages or salaries (2002 est); agriculture 90%, industry and commerce 6%, government 4%. **Industries:** uranium mining, cement, brick, textiles, food processing, chemicals, slaughterhouses. **Natural resources:** uranium, coal, iron ore, tin, phosphates, gold, petroleum. **Exports:** $280 million (f.o.b., 2002 est.): uranium ore, livestock, cowpeas, onions. **Imports:** $400 million (f.o.b., 2002 est.): foodstuffs, machinery, vehicles and parts, petroleum, cereals. **Major trading partners:** France, Nigeria, Japan, Côte d'Ivoire, China, U.S., India.

Geography Niger, in West Africa's Sahara region, is four-fifths the size of Alaska. It is surrounded by Mali, Algeria, Libya, Chad, Nigeria, Benin, and Burkina Faso. The Niger River in the southwest flows through the country's only fertile area. Elsewhere the land is semiarid.

Government Republic, emerging from military rule.

History The nomadic Tuaregs were the first inhabitants in the Sahara region. The Hausa (14th century), the Zerma (17th century), the Gobir (18th century), and Fulani (19th century) also established themselves in the region now called Niger.

Niger was incorporated into French West Africa in 1896. There were frequent rebellions, but when order was restored in 1922, the French made the area a colony. In 1958, the voters approved the French constitution and voted to make the territory an autonomous republic within the French Community. The republic adopted a constitution in 1959 but the next year withdrew from the Community, proclaiming its independence.

During the 1970s, the country's economy flourished from uranium production, but when uranium prices fell in the 1980s, its brief period of prosperity ended. The 1974 army coup ousted President Hamani Diori, who had held office since 1960. An estimated 2 million people were starving in Niger, but 200,000 tons of imported food, half U.S.-supplied, substantially ended famine conditions by the year's end. The new president, Lt. Col. Seyni Kountché, chief of staff of the army, installed a 12-man military government. A predominantly civilian government was formed by Kountché in 1976.

In 1993, the country's first multiparty election resulted in the presidency of Ousmane Mahamane, who was then deposed in a Jan. 1996 coup. In July, the military leader of the coup, Ibrahim Baré Maïnassara, was declared president in a rigged election. Considered a corrupt and ineffectual president, Maïnassara was assassinated in April 1999 by his own guards. The National Reconciliation Council, responsible for the coup, kept its promise and held democratic elections; in Nov. 1999, Tandja Mamadou was elected president. As a result, foreign aid, primarily from France, was restored.

The nomadic Tuaregs, of Berber and Arab descent, have a fiercely insular culture and share little affinity with the black African majority of Niger. Conflict between the Tuaregs and the other tribes of Niger first surfaced in the early 20th century. Cease-fires between the government and various Tuareg rebel groups went into effect in 1995 and 1997. The impoverished Tuaregs have received little of the economic aid they were promised, which is not surprising given Niger's political instability and desperate poverty.

Niger found itself a pawn in the war against Iraq when both the U.S. and Britain claimed that Iraq sought to buy uranium from Niger and cited this as evidence that Saddam Hussein was reconstituting his country's nuclear weapons program. While the U.S. evidence for the Iraq-Niger uranium connection was quickly exposed as a forgery, British prime minister Tony Blair continued to insist on the veracity of the claim based on separate intelligence, which Britain's Butler report concluded was "credible." In July 2003, Prime Minister Amadou demanded that "If Britain has evidence to support its claim then it has only to produce it for everybody to see. . . . Everybody knows that the claims are untrue."

Nigeria

FEDERAL REPUBLIC OF NIGERIA

President: Olusegun Obasanjo (1999)
Area: 356,667 sq mi (923,768 sq km)
Population (2004 est.): 137,253,133 (growth rate: 2.5%); birth rate: 38.2/1000; infant mortality rate: 70.5/1000; life expectancy: 50.5; density per sq mi: 385
Capital (2003 est.): Abuja, 590,400 (metro. area), 165,700 (city proper). **Largest cities:** Lagos (2003 est.), 9,529,700 (metro. area), 8,349,700 (city proper); Kano, 3,329,900; Ibadan, 3,139,500; Kaduna, 1,510,300. **Monetary unit:** Naira. **Languages:** English (official), Hausa, Yoruba, Ibo, Fulani, and more than 200 others. **Ethnicity/race:** More than 250 ethnic groups, including Hausa and Fulani 29%, Yoruba 21%, Ibo 18%, Ijaw 10%, Kanuri 4%, Ibibio 3.5%, Tiv 2.5%. **Religions:** Islam 50%, Christian 40%, indigenous beliefs 10%. **Literacy rate:** 68% (2003 est.)
Economic summary: GDP/PPP (2003 est.): $110.8 billion; per capita $800. **Real growth rate:** 3.4%. **Inflation:** 11.7% (2002 est.). **Unemployment:** 28% (1992 est.). **Arable land:** 31%. **Agriculture:** cocoa, peanuts, palm oil, corn, rice, sorghum, millet, cassava (tapioca), yams, rubber; cattle, sheep, goats, pigs; timber; fish. **Labor force:** 66 million; agriculture 70%, industry 10%, services 20% (1999 est.). **Industries:** crude oil, coal, tin, columbite, palm oil, peanuts, cotton, rubber, wood, hides and skins, textiles, cement and other construction materials, food products, footwear, chemicals, fertilizer, printing, ceramics, steel. **Natural resources:** natural gas, petroleum, tin, columbite, iron ore, coal, limestone, lead, zinc, arable land. **Exports:** $21.8 billion (f.o.b., 2003 est.): petroleum and petroleum products 95%, cocoa, rubber. **Imports:** $14.54 billion (f.o.b., 2003 est.): machinery, chemicals, transport equipment, manufactured goods, food and live animals. **Major trading partners:** U.S., Brazil, Spain, Indonesia, France, India, UK, China, Germany, South Korea, Netherlands, Italy. **Member of Commonwealth of Nations**

Geography Nigeria, one-third larger than Texas and the most populous country in Africa, is situated on the Gulf of Guinea in West Africa. Its neighbors are Benin, Niger, Cameroon, and Chad. The lower course of the Niger River flows south through the western part of the country into the Gulf of Guinea. Swamps and mangrove forests border the southern coast; inland are hardwood forests.

Government Multiparty government transitioning from military to civilian rule.

History The first inhabitants of what is now Nigeria were thought to have been the Nok people (500 B.C.–c. A.D. 200). The Kanuri, Hausa, and Fulani peoples subsequently migrated there. Islam was introduced in the 13th century, and the empire of Kanem controlled the area from the end of the 11th century to the 14th.

The Fulani empire ruled the region from the beginning of the 19th century until the British annexed Lagos in 1851 and seized control of the rest of the region by 1886. It formally became the Colony and Protectorate of Nigeria in 1914. During World War I, native troops of the West African frontier force joined with French forces to defeat the German garrison in the Cameroons.

On Oct. 1, 1960, Nigeria gained independence, becoming a member of the Commonwealth of Nations and joining the United Nations. Organized as a loose federation of self-governing states, the independent nation faced an overwhelming task of unifying a country with 250 ethnic and linguistic groups.

Rioting broke out in 1966, and military leaders, primarily of Ibo ethnicity, seized control. In July, a second military coup put Col. Yakubu Gowon in power, a choice unacceptable to the Ibos. Also in that year, the Muslim Hausas in the north massacred the predominantly Christian Ibos in the east, many of whom had been driven from the north. Thousands of Ibos took refuge in the eastern region, which declared its independence as the Republic of Biafra on May 30, 1967. Civil war broke out. In Jan. 1970, after 31 months of civil war, Biafra surrendered to the federal government.

Gowon's nine-year rule was ended in 1975 by a bloodless coup that made Army Brig. Muritala Rufai Mohammed the new chief of state. The return of civilian leadership was established with the election of Alhaji Shehu Shagari as president in 1979. An oil boom in the 1970s buoyed the economy and by the 1980s Nigeria was considered an exemplar of African democracy and economic well being.

The military again seized power in 1984, only to be followed by another military coup the following year. Maj. Gen. Ibrahim Babangida announced that the country would be returned to civilian rule, but after the presidential election of June 12, 1993, he voided the results. Nevertheless, Babangida resigned as president in August. In November the military, headed by defense minister Sani Abacha, seized power again.

Corruption and notorious governmental inefficiency as well as a harshly repressive military regime characterized Abacha's reign over this oil-rich country, turning it into an international pariah. A UN fact-finding mission in 1996 reported that Nigeria's "problems of human rights are terrible and the political problems are terrifying." During the 1970s, Nigeria had the 33rd highest per-capita income in the world, but by 1997 it had dropped to the 13th poorest. The hanging of writer Ken Saro-Wiwa in 1995 because he protested against the government was condemned around the world.

As leader of the multination peacekeeping force ECOMOG, Nigeria has established itself as West Africa's superpower, intervening militarily in the civil wars of Liberia and Sierra Leone. But Nigeria's costly war efforts have been unpopular with its own people, who feel Nigeria's limited economic resources are being unnecessarily drained.

Abacha died of a heart attack in 1998, and was succeeded by another military ruler, Gen. Abdulsalam Abubakar, who pledged to step aside for an elected leader by May 1999. The suspicious death of opposition leader Mashood Abiola, who had been imprisoned by the military ever since he legally won the 1993 presidential election, was a crushing blow to democratic proponents. In Feb. 1999, free presidential elections led to an overwhelming victory for Gen. Olusegun Obasanjo, a former member of the military elite who was imprisoned for three years for criticizing the military rule. Obasanjo's commitment to democracy, his anticorruption drives, and his desire to recover billions allegedly stolen by the family and cronies of Abacha initially gained him high praise from the populace as well as the international community. But within two years, the hope of reform seemed doomed as economic mismanagement and rampant corruption persisted. Obasanjo's priorities in 2001 were symbolized by his plans to build a $330 million national soccer stadium, an extravagance that exceeded the combined budget for both health and education. In April 2003, he was reelected.

Nigeria's stability has been repeatedly threatened by fighting between fundamentalist Muslims and Christians over the spread of Islamic law (sharia) across the heavily Muslim north. About one-third of Nigeria's 36 states are ruled by sharia law. More than 10,000 people have died in religious clashes since military rule ended in 1999.

In 2003, after religious and political leaders in the Kano region banned polio immunization, contending that it sterilized girls and spread HIV, an outbreak of polio spread through Nigeria and into neighboring countries the following year. The Kano region lifted its ten-month ban against vaccination in July 2004. On Aug. 24, there were 602 polio cases worldwide, 79% of which were in Nigeria.

In Sept. 2004, violence broke out in the Niger Delta, Nigeria's oil producing region. A rebel group, the Niger Delta People's Volunteer Force, threatened to shut down oil production unless the desperately impoverished local residents, the Ijaw people, begin to see some benefit from Nigeria's oil riches. The conflict caused world oil prices to soar.

Norway

KINGDOM OF NORWAY

National name: Kongeriket Norge
Sovereign: King Harald V (1991)
Prime Minister: Kjell Magne Bondevik (2001)
Area: 125,181 sq mi (324,220 sq km)
Population (2004 est.): 4,574,560 (growth rate: 0.4%); birth rate: 11.9/1000; infant mortality rate: 3.7/1000; life expectancy: 79.3; density per sq mi: 37
Capital and largest city (2003 est.): Oslo, 791,500. **Other large cities:** Bergen, 211,200; Stavanger, 168,600; Trondheim, 144,000. **Monetary unit:** Norwegian krone. **Languages:** Bokmål Norwegian, Nynorsk Norwegian (both official); small Sami- and Finnish-speaking minorities. **Ethnicity/race:** Norwegian, Sami 20,000. **Religions:** Evangelical Lutheran 86% (state church), other Protestant and Roman Catholic 3%, other 1%, none and unknown 10%. **Literacy rate:** 100% (2003 est.)
Economic summary: GDP/PPP (2003 est.): $171.6 billion; per capita $37,700. **Real growth rate:** 0.5%. **Inflation:** 2.6%. **Unemployment:** 4.5%. **Arable land:** 3%. **Agriculture:** barley, wheat, potatoes; pork, beef, veal, milk; fish. **Labor force:** 2.4 million (2000 est.); services 74%, industry 22%, agriculture, forestry, and fishing 4% (1995). **Industries:** petroleum and gas, food processing, shipbuilding, pulp and paper products, metals, chemicals, timber, mining, textiles, fishing. **Natural resources:** petroleum, copper, natural gas, pyrites, nickel, iron ore, zinc, lead, fish, timber, hydropower. **Exports:** $67.27 billion (f.o.b., 2003 est.): petroleum and petroleum products, machinery and equipment, metals, chemicals, ships, fish. **Imports:** $40.19 billion (f.o.b., 2003 est.): machinery and equipment, chemicals, metals, foodstuffs. **Major trading partners:** UK, Germany, France, U.S., Netherlands, Sweden, Denmark, Italy.

Geography Norway is situated in the western part of the Scandinavian peninsula. It extends about 1,100 mi (1,770 km) from the North Sea along the Norwegian Sea to more than 300 mi (483 km) above the Arctic Circle, the farthest north of any European country. It is slightly larger than New Mexico. Nearly 70% of Norway is uninhabitable and covered by mountains, glaciers, moors, and rivers. The hundreds of deep fjords that cut into the coastline give Norway an overall oceanfront of more than 12,000 mi (19,312 km). Galdhø Peak, at 8,100 ft (2,469 m), is Norway's highest point and the Glåma (Glomma) is the principal river, at 372 mi (598 km) long.

Government Constitutional monarchy.

History Norwegians, like the Danes and Swedes, are of Teutonic origin. The Norsemen, also known as Vikings, ravaged the coasts of northwest Europe from the 8th to the 11th century and were ruled by local chieftains. Olaf II Haraldsson became the first effective king of all Norway in 1015 and began converting the Norwegians to Christianity. After 1442, Norway was ruled by Danish kings until 1814, when it was united with Sweden—although retaining a degree of independence and receiving a new constitution—in an uneasy partnership. In 1905, the Norwegian Parliament arranged a peaceful separation and invited a

Danish prince to the Norwegian throne—King Haakon VII. A treaty with Sweden provided that all disputes be settled by arbitration and that no fortifications be erected on the common frontier.

When World War I broke out, Norway joined with Sweden and Denmark in a decision to remain neutral and to cooperate in the joint interest of the three countries. In World War II, Norway was invaded by the Germans on April 9, 1940. It resisted for two months before the Nazis took complete control. King Haakon and his government fled to London, where they established a government-in-exile. Maj. Vidkun Quisling, who served as Norway's premier during the war, was the most notorious of the Nazi collaborators. The word for traitor, *quisling*, bears his name. He was executed by the Norwegians on Oct. 24, 1945. Despite severe losses in the war, Norway recovered quickly as its economy expanded. It joined NATO in 1949.

In the late 20th century, the Labor Party and the Conservative Party seesawed for control, each sometimes having to lead minority governments. An important debate has been over Norway's membership in the European Union. In an advisory referendum held in Nov. 1994, voters rejected seeking membership for their nation in the EU. The country became the second-largest net oil exporter after Saudi Arabia in 1995. Norway continued to experience rapid economic growth into the new millennium.

In March 2000, Prime Minister Kjell Magne Bondevik resigned after parliament voted to build the country's first gas-fired power stations. Bondevik had objected to the project, asserting that the plants would emit too much carbon dioxide. Labor Party leader Jens Stoltenberg succeeded Bondevik. Stoltenberg and the Labor Party were defeated in Sept. 2001 elections, and no party emerged with a clear majority. After a month of talks, the Conservatives, the Christian People's Party, and the Liberals formed a coalition with Bondevik as prime minister. The governing coalition was backed by the far-right Progress Party.

For several years running, the UN's Human Development Index has rated Norway the world's "most livable" country. The index ranks nations according to their citizens' quality of life.

Dependencies of Norway

Svalbard (23,957 sq mi; 62,049 sq km), in the Arctic Ocean about 360 mi north of Norway, consists of the Spitsbergen group and several smaller islands, including Bear Island, Hope Island, King Charles Land, and White Island (or Gillis Land). The capital is Longyearbyen. It came under Norwegian administration in 1925. **Population:** 2,811 (2003 est.). 62% of the population is Russian and Ukrainian; 38% are Norwegian. Coal mining is the major economic activity.

Bouvet Island (23 sq mi; 58.5 sq km), an island nature reserve in the South Atlantic about 1,600 mi south-southwest of the Cape of Good Hope, came under Norwegian administration in 1928. It is uninhabited.

Jan Mayen Island (144 sq mi; 373 sq km), in the Arctic Ocean between Norway and Greenland, came under Norwegian administration in 1929. There are no permanent inhabitants, just workers at the navigation base and weather/radio station.

Oman

SULTANATE OF OMAN

National name: Saltonat Uman
Sultan: Qabus ibn Sa'id (1970)
Area: 82,031 sq mi (212,460 sq km)[1]
Population (2004 est.): 2,903,165 (growth rate: 3.3%);

birth rate: 37.1/1000; infant mortality rate: 20.3/1000; life expectancy: 72.9; density per sq mi: 35
Capital (2003 est.): Muscat, 797,000 (metro.area), 54,800 (city proper). **Monetary unit:** Omani rial.
Languages: Arabic (official), English, Baluchi, Urdu, Indian dialects. **Ethnicity/race:** Arab, Baluchi, South Asian (Indian, Pakistani, Sri Lankan, Bangladeshi), African. **Religion:** Islam: Ibadhi 75%, Sunni, Shi'a; Hindu. **Literacy rate:** 76% (2003 est.)
Economic summary: GDP/PPP (2003 est.): $37.5 billion; per capita $13,400. **Real growth rate:** 3.3%. **Inflation:** 0.3%. **Unemployment:** n.a. **Arable land:** 0%. **Agriculture:** dates, limes, bananas, alfalfa, vegetables; camels, cattle; fish. **Labor force:** 920,000 (2002 est.); agriculture n.a., industry n.a., services n.a. **Industries:** crude oil production and refining, natural gas production, construction, cement, copper. **Natural resources:** petroleum, copper, asbestos, some marble, limestone, chromium, gypsum, natural gas. **Exports:** $11.7 billion (f.o.b., 2003 est.): petroleum, reexports, fish, metals, textiles. **Imports:** $5.659 billion (f.o.b., 2003 est.): machinery and transport equipment, manufactured goods, food, livestock, lubricants. **Major trading partners:** Japan, South Korea, China, Thailand, UAE, Singapore, U.S., UK, Germany.

1. Excluding the Kuria Muria Islands.

Geography Oman is a 1,000-mile-long (1,700-km) coastal plain at the southeast tip of the Arabian peninsula lying on the Arabian Sea and the Gulf of Oman. It is bordered by the United Arab Emirates, Saudi Arabia, and Yemen. The country is the size of Kansas.

Government Absolute monarchy.

History Arabs migrated to Oman from the 9th century B.C. onward, and conversion to Islam occurred in the 7th century A.D. Muscat, the capital of the geographical area known as Oman, was occupied by the Portuguese from 1508 to 1648. Then it fell to Ottoman Turks, but in 1741 Ahmad ibn Sa'id forced them out. The descendants of Sultan Ahmad rule Oman today.

Ahmad expanded his empire to East Africa, and for a time the Omani capital was in Zanzibar. After 1861, however, Zanzibar fell from Omani control.

The sultans and imams of Oman clashed continuously throughout the 20th century until 1959, when the last Ibadi imam was evicted from the country. In a palace coup on July 23, 1970, the sultan, Sa'id bin Taimur, who had ruled since 1932, was overthrown by his son, Qabus ibn Sa'id, who promised to establish a modern government and use newfound oil wealth to aid the people of this very isolated state. Oman joined the Arab League and the United Nations in 1971.

A long border dispute with Yemen was resolved in Oct. 1992; in 1997, the countries agreed to new maps defining the border.

In 1997, Sultan Qabus granted women the right to be elected to the country's consultative body, the Shura Council (Majlis al-Shura). In 2003, the sultan extended voting rights to everyone over 21; previously, voters were selected from among the elite, and only about a quarter of the population was allowed to vote.

Pakistan

ISLAMIC REPUBLIC OF PAKISTAN

President: Gen. Pervez Musharraf (2001)
Prime minister (caretaker): Shaukat Aziz (2004)
Area: 310,401 sq mi (803,940 sq km)[1]
Population (2004 est.): 159,196,336 (growth rate: 2.0%); birth rate: 31.2/1000; infant mortality rate: 74.4/1000; life expectancy: 62.6; density per sq mi: 513
Capital (2003 est.): Islamabad, 601,600. **Largest cities:**

Karachi, 10,573,200; Lahore, 5,756,100; Faisalabad (Lyallpur), 2,247,700; Rawalpindi, 1,598,600; Gujranwala, 1,384,100. **Monetary unit:** Pakistan rupee. **Principal languages:** Punjabi 48%, Sindhi 12%, Siraiki (a Punjabi variant) 10%, Pashtu 8%, Urdu (official) 8%, Balochi 3%, Hindko 2%, Brahui 1%, English, Burushaski, and others 8%. **Ethnicity/race:** Punjabi, Sindhi, Pashtun (Pathan), Baloch, Muhajir (immigrants from India and their descendants). **Religions:** Islam 97% (Sunni 77%, Shiite 20%); Christian, Hindu, and other 3%. **Literacy rate:** 46% (2003 est.)

Economic summary GDP/PPP (2003 est.): $317.7 billion; per capita $2,100. **Real growth rate:** 5.4%. **Inflation:** 3.1% (FY 02/03 est.). **Unemployment:** 7.7% plus substantial underemployment. **Arable land:** 28%. **Agriculture:** cotton, wheat, rice, sugarcane, fruits, vegetables; milk, beef, mutton, eggs. **Labor force:** 40.4 million; note: extensive export of labor, mostly to the Middle East, and use of child labor (2000); agriculture 44%, industry 17%, services 39% (1999 est.). **Industries:** textiles, and apparel, food processing, beverages, construction materials, paper products, fertilizer, shrimp. **Natural resources:** land, extensive natural gas reserves, limited petroleum, poor quality coal, iron ore, copper, salt, limestone. **Exports:** $11.7 billion (f.o.b., 2003 est.): textiles (garments, cotton cloth, and yarn), rice, leather, sports goods, and carpets and rugs. **Imports:** $12.51 billion (f.o.b., 2003 est.): petroleum, petroleum products, machinery, chemicals, transportation equipment, edible oils, pulses, iron and steel, tea. **Major trading partners:** U.S. UAE, UK, Germany, Hong Kong, Saudi Arabia, Kuwait, China, Japan, Malaysia.

1. Excluding Kashmir and Jammu.

Geography Pakistan is situated in the western part of the Indian subcontinent, with Afghanistan and Iran on the west, India on the east, and the Arabian Sea on the south. The name *Pakistan* is derived from the Urdu words *Pak* (meaning pure) and *stan* (meaning country). It is nearly twice the size of California.

The northern and western highlands of Pakistan contain the towering Karakoram and Pamir mountain ranges, which include some of the world's highest peaks: K2 (28,250 ft; 8,611 m) and Nanga Parbat (26,660 ft; 8,126 m). The Baluchistan Plateau lies to the west, and the Thar Desert and an expanse of alluvial plains, the Punjab and Sind, lie to the east. The 1,000-mile-long (1,609 km) Indus River and its tributaries flow through the country from the Kashmir region to the Arabian Sea.

Government Military rule was instituted Oct. 1999; a nominal democracy was declared in June 2001 by the ruling military leader, Pervez Musharraf.

History Pakistan was one of the two original successor states to British India, which was partitioned along religious lines in 1947. For almost 25 years following independence, it consisted of two separate regions, East and West Pakistan, but now is made up only of the western sector. Both India and Pakistan have laid claim to the Kashmir region, and this territorial dispute led to war in 1949, and again in 1965, 1971, and 1999, and remains unresolved today.

What is now Pakistan was in prehistoric times the Indus Valley civilization (c. 2500–1700 B.C.). A series of invaders—Aryans, Persians, Greeks, Arabs, Turks, and others—controlled the region for the next several thousand years. Islam, the dominant religion, was introduced in 711. In 1526, the land became part of the Mogul Empire, which ruled most of the Indian subcontinent from the 16th to the mid-18th century. By 1857, the British became the dominant power in the region.

With Hindus holding most of the economic, social, and political advantages, the Muslim minority's dissatisfaction grew, leading to the formation of the nationalist Muslim League in 1906 by Mohammed Ali Jinnah (1876–1949). The league supported Britain in the Second World War while the Hindu nationalist leaders, Nehru and Gandhi, refused. In return for the league's support of Britain, Jinnah expected British backing for Muslim autonomy. Britain agreed to the formation of Pakistan as a separate dominion within the Commonwealth in Aug. 1947, a bitter disappointment to India's dream of a unified subcontinent. Jinnah became governor-general. The partition of Pakistan and India along religious lines resulted in the largest migration in human history, with 17 million people fleeing across the borders in both directions to escape the sectarian violence accompanying the partition.

Pakistan became a republic on March 23, 1956, with Maj. Gen. Iskander Mirza becoming the first president. Military rule prevailed for the next two decades. Tensions between East and West Pakistan existed from the outset. Separated by more than a thousand miles, the two regions shared few cultural and social traditions other than religion. To the growing resentment of East Pakistan, the West monopolized the country's political and economic power. In 1970, East Pakistan's Awami League, led by the Bengali leader Sheik Mujibur Rahman, secured a majority of the seats in the National Assembly. President Yahya Khan postponed the opening of the National Assembly to skirt East Pakistan's demand for greater autonomy, provoking civil war. The independent state of Bangladesh, or Bengali nation, was proclaimed on March 26, 1971. Indian troops entered the war in its last weeks fighting on the side of the new state. Pakistan was defeated on Dec. 16, 1971, and President Yahya Khan stepped down. Zulfikar Ali Bhutto took over Pakistan and accepted Bangladesh as an independent entity. In 1976, formal relations between India and Pakistan resumed.

Pakistan's first elections under civilian rule took place in March 1977, and the overwhelming victory of Bhutto's Pakistan People's Party (PPP) was denounced as fraudulent. A rising tide of violent protest and political deadlock led to a military takeover on July 5 by Gen. Mohammed Zia ul-Haq. Bhutto was tried and convicted for the 1974 murder of a political opponent, and despite worldwide protests was executed on April 4, 1979, touching off riots by his supporters. Zia declared himself president on Sept. 16, 1978, and ruled by martial law until Dec. 30, 1985, when a measure of representative government was restored. On Aug. 19, 1988, Zia was killed in a midair explosion of a Pakistani Air Force plane. Elections at the end of 1988 brought longtime Zia opponent Benazir Bhutto, daughter of Zulfikar Bhutto, into office as prime minister.

In the 1990s, Pakistan saw a shaky succession of governments—Benazir Bhutto was prime minister twice and Nawaz Sharif three times, until he was deposed in a coup on Oct. 12, 1999, by Gen. Pervez Musharraf. The Pakistani public, familiar with military rule for 25 of the nation's 52-year history, generally viewed the coup as a positive step, and hoped it would bring a badly needed economic upswing.

To the surprise of much of the world, two new nuclear powers suddenly emerged in May 1998 when India, followed by Pakistan just weeks later, conducted nuclear tests. Fighting with India again broke out in the disputed territory of Kashmir in May 1999.

Close ties with Afghanistan's Taliban government thrust Pakistan into a difficult position following the Sept. 11 terrorist attacks on the U.S. Under U.S. pressure, Pakistan broke with its neighbor to become the

United States' chief ally in the region. In return, President Bush ended sanctions (instituted after Pakistan's testing of nuclear weapons in 1998), rescheduled its debt, and helped to bolster the legitimacy of Pervez Musharraf's rule, who appointed himself president in 2001.

On Dec. 13, 2001, suicide bombers attacked the Indian parliament, killing 14 people, including 5 assailants. Indian officials blamed the attack on Islamic militants supported by Pakistan. Both sides assembled hundreds of thousands of troops along the Indian-Pakistani border, bringing the two nuclear powers to the brink of war.

In April 2002, voters overwhelmingly approved a referendum to extend Musharraf's presidency for another five years. The vote, however, outraged opposing political parties and human rights groups that said the process was rigged. In August, he unveiled 29 constitutional amendments that strengthened his grip on the country.

Pakistani officials dealt a heavy blow to al-Qaeda in March 2003, arresting Khalid Shaikh Mohammed, the top aide to Osama bin Laden, who organized the 2001 terrorist attacks against the U.S. The search for bin Laden intensified in northern Pakistan following Mohammed's arrest.

In Nov. 2003, Pakistan and India declared the first formal cease-fire in Kashmir in 14 years. Three rounds of bilateral talks followed in 2004.

Musharraf narrowly survived two assassination attempts in Dec. 2003; four attempts on his life have been made in the past two years. Al-Qaeda and other Islamic radical groups are believed responsible.

Abdul Qadeer Khan, the father of Pakistan's nuclear bomb, was exposed in Feb. 2004 for having sold nuclear secrets to North Korea, Iran, and Libya. Musharraf had him apologize publicly, and then pardoned him. While much of the world reviled him for this unconscionable act of nuclear proliferation, the scientist remains a national hero in Pakistan. Khan claimed that he alone and not Pakistan's military or government was involved in the selling of these ultra-classified secrets; few in the international community have accepted this explanation.

In March 2004, Pakistan launched an assault on hundreds of foreign militants holed up along the mountainous South Waziristan region, which borders Afghanistan. The Pakistani Army intensified its assault on the militants through the summer, prompting thousands of Afghan refugees to flee back into Afghanistan. Factional violence prevailed elsewhere in Pakistan. In May, Sunni militants killed more than 70 people in coordinated suicide bombings at Shiite mosques in Karachi.

Musharraf suggested in September that he would retain his post as head of the armed forces, despite an earlier promise to step aside by the end of 2004.

Palau

REPUBLIC OF PALAU

President: Tommy Remengesau (2001)
Total area: 177 sq mi (458 sq km)
Population (2004 est.): 20,016 (growth rate: 1.5%); birth rate: 18.7/1000; infant mortality rate: 15.3/1000; life expectancy: 69.8; density per sq mi: 113
Capital and largest city (2003 est.): Koror, 11,100.
  Monetary unit: U.S. dollar used. **Languages:** English (official everywhere); Palau (official in all states but those following); Sonsoralese (official in Sonsoral); Tobi (official in Tobi); Angaur and Japanese (official in Angaur). **Ethnicity/race:** Palauan (Micronesian with Malayan and Melanesian admixtures) 70%, Asian

(mainly Filipinos, followed by Chinese, Taiwanese, and Vietnamese) 28%, white 2% (2000 est.). **Religions:** Christian (Roman Catholics 49%, Seventh-Day Adventists, Jehovah's Witnesses, the Assembly of God, the Liebenzell Mission, and Latter-Day Saints), Modekngei (one-third observes this indigenous religion). **Literacy rate:** 92% (1980 est.)
Economic summary: GDP/PPP (2001 est.): $174 million; note: GDP numbers reflect U.S. spending; per capita $9,000. **Real growth rate:** 1%. **Inflation:** 3.4% (2000 est.). **Unemployment:** 2.3% (2000 est.). **Arable land:** 22%. **Agriculture:** coconuts, copra, cassava (tapioca), sweet potatoes. **Labor force:** 9,845 (2000); agriculture 20%, industry n.a., services n.a. (1990). **Industries:** tourism, craft items (from shell, wood, pearls), construction, garment making. **Natural resources:** forests, minerals (especially gold), marine products, deep-seabed minerals. **Exports:** $18 million (f.o.b., 2001 est.): shellfish, tuna, copra, garments. **Imports:** $99 million (f.o.b., 2001 est.): machinery and equipment, fuels, metals; foodstuffs. **Major trading partners:** U.S., Japan, Singapore, Guam, Korea.

Geography The Palau island chain consists of about 200 islands located in the western Pacific Ocean, 528 mi (650 km) southeast of the Philippines. Only eight of the islands are permanently inhabited.

Government Constitutional republic.

History The original settlers of Palau are believed to have arrived from Indonesia as early as 2500 B.C. The Palau islands' position on the western threshold of Oceania and their proximity to Southeast Asia have led to the population being a mixture of Malay, Melanesian, Filipino, and Polynesian ancestry.

Explored by the Spanish navigator Ruy López de Villalobos in 1543, the islands remained under nominal Spanish ownership for more than 300 years before Spain sold them to Germany in 1899. Japan occupied Palau during World War I and received a mandate over them from the League of Nations in 1920. They remained in Japanese control and served as an important naval base until the U.S. seized them during World War II. After the war they became a UN trusteeship (1947), administered by the United States. Palau signed a Compact of Free Association with the U.S. in 1992, requiring the United States to provide economic aid in exchange for the right to build and maintain U.S. military facilities in Palau. Palau became a sovereign state in 1994. In 2000, former vice president Tommy Remengesau won the presidential election.

Palestinian State (proposed)

WEST BANK AND GAZA STRIP

President: Yasir Arafat (1994)
Prime Minister: Ahmed Qurei (2003)
Area: West Bank: 2,263 sq mi (5,860 sq km); Gaza Strip: 139 sq mi (360 sq km)
Population (2004 est.): West Bank: 2,311,204, Gaza Strip: 1,324,991 (growth rate: West Bank: 3.2%, Gaza Strip: 3.8%); birth rate: West Bank: 33.2/1000, Gaza Strip: 40.6/1000; infant mortality rate: West Bank: 20.2/1,000, Gaza Strip: 23.5/1000; life expectancy: West Bank: 72.9, Gaza Strip: 71.6; density per sq mi: West Bank: 1,022, Gaza Strip: 9,533
Capital: Undetermined. **Large cities (2003 est.):** Gaza, 1,331,600 (metro. area), 407,600 (city proper), Hebron, 137,000; Nablus, 115,400. **Monetary units:** New Israeli shekels, Jordanian dinars, U.S. dollars. **Languages:** Arabic, Hebrew, English. **Ethnicity/race:** West Bank: Palestinian Arab and other 83%, Jewish

17%; Gaza Strip: Palestinian Arab and other 99.4%, Jewish 0.6%. **Religions:** West Bank: Islam 75% (predominantly Sunni), Jewish 17%, Christian and other 8%; Gaza Strip: Islam 98.7% (predominantly Sunni), Christian 0.7%, Jewish 0.6%

Economic summary: Gaza Strip: GDP/PPP (2003 est.): $768 million; $600 per capita. **Real growth rate:** 4.5%. **Inflation:** 2.2% (includes West Bank) (2001 est.). **Unemployment:** 50% (includes West Bank). **Arable land:** 26%. **Agriculture:** olives, citrus, vegetables; beef, dairy products. **Labor force:** n.a.; services 66%, industry 21%, agriculture 13% (1996). **Industries:** generally small family businesses that produce textiles, soap, olive-wood carvings, and mother-of-pearl souvenirs; the Israelis have established some small-scale modern industries in an industrial center. **Natural resources:** arable land, natural coast. **Exports:** $603 million (f.o.b.; includes West Bank): citrus, flowers. **Imports:** $1.9 billion (c.i.f.; includes West Bank): food, consumer goods, construction materialss. **Major trading partners:** Israel, Egypt, West Bank. **West Bank: GDP/PPP** (2002 est.): $1.7 billion; $800 per capita. **Real growth rate:** –22%. **Arable land:** negl. **Agriculture:** olives, citrus, vegetables; beef, dairy products. **Labor force:** n.a.; services 66%, industry 21%, agriculture 13% (1996). **Natural resources:** arable land. **Major trading partners:** Israel, Jordan, Gaza Strip.

Geography The West Bank is located to the east of Israel and the west of Jordan. The Gaza Strip is located between Israel and Egypt on the Mediterranean coast.

Government The Palestinian Authority (PA), with Arafat its elected leader, took control of the newly non-Israeli-occupied areas, assuming governmental duties in 1994.

History The history of the proposed modern Palestinian state, which is expected to be formed from the territories of the West Bank and Gaza Strip, began with the British Mandate of Palestine. From Sept. 29, 1923, until May 14, 1948, Britain controlled the region, but by 1947, Britain had appealed to the UN to solve the complex problem of competing Palestinian and Jewish claims to the land. In Aug. 1947, the UN proposed dividing Palestine into a Jewish state, an Arab state, and a small international zone. Arabs rejected the idea. As soon as Britain pulled out of Palestine in 1948, neighboring Arab nations invaded, intent on crushing the newly declared State of Israel. Israel emerged victorious, affirming its sovereignty. The remaining areas of Palestine were divided between Transjordan (now Jordan), which annexed the West Bank, and Egypt, which gained control of the Gaza Strip.

Through a series of political and social policies, Jordan sought to consolidate its control over the political future of Palestinians and to become their speaker. Jordan even extended citizenship to Palestinians in 1949—Palestinians constituted about two-thirds of the country's population. In the Gaza Strip, administered by Egypt from 1948–1967, poverty and unemployment were high, and most of the Palestinians lived in refugee camps.

In the Arab-Israeli war of 1967, Israel, over a period of six days, defeated the military forces of Egypt, Syria, and Jordan, and annexed the territories of East Jerusalem, the Golan Heights, the West Bank, the Gaza Strip, and all of the Sinai peninsula. The Palestinian Liberation Organization (PLO), formed in 1964, was a terrorist organization bent on Israel's annihilation. Palestinian rioting, demonstrations, and terrorist acts against Israelis became chronic. In 1974, PLO leader

Yasir Arafat addressed the UN General Assembly, the first stateless government to do so. Violence again escalated in 1987 during the *intifada* ("shaking off"), a new era in Palestinian mass mobilization. In 1988, Yasir Arafat publicly eschewed terrorism and officially recognized the state of Israel.

In 1993, highly secretive talks in Norway between the PLO and the Israeli government resulted in the Oslo Agreement. The accord stipulated a five-year plan in which Palestinians of the West Bank and the Gaza Strip would gradually become self-governing. On Sept. 13, 1993, Arafat and Israeli prime minister Yitzak Rabin signed the historic "Declaration of Principles." As part of the agreement, Israel pulled out of the Gaza Strip and Jericho in the West Bank in 1994. The Palestinian Authority (PA), with Arafat as its elected leader, took control of the newly non-Israeli-occupied areas, assuming all governmental duties.

Intensive negotiations between Barak and Arafat in 2000 remained deadlocked over Israeli-occupied East Jerusalem, which Arafat insisted must be the capital of the future Palestinian state. At the end of September, however, the stalemate disintegrated into the worst violence between Israelis and Palestinians in years, provoked by Likud hardliner Ariel Sharon's visit to the compound called Temple Mount by Jews and Haram al-Sharif by Muslims, a fiercely contested site that is sacred to both faiths. The intensified violence, which included an unprecedented number of Palestinian suicide attacks against Israeli civilians, and the inevitable Israeli military reprisals, was dubbed the al-Aksa intifada. In four years (2000–2004), the intifada had led to the deaths of almost 4,000, including nearly 3,000 Palestinians.

For five months in 2002, Israeli troops surrounded Yasir Arafat at the Palestinian Authority headquarters in Ramallah. Prime Minister Sharon, blaming Arafat directly for inciting terror, called for his expulsion from the territories. Washington echoed Israel's view that Arafat had become "irrelevant," and announced that the U.S. would not recognize an independent Palestinian state until Arafat was replaced. Throughout the summer, Palestinian suicide bombings (Hamas and the Al-Aksa Martyr Brigade claimed responsibility for the majority of them) and Israeli reprisals continued.

In March 2003, Arafat agreed to political reforms—his rule, to the disillusionment of many Palestinians, is rife with corruption. He also agreed to share power with a prime minister. Mahmoud Abbas, second-in-command of the PLO, assumed the post on April 30. Unlike Arafat, Abbas emphatically rejected the Palestinian intifada, but he had no influence or control over Palestinian militant groups the way Arafat did. On May 1, the Quartet (the U.S., UN, EU, and Russia) unfurled its "road map" for peace, which called on both sides to make concessions and end the wave of deadly violence. But the road map quickly led nowhere: Abbas, with little real political power, could not disable terrorist organizations, and Israel did not dismantle settlements, much less prevent new ones from cropping up. Sharon also continued to build the controversial security barrier that divides Israeli and Palestinian areas (in Oct. 2003, a UN resolution condemned the barrier by 144–4). Abbas resigned in September, and Arafat appointed a new prime minister, Ahmed Qurei.

On March 22, 2004, Israel assassinated Sheik Ahmed Yassin, the founder and spiritual leader of Hamas. Outrage and protest throughout the Arab world followed. Since September 2003, Israel has killed more than 20 Hamas officials, and has vowed to destroy the entire leadership. Within months, Israel had assassinated Yassin's successor as well.

On April 14, Palestinians were infuriated when President Bush endorsed Sharon's unilateral withdrawal plan: Israel stated it would withdraw from the Gaza Strip, but would hold on to large blocks of land in the West Bank and reject the "right of return" for Palestinian refugees. While Palestinians might have eventually given up both these claims during peace talks, the fact that Sharon made these decisions without negotiating plunged Israeli-Palestinian relations to a new low.

In July 2004, Israel revised the route of its security barrier so that it no longer cut into Palestinian land—the UN estimated that the original route would have taken almost 15% of West Bank territory for Israel. The new route will attempt to insure that Palestinians aren't subject to undue hardships—separating villagers from their farmland, for example.

Panama

REPUBLIC OF PANAMA

National name: República de Panamá
President: Mireya Moscoso (1999)
Area: 30,193 sq mi (78,200 sq km)
Population (2004 est.): 3,000,463 (growth rate: 1.3%); birth rate: 20.4/1000; infant mortality rate: 21.0/1000; life expectancy: 72.1; density per sq mi: 99
Capital and largest city (2003 est.): Panama City, 1,053,500 (metro.area), 437,200 (city proper). **Other large cities:** San Miguelito, 309,500; Colón, 44,400.
Monetary unit: balboa; U.S. dollar. **Languages:** Spanish (official), English 14%, many bilingual.
Ethnicity/race: mestizo 70%, Amerindian and mixed (West Indian) 14%, white 10%, Indian 6%. **Religions:** Roman Catholic 85%, Protestant 15%. **Literacy rate:** 93% (2003 est.).
Economic summary: GDP/PPP (2003 est.): $18.62 billion; per capita $6,300. **Real growth rate:** 3.2%. **Inflation:** 1.3%. **Unemployment:** 14.5%. **Arable land:** 7%. **Agriculture:** bananas, rice, corn, coffee, sugarcane, vegetables; livestock; shrimp. **Labor force:** 1.1 million (2000 est.); note: shortage of skilled labor, but an oversupply of unskilled labor; agriculture 20.8%, industry 18%, services 61.2% (1995 est.). **Industries:** construction, petroleum refining, brewing, cement and other construction materials, sugar milling. **Natural resources:** copper, mahogany forests, shrimp, hydropower. **Exports:** $5.237 billion (f.o.b., 2003 est.): bananas, shrimp, sugar, coffee, clothing. **Imports:** $6.622 billion (f.o.b., 2003 est.): capital goods, crude oil, foodstuffs, consumer goods, chemicals. **Major trading partners:** U.S., Sweden, Costa Rica, Honduras, Colombia, Japan, Venezuela.

Geography The southernmost of the Central American nations, Panama is south of Costa Rica and north of Colombia. The Panama Canal bisects the isthmus at its narrowest and lowest point, allowing passage from the Caribbean Sea to the Pacific Ocean. Panama is slightly smaller than South Carolina. It is marked by a chain of mountains in the west, moderate hills in the interior, and a low range on the east coast. There are extensive forests in the fertile Caribbean area.

Government Constitutional democracy.

History Explored by Columbus in 1502 and by Balboa in 1513, Panama was the principal shipping point to and from South and Central America in colonial days. In 1821, when Central America revolted against Spain, Panama joined Colombia, which had already declared its independence. For the next 82 years, Panama attempted unsuccessfully to break away from Colombia. Between 1850 and 1900 Panama had 40 administrations, 50 riots, 5 attempted secessions, and 13 U.S. interventions. After a U.S. proposal for canal rights over the narrow isthmus was rejected by Colombia, Panama proclaimed its independence with U.S. backing in 1903.

For canal rights in perpetuity, the U.S. paid Panama $10 million and agreed to pay $250,000 each year, which was increased to $430,000 in 1933, and to $1,930,000 in 1955. In exchange, the U.S. got the Canal Zone—a 10-mile-wide strip across the isthmus—and considerable influence in Panama's affairs. On Sept. 7, 1977, Gen. Omar Torrijos Herrera and President Jimmy Carter signed treaties giving Panama gradual control of the canal, phasing out U.S. military bases, and guaranteeing the canal's neutrality.

Nicolas Ardito Barletta, Panama's first directly elected president in 16 years, was inaugurated on Oct. 11, 1984, for a five-year term. He was a puppet of strongman Gen. Manuel Noriega, a former CIA operative and head of the secret police. Noriega replaced Barletta with vice president Eric Arturo Delvalle a year later. In 1988, Noriega was indicted in the U.S. for drug trafficking, but when Delvalle attempted to fire him, Noriega forced the National Assembly to replace Delvalle with Manuel Solis Palma. In Dec. 1989, the assembly named Noriega "maximum leader" and declared the U.S. and Panama to be in a state of war. In Dec. 1989, 24,000 U.S. troops seized control of Panama City in an attempt to capture Noriega after a U.S. soldier was killed in Panama. On Jan. 3, 1990, Noriega surrendered himself to U.S. custody and was transported to Miami, where he was later convicted of drug trafficking. Guillermo Endara, who probably would have won an election suppressed earlier by Noriega, was installed as president.

On Dec. 31, 1999, the U.S. formally handed over control of the Panama Canal to Panama. Meanwhile, Colombian rebels and paramilitary forces have made periodic incursions into Panamanian territory, raising security concerns. Panama has also faced increased drug and arms smuggling.

In May 2004 presidential elections, Martín Torrijos, the son of former dictator Omar Torrijos, won 47.5% of the vote. He took office in September.

Panama Canal. In 1524, King Charles V of Spain ordered a survey of a waterway across the isthmus in consideration of building a canal. In 1878, the Colombian government gave a construction concession to the French Canal Company. The effort ended in bankruptcy nine years later, and the United States ultimately paid the French $40 million for their rights and assets. The U.S. project, built on territory controlled by the United States, began in 1904 and was completed in 1914.

Papua New Guinea

Sovereign: Queen Elizabeth II (1952)
Governor-General: Paulias Matane (2004)
Prime Minister: Sir Michael Somare (2002)
Area: 178,703 sq mi (462,840 sq km)
Population (2004 est.): 5,420,280 (growth rate: 2.3%); birth rate: 30.5/1000; infant mortality rate: 53.2/1000; life expectancy: 64.6; density per sq mi: 30
Capital and largest city (2003 est.): Port Moresby, 324,900. **Monetary unit:** Kina. **Languages:** Tok Pisin (Melanesian Pidgin, the lingua franca), Hiri Motu (in Papua region), English 1–2%; 715 indigenous languages. **Ethnicity/race:** Melanesian, Papuan, Negrito, Micronesian, Polynesian. **Religions:** Roman Catholic 22%, Lutheran 16%, Presbyterian/Methodist/

London Missionary Society 8%, Anglican 5%, Evangelical Alliance 4%, Seventh-Day Adventist 1%, other Protestant 10%, indigenous beliefs 34%. **Literacy rate:** 66% (2003 est.)
Economic summary: GDP/PPP (2003 est.): $11.4 billion; per capita $2,200. **Real growth rate:** 0.7%. **Inflation:** 17.2%. **Unemployment:** n.a. **Arable land:** 0%. **Agriculture:** coffee, cocoa, coconuts, palm kernels, tea, rubber, sweet potatoes, fruit, vegetables; poultry, pork. **Labor force:** 2.3 million (1999). **Industries:** copra crushing, palm oil processing, plywood production, wood chip production; mining of gold, silver, and copper; crude oil production; construction, tourism. **Natural resources:** gold, copper, silver, natural gas, timber, oil, fisheries. **Exports:** $1.938 billion (f.o.b., 2003 est.): oil, gold, copper ore, logs, palm oil, coffee, cocoa, crayfish, prawns. **Imports:** $967 million (f.o.b., 2003 est.): machinery and transport equipment, manufactured goods, food, fuels, chemicals. **Major trading partners:** Australia, Japan, China, Singapore, New Zealand. **Member of Commonwealth of Nations**

Geography Papua New Guinea occupies the eastern half of the island of New Guinea, just north of Australia, and many outlying islands. The Indonesian province of West Papua (Irian Jaya) is to the west. To the north and east are the islands of Manus, New Britain, New Ireland, and Bougainville, all part of Papua New Guinea. About one-tenth larger than California, its mountainous interior has only recently been explored. Two major rivers, the Sepik and the Fly, are navigable for shallow-draft vessels.

Government Constitutional monarchy with parliamentary democracy.

History The first inhabitants of the island New Guinea were Papuan, Melanesian, and Negrito tribes, who altogether spoke more than 700 distinct languages. The eastern half of New Guinea was first explored by Spanish and Portuguese explorers in the 16th century. In 1828, the Dutch formally took possession of the western half of the island (now the province of West Papua [Irian Jaya], Indonesia). In 1885, Germany formally annexed the northern coast and Britain took similar action in the south. In 1906, Britain transferred its rights to British New Guinea to a newly independent Australia, and the name of the territory was changed to the Territory of Papua. Australian troops invaded German New Guinea (called Kaiser-Wilhelmsland) in World War I and gained control of the territory under a League of Nations mandate. New Guinea and some of Papua were invaded by Japanese forces in 1942. After being liberated by the Australians in 1945, it became a United Nations trusteeship, administered by Australia. The territories were combined and called the Territory of Papua and New Guinea.

Australia granted limited home rule in 1951. Autonomy in internal affairs came nine years later, and in Sept. 1975, Papua New Guinea achieved complete independence from Britain.

A violent nine-year secessionist movement took place on the island of Bougainville. In 1989, guerrillas of the Bougainville Revolutionary Army (BRA) shut down the island's Australian-owned copper mine, a major source of revenue for the country. The rebels believed that Bougainville deserved a greater share of the earnings for its copper. In 1990, the BRA declared Bougainville's independence, whereupon the government blockaded the island until Jan. 1991, when a peace treaty was signed. In 1997, Papua New Guinea's government hired South African mercenary soldiers to fight on Bougainville in order to end the long-running crisis, but this action led to massive demonstrations and the mercenary contract was rescinded. In April 1998, a cease-fire was declared.

On July 17, 1998, an earthquake-triggered tsunami (tidal wave) off the northeast coast of Papua New Guinea killed at least 1,500 people and left thousands more injured and homeless.

Paraguay

REPUBLIC OF PARAGUAY

National name: República del Paraguay
President: Nicanor Duarte Frutos (2003)
Area: 157,046 sq mi (406,750 sq km)
Population (2004 est.): 6,191,368 (growth rate: 2.5%); birth rate: 29.8/1000; infant mortality rate: 26.7/1000; life expectancy: 74.6; density per sq mi: 39
Capital and largest city (2003 est.): Asunción, 1,482,200 (metro. area), 525,100. **Other large cities:** Ciudad del Este, 239,500; San Lorenzo, 210,000.
Monetary unit: Guaraní. **Languages:** Spanish, Guaraní (both official). **Ethnicity/race:** mestizo 95%. **Religion:** Roman Catholic 90%, Mennonite, other Protestant. **Literacy rate:** 94% (2003 est.)
Economic summary: GDP/PPP (2003 est.): $28.03 billion; per capita $4,600. **Real growth rate:** 1.3%. **Inflation:** 10.5% (2002 est.). **Unemployment:** 16.4% (2002 est.). **Arable land:** 6%. **Agriculture:** cotton, sugarcane, soybeans, corn, wheat, tobacco, cassava (tapioca), fruits, vegetables; beef, pork, eggs, milk; timber. **Labor force:** 2.5 million (2002 est.); agriculture 45%. **Industries:** sugar, cement, textiles, beverages, wood products. **Natural resources:** hydropower, timber, iron ore, manganese, limestone. **Exports:** $2.727 billion (f.o.b., 2003 est.): soybeans, feed, cotton, meat, edible oils, electricity. **Imports:** $2.77 billion (f.o.b., 2003 est.): road vehicles, consumer goods, tobacco, petroleum products, electrical machinery. **Major trading partners:** Brazil, Argentina, Chile, Bermuda, U.S., Hong Kong. **International conflicts:** unruly region at convergence of Argentina-Brazil-Paraguay borders is locus of money laundering, smuggling, arms and drug trafficking, and harbors Islamist militants.

Geography California-size Paraguay is surrounded by Brazil, Bolivia, and Argentina in south-central South America. Eastern Paraguay, between the Paraná and Paraguay rivers, is upland country with the thickest population settled on the grassy slope that inclines toward the Paraguay River. The greater part of the Chaco region to the west is covered with marshes, lagoons, dense forests, and jungles.

Government Constitutional republic.

History Indians speaking Guaraní—the most common language in Paraguay today, after Spanish—were the country's first inhabitants. In 1526 and again in 1529, Sebastian Cabot explored Paraguay when he sailed up the Paraná and Paraguay Rivers. From 1608 until their expulsion from the Spanish dominions in 1767, the Jesuits maintained an extensive establishment in the south and east of Paraguay. In 1811, Paraguay revolted against Spanish rule and became a nominal republic under two consuls.

Paraguay was governed by three dictators during the first 60 years of independence. The third, Francisco López, waged war against Uruguay, Brazil, and Argentina in 1865–1870, a conflict in which half the male population was killed. A new constitution in 1870, designed to prevent dictatorships and internal strife, failed to do so, and not until 1912 did a period of comparative economic and political stability begin. The Chaco War (1932–1935) with Bolivia won Paraguay more western territory.

After World War II, politics became particularly unstable. Alfredo Stroessner was dictator from 1954 until 1989, during which he was accused of the torture and murder of thousands of political opponents. Despite Paraguay's human rights record, the U.S. continuously supported Stroessner.

Stroessner was overthrown by army leader Gen. Andres Rodriguez in 1989. Rodriguez went on to win Paraguay's first multicandidate election in decades. Paraguay's new constitution went into effect in 1992. In 1993, Juan Carlos Wasmosy, a wealthy businessman and the candidate of the governing Colorado Party, won a five-year term in free elections.

Raúl Cubas Grau was elected president in May 1998. In 1999, Cubas was forced from office for his alleged involvement in the assassination of Vice President Luis María Argaña. The vice president had criticized Cubas for refusing to jail his mentor, Gen. Lino Oviedo, who had been convicted of leading a failed 1996 coup against Wasmosy.

The new president, Luis Ángel González Macchi, undertook a governmental overhaul, and for the first time since Stroessner was overthrown, political and economic power was no longer entirely within the hands of the corrupt and military-backed Colorado Party. The U.S. has accused the Colorado Party of smuggling, money laundering, trafficking Bolivian cocaine, and supporting international terrorist organizations.

In Aug. 2000, the opposition Liberal Party won its first major victory in more than 50 years with the election of Julio Cesar Franco as vice president. He narrowly defeated the son of the previous vice president, Argaña. Paraguay's government sought to clean up the political system by bringing to trial political and military figures suspected of human rights violations, corruption, or other crimes.

In 2002, anti-government rioters demanded that President González Macchi resign, blaming him for Paraguay's protracted recession since the late 1990s. In Dec. 2002, González Macchi was accused of mishandling $16 million in state funds. He was acquitted in an impeachment trial in Feb. 2003. Former journalist Nicanor Duarte Frutos became president on August 15, 2003. He has pledged to clean up the pervasive corruption in his nearly bankrupt country.

A fire at a massive supermarket near the capital killed nearly 400 shoppers and injured hundreds more on Aug. 1, 2004. Security guards had barred the exits to prevent looting. The supermarket's owners have been charged with manslaughter.

Peru

REPUBLIC OF PERU

National name: República del Perú
President: Alejandro Toledo (2001)
Prime Minister: Carlos Ferrero Costa (2003)
Area: 496,223 sq mi (1,285,220 sq km)
Population (2004 est.): 27,544,305 (growth rate: 1.4%); birth rate: 21.3/1000; infant mortality rate: 33.0/1000; life expectancy: 69.2; density per sq mi: 56
Capital and largest city (2003 est.): Lima, 8,113,000 (metro. area). **Other large cities:** Arequipa, 837,300; Trujillo, 725,200; Chiclayo, 598,400. **Monetary unit:** Nuevo sol (1991). **Languages:** Spanish, Quéchua (both official); Aymara; many minor Amazonian languages. **Ethnicity/race:** Amerindian 45%, mestizo 37%, white 15%, black, Japanese, Chinese, and other 3%. **Religion:** Roman Catholic 90%. **Literacy rate:** 91% (2003 est.)
Economic summary: GDP/PPP (2003 est.): $146.9 billion; per capita $5,200. **Real growth:** 5.4%. **Inflation:** 2.2%. **Unemployment:** 13.4%; widespread underemployment. **Arable land:** 3%. **Agriculture:** coffee, cotton, sugarcane, rice, wheat, potatoes, corn, plantains, coca; poultry, beef, dairy products, wool; fish. **Labor force:** 7.5 million (2000 est.); agriculture, mining and quarrying, manufacturing, construction, transport, services. **Industries:** mining of metals, petroleum, fishing, textiles, clothing, food processing, cement, auto assembly, steel, shipbuilding, metal fabrication. **Natural resources:** copper, silver, gold, petroleum, timber, fish, iron ore, coal, phosphate, potash, hydropower, natural gas. **Exports:** $8.954 billion (f.o.b., 2003 est.): fish and fish products, gold, copper, zinc, crude petroleum and byproducts, lead, coffee, sugar, cotton. **Imports:** $8.244 billion (f.o.b., 2003 est.): machinery, transport equipment, foodstuffs, petroleum, iron and steel, chemicals, pharmaceuticals. **Major trading partners:** U.S., China, UK, Switzerland, Japan, Chile, Spain, Colombia, Brazil, Venezuela, Argentina.

Geography Peru, in western South America, extends for nearly 1,500 mi (2,414 km) along the Pacific Ocean. Colombia and Ecuador are to the north, Brazil and Bolivia to the east, and Chile to the south. Five-sixths the size of Alaska, Peru is divided by the Andes Mountains into three sharply differentiated zones. To the west is the coastline, much of it arid, extending 50 to 100 mi (80 to 160 km) inland. The mountain area, with peaks over 20,000 ft (6,096 m), lofty plateaus, and deep valleys, lies centrally. Beyond the mountains to the east is the heavily forested slope leading to the Amazonian plains.

Government Constitutional republic.

History Peru was once part of the great Incan empire and later the major vice-royalty of Spanish South America. It was conquered in 1531–1533 by Francisco Pizarro. On July 28, 1821, Peru proclaimed its independence, but the Spanish were not finally defeated until 1824. For a hundred years thereafter, revolutions were frequent; a new war was fought with Spain in 1864–1866, and an unsuccessful war was fought with Chile from 1879 to 1883 (the War of the Pacific).

Peru emerged from 20 years of dictatorship in 1945 with the inauguration of President José Luis Bustamente y Rivero after the first free election in many decades. But he served for only three years and was succeeded in turn by Gen. Manuel A. Odria, Manuel Prado y Ugarteche, and Fernando Belaúnde Terry. On Oct. 3, 1968, Belaúnde was overthrown by Gen. Juan Velasco Alvarado. In 1975, Velasco was replaced in a bloodless coup by his premier, Gen. Francisco Morales Bermudez, who promised to restore civilian government. In elections held on May 18, 1980, Belaúnde Terry, the last civilian president, was elected president again. Maoist guerrilla group Shining Path, or Sendero Luminoso, began their brutal campaign to overthrow the government. The military's subsequent crackdown led to further civilian human rights abuses and disappearances. A smaller rebel group, Tupac Amaru, also fought against the government.

Peru's fragile democracy survived. In 1985, Belaúnde Terry was the first elected president to turn over power to a constitutionally elected successor since 1945. Alberto Fujimori won the 1990 elections. Citing continuing terrorism, drug trafficking, and corruption, Fujimori dissolved Congress, suspended the constitution, and imposed censorship in April 1992. By September, most of Shining Path had been vanquished. A new constitution was approved in 1993.

Fujimori was reelected in 1995, and again in May 2000 to a third five-year term, after his opponent, Alejandro Toledo, withdrew from the contest, charging fraud. In Sept. 2000, Fujimori's intelligence chief, Vladimiro Montesinos, was videotaped bribing a congressman. Fujimori announced he would dismantle the powerful National Intelligence Service, which has been accused of human rights violations. Two months later, he stunned his nation by resigning during a trip to Japan. Revelations that Fujimori secretly held Japanese citizenship—and could not be extradited to face corruption charges—enraged the populace.

In 2001, the centrist Alejandro Toledo was elected president with 53% of the vote, narrowly defeating former president Alan García. His rags-to-riches story and mixed Indian and Latino heritage made him popular among the poor. Inheriting a country wracked by economic troubles and corruption, Toledo did little, however, to restore confidence in the government. Early in his presidency, he gave himself a significant pay raise while at the same time calling for economic austerity. In June 2002, a popular revolt took place in the cities of Arequipa and Tacna, and other areas of southern Peru after the sale of two state-run electricity firms to a Belgian company, Tractebel—Toledo had specifically promised during his campaign not to sell these firms. Opinion polls have revealed that more than 60% of Peruvians are adamantly opposed to privatization and foreign investment, which in the past has led to price increases, mass layoffs, corruption, and few discernible benefits for the populace. To quell the rioting, Toledo suspended the decision to privatize, apologized publicly, and reshuffled his government.

In Aug. 2003, a truth commission report revealed that 69,000 people were killed during the 1980–2000 wars between rebel groups and the government, about twice the original estimate. The deaths were carried out by the rebels (54%) as well as the military (30%); other militias were responsible for the remainder.

Since Toledo took office in 2001, the economy has grown annually by about 4%, but this growth, centered on mining and the gas industry, has not yet created new jobs. A series of scandals and political missteps have continued to cause Toledo's approval ratings to drop—according to 2004 polls cited in *The Economist*, he is Latin America's least popular leader.

The Philippines

REPUBLIC OF THE PHILIPPINES

National name: Republika ng Pilipinas
President: Gloria Macapagal Arroyo (2001)
Area: 115,830 sq mi (300,000 sq km)
Population (2004 est.): 86,241,697 (growth rate: 1.9%); birth rate: 25.8/1000; infant mortality rate: 24.2/1000; life expectancy: 69.6; density per sq mi: 745
Capital and largest city (2003 est.): Manila, 13,790,900 (metro. area), 10,232,900 (city proper). **Other large cities:** Quezon City (2000 est.), 1,669,776 (part of Manila metro. area); Cebu (2003 est.), 761,900.
Monetary unit: Peso. **Languages:** Filipino (based on Tagalog), English (both official); eight major dialects: Tagalog, Cebuano, Ilocano, Hiligaynon or Ilonggo, Bicol, Waray, Pampango, and Pangasinense.
Ethnicity/race: Christian Malay 91.5%, Muslim Malay 4%, Chinese 1.5%, other 3%. **Religions:** Roman Catholic 83%, Protestant 9%, Islam 5%, Buddhist and other 3%. **Literacy rate:** 96% (2003 est.)
Economic summary: GDP/PPP (2003 est.): $390.7 billion; per capita $4,600. **Real growth rate:** 4.5%. **Inflation:** 3.1%. **Unemployment:** 11.4%. **Arable land:** 18%. **Agriculture:** rice, coconuts, corn, sugarcane, bananas, pineapples, mangoes; pork, eggs, beef; fish.

Labor force: 34.6 million; agriculture 45%, industry 15%, services 40% (2003 est.). **Industries:** textiles, pharmaceuticals, chemicals, wood products, food processing, electronics assembly, petroleum refining, fishing. **Natural resources:** timber, petroleum, nickel, cobalt, silver, gold, salt, copper. **Exports:** $34.56 billion (f.o.b., 2003 est.): electronic equipment, machinery and transport equipment, garments, coconut products, chemicals. **Imports:** $35.97 billion (f.o.b., 2003 est.): raw materials, machinery and equipment, fuels, chemicals. **Major trading partners:** U.S., Japan, China, Taiwan, Singapore, Hong Kong, Malaysia, Netherlands, Germany, South Korea.

Geography The Philippine Islands are an archipelago of over 7,000 islands lying about 500 mi (805 km) off the southeast coast of Asia. The overall land area is comparable to that of Arizona. Only about 7% of the islands are larger than one square mile, and only one-third have names. The largest are Luzon in the north (40,420 sq mi; 104,687 sq km), Mindanao in the south (36,537 sq mi; 94,631 sq km), and Samar (5,124 sq mi; 13,271 sq km). The islands are of volcanic origin, with the larger ones crossed by mountain ranges. The highest peak is Mount Apo (9,690 ft; 2,954 m) on Mindanao.

Government Republic.

History Ferdinand Magellan, the Portuguese navigator in the service of Spain, explored the Philippines in 1521. Twenty-one years later, a Spanish exploration party named the group of islands in honor of Prince Philip, who was later to become Philip II of Spain. Spain retained possession of the islands for the next 350 years.

The Philippines were ceded to the U.S. in 1899 by the Treaty of Paris after the Spanish-American War. Meanwhile, the Filipinos, led by Emilio Aguinaldo, had declared their independence. They initiated guerrilla warfare against U.S. troops that persisted until the capture of Aguinaldo in 1901. By 1902, peace was established except among the Islamic Moros on the southern island of Mindanao.

The first U.S. civilian governor-general was William Howard Taft (1901–1904). The Jones Law (1916) provided for the establishment of a Philippine Legislature composed of an elective Senate and House of Representatives. The Tydings-McDuffie Act (1934) provided for a transitional period until 1946, at which time the Philippines would become completely independent. Under a constitution approved by the people of the Philippines in 1935, the Commonwealth of the Philippines came into being with Manuel Quezon y Molina as president.

On Dec. 8, 1941, the islands were invaded by Japanese troops. Following the fall of Gen. Douglas MacArthur's forces at Bataan and Corregidor, Quezon established a government-in-exile that he headed until his death in 1944. He was succeeded by Vice President Sergio Osmeña. U.S. forces under MacArthur reinvaded the Philippines in Oct. 1944 and, after the liberation of Manila in Feb. 1945, Osmeña reestablished the government.

The Philippines achieved full independence on July 4, 1946. Manuel A. Roxas y Acuña was elected its first president, succeeded by Elpidio Quirino (1948–1953), Ramón Magsaysay (1953–1957), Carlos P. García (1957–1961), Diosdado Macapagal (1961–1965), and Ferdinand E. Marcos (1965–1986).

Under Marcos, civil unrest broke out in opposition to the leader's despotic rule. Martial law was declared on Sept. 21, 1972, and Marcos proclaimed a new constitution that ensconced himself as president. Martial law was officially lifted on Jan. 17, 1981, but Marcos and his wife, Imelda, retained broad powers.

In an attempt to resecure American support, Marcos set presidential elections for Feb. 7, 1986. With the support of the Catholic Church, Corazon Aquino declared her candidacy. Marcos was declared the official winner, but independent observers reported widespread election fraud and vote-rigging. Anti-Marcos protests exploded in Manila, Defense Minister Juan Enrile and Lt. Gen. Fidel Ramos defected to the opposition, and Marcos lost virtually all support; he was forced to flee into exile and entered the U.S. on Feb. 25, 1986.

The Aquino government survived coup attempts by Marcos supporters and other right-wing elements, including one in November by Enrile. Legislative elections on May 11, 1987, gave pro-Aquino candidates a large majority. Negotiations on renewal of leases for U.S. military bases threatened to sour relations between the two countries. Volcanic eruptions from Mount Pinatubo, however, severely damaged Clark Air Base, and in July 1991, the U.S. decided simply to abandon it.

In elections in May 1992, Gen. Fidel Ramos, who had the support of the outgoing Aquino, won the presidency in a seven-way race. In Sept. 1992, the U.S. Navy turned over the Subic Bay naval base to the Philippines, ending its long-standing U.S. military presence.

Meanwhile, the separatist Moro National Liberation Front was fighting a protracted war for an Islamic homeland on Mindanao, the southernmost of the two main islands. The Philippine army also battled another rebel group, the Moro Islamic Liberation Front. In Aug. 2001, both rebel groups signed unity agreements with the Philippine government. Frequent and violent clashes with these and other terrorist groups have continued, however. Abu Sayyaf, a small group of guerrillas that has been fighting since the 1970s for an independent Islamic state and reportedly has links to Osama bin Laden, gained international notoriety throughout 2000 and 2001 with its spree of kidnappings and murders. The Philippine military has also battled the New People's Army, a group of communist guerrillas that have targeted Philippine security forces since 1969. International officials reported in June 2003 that Jemaah Islamiyah, an affiliate of al-Qaeda, was training recruits in Mindanao, in the southern Philippines. About 120,000 people have died in the conflicts with rebel groups, and more than 3 million have been displaced.

In May 1998, 61-year-old former action film star Joseph Estrada was elected president of the Philippines. Within two years, however, the Philippine Senate began to impeach Estrada on corruption charges. Massive street demonstrations and the loss of political support eventually forced Estrada from office. Vice President Gloria Macapagal Arroyo, daughter of former president Diosdado Macapagal, became president in Jan. 2001.

In July 2003, dozens of mutinous soldiers took over a Manila shopping complex, protesting low pay and demanding the resignation of President Arroyo and the defense secretary. The demonstration ended peacefully.

In May 2004 elections, President Arroyo narrowly defeated film star Fernando Poe. Poe alleged voter fraud and warned of a revolt by his supporters.

Islamic militants in Iraq kidnapped Filipino truck driver Angelo de la Cruz in July. The Philippine government angered many foreign officials when it agreed to withdraw its troops from Iraq to spare his life.

Poland
REPUBLIC OF POLAND
National name: Rzeczpospolita Polska
President: Aleksander Kwasniewski (1995)
Prime Minister: Marek Belka (2004)
Area: 120,728 sq mi (312,685 sq km)
Population (2004 est.): 38,626,349 (growth rate: 0%); birth rate: 10.6/1000; infant mortality rate: 8.7/1000; life expectancy: 74.2; density per sq mi: 320
Capital and largest city (2003 est.): Warsaw, 2,201,900 (metro. area), 1,607,600 (city proper). **Other large cities:** Lodz, 778,200; Krakow, 733,100; Wroclaw, 632,200; Poznan, 581,200; Gdansk, 456,700; Szczecin, 415,700. **Monetary unit:** Zloty. **Language:** Polish. **Ethnicity:** Polish 96.7%, German 0.4%, Belorussian 0.1% Ukrainian 0.1%, other 2.7% (2002). **Religions:** Roman Catholic 95% (about 75% practicing), Eastern Orthodox, Protestant, and other 5%. **Literacy rate:** 100% (2003 est.)
Economic summary: GDP/PPP (2003 est.): $426.7 billion; per capita $11,000. **Real growth rate:** 3.6%. **Inflation:** 0.7%. **Unemployment:** 18%. **Arable land:** 46%. **Agriculture:** potatoes, fruits, vegetables, wheat; poultry, eggs, pork. **Labor force:** 17.6 million (2000 est.); industry 22.1%, agriculture 27.5%, services 50.4% (1999). **Industries:** machine building, iron and steel, coal mining, chemicals, shipbuilding, food processing, glass, beverages, textiles. **Natural resources:** coal, sulfur, copper, natural gas, silver, lead, salt, amber, arable land. **Exports:** $57.6 billion (f.o.b., 2003 est.): machinery and transport equipment 30.2%, intermediate manufactured goods 25.5%, miscellaneous manufactured goods 20.9%, food and live animals 8.5% (1999). **Imports:** $63.65 billion (f.o.b., 2003 est.): machinery and transport equipment 38.2%, intermediate manufactured goods 20.8%, chemicals 14.3%, miscellaneous manufactured goods 9.5% (1999). **Major trading partners:** Germany, Italy, France, UK, Czech Republic, Russia, Netherlands.

Geography Poland, a country the size of New Mexico, is in north-central Europe. Most of the country is a plain with no natural boundaries except the Carpathian Mountains in the south and the Oder and Neisse rivers in the west. Other major rivers, which are important to commerce, are the Vistula, Warta, and Bug.

Government Democratic republic.

History Great (north) Poland was founded in 966 by Mieszko I, who belonged to the Piast dynasty. The tribes of southern Poland then united to form Little Poland. In 1047, both Great Poland and Little Poland united under the rule of Casimir I the Restorer. Poland merged with Lithuania by royal marriage in 1386. The Polish-Lithuanian state reached the peak of its power between the 14th and 16th century, scoring military successes against the (Germanic) Knights of the Teutonic Order, the Russians, and the Ottoman Turks.

Lack of a strong monarchy enabled Russia, Prussia, and Austria to carry out a first partition of the country in 1772, a second in 1792, and a third in 1795. For more than a century thereafter, there was no Polish state, just Austrian, Prussian, and Russian sectors, but the Poles never ceased their efforts to regain their independence. The Polish people revolted against Russian, Prussian, and Austrian dominance throughout the 19th century. Poland was formally reconstituted in Nov. 1918, with Marshal Josef Pilsudski as chief of state. In 1919, Ignace Paderewski, the famous pianist and patriot, became the first premier. In 1926, Pilsudski seized complete power in a coup and ruled dictatorially until his death on May 12, 1935.

Despite a ten-year nonaggression pact signed in 1934, Hitler attacked Poland on Sept. 1, 1939. Soviet troops invaded from the east on Sept. 17, and on Sept. 28, a German-Soviet agreement divided Poland between the USSR and Germany. Wladyslaw Raczkiewicz formed a government-in-exile in France, which moved to London after France's defeat in 1940. All of Poland was occupied by Germany after the Nazi attack on the USSR in June 1941. Nazi Germany's occupation policy in Poland was designed to eradicate Polish culture through mass executions and to exterminate the country's large Jewish minority.

The Polish government-in-exile was replaced with the Communist-dominated Polish Committee of National Liberation by the Soviet Union in 1944. Moving to Lublin after that city's liberation, it proclaimed itself the Provisional Government of Poland. Some former members of the Polish government in London joined with the Lublin government to form the Polish Government of National Unity, which Britain and the U.S. recognized. On Aug. 2, 1945, in Berlin, President Harry S. Truman, Joseph Stalin, and Prime Minister Clement Attlee of Britain established a new de facto western frontier for Poland along the Oder and Neisse rivers. (The border was finally agreed to by West Germany in a nonaggression pact signed on Dec. 7, 1970.) On Aug. 16, 1945, the USSR and Poland signed a treaty delimiting the Soviet-Polish frontier. Under these agreements, Poland was shifted westward. In the east, it lost 69,860 sq mi (180,934 sq km); in the west, it gained (subject to final peace-conference approval) 38,986 sq mi (100,973 sq km).

A new constitution in 1952 made Poland a "people's democracy" of the Soviet type. In 1955, Poland became a member of the Warsaw Treaty Organization, and its foreign policy became identical to that of the USSR. The government undertook persecution of the Roman Catholic Church as a remaining source of opposition. Wladyslaw Gomulka was elected leader of the United Workers (Communist) Party in 1956. He denounced the Stalinist terror, ousted many Stalinists, and improved relations with the church. Most collective farms were dissolved, and the press became freer. A strike that began in shipyards and spread to other industries in Aug. 1980 produced a stunning victory for workers when the economically hard-pressed government accepted for the first time in a Marxist state the right of workers to organize in independent unions.

Led by Solidarity, a free union founded by an electrician, Lech Walesa, workers launched a drive for liberty and improved conditions. A national strike for a five-day workweek in Jan. 1981 led to the dismissal of Premier Pinkowski and the naming of the fourth premier in less than a year, Gen. Wojciech Jaruzelski. Martial law was declared on Dec. 13, when Walesa and other Solidarity leaders were arrested. It formally ended in 1984 but the government retained emergency powers. Increasing opposition to the government because of the failing economy led to a new wave of strikes in 1988. Unable to totally quell the dissent, the government re-legalized Solidarity and allowed it to compete in elections.

Solidarity members won a stunning victory in 1989, taking almost all the seats in the Senate and all of the 169 seats they were allowed to contest in the Sejm. This gave them substantial influence in the new government. Tadeusz Mazowiecki was appointed prime minister. Lech Walesa won the presidential election of 1990 with 74% of the vote. In 1991, the first fully free parliamentary election since World War II resulted in representation for 29 political parties. Efforts to turn Poland into a market economy, however, led to economic difficulties and widespread discontent. In the second democratic parliamentary election of Sept. 1993, voters returned power to ex-Communists and their allies. Solidarity's popularity and influence continued to wane. In 1995, Aleksander Kwasniewski, leader of the successor to the Communist Party, the Democratic Left, won the presidency over Walesa in a landslide.

In 1999, Poland became part of NATO, along with the Czech Republic and Hungary.

In Sept. 2001 parliamentary elections, former Communists, reconstituted as the center-left Democratic Left Alliance, won 41% of the vote. The election seemed to mark the demise of Solidarity, which did not win a single seat.

Poland was a staunch supporter of the United States and Britain during the 2003 Iraq war, and sent 200 troops to Iraq (60 were combat soldiers). In Sept. 2003, Poland became the leader of a 9,000-strong, multinational stabilizing force in Iraq. It contributed 2,000 of its own soldiers.

On May 1, 2004, Poland joined the EU. Prime Minister Leszek Miller resigned on May 2, 2004. His popularity had plummeted to 10% because of the country's continued economic troubles and because of a number of corruption scandals.

Portugal

REPUBLIC OF PORTUGAL

National name: República Portuguesa
President: Jorge Sampaio (1996)
Prime Minister: Pedro Santana Lopes (2004)
Area: 35,672 sq mi (92,391 sq km)
Population (2004 est.): 10,524,145 (growth rate: 0.4%); birth rate: 10.9/1000; infant mortality rate: 5.1/1000; life expectancy: 77.4; density per sq mi: 295
Capital and largest city (2003 est.): Lisbon, 2,618,100 (metro. area), 559,400. **Other large city:** Oporto, 264,200. **Monetary units:** Euro (formerly escudo). **Language:** Portuguese (official), Mirandese (official, but locally used). **Ethnicity/race:** homogeneous Mediterranean stock; less than 100,000 citizens of black African descent who immigrated to mainland during decolonization; East Europeans have entered since 1990. **Religions:** Roman Catholic 94%, Protestant (1995). **Literacy rate:** 93% (2003 est.).
Economic summary: GDP/PPP (2003 est.): $182.3 billion; per capita $18,000. **Real growth rate:** −1%. **Inflation:** 3.1%. **Unemployment:** 6%. **Arable land:** 21%. **Agriculture:** grain, potatoes, olives, grapes; sheep, cattle, goats, poultry, beef, dairy products. **Labor force:** 5.1 million (2000); services 60%, industry 30%, agriculture 10% (1999 est.). **Industries:** textiles and footwear; wood pulp, paper, and cork; metalworking; oil refining; chemicals; fish canning; wine; tourism. **Natural resources:** fish, forests (cork), tungsten, iron ore, uranium ore, marble, arable land, hydropower. **Exports:** $31.13 billion (f.o.b., 2003 est.): clothing and footwear, machinery, chemicals, cork and paper products, hides. **Imports:** $43.73 billion (f.o.b., 2003 est.): machinery and transport equipment, chemicals, petroleum, textiles, agricultural products. **Major trading partners:** Spain, Germany, France, UK, U.S., Italy, Belgium, Netherlands. **International disputes:** Portugal has periodically reasserted claims to territories around the town of Olivenza, Spain.

Geography Portugal occupies the western part of the Iberian Peninsula and is slightly smaller than Indiana. The country is crossed by three large rivers that rise in Spain, flow into the Atlantic, and divide the country into three geographic areas. The Minho

River, part of the northern boundary, cuts through a mountainous area that extends south to the vicinity of the Douro River. South of the Douro, the mountains slope to the plains around the Tejo River. The remaining division is the southern one of Alentejo. The Azores stretch over 340 mi (547 km) in the Atlantic, and consist of nine islands with a total area of 902 square mi (2,335 sq km). Madeira, consisting of two inhabited islands, Madeira and Porto Santo, and two groups of uninhabited islands, lie in the Atlantic about 535 mi (861 km) southwest of Lisbon.

Government Parliamentary democracy.

History An early Celtic tribe, the Lusitanians, are believed to have been the first inhabitants of Portugal. The Roman Empire conquered the region in about 140 B.C. Toward the end of the Roman Empire, the Visigoths had invaded the entire Iberian peninsula.

Portugal won its independence from Moorish Spain in 1143. King John I (1385–1433) unified his country at the expense of the Castilians and the Moors of Morocco. The expansion of Portugal was brilliantly coordinated by John's son, Prince Henry the Navigator. In 1488, Bartolomeu Dias reached the Cape of Good Hope, proving that Asia was accessible by sea. In 1498, Vasco da Gama reached the west coast of India. By the middle of the 16th century, the Portuguese Empire extended to West and East Africa, Brazil, Persia, Indochina, and the Malayan peninsula.

In 1581, Philip II of Spain invaded Portugal and held it for 60 years, precipitating a catastrophic decline in Portuguese commerce. Courageous and shrewd explorers, the Portuguese proved to be inefficient and corrupt colonizers. By the time the Portuguese monarchy was restored in 1640, Dutch, English, and French competitors began to seize the lion's share of the world's colonies and commerce. Portugal retained Angola and Mozambique in Africa, and Brazil (until 1822).

The corrupt King Carlos, who ascended the throne in 1889, made João Franco the premier with dictatorial power in 1906. In 1908, Carlos and his heir were shot dead on the streets of Lisbon. The new king, Manoel II, was driven from the throne in the revolution of 1910, and Portugal became a French-style republic. Traditionally friendly to Britain, Portugal fought in World War I on the Allied side in Africa as well as on the Western Front. Weak postwar governments and a revolution in 1926 brought Antonio de Oliveira Salazar to power. As minister of finance (1928–1940) and premier (1932–1968), Salazar ruled Portugal as a virtual dictator. He kept Portugal neutral in World War II but gave the Allies naval and air bases after 1943. Portugal joined NATO as a founding member in 1949 but did not gain admission to the United Nations until 1955.

Portugal's foreign and colonial policies met with increasing difficulty both at home and abroad beginning in the 1950s—the bloodiest and most protracted wars against colonialism in Africa were fought against the Portuguese. Portugal lost the tiny remnants of its Indian empire—Goa, Daman, and Diu—to Indian military occupation in 1961, the year an insurrection broke out in Angola. For the next 13 years, Salazar, who died in 1970, and his successor, Marcello Caetano, fought independence movements amid growing world criticism. Leftists in the armed forces, weary of a losing battle, launched a successful revolution on April 25, 1974. After the 1974 revolution, the new military junta gave up its territories, beginning with Portuguese Guinea in Sept. 1974, which became the Republic of Guinea-Bissau. The decolonization of the Cape Verde Islands and Mozambique was effected in July 1975. Angola achieved independence later that same year, thus end-

ing a colonial involvement in that continent that had begun in 1415. Full-scale, internationalized civil war, however, followed Portugal's departure from Angola, and Indonesia forcibly annexed independent East Timor. Also in that year, the government nationalized banking, transport, heavy industries, and the media. Portugal continued to experience social, economic, and political upheavals for the next decade.

Portugal was admitted to the European Economic Community (now European Union) on Jan. 1, 1986, and on Feb. 16, Mario Soares became the country's first civilian president in 60 years. Aníbal Cavaço Silva, an advocate of free-market economics and the Social Democratic candidate, had been elected as prime minister in 1985, signaling a more politically stable era. General elections in Oct. 1995 went to the Socialist Party, which fell just short of an absolute majority in the assembly. Lisbon mayor Jorge Sampaio, a Socialist, won the race for president in Jan. 1996. Portugal's Socialist government continued to take advantage of rosy economic conditions in 1997, and in 1999, it became a founding member of the European Economic and Monetary Union (EMU).

Portugal gave up its last colony, Macao, on Dec. 20, 1999, turning the small Asian seaport over to China.

In 2002, center-right Social Democrat leader José Manuel Durão Barroso became prime minister, after the Socialist Party suffered defeats. In the summer of 2003, more than a thousand people died during an unprecedented heat wave that caused fires to ravage Portugal's forests. Prime Minister Barroso resigned in July 2004 to become president of the European Commission. Pedro Santana Lopes, the new leader of the Social Democrats, succeeded him as prime minister.

Qatar

STATE OF QATAR

Emir: Sheik Hamad bin Khalifa al-Thani (1995)
Prime Minister: Abdullah bin Khalifa al-Thani (1996)
Area: 4,416 sq mi (11,437 sq km)
Population (2004 est.): 840,290 (growth rate: 2.7%); birth rate: 15.6/1000; infant mortality rate: 19.3/1000; life expectancy: 73.4; density per sq mi: 190
Capital (2003 est.): Doha, 550,700 (metro. area), 318,500 (city proper). **Monetary unit:** Qatari riyal. **Languages:** Arabic (official); English a common second language. **Ethnicity/race:** Arab 40%, Pakistani 18%, Indian 18%, Iranian 10%, other 14%. **Religion:** Islam 95%. **Literacy rate:** 83% (2003 est.)
Economic summary: GDP/PPP (2003 est.): $17.54 billion; per capita $21,500. **Real growth rate:** 8.5%. **Inflation:** 2%. **Unemployment:** 2.7% (2001). **Arable land:** 1%. **Agriculture:** fruits, vegetables; poultry, dairy products, beef; fish. **Labor force:** 280,122 (1997 est.). **Industries:** crude oil production and refining, fertilizers, petrochemicals, steel reinforcing bars, cement. **Natural resources:** petroleum, natural gas, fish. **Exports:** $12.36 billion (f.o.b., 2003 est.): petroleum products, fertilizers, steel. **Imports:** $5.711 billion (f.o.b., 2003 est.): machinery and transport equipment, food, chemicals. **Major trading partners:** Japan, South Korea, Singapore, U.S., France, UK, Germany, Italy, UAE, Saudi Arabia.

Geography Qatar (pronounced KAH-tar) occupies a small peninsula that extends into the Persian Gulf from the east side of the Arabian Peninsula. Saudi Arabia is to the west and the United Arab Emirates to the south. The country is mainly barren.

Government Traditional monarchy.

History Qatar was once controlled by the sheikhs of Bahrain, but in 1867, war broke out between the people and their absentee rulers. To keep the peace in the Gulf, the British installed Muhammad ibn Thani al-Thani, head of a leading Qatari family, as the region's ruler. In 1893, the Ottoman Turks made incursions into Qatar, but the emir successfully deflected them. In 1916, the emir agreed to allow Qatar to become a British protectorate.

Oil was discovered in the 1940s, bringing wealth to the country in the 1950s and 1960s. About 85% of Qatar's income from exports comes from oil. Its people have one of the highest per capita incomes in the world. In 1971, Qatar was to join the other emirates of the Trucial Coast to become part of the United Arab Emirates. But both Qatar and Bahrain decided against the merger and instead became independent nations.

Qatar permitted the international forces to use Qatar as a base during the 1991 Persian Gulf War. A border dispute erupted with Saudi Arabia that was settled in Dec. 1992. A territorial dispute with Bahrain over the Hawar Islands remains unresolved, however. In 1994, Qatar signed a defense pact with the U.S., becoming the third Gulf state to do so.

In June 1995, Crown Prince Hamad bin Khalifa al-Thani deposed his father, primarily because the king was out of step with the country's economic reforms. The emir was not stripped of his title, and much of the power was already in his son's hands. The new emir lifted press censorship and instituted other liberal reforms, including democratic elections and women's suffrage (1999). In 2003 Crown Prince Jassim, who declared he had never wanted to be king, abdicated in favor of his younger brother, Prince Tamim.

Qatar is the home of Al Jazeera, the Arabic satellite television network that has broadcast exclusive video footage of and statements by Osama bin Laden. The independent station is immensely popular in the Middle East, but has been criticized by many Arab countries for running interviews with controversial and opposition figures.

Qatar served as the headquarters for U.S. Central Command (CENTCOM) during the 2003 war in Iraq.

Romania

REPUBLIC OF ROMANIA

President: Ion Iliescu (2000)
Prime Minister: Adrian Nastase (2000)
Area: 91,699 sq mi (237,500 sq km)
Population (2004 est.): 22,355,551 (growth rate: –0.1%); birth rate: 10.7/1000; infant mortality rate: 27.2/1000; life expectancy: 71.1; density per sq mi: 244
Capital and largest city (2003 est.): Bucharest, 2,210,800 (metro. area), 1,906,800 (city proper).
Other large cities: Iasi, 320,000; Cluj-Napoca, 316,400; Timisoara, 316,100; Constanta, 309,000; Craiova, 301,100, Galati, 297,100; Brasov, 282,500.
Monetary unit: Leu. **Languages:** Romanian (official), Hungarian, German. **Ethnicity/race:** Romanian 89.5%, Hungarian 6.6%, Roma (Gyspy) 2.5%, Ukrainian 0.3%, German 0.3%, Russian 0.2%, Turkish 0.2%, other 0.4% (2002). **Religions:** Romanian Orthodox 87%, Protestant 6.8%, Roman Catholic 5.6%, other (mostly Islam) 0.4%, unaffiliated 0.2% (2002). **Literacy rate:** 98% (2003 est.)
Economic summary: GDP/PPP (2003 est.): $154.4 billion; per capita $6,900. **Real growth rate:** 4.5%. **Inflation:** 14.3%. **Unemployment:** 7.3%. **Arable land:** 41%. **Agriculture:** wheat, corn, barley, sugar beets, sunflower seed, potatoes, grapes; eggs, sheep. **Labor force:** 9.9 million (1999 est.); agriculture 40%, industry 25%, services 35% (1998). **Industries:** textiles and footwear, light machinery and auto assembly, mining, timber, construction materials, metallurgy, chemicals, food processing, petroleum refining. **Natural**

resources: petroleum (reserves declining), timber, natural gas, coal, iron ore, salt, arable land, hydropower. **Exports:** $17.63 billion (f.o.b., 2003 est.): textiles and footwear, metals and metal products, machinery and equipment, minerals and fuels. **Imports:** $22.17 billion (f.o.b., 2003 est.): machinery and equipment 23%, fuels and minerals 12%, chemicals 9%, textile and products 19% (1999). **Major trading partners:** Italy, Germany, France, UK, U.S., Turkey, Russia, Austria, Hungary.

Geography Romania is in southeast Europe and is slightly smaller than Oregon. The Carpathian Mountains divide Romania's upper half from north to south and connect near the center of the country with the Transylvanian Alps, running east and west. North and west of these ranges lies the Transylvanian plateau, and to the south and east are the plains of Moldavia and Walachia. In its last 190 mi (306 km), the Danube River flows through Romania only. It enters the Black Sea in northern Dobruja, just south of the border with the Ukraine.

Government Republic.

History Most of Romania was the Roman province of Dacia from about A.D. 100 to 271. From the 3rd to the 12th century, wave after wave of barbarian conquerors overran the native Daco-Roman population. Subjection to the first Bulgarian empire (8th–10th century) brought Eastern Orthodox Christianity to the Romanians. In the 11th century, Transylvania was absorbed into the Hungarian empire. By the 16th century, the main Romanian principalities of Moldavia and Walachia had become satellites within the Ottoman Empire, although they retained much independence. After the Russo-Turkish War of 1828–1829, they became Russian protectorates. The nation became a kingdom in 1881 after the Congress of Berlin.

At the start of World War I, Romania proclaimed its neutrality, but later joined the Allied side and in 1916 declared war on the Central Powers. The armistice of Nov. 11, 1918, gave Romania vast territories from Russia and the Austro-Hungarian Empire, doubling its size. The areas acquired included Bessarabia, Transylvania, and Bukovina. The Banat, a Hungarian area, was divided with Yugoslavia. King Carol II was crowned in 1930 and transformed the throne into a royal dictatorship. In 1938, he abolished the democratic constitution of 1923. In 1940, the country was reorganized along Fascist lines, and the Fascist Iron Guard became the nucleus of the new totalitarian party. On June 27, the Soviet Union occupied Bessarabia and northern Bukovina. King Carol II dissolved Parliament, granted the new premier, Ion Antonescu, full power, abdicated his throne, and went into exile.

Romania subsequently signed the Axis Pact on Nov. 23, 1940, and the following June joined in Germany's attack on the Soviet Union, reoccupying Bessarabia. About 270,000 Jews were massacred in Fascist Romania. Following the invasion of Romania by the Red Army in Aug. 1944, King Michael led a coup that ousted the Antonescu government. An armistice with the Soviet Union was signed in Moscow on Sept. 12, 1944. A Communist-dominated government bloc won elections in 1946, Michael abdicated on Dec. 30, 1947, and in 1955 Romania joined the Warsaw Treaty Organization and the United Nations.

Running a neo-Stalinist police state from 1967–1989, Nicolae Ceausescu wound the iron curtain tightly around Romania, turning a moderately prosperous country into one at the brink of starvation. To repay his $10 billion foreign debt in 1982, he ransacked the Romanian economy of everything that could be exported, leaving the country with desperate shortages of food, fuel, and other essentials. An army-assisted rebellion in Dec. 1989 led to Ceausescu's overthrow, trial, and execution.

An ex-Communist, Ion Iliescu of the National Salvation Front, served as president from 1990–1995. Emil Constantinescu of the Democratic Convention Party served as president from 1996–2000. The post-Communist governments' conflicted and half-hearted attempts to change to a free-market economy have been largely unrealized. In 2000 former president Iliescu returned to power with a landslide victory, easily defeating a xenophobic nationalist opponent. Discrimination against the Magyars (ethnic Hungarians) and the Roma (gypsies) continues, fueled by several ultra-nationalist political parties.

The country applied for membership in the EU in June 1995, but it is doubtful that Romania will be able to join the Union before at least 2007. Economic reform has proceeded at a glacial pace, and growing dissatisfaction with the government's inefficiencies and economic policies led to a wave of protests by workers, students, and others that peaked in 1997, and again in 1999, when coal miners striked.

Romania deployed 650 peacekeeping forces to Iraq in 2003, and joined NATO in 2004.

Russia

RUSSIAN FEDERATION

President: Vladimir Putin (2000)
Prime Minister: Mikhail Fradkov (2004)
Area: 6,592,735 sq mi (17,075,200 sq km)
Population (2004 est.): 143,782,3383 (growth rate: –0.5%); birth rate: 9.6/1000; infant mortality rate: 17.0/1000; life expectancy: 66.4; density per sq mi: 22
Capital and largest city (2003 est.): Moscow, 11,970,500 (metro. area), 8,368,200 (city proper). **Other large cities:** St. Petersburg, 4,582,300; Novosibirsk, 1,395,500; Nizhny Novgorod, 1,340,900; Yekaterinburg, 1,256,600; Samara, 1,146,800; Kazan, 1,113,600; Ufa, 1,096,600; Chelyabinsk, 1,080,000; Perm, 998,800; Volgograd, 984,200. **Monetary unit:** Ruble. **Languages:** Russian, others. **Ethnicity/race:** Russian 81.5%, Tatar 3.8%, Ukrainian 3%, Chuvash 1.2%, Bashkir 0.9%, Byelorussian 0.8%, Moldavian 0.7%, other 8.1% (1989). **Religions:** Russian Orthodox, Islam, others. **Literacy rate:** 100% (2003 est.)
Economic summary: GDP/PPP (2003 est.): $1.287 trillion; per capita $8,900. **Real growth rate:** 7.3%. **Inflation:** 12%. **Unemployment:** 8.4%, plus considerable underemployment. **Arable land:** 7%. **Agriculture:** grain, sugar beets, sunflower seed, vegetables, fruits; beef, milk. **Labor force:** 71.5 million; agriculture 12.3%, industry 22.7%, services 65%. **Industries:** complete range of mining and extractive industries producing coal, oil, gas, chemicals, and metals; all forms of machine building from rolling mills to high-performance aircraft and space vehicles; shipbuilding; road and rail transportation equipment; communications equipment; agricultural machinery, tractors, and construction equipment; electric power generating and transmitting equipment; medical and scientific instruments; consumer durables, textiles, foodstuffs, handicrafts. **Natural resources:** wide natural resource base including major deposits of oil, natural gas, coal, and many strategic minerals; timber; note: formidable obstacles of climate, terrain, and distance hinder exploitation of natural resources. **Exports:** $134.4 billion (2003 est.): petroleum and petroleum products, natural gas, wood and wood products, metals, chemicals, and a wide variety of civilian and military manufactures. **Imports:** $74.8 billion (2003 est.):

machinery and equipment, consumer goods, medicines, meat, sugar, semifinished metal products. **Major trading partners:** Germany, Italy, Netherlands, China, U.S., Ukraine, Belarus, Switzerland, Kazakhstan, France.

Geography The Russian Federation is the largest of the 21 republics that make up the Commonwealth of Independent States. It occupies most of eastern Europe and north Asia, stretching from the Baltic Sea in the west to the Pacific Ocean in the east, and from the Arctic Ocean in the north to the Black Sea and the Caucasus in the south. It is bordered by Norway and Finland in the northwest; Estonia, Latvia, Belarus, Ukraine, Poland, and Lithuania in the west; Georgia and Azerbaijan in the southwest; and Kazakhstan, Mongolia, China, and North Korea along the southern border.

Government Constitutional federation.

History Tradition says the Viking Rurik came to Russia in 862 and founded the first Russian dynasty in Novgorod. The various tribes were united by the spread of Christianity in the 10th and 11th centuries; Vladimir "the Saint" was converted in 988. During the 11th century, the grand dukes of Kiev held such centralizing power as existed. In 1240, Kiev was destroyed by the Mongols, and the Russian territory was split into numerous smaller dukedoms. Early dukes of Moscow extended their dominion over other Russian cities through their office of tribute collector for the Mongols and because of Moscow's role as an administrative and trade center.

In the late 15th century, Duke Ivan III acquired Novgorod and Tver and threw off the Mongol yoke. Ivan IV, the Terrible (1533–1584), first Muscovite czar, is considered to have founded the Russian state. He crushed the power of rival princes and boyars (great landowners), but Russia remained largely medieval until the reign of Peter the Great (1689–1725), grandson of the first Romanov czar, Michael (1613–1645). Peter made extensive reforms aimed at westernization and, through his defeat of Charles XII of Sweden at the Battle of Poltava in 1709, he extended Russia's boundaries to the west. Catherine the Great (1762–1796) continued Peter's westernization program and also expanded Russian territory, acquiring the Crimea, Ukraine, and part of Poland. During the reign of Alexander I (1801–1825), Napoléon's attempt to subdue Russia was defeated (1812–1813), and new territory was gained, including Finland (1809) and Bessarabia (1812). Alexander originated the Holy Alliance, which for a time crushed Europe's rising liberal movement.

Alexander II (1855–1881) pushed Russia's borders to the Pacific and into central Asia. Serfdom was abolished in 1861, but heavy restrictions were imposed on the emancipated class. Revolutionary strikes, following Russia's defeat in the war with Japan, forced Nicholas II (1894–1917) to grant a representative national body (Duma), elected by narrowly limited suffrage. It met for the first time in 1906, but had little influence on Nicholas.

World War I demonstrated czarist corruption and inefficiency, and only patriotism held the poorly equipped army together for a time. Disorders broke out in Petrograd (renamed Leningrad and now St. Petersburg) in March 1917, and defection of the Petrograd garrison launched the revolution. Nicholas II was forced to abdicate on March 15, 1917, and he and his family were killed by revolutionists on July 16, 1918. A provisional government under the successive premierships of Prince Lvov and a moderate, Alexander Kerensky, lost ground to the radical, or Bolshevik, wing of the Socialist Democratic Labor Party. On Nov.

7, 1917, the Bolshevik Revolution, engineered by Vladimir Lenin and Leon Trotsky, overthrew the Kerensky government and authority was vested in a Council of People's Commissars, with Lenin as premier.

The humiliating Treaty of Brest-Litovsk (March 3, 1918) concluded the war with Germany, but civil war and foreign intervention delayed Communist control of all Russia until 1920. A brief war with Poland in 1920 resulted in Russian defeat.

Emergence of the USSR The Union of Soviet Socialist Republics was established as a federation on Dec. 30, 1922. The death of Lenin on Jan. 21, 1924, precipitated an intraparty struggle between Joseph Stalin, general secretary of the party, and Trotsky, who favored swifter socialization at home and fomentation of revolution abroad. Trotsky was dismissed as commissar of war in 1925 and banished from the Soviet Union in 1929. He was murdered in Mexico City on Aug. 21, 1940, by a political agent. Stalin further consolidated his power by a series of purges in the late 1930s, liquidating prominent party leaders and military officers. Stalin assumed the premiership on May 6, 1941.

The term "Stalinism" has become the definition of an inhumane, draconian socialism. Stalin sent millions of Soviets who did not conform to the Stalinist ideal to forced-labor camps, and he persecuted his country's vast number of ethnic groups—reserving particular vitriol for Jews and Ukranians. Soviet historian Roy Medvedev estimated that about 20 million died from starvation, executions, forced collectivization, and life in the labor camps under Stalin's rule.

Soviet foreign policy, at first friendly toward Germany and antagonistic toward Britain and France and then, after Hitler's rise to power in 1933, becoming anti-Fascist and pro–League of Nations, took an abrupt turn on Aug. 24, 1939, with the signing of a nonaggression pact with Nazi Germany. The next month, Moscow joined in the German attack on Poland, seizing territory later incorporated into the Ukrainian and Belorussian SSRs. The Russo-Finnish War (1939–1940) added territory to the Karelian SSR set up on March 31, 1940; the annexation of Bessarabia and Bukovina from Romania became part of the new Moldavian SSR on Aug. 2, 1940; and the annexation of the Baltic republics of Estonia, Latvia, and Lithuania in June 1940 created the 14th, 15th, and 16th Soviet republics. The Soviet-German collaboration ended abruptly with a lightning attack by Hitler on June 22, 1941, which seized 500,000 sq mi of Russian territory before Soviet defenses, aided by U.S. and British arms, could halt it. The Soviet resurgence at Stalingrad from Nov. 1942 to Feb. 1943 marked the turning point in a long battle, ending in the final offensive of Jan. 1945. Then, after denouncing a 1941 nonaggression pact with Japan in April 1945, when Allied forces were nearing victory in the Pacific, the Soviet Union declared war on Japan on Aug. 8, 1945, and quickly occupied Manchuria, Karafuto, and the Kuril Islands.

After the war, the Soviet Union, United States, Great Britain, and France divided Berlin and Germany into four zones of occupation, which led to immediate antagonism between the Soviet and Western powers, culminating in the Berlin blockade in 1948. The USSR's tightening control over a cordon of Communist states, running from Poland in the north to Albania in the south, was dubbed the "iron curtain" by Churchill and would later become the Warsaw Pact. It marked the beginning of the cold war, the simmering hostility that pitted the world's two superpowers, the U.S. and the USSR—and their competing political ideologies—against each other for the next 45 years. Stalin died on March 6, 1953.

The new power emerging in the Kremlin was Nikita S. Khrushchev (1958–1964), first secretary of the party. Khrushchev formalized the eastern European system into a Council for Mutual Economic Assistance (Comecon) and a Warsaw Pact Treaty Organization as a counterweight to NATO. The Soviet Union exploded a hydrogen bomb in 1953, developed an intercontinental ballistic missile by 1957, sent the first satellite into space (Sputnik I) in 1957, and put Yuri Gagarin in the first orbital flight around Earth in 1961. Khrushchev's downfall stemmed from his decision to place Soviet nuclear missiles in Cuba and then, when challenged by the U.S., backing down and removing the weapons. He was also blamed for the ideological break with China after 1963. Khrushchev was forced into retirement on Oct. 15, 1964, and was replaced by Leonid I. Brezhnev as first secretary of the party and Aleksei N. Kosygin as premier.

U.S. president Jimmy Carter and Brezhnev signed the SALT II treaty in Vienna on June 18, 1979, setting ceilings on each nation's arsenal of intercontinental ballistic missiles. The U.S. Senate refused to ratify the treaty because of the invasion of Afghanistan by Soviet troops on Dec. 27, 1979. On Nov. 10, 1982, Leonid Brezhnev died. Yuri V. Andropov, who had formerly headed the KGB, became his successor, but died less than two years later, in Feb. 1984. Konstantin U. Chernenko, a 72-year-old party stalwart who had been close to Brezhnev, succeeded him. After 13 months in office, Chernenko died on March 10, 1985. Chosen to succeed him as Soviet leader was Mikhail S. Gorbachev, who led the Soviet Union in its long-awaited shift to a new generation of leadership. Unlike his immediate predecessors, Gorbachev did not also assume the title of president but wielded power from the post of party general secretary.

Gorbachev introduced sweeping political and economic reforms, bringing "glasnost" and "perestroika," openness and restructuring, to the Soviet system. He established much warmer relations with the West, ended the Soviet occupation of Afghanistan, and announced that the Warsaw pact countries were free to pursue their own political agendas. Gorbachev's revolutionary steps ushered in the end of the cold war, and in 1990 he was awarded the Nobel Peace Prize for his contributions to ending the 45-year conflict between East and West.

The Soviet Union took much criticism in early 1986 over the April 24 meltdown at the Chernobyl nuclear plant and its reluctance to give out any information on the accident.

Dissolution of the USSR Gorbachev's promised reforms, however, began to falter, and he soon had a formidable political opponent agitating for even more radical restructuring. Boris Yeltsin, president of the Russian SSR, began challenging the authority of the federal government, and resigned from the Communist Party along with other dissenters in 1990. On Aug. 29, 1991, an attempted coup d'état against Gorbachev was orchestrated by a group of hardliners. Yeltsin's defiant actions during the coup—he barricaded himself in the Russian parliament and called for national strikes—resulted in Gorbachev's reinstatement. But from then on, power had effectively shifted from Gorbachev to Yeltsin, and away from centralized power to greater power for the individual Soviet republics. In his last months as the head of the Soviet Union, Gorbachev dissolved the Communist Party and proposed the formation of the Commonwealth of Independent States

Rulers of Russia Since 1533

Name	Ruled[1]	Name	Ruled[1]	Name	Ruled[1]
Ivan IV the Terrible	1533–1584	Ivan VI	1740–1741[6]	**POLITICAL LEADERS OF USSR**	
Theodore I	1584–1598	Elizabeth	1741–1762	Vladimir Ilyich Lenin	1917–1924
Boris Godunov	1598–1605	Peter III	1762–1762	Aleksei Rykov	1924–1930
Theodore II	1605–1605	Catherine II the Great	1762–1796	Vyacheslav Molotov	1930–1941
Demetrius I[2]	1605–1606	Paul I	1796–1801	Joseph Stalin[8]	1941–1953
Basil IV Shuiski	1606–1610[3]	Alexander I	1801–1825	Georgi M. Malenkov	1953–1955
"Time of Troubles"	1610–1613	Nicholas I	1825–1855	Nikolai A. Bulganin	1955–1958
Michael Romanov	1613–1645	Alexander II	1855–1881	Nikita S. Khrushchev	1958–1964
Alexis I	1645–1676	Alexander III	1881–1894	Leonid I. Brezhnev	1964–1982
Theodore III	1676–1682	Nicholas II	1894–1917[7]	Yuri V. Andropov	1982–1984
Ivan V[4]	1682–1689[5]	**PROVISIONAL GOVERNMENT**		Konstantin U.	1984–1985
Peter I the Great[4]	1682–1725	**(PREMIERS)**		Chernenko	
Catherine I	1725–1727	Prince Georgi Lvov	1917–1917	Mikhail S. Gorbachev	1985–1991
Peter II	1727–1730	Alexander Kerensky	1917–1917	**PRESIDENTS OF RUSSIA**	
Anna	1730–1740			Boris Yeltsin	1991–1999
				Vladimir Putin	2000–

1. For czars through Nicholas II, year of end of rule is also that of death, unless otherwise indicated. 2. Also known as Pseudo-Demetrius. 3. Died 1612. 4. Ivan V and Peter I the Great ruled jointly until 1689, when Ivan was deposed. 5. Died 1696. 6. Died 1764. 7. Killed 1918. 8. General secretary of Communist Party, 1924–1953.

(CIS), which, when implemented, gave most of the Soviet Socialist Republics their independence, binding them together in a loose, primarily economic, federation. Russia and ten other former Soviet republics joined the CIS on Dec. 21, 1991. Gorbachev resigned on Dec. 25, and Yeltsin, who had been the driving force behind the Soviet dissolution, became president of the newly established Russian Republic.

At the start of 1992, Russia embarked on a series of dramatic economic reforms, including the freeing of prices on most goods, which led to an immediate downturn. A national referendum on confidence in Yeltsin and his economic program took place in April 1993. To the surprise of many, the president and his shock-therapy program won by a resounding margin. In September, Yeltsin dissolved the legislative bodies left over from the Soviet era.

The president of the southern republic of Chechnya accelerated his region's drive for independence in 1994. In December, Russian troops closed the borders and sought to squelch the independence drive. The Russian military forces met firm and costly resistance. In May 1997, the two-year war formally ended with the signing of a peace treaty that adroitly avoided the issue of Chechen independence.

In March 1998 Yeltsin dismissed his entire government and replaced Prime Minister Viktor Chernomyrdin with fuel and energy minister Sergei Kiriyenko. On Aug. 28, 1998, amid the Russian stock market's free fall, the Russian government halted trading of the ruble on international currency markets. This financial crisis led to a long-term economic downturn and to political upheaval. Yeltsin then sacked Kiriyenko and reappointed Chernomyrdin. The Duma rejected Chernomyrdin and on Sept. 11 elected foreign minister Yevgeny Primakov as prime minister. The repercussions of Russia's financial emergency were felt throughout the Commonwealth of Independent States.

Impatient with Yeltsin's increasingly erratic behavior, the Duma attempted to impeach him in May 1999. But the impeachment motion was quickly quashed and soon Yeltsin was on the ascendancy again. In keeping with his capricious style, Yeltsin dismissed Prime Minister Primakov and replaced him with Interior Minister Sergei Stepashin. Just three months later, however, Yeltsin ousted Stepashin and replaced him with Vladimir Putin on Aug. 9, 1999, announcing that in addition to serving as

prime minister, the former KGB agent was his choice as a successor in the 2000 presidential election.

In a decision that took Russia and the world by surprise, Boris Yeltsin resigned on Dec. 31, 1999, and Vladimir Putin became the acting president. On March 26, 2000, Putin won the presidential election with about 53% of the vote. Since then Putin has moved to centralize power in Moscow and has attempted to limit the power and influence of both the regional governors and wealthy business leaders. Although Russia remains economically stagnant, Putin has brought his nation a measure of political stability it never had under the mercurial and erratic Yeltsin.

Just three years after the bloody 1994–1996 Chechen-Russian war ended in devastation and stalemate, the fighting started again in 1999, with Russia launching air strikes and following up with ground troops. By the end of November, Russian troops had surrounded Chechnya's capital, Grozny, and about 215,000 Chechen refugees had fled to neighboring Ingushetia. Russia maintained that a political solution was impossible until Islamic militants in Chechnya had been vanquished. In Feb. 2000, after almost five months of fighting, Russian troops captured Grozny. The control of Grozny was a political as well as a military victory for Putin, whose hard-line stance against Chechnya has greatly contributed to his political popularity.

In 1999, the former Russian satellites of Poland, Hungary, and the Czech Republic joined NATO, raising Russia's hackles. The desire of Lithuania, Latvia, and Estonia, all of which were once part of the Soviet Union, to join the organization in the future has further antagonized Russia.

In Aug. 2000 the Russian government was severely criticized for its handling of the *Kursk* disaster, a nuclear submarine accident that left 118 sailors dead.

Russia was initially alarmed in 2001 when the U.S. announced its rejection of the Anti-Ballistic Missile Treaty of 1972, which for 30 years had been viewed as a crucial force in keeping the nuclear arms race under control. But Putin was eventually placated by Bush's reassurances, and in May 2002, the U.S. and Russian leaders announced a landmark pact to cut both countries' nuclear arsenals by up to two-thirds over the next ten years.

On Oct. 23, 2002, Chechen rebels seized a crowded Moscow theater and detained 763 people, including 3 Americans. Armed and wired with explosives, the rebels demanded that the Russian government end the war in Chechnya. Government forces stormed the theater the next day, after releasing a gas into the theater, which killed not only all the rebels but more than 100 hostages.

In March 2003, Chechens voted in a referendum that approved a new regional constitution making Chechnya a separatist republic within Russia. Agreeing to the constitution meant abandoning claims for complete independence, and the new powers accorded the republic were little more than cosmetic. During 2003, there were 11 bomb attacks against Russia that were believed to have been orchestrated by Chechen rebels.

In April 2003 reformist politician Sergei Yushenkov became the third outspoken critic of the Kremlin to be assassinated in the last five years. Just hours before he was gunned down, Yushenkov had officially registered his new political party, Liberal Russia. In Nov. 2003, billionaire Mikhail Khodorkovskiy, president of the Yukos oil company, was arrested on charges of fraud and tax evasion. Khodorkovskiy supported liberal opposition parties, which has led many to suspect that President Putin may have called for his arrest on trumped-up charges.

On Feb. 24, 2004, Putin suddenly dismissed his prime minister and cabinet. He offered no explanation for the purge, and his motives remain unclear. To no one's surprise, Putin was reelected president in March, with 70% of the vote. International election observers considered the process less than democratic.

On May 9, Chechnya's Moscow-backed leader, Akhmad Kadyrov, was killed in a bombing. The assassination undermined Russian claims that Chechnya has been growing more secure. At the end of August, another Russian-supported leader, Alu Alkhanov, was elected president of Chechnya with 73.5% of the vote. Days before the election, Chechen terrorists blew up two planes, killing all 90 passengers. Following the elections, a Chechen terrorist attack at a Moscow subway stop killed nine. On Sept. 1–3, dozens of heavily armed guerrillas seized a school in Beslan, near Chechnya, and held about 1,100 young schoolchildren, teachers, and parents hostage. At least 335 hostages were killed, including about 156 children, and more than 550 were wounded. Chechen warlord Shamil Basayev claimed responsibility. In the aftermath of the horrific attack, Putin announced that he would radically restructure the government to fight terrorism more effectively. The world community expressed deep concern that Putin's plans would consolidate his power and roll back democracy in Russia.

In Sept. 2004, Russia endorsed the Kyoto Protocol on climate change. It was the final endorsement needed to put the protocol into effect worldwide.

Rwanda

RWANDESE REPUBLIC

National name: Republika y'u Rwanda
President: Paul Kagame (2000)
Prime Minister: Bernard Makuza (2000)
Area: 10,169 sq mi (26,338 sq km)
Population (2004 est.): 7,954,013 (growth rate: 1.8%); birth rate: 40.0/1000; infant mortality rate: 101.7/1000; life expectancy: 39.2; density per sq mi: 782
Capital and largest city (2003 est.): Kigali, 298,100.
Monetary unit: Rwanda franc. **Languages:** Kinyarwanda, French, and English (all official); Kiswahili in commercial centers. **Ethnicity/race:** Hutu 84%, Tutsi 15%, Twa (Pygmoid) 1%. **Religions:**
Roman Catholic 56.5%, Protestant 26%, Adventist 11.1%, Islam 4.6%, indigenous beliefs 0.1%, none 1.7% (2001). **Literacy rate:** 70% (2003 est.)
Economic summary: GDP/PPP (2003 est.): $10.11 billion; per capita $1,300. **Real growth rate:** 3.5%. **Inflation:** 5.5% (2002 est.). **Unemployment:** n.a. **Arable land:** 32%. **Agriculture:** coffee, tea, pyrethrum (insecticide made from chrysanthemums), bananas, beans, sorghum, potatoes; livestock. **Labor force:** 4.6 million (2000); agriculture 90%. **Industries:** cement, agricultural products, small-scale beverages, soap, furniture, shoes, plastic goods, textiles, cigarettes. **Natural resources:** gold, cassiterite (tin ore), wolframite (tungsten ore), methane, hydropower, arable land. **Exports:** $73.33 million (f.o.b., 2003 est.): coffee, tea, hides, tin ore. **Imports:** $245.8 million (f.o.b., 2003 est.): foodstuffs, machinery and equipment, steel, petroleum products, cement and construction material. **Major trading partners:** Indonesia, Germany, Hong Kong, South Africa, Kenya, Belgium, Israel.

Geography Rwanda, in east-central Africa, is surrounded by the Democratic Republic of the Congo, Uganda, Tanzania, and Burundi. It is slightly smaller than Maryland. Steep mountains and deep valleys cover most of the country. Lake Kivu in the northwest, at an altitude of 4,829 ft (1,472 m), is the highest lake in Africa. Extending north of it are the Virunga Mountains, which include the volcano Karisimbi (14,187 ft; 4,324 m), Rwanda's highest point.

Government Republic.

History The original inhabitants of Rwanda were the Twa, a Pygmy people who now make up only 1% of the population. While the Hutu and Tutsi are often considered to be two separate ethnic groups, scholars point out that they speak the same language, have a history of intermarriage, and share many cultural characteristics. Traditionally, the differences between the two groups were occupational rather than ethnic. Agricultural people were considered Hutu, while the cattle-owning elite were identified as Tutsi. Supposedly Tutsi were tall and thin, while Hutu were short and square, but it is often impossible to tell one from the other. The 1933 requirement by the Belgians that everyone carry an identity card indicating tribal identity as Tutsi or Hutu increased the distinction. Since independence, repeated violence in both Rwanda and Burundi has increased ethnic differentiation between the groups.

Rwanda, which became a part of German East Africa in 1890, was first visited by European explorers in 1854. During World War I, it was occupied in 1916 by Belgian troops. After the war, it became a Belgian League of Nations mandate, along with Burundi, under the name of Ruanda-Urundi. The mandate was made a UN trust territory in 1946. Until the Belgian Congo achieved independence in 1960, Ruanda-Urundi was administered as part of that colony. Belgium at first maintained Tutsi dominance but eventually encouraged power sharing between Hutu and Tutsi. Ethnic tensions led to civil war, forcing many Tutsi into exile. When Ruanda became the independent nation of Rwanda on July 1, 1962, it was under Hutu rule.

In Oct. 1990, the Rwandan Patriotic Front (RPF), Tutsi rebels in exile in Uganda, invaded in an attempt to overthrow the Hutu-led Rwandan government. Peace accords were signed in Aug. 1993, calling for a coalition government. But after the downing of a plane in April 1994 that killed the presidents of both Rwanda and Burundi, deep-seated ethnic violence erupted. (Who is responsible for shooting down the plane is unclear. One theory suggests it was Hutu extremists who rejected the Hutu-Tutsi power-sharing plan proposed by President Juvénal Habyarimana, a Hutu moderate. In 2004, a French judge asserted that it was the current Tutsi president, Paul Kagame, who has vehemently denied the charge.)

The presidential guard began murdering Tutsi opposition leaders, and soon policemen and soldiers began attempting to murder the entire Tutsi population. In 100 days, beginning in April 1994, Hutu rampaged through the country and slaughtered an estimated 800,000 Tutsi and their moderate Hutu sympathizers. A 30,000-member militia group, the Interahamwe, led much of the murderous spree, but, goaded by radio propaganda, ordinary Hutu joined in massacring their Tutsi neighbors. Although the genocidal slaughter seemed a spontaneous eruption of hatred, it has in fact been shown to have been carefully orchestrated by the Hutu government.

In response, the Tutsi rebel force, the Rwandan Patriotic Front, swept across the country in a 14-week civil war, routing the largely Hutu government. Despite horrific reports of genocide, no country came to the Tutsi's assistance. The UN, already stationed in Rwanda at the time of the killing, withdrew entirely after ten of its soldiers were killed.

In the aftermath of the genocide, an estimated 1.7 million Hutu fled across the border into neighboring Zaire (now the Democratic Republic of the Congo). Although Tutsi rebels took control of the government, they permitted a Hutu, Pasteur Bizimungu, to serve as president, attempting to deflect accusations of a resurgence in Tutsi elitism and to foster national unity. Paul Kagame, the Tutsi rebel leader, became vice president and *eminence gris*.

Amid the legitimate refugees from the genocide were Hutu militiamen, who began waging guerrilla warfare from refugee camps in Zaire. The Hutu guerrillas in Zaire, as well as Zaire's threat to exile their own ethnic Tutsi, led to Rwanda's support of rebel forces, headed by Laurent Kabila, bent on overthrowing Zaire's Mobutu Sese Seko. But Rwanda soon grew disenchanted with the new regime of Kabila. The Kabila government was not able to prevent the raids from Hutu guerrillas that continued to traumatize the country and destabilize the region. In Aug. 1998, a little more than a year after Kabila took over, a rebellion began against his reign, instigated by Rwanda and Uganda.

Refugee problems, continued massacres, and the horrific legacy of genocide continued to haunt the national psyche. In Sept. 1998, a UN tribunal sentenced Jean Kambanda, a former prime minister of Rwanda, to life in prison for his part in the 1994 genocide. He became the first person in history to be convicted for the crime of genocide, first defined in the 1948 Genocide Convention after World War II. By 2001, eight others had also been convicted of the same charge. The UN tribunal, however, has been criticized for its inefficiency and slow pace. In Dec. 1999, an independent report, commissioned by the UN, took Kofi Annan and other UN officials to task for not intervening effectively in the genocide.

In April 2000, President Bizimungu resigned and Vice President Paul Kagame became the first Tutsi president of the nation. It was Kagame's rebel force that seized Rwanda's capital and put an end to the genocide in 1994.

Rwanda continued fighting against the Democratic Republic of the Congo throughout its four-year civil war. Finally, in July 2002, the two countries signed a peace accord: Rwanda promised to withdraw its 35,000 troops from the Congolese border; Congo in turn agreed to disarm the thousands of Hutu militiamen in its territory, who threatened Rwandan security.

In May 2003, 93% of Rwandans voted to approve a new constitution that instituted a balance of political power between Hutu and Tutsi—no party, for example, can hold more than half the seats in parliament. It also outlawed the incitement of ethnic hatred. In the Aug. 26 presidential elections, the first since the Rwandan genocide, Paul Kagame, who had served as president since 2000, won a landslide victory. In June 2004, Pasteur Bizimungu, the Hutu who had served as president between 1994 and 2000 (then-vice president Kagame held the real power), was sentenced to 15 years in prison on charges of inciting ethnic hatred. Many consider the trial politically motivated.

St. Kitts and Nevis

FEDERATION OF ST. KITTS AND NEVIS

Sovereign: Queen Elizabeth II (1952)
Governor-General: Sir Cuthbert Sebastian (1996)
Prime Minister: Denzil Douglas (1995)
Area: St. Kitts, 65 sq mi (168 sq km); Nevis, 36 sq mi (93 sq km)
Population (2004 est.): 38,836 (growth rate: 0.3%); birth rate: 18.3/1000; infant mortality rate: 14.9/1000; life expectancy: 71.9; density per sq mi: 385
Capital (2003 est.): Basseterre (on St. Kitts), 11,500. **Largest town on Nevis:** Charlestown, 1,300. **Monetary unit:** East Caribbean dollar. **Languages:** English. **Ethnicity/race:** predominantly black; some British, Portuguese, and Lebanese. **Religions:** Anglican, other Protestant, Roman Catholic. **Literacy rate:** 97% (1980 est.)
Economic summary: GDP/PPP (2002 est.): $339 million; per capita $8,800. **Real growth rate:** –1.9%. **Inflation:** 1.7% (2001 est.). **Unemployment:** 4.5% (1997). **Arable land:** 17%. **Agriculture:** sugarcane, rice, yams, vegetables, bananas; fish. **Labor force:** 18,172 (June 1995). **Industries:** sugar processing, tourism, cotton, salt, copra, clothing, footwear, beverages. **Natural resources:** arable land. **Exports:** $70 million (2002 est.): machinery, food, electronics, beverages, tobacco. **Imports:** $195 million (2002 est.): machinery, manufactures, food, fuels. **Major trading partners:** U.S., UK, Canada, Portugal, Trinidad and Tobago, Japan.

Geography St. Kitts, the larger of the two islands, is roughly oval in shape except for a long, narrow peninsula to the southeast. Its highest point is Mount Liamuiga (3,792 ft [1,156 m]). The Narrows, a 2-mile- (3-km-) wide channel, separates the two islands. The circularly shaped Nevis is surrounded by coral reefs and the island is almost entirely a single mountain, Nevis Peak (3,232 ft [985 m]). A volcanic mountain chain dominates the center of both islands.

Government Constitutional monarchy.

History When Christopher Columbus explored the islands in 1493, they were inhabited by the Carib people. Today, most of the inhabitants are the descendants of African slaves. St. Kitts, formerly St. Christopher, was settled by the British in 1623; Nevis in 1628. The French settled on St. Kitts in 1627, and an Anglo-French rivalry lasted for more than 100 years. After a decisive British victory over the French at Brimstone Hill in 1782, the islands came under permanent British control. The islands, along with nearby Anguilla, were united in 1882. They joined the West Indies federation in 1958 and remained in that association until its dissolution in 1962. St. Kitts–Nevis-Anguilla became an associated state of the United Kingdom in 1967. Anguilla seceded in 1980, and St. Kitts and Nevis became independent on Sept. 19, 1983.

A drop in world sugar prices hurt the nation's economy through the mid-1980s, and the government sought to reduce the islands' dependence on sugar production and to diversify the economy, promoting tourism and financial services. In 1990, the premier of Nevis announced that he intended to seek an end to the federation with St. Kitts by 1992, but a local election in June 1992 postponed the idea. In Aug. 1998, 62% of the population voted for Nevis to secede, but the vote fell short of the two-thirds majority required.

The country had been blacklisted by various international financial agencies for improprieties in its offshore financial services industry, but by 2002 it had been removed from all such lists.

St. Lucia

Sovereign: Queen Elizabeth II (1952)
Governor-General: Dame Pearlette Louisy (1997)
Prime Minister: Kenny D. Anthony (1997)
Area: 238 sq mi (616 sq km)
Population (2004 est.): 164,213 (growth rate: 1.3%); birth rate: 20.5/1000; infant mortality rate: 14.0/1000; life expectancy: 73.3; density per sq mi: 690
Capital and largest city (2003 est.): Castries, 60,300.
Monetary unit: East Caribbean dollar. **Languages:** English (official), French patois. **Ethnicity/race:** black 90%, mixed 6%, East Indian 3%, white 1%.
Religions: Roman Catholic 90%, Anglican 3%, other Protestant 7%. **Literacy rate:** 67% (1980 est.)
Economic summary: GDP/PPP (2002 est.): $866 million; per capita $5,400. **Real growth rate:** 3.3%. **Inflation:** 3% (2001 est.). **Unemployment:** 16.5% (1997 est.). **Arable land:** 5%. **Agriculture:** bananas, coconuts, vegetables, citrus, root crops, cocoa. **Labor force:** 43,800 (2001 est.); agriculture 21.7%, services 53.6%, industry, commerce, and manufacturing 24.7%. **Industries:** clothing, assembly of electronic components, beverages, corrugated cardboard boxes, tourism, lime processing, coconut processing. **Natural resources:** forests, sandy beaches, minerals (pumice), mineral springs, geothermal potential. **Exports:** $66 million (2002 est.): bananas 41%, clothing, cocoa, vegetables, fruits, coconut oil. **Imports:** $267 million (2002 est.): food 23%, manufactured goods 21%, machinery and transportation equipment 19%, chemicals, fuels. **Major trading partners:** UK, U.S., Barbados, Brazil, Trinidad and Tobago. **Member of Commonwealth of Nations**

Geography One of the Windward Islands of the eastern Caribbean, St. Lucia lies just south of Martinique. It is of volcanic origin. A chain of wooded mountains runs from north to south, and from them flow many streams into fertile valleys.

Government Parliamentary democracy. A governor-general represents the sovereign, Queen Elizabeth II.

History The first inhabitants of St. Lucia were the Arawak Indians, who were forced off the island by the Caribs. Explored by Spain and then France, St. Lucia became a British territory in 1814 and one of the Windward Islands in 1871. With other Windward Islands, St. Lucia was granted home rule in 1967 as one of the West Indies Associated States. On Feb. 22, 1979, St. Lucia achieved full independence in ceremonies boycotted by the opposition St. Lucia Labour Party, which had advocated a referendum before cutting ties with Britain. The United Workers Party (UWP), then in power, called for new elections and was defeated by the St. Lucia Labour Party

(SLP). The UWP was returned to power in the elections of 1982, 1987, and 1992.

Kenny Anthony became prime minister in 1997, when his St. Lucia Labour Party won 16 of the 17 parliamentary seats.

The 1999 European Union decision to end its preferential treatment of bananas imported from former colonies has led St. Lucia to try to diversify its agricultural crops. In 2002, tropical storm Lili devasted the banana crop.

St. Vincent and the Grenadines

Sovereign: Queen Elizabeth II (1952)
Governor-General: Frederick Ballantyne (2002)
Prime Minister: Ralph Gonsalves (2001)
Area: 150 sq mi (389 sq km)
Population (2004 est.): 117,193 (growth rate: 0.3%); birth rate: 16.8/1000; infant mortality rate: 15.2/1000; life expectancy: 73.4; density per sq mi: 780
Capital and largest city (2003 est.): Kingstown, 17,600.
Monetary unit: East Caribbean dollar. **Languages:** English, French patois. **Ethnicity/race:** black 66%, mixed 19%, East Indian 6%, Carib Amerindian 2%, other 7%. **Religions:** Anglican 47%, Methodist 28%, Roman Catholic 13%, Hindu, Seventh-Day Adventist, other Protestant. **Literacy rate:** 96% (1970 est.)
Economic summary: GDP/PPP (2002 est.): $339 million; per capita $2,900. **Real growth rate:** –0.5%. **Inflation:** –0.4% (2001 est.). **Unemployment:** 22% (1997 est.). **Arable land:** 10%. **Agriculture:** bananas, coconuts, sweet potatoes, spices; small numbers of cattle, sheep, pigs, goats; fish. **Labor force:** 67,000 (1984 est.); agriculture 26%, industry 17%, services 57% (1980 est.). **Industries:** food processing, cement, furniture, clothing, starch. **Natural resources:** hydropower, cropland. **Exports:** $38 million (2002 est.): bananas 39%, eddoes and dasheen (taro), arrowroot starch, tennis racquets. **Imports:** $174 million (2002 est.): foodstuffs, machinery and equipment, chemicals and fertilizers, minerals and fuels. **Major trading partners:** France, Greece, Spain, UK, U.S., Trinidad and Tobago, Singapore. **Member of Commonwealth of Nations**

Geography St. Vincent, chief island of the chain, is 18 mi (29 km) long and 11 mi (18 km) wide, and is located 100 mi (161 km) west of Barbados. The island is mountainous and well forested. St. Vincent is dominated by the volcano Mount Soufrière, which rises to 4,048 ft (1,234 m). The Grenadines, a chain of nearly 600 islets with a total area of only 17 sq mi (27 sq km), extend for 60 mi (96 km) between St. Vincent and Grenada. The main islands in the Grenadines are Bequia, Balliceau, Canouan, Mayreau, Mustique, Isle D'Quatre, Petit Saint Vincent, and Union Island.

Government Parliamentary democracy.

History The Carib Indians inhabited St. Vincent before the Europeans arrived, and the island still sports a sizable number of Carib artifacts. Explored by Columbus in 1498, and alternately claimed by Britain and France, St. Vincent became a British colony by the Treaty of Paris in 1763. In 1773, the island was divided between the Caribs and the British, but conflicts between the groups persisted. In 1776, the Caribs revolted and were subdued. Thereafter the British deported most of them to islands in the Gulf of Honduras. Sugarcane cultivation brought thousands of African slaves and, later, Portuguese and East Indian laborers.

The islands belonged to the West Indies Federation from 1958 until its dissolution in 1962, won home rule in 1969 as part of the West Indies Associated States, and achieved full independence Oct. 26, 1979. Prime Minister Milton Cato's government quelled a brief rebellion on Dec. 8, 1979, attributed to economic problems following the eruption of Mount Soufrière in April 1979 (which had caused the evacuation of the northern two-thirds of the island). The eruption, followed by Hurricane Allen in 1980, seriously damaged the nation's economy, particularly the important banana crop, in the 1980s. But by the 1990s the economy had begun to rebound. With the 1999 decision by the European Union to end its preferential treatment of bananas imported from former colonies, St. Vincent sought to diversify its economy, primarily through expanding tourism.

In March 2001 elections, the Unity Labour Party (ULP) won a landslide upset, capturing 12 of the 15 contested parliamentary seats. Ralph Gonsalves, a lawyer, became the new prime minister.

Samoa

INDEPENDENT STATE OF SAMOA

Head of State: Malietoa Tanumafili II (1963)
Prime Minister: Tuilaepa Sailele Malielegaoi (1998)
Area: 1,137 sq mi (2,944 sq km)
Population (2004 est.): 177,714 (growth rate: –0.2%); birth rate: 15.7/1000; infant mortality rate: 28.7/1000; life expectancy: 70.4; density per sq mi: 156
Capital and largest city (2003 est.): Apia, 35,900. **Monetary unit:** Tala. **Languages:** Samoan, English. **Ethnicity/race:** Samoan 92.6%, Euronesians 7% (persons of European and Polynesian blood), Europeans 0.4%. **Religion:** Christian 99.7% (about half associated with the London Missionary Society; includes Congregational, Roman Catholic, Methodist, Latter-Day Saints, Seventh-Day Adventist). **Literacy rate:** 100% (2003 est.)
Economic summary: GDP/PPP (2002 est.): $1 billion; per capita $5,600. **Real growth rate:** 5%. **Inflation:** 4% (2001 est.). **Unemployment:** n.a.; note: substantial underemployment. **Arable land:** 19%. **Agriculture:** coconuts, bananas, taro, yams, coffee, cocoa. **Labor force:** 90,000 (2000 est.). **Industries:** food processing, building materials, auto parts. **Natural resources:** hardwood forests, fish, hydropower. **Exports:** $14 million (f.o.b., 2002): fish, coconut oil and cream, copra, taro, automotive parts, garments, beer. **Imports:** $113 million (f.o.b., 2002): machinery and equipment, industrial supplies, foodstuffs. **Major trading partners:** Australia, U.S., Japan, New Zealand, Fiji, Taiwan.

Geography Samoa, formerly Western Samoa, is in the South Pacific Ocean about 2,200 mi (3,540 km) south of Hawaii. The larger islands in the Samoan chain, Upolu and Savai'i, are mountainous and of volcanic origin. There is little level land except in the coastal areas, where most cultivation takes place.

Government Constitutional monarchy under a native chief.

History Polynesians, possibly from Tonga, first settled in the Samoan islands about 1000 B.C. Samoa was explored by Dutch and French traders in the 18th century. Toward the end of the 19th century, conflicting interests of the U.S., Britain, and Germany resulted in an 1899 treaty that recognized the paramount interests of the U.S. in those islands west of 171°W (American Samoa) and Germany's interests in the other islands (Western Samoa).

New Zealand seized Western Samoa from Germany in 1914, and in 1946 it became a UN trust territory administered by New Zealand. A resistance movement to both German and New Zealand rule, known as the

Mau ("strongly held view") movement, helped to edge the islands toward independence on Jan. 1, 1962. A constitutional monarchy, Samoa has a legislative assembly whose members are from the *matai*, or titled class.

Barraged regularly by cyclones that have wreaked havoc on the country's primarily agrarian economy, Samoa has begun stepping up its tourism industry—not such a difficult undertaking in this archetypal South Pacific paradise.

A referendum in 1990 gave most women the right to vote for the first time. In 1997, a new constitutional amendment changed the country's name to Samoa. In 2002, the prime minister of New Zealand apologized to Samoa for the injustices that occurred under New Zealand rule.

San Marino

MOST SERENE REPUBLIC OF SAN MARINO

National name: Repubblica di San Marino
Captains Regent: Giuseppe Arzilli and Roberto Raschi (2004)
Area: 24 sq mi (61.2 sq km)
Population (2004 est.): 28,503 (growth rate: 1.3%); birth rate: 10.3/1000; infant mortality rate: 5.9/1000; life expectancy: 81.5; density per sq mi: 1,206
Capital (2003 est.): San Marino, 4,300. **Largest city:** Serravalle, 8,700. **Monetary unit:** Euro. **Language:** Italian. **Ethnicity/race:** Sammarinese, Italian. **Religion:** Roman Catholic. **Literacy rate:** 96% (1976 est.)
Economic summary: GDP/PPP (2001 est.): $940 million; per capita $34,600. **Real growth rate:** 7.5%. **Inflation:** 3.3%. **Unemployment:** 2.6%. **Arable land:** 17%. **Agriculture:** wheat, grapes, corn, olives; cattle, pigs, horses, beef, cheese, hides. **Labor force:** 18,500 (1999); services 57%, industry 42%, agriculture 1% (2000 est.). **Industries:** tourism, banking, textiles, electronics, ceramics, cement, wine. **Natural resources:** building stone. **Exports:** trade data are included with the statistics for Italy: building stone, lime, wood, chestnuts, wheat, wine, baked goods, hides, ceramics. **Imports:** trade data are included with the statistics for Italy: wide variety of consumer manufactures, food.

Geography One-tenth the size of New York City, San Marino is surrounded by Italy. It is situated in the Apennines, a little inland from the Adriatic Sea near Rimini.

Government Republic.

History According to tradition, San Marino was founded about A.D. 350 and had the good luck for centuries to stay out of the many wars and feuds on the Italian peninsula. It is the oldest republic in the world. San Marino has survived, completely intact, attacks by other self-governing Italian city-states, the Napoleonic Wars, the unification of Italy, and two world wars. Those born in San Marino remain citizens and can vote no matter where they live. Throughout the 1990s San Marino has taken a more active role in international diplomacy, establishing strong diplomatic and economic ties to a host of other countries. It joined the United Nations in 1992.

São Tomé and Príncipe

DEMOCRATIC REPUBLIC OF SÃO TOMÉ AND PRÍNCIPE

President: Fradique de Menezes (2003)
Prime Minister: Damião Vaz d'Almeida (2004)
Area: 386 sq mi (1,001 sq km)
Population (2004 est.): 181,565 (growth rate: 3.2%);

birth rate: 41.4/1000; infant mortality rate: 44.6/1000;
life expectancy: 66.6; density per sq mi: 470
Capital and largest city (2003 est.): São Tomé, 53,300.
Monetary unit: Dobra. **Language:** Portuguese
(official). **Ethnicity/race:** mestico (mixed European
and native African), angolares (descendants of
Angolan slaves), forros (descendants of freed slaves),
servicais (contract laborers from Angola, Mozambique,
and Cape Verde), tongas (children of servicais born on
the islands), Europeans (primarily Portuguese).
Religions: Christian 80% (Roman Catholic,
Evangelical Protestant, Seventh-Day Adventist).
Literacy rate: 79% (1991 est.)
Economic summary: GDP/PPP (2002 est.): $200
million; per capita $1,200. **Real growth rate:** 4%.
Inflation: 9%. **Unemployment:** n.a. **Arable land:** 2%.
Agriculture: cocoa, coconuts, palm kernels, copra,
cinnamon, pepper, coffee, bananas, papayas, beans;
poultry; fish. **Labor force:** n.a.; population mainly
engaged in subsistence agriculture and fishing; note:
shortages of skilled workers. **Industries:** light
construction, textiles, soap, beer; fish processing;
timber. **Natural resources:** fish, hydropower. **Exports:**
$6.479 million (f.o.b., 2003 est.): cocoa 80%, copra,
coffee, palm oil. **Imports:** $30.03 million (f.o.b., 2003
est.): machinery and electrical equipment, food
products, petroleum products. **Major trading partners:**
Netherlands, Poland, Canada, Germany, Philippines,
Spain, Belgium, France, Portugal, UK.

Geography The tiny volcanic islands of São Tomé
and Príncipe lie in the Gulf of Guinea about 150 mi
(240 km) off West Africa. São Tomé (about 330 sq mi;
859 sq km) is covered by a dense mountainous jungle,
out of which have been carved large plantations.
Príncipe (about 40 sq mi; 142 sq km) consists of
jagged mountains. Other islands in the republic are
Pedras Tinhosas and Rolas. About 95% of the population lives on São Tomé.

Government Republic.

History São Tomé and Príncipe, believed to have
been originally uninhabited, were explored by Portuguese navigators in 1471 and settled by the end of the
century. Intensive cultivation by slave labor made the
islands a major producer of sugar during the 17th century but output declined until the introduction of coffee and cocoa in the 19th century brought new prosperity. The island of São Tomé was the world's largest
producer of cocoa in 1908, and the crop is still its
most important. Working conditions for laborers, however, were horrendous, and in 1909 British and German chocolate manufacturers boycotted São Tomé
cocoa in protest. An exile liberation movement was
formed in 1953 after Portuguese landowners quelled
labor riots by killing several hundred African workers.
  The Portuguese revolution of 1974 brought the end
of the overseas empire, and on July 12, 1975, Lisbon
granted São Tomé independence. Manuel Pinto da
Costa, leader of the only legal political party (Movement for the Liberation of São Tomé and Príncipe
[MLSTP]) became president and Miguel Trovoada
served as prime minister. After a 1978 coup attempt
failed, Trovoada was accused of participating in the
conspiracy and exiled. In 1990 a new constitution
instituted multi-party rule. Trovoada returned and in
March 1991 became president in the country's first
free elections. Príncipe became autonomous in 1995.
  Protests and unrest erupted throughout the 1990s
over unemployment and soaring inflation. One of Africa's poorest countries, São Tomé has what is believed
to be enormous untapped off-shore oil reserves—an
estimated 6 billion barrels that are expected to begin
flowing by 2007 or 2008. Businessman Fradique de

Menezes won the presidential election in 2001. In July
2003, a military coup deposed Menezes while he was
out of the country. Major Fernando Pereira, head of the
country's military school, seized power, but relinquished it a week later under international pressure.
Menezes again assumed the presidency.

Saudi Arabia
KINGDOM OF SAUDI ARABIA

National name: Al-Mamlaka al-'Arabiya as-Sa'udiya
Sovereign: King Fahd bin 'Abdulaziz (1982)
Area: 756,981 sq mi (1,960,582 sq km)
Population (2004 est.): 25,795,938 (growth rate: 2.4%);
birth rate: 29.7/1000; infant mortality rate: 13.7/1000;
life expectancy: 75.2; density per sq mi: 34
Capital and largest city (2003 est.): Riyadh, 3,724,100.
Other large cities: Jeddah, 2,745,000; Makkah
(Mecca), 1,614,800. **Monetary unit:** Riyal.
Languages: Arabic. **Ethnicity/race:** Arab 90%,
Afro-Asian 10%. **Religion:** Islam 100%. **Literacy rate:**
79% (2003 est.)
Economic summary: GDP/PPP (2003 est.): $286.2
billion; per capita $11,800. **Real growth rate:** 4.7%.
Inflation: 1%. **Unemployment:** 25%. **Arable land:**
2%. **Agriculture:** wheat, barley, tomatoes, melons,
dates, citrus; mutton, chickens, eggs, milk. **Labor
force:** 7 million; note: 35% of the population in the
15–64 age group is non-national (1999); agriculture
12%, industry 25%, services 63% (1999 est.).
Industries: crude oil production, petroleum refining,
basic petrochemicals, cement, construction, fertilizer,
plastics. **Natural resources:** petroleum, natural gas,
iron ore, gold, copper. **Exports:** $86.53 billion (f.o.b.,
2003 est.): petroleum and petroleum products 90%.
Imports: $30.38 billion (f.o.b., 2003 est.): machinery
and equipment, foodstuffs, chemicals, motor vehicles,
textiles. **Major trading partners:** U.S., Japan, South
Korea, Singapore, China, Germany, UK, France, Italy.

Geography Saudi Arabia occupies most of the Arabian Peninsula, with the Red Sea and the Gulf of
Aqaba to the west, and the Arabian Gulf to the east.
Neighboring countries are Jordan, Iraq, Kuwait, Qatar,
the United Arab Emirates, the Sultanate of Oman,
Yemen, and Bahrain, connected to the Saudi mainland
by a causeway. Saudi Arabia contains the world's largest continuous sand desert, the Rub Al-Khali, or
Empty Quarter. Its oil region lies primarily in the eastern province along the Arabian Gulf.

Government Saudi Arabia was an absolute monarchy until 1992, at which time the Saud royal
family introduced the country's first constitution.
The legal system is based on the *sharia* (Islamic
law).

History Saudi Arabia is not only the homeland of
the Arab peoples—it is thought that the first Arabs
originated on the Arabian peninsula—but also the
homeland of Islam, the world's second-largest
religion. Muhammad founded Islam there, and it
is the location of the two holy pilgrimage cities of
Mecca and Medina. The Islamic calendar begins
in 622, the year of the hegira, or Muhammad's
flight from Mecca. A succession of invaders
attempted to control the peninsula, but by 1517
the Ottoman Empire dominated, and in the middle
of the 18th century, it was divided into separate
principalities. In 1745 Muhammad ibn 'Abd
al-Wahhab began calling for the purification and
reform of Islam, and the Wahhabi movement
swept across Arabia. By 1811, Wahhabi leaders
had waged a *jihad*—a holy war—against other

forms of Islam on the peninsula, and succeeded in uniting much of it. By 1818, however, the Wahhabis had been driven out of power again by the Ottomans and their Egyptian allies.

The kingdom of Saudi Arabia is almost entirely the creation of King Ibn Saud (1882–1953). A descendant of Wahhabi leaders, he seized Riyadh in 1901 and set himself up as leader of the Arab nationalist movement. By 1906 he had established Wahhabi dominance in Nejd and conquered Hejaz in 1924–1925. The Hejaz and Nejd regions were merged to form the kingdom of Saudi Arabia in 1932, which was an absolute monarchy ruled by sharia, Islamic law. A year later the region of Asir was incorporated into the kingdom.

Oil was discovered in 1936, and commercial production began during World War II. Its wealth allowed the country to provide free health care and education while not collecting any taxes from its people. Saudi Arabia was neutral until nearly the end of the war, but it was permitted to be a charter member of the United Nations. The country joined the Arab League in 1945 and took part in the 1948–1949 war against Israel. Saudi Arabia still does not recognize the state of Israel. On Ibn Saud's death in 1953, his eldest son, Saud, began an 11-year reign marked by an increasing hostility toward the radical Arabism of Egypt's Gamal Abdel Nasser. In 1964, the ailing Saud was deposed and replaced by the premier, Crown Prince Faisal, who gave vocal support but no military help to Egypt in the 1967 Arab-Israeli war.

Faisal's assassination by a deranged kinsman in 1975 shook the Middle East, but it failed to alter his kingdom's course. His successor was his brother, Prince Khalid. Khalid gave influential support to Egypt during negotiations on Israeli withdrawal from the Sinai Desert. King Khalid died of a heart attack in 1982, and was succeeded by his half-brother, Prince Fahd bin 'Abdulaziz, who had exercised the real power throughout Khalid's reign. King Fahd, a pro-Western modernist, chose his 58-year-old half-brother, Abdullah, as crown prince.

Saudi Arabia and the smaller, oil-rich Arab states on the Persian Gulf, fearful that they might become Ayatollah Ruhollah Khomeini's next targets if Iran conquered Iraq, made large financial contributions to the Iraqi war effort during the 1980s. At the same time, cheating by other members of the Organization of Petroleum Exporting Countries (OPEC), competition from nonmember oil producers, and conservation efforts by consuming nations combined to drive down the world price of oil. Saudi Arabia has one-third of all known oil reserves, but falling demand and rising production outside OPEC combined to reduce its oil revenues from $120 billion in 1980 to less than $25 billion in 1985, threatening the country with domestic unrest and undermining its influence in the Gulf area.

At the start of 1996, King Fahd passed authority to Crown Prince Abdullah, saying he needed rest. Although not an abdication, it was unclear how long the king would be absent. In 1998 the country's oil income fell by 40% because of a worldwide decline in prices, and it entered its first recession in 6 years.

In 2000, Saudi Arabia, along with other OPEC nations experiencing a recession, decided to reduce production to raise oil prices. In 2001, OPEC cut oil production three additional times.

Saudi Arabia's relations with the U.S. were strained after the Sept. 11, 2001, terrorist attacks—15 of the suicide bombers involved were Saudis. Despite the monarchy's close ties to the West, much of the extremely influential religious establishment has supported anti-Americanism and Islamic militancy. In Aug. 2003, following the U.S.-led war on Iraq in March and April 2003, the United States withdrew its troops stationed in Saudi Arabia. The U.S. had maintained troops in the country for the past decade, a source of great controversy in the strongly conservative Islamic country. One of the major reasons for the Sept. 11 attacks, according to Saudi terrorist Osama bin Laden, was the presence of U.S. troops in the home of Islam's holiest sites, Medina and Mecca. On May 12, 2003, suicide bombers killed 34, including eight Americans, at housing compounds for Westerners in Riyadh. Al-Qaeda was suspected. Saudi Arabia's commitment to antiterrorist measures was again called into question by the U.S. and other countries. In July, the U.S. Congress bitterly criticized Saudi Arabia's alleged financing of terrorist organizations. While the Saudi government arrested a sizable number of suspected terrorists in 2003 and 2004, little has been done to quell Islamic militancy in the kingdom. On Nov. 9, 2003, 17 Westerners were killed in a suicide bombing in Riyadh. In the first attack on a Saudi government target, on April 21, 2004, a bomb destroyed a Saudi security forces building in Riyadh, killing 4 and wounding more than 100. On May 29, a Western complex in Khobar was attacked, killing 22. In 4 separate attacks in June, 4 foreign workers were killed by militants.

Senegal

REPUBLIC OF SENEGAL

National name: République du Sénegal
President: Abdoulaye Wade (2000)
Prime Minister: Macky Sall (2004)
Area: 75,749 sq mi (196,190 sq km)
Population (2004 est.): 10,852,147 (growth rate: 2.5%); birth rate: 35.7/1000; infant mortality rate: 56.5/1000; life expectancy: 56.6; density per sq mi: 143
Capital and largest city (2003 est.): Dakar, 2,476,400.
Monetary unit: CFA Franc. **Languages:** French (official); Wolof, Pulaar, Jola, Mandinka. **Ethnicity/ race:** Wolof 43.3%, Fulani 23.8%, Serer 14.7%, Diola 3.7%, Mandingo 3%, Soninke 1.1%, European and Lebanese 1%, other 9.4%. **Religions:** Islam 94%, Christian 5% (mostly Roman Catholic), indigenous 1%.
Literacy rate: 40% (2003 est.)
Economic summary: GDP/PPP (2003 est.): $16.93 billion; per capita $1,600. **Real growth rate:** 4.5%. **Inflation:** 3% (2002 est.). **Unemployment:** 48% (urban youth 40%) (2001 est.). **Arable land:** 12%. **Agriculture:** peanuts, millet, corn, sorghum, rice, cotton, tomatoes, green vegetables; cattle, poultry, pigs; fish. **Labor force:** n.a.; agriculture 70%. **Industries:** agricultural and fish processing, phosphate mining, fertilizer production, petroleum refining, construction materials. **Natural resources:** fish, phosphates, iron ore. **Exports:** $1.23 billion (f.o.b., 2003 est.): fish, groundnuts (peanuts), petroleum products, phosphates, cotton. **Imports:** $1.753 billion (f.o.b., 2003 est.): foods and beverages, capital goods, fuels. **Major trading partners:** India, France, Mali, Greece, Italy, Nigeria, Thailand, U.S., Germany, Spain.

Geography The capital of Senegal, Dakar, is the westernmost point in Africa. The country, slightly smaller than South Dakota, surrounds Gambia on three sides and is bordered on the north by Mauritania, on the east by Mali, and on the south by Guinea and Guinea-Bissau.

Senegal is mainly a low-lying country, with a semi-desert area in the north and northeast and forests in the southwest. The largest rivers include the Senegal in the north and the Casamance in the southern tropical climate region.

Government Multiparty democractic republic.

History The Toucouleur people, among the early inhabitants of Senegal, converted to Islam in the 11th century, although their religious beliefs retained strong elements of animism. The Portuguese had some stations on the banks of the Senegal River in the 15th century, and the first French settlement was made at Saint-Louis in 1659. Gorée Island became a major center for the Atlantic slave trade through the 1700s, and millions of Africans were shipped from there to the New World. The British took parts of Senegal at various times, but the French gained possession in 1840 and made it part of French West Africa in 1895. In 1946, together with other parts of French West Africa, Senegal became an overseas territory of France. On June 20, 1960, it became an independent republic federated with Mali, but the federation collapsed within four months.

Although Senegal is neither a large nor a strategically located country, it has nonetheless played a prominent role in African politics since its independence. As a black nation that is more than 90% Muslim, Senegal has been a diplomatic and cultural bridge between the Islamic and black African worlds. Senegal has also maintained closer economic, political, and cultural ties to France than probably any other former French African colony.

Senegal's first president, Léopold Sédar Senghor, towered over the country's political life until his voluntary retirement in 1981. He replaced multiparty democracy with an authoritarian regime. An acclaimed poet, Senghor sought to become a "black-skinned Frenchman," a quest he ultimately discovered to be impossible. An advocate of "African socialism," Senghor increased government involvement in the economy through a series of four-year plans.

In 1973 Senegal and six other nations created the West African Economic Community. When rising oil prices and fluctuations in the price of peanuts, a major export crop, ruined the economy in the 1970s, Senghor reversed course. He emphasized new industries such as tourism and fishing. Politically, the so-called passive revolution allowed limited opposition.

When the economy continued to stagnate, and with it Senghor's popularity, he resigned after 20 years at the helm in favor of his protégé, Abdou Diouf. Diouf, who led the country for the next 20 years, initiated further economic and political liberalization, including the sale of government companies and permitting the existence of political parties. In March 2000, opposition party challenger Abdoulaye Wade won 60% of the vote in multiparty elections. Diouf stepped aside in what was hailed as a rare smooth transition of power in Africa. In Jan. 2001, the Senegalese voted in a new constitution that legalized opposition parties and granted women equal property rights with men. In Sept. 2002, more than 1,100 passengers were killed when the state-owned *Joola* ferry sank. The government accepted responsibility for the disaster.

The president removed Prime Minister Idrissa Seck in April 2004. Seck was considered Wade's rival.

Serbia and Montenegro

SERBIA AND MONTENEGRO

Federal President: Svetozar Marovic (2003)
Presidents: Boris Tadic, Serbia (2004); Filip Vujanovic, Montenegro (2003)
Prime Ministers: Vojislav Kostunica, Serbia (2004); Milo Djukanovic, Montenegro (2002)
Area: 39,517 sq mi (102,350 sq km)
Population (2004 est.): 10,825,900 (growth rate: 0.0%); birth rate: 12.1/1000; infant mortality rate: 13.4/1000; life expectancy: 74.4; density per sq mi: 274

Capital and largest city (2003 est.): Belgrade, 1,717,800 (metro. area), 1,285,200 (city proper). **Other large cities:** Pristina, 204,500; Novi Sad, 191,300; Nis, 174,000. **Monetary unit:** Yugoslav new dinar. **Languages:** Serbian (official) 95%, Albanian 5%. **Ethnicity/race:** Serbs 62.6%, Albanians 16.5%, Montenegrins 5%, Hungarians 3.3%, other 12.6% (1991). **Religions:** Orthodox 65%, Islam 19%, Roman Catholic 4%, Protestant 1%, other 11%. **Literacy rate:** 93% (1991)
Economic summary: GDP/PPP (2003 est.): $24.01 billion; per capita $2,300. **Real growth rate:** 2%. **Inflation:** 11.6%. **Unemployment:** 34.5%. **Arable land:** 36%. **Agriculture:** cereals, fruits, vegetables, tobacco, olives; cattle, sheep, goats. **Labor force:** 3 million (2001 est.); agriculture n.a., industry n.a., services n.a. **Industries:** machine building (aircraft, trucks, and automobiles; tanks and weapons; electrical equipment; agricultural machinery); metallurgy (steel, aluminum, copper, lead, zinc, chromium, antimony, bismuth, cadmium); mining (coal, bauxite, nonferrous ore, iron ore, limestone); consumer goods (textiles, footwear, foodstuffs, appliances); electronics, petroleum products, chemicals, and pharmaceuticals. **Natural resources:** oil, gas, coal, antimony, copper, lead, zinc, nickel, gold, pyrite, chrome, hydropower, arable land. **Exports:** $2.667 billion (f.o.b., 2003 est.): manufactured goods, food and live animals, raw materials. **Imports:** $7.144 billion (f.o.b., 2003 est.): machinery and transport equipment, fuels and lubricants, manufactured goods, chemicals, food and live animals, raw materials. **Major trading partners:** Italy, Germany, Greece, Austria, France, Slovenia, Bulgaria, Romania.

Geography Serbia and Montenegro together are about the size of the state of Kentucky. They are largely mountainous. The northeast section of Serbia is part of the rich, fertile Danubian Plain drained by the Danube, Tisa, Sava, and Morava river systems. Montenegro is a jumbled mass of mountains, containing also some grassy slopes and fertile river valleys.

Government In Feb. 2003, the Federal Republic of Yugoslavia was renamed Serbia and Montenegro. The former Yugoslavia, once an often volatile union of six republics, splintered in the 1990s from a brutal ten-year civil war. The renaming reflects the two remaining republics, Serbia and Montenegro. The new government is a loose union, linked only by a small joint administration in charge of defense and foreign affairs.

History Renamed Serbia and Montenegro in 2003, the former Yugoslavia was formed on Dec. 4, 1918, from the patchwork of Balkan states and territories. World War I began there with the assassination of Archduke Franz Ferdinand of Austria at Sarajevo on June 28, 1914. The new kingdom of Serbs, Croats, and Slovenes included the former kingdoms of Serbia and Montenegro; Bosnia-Herzegovina, previously administered jointly by Austria and Hungary; Croatia-Slavonia, a semiautonomous region of Hungary; and Dalmatia, formerly administered by Austria. King Peter I of Serbia became the first monarch; his son, Alexander I, succeeded him on Aug. 16, 1921. Croatian demands for a federal state forced Alexander to assume dictatorial powers in 1929 and to change the country's name to Yugoslavia. Serbian dominance continued despite his efforts, amid the resentment of other regions. A Macedonian associated with Croatian dissidents assassinated Alexander in Marseilles, France, on Oct. 9, 1934, and his cousin, Prince Paul, became regent for the king's son, Prince Peter.

Paul's pro-Axis policy brought Yugoslavia to sign the Axis Pact on March 25, 1941, and opponents overthrew the government two days later. On April 6 the Nazis occupied the country, and the young king and his government fled. Two guerrilla armies—the Chetniks under Draza Mihajlovic supporting the monarchy, and the Partisans under Tito (Josip Broz) leaning toward the USSR—fought the Nazis for the duration of the war. In 1943, Tito established an Executive National Committee of Liberation to function as a provisional government. Tito won the election held in the fall of 1945, as monarchists boycotted the vote. A new Assembly abolished the monarchy and proclaimed the Federal People's Republic of Yugoslavia, with Tito as prime minister. Tito ruthlessly eliminated the opposition and broke with the Soviet bloc in 1948. Yugoslavia followed a middle road, combining orthodox Communist control of politics and general overall economic policy with a varying degree of freedom in the arts, travel, and individual enterprise. Tito became president in 1953 and president-for-life under a revised constitution adopted in 1963.

After Tito's death on May 4, 1980, a rotating presidency designed to avoid internal dissension was put into effect immediately, and the feared clash of Yugoslavia's multiple nationalities and regions appeared to have been averted. In May 1991 Croatian voters supported a referendum calling for their republic to become an independent nation. A similar referendum passed in December in Slovenia. In June the respective Parliaments in both republics passed declarations of independence. Ethnic violence flared almost immediately. The largely Serbian-led Yugoslav military pounded breakaway Bosnia and Herzegovina, leading the UN Security Council in May 1992 to impose economic sanctions on the Belgrade government.

Despite rampant inflation reaching approximately 3,000% per month in Dec. 1993, the Serbian government of Slobodan Milosevic maintained its effective control over the remainder of Yugoslavia. Trade sanctions were lifted in Dec. 1995 following the signing of the Dayton Accords. In June 1996, the UN Security Council lifted its heavy weapons embargo. Large groups of demonstrators in 1996–1997 engaged in several months of daily protests after Slobodan Milosevic refused to recognize opposition victories in local elections and in elections in Montenegro. Constitutionally barred from another term as president of Serbia, Milosevic became president of the Federal Republic of Yugoslavia (Serbia and Montenegro) in July 1997.

In Feb. 1998 the Yugoslav army and Serbian police began fighting against the separatist Kosovo Liberation Army, but their scorched-earth tactics were concentrated on ethnic Albanian civilians—Muslims who make up 90% of Kosovo's population. More than 900 Kosovars were killed in the fighting, and the hundreds of thousands forced to flee their homes were without adequate food and shelter. Although Serbs make up only 10% of Kosovo's population, the region figures strongly in Serbian nationalist mythology.

NATO was reluctant to intervene because Kosovo—unlike Bosnia in 1992—was legally a province of Yugoslavia. The proof of civilian massacres finally gave NATO the impetus to intervene for the first time ever in the dealings of a sovereign nation with its own people. After months of negotiations led nowhere, on March 24, 1999, NATO began launching air strikes. Weeks of daily bombings destroyed significant Serbian

military targets, yet Milosevic showed no signs of relenting. In fact, Serbian militia stepped up civilian massacres and deportations in Kosovo—by the end of the conflict, the UN high commissioner for refugees estimated that at least 850,000 people had fled Kosovo. The refugee crisis put a heavy burden on neighboring countries such as Albania and Macedonia. As effective as NATO airpower might have been against Serbian targets, it was utterly helpless in preventing Serb soldiers and paramilitaries from wreaking havoc on Kosovo's civilians. The initial reason NATO gave for involvement in Kosovo was to avoid a wider Balkan war, but once Serbia began accelerating its campaign of ethnic cleansing in Kosovo, NATO's reason for fighting changed to preventing a human rights calamity. Yet without a concomitant change in military strategy—sending in ground troops—many wondered whether there would be any Kosovars left to save. NATO's hesitation in committing to a land battle—and therefore putting its troops at greater risk—ultimately paid off. Serbia finally agreed to sign a UN-approved peace agreement with NATO on June 3, ending the 11-week war.

In the Sept. 2000 federal elections, Vojislav Kostunica, a constitutional law professor and political outsider, won the presidency in spite of widespread reports of fraud and voter intimidation. His election formally ended the autocratic rule of Milosevic, who had entangled his country in almost continuous war, first with the breakaway republics of Croatia and Bosnia (1991–1995) and then in the Serbian province of Kosovo in 1998. He had dragged Yugoslavia into economic collapse and relegated it to pariah status throughout much of the world. When Milosevic refused to honor the election results and demanded a runoff election, the country erupted in massive public demonstrations, ultimately forcing Milosevic to step down on Oct. 5. But Kostunica was quick to assert himself as a true-believing Serb nationalist with no plans for becoming the darling of the West.

In 2001, Milosevic was turned over to the United Nations International Criminal Tribunal for the former Yugoslavia in The Hague, charged with genocide and crimes against humanity. His lengthy trial continued through 2004.

In March 2002, the nation agreed to form a new state, replacing Yugoslavia with a loose federation called Serbia and Montenegro, which went into effect Feb. 2003. The new arrangement was made to placate Montenegro's restive stirrings for independence and allowed Montenegro to hold a referendum on independence after three years. In May 2003, Filip Vujanovic, a strong advocate of Montenegran independence, was elected Montenegro's president.

The prime minister of the Serbian state, Zoran Djindjic, a reformer who helped bring about the fall of Milosevic, was assassinated in March 2003. Extreme nationalists, organized crime, and Serbia's own police and security services were implicated. Ultranationalists made a resurgence in December parliamentary elections—Milosevic's Socialist party received 7% of the vote, and the Radical party, whose leader, like Milosevic, is an indicted war criminal jailed in the Hague, received 27% of the vote.

On March 17, 2004, Mitrovica, in Kosovo, experienced the worst ethnic violence in the region since the 1999 war. At least 19 people were killed, another 500 were injured, and about 4,000 Serbs lost their homes. NATO sent in an extra 1,000 troops to restore order.

Seychelles

REPUBLIC OF SEYCHELLES

President: James Michel (2004)
Area: 176 sq mi (455 sq km)
Population (2004 est.): 80,832 (growth rate: 0.4%); birth rate: 16.6/1000; infant mortality rate: 16.0/1000; life expectancy: 71.5; density per sq mi: 460
Capital and largest city (2003 est.): Victoria, 23,000. **Monetary unit:** Seychelles rupee. **Languages:** Seselwa Creole, English, French (all official). **Ethnicity/race:** mixed French, African, Indian, Chinese, and Arab. **Religions:** Roman Catholic 86.6%, Anglican 6.8%, other Christian 2.5%, other 4.1%. **Literacy rate:** 58% (1971 est.)
Economic summary: GDP/PPP (2002 est.): $626 million; per capita $7,800. **Real growth rate:** 1.5%. **Inflation:** 0.5%. **Unemployment:** n.a. **Arable land:** 2%. **Agriculture:** coconuts, cinnamon, vanilla, sweet potatoes, cassava (tapioca), bananas; broiler chickens; tuna fish. **Labor force:** 30,900 (1996); industry 19%, services 71%, agriculture 10% (1989). **Industries:** fishing; tourism; processing of coconuts and vanilla, coir (coconut fiber) rope, boat building, printing, furniture; beverages. **Natural resources:** fish, copra, cinnamon trees. **Exports:** $250 million (f.o.b., 2003 est.): canned tuna, frozen fish, cinnamon bark, copra, petroleum products (reexports). **Imports:** $383.7 million (f.o.b., 2003 est.): machinery and equipment, foodstuffs, petroleum products, chemicals. **Major trading partners:** UK, France, Italy, U.S., Spain, Japan, Netherlands, Thailand, Saudi Arabia, South Africa, Singapore, Taiwan. **Member of Commonwealth of Nations**

Geography The Seychelles consist of an archipelago of about 100 islands in the Indian Ocean northeast of Madagascar. The principal islands are Mahé (55 sq mi; 142 sq km), Praslin (15 sq mi; 38 sq km), and La Digue (4 sq mi; 10 sq km). The Aldabra, Farquhar, and Desroches groups are included in the territory of the republic.

Government Socialist multiparty republic.

History The Seychelles were uninhabited when the British East India Company became the first visitors to the archipelago in 1609. Thereafter, they became a favorite pirate haven. The French claimed the islands in 1756 and administered them as part of the colony of Mauritius. The British gained control of the islands through the Treaty of Paris (1814), and changed the islands' name from the French Séchelles to the Anglicized Seychelles.

The islands became self-governing in 1975 and independent on June 29, 1976. They have remained a member of the Commonwealth of Nations. Their first president, James Mancham, was overthrown in 1977 by the prime minister, France-Albert René. At first René created a socialist state with a one-party system, but later he reintroduced a multiparty system as well as various reforms.

To increase revenue, in 1996 the government quietly initiated an Economic Citizenship Program that provides foreigners with the opportunity to obtain a Seychelles passport upon payment of $25,000. A new law in late 1995 had granted immunity from criminal prosecution to anyone investing $10 million in the country.

In elections held in March 1998, President France-Albert René was reelected with 66.6% of the vote.

In Sept. 2001, President René was reelected for another five years, defeating Wavel Ramkalawan, an Anglican priest. In April 2004, he stepped down after 27 years in power. His vice president, James Michel, who had also served in the government for 27 years, assumed the presidency.

Sierra Leone

REPUBLIC OF SIERRA LEONE

President: Ahmad Tejan Kabbah (1998)
Area: 27,699 sq mi (71,740 sq km)
Population (2004 est.): 5,883,889 (growth rate: 2.3%); birth rate: 43.3/1000; infant mortality rate: 145.2/1000; life expectancy: 42.7; density per sq mi: 212
Capital and largest city (2003 est.): Freetown, 1,051,000. **Monetary unit:** Leone. **Languages:** English (official), Mende (southern vernacular), Temne (northern vernacular), Krio (lingua franca). **Ethnicity/race:** 20 native African tribes 90% (Temne 30%, Mende 30%, other 30%); Creole (Krio) 10%; refugees from Liberia's recent civil war, small numbers of Europeans, Lebanese, Pakistanis, and Indians. **Religions:** Islam 60%, indigenous 30%, Christian 10%. **Literacy rate:** 31% (1995 est.)
Economic summary: GDP/PPP (2003 est.): $3.057 billion; per capita $500. **Real growth rate:** 6.5%. **Inflation:** 1% (2002 est.). **Unemployment:** n.a. **Arable land:** 7%. **Agriculture:** rice, coffee, cocoa, palm kernels, palm oil, peanuts; poultry, cattle, sheep, pigs; fish. **Labor force:** 1.369 million (1981 est.). **Industries:** mining (diamonds); small-scale manufacturing (beverages, textiles, cigarettes, footwear); petroleum refining. **Natural resources:** diamonds, titanium ore, bauxite, iron ore, gold, chromite. **Exports:** $49 million (f.o.b., 2002 est.): diamonds, rutile, cocoa, coffee, fish. **Imports:** $264 million (f.o.b., 2002 est.): foodstuffs, machinery and equipment, fuels and lubricants, chemicals. **Major trading partners:** Belgium, Germany, UK, Netherlands, U.S., Côte d'Ivoire, Italy. **Member of Commonwealth of Nations**

Geography Sierra Leone, on the Atlantic Ocean in West Africa, is half the size of Illinois. Guinea, in the north and east, and Liberia, in the south, are its neighbors. Mangrove swamps lie along the coast, with wooded hills and a plateau in the interior. The eastern region is mountainous.

Government Constitutional democracy.

History The Bulom people were thought to have been the earliest inhabitants of Sierra Leone, followed by the Mende and Temne peoples in the 15th century, and thereafter the Fulani. The Portuguese were the first Europeans to explore the land and gave Sierra Leone its name, which means "lion mountains." Freetown, on the coast, was ceded to English settlers in 1787 as a home for blacks discharged from the British armed forces and also for runaway slaves who had found asylum in London. In 1808 the coastal area became a British colony, and in 1896 a British protectorate was proclaimed over the hinterland.

Sierra Leone became an independent nation on April 27, 1961. A military coup overthrew the civilian government in 1967, which was in turn replaced by civilian rule a year later. The country declared itself a republic on April 19, 1971.

A coup attempt early in 1971 led to then prime minister Siaka Stevens calling in troops from neighboring Guinea's army, which remained for two years. Stevens turned the government into a one-party state under the aegis of the All People's Congress Party in April 1978. In 1992 rebel soldiers overthrew Stevens's successor, Joseph Momoh, calling for a return to a multiparty system. In 1996, another military coup ousted the country's military leader and president. Nevertheless, a multiparty presidential election proceeded in 1996, and People's Party candidate Ahmad Tejan Kabbah won with 59.4% of the vote, becoming Sierra Leone's first democratically elected president.

But a violent military coup ousted President Kabbah's civilian government in May 1997. The leader of the coup, Lieut. Col. Johnny Paul Koroma, assumed the title "Head of the Armed Forces Revolutionary Council" (AFRC). Koroma began a reign of terror, destroying the economy and murdering enemies. The Commonwealth of Nations demanded the reinstatement of Kabbah, and ECOMOG, the Nigerian-led peacekeeping force, intervened. On March 10, 1998, after ten months in exile, Kabbah resumed his rule over Sierra Leone. The ousted junta and other rebel forces continued to wage attacks, many of which included the torture, rape, and brutal maimings of thousands of civilians, including countless children—amputation by machete is the horrific signature of the rebels. In addition to political power, the rebels are after control of Sierra Leone's rich diamond fields.

In Jan. 1999, rebels and Liberian mercenaries stormed the capital, demanding the release of the imprisoned Revolutionary United Front (RUF) leader, Foday Sankoh. ECOMOG regained control of Freetown, but President Kabbah later released Sankoh so he could participate in peace negotiations. Pressured by Nigeria and the U.S., among other countries, Kabbah agreed to an untenable power-sharing agreement in July 1999, which made Sankoh vice president of the country—and in charge of the diamond mines. The accord dissolved in May 2000 after the RUF abducted about 500 UN peacekeepers and attacked Freetown. Sankoh was captured and died in government custody in 2003, while awaiting trial for war crimes.

The conflict was officially declared over in Jan. 2002. An estimated 50,000 people were killed in the decade-long civil war. The UN installed its largest peacekeeping force in the country (17,000 troops). In May 2002, President Kabbah was reelected with 70% of the vote.

Singapore

REPUBLIC OF SINGAPORE

President: S. R. Nathan (1999)
Prime Minister: Lee Hsien Loong (2004)
Area: 267 sq mi (692.7 sq km)
Population (2004 est.): 4,353,893 (growth rate: 1.7%); birth rate: 9.6/1000; infant mortality rate: 2.3/1000; life expectancy: 81.5; density per sq mi: 16,279
Capital and largest city (2003 est.): Singapore, 3,438,600. **Monetary unit:** Singapore dollar.
Languages: Malay (national), Mandarin Chinese, Tamil, English (all official). **Ethnicity/race:** Chinese 76.7%, Malay 14%, Indian 7.9%, other 1.4%.
Religions: Buddhist (Chinese), Islam (Malays), Christian, Hindu, Sikh, Taoist, Confucianist. **Literacy rate:** 93% (2003 est.)
Economic summary: GDP/PPP (2003 est.): $109.1 billion; per capita $23,700. **Real growth rate:** 0.8%. **Inflation:** 0.7%. **Unemployment:** 5%. **Arable land:** 2%. **Agriculture:** rubber, copra, fruit, orchids, vegetables; poultry, eggs, fish, ornamental fish. **Labor force:** 2 million; financial, business, and other services 35%, manufacturing 21%, construction 13%, transportation and communication 9%, other 22%. **Industries:** electronics, chemicals, financial services, oil drilling equipment, petroleum refining, rubber processing and rubber products, processed food and beverages, ship repair, entrepôt trade, biotechnology. **Natural resources:** fish, deepwater ports. **Exports:** $142.4 billion (f.o.b., 2003 est.): machinery and equipment (including electronics), consumer goods, chemicals, mineral fuels. **Imports:** $121.6 billion (2003

est.): machinery and equipment, mineral fuels, chemicals, foodstuffs. **Major trading partners:** Malaysia, U.S., Hong Kong, Japan, China, Taiwan, Thailand, South Korea. **Member of Commonwealth of Nations**

Geography The Republic of Singapore consists of the main island of Singapore, off the southern tip of the Malay Peninsula between the South China Sea and the Indian Ocean, and 58 nearby islands.

Government Parliamentary republic.

History Inhabitants of the Malaysian peninsula and the island of Singapore migrated to the area between 2500 and 1500 B.C. (*see* Malaysia). British and Dutch interest in the region grew with the spice trade, and the trading post of Singapore was founded in 1819 by Sir Stamford Raffles. It was made a separate Crown colony of Britain in 1946, when the former colony of the Straits Settlements was dissolved. The other two settlements on the peninsula—Penang and Malacca—became part of the Union of Malaya, and the small island of Labuan was transferred to North Borneo. The Cocos (or Keeling) Islands and Christmas Island were transferred to Australia in 1955 and in 1958, respectively.

Singapore attained full internal self-government in 1959, and Lee Kwan Yew, an economic visionary with an authoritarian streak, took the helm as prime minister. On Sept. 16, 1963, Singapore joined Malaya, Sabah (North Borneo), and Sarawak in the Federation of Malaysia. It withdrew from the Federation on Aug. 9, 1965, and a month later proclaimed itself a republic.

Under Lee, Singapore developed into one of the cleanest, safest, and most economically prosperous cities in Asia. However, Singapore's strict rules of civil obedience also drew criticism from those who said the nation's prosperity was achieved at the expense of individual freedoms.

S. R. Nathan was declared president without an election when he was certified as the only candidate eligible to run in 1999 elections. In August 2004, Lee Hsien Loong became the country's third premier since it gained independence from Britain in 1965.

Slovakia

REPUBLIC OF SLOVAKIA

President: Ivan Gasparovic (2004)
Prime Minister: Mikulás Dzurinda (1998)
Area: 18,859 sq mi (48,845 sq km)
Population (2004 est.): 5,423,567 (growth rate: 0.1%); birth rate: 10.6/1000; infant mortality rate: 7.6/1000; life expectancy: 74.2; density per sq mi: 288
Capital and largest city (2003 est.): Bratislava, 428,800. **Other large city:** Kosice, 233,600. **Monetary unit:** Koruna. **Languages:** Slovak (official), Hungarian. **Ethnicity/race:** Slovak 85.7%, Hungarian 10.6%, Roma 1.6%, Czech, Moravian, Silesian 1%, Ruthenian and Ukrainian 0.6%, German 0.1%, Polish 0.1%, other 0.2% (1996). **Religions:** Roman Catholic 60.3%, atheist 9.7%, Protestant 8.4%, Orthodox 4.1%, other 17.5%. **Literacy rate:** n.a
Economic summary: GDP/PPP (2003 est.): $72.29 billion; per capita $13,300. **Real growth rate:** 3.9%. **Inflation:** 8.6%. **Unemployment:** 15%. **Arable land:** 31%. **Agriculture:** grains, potatoes, sugar beets, hops, fruit; pigs, cattle, poultry; forest products. **Labor force:** 3 million (1999); industry 29.3%, agriculture 8.9%, construction 8%, transport and communication 8.2%, services 45.6% (1994). **Industries:** metal and metal products; food and beverages; electricity, gas, coke, oil, nuclear fuel; chemicals and manmade fibers;

machinery; paper and printing; earthenware and ceramics; transport vehicles; textiles; electrical and optical apparatus; rubber products. **Natural resources:** brown coal and lignite; small amounts of iron ore, copper and manganese ore; salt; arable land. **Exports:** $21.25 billion (f.o.b., 2003 est.): machinery and transport equipment 39.4%, intermediate manufactured goods 27.5%, miscellaneous manufactured goods 13%, chemicals 8% (1999). **Imports:** $21.9 billion (f.o.b., 2003 est.): machinery and transport equipment 37.7%, intermediate manufactured goods 18%, fuels 13%, chemicals 11%, miscellaneous manufactured goods 9.5% (1999). **Major trading partners:** Germany, Czech Republic, Austria, Italy, Poland, Hungary, Russia, France.

Geography Slovakia is located in central Europe. The land has rugged mountains, rich in mineral resources, with vast forests and pastures. The Carpathian Mountains dominate the topography of Slovakia, with lowland areas in the southern region. Slovakia is about twice the size of the state of Maryland.

Government Parliamentary democracy.

History Present-day Slovakia was settled by Slavic Slovaks about the 6th century. They were politically united in the Moravian empire in the 9th century. In 907, the Germans and the Magyars conquered the Moravian state, and the Slovaks fell under Hungarian control from the 10th century up until 1918. When the Hapsburg-ruled empire collapsed in 1918 following World War I, the Slovaks joined the Czech lands of Bohemia, Moravia, and part of Silesia to form the new joint state of Czechoslovakia. In March 1939, Germany occupied Czechoslovakia, established a German "protectorate," and created a puppet state out of Slovakia with Monsignor Josef Tiso as premier. The country was liberated from the Germans by the Soviet army in the spring of 1945, and Slovakia was restored to its prewar status and rejoined to a new Czechoslovakian state.

After the Communist Party took power in Feb. 1948, Slovakia was again subjected to a centralized Czech-dominated government, and antagonism between the two republics developed. On Jan. 1969, the nation became the Slovak Socialist Republic of Czechoslovakia.

Nearly 42 years of Communist rule for Slovakia ended when Vaclav Havel became president of Czechoslovakia in 1989 and democratic political reform began. However, with the demise of Communist power, a strong Slovak nationalist movement resurfaced, and the rival relationship between the two states increased. By the end of 1991, discussions between Slovak and Czech political leaders turned to whether the Czech and Slovak republics should continue to coexist within the federal structure or be divided into two independent states.

After the general election in June 1992, it was decided that two fully independent republics would be created. The Republic of Slovakia came into existence on Jan. 1, 1993. The Parliament in February elected Michal Kovac as president.

Populist Vladimir Meciar, who served three times as Slovakia's prime minister, exhibited increasingly authoritarian behavior, and was cited as the reason Slovakia was eliminated from consideration for both the EU and NATO. Slovakia's very low influx of foreign capital during Meciar's tenure was the result of his government's lack of transparency. Meciar was unseated in 1998 elections by the reformist government of Mikulás Dzurinda. In April 2000 he was arrested and charged with paying illegal bonuses to his cabinet ministers while in office. A three-week standoff with police preceded the arrest, ending only when police commandos blew open the door on Meciar's house and seized him. He was also questioned about his alleged involvement in the 1995 kidnapping of the son of Slovakia's former president, Michal Kovac.

Dzurinda has improved Slovakia's reputation in the West, but his tough economic measures have made him unpopular within the country. Meciar, on the other hand, has proven oddly resilient. In Sept. 2002 elections, the ruling coalition held onto power, despite Meciar coming out ahead in the vote. In April 2004, Meciar ran for the presidency against his former righthand man, Ivan Gasparovic. Gasparovic won the largely ceremonial post by a wide majority. In 2004, Slovakia joined the EU and NATO.

Slovenia

REPUBLIC OF SLOVENIA

President: Janez Drnovsek (2002)
Prime Minister: Anton Rop (2002)
Area: 7,827 sq mi (20,273 sq km)
Population (2004 est.): 2,011,473 (growth rate: 0.0%); birth rate: 8.9/1000; infant mortality rate: 4.5/1000; life expectancy: 75.9; density per sq mi: 257
Capital and largest city (2003 est.): Ljubljana, 258,000.
Other large city: Maribor, 92,400. **Monetary unit:** Slovenian tolar. **Languages:** Slovenian 92%, Serbo-Croatian 6.2%, other 1.8%. **Ethnicity/race:** Slovene 92%, Croat 1%, Serb 0.5%, Hungarian 0.4%, Bosniak 0.3%, other 5.8% (1991). **Religions:** Roman Catholic 70.8% (including 2% Uniate), Lutheran 1%, Islam 1%, atheist 4.3%, other 22.9%. **Literacy rate:** 100% (2003 est.)
Economic summary: GDP/PPP (2003 est.): $36.89 billion; per capita $18,300. **Real growth rate:** 2.5%. **Inflation:** 5.6%. **Unemployment:** 11.2%. **Arable land:** 11%. **Agriculture:** potatoes, hops, wheat, sugar beets, corn, grapes; cattle, sheep, poultry. **Labor force:** 876,100; agriculture n.a., industry n.a., services n.a. **Industries:** ferrous metallurgy and aluminum products, lead and zinc smelting, electronics (including military electronics), trucks, electric power equipment, wood products, textiles, chemicals, machine tools. **Natural resources:** lignite coal, lead, zinc, mercury, uranium, silver, hydropower, forests. **Exports:** $11.98 billion (f.o.b., 2003 est.): manufactured goods, machinery and transport equipment, chemicals, food. **Imports:** $12.63 billion (f.o.b., 2003 est.): machinery and transport equipment, manufactured goods, chemicals, fuels and lubricants, food. **Major trading partners:** Germany, Italy, Austria, Croatia, France, Bosnia and Herzegovina.

Geography Slovenia occupies an area about the size of the state of Massachusetts. It is largely a mountainous republic and almost half of the land is forested, with hilly plains spread across the central and eastern regions. Mount Triglav, the highest peak, rises to 9,393 ft (2,864 m).

Government Parliamentary democractic republic.

History Slovenia was originally settled by Illyrian and Celtic peoples. It became part of the Roman empire in the first century B.C.

The Slovenes were a south Slavic group that settled in the region during the 6th century A.D. During the 7th century, the Slavs established the Slavic state of Samu, which owed its allegiance to the Avars, who dominated the Hungarian plain until Charlemagne defeated them in the late 8th century.

When the Hungarians were defeated by the Turks in 1526, Hungary accepted Austrian Hapsburg rule in order to escape Turkish domination; the Hapsburg monarchy was the first to include all of the Slovene regions. Thus, Slovenia and Croatia became part of the Austro-Hungarian kingdom when the dual monarchy was established in 1867. Like Croatia and unlike the other Balkan states, it is primarily Roman Catholic.

Following the defeat and collapse of Austria-Hungary in World War I, Slovenia declared its independence. It formally joined with Montenegro, Serbia, and Croatia on Dec. 4, 1918, to form the new nation called the Kingdom of the Serbs, Croats, and Slovenes. The name was later changed to Yugoslavia in 1929.

During World War II, Germany occupied Yugoslavia, and Slovenia was divided among Germany, Italy, and Hungary. For the duration of the war many Slovenes fought a guerrilla war against the Nazis under the leadership of the Croatian-born Communist resistance leader, Marshal Tito. After the final defeat of the Axis powers in 1945, Slovenia was again made into a republic of the newly established Communist nation of Yugoslavia.

In the 1980s, Slovenia agitated for greater autonomy and occasionally threatened to secede. It introduced a multiparty system and in 1990 elected a non-Communist government. Slovenia declared its independence from Yugoslavia on June 25, 1991. The Serbian-dominated Yugoslavian army tried to keep Slovenia in line and some brief fighting took place, but the army then withdrew its forces. Unlike Croatia and Bosnia, Slovenia was able to sever itself from Yugoslavia with relatively little violence. With recognition of its independence granted by the European Community in 1992, the country began realigning its economy and society toward western Europe. Slovenia joined the EU and NATO in 2004.

Solomon Islands

Sovereign: Queen Elizabeth II (1952)
Governor-General: Nathaniel Waena (2004)
Prime Minister: Sir Allan Kemakeza (2001)
Area: 10,985 sq mi (28,450 sq km)
Population (2004 est.): 523,617 (growth rate: 2.8%); birth rate: 31.6/1000; infant mortality rate: 22.1/1000; life expectancy: 72.4; density per sq mi: 48
Capital and largest city (2003 est.): Honiara (on Guadalcanal), 54,600. **Monetary unit:** Solomon Islands dollar. **Languages:** English 1%–2% (official), Melanesian pidgin (lingua franca), 120 indigenous languages. **Ethnicity/race:** Melanesian 93%, Polynesian 4%, Micronesian 1.5%, European 0.8%, Chinese 0.3%, other 0.4%. **Religions:** Anglican 45%, Roman Catholic 18%, United (Methodist/Presbyterian) 12%, Baptist 9%, Seventh-Day Adventist 7%, other Protestant 5%, indigenous beliefs 4%. **Literacy rate:** n.a
Economic summary: GDP/PPP (2001 est.): $800 million; per capita $1,700. **Real growth rate:** –10%. **Inflation:** 9% (2002 est.). **Unemployment:** n.a. **Arable land:** 2%. **Agriculture:** cocoa beans, coconuts, palm kernels, rice, potatoes, vegetables, fruit; cattle, pigs; timber; fish. **Labor force:** 26,842 (1999); agriculture 75%, industry 5%, services 20% (2000 est.). **Industries:** fish (tuna), mining, timber. **Natural resources:** fish, forests, gold, bauxite, phosphates, lead, zinc, nickel. **Exports:** $90 million (f.o.b., 2002 est.): timber, fish, copra, palm oil, cocoa. **Imports:** $100 million (f.o.b., 2002 est.): food, equipment, manufactured goods, fuels, chemicals. **Major trading partners:** Japan, China, South Korea, Philippines, Thailand, Singapore, Australia, New Zealand, Fiji, Papua New Guinea. **Member of British Commonwealth**

Geography A scattered archipelago of about 1,000 mountainous islands and low-lying coral atolls, the Solomon Islands lie east of Papua New Guinea and northeast of Australia in the south Pacific. The islands include Guadalcanal, Malaita, Santa Isabel, San Cristóbal, Choiseul, New Georgia, and the Santa Cruz group.

Government Parliamentary democracy.

History It is thought that people have lived in the Solomon Islands since at least 2000 B.C. Explored in 1568 by Alvaro de Mendana of Spain, the Solomons were not visited again for about 200 years. In 1886, Great Britain and Germany divided the islands between them, but later Britain was given control of the entire territory. The Japanese invaded the islands in World War II, and they became the scene of some of the bloodiest battles in the Pacific theater, most famously the battle of Guadalcanal. The British gained control of the island again in 1945. In 1976 the islands became self-governing, and gained independence in 1978.

Since early 1999, the Isatabu Freedom Movement, a militia group made up of indigenous Isatabus from Guadalcanal, have expelled more than 20,000 Malaitans from the island. The Malaitans had migrated from nearby Malaita, and many secured jobs in the capital, Honiara, stirring resentment among Isatabus that has grown steadily since independence. In response to the ethnic violence and expulsions, a rival Malaitan militia group was founded, the Malaita Eagle Force. In June 2000, the Malaita Eagle Force stole police weapons, forced Prime Minister Bartholomew Ulufa'alu to resign, and seized control of Honiara. The rival groups agreed to a cease-fire in June 2000, barely averting a civil war. Although a peace agreement has been signed and elections have taken place, the country continues to suffer from lawlessness. In July 2003, at the request of the prime minister, a 2,250-strong international peace-keeping force led by Australia arrived on the island to restore order, disarm the militias, and expel the "thieves, drunkards, and extortionists" from the notoriously corrupt police force. The warlord Harold Keke surrendered to Australian forces in August 2003. Australia's intervention was highly successful, and a year after troops arrived, the country remained relatively stable.

Somalia

SOMALI DEMOCRATIC REPUBLIC

National name: Jamhuuriyadda Soomaaliya
Prime Minister: Abdullahi Yusuf Ahmed (2004)
Area: 246,199 sq mi (637,657 sq km)
Population (2004 est.): 8,304,601 (growth rate: 3.4%); birth rate: 46.0/1000; infant mortality rate: 118.5/1000; life expectancy: 47.7; density per sq mi: 34
Capital and largest city (2003 est.): Mogadishu, 1,208,800. **Monetary unit:** Somali shilling. **Languages:** Somali (official), Arabic, English, Italian. **Ethnicity/race:** Somali 85%, Bantu and others 15% (including Arabs 30,000). **Religion:** Islam (Sunni). **Literacy rate:** 38% (2001 est.)
Economic summary: GDP/PPP (2003 est.): $4.361 billion; per capita $500. **Real growth rate:** 2.1% (2002 est.). **Inflation:** over 100% (businesses print their own money). **Unemployment:** n.a. **Arable land:** 2%. **Agriculture:** cattle, sheep, goats; bananas, sorghum, corn, coconuts, rice, sugarcane, mangoes, sesame seeds, beans; fish. **Labor force:** 3.7 million (very few are skilled laborers); agriculture (mostly pastoral nomadism) 71%, industry and services 29%. **Industries:** a few light industries, including sugar

refining, textiles, petroleum refining (mostly shut down), wireless communication. **Natural resources:** uranium and largely unexploited reserves of iron ore, tin, gypsum, bauxite, copper, salt, natural gas, likely oil reserves. **Exports:** $79 million (f.o.b., 2002 est.): livestock, bananas, hides, fish, charcoal, scrap metal. **Imports:** $344 million (f.o.b., 2002 est.): manufactures, petroleum products, foodstuffs, construction materials, qat. **Major trading partners:** UAE, Yemen, Oman, Djibouti, Kenya, Brazil, Thailand, UK.

Geography Somalia, situated in the Horn of Africa, lies along the Gulf of Aden and the Indian Ocean. It is bounded by Djibouti in the northwest, Ethiopia in the west, and Kenya in the southwest. In area it is slightly smaller than Texas. Generally arid and barren, Somalia has two chief rivers, the Shebelle and the Juba.

Government Between Jan. 1991 and Aug. 2000, Somalia had no working government. A fragile parliamentary government was formed in 2000, but expired in 2003 without establishing control of the country. In 2004, a new transitional parliament was instituted and which elected a president.

History From the 7th to the 10th century, Arab and Persian trading posts were established along the coast of present-day Somalia. Nomadic tribes occupied the interior, occasionally pushing into Ethiopian territory. In the 16th century, Turkish rule extended to the northern coast, and the Sultans of Zanzibar gained control in the south.

After British occupation of Aden in 1839, the Somali coast became its source of food. The French established a coal mining station in 1862 at the site of Djibouti, and the Italians planted a settlement in Eritrea. Egypt, which for a time claimed Turkish rights in the area, was succeeded by Britain. By 1920, a British protectorate and an Italian protectorate occupied what is now Somalia. The British ruled the entire area after 1941, with Italy returning in 1950 to serve as United Nations trustee for its former territory.

By 1960, Britain and Italy granted independence to their respective sectors, enabling the two to join as the Republic of Somalia on July 1, 1960. Somalia broke diplomatic relations with Britain in 1963 when the British granted the Somali-populated Northern Frontier District of Kenya to the Republic of Kenya.

On Oct. 15, 1969, President Abdi Rashid Ali Shermarke was assassinated and the army seized power, dissolving the legislature and arresting all government leaders. Maj. Gen. Mohamed Siad Barre, as president of a renamed Somali Democratic Republic, leaned heavily toward the USSR. In 1977, Somalia openly backed rebels in the easternmost area of Ethiopia, the Ogaden Desert, which had been seized by Ethiopia at the turn of the century. Somalia acknowledged defeat in an eight-month war against the Ethiopians that year, having lost much of its 32,000-man army and most of its tanks and planes. President Siad Barre fled the country in late Jan. 1991. His departure left Somalia in the hands of a number of clan-based guerrilla groups, none of which trusted each other.

Africa's worst drought occurred in 1992, and coupled with the devastation of civil war, Somalia was plunged into a severe famine—an estimated one-third of the population was in danger of dying from starvation. U.S. troops were sent in to protect the delivery of food in Dec. 1992. In May 1993 the UN took control of the relief efforts from the U.S. The warlord Mohamed Farah Aidid ambushed UN troops and dragged American bodies through the streets, causing an about-face in America's willingness to involve itself in the fate of this anarchic country. Peace talks in Kenya appeared to be moving slowly but steadily toward an agreement on an interim government, at least in principle, when on March 23, 1994, they collapsed. The last of the U.S. troops left in late March, leaving 19,000 UN troops behind.

Since 1991 Somalia has been engulfed in anarchy. Years of peace negotiations between the various factions were fruitless, and warlords and militias ruled over individual swathes of land. In 1991, a breakaway nation, the Somaliland Republic, proclaimed its independence. Since then several warlords have set up their own ministates in Puntland and Jubaland. Although internationally unrecognized, these states have been peaceful and stable.

In Aug. 2000, a parliament convened in nearby Djibouti and elected Somalia's first government in nearly a decade. After its first year in office, the new government still controlled only 10% of the country, and in Aug. 2003, its mandate expired. But it had made advances for a country starting over: a national police force and army are in place and half of the 20,000 militias roaming the country have been demobilized.

In Oct. 2002, new talks to establish a government began; in Aug. 2004 a new 275-member transitional parliament was inaugurated for a five-year term. Parliament selected a national president in September, Abdullahi Yusuf Ahmed, the president of the breakaway region of Puntland.

South Africa

REPUBLIC OF SOUTH AFRICA

National name: Republic of South Africa
President: Thabo Mbeki (1999)
Area: 471,008 sq mi (1,219,912 sq km)
Population (2004 est.): 42,718,530 (growth rate: –0.2%); birth rate: 18.4/1000; infant mortality rate: 62.2/1000; life expectancy: 44.2; density per sq mi: 91
Administrative capital (2003 est.): Pretoria, 1,541,300 (metro. area), 1,249,700 (city proper); **Legislative capital and largest city:** Cape Town, 3,140,600 (metro. area), 2,733,000 (city proper); **Judicial capital:** Bloemfontein, 378,000. No decision has been made to relocate the seat of government. South Africa is demarcated into nine provinces, consisting of the Gauteng, Northern Province, Mpumalanga, North West, KwaZulu/Natal, Eastern Cape, Western Cape, Northern Cape, and Free State. Each province has its own capital. **Other large cities:** Durban/Pinetown, 2,396,100; Johannesburg, 1,675,200; East Rand, 1,378,792 (part of Johannesburg metro. area, 2000 est.). **Monetary unit:** Rand. **Languages:** Afrikaans, English, Ndebele, Pedi, Sotho, Swazi, Tsonga, Tswana, Venda, Xhosa, Zulu (all 11 official). **Ethnicity/ race:** black 75.2%, white 13.6%, Colored 8.6%, Indian 2.6%. **Religions:** Christian 68% (includes most whites and Coloreds, about 60% of blacks, and about 40% of Indians), indigenous beliefs and animist 28.5%, Islam 2%, Hindu 1.5% (60% of Indians). **Literacy rate:** 86% (2003 est.)
Economic summary: GDP/PPP (2003 est.): $456.7 billion; per capita $10,700. **Real growth rate:** 1.9%. **Inflation:** 9.9% (2002 est.). **Unemployment:** 37% (includes workers no longer looking for employment) (2001 est.). **Arable land:** 12%. **Agriculture:** corn, wheat, sugarcane, fruits, vegetables; beef, poultry, mutton, wool, dairy products. **Labor force:** 17 million economically active (1998 est); agriculture 30%,

industry 25%, services 45% (1999 est.). **Industries:** mining (world's largest producer of platinum, gold, chromium), automobile assembly, metalworking, machinery, textile, iron and steel, chemicals, fertilizer, foodstuffs. **Natural resources:** gold, chromium, antimony, coal, iron ore, manganese, nickel, phosphates, tin, uranium, gem diamonds, platinum, copper, vanadium, salt, natural gas. **Exports:** $36.77 billion (f.o.b., 2003 est.): gold, diamonds, platinum, other metals and minerals, machinery and equipment. **Imports:** $33.89 billion (f.o.b., 2003 est.): machinery, foodstuffs and equipment, chemicals, petroleum products, scientific instruments. **Major trading partners:** UK, U.S., Germany, Japan, Italy, Saudi Arabia, France, China, Iran.

Geography South Africa, on the continent's southern tip, is bordered by the Atlantic Ocean on the west and by the Indian Ocean on the south and east. Its neighbors are Namibia in the northwest, Zimbabwe and Botswana in the north, and Mozambique and Swaziland in the northeast. The kingdom of Lesotho forms an enclave within the southeast part of South Africa, which occupies an area nearly three times that of California.

The southernmost point of Africa is Cape Agulhas, located in the Western Cape Province about 100 mi (161 km) southeast of the Cape of Good Hope.

Government Republic.

History The San people were the first settlers; the Khoikhoi and Bantu-speaking tribes followed. The Dutch East India Company landed the first European settlers on the Cape of Good Hope in 1652, launching a colony that by the end of the 18th century numbered only about 15,000. Known as Boers or Afrikaners, speaking a Dutch dialect known as Afrikaans, the settlers as early as 1795 tried to establish an independent republic.

After occupying the Cape Colony in that year, Britain took permanent possession in 1815 at the end of the Napoleonic Wars, bringing in 5,000 settlers. Anglicization of government and the freeing of slaves in 1833 drove about 12,000 Afrikaners to make the "great trek" north and east into African tribal territory, where they established the republics of the Transvaal and the Orange Free State.

The discovery of diamonds in 1867 and gold nine years later brought an influx of "outlanders" into the republics and spurred Cape Colony prime minister Cecil Rhodes to plot annexation. Rhodes's scheme of sparking an "outlander" rebellion, to which an armed party under Leander Starr Jameson would ride to the rescue, misfired in 1895, forcing Rhodes to resign. What British expansionists called the "inevitable" war with the Boers eventually broke out on Oct. 11, 1899. The defeat of the Boers in 1902 led in 1910 to the Union of South Africa, composed of four provinces, the two former republics, and the old Cape and Natal colonies. Louis Botha, a Boer, became the first prime minister. Organized political activity among Africans started with the establishment of the African National Congress in 1912.

Jan Christiaan Smuts brought the nation into World War II on the Allied side against Nationalist opposition, and South Africa became a charter member of the United Nations in 1945, but refused to sign the Universal Declaration of Human Rights. Apartheid—racial separation—dominated domestic politics as the Nationalists gained power and imposed greater restrictions on Bantus (black Africans), Asians, and Coloreds (in South Africa the term meant any nonwhite person). Black voters were removed from the voter rolls in 1936. Over the next half-century, the nonwhite population of South Africa was forced out of designated white areas. The Group Areas Acts of 1950 and 1986 forced about 1.5 million Africans to move from cities to rural townships, where they lived in abject poverty under repressive laws.

South Africa declared itself a republic in 1961 and severed its ties with the Commonwealth, which strongly objected to the country's racist policies. The white supremacist National party, which had first come to power in 1948, would continue its rule for the next three decades.

In 1960, 70 black protestors were killed during a peaceful demonstration in Sharpesville. The African National Congress (ANC), the principal anti-apartheid organization, was banned that year, and in 1964 its leader, Nelson Mandela, was sentenced to life imprisonment. Black protests against apartheid grew stronger and more violent. In 1976, an uprising in the black township of Soweto spread to other black townships and left 600 dead. Beginning in the 1960s, international opposition to apartheid intensified. The UN imposed sanctions, and many countries divested of their South African holdings.

Apartheid's grip on South Africa began to give way when F. W. de Klerk replaced P. W. Botha as president in 1989. De Klerk removed the ban on the ANC, and released its leader, Nelson Mandela, after 27 years of imprisonment. The Inkatha Freedom Party, a black opposition group led by Mangosuthu Buthelezi, which was seen as collaborating with the apartheid system, frequently clashed with the ANC during this period.

In 1991, a multiracial forum led by de Klerk and Mandela, the Convention for a Democratic South Africa (CODESA), began working on a new constitution. In 1993, an interim constitution was passed, which dismantled apartheid and provided for a multiracial democracy with majority rule. The peaceful transition of South Africa from one of the world's most repressive societies into a democracy is one of the 20th century's most remarkable success stories. Mandela and de Klerk were jointly awarded the Nobel peace prize in 1993.

The 1994 election, the country's first multiracial one, resulted in a massive victory for Mandela and his ANC. The new government included six ministers from the National Party and three from the Inkatha Freedom Party. A new national constitution was approved and adopted in May 1996.

In 1997 the Truth and Reconciliation Commission, chaired by Desmond Tutu, began hearings regarding human rights violations between 1960 and 1993. The commission promised amnesty to those who confessed their crimes under the apartheid system. In 1998, F. W. de Klerk, P. W. Botha, and leaders of the ANC appeared before the commission, and the nation continued to grapple with its enlightened but often painful and divisive process of national recovery.

Nelson Mandela, whose term as president cemented his reputation as one of the world's most far-sighted and magnanimous statesmen, retired in 1999. On June 2, 1999, Thabo Mbeki, the pragmatic deputy president of South Africa and leader of the ANC, was elected president in a landslide, having already assumed many of Mandela's governing responsibilities.

In his first term, Mbeki wrestled with a slumping economy, a skyrocketing crime rate, and the country's rising AIDS epidemic. South Africa, which has the highest number of HIV-positive people in the world (nearly 5 million, about 12% of the population), has been hampered in fighting the epidemic by its president's highly controversial views. Mbeki has denied the link between HIV and AIDS, and claimed that the West has exaggerated the epidemic to sell drugs. The international community as well as most South African leaders, including Nelson Mandela and Desmond Tutu, have condemned Mbeki's stance. Finally, in Aug. 2003, after years of delay, Mbeki reversed his hands-off AIDS policy, but the government's deep ambivalence toward combating the epidemic persists.

As expected, on April 15, 2004, the African National Congress won South Africa's general election in a landslide, taking about 70% of the vote, and Thabo Mbeki was sworn in for a second term.

Spain

KINGDOM OF SPAIN

National name: Reino de España
Ruler: King Juan Carlos I (1975)
Prime Minister: José Luis Rodríguez Zapatero (2004)
Area: 194,896 sq mi (504,782 sq km)[1]
Population (2004 est.): 40,280,780 (growth rate: 0.2%); birth rate: 10.1/1000; infant mortality rate: 4.5/1000; life expectancy: 79.4; density per sq mi: 207
Capital and largest city (2003 est.): Madrid, 5,130,000 (metro. area), 3,169,400 (city proper). **Other large cities:** Barcelona, 1,528,800; Valencia, 741,100; Seville, 679,100. **Monetary units:** Euro (formerly peseta). **Languages:** Castilian Spanish 74% (official nationwide); Catalan 17%, Galician 7%, Basque 2% (each official regionally). **Ethnicity/race:** composite of Mediterranean and Nordic types. **Religion:** Roman Catholic 94%, other 6%. **Literacy rate:** 98% (2003 est.)
Economic summary: GDP/PPP (2003 est.): $885.5 billion; per capita $22,000. **Real growth rate:** 2.4%. **Inflation:** 2.6%. **Unemployment:** 11.7%. **Arable land:** 29%. **Agriculture:** grain, vegetables, olives, wine grapes, sugar beets, citrus; beef, pork, poultry, dairy products; fish. **Labor force:** 17.1 million (2001); services 64%, manufacturing, mining, and construction 29%, agriculture 7% (2001 est.). **Industries:** textiles and apparel (including footwear), food and beverages, metals and metal manufactures, chemicals, shipbuilding, automobiles, machine tools, tourism. **Natural resources:** coal, lignite, iron ore, uranium, mercury, pyrites, fluorspar, gypsum, zinc, lead, tungsten, copper, kaolin, potash, hydropower, arable land. **Exports:** $159.4 billion (f.o.b., 2003 est.): machinery, motor vehicles; foodstuffs, other consumer goods. **Imports:** $197.1 billion (f.o.b., 2003 est.): machinery and equipment, fuels, chemicals, semifinished goods; foodstuffs, consumer goods. **Major trading partners:** France, Germany, UK, Portugal, Italy, U.S., Netherlands.

1. Including the Balearic and Canary Islands.

Geography Spain occupies 85% of the Iberian Peninsula, which it shares with Portugal, in southwest Europe. Africa is less than 10 mi (16 km) south at the Strait of Gibraltar. A broad central plateau slopes to the south and east, crossed by a series of mountain ranges and river valleys. Principal rivers are the Ebro in the northeast, the Tajo in the central region, and the Guadalquivir in the south. Off Spain's east coast in the Mediterranean are the Balearic Islands (1,936 sq mi; 5,014 sq km), the largest of which is Majorca. Sixty mi (97 km) west of Africa are the Canary Islands (2,808 sq mi; 7,273 sq km).

Government Parliamentary monarchy.

History Spain, originally inhabited by Celts, Iberians, and Basques, became a part of the Roman Empire in 206 B.C., when it was conquered by Scipio Africanus. In A.D. 412, the barbarian Visigothic leader Ataulf crossed the Pyrenees and ruled Spain, first in the name of the Roman emperor and then independently. In 711, the Muslims under Tariq entered Spain from Africa and within a few years completed the subjugation of the country. In 732, the Franks, led by Charles Martel, defeated the Muslims near Poitiers, thus preventing the further expansion of Islam in southern Europe. Internal dissension of Spanish Islam invited a steady Christian conquest from the north.

Aragon and Castile were the most important Spanish states from the 12th to the 15th century, consolidated by the marriage of Ferdinand II and Isabella I in 1469. The last Muslim stronghold, Granada, was captured in 1492. Roman Catholicism was established as the official state religion and most Jews (1492) and Muslims (1502) were expelled. In the era of exploration, discovery, and colonization, Spain amassed tremendous wealth and a vast colonial empire through the conquest of Mexico by Cortés (1519–1521) and Peru by Pizarro (1532–1533). The Spanish Hapsburg monarchy became for a time the most powerful in the world. In 1588, Philip II sent his invincible Armada to invade England, but its destruction cost Spain its supremacy on the seas and paved the way for England's colonization of America. Spain then sank rapidly to the status of a second-rate power under the rule of weak Hapsburg kings, and never again played a major role in European politics. The War of the Spanish Succession (1701–1714) resulted in Spain's loss of Belgium, Luxembourg, Milan, Sardinia, and Naples. Its colonial empire in the Americas and the Philippines vanished in wars and revolutions during the 18th and 19th centuries.

In World War I, Spain maintained a position of neutrality. In 1923, Gen. Miguel Primo de Rivera became dictator. In 1930, King Alfonso XIII revoked the dictatorship, but a strong antimonarchist and republican movement led to his leaving Spain in 1931. The new constitution declared Spain a workers' republic, broke up the large estates, separated church and state, and secularized the schools. The elections held in 1936 returned a strong Popular Front majority, with Manuel Azaña as president.

On July 18, 1936, a conservative army officer in Morocco, Francisco Franco Bahamonde, led a mutiny against the government. The civil war that followed lasted three years and cost the lives of nearly a million people. Franco was aided by Fascist Italy and Nazi Germany, while Soviet Russia helped the Loyalist side. Several hundred leftist Americans served in the Abraham Lincoln Brigade on the side of the republic. The war ended when Franco took Madrid on March 28, 1939. Franco became head of the state, national chief of the Falange Party (the governing party), and premier and caudillo (leader). In a referendum in 1947, the Spanish people approved a Franco-drafted succession law declaring Spain a monarchy again. Franco, however, continued as chief of state.

In 1969, Franco and the Cortes (states) designated Prince Juan Carlos Alfonso Victor María de Borbón (who married Princess Sophia of Greece on May 14, 1962) to become king of Spain when the provisional government headed by Franco came to an end. Franco died of a heart attack on Nov. 20, 1975, after more than a year of ill health, and Juan Carlos was proclaimed king on Nov. 22.

Under pressure from Catalonian and Basque nationalists, Premier Adolfo Suárez granted home rule to these regions in 1979. Basque separatists committed hundreds of terrorist bombings and kidnappings that continue to the present. With the overwhelming election of Prime Minister Felipe González Márquez and his Spanish Socialist Workers Party in the Oct. 20, 1982, parliamentary elections, the Franco past was finally buried.

Spain entered NATO in 1982. A treaty admitting Spain, along with Portugal, to the European Economic Community, now the European Union, took effect on Jan. 1, 1986. General elections in March 1996 produced a victory for the conservative Popular Party, and its leader, José María Aznar, became prime minister. He and his party easily won reelection in 2000.

In Aug. 2002, Batasuna, the political wing of the Basque terrorist organization ETA, was banned. The wisdom of driving the party underground instead of permitting it a legitimate political outlet has been questioned.

Aznar's backing of the U.S. war in Iraq was highly unpopular—90% of Spaniards opposed the war. (Spain sent no troops to Iraq during the war, but contributed 1,300 peacekeeping forces during the reconstruction period.) Yet his People's Party did extremely well in municipal elections in May 2003. The country's relative prosperity and the prime minister's tough stance against the ETA were thought to be responsible for the strong showing.

On March 11, 2004, Spain's most horrific terrorist attack occurred: 202 people were killed and 1,400 were injured in bombings at Madrid's railway station. The government at first blamed ETA, but soon evidence emerged that al-Qaeda was responsible. When record numbers of voters went to the polls days later, Aznar's Popular Party suffered a stinging defeat, and José Luis Rodríguez Zapatero of the Socialist Party became the new prime minister. Many Spaniards blamed Aznar's staunch support of the U.S. and the war in Iraq for making Spain an al-Qaeda target. Others were angered by what they saw as the government's politically motivated insistence that ETA was to blame for the attacks at the same time that links to al-Qaeda were emerging. By April, a dozen suspects, most of them Moroccan, were arrested for the bombings. On April 4, several suspects blew themselves up during a police raid to avoid capture. In May, the new prime minister made good on his campaign promise, recalling Spain's 1,300 soldiers from Iraq, much to the displeasure of the United States, which said Spain was appeasing terrorists.

Sri Lanka

DEMOCRATIC SOCIALIST REPUBLIC OF SRI LANKA

President: Chandrika B. Kumaratunga (1994)
Prime Minister: Mahinda Rajapakse (2004)
Area: 25,332 sq mi (65,610 sq km)
Population (2004 est.): 19,905,165 (growth rate: 0.8%); birth rate: 15.9/1000; infant mortality rate: 14.8/1000; life expectancy: 72.9; density per sq mi: 786
Capital and largest city (2003 est.): Colombo, 2,436,000 (metro. area), 656,100 (city proper); **Legislative and judicial capital:** Sri Jayawardenepura Kotte, 118,300. **Other large cities:** Dehiwala-Mount Lavinia 214,300; Moratuwa, 181,000; Kandy, 112,400. **Monetary unit:** Sri Lanka rupee. **Languages:** Sinhala 74% (official and national), Tamil 18% (national), other 8%; English is commonly used in government and spoken competently by about 10%. **Ethnicity/race:** Sinhalese 74%, Tamil 18%, Moor 7%, Burgher, Malay, and Vedda 1%. **Religions:** Buddhist 70%, Hindu 15%, Christian 8%, Islam 7% (1999). **Literacy rate:** 92% (2003 est.)
Economic summary: GDP/PPP (2003 est.): $73.49

billion; per capita $3,700. **Real growth rate:** 5.2%. **Inflation:** 9%. **Unemployment:** 8%. **Arable land:** 13%. **Agriculture:** rice, sugarcane, grains, pulses, oilseed, spices, tea, rubber, coconuts; milk, eggs, hides, beef. **Labor force:** 6.6 million (1998); services 45%, agriculture 38%, industry 17% (1998 est.). **Industries:** rubber processing, tea, coconuts, and other agricultural commodities; clothing, cement, petroleum refining, textiles, tobacco. **Natural resources:** limestone, graphite, mineral sands, gems, phosphates, clay, hydropower. **Exports:** $5.269 billion (f.o.b., 2003 est.): textiles and apparel, tea, diamonds, coconut products, petroleum products. **Imports:** $6.626 billion (f.o.b., 2003 est.): textiles, mineral products, petroleum, foodstuffs, machinery and equipment. **Major trading partners:** U.S., UK, Belgium, Germany, India, Hong Kong, Singapore, China, Taiwan, South Korea, Japan, Iran. **Member of Commonwealth of Nations**

Geography An island in the Indian Ocean off the southeast tip of India, Sri Lanka is about half the size of Alabama. Most of the land is flat and rolling; mountains in the south-central region rise to over 8,000 ft (2,438 m).

Government Republic.

History Indo-Aryan emigration from India in the 5th century B.C. came to form the largest ethnic group on Sri Lanka today, the Sinhalese. Tamils, the second-largest ethnic group on the island, were originally from the Tamil region of India, and emigrated between the 3rd century B.C. and A.D. 1200. Until colonial powers controlled Ceylon (the country's name until 1972), Sinhalese and Tamil rulers fought for dominance over the island. The Tamils, primarily Hindus, claimed the northern section of the island and the Sinhalese, who are predominantly Buddhist, controlled the south. In 1505 the Portuguese took possession of Ceylon until the Dutch India Company usurped control (1658–1796). The British took over in 1796, and Ceylon became an English Crown colony in 1802. The British developed coffee, tea, and rubber plantations. On Feb. 4, 1948, after pressure from Ceylonese nationalist leaders (which briefly unified the Tamil and Sinhalese), Ceylon became a self-governing dominion of the Commonwealth of Nations.

S.W.R.D. Bandaranaike became prime minister in 1956 and championed Sinhalese nationalism, making Sinhala the country's only official language and including state support of Buddhism, further marginalizing the Tamil minority. He was assassinated in 1959 by a Buddhist monk. His widow, Sirimavo Bandaranaike, became the world's first female prime minister in 1960. The name *Ceylon* was changed to Sri Lanka on May 22, 1972, which was its original name and means "resplendent island."

The Tamil minority's mounting resentment toward the Sinhalese majority's monopoly on political and economic power, exacerbated by cultural and religious differences, erupted in bloody violence in 1983. Tamils make up about 18% of the population in Sri Lanka, whereas approximately three-quarters of Sri Lanka's 18 million people are Sinhalese. Tamil rebel groups, the strongest of which are the Liberation Tigers of Tamil Eelam, or Tamil Tigers, are fighting for a separate nation.

President Ranasinghe Premadasa was assassinated at a May Day political rally in 1993, when a Tamil rebel detonated explosives strapped to himself. Tamil extremists have frequently resorted to terrorist attacks against civilians and are renowned for suicide bombers that target government officials. The next president, Chandrika Kumaratunga, vowed to restore peace to the country. In Dec. 1999, she was herself wounded in a terrorist attack. By early 2000, 18 years of war had claimed the lives of more than 64,000, mostly civilians.

After Dec. 2001 elections, Ranil Wickremesinghe, a longtime bitter rival of President Kumaratunga, was sworn in as prime minister. Wickremesinghe's victory precipitated a formal cease-fire with the Tamil rebels, signed in Feb. 2002. In September talks, the government lifted its ban on the group, and the Tigers dropped their demand for an independent Tamil state. Another significant breakthrough came in December when the Tigers and the government struck a power-sharing deal that would give the rebels regional autonomy. But negotiations in 2003 achieved little.

Intense political rivalry threatened the peace process. In Nov. 2003, President Kumaratunga, convinced that Prime Minister Wickremesinghe was too soft in his negotiations with the Tigers, wrested away some of his powers. In Feb. 2004, the president dissolved parliament and called for elections in the hope of further eroding the power of the prime minister. The gamble paid off for Kumaratunga—her United People's Freedom Alliance won April's parliamentary elections, and Wickremesinghe was replaced by a new prime minister, Mahinda Rajapakse, a high-ranking member of Kumaratunga's party.

A suicide bomber killed herself and four policemen in the capital, Colombo, in July. It was the first such attack since the government and the Tigers signed a cease-fire in 2002.

Sudan

REPUBLIC OF THE SUDAN

National name: Jamhuryat es-Sudan
President: Lt. Gen. Omar Hassan Ahmad al-Bashir (1989)
Area: 967,493 sq mi (2,505,810 sq km)
Population (2004 est.): 39,148,162 (growth rate: 2.6%); birth rate: 35.8/1000; infant mortality rate: 64.1/1000; life expectancy: 58.1; density per sq mi: 40
Capital (2003 est.): Khartoum, 5,717,300 (metro. area), 1,397,900 (city proper). **Largest cities:** Omdurman, 2,103,900; Port Sudan, 450,400. **Monetary unit:** Dinar. **Languages:** Arabic (official), Nubian, Ta Bedawie, diverse dialects of Nilotic, Nilo-Hamitic, Sudanic languages, English. **Ethnicity/race:** black 52%, Arab 39%, Beja 6%, foreigners 2%, other 1%. **Religions:** Islam (Sunni) 70% (in north), indigenous 25%, Christian 5% (mostly in south and Khartoum). **Literacy rate:** 61% (2003 est.)
Economic summary: GDP/PPP (2003 est.): $70.75 billion; per capita $1,900. **Real growth rate:** 6.1%. **Inflation:** 8.8%. **Unemployment:** 18.7%. **Arable land:** 7%. **Agriculture:** cotton, groundnuts (peanuts), sorghum, millet, wheat, gum arabic, sugarcane, cassava (tapioca), mangos, papaya, bananas, sweet potatoes, sesame; sheep, livestock. **Labor force:** 11 million (1996 est.); agriculture 80%, industry and commerce 7%, government 13% (1998 est.). **Industries:** oil, cotton ginning, textiles, cement, edible oils, sugar, soap distilling, shoes, petroleum refining, pharmaceuticals, armaments, automobile/light truck assembly. **Natural resources:** petroleum; small reserves of iron ore, copper, chromium ore, zinc, tungsten, mica, silver, gold, hydropower. **Exports:** $2.45 billion (f.o.b., 2003 est.): oil and petroleum products, cotton, sesame, livestock, groundnuts, gum arabic, sugar. **Imports:** $2.383 billion (f.o.b., 2003 est.): foodstuffs, manufactured goods, refinery and transport equipment, medicines and chemicals, textiles, wheat. **Major trading partners:** China, Japan, Saudi Arabia, Germany, India, UK, Indonesia, Australia.

Geography The Sudan, in northeast Africa, is the largest country on the continent, measuring about one-fourth the size of the United States. Its neighbors are Chad and the Central African Republic on the west, Egypt and Libya on the north, Ethiopia and Eritrea on the east, and Kenya, Uganda, and Democratic Republic of the Congo on the south. The Red Sea washes about 500 mi of the eastern coast. It is traversed from north to south by the Nile.

Government Military government.

History What is now northern Sudan was in ancient times the kingdom of Nubia, which came under Egyptian rule after 2600 B.C. An Egyptian and Nubian civilization called Kush flourished until A.D. 350. Missionaries converted the region to Christianity in the 6th century, but an influx of Muslim Arabs, who had already conquered Egypt, eventually controlled the area and replaced Christianity with Islam. During the 1500s a people called the Funj conquered much of Sudan, and several other black African groups settled in the south, including the Dinka, Shilluk, Nuer, and Azande. Egyptians again conquered the Sudan in 1874, and after Britain occupied Egypt in 1882, it took over Sudan in 1898, ruling the country in conjunction with Egypt. It was known as the Anglo-Egyptian Sudan between 1898 and 1955.

The 20th century saw the growth of Sudanese nationalism, and in 1953 Egypt and Britain granted the Sudan self-government. Independence was proclaimed on Jan. 1, 1956. Since independence, the Sudan has been ruled by a series of unstable parliamentary governments and military regimes. Under Maj. Gen. Gaafar Mohamed Nimeiri, the Sudan instituted fundamentalist Islamic law in 1983. This exacerbated the rift between the Arab North, the seat of the government, and the black African animists and Christians in the South. Differences in language, religion, ethnicity, and political power erupted in an unending civil war between government forces, strongly influenced by the National Islamic Front (NIF), and the southern rebels, whose most influential faction is the Sudan People's Liberation Army (SPLA). Human rights violations, religious persecution, and allegations that the Sudan had been a safe haven for terrorists isolated the country from most of the international community. In 1995, the UN imposed sanctions against it.

On Aug. 20, 1998, the United States launched cruise missiles that destroyed a pharmaceutical manufacturing facility in Khartoum that allegedly manufactured chemical weapons. The U.S. contended that the Sudanese factory was financed by Islamic militant Osama bin Laden.

Since 1999 international attention has been focused on evidence that slavery is widespread throughout Sudan. Arab raiders from the north of the country have enslaved thousands of southerners, who are black. The Dinka people have been the hardest hit. Some sources point out that the raids intensified in the 1980s along with the civil war between north and south.

Ever since Lt. Gen. Omar Bashir's military coup in 1989, the de facto ruler of Sudan had been Hassan el-Turabi, a cleric and political leader who is a major figure in the pan-Arabic Islamic fundamentalist resurgence. In 1999, however, Bashir ousted Turabi and placed him under house arrest. (He was freed in Oct. 2003.) Since then Bashir has made overtures to the West, and in Sept. 2001, the UN lifted its six-year-old sanctions. The U.S., however, still officially considers it a terrorist state.

A cease-fire was declared between the Sudanese government and the Sudan People's Liberation Army

(SPLA) in July 2002. During peace talks, which continued through 2003, the government agreed to a power-sharing government for six years, to be followed by a referendum on self-determination for the south. Fighting on both sides continued throughout the peace negotiations. In May 2004, a peace deal between the government and the SPLA was signed, ending 20 years of brutal civil war that resulted in the deaths of 2 million people.

Just as Sudan's civil war seemed to be coming to an end, another war intensified in the northwestern Darfur region. After the government quelled a rebellion in Darfur in Jan. 2004, it allowed pro-government militias called the Janjaweed to carry out massacres against black villagers and rebel groups in the region. These Arab militias, believed to have been armed by the government, have killed more than 30,000 and displaced more than 1 million. While the war in the south was fought against black Christians and animists, the Darfur conflict is being fought against black Muslims. Although the international community has reacted with alarm to the humanitarian disaster—unmistakably the world's worst—it has been ineffective in persuading the Sudanese government to rein in the Janjaweed. Despite the EU and the U.S. describing the killing as genocide, and despite a UN Security Council resolution demanding that Sudan stop the Arab militias, the killing continued throughout the summer and fall of 2004.

Suriname

REPUBLIC OF SURINAME

President: Ronald Venetiaan (2000)
Prime Minister: Jules Ajodhia (2000)
Area: 63,039 sq mi (163,270 sq km)
Population (2004 est.): 436,935 (growth rate: 0.3%); birth rate: 18.9/1000; infant mortality rate: 24.2/1000; life expectancy: 69.1; density per sq mi: 7
Capital and largest city (2003 est.): Paramaribo, 217,300. **Monetary unit:** Surinamese dollar.
Languages: Dutch (official), Surinamese (lingua franca), English widely spoken, Hindustani, Javanese. **Ethnicity/race:** East Indians (also known locally as Hindustanis) 37%, Creole (mixed white and black) 31%, Javanese 15%, "Bush Negroes" (also known as Maroons) 10%, Amerindian 2%, Chinese 2%, Europeans 1%, other 2%. **Religions:** Hindu 27.4%, Protestant 25.2% (predominantly Moravian), Roman Catholic 22.8%, Islam 19.6%, indigenous 5%. **Literacy rate:** 93% (1995 est.)
Economic summary: GDP/PPP (2003 est.): $1.533 billion; per capita $3,500. **Real growth rate:** 1.5%. **Inflation:** 17% (2002 est.). **Unemployment:** 17% (2000). **Arable land:** 0%. **Agriculture:** paddy rice, bananas, palm kernels, coconuts, plantains, peanuts; beef, chickens; forest products; shrimp. **Labor force:** 100,000; agriculture n.a., industry n.a., services n.a. **Industries:** bauxite and gold mining, alumina production, oil, lumbering, food processing, fishing. **Natural resources:** timber, hydropower, fish, kaolin, shrimp, bauxite, gold, and small amounts of nickel, copper, platinum, iron ore. **Exports:** $495 million (f.o.b., 2002): alumina, crude oil, lumber, shrimp and fish, rice, bananas. **Imports:** $604 million (f.o.b., 2002): capital equipment, petroleum, foodstuffs, cotton, consumer goods. **Major trading partners:** U.S., Norway, France, Trinidad and Tobago, Iceland, Canada, Netherlands, China, Netherlands Antilles, Japan.

Geography Suriname lies on the northeast coast of South America, with Guyana to the west, French Guiana to the east, and Brazil to the south. It is about one-tenth larger than Michigan. The principal rivers are the Corantijn on the Guyana border, the Marowijne

in the east, and the Suriname, on which the capital city of Paramaribo is situated.

Government Constitutional democracy.

History Suriname's earliest inhabitants were the Surinen Indians, after whom the country is named. By the 16th century they had been supplanted by other South American Indians. Spain explored Suriname in 1593, but by 1602 the Dutch began to settle the land, followed by the English. The English transferred sovereignty to the Dutch in 1667 (the Treaty of Breda) in exchange for New Amsterdam (New York). Colonization was confined to a narrow coastal strip, and until the abolition of slavery in 1863, African slaves furnished the labor for the coffee and sugarcane plantations. Escaped African slaves fled into the interior, reconstituted their western African culture, and came to be called "Bush Negroes" by the Dutch. After 1870, East Indian laborers were imported from British India and Javanese from the Dutch East Indies.

Known as Dutch Guiana, the colony was integrated into the kingdom of the Netherlands in 1948. Two years later Dutch Guiana was granted home rule, except for foreign affairs and defense. After race rioting over unemployment and inflation, the Netherlands granted Suriname complete independence on Nov. 25, 1975. A coup d'état in 1980 brought military rule. During much of the 1980s Suriname was under the repressive control of Lieut. Col. Dési Bouterse. The Netherlands stopped all aid in 1982 when Suriname soldiers killed 15 journalists, politicians, lawyers, and union officials. Defense spending increased significantly, and the economy suffered. A guerrilla insurgency by the Jungle Commando (a Bush Negro guerrilla group) threatened to destabilize the country and was harshly suppressed by Bouterse. Free elections were held on May 25, 1991, depriving the military of much of its political power. In 1992 a peace treaty was signed between the government and several guerrilla groups. In March 1997, the president announced new economic measures, including eliminating import tariffs on most basic goods coupled with strict price controls. Later that year, the Netherlands said it would prosecute Bouterse for cocaine trafficking.

Public discontent over the 70% inflation rate prompted President Jules Wijdenbosch to hold elections in May 2000, one year ahead of schedule. The New Front for Democracy and Development, a coalition led by former president Ronald Venetiaan, won the election. Suriname has earned a reputation as a center for drug trafficking; in 1998, former dictator Bouterse was sentenced in absentia in the Netherlands for transporting cocaine. As of Jan. 2004, Suriname changed the name of its currency from the guilder to the dollar.

Swaziland

KINGDOM OF SWAZILAND

Ruler: King Mswati III (1986)
Prime Minister: Barnabas Sibusiso Dlamini (1996)
Area: 6,704 sq mi (17,363 sq km)
Population (2004 est.): 1,169,241 (growth rate: 0.5%); birth rate: 28.6/1000; infant mortality rate: 68.4/1000; life expectancy: 37.5; density per sq mi: 174
Capital (2003 est.): Mbabane 69,000. **Largest city:** Manzini, 75,000. **Monetary unit:** Lilangeni.
Languages: English, siSwati (both official). **Ethnicity/race:** African 97%, European 3%. **Religions:** Zionist (a blend of Christianity and indigenous ancestral worship) 40%; Roman Catholic 20%; Muslim 10%; Anglican, Bahai, Methodist, Mormon, Jewish, and other 30%. **Literacy rate:** 82% (2003 est.)
Economic summary: GDP/PPP (2003 est.): $5.702 billion; per capita $4,900. **Real growth rate:** 2.2%.

Inflation: 11.8% (2002 est.). **Unemployment:** 34% (2000 est.). **Arable land:** 10%. **Agriculture:** sugarcane, cotton, corn, tobacco, rice, citrus, pineapples, sorghum, peanuts; cattle, goats, sheep. **Labor force:** 383,200 (2000). **Industries:** mining (coal), wood pulp, sugar, soft drink concentrates, textile and apparel. **Natural resources:** asbestos, coal, clay, cassiterite, hydropower, forests, small gold and diamond deposits, quarry stone, talc. **Exports:** $905.6 million (f.o.b., 2003 est.): soft drink concentrates, sugar, wood pulp, cotton yarn, refrigerators, citrus and canned fruit. **Imports:** $1.088 million (f.o.b., 2003 est.): motor vehicles, machinery, transport equipment, foodstuffs, petroleum products, chemicals. **Major trading partners:** South Africa, EU, Mozambique, U.S., UK, Japan, Singapore. **Member of Commonwealth of Nations**

Geography Swaziland, which is about 85% the size of New Jersey, is surrounded by South Africa and Mozambique. The country consists of a high veld in the west and a series of plateaus descending from 6,000 ft (1,829 m) to a low veld of 1,500 ft (457 m).

Government Absolute monarchy.

History Bantu peoples migrated southwest to the area of Mozambique in the 16th century. A number of clans broke away from the main body in the 18th century and settled in Swaziland. In the 19th century these clans organized as a tribe, partly because they were in constant conflict with the Zulu. Their ruler, Mswazi, appealed to the British in the 1840s for help against the Zulu. The British and the Transvaal governments guaranteed the independence of Swaziland in 1881.

South Africa held Swaziland as a protectorate from 1894 to 1899, but after the Boer War, in 1902, Swaziland was transferred to British administration. The paramount chief was recognized as the native authority in 1941. In 1963, the territory was constituted a protectorate, and on Sept. 6, 1968, it became the independent nation of Swaziland.

Since 1986, King Mswati III has ruled as sub-Saharan Africa's last absolute monarch. Political parties are banned and the king appoints 10 of the 65 members of Parliament as well as the prime minister. King Mswati can veto any law passed by the legislature and frequently rules by decree.

In 2002, hundreds of thousands of Swazis faced starvation. Two years of drought as well as bad planning and agricultural practices were blamed for the crisis. The government came under criticism for buying the king a $50 million luxury jet—a quarter of the national budget—while famine loomed. In 2002, the country's judges resigned en masse in protest of the government's refusal to comply with court decisions. In April 2003, the government information minister announced that the media was banned from making negative remarks about the government—criticism of the king's new luxury jet in particular would not be tolerated. In 2004, a third year of drought befell the country. International donor agencies and human rights groups condemned the king's plans to build new multimillion-dollar palaces for each of his 11 wives while his people faced starvation and the country's AIDS epidemic spiraled out of control—30% of the population is infected.

Sweden

KINGDOM OF SWEDEN

National name: Konungariket Sverige
Sovereign: King Carl XVI Gustaf (1973)
Prime Minister: Göran Persson (1996)
Area: 173,731 sq mi (449,964 sq km)

Population (2004 est.): 8,986,400 (growth rate: 0.2%); birth rate: 10.5/1000; infant mortality rate: 2.8/1000; life expectancy: 80.3; density per sq mi: 52
Capital and largest city (2003 est.): Stockholm, 1,622,300 (metro. area), 1,251,900 (city proper). **Other large cities:** Göteborg, 506,600; Malmö, 245,300; Uppsala, 127,300. **Monetary unit:** Krona. **Language:** Swedish, small Sami- and Finnish-speaking minorities. **Ethnicity/race:** indigenous population: Swedes and Finnish and Sami minorities; foreign-born or first-generation immigrants: Finns, Yugoslavs, Danes, Norwegians, Greeks, Turks. **Religions:** Lutheran 87%, Roman Catholic, Orthodox, Baptist, Muslim, Jewish, Buddhist. **Literacy rate:** 99% (1979 est.)
Economic summary: GDP/PPP (2003 est.): $238.1 billion; per capita $26,800. **Real growth rate:** 1.6%. **Inflation:** 2.3%. **Unemployment:** 4.6%. **Arable land:** 7%. **Agriculture:** barley, wheat, sugar beets; meat, milk. **Labor force:** 4.4 million (2000 est.); agriculture 2%, industry 24%, services 74% (2000 est.). **Industries:** iron and steel, precision equipment (bearings, radio and telephone parts, armaments), wood pulp and paper products, processed foods, motor vehicles. **Natural resources:** zinc, iron ore, lead, copper, silver, timber, uranium, hydropower. **Exports:** $102.8 billion (f.o.b., 2003 est.): machinery 35%, motor vehicles, paper products, pulp and wood, iron and steel products, chemicals. **Imports:** $83.27 billion (f.o.b., 2003 est.): machinery, petroleum and petroleum products, chemicals, motor vehicles, iron and steel; foodstuffs, clothing. **Major trading partners:** U.S., Germany, Norway, UK, Denmark, Finland, Netherlands, France, Belgium.

Geography Sweden, which occupies the eastern part of the Scandinavian peninsula, is the fourth-largest country in Europe, and is one-tenth larger than California. The country slopes eastward and southward from the Kjólen Mountains along the Norwegian border, where the peak elevation is Kebnekaise at 6,965 ft (2,123 m) in Lapland. In the north are mountains and many lakes. To the south and east are central lowlands and south of them are fertile areas of forest, valley, and plain. Along Sweden's rocky coast, chopped up by bays and inlets, are many islands, the largest of which are Gotland and Öland.

Government Constitutional monarchy.

History The earliest historical mention of Sweden is found in Tacitus's *Germania*, where reference is made to the powerful king and strong fleet of the Sviones. In the 11th century, Olaf Sköttkonung became the first Swedish king to be baptized as a Christian. Around 1400, an attempt was made to unite Sweden, Norway, and Denmark into one kingdom, but this led to bitter strife between the Danes and the Swedes. In 1520, the Danish king Christian II conquered Sweden and in the "Stockholm Bloodbath" put leading Swedish personages to death. Gustavus Vasa (1523–1560) broke away from Denmark and fashioned the modern Swedish state. He also confiscated property from the Roman Catholic Church in Sweden to pay Sweden's war debts. The king justified his actions on the basis of Martin Luther's doctrines, which were being accepted nationwide with royal encouragement. The Lutheran Swedish church was eventually adopted as the state church.

Sweden played a leading role in the second phase (1630–1635) of the Thirty Years' War (1618–1648). By the Treaty of Westphalia (1648), Sweden obtained western Pomerania and some neighboring territory on the Baltic. In 1700, a coalition of Russia, Poland, and Denmark united against Sweden and by the Peace of

Nystad (1721) forced it to relinquish Livonia, Ingria, Estonia, and parts of Finland. Sweden emerged from the Napoleonic Wars with the acquisition of Norway from Denmark and with a new royal dynasty stemming from Marshal Jean Bernadotte of France, who became King Charles XIV (1818–1844). The artificial union between Sweden and Norway led to an uneasy relationship, and the union was finally dissolved in 1905. Sweden maintained a position of neutrality in both world wars.

An elaborate structure of welfare legislation, imitated by many larger nations, began with the establishment of old-age pensions in 1911. Economic prosperity based on its neutralist policy enabled Sweden, together with Norway, to pioneer in public health, housing, and job security programs. Forty-four years of Socialist government were ended in 1976 with the election of a conservative coalition headed by Thorbjörn Fälldin. The Socialists were returned to power in the election of 1982, but Prime Minister Olof Palme, a Socialist, was assassinated by a gunman on Feb. 28, 1986, leaving Sweden stunned. Palme's Socialist domestic policies were carried out by his successor, Ingvar Carlsson. Elections in Sept. 1991 ousted the Social Democrats (Socialists) from power. The new coalition of four conservative parties pledged to reduce taxes and cut back on the welfare state but not alter Sweden's traditional neutrality. In Sept. 1994 the Social Democrats emerged again after three years as the opposition party.

In a 1994 referendum voters approved joining the European Union. Although supportive of a European monetary union, Sweden decided not to adopt the euro when it debuted in 1999 and rejected it again overwhelmingly in a referendum in Sept. 2003.

The Social Democrat party, and its leader, Prime Minister Persson, easily won the Sept. 2002 elections. The center-left Social Democrats have run the government for six out of the last seven decades.

Switzerland

SWISS CONFEDERATION

National name: Schweiz/Suisse/Svizzera/Svizra
President: Joseph Deiss (2004)
Area: 15,942 sq mi (41,290 sq km)
Population (2004 est.): 7,450,867 (growth rate: 0.5%); birth rate: 9.8/1000; infant mortality rate: 4.4/1000; life expectancy: 80.3; density per sq mi: 467
Capital (2003 est.): Bern, 122,700. **Largest cities:** Zurich, 971,800 (metro. area), 348,100 (city proper); Geneva, 178,900; Basel, 162,800; Lausanne, 117,400.
Monetary unit: Swiss franc. **Languages:** German 63.7%, French 12.9%, Italian 7.6%, Romansch 0.6% (all official); other 8.9%. **Ethnicity/race:** German 65%, French 18%, Italian 10%, Romansch 1%, other 6%. **Religions:** Roman Catholic 46.1%, Protestant 40%, other 5%, no religion 8.9% (1990). **Literacy rate:** 99% (1980 est.)
Economic summary: GDP/PPP (2003 est.): $239.8 billion; per capita $32,800. **Real growth rate:** –0.3%. **Inflation:** 0.5%. **Unemployment:** 3.9%. **Arable land:** 11%. **Agriculture:** grains, fruits, vegetables; meat, eggs. **Labor force:** 4 million (2001); services 69%, industry 26%, agriculture 5% (1998). **Industries:** machinery, chemicals, watches, textiles, precision instruments. **Natural resources:** hydropower potential, timber, salt. **Exports:** $110 billion (f.o.b., 2003 est.): machinery, chemicals, metals, watches, agricultural products. **Imports:** $102.2 billion (f.o.b., 2003 est.): machinery, chemicals, vehicles, metals; agricultural

products, textiles. **Major trading partners:** Germany, U.S., Italy, France, UK, Russia, Austria, Netherlands.

Geography Switzerland, in central Europe, is the land of the Alps. Its tallest peak is the Dufourspitze at 15,203 ft (4,634 m) on the Swiss side of the Italian border, one of 10 summits of the Monte Rose massif. The tallest peak in all of the Alps, Mont Blanc (15,771 ft; 4,807 m), is actually in France. Most of Switzerland is composed of a mountainous plateau bordered by the great bulk of the Alps on the south and by the Jura Mountains on the northwest. The country's largest lakes—Geneva, Constance (Bodensee), and Maggiore—straddle the French, German-Austrian, and Italian borders, respectively. The Rhine, navigable from Basel to the North Sea, is the principal inland waterway.

Government Federal republic.

History Called Helvetia in ancient times, Switzerland in 1291 was a league of cantons in the Holy Roman Empire. Fashioned around the nucleus of three German forest districts of Schwyz, Uri, and Unterwalden, the Swiss Confederation slowly added new cantons. In 1648 the Treaty of Westphalia gave Switzerland its independence from the Holy Roman Empire.

French revolutionary troops occupied the country in 1798 and named it the Helvetic Republic, but Napoleon in 1803 restored its federal government. By 1815, the French- and Italian-speaking peoples of Switzerland had been granted political equality.

In 1815, the Congress of Vienna guaranteed the neutrality and recognized the independence of Switzerland. In the revolutionary period of 1847, the Catholic cantons seceded and organized a separate union called the *Sonderbund*, but they were defeated and rejoined the federation.

In 1848, the new Swiss constitution established a union modeled upon that of the U.S. The federal constitution of 1874 established a strong central government while giving large powers of control to each canton. National unity and political conservatism grew as the country prospered from its neutrality. Its banking system became the world's leading repository for international accounts.

Strict neutrality was its policy in both world wars. Geneva was the seat of the League of Nations (later the European headquarters of the United Nations) and of a number of international organizations.

Allegations in the 1990s concerning secret assets of Jewish Holocaust victims deposited in Swiss banks led to international criticism and the establishment of a fund to reimburse the victims and their families.

Surprisingly, women were not given the right to vote or to hold office until 1971. Switzerland's first woman president—as well as the first Jew to assume the position—was Ruth Dreifuss in 1999.

In Sept. 2000, the Swiss voted against a plan to cut the number of foreigners in the country to 18% of the population (in 2000 foreigners made up 19.3%). Since 1970, four similar anti-immigration plans have failed.

On Sept 10, 2002, the Swiss abandoned their longheld neutrality to become the 190th member of the UN.

In Oct. 2003, Switzerland took a turn to the right when the far-right Swiss People's party (SVP) had the strongest showing in parliamentary elections, garnering 28% of the vote. Its virulently anti-immigration, anti-EU leader, Christopher Blocher, was given a cabinet position.

Syria

SYRIAN ARAB REPUBLIC

National name: Al-Jamhouriya al Arabiya As-Souriya
President: Bashar al-Assad (2000)
Prime Minister: Muhammad Naji al-Otari (2003)
Area: 71,498 sq mi (185,180 sq km)
Population (2004 est.): 18,016,874 (growth rate: 2.4%);
birth rate: 28.9/1000; infant mortality rate: 30.6/1000;
life expectancy: 69.7; density per sq mi: 252
Capital (2003 est.): Damascus, 2,381,800 (metro. area),
1,861,900. **Largest cities:** Aleppo, 2,492,100 (metro.
area), 1,933,700 (city proper); Homs, 751,500;
Latakia, 417,100; Hama, 380,200. **Monetary unit:**
Syrian pound. **Languages:** Arabic (official); Kurdish,
Armenian, Aramaic, Circassian widely understood;
French, English somewhat understood. **Ethnicity/
race:** Arab 90.3%, Kurds, Armenians, and other 9.7%.
Religions: Islam (Sunni) 74%; Alawite, Druze, and
other Islamic sects 16%; Christian (various sects)
10%; Jewish (tiny communities in Damascus, Al
Qamishli, and Aleppo). **Literacy rate:** 77% (2003 est.)
Economic summary: GDP/PPP (2003 est.): $58.01
billion; per capita $3,300. **Real growth rate:** 0.9%.
Inflation: 1.5%. **Unemployment:** 20% (2002 est.).
Arable land: 26%. **Agriculture:** wheat, barley, cotton,
lentils, chickpeas, olives, sugar beets; beef, mutton,
eggs, poultry, milk. **Labor force:** 5.2 million (2000 est.).
Industries: petroleum, textiles, food processing,
beverages, tobacco, phosphate rock mining. **Natural
resources:** petroleum, phosphates, chrome and
manganese ores, asphalt, iron ore, rock salt, marble,
gypsum, hydropower. **Exports:** $5.143 billion (f.o.b.,
2003 est.): crude oil 70%, petroleum products 7%, fruits
and vegetables 5%, cotton fiber 4%, clothing 3%, meat
and live animals 2% (2000 est.). **Imports:** $4.845
billion (f.o.b., 2003 est.): machinery and transport
equipment 21%, food and livestock 18%, metal and
metal products 15%, chemicals and chemical products
10% (2000 est.). **Major trading partners:** Germany,
Italy, Turkey, France, Lebanon, China, South Korea,
U.S.

Geography Slightly larger than North Dakota, Syria
lies at the eastern end of the Mediterranean Sea. It is
bordered by Lebanon and Israel on the west, Turkey
on the north, Iraq on the east, and Jordan on the south.
Coastal Syria is a narrow plain, in back of which is a
range of coastal mountains, and still farther inland a
steppe area. In the east is the Syrian Desert, and in the
south is the Jebel Druze Range. The highest point in
Syria is Mount Hermon (9,232 ft; 2,814 m) on the
Lebanese border.

Government Republic under a military regime since
March 1963.

History Ancient Syria was conquered by Egypt
about 1500 B.C., and after that by Hebrews, Assyrians,
Chaldeans, Persians, and Alexander the Great of
Macedonia. From 64 B.C. until the Arab conquest in
A.D. 636, it was part of the Roman Empire except during brief periods. The Arabs made it a trade center for
their extensive empire, but it suffered severely from
the Mongol invasion in 1260 and fell to the Ottoman
Turks in 1516. Syria remained a Turkish province
until World War I.

A secret Anglo-French pact of 1916 put Syria in
the French zone of influence. The League of
Nations gave France a mandate over Syria after
World War I, but the French were forced to put
down several nationalist uprisings. In 1930, France
recognized Syria as an independent republic but
still subject to the mandate. After nationalist demonstrations in 1939, the French high commissioner
suspended the Syrian constitution. In 1941, British
and Free French forces invaded Syria to eliminate
Vichy control. During the rest of World War II,
Syria was an Allied base. Again in 1945, nationalist demonstrations broke into actual fighting, and
British troops had to restore order. Syrian forces
met a series of reverses while participating in the
Arab invasion of Palestine in 1948. In 1958, Egypt
and Syria formed the United Arab Republic, with
Gamal Abdel Nasser of Egypt as president. However, Syria became independent again on Sept. 29,
1961, following a revolution.

In the Arab-Israeli War of 1967, Israel quickly vanquished the Syrian army. Before acceding to the UN
cease-fire, the Israeli forces took control of the fortified
Golan Heights. Syria joined Egypt in attacking Israel in
Oct. 1973 in the fourth Arab-Israeli war, but was
pushed back from initial successes on the Golan
Heights and ended up losing more land. However, in
the settlement worked out by U.S. secretary of state
Henry A. Kissinger in 1974, the Syrians recovered all
the territory lost in 1973.

In the mid-1970s Syria sent some 20,000 troops to
support Muslim Lebanese in their armed conflict with
Christian militants supported by Israel during the civil
war in Lebanon. Syrian troops frequently clashed with
Israeli troops during Israel's 1982 invasion of Lebanon
and remained thereafter as occupiers of large portions
of Lebanon.

In 1990, President Assad ruled out any possibility of
legalizing opposition political parties. In Dec. 1991
voters approved a fourth term for Assad, giving him
99.98% of the vote.

In the 1990s, the slowdown in the Israeli-
Palestinian peace process was echoed in the lack of
progress in Israeli-Syrian relations. Confronted with
a steadily strengthening strategic partnership
between Israel and Turkey, Syria took steps to con-
struct a countervailing alliance by improving relations with Iraq, strengthening ties with Iran, and collaborating more closely with Saudi Arabia. In Dec.
1999, Israeli-Syrian talks resumed after a nearly
four-year hiatus, but soon broke down over discussions about the Golan Heights.

On June 10, 2000, President Hafez al-Assad died.
He had ruled with an iron fist since taking power in a
military coup in 1970. His son, Bashar al-Assad, an
ophthalmologist by training, succeeded him. He has
emulated his father's autocratic rule.

In the summer of 2001, Syria withdrew nearly all of
its 25,000 troops from Beirut. Syrian soldiers, however,
remain in the Lebanese countryside.

In April 2003, shortly after the Iraq war seemed to
be winding down, the Bush administration turned its
ire on Syria, calling the country a rogue nation that
harbored members of Saddam Hussein's regime and
possessed chemical weapons.

In March 2004, Syrian Kurds rioted and clashed
with police for several days after a brawl at a soccer
game. It was Syria's worst unrest in decades.

The U.S. imposed economic sanctions on the country in May, accusing it of continuing to support terrorism.

In Sept. 2004, a UN Security Council resolution
asked Syria to withdraw its 15,000 remaining troops
from Lebanon. Syria responded by moving about 3,000
troops from the vicinity of Beirut to eastern Lebanon,
a gesture viewed by many as merely cosmetic.

Taiwan

REPUBLIC OF CHINA

President: Chen Shui-bian (2000)
Prime Minister: Yu Shyi-kun (2002)
Area: 13,892 sq mi (35,980 sq km)
Population (2004 est.): 22,749,838 (growth rate: 0.6%);
birth rate: 12.7/1000; infant mortality rate: 6.5/1000; life
expectancy: 77.1; density per sq mi: 1,638
Capital and largest city (2003 est.): Taipei, 7,871,900
(metro. area), 2,722,600 (city proper). **Other large
cities:** Kaohsiung, 1,514,900; Tai Chung, 1,069,900;
Tainan, 755,800; Keelung, 410,500. **Monetary unit:**
Taiwan dollar. **Language:** Chinese (Mandarin, official),
Taiwanese (Min), Hakka dialects. **Ethnicity/race:**
Taiwanese (including Hakka) 84%, mainland Chinese
14%, aborigine 2%. **Religions:** mixture of Buddhist,
Confucian, and Taoist 93%, Christian 4.5%, other
2.5%. **Literacy rate:** 86% (1980)
Economic summary: GDP/PPP (2003 est.): $528.6
billion; per capita $23,400. **Real growth rate:** 3.2%.
Inflation: −0.2% (2002 est.). **Unemployment:** 5.1%.
Arable land: 24%. **Agriculture:** rice, corn,
vegetables, fruit, tea; pigs, poultry, beef, milk; fish.
Labor force: 10 million (2003); services 58%, industry
35%, agriculture 7% (2001 est.). **Industries:**
electronics, petroleum refining, chemicals, textiles, iron
and steel, machinery, cement, food processing.
Natural resources: small deposits of coal, natural
gas, limestone, marble, asbestos. **Exports:** $143
billion (f.o.b., 2003 est.): machinery and electrical
equipment 54%, metals, textiles, plastics, chemicals.
Imports: $119.6 billion (f.o.b., 2003 est.): machinery
and electrical equipment 44.5%, minerals, precision
instruments. **Major trading partners:** Hong Kong,
U.S., Japan, China, South Korea.

Geography The Republic of China today consists
of the island of Taiwan, an island 100 mi (161 km)
off the Asian mainland in the Pacific; two off-shore
islands, Kinmen (Quemoy) and Matsu; and the
nearby islets of the Pescadores chain. It is slightly
larger than the combined areas of Massachusetts
and Connecticut.

Government Multiparty democracy.

History Taiwan was inhabited by aborigines of
Malayan descent when Chinese from the areas now
designated as Fukien and Kwangtung began settling it
in the 7th century, becoming the majority. The Portuguese explored the area in 1590, naming it "the Beautiful" (Formosa). In 1624 the Dutch set up forts in the
south, the Spanish in the north. The Dutch forced out
the Spanish in 1641 and controlled the island until
1661, when Chinese general Koxinga took it over and
established an independent kingdom. The Manchus
seized the island in 1683 and held it until 1895, when
it passed to Japan after the first Sino-Japanese War.
Japan developed and exploited Formosa. It was the
target of heavy American bombing during World War
II, and at the close of the war the island was restored
to China.

After the defeat of its armies on the mainland, the
Nationalist government of Generalissimo Chiang Kai-
shek retreated to Taiwan in Dec. 1949. Chiang dominated the island, even though only 15% of the population consisted of the 1949 immigrants, the
Kuomintang. He maintained a 600,000-man army in
the hope of eventually recovering the mainland.
Beijing viewed the Taiwanese government with suspicion and anger, referring to Taiwan as a breakaway
province of China.

The UN seat representing all of China was held by
the Nationalists for over two decades before being lost
in Oct. 1971, when the People's Republic of China was
admitted and Taiwan was forced to abdicate its seat to
Beijing.

Chiang died at 87 of a heart attack on April 5, 1975.
His son, Chiang Ching-kuo, continued as premier and
was a dominant figure in the Taipei regime. In April
1991, President Lee Teng-hui formally declared an end
to emergency rule, which had existed since Chiang's
forces originally occupied the island. In the first full
election in many decades, the governing Kuomintang
in Dec. 1991 won 71% of the vote, affirming the
island's opposition to reunification with China. In Feb.
1993 the president, himself a native Taiwanese, nominated Lien Chan, another native, to be prime minister,
marking a further generational shift away from the
mainland exiles.

In the island's first free presidential election, voters
defied mainland intimidation and gave 54% of the vote
to incumbent president Lee Teng-hui.

President Lee Teng-hui rankled mainland China by
announcing in July 1999 that he was abandoning the
longstanding "One China" policy that has kept the
peace between the small island and its powerful neighbor, and would from now on deal with China on a
"state-to-state basis." China, which has vowed to
someday unite Taiwan with the mainland, retaliated by
conducting submarine warfare exercises and missile
tests near the island in an effort to intimidate its tiny
brazen neighbor, as it had once before in 1996.

In the March 2000 presidential race, voters elected
pro-independence candidate Chen Shui-bian of the
Democratic Progressive Party, ending more than 50
years of Nationalist rule.

The day before March 20, 2004, elections, President
Chen Shui-bian and Vice President Annette Lu survived an assassination attempt. Chen won the election
over Lien Chan by just 30,000 votes out of 13 million
cast. The country's first-ever referendum failed because
less than 50% of eligible voters weighed in on its questions. The referendum asked if Taiwan should arm
itself with additional defensive weapons if China does
not withdraw its missiles and if Taiwan should continue to negotiate with China.

Tajikistan

REPUBLIC OF TAJIKISTAN

President: Imomali Rakhmonov (1992)
Prime Minister: Akil Akilov (1999)
Area: 55,251 sq mi (143,100 sq km)
Population (2004 est.): 7,011,556 (growth rate: 2.1%);
birth rate: 32.6/1000; infant mortality rate: 112.1/1000;
life expectancy: 64.5; density per sq mi: 127
Capital and largest city (2003 est.): Dushanbe, 817,100
(metro. area), 590,300 (city proper). **Other large city:**
Khodzhent (Leninabad), 156,500. **Monetary unit:** Tajik
ruble. **Language:** Tajik (official), Russian widely used in
government and business. **Ethnicity/race:** Tajik 64.9%,
Uzbek 25%, Russian 3.5% (declining because of
emigration), other 6.6%. **Religion:** Islam: Sunni 85%,
Shiite 5%; other 10% (2003 est.). **Literacy rate:** 99%
(2003 est.)
Economic summary: GDP/PPP (2003 est.): $6.996
billion; per capita $1,000. **Real growth rate:** 9.9%.
Inflation: 16%. **Unemployment:** 40% (2002 est.).
Arable land: 5%. **Agriculture:** cotton, grain, fruits,
grapes, vegetables; cattle, sheep, goats. **Labor force:**
3.187 million (2000); agriculture 67%, industry 8%,
services 25% (2000 est.). **Industries:** aluminum, zinc,
lead, chemicals and fertilizers, cement, vegetable oil,
metal-cutting machine tools, refrigerators and freezers.
Natural resources: hydropower, some petroleum,
uranium, mercury, brown coal, lead, zinc, antimony,

tungsten, silver, gold. **Exports:** $750 million (f.o.b., 2003 est.): aluminum, electricity, cotton, fruits, vegetable oil, textiles. **Imports:** $890 million (f.o.b., 2003 est.): electricity, petroleum products, aluminum oxide, machinery and equipment, foodstuffs. **Major trading partners:** Netherlands, Turkey, Russia, Uzbekistan, Switzerland, Hungary, Latvia, Ukraine, Kazakhstan, Turkmenistan, Azerbaijan, India.

Geography Ninety-three percent of Tajikistan's territory is mountainous, and the mountain glaciers are the source of its rivers. Tajikistan is an earthquake-prone area. The republic is bounded by China in the east, Afghanistan to the south, and Uzbekistan and Kyrgyzstan to the west and north. The central Asian republic also includes the Gorno-Badakh Shan Autonomous region. Tajikistan is slightly larger than the state of Illinois.

Government Republic.

History The Tajiks, whose language is nearly identical with Persian, were part of the ancient Persian empire that was ruled by Darius I and later conquered by Alexander the Great (333 B.C.). In the 7th and 8th centuries, Arabs conquered the region and brought Islam. The Tajiks were successively ruled by Uzbeks and then Afghans until claimed by Russia in the 1860s. In 1924, Tajikistan was consolidated into a newly formed Tajik Autonomous Soviet Socialist Republic, which was administratively part of the Uzbek SSR until the Tajik ASSR gained full-fledged republic status in 1929.

Tajikistan declared its sovereignty in Aug. 1990. In 1991, the republic's Communist leadership supported the attempted coup against Soviet president Mikhail Gorbachev. Tajikistan joined with ten other former Soviet republics in the Commonwealth of Independent States on Dec. 21, 1991. A parliamentary republic was proclaimed and presidential rule abolished in Nov. 1992. After independence, Tajikistan experienced sporadic conflict as the Communist-dominated government struggled to combat an insurgency by Islamic and democratic opposition forces. Despite continued international efforts to end the civil war, periodic fighting continued. About 60,000 people lost their lives in Tajikistan's civil war. The conflict ended officially on June 27, 1997, with the signing in Moscow of peace accords between the government of President Imomali Rakhmonov and the United Tajik Opposition (UTO), a coalition of largely Islamic groups. Since then, however, peace has been tenuous, marred regularly by killing sprees by various opposition groups.

A referendum in June 2003 extended the president's term in office for an additional 14 years. Opposition parties cried foul.

Tanzania

UNITED REPUBLIC OF TANZANIA

President: Benjamin William Mkapa (1995)
Prime Minister: Frederick Tluway Sumaye (1995)
Area: 364,898 sq mi (945,087 sq km)[1]
Population (2004 est.): 36,588,225 (growth rate: 2.0%); birth rate: 39.0/1000; infant mortality rate: 102.1/1000; life expectancy: 44.4; density per sq mi: 100
Administrative capital and largest city (2003 est.): Dar es Salaam, 2,489,800; **Official capital:** Dodoma, 164,500. **Monetary unit:** Tanzanian shilling.
Languages: Swahili, English (both official); Arabic; many local languages. **Ethnicity/race:** native African 99% (includes 95% Bantu, consisting of well over 100 tribes), Asian, European, and Arab 1%. **Religions:** mainland: Christian 30%, Islam 35%, indigenous 35%; Zanzibar: more than 99% Islam. **Literacy rate:** 78% (2003 est.)

Economic summary: GDP/PPP (2003 est.): $21.58 billion; per capita $600. **Real growth rate:** 5.2%. **Inflation:** 4.6% **Unemployment:** n.a. **Arable land:** 4%. **Agriculture:** coffee, sisal, tea, cotton, pyrethrum (insecticide made from chrysanthemums), cashew nuts, tobacco, cloves, corn, wheat, cassava (tapioca), bananas, fruits, vegetables; cattle, sheep, goats. **Labor force:** 13.495 million; agriculture 80%, industry and services 20% (2002 est.). **Industries:** agricultural processing (sugar, beer, cigarettes, sisal twine), diamond and gold mining, oil refining, shoes, cement, textiles, wood products, fertilizer, salt. **Natural resources:** hydropower, tin, phosphates, iron ore, coal, diamonds, gemstones, gold, natural gas, nickel. **Exports:** $978 million (f.o.b., 2003 est.): gold, coffee, cashew nuts, manufactures, cotton. **Imports:** $1.674 billion (f.o.b., 2003 est.): consumer goods, machinery and transportation equipment, industrial raw materials, crude oil. **Major trading partners:** India, Japan, Netherlands, UK, Belgium, Kenya, Germany, South Africa, China, U.S., Australia. **Member of Commonwealth of Nations**

1. Including Zanzibar.

Geography Tanzania is in East Africa on the Indian Ocean. To the north are Uganda and Kenya; to the west, Burundi, Rwanda, and Congo; and to the south, Mozambique, Zambia, and Malawi. Its area is three times that of New Mexico. Tanzania contains three of Africa's best-known lakes—Victoria in the north, Tanganyika in the west, and Nyasa in the south. Mount Kilimanjaro in the north, 19,340 ft (5,895 m), is the highest point on the continent. The island of Zanzibar is separated from the mainland by a 22-mile channel.

Government Republic.

History Arab traders first began to colonize the area in 700. Portuguese explorers reached the coastal regions in 1500 and held some control until the 17th century, when the sultan of Oman took power. With what are now Burundi and Rwanda, Tanganyika became the colony of German East Africa in 1885. After World War I, it was administered by Britain under a League of Nations mandate and later as a UN trust territory.

Although not mentioned in old histories until the 12th century, Zanzibar was always believed to have had connections with southern Arabia. The Portuguese made it one of their tributaries in 1503 and later established a trading post, but they were driven from Oman by Arabs in 1698. Zanzibar was declared independent of Oman in 1861 and, in 1890, it became a British protectorate.

Tanganyika became independent on Dec. 9, 1961; Zanzibar on Dec. 10, 1963. On April 26, 1964, the two nations merged into the United Republic of Tanganyika and Zanzibar. The name was changed to Tanzania six months later.

An invasion by Ugandan troops in Nov. 1978 was followed by a counterattack in Jan. 1979, in which 5,000 Tanzanian troops were joined by 3,000 Ugandan exiles opposed to President Idi Amin. Within a month, full-scale war developed. Tanzanian president Julius Nyerere kept troops in Uganda in open support of former Ugandan president Milton Obote, despite protests from opposition groups, until the national elections in Dec. 1980.

In Nov. 1985, Nyerere stepped down as president. Ali Hassan Mwinyi, his vice president, succeeded him.

Running unopposed, Mwinyi was elected president in October. Shortly thereafter plans were announced to study the benefits of instituting a multiparty democracy, and in Oct. 1995 the country's first multiparty elections since independence took place.

On Aug. 7, 1998, the U.S. embassy in Dar es Salaam was bombed by terrorists, killing ten. The same day an even more devastating explosion destroyed the U.S. embassy in neighboring Kenya.

Since taking office in 1995 President Benjamin William Mkapa has sought to increase economic productivity while dealing with serious pollution problems and deforestation. With more than one million people infected with HIV, AIDS care and prevention have been major public health issues. On foreign policy, Tanzania has taken a leading diplomatic role in East Africa, hosting peace talks for the factions fighting in neighboring Burundi. The UN International Criminal Tribunal for Rwanda (ICTR) is located in the town of Arusha. In Oct. 2000, Mkapa was easily reelected. In 2002, opposition leaders and foreign donors criticized the president's costly new $21 million personal jet.

Thailand

KINGDOM OF THAILAND

Ruler: King Bhumibol Adulyadej (1946)
Prime Minister: Thaksin Shinawatra (2001)
Area: 198,455 sq mi (514,000 sq km)
Population (2004 est.): 64,865,523 (growth rate: 0.9%); birth rate: 16.0/1000; infant mortality rate: 21.1/1000; life expectancy: 71.4; density per sq mi: 327
Capital and largest city (2003 est.): Bangkok, 8,838,500 (metro. area), 6,610,800 (city proper). **Other large cities:** Nonthanburi, 304,700; Chiang Mai, 175,500. **Monetary unit:** baht. **Languages:** Thai (Siamese), English (secondary language of the elite), ethnic and regional dialects. **Ethnicity/race:** Thai 75%, Chinese 14%, other 11%. **Religions:** Buddhist 95%, Islam 3.8%, Christian 0.5%, Hindu 0.1%, other 0.6% (1991). **Literacy rate:** 96% (2003 est.)
Economic summary: GDP/PPP (2003 est.): $475.7 billion; per capita $7,400. **Real growth rate:** 6.3%. **Inflation:** 1.8%. **Unemployment:** 2.2%. **Arable land:** 33% (2001 est.). **Agriculture:** rice, cassava (tapioca), rubber, corn, sugarcane, coconuts, soybeans. **Labor force:** 33.4 million (2001 est.); agriculture 54%, industry 15%, services 31% (1996 est.). **Industries:** tourism; textiles and garments, agricultural processing, beverages, tobacco, cement, light manufacturing, such as jewelry; electric appliances and components, computers and parts, integrated circuits, furniture, plastics; world's second-largest tungsten producer and third-largest tin producer. **Natural resources:** tin, rubber, natural gas, tungsten, tantalum, timber, lead, fish, gypsum, lignite, fluorite, arable land. **Exports:** $75.99 billion (f.o.b., 2003 est.): computers, transistors, seafood, clothing, rice. **Imports:** $65.3 billion (f.o.b., 2003 est.): capital goods, intermediate goods and raw materials, consumer goods, fuels. **Major trading partners:** U.S., Japan, Singapore, Hong Kong, China, Malaysia.

Geography Thailand occupies the western half of the Indochinese peninsula and the northern two-thirds of the Malay Peninsula in southeast Asia. Its neighbors are Burma (Myanmar) on the north and west, Laos on the north and northeast, Cambodia on the east, and Malaysia on the south. Thailand is about the size of France.

Government Constitutional monarchy.

History The Thais first began settling their present homeland in the 6th century, and by the end of the 13th century ruled most of the western portion. During the next 400 years, they fought sporadically with the Cambodians to the east and Burmese to the west. Formerly called Siam, Thailand has never experienced foreign rule. The British gained a colonial foothold in the region in 1824, but by 1896 an Anglo-French accord guaranteed the independence of Thailand. A coup in 1932 demoted the monarchy to titular status and established representative government with universal suffrage.

At the outbreak of World War II, Japanese forces attacked Thailand. After five hours of token resistance Thailand yielded to Japan on Dec. 8, 1941, subsequently becoming a staging area for the Japanese campaign against Malaya. Following the demise of a pro-Japanese puppet government in July 1944, Thailand repudiated the declaration of war it had been forced to make in 1942 against Britain and the U.S.

By the late 1960s the nation's problems largely stemmed from conflicts brewing in neighboring Cambodia and Vietnam. Although Thailand had received $2 billion in U.S. economic and military aid since 1950, and had sent troops (paid by the U.S.) to Vietnam while permitting U.S. bomber bases on its territory, the collapse of South Vietnam and Cambodia in spring 1975 brought rapid changes in the country's diplomatic posture. At the Thai government's insistence, the U.S. agreed to withdraw all 23,000 U.S. military personnel remaining in Thailand by March 1976.

Three years of civilian government ended with a military coup on Oct. 6, 1976. Political parties, banned after the coup, gained limited freedom in 1980. The same year, the National Assembly elected Gen. Prem Tinsulanonda as prime minister. Prem continued as prime minister following 1983 and 1986 elections.

Fleeing from Laos, Vietnam, and the murderous regime of Cambodia's Pol Pot, refugees flooded into Thailand in 1978 and 1979. Despite efforts by the United States and other Western countries to resettle them, a total of 130,000 Laotians and Vietnamese were living in camps along the Cambodian border in mid-1980.

On April 3, 1981, a military coup against the Prem government failed. Another coup attempt on Sept. 9, 1985, was crushed by loyal troops after ten hours of fighting in Bangkok. In Feb. 1991, yet another coup yielded another junta, which declared a state of emergency and abolished the constitution. A scandal over a land-reform program caused the fall of the government in May 1995. A succession of governments followed.

Following several years of unprecedented economic growth, Thailand's economy, once one of the strongest in the region, collapsed under the weight of foreign debt in 1997. The Thai economy's downfall set off a chain reaction in the region, sparking the Asian currency crisis. The Thai government quickly accepted restructuring guidelines as a condition of the International Monetary Fund's $17 billion bailout. Thailand's economy, while far from completely recovered, continued to improve over the next several years. The Thai Rak Thai ("Thais Love Thais") party won elections in Jan. 2001 and formed a coalition government with the Chart Thai and New Aspiration Parties. Thaksin Shinawatra became prime minister. The hugely popular Thaksin, a billionaire telecommunications mogul, was indicted in Dec. 2000 on corruption charges but was acquitted in August 2001.

A high-ranking member of al-Qaeda, Riduan Isamuddin, known as Hambali, was captured in Aug. 2003 in Thailand in a joint operation between the CIA and Thai police. Officials believe Hambali, an Indonesian, organized the 2002 bombing of a Bali nightclub and the Aug. 2003 attack on the Marriott hotel in Jakarta.

Violence has plagued Thailand's Muslim-dominated southern provinces since the beginning of 2004, with armed insurgents attacking police stations, security stations, and military depots. Nearly 200 people have been killed in the attacks, which officials attribute to Islamic militants.

Togo

REPUBLIC OF TOGO

National name: République Togolaise
President: Gen. Gnassingbé Eyadema (1967)
Prime Minister: Koffi Sama (2002)
Area: 21,925 sq mi (56,785 sq km)
Population (2004 est.): 5,556,812 (growth rate: 2.3%); birth rate: 34.4/1000; infant mortality rate: 67.7/1000; life expectancy: 53.1; density per sq mi: 253
Capital and largest city (2003 est.): Lomé, 749,700 (metro. area), 676,400 (city proper). **Monetary unit:** CFA Franc. **Languages:** French (official, commerce); Ewé, Mina (south); Kabyé, Cotocoli (north); and many dialects. **Ethnicity/race:** native African (37 tribes; largest and most important are Ewe, Mina, and Kabre) 99%, European and Syrian-Lebanese less than 1%. **Religions:** Indigenous beliefs 51%, Christian 29%, Islam 20%. **Literacy rate:** 61% (2003 est.)
Economic summary: GDP/PPP (2003 est.): $8.232 billion; per capita $1,500. **Real growth rate:** 3.2%. **Inflation:** 4% (2002 est.). **Unemployment:** n.a. **Arable land:** 41%. **Agriculture:** coffee, cocoa, cotton, yams, cassava (tapioca), corn, beans, rice, millet, sorghum; livestock; fish. **Labor force:** 1.74 million (1996); agriculture 65%, industry 5%, services 30% (1998 est.). **Industries:** phosphate mining, agricultural processing, cement; handicrafts, textiles, beverages. **Natural resources:** phosphates, limestone, marble, arable land. **Exports:** $398.1 million (f.o.b., 2003 est.): reexports, cotton, phosphates, coffee, cocoa. **Imports:** $501.3 million (f.o.b., 2003 est.): machinery and equipment, foodstuffs, petroleum products. **Major trading partners:** Ghana, Benin, Burkina Faso, Philippines, Niger, France, China, Netherlands, Germany, UK, Italy.

Geography   Togo, twice the size of Maryland, is on the south coast of West Africa bordering on Ghana to the west, Burkina Faso to the north, and Benin to the east. The Gulf of Guinea coastline, only 32 mi long (51 km), is low and sandy. The only port is at Lomé. The Togo hills traverse the central section.

Government   Republic transitioning to multiparty democratic rule.

History   The Voltaic peoples and the Kwa were the earliest known inhabitants. The Ewe followed in the 14th century, and the Ane in the 18th century. The Danish claimed the land in the 18th century, but by 1884 it was established as a German colony (Togoland). The area was split between the British and the French under League of Nations mandates after World War I and subsequently administered as UN trusteeships. The British portion voted for incorporation with Ghana. The French portion became Togo, which declared its independence on April 27, 1960.

Togo's first democratically elected president, Sylvano Olympius, was overthrown in 1963. He was shot and killed by Sgt. Etienne Eyadema while he attempted to scale the walls of the American Embassy to seek asylum. The government of Nicolas Grunitzky was overthrown in a bloodless coup on Jan. 13, 1967, led by Lt. Col. Etienne Eyadema (now called Gen. Gnassingbé Eyadema). A National Reconciliation Committee was set up to rule the country, but in April, Eyadema dissolved the committee and took over as president. He suspended the constitution, banned political parties, and created a cult of personality around his presidency—his official biography describes him as a "force of nature." Under pressure from the West, Eyadema legalized opposition parties in 1993, but the first multiparty presidential election in Aug. 1993 (which gave Eyadema more than 96% of the vote) was considered fraudulent, as was his 1998 reelection. In 2003, Eyadema was reelected, continuing his tenure as the longest-serving ruler in Africa—in 2004, it had been 37 years.

Tonga

KINGDOM OF TONGA

Sovereign: King Taufa'ahau Tupou IV (1965)
Prime Minister: Prince Lavaka Ata Ulukalala (2000)
Area: 289 sq mi (748 sq km)
Population (2004 est.): 110,237 (growth rate: 1.9%); birth rate: 24.9/1000; infant mortality rate: 13.0/1000; life expectancy: 69.2; density per sq mi: 382
Capital and largest city (2003 est.): Nuku'alofa, 24,500. **Monetary unit:** Pa'anga. **Languages:** Tongan (an Austronesian language), English. **Ethnicity/race:** Polynesian, European (about 300). **Religions:** Christian (Free Wesleyan Church claims over 30,000 adherents). **Literacy rate:** 99% (1996 est.)
Economic summary: GDP/PPP (2001 est.): $236 million; per capita $2,200. **Real growth rate:** 3%. **Inflation:** 10.3% (1996 est.). **Unemployment:** 13.3% (1996 est.). **Arable land:** 24%. **Agriculture:** squash, coconuts, copra, bananas, vanilla beans, cocoa, coffee, ginger, black pepper; fish. **Labor force:** 33,908 (1996); agriculture 65% (1997 est.). **Industries:** tourism, fishing. **Natural resources:** fish, fertile soil. **Exports:** $27 million (f.o.b., 2002 est.): squash, fish, vanilla beans, root crops. **Imports:** $86 million (f.o.b., 2002 est.): foodstuffs, machinery and transport equipment, fuels, chemicals. **Major trading partners:** Japan, U.S., Greece, New Zealand, Fiji, Australia, China. **Member of Commonwealth of Nations**

Geography   Situated east of the Fiji Islands in the South Pacific, Tonga (also called the Friendly Islands) consists of some 150 islands, of which 36 are inhabited. Most of the islands contain active volcanic craters; others are coral atolls.

Government   Hereditary constitutional monarchy.

History   Polynesians have lived on Tonga for at least 3,000 years. The Dutch were the first to explore the islands, landing on Tafahi in 1616. British explorer James Cook landed on islands in 1773 and 1777, and dubbed them the Friendly Islands. The current royal dynasty of Tonga was founded in 1831 by Taufa'ahau Tupou, who took the name George I. He consolidated the kingdom by conquest and in 1875 granted a constitution. In 1900, his great-grandson, George II, signed a treaty of friendship with Britain, and the country became a British protected state. The treaty was revised in 1959. Tonga became independent on June 4, 1970.

The government is largely controlled by the king, his nominees, and a small group of hereditary nobles. In the 1990s a movement began aimed at curtailing the powers of the monarchy, and the Tongan Pro-Democracy Movement (TPDM) has continued to gain in popular support. In 1999, Tonga gained UN membership.

The king's official court jester, American Jesse Bogdonoff, a former salesman of magnets to relieve back pain, was sued by the government in 2002 for squandering $26 million of Tonga's money (40% of its annual revenue) in unsound investment schemes. In 2004, he agreed to pay a $1 million settlement.

The king, who celebrated his 85th birthday in 2003, has grown increasingly authoritarian and has curtailed press freedom.

In 2004, the national airline was forced to close after running out of money for repairs.

Trinidad and Tobago

REPUBLIC OF TRINIDAD AND TOBAGO

President: Maxwell Richards (2003)
Prime Minister: Patrick Manning (2001)
Area: 1,980 sq mi (5,128 sq km)
Population (2004 est.): 1,096,585 (growth rate: –0.7%); birth rate: 12.8/1000; infant mortality rate: 24.6/1000; life expectancy: 69.3; density per sq mi: 554
Capital and largest city (2003 est.): Port-of-Spain, 263,800 (metro. area), 45,300 (city proper). **Monetary unit:** Trinidad and Tobago dollar. **Languages:** English (official), Hindi, French, Spanish, Chinese. **Ethnicity/ race:** East Indian (a local term—primarily immigrants from northern India) 40.3%, black 39.5%, mixed 18.4%, white 0.6%, Chinese and other 1.2%. **Religions:** Roman Catholic 29.4%, Hindu 23.8%, Anglican 10.9%, Islam 5.8%, Presbyterian 3.4%, other 26.7%. **Literacy rate:** 99% (2003 est.)
Economic summary: GDP/PPP (2003 est.): $10.6 billion; per capita $9,600. **Real growth rate:** 4.5%. **Inflation:** 3.7%. **Unemployment:** 10.9%. **Arable land:** 15%. **Agriculture:** cocoa, sugarcane, rice, citrus, coffee, vegetables; poultry. **Labor force:** 564,000 (2000); construction and utilities 12.4%, manufacturing, mining, and quarrying 14%, agriculture 9.5%, services 64.1% (1997 est.). **Industries:** petroleum, chemicals, tourism, food processing, cement, beverages, cotton textiles. **Natural resources:** petroleum, natural gas, asphalt. **Exports:** $4.9 billion (f.o.b., 2003 est.): petroleum and petroleum products, chemicals, steel products, fertilizer, sugar, cocoa, coffee, citrus, flowers. **Imports:** $3.917 billion (f.o.b., 2003 est.): machinery, transportation equipment, manufactured goods, food, live animals. **Major trading partners:** U.S., Jamaica, France, Côte d'Ivoire, UK, Japan, Brazil. **Member of Commonwealth of Nations**

Geography Trinidad and Tobago lie in the Caribbean Sea off the northeast coast of Venezuela. Trinidad, the larger at 1,864 sq mi (4,828 sq km), is mainly flat and rolling, with mountains in the north that reach a height of 3,085 ft (940 m) at Mount Aripo. Tobago, at just 116 sq mi (300 sq km), is heavily forested with hardwood trees.

Government Parliamentary democracy.

History When Trinidad was explored by Columbus in 1498, it was inhabited by the Arawaks; Carib Indians inhabited Tobago. Trinidad remained in Spanish possession, despite raids by other European nations, until it was ceded to Britain in 1802. Tobago passed between Britain and France several times, but it was ultimately given to Britain in 1814. Slavery was abolished in 1834. Between 1845 and 1917, thousands of indentured workers were brought from India to work on sugarcane plantations. In 1889 Trinidad and Tobago were made a single colony.

Partial self-government was instituted in 1925, and from 1958 to 1962 the nation was part of the West Indies Federation. On Aug. 31, 1962, it became independent and on Aug. 1, 1976, Trinidad and Tobago became a republic, remaining within the Commonwealth. While the country is a stable democracy and enjoys the highest living standards in the Caribbean thanks to oil revenue, tension between East Indians and blacks has underlined much of political life. In 1970 rioting and an army mutiny against the East Indian population prompted a state of emergency, which lasted for two years.

Eric Williams, "Father of the Nation" and leader of the People's National Movement (PNM), which is largely supported by blacks, governed from 1956 until his death in 1981. In Dec. 1986 the multiracial National Alliance for Reconstruction (NAR), based in Tobago, won a parliamentary majority, promising to sell most state-owned companies, reorganize the civil service, and reduce dependence on oil.

In 1990, to protest the NAR government, some 100 radical black Muslims blew up the police station in an attempted coup, in which the prime minister and other officials were held hostage for six days. The NAR was defeated in 1991, and the PNM returned to power. In 1995, the East Indian–based party, the United National Congress (UNC), led by Basdeo Panday, formed a coalition government with the NAR. In 2000, Panday narrowly won another term.

In Dec. 2001 elections, both the governing UNC party and the People's National Movement (PNM) party gained 18 seats each. The two parties agreed to allow President Robinson to select the prime minister to end the impasse. But when Robinson selected Patrick Manning of the PNM because of his "moral and spiritual values," the opposition angrily called for new elections. In Oct. 2002 elections, Manning's party declared victory. Maxwell Richards, a university dean, was selected president by Parliament in 2003. In Aug. 2004, Caroni, the state-owned sugar company, closed down; more than 8,000 lost their jobs.

Tunisia

REPUBLIC OF TUNISIA

National name: Al-Joumhouria Attunisia
President: Zine al-Abidine Ben Ali (1987)
Prime Minister: Mohamed Ghannouchi (1999)
Area: 63,170 sq mi (163,610 sq km)
Population (2004 est.): 9,974,722 (growth rate: 1.0%); birth rate: 15.7/1000; infant mortality rate: 25.8/1000; life expectancy: 74.7; density per sq mi: 158
Capital and largest city (2003 est.): Tunis, 1,660,300 (metro. area), 699,700 (city proper). **Monetary unit:** Tunisian dinar. **Languages:** Arabic (official, commerce), French (commerce). **Ethnicity/race:** Arab-Berber 98%, European 1%, Jewish and other 1%. **Religions:** Islam (Sunni) 98%, Christian 1%, Jewish and other 1%. **Literacy rate:** 74% (2003 est.)
Economic summary: GDP/PPP (2003 est.): $68.78 billion; per capita $6,900. **Real growth rate:** 6%. **Inflation:** 2.7%. **Unemployment:** 14.3%. **Arable land:** 19%. **Agriculture:** olives, olive oil, grain, dairy products, tomatoes, citrus fruit, beef, sugar beets, dates, almonds. **Labor force:** 3.5 million; note: shortage of skilled labor (2001 est.); services 55%, industry 23%, agriculture 22% (1995 est.). **Industries:** petroleum, mining (particularly phosphate and iron ore), tourism, textiles, footwear, agribusiness, beverages. **Natural resources:** petroleum, phosphates, iron ore, lead, zinc, salt. **Exports:** $8.035 billion (f.o.b., 2003 est.): textiles, mechanical goods,

phosphates and chemicals, agricultural products, hydrocarbons. **Imports:** $10.3 billion (f.o.b., 2003): textiles, machinery and equipment, hydrocarbons, chemicals, food. **Major trading partners:** France, Italy, Germany, spain, Libya, Belgium.

Geography Tunisia, at the northernmost bulge of Africa, thrusts out toward Sicily to mark the division between the eastern and western Mediterranean Sea. Twice the size of South Carolina, it is bordered on the west by Algeria and by Libya on the south. Coastal plains on the east rise to a north-south escarpment that slopes gently to the west. The Sahara Desert lies in the southernmost part. Tunisia is more mountainous in the north, where the Atlas range continues from Algeria.

Government Republic.

History Tunisia was settled by the Phoenicians in the 12th century B.C. By the sixth and fifth centuries B.C., the great city-state of Carthage (derived from the Phoenician name for "new city") dominated much of the western Mediterranean. The three Punic Wars between Rome and Carthage (the second was the most famous, pitting the Roman general Scipio Africanus against Carthage's Hannibal) led to the complete destruction of Carthage by 146 B.C.

Except for an interval of Vandal conquest in A.D. 439–533, Carthage was part of the Roman Empire until the Arab conquest of 648–669. It was then ruled by various Arab and Berber dynasties, followed by the Turks, who took it in 1570–1574 and made it part of the Ottoman Empire until the 19th century. In the late 16th century, it was a stronghold for the Barbary pirates. French troops occupied the country in 1881, and the bey, the local Tunisian ruler, signed a treaty acknowledging it as a French protectorate.

Nationalist agitation forced France to recognize Tunisian independence and sovereignty in 1956. The Constituent Assembly deposed the bey on July 25, 1957, declared Tunisia a republic, and elected Habib Bourguiba as president. Bourguiba maintained a pro-Western foreign policy that earned him enemies. Tunisia refused to break relations with the U.S. during the Arab-Israeli War in June 1967. Concerned with Islamic fundamentalist plots against the state, the government stepped up efforts to eradicate the movement, including censorship and frequent detention of suspects.

In 1987, the aged Bourguiba was declared mentally unfit to continue as president and was removed from office in a bloodless coup. He was succeeded by Gen. Zine al-Abidine Ben Ali, whose tenure has been marked by repression, a poor human rights record, the rise in Islamic fundamentalism, and growing anti-Western sentiments among the populace. Ben Ali was reelected in Oct. 1999 with 99% of the vote in an election criticized by many human rights observers. In May 2000 Ben Ali's Constitutional Democratic Assembly Party swept local elections with 92% of the vote, in a contest many opposition leaders boycotted. However, Tunisia's economy continued to improve in the late 1990s, making the country one of the most attractive in Africa for foreign investors. In May 2002, a referendum passed that ended the three-term limit for the presidency. It permitted Ben Ali, who has served as president for more than 15 years, to run for two more terms. Opposition parties protested. In 2004, Human Rights Watch accused Tunisia of keeping 40 political prisoners in solitary confinement for years, some for up to 13 years. The government has denied the accusations.

Turkey

REPUBLIC OF TURKEY

National name: Türkiye Cumhuriyeti
President: Ahmet Necdet Sezer (2000)
Prime Minister: Recep Tayyip Erdogan (2003)
Area: 301,382 sq mi (incl. 9,121 in Europe) (780,580 sq km)
Population (2004 est.): 68,893,918 (growth rate: 1.1%); birth rate: 17.2/1000; infant mortality rate: 42.6/1000; life expectancy: 72.1; density per sq mi: 229
Capital (2003 est.): Ankara, 3,582,000 (metro. area), 3,456,100 (city proper). **Largest cities:** Istanbul, 10,048,900 (metro. area), 9,419,000 (city proper); Izmir, 2,398,200; Bursa, 1,288,900; Adana, 1,219,900; Gaziantep, 979,500. **Monetary unit:** Turkish lira.
Language: Turkish (official), Kurdish, Arabic, Armenian, Greek. **Ethnicity/race:** Turkish 80%, Kurdish 20% (estimated). **Religion:** Islam (mostly Sunni) 99.8%, other 0.2% (mostly Christians and Jews). **Literacy rate:** 87% (2003 est.)
Economic summary: GDP/PPP (2003 est.): $455.3 billion; per capita $6,700. **Real growth rate:** 5%. **Inflation:** 18.4%. **Unemployment:** 11.3% (plus underemployment of 6.1%). **Arable land:** 35%. **Agriculture:** tobacco, cotton, grain, olives, sugar beets, pulses, citrus; livestock. **Labor force:** 23.8 million (2001 3rd quarter); note: about 1.2 million Turks work abroad; agriculture 40%, services 38%, industry 22% (2001). **Industries:** textiles, food processing, autos, mining (coal, chromite, copper, boron), steel, petroleum, construction, lumber, paper. **Natural resources:** antimony, coal, chromium, mercury, copper, borate, sulfur, iron ore, arable land, hydropower. **Exports:** $49.12 billion (f.o.b., 2003 est.): apparel, foodstuffs, textiles, metal manufactures, transport equipment. **Imports:** $62.43 billion (f.o.b., 2003 est.): machinery, chemicals, semi-finished goods, fuels, transport equipment. **Major trading partners:** Germany, U.S., UK, Italy, France, Russia, Switzerland.

Geography Turkey is at the northeast end of the Mediterranean Sea in southeast Europe and southwest Asia. To the north is the Black Sea and to the west is the Aegean Sea. Its neighbors are Greece and Bulgaria to the west, Russia and Ukraine to the north (through the Black Sea), Georgia, Armenia, Azerbaijan, and Iran to the east, and Syria and Iraq to the south. The Dardanelles, the Sea of Marmara, and the Bosporus divide the country. Turkey in Europe comprises an area about equal to the state of Massachusetts. Turkey in Asia is about the size of Texas. Its center is a treeless plateau rimmed by mountains.

Government Republican parliamentary democracy.

History Anatolia (Turkey in Asia) was occupied in about 1900 B.C. by the Indo-European Hittites and, after the Hittite Empire's collapse in 1200 B.C., by Phrygians and Lydians. The Persian Empire occupied the area in the 6th century B.C., giving way to the Roman Empire, then later the Byzantine Empire. The Ottoman Turks first appeared in the early 13th century, subjugating Turkish and Mongol bands pressing against the eastern borders of Byzantium and making the Christian Balkan states their vassals. They gradually spread through the Near East and Balkans, capturing Constantinople in 1453 and storming the gates of Vienna two centuries later. At its height, the Ottoman Empire stretched from the Persian Gulf to western Algeria. Lasting for 600 years, the Ottoman Empire was not only one of the most powerful empires in the history of the Mediterranean region, but it generated a great cultural outpouring of Islamic art, architecture, and literature.

After the reign of Sultan Süleyman I the Magnificent (1494–1566), the Ottoman Empire began to decline politically, administratively, and economically. By the 18th century, Russia was seeking to establish itself as the protector of Christians in Turkey's Balkan territories. Russian ambitions were checked by Britain and France in the Crimean War (1854–1856), but the Russo-Turkish War (1877–1878) gave Bulgaria virtual independence and Romania and Serbia liberation from their nominal allegiance to the sultan. Turkish weakness stimulated a revolt of young liberals known as the Young Turks in 1909. They forced Sultan Abdul Hamid to grant a constitution and install a liberal government. However, reforms were no barrier to further defeats in a war with Italy (1911–1912) and the Balkan Wars (1912–1913). Turkey sided with Germany in World War I, and, as a result, lost territory at the conclusion of the war.

Turkey's current boundaries were drawn in 1923 at the Conference of Lausanne, and Turkey became a republic with Kemal Atatürk as the first president. The Ottoman sultanate and caliphate were abolished, and modernization, reform, and industrialization began under Atatürk's direction. He secularized Turkish society, reducing Islam's dominant role and replacing Arabic with the Latin alphabet for writing the Turkish language. After Atatürk's death in 1938, parliamentary government and a multiparty system gradually took root in Turkey, despite periods of instability and brief intervals of military rule. Neutral during most of World War II, Turkey, on Feb. 23, 1945, declared war on Germany and Japan, but it took no active part in the conflict. Turkey became a full member of NATO in 1952, was a signatory in the Balkan Entente (1953), joined the Baghdad Pact (1955; later CENTO), joined the Organization for European Economic Cooperation (OEEC) and the Council of Europe, and became an associate member of the European Common Market in 1963.

Turkey invaded Cyprus by sea and air on July 20, 1974, following the failure of diplomatic efforts to resolve conflicts between Turkish and Greek Cypriots. Turkey unilaterally announced a cease-fire on Aug. 16, after having gained control of 40% of the island. Turkish Cypriots established their own state in the north on Feb. 13, 1975. In July 1975, after a 30-day warning, Turkey took control of all the U.S. installations except the joint defense base at Incirlik, which it reserved for "NATO tasks alone."

The establishment of military government in Sept. 1980 stopped the slide toward anarchy and brought some improvement in the economy. A Constituent Assembly, consisting of the six-member National Security Council and members appointed by them, drafted a new constitution that was approved by an overwhelming (91.5%) majority of the voters in a Nov. 6, 1982, referendum. Martial law was gradually lifted. The military, however, effectively continues to control the country.

About 12 million Kurds, roughly 20% of Turkey's population, live in the southeast region of Turkey. Turkey, however, does not officially recognize Kurds as a minority group and is therefore exempted from protecting their rights. Oppression of Kurds and Kurdish culture led to the emergence in 1984 of the Kurdistan Workers' Party (PKK), a militant Kurdish terrorist campaign under the leadership of Abdullah Ocalan. Although the guerrilla movement sought independence at first, by the late 1980s the rebel Kurds were willing to accept an autonomous state or a federation with Turkey. About 35,000 have died in clashes between the military and the PKK during the 1980s and 1990s. On Feb. 16, 1999, Ocalan was captured. He was tried and convicted of treason and separatism on June 2, 1999, and sentenced to death.

On Aug. 17, 1999, western Turkey was devastated by an earthquake (magnitude 7.4) that left more than 17,000 dead and 200,000 homeless. Another huge earthquake struck in November.

Construction on a $3 billion, 1,000-mile oil pipeline running from Baku, Azerbaijan, to the Mediterranean port city of Ceyhan began in Sept. 2002. It is expected to bolster the economy.

In Nov. 2002 elections, the recently formed Justice and Development Party (AK) won. Its leader, Recep Tayyip Erdogan, was barred from becoming prime minister, however, because of a conviction for "inciting religious hatred" by reciting an Islamic poem at a rally in 1998. Another popular AK leader, Abdullah Gul, served as prime minister until Turkish law was amended to permit Erdogan to run for a seat in parliament again, which he easily won. Gul resigned as prime minister, making way for Erdogan.

In March 2003, U.S.-Turkish relations were severely strained when Turkey's parliament narrowly failed to pass a resolution permitting the U.S. to use Turkish bases as a launching pad for the pending war against Iraq. Turkish opinion polls reported that an overwhelming 90% of Turks were against war in Iraq, but the U.S. had promised the country much-needed economic aid.

In Nov. 2003, two terrorist attacks rocked Istanbul. On Nov. 17, truck bombs exploded near two synagogues; on Nov. 22, the British Consulate and a British bank were targeted. More than 50 were killed and hundreds were wounded in the attacks; al-Qaeda is believed to be responsible.

In an effort to make itself more attractive for potential EU membership, Turkey has begun revamping some of its repressive laws and policies. In 2003, its parliament passed a law reducing the military's role in political life, and offered partial amnesty to PKK members, many of whom have sought refuge in northern Iraq. In 2004, Turkish state television broadcast the first Kurdish language program and the government freed four Kurdish activists from prison. Turkey also abolished the death penalty in all but exceptional cases.

Turkmenistan

TURKMENISTAN

President-for-Life: Saparmurad A. Niyazov (1990)
Area: 188,455 sq mi (488,100 sq km)
Population (2004 est.): 4,863,169 (growth rate: 1.8%); birth rate: 27.8/1000; infant mortality rate: 73.1/1000; life expectancy: 61.3; density per sq mi: 26
Capital and largest city (2003 est.): Ashgabat, 727,700. **Other large cities:** Chardzhou, 213,500; Tashauz, 160,400. **Monetary unit:** Manat.
Languages: Turkmen 72%; Russian 12%; Uzbek 9%, other 7%. **Ethnicity/race:** Turkmen 85%, Uzbek 5%, Russian 4%, other 6% (2003). **Religions:** Islam 89%, Eastern Orthodox 9%, unknown 2%. **Literacy rate:** 98% (1989 est.)
Economic summary: GDP/PPP (2003 est.): $27.07 billion; per capita $5,700. **Real growth rate:** 20%. **Inflation:** 11%. **Unemployment:** n.a. **Arable land:** 3%. **Agriculture:** cotton, grain; livestock. **Labor force:** 2.34 million (1996); agriculture 48%, industry 15%, services 37% (1998 est.). **Industries:** natural gas, oil, petroleum products, textiles, food processing. **Natural resources:** petroleum, natural gas, coal, sulfur, salt. **Exports:** $3.355 billion (f.o.b., 2003 est.): gas 57%, oil 26%, cotton fiber 3%, textiles 2% (2001). **Imports:** $2.472 billion (f.o.b., 2003 est.): machinery and equipment 60%, foodstuffs 15% (1999). **Major trading partners:** Ukraine, Italy, Iran, Turkey, Russia, UAE, U.S., China, Germany.

Geography Turkmenistan (formerly Turkmenia) is bounded by the Caspian Sea in the west, Kazakhstan in the north, Uzbekistan in the east, and Iran and Afghanistan in the south. About nine-tenths of Turkmenistan is desert, chiefly the Kara-Kum. One of the world's largest sand deserts, it is approximately 138,966 sq mi (360,000 sq km).

Government One-party republic.

History Turkmenistan was once part of the ancient Persian Empire. The Turkmen people were originally pastoral nomads and some of them continued this way of life up into the 20th century, living in transportable dome-shaped felt tents. The territory was ruled by the Seljuk Turks in the 11th century. The Mongols of Ghenghis Khan conquered the land in the 13th century and dominated the area for the next two centuries until they were deposed in the late 15th century by invading Uzbeks. Prior to the 19th century, Turkmenia was divided into two lands, one belonging to the khanate of Khiva and the other belonging to the khanate of Bukhara. In 1868, the khanate of Khiva was made part of the Russian empire and Turkmenia became known as the Transcaspia Region of Russian Turkistan. Turkmenistan was later formed out of the Turkistan Autonomous Soviet Socialist Republic, founded in 1922, and was made an independent Soviet Socialist Republic on May 13, 1925. It was the poorest of the Soviet republics.

Turkmenistan declared its sovereignty in Aug. 1990 and became a member of the Commonwealth of Independent States on Dec. 21, 1991, together with ten other former Soviet republics. It established a government more authoritarian than those functioning in the other newly independent central Asian republics. President Saparmurad A. Niyazov, also called the Turkmenbashi (Leader of All Turkmens), has attempted to create a cult of personality through extravagant self-promotion. Cities, aftershave, and a meteor now bear his name. In 2002, he renamed all the months of the calendar—April is now named after his mother. Niyazov was voted president-for-life by his rubber-stamp Parliament in 1999.

In the 1990s, Turkmenistan exported gas through a Russian pipeline, bringing in about $1 billion per year. But in 1993, Russia closed down Turkmenistan's only pipeline because it competed with Russia's own gas exportation. Turkmenistan was limited to exporting gas to its impoverished central Asian neighbors, who were unable to pay their bills. The nation then opened a pipeline route to Iran, generally agreed to be the most economical route for exporting Caspian oil, and thus ruffled the feathers of Iran's enemy, the U.S. So far, the new plan has not brought in money, and the country is living off loans from Western countries such as Germany who hope to partner with the oil-rich, money-poor country. In 2003, Russia agreed to buy 60 billion cubic meters of gas from Turkmenistan annually. At the time of the deal, Turkmenistan began to restrict the rights of its ethnic Russian citizens, infuriating Russia.

An alleged assassination attempt against Niyazov in Nov. 2002 (thought by outsiders to have been staged) resulted in the conviction of 46 opposition leaders and critics of the government.

In recent years, the country's educational system has degenerated significantly—the number of years of school required has been reduced, the curriculum has grown increasingly vocational, and substantial classroom time is devoted to political propaganda, including the president's own book, *Rukhnama* (Book of the Soul).

Tuvalu

Sovereign: Queen Elizabeth II (1952)
Governor-General: Faimalaga Luka (2003)
Prime Minister: Maatia Toafa (2004)
Area: 10 sq mi (26 sq km)
Population (2004 est.): 11,468 (growth rate: 1.4%); birth rate: 21.6/1000; infant mortality rate: 20.7/1000; life expectancy: 67.7; density per sq mi: 1,142
Capital and largest city (2003 est.): Funafuti, 5,300.
   Monetary unit: Australian dollar. **Languages:** Tuvaluan, English, Samoan, Kiribati (on the island of Nui). **Ethnicity/race:** Polynesian 96%, Micronesian 4%. **Religion:** Church of Tuvalu (Congregationalist) 97%, Seventh-Day Adventist 1.4%, Baha'i 1%, other 0.6%. **Literacy rate:** n.a
Economic summary: GDP/PPP (2000 est.): n.a.; per capita $1,100. **Real growth rate:** 3%. **Inflation:** 5%. **Unemployment:** n.a. **Arable land:** 0%. **Agriculture:** coconuts; fish. **Labor force:** 7,000 (2001 est.); people make a living mainly through exploitation of the sea, reefs, and atolls and from wages sent home by those working abroad (mostly workers in the phosphate industry and sailors). **Industries:** fishing, tourism, copra. **Natural resources:** fish. **Exports:** $1 million (f.o.b., 2002): copra, fish. **Imports:** $79 million (c.i.f., 2002): food, animals, mineral fuels, machinery, manufactured goods. **Major trading partners:** UK, Italy, Denmark, Fiji, Hungary, Japan. **Member of Commonwealth of Nations**

Geography Tuvalu consists of nine small islands scattered over 500,000 sq mi of the western Pacific, just south of the equator. The islands include Niulakita, Nukulaelae, Funafuti, Nukufetau, Vaitupu, Nui, Niutao, Nanumaga (Nanumanga), and Nanumea.

Government Constitutional monarchy with a parliamentary democracy.

History Formerly the Ellice Islands, Tuvalu's first Polynesian settlers were probably Samoans or Tongans. The Ellice Islands became a British protectorate in 1892 and were annexed by Britain in 1915–1916 as part of the Gilbert and Ellice Islands Colony. The Ellice Islands were separated from the Gilberts in 1975, given home rule, and renamed Tuvalu. Full independence was granted on Sept. 30, 1978, but it remained part of the Commonwealth. In 1979, the U.S. gave Tuvalu four islands that had been U.S. territory.

In 1997, the government adopted a strong stance on the need to control emissions of greenhouse gases in order to ensure the survival of low-lying island nations, which are threatened by rising sea levels—Tuvalu's highest point is just 16 ft above sea level. In 2000, Tuvalu became a member of the United Nations.

Uganda

REPUBLIC OF UGANDA

President: Yoweri Museveni (1986)
Prime Minister: Apolo Nsibambi (1999)
Area: 91,135 sq mi (236,040 sq km)
Population (2004 est.): 26,404,543 (growth rate: 3.0%); birth rate: 46.3/1000; infant mortality rate: 86.2/1000; life expectancy: 45.3; density per sq mi: 290
Capital and largest city (2003 est.): Kampala, 1,461,600 (metro. area), 1,244,000 (city proper).
   Monetary unit: Ugandan new shilling. **Languages:** English (official), Ganda or Luganda, other Niger-Congo languages, Nilo-Saharan languages, Swahili, Arabic. **Ethnicity/race:** Baganda 17%, Ankole 8%, Basoga 8%, Iteso 8%, Bakiga 7%, Langi 6%, Rwanda 6%, Bagisu 5%, Acholi 4%, Lugbara 4%,

Batoro 3%, Bunyoro 3%, Alur 2%, Bagwere 2%, Bakonjo 2%, Jopodhola 2%, Karamojong 2%, Rundi 2%, non-African (European, Asian, Arab) 1%, other 8%. **Religions:** Roman Catholic 33%, Protestant 33%, Islam 16%, indigenous beliefs 18%. **Literacy rate:** 70% (2003 est.)

Economic summary: GDP/PPP (2003 est.): $36.1 billion; per capita $1,400. **Real growth rate:** 4.4%. **Inflation:** 0.1% (2002 est.). **Unemployment:** n.a. **Arable land:** 25%. **Agriculture:** coffee, tea, cotton, tobacco, cassava (tapioca), potatoes, corn, millet, pulses; beef, goat meat, milk, poultry; cut flowers. **Labor force:** 12 million (2001 est.); agriculture 82%, industry 5%, services 13% (1999 est.). **Industries:** sugar, brewing, tobacco, cotton textiles, cement. **Natural resources:** copper, cobalt, hydropower, limestone, salt, arable land. **Exports:** $495 million (f.o.b., 2003 est.): coffee, fish and fish products, tea; gold, cotton, flowers, horticultural products. **Imports:** $1.179 billion (f.o.b., 2003 est.): capital equipment, vehicles, petroleum, medical supplies; cereals. **Major trading partners:** Belgium, Netherlands, Germany, Spain, Hong Kong, U.S., UK, Italy, Portugal, Kenya, South Africa, India. **Member of the Commonwealth of Nations**

Geography Uganda, twice the size of Pennsylvania, is in East Africa. It is bordered on the west by Congo, on the north by the Sudan, on the east by Kenya, and on the south by Tanzania and Rwanda. The country, which lies across the equator, is divided into three main areas—swampy lowlands, a fertile plateau with wooded hills, and a desert region. Lake Victoria forms part of the southern border.

Government Multiparty democractic republic.

History About 500 B.C. Bantu-speaking peoples migrated to the area now called Uganda. By the 14th century, three kingdoms dominated, Buganda (meaning "state of the Gandas"), Bunyoro, and Ankole. Uganda was first explored by Europeans as well as Arab traders in 1844. An Anglo-German agreement of 1890 declared it to be in the British sphere of influence in Africa, and the Imperial British East Africa Company was chartered to develop the area. The company did not prosper financially, and in 1894 a British protectorate was proclaimed. Few Europeans permanently settled in Uganda, but it attracted many Indians, who became important players in Ugandan commerce.

Uganda became independent on Oct. 9, 1962. Sir Edward Mutesa, the king of Buganda (Mutesa II), was elected the first president, and Milton Obote the first prime minister, of the newly independent country. With the help of a young army officer, Col. Idi Amin, Prime Minister Obote seized control of the government from President Mutesa four years later.

On Jan. 25, 1971, Colonel Amin deposed President Obote. Obote went into exile in Tanzania. Amin expelled Asian residents and launched a reign of terror against Ugandan opponents, torturing and killing tens of thousands. In 1976, he had himself proclaimed "President for Life." In 1977, Amnesty International estimated that 300,000 may have died under his rule, including church leaders and recalcitrant cabinet ministers.

After Amin held military exercises on the Tanzanian border in 1978, angering Tanzania's president, Julius Nyerere, a combined force of Tanzanian troops and Ugandan exiles loyal to former president Obote invaded Uganda and chased Amin into exile in Saudi Arabia in 1979. After a series of interim administrations, President Obote led his People's Congress Party to victory in 1980 elections that opponents charged

were rigged. On July 27, 1985, army troops staged a coup and took over the government. Obote fled into exile. The military regime installed Gen. Tito Okello as chief of state.

The National Resistance Army (NRA), an anti-Obote group led by Yoweri Museveni, kept fighting after it had been excluded from the new regime. It seized Kampala on Jan. 29, 1986, and Museveni was declared president. Museveni has transformed the ruins of Idi Amin and Milton Obote's Uganda into an economic miracle, preaching a philosophy of self-sufficiency and anticorruption. Western countries have flocked to assist him in the country's transformation. Nevertheless, it remains one of Africa's poorest countries. A ban on political parties was lifted in 1996, and the incumbent Museveni won 72% of the vote, reflecting his popularity due to the country's economic recovery.

Uganda has waged an enormously successful campaign against AIDS, dramatically reducing the rate of new infections through an intensive public health and education campaign. Museveni won reelection in March 2001 with 70% of the vote, following a nasty and spirited campaign.

Close ties with Rwanda (many Rwandan Tutsi exiles helped Museveni come to power) led to the cooperation of Uganda and Rwanda in the ousting of Zaire's Mobutu Sese Seko in 1997, and a year later, in efforts to unseat his successor, Laurent Kabila, whom both countries originally supported but from whom they grew estranged. But in 1999, Uganda and Rwanda quarreled over strategy in the Democratic Republic of the Congo, and began fighting each other. The two countries mended their differences in 2002. Uganda also signed a peace accord with the Congo in Sept. 2002, and finally withdrew its remaining troops from the country in May 2003.

In 2004, Uganda continued its 17-year battle against the Lord's Resistance Army (LRA), an extremist rebel group based in Sudan. Between 8,000 and 10,000 children have been abducted by the LRA and form the army of "prophet" Joseph Kony, whose aim is to take over Uganda and run it according to his vision of Christianity. Up to 1.5 million people in northern Uganda have been displaced because of the fighting and the fear that their children will be abducted.

Ukraine

UKRAINE

President: Leonid D. Kuchma (1994)
Prime Minister: Viktor Yanukovich (2002)
Area: 233,089 sq mi (603,700 sq km)
Population (2004 est.): 47,732,079 (growth rate: −0.7%); birth rate: 10.2/1000; infant mortality rate: 20.6/1000; life expectancy: 66.7; density per sq mi: 205
Capital (2003 est.): Kyiv (Kiev), 3,296,100 (metro. area), 2,588,400 (city proper). **Other large cities:** Kharkiv, 1,435,200; Odessa, 1,022,300; Donetske, 984,900; Lvov, 700,100. **Monetary unit:** Hryvna. **Language:** Ukrainian, Russian, Romanian, Polish, Hungarian. **Ethnicity/race:** Ukrainian 77.8%, Russian 17.3%, Belorussian 0.6%, Moldovan 0.5%, Crimean Tatar 0.5%, Bulgarian 0.4%, Hungarian 0.3%, Romanian 0.3%, Polish 0.3%, Jewish 0.2%, other 1.8% (2001). **Religions:** Ukrainian Orthodox (Moscow Patriarchate, Kiev Patriarchate), Ukrainian Autocephalous Orthodox, Ukrainian Catholic (Uniate), Protestant, Jewish. **Literacy rate:** 100% (2003 est.)
Economic summary: GDP/PPP (2003 est.): $256.5 billion; per capita $5,300. **Real growth rate:** 8.2%. **Inflation:** 8.2%. **Unemployment:** 4% officially registered; large number of unregistered or underemployed workers. **Arable land:** 57%.

Agriculture: grain, sugar beets, sunflower seeds, vegetables; beef, milk. **Labor force:** 22.8 million (year-end 1997); industry 32%, agriculture 24%, services 44% (1996). **Industries:** coal, electric power, ferrous and nonferrous metals, machinery and transport equipment, chemicals, food processing (especially sugar). **Natural resources:** iron ore, coal, manganese, natural gas, oil, salt, sulfur, graphite, titanium, magnesium, kaolin, nickel, mercury, timber, arable land. **Exports:** $23.58 billion (2003 est.): ferrous and nonferrous metals, fuel and petroleum products, chemicals, machinery and transport equipment, food products. **Imports:** $23.58 billion (2003 est.): energy, machinery and equipment, chemicals. **Major trading partners:** Russia, Italy, Turkey, Germany, China, Turkmenistan, Poland.

Geography Located in southeast Europe, the country consists largely of fertile black soil steppes. Mountainous areas include the Carpathians in the southwest and the Crimean chain in the south. There are forest lakes in the north. Ukraine is bordered by Belarus on the north, by Russia on the north, northeast, and east, by the Sea of Azov and the Black Sea on the south, by Moldova and Romania on the southwest, and by Hungary, Slovakia, and Poland on the west.

Government Constitutional republic.

History Ukraine was known as "Kievan Rus" (from which *Russia* is a derivative) up until the 16th century. In the 9th century, Kiev was the major political and cultural center in eastern Europe. Kievan Rus reached the height of its power in the 10th century and adopted Byzantine Christianity, the Church Slavonic written language, and the Cyrillic alphabet during that period. The Mongol conquest in 1240 ended Kievan power. From the 13th to the 16th century, Kiev was under the influence of Poland and western Europe. The negotiation of the Union of Brest-Litovsk in 1596 divided the Ukrainians into Orthodox and Ukrainian Catholic faithful. In 1654, Ukraine asked the czar of Moscovy for protection against Poland, and the Treaty of Pereyasav signed that year recognized the suzerainty of Moscow. The agreement was interpreted by Moscow as an invitation to take over Kiev, and the Ukrainian state was eventually absorbed into the Russian empire.

After the Russian Revolution, Ukraine declared its independence from Russia on Jan. 28, 1918, and several years of warfare ensued with several groups. The Red Army finally was victorious over Kiev, and in 1920 Ukraine became a Soviet republic. In 1922, Ukraine became one of the founders of the Union of Soviet Socialist Republics. In the 1930s, the Soviet government's enforcement of collectivization met with peasant resistance, which in turn prompted the confiscation of grain from Ukrainian farmers by Soviet authorities; the resulting famine took an estimated 5 million lives. Ukraine was one of the most devastated Soviet republics after World War II. (For details on World War II, *see* Headline History, World War II.) On April 26, 1986, the nation's nuclear power plant at Chernobyl was the site of the world's worst nuclear accident. On Oct. 29, 1991, the Ukrainian Parliament voted to shut down the reactor within two years' time and asked for international assistance in dismantling it.

When President Leonid Kravchuk was elected by the Ukrainian Parliament in 1990, he vowed to seek Ukrainian sovereignty. Ukraine declared its independence on Aug. 24, 1991. In Dec. 1991, Ukrainian, Russian, and Belorussian leaders cofounded a new Commonwealth of Independent States with the new capital to be situated in Minsk, Belarus. The new country's government was slow to reform the Soviet-era state-run economy,

which was plagued by declining production, rising inflation, and widespread unemployment in the years following independence. The U.S. announced in Jan. 1994 that an agreement had been reached with Russia and Ukraine for the destruction of Ukraine's entire nuclear arsenal. In Oct. 1994, Ukraine began a program of economic liberalization and moved to reestablish central authority over Crimea. In 1995, Crimea's separatist leader was removed and the Crimean constitution revoked.

In June 1996, the last strategic nuclear warhead was removed to Russia. Also that month Parliament approved a new constitution that allowed for private ownership of land. An agreement was signed in May 1997 on the future of the Black Sea fleet, by which Ukrainian and Russian ships will share the port of Sevastopol for 20 years.

The Russian financial crisis in fall 1998 led to severe problems for the Ukrainian economy, which is dependent on Russia for 40% of its foreign trade. Ukraine remains saddled with its Soviet-era economy, and most of its major industries are still under state control. Corruption is rampant, and as a result, Western investors have shown only minimal interest. The election of the reform-minded Viktor Yushchenko as prime minister in Dec. 1999, however, was greeted with optimism by the West. He was also highly popular among Ukrainians. But in April 2001, he was dismissed in a no-confidence vote engineered by Communist hardliners and Ukrainian big business.

In the winter of 2001 violent demonstrations rocked Ukraine, with protesters demanding the resignation and impeachment of authoritarian president Leonid Kuchma. Critics accused Kuchma of involvement in the murder of a journalist critical of government corruption. Kuchma was recorded on tape urging that the journalist be disposed of.

In 2004, Kuchma announced he would be retiring. A presidential election on Oct. 31, 2004, will pit Viktor Yushchenko, the former reformist prime minister, against Viktor Yanukovich, current prime minister and Kuchma's choice. The campaign was an especially dirty one. Yushchenko was allegedly poisoned and had to be hospitalized for several weeks shortly before the election.

United Arab Emirates

President: Sheikh Zayed bin Sultan al-Nahyan (1971)
Prime Minister: Sheikh Maktoum bin Rashid al-Maktoum (1990)
Area: 32,000 sq mi (82,880 sq km)
Population (2004 est.): 2,523,915 (growth rate: 1.6%); birth rate: 18.7/1000; infant mortality rate: 15.1/1000; life expectancy: 75.0; density per sq mi: 79
Capital (2003 est.): Abu Dhabi, 539,800. **Largest city:** Dubai, 1,511,700 (metro. area), 906,100 (city proper). **Monetary unit:** U.A.E. dirham. **Languages:** Arabic (official), Persian, English, Hindi, Urdu. **Ethnicity/race:** Emiri 19%, other Arab and Iranian 23%, South Asian 50%, other expatriates (includes Westerners and East Asians) 8% (1982). **Religions:** Islam 96% (Sunni 80%, Shiite 16%) , Christian, Hindu, and other 4%. **Literacy rate:** 78% (2003 est.)
Economic summary: GDP/PPP (2003 est.): $57.7 billion; per capita $23,200. **Real growth rate:** 5.2%. **Inflation:** 3.2%. **Unemployment:** 2.4% (2001). **Arable land:** 0%. **Agriculture:** dates, vegetables, watermelons; poultry, eggs, dairy products; fish. **Labor force:** 2.1 million; note: 73.9% of the population in the 15–64 age group is non-national (2001); services 78%, industry 15%, agriculture 7% (2000 est.). **Industries:** petroleum, fishing, petrochemicals, construction materials, some boat building,

handicrafts, pearling. **Natural resources:** petroleum, natural gas. **Exports:** $56.73 billion (f.o.b., 2003 est.): crude oil 45%, natural gas, reexports, dried fish, dates. **Imports:** $37.16 billion (f.o.b., 2003 est.): machinery and transport equipment, chemicals, food. **Major trading partners:** Japan, South Korea, Singapore, U.S., China, Germany, India, France, UK, Iran.

Geography The United Arab Emirates, in the eastern part of the Arabian Peninsula, extends along part of the Gulf of Oman and the southern coast of the Persian Gulf. The nation is the size of Maine. Its neighbors are Saudi Arabia to the west and south, Qatar to the north, and Oman to the east. Most of the land is barren and sandy.

Government Federation formed in 1971 by seven emirates known as the Trucial States—Abu Dhabi (the largest), Dubai, Sharjah, Ajman, Fujairah, Ras al-Khaimah, and Umm al-Qaiwain.

History Originally the area was inhabited by a seafaring people who were converted to Islam in the 7th century. Later, a dissident sect, the Carmathians, established a powerful sheikdom, and its army conquered Mecca. After the sheikdom disintegrated, its people became pirates. Threatening the Sultanate of Muscat and Oman early in the 19th century, the pirates provoked the intervention of the British, who in 1820 enforced a partial truce and in 1853 a permanent truce. Thus what had been called the Pirate Coast was renamed the Trucial Coast. The British provided the nine Trucial states with protection but did not formally administer them as a colony.

The British withdrew from the Persian Gulf in 1971, and the Trucial states became a federation called the United Arab Emirates (UAE). Two of the Trucial states, Bahrain and Oman, chose not to join the federation, reducing the number of states to seven.

The country signed a military defense agreement with the U.S. in 1994 and one with France in 1995.

After the Sept. 11 terrorist attacks on the U.S., the UAE was identified as a major financial center used by al-Qaeda in transferring money to the hijackers. The nation immediately cooperated with the U.S., freezing accounts tied to suspected terrorists and strongly clamping down on money laundering. The U.S. stationed troops in the UAE during the 2003 Iraq war.

United Kingdom

UNITED KINGDOM OF GREAT BRITAIN AND NORTHERN IRELAND

Sovereign: Queen Elizabeth II (1952)
Prime Minister: Tony Blair (1997)
Area: 94,525 sq mi (244,820 sq km)
Population (2004 est.): 60,270,708 (growth rate: 0.3%); birth rate: 10.9/1000; infant mortality rate: 5.2/1000; life expectancy: 78.3; density per sq mi: 638
Capital and largest city (2003 est.): London, 11,219,000 (metro. area), 7,417,700 (city proper). **Other large cities:** Glasgow, 1,099,400; Birmingham, 971,800; Liverpool, 461,900; Edinburgh, 460,000; Leeds, 417,000; Bristol, 406,500; Manchester, 390,700; Bradford, 288,400. **Monetary unit:** Pound sterling (£). **Languages:** English, Welsh, Scots Gaelic. **Ethnicity/race:** English 81.5%; Scottish 9.6%; Irish 2.4%; Welsh 1.9%; Ulster 1.8%; West Indian, Indian, Pakistani, and other 2.8%. **Religions:** Anglican and Roman Catholic 40 million, Muslim 1.5 million, Presbyterian 800,000, Methodist 760,000, Sikh 500,000, Hindu 500,000, Jewish 350,000. **Literacy rate:** 99% (2000 est.)

Economic summary: GDP/PPP (2003 est.): $1.664 trillion; per capita $27,700. **Real growth rate:** 2.1%. **Inflation:** 3%. **Unemployment:** 5.1%. **Arable land:** 26%. **Agriculture:** cereals, oilseed, potatoes, vegetables; cattle, sheep, poultry; fish. **Labor force:** 29.7 million (2001); agriculture 1%, industry 25%, services 74% (1999). **Industries:** machine tools, electric power equipment, automation equipment, railroad equipment, shipbuilding, aircraft, motor vehicles and parts, electronics and communications equipment, metals, chemicals, coal, petroleum, paper and paper products, food processing, textiles, clothing, other consumer goods. **Natural resources:** coal, petroleum, natural gas, tin, limestone, iron ore, salt, clay, chalk, gypsum, lead, silica, arable land. **Exports:** $304.5 billion (f.o.b., 2003 est.): manufactured goods, fuels, chemicals; food, beverages, tobacco. **Imports:** $363.6 billion (f.o.b., 2003 est.): manufactured goods, machinery, fuels; foodstuffs. **Major trading partners:** U.S., Germany, France, Ireland, Netherlands, Belgium, Italy, Spain.

Geography The United Kingdom, consisting of Great Britain (England, Wales, and Scotland) and Northern Ireland, is twice the size of New York State. England, in the southeast part of the British Isles, is separated from Scotland on the north by the granite Cheviot Hills; from them the Pennine chain of uplands extends south through the center of England, reaching its highest point in the Lake District in the northwest. To the west along the border of Wales—a land of steep hills and valleys—are the Cambrian Mountains, while the Cotswolds, a range of hills in Gloucestershire, extend into the surrounding shires.

Important rivers flowing into the North Sea are the Thames, Humber, Tees, and Tyne. In the west are the Severn and Wye, which empty into the Bristol Channel and are navigable, as are the Mersey and Ribble.

Government The United Kingdom is a constitutional monarchy and parliamentary democracy, with a queen and a Parliament that has two houses: the House of Lords, with 574 life peers, 92 hereditary peers, and 26 bishops; and the House of Commons, which has 651 popularly elected members. Supreme legislative power is vested in Parliament, which sits for five years unless sooner dissolved. The House of Lords was stripped of most of its power in 1911, and now its main function is to revise legislation. In Nov. 1999 hundreds of hereditary peers were expelled in an effort to make the body more democratic. The executive power of the Crown is exercised by the cabinet, headed by the prime minister.

Ruler Queen Elizabeth II, born April 21, 1926, elder daughter of King George VI and Queen Elizabeth, succeeded to the throne on the death of her father on Feb. 6, 1952. On Nov. 20, 1947, she married Prince Philip, duke of Edinburgh, born June 10, 1921. Their children are Prince Charles[1] (her apparent), born Nov. 14, 1948; Princess Anne, born Aug. 15, 1950; Prince Andrew, born Feb. 19, 1960; and Prince Edward, born March 10, 1964. Prince William Arthur Philip Louis, son of Prince Charles and the late princess of Wales and second in line to the throne, was born June 21, 1982. A second son, Prince Henry Charles Albert David, was born Sept. 15, 1984, and is third in line.

---

1. The title Prince of Wales, which is not inherited, was conferred on Prince Charles by his mother on July 26, 1958. The investiture ceremony took place on July 1, 1969. The previous Prince of Wales was Prince Edward Albert, who held the title from 1911 to 1936 before he became Edward VIII.

History Stonehenge and other examples of prehistoric culture are what remains of the earliest inhabitants of Britain. Celtic peoples followed. Roman invasions of the 1st century B.C. brought Britain into contact with continental Europe. When the Roman legions withdrew in the 5th century A.D., Britain fell easy prey to the invading hordes of Angles, Saxons, and Jutes from Scandinavia and the Low Countries. The invasions had little effect on the Celtic peoples of Wales and Scotland. Seven large Anglo-Saxon kingdoms were established, and the original Britons were forced into Wales and Scotland. It was not until the 10th century that the country finally became united under the kings of Wessex. Following the death of Edward the Confessor (1066), a dispute about the succession arose, and William, duke of Normandy, invaded England, defeating the Saxon king, Harold II, at the Battle of Hastings (1066). The Norman conquest introduced Norman French law and feudalism.

The reign of Henry II (1154–1189), first of the Plantagenets, saw an increasing centralization of royal power at the expense of the nobles, but in 1215 King John (1199–1216) was forced to sign the Magna Carta, which awarded the people, especially the nobles, certain basic rights. Edward I (1272–1307) continued the conquest of Ireland, reduced Wales to subjection, and made some gains in Scotland. In 1314, however, English forces led by Edward II were ousted from Scotland after the Battle of Bannockburn. The late 13th and early 14th centuries saw the development of a separate House of Commons with tax-raising powers. Edward III's claim to the throne of France led to the Hundred Years' War (1338–1453) and the loss of almost all the large English territory in France. In England, the great poverty and discontent caused by the war were intensified by the Black Death, a plague that reduced the population by about one-third. The Wars of the Roses (1455–1485), a struggle for the throne between the House of York and the House of Lancaster, ended in the victory of Henry Tudor (Henry VII) at Bosworth Field (1485).

During the reign of Henry VIII (1509–1547), the church in England asserted its independence from the Roman Catholic Church. Under Edward VI and Mary, the two extremes of religious fanaticism were reached, and it remained for Henry's daughter, Elizabeth I (1558–1603), to set up the Church of England on a moderate basis. In 1588, the Spanish Armada, a fleet sent out by Catholic King Philip II of Spain, was defeated by the English and destroyed during a storm. During Elizabeth's reign, England became a world power. Elizabeth's heir was a Stuart—James VI of Scotland—who joined the two crowns as James I (1603–1625). The Stuart kings incurred large debts and were forced either to depend on Parliament for taxes or to raise money by illegal means. In 1642, war broke out between Charles I and a large segment of the Parliament; Charles was defeated and executed in 1649, and the monarchy then was abolished. After the death in 1658 of Oliver Cromwell, the lord protector, the Puritan Commonwealth fell to pieces and Charles II was placed on the throne in 1660. The struggle between the king and Parliament continued, but Charles II knew when to compromise. His brother, James II (1685–1688), possessed none of his ability and was ousted by the Revolution of 1688, which confirmed the primacy of Parliament. James's daughter, Mary, and her husband, William of Orange, then became the rulers.

Queen Anne's reign (1702–1714) was marked by the duke of Marlborough's victories over France at Blenheim, Oudenarde, and Malplaquet in the War of the Spanish Succession. England and Scotland meanwhile were joined by the Act of Union (1707). Upon the death of Anne, the distant claims of the elector of Hanover were recognized, and he became king of Great Britain and Ireland as George I. The unwillingness of the Hanoverian kings to rule resulted in the formation by the royal ministers of a cabinet, headed by a prime minister, which directed all public business. Abroad, the constant wars with France expanded the British Empire all over the globe, particularly in North America and India. This imperial growth was checked by the revolt of the American colonies (1775–1781). Struggles with France broke out again in 1793 and during the Napoleonic Wars, which ended at Waterloo in 1815.

The Victorian era, named after Queen Victoria (1837–1901), saw the growth of a democratic system of government that had begun with the Reform Bill of 1832. The two important wars in Victoria's reign were the Crimean War against Russia (1853–1856) and the Boer War (1899–1902), the latter enormously extending Britain's influence in Africa. Increasing uneasiness at home and abroad marked the reign of Edward VII (1901–1910). Within four years after the accession of George V in 1910, Britain entered World War I when Germany invaded Belgium. The nation was led by coalition cabinets, headed first by Herbert Asquith and then, starting in 1916, by the Welsh statesman David Lloyd George. Postwar labor unrest culminated in the general strike of 1926.

King Edward VIII succeeded to the throne on Jan. 20, 1936, at his father's death, but abdicated on Dec. 11, 1936 (in order to marry an American divorcée, Wallis Warfield Simpson), in favor of his brother, who became George VI.

The efforts of Prime Minister Neville Chamberlain to stem the rising threat of Nazism in Germany failed with the German invasion of Poland on Sept. 1, 1939, which was followed by Britain's entry into World War II on Sept. 3. Allied reverses in the spring of 1940 led to Chamberlain's resignation and the formation of another coalition war cabinet by the Conservative leader, Winston Churchill, who led Britain through most of World War II. Churchill resigned shortly after V-E Day, May 8, 1945, but then formed a "caretaker" government that remained in office until after the parliamentary elections in July, which the Labour Party won overwhelmingly. The new government, formed by Clement R. Attlee, began a moderate socialist program.

In 1951, Churchill again became prime minister at the head of a Conservative government. George VI died on Feb. 6, 1952, and was succeeded by his daughter, Elizabeth II. Churchill stepped down in 1955 in favor of Sir Anthony Eden, who resigned on grounds of ill health in 1957 and was succeeded by Harold Macmillan and Sir Alec Douglas-Home. In 1964, Harold Wilson led the Labour Party to victory. A lagging economy brought the Conservatives back to power in 1970. Prime Minister Edward Heath won Britain's admission to the European Community. Margaret Thatcher became Britain's first woman prime minister as the Conservatives won 339 seats on May 3, 1979.

An Argentine invasion of the Falkland Islands on April 2, 1982, involved Britain in a war 8,000 mi from the home islands. Argentina had long claimed the Falklands, known as the *Malvinas* in Spanish, which had been occupied by the British since 1832. Britain won a decisive victory within six weeks when more than 11,000 Argentine troops on the Falklands surrendered on June 14, 1982.

Although there were continuing economic problems and foreign policy disputes, an upswing in the

Rulers of England and Great Britain

Name	Born	Ruled[1]	Name	Born	Ruled[1]
SAXONS[2]			Henry VI	1421	1422–1461[5]
Egbert[3]	c. 775	802–839	**HOUSE OF YORK**		
Ethelwulf	?	839–858	Edward IV	1442	1461–1483[5]
Ethelbald	?	858–860	Edward V	1470	1483–1483
Ethelbert	?	860–865	Richard III	1452	1483–1485
Ethelred I	?	865–871	**HOUSE OF TUDOR**		
Alfred the Great	849	871–899	Henry VII	1457	1485–1509
Edward the Elder	c. 870	899–924	Henry VIII	1491	1509–1547
Athelstan	895	924–939	Edward VI	1537	1547–1553
Edmund I the Deed-doer	921	939–946	Jane (Lady Jane Grey)[6]	1537	1553–1553
Edred	c. 925	946–955	Mary I ("Bloody Mary")	1516	1553–1558
Edwy the Fair	c. 943	955–959	Elizabeth I	1533	1558–1603
Edgar the Peaceful	943	959–975	**HOUSE OF STUART**		
Edward the Martyr	c. 962	975–978	James I[7]	1566	1603–1625
Ethelred II the Unready	968	978–1016	Charles I	1600	1625–1649
Edmund II Ironside	c. 993	1016	**COMMONWEALTH**		
DANES			Council of State	—	1649–1653
Canute	995	1016–1035	Oliver Cromwell[8]	1599	1653–1658
Harold I Harefoot	c.1016	1035–1040	Richard Cromwell[8]	1626	1658–1659[9]
Hardecanute	c.1018	1040–1042	**RESTORATION OF HOUSE OF STUART**		
SAXONS			Charles II	1630	1660–1685
Edward the Confessor	c.1004	1042–1066	James II	1633	1685–
Harold II	c.1020	1066			1688[10]
HOUSE OF NORMANDY			William III[11]	1650	1689–1702
William I the Conqueror	1027	1066–1087	Mary II[11]	1662	1689–1694
William II Rufus	c.1056	1087–1100	Anne	1665	1702–1714
Henry I Beauclerc	1068	1100–1135	**HOUSE OF HANOVER**		
Stephen of Boulogne	c.1100	1135–1154	George I	1660	1714–1727
HOUSE OF PLANTAGENET			George II	1683	1727–1760
Henry II	1133	1154–1189	George III	1738	1760–1820
Richard I Coeur de Lion	1157	1189–1199	George IV	1762	1820–1830
John Lackland	1167	1199–1216	William IV	1765	1830–1837
Henry III	1207	1216–1272	Victoria	1819	1837–1901
Edward I Longshanks	1239	1272–1307	**HOUSE OF SAXE-COBURG[12]**		
Edward II	1284	1307–1327	Edward VII	1841	1901–1910
Edward III	1312	1327–1377	**HOUSE OF WINDSOR[12]**		
Richard II	1367	1377–1399[4]	George V	1865	1910–1936
HOUSE OF LANCASTER			Edward VIII	1894	1936[13]
Henry IV Bolingbroke	1367	1399–1413	George VI	1895	1936–1952
Henry V	1387	1413–1422	Elizabeth II	1926	1952–

1. Year of end of rule is also that of death, unless otherwise indicated. 2. Dates for Saxon kings are still subject of controversy. 3. Became king of West Saxons in 802; considered (from 828) first king of all England. 4. Died 1400. 5. Henry VI reigned again briefly 1470–1471. 6. Nominal queen for 9 days; not counted as queen by some authorities. She was beheaded in 1554. 7. Ruled in Scotland as James VI (1567–1625). 8. Lord Protector. 9. Died 1712. 10. Died 1701. 11. Joint rulers (1689–1694). 12. Name changed from Saxe-Coburg to Windsor in 1917. 13. Was known after his abdication as the duke of Windsor, died 1972.

economy in 1986–1987 led Thatcher to call elections in June, and she won a near-unprecedented third consecutive term. The unpopularity of Thatcher's poll tax together with an uncompromising position toward further European integration eroded support within her own party. When John Major won the Conservative Party leadership in November, Thatcher resigned, paving the way for Major to form a government.

Eighteen years of Conservative rule ended in May 1997 when Tony Blair and the Labour Party triumphed in the British elections. Blair has been compared to former U.S. president Bill Clinton for his youthful, telegenic personality and centrist views. He produced constitutional reform that partially decentralized the UK, leading to the formation of separate Parliaments in Wales and Scotland by 1999. Britain turned over its colony Hong Kong to China in July 1997.

Blair's controversial meeting in Oct. 1997 with Sinn Fein's president, Gerry Adams, was the first meeting in 76 years between a British prime minister and a Sinn Fein leader. It infuriated numerous factions but was a symbolic gesture in support of the nascent peace talks in Northern Ireland. In 1998 the Good Friday Agreement, strongly supported by Tony Blair, led to the first promise of peace between so-called Catholics and Protestants since the beginning of the so-called Troubles.

Along with the U.S., Britain launched air strikes against Iraq in Dec. 1998 after Saddam Hussein expelled UN arms inspectors. In the spring of 1999, Britain spearheaded the NATO operation in Kosovo, which resulted in Yugoslavian president Slobodan Milosevic's withdrawal from the territory.

In Feb. 2001, foot-and-mouth disease broke out among British livestock, prompting other nations to ban British meat imports and forcing the slaughter of thousands of cattle, pigs, and sheep in an effort to stem the highly contagious disease. The episode cost farmers and the tourist industry billions of dollars.

In June 2001, Blair won a second landslide victory, with the Labour Party capturing 413 seats in Parliament.

Britain became the U.S.'s staunchest ally after the Sept. 11 attacks. British troops joined the U.S. in the bombing campaign against Afghanistan in Oct. 2001,

British Prime Ministers Since 1770

Name	Term	Name	Term
Lord North (Tory)	1770–1782	William E. Gladstone (Liberal)	1886–1886
Marquis of Rockingham (Whig)	1782–1782	Marquis of Salisbury (Conservative)	1886–1892
Earl of Shelburne (Whig)	1782–1783	William E. Gladstone (Liberal)	1892–1894
Duke of Portland (Coalition)	1783–1783	Earl of Rosebery (Liberal)	1894–1895
William Pitt, the Younger (Tory)	1783–1801	Marquis of Salisbury (Conservative)	1895–1902
Henry Addington (Tory)	1801–1804	Arthur James Balfour (Conservative)	1902–1905
William Pitt, the Younger (Tory)	1804–1806	Sir H. Campbell-Bannerman (Liberal)	1905–1908
Baron Grenville (Whig)	1806–1807	Herbert H. Asquith (Liberal)	1908–1915
Duke of Portland (Tory)	1807–1809	Herbert H. Asquith (Coalition)	1915–1916
Spencer Perceval (Tory)	1809–1812	David Lloyd George (Coalition)	1916–1922
Earl of Liverpool (Tory)	1812–1827	Andrew Bonar Law (Conservative)	1922–1923
George Canning (Tory)	1827–1827	Stanley Baldwin (Conservative)	1923–1924
Viscount Goderich (Tory)	1827–1828	James Ramsay MacDonald (Labour)	1924–1924
Duke of Wellington (Tory)	1828–1830	Stanley Baldwin (Conservative)	1924–1929
Earl Grey (Whig)	1830–1834	James Ramsay MacDonald (Labour)	1929–1931
Viscount Melbourne (Whig)	1834–1834	James Ramsay MacDonald (Coalition)	1931–1935
Sir Robert Peel (Tory)	1834–1835	Stanley Baldwin (Coalition)	1935–1937
Viscount Melbourne (Whig)	1835–1841	Neville Chamberlain (Coalition)	1937–1940
Sir Robert Peel (Tory)	1841–1846	Winston Churchill (Coalition)	1940–1945
Earl Russell (Whig)	1846–1852	Clement R. Attlee (Labour)	1945–1951
Earl of Derby (Tory)	1852–1852	Sir Winston Churchill (Conservative)	1951–1955
Earl of Aberdeen (Coalition)	1852–1855	Sir Anthony Eden (Conservative)	1955–1957
Viscount Palmerston (Liberal)	1855–1858	Harold Macmillan (Conservative)	1957–1963
Earl of Derby (Conservative)	1858–1859	Sir Alec Frederick Douglas-Home (Conservative)	1963–1964
Viscount Palmerston (Liberal)	1859–1865		
Earl Russell (Liberal)	1865–1866	Harold Wilson (Labour)	1964–1970
Earl of Derby (Conservative)	1866–1868	Edward Heath (Conservative)	1970–1974
Benjamin Disraeli (Conservative)	1868–1868	Harold Wilson (Labour)	1974–1976
William E. Gladstone (Liberal)	1868–1874	James Callaghan (Labour)	1976–1979
Benjamin Disraeli (Conservative)	1874–1880	Margaret Thatcher (Conservative)	1979–1990
William E. Gladstone (Liberal)	1880–1885	John Major (Conservative)	1990–1997
Marquis of Salisbury (Conservative)	1885–1886	Tony Blair (Labour)	1997–

after the Taliban-led government refused to turn over the prime suspect in the terrorist attacks, Osama bin Laden.

Blair again proved himself to be the U.S.'s strongest international supporter in Sept. 2002, when he became President Bush's major ally in calling for a war against Iraq. Blair maintained that military action was justified because Iraq was developing weapons of mass destruction that were a direct threat to its enemies. He continued to support the Bush administration's hawkish policies despite significant opposition in his own party and the British public: in March 2003, a *Times of London* newspaper poll indicated that only 19% of respondents approved of military action without a UN mandate. As the inevitability of the U.S. strike on Iraq grew nearer, Blair announced that he would join the U.S. in fighting Iraq with or without a second UN resolution. Three of his ministers resigned as a result. Britain entered the war on March 20, supplying 45,000 troops who fought mostly in Basra, in the southern portion of the country.

In the aftermath of the war, Blair came under fire from government officials for allegedly exaggerating Iraq's possession of weapons of mass destruction. In July 2003 Blair announced that "history will forgive" the UK and U.S. "if we are wrong"—the end to the "inhuman carnage and suffering" caused by Saddam Hussein was justification enough for the war. The arguments about the war grew so vociferous between the Blair government and the BBC that a prominent weapons scientist, David Kelly, who was caught in the middle, committed suicide. In Jan. 2004, the Hutton Report exonerated the Blair administration of any misconduct concerning the weapons inspections and concluded that it had not "sexed-up" the intelligence dossier, an accusation put forth by BBC reporter Andrew Gilligan. The report strongly criticized the BBC for its "defective" editorial policies, and as a consequence, the BBC's top management resigned. That same week, Blair was also victorious in averting a parliamentary revolt over his proposal to hike university tuition fees.

In July 2004, the Butler Report on pre–Iraq war British intelligence was released. It echoed the findings of the U.S. Senate Intelligence Committee of the week before that the intelligence had vastly exaggerated Saddam Hussein's threat. The famous claim that Iraq's chemical and biological weapons "are deployable within 45 minutes of an order to use them" was especially singled out as highly misleading, and "led to suspicions that it had been included because of its eye-catching character." Referring to the intelligence as "insufficiently robust," the report had a far milder tone than its American counterpart, which excoriated U.S. intelligence agencies for their failings. But like the U.S. report, it cleared the government of any role in manipulating the intelligence.

Northern Ireland

Status: Part of United Kingdom
First Minister: (suspended Oct. 14, 2002)
Area: 5,452 sq mi (14,121 sq km)
Population (1998 est.): 1,688,600
Capital and largest city (2003 est.): Belfast, 484,800 (metro. area), 246,200 (city proper). **Monetary unit:** British pound sterling (£). **Language:** English. **Religions:** Presbyterian, Church of Ireland, Roman Catholic, Methodist.

Geography Northern Ireland is composed of 26 districts, derived from the boroughs of Belfast and Londonderry and the counties of Antrim, Armagh, Down, Fermanagh, Londonderry, and Tyrone. Together they are commonly called Ulster, though the territory does not include the entire ancient province of Ulster. It is slightly larger than Connecticut.

Government Northern Ireland is an integral part of the United Kingdom (it has 12 representatives in the British House of Commons), but under the terms of the Government of Ireland Act in 1920, it had a semiautonomous government. In 1972, however, after three years of sectarian violence between Protestants and Catholics that resulted in more than 400 dead and thousands injured, Britain suspended the Ulster Parliament. The Ulster counties were governed directly from London after an attempt to return certain powers to an elected assembly in Belfast.

As a result of the Good Friday Agreement of 1998, a new coalition government was formed on Dec. 2, 1999, with the British government formally transferring governing power to the Northern Irish Parliament. David Trimble, Protestant leader of the Ulster Unionist Party (UUP) and winner of the 1998 Nobel Peace Prize, became first minister. The government has been suspended four times since then; it has remained suspended since Oct. 14, 2002.

History Ulster was part of Catholic Ireland until the reign of Elizabeth I (1558–1603) when, after suppressing three Irish rebellions, the Crown confiscated lands in Ireland and settled the Scots Presbyterians in Ulster. Another rebellion in 1641–1651, brutally crushed by Oliver Cromwell, resulted in the settlement of Anglican Englishmen in Ulster. Subsequent political policy favoring Protestants and disadvantaging Catholics encouraged further Protestant settlement in Northern Ireland.

Northern Ireland did not separate from the South until William Gladstone presented, in 1886, his proposal for home rule in Ireland. The Protestants in the North feared domination by the Catholic majority. Industry, moreover, was concentrated in the North and dependent on the British market. When World War I began, civil war threatened between the regions. Northern Ireland, however, did not become a political entity until the six counties accepted the Home Rule Bill of 1920. This set up a semiautonomous Parliament in Belfast and a Crown-appointed governor advised by a cabinet of the prime minister and 8 ministers, as well as a 12-member representation in the House of Commons in London.

When the Republic of Ireland gained sovereignty in 1922, relations improved between North and South, although the Irish Republican Army (IRA), outlawed in recent years, continued the struggle to end the partition of Ireland. In 1966–1969, rioting and street fighting between Protestants and Catholics occurred in Londonderry, fomented by extremist nationalist Protestants, who feared the Catholics might attain a local majority, and by Catholics demonstrating for civil rights. These confrontations became known as "the Troubles."

The religious communities, Catholic and Protestant, became hostile armed camps. British troops were brought in to separate them, but themselves became a target of Catholics, particularly by the IRA, which by this time had turned into a full-fledged terrorist movement. The goal of the IRA was to eject the British and unify Northern Ireland with the Irish Republic to the south. The Protestants remained tenaciously loyal to the United Kingdom, and various Protestant terrorist organizations pursued the Unionist cause through violence. Various attempts at representational government and power-sharing foundered during the 1970s, and both sides were further polarized. Direct rule from London and the presence of British troops failed to stop the violence.

In Oct. 1977, the 1976 Nobel Peace Prize was awarded to Mairead Corrigan and Betty Williams, founders of the Community of Peace People, a nonsectarian organization dedicated to creating peace in Northern Ireland. Intermittent violence continued, however, and on Aug. 27, 1979, an IRA bomb killed Lord Mountbatten as he was sailing off southern Ireland, heightening tensions. Catholic protests over the death of IRA hunger striker Bobby Sands in 1981 fueled more violence. Riots, sniper fire, and terrorist attacks killed more than 3,200 people between 1969 and 1998. Among the attempts at reconciliation undertaken during the 1980s was the Anglo-Irish Agreement (1985), which, to the dismay of Unionists, marked the first time the Republic of Ireland had been given an official consultative role in the affairs of the province.

In 1997, Northern Ireland made a significant step in the direction of stemming sectarian strife. The first formal peace talks began on Oct. 6 with representatives of eight major Northern Irish political parties participating, a feat that in itself required three years of negotiations. Two smaller Protestant parties, including hard-liner Ian Paisley's Democratic Unionists, boycotted the talks. For the first time, Sinn Fein, the political wing of the IRA, won two seats in the British Parliament, which went to Sinn Fein president Gerry Adams and his second-in-command, Martin McGuinness. Although the election strengthened the IRA's political legitimacy, it was the IRA's resumption of the 17-month cease-fire, which had collapsed in Feb. 1996, that gained them a place at the negotiating table.

A landmark settlement, the Good Friday Agreement of April 10, 1998, came after 19 months of intensive negotiations that involved 8 of the 10 Northern Irish political parties. The accord called for Protestants to share political power with the minority Catholics, and it gave the Republic of Ireland a voice in Northern Ireland affairs. In turn, Catholics were to suspend the goal of a united Ireland—a territorial claim that was the raison d'être of the IRA and was written into the Irish Republic's constitution—unless the largely Protestant North voted in favor of such an arrangement, an unlikely occurrence.

The resounding commitment to the settlement was demonstrated in a dual referendum on May 22, 1998: the North approved the accord by a vote of 71% to 29%, and in the Irish Republic 94% favored it. In October, the Nobel Peace Prize was awarded to John Hume and David Trimble, leaders of the largest Catholic and Protestant political parties, an incentive for all sides to ensure that this time the peace would last.

In Dec. 1998 the rival Northern Ireland politicians agreed on the organization and contents of the new coalition government, but in June 1999 the peace process again hit an impasse when the IRA refused to disarm prior to the assembly of Northern Ireland's new provincial cabinet. Sinn Fein insisted the IRA would only begin giving up its illegal weapons after the formation of the new government; Unionists demanded disarmament first. As a result, the Ulster Unionists boycotted the assembly session that would have nominated the cabinet to run the new coalition government. The nascent Northern Irish government was stillborn in July 1999.

Subsequent talks on the agreement, which would have ended three decades of direct rule from London, seemed to go nowhere. Finally, at the end of November, David Trimble, leader of the Ulster Unionists, abandoned the seemingly sacrosanct "no guns, no government" position, and took a difficult leap of faith in agreeing to form a government prior to Sinn Fein's disarmament. If the IRA did not begin the destruction of their weapons by Jan. 31, 2000, however, the Ulster Unionists threatened they would withdraw from the Northern Irish Parliament, shutting down the new government. With this compromise in place, the new government was quickly formed, and on Dec. 2, 1999, the British government formally transferred governing power to the Northern Irish Parliament. David Trimble became first minister. Two leaders of Sinn Fein, Gerry Adams and Martin McGuinness, received seats in the 4-party, 12-member Parliament. But by the deadline, Sinn Fein had made little progress toward disarmament, and claimed it had not made any such commitment. As a result, the British government suspended Parliament on Feb. 12, 2000, and once again imposed direct rule. In July 2001, after issuing one last ultimatum to the IRA to begin destroying its weapons stores, Ulster Unionist leader David Trimble resigned his post as first minister.

Following Trimble's departure, the IRA offered another vague and open-ended disarmament plan, only to withdraw it. But on Oct. 23, days before Britain was to suspend the assembly, Sinn Fein leader Gerry Adams dramatically announced that the IRA had indeed begun disarming. Partially in response to the Sept. 11 attacks, which made the IRA's claim to weapons of terror seem even more senselessly brutal, Sinn Fein chose to embrace the promise of a political solution to the Northern Irish troubles. On Nov. 6, David Trimble was reelected as first minister.

On April 8, 2002, international weapons inspectors announced that the IRA had put more stockpiled munitions "beyond use," the euphemistic phrase used in the negotiations to mean disarmament. British and Irish leaders hoped that Protestant guerrilla groups would also begin to surrender their weapons. However, in mid-June British and Irish political leaders called emergency talks to stem the rising tide of violence in Belfast. On July 16, the IRA issued a public apology to the families of the 650 civilians killed by the IRA since the late 1960s.

On Oct. 14, the British government again assumed direct rule of Northern Ireland, after the Unionists threatened to quit the Assembly in protest of suspected spying activity by the IRA. In March and April 2003, negotiations were again underway to reinstate the Northern Ireland assembly. But Sinn Fein's vague language, weakly pledging that its "strategies and disciplines will not be inconsistent with the Good Friday Agreement," caused Tony Blair to challenge Sinn Fein to once and for all make a clear, unambiguous pledge to renounce paramilitary for political means. According to the *New York Times* (April 24, 2003), "virtually every newspaper in Britain and Ireland has editorialized in favor of full disarmament, and the Irish government, traditionally sympathetic to Sinn Fein, is almost as adamant about the matter as London is."

In Nov. 2003 legislative elections, the Ulster Unionists and other moderates lost out to Northern Ireland's extremist parties: Ian Paisley's Democratic Unionists and Sinn Fein. The prospect of power-sharing between these antithetical parties looked dim. An effort to revive the deadlocked power-sharing negotiations was broached in March 2004 by Tony Blair and Ireland's Bertie Ahern, who announced, "The elections were in November, this is March, we must move on." In Sept.

2004, another round of talks, aimed at ending the impasse, broke up with no significant progress.

Scotland

Status: Part of United Kingdom
First Minister: Jack McConnell (2001)
Area: 30,414 sq mi (78,772 sq km)
Population (1996 est.): 5,128,000; density per sq mi: 168.6
Capital (2003 est.): Edinburgh, 663,700 (metro. area), 460,000 (city proper). **Largest city:** Glasgow, 1,361,000 (metro. area), 1,099,400 (city proper).
Monetary unit: British pound sterling (£). **Languages:** English, Scots Gaelic. **Religions:** Church of Scotland (established church—Presbyterian), Roman Catholic, Scottish Episcopal Church, Baptist, Methodist

Geography Scotland occupies the northern third of the island of Great Britain. It is bounded by England in the south and on the other three sides by water: by the Atlantic Ocean on the west and north and by the North Sea on the east. Scotland is divided into three physical regions—the Highlands; the Central Lowlands, containing two-thirds of the population; and the Southern Uplands. The western Highland coast is intersected throughout by long, narrow sea lochs, or fjords. Scotland also includes the Outer and Inner Hebrides and other islands off the west coast and the Orkney and Shetland Islands off the north coast.

Government England and Scotland have shared a monarch since 1603 and a Parliament since 1707, but in May 1999, Scotland elected its own Parliament for the first time in three centuries. The new Scottish legislature was in part the result of British prime minister Tony Blair's campaign promise to permit devolution, the transfer of local powers from London to Edinburgh. In a Sept. 1997 referendum, 74% of Scotland voted in favor of their own Parliament, which controls most domestic affairs, including health, education, and transportation, and has powers to legislate and raise taxes. Queen Elizabeth opened the new Parliament on July 2, 1999.

History The first inhabitants of Scotland were the Picts, a Celtic tribe. Between A.D. 82 and A.D. 208, the Romans invaded Scotland, naming it Caledonia. Roman influence over the land, however, was minimal.

The Scots, a Celtic tribe from Ireland, migrated to the west coast of Scotland in about 500. Kenneth McAlpin, King of the Scots, ascended the throne of the Pictish kingdom in about 843, thereby uniting the various Scots and Pictish tribes under one kingdom called Dal Riada. By the 11th century, the monarchy had extended its borders to include much of what is Scotland today.

English influence in the region expanded when Malcolm III, king of Scotland from 1057–1093, married an English princess. England's appetite for Scottish land began to grow over the 12th and 13th centuries, and in 1296 King Edward I of England successfully invaded Scotland. The following year Robert the Bruce led a revolt for independence, was crowned king of Scotland (Robert I) in 1306, and after years of battle defeated the English in 1314 at the Battle of Bannockburn. In 1328 the English finally recognized Scottish independence.

In the 16th century John Knox introduced the Scottish reformation, and the Presbyterian church replaced Catholicism as the official religion. In 1567, Mary, Queen of Scots, a Catholic, was forced to abdicate the Scottish throne, and was later executed by Elizabeth I of England. Mary's son, James VI, was raised as a Protestant, and in 1603 he succeeded Elizabeth on the English throne as King James I of England. James thus became ruler of both Scotland and England, though the countries remained separate. In 1707, after a century of turmoil, Scotland and England passed the Act of Union, which united Scotland, England, and Wales under one rule as the Kingdom of Great Britain. The House of Hanover replaced the Stuart lineage on the throne in 1714, which caused a rebellion among Scots who still supported the Stuarts. The Jacobites, as the rebels were called, led two uprisings, in 1715 and again in 1745.

With the advent of the Industrial Revolution, Scotland, whose chief product had been textiles, began developing the industries of shipbuilding, coal mining, iron, and steel. In the late 20th century Scotland concentrated on electronics and high-tech industries. The North Sea has also become an important source of oil and gas.

In May 1999, Scotland elected its first separate Parliament in three centuries. Labour won the largest number of seats, defeating the Scottish National Party (SNP), which supports Scotland's independence from Britain.

Wales

Status: Part of United Kingdom
First Secretary: Rhodri Morgan (2000)
Area: 8,019 sq mi (20,768 sq km)
Population (1993 est.): 2,906,500
Capital and largest city (2003 est.): Cardiff, 676,400 (metro. area), 280,800 (city proper). **Monetary unit:** British pound sterling (£). **Languages:** English, Welsh. **Religions:** Calvinistic Methodist, Church of Wales (disestablished—Anglican), Roman Catholic

Geography Wales lies west of England and is separated from England by the Cambrian Mountains. It is bordered on the northwest, west, and south by the Irish Sea and on the northeast and east by England. Wales is generally hilly; the Snowdon range in the northern part culminates in Mount Snowdon (3,560 ft, 1,085 m), Wales's highest peak.

Government Until 1999, Wales was ruled solely by the UK government and a secretary of state. In the referendum of Sept. 18, 1997, Welsh citizens voted to establish a National Assembly. Wales will remain part of the UK, and the secretary of state for Wales and members of Parliament from Welsh constituencies will continue to have seats in Parliament. Unlike Scotland, which in 1999 voted to have its own Parliament, the National Assembly will not be able to legislate and raise taxes. Wales will, however, control most of its local affairs. The Welsh assembly officially opened on July 1, 1999.

History The prehistoric peoples of Wales left behind megaliths and other impressive monuments. They were followed by settlements of Celts in the region. The Romans occupied the region from the 1st to the 5th century A.D. Thereafter Angles, Saxons, and Jutes invaded the British island, but they left Wales virtually untouched. Beginning in the 8th century, the various Welsh tribes fought with their Anglo-Saxon neighbors to the east, but the Welsh were able to thwart attempted invasions. After William the Conqueror subdued England in 1066, however, his Norman armies marched into Wales in 1093 and occupied portions of it. By 1282, the English conquest of Wales was complete, and in 1284, the Statute of Rhuddlan formalized England's sovereignty over Wales. In 1301, King Edward I gave his son, who later became Edward II, the title Prince of Wales, a gesture meant to indicate the unity and relationship between the two lands. With the exception of Edward II, all subsequent British monarchs have given this title to their eldest son.

In 1400, the Welsh prince Owen Glendower led a revolt against the English, expelling them from much of Wales in just four years. By 1410, however, his rebellion was crushed. In 1485, Henry VII became king of England. A Welshman and the first in the Tudor line, Henry's reign, and that of subsequent Tudors, made English rule more palatable to the Welsh. His son, King Henry VIII, joined England and Wales under the Act of Union in 1536.

The Industrial Revolution of the 19th century transformed Wales and threatened the traditional livelihood of farmers and shepherds. In the 20th century, the economy of Wales was based primarily on coal production. After World War I, coal prices dropped; this, coupled with the Great Depression, fueled high unemployment rates and economic uncertainty.

In recent years, a resurgence of the Welsh language and culture has demonstrated a stronger national identity among the Welsh, and politically the country moved toward greater self-government (devolution). In 1999, with the strong support of Britain's prime minister, Tony Blair, Wales opened the Welsh National Assembly, the first real self-government Wales has had in more than 600 years.

Overseas Territories and Crown Dependencies of the United Kingdom

Anguilla

Status: Overseas territory
Governor: Alan Huckle (2004)
Chief Minister: Osbourne Fleming (2000)
Area: 39.38 sq mi (102 sq km)
Population (2004 est.): 13,008 (growth rate: 2.0%); birth rate: 14.5/1000; infant mortality rate: 21.9/1000; life expectancy: 76.9; density per sq mi: 330
Capital (2003 est.): The Valley, 830. **Monetary unit:** East Caribbean dollar. **Ethnicity/race:** black African. **Literacy:** 95% (1984 est.)
Economic summary: GDP/PPP (2001 est.): $104 million; per capita $8,600. **Real growth rate:** 2.8%. **Inflation:** 2.3%. **Unemployment:** 6.7% (2001). **Arable land:** 0%. **Agriculture:** small quantities of tobacco, vegetables; cattle raising. **Labor force:** 6,049 (2001); commerce 36%, services 29%, construction 18%, transportation and utilities 10%, manufacturing 3%, agriculture/fishing/forestry/mining 4% (2000 est.). **Industries:** tourism, boat building, offshore financial services. **Natural resources:** salt, fish, lobster. **Exports:** $2.6 million (1999): lobster, fish, livestock, salt, concrete blocks, rum. **Imports:** $80.9 million (1999): fuels, foodstuffs, manufactures, chemicals, trucks, textiles. **Major trading partners:** UK, U.S., Puerto Rico, Saint Martin.

Anguilla was first colonized in 1650 by English settlers from St. Christopher (St. Kitts) and has since remained a British territory. It was originally part of the West Indies Associated States as a component of the St. Kitts–Nevis-Anguilla Federation. In 1967, Anguilla declared its independence from the federation but Britain did not recognize this action. In Feb. 1969, Anguilla voted to cut all ties with Britain and become an independent republic. In March, Britain landed troops on the island and, on March 30, a truce was signed. In July 1971, Anguilla became a dependency of Britain and two months later Britain ordered the withdrawal of all its troops. A new constitution for Anguilla, effective in Feb. 1976, provided for separate administration and a government of elected representatives. The Associated State of St. Kitts–Nevis-Anguilla ended in 1980, and in 1982 a new Anguillan constitution took effect.

Bermuda

Status: Overseas territory
Governor: Sir John Vereker (2002)
Premier: Alex Scott (2003)
Area: 21 sq mi (53.3 sq km)
Population (2004 est.): 64,935 (growth rate: 0.7%); birth rate: 11.8/1000; infant mortality rate: 8.8/1000; life expectancy: 77.6; density per sq mi: 3,155
Capital (2003 est.): Hamilton, 970. **Monetary unit:** Bermuda dollar. **Ethnicity/race:** black African 58%, white and other 42%. **Literacy rate:** 98% (1970 est.)
Economic summary: GDP/PPP (2003 est.): $2.33 billion; per capita $36,000. **Real growth rate:** 2%. **Inflation:** 3.3% (mid-2003 est.). **Unemployment:** 5% (2002 est.). **Arable land:** 6%. **Agriculture:** bananas, vegetables, citrus, flowers; dairy products. **Labor force:** 37,472 (2000); clerical 22%, services 20%, laborers 17%, professional and technical 17%, administrative and managerial 13%, sales 8%, agriculture and fishing 3%. **Industries:** tourism, international business, light manufacturing. **Natural resources:** limestone, pleasant climate fostering tourism. **Exports:** $879 million (2002): reexports of pharmaceuticals. **Imports:** $5.523 billion (2002): machinery and transport equipment, construction materials, chemicals, food and live animals. **Major trading partners:** France, UK, U.S., Kazakhstan, Italy, South Korea, Mexico.

Bermuda is an archipelago of about 360 small islands, 580 mi (934 km) east of North Carolina. The largest is (Great) Bermuda, or Main Island. Explored by Juan de Bermúdez, a Spaniard, the islands were settled in 1612 by an offshoot of the Virginia Company. Bermuda became a Crown colony in 1684.

In 1968, Bermuda was granted a new constitution, its first prime minister, and autonomy, except for foreign relations, defense, and internal security. The predominantly white United Bermuda Party has retained power in four elections against the opposition—the black-led Progressive Labour Party—although Bermuda's population is 58% black. U.S. air and navy bases, which had been leased in 1941 for 99-year terms, closed in 1995, along with Canadian, British army, and Royal Navy bases. In a referendum held in Aug. 1995, nearly three-fourths of those voting opposed independence.

British Indian Ocean Territory

Status: Overseas territory
Commissioner: John White (1998)
Administrative headquarters: Victoria, Seychelles
Area: 85 sq mi (220 sq km)

This territory, consisting of the Chagos Archipelago and other small island groups, was formed in 1965 by agreement with Mauritius and the Seychelles. One of its islands, Diego Garcia (17 sq mi), is a joint U.S.-UK refueling and support station that was used during the Persian Gulf War (1991), the war against Afghanistan (1991), and the second Iraq war (2003). The island's small native population, known as the Ilois, were forced to relocate (1967–1973) to Mauritius and the Seychelles, where the majority of these former agricultural workers live in poverty in urban slums. In 2000, a British court ruled that the immigration order was invalid, but upheld the island's military status. The Ilois sued the British government for compensation and the right to repatriation, but in Oct. 2003 a British judge ruled that although the Ilois had been treated "shamefully" by the government, their claims were unfounded. The Ilois are expected to appeal.

British Virgin Islands

VIRGIN ISLANDS
Status: Overseas territory
Governor: Tom Macan (2002)
Chief Minister: Orlando Smith (2003)
Area: 59 sq mi (153 sq km)
Population (2004 est.): 22,187 (growth rate: 2.1%); birth rate: 15.0/1000; infant mortality rate: 18.1/1000; life expectancy: 76.3; density per sq mi: 376
Capital (2003 est.): Road Town (on Tortola): 9,100. **Monetary unit:** U.S. dollar. **Literacy rate:** 97.8% (1991 est.)
Economic summary: GDP/PPP (2002 est.): $320 million; per capita $16,000. **Real growth rate:** 1%. **Inflation:** 2.5% (2002). **Unemployment:** 3% (1995). **Arable land:** 20%. **Agriculture:** fruits, vegetables; livestock, poultry; fish. **Labor force:** 4,911 (1980). **Industries:** tourism, light industry, construction, rum, concrete block, offshore financial center. **Natural resources:** negl. **Exports:** $25.3 million (2002): rum, fresh fish, fruits, animals; gravel, sand. **Imports:** $187 million (2002 est.): building materials, automobiles, foodstuffs, machinery. **Major trading partners:** U.S. Virgin Islands, Puerto Rico, U.S.

Some 36 islands (more than 20 are uninhabited) in the Caribbean Sea northeast of Puerto Rico and west of the Leeward Islands, the British Virgin Islands are economically interdependent with the U.S. Virgin Islands to the south. The principal islands are Tortola, Virgin Gorda, Anegada, and Jost Van Dyke. When Christopher Columbus explored the islands in 1493, he found the Carib people living there. By 1596 most of the Caribs had fled or been killed.

The British Virgin Islands were annexed in 1672. The English planters' slave-based sugar plantations declined after slavery was abolished in the first half of the 19th century. The islands received a separate administration in 1956 as a Crown colony. Tourism is the islands' mainstay.

Cayman Islands

Status: Overseas territory
Governor: Bruce Dinwiddy (2002)
Area: 101 sq mi (262 sq km)
Population (2004 est.): 43,103 (growth rate: 2.7%); birth rate: 13.1/1000; infant mortality rate: 8.4/1000; life expectancy: 79.8; density per sq mi: 426
Capital (2003 est.): George Town (on Grand Cayman), 29,400. **Monetary unit:** Cayman Islands dollar. **Literacy rate:** 98% (1970 est.)
Economic summary: GDP/PPP (2002 est.): $1.27 billion; per capita $35,000. **Real growth rate:** 1.7%. **Inflation:** 2.8% (2002). **Unemployment:** 4.1% (1997). **Arable land:** 0%. **Agriculture:** vegetables, fruit; livestock, turtle farming. **Labor force:** 19,820 (1995); agriculture 1.4%, industry 12.6%, services 86% (1995). **Industries:** tourism, banking, insurance and finance, construction, construction materials, furniture. **Natural resources:** fish, climate and beaches that foster tourism. **Exports:** $1.2 million (1999): turtle products, manufactured consumer goods. **Imports:** $457.4 million (1999): foodstuffs, manufactured goods. **Major trading partners:** U.S., Trinidad and Tobago, UK, Netherlands Antilles, Japan.

The Caymans consist of three islands—Grand Cayman (76 sq mi; 197 sq km), Cayman Brac (22 sq mi; 57 sq km), and Little Cayman (20 sq mi; 52 sq km)—situated about 180 mi (290 km) northwest of Jamaica. They were dependencies of Jamaica until 1959, when they became a unit territory within the Federation of the West Indies. In 1962, upon the dissolution of the federation, the Cayman Islands became a British dependency, and a new constitution approved in 1972 provided for a greater degree of autonomy. Tourism and finance are the Cayman Islands' major industries. For a time, the Cayman Islands were blacklisted by the Paris-based Financial Action Task Force (FATF) for its allegedly loose policy concerning money laundering. It was removed from the list in 2001.

Channel Islands: Jersey and Guernsey

Status: Crown dependencies
Lieutenant Governor of Jersey: Sir Michael Wilkes (1995)
Lieutenant Governor of Guernsey: Vice Adm. Sir John Coward (1994)
Area: 45 sq mi (116 sq km) (Jersey), 30 sq mi (78 sq km) (Guernsey)
Populations (2004 est.): Jersey, 90,502; Guernsey, 65,031
Capital of Jersey (2003 est.): St. Helier, 28,600
Capital of Guernsey (2003 est.): St. Peter Port, 16,600.
 Monetary units: Guernsey pound; Jersey pound

This group of islands, lying in the English Channel off the northwest coast of France, belonged to the Duchy of Normandy until it passed to the English Crown with the Norman conquest of 1066. It was the only British possession occupied by Germany during World War II. English and French are commonly spoken (though use of the latter is declining), and a Norman-French patois survives.

For administrative purposes, the islands are divided into the Bailiwick of Jersey (45 sq mi; 116 sq km), including the Ecrehous rocks and Les Minquiers, and the Bailiwick of Guernsey (30 sq mi; 78 sq km), including Alderney (3 sq mi; 7.8 sq km), Sark (2 sq mi; 5.2 sq km), Herm, Jethou, Brechou, and other smaller islands. The Channel Islands enjoy tax sovereignty, and their exports are protected by British tariff barriers. Financial services, tourism, market gardening, and dairy farming are important industries.

Falkland Islands

Status: Overseas territory
Governor: Howard Pearce (2002)
Chief Executive: A. M. Gurr
Area: 4,700 sq mi (12,173 sq km)
Population (July 2003 est.): 2,967
Capital (2003 est.): Stanley (on East Falkland), 2,100.
 Monetary unit: Falkland Island pound
Economic summary: GDP/PPP (2002 est.): $75 million; per capita $25,000. **Real growth rate:** n.a. **Inflation:** 3.6% (1998). **Unemployment:** full employment; labor shortage (2001). **Arable land:** 0%. **Agriculture:** fodder and vegetable crops; sheep, dairy products. **Labor force:** 1,100 (est.); agriculture 95% (mostly sheepherding and fishing). **Industries:** fish and wool processing; tourism. **Natural resources:** fish, squid, wildlife, calcified seaweed, sphagnum moss. **Exports:** $82 million (2002): wool, hides, meat. **Imports:** $53 million (2002): fuel, food and drink, building materials, clothing. **Major trading partners:** Spain, UK, U.S., Italy.

This sparsely inhabited dependency consists of a group of islands in the South Atlantic, about 250 mi (402 km) east of the South American mainland. The largest islands are East Falkland and West Falkland. The English captain John Strong made the first recorded landing in the Falklands in 1690. The islands passed among the French, Spanish, and British until 1820, when the Argentine government proclaimed its sovereignty. In 1833 a British force expelled the few remaining Argentine officials from the island without firing a shot, and in 1841 a British civilian lieutenant-governor was appointed for the Falklands. Colonial sta-

tus was granted to the Falklands in 1892. Argentina, calling the islands *Las Islas Malvinas*, regularly protested Britain's occupation of the islands. On April 2, 1982, Argentina's military government invaded the Falklands. The Falkland Islands war ended ten weeks later with the surrender of the Argentine forces at Stanley to British troops, who had forcibly reoccupied the islands. Argentina still claims the islands. But an agreement between Argentina and the United Kingdom in 1995 sought to defuse licensing and sovereignty conflicts that would dampen foreign interest in exploiting the Falkland Islands' potential oil reserves.

Gibraltar

Status: Overseas territory
Governor: Francis Richards (2003)
Chief Minister: Peter Caruana (1996)
Area: 2.51 sq mi (6.5 sq km)
Population (2004 est.): 27,833 (growth rate: 0.2%); birth rate: 11.0/1000; infant mortality rate: 5.2/1000; life expectancy: 79.5; density per sq mi: 11,090. **Monetary unit:** Gibraltar pound. **Literacy rate:** above 80% (2003 est.)
Economic summary: GDP/PPP (1997 est.): $500 million; per capita $17,500. **Real growth rate:** n.a. **Inflation:** 1.5% (1998). **Unemployment:** 2% (2001 est.). **Arable land:** 0%. **Agriculture:** none. **Labor force:** 14,800 (including non-Gibraltar laborers); services 60%, industry 40%, agriculture negl. **Industries:** tourism, banking and finance, ship repairing, tobacco. **Natural resources:** negl. **Exports:** $136 million (2002): (principally reexports) petroleum 51%, manufactured goods 41%, other 8%. **Imports:** $1.743 billion (c.i.f., 2002): fuels, manufactured goods, and foodstuffs. **Major trading partners:** UK, Switzerland, Germany, France, Spain, Turkmenistan, Ukraine, Italy.

Gibraltar, at the south end of the Iberian Peninsula, is a rocky promontory commanding the western entrance to the Mediterranean. Aside from its strategic importance, it is also a free port, naval base, and coaling station. It was captured by the Moorish leader Tarik, crossing from Africa into Spain in 711, and its name is derived from the Arabic, *Jabal-al-Tarik* (Mount of Tarik). In the 15th century, it passed to the Moorish ruler of Granada and later became Spanish. It was captured by an Anglo-Dutch force in 1704 during the War of the Spanish Succession and passed to Great Britain by the Treaty of Utrecht in 1713. Since then Spain has continually laid claims to it. Most of the inhabitants of Gibraltar are of Spanish, Italian, and Maltese descent, and in 1981 Gibraltarians were granted full British citizenship. Spanish efforts to recover Gibraltar culminated in a referendum in 1967, in which the residents voted overwhelmingly to retain their link with Britain. In response, Spain sealed Gibraltar's land border between 1969 and 1985. In 2002, Britain and Spain discussed sharing the sovereignty of Gibraltar. In response, the government of Gibraltar held a referendum in Nov. 2002 in which the population voted almost unanimously against shared sovereignty.

Isle of Man

Status: Crown dependency
Lieutenant Governor: Ian David Macfadyen (2000)
Chief Minister: Donald James Gelling (1996)
Area: 221 sq mi (572 sq km)
Population (2004 est.): 74,655 (growth rate: 0.5%); birth rate: 11.3/1000; infant mortality rate: 6.1/1000; life expectancy: 78.2; density per sq mi: 338
Capital (2003 est.): Douglas, 25,400. **Monetary unit:** Isle of Man pound

The Isle of Man is situated in the Irish Sea, equidistant from Scotland, Ireland, and England. Among its earliest inhabitants were Celts, and their language, Manx, which is closely related to Irish and Scottish Gaelic, remained the everyday speech of the people until the first half of the 19th century. Manx now has no native speakers. Norse (Viking) invasions began about 800, and the island was a dependency of Norway until 1266. During this period the Isle of Man came under a Scandinavian system of government that has remained practically unchanged ever since. The island came under the control of England in 1341. After allowing a succession of feudal lords to rule the island, the British Parliament purchased sovereignty over the island in 1765. The Isle of Man continues to be administered according to its own laws by a government composed of the lieutenant governor, a legislative council, and a House of Keys, one of the most ancient legislative assemblies in the world.

Montserrat

Status: Overseas territory
Governor: Deborah Barnes Jones (2004)
Chief Minister: John Osborne (2001)
Area: 39 sq mi (102 sq km)
Population (2004 est.): 9,245 (growth rate: 1.0%); birth rate: 17.6/1000; infant mortality rate: 7.6/1000; life expectancy: 78.5; density per sq mi: 235
Capital (2003 est.): Plymouth. The city was abandoned in 1997 due to volcanic activity. Interim government buildings have been built at Brades Estate, in the Carr's Bay/Little Bay vicinity at the northwest end of Montserrat. **Monetary unit:** East Caribbean dollar
Economic summary: GDP/PPP (2002 est.): $29 million; per capita $3,400. **Real growth rate:** –1%. **Inflation:** 2.6% (2002 est.). **Unemployment:** 6% (1998 est.). **Arable land:** 20%. **Agriculture:** cabbages, carrots, cucumbers, tomatoes, onions, peppers; livestock products. **Labor force:** 4,521; note—recently lowered by flight of people from volcanic activity (2000 est); agriculture n.a., industry n.a., services n.a. **Industries:** tourism, rum, textiles, electronic appliances. **Natural resources:** negl. **Exports:** $700,000 (2001): electronic components, plastic bags, apparel, hot peppers, live plants, cattle. **Imports:** $17 million (2001): machinery and transportation equipment, foodstuffs, manufactured goods, fuels, lubricants and related materials. **Major trading partners:** U.S., Antigua and Barbuda, UK, Trinidad and Tobago, Japan, Canada.

The island of Montserrat is in the Lesser Antilles of the West Indies. Until 1956, it was a division of the Leeward Islands. In 1958 Montserrat joined the Federation of the West Indies, remaining a member until that organization's dissolution in 1962. Unlike most other British West Indies possessions, Montserrat, with its weak economy, has not vigorously sought independence. The Soufrière Hills volcano began erupting in 1995, and the situation continued to worsen through 1998, with the capital, Plymouth, destroyed and the southern and central parts of the British colony having been evacuated. Thousands had moved to nearby Antigua, Britain, or other parts of the Caribbean. In 2004, the U.S. Dept. of Homeland Security announced that it was revoking the "temporary protected status" of its 292 Montserrat refugees, a number of whom have lived in the U.S. for years and rebuilt their lives there. A *Washington Post* editorial called the decision "absurd and cruel."

Pitcairn Island

Status: Overseas territory
Governor: Richard Fell (nonresident) (2001)
Island Mayor: Steve Christian (1999)
Area: 18.15 sq mi (47 sq km)
Population (2004): 47; density per sq mi: 3
Capital: Adamstown

Pitcairn Island, in the South Pacific about midway between Australia and South America, consists of the island of Pitcairn and the three uninhabited islands of Henderson, Duicie, and Oeno. Pitcairn was settled in 1790 by British mutineers from the ship *Bounty,* commanded by Capt. William Bligh. One of the most remote islands in the world, it was annexed as a British colony in 1838. Overpopulation forced removal of the settlement to Norfolk Island in 1856, but about 40 persons soon returned.

The descendants of First Mate Fletcher Christian, the eight other mutineers, and the dozen or so Tahitians who accompanied them still inhabit the island. In addition to English, the residents of Pitcairn speak a dialect that is a mixture of Tahitian and 18th-century English.

St. Helena

Status: Overseas territory
Governor: David Hollamby (1999)
Area: 158 sq mi (410 sq km)
Population (2004 est.): 7,415 (growth rate: 0.6%); birth rate: 12.7/1000; infant mortality rate: 19.9/1000; life expectancy: 77.6; density per sq mi: 47
Capital (2003 est.): Jamestown, 1,500. **Monetary unit:** Pound sterling. **Literacy rate:** 97% (1987 est.)

St. Helena is a remote volcanic island in the South Atlantic about 1,100 mi (1,770 km) from the west coast of Africa. It is famous as Napoleon's place of exile (1815–1821). The island was discovered in 1502 by João da Nova, a Spanish navigator in the service of Portugal. It was taken for England in 1659 by the East India Company and was brought under the direct government of the Crown in 1834. After the opening of the Suez Canal in 1870, St. Helena's importance as a port of call diminished. About two-thirds of the colony's budget is provided by the United Kingdom in the form of a subsidy.

St. Helena has two dependencies: Ascension (34 sq mi; 88 sq km), an island about 700 mi (1,127 km) northwest of St. Helena; and Tristan da Cunha (40 sq mi; 104 sq km), a group of six islands about 1,500 mi (2,414 km) south-southwest of St. Helena.

South Georgia and the South Sandwich Islands

Status: Overseas territory
Commissioner: Donald A. Lamont (1999)
Area: 1,506 sq mi (3,903 sq km)
Population: no indigenous inhabitants

The islands are located in the South Atlantic Ocean, east of the tip of South America, approximately 1,000 km east of the Falkland Islands, from which they are administered. In addition to South Georgia Island and the nine South Sandwich Islands, the island group includes Shag Rocks, Black Rock, Clerke Rocks, and Bird Island. A small military garrison on South Georgia withdrew in March 2001 and was replaced by a permanent group of scientists of the British Antarctic Survey.

Turks and Caicos Islands

Status: Overseas territory
Governor: Jim Poston (2002)
Chief Minister: Derek H. Taylor (1995)
Area: 166 sq mi (430 sq km)
Population (2004 est.): 19,956 (growth rate: 3.0%); birth rate: 22.9/1000; infant mortality rate: 16.3/1000; life expectancy: 74.3; density per sq mi: 120
Capital (2003 est.): Cockburn Town, 5,000. **Monetary unit:** U.S. dollar. **Literacy rate:** 98% (1970 est.)
Economic summary: GDP/PPP (2000 est.): $231 million; per capita $9,600. **Real growth rate:** 4.9%. **Inflation:** 4% (1995). **Unemployment:** 10% (1997 est.). **Arable land:** 2%. **Agriculture:** products: corn, beans, cassava (tapioca), citrus fruits; fish. **Labor force:** 4,848 (1990 est.); about 33% in government and 20% in agriculture and fishing; significant numbers in tourism, financial, and other services (1997 est.). **Industries:** tourism, offshore financial services. **Natural resources:** spiny lobster, conch. **Exports:** $169.2 million (2000): lobster, dried and fresh conch, conch shells. **Imports:** $175.6 million (2000): food and beverages, tobacco, clothing, manufactures, construction materials. **Major trading partners:** U.S., UK.

These two groups of islands are near the Bahamas in the Caribbean. The principal islands in the Turks group are Grand Turk and Salt Cay; the principal islands in the Caicos group are South Caicos, East Caicos, Middle (or Grand) Caicos, North Caicos, Providenciales, and West Caicos. The islands were not settled by Europeans until 1678, when British colonists from Bermuda established a salt-panning industry. The islands were at first placed under the Bahamian government, but in 1874 they became dependencies of the colony of Jamaica. Following Jamaica's independence, they became a British Crown colony. The salt production industry, the islands' economic mainstay, ceased in 1964 and gave way to tourism, offshore financial services, and fishing.

United States

THE UNITED STATES OF AMERICA

President: George W. Bush (2001)
Vice President: Richard B. Cheney (2001)
Area (2003): 3,717,792 sq mi (9,629,091 sq km)
Population (2004 est.): 293,027,571
Population (2000 census): 280,562,489 (change 1990–2000: 13.2%) (growth rate: 0.9%); birth rate: 14.1/1000; infant mortality rate: 6.6/1000; life expectancy: 77.4; density per sq mi: 79
Capital (2003 est.): Washington, DC, 570,898. **Largest cities (2003 est.):** New York, 8,085,742 (city proper); Los Angeles, 3,819,951; Chicago, 2,869,121; Houston, 2,009,960; Philadelphia, 1,479,339; Phoenix, 1,388,416; San Diego, 1,226,753; San Antonio, 1,214,725; Dallas, 1,208,318; Detroit, 911,402.
Monetary unit: dollar. **Languages:** English, sizable Spanish-speaking minority. **Ethnicity/race:** White: 211,460,626 (75.1%); Black: 34,658,190 (12.3%); Asian: 10,242,998 (3.6%); American Indian and Alaska Native: 2,475,956 (0.9%); Native Hawaiian and other Pacific Islander: 398,835 (0.1%); other race: 15,359,073 (5.5%); Hispanic origin:[1] 35,305,818 (12.5%). **Religions:** Protestant 56%; Roman Catholic 28%; Jewish 2%; other 4%; none 10% (1989).
Literacy rate: 97% (1979 est.)
Economic summary: GDP/PPP (2003 est.): $10.98 trillion; per capita $37,800. **Real growth rate:** 3.1%. **Inflation:** 2.1% (2003). **Unemployment:** 6.2%. **Arable land:** 19%. **Agriculture:** wheat, corn, other grains, fruits, vegetables, cotton; beef, pork, poultry, dairy products; forest products; fish. **Labor force:** 141.8 million (includes unemployed) (2003); managerial and professional 31%, technical, sales, and administrative support 28.9%, services 13.6%, manufacturing, mining, transportation, and crafts 24.1%, farming, forestry, and fishing 2.4%; note: figures exclude the unemployed (2001) **Industries:** leading industrial power in the world, highly diversified and technologically advanced; petroleum, steel, motor vehicles, aerospace, telecommunications, chemicals, electronics, food processing, consumer goods, lumber, mining. **Natural resources:** coal, copper, lead, molybdenum, phosphates, uranium, bauxite, gold, iron, mercury, nickel, potash, silver, tungsten, zinc, petroleum, natural gas, timber. **Exports:** $714.5 billion (f.o.b., 2003 est.): capital goods, automobiles, industrial supplies and raw materials, consumer goods, agricultural products. **Imports:** $1.26 trillion (f.o.b., 2003 est.): crude oil and refined petroleum products, machinery, automobiles, consumer goods, industrial raw materials, food and beverages. **Major trading partners:** Canada, Mexico, Japan, UK, China, Germany.

1. Persons of Hispanic origin can be of any race.
Government Federal republic.

The president is elected for a four-year term and may be reelected only once. The bicameral Congress consists of the 100-member Senate, elected to a six-year term with one-third of the seats becoming vacant every two years, and the 435-member House of Representatives, elected every two years. The minimum voting age is 18. (*See also* Profile of the United States, U.S. States, U.S. Cities, U.S. Statistics, and U.S. Government and History.)

U.S. Territories and Outlying Areas

Puerto Rico

COMMONWEALTH OF PUERTO RICO

Status: Commonwealth
Governor: Sila María Calderón (2001)
Capital and largest city (2002 est.): San Juan, 433,412. **Other large cities:** Bayamón, 224,670; Ponce, 186,112; Carolina, 187,468
Land area: 3,515 sq mi (9,104 sq km)
Population (2004 est.): 3,897,960 (growth rate: 0.5%); birth rate: 14.1/1000; infant mortality rate: 8.4/1000; life expectancy: 77.5; density per sq mi: 1,109. **Currency:** U.S. dollar. **Languages:** Spanish and English (both official). **Ethnicity/race:** Almost entirely Hispanic. **Religions:** Roman Catholic 85%, Protestant denominations and other 15%. **Literacy rate:** 94% (2001)
Economic summary: GDP/PPP (2003 est.): $65.28 billion; per capita $16,800. **Real growth rate:** 1.6%. **Inflation:** 6.5%. **Unemployment:** 12% (2002). **Arable land:** 4%. **Agriculture:** sugarcane, coffee, pineapples, plantains, bananas; livestock products, chickens. **Labor force:** 1.3 million (2002); agriculture 3%, industry 20%, services 77% (2000 est.). **Industries:** pharmaceuticals, electronics, apparel, food products; tourism. **Natural resources:** some copper and nickel; potential for onshore and offshore oil. **Exports:** $46.22 billion (f.o.b., 2002): chemicals, electronics, apparel, canned tuna, rum, beverage concentrates, medical equipment. **Imports:** $26.46 billion (c.i.f., 2002): chemicals, machinery and equipment, clothing, food, fish, petroleum products. **Major trading partner:** U.S., UK, Dominican Republic, Ireland, Japan.

The Commonwealth of Puerto Rico is located in the Caribbean Sea, about 1,000 mi east-southeast of Miami, Fla. A possession of the United States, it consists of the island of Puerto Rico plus the adjacent islets of Vieques, Culebra, and Mona. Puerto Rico has a mountainous, tropical ecosystem with very little flat land and few mineral resources.

Puerto Rico's governor is elected directly for a four-year term. A bicameral legislature consists of a 27-member Senate and a 51-member House of Representatives, all elected for four-year terms. From 1940 to 1968, Puerto Rican politics was dominated by a party advocating voluntary association with the U.S. Since then, the New Progressive Party, a party favoring U.S. statehood, has won five of the last eight gubernatorial elections. Puerto Ricans have twice voted to determine their political status. In 1967, the outcome was Commonwealth 60%; statehood 39%; independence 1%. In 1993, Commonwealth dropped to 48.6%; statehood rose to 46.3%; independence polled 4.4%; and 0.6% of the ballots were blank or spoiled.

Under the Commonwealth formula, residents of Puerto Rico lack voting representation in Congress and do not participate in presidential elections. As U.S. citizens, Puerto Ricans are subject to military service and most federal laws. Residents of the Commonwealth pay no federal income tax on locally generated earnings, but Puerto Rico government income-tax rates are set at a level that closely parallels federal-plus-state levies on the mainland.

When Christopher Columbus arrived there in 1493, the island was inhabited by the peaceful Arawak Indians, who were being challenged by the warlike Carib Indians. Puerto Rico remained economically undeveloped until 1830, when sugarcane, coffee, and tobacco plantations were gradually developed. After Puerto Ricans began to press for independence, Spain granted the island broad powers of self-government in 1897. But during the Spanish-American War of 1898 American troops invaded the island and Spain ceded it to the U.S. Since then, Puerto Rico has remained an unincorporated U.S. territory. Its people were granted American citizenship under the Jones Act in 1917; were permitted to elect their own governor, beginning in 1948; and now fully administer their internal affairs under a constitution approved by the U.S. Congress in 1952. In spite of broad popular support for the autonomy of the Commonwealth government and a rapidly modernizing industrial society, there were expressions of dissatisfaction. Puerto Rican extremists dramatized their desire for independence with an attempt to assassinate President Truman on Nov. 1, 1950, and on March 1, 1954, they wounded five congressmen in an attack on the U.S. Capitol.

A self-help program of economic development and social welfare (called "Operation Bootstrap") was forged in the 1940s by four-time governor Luis Muñoz Marín. In a little more than four decades, much of the island's crushing poverty was eliminated. This was done partly through the development of manufacturing and service industries, the latter related to an enormous growth in tourism. Also, many Puerto Ricans migrated to large cities on the mainland U.S.

Puerto Rico is a major hub of Caribbean commerce, finance, tourism, and communications. San Juan is one of the world's busiest cruise-ship ports, and Puerto Rico's standard of living continues to be among the highest in the hemisphere. Its future political status, however, remains unclear. On March 4, 1998, the U.S. House of Representatives passed a bill that called for binding elections in Puerto Rico to decide the island's permanent political status.

Since the 1940s, the U.S. Navy has used Vieques island as a bombing range. Protests against the exercises grew in recent years, and in a July 2001 referendum residents of the island voted overwhelmingly to close the base. The navy withdrew from Vieques in May 2003.

Guam

TERRITORY OF GUAM

Status: Territory
Governor: Felix Camacho (2003)
Capital (2000 est.): Agaña, 1,100
Land area: 212 sq mi (549 sq km)
Population (2004 est.): 166,090 (growth rate: 1.5%); birth rate: 19.3/1000; infant mortality rate: 7.2/1000; life expectancy: 78.1; density per sq mi: 784. **1996 est. net migration:** 3 migrants per 1,000 population. **Languages:** English and Chamorro; note: most residents are bilingual; Japanese also widely spoken. **Ethnicity/race:** Chamorro 37%, Filipino 26%, Caucasian 10%, Chinese, Japanese, Korean, and other, 27%. **Religions:** Roman Catholic 85%, other 15% (1999 est.). **Literacy rate:** 99% (1990 est.). **Currency:** U.S. dollar
Economic summary: GDP/PPP (2000 est.): $3.2 billion; per capita $21,000. **Real growth rate:** n.a. **Inflation:** 0% (1999 est.). **Unemployment:** 15% (2000 est.). **Arable land:** 11%. **Agriculture:** fruits, copra, vegetables; eggs, pork, poultry, beef. **Labor force:** 60,000 (2000 est.); federal and territorial government 26%, private 74% (trade 24%, other services 40%, industry 10%) (2000 est.). **Industries:** U.S. military, tourism, construction, transshipment services, concrete products, printing and publishing, food processing, textiles. **Natural resources:** fishing (largely undeveloped), tourism (especially from Japan). **Exports:** $38 million (f.o.b., 2002 est.): mostly transshipments of refined petroleum products; construction materials, fish, food and beverage products. **Imports:** $462 million (f.o.b., 2002 est.): petroleum and petroleum products, food, manufactured goods. **Major trading partners:** Japan, South Korea, Canada, Singapore, Hong Kong.

Guam is the largest and southernmost island in the Marianas Archipelago. The island is divided into a northern coralline limestone plateau and a southern chain of volcanic hills. Today Guam is an unincorporated, organized territory of the United States. The people of Guam have been U.S. citizens since 1950. They have been represented in the U.S. Congress since 1973 by a nonvoting delegate, but do not participate in presidential elections. The executive branch includes a popularly elected governor, who serves a four-year term. The legislative branch is a 21-member unicameral legislature whose members are elected every two years.

Guam was probably explored by the Portuguese navigator Ferdinand Magellan (sailing for Spain) in 1521. The island was formally claimed by Spain in 1565, and its people were forced into submission and conversion to Roman Catholicism beginning in 1668. After the Spanish-American War of 1898, Spain ceded Guam to the United States. From 1899 to 1949, the U.S. Navy administered Guam, except during the Japanese occupation from 1941–1944. Guam was liberated by American military forces in the summer of 1944. Guam's economy is based on tourism and U.S. military spending (U.S. naval and air force bases occupy one-third of the land on Guam).

U.S. Virgin Islands

VIRGIN ISLANDS OF THE UNITED STATES

Status: Territory
Governor: Charles Turnbull (1999)
Capital (2000 est.): Charlotte Amalie (on St. Thomas), 11,004
Land area: 136 sq mi (352 sq km)

Population (2004 est.): 108,775 (growth rate: –0.1%); birth rate: 14.5/1000; infant mortality rate: 8.2/1000; life expectancy: 78.8; density per sq mi: 800. **Languages:** English (official), but Spanish and French are also spoken. **Ethnicity/race:** West Indian 74% (45% born in the Virgin Islands and 29% born elsewhere in the West Indies), U.S. mainland 13%, Puerto Rican 5%, other 8%, black 80%, white 15%, other 5%, 14% of Hispanic origin. **Religions:** Baptist 42%, Roman Catholic 34%, Episcopalian 17%, other 7%. **Literacy rate:** n.a. **Currency:** U.S. dollar
Economic summary: GDP/PPP (2001 est.): $2.4 billion; per capita $19,000. **Real growth rate:** 2%. **Inflation:** 2% (1992). **Unemployment:** 8.7% (2002 est.). **Arable land:** 15%. **Agriculture:** fruit, vegetables, sorghum; Senepol cattle. **Labor force:** 49,000 (2002 est.); agriculture 1%, industry 20%, services 79% (1990 est.). **Industries:** tourism, petroleum refining, watch assembly, rum distilling, construction, pharmaceuticals, textiles, electronics. **Natural resources:** sun, sand, sea, surf. **Exports:** $ n.a.: refined petroleum products. **Imports:** $ n.a.: crude oil, foodstuffs, consumer goods, building materials. **Major trading partners:** U.S., Puerto Rico.

The Virgin Islands, consisting of nine main islands and some 75 islets, were explored by Columbus in 1493. They were originally inhabited by the Carib Indians. Since 1666, England has held six of the main islands; the remaining three (St. Croix, St. Thomas, and St. John), as well as about 50 of the islets, were eventually acquired by Denmark, which named them the Danish West Indies. In 1917, these islands were purchased by the U.S. from Denmark for $25 million.

Congress granted U.S. citizenship to Virgin Islanders in 1927. Universal suffrage was given in 1936 to all persons who could read and write English. The governor was elected by popular vote for the first time in 1970; previously he had been appointed by the U.S. president. A unicameral 15-person legislature serves the Virgin Islands, and congressional legislation gave the islands a nonvoting representative in Congress. Residents of the islands substantially enjoy the same rights as those enjoyed by mainlanders, but they may not vote in presidential elections.

Tourism is the primary economic activity, accounting for most of the GDP and 70% of employment. All goods made in the Virgin Islands qualify for duty-free entry into the United States.

American Samoa
TERRITORY OF AMERICAN SAMOA

Status: Territory
Governor: Togiola Tulafono (2003)
Capital (2003 est.): Pago Pago, 4,100
Land area: 77 sq mi (199 sq km)
Population (2004 est.): 57,902 (growth rate: 0.0%); birth rate: 24.5/1000; infant mortality rate: 9.5/1000; life expectancy: 75.6; density per sq mi: 754. **Languages:** Samoan (closely related to Hawaiian and other Polynesian languages) and English; most people are bilingual. **Ethnicity/race:** Samoan (Polynesian) 89%, Tongan 4%, Caucasian 2%, other 5%. **Religions:** Christian Congregationalist 50%, Roman Catholic 20%, Protestant denominations and other 30%. **Literacy rate:** 97% (1980 est.). **Currency:** U.S. dollar
Economic summary: GDP/PPP (2000 est.): $500 million; per capita $8,000. **Real growth rate:** n.a. **Inflation:** n.a. **Unemployment:** 6% (2000). **Arable land:** 5%. **Agriculture:** bananas, coconuts, vegetables, taro, breadfruit, yams, copra, pineapples, papayas; dairy products, livestock. **Labor force:** 14,000 (1996); government 33%, tuna canneries 34%, other 33% (1990). **Industries:** tuna canneries (largely dependent on foreign fishing vessels), handicrafts.

Natural resources: pumice, pumicite. **Exports:** $30 million (2002): canned tuna 93%. **Imports:** $123 million (2002): materials for canneries 56%, food 8%, petroleum products 7%, machinery and parts 6%. **Major trading partners:** Indonesia, Japan, Samoa, Australia, New Zealand, South Korea.

American Samoa, a group of five volcanic islands and two coral atolls located some 2,600 mi south of Hawaii in the South Pacific, is an unincorporated, unorganized territory of the U.S. It includes the eastern Samoan islands of Tutuila, Aunu'u, and Rose; three islands (Ta'u, Olosega, and Ofu) of the Manu'a group; and Swains Island. Around 1000 B.C. Protopolynesians established themselves in the islands, and their descendants are one of the few remaining Polynesian societies. The Dutch navigator Jacob Roggeveen sighted the Manu'a Islands in 1722. American Samoa has been a territory of the United States since April 17, 1900, when the High Chiefs of Tutuila signed the first of two Deeds of Cession for the islands to the U.S. (Congress ratified the Deeds in 1929.) Swains Island, which is privately owned, came under U.S. administration in 1925.

Until World War II the United States operated a coaling station and naval base in Pago Pago. During the war, the islands were an important U.S. Marines staging area. In 1960 American Samoa ratified its territorial constitution and has since developed a modern, self-governing political system. American Samoans elect a governor, lieutenant governor, and legislature. The legislature (Fono) consists of two houses: the Senate, selected by village chiefs (matai) for four-year terms, and the House of Representatives, elected by the general population for two-year terms. The people of American Samoa are U.S. nationals, not U.S. citizens, but many have become naturalized American citizens. American Samoa does 80%–90% of its foreign trade with the U.S. Canned tuna is the primary export, earning $300 million annually. Transfers from the U.S. government add substantially to American Samoa's economic well-being.

Northern Mariana Islands
THE COMMONWEALTH OF THE NORTHERN MARIANA ISLANDS, OR CNMI

Status: Commonwealth
Governor: Juan N. Babautu (2002)
Capital: Chalan Kanoa (on Saipan)
Total area: 184 sq mi (477 sq km)
Population (2004 est.): 78,252 (growth rate: 2.7%); birth rate: 19.8/1000; infant mortality: 7.3/1000; life expectancy: 75.7; density per sq mi: 425. **Languages:** English (official), Chamorro, Carolinian. **Ethnicity/race:** Chamorro, Carolinian, other Micronesian, Caucasian, Japanese, Chinese, Korean. **Religion:** Primarily Roman Catholic. **Literacy rate:** 97% (1980 est.). **Currency:** U.S. dollar
Economic summary: GDP/PPP (2000 est.): $900 million; note: GDP numbers reflect U.S. spending; per capita $12,500. **Real growth rate:** n.a. **Inflation:** 1.2% (1997 est.). **Unemployment:** n.a. **Arable land:** 15%. **Agriculture:** coconuts, fruits, vegetables; cattle. **Labor force:** 6,006 total indigenous labor force; 2,699 unemployed; 28,717 foreign workers (June 1995). **Industries:** tourism, construction, garments, handicrafts. **Natural resources:** arable land, fish. **Exports:** $ n.a.: garments. **Imports:** $ n.a.: food, construction equipment and materials, petroleum products. **Major trading partners:** U.S., Japan.

The Northern Mariana Islands, east of the Philippines and south of Japan, include the islands of Rota,

Saipan, Tinian, Pagan, Guguan, Agrihan, and Aguijan. Although sighted by Ferdinand Magellan in 1521 as he sailed for Spain, the islands were not settled by Europeans until 1668, when missionaries converted the indigenous Chamorro people to Catholicism. They were ruled successively by Spain, Germany, and Japan before they became a UN Trusteeship (administered by the U.S.) after World War II. The Commonwealth of the Northern Mariana Islands (CNMI) became part of the United States in Nov. 1986. Spanish cultural traditions remain strong.

In recent years, Saipan's garment industry has been accused of exploiting thousands of Asian immigrants. Saipan's territorial status enables its employers to claim their clothing is "Made in the USA," while paying workers low wages and sidestepping import duties and tariffs.

Midway Islands

Status: Territory
Total area: 2 sq mi (5 sq km)
Population (July 2003 est.): no indigenous inhabitants; approx. 40 U.S. Fish and Wildlife Service staff.

The Midway Islands consist of a circular atoll, 6 mi in diameter, that encloses two islands. Lying about 1,150 mi west-northwest of Hawaii, the islands were first explored by Captain N. C. Brooks on July 5, 1859, in the name of the U.S. The atoll was declared a U.S. possession in 1867, and in 1903 Theodore Roosevelt made it a naval reservation. The island was renamed "Midway" by the U.S. Navy in recognition of its geographic location on the route between California and Japan. Air traffic across the Pacific increased the island's importance in the mid-1930s; the San Francisco–Manila mail route included a regular stop on Midway. Its military importance was soon recognized, and the navy began building an air and submarine base there in 1940. The Battle of Midway, which took place from June 3–6, 1942, was considered a turning point in World War II. After the war, the strategic importance of the island declined; the Midway stop for commercial air traffic was eliminated in 1950, and the air base closed in 1992.

Wake Island

Status: Territory
Total area: 2.51 sq mi (6.5 sq km)
Comparative size: about 11 times the size of the Mall in Washington, DC
Population (July 2003 est.): no indigenous inhabitants; 200 civilian contractors.
Economy: The economic activity is limited to providing services to U.S. military personnel and contractors on the island. All food and manufactured goods must be imported.

Wake Island, about halfway between Midway and Guam, is an atoll consisting of the three islets of Wilkes, Peale, and Wake. They were discovered by the British in 1796 and annexed by the U.S. in 1899. In 1938, Pan American Airways established a seaplane base, and Wake Island was used as a commercial base for several years. On Dec. 8, 1941, it was attacked by the Japanese, who finally took possession on Dec. 23. It was surrendered by the Japanese on Sept. 4, 1945.

Johnston Atoll

Status: Territory
Land area: 1.08 sq mi (2.8 sq km); density per sq mi: 1,111
Population (Jan. 2004 est.): no indigenous inhabitants; 396 U.S. military and civilian personnel

Johnston is a coral atoll about 700 mi southwest of Hawaii. It consists of four small islands—Johnston Island, Sand Island, Hikina Island, and Akau Island—which lie on a 9-mile-long reef. The atoll was discovered by Capt. Charles James Johnston of HMS *Cornwallis* in 1807. In 1858 it was claimed by Hawaii, and later became a U.S. possession. Johnston Atoll was used by the U.S. Air Force to conduct test launchings of nuclear missiles and contains a landfill of plutonium-contaminated waste. More than 4 million pounds of chemical weapons have been destroyed on Johnston since 1990, and the U.S. military had been fined several times since then for improperly handling VX and sarin gas and releasing the deadly substances on the atoll. The military is gradually departing and the atoll will be turned into a wildlife refuge. However, the U.S. Fish and Wildlife Service, the atoll's inheritor, is concerned about the possibility of eventual radioactive leakage.

Baker, Howland, and Jarvis Islands

Status: Territory

These Pacific islands were claimed by the United States under the Guano Act of 1856 on May 13, 1936. Guano, composed of phosphates, was used as fertilizer in the 19th century, and its collection was highly lucrative. Through the Guano Act the U.S. gained 79 tiny territories around the world; it still controls eight of them. Baker Island is an atoll with an area of approximately one square mile about 1,650 mi from Hawaii. Howland Island, 36 mi to the northwest, is 1 mile long and half a mile wide. On their round-the-world flight in 1937, Amelia Earhart and Fred J. Noonan were headed for Howland when they disappeared. Jarvis Island is several hundred miles to the east.

Kingman Reef

Status: Territory

Kingman Reef, located about 1,000 mi south of Hawaii, was discovered by Capt. E. Fanning in 1798 but named for Capt. W. E. Kingman, who rediscovered it in 1853. Triangular in shape, it is about 9.5 mi long. A U.S. possession since 1922, Kingman Reef is a Naval Defensive Sea Area and Airspace Reservation and is closed to the public.

Navassa Island

Status: Territory

Navassa Island is located in the Caribbean Sea 99.4 mi (160 km) south of the U.S. naval base at Guantánamo, Cuba, between Cuba, Haiti, and Jamaica. The island has a total area of 2.01 sq mi (5.2 sq km). It was claimed for the U.S. under the Guano Act in 1857. The Navassa Phosphate Company mined the island until 1900, enlisting hundreds of freed American slaves to dig out several tons of guano. Working conditions were so brutal that the laborers finally revolted in 1889, killing their supervisors. The island is also claimed by Haiti.

Palmyra Atoll

Status: Territory

Palmyra Atoll is an incorporated territory of the U.S. and privately owned. The atoll has a total area of 4.6 sq mi (11.9 sq km) and is located in the North Pacific Ocean, 994 mi (1,600 km) southwest of Honolulu. It was a U.S. military base during World War II but was not attacked.

Uruguay

ORIENTAL REPUBLIC OF URUGUAY

National name: República Oriental del Uruguay
President: Jorge Batlle (2000)
Area: 68,039 sq mi (176,220 sq km)
Population (2004 est.): 3,399,237 (growth rate: 0.5%);
birth rate: 14.4/1000; infant mortality rate: 12.3/1000;
life expectancy: 75.9; density per sq mi: 50
Capital and largest city (2003 est.): Montevideo,
1,745,100 (metro. area), 1,347,600 (city proper).
Monetary unit: Uruguay peso. **Language:** Spanish,
Portunol, or Brazilero. **Ethnicity/race:** white 88%,
mestizo 8%, black 4%. **Religions:** Roman Catholic
66%, Protestant 2%, Jewish 1%, nonprofessing or
other 31%. **Literacy rate:** 98% (2003 est.)
Economic summary: GDP/PPP (2003 est.): $42.94
billion; per capita $12,600. **Real growth rate:** 0.3%.
Inflation: 10.2%. **Unemployment:** 16.1%. **Arable
land:** 7%. **Agriculture:** rice, wheat, corn, barley;
livestock; fish. **Labor force:** 1.3 million (2002);
agriculture 14%, industry 16%, services 70%.
Industries: food processing, electrical machinery,
transportation equipment, petroleum products, textiles,
chemicals, beverages. **Natural resources:** arable
land, hydropower, minor minerals, fisheries. **Exports:**
$2.164 billion (f.o.b., 2003 est.): meat, rice, leather
products, wool, vehicles, dairy products. **Imports:**
$1.989 billion (f.o.b., 2003 est.): machinery, chemicals,
road vehicles, crude petroleum. **Major trading
partners:** Brazil, Argentina, U.S., Germany, Italy,
Venezuela.

Geography Uruguay, on the east coast of South
America south of Brazil and east of Argentina, is comparable in size to Oklahoma. The country consists of a
low, rolling plain in the south and a low plateau in the
north. It has a 120-mile (193 km) Atlantic shoreline, a
235-mile (378 km) frontage on the Rio de la Plata, and
270 mi (435 km) on the Uruguay River, its western
boundary.

Government Constitutional republic.

History Prior to European settlement, Uruguay was
inhabited by indigenous people, the Charrúas. Juan
Díaz de Solís, a Spaniard, visited Uruguay in 1516,
but the Portuguese were first to settle it when they
founded the town of Colonia del Sacramento in 1680.
After a long struggle, Spain wrested the country from
Portugal in 1778, by which time almost all of the
indigenous people had been exterminated. Uruguay
revolted against Spain in 1811, only to be conquered
in 1817 by the Portuguese from Brazil. Independence
was reasserted with Argentine help in 1825, and the
republic was set up in 1828.

A revolt in 1836 touched off nearly 50 years of factional strife, including an inconclusive civil war (1839–
1851) and a war with Paraguay (1865–1870), accompanied by occasional armed intervention by Argentina
and Brazil. Uruguay, made prosperous by meat and
wool exports, founded a welfare state early in the 20th
century under President José Batlle y Ordóñez, who
ruled from 1903 to 1929. A decline began in the 1950s
as successive governments struggled to maintain a
large bureaucracy and costly social benefits. Economic
stagnation and left-wing terrorist activity followed.

A military coup ousted the civilian government in
1973. The military dictatorship that followed used fear
and terror to demoralize the population, taking thousands of political prisoners. After ruling for 12 years,
the brutal military regime permitted election of a civil-

ian government in Nov. 1984 and relinquished rule in
March 1985; full political and civil rights were then
restored.

Subsequent leaders contended with high inflation
and a mammoth national debt. Presidential and legislative elections in Nov. 1994 resulted in a narrow victory
for the center-right Colorado Party and its presidential
candidate, Julio Sanguinetti Cairolo, who had been
president in 1985–1990. He pushed for constitutional
and economic reforms aimed at reducing inflation and
the size of the public sector, including tax increases
and privatization. In Nov. 1999 Jorge Batlle, of the
center-right Colorado Party, won the presidency.

In 2002, Uruguay entered its fourth year of recession. Economic troubles in neighboring Argentina
caused a staggering 90% drop in tourism. Batlle also
faced a sizable budget deficit, a growing public debt,
and a weakening of the peso on international markets.
The country's economic outlook began improving in
2003. In a Dec. 2003 referendum, 60% of the electorate voted against opening up the state oil monopoly to
foreign investment.

Uzbekistan

REPUBLIC OF UZBEKISTAN

National name: Uzbekiston Respublikasi
President: Islam A. Karimov (1990)
Prime Minister: Shavkat Mirziyayev (2003)
Area: 172,741 sq mi (447,400 sq km)
Population (2004 est.): 26,410,416 (growth rate: 1.6%);
birth rate: 26.1/1000; infant mortality rate: 71.3/1000;
life expectancy: 64.1; density per sq mi: 153
Capital and largest city (2003 est.): Tashkent,
3,457,500 (metro. area), 2,155,400 (city proper).
Other large cities: Samarkand, 374,900; Andijon,
354,500. **Monetary unit:** Uzbekistani sum.
Languages: Uzbek 74.3%, Russian 14.2%, Tajik
4.4%, other 7.1%. **Ethnicity/race:** Uzbek 80%,
Russian 5.5%, Tajik 5%, Kazak 3%, Karakalpak 2.5%,
Tatar 1.5%, other 2.5% (1996 est.). **Religions:** Islam
(mostly Sunnis) 88%, Eastern Orthodox 9%, other 3%.
Literacy rate: 99% (2003 est.)
Economic summary: GDP/PPP (2003 est.): $44.11
billion; per capita $1,700. **Real growth rate:** 3.4%.
Inflation: 21.9%. **Unemployment:** 10% plus another
20% underemployed (2001 est.). **Arable land:** 11%.
Agriculture: cotton, vegetables, fruits, grain; livestock.
Labor force: 11.9 million (1998 est.); agriculture 44%,
industry 20%, services 36% (1995). **Industries:**
textiles, food processing, machine building, metallurgy,
natural gas, chemicals. **Natural resources:** natural
gas, petroleum, coal, gold, uranium, silver, copper,
lead and zinc, tungsten, molybdenum. **Exports:** $2.83
billion (f.o.b., 2003 est.): cotton 41.5%, gold 9.6%,
energy products 9.6%, mineral fertilizers, ferrous
metals, textiles, food products, automobiles (1998
est.). **Imports:** $2.31 billion (f.o.b., 2003 est.):
machinery and equipment 49.8%, foodstuffs 16.4%,
chemicals, metals (1998 est.). **Major trading
partners:** Russia, Ukraine, Italy, Tajikistan, Poland,
South Korea, Kazakhstan, U.S., Germany, China,
Turkey.

Geography Uzbekistan is situated in central Asia
between the Amu Darya and Syr Darya Rivers, the
Aral Sea, and the slopes of the Tien Shan Mountains.
It is bounded by Kazakhstan in the north and northwest, Kyrgyzstan and Tajikistan in the east and southeast, Turkmenistan in the southwest, and Afghanistan
in the south. The republic also includes the Karakal-
pakstan Autonomous Republic, with its capital, Nukus
(1992 est. pop., 182,000). The country is about one-
tenth larger in area than the state of California.

Government Republic; authoritarian presidential rule.

History The Uzbekistan land was once part of the ancient Persian empire and was later conquered by Alexander the Great in the 4th century B.C. During the 8th century, the nomadic Turkic tribes living there were converted to Islam by invading Arab forces who dominated the area. The Mongols under Ghengis Khan took over the region from the Seljuk Turks in the 13th century, and it later became part of Tamerlane the Great's empire and that of his successors until the 16th century. The Uzbeks invaded the territory in the early 16th century and merged with the other inhabitants in the area. Their empire broke up into separate Uzbek principalities, the khanates of Khiva, Bukhara, and Kokand. These city-states resisted Russian expansion into the area but were conquered by the Russian forces in the mid-19th century.

The territory was made into the Uzbek Republic in 1924 and became the independent Uzbekistan Soviet Socialist Republic in 1925. Under Soviet rule, Uzbekistan concentrated on growing cotton with the help of irrigation, mechanization, and chemical fertilizers and pesticides, causing serious environmental damage.

In June 1990, Uzbekistan became the first central Asian republic to declare that its own laws had sovereignty over those of the central Soviet government. Uzbekistan became fully independent and joined with ten other former Soviet republics on Dec. 21, 1991, in the Commonwealth of Independent States.

Vozrozhdeniye, an island in the Aral Sea, was a secret test site for biological weapons during the Soviet era. In 1988, the Soviets attempted to bury the evidence on the island, a frightening legacy that Uzbekistan inherited upon independence. U.S. scientists have confirmed that the island contains live anthrax and other deadly poisons.

President Karimov, a former Communist Party boss, has effectively suppressed opposition parties. Human rights abuses have grown at an alarming rate over the years, and torture is used as a routine investigation technique.

In 1999, the country battled against militant Islamic groups bent on the overthrow of the secular government. Fighting against the Islamic Movement of Uzbekistan (IMU) continued for the next few years. In 2000, Russia offered to help Uzbekistan "liquidate" the Islamic extremists. Several terrorist bombings took place in March 2004, killing 40. A trial in Aug. 2004 sentenced 15 accused Islamic militants to prison, but human rights groups questioned the trial's fairness.

In 2001, Uzbekistan provided the United States and the UK with a base to fight against Taliban and al-Qaeda forces in neighboring Afghanistan, and became the United States' main regional partner in the war on terror. As a strategic partner, the U.S. was initially reluctant to take a firm stand regarding Uzbekistan's dismal human rights record. The repressive country's 6,000 political and religious prisoners are subject to horrific torture and appalling conditions. But in July 2004, the U.S. State Department announced it would cut $18 million in military and economic aid to Uzbekistan because it had failed to improve its human rights record.

Vanuatu

REPUBLIC OF VANUATU

President: Kalkot Mataskelekele (2004)
Prime Minister: Serge Vohor (2004)
Area: 4,710 sq mi (12,200 sq km)
Population (2004 est.): 202,609 (growth rate: 1.6%);
birth rate: 23.7/1000; infant mortality rate: 56.6/1000; life expectancy: 62.1; density per sq mi: 43
Capital and largest city (2003 est.): Port Vila, 35,300.
Monetary unit: Vatu. **Languages:** Bislama (a Melanesian pidgin English), English, French (all 3 official); more than 100 local languages. **Ethnicity/ race:** indigenous Melanesian 98%, French, Vietnamese, Chinese, other Pacific Islanders. **Religions:** Presbyterian 36.7%, Anglican 15%, Roman Catholic 15%, indigenous beliefs 7.6%, Seventh-Day Adventist 6.2%, Church of Christ 3.8%, other 15.7% (including Jon Frum Cargo cult). **Literacy rate:** 53% (1979 est.)
Economic summary: GDP/PPP (2002 est.): $563 million; per capita $2,900. **Real growth rate:** −0.3%. **Inflation:** 2% (2002 est.). **Unemployment:** n.a. **Arable land:** 2%. **Agriculture:** copra, coconuts, cocoa, coffee, taro, yams, coconuts, fruits, vegetables; fish, beef. **Labor force:** n.a.; agriculture 65%, services 30%, industry 5% (2000 est.). **Industries:** food and fish freezing, wood processing, meat canning. **Natural resources:** manganese, hardwood forests, fish. **Exports:** $79 million (f.o.b., 2003): copra, beef, cocoa, timber, kava, coffee. **Imports:** $138 million (f.o.b., 2003): machinery and equipment, foodstuffs, fuels. **Major trading partners:** India, Thailand, South Korea, Indonesia, Japan, Australia, New Zealand, Singapore, Fiji, Taiwan.

Geography Vanuatu is an archipelago of 83 islands lying between New Caledonia and Fiji in the South Pacific. Largest of the islands is Espiritu Santo (875 sq mi; 2,266 sq km); others are Efate, Malekula, Malo, Pentecost, and Tanna.

Government Republic.

History The first settlers are believed to have arrived approximately 3,500 years ago from New Guinea and the Solomon Islands by canoe. The islands were sighted by Pedro Fernandes de Queiros of Portugal in 1606 and were charted by the British navigator James Cook in 1774, who named the archipelago New Hebrides, after the northern Scottish islands. Competing British and French claims to the islands led to the formation of a condominium government, allowing for joint British-French rule in 1906. The islands' plantation economy, based on imported Vietnamese labor, was prosperous until the 1920s, when markets for its products declined. Diseases brought by missionaries, sandalwood traders, and others helped reduce the population from approximately 1 million in 1800 to 45,000 in 1935. The islands served as a major Allied base in World War II. After World War II, the indigenous Melanesians began lobbying for independence. In 1980 the country achieved independence and was renamed Vanuatu.

A brief rebellion by French settlers and plantation workers on Espiritu Santo took place in May 1980. Britain, France, and Papua New Guinea sent soldiers, who quelled the revolt, which the new government said was financed by the Phoenix Foundation, a right-wing U.S. group.

In July 2002, former prime minister Barak Sope was convicted of forgery. Alfred Maseng was elected president in April 2004, but was forced to step down when his criminal record was revealed. In Aug. 2004, Kalkot Mataskelekele was selected from 16 candidates as the new president. He is the country's first president to hold a university degree.

Vatican City (Holy See)

National name: Stato della Città del Vaticano
Ruler: Pope John Paul II (1978)
Area: 0.17 sq mi (0.44 sq km)
Population (July 2003 est.): 911; density per sq mi:
5,362. **Monetary unit:** Euro. **Languages:** Italian, Latin,
French, various other languages. **Ethnicity/race:**
Italian, Swiss, other. **Religion:** Roman Catholic.
Labor force: dignitaries, priests, nuns, guards, and 3,000
lay workers who live outside the Vatican.
Budget (2001): Revenues: $173.5 million; expenditures:
$176.6 million, including capital expenditures.

Geography The Vatican City State is situated on the
Vatican hill, on the right bank of the Tiber River,
within the city of Rome.

Government The pope has full legal, executive, and
judicial powers. Executive power over the area is in
the hands of a commission of cardinals appointed by
the pope. The College of Cardinals is the pope's chief
advisory body, and upon his death the cardinals elect
his successor for life.

History The Vatican City State, sovereign and independent, is the survivor of the papal states that in
1859 comprised an area of some 17,000 sq mi
(44,030 sq km). During the struggle for Italian unification, from 1860 to 1870, most of this area became
part of Italy. By an Italian law of May 13, 1871, the
temporal power of the pope was abrogated, and the
territory of the papacy was confined to the Vatican
and Lateran palaces and the villa of Castel Gandolfo.
The popes consistently refused to recognize this
arrangement. The Lateran Treaty of Feb. 11, 1929,
between the Vatican and the kingdom of Italy established the autonomy of the Holy See.

The first session of Ecumenical Council Vatican
II was opened by John XXIII on Oct. 11, 1962, to
plan and set policies for the modernization of the
Roman Catholic Church. Pope Paul VI continued
the council, presiding over the last three sessions.
Vatican II, as it is called, revolutionized some of the
church's practices. Power was decentralized, giving
bishops a larger role, the liturgy was vernacular-
ized, and laymen were given a larger part in church
affairs.

On Aug. 26, 1978, Cardinal Albino Luciani was
chosen by the College of Cardinals to succeed Paul
VI, who had died of a heart attack on Aug. 6. The
new pope took the name John Paul I. Only 34 days
after his election, John Paul I died of a heart attack,
ending the shortest reign in 373 years. On Oct. 16,
Cardinal Karol Wojtyla, 58, was chosen pope and
took the name John Paul II. Pope John Paul II became
the first Polish pope and the first non-Italian pope
since the 16th century. His rule has been characterized by conservatism regarding church doctrine. He
has been the Vatican's greatest ambassador, traveling
to more than 115 countries.

On May 13, 1981, a Turkish terrorist shot the pope
in St. Peter's Square, the first assassination attempt
against the pontiff in modern times. On June 3, 1985,
the Vatican and Italy ratified a new church-state treaty,
known as a concordat, replacing the Lateran Pact of
1929. The new accord affirmed the independence of
Vatican City but ended a number of privileges the
Catholic Church had in Italy, including its status as the
state religion.

In March 2000, the pope issued an apology for sins
committed by Catholics over the past 2,000 years,
including religious persecutions and discrimination
against women. Several groups criticized the vague-
ness of the apology, wishing the pope had specified the
church's particularly egregious sins. The pope also
remained circumspect about the U.S. church's sexual
abuse scandals in 2002. In 2003, the Vatican launched
an international campaign against legalizing same-sex
marriage.

For a list of all the popes, *see* pp. 366–368.

Venezuela

REPUBLIC OF VENEZUELA

National name: Republica de Venezuela
President: Hugo Chavez (1999)
Area: 352,143 sq mi (912,050 sq km)
Population (2004 est.): 25,017,387 (growth rate: 1.4%);
birth rate: 19.3/1000; infant mortality rate: 23.0/1000;
life expectancy: 74.1; density per sq mile: 71
Capital (2003 est.): Caracas, 3,517,300 (metro. area),
1,741,400 (city proper). **Largest cities:** Maracaibo,
1,889,000 (metro. area), 1,854,300 (city proper);
Valencia, 1,515,400; Barquisimeto, 948,900. **Monetary
unit:** Bolivar. **Languages:** Spanish (official), numerous
indigenous dialects. **Ethnicity/race:** Spanish, Italian,
Portuguese, Arab, German, African, indigenous
people. **Religions:** Roman Catholic 96%, Protestant
2%, other 2%. **Literacy rate:** 93% (2003 est.)
Economic summary: GDP/PPP (2003 est.): $117.9
billion; per capita $4,800. **Real growth rate:** –9.2%.
Inflation: 31.1%. **Unemployment:** 18%. **Arable land:**
3%. **Agriculture:** corn, sorghum, sugarcane, rice,
bananas, vegetables, coffee; beef, pork, milk, eggs;
fish. **Labor force:** 9.9 million (1999); services 64%,
industry 23%, agriculture 13% (1997 est.). **Industries:**
petroleum, iron ore mining, construction materials,
food processing, textiles, steel, aluminum, motor
vehicle assembly. **Natural resources:** petroleum,
natural gas, iron ore, gold, bauxite, other minerals,
hydropower, diamonds. **Exports:** $25.86 billion (f.o.b.,
2003 est.): petroleum, bauxite and aluminum, steel,
chemicals, agricultural products, basic manufactures.
Imports: $10.71 billion (f.o.b., 2003 est.): raw
materials, machinery and equipment, transport
equipment, construction materials. **Major trading
partners:** U.S., Netherlands Antilles, Canada,
Colombia, Brazil, Mexico.

Geography Venezuela, a third larger than Texas,
occupies most of the northern coast of South
America on the Caribbean Sea. It is bordered by
Colombia to the west, Guyana to the east, and Brazil
to the south. Mountain systems break Venezuela into
four distinct areas: (1) the Maracaibo lowlands; (2)
the mountainous region in the north and northwest;
(3) the Orinoco basin, with the llanos (vast grass-
covered plains) on its northern border and great forest areas in the south and southeast; and (4) the Guiana Highlands, south of the Orinoco, accounting for
nearly half the national territory.

Government Federal republic.

History When Columbus explored Venezuela on his
third voyage in 1498, the area was inhabited by
Arawak, Carib, and Chibcha Indians. A subsequent
Spanish explorer gave the country its name, meaning
"Little Venice." Caracas was founded in 1567. Simón
Bolívar, who led the liberation of much of the conti-
nent from Spain, was born in Caracas in 1783. With
Bolívar taking part, Venezuela was one of the first
South American colonies to revolt in 1810, winning
independence in 1821. Federated at first with Colom-
bia and Ecuador as the Republic of Greater Colombia,
Venezuela became a republic in 1830. A period of

unstable dictatorships followed. Antonio Guzman Blanco governed from 1870 to 1888, developing an infrastructure, expanding agriculture, and welcoming foreign investment.

Gen. Juan Vicente Gómez was dictator from 1908 to 1935, when Venezuela became a major oil exporter. A military junta ruled after his death. Leftist Dr. Rómulo Betancourt and the Democratic Action Party won a majority of seats in a constituent assembly to draft a new constitution in 1946. A well-known writer, Rómulo Gallegos, candidate of Betancourt's party, became Venezuela's first democratically elected president in 1947. Within eight months, Gallegos was overthrown by a military-backed coup led by Marcos Peréz Jiménez, who was ousted himself in 1958. Since 1959, Venezuela has been one of the most stable democracies in Latin America. Betancourt served from 1959–1964, while Rafael Caldera Rodríguez, president from 1969 to 1974, legalized the Communist Party and established diplomatic relations with Moscow.

Venezuela benefited from the oil boom of the early 1970s. In 1974, President Carlos Andrés Pérez took office, and in 1976 Venezuela nationalized foreign-owned oil and steel companies, offering compensation. Luis Herrera Campíns took office in 1978. Declining world oil prices sent Venezuela's economy into a tailspin, increasing the country's foreign debt. Pérez was reelected to a nonconsecutive term in 1988 and launched an unpopular austerity program. Military officers staged two unsuccessful coup attempts in 1992, while the following year Congress impeached Pérez on corruption charges. President Rafael Caldera Rodríguez was elected in Dec. 1993 to face the 1994 collapse of half of the country's banking sector, falling oil prices, foreign debt repayment, and inflation. In 1997, the government announced an expansion of gold and diamond mining to reduce reliance on oil.

Leftist president Hugo Chavez took office in 1999, pledging political and economic reforms to give the poor a greater share of the country's oil wealth. A constituent assembly was formed to rewrite the constitution in July 1999, followed by the creation of a constitutional assembly made up of Chavez's allies that replaced the democratically elected Congress. Chavez's assumption of greater power prompted charges that he is establishing a left-wing dictatorship.

Chavez was reelected to a six-year term in July 2000. Troops were called in to quell serious protests over the election in several cities. In 2000 Chavez visited other OPEC countries, becoming the first foreign head of state to visit Iraq since the 1991 Gulf War. He is close to President Fidel Castro of Cuba, which receives Venezuelan oil at reduced prices.

In Dec. 2001, business and labor organizations held a work stoppage to protest Chavez's increasingly authoritarian government. In April 2002, tensions reached a boiling point as workers reduced oil production to protest Chavez policies. Following a massive anti-Chavez demonstration during which 12 people were killed, a coalition of business and military leaders forced Chavez from power. But international criticism of the coup, especially in Latin America, and an outpouring of support from the president's followers, returned Chavez to power just two days later. After the coup, Chavez remained highly popular among the poor, despite the desperate state of the economy. Venezuelan labor unions, business organizations, the media, and a good part of the military remained substantially less enchanted.

Beginning in early Dec. 2002, a general strike was called by business and labor leaders. By Jan. 2003 it had virtually brought the economy, including the oil industry, to a halt. Strike leaders pledged to continue until Chavez resigned or agreed to early elections. But in Feb. 2003, after nine weeks, the strikers conceded defeat. In Aug. 2003, a petition with 3.2 million signatures was delivered to the country's election commission, demanding a recall referendum on Chavez. The Chavez government challenged the referendum process every step of the way, and petitions submitted in Sept. 2003 and Feb. 2004 were rejected as invalid. The electoral board finally accepted a petition in June 2004 and scheduled the referendum for August 15. Chavez, who had been shoring up his standing with the Venezuelan poor during the delays, won the referendum with an overwhelming 58% of the vote. The opposition alleged fraud, but international observers confirmed that there had been no irregularities. While Chavez's hand is clearly strengthened, the results are likely to fracture the country even further.

Vietnam

SOCIALIST REPUBLIC OF VIETNAM

National name: Công Hòa Xa Hôi Chú Nghia Viêt Nam
President: Tran Duc Luong (1997)
Prime Minister: Phan Van Khai (1997)
Area: 127,243 sq mi (329,560 sq km)
Population (2004 est.): 82,689,518 (growth rate: 1.3%); birth rate: 19.6/1000; infant mortality rate: 29.9/1000; life expectancy: 70.4; density per sq mi: 650
Capital (2003 est.): Hanoi, 2,543,700 (metro. area), 1,396,500 (city proper). **Largest cities:** Ho Chi Minh City (Saigon), 5,894,100 (metro. area), 3,415,300 (city proper); Haiphong, 581,600; Da Nang, 452,700; Hué 271,900; Nha Trang, 270,100; Qui Nho'n, 199,700.
Monetary unit: Dong. **Languages:** Vietnamese (official); English (increasingly favored as a second language); some French, Chinese, Khmer; mountain area languages (Mon-Khmer and Malayo-Polynesian). **Ethnicity/race:** Vietnamese 85%–90%, Chinese, Hmong, Thai, Khmer, Cham, mountain groups. **Religions:** Buddhist, Hoa Hao, Cao Dai, Christian (predominantly Roman Catholic, some Protestant), indigenous beliefs, Muslim. **Literacy rate:** 94% (2003 est.)
Economic summary: GDP/PPP (2003 est.): $203.9 billion; per capita $2,500. **Real growth rate:** 7.3%. **Inflation:** 3.9% (2002 est.). **Unemployment:** 25% (1995 est.). **Arable land:** 17%. **Agriculture:** paddy rice, corn, potatoes, rubber, soybeans, coffee, tea, bananas, sugar; poultry, pigs; fish. **Labor force:** 38.2 million (1998 est.); agriculture 63%, industry and services 37% (2000 est.). **Industries:** food processing, garments, shoes, machine-building, mining, cement, chemical fertilizer, glass, tires, oil, coal, steel, paper. **Natural resources:** phosphates, coal, manganese, bauxite, chromate, offshore oil and gas deposits, forests, hydropower. **Exports:** $19.88 billion (f.o.b., 2003 est.): crude oil, marine products, rice, coffee, rubber, tea, garments, shoes. **Imports:** $22.5 billion (f.o.b., 2003 est.): machinery and equipment, petroleum products, fertilizer, steel products, raw cotton, grain, cement, motorcycles. **Major trading partners:** U.S., Japan, Australia, China, Germany, Singapore, UK, South Korea, Taiwan, Thailand.

Geography   Vietnam occupies the eastern and southern part of the Indochinese peninsula in Southeast Asia, with the South China Sea along its entire coast. China is to the north and Laos and Cambodia are to the west. Long and narrow on a north-south axis, Vietnam is about twice the size of Arizona. The Mekong River delta lies in the south.

Government   Communist state.

History The Vietnamese are descendants of nomadic Mongols from China and migrants from Indonesia. According to mythology, the first ruler of Vietnam was Hung Vuong, who founded the nation in 2879 B.C. China ruled the nation then known as Nam Viet as a vassal state from 111 B.C. until the 15th century, an era of nationalistic expansion, when Cambodians were pushed out of the southern area of what is now Vietnam.

A century later, the Portuguese were the first Europeans to enter the area. France established its influence early in the 19th century, and within 80 years conquered the three regions into which the country was then divided—Cochin-China in the south, Annam in the central region, and Tonkin in the north.

France first unified Vietnam in 1887, when a single governor-generalship was created, followed by the first physical links between north and south—a rail and road system. Even at the beginning of World War II, however, there were internal differences among the three regions. Japan took over military bases in Vietnam in 1940, and a pro-Vichy French administration remained until 1945. Veteran Communist leader Ho Chi Minh organized an independence movement known as the Vietminh to exploit the confusion surrounding France's weakened influence in the region. At the end of the war, Ho's followers seized Hanoi and declared a short-lived republic, which ended with the arrival of French forces in 1946.

Paris proposed a unified government within the French Union under the former Annamite emperor, Bao Dai. Cochin-China and Annam accepted the proposal, and Bao Dai was proclaimed emperor of all Vietnam in 1949. Ho and the Vietminh withheld support, and the revolution in China gave them the outside help needed for a war of resistance against French and Vietnamese troops armed largely by a United States worried about cold war Communist expansion.

A bitter defeat at Dien Bien Phu in northwest Vietnam on May 5, 1954, broke the French military campaign and resulted in the division of Vietnam. In the new South, Ngo Dinh Diem, premier under Bao Dai, deposed the monarch in 1955 and made himself president. Diem used strong U.S. backing to create an authoritarian regime that suppressed all opposition but could not eradicate the Northern-supplied Communist Viet Cong.

Skirmishing grew into a full-scale war, with escalating U.S. involvement. A military coup, U.S.-inspired in the view of many, ousted Diem on Nov. 1, 1963, and a kaleidoscope of military governments followed. The most savage fighting of the war occurred in early 1968 during the Vietnamese New Year, known as Tet. Although the so-called Tet Offensive ended in a military defeat for the North, its psychological impact changed the course of the war.

U.S. bombing and an invasion of Cambodia in the summer of 1970—an effort to destroy Viet Cong bases in the neighboring state—marked the end of major U.S. participation in the fighting. Most American ground troops were withdrawn from combat by mid-1971 when the U.S. conducted heavy bombing raids on the Ho Chi Minh Trail—a crucial North Vietnamese supply line. In 1972, secret peace negotiations led by Secretary of State Henry A. Kissinger took place, and a peace settlement was signed in Paris on Jan. 27, 1973.

By April 9, 1975, Hanoi's troops marched within 40 miles of Saigon, the South's capital. South Vietnam's president Thieu resigned on April 21 and fled. Gen. Duong Van Minh, the new president, surrendered Saigon on April 30, ending a war that claimed the lives of 1.3 million Vietnamese and 58,000 Americans.

In 1977, border clashes between Vietnam and Cambodia intensified, as well as accusations by its former ally Beijing that Chinese residents of Vietnam were being subjected to persecution. Beijing cut off all aid and withdrew 800 technicians.

Hanoi was also preoccupied with a continuing war in Cambodia, where 60,000 Vietnamese troops had invaded and overthrown the country's Communist leader Pol Pot and his pro-Chinese regime. In early 1979, Vietnam was conducting a two-front war: defending its northern border against a Chinese invasion, and supporting its army in Cambodia, which was still fighting Pol Pot's Khmer Rouge guerrillas. Hanoi's Marxist policies combined with the destruction of the country's infrastructure during the decades of fighting devastated Vietnam's economy. However, it started to pick up in 1986 under *do Maui* (economic renovation), an effort at limited privatization. Vietnamese troops began limited withdrawals from Laos and Cambodia in 1988, and Vietnam supported the Cambodian peace agreement signed in Oct. 1991.

The U.S. lifted a Vietnamese trade embargo in Feb. 1994 that had been in place since U.S. involvement in the war. Full diplomatic relations were announced between the two countries in July 1995. In April 1997, a pact was signed with the U.S. concerning repayment of the $146 million wartime debt incurred by the South Vietnamese government, and the following year the nation began a drive to eliminate inefficient bureaucrats and streamline the approval process for direct foreign investment. Efforts of reform-minded officials toward political and economic change have been thwarted by Vietnam's ruling Communist Party. In April 2001, however, the progressive Nong Duc Manh was appointed general secretary of the ruling Communist Party, succeeding Le Kha Phieu. Even with a reformer at the helm of the party, change has been slow and cautious.

In Nov. 2001, Vietnam's National Assembly approved a trade agreement that opened U.S. markets to Vietnam's goods and services. Tariffs on Vietnam's products dropped to about 4% from rates as high as 40%. Vietnam in return opened its state markets to foreign competition.

The government highlighted its efforts to crack down on corruption and crime with the June 2003 conviction of notorious criminal syndicate boss Truong Van Cam, known as Nam Cam. He was sentenced to death, along with 155 other defendants, and executed in June 2004.

(For a Vietnam War chronology, *see* Headline History.)

Western Sahara (proposed state)

WESTERN SAHARA
Area: 102,703 sq mi (266,000 sq km)
Population (2004 est.): 267,405 (growth rate: 2.3%); birth rate: 45.1/1000; infant mortality rate: 133.6/1000; life expectancy: 49.8; density per sq mi: 3
Largest cities (2003 est.): El Aaiun 198,200. **Monetary unit:** Tala. **Languages:** Hassaniya Arabic, Moroccan Arabic. **Ethnicity/race:** Saharawi, Arab, Berber. **Religion:** Islam
Economic summary: GDP/PPP: n.a. **Arable land:** 0%. **Agriculture:** fruits and vegetables (grown in the few oases); camels, sheep, goats (kept by nomads). **Labor force:** 12,000; animal husbandry and subsistence farming 50%. **Industries:** phosphate mining, handicrafts. **Natural resources:** phosphates, iron ore. **Exports:** n.a.: phosphates 62%. **Imports:** n.a.: fuel for fishing fleet, foodstuffs. **Major trading partners:** Morocco claims and administers Western Sahara, so trade partners are included in overall Moroccan accounts.

Geography Located in northern Africa on the Atlantic Ocean, Western Sahara is surrounded by Algeria to the east, Morocco to the north, and Mauritania to the south. About the size of Colorado, it is mostly low, flat desert with some small mountains in the south and northeast.

Government Legal status of the territory is disputed and sovereignty unresolved; a UN referendum on the issue is planned. The territory is contested by Morocco and the Polisario Front, which in Feb. 1976 formally proclaimed a government-in-exile of the Saharawi Arab Democratic Republic, now officially recognized by about 55 countries.

History Little is known about Western Sahara before the 4th century B.C., when trade with Europe began. During the Middle Ages it was occupied first by Berbers and then by the Arabic-speaking Muslim Bedouins. In the 19th century the Spanish laid claim to the southern coastal region, called Rio de Oro, and later occupied the northern interior region, Saguia el Hamra, in 1934. The Spanish formally united the two regions, and it became known as Spanish Sahara in 1958. Both Morocco and Mauritania sought to control the territory, and when the Spanish departed in 1976 they divided the territory between them. In the meantime, the indigenous Saharawis began fighting for independence. In 1976, the insurgents, called the Polisario Front, declared a government-in-exile (the Saharawi Arab Democratic Republic) from their base in Algeria. Mauritania reached a peace agreement with the Polisario in 1979, but Morocco then seized the land given up by Mauritania and now exerts administrative control over the entire region. The Polisario Front fought Morocco to a stalemate, and agreed in Sept. 1991 to a cease-fire, which was contingent on a referendum regarding independence. For more than a decade, however, the UN has failed to hold the referendum; disputes over voter eligibility have been the major stumbling block, as well as Morocco's opposition to the referendum. In Aug. 2001, former secretary of state James A. Baker, special UN envoy to the Western Sahara, proposed that instead of a referendum on independence, Western Sahara consider becoming an autonomous region of Morocco. The Polisario rejected the new proposal, which it saw as a reversal of the UN's decade-old promise to hold a referendum on self-determination. In 2002, King Mohammed VI of Morocco reasserted that he will not "renounce an inch of" the Western Sahara.

In August 2003, a UN Security Council resolution adopted a new peace plan that would turn Western Sahara into a semi-autonomous region of Morocco for five years, after which a referendum would be held to determine independence, autonomy, or integration into Morocco. The Polisario agreed to the plan; Morocco refused to consider it. In June 2004, a frustrated James Baker resigned after seven years as UN envoy. His successor has vowed to achieve a resolution. The UN has spent more than $600 million on peacekeeping efforts in Western Sahara over the last 13 years.

Yemen

REPUBLIC OF YEMEN

National name: Al Jumhuriyahal Yamaniyah
President: Ali Abdullah Saleh (1990)
Prime Minister: Abdul Qader Bajamal (2001)
Area: 203,849 sq mi (527,970 sq km)
Population (2004 est.): 20,024,867 (growth rate: 3.4%); birth rate: 43.2/1000; infant mortality rate: 65.0/1000; life expectancy: 61.0; density per sq mi: 98

Capital and largest city (2003 est.): Sanaá, 1,778,900. **Other large cities:** Aden, 568,700; Hodiedah, 426,100; Tiaz, 317,600. **Monetary unit:** Rial.
Language: Arabic. **Ethnicity/race:** predominantly Arab; but also Afro-Arab, South Asians, Europeans. **Religion:** Islam (including Sunni and Shiite), small numbers of Jewish, Christian, and Hindu. **Literacy rate:** 50% (2003 est.)
Economic summary: GDP/PPP (2003 est.): $15.22 billion; per capita $800. **Real growth rate:** 3.1%. **Inflation:** 12.3%. **Unemployment:** 35%. **Arable land:** 3%. **Agriculture:** grain, fruits, vegetables, pulses, qat (mildly narcotic shrub), coffee, cotton; dairy products, livestock (sheep, goats, cattle, camels), poultry; fish. **Labor force:** 3.7 million; most people are employed in agriculture and herding or as expatriate laborers; services, construction, industry, and commerce account for less than one-half of the labor force. **Industries:** crude oil production and petroleum refining; small-scale production of cotton textiles and leather goods; food processing; handicrafts; small aluminum products factory; cement. **Natural resources:** petroleum, fish, rock salt, marble, small deposits of coal, gold, lead, nickel, copper, fertile soil in west. **Exports:** $3.92 billion (f.o.b., 2003 est.): crude oil, coffee, dried and salted fish. **Imports:** $3.042 billion (f.o.b., 2003 est.): food and live animals, machinery and equipment, chemicals. **Major trading partners:** India, Thailand, South Korea, China, Malaysia, U.S., Singapore, Saudi Arabia, UAE, Russia, France.

Geography Formerly divided into two nations, the People's Democratic Republic of Yemen and the Yemen Arab Republic, the Republic of Yemen occupies the southwest tip of the Arabian Peninsula on the Red Sea opposite Ethiopia, and extends along the southern part of the Arabian Peninsula on the Gulf of Aden and the Indian Ocean. Saudi Arabia is to the north and Oman is to the east. The country is about the size of France. A 700-mile (1,130-km) narrow coastal plain in the south gives way to a mountainous region and then a plateau area.

Government Parliamentary republic.

History The history of Yemen dates back to the Minaean (1200–650 B.C.) and Sabaean (750–115 B.C.) kingdoms. Ancient Yemen (centered around the port of Aden) engaged in the lucrative myrrh and frankincense trade. It was invaded by the Romans (1st century A.D.) as well as the Ethiopians and Persians (6th century A.D.). In A.D. 628 it converted to Islam and in the 10th century came under the control of the Rassite dynasty of the Zaidi sect, which remained involved in North Yemeni politics until 1962. The Ottoman Turks nominally occupied the area from 1538 to the decline of their empire in 1918.

The northern portion of Yemen was ruled by imams until a pro-Egyptian military coup took place in 1962. The junta proclaimed the Yemen Arab Republic, and after a civil war in which Egypt's Nasser and the USSR supported the revolutionaries, and King Saud of Saudi Arabia and King Hussein of Jordan supported the royalists, the royalists were finally defeated in mid-1969.

The southern port of Aden, strategically located at the opening of the Red Sea, was colonized by Britain in 1839, and by 1937, with an expansion of its territory, it was known as the Aden Protectorate. In the 1960s the Nationalist Liberation Front (NLF) fought against British rule, which led to the establishment of the People's Republic of Southern Yemen on Nov. 30, 1967. In 1979, under strong Soviet influence, the country became the only Marxist state in the Arab world.

The Republic of Yemen was established on May 22, 1990, when pro-Western Yemen and the Marxist Yemen Arab Republic merged after 300 years of separation to form the new nation. The poverty and decline in Soviet economic support in the south was an important incentive for the merger. The new president, Ali Abdullah Saleh, was elected by the Parliaments of both countries.

Differences over power sharing and the pace of integration between the north and the south came to a head in 1994, resulting in a civil war. The north's superior forces quickly overwhelmed the south in May and early June despite the south's brief declaration of succession. The victorious north presented a reconciliation plan providing for a general amnesty and pledges to protect political democracy.

The president's party, the General People's Congress, won an enormous victory in the April 1997 parliamentary elections, the first since the civil war. In 1998–1999, a militant Islamic group, the Aden-Abyan Islamic Army, kidnapped several groups of Western tourists, which led to the deaths of several during a poorly orchestrated rescue attempt. The group's leader, Zein al-Abidine al-Mihdar, threatened to continue attacks on tourists and government officials. The goal of the militants is to overthrow the government and turn Yemen into an Islamic state.

On Oct. 12, 2000, 17 Americans died and 37 were wounded when suicide bombers attacked the U.S. Navy destroyer *Cole,* which was refueling in Aden, Yemen. The U.S. has had numerous clashes with Yemeni authorities during the investigation of the terrorist act. After the Sept. 11 terrorist attacks on the U.S., however, Yemen increased its cooperation with the U.S. and assisted in antiterrorism measures. In Oct. 2002, a French tanker, the *Limburg,* was also the victim of a terrorist attack off the coast of Yemen. Ten suspects of the *Cole* bombing escaped from prison in April 2003; seven, including the two suspected masterminds of the attack, were recaptured in 2004. Fifteen militants were convicted in Aug. 2004 on a variety of charges, including the attack on the *Limburg.* In September, two key al-Qaeda operatives involved in the *Cole* bombing were sentenced to death.

Yugoslavia

SEE SERBIA AND MONTENEGRO.

Zaire

SEE CONGO, DEMOCRATIC REPUBLIC OF.

Zambia

REPUBLIC OF ZAMBIA

President: Levy Mwanawasa (2002)
Area: 290,584 sq mi (752,614 sq km)
Population (2004 est.): 10,462,436 (growth rate: 1.5%); birth rate: 39.0/1000; infant mortality rate: 98.4/1000; life expectancy: 35.2; density per sq mi: 36
Capital and largest city (2003 est.): Lusaka, 1,773,300 (metro. area), 1,265,000 (city proper). **Other large cities:** Ndola, 349,300; Kitwe, 306,200; Kabwe, 219,600; Chingola, 151,100. **Monetary unit:** Kwacha.
Languages: English (official); major vernaculars: Bemba, Kaonda, Lozi, Lunda, Luvale, Nyanja, Tonga; about 70 other indigenous languages. **Ethnicity/race:** African 98.7%, European 1.1%, other 0.2%.
Religions: Christian 50%–75%, Islam and Hindu 24%–49%, indigenous beliefs 1%. **Literacy rate:** 81% (2003 est.)
Economic summary: GDP/PPP (2003 est.): $8.596 billion; per capita $800. **Real growth rate:** 4%.

Inflation: 21.5%. **Unemployment:** 50% (2000 est.). **Arable land:** 7%. **Agriculture:** corn, sorghum, rice, peanuts, sunflower seed, vegetables, flowers, tobacco, cotton, sugarcane, cassava (tapioca), coffee; cattle, goats, pigs, poultry, milk, eggs, hides. **Labor force:** 4.29 million (2000); agriculture 85%, industry 6%, services 9%. **Industries:** copper mining and processing, construction, foodstuffs, beverages, chemicals, textiles, fertilizer, horticulture. **Natural resources:** copper, cobalt, zinc, lead, coal, emeralds, gold, silver, uranium, hydropower. **Exports:** $1.039 billion (f.o.b., 2003 est.): copper 55%, cobalt, electricity, tobacco, flowers, cotton. **Imports:** $1.128 billion (f.o.b., 2003 est.): machinery, transportation equipment, petroleum products, electricity, fertilizer; foodstuffs, clothing. **Major trading partners:** Malawi, Thailand, Japan, Saint Pierre and Miquelon, Taiwan, South Africa, Egypt, China, Netherlands, U.S. **International conflicts:** dormant dispute remains where Botswana, Namibia, Zambia, and Zimbabwe boundaries converge.

Geography Zambia, a landlocked country in south-central Africa, is about one-tenth larger than Texas. It is surrounded by Angola, Zaire, Tanzania, Malawi, Mozambique, Zimbabwe, Botswana, and Namibia. The country is mostly a plateau that rises to 8,000 ft (2,434 m) in the east.

Government Republic.

History Early humans inhabited present-day Zambia between one and two million years ago. Today the country is made up almost entirely of Bantu-speaking peoples. Empire builder Cecil Rhodes obtained mining concessions in 1889 from King Lewanika of the Barotse and sent settlers to the area soon thereafter. The region was ruled by the British South Africa Company, which he established, until 1924, when the British government took over the administration.

From 1953 to 1964, Northern Rhodesia was federated with Southern Rhodesia (now Zimbabwe) and Nyasaland (now Malawi) in the Federation of Rhodesia and Nyasaland. On Oct. 24, 1964, Northern Rhodesia became the independent nation of Zambia.

Kenneth Kaunda, the first president, kept Zambia within the Commonwealth of Nations. The country's economy, dependent on copper exports, was threatened when Rhodesia declared its independence from British rule in 1965 and defied UN sanctions, which Zambia supported, an action that deprived Zambia of its trade route through Rhodesia. The U.S., Britain, and Canada organized an airlift in 1966 to ship gasoline into Zambia.

In 1972 Kaunda outlawed all opposition political parties. The world copper market collapsed in 1975. The Zambian economy was devastated—it had been the third-largest miner of copper in the world after the United States and Soviet Union. With a soaring debt and inflation rate in 1991, riots took place in Lusaka, resulting in a number of killings. Mounting domestic pressure forced Kaunda to move Zambia toward multiparty democracy. National elections on Oct. 31, 1991, brought a stunning defeat to Kaunda. The new president, Frederick Chiluba, called for sweeping economic reforms, including privatization and the establishment of a stock market. He was reelected in Nov. 1996. Chiluba declared martial law in 1997 and arrested Kaunda following a failed coup attempt. The 1999 slump in world copper prices again depressed the economy since copper provides 80% of Zambia's export earnings.

In 2001 Chiluba contemplated changing the constitution to allow him to run for another presidential term. After protests he relented, and selected Levy Mwanawasa, a former vice president with whom he had fallen out, as his successor. Mwanawasa became president in Jan. 2002; opposition parties protested over alleged fraud. In June 2002, Mwanawasa, once seen as a pawn of Chiluba, accused the former president of stealing millions from the government while in office. Chiluba was arrested and charged in Feb. 2003.

Although the country faced the threat of famine in 2002, the president refused to accept any international donations of food that had been genetically modified, which Mwanawasa considered "poison." In Aug. 2003, impeachment proceedings against the president for corruption were rejected by Parliament.

Zimbabwe

REPUBLIC OF ZIMBABWE

President: Robert Mugabe (1980)
Area: 150,803 sq mi (390,580 sq km)
Population (2004 est.): 12,671,860 (growth rate: 0.7%); birth rate: 30.1/1000; infant mortality rate: 67.1/1000; life expectancy: 37.8; density per sq mi: 84
Capital and largest city (2003 est.): Harare, 2,331,400 (metro. area), 1,919,700 (city proper). **Other large cities:** Bulawayo, 965,000; Chitungwiza, 411,700.
Monetary unit: Zimbabwean dollar. **Languages:** English (official), Shona, Ndebele (Sindebele), numerous minor tribal dialects. **Ethnicity/race:** African 98% (Shona 82%, Ndebele 14%, other 2%), mixed and Asian 1%, white less than 1%. **Religions:** syncretic (part Christian, part indigenous beliefs) 50%, Christian 25%, indigenous beliefs 24%, Muslim and other 1%. **Literacy rate:** 91% (2003 est.).
Economic summary: GDP/PPP (2003 est.): $24.03 billion; per capita $1,900. **Real growth rate:** –13.6%. **Inflation:** 383.4%. **Unemployment:** 70% (2002 est.). **Arable land:** 8%. **Agriculture:** corn, cotton, tobacco, wheat, coffee, sugarcane, peanuts; cattle, sheep, goats, pigs. **Labor force:** 5.8 million (2000 est.); agriculture 66%, services 24%, industry 10% (1996). **Industries:** mining (coal, gold, copper, nickel, tin, clay, numerous metallic and nonmetallic ores), steel, wood products, cement, chemicals, fertilizer, clothing and footwear, foodstuffs, beverages. **Natural resources:** coal, chromium ore, asbestos, gold, nickel, copper, iron ore, vanadium, lithium, tin, platinum group metals. **Exports:** $1.261 billion (f.o.b., 2003 est.): tobacco, gold, ferroalloys, textiles/clothing. **Imports:** $1.691 billion (f.o.b., 2003 est.): machinery and transport equipment, other manufactures, chemicals, fuels. **Major trading partners:** China, South Africa, Germany, UK, Japan, Netherlands, U.S., Democratic Republic of the Congo, Mozambique. **International disputes:** dormant dispute remains where Botswana, Namibia, Zambia, and Zimbabwe boundaries converge.

Geography Zimbabwe, a landlocked country in south-central Africa, is slightly smaller than California. It is bordered by Botswana on the west, Zambia on the north, Mozambique on the east, and South Africa on the south.

Government Parliamentary democracy.

History The remains of early humans, dating back 500,000 years, have been discovered in present-day Zimbabwe. The land's earliest settlers, the Khoisan, date back to 200 B.C. After a period of Bantu domination, the Shona people ruled, followed by the Nguni and Zulu peoples. By the mid-19th century the descendants of the Nguni and Zulu, the Ndebele, had established a powerful warrior kingdom.

The first British explorers, colonists, and missionaries arrived in the 1850s, and the massive influx of foreigners led to the establishment of the territory Rho-

desia, named after Cecil Rhodes of the British South Africa Company. In 1923, European settlers voted to become the self-governing British colony of Southern Rhodesia. After a brief federation with Northern Rhodesia (now Zambia) and Nyasaland (now Malawi) in the post–World War II period, Southern Rhodesia (also known as Rhodesia) chose to remain a colony when its two partners voted for independence in 1963.

On Nov. 11, 1965, the conservative white-minority government of Rhodesia declared its independence from Britain. The country resisted the demands of black Africans, and Prime Minister Ian Smith withstood British pressure, economic sanctions, and guerrilla attacks to uphold white supremacy. On March 1, 1970, Rhodesia formally proclaimed itself a republic. Heightened guerrilla war and a withdrawal of South African military aid in 1976 marked the beginning of the collapse of Smith's 11 years of resistance.

Black nationalist movements were led by Bishop Abel Muzorewa of the African National Congress and Ndabaningi Sithole, who were moderates, and guerrilla leaders Robert Mugabe of the Zimbabwe African National Union (ZANU) and Joshua Nkomo of the Zimbabwe African People's Union (ZAPU), who advocated revolution.

On March 3, 1978, Smith, Muzorewa, Sithole, and Chief Jeremiah Chirau signed an agreement to transfer power to the black majority by Dec. 31, 1978. They constituted themselves an Executive Council, with chairmanship rotating but with Smith retaining the title of prime minister. Blacks were named to each cabinet ministry, serving as coministers with the whites already holding these posts. African nations and rebel leaders immediately denounced the action, but Western governments were more reserved, although none granted recognition to the new regime.

The white minority finally consented to hold multiracial elections in 1980, and Robert Mugabe won a landslide victory. The country achieved independence on April 17, 1980, under the name Zimbabwe. Mugabe eventually established a one-party socialist state, but by 1990 he had instituted multiparty elections and in 1991 deleted all references to Marxism-Leninism and scientific socialism from the constitution. Parliamentary elections in April 1995 gave Mugabe's party a stunning victory with 63 of the 65 contested seats, and in 1996 Mugabe won another six-year term as president.

In 2000, veterans of Zimbabwe's war for independence in the 1970s began squatting on land owned by white farmers in an effort to reclaim land taken under British colonization—one-third of Zimbabwe's arable land was owned by 4,000 whites. In Aug. 2002, Mugabe ordered all white commercial farmers to leave their land without compensation; by November most of the farmers had been forced to leave. Mugabe's support for the squatters and his repressive rule has led to foreign sanctions against Zimbabwe. Once heralded as a champion of the anticolonial movement, Mugabe is now viewed by much of the international community as an authoritarian ruler responsible for egregious human rights abuses and for running the economy of his country into the ground.

In March 2002, Zimbabwe was suspended from the Commonwealth of Nations. That month Mugabe was reelected president for another six years in a blatantly rigged election whose results were enforced by the president's militia. In 2003, inflation hit 300%, the country faced severe food shortages, and the farming system had been destroyed. In 2004, the IMF estimated that the country had grown one-third poorer in the last five years.

United Nations

Preamble of the United Nations Charter

The Charter of the United Nations was adopted at the San Francisco Conference of 1945. The complete text is available on the UN website, www.un.org/aboutun/charter.

We the peoples of the United Nations determined to save succeeding generations from the scourge of war, which twice in our lifetime has brought untold sorrow to mankind, and

To reaffirm faith in fundamental human rights, in the dignity and worth of the human person, in the equal rights of men and women and of nations large and small, and

To establish conditions under which justice and respect for the obligations arising from treaties and other sources of international law can be maintained, and

To promote social progress and better standards of life in larger freedom, and for these ends

To practice tolerance and live together in peace with one another as good neighbors, and

To unite our strength to maintain international peace and security, and

To insure, by the acceptance of principles and the institution of methods, that armed force shall not be used, save in the common interest, and

To employ international machinery for the promotion of the economic and social advancement of all peoples, have resolved to combine our efforts to accomplish these aims.

Accordingly, our respective Governments, through representatives assembled in the city of San Francisco, who have exhibited their full powers found to be in good and due form, have agreed to the present Charter of the United Nations and do hereby establish an international organization to be known as the United Nations.

Principal Organs of the United Nations

Secretariat

This is the directorate on UN operations, apart from political decisions. The staff works under the secretary-general, whom it assists and advises.

Secretaries-General
Kofi Annan, Ghana, Jan. 1, 1997.
Boutros Boutros-Ghali, Egypt, 1992–1996.
Javier Pérez de Cuéllar, Peru, 1982–1991.
Kurt Waldheim, Austria, 1972–1981.
U Thant, Burma (Myanmar), 1961–1971.
Dag Hammarskjöld, Sweden, 1953–1961.
Trygve Lie, Norway, 1946–1953.

General Assembly

The General Assembly is the world's forum for discussing matters affecting world peace and security, and for making recommendations concerning them. It has no power to enforce decisions. It is composed of the 51 original member nations and those admitted since, totaling 191. On important questions, including international peace and security, a two-thirds majority of those present and voting is required. Decisions on other questions are made by a simple majority. Emphasis is given to questions relating to international peace and security brought before it by members, the Security Council, or nonmembers. It also maintains a broad program of international cooperation in economic, social, cultural, educational, and health fields, and for assisting in human rights and freedoms.

International Court of Justice

The International Court of Justice is the UN's principal judicial organ. Based in The Hague, Netherlands, the Court pursues two primary objectives:

(1) settling legal disputes submitted by states in accordance with international law, and (2) advising on legal questions brought by authorized international organs and agencies. The Court consists of 15 judges elected to nine-year terms by the United Nations General Assembly and the Security Council during independent sittings.

Security Council

The Security Council is the primary instrument for establishing and maintaining international peace. Its main purpose is to prevent war by settling disputes between nations. Under the charter, the council is permitted to dispatch a UN force to stop aggression. All member nations undertake to make available armed forces, assistance, and facilities to maintain international peace and security (see p. 907 for list of UN Peacekeeping Operations).

The Security Council has 15 members. There are five permanent members: the United States, the Russian Federation, Britain, France, and China; and ten temporary members elected by the General Assembly for two-year terms, from five different regions of the world. Voting on procedural matters requires a nine-vote majority to carry. However, on questions of substance, the vote of each of the five permanent members is required. As of Jan. 2004, the ten elected nonpermanent members were Algeria, Angola, Benin, Brazil, Chile, Germany, Pakistan, the Philippines, Romania, and Spain. In Jan. 2005 the terms of Angola, Chile, Germany, Pakistan, and Spain will expire.

Economic and Social Council

This council is composed of 54 members elected by the General Assembly to three-year terms. It works under the authority of the General Assembly and seeks to promote progress in terms of higher standards of living, full employment, and economic and social viability; it also seeks solutions to international socioeconomic, health, and other problems through international and cultural cooperation. Finally, it advocates for the universal respect for and observance of human rights and fundamental freedoms for all.

Trusteeship Council

The UN charter originally established the Trusteeship Council as a main organ of the UN and entrusted it with the administration of territories placed under the trusteeship system.

The Trusteeship Council suspended operations on Nov. 1, 1994, after the October independence of Palau, the last UN territory.

UN Peacekeeping Missions

Since 1948 there have been 59 UN peacekeeping operations, of which 46 have been created by the United Nations Security Council since 1988. Close to 130 nations have contributed personnel at various times, and 94 are currently providing peacekeepers. As of May 31, 2004, there were 16 peacekeeping operations underway with a total of 55,457 personnel, and the top contributors of military and civilian personnel to current missions were Pakistan (7,997), Bangladesh (6,753), Nigeria (3,424), and Ghana (3,259).

Current UN Peacekeeping Operations

Region/Country	Began	Region/Country	Began
AFRICA		**ASIA**	
Western Sahara	April 1991	India/Pakistan	Jan. 1949
Sierra Leone	Oct. 1999	East Timor	May 2002
Democratic Republic	Nov. 1999	**EUROPE**	
of the Congo		Cyprus	March 1964
Ethiopia and Eritrea	July 2000	Georgia	Aug. 1993
Côte d'Ivoire	May 2003	Kosovo	June 1999
Liberia	Oct. 2003	**MIDDLE EAST**	
Burundi	May 2004	Middle East	May 1948
AMERICA		Golan Heights	June 1974
Haiti	April 2004	Lebanon	March 1978

Completed UN Peacekeeping Operations

Region/Country	Duration	Region/Country	Duration
AFRICA		**AMERICAS**	
Congo	July 1960–June 1964	Dominican Republic	May 1965–Oct. 1966
Angola	Dec. 1988–May 1991	Central America	Nov. 1989–Jan. 1992
Namibia	April 1989–March 1990	Observer Group	
Angola	May 1991–Feb. 1995	El Salvador	July 1991–April 1995
Somalia	April 1992–March 1993	Haiti	Sept. 1993–June 1996
Mozambique	Dec. 1992–Dec. 1994	Haiti	July 1996–July 1997
Somalia	March 1993–March 1995	Guatemala	Jan.–May 1997
Rwanda/Uganda	June 1993–Sept. 1994	Haiti	Aug.–Nov. 1997
Liberia	Sept. 1993–Sept. 1997	Haiti	Dec. 1997–March 2000
Rwanda	Oct. 1993–March 1996	**ASIA**	
Chad/Libya	May–June 1994	West New Guinea	Oct. 1962–April 1963
Angola	Feb. 1995–June 1997	India/Pakistan	Sept. 1965–March 1966
Angola	June 1997–Feb. 1999	Afghanistan/Pakistan	May 1988–March 1990
Sierra Leone	July 1998–Oct. 1999	Cambodia	Oct. 1991–March 1992
Central African Republic	April 1998–Feb. 2000	Cambodia	March 1992–Sept. 1993
MIDEAST		Tajikistan	Dec. 1994–May 2000
Middle East—1st UN	Nov. 1956–June 1967	East Timor	Oct. 1999–May 2002
Emergency Force		**EUROPE**	
Lebanon	June–Dec. 1958	Former Yugoslavia	Feb. 1992–March 1995
Yemen	July 1963–Sept. 1964	Croatia	March 1995–Jan. 1996
Middle East—2nd UN	Oct. 1973–July 1979	Former Yugoslavia	March 1995–Feb. 1999
Emergency Force		Rep. of Macedonia	
Iran/Iraq	Aug. 1988–Feb. 1991	Bosnia & Herzegovina	Dec. 1995–Dec. 2002
Iraq/Kuwait	April 1991–Oct. 2003	Croatia	Jan. 1996–Jan. 1998
		Prevlaka Peninsula	Feb. 1996–Dec. 2002
		Croatia	Jan. 1998–Oct. 1998

Source: United Nations Dept. of Public Information.

Members of the United Nations (191 nations)

Country	Joined UN[1]	Country	Joined UN[1]	Country	Joined UN[1]
Afghanistan	1946	Georgia	1992	Norway	1945
Albania	1955	Germany	1973	Oman	1971
Algeria	1962	Ghana	1957	Pakistan	1947
Andorra	1993	Greece	1945	Palau	1994
Angola	1976	Grenada	1974	Panama	1945
Antigua and Barbuda	1981	Guatemala	1945	Papua New Guinea	1975
Argentina	1945	Guinea	1958	Paraguay	1945
Armenia	1992	Guinea-Bissau	1974	Peru	1945
Australia	1945	Guyana	1966	Philippines	1945
Austria	1955	Haiti	1945	Poland	1945
Azerbaijan	1992	Honduras	1945	Portugal	1955
Bahamas	1973	Hungary	1955	Qatar	1971
Bahrain	1971	Iceland	1946	Romania	1955
Bangladesh	1974	India	1945	Russian Federation	1945
Barbados	1966	Indonesia	1950	Rwanda	1962
Belarus	1945	Iran	1945	St. Kitts and Nevis	1983
Belgium	1945	Iraq	1945	St. Lucia	1979
Belize	1981	Ireland	1955	St. Vincent and the	
Benin	1960	Israel	1949	Grenadines	1980
Bhutan	1971	Italy	1955	Samoa, Western	1976
Bolivia	1945	Jamaica	1962	San Marino	1992
Bosnia and Herzegovina	1992	Japan	1956	São Tomé and Príncipe	1975
Botswana	1966	Jordan	1955	Saudi Arabia	1945
Brazil	1945	Kazakhstan	1992	Senegal	1960
Brunei Darussalam	1984	Kenya	1963	Serbia and Montenegro[6]	2000
Bulgaria	1955	Kiribati	1999	Seychelles	1976
Burkina Faso	1960	North Korea	1991	Sierra Leone	1961
Burma (Myanmar)	1948	South Korea	1991	Singapore	1965
Burundi	1962	Kuwait	1963	Slovakia[3]	1993
Cambodia	1955	Kyrgyzstan	1992	Slovenia	1992
Cameroon	1960	Laos	1955	Solomon Islands	1978
Canada	1945	Latvia	1991	Somalia	1960
Cape Verde	1975	Lebanon	1945	South Africa	1945
Central African Republic	1960	Lesotho	1966	Spain	1955
Chad	1960	Liberia	1945	Sri Lanka	1955
Chile	1945	Libya	1955	Sudan	1956
China[2]	1945	Liechtenstein	1990	Suriname	1975
Colombia	1945	Lithuania	1991	Swaziland	1968
Comoros	1975	Luxembourg	1945	Sweden	1946
Congo	1960	Macedonia[5]	1993	Switzerland[4]	2002
Congo, Dem. Rep.	1960	Madagascar	1960	Syria	1945
Costa Rica	1945	Malawi	1964	Tajikistan	1992
Côte d'Ivoire	1960	Malaysia	1957	Tanzania	1961
Croatia	1992	Maldives	1965	Thailand	1946
Cuba	1945	Mali	1960	Togo	1960
Cyprus	1960	Malta	1964	Tonga	1999
Czech Republic[3]	1993	Marshall Islands	1991	Trinidad and Tobago	1962
Denmark	1945	Mauritania	1961	Tunisia	1956
Djibouti	1977	Mauritius	1968	Turkey	1945
Dominica	1978	Mexico	1945	Turkmenistan	1992
Dominican Republic	1945	Micronesia	1991	Tuvalu	2000
East Timor[4]	2002	Moldova	1992	Uganda	1962
Ecuador	1945	Monaco	1993	Ukraine	1945
Egypt	1945	Mongolia	1961	United Arab Emirates	1971
El Salvador	1945	Morocco	1956	United Kingdom	1945
Equatorial Guinea	1968	Mozambique	1975	United States	1945
Eritrea	1993	Namibia	1990	Uruguay	1945
Estonia	1991	Nauru	1999	Uzbekistan	1992
Ethiopia	1945	Nepal	1955	Vanuatu	1981
Fiji	1970	Netherlands	1945	Venezuela	1945
Finland	1955	New Zealand	1945	Vietnam	1977
France	1945	Nicaragua	1945	Yemen, Republic of	1947
Gabon	1960	Niger	1960	Zambia	1964
Gambia	1965	Nigeria	1960	Zimbabwe	1980

1. The UN officially came into existence on Oct. 24, 1945. 2. On Oct. 25, 1971, the UN voted membership to the People's Republic of China, which replaced the Republic of China (Taiwan) in the world body. 3. Czechoslovakia was an original member of the United Nations from Oct. 24, 1945. As of Dec. 31, 1992, it ceased to exist and the Czech Republic and Slovakia as successor states were admitted Jan. 19, 1993. 4. Newest members. 5. The General Assembly on April 8, 1993, decided to admit the state provisionally being referred to as "The Former Yugoslav Republic of Macedonia" pending settlement of the difference that has arisen over its name. 6. The Socialist Federal Republic of Yugoslavia was a charter member; after its dissolution, the Federal Republic of Yugoslavia was admitted Nov. 1, 2000. On Feb. 4, 2003, the name of the Federal Republic of Yugoslavia was changed to Serbia and Montenegro.

U.S. Representatives to the United Nations

Year	Ambassador	Year	Ambassador
1946	Edward R. Stettinius, Jr.	1977–1979	Andrew Young
1946–1947	Herschel V. Johnson (acting)	1979–1981	Donald McHenry
1947–1953	Warren R. Austin	1981–1985	Jeane J. Kirkpatrick
1953–1960	Henry Cabot Lodge, Jr.	1985–1989	Vernon A. Walters
1960–1961	James J. Wadsworth	1989–1992	Thomas J. Pickering
1961–1965	Adlai E. Stevenson	1992–1993	Edward J. Perkins
1965–1968	Arthur J. Goldberg	1993–1996	Madeleine K. Albright
1968	George W. Ball	1997–1998	Bill Richardson
1968–1969	James Russell Wiggins	1998–1999	A. Peter Burleigh (acting)
1969–1971	Charles W. Yost	1999–2001	Richard Holbrooke
1971–1973	George H. W. Bush	2001	James B. Cunningham (acting)
1973–1975	John A. Scali	2001–2004	John D. Negroponte
1975–1976	Daniel P. Moynihan	2004–	John Danforth
1976–1977	William W. Scranton		

Selected International Organizations

Arab League (AL)

Members: (21 plus the Palestine Liberation Organization) Algeria, Bahrain, Comoros, Djibouti, Egypt, Iraq, Jordan, Kuwait, Lebanon, Libya, Mauritania, Morocco, Oman, Qatar, Saudi Arabia, Somalia, Sudan, Syria, Tunisia, UAE, Yemen, Palestine Liberation Organization

Association of Southeast Asian Nations (ASEAN)

Members: (10) Brunei, Burma, Cambodia, Indonesia, Laos, Malaysia, Philippines, Singapore, Thailand, Vietnam
Associate Member: (1) Papua New Guinea

Group of 8 (G-8)

Members: (9) Canada, EU (as one member), France, Germany, Italy, Japan, Russia, UK, U.S.

Commonwealth of Nations

Members: (54) Antigua and Barbuda, Australia, the Bahamas, Bangladesh, Barbados, Belize, Botswana, Brunei, Cameroon, Canada, Cyprus, Dominica, Fiji, the Gambia, Ghana, Grenada, Guyana, India, Jamaica, Kenya, Kiribati, Lesotho, Malawi, Malaysia, Maldives, Malta, Mauritius, Mozambique, Namibia, Nauru, New Zealand, Nigeria, Pakistan, Papua New Guinea, Saint Kitts and Nevis, Saint Lucia, Saint Vincent and the Grenadines, Samoa, Seychelles, Sierra Leone, Singapore, Solomon Islands, South Africa, Sri Lanka, Swaziland, Tanzania, Tonga, Trinidad and Tobago, Tuvalu, Uganda, UK, Vanuatu, Zambia, Zimbabwe (suspended)

Commonwealth of Independent States (CIS)

Members: (12) Armenia, Azerbaijan, Belarus, Georgia, Kazakhstan, Kyrgyzstan, Moldova, Russia, Tajikistan, Turkmenistan, Ukraine, Uzbekistan

European Union (EU)

Members: (15) Austria, Belgium, Denmark, Finland, France, Germany, Greece, Ireland, Italy, Luxembourg, Netherlands, Portugal, Spain, Sweden, UK **New Members in 2004:** (10) Cyprus, Czech Republic, Estonia, Hungary, Latvia, Lithuania, Malta, Poland, Slovakia, Slovenia

North Atlantic Treaty Organization (NATO)

Members: (19) Belgium, Canada, Czech Republic, Denmark, France, Germany, Greece, Hungary, Iceland, Italy, Luxembourg, Netherlands, Norway, Poland, Portugal, Spain, Turkey, UK, U.S. **New members in 2004:** (7) Bulgaria, Estonia, Latvia, Lithuania, Romania, Slovakia, Slovenia

African Union (AU)[1]

Members: (53) Algeria, Angola, Benin, Botswana, Burkina Faso, Burundi, Cameroon, Cape Verde, Central African Republic, Chad, Comoros, Congo, Côte d'Ivoire, Democratic Republic of the Congo, Djibouti, Egypt, Equatorial Guinea, Eritrea, Ethiopia, Gabon, The Gambia, Ghana, Guinea, Guinea-Bissau, Kenya, Lesotho, Liberia, Libya, Madagascar, Malawi, Mali, Mauritania, Mauritius, Mozambique, Namibia, Niger, Nigeria, Rwanda, São Tomé and Príncipe, Senegal, Seychelles, Sierra Leone, Somalia, South Africa, Sudan, Swaziland, Tanzania, Togo, Tunisia, Uganda, Western Sahara, Zambia, Zimbabwe

Organization of Petroleum Exporting Countries (OPEC)

Members: (11) Algeria, Indonesia, Iran, Iraq, Kuwait, Libya, Nigeria, Qatar, Saudi Arabia, UAE, Venezuela

1. The Organization of African Unity (OAU), the African Union's predecessor, was formally disbanded on July 8, 2002. The AU was inaugurated July 9, 2002. The 53 member nations remain the same.

Foreign Embassies in the United States

Source: U.S. Department of State

Embassy of Afghanistan, 2341 Wyoming Ave., N.W.,Washington, D.C. 20008. Phone: 202-483-6410.

Embassy of the Republic of Albania, 2100 S St., N.W., Washington, D.C. 20008. Phone: 202-223-4942.

Embassy of the Democratic & Popular Republic of Algeria, 2118 Kalorama Rd., N.W., Washington, D.C. 20008. Phone: 202-265-2800.

Embassy of Andorra/Permanent Mission to the UN, 2 United Nations Plaza, 25th flr., New York, N.Y. 10017. Phone: 212-750-8064.

Embassy of the Republic of Angola, 2100–2108 16th St., N.W., Washington, D.C. 20009. Phone: 202-785-1156.

Embassy of Antigua & Barbuda, 3216 New Mexico Ave., N.W., Washington, D.C. 20016. Phone: 202-362-5122.

Embassy of the Argentine Republic, 1600 New Hampshire Ave., N.W., Washington, D.C. 20009. Phone: 202-238-6401.

Embassy of the Republic of Armenia, 2225 R Street, N.W., Washington, D.C. 20008. Phone: 202-319-1976.

Embassy of Australia, 1601 Massachusetts Ave., N.W., Washington, D.C. 20036. Phone: 202-797-3000.

Embassy of Austria, 3524 International Court, N.W., Washington, D.C. 20008-3027. Phone: 202-895-6700.

Embassy of the Republic of Azerbaijan, 2741 34th St., N.W., Washington, D.C. 20008. Phone: 202-337-3500.

Embassy of the Commonwealth of the Bahamas, 2220 Massachusetts Ave., N.W., Washington, D.C. 20008. Phone: 202-319-2660.

Embassy of the Kingdom of Bahrain, 3502 International Dr., N.W., Washington, D.C. 20008. Phone: 202-342-1111.

Embassy of the People's Republic of Bangladesh, 3510 International Drive, N.W., Washington, D.C. 20008. Phone: 202-244-0183.

Embassy of Barbados, 2144 Wyoming Ave., N.W., Washington, D.C. 20008. Phone: 202-939-9200.

Embassy of the Republic of Belarus, 1619 New Hampshire Ave., N.W., Washington, D.C. 20009. Phone: 202-986-1604.

Embassy of Belgium, 3330 Garfield St., N.W., Washington, D.C. 20008. Phone: 202-333-6900.

Embassy of Belize, 2535 Massachusetts Ave., N.W., Washington, D.C. 20008. Phone: 202-332-9636.

Embassy of the Republic of Benin, 2124 Kalorama Road, N.W., Washington, D.C. 20008. Phone: 202-232-6656.

Bhutan Permanent Mission to the UN, 2 UN Plaza, 27th Floor, New York NY 10017. Phone: 212-826-1919.

Embassy of Bolivia, 3014 Massachusetts Ave., N.W., Washington, D.C. 20008. Phone: 202-483-4410.

Embassy of Bosnia and Herzegovina, 2109 E St. N.W., Washington, D.C. 20037. Phone: 202-337-6473.

Embassy of Botswana, 1531-1533 New Hampshire Ave., N.W., Washington, D.C. 20036. Phone: 202-244-4990.

Brazilian Embassy, 3006 Massachusetts Ave., N.W., Washington, D.C. 20008. Phone: 202-238-2700.

Embassy of Brunei Darussalam, 3520 International Court, N.W., Washington, D.C. 20008. Phone: 202-237-1838.

Embassy of the Republic of Bulgaria, 1621 22nd St., N.W., Washington, D.C. 20008. Phone: 202-387-0174.

Embassy of Burkina Faso, 2340 Massachusetts Ave., N.W., Washington, D.C. 20008. Phone: 202-332-5577.

Embassy of the Republic of Burundi, 2233 Wisconsin Ave., N.W., Suite 212, Washington, D.C. 20007. Phone: 202-342-2574.

Embassy of the Kingdom of Cambodia, 4530 16th St., N.W., Washington, D.C. 20011. Phone: 202-726-7742.

Embassy of the Republic of Cameroon, 2349 Massachusetts Ave., N.W., Washington, D.C. 20008. Phone: 202-265-8790.

Embassy of Canada, 501 Pennsylvania Ave., N.W., Washington, D.C. 20001. Phone: 202-682-1740.

Embassy of the Republic of Cape Verde, 3415 Massachusetts Ave., N.W., Washington, D.C. 20007. Phone: 202-965-6820.

Embassy of Central African Republic, 1618 22nd St. N.W., Washington, D.C. 20008. Phone: 202-483-7800.

Embassy of the Republic of Chad, 2002 R St., N.W., Washington, D.C. 20009. Phone: 202-462-4009.

Embassy of Chile, 1732 Massachusetts Ave., N.W., Washington, D.C. 20036. Phone: 202-785-1746.

Embassy of the People's Republic of China, 2300 Connecticut Ave., N.W., Washington, D.C. 20008. Phone: 202-328-2500.

Embassy of Colombia, 2118 Leroy Pl., N.W., Washington, D.C. 20008. Phone: 202-387-8338.

Embassy of the Federal and Islamic Republic of Comoros, c/o Permanent Mission of the Federal and Islamic Republic of Comoros to the United Nations, 420 E. 50th St., New York, N.Y. 10022. Phone: 212-972-8010.

Embassy of the Democratic Republic of Congo, 1800 New Hampshire Ave., N.W., Washington, D.C. 20009. Phone: 202-234-7690.

Embassy of the Republic of Congo, 4891 Colorado Ave., N.W., Washington, D.C. 20011. Phone: 202-726-5500.

Embassy of Costa Rica, 2114 S St., N.W., Washington, D.C. 20008. Phone: 202-234-2945.

Embassy of the Republic of Côte d'Ivoire, 2424 Massachusetts Ave., N.W., Washington, D.C. 20007. Phone: 202-797-0300.

Embassy of the Republic of Croatia, 2343 Massachusetts Ave., N.W., Washington, D.C. 20008-2853. Phone: 202-588-5899.

Cuban Interests Section, 2630 16th St., N.W., Washington, D.C. 20009. Phone: 202-797-8518.

Embassy of the Republic of Cyprus, 2211 R St. N.W., Washington, D.C. 20008. Phone: 202-462-5772.

Embassy of the Czech Republic, 3900 Spring of Freedom St., N.W., Washington, D.C. 20008. Phone: 202-274-9100.

Royal Danish Embassy, 3200 Whitehaven St., N.W., Washington, D.C. 20008. Phone: 202-234-4300.

Embassy of the Republic of Djibouti, 1156 15th St., N.W., Suite 515, Washington, D.C. 20005. Phone: 202-331-0270.

Embassy of the Commonwealth of Dominica, 3216 New Mexico Ave., N.W., Washington, D.C. 20016. Phone: 202-364-6781/2.

Embassy of the Dominican Republic, 1715 22nd St., N.W., Washington, D.C. 20008. Phone: 202-332-6280.

Embassy of Ecuador, 2535 15th St., N.W., Washington, D.C. 20009. Phone: 202-234-7200.

Embassy of the Arab Republic of Egypt, 3521 International Court, N.W., Washington, D.C. 20008. Phone: 202-895-5400.

Embassy of El Salvador, 2308 California St., N.W., Washington, D.C. 20008. Phone: 202-265-9671.

Embassy of Equatorial Guinea, 2020 16th Street, N.W., Washington, D.C. 20009. Phone: 202-518-5700.

Embassy of the State of Eritrea, 1708 New Hampshire Ave., N.W., Washington, D.C., 20009. Phone: 202-319-1991.

Embassy of Estonia, 2131 Massachusetts Ave., N.W., Washington, D.C. 20008. Phone: 202-588-0101.

Embassy of Ethiopia, 3506 International Dr., N.W., Washington, D.C. 20008. Phone: 202-364-1200.

European Union Delegation, 2300 M St., N.W., Washington, D.C. 20037. Phone: 202-862-9500.

Embassy of Fiji, 2233 Wisconsin Ave., N.W., Suite 240, Washington, D.C. 20007. Phone: 202-337-8320.

Embassy of Finland, 3301 Massachusetts Ave., N.W., Washington, D.C. 20008. Phone: 202-298-5800.

Embassy of France, 4101 Reservoir Rd., N.W., Washington, D.C. 20007. Phone: 202-944-6000.

Embassy of the Gabonese Republic, 2034 20th St., N.W., Suite 200, Washington, D.C. 20009. Phone: 202-797-1000.

Embassy of the Republic of the Gambia, 1156 15th St., N.W., Suite 905, Washington, D.C. 20005-2076. Phone: 202-785-1399.

Embassy of the Republic of Georgia, 1615 New Hampshire Ave., N.W., Suite 300, Washington, D.C. 20009. Phone: 202-387-2390.

Embassy of Germany, 4645 Reservoir Rd., N.W., Washington, D.C. 20007-1998. Phone: 202-298-4000.

Embassy of Ghana, 3512 International Dr., N.W., Washington, D.C. 20008. Phone: 202-686-4520.

Embassy of Greece, 2221 Massachusetts Ave., N.W., Washington, D.C. 20008. Phone: 202-939-1300.

Embassy of Grenada, 1701 New Hampshire Ave., N.W., Washington, D.C. 20009. Phone: 202-265-2561.

Embassy of Guatemala, 2220 R St., N.W., Washington, D.C. 20008. Phone: 202-745-4952.

Embassy of the Republic of Guinea, 2112 Leroy Pl., N.W., Washington, D.C. 20008. Phone: 202-986-4300.

Embassy of the Republic of Guinea-Bissau, 15929 Yukon Lane, Rockville, MD 20855. Phone: 301-947-3958.

Embassy of Guyana, 2490 Tracy Pl., N.W., Washington, D.C. 20008. Phone: 202-265-6900.

Embassy of the Republic of Haiti, 2311 Massachusetts Ave., N.W., Washington, D.C. 20008. Phone: 202-332-4090.

Apostolic Nunciature of the Holy See, 3339 Massachusetts Ave., N.W., Washington, D.C. 20008. Phone: 202-333-7121.

Embassy of Honduras, 3007 Tilden St., N.W., Suite 4-M, Washington, D.C. 20008. Phone: 202-966-7702.

Embassy of the Republic of Hungary, 3910 Shoemaker St., N.W., Washington, D.C. 20008. Phone: 202-364-8218.

Embassy of Iceland, 1156 15th St., N.W., Suite 1200, Washington, D.C. 20005-1704. Phone: 202-265-6653.

Embassy of India, 2107 Massachusetts Ave., N.W., Washington, D.C. 20008. Phone: 202-939-7000.

Embassy of the Republic of Indonesia, 2020 Massachusetts Ave., N.W., Washington, D.C. 20036. Phone: 202-775-5200.

Iranian Interests Section, 2209 Wisconsin Ave., N.W., Washington, D.C. 20007. Phone: 202-965-4990.

Iraqi Interests Section, 1801 P St., N.W., Washington, D.C. 20036. Phone: 202-483-7500.

Embassy of Ireland, 2234 Massachusetts Ave., N.W., Washington, D.C. 20008. Phone: 202-462-3939.

Embassy of Israel, 3514 International Dr., N.W., Washington, D.C. 20008. Phone: 202-364-5500.

Embassy of Italy, 3000 Whitehaven St., N.W., Washington, D.C. 20008. Phone: 202-612-4400.

Embassy of Jamaica, 1520 New Hampshire Ave., N.W., Washington, D.C. 20036. Phone: 202-452-0660.

Embassy of Japan, 2520 Massachusetts Ave., N.W., Washington, D.C. 20008. Phone: 202-238-6700.

Embassy of the Hashemite Kingdom of Jordan, 3504 International Dr., N.W., Washington, D.C. 20008. Phone: 202-966-2664.

Embassy of the Republic of Kazakhstan, (temporary) 1401 16th St., N.W., Washington, D.C. 20036. Phone: 202-232-5488.

Embassy of the Republic of Kenya, 2249 R St., N.W., Washington, D.C. 20008. Phone: 202-387-6101.

Embassy of the Republic of Korea, 2450 Massachusetts Ave., N.W., Washington, D.C. 20008. Phone: 202-939-5600.

Kuwait Information Office, 2600 Virginia Ave., N.W., Suite 404, Washington, D.C. 20037. Phone: 202-338-0211.

Embassy of the Kyrgyz Republic, 1732 Wisconsin Ave., Washington, D.C. 20007. Phone: 202-338-5141.

Embassy of the Lao People's Democratic Republic, 2222 S St., N.W., Washington, D.C. 20008. Phone: 202-332-6416.

Embassy of Latvia, 4325 17th St., N.W., Washington, D.C. 20011. Phone: 202-726-8213.

Embassy of Lebanon, 2560 28th St., N.W., Washington, D.C. 20008. Phone: 202-939-6300.

Embassy of the Kingdom of Lesotho, 2511 Massachusetts Ave., N.W., Washington, D.C. 20008. Phone: 202-797-5533.

Embassy of the Republic of Liberia, 5201 16th St., N.W., Washington, D.C. 20011. Phone: 202-723-0437.

Embassy of the Republic of Lithuania, 2622 16th St., N.W., Washington, D.C. 20009. Phone: 202-234-5860.

Embassy of Luxembourg, 2200 Massachusetts Ave., N.W., Washington, D.C. 20008. Phone: 202-265-4171.

Embassy of the Republic of Macedonia, 1101 30th St., N.W., Suite 302, Washington, D.C. 20007. Phone: 202-337-3063.

Embassy of the Republic of Madagascar, 2374 Massachusetts Ave., N.W., Washington, D.C. 20008. Phone: 202-265-5525, 5526.

Embassy of Malawi, 2408 Massachusetts Ave., N.W., Washington, D.C. 20008. Phone: 202-797-1007.

Embassy of Malaysia, 3516 International Ct., N.W., Washington, D.C. 20008. Phone: 202-572-9700.

Embassy of the Republic of Mali, 2130 R St., N.W., Washington, D.C. 20009. Phone: 202-332-2249.

Embassy of Malta, 2017 Connecticut Ave., N.W., Washington, D.C. 20008. Phone: 202-462-3611.

Embassy of the Republic of the Marshall Islands, 2433 Massachusetts Ave., N.W., Washington, D.C. 20008. Phone: 202-234-5414.

Embassy of the Islamic Republic of Mauritania, 2129 Leroy Pl., N.W., Washington, D.C. 20008. Phone: 202-232-5700.

Embassy of the Republic of Mauritius, 4301 Connecticut Ave., N.W., Suite 441, Washington, D.C. 20008. Phone: 202-244-1491.

Embassy of Mexico, 1911 Pennsylvania Ave., N.W., Washington, D.C. 20006. Phone: 202-728-1600.

Embassy of the Federated States of Micronesia, 1725 N St., N.W., Washington, D.C. 20036. Phone: 202-223-4383.

Embassy of the Republic of Moldova, 2101 S St., N.W., Washington, D.C. 20008. Phone: 202-667-1130, 1131, 1137.

Embassy of Mongolia, 2833 M St., N.W., Washington, D.C. 20007. Phone: 202-333-7117.

Embassy of the Kingdom of Morocco, 1601 21st St., N.W., Washington, D.C. 20009. Phone: 202-462-7979 to 7982, inclusive.

Embassy of the Republic of Mozambique, 1990 M St., N.W., Suite 570, Washington, D.C. 20036. Phone: 202-293-7146.

Embassy of the Union of Myanmar (Burma), 2300 S St., N.W., Washington, D.C. 20008. Phone: 202-332-9044.

Embassy of the Republic of Namibia, 1605 New Hampshire Ave., N.W., Washington, D.C. 20009. Phone: 202-986-0540.

Embassy of Nepal, 2131 Leroy Pl., N.W., Washington, D.C. 20008. Phone: 202-667-4550.

Embassy of the Netherlands, 4200 Linnean Ave., N.W., Washington, D.C. 20008. Phone: 202-244-5300.

Embassy of New Zealand, 37 Observatory Circle, N.W., Washington, D.C. 20008. Phone: 202-328-4800.

Embassy of Nicaragua, 1627 New Hampshire Ave., N.W., Washington, D.C. 20009. Phone: 202-939-6570.

Embassy of the Republic of Niger, 2204 R St., N.W., Washington, D.C. 20008. Phone: 202-483-4224 to 4227, inclusive.

Embassy of the Federal Republic of Nigeria, 3519 International Ct., N.W., Washington, D.C. 20008. Phone: 202-986-8400.

Royal Embassy of Norway, 2720 34th St., N.W., Washington, D.C. 20008. Phone: 202-333-6000.

Embassy of the Sultanate of Oman, 2535 Belmont Rd., N.W., Washington, D.C. 20008. Phone: 202-387-1980.

Embassy of the Islamic Republic of Pakistan, 3517 International Ct., N.W., Washington, D.C. 20008. Phone: 202-243-6500.

Embassy of the Republic of Palau, 1800 K St., N.W., #714, Washington, D.C. 20036. Phone: 202-452-6814.

Embassy of the Republic of Panama, 2862 McGill Terrace, N.W., Washington, D.C. 20008. Phone: 202-483-1407.

Embassy of Papua New Guinea, 1779 Massachusetts Ave., N.W., Suite 805, Washington, D.C. 20036. Phone: 202-745-3680.

Embassy of Paraguay, 2400 Massachusetts Ave., N.W., Washington, D.C. 20008. Phone: 202-483-6960.

Embassy of Peru, 1700 Massachusetts Ave., N.W., Washington, D.C. 20036. Phone: 202-833-9860.

Embassy of the Philippines, 1600 Massachusetts Ave., N.W., Washington, D.C. 20036. Phone: 202-467-9300.

Embassy of the Republic of Poland, 2640 16th St., N.W., Washington, D.C. 20009. Phone: 202-234-3800.

Embassy of Portugal, 2125 Kalorama Rd., N.W., Washington, D.C. 20008. Phone: 202-328-8610.

Embassy of the State of Qatar, 4200 Wisconsin Ave., N.W., Suite #200, Washington, D.C. 20016. Phone: 202-274-1603.

Embassy of Romania, 1607 23rd St., N.W., Washington, D.C. 20008. Phone: 202-332-2879.

Embassy of the Russian Federation, 2650 Wisconsin Ave., N.W., Washington, D.C. 20007. Phone: 202-298-5700.

Embassy of the Republic of Rwanda, 1714 New Hampshire Ave., N.W., Washington, D.C. 20009. Phone: 202-232-2882.

Embassy of Saint Kitts and Nevis, 3216 New Mexico Ave., N.W., Washington, D.C. 20016. Phone: 202-686-2636.

Embassy of Saint Lucia, 3216 New Mexico Ave., N.W., Washington, D.C. 20016. Phone: 202-364-6792 to 6795.

Embassy of Saint Vincent and the Grenadines, 3216 New Mexico Ave., N.W., Washington, D.C. 20016. Phone: 202-364-6730.

Royal Embassy of Saudi Arabia, 601 New Hampshire Ave., N.W., Washington, D.C. 20037. Phone: 202-337-4076/4134.

Embassy of the Republic of Senegal, 2112 Wyoming Ave., N.W., Washington, D.C. 20008. Phone: 202-234-0540.

Embassy of Serbia and Montenegro, 2134 Kalorama Rd., N.W., Washington, D.C. 20008. Phone: 202-332-0333.

Embassy of the Republic of Seychelles, 800 Second Ave., Suite 400C, New York, N.Y. 10017. Phone: 212-972-1785.

Embassy of Sierra Leone, 1701 19th St., N.W., Washington, D.C. 20009. Phone: 202-939-9261.

Embassy of the Republic of Singapore, 3501 International Pl., N.W., Washington, D.C. 20008. Phone: 202-537-3100.

Embassy of the Slovak Republic, 3523 International Ct., N.W., Washington, D.C. 20008. Phone: 202-237-1054.

Embassy of the Republic of Slovenia, 1525 New Hampshire Ave., N.W., Washington, D.C. 20036. Phone: 202-667-5363.

Embassy of the Republic of South Africa, 3051 Massachusetts Ave., N.W., Washington, D.C. 20008. Phone: 202-232-4400.

Embassy of Spain, 2375 Pennsylvania Ave., N.W., Washington, D.C. 20037. Phone: 202-728-2330.

Embassy of Sri Lanka, 2148 Wyoming Ave., N.W., Washington, D.C. 20008. Phone: 202-483-4025 to 4028.

Embassy of the Republic of the Sudan, 2210 Massachusetts Ave., N.W., Washington, D.C. 20008. Phone: 202-338-8565.

Embassy of the Republic of Suriname, 4301 Connecticut Ave., N.W., Suite 460, Washington, D.C. 20008. Phone: 202-244-7488.

Embassy of the Kingdom of Swaziland, 1712 New Hampshire Ave., N.W., Washington, D.C. 20009. Phone: 202-234-5002.

Embassy of Sweden, 1501 M St., N.W., Suite 900, Washington, D.C. 20005. Phone: 202-467-2600.

Embassy of Switzerland, 2900 Cathedral Ave., N.W., Washington, D.C. 20008. Phone: 202-745-7900.

Embassy of the Syrian Arab Republic, 2215 Wyoming Ave., N.W., Washington, D.C. 20008. Phone: 202-232-6313.

Taipei Economic and Cultural Representation Office (Taiwan), 4201 Wisconsin Ave., N.W., Washington, D.C. 20016. Phone: 202-895-1800.

Embassy of the United Republic of Tanzania, 2139 R St., N.W., Washington, D.C. 20008. Phone: 202-884-1080.

Royal Thai Embassy, 1024 Wisconsin Ave., N.W., Washington, D.C. 20007. Phone: 202-944-3600.

Embassy of the Republic of Togo, 2208 Massachusetts Ave., N.W., Washington, D.C. 20008. Phone: 202-234-4212.

Embassy of the Republic of Trinidad and Tobago, 1708 Massachusetts Ave., N.W., Washington, D.C. 20036. Phone: 202-467-6490.

Embassy of Tunisia, 1515 Massachusetts Ave., N.W., Washington, D.C. 20005. Phone: 202-862-1850.

Embassy of the Republic of Turkey, 2525 Massachusetts Ave., N.W., Washington, D.C. 20008. Phone: 202-612-6700.

Embassy of Turkmenistan, 2207 Massachusetts Ave., N.W., Washington, D.C. 20008. Phone: 202-588-1500.

Embassy of the Republic of Uganda, 5911 16th St., N.W., Washington, D.C. 20011. Phone: 202-726-7100.

Embassy of Ukraine, 3350 M St., N.W., Washington, D.C. 20007. Phone: 202-333-7505.

Embassy of the United Arab Emirates, 3522 International Ct., N.W., Washington, D.C. 20008. Phone: 202-243-2400.

United Kingdom of Great Britain & Northern Ireland— British Embassy, 3100 Massachusetts Ave., N.W., Washington, D.C. 20008. Phone: 202-588-7800.

Embassy of Uruguay, 1913 I St., N.W., Washington, D.C. 20006. Phone: 202-331-1313.

Embassy of the Republic of Uzbekistan, 1746 Massachusetts Ave., N.W., Washington, D.C. 20036. Phone: 202-887-5300.

Embassy of the Republic of Venezuela, 1099 30th St., N.W., Washington D.C. 20007. Phone: 202-342-2214.

Embassy of the Socialist Republic of Vietnam, 1233 20th St., N.W., Suite 400, Washington, D.C. 20036. Phone: 202-861-0737.

Embassy of the Republic of Yemen, 2600 Virginia Ave., N.W., Suite 705, Washington, D.C. 20037. Phone: 202-965-4760.

Embassy of the Republic of Zambia, 2419 Massachusetts Ave., N.W., Washington, D.C. 20008. Phone: 202-265-9717.

Embassy of the Republic of Zimbabwe, 1608 New Hampshire Ave., N.W., Washington, D.C. 20009. Phone: 202-332-7100.

Diplomatic Personnel to and from the U.S.

Country	U.S. Representative to[1]	Rank	Representative from[1]	Rank
Afghanistan	Zalmay Khalilzad	Amb.	Seyyed Tayeb Jawad	Amb.
Albania	James F. Jeffrey	Amb.	Fatos Tarifa	Amb.
Algeria	Richard W. Erdman	Amb.	Idriss Jazairy	Amb.
Andorra	George Argyros	Amb.	Jelena V. Pia Comella	Cd'A
Angola	Christopher Dell	Amb.	Josefina Pitra Diakité	Amb.
Antigua and Barbuda	Mary E. Kramer[2]	Amb.	Lionel Alexander Hurst	Amb.
Argentina	Lino Gutierrez	Amb.	Jose Octavio Bordon	Amb.
Armenia	John M. Ordway	Amb.	Arman Kirakossian	Amb.
Australia	John Thomas Schieffer	Amb.	Michael J. Thawley	Amb.
Austria	William Lyons Brown, Jr.	Amb.	Eva Nowotny	Amb.
Azerbaijan	Reno Harnish	Amb.	Hafiz Pashayev	Amb.
Bahamas	Robert M. Witajewski	Cd'A.	Joshua Sears	Amb.
Bahrain	Ronald E. Neumann	Amb.	Khalifa bin Ali Al-Khalifa	Amb.
Bangladesh	Harry K. Thomas, Jr.	Amb.	Syed Hasan Ahmad	Amb.
Barbados	Mary E. Kramer[2]	Amb.	Michael Ian King	Amb.
Belarus	George A. Krol	Amb.	Mikhail Khvostov	Amb.
Belgium	Brenda B. Schoonover	Cd'A	Franciskus van Daele	Amb.
Belize	Russell F. Freeman	Amb.	Lisa M. Shoman	Amb.
Benin	Wayne Neill	Amb.	Segbe Cyrille Oguin	Amb.
Bermuda	Denis Patrick Coleman, Jr.	C.G.	—	—
Bolivia	David N. Greenlee	Amb.	Jaime Aparicio Otero	Amb.
Bosnia-Herzegovina	Clifford G. Bond	Amb.	Igor Davidovic	Amb.
Botswana	Joseph Huggins	Amb.	Lapologang Caesar Lekoa	Amb.
Brazil	Donna J. Hrinak	Amb.	Roberto Abdenur	Amb.
Brunei	Gene B. Christy	Amb.	Pengiran Anak Dato Puteh	Amb.
Bulgaria	James W. Pardew	Amb.	Elena Poptodorova	Amb.
Burkina Faso	Anthony Holmes	Amb.	Tertius Zongo	Amb.
Burundi	James Howard Yellin	Amb.	Antoine Ntamobwa	Amb.
Cambodia	Charles Aaron Ray	Amb.	Roland Eng	Amb.
Cameroon	George M. Staples	Amb.	Jerome Mendouga	Amb.
Canada	Paul Cellucci	Amb.	Michael F. Kergin	Amb.
Cape Verde	Donald C. Johnson	Amb.	Jose Brito	Amb.
Central African Republic	—	—	Emmanuel Touaboy	Amb.
Chad	Christopher E. Goldthwait	Amb.	Ahmat Hassaballah Soubiane	Amb.
Chile	William R. Brownfield	Amb.	Andrés Bianchi	Amb.
China	Clark J. Randt, Jr.	Amb.	Yang Jiechi	Amb.
Colombia	William B. Wood	Amb.	Luis Alberto Moreno	Amb.
Comoros	John Price	Amb.	Mahmoud M. Aboud	Amb.
Congo, Dem. Rep. of	Aubrey Hooks	Amb.	Faida Mitifu	Amb.
Congo, Rep. of	Robin R. Sanders	Amb.	Serge Mombouli	Amb.
Costa Rica	John J. Danilovich	Amb.	Jaime Daremblum	Amb.
Côte d'Ivoire	Arlene Render	Amb.	Daouda Diabate	Amb.
Croatia	Ralph Frank	Amb.	Ivan Grdesic	Amb.
Cuba	James C. Cason	P.O.	Dagoberto Rodriguez Barrera	P.O.
Cyprus	Michael Klosson	Amb.	Euripides L. Evriviades	Amb.
Czech Republic	William J. Cabaniss	Amb.	Martin Palous	Amb.
Denmark	Stuart A. Bernstein	Amb.	Ulrik Andreas Federspiel	Amb.
Djibouti	Marguerita Ragsdale	Amb.	Roble Olhaye	Amb.
Dominica	Mary E. Kramer[2]	Amb.	Swinburne Lestrade	Amb.
Dominican Republic	Hans H. Hertell	Amb.	Hugo Guiliani Cury	Amb.
East Timor	Grover Joseph Rees	Amb.	Jose Luis Guterrés	Amb.
Ecuador	Kristie Anne Kenney	Amb.	Raul Gangotena Rivadeneira	Amb.
Egypt	C. David Welch	Amb.	M. Nabil Fahmy	Amb.
El Salvador	H. Douglas Barclay	Amb.	Rene A. León Rodríguez	Amb.
Equatorial Guinea	George M. Staples	Amb.	Teodoro Biyoga Nsue	Amb.
Eritrea	Donald J. McConnell	Amb.	Girma Asmerom	Amb.
Estonia	Joseph M. DeThomas	Amb.	Juri Luik	Amb.
Ethiopia	Aurelia A. Brazeal	Amb.	Kassahun Ayele	—
EU Delegation	Rockwell Schnabel	Amb.	Günther Burghardt	Amb.
Fiji	David L. Lyon[3]	Amb.	Paula Bolaqace Navunisaravj	S.S.
Finland	Earle I. Mack	Amb.	Jukka Valtasaari	Amb.
France	Howard H. Leach	Amb.	John-David Levitte	Amb.
Gabon	Kenneth P. Moorefield	Amb.	Jules Marius Ogouebandja	Amb.
Gambia, The	Jackson McDonald	Amb.	Dodou Bammy Jagne	Amb.
Georgia	Richard M. Miles	Amb.	Levan Mikeladze	Amb.
Germany	Daniel R. Coats	Amb.	Wolfgang Friedrich Ischinger	Amb.
Ghana	Mary Carlin Yates	Amb.	Isaac Aggrey	Cd'A

Country	U.S. Representative to[1]	Rank	Representative from[1]	Rank
Greece	Thomas J. Miller	Amb.	Yeoryious Savvaides	Amb.
Grenada	Mary E. Kramer[2]	Amb.	Denis G. Antoine	Amb.
Guatemala	John Randle Hamilton	Amb.	Jose Guillermo Castillo	Amb.
Guinea	Barrie R. Walkley	Amb.	Raflou Alpha Oumar Barry	Amb.
Guinea-Bissau	—	—	Henrique Adriano Da Silva	Cd'A.
Guyana	Ronald D. Godard	Amb.	Dr. Ali Odeen Ishmael	Amb.
Haiti	James B. Foley	Amb.	Raymond Valcin	Amb.
Holy See	Jim Nicholson	Amb.	Gabriel Montalvo	Pap. Nun.
Honduras	Larry Leon Palmer	Amb.	Mario Miguel Cunahuati	Amb.
Hong Kong	James Keith	C.G.	—	—
Hungary	George Herbert Walker	Amb.	Andras Simonyi	Amb.
Iceland	James I. Gadsden	Amb.	Helgi Agustsson	Amb.
India	David C. Mulford	Amb.	Rakesh Sood	Cd'A
Indonesia	Ralph L. Boyce	Amb.	Soemadi D. M. Brotodiningrat	Amb.
Iran	—	—	—	—
Iraq	John Negroponte	Amb.	—	—
Ireland	James C. Kenny	Amb.	Noel Fahey	Amb.
Israel	Daniel C. Kurtzer	Amb.	Daniel Ayalon	Amb.
Italy	Melvin F. Sembler	Amb.	Sergio Vento	Amb.
Jamaica	Sue McCourt Cobb	Amb.	Earle Courtenay Rattray	Cd'A
Japan	Howard H. Baker, Jr.	Amb.	Ryozo Kato	Amb.
Jordan	Edward William Gnehm, Jr.	Amb.	Karim Tawiq Kawar	Amb.
Kazakhstan	Larry C. Napper	Amb.	Kanat B. Saudabayev	Amb.
Kenya	Johnnie Carson	Amb.	Leonard Njogu Ngaithe	Amb.
Kiribati, Republic of	Michael J. Senko[4]	Amb.	—	—
Korea, South	Thomas C. Hubbard	Amb.	Sung-Joo Han	Amb.
Kuwait	Richard H. Jones	Amb.	Salem Abdullah Al-Jaber Al-Sabah	Amb.
Kyrgyz Republic	Stephen M. Young	Amb.	Baktybek Abdrisaev	Amb.
Laos	Douglas A. Hartwick	Amb.	Phanthong Phommahaxay	Amb.
Latvia	Brian E. Carlson	Amb.	Aivis Ronis	Amb.
Lebanon	Vincent Martin Battle	Amb.	Farid Abboud	Amb.
Lesotho	Robert G. Loftis	Amb.	Molelekeng E. Rapolaki	Amb.
Liberia	John William Blaney III	Amb.	Charles A. Minor	Amb.
Liechtenstein	Pamela Willeford[5]	Amb.	Claudia Fritsche	Amb.
Lithuania	Stephen D. Mull	Amb.	Vygaudas Usackas	Amb.
Luxembourg	Peter Terpeluk, Jr.	Amb.	Arlette Conzemius-Paccourd	Amb.
Macedonia	Lawrence Edward Butler	Amb.	Nikola Dimitrov	Amb.
Madagascar	Wanda L. Nesbitt	Amb.	Rajaonarivony Narisoa	Amb.
Malawi	Stephen Browning	Amb.	Bernardo Sande	Amb.
Malaysia	Marie T. Huhtala	Amb.	Ghazzali bin Sheikh Abdul Khalid	Amb.
Maldives	Jeffrey J. Lunstead[6]	Amb.	Mohamed Latheef	Amb.
Mali	Vicki Huddlestone	Amb.	Abdoulaye Diop	Amb.
Malta	Anthony H. Gioia	Amb.	John Lowell	Amb.
Marshall Islands	Michael J. Senko[4]	Amb.	Banny de Brum	Amb.
Mauritania	Joseph E. Lebaron	Amb.	Tijani Ould M. E. Kerim	Amb.
Mauritius	John Price	Amb.	Usha Jeetah	Amb.
Mexico	Antonio O. Garza	Amb.	Carlos Alberto de Icaza Gonzalez	Amb.
Micronesia	Larry Miles Dinger	Amb.	Jesse B. Marehalau	Amb.
Moldova	Heather M. Hodges	Amb.	Mihai Manoli	Amb.
Mongolia	Pamela J. Slutz	Amb.	Ravdangiyn Bold	Amb.
Morocco	Thomas T. Riley	Amb.	Aziz Mekouar	Amb.
Mozambique	Sharon P. Wilkinson	Amb.	Armando A. Panguene	Amb.
Myanmar (Burma)	Carmen M. Martinez	Cd'A	Linn Myaing	Amb.
Namibia	Kevin J. McGuire	Amb.	Leonard Nangolo Iipumbu	Amb.
Nauru	David L. Lyon[3]	Amb.	—	—
Nepal	Michael E. Malinowski	Amb.	Rudra Kumar Nepal	Cd'A
Netherlands	Clifford M. Sobel	Amb.	Boudewijn Johannes Van Eenennaam	Amb.
Netherlands Antilles	Deborah A. Bolton	C.G.	—	—
New Zealand	Charles J. Swindells	Amb.	John Wood	Amb.
Nicaragua	Barbara Calandra Moore	Amb.	Salvador Stadthagen	Amb.
Niger	Gail Dennise Thomas Mathieu	Amb.	Joseph Diatta	Amb.
Nigeria	Howard Franklin Jeter	Amb.	George Achulike Obiozor	Amb.
Norway	John Doyle Ong	Amb.	Knut VolleBaek	Amb.
Oman	Richard Lewis Baltimore III	Amb.	Mohamed Ali Al-Khusaiby	Amb.
Pakistan	Nancy J. Powell	Amb.	Ashraf Jehangir Qazi	Amb.

Country	U.S. Representative to[1]	Rank	Representative from[1]	Rank
Palau	Francis J. Ricciardone, Jr.	Amb.	Hersey Kyota	Amb.
Panama	Linda Ellen Watt	Amb.	Roberto Alfaro Estripeaut	Amb.
Papua New Guinea	Robert W. Fitts	Amb.	Evan Jeremy Paki	Amb.
Paraguay	John F. Keane	Amb.	James Spalding Hellmers	Amb.
Peru	J. Curtis Struble	Amb.	Eduardo Ferrero Costa	Amb.
Philippines	Francis J. Ricciardone, Jr.	Amb.	Albert Del Rosario	Amb.
Poland	Christopher R. Hill	Amb.	Przemyslaw Grudzinski	Amb.
Portugal	John N. Palmer	Amb.	Pedro M. Dos Reis Alves Catarino	Amb.
Qatar	Maureen E. Quinn	Amb.	Bader Omar Al-Dafa	Amb.
Romania	Michael E. Guest	Amb.	Sorin Dumitru Ducaru	Amb.
Russia	Alexander Vershbow	Amb.	Yuriy Viktorovich Ushakov	Amb.
Rwanda	Margaret K. McMillion	Amb.	Zac Nsenga	Amb.
Saint Kitts and Nevis	Mary E. Kramer[2]	Amb.	Izben Cordinal Williams	Amb.
Saint Lucia	Mary E. Kramer[2]	Amb.	Sonia Merlyn Johnny	Amb.
Saint Vincent and the Grenadines	Mary E. Kramer[2]	Amb.	Ellsworth I. A. John	Amb.
Samoa, Western	Charles J. Swindells	Amb.	Aliioaiga Feturi Elisaia	Amb.
São Tomé and Príncipe, Dem. Rep. of	Kenneth P. Moorefield	Amb.	Domingos Augusto Ferreira	UN PM
Saudi Arabia	James Curtis Oberwetter	Amb.	Bandar bin Sultan	Amb.
Senegal	Harriet L. Elam-Thomas	Amb.	Amadou Lamine Ba	Amb.
Serbia and Montenegro	Michael C. Polt	Amb.	Ivan Vujacic	Amb.
Seychelles	John Price	Amb.	Claude Sylvestre Morel	Amb.
Sierra Leone	Peter Russell Chaveas	Amb.	Ibrahim M. Kamara	Amb.
Singapore	Franklin L. Lavin	Amb.	Heng Chee Chan	Amb.
Slovakia	Ronald Weiser	Amb.	Rastislav Kacer	Amb.
Slovenia	Johnny Young	Amb.	Jasna Gersak	Cd'A
Solomon Islands	Robert W. Fitts	Amb.	Colin David Beck	Amb.
South Africa	Cameron H. Hume	Amb.	Barbara Joyce Mosima Masekela	Amb.
Spain	George L. Argyros	Amb.	Carlos Westendorp	Amb.
Sri Lanka	Jeffrey J. Lunstead[6]	Amb.	Devinda R. Subasinghe	Amb.
Sudan	Gerard M. Gallucci	Cd'A	Khidr Haroun Ahmed	Cd'A
Suriname	Marsha E. Barnes	Amb.	Henry Lothar Illes	Amb.
Swaziland	James D. McGee	Amb.	Mary Madzandza Kanya	Amb.
Sweden	Charles A. Heimbold, Jr.	Amb.	Jan Eliasson	Amb.
Switzerland	Pamela Willeford[5]	Amb.	Christian Blickenstorfer	Amb.
Syria	Margaret Scobey	Amb.	Imad Mustafa	Amb.
Tajikistan	Richard E. Hoagland	Amb.	Khamrokhon Zaripov	Amb.
Tanzania	Robert V. Royall	Amb.	Andrew Mhando Daraja	Amb.
Thailand	Darryl N. Johnson	Amb.	Chirachai Punkrasin	Cd'A
Togo	Gregory Engle	Amb.	Akoussoulelou Bodjona	Amb.
Tonga	David L. Lyon[3]	Amb.	Sonatane T. T. Tupou	Amb.
Trinidad and Tobago	Roy L. Austin	Amb.	Marina Annette Valere	Amb.
Tunisia	William J. Hudson	Amb.	Hatem Atallah	Amb.
Turkey	Eric S. Edelman	Amb.	Osman Faruk Logoglu	Amb.
Turkmenistan	Tracey A. Jacobson	Amb.	Meret Bairamovich Orazov	Amb.
Tuvalu	David L. Lyon[3]	Amb.	—	—
Uganda	Jimmy Kolker	Amb.	Edith Grace Ssempala	Amb.
Ukraine	John E. Herbst	Amb.	Mykhailo B. Reznik	Amb.
United Arab Emirates	Marcelle M. Wahba	Amb.	Al Asri Saeed Ahmed Al Dhahri	Amb.
United Kingdom	William S. Farish	Amb.	David G. Manning	Amb.
Uruguay	Martin J. Silverstein	Amb.	Hugo Fernandez-Faingold	Amb.
Uzbekistan	Jon Purnell	Amb.	Abdulaziz Kamilov	Amb.
Vanuatu	Robert W. Fitts	Amb.	—	—
Venezuela	Charles S. Shapiro	Amb.	Bernardo Alvarez	Amb.
Vietnam	Raymond F. Burghardt	Amb.	Nguyen Tam Chien	Amb.
Yemen	Edmund J. Hull	Amb.	Abdulwahab A. Al-Hajjri	Amb.
Zambia	Martin George Brennan	Amb.	Inonge Mbikusita-Lewanika	Amb.
Zimbabwe	Joseph G. Sullivan	Amb.	Simbi Veke Mubako	Amb.

1. As of June 2004. 2. The U.S. embassy in Barbados currently serves seven independent nations of the Eastern Caribbean (Barbados, Antigua and Barbuda, Dominica, Grenada, St. Kitts and Nevis, St. Lucia, and St. Vincent and the Grenadines) and provides consular services to American citizens in the nearby European dependent territories. 3. Ambassador to Fiji, Nauru, Tonga, and Tuvalu. 4. Ambassador to Marshall Islands and Republic of Kiribati. 5. Ambassador to Liechtenstein and Switzerland. 6. Ambassador to the Maldives and Sri Lanka. NOTE: Amb.=Ambassador; Cd'A=Charge d'Affaires; C.G.=Consul General; Pap. Nun.=Papal Nuncio; P.O.=Principal Officer; UN PM=head of Permanent Mission to U.N.; S.S.=Second Secretary *Sources:* U.S. Department of State, CIA World Factbook.

The Olympic Games

1896 Athens, Greece	1948 London, Great Britain (S)	1984 Sarajevo, Yugoslavia (W)
1900 Paris, France	1952 Oslo, Norway (W)	1984 Los Angeles, United States (S)
1904 St. Louis, United States	1952 Helsinki, Finland (S)	1988 Calgary, Canada (W)
1906 Athens, Greece	1956 Cortina d'Ampezzo, Italy (W)	1988 Seoul, South Korea (S)
1908 London, Great Britain	1956 Melbourne, Australia (S)	1992 Albertville, France (W)
1912 Stockholm, Sweden	1960 Squaw Valley, United States (W)	1992 Barcelona, Spain (S)
1920 Antwerp, Belgium	1960 Rome, Italy (S)	1994 Lillehammer, Norway (W)
1924 Chamonix, France (W)	1964 Innsbruck, Austria (W)	1996 Atlanta, United States (S)
1924 Paris, France (S)	1964 Tokyo, Japan (S)	1998 Nagano, Japan (W)
1928 St. Moritz, Switzerland (W)	1968 Grenoble, France (W)	2000 Sydney, Australia (S)
1928 Amsterdam, Netherlands (S)	1968 Mexico City, Mexico (S)	2002 Salt Lake City, United States (W)
1932 Lake Placid, United States (W)	1972 Sapporo, Japan (W)	2004 Athens, Greece (S)
1932 Los Angeles, United States (S)	1972 Munich, Germany (S)	2006 Turin, Italy (W)
1936 Garmisch-Partenkirchen,	1976 Innsbruck, Austria (W)	2008 Beijing, China (S)
Germany (W)	1976 Montreal, Canada (S)	2010 Vancouver, Canada (W)
1936 Berlin, Germany (S)	1980 Lake Placid, United States (W)	
1948 St. Moritz, Switzerland (W)	1980 Moscow, USSR (S)	

(W)—Site of Winter Games. (S)—Site of Summer Games. The nine cities bidding for the 2012 Olympic Summer Games are: Paris, London, Moscow, Madrid, New York, Istanbul, Leipzig, Rio de Janeiro and Havana. The IOC will select the host city for the 2012 games on July 6, 2005.

The first Olympic Games of which there is record were held in 776 B.C., and consisted of one event, a great foot race of about 200 yards held on a plain by the River Alpheus (now the Ruphia) just outside the little town of Olympia in Greece. It was from that date the Greeks began to keep their calendar by "Olympiads," the four-year spans between the celebrations of the famous games.

The modern Olympic Games, which started in Athens in 1896, are the result of the devotion of a French educator, Baron Pierre de Coubertin, to the idea that, since young people and athletics have gone together through the ages, education and athletics might go hand-in-hand toward a better international understanding.

The principal organization responsible for the staging of the Games is the International Olympic Committee (IOC). Other important roles are played by the National Olympic Committees in each participating country, international sports federations, and the organizing committee of the host city.

The Olympic motto is "Citius, Altius, Fortius,"—"Faster, Higher, Stronger." The Olympic symbol is five interlocking circles colored blue, yellow, black, green, and red, on a white background, representing the five continents. At least one of those colors appears in the national flag of every country.

Beginning in 1994, the IOC decided to change the format of having both the Summer and Winter Games in the same year. Summer and Winter Olympics now alternate every two years.

In Feb. 1998 the IOC announced that new sports added to the games must include women's events.

Summer Games: Gold Medals

TRACK AND FIELD–MEN

100-Meter Dash

1896	Thomas Burke, United States	12.00
1900	Francis W. Jarvis, United States	10.80
1904	Archie Hahn, United States	11.00
1906	Archie Hahn, United States	11.20
1908	Reginald Walker, South Africa	10.80
1912	Ralph Craig, United States	10.80
1920	Charles Paddock, United States	10.80
1924	Harold Abrahams, Great Britain	10.60
1928	Percy Williams, Canada	10.80
1932	Eddie Tolan, United States	10.30
1936	Jesse Owens, United States	10.30[1]
1948	Harrison Dillard, United States	10.30
1952	Lindy Remigino, United States	10.40
1956	Bobby Morrow, United States	10.50
1960	Armin Hary, Germany	10.20
1964	Robert Hayes, United States	10.00
1968	James Hines, United States	09.90
1972	Valery Borzov, USSR	10.14
1976	Hasely Crawford, Trinidad and Tobago	10.06
1980	Allan Wells, Britain	10.25
1984	Carl Lewis, United States	09.99

1988	Carl Lewis, United States	09.92[2]
1992	Linford Christie, Great Britain	09.96
1996	Donovan Bailey, Canada	09.84[3]
2000	Maurice Greene, United States	09.87
2004	Justin Gatlin, United States	09.85

1. Wind assisted. 2. Lewis was awarded the gold medal when Ben Johnson of Canada, the original winner in 09.79s, was stripped of the medal after testing positive for steroid use. 3. World record.

200-Meter Dash

1900	John Tewksbury, United States	22.20
1904	Archie Hahn, United States	21.60
1908	Robert Kerr, Canada	22.60
1912	Ralph Craig, United States	21.70
1920	Allan Woodring, United States	22.00
1924	Jackson Scholz, United States	21.60
1928	Percy Williams, Canada	21.80
1932	Eddie Tolan, United States	21.20
1936	Jesse Owens, United States	20.70
1948	Melvin E. Patton, United States	21.10
1952	Andrew Stanfield, United States	20.70
1956	Bobby Morrow, United States	20.60
1960	Livio Berruti, Italy	20.50

1964	Henry Carr, United States	20.30
1968	Tommie Smith, United States	19.80
1972	Vallery Borzov, USSR	20.00
1976	Don Quarrie, Jamaica	20.23
1980	Pietro Mennea, Italy	20.19
1984	Carl Lewis, United States	19.80
1988	Joe DeLoach, United States	19.75
1992	Mike Marsh, United States	20.01
1996	Michael Johnson, United States	19.32[1]
2000	Konstantinos Kenteris, Greece	20.09
2004	Shawn Crawford, United States	19.79

1. World record.

400-Meter Dash

1896	Thomas Burke, United States	54.20
1900	Maxwell Long, United States	49.40
1904	Harry Hillman, United States	49.20
1906	Paul Pilgrim, United States	53.20
1908	Wyndham Halswelle, Great Britain (walkover)	50.00
1912	Charles Reidpath, United States	48.20
1920	Bevil Rudd, South Africa	49.60
1924	Eric Liddell, Great Britain	47.60
1928	Ray Barbuti, United States	47.80
1932	William Carr, United States	46.20
1936	Archie Williams, United States	46.50
1948	Arthur Wint, Jamaica, B.W.I.	46.20
1952	George Rhoden, Jamaica, B.W.I.	45.90
1956	Charles Jenkins, United States	46.70
1960	Otis Davis, United States	44.90
1964	Mike Larrabee, United States	45.10
1968	Lee Evans, United States	43.80
1972	Vincent Matthews, United States	44.66
1976	Alberto Juantorena, Cuba	44.26
1980	Viktor Markin, USSR	44.60
1984	Alonzo Babers, United States	44.27
1988	Steve Lewis, United States	43.87
1992	Quincy Watts, United States	43.50
1996	Michael Johnson, United States	43.49
2000	Michael Johnson, United States	43.84
2004	Jeremy Wariner, United States	44.00

800-Meter Run

1896	Edwin Flack, Australia	2:11.00
1900	Alfred Tysoe, Great Britain	2:01.40
1904	James Lightbody, United States	1:56.00
1906	Paul Pilgrim, United States	2:01.20
1908	Mel Sheppard, United states	1:52.80
1912	Ted Meredith, United States	1:51.90
1920	Albert Hill, Great Britain	1:53.40
1924	Douglas Lowe, Great Britain	1:52.40
1928	Douglas Lowe, Great Britain	1:51.80
1932	Thomas Hampson, Great Britain	1:49.80
1936	John Woodruff, United States	1:52.90
1948	Malvin Whitfield, United States	1:49.20
1952	Malvin Whitfield, United States	1:49.20
1956	Tom Courtney, United States	1:47.70
1960	Peter Snell, New Zealand	1:46.30
1964	Peter Snell, New Zealand	1:45.10
1968	Ralph Doubell, Australia	1:44.30
1972	David Wottle, United States	1:45.90
1976	Alberto Juantorena, Cuba	1:43.50
1980	Steve Ovett, Britain	1:45.40
1984	Joaquin Cruz, Brazil	1:43.00
1988	Paul Ereng, Kenya	1:43.45
1992	William Tanui, Kenya	1:43.66
1996	Vebjoern Rodal, Norway	1:42.58
2000	Nils Schumann, Germany	1:45.08
2004	Yuriy Borzakovskiy, Russia	1:44.45

1,500-Meter Run

1896	Edwin Flack, Australia	4:33.20
1900	Charles Bennett, Great Britain	4:06.00
1904	James Lightbody, United States	4:05.40
1906	James Lightbody, United States	4:12.00
1908	Mel Sheppard, United States	4:03.40
1912	Arnold Jackson, Great Britain	3:56.80

1920	Albert Hill, Great Britain	4:01.80
1924	Paavo Nurmi, Finland	3:53.60
1928	Harry Larva, Finland	3:53.20
1932	Luigi Becali, Italy	3:51.20
1936	Jack Lovelock, New Zealand	3:47.80
1948	Henri Eriksson, Sweden	3:49.80
1952	Joseph Barthel, Luxembourg	3:45.20
1956	Ron Delany, Ireland	3:41.20
1960	Herb Elliott, Australia	3:35.60
1964	Peter Snell, New Zealand	3:38.10
1968	Kipchoge Keino, Kenya	3:34.90
1972	Pekka Vasala, Finland	3:36.30
1976	John Walker, New Zealand	3:39.17
1980	Sebastian Coe, Britain	3:38.40
1984	Sebastian Coe, Britain	3:32.53
1988	Peter Rono, Kenya	3:35.96
1992	Fermin Cacho Ruiz, Spain	3:40.12
1996	Noureddine Morceli, Algeria	3:35.78
2000	Noah Ngeny, Kenya	3:32.07
2004	Hicham El Guerrouj, Morocco	3:34.18

5,000-Meter Run

1912	Hannes Kolehmainen, Finland	14:36.60
1920	Joseph Guillemot, France	14:55.60
1024	Paavo Nurmi, Finland	14:31.20
1928	Willie Ritola, Finland	14:38.00
1932	Lauri Lehtinen, Finland	14:30.00
1936	Gunnar Hockert, Finland	14:22.20
1948	Gaston Reiff, Belgium	14:17.60
1952	Emil Zatopek, Czechoslovakia	14:06.60
1956	Vladimir Kuts, USSR	13:39.60
1960	Murray Halberg, New Zealand	13:43.40
1964	Bob Schul, United States	13:48.80
1968	Mohamed Gammoudi, Tunisia	14:05.00
1972	Lasse Viren, Finland	13:26.40
1976	Lasse Viren, Finland	13:24.76
1980	Miruts Yifter, Ethiopia	13:21.00
1984	Saud Aouita, Morocco	13:05.59
1988	John Ngugi, Kenya	13:11.70
1992	Dieter Baumann, Germany	13:12.52
1996	Venuste Niyongabo, Burundi	13:07.96
2000	Millon Wolde, Ethiopia	13:35.49
2004	Hicham El Guerrouj, Morocco	13:14.39

10,000-Meter Run

1912	Hannes Kolehmainen, Finland	31:20.80
1920	Paavo Nurmi, Finland	31:45.80
1924	Willie Ritola, Finland	30:23.20
1928	Paavo Nurmi, Finland	30:18.80
1932	Janusz Kusocinski, Poland	30:11.40
1936	Ilmari Salminen, Finland	30:15.40
1948	Emil Zatopek, Czechoslovakia	29:59.60
1952	Emil Zatopek, Czechoslovakia	29:17.00
1956	Vladimir Kuts, USSR	28:45.60
1960	Peter Bolotnikov, USSR	28:32.20
1964	Billy Mills, United States	28:24.40
1968	Nartali Temu, Kenya	29:27.40
1972	Lasse Viren, Finland	27:38.40
1976	Lasse Viren, Finland	27:40.38
1980	Miruts Yifter, Ethiopia	27:42.70
1984	Alberto Cova, Italy	27:47.50
1988	Mly Brahim Boutaib, Morocco	27:21.46
1992	Khalid Skah, Morocco	27:47.70
1996	Haile Gebrselassie, Ethiopia	27:07.34
2000	Haile Gebrselassie, Ethiopia	27:18.20
2004	Kenenisa Bekele, Ethiopia	27:05.10

Marathon

1896	Spiridon Loues, Greece	2:58:50.00
1900	Michel Teato, France	2:59:45.00
1904	Thomas Hicks, United States	3:28:53.00
1906	William J. Sherring, Canada	2:51:23.65
1908	John J. Hayes, United States	2:55:18.40
1912	Kenneth McArthur, South Africa	2:36:54.80
1920	Hannes Kolehmainen, Finland	2:32:35.80
1924	Albin Stenroos, Finland	2:41:22.60

1928	A. B. El Quafi, France	2:32:57.00
1932	Juan Zabala, Argentina	2:31:36.00
1936	Kitei Son, Japan	2:29:19.20
1948	Delfo Cabrera, Argentina	2:34:51.60
1952	Emil Zatopek, Czechoslovakia	2:23:30.20
1956	Alain Mimoun, France	2:25:00.00
1960	Abebe Bikila, Ethiopia	2:15:16.20
1964	Abebe Bikila, Ethiopia	2:12:11.20
1968	Mamo Wold, Ethiopia	2:20:26.40
1972	Frank Shorter, United States	2:12:19.80
1976	Walter Cierpinski, East Germany	2:09:55.00
1980	Walter Cierpinski, East Germany	2:11:30.00
1984	Carlos Lopes, Portugal	2:09:21.00
1988	Gelindo Bordin, Italy	2:10:47.00
1992	Hwang Young-Cho, South Korea	2:13:23.00
1996	Josia Thugwane, South Africa	2:12:36.00
2000	Gezahgne Abera, Ethiopia	2:10:11.00
2004	Stefano Baldini, Italy	2:10:55.00

110-Meter Hurdles

1896	Thomas Curtis, United States	17.60
1900	Alvin Kraenzlein, United States	15.40
1904	Frederick Schule, United States	16.00
1906	R.G. Leavitt, United States	16.20
1908	Forrest Smithson, United States	15.00
1912	Frederick Kelly, United States	15.10
1920	Earl Thomson, Canada	14.80
1924	Daniel Kinsey, United States	15.00
1928	Sydney Atkinson, South Africa	14.80
1932	George Saling, United States	14.60
1936	Forrest Towns, United States	14.20
1948	William Porter, United States	13.90
1952	Harrison Dillard, United States	13.70
1956	Lee Calhoun, United States	13.50
1960	Lee Calhoun, United States	13.80
1964	Hayes Jones, United States	13.60
1968	Willie Davenport, United States	13.30
1972	Rodney Milburn, United States	13.24
1976	Guy Drut, France	13.30
1980	Thomas Munkett, East Germany	13.20
1984	Roger Kingdom, United States	13.20
1988	Roger Kingdom, United States	12.98
1992	Mark McCoy, Canada	13.12
1996	Allen Johnson, United States	12.95
2000	Anier Garcia, Cuba	13.00
2004	Xiang Liu, China	12.91

200-Meter Hurdles

1900	Alvin Kraenzlein, United States	25.40
1904	Harry Hillman, United States	24.60

400-Meter Hurdles

1900	John Tewksbury, United States	57.60
1904	Harry Hillman, United States	53.00
1908	Charles Bacon, United States	55.00
1920	Frank Loomis, United States	54.00
1924	F. Morgan Taylor, United States	52.60
1928	Lord David Burghley, Great Britain	53.40
1932	Robert Tisdall, Ireland	51.80[1]
1936	Glenn Hardin, United States	52.40
1948	Roy Cochran, United States	51.10
1952	Charles Moore, United States	50.80
1956	Glenn Davis, United States	50.10
1960	Glenn Davis, United States	49.30
1964	Rex Cawley, United States	49.60
1968	David Hemery, Great Britain	48.10
1972	John Akii-Bua, Uganda	47.80
1976	Edwin Moses, United States	47.64
1980	Volker Beck, East Germany	48.70
1984	Edwin Moses, United States	47.75
1988	Andre Phillips, United States	47.19
1992	Kevin Young, United States	46.78
1996	Derrick Adkins, United States	47.54
2000	Angelo Taylor, United States	47.50
2004	Felix Sanchez, Dominican Republic	47.63

1. Record not allowed.

2,500-Meter Steeplechase

1900	George Orton, United States	7:34.00
1904	James Lightbody, United States	7:39.60

3,000-Meter Steeplechase

1920	Percy Hodge, Great Britain	10:00.40
1924	Willie Ritola, Finland	09:33.60
1928	Toivo Loukola, Finland	09:21.80
1932	Volmari Iso-Hollo, Finland	10:33.40[1]
1936	Volmari Iso-Hollo, Finland	09:03.80
1948	Thure Sjoestrand, Sweden	09:04.60
1952	Horace Ashenfelter, United States	08:45.40
1956	Chris Brasher, Great Britain	08:41.20
1960	Zdzislaw Krzyskowiak, Poland	08:34.20
1964	Gaston Roelants, Belgium	08:30.80
1968	Amos Biwott, Kenya	08:51.00
1972	Kipchoge Keino, Kenya	08:23.60
1976	Anders Gardervd, Sweden	08:08.02
1980	Bronislaw Malinowski, Poland	08:09.70
1984	Julius Korir, Kenya	08:11.80
1988	Julius Karluki, Kenya	08:05.51
1992	Matthew Birir, Kenya	08:08.84
1996	Joseph Keter, Kenya	08:07.12
2000	Reuben Kosgei, Kenya	08:21.43
2004	Ezekiel Kemboi, Kenya	08:05.81

1. About 3,450 meters-extra lap by error.

10,000-Meter Walk

1912	George Goulding, Canada	46:28.40
1920	Ugo Frigerio, Italy	48:06.20
1924	Ugo Frigerio, Italy	47:49.00
1948	John Mikaelsson, Sweden	45:13.20
1952	John Mikaelsson, Sweden	45:02.80

20,000-Meter Walk

1956	Leonid Spirin, USSR	1:31:27.40
1960	Vladimir Golubnichy, USSR	1:34:07.20
1964	Ken Mathews, Great Britain	1:29:34.00
1968	Vladimir Golubnichy, USSR	1:33:58.40
1972	Peter Frenkel, East Germany	1:26:42.40
1976	Daniel Bautista, Mexico	1:24:40.60
1980	Maurizio Damiliano, Italy	1:23:35.50
1984	Ernesto Conto, Mexico	1:23:13.00
1988	Jozef Pribilinec, Czechoslovakia	1:19:57.00
1992	Daniel Plaza, Spain	1:21:45.00
1996	Jefferson Perez, Ecuador	1:20:07.00
2000	Robert Korzeniowski, Poland	1:18:59.00
2004	Ivano Brugnetti, Italy	1:19:40.00

50,000-Meter Walk

1932	Thomas W. Green, Great Britain	4:50:10.00
1936	Harold Whitlock, Great Britain	4:30:41.10
1948	John Ljunggren, Sweden	4:41:52.00
1952	Giuseppe Dordoni, Italy	4:28:07.80
1956	Norman Read, New Zealand	4:30:42.80
1960	Donald Thompson, Great Britain	4:25:30.00
1964	Abdon Pamich, Italy	4:11:12.40
1968	Christoph Hohne, East Germany	4:20:13.60
1972	Bern Kannernberg, West Germany	3:56:11.60
1980	Hartwig Guader, East Germany	3:49:24.00
1984	Raul Gonzalez, Mexico	3:37:26.00
1988	Viacheslav Ivanenko, USSR	3:48:29.00
1992	Andrei Perlov, Unified Team[1]	3:50:13.00
1996	Robert Korzeniowski, Poland	3:43:30.00
2000	Robert Korzeniowski, Poland	3:42:22.00
2004	Robert Korzeniowski, Poland	3:38:46.00

1. Former Soviet Union team.

400-Meter Relay (4x100)

1912	Great Britain	42.40
1920	United States	42.20
1924	United States	41.00
1928	United States	41.00
1932	United States	40.00
1936	United States	39.80
1948	United States	40.60
1952	United States	40.10
1956	United States	39.50

1960	Germany	39.50
1964	United States	39.00
1968	United States	38.20
1972	United States	38.19
1976	United States	38.33
1980	USSR	38.26
1984	United States	37.83
1988	USSR	38.19
1992	United States	37.40[1]
1996	Canada	37.69
2000	United States	37.61
2004	Great Britain	38.07

1. World record.

1,600-Meter Relay (4x400)

1912	United States	3:16.60
1920	Great Britain	3:22.20
1924	United States	3:16.00
1928	United States	3:14.20
1932	United States	3:08.20
1936	Great Britain	3:09.00
1948	United States	3:10.40
1952	Jamaica, B.W.I.	3:03.90
1956	United States	3:04.80
1960	United States	3:02.20
1964	United States	3:00.70
1968	United States	2:56.10
1972	Kenya	2:59.80
1976	United States	2:58.65
1980	USSR	3:01.10
1984	United States	2:57.91
1988	United States	2:56.16
1992	United States	2:55.74[1]
1996	United States	2:55.99
2000	United States	2:56.35
2004	United States	2:55.91

1. World record.

Team Race

		Pts
1900	Great Britain (5,000 meters)	26
1904	United States (4 miles)	27
1908	Great Britain (3 miles)	6
1912	United States (3,000 meters)	9
1920	United States (3,000 meters)	10
1924	Finland (3,000 meters)	9

Standing High Jump

1900	Ray Ewry, United States	5 ft 5 in
1904	Ray Ewry, United States	4 ft 11 in
1906	Ray Ewry, United States	5 ft 1.625 in
1908	Ray Ewry, United States	5 ft 2 in
1912	Platt Adams, United States	5 ft 4.125 in

Running High Jump

1896	Ellery Clark, United States	5 ft 11.25 in
1900	Irving Baxter, United States	6 ft 2.75 in
1904	Samuel Jones, United States	5 ft 11 in
1906	Con Leahy, Ireland	5 ft 9.875 in
1908	Harry Porter, United States	6 ft 3 in
1912	Alma Richards, United States	6 ft 4 in
1920	Richmond Landon, United States	6 ft 4.25 in
1924	Harold Osborn, United States	6 ft 5.9375 in
1928	Robert W. King, United States	6 ft 4.375 in
1932	Duncan McNaughton, Canada	6 ft 5.625 in
1936	Cornelius Johnson, United States	6 ft 7.9375 in
1948	John Winter, Australia	6 ft 6 in
1952	Walter David, United States	6 ft 8.9375 in
1956	Charles Damas, United States	6 ft 11.25 in
1960	Robert Shavlakadze, USSR	7 ft 1 in
1964	Valeri Brumel, USSR	7 ft 1.75 in
1968	Dick Fosbury, United States	7 ft 4.25 in
1972	Yuri Tarmak, USSR	7 ft 3.75 in
1976	Jacek Wszola, Poland	7 ft 4.5 in
1980	Gerd Wessig, East Germany	7 ft 8.75 in
1984	Dietmar Mogenburg, West Germany	7 ft 8.5 in
1988	Guennadi Avdeenko, USSR	7 ft 0.5 in
1992	Javier Sotomayor, Cuba	7 ft 8.5 in
1996	Charles Austin, United States	7 ft 10 in
2000	Sergey Kliugin, Russia	7 ft 8.5 in
2004	Stefan Holm, Sweden	7 ft 8.91 in

Long Jump

1896	Ellery Clark, United States	20 ft 9.75 in
1900	Alvin Kraenzlein, United States	23 ft 6.875 in
1904	Myer Prinstein, United States	24 ft 1 in
1906	Myer Prinstein, United States	23 ft 7.5 in
1908	Frank Irons, United States	24 ft 6.5in
1912	Albert Gutterson, United States	24 ft 11.25 in
1920	William Pettersen, Sweden	23 ft 5.5 in
1924	DeHart Hubbard, United States	24 ft 5.125 in
1928	Edward B. Hamm, United States	25 ft 4.75 in
1932	Edward Gordon, United States	25 ft 0.75 in
1936	Jesse Owens, United States	26 ft 5.3125 in
1948	Willie Steele, United States	25 ft 8 in
1952	Jerome Biffle, United States	24 ft 10 in
1956	Gregory Bell, United States	25 ft 8.25 in
1960	Ralph Boston, United States	26 ft 7.75 in
1964	Lynn Davies, Great Britain	26 ft 5.75 in
1968	Bob Beamon, United States	29 ft 2.5 in
1972	Randy Williams, United States	27 ft 0.5 in
1976	Arnie Robinson, United States	24 ft 7.75 in
1980	Lutz Dombrowski, E. Germany	28 ft 0.25 in
1984	Carl Lewis, United States	28 ft 0.25 in
1988	Carl Lewis, United States	28 ft 7.25 in
1992	Carl Lewis, United States	28 ft 5.5 in
1996	Carl Lewis, United States	27 ft 10.75 in
2000	Ivan Pedroso, Cuba	28 ft 0.75 in
2004	Dwight Phillips, United States	28 ft 2.19 in

Triple Jump

1896	James B. Connolly, United States	45 ft
1900	Myer Prinstein, United States	47 ft 4.25 in
1904	Myer Prinstein, United States	47 ft
1906	P.G. O'Connor, Ireland	46 ft 2 in
1908	Timothy Ahearne, Great Britain	48 ft 1.25 in
1912	Gustaf Lindblom, Sweden	48 ft 5.125 in
1920	Vilho Tuulos, Finland	47 ft 6.875 in
1924	Archie Winter, Australia	50 ft 11.125 in
1928	Mikio Oda, Japan	49 ft 10.8125 in
1932	Chuhei Nambu, Japan	51 ft 7 in
1936	Naoto Tajima, Japan	52 ft 5.875 in
1948	Arne Ahman, Sweden	50 ft 6.25 in
1952	Adhemar da Silva, Brazil	53 ft 2.5 in
1956	Adhemar da Silva, Brazil	53 ft 7.5 in
1960	Jozef Schmidt, Poland	55 ft 1.75 in
1964	Jozef Schmidt, Poland	55 ft 3.25 in
1968	Viktor Saneyev, USSR	57 ft 0.75 in
1972	Viktor Saneyev, USSR	56 ft 11 in
1976	Viktor Saneyev, USSR	56 ft 8.75 in
1980	Jaak Uudmae, USSR	56 ft 11.125 in
1984	Al Joyner, United States	56 ft 7.5 in
1988	Hristo Markov, Bulgaria	57 ft 9.25 in
1992	Mike Conley, United States	59 ft 7.5 in
1996	Kenny Harrison, United States	59 ft 4.25 in
2000	Jonathan Edwards, Great Britain	58 ft 1.25 in
2004	Christian Olsson, Sweden	58 ft 4.39 in

Pole Vault

1896	William Hoyt, United States	10 ft 9.75 in
1900	Irving Baxter, United States	10 ft 9.875 in
1904	Charles Dvorak, United States	11 ft 6 in
1906	Fernand Gouder, France	11 ft 6 in
1908	Alfred Gilbert, United States, and Edward Cook, United States (tie)	12 ft 2 in
1912	Harry Babcock, United States	12 ft 11.5 in
1920	Frank Foss, United States	13 ft 5.5625 in
1924	Lee Barnes, United States	12 ft 11.5 in
1928	Sabin W. Carr, United States	13 ft 9.375 in
1932	William Miller, United States	14 ft 1.875 in
1936	Earle Meadows, United States	14 ft 3.25 in
1948	Guinn Smith, United States	14 ft 0.25 in
1952	Robert Richards, United States	14 ft 11.125 in
1956	Robert Richards, United States	14 ft 11.5 in

1960	Don Bragg, United States	15 ft 5.125 in
1964	Fred Hansen, United States	16 ft 8.75 in
1968	Bob Seagren, United States	17 ft 8.5 in
1972	Wolfgang Nordwig, East Germany	18 ft 0.5 in
1976	Tadeusz Slusarski, Poland	18 ft 0.5 in
1980	Wladyslaw Kozakiewics, Poland	18 ft 11.5 in
1984	Pierre Quinon, France	18 ft 10.25 in
1988	Sergei Bubka, USSR	19 ft 4.25 in
1992	Maxim Tarassov, Unified Team[1]	19 ft 0.25 in
1996	Jean Galfione, France	19 ft 5.25 in
2000	Nick Hysong, United States	19 ft 4.25 in
2004	Tim Mack, United States	19 ft 6.25 in

1. Former Soviet Union team.

16-lb Shot-Put

1896	Robert Garrett, United States	36 ft 9.75 in
1900	Richard Sheldon, United States	46 ft 3.125 in
1904	Ralph Rose, United States	48 ft 7 in
1906	Martin Sheridan, United States	40 ft 4.8 in
1908	Ralph Rose, United States	46 ft 7.5 in
1912	Pat McDonald, United States	50 ft 4 in
1920	Ville Porhola, Finland	48 ft 7.125 in
1924	Clarence Houser, United States	49 ft 2.5 in
1928	John Kuck, United States	52 ft 11.6875 in
1932	Leo Sexton, United States	52 ft 6.1875 in
1936	Hans Woellke, Germany	53 ft 1.75 in
1948	Wilbur Thompson, United States	56 ft 2 in
1952	Parry O'Brien, United States	57 ft 1.5 in
1956	Parry O'Brien, United States	60 ft 11 in
1960	Bill Nieder, United States	64 ft 6.75 in
1964	Dallas Long, United States	66 ft 8.25 in
1968	Randy Matson, United States	67 ft 4.75 in
1972	Wladyslaw Komar, Poland	69 ft 6 in
1976	Udo Beyer, East Germany	69 ft 0.75 in
1980	Vladmir Klselyov, USSR	70 ft 0.5 in
1984	Alessandro Andrei, Italy	69 ft 9 in
1988	Uhf Timmerman, East Germany	73 ft 8.75 in
1992	Michael Stulze, United States	71 ft 2.5 in
1996	Randy Barnes, United States	70 ft 11.25 in
2000	Arsi Harju, Finland	69 ft 10.25 in
2004	Yuriy Bilonog, Ukraine	69 ft 5.07 in

Discus Throw

1896	Robert Garrett, United States	95 ft 7.5 in
1900	Rudolf Bauer, Hungary	118 ft 2.875 in
1904	Martin Sheridan, United States	128 ft 10.5 in
1906	Martin Sheridan, United States	136 ft 0.3 in
1908	Martin Sheridan, United States	134 ft 2 in
1912	Armas e, Finland	145 ft 0.5625 in
1920	Elmer Niklander, Finland	146 ft 7 in
1924	Clarence Houser, United States	151 ft 5.25 in
1928	Clarence Houser, United States	155 ft 2.8 in
1932	John Anderson, United States	162 ft 4.875 in
1936	Ken Carpenter, United States	165 ft 7.375 in
1948	Adolfo Consolini, Italy	173 ft 2 in
1952	Simeon Iness, United States	180 ft 6.5 in
1956	Al Oerter, United States	184 ft 10.5 in
1960	Al Oerter, United States	194 ft 2 in
1964	Al Oerter, United States	200 ft 1.5 in
1968	Al Oerter, United States	212 ft 6 in
1972	Ludvik Danek, Czechoslovakia	211 ft 3 in
1976	Mac Wilkins, United States	221 ft 5 in
1980	Viktor Rashchupkin, USSR	218 ft 8 in
1984	Rolf Dannenberg, West Germany	218 ft 6 in
1988	Jurgen Schult, East Germany	225 ft 9.25 in
1992	Romas Ubartas, Lithuania	213 ft 7.75 in
1996	Lars Riedel, Germany	227 ft 8 in
2000	Virgilijus Alekna, Lithuania	227 ft 4 in
2004	Virgilijus Alekna, Lithuania	229 ft 3.57 in

Javelin Throw

1906	Eric Lemming, Sweden	175 ft 6 in
1908	Eric Lemming, Sweden	179 ft 10.5 in
1912	Eric Lemming, Sweden	198 ft 11.25 in
1920	Jonni Myyra, Finland	215 ft 9.75 in
1924	Jonni Myyra, Finland	206 ft 6.75 in

1928	Eric Lundquist, Sweden	218 ft 6.125 in
1932	Matti Jarvinen, Finland	238 ft 7 in
1936	Gerhard Stoeck, Germany	235 ft 8.3125 in
1948	Kaj Rautavaara, Finland	228 ft 10.5 in
1952	Cy Young, United States	242 ft 0.75 in
1956	Egil Danielsen, Norway	281 ft 2.25 in
1960	Viktor Tsibuelnko, USSR	277 ft 8.375 in
1964	Pauli Nevala, Finland	271 ft 2.25 in
1968	Janis Lusis, USSR	295 ft 7 in
1972	Klaus Wolfermann, West Germany	296 ft 10 in
1976	Miklos Nemeth, Hungary	310 ft 4 in
1980	Dainis Kula, USSR	299 ft 2.375 in
1984	Arto Haerkoenen, Finland	284 ft 8 in
1988	Tapio Korjus, Finland	276 ft 6 in
1992	Jan Zelezny, Czechoslovakia	294 ft 2 in
1996	Jan Zelezny, Czech Republic	289 ft 3 in
2000	Jan Zelezny, Czech Republic	295 ft 9.5 in
2004	Andreas Thorkildsen, Norway	283 ft 9.51 in

16-lb Hammer Throw

1900	John Flanagan, United States		167 ft 4 in
1904	John Flanagan, United States		168 ft 1 in
1908	John Flanagan, United States		170 ft 4.25 in
1912	Matt McGrath, United States		179 ft 7.125 in
1920	Pat Ryan, United States		173 ft 5.625 in
1924	Fred Tootell, United States		174 ft 10.25 in
1928	Patrick O'Callaghan, Ireland		168 ft 7.5 in
1932	Patrick O'Callaghan, Ireland		176 ft 11.125 in
1936	Karl Hein, Germany		185 ft 4 in
1948	Imre Nemeth, Hungary		183 ft 11.5 in
1952	Jozsef Csermak, Hungary		197 ft 11.5625 in
1956	Harold Connolly, United States		207 ft 2.75 in
1960	Vasily Rudenkov, USSR		220 ft 1.625 in
1964	Romuald Klim, USSR		228 ft 9.5 in
1968	Gyula Zsivotzky, Hungary		240 ft 8 in
1972	Anatoly Bondarchuk, USSR		247 ft 8.5 in
1976	Yuri Sedykh, USSR		254 ft 4 in
1980	Yuri Sedykh, USSR	(81.80m)	268 ft 4.5 in
1984	Juha Tiainen, Finland		256 ft 2 in
1988	Sergei Litvinov, USSR		278 ft 2.5 in
1992	Andrey Abduvaliyev, Unified Team[1]		270 ft 9.5 in
1996	Balazs Kiss, Hungary		266 ft 6 in
2000	Szymon Ziolkowski, Poland		262 ft 6 in
2004	Koji Murofushi, Japan		272 ft 0.17 in

1. Former Soviet Union team.

Decathlon

1912	Jim Thorpe, United States	—
	Hugo Wieslander, Sweden	—
1920	Helge Lovland, Norway	6,804.35 pts.
1924	Harold Osborn, United States	7,710.775 pts.
1928	Paavo Yrjola, Finland	8,053.29 pts.
1932	James Bausch, United States	8,462.23 pts.
1936	Glenn Morris, United States	7,900 pts.[1]
1948	Robert B. Mathias, United States	7,139 pts.
1952	Robert B. Mathias, United States	7,887 pts.
1956	Milton Campbell, United States	7,937 pts.
1960	Rafer Johnson, United States	8,392 pts.
1964	Willi Holdorf, Germany	7,887 pts.[1]
1968	Bill Toomey, United States	8,193 pts.
1972	Nikolai Avilov, USSR	8,454 pts.
1976	Bruce Jenner, United States	8,618 pts.
1980	Daley Thompson, Great Britain	8,495 pts.
1984	Daley Thompson, Great Britain	8,797 pts.
1988	Christian Schenk, East Germany	8,488 pts.
1992	Robert Zmelik, Czechoslovakia	8,611 pts.
1996	Dan O'Brien, United States	8,824 pts.
2000	Erki Nool, Estonia	8,641 pts.
2004	Roman Sebrle, Czech Republic	8,893 pts.

1. Point system revised.

TRACK AND FIELD–WOMEN

100-Meter Dash
1928	Elizabeth Robinson, United States	12.20
1932	Stella Walsh, Poland	11.90
1936	Helen Stephens, United States	11.50
1948	Fanny Blankers-Koen, Netherlands	11.90
1952	Marjorie Jackson, Australia	11.50
1956	Betty Cuthbert, Australia	11.50
1960	Wilma Rudolph, United States	11.00
1964	Wyomia Tyus, United States	11.40
1968	Wyomia Tyus, United States	11.00
1972	Renate Stecher, East Germany	11.07
1976	Annegret Richter, West Germany	11.08
1980	Lyudmila Kondratyeva, USSR	11.06
1984	Evelyn Ashford, United States	10.97
1988	Florence Griffith-Joyner, United States	10.54
1992	Gail Devers, United States	10.82
1996	Gail Devers, United States	10.94
2000	Marion Jones, United States	10.75
2004	Yuliya Nesterenko, Belarus	10.93

200-Meter Dash
1948	Fanny Blankers-Koen, Netherlands	24.40
1952	Marjorie Jackson, Australia	23.70
1956	Betty Cuthbert, Australia	23.40
1960	Wilma Rudolph, United States	24.00
1964	Edith McGuire, United States	23.00
1968	Irena Szewinska, Poland	22.50
1972	Renate Stecher, East Germany	22.40
1976	Baerbel Eckert, East Germany	22.37
1980	Barbara Wockel, East Germany	22.03
1984	Valerie Brisco-Hooks, United States	21.81
1988	Florence Griffith-Joyner, United States	21.34
1992	Gwen Torrence, United States	21.81
1996	Marie-Jose Perec, France	22.12
2000	Marion Jones, United States	21.84
2004	Veronica Campbell, Jamaica	22.05

400-Meter Dash
1964	Betty Cuthbert, Australia	52.00
1968	Colette Besson, France	52.00
1972	Monika Zehrt, East Germany	51.08
1976	Irena Szewinska, Poland	49.29
1980	Marita Koch, East Germany	48.88
1984	Valerie Brisco-Hooks, United States	48.83
1988	Olga Bryzguina, USSR	48.65
1992	Marie Jose-Perec, France	48.83
1996	Marie Jose-Perec, France	48.25
2000	Cathy Freeman, Australia	49.11
2004	Tonique Williams-Darling, Bahamas	49.41

800-Meter Run
1928	Lina Radke, Germany	2:16.80
1960	Ljudmila Shevcova, USSR	2:04.30
1964	Ann Packer, Great Britain	2:01.10
1968	Madeline Manning, United States	2:00.90
1972	Hildegard Falck, West Germany	1:58.60
1976	Tatiana Kazankina, USSR	1:54.94
1980	Nadezhda Olizarenko, USSR	1:53.50
1984	Doina Melinte, Romania	1:57.60
1988	Sigrun Wodars, East Germany	1:56.10
1992	Ellen Van Langen, Netherlands	1:55.54
1996	Svetlana Masterkova, Russia	1:57.73
2000	Maria Mutola, Mozambique	1:56.15
2004	Kelly Holmes, Great Britain	1:56.38

1,500-Meter Run
1972	Ludmila Bragina, USSR	4:01.40
1976	Tatiana Kazankina, USSR	4:05.48
1980	Tatiana Kazankina, USSR	3:56.60
1984	Gabriella Dorio, Italy	4:03.25
1988	Paula Ivan, Romania	3:53.96
1992	Hassiba Boulmerka, Algeria	3:55.30
1996	Svetlana Masterkova, Russia	4:00.83
2000	Nouria Merah-Benida, Algeria	4:05.10
2004	Kelly Holmes, Great Britain	3:57.90

5,000-Meter Run
1996	Wang, Jun-Xia, China	14:59.88
2000	Gabriela Szabo, Romania	14:40.79
2004	Meseret Defar, Ethiopia	14:45.65

10,000-Meter Run
1992	Derartu Tulu, Ethiopia	31:60.02
1996	Fernanda Ribeiro, Portugal	31:01.63
2000	Derartu Tulu, Ethiopia	30:17.49
2004	Huina Xing, China	30:24.36

Marathon
1984	Joan Benoit, United States	2:24:52
1988	Rose Mota, Portugal	2:25.40
1992	Valentina Yegorova, Unified Team	2:32.41
1996	Fatuma Roba, Ethiopia	2:26.05
2000	Naoko Takahashi, Japan	2:23.14
2004	Mizuki Noguchi, Japan	2:26.20

80-Meter Hurdles
1932	Mildred Didrikson, United States	11.70
1936	Trebisonda Valla, Italy	11.70
1948	Fanny Blankers-Koen, Netherlands	11.20
1952	Shirley S. de la Hunty, Australia	10.90
1956	Shirley S. de la Hunty, Australia	10.70
1960	Irina Press, USSR	10.80
1964	Karin Balzer, Germany	10.50[1]
1968	Maureen Caird, Australia	10.30

1. Wind assisted.

100-Meter Hurdles
1972	Annelie Ehrhardt, East Germany	12.59
1976	Johanna Schaller, East Germany	12.77
1980	Vera Komisova, USSR	12.56
1984	Benita Fitzgerald-Brown, United States	12.84
1988	Jordanka Donkova, Bulgaria	12.38
1992	Paraskevi Patoulidou, Greece	12.64
1996	Ludmila Engquist, Sweden	12.58
2000	Olga Shishigina, Kazakhstan	12.65
2004	Joanna Hayes, United States	12.37

400-Meter Hurdles
1984	Nawai El Moutawakel, Morocco	54.61
1988	Debra Flintoff-King, Australia	53.17
1992	Sally Gunnell, Great Britain	53.23
1996	Deon Hemmings, Jamaica	52.82
2000	Irina Privalova, Russia	53.02
2004	Fani Halkia, Greece	52.82

400-Meter Relay (4 × 100)
1928	Canada	48.40
1932	United States	47.00
1936	United States	46.90
1948	Netherlands	47.50
1952	United States	45.90
1956	Australia	44.50
1960	United States	44.50
1964	Poland	43.60
1968	United States	42.80
1972	West Germany	42.81
1976	East Germany	42.50
1980	East Germany	41.60
1984	United States	41.65
1988	United States	41.98
1992	United States	42.11
1996	United States	41.95
2000	Bahamas	41.95
2004	Jamaica	41.73

1,600-Meter Relay (4 × 400)
1972	East Germany	3:23.00
1976	East Germany	3:19.23
1980	USSR	3:20.20
1984	United States	3:18.29
1988	USSR	3:15.18
1992	Unified Team[1]	3:20.20
1996	United States	3:20.91
2000	United States	3:22.62
2004	United States	3:19.01

1. Former Soviet Union team.

10,000-Meter Walk
1992	ChenYue-Ling, China	44:32
1996	Yelena Nikolayeva, Russia	41:49

20,000-Meter Walk
2000	Liping Wang, China	1:29:05
2004	Athanasia Tsoumeleka, Greece	1:29:12

Running High Jump
1928	Ethel Catherwood, Canada	5 ft 3 in
1932	Jean Shiley, United States	5 ft 5.25 in
1936	Ibolya Csak, Hungary	5 ft 3 in
1948	Alice Coachman, United States	5 ft 6.125 in
1952	Ester Brand, South Africa	5 ft 5.75 in
1956	Mildred McDaniel, United States	5 ft 9.25 in
1960	Iolanda Balas, Romania	6 ft 0.75 in
1964	Iolanda Balas, Romania	6 ft 2.75 in
1968	Miloslava Rezkova, Czechoslovakia	5 ft 11.75 in
1972	Ulrike Meyfarth, West Germany	6 ft 3.625 in
1976	Rosemarie Ackerman, E. Germany	6 ft 4 in
1980	Sara Simeoni, Italy	6 ft 5.5 in
1984	Ulrike Meyfarth, West Germany	6 ft 7.5 in
1988	Louise Ritter, United States	6 ft 8 in
1992	Heike Henkel, Germany	6 ft 7.5 in
1996	Stefka Kostadinova, Bulgaria	6 ft 8.75 in
2000	Yelena Yelesina, Russia	6 ft 7 in
2004	Yelena Slesarenko, Russia	6 ft 9.1 in

Long Jump
1948	Olga Gyarmati, Hungary	18 ft 8.25 in
1952	Yvette Williams, New Zealand	20 ft 5.75 in
1956	Elzbieta Krzesinska, Poland	20 ft 9.75 in
1960	Vera Krepkina, USSR	20 ft 10.75 in
1964	Mary Rand, Great Britain	22 ft 2 in
1968	Viorica Ciscopoleanu, Romania	22 ft 4.5 in
1972	Heidemarie Rosendahl, West Germany	22 ft 3 in
1976	Angela Voigt, East Germany	22 ft. 0.5 in
1980	Tatiana Kolpakova, USSR	23 ft 2 in
1984	Anisoara Stanciu, Romania	22 ft 10 in
1988	Jackie Joyner-Kersee, United States	24 ft 3.5 in
1992	Heike Drechsler, Germany	23 ft 5.25 in
1996	Chioma Ajunwa, Nigeria	23 ft 4.5 in
2000	Heike Drechsler, Germany	22 ft 11.25 in
2004	Tatyana Lebedeva, Russia	23 ft 2.35 in

Triple Jump
1996	Inessa Kravets, Ukraine	50 ft 1.5 in
2000	Tereza Marinova, Belarus	49 ft 10.5 in
2004	Francoise Mbango Etone, Cameroon	50 ft 2.36 in

Shot-Put
1948	Micheline Ostermeyer, France	45 ft 1.5 in
1952	Galina Zybina, USSR	50 ft 1.5 in
1956	Tamara Tishkyevich, USSR	54 ft 5 in
1960	Tamara Press, USSR	56 ft 9.875 in
1964	Tamara Press, USSR	59 ft 6 in
1968	Margitta Gummel, East Germany	64 ft 4 in
1972	Nadezhda Chizhova, USSR	69 ft
1976	Ivanka Christova, Bulgaria	69 ft 5 in
1980	Ilona Sluplanek, East Germany	73 ft 6 in
1984	Claudia Losch, West Germany	67 ft 2.25 in
1988	Natalya Lisovskaya, USSR	72 ft 11.5 in
1992	Svetlana Kriveleva, Unified Team[1]	69 ft 1.25 in
1996	Astrid Kumbernuss, Germany	67 ft 5.5 in
2000	Yanina Korolchik, Belarus	67 ft 5.5 in
2004	Yumileidi Cumba, Cuba	64 ft 3.26 in

1. Former Soviet Union team.

Discus Throw
1928	Helena Konopacka, Poland	129 ft 11.875 in
1932	Lillian Copeland, United States	133 ft 2 in
1936	Gisela Mauermayer, Germany	156 ft 3.175 in
1948	Micheline Ostermeyer, France	137 ft 6.5 in
1956	Olga Fikotova, Czechoslovakia	176 ft 1.5 in
1960	Nina Ponomareva, USSR	180 ft 8.25 in
1964	Tamara Press, USSR	187 ft 10.75 in
1968	Lia Manoliu, Romania	191 ft 2.5 in
1972	Faina Melnik, USSR	218 ft 7 in

1976	Evelin Schlaak, East Germany	226 ft 4 in
1980	Evelin Jahl, East Germany	229 ft 6.5 in
1984	Ria Stalman, Netherlands	214 ft 5 in
1988	Martina Hellmann, East Germany	237 ft 2.25 in
1992	Maritza Marten, Cuba	229 ft 10.25 in
1996	Ilke Wyludda, Germany	228 ft 6.5 in
2000	Ellina Zvereva, Belarus	224 ft 5 in
2004	Natalya Sadova, Russia	219 ft 10.58 in

Javelin Throw
1932	Mildred Didrikson, United States	143 ft 4 in
1936	Tilly Fleischer, Germany	148 ft 2.75 in
1948	Herma Bauma, Austria	149 ft 6 in
1952	Dana Zatopek, Czechoslovakia	165 ft 7 in
1956	Inessa Janzeme, USSR	176 ft 8 in
1960	Elvira Ozolina, USSR	183 ft 8 in
1964	Mihaela Penes, Romania	198 ft 7.5 in
1968	Angela Nemeth, Hungary	198 ft
1972	Ruth Fuchs, East Germany	209 ft 7 in
1976	Ruth Fuchs, East Germany	216 ft 4 in
1980	Maria Colon, Cuba	224 ft 5 in
1984	Tessa Sanderson, Britain	228 ft 2 in
1988	Petra Felke, East Germany	245 ft
1992	Silke Renke, Germany	224 ft 2.5 in
1996	Heli Rantanen, Finland	222 ft 11 in
2000	Trine Hattestad, Norway	226 ft 1 in
2004	Osleidys Menendez, Cuba	234 ft 8.14 in

Hammer Throw
2000	Kamila Skolimowska, Poland	233 ft 5.75 in
2004	Olga Kuzenkova, Russia	246 ft 1.54 in

Pole Vault
2000	Stacy Dragila, United States	15 ft 1 in
2004	Yelena Isinbayeva, Russia	16 ft 1.31 in[1]

1. World record.

Pentathlon
1964	Irina Press, USSR	5,246 pts.
1968	Ingrid Becker, West Germany	5,098 pts.
1972	Mary Peters, Britain	4,801 pts.
1976	Siegrun Siegl, East Germany	4,745 pts.
1980	Nadyeshda Tkachenko, USSR	5,083 pts.
1984	Daniele Masala, Italy	5,469 pts.
1988	Jackie Joyner-Kersee, United States	7,291 pts.

Heptathlon
1992	Jackie Joyner-Kersee, United States	7,044 pts.
1996	Ghada Shouaa, Syria	6,780 pts.
2000	Denise Lewis, Great Britain	6,584 pts.
2004	Carolina Kluft, Sweden	6,952 pts.

SWIMMING–MEN

50-Meter Freestyle
1988	Matt Biondi, United States	22.14
1992	Alexander Popov, Unified Team[1]	21.91
1996	Alexander Popov, Russia	22.13
2000	Anthony Ervin and Gary Hall, Jr., United States	21.98
2004	Gary Hall, Jr., United States	21.93

1. Former Soviet Union team.

100-Meter Freestyle
1896	Alfred Hajos, Hungary	1:22.20
1904	Zoltan de Halmay, Hungary	1:02.80[1]
1906	Charles Daniels, United States	1:13.00
1908	Charles Daniels, United States	1:05.60
1912	Duke P. Kahanamoku, United States	1:03.40
1920	Duke P. Kahanamoku, United States	1:01.40
1924	John Weissmuller, United States	0:59.00
1928	John Weissmuller, United States	0:58.60
1932	Yasuji Miyazaki, Japan	0:58.20
1936	Ferenc Csik, Hungary	0:57.60
1948	Walter Ris, United States	0:57.30
1952	Clarke Scholes, United States	0:57.40
1956	Jon Henricks, Australia	0:55.40
1960	John Devitt, Australia	0:55.20
1964	Don Schollander, United States	0:53.40

1968	Michael Wenden, Australia	0:52.20
1972	Mark Spitz, United States	0:51.22
1976	Jim Montgomery, United States	0:49.99
1980	Jorg Woithe, East Germany	0:50.40
1984	Rowdy Gaines, United States	0:49.80
1988	Matt Biondi, United States	0:48.63
1992	Alexander Popov, Unified Team[2]	0:49.02
1996	Alexander Popov, Russia	0:48.74
2000	Pieter van den Hoogenband, Netherlands	0:48.30
2004	Pieter van den Hoogenband, Netherlands	0:48.17

1. 100 yards. 2. Former Soviet Union team.

200-Meter Freestyle

1900	Frederick Lane, Australia	2:25.20
1904	Charles Daniels, United States	2:44.20[1]
1968	Michael Wenden, Australia	1:55.20
1972	Mark Spitz, United States	1:52.78
1976	Bruce Furniss, United States	1:50.29
1980	Sergei Kopiliakov, USSR	4:49.81
1984	Michael Gross, West Germany	1:47.44
1988	Duncan Armstrong, Australia	1:47.25
1992	Evgueni Sadovyi, Unified Team[2]	1:46.70
1996	Danyon Loader, New Zealand	1:47.63
2000	Pieter van den Hoogenband, Netherlands	1:45.35[3]
2004	Ian Thorpe, Australia	1:44.71

1. 220 yards 2. Former Soviet Union team. 3. World record.

400-Meter Freestyle

1896	Paul Neumann, Austria	8:12.60[1]
1904	Charles Daniels, United States	6:16.20[2]
1906	Otto Sheff, Austria	6:23.80
1908	Henry Taylor, Great Britain	5:36.80
1912	George Hodgson, Canada	5:24.40
1920	Norman Ross, United States	5:26.80
1926	John Weissmuller, United States	5:04.20
1928	Albert Zorilla, Argentina	5:01.60
1932	Clarence Crabbe, United States	4:48.40
1936	Jack Medica, United States	4:44.50
1948	William Smith, United States	4:41.00
1952	Jean Boiteux, France	4:30.70
1956	Murray Rose, Australia	4:27.30
1960	Murray Rose, Australia	4:18.30
1964	Don Schollander, United States	4:12.20
1968	Mike Burton, United States	4:09.00
1972	Bradford Cooper, Australia	4:00.27[3]
1976	Brian Goodell, United States	3:51.93
1980	Vladimir Salnikov, USSR	3:51.31
1984	George DiCarlo, United States	3:51.23
1988	Uwe Dassier, East Germany	3:46.95
1992	Evgueni Sadovyi, Unified Team	3:45.00[4]
1996	Danyon Loader, New Zealand	3:47.97
2000	Ian Thorpe, Australia	3:40.59[4]
2004	Ian Thorpe, Australia	3:43.10

1. 500 meters. 2. 440 yards. 3. Rich DeMont, United States, won but was disqualified following day for medical reasons. 4. World record.

1,500-Meter Freestyle

1904	Emil Rausch, Germany	27:18.20[1]
1906	Henry Taylor, Great Britain	28:28.00[2]
1908	Henry Taylor, Great Britain	22:48.40
1912	George Hodgson, Canada	22:00.00
1920	Norman Ross, United States	22:23.20
1924	Andrew Charlton, Australia	20:06.60
1928	Arne Borg, Sweden	19:51.80
1932	Kusuo Kitamura, Japan	19:12.40
1936	Noboru Terada, Japan	19:13.70
1948	James McLane, United States	19:18.50
1952	Ford Konno, United States	18:30.00
1956	Murray Rose, Australia	17:58.90
1960	Jon Konrads, Australia	17:19.60
1964	Robert Windle, Australia	17:01.70
1968	Michael Burton, United States	16:38.90
1972	Michael Burton, United States	15:52.58
1976	Brian Goodell, United States	15:02.40
1980	Vladimir Salnikov, USSR	14:58.27
1984	Michael O'Brien, United States	15:05.20
1988	Vladimir Salnikov, USSR	15:00.40
1992	Kieren Perkins, Australia	14:43.48
1996	Kieren Perkins, Australia	14:56.40
2000	Grant Hackett, Australia	14:48.33
2004	Grant Hackett, Australia	14:43.40

1. One mile. 2. 1,600 meters

100-Meter Backstroke

1904	Walter Brack, Germany	1:16.80[1]
1908	Arno Bieberstein, Germany	1:24.60
1912	Harry Hebner, United States	1:21.20
1920	Warren Kealoha, United States	1:15.20
1924	Warren Kealoha, United States	1:13.20
1928	George Kojac, United States	1:08.20
1932	Masaji Kiyokawa, Japan	1:08.60
1936	Adolph Kiefer, United States	1:05.90
1948	Allen Stack, United States	1:06.40
1952	Yoshinobu Oyakawa, United States	1:05.40
1956	David Thiele, Australia	1:02.20
1960	David Thiele, Australia	1:01.90
1968	Roland Matthes, East Germany	0:58.70
1972	Roland Matthes, East Germany	0:56.58
1976	John Naber, United States	0:55.49
1980	Bengt Baron, Sweden	0:56.53
1984	Rick Carey, United States	0:55.79
1988	Daichi Suzuki, Japan	0:55.05
1992	Mark Tewksbury, Canada	0:53.98
1996	Jeff Rouse, United States	0:54.10
2000	Lenny Krayzelburg, United States	0:53.72
2004	Aaron Peirsol, United States	0:54.06

1. 100 yards

200-Meter Backstroke

1900	Ernst Hoppenberg, Germany	2:47.00
1964	Jed Graef, United States	2:10.30
1968	Roland Matthes, East Germany	2:09.60
1972	Roland Matthes, East Germany	2:02.82
1976	John Naber, United States	1:59.19
1980	Sandor Wladar, Hungary	2:01.93
1984	Rick Carey, United States	2:00.23
1988	Igor Polianski, USSR	1:59.37
1992	Martin Lopez Zubero, Spain	1:58.47
1996	Brad Bridgewater, United States	1:58.54
2000	Lenny Krayzelburg, United States	1:56.76
2004	Aaron Peirsol, United States	1:54.95

100-Meter Breaststroke

1968	Donald McKenzie, United States	1:07.70
1972	Nobutaka Taguchi, Japan	1:04.94
1976	John Hencken, United States	1:03.11
1980	Duncan Goodhew, Britain	1:03.34
1984	Steve Lindquist, United States	1:01.65
1988	Adrian Moorhouse, Great Britain	1:02.04
1992	Nelson Diebel, United States	1:01.50
1996	Fred Deburghgraeve, Belgium	1:00.60[1]
2000	Domenico Fioravanti, Italy	1:00.46
2004	Kosuke Kitajima, Japan	1:00.08

1. World record.

200-Meter Breaststroke

1908	Frederick Holman, Great Britain	3:09.20
1912	Walter Bathe, Germany	3:01.80
1920	Haken Malmroth, Sweden	3:04.40
1924	Robert Skelton, United States	2:56.60
1928	Yoshiyuki Tsuruta, Japan	2:48.80
1932	Yoshiyuki Tsuruta, Japan	2:45.40
1936	Tetsuo Hamuro, Japan	2:41.50
1948	Joseph Verdeur, United States	2:39.30
1952	John Davies, Australia	2:34.40
1956	Masaura Furukawa, Japan	2:34.70
1960	Bill Muliken, United States	2:37.40
1964	Ian O'Brien, Australia	2:07.80
1968	Felipe Munoz, Mexico	2:28.70
1972	John Hencken, United States	2:21.55
1976	David Willkie, Britain	2:15.11
1980	Robertas Zulpa, USSR	2:15.85

1984	Victor Davis, Canada	2:13.34
1988	Jozef Szabo, Hungary	2:13.52
1992	Mike Barrowman, United States	2:10.16
1996	Norbert Rozsa, Hungary	2:12.57
2000	Domenico Fioravanti, Italy	2:10.87
2004	Kosuke Kitajima, Japan	2:09.44

100-Meter Butterfly

1968	Douglas Russell, United States	55.90
1972	Mark Spitz, United States	54.27
1976	Matt Vogel, United States	54.35
1980	Par Arvidsson, Sweden	54.92
1984	Michael Gross, West Germany	53.08
1988	Anthony Nesty, Surinam	53.00
1992	Pablo Morales, United States	53.32
1996	Denis Pankratov, Russia	52.27[1]
2000	Lars Froelander, Sweden	52.00
2004	Michael Phelps, United States	51.25

1. World record.

200-Meter Butterfly

1956	Bill Yorzyk, United States	2:19.30
1960	Mike Troy, United States	2:12.80
1964	Kevin Berry, Australia	2:06.60
1968	Carl Robie, United States	2:08.70
1972	Mark Spitz, United States	2:00.70
1976	Mike Bruner, United States	1:59.23
1980	Sergei Fesenko, USSR	1:59.76
1984	Jon Sieben, Australia	1:57.00
1988	Michael Gross, East Germany	1:56.94
1992	Mel Stewart, United States	1:56.26
1996	Denis Pankratov, Russia	1:56.51
2000	Tom Malchow, United States	1:55.35
2004	Michael Phelps, United States	1:54.04

200-Meter Individual Medley

1968	Charles Hickcox, United States	2:12.00
1972	Gunnar Larsson, Sweden	2:07.17
1988	Tamas Darnyi, Hungary	2:00.17
1992	Tamas Darnyi, Hungary	2:00.76
1996	Attila Czene, Hungary	1:59.91
2000	Massimiliano Rosolino, Italy	1:58.98
2004	Michael Phelps, United States	1:57.14

400-Meter Individual Medley

1964	Dick Roth, United States	4:45.40
1968	Charles Hickcox, United States	4:48.40
1972	Gunnar Larsson, Sweden	4:31.98
1976	Rod Strachan, United States	4:23.68
1980	Aleksandr Sidorenko, USSR	4:22.80
1984	Alex Baumann, Canada	4:17.41
1988	Tamas Darnyi, Hungary	4:14.75
1992	Tamas Darnyi, Hungary	4:14.23
1996	Tom Dolan, United States	4:14.90
2000	Tom Dolan, United States	4:11.76
2004	Michael Phelps, United States	4:08.26[1]

1. World record.

400-Meter Freestyle Relay (4 × 100)

1964	United States	3:32.20
1968	United States	3:31.70
1972	United States	3:26.42
1988	United States	3:16.52
1992	United States	3:16.74
1996	United States	3:15.41
2000	Australia	3:13.67
2004	South Africa	3:13.17[1]

1. World record.

800-Meter Freestyle Relay (4 × 200)

1908	Great Britain	10:55.60
1912	Australia	10:11.20
1920	United States	10:04.40
1924	United States	09:53.40
1928	United States	09:36.20
1932	Japan	08:58.40
1936	Japan	08:51.50
1948	United States	08:46.10
1952	United States	08:31.10

1956	Australia	08:23.60
1960	United States	08:10.20
1964	United States	07:52.10
1968	United States	07:52.30
1972	United States	07:35.78
1976	United States	07:23.22
1980	USSR	07:23.50
1984	United States	07:16.59
1988	United States	07:12.51
1992	Unified Team[1]	07:11.95
1996	United States	07:14.84
2000	Australia	07:07.05[2]
2004	United States	07:07.33

1. Former Soviet Union team. 2. World record.

400-Meter Medley Relay (4 × 100)

1960	United States	4:05.40
1964	United States	3:58.40
1968	United States	3:54.90
1972	United States	3:48.16
1976	United States	3:42.22
1980	Australia	3:45.70
1984	United States	3:39.30
1988	United States	3:36.93
1992	United States	3:36.93
1996	United States	3:34.84
2000	United States	3:33.73
2004	United States	3:30.68[1]

1. World record.

Springboard Dive		**Points**
1908	Albert Zuerner, Germany	85.50
1912	Paul Guenther, Germany	79.23
1920	Louis Kuehn, United States	675.00
1924	Albert White, United States	696.40
1928	Pete Desjardins, United States	185.04
1932	Michael Galitzen, United States	161.38
1936	Richard Degener, United States	163.57
1948	Bruce Harlan, United States	163.64
1952	David Browning, United States	205.59
1956	Robert Clotworthy, United States	159.56
1960	Gary Tobian, United States	170.00
1964	Ken Sitzberger, United States	159.90
1968	Bernard Wrightson, United States	170.15
1972	Vladimir Vasin, USSR	594.09
1976	Phil Boggs, United States	619.05
1980	Aleksandr Portnov, USSR	905.02
1984	Greg Louganis, United States	754.41
1988	Greg Louganis, United States	730.80
1992	Mark Lenzi, United States	676.53
1996	Xiong Ni, China	701.46
2000	Xiong Ni, China	708.72
2004	Bo Peng, China	787.38

Platform Dive		**Points**
1904	G.E. Sheldon, United States	12.75
1906	Gottlob Walz, Germany	156.00
1908	Hialmar Johansson, Sweden	83.75
1912	Erik Adlerz, Sweden	73.94
1920	Clarence Pinkston, United States	100.67
1924	Albert White, United States	487.30
1928	Pete Desjardins, United States	98.74
1932	Harold Smith, United States	124.80
1936	Marshall Wayne, United States	113.58
1948	Samuel Lee, United States	130.05
1952	Samuel Lee, United States	156.28
1956	Joaquin Capilla, Mexico	152.44
1960	Bob Webster, United States	165.56
1964	Bob Webster, United States	148.58
1968	Klaus Dibiasi, Italy	164.18
1972	Klaus Dibiasi, Italy	504.12
1976	Klaus Dibiasi, Italy	600.51
1980	Falk Hoffman, East Germany	835.65
1984	Greg Louganis, United States	710.91
1988	Greg Louganis, United States	638.61
1992	Sun, Shu-Wei, China	677.31

1996	Dmitri Saoutine, Russia	692.34
2000	Tian Liang, China	724.53
2004	Jia Hu, China	748.08

Synchronized 3m Springboard Dive — Points

2000	Xiao Hailiang and Xiong Ni, China	365.58
2004	Nikolaos Siranidis and Thomas Bimis, Greece	353.34

Synchronized 10m Platform Dive — Points

2000	Igor Loukachine and Dmitri Saoutine, Russia	365.04
2004	Liang Tian and Jinghui Yang, China	383.88

SWIMMING–WOMEN

50-Meter Freestyle

1988	Kristin Otto, East Germany	25.49
1992	Yang, Wen-Yi, China	24.79
1996	Amy Van Dyken, United States	24.87
2000	Inge de Bruijn, Netherlands	24.32
2004	Inge de Bruijn, Netherlands	24.58

100-Meter Freestyle

1912	Fanny Durack, Australia	1:22.20
1920	Ethelda Bleibtrey, United States	1:13.60
1924	Ethel Lackie, United States	1:12.40
1928	Albina Osipowich, United States	1:11.00
1932	Helene Madison, United States	1:06.80
1936	Hendrika Mastenbroek, Netherlands	1:05.90
1948	Greta Andersen, Denmark	1:06.30
1952	Katalin Szoke, Hungary	1:06.80
1956	Dawn Fraser, Australia	1:02.00
1960	Dawn Fraser, Australia	1:01.20
1964	Dawn Fraser, Australia	0:59.50
1968	Marge Jan Henne, United States	1:00.00
1972	Sandra Neilson, United States	0:58.59
1976	Kornelia Ender, East Germany	0:55.65
1980	Barbara Krause, East Germany	0:54.79
1984	Carrie Steinseifer, United States	0:55.92
1988	Kristin Otto, East Germany	0:54.93
1992	Zhuang Yong, China	0:54.64
1996	Le Jingyi, China	0:54.50
2000	Inge de Bruijn, Netherlands	0:58.83
2004	Jodie Henry, Australia	0.53.84

200-Meter Freestyle

1968	Debbie Meyer, United States	2:10.50
1972	Shane Gould, Australia	2:03.56
1976	Kornelia Ender, East Germany	1:59.26
1980	Barbara Krause, East Germany	1:58.33
1984	Mary Wayle, United States	1:59.23
1988	Heike Friedrich, East Germany	1:57.65
1992	Nicole Haislett, United States	1:57.90
1996	Claudia Poll, Costa Rica	1:58.16
2000	Susie O'Neill, Australia	1:58.24
2004	Camelia Potec, Romania	1:58.03

400-Meter Freestyle

1920	Ethelda Bleibtrey, United States	4:34.00[1]
1924	Martha Norelius, United States	6:02.20
1928	Martha Norelius, United States	5:42.80
1932	Helene Madison, United States	5:28.50
1936	Hendrika Mastenbroek, Netherlands	5:26.40
1948	Ann Curtis, United States	5:17.80
1952	Valerie Gyenge, Hungary	5:12.10
1956	Lorraine Crapp, Australia	4:54.60
1960	Chris von Saltza, United States	4:50.60
1964	Ginny Duenkel, United States	4:43.30
1968	Debbie Meyer, United States	4:31.80
1972	Shane Gould, Australia	4:19.04
1976	Petra Thumer, East Germany	4:09.89
1980	Ines Diers, East Germany	4:08.76
1984	Tiffany Cohen, United States	4:07.10
1988	Janet Evans, United States	4:03.85
1992	Dagmar Hase, Germany	4:07.18
1996	Michelle Smith, Ireland	4:07.25
2000	Brooke Bennett, United States	4:05.80

2004	Laure Manaudou, France	4:05.34

1. 300 meters.

800-Meter Freestyle

1968	Debbie Meyer, United States	9:24.00
1972	Keena Rothhammer, United States	8:53.68
1976	Petra Thumer, East Germany	8:37.14
1980	Michelle Ford, Australia	8:28.90
1984	Tiffany Cohen, United States	8:24.95
1988	Janet Evans, United States	8:20.20
1992	Janet Evans, Unites States	8:25.52
1996	Brooke Bennett, Unites States	8:27.89
2000	Brooke Bennett, United States	8:19.67
2004	Ai Shibata, Japan	8:24.54

100-Meter Backstroke

1924	Sybil Bauer, United States	1:23.20
1928	Marie Braun, Netherlands	1:22.00
1932	Eleanor Holm, United States	1:19.40
1936	Dina Senff, Netherlands	1:18.90
1948	Karen Harup, Denmark	1:14.40
1952	Joan Harrison, South Africa	1:14.30
1956	Judy Grinham, Great Britain	1:12.90
1960	Lynn Burke, United States	1:09.30
1964	Cathy Ferguson, United States	1:07.70
1968	Kaye Hall, United States	1:06.20
1972	Melissa Belote, United States	1:05.78
1976	Ulrike Richter, East Germany	1:01.83
1980	Rica Reinisch, East Germany	1:00.86
1984	Theresa Andrews, United States	1:02.55
1988	Kristin Otto, East Germany	1:00.89
1992	Krisztina Egerszegi, Hungary	1:00.68
1996	Beth Botsford, United States	1:01.19
2000	Diana Mocanu, Romania	1:00.21
2004	Natalie Coughlin, United States	1:00.37

200-Meter Backstroke

1968	Pokey Watson, United States	2:24.80
1972	Melissa Belote, United States	2:19.19
1976	Ulrike Richter, East Germany	2:13.43
1980	Rica Reinisch, East Germany	2:11.77
1984	Jolanda DeRover, Netherlands	2:12.38
1988	Krisztina Egerszegi, Hungary	2:09.29
1992	Krisztina Egerszegi, Hungary	2:07.06
1996	Krisztina Egerszegi, Hungary	2:07.83
2000	Diana Mocanu, Romania	2:08.16
2004	Kirsty Coventry, Zimbabwe	2:09.19

100-Meter Breaststroke

1968	Djurdjica Bjedov, Yugoslavia	1:15.80
1972	Catherine Carr, United States	1:13.58
1976	Hannelore Anke, East Germany	1:11.16
1980	Ute Geweniger, East Germany	1:10.22
1984	Petra Van Staveren, Netherlands	1:09.88
1988	Tainia Dangalakova, Bulgaria	1:07.95
1992	Elena Roudkovskaia, Unified Team	1:08.00
1996	Penny Heyns, South Africa	1:07.73
2000	Megan Quann, United States	1:07.05
2004	Xuejuan Luo, China	1:06.64

200-Meter Breaststroke

1924	Lucy Morton, Great Britain	3:33.20
1928	Hilde Schrader, Germany	3:12.60
1932	Clare Dennis, Australia	3:06.30
1936	Hideko Maehata, Japan	3:03.60
1948	Nel van Vliet, Netherlands	2:57.20
1952	Eva Szekely, Hungary	2:51.70
1956	Ursala Happe, Germany	2:53.10
1960	Anita Lonsbrough, Great Britain	2:49.50
1964	Galina Prozumenschikova, USSR	2:46.40
1968	Sharon Wichman, United States	2:44.40
1972	Beverly Whitfield, Australia	2:41.71
1976	Marina Koshevaia, USSR	2:33.35
1980	Lina Kachushite, USSR	2:29.54
1984	Anne Ottenbrite, Canada	2:30.38
1988	Silke Hoerner, East Germany	2:26.71
1992	Kyoko Iwasaki, Japan	2:26.65
1996	Penny Heyns, South Africa	2:25.41

2000	Agnes Kovacs, Hungary	2:24.35
2004	Amanda Beard, United States	2:23.37

100-Meter Butterfly

1956	Shelley Mann, United States	1:11.00
1960	Carolyn Schuler, United States	1:09.50
1964	Sharon Stouder, United States	1:04.70
1968	Lynn McClements, Australia	1:05.50
1972	Mayumi Aoki, Japan	1:03.34
1976	Kornelia Ender, East Germany	1:00.13
1980	Caren Metschuck, East Germany	1:00.42
1984	Mary Meagher, United States	0:59.26
1988	Kristin Otto, East Germany	0:59.00
1992	Qian Hong, China	0:58.62
1996	Amy Van Dyken, United States	0:59.13
2000	Inge de Bruijn, Netherlands	0:56.61[1]
2004	Petria Thomas, Australia	0:57.72

1. World record.

200-Meter Butterfly

1968	Ada Kok, Netherlands	2:24.70
1972	Karen Moe, United States	2:15.57
1976	Andrea Pollack, East Germany	2:11.41
1980	Ines Geissler, East Germany	2:10.44
1984	Mary Meagher, United States	2:06.90
1988	Kathleen Nord, East Germany	2:09.51
1992	Summer Sanders, United States	2:08.67
1996	Susan O'Neill, Australia	2:07.76
2000	Misty Hyman, United States	2:05.88
2004	Otylia Jedrzejczak, Poland	2:06.05

200-Meter Individual Medley

1968	Claudia Kolb, United States	2:24.70
1972	Shane Gould, Australia	2:23.07
1984	Tracy Caulkins, United States	2:12.64
1988	Daniela Hunger, East Germany	2:12.59
1992	Lin Lee, China	2:11.55[1]
1996	Michelle Smith, Ireland	2:13.93
2000	Yana Klochkova, Ukraine	2:10.68
2004	Yana Klochkova, Ukraine	2:11.14

1. World record.

400-Meter Individual Medley

1964	Donna de Varona, United States	5:18.70
1968	Claudia Kolb, United States	5:08.50
1972	Gail Neall, Australia	5:02.97
1976	Ulrike Tauber, East Germany	4:42.77
1980	Petra Schneider, East Germany	4:36.29
1984	Tracy Caulkins, United States	4:39.21
1988	Janet Evans, United States	4:37.76
1992	Krisztina Egerszegi, Hungary	4:36.54
1996	Michelle Smith, Ireland	4:39.18
2000	Yana Klochkova, Ukraine	4:33.59[1]
2004	Yana Klochkova, Ukraine	4:34.83

1. World record.

400-Meter Freestyle Relay (4 × 100)

1912	Great Britain	5:52.80
1920	United States	5:11.60
1924	United States	4:58.80
1928	United States	4:47.60
1932	United States	4:38.00
1936	Netherlands	4:36.00
1948	United States	4:29.20
1952	Hungary	4:24.40
1956	Australia	4:17.10
1960	United States	4:08.90
1964	United States	4:03.80
1968	United States	4:02.50
1972	United States	3:55.19
1976	United States	3:44.82
1980	East Germany	3:42.71
1984	United States	3:44.43
1988	East Germany	3:40.63
1992	United States	3:39.46
1996	United States	3:39.29
2000	United States	3:36.61
2004	Australia	3:35.94[1]

1. World record.

800-Meter Freestyle Relay (4 × 200)

1996	United States	7:59.87
2000	United States	7:57.80
2004	United States	7:53.42[1]

1. World record.

400-Meter Medley Relay (4 × 100)

1960	United States	4:41.10
1964	United States	4:33.90
1968	United States	4:28.30
1972	United States	4:20.75
1976	East Germany	4:07.95
1980	East Germany	4:06.67
1984	United States	4:08.34
1988	East Germany	4:03.74
1992	United States	4:02.54
1996	United States	4:02.88
2000	United States	3:58.30
2004	Australia	3:57.32[1]

1. World record.

Springboard Dive	**Points**
1920 Aileen Riggin, United States	539.90
1924 Elizabeth Becker, United States	474.50
1928 Helen Meany, United States	78.62
1932 Georgia Coleman, United States	87.52
1936 Marjorie Gestring, United States	89.27
1948 Victoria M. Draves, United States	108.74
1952 Patricia McCormick, United States	147.30
1956 Patricia McCormick, United States	142.36
1960 Ingrid Kramer, Germany	155.81
1964 Ingrid Kramer Engel, Germany	145.00
1968 Sue Gossick, United States	150.77
1972 Micki King, United States	450.03
1976 Jennifer Chandler, United States	506.19
1980 Irina Kalinina, USSR	725.91
1984 Sylvie Bernier, Canada	530.70
1988 Gao Min, China	580.23
1992 Gao Min, China	572.40
1996 Fu Ming-Xia, China	547.68
2000 Fu Ming-Xia, China	609.42
2004 Jingjing Guo, China	633.15

Platform Dive	**Points**
1912 Greta Johansson, Sweden	39.90
1920 Stefani Fryland, Denmark	34.60
1924 Caroline Smith, United States	166.00
1928 Elizabeth B. Pinkston, United States	31.60
1932 Dorothy Poynton, United States	40.26
1936 Dorothy Poynton Hill, United States	33.92
1948 Victoria M. Draves, United States	68.87
1952 Patricia McCormick, United States	79.37
1956 Patricia McCormick, United States	84.85
1960 Ingrid Kramer, Germany	91.28
1964 Lesley Bush, United States	99.80
1968 Milena Duchkova, Czechoslovakia	109.59
1972 Ulrika Knape, Sweden	390.00
1976 Elena Vaytsekhovskaia, USSR	406.59
1980 Martina Jaschke, East Germany	596.25
1984 Zhou Ji-Hong, China	435.51
1988 Xu Yan-Mei, China	445.20
1992 Fu Ming-Xia, China	461.43
1996 Fu Ming-Xia, China	521.58
2000 Laura Wilkinson, United States	543.75
2004 Chantelle Newbery, Australia	590.31

Synchronized 3m Springboard Dive	**Points**
2000 Vera Ilina and Ioulia Pakhalina, Russia	332.64
2004 Minxia Wu and Jingjing Guo, China	336.90

Synchronized 10m Platform Dive	**Points**
2000 Li Na and Sang Xue, China	345.12
2004 Lishi Lao and Ting Li, China	352.14

DISTRIBUTION OF MEDALS—2004 SUMMER GAMES

Country	Gold	Silver	Bronze	Total	Country	Gold	Silver	Bronze	Total
United States	35	39	29	103	Jamaica	2	1	2	5
Russia	27	27	38	92	Uzbekistan	2	1	2	5
China	32	17	14	63	Croatia	1	2	2	5
Australia	17	16	16	49	Egypt	1	1	3	5
Germany	14	16	18	48	Switzerland	1	1	3.	5
Japan	16	9	12	37	Azerbaijan	1	0	4	5
France	11	9	13	33	North Korea	0	4	1	5
Italy	10	11	11	32	Georgia	2	2	0	4
South Korea	9	12	9	30	Indonesia	1	1	2	4
Great Britain	9	9	12	30	Latvia	0	4	0	4
Cuba	9	7	11	27	Mexico	0	3	1	4
Ukraine	9	5	9	23	Slovenia	0	1	3	4
Netherlands	4	9	9	22	Morocco	2	1	0	3
Romania	8	5	6	19	Chile	2	0	1	3
Spain	3	11	5	19	Lithuania	1	2	0	3
Hungary	8	6	3	17	Zimbabwe	1	1	1	3
Greece	6	6	4	16	Belgium	1	0	2	3
Belarus	2	6	7	15	Portugal	0	2	1	3
Canada	3	6	3	12	Estonia	0	1	2	3
Bulgaria	2	1	9	12	Bahamas	1	0	1	2
Brazil	4	3	3	10	Israel	1	0	1	2
Turkey	3	3	4	10	Finland	0	2	0	2
Poland	3	2	5	10	Serbia/Montenegro	0	2	0	2
Thailand	3	1	4	8	Nigeria	0	0	2	2
Denmark	2	0	6	8	Venezuela	0	0	2	2
Kazakhstan	1	4	3	8	Cameroon	1	0	0	1
Czech Republic	1	3	4	8	Dominican Rep.	1	0	0	1
Sweden	4	1	2	7	Ireland	1	0	0	1
Austria	2	4	1	7	United Arab Emirates	1	0	0	1
Ethiopia	2	3	2	7					
Kenya	1	4	2	7	Hong Kong	0	1	0	1
Norway	5	0	1	6	India	0	1	0	1
Iran	2	2	2	6	Paraguay	0	1	0	1
Slovakia	2	2	2	6	Colombia	0	0	1	1
Argentina	2	0	4	6	Eritrea	0	0	1	1
South Africa	1	3	2	6	Mongolia	0	0	1	1
New Zealand	3	2	0	5	Syria	0	0	1	1
Taiwan	2	2	1	5	Trinidad/Tobago	0	0	1	1

BOXING

(U.S. winners only)

NOTE: U.S. boycotted Olympics in 1980.

Flyweight-112 pounds (51 kg)

1904	George Finnegan	1952	Nate Brooks
1920	Frank De Genaro	1976	Leo Randolph
1924	Fidel La Barba	1984	Steve McCrory

Bantamweight-119 (54 kg)

1904	O.L. Kirk	1988	Kennedy McKinney

Featherweight-126 pounds (57 kg)

1904	O.L. Kirk	1984	Meldrick Taylor
1924	Jackie Fields		

Lightweight-132 pounds (60 kg)

1904	H.J. Spanger	1976	Howard Davis
1920	Samuel Mosberg	1984	Pernell Whitaker
1968	Ronnie Harris	1992	Oscar De La Hoya

Light Welterweight-140 pounds (63.5 kg)

1952	Charles Adkins	1976	Ray Leonard
1972	Ray Seales	1984	Jerry Page

Welterweight-148 pounds (67 kg)

1904	Al Young	1984	Mark Breland
1932	Edward Flynn		

Light Middleweight-157 pounds (71 kg)

1960	Wilbert McClure	1996	David Reid
1984	Frank Tate		

Middleweight-165 pounds (75 kg)

1904	Charles Mayer	1960	Eddie Cook
1932	Carmen Barth	1976	Michael Spinks
1952	Floyd Patterson		

Light Heavyweight-179 pounds (81 kg)

1920	Edward Eagan	1976	Leon Spinks
1952	Norvel Lee	1988	Andrew Maynard
1956	James Boyd	2004	Andre Ward
1960	Cassius Clay		

Heavyweight-201 pounds (91 kg)

1904	Sam Berger	1968	George Foreman
1952	Edward Sanders	1984	Henry Tilman
1956	Pete Rademacher	1988	Ray Mercer
1964	Joe Frazier		

Super Heavyweight (unlimited)

1984	Tyrell Biggs

BASKETBALL–MEN

1904 United States	1976 United States
1936 United States	1980 Yugoslavia
1948 United States	1984 United States
1952 United States	1988 USSR
1956 United States	1992 United States
1960 United States	1996 United States
1964 United States	2000 United States
1968 United States	2004 Argentina
1972 USSR	

BASKETBALL–WOMEN

1976 USSR	1992 Unified Team[1]
1980 USSR	1996 United States
1984 United States	2000 United States
1988 United States	2004 United States
1. Former Soviet Union team.	

Other 2004 Summer Olympic Games Champions

Archery

Men's individual—Marco Galiazzo, Italy
Men's team—South Korea
Women's individual—Sung Hyun Park, South Korea
Women's team—South Korea

Badminton

Men's singles—Taufik Hidayat, Indonesia
Men's doubles—South Korea (Dong Moon Kim, Tae Kwon Ha)
Women's singles—Ning Zhang, China
Women's doubles—China (Jiewen Zhang, Wei Yang)
Mixed doubles—China (Jun Zhang, Ling Gao)

Baseball

Men—Cuba

Beach Volleyball

Women—United States (Kerri Walsh, Misti May)
Men—Brazil (Ricardo Santos, Emanuel Rega)

Boxing

Light flyweight—Yan Bhartelemy Varela, Cuba
Flyweight—Yuriorkis Gamboa Toledano, Cuba
Bantamweight—Guillermo Rigondeaux Ortiz, Cuba
Featherweight—Alexei Tichtchenko, Russia
Lightweight—Mario Cesar Kindelan Mesa, Cuba
Light welterweight—Manus Boonjumnong, Thailand
Welterweight—Bakhtiyar Artayev, Kazakhstan
Middleweight—Gaydarbek Gaydarbekov, Russia
Light heavyweight—Andre Ward, United States
Heavyweight—Odlanier Solis Fonte, Cuba
Super heavyweight—Alexander Povetkin, Russia

Cycling—Men

Individual sprint (track)—Ryan Bayley, Australia
Individual pursuit (track)—Bradley Wiggins, Great Britain
Team pursuit (track)—Australia
Team sprint (track)—Germany
1 km time trial (track)—Chris Hoy, Great Britain
Individual points race (track)—Mikhail Ignatyev, Russia

Keirin (track)—Ryan Bayley, Australia
Madison (track)—Australia
Individual time trial (road)—Tyler Hamilton, United States
Road race—Paolo Bettini, Italy
Mountain bike—Julien Absalon, France

Cycling—Women

Sprint (track)—Lori-Ann Muenzer, Canada
Individual pursuit (track)—Sarah Ulmer, New Zealand
500m time trial (track)—Anna Meares, Australia
Points race (track)—Olga Slyusareva, Russia
Individual time trial (road)—Leontien Zijlaard-Van Moorsel, Netherlands
Road race—Sara Carrigan, Australia
Mountain bike—Gunn-Rita Dahle, Norway

Equestrian

Individual three-day—Leslie Law, Great Britain
Three-day team event—France
Individual dressage—Anky van Grunsven, Netherlands
Team dressage—Germany
Individual jumping—Cian O'Connor, Ireland
Team jumping—Germany

Fencing—Men

Individual epee—Marcel Fischer, Switzerland
Individual foil—Brice Guyart, France
Individual sabre—Aldo Montano, Italy
Team epee—France
Team foil—Italy
Team sabre—France

Fencing—Women

Individual epee—Timea Nagy, Hungary
Individual foil—Valentina Vezzali, Italy
Individual sabre—Mariel Zagunis, United States
Team epee—Russia

Field Hockey

Men—Australia
Women—Germany

Gymnastics (Artistic)—Men

All-around—Paul Hamm, United States
Floor exercise—Kyle Shewfelt, Canada
Pommel horse—Haibin Teng, China
Rings—Dimosthenis Tampakos, Greece
Horizontal bar—Igor Cassina, Italy
Parallel bars—Valeri Goncharov, Ukraine
Vault—Gervasio Deferr, Spain
Team—Japan

Gymnastics (Artistic)—Women

All-around—Carly Patterson, United States
Uneven bars—Emilie Lepennec, France
Balance beam—Catalina Ponor, Romania
Floor exercise—Catalina Ponor, Romania
Vault—Monica Rosu, Romania
Team—Romania

Gymnastics (Rhythmic)

Individual—Alina Kabaeva, Russia
Team—Russia

Judo—Men

Extra-lightweight (60kg)—Tadahiro Nomura, Japan
Half-lightweight (66kg)—Masato Uchishiba, Japan
Lightweight (73kg)—Won Hee Lee, South Korea
Half-middleweight (81kg)—Ilias Iliadis, Greece
Middleweight (90kg)—Zurab Zviadauri, Georgia
Half-heavyweight (100kg)—Ihar Makarau, Belarus
Heavyweight (100kg+)—Keiji Suzuki, Japan

Judo—Women

Extra-lightweight (48kg)—Ryoko Tani, Japan
Half-lightweight (52kg)—Dongmei Xian, China
Lightweight (57kg)—Yvonne Boenisch, Germany
Half-middleweight (63kg)—Ayumi Tanimoto, Japan
Middleweight (70kg)—Masae Ueno, Japan
Half-heavyweight (78kg)—Noriko Anno, Japan
Heavyweight (78kg+)—Maki Tsukada, Japan

Kayak-Canoe—Men

Kayak pairs 500m—Germany
Canoe singles 500m—Andreas Dittmer, Germany
Canoe pairs 500m—China
Kayak singles 500m—Adam Van Koeverden, Canada
Kayak singles 1,000m—Eirik Veraas Larsen, Norway
Kayak fours 1,000m—Hungary
Canoe singles 1,000m—David Cal, Spain
Canoe pairs 1,000m—Germany
Canoe slalom pairs—Slovakia

Kayak slalom singles—Benoit Peschier, France
Canoe slalom singles—Tony Estanguet, France

Kayak—Women
Pairs 500m—Hungary
Singles 500m—Natasa Janics, Hungary
Fours 500m—Germany
Slalom singles—Elena Kaliska, Slovakia

Modern Pentathlon
Men—Andrey Moiseev, Russia
Women—Zsuzsanna Voros, Hungary

Rowing—Men
Single sculls—Olaf Tufte, Norway
Lightweight double sculls—Poland
Heavyweight double sculls—France
Quadruple sculls—Russia
Coxless pair—Australia
Lightweight coxless four—Denmark
Heavyweight coxless four—Great Britain
Eight—United States

Rowing—Women
Single sculls—Katrin Rutschow-Stomporowski, Germany
Lightweight double sculls—Romania
Heavyweight double sculls—New Zealand
Quadruple sculls—Germany
Coxless pair—Romania
Eight—Romania

Sailing
Open Tornado—Austria
Open 49er—Spain
Open Laser—Brazil
Men's Star—Brazil
Men's Mistral—Israel
Men's Finn—Great Britain
Men's 470—United States
Women's Mistral—France
Women's Europe—Norway
Women's Yngling—Great Britain
Women's 470—Greece

Shooting—Men
Skeet—Andrea Benelli, Italy
Rifle 3-position—Zhanbo Jia, China
Rapid fire pistol—Ralf Schumann, Germany
Rifle prone—Matt Emmons, United States
Running target—Manfred Kurzer, Germany (World record)

Double trap—Ahmed Almaktoum, United Arab Emirates
50m pistol—Mikhail Nestruev, Russia
Air rifle—Qinan Zhu, China
Trap—Alexei Alipov, Russia
Air pistol—Yifu Wang, China

Shooting—Women
Rifle 3-position—Lioubov Galkina, Russia
Skeet—Diana Igaly, Hungary
25m Pistol—Mariya Grozdeva, Bulgaria
Double trap—Kim Rhode, United States
Trap—Suzanne Balogh, Australia
Air pistol—Olena Kostevych, Ukraine
Air rifle—Li Du, China

Soccer
Men—Argentina
Women—United States

Softball
United States

Synchronized Swimming
Duet—Russia
Team—Russia

Table Tennis
Men's singles—Seung Min Ryu, South Korea
Men's doubles—China
Women's singles—Zhang Yining, China
Women's doubles—China

Taekwondo
Men 58kg—Mu Yen Chu, Taiwan
Men 68kg—Hadi Saei Bonehkohal, Iran
Men 80kg—Steven Lopez, United States
Men 80kg+—Dae Sung Moon, South Korea
Women 49kg—Shih Hsin Chen, Taiwan
Women 57kg—Ji Won Jang, South Korea
Women 67kg—Wei Luo, China
Women 67kg+—Zhong Chen, China

Team Handball
Men—Croatia
Women—Denmark

Tennis
Men's singles—Nicolas Massu, Chile
Men's doubles—Chile
Women's singles—Justine Henin-Hardenne, Belgium
Women's doubles—China

Trampoline
Men—Yuri Nikitin, Russia
Women—Anna Dogonadze, Germany

Triathlon
Men—Hamish Carter, New Zealand
Women—Kate Allen, Austria

Volleyball
Men—Brazil
Women—China

Water Polo
Men—Hungary
Women—Italy

Weightlifting—Men
56kg—Halil Mutlu, Turkey
62kg—Zhiyong Shi, China
69kg—Guozheng Zhang, China
77kg—Taner Sagir, Turkey
85kg—George Asanidze, Georgia
94kg—Milen Dobrev, Bulgaria
105kg—Dmitry Berestov, Russia
105kg+—Hossein Reza Zadeh, Iran

Weightlifting—Women
48kg—Taylan Nurcan, Turkey
53kg—Udomporn Polsak, Thailand
58kg—Yanqing Chen, China
63kg—Natalia Skakun, Ukraine
69kg—Chunhong Liu, China
75kg—Pawina Thongsuk, Thailand
75kg+—Gonghong Tang, China

Wrestling—Men's Freestyle
55kg—Mavlet Batirov, Russia
60kg—Yandro Miguel Quintana, Cuba
66kg—Elbrus Tedeyev, Ukraine
74kg—Buvaysa Saytiev, Russia
84kg—Cael Sanderson, United States
96kg—Khadjimourat Gatsalov, Russia
120kg—Artur Taymazov, Uzbekistan

Wrestling—Women's Freestyle
48kg—Irini Merleni, Ukraine
55kg—Saeori Yoshida, Japan
63kg—Kaori Icho, Japan
72kg—Xu Wang, China

Wrestling—Men's Greco-Roman
55kg—Istvan Majoros, Hungary
60kg—Ji Hyun Jung, South Korea
66kg—Farid Mansurov, Azerbaijan
74kg—Alexandr Dokturishivili, Uzbekistan
84kg—Alexei Michine, Russia
96kg—Karam Ibrahim, Egypt
120kg—Khasan Baroev, Russia

Winter Games: Gold Medals

FIGURE SKATING—MEN

1908 Ulrich Salchow, Sweden
1920 Gillis Grafström, Sweden
1924 Gillis Grafström, Sweden
1928 Gillis Grafström, Sweden
1932 Karl Schäfer, Austria
1936 Karl Schäfer, Austria
1948 Dick Button, United States
1952 Dick Button, United States
1956 Hayes Alan Jenkins, United States
1960 David Jenkins, United States
1964 Manfred Schnelldorfer, Germany

1968 Wolfgang Schwarz, Austria
1972 Ondrej Nepela, Czechoslovakia
1976 John Curry, Great Britain
1980 Robin Cousins, Great Britain
1984 Scott Hamilton, United States
1988 Brian Boitano, United States
1992 Viktor Petrenko, Unified Team*
1994 Alexei Urmanov, Russia
1998 Ilia Kulik, Russia
2002 Alexei Yagudin, Russia

*Former Soviet Union team.

FIGURE SKATING–WOMEN

1908	Madge Syers, Britain
1920	Magda Julin-Mauroy, Sweden
1924	Herma Planck-Szabö, Austria
1928	Sonja Henie, Norway
1932	Sonja Henie, Norway
1936	Sonja Henie, Norway
1948	Barbara Ann Scott, Canada
1952	Jeanette Altwegg, Great Britain
1956	Tenley Albright, United States
1960	Carol Heiss, United States
1964	Sjoukje Dijkstra, Netherlands
1968	Peggy Fleming, United States
1972	Beatrix Schuba, Austria
1976	Dorothy Hamill, United States
1980	Anett Pötzsch, East Germany
1984	Katarina Witt, East Germany
1988	Katarina Witt, East Germany
1992	Kristi Yamaguchi, United States
1994	Oksana Baiul, Ukraine
1998	Tara Lipinski, United States
2002	Sarah Hughes, United States

SPEED SKATING–MEN

(U.S. winners only)

500 Meters

1924	Charles Jewtraw	44.00
1932	Jack Shea	43.40
1952	Ken Henry	43.20
1964	Terry McDermott	40.10
1980	Eric Heiden	38.03
2002	Casey FitzRandolph	69.23[1]

1,000 Meters

1976	Peter Mueller	1:19.32
1980	Eric Heiden	1:15.18
1994	Dan Jansen	1:12.43[2]

1,500 Meters

1932	Jack Shea	2:57.50
1980	Eric Heiden	1:55.44
2002	Derek Parra	1:43.95[2]

5,000 Meters

| 1932 | Irving Jaffee | 9:40.80 |
| 1980 | Eric Heiden | 7:02.29 |

10,000 Meters

| 1932 | Irving Jaffee | 19:13.60 |
| 1980 | Eric Heiden | 14:28.13 |

1. Combined time of two races. 2. World record.

SPEED SKATING–WOMEN

(U.S. winners only)

500 Meters

1972	Anne Henning	43.33
1976	Sheila Young	42.76
1988	Bonnie Blair	39.10
1992	Bonnie Blair	40.33
1994	Bonnie Blair	39.25

1,000 Meters

1992	Bonnie Blair	1:21.90
1994	Bonnie Blair	1:18.74
2002	Chris Witty	1:13.83[1]

1,500 Meters

| 1972 | Dianne Holum | 2:20.85 |

1. World record.

SKIING, ALPINE–MEN

Downhill

1948	Henri Oreiller, France	2:55.00
1952	Zeno Colò, Italy	2:30.80
1956	Toni Sailer, Austria	2:52.20
1960	Jean Vuarnet, France	2:06.00
1964	Egon Zimmermann, Austria	2:18.16

1968	Jean-Claude Killy, France	1:59.85
1972	Bernhard Russi, Switzerland	1:51.43
1976	Franz Klammer, Austria	1:45.73
1980	Leonhard Stock, Austria	1:45.50
1984	Bill Johnson, United States	1:45.59
1988	Pirmin Zurbriggen, Switzerland	1:59.63
1992	Patrick Ortlieb, Austria	1:50.37
1994	Tommy Moe, United States	1:45.75
1998	Jean-Luc Cretier, France	1:50.11
2002	Fritz Strobl, Austria	1:39.13

Slalom

1948	Edi Reinalter, Switzerland	2:10.30
1952	Othmar Schneider, Austria	2:00.00
1956	Toni Sailer, Austria	3:14.70
1960	Ernst Hinterseer, Austria	2:08.90
1964	Pepi Stiegler, Austria	2:11.13
1968	Jean-Claude Killy, France	1:39.73
1972	Francisco Ochoa, Spain	1:49.27
1976	Piero Gros, Italy	2:03.29
1980	Ingemar Stenmark, Sweden	1:44.26
1984	Phil Mahre, United States	1:39.41
1988	Alberto Tomba, Italy	1:39.47
1992	Finn Christian Jagge, Norway	1:44.39
1994	Thomas Stangassinger, Austria	2:02.02
1998	Hans-Petter Buraas, Norway	1:49.31
2002	Jean-Pierre Vidal, France	1:41.06

Giant Slalom

1952	Stein Eriksen, Norway	2:25.00
1956	Toni Sailer, Austria	3:00.10
1960	Roger Staub, Switzerland	1:48.30
1964	François Bonlieu, France	1:46.71
1968	Jean-Claude Killy, France	3:29.28
1972	Gustav Thöni, Italy	3:09.62
1976	Heini Hemmi, Switzerland	3:26.97
1980	Ingemar Stenmark, Sweden	2:40.74
1984	Max Julen, Switzerland	2:41.18
1988	Alberto Tomba, Italy	2:06.37
1992	Alberto Tomba, Italy	2:06.98
1994	Markus Wasmeier, Germany	2:52.46
1998	Hermann Maier, Austria	2:38.51
2002	Stephan Eberharter, Austria	2:23.28

Super Giant Slalom

1988	Frank Piccard, France	1:39.66
1992	Kjetil Andre Aamodt, Norway	1:13.04
1994	Markus Wasmeier, Germany	1:32.53
1998	Hermann Maier, Austria	1:34.84
2002	Kjetil Andre Aamodt, Norway	1:21.58

Men's Combined (Downhill and Slalom)

		Points
1936	Franz Pfnür, Germany	99.25
1948	Henri Oreiller, France	3.27
1952–1984	Not held	
1988	Hubert Strolz, Austria	36.55
1992	Josef Polig, Italy	14.58
		Time
1994	Lasse Kjus, Norway	3:17.53
1998	Mario Reiter, Austria	3:08.06
2002	Kjetil Andre Aamodt, Norway	3:17.56

SKIING, ALPINE–WOMEN

Downhill

1948	Hedy Schlunegger, Switzerland	2:28.30
1952	Trude Jochum-Beiser, Austria	1:47.10
1956	Madeleine Berthod, Switzerland	1:40.70
1960	Heidi Biebl, Germany	1:37.60
1964	Christl Haas, Austria	1:55.39
1968	Olga Pall, Austria	1:40.87
1972	Marie-Theres Nadig, Switzerland	1:36.68
1976	Rosi Mittermaier, West Germany	1:46.16
1980	Annemarie Moser-Pröll, Austria	1:37.52
1984	Michela Figini, Switzerland	1:13.36
1988	Marina Kiehl, West Germany	1:25.86
1992	Kerrin Lee-Gartner, Canada	1:52.55

1994	Katja Seizinger, Germany	1:35.93
1998	Katja Seizinger, Germany	1:28.89
2002	Carole Montillet, France	1:39.56

Slalom

1948	Gretchen Fraser, United States	1:57.20
1952	Andrea Mead Lawrence, United States	2:10.60
1956	Renée Colliard, Switzerland	1:52.30
1960	Anne Heggtveit, Canada	1:49.60
1964	Christine Goitschel, France	1:29.86
1968	Marielle Goitschel, France	1:25.86
1972	Barbara Cochran, United States	1:31.24
1976	Rosi Mittermaier, West Germany	1:30.54
1980	Hanni Wenzel, Liechtenstein	1:25.09
1984	Paoletta Magoni, Italy	1:36.47
1988	Vreni Schneider, Switzerland	1:36.69
1992	Petra Kronberger, Austria	1:32.68
1994	Vreni Schneider, Switzerland	1:56.01
1998	Hilde Gerg, Germany	1:32.40
2002	Janica Kostelic, Croatia	1:46.10

Giant Slalom

1952	Andrea Mead Lawrence, United States	2:06.80
1956	Ossi Reichert, Germany	1:56.50
1960	Yvonne Rügg, Switzerland	1:39.90
1964	Marielle Goitschel, France	1:52.24
1968	Nancy Greene, Canada	1:51.97
1972	Marie-Theres Nadig, Switzerland	1:29.90
1976	Kathy Kreiner, Canada	1:29.13
1980	Hanni Wenzel, Liechtenstein	2:41.66
1984	Debbie Armstrong, United States	2:20.98
1988	Vreni Schneider, Switzerland	2:06.49
1992	Pernilla Wiberg, Sweden	2:12.74
1994	Deborah Compagnoni, Italy	2:30.97
1998	Deborah Compagnoni, Italy	2:50.59
2002	Janica Kostelic, Croatia	2:30.01

Super Giant Slalom

1988	Sigrid Wolf, Austria	1:19.03
1992	Deborah Compagnoni, Italy	1:21.22
1994	Diann Roffe-Steinrotter, United States	1:22.15
1998	Picabo Street, United States	1:18.02
2002	Daniela Ceccarelli, Italy	1:13.59

Combined (Downhill and Slalom)   **Points**

1936	Christl Cranz, Germany	97.06
1948	Trude Beiser, Austria	6.58
1952-84	Not held	
1988	Anita Wachter, Austria	29.25
1992	Petra Kronberger, Austria	2.55
		Time
1994	Pernilla Wiberg, Sweden	3:05.16
1998	Katja Seizinger, Germany	2:40.74
2002	Janica Kostelic, Croatia	2:43.28

ICE HOCKEY

MEN

1920	Canada	1976	USSR
1924	Canada	1980	United States
1928	Canada	1984	USSR
1932	Canada	1988	USSR
1936	Great Britain	1992	Unified Team*
1948	Canada	1994	Sweden
1952	Canada	1998	Czech Republic
1956	USSR	2002	Canada
1960	United States		
1964	USSR	**WOMEN**	
1968	USSR	1998	United States
1972	USSR	2002	Canada
		*Former Soviet Union team.	

2002 Men's Championship
Canada 5, United States 2
2002 Women's Championship
Canada 3, United States 2

FREESTYLE SKIING—MEN

Moguls

1992	Edgar Grospiron, France
1994	Jean-Luc Brassard, Canada
1998	Jonny Moseley, United States
2002	Janne Lahtela, Finland

Aerials

1994	Andreas Schoenbaechler, Switzerland
1998	Eric Bergoust, United States
2002	Ales Valenta, Czech Republic

FREESTYLE SKIING—WOMEN

Moguls

1992	Donna Weinbrecht, United States
1994	Stine Lise Hattestad, Norway
1998	Tae Satoya, Japan
2002	Kari Traa, Norway

Aerials

1994	Lina Cherjazova, Uzbekistan
1998	Nikki Stone, United States
2002	Alisa Camplin, Australia

DISTRIBUTION OF MEDALS
2002 WINTER OLYMPIC GAMES

(Salt Lake City, Utah)

Country	Gold	Silver	Bronze	Total
Germany	12	16	7	35
United States	10	13	11	34
Norway	11	7	6	24
Canada	6	3	8	17
Austria	2	4	10	16
Russia	6	6	4	16
Italy	4	4	4	12
France	4	5	2	11
Switzerland	3	2	6	11
China	2	2	4	8
Netherlands	3	5	0	8
Finland	4	2	1	7
Sweden	0	2	4	6
Croatia	3	1	0	4
Korea	2	2	0	4
Bulgaria	0	1	2	3
Estonia	1	1	1	3
Great Britain	1	0	2	3
Australia	2	0	0	2
Czech Republic	1	0	1	2
Japan	0	1	1	2
Poland	0	1	1	2
Spain	0	0	1	1
Belarus	0	0	1	1
Slovenia	0	0	1	1

2002 UNITED STATES MEDALISTS

Alpine Skiing
Men's Combined—SILVER—Bode Miller
Men's Giant Slalom—SILVER—Bode Miller

Bobsleigh
Four-Man—SILVER—Todd Hayes, Bill Schuffenhauer, Garrett Hines, Randy Jones
Four-Man—BRONZE—Mike Kohn, Doug Sharp, Brian Shimer, Dan Steele
Women—GOLD—Jill Bakken, Vonetta Flowers

Figure Skating
Women—GOLD—Sarah Hughes
Women—BRONZE—Michelle Kwan
Men—BRONZE—Timothy Goebel

Freestyle Skiing
Men's Aerials—SILVER—Joe Pack
Men's Moguls—SILVER—Travis Mayer
Women's Moguls—SILVER—Shannon Bahrke

Hockey
Men—SILVER—Tom Barrasso, Brian Rolston, Mike York, Tony Amonte, Chris Chelios, Chris Drury, Mike Dunham, Bill Guerin, Brett Hull, John LeClair, Brian Leetch, Mike Modano, Brian Rafalski, Jeremy Roenick, Gary Suter, Keith Tkachuk, Doug Weight, Scott Young, Tom Poti, Mike Richter, Phil Housley, Adam Deadmarsh, Aaron Miller
Women—Silver—Chris Bailey, Laurie Baker, Karyn Bye, Julie Chu, Natalie Darwitz, Sara DeCosta, Tricia Dunn, Cammi Granato, Courtney Kennedy, Andrea Kilbourne, Katie King, Shelley Looney, Sue Merz, Allison Mleczko, Tara Mounsey, Jenny Potter, Angela Ruggiero, Sara Tueting, Lyndsay Wall, Krissy Wendell

Luge
Men's Doubles—SILVER—Brian Martin, Mark Grimmette
Men's Doubles—BRONZE—Clay Ives

Short Track Speed Skating
Men's 1,000 m—SILVER—Apolo Anton Ohno
Men's 1,500 m—GOLD—Apolo Anton Ohno
Men's 500 m—BRONZE—Rusty Smith

Skeleton
Men—GOLD—Jim Shea
Women—GOLD—Tristan Gale
Women—SILVER—Lea Ann Parsley

Snowboarding
Men's Halfpipe—GOLD—Ross Powers
Men's Halfpipe—SILVER—Danny Kass
Men's Halfpipe—BRONZE—Jarret Thomas
Men's Parallel Giant Slalom—BRONZE—Chris Klug
Women's Halfpipe—GOLD—Kelly Clark

Speed Skating
Women's 1,000 m—GOLD—Chris Witty
Women's 1,000 m—BRONZE—Jennifer Rodriguez
Women's 1,500 m—BRONZE—Jennifer Rodriguez
Men's 1,000 m—BRONZE—Joey Cheek
Men's 1,500 m—GOLD—Derek Parra
Men's 500 m—GOLD—Casey FitzRandolph
Men's 500 m—BRONZE—Kip Carpenter
Men's 5,000 m—SILVER—Derek Parra

Other 2002 Winter Olympic Games Champions

Biathlon
Men's 10 km Sprint—Ole Einar Bjoerndalen, Norway
Men's 12.5 km Pursuit—Ole Einar Bjoerndalen, Norway
Men's 20 km Individual—Ole Einar Bjoerndalen, Norway
Men's 4 × 7.5 km Relay—Norway
Women's 10 km Pursuit—Olga Pyleva, Russia
Women's 15 km Individual—Andrea Henkel, Germany
Women's 4 × 7.5 km Relay—Germany
Women's 7.5 km Sprint—Kati Wilhelm, Germany

Bobsledding
2-man—Germany
4-man—Germany
Women—United States

Cross-Country Skiing
Men's 10 km Free Pursuit—Johann Muehlegg, Spain
Men's 15 km Classical—Andrus Veerpalu, Estonia
Men's 30 km Free Mass Start—Johann Muehlegg, Spain
Men's 4 × 10 km Relay—Norway
Men's 50 km Classical—Mikhail Ivanov, Russia
Men's Sprint—Tor Arne Hetland, Norway
Women's 10 km Classical—Bente Skari, Norway
Women's 15 km Free Mass Start—Stefania Belmondo, Italy
Women's 30 km Classical—Gabriella Paruzzi, Italy
Women's 4 × 5 km Relay—Germany
Women's 5 km Free Pursuit—Olga Danilova, Russia
Women's Sprint—Julija Tchepalova, Russia

Curling
Men—Norway
Women—Germany

Figure Skating
Pairs—David Pelletier and Jamie Sale, Canada; Elena Berezhnaya and Anton Sikharulidze, Russia
Ice dancing—Marina Anissina and Gwendal Peizerat, France

Skeleton
Men—Jim Shea, United States
Women—Tristan Gale, United States

Luge
Men's Doubles—Germany
Men's Singles—Armin Zoeggeler, Italy
Women's Singles—Sylke Otto, Germany

Nordic Combined
Individual 15 km—Samppa Lajunen, Finland
Sprint 7.5 km—Samppa Lajunen, Finland
Team 4 × 5 km Relay—Finland

Short Track Speed Skating
Women's 1,000 km—Yang Yang (A), China
Women's 1,500 km—Gi-Hyun Ko, Korea
Women's 3,000 km Relay—Korea
Women's 500 m—Yang Yang (A), China
Men's 1,000 m—Steven Bradbury, Australia
Men'1 1,500 m—Apolo Anton Ohno, United States
Men's 500 m—Marc Gagnon, Canada
Men's 5,000 m Relay—Canada

Ski Jumping
Individual K120—Simon Ammann, Switzerland
Individual K90—Simon Ammann, Switzerland
Team K120—Germany

Snowboarding
Men's Halfpipe—Ross Powers, United States
Men' Parallel Giant Slalom—Philipp Schoch, Switzerland
Women's Halfpipe—Kelly Clark, United States
Women's Parallel Giant Slalom—Isabelle Blanc, France

Speed Skating
Women's 1,500 m—Anni Friesinger, Germany
Women's 3,000 m—Claudia Pechstein, Germany
Women's 500 m—Catriona LeMay Doan, Canada
Women's 5,000 m—Claudia Pechstein, Germany
Men's 1,000 m—Gerard van Velde, Netherlands
Men's 10,000 m—Jochem Uytdehaage, Netherlands
Men's 5,000 m—Jochem Uytdehaage, Netherlands

Football

The pastime of kicking around a ball goes back beyond the limits of recorded history. Ancient savage tribes played football of a primitive kind. There was a ball-kicking game played by Athenians, Spartans, and Corinthians 2,500 years ago, which the Greeks called *Episkuros*. The Romans had a somewhat similar game called *Harpastum* and are supposed to have carried the game with them when they invaded the British Isles in the first century B.C.

Undoubtedly the game known in the United States as football traces directly to the English game of rugby, though the modifications have been many. Informal football was played on college lawns well over a century ago, and an annual freshman-sophomore series of "scrimmages" began at Yale in 1840. The first formal intercollegiate football game was the Princeton-Rutgers contest at New Brunswick, N.J., on Nov. 6, 1869, with Rutgers winning by 6 goals to 4.

In those days, games were played with 25, 20, 15, or 11 men on a side. In 1880, there was a convention at which Walter Camp of Yale persuaded the delegates to agree to 11 players on a side.

The first professional game was played in 1895 at Latrobe, Pa. The National Football League was founded in 1920, as the American Professional Football Association (the name changed to NFL in 1922). The All-American Conference went into action in 1946. At the end of the 1949 season the two circuits merged, retaining the name of the older league. In 1960, the American Football League began operations. In 1970, the leagues merged. The United States Football League played its first season in 1983, from March to July. It suspended spring operations after the 1985 season, and planned a 1986 move to fall, but suspended operations again.

In March 1991, another effort at spring football was launched. This time the ten-team World League of American Football had the backing of the National Football League. After two seasons it was suspended. The league returned in 1995, with six teams in Europe. In 1998, it was renamed the NFL Europe League.

In 2002 the NFL divisions were realigned. National and American Conferences were split into four divisions with four teams per division. Scheduling has also been changed and every team will meet every other team at least once every four years.

College Football

NATIONAL COLLEGE FOOTBALL CHAMPIONS

The "National Collegiate Athletic Association Football Guide" recognizes as unofficial national champion the team selected each year by press association polls of writers and coaches.

1936 Minnesota	1952 Mich. State	1965 Alabama and	1977 Notre Dame	1991 Miami (Fla.) and
1937 Pittsburgh	1953 Maryland	Mich. State	1978 Alabama and	Washington
1938 Texas Christian	1954 Ohio State and	1966 Notre Dame	So. Calif.	1992 Alabama
1939 Texas A & M	UCLA	1967 So. Calif.	1979 Alabama	1993 Florida State
1940 Minnesota	1955 Oklahoma	1968 Ohio State	1980 Georgia	1994 Nebraska
1941 Minnesota	1956 Oklahoma	1969 Texas	1981 Clemson	1995 Nebraska
1942 Ohio State	1957 Auburn and	1970 Texas and	1982 Penn State	1996 Univ. of Florida
1943 Notre Dame	Ohio State	Nebraska	1983 Miami (Fla.)	1997 Michigan and
1944 Army	1958 Louisiana State	1971 Nebraska	1984 Brigham Young	Nebraska
1945 Army	1959 Syracuse	1972 So. Calif.	1985 Oklahoma	1998 Tennessee
1946 Notre Dame	1960 Minnesota	1973 Notre Dame	1986 Penn State	1999 Florida State
1947 Notre Dame	1961 Alabama	and U. of Ala.	1987 Miami (Fla.)	2000 Oklahoma
1948 Michigan	1962 So. Calif.	1974 Oklahoma and	1988 Notre Dame	2001 Miami (Fla.)
1949 Notre Dame	1963 Texas	So. Calif.	1989 Miami (Fla.)	2002 Ohio State
1950 Oklahoma	1964 Alabama	1975 Oklahoma	1990 Colorado and	2003 Louisiana State
1951 Tennessee		1976 Pittsburgh	Georgia Tech	and So. Calif.

RECORD OF ANNUAL MAJOR COLLEGE FOOTBALL BOWL GAMES

Rose Bowl (At Pasadena, Calif.)

1902 Michigan 49, Stanford 0	1927 Alabama 7, Stanford 7	1944 So. Calif. 29, Washington 0
1916 Washington State 14, Brown 0	1928 Stanford 7, Pittsburgh 6	1945 So. Calif. 25, Tennessee 0
1917 Oregon 14, Pennsylvania 0	1929 Georgia Tech 8, California 7	1946 Alabama 34, So. Calif. 14
1918 Mare Island Marines 19, Camp Lewis 7	1930 So. Calif. 47, Pittsburgh 14	1947 Illinois 45, UCLA 14
1919 Great Lakes 17, Mare Island Marines 0	1931 Alabama 24, Wash. State 0	1948 Michigan 49, So. Calif. 0
	1932 So. Calif. 21, Tulane 12	1949 Northwestern 20, California 14
1920 Harvard 7, Oregon 6	1933 So. Calif. 35, Pittsburgh 0	1950 Ohio State 17, California 14
1921 California 28, Ohio State 0	1934 Columbia 7, Stanford 0	1951 Michigan 14, California 6
1922 Washington and Jefferson 0, California 0	1935 Alabama 29, Stanford 13	1952 Illinois 40, Stanford 7
1923 So. Calif. 14, Penn State 3	1936 Stanford 7, So. Methodist 0	1953 So. Calif. 7, Wisconsin 0
1924 Navy 14, Washington 14	1937 Pittsburgh 21, Washington 0	1954 Michigan State 28, UCLA 20
1925 Notre Dame 27, Stanford 10	1938 California 13, Alabama 0	1955 Ohio State 20, So. Calif. 7
1926 Alabama 20, Washington 19	1939 So. Calif. 7, Duke 3	1956 Michigan State 17, UCLA 14
	1940 So. Calif. 14, Tennessee 0	1957 Iowa 35, Oregon State 19
	1941 Stanford 21, Nebraska 13	1958 Ohio State 10, Oregon 7
	1942 Oregon State 20, Duke 16[1]	1959 Iowa 38, California 12
	1943 Georgia 9, UCLA 0	1960 Washington 44, Wisconsin 8

1961 Washington 17, Minnesota 7
1962 Minnesota 21, UCLA 3
1963 So. Calif. 42, Wisconsin 37
1964 Illinois 17, Washington 7
1965 Michigan 34, Oregon State 7
1966 UCLA 14, Michigan State 12
1967 Purdue 14, So. Calif. 13
1968 So. Calif. 14, Indiana 3
1969 Ohio State 27, So. Calif. 16
1970 So. Calif. 10, Michigan 3
1971 Stanford 27, Ohio State 17
1972 Stanford 13, Michigan 12
1973 So. Calif. 42, Ohio State 17
1974 Ohio State 42, So. Calif. 21
1975 So. Calif. 18, Ohio State 17
1976 UCLA 23, Ohio State 10
1977 So. Calif. 14, Michigan 6
1978 Washington 27, Michigan 20
1979 So. Calif. 17, Michigan 10
1980 So. Calif. 17, Ohio State 16
1981 Michigan 23, Washington 6
1982 Washington 28, Iowa 0
1983 UCLA 24, Michigan 14
1984 UCLA 45, Illinois 9
1985 So. Calif. 20, Ohio St. 17
1986 UCLA 45, Iowa 28
1987 Arizona State 22, Michigan 15
1988 Michigan State 20, So. Calif. 17
1989 Michigan 22, So. Calif. 14
1990 So. Calif. 17, Michigan 10
1991 Washington 46, Iowa 34
1992 Washington 34, Michigan 14
1993 Michigan 38, Washington 31
1994 Wisconsin 21, UCLA 16
1995 Penn State 38, Oregon 20
1996 So. Calif. 41, Northwestern 32
1997 Ohio State 20, Arizona State 17
1998 Michigan 21, Washington State 16
1999 Wisconsin 38, UCLA 31
2000 Wisconsin 17, Stanford 9
2001 Washington 34, Purdue 24
2002 Miami 37, Nebraska 14
2003 Oklahoma 34, Washington State 14 ·
2004 So. Calif. 28, Michigan 14
1. Played at Durham, N.C.

Orange Bowl (At Miami)

1933 Miami (Fla.) 7, Manhattan 0
1934 Duquesne 33, Miami (Fla.) 7
1935 Bucknell 26, Miami (Fla.) 0
1936 Catholic 20, Mississippi 19
1937 Duquesne 13, Mississippi State 12
1938 Auburn 6, Michigan State 0
1939 Tennessee 17, Oklahoma 0
1940 Georgia Tech 21, Missouri 7
1941 Mississippi State 14, George-town 7
1942 Georgia 40, Texas Christian 26
1943 Alabama 37, Boston College 21
1944 Louisiana State 19, Texas A & M 14
1945 Tulsa 26, Georgia Tech 12
1946 Miami (Fla.) 13, Holy Cross 6
1947 Rice 8, Tennessee 0
1948 Georgia Tech 20, Kansas 14
1949 Texas 41, Georgia 28
1950 Santa Clara 21, Kentucky 13

1951 Clemson 15, Miami (Fla.) 14
1952 Georgia Tech 17, Baylor 14
1953 Alabama 61, Syracuse 6
1954 Oklahoma 7, Maryland 0
1955 Duke 34, Nebraska 7
1956 Oklahoma 20, Maryland 6
1957 Colorado 27, Clemson 21
1958 Oklahoma 48, Duke 21
1959 Oklahoma 21, Syracuse 6
1960 Georgia 14, Missouri 0
1961 Missouri 21, Navy 14
1962 Louisiana State 25, Colorado 7
1963 Alabama 17, Oklahoma 0
1964 Nebraska 13, Auburn 7
1965 Texas 21, Alabama 17
1966 Alabama 39, Nebraska 28
1967 Florida 27, Georgia Tech 12
1968 Oklahoma 26, Tennessee 24
1969 Penn State 15, Kansas 14
1970 Penn State 10, Missouri 3
1971 Nebraska 17, Louisiana State 12
1972 Nebraska 38, Alabama 6
1973 Nebraska 40, Notre Dame 6
1974 Penn State 16, Louisiana State 9
1975 Notre Dame 13, Alabama 11
1976 Oklahoma 14, Michigan 6
1977 Ohio State 27, Colorado 10
1978 Arkansas 31, Oklahoma 6
1979 Oklahoma 31, Nebraska 24
1980 Oklahoma 24, Florida State 7
1981 Oklahoma 18, Florida State 17
1982 Clemson 22, Nebraska 15
1983 Nebraska 21, Louisiana State 20
1984 Miami (Fla.) 31, Nebraska 30
1985 Washington 28, Oklahoma 17
1986 Oklahoma 25, Penn State 10
1987 Oklahoma 42, Arkansas 8
1988 Miami (Fla.) 20, Oklahoma 14
1989 Miami (Fla.) 23, Nebraska 3
1990 Notre Dame 21, Colorado 6
1991 Colorado 10, Notre Dame 9
1992 Miami (Fla.) 22, Nebraska 0
1993 Florida State 27, Nebraska 14
1994 Florida State 18, Nebraska 16
1995 Nebraska 24, Miami (Fla.) 17
1996 Florida State 31, Notre Dame 26
1997 Nebraska 41, Virginia Tech 21
1998 Nebraska 42, Tennessee 17
1999 Florida 31, Syracuse 10
2000 Michigan 35, Alabama 34
2001 Oklahoma 13, Florida State 2
2002 Florida 56, Maryland 23
2003 So. Calif. 38, Iowa 17
2004 Miami 16, Florida State 14

Sugar Bowl (At New Orleans)

1935 Tulane 20, Temple 14
1936 Texas Christian 3, Louisiana State 2
1937 Santa Clara 21, Louisiana State 14
1938 Santa Clara 6, Louisiana State 0
1939 Texas Christian 15, Carnegie Tech 7
1940 Texas A & M 14, Tulane 13

1941 Boston College 19, Tennessee 13
1942 Fordham 2, Missouri 0
1943 Tennessee 14, Tulsa 7
1944 Georgia Tech 20, Tulsa 18
1945 Duke 29, Alabama 26
1946 Oklahoma A & M 33, St. Mary's (Calif.) 13
1947 Georgia 20, North Carolina 10
1948 Texas 27, Alabama 7
1949 Oklahoma 14, North Carolina 6
1950 Oklahoma 35, Louisiana State 0
1951 Kentucky 13, Oklahoma 7
1952 Maryland 28, Tennessee 13
1953 Georgia Tech 24, Mississippi 7
1954 Georgia Tech 42, West Virginia 19
1955 Navy 21, Mississippi 0
1956 Georgia Tech 7, Pittsburgh 0
1957 Baylor 13, Tennessee 7
1958 Mississippi 39, Texas 7
1959 Louisiana State 7, Clemson 0
1960 Mississippi 21, Louisiana State 0
1961 Mississippi 14, Rice 6
1962 Alabama 10, Arkansas 3
1963 Mississippi 17, Arkansas 13
1964 Alabama 12, Mississippi 7
1965 Louisiana State 13, Syracuse 10
1966 Missouri 20, Florida 18
1967 Alabama 34, Nebraska 7
1968 Louisiana State 20, Wyoming 13
1969 Arkansas 16, Georgia 2
1970 Mississippi 27, Arkansas 22
1971 Tennessee 34, Air Force Academy 13
1972 Oklahoma 40, Auburn 22
1973 Oklahoma 14, Penn State 0
1974 Notre Dame 24, Alabama 23
1975 Nebraska 13, Florida 10
1976 Alabama 13, Penn State 6
1977 Pittsburgh 27, Georgia 3
1978 Alabama 35, Ohio State 6
1979 Alabama 14, Penn State 7
1980 Alabama 24, Arkansas 9
1981 Georgia 17, Notre Dame 10
1982 Pittsburgh 24, Georgia 20
1983 Penn State 27, Georgia 23
1984 Auburn 9, Michigan 7
1985 Nebraska 28, Louisiana State 10
1986 Tennessee 35, Miami (Fla.) 7
1987 Nebraska 30, Louisiana State 15
1988 Syracuse 16, Auburn 16 (tie)
1989 Florida State 13, Auburn 7
1990 Miami (Fla.) 33, Alabama 25
1991 Tennessee 23, Virginia 22
1992 Notre Dame 39, Florida 28
1993 Alabama 34, Miami (Fla.) 13
1994 Florida 41, West Virginia 7
1995 Florida State 23, Florida 17
1996 Virginia Tech 28, Texas 10
1997 Florida 52, Florida State 20
1998 Florida State 31, Ohio State 14
1999 Ohio State 24, Texas A & M 14
2000 Florida State 46, Virginia Tech. 29

2001   Miami (Fla.) 37, Florida 20
2002   Louisiana State 47, Illinois 34
2003   Georgia 26, Florida State 13
2004   Louisiana State 21, Oklahoma
         14

Cotton Bowl (At Dallas)

1937   Texas Christian 16, Marquette 6
1938   Rice 28, Colorado 14
1939   St. Mary's (Calif.) 20, Texas
         Tech. 13
1940   Clemson 6, Boston College 3
1941   Texas A & M 13, Fordham 12
1942   Alabama 29, Texas A & M 21
1943   Texas 14, Georgia Tech 7
1944   Randolph Field 7, Texas 7
1945   Oklahoma A & M 34, Texas
         Christian 0
1946   Texas 40, Missouri 27
1947   Louisiana State 0, Arkansas 0
1948   So. Methodist 13, Penn State 13
1949   So. Methodist 21, Oregon 13
1950   Rice 27, North Carolina 13
1951   Tennessee 20, Texas 14
1952   Kentucky 20, Texas Christian 7
1953   Texas 16, Tennessee 0
1954   Rice 28, Alabama 6
1955   Georgia Tech 14, Arkansas 6
1956   Mississippi 14, Texas
         Christian 13
1957   Texas Christian 28,
         Syracuse 27
1958   Navy 20, Rice 7
1959   Air Force 0, Texas Christian 0
1960   Syracuse 23, Texas 14
1961   Duke 7, Arkansas 6
1962   Texas 12, Mississippi 7
1963   Louisiana State 13, Texas 0
1964   Texas 28, Navy 6
1965   Arkansas 10, Nebraska 7
1966   Louisiana State 14, Arkansas 7
1967   Georgia 24, So. Methodist 9
1968   Texas A & M 20, Alabama 16
1969   Texas 36, Tennessee 13
1970   Texas 21, Notre Dame 17
1971   Notre Dame 24, Texas 11
1972   Penn State 30, Texas 6
1973   Texas 17, Alabama 13
1974   Nebraska 19, Texas 3
1975   Penn State 41, Baylor 20

1976   Arkansas 31, Georgia 10
1977   Houston 30, Maryland 21
1978   Notre Dame 38, Texas 10
1979   Notre Dame 35, Houston 34
1980   Houston 17, Nebraska 14
1981   Alabama 30, Baylor 2
1982   Texas 14, Alabama 12
1983   So. Meth. 7, Pittsburgh 3
1984   Georgia 10, Texas 9
1985   Boston College 45, Houston 28
1986   Texas A & M 36, Auburn 16
1987   Ohio State 28, Texas A & M 12
1988   Texas A & M 35, Notre
         Dame 10
1989   UCLA 17, Arkansas 3
1990   Tennessee 31, Arkansas 27
1991   Miami (Fla.) 46, Texas 3
1992   Florida State 10, Texas A & M 2
1993   Notre Dame 28, Texas A & M 3
1994   Notre Dame 24, Texas A & M 21
1995   So. Calif. 55, Texas Tech 14
1996   Colorado 38, Oregon 6
1997   Brigham Young 19, Kansas
         State 15
1998   UCLA 29, Texas A & M 23
1999   Texas 38, Mississippi State 11
2000   Arkansas 27, Texas 6
2001   Kansas State 35, Tennessee 21
2002   Oklahoma 10, Arkansas 3
2003   Texas 35, Louisiana State 20
2004   Mississippi 31, Oklahoma State
         28

Gator Bowl (At Jacksonville, Fla.)

1953   Florida 14, Tulsa 13
1954   Texas Tech 35, Auburn 13
1955   Auburn 33, Baylor 13
1956   Vanderbilt 25, Auburn 13
1957   Georgia Tech 21, Pittsburgh 14
1958   Tennessee 3, Texas A & M 0
1959   Mississippi 7, Florida 3
1960   Arkansas 14, Georgia Tech 7
1961   Florida 13, Baylor 12
1962   Penn State 30, Georgia
         Tech 15
1963   Florida 17, Penn State 7
1964   No. Carolina 35, Air Force 0
1965   Florida State 36, Oklahoma 19

1966   Georgia Tech 31, Texas
         Tech 21
1967   Tennessee 18, Syracuse 12
1968   Penn State 17, Florida
         State 17 (tie)
1969   Missouri 35, Alabama 10
1970   Florida 14, Tennessee 13
1971   Auburn 35, Mississippi 28
1972   Georgia 7, North Carolina 3
1973   Auburn 24, Colorado 3
1974   Texas Tech 28, Tennessee 19
1975   Auburn 27, Texas 3
1976   Maryland 13, Florida 0
1977   Notre Dame 20, Penn State 9
1978   Pittsburgh 34, Clemson 3
1979   Clemson 17, Ohio State 15
1980   North Carolina 17, Michigan 15
1981   Pittsburgh 37, South Carolina 9
1982   North Carolina 31, Arkansas 27
1983   Florida State 31, West
         Virginia 12
1984   Florida 14, Iowa 6
1985   Oklahoma State 21,
         South Carolina 14
1986   Florida State 34, Oklahoma
         State 23
1987   Clemson 27, Stanford 21
1988   Louisiana State 30, South
         Carolina 13
1989   Georgia 34, Mich. State 27
1990   Clemson 27, West Virginia 7
1991   Michigan 35, Mississippi 3
1992   Oklahoma 38, Virginia 14
1993   Florida 27, No. Carolina St. 10
1994   Alabama 24, No. Carolina 10
1995   Tennessee 45, Virginia Tech 23
1996   Syracuse 41, Clemson 0
1997   North Carolina 20, West
         Virginia 13
1998   North Carolina 42, Virginia
         Tech 3
1999   Georgia Tech 35, Notre
         Dame 28
2000   Miami (Fla.) 28, Georgia
         Tech 13
2001   Virginia Tech 41, Clemson 20
2002   Florida State 30, Virginia Tech 17
2003   North Carolina State 28, Notre
         Dame 6
2004   Maryland 41, West Virginia 7

RESULTS OF OTHER 2003–2004 BOWL GAMES

New Orleans Bowl—Memphis 27, North Texas 17
GMAC Bowl—Miami (Ohio) 49, Louisville 28
Plains Capital Fort Worth Bowl—Boise State 34, Texas
   Christian 31
Mazda Tangerine Bowl—North Carolina State 56, Kansas
   26
Las Vegas Bowl—Oregon State 55, New Mexico 14
Sheraton Hawaii Bowl—Hawaii 54, Houston 48
Motor City Bowl—Bowling Green 28, Northwestern 24
Insight Bowl—California 52, Virginia Tech 49
Continental Tire Bowl—Virginia 23, Pittsburgh 16
Mastercard Alamo Bowl—Nebraska 17, Michigan State 3
EV1.net Houston Bowl—Texas Tech 38, Navy 14

Pacific Life Holiday Bowl—Washington State 28, Texas 20
Silicon Valley Football Classic—Fresno State 17, UCLA 9
Gaylord Hotels Music City Bowl—Auburn 28, Wisconsin 14
Wells Fargo Sun Bowl—Minnesota 31, Oregon 30
Mainstay Independence Bowl—Arkansas 27, Missouri 14
Axa Liberty Bowl—Utah 17, Southern Miss 0
Diamond Walnut San Francisco Bowl—Boston College 35,
   Colorado State 21
Outback Bowl—Iowa 37, Florida 17
Capital One Bowl—Georgia 34, Purdue 27
Chick-Fil-A Peach Bowl—Clemson 27, Tennessee 14
Tostitos Fiesta Bowl—Ohio State 35, Kansas State 28
Humanitarian Bowl—Georgia Tech 52, Tulsa 10

HEISMAN MEMORIAL TROPHY WINNERS

The Heisman Memorial Trophy is presented annually by the Downtown Athletic Club of New York City to the nation's outstanding college football player, as determined by a poll of sportswriters and sportscasters.

1935 Jay Berwanger, Chicago	1959 Billy Cannon, Louisiana State	1984 Doug Flutie, Boston College
1936 Larry Kelley, Yale	1960 Joe Bellino, Navy	1985 Bo Jackson, Auburn
1937 Clinton Frank, Yale	1961 Ernie Davis, Syracuse	1986 Vinny Testaverde, Miami
1938 Davey O'Brien, Texas Christian	1962 Terry Baker, Oregon State	1987 Tim Brown, Notre Dame
1939 Nile Kinnick, Iowa	1963 Roger Staubach, Navy	1988 Barry Sanders, Oklahoma State
1940 Tom Harmon, Michigan	1964 John Huarte, Notre Dame	1989 Andre Ware, Houston
1941 Bruce Smith, Minnesota	1965 Mike Garrett, So. Calif.	1990 Ty Detmer, Brigham Young
1942 Frank Sinkwich, Georgia	1966 Steve Spurrier, Florida	1991 Desmond Howard, Michigan
1943 Angelo Bertelli, Notre Dame	1967 Gary Beban, UCLA	1992 Gino Torretta, Miami
1944 Leslie Horvath, Ohio State	1968 O. J. Simpson, So. Calif.	1993 Charlie Ward, Florida State
1945 Felix Blanchard, Army	1969 Steve Owens, Oklahoma	1994 Rashaan Salaam, Colorado
1946 Glenn Davis, Army	1970 Jim Plunkett, Stanford	1995 Eddie George, Ohio State
1947 Johnny Lujack, Notre Dame	1971 Pat Sullivan, Auburn	1996 Danny Wuerffel, Florida
1948 Doak Walker, So. Methodist	1972 Johnny Rodgers, Nebraska	1997 Charles Woodson, Michigan
1949 Leon Hart, Notre Dame	1973 John Cappelletti, Penn State	1998 Ricky Williams, Texas
1950 Vic Janowicz, Ohio State	1974-75 Archie Griffin, Ohio State	1999 Ron Dayne, Wisconsin
1951 Dick Kazmaier, Princeton	1976 Tony Dorsett, Pittsburgh	2000 Chris Weinke, Florida State
1952 Billy Vessels, Oklahoma	1977 Earl Campbell, Texas	2001 Eric Crouch, University of
1953 Johnny Lattner, Notre Dame	1978 Billy Sims, Oklahoma	Nebraska
1954 Alan Ameche, Wisconsin	1979 Charles White, So. Calif.	2002 Carson Palmer, University of
1955 Howard Cassady, Ohio State	1980 George Rogers, South Carolina	Southern California
1956 Paul Hornung, Notre Dame	1981 Marcus Allen, So. Calif.	2003 Jason White, Oklahoma
1957 John Crow, Texas A & M	1982 Herschel Walker, Georgia	
1958 Pete Dawkins, Army	1983 Mike Rozier, Nebraska	

2003 NCAA CHAMPIONSHIP PLAYOFFS

DIVISION I-AA

Quarterfinals
(Dec. 6, 2003)
Delaware 37, Northern Iowa 7
Colgate 28, Western Illinois 27
Wofford 34, Western Kentucky 17
Florida Atlantic 48, Northern Arizona 25

Semifinals
(Dec. 13, 2003)
Colgate 36, Florida Atlantic 24
Delaware 24, Wofford 9

Championship
(Dec. 19, 2003)
Delaware 40, Colgate 0

DIVISION II

Quarterfinals
(Nov. 29, 2003)
North Dakota 36, Winona State 29
Grand Valley State 10, Saginaw Valley
State 3
North Alabama 41, Carson-Newman 9
Texas A&M-Kingsville 49, Central
Oklahoma 6

Semifinals
(Dec. 6, 2003)
North Dakota 29, North Alabama 22
Grand Valley State 31, Texas
A&M-Kingsville 3

Championship
(Dec. 13, 2003)
Grand Valley State 10, North Dakota 3

DIVISION III

Quarterfinals
(Dec. 7, 2003)
Bridgewater 13, Lycoming 9
Mount Union 56, Wheaton 10
Rensselaer 21, Ithaca 16
St. John's (Minn.) 31, Linfield 25

Semifinals
(Dec. 13, 2003)
Mount Union 66, Bridgewater 0
St. John's (Minn.) 38, Rensselaer 10

Championship
(Dec. 20, 2003)
St. John's (Minn.) 24, Mount Union 6

2003 NATIONAL ASSOCIATION OF INTERCOLLEGIATE ATHLETICS CHAMPIONSHIPS

Quarterfinals
(Nov. 29, 2003)
St. Francis (Ind.) 41, St. Ambrose (Iowa) 14
Carroll (Mont.) 49, Mary (N.D.) 7
Northwestern Oklahoma State 24, Dickinson State (N.D.)
17
Sioux Falls (S.D.) 33, Northwestern (Iowa) 7

Semifinals
(Dec. 6, 2003)
Carroll (Mont.) 38, St. Francis (Ind.) 14
Northwestern Oklahoma State 16, Sioux Falls (S.D.) 13
Championship
(Dec. 20, 2003)
Carroll (Mont.) 41, Northwestern Oklahoma State 28

COLLEGE FOOTBALL HALL OF FAME

(P.O. Box 11146, South Bend, Indiana)
NOTE: Date given is player's last year of competition.

Players

Abell, Earl—Colgate, 1915	Anderson, Bob P.—Army, 1959	Baker, John—So. Calif., 1931
Agase, Alex—Purdue/Illinois, 1946	Anderson, Dick—Colorado, 1967	Baker, Terry—Oregon State, 1962
Agganis, Harry—Boston Univ., 1952	Anderson, Donny—Texas Tech, 1965	Ballin, Harold—Princeton, 1914
Albert, Frank—Stanford, 1941	Anderson, H. (Hunk)—Notre Dame, 1921	Banker, Bill—Tulane, 1929
Aldrich, Chas. (Ki)—Texas Christian, 1938	Arnett, Jon—So. Calif., 1956	Banonis, Vince—Detroit, 1941
Aldrich, Malcolm—Yale, 1921	Atkins, Doug—Tennessee, 1952	Barnes, Stanley—So. Calif., 1921
Alexander, Joseph—Syracuse, 1920	Babich, Bob—Miami-Ohio, 1968	Barrett, Charles—Cornell, 1915
Allen, Marcus—So. Calif., 1981	Bacon, C. Everett—Wesleyan, 1912	Baston, Bert—Minnesota, 1916
Alworth, Lance—Arkansas, 1961	Bagnell, Francis (Reds)—Pennsylvania, 1950	Battles, Cliff—W. Va. Wesleyan, 1931
Ameche, Alan (Horse)—Wisconsin, 1954	Bailey, Johnny—Texas A&M, 1989	Baugh, Sammy—Texas Christian, 1936
Amling, Warren—Ohio State, 1946	Baker, Hobart (Hobey)—Princeton, 1913	Baughan, Maxie—Georgia Tech, 1959
		Bausch, James—Kansas, 1930

Beagle, Ron—Navy, 1955
Beasley, Terry—Auburn, 1971
Beban, Gary—UCLA, 1967
Bechtol, Hub—Texas Tech, 1946
Beck, Ray—Georgia Tech, 1951
Beckett, John—Oregon, 1913
Bednarik, Chuck—Pennsylvania 1948
Behm, Forrest—Nebraska, 1940
Bell, Bobby—Minnesota, 1962
Bell, Ricky—Southern California, 1976
Bellino, Joe—Navy, 1960
Below, Marty—Wisconsin, 1923
Benbrook, A.—Michigan, 1911
Bentrim, Jeff—North Dakota State, 1986
Bertelli, A.—Notre Dame, 1943
Berry, Charlie—Lafayette, 1924
Berwanger, John (Jay)—Chicago, 1935
Bettencourt, Larry—St. Mary's, 1927
Biletnikoff, Fred—Florida State, 1964
Blanchard, Felix (Doc)—Army, 1946
Blazine, Tony—Ill. Wesleyan, 1934
Bock, Ed—Iowa State, 1938
Bomar, Lynn—Vanderbilt, 1924
Bomeisler, Doug (Bo)—Yale, 1913
Booth, Albie—Yale, 1931
Bork, George—Northern Illinois, 1963
Borries, Fred—Navy, 1934
Bosely, Bruce—West Virginia, 1955
Bosseler, Don—Miami (Fla.), 1956
Bottari, Vic—California, 1939
Bowden, Murry—Dartmouth, 1970
Boynton, Ben—Williams, 1920
Bozis, Al—Georgetown, 1941
Bradshaw, Terry—Louisiana Tech, 1969
Brewer, Charles—Harvard, 1895
Bright, John—Drake, 1951
Brodie, John—Stanford, 1956
Brooke, George—Pennsylvania, 1895
Brosky, Al—Illinois, 1952
Brown, Bob—Nebraska, 1963
Brown, George—Navy/San Diego State, 1947
Brown, Gordon—Yale, 1900
Brown, Jim—Syracuse, 1956
Brown, John, Jr.—Navy, 1913
Brown, Johnny Mack—Alabama, 1925
Brown, Raymond (Tay)—So. Calif., 1932
Brown, Tom—Minnesota, 1960
Browner, Ross—Notre Dame, 1977
Bruner, Teel—Centre College (Ky.), 1985
Buchanan, Buck—Grambling State, 1962
Budde, Brad—So. Calif., 1979
Bunker, Paul—Army, 1902
Burford, Chris—Stanford, 1959
Burris, Kurt—Oklahoma, 1954
Burton, Ron—Northwestern, 1956
Butkus, Dick—Illinois, 1964
Butler, Kevin—Georgia, 1984
Butler, Robert—Wisconsin, 1912
Cafego, George—Tennessee, 1939
Cagle, Chris—SW La./Army, 1929
Cain, John—Alabama, 1932
Calip, Brad—East Central (Okla.), 1984
Cameron, Eddie—Wash. & Lee, 1924
Campbell, David C.—Harvard, 1901
Campbell, Earl—Texas, 1977
Cannon, Billy—Louisiana State, 1959
Cannon, Jack—Notre Dame, 1929
Cappelletti, John—Penn State, 1973
Carideo, Frank—Notre Dame, 1930
Caroline, J.C.—Illinois, 1954
Carney, Charles—Illinois, 1921
Carpenter, Bill—Army, 1959
Carpenter, C. Hunter—VPI, 1905
Carroll, Charles—Washington, 1928
Carson, Harry—So. Carolina State, 1975
Carter, Anthony—Michigan, 1982
Casanova, Tommy—Louisiana State, 1971
Casey, Edward L.—Harvard, 1919
Cason, Rod—Angelo State, 1971
Cassady, Howard—Ohio State, 1955

Casillas, Tony—Oklahoma, 1985
Chamberlain, Guy—Nebraska, 1915
Chapman, Sam—Cal.-Berkeley, 1938
Chappuis, Bob—Michigan, 1947
Christman, Paul—Missouri, 1940
Cichy, Joe—North Dakota State, 1970
Clark, Earl (Dutch)—Colo. College, 1929
Cleary, Paul—So. Calif., 1947
Clevenger, Zora—Indiana, 1903
Cloud, Jack—William & Mary, 1948
Cochran, Gary—Princeton, 1895
Cody, Josh—Vanderbilt, 1920
Coleman, Don—Mich. State, 1951
Conerly, Chuck—Mississippi, 1947
Connor, George—Notre Dame, 1947
Cooper, Bill—Muskingum (Ohio), 1960
Corbin, W.—Yale, 1888
Corbus, William—Stanford, 1933
Cowan, Hector—Princeton, 1889
Covert, Jimbo—Pittsburgh, 1983
Coy, Edward H. (Tad)—Yale, 1909
Crawford, Brad—Franklin (Ind.), 1977
Crawford, Fred—Duke, 1933
Crow, John D.—Texas A & M, 1957
Crowley, James—Notre Dame, 1924
Csonka, Larry—Syracuse, 1967
Cutter, Slade—Navy, 1934
Czarobski, Ziggie—Notre Dame, 1947
Dale, Carroll—Virginia Tech, 1959
Dalrymple, Gerald—Tulane, 1931
Dalton, John—Navy, 1912
Daly, Charles—Harvard/Army, 1902
Daniell, Averell—Pittsburgh, 1936
Daniell, James—Ohio State, 1941
Davies, Tom—Pittsburgh, 1921
Davis, Ernest—Syracuse, 1961
Davis, Glenn—Army, 1946
Davis, Harold—Westminster (Pa.), 1956
Davis, Robert T.—Georgia Tech, 1947
Dawkins, Pete—Army, 1958
Delaney, Joe—Northwestern State, 1980
Deery, Tom—Widener, 1981
DeLong, Steve—Tennessee, 1964
Dement, Kenneth—SE Missouri, 1954
Den Herder, Vern—Central (Iowa), 1970
De Rogatis, Al—Duke, 1940
DesJardien, Paul—Chicago 1914
Devino, Aubrey—Iowa, 1921
DeWitt, John—Princeton, 1903
Dial, Buddy—Rice, 1958
Dicus, Chuck—Arkansas, 1970
Dierdorf, Dan—Michigan, 1970
Ditka, Mike—Pittsburgh, 1960
Dobbs, Glenn—Tulsa, 1942
Dodd, Bobby—Tennessee, 1930
Donan, Holland—Princeton, 1950
Donchess, Joseph—Pittsburgh, 1929
Dorsett, Tony—Pittsburgh, 1976
Dougherty, Nathan—Tennessee, 1909
Dove, Bob—Notre Dame, 1942
Drahos, Nick—Cornell, 1940
Driscoll, Paddy—Northwestern, 1917
Drury, Morley—So. Calif., 1927
Dryer, Fred—San Diego State, 1968
Dudek, Joe—Plymouth State, 1985
Duden, Dick—Navy, 1945
Dudley, William (Bill)—Virginia, 1941
Duncan, Randy—Iowa, 1958
Easley, Ken—UCLA, 1980
Eckersall, Walter—Chicago, 1906
Edwards, Turk—Washington State, 1931
Edwards, William—Princeton, 1900
Eichenlaub, R.—Notre Dame, 1913
Eisenhauer, Steve—Navy, 1953
Elking, Larry—Baylor, 1964
Elliott, Chalmers—Purdue, 1944 & Mich., 1947
Elliott, Pete—Michigan, 1948
Elmendorf, Dave—Texas A & M, 1970
Elway, John—Stanford, 1982
Emanuel, Frank—Tennessee, 1965
Evans, Ray—Kansas, 1947
Exendine, Albert—Carlisle, 1908

Falaschi, Nello—Santa Clara, 1937
Fears, Tom—Santa Clara/UCLA, 1947
Feathers, Beattie—Tennessee, 1933
Fenimore, Robert—Oklahoma State, 1947
Fenton, G.E. (Doc)—Louisiana State, 1910
Ferguson, Bob—Ohio State, 1961
Ferraro, John—So. Calif., 1944
Fesler, Wesley—Ohio State, 1930
Fincher, Bill—Georgia Tech, 1920
Fischer, Bill—Notre Dame, 1948
Fish, Hamilton—Harvard, 1909
Fisher, Robert—Harvard, 1911
Flowers, Abe—Georgia Tech, 1920
Flowers, Charlie—Mississippi, 1959
Floyd, George—Eastern Kentucky, 1981
Fortmann, Daniel—Colgate, 1935
Fralic, Bill—Pittsburgh, 1984
Francis, Sam—Nebraska, 1936
Franck, George (Sonny)—Minnesota, 1940
Franco, Edmund (Ed)—Fordham, 1937
Frank, Clint—Yale, 1937
Franz, Rodney—California, 1949
Frederickson, Tucker—Auburn, 1964
Friedman, Benny—Michigan, 1926
Gabriel, Roman—North Carolina St., 1961
Gain, Bob—Kentucky, 1950
Galiffa, Arnold—Army, 1949
Galimore, Willie—Florida A & M, 1956
Gallarneau, Hugh—Stanford, 1941
Gamble, Kenny—Colgate, 1987
Garbisch, Edgar—Army, 1924
Garrett, Mike—So. Calif., 1965
Gelbert, Charles—Pennsylvania, 1896
Geyer, Forest—Oklahoma, 1915
Gibbs, Jake—Mississippi, 1960
Giel, Paul—Minnesota, 1953
Gifford, Frank—So. Calif., 1951
Gilbert, Chris—Texas, 1968
Gilbert, Walter—Auburn, 1936
Gilmer, Harry—Alabama, 1947
Gipp, George—Notre Dame, 1920
Gladchuk, Chet—Boston College, 1940
Glass, Bill—Baylor, 1956
Glover, Rich—Nebraska, 1972
Goldberg, Marshall—Pittsburgh, 1938
Goodreault, Gene—Boston College, 1940
Gordon, Walter—California, 1918
Governale, Paul—Columbia, 1942
Grabowski, Jim—Illinois, 1965
Graham, Otto—Northwestern, 1943
Gradishar, Randy—Ohio State, 1973
Grange, Harold (Red)—Illinois, 1925
Grayson, Roberty—Stanford, 1935
Green, Charles—Wittenberg, 1964
Green, Darrell—Texas A&I, 1982
Green, Hugh—Pittsburgh, 1980
Green, Joe—North Texas State, 1968
Green, Tim—Syracuse, 1985
Griese, Bob—Purdue, 1966
Griffin, Archie—Ohio State, 1975
Grinnell, William—Tufts, 1934
Groom, Jerry—Notre Dame, 1950
Guglielmi, Ralph—Notre Dame, 1954
Gulick, Merel—Hobart, 1929
Guy, Ray—So. Mississippi, 1972
Guyon, Joe—Georgia Tech, 1919
Hadl, John—Kansas, 1961
Hale, Edwin—Mississippi Col., 1921
Hall, Parker—Mississippi, 1938
Ham, Jack—Penn State, 1970
Hamilton, Robert (Bones)—Stanford, 1935
Hamilton, Tom—Navy, 1925
Hannah, John—Alabama, 1972
Hanson, Vic—Syracuse, 1926
Harder, Pat—Wisconsin, 1942
Hardwick, H. (Tack)—Harvard, 1914
Hare, T. Truxton—Pennsylvania, 1900

Harley, Chick—Ohio State, 1919
Harmon, Tom—Michigan, 1940
Harpster, Howard—Carnegie Tech, 1928
Harris, Wayne—Arkansas, 1960
Hart, Edward J. Princeton, 1911
Hart, Leon—Notre Dame, 1949
Hartman, Bill—Georgia, 1937
Haslett, Jim—Indiana (Pa.), 1978
Hawkins, Frank—Nevada, 1980
Haynes, Michael—Arizona State, 1975
Hazel, Homer—Rutgers, 1924
Healey, Ed—Dartmouth, 1916
Heffelfiner, W. (Pudge)—Yale, 1891
Hein, Mel—Washington State, 1930
Heinrich, Don—Washington, 1952
Hendricks, Ted—Miami, 1968
Henley, Garney—Huron, 1959
Henry, Wilbur—Wash. & Jefferson, 1919
Herschberger, Clarence—Chicago, 1899
Herwig, Robert—California, 1937
Heston, Willie—Michigan, 1904
Hickman, Herman—Tennessee, 1931
Hickok, William—Yale, 1895
Hicks, John—Ohio State, 1973
Hill, Dan—Duke, 1938
Hillebrand, A.R. (Doc)—Princeton, 1900
Hinkey, Frank—Yale, 1894
Hinkle, Carl—Vanderbilt, 1937
Hinkle, Clark—Bucknell, 1932
Hirsch, Elroy—Wisconsin/Michigan, 1943
Hitchcock, James—Auburn, 1932
Hoage, Terry—Georgia, 1983
Hoffman, Frank—Notre Dame, 1931
Hogan, James J.—Yale, 1904
Holland, Jerome (Brud)—Cornell, 1938
Holleder, Don—Army, 1955
Hollenbeck, William—Pennsylvania, 1908
Holovak, Michael—Boston College, 1942
Holt, Pierce—Angelo State, 1980
Holub, E.J.—Texas Tech, 1960
Hornung, Paul—Notre Dame, 1956
Horrell, Edwin—California, 1924
Horvath, Les—Ohio State, 1944
Howe Arthur—Yale, 1911
Howell, Millard (Dixie)—Alabama, 1934
Hubbard, Cal—Centenary, 1926
Hubbard, John—Amherst, 1906
Hubert, Allison—Alabama, 1925
Huff, Robert Lee (Sam)—W. Va., 1955
Humble, Weldon G.—Rice, 1946
Hunley, Ricky—Arizona, 1983
Hunt, Jackie—Marshall, 1941
Hunt, Joel—Texas A & M, 1927
Huntington, Ellery—Colgate, 1914
Hutson, Don—Alabama, 1934
Ingram, James—Navy, 1906
Iacavazzi, Cosmo—Princeton, 1964
Isbell, Cecil—Purdue, 1937
Jablonsky, Harvey—Wash. U./Army, 1933
Jackson, Bo—Auburn, 1985
Jackson, Keith—Oklahoma, 1987
Janowicz, Vic—Ohio State, 1951
Jefferson, John—Arizona State, 1977
Jenkins, Darold—Missouri, 1941
Jensen, Jack—Cal.-Berkeley, 1948
Joesting, Herbert—Minnesota, 1927
Johnson, Billy—Widener, 1973
Johnson, Gary—Grambling State, 1974
Johnson, James—Carlisle, 1903
Johnson, Robert—Tennessee, 1967
Johnson, Ron—Michigan, 1968
Jones, Brent—Santa Clara, 1985
Jones, Calvin—Iowa, 1955
Jones, Gormer—Ohio State, 1935
Jones, Stan—Maryland, 1953
Jordan, Lee Roy—Alabama, 1962
Juhan, Frank—Univ. of South, 1910
Justice, Charlie—North Carolina, 1949
Kaer, Mort—So. Calif., 1926
Kapp, Joe—California, 1958

Karras, Alex—Iowa, 1957
Kavanaugh, Kenneth—Louisiana State, 1939
Kaw, Edgar—Cornell, 1922
Kazmaier, Richard—Princeton, 1951
Keck, James—Princeton, 1921
Kelley, Larry—Yale, 1936
Kelly, William—Montana, 1926
Kenna, Ed—Syracuse, 1966
Kern, George—Boston College, 1941
Ketcham, Henry—Yale, 1913
Keyes, Leroy—Purdue, 1968
Killinger, William—Penn State, 1922
Kilmer, Billy—UCLA, 1960
Kimbrough, John—Texas A & M, 1940
Kinard, Frank—Mississippi, 1937
Kinard, Terry—Clemson, 1982
Kiner, Steve—Tennessee, 1969
King, Philip—Princeton, 1893
Kinnick, Nile—Iowa, 1939
Kipke, Harry—Michigan, 1923
Kirkpatrick, John Reed—Yale, 1910
Kitzmiller, John—Oregon, 1929
Koch, Barton—Baylor, 1931
Kitner, Malcolm—Texas, 1942
Kramer, Ron—Michigan, 1956
Kroll, Alex—Rutgers, 1961
Krueger, Charlie—Texas A & M, 1957
Kwalick, Ted—Penn State, 1968
Lach, Steve—Duke, 1941
Lane, Myles—Dartmouth, 1927
Lanier, Sr., Willie—Morgan State, 1966
Lattner, Joseph J.—Notre Dame, 1953
Lauricella, Hank—Tennessee, 1952
Lautenschlaeger—Tulane, 1925
Layden, Elmer—Notre Dame, 1924
Layne, Bobby—Texas, 1947
Lea, Langdon—Princeton, 1895
LeBaron, Eddie—Univ. of Pacific, 1949
LeClair, Jim—North Dakota, 1971
Leech, James—Va. Mil. Inst., 1920
Lester, Darrell—Texas Christian, 1935
Levias, Jerry—Southern Methodist, 1968
Lewis, D. D.—Mississippi State, 1968
Lilly, Bob—Texas Christian, 1960
Lio, Augie—Georgetown, 1940
Lockbaum, Gordie—Holy Cross, 1987
Locke, Gordon—Iowa, 1922
Lomax, Neil—Portland (Ore.) State, 1980
Long, Chuck—Iowa, 1985
Long, Mel—Toledo, 1971
Loria, Frank—Virginia Tech, 1967
Lott, Ronnie—So. Calif., 1980
Lourie, Don—Princeton, 1921
Lucas, Richard—Penn State, 1959
Luckman, Sid—Columbia, 1938
Lujack, John—Notre Dame, 1947
Lund, J. L. (Pug)—Minnesota, 1934
Lynch, Jim—Notre Dame, 1966
MacAfee, Ken—Notre Dame, 1977
Macomber, Bart—Illinois, 1915
MacLeod, Robert—Dartmouth, 1938
Maegle, Dick—Rice, 1954
Mahan, Edward W.—Harvard, 1915
Majors, John—Tennessee, 1956
Mallory, William—Yale, 1893
Mancha, Vaughn—Alabama, 1947
Mandich, James—Michigan, 1969
Mann, Gerald—So. Methodist, 1927
Manning, Archie—Mississippi, 1970
Manske, Edgar—Northwestern, 1933
Marinaro, Ed—Cornell, 1971
Marino, Dan—Pittsburgh, 1982
Markov, Vic—Washington, 1937
Marshall, Robert—Minnesota, 1907
Martin, Jim—Notre Dame, 1949
Matson, Ollie—San Fran. U., 1952
Matthews, Ray—Texas Christian, 1928
Maulbetsch, John—Michigan, 1914
Mauthe, J. L. (Pete)—Penn State, 1912

Maxwell, Robert—Chicago/Swarthmore, 1906
McAfee, George—Duke, 1939
McCallum, Napoleon—Navy, 1985
McCauley, Don—North Carolina, 1970
McClung, Thomas L.—Yale, 1891
McColl, William F.—Stanford, 1951
McCormick, James B.—Princeton, 1907
McDonald, Tom—Oklahoma, 1956
McDowall, Jack—No. Carolina State, 1927
McElhenny, Hugh—Washington, 1951
McEver, Gene—Tennessee, 1931
McEwan, John—Minn./Army, 1916
McFadden, J. B.—Clemson, 1939
McFadin, Bud—Texas, 1950
McGee, Mike—Duke, 1959
McGinley, Edward—Pennsylvania, 1924
McGovern, J.—Minnesota, 1910
McGraw, Thurman—Colorado State, 1949
McGriff, Tyrone—Florida A & M, 1979
McKeever, Mike—So. Calif., 1960
McKenzie, Reggie—Michigan, 1971
McLaren, George—Pittsburgh, 1918
McMahon, Jim—Brigham Young, 1981
McMillan, Dan—So. Calif./California, 1922
McMillin, A. N. (Bo)—Centre, 1921
McWhorter, Robert—Georgia, 1913
Mercer, Leroy—Pennsylvania, 1912
Meredith, Don—So. Methodist, 1959
Merritt, Frank—Army, 1943
Metzger, Bert—Notre Dame, 1930
Meyland, Wayne—Nebraska, 1967
Michaels, Lou—Kentucky, 1957
Michels, John—Tennessee, 1952
Mickal, Abe—Louisiana State, 1935
Miller, Creighton—Notre Dame, 1943
Miller, Don—Notre Dame, 1925
Miller, Edgar (Rip)—Notre Dame, 1924
Miller, Eugene—Penn State, 1913
Miller, Fred—Notre Dame, 1928
Millner, Wayne—Notre Dame, 1935
Milstead, Century—Wabash/Yale, 1923
Minds, John—Pennsylvania, 1897
Minisi, Anthony—Navy/Pennsylvania, 1947
Mitchell, Lydell—Penn State, 1971
Modzelewski, Dick—Maryland, 1952
Moffatt, Alex—Princeton, 1884
Molinski, Ed—Tennessee, 1940
Montgomery, Cliff—Columbia, 1933
Montgomery, Wilbert—Abilene Christian, 1976
Moomaw, Donn—UCLA, 1952
Morley, William—Columbia, 1903
Morris, George—Georgia Tech, 1952
Morris, Larry—Georgia Tech, 1954
Morton, Craig—California, 1964
Morton, William—Dartmouth, 1931
Moscrip, Monk—Stanford, 1935
Muller, Harold (Brick)—Calif., 1922
Musso, Johnny—Alabama, 1971
Nagurski, Bronko—Minnesota, 1929
Neighbors, Billy—Alabama, 1961
Nevers, Ernie—Stanford, 1925
Newell, Marshall—Harvard, 1893
Newman, Harry—Michigan, 1932
Newsome, Ozzie—Alabama, 1977
Nielsen, Gifford—Brigham Young, 1976
Nix, Dwayne, Texas A&M-Kingsville, 1968
Nobis, Tommy—Texas, 1965
Nomellini, Leo—Minnesota, 1949
Oberland, Andrew—Dartmouth, 1925
O'Brien, Davey—Texas Christian, 1938
O'Brien, Ken—Cal.-Davis, 1982
O'Dea, Pat—Wisconsin, 1899
Odell, Robert—Pennsylvania, 1943
O'Hearn, J.—Cornell, 1915
Olds, Robin—Army, 1942

Oliphant, Elmer—Purdue/Army, 1917
Olsen, Merlin—Utah State, 1961
Onkotz, Dennis—Penn State, 1969
Oosterbaan, Ben—Michigan, 1927
O'Rourke, Charles—Boston College, 1940
Orsi, John—Colgate, 1931
Osgood, W. D.—Cornell/Pennsylvania, 1895
Osmanski, William—Holy Cross, 1938
Outland, John—Kansas/Pennsylvania, 1899
Owen, George—Harvard, 1922
Owens, Jim—Oklahoma, 1949
Owens, Steve—Oklahoma, 1969
Page, Alan—Notre Dame, 1966
Palumbo, Joe—U. of Virginia, 1951
Pardee, Jack—Texas A & M, 1956
Parilli, Vito (Babe)—Kentucky, 1951
Parker, Clarence (Ace)—Duke, 1936
Parker, Jackie—Miss. State, 1953
Parker, James—Ohio State, 1956
Payton, Walter—Jackson State, 1974
Pazzetti, V. J.—Wesleyan/Lehigh, 1912
Peabody, Endicott—Harvard, 1941
Peck, Robert—Pittsburgh, 1916
Pellegrini, Bob—Maryland, 1955
Pennock, Stanley B.—Harvard, 1914
Pfann, George—Cornell, 1923
Phillips, H. D.—Univ. of South, 1904
Phillips, Loyd—Arkansas, 1966
Pingel, John—Michigan State, 1938
Pihos, Pete—Indiana, 1945
Pinckert, Ernie—So. Calif., 1931
Plunkett, Jim—Stanford, 1970
Poe, Arthur—Princeton, 1899
Pollard, Fritz—Brown, 1916
Poole, Barney—Miss./Army, 1947
Powell, Marvin—So. Calif., 1976
Pregulman, Merv—Michigan, 1943
Price, Eddie—Tulane, 1949
Pritchard, Ron—Arizona State, 1968
Pruitt, Greg—Oklahoma, 1972
Pugh, Larry—Westminster, Pa., 1964
Pund, Henry—Georgia Tech, 1928
Ramsey, Gerrard—Wm. & Mary, 1942
Rauch, John—Georgia, 1948
Reasons, Gary—Northwestern State (La.), 1983
Redell, Bill—Occidental, 1963
Redman, Rick—Washington, 1964
Reeds, Claude—Oklahoma, 1913
Reid, Mike—Penn State, 1970
Reid, Steve—Northwestern, 1936
Reid, William—Harvard, 1900
Reifsnyder, Bob—Navy, 1958 ˙
Renfro, Mel—Oregon, 1963
Rentner, Ernest—Northwestern, 1932
Reppert, Scott—Lawrence (Wis.), 1982
Ressler, Glenn—Penn State, 1964
Reynolds, Robert—Nebraska, 1952
Reynolds, Robert—Stanford, 1935
Rhino, Randy—Georgia Tech, 1974
Rhome, Jerry—Tulsa, 1964
Richardson, Willie—Jackson State (Miss.), 1962
Richter, Les—California, 1951
Richter, Pat—Wisconsin, 1962
Riley, John—Northwestern, 1931
Rimington, Dave—Nebraska, 1982
Rinehart, Charles—Lafayette, 1897
Ritchie, Richard—Texas A & M, 1977
Ritcher, Jim—No. Carolina St., 1979
Roberts, Calvin—Gustavus Adolphus (Minn.), 1952
Roberts, J. D.—Oklahoma, 1953
Robeson, Paul—Rutgers, 1918
Robinson, Dave—Penn State, 1962
Robinson, Jerry—UCLA, 1978
Rocker, Tracy—Auburn, 1988
Rodgers, Ira—West Virginia, 1919
Rodgers, Johnny—Nebraska, 1972
Rogers, Edward L.—Minnesota, 1903

Rogers, George—South Carolina, 1980
Roland, Johnny—Missouri, 1965
Romig, Joe—Colorado, 1961
Rosenberg, Aaron—So. Calif., 1934
Ross, Dan—Northeastern, 1978
Rote, Kyle—So. Methodist, 1950
Routt, Joe—Texas A & M, 1937
Salmon, Louis—Notre Dame, 1904
Sanders, Barry—Oklahoma State, 1988
Sarkisian, Alex—Northwestern, 1948
Sauer, George—Nebraska, 1933
Savitsky, George—Pennsylvania, 1947
Saxon, Jimmy—Texas, 1961
Sayers Gale—Kansas, 1964
Scarbath, Jack—Maryland, 1952
Scarlett, Hunter—Pennsylvania, 1909
Schloredt, Bob—Washington, 1960
Schmidt, Joe—Pittsburgh, 1952
Schoonover, Wear—Arkansas, 1929
Schreiner, Dave—Wisconsin, 1942
Schultz, Adolf (Germany)—Mich., 1908
Schwab, Frank—Lafayette, 1922
Schwartz, Marchmont—Notre Dame, 1931
Schwegler, Paul—Washington, 1931
Scott, Clyde—Arkansas, 1949
Scott, Freddie—Amherst, 1973
Scott, Richard—Navy, 1947
Scott, Tom—Virginia, 1953
Seibels, Henry—Sewanee, 1899
Sellers, Ron—Florida State, 1968
Selmon, Lee Roy—Oklahoma, 1975
Sewell, Harley—Texas, 1952
Shakespeare, Bill—Notre Dame, 1935
Shell, Donnie—So. Carolina St., 1973
Shelton, Murray—Cornell, 1915
Shevlin, Tom—Yale, 1905
Shively, Bernie—Illinois, 1926
Simons, Claude—Tulane, 1934
Sims, Billy—Oklahoma, 1979
Simpson, O. J.—So. Calif., 1968
Singletary, Mike—Baylor, 1980
Sington, Fred—Alabama, 1930
Sinkwich, Frank—Georgia, 1942
Sisemore, Jerry—Texas, 1972
Sitko, Emil—Notre Dame, 1949
Skladany, Joe—Pittsburgh, 1933
Slater, F.F. (Duke)—Iowa, 1921
Smith, Billy Ray—Arkansas, 1982
Smith, Bruce—Minnesota, 1941
Smith, Bubba—Michigan State, 1966
Smith, Ernie—So. Calif., 1932
Smith, Harry—So. Calif., 1939
Smith, Jim Ray—Baylor, 1954
Smith, John (Clipper)—Notre Dame, 1927
Smith, Riley—Alabama, 1935
Smith, Vernon—Georgia, 1931
Snow, Neil—Michigan, 1901
Spani, Gary—Kansas State, 1977
Sparlis, Al—UCLA, 1945
Spears, Clarence W.—Dartmouth, 1915
Spears, W.D.—Vanderbilt, 1927
Sprackling, William—Brown, 1911
Sprague, M. (Bud)—Texas/Army, 1928
Spurrier, Steve—Florida, 1966
Stafford, Harrison—Texas, 1932
Stagg, Amos Alonzo—Yale, 1889
Stanfill, Bill—Georgia, 1968
Starcevich, Max—Washington, 1936
Staubach, Roger—Navy, 1963
Steffen, Walter—Chicago, 1908
Steffy, Joe—Army, 1947
Stein, Herbert—Pittsburgh, 1921
Steuber, Robert—Missouri, 1943
Stevens, Mal—Yale, 1923
Stevenson, Ben—Tuskegee (Ala.), 1930
Stevenson, Vincent—Pennsylvania, 1905
Stillwagon, Jim—Ohio State, 1970
Stinchcomb, Gaylord—Ohio State, 1920
Strom, Brock—Air Force, 1959
Stromberg, William—Johns Hopkins, 1981

Strong, Ken—New York Univ., 1928
Strupper, George—Georgia Tech, 1917
Stuhldreher, Harry—Notre Dame, 1924
Stydahar, Joe—West Virginia, 1935
Suffridge, Robert—Tennessee, 1940
Suhey, Steve—Penn State, 1947
Sullivan, Pat—Auburn, 1971
Sundstrom, Frank—Cornell, 1923
Swann, Lynn—So. Calif., 1973
Swanson, Clarence—Nebraska, 1921
Swiacki, Bill—Holy Cross/Colombia, 1947
Swink, Jim—Texas Christian, 1956
Talboom, Eddie—Wyoming, 1950
Taliafarro, George—Indiana, 1948
Tarkenton, Fran—Georgia, 1960
Tatum, Jack—Ohio State, 1970
Tavener, John—Indiana, 1944
Taylor, Bruce—Boston Univ., 1969
Taylor, Charles—Stanford, 1942
Theismann, Joe—Notre Dame, 1970
Thomas, Aurelius—Ohio State, 1957
Thompson, Joe—Pittsburgh, 1907
Thomsen, Lynn—Austana, 1986
Thorne, Samuel B.—Yale, 1906
Thorpe, Jim—Carlisle, 1912
Ticknor, Ben—Harvard, 1930
Tigert, John—Vanderbilt, 1904
Tinsley, Gaynell—Louisiana State, 1936
Tipton, Eric—Duke, 1938
Tonnemaker, Clayton—Minnesota, 1949
Torrey, Robert—Pennsylvania, 1906
Trautman, Randy—Boise State, 1981
Travis, Ed Tarkio—Missouri, 1920
Trippi, Charles—Georgia, 1946
Tryon, J. Edward—Colgate, 1925
Tubbs, Jerry—Oklahoma, 1956
Utay, Joe—Texas A & M, 1907
Van Brocklin, Norm—Oregon, 1948
Van Pelt, Brad—Michigan State, 1972
Van Sickel, Dale—Florida, 1929
Van Surdam, Henderson—Wesleyan, 1905
Very, Dexter—Penn State, 1912
Vessels, Billy—Oklahoma, 1952
Vick, Ernie—Michigan, 1921
Wagner, Huber—Pittsburgh, 1913
Walker; Doak—So. Methodist, 1949
Walker, Herschel—Georgia, 1982
Wallace, Bill—Rice, 1935
Walsh, Adam—Notre Dame, 1924
Warburton, I. (Cotton)—So. Calif., 1934
Ward, Robert (Bob)—Maryland, 1951
Ware, Andre—Houston, 1989
Warner, William—Cornell, 1903
Washington, Ken—UCLA, 1939
Weatherall, Jim—Oklahoma, 1951
Webster, George—Mich. State, 1966
Wedemeyer, Herman J.—St. Mary's, 1947
Weekes, Harold—Columbia, 1902
Wehrli, Roger—Missouri, 1968
Weiner, Art—North Carolina, 1949
Weir, Ed—Nebraska, 1925
Welch, Gus—Carlisle, 1914
Weller, John—Princeton, 1935
Wendell, Percy—Harvard, 1913
West, D. Belford—Colgate, 1919
Westfall, Bob—Michigan, 1941
Weyand, Alex—Army, 1915
Wharton, Charles—Pennsylvania, 1896
Wheeler, Arthur—Princeton, 1894
White, Byron (Whizzer)—Colorado, 1937
White, Charles—So. Calif., 1979
White, Danny—Arizona State, 1973
White, Ed—California-Berkeley, 1968
White, Randy—Maryland, 1974
White, Reggie—Tennessee, 1983
Whitmire, Don—Alabama/Navy, 1944
Wickhorst, Frank—Navy, 1926
Widseth, Ed—Minnesota, 1936
Wildung, Richard—Minnesota, 1942
Williams, Bob—Notre Dame, 1950

Williams, Doug—Grambling, 1977
Williams, James—Rice, 1949
Willis, William—Ohio State, 1945
Wilson, George—Washington, 1925
Wilson, George—Lafayette, 1928
Wilson, Harry—Penn State/Army, 1923
Wilson, Marc—Brigham Young, 1979
Winslow, Kellen—Missouri, 1978
Wistert, Albert A.—Michigan, 1942

Wistert, Al—Michigan, 1942
Wistert, Frank (Whitey)—Michigan, 1933
Wood, Barry—Harvard, 1931
Wojciechowicz, Alex—Fordham, 1936
Wyant, Andrew—Bucknell/Chicago, 1894
Wyatt, Bowden—Tennessee, 1938
Wyckoff, Clint—Cornell, 1896
Yarr, Tom—Notre Dame, 1931
Yary, Ron—So. Calif., 1968

Yoder, Lloyd—Carnegie Tech, 1926
Young, Charles—So. Calif., 1972
Young, Claude (Buddy)—Illinois, 1946
Young, Harry—Wash. & Lee, 1916
Young, Steve—Brigham Young, 1983
Young, Walter—Oklahoma, 1938
Youngblood, Jack—Florida, 1970
Youngblood, Jim—Tennessee, 1972
Zarnas, Gus—Ohio State, 1937

Coaches

Bill Alexander
Dr. Ed Anderson
Ike Armstrong
Chris Ault
Earl Banks
Harry Baujan
Thomas Beck
Matty Bell
Hugo Bezdek
Dana X. Bible
Bernie Bierman
Bob Blackman
Earl (Red) Blaik
Frank Broyles
Earle Bruce
Paul "Bear" Bryant
Harold Burry
Jim Butterfield
James "Wally" Butts
Charles W. Caldwell
Walter Camp
Len Casanova
Marino Casem
Frank Cavanaugh
Jerry Claiborne
Richard Colman
Don Coryell
Carmen Cozza
Fritz Crisler
Duffy Daugherty
Bob Devaney
Dan Devine
Doug Dickey

Gil Dobie
Bobby Dodd
Terry Donahue
Michael Donohue
Vince Dooley
Gus Dorais
Bill Edwards
LaVell Edwards
Charles (Rip) Engle
Forest Evashevski
Don Faurot
Hayden Fry
Joseph Fusco
Jake Gaither
Sid Gillman
Ernest Godfrey
Ray Graves
Andy Gustafson
Jack Harding
Edward K. Hall
Richard Harlow
Jesse Harper
Percy Haughton
Woody Hayes
John W. Heisman
R.A. (Bob) Higgins
Paul Hoernemann
Orin E. Hollingberry
Frank Howard
Marcelino (Chelo)
   Huerta
William Ingram
Don James

Morley Jennings
Howard Jones
L. (Biff) Jones
Thomas (Tad) Jones
Ralph (Shug) Jordan
Bob Keade
Andy Kerr
Roy Kidd
Chuck Klausing
Frank Kush
Frank Leahy
George E. Little
Lou Little
El (Slip) Madigan
Fred Martinelli
Dave Maurer
Charley McClendon
Herbert McCracken
Daniel McGugin
John McKay
Allyn McKeen
DeOrmond (Tuss)
   McLaughry
John Merritt
L.R. (Dutch) Meyer
Bernie Moore
Scrappy Moore
Jack Mollenkopf
Ray Morrison
Darrell Mudra
Arnett "Ace" Mumford
George A. Munger
Clarence Munn

Frank Murray
William Murray
Ed (Hooks) Mylin
Earle (Greasy) Neale
Jess Neely
David Nelson
Robert Neyland
Billy Nicks
Homer Norton
Frank (Buck) O'Neill
Tom Osborne
Bennie Owen
Ara Parseghian
Doyt Perry
James Phalea
Tommy Prothro
John Ralston
Harold "Tubby" Ray-
   mond
Charlie Richard
E.N. Robinson
Knute Rockne
E. L. (Dick) Romney
William W. Roper
Darrell Royal
Ad Rutschman
Henry (Red) Sanders
George F. Sanford
Bo Schembechler
Ron Schipper
Francis A. Schmidt
Floyd (Ben)
   Schwartzwalder

Clark Shaughnessy
Buck Shaw
Edgar Sherman
Andrew L. Smith
Carl Snavely
Jim Sochor
Amos A. Stagg
Gilbert Steinke
Dick Strahm
Jock Sutherland
Barry Switzer
James Tatum
Grant Teaff
Frank W. Thomas
Lee Tressell
Thad Vann
John H. Vaught
Wallace Wade
Lynn Waldorf
Glenn (Pop) Warner
Frank Waters
George Welsh
E.E. (Tad) Wieman
John W. Wilce
Bud Wilkinson
Henry L. Williams
George W. Woodruff
Warren Woodson
Bowden Wyatt
Bill Yeoman
Fielding H. Yost
Jim Young
Robert Zuppke

Professional Football

SUPER BOWLS I-XXXVIII

Game	Date	Winner	Loser	Site	Attendance
XXXVIII	Feb. 1, 2004	New England (AFC) 32	Carolina (NFC) 29	Reliant Stadium, Houston, Tex.	71,525
XXXVII	Jan. 26, 2003	Tampa Bay (NFC) 48	Oakland Raiders (AFC) 21	Qualcomm Stadium, San Diego, Calif.	67,603
XXXVI	Feb. 3, 2002	New England (AFC) 20	St. Louis (NFC) 17	Superdome, New Orleans	72,922
XXXV	Jan. 28, 2001	Baltimore (AFC) 34	New York Giants (NFC) 7	Raymond James Stadium, Tampa, Fla.	71,921
XXXIV	Jan. 30, 2000	St. Louis (NFC) 23	Tennessee (AFC) 16	Georgia Dome, Atlanta, Ga.	72,625
XXXIII	Jan. 31, 1999	Denver (AFC) 34	Atlanta (NFC) 19	Pro Player Stadium, Miami, Fla.	74,803
XXXII	Jan. 25, 1998	Denver (AFC) 31	Green Bay (NFC) 24	Qualcomm Stadium, San Diego, Calif.	68,912
XXXI	Jan. 26, 1997	Green Bay (NFC) 35	New England (AFC) 21	Superdome, New Orleans, La.	72,301
XXX	Jan. 28, 1996	Dallas (NFC) 27	Pittsburgh (AFC) 17	Sun Devil Stadium, Tempe, Ariz.	76,347
XXIX	Jan. 29, 1995	San Francisco (NFC) 49	San Diego (AFC) 26	Joe Robbie Stadium, Miami, Fla.	74,107
XXVIII	Jan. 30, 1994	Dallas (NFC) 30	Buffalo (AFC) 13	Georgia Dome, Atlanta, Ga.	72,817
XXVII	Jan. 31, 1993	Dallas (NFC) 52	Buffalo (AFC) 17	Rose Bowl, Pasadena, Calif.	98,374
XXVI	Jan. 26, 1992	Washington (NFC) 37	Buffalo (AFC) 24	Metrodome, Minneapolis, Minn.	63,130
XXV	Jan. 27, 1991	Giants (NFC) 20	Buffalo (AFC) 19	Tampa Stadium, Tampa, Fla.	73,813
XXIV	Jan. 28, 1990	San Francisco (NFC) 55	Denver (AFC) 10	Superdome, New Orleans	72,919
XXIII	Jan. 22, 1989	San Francisco (NFC) 20	Cincinnati (AFC) 16	Joe Robbie Stadium, Miami, Fla.	75,179
XXII	Jan. 31, 1988	Washington (NFC) 42	Denver (AFC) 10	Jack Murphy Stadium, San Diego, Calif.	73,302
XXI	Jan. 25, 1987	Giants (NFC) 39	Denver (AFC) 20	Rose Bowl, Pasadena, Calif.	101,063
XX	Jan. 26, 1986	Chicago (NFC) 46	New England (AFC) 10	Superdome, New Orleans	73,818
XIX	Jan. 20, 1985	San Francisco (NFC) 38	Miami (AFC) 16	Stanford Stadium, Palo Alto, Calif.	84,059
XVIII	Jan. 22, 1984	Los Angeles Raiders (AFC) 38	Washington (NFC) 9	Tampa Stadium, Tampa, Fla	72,920
XVII	Jan. 30, 1983	Washington (NFC) 27	Miami (AFC) 17	Rose Bowl, Pasadena, Calif.	103,667
XVI	Jan. 24, 1982	San Francisco (NFC) 26	Cincinnati (AFC) 21	Silverdome, Pontiac, Mich.	81,270
XV	Jan. 25, 1981	Oakland (AFC) 27	Philadelphia (NFC) 10	Superdome, New Orleans	75,500

Game	Date	Winner	Loser	Site	Attendance
XIV	Jan. 20, 1980	Pittsburgh (AFC) 31	Los Angeles (NFC) 19	Rose Bowl, Pasadena	103,985
XIII	Jan. 21, 1979	Pittsburgh (AFC) 35	Dallas (NFC) 31	Orange Bowl, Miami	79,484
XII	Jan. 15, 1978	Dallas (NFC) 27	Denver (AFC) 10	Superdome, New Orleans	75,583
XI	Jan. 9, 1977	Oakland (AFC) 32	Minnesota (NFC) 14	Rose Bowl, Pasadena	103,424
X	Jan. 18, 1976	Pittsburgh (AFC) 21	Dallas (NFC) 17	Orange Bowl, Miami	80,187
IX	Jan. 12, 1975	Pittsburgh (AFC) 16	Minnesota (NFC) 6	Tulane Stadium, New Orleans	80,997
VIII	Jan. 13, 1974	Miami (AFC) 24	Minnesota (NFC) 7	Rice Stadium, Houston	71,882
VII	Jan. 14, 1973	Miami (AFC) 14	Washington (NFC) 7	Memorial Coliseum, Los Angeles	90,182
VI	Jan. 16, 1972	Dallas (NFC) 24	Miami (AFC) 3	Tulane Stadium, New Orleans	81,591
V	Jan. 17, 1971	Baltimore (AFC) 16	Dallas (NFC) 13	Orange Bowl, Miami	79,204
IV	Jan. 11, 1970	Kansas City (AFL) 23	Minnesota (NFL) 7	Tulane Stadium, New Orleans	80,562
III	Jan. 12, 1969	New York (AFL) 16	Baltimore (NFL) 7	Orange Bowl, Miami	75,389
II	Jan. 14, 1968	Green Bay (NFL) 33	Oakland (AFL) 14	Orange Bowl, Miami	75,546
I	Jan. 15, 1967	Green Bay (NFL) 35	Kansas City (AFL) 10	Memorial Coliseum, Los Angeles	61,946

NOTE: Super Bowls I to IV were played before the American Football League and National Football League merged into the NFL, which was divided into two conferences, the NFC and AFC.

NATIONAL FOOTBALL LEAGUE FINAL STANDINGS 2003

AMERICAN FOOTBALL CONFERENCE

	W	L	T	Pct	PF	PA
East						
New England Patriots[1]	14	2	0	.875	348	238
Miami Dolphins	10	6	0	.625	311	261
Buffalo Bills	6	10	0	.375	243	279
New York Jets	6	10	0	.375	283	299
North						
Baltimore Ravens[1]	10	6	0	.625	391	281
Cincinnati Bengals	8	8	0	.500	346	384
Pittsburgh Steelers	6	10	0	.375	300	327
Cleveland Browns	5	11	0	.312	254	322
South						
Indianapolis Colts[1]	12	4	0	.750	447	336
Tennessee Titans[2]	12	4	0	.750	435	324
Jacksonville Jaguars	5	11	0	.312	276	331
Houston Texans	5	11	0	.312	255	380
West						
Kansas City Chiefs[1]	13	3	0	.812	484	332
Denver Broncos[2]	10	6	0	.625	381	301
Oakland Raiders	4	12	0	.250	270	379
San Diego Chargers	4	12	0	.250	313	441

1. Division champion. 2. Wild card qualifier for playoffs. **Wild card:** Jan. 3, 2004: Tennessee 20, Baltimore 17; Jan. 4: Indianapolis 41, Denver 10. **Division:** Jan. 10, 2004: New England 17, Tennessee 14; Jan. 11: Indianapolis 38, Kansas City 31. **Conference:** Jan. 18: New England 24, Indianapolis 14.

NATIONAL FOOTBALL CONFERENCE

	W	L	T	Pct	PF	PA
East						
Philadelphia Eagles[1]	12	4	0	.750	374	287
Dallas Cowboys[2]	10	6	0	.625	289	260
Washington Redskins	5	11	0	.312	287	372
New York Giants	4	12	0	.250	243	387
North						
Green Bay Packers[1]	10	6	0	.625	442	307
Minnesota Vikings	9	7	0	.562	416	353
Chicago Bears	7	9	0	.438	283	346
Detroit Lions	5	11	0	.312	270	379
South						
Carolina Panthers [1]	11	5	0	.688	325	304
New Orleans Saints	8	8	0	.500	340	326
Tampa Bay Buccaneers	7	9	0	.438	301	264
Atlanta Falcons	5	11	0	.312	299	422
West						
St. Louis Rams[1]	12	4	0	.750	447	328
Seattle Seahawks[2]	10	6	0	.625	404	327
San Francisco 49ers	7	9	0	.438	384	337
Arizona Cardinals	4	12	0	.250	225	452

1. Division champion. 2. Wild card qualifier for playoffs. **Wild card:** Jan. 3, 2004: Carolina 29, Dallas 10; Jan. 4: Green Bay 33, Seattle 27 (OT). **Division:** Jan. 10, 2004: Carolina 29, St. Louis 23 (2OT); Jan. 11: Philadelphia 20, Green Bay 17 (OT). **Conference:** Jan. 18: Carolina 14, Philadelphia 3.

LEAGUE CHAMPIONSHIP—SUPER BOWL XXXVIII

(Feb. 1, 2004, Reliant Stadium, Houston, Tex. Attendance: 71,525. Time: 4:05)

Scoring

	1st Q	2nd Q	3rd Q	4th Q	Final
Carolina	0	10	0	19	**29**
New England	0	14	0	18	**32**

2nd: NE—TD: Branch 5-yd pass from Brady (Vinatieri kick), 11:55. TD: Givens 5-yd pass from Brady (Vinatieri kick), 14:42. CAR—TD: S. Smith 39-yd pass from Delhomme (Kasay kick), 13:51. FG: Kasay 50-yd, 15:00.

4th: NE—TD: A. Smith 2-yd run (Vinatieri kick), 0:11. TD: Vrabel 1-yd pass from Brady (Faulk run for 2-pt conversion), 12:09. FG: Vinatieri 41-yd, 14:56. CAR—TD: Foster 33-yd run (2-pt pass conversion failed), 2:21. TD: Muhammad 85-yd pass from Delhomme (2-pt pass conversion failed), 8:07. TD: Proehl 12-yd pass from Delhomme (Kasay kick), 13:52.

Individual Statistics

Passing: CAR—Delhomme 16–33 for 323 yds. NE—Brady 32–48 for 354 yds.

Rushing: CAR—Davis 13 for 49 yds, Foster 3 for 43 yds. NE—A. Smith 26 for 83 yds, Faulk 6 for 42 yds, Brady 2 for 12 yds, T. Brown 1 for −10 yds.

Receiving: CAR—Muhammad 4 for 140 yds, S. Smith 4 for 80 yds, Proehl 4 for 71 yds, Wiggins 2 for 21 yds, Foster 1 for 9 yds, Mangum 1 for 2 yds. NE—Branch 10 for 143 yds, T. Brown 8 for 76 yds, Givens 5 for 69 yds, Graham 4 for 46 yds, Faulk 4 for 19 yds, Brabel 1 for 1 yd.

Field goals: CAR—Kasay 1–1. NE—Vinatieri 1–3.

Punting: CAR—Sauerbrun 7. NE—Walter 5.

Kickoff Returns: CAR—Mangum 1, Smart 4, S. Smith 1. NE—B. Johnson 4.

Punt Returns: CAR—S. Smith 1. NE—Branch 1, T. Brown 4.

MVP: Tom Brady, New England quarterback.

Statistics of the Game

	Panthers	Patriots		Panthers	Patriots
First downs	17	29	Completions/attempts	16–33	32–48
3rd down efficiency	4–12	8–17	Yards per pass	8.0	7.4
Total offense (net yards)	387	481	Yards lost to sacks	4–28	0–0
Plays	53	83	Had intercepted	0	1
Average gain	7.3	5.8	Punts/average	7–44.3	5–34.6
Rushing yards (net)	92	127	Return/yardage	14	42
Rushes	16	35	Penalties/yards	12–73	8–60
Average per rush	5.8	3.6	Fumbles/lost	1–1	1–0
Passing yards (net)	295	354	Time of possession	21:02	38:58

NATIONAL LEAGUE CHAMPIONS

Year	Champion	(W-L-T)	Year	Champion	(W-L-T)	Year	Champion	(W-L-T)
1920	Akron Pros	(6–0–3)	1925	Chicago Cardinals	(11-2-1)	1928	Providence	(8-1-2)
1921	Chicago Staleys)	(10-1-1)	1926	Frankford Yellow	(14-1-1)		Steam Roller	
1922	Canton Bulldogs	(10-0-2)		Jackets		1929	Green Bay Packers	(12-0-1)
1923	Canton Bulldogs	(11-0-1)	1927	New York Giants	(11-1-1)	1930	Green Bay Packers	(10-3-1)
1924	Cleveland Bulldogs	(7-1-1)				1931	Green Bay Packers	(12-2-0)
						1932	Chicago Bears	(7-1-6)

Year	Eastern Conference winners (W-L-T)	Western Conference winners (W-L-T)	League champion playoff results
1933	New York Giants (11-3-0)	Chicago Bears (10-2-1)	Chicago Bears 23, New York 21
1934	New York Giants (8-5-0)	Chicago Bears (13-0-0)	New York 30, Chicago Bears 13
1935	New York Giants (9-3-0)	Detroit Lions (7-3-2)	Detroit 26, New York 7
1936	Boston Redskins (7-5-0)	Green Bay Packers (10-1-1)	Green Bay 21, Boston 6
1937	Washington Redskins (8-3-0)	Chicago Bears (9-1-1)	Washington 28, Chicago Bears 21
1938	New York Giants (8-2-1)	Green Bay Packers (8-3-0)	New York 23, Green Bay 17
1939	New York Giants (9-1-1)	Green Bay Packers (9-2-0)	Green Bay 27, New York 0
1940	Washington Redskins (9-2-0)	Chicago Bears (8-3-0)	Chicago Bears 73, Washington 0
1941	New York Giants (8-3-0)	Chicago Bears (10-1-1)²	Chicago Bears 37, New York 9
1942	Washington Redskins (10-1-1)	Chicago Bears (11-0-0)	Washington 14, Chicago Bears 6
1943	Washington Redskins (6-3-1)²	Chicago Bears (8-1-1)	Chicago Bears 41, Washington 21
1944	New York Giants (8-1-1)	Green Bay Packers (8-2-0)	Green Bay 14, New York 7
1945	Washington Redskins (8-2-0)	Cleveland Rams (9-1-0)	Cleveland 15, Washington 14
1946	New York Giants (7-3-1)	Chicago Bears (8-2-1)	Chicago Bears 24, New York 14
1947	Philadelphia Eagles (8-4-0)²	Chicago Cardinals (9-3-0)	Chicago Cardinals 28, Philadelphia 21
1948	Philadelphia Eagles (9-2-1)	Chicago Cardinals (11-1-0)	Philadelphia 7, Chicago Cardinals 0
1949	Philadelphia Eagles (11-1-0)	Los Angeles Rams (8-2-2)	Philadelphia 14, Los Angeles 0
1950¹	Cleveland Browns (10-2-0)²,³	Los Angeles Rams (9-3-0)²	Cleveland 30, Los Angeles 28
1951¹	Cleveland Browns (11-1-0)	Los Angeles Rams (8-4-0)	Los Angeles 24, Cleveland 17
1952¹	Cleveland Browns (8-4-0)	Detroit Lions (9-3-0)²	Detroit 17, Cleveland 7
1953	Cleveland Browns (11-1-0)	Detroit Lions (10-2-0)	Detroit 17, Cleveland 16
1954	Cleveland Browns (9-3-0)	Detroit Lions (9-2-1)	Cleveland 56, Detroit 10
1955	Cleveland Browns (9-2-1)	Los Angeles Rams (8-3-1)	Cleveland 38, Los Angeles 14
1956	New York Giants (8-3-1)	Chicago Bears (9-2-1)	New York 47, Chicago Bears 7
1957	Cleveland Browns (9-2-1)	Detroit Lions (8-4-0)²	Detroit 59, Cleveland 14
1958	New York Giants (9-3-0)²	Baltimore Colts (9-3-0)	Baltimore 23, New York 17⁴
1959	New York Giants (10-2-0)	Baltimore Colts (9-3-0)	Baltimore 31, New York 16
1960	Philadelphia Eagles (10-2-0)	Green Bay Packers (8-4-0)	Philadelphia 17, Green Bay 13
1961	New York Giants (10-3-1)	Green Bay Packers (11-3-0)	Green Bay 37, New York 0
1962	New York Giants (12-2-0)	Green Bay Packers (13-1-0)	Green Bay 16, New York 7
1963	New York Giants (11-3-0)	Chicago Bears (11-1-2)	Chicago 14, New York 10
1964	Cleveland Browns (10-3-1)	Baltimore Colts (12-2-0)	Cleveland 27, Baltimore 0
1965	Cleveland Browns (11-3-0)	Green Bay Packers (11-3-1)²	Green Bay 23, Cleveland 12
1966	Dallas Cowboys (10-3-1)	Green Bay Packers (12-2-0)	Green Bay 34, Dallas 27
1967	Dallas Cowboys (9-5-0)²	Green Bay Packers (9-4-1)²	Green Bay 21, Dallas 17
1968	Cleveland Browns (10-4-0)²	Baltimore Colts (13-1-0)²	Baltimore 34, Cleveland 0
1969	Cleveland Browns (10-3-1)²	Minnesota Vikings (12-2-0)²	Minnesota 27, Cleveland 7

1. League was divided into American and National Conferences, 1950-52 and again in 1970, when leagues merged. 2. Won divisional playoff. 3. Cleveland Browns and San Francisco 49ers joined league after All-America Football Conference (1946–1949) folded. 4. Won at 8:15 of sudden death overtime period.

NATIONAL CONFERENCE CHAMPIONS

Year	Eastern Division	Central Division	Western Division	Champion
1970	Dallas Cowboys (10-4-0)	Minnesota Vikings (12-2-0)	San Francisco 49ers (10-3-1)	Dallas
1971	Dallas Cowboys (11-3-0)	Minnesota Vikings (11-3-0)	San Francisco 49ers (9-5-0)	Dallas
1972	Washington Redskins (11-3-0)	Green Bay Packers (10-4-0)	San Francisco 49ers (8-5-1)	Washington
1973	Dallas Cowboys (10-4-0)	Minnesota Vikings (12-2-0)	Los Angeles Rams (12-2-0)	Minnesota
1974	St. Louis Cardinals (10-4-0)	Minnesota Vikings (10-4-0)	Los Angeles Rams (10-4-0)	Minnesota
1975	St. Louis Cardinals (11-3-0)	Minnesota Vikings (12-2-0)	Los Angeles Rams (12-2-0)	Dallas¹
1976	Dallas Cowboys (11-3-0)	Minnesota Vikings (11-2-1)	Los Angeles Rams (10-3-1)	Minnesota
1977	Dallas Cowboys (12-2-0)	Minnesota Vikings (9-5-0)	Los Angeles Rams (10-4-0)	Dallas

Year	Eastern Division	Central Division	Western Division	Champion
1978	Dallas Cowboys (12-4-0)	Minnesota Vikings (8-7-1)	Los Angeles Rams (12-4-0)	Dallas
1979	Dallas Cowboys (11-5-0)	Tampa Bay Buccaneers (10-6-0)	Los Angeles Rams (9-7-0)	Los Angeles
1980	Philadelphia Eagles (12-4-0)	Minnesota Vikings (9-7-0)	Atlanta Falcons (12-4-0)	Philadelphia
1981	Dallas Cowboys (12-4-0)	Tampa Bay Buccaneers (9-7-0)	San Francisco 49ers (13-3-0)	San Francisco
1982[2]				Washington
1983	Washington Redskins (14-2-0)	Detroit Lions (8-8-0)	San Francisco 49ers (10-6-0)	Washington
1984	Washington Redskins (11-5-0)	Chicago Bears (10-6-0)	San Francisco 49ers (15-1-0)	San Francisco
1985	Dallas Cowboys (10-6-0)	Chicago Bears (15-1-0)	Los Angeles Rams (11-5-0)	Chicago
1986	New York Giants (14-2-0)	Chicago Bears (14-2-0)	San Francisco 49ers (10-5-1)	New York
1987	Washington Redskins (11-4-0)	Chicago Bears (11-4-0)	San Francisco 49ers (13-2-0)	Washington
1988	Philadelphia Eagles (10-6-0)	Chicago Bears (12-4-0)	San Francisco 49ers (10-6-0)	San Francisco
1989	New York Giants (12-4-0)	Minnesota Vikings (10-6-0)	San Francisco 49ers (14-2-0)	San Francisco
1990	New York Giants (13-3-0)	Chicago Bears (11-5-0)	San Francisco 49ers (14-2-0)	New York
1991	Washington (14-2-0)	Detroit Lions (12-4-0)	New Orleans Saints (11-5-0)	Washington
1992	Dallas Cowboys (13-3-0)	Minnesota Vikings (11-5-0)	San Francisco 49ers (14-2-0)	Dallas
1993	Dallas Cowboys (12-4-0)	Detroit Lions (10-6-0)	San Francisco 49ers (10-6-0)	Dallas
1994	Dallas Cowboys (12-4-0)	Minnesota Vikings (10-6-0)	San Francisco 49ers (13-3-0)	San Francisco
1995	Dallas Cowboys (12-4-0)	Green Bay Packers (11-5-0)	San Francisco 49ers (11-5-0)	Dallas
1996	Dallas Cowboys (10-6-0)	Green Bay Packers (13-3-0)	Carolina Panthers (12-4-0)	Green Bay
1997	New York Giants (10-5-1)	Green Bay Packers (13-3-0)	San Francisco 49ers (13-3-0)	Green Bay
1998	Dallas Cowboys (10-6-0)	Minnesota Vikings (15-1-0)	Atlanta Falcons (14-2-0)	Atlanta
1999	Washington Redskins (10-6-0)	Tampa Bay Buccaneers (11-5-0)	St. Louis Rams (13-3-0)	St. Louis
2000	New York Giants (12-4-0)	Minnesota Vikings (11-5-0)	New Orleans Saints (10-6-0)	New York
2001	Philadelphia Eagles (11-5-0)	Chicago Bears (13-3-0)	St. Louis Rams (14-2-0)	St. Louis

Year	East	North	South	West	Champion
2002	Philadelphia (12-4-0)	Green Bay (12-4-0)	Tampa Bay (12-4-0)	San Francisco (10-6-0)	Tampa Bay
2003	Philadelphia (12-4-0)	Green Bay (10-6-0)	Carolina (11-5-0)	St. Louis (12-4-0)	Carolina

1. Wild card. 2. Schedule reduced to 9 games from usual 16, with no standings kept in Eastern, Central, and Western Divisions because of 57-day player strike. Washington Redskins won conference title and also had best regular-season record (8-1-0).

AMERICAN LEAGUE CHAMPIONS

Year	Eastern Division (W-L-T)	Western Division (W-L-T)	League champion, playoff results
1960	Houston Oilers (10-4-0)	Los Angeles Chargers (10-4-0)	Houston 24, Los Angeles 16
1961	Houston Oilers (10-3-1)	San Diego Chargers (12-2-0)	Houston 10, San Diego 3
1962	Houston Oilers (11-3-0)	Dallas Texans (11-3-0)	Dallas 20, Houston 17[1]
1963	Boston Patriots (8-6-1)[2]	San Diego Chargers (11-3-0)	San Diego 51, Boston 10
1964	Buffalo Bills (12-2-0)	San Diego Chargers (8-5-1)	Buffalo 20, San Diego 7
1965	Buffalo Bills (10-3-1)	San Diego Chargers (9-2-3)	Buffalo 23, San Diego 0
1966	Buffalo Bills (9-4-1)	Kansas City Chiefs (11-2-1)	Kansas City 31, Buffalo 7
1967	Houston Oilers (9-4-1)	Oakland Raiders (13-1-0)	Oakland 40, Houston 7
1968	New York Jets (11-3-0)	Oakland Raiders (12-2-0)[2]	New York 27, Oakland 23
1969	New York Jets (10-4-0)	Oakland Raiders (12-1-1)	Kansas City 17, Oakland 7[3]

1. Won at 2:45 of second sudden death overtime period. 2. Won divisional playoff. 3. Kansas City defeated New York, 13-6, and Oakland defeated Houston, 56-7, in interdivisional playoffs.

AMERICAN CONFERENCE CHAMPIONS

Year	Eastern Division	Central Division	Western Division	Champion
1970	Baltimore Colts (11-2-1)	Cincinnati Bengals (8-6-0)	Oakland Raiders (8-4-2)	Baltimore
1971	Miami Dolphins (10-3-1)	Cleveland Browns (9-5-0)	Kansas City Chiefs (10-3-1)	Miami
1972	Miami Dolphins (14-0-0)	Pittsburgh Steelers (11-3-0)	Oakland Raiders (10-3-1)	Miami
1973	Miami Dolphins (12-2-0)	Cincinnati Bengals (10-4-0)	Oakland Raiders (9-4-1)	Miami
1974	Miami Dolphins (11-3-0)	Pittsburgh Steelers (10-3-1)	Oakland Raiders (12-2-0)	Pittsburgh
1975	Baltimore Colts (10-4-0)	Pittsburgh Steelers (12-2-0)	Oakland Raiders (11-3-0)	Pittsburgh
1976	Baltimore Colts (11-3-0)	Pittsburgh Steelers (10-4-0)	Oakland Raiders (13-1-0)	Oakland
1977	Baltimore Colts (10-4-0)	Pittsburgh Steelers (9-5-0)	Denver Broncos (12-2-0)	Denver
1978	New England Patriots (11-5-0)	Pittsburgh Steelers (14-2-0)	Denver Broncos (10-6-0)	Pittsburgh
1979	Miami Dolphins (10-6-0)	Pittsburgh Steelers (12-4-0)	San Diego Chargers (12-4-0)	Pittsburgh
1980	Buffalo Bills (11-5-0)	Cleveland Browns (11-5-0)	San Diego Chargers (11-5-0)	Oakland[1]
1981	Miami Dolphins (11-4-1)	Cincinnati Bengals (12-4-0)	San Diego Chargers (10-6-0)	Cincinnati
1982[2]	Miami Dolphins won the conference title, but the Los Angeles Raiders had best regular-season record (8-1-0).			
1983	Miami Dolphins (12-4-0)	Pittsburgh Steelers (10-6-0)	Los Angeles Raiders (12-4-0)	Los Angeles
1984	Miami Dolphins (14-2-0)	Pittsburgh Steelers (9-7-0)	Denver Broncos (13-3-0)	Miami
1985	Miami Dolphins (12-4-0)	Cleveland Browns (8-8)	Los Angeles Raiders (12-4-0)	New England[1]
1986	New England Patriots (11-5-0)	Cleveland Browns (12-4-0)	Denver Broncos (11-5-0)	Denver
1987	Indianapolis Colts (9-6-0)	Cleveland Browns (10-5-0)	Denver Broncos (10-4-1)	Denver
1988	Buffalo Bills (12-4-0)	Cincinnati Bengals (12-4-0)	Seattle Seahawks (9-7-0)	Cincinnati
1989	Buffalo Bills (9-7-0)	Cleveland Browns (9-6-1)	Denver Broncos (11-5-0)	Denver
1990	Buffalo Bills (13-3-0)	Cincinnati Bengals (9-7-0)	Los Angeles Raiders (12-4-0)	Buffalo
1991	Buffalo Bills (13-3-0)	Houston Oilers (11-5-0)	Denver Broncos (12-4-0)	Buffalo
1992	Miami Dolphins (11-5-0)	Pittsburgh Steelers (11-5-0)	San Diego Chargers (11-5-0)	Buffalo[1]

Year	Eastern Division	Central Division	Western Division	Champion
1993	Buffalo Bills (12-4-0)	Houston Oilers (12-4-0)	Kansas City Chiefs (11-5-0)	Buffalo
1994	Miami Dolphins (10-6-0)	Pittsburgh Steelers (12-4-0)	San Diego Chargers (11-5-0)	San Diego
1995	Buffalo Bills (10-6-0)	Pittsburgh Steelers (11-5-0)	Kansas City Chiefs (13-3-0)	Pittsburgh
1996	New England Patriots (11-5-0)	Pittsburgh Steelers (10-6-0)	Denver Broncos (13-3-0)	New England
1997	New England Patriots (10-6-0)	Pittsburgh Steelers (11-5-0)	Kansas City Chiefs (13-3-0)	Denver[1]
1998	New York Jets (12-4-0)	Jacksonville Jaguars (11-5-0)	Denver Broncos (14-2-0)	Denver
1999	Indianapolis Colts (13-3-0)	Jacksonville Jaguars (14-2-0)	Seattle Seahawks (9-7-0)	Tennessee[1]
2000	Miami Dolphins (11-5-0)	Tennessee Titans (13-3-0)	Oakland Raiders (12-4-0)	Baltimore[1]
2001	New England Patriots (11-5-0)	Pittsburgh Steelers (13-3-0)	Oakland Raiders (10-6-0)	New England

Year	East	North	South	West	Champion
2002	N.Y. Jets (9-7-0)	Pittsburgh (10-5-1)	Tennessee (11-5-0)	Oakland (11-5-0)	Oakland
2003	New England (14-2-0)	Baltimore (10-6-0)	Indianapolis (12-4-0)	Kansas City (13-3-0)	New England

1. Wild card. 2. Schedule reduced to 9 games from usual 16, with no standings kept in Eastern, Central, and Western Divisions, because of 57-day player strike.

NFL INDIVIDUAL LIFETIME, SEASON, AND GAME RECORDS

(American Football League records were incorporated into NFL records after merger of the leagues.) Players listed in boldface were active during the 2003 season. The NFL does not recognize records from the All-American Football Conference (AAFC), which existed from 1946 to 1949. The 49ers, Browns, and Colts merged with the NFL in 1949.

All-Time Scoring Leaders (Through 2003)

Rank	Player	Touch-downs	Player	Points
1.	Jerry Rice	205	Gary Anderson	2,348
2.	Emmitt Smith	165	Morten Andersen	2,257
3.	Marcus Allen	145	George Blanda	2,002
4.	Marshall Faulk	131	Norm Johnson	1,736
4.	Cris Carter	131	Nick Lowery	1,711
6.	Jim Brown	126	Jan Stenerud	1,699
7.	Walter Payton	125	Eddie Murray	1,594
8.	John Riggins	116	Al Del Greco	1,584
9.	Lenny Moore	113	Pat Leahy	1,470
10.	Barry Sanders	109	Jim Turner	1,439

All-Time Leading Receivers (Through 2003)

Rank	Player	Number of receptions	Player	Yards
1.	Jerry Rice	1,520	Jerry Rice	22,458
2.	Cris Carter	1,101	Tim Brown	15,761
3.	Tim Brown	1,068	James Lofton	14,004
4.	Andre Reed	951	Cris Carter	13,899
5.	Art Monk	940	Henry Ellard	13,777
6.	Irving Fryar	851	Andre Reed	13,198
7.	Larry Centers	825	Steve Largent	13,089
8.	Steve Largent	819	Irving Fryar	12,785
9.	Henry Ellard	814	Art Monk	12,721
10.	James Lofton	764	Charlie Joiner	12,146

All-Time Leading Passers (Through 2003)

Rank	Player	Yards	Player	Number completed	Player	Number of touchdowns
1.	Dan Marino	61,361	Dan Marino	4,967	Dan Marino	420
2.	John Elway	51,475	John Elway	4,123	Brett Favre	346
3.	Warren Moon	49,325	Warren Moon	3,985	Fran Tarkenton	342
4.	Fran Tarkenton	47,003	Brett Favre	3,960	John Elway	300
5.	Brett Favre	45,726	Fran Tarkenton	3,686	Warren Moon	291
6.	Dan Fouts	43,040	Joe Montana	3,409	Johnny Unitas	290
7.	Vinny Testaverde	40,943	Vinny Testaverde	3,319	Joe Montana	273
8.	Joe Montana	40,551	Dan Fouts	3,297	Dave Krieg	261
9.	Johnny Unitas	40,239	Drew Bledsoe	3,183	Sonny Jurgensen	255
10.	Dave Krieg	38,147	Dave Krieg	3,105	Dan Fouts	254

All-Time Interception Leaders (Through 2003)

		Amount
1.	Paul Krause	81
2.	Emlen Tunnell	79
3.	Rod Woodson	71
4.	Dick Lane	68
5.	Ken Riley	65
6.	Ronnie Lott	63
7.	Dave Brown	62
	Dick LeBeau	62
9.	Emmitt Thomas	58
10.	Mel Blount	57
	Bobby Boyd	57
	Johnny Robinson	57
	Everson Walls	57
	Eugene Robinson	57

All-Time Sack Leaders (Through 2003)

		Amount
1.	Bruce Smith	200.0
2.	Reggie White	198.0
3.	Kevin Greene	157.0
4.	Chris Doleman	150.5
5.	John Randle	137.5
	Richard Dent	137.5
7.	Lawrence Taylor	132.5
	Leslie O'Neal	132.5
9.	Rickey Jackson	128.0
10.	Derrick Thomas	126.5

All-Time Leading Rushers (Through 2003)

		Yards
1.	Emmitt Smith	17,403
2.	Walter Payton	16,726
3.	Barry Sanders	15,269
4.	Eric Dickerson	13,259
5.	Tony Dorsett	12,739
6.	Jerome Bettis	12,353
7.	Jim Brown	12,312
8.	Marcus Allen	12,243
9.	Franco Harris	12,120
10.	Thurman Thomas	12,074

Scoring

Most points scored, lifetime—2,348, Gary Anderson, Pittsburgh, 1982–94; Philadelphia, 1995–96; San Francisco, 1997; Minnesota, 1998–2002; Tennessee, 2003.

Most points, season—176, Paul Hornung, Green Bay, 1960 (15 td, 41 pat, 15 fg).

Most points, game—40, Ernie Nevers, Chicago Cardinals, 1929 (6 td, 4 pat).

Most touchdowns, lifetime—205, Jerry Rice, San Francisco, 1985–2000; Oakland 2001–2003.

Most points after touchdown, lifetime—943, George Blanda, Chicago Bears, 1949–58; Baltimore, 1950; Houston, 1960–66; Oakland, 1967–75.

Most field goals, lifetime—521, Gary Anderson, Pittsburgh, 1982–94; Philadelphia, 1995–96; San Francisco, 1997; Minnesota, 1998–2002; Tennessee, 2003.

Most field goals, season—39, Olindo Mare, Miami, 1999; Jeff Wilkins, St. Louis, 2003.

Most field goals, game—7, Jim Bakken, St. Louis, 1967; Rich Karlis, Minnesota, 1989; and Chris Boniol, Dallas, 1996.

Longest field goal—63 yards, Tom Dempsey, New Orleans, 1970; Jason Elam, Denver, 1998.

Rushing

Most yards gained, lifetime—17,418, Emmitt Smith, Dallas Cowboys, 1990–2002; Arizona, 2003.

Most yards gained, season—2,105, Eric Dickerson, Los Angeles, 1984.

Most yards gained, game—278, Corey Dillon, Cincinnati, 2000.

Most touchdowns, lifetime—155, Emmitt Smith, Dallas, 1990–2002; Arizona, 2003.

Most touchdowns, season—25, Emmitt Smith, Dallas, 1995.

Most touchdowns, game—6, Ernie Nevers, Chicago Cardinals, 1929.

Longest run from scrimmage—99 yards, Tony Dorsett, Dallas, 1983.

Receiving

Most pass receptions, lifetime—1,520, Jerry Rice, San Francisco, 1985–2000; Oakland 2001–2003.

Most pass receptions, season—123, Herman Moore, Detroit, 1995.

Most pass receptions, game—20, Terrell Owens, San Francisco, 2000.

Most yards gained, pass receptions, lifetime—22,458, Jerry Rice, San Francisco, 1985–2000; Oakland 2001–2003.

Most yards gained, receptions, season—1,848, Jerry Rice, San Francisco, 1995.

Most yards gained, receptions, game—336, Flipper Anderson, Los Angeles Rams, 1989.

Most touchdown receptions, lifetime—194, Jerry Rice, San Francisco, 1985–2000; Oakland 2001–2003.

Most touchdown pass receptions, season—22, Jerry Rice, San Francisco, 1987.

Most touchdown pass receptions, game—5, Bob Shaw, Chicago Cards, 1950; Kellen Winslow, San Diego, 1981; Jerry Rice, San Francisco, 1990.

Interceptions

Most pass interceptions, lifetime—81, Paul Krause, Washington, 1964-67; Minnesota, 1968–79.

Most pass interceptions, season—14, Richard (Night Train) Lane, Detroit, 1952.

Most pass interceptions, game—4, by 18 players.

Longest pass interception return—104 yards, James Willis, Philadelphia, 1996.

Kicking

Highest average punting, lifetime—45.1 yards, Sammy Baugh, Washington, 1937–52.

Longest punt return—103 yards, Robert Bailey, L.A. Rams, 1994.

Longest kick-off return—106 yards, Roy Green, St. Louis, 1979; Al Carmichael, Green Bay, 1956; Noland Smith, Kansas City, 1967.

Passing

Most touchdown passes, lifetime—420, Dan Marino, Miami, 1983–99.

Most touchdown passes, season—48, Dan Marino, Miami, 1984.

Most touchdown passes, game—7, Sid Luckman, Chicago Bears, 1943; Adrian Burk, Philadelphia, 1954; George Blanda, Houston, 1961; Y. A. Tittle, N.Y. Giants, 1962; Joe Kapp, Minnesota, 1969.

Longest pass completion—99 yards, Frank Filchock (to Andy Farkas), Washington, 1939; George Izo (to Bob Mitchell), Washington, 1963; Karl Sweetan (to Pat Studstill), Detroit, 1966; Sonny Jurgensen (to Gerry Allen), Washington, 1968; Jim Plunkett (to Cliff Branch) L.A. Raiders, 1983; Ron Jaworski (to Mike Quick), Philadelphia, 1985; Stan Humphries (to Tony Martin), San Diego, 1994; Brett Favre (to Robert Brooks), Green Bay, 1995.

Most passes completed, lifetime—4,967, Dan Marino, Miami, 1983–99.

Most passes completed, season—404, Warren Moon, 1991.

Most passes completed, game—45, Drew Bledsoe, New England, 1994.

Most yards gained, lifetime—61,361, Dan Marino, Miami, 1983–99.

Most yards gained, season—5,084, Dan Marino, Miami, 1984.

Most yards gained, game—554, Norm Van Brocklin, Los Angeles, 1951.

PRO FOOTBALL HALL OF FAME

(National Football Museum, Canton, Ohio)

Teams named are those with which player is best identified; figures in parentheses indicate number of playing seasons.

Adderley, Herb, defensive back, Packers, Cowboys (12)	1961–72
Allen, George, coach, Rams, Redskins (12)	1966–77
Allen, Marcus, running back, Raiders, Chiefs (16)	1982–97
Alworth, Lance, wide receiver, Chargers, Cowboys (12)	1961–72
Atkins, Doug, defensive end, Browns, Bears, Saints (17)	1953–69
Badgro, Morris, end, N.Y. Yankees, Giants, Brooklyn Dodgers (8)	1927, 1930–36
Barney, Lem, defensive back, Lions (11)	1967–78
Battles, Cliff, back, Redskins (6)	1932–37
Baugh, Sammy, quarterback, Redskins (16)	1936–52
Bednarik, Chuck, center-lineback, Eagles (14)	1949–62
Bell, Bert, NFL founder, Eagles and Steelers, NFL Commissioner	1946–59
Bell, Bobby, linebacker, Chiefs (12)	1963–74
Berry, Raymond, end, Colts (13)	1955–67
Bethea, Elvin, defensive end, Oilers (16)	1968–83
Bidwell, Charles W., owner, Chicago Cardinals	1933–47
Biletnikoff, Fred, wide receiver, Raiders (14)	1965–78
Blanda, George, quarterback-kicker, Bears, Oilers, Raiders (27)	1949–75
Blount, Mel, cornerback, Pittsburgh Steelers (14)	1970–83
Bradshaw, Terry, quarterback, Pittsburgh Steelers (14)	1970–83
Brown, Bob, tackle, Eagles, Rams, Raiders (10)	1964–73
Brown, Jim, fullback, Browns (9)	1957–65
Brown, Paul E., coach, Browns (1946–62), Bengals (1968–75)	1946–75

Brown, Roosevelt, tackle, Giants (13) — 1953–65
Brown, Willie, cornerback, Broncos, Raiders (16) — 1963–78
Buchanan, Buck, tackle, Chiefs (11) — 1963–73
Buoniconti, Nick, linebacker, Patriots, Dolphins (14) — 1962–74, 1976
Butkus, Dick, linebacker, Bears (9) — 1965–73
Campbell, Earl, running back, Oilers, Saints (8) — 1978–85
Canadeo, Tony, back, Packers (11) — 1941–52
Carr, Joe, NFL president (18) — 1921–39
Casper, Dave, tight end, Raiders, Oilers, Vikings (11) — 1974–84
Chamberlin, Guy, end, 4 teams (9) — 1919–27
Christiansen, Jack, defensive back, Lions (8) — 1951–58
Clark, Earl (Dutch), quarterback, Spartans, Lions (7) — 1931–38
Connor, George, tackle, linebacker, Bears (8) — 1948–55
Conzelman, Jimmy, quarterback, 5 teams (10), owner, Detroit Panthers — 1921–48
Creekmur, Lou, offensive tackle/guard, Lions (10) — 1950–59
Csonka, Larry, back, Dolphins, Giants (11) — 1968–79
Davis, Al, owner, Raiders, coach, general manager — 1963–
Davis, Willie, defensive end, Packers (10) — 1960–69
Dawson, Len, quarterback, Steelers, Browns, Texans, Chiefs (19) — 1957–75
DeLamielleure, guard, Bills, Browns (13) — 1973–84
Dickerson, Eric, running back, Rams, Colts, Raiders, Falcons (11) — 1983–93
Dierdorf, Dan, tackle/center, Cardinals (13) — 1971–83
Ditka, Mike, tight end, Bears, Eagles, Cowboys (12) — 1961–72
Donovan, Art, defensive tackle, Colts (12) — 1950–61
Dorsett, Tony, running back, Cowboys, Broncos (12) — 1977–88
Driscoll, John (Paddy), quarterback, Cards, Bears (11) — 1919–29
Dudley, Bill, back, Steelers, Lions, Redskins (9) — 1942–53
Edwards, Albert Glen (Turk), tackle, Redskins (9) — 1932–40
Eller, Carl, defensive end, Vikings, Seahawks (16) — 1964–79
Elway, John, quarterback, Broncos (16) — 1983–98
Ewbank, Weeb, coach, Colts, Jets (20) — 1954–73
Fears, Tom, end, Rams (9); coach, Saints — 1948–56
Finks, Jim, administrator/general manager, Vikings, Bears, Saints — 1964–93
Flaherty, Ray, end, Yankees, Giants (9); coach, Redskins, Yankees (14) — 1928–49
Ford, Len, end, defensive end, Browns, Packers (11) — 1948–58
Fouts, Dan, quarterback, Chargers (15) — 1973–87
Fortmann, Daniel J., guard, Bears (8) — 1936–43
Gatski, Frank, offensive lineman, Browns (12) — 1946–57
George, Bill, linebacker, Bears, Rams (15) — 1952–66
Gibbs, Joe, coach, Redskins (11) — 1981–92
Gifford, Frank, back, Giants (12) — 1952–64
Gillman, Sid, coach, Rams, Chargers, Oilers (18) — 1955–70, 73–74
Graham, Otto, quarterback, Browns (10) — 1946–55
Grange, Harold (Red), back, Bears, Yankees (9) — 1925–34
Grant, Bud, coach, Vikings (18) — 1967–85
Greene, Joe, defensive tackle, Steelers (13) — 1968–81
Gregg, Forrest, tackle, Packers (15) — 1956–71
Griese, Bob, quarterback, Dolphins (14) — 1967–80
Groza, Lou, place-kicker, tackle, Browns (21) — 1946–67
Guyon, Joe, back, 6 teams (8) — 1919–27
Halas, George, NFL founder, owner and coach, Staleys and Bears, end (11) — 1919–27
Ham, Jack, linebacker, Steelers (13) — 1970–82
Hampton, Dan, defensive end, defensive tackle, Bears (12) — 1979–90
Hannah, John, guard, Patriots (13) — 1973–85
Harris, Franco, running back, Steelers, Seahawks (13) — 1972–84
Haynes, Mike, defensive back, Patriots, Raiders (10) — 1976–85
Healey, Ed, tackle, Bears (8) — 1920–27
Hein, Mel, center, Giants (15) — 1931–45
Hendricks, Ted, linebacker, Colts, Packers, Raiders (15) — 1969–83
Henry, Wilbur (Pete), tackle, Bulldogs, Giants (8) — 1920–28
Herber, Arnie, quarterback, Packers, Giants (13) — 1930–45
Hewitt, Bill, end, Bears, Eagles (9) — 1932–43
Hinkle, Clarke, fullback, Packers (10) — 1932–41
Hirsch, Elroy (Crazy Legs), back, end, Rams (12) — 1946–57
Hornung, Paul, running back, Packers (9) — 1957–62, 64–66
Houston, Ken, defensive back, Oilers, Redskins (14) — 1967–80
Hubbard, R. (Cal), tackle, Giants, Packers (9) — 1927–36
Huff, Sam, linebacker, Giants, Redskins (13) — 1956–67, 1969
Hunt, Lamar, founder A.F.L., owner Texans, Chiefs — 1959–
Hutson, Don, end, Packers (11) — 1935–45
Johnson, John Henry, back, 49ers, Lions, Steelers, Oilers (13) — 1954–66
Johnson, Jimmy, cornerback, 49ers (16) — 1961–76

Joiner, Charlie, receiver, Oilers, Bengals, Chargers (18) — 1969–86
Jones, David (Deacon), defensive end, Rams, Chargers, Redskins (14) — 1961–74
Jones, Stan, defensive tackle, Bears, Redskins (13) — 1954–66
Jordan, Henry, defensive tackle, Browns, Packers (13) — 1957–69
Jurgensen, Sonny, quarterback, Eagles, Redskins (18) — 1957–74
Kelly, Jim, quarterback, Bills (11) — 1986–96
Kelly, Leroy, running back, Browns (10) — 1964–73
Kiesling, Walt, guard, 6 teams (13) — 1926–38
Kinard, Frank (Bruiser), tackle, Dodgers (9) — 1938–47
Krause, Paul, safety, Redskins, Vikings (16) — 1964–79
Lambeau, Earl (Curly), NFL founder, coach, end, back, Packers (11) — 1919–53
Lambert, Jack, linebacker, Steelers (11) — 1974–84
Landry, Tom, coach, Cowboys (29) — 1960–88
Lane, Richard (Night Train), defensive back, Rams, Cardinals, Lions (14) — 1952–65
Langer, Jim, center, Dolphins, Vikings (12) — 1970–81
Lanier, Willie, linebacker, Chiefs (11) — 1967–77
Largent, Steve, receiver, Seahawks (14) — 1976–89
Lary, Yale, defensive back, punter, Lions (11) — 1952–64
Laveill, Dante, end, Browns (11) — 1946–56
Layne, Bobby, quarterback, Bears, Lions, Steelers (15) — 1948–62
Leemans, Alphonse (Tuffy), back, Giants (8) — 1936–43
Levy, Marv, coach, Chiefs, Bills (17) — 1978–97
Lilly, Bob, defensive tackle, Cowboys (14) — 1961–74
Little, Larry, guard, Dolphins, Chargers (14) — 1967–80
Lofton, James, wide receiver, Packers, Raiders, Bills, Rams, Eagles (14) — 1978–93
Lombardi, Vince, coach, Packers, Redskins (11) — 1959–70
Long, Howie, defensive end, Raiders (13) — 1981–93
Lott, Ronnie, cornerback, safety, 49ers, Raiders, Jets (14) — 1981–94
Luckman, Sid, quarterback, Bears (12) — 1939–50
Lyman, Roy (Link), tackle, Bulldogs, Bears (11) — 1922–34
Mack, Tom, guard, Rams (13) — 1966–78
Mackey, John, tight end, Colts, Chargers (10) — 1963–72
Mara, Tim, NFL founder, owner, Giants — 1925–59
Mara, Wellington, NFL executive, owner, Giants — 1937–
Marchetti, Gino, defensive end, Colts (14) — 1952–66
Marshall, George P., NFL founder, owner, Redskins — 1932–65
Matson, Ollie, back, Cardinals, Rams, Lions, Eagles (14) — 1952–66
Maynard, Don, receiver, Giants, Jets, Cardinals (15) — 1958–73
McAfee, George, back, Bears (8) — 1940–50
McCormack, Mike, tackle, N.Y. Yanks, Cleveland Browns (10) — 1951–62
McDonald, Tommy, wide receiver, Eagles, Cowboys, Rams, Falcons, Browns (12) — 1957–68
McElhenny, Hugh, back, 49ers, Vikings, Giants (13) — 1952–64
McNally, John (Blood), back, 7 teams (15) — 1925–39
Michalske, August, guard, Yankees, Packers (11) — 1926–37
Millner, Wayne, end, Redskins (7) — 1936–45
Mitchell, Bobby, wide receiver, Browns, Redskins (11) — 1958–68
Mix, Ron, tackle, Chargers (11) — 1960–71
Montana, Joe, quarterback, 49ers, Chiefs (15) — 1979–94
Moore, Lenny, back, Colts (12) — 1956–67
Motley, Marion, fullback, Browns, Steelers (9) — 1946–55
Munchak, Mike, guard, Oilers (12) — 1982–93
Munoz, Anthony, tackle, Bengals (13) — 1980–92
Musso, George, guard-tackle, Bears (12) — 1933–44
Nagurski, Bronko, fullback, Bears (9) — 1930–43
Namath, Joe, quarterback, Jets, Rams (13) — 1965–77
Neale, Earle (Greasy), coach, Eagles — 1941–50
Nevers, Ernie, fullback, Chicago Cardinals (5) — 1926–31
Newsome, Ozzie, tight end, Browns (13) — 1978–90
Nitschke, Ray, linebacker, Packers (15) — 1958–72
Noll, Chuck, coach, Steelers (23) — 1969–81
Nomellini, Leo, defensive tackle, 49ers (14) — 1950–63
Olsen, Merlin, defensive tackle, Rams (15) — 1962–76
Otto, Jim, center, Raiders (15) — 1960–74
Owen, Steve, tackle, Giants (9), coach, Giants (13) — 1924–53
Page, Alan, defensive tackle, Vikings, Bears (15) — 1967–81
Parker, Clarence (Ace), quarterback, Dodgers (7) — 1937–46
Parker, Jim, guard, tackle, Colts (11) — 1957–67
Payton, Walter, running back, Bears (13) — 1977–89
Perry, Joe, fullback, 49ers, Colts (16) — 1948–63
Pihos, Pete, end, Eagles (9) — 1947–55
Ray, Hugh (Shorty), NFL advisor — 1938–52
Reeves, Dan, owner, Rams — 1941–71
Renfro, Mel, cornerback, safety, Cowboys (14) — 1964–77

Riggins, John, running back, Jets, Redskins (14)	1971–84
Ringo, Jim, center, Packers (15)	1953–67
Robustelli, Andy, defensive end, Rams, Giants (14)	1951–64
Rooney, Art, NFL founder, owner, Steelers	1933–88
Rooney, Dan, contributor, Steelers	1955–
Rozelle, Pete, commissioner, NFL	1960–89
St. Claire, Bob, tackle, 49ers (11)	1953–63
Sanders, Barry, running back, Lions (10)	1989–98
Sayers, Gale, back, Bears (7)	1965–71
Schmidt, Joe, linebacker, Lions (13)	1953–65
Schramm, Tex, administrator, Rams, Cowboys (42)	1947–89
Selmon, Lee Roy, defensive end, Buccaneers (13)	1976–84
Shaw, Billy, guard, Bills (9)	1961–69
Shell, Art, tackle, Raiders (15)	1968–82
Shula, Don, coach, Colts, Dolphins (33)	1963–95
Simpson, O.J., back, Bills, 49ers (11)	1969–79
Singletary, Mike, linebacker, Bears (12)	1981–92
Slater, Jackie, tackle, Rams (20)	1976–95
Smith, Jackie, tight end, Cardinals, Cowboys (16)	1963–78
Stallworth, John, wide receiver, Steelers (14)	1974–87
Starr, Bart, quarterback, coach, Packers (16)	1956–71
Staubach, Roger, quarterback, Cowboys (11)	1969–79
Stautner, Ernie, defensive tackle, Steelers (14)	1950–63
Stenerud, Jan, placekicker, Chiefs, Packers, Vikings (19)	1967–85
Stephenson, Dwight, center, Dolphins (8)	1980–87
Stram, Hank, coach, Texans/Chiefs, Saints (17)	1960–74, 1976–77
Strong, Ken, back, Giants, Yankees (14)	1929–47
Stydahar, Joe, tackle, Bears (9); coach, Rams, Cardinals (5)	1936–54
Swann, Lynn, wide receiver, Steelers (9)	1974–82
Tarkenton, Fran, quarterback, Vikings, Giants (18)	1961–78
Taylor, Charlie, wide receiver, Redskins (14)	1964–77
Taylor, Jim, fullback, Packers, Saints (10)	1958–67
Taylor, Lawrence, linebacker, Giants (13)	1981–93
Thorpe, Jim, back, 7 teams (12)	1915–28
Tittle, Y.A., quarterback, Colts, 49ers, Giants (17)	1948–64
Trafton, George, center, Bears (13)	1920–32
Trippi, Charley, back, Chicago Cardinals (9)	1947–55
Tunnell, Emlen, defensive back, Giants, Packers (14)	1948–61
Turner, Clyde (Bulldog), center, Bears (13)	1940–52
Unitas, John, quarterback, Colts (18)	1956–73
Upshaw, Gene, guard, Raiders (15)	1967–81
Van Brocklin, Norm, quarterback, Rams, Eagles (12)	1949–60
Van Buren, Steve, back, Eagles (8)	1944–51
Walker, Doak, running back, def. back, kicker, Lions (6)	1950–55
Walsh, Bill, coach, 49ers (10)	1979–88
Warfield, Paul, wide receiver, Browns, Dolphins (13)	1964–74, 76–77
Waterfield, Bob, quarterback, Rams (8)	1945–52
Webster, Mike, center, Steelers, Chiefs (17)	1974–90
Weinmeister, Arnie, tackle, N.Y. Yankees, Giants (6)	1948–53
White, Randy, defensive tackle, Cowboys (14)	1975–88
Wilcox, Dave, linebacker, 49ers (11)	1964–74
Willis, Bill, guard, Browns (8)	1946–53
Wilson, Larry, defensive back, Cardinals (13)	1960–72
Winslow, Kellen, tight end, Chargers (9)	1979–87
Wood, Willie, safety, Packers (12)	1960–71
Wojciechowicz, Alex, center, Lions, Eagles (13)	1938–50
Yary, Ron, tackle, Vikings, Rams (15)	1968–82
Youngblood, Jack, defensive end, Rams (14)	1971–84

Basketball

Basketball is one of the few sports whose exact origin is definitely known. In the winter of 1891–1892, Dr. James Naismith, an instructor in the YMCA Training College (now Springfield College) at Springfield, Mass., deliberately invented the game of basketball in order to provide indoor exercise and competition for the students between the closing of the football season and the opening of the baseball season. He affixed peach baskets overhead ·on the walls at opposite ends of the gymnasium and organized teams to play his new game in which the purpose was to toss an association (soccer) ball into one basket and prevent the opponents from tossing the ball into the other basket. Because Dr. Naismith had eighteen available players when he invented the game, the first rule was: "There shall be nine players on each side." Later the number of players became optional, depending upon the size of the available court, but the five-player standard was adopted when the game spread over the country. U.S. soldiers brought basketball to Europe in World War I, and it soon became a worldwide sport.

College Basketball
NCAA CHAMPIONS

1939 Oregon	1951 Kentucky	1964 UCLA	1983 North Carolina State	1996 Kentucky
1940 Indiana & USC	1952 Kansas	1965 UCLA		1997 Arizona
1941 Wisconsin	1953 Indiana	1966 Texas Western	1984 Georgetown	1998 Kentucky
1942 Stanford	1954 La Salle	1967–73 UCLA	1985 Villanova	1999 Connecticut
1943 Wyoming	1955 San Francisco	1974 North Carolina State	1986 Louisville	2000 Michigan State
1944 Utah	1956 San Francisco		1987 Indiana	2001 Duke
1945 Oklahoma A & M	1957 North Carolina	1975 UCLA	1988 Kansas	2002 Maryland
	1958 Kentucky	1976 Indiana	1989 Michigan	2003 Syracuse
1946 Oklahoma A & M	1959 California	1977 Marquette	1990 UNLV	2004 Connecticut
	1960 Ohio State	1978 Kentucky	1991 Duke	
1947 Holy Cross	1961 Cincinnati	1979 Michigan State	1992 Duke	
1948 Kentucky	1962 Cincinnati	1980 Louisville	1993 North Carolina	
1949 Kentucky	1963 Loyola (Chicago)	1981 Indiana	1994 Arkansas	
1950 C.C.N.Y.		1982 North Carolina	1995 UCLA	

NATIONAL INVITATION TOURNAMENT (NIT) CHAMPIONS

1938	Temple	1953	Seton Hall	1965	St. John's (N.Y.C.)	1978	Texas
1939	Long Island U.	1954	Holy Cross	1966	Brigham Young	1979	Indiana
1940	Colorado	1955	Duquesne	1967	So. Illinois	1980	Virginia
1941	Long Island U.	1956	Louisville	1968	Dayton	1981	Tulsa
1942	West Virginia	1957	Bradley	1969	Temple	1982	Bradley
1943–44	St. John's (N.Y.C.)	1958	Xavier (Cincinnati)	1970	Marquette	1983	Fresno State
1945	DePaul	1959	St. John's (N.Y.C.)	1971	North Carolina	1984	Michigan
1946	Kentucky			1972	Maryland	1985	UCLA
1947	Utah	1960	Bradley	1973	Virginia Tech	1986	Ohio State
1948	St. Louis	1961	Providence	1974	Purdue	1987	So. Mississippi
1949	San Francisco	1962	Dayton	1975	Princeton	1988	Connecticut
1950	C.C.N.Y.	1963	Providence	1976	Kentucky	1989	St. John's (N.Y.C.)
1951	Brigham Young	1964	Bradley	1977	St. Bonaventure	1990	Vanderbilt
1952	La Salle					1991	Stanford
						1992	Virginia
						1993	Minnesota
						1994	Villanova
						1995	Virginia Tech
						1996	Nebraska
						1997	Michigan
						1998	Minnesota
						1999	California
						2000	Wake Forest
						2001	Tulsa
						2002	Memphis
						2003	St. John's (N.Y.C.)
						2004	Michigan

MEN'S NCAA BASKETBALL CHAMPIONSHIPS, 2004

Division I

First Round—St. Louis
Kentucky 96, Florida A&M 76
Washington 100, Univ. of Alabama-Birmingham 102
Providence 58, Univ. of the Pacific 66
Kansas 78, Illinois-Chicago 53
Boston College 58, Utah 51
Georgia Tech 65, No. Iowa 60
Michigan State 66, Nevada 72
Gonzaga 76, Valparaiso 49

First Round—East Rutherford
St. Joseph's 82, Liberty 63
Texas Tech 76, Charlotte 73
Florida 60, Manhattan 75
Wake Forest 79, Va. Common 78
Wisconsin 76, Richmond 64
Pittsburgh 53, Central Florida 44
Memphis 59, South Carolina 43
Oklahoma State 75, Eastern Washington 56

First Round—Atlanta
Duke 96, Alabama State 61
Seton Hall 80, Arizona 76
Illinois 72, Murray State 53
Cincinnati 80, East Tennessee State 77
Univ. of North Carolina 63, Air Force 52
Texas 66, Princeton 49
Xavier 80, Louisville 70
Mississippi State 85, Monmouth 52

First Round—Phoenix
Stanford 71, Texas-San Antonio 45
Alabama 65, Southern Illinois 64
Syracuse 80, Brigham Young 75
Maryland 86, Texas-El Paso 83
Vanderbilt 71, Western Michigan 58
North Carolina State 61, Louisiana Lafayette 52
DePaul 76, Dayton 69
Connecticut 70, Vermont 53

Second Round—St. Louis
Kentucky 75, Univ. of Alabama-Birmingham 76
Univ. of the Pacific 63, Kansas 78
Boston College 54, Georgia Tech 57
Nevada 91, Gonzaga 72

Second Round—East Rutherford
St. Joseph 70, Texas Tech 65
Manhattan 80, Wake Forest 84
Wisconsin 55, Pittsburgh 59
Memphis 53, Oklahoma State 70

Second Round—Atlanta
Duke 90, Seton Hall 62
Illinois 92, Cincinnati 68
Univ. of North Carolina 75, Texas 78
Xavier 89, Mississippi State 74

Second Round—Phoenix
Stanford 67, Alabama 70
Syracuse 72, Maryland 70
Vanderbilt 75, North Carolina State 73
DePaul 55, Connecticut 72

Third Round—St. Louis
Univ. of Alabama-Birmingham 74, Kansas 100
Georgia Tech 72, Nevada 67

Third Round—East Rutherford
St. Joseph 84, Wake Forest 80
Pittsburgh 51, Oklahoma State 63

Third Round—Atlanta
Duke 72, Illinois 63
Texas 71, Xavier 79

Third Round—Phoenix
Alabama 80, Syracuse 71
Vanderbilt 53, Connecticut 73

Regional Finals
St. Louis—Kansas 71, Georgia Tech 79
East Rutherford—St. Joseph 62, Oklahoma State 64
Atlanta—Duke 66, Xavier 63
Phoenix—Alabama 71, Connecticut 87

Final Four
(April 3, 2004, San Antonio, Tex.)
Georgia Tech 67, Oklahoma State 65
Duke 78, Connecticut 79

National Final
(April 5, 2004, San Antonio, Tex.)
Georgia Tech 73, Connecticut 82

Division II
Championship
Southern Indiana 59, Kennesaw State 84

Division III
Championship
Williams 82, Wisconsin-Stevens Point 84

LEADING NCAA DIVISION I MEN, 2003–2004

POINTS PER GAME

	FGM	3FG	FT	PTS	PPG
Keydren Clark, St. Peter's	233	112	197	775	26.7
Kevin Martin, Western Carolina	208	51	206	673	24.9
David Hawkins, Temple	224	84	177	709	24.4
Taylor Coppenrath, Vermont	203	14	159	579	24.1
Luis Flores, Manhattan	234	68	208	744	24.0

FIELD-GOAL PERCENTAGE

	G	FGM	FGA	FG%
Nigel Dixon, Western Kentucky	28	179	264	67.8
Sean Finn, Dayton	33	175	264	66.3
Adam Mark, Belmont	30	233	352	66.2
David Harrison, Colorado	29	186	295	63.1
Cuthbert Victor, Murray State	34	190	302	62.9

REBOUNDING

	G	REB	RPG
Paul Millsap, Louisiana Tech	30	374	12.5
Jaime Lioreda, Louisiana State	22	256	11.6
Emeka Okafor, Connecticut	36	415	11.5
Nate Lofton, Southeastern Louisiana	29	315	10.9
Nigel Wyatte, Wagner	28	292	10.4

ASSISTS

	G	AST	APG
Greg Davis, Troy State	31	256	8.3
Martell Bailey, Illinois-Chicago	32	250	7.8
Aaron Miles, Kansas	33	242	7.3
Andres Rodriguez, American	31	225	7.3
Raymond Felton, North Carolina	30	212	7.1

FREE-THROW PERCENTAGE

	G	FT	FTA	FT%
Blake Ahearn, SW Missouri State	33	117	120	97.5
J. J. Redick, Duke	37	143	150	95.3
Jake Sullivan, Iowa State	33	83	89	93.3
Steve Drabyn, Belmont	30	96	105	91.4
Chris Hernandez, Stanford	30	96	105	91.4

THREE-PT FIELD-GOAL PERCENTAGE

	G	3FG	3FGA	3FG%
Brad Lechtenberg, San Diego	23	71	139	51.1
James Odoms, Mercer	23	59	121	48.8
Tyson Dorsey, Samford	28	74	152	48.7
Antonio Burks, Stephen F. Austin	30	78	164	47.6
Trey Guidry, Illinois State	29	86	187	46.0

NCAA DIVISION I SINGLE-GAME SCORING MARKS[1]

	Year	Pts
Kevin Bradshaw, US Int'l vs. Loyola-CA	1991	72
Pete Maravich, LSU vs. Alabama	1970	69
Calvin Murphy, Niagara vs. Syracuse	1969	68
Jay Handlan, Wash. & Lee vs. Furman	1951	66
Pete Maravich, LSU vs. Tulane	1969	66
Anthony Roberts, Oral Rbts. vs. N.C. A&T.	1977	66

	Year	Pts
Anthony Roberts, Oral Rbts. vs. Oregon	1977	65
Scott Haffner, Evansville vs. Dayton	1989	65
Pete Maravich, LSU vs. Kentucky	1970	64
Johnny Neumann, Ole Miss vs. LSU	1971	63
Hersey Hawkins, Bradley vs. Detroit	1988	63

1. Scored against a Division I opponent.

NCAA DIVISION I INDIVIDUAL CAREER RECORDS

SCORING—TOTAL POINTS

	Yrs	Last	Gm	Pts
Pete Maravich, LSU	3	1970	83	3,667
Freeman Williams, Port. St.	4	1978	106	3,249
Lionel Simmons, La Salle	4	1990	131	3,217
Alphonso Ford, Miss. Val. St.	4	1993	109	3,165
Harry Kelly, Texas Southern	4	1983	110	3,066
Hersey Hawkins, Bradley	4	1988	125	3,008
Oscar Robertson, Cincinnati	3	1960	88	2,973
Danny Manning, Kansas	4	1988	147	2,951
Alfredrick Hughes, Loyola-Ill.	4	1985	120	2,914
Elvin Hayes, Houston	4	1968	93	2,884

SCORING—AVERAGE POINTS

	Yrs	Last	Pts	Avg
Pete Maravich, LSU	3	1970	3,667	44.2
Austin Carr, Notre Dame	3	1971	2,560	34.6
Oscar Robertson, Cinn.	3	1960	2,973	33.8
Calvin Murphy, Niagara	3	1970	2,548	33.1
Dwight Lamar, SW La.	2	1973	1,862	32.7
Frank Selvy, Furman	3	1954	2,538	32.5
Rick Mount, Purdue	3	1970	2,323	32.3
Darrell Floyd, Furman	3	1956	2,281	32.1
Nick Werkman, Seton Hall	3	1964	2,273	32.0
Willie Humes, Idaho St.	2	1971	1,510	31.5

BLOCKED SHOTS—AVERAGE

	Yrs	Last	No	Avg
Keith Closs, Cen. Conn. St.	2	1996	317	5.87
Adonal Foyle, Colgate	3	1997	492	5.66
David Robinson, Navy	2	1987	351	5.24
Wojciech Mydra, La.-Monroe	4	2002	535	4.65
Shaquille O'Neal, LSU	3	1992	412	4.58

Note: minimum 225 blocked shots.

ASSISTS—TOTAL

	Yrs	Last	Gm	No
Bobby Hurley, Duke	4	1993	140	1,076
Chris Corchiani, N.C. State	4	1991	124	1,038
Ed Cota, N. Carolina	4	2000	138	1,030
Keith Jennings, E. Tenn. St.	4	1991	127	983
Steve Blake, Maryland	4	2003	138	972
Sherman Douglas, Syracuse	4	1989	138	960
Tony Miller, Marquette	4	1995	123	956
Greg Anthony, Portland/UNLV	4	1991	138	950
Doug Gottlieb, ND/Okla St.	4	2000	124	947
Gary Payton, Oregon St.	4	1990	120	939

STEALS—AVERAGE

	Yrs	Last	No	Avg
Desmond Cambridge, Alabama A&M	3	2002	330	3.93
Mookie Blaylock, Oklahoma	2	1989	281	3.80
Ronn McMahon, Eastern Wash.	3	1990	225	3.52
Eric Murdock, Providence	4	1991	376	3.21
Van Usher, Tennessee Tech	3	1992	270	3.18

Note: minimum 225 steals.

REBOUNDS—TOTAL, SINCE 1973

	Yrs	Last	Gm	No
Tim Duncan, Wake Forest	4	1997	128	1,570
Derrick Coleman, Syracuse	4	1990	143	1,537
Malik Rose, Drexel	4	1996	120	1,514
Ralph Sampson, Virginia	4	1983	132	1,511
Pete Padgett, Nevada-Reno	4	1976	104	1,464
Lionel Simmons, La Salle	4	1990	131	1,429
Anthony Bonner, St. Louis	4	1990	133	1,424
Tyrone Hill, Xavier-Ohio	4	1990	126	1,380
Popeye Jones, Murray St.	4	1992	123	1,374
Michael Brooks, La Salle	4	1980	114	1,372

WOMEN'S NCAA CHAMPIONSHIPS, 2004

Division I

First Round—Mideast
Duke 103, Northwestern State 51
Old Dominion 64, Marquette 67
Louisiana Tech 81, Montana 77
Texas Tech 60, Maine 50
Ohio State 73, West Virginia 67
Boston College 58, Eastern Michigan 56
Minnesota 92, UCLA 81
Kansas State 71, Valparaiso 63

First Round—Midwest
Tennessee 77, Colgate 54
George Washington 46, DePaul 83
Florida 68, New Mexico 56
Baylor 71, Loyola-Marymount 60
Stanford 68, Missouri 44
Oklahoma 58, Marist 45
Rutgers 69, Chattanooga 74
Vanderbilt 76, Lipscomb 45

First Round—East
Penn State 79, Hampton 42
Virginia Tech 89, Iowa 76
Notre Dame 69, SW Missouri State 65
North Carolina 62, Middle Tennessee 67
Colorado 49, UC-Santa Barbara 76
Houston 62, Wis.-Green Bay 47
Auburn 79, N.C. State 59
Connecticut 91, Pennsylvania 55

First Round—West
Texas 92, Southern 57
Michigan State 72, Arizona 60
Miami (Fla.) 85, Maryland 86
Louisiana State 83, Austin Peay 66
Texas Christian 70, Temple 57
Georgia 78, Liberty 53
Villanova 66, Ole Miss 63
Purdue 78, St. Francis (Pa.) 59

Second Round—Mideast
Duke 76, Marquette 67
Louisiana Tech 81, Texas Tech 64
Ohio State 48, Boston College 63
Minnesota 80, Kansas State 61

Second Round—Midwest
Florida 76, Baylor 91
Tennessee 79, DePaul 59
Stanford 68, Oklahoma 43
Chattanooga 44, Vanderbilt 60

Second Round—East
Penn State 61, Virginia Tech 48
Notre Dame 59, Middle Tennessee 46
UC-Santa Barbara 56, Houston 52
Auburn 53, Connecticut 79

Second Round—West
Texas 80, Michigan State 61
Maryland 61, Louisiana State 76
Texas Christian 71, Georgia 85
Villanova 42, Purdue 60

Third Round—Mideast
Duke 63, Louisiana Tech 49
Boston College 63, Minnesota 76

Third Round—Midwest
Tennessee 71, Baylor 69
Stanford 57, Vanderbilt 55

Third Round—East
Penn State 55, Notre Dame 49
UC-Santa Barbara 55, Connecticut 63

Third Round—West
Texas 55, Louisiana State 71
Georgia 66, Purdue 64

Regional Finals
Mideast—Duke 75, Minnesota 82
Midwest—Tennessee 62, Stanford 60
East—Penn State 49, Connecticut 66
West—Louisiana State 62, Georgia 60

Final Four
(April 4, 2004, New Orleans, La.)
Minnesota 58, Connecticut 67
Tennessee 52, Louisiana State 50

National Championship
(April 6, 2004, New Orleans, La.)
Connecticut 70, Tennessee 61

Division II
Championship
Drury 72, California (Pa.) 75

Division III
Championship
Wilmington (Ohio) 59, Bowdoin 53

LEADING NCAA DIVISION I WOMEN, 2003–2004

POINTS PER GAME

	FGM	3FG	FT	PTS	PPG
Emily Faurholt, Idaho	261	43	172	737	25.4
Hana Peljito, Harvard	246	37	112	641	23.7
Chandi Jones, Houston	255	71	146	727	22.7
Cyndi Wilks, Va. Commonwealth	215	58	130	618	22.1
Shameka Christon, Arkansas	219	47	126	611	21.8

FIELD-GOAL PERCENTAGE

	G	FGM	FGA	FG%
Katie Feenstra, Liberty	32	291	443	65.7
Janel McCarville, Minnesota	34	212	344	61.6
Gerlonda Hardin, Austin Peay	31	223	367	60.8
Le'Coe Willingham, Auburn	31	192	316	60.8
Khara Smith, DePaul	30	261	430	60.7

THREE-POINT FIELD-GOAL PERCENTAGE

	G	3FG	3FGA	3FG%
Marion Crandall, Eastern Michigan	30	77	152	50.7
K. C. Cowgill, SW Missouri State	32	65	138	47.1
Stefanie Collins, St. Bonaventure	26	75	161	46.6
Tory Mauseth, Yale	27	55	120	45.8
Cathy Joens, George Washington	30	96	218	44.0

FREE-THROW PERCENTAGE

	G	FT	FTA	FT%
Shanna Zolman, Tennessee	35	88	92	95.7
Cyndi Valentin, Indiana	29	99	107	92.5
Seimone Augustus, Louisiana State	35	100	111	90.1
Jill Marano, La Salle	28	95	106	89.6
Kari Koch, SW Missouri State	32	107	120	89.2

REBOUNDS PER GAME

	G	REB	RPG
Ashlee Kelly, Quinnipiac	29	392	13.5
Desire Almind, Bucknell	29	390	13.4
Sandora Irvin, Texas Christian	30	366	12.2
Rebekkah Brunson, Georgetown	28	336	12.0
Khara Smith, DePaul	30	351	11.7

ASSISTS PER GAME

	G	AST	APG
La'Terrica Dobin, Northwestern State	26	249	9.6
Temeka Johnson, Louisiana State	35	289	8.3
Leah Cannon, Oral Roberts	28	321	8.3
Yolanda Paige, West Virginia	32	253	7.9
Brooklynn Lorenzen, Montana	32	251	7.8

OTHER TOURNAMENTS, 2003–2004

MEN
NIT—Michigan 62, Rutgers 55
NAIA Div. I—Mountain State (W. Va.) 74, Concordia 70
NAIA Div. II—Oregon Tech 81, Bellevue (Neb.) 72

WOMEN
NIT—Creighton 72, Nevada-Las Vegas 53
NAIA Div. I—Southern Nazarene 77, Oklahoma City 61
NAIA Div. II—Morningside 87, Cedarville (Ohio) 74

Professional Basketball

NATIONAL BASKETBALL ASSOCIATION CHAMPIONS

The National Basketball Association was originally the Basketball Association of America. It took its current name in 1949 when it merged with the National Basketball League.

Year	Eastern Conference	Western Conference	Winner (Series)
1947	Philadelphia Warriors	Chicago Stags	Philadelphia Warriors (4–1)
1948	Philadelphia Warriors	Baltimore Bullets	Baltimore Bullets (4–2)
1949	Washington Capitols	Minneapolis Lakers	Minneapolis Lakers (4–2)
1950	Syracuse Nationals	Minneapolis Lakers	Minneapolis Lakers (4–2)
1951	New York Knickerbockers	Rochester Royals	Rochester Royals (4–3)
1952	New York Knickerbockers	Minneapolis Lakers	Minneapolis Lakers (4–3)
1953	New York Knickerbockers	Minneapolis Lakers	Minneapolis Lakers (4–1)
1954	Syracuse Nationals	Minneapolis Lakers	Minneapolis Lakers (4–3)
1955	Syracuse Nationals	Ft. Wayne Pistons	Syracuse Nationals (4–3)
1956	Philadelphia Warriors	Ft. Wayne Pistons	Philadelphia Warriors (4–1)
1957	Boston Celtics	St. Louis Hawks	Boston Celtics (4–3)
1958	Boston Celtics	St. Louis Hawks	St. Louis Hawks (4–2)
1959	Boston Celtics	Minneapolis Lakers	Boston Celtics (4–0)
1960	Boston Celtics	St. Louis Hawks	Boston Celtics (4–3)
1961	Boston Celtics	St. Louis Hawks	Boston Celtics (4–1)
1962	Boston Celtics	Los Angeles Lakers	Boston Celtics (4–3)
1963	Boston Celtics	Los Angeles Lakers	Boston Celtics (4–2)
1964	Boston Celtics	San Francisco Warriors	Boston Celtics (4–1)
1965	Boston Celtics	Los Angeles Lakers	Boston Celtics (4–1)
1966	Boston Celtics	Los Angeles Lakers	Boston Celtics (4–3)
1967	Philadelphia 76ers	San Francisco Warriors	Philadelphia 76ers (4–2)
1968	Boston Celtics	Los Angeles Lakers	Boston Celtics (4–2)
1969	Boston Celtics	Los Angeles Lakers	Boston Celtics (4–3)
1970	New York Knickerbockers	Los Angeles Lakers	New York Knickerbockers (4–3)
1971	Baltimore Bullets	Milwaukee Bucks	Milwaukee Bucks (4–0)
1972	New York Knickerbockers	Los Angeles Lakers	Los Angeles Lakers (4–1)
1973	New York Knickerbockers	Los Angeles Lakers	New York Knickerbockers (4–1)
1974	Boston Celtics	Milwaukee Bucks	Boston Celtics (4–3)
1975	Washington Bullets	Golden State Warriors	Golden State Warriors (4–0)
1976	Boston Celtics	Phoenix Suns	Boston Celtics (4–2)
1977	Philadelphia 76ers	Portland Trail Blazers	Portland Trail Blazers (4–2)
1978	Washington Bullets	Seattle SuperSonics	Washington Bullets (4–3)
1979	Washington Bullets	Seattle SuperSonics	Seattle SuperSonics (4–1)
1980	Philadelphia 76ers	Los Angeles Lakers	Los Angeles Lakers (4–2)
1981	Boston Celtics	Houston Rockets	Boston Celtics (4–2)
1982	Philadelphia 76ers	Los Angeles Lakers	Los Angeles Lakers (4–2)
1983	Philadelphia 76ers	Los Angeles Lakers	Philadelphia 76ers (4–0)
1984	Boston Celtics	Los Angeles Lakers	Boston Celtics (4–3)
1985	Boston Celtics	Los Angeles Lakers	Los Angeles Lakers (4–2)
1986	Boston Celtics	Houston Rockets	Boston Celtics (4–2)
1987	Boston Celtics	Los Angeles Lakers	Los Angeles Lakers (4–2)
1988	Detroit Pistons	Los Angeles Lakers	Los Angeles Lakers (4–3)
1989	Detroit Pistons	Los Angeles Lakers	Detroit Pistons (4–0)
1990	Detroit Pistons	Portland Trail Blazers	Detroit Pistons (4–1)
1991	Chicago Bulls	Los Angeles Lakers	Chicago Bulls (4–1)
1992	Chicago Bulls	Portland Trail Blazers	Chicago Bulls (4–2)
1993	Chicago Bulls	Phoenix Suns	Chicago Bulls (4–2)
1994	New York Knickerbockers	Houston Rockets	Houston Rockets (4–3)
1995	Orlando Magic	Houston Rockets	Houston Rockets (4–0)
1996	Chicago Bulls	Seattle SuperSonics	Chicago Bulls (4–2)
1997	Chicago Bulls	Utah Jazz	Chicago Bulls (4–2)
1998	Chicago Bulls	Utah Jazz	Chicago Bulls (4–2)
1999	New York Knickerbockers	San Antonio Spurs	San Antonio Spurs (4–1)
2000	Indiana Pacers	Los Angeles Lakers	Los Angeles Lakers (4–2)
2001	Philadelphia 76ers	Los Angeles Lakers	Los Angeles Lakers (4–1)
2002	New Jersey Nets	Los Angeles Lakers	Los Angeles Lakers (4–0)
2003	New Jersey Nets	San Antonio Spurs	San Antonio Spurs (4–2)
2004	Detroit Pistons	Los Angeles Lakers	Detroit Pistons (4–1)

INDIVIDUAL NBA SCORING CHAMPIONS

Season	Player, Team	G	FG	FT	Pts	Avg
1953–54	Neil Johnston, Philadelphia Warriors	72	591	577	1,759	24.4
1954–55	Neil Johnston, Philadelphia Warriors	72	521	589	1,631	22.7
1955–56	Bob Pettit, St. Louis Hawks	72	646	557	1,849	25.7
1956–57	Paul Arizin, Philadelphia Warriors	71	613	591	1,817	25.6
1957–58	George Yardley, Detroit Pistons	72	673	655	2,001	27.8
1958–59	Bob Pettit, St. Louis Hawks	72	719	667	2,105	29.2
1959–60	Wilt Chamberlain, Philadelphia Warriors	72	1,065	577	2,707	37.6
1960–61	Wilt Chamberlain, Philadelphia Warriors	79	1,251	531	3,033	38.4
1961–62	Wilt Chamberlain, Philadelphia Warriors	80	1,597	835	4,029	50.4
1962–63	Wilt Chamberlain, San Francisco Warriors	80	1,463	660	3,586	44.8
1963–64	Wilt Chamberlain, San Francisco Warriors	80	1,204	540	2,948	36.9
1964–65	Wilt Chamberlain, San Francisco Warriors/Phila. 76ers	73	1,063	408	2,534	34.7
1965–66	Wilt Chamberlain, Philadelphia 76ers	79	1,074	501	2,649	33.5
1966–67	Rick Barry, San Francisco Warriors	78	1,011	753	2,775	35.6
1967–68	Dave Bing, Detroit Pistons	79	835	472	2,142	27.1
1968–69	Elvin Hayes, San Diego Rockets	82	930	467	2,327	28.4
1969–70	Jerry West, Los Angeles Lakers	74	831	647	2,309	31.2
1970–71	Lew Alcindor,[1] Milwaukee Bucks	82	1,063	470	2,596	31.7
1971–72	Kareem Abdul-Jabbar, Milwaukee Bucks	81	1,159	504	2,822	34.8
1972–73	Nate Archibald, Kansas City/Omaha Kings	80	1,028	663	2,719	34.0
1973–74	Bob McAdoo, Buffalo Braves	74	901	459	2,261	30.8
1974–75	Bob McAdoo, Buffalo Braves	82	1,095	641	2,831	34.5
1975–76	Bob McAdoo, Buffalo Braves	78	934	559	2,427	31.1
1976–77	Pete Maravich, New Orleans Jazz	73	886	501	2,273	31.1
1977–78	George Gervin, San Antonio Spurs	82	864	504	2,232	27.2
1978–79	George Gervin, San Antonio Spurs	80	947	471	2,365	29.6
1979–80	George Gervin, San Antonio Spurs	78	1,024	505	2,585	33.1
1980–81	Adrian Dantley, Utah Jazz	80	909	632	2,452	30.7
1981–82	George Gervin, San Antonio Spurs	79	993	555	2,551	32.3
1982–83	Alex English, Denver Nuggets	82	959	406	2,326	28.4
1983–84	Adrian Dantley, Utah Jazz	79	802	813	2,418	30.6
1984–85	Bernard King, New York Knicks	55	691	426	1,809	32.9
1985–86	Dominique Wilkins, Atlanta Hawks	78	888	527	2,366	30.3
1986–87	Michael Jordan, Chicago Bulls[2]	82	1,098	833	3,041	37.1
1987–88	Michael Jordan, Chicago Bulls[3]	82	1,069	723	2,868	35.0
1988–89	Michael Jordan, Chicago Bulls[4]	81	966	674	2,633	32.5
1989–90	Michael Jordan, Chicago Bulls[5]	82	1,034	593	2,753	33.6
1990–91	Michael Jordan, Chicago Bulls[6]	82	990	571	2,580	31.5
1991–92	Michael Jordan, Chicago Bulls[7]	80	943	491	2,404	30.1
1992–93	Michael Jordan, Chicago Bulls[8]	78	992	476	2,541	32.6
1993–94	David Robinson, San Antonio Spurs[9]	80	840	693	2,383	29.8
1994–95	Shaquille O'Neal, Orlando Magic[10]	79	930	455	2,315	29.3
1995–96	Michael Jordan, Chicago Bulls[11]	82	916	548	2,491	30.4
1996–97	Michael Jordan, Chicago Bulls[11]	82	920	480	2,431	29.6
1997–98	Michael Jordan, Chicago Bulls[12]	82	881	565	2,357	28.7
1998–99	Allen Iverson, Philadelphia 76ers[13]	48	435	356	1,284	26.8
1999–2000	Shaquille O'Neal, L.A. Lakers	79	956	432	2,344	29.7
2000–01	Allen Iverson, Philadelphia 76ers[14]	71	762	585	2,207	31.1
2001–02	Allen Iverson, Philadelphia 76ers[15]	60	665	475	1,883	31.4
2002–03	Tracy McGrady, Orlando Magic	75	829	576	2,407	32.1
2003–04	Tracy McGrady, Orlando Magic	67	653	398	1,878	28.0

1. (Kareem Abdul-Jabbar). 2. Also had 12 3-point field goals. 3. Also had 7 3-point field goals. 4. Also had 27 3-point field goals. 5. Also had 92 3-point field goals. 6. Also had 29 3-point field goals. 7. Attempted 27 3-point field goals. 8. Also had 81 3-point field goals. 9. Also had 10 3-point field goals. 10. O'Neal scored no 3-point field goals in 1994–1995. 11. Also had 111 3-point field goals in both 1995–1996 and 1996–1997. 12. Also had 30 3-point field goals. 13. Also had 58 3-point field goals. 14. Also had 98 3-point field goals. 15. Also had 78 3-point field goals.

NBA INDIVIDUAL RECORDS, GAME

(Through 2003–2004 season)

Most points, game—100, Wilt Chamberlain, Philadelphia vs. New York, 1962

Most free throws, game—28, Wilt Chamberlain, Philadelphia vs. New York, 1962; 28, Adrian Dantley, Utah vs. Houston, 1984

Most field goals, game—36, Wilt Chamberlain, Philadelphia vs. New York, 1962

Most assists, game—30, Scott Skiles, Orlando vs. Denver, 1990

Most rebounds, game—55, Wilt Chamberlain, Philadelphia vs. Boston, 1960

Most 3-pt. field goals, game—11, Dennis Scott, Orlando vs. Atlanta, 1996

Most blocked shots, game—17, Elmore Smith, Los Angeles vs. Portland, 1973

Most steals, game—11, Larry Kenon, San Antonio vs. Kansas City, 1976; 11, Kendall Gill, New Jersey vs. Miami, 1999

NBA MOST VALUABLE PLAYERS

1956 Bob Pettit, St. Louis
1957 Bob Cousy, Boston
1958 Bill Russell, Boston
1959 Bob Pettit, St. Louis
1960 Wilt Chamberlain, Philadelphia
1961–63 Bill Russell, Boston
1964 Oscar Robertson, Cincinnati
1965 Bill Russell, Boston
1966–68 Wilt Chamberlain, Philadelphia
1969 Wes Unseld, Baltimore
1970 Willis Reed, New York
1971–72 Lew Alcindor
 (Kareem Abdul-Jabbar), Milwaukee
1973 Dave Cowens, Boston
1974 Kareem Abdul-Jabbar,
 Milwaukee

1975 Bob McAdoo, Buffalo
1976–77 Kareem Abdul-Jabbar,
 L.A. Lakers
1978 Bill Walton, Portland
1979 Moses Malone, Houston
1980 Kareem Abdul-Jabbar,
 L.A. Lakers
1981 Julius Erving, Philadelphia
1982 Moses Malone, Houston
1983 Moses Malone, Philadelphia
1984 Larry Bird, Boston
1985 Larry Bird, Boston
1986 Larry Bird, Boston
1987 Magic Johnson, L.A. Lakers
1988 Michael Jordan, Chicago
1989 Magic Johnson, L.A. Lakers

1990 Magic Johnson, L.A. Lakers
1991 Michael Jordan, Chicago
1992 Michael Jordan, Chicago
1993 Charles Barkley, Phoenix
1994 Hakeem Olajuwon, Houston
1995 David Robinson, San Antonio
1996 Michael Jordan, Chicago
1997 Karl Malone, Utah
1998 Michael Jordan, Chicago
1999 Karl Malone, Utah
2000 Shaquille O'Neal, L.A. Lakers
2001 Allen Iverson, Philadelphia
2002 Tim Duncan, San Antonio
2003 Tim Duncan, San Antonio
2004 Kevin Garnett, Minnesota

NBA LIFETIME LEADERS

(through 2004 season)
Players in bold face active in 2003–2004 season

POINTS

	Yrs	Gm	Pts	Avg
Kareem Abdul-Jabbar	20	1,560	38,387	24.6
Karl Malone	19	1,476	36,928	25.0
Michael Jordan	15	1,072	32,292	30.1
Wilt Chamberlain	14	1,045	31,419	30.1
Moses Malone	19	1,329	27,409	20.6
Elvin Hayes	16	1,303	27,313	21.0
Hakeem Olajuwon	18	1,238	26,946	21.8
Oscar Robertson	14	1,040	26,710	25.7
Dominique Wilkins	15	1,074	26,668	24.8
John Havlicek	16	1,270	26,395	20.8

SCORING AVERAGE

Minimum of 400 games or 10,000 points

	Yrs	Gm	Pts	Avg
Michael Jordan	15	1,072	32,292	30.1
Wilt Chamberlain	14	1,045	31,419	30.1
Elgin Baylor	14	846	23,149	27.4
Shaquille O'Neal	12	809	21,914	27.1
Jerry West	14	932	25,192	27.0
Allen Iverson	8	535	14,436	27.0
Bob Pettit	11	792	20,880	26.4
George Gervin	10	791	20,708	26.2
Oscar Robertson	14	1,040	26,710	25.7
Karl Malone	19	1,476	36,928	25.0

FIELD GOALS MADE

	Yrs	FG	Att	Pct
Kareem Abdul-Jabbar	20	15,837	28,307	.559
Karl Malone	19	13,528	26,210	.516
Wilt Chamberlain	14	12,681	23,497	.540
Michael Jordan	15	12,192	24,537	.497
Elvin Hayes	16	10,976	24,272	.452
Hakeem Olajuwon	18	10,749	20,991	.512
Alex English	15	10,659	21,036	.507
John Havlicek	16	10,513	23,930	.439
Dominique Wilkins	15	9,963	21,589	.461
Patrick Ewing	15	9,702	19,241	.504

FREE THROWS

	Yrs	FT	Att	Pct
Karl Malone	19	9,787	13,188	.742
Moses Malone	19	8,531	11,090	.769
Oscar Robertson	14	7,694	9,185	.838
Michael Jordan	15	7,327	8,772	.835
Jerry West	14	7,160	8,801	.814
Dolph Schayes	16	6,979	8,274	.843
Adrian Dantley	15	6,832	8,351	.818
Kareem Abdul-Jabbar	20	6,712	9,304	.721
Charles Barkley	16	6,349	8,643	.735
Bob Pettit	11	6,182	8,119	.761

3–PT FIELD GOALS MADE

Reggie Miller	2,464
Dale Ellis	1,719
Glen Rice	1,559
Tim Hardaway	1,542
Nick Van Exel	1,373

TOTAL MINUTES PLAYED

Kareem Abdul-Jabbar	57,446
Karl Malone	54,852
Elvin Hayes	50,000
Wilt Chamberlain	47,859
John Stockton	47,764

BLOCKED SHOTS

Hakeem Olajuwon	3,830
Kareem Abdul-Jabbar	3,189
Mark Eaton	3,064
Dikembe Mutombo	2,996
David Robinson	2,954

STEALS

John Stockton	3,265
Michael Jordan	2,514
Maurice Cheeks	2,310
Scottie Pippen	2,307
Gary Payton	2,243

REBOUNDS

Wilt Chamberlain	23,924	**Karl Malone**	14,968
Bill Russell	21,620	Robert Parish	14,715
Kareem Abdul-Jabbar	17,440	Nate Thurmond	14,464
Elvin Hayes	16,279	Walt Bellamy	14,241
Moses Malone	16,212	Wes Unseld	13,769

ASSISTS

John Stockton	15,806	**Gary Payton**	8,039
Mark Jackson	10,334	**Rod Strickland**	7,948
Magic Johnson	10,141	Maurice Cheeks	7,392
Oscar Robertson	9,887	Lenny Wilkens	7,211
Isiah Thomas	9,061	Terry Porter	7,160

NATIONAL BASKETBALL ASSOCIATION FINAL STANDINGS, 2003–2004

EASTERN CONFERENCE

Atlantic Division[1]	W	L	Pct	GB
New Jersey Nets[1]	47	35	.573	—
Miami Heat[2]	42	40	.512	5
New York Knicks[2]	39	43	.476	8
Boston Celtics[2]	36	46	.439	11
Philadelphia 76ers	33	49	.402	14
Washington Wizards	25	57	.305	22
Orlando Magic	21	61	.256	26

Central Division[1]	W	L	Pct	GB
Indiana Pacers[2]	61	21	.744	—
Detroit Pistons[2]	54	28	.659	7
New Orleans Hornets[2]	41	41	.500	20
Milwaukee Bucks[2]	41	41	.500	20
Cleveland Cavaliers	35	47	.427	26
Toronto Raptors	33	49	.402	28
Atlanta Hawks	28	54	.341	33
Chicago Bulls	23	59	.280	38

1: Division champion. 2. Playoff qualifier.

WESTERN CONFERENCE

Midwest Division	W	L	Pct	GB
Minnesota Timberwolves[1]	58	24	.707	—
San Antonio Spurs[2]	57	25	.695	1
Dallas Mavericks[2]	52	30	.634	6
Memphis Grizzlies[2]	50	32	.610	8
Houston Rockets[2]	45	37	.549	13
Denver Nuggets[2]	43	39	.524	15
Utah Jazz[2]	42	40	.512	16

Pacific Division	W	L	Pct	GB
L.A. Lakers[1]	56	26	.683	—
Sacramento Kings[2]	55	27	.671	1
Portland Trail Blazers	41	41	.500	15
Golden State Warriors	37	45	.451	19
Seattle SuperSonics	37	45	.451	19
Phoenix Suns	29	53	.354	27
L.A. Clippers	28	54	.341	28

1. Division champion. 2. Playoff qualifier.

NBA PLAYOFFS, 2004

EASTERN CONFERENCE

First Round
(Best of 7)
Indiana Pacers defeated Boston Celtics, 4 games to 0
New Jersey Nets defeated New York Knicks, 4 games to 0
Detroit Pistons defeated Milwaukee Bucks, 4 games to 1
Miami Heat defeated New Orleans Hornets, 4 games to 3

Conference Semifinals
(Best of 7)
Indiana Pacers defeated Miami Heat 4 games to 2
Detroit Pistons defeated New Jersey Nets, 4 games to 3

Conference Finals
(Best of 7)
Detroit Pistons defeated Indiana Pacers, 4 games to 2

WESTERN CONFERENCE

First Round
(Best of 7)
Minnesota Timberwolves defeated Denver Nuggets, 4 games to 1
L.A. Lakers defeated Houston Rockets, 4 games to 1
San Antonio Spurs defeated Memphis Grizzlies, 4 games to 0
Sacramento Kings defeated Dallas Mavericks, 4 games to 1

Conference Semifinals
(Best of 7)
Minnesota Timberwolves defeated Sacramento Kings, 4 games to 3
L.A. Lakers defeated San Antonio Spurs, 4 games to 2

Conference Finals
(Best of 7)
L.A. Lakers defeated Minnesota Timberwolves, 4 games to 2

NBA CHAMPIONSHIPS

Detroit Pistons defeated L.A. Lakers, 4 games to 1
Chauncey Billups, Detroit, named Finals MVP

June 6—Detroit 87, Los Angeles 75
June 8—Los Angeles 99, Detroit 91 (OT)
June 10—Detroit 88, Los Angeles 68

June 13—Detroit 88, Los Angeles 80

June 15—Detroit 100, Los Angeles 87

NBA INDIVIDUAL LEADERS, 2003–2004 SEASON

POINTS PER GAME
Minimum of 49 games played

	Gm	Pts	PPG
Tracy McGrady, Orlando	67	1,878	28.0
Predrag Stojakovic, Sacramento	81	1,964	24.2
Kevin Garnett, Minnesota	82	1,987	24.2
Kobe Bryant, L.A. Lakers	65	1,557	24.0
Paul Pierce, Boston	80	1,836	23.0
Baron Davis, New Orleans	67	1,532	22.9
Vince Carter, Toronto	73	1,645	22.5
Tim Duncan, San Antonio	69	1,538	22.3
Dirk Nowitzki, Dallas	77	1,680	21.8
Michael Redd, Milwaukee	82	1,776	21.7

ASSISTS PER GAME
Minimum of 49 games played

	Gm	Ast	APG
Jason Kidd, New Jersey	67	618	9.2
Stephon Marbury, New York	81	719	8.9
Steve Nash, Dallas	78	687	8.8
Baron Davis, New Orleans	67	501	7.5
Sam Cassell, Minnesota	81	592	7.3
Eric Snow, Philadelphia	82	563	6.9
Jason Williams, Memphis	72	492	6.8
Kirk Hinrich, Chicago	76	517	6.8
Steve Francis, Houston	79	493	6.2
Jeff McInnis, Cleveland	70	430	6.1
Andre Miller, Denver	82	501	6.1
Damon Stoudamire, Portland	82	500	6.1

REBOUNDS PER GAME
Minimum of 49 games played

	Gm	Reb	RPG
Kevin Garnett, Minnesota	82	1,139	13.9
Tim Duncan, San Antonio	69	859	12.4
Ben Wallace, Detroit	81	1,006	12.4
Erick Dampier, Golden State	74	887	12.0
Carlos Boozer, Cleveland	75	857	11.4
Zach Randolph, Portland	81	851	10.5
Jamaal Magloire, New Orleans	82	847	10.3
Brad Miller, Sacramento	72	743	10.3
Kenny Thomas, Philadelphia	74	750	10.1
Marcus Camby, Denver	72	727	10.1

FIELD GOAL PERCENTAGE
Minimum of 288 field goals made

	FGM	FGA	Pct
Shaquille O'Neal, L.A. Lakers	554	948	.584
Mark Blount, Boston	342	604	.566
Erick Dampier, Golden State	348	650	.535
Antawn Jamison, Dallas	488	913	.535
Nenê, Denver	334	630	.530
Carlos Boozer, Cleveland	471	900	.523
Yao Ming, Houston	535	1,025	.522
Brad Miller, Sacramento	373	731	.510
Corliss Williamson, Detroit	304	602	.505
Tim Duncan, San Antonio	592	1,181	.501

FREE-THROW PERCENTAGE
Minimum of 120 free throws made

	FTM	FTA	Pct
Predrag Stojakovic, Sacramento	394	425	.927
Steve Nash, Dallas	230	251	.916
Allan Houston, New York	157	172	.913
Ray Allen, Seattle	245	271	.904
Reggie Miller, Indiana	146	165	.885
Chauncey Billups, Detroit	404	460	.878
Brian Cardinal, Golden State	238	271	.878
Dirk Nowitzki, Dallas	371	423	.877
Earl Boykins, Denver	142	162	.877
Damon Stoudamire, Portland	127	145	.876

3-POINT FIELD GOAL PERCENTAGE
Minimum of 55 3-point field goals made

	3FGM	3FGA	Pct
Anthony Peeler, Sacramento	68	141	.482
Brent Barry, Seattle	114	252	.452
Brian Cardinal, Golden State	55	124	.444
Fred Hoiberg, Minnesota	76	172	.442
Aaron McKie, Philadelphia	75	172	.436
Predrag Stojakovic, Sacramento	240	554	.433
Allan Houston, New York	87	202	.431
Hidayet Turkoglu, San Antonio	101	241	.419
Casey Jacobsen, Phoenix	75	180	.417
Charlie Ward, San Antonio	84	206	.408

BLOCKED SHOTS PER GAME
Minimum of 49 games played or 96 block shots

	Gm	Blk	BPG
Theo Ratliff, Portland	85	307	3.61
Ben Wallace, Detroit	81	246	3.04
Andrei Kirilenko, Utah	78	215	2.76
Tim Duncan, San Antonio	69	185	2.68
Marcus Camby, Denver	72	187	2.60
Jermaine O'Neal, Indiana	78	199	2.55
Zydrunas Ilgauskas, Cleveland	81	201	2.48
Shaquille O'Neal, L.A. Lakers	67	166	2.48
Samuel Dalembert, Philadelphia	82	189	2.30
Elton Brand, L.A. Clippers	69	154	2.23

STEALS PER GAME
Minimum of 49 games played or 120 steals

	Gm	Stl	SPG
Baron Davis, New Orleans	67	158	2.36
Shawn Marion, Phoenix	79	167	2.11
Ron Artest, Indiana	73	152	2.08
Andrei Kirilenko, Utah	78	150	1.92
Doug Christie, Sacramento	82	151	1.84
Stephen Jackson, Atlanta	80	142	1.78
Emanuel Ginobili, San Antonio	77	136	1.77
Ben Wallace, Detroit	81	143	1.77
Steve Francis, Houston	79	139	1.76
Andre Miller, Denver	82	142	1.73

Women's Professional Basketball
WOMEN'S NATIONAL BASKETBALL ASSOCIATION, 2004 SEASON

Eastern Conference

	W	L	Pct	GB	Home	Road
Connecticut Sun	18	16	.529	—	10–7	8–9
New York Liberty	18	16	.529	—	11–6	7–10
Detroit Shock	17	17	.500	1	8–9	9–8
Washington Mystics	17	17	.500	1	11–6	6–11
Charlotte Sting	16	18	.471	2	10–7	6–11
Indiana Fever	15	19	.441	3	10–7	5–12

Western Conference

	W	L	Pct	GB	Home	Road
Los Angeles Sparks	25	9	.735	—	15–2	10–7
Seattle Storm	20	14	.588	5	13–4	7–10
Sacramento Monarchs	18	16	.529	7	10–7	8–9
Minnesota Lynx	18	16	.529	7	11–6	7–10
Phoenix Mercury	17	17	.500	8	10–7	7–10
Houston Comets	13	21	.382	12	9–8	4–13
San Antonio Silver Stars	9	25	.265	16	6–11	3–14

NOTE: GB refers to Games Behind leader.

Conference Championship Series (Best of 3)

EASTERN CONFERENCE

Date	Result
Oct. 1	Connecticut 61, New York 51
Oct. 3	Connecticut 60, New York 57

Connecticut wins series, 2–0

WESTERN CONFERENCE

Date	Result
Oct. 1	Sacramento 74, Seattle 72
Oct. 3	Seattle 66, Sacramento 54
Oct. 5	Seattle 82, Sacramento 62

Seattle wins series, 2–1

League Championship Series (Best of 3)
Seattle wins championship, 2 games to 1

Date	Result
Oct. 8	Connecticut 68, Seattle 64
Oct. 10	Seattle 67, Connecticut 65
Oct. 12	Seattle 74, Connecticut 60

WNBA ANNUAL AWARDS, 2004 SEASON

Most Valuable Player: Lisa Leslie, Los Angeles
Rookie of the Year: Diana Taurasi, Phoenix
Coach of the Year: Suzie McConnell Serio, Minnesota
Defensive Player of the Year: Lisa Leslie, Los Angeles
Most Improved Players of the Year: Wendy Palmer, Connecticut and Kelly Miller, Indiana

Kim Perrot Sportsmanship Award: Teresa Edwards, Minnesota
Cascade Dish and Assist Award: Nikki Teasley, Los Angeles
Bud Light Peak Performers: Lisa Leslie, Los Angeles and Lauren Jackson, Seattle

2004 WNBA LEAGUE LEADERS

POINTS PER GAME

	Gm	Pts	PPG
Lauren Jackson, Seattle	31	634	20.5
Tina Thompson, Houston	26	520	20.0
Lisa Leslie, Los Angeles	34	598	17.6
Diana Taurasi, Phoenix	34	578	17.0
Tamika Catchings, Indiana	34	568	16.7

REBOUNDS PER GAME

	Gm	Reb	RPG
Lisa Leslie, Los Angeles	34	336	9.9
Cheryl Ford, Detroit	31	297	9.6
Michelle Snow, Houston	31	239	7.7
Tamika Catchings, Indiana	34	249	7.3
Elena Baranova, New York	34	246	7.2
Yolanda Griffith, Sacramento	34	246	7.2
Taj McWilliams-Franklin, Connecticut	34	244	7.2

ASSISTS PER GAME

	Gm	Ast	APG
Nikki Teasley, Los Angeles	34	207	6.1
Sue Bird, Seattle	34	184	5.4
Dawn Staley, Charlotte	34	171	5.0
Ticha Penicheiro, Sacramento	33	163	4.9
Lindsay Whalen, Connecticut	31	148	4.8

BLOCKS PER GAME

	Gm	Blk	BPG
Lisa Leslie, Los Angeles	34	98	2.88
Tammy Sutton-Brown, Charlotte	34	71	2.09
Lauren Jackson, Seattle	31	62	2.00
Elena Baranova, New York	34	58	1.71
Ruth Riley, Detroit	34	53	1.56

STEALS PER GAME

	Gm	Stl	SPG
Yolanda Griffith, Sacramento	34	75	2.21
Nykesha Sales, Connecticut	34	75	2.21
Alana Beard, Washington	34	69	2.03
Tamika Catchings, Indiana	34	67	1.97
Deanna Nolan, Detroit	34	66	1.94
Ticha Penicheiro, Sacramento	33	64	1.94

FIELD GOAL PERCENTAGE

	FGM	FGA	FG%
Tamika Williams, Minnesota	102	189	.540
Yolanda Griffith, Sacramento	177	341	.519
Lisa Leslie, Los Angeles	223	451	.494
LaToya Thomas, San Antonio	171	350	.489
Penny Taylor, Phoenix	150	310	.484

3-POINT FIELD GOAL PERCENTAGE

	3FGM	3FGA	3FG%
Charlotte Smith-Taylor, Charlotte	29	58	.500
Elena Baranova, New York	53	115	.461
Lauren Jackson, Seattle	52	115	.452
Sue Bird, Seattle	64	146	.438
Katie Smith, Minnesota	60	139	.432

FREE THROW PERCENTAGE

	FTM	FTA	FT%
Katie Smith, Minnesota	98	109	.899
Vickie Johnson, New York	62	70	.886
Kelly Miller, Indiana	50	57	.877
Allison Feaster, Charlotte	79	91	.868
Anna DeForge, Phoenix	88	102	.863

Sports Personalities

A name in parentheses is the original name or form of name. Localities are places of birth. Dates of birth appear as month/day/year. **Boldface** years in parentheses are dates of (**birth–death**).

Information has been gathered from many sources, including the individuals themselves. However, the almanac cannot guarantee the accuracy of every individual item.

Aaron, Hank (Henry) (baseball); Mobile, Ala., 2/5/34
Abdul-Jabbar, Kareem (Lewis Ferdinand Alcindor, Jr.) (basketball); New York City, 4/16/47
Affleck, Francis (auto racing) **(1951–1985)**
Agassi, Andre (tennis); Las Vegas, Nev., 4/29/70
Aikman, Troy (football); Henryetta, Okla., 11/21/66
Ali, Muhammad (Cassius Clay) (boxing); Louisville, Ky., 1/18/42
Allen, Dick (Richard Anthony) (baseball); Wampum, Pa., 3/8/42
Allen, George (football) **(1918–1990)**
Allison, Bobby (Robert Arthur) (auto racing); Hueytown, Ala., 12/3/37
Allison, Davey (auto racing); Hueytown, Ala. **(1961–1993)**
Alston, Walter (baseball); Venice, Ohio **(1911–1984)**
Alworth, Lance (football); Houston, 8/3/40
Ameche, Alan (football); Houston, Tex. **(1933–1988)**
Anderson, Sparky (George) (baseball); Bridgewater, S.D., 2/22/34
Andretti, Mario (auto racing); Montona, Trieste, Italy, 2/28/40
Anthony, Earl (bowling); Kent, Wash. **(1939–2001)**
Appling, Luke (baseball); High Point, N.C. **(1907–1990)**
Arcaro, Eddie (George Edward) (jockey); Cincinnati **(1916–1997)**
Armstrong, Lance (bicycling); Plano, Tex., Sept. 18, 1971
Ashe, Arthur (tennis); Richmond, Va. **(1943–1993)**
Ashford, Evelyn (track & field) (sprinter); Shreveport, La., 4/15/57
Austin, Tracy (tennis); Rolling Hills, Calif., 12/2/62
Averill, Earl (baseball); Everett, Wash. **(1915–1983)**
Babashoff, Shirley (swimming); Whittier, Calif., 1/31/57
Baer, Max (boxing); Omaha, Neb. **(1909–1959)**

Bailey, Donovan (track); Canada, 12/16/67
Banks, Ernie (baseball); Dallas, 1/31/31
Bannister, Roger (runner); Harrow, England, 3/24/29
Barkley, Charles (basketball); Leeds, Ala., 2/20/63
Barry, Rick (Richard) (basketball); Elizabeth, N.J., 3/28/44
Bauer, Hank (Henry) (baseball); East St. Louis, Ill., 7/31/22
Baugh, Sammy (football); Temple, Tex., 3/17/14
Baylor, Elgin (basketball); Washington, D.C., 9/16/34
Beamon, Bob (long jumper); New York City, 8/29/46
Becker, Boris (tennis); Leiman, W. Germany, 11/22/67
Beckham, David (soccer); Leytonstone, England, 5/2/75
Bee, Clair (basketball); Cleveland, Ohio **(1896–1983)**
Beliveau, Jean (hockey); Three Rivers, Quebec, Canada, 8/31/31
Belle, Albert (baseball); Shreveport, La., 8/25/66
Beman, Deane (golf); Washington, D.C., 4/22/38
Bench, Johnny (Johnny Lee) (baseball); Oklahoma City, 12/7/47
Berg, Patty (Patricia Jane) (golf); Minneapolis, 2/13/18
Berra, Yogi (Lawrence) (baseball); St. Louis, 5/12/25
Biletnikoff, Frederick (football); Erie, Pa., 2/23/43
Bing, Dave (basketball); Washington, D.C., 11/24/43
Bird, Larry (basketball); French Lick, Ind., 12/7/56
Blaik, Earl H. (football); Detroit **(1897–1989)**
Blanda, George Frederick (football); Youngwood, Pa., 9/17/27
Bledsoe, Drew (football); Walla Walla, Wash., 2/14/72
Blue, Vida (baseball); Mansfield, La., 7/28/49
Bodine, Brett (auto racing); Chemung, N.Y., 1/11/59

Bodine, Geoff (auto racing); Chemung, N.Y., 4/18/49
Boggs, Wade (baseball); Omaha, Neb., 6/15/58
Bonds, Barry (baseball); Riverside, Calif., 7/24/64
Borg, Björn (tennis); Stockholm, Sweden, 6/6/56
Boros, Julius (golf); Fairfield, Conn. **(1920–1994)**
Bossy, Mike (hockey); Montreal, 1/22/57
Boston, Ralph (long jumper); Laurel, Miss., 5/9/39
Bourque, Ray (hockey); Montreal, Que., 12/28/60
Bradley, Bill (William Warren) (basketball); Crystal City, Mo., 7/28/43
Bradley, Pat (golf); Westford, Mass., 3/24/51
Bradshaw, Terry (football); Shreveport, La., 9/2/48
Breedlove, Craig (Norman) (speed driving); Los Angeles, 3/23/38
Brett, George (baseball); Glendale, W. Va., 5/15/53
Brock, Louis Clark (baseball); El Dorado, Ark., 6/18/39
Brown, Jim (football); St. Simon Island, Ga., 2/17/36
Brumel, Valeri (high jumper); Tolbuzino, Siberia, 4/14/42
Bryant, Paul "Bear" (football); Morro Bottom, Ark. **(1913–1983)**
Bryant, Rosalyn Evette (track); Chicago, 1/7/56
Burton, Michael (swimming); Des Moines, Iowa, 7/3/47
Butkus, Dick (Richard Marvin) (football); Chicago, 12/9/42
Calipari, John (basketball); Moon, Pa., 2/10/59
Campanella, Roy (baseball); Homestead, Pa. **(1921–1993)**
Campbell, Earl (football); Tyler, Tex., 3/29/55
Canseco, Jose (baseball); Havana, Cuba, 7/2/64
Caponi, Donna Maria (golf); Detroit, 1/29/45
Cappelletti, Gino (football); Keewatin, Minn., 3/26/34
Capriati, Jennifer (tennis); New York, N.Y., 3/29/76
Carew, Rod (Rodney Cline) (baseball); Gatun, Panama, 10/1/45
Carlos, John (sprinter); New York City, 6/5/45
Carlton, Steven Norman (baseball); Miami, Fla., 12/22/44
Carner, Joanne Gunderson, Mrs. Don (golf); Kirkland, Wash., 3/4/39
Casals, Rosemary (tennis); San Francisco, 9/16/48
Casper, Billy (golf); San Diego, Calif., 6/24/31
Caulkins, Tracy (swimming); Winona, Minn., 1/11/63
Cauthen, Steve (jockey); Covington, Ky., 5/1/60
Chamberlain, Wilt (Wilton) (basketball); Philadelphia **(1936–1999)**
Chandler, A. B. (Happy) (baseball); Louisville, Ky. **(1898–1991)**
Chandler, Spud (baseball); Commerce, Ga. **(1907–1990)**
Chang, Michael (tennis); Hoboken, N.J., 2/22/72
Chapot, Frank (equestrian); Camden, N.J., 2/24/34
Chastain, Brandi (soccer); San Jose, Calif., 7/21/68
Chinaglia, Giorgio (soccer); Carrara, Italy, 1/24/47
Clarke, Bobby (Robert Earle) (hockey); Flin Flon, Manitoba, Canada, 8/13/49
Clemens, Roger (baseball); Dayton, Ohio, 8/4/62
Clemente, Roberto Walker (baseball); Carolina, Puerto Rico **(1934–1972)**
Cobb, Ty (Tyrus Raymond) (baseball); Narrows, Ga. **(1886–1961)**
Cochran, Barbara Ann (skiing); Claremont, N.H., 1/14/51
Cochran, Marilyn (skiing); Burlington, Vt., 2/7/50
Cochran, Robert (skiing); Claremont, N.H., 12/11/51
Coe, Sebastian Newbold (track); London, England, 9/29/56
Coffey, Paul (hockey); Weston, Ont., 6/1/61
Colavito, Rocky (Rocco Domenico) (baseball); New York City, 8/10/33
Coleman, Derrick (basketball); Mobile, Ala., 6/21/67
Comaneci, Nadia (gymnast); Onesti, Romania, 11/12/61
Conigliaro, Tony (baseball); Revere, Mass. **(1945–1990)**
Connors, Jimmy (James Scott) (tennis); East St. Louis, Ill., 9/2/52
Cooper, Cynthia (basketball); Chicago, Ill., 4/14/63
Cordero, Angel (jockey); Santurce, Puerto Rico, 5/8/42
Cosell, Howard (broadcaster); Winston-Salem, N.C. **(1918–1995)**
Courier, Jim (tennis); Sanford, Fla., 8/17/70
Cournoyer, Yvan Serge (hockey); Drummondville, Quebec, Canada, 11/22/43
Court, Margaret Smith (tennis); Albury, New South Wales, Australia, 7/16/42
Cousy, Bob (basketball); New York City, 8/9/28
Crabbe, Buster (swimming); Scottsdale, Ariz. **(1908–1983)**
Crenshaw, Ben (golf); Austin, Tex., 1/11/52
Cronin, Joe (baseball executive); San Francisco **(1906–1984)**
Cruyff, Johan (soccer); Amsterdam, Netherlands, 4/25/47
Csonka, Larry (Lawrence Richard) (football); Stow, Ohio, 12/25/46
Dancer, Stanley (harness racing); New Egypt, N.J., 7/25/27
Dark, Alvin (baseball); Comanche, Okla., 1/7/22
Davenport, Willie (track); Troy, Ala. **(1943–2002)**
Dawson, Andre (baseball); Miami, Fla., 7/10/54
Dawson, Leonard Ray (football); Alliance, Ohio, 6/20/35
Dean, Dizzy (Jay Hanna) (baseball); Lucas, Ark. **(1911–1974)**
DeBusschere, Dave (basketball); Detroit **(1940–2003)**
De La Hoya, Oscar (boxing); East Los Angeles, Calif., 2/4/73
Delvecchio, Alex Peter (hockey); Fort William, Ontario, Canada, 12/4/31
Demaret, Jim (golf); Houston **(1910–1983)**
Dempsey, Jack (William H.) (boxing); Manassa, Colo. **(1895–1983)**
DeVicenzo, Roberto (golf); Buenos Aires, 4/14/23
Dibbs, Edward George (tennis); Brooklyn, New York, 2/23/51
Dietz, James W. (rowing); New York, N.Y., 1/12/49

DiMaggio, Joe (baseball); Martinez, Calif. **(1914–1999)**
Dionne, Marcel (hockey); Drummondville, Quebec, Canada, 8/3/51
Dorsett, Tony (football); Rochester, Pa., 4/7/54
Dryden, Kenneth (hockey); Hamilton, Ontario, Canada, 8/4/47
Drysdale, Don (baseball); Van Nuys, Calif. **(1936–1993)**
Duran, Roberto (boxing); Panama City, 6/16/51
Durocher, Leo (baseball); West Springfield, Mass. **(1906–1991)**
Durr, Francois (tennis); Algiers, Algeria, 12/25/42
Earnhardt, Dale (auto racing); Concord, N.C. **(1951–2001)**
Eckersley, Dennis (baseball); Oakland, Calif., 10/3/54
Elder, Lee (golf); Dallas, 7/14/34
Elway, John (football); Port Angeles, Wash., 6/28/60
Emerson, Roy (tennis); Kingsway, Australia, 11/3/36
Ender, Kornelia (swimming); Plauen, East Germany, 10/25/58
Erving, Julius ("Dr. J") (basketball); Roosevelt, N.Y., 2/22/50
Esposito, Phil (Philip Anthony) (hockey); Sault Ste. Marie, Ontario, Canada, 2/20/42
Evans, Lee (runner); Mandena, Calif., 2/25/47
Evert, Chris (Christine Marie) (tennis); Fort Lauderdale, Fla., 12/21/54
Ewbank, Weeb (football); Richmond, Ind. **(1907–1998)**
Ewing, Patrick (basketball); Kingston, Jamaica, 8/5/62
Favre, Brett (football); Gulfport, Miss., 10/10/69
Feller, Robert (Bob) (baseball); Van Meter, Iowa, 11/3/18
Feuerbach, Allan Dean (track); Preston, Iowa, 1/12/48
Finley, Charles O. (sportsman); Ensley, Ala. **(1918–1996)**
Fischer, Bobby (chess); Chicago, 3/9/43
Fitzsimmons, Bob (Robert Prometheus) (boxing); Cornwall, England **(1862–1917)**
Fleming, Peggy Gale (ice skating); San Jose, Calif., 7/27/48
Ford, Whitey (Edward) (baseball); New York City, 10/21/28
Foreman, George (boxing); Marshall, Tex., 1/10/49
Fosbury, Richard (high jumper); Portland, Ore., 3/6/47
Fox, Nellie (Jacob Nelson) (baseball); St. Thomas, Pa. **(1927–1975)**
Foxx, James Emory (baseball); Sudlersville, Md. **(1907–1967)**
Foyt, A. J. (auto racing); Houston, 1/16/35
Frazier, Joe (boxing); Beaufort, S.C., 1/12/44
Frazier, Walt (basketball); Atlanta, 3/29/45
Freeman, Cathy (track & field); Mackay, Queensland, Australia, 2/16/73
Frick, Ford C. (baseball); Wawaka, Ind. **(1894–1978)**
Furniss, Bruce (swimming); Fresno, Calif., 5/27/57
Gable, Dan (wrestling); Waterloo, Iowa, 10/25/45
Gabriel, Roman (football); Wilmington, N.C., 8/5/40
Gallagher, Michael Donald (skiing); Yonkers, N.Y., 10/3/41
Garvey, Steve (baseball); Tampa, Fla., 12/22/48
Gehrig, Lou (Henry Louis) (baseball); New York City **(1903–1941)**
Gehringer, Charlie (baseball); Fowlerville, Mich. **(1903–1993)**
Geoffrion, "Boom Boom" (Bernie) (hockey); Montreal, 2/14/31
Gerulaitis, Vitas (tennis); Brooklyn, N.Y. **(1954–1994)**
Gervin, George (basketball); Long Beach, Calif., 4/27/52
Giacomin, Ed (hockey); Sudbury, Ontario, Canada, 6/6/39
Giamatti, A. Bartlett (baseball); South Hadley, Mass. **(1938–1989)**
Gibson, Bob (baseball); Omaha, Neb., 11/9/35
Gifford, Frank (football); Santa Monica, Calif., 8/16/30
Gilbert, Rod (Rodrique) (hockey); Montreal, 7/1/41
Gilmore, Artis (basketball); Chipley, Fla., 9/21/49
Glance, Harvey (track); Phenix City, Ala., 3/28/57
Gonzalez, Pancho (tennis); Los Angeles **(1928–1995)**
Goodell, Brian Stuart (swimming); Stockton, Calif., 4/2/59
Gooden, Dwight (baseball); Tampa, Fla., 11/16/64
Goodrich, Gail (basketball); Los Angeles, 4/23/43
Goolagong, Cawley, Evonne (tennis); Griffith, Australia, 7/31/51
Gordon, Jeff (auto racing); Vallejo, Calif., 8/4/71
Gossage, "Goose" (Rich) (baseball); Colorado Springs, Colo., 4/5/51
Graf, Steffi (tennis); Mannheim, W. Germany, 6/14/69
Graham, David (golf); Windson, Australia, 5/23/46
Graham, Otto Everett (football); Waukegan, Ill., 12/6/21
Grange, Red (Harold) (football); Forksville, Pa. **(1904–1991)**
Green, Hubert (golf); Birmingham, Ala., 12/28/46
Greene, Charles E. (sprinter); Pine Bluff, Ark., 3/21/45
Greene, "Mean" (Joe) (football); Temple, Tex., 9/24/46
Gretzky, Wayne (hockey); Brantford, Ont., 1/26/61
Griese, Bob (Robert Allen) (football); Evansville, Ind., 2/3/45
Griffey, Ken, Jr. (baseball); Donora, Pa., 11/21/69
Grove, Lefty (Robert Moses) (baseball); Lonaconing, Md. **(1900–1975)**
Groza, Lou (football); Martins Ferry Ohio **(1924–2000)**
Guidry, Ronald Ames (baseball); Lafayette, La., 8/28/50
Gwynn, Tony (baseball); Los Angeles, Calif., 5/9/60
Halas, George (football); Chicago **(1895–1983)**
Hall, Gary (swimming); Fayetteville, N.C., 8/7/51
Hamill, Dorothy (figure skating); Chicago, 7/26/56
Hamilton, Scott (figure skating); Bowling Green, Ohio, 8/28/58
Hamm, Mia (soccer); Selma, Ala., 3/17/72
Hammond, Kathy (runner); Sacramento, Calif., 11/2/51
Hardaway, Anfernee (basketball); Memphis, Tenn., 7/18/72
Harding, Tonya (figure skating); Portland, Ore., 11/12/70
Harris, Franco (football); Ft. Dix, N.J., 3/7/50
Hartack, William, Jr. (jockey); Colver, Pa., 12/9/32

Hasek, Dominik (hockey); Pardubice, Czechoslovakia, 1/29/65
Haughton, William (harness racing); Gloversville, N.Y. **(1923–1986)**
Havlicek, John (basketball); Martins Ferry, Ohio, 4/8/40
Hayes, Elvin (basketball); Rayville, La., 11/17/45
Hayes, Woody (football); Upper Arlington, Ohio **(1913–1987)**
Heiden, Eric (speed skating); Madison, Wis., 6/14/58
Hencken, John (swimming); Culver City, Calif., 5/29/54
Henderson, Rickey (baseball); Chicago, 12/25/58
Henie, Sonja (ice skater); Oslo **(1912–1969)**
Herman, Floyd Caves (Babe) (baseball); Buffalo, N.Y. **(1903–1987)**
Hernandez, Keith (baseball); San Francisco, 10/20/53
Hershiser, Orel (baseball); Buffalo, N.Y., 9/16/58
Hickcox, Charles (swimming); Phoenix, Ariz., 2/6/47
Hines, James (sprinter); Dumas, Ark., 9/10/46
Hingis, Martina (tennis); Kosice, Slovakia, 9/30/80
Hodges, Gil (baseball); Princeton, Ind. **(1924–1972)**
Hogan, Ben (golf); Dublin, Tex. **(1912–1997)**
Holmes, Larry (boxing); Cuthert, Ga., 11/3/49
Holyfield, Evander (boxing); Atlanta, Ga., 10/19/62
Hornsby, Rogers (baseball); Winters, Tex. **(1896–1963)**
Hornung, Paul (football); Louisville, Ky., 12/23/35
Houk, Ralph (baseball); Lawrence, Kan., 8/9/19
Howard, Elston (baseball); St. Louis **(1929–1980)**
Howe, Gordon (hockey); Floral, Sask., Canada, 3/31/28
Howell, Jim Lee (football); Lonoke, Ark. **(1914–1995)**
Howser, Dick (baseball); Miami, Fla. **(1937–1987)**
Hubbell, Carl (baseball); Carthage, Mo. **(1903–1988)**
Huff, Sam (Robert Lee) (football); Morgantown, W. Va., 10/4/34
Hull, Bobby (hockey); Point Anne, Ontario, Canada, 1/3/39
Hunter, "Catfish" (Jim) (baseball); Hertford, N.C. **(1946–1999)**
Hutson, Donald (football); Pine Bluff, Ark. **(1913–1997)**
Irwin, Hale (golf); Joplin, Mo., 6/3/45
Jacobs, Helen Hull (tennis); Globe, Ariz. **(1908–1997)**
Jackson, Phil (basketball coach); Deer Lodge, Mont., 9/17/45
Jackson, Reggie (baseball); Wyncote, Pa., 5/18/46
Jagr, Jaromir (hockey); Kladno, Czechoslovakia, 2/15/72
Jeffries, James J. (boxing); Carroll, Ohio **(1875–1953)**
Jenkins, Ferguson Arthur (baseball); Chatham, Ontario, Canada, 12/13/43
Jenner, (W.) Bruce (track); Mt. Kisco, N.Y., 10/28/49
Jezek, Linda (swimming); Palo Alto, Calif., 3/10/60
Johnson, Anthony (rowing); Washington, D.C., 11/16/40
Johnson, Jack (John Arthur) (boxing); Galveston, Tex. **(1876–1946)**
Johnson, Jimmy (football); Port Arthur, Tex., 8/14/43
Johnson, "Magic" (Earvin) (basketball); E. Lansing, Mich., 8/14/59
Johnson, Michael (track); Dallas, Tex., 9/13/67
Johnson, Rafer (decathlon); Hillsboro, Tex., 8/18/35
Johnson, Randy (baseball); Walnut Creek, Calif., 9/10/63
Johnson, Wilham Julius (Judy) (baseball); Wilmington, Del. **(1899–1989)**
Jones, Cobi (soccer); Detroit, Mich., 6/16/70
Jones, Deacon (David) (football); Eatonville, Fla., 12/9/38
Jones, Marion (track & field); Los Angeles, Calif., 10/12/75
Jordan, Michael (basketball); Brooklyn, N.Y., 2/17/63
Joyner, Florence Griffith (sprinter); Mojave Desert, Calif. **(1959–1998)**
Joyner-Kersee, Jackie (track); East St. Louis, Ill., 3/3/62
Juantoreno, Alberto (track); Santiago, Cuba, 12/3/51
Jurgensen, Sonny (football); Wilmington, N.C., 8/23/34
Justice, Dave (baseball); Cincinnati, Ohio, 4/14/66
Kaat, Jim (baseball); Zeeland, Mich., 11/7/38
Kaline, Al (Albert) (baseball); Baltimore, 12/19/34
Keino, Kipchoge (runner); Kapchemoiymo, Kenya, 1/17/40
Kelly, Leroy (football); Philadelphia, 5/20/42
Kelly, Red (Leonard Patrick) (hockey); Simcoe, Ontario, Canada, 7/9/27
Kerrigan, Nancy (figure skating); Woburn, Mass., 10/13/69
Killebrew, Harmon (baseball); Payette, Idaho, 6/29/36
Killy, Jean-Claude (skiing); Saint-Cloud, France, 8/30/43
Kilmer, Bill (William Orland) (football); Topeka, Kan., 9/5/39
King, Bille Jean (Bille Jean Moffitt) (tennis); Long Beach, Calif., 11/22/43
Kinsella, John (swimming); Oak Park, Ill., 8/26/52
Kluszewski, Ted (baseball); Argo, Ill. **(1924–1988)**
Kodes, Jan (tennis); Prague, 3/1/46
Kolb, Claudia (swimming); Hayward, Calif., 12/19/49
Korbut, Olga (gymnast); Grodno, Byelorussia, USSR, 5/16/55
Koufax, Sandy (Sanford) (baseball); Brooklyn, N.Y., 12/30/35
Kramer, Jack (tennis); Las Vegas, Nev., 8/1/21
Kramer, Jerry (football); Jordan, Mont., 1/23/36
Krayzelburg, Lenny (swimming); Odessa, Ukraine, 9/28/75
Kuenn, Harvey (baseball); West Allis, Wis. **(1930–1988)**
Kuhn, Bowie Kent (baseball); Takoma Park, Md., 10/28/26
Kwan, Michelle (figure skating); Torrance, Calif., 7/7/80
Lafleur, Guy Damien (hockey); Thurso, Quebec, Canada, 9/20/51
Laird, Ronald (walker); Louisville, Ky., 5/31/35
Lalas, Alexi (soccer); Birmingham, Mich., 6/1/70
Lamonica, Daryle (football); Fresno, Calif., 7/17/41

Landis, Kenesaw Mountain (1st baseball commissioner); Millville, Ohio **(1866–1944)**
Landry, Tom (football); Mission, Tex. **(1924–2000)**
Landy, John (runner, governor of Victoria); Australia, 4/12/30
Larrieu, Francie (track); Palo Alto, Calif., 11/28/52
La Russa, Tony (baseball); Tampa, Fla., 10/4/44
Lasorda, Tom (baseball); Norristown, Pa., 9/22/27
Laver, Rod (tennis); Rockhampton, Australia, 8/9/38
Layne, Bobby (football); Lubbock, Texas **(1927–1986)**
Leetch, Brian (hockey); Corpus Christi, Tex., 3/3/68
Lemieux, Mario (hockey); Montreal, Quebec, Canada, 10/5/65
Lendl, Ivan (tennis); Prague, 3/7/60
Leonard, Benny (Benjamin Leiner) (boxing); New York City **(1896–1947)**
Leonard, Sugar Ray (boxing); Wilmington, N.C., 5/17/56
Lewis, Carl (track); Willingboro, N.J., 7/1/61
Lindros, Eric (hockey); London, Ont., 2/28/73
Lipinski, Tara (figure skating); Philadelphia, Pa., 6/10/82
Liquori, Marty (runner); Montclair, N.J., 9/11/49
Little, Lou (football); Leominster, Mass. **(1893–1979)**
Littler, Gene (golf); La Jolla, Calif., 7/21/30
Lobo, Rebecca (basketball); Southwick, Mass., 10/6/73
Lombardi, Vince (football); Brooklyn, N.Y. **(1913–1970)**
Longden, Johnny (horse racing); Wakefield, England **(1907–2003)**
Lopat, Eddie (baseball); New York, N.Y. **(1918–1992)**
Lopez, Al (baseball); Tampa, Fla., 8/20/08
Lopez, Nancy (golf); Torrance, Calif., 1/6/57
Louis, Joe (Joe Louis Barrow) (boxing); Lafayette, Ala. **(1914–1981)**
Lukas, D. Wayne (horse racing); Antigo, Wis., 9/2/35
Lynn, Frederic Michael (baseball); Chicago, Ill., 2/3/52
Lynn, Janet (figure skating); Rockford, Ill., 4/6/53
Mack, Connie (Cornelius Alexander McGillicuddy) (baseball executive); East Brookfield, Mass. **(1862–1956)**
Mackey, John (football); New York City, 9/24/41
Maddux, Greg (baseball); San Angelo, Texas, 4/14/66
Mahovlich, Frank (Francis William) (hockey); Timmins, Ontario, Canada, 1/10/38
Mahre, Phil (skiiing); White Pass, Wash., 5/10/57
Malone, Karl (basketball); Summerfield, La., 7/24/63
Malone, Moses (basketball); Petersburg, Va., 3/23/55
Mandlikova, Hana (tennis); Prague, Czechoslovakia, 2/62
Mann, Carol (golf); Buffalo, N.Y., 2/3/41
Manning, Madeline (runner); Cleveland, 1/11/48
Mantle, Mickey Charles (baseball); Spavinaw, Okla. **(1931–1995)**
Maravich, "Pistol Pete" (Peter) Aliquippa, Pa. **(1948–1988)**
Marble, Alice (tennis); Palm Springs, Calif. **(1913–1990)**
Marciano, Rocky (boxing); Brockton, Mass. **(1923–1969)**
Marichal, Juan (baseball); Laguna Verde, Montecristi, Dominican Republic, 10/20/37
Marino, Dan (football); Pittsburgh, Pa., 9/15/61
Maris, Roger (baseball); Hibbing, Minn. **(1934–1985)**
Martin, Billy (Alfred Manuel) (baseball); Berkeley, Calif. **(1928–1989)**
Martin, Christy (boxing); Mullers, W.Va., 6/12/68
Martin, Rick (Richard Lionel) (hockey); Verdun, Quebec, Canada, 7/26/51
Martinez, Pedro (baseball); Manoguayabo, Dominican Republic, 10/25/71
Mathews, Ed (Edwin) (baseball); Texarkana, Tex. **(1931–2001)**
Mattingly, Don (baseball); Evansville, Ind., 4/20/61
Matson, Randy (shot putter); Kilgore, Tex., 3/5/45
Mays, Willie (baseball); Westfield, Ala., 5/6/31
McAdoo, Bob (basketball); Greensboro, N.C., 9/25/51
McCarthy, Joe (Joseph Vincent) (baseball); Philadelphia **(1887–1978)**
McCovey, Willie Lee (baseball); Mobile, Ala., 1/10/38
McDonald, Lanny (hockey); Hanna, Alberta, Canada, 2/16/53
McDowell, Jack (baseball); Van Nuys, Calif., 1/16/66
McEnroe, John Patrick, Jr. (tennis); Wiesbaden, Germany, 2/16/59
McGraw, John Joseph (baseball); Truxton, N.Y. **(1873–1934)**
McGwire, Mark (baseball); Pomona, Calif., 10/1/63
McLain, Dennis (baseball); Chicago, 3/24/44
McMillan, Kathy Laverne (track); Raeford, N.C., 11/7/57
Merrill, Janice (track); New London, Conn., 6/18/62
Messier, Mark (hockey); Edmonton, Alberta, Canada, 1/18/61
Meyer, Deborah (swimming); Haddonfield, N.J., 8/14/52
Meyers, Ann (basketball); San Diego, Calif., 3/26/55
Middlecoff, Cary (golf); Halls, Tenn. **(1921–1998)**
Mikita, Stan (hockey); Sokolce, Czechoslovakia, 5/20/40
Milburn, Rodney, Jr. (hurdler); Opelousas, La., 5/18/50
Miller, Cheryl (basketball); Riverside, Calif., 1/3/64
Miller, Johnny (golf); San Francisco, 4/29/47
Miller, Reggie (basketball); Riverside, Calif., 8/24/65
Montana, Joe (football); New Eagle, Pa., 6/11/56
Montgomery, Jim (swimming); Madison, Wis., 1/24/55
Montgomery, Tim (track); Gaffney, S.C., 1/25/75
Moody, Helen Wills (tennis); Centerville, Calif. **(1906–1998)**
Moore, Archie (boxing); Benoit, Miss. **(1916–1998)**

Morgan, Joe Leonard (baseball); Bonham, Tex., 9/19/43
Morrall, Earl (football); Muskegon, Mich., 5/17/34
Morton, Craig L. (football); Flint, Mich., 2/5/43
Mosconi, Willie (pocket billiards); Philadelphia **(1913–1993)**
Moses, Edwin Corley (track); Dayton, Ohio, 8/31/55
Mungo, Van Lingo (baseball); Pageland, S.C. **(1911–1985)**
Munson, Thurman (baseball); Akron, Ohio **(1947–1979)**
Murphy, Calvin (basketball); Norwalk, Conn., 5/9/48
Murray, Eddie (baseball); Los Angeles, Calif., 2/24/56
Musial, Stan (baseball); Donora, Pa., 11/21/20
Myers, Linda (archery); York, Pa., 6/19/47
Naber, John (swimming); Evanston, Ill., 1/20/56
Namath, Joe (Joseph William) (football); Beaver Falls, Pa., 5/31/43
Nastase, Ilie (tennis); Bucharest, 7/19/46
Navratilova, Martina (tennis); Prague, 10/18/56
Nehemiah, Renaldo (track); Newark, N.J., 3/24/59
Nelson, Cindy (skiing); Lutsen, Minn., 8/19/55
Newcombe, John (tennis); Sydney, Australia, 5/23/44
Niekro, Phil (baseball); Lansing, Ohio, 4/1/39
Nicklaus, Jack (golf); Columbus, Ohio, 1/21/40
Norman, Gregory (golf); Mount Isa, Australia, 2/10/55
Oerter, Al (discus thrower); New York City, 9/19/36
Olajuwon, Hakeem (basketball); Lagos, Nigeria, 1/21/63
Oldfield, Barney (racing driver); Fulton County, Ohio **(1878–1946)**
Oliva, Tony (Pedro) (baseball); Pinar Del Rio, Cuba, 7/20/40
Olsen, Merlin Jay (football); Logan, Utah, 9/15/40
O'Malley, Walter (baseball executive); New York City **(1903–1979)**
O'Neal, Shaquille (basketball); Newark, N.J., 3/6/72
Orantes, Manuel (tennis); Granada, Spain, 2/6/49
Orr, Bobby (hockey); Parry Sound, Ontario, Canada, 3/20/48
Ovett, Steve (track); Brighton, England, 10/9/55
Owens, Jesse (track); Decatur, Ala. **(1913–1980)**
Paige, Satchel (Leroy) (baseball); Mobile, Ala. **(1906–1982)**
Palmer, Arnold (golf); Latrobe, Pa., 9/10/29
Palmer, James Alvin (baseball); New York City, 10/15/45
Parcells, Bill (football coach); Englewood, N.J., 8/22/41
Parent, Bernard Marcel (hockey); Montreal, 4/3/45
Parseghian, Ara (football); Akron, Ohio, 5/21/23
Pasarell, Charles (tennis); San Juan, Puerto Rico, 2/12/44
Patterson, Floyd (boxing); Waco, N.C., 1/4/35
Peete, Calvin (golf); Detroit, Mich., 7/18/43
Pelé (Edson Arantes do Nascimento) (soccer); Tres Coracoes, Brazil, 10/23/40
Perry, Gaylord (baseball); Williamston, N.C., 9/15/38
Perry, Jim (baseball); Williamston, N.C., 10/30/36
Pettit, Bob (basketball); Baton Rouge, La., 12/12/32
Petty, Richard Lee (auto racing); Randleman, N.C., 7/2/37
Pincay, Laffit, Jr. (jockey); Panama City, Panama, 12/29/46
Pippen, Scottie (basketball); Trenton, N.J., 9/25/65
Plager, Barclay (ice hockey); Kirkland Lake, Ontario **(1941–1988)**
Plante, Jacques (hockey); Sahwinigan Falls, Quebec, Canada **(1929–1986)**
Player, Gary (golf); Johannesburg, South Africa, 11/1/35
Plunkett, Jim (football); San Jose, Calif., 12/5/47
Potvin, Denis Charles (hockey); Hull, Quebec, Canada, 10/29/53
Powell, Boog (John) (baseball); Lakeland, Fla., 8/17/41
Powell, Mike (track); Philadelphia, 11/10/63
Prefontaine, Steve Roland (runner); Coos Bay, Ore. **(1951–1975)**
Prince, Bob (baseball announcer); Pittsburgh **(1917–1985)**
Proell, Annemarie Moser (Alpine skier); Kleinarl, Austria, 3/27/53
Rafter, Patrick (tennis); Brisbane, Australia, 12/28/72
Ralston, Dennis (tennis); Bakersfield, Calif., 7/27/42
Rankin, Judy Torluemke (golf); St. Louis, Mo., 2/18/45
Raschi, Vic (baseball); West Springfield, Mass. **(1919–1988)**
Ratelle, Jean (Joseph Gilbert Yvon Jean) (hockey); St. Jean, Quebec, Canada, 10/29/53
Rawls, Betsy (Elizabeth Earle) (golf); Spartanburg, S.C., 5/4/28
Reed, Willis (basketball); Hico, La., 6/25/42
Reese, Pee Wee (Harold) (baseball); Ekron, Ky. **(1919–1999)**
Resch, Glenn "Chico". (hockey); Moose Jaw, Saskatchewan, Canada, 7/10/48
Rice, Jerry (football); Crawford, Miss., 10/13/62
Richard, Maurice (hockey); Montreal, 8/14/24
Riessen, Martin (tennis); Hinsdale, Ill., 12/4/41
Rigney, William (baseball); Alameda, Calif. **(1918–2001)**
Rios, Marcelo (tennis); Santiago, Chile, 12/26/75
Ripken, Cal, Jr. (baseball); Havre de Grace, Md., 8/24/60
Rizzuto, Phil (baseball); New York City, 9/25/18
Robertson, Oscar (basketball); Charlotte, Tenn., 11/24/38
Robinson, Arnie (track); San Diego, Calif., 4/7/48
Robinson, Brooks (baseball); Little Rock, Ark., 5/18/37
Robinson, David (basketball); Key West, Fla., 8/6/65
Robinson, Frank (baseball); Beaumont, Tex., 8/31/35
Robinson, Jackie (baseball); Cairo, Ga. **(1919–1972)**
Robinson, Larry Clark (hockey); Marvelville, Ontario, Canada, 6/2/51

Robinson, "Sugar" Ray (boxing); Detroit **(1921–1989)**
Rockne, Knute Kenneth (football); Voss, Norway **(1888–1931)**
Rockwell, Martha (skiing); Providence, R.I., 4/26/44
Rodman, Dennis (basketball); Trenton, N.J., 5/13/61
Ronaldo (soccer); Bento Ribeiro, Brazil, 9/22/76
Rono, Henry (track); Kiptaragon, Kenya, 2/12/52
Rooney, Art (football); Pittsburgh, Pa. **(1901–1988)**
Rose, Pete (Peter Edward) (baseball); Cincinnati, 4/14/41
Rosenbloom, Maxie (boxing); New York City **(1904–1976)**
Rosewall, Ken (tennis); Sydney, Australia, 11/2/34
Rote, Kyle (football); San Antonio **(1928–2002)**
Roush, Edd (baseball); Oakland City, Ind. **(1893–1988)**
Rozelle, Pete (Alvin Ray) (commissioner of National Football League); South Gate, Calif. **(1926–1996)**
Rudolph, Wilma Glodean (sprinter); St. Bethlehem, Tenn. **(1940–1994)**
Russell, Bill (basketball); Monroe, La., 2/12/34
Ruth, Babe (George Herman Ruth) (baseball); Baltimore **(1895–1948)**
Rutherford, Johnny (auto racing); Fort Worth, 3/12/38
Ryan, Nolan (Lynn Nolan, Jr.) (baseball); Refugio, Tex., 1/31/47
Ryon, Luann (archery); Long Beach, Calif., 1/13/53
Ryun, Jim (runner); Wichita, Kan., 4/29/47
Salazar, Alberto (track); Havana, 8/7/58
Sampras, Pete (tennis); Washington, D.C., 8/12/71
Samuels, Howard (horse racing soccer); New York City **(1920–1984)**
Sanders, Barry (football); Wichita, Kan., 7/16/68
Sanders, Deion (baseball/football); Ft. Myers, Fla., 8/9/67
Santana, Manuel (Manuel Martinez Martinez) (tennis); Chamartin, Spain, 5/10/38
Sayers, Gale (football); Wichita, Kan., 5/30/43
Schmidt, Mike (baseball); Dayton, Ohio, 9/27/49
Schoendienst, Red (Albert) (baseball); Germantown, Ill., 2/2/23
Schollander, Donald (swimming); Charlotte, N.C., 4/30/46
Scurry, Briana (soccer); Minneapolis, Minn., 9/7/71
Seagren, Bob (Robert Lloyd) (pole vaulter); Pomona, Calif., 10/17/46
Seau, Junior (football); Oceanside, Calif., 1/19/69
Seaver, Tom (baseball); Fresno, Calif., 11/17/44
Seidler, Maren (track); Brooklyn, N.Y., 6/11/51
Seles, Monica (tennis); Novi Sad, Yugoslavia, 12/2/73
Selke, Frank (ice hockey); Canada **(1893–1985)**
Sewell, Joe (baseball); Titus, Ala. **(1898–1990)**
Shepherd, Lee (auto racing) **(1945–1985)**
Shero, Fred (hockey); Camden, N.J. **(1925–1990)**
Shoemaker, Willie (jockey); Fabens, Tex. **(1931–2003)**
Shore, Eddie (ice hockey); Saskatchewan, Canada **(1902–1985)**
Shorter, Frank (runner); Munich, Germany, 10/31/47
Shriver, Pam (tennis); Baltimore, 7/4/62
Shula, Don (Donald Francis) (football); Grand River, Ohio, 1/4/30
Silvester, Jay (discus thrower); Tremonton, Utah, 2/27/37
Simpson, O.J. (Orenthal James) (football); San Francisco, 7/9/47
Sims, Billy (football); St. Louis, 9/18/55
Smith, Bubba (Charles Aaron) (football); Orange, Tex., 2/28/45
Smith, Emmitt (football); Pensacola, Fla., 5/15/69
Smith, Ozzie (baseball); Mobile, Ala., 12/26/54
Smith, Ronnie Ray (sprinter); Los Angeles, 3/28/49
Smith, Stanley Roger (tennis); Pasadena, Calif., 12/14/46
Smith, Tommie (sprinter); Clarksville, Tex., 6/5/44
Smoke, Marcia Jones (canoeing); Oklahoma City, 7/18/41
Snead, Sam (golf); Hot Springs, Va. **(1912–2002)**
Sneva, Tom (auto racing); Spokane, Wash., 6/1/48
Snider, Duke (Edwin) (baseball); Los Angeles, 9/19/26
Solomon, Harold (tennis); Washington, D.C., 9/17/52
Sosa, Sammy (Samuel) (baseball); San Pedro de Macoris, Dominican Republic, 11/12/68
Spahn, Warren (baseball); Buffalo, N.Y. **(1921–2003)**
Speaker, Tristram (baseball); Hubbard City, Tex. **(1888–1958)**
Spencer, Brian (ice hockey); Fort St. James, British Columbia **(1949–1988)**
Spinks, Leon (boxing); St. Louis, 7/11/53
Spitz, Mark (swimming); Modesto, Calif., 2/10/50
Stabler, Kenneth (football); Foley, Ala., 12/25/45
Stagg, Amos Alonzo (football); West Orange, N.J. **(1862–1965)**
Stargell, Willie (Wilver Dornell) (baseball); Earlsboro, Okla. **(1941–2001)**
Starr, Bart (football); Montgomery, Ala., 1/9/34
Staub, "Rusty" (Daniel) (baseball); New Orleans, 4/4/44
Staubach, Roger (football); Cincinnati, 2/5/42
Steinkraus, William C. (equestrian); Cleveland, 10/12/25
Stenerud, Jan (football); Fetsund, Norway, 11/26/42
Stengel, Casey (Charles Dillon) (baseball); Kansas City, Mo. **(1891–1975)**
Stenmark, Ingemar (Alpine skier); Tarnaby, Sweden, 3/18/56
Stevens, Scott (hockey); Completon, New Brunswick, 5/4/66
Stockton, Richard LaClede (tennis); New York City, 2/18/51
Stones, Dwight Edwin (track); Los Angeles, 12/6/53
Strawberry, Darryl (baseball); Los Angeles, 3/12/62
Street, Picabo (skiing); Triumph, Idaho, 4/3/71
Sullivan, John Lawrence (boxing); Boston **(1858–1918)**
Summitt, Pat (basketball); Henrietta, Tenn., 6/14/52

Sutton, Don (Donald Howard) (baseball); Clio, Ala., 4/2/45
Swann, Lynn (football); Alcoa, Tenn., 3/7/52
Swoopes, Sheryl (basketball); Brownfield, Tex., 3/25/71
Tanner, Leonard Roscoe III (tennis); Chattanooga, Tenn., 10/15/51
Tarkenton, Fran (Francis) (football); Richmond, Va., 2/3/40
Tebbetts, Birdie (George R.) (baseball); Nashua, N.H. **(1914–1999)**
Theismann, Joe (football); New Brunswick, N.J., 9/9/46
Thomas, Frank (baseball); Columbus, Ga., 5/27/68
Thomas, Isiah (basketball); Chicago, Ill., 4/30/61
Thomas, Thurman (football); Houston, Texas, 5/16/66
Thompson, David (basketball); Shelby, N.C., 7/13/54
Thorpe, Ian (swimming); Sydney, New South Wales, Australia, 10/13/82
Thorpe, Jim (James Francis) (all-around athlete); nr. Prague, Okla. **(1888–1953)**
Tilden, William Tatem II (tennis); Philadelphia **(1893–1953)**
Tittle, Y. A. (Yelberton Abraham) (football); Marshall, Tex., 10/24/26
Toomey, William (decathlon); Philadelphia, 1/10/39
Trevino, Lee (golf); Dallas, 12/1/39
Trottier, Bryan (hockey); Val Marie, Sask., Canada, 7/17/56
Tunney, Gene (James J.) (boxing); New York City **(1898–1978)**
Tyson, Mike (boxing); Brooklyn, N.Y., 6/30/66
Tyus, Wyomia (runner); Griffin, Ga., 8/29/45
Ueberroth, Peter (baseball); Evanston, Ill., 9/2/37
Unitas, John (football); Pittsburgh **(1933–2002)**
Unser, Al (auto racing); Albuquerque, N. Mex., 5/29/39
Unser, Bobby (auto racing); Albuquerque, N. Mex., 2/20/34
Valenzuela, Fernando (baseball); Sonora, Mexico, 11/1/60
Valvano, Jim (basketball); New York, N.Y. **(1946–1993)**
Van Brocklin, Norm (football); Eagle Butte, S. Dak. **(1926–1983)**
Vaughn, Mo (baseball); Norwalk, Conn., 12/15/67
Vilas, Guillermo (tennis); Mar del Plata, Argentina, 8/17/52
Viola, Frank (baseball); Hempstead, N.Y., 4/19/60
Viren, Lasse (track); Myrskyla, Finland, 7/22/49
Vitale, Dick (basketball); E. Rutherford, N.J., 6/9/39
Wade, Virginia (tennis); Bournemouth, England, 7/10/45
Wagner, Honus (John Peter Honus) (baseball); Carnegie, Pa. **(1867–1955)**
Waitz, Grete (Andersen) (running); Oslo, Norway, 10/1/53
Walcott, Jersey Joe (Arnold Cream) (boxing); Merchantville, N.J. **(1914–1994)**

Wallace, Rusty (auto racing); St. Louis, Mo., 8/14/56
Walsh, Adam (football) **(1902–1985)**
Walton, Bill (basketball); La Mesa, Calif., 11/5/52
Waterfield, Bob (football); Burbank, Calif **(1921–1983)**
Watson, Martha Rae (track); Long Beach, Calif., 8/19/46
Watson, Tom (golf); Kansas City, Mo., 9/4/49
Weaver, Earl (baseball); St. Louis, 8/14/30
Weiskopf, Tom (golf); Massillon, Ohio, 11/9/42
Weiss, George (baseball executive); New Haven, Conn. **(1895–1972)**
Weissmuller, Johnny (swimmer and actor); Freidorf, Romania **(1904–1984)**
West, Jerry (basketball); Cheylan, W. Va., 5/28/38
White, Reggie (football); Chattanooga, Tenn., 12/19/61
White, Willye B. (long jumper); Money, Miss., 1/1/36
Whitworth, Kathy (golf); Monahans, Tex., 9/27/39
Wilkens, Mac Maurice (track); Eugene, Ore., 11/15/50
Wilkins, Lennie (basketball) 11/25/37
Wilkinson, Bud (football); Minneapolis **(1916–1994)**
Williams, Dick (baseball); St. Louis, 5/7/29
Williams, Serena (tennis); Saginaw, Mich., 9/26/81
Williams, Ted (baseball); San Diego, Calif. **(1918–2002)**
Williams, Venus (tennis); Lynnwood, Calif., 6/17/80
Wills, Maury (baseball); Washington, D.C., 10/2/32
Winfield, Dave (baseball); St. Paul, Minn., 10/3/51
Wohlhuter, Richard C. (runner); Geneva, Ill., 12/23/45
Wood, "Smokey Joe" (Joseph) (baseball); Kansas City, Mo. **(1890–1985)**
Woods, Tiger (Eldrick) (golf); Long Beach, Calif., 12/30/75
Wottle, David James (runner); Canton, Ohio, 8/7/50
Wright, Mickey (Mary Kathryn) (golf); San Diego, Calif., 2/14/35
Yarborough, Cale (William Caleb) (auto racing); Timmonsville, S.C., 3/27/39
Yastrzemski, Carl (baseball); Southampton, N.Y., 8/22/39
Young, Cy (Denton True) (baseball); Gilmore, Ohio **(1867–1955)**
Young, Sheila (speed skater, bicycle racer); Detroit, 10/14/50
Young, Steve (football); Salt Lake City, Utah, 10/11/61
Zaharias, Babe Didrikson (golf); Port Arthur, Tex. **(1913–1956)**

Sullivan Awards

JAMES E. SULLIVAN MEMORIAL AWARD WINNERS
(Amateur Athlete of the Year Chosen in Amateur Athletic Union Poll)

1930	Robert Tyre Jones, Jr.	Golf	1957	Bobby Jo Morrow	Track and field
1931	Bernard E. Berlinger	Track and field	1958	Glenn Davis	Track and field
1932	James A. Bausch	Track and field	1959	Parry O'Brien	Track and field
1933	Glenn Cunningham	Track and field	1960	Rafer Johnson	Track and field
1934	William R. Bonthron	Track and field	1961	Wilma Rudolph Ward	Track and field
1935	W. Lawson Little, Jr.	Golf	1962	Jim Beatty	Track and field
1936	Glenn Morris	Track and field	1963	John Pennel	Track and field
1937	J. Donald Budge	Tennis	1964	Don Schollander	Swimming
1938	Donald R. Lash	Track and field	1965	Bill Bradley	Basketball
1939	Joseph W. Burk	Rowing	1966	Jim Ryun	Track and field
1940	J. Gregory Rice	Track and field	1967	Randy Matson	Track and field
1941	Leslie MacMitchell	Track and field	1968	Debbie Meyer	Swimming
1942	Cornelius Warmerdam	Track and field	1969	Bill Toomey	Decathlon
1943	Gilbert L. Dodds	Track and field	1970	John Kinsella	Swimming
1944	Ann Curtis	Swimming	1971	Mark Spitz	Swimming
1945	Felix (Doc) Blanchard	Football	1972	Frank Shorter	Marathon
1946	Y. Arnold Tucker	Football	1973	Bill Walton	Basketball
1947	John B. Kelly, Jr.	Rowing	1974	Rick Wohlhuter	Track and field
1948	Robert B. Mathias	Track and field	1975	Tim Shaw	Swimming
1949	Richard T. Button	Figure skating	1976	Bruce Jenner	Track and field
1950	Fred Wilt	Track and field	1977	John Naber	Swimming
1951	Robert E. Richards	Track and field	1978	Tracy Caulkins	Swimming
1952	Horace Ashenfelter	Track and field	1979	Kurt Thomas	Gymnastics
1953	Sammy Lee	Diving	1980	Eric Heiden	Speed skating
1954	Malvin Whitfield	Track and field	1981	Carl Lewis	Track and field
1955	Harrison Dillard	Track and field	1982	Mary Decker Tabb	Track and field
1956	Patricia McCormick	Diving	1983	Edwin Moses	Track and field

1984	Greg Louganis	Diving	1994	Dan Jansen	Speed skating
1985	Joan Benoit-Samuelson	Marathon	1995	Bruce Baumgartner	Wrestling
1986	Jackie Joyner-Kersee	Heptathlon	1996	Michael Johnson	Track and field
1987	Jim Abbott	Baseball	1997	Peyton Manning	Football
1988	Florence Griffith-Joyner	Track and field	1998	Chamique Holdsclaw	Basketball
1989	Janet Evans	Swimming	1999	Kelly and Coco Miller	Basketball
1990	John Smith	Wrestling	2000	Rulon Gardner	Wrestling
1991	Mike Powell	Track and field	2001	Michelle Kwan	Figure skating
1992	Bonnie Blair	Speed skating	2002	Sarah Hughes	Figure skating
1993	Charles Ward	Football/Basketball	2003	Michael Phelps	Swimming

Hockey

Ice hockey, by birth and upbringing a Canadian game, is an offshoot of field hockey. Some historians say that the first ice hockey game was played in Montreal in Dec. 1879 between two teams composed almost exclusively of McGill University students, but others assert that earlier hockey games took place in Kingston, Ontario, or Halifax, Nova Scotia. In the Montreal game of 1879, there were fifteen players on a side, who used an assortment of crude sticks to keep the puck in motion. Early rules allowed nine men on a side, but the number was reduced to seven in 1886 and later to six.

The first governing body of the sport was the Amateur Hockey Association of Canada, organized in 1887. In the winter of 1894–1895, a group of college students from the United States visited Canada and saw hockey played. They became enthusiastic about the game and introduced it as a winter sport when they returned home. The first professional league was the International Hockey League, which operated in northern Michigan in 1904–1906.

Until 1910, professionals and amateurs were allowed to play together on "mixed teams," but this arrangement ended with the formation of the first "big league," the National Hockey Association, in eastern Canada in 1910. The Pacific Coast League was organized in 1911 for western Canadian hockey. The league included Seattle and later other American cities. The National Hockey League replaced the National Hockey Association in 1917. Boston, in 1924, was the first American city to join that circuit.

The league expanded to include western cities in 1967. The Stanley Cup was competed for by "mixed teams" from 1894 to 1910, thereafter by professionals. It was awarded to the winner of the NHL playoffs from 1926–1967 and now to the league champion. The World Hockey Association was organized in Oct. 1972 and was dissolved after the 1978–1979 season when the NHL absorbed four of the teams.

Rule changes have been implemented to steer the league from its violent reputation in order to better showcase the world's most talented stars.

Hockey, once considered a cold-weather sport, has taken major strides in increasing its fan base to the southern and western part of the United States as well. In the 1995–1996 season, Florida and Colorado battled in the Stanley Cup Finals, the San Jose Sharks sold out all 41 of their home games, and the second team in two years (Winnipeg) migrated from Canada to the Southwest region of the U.S. (Phoenix).

The NHL continued to expand when the Nashville Predators joined the league in the 1998–1999 season. The 1999–2000 season included the new Atlanta Thrashers and the 2000–2001 season introduced the Columbus Blue Jackets and the Minnesota Wild.

The collective agreement between the NHL and the NHL Players Association (NHLPA) expired on Sept. 15, 2004 and a lockout began. The NHLPA was adamant about refusing a salary cap while the troubled league saw the need for economic tightening. October games were cancelled and the entire season was in jeopardy.

STANLEY CUP WINNERS

Emblematic of World Professional Championship; NHL Championship after 1967

1893	Montreal A.A.A.	1914	Toronto Blueshirts	1934	Chicago Blackhawks
1894	Montreal A.A.A.	1915	Vancouver Millionaries	1935	Montreal Maroons
1895	Montreal Victorias	1916	Montreal Canadiens	1936–37	Detroit Red Wings
1896	(Feb.) Winnipeg Victorias	1917	Seattle Metropolitans	1938	Chicago Red Hawks
1896	(Dec.) Montreal Victorias	1918	Toronto Arenas	1939	Boston Bruins
1897–99	Montreal Victorias	1919	No champion	1940	N.Y. Rangers
1899–1900	Montreal Shamrocks	1920–21	Ottawa Senators	1941	Boston Bruins
1901	Winnipeg Victorias	1922	Toronto St. Patricks	1942	Toronto Maple Leafs
1902	Montreal A.A.A.	1923	Ottawa Senators	1943	Detroit Red Wings
1903–05	Ottawa Silver Seven	1924	Montreal Canadiens	1944	Montreal Canadiens
1906	Montreal Wanderers	1925	Victoria Cougars	1945	Toronto Maple Leafs
1907	(Jan.) Kenora Thistles	1926	Montreal Maroons	1946	Montreal Canadiens
1907	(March) Montreal Wanderers	1927	Ottawa Senators	1947–49	Toronto Maple Leafs
1908	Montreal Wanderers	1928	N.Y. Rangers	1950	Detroit Red Wings
1909	Ottawa Senators	1929	Boston Bruins	1951	Toronto Maple Leafs
1910	Montreal Wanderers	1930–31	Montreal Canadiens	1952	Detroit Red Wings
1911	Ottawa Senators	1932	Toronto Maple Leafs	1953	Montreal Canadiens
1912–13	Quebec Bulldogs	1933	N.Y. Rangers	1954–55	Detroit Red Wings

1956–60 Montreal Canadiens	1974–75 Philadelphia Flyers	1994 N.Y. Rangers
1961 Chicago Blackhawks	1976–79 Montreal Canadiens	1995 N.J. Devils
1962–64 Toronto Maple Leafs	1980–83 N.Y. Islanders	1996 Colorado Avalanche
1965–66 Montreal Canadiens	1984–85 Edmonton Oilers	1997–98 Detroit Red Wings
1967 Toronto Maple Leafs	1986 Montreal Canadiens	1999 Dallas Stars
1968–69 Montreal Canadiens	1987–88 Edmonton Oilers	2000 N.J. Devils
1970 Boston Bruins	1989 Calgary Flames	2001 Colorado Avalanche
1971 Montreal Canadiens	1990 Edmonton Oilers	2002 Detroit Red Wings
1972 Boston Bruins	1991–92 Pittsburgh Penguins	2003 N.J. Devils
1973 Montreal Canadiens	1993 Montreal Canadiens	2004 Tampa Bay Lightning

NHL CHAMPIONS

Wales Trophy
1939–41 Boston	1963 Toronto	1974 Boston	1987 Philadelphia	1998 Washington
1942 New York	1964 Montreal	**Eastern Conference**[1]	1988 Boston	1999 Buffalo
1943 Detroit	1965 Detroit	1975 Buffalo	1989 Montreal	2000–01 New
1944–47 Montreal	1966 Montreal	1976–79 Montreal	1990 Boston	Jersey
1948 Toronto	1967 Chicago	1980 Buffalo	1991–92 Pittsburgh	2002 Carolina
1948–55 Detroit	**Eastern Division**	1981 Montreal	1993 Montreal	2003 New Jersey
1956 Montreal	1968–69 Montreal	1982–84 N.Y.	1994 N.Y. Rangers	2004 Tampa Bay
1957 Detroit	1970 Chicago	Islanders	1995 New Jersey	
1958–62 Montreal	1971–72 Boston	1985 Philadelphia	1996 Florida	
	1973 Montreal	1986 Montreal	1997 Philadelphia	

1. Prior to 1994 was the Wales Conference.

CAMPBELL BOWL

Western Division
1968–70 St. Louis	1980 Philadelphia	1991 Minnesota	1999–2000 Dallas
1971–73 Chicago	1981 N.Y. Islanders	1992 Chicago	2001 Colorado
1974 Philadelphia	1982–85 Edmonton	1993 Los Angeles	2002 Detroit
Western Conference[2]	1986 Calgary	1994 Vancouver	2003 Anaheim
1975–77 Philadelphia	1987–88 Edmonton	1995 Detroit	2004 Calgary
1978–79 N.Y. Islanders	1989 Calgary	1996 Colorado	
	1990 Edmonton	1997–98 Detroit	

2. Prior to 1994 was the Campbell Conference.

NATIONAL HOCKEY LEAGUE YEARLY TROPHY WINNERS

The Hart Trophy—Most Valuable Player

1924 Frank Nighbor, Ottawa	1949 Sid Abel, Detroit	1993 Mario Lemieux, Pittsburgh
1925 Billy Burch, Hamilton	1950 Chuck Rayner, N.Y. Rangers	1994 Sergei Fedorov, Detroit
1926 Nels Stewart, Montreal Maroons	1951 Milt Schmidt, Boston	1995 Eric Lindros, Philadelphia
1927 Herb Gardiner, Montreal Canadiens	1952–53 Gordie Howe, Detroit	1996 Mario Lemieux, Pittsburgh
1928 Howie Morenz, Montreal Canadiens	1954 Al Rollins, Chicago	1997–98 Dominik Hasek, Buffalo
1929 Roy Worters, N.Y. Americans	1955 Ted Kennedy, Toronto	1999 Jaromir Jagr, Pittsburgh
1930 Nels Stewart, Montreal Maroons	1956 Jean Belveau, Montreal Canadiens	2000 Chris Pronger, St. Louis
1931–32 Howie Morenz, Montreal Canadiens	1957–58 Gordie Howe, Detroit	2001 Joe Sakic, Colorado
1933 Eddie Shore, Boston	1959 Andy Bathgate, N.Y. Rangers	2002 Jose Theodore, Montreal
1934 Aurel Joliat, Montreal Canadiens	1960 Gordie Howe, Detroit	2003 Peter Forsberg, Colorado
1935–36 Eddie Shore, Boston	1961 Bernie Geoffrion, Montreal Canadiens	2004 Martin St. Louis, Tampa Bay
1937 Babe Siebert, Montreal Canadiens	1962 Jacques Plante, Montreal Canadiens	
1938 Eddie Shore, Boston	1963 Gordon Howe, Detroit	**Vezina Trophy—Leading Goalkeeper**
1939 Toe Blake, Montreal Canadiens	1964 Jean Beliveau, Montreal Canadiens	1956–60 Jacques Plante, Montreal
1940 Ebbie Goodfellow, Detroit	1965–66 Bobby Hull, Chicago	1961 Johnny Bower, Toronto
1941 Bill Cowley, Boston	1967–68 Stan Mikita, Chicago	1962 Jacques Plante, Montreal
1942 Tommy Anderson, N.Y. Americans	1969 Phil Esposito, Boston	1963 Glenn Hall, Chicago
1943 Bill Cowley, Boston	1970–72 Bobby Orr, Boston	1964 Charlie Hodge, Montreal
1944 Babe Pratt, Toronto	1973 Bobby Clarke, Philadelphia	1965 Terry Sawchuk—Johnny Bower, Toronto
1945 Elmer Lach, Montreal Canadiens	1974 Phil Esposito, Boston	1966 Gump Worsley—Charlie Hodge, Montreal
1946 Max Bentley, Chicago	1975–76 Bobby Clarke, Philadelphia	1967 Glen Hall—Denis Dejordy, Chicago
1947 Maurice Richard, Montreal Canadiens	1977–78 Guy Lafleur, Montreal	1968 Gump Worsley—Rogie Vachon, Montreal
1948 Buddy O'Connor, N.Y. Rangers	1979 Bryan Trottier, N.Y. Islanders	1969 Glenn Hall—Jacques Plante, St. Louis
	1980–87 Wayne Gretzky, Edmonton	1970 Tony Esposito, Chicago
	1988 Mario Lemieux, Pittsburgh	1971 Ed Giacomin—Gilles Villemure, N.Y. Rangers
	1989 Wayne Gretzky, Los Angeles	
	1990 Mark Messier, Edmonton	
	1991 Brett Hull, St. Louis	
	1992 Mark Messier, N.Y. Rangers	

1972 Tony Esposito—Gary Smith, Chicago	1999 Al MacInnis, St. Louis	1975 Eric Vail, Atlanta
1973 Ken Dryden, Montreal	2000 Chris Pronger, St. Louis	1976 Bryan Trottier, N.Y. Islanders
1974 Bernie Parent, Philadelphia and Tony Esposito, Chicago	2001–2003 Nicklas Lidstrom, Detroit	1977 Willi Plett, Atlanta
	2004 Scott Niedermayer, New Jersey	1978 Mike Bossy, N.Y. Islanders
1975 Bernie Parent, Philadelphia		1979 Bobby Smith, Minnesota

1972 Tony Esposito—Gary Smith, Chicago
1973 Ken Dryden, Montreal
1974 Bernie Parent, Philadelphia and Tony Esposito, Chicago
1975 Bernie Parent, Philadelphia
1976 Ken Dryden, Montreal
1977–79 Ken Dryden—Bunny Larocque, Montreal
1980 Bob Sauve—Don Edwards, Buffalo
1981 Richard Sevigny—Denis Herron—Bunny Larocque, Montreal
1982 Billy Smith, N.Y. Islanders
1983 Pete Peeters, Boston
1984 Tom Barrasso, Buffalo
1985 Pelle Lindbergh, Philadelphia
1986 John Vanbiesbrouck, N.Y. Rangers
1987 Ron Hextall, Philadelphia
1988 Grant Fuhr, Edmonton
1989–90 Patrick Roy, Montreal
1991 Ed Belfour, Chicago
1992 Patrick Roy, Montreal
1993 Ed Belfour, Chicago
1994–95 Dominik Hasek, Buffalo
1996 Jim Carey, Washington
1997–99 Dominik Hasek, Buffalo
2000 Olaf Kolzig, Washington
2001 Dominik Hasek, Buffalo
2002 Jose Theodore, Montreal
2003–04 Martin Brodeur, New Jersey

James Norris Trophy— Defenseman

1954 Red Kelly, Detroit
1955–58 Doug Harvey, Montreal
1959 Tom Johnson, Montreal
1960–62 Doug Harvey, Montreal, N.Y. Rangers (62)
1963–65 Pierre Pilote, Chicago
1966 Jacques Laperriere, Montreal
1967 Harry Howell, N.Y. Rangers
1968–75 Bobby Orr, Boston
1976 Denis Potvin, N.Y. Islanders
1977 Larry Robinson, Montreal
1978–79 Denis Potvin, N.Y. Islanders
1980 Larry Robinson, Montreal
1981 Randy Carlyle, Pittsburgh
1982 Doug Wilson, Chicago
1983–84 Rod Langway, Washington
1985–86 Paul Coffey, Edmonton
1987–88 Ray Bourque, Boston
1989 Chris Chelios, Montreal
1990–91 Ray Bourque, Boston
1992 Brian Leetch, N.Y. Rangers
1993 Chris Chelios, Chicago
1994 Ray Bourque, Boston
1995 Paul Coffey, Detroit
1996 Chris Chelios, Chicago
1997 Brian Leetch, N.Y. Rangers
1998 Rob Blake, Los Angeles

1999 Al MacInnis, St. Louis
2000 Chris Pronger, St. Louis
2001–2003 Nicklas Lidstrom, Detroit
2004 Scott Niedermayer, New Jersey

Lady Byng Trophy— Sportsmanship

1960 Don McKenney, Boston
1961 Red Kelly, Toronto
1962–63 Dave Keon, Toronto
1964 Ken Wharram, Chicago
1965 Bobby Hull, Chicago
1966 Alex Delvecchio, Detroit
1967–68 Stan Mikita, Chicago
1969 Alex Delvecchio, Detroit
1970 Phil Goyette, St. Louis
1971 Johnny Bucyk, Boston
1972 Jean Ratelle, N.Y. Rangers
1973 Gilbert Perreault, Buffalo
1974 Johnny Bucyk, Boston
1975 Marcel Dionne, Detroit
1976 Jean Ratelle, N.Y. Rangers, Boston
1977 Marcel Dionne, Los Angeles
1978 Butch Goring, Los Angeles
1979 Bob MacMillan, Atlanta
1980 Wayne Gretzky, Edmonton
1981 Rick Kehoe, Pittsburgh
1982 Rick Middleton, Boston
1983–84 Mike Bossy, N.Y. Islanders
1985 Jari Kurri, Edmonton
1986 Mike Bossy, N.Y. Islanders
1987 Joey Mullen, Calgary
1988 Mats Naslund, Montreal
1989 Joey Mullen, Calgary
1990 Brett Hull, St. Louis
1991–92 Wayne Gretzky, Los Angeles
1993 Pierre Turgeon, N.Y. Islanders
1994 Wayne Gretzky, Los Angeles
1995 Ron Francis, Pittsburgh
1996–97 Paul Kariya, Anaheim
1998 Ron Francis, Pittsburgh
1999 Wayne Gretzky, N.Y. Rangers
2000 Pavol Demitra, St. Louis
2001 Joe Sakic, Colorado
2002 Ron Francis, Carolina
2003 Alexander Mogilny, Toronto
2004 Brad Richards, Tampa Bay

Calder Trophy—Rookie

1962 Bobby Rousseau, Montreal
1963 Kent Douglas, Toronto
1964 Jacques Laperriere, Montreal
1965 Roger Crozier, Detroit
1966 Brit Selby, Toronto
1967 Bobby Orr, Boston
1968 Derek Sanderson, Boston
1969 Danny Grant, Minnesota
1970 Tony Esposito, Chicago
1971 Gilbert Perreault, Buffalo
1972 Ken Dryden, Montreal
1973 Steve Vickers, N.Y. Rangers
1974 Denis Potvin, N.Y. Islanders

1975 Eric Vail, Atlanta
1976 Bryan Trottier, N.Y. Islanders
1977 Willi Plett, Atlanta
1978 Mike Bossy, N.Y. Islanders
1979 Bobby Smith, Minnesota
1980 Ray Bourque, Boston
1981 Peter Stastny, Quebec
1982 Dale Hawerchuk, Winnipeg
1983 Steve Larmer, Chicago
1984 Tom Barrasso, Buffalo
1985 Mario Lemieux, Pittsburgh
1986 Gary Suter, Calgary
1987 Luc Robitaille, Los Angeles
1988 Joe Nieuwendyk, Calgary
1989 Brian Leetch, N.Y. Rangers
1990 Sergei Makarov, Calgary
1991 Ed Belfour, Chicago
1992 Pavel Bure, Vancouver
1993 Teemu Selanne, Winnipeg
1994 Martin Brodeur, N.J. Devils
1995 Peter Forsberg, Quebec
1996 Daniel Alfredsson, Ottawa
1997 Bryan Berard, N.Y. Islanders
1998 Sergei Samsonov, Boston
1999 Chris Drury, Colorado
2000 Scott Gomez, New Jersey
2001 Evgeni Nabokov, San Jose
2002 Dany Heatley, Atlanta
2003 Barret Jackman, St. Louis
2004 Andrew Raycroft, Boston

Art Ross Trophy—Leading Scorer

1955 Bernie Geoffrion, Montreal
1956 Jean Beliveau, Montreal
1957 Gordie Howe, Detroit
1958–59 Dickie Moore, Montreal
1960 Bobby Hull, Chicago
1961 Bernie Geoffrion, Montreal
1962 Bobby Hull, Chicago
1963 Gordie Howe, Detroit
1964–65 Stan Mikita, Chicago
1966 Bobby Hull, Chicago
1967–68 Stan Mikita, Chicago
1969 Phil Esposito, Boston
1970 Bobby Orr, Boston
1971–74 Phil Esposito, Boston
1975 Bobby Orr, Boston
1976–78 Guy Lafleur, Montreal
1979 Bryan Trottier, N.Y. Islanders
1980 Marcel Dionne, Los Angeles
1981–87 Wayne Gretzky, Edmonton
1988–89 Mario Lemieux, Pittsburgh
1990–91 Wayne Gretzky, Los Angeles
1992–93 Mario Lemieux, Pittsburgh
1994 Wayne Gretzky, Los Angeles
1995 Jaromir Jagr, Pittsburgh
1996–97 Mario Lemieux, Pittsburgh
1998–2001 Jaromir Jagr, Pittsburgh
2002 Jarome Iginla, Calgary
2003 Peter Forsberg, Colorado
2004 Martin St. Louis, Tampa Bay

OTHER NHL AWARDS—2004

Frank Selke Trophy (Top defensive forward)—Kris Draper, Detroit

King Clancy Trophy (Humanitarian community involvement)—Jarome Iginla, Calgary

Jack Adams Award (Coach of the Year)—John Tortorella, Tampa Bay

Bill Masterson Trophy (Perseverance, sportsmanship, and dedication to hockey)—Bryan Berard, Chicago

Maurice Richard Trophy (Goal-scoring leader)—Rick Nash, Columbus; Ilya Kovalchuk, Atlanta; and Jarome Iginla, Calgary

STANLEY CUP PLAYOFFS—2004

NOTE: Home teams are in capitals.

EASTERN CONFERENCE

Quarterfinals
Tampa Bay Lightning defeated New York Islanders,
  4 games to 1
Montreal Canadiens defeated Boston Bruins,
  4 games to 3
Philadelphia Flyers defeated New Jersey Devils,
  4 games to 1
Toronto Maple Leafs defeated Ottawa Senators,
  4 games to 3

Semifinals
Tampa Bay Lightning defeated Montreal Canadiens,
  4 games to 0
Philadelphia Flyers defeated Toronto Maple Leafs,
  4 games to 0

Finals
Tampa Bay Lightning defeated Philadelphia Flyers,
  4 games to 3
  May 8—TAMPA BAY 3, Philadelphia 1
  May 10—Philadelphia 6, TAMPA BAY 2
  May 13—Tampa Bay 4, PHILADELPHIA 1
  May 15—PHILADELPHIA 3, Tampa Bay 2
  May 18—TAMPA BAY 4, Philadelphia 2
  May 20—PHILADELPHIA 5, Tampa Bay 4 (OT)
  May 22—TAMPA BAY 2, Philadelphia 1

WESTERN CONFERENCE

Quarterfinals
Detroit Red Wings defeated Nashville Predators,
  4 games to 2
San Diego Sharks defeated St. Louis Blues,
  4 games to 1
Calgary Flames defeated Vancouver Canucks,
  4 games to 3
Colorado Avalanche defeated Dallas Stars,
  4 games to 1

Semifinals
Calgary Flames defeated Detroit Red Wings,
  4 games to 2
San Diego Sharks defeated Colorado Avalanche,
  4 games to 2

Finals
Calgary Flames defeated San Diego Sharks,
  4 games to 2
  May 9—Calgary 4, SAN JOSE 3 (OT)
  May 11—Calgary 4, SAN JOSE 1
  May 13—San Jose 3, CALGARY 0
  May 16—San Jose 4, CALGARY 2
  May 17—Calgary 3, SAN JOSE 0
  May 19—CALGARY 3, San Jose 1

STANLEY CUP CHAMPIONSHIP FINALS
Tampa Bay Lightning defeated Calgary Flames, 4 games to 3.

May 25—Calgary 4, TAMPA BAY 1
May 27—TAMPA BAY 4, Calgary 1
May 29—CALGARY 3, Tampa Bay 0
May 31—Tampa Bay 1, CALGARY 0

June 3—Calgary 3, TAMPA BAY 2 (OT)

June 5—Tampa Bay 3, CALGARY 2 (OT)

June 7—TAMPA BAY 2, Calgary 1

Conn Smythe Trophy for most valuable player in the playoffs: Brad Richards, Tampa Bay

NATIONAL HOCKEY LEAGUE FINAL STANDINGS OF THE CLUBS: 2003–2004

EASTERN CONFERENCE

Atlantic Division

	W	L	T	Pts	GF	GA
Philadelphia Flyers[1]	40	21	15	101	229	186
New Jersey Devils[2]	43	25	12	100	213	164
N.Y. Islanders[2]	38	29	11	91	237	210
N.Y. Rangers	27	40	7	69	206	250
Pittsburgh Penguins	23	47	8	58	190	303

Northeast Division

	W	L	T	Pts	GF	GA
Boston Bruins[1]	41	19	15	104	209	188
Toronto Maple Leafs[2]	45	24	10	103	242	204
Ottawa Senators[2]	43	23	10	102	262	189
Montreal Canadiens[2]	41	30	7	93	208	192
Buffalo Sabres	37	34	7	85	220	221

Southeast Division

	W	L	T	Pts	GF	GA
Tampa Bay Lightning[1]	46	22	8	106	245	192
Atlanta Thrashers	33	37	8	78	214	243
Carolina Hurricanes	28	34	14	76	172	209
Florida Panthers	28	35	15	75	188	221
Washington Capitals	23	46	10	59	186	253

WESTERN CONFERENCE

Central Division

	W	L	T	Pts	GF	GA
Detroit Red Wings[1]	48	21	11	109	255	189
St. Louis Blues[2]	39	30	11	91	191	198
Nashville Predators[2]	38	29	11	91	216	217
Columbus Blue Jackets	25	45	8	62	177	238
Chicago Blackhawks	20	43	11	59	188	259

Northwest Division

	W	L	T	Pts	GF	GA
Vancouver Canucks[1]	43	24	10	101	235	194
Colorado Avalanche[1]	40	22	13	100	236	198
Calgary Flames[1]	42	30	7	94	200	176
Edmonton Oilers	36	29	12	89	221	208
Minnesota Wild	30	29	20	83	188	183

Pacific Division

	W	L	T	Pts	GF	GA
San Jose Sharks[1]	43	21	12	104	219	183
Dallas Stars[2]	41	26	13	97	194	175
Los Angeles Kings	28	29	16	81	205	217
Anaheim Mighty Ducks	29	35	10	76	184	213
Phoenix Coyotes	22	36	18	68	188	245

1. Clinched division. 2. Playoff qualifier.

NHL LEADING SCORERS: 2003–2004

	Gm	G	A	Pts
Martin St. Louis, Tampa Bay	82	38	56	94
Ilya Kovalchuk, Atlanta	81	41	46	87
Joe Sakic, Colorado	81	33	54	87
Markus Naslund, Vancouver	78	35	49	84
Marian Hossa, Ottawa	81	36	46	82
Patrik Elias, New Jersey	82	38	43	81
Daniel Alfredsson, Ottawa	77	32	48	80
Cory Stillman, Tampa Bay	81	25	55	80
Robert Lang, Detroit	69	30	49	79
Brad Richards, Tampa Bay	82	26	53	79

NHL CAREER SCORING LEADERS

(Through 2003–2004 season)

		Yrs	Gm	G	A	Pts
1.	Wayne Gretzky	20	1,487	894	1,963	2,857
2.	**Mark Messier**	25	1,756	694	1,193	1,887
3.	Gordie Howe	26	1,767	801	1,049	1,850
4.	**Ron Francis**	24	1,731	549	1,249	1,798
5.	Marcel Dionne	18	1,348	731	1,040	1,771
6.	**Steve Yzerman**	21	1,453	678	1,043	1,721
7.	**Mario Lemieux**	16	889	683	1,018	1,701
8.	Phil Esposito	18	1,282	717	873	1,590
9.	Ray Bourque	22	1,612	410	1,169	1,579
10.	Paul Coffey	21	1,409	396	1,135	1,531

Players active during 2003–2004 season in **bold** type.

NHL LEADING GOALTENDERS: 2003–2004

(Minimum 26 games played)

	Gm	GAA	W	L	T
Miikka Kiprusoff, Calgary	38	1.69	24	10	4
Dwayne Roloson, Minnesota	48	1.88	19	18	11
Marty Turco, Dallas	73	1.98	37	21	13
Martin Brodeur, New Jersey	75	2.03	38	26	11
Robert Esche, Philadelphia	40	2.04	21	11	7
Andrew Raycroft, Boston	57	2.05	29	18	9
Vesa Toskala, San Diego	28	2.06	12	8	4
John Grahame, Tampa Bay	29	2.06	18	9	1
David Aebischer, Colorado	62	2.09	32	19	9
Manny Legace, Detroit	41	2.12	23	10	5

NHL CAREER GOALTENDING WINS LEADERS

(Through 2003–2004 season)

		Yrs	Gm	W	L	T
1.	Patrick Roy	20	1,029	551	315	131
2.	Terry Sawchuk	21	971	447	330	172
3.	Jacques Plante	18	837	435	247	146
4.	**Ed Belfour**	16	856	435	281	111
5.	Tony Esposito	16	886	423	306	152
6.	Glenn Hall	18	906	407	326	163
7.	Grant Fuhr	19	868	403	295	114
8.	**Martin Brodeur**	12	740	403	217	105
9.	**Curtis Joseph**	15	798	396	289	90
10.	Mike Vernon	19	781	385	273	92

Players active during 2003–2004 season in **bold** type.

Bowling

The game of bowling in the United States is an indoor development of the more ancient outdoor game that survives as lawn bowling. The outdoor game is prehistoric in origin and probably goes back to primitive man and round stones that were rolled at some target. It is believed that a game something like nine-pins was popular among the Dutch, Swiss, and Germans as long ago as A.D. 1200. The game was played outdoors with an alley consisting of a single plank 12 to 18 inches wide, along which a ball was rolled toward three rows of three pins each placed at the far end of the alley. When the first indoor alleys were built and how the game was modified from time to time are matters of dispute.

It is supposed that the early settlers of New Amsterdam (New York City), being Dutch, brought their two bowling games with them. About a century ago the game of nine-pins was flourishing in the United States but was so corrupted by gambling on matches that it was barred by law in New York and Connecticut. Since the law specifically barred "nine-pins," it was eventually evaded by adding another pin and thus legally making it a new game.

Various organizations were formed to make rules for bowling and supervise competition in the United States, but none was successful until the American Bowling Congress, organized Sept. 9, 1895, became the ruling body.

AMERICAN BOWLING CONGRESS CHAMPIONS

Year	Singles	All events
1959	Ed Lubanski	Ed Lubanski
1960	Paul Kulbaga	Vince Lucci
1961	Lyle Spooner	Luke Karen
1962	Andy Renaldo	Billy Young
1963	Fred Delello	Bus Owalt
1964	Jim Stefanich	Les Zikes, Jr.
1965	Ken Roeth	Tom Hathaway
1966	Don Chapman	John Wilcox
1967	Frank Perry	Gary Lewis
1968	Wayne Kowalski	Vince Mazzanti
1969	Greg Campbell	Eddie Jackson
1970	Jake Yoder	Mike Berlin
1971	Al Cohn	Al Cohn
1972	Bill Pointer	Mac Lowry
1973	Ed Thompson	Ron Woolet

Year	Singles	All events
1974	Gene Krause	Bob Hart
1975	Jim Setser	Bobby Meadows
1976	Mike Putzer	Jim Lindquist
1977	Frank Gadaleto	Bud Debenham
1978	Rich Mersek	Chris Cobus
1979	Rick Peters	Bob Basacchi
1980	Mike Eaton	Steve Fehr
1981	Rob Vital	Rod Toft
1982	Bruce Bohm	Rich Wonders
1983	Rick Kendrick	Tony Cariello
1984	Bob Antczak and Neal Young (tie)	
		Bob Goike
1985	Glen Harbison	Barry Asher
1986	Jess Mackey	Ed Marazka
1987	Terry Taylor	Ryan Schafer

Year	Singles	All events	Year	Singles	All events
1988	Steve Hutkowski	Rick Steelsmith	1996	Donald Scudder, Jr.	Scott Kurtz
1989	Paul Tetreault	George Hall	1997	John Socha	Jeff Richgels
1990	Bob Hochrein	Mike Neumann	1998	John Gaines	Chris Barnes
1991	Ed Deines	Tom Howery	1999	Dan Winter	Thomas A. Jones
1992	Bob Youker and Gary		2000	Garran Hein	Roy Daniels
	Blatchford (tie)	Mike Tucker	2001	Nicholas Hoagland	D. J. Archer
1993	Dan Bock	Jeff Nimke	2002	Mark Millsap	Stephen A. Hardy
1994	John Weltzien	Thomas Holt	2003	Ron R. Bahr	Steve P. Kloempken
1995	Matt Surina	Jeff Kwiatkowski	2004	John Janawicz	John Janawicz

PROFESSIONAL BOWLERS ASSOCIATION

PBA World Championship[1]

1960	Don Carter	1972	Johnny Guenther	1984	Bob Chamberlain	1996	Butch Soper
1961	Dave Soutar	1973	Earl Anthony	1985	Mike Aulby	1997	Rich Steelsmith
1962	Carmen Salvino	1974	Earl Anthony	1986	Tom Crites	1998	Pete Weber
1963	Billy Hardwick	1975	Earl Anthony	1987	Randy Pedersen	1999	Tim Criss
1964	Bob Strampe	1976	Paul Colwell	1988	Brian Voss	2000	Norm Duke
1965	Dave Davis	1977	Tommy Hudson	1989	Pete Weber	2001	Walter Ray Williams, Jr.
1966	Wayne Zahn	1978	Warren Nelson	1990	Jim Pencak	2002	Doug Kent
1967	Dave Davis	1979	Mike Aulby	1991	Mike Miller	2003	Walter Ray Williams, Jr.
1968	Wayne Zahn	1980	Johnny Petraglia	1992	Eric Forkel	2004	Tom Baker
1969	Mike McGrath	1981	Earl Anthony	1993	Ron Palombi		
1970	Mike McGrath	1982	Earl Anthony	1994	David Traber		
1971	Mike Lemongello	1983	Earl Anthony	1995	Scott Alexander		

1. Formerly National Championship Tournament.

BOWLING PROPRIETORS' ASSOCIATION OF AMERICA—MEN

United States Open[1]

1971	Mike Lemongello	1980	Steve Martin	1989	Mike Aulby	1998	Walter Ray Williams, Jr.
1972	Don Johnson	1981	Marshall Holman	1990	Ron Palumbi, Jr.		
1973	Mike McGrath	1982	Dave Husted	1991	Pete Weber	1999	Bob Learn, Jr.
1974	Larry Laub	1983	Gary Dickinson	1992	Robert Lawrence	2000	Robert Smith
1975	Steve Neff	1984	Mark Roth	1993	Del Ballard, Jr.	2001	Mika Koivuniemi
1976	Paul Moser	1985	Marshall Holman	1994	Justin Hromek	2002–	Walter Ray Williams,
1977	Johnny Petraglia	1986	Steve Cook	1995	Dave Husted	2003[2]	Jr.
1978	Nelson Burton, Jr.	1987	Del Ballard	1996	Dave Husted	2004	Pete Weber
1979	Joe Berardi	1988	Pete Weber	1997	Not held		

1. Replaced All-Star tournament and is rolled as part of PBA tour. 2. 2002 and 2003 tournaments combined.

WOMEN'S INTERNATIONAL BOWLING CONGRESS CHAMPIONS

Year	Singles	All events	Year	Singles	All events
1959	Mae Bolt	Pat McBride	1984	Freida Gates	Shinobu Saitoh
1960	Marge McDaniels	Judy Roberts	1985	Polly Schwarzel	Aleta Sill
1961	Elaine Newton	Evelyn Teal	1986	Dana Stewart	Robin Romeo and Maria
1962	Martha Hoffman	Flossie Argent			Lewis (tie)
1963	Dot Wilkinson	Helen Shablis	1987	Regi Junak	Leanne Barrette
1964	Jean Havlish	Jean Havlish	1988	Michelle Meyer-Welty	Lisa Wagner
1965	Doris Rudell	Donna Zimmerman	1989	Lorraine Anderson	Nancy Fehn
1966	Gloria Bouvia	Kate Helbig	1990	Dana Miller-Mackie and	Carol Norman
1967	Gloria Paeth	Carol Miller		Paula Carter (tie)	
1968	Norma Parks	Susie Reichley	1991	Debbie Kuhn	Debbie Kuhn
1969	Joan Bender	Helen Duval	1992	Patty Ann	Mitsuko Tokimoto
1970	Dorothy Fothergill	Dorothy Fothergill	1993	Karen Collurs and Kari	Bertha Blackshur and
1971	Mary Scruggs	Lorrie Nichols		Murph (tie)	Sharon Davis (tie)
1972	D. D. Jacobson	Mildred Martorella	1994	Vicki Fifield	Wendy Macpherson-
1973	Bobby Buffaloe	Toni Calvery			Papanos
1974	Shirley Garms	Judy C. Soutar	1995	Beth Owen	Beth Owen
1975	Barbara Leicht	Virginia Norton	1996	Cindy Berlanga	Lorrie Nichols
1976	Bev Shonk	Betty Morris	1997	Jean Schmidt	Kendra Cameron
1977	Akiko Yamaga	Akiko Yamaga	1998	Nellie Glandon	Liz Johnson
1978	Mae Bolt	Annese Kelly	1999	Maggie Matheson	Marlene Walls
1979	Betty Morris	Betty Morris	2000	Cathy Krasner	Carolyn Dorin-Ballard
1980	Betty Morris	Cheryl Robinson	2001	Lisa Wagner	Jonquay Armon
1981	Virginia Norton	Virginia Norton	2002	Theresa Smith	Cara Honeychurch
1982	Gracie Freeman	Aleta Rzepecki	2003	Michelle Feldman	Michelle Feldman
1983	Aleta Rzepecki	Virginia Norton	2004	Sharon Smith	Kim Adler

BOWLING PROPRIETORS' ASSOCIATION OF AMERICA—WOMEN

United States Open[1]

1971	Paula Carter	1981	Donna Adamek	1991	Anne Marie Duggan	2001	Kim Terrell
1972	Lorrie Nichols	1982	Shinobu Saitoh	1992	Tish Johnson	2002–	Kelly Kulick
1973	Mildred Martorella	1983	Dana Miller	1993	Dede Davidson	2003[2]	
1974	Pat Costello (Calif.)	1984	Karen Ellingsworth	1994	Aleta Sill		
1975	Paula Carter	1985	Pat Mercatanti	1995	Tish Johnson		
1976	Patty Costello (Pa.)	1986	Wendy Macpherson	1996	Liz Johnson		
1977	Betty Morris	1987	Carol Nurman	1997	Not held		
1978	Donna Adamek	1988	Lisa Wagner	1998	Aleta Sill		
1979	Diana Silva	1989	Robin Romeo	1999	Kim Adler		
1980	Pat Costello (Calif.)	1990	Dana Miller-Mackie	2000	Tennelle Grijalva		

1. Rolled as part of PWBA tour. 2. 2002 and 2003 tournaments combined. PWBA joined WIBC in 2004.

WIBC QUEENS TOURNAMENT CHAMPIONS

1961	Janet Harman	1973	Dorothy Fothergill	1985	Aleta Sill	1997	Sandra-Jo Shiery-Odom
1962	Dorothy Wilkinson	1974	Judy Soutar	1986	Cora Fiebig		
1963	Irene Monterosso	1975	Cindy Powell	1987	Cathy Almeida	1998	Lynda Norry
1964	D.D. Jacobson	1976	Pamela Buckner	1988	Wendy Macpherson	1999	Leanne Barrette
1965	Betty Kuczynski	1977	Dana Stewart	1989	Carol Gianotti	2000	Wendy Macpherson
1966	Judy Lee	1978	Loa Boxberger	1990	Patty Ann	2001	Carolyn Dorin-Ballard
1967	Mildred Martorella	1979	Donna Adamek	1991	Dede Davidson	2002	Kim Terrell
1968	Phyllis Massey	1980	Donna Adamek	1992	Cindy Coburn-Carroll	2003	Wendy Macpherson
1969	Ann Feigel	1981	Katsuko Sugimoto	1993	Jan Schmidt	2004	Marianne DiRupo
1970	Mildred Martorella	1982	Katsuko Sugimoto	1994	Anne Marie Duggan		
1971	Mildred Martorella	1983	Aleta Rzepecki	1995	Sandy Postma		
1972	Dorothy Fothergill	1984	Kazue Inahashi	1996	Lisa Wagner		

PBA WORLD CHAMPIONSHIP—2004

(March 15–21, 2004, Taylor, Mich.)

Winner—Tom Baker, Buffalo, N.Y., defeated Mika Koivuniemi, Finland, 246–239, in title match.

3. Wes Malott, Austin, Texas

4. Brad Angelo, Lockport, N.Y.

AMERICAN BOWLING CONGRESS TOURNAMENT—2004

(June 28, Reno, Nev.)

Singles—John Janawicz, Winter Haven, Fla.	858
Doubles—Mike Vasey and Joseph Crocco, Racine, Wis.	1,477
Team—S & B Pro Shop, Clinton Township, Mich.	3,268
All events—John Janawicz, Winter Haven, Fla.	2,224

WOMEN'S INTERNATIONAL BOWLING CONGRESS TOURNAMENT—2004

(April 15–July 6, 2004, Wichita, Kans.)

Singles—Sharon Smith, Bowling Green, N.Y.	754
Doubles—Lynda Barnes, Flower Mound, Tex., and Carolyn Dorin-Ballard, N. Richland Hills, Tex.	1,498
Team—High Roller, Henderson, Nev.	3,320
All events—Kim Adler, Merritt Island, Fla.	2,133

WOMEN'S INTERNATIONAL BOWLING CONGRESS QUEENS TOURNAMENT—2004

(May 15–19, 2004, Wichita, Kans.)

Winner—Marianne DiRupo, Succasunna, N.J., defeated Michelle Feldman, Skaneateles, N.Y., 226–202, in title match.

3. Olivia Sandham, Wichita, Kans.

4. Takiko Naganawa, Funabashi, Japan

5. Liz Johnson, Cheektowaga, N.Y.

Skiing

HISTORY OF SKIING IN THE UNITED STATES

Skis were devised for utility, to aid those who had to travel over snow. The Norwegians, Swedes, Lapps, and other inhabitants of northern lands used skis for many centuries before skiing became a sport. Emigrants from these countries brought skis to the United States with them. The first skier of record in the United States was a mailman by the name of "Snowshoe" Thompson, born and raised in Telemarken, Norway, who came to the United States and, beginning in 1850, used skis through 20 successive winters in carrying mail from northern California to Carson Valley, Idaho.

Ski clubs sprang up over 100 years ago where there were Norwegian and Swedish settlers in Wisconsin and Minnesota, and ski contests were held in that territory in 1886. On Feb. 21, 1904, at Ishpenning, Mich., a small group of skiers organized the National Ski Association. In 1961 it was renamed the United States Ski Association. In the 1990s it became the United States Ski and Snowboard Association and included freestyle and disabled skiing.

ALPINE SKIING
2004 Chevy Truck U.S. Alpine Championships
(March 18–23, 2004, Alyeska Resort, Girdwood, Alaska)

Men

Downhill—1. Bryon Friedman, Park City, Utah; 2. Jeremy Transue, Hunter, N.Y.; 3. Daron Rahlves, Sugar Bowl, Calif.

Slalom—1. Jimmy Cochran, Keene, N.H.; 2. Jesse Marshall, Pittsfield, Vt.; 3. Chip Knight, Stowe, Vt.

Super G—1. Daron Rahlves, Sugar Bowl, Calif.; 2. Dane Spencer, Boise, Idaho; 3. Jake Fiala, Frisco, Colo.

Giant Slalom—1. Jimmy Cochran, Keene, N.H.; 2. Jake Zamansky, Aspen, Colo.; 3. Tom Rothrock, Cashmere, Wash.

Combined—1. Bryon Friedman, Park City, Utah; 2. Jake Zamansky, Aspen, Colo.; 3. Roger Brown, Norwich, Vt.

Women

Downhill—1. Jonna Mendes, Heavenly, Calif.; 2. Julia Mancuso, Olympic Valley, Calif.; 3. Libby Ludlow, Bellevue, Wash.

Slalom—1. Lindsey Kildow, Vail, Colo.; 2. Julia Mancuso, Olympic Valley, Calif.; 3. Katie Hitchcock, Sugar Bowl, Calif.

Super G—1. Lindsey Kildow, Vail, Colo.; 2. Julia Mancuso, Olympic Valley, Calif.; 3. Libby Ludlow, Bellevue, Wash.

Giant Slalom—1. Libby Ludlow, Bellevue, Wash; 2. Julia Mancuso, Olympic Valley, Calif.; 3. Jessica Kelley, Starksboro, Vt.

Combined —1. Julia Mancuso, Olympic Valley, Calif.; 2. Megan Hughes, Killington, Vt.; 3. Bryna McCarty, Concord, Vt.

2004 Alpine World Cup Champions

Men	Pts	Women	Pts
Overall—Hermann Maier, Austria	1,265	Overall—Anja Paerson, Sweden	1,561
Downhill—Stephan Eberharter, Austria	831	Downhill—Renate Goetschl, Austria	680
Slalom—Rainer Schoenfelder, Austria	630	Slalom—Anja Paerson, Sweden	770
Giant Slalom—Bode Miller, United States	410	Giant Slalom—Anja Paerson, Sweden	630
Super G—Hermann Maier, Austria	580	Super G—Renate Goetschl, Austria	467
Combined—Bode Miller, United States	200		

2004 Disabled World Cup

Skiers are placed in categories appropriate to their disability. There are 3 blind classes, 11 standing classes, and 5 sitting classes. When several classes combine in competition, a factor system is used to calculate results.

Men

Downhill—**Blind:** Erik Villalon, Spain. **Sitting:** Martin Braxenthaler, Germany. **Standing:** Robert Meusburger, Austria.

Slalom—**Blind:** Erik Villalon, Spain. **Sitting:** Martin Braxenthaler, Germany. **Standing:** Thomas Pfyl, Switzerland.

Giant Slalom—**Blind:** Erik Villalon, Spain. **Sitting:** Andreas Schiestl, Austria. **Standing:** Romain Riboud, France.

Super G—**Blind:** Radomir Dudas, Slovak Republic. **Sitting:** Andreas Schiestl, Austria. **Standing:** Gerd Schönfelder, Germany.

Combined—**Blind:** Erik Villalon, Spain. **Sitting:** Andreas Schiestl, Austria. **Standing:** Romain Riboud, France.

Women

Downhill—**Blind:** Pascale Casanova, France. **Sitting:** Lacey Heward, United States. **Standing:** Solene Jambaque, France.

Slalom—**Blind:** Pascale Casanova, France. **Sitting:** Stephani Victor, United States. **Standing:** Csilla Kristof, United States.

Giant Slalom—**Blind:** Pascale Casanova, France. **Sitting:** Laurie Stephens, United States. **Standing:** Solene Jambaque, France.

Super G—**Blind:** Pascale Casanova, France. **Sitting:** Lacey Heward, United States. **Standing:** Lauren Woolstencroft, Canada.

Combined—**Blind:** Pascale Casanova, France. **Sitting:** Stephani Victor, United States. **Standing:** Csilla Kristof, United States.

FREESTYLE SKIING

2004 Freestyle Skiing World Cup Champions
Men

Aerials—Steve Omischl, Canada
Moguls—Janne Lahtela, Finland
Ski-Cross—Jesper Brugge, Sweden
Halfpipe—Mathias Wecxsteen, France
Overall—Steve Omischl, Canada

Women

Aerials—Alisa Camplin, Australia
Moguls—Jennifer Heil, Canada
Ski-Cross—Ophelie David, France
Halfpipe—Marie Martinod, France
Overall—Kari Traa, Norway

2004 Chevy Truck U.S. Freestyle Championships

(March 26–28, 2004, Heavenly, Calif.)

Men

Aerials—Jeret Peterson, Boise, Idaho
Moguls—Travis Cabral, South Lake Tahoe, Calif.
Dual Moguls—Travis Cabral, South Lake Tahoe, Calif.

Women

Aerials—Kelly Hilliman, Tonawanda, N.Y.
Moguls—Jillian Vogtli, Ellicotville, N.Y.
Dual Moguls—Shelly Robertson, Reno, Nev.

SNOWBOARDING
2004 World Cup Snowboard Champions

Men

Big Air—Simon Ax, Sweden
Halfpipe—Risto Mattila, Finland
Parallel Slalom—Siegfried Grabner, Austria
Snowboard Cross—Xavier Delerue, France
Overall—Jasey Jay Anderson, Canada

Women

Halfpipe—Soko Yamaoka, Japan
Parallel Slalom—Daniela Meuli, Switzerland
Snowboard Cross—Karine Ruby, France
Overall—Julie Pomagalski, France

2004 Philips U.S. Snowboard Open
(Stratton, Vermont)

Men
Rail Jam—Rahm Klampert
Halfpipe—Danny Kass
Slopestyle—Jake Blauvelt

Women
Rail Jam—Leanne Pelosi
Halfpipe—Kelly Clark
Slopestyle—Priscilla Levac

NORDIC SKIING/SKI JUMPING/CROSS COUNTRY

2004 Chevy Truck U.S. Ski Jumping/Nordic Combined Championships
(March 20–21, 2004, Steamboat Springs, Colo.)

Men
Nordic Combined (K90m jumping–10k race)—1. Todd Lodwick, Steamboat Springs, Colo.; 2. Johnny Spillane, Steamboat Springs, Colo.; 3. Eric Camerota, Park City, Utah.

Normal Hill (K90m)—1. Todd Lodwick, Steamboat Springs, Colo.; 2. Clint Jones, Steamboat Springs, Colo.; 3. Johnny Spillane, Steamboat Springs, Colo.

Large Hill (K114m)—1. Todd Lodwick, Steamboat Springs, Colo.; 2. Johnny Spillane, Steamboat Springs, Colo.; 3. Tommy Schwall, Steamboat Springs, Colo.

Women
Normal Hill (K90m)—1. Lindsey Van, Park City, Utah; 2. Jessica Jerome, Park City, Utah; 3. Alissa Johnson, Park City, Utah.

Large Hill (K114m)—1. Lindsey Van, Park City, Utah; 2. Jessica Jerome, Park City, Utah; 3. Alissa Johnson, Park City, Utah.

2004 Chevy Truck U.S. Cross Country Championships
(Jan. 3–11, 2004, Rumford, Maine)

Men
30km Classic—Carl Swenson, Boulder, Colo.
10km Free—Carl Swenson, Boulder, Colo.
10km Classic—Carl Swenson, Boulder, Colo.
1km Free Sprints—Leif Zimmerman, Bozeman, Mont.
50km Free Sprints—Lars Flora, Anchorage, Alaska

Women
15km Classic—Rebecca Dussault, Gunnison, Colo.
5km Free—Rebecca Dussault, Gunnison, Colo.
5km Classic—Rebecca Dussault, Gunnison, Colo.
1km Free Sprints—Kikkan Randall, Anchorage, Alaska
30km Free Sprints—Sarah Konrad, Laramie, Wyo.

Speed Skating

WORLD SPEED SKATING RECORDS (LONG TRACK)

Distance	Time	Skater	Place	Date
Men				
500 m	34.32	Hiroyasu Shimizu, Japan	Salt Lake City	March 10, 2001
1,000 m	1:07.18	Gerard van Velde, Netherlands	Salt Lake City	Feb. 16, 2002
1,500 m	1:43.95	Derek Parra, United States	Salt Lake City	Feb. 19, 2002
3,000 m	3:42.75	Gianni Romme, Netherlands	Calgary, Canada	Aug. 11, 2000
5,000 m	6:14.66	Jochem Uytdehaage, Netherlands	Salt Lake City	Feb. 9, 2002
10,000 m	12:58.92	Jochem Uytdehaage, Netherlands	Salt Lake City	Feb. 22, 2002
Women				
500 m	37.22	Catriona LeMay Doan, Canada	Calgary, Canada	Dec. 9, 2001
1,000 m	1:13.83	Chris Witty, United States	Salt Lake City	Feb. 17, 2002
1,500 m	1:54.02	Anna "Anni" Friesinger, Germany	Salt Lake City	Feb. 20, 2002
3,000 m	3:57.70	Claudia Pechstein, Germany	Salt Lake City	Feb. 10, 2002
5,000 m	6:46.91	Claudia Pechstein, Germany	Salt Lake City	Feb. 23, 2002

WORLD SPEED SKATING RECORDS (SHORT TRACK)

Distance	Time	Skater	Place	Date
Men				
500 m	41.184	Jean-Francois Monette, Canada	Calgary, Canada	Oct. 18, 2003
1,000 m	1:24.674	Jiajun Li, China	Bormio, Italy	Feb. 14, 2004
1,500 m	2:10.639	Hyun-Soo Ahn, Korea	Marquette, Mich.	Oct. 24, 2003
3,000 m	4:32.646	Hyun-Soo Ahn, Korea	Beijing, China	Dec. 7, 2003
5,000 m relay	6:42.893	Republic of Korea	Calgary, Canada	Oct. 18, 2003
Women				
500 m	43.671	Evgenia Radanova, Bulgaria	Calgary, Canada	Oct. 19, 2001
1,000 m	1:30.483	Chun-Sa Byun, Korea	Budapest, Hungary	Jan. 12, 2003
1,500 m	2:18.861	Eun-Ju Jung, Korea	Beijing, China	Jan. 11, 2004
3,000 m	5:01.976	Eun-Kyung Choi, Korea	Calgary, Canada	Oct. 22, 2000
3,000 m relay	4:11.742	Republic of Korea	Calgary, Canada	Oct. 19, 2003

WORLD SINGLE DISTANCE SPEED SKATING CHAMPIONSHIPS—2004
(March 12–14, 2004, Seoul, Korea)

Men	Time	Women	Time
500 m—Mike Ireland, Canada	35.40	500 m—Manli Wang, China	38.65
1,000 m—Erben Wennemars, Netherlands	1:10.66	1,000 m—Anni Friesinger, Germany	1:17.82
1,500 m—Shani Davis, United States	1:48.64	1,500 m—Anni Friesinger, Germany	2:00.48
5,000 m—Chad Hedrick, United States	6:34.37	3,000 m—Claudia Pechstein, Germany	4:13.46
10,000 m—Carl Verheijen, Netherlands	13:37.15	5,000 m—Clara Hughes, Canada	7:10.66

WORLD SHORT TRACK CHAMPIONSHIPS—2004
(March 19–21, 2004, Gothenburg, Sweden)

Men	Time	Women	Time
500 m—Suk-Woo Song, Korea	42.599	500 m—Meng Wang, China	45.332
1,000 m—Hyun-Soo Ahn, Korea	1:26.813	1,000 m—Eun-Kyung Choi, Korea	1:34.724
1,500 m—Hyun-Soo Ahn, Korea	2:16.376	1,500 m—Eun-Kyung Choi, Korea	2:28.048
3,000 m—Hyun-Soo Ahn, Korea	5:03.670	3,000 m—Chun-Sa Byun, Korea	5:58.035
Overall—Hyun-Soo Ahn, Korea	102 pts	Overall—Eun-Kyung Choi, Korea	84 pts
5,000 m Relay—Korea	6:48.133	3,000 m Relay—Korea	4:20.985

Figure Skating

WORLD CHAMPIONS

Men
1960	Alain Giletti, France
1961	No competition
1962	Donald Jackson, Canada
1963	Don McPherson, Canada
1964	Manfred Schnelldorfer, West Germany
1965	Alain Calmat, France
1966–68	Emmerich Danzer, Austria
1969–70	Tim Wood, United States
1971–73	Ondrej Nepela, Czechoslovakia
1974	Jan Hoffman, East Germany
1975	Sergei Yolkov, USSR
1976	John Curry, Britain
1977	Vladimir Kovalev, USSR
1978	Charles Tickner, United States
1979	Vladimir Kovalev, USSR
1980	Jan Hoffman, East Germany
1981–84	Scott Hamilton, United States
1985	Alexandr Fadeev, USSR
1986	Brian Boitano, United States
1987	Brian Orser, Canada
1988	Brian Boitano, United States
1989–91	Kurt Browning, Canada
1992	Viktor Petrenko, Unified Team
1993	Kurt Browning, Canada
1994–95	Elvis Stojko, Canada

1996	Todd Eldredge, United States
1997	Elvis Stojko, Canada
1998– 2000	Alexei Yagudin, Russia
2001	Evgeni Plushenko, Russia
2002	Alexei Yagudin, Russia
2003–04	Evgeni Plushenko, Russia

Women
1956–60	Carol Heiss, United States
1961	No competition
1962–64	Sjoukje Dijkstra, Netherlands
1965	Petra Burka, Canada
1966–68	Peggy Fleming, United States
1969–70	Gabriele Seyfert, East Germany
1971–72	Beatrix Schuba, Austria
1973	Karen Magnusson, Canada
1974	Christine Errath, East Germany
1975	Dianne de Leeuw, Netherlands
1976	Dorothy Hamill, United States
1977	Linda Fratianne, United States
1978	Anett Poetzsch, East Germany
1979	Linda Fratianne, United States

1980	Anett Poetzsch, East Germany
1981	Denise Beillmann, Switzerland
1982	Elaine Zayak, United States
1983	Rosalynn Sumners, United States
1984–85	Katarina Witt, East Germany
1986	Debi Thomas, United States
1987–88	Katarina Witt, East Germany
1989	Midori Ito, Japan
1990	Jill Trenary, United States
1991–92	Kristi Yamaguchi, United States
1993	Oksana Baiul, Ukraine
1994	Yuka Sato, Japan
1995	Chen Lu, China
1996	Michelle Kwan, United States
1997	Tara Lipinski, United States
1998	Michelle Kwan, United States
1999	Maria Butyrskaya, Russia
2000–01	Michelle Kwan, United States
2002	Irina Slutskaya, Russia
2003	Michelle Kwan, United States
2004	Shizuka Arakawa, Japan

U.S. CHAMPIONS

Men
1946–52	Richard Button
1953–56	Hayes Jenkins
1957–60	David Jenkins
1961	Bradley Lord
1962	Monty Hoyt
1963	Tommy Liz
1964	Scott Allen
1965	Gary Visconti
1966	Scott Allen
1967	Gary Visconti

1968–70	Tim Wood
1971	John M. Petkevich
1972	Ken Shelley
1973–75	Gordon McKellen
1976	Terry Kubicka
1977–80	Charles Tickner
1981–84	Scott Hamilton
1985–88	Brian Boitano
1989	Christopher Bowman
1990–91	Todd Eldredge
1992	Christopher Bowman

1993–94	Scott Davis
1995	Todd Eldredge
1996	Rudy Galindo
1997–98	Todd Eldredge
1999–2000	Michael Weiss
2001	Timothy Goebel
2002	Todd Eldredge
2003	Michael Weiss
2004	Johnny Weir

Women					
1943–48	Gretchen Merrill	1969–73	Janet Lynn	1991	Tonya Harding
1949–50	Yvonne Sherman	1974–76	Dorothy Hamill	1992	Kristi Yamaguchi
1951	Sonya Klopfer	1977–80	Linda Fratianne	1993	Nancy Kerrigan
1952–56	Tenley Albright	1981	Elaine Zayak	1994	Tonya Harding
1957–60	Carol Heiss	1982–84	Rosalynn Sumners	1995	Nicole Bobek
1961	Laurence Owen	1985	Tiffany Chin	1996	Michelle Kwan
1962	Barbara Roles Pursley	1986	Debi Thomas	1997	Tara Lipinski
1963	Lorraine Hanlon	1987	Jill Trenary	1998–2004	Michelle Kwan
1964–68	Peggy Fleming	1988	Debi Thomas		
		1989–90	Jill Trenary		

2004 UNITED STATES CHAMPIONSHIPS

(Jan. 3–11, 2004, Atlanta, Ga.)

Men's singles
1. Johnny Weir, Newark, Del.
2. Michael Weiss, McLean, Va.
3. Matthew Savoie, Peoria, Ill.

Pairs
1. Rena Inoue and John Baldwin, both Santa Monica, Calif.
2. Katie Orscher, Glastonbury, Conn., and Garrett Lucash, Granby, Conn.
3. Tiffany Scott, Hanson, Mass., and Philip Dulebohn, Germantown, Md.

Women's singles
1. Michelle Kwan, Manhattan Beach, Calif.
2. Sasha Cohen, New York, N.Y.
2. Jennifer Kirk, Newton, Mass.

Dance
1. Tanith Belbin, Kirkland, Quebec, and Ben Agosto, Chicago, Ill.
2. Melissa Gregory and Denis Petukhov, both Northbrook, Ill.
2. Loren Galler-Rabinowitz, Brookline, Mass., and David Mitchell, Cortland, N.Y.

2004 WORLD CHAMPIONSHIPS

(March 22–28, Dortmund, Germany)

Men's singles
1. Evgeni Plushenko, Russia
2. Brian Joubert, France
3. Stefan Lindemann, Germany

Women's singles
1. Shizuka Arakawa, Japan
2. Sasha Cohen, United States
3. Michelle Kwan, United States

Pairs
1. Tatiana Totmianina and Maxim Marinin, Russia
2. Xue Shen and Hongbo Zhao, China
3. Qing Pang and Jian Tong, China

Dance
1. Tatiana Navka and Roman Kostomarov, Russia
2. Albena Denkova and Maxim Staviski, Bulgaria
2. Kati Winkler and Rene Lohse, Germany

Swimming

WORLD LONG COURSE RECORDS—MEN

(Through Aug. 28, 2004)

Distance	Record	Holder	Country	Date
Freestyle				
50 m	0:21.64	Alexander Popov	Russia	June 16, 2000
100 m	0:47.84	Pieter van den Hoogenband	Netherlands	Sept. 19, 2000
200 m	1:44.06	Ian Thorpe	Australia	July 25, 2001
400 m	3:40.08	Ian Thorpe	Australia	July 30, 2002
800 m	7:39.16	Ian Thorpe	Australia	July 24, 2001
1,500 m	14:34.56	Grant Hackett	Australia	July 29, 2001
Backstroke				
50 m	0:24.80	Thomas Rupprath	Germany	July 27, 2003
100 m	0:53.45	Aaron Peirsol	United States	Aug. 21, 2004
200 m	1:54.74	Aaron Peirsol	United States	July 12, 2004
Breaststroke				
50 m	0:27.18	Oleg Lisog0r	Ukraine	Aug. 2, 2002
100 m	0:59.30	Brendan Hansen	United States	July 8, 2004
200 m	2:09.04	Brendan Hansen	United States	July 11, 2004
Butterfly				
50 m	0:23.30	Ian Crocker	United States	Feb. 29, 2004
100 m	0:50.76	Ian Crocker	United States	July 13, 2004
200 m	1:53.93	Michael Phelps	United States	July 22, 2003
Individual medley				
200 m	1:55.94	Michael Phelps	United States	Aug. 9, 2003
400 m	4:08.26	Michael Phelps	United States	Aug. 14, 2004
Medley relay				
400 m	3:30.68	Olympic Team	United States	Aug. 21, 2004
Freestyle relay				
400 m	3:13.17	Olympic Team	South Africa	Aug. 15, 2004
800 m	7:04.66	National Team	Australia	July 27, 2001

NOTE: International Swimming Federation (FINA) discontinued acceptance of records in yards in 1968. *Source:* FINA.

WORLD LONG COURSE RECORDS—WOMEN
(Through Aug. 28, 2004)

Distance	Record	Holder	Country	Date
Freestyle				
50 m	0:24.13	Inge de Bruijn	Netherlands	Sept. 22, 2000
100 m	0:53.52	Jodie Henry	Australia	Aug. 18, 2004
200 m	1:56.64	Franziska van Almsick	Germany	Aug. 3, 2002
400 m	4:03.85	Janet Evans	United States	Sept. 22, 1988
800 m	8:16.22	Janet Evans	United States	Aug. 20, 1989
1,500 m	15:52.10	Janet Evans	United States	March 26, 1988
Backstroke				
50 m	0:28.25	Sandra Voelker	Germany	June 17, 2000
100 m	0:59.58	Natalie Coughlin	United States	Aug. 13, 2002
200 m	2:06.62	Kristina Egerszegi	Hungary	Aug. 25, 1991
Breaststroke				
50 m	0:30.57	Zoe Baker	Great Britain	July 30, 2002
100 m	1:06.37	Leisel Jones	Australia	July 21, 2003
200 m	2:22.44	Amanda Beard	United States	July 12, 2004
Butterfly				
50 m	0:25.57	Anna-Karin Kammerling	Sweden	July 30, 2000
100 m	0:56.61	Inge de Bruijn	Netherlands	Sept. 17, 2000
200 m	2:05.78	Otylia Jedrzejczak	Poland	Aug. 4, 2002
Individual medley				
200 m	2:09.72	Yanyan Wu	China	Oct. 17, 1997
400 m	4:33.59	Yana Klochkova	Ukraine	Sept. 16, 2000
Medley relay				
400 m	3:57.32	Olympic Team	Australia	Agu. 21, 2004
Freestyle relay				
400 m	3:35.94	Olympic Team	Australia	Aug. 14, 2004
800 m	7:53.42	Olympic Team	United States	Aug. 18, 2004

NOTE: International Swimming Federation (FINA) discontinued acceptance of records in yards in 1968. *Source:* FINA.

AMERICAN LONG COURSE SWIMMING RECORDS
(Through Aug. 28, 2004)

MEN

Distance	Record	Holder	Date
Freestyle			
50 m	0:21.76	Gary Hall, Jr.	Aug. 15, 2000
100 m	0:48.33	Anthony Ervin	July 27, 2001
200 m	1:45.32	Michael Phelps	Aug. 16, 2004
400 m	3:44.11	Klete Keller	Aug. 14, 2004
800 m	7:48.09	Larsen Jensen	July 25, 2003
1,500 m	14:45.29	Larsen Jensen	Aug. 21, 2004
Backstroke			
50 m	0:24.99	Lenny Krayzelburg	Aug. 28, 1999
100 m	0:53.45	Aaron Peirsol	Aug. 21, 2004
200 m	1:54.74	Aaron Peirsol	July 12, 2004
Breaststroke			
50 m	0:27.39	Ed Moses	March 31, 2001
100 m	0:59.30	Brendan Hansen	July 8, 2004
200 m	2:09.04	Brendan Hansen	July 11, 2004
Butterfly			
50 m	0:23.30	Ian Crocker	Feb. 29, 2004
100 m	0:50.76	Ian Crocker	July 13, 2004
200 m	1:53.93	Michael Phelps	July 22, 2003
Individual medley			
200 m	1:55.94	Michael Phelps	Aug. 9, 2003
400 m	4:08.26	Michael Phelps	Aug. 14, 2004
Medley relay			
400 m	3:30.68	U.S. Olympic Team	Aug. 21, 2004
Freestyle relay			
400 m	3:13.86	U.S. Olympic Team	Sept. 16, 2000
800 m	7:07.33	U.S. Olympic Team	Aug. 17, 2004

WOMEN

Distance	Record	Holder	Date
Freestyle			
50 m	0:24.63	Dara Torres	Sept. 23, 2000
100 m	0:53.99	Natalie Coughlin	Aug. 29, 2002
200 m	1:57.41	Lindsay Benko	July 24, 2003
400 m	4:03.85	Janet Evans	Sept. 22, 1988
800 m	8:16.22	Janet Evans	Aug. 20, 1989
1,500 m	15:52.10	Janet Evans	March 26, 1988
Backstroke			
50 m	0:28.49	Natalie Coughlin	July 23, 2001
100 m	0:59.58	Natalie Coughlin	Aug. 13, 2002
200 m	2:08.53	Natalie Coughlin	Aug. 16, 2002
Breaststroke			
50 m	0:31.34	Megan Quann	Aug. 11, 2000
100 m	1:07.05	Megan Quann	Sept. 18, 2000
200 m	2:22.44	Amanda Beard	July 12, 2004
Butterfly			
50 m	0:26.50	Dara Torres	Aug. 9, 2000
100 m	0:57.58	Dara Torres	Aug. 9, 2000
200 m	2:05.88	Misty Hyman	Sept. 20, 2000
Individual medley			
200 m	2:11.91	Summer Sanders	July 30, 1992
400 m	4:37.58	Summer Sanders	July 26, 1992
Medley relay			
400 m	3:58.30	U.S. Olympic Team	Sept. 23, 2000
Freestyle relay			
400 m	3:36.38	U.S. Olympic Team	Aug. 14, 2004
800 m	7:53.42	U.S. Olympic Team	Aug. 18, 2004

Source: United States Swim Team, FINA.

UNITED STATES SUMMER NATIONAL CHAMPIONSHIPS, 2004
(Stanford, Calif., Aug. 3–7, 2004)

Men	Time	Women	Time
50 m freestyle—Randall Bal	0:22.75	50 m freestyle—Brooke Bishop	0:26.10
100 m freestyle—Garrett Weber-Gale	0:49.91	100 m freestyle—Tanica Jamison	0:55.96
200 m freestyle—Justin Mortimer	1:50.18	200 m freestyle—Lauren Medina	2:01.89
400 m freestyle—John Koehler	3:57.04	400 m freestyle—Kate Ziegler	4:12.06
800 m freestyle—Justin Mortimer	8:02.90	800 m freestyle—Alyssa Kiel	8:33.08
1500 m freestyle—Justin Mortimer	15:23.96	1500 m freestyle—Kate Ziegler	16:22.03
100 m backstroke—Randall Bal	0:54.67	100 m backstroke—Hayley McGregory	1:02.55
200 m backstroke—Trent Staley	2:02.02	200 m backstroke—Hayley McGregory	2:13.59
100 m breaststroke—Julien Nicolardot	1:03.08	100 m breaststroke—Jessica Hardy	1:08.33
200 m breaststroke—Julien Nicolardot	2:14.52	200 m breaststroke—Lindsey Ertter	2:30.64
100 m butterfly—Daniel Rohleder	0:54.17	100 m butterfly—Tanica Jamison	0:59.23
200 m butterfly—William Stovall	2:00.03	200 m butterfly—Kimberly Vandenberg	2:11.08
200 m individual medley—Mark Stephens	2:04.34	200 m individual medley—Danielle Townsend	2:15.75
400 m individual medley—Justin Mortimer	4:21.15	400 m individual medley—Ariana Kukors	4:45.41
400 m medley relay—Longhorn Aquatic	3:46.02	400 m medley relay—Longhorn Aquatic	4:10.34
400 m freestyle relay—Longhorn Aquatic	3:25.59	400 m freestyle relay—Longhorn Aquatic	3:48.76
800 m freestyle relay—Mecklenburg	7:35.84	800 m freestyle relay—Longhorn Aquatic	8:18.05

NCAA DIV. I CHAMPIONSHIPS, 2004

Men (East Meadow, N.Y. March 25–27, 2004)	Time	Women (College Station, Tex., March 18–20, 2004) Points	
50 m freestyle—Fred Bousquet, Auburn	0:21.10	50 m freestyle—Kara Lynn Joyce, Georgia	0:24.24
100 m freestyle—Ian Crocker, Texas	0:46.25	100 m freestyle—Kara Lynn Joyce, Georgia	0:53.15
200 m freestyle—Jayme Cramer, Stanford	1:45.04	200 m freestyle—Margaret Hoelzer, Auburn	1:56.16
400 m freestyle—Peter Vanderkaay, Michigan	3:40.78	400 m freestyle—Emily Mason, Arizona	4:01.58
1500 m freestyle—Peter Vanderkaay, Michigan	14:44.53	1500 m freestyle—Kalyn Keller, Southern Calif.	15:49.14
100 m backstroke—Peter Marshall, Stanford	0:50.32	100 m backstroke—Natalie Coughlin, California	0:57.51
200 m backstroke—Aaron Peirsol, Texas	1:50.64	200 m backstroke—Kirsty Coventry, Auburn	2:03.86
100 m breaststroke—Brendan Hansen, Texas	0:58.19	100 m breaststroke—Tara Kirk, Stanford	1:04.79
200 m breaststroke—Brendan Hansen, Texas	2:04.73	200 m breaststroke—Tara Kirk, Stanford	2:20.70
100 m butterfly—Ian Crocker, Texas	0:49.07	100 m butterfly—Natalie Coughlin, California	0:56.88
200 m butterfly—Rainer Kendrick, Texas	1:54.97	200 m butterfly—Mary Descenza, Georgia	2:06.02
200 m individual medley—George Bovell, Auburn	1:53.93	200 m individual medley—Kaitlin Sandeno, Southern Calif.	2:08.11
400 m individual medley—Ryan Lochte, Florida	4:04.52	400 m individual medley—Kaitlin Sandeno, Southern Calif.	4:30.44
200 m freestyle relay—Auburn	1:23.75	200 m freestyle relay—Georgia	1:37.27
200 m medley relay—Auburn	1:34.25	200 m medley relay—Auburn	1:49.02
4×100 m medley relay—Texas	3:25.38	4×100 m medley relay—Georgia	3:56.48
4×100 m freestyle relay—Auburn	3:08.85	4×100 m freestyle relay—Georgia	3:35.14
4×200 m freestyle relay—Michigan	7:01.42	4×200 m freestyle relay—California	7:50.94
1 m springboard dive—Jevon Tarantino, Tennessee	388.65 pts	1 m springboard dive—Allison Brennan, South Carolina	307.20 pts
3 m springboard dive—Joona Puhakka, Arizona State	647.30 pts	3 m springboard dive—Lane Bassham, Alabama	557.75 pts
Platform dive—Caesar Garcia, Auburn	635.05 pts	Platform dive—Nicole Pohorenec, Texas	482.20 pts

Boxing

Whether it be called pugilism, prize fighting, or boxing, there is no tracing "the Sweet Science" to any definite source. Tales of rivals exchanging blows for fun, fame, or money go back to earliest recorded history and classical legend. There was a mixture of boxing and wrestling called the "pancratium" in the ancient Olympic Games; in such contests rivals belabored one another with hands fortified by heavy leather wrappings that were sometimes studded with metal. More than one Olympic competitor lost his life in this brutal exercise.

There was little law or order in pugilism until Jack Broughton, one of the early champions of England, drew up a set of rules for the game in 1743. Broughton, called "the father of English boxing," also is credited with having invented boxing

gloves. However, these gloves—or "mufflers" as they were called—were used only in teaching "the manly art of self-defense" or in training bouts. All professional championship fights were contested with bare knuckles until 1892, when John L. Sullivan lost the heavyweight championship of the world to James J. Corbett in New Orleans in a bout in which both contestants wore regulation gloves.

The Broughton Rules were superseded by the London Prize Ring Rules of 1838. In 1884 the eighth marquis of Queensberry, with the help of John G. Chambers, put forward the Queensberry Rules, a code that called for gloved contests. Amateurs took to the Queensberry Rules more quickly than the professionals did.

HISTORY OF WORLD HEAVYWEIGHT CHAMPIONSHIP FIGHTS (WBC, WBA, IBF)

(Bouts in which a new champion was crowned)

Date	Where held	Winner, weight (age)	Loser, weight (age)	Rounds
Sept. 7, 1892	New Orleans, La.	James J. Corbett, 178 (26)	John L. Sullivan, 212 (33)	21
March 17, 1897	Carson City, Nev.	Bob Fitzsimmons, 167 (34)	James J. Corbett, 183 (30)	KO 14
June 9, 1899	Coney Island, N.Y.	James J. Jeffries, 206 (24)[1]	Bob Fitzsimmons, 167 (37)	KO 11
July 3, 1905	Reno, Nev.	Marvin Hart 190 (28)	Jack Root 171 (29)	TKO 12
Feb. 23, 1906	Los Angeles	Tommy Burns, 180 (24)[2]	Marvin Hart, 188 (29)	20
Dec. 26, 1908	Sydney, Australia	Jack Johnson, 196 (30)	Tommy Burns, 176 (27)	KO 14
April 5, 1915	Havana, Cuba	Jess Willard, 230 (33)	Jack Johnson, 205½ (37)	KO 26
July 4, 1919	Toledo, Ohio	Jack Dempsey, 187 (24)	Jess Willard, 245 (37)	KO 3
Sept. 23, 1926	Philadelphia	Gene Tunney, 189 (28)[3]	Jack Dempsey, 190 (31)	10
June 12, 1930	New York	Max Schmeling, 188 (24)	Jack Sharkey, 197 (27)	WF 4
June 21, 1932	Long Island City	Jack Sharkey, 205 (29)	Max Schmeling, 188 (26)	15
June 29, 1933	Long Island City	Primo Carnera, 260½ (26)	Jack Sharkey, 201 (30)	KO 6
June 14, 1934	Long Island City	Max Baer, 209½ (25)	Primo Carnera, 263¼ (27)	KO 11
June 13, 1935	Long Island City	Jim Braddock, 193¾ (29)	Max Baer, 209½ (26)	15
June 22, 1937	Chicago	Joe Louis, 197¼ (23)	Jim Braddock, 197 (31)	KO 8
June 22, 1949	Chicago	Ezzard Charles, 181¾ (27)[4]	Joe Walcott, 195½ (35)	15
Sept. 27, 1950	New York	Ezzard Charles, 184½ (29)[5]	Joe Louis, 218 (36)	15
July 18, 1951	Pittsburgh	Joe Walcott, 194 (37)	Ezzard Charles, 182 (30)	KO 7
Sept. 23, 1952	Philadelphia	Rocky Marciano, 184 (29)[6]	Joe Walcott, 196 (38)	KO13
Nov. 30, 1956	Chicago	Floyd Patterson, 182¼ (21)	Archie Moore, 187¾ (42)	KO 5
June 26, 1959	New York	Ingemar Johansson, 196 (26)	Floyd Patterson, 182 (24)	KO 3
June 20, 1960	New York	Floyd Patterson, 190 (25)	Ingemar Johansson, 194¾ (27)	KO 5
Sept. 25, 1962	Chicago	Sonny Liston, 214 (28)	Floyd Patterson, 189 (27)	KO 1
Feb. 25, 1964	Miami Beach, Fla.	Cassius Clay (Muhammad Ali), 210 (22)[7]	Sonny Liston, 218 (30)	KO 7
March 4, 1968	New York	Joe Frazier, 204½ (24)[8]	Buster Mathis, 243½ (23)	KO 11
April 27, 1968	Oakland, Calif.	Jimmy Ellis, 197 (28)[9]	Jerry Quarry, 195 (22)	15
Feb. 16, 1970	New York	Joe Frazier, 205 (26)[10]	Jimmy Ellis, 201 (29)	KO 5
Jan. 22, 1973	Kingston, Jamaica	George Foreman, 217½ (24)	Joe Frazier, 214 (29)	KO 2
Oct. 30, 1974	Kinshasa, Zaire	Muhammad Ali, 216½ (32)	George Foreman, 220 (26)	KO 8
Feb. 15, 1978	Las Vegas, Nev.	Leon Spinks, 197 (25)	Muhammad Ali, 224½ (36)	15
June 9, 1978	Las Vegas, Nev.	Larry Holmes, 212 (28)[11]	Ken Norton, 220 (32)	15
Sept. 15, 1978	New Orleans	Muhammad Ali, 221 (36)[12]	Leon Spinks, 201 (25)	15
Oct. 20, 1979	Pretoria, S. Africa	John Tate, 240 (24)[13]	Gerrie Coetzee, 222 (24)	15
March 31, 1980	Knoxville, Tenn.	Mike Weaver, 207½ (27)	John Tate, 232 (25)	KO 15
Dec. 10, 1982	Las Vegas, Nev.	Michael Dokes, 216 (24)	Mike Weaver, 209½ (30)	KO 1
Sept. 23, 1983	Richfield, Ohio	Gerrie Coetzee, 215 (28)	Michael Dokes, 217 (25)	KO 10
March 9, 1984	Las Vegas, Nev.	Tim Witherspoon, 220½ (26)[14]	Greg Page, 239½ (25)	12
Aug. 31, 1984	Las Vegas, Nev.	Pinklon Thomas, 216 (26)	Tim Witherspoon, 217 (26)	12
Nov. 9, 1984	Las Vegas, Nev.	Larry Holmes, 221½ (35)[15]	James Smith, 227 (31)	KO 12
Dec. 1, 1984	Sun City, S. Africa	Greg Page, 236 (25)[16]	Gerry Coetzee, 217 (29)	KO 8
April 29, 1985	Buffalo, N.Y.	Tony Tubbs, 229 (26)[16]	Greg Page, 239½ (26)	15
Sept. 21,1985	Las Vegas, Nev.	Michael Spinks, 200 (29)	Larry Holmes, 221 (35)	15
Jan. 17, 1986	Atlanta, Ga.	Tim Witherspoon, 227 (28)	Tony Tubbs, 229 (27)	15
Nov. 23, 1986	Las Vegas, Nev.	Mike Tyson, 217 (20)[17]	Trevor Berbick, 220 (29)	KO 2
Dec. 12, 1986	New York, N.Y.	James Smith, 230 (33)[16]	Tim Witherspoon, 218 (29)	KO 1
March 7, 1987	Las Vegas, Nev.	Mike Tyson, 217 (20)[16]	James Smith, 230 (33)	12
Feb. 10, 1990	Tokyo	James "Buster" Douglas, 231½ (29)[18]	Mike Tyson, 220 (23)	KO 10
Oct. 25, 1990	Las Vegas, Nev.	Evander Holyfield, 208 (28)	James "Buster" Douglas, 246 (30)	KO 3
Nov. 13, 1992	Las Vegas, Nev.	Riddick Bowe,[19] 235 (25)	Evander Holyfield, 205 (30)	12
Nov. 6, 1993	Las Vegas, Nev.	Evander Holyfield, 217 (30)	Riddick Bowe, 246 (26)	12
April 22, 1994	Las Vegas, Nev.	Michael Moorer, 214 (26)	Evander Holyfield,[20] 214 (31)	12
Sept 24, 1994	London	Oliver McCall,[21] 228 (29)	Lennox Lewis, 238 (28)	2
Nov. 5, 1994	Las Vegas, Nev.	George Foreman,[22] 250 (45)	Michael Moorer, 222 (26)	10
April 8, 1995	Las Vegas, Nev.	Bruce Seldon,[23] 232 (28)	Tony Tucker, 238 (36)	7
Dec.9, 1995	Stuttgart, Ger.	Frans Botha,[24] 227 (28)	Axel Schulz, 222 (27)	12
March 16, 1996	Las Vegas, Nev.	Mike Tyson,[25] 220 (29)	Frank Bruno, 247 (34)	3
June 22, 1996	Dortmund, Ger.	Michael Moorer, 222 (28)	Axel Schulz, 222 (27)	12
Sept. 7, 1996	Las Vegas, Nev.	Mike Tyson, 219 (30)	Bruce Seldon, 229 (29)	1
Nov. 9, 1996	Las Vegas, Nev.	Evander Holyfield,[23] 215 (34)	Mike Tyson, 222 (30)	11
Feb. 7, 1997	Las Vegas, Nev.	Lennox Lewis,[25] 251 (31)	Oliver McCall, 237 (30)	5
Nov. 8, 1997	Las Vegas, Nev.	Evander Holyfield,[26] 214 (35)	Michael Moorer, 223 (30)	8
Nov. 13, 1999	Las Vegas, Nev.	Lennox Lewis,[23, 27] 240 (33)	Evander Holyfield, 217 (36)	12
Aug. 12, 2000	Las Vegas, Nev.	Evander Holyfield,[23] 221 (37)	John Ruiz, 224 (24)	12
March 3, 2001	Las Vegas, Nev.	John Ruiz,[23] 227 (27)	Evander Holyfield, 217 (38)	12
Apr. 21, 2001	South Africa	Hasim Rahman,[25, 26] 237 (28)	Lennox Lewis, 253 (35)	KO 5
Nov. 17, 2001	Las Vegas, Nev.	Lennox Lewis,[25, 26, 28] 246 (36)	Hasim Rahman, 236 (29)	KO 4
Dec. 14, 2002	Atlantic City, N.J.	Chris Byrd,[26] 214 (32)	Evander Holyfield, 220 (40)	12
March 1, 2003	Las Vegas, Nev.	Roy Jones, Jr.,[23] 193 (34)	John Ruiz, 226 (31)	12
April 17, 2004	New York, N.Y.	John Ruiz,[23] 240 (32)	Fres Oquendo, 222 (31)	11
April 24, 2004	Los Angeles, Calif.	Vitali Klitschko,[25] 245 (33)	Corrie Sanders, 235 (32)	8

1. Jeffries retired as champion in March 1905. He named Marvin Hart and Jack Root as leading contenders and agreed to referee their fight in Reno, Nev., on July 3, 1905, with the stipulation that he would term the winner the champion. Hart, 190 (28), knocked out Root, 171 (29), in the 12th round. 2. Burns claimed the title after defeating Hart. 3. Tunney retired as champion after defeating Tom Heeney on July 26, 1928. 4. After Louis announced his retirement as champion on March 1, 1949, Charles won recognition from the National Boxing Association as champion by defeating Walcott. 5. Charles gained undisputed recognition as champion by defeating Louis, who came out of retirement. 6. Retired as champion April 27, 1956. 7. The World Boxing Association (WBA) later withdrew its recognition of Clay as champion and declared the winner of a bout between Ernie Terrell and Eddie Machen would gain its version of the title. Terrell, 199 (25), won a 15-round decision from Machen, 192 (32), in Chicago on March 5, 1965. Clay, 212¼ (25) and Terrell, 212½ (27), met in Houston on Feb. 6, 1967, Clay winning a 15-round decision. 8. Winner recognized by N.Y., Mass., Maine, Ill., Tex. and Pa. to fill vacated title when Clay was stripped of championship for failing to accept U.S. Induction. 9. Bout was final of eight-man tournament to fill Clay's place and is recognized by World Boxing Association. 10. Bout settled controversy over title. 11. Holmes won World Boxing Council title after WBC had withdrawn recognition of Spinks, March 18, 1978, and awarded its title to Norton. WBC said Spinks had reneged on agreement to fight Norton. 12. Ali regained World Boxing Association championship. 13. Tate won WBA title after Ali retired and left it vacant. 14. Tim Witherspoon and Greg Page fought for the WBC heavyweight title vacated by Larry Holmes, who could not come to agreement on a deal to fight Page, the No. 1 contender. Holmes declared he would fight under the banner of the International Boxing Federation (IBF). Several dates were set and postponed for fights between Holmes and Gerry Coetzee, the WBA champ, the latest being Nov. 16, 1984. 15. First fight under banner of International Boxing Federation. 16. New WBA champion. 17. New WBC champion. 18. New undisputed champion. 19. The WBC stripped Bowe of its version of the title in December 1992 and named Lennox Lewis champion. 20. After the loss, Holyfield retired. 21. New WBC champion. Lennox Lewis had been named champion in 1992 and had won three title defenses before losing to McCall. 22. For combined WBA/IBF titles. Later WBA stripped Foreman of title for failing to fight no. 1 contender Tony Tucker. IBF also stripped Foreman on June 29, 1995. 23. New WBA champion. 24. Botha later tested positive for steroids and was stripped of the title. 25. New WBC champion. 26. New IBF champion. 27. Surrendered WBA title to fight Michael Grant in unsanctioned bout. 28. Lewis surrendered his IBF title in 2002.

OTHER WORLD BOXING TITLEHOLDERS

Light Heavyweight

(Through Sept. 29, 2004)

1903	Jack Root, George Gardner	
1903–05	Bob Fitzsimmons	
1905–12	Philadelphia Jack O'Brien[1]	
1912–16	Jack Dillon	
1916–20	Battling Levinsky	
1920–22	Georges Carpentier	
1923	Battling Siki	
1923–25	Mike McTigue	
1925–26	Paul Berlenbach	
1926–27	Jack Delaney[2]	
1927	Mike McTigue	
1927–29	Tommy Loughran	
1930	Jimmy Slattery	
1930–34	Maxie Rosenbloom	
1934–35	Bob Olin	
1935–39	John Henry Lewis	
1939	Melio Bettina	
1939–41	Billy Conn[2]	
1941	Anton Christoforidis (NBA)	
1941–48	Gus Lesnevich	
1948–50	Freddie Mills	
1950–52	Joey Maxim	
1952–61	Archie Moore[3]	
1961–63	Harold Johnson	
1963–65	Willie Pastrano	
1965–66	José Torres	
1966–67	Dick Tiger	
1968	Dick Tiger, Bob Foster	
1969–70	Bob Foster	
1971	Vicente Rondon (WBA), Bob Foster (WBC)	
1972–73	Bob Foster (WBA, WBC)	
1974	John Conteh (WBA), Bob Foster (WBC)[1, 4]	
1975–76	Victor Galindez (WBA), John Conteh (WBC)	
1977	Victor Galindez (WBA), John Conteh (WBC),[4] Miguel Cuello (WBC)	
1978	Victor Galindez (WBA), Mike Rossman (WBA), Miguel Cuello (WBC), Mate Parlov (WBC), Marvin Johnson (WBC)	
1979	Mike Rossman (WBA), Victor Galindez (WBA), Marvin Johnson (WBC), Matthew (Franklin) Saad Muhammad (WBC)	

1980	Matthew Saad Muhammad (WBC), Marvin Johnson (WBA), Eddie (Gregory) Mustafa Muhammad (WBA)	
1981	Matthew Saad Muhammad (WBC), Eddie Mustafa Muhammad (WBA), Michael Spinks (WBA), Dwight Braxton (WBC)	
1982	Dwight Braxton (WBC), Michael Spinks (WBA)	
1983	Michael Spinks (undisputed)	
1984	Michael Spinks (undisputed)	
1985	Michael Spinks (undisputed)[5]	
1986	Marvin Johnson (WBA), Dennis Andries (WBC)	
1987	Thomas Hearns (WBC), Virgil Hill (WBA), Bobby Czyz (IBF)	
1988	Charles Williams (IBF), Virgil Hill (WBA), Donny LaLonde (WBC), Sugar Ray Leonard (WBC)	
1989	Dennis Andries (WBC), Virgil Hill (WBA), Charles Williams (IBF), Jeff Harding (WBC)	
1990	Virgil Hill (WBA), Charles Williams (IBF), Jeff Harding (WBC), Dennis Andries (WBC)	
1991	Virgil Hill (WBA), Thomas Hearns (WBA), Dennis Andries (WBC), Charles Williams (IBF)	
1992	Charles Williams (IBF), James Waring (IBF), Jeff Harding (WBC)	
1993	Virgil Hill (WBA), Jeff Harding (WBC), Henry Maske (IBF)	
1994	Virgil Hill (WBA), Mike McCallum (WBC), Henry Maske (IBF)	
1995	Virgil Hill (WBA), Fabio Tiozzo (WBC), Henry Maske (IBF)	

1996–97	Virgil Hill (WBA), Fabio Tiozzo (WBC), Henry Maske (IBF)	
1998	Roy Jones (WBA, WBC), Reggie Johnson (IBF)	
1999– 2001	Roy Jones (WBA, WBC, IBF)	
2002	Bruno Girard (WBA), Roy Jones (WBC, IBF)	
2003	Vacant (WBA), Antonio Tarver (WBC, IBF)	
2004	Antonio Tarver (WBC), Fabrice Tiozzo (WBA), Glen Johnson (IBF)	

1. Retired. 2. Abandoned title. 3. NBA withdrew recognition in 1961, New York Commission in 1962; recognized thereafter only by California and Europe. 4. WBC withdrew recognition. 5. Spinks relinquished title in 1985 to fight for heavyweight title.

Middleweight

1867–72	Tom Chandler
1872–81	George Rooke
1881–82	Mike Donovan[1]
1884–91	Jack (Nonpareil) Dempsey
1891–97	Bob Fitzsimmons[2]
1908	Stanley Ketchel, Billy Papke
1908–10	Stanley Ketchel[3]
1913	Frank Klaus
1913–14	George Chip
1914–17	Al McCoy
1917–20	Mike O'Dowd
1920–23	Johnny Wilson
1923–26	Harry Greb
1926	Tiger Flowers
1926–31	Mickey Walker[2]
1931–41	Gorilla Jones, Ben Jeby, Marcel Thil, Lou Brouillard, Vince Dundee, Teddy Yarosz, Babe Risko, Freddy Steele, Al Hostak, Solly Kreiger, Fred Apostoli, Cerferino Garcia, Ken Overlin, Billy Soose, Tony Zale[4]
1941–47	Tony Zale
1947–48	Rocky Graziano
1948	Tony Zale
1948–49	Marcel Cerdan
1949–51	Jake LaMotta

1951–52	Ray Robinson[1]
1952	Ray Robinson, Randy Turpin
1953–55	Carl Olson
1955–57	Ray Robinson[5]
1957	Gene Fullmer, Ray Robinson
1957–58	Carmen Basilio
1958–60	Ray Robinson[6]
1959–62	Gene Fullmer (NBA)
1960–61	Paul Pender[7]
1961–62	Terry Downes[1]
1962	Paul Pender[1]
1962–63	Dick Tiger
1963–65	Joey Giardello
1965–66	Dick Tiger
1966	Emile Griffith
1967	Nino Benvenuti, Emile Griffith
1968	Emile Griffith, Nino Benvenuti
1969	Nino Benvenuti
1970	Nino Benvenuti, Carlos Monzon
1971–73	Carlos Monzon
1974–75	Carlos Monzon (WBA), Rodrigo Valdez (WBC)
1976	Carlos Monzon (WBA, WBC), Rodrigo Valdez (WBC)
1977	Carlos Monzon (WBA, WBC),[1] Rodrigo Valdez (WBA, WBC)
1978	Rodrigo Valdez, Hugo Corro
1979	Hugo Corro, Vito Antuofermo
1980	Vito Antuofermo, Alan Minter, Marvin Hagler
1981	Marvin Hagler
1982–86	Marvin Hagler (undisputed)
1987	Marvin Hagler (undisputed), Sugar Ray Leonard (undisputed)
1988	Sumbu Kalambay (WBA), Thomas Hearns (WBC), Iran Barkley (WBC), Frank Tate (IBF), Michael Nunn (IBF), James Kinchen (NABF)
1989	Michael Nunn (IBF), Mike McCallum (WBA), Iran Barkley (WBC), Roberto Duran (WBC)
1990	Michael McCallum (WBA), Michael Nunn (IBF), Iran Barkley (WBC)
1991	Michael Nunn (IBF), James Toney (IBF), Michael McCallum (WBA)
1992	James Toney (IBF), Julian Jackson (WBC), Reggie Johnson (WBA)
1993	Reggie Johnson (WBA), Gerald McClellan (WBC), Roy Jones (IBF)
1994	Julian Jackson (WBA), Gerald McClellan (WBC), Roy Jones (IBF)
1995	Jorge Castro (WBA), Julian Jackson (WBC), Bernard Hopkins (IBF)
1996	William Joppy (WBA), Keith Holmes (WBC), Bernard Hopkins (IBF)
1997	Shinji Takehara (WBA), Quincy Taylor (WBC), Bernard Hopkins (IBF)

1998	William Joppy (WBA), Hassine Cherifi (WBC), Bernard Hopkins (IBF)
1999–	William Joppy (WBA),
2000	Keith Holmes (WBC), Bernard Hopkins (IBF)
2001	Felix Trinidad (WBA), Bernard Hopkins (WBC, IBF)
2002	William Joppy (WBA), Bernard Hopkins (WBC, IBF)
2003–04	Bernard Hopkins (WBA, WBC, IBF)

1. Retired. 2. Abandoned title. 3. Died. 4. National Boxing Association and New York Commission disagreed on champions. Those listed were accepted by one or the other until Zale gained world-wide recognition. 5. Ended retirement in 1954. 6. NBA withdrew recognition. 7. Recognized by New York, Massachusetts, and Europe.

Welterweight

1892–94	Mysterious Billy Smith
1894–96	Tommy Ryan
1896	Kid McCoy[1]
1896–	
1900	Mysterious Billy Smith
1900	Rube Ferns
1900–01	Matty Matthews
1901	Ruby Ferns
1901–04	Joe Walcott
1904	Dixie Kid[1]
1904–06	Joe Walcott
1906–07	Honey Mellody
1907	Mike (Twin) Sullivan[1]
1915–19	Ted Lewis
1919–22	Jack Britton
1922–26	Mickey Walker
1926–27	Pete Latzo
1927–29	Joe Dundee
1929–30	Jackie Fields
1930	Young Jack Thompson
1930–31	Tommy Freeman
1931	Young Jack Thompson
1931–32	Lou Brouillard
1932–33	Jackie Fields
1933	Young Corbett 3rd
1933–34	Jimmy McLarnin, Barney Ross
1934–35	Jimmy McLarnin
1935–38	Barney Ross
1938–40	Henry Armstrong
1940–41	Fritzie Zivic
1941–46	Freddie Cochrane
1946	Marty Servo[2]
1946–51	Ray Robinson[1]
1951	Johnny Bratton (NBA)
1951–54	Kid Gavilan
1954–55	Johnny Saxton
1955	Tony DeMarco
1955–56	Carmen Basilio
1956	Johnny Saxton
1956–57	Carmen Basilio[1]
1958	Virgil Akins
1959–60	Don Jordan
1960–61	Benny (Kid) Paret
1961	Emile Griffith
1961–62	Benny (Kid) Paret
1962–63	Emile Griffith, Luis Rodriguez
1963–66	Emile Griffith[1]
1966–69	Curtis Cokes
1969	Curtis Cokes, José Napoles
1970	José Napoles, Billy Backus

1971	Billy Backus, José Napoles
1972–74	José Napoles
1975	José Napoles (WBA, WBC),[3] Angel Espada (WBA), John Stracey (WBC)
1976	Angel Espada (WBA), José Cuevas (WBA), John Stracey (WBC), Carlos Palomino
1977–78	José Cuevas (WBA), Carlos Palomino (WBC)
1979	José Cuevas (WBA), Carlos Palomino (WBC), Wilfredo Benitez (WBC)
1980	José Cuevas (WBA), Ray Leonard (WBC), Roberto Duran (WBC), Thomas Hearns (WBA)
1981	Ray Leonard (WBC), Thomas Hearns (WBA), Ray Leonard (WBC, WBA)
1982	Ray Leonard
1983–85	Donald Curry (WBA), Milton McCrory (WBC)
1985–86	Donald Curry (undisputed)
1987	Mark Breland (WBA), Marlon Starling (WBA), Lloyd Honeyghan (IBF)
1988	Marlon Starling (WBA), Tomas Molinares (WBA), Lloyd Honeyghan (WBC), Simon Brown (IBF)
1989	Mark Breland (WBA), Marlon Starling (WBC), Simon Brown (IBF)
1990	Mark Breland (WBA), Aaron Davis (WBA), Simon Brown (IBF), Marlon Starling (WBC), Maurice Blocker (WBC)
1991	Meldrick Taylor (WBA), Simon Brown (IBF, WBC)
1992	Meldrick Taylor (WBA), James "Buddy" McGirt (WBC), Maurice Blocker (IBF)
1993	Cristiano Espana (WBA), Pernell Whitaker (WBC), Felix Trinidad (IBF)
1994	Ike Quartey (WBA), Pernell Whitaker (WBC), Felix Trinidad (IBF)
1995	Ike Quartey (WBA), Pernell Whitaker (WBC), Felix Trinidad (IBF)
1996–97	Ike Quartey (WBA), Pernell Whitaker (WBC), Felix Trinidad (IBF)
1998	Ike Quartey (WBA), Oscar De La Hoya (WBC), Felix Trinidad (IBF)
1999	James Page (WBA), Oscar De La Hoya (WBC), Felix Trinidad (IBF, WBC)
2000	James Page (WBA), Shane Mosley (WBC), Vacant (IBF)
2001	Andrew Lewis (WBA), Shane Mosley (WBC), Vernon Forrest (IBF)
2002	Ricardo Mayorga (WBA), Vernon Forrest (WBC), Michele Piccirillo (IBF)
2003	Ricardo Mayorga (WBA, WBC), Cory Spinks (IBF)
2004	Cory Spinks (WBC, WBA, IBF)

1. Retired. 2. Abandoned title. 3. WBA withdrew recognition.

Lightweight

1869–99	Kid Lavigne
1899–	
1902	Frank Erne
1902–08	Joe Gans
1908–10	Battling Nelson
1910–12	Ad Wolgast
1912–14	Willie Ritchie
1914–17	Freddy Welsh
1917–25	Benny Leonard[1]
1925	Jimmy Goodrich
1925–26	Rocky Kansas
1926–30	Sammy Mandell
1930	Al Singer
1930–33	Tony Canzoneri
1933–35	Barney Ross[2]
1935–36	Tony Canzoneri
1936–38	Lou Ambers
1938–39	Henry Armstrong
1939–40	Lou Ambers
1940–41	Lew Jenkins
1941–42	Sammy Angott[1]
1943–47	Beau Jack (N.Y.),
	Bob Montgomery (N.Y.),
	Sammy Angott (NBA),
	Juan Zurita (NBA),
	Ike Williams (NBA)
1947–51	Ike Williams
1951–52	James Carter
1952	Lauro Salas
1952–54	James Carter
1954	Paddy DeMarco
1954–55	James Carter
1955–56	Wallace Smith
1956–62	Joe Brown
1962–65	Carlos Ortiz
1965	Ismael Laguna
1965–68	Carlos Ortiz
1968	Teo Cruz
1969	Teo Cruz,
	Mando Ramos
1970	Mando Ramos,
	Ismael Laguna,
	Ken Buchanan
1971	Ken Buchanan (WBA),
	Mando Ramos (WBC),
	Pedro Carrasco (WBC)
1972	Ken Buchanan (WBA),
	Roberto Duran (WBA),
	Pedro Carrasco (WBC),
	Mando Ramos (WBC),
	Chango Carmona (WBC),
	Rodolfo Gonzalez (WBC)
1973	Roberto Duran (WBA),
	Rodolfo Gonzalez (WBC)
1974	Roberto Duran (WBA),
	Rodolfo Gonzalez (WBC),
	Guts Ishimatsu (WBC)
1975	Roberto Duran (WBA),
	Guts Ishimatsu (WBC)
1976	Roberto Duran (WBA),
	Guts Ishimatsu (WBC),
	Esteban De Jesus (WBC)
1977	Roberto Duran (WBA),
	Esteban De Jesus (WBC)
1978	Roberto Duran (WBA, WBC)
1979	Roberto Duran,[2]
	Jim Watt (WBC),
	Ernesto Espana (WBA)
1980	Ernesto Espana (WBA),
	Hilmer Kenty (WBA),
	Jim Watt (WBC)
1981	Hilmer Kenty (WBA),
	Sean O'Grady (WBA),
	James Watt (WBC),
	Alexis Arguello (WBC),
	Arturo Frias (WBA)
1982	Arturo Frias (WBA),
	Ray Mancini (WBA),
	Alexis Arguello (WBC)
1983	Edwin Rosario (WBC),
	Ray Mancini (WBA)
1984	Edwin Rosario (WBC),
	Livingstone Bramble (WBA)
1985	Jose Luis Ramirez (WBC),
	Hector Camacho (WBC),
	Livingstone Bramble (WBA)
1986	Hector Camacho (WBC),
	Livingstone Bramble (WBA),
	Jim Paul (IBF)
1987	Edwin Rosario (WBA),
	Jose Luis Ramirez (WBC),
	Greg Haugen (IBF)
1988	Jose Luis Ramirez (WBC),
	Julio Cesar Chavez (WBA),
	Greg Haugen (IBF),
	Julio Cesar Chavez (WBC & WBA title unified)
1989	Pernell Whitaker (IBF, WBC),
	Edwin Rosario (WBA)
1990	Pernell Whitaker (IBF, WBC),
	Juan Nazario (WBA)
1991	Pernell Whitaker (IBF, WBA, WBC)
1992	Pernell Whitaker (IBF, WBA, WBC),[3]
	Joey Gamache (WBA)
1993	Dingaan Thobela (WBA),
	Angel Gonzalez (WBC),
	Freddie Pendleton (IBF)
1994	Orzubek Nazarov (WBA),
	Angel Gonzalez (WBC),
	Rafael Ruelas (IBF)
1995	Orzubek Nazarov (WBA),
	Angel Gonzalez (WBC),
	Oscar De La Hoya (IBF)
1996	Gusshie Nazarov (WBA),
	Jean Baptiste Mendy (WBC),
	Phillip Holiday (IBF)
1997	Orzubek Nazarov (WBA),
	Jean Baptiste Mendy (WBC),
	Philip Holiday (IBF)
1998	Jean Baptiste Mendy (WBA),
	Cesar Bazan (WBC),
	Shane Mosley (IBF)
1999	Stefano Zoff (WBA),
	Stevie Johnston (WBC),
	Paul Spadafora (IBF)
2000	Takanori Hatakeyama (WBA), Jose Luis Castillo (WBC), Paul Spadafora (IBF)
2001	Julien Lorcy (WBA), Jose Luis Castillo (WBC), Paul Spadafora (IBF)
2002	Leonard Dorin (WBA), Floyd Mayweather (WBC), Paul Spadafora (IBF)
2003	Leonard Dorin (WBA), Floyd Mayweather (WBC), Vacant (IBF)
2004	Jose Luis Castillo (WBC), Juan Diaz (WBA, IBF)

1. Retired. 2. Abandoned title. 3. Moving up in weight class, so resigned titles.

Featherweight

1889	Dal Hawkins[1]
1890	Billy Murphy
1892–	
1900	George Dixon
1900–01	Terry McGovern
1901	Young Corbett[1]
1901–12	Abe Attell
1912–23	Johnny Kilbane
1923	Eugene Criqui
1923–25	Johnny Dundee[1]
1925–27	Louis (Kid) Kaplan[1]
1927–28	Benny Bass
1928	Tony Canzoneri
1928–29	Andre Routis
1929–32	Battling Battalino[1]
1932	Tommy Paul (NBA), Kid Chocolate (N.Y.)
1933–36	Freddie Miller
1936–37	Petey Sarron
1937–38	Henry Armstrong[1]
1938–40	Joey Archibald
1940–41	Harry Jefra, Joey Archibald
1941–42	Chalky Wright
1942–48	Willie Pep
1948–49	Sandy Saddler[2]
1949–50	Willie Pep
1950–57	Sandy Saddler
1957–59	Kid Bassey
1959–63	Davey Moore
1963–64	Sugar Ramos
1964–67	Vicente Saldivar[2]
1968	Howard Winstone, José Legra,[3] Paul Rojas (WBA), Sho Saijo (WBA)
1969	Sho Saijo (WBA), Johnny Famechon[3]
1970	Sho Saijo (WBA), Johnny Famechon,[3] Vicente Saldivar,[3] Kuniaki Shibata[3]
1971	Sho Saijo (WBA), Antonio Gomez (WBA), Kuniaki Shibata (WBC)
1972	Antonio Gomez (WBA), Ernesto Marcel (WBA), Kuniaki Shibata (WBC), Clemente Sanchez (WBC), José Legra (WBC)
1973	Ernesto Marcel (WBA), José Legra (WBC), Eder Jofre (WBC)
1974	Ernesto Marcel (WBA),[2] Ruben Olivares (WBA), Alexis Arguello (WBA), Eder Jofre (WBC), Bobby Chacon (WBC)
1975	Alexis Arguello (WBA), Bobby Chacon (WBC), Ruben Olivares (WBC), David Kotey (WBC)
1976	Alexis Arguello (WBA),[2] David Kotey (WBC), Danny Lopez (WBC)
1977	Rafael Ortega (WBA), Danny Lopez (WBC)
1978	Rafael Ortega (WBA), Cecilio Lastra (WBA), Eusebio Pedroza (WBA), Danny Lopez (WBC)
1979	Eusebio Pedroza (WBA), Danny Lopez (WBC)
1980	Eusebio Pedroza (WBA), Danny Lopez (WBC), Salvador Sanchez (WBC)
1981	Eusebio Pedroza (WBA), Salvador Sanchez (WBC)
1982	Eusebio Pedroza (WBA), Salvador Sanchez (WBC)[4]
1983	Juan Laporte (WBC), Eusebio Pedroza (WBA)
1984	Wilfred Gomez (WBC), Eusebio Pedroza (WBA)

1985	Eusebio Pedroza (WBA), Barry McGuigan (WBA), Azumah Nelson (WBC)
1986	Barry McGuigan (WBA), Stevie Cruz (WBA), Azumah Nelson (WBC)
1987	Azumah Nelson (WBC), Antonio Esparragoza (WBA)
1988	Calvin Grove (IBF), Jorge Paez (IBF), Antonio Esparragoza (WBA), Jeff Fenech (WBC)
1989	Jorge Paez (IBF), Antonio Esparragoza (WBA), Jeff Fenech (WBC)
1990	Marcos Villasana (WBC), Antonio Esparragoza (WBA), Jorge Paez (IBF)
1991	Yung-Kyun Park (WBA), Troy Dorsey (IBF), Marcos Villagana (WBC)
1992	Paul Hodkinson (WBC), Manuel Medina (IBF), Yung-Kyun Park (WBA)
1993	Yung-Kyun Park (WBA), Goyo Vargas (WBC), Tom Johnson (IBF)
1994	Eloy Rojas (WBA), Kevin Kelley (WBC), Tom Johnson (IBF)
1995	Eloy Rojas (WBA), Alejandro Gonzalez (WBC), Tom Johnson (IBF)
1996	Wilfredo Vázquez (WBA), Luisto Espinoza (WBC), Tom Johnson (IBF)
1997	Elroy Rojas (WBA), Luisito Espinoza (WBC), Tom Johnson (IBF)
1998	vacant (WBA), Luisito Espinoza (WBC), Manuel Medina (IBF)
1999	Freddie Norwood (WBA), Cesar Soto (WBC), Manuel Medina (IBF)
2000	Freddie Norwood (WBA), Guty Espadas (WBC), Paul Ingle (IBF)
2001	Derrick Gainer (WBA), Erik Morales (WBC), Frankie Toledo (IBF)
2002	Derrick Gainer (WBA), vacant (WBC), Johnny Tapia (IBF)
2003	Derrick Gainer (WBA), Erik Morales (WBC), Manuel Marquez (IBF)
2004	Injin Chi (WBC), Juan Manuel Marquez (WBA, IBF)

1. Abandoned title. 2. Retired. 3. Recognized in Europe, Mexico, and Asia. 4. Killed in auto accident.

Bantamweight

1890–92	George Dixon[1]
1894–99	Jimmy Barry[2]
1899–	
1900	Terry McGovern[1]
1901	Harry Harris[1]
1902–03	Harry Forbes[1]
1903–04	Frankie Neil
1904	Joe Bowker[1]
1905–07	Jimmy Walsh[1]
1910–14	Johnny Coulon
1914–17	Kid Williams
1917–20	Pete Herman
1920	Joe Lynch
1920–21	Joe Lynch, Pete Herman, Johnny Buff
1922	Johnny Buff, Joe Lynch
1923	Joe Lynch
1924	Joe Lynch, Abe Goldstein, Eddie "Cannonball" Martin
1925	Eddie "Cannonball" Martin, Charlie (Phil) Rosenberg[3]
1927–28	Bud Taylor (NBA)[1]
1929–34	Al Brown
1935	Al Brown, Baltazar Sangchili
1936	Baltazar Sangchili, Tony Marino, Sixto Escobar
1937	Sixto Escobar, Harry Jeffra
1938	Harry Jeffra, Sixto Escobar
1939–40	Sixto Escobar[2]
1940–42	Lou Salica
1942–46	Manuel Ortiz
1947	Manuel Ortiz, Harold Dade
1948–50	Manuel Ortiz
1950–52	Vic Toweel
1952–54	Jimmy Carruthers[2]
1954–55	Robert Cohen
1956	Robert Cohen, Mario D'Agata, Raul Macias (NBA)
1957	Mario D'Agata, Alphonse Halimi
1958–59	Alphonse Halimi
1959–60	Jose Becerra[2]
1960–61	Alphonse Halimi[4]
1961–62	Johnny Caldwell[4]
1961–65	Eder Jofre
1965–68	Masahika "Fighting" Harada
1968	Masahika "Fighting" Harada, Lionel Rose
1969	Lionel Rose, Ruben Olivares
1970	Ruben Olivares, Chucho Castillo
1971	Chucho Castillo, Ruben Olivares
1972	Ruben Olivares, Rafael Herrera, Enrique Pinder
1973	Enrique Pinder (WBA), Romeo Anaya (WBA), Arnold Taylor (WBA), Rodolfo Martinez (WBC), Rafael Herrera
1974	Arnold Taylor (WBA), Soo Hwan Hong (WBA), Rafael Herrera (WBC), Rodolfo Martinez (WBC)
1975	Soo Hwan Hong (WBA), Alfonso Zamora (WBA), Rodolfo Martinez (WBC)
1976	Alfonso Zamora (WBA), Rodolfo Martinez (WBC), Carlos Zarate (WBC)
1977	Alfonso Zamora (WBA), Jorge Lujan (WBA), Carlos Zarate (WBC)

1978	Jorge Lujan (WBA), Carlos Zarate (WBC)
1979	Jorge Lujan (WBA), Carlos Zarate (WBC), Lupe Pintor (WBC)
1980	Jorge Lujan (WBA), Lupe Pintor (WBC), Julian Solis (WBA), Jeff Chandler (WBA)
1981	Lupe Pintor (WBC), Jeff Chandler (WBA)
1982	Lupe Pintor (WBC), Jeff Chandler (WBA)
1983	Jeff Chandler (WBA), Albert Dauila (WBC)
1984	Richie Sandqual (WBA), Albert Dauila (WBC)
1985	Richard Sandoval (WBA), Daniel Zaragoza (WBC), Miguel Lora (WBC)
1986	Richard Sandoval (WBA), Bernardo Pinango (WBA), Jeff Fenech (IBF)
1987	Bernardo Pinango (WBA), Takuya Muguruma (WBA), Miguel Lora (WBC)
1988	Wilfredo Vásquez (WBA), Jibaro Perez (WBC), Moon Sung-gil (WBA), Orlando Canizales (IBF)
1989	Jibaro Perez (WBC), Moon Sung-gil (WBA), Orlando Canizales (IBF), Kaokor Galaxy (WBA), Luis Espinosa (WBA)
1990	Orlando Canizales (IBF), Jibaro Perez (WBC), Luis Espinosa (WBA)
1991	Greg Richardson (WBC), Orlando Canizales (IBF), Luis Espinosa (WBA)
1992	Joichiro Tatsuyoshi (WBC), Victor Manuel Rabanales (WBC), Eddie Cook (WBA), Orlando Gonzales (IBF)
1993	Jorge Julio (WBA), Byun-Jong-il (WBC), Orlando Canizales (IBF)
1994	John Michael Johnson (WBA), Yasuei Yakushiji (WBC), Orlando Canizales (IBF)
1995	Daorun Chuwatang (WBA), Yasuei Yakushiji (WBC), Mbulelo Botile (IBF)
1996–97	Nana Konadu (WBA), Wayne McCullough (WBC), Mbulelo Botile (IBF)
1998	Nana Konadu (WBA), Joichiro Tatsuyoshi (WBC), Tim Austin (IBF)
1999– 2001	Paulie Ayala (WBA), Veeraphol Sahaprom (WBC), Tim Austin (IBF)
2002	Johnny Bredahl (WBA), Veeraphol Sahaprom (WBC), Tim Austin (IBF)
2003–04	Johnny Bredahl (WBA), Veerapol Sahaprom (WBC), Rafael Marquez (IBF)

1. Abandoned title. 2. Retired. 3. Deprived of title for failing to make weight. 4. Recognized in Europe.

Horse Racing

Ancient drawings on stone and bone prove that horse racing is at least 3,000 years old, but thoroughbred racing is a modern development. Practically every thoroughbred in training today traces its registered ancestry back to one or more of three sires that arrived in England about 1728 from the Near East and became known, from the names of their owners, as the Byerly Turk, the Darley Arabian, and the Godolphin Arabian. The Jockey Club (English) was founded at Newmarket in 1750 or 1751 and became the custodian of the Stud Book as well as the court of last resort in deciding turf affairs.

Horse racing took place in this country before the Revolution, but the great lift to the breeding industry came with the importation in 1798, by Col. John Hoomes of Virginia, of Diomed, winner of the Epsom Derby of 1780. Diomed's lineal descendants included such famous 19th-century stars of the American turf as American Eclipse, Sir Archy, and Lexington. From 1800 to the time of the Civil War there were race courses and breeding establishments plentifully scattered through Virginia, North Carolina, South Carolina, Tennessee, Kentucky, and Louisiana.

The oldest stake event in North America is the Queen's Plate, a Canadian fixture that was first run in the Province of Quebec in 1836. The oldest stake event in the United States is the Travers, which was first run at Saratoga in 1864. The gambling that goes with horse racing and trickery by jockeys, trainers, owners, and track officials caused attacks on the sport by reformers and a demand among horse racing enthusiasts for an honest and effective control of some kind, but nothing of lasting value to racing came of this until the formation in 1894 of the Jockey Club (American).

"TRIPLE CROWN" WINNERS IN THE UNITED STATES

(Kentucky Derby, Preakness, and Belmont Stakes)

Year	Horse	Owner	Year	Horse	Owner
1919	Sir Barton	J. K. L. Ross	1946	Assault	Robert J. Kleberg
1930	Gallant Fox	William Woodward	1948	Citation	Warren Wright
1935	Omaha	William Woodward	1973	Secretariat	Meadow Stable
1937	War Admiral	Samuel D. Riddle	1977	Seattle Slew	Karen Taylor
1941	Whirlaway	Warren Wright	1978	Affirmed	Louis Wolfson
1943	Count Fleet	Mrs. John Hertz			

KENTUCKY DERBY

Churchill Downs; 3-year-olds; 1¼ mi

Year	Winner	Jockey	Year	Winner	Jockey	Year	Winner	Jockey
1875	Aristides	O. Lewis	1907	Pink Star	A. Minder	1938	Lawrin	E. Arcaro
1876	Vagrant	R. Swim	1908	Stone Street	A. Pickens	1939	Johnstown	J. Stout
1877	Baden Baden	W. Walker	1909	Wintergreen	V. Powers	1940	Gallahadion	C. Bierman
1878	Day Star	J. Carter	1910	Donau	F. Herbert	1941	Whirlaway	E. Arcaro
1879	Lord Murphy	C. Shauer	1911	Meridian	G. Archibald	1942	Shut Out	W. D. Wright
1880	Fonso	G. Lewis	1912	Worth	C. H. Shilling	1943	Count Fleet	J. Longden
1881	Hindoo	J. McLaughlin	1913	Donerail	R. Goose	1944	Pensive	C. McCreary
1882	Apollo	B. Hurd	1914	Old Rosebud	J. McCabe	1945	Hoop Jr.	E. Arcaro
1883	Leonatus	W. Donohue	1915	Regret	J. Notter	1946	Assault	W. Mehrtens
1884	Buchanan	I. Murphy	1916	George Smith	J. Loftus	1947	Jet Pilot	E. Guerin
1885	Joe Cotton	B. Henderson	1917	Omar Khayyam	C. Borel	1948	Citation	E. Arcaro
1886	Ben Ali	P. Duffy	1918	Exterminator	W. Knapp	1949	Ponde	S. Brooks
1887	Montrose	I. Lewis	1919	Sir Barton	J. Loftus	1950	Middleground	W. Boland
1888	Macbeth II	G. Covington	1920	Paul Jones	T. Rice	1951	Count Turf	C. McCreary
1889	Spokane	T. Kiley	1921	Behave Yourself	C. Thompson	1952	Hill Gail	E. Arcaro
1890	Riley	I. Murphy	1922	Morvich	A. Johnson	1953	Dark Star	H. Moreno
1891	Kingman	I. Murphy	1923	Zev	E. Sande	1954	Determine	R. York
1892	Azra	L. Clayton	1924	Black Gold	J. D. Mooney	1955	Swaps	W. Shoemaker
1893	Lookout	E. Kunze	1925	Flying Ebony	E. Sande	1956	Needles	D. Erb
1894	Chant	F. Goodale	1926	Bubbling Over	A. Johnson	1957	Iron Liege	W. Hartack
1895	Halma	S. Perkins	1927	Whiskery	L. McAtee	1958	Tim Tam	I. Valenzuela
1896	Ben Brush	W. Simms	1928	Reigh Count	C. Lang	1959	Tomy Lee	W. Shoemaker
1897	Typhoon II	B. Garner	1929	Clyde Van Dusen	L. McAtee	1960	Venetian Way	W. Hartack
1898	Plaudit	W. Simms	1930	Gallant Fox	E. Sande	1961	Carry Back	J. Sellers
1899	Manuel	F. Taral	1931	Twenty Grand	C. Kurtsinger	1962	Decidedly	W. Hartack
1900	Lieut. Gibson	J. Boland	1932	Burgoo King	E. James	1963	Chateaugay	B. Baeza
1901	His Eminence	J. Winkfield	1933	Brokers Tip	D. Meade	1964	Northern Dancer	W. Hartack
1902	Alan-a-Dale	J. Winkfield	1934	Cavalcade	M. Garner	1965	Lucky Debonair	W. Shoemaker
1903	Judge Himes	H. Booker	1935	Omaha	W. Saunders	1966	Kauai King	D. Brumfield
1904	Elwood	F. Prior	1936	Bold Venture	I. Hanford	1967	Proud Clarion	R. Ussery
1905	Agile	J. Martin	1937	War Admiral	C. Kurtsinger	1968	Forward Pass[1]	I. Valenzuela
1906	Sir Huon	R. Troxler						

Year	Winner	Jockey	Year	Winner	Jockey	Year	Winner	Jockey
1969	Majestic Prince	W. Hartack	1981	Pleasant Colony	J. Velasquez	1995	Thunder Gulch	G. Stevens
1970	Dust Commander	M. Manganello	1982	Gato del Sol	E. Delahoussaye	1996	Grindstone	J. Bailey
1971	Canonero II	G. Avila	1983	Sunny's Halo	E. Delahoussaye	1997	Silver Charm	G. Stevens
1972	Riva Ridge	R. Turcotte	1984	Swale	L. Pincay, Jr.	1998	Real Quiet	K. Desormeaux
1973	Secretariat	R. Turcotte	1985	Spend a Buck	A. Cordero, Jr.	1999	Charismatic	C. Antley
1974	Cannonade	A. Cordero, Jr.	1986	Ferdinand	W. Shoemaker	2000	Fusaichi Pegasus	K. Desormeaux
1975	Foolish Pleasure	J. Vasquez	1987	Alysheba	C. McCarron	2001	Monarchos	J. Chavez
1976	Bold Forbes	A. Cordero, Jr.	1988	Winning Colors	G. Stevens	2002	War Emblem	V. Espinoza
1977	Seattle Slew	J. Cruguet	1989	Sunday Silence	P. Valenzuela	2003	Funny Cide	J. Santos
1978	Affirmed	S. Cauthen	1990	Unbridled	C. Perret	2004	Smarty Jones	S. Elliott
1979	Spectacular Bid	R. Franklin	1991	Strike the Gold	C. Antley			
1980	Genuine Risk	J. Vasquez	1992	Lil E. Tee	P. Day			
			1993	Sea Hero	J. Bailey			
			1994	Go For Gin	C. McCarron			

1. Dancer's Image finished first but was disqualified after traces of drugs were found in his system.

PREAKNESS STAKES
Pimlico; 3-year-olds; 1³⁄₁₆ mi

Year	Winner	Jockey	Year	Winner	Jockey	Year	Winner	Jockey
1873	Survivor	G. Barbee	1918	Jack Hare Jr.	C. Peak	1962	Greek Money	J. Rotz
1874	Culpepper	W. Donohue	1919	Sir Barton	J. Loftus	1963	Candy Spots	W. Shoemaker
1875	Tom Ochiltree	L. Hughes	1920	Man o' War	C. Kummer	1964	Northern Dancer	W. Hartack
1876	Shirley	G. Barbee	1921	Broomspun	F. Coltiletti	1965	Tom Rolfe	R. Turcotte
1877	Cloverbrook	C. Holloway	1922	Pillory	L. Morris	1966	Kauai King	D. Brumfield
1878	Duke of Magenta	C. Holloway	1923	Vigil	B. Marinelli	1967	Damascus	W. Shoemaker
1879	Harold	L. Hughes	1924	Nellie Morse	J. Merimee	1968	Forward Pass	I. Valenzuela
1880	Grenada	L. Hughes	1925	Coventry	C. Kummer	1969	Majestic Prince	W. Hartack
1881	Saunterer	T. Costello	1926	Display	J. Maiben	1970	Personality	E. Belmonte
1882	Vanguard	T. Costello	1927	Bostonian	W. Abel	1971	Canonero II	G. Avila
1883	Jacobus	G. Barbee	1928	Victorian	S. Workman	1972	Bee Bee Bee	E. Nelson
1884	Knight of Ellerslie	S. Fisher	1929	Dr. Freeland	L. Schaefer	1973	Secretariat	R. Turcotte
1885	Tecumseh	J. McLaughlin	1930	Gallant Fox	E. Sande	1974	Little Current	M. Rivera
1886	The Bard	S. Fisher	1931	Mate	G. Ellis	1975	Master Derby	D. McHargue
1887	Dunboyne	W. Donohue	1932	Burgoo King	E. James	1976	Elocutionist	J. Lively
1888	Refund	F. Littlefield	1933	Head Play	C. Kurtsinger	1977	Seattle Slew	J. Cruguet
1889	Buddhist	W. Anderson	1934	High Quest	R. Jones	1978	Affirmed	S. Cauthen
1890	Montague	W. Martin	1935	Omaha	W. Saunders	1979	Spectacular Bid	R. Franklin
1891-93	Not held		1936	Bold Venture	G. Woolf	1980	Codex	A. Cordero
1894	Assignee	F. Taral	1937	War Admiral	C. Kurtsinger	1981	Pleasant Colony	J. Velasquez
1895	Belmar	F. Taral	1938	Dauber	M. Peters	1982	Aloma's Ruler	J. Kaenel
1896	Margrave	H. Griffin	1939	Challedon	G. Seabo	1983	Deputed Testamony	D. Miller
1897	Paul Kauvar	T. Thorpe	1940	Bimelech	F.A. Smith	1984	Gate Dancer	A. Cordero
1898	Sly Fox	W. Simms	1941	Whirlaway	E. Arcaro	1985	Tank's Prospect	P. Day
1899	Half Time	R. Clawson	1942	Alsab	B. James	1986	Snow Chief	A. Solis
1900	Hindus	H. Spencer	1943	Count Fleet	J. Longden	1987	Alysheba	C. McCarron
1901	The Parader	F. Landry	1944	Pensive	C. McCreary	1988	Risen Star	E. Delahoussaye
1902	Old England	L. Jackson	1945	Polynesian	W.D. Wright	1989	Sunday Silence	P. Valenzuela
1903	Flocarline	W. Gannon	1946	Assault	W. Mehrtens	1990	Summer Squall	P. Day
1904	Bryn Mawr	E. Hildebrand	1947	Faultless	D. Dodson	1991	Hansel	J. Bailey
1905	Cairngorm	W. Davis	1948	Citation	E. Arcaro	1992	Pine Bluff	C. McCarron
1906	Whimsical	W. Miller	1949	Capot	T. Atkinson	1993	Prairie Bayou	M. Smith
1907	Don Enrique	G. Mountain	1950	Hill Prince	E. Arcaro	1994	Tabasco Cat	P. Day
1908	Royal Tourist	E. Dugan	1951	Bold	E. Arcaro	1995	Timber Country	P. Day
1909	Effendi	W. Doyle	1952	Blue Man	C. McCreary	1996	Louis Quatorze	P. Day
1910	Layminster	R. Estep	1953	Native Dancer	E. Guerin	1997	Silver Charm	G. Stevens
1911	Watervale	E. Dugan	1954	Hasty Road	J. Adams	1998	Real Quiet	K. Desormeaux
1912	Colonel Holloway	C. Turner	1955	Nashua	E. Arcaro	1999	Charismatic	C. Antley
1913	Buskin	J. Butwell	1956	Fabius	W. Hartack	2000	Red Bullet	J. Bailey
1914	Holiday	A. Schuttinger	1957	Bold Ruler	E. Arcaro	2001	Point Given	G. Stevens
1915	Rhine Maiden	D. Hoffman	1958	Tim Tam	I. Valenzuela	2002	War Emblem	V. Espinoza
1916	Damrosch	L. McAtee	1959	Royal Orbit	W. Harmatz	2003	Funny Cide	J. Santos
1917	Kalitan	E. Haynes	1960	Bally Ache	R. Ussery	2004	Smarty Jones	S. Elliott
1918	War Cloud	J. Loftus	1961	Carry Back	J. Sellers			

BELMONT STAKES

Belmont Park; 3-year-olds; 1½ mi

Run at Jerome Park 1867 to 1890; at Morris Park 1890–94; at Belmont Park 1905–62; at Aqueduct 1963–67. Distance 1⅝ mi prior to 1874; reduced to 1½ mi, 1874; reduced to 1¼ mi, 1890; reduced to 1⅛ mi, 1893; increased to 1¼ mi, 1895; increased to 1⅜ mi, 1896; reduced to 1¼ mi in 1904; increased to 1½ mi, 1926.

Year	Winner	Jockey
1867	Ruthless	J. Gilpatrick
1868	General Duke	B. Swim
1869	Fenian	C. Miller
1870	Kingfisher	W. Dick
1871	Harry Bassett	W. Miller
1872	Joe Daniels	J. Roe
1873	Springbok	J. Roe
1874	Saxon	G. Barbee
1875	Calvin	B. Swim
1876	Algerine	B. Donohue
1877	Cloverbrook	C. Holloway
1878	Duke of Magenta	L. Hughes
1879	Spendthrift	G. Evans
1880	Grenada	L. Hughes
1881	Saunterer	T. Costello
1882	Forester	J. McLaughlin
1883	George Kinney	J. McLaughlin
1884	Panique	J. McLaughlin
1885	Tyrant	P. Duffy
1886	Inspector B	J. McLaughlin
1887	Hanover	J. McLaughlin
1888	Sir Dixon	J. McLaughlin
1889	Eric	W. Hayward
1890	Burlington	P. Barnes
1891	Foxford	E. Garrison
1892	Patron	W. Hayward
1893	Commanche	W. Simms
1894	Henry of Navarre (11/2)	W. Simms
1895	Belmar	F. Taral
1896	Hastings	H. Griffin
1897	Scottish Chieftain	J. Scherrer
1898	Bowling Brook	F. Littlefield
1899	Jean Beraud	R. Clawson
1900	Ildrim	N. Turner
1901	Commando	H. Spencer
1902	Masterman	J. Bullman
1903	Africander	J. Bullman
1904	Delhi	G. Odom
1905	Tanya	E. Hildebrand
1906	Burgomaster	L. Lyne
1907	Peter Pan	G. Mountain
1908	Colin	J. Notter
1909	Joe Madden	E. Dugan
1910	Sweep	J. Butwell
1911-12	Not held	
1913	Prince Eugene	R. Troxler
1914	Luke McLuke	M. Buxton
1915	The Finn	G. Byrne
1916	Friar Rock	E. Haynes
1917	Hourless	J. Butwell
1918	Johren	F. Robinson
1919	Sir Barton	J. Loftus
1920	Man o' War	C. Kummer
1921	Grey Lag	E. Sande
1922	Pillory	C.H. Miller
1923	Zev	E. Sande
1924	Mad Play	E. Sande
1925	American Flag	A. Johnson
1926	Crusader	A. Johnson
1927	Chance Shot	E. Sande
1928	Vito	C. Kummer
1929	Blue Larkspur	M. Garner
1930	Gallant Fox	E. Sande
1931	Twenty Grand	C. Kurtsinger
1932	Faireno	T. Malley
1933	Hurryoff	M. Garner
1934	Peace Chance	W. D. Wright
1935	Omaha	W. Saunders
1936	Granville	J. Stout
1937	War Admiral	C. Kurtsinger
1938	Pasteurized	J. Stout
1939	Johnstown	J. Stout
1940	Bimelech	F.A. Smith
1941	Whirlaway	E. Arcaro
1942	Shut Out	E. Arcaro
1943	Count Fleet	J. Longden
1944	Bounding Home	G.L. Smith
1945	Pavot	E. Arcaro
1946	Assault	W. Mehrtens
1947	Phalanx	R. Donoso
1948	Citation	E. Arcaro
1949	Capot	T. Atkinson
1950	Middleground	W. Boland
1951	Counterpoint	D. Gorman
1952	One Count	E. Arcaro
1953	Native Dancer	E. Guerin
1954	High Gun	E. Guerin
1955	Nashua	E. Arcaro
1956	Needles	D. Erb
1957	Gallant Man	W. Shoemaker
1958	Cavan	P. Anderson
1959	Sword Dancer	W. Shoemaker
1960	Celtic Ash	W. Hartack
1961	Sherluck	B. Baeza
1962	Jaipur	W. Shoemaker
1963	Chateaugay	B. Baeza
1964	Quadrangle	M. Ycaza
1965	Hail to All	J. Sellers
1966	Amberoid	W. Boland
1967	Damascus	W. Shoemaker
1968	Stage Door Johnny	H. Gustines
1969	Arts and Letters	B. Baeza
1970	High Echelon	J. Rotz
1971	Pass Catcher	R. Blum
1972	Riva Ridge	R. Turcotte
1973	Secretariat	R. Turcotte
1974	Little Current	M. Rivera
1975	Avatar	W. Shoemaker
1976	Bold Forbes	A. Cordero, Jr.
1977	Seattle Slew	J. Cruguet
1978	Affirmed	S. Cauthen
1979	Coastal	R. Hernandez
1980	Temperence Hill	E. Maple
1981	Summing	G. Martens
1982	Conquistador Cielo	L. Pincay, Jr.
1983	Caveat	L. Pincay, Jr.
1984	Swale	L. Pincay, Jr.
1985	Creme Fraiche	E. Maple
1986	Danzig Connection	C. McCarron
1987	Bet Twice	C. Perret
1988	Risen Star	E. Delahoussaye
1989	Easy Goer	P. Day
1990	Go And Go	M. Kinane
1991	Hansel	J. Bailey
1992	A.P. Indy	E. Delahoussaye
1993	Colonial Affair	J. Krone
1994	Tabasco Cat	P. Day
1995	Thunder Gulch	G.Stevens
1996	Editor's Note	R. Douglas
1997	Touch Gold	C. McCarron
1998	Victory Gallop	G. Stevens
1999	Lemon Drop Kid	J. Santos
2000	Commendable	P. Day
2001	Point Given	G. Stevens
2002	Sarava	E. Prado
2003	Empire Maker	J. Bailey
2004	Birdstone	E. Prado

TRIPLE CROWN RACES—2004

Kentucky Derby (Churchill Downs, Louisville, Ky., May 1, 2004.) Purse: $1,000,000. Distance: 1¼ mi. Order of finish: 1. Smarty Jones (Elliott), mutuel returns: $10.20, $6.20, $4.80. 2. Lion Heart (Smith), $8.20, $5.80. 3. Imperialism (Desormeaux), $6.20. 4. Limehouse (Santos). 5. The Cliff's Edge (Sellers). 6. Action This Day (Flores). 7. Read the Footnotes (Albarado). 8. Birdstone (Prado). 9. Tapit (Dominguez). 10. Borrego (Espinoza). 11. Song of the Sword (Arroyo, Jr.). 12. Master David (Solis). 13. Pro Prado (McKee). 14. Castledale (IRE) (Valdivia, Jr.). 15. Friends Lake (Migliore). 16. Minister Eric (Day). 17. Pollard's Vision (Velazquez). 16. Quintons Gold Rush (Nakatani). Winner's purse: $5,854,800. Margin of victory: 2¾ lengths. Time of race: 2:04.06.

Preakness Stakes (Pimlico, Baltimore, Md., May 15, 2004.) Purse: $1,000,000. Distance: 1³⁄₁₆ mi. Order of finish: 1. Smarty Jones (Elliott), mutuel returns: $3.40, $3.00, $2.60. 2. Rock Hard Ten (Stevens), $5.00, $4.00. 3. Eddington (Bailey), $5.20. 4. Lion Heart (Smith). 5. Imperialism (Desormeaux). 6. Sir Shackleton (Bejarano). 7. Borrego (Espinoza). 8. Little Matth Man (Migliore). 9. Song of the Sword (Chavez). 10. Water Cannon (Fogelsonger). Winner's purse: $650,000. Margin of victory: 11½ lengths. Time of race: 1:55.59.

Belmont Stakes (Belmont Park, Elmont, N.Y., June 5, 2004.) Gross purse: $1,000,000. Distance: 1½ mi. Order of finish: 1. Birdstone (Prado), mutuel returns: $74.00, $14.00, $8.60. 2. Smarty Jones (Elliott), $3.30, $2.60.

3. Royal Assault (Day), $6.10. 4. Eddington (Bailey). 5. Rock Hard Ten (Solis). 6. Tap Dancer (Castellano). 7. Master David (Santos). 8. Caiman (Dominguez). 9. Purge (Velazquez). Winner's purse: $600,000. Margin of victory: 1 length. Time of race: 2:27.50.

ECLIPSE AWARDS—2003

(Presented on Jan. 26, 2004)

Horse of the Year	Mineshaft
2-year-old colt	Action This Day
2-year-old filly	Halfbridled
3-year-old colt	Funny Cide
3-year-old filly	Bird Town
Older male	Mineshaft
Older female	Azeri
Sprinter	Aldebaran
Male turf	High Chaparral
Female turf	Islington
Steeplechase	McDynamo
Owner	Juddmonte Farms
Breeder	Juddmonte Farms
Jockey	Jerry Bailey
Apprentice jockey	Eddie Castro
Trainer	Robert Frankel

(Based on vote by the Thoroughbred Racing Associations, the *Daily Racing Form,* and the National Turf Writers Association.)

Track and Field

WORLD OUTDOOR RECORDS—MEN

(Through Sept. 27, 2004)

Recognized by the International Athletic Federation. The IAAF decided late in 1976 not to recognize records in yards except for the one-mile run.

The IAAF also requires automatic timing for all records for races of 400 meters or less.

Event	Record	Holder	Home country	Where made	Date
Running					
100 m	0:09.78	Tim Montgomery	United States	Paris, France	Sept. 14, 2002
200 m	0:19.32	Michael Johnson	United States	Atlanta, Ga.	Aug. 1, 1996
400 m	0:43.18	Michael Johnson	United States	Seville, Spain	Aug. 26, 1999
800 m	1:41.11	Wilson Kipketer	Denmark	Köln, Germany	Aug. 24, 1997
1,000 m	2:11.96	Noah Ngeny	Kenya	Rieti, Italy	Sept. 5, 1999
1,500 m	3:26.00	Hicham El Guerrouj	Morocco	Rome, Italy	July 14, 1998
1 mile	3:43.13	Hicham El Guerrouj	Morocco	Rome, Italy	July 7, 1999
2,000 m	4:44.79	Hicham El Guerrouj	Morocco	Berlin, Germany	Sept. 7, 1999
3,000 m	7:20.67	Daniel Komen	Kenya	Rieti, Italy	Sept. 1, 1996
3,000 m steeplechase	7:53.63[1]	Saif Saaeed Shaheen	Qatar	Brussels, Belgium	Sept. 3, 2004
5,000 m	12:37.35	Kenenisa Bekele	Ethiopia	Hengelo, Netherlands	May 31, 2004
10,000 m	26:20.31	Kenenisa Bekele	Ethiopia	Ostrava, Czech Republic	June 8, 2004
20,000 m	56:55.60	Arturo Barrios	Mexico	La Fléche, France	March 30, 1991
25,000 m	1:13:55.80	Toshihiko Seko	Japan	Christchurch, N.Z.	March 22, 1981
30,000 m	1:29:18.80	Toshihiko Seko	Japan	Christchurch, N.Z.	March 22, 1981
1 hour	21,101 m	Arturo Barrios	Mexico	La Fleche, France	March 30, 1991
Marathon[2]	2:04.55	Paul Tergat	Kenya	Berlin, Germany	Sept. 28, 2003
Walking					
20,000 m	1:17:21.00	Jefferson Pérez	Ecuador	Paris, France	Aug. 23, 2003
30,000 m	2:01:44.10	Maurizio Damilano	Italy	Cuneo, Italy	Oct. 3, 1992
50,000 m	3:35:29.00	Denis Nizhegorodov	Russia	Cheboksary, Russia	June 13, 2004
2 hours	29,572 m	Maurizio Damilano	Italy	Cuneo, Italy	Oct. 3, 1992
Hurdles					
110 m	0:12.91	Colin Jackson	Great Britain	Stuttgart, Germany	Aug. 20, 1993
	0:12.91[1]	Xiang Liu	China	Athens, Greece	Aug. 27, 2004
400 m	0:46.78	Kevin Young	United States	Barcelona, Spain	Aug. 6, 1992

Event	Record	Holder	Home country	Where made	Date
Relay races					
400 m (4 × 100)	0:37.40	National Team	United States	Barcelona, Spain	Aug. 8, 1992
	0:37.40	National Team	United States	Stuttgart, Germany	Aug. 21, 1993
800 m (4 × 200)	1:18.68	Santa Monica T.C.	United States	Walnut, Calif.	April 17, 1994
1,600 m					
(4 × 400)	2:54.20	National Team	United States	New York, N.Y.	July 22, 1998
3,200 m					
(4 × 800)	7:03.89	National Team	Britain	London, England	Aug. 30, 1982
6,000 m	14:38.80	National Team	West Germany	Köln, Germany	Aug. 17, 1977
Field events					
High jump	2.45 m	Javier Sotomayor	Cuba	Salamanca, Spain	July 27, 1993
Long jump	8.95 m	Mike Powell	United States	Tokyo, Japan	Aug. 30, 1991
Triple jump	18.29 m	Jonathan Edwards	Great Britain	Goteborg, Sweden	Aug. 7, 1995
Pole vault	6.14 m	Sergey Bubka	Ukraine	Sestriere, Italy	July 31, 1994
Shot-put	23.12 m	Randy Barnes	United States	Los Angeles, Calif.	May 20, 1990
Discus throw	74.08 m	Jürgen Schult	East Germany	Neubrandenburg, E. Germany	June 6, 1986
Hammer throw	86.74 m	Yuriy Sedykh	USSR	Stuttgart, Germany	Aug. 30, 1986
Javelin throw	98.48 m	Jan Zelezny	Czech Republic	Jena, Germany	May 25, 1996
Decathlon	9,026 pts.	Roman Sebrle	Czech Republic	Götzis, Austria	May 27, 2001

1. Awaiting IAAF ratification. 2. Not recognized by IAAF as world record, but considered to be "world-best performance."
Source: IAAF.

WORLD OUTDOOR RECORDS—WOMEN

(Through Sept. 27, 2004)

Event	Record	Holder	Home country	Where made	Date
Running					
100 m	0:10.49	Florence Griffith-Joyner	United States	Indianapolis, Ind.	July 16, 1988
200 m	0:21.34	Florence Griffith-Joyner	United States	Seoul, South Korea	Sept. 29, 1988
400 m	0:47.60	Martina Koch	East Germany	Canberra, Australia	Oct. 6, 1985
800 m	1:53.28	Jarmila Kratochvilova	Czechoslovakia	Munich, W. Germany	July 26, 1983
1000 m	2:28.98	Svetlana Masterkova	Russia	Brussels, Belgium	Aug. 23, 1996
1,500 m	3:50.46	Qu Yunxia	China	Beijing, China	Sept. 11, 1993
1 mile	4:12.56	Svetlana Masterkova	Russia	Zurich, Switzerland	Aug. 14, 1996
2,000 m	5:25.36	Sonia O'Sullivan	Ireland	Edinburgh, Scotland	July 8, 1994
3,000 m	8:06.11	Wang Junxia	China	Beijing, China	Sept. 13, 1993
5,000 m	14:24.68	Elvan Abeylegesse	Turkey	Bergen, Norway	June 11, 2004
10,000 m	29:31.78	Wang Junxia	China	Beijing, China	Sept. 8, 1993
20,000 m	1:05:26.60	Tegla Loroupe	Kenya	Borgholzhausen, Germany	Sept. 3, 2000
25,000 m	1:27:05.90	Tegla Loroupe	Kenya	Mengerskirchen, Germany	Sept. 21, 2002
30,000 m	1:45:50.00	Tegla Loroupe	Kenya	Warstein, Germany	June 6, 2003
1 hour	18.340	Tegla Loroupe	Kenya	Borgholzhausen, Germany	July 8, 1998
3,000 m steeplechase	9:01.59	Gulnara Samitova	Russia	Iráklio, Greece	July 4, 2004
Marathon[1]	2:15:25	Paula Radcliffe	Great Britain	London, England	April 13, 2003
Walking					
5,000 m	20:02.60	Gillian O'Sullivan	Ireland	Dublin, Ireland	July 13, 2002
10,000 m	41:56.23	Nadezhda Ryashkina	Russia	Seattle, Wash.	July 24, 1990
20,000 m	1:26:22.00	Yan Wang	China	Guangzhou, China	Nov. 19, 2001
	1:26:22.00	Yelena Nikolayeva	Russia	Cheboksary, Russia	May 18, 2003
Hurdles					
100 m	0:12.21	Yordanka Donkova	Bulgaria	Stara Zagora, Bulgaria	Aug. 20, 1988
400 m	0:52.34	Yuliya Pechonkina	Russia	Tula, Russia	Aug. 8, 2003
Relay races					
400 m (4 × 100)	0:41.37	East Germany	E. Germany	Canberra, Australia	Oct. 6, 1985
800 m (4 × 200)	1:27.46	United States "Blue"	United States	Philadelphia, Pa.	April 29, 2000
1,600 m (4 × 400)	3:15.17	USSR	USSR	Seoul, South Korea	Oct. 1, 1988
3,200 m (4 × 800)	7:50.17	USSR	USSR	Moscow, USSR	Aug. 5, 1984
Field events					
High jump	2.09 m	Stefka Kostadinova	Bulgaria	Rome, Italy	Aug. 30, 1987
Pole vault	4.92 m[2]	Yelena Isinbayeva	Russia	Brussels, Belgium	Sept. 3, 2004
Long jump	7.52 m	Galina Chistyakova	USSR	Leningrad, Russia	June 11, 1988
Triple jump	15.50 m	Inessa Kravets	Ukraine	Goteborg, Sweden	Aug. 10, 1995
Shot-put	22.63 m	Natalya Lisovskaya	USSR	Moscow, Russia	June 7, 1987
Discus throw	76.80 m	Gabriele Reinsch	East Germany	Neubrandenburg, E. Ger.	July 9, 1988
Hammer throw	76.07 m	Mihaela Melinte	Romania	Rüdlingen, Switzerland	Aug. 29, 1999

Event	Record	Holder	Home country	Where made	Date
Javelin throw	71.54 m	Osleidys Menéndez	Cuba	Réthymno, Greece	July 1, 2001
Heptathlon	7,291 pts	Jackie Joyner-Kersee	United States	Seoul, South Korea	Sept. 24, 1988
Decathlon	8,150[2]	Marie Collonvillé	France	Talence, France	Sept. 26, 2004

1. Not recognized by IAAF as world record, but considered to be "world-best performance." 2. Awaiting IAAF ratification.
Source: IAAF.

AMERICAN OUTDOOR RECORDS—MEN
(Through Sept. 27, 2004)

Event	Record	Holder	Where made	Date
Running				
100 m	0:09.78	Tim Montgomery	Paris, France	Sept. 14, 2002
200 m	0:19.32	Michael Johnson	Atlanta, Ga.	Aug. 1, 1996
400 m	0:43.18	Michael Johnson	Seville, Spain	Aug. 26, 1999
800 m	1:42.60	Johnny Gray	Koblenz, W. Germany	Aug. 29, 1985
1,000 m	2:13.90	Richard Wohlhuter	Oslo, Norway	July 30, 1974
1,500 m	3:29.77	Sydney Maree	Cologne, W. Germany	Aug. 25, 1985
1 mile	3:47.69	Steve Scott	Oslo, Norway	July 7, 1982
2,000 m	4:52.44	Jim Spivey	Lausanne, Switzerland	Sept. 15, 1987
3,000 m	7:30.84	Bob Kennedy	Monaco	Aug. 8, 1998
5,000 m	12:58.21	Bob Kennedy	Zurich, Switzerland	Aug. 14, 1996
10,000 m	27:13.98	Meb Keflezighi	Stanford, Calif.	May 4, 2001
3,000-m steeplechase	8:09.17	Henry Marsh	Koblenz, W. Ger.	Aug. 29, 1985
Marathon	2:05:38	Khalid Khannouchi	London, England	April 14, 2002
Hurdles				
110 m	0:12.92	Roger Kingdom	Berlin, Germany	Aug. 16, 1989
		Allen Johnson	Atlanta, Ga.	June 23, 1996
400 m	0:46.78	Kevin Young	Barcelona	Aug. 6, 1992
Relay races				
400 m (4 × 100)	0:37.40	Olympic Team	Barcelona, Spain	Aug. 8, 1992
		USA National Team	Stuttgart, Germany	Aug. 21, 1993
800 m (4 × 200)	1:18.68	Santa Monica T.C.	Walnut, Calif.	April 17, 1994
1,600 m (4 × 400)	2:54.20	USA National Team	New York, N.Y.	July 22, 1998
3,200 m (4 × 800)	7:06.50	Santa Monica T.C.	Walnut, Calif.	Apr. 26, 1986
6,000 m (4 × 1,500)	14:46.30	National Team	Bourges, France	June 24, 1979
Field events				
High jump	2.45 m	Charles Austin	Zurich, Switzerland	Aug. 7, 1991
Long jump	8.95 m	Mike Powell	Tokyo, Japan	Aug. 30, 1991
Triple jump	18.09 m	Kenny Harrison	Atlanta, Ga.	July 27, 1996
Pole vault	6.03 m	Jeff Hartwig	Jonesboro, Ark.	June 14, 2000
Shot-put	23.12 m	Randy Barnes	Los Angeles	May 20, 1990
Discus throw	71.32 m	Ben Plucknett	Stockholm, Swe.	July 7, 1981
Javelin throw	87.68 m	Breaux Greer	Monaco	Sept. 19, 2004
Hammer throw	82.52 m	Lance Deal	Milan, Italy	July 9, 1996
Decathlon	8,891 pts	Dan O'Brien	Talence, France	Sept. 4–5, 1992

AMERICAN OUTDOOR RECORDS—WOMEN
(Through Sept. 27, 2004)

Event	Record	Holder	Where made	Date
Running				
100 m	0:10.49	Florence Griffith Joyner	Indianapolis, Ind.	July 16, 1988
200 m	21.34	Florence Griffith Joyner	Seoul, South Korea	Sept. 29, 1988
400 m	0:48.83	Valerie Brisco	Los Angeles, Calif.	Aug. 6, 1984
800 m	1:56.40	Jearl Miles-Clark	Zurich, Switzerland	Aug. 11, 1999
1,000 m	2:31.80	Regina Jacobs	Brunswick, Maine	July 3, 1999
1,500 m	3:57.12	Mary Slaney	Stockholm, Sweden.	July 26, 1983
2,000 m	5:32.70	Mary Slaney	Eugene, Ore.	Aug. 3, 1984
1 mile	4:16.71	Mary Decker Slaney	Zurich, Switzerland	Aug. 21, 1985
3,000 m	8:29.69	Mary Decker Slaney	Cologne, Germany	Aug. 25, 1985
5,000 m	14:45.35	Regina Jacobs	Sacramento, Calif.	July 21, 2000
10,000 m	30:50.32	Deena Drossin Kastor	Palo Alto, Calif.	May 3, 2002
3,000 m steeplechase	9:29.32	Briana Shook	Heusden-Zolder, Belgium	July 31, 2004
Marathon	2:21:16	Deena Drossin Kastor	London, England	April 13, 2003
Hurdles				
100 m	0:12.33	Gail Devers	Sacramento, Calif.	July 23, 2000
400 m	0:52.61	Kim Batten	Gotebörg, Sweden	Aug. 11, 1995
Relay races				
400 m (4 × 100)	41.47	U.S.A. National Team	Athens, Greece	Aug. 9, 1997
800 m (4 × 200)	1:27.46	United States Blue Team	Philadelphia, Pa.	April 29, 2000
1,600 m (4 × 400)	3:15.51	U.S. Olympic Team	Seoul, South Korea	Oct. 1, 1988
3,200 m (4 × 800)	8:33.49	University of Texas	Austin, Tex.	Jan. 4, 2004

Event	Record	Holder	Where made	Date
Field events				
Pole vault	4.83 m	Stacy Dragila	Ostrava, Czech Republic	June 8, 2004
High jump	2.03 m	Louise Ritter	Austin, Tex.	July 9, 1988
Long jump	7.49 m	Jackie Joyner-Kersee	New York, N.Y.	May 22, 1994
Triple jump	14.42 m	Sheila Hudson	Stockholm, Sweden	July 8, 1996
Shot-put	21.18 m	Ramona Pagel	San Diego, Calif.	June 25, 1988
Discus throw	69.44 m	Suzy Powell	La Jolla, Calif.	April 27, 2002
Hammer throw	72.01 m	Anna Norgren-Mahon	Walnut, Calif.	July 27, 2002
Javelin throw (old)	69.32 m	Kate Schmidt	Fürth, W. Ger.	Sept. 10, 1977
Javelin throw (new)	60.86 m	Kim Kreiner	Santo Domingo, Dom. Rep.	Aug. 7, 2003
Heptathlon	7,291 pts	Jackie Joyner-Kersee	Seoul, South Korea	Sept. 23–24, 1988

HISTORY OF THE RECORD FOR THE MILE RUN
(Under 4 minutes)

Time	Athlete	Country	Year	Location
3:59.4	Roger Bannister	England	1954	Oxford, England
3:58.0	John Landy	Australia	1954	Turku, Finland
3:57.2	Derek Ibbotson	England	1957	London
3:54.5	Herb Elliott	Australia	1958	Dublin
3:54.4	Peter Snell	New Zealand	1962	Wanganui, N.Z.
3:54.1	Peter Snell	New Zealand	1964	Auckland, N.Z.
3:53.6	Michel Jazy	France	1965	Rennes, France
3:51.3	Jim Ryun	United States	1966	Berkeley, Calif.
3:51.1	Jim Ryun	United States	1967	Bakersfield, Calif.
3:51.0	Filbert Bayi	Tanzania	1975	Kingston, Jamaica
3:49.4	John Walker	New Zealand	1975	Goteborg, Sweden
3:49.0	Sebastian Coe	England	1979	Oslo
3:48.8	Steve Ovett	England	1980	Oslo
3:48.53	Sebastian Coe	England	1981	Zurich, Switzerland
3:48.40	Steve Ovett	England	1981	Koblenz, W. Ger.
3:47.33	Sebastian Coe	England	1981	Brussels
3:46.31	Steve Cram	England	1985	Oslo
3:44.39	Noureddine Morceli	Algeria	1993	Rieti, Italy
3:43.13	Hicham El Guerrouj	Morocco	1999	Rome, Italy

Source: USA Track & Field.

WORLD INDOOR RECORDS—MEN
(Through Sept. 27, 2004)

Event	Record	Holder	Home country	Where made	Date
Running					
50 m	0:05.56	Donovan Bailey	Canada	Reno, Nev.	Feb. 9, 1996
60 m	0:06.39	Maurice Greene	United States	Madrid, Spain	Feb. 3, 1998
	0:06.39	Maurice Greene	United States	Atlanta, Ga.	March 3, 2001
200 m	0:19.92	Frank Fredericks	Namibia	Liévin, France	Feb. 18, 1996
400 m	0:44.63	Michael Johnson	United States	Atlanta, Ga.	March 4, 1995
800 m	1:42.67	Wilson Kipketer	Denmark	Paris, France	March 9, 1997
1,000 m	2:14.96	Wilson Kipketer	Denmark	Birmingham, England	Feb. 20, 2000
1,500 m	3:31.18	Hicham El Guerrouj	Morocco	Stuttgart, Germany	Feb. 2, 1997
1 mile	3:48.45	Hicham El Guerrouj	Morocco	Ghent, Belgium	Feb. 12, 1997
3,000 m	7:24.90	Daniel Komen	Kenya	Budapest, Hungary	Feb. 6, 1998
5,000 m	12:49.60	Kenenisa Bekele	Ethiopia	Birmingham, England	Feb. 20, 2004
5,000 m race walking	18:07.08	Mikhail Shchennikov	Russia	Moscow, Russia	Feb. 14, 1995
Hurdles					
50 m	0:06.25	Mark McKoy	Canada	Kobe, Japan	March 5, 1986
60 m	0:07.30	Colin Jackson	Great Britain	Sindelfingen, Germany	March 6, 1994
Relay races					
800 m (4 × 200)	1:22.11	Great Britain & Northern Ireland	Great Britain	Glasgow, Scotland	March 3, 1991
1,600 m (4 × 400)	3:02.83	National Team	United States	Maebashi, Japan	March 7, 1999
3,200 m (4 × 800)	7:13.94	Global Athletics & Marketing	United States	Boston, Mass.	Feb. 6, 2000
Field events					
High jump	2.43 m	Javier Sotomayor	Cuba	Budapest, Hungary	March 4, 1989
Pole vault	6.15 m	Sergey Bubka	Ukraine	Donetsk, Ukraine	Feb. 21, 1993
Long jump	8.79 m	Carl Lewis	United States	New York, N.Y.	Jan. 27, 1984
Triple jump	17.83 m	Aliecer Urrutia	Cuba	Sindelfingen, Germany	March 1, 1997
	17.83 m	Christian Olsson	Sweden	Budapest, Hungary	March 7, 2004
Shot-put	22.66 m	Randy Barnes	United States	Los Angeles, Calif.	Jan. 20, 1989
Heptathlon	6,476 pts.	Dan O'Brien	United States	Toronto, Canada	March 14, 1993

Source: IAAF.

WORLD INDOOR RECORDS—WOMEN

(Through Sept. 27, 2004)

Event	Record	Holder	Home country	Where made	Date
Running					
50 m	0:05.96	Irina Privalova	Russia	Madrid, Spain	Feb. 9, 1995
60 m	0:06.92	Irina Privalova	Russia	Madrid, Spain	Feb. 11, 1993
	0:06.92	Irina Privalova	Russia	Madrid, Spain	Feb. 9, 1995
200 m	0:21.87	Merlene Ottey	Jamaica	Liévin, France	Feb. 13, 1993
400 m	0:49.59	Jarmila Kratochvílová	Czechoslovakia	Milan, Italy	March 7, 1982
800 m	1:55.82	Jolanda Ceplak	Slovak Republic	Vienna, Austria	March 3, 2002
1,000 m	2:30.94	Maria de Lurdes Mutola	Mozambique	Stockholm, Sweden	Feb. 25, 1999
1,500 m	3:59.98	Regina Jacobs	United States	Boston, Mass.	Feb. 1, 2003
1 mile	4:17.14	Doina Melinte	Romania	East Rutherford, N.J.	Feb. 9, 1990
3,000 m	8:29.15	Berhane Adere	Ethiopia	Stuttgart, Germany	Feb. 3, 2002
5,000 m	14:39.29	Berhane Adere	Ethiopia	Stuttgart, Germany	Jan. 31, 2004
3,000 m race walking	11:40.33	Claudia Stef	Romania	Bucharest, Romania	Jan. 30, 1999
Hurdles					
50 m	0:06.58	Cornelia Oschkenat	East Germany	Berlin, Germany	Feb. 20, 1988
60 m	0:07.69	Ludmila Engquist	Soviet Union	Chelyabinsk, Russia	Feb. 4, 1990
Relay races					
800 m (4 × 200)	1:32.55	Sc Eintracht Hamm	West Germany	Dortmund, Germany	Feb. 20, 1988
	1:32.55	LG Olympia Dortmund	Germany	Karlsruhe, Germany	Feb. 21, 1999
1,600 m (4 × 400)	3:23.88	National Team	Russia	Budapest, Hungary	March 7, 2004
3,200 m (4 × 800)	8:18.71	National Team	Russia	Moscow, Russia	Feb. 4, 1994
Field events					
High jump	2.07 m	Heike Henkel	Germany	Karlsruhe, Germany	Feb. 8, 1992
Pole vault	4.86 m	Yelena Isinbayeva	Russia	Budapest, Hungary	March 6, 2004
Long jump	7.37 m	Heike Dreschler	East Germany	Vienna, Austria	Feb. 13, 1988
Triple jump	15.36 m	Tatyana Lebedeva	Russia	Budapest, Hungary	March 6, 2004
Shot-put	22.50 m	Helena Fibingerová	Czechoslovakia	Jablonec, Czechoslovakia	Feb. 19, 1977
Pentathlon	4,991 pts.	Irina Belova	Unified Team	Berlin, Germany	Feb. 15, 1992

Source: IAAF.

Tennis

Lawn tennis is a comparatively modern modification of the ancient game of court tennis. Maj. Walter Clopton Wingfield thought that something like court tennis might be played outdoors on lawns, and in Dec. 1873, at Nantclwyd, Wales, he introduced his new game under the name of *Sphairistike* at a lawn party. The game was a success and spread rapidly, but the name was a total failure and almost immediately disappeared when all the players and spectators began to refer to the new game as *lawn tennis.* In the early part of 1874, a young lady named Mary Ewing Outerbridge returned from Bermuda to New York, bringing with her the implements and necessary equipment of the new game, which she had obtained from a British Army supply store in Bermuda. Miss Outerbridge and friends played the first game of lawn tennis in the United States on the grounds of the Staten Island Cricket and Baseball Club in the spring of 1874.

For a few years, the new game went along in haphazard fashion until about 1880, when standard measurements for the court and standard equipment within definite limits became the rule. In 1881, the U.S. Lawn Tennis Association (whose name was changed in 1975 to the U.S. Tennis Association) was formed and conducted the first national championship at Newport, R.I. The international matches for the Davis Cup began with a series between the British and U.S. players on the courts of the Longwood Cricket Club, Chestnut Hill, Mass., in 1900, with the home players winning.

Professional tennis, which got its start in 1926 when the French star Suzanne Lenglen was paid $50,000 for a tour, received full recognition in 1968. Staid old Wimbledon, the London home of what are considered the world championships, let the pros compete. This decision ended a long controversy over open tennis and changed the format of the competition. The U.S. championships were also opened to the pros and the site of the event, long held at Forest Hills, N.Y., was shifted to the National Tennis Center in Flushing Meadows, N.Y., in 1978. Pro tours for men and women became worldwide in play that continued throughout the year.

DAVIS CUP CHAMPIONSHIPS

No matches in 1901, 1910, 1915–1918, and 1940–1945

1900 United States 3, British Isles 0	1937 United States 4, Great Britain 1	1973 Australia 5, United States 0
1902 United States 3, British Isles 2	1938 United States 3, Australia 2	1974 South Africa (Default by India)
1903 British Isles 4, United States 1	1939 Australia 3, United States 2	1975 Sweden 3, Czechoslovakia 2
1904 British Isles 5, Belgium 0	1946 United States 5, Australia 0	1976 Italy 4, Chile 1
1905 British Isles 5, United States 0	1947 United States 4, Australia 1	1977 Australia 3, Italy 1
1906 British Isles 5, United States 0	1948 United States 5, Australia 0	1978 United States 4, Britain 1
1907 Australasia 3, British Isles 2	1949 United States 4, Australia 1	1979 United States 5, Italy 0
1908 Australasia 3, United States 2	1950 Australia 4, United States 1	1980 Czechoslovakia 3, Italy 2
1909 Australasia 5, United States 0	1951 Australia 3, United States 2	1981 United States 3, Argentina 1
1911 Australasia 5, United States 0	1952 Australia 4, United States 1	1982 United States 3, France 0
1912 British Isles 3, Australasia 2	1953 Australia 3, United States 2	1983 Australia 3, Sweden 2
1913 United States 3, British Isles 2	1954 United States 3, Australia 2	1984 Sweden 4, United States 1
1914 Australasia 3, United States 2	1955 Australia 5, United States 0	1985 Sweden 3, West Germany 2
1919 Australasia 4, British Isles 1	1956 Australia 5, United States 0	1986 Australia 3, Sweden 2
1920 United States 5, Australasia 0	1957 Australia 3, United States 2	1987 Sweden 5, India 0
1921 United States 5, Japan 0	1958 United States 3, Australia 2	1988 West Germany 4, Sweden 1
1922 United States 4, Australasia 1	1959 Australia 3, United States 2	1989 West Germany 3, Sweden 2
1923 United States 4, Australasia 1	1960 Australia 4, Italy 1	1990 United States 3, Australia 2
1924 United States 5, Australasia 0	1961 Australia 5, Italy 0	1991 France 3, United States 1
1925 United States 5, France 0	1962 Australia 5, Mexico 0	1992 United States 3, Switzerland 1
1926 United States 4, France 1	1963 United States 3, Australia 2	1993 Germany 4, Australia 1
1927 France 3, United States 2	1964 Australia 3, United States 2	1994 Sweden 4, Russia 1
1928 France 4, United States 1	1965 Australia 4, Spain 1	1995 United States 3, Russia 1
1929 France 3, United States 2	1966 Australia 4, India 1	1996 France 3, Sweden 2
1930 France 4, United States 1	1967 Australia 4, Spain 1	1997 Sweden 5, United States 0
1931 France 3, Great Britain 2	1968 United States 4, Australia 1	1998 Sweden 4, Italy 1
1932 France 3, United States 2	1969 United States 5, Romania 0	1999 Australia 3, France 2
1933 Great Britain 3, France 2	1970 United States 5, West	2000 Spain 3, Australia 1
1934 Great Britain 4, United States 1	Germany 0	2001 France 3, Australia 2
1935 Great Britain 5, United States 0	1971 United States 3, Romania 2	2002 Russia 3, France 2
1936 Great Britain 3, Australia 2	1972 United States 3, Romania 2	2003 Australia 3, Spain 1

FEDERATION CUP CHAMPIONSHIPS

World team competition for women conducted by International Lawn Tennis Federation

1963 United States 2, Australia 1	1978 United States 2, Australia 1	1989 United States 3, Spain 0
1964 Australia 2, United States 1	1979 United States 3, Australia 0	1990 United States 2, Soviet Union 1
1965 Australia 2, United States 1	1980 United States 3, Australia 0	1991 Spain 2, United States 1
1966 United States 3, West Germany 0	1981 United States 3, Britain 0	1992 Germany 2, Spain 1
1967 United States 2, Britain 0	1982 United States 3, West Germany 0	1993 Spain 3, Australia 0
1968 Australia 3, Netherlands 0	1983 Czechoslovakia 2, West	1994 Spain 3, United States 0
1969 United States 2, Australia 1	Germany 1	1995 Spain 3, United States 2
1970 Australia 3, West Germany 0	1984 Czechoslovakia 2, Australia 1	1996 United States 5, Spain 0
1971 Australia 3, Britain 0	1985 Czechoslovakia 2, United	1997 France 4, Netherlands 1
1972 South Africa 2, Britain 1	States 1	1998 Spain 3, Switzerland 2
1973 Australia 3, South Africa 0	1986 United States 3,	1999 United States 4, Russia 1
1974 Australia 2, United States 1	Czechoslovakia 0	2000 United States 5, Spain 0
1975 Czechoslovakia 3, Australia 0	1987 West Germany 2, United States 1	2001 Belgium 2, Russia 1
1976 United States 3, Australia 1	1988 Czechoslovakia 2, Soviet Union 1	2002 Slovak Republic 3, Spain 1
1977 United States 2, Australia 1		2003 France 4, United States 1

U.S. NATIONAL AND OPEN CHAMPIONS

SINGLES—MEN

NATIONAL	1906 William J. Clothier	1930 John H. Doeg	1948–49 Richard Gonzales
1881–87 Richard D. Sears	1907–11 William A. Larned	1931–32 Ellsworth Vines	1950 Arthur Larsen
1888–89 Henry Slocum, Jr.	1912–13 Maurice McLough-	1933–34 Fred J. Perry	1951–52 Frank Sedgman
1890–92 Oliver S. Campbell	lin[1]	1935 Wilmer L. Allison	1953 Tony Trabert
1893–94 Robert D. Wrenn	1914 R. N. Williams II	1936 Fred J. Perry	1954 Vic Seixas
1895 Fred H. Hovey	1915 William Johnston	1937–38 Don Budge	1955 Tony Trabert
1896–97 Robert D. Wrenn	1916 R. N. William II	1939 Robert L. Riggs	1956 Ken Rosewall
1898–	1917–18 R. Lindley Murray[2]	1940 Donald McNeill	1957 Mal Anderson
1900 Malcolm Whitman	1919 William Johnston	1941 Robert L. Riggs	1958 Ashley Cooper
1901–02 William A. Larned	1920–25 Bill Tilden	1942 Fred Schroeder	1959–60 Neale Fraser
1903 Hugh L. Doherty	1926–27 Jean Rene Lacoste	1943 Joseph Hunt	1961 Roy Emerson
1904 Holcombe Ward	1928 Henri Cochet	1944–45 Frank Parker	1962 Rod Laver
1905 Beals C. Wright	1929 Bill Tilden	1946–47 Jack Kramer	1963 Rafael Osuna

1964	Roy Emerson	1971	Stan Smith	1983	Jimmy Connors	1996	Pete Sampras
1965	Manuel Santana	1972	Ilie Nastase	1984	John McEnroe	1997–98	Patrick Rafter
1966	Fred Stolle	1973	John Newcombe	1985–87	Ivan Lendl	1999	Andre Agassi
1967	John Newcombe	1974	Jimmy Connors	1988	Mats Wilander	2000	Marat Safin
1968	Arthur Ashe	1975	Manuel Orantes	1989	Boris Becker	2001	Lleyton Hewitt
1969	Rod Laver	1976	Jimmy Connors	1990	Pete Sampras	2002	Pete Sampras
		1977	Guillermo Vilas	1991	Stefan Edberg	2003	Andy Roddick
OPEN		1978	Jimmy Connors	1992	Stefan Edberg	2004	Roger Federer
1968	Arthur Ashe	1979	John McEnroe	1993	Pete Sampras		
1969	Rod Laver	1980–81	John McEnroe	1994	Andre Agassi		
1970	Ken Rosewall	1982	Jimmy Connors	1995	Pete Sampras		

1. Challenge Round abandoned in 1912. 2. Patriotic Tournament in 1917.

SINGLES—WOMEN

NATIONAL		1915–18	Molla Bjurstedt	1954–55	Doris Hart	1982	Chris Evert-Lloyd
1887	Ellen F. Hansel	1919	Hazel Hotchkiss	1956	Shirley Fry	1983–84	Martina Navratilova
1888–89	Bertha Townsend		Wightman	1957–58	Althea Gibson	1985	Hana Mandlikova
1890	Ellen C. Roosevelt	1920–22	Molla Bjurstedt	1959	Maria Bueno	1986–87	Martina Navratilova
1891–92	Mabel E. Cahill		Mallory	1960–61	Darlene Hard	1988	Steffi Graf
1893	Aline M. Terry	1923–25	Helen N. Wills	1962	Margaret Smith	1989	Steffi Graf
1894	Helen R. Helwig	1926	Molla B. Mallory	1963–64	Maria Bueno	1990	Gabriela Sabatini
1895	Juliette P. Atkinson	1927–29	Helen N. Wills	1965	Margaret Smith	1991	Monica Seles
1896	Elisabeth H. Moore	1930	Betty Nuthall	1966	Maria Bueno	1992	Monica Seles
1897–98	Juliette P. Atkinson	1931	Helen Wills Moody	1967	Billie Jean King	1993	Steffi Graf
1899	Marion Jones	1932–35	Helen Jacobs	1968–69	Margaret Smith	1994	Arantxa Sanchez
1900	Myrtle McAteer	1936	Alice Marble		Court[1]		Vicario
1901	Elisabeth H. Moore	1937	Anita Lizana			1995	Steffi Graf
1902	Marion Jones	1938–40	Alice Marble	**OPEN**		1996	Steffi Graf
1903	Elisabeth H. Moore	1941	Sarah Palfrey	1968	Virginia Wade	1997	Martina Hingis
1904	May Sutton		Cooke	1969–70	Margaret Court	1998	Lindsay Davenport
1905	Elisabeth H. Moore	1942–44	Pauline Betz	1971–72	Billie Jean King	1999	Serena Williams
1906	Helen Homans	1945	Sarah Cooke	1973	Margaret Court	2000–01	Venus Williams
1907	Evelyn Sears	1946	Pauline Betz	1974	Billie Jean King	2002	Serena Williams
1908	Maud	1947	Louise Brough	1975–78	Chris Evert	2003	Justine
	Bargar-Wallach	1948–50	Margaret Osborne	1979	Tracy Austin		Henin-Hardenne
1909–11	Hazel V. Hotchkiss		duPont	1980	Chris Evert-Lloyd	2004	Svetlana
1912–14	Mary K. Browne	1951–53	Maureen Connolly	1981	Tracy Austin		Kuznetsova

1. With the inaugural of the Open Tournament in 1968, the United States Lawn Tennis Association held a championship at Longwood, Chestnut Hill, Mass., which barred contract professionals in 1968 and 1969.

DOUBLES—MEN

NATIONAL		1950	John Bromwich–Frank	1971	John Newcombe–Roger
1920	Bill Johnston–C. J. Griffin		Sedgman		Taylor
1921–22	Bill Tilden–Vincent Richards	1951	Frank Sedgman–Ken	1972	Cliff Drysdale–Roger Taylor
1923	Bill Tilden–B. I. C. Norton		McGregor	1973	John Newcombe–Owen
1924	H. O. Kinsey–R. G. Kinsey	1952	Vic Seixas–Mervyn Rose		Davidson
1925–26	Vincent Richards–R. N.	1953	Mervyn Rose–Rex Hartwig	1974	Bob Lutz–Stan Smith
	Williams II	1954	Vic Seixas–Tony Trabert	1975	Jimmy Connors–Ilie Nastase
1927	Bill Tilden–Frank Hunter	1955	Kosei Kamo–Atsushi Miyagi	1976	Marty Riessen–Tom Okker
1928	G. M. Lott, Jr.–V. Hennessy	1956	Lewis Hoad–Ken Rosewall	1977	Frew McMillan–Bob Hewitt
1929–30	G. M. Lott, Jr.–J. H. Doeg	1957	Ashley Cooper–Neale Fraser	1978	Bob Lutz–Stan Smith
1931	W. L. Allison–John Van Ryn	1958	Ham Richardson–Alex	1979	John McEnroe–Peter
1932	E. H. Vines, Jr.–Keith Gledh		Olmedo		Fleming
1933–34	G. M. Lott, Jr.–L. R. Stoefen	1959–60	Neale Fraser–Roy Emerson	1980	Stan Smith–Bob Lutz
1935	W. L. Allison–John Van Ryn	1961	Chuck McKinley–Dennis	1981	John McEnroe–Peter
1936	Don Budge–Gene Mako		Ralston		Fleming
1937	G. von Cramm–H. Henkel	1962	Rafael Osuna–Antonio	1982	Kevin Curren–Steve Denton
1938	Don Budge–Gene Mako		Palafox	1983	John McEnroe–Peter
1939	A. K. Quist–J. E. Bromwich	1963–64	Chuck McKinley–Dennis		Fleming
1940–41	Jack Kramer–F. R.		Ralston	1984	John Fitzgerald–Tomas Smid
	Schroeder	1965–66	Fred Stolle–Roy Emerson	1985	Ken Flach–Robert Seguso
1942	Gardnar Mulloy–Bill Talbert	1967	John Newcombe–Tony Roche	1986	Andres Gomez–Slobodan
1943	Jack Kramer–Frank Parker	1968	Stan Smith–Bob Lutz[1]		Zivojinovic
1944	Don McNeill–Bob Falkenburg	1969	Richard Crealy–Allan Stone[1]	1987	Stefan Edberg–Anders
1945	Gardnar Mulloy–Bill Talbert				Jarryd
1946	Gardnar Mulloy–Bill Talbert	**OPEN**		1988	Sergio Casal–Emilio Sanchez
1947	Jack Kramer–Fred Schroeder	1968	Stan Smith–Bob Lutz	1989	John McEnroe–Mark
1948	Gardnar Mulloy–Bill Talbert	1969	Fred Stolle–Ken Rosewall		Woodforde
1949	John Bromwich–William	1970	Nikki Pilic–Fred Barthes	1990	Pieter Aldrich–Danie Visser
	Sidwell				

1991	John Fitzgerald–Anders Jarryd	1997	Yevgeny Kafelnikov–Daniel Vacek	2002	Mahesh Bhupathi–Max Mirnyi
1992	Jim Grabb–Richey Reneberg	1998	Sandon Stolle–Cyril Zuk	2003	Jonas Bjorkman–Todd Woodbridge
1993	Ken Flach–Rick Leach	1999	Sebastien Lareau–Alex O'Brien	2004	Mark Knowles–Daniel Nestor
1994	Jacco Hingh–Paul Haarhuis	2000	Lleyton Hewitt–Max Mirnyi		
1995–96	Todd Woodbridge–Mark Woodforde	2001	Wayne Black–Kevin Ullyett		

1. With the inaugural of the Open Tournament in 1968, the United States Lawn Tennis Association held a national championship at Longwood, Chestnut Hill, Mass., which barred contract professionals in 1968 and 1969.

DOUBLES—WOMEN

NATIONAL

1924	G. W. Wightman–Helen Wills	1963	Margaret Smith–Robyn Ebbern	1982	Rosemary Casals–Wendy Turnbull
1925	Mary K. Browne–Helen Wills	1964	Karen Hantze Susman–Billie Jean Moffitt	1983–84	Martina Navratilova–Pam Shriver
1926	Elizabeth Ryan–Eleanor Goss	1965	Nancy Richey–Carole Caldwell Graebner	1985	Claudia Khode-Kilsch–Helena Sukova
1927	L. A. Godfree–Ermyntrude Harvey	1966	Nancy Richey–Maria Bueno	1986–87	Martina Navratilova–Pam Shriver
1928	Hazel Hotchkiss Wightman–Helen Wills	1967	Billie Jean King–Rosemary Casals	1988	Gigi Fernandez–Robin White
1929	Phoebe Watson–L. R. C. Michell	1968	Margaret Court–Maria Bueno[1]	1989	Hana Mandlikova–Martina Navratilova
1930	Betty Nuthall–Sarah Palfrey	1969	Margaret Court–Virginia Wade[1]	1990	Gigi Fernandez–Martina Navratilova
1931	Betty Nuthall–E. B. Wittingstall	**OPEN**		1991	Pam Shriver–Natalia Zvereva
1932	Helen Jacobs–Sarah Palfrey	1968	Maria Bueno–Margaret Court	1992	Gigi Fernandez–Natalia Zvereva
1933	Betty Nuthall–Freda James	1969	Darlene Hard–Francoise Durr		
1934	Helen Jacobs–Sarah Palfrey	1970	Margaret Court–Judy Dalton	1993	Arantxa Sanchez Vicario–Helena Sukova
1935	Helen Jacobs–Sarah Palfrey Fabyan	1971	Rosemary Casals–Judy Dalton	1994	Jana Novotna–Arantxa Sanchez Vicario
1936	Marjorie G. Van Ryn–Carolin Babcock	1972	Francoise Durr–Betty Stove	1995	Gigi Fernandez–Natasha Zvereva
1937–40	Sarah Palfrey Fabyan–Alice Marble	1973	Margaret Court–Virginia Wade		
1941	Sarah Palfrey Cooke–Margaret Osborne	1974	Billie Jean King–Rosemary Casals	1996	Gigi Fernandez–Natasha Zvereva
1942–47	A. Louise Brough–Margaret Osborne	1975	Margaret Court–Virginia Wade	1997	Lindsay Davenport–Jana Novotna
1948–50	A. Louise Brough–Margaret O. duPont	1976	Linky Boshoff–Ilana Kloss	1998	Martina Hingis–Jana Novotna
1951–54	Doris Hart–Shirley Fry	1977	Martina Navratilova–Betty Stove	1999	Serena Williams–Venus Williams
1955–57	A. Louise Brough–Margaret O. duPont	1978	Billie Jean King–Martina Navratilova	2000	Julie-Halard Decugis–Ai Sugiyama
1958–59	Darlene Hard–Jeanne Arth	1979	Betty Stove–Wendy Turnbull	2001	Lisa Raymond–Renae Stubbs
1960	Darlene Hard–Maria Bueno	1980	Billie Jean King–Martina Navratilova	2002–04	Virginia Ruano Pascual–Paola Suarez
1961	Darlene Hard–Lesley Turner	1981	Kathy Jordan–Anne Smith		
1962	Darlene Hard–Maria Bueno				

1. With the inaugural of the Open Tournament in 1968, the United States Lawn Tennis Association held a national championship at Longwood, Chestnut Hill, Mass., which barred contract professionals in 1968 and 1969.

U.S. OPEN, 2004
(Flushing Meadow, N.Y., Aug. 30–Sept. 12, 2004)

Men's singles—Roger Federer defeated Lleyton Hewitt, 6–0, 7–6 (7–3), 6–0.

Women's singles—Svetlana Kuznetsova defeated Elena Dementieva 6–3, 7–5.

Men's doubles—Mark Knowles and Daniel Nestor defeated Leander Paes and David Rikl, 6–3, 6–3.

Women's doubles—Virginia Ruano Pascual and Paola Suarez defeated Svetlana Kuznetsova and Elena Likhovtseva, 6–4, 7–5.

Mixed doubles—Vera Zvonareva and Bob Bryan defeated Alicia Molik and Todd Woodbridge, 6–3, 6–4.

BRITISH (WIMBLEDON) CHAMPIONS
(Amateur from inception in 1877 through 1967)
SINGLES—MEN

1908–09	Arthur Gore	1923	William Johnston	1929	Jean Cochet	1937–38	Don Budge
1910–13	A. F. Wilding	1924	Jean Borotra	1930	Bill Tilden	1939	Robert L. Riggs
1914	N. E. Brookes	1925	Rene Lacoste	1931	S. B. Wood	1946	Yvon Petra
1919	G. L. Patterson	1926	Jean Borotra	1932	Ellsworth Vines	1947	Jack Kramer
1920–21	Bill Tilden	1927	Henri Cochet	1933	J. H. Crawford	1948	R. Falkenburg
1922	G. L. Patterson	1928	Rene Lacoste	1934–36	Fred Perry	1949	Fred Schroeder

1950	Budge Patty	1961–62	Rod Laver	1975	Arthur Ashe	1991	Michael Stich
1951	Richard Savitt	1963	Chuck McKinley	1976–80	Bjorn Borg	1992	Andre Agassi
1952	Frank Sedgman	1964–65	Roy Emerson	1981	John McEnroe	1993–95	Pete Sampras
1953	Vic Siexas	1966	Manuel Santana	1982	Jimmy Connors	1996	Richard Krajicek
1954	Jaroslav Drobny	1967	John Newcombe	1983–84	John McEnroe	1997–	
1955	Tony Trabert	1968–69	Rod Laver	1985–86	Boris Becker		
1956–57	Lewis Hoad	1970–71	John Newcombe	1987	Pat Cash	2000	Pete Sampras
1958	Ashley Cooper	1972	Stan Smith	1988	Stefan Edberg	2001	Goran Ivanisevic
1959	Alex Olmedo	1973	Jan Kodes	1989	Boris Becker	2002	Lleyton Hewitt
1960	Neale Fraser	1974	Jimmy Connors	1990	Stefan Edberg	2003–04	Roger Federer

SINGLES—WOMEN

1919–23	Suzanne Lenglen	1946	Pauline M. Betz	1966–68	Billie Jean King	1988–89	Steffi Graf
1924	Kathleen McKane	1947	Margaret Osborne	1969	Ann Jones	1990	Martina Navratilova
1925	Suzanne Lenglen	1948–50	A. Louise Brough	1970	Margaret Court	1991–93	Steffi Graf
1926	Kathleen Godfree	1951	Doris Hart	1971	Evonne Goolagong	1994	Conchita Martinez
1927–29	Helen Wills	1952–54	Maureen Connolly	1972–73	Billie Jean King	1995–96	Steffi Graf
1930	Helen Wills Moody	1955	A. Louise Brough	1974	Chris Evert	1997	Martina Hingis
1931	Cilly Aussem	1956	Shirley Fry	1975	Billie Jean King	1998	Jana Novotna
1932–33	Helen Wills Moody	1957–58	Althea Gibson	1976	Chris Evert	1999	Lindsay Davenport
1934	D. E. Round	1959–60	Maria Bueno	1977	Virginia Wade	2000–01	Venus Williams
1935	Helen Wills Moody	1961	Angela Mortimer	1978–79	Martina Navratilova	2002–03	Serena Williams
1936	Helen Jacobs	1962	Karen Susman	1980	Evonne Goolagong Cawley	2004	Maria Sharapova
1937	D. E. Round	1963	Margaret Smith				
1938	Helen Wills Moody	1964	Maria Bueno	1981	Chris Evert-Lloyd		
1939	Alice Marble	1965	Margaret Smith	1982–87	Martina Navratilova		

DOUBLES—MEN

1953	K. Rosewall–L. Hoad	1972	Bob Hewitt–Frew McMillan	1986	Joakim Nystrom–Mats Wilander
1954	R. Hartwig–M. Rose	1973	Jimmy Connors–Ilie Nastase		
1955	R. Hartwig–L. Hoad	1974	John Newcombe–Tony Roche	1987	Ken Flach–Robert Seguso
1956	L. Hoad–K. Rosewall			1988	Ken Flach–Robert Seguso
1957	Gardnar Mulloy–Budge Patty	1975	Vitas Gerulaitis–Sandy Mayer	1989	John Fitzgerald–Anders Jarryd
1958	Sven Davidson–Ulf Schmidt	1976	Brian Gottfried–Raul Ramirez		
1959	Roy Emerson–Neale Fraser			1990	Rick Leach–Jim Pugh
1960	Dennis Ralston–Rafael Osuna	1977	Ross Case–Geoff Masters	1991	Anders Jarryd–John Fitzgerald
1961	Roy Emerson–Neale Fraser	1978	Fred McMillan–Bob Hewitt	1992	John McEnroe–Michael Stich
1962	Fred Stolle–Bob Hewitt	1979	Peter Fleming–John McEnroe		
1963	Rafael Osuna–Antonio Palafox	1980	Peter McNamara–Paul McNamee	1993–97	Todd Woodbridge–Mark Woodforde
1964	Fred Stolle–Bob Hewitt	1981	John McEnroe–Peter Fleming	1998	Jacco Eltingh–Paul Haarhuis
1965	John Newcombe–Tony Roche	1982	Paul McNamee–Peter McNamara	1999	Mahesh Bhupathi–Leander Paes
1966	John Newcombe–Ken Fletcher	1983–84	John McEnroe–Peter Fleming	2000	Todd Woodbridge–Mark Woodforde
1967	Bob Hewitt–Frew McMillan	1985	Heinz Gunthardt–Balazs Taroczy	2001	Donald Johnson–Jared Palmer
1968–70	John Newcombe–Tony Roche			2002–04	Todd Woodbridge–Jonas Bjorkman
1971	Rod Laver–Roy Emerson				

DOUBLES—WOMEN

1956	Althea Gibson–Angela Buxton	1970–71	Billie Jean King–Rosemary Casals	1982–84	Pam Shriver–Martina Navratilova
1957	Althea Gibson–Darlene Hard	1972	Billie Jean King–Betty Stove	1985	Kathy Jordan–Elizabeth Smylie
1958	Althea Gibson–Maria Bueno	1973	Billie Jean King–Rosemary Casals	1986	Pam Shriver–Martina Navratilova
1959	Darlene Hard–Jeanne Arth	1974	Evonne Goolagong–Peggy Michel	1987	Claudia Khode-Kilsch–Helena Sukova
1960	Darlene Hard–Maria Bueno				
1961	Karen Hantze–Billie Jean Moffitt	1975	Ann Kiyomura–Kazuko Sawamatsu	1988	Steffi Graf–Gabriela Sabatini
1962	Karen Hantze Susman–Billie Jean Moffitt	1976	Chris Evert–Martina Navratilova	1989	Jana Novotna–Helena Sukova
1963	Darlene Hard–Maria Bueno	1977	Helen Cawley–JoAnne Russell	1990	Jana Novotna–Helena Sukova
1964	Margaret Smith–Les Turnerley	1978	Wendy Turnbull–Kerry Reid	1991	Pam Shriver–Natalia Zvereva
1965	Billie Jean Moffitt–Maria Bueno	1979	Billie Jean King–Martina Navratilova	1992	Gigi Fernandez–Natalia Zvereva
1966	Nancy Richey–Maria Bueno	1980	Kathy Jordan–Anne Smith	1993	Gigi Fernandez–Natalia Zvereva
1967–68	Billie Jean King–Rosemary Casals	1981	Martina Navratilova–Pam Shriver		
1969	Margaret Court–Judy Tegart				

1994	Gigi Fernandez–Natalia Zvereva	1998	Martina Hingis–Jana Novotna	2002	Serena Williams–Venus Williams
1995	Jana Novotna–Arantxa Sanchez Vicario	1999	Lindsay Davenport–Corina Morariu	2003	Kim Clijsters–Ai Sugiyama
1996	Martina Hingis–Helena Sukova	2000	Venus Williams–Serena Williams	2004	Cara Black–Rennae Stubbs
1997	Gigi Fernandez–Natasha Zvereva	2001	Lisa Raymond–Rennae Stubbs		

WIMBLEDON CHAMPIONS, 2004

(Wimbledon, England, June 21–July 4, 2004)

Men's singles—Roger Federer defeated Andy Roddick, 4–6, 7–5, 7–6 (7–3), 6–4.

Women's singles—Maria Sharapova defeated Serena Williams, 6–1, 6–4.

Men's doubles—Todd Woodbridge and Jonas Bjorkman defeated Julian Knowle and Nenad Zimonjic, 6–1, 6–4, 4–6, 6–4.

Women's doubles—Cara Black and Rennae Stubbs defeated Liezel Huber and Ai Sugiyama, 6–3, 7–6 (7–5).

Mixed doubles—Wayne Black and Cara Black defeated Todd Woodbridge and Alicia Molik, 3–6, 7–6 (10–8), 6–4.

OTHER 2004 GRAND SLAM CHAMPIONS

French Open

(Paris, May 24–June 6, 2004)

Men's singles—Gaston Gaudio defeated Guillermo Coria, 8–6, 0–6, 3–6, 6–4, 6–1.

Women's singles—Anastasia Myskina defeated Elena Dementieva, 6–1, 6–2.

Men's doubles—Xavier Malisse and Olivier Rochus defeated Michael Llodra and Fabrice Santoro, 7–5, 7–5.

Women's doubles—Virginia Ruano Pascual and Paola Suarez defeated Svetlana Kuznetsova and Elena Likhovtseva, 6–0, 6–3.

Mixed doubles—Tatiana Golovin and Richard Gasquet defeated Cara Black and Wayne Black, 6–3, 6–4.

Australian Open

(Melbourne, Australia, Jan. 19–Feb. 1, 2004)

Men's singles—Roger Federer defeated Marat Safin, 7–6 (7–3), 6–4. 6–2.

Women's singles—Justine Henin-Hardenne defeated Kim Clijsters, 6–3, 4–6, 6–3.

Men's doubles—Michael Llodra and Fabrice Santoro defeated Bob Bryan and Mike Bryan, 7–6 (7–4), 6–3.

Women's doubles—Virginia Ruano Pascual and Paola Suarez defeated Svetlana Kuznetsova and Elena Likhovtseva, 6–4, 6–3.

Mixed doubles—Nenad Zimonjic and Elena Bovina defeated Leander Paes and Martina Navratilova, 6–1, 7–6 (7–3).

OTHER WTA TOURNAMENTS, 2004

Tournament	Singles champion
adidas International, Sydney, Australia	Justine Henin-Hardenne
Toray Pan Pacific Open, Tokyo, Japan	Lindsay Davenport
Open Gaz de France, Paris, France	Kim Clijsters
Proximus Diamond Games, Antwerp, Belgium	Kim Clijsters
Qatar Total Open, UAE	Anastasia Myskina
Pacific Life Open, Indian Wells, Calif.	Justine Henin-Hardenne
NASDAQ-100 Open, Miami, Fla.	Serena Williams
Bausch & Lomb Championships, Amelia Island, Fla.	Lindsay Davenport
Grand Prix de S.A.R. la Princesse, Casablanca, Morocco	Emilie Loit
Family Circle Cup, Charleston, S.C.	Venus Williams
J&S Cup, Warsaw, Poland	Venus Williams
Ladies German Open, Berlin, Germany	Amelie Mauresmo
Telecom Italia Masters, Rome, Italy	Amelie Mauresmo
Hastings Direct Int'l Championships, Eastbourne, England	Svetlana Kuznetsova
Bank of the West Classic, Stanford, Calif.	Lindsay Davenport
JP Morgan Chase Open, Los Angeles, Calif.	Lindsay Davenport
Acura Classic, San Diego, Calif.	Lindsay Davenport
Rogers AT&T Cup, Montreal, Canada	Amelie Mauresmo
Pilot Pen, New Haven, Conn.	Elena Bovina

Source: www.wtatour.com.

OTHER ATP TOURNAMENTS, 2004

Tournament	Singles champion
Exxon Mobil Open, Doha, Qatar	Nicolas Escude
Kroger St. Jude, Memphis, Tenn.	Joachim Johansson
ABN AMRO World Tennis, Rotterdam, Netherlands	Lleyton Hewitt
Dubai Duty Free, Dubai, UAE	Roger Federer
Abierto Mexicano Telefonica Movistar, Acapulco, Mexico	Carlos Moya
Pacific Life Open, Indian Wells, Calif.	Roger Federer
NASDAQ-100 Open, Miami, Fla.	Andy Roddick
Estoril Open, Estoril, Portugal	Juan Ignacio Chela
Tennis Masters, Monte Carlo, Monaco	Guillermo Coria
Open Seat Godo 2004, Barcelona, Spain	Tommy Robredo
Telecom Italia Masters, Rome, Italy	Carlos Moya
Masters Series, Hamburg, Germany	Roger Federer
Stella Artois, London, England	Andy Roddick
Allianz Suisse Open, Gstaad, Switzerland	Roger Federer
Mercedes Cup, Stuttgart, Germany	Guillermo Canas
RCA Championships, Indianapolis, Ind.	Andy Roddick
Generali Open, Kitzbuhel, Austria	Nicolas Massu
Tennis Masters, Toronto, Canada	Roger Federer
Western & Southern Financial Group Masters, Cincinnati, Ohio	Andre Agassi
Legg Mason Tennis Classic, Washington, DC	Lleyton Hewitt
China Open, Beijing, China	Marat Safin

Source: www.atptennis.com.

WOMEN'S TOP 5 MONEY WINNERS, 2004

1.	Svetlana Kuznetsova	$1,779,378
2.	Lindsay Davenport	1,697,011
3.	Anastasia Myskina	1,481,863
4.	Justine Henin-Hardenne	1,425,406
5.	Elena Dementieva	1,391,420

As of Sept. 20, 2004. *Source:* www.wtatour.com.

MEN'S TOP 5 MONEY WINNERS, 2004

1.	Roger Federer	$4,753,222
2.	Andy Roddick	2,081,440
3.	Lleyton Hewitt	1,977,421
4.	Guillermo Coria	1,607,155
5.	Gaston Gaudio	1,514,589

As of Sept. 20, 2004 . *Source:* www.atptennis.com.

Harness Racing

Oliver Wendell Holmes, the famous Autocrat of the Breakfast Table, wrote that the running horse was a gambling toy but the trotting horse was useful and, furthermore, "horse-racing is not a republican institution; horse-trotting is." Oliver Wendell Holmes was a born-and-bred New Englander, and New England was the nursery of the harness racing sport in America. Pacers and trotters were matters of local pride and prejudice in colonial New England, and, shortly after the Revolution, the Messenger and Justin Morgan strains produced many winners in harness racing "matches" along the turnpikes of New York, Connecticut, Rhode Island, Massachusetts, Vermont, and New Hampshire.

There was English thoroughbred blood in Messenger and Justin Morgan, and, many years later, it was blended in Rysdyk's Hambletonian, foaled in 1849. Hambletonian was not particularly fast under harness but his descendants have had almost a monopoly of prizes, titles, and records in the harness racing game. Hambletonian was purchased as a foal with its dam for a total of $124 by William Rysdyk of Goshen, N.Y., and made a modest fortune for the purchaser.

Trotters and pacers often were raced under saddle in the old days, and, in fact, the custom still survives in some places in Europe. Dexter, the great trotter that lowered the mile record from 2:19¾ to 2:17¼ in 1867, was said to handle just as well under saddle as when pulling a sulky. But as sulkies were lightened in weight and improved in design, trotting under saddle became less common and finally faded out in this country.

HISTORY OF TRADITIONAL HARNESS RACING STAKES

THE HAMBLETONIAN

Year	Winner	Driver	Best time	Total purse
1967	Speedy Streak	Del Cameron	2:00	$122,650
1968	Nevele Pride	Stanley Dancer	1:59.2	116,190
1969	Lindy's Pride	Howard Beissinger	1:57 .3	124,910
1970	Timothy T.	John Simpson, Jr.	1:58.2[1]	143,630
1971	Speedy Crown	Howard Beissinger	1:57.2	129,770
1972	Super Bowl	Stanley Dancer	1:56.2	119,090
1973	Flirth	Ralph Baldwin	1:57.1	144,710
1974	Christopher T	Billy Haughton	1:58.3	160,150
1975	Bonefish	Stanley Dancer	1:59[2]	232,192
1976	Steve Lobell	Billy Haughton	1:56.2	263,524
1977	Green Speed	Billy Haughton	1:55.3	284,131
1978	Speedy Somolli	Howard Beissinger	1:55[3]	241,280
1979	Legend Hanover	George Sholty	1:56.1	300,000
1980	Burgomeister	Billy Haughton	1:56.3	293,570
1981	Shiaway St. Pat	Ray Remmen	2:01.1[4]	838,000
1982	Speed Bowl	Tommy Haughton	1:56.4	875,750
1983	Duenna	Stanley Dancer	1:57.2	1,000,000
1984	Historic Freight	Ben Webster	1:56.2[5]	1,219,000
1985	Prakas	Bill O'Donnell	1:54.3	1,272,000
1986	Nuclear Kosmos	Ulf Thoresen	1:55.2[6]	1,172,082
1987	Mack Lobell	John Campbell	1:53.3	1,046,300
1988	Armbro Goal	John Campbell	1:54.3	1,156,800
1989	Park Avenue Joe and Probe*	Ron Wayples Bill Fahy	1:54.3	1,131,000
1990	Harmonious	John Campbell	1:54.1	1,346,000
1991	Giant Victory	Jack Moiseyev	1:54.4	1,238,000
1992	Alf Palema	Mickey McNichol	1:56.2[7]	1,288,000
1993	American Winner	Ron Pierce	1:53.1	1,200,000
1994	Victory Dream	Mike Lachance	1:53.4	1,200,000
1995	Tagliabue	John Campbell	1:54.4	1,200,000
1996	Continentalvictory	Mike Lachance	1:52.1	1,200,000
1997	Malabar Man	Malvern Burroughs	1:53.4	1,000,000
1998	Muscles Yankee	John Campbell	1:52.2	1,000,000
1999	Self Possessed	Mike Lachance	1:51.3	1,000,000

Year	Winner	Driver	Best time	Total purse
2000	Yankee Paco	Travor Ritchie	1:53.2	1,000,000
2001	Scarlet Knight	Stefan Melander	1:53.4	1,000,000
2002	Chip Chip Hooray	Eric Ledford	1:53.3	1,000,000
2003	Amigo Hall	Mike Lachance	1:54.0	1,000,000
2004	Windsong's Legacy	Trond Smedshammer	1:54.1	1,000,000

Three-year-old trotters. One mile. Guy McKinney won first race at Syracuse in 1926; held at Goshen, N.Y., 1930–1942, 1944–1956; at Yonkers, N.Y., 1943; at Du Quoin, Ill., 1957–1980. Since 1981, the race has been held at The Meadowlands in East Rutherford, N.J. *Cowinners. Fastest heat won by: 1. By Formal Notice. 2. By Yankee Bambino. 3. By Speedy Somolli and Florida Pro. 4. By Super Juan. 5. Delvin G. Hanover. 6. Royal Prestige. 7. Baltic Sonata.

LITTLE BROWN JUG

Year	Winner	Driver	Best time	Total purse
1967	Best of All	Jim Hackett	1:59[1]	$84,778
1968	Rum Customer	Billy Haughton	1:59.3	104,226
1969	Laverne Hanover	Billy Haughton	2:00.2	109,731
1970	Most Happy Fella	Stanley Dancer	1:57.1	100,110
1971	Nansemond	Herve Filion	1:57.2	102,994
1972	Strike Out	Keith Waples	1:56.3	104,916
1973	Melvin's Woe	Joe O'Brien	1:57.3	120,000
1974	Ambro Omaha	Billy Haughton	1:57	132,630
1975	Seatrain	Ben Webster	1:57[2]	147,813
1976	Keystone Ore	Stanley Dancer	1:56.4[3]	153,799
1977	Governor Skipper	John Chapman	1:56.1	150,000
1978	Happy Escort	William Popfinger	1:55.2[4]	186,760
1979	Hot Hitter	Herve Filion	1:55.3	226,455
1980	Niatross	Clint Galbraith	1:54.4	207,361
1981	Fan Hanover	Glen Garnsey	1:56[5]	243,799
1982	Merger	John Campbell	1:56.3	328,900
1983	Ralph Hanover	Ron Waples	1:55.3	358,800
1984	Colt 46	Norman Boring	1:53.3	366,717
1985	Nihilator	Bill O'Donnell	1:52.1	350,730
1986	Barberry Spur	Bill O'Donnell	1:52.4	407,684
1987	Jaguar Spur	Richard Stillings	1:55.3	412,330
1988	B.J. Scoot	Mike Lachance	1:52.3	486,050
1989	Goalie Jeff	Mike Lachance	1:54.1	500,200
1990	Beach Towel	Ray Remmen	1:53.3	253,049
1991	Precious Bunny	Jack Moiseyev	1:54.1	575,150
1992	Fake Left	Ron Waples	1:54.2	556,210
1993	Life Sign	John Campbell	1:52	465,500
1994	Magical Mike	Mike Lachance	1:52.3	512,830
1995	Nick's Fantasy	John Campbell	1:51.2	543,670
1996	Armbro Operative	Jack Moiyesev	1:52.3	542,220
1997	Western Dreamer	Mike Lachance	1:51.1	605,210
1998	Shady Character	Ron Pierce	1:52.3	566,630
1999	Blissfull Hall	Ron Pierce	1:55.3	543,980
2000	Astreos	Chris Christoforou	1:55.3	547,972
2001	Bettor's Delight	Mike Lachance	1:51.4	646,050
2002	Million Dollar Cam	Luc Ouellette	1:50.2	618,625
2003	No Pan Intended	David Miller	1:50.0	605,050
2004	Timesareachanging	Ron Pierce	1:51.3	571,500

Three-year-old pacers. One Mile. Raced at Delaware County Fair Grounds, Delaware, Ohio. 1. By Nardin's Byrd. 2. By Albert's Star. 3. By Armbro Ranger. 4. By Falcon Almahurst. 5. By Seahawk Hanover.

HARNESS HORSE OF THE YEAR

1959	Bye Bye Byrd, Pacer	1977	Green Speed, Trotter	1992	Artsplace
1960–61	Adios Butler, Pacer	1978	Abercrombie, Pacer	1993	Staying Together
1962	Su Mac Lad, Trotter	1979–80	Niatross, Pacer	1994	Cam's Card Shark
1963	Speedy Scot, Trotter	1981	Fan Hanover, Pacer	1995	CR Kay Suzie
1964–66	Bret Hanover, Pacer	1982–83	Cam Fella, Pacer	1996	Continentalvictory
1967–69	Nevele Pride, Trotter	1984	Fancy Crown, Trotter	1997	Malabar Man
1970	Fresh Yankee, Trotter	1985	Nihilator, Trotter	1998–99	Moni Maker
1971–72	Albatross, Pacer	1986	Forrest Skipper	2000	Gallo Blue Chip
1973	Sir Dalrae, Pacer	1987–88	Mack Lobell	2001	Bunny Lake
1974	Delmonica Hanover, Trotter	1989	Matt's Scooter	2002	Real Desire
1975	Savoir, Trotter	1990	Beach Towell	2003	No Pan Intended
1976	Keystone Ore, Pacer	1991	Precious Bunny		

Chosen in poll conducted by U.S. Trotting Association in conjunction with the U.S. Harness Writers Association.

Golf

It may be that golf originated in Holland—historians believe it did—but certainly Scotland fostered the game and is famous for it. In fact, in 1457 the Scottish Parliament, disturbed because football and golf had lured young Scots from the more soldierly exercise of archery, passed an ordinance that "futeball and golf be utterly cryit doun and nocht usit." James I and Charles I of the royal line of Stuarts were golf enthusiasts, whereby the game came to be known as "the royal and ancient game of golf."

The golf balls used in the early games were leather-covered and stuffed with feathers. Clubs of all kinds were fashioned by hand to suit individual players. The great step in spreading the game came with the change from the feather ball to the gutta-percha ball about 1850. In 1860, formal competition began with the establishment of an annual tournament for the British Open championship. There are records of "golf clubs" in the United States as far

back as colonial days but no proof of actual play before John Reid and some friends laid out six holes on the Reid lawn in Yonkers, N.Y., in 1888 and played there with golf balls and clubs brought over from Scotland by Robert Lockhart. This group then formed the St. Andrews Golf Club of Yonkers, and golf was established in this country.

However, it remained a rather sedate and almost aristocratic pastime until a 20-year-old ex-caddy, Francis Ouimet of Boston, defeated two great British professionals, Harry Vardon and Ted Ray, in the United States Open championship at Brookline, Mass., in 1913. This feat put the game and Francis Ouimet on the front pages of the newspapers and stirred a wave of enthusiasm for the sport. The greatest feat so far in golf history is that of Robert Tyre Jones, Jr., of Atlanta, who won the British Open, the British Amateur, the U.S. Open, and the U.S. Amateur titles in one year, 1930.

THE MASTERS TOURNAMENT WINNERS

Augusta National Golf Club, Augusta, Ga.

Year	Winner	Score	Year	Winner	Score	Year	Winner	Score
1934	Horton Smith	284	1959	Art Wall, Jr.	284	1982	Craig Stadler[1]	284
1935	Gene Sarazen[1]	282	1960	Arnold Palmer	282	1983	Severiano Ballesteros	280
1936	Horton Smith	285	1961	Gary Player	280	1984	Ben Crenshaw	277
1937	Byron Nelson	283	1962	Arnold Palmer[1]	280	1985	Bernhard Langer	282
1938	Henry Picard	285	1963	Jack Nicklaus	286	1986	Jack Nicklaus	279
1939	Ralph Guldahl	279	1964	Arnold Palmer	276	1987	Larry Mize[1]	285
1940	Jimmy Demaret	280	1965	Jack Nicklaus	271	1988	Sandy Lyle	281
1941	Craig Wood	280	1966	Jack Nicklaus[1]	288	1989	Nick Faldo[1]	283
1942	Byron Nelson[1]	280	1967	Gay Brewer, Jr.	280	1990	Nick Faldo	278
1943–45 No Tournaments			1968	Bob Goalby	277	1991	Ian Woosnam	277
1946	Herman Keiser	282	1969	George Archer	281	1992	Fred Couples	275
1947	Jimmy Demaret	281	1970	Billy Casper[1]	279	1993	Bernard Langer	277
1948	Claude Harmon	279	1971	Charles Coody	279	1994	Jose Maria Olazabal	279
1949	Sam Snead	282	1972	Jack Nicklaus	286	1995	Ben Crenshaw	274
1950	Jimmy Demaret	283	1973	Tommy Aaron	283	1996	Nick Faldo	276
1951	Ben Hogan	280	1974	Gary Player	278	1997	Tiger Woods	270
1952	Sam Snead	286	1975	Jack Nicklaus	276	1998	Mark O'Meara	279
1953	Ben Hogan	274	1976	Ray Floyd	271	1999	Jose Maria Olazabal	280
1954	Sam Snead[1]	289	1977	Tom Watson	276	2000	Vijay Singh	278
1955	Cary Middlecoff	279	1978	Gary Player	277	2001	Tiger Woods	272
1956	Jack Burke	289	1979	Fuzzy Zoeller[1]	280	2002	Tiger Woods	276
1957	Doug Ford	283	1980	Severiano Ballesteros	275	2003	Mike Weir	281
1958	Arnold Palmer	284	1981	Tom Watson	280	2004	Phil Mickelson	279

1. Winner in playoff.

U.S. OPEN CHAMPIONS

Year	Winner	Score	Where played	Year	Winner	Score	Where played
1895	Horace Rawlins	173	Newport	1912	John McDermott	294	Buffalo
1896	James Foulis	152	Shinnecock Hills	1913	Francis Ouimet[1, 2]	304	Brookline
1897	Joe Lloyd	162	Chicago	1914	Walter Hagen	290	Midlothian
1898[3]	Fred Herd	328	Myopia	1915	Jerome D. Travers[2]	297	Baltusrol
1899	Willie Smith	315	Baltimore	1916	Charles Evans, Jr.[2]	286	Minikahda
1900	Harry Vardon	313	Chicago	1917–18	No tournaments[4]		
1901	Willie Anderson[1]	331	Myopia	1919	Walter Hagen[2]	301	Brae Burn
1902	Laurie Auchterlonie	307	Garden City	1920	Edward Ray	295	Inverness
1903	Willie Anderson[1]	307	Baltusrol	1921	Jim Barnes	289	Columbia
1904	Willie Anderson	303	Glen View	1922	Gene Sarazen	288	Skokie
1905	Willie Anderson	314	Myopia	1923	R. T. Jones, Jr.[1, 2]	296	Inwood
1906	Alex Smith	295	Onwentsia	1924	Cyril Walker	297	Oakland Hills
1907	Alex Ross	302	Philadelphia	1925	Willie Macfarlane[1]	291	Worcester
1908	Fred McLeod[1]	322	Myopia	1926	R. T. Jones, Jr.[2]	293	Scioto
1909	George Sargent	290	Englewood	1927	Tommy Armour[1]	301	Oakmont
1910	Alex Smith[1]	298	Philadelphia	1928	Johnny Farrell[1]	294	Olympia Fields
1911	John McDermott[1]	307	Chicago	1929	R. T. Jones, Jr.[1, 2]	294	Winged Foot

Year	Winner	Score	Where played	Year	Winner	Score	Where played
1930	R. T. Jones, Jr.[2]	287	Interlachen	1970	Tony Jacklin	281	Hazeltine
1931	Billy Burke[1]	292	Inverness	1971	Lee Trevino[1]	280	Merion
1932	Gene Sarazen	286	Fresh Meadow	1972	Jack Nicklaus	290	Pebble Beach
1933	John Goodman[2]	287	North Shore	1973	Johnny Miller	279	Oakmont
1934	Olin Dutra	293	Merion	1974	Hale Irwin	287	Winged Foot
1935	Sam Parks, Jr.	299	Oakmont	1975	Lou Graham[1]	287	Medinah
1936	Tony Manero	282	Baltusrol	1976	Jerry Pate	277	Atlanta A.C.
1937	Ralph Guldahl	281	Oakland Hills	1977	Hubert Green	278	Southern Hills
1938	Ralph Guldahl	284	Cherry Hills	1978	Andy North	285	Cherry Hills
1939	Byron Nelson[1]	284	Philadelphia	1979	Hale Irwin	284	Inverness
1940	Lawson Little[1]	287	Canterbury	1980	Jack Nicklaus	272	Baltusrol
1941	Craig Wood	284	Colonial	1981	David Graham	273	Merion
1942–45	No tournaments[5]			1982	Tom Watson	282	Pebble Beach
1946	Lloyd Mangrum[1]	284	Canterbury	1983	Larry Nelson	280	Oakmont
1947	Lew Worsham[1]	282	St. Louis	1984	Fuzzy Zoeller[1]	276	Winged Foot
1948	Ben Hogan	276	Riviera	1985	Andy North	279	Oakland Hills
1949	Cary Middlecoff	286	Medinah	1986	Ray Floyd	279	Shinnecock Hills
1950	Ben Hogan[1]	287	Merion	1987	Scott Simpson	277	Olympic Golf Club
1951	Ben Hogan	287	Oakland Hills	1988	Curtis Strange[1]	278	The Country Club
1952	Julius Boros	281	Northwood	1989	Curtis Strange	278	Oak Hill Country
1953	Ben Hogan	283	Oakmont				Club
1954	Ed Furgol	284	Baltusrol	1990	Hale Irwin[1]	280	Medinah C.C.
1955	Jack Fleck[1]	287	Olympic	1991	Payne Stewart[1]	282	Hazeltine
1956	Cary Middlecoff	281	Oak Hill	1992	Tom Kite	285	Pebble Beach
1957	Dick Mayer[1]	298	Inverness	1993	Lee Janzen	272	Baltusrol
1958	Tommy Bolt	283	Southern Hills	1994	Ernie Els	279	Oakmont
1959	Bill Casper, Jr.	282	Winged Foot	1995	Corey Pavin	280	Shinnecock Hills
1960	Arnold Palmer	280	Cherry Hills	1996	Steve Jones	278	Oakland Hills
1961	Gene Littler	281	Oakland Hills	1997	Ernie Els	276	Congressional C.C.
1962	Jack Nicklaus[1]	283	Oakmont	1998	Lee Janzen	280	Olympic Country
1963	Julius Boros[1]	293	Country Club				Club
1964	Ken Venturi	278	Congressional	1999	Payne Stewart	279	Pinehurst
1965	Gary Player[1]	282	Bellerive	2000	Tiger Woods	272	Pebble Beach
1966	Bill Casper[1]	278	Olympic	2001	Retief Goosen	276	Southern Hills
1967	Jack Nicklaus	275	Baltusrol	2002	Tiger Woods	277	Bethpage Black
1968	Lee Trevino	275	Oak Hill	2003	Jim Furyk	272	Olympia Fields
1969	Orville Moody	281	Champions G.C.	2004	Retief Goosen	276	Shinnecock Hills

1. Winner in playoff. 2. Amateur. 3. In 1898, competition was extended to 72 holes. 4. In 1917, Jock Hutchison, with a 292, won an Open Patriotic Tournament for the benefit of the American Red Cross at Whitemarsh Valley Country Club. 5. In 1942, Ben Hogan, with a 271, won a Hale American National Open Tournament for the benefit of the Navy Relief Society and USO at Ridgemoor Country Club.

U.S. AMATEUR CHAMPIONS

1895	Charles B. Macdonald	1926	George Von Elm	1957	Hillman Robbins	1981	Nathaniel Crosby
1896–97	H. J. Whigham	1927–28	R. T. Jones, Jr.	1958	Charles Coe	1982	Jay Sigel
1898	Findlay S. Douglas	1929	H. R. Johnston	1959	Jack Nicklaus	1983	Jay Sigel
1899	H. M. Harriman	1930	R. T. Jones, Jr.	1960	Deane Beman	1984	Scott Verplank
1900–01	Walter J. Travis	1931	Francis Ouimet	1961	Jack Nicklaus	1985	Sam Randolph
1902	Louis N. James	1932	Ross Somerville	1962	Labron Harris, Jr.	1986	Buddy Alexander
1903	Walter J. Travis	1933	G. T. Dunlap, Jr.	1963	Deane Beman	1987	Bill Mayfair
1904–05	H. Chandler Egan	1934–35	Lawson Little	1964	Bill Campbell	1988	Eric Meeks
1906	Eben M. Byers	1936	John W. Fischer	1965[2]	Robert Murphy, Jr.	1989	Chris Patton
1907–08	Jerome D. Travers	1937	John Goodman	1966	Gary Cowan[1]	1990	Phil Mickelson
1909	Robert A. Gardner	1938	Willie Turnesa	1967	Bob Dickson	1991	Mitch Voges
1910	W. C. Fownes, Jr.	1939	Marvin H. Ward	1968	Bruce Fleisher	1992	Justin Leonard
1911	Harold H. Hilton	1940	R. D. Chapman	1969	Steven Melnyk	1993	John Harris
1912–13	Jerome D. Travers	1941	Marvin H. Ward	1970	Lanny Wadkins	1994–96	Tiger Woods
1914	Francis Ouimet	1946	Ted Bishop	1971	Gary Cowan	1997	Matthew Kuchar
1915	Robert A. Gardner	1947	Robert Riegel	1972	Vinny Giles 3d	1998	Hank Kuehne
1916	Charles Evans, Jr.	1948	Willie Turnesa	1973[3]	Craig Stadler	1999	David Gossett
1919	S. D. Herron	1949	Charles Coe	1974	Jerry Pate	2000	Jeff Quinney
1920	Charles Evans, Jr.	1950	Sam Urzetta	1975	Fred Ridley	2001	Bubba Dickerson
1921	Jesse P. Guilford	1951	Billy Maxwell	1976	Bill Sander	2002	Ricky Barnes
1922	Jess W. Sweetser	1952	Jack Westland	1977	John Fought	2003	Nick Flanagan
1923	Max R. Marston	1953	Gene Littler	1978	John Cook	2004	Ryan Moore
1924–25	R. T. Jones, Jr.	1954	Arnold Palmer	1979	Mark O'Meara		
		1955–56	Harvie Ward	1980	Hal Sutton		

1. Winner in playoff. 2. Tourney switched to medal play through 1972. 3. Return to match play.

U.S. PGA CHAMPIONS

Year	Winner	Year	Winner	Year	Winner	Year	Winner
1916	Jim Barnes	1945	Byron Nelson	1965	Dave Marr	1985	Hubert Green
1919	Jim Barnes	1946	Ben Hogan	1966	Al Geiberger	1986	Bob Tway
1920	Jock Hutchison	1947	Jim Ferrier	1967	Don January[1]	1987	Larry Nelson
1921	Walter Hagen	1948	Ben Hogan	1968	Julius Boros	1988	Jeff Sluman
1922–23	Gene Sarazen	1949	Sam Snead	1969	Ray Floyd	1989	Payne Stewart
1924–27	Walter Hagen	1950	Chandler Harper	1970	Dave Stockton	1990	Wayne Grady
1928–29	Leo Diegel	1951	Sam Snead	1971	Jack Nicklaus	1991	John Daly
1930	Tommy Armour	1952	Jim Turnesa	1972	Gary Player	1992	Nick Price
1931	Tom Creavy	1953	Walter Burkemo	1973	Jack Nicklaus	1993	Paul Azinger[1]
1932	Olin Dutra	1954	Chick Harbert	1974	Lee Trevino	1994	Nick Price
1933	Gene Sarazen	1955	Doug Ford	1975	Jack Nicklaus	1995	Steve Elkington
1934	Paul Runyan	1956	Jack Burke, Jr.	1976	Dave Stockton	1996	Mark Brooks[1]
1935	Johnny Revolta	1957	Lionel Hebert	1977	Lanny Wadkins[1]	1997	Davis Love III
1936–37	Denny Shute	1958[2]	Dow Finsterwald	1978	John Mahaffey	1998	Vijay Singh
1938	Paul Runyan	1959	Bob Rosburg	1979	David Graham[1]	1999–	
1939	Henry Picard	1960	Jay Hebert	1980	Jack Nicklaus	2000	Tiger Woods
1940	Byron Nelson	1961	Jerry Barber[1]	1981	Larry Nelson	2001	David Toms
1941	Victor Ghezzi	1962	Gary Player	1982	Ray Floyd	2002	Rich Beem
1942	Sam Snead	1963	Jack Nicklaus	1983	Hal Sutton	2003	Shaun Micheel
1944	Bob Hamilton	1964	Bobby Nichols	1984	Lee Trevino	2004	Vijay Singh

1. Winner in playoff. 2. Switched to medal play.

U.S. WOMEN'S AMATEUR CHAMPIONS

Year	Winner	Year	Winner	Year	Winner	Year	Winner
1916	Alexa Stirling	1947	Louise Suggs	1967	Lou Dill	1987	Kay Cockerill
1919–20	Alexa Stirling	1948	Grace Lenczyk	1968	JoAnne G. Carner	1988	Pearl Sinn
1921	Marion Hollins	1949	Mrs. D. G. Porter	1969	Catherine LaCoste	1989	Vicki Goetze
1922	Glenna Collett	1950	Beverly Hanson	1970	Martha Wilkinson	1990	Pat Hurst
1923	Edith Cummings	1951	Dorothy Kirby	1971	Laura Baugh	1991	Amy Fruhwirth
1924	Dorothy Campbell Hurd	1952	Jacqueline Pung	1972	Mary Ann Budke	1992	Vicki Goetze
		1953	Mary Lena Faulk	1973	Carol Semple	1993	Jill McGill
1925	Glenna Collett	1954	Barbara Romack	1974	Cynthia Hill	1994	Wendy Ward
1926	Helen Stetson	1955	Patricia Lesser	1975	Beth Daniel	1995	Kelli Kuehne
1927	Mrs. M. B. Horn	1956	Marlene Stewart	1976	Donna Horton	1996	Kelli Kuehne
1928–30	Glenna Collett	1957	JoAnne Gunderson	1977	Beth Daniel	1997	Silvia Cavalleri
1931	Helen Hicks	1958	Anne Quast	1978	Cathy Sherk	1998	Grace Park
1932–34	Virginia Van Wie	1959	Barbara McIntire	1979	Carolyn Hill	1999	Dorothy Delasin
1935	Glenna Collett Vare	1960	JoAnne Gunderson	1980	Juli Inkster	2000	Marcy Newton
1936	Pamela Barton	1961	Anne Quast Decker	1981	Juli Inkster	2001	Meredith Duncan
1937	Mrs. J. A. Page, Jr.	1962	JoAnne Gunderson	1982	Juli Inkster	2002	Becky Lucidi
1938	Patty Berg	1963	Anne Quast Welts	1983	Joanne Pacillo	2003	Virada Nirapath-pongporn
1939–40	Betty Jameson	1964	Barbara McIntire	1984	Deb Richard		
1941	Mrs. Frank Newell	1965	Jean Ashley	1985	Michiko Hattori	2004	Jane Park
1946	Mildred Zaharias	1966	JoAnne Gunderson	1986	Kay Cockerill		

U.S. WOMEN'S OPEN CHAMPIONS

Year	Winner	Score	Year	Winner	Score	Year	Winner	Score
1946	Patty Berg (match play)	—	1965	Carol Mann	290	1985	Kathy Baker	280
			1966	Sandra Spuzich	297	1986	Jane Geddes[1]	287
1947	Betty Jameson	295	1967	Catherine LaCoste[2]	294	1987	Laura Davies[1]	285
1948	Mildred D. Zaharias	300	1968	Susie Berning	289	1988	Liselotte Neumann	277
1949	Louise Suggs	291	1969	Donna Caponi	294	1989	Betsy King	278
1950	Mildred D. Zaharias	291	1970	Donna Caponi	287	1990	Betsy King	284
1951	Betsy Rawls	293	1971	JoAnne Carner	288	1991	Meg Mallon	283
1952	Louise Suggs	284	1972	Susie Berning	299	1992	Patty Sheehan	280
1953	Betsy Rawls[1]	302	1973	Susie Berning	290	1993	Lauri Merten	280
1954	Mildred D. Zaharias	291	1974	Sandra Haynie	295	1994	Patty Sheehan	277
1955	Fay Crocker	299	1975	Sandra Palmer	295	1995	Annika Sorenstam	278
1956	Katherine Cornelius[1]	302	1976	JoAnne Carner[1]	292	1996	Annika Sorenstam	272
1957	Betsy Rawls	299	1977	Hollis Stacy	292	1997	Alison Nicholas	274
1958	Mickey Wright	290	1978	Hollis Stacy	289	1998	Se Ri Pak	290
1959	Mickey Wright	287	1979	Jerilyn Britz	284	1999	Juli Inkster	272
1960	Betsy Rawls	291	1980	Amy Alcott	280	2000	Karrie Webb	282
1961	Mickey Wright	293	1981	Pat Bradley	279	2001	Karrie Webb	273
1962	Murle Lindstrom	301	1982	Janet Alex	283	2002	Juli Inkster	276
1963	Mary Mills	289	1983	Jan Stephenson	290	2003	Hilary Lunke[1]	353
1964	Mickey Wright[1]	290	1984	Hollis Stacy	290	2004	Meg Mallon	274

1. Winner in playoff. 2. Amateur.

BRITISH OPEN CHAMPIONS

(First tournament, held in 1860, was won by Willie Park, Sr.)

Year	Winner	Score	Year	Winner	Score	Year	Winner	Score
1920	George Duncan	303	1953	Ben Hogan	282	1980	Tom Watson	271
1921	Jock Hutchison	296	1954	Peter Thomson	283	1981	Bill Rogers	276
1922	Walter Hagen	300	1955	Peter Thomson	281	1982	Tom Watson	284
1923	A. G. Havers	295	1956	Peter Thomson	286	1983	Tom Watson	275
1924	Walter Hagen	301	1957	Bobby Locke	279	1984	Severiano Ballesteros	276
1925	Jim Barnes	300	1958	Peter Thomson	278	1985	Sandy Lyle	282
1926	R. T. Jones, Jr.	291	1959	Gary Player	284	1986	Greg Norman	280
1927	R. T. Jones, Jr.	285	1960	Kel Nagle	278	1987	Nick Faldo	279
1928	Walter Hagen	292	1961	Arnold Palmer	284	1988	Seve Ballesteros	273
1929	Walter Hagen	292	1962	Arnold Palmer	276	1989	Mark Calcavecchia	275
1930	R. T. Jones, Jr.	291	1963	Bob Charles	277	1990	Nick Faldo	270
1931	Tommy Armour	296	1964	Tony Lema	279	1991	Ian Baker-Finch	272
1932	Gene Sarazen	283	1965	Peter Thomson	285	1992	Nick Faldo	272
1933	Denny Shute	292	1966	Jack Nicklaus	282	1993	Greg Norman	267
1934	Henry Cotton	283	1967	Roberto de Vicenzo	278	1994	Nick Price	268
1935	A. Perry	283	1968	Gary Player	289	1995	John Daly	282
1936	A. H. Padgham	287	1969	Tony Jacklin	280	1996	Tom Lehman	271
1937	Henry Cotton	290	1970	Jack Nicklaus	283	1997	Justin Leonard	272
1938	R. A. Whitcombe	295	1971	Lee Trevino	278	1998	Mark O'Meara	280
1939	R. Burton	290	1972	Lee Trevino	278	1999	Paul Lawrie	290
1940	Sam Snead	290	1973	Tom Weiskopf	276	2000	Tiger Woods	269
1947	Fred Daly	294	1974	Gary Player	282	2001	David Duval	274
1948	Henry Cotton	283	1975	Tom Watson	279	2002	Ernie Els	278
1949	Bobby Locke	283	1976	Johnny Miller	279	2003	Ben Curtis	283
1950	Bobby Locke	279	1977	Tom Watson	268	2004	Todd Hamilton	274
1951	Max Faulkner	285	1978	Jack Nicklaus	281			
1952	Bobby Locke	287	1979	Severiano Ballesteros	283			

OTHER 2004 PGA TOUR WINNERS

(Through Oct. 3, 2004)

Tournament—winner	First place prize money
Mercedes Championship—Stuart Appleby	$1,060,000
Sony Open in Hawaii—Ernie Els	864,000
Bob Hope Chrysler Classic—Phil Mickelson	810,000
AT&T Pebble Beach National Pro-Am—Vijay Singh	954,000
Buick Invitational—John Daly	810,000
WGC-Accenture Match Play Championship—Tiger Woods	1,200,000
Ford Championship at Doral—Craig Parry	900,000
The Honda Classic—Todd Hamilton	900,000
THE PLAYERS Championship—Adam Scott	1,440,000
BellSouth Classic—Zach Johnson	810,000
MCI Heritage—Stewart Cink	864,000
Shell Houston Open—Vijay Singh	900,000
HP Classic of New Orleans—Vijay Singh	918,000
Wachovia Championship—Joey Sindelar	1,008,000
EDS Byron Nelson Championship—Sergio Garcia	1,044,000
Bank of America Colonial—Steve Flesch	954,000
Buick Classic—Sergio Garcia	945,000
FedEx St. Jude Classic—David Toms	846,000
The INTERNATIONAL—Rod Pampling	900,000
WGC-NEC Invitational—Stewart Cink	1,200,000
Deutsche Bank Championship—Vijay Singh	900,000
Bell Canadian Open—Vijay Singh	810,000
WGC-American Express Championship—Ernie Els	1,200,000
The Ryder Cup—Team Europe	

Source: www.pgatour.com.

OTHER 2004 LPGA TOUR WINNERS

(Through Oct. 3, 2004)

Tournament—winner	First place prize money
Welch's/Fry's Championship—Karen Stupples	$120,000
Safeway International—Annika Sorenstam	180,000
Kraft Nabisco Championship—Grace Park	240,000
The Office Depot—Annika Sorenstam	262,500
Takefuji Classic—Cristie Kerr	165,000
Chick-fil-A Charity Championship—Jennifer Rosales	240,000
Michelob ULTRA Open—Se Ri Pak	330,000
Franklin American Mortgage Championship—Lorena Ochoa	135,000
Sybase Classic—Sherri Steinhauer	187,500
Corning Classic—Annika Sorenstam	150,000
Kellogg-Keebler Classic—Karrie Webb	180,000
McDonald's LPGA Championship—Annika Sorenstam	240,000
ShopRite LPGA Classic—Cristie Kerr	195,000
Wegman's Rochester LPGA—Kim Saiki	225,000
Canadian Women's Open—Meg Mallon	195,000
Giant Eagle LPGA Classic—Moira Dunn	150,000
Evian Masters—Wendy Doolan	375,000
Women's British Open—Karen Stupples	290,880
Jamie Farr Classic—Meg Mallon	165,000
Wendy's Championship—Catriona Matthew	165,000
Wachovia LPGA Classic—Lorena Ochoa	150,000
John Q. Hammons Classic—Annika Sorenstam	150,000
Safeway Classic—Hee-Won Han	180,000
Longs Drugs Challenge—Christina Kim	150,000

Source: Ladies Professional Golf Association. Web: www.lpga.com.

Auto Racing

INDIANAPOLIS 500

Year	Winner	Car	Time	mph	Second place
1911	Ray Harroun	Marmon	6:42:08.000	74.590	Ralph Mulford
1912	Joe Dawson	National	6:21:06.000	78.720	Teddy Tetzloff
1913	Jules Goux	Peugeot	6:35:05.000	75.930	Spencer Wishart
1914	René Thomas	Delage	6:03:45.000	82.470	Arthur Duray
1915	Ralph DePalma	Mercedes	5:33:55.510	89.840	Dario Resta
1916[1]	Dario Resta	Peugeot	3:34:17.000	84.000	Wilbur D'Alene
1919	Howard Wilcox	Peugeot	5:40:42.870	88.050	Eddie Hearne
1920	Gaston Chevrolet	Monroe	5:38:32.000	88.620	René Thomas
1921	Tommy Milton	Frontenac	5:34:44.650	89.620	Roscoe Sarles
1922	Jimmy Murphy	Murphy Special	5:17:30.790	94.480	Harry Hartz
1923	Tommy Milton	H. C. S. Special	5:29:50.170	90.950	Harry Hartz
1924	L. L. Corum-Joe Boyer	Dusenberg Special	5:05:23.510	98.230	Earl Cooper
1925	Peter DePaolo	Dusenberg Special	4:56:39.450	101.130	Dave Lewis
1926[2]	Frank Lockhart	Miller Special	4:10:14.950	95.904	Harry Hartz
1927	George Souders	Dusenberg Special	5:07:33.080	97.540	Earl DeVore
1928	Louis Meyer	Miller Special	5:01:33.750	99.480	Lou Moore
1929	Ray Keech	Simplex Special	5:07:25.420	97.580	Louis Meyer
1930	Billy Arnold	Miller-Hartz Special	4:58:39.720	100.448	Shorty Cantlon
1931	Louis Schneider	Bowes Special	5:10:27.930	96.629	Fred Frame
1932	Fred Frame	Miller-Hartz Special	4:48:03.790	104.144	Howard Wilcox
1933	Louis Meyer	Tydol Special	4:48:00.750	104.162	Wilbur Shaw
1934	Bill Cummings	Boyle Products Special	4:46:05.200	104.863	Mauri Rose
1935	Kelly Petillo	Gilmore Special	4:42:22.710	106.240	Wilbur Shaw
1936	Louis Meyer	Ring Free Special	4:35:03.390	109.069	Ted Horn
1937	Wilbur Shaw	Shaw-Gilmore Special	4:24:07.800	113.580	Ralph Hepburn
1938	Floyd Roberts	Burd Piston Ring Special	4:15:58.400	117.200	Wilbur Shaw
1939	Wilbur Shaw	Boyle Special	4:20:47.390	115.035	Jimmy Snyder
1940	Wilbur Shaw	Boyle Special	4:22:31.170	114.277	Rex Mays
1941	Floyd Davis-Mauri Rose	Noc-Out Hose Clamp Special	4:20:36.240	115.117	Rex Mays
1946	George Robson	Thorne Engineering Special	4:21:26.710	114.820	Jimmy Jackson
1947	Mauri Rose	Blue Crown Special	4:17:52.170	116.338	Bill Holland
1948	Mauri Rose	Blue Crown Special	4:10:23.330	119.814	Bill Holland
1949	Bill Holland	Blue Crown Special	4:07:15.970	121.327	Johnny Parsons
1950[3]	Johnnie Parsons	Wynn's Friction Proof Special	2:46:55.970	124.002	Bill Holland
1951	Lee Wallard	Belanger Special	3:57:38.050	126.244	Mike Nazaruk
1952	Troy Ruttman	Agajanian Special	3:52:41.880	128.922	Jim Rathmann
1953	Bill Vukovich	Fuel Injection Special	3:53:01.690	128.740	Art Cross
1954	Bill Vukovich	Fuel Injection Special	3:49:17.270	130.840	Jim Bryan
1955	Bob Sweikert	John Zink Special	3:53:59.130	128.209	Tony Bettenhausen
1956	Pat Flaherty	John Zink Special	3:53:28.840	128.490	Sam Hanks
1957	Sam Hanks	Belond Exhaust Special	3:41:14.250	135.601	Jim Rathmann
1958	Jimmy Bryan	Belond A-P Special	3:44:13.800	133.791	George Amick
1959	Rodger Ward	Leader Card 500 Roadster	3:40:49.200	135.857	Jim Rathmann
1960	Jim Rathmann	Ken-Paul Special	3:36:11.360	138.767	Rodger Ward
1961	A. J. Foyt	Bowes Special	3:35:37.490	139.130	Eddie Sachs
1962	Rodger Ward	Leader Card Special	3:33:50.330	140.293	Len Sutton
1963	Parnelli Jones	Agajanian Special	3:29:35.400	143.137	Jim Clark
1964	A. J. Foyt	Sheraton-Thompson Spl.	3:23:35.830	147.350	Rodger Ward
1965	Jim Clark	Lotus-Ford	3:19:05.340	150.686	Parnelli Jones
1966	Graham Hill	Red Ball Lola-Ford	3:27:52.530	144.317	Jim Clark
1967[4]	A. J. Foyt	Sheraton-Thompson Coyote-Ford	3:18:24.220	151.207	Al Unser
1968	Bobby Unser	Rislone Eagle-Offenhauser	3:16:13.760	152.882	Dan Gurney
1969	Mario Andretti	STP Hawk-Ford	3:11:14.710	156.867	Dan Gurney
1970	Al Unser	Johnny Lightning P. J. Colt-Ford	3:12:37.040	155.749	Mark Donohue
1971	Al Unser	Johnny Lightning P. J. Colt-Ford	3:10:11.560	157.735	Peter Revson
1972	Mark Donohue	Sunoco McLaren-Offenhauser	3:04:05.540	162.962	Al Unser
1973[5]	Gordon Johncock	STP Eagle-Offenhauser	2:05:26.590	159.036	Bill Vukovich, Jr.
1974	Johnny Rutherford	McLaren-Offenhauser	3:09:10.060	158.589	Bobby Unser
1975[6]	Bobby Unser	Jorgensen Eagle-Offenhauser	2:54:55.080	149.213	Johnny Rutherford
1976[7]	Johnny Rutherford	Hy-gain McLaren-Offenhauser	1:42:52.000	148.725	A. J. Foyt
1977	A. J. Foyt	Gilmore Coyote-Foyt	3:05:57.160	161.331	Tom Sneva
1978	Al Unser	1st Nat'l City Lola-Cosworth	3:05:54.990	161.363	Tom Sneva
1979	Rick Mears	Gould Penske-Cosworth	3:08:47.970	158.899	A. J. Foyt
1980	Johnny Rutherford	Pennzoil Chaparral-Cosworth	3:29:59.560	142.862	Tom Sneva
1981[8]	Bobby Unser	Norton Penske-Cosworth	3:35:41.780	139.029	Mario Andretti
1982	Gordon Johncock	STP Wildcat-Cosworth	3:05:09.140	162.084	Rick Mears
1983	Tom Sneva	Texaco Star March-Cosworth	3:05:03.066	162.117	Al Unser
1984	Rick Mears	Pennzoil March-Cosworth	3:03:21.660	163.612	Roberto Guerrero
1985	Danny Sullivan	Miller March-Cosworth	3:16:06.069	152.982	Mario Andretti
1986	Bobby Rahal	Budweiser March-Cosworth	2:55:43.480	170.722	Kevin Cogan

Year	Winner	Car	Time	mph	Second place
1987	Al Unser, Sr.	Cummins March-Cosworth	3:04:59.147	162.175	Roberto Guerrero
1988	Rick Mears	Pennzoil Penske P.C.17-Chevrolet	3:27:10.204	144.809	Emerson Fittipaldi
1989	Emerson Fittipaldi	Marlboro Penske-Cosworth	2:59:01.049	167.581	Al Unser, Jr.
1990	Arie Luyendyk	Domino's Pizza Lola-Cosworth	2:41:18.404	185.981	Bobby Rahal
1991	Rick Mears	Marlboro Penske-Cosworth	2:50:00.791	176.457	Michael Andretti
1992	Al Unser, Jr.	Valvoline-Chevrolet	3:43.05.148	134.477	Scott Goodyear
1993	Emerson Fittipaldi	Penske-Chevrolet	3:10:49.860	157.207	Arie Luyendyk
1994	Al Unser, Jr.	Penske-Mercedes	3:06:29.006	160.872	Jacques Villeneuve
1995	Jacques Villeneuve	Reynard-Ford	3:15:17.561	153.616	Christian Fittipaldi
1996	Buddy Lazier	Reynard-Ford	3:22:45.753	147.956	Davy Jones
1997	Arie Luyendyk	G Force-Aurora	3:25:43.388	145.827	Scott Goodyear
1998	Eddie Cheever	Dallara-Aurora	3:26:40.524	145.155	Buddy Lazier
1999	Kenny Brack	Dallara-Aurora-Goodyear	3:15:51.182	153.176	Jeff Ward
2000	Juan Montoya	GForce-Aurora-Firestone	2:58:59.431	167.607	Buddy Lazier
2001	Helio Castroneves	Dallara-Aurora-Firestone	3:31:54.180	141.574	Gil de Ferran
2002	Helio Castroneves	Dallara-Chevrolet-Firestone	3:00:10.871	166.499	Paul Tracy
2003	Gil de Ferran	Panoz G Force-Toyota-Firestone	3:11:56.989	156.291	Helio Castroneves
2004[9]	Buddy Rice	Rahal-Letterman Argent/Pioneer	3:14:55.240	138.518	Tony Kanaan

1. 300 miles. 2. Race ended at 400 miles because of rain. 3. Race ended at 345 miles because of rain. 4. Race, postponed after 18 laps because of rain on May 30, was finished on May 31. 5. Race postponed May 28 and 29 was cut to 332.5 miles because of rain, May 30. 6. Race ended at 435 miles because of rain. 7. Race ended at 255 miles because of rain. 8. Andretti was awarded the victory the day after the race after Bobby Unser, whose car finished first, was penalized one lap and dropped from first place to second for passing other cars illegally under a yellow caution flag. Unser appealed the decision to the U.S. Auto Club but it was upheld. A panel ruled the penalty was too severe and instead fined Unser $40,000, but restored the victory to him. 9. Race ended with 20 laps to go because of rain.

2004 NASCAR NEXTEL CUP RACES

Date	Race	Raceway	Winner
Feb. 15	Daytona 500	Daytona International Speedway	Dale Earnhardt, Jr.
Feb. 22	Subway 400	North Carolina Speedway	Matt Kenseth
March 7	UAW-DaimlerChrysler 400	Las Vegas Motor Speedway	Matt Kenseth
March 14	Golden Corral 500	Atlanta Motor Speedway	Dale Earnhardt, Jr.
March 21	Carolina Dodge Dealers 400	Darlington Raceway	Jimmie Johnson
March 28	Food City 500	Bristol Motor Speedway	Kurt Busch
April 4	Samsung/RadioShack 500	Texas Motor Speedway	Elliott Sadler
April 18	Advance Auto Parts 500	Martinsville Speedway	Rusty Wallace
April 25	Aaron's 499	Talladega Superspeedway	Jeff Gordon
May 2	Auto Club 500	California Speedway	Jeff Gordon
May 15	Chevy American Revolution 400	Richmond International Raceway	Dale Earnhardt, Jr.
May 30	Coca-Cola 600	Lowe's Motor Speedway	Jimmie Johnson
June 6	MBNA 400 "A Salute to Heroes"	Dover International Speedway	Mark Martin
June 13	Pocono 500	Pocono Raceway	Jimmie Johnson
June 20	DHL 400	Michigan International Speedway	Ryan Newman
June 27	Dodge/Save Mart 350	Infineon Raceway	Jeff Gordon
July 3	Pepsi 400	Daytona International Speedway	Jeff Gordon
July 11	Tropicana 400	Chicagoland Speedway	Tony Stewart
July 25	Siemens 300	New Hampshire International Speedway	Kurt Busch
Aug. 1	Pennsylvania 500	Pocono Raceway	Jimmie Johnson
Aug. 8	Brickyard 400	Indianapolis Motor Speedway	Jeff Gordon
Aug. 15	Sirius at The Glen	Watkins Glen International	Tony Stewart
Aug. 22	GFS Marketplace 400	Michigan International Speedway	Greg Biffle
Aug. 28	Sharpie 500	Bristol Motor Speedway	Dale Earnhardt, Jr.
Sept. 5	Pop Secret 500	California Speedway	Elliott Sadler
Sept. 11	Chevy Rock and Roll 400	Richmond International Raceway	Jeremy Mayfield
Sept. 19	Sylvania 300	New Hampshire International Speedway	Kurt Busch
Sept. 26	MBNA America 400	Dover International Speedway	Ryan Newman
Oct. 3	EA Sports 500	Talladega Superspeedway	Dale Earnhardt, Jr.
Oct. 10	Banquet 400	Kansas Speedway	Joe Nemechek

NASCAR NEXTEL CUP CHAMPIONS

1949	Red Byron	1964	Richard Petty	1981	Darrell Waltrip	1993	Dale Earnhardt
1950	Bill Rexford	1965	Ned Jarrett	1982	Darrell Waltrip	1994	Dale Earnhardt
1951	Herb Thomas	1966	David Pearson	1983	Bobby Allison	1995	Jeff Gordon
1952	Tim Flock	1967	Richard Petty	1984	Terry Labonte	1996	Terry Labonte
1953	Herb Thomas	1968–69	David Pearson	1985	Darrell Waltrip	1997–98	Jeff Gordon
1954	Lee Petty	1970	Bobby Isaac	1986	Dale Earnhardt	1999	Dale Jarrett
1955	Tim Flock	1971–72	Richard Petty	1987	Dale Earnhardt	2000	Bobby Labonte
1956–57	Buck Baker	1973	Benny Parsons	1988	Bill Elliott	2001	Jeff Gordon
1958–59	Lee Petty	1974–75	Richard Petty	1989	Rusty Wallace	2002	Tony Stewart
1960	Rex White	1976–78	Cale Yarborough	1990	Dale Earnhardt	2003	Matt Kenseth
1961	Ned Jarrett	1979	Richard Petty	1991	Dale Earnhardt	2004	Kurt Busch[1]
1962–63	Joe Weatherly	1980	Dale Earnhardt	1992	Alan Kulwicki		

1. As of Oct. 11, 2004. Six races left in season.

2004 NASCAR BUSCH SERIES POINT STANDINGS[1]

Driver	Pts	Winnings	Driver	Pts	Winnings
1. Martin Truex, Jr.	4,212	$932,820	11. David Stremme	3,092	712,000
2. Kyle Busch[2]	4,063	1,115,800	12. Kenny Wallace	3,089	608,325
3. Greg Biffle	3,732	857,770	13. Casey Atwood	3,027	609,700
4. Jason Leffler	3,661	832,530	14. Michael Waltrip	3,007	494,710
5. Ron Hornaday	3,542	908,115	15. Stacy Compton	2,987	680,385
6. David Green	3,524	889,450	16. Johnny Sauter	2,983	632,005
7. Jason Keller	3,492	886,800	17. Tim Fedewa	2,922	616,050
8. Mike Bliss	3,314	691,425	18. Robert Pressley	2,921	597,960
9. Ashton Lewis	3,135	643,745	19. Bobby Hamilton, Jr.	2,896	738,054
10. Kasey Kahne	3,119	594,411	20. Mike Wallace	2,890	738,905

1. As of Oct. 11, 2004. Six races left in season. 2. Rookie.

INDYCAR/CART/CHAMP CAR CHAMPIONS

1910	Ray Harroun	1933	Louis Meyer	1962	Rodger Ward	1986–87	Bobby Rahal
1911	Ralph Mulford	1934	Bill Cummings	1963–64	A. J. Foyt	1988	Danny Sullivan
1912	Ralph DePalma	1935	Kelly Petillo	1965–66	Mario Andretti	1989	Emerson Fittipaldi
1913	Earl Cooper	1936	Mauri Rose	1967	A. J. Foyt		
1914	Ralph DePalma	1937	Wilbur Shaw	1968	Bobby Unser	1990	Al Unser, Jr.
1915	Earl Cooper	1938	Floyd Roberts	1969	Mario Andretti	1991	Michael Andretti
1916	Dario Resta	1939	Wilbur Shaw	1970	Al Unser	1992	Bobby Rahal
1917	Earl Cooper	1940–41	Rex Mays	1971–72	Joe Leonard	1993	Nigel Mansell
1918	Ralph Mulford	1946–48	Ted Horn	1973	Roger McCluskey	1994	Al Unser, Jr.
1919	Howard Wilcox	1949	Johnnie Parsons	1974	Bobby Unser	1995	Jacques Villeneuve
1920	Gaston Chevrolet	1950	Henry Banks	1975	A. J. Foyt		
1921	Tommy Milton	1951	Tony Bettenhausen	1976	Gordon Johncock	1996	Jimmy Vasser
1922	James Murphy			1977–78	Tom Sneva	1997–98	Alessandro Zanardi
1923	Eddie Hearne	1952	Chuck Stevenson	1979	Rick Mears		
1924	James Murphy	1953	Sam Hanks		(CART), A. J.	1999	Juan Montoya
1925	Peter DePaolo	1954	Jimmy Bryan		Foyt (USAC)[1]	2000	Gil de Ferran
1926	Harry Hartz	1955	Bob Sweikert	1980	Johnny Rutherford	2001	Gil de Ferran
1927	Peter DePaolo	1956–57	Jimmy Bryan			2002	Cristiano da Matta
1928–29	Louis Meyer	1958	Tony Bettenhausen	1981–82	Rick Mears		
1930	Billy Arnold			1983	Al Unser	2003	Paul Tracy
1931	Louis Schneider	1959	Rodger Ward	1984	Mario Andretti	2004	Sebastien Bourdais[2]
1932	Bob Carey	1960–61	A. J. Foyt	1985	Al Unser		

NOTE: There have been three sanctioning bodies for the series: the Automobile Association of America (1909–1955), the U.S. Auto Club (1956–1979), and the Championship Auto Racing Team (CART), 1979–2003. Open Wheel Racing Series acquired CART in Dec. 2003. 1. Two separate series were held in 1979. 2. As of Oct. 11, 2004. Two races left in season.

2004 INDY RACING LEAGUE POINT STANDINGS

Driver	Pts	Driver	Pts	Driver	Pts
1. Tony Kannan	618	9. Bryan Herta	362	17. A. J. Foyt IV	232
2. Dan Wheldon	533	10. Scott Dixon	355	17. Mark Taylor	232
3. Buddy Rice	485	11. Darren Manning	323	19. Tomas Scheckter	230
4. Helio Castroneves	446	12. Alex Barron	310	20. Felipe Giaffone	214
5. Adrian Fernandez	445	13. Scott Sharp	282	21. Townsend Bell	193
6. Dario Franchitti	409	14. Kosuke Matsuura	280	22. Jaques Lazier	104
7. Sam Hornish, Jr.	387	15. Tora Takagi	263	23. Greg Ray	99
8. Vitor Meira	376	16. Ed Carpenter	245	24. Robbie Buhl	44

FORMULA 1/WORLD GRAND PRIX DRIVER CHAMPIONS

1950	Giuseppe Farina, Italy, Alfa Romeo	1966	Jack Brabham, Australia, Brabham-Repco
1951	Juan Fangio, Argentina, Alfa Romeo	1967	Denis Hulme, New Zealand, Brabham-Repco
1952	Alberto Ascari, Italy, Ferrari	1968	Graham Hill, England, Lotus-Ford
1953	Alberto Ascari, Italy, Ferrari	1969	Jackie Stewart, Scotland, Matra-Ford
1954	Juan Fangio, Argentina, Maserati, Mercedes-Benz	1970	Jochen Rindt, Austria, Lotus-Ford
1955	Juan Fangio, Argentina, Mercedes-Benz	1971	Jackie Stewart, Scotland, Tyrrell-Ford
1956	Juan Fangio, Argentina, Lancia-Ferrari	1972	Emerson Fittipaldi, Brazil, Lotus-Ford
1957	Juan Fangio, Argentina, Maserati	1973	Jackie Stewart, Scotland, Tyrrell-Ford
1958	Mike Hawthorn, England, Ferrari	1974	Emerson Fittipaldi, Brazil, McLaren-Ford
1959	Jack Brabham, Australia, Cooper	1975	Niki Lauda, Austria, Ferrari
1960	Jack Brabham, Australia, Cooper	1976	James Hunt, Britain, McLaren-Ford
1961	Phil Hill, United States, Ferrari	1977	Niki Lauda, Austria, Ferrari
1962	Graham Hill, England, BRM	1978	Mario Andretti, United States, Lotus
1963	Jim Clark, Scotland, Lotus-Ford	1979	Jody Scheckter, South Africa, Ferrari
1964	John Surtees, England, Ferrari	1980	Alan Jones, Australia, Williams-Ford
1965	Jim Clark, Scotland, Lotus-Ford	1981	Nelson Piquet, Brazil, Brabham-Ford

1982 Keke Rosberg, Finland, Williams-Ford	1994 Michael Schumacher, Germany, Benetton
1983 Nelson Piquet, Brazil. Brabham-BMW	1995 Michael Schumacher, Germany, Benetton Renault
1984 Niki Lauda, Austria, McLaren-Porsche	1996 Damon Hill, Britain, Williams
1985 Alain Prost, France, McLaren-Porsche	1997 Jacques Villeneuve, Canada, Williams-Renault
1986 Alain Prost, France, McLaren-Porsche	1998 Mika Hakkinen, Finland, McLaren-Mercedes
1987 Nelson Piquet, Brazil, Williams-Honda	1999 Mika Hakkinen, Finland, McLaren-Mercedes
1988 Aryton Senna, Brazil, McLaren-Honda	2000 Michael Schumacher, Germany, Ferrari
1989 Alain Prost, France, McLaren-Porsche	2001 Michael Schumacher, Germany, Ferrari
1990 Ayrton Senna, Brazil, McLaren-Honda	2002 Michael Schumacher, Germany, Ferrari
1991 Aryton Senna, Brazil, McLaren-Honda	2003 Michael Schumacher, Germany, Ferrari
1992 Nigel Mansell, Britain, Williams-Renault	2004 Michael Schumacher, Germany, Ferrari
1993 Alain Prost, France, Williams-Renault	

Bicycling

TOUR DE FRANCE–2004

(July 3–25, 2004)

	Team	Behind		Team	Behind
1. Lance Armstrong, United States	U.S. Postal-Berry Floor	([1])	6. Francisco Mancebo, Spain	Illes Balears-B. Santander	18:01
2. Andréas Klöden, Germany	T-Mobile	06:19	7. Georg Totschnig, Austria	Gerolsteiner	18:27
3. Ivan Basso, Italy	Team CSC	06:40	8. Carlos Sastre, Spain	Team CSC	19:51
4. Jan Ullrich, Germany	T-Mobile	08:50	9. Levi Leipheimer, United States	Rabobank	20:12
5. José Azevedo, Portugal	U.S. Postal-Berry Floor	14:30	10. Oscar Pereiro Sio, Spain	Phonak Hearing Systems	22:54

1. Completed course in 83 hours, 36 minutes, 2 seconds.

Marathons

BOSTON MARATHON

(April 19, 2004)

Men	Time	Women	Time
Timothy Cherigat, Kenya	2:10:37	Catherine Ndereba, Kenya	2:24:27
Wheelchair—Ernst Van Dyk, South Africa	1:18:27	Wheelchair—Cheri Blauwet, United States	1:39:53

OTHER 2004 MARATHONS

Berlin (Sept. 25–26, 2004)		Los Angeles (March 7, 2004)	
Men	**Time**	**Men**	**Time**
Felix Limo, Kenya	2:06:44	David Kirui, Kenya	2:13:41
Wheelchair—Thomas Gerlach, Denmark	1:33:49	Wheelchair—Joel Jeannot, France	1:27:08
Handbiker—Errol Marklein, Germany	1:17:02	**Women**	
Women		Tatyana Pozdnyakova, Ukraine	2:30:17
Yoko Shibui, Japan	2:19:41	Wheelchair—Cheri Blauwet, United States	1:54:02
Handbiker—Monique Vorst, Netherlands	1:24:43	**London (April 18, 2004)**	
Paris (April 4, 2004)		**Men**	**Time**
Men	**Time**	Rutto Evans, Kenya	2:06:18
Ambesa Tolosa, Ethiopia	2:08:56	Wheelchair—Saul Mendoza, Mexico	1:36:56
Wheelchair—Heinz Frei, Switzerland	1:37:43	**Women**	
Women		Margaret Okayo, Kenya	2:22:35
Salina Kosgei, Kenya	2:24:32	Wheelchair—Francesca Porcellato, Italy	2:04:59

Little League

LITTLE LEAGUE WORLD SERIES CHAMPIONS

Year	Champion	Runner-up	Score	Year	Champion	Runner-up	Score
1947	Williamsport, Pa.	Lock Haven, Pa.	16–7	1957	Monterrey, Mex.	LaMesa, Calif.	4–0
1948	Lock Haven, Pa.	St. Petersburg, Fla.	6–5	1958	Monterrey, Mex.	Kankakee, Ill.	10–1
1949	Hammontown, N.J.	Pensacola, Fla.	5–0	1959	Hamtramck, Mich.	Auburn, Calif.	12–0
1950	Houston, Tex.	Bridgeport, Conn.	2–1	1960	Levittown, Pa.	Ft. Worth, Tex.	5–0
1951	Stamford, Conn.	Austin, Tex.	3–0	1961	El Cajon, Calif.	El Campo, Tex.	4–2
1952	Norwalk, Conn.	Monongahela, Pa.	4–3	1962	San Jose, Calif.	Kankakee, Ill.	3–0
1953	Birmingham, Ala.	Schenectady, N.Y.	1–0	1963	Granada Hills, Calif.	Stratford, Conn.	2–1
1954	Schenectady, N.Y.	Colton, Calif.	7–5	1964	Staten Island, N.Y.	Monterrey, Mex.	4–0
1955	Morrisville, Pa.	Merchantville, N.J.	4–3	1965	Windsor Locks, Conn.	Stoney Creek, Can.	3–1
1956	Roswell, N.M.	Merchantville, N.J.	3–1	1966	Houston, Tex.	W. New York, N.J.	8–2

Year	Champion	Runner-up	Score	Year	Champion	Runner-up	Score
1967	West Tokyo, Japan	Chicago, Ill.	4–1	1990	Taipei, Taiwan	Shippensburg, Pa.	9–0
1968	Osaka, Japan	Richmond, Va.	1–0	1991	Tai-Chung, Taiwan	San Ramon Valley, Calif.	11–0
1969	Taipei, Taiwan	Santa Clara, Calif.	5–0				
1970	Wayne, N.J.	Campbell, Calif.	2–0	1992*	Long Beach, Calif.	Zamboanga, Phil.	6–0
1971	Tainan, Taiwan	Gary, Ind.	12–3	1993	Long Beach, Calif.	David Chiriqui, Pan.	3–2
1972	Taipei, Taiwan	Hammond, Ind.	6–0	1994	Maracaibo, Venezuela	Northridge, Calif.	4–3
1973	Tainan City, Taiwan	Tucson, Ariz.	12–0	1995	Tainan, Taiwan	Spring, Texas	17–3
1974	Kao Hsiung, Taiwan	El Cajon, Calif.	7–2	1996	Kao-Hsuing City, Taipei	Cranston, R.I.	13–3
1975	Lakewood, N.J.	Tampa, Fla.	4–3				
1976	Tokyo, Japan	Campbell, Calif.	10–3	1997	Guadalupe, Mexico	South Mission Viejo, Calif.	5–4
1977	Kao Hsiung, Taiwan	El Cajon, Calif.	7–2				
1978	Pin-Tung, Taiwan	Danville, Calif.	11–1	1998	Toms River, N.J.	Kashima, Japan	12–9
1979	Hsien, Taiwan	Campbell, Calif.	2–1	1999	Hirakata, Osaka, Japan	Phenix City, Ala.	5–0
1980	Hua Lian, Taiwan	Tampa, Fla.	4–3				
1981	Tai-Chung, Taiwan	Tampa, Fla.	4–2	2000	Maracaibo, Venezuela	Bellaire, Tex.	3–2
1982	Kirkland, Wash.	Hsien, Taiwan	6–0	2001	Tokyo Kitasuna, Tokyo, Japan	Apopka, Fla.	2–1
1983	Marietta, Ga.	Barahona, Dom. Rep.	3–1				
1984	Seoul, S. Korea	Altamonte Springs, Fla.	6–2	2002	Louisville, Ky.	Sendai, Japan	1–0
1985	Seoul, S. Korea	Mexicali, Mex.	7–1	2003	Musashi-Fuchu, Tokyo, Japan	East Boynton Beach, Fla.	10–1
1986	Tianan Park, Taiwan	Tucson, Ariz.	12–0				
1987	Hua Lian, Taiwan	Irvine, Calif.	21–1	2004	Pabao Little League, Willemstad, Curaçao	Conejo Valley East, Thousand Oaks, Calif.	5–2
1988	Tai-Chung, Taiwan	Pearl City, Haw.	10–0				
1989	Trumbull, Conn.	Kaohsiung, Taiwan	5–2				

* Long Beach declared a 6–0 winner after the international tournament committee determined that Zamboanga City had used players that were not within its city limits.

Baseball

The popular tradition that baseball was invented by Abner Doubleday at Cooperstown, N.Y., in 1839 has been enshrined in the Hall of Fame and National Museum of Baseball erected in that town, but research has proved that a game called "Base Ball" was played in this country and England before 1839. The first team baseball as we know it was played at the Elysian Fields, Hoboken, N.J., on June 19, 1846, between the Knickerbockers and the New York Nine. The next fifty years saw a gradual growth of baseball and an improvement of equipment and playing skill.

Historians have it that the first pitcher to throw a curve was William A. (Candy) Cummings in 1867. The Cincinnati Red Stockings were the first all-professional team, and in 1869 they played 64 games without a loss. The standard ball of the same size and weight, still the rule, was adopted in 1872.

The first catcher's mask was worn in 1875. The National League was organized in 1876. The first chest protector was worn in 1885. The three-strike rule was put on the books in 1887, and the four-ball ticket to first base was instituted in 1889. The pitching distance was lengthened to 60 feet 6 inches in 1893, and the rules have been modified only slightly since that time.

The American League, under the vigorous leadership of B. B. Johnson, became a major league in 1901. Judge Kenesaw Mountain Landis, by action of the two major leagues, became Commissioner of Baseball in 1921.

In Sept. 2004, Major League Baseball announced that the Montreal Expos would move to Washington, DC in time for the 2005 season.

MAJOR LEAGUE ALL-STAR GAME

Year	Date	Winning league (manager)	Runs	Losing league (manager)	Runs	Winning pitcher	Losing pitcher	Site	Paid attendance
1933	July 6	A.L. (Mack)	4	N.L. (McGraw)	2	Gomez	Hallahan	Chicago A.L.	47,595
1934	July 10	A.L. (Cronin)	9	N.L. (Terry)	7	Harder	Mungo	New York N.L.	48,363
1935	July 8	A.L. (Cochrane)	4	N.L. (Frisch)	1	Gomez	Walker	Cleveland A.L.	69,831
1936	July 7	N.L. (Grimm)	4	A.L. (McCarthy)	3	J. Dean	Grove	Boston N.L.	25,556
1937	July 7	A.L. (McCarthy)	8	N.L. (Terry)	3	Gomez	J. Dean	Washington A.L.	31,391
1938	July 6	N.L. (Terry)	4	A.L. (McCarthy)	1	Vander Meer	Gomez	Cincinnati N.L.	27,067
1939	July 11	A.L. (McCarthy)	3	N.L. (Hartnett)	1	Bridges	Lee	New York A.L.	62,892
1940	July 9	N.L. (McKechnie)	4	A.L. (Cronin)	0	Derringer	Ruffing	St. Louis N.L.	32,373
1941	July 8	A.L. (Baker)	7	N.L. (McKechnie)	5	E. Smith	Passeau	Detroit A.L.	54,674
1942	July 6	A.L. (McCarthy)	3	N.L. (Durocher)	1	Chandler	Cooper	New York N.L.	34,178
1943	July 13	A.L. (McCarthy)	5	N.L. (Southworth)	3	Leonard	Cooper	Philadelphia A.L.	31,938
1944	July 11	N.L. (Southworth)	7	A.L. (McCarthy)	1	Raffensberger	Hughson	Pittsburgh N.L.	29,589
1946	July 9	A.L. (O'Neill)	12	N.L. (Grimm)	0	Feller	Passeau	Boston A.L.	34,906
1947	July 8	A.L. (Cronin)	2	N.L. (Dyer)	1	Shea	Sain	Chicago N.L.	41,123
1948	July 13	A.L. (Harris)	5	N.L. (Durocher)	2	Raschi	Schmitz	St. Louis A.L.	34,009
1949	July 12	A.L. (Boudreau)	11	N.L. (Southworth)	7	Trucks	Newcombe	Brooklyn N.L.	32,577
1950	July 11	N.L. (Shotton)	4	A.L. (Stengel)	3[1]	Blackwell	Gray	Chicago A.L.	46,127
1951	July 10	N.L. (Sawyer)	8	A.L. (Stengel)	3	Maglie	Lopat	Detroit A.L.	52,075
1952	July 8	N.L. (Durocher)	3	A.L. (Stengel)	2[2]	Rush	Lemon	Philadelphia N.L.	32,785
1953	July 14	N.L. (Dressen)	5	A.L. (Stengel)	1	Spahn	Reynolds	Cincinnati N.L.	30,846
1954	July 13	A.L. (Stengel)	11	N.L. (Alston)	9	Stone	Conley	Cleveland A.L.	68,751

Year	Date	Winning league (manager)	Runs	Losing league (manager)	Runs	Winning pitcher	Losing pitcher	Site	Paid attendance
1955	July 12	N.L. (Durocher)	6	A.L. (Lopez)	5[3]	Conley	Sullivan	Milwaukee N.L.	45,643
1956	July 10	N.L. (Alston)	7	A.L. (Stengel)	3	Friend	Pierce	Washington A.L.	28,843
1957	July 9	A.L. (Stengel)	6	N.L. (Alston)	5	Bunning	Simmons	St. Louis N.L.	30,693
1958	July 8	A.L. (Stengel)	4	N.L. (Haney)	3	Wynn	Friend	Baltimore A.L.	48,829
1959[4]	July 7	N.L. (Haney)	5	A.L. (Stengel)	4	Antonelli	Ford	Pittsburgh N.L.	35,277
	Aug. 3	A.L. (Stengel)	5	N.L. (Haney)	3	Walker	Drysdale	Los Angeles N.L.	55,105
1960[4]	July 11	N.L. (Alston)	5	A.L. (Lopez)	3	Friend	Monbouquette	Kansas City A.L.	30,619
	July 13	N.L. (Alston)	6	A.L. (Lopez)	0	Law	Ford	New York A.L.	38,362
1961[4]	July 11	N.L. (Murtaugh)	5	A.L. (Richards)	4[5]	Miller	Wilhelm	San Francisco N.L.	44,115
	July 31	N.L. (Murtaugh)	1	A.L. (Richards)	1[6]	—	—	Boston A.L.	31,851
1962[4]	July 10	N.L. (Hutchinson)	3	A.L. (Houk)	1	Marichal	Pascual	Washington A.L.	45,480
	July 30	A.L. (Houk)	9	N.L. (Hutchinson)	4	Herbert	Mahaffey	Chicago N.L.	38,359
1963	July 9	N.L. (Dark)	5	A.L. (Houk)	3	Jackson	Bunning	Cleveland A.L.	44,160
1964	July 7	N.L. (Alston)	7	A.L. (Lopez)	4	Marichal	Radatz	New York A.L.	50,850
1965	July 13	N.L. (March)	6	A.L. (Lopez)	5	Koufax	McDowell	Minnesota A.L.	46,706
1966	July 12	N.L. (Alston)	2	A.L. (Mele)	1[5]	Perry	Rickert	St. Louis N.L.	49,926
1967	July 11	N.L. (Alston)	2	A.L. (Bauer)	1[7]	Drysdale	Hunter	Anaheim A.L.	46,309
1968	July 9	N.L. (Schoendienst)	1	A.L. (Williams)	0	Drysdale	Tiant	Houston N.L.	48,321
1969	July 23	N.L. (Schoendienst)	9	A.L. (M. Smith)	3	Carlton	Stottlemyre	Washington A.L.	45,259
1970	July 14	N.L. (Hodges)	5	A.L. (Weaver)	4	Osteen	Wright	Cincinnati N.L.	51,838
1971	July 13	A.L. (Weaver)	6	N.L. (Anderson)	4	Blue	Ellis	Detroit A.L.	53,559
1972	July 25	N.L. (Murtaugh)	4	A.L. (Weaver)	3[5]	McGraw	McNally	Atlanta N.L.	53,107
1973	July 24	N.L. (Anderson)	7	A.L. (Williams)	1	Wise	Blyleven	Kansas City A.L.	40,849
1974	July 23	N.L. (Berra)	7	A.L. (Williams)	2	Brett	Tiant	Pittsburgh N.L.	50,706
1975	July 15	N.L. (Alston)	6	A.L. (Dark)	3	Matlack	Hunter	Milwaukee A.L.	51,540
1976	July 13	N.L. (Anderson)	7	A.L. (D. Johnson)	1	R. Jones	Fidrych	Philadelphia N.L.	63,974
1977	July 19	N.L. (Anderson)	7	A.L. (Martin)	5	Sutton	Palmer	New York A.L.	56,683
1978	July 11	N.L. (Lasorda)	7	A.L. (Martin)	3	Sutter	Gossage	San Diego N.L.	51,549
1979	July 17	N.L. (Lasorda)	7	A.L. (Lemon)	6	Sutter	Kern	Seattle A.L.	58,905
1980	July 8	N.L. (Tanner)	4	A.L. (Weaver)	2	Reuss	John	Los Angeles N.L.	56,088
1981[8]	Aug. 9	N.L. (Green)	5	A.L. (Frey)	4	Blue	Fingers	Cleveland A.L.	72,086
1982	July 13	N.L. (Lasorda)	4	A.L. (Martin)	1	Rogers	Eckersley	Montreal N.L.	59,057
1983	July 6	A.L. (Kuenn)	13	N.L. (Herzog)	3	Steib	Soto	Chicago A.L.	43,801
1984	July 11	N.L. (Owens)	3	A.L. (Altobelli)	1	Lea	Steib	San Francisco N.L.	57,756
1985	July 16	N.L. (Williams)	6	A.L. (Anderson)	1	Hoyt	Morris	Minneapolis A.L.	54,960
1986	July 15	A.L. (Howser)	3	N.L. (Herzog)	2	Clemens	Gooden	Houston N.L.	45,774
1987	July 14	N.L. (Johnson)	2	A.L. (McNamara)	0[9]	Smith	Howell	Oakland A.L.	49,671
1988	July 12	A.L. (Kelly)	2	N.L. (Herzog)	1	Viola	Gooden	Cincinnati, A.L.	55,837
1989	July 11	A.L. (LaRussa)	5	N.L. (Lasorda)	3	Ryan	Smoltz	California A.L.	64,036
1990	July 10	A.L. (LaRussa)	2	N.L. (Craig)	0	Saberhagen	Brantley	Chicago N.L.	39,071
1991	July 9	A.L. (LaRussa)	4	N.L. (Piniella)	2	Key	Martinez	Toronto A.L.	52,383
1992	July 14	A.L. (Kelly)	13	N.L. (Cox)	6	Brown	Glavine	San Diego N.L.	59,372
1993	July 13	A.L. (Gaston)	9	N.L. (Cox)	3	McDowell	Burkett	Baltimore A.L.	48,147
1994	July 12	N.L. (Fregosi)	8	A.L. (Gaston)	7[5]	Jones	Bere	Pittsburgh N.L.	59,568
1995	July 11	N.L. (Alou)	3	A.L. (Showalter)	2	Slocumb	Rogers	Texas A.L.	50,920
1996	July 9	N.L. (Cox)	6	A.L. (Hargrove)	0	Smoltz	Nagy	Philadelphia N.L.	62,670
1997	July 8	A.L. (Torre)	3	N.L. (Cox)	1	Johnson	Maddux	Cleveland A.L.	44,916
1998	July 7	A.L. (Hargrove)	13	N.L. (Leyland)	8	Colon	Urbina	Denver N.L.	51,267
1999	July 13	A.L. (Torre)	4	N.L. (Bochy)	1	P. Martinez	Schilling	Boston A.L.	34,187
2000	July 11	A.L. (Torre)	6	N.L. (Cox)	3	Baldwin	Leiter	Atlanta N.L.	51,323
2001	July 10	A.L. (Torre)	4	N.L. (Valentine)	1	Garcia	Park	Seattle A.L.	47,364
2002	July 9	7–7 tie after 11 innings. Bob Brenley, N.L. manager, Joe Torre, A.L. manager						Milwaukee N.L.	41,871
2003	July 15	A.L. (Scioscia)	7	N.L. (Baker)	6	Donnelly	Gagne	Chicago A.L.	47,609
2004	July 13	A.L. (Torre)	9	N.L. (McKeon)	4	Mulder	Clemens	Houston, N.L.	41,866

1. Fourteen innings. 2. Five innings, rain. 3. Twelve innings. 4. Two games. 5. Ten innings. 6. Called because of rain after nine innings. 7. Fifteen innings. 8. Game was originally scheduled for July 14, but was put off because of players' strike. 9. Thirteen innings. NOTE: No game in 1945.

NATIONAL BASEBALL HALL OF FAME
Cooperstown, N.Y.

Fielders

Member	Active years	Member	Active years	Member	Active years
Aaron, Henry (Hank)	1954–1976	Beckley, Jacob	1888–1907	Brouthers, Dennis	1879–1896
Anson, Adrian (Cap)	1876–1897	Bell, James (Cool Papa)[1]	1920–1947	Burkett, Jesse	1890–1905
Aparicio, Luis	1956–1973	Bench, John	1967–1983	Campanella, Roy	1948–1957
Appling, Lucius (Luke)	1930–1950	Berra, Lawrence (Yogi)	1946–1965	Carew, Rod	1967–1985
Ashburn, Richie	1948–1962	Bottomley, James	1922–1937	Carey, Max	1910–1929
Averill, H. Earl	1929–1941	Boudreau, Louis	1938–1952	Carter, Gary	1974–1991
Baker, J. Frank (Home Run)	1908–1922	Bresnahan, Roger	1897–1915	Cepeda, Orlando	1958–1974
Bancroft, David	1915–1930	Brett, George	1973–1993	Chance, Frank	1898–1914
Banks, Ernest	1953–1971	Brock, Lou	1961–1980	Charleston, Oscar[1]	1915–1954

Member	Active years	Member	Active years	Member	Active years
Clarke, Fred	1894–1915	Irvin, Monford (Monte)[1]	1939–1956	Puckett, Kirby	1984–1995
Clemente, Roberto	1955–1972	Jackson, Reggie	1967–1987	Reese, Harold (Pee Wee)	1940–1958
Cobb, Tyrus	1905–1928	Jackson, Travis	1922–1936	Rice, Edgar (Sam)	1915–1934
Cochrane, Gordon (Mickey)	1925–1937	Jennings, Hugh	1891–1918	Rizzuto, Phil	1941–1956
Collins, Edward	1906–1930	Johnson, William (Judy)[1]	1921–1937	Robinson, Brooks	1955–1977
Collins, James	1895–1908	Kaline, Albert W.	1953–1974	Robinson, Frank	1956–1976
Comiskey, Charles	1882–1894	Keeler, William (Wee Willie)	1892–1910	Robinson, Jack	1947–1956
Combs, Earle	1924–1935	Kell, George	1943–1957	Robinson, Wilbert	1886–1902
Connor, Roger	1880–1897	Kelley, Joseph	1891–1908	Roush, Edd	1913–1931
Crawford, Samuel	1899–1917	Kelly, George	1915–1932	Ruth, Babe	1914–1935
Cronin, Joseph	1926–1945	Kelly, Michael (King)	1878–1893	Schalk, Raymond	1912–1929
Cuyler, Hazen (Kiki)	1921–1938	Killebrew, Harmon	1954–1975	Schoendienst, Red	1945–1963
Dandridge, Ray[1]	1933–1953	Kiner, Ralph	1946–1955	Schmidt, Mike	1973–1989
Davis, George	1890–1909	Klein, Charles H. (Chuck)	1928–1944	Sewell, Joseph	1920–1933
Delahanty, Edward	1888–1903	Lajoie, Napoleon	1896–1916	Simmons, Al	1924–1944
Dickey, William	1928–1946	Lazzeri, Tony	1926–1939	Sisler, George	1915–1930
Dihigo, Martin[1]	1923–1945	Leonard, Walter (Buck)[1]	1933–1955	Slaughter, Enos	1938–1959
DiMaggio, Joseph	1936–1951	Lindstrom, Frederick	1924–1936	Smith, Ozzie	1978–1996
Doby, Larry	1947–1959	Lloyd, John Henry (Pop)[1]	1905–1931	Snider, Edwin D. (Duke)	1947–1964
Doerr, Bobby	1937–1951	Lombardi, Ernie	1932–1947	Speaker, Tristram	1907–1928
Duffy, Hugh	1888–1906	Mantle, Mickey	1951–1968	Stargell, Willie	1962–1982
Ewing, William	1880–1897	Manush, Henry (Heinie)	1923–1939	Stearnes, Norman (Turkey)	1921–1942
Evers, John	1902–1919	Maranville, Walter (Rabbit)	1912–1935	Terry, William	1923–1936
Ferrell, Rick	1929–1947	Matthews, Edwin	1952–1968	Thompson, Samuel	1885–1906
Fisk, Carlton	1969–1991	Mays, Willie	1951–1973	Tinker, Joseph	1902–1916
Flick, Elmer	1898–1910	Mazeroski, William Stanley (Maz)	1956–1972	Traynor, Harold (Pie)	1920–1937
Fox, Nellie	1947–1965	McCarthy, Thomas	1884–1896	Vaughan, Arky	1932–1948
Foxx, James	1925–1945	McCovey, Willie	1959–1980	Wagner, John (Honus)	1897–1917
Frisch, Frank	1919–1937	McGraw, John J.	1891–1906	Wallace, Roderick (Bobby)	1894–1918
Gehrig, H. Louis (Lou)	1923–1939	McPhee, John Alexander (Bid)	1882–1899	Waner, Lloyd	1927–1945
Gehringer, Charles	1924–1942			Waner, Paul	1926–1945
Gibson, Josh[1]	1929–1946	Medwick, Joseph (Ducky)	1932–1948	Ward, John (Monte)	1878–1894
Goslin, Leon (Goose)	1921–1938	Mize, John (The Big Cat)	1936–1953	Wells, Willie	1924–1949
Greenberg, Henry (Hank)	1933–1947	Molitor, Paul	1978–1998	Wheat, Zachariah	1909–1927
Hafey, Charles (Chick)	1924–1937	Morgan, Joe	1963–1984	Williams, Billy	1959–1976
Hamilton, William	1888–1901	Murray, Eddie	1977–1997	Williams, Theodore	1939–1960
Hartnett, Charles (Gabby)	1922–1941	Musial, Stanley	1941–1963	Wilson, Lewis R. (Hack)	1923–1934
Heilmann, Harry	1914–1932	O'Rourke, James	1876–1894	Winfield, David Mark	1973–1995
Herman, William	1931–1947	Ott, Melvin	1926–1947	Yastrzemski, Carl	1961–1983
Hooper, Harry	1909–1925	Perez, Tony	1964–1983	Youngs, Ross (Pep)	1917–1926
Hornsby, Rogers	1915–1937			Yount, Robin	1974–1993

1. Negro League player selected by special committee.

Pitchers

Alexander, Grover	1911–1930	Grove, Robert (Lefty)	1925–1941	Plank, Edward	1901–1917
Bender, Charles (Chief)	1903–1925	Haines, Jesse	1918–1937	Radbourn, Charles (Hoss)	1880–1891
Brown, Mordecai (3-Finger)	1903–1916	Hoyt, Waite	1918–1938	Rixey, Eppa	1912–1933
Bunning, Jim	1955–1971	Hubbell, Carl	1928–1943	Roberts, Robert (Robin)	1948–1966
Carlton, Steve	1965–1988	Hunter, Jim (Catfish)	1965–1979	Rogan, Wilber	1920–1938
Chesbro, John	1899–1909	Jenkins, Ferguson	1965–1983	Ruffing, Charles (Red)	1924–1947
Clarkson, John	1882–1894	Johnson, Walter	1907–1927	Rusie, Amos	1889–1901
Coveleski, Stanley	1912–1928	Joss, Adrian	1902–1910	Ryan, Nolan, Jr.	1966–1993
Day, Leon	1935–1955	Keefe, Timothy	1880–1893	Seaver, Tom	1967–1986
Dean, Jerome (Dizzy)	1930–1947	Koufax, Sanford (Sandy)	1955–1966	Smith, Hilton Lee	1932–1948
Drysdale, Don	1956–1969	Lemon, Robert	1946–1958	Spahn, Warren	1942–1965
Eckersley, Dennis	1975–1998	Lyons, Theodore	1923–1946	Sutton, Don	1966–1988
Faber, Urban (Red)	1914–1933	Marichal, Juan	1960–1975	Vance, Arthur (Dazzy)	1915–1935
Feller, Robert	1936–1956	Marquard, Richard (Rube)	1908–1924	Waddell, Rube	1897–1910
Fingers, Rollie	1968–1985	Mathewson, Christopher	1900–1916	Walsh, Edward	1904–1917
Ford, Edward (Whitey)	1950–1967	McGinnity, Joseph	1899–1908	Welch, Michael (Mickey)	1880–1892
Foster, Andrew (Rube)	1897–1926	Newhouser, Hal	1939–1955	Wilhelm, Hoyt	1952–1972
Foster, Bill	1923–1937	Nichols, Charles (Kid)	1890–1906	Williams, Joseph	1910–1932
Galvin, James (Pud)	1876–1892	Niekro, Phil	1959–1987	Willis, Vic	1898–1910
Gibson, Bob	1959–1975	Paige, Leroy (Satchel)[1]	1926–1965	Wynn, Early	1939–1963
Gomez, Vernon (Lefty)	1930–1943	Palmer, Jim	1965–1984	Young, Denton (Cy)	1890–1911
Griffith, Clark	1891–1914	Pennock, Herbert	1912–1934		
Grimes, Burleigh	1916–1934	Perry, Gaylord	1962–1983		

1. Negro League player selected by special committee.

Officials and Others

Alston, Walter[1]	Comiskey, Charles[1]	Hanlon, Ned[3]	Lasorda, Tommy[1]	Selee, Frank G.[1]
Anderson, Sparky[1]	Conlan, John[3]	Harridge, William[3]	Lopez, Alfonso R.[7]	Spalding, Albert G.[2]
Barlick, Al[2]	Connolly, Thomas[2]	Harris, Stanley R.[7]	Mack, Connie[1, 3]	Stengel, Charles D.[7]
Barrow, Edward[1, 3]	Cummings, William A.[6]	Hubbard, R. Calvin[2]	MacPhail, Lee, Jr.[3]	Veeck, Bill[3]
Bulkeley, Morgan G.[3]	Durocher, Leo[1]	Huggins, Miller J.[1]	MacPhail, Leland S.[3]	Weaver, Earl[1]
Cartwright, Alexander[3]	Evans, William G.[2, 3]	Hulbert, William[3]	McCarthy, Joseph V.[1]	Weiss, George M.[3]
Chadwick, Henry[4]	Foster, Rube[3]	Johnson, B. Bancroft[3]	McGowan, Bill[2]	Wright, George[6]
Chandler, A. B.[5]	Frick, Ford C.[3, 5]	Klem, William[2]	McKechnie, William B.[1]	Wright, Harry[1, 6]
Chylak, Nestor, Jr.[2]	Giles, Warren C.[3]	Landis, Kenesaw M.[5]	Rickey, W. Branch[1, 3]	Yawkey, Thomas[3]

1. Manager. 2. Umpire. 3. Executive. 4. Writer-statistician. 5. Commissioner. 6. Early player. 7. Player-manager.

RECORD OF WORLD SERIES GAMES
(through 2003)

Figures in parentheses for winning pitchers (WP) and losing pitchers (LP) indicate the game number in the series.

1903—Boston A.L. 5 (Jimmy Collins); Pittsburgh N.L. 3 (Fred Clarke). WP—Boston: Dinneen (2, 6, 8), Young (5, 7); Pittsburgh: Phillippe (1, 3, 4). LP—Boston: Young (1), Hughes (3), Dinneen (4); Pittsburgh: Leever (2, 6), Kennedy (5) Phillippe (7, 8).

1904—No series.

1905—New York N.L. 4 (John J. McGraw); Philadelphia A.L. 1 (Connie Mack). WP—New York: Mathewson (1, 3, 5); McGinnity (4); Phila.: Bender (2). LP—New York: McGinnity (2); Phila.: Plank (1, 4), Coakley (3), Bender (5).

1906—Chicago A.L. 4 (Fielder Jones); Chicago N.L. 2 (Frank Chance). WP—Chicago: A.L.: Altrock (1), Walsh (3, 5), White (6); Chicago: N.L.: Reulbach (2), Brown (4). LP—Chicago A.L.: White (3), Altrock. (4); Chicago: N.L.: Brown (1, 6), Pfeister (3, 5).

1907—Chicago N.L. 4 (Frank Chance); Detroit A.L. 0 (Hugh Jennings). First game tied 3–3, 12 innings. WP—Pfeister (2), Reulbach (3), Overall (4), Brown (5). LP—Mullin (2, 4), Siever (3), Donovan (4).

1908—Chicago N.L. 4 (Frank Chance); Detroit A.L. 1 (Hugh Jennings). WP—Chicago: Brown (1, 4), Overall (2, 5); Det.: Mullin (3). LP—Chicago: Pfeister (3); Det.: Summers (1, 4), Donovan (2, 5).

1909—Pittsburgh N.L. 4 (Fred Clarke); Detroit A.L. 3 (Hugh Jennings). WP—Pittsburgh: Adams (1, 5, 7), Maddox (3); Det.: Donovan (2), Mullin (4, 6). LP—Pittsburgh: Camnitz (2), Leifield (4), Willis (6); Det.: Mullin (1), Summers (3, 5), Donovan (7).

1910—Philadelphia A.L. 4 (Connie Mack); Chicago N.L. 1 (Frank Chance). WP—Phila.: Bender (1), Coombs (2, 3, 5); Chicago: Brown (4). LP—Phila.: Bender (4); Chicago: Overall (1), Brown (2, 5), McIntyre (3).

1911—Philadelphia A.L. 4 (Connie Mack); New York N.L. 2 (John J. McGraw). WP—Phila.: Plank (2), Coombs (3), Bender (4, 6); New York: Mathewson (1), Crandall (5). LP—Phila.: Bender (1), Plank (5); New York: Marquard (2), Mathewson (3, 4), Ames (6).

1912—Boston A.L. 4 (J. Garland Stahl); New York N.L. 3 (John J. McGraw). Second game tied, 6–6, 11 innings. WP—Boston: Wood (1, 4, 8), Bedient (5); New York: Marquard (3, 6), Tesreau (7). LP—Boston: O'Brien (3, 6), Wood (7); New York: Tesreau (1, 4), Mathewson (5, 8).

1913—Philadelphia A.L. 4 (Connie Mack); New York N.L. 1 (John J. McGraw). WP—Phila.: Bender (1, 4), Bush (3), Plank (5); New York: Mathewson (2); LP—Phila.: Plank (2); New York: Marquard (1), Tesreau (3), Demaree (4), Mathewson (5).

1914—Boston N.L. 4 (George Stallings); Philadelphia A.L. 0 (Connie Mack). WP—Rudolph (1, 4), James (2, 3). LP—Bender (1), Plank (2), Bush (3), Shawkey (4).

1915—Boston A.L. 4 (Bill Carrigan); Philadelphia N.L. 1 (Pat Moran). WP—Boston: Foster (2, 5), Leonard (3), Shore (4); Phila.: Alexander (1). LP—Boston: Shore (1); Phila.: Mayer (2), Alexander (3), Chalmers (4), Rixey (5).

1916—Boston A.L. 4 (Bill Carrigan); Brooklyn N.L. 1 (Wilbert Robinson). WP—Boston: Shore (1; 5), Ruth (2), Leonard (4),

Brooklyn: Coombs (3). LP—Boston: Mays (3); Brooklyn: Marquard (1, 4), Smith (2), Pfeffer (5).

1917—Chicago A.L. 4 (Clarence Rowland); New York N.L. 2 (John J. McGraw). WP—Chicago: Cicotte (1), Faber (2, 5, 6); New York: Benton (3), Schupp (4), LP—Chicago: Cicotte (3), Faber (4); New York: Sallee (1, 5), Anderson (2), Benton (6).

1918—Boston A.L. 4 (Ed Barrow); Chicago N.L. 2 (Fred Mitchell). WP—Boston: Ruth (1, 4), Mays (3, 6); Chicago: Tyler (2), Vaughn (5). LP—Boston: Bush (2), Jones (5); Chicago: Vaughn (1, 3), Douglas (4), Tyler (6).

1919—Cincinnati N.L. 5 (Pat Moran); Chicago A.L. 3 (William Gleason). WP—Cincinnati: Ruether (1), Sallee (2), Ring (4), Eller (5, 8); Chicago: Kerr (3, 6), Cicotte (7). LP—Cincinnati: Fisher (3), Ring (6), Sallee (7); Chicago: Cicotte (1, 4), Williams (2, 5, 8).

1920—Cleveland A.L. 5 (Tris Speaker); Brooklyn N.L. 2 (Wilbert Robinson). WP—Cleve.: Coveleski (1, 4, 7), Bagby (5), Mails (6); Brooklyn: Grimes (2), Smith (3). LP—Cleve.: Bagby (2), Caldwell (3). Brooklyn: Marquard (1), Cadore (4), Grimes (5, 7), Smith (6).

1921—New York N.L. 5 (John J. McGraw); New York A.L. 3 (Miller Huggins). WP—New York N.L.: Barnes (3, 6), Douglas (4, 7), Nehf (8); New York A.L.: Mays (1), Hoyt (2, 5). LP—New York N.L.: Nehf (2, 5), Douglas (1). New York A.L.: Quinn (3), Mays (4, 7), Shawkey (6), Hoyt (8).

1922—New York N.L. 4 (John J. McGraw); New York A.L. 0 (Miller Huggins). Second game tied 3–3, 10 innings. WP—Ryan (1), Scott (3), McQuillan (4), Nehf (5); LP—Bush (1, 5), Hoyt (3), Mays (4).

1923—New York A.L. 4 (Miller Huggins); New York N.L. 2 (John J. McGraw). WP—New York A.L.: Pennock (2, 6), Shawkey (4), Bush (5); New York N.L.: Ryan (1), Nehf (3). LP—New York A.L.: Bush (1), Jones (3); New York N.L.: McQuillan (2), Scott (4), Bentley (5), Nehf (6).

1924—Washington A.L. 4 (Bucky Harris); New York N.L. 3 (John J. McGraw). WP—Washington: Zachary (2, 6), Mogridge (4), Johnson (7); New York: Nehf (1), McQuillan (3), Bentley (5). LP—Washington: Johnson (1, 5), Marberry (3); New York: Bentley (2, 7), Barnes (4), Nehf (6).

1925—Pittsburgh N.L. 4 (Bill McKechnie); Washington A.L. 3 (Bucky Harris). WP—Pittsburgh: Aldridge (2, 5), Kremer (6, 7); Washington: Johnson (1, 4), Ferguson (3). LP—Pittsburgh: Meadows (1), Kremer (3), Yde (4); Washington: Coveleski (2, 5), Ferguson (6), Johnson (7).

1926—St. Louis N.L. 4 (Rogers Hornsby); New York A.L. 3 (Miller Huggins). WP—St. Louis: Alexander (2, 6), Haines (3, 7); New York: Pennock (1, 5), Hoyt (4). LP—St. Louis: Sherdel (1, 5), Reinhart (4); New York: Shocker (2), Ruether (3), Shawkey (6), Hoyt (7).

1927—New York A.L. 4 (Miller Huggins); Pittsburgh N.L. 0 (Donie Bush). WP—Hoyt (1), Pipgras (2), Pennock (3), Moore (4). LP—Kremer (1), Aldridge (2), Meadows (3), Miljus (4).

1928—New York A.L. 4 (Miller Huggins); St. Louis N.L. 0 (Bill McKechnie). WP—Hoyt (1, 4), Pipgras (2), Zachary (3).

LP—Sherdel (1, 4), Alexander (2), Haines (3).

1929—Philadelphia A.L. 4 (Connie Mack); Chicago N.L. 1 (Joe McCarthy). WP—Phila.: Ehmke (1), Earnshaw (2), Rommel (4), Walberg (5); Chicago: Bush (3). LP—Phila.: Earnshaw (3) Chicago: Root (1), Malone (2, 5), Blake (4).

1930—Philadelphia A.L. 4 (Connie Mack); St. Louis N.L. 2 (Gabby Street). WP—Phila.: Grove (1, 5), Earnshaw (2, 6); St. Louis: Hallahan (3), Haines (4). LP—Phila.: Walberg (3), Grove (4); St. Louis: Grimes (1, 5), Rhem (2), Hallahan (6).

1931—St. Louis N.L. 4 (Gabby Street); Philadelphia A.L. 3 (Connie Mack). WP—St. Louis: Hallahan (2, 5), Grimes (3, 7); Phila.: Grove (1, 6), Earnshaw (4); St. Louis: Derringer (1, 6), Johnson (4); Phila.: Earnshaw (2, 7), Grove (3), Hoyt (5).

1932—New York A.L. (Joe McCarthy); Chicago N.L. 0 (Charles Grimm). WP—Ruffing (1), Gomez (2), Pipgras (3), Moore (4). LP—Bush (1), Warneke (2), Root (3), May (4).

1933—New York N.L. 4 (Bill Terry); Washington A.L. 1 (Joe Cronin.). WP—New York: Hubbell (1, 4), Schumacher (2), Luque (5); Washington: Whitehill (3). LP—New York: Fitzsimmons (3); Washington: Stewart (1), Crowder (2), Weaver (4), Russell (5).

1934—St. Louis N.L. 4 (Frank Frisch); Detroit A.L. 3 (Mickey Cochrane). WP—St. Louis: J. Dean (1, 7), P. Dean (3, 6); Det.: Rowe (2), Auker (4), Bridges (5). LP—St. Louis: W. Walker (2, 4), J. Dean (5); Det.: Crowder (1), Bridges (3), Rowe (6), Auker (7).

1935—Detroit A.L. 4 (Mickey Cochrane); Chicago N.L. 2 (Charles Grimm). WP—Det.: Bridges (2, 6), Rowe (3), Crowder (4); Chicago: Warneke (1, 5); LP—Det.: Rowe (1, 5), Chicago: Root (2), French (3, 6), Carleton (4).

1936—New York A.L. 4 (Joe McCarthy); New York N.L. 2 (Bill Terry). WP—New York A.L.: Gomez (2, 6), Hadley (3), Pearson (4); New York N.L.: Hubbell (1), Schumacher (5); LP—New York A.L.: Ruffing (1), Malone (5); New York N.L.: Schumacher (2), Fitzsimmons (3, 6), Hubbell (4).

1937—New York A.L. 4 (Joe McCarthy); New York N.L. 1 (Bill Terry). WP—New York A.L.: Gomez (1, 5), Ruffing (2), Pearson (3); New York N.L.: Hubbell (4). LP—New York A.L.: Hadley (4); New York N.L.: Hubbell (1), Melton (2, 5), Schumacher (3).

1938—New York A.L. 4 (Joe McCarthy); Chicago N.L. 0 (Gabby Hartnett). WP—Ruffing (1, 4), Gomez (2), Pearson (3) LP—Lee (1, 4), Dean (2), Bryant (3).

1939—New York A.L. 4 (Joe McCarthy); Cincinnati N.L. 0 (Bill McKechnie). WP—Ruffing (1), Pearson (2), Hadley (3), Murphy (4). LP—Derringer (1), Walters (2), Thompson (3).

1940—Cincinnati N.L. 4 (Bill McKechnie; Detroit A.L. 3 (Del Baker). WP—Cincinnati: Walters (2, 6), Derringer (4, 7); Det.: Newsom (1), Bridges (3). LP—Cincinnati: Derringer (1), Turner (3), Thompson (5); Det.: Rowe (2, 6), Trout (4), Newsom (7).

1941—New York A.L. 4 (Joe McCarthy); Brooklyn N.L. 1 (Leo Durocher). WP—New York: Ruffing (1), Russo (3), Murphy (4), Bonham (5); Bklyn: Wyatt (2). LP—New York: Chandler (2); Bklyn: Davis (1), Casey (3, 4), Wyatt (5).

1942—St. Louis N.L. 4 (Billy Southworth; New York A.L. 1 (Joe McCarthy). WP—St. Louis: Beazley (2, 5), White (3), Lanier (4); New York: Ruffing (1). LP—St. Louis: Cooper (1); New York: Bonham (2), Chandler (3), Donald (4), Ruffing (5).

1943—New York A.L. 4 (Joe McCarthy); St. Louis N.L. 1 (Billy Southworth). WP—New York: Chandler (1, 5), Borowy (3), Russo (4); St. Louis: Cooper (2). LP—New York: Bonham (2); St. Louis: Lanier (1), Brazle (3), Brecheen (4), Cooper (5).

1944—St. Louis N.L. 4 (Billy Southworth); St. Louis A.L. 2 (Luke Sewell). WP—St. Louis N.L.: Donnelly (2), Brecheen (4), Cooper (5), Lanier (6); St. Louis A.L.: Galehouse (1), Kramer (3). LP—St. Louis N.L.: Cooper (1), Wilks (3); St. Louis A.L.: Muncrief (2), Jakucki (4), Galehouse (5), Potter (6).

1945—Detroit A.L. 4 (Steve O'Neill); Chicago N.L. 3 (Charles Grimm). WP—Det.: Trucks (2), Trout (4), Newhouser (5, 7); Chicago: Borowy (1, 6), Passeau (3). LP—Det.: Newhouser

(1), Overmire (3), Trout (6); Chicago: Wyse (2), Prim (4), Borowy (5, 7).

1946—St. Louis N.L. 4 (Eddie Dyer); Boston A.L. 3 (Joe Cronin). WP—St. Louis: Brecheen (2, 6, 7), Munger (4); Boston: Johnson (1), Ferriss (3), Dobson (5). LP—St. Louis: Pollet (1), Dickson (3), Brazle (5); Boston: Harris (2, 6), Hughson (4), Klinger (7).

1947—New York A.L. 4 (Bucky Harris); Brooklyn N.L. 3 (Burt Shotton). WP—New York: Shea (1, 5), Reynolds (2), Page (7); Brooklyn: Casey (3, 4), Branca (6). LP—New York: Newsom (3), Bevens (4), Page (6); Brooklyn: Branca (1), Lombardi (2), Barney (5), Gregg (7).

1948—Cleveland A.L. 4 (Lou Boudreau); Boston N.L. 2 (Billy Southworth). WP—Cleve.: Lemon (2, 6), Bearden (3), Gromek (4); Boston: Sain (1), Spahn (5). LP—Cleve.: Feller (1, 5); Boston: Spahn (2), Bickford (3), Sain (4), Voiselle (6).

1949—New York A.L. 4 (Casey Stengel); Brooklyn N.L. 1 (Burt Shotton). WP—New York: Reynolds (1), Page (5), Lopat (4), Raschi (5); Brooklyn: Roe (2). LP—New York: Raschi (2); Brooklyn: Newcombe (1, 4), Branca (3), Barney (5).

1950—New York A.L. 4 (Casey Stengel); Philadelphia N.L. 0 (Eddie Sawyer). WP—Raschi (1), Reynolds (2), Ferrick (3), Ford (4). LP—Konstanty (1), Roberts (2), Meyer (3), Miller (4).

1951—New York A.L. 4 (Casey Stengel); New York N.L. 2 (Leo Durocher). WP—New York A.L.: Lopat (2, 5), Reynolds (4), Raschi (6); New York N.L.: Koslo (1), Hearn (3). LP—New York A.L.: Reynolds (1), Raschi (3); New York N.L.: Jansen (2, 5), Maglie (4), Koslo (6).

1952—New York A.L. 4 (Casey Stengel); Brooklyn N.L. 3 (Chuck Dressen). WP—New York: Raschi (2, 6), Reynolds (4, 7); Brooklyn: Black (4), Roe (3), Erskine (5); New York: Reynolds (1), Lopat (3), Sain (5); Brooklyn: Erskine (2), Black (4, 7), Loes (6).

1953—New York A.L. 4 (Casey Stengel); Brooklyn N.L. 2 (Chuck Dressen). WP—New York: Sain (1), Lopat (2), McDonald (4), Reynolds (6); Brooklyn: Erskine (3), Loes (4). LP—New York: Raschi (1), Ford (4); Brooklyn: Labine (1, 6), Roe (2), Podres (5).

1954—New York N.L. 4 (Leo Durocher); Cleveland A.L. 0 (Al Lopez). WP—Grissom (1), Antonelli (2), Gomez (3), Liddie (4). LP—Lemon (1, 4), Wynn (2), Garcia (3).

1955—Brooklyn N.L. 4 (Walter Alston); New York A.L. 3 (Casey Stengel). WP—Brooklyn: Podres (3, 7), Labine (4), Craig (5); New York: Ford (1, 6), Byrne (2). LP—Brooklyn: Newcombe (1), Loes (2), Spooner (6); New York: Turley (3), Larsen (4), Grim (5), Byrne (7).

1956—New York A.L. 4 (Casey Stengel); Brooklyn N.L. 3 (Walter Alston). WP—New York: Ford (3), Sturdivant (4), Larsen (5), Kucks (7); Brooklyn: Maglie (1), Bessent (2), Labine (6). LP—New York: Ford (1), Morgan (2), Turley (6); Brooklyn: Craig (3), Erskine (4), Maglie (5), Newcombe (7).

1957—Milwaukee N.L. 4 (Fred Haney); New York A.L. 3 (Casey Stengel). WP—Milwaukee: Burdette (2, 5, 7), Spahn (4); New York: Ford (1), Larsen (3), Turley (6). LP—Milwaukee: Spahn (1), Buhl (3), Johnson (6); New York: Shantz (2), Grim (4), Ford (5), Larsen (7).

1958—New York A.L. 4 (Casey Stengel); Milwaukee N.L. 3 (Fred Haney). WP—New York: Larsen (3), Turley (5, 7), Duren (6); Milwaukee: Spahn (1, 4), Burdette (2). LP—New York: Duren (1), Turley (2), Ford (4); Milwaukee: Rush (3), Burdette (5, 7), Spahn (6).

1959—Los Angeles N.L. 4 (Walter Alston); Chicago A.L. 2 (Al Lopez). WP—Los Angeles: Podres (2), Drysdale (3), Sherry (4, 6); Chicago: Wynn (1), Shaw (5). LP—Los Angeles: Craig (1), Koufax (5); Chicago: Shaw (2), Donovan (4), Staley (4), Wynn (6).

1960—Pittsburgh N.L. 4 (Danny Murtaugh); New York A.L. 3 (Casey Stengel). WP—Pittsburgh: Law (1, 4), Haddix (5, 7); New York: Turley (2), Ford (3, 6). LP—Pittsburgh: Friend (2, 6), Mizell (3); New York: Ditmar (1, 5), Terry (4, 7).

1961—New York A.L. 4 (Ralph Houk); Cincinnati N.L. 1 (Fred Hutchinson). WP—New York: Ford (1, 4), Arroyo (3), Daley (5); Cincinnati: Jay (2). LP—New York: Terry (2); Cincinnati:

O'Toole (1, 4), Purkey (3), Jay (5).

1962—New York A.L. 4 (Ralph Houk); San Francisco N.L. 3 (Al Dark). WP—New York: Ford (1), Stafford (3), Terry (5, 7); San Francisco Sanford (2), Larsen (4), Pierce (6). LP—New York: Terry (2), Coates (4), Ford (6); San Francisco: O'Dell (1), Pierce (3), Sanford (5, 7).

1963—Los Angeles N.L. 4 (Walter Alston); New York A.L. 0 (Ralph Houk). WP—Koufax (1, 4), Podres (3), Drysdale (3). LP—Ford (1, 4), Downing (2), Bouton (3).

1964—St. Louis N.L. 4 (Johnny Keane); New York A.L. 3 (Yogi Berra). WP—St. Louis: Sadecki (1), Craig (4), Gibson (5, 7); New York: Stottlemyre (2), Bouton (3, 6). LP—St. Louis: Gibson (2), Schultz (3), Simmons (6); New York: Ford (1), Downing (4), Mikkelsen (5), Stottlemyre (7).

1965—Los Angeles N.L. 4 (Walter Alston); Minnesota A.L. 3 (Sam Mele). WP—Los Angeles: Osteen (3), Drysdale (4), Koufax (5, 7); Minnesota: Grant (1, 6), Kaat (2). LP—Los Angeles: Drysdale (1), Koufax (2), Osteen (6); Minnesota: Pascual (3), Grant (4), Kaat (5, 7).

1966—Baltimore A.L. 4 (Hank Bauer); Los Angeles N.L. 0 (Walter Alston). WP—Drabowsky (1), Palmer (2), Bunker (3), McNally (4). LP—Drysdale (1, 4), Koufax (2), Osteen (3).

1967—St. Louis N.L. 4 (Red Schoendienst); Boston A.L. 3 (Dick Williams). WP—St. Louis: Gibson (1, 4, 7), Briles (3); Boston: Lonborg (2, 5), Wyatt (6). LP—St. Louis: Hughes (2), Carlton (5), Lamabe (6); Boston: Santiago (1, 4), Bell (3), Lonborg (7).

1968—Detroit A.L. 4 (Mayo Smith); St. Louis N.L. 3 (Red Schoendienst). WP—Det.: Lolich (2, 5, 7), McLain (6); St. Louis: Gibson (1, 4), Washburn (3), LP—Det.: McLain (1, 4), Wilson (3); St. Louis: Briles (2), Hoerner (5), Washburn (6), Gibson (7).

1969—New York N.L. 4 (Gil Hodges); Baltimore A.L. 1 (Earl Weaver). WP—New York: Koosman (2, 5), Gentry (3), Seaver (4); Baltimore: Cuellar (1). LP—New York: Seaver (1); Baltimore: McNally (2), Palmer (3), Hall (4), Watt (5).

1970—Baltimore A.L. 4 (Earl Weaver); Cincinnati N.L. 1 (Sparky Anderson) 1. WP—Baltimore: Palmer (1), Phoebus (2), McNally (3), Cuellar (5); Cincinnati: Carroll (4). LP—Cincinnati: Nolan (1), Wilcox (2), Cloninger (3), Merritt (5); Baltimore: Watt (4).

1971—Pittsburgh N.L. 4 (Danny Murtaugh); Baltimore A.L. 3 (Earl Weaver). WP—Pittsburgh: Blass (3, 7), Kison (4), Briles (5); Baltimore: McNally (1, 6), Palmer (2). LP—Pittsburgh: Ellis (1), R. Johnson (2), Miller (6); Baltimore: Cuellar (3, 7), Watt (4) McNally (5).

1972—Oakland A.L. 4 (Dick Williams); Cincinnati N.L. (Sparky Anderson) 3. WP—Oakland: Holtzman (2), Hunter (2, 7), Fingers (4); Cincinnati: Billingham (3), Grimsley (5). LP—Oakland: Odom (3), Fingers (5), Blue (6); Cincinnati: Nolan (1), Grimsley (2), Carroll (4), Borbon (7).

1973—Oakland A.L. 4 (Dick Williams); New York N.L. 3 (Yogi Berra). WP—Oakland: Holtzman (1, 7), Lindblad (3), Hunter (6). New York: McGraw (2), Matlack (4), Koosman (5). LP—Oakland: Fingers (2), Holtzman (4), Blue (5). New York: Matlack (1, 7) Parker (3), Seaver (6).

1974—Oakland A.L. 4 (Al Dark); Los Angeles N.L. 1 (Walter Alston). WP—Oakland: Fingers (1), Hunter (3), Holtzman (4), Odom (5). Los Angeles: Sutton (2). LP—Oakland: Blue (2), Los Angeles: Messersmith (1, 4), Downing (3), Marshall (5).

1975—Cincinnati N.L. 4 (Sparky Anderson); Boston A.L. 3 (Darrell Johnson). WP—Cincinnati: Eastwick (2, 3), Gullett (5), Carroll (7); Boston: Tiant (1, 4), Wise (6). LP—Cincinnati: Gullett (1), Norman (4), Darcy (6); Boston: Drago (5), Willoughby (3), Cleveland (5), Burton (7).

1976—Cincinnati N.L. 4 (Sparky Anderson); New York A.L. 0 (Billy Martin). WP—Gullett (1), Billingham (2), Zachry (3), Nolan (4). LP—Alexander (1), Hunter (2), Ellis (3), Figueroa (4).

1977—New York A.L. 4 (Billy Martin); Los Angeles N.L. 2 (Tom Lasorda). WP—New York: Lyle (1), Torrez (3, 6), Guidry (4); Los Angeles: Hooton (2), Sutton (5). LP—New York: Hunter (2), Gullett (5); Los Angeles: Rhoden (1), John (3), Rau (4), Hooton (6).

1978—New York A.L. 4 (Bob Lemon), Los Angeles N.L. 2 (Tom Lasorda); WP—New York: Guidry (3), Gossage (4); Beattie (5), Hunter (6); Los Angeles: John (1), Hooton (2). LP—New York: Figueroa (1), Hunter (2); Los Angeles: Sutton (3, 6), Welch (4), Hooton (5).

1979—Pittsburgh N.L. 4 (Chuck Tanner), Baltimore A.L. 3 (Earl Weaver); WP—Pittsburgh: D. Robinson (2), Blyleven (5), Candelaria (6), Jackson (7); Baltimore: Flanagan (1), McGregor (3), Stoddard (4). LP—Pittsburgh: Kison (1), Candelaria (3), Tekulve (4); Baltimore: Stanhouse (2), Flanagan (5), Palmer (6), McGregor (7).

1980—Philadelphia N.L. 4 (Dallas Green), Kansas City A.L. 2 (Jim Frey); WP—Philadelphia: Walk (1), Carlton (2), McGraw (5), Carlton (6); Kansas City: Quisenberry (3), Leonard (4). LP—Philadelphia: McGraw (3), Christenson (4); Kansas City: Leonard (1), Quisenberry (2) Quisenberry (5), Gale (6).

1981—Los Angeles N.L. 4 (Tom Lasorda), New York N.L. 2 (Bob Lemon); WP—Los Angeles: Valenzuela (3), Howe (4), Reuss (5), Hooton (6); New York: Guidry (1), John (2). LP—Los Angeles: Reuss (1), Hooton (2); New York: Frazier (3), Frazier (4), Guidry (5), Frazier (6).

1982—St. Louis N.L. 4 (Whitey Herzog), Milwaukee A.L. 3 (Harvey Kuenn); WP—St. Louis: Sutter (2), Andujar (3), Stuper (6), Andujar (7). Milwaukee: Caldwell (1), Slaton (4), Caldwell (5). LP—St. Louis: Forsch (1), Bair (4), Forsch (5). Milwaukee: McClure (3), Vuckovich (3), Sutton (6), McClure (7).

1983—Baltimore A.L. 4 (Joe Altobelli), Philadelphia N.L. 1 (Paul Owens); WP—Baltimore: Boddicker (2), Palmer (3), Davis (4), McGregor (5). Philadelphia: Denny (1).

1984—Detroit A.L. 4 (Sparky Anderson), San Diego N.L. 1 (Dick Williams); WP—Det.: Morris (1,4), Wilcox (3), Lopez (5), San Diego: Hawkins (2). LP—Det.: Petry (2), San Diego: Thurmond (1), Lollar (3), Show (4), Hawkins (5).

1985—Kansas City A.L. 4 (Dick Howser), St. Louis N.L. 3 (Whitey Herzog); WP—KC: Saberhagen (3,7) Quisenberry (6), Jackson (5). St. Louis: Tudor (1,4) Dayley (2). LP—KC: Jackson (5), Leibrandt (2), Black (4); St. Louis: Andujar (3), Forsch (5), Worrell (6), Tudor (7).

1986—New York N.L. 4 (Dave Johnson); Boston A.L. (John McNamara) 3 WP—New York—Ojeda (3), Darling (4), Aguilera (6), McDowell (7), Bos: Hurst (1), (5), Crawford (2). LP—New York Darling (1), Gooden (2, 5).

1987—Minnesota A.L. 4 (Tom Kelly); St. Louis N.L. (Whitey Herzog) 3. WP—Minnesota Viola (1, 7), Blyleven (2), Schatzeder (6), St. Louis: Tudor (3), Forsch (4), Cox (5). LP—Minnesota Berenguer (3), Viola (4), Blyleven (5); St. Louis: Magrane (1), Cox (2, 7), Tudor (6).

1988—Los Angeles N.L. 4 (Tommy Lasorda); Oakland A.L. (Tony LaRussa) 1. WP—Los Angeles: Hershiser (2, 5), Pena (1), Belcher (4); Oakland: Honeycutt (3). LP—Los Angeles: Howell (3); Oakland: Davis (2, 5), Eckersley (1), Stewart (4).

1989—Oakland A.L. 4 (Tony LaRussa); San Francisco N.L. 0 (Roger Craig). WP—Oakland: Dave Stewart (1, 3), Mike Moore (2, 4). LP—San Francisco: Scott Garrelts (1, 3), Don Robinson (4), Rick Reuschel (2).

1990—Cincinnati N.L. 4 (Lou Piniella); Oakland A.L. 0 (Tony LaRussa). WP—Cincinnati: Jose Rijo (1, 4), Rob Dibble (2), Tom Browning (3). LP—Oakland: Dave Stewart (1, 4), Dennis Eckersley (2), Mike Moore (3).

1991—Minnesota A.L. 4 (Tom Kelly); Atlanta N.L. 3 (Bobby Cox). WP—Minnesota: Morris (1,7), Tapani (2), Aguilera (6). Atlanta: Clancy (3), Stanton (4), Glavine (5). LP—Minnesota: Aguilera (3), Guhrtie (4), Tapani (5). Atlanta: Leibrandt (1, 6), Glavine (2), Pena (7).

1992—Toronto A.L. 4 (Cito Gaston); Atlanta N.L. 2 (Bobby Cox). WP—Toronto: Ward (2, 3), Key (4, 6). Atlanta: Glavine (1), Smoltz (5). LP—Toronto: Morris (1, 5). Atlanta: Leibrandt (6), Reardon (2), Avery (3), Glavine (4).

1993—Toronto A.L. 4 (Cito Gaston); Philadelphia N.L. 2 (Jim Fregosi). WP—Toronto: Leiter (1), Hentgen (3), Castillo (4), Ward (6). Philadelphia: Mullholland (2), Schilling (5). LP—Toronto: Stewart (2), Guzman (5). Philadelphia: Schilling (1), Jackson (3), Williams (4, 6).

1994—World Series cancelled due to players' strike.

1995—Atlanta N.L. 4 (Bobby Cox); Cleveland A.L. 2 (Mike Hargrove). WP—Atlanta: Maddux (1), Glavine (2,6), Avery (4). Cleveland: Mesa (3), Hershiser (5). LP—Atlanta: Pena (3), Maddux (5). Cleveland: Hershiser (1), Martinez (2), Hill (4), Poole (4).

1996—New York A.L. 4 (Joe Torre); Atlanta N.L. 2 (Bobby Cox). WP—New York: Cone (3), Lloyd (4), Pettitte (5), Key (6). Atlanta: Smoltz (1), Maddux (2). LP—New York: Pettitte (1), Key (2). Atlanta: Glavine (3), Avery (4), Smoltz (5), Maddux (6).

1997—Florida N.L. 4 (Jim Leyland); Cleveland A.L. 3 (Mike Hargrove). WP—Florida: Hernandez (1, 5), Cook (3), Powell (7). Cleveland: Ogea (2, 6), Wright (4). LP—Florida: Brown (2, 6), Saunders (4). Cleveland: Hershiser (1, 5), Plunk (4), Nagy (7).

1998—New York A.L. 4 (Joe Torre); San Diego N.L. 0 (Bruce Bochy). WP—New York: Wells (1), Hernandez (2), Mendoza (3), Pettitte (4). LP—San Diego: Wall (1), Ashby (2), Hoffman (3), Brown (4).

1999—New York A.L. 4 (Joe Torre); Atlanta N.L. 0 (Bobby Cox). WP—New York: Hernandez (1), Cone (2), Rivera (3), Clemens (4). LP—Atlanta: Maddux (1), Millwood (2), Remlinger (3), Smoltz (4).

2000—New York Yankees A.L. 4 (Joe Torre); New York Mets N.L. 1 (Bobby Valentine). WP—Yankees: Stanton (1, 5), Clemens (2), Nelson (3). Mets: Franco (3). LP—Wendell (1), Hampton (2), Jones (4), Leiter (5). Yankees: Hernandez (3).

2001—Arizona Diamondbacks N.L. 4 (Bob Brenly); New York Yankees A.L. 3 (Joe Torre). WP—Arizona: Schilling (1), Johnson (2, 6, 7). New York: Clemens (3), Rivera (4), Hitchcock (5). LP—New York: Mussina (1), Pettitte (2, 6), Rivera (7). Arizona: Anderson (3), Kim (4), Lopez (5).

2002—Anaheim Angels A.L. 4 (Scioscia); San Francisco Giants N.L. 3 (Baker). WP—Anaheim: Rodriguez (2), Ortiz (3), Donnelly (6), Lackey (7). San Francisco: Schmidt (1), Worrell (4), Zerbe (5). LP—Anaheim: Washburn (1, 5), Rodriguez (4). San Francisco: Rodriguez (2), Hernandez (3, 7), Worrell (6).

2003—Florida Marlins 4 (McKeon); New York Yankees A.L. 2 (Torre). WP—Florida: Penny (1, 5), Looper (4), Beckett (6). New York: Pettitte (2), Mussina (3). LP—Florida: Redman (2), Beckett (3). New York: Wells (1), Weaver (4), Contreras (5), Pettitte (6).

WORLD SERIES CLUB STANDINGS
(through 2004)

	Series	Won	Lost	Pct.		Series	Won	Lost	Pct.
Toronto (A)	2	2	0	1.000	Kansas City (A)	2	1	1	.500
Florida (N)	2	2	0	1.000	Detroit (A)	9	4	5	.444
Arizona (N)	1	1	0	1.000	Cleveland (A)	5	2	3	.400
Anaheim (A)	1	1	0	1.000	New York (N-Giants)	14	5	9	.357
Pittsburgh (N)	7	5	2	.714	Washington (A)	3	1	2	.333
New York (A)	39	26	13	.667	Atlanta (N)	5	1	4	.200
Oakland (A)	6	4	2	.667	Philadelphia (N)	5	1	4	.200
Minnesota (A)	3	2	1	.667	Chicago (N)	10	2	8	.200
Philadelphia (A)	8	5	3	.625	Brooklyn (N)	9	1	8	.111
Boston (A)	10	6	4	.600	St. Louis (A)	1	0	1	.000
St. Louis (N)	16	9	7	.563	San Francisco (N)	3	0	3	.000
Los Angeles (N)	9	5	4	.556	Milwaukee (A)	1	0	1	.000
Cincinnati (N)	9	5	4	.556	San Diego (N)	2	0	2	.000
New York (N-Mets)	4	2	2	.500					
Milwaukee (N)	2	1	1	.500	**Recapitulation**				**Won**
Boston (N)	2	1	1	.500	American League				58
Chicago (A)	4	2	2	.500	National League				40
Baltimore (A)	6	3	3	.500					

WORLD SERIES SINGLE GAME AND SINGLE SERIES RECORDS
(through 2004)

Most hits game—5, Paul Molitor, Milwaukee A.L., first game vs. St. Louis N.L., 1982.

Most 4-hit games, series—2, Robin Yount, Milwaukee A.L., first and fifth games vs. St. Louis N.L., 1982.

Most hits inning—2, held by 17 players.

Most hits series—13 (7 games) Bobby Richardson, New York A.L., 1964; Lou Brock, St. Louis N.L., 1968; Marty Barrett, Boston A.L., 1986.

Most home runs, series—5 (6 games) Reggie Jackson, New York A.L., 1977; 4 (4 games) Lou Gehrig, New York A.L., 1928; 4 (6 games) Willie Aikens, Kansas City A.L., 1980; 4 (7 games) Babe Ruth, New York A.L., 1926; Duke Snider, Brooklyn N.L., 1952, 1955; Hank Bauer, New York A.L., 1958; Gene Tenace, Oakland A.L., 1972; 4 Barry Bonds, San Francisco N.L., 2002.

Most home runs, game—3, Babe Ruth, New York A.L., 1926 and 1928; Reggie Jackson, New York A.L., 1977.

Most strikeouts, series—12 (6 games) Willie Wilson, Kansas City A.L., 1980; 11 (7 games) Ed Mathews, Milwaukee N.L., 1958; Wayne Garrett, New York N.L., 1973; 9 (5 games) Carmelo Martinez, San Diego N.L., 1984; 7 (4 games) Bob Muesel, New York A.L., 1927; Ken Caminiti, San Diego N.L., 1998.

Most stolen bases, game—3, Honus Wagner, Pittsburgh N.L., 1909; Willie Davis, Los Angeles N.L., 1965; Lou Brock, St. Louis N.L., 1967 and 1968.

Most strikeouts by pitcher, game—17, Bob Gibson, St. Louis N.L. 1968.

Most strikeouts by pitcher in succession—6, Horace Eller, Cincinnati N.L., 1919; Moe Drabowsky, Baltimore A.L., 1966.

Most strikeouts by pitcher, series—35 (7 games) Bob Gibson, St. Louis N.L., 1968; 23 (4 games) Sandy Koufax, Los Angeles, 1963; 20 (6 games) Chief Bender, Philadelphia A.L., 1911; 18 (5 games) Christy Mathewson, New York N.L., 1905.

Most bases on balls, series—13 (7 games) Barry Bonds, San Francisco N.L., 2002; 11 (7 games) Babe Ruth, New York A.L., 1926; Gene Tenace, Oakland A.L., 1973; 9 (6 games) Willie Randolph, New York A.L., 1981; 7 (5 games) James Sheckard, Chicago N.L., 1910; Mickey Cochrane, Philadelphia A.L., 1929; Joe Gordon, New York A.L., 1941; 7 (4 games) Hank Thompson, New York N.L., 1954.

Most consecutive scoreless innings one series—27, Christy Mathewson, New York N.L., 1905.

LIFETIME WORLD SERIES RECORDS
(through 2004)

Most hits—71, Yogi Berra, New York A.L., 1947, 1949–53, 1955–58, 1960–63.

Most runs—42, Mickey Mantle, New York A.L., 1951–53, 1955–58, 1960–64.

Most runs batted in—40, Mickey Mantle, New York A.L., 1951–53, 1955–58, 1960–64.

Most home runs—18, Mickey Mantle, New York A.L., 1951–53, 1955–58, 1960–64.

Most bases on balls—43, Mickey Mantle, New York A.L., 1951–53, 1955–58, 1960–64.

Most strikeouts—54, Mickey Mantle, New York A.L., 1951–53, 1955–58, 1960–64.

Most stolen bases—14, Eddie Collins, Philadelphia A.L. 1910–11, 13–14; Chicago A.L., 1917, 1919. Lou Brock, St. Louis N.L., 1964, 67–68.

Most victories, pitcher—10, Whitey Ford, New York A.L., 1950, 1953, 1955–58, 1960–64.

Most times member of winning team—10, Yogi Berra, New York A.L., 1947, 1949–53, 1956, 1958, 1961–62.

Most victories, no defeats—6, Vernon Gomez, New York A.L., 1932, 1936(2), 1937(2), 1938.

Most shutouts—4, Christy Mathewson, New York N.L., 1905 (3), 1913.

Most innings pitched—146, Whitey Ford, New York A.L., 1950, 1953, 1955–58, 1960–1964

Most consecutive scoreless innings—33⅔, Whitey Ford, New York A.L., 1960 (18), 1961 (14), 1962 (1⅔).

Most strikeouts by pitcher—94, Whitey Ford, New York A.L., 1950, 1953, 1955–58, 1960–1964

BASEBALL'S PERFECTLY PITCHED GAMES[1]
(no opposing runner reached base)

Lee Richmond—Worcester vs. Cleveland (N.L.) June 12, 1880 (1–0)

John M. Ward—Providence vs. Buffalo (N.L.) June 17, 1880 (5–0)

Cy Young—Boston vs. Philadelphia (A.L.) May 5, 1904 (3–0)

Addie Joss—Cleveland vs. Chicago (A.L.) Oct. 2, 1908 (1–0)

Ernest Shore[2]—Boston vs. Washington (A.L.) June 23, 1917 (4–0)

Charles Robertson—Chicago vs. Detroit (A.L.) April 30, 1922 (2–0)

Don Larsen[3]—New York (A.L.) vs. Brooklyn (N.L.) Oct. 8, 1956 (2–0)

Jim Bunning—Philadelphia vs. New York (N.L.) June 21, 1964 (6–0)

Sandy Koufax—Los Angeles vs. Chicago (N.L.) Sept. 9, 1965 (1–0)

Jim Hunter—Oakland vs. Minnesota (A.L.) May 8, 1968 (4–0)

Len Barker—Cleveland vs. Toronto (A.L.) May 15, 1981 (3–0)

Mike Witt—California vs. Texas (A.L.) Sept. 30, 1984 (1–0)

Tom Browning—Cincinnati vs. Los Angeles (N.L.) Sept. 16, 1988 (1–0)

Dennis Martinez—Montreal vs. Los Angeles (N.L.) July 28, 1991 (2–0)

Kenny Rogers—Texas vs. California (A.L.) July 28, 1994 (4–0)

David Wells—New York vs. Minnesota (A.L.) May 17, 1998 (4–0)

David Cone[4]—New York (A.L.) vs. Montreal (N.L.) July 18, 1999 (6–0)

Randy Johnson—Arizona vs. Atlanta (N.L.) May 18, 2004 (2–0)

1. Harvey Haddix, of Pittsburgh, pitched 12 perfect innings against Milwaukee (N.L.), May 26, 1959, but lost game in 13th on error and hit. Montreal's Pedro Martinez pitched nine perfect innings against the San Diego Padres on June 3, 1995 before surrendering a leadoff double to Bip Roberts in the 10th. Mel Rojas finished the game, which Montreal won, 1–0. 2. Shore, relief pitcher for Babe Ruth who walked first batter before being ejected by umpire, retired 26 batters who faced him and base-runner was out stealing. 3. World Series. 4. Interleague game.

LIFETIME BATTING, PITCHING, AND BASE-RUNNING RECORDS
(Records through 2004. Boldface indicates player active in 2004 season.)

Hits (3,000+)

Pete Rose	4,256
Ty Cobb	4,189
Hank Aaron	3,771
Stan Musial	3,630
Tris Speaker	3,514
Carl Yastrzemski	3,419
Cap Anson	3,418
Honus Wagner	3,415
Paul Molitor	3,319
Eddie Collins	3,315
Willie Mays	3,283
Eddie Murray	3,255
Nap Lajoie	3,242
Cal Ripken, Jr.	3,184
George Brett	3,154
Paul Waner	3,152
Robin Yount	3,142
Tony Gwynn	3,141
Dave Winfield	3,110
Rickey Henderson	3,055
Rod Carew	3,053
Lou Brock	3,023
Wade Boggs	3,010
Al Kaline	3,007
Roberto Clemente	3,000

Earned Run Average
(Minimum 1,500 innings pitched)

Ed Walsh	1.82
Addie Joss	1.89
Al Spalding	2.04
Mordecai Brown	2.06
John Ward	2.10
Christy Mathewson	2.13
Tommy Bond	2.14
Rube Waddell	2.16
Walter Johnson	2.17
Ed Reulbach	2.28
Will White	2.28
Ed Plank	2.35
Larry Corcoran	2.36
Ed Cicotte	2.38
Candy Cummings	2.39
Doc White	2.39
Nap Rucker	2.42
George Bradley	2.43
Jim McCormick	2.43

Runs Scored

Rickey Henderson	2,295
Ty Cobb	2,246
Hank Aaron	2,174
Babe Ruth	2,174
Pete Rose	2,165
Barry Bonds	2,070
Willie Mays	2,062
Cap Anson	1,996
Stan Musial	1,949
Lou Gehrig	1,888
Tris Speaker	1,882
Mel Ott	1,859
Frank Robinson	1,829
Eddie Collins	1,821
Carl Yastrzemski	1,816
Ted Williams	1,798
Paul Molitor	1,782
Charlie Gehringer	1,774
Jimmie Foxx	1,751
Honus Wagner	1,736

Jim O'Rourke	1,729
Jesse Burkett	1,720
Willie Keeler	1,719
Billy Hamilton	1,691
Bid McPhee	1,678
Mickey Mantle	1,677
Dave Winfield	1,669
Joe Morgan	1,650

Strikeouts, Pitching

Nolan Ryan	5,714
Roger Clemens	4,317
Randy Johnson	4,161
Steve Carlton	4,136
Bert Blyleven	3,701
Tom Seaver	3,640
Don Sutton	3,574
Gaylord Perry	3,534
Walter Johnson	3,508
Phil Niekro	3,342
Ferguson Jenkins	3,192
Bob Gibson	3,117
Greg Maddux	2,916
Jim Bunning	2,855

Player	No.
Mickey Lolich	2,832
Cy Young	2,803
Frank Tanana	2,773
Curt Schilling	**2,745**
David Cone	2,668
Pedro Martinez	**2,653**
Chuck Finley	2,610
Warren Spahn	2,583
Bob Feller	2,581
Tim Keefe	2,564
Jerry Koosman	2,556

Home Runs

Player	No.
Hank Aaron	755
Babe Ruth	714
Barry Bonds	**703**
Willie Mays	660
Frank Robinson	586
Mark McGwire	583
Sammy Sosa	**574**
Harmon Killebrew	573
Reggie Jackson	563
Rafael Palmeiro	**551**
Mike Schmidt	548
Mickey Mantle	536
Jimmie Foxx	534
Willie McCovey	521
Ted Williams	521
Ernie Banks	512
Eddie Mathews	512
Mel Ott	511
Eddie Murray	504
Ken Griffey, Jr.	**501**
Lou Gehrig	493
Fred McGriff	**493**
Stan Musial	475
Willie Stargell	475
Dave Winfield	465
Jose Canseco	462
Carl Yastrzemski	452
Jeff Bagwell	**446**
Dave Kingman	442
Andre Dawson	438
Frank Thomas	**436**
Juan Gonzalez	**434**
Cal Ripken, Jr.	431
Billy Williams	426
Jim Thome	**423**
Gary Sheffield	**415**
Darrell Evans	414
Duke Snider	407
Al Kaline	399
Andres Galarraga	**399**
Dale Murphy	398
Joe Carter	396
Graig Nettles	390
Manny Ramirez	**390**
Johnny Bench	389
Dwight Evans	385
Harold Baines	384
Frank Howard	382
Jim Rice	382
Albert Belle	381
Alex Rodriquez	**381**
Orlando Cepeda	379
Tony Perez	379

Shutouts

Player	No.
Walter Johnson	110
Grover Alexander	90
Christy Mathewson	79
Cy Young	76
Ed Plank	69
Warren Spahn	63
Nolan Ryan	61
Tom Seaver	61
Bert Blyleven	60
Don Sutton	58
Pud Galvin	57
Ed Walsh	57
Bob Gibson	56
Mordecai Brown	55
Steve Carlton	55
Jim Palmer	53
Gaylord Perry	53

Strikeouts, Batting

Player	No.
Reggie Jackson	2,597
Sammy Sosa	2,110
Andres Galarraga	**2,003**
Jose Canseco	1,942
Willie Stargell	1,936
Mike Schmidt	1,883
Fred McGriff	**1,882**
Tony Perez	1,867
Dave Kingman	1,816
Bobby Bonds	1,757
Dale Murphy	1,748
Lou Brock	1,730
Mickey Mantle	1,710
Jim Thome	**1,703**
Harmon Killebrew	1,699
Chili Davis	1,698
Dwight Evans	1,697
Rickey Henderson	1,694
Dave Winfield	1,686
Gary Gaetti	1,602
Mark McGwire	1,596
Lee May	1,570
Dick Allen	1,556
Willie McCovey	1,550
Ray Lankford	**1,550**
Dave Parker	1,537
Jeff Bagwell	**1,537**
Frank Robinson	1,532
Lance Parrish	1,527

Walks

Player	No.
Barry Bonds	**2,302**
Rickey Henderson	2,190
Babe Ruth	2,062
Ted Williams	2,019
Joe Morgan	1,865
Carl Yastrzemski	1,845
Mickey Mantle	1,733
Mel Ott	1,708
Eddie Yost	1,614
Darrell Evans	1,605
Stan Musial	1,599
Pete Rose	1,566
Harmon Killebrew	1,559
Lou Gehrig	1,508
Mike Schmidt	1,507
Eddie Collins	1,499
Willie Mays	1,464
Jimmie Foxx	1,452
Frank Thomas	**1,450**
Eddie Mathews	1,444
Frank Robinson	1,420
Wade Boggs	1,412
Hank Aaron	1,402

AMERICAN LEAGUE HOME RUN CHAMPIONS

Year	Player, team	No.
1901	Nap Lajoie, Philadelphia	13
1902	Ralph Seybold, Philadelphia	16
1903	Buck Freeman, Boston	13
1904	Harry Davis, Philadelphia	10
1905	Harry Davis, Philadelphia	8
1906	Harry Davis, Philadelphia	12
1907	Harry Davis, Philadelphia	8
1908	Sam Crawford, Detroit	7
1909	Ty Cobb, Detroit	9
1910	J. Garland Stahl, Boston	10
1911	Franklin Baker, Philadelphia	9
1912	Franklin Baker, Philadelphia	10
1913	Franklin Baker, Philadelphia	12
1914	Franklin Baker, Philadelphia; Sam Crawford, Detroit	8
1915	Robert Roth, Chicago-Cleveland	7
1916	Wally Pipp, New York	12
1917	Wally Pipp, New York	9
1918	Babe Ruth, Boston; Clarence Walker, Philadelphia	11
1919	Babe Ruth, Boston	29
1920	Babe Ruth, New York	54
1921	Babe Ruth, New York	59
1922	Ken Williams, St. Louis	39
1923	Babe Ruth, New York	41
1924	Babe Ruth, New York	46
1925	Bob Meusel, New York	33
1926	Babe Ruth, New York	47
1927	Babe Ruth, New York	60
1928	Babe Ruth, New York	54
1929	Babe Ruth, New York	46
1930	Babe Ruth, New York	49
1931	Lou Gehrig, New York; Babe Ruth, New York	46
1932	Jimmie Foxx, Philadelphia	58
1933	Jimmie Foxx, Philadelphia	48
1934	Lou Gehrig, New York	49
1935	Jimmie Foxx, Philadelphia; Hank Greenberg, Detroit	36
1936	Lou Gehrig, New York	49
1937	Joe DiMaggio, New York	46
1938	Hank Greenberg, Detroit	58
1939	Jimmie Foxx, Boston	35
1940	Hank Greenberg, Detroit	41
1941	Ted Williams, Boston	37
1942	Ted Williams, Boston	36
1943	Rudy York, Detroit	34
1944	Nick Etten, New York	22
1945	Vern Stephens, St. Louis	24
1946	Hank Greenberg, Detroit	44
1947	Ted Williams, Boston	32
1948	Joe DiMaggio, New York	39
1949	Ted Williams, Boston	43
1950	Al Rosen, Cleveland	37
1951	Gus Zernial, Chicago-Philadelphia	33
1952	Larry Doby, Cleveland	32
1953	Al Rosen, Cleveland	43
1954	Larry Doby, Cleveland	32
1955	Mickey Mantle, New York	37
1956	Mickey Mantle, New York	52
1957	Roy Sievers, Washington	42
1958	Mickey Mantle, New York	42
1959	Rocky Colavito, Cleveland; Harmon Killebrew, Washington	42
1960	Mickey Mantle, New York	40
1961	Roger Maris, New York	61
1962	Harmon Killebrew, Minnesota	48
1963	Harmon Killebrew, Minnesota	45
1964	Harmon Killebrew, Minnesota	49
1965	Tony Conigliaro, Boston	32
1966	Frank Robinson, Baltimore	49
1967	Carl Yastrzemski, Boston; Harmon Killebrew, Minnesota	44
1968	Frank Howard, Washington	44
1969	Harmon Killebrew, Minnesota	49
1970	Frank Howard, Washington	44
1971	Bill Melton, Chicago	33
1972	Dick Allen, Chicago	37
1973	Reggie Jackson, Oakland	32
1974	Dick Allen, Chicago	32
1975	Reggie Jackson, Oakland; George Scott, Milwaukee	36
1976	Graig Nettles, New York	32

Year	Player, team	No.	Year	Player, team	No.	Year	Player, team	No.
1977	Jim Rice, Boston	39	1983	Jim Rice, Boston	39	1994[2]	Ken Griffey, Jr., Seattle	40
1978	Jim Rice, Boston	46	1984	Tony Armas, Boston	43	1995	Albert Belle, Cleveland	50
1979	Gorman Thomas, Milwaukee	45	1985	Darrell Evans, Detroit	40	1996	Mark McGwire, Oakland	52
1980	Reggie Jackson, New York; Ben Oglivie, Milwaukee	41	1986	Jesse Barfield, Toronto	40	1997	Ken Griffey, Jr., Seattle	56
			1987	Mark McGwire, Oakland	49	1998	Ken Griffey, Jr., Seattle	56
1981[1]	Tony Armas, Oakland; Dwight Evans, Boston; Bobby Grich, California; Eddie Murray, Baltimore (tie)	22	1988	Jose Canseco, Oakland	42	1999	Ken Griffey, Jr., Seattle	48
			1989	Fred McGriff, Toronto	36	2000	Troy Glaus, Anaheim	47
			1990	Cecil Fielder, Detroit	51	2001	Alex Rodriguez, Texas	52
			1991	Jose Canseco, Oakland; Cecil Fielder, Detroit (tie)	44	2002	Alex Rodriguez, Texas	57
1982	Gorman Thomas, Milwaukee; Reggie Jackson, California	39				2003	Alex Rodriguez, Texas	47
			1992	Juan Gonzalez, Texas	43	2004	Manny Ramirez, Boston	43
			1993	Juan Gonzalez, Texas	46			

1. Split season because of players' strike. 2. Season ended on Aug. 12 because of players' strike.

AMERICAN LEAGUE BATTING CHAMPIONS

Year	Player, team	Avg.	Year	Player, team	Avg.	Year	Player, team	Avg.
1901	Nap Lajoie, Philadelphia	.422	1936	Luke Appling, Chicago	.388	1971	Tony Oliva, Minnesota	.337
1902	Ed Delahanty, Washington	.376	1937	Charley Gehringer, Detroit	.371	1972	Rod Carew, Minnesota	.318
1903	Nap Lajoie, Cleveland	.355	1938	Jimmie Foxx, Boston	.349	1973	Rod Carew, Minnesota	.350
1904	Nap Lajoie, Cleveland	.381	1939	Joe DiMaggio, New York	.381	1974	Rod Carew, Minnesota	.364
1905	Elmer Flick, Cleveland	.306	1940	Joe DiMaggio, New York	.352	1975	Rod Carew, Minnesota	.359
1906	George Stone, St. Louis	.358	1941	Ted Williams, Boston	.406	1976	George Brett, Kansas City	.333
1907	Ty Cobb, Detroit	.350	1942	Ted Williams, Boston	.356	1977	Rod Carew, Minnesota	.388
1908	Ty Cobb, Detroit	.324	1943	Luke Appling, Chicago	.328	1978	Rod Carew, Minnesota	.333
1909	Ty Cobb, Detroit	.377	1944	Lou Boudreau, Cleveland	.327	1979	Fred Lynn, Boston	.333
1910	Ty Cobb, Detroit	.385	1945	George Stirnweiss, New York	.309	1980	George Brett, Kansas City	.390
1911	Ty Cobb, Detroit	.420				1981[1]	Carney Lansford, Boston	.336
1912	Ty Cobb, Detroit	.410	1946	Mickey Vernon, Washington	.353	1982	Willie Wilson, Kansas City	.332
1913	Ty Cobb, Detroit	.390	1947	Ted Williams, Boston	.343	1983	Wade Boggs, Boston	.361
1914	Ty Cobb, Detroit	.368	1948	Ted Williams, Boston	.369	1984	Don Mattingly, New York	.343
1915	Ty Cobb, Detroit	.369	1949	George Kell, Detroit	.343	1985	Wade Boggs, Boston	.368
1916	Tris Speaker, Cleveland	.386	1950	Billy Goodman, Boston	.354	1986	Wade Boggs, Boston	.357
1917	Ty Cobb, Detroit	.383	1951	Ferris Fain, Philadelphia	.344	1987	Wade Boggs, Boston	.363
1918	Ty Cobb, Detroit	.382	1952	Ferris Fain, Philadelphia	.327	1988	Wade Boggs, Boston	.366
1919	Ty Cobb, Detroit	.384	1953	Mickey Vernon, Washington	.337	1989	Kirby Puckett, Minnesota	.339
1920	George Sisler, St. Louis	.407	1954	Bobby Avila, Cleveland	.341	1990	George Brett, Kansas City	.328
1921	Harry Heilmann, Detroit	.394	1955	Al Kaline, Detroit	.340	1991	Julio Franco, Texas	.341
1922	George Sisler, St. Louis	.420	1956	Mickey Mantle, New York	.353	1992	Edgar Martinez, Seattle	.343
1923	Harry Heilmann, Detroit	.403	1957	Ted Williams, Boston	.388	1993	John Olerud, Toronto	.363
1924	Babe Ruth, New York	.378	1958	Ted Williams, Boston	.328	1994[2]	Paul O'Neill, New York	.359
1925	Harry Heilmann, Detroit	.393	1959	Harvey Kuenn, Detroit	.353	1995	Edgar Martinez, Seattle	.356
1926	Heinie Manush, Detroit	.378	1960	Pete Runnels, Boston	.320	1996	Alex Rodriguez, Seattle	.358
1927	Harry Heilmann, Detroit	.398	1961	Norman Cash, Detroit	.361	1997	Frank Thomas, Chicago	.347
1928	Goose Goslin, Washington	.379	1962	Pete Runnels, Boston	.326	1998	Bernie Williams, New York	.339
1929	Lew Fonseca, Cleveland	.369	1963	Carl Yastrzemski, Boston	.321	1999	Nomar Garciaparra, Boston	.357
1930	Al Simmons, Philadelphia	.381	1964	Tony Oliva, Minnesota	.323	2000	Nomar Garciaparra, Boston	.372
1931	Al Simmons, Philadelphia	.390	1965	Tony Oliva, Minnesota	.321	2001	Ichiro Suzuki, Seattle	.350
1932	Dale Alexander, Detroit-Boston	.367	1966	Frank Robinson, Baltimore	.316	2002	Manny Ramirez, Boston	.349
			1967	Carl Yastrzemski, Boston	.326	2003	Bill Mueller, Boston	.326
1933	Jimmie Foxx, Philadelphia	.356	1968	Carl Yastrzemski, Boston	.301	2004	Ichiro Suzuki, Seattle	.372
1934	Lou Gehrig, New York	.363	1969	Rod Carew, Minnesota	.332			
1935	Buddy Myer, Washington	.349	1970	Alex Johnson, California	.329			

1. Split season because of players' strike. 2. Season ended on Aug. 12 because of players' strike.

NATIONAL LEAGUE HOME RUN CHAMPIONS

Year	Player, team	No.	Year	Player, team	No.	Year	Player, team	No.
1876	George Hall, Philadelphia Athletics	5	1887	Roger Connor, New York; Wm. O'Brien, Washington	17	1895	Bill Joyce, Washington	17
						1896	Ed Delahanty, Philadelphia; Sam Thompson, Philadelphia	13
1877	George Shaffer, Louisville	3	1888	Roger Connor, New York	14			
1878	Paul Hines, Providence	4	1889	Sam Thompson, Philadelphia	20			
1879	Charles Jones, Boston	9				1897	Nap Lajoie, Philadelphia	10
1880	James O'Rourke, Boston; Harry Stovey, Worcester	6	1890	Tom Burns, Brooklyn; Mike Tiernan, New York	13	1898	James Colins, Boston	14
						1899	John Freeman, Washington	25
1881	Dan Brouthers, Buffalo	8	1891	Harry Stovey, Boston; Mike Tiernan, New York	16	1900	Herman Long, Boston	12
1882	George Wood, Detroit	7				1901	Sam Crawford, Cincinnati	16
1883	William Ewing, New York	10	1892	Jim Holliday, Cincinnati	13	1902	Tom Leach, Pittsburgh	6
1884	Ed Williamson, Chicago	27	1893	Ed Delahanty, Philadelphia	19	1903	James Sheckard, Brooklyn	9
1885	Abner Dalrymple, Chicago	11	1894	Hugh Duffy, Boston; Robert Lowe, Boston	18	1904	Harry Lumley, Brooklyn	9
1886	Arthur Richardson, Detroit	11				1905	Fred Odwell, Cincinnati	9

Year	Player, team	No.	Year	Player, team	No.	Year	Player, team	No.
1906	Tim Jordan, Brooklyn	12	1938	Mel Ott, New York	36	1970	Johnny Bench, Cincinnati	45
1907	David Brain, Boston	10	1939	John Mize, St. Louis	28	1971	Willie Stargell, Pittsburgh	48
1908	Tim Jordan, Brooklyn	12	1940	John Mize, St. Louis	43	1972	Johnny Bench, Cincinnati	40
1909	John Murray, New York	7	1941	Dolph Camilli, Brooklyn	34	1973	Willie Stargell, Pittsburgh	44
1910	Fred Beck, Boston; Frank Schulte, Chicago	10	1942	Mel Ott, New York	30	1974	Mike Schmidt, Philadelphia	36
			1943	Bill Nicholson, Chicago	29	1975	Mike Schmidt, Philadelphia	38
1911	Frank Schulte, Chicago	21	1944	Bill Nicholson, Chicago	33	1976	Mike Schmidt, Philadelphia	38
1912	Henry Zimmerman, Chicago	14	1945	Tommy Holmes, Boston	28	1977	George Foster, Cincinnati	52
1913	Cliff Cravath, Philadelphia	19	1946	Ralph Kiner, Pittsburgh	23	1978	George Foster, Cincinnati	40
1914	Cliff Cravath, Philadelphia	19	1947	Ralph Kiner, Pittsburgh;	51	1979	Dave Kingman, Chicago	48
1915	Cliff Cravath, Philadelphia	24		John Mize, New York		1980	Mike Schmidt, Philadelphia	48
1916	Davis Robertson, New York; Fred Williams, Chicago	12	1948	Ralph Kiner, Pittsburgh; John Mize, New York	40	1981[1]	Mike Schmidt, Philadelphia	31
						1982	Dave Kingman, New York	37
1917	Davis Robertson, New York; Cliff Cravath, Philadelphia	12	1949	Ralph Kiner, Pittsburgh	54	1983	Mike Schmidt, Philadelphia	40
			1950	Ralph Kiner, Pittsburgh	47	1984	Mike Schmidt, Philadelphia;	36
1918	Cliff Cravath, Philadelphia	8	1951	Ralph Kiner, Pittsburgh	42		Dale Murphy, Atlanta	
1919	Cliff Cravath, Philadelphia	12	1952	Ralph Kiner, Pittsburgh;	37	1985	Dale Murphy, Atlanta	37
1920	Cy Williams, Philadelphia	15		Hank Sauer, Chicago		1986	Mike Schmidt, Philadelphia	37
1921	George Kelly, New York	23	1953	Ed Mathews, Milwaukee	47	1987	Andre Dawson, Chicago	49
1922	Rogers Hornsby, St. Louis	42	1954	Ted Kluszewski, Cincinnati	49	1988	Darryl Strawberry, New York	39
1923	Cy Williams, Philadelphia	41	1955	Willie Mays, New York	51	1989	Kevin Mitchell, San Francisco	47
1924	Jacques Fournier, Brooklyn	27	1956	Duke Snider, Brooklyn	43			
1925	Rogers Hornsby, St. Louis	39	1957	Hank Aaron, Milwaukee	44	1990	Ryne Sandberg, Chicago	40
1926	Hack Wilson, Chicago	21	1958	Ernie Banks, Chicago	47	1991	Howard Johnson, New York	38
1927	Hack Wilson, Chicago; Cy Williams, Philadelphia	30	1959	Ed Mathews, Milwaukee	46	1992	Fred McGriff, San Diego	35
			1960	Ernie Banks, Chicago	41	1993	Barry Bonds, San Francisco	46
1928	Hack Wilson, Chicago; Jim Bottomley, St. Louis	31	1961	Orlando Cepeda, San Francisco	46	1994[2]	Matt Williams, San Francisco	43
						1995	Dante Bichette, Colorado	40
1929	Chuck Klein, Philadelphia	43	1962	Willie Mays, San Francisco	49	1996	Andres Galarraga, Colorado	47
1930	Hack Wilson, Chicago	56	1963	Hank Aaron, Milwaukee;	44	1997	Larry Walker, Colorado	49
1931	Chuck Klein, Philadelphia	31		Willie McCovey, San Francisco		1998	Mark McGwire, St. Louis	70
1932	Chuck Klein, Philadelphia; Mel Ott, New York	38	1964	Willie Mays, San Francisco	47	1999	Mark McGwire, St. Louis	65
1933	Chuck Klein, Philadelphia	28	1965	Willie Mays, San Francisco	52	2000	Sammy Sosa, Chicago	50
1934	Mel Ott, New York; Rip Collins, St. Louis	35	1966	Hank Aaron, Atlanta	44	2001	Barry Bonds, San Francisco	73
			1967	Hank Aaron, Atlanta	39	2002	Sammy Sosa, Chicago	49
1935	Wally Berger, Boston	34	1968	Willie McCovey, San Francisco	36	2003	Jim Thome, Philadelphia	47
1936	Mel Ott, New York	33				2004	Adrian Beltre, Los Angeles	48
1937	Mel Ott, New York; Joe Medwick, St. Louis	31	1969	Willie McCovey, San Francisco	45			

1. Split season because of players' strike. 2. Season ended on Aug. 12 because of players' strike.

NATIONAL LEAGUE BATTING CHAMPIONS

Year	Player, team	Avg.	Year	Player, team	Avg.	Year	Player, team	Avg.
1876	Roscoe Barnes, Chicago	.404	1901	Jesse Burkett, St. Louis	.382	1926	Gene Hargrave, Cincinnati	.353
1877	Jim White, Boston	.385	1902	Clarence Beaumont, Pittsburgh	.357	1927	Paul Waner; Pittsburgh	.380
1878	Abner Dalrymple, Milwaukee	.356				1928	Rogers Hornsby, Boston	.387
1879	Cap Anson, Chicago	.407	1903	Honus Wagner, Pittsburgh	.355	1929	Lefty O'Doul, Philadelphia	.398
1880	George Gore, Chicago	.365	1904	Honus Wagner, Pittsburgh	.349	1930	Bill Terry, New York	.401
1881	Cap Anson, Chicago	.399	1905	Cy Seymour, Cincinnati	.377	1931	Chick Hafey, St. Louis	.349
1882	Dan Brouthers, Buffalo	.367	1906	Honus Wagner, Pittsburgh	.339	1932	Lefty O'Doul, Brooklyn	.368
1883	Dan Brouthers, Buffalo	.371	1907	Honus Wagner, Pittsburgh	.350	1933	Chuck Klein, Philadelphia	.368
1884	James O'Rourke, Buffalo	.350	1908	Honus Wagner, Pittsburgh	.354	1934	Paul Waner, Pittsburgh	.362
1885	Roger Connor, New York	.371	1909	Honus Wagner, Pittsburgh	.339	1935	Arky Vaughan, Pittsburgh	.385
1886	King Kelly, Chicago	.388	1910	Sherwood Magee, Philadelphia	.331	1936	Paul Waner, Pittsburgh	.373
1887	Cap Anson, Chicago	.421				1937	Joe Medwick, St. Louis	.374
1888	Cap Anson, Chicago	.343	1911	Honus Wagner, Pittsburgh	.334	1938	Ernie Lombardi, Cincinnati	.342
1889	Dan Brouthers, Boston	.373	1912	Henry Zimmerman, Chicago	.372	1939	John Mize, St. Louis	.349
1890	John Glasscock, New York	.336	1913	Jake Daubert, Brooklyn	.350	1940	Debs Garms, Pittsburgh	.355
1891	William Hamilton, Philadelphia	.338	1914	Jake Daubert, Brooklyn	.329	1941	Pete Reiser, Brooklyn	.343
			1915	Larry Doyle, New York	.320	1942	Ernie Lombardi, Boston	.330
1892	Dan Brouthers, Brooklyn; Clarence Childs, Cleveland	.335	1916	Hal Chase, Cincinnati	.339	1943	Stan Musial, St. Louis	.357
			1917	Edd Roush, Cincinnati	.341	1944	Dixie Walker, Brooklyn	.357
1893	Hugh Duffy, Boston	.378	1918	Zack Wheat, Brooklyn	.335	1945	Phil Cavarretta, Chicago	.355
1894	Hugh Duffy, Boston	.438	1919	Edd Roush, Cincinnati	.321	1946	Stan Musial, St. Louis	.365
1895	Jesse Burkett, Cleveland	.423	1920	Rogers Hornsby, St. Louis	.370	1947	Harry Walker, St. Louis-Philadelphia	.363
1896	Jesse Burkett, Cleveland	.410	1921	Rogers Hornsby, St. Louis	.397			
1897	Willie Keeler, Baltimore	.432	1922	Rogers Hornsby, St. Louis	.401	1948	Stan Musial, St. Louis	.376
1898	Willie Keeler, Baltimore	.379	1923	Rogers Hornsby, St. Louis	.384	1949	Jackie Robinson, Brooklyn	.342
1899	Ed Delahanty, Philadelphia	.408	1924	Rogers Hornsby, St. Louis	.424	1950	Stan Musial, St. Louis	.346
1900	Honus Wagner, Pittsburgh	.381	1925	Rogers Hornsby, St. Louis	.403	1951	Stan Musial, St. Louis	.355

Year	Player, team	Avg.	Year	Player, team	Avg.	Year	Player, team	Avg.
1952	Stan Musial, St. Louis	.336	1970	Rico Carty, Atlanta	.366	1988	Tony Gwynn, San Diego	.313
1953	Carl Furillo, Brooklyn	.344	1971	Joe Torre, St. Louis	.363	1989	Tony Gwynn, San Diego	.336
1954	Willie Mays, New York	.345	1972	Billy Williams, Chicago	.333	1990	Willie McGee, St. Louis	.335
1955	Richie Ashburn, Philadelphia	.338	1973	Pete Rose, Cincinnati	.338	1991	Terry Pendleton, Atlanta	.319
1956	Hank Aaron, Milwaukee	.328	1974	Ralph Garr, Atlanta	.353	1992	Gary Sheffield, San Diego	.330
1957	Stan Musial, St. Louis	.351	1975	Bill Madlock, Chicago	.354	1993	Andres Galarraga, Colorado	.370
1958	Richie Ashburn, Philadelphia	.350	1976	Bill Madlock, Chicago	.339	1994²	Tony Gwynn, San Diego	.394
1959	Hank Aaron, Milwaukee	.355	1977	Dave Parker, Pittsburgh	.338	1995	Tony Gwynn, San Diego	.368
1960	Dick Groat, Pittsburgh	.325	1978	Dave Parker, Pittsburgh	.334	1996	Tony Gwynn, San Diego	.353
1961	Roberto Clemente, Pittsburgh	.351	1979	Keith Hernandez, St. Louis	.344	1997	Tony Gwynn, San Diego	.372
1962	Tommy Davis, Los Angeles	.346	1980	Bill Buckner, Chicago	.324	1998	Larry Walker, Colorado	.363
1963	Tommy Davis, Los Angeles	.326	1981¹	Bill Madlock, Pittsburgh	.341	1999	Larry Walker, Colorado	.379
1964	Roberto Clemente, Pittsburgh	.339	1982	Al Oliver, Montreal	.331	2000	Todd Helton, Colorado	.372
1965	Roberto Clemente, Pittsburgh	.329	1983	Bill Madlock, Pittsburgh	.323	2001	Larry Walker, Colorado	.350
1966	Matty Alou, Pittsburgh	.342	1984	Tony Gwynn, San Diego	.351	2002	Barry Bonds, San Francisco	.370
1967	Roberto Clemente, Pittsburgh	.357	1985	Willie McGee, St. Louis	.353	2003	Albert Pujols, St. Louis	.359
1968	Pete Rose, Cincinnati	.335	1986	Tim Raines, Montreal	.334	2004	Barry Bonds, San Francisco	.362
1969	Pete Rose, Cincinnati	.348	1987	Tony Gwynn, San Diego	.370			

1. Split season because of players' strike. 2. Season ended on Aug. 12 because of players' strike.

MOST VALUABLE PLAYERS
(Baseball Writers' Association selections)

American League

Year	Player, team
1931	Lefty Grove, Philadelphia
1932–33	Jimmie Foxx, Philadelphia
1934	Mickey Cochrane, Detroit
1935	Hank Greenberg, Detroit
1936	Lou Gehrig, New York
1937	Charlie Gehringer, Detroit
1938	Jimmie Foxx, Boston
1939	Joe DiMaggio, New York
1940	Hank Greenberg, Detroit
1941	Joe DiMaggio, New York
1942	Joe Gordon, New York
1943	Spurgeon Chandler, New York
1944–45	Hal Newhouser, Detroit
1946	Ted Williams, Boston
1947	Joe DiMaggio, New York
1948	Lou Boudreau, Cleveland
1949	Ted Williams, Boston
1950	Phil Rizzuto, New York
1951	Yogi Berra, New York
1952	Bobby Shantz, Philadelphia
1953	Al Rosen, Cleveland
1954–55	Yogi Berra, New York
1956–57	Mickey Mantle, New York
1958	Jackie Jensen, Boston
1959	Nellie Fox, Chicago
1960–61	Roger Maris, New York
1962	Mickey Mantle, New York
1963	Elston Howard, New York
1964	Brooks Robinson, Baltimore
1965	Zoilo Versalles, Minnesota
1966	Frank Robinson, Baltimore
1967	Carl Yastrzemski, Boston
1968	Dennis McLain, Detroit
1969	Harmon Killebrew, Minnesota
1970	John (Boog) Powell, Baltimore
1971	Vida Blue, Oakland
1972	Dick Allen, Chicago
1973	Reggie Jackson, Oakland
1974	Jeff Burroughs, Texas
1975	Fred Lynn, Boston
1976	Thurman Munson, New York
1977	Rod Carew, Minnesota
1978	Jim Rice, Boston
1979	Don Baylor, California
1980	George Brett, Kansas City
1981	Rollie Fingers, Milwaukee
1982	Robin Yount, Milwaukee
1983	Cal Ripken, Jr., Baltimore
1984	Willie Hernandez, Detroit
1985	Don Mattingly, New York
1986	Roger Clemens, Boston
1987	George Bell, Toronto
1988	Jose Canseco, Oakland
1989	Robin Yount, Milwaukee
1990	Rickey Henderson, Oakland
1991	Cal Ripken, Jr., Baltimore
1992	Dennis Eckersley, Oakland
1993	Frank Thomas, Chicago
1994	Frank Thomas, Chicago
1995	Mo Vaughn, Boston
1996	Juan Gonzalez, Texas
1997	Ken Griffey, Jr., Seattle
1998	Juan Gonzalez, Texas
1999	Ivan Rodriguez, Texas
2000	Jason Giambi, Oakland
2001	Ichiro Suzuki, Seattle
2002	Miguel Tejada, Oakland
2003	Alex Rodriguez, Texas

National League

Year	Player, team
1931	Frank Frisch, St. Louis
1932	Chuck Klein, Philadelphia
1933	Carl Hubbell, New York
1934	Dizzy Dean, St. Louis
1935	Gabby Hartnett, Chicago
1936	Carl Hubbell, New York
1937	Joe Medwick, St. Louis
1938	Ernie Lombardi, Cincinnati
1939	Bucky Walters, Cincinnati
1940	Frank McCormick, Cincinnati
1941	Dolph Camilli, Brooklyn
1942	Mort Cooper, St. Louis
1943	Stan Musial, St. Louis
1944	Marty Marion, St. Louis
1945	Phil Cavarretta, Chicago
1946	Stan Musial, St. Louis
1947	Bob Elliott, Boston
1948	Stan Musial, St. Louis
1949	Jackie Robinson, Brooklyn
1950	Jim Konstanty, Philadelphia
1951	Roy Campanella, Brooklyn
1952	Hank Sauer, Chicago
1953	Roy Campanella, Brooklyn
1954	Willie Mays, New York
1955	Roy Campanella, Brooklyn
1956	Don Newcombe, Brooklyn
1957	Hank Aaron, Milwaukee
1958–59	Ernie Banks, Chicago
1960	Dick Groat, Pittsburgh
1961	Frank Robinson, Cincinnati
1962	Maury Wills, Los Angeles
1963	Sandy Koufax, Los Angeles
1964	Ken Boyer, St. Louis
1965	Willie Mays, San Francisco
1966	Roberto Clemente, Pittsburgh
1967	Orlando Cepeda, St. Louis
1968	Bob Gibson, St. Louis
1969	Willie McCovey, San Francisco
1970	Johnny Bench, Cincinnati
1971	Joe Torre, St. Louis
1972	Johnny Bench, Cincinnati
1973	Pete Rose, Cincinnati
1974	Steve Garvey, Los Angeles
1975–76	Joe Morgan, Cincinnati
1977	George Foster, Cincinnati
1978	Dave Parker, Pittsburgh
1979	Willie Stargell, Pittsburgh
1979	Keith Hernandez, St. Louis
1980	Mike Schmidt, Philadelphia
1981	Mike Schmidt, Philadelphia
1982	Dale Murphy, Atlanta
1983	Dale Murphy, Atlanta
1984	Ryne Sandberg, Chicago
1985	Willie McGee, St. Louis
1986	Mike Schmidt, Philadelphia
1987	Andre Dawson, Chicago
1988	Kirk Gibson, Los Angeles
1989	Kevin Mitchell, San Francisco
1990	Barry Bonds, Pittsburgh
1991	Terry Pendleton, Atlanta
1992	Barry Bonds, Pittsburgh
1993	Barry Bonds, San Francisco
1994	Jeff Bagwell, Houston
1995	Barry Larkin, Cincinnati
1996	Ken Caminiti, San Diego
1997	Larry Walker, Colorado
1998	Sammy Sosa, Chicago
1999	Chipper Jones, Atlanta
2000	Jeff Kent, San Francisco
2001–03	Barry Bonds, San Francisco

MAJOR LEAGUE LIFETIME RECORDS

(through 2004)

Pitching Wins
(Boldface indicates player active in 2004)

		W	L	ERA	G
1.	Cy Young	511	316	2.63	906
2.	Walter Johnson	417	279	2.17	802
3.	Grover Alexander	373	208	2.56	696
4.	Christy Mathewson	373	188	2.13	635
5.	Pud Galvin	365	310	2.85	705
6.	Warren Spahn	363	245	3.09	750
7.	Kid Nichols	361	208	2.95	620
8.	Tim Keefe	342	225	2.62	600
9.	Steve Carlton	329	244	3.22	741
10.	**Roger Clemens**	**328**	**164**	**3.18**	**640**
11.	John Clarkson	328	178	2.81	531
12.	Eddie Plank	326	194	2.35	623
13.	Nolan Ryan	324	292	3.19	807
14.	Don Sutton	324	256	3.26	774
15.	Phil Niekro	318	274	3.35	864
16.	Gaylord Perry	314	265	3.11	777
17.	Tom Seaver	311	205	2.86	656
18.	Charley Radbourn	309	195	2.67	528
19.	Mickey Welch	307	210	2.71	565
20.	**Greg Maddux**	**305**	**174**	**2.95**	**608**
21.	Lefty Grove	300	141	3.06	616
22.	Early Wynn	300	244	3.54	691
23.	Bobby Mathews	297	248	2.85	578
24.	Tommy John	288	231	3.34	760
25.	Bert Blyleven	287	250	3.31	692

Pitchers Active in 2004

		W	L	ERA	G
1.	Roger Clemens	328	164	3.18	640
2.	Greg Maddux	305	174	2.95	608
3.	Tom Glavine	262	171	3.44	570
4.	Randy Johnson	246	128	3.07	489
5.	David Wells	212	136	4.03	588
6.	Mike Mussina	211	119	3.59	413
7.	Kevin Brown	207	137	3.20	473
8.	Chuck Finley	200	173	3.85	524
9.	Jamie Moyer	192	145	4.15	506
10.	Curt Schilling	184	123	3.32	482

Leading Batters, by Batting Average

		G	AB	H	Avg.
1.	Ty Cobb	3,035	11,429	4,191	.367
2.	Rogers Hornsby	2,259	8,173	2,930	.358
3.	Ed Delahanty	1,835	7,505	2,596	.346
4.	Tris Speaker	2,789	10,195	3,514	.345
5.	Billy Hamilton	1,591	6,269	2,159	.344
5.	Ted Williams	2,292	7,706	2,654	.344
7.	Dan Brouthers	1,673	6,711	2,296	.342
7.	Harry Heilmann	2,147	7,787	2,660	.342
7.	Babe Ruth	2,503	8,399	2,873	.342
10.	Willie Keeler	2,123	8,591	2,932	.341
10.	Bill Terry	1,721	6,428	2,193	.341
12.	Lou Gehrig	2,164	8,001	2,721	.340
13.	George Sisler	2,055	8,267	2,812	.340
14.	Jesse Burkett	2,066	8,421	2,850	.338
15.	Tony Gwynn	2,440	9,288	3,141	.338
16.	Nap Lajoie	2,480	9,589	3,242	.338
17.	Al Simmons	2,215	8,759	2,927	.334
18.	Cap Anson	2,523	10,278	3,418	.333
19.	Eddie Collins	2,826	9,949	3,315	.333
20.	Paul Waner	2,549	9,459	3,152	.333
21.	Stan Musial	3,026	10,972	3,630	.331
22.	Sam Thompson	1,407	5,984	1,979	.331
23.	Heinie Manush	2,008	7,654	2,524	.330
24.	Wade Boggs	2,440	9,180	3,010	.328
25.	Rod Carew	2,469	9,315	3,053	.328

Players Active in 2004 (3,000 at-bats minimum)

		G	AB	H	Avg.
1.	Todd Helton	1,135	4,051	1,372	.339
2	Vladimir Guerrero	1,160	4,375	1,421	.325
3.	Nomar Garciaparra	1,009	4,133	1,330	.322
4.	Manny Ramirez	1,535	5,572	1,760	.316
5.	Derek Jeter	1,366	5,513	1,734	.315
6.	Mike Piazza	1,590	5,805	1,829	.315
7.	Larry Walker	1,888	6,592	2,069	.314
8.	Edgar Martinez	2,055	7,213	2,247	.312
9.	Frank Thomas	1,925	6,851	2,113	.308
10.	Magglio Ordonez	1,001	3,807	1,167	.307

MAJOR LEAGUE ALL-TIME PITCHING RECORDS

(through 2004)

Most Games Won—511, Cy Young, Cleveland N.L., 1890–98, St. Louis N.L., 1899–1900, Boston A.L., 1901–08, Cleveland A.L., 1909–11, Boston N.L., 1911.

Most Games Won, Season—54, Al Spalding, Boston N.A., 1875. (Since 1900—41, Jack Chesbro, New York A.L., 1904.)

Most Consecutive Games Won—24, Carl Hubbell, New York N.L., 1936 (16) and 1937 (8).

Most Consecutive Games Won, Season—19, Tim Keefe, New York N.L., 1888; Rube Marquard, New York N.L., 1912.

Most Years Won 20 or More Games—16, Cy Young, Cleveland N.L., 1891–98, St. Louis N.L., 1899–1900, Boston A.L., 1901–04, 1907–08.

Most Shutouts—110, Walter Johnson, Washington A.L., 1907–27.

Most Shutouts, Season—16, Grover Alexander, Philadelphia N.L., 1916.

Most Consecutive Shutouts—6, Don Drysdale, Los Angeles N.L., 1968.

Most Consecutive Scoreless Innings—59, Orel Hershiser, Los Angeles Dodgers, 1988.

Most Strikeouts—5,714, Nolan Ryan, New York N.L., California A.L., Houston N.L., 1968–1988 Texas, 1989–93.

Most Strikeouts, Season—513, Matthew Kilroy, Baltimore A.A., 1886. (Since 1900—383, Nolan Ryan, California A.L., 1973.)

Most Strikeouts, Game—21, Tom Cheney, Washington A.L., 1962, 16 innings. 20, Roger Clemens, Boston A.L., 1986, nine innings; Kerry Wood, Chicago N.L., 1998, nine innings.

Most Consecutive Strikeouts—10, Tom Seaver, New York N.L. vs. San Diego, April 22, 1970.

Most Games, Season—106, Mike Marshall, Los Angeles N.L., 1974.

Most Complete Games, Season—75, William White, Cincinnati N.L., 1879. (Since 1900—48, Jack Chesbro, New York A.L., 1904.)

CY YOUNG AWARD

1956   Don Newcombe, Brooklyn N.L.
1957   Warren Spahn, Milwaukee N.L.
1958   Bob Turley, New York A.L.
1959   Early Wynn, Chicago A.L.
1960   Vernon Law, Pittsburgh N.L
1961   Whitey Ford, New York A.L.
1962   Don Drysdale, Los Angeles N.L.
1963   Sandy Koufax, Los Angeles N.L.
1964   Dean Chance, Los Angeles A.L.
1965   Sandy Koufax, Los Angeles N.L.
1966   Sandy Koufax, Los Angeles N.L.
1967   Jim Lonborg, Boston A.L.;
         Mike McCormick, San Francisco
         N.L.
1968   Dennis McLain, Detroit A.L.;
         Bob Gibson, St. Louis N.L.
1969   Mike Cuellar, Baltimore A.L. and
         Dennis McLain, Detroit A.L.
         (tied); Tom Seaver, New York N.L.
1970   Jim Perry, Minnesota A.L.;
         Bob Gibson, St. Louis N.L.
1971   Vida Blue, Oakland A.L.;
         Ferguson Jenkins, Chicago N.L.
1972   Gaylord Perry, Cleveland A.L.;
         Steve Carlton, Philadelphia N.L.
1973   Jim Palmer, Baltimore A.L.;
         Tom Seaver, New York N.L.
1974   Catfish Hunter, Oakland A.L.;
         Mike Marshall, Los Angeles N.L.

1975   Jim Palmer, Baltimore A.L.;
         Tom Seaver, New York N.L.
1976   Jim Palmer, Baltimore A.L.;
         Randy Jones, San Diego N.L.
1977   Sparky Lyle, New York A.L.;
         Steve Carlton, Philadelphia N.L.
1978   Ron Guidry, New York A.L.;
         Gaylord Perry, San Diego N.L.
1979   Mike Flanagan, Baltimore A.L.;
         Bruce Sutter, Chicago N.L.
1980   Steve Stone, Baltimore A.L.;
         Steve Carlton, Philadelphia N.L.
1981   Rollie Fingers, Milwaukee A.L.;
         Fernando Valenzuela, Los
         Angeles N.L.
1982   Pete Vuckovich, Milwaukee A.L.;
         Steve Carlton, Philadelphia N.L.
1983   LaMarr Hoyt, Chicago A.L.;
         John Denny, Philadelphia N.L.
1984   Willie Hernandez, Detroit A.L.;
         Rick Sutcliffe, Chicago N.L.
1985   Bret Saberhagen, Kansas City A.L.;
         Dwight Gooden, New York N.L.
1986   Roger Clemens, Boston A.L.;
         Mike Scott, Houston N.L.
1987   Roger Clemens, Boston A.L.;
         Steve Bedrosian, Philadelphia N.L.
1988   Frank Viola, Minnesota A.L.;
         Orel Hershiser, Los Angeles, N.L.

1989   Bret Saberhagen, Kansas A.L.;
         Mark Davis, San Diego N.L.
1990   Bob Welch, Oakland A.L.;
         Doug Drabek, Pittsburgh N.L.
1991   Roger Clemens, Boston A.L.;
         Tom Glavine, Atlanta N.L.
1992   Dennis Eckersley, Oakland A.L.;
         Greg Maddux, Chicago N.L.
1993   Jack McDowell, Chicago A.L.;
         Greg Maddux, Atlanta N.L.
1994   David Cone, Kansas A.L.;
         Greg Maddux, Atlanta N.L.
1995   Randy Johnson, Seattle A.L.;
         Greg Maddux, Atlanta N.L.
1996   Pat Hentgen, Toronto A.L.;
         John Smoltz, Atlanta N.L.
1997   Roger Clemens, Toronto A.L.;
         Pedro Martinez, Montreal N.L.
1998   Roger Clemens, Toronto A.L.;
         Tom Glavine, Atlanta N.L.
1999– Pedro Martinez, Boston A.L.;
2000   Randy Johnson, Arizona N.L.
2001   Roger Clemens, New York A.L.;
         Randy Johnson, Arizona N.L.
2002   Barry Zito, Oakland A.L.;
         Randy Johnson, Arizona N.L.
2003   Roy Halladay, Toronto A.L.
         Eric Gagne, Los Angeles N.L.

ROOKIE OF THE YEAR
(Baseball Writers' Association selections)

American League

1949   Roy Sievers, St. Louis
1950   Walt Dropo, Boston
1951   Gil McDougald, New York
1952   Harry Byrd, Philadelphia
1953   Harvey Kuenn, Detroit
1954   Bob Grim, New York
1955   Herb Score, Cleveland
1956   Luis Aparicio, Chicago
1957   Tony Kubek, New York
1958   Albie Pearson, Washington
1959   Bob Allison, Washington
1960   Ron Hansen, Baltimore
1961   Don Schwall, Boston
1962   Tom Tresh, New York
1963   Gary Peters, Chicago
1964   Tony Oliva, Minnesota
1965   Curt Blefary, Baltimore
1966   Tommy Agee, Chicago
1967   Rod Carew, Minnesota

1968   Stan Bahnsen, New York
1969   Lou Piniella, Kansas City
1970   Thurman Munson, New York
1971   Chris Chambliss, Cleveland
1972   Carlton Fisk, Boston
1973   Alonzo Bumbry, Baltimore
1974   Mike Hargrove, Texas
1975   Fred Lynn, Boston
1976   Mark Fidrych, Detroit
1977   Eddie Murray, Baltimore
1978   Lou Whitaker, Detroit
1979   Alfredo Griffin, Toronto
1979   John Castino, Minnesota
1980   Joe Charboneau, Cleveland
1981   Dave Righetti, New York
1982   Cal Ripken, Jr., Baltimore
1983   Ron Kittle, Chicago
1984   Alvin Davis, Seattle
1985   Ozzie Guillen, Chicago

1986   Jose Canseco, Oakland
1987   Mark McGwire, Oakland
1988   Walter Weiss, Oakland
1989   Gregg Olson, Baltimore
1990   Sandy Alomar Jr., Cleveland
1991   Chuck Knoblauch, Minnesota
1992   Pat Listach, Milwaukee
1993   Tim Salmon, California
1994   Bob Hamelin, Kansas City
1995   Marty Cordova, Minnesota
1996   Derek Jeter, New York
1997   Nomar Garciaparra, Boston
1998   Ben Grieve, Oakland
1999   Carlos Beltran, Kansas City
2000   Kazuhiro Sasaki, Seattle
2001   Ichiro Suzuki, Seattle
2002   Eric Hinske, Toronto
2003   Angel Berroa, Kansas City

National League

1949   Don Newcombe, Brooklyn
1950   Sam Jethroe, Boston
1951   Willie Mays, New York
1952   Joe Black, Brooklyn
1953   Jim Gilliam, Brooklyn
1954   Wally Moon, St. Louis
1955   Bill Virdon, St. Louis
1956   Frank Robinson, Cincinnati
1957   Jack Sanford, Philadelphia
1958   Orlando Cepeda, San Francisco
1959   Willie McCovey, San Francisco
1960   Frank Howard, Los Angeles
1961   Billy Williams, Chicago
1962   Ken Hubbs, Chicago
1963   Pete Rose, Cincinnati
1964   Richie Allen, Philadelphia
1965   Jim Lefebvre, Los Angeles
1966   Tommy Helms, Cincinnati
1967   Tom Seaver, New York

1968   Johnny Bench, Cincinnati
1969   Ted Sizemore, Los Angeles
1970   Carl Morton, Montreal
1971   Earl Williams, Atlanta
1972   Jon Matlack, New York
1973   Gary Matthews, San Francisco
1974   Bake McBride, St. Louis
1975   John Montefusco, San Francisco
1976   Pat Zachry, Cincinnati
1976   Bruce Metzger, San Diego
1977   Andre Dawson, Montreal
1978   Bob Horner, Atlanta
1979   Rick Sutcliffe, Los Angeles
1980   Steve Howe, Los Angeles
1981   Fernando Valenzuela, Los Angeles
1982   Steve Sax, Los Angeles
1983   Darryl Strawberry, New York
1984   Dwight Gooden, New York
1985   Vince Coleman, St. Louis

1986   Todd Worrell, St. Louis
1987   Benito Santiago, San Diego
1988   Chris Sabo, Cincinnati
1989   Jerome Walton, Chicago
1990   Dave Justice, Atlanta
1991   Jeff Baguell, Houston
1992   Eric Karros, Los Angeles
1993   Mike Piazza, Los Angeles
1994   Raul Mondesi, Los Angeles
1995   Hideo Nomo, Los Angeles
1996   Todd Hollandsworth, Los Angeles
1997   Scott Rolen, Philadelphia
1998   Kerry Wood, Chicago
1999   Scott Williamson, Cincinnati
2000   Rafael Furcal, Atlanta
2001   Albert Pujols, St. Louis
2002   Jason Jennings, Colorado
2003   Dontrelle Willis, Florida

MAJOR LEAGUE INDIVIDUAL ALL-TIME HITTING RECORDS
(through 2004)

Highest Batting Average, Season—.440, Hugh Duffy, Boston N.L., 1894; .435, Tip O'Neill, St. Louis, A.A., 1887. (Since 1900—.426, Nap Lajoie, Phil. A.L., 1901); 424, Rogers Hornsby, St. Louis N.L., 1924.

Most Times at Bat—14,053, Pete Rose, Cincinnati N.L., 1963–78; Philadelphia N.L., 1979–83; Montreal N.L., 1984; Cincinnati N.L., 1984–86.

Most Years Batted .300 or Better—23, Ty Cobb, Detroit A.L., 1906–26, Philadelphia A.L., 1927–28.

Most Hits—4,256, Pete Rose, Cincinnati 1963–79, Philadelphia 1980–83, Montreal 1984, Cincinnati 1984–86.

Most Hits, Season—262, Ichiro Suzuki, Seattle A.L., 2004.

Most Hits in Succession—12, Mike Higgins, Boston A.L., in four games, 1938; Walt Dropo, Detroit A.L., in three games, 1952.

Most Consecutive Games Batted Safely—56, Joe DiMaggio, New York A.L., 1941.

Most Runs—2,295, Rickey Henderson, Oakland A.L., 1979–84, 1989–93, 1994–95, 1998; New York A.L., 1985–89; Toronto A.L., 1993; San Diego N.L., 1996, 1997, 2001; Anaheim A.L., 1997; New York N.L., 1999–2000; Seattle A.L., 2000; Boston A.L., 2002; Los Angeles N.L., 2003.

Most Runs, Season—192, William Hamilton, Philadelphia N.L., 1894. (Since 1900—177, Babe Ruth, New York A.L., 1921.)

Most Runs Batted in—2,297, Hank Aaron, Milwaukee N.L., 1954–1965; Atlanta N.L., 1966–74; Milwaukee A.L., 1975–76.

Most Runs Batted in, Season—191, Hack Wilson, Chicago N.L., 1930.

Most Home Runs—755, Hank Aaron, Milwaukee N.L., 1954–1965; Atlanta N.L., 1966–74; Milwaukee A.L., 1975–76.

Most Home Runs, Season—162-game season: 73, Barry Bonds, San Francisco N.L., 2001; 70, Mark McGwire, St. Louis N.L., 1998; 66, Sammy Sosa, Chicago N.L., 1998; 65, Mark McGwire, St. Louis N.L., 1999; 64, Sammy Sosa, Chicago N.L., 2001; 63, Sammy Sosa, Chicago N.L., 1999; 61, Roger Maris, New York A.L., 1961. 154-game season: 60, Babe Ruth, New York A.L., 1927.

Most Home Runs with Bases Filled—23, Lou Gehrig, New York A.L., 1927–39.

Most 2-Base Hits—792, Tris Speaker, Boston A.L., 1907–15, Cleveland A.L., 1916–26, Washington A.L., 1927, Philadelphia A.L., 1928.

Most 2-Base Hits, Season—67, Earl Webb, Boston A.L., 1931.

Most 3-Base Hits—309, Sam Crawford, Cincinnati N.L., 1899–1902, Detroit A.L., 1903–17.

Most 3-Base Hits, Season—36, Owen Wilson, Pittsburgh N.L., 1912.

Most Games Played—3,562, Pete Rose, Cincinnati N.L., Philadelphia N.L., Montreal N.L., 1964–86.

Most Consecutive Games Played—2,632, Cal Ripken, Jr., Baltimore Orioles A.L., 1981–1998.

Most Bases on Balls—2,302, Barry Bonds, Pittsburgh N.L., 1986–92; San Francisco N.L., 1993–.

Most Bases on Balls, Season—232, Barry Bonds, San Francisco N.L., 2004.

Most Strikeouts, Season—195, Adam Dunn, Cincinnati N.L., 2004.

Most Stolen Bases, Lifetime—1,406, Rickey Henderson, Oakland A.L., 1979–84, 1989–93, 1994–95, 1998; New York A.L., 1985–89; Toronto A.L., 1993; San Diego N.L., 1996, 1997, 2001; Anaheim A.L., 1997; New York N.L., 1999–2000; Seattle A.L., 2000; Boston A.L., 2002; Los Angeles N.L., 2003.

Most Stolen Bases, Season—138, Hugh Nicol, Cincinnati A.A., 1887. Since 1900: 130, Rickey Henderson, Oakland A.L., 1982; 118, Lou Brock, St. Louis N.L., 1974.

Most Stolen Bases, Game—7, George Gore, Chicago N.L. 1881; William Hamilton, Philadelphia N.L. 1894. (Since 1900—6, Eddie Collins, Philadelphia A.L., 1912.) and Otis Nixon, Atlanta N.L., 1991.

Most Times Stealing Home, Lifetime—50, Ty Cobb, Detroit-Phil. A.L., 1905–28.

MOST HOME RUNS IN ONE SEASON—45 OR MORE

HR	Player/Team	Year
73	Barry Bonds, San Francisco (N.L.)	2001
70	Mark McGwire, St. Louis (N.L.)	1998
66	Sammy Sosa, Chicago (N.L.)	1998
65	Mark McGwire, St. Louis (N.L.)	1999
64	Sammy Sosa, Chicago (N.L.)	2001
63	Sammy Sosa, Chicago (N.L.)	1999
61	Roger Maris, New York (A.L.)	1961
60	Babe Ruth, New York (A.L.)	1927
59	Babe Ruth, New York (A.L.)	1921
58	Jimmie Foxx, Philadelphia (A.L.)	1932
58	Hank Greenberg, Detroit (A.L.)	1938
58	Mark McGwire, Oakland (A.L.), St. Louis (N.L.)	1997
57	Luis Gonzalez, Arizona (N.L.)	2001
57	Alex Rodriguez, Texas (A.L.)	2002
56	Hack Wilson, Chicago (N.L.)	1930
56	Ken Griffey, Jr., Seattle (A.L.)	1997
56	Ken Griffey, Jr., Seattle (A.L.)	1998
54	Babe Ruth, New York (A.L.)	1920
54	Babe Ruth, New York (A.L.)	1928
54	Ralph Kiner, Pittsburgh (N.L.)	1949
54	Mickey Mantle, New York (A.L.)	1961
52	Mickey Mantle, New York (A.L.)	1956
52	Willie Mays, San Francisco (N.L.)	1965
52	George Foster, Cincinnati (N.L.)	1977
52	Mark McGwire, Oakland (A.L.)	1996
52	Alex Rodriguez, Texas (A.L.)	2001
52	Jim Thome, Cleveland (A.L.)	2002
51	Ralph Kiner, Pittsburgh (N.L.)	1947
51	John Mize, New York (N.L.)	1947
51	Willie Mays, New York (N.L.)	1955
51	Cecil Fielder (A.L.)	1990
50	Jimmie Foxx, Boston (A.L.)	1938
50	Albert Belle, Cleveland (A.L.)	1995
50	Brady Anderson, Baltimore (A.L.)	1996
50	Sammy Sosa, Chicago (N.L.)	2000
50	Greg Vaughn, San Diego (N.L.)	1998
49	Babe Ruth, New York (A.L.)	1930
49	Lou Gehrig, New York (A.L.)	1934
49	Lou Gehrig, New York (A.L.)	1936
49	Ted Kluszewski, Cincinnati (N.L.)	1954
49	Willie Mays, San Francisco (N.L.)	1962
49	Harmon Killebrew, Minnesota (A.L.)	1964
49	Frank Robinson, Baltimore (A.L.)	1966
49	Harmon Killebrew, Minnesota (A.L.)	1969
49	Mark McGwire, Oakland (A.L.)	1987
49	Andre Dawson, Chicago (N.L.)	1987
49	Ken Griffey, Jr., Seattle (A.L.)	1996
49	Larry Walker, Colorado (N.L.)	1997
49	Albert Belle, Chicago (A.L.)	1998
49	Barry Bonds, San Francisco (N.L.)	2000
49	Shawn Green, Los Angeles (N.L.)	2001
49	Todd Helton, Colorado (N.L.)	2001
49	Jim Thome, Cleveland (A.L.)	2001
49	Sammy Sosa, Chicago (N.L.)	2002
48	Jimmie Foxx, Philadelphia (A.L.)	1933
48	Harmon Killebrew, Minnesota (A.L.)	1962
48	Frank Howard, Washington (A.L.)	1969
48	Willie Stargell, Pittsburgh (N.L.)	1971

HR	Player/Team	Year
48	Dave Kingman, Chicago (N.L.)	1979
48	Mike Schmidt, Philadelphia (N.L.)	1980
48	Albert Belle, Cleveland (A.L.)	1996
48	Ken Griffey, Jr., Seattle (A.L.)	1999
48	Adrian Beltre, Los Angeles (N.L.)	2004
47	Babe Ruth, New York (A.L.)	1926
47	Ralph Kiner, Pittsburgh (N.L.)	1950
47	Ed Mathews, Milwaukee (N.L.)	1953
47	Ernie Banks, Chicago (N.L.)	1958
47	Willie Mays, San Francisco (N.L.)	1964
47	Hank Aaron, Atlanta (N.L.)	1971
47	Reggie Jackson, Oakland (A.L.)	1969
47	George Bell, Toronto (A.L.)	1987
47	Kevin Mitchell, San Francisco (N.L.)	1989
47	Andres Galarraga, Colorado (N.L.)	1996
47	Juan Gonzalez, Texas (A.L.)	1996
47	Rafael Palmeiro, Texas (A.L.)	1999
47	Jeff Bagwell, Houston (N.L.)	2000
47	Troy Glaus, Anaheim (A.L.)	2000
47	Rafael Palmeiro, Texas (A.L.)	2001
47	Alex Rodriguez, Texas (A.L.)	2003
47	Jim Thome, Philadelphia (N.L.)	2003
46	Babe Ruth, New York (A.L.)	1924
46	Babe Ruth, New York, (A.L.)	1929
46	Babe Ruth, New York (A.L.)	1931
46	Lou Gehrig, New York (A.L.)	1931

HR	Player/Team	Year
46	Joe DiMaggio, New York (A.L.)	1937
46	Ed Mathews, Milwaukee (N.L.)	1959
46	Orlando Cepeda, San Francisco (N.L.)	1961
46	Jim Rice, Boston (A.L.)	1978
46	Juan Gonzalez, Texas (A.L.)	1993
46	Barry Bonds, San Francisco (N.L.)	1993
46	Jose Canseco, Toronto (A.L.)	1998
46	Vinnie Castilla, Colorado (N.L.)	1998
46	Barry Bonds, San Francisco (N.L.)	2002
46	Adam Dunn, Cincinnati (N.L.)	2004
46	Albert Pujols, St. Louis (N.L.)	2004
45	Ernie Banks, Chicago (N.L.)	1959
45	Harmon Killebrew, Minnesota (A.L.)	1963
45	Willie McCovey, San Francisco (N.L.)	1969
45	Johnny Bench, Cincinnati (N.L.)	1970
45	Gorman Thomas, Milwaukee (A.L.)	1979
45	Hank Aaron, Milwaukee (N.L.)	1962
45	Ken Griffey, Jr., Seattle (A.L.)	1993
45	Juan Gonzalez, Texas (A.L.)	1998
45	Manny Ramirez, Cleveland (A.L.)	1998
45	Chipper Jones, Atlanta (N.L.)	1999
45	Greg Vaughn, Cincinnati (N.L.)	1999
45	Barry Bonds, San Francisco (N.L.)	2003
45	Richie Sexson, Milwaukee (N.L.)	2003
45	Barry Bonds, San Francisco (N.L.)	2004

MAJOR LEAGUE BASEBALL—2004

AMERICAN LEAGUE FINAL STANDINGS

EASTERN DIVISION

Team	W	L	Pct	GB
New York Yankees	101	61	.623	—
Boston Red Sox[1]	98	64	.605	3.0
Baltimore Orioles	78	84	.481	23.0
Tampa Bay Devil Rays	70	91	.435	30.5
Toronto Blue Jays	67	94	.416	33.5

CENTRAL DIVISION

Team	W	L	Pct	GB
Minnesota Twins	92	70	.568	—
Chicago White Sox	83	79	.512	9.0
Cleveland Indians	80	82	.494	12.0
Detroit Tigers	72	90	.444	20.0
Kansas City Royals	58	104	.358	34.0

WESTERN DIVISION

Team	W	L	Pct	GB
Anaheim Angels	92	70	.568	—
Oakland Athletics	91	71	.562	1.0
Texas Rangers	89	73	.549	3.0
Seattle Mariners	63	99	.389	29.0

1. Wild card.

AMERICAN LEAGUE LEADERS, 2004

Batting—Ichiro Suzuki, Seattle	.372
Home runs—Manny Ramirez, Boston	43
Runs batted in—Miguel Tejada, Baltimore	150
Runs—Vladimir Guerrero, Anaheim	124
Hits—Ichiro Suzuki, Seattle	262
Stolen bases—Carl Crawford, Tampa Bay	59
Doubles—Brian Roberts, Baltimore	50
Triples—Carl Crawford, Tampa Bay	19
Slugging percentage—Manny Ramirez, Boston	.613

A.L. Pitching

Wins—Curt Schilling, Boston	21
Earned run average—Johan Santana, Minnesota	2.61
Strikeouts—Johan Santana, Minnesota	265
Innings pitched—Mark Buehrle, Chicago	245.1
Complete games—Mark Mulder, Oakland; Sidney Ponson, Baltimore; Jake Westbrook, Cleveland	5
Shutouts—Jeremy Bonderman, Detroit; Tim Hudson, Oakland; Sidney Ponson, Baltimore	2
Saves—Mariano Rivera, New York	53

NATIONAL LEAGUE FINAL STANDINGS

EASTERN DIVISION

Team	W	L	Pct	GB
Atlanta Braves	96	66	.593	—
Philadelphia Phillies	86	76	.531	10.0
Florida Marlins	83	79	.512	13.0
New York Mets	71	91	.438	25.0
Montreal Expos	67	95	.414	29.0

CENTRAL DIVISION

Team	W	L	Pct	GB
St. Louis Cardinals	105	57	.648	—
Houston Astros[1]	92	70	.568	13.0
Chicago Cubs	89	73	.549	16.0
Cincinnati Reds	76	86	.469	29.0
Pittsburgh Pirates	72	89	.447	32.5
Milwaukee Brewers	67	94	.416	37.5

WESTERN DIVISION

Team	W	L	Pct	GB
Los Angeles Dodgers	93	69	.574	—
San Francisco Giants	91	71	.562	2.0
San Diego Padres	87	75	.537	6.0
Colorado Rockies	68	94	.420	25.0
Arizona Diamondbacks	51	111	.315	42.0

1. Wild card.

NATIONAL LEAGUE LEADERS, 2004

Batting—Barry Bonds, San Francisco	.362
Home runs—Adrian Beltre, Los Angeles	48
Runs batted in—Vinny Castilla, Colorado	131
Runs—Albert Pujols, St. Louis	133
Hits—Juan Pierre, Florida	221
Stolen bases—Scott Podsednik, Milwaukee	70
Doubles—Lyle Overbay, Milwaukee	53
Triples—Juan Pierre, Florida	12
Slugging percentage—Barry Bonds, San Francisco	.812

N.L. Pitching

Wins—Roy Oswalt, Houston	20
Earned run average—Jake Peavy, San Diego	2.27
Strikeouts—Randy Johnson, Arizona	290
Innings pitched—Livan Hernandez, Montreal	255.0
Complete games—Livan Hernandez, Montreal	9
Shutouts—Cory Lidle, Philadelphia	3
Saves—Armando Benitez, Florida	47

AMERICAN LEAGUE STATISTICS, 2004

Team Pitching

	W	L	ERA	SHO	H	R	SO
Minnesota	92	70	4.03	9	1,523	715	1,123
Oakland	91	71	4.17	8	1,466	742	1,034
Boston	98	64	4.18	12	1,430	768	1,132
Anaheim	92	70	4.28	11	1,476	734	1,164
Texas	89	73	4.53	9	1,536	794	979
New York	101	61	4.69	5	1,532	808	1,058
Baltimore	78	84	4.70	10	1,488	830	1,090
Seattle	63	99	4.76	7	1,498	823	1,036
Cleveland	80	82	4.81	8	1,553	857	1,115
Tampa Bay	70	91	4.81	5	1,459	842	923
Chicago	83	79	4.91	8	1,505	831	1,013
Toronto	67	94	4.91	11	1,505	823	956
Detroit	72	90	4.93	9	1,542	844	995
Kansas City	58	104	5.15	3	1,638	905	887

Team Batting

	Avg.	AB	R	H	HR	RBI
Anaheim	.282	5,675	836	1,603	162	783
Boston	.282	5,720	949	1,613	222	912
Baltimore	.281	5,736	842	1,614	169	803
Cleveland	.276	5,676	858	1,565	184	820
Detroit	.272	5,623	827	1,531	201	800
Oakland	.270	5,728	793	1,545	189	752
Seattle	.270	5,722	698	1,544	136	658
Chicago	.268	5,534	865	1,481	242	823
New York	.268	5,527	897	1,483	242	863
Minnesota	.266	5,623	780	1,494	191	735
Texas	.266	5,615	860	1,492	227	825
Toronto	.260	5,531	719	1,438	145	680
Kansas City	.259	5,538	720	1,432	150	675
Tampa Bay	.258	5,483	714	1,416	145	685

Individual Pitching
(based on 10 decisions)

	W	L	ERA	IP	H	BB	SO
C. Schilling, Boston	21	6	3.26	226.2	206	35	203
J. Santana, Minnesota	20	6	2.61	228.0	156	54	265
B. Colon, Anaheim	18	12	5.01	208.1	215	71	158
K. Rogers, Texas	18	9	4.76	211.2	248	66	126
M. Mulder, Oakland	17	8	4.43	225.2	223	83	140
M. Buehrle, Chicago	16	10	3.89	245.1	257	51	165
P. Martinez, Boston	16	9	3.90	217.0	193	61	227
R. Drese, Texas	14	10	4.20	207.2	233	58	98
J. Lackey, Anaheim	14	13	4.67	198.1	215	60	144
C. Lee, Cleveland	14	8	5.43	179.0	188	81	161
J. Lieber, New York	14	8	4.33	176.2	216	18	102
R. Lopez, Baltimore	14	9	3.59	170.2	164	54	121
D. Lowe, Boston	14	12	5.42	182.2	224	71	105
C. Silva, Minnesota	14	8	4.21	203.0	255	35	76
J. Vazquez, New York	14	10	4.91	198.0	195	60	150
J. Westbrook, Cleveland	14	9	3.38	215.2	208	61	116
J. Contreras, Chicago	13	9	5.50	170.1	166	84	150
F. Garcia, Chicago	13	11	3.81	210.0	192	64	184
D. Cabrera, Baltimore	12	8	5.00	147.2	145	89	76
J. Garland, Chicago	12	11	4.89	217.0	223	76	113

Individual Batting
(based on 300 plate appearances)

	Avg.	AB	R	H	HR	RBI
I. Suzuki, Seattle	.372	704	101	262	8	60
M. Mora, Baltimore	.340	550	111	187	27	104
V. Guerrero, Anaheim	.337	612	124	206	39	126
I. Rodriguez, Detroit	.334	527	72	176	19	86
E. Durazo, Oakland	.321	511	80	164	22	88
C. Guillen, Detroit	.318	522	97	166	20	97
J. Lopez, Baltimore	.316	579	83	183	23	86
M. Kotsay, Oakland	.314	606	78	190	15	63
M. Young, Texas	.313	690	114	216	22	99
T. Hafner, Cleveland	.311	482	96	150	28	109
M. Tejada, Baltimore	.311	653	107	203	34	150
A. Rowand, Chicago	.310	487	94	151	24	69
M. Ramirez, Boston	.308	568	108	175	43	130
C. Lee, Chicago	.305	591	103	180	31	99
J. Damon, Boston	.304	621	123	189	20	94
R. Ibanez, Seattle	.304	481	67	146	16	62
D. Ortiz, Boston	.301	582	94	175	41	139
L. Ford, Minnesota	.299	569	89	170	15	72
H. Matsui, New York	.298	584	109	174	31	108
C. Crisp, Cleveland	.297	491	78	146	15	71
A. Huff, Tampa Bay	.297	600	92	178	29	104
K. Millar, Boston	.297	508	74	151	18	74

NATIONAL LEAGUE STATISTICS, 2004

Team Pitching

	W	L	ERA	SHO	H	R	SO
Atlanta	96	66	3.74	13	1,475	668	1,025
St. Louis	105	57	3.75	12	1,378	659	1,041
Chicago	89	73	3.81	6	1,363	665	1,346
Los Angeles	93	69	4.01	6	1,386	684	1,066
San Diego	87	75	4.03	3	1,460	705	1,079
Houston	92	70	4.05	13	1,416	698	1,282
New York	71	91	4.09	6	1,452	731	977
Florida	83	79	4.10	14	1,395	700	1,116
Milwaukee	67	94	4.24	10	1,440	757	1,098
Pittsburgh	72	89	4.29	8	1,451	744	1,079
San Francisco	91	71	4.29	8	1,481	770	1,020
Montreal	67	95	4.33	11	1,477	769	1,032
Philadelphia	86	76	4.45	5	1,488	781	1,070
Arizona	51	111	4.98	6	1,480	899	1,153
Cincinnati	76	86	5.19	8	1,595	907	992
Colorado	68	94	5.54	2	1,634	923	947

Team Batting

	Avg.	AB	R	H	HR	RBI
St. Louis	.278	5,555	855	1,544	214	817
Colorado	.275	5,577	833	1,531	202	795
San Diego	.273	5,573	768	1,521	139	722
Atlanta	.270	5,570	803	1,503	178	767
San Francisco	.270	5,546	850	1,500	183	805
Chicago	.268	5,628	789	1,508	235	755
Houston	.267	5,468	803	1,458	187	756
Philadelphia	.267	5,643	840	1,505	215	802
Florida	.264	5,486	718	1,447	148	677
Los Angeles	.262	5,542	761	1,450	203	731
Pittsburgh	.260	5,483	680	1,428	142	648
Arizona	.253	5,544	615	1,401	135	582
Cincinnati	.250	5,518	750	1,380	194	713
Montreal	.249	5,474	635	1,361	151	605
New York	.249	5,532	684	1,376	185	658
Milwaukee	.248	5,483	634	1,358	135	601

Individual Pitching (based on 10 decisions)

	W	L	ERA	IP	H	BB	SO
R. Oswalt, Houston	20	10	3.49	237.0	233	62	206
R. Clemens, Houston	18	4	2.98	214.1	169	79	218
C. Pavano, Florida	18	8	3.00	222.1	212	49	139
J. Schmidt, San Francisco	18	7	3.20	225.0	165	77	251
R. Johnson, Arizona	16	14	2.60	245.2	177	44	290
G. Maddux, Chicago	16	11	4.02	212.2	218	33	151
J. Suppan, St. Louis	16	9	4.16	188.0	192	65	110
C. Zambrano, Chicago	16	8	2.75	209.2	174	81	188
C. Carpenter, St. Louis	15	5	3.46	182.0	169	38	152
S. Estes, Colorado	15	8	5.84	202.0	223	105	117
B. Lawrence, San Diego	15	14	4.12	203.0	226	55	121
J. Marquis, St. Louis	15	7	3.71	201.1	215	70	138
M. Morris, St. Louis	15	10	4.72	202.0	205	56	131
R. Ortiz, Atlanta	15	9	4.13	204.2	197	112	143
J. Peavy, San Diego	15	6	2.27	166.1	146	53	173
J. Wright, Atlanta	15	8	3.28	186.1	168	70	159
E. Milton, Philadelphia	14	6	4.75	201.0	196	75	161
J. Thomson, Atlanta	14	8	3.72	198.1	210	52	133
I. Valdez, Florida	14	9	5.19	170.0	202	49	67

Individual Batting (based on 300 plate appearances)

	Avg.	AB	R	H	HR	RBI
B. Bonds, San Francisco	.362	373	129	135	45	101
T. Helton, Colorado	.347	547	115	190	32	96
M. Loretta, San Diego	.335	620	108	208	16	76
A. Beltre, Los Angeles	.334	598	104	200	48	121
A. Pujols, St. Louis	.331	592	133	196	46	123
J. Pierre, Florida	.326	678	100	221	3	49
S. Casey, Cincinnati	.324	571	101	185	24	99
J. Kendall, Pittsburgh	.319	574	86	183	3	51
A. Ramirez, Chicago	.318	547	99	174	36	103
L. Berkman, Houston	.316	544	104	172	30	106
J. Estrada, Atlanta	.314	462	56	145	9	76
S. Rolen, St. Louis	.314	500	109	157	34	124
S. Hillenbrand, Arizona	.310	562	68	174	15	80
J. Wilson, Pittsburgh	.308	652	82	201	11	59
T. Womack, St. Louis	.307	553	91	170	5	38
J. Drew, Atlanta	.305	518	118	158	31	93
B. Abreu, Philadelphia	.301	574	118	173	30	105
J. Edmonds, St. Louis	.301	498	102	150	42	111
L. Overbay, Milwaukee	.301	579	83	174	16	87

AMERICAN LEAGUE DIVISION SERIES—2004

New York Yankees defeated Minnesota Twins
　3 games to 1
　Oct. 5—Minnesota 2, New York 0
　Oct. 6—New York 7, Minnesota 6
　Oct. 8—New York 8, Minnesota 4
　Oct. 9—New York 6, Minnesota 5

Boston Red Sox defeated Anaheim Angels,
　3 games to 0
　Oct. 5—Boston 9, Anaheim 3
　Oct. 6—Boston 8, Anaheim 3
　Oct. 8—Boston 8, Anaheim 6

NATIONAL LEAGUE DIVISION SERIES—2004

St. Louis Cardinals defeated Los Angeles Dodgers,
　3 games to 1
　Oct. 5—St. Louis 8, Los Angeles 3
　Oct. 7—St. Louis 8, Los Angeles 3
　Oct. 9—Los Angeles 4, St. Louis 0
　Oct. 10—St. Louis 6, Los Angeles 2
Houston Astros defeated Atlanta Braves,
　3 games to 2
　Oct. 6—Houston 9, Atlanta 3
　Oct. 7—Atlanta 4, Houston 2
　Oct. 9—Houston 8, Atlanta 5
　Oct. 10—Atlanta 6, Houston 5
　Oct. 11—Houston 12, Atlanta 3

AMERICAN LEAGUE CHAMPIONSHIP SERIES—2004

Boston Red Sox defeated New York Yankees, 4 games to 3
Series MVP—David Ortiz, Boston

1st Game, at New York, Oct. 12, 2004

								R	H	E
Boston	000	000	520	—				7	10	0
New York	204	002	02x	—				10	14	0

Pitchers—Boston: Schilling, Leskanic, Mendoza, Wakefield, Embree, Timlin, Foulke. New York: Mussina, Sturtze, Gordon, Rivera. Winner: Mussina. Loser: Schilling. Save: Rivera. Attendance: 56,135.

2nd Game, at New York, Oct. 13, 2004

						R	H	E
Boston	000	000	010	—		1	5	0
New York	100	002	00x	—		3	7	0

Pitchers—Boston: Martinez, Timlin, Embree, Foulke. New York: Lieber, Gordon, Rivera. Winner: Lieber. Loser: Martinez. Save: Rivera. Attendance: 56,136.

3rd Game, at Boston, Oct. 16, 2004

						R	H	E
New York	303	520	402	—		19	22	1
Boston	042	000	200	—		8	15	0

Pitchers—New York: Brown, Vazquez, Quantrill, Gordon. Boston: Arroyo, Mendoza, Leskanic, Wakefield, Embree, Myers. Winner: Vazquez. Loser: Mendoza. Attendance: 35,126

4th Game, at Boston, Oct. 17, 2004

						R	H	E
New York	002	002	000	000		4	12	1
Boston	000	030	001	002		6	8	0

Pitchers—New York: Hernandez, Sturtze, Rivera, Gordon, Quantrill. Boston: Lowe, Timlin, Foulke, Embree, Myers, Leskanic. Winner: Leskanic. Loser: Quantrill. Attendance: 34,826.

5th Game, at Boston, Oct. 18, 2004

						R	H	E
New York	010	003	000	000	00	4	12	1
Boston	200	000	020	000	01	5	13	1

Pitchers—New York: Mussina, Sturtze, Gordon, Rivera, Heredia, Quantrill, Loaiza. Boston: Martinez, Timlin, Foulke, Arroyo, Myers, Embree, Wakefield. Winner: Wakefield. Loser: Loaiza. Attendance: 35,120.

6th Game, at New York, Oct. 19, 2004

						R	H	E
Boston	000	400	000	—		4	11	0
New York	000	000	110	—		2	6	0

Pitchers—Boston: Schilling, Arroyo, Foulke. New York: Lieber, Heredia, Quantrill, Sturtze. Winner: Schilling. Loser: Lieber. Save: Foulke. Attendance: 56,128.

7th Game, at New York, Oct. 20, 2004

						R	H	E
Boston	240	200	011	—		10	13	0
New York	001	000	200	—		3	5	1

Pitchers—Boston: Lowe, Martinez, Timlin, Embree. New York: Brown, Vazquez, Loaiza, Heredia, Gordon, Rivera.

Winner: Lowe. Loser: Brown. Attendance: 56,129.

NATIONAL LEAGUE CHAMPIONSHIP SERIES—2004
St. Louis Cardinals defeated the Houston Astros, 4 games to 3
Series MVP—Albert Pujols

1st Game, at St. Louis, Oct. 13, 2004

								R	H	E
Houston	2 0 0	2 0 0	0 2 1	—	7	10	1
St. Louis	2 0 0	0 2 6	0 0 x	—	10	12	0

Pitchers—Houston: Backe, Qualls, Harville, Wheeler. St. Louis: Williams, Calero, Haren, King, Tavarez, Isringhausen. Winner: Williams. Loser: Qualls. Save: Isringhausen. Attendance: 52,323.

2nd Game, at St. Louis, Oct. 14, 2004

								R	H	E
Houston	1 0 0	1 1 0	1 0 0	—	4	10	1
St. Louis	0 0 0	0 4 0	0 2 x	—	6	9	0

Pitchers—Houston: Munro, Harville, Wheeler, Miceli. St. Louis: Morris, Kline, Calero, Tavarez, Isringhausen Winner: Tavarez. Loser: Miceli. Save: Isringhausen. Attendance: 52,347.

3rd Game, at Houston, Oct. 16, 2004

								R	H	E
St. Louis	1 1 0	0 0 0	0 0 0	—	2	5	0
Houston	3 0 0	0 0 0	0 2 x	—	5	8	0

Pitchers—St. Louis: Suppan, Haren, King, Eldred. Houston: Clemens, Lidge. Winner: Clemens. Loser: Suppan. Save: Lidge. Attendance: 42,896.

4th Game, at Houston, Oct. 17, 2004

								R	H	E
St. Louis	3 0 1	1 0 0	0 0 0	—	5	9	0
Hosuton	1 0 2	0 0 2	1 0 x	—	6	9	0

Pitchers—St. Louis: Marquis, Calero, King, Tavarez, Isringhausen. Houston: Oswalt, Wheeler, Lidge. Winner: Wheeler. Loser: Tavarez. Save: Lidge. Attendance: 47,760.

5th Game, at Houston, Oct. 18, 2004

								R	H	E
St. Louis	0 0 0	0 0 0	0 0 0	—	0	1	0
Houston	0 0 0	0 0 0	0 0 3	—	3	3	0

Pitchers—St. Louis: Williams, Isringhausen. Houston: Backe, Lidge. Winner: Lidge. Loser: Isringhausen. Attendance: 43,045.

6th Game, at St. Louis, Oct. 20, 2004

									R	H	E
Houston	1 0 1	1 0 0	0 0 1	0 0 0	—	4	10	0
St. Louis	2 0 2	0 0 0	0 0 0	0 0 2	—	6	15	0

Pitchers—Houston: Munro, Harville, Qualls, Wheeler, Lidge, Miceli. St. Louis: Morris, King, Calero, Isringhausen, Tavarez. Winner: Tavarez. Loser: Miceli. Attendance: 52,144.

7th Game, at St. Louis, Oct. 21, 2004

								R	H	E
Houston	1 0 1	0 0 0	0 0 0	—	2	3	0
St. Louis	0 0 1	0 0 3	0 1 x	—	5	9	1

Pitchers—Houston: Clemens, Oswalt. St. Louis: Suppan, Calero, Tavarez, Isringhausen. Winner: Suppan. Loser: Clemens. Save: Isringhausen. Attendance: 52,140,

AMERICAN LEAGUE PENNANT WINNERS

Year	Club	Manager	Won	Lost	Pct	Year	Club	Manager	Won	Lost	Pct
1901	Chicago	Clark C. Griffith	83	53	.610	1935	Detroit[1]	Gordon Cochrane	93	58	.616
1902	Philadelphia	Connie Mack	83	53	.610	1936	New York[1]	Joseph V. McCarthy	102	51	.667
1903	Boston[1]	Jimmy Collins	91	47	.659	1937	New York[1]	Joseph V. McCarthy	102	52	.662
1904	Boston[2]	Jimmy Collins	95	59	.617	1938	New York[1]	Joseph V. McCarthy	99	53	.651
1905	Philadelphia	Connie Mack	92	56	.622	1939	New York[1]	Joseph V. McCarthy	106	45	.702
1906	Chicago[1]	Fielder A. Jones	93	58	.616	1940	Detroit	Delmar D. Baker	90	64	.584
1907	Detroit	Hugh A. Jennings	92	58	.613	1941	New York[1]	Joseph V. McCarthy	101	53	.656
1908	Detroit	Hugh A. Jennings	90	63	.588	1942	New York	Joseph V. McCarthy	103	51	.669
1909	Detroit	Hugh A. Jennings	98	54	.645	1943	New York[1]	Joseph V. McCarthy	98	56	.636
1910	Philadelphia[1]	Connie Mack	102	48	.680	1944	St. Louis	Luke Sewell	89	65	.578
1911	Philadelphia[1]	Connie Mack	101	50	.669	1945	Detroit[1]	Steve O'Neill	88	65	.575
1912	Boston[1]	J. Garland Stahl	105	47	.691	1946	Boston	Joseph E. Cronin	104	50	.675
1913	Philadelphia[1]	Connie Mack	96	57	.627	1947	New York[1]	Stanley R. Harris	97	57	.630
1914	Philadelphia	Connie Mack	99	53	.651	1948	Cleveland[1]	Lou Boudreau	97	58	.626
1915	Boston[1]	William F. Carrigan	101	50	.669	1949	New York[1]	Casey Stengel	97	57	.630
1916	Boston[1]	William F. Carrigan	91	63	.591	1950	New York [1]	Casey Stengel	98	56	.636
1917	Chicago[1]	Clarence H. Rowland	100	54	.649	1951	New York[1]	Casey Stengel	98	56	.636
1918	Boston[1]	Ed Barrow	75	51	.595	1952	New York[1]	Casey Stengel	95	59	.617
1919	Chicago	William Gleason	88	52	.629	1953	New York[1]	Casey Stengel	99	52	.656
1920	Cleveland[1]	Tris Speaker	98	56	.636	1954	Cleveland	Al Lopez	111	43	.721
1921	New York	Miller J. Huggins	98	55	.641	1955	New York[1]	Casey Stengel	96	58	.623
1922	New York	Miller J. Huggins	94	60	.610	1956	New York[1]	Casey Stengel	97	57	.630
1923	New York[1]	Miller J. Huggins	98	54	.645	1957	New York	Casey Stengel	98	56	.636
1924	Washington	Stanley R. Harris	92	62	.597	1958	New York[1]	Casey Stengel	92	62	.597
1925	Washington	Stanley R. Harris	96	55	.636	1959	Chicago	Al Lopez	94	60	.610
1926	New York	Miller J. Huggins	91	63	.591	1960	New York	Casey Stengel	97	57	.630
1927	New York[1]	Miller J. Huggins	110	44	.714	1961	New York[1]	Ralph Houk	109	53	.673
1928	New York[1]	Miller J. Huggins	101	53	.656	1962	New York[1]	Ralph Houk	96	66	.593
1929	Philadelphia[1]	Connie Mack	104	46	.693	1963	New York	Ralph Houk	104	57	.646
1930	Philadelphia[1]	Connie Mack	102	52	.662	1964	New York	Yogi Berra	99	63	.611
1931	Philadelphia	Connie Mack	107	45	.704	1965	Minnesota	Sam Mele	102	60	.630
1932	New York[1]	Joseph V. McCarthy	107	47	.695	1966	Baltimore[1]	Hank Bauer	97	53	.606
1933	Washington	Joseph E. Cronin	99	53	.651	1967	Boston	Dick Williams	92	70	.568
1934	Detroit	Gordon Cochrane	101	53	.656	1968	Detroit[1]	Mayo Smith	103	59	.636

Year	Club	Manager	Won	Lost	Pct	Year	Club	Manager	Won	Lost	Pct
1969	Baltimore[3]	Earl Weaver	109	53	.673	1987	Minnesota[5]	Tom Kelly	85	77	.525
1970	Baltimore[1,3]	Earl Weaver	108	54	.667	1988	Oakland[12]	Tony LaRussa	104	58	.642
1971	Baltimore[4]	Earl Weaver	101	57	.639	1989	Oakland[1,11]	Tony LaRussa	99	63	.611
1972	Oakland[1,5]	Dick Williams	93	62	.600	1990	Oakland[12]	Tony LaRussa	103	59	.636
1973	Oakland[1,6]	Dick Williams	94	68	.580	1991	Minnesota[1,11]	Tom Kelly	95	67	.586
1974	Oakland[1,6]	Alvin Dark	90	72	.556	1992	Toronto[1,4]	Cito Gaston	96	66	.593
1975	Boston[4]	Darrell Johnson	95	65	.594	1993	Toronto[1,10]	Cito Gaston	95	67	.586
1976	New York[7]	Billy Martin	97	62	.610	1994	Strike ended season Aug. 11. No playoffs, no pennant winner.				
1977	New York[1, 7]	Billy Martin	100	62	.617						
1978	New York[1,7]	Billy Martin and Bob Lemon	100	63	.613	1995	Cleveland[13]	Mike Hargrove	100	44	.694
						1996	New York[1,6]	Joe Torre	92	70	.568
1979	Baltimore[4]	Earl Weaver	102	57	.642	1997	Cleveland[6]	Mike Hargrove	86	75	.534
1980	Kansas City[9]	Jim Frey	97	65	.599	1998	New York[1, 14]	Joe Torre	114	48	.704
1981*	New York[4]	Gene Michaeland Bob Lemon	59	48	.551	1999	New York[1, 15]	Joe Torre	98	64	.605
						2000	New York[1, 16]	Joe Torre	87	74	.540
1982	Milwaukee[8]	Harvey Kuenn	95	67	.586	2001	New York[15]	Joe Torre	95	65	.594
1983	Baltimore[1, 10]	Joe Altobelli	98	64	.605	2002	Anaheim[17]	Mike Scioscia	99	63	.611
1984	Detroit[1,7]	Sparky Anderson	104	58	.642	2003	New York[15]	Joe Torre	101	61	.623
1985	Kansas City[1,11]	Dick Howser	91	71	.562	2004	Boston[1, 9]	Terry Francona	98	64	.605
1986	Boston[8]	John McNamara	95	66	.590						

*Split season because of players' strike. 1. World Series winner. 2. No World Series. 3. Defeated Minnesota, Western Division winner, in playoff. 4. Defeated Oakland, Western Division Leader, in playoff. 5. Defeated Detroit, Eastern Division winner, in playoff. 6. Defeated Baltimore, Eastern Division winner, in playoff. 7. Defeated Kansas City, Western Division winner, in playoff. 8. Defeated California, Western Division winner, in playoff. 9. Defeated New York, Eastern Division winner, in playoff. 10. Defeated Chicago, Western Division winner, in playoff. 11. Defeated Toronto, Eastern Division winner, in playoff. 12. Defeated Boston, Eastern division winner, in playoffs. 13. Defeated Seattle Mariners, Western Division winner, in playoff. 14. Defeated Cleveland Indians, Central Division winner, in playoff. 15. Defeated Boston Red Sox, Eastern Division wild-card team, in playoffs. 16. Defeated Seattle Mariners, Western Division wild-card team, in playoff. 17. Defeated Minnesota Twins, Central Division winner, in playoff.

NATIONAL LEAGUE PENNANT WINNERS

Year	Club	Manager	Won	Lost	Pct	Year	Club	Manager	Won	Lost	Pct
1876	Chicago	Albert G. Spalding	52	14	.788	1918	Chicago	Fred L. Mitchell	84	45	.651
1877	Boston	Harry Wright	31	17	.646	1919	Cincinnati[2]	Patrick J. Moran	96	44	.686
1878	Boston	Harry Wright	41	19	.683	1920	Brooklyn	Wilbert Robinson	93	61	.604
1879	Providence	George Wright	55	23	.705	1921	New York[2]	John J. McGraw	94	59	.614
1880	Chicago	Adrian C. Anson	67	17	.798	1922	New York[2]	John J. McGraw	93	61	.604
1881	Chicago	Adrian C. Anson	56	28	.667	1923	New York	John J. McGraw	95	58	.621
1882	Chicago	Adrian C. Anson	55	29	.655	1924	New York	John J. McGraw	93	60	.608
1883	Boston	John F. Morrill	63	35	.643	1925	Pittsburgh[2]	Wm. B. McKechnie	95	58	.621
1884	Providence	Frank C. Bancroft	84	28	.750	1926	St. Louis[2]	Rogers Hornsby	89	65	.578
1885	Chicago	Adrian C. Anson	87	25	.777	1927	Pittsburgh	Donie Bush	94	60	.610
1886	Chicago	Adrian C. Anson	90	34	.726	1928	St. Louis	Wm. B. McKechnie	95	59	.617
1887	Detroit	W. H. Watkins	79	45	.637	1929	Chicago	Joseph V. McCarthy	98	54	.645
1888	New York	James J. Mutrie	84	47	.641	1930	St. Louis	Gabby Street	92	62	.597
1889	New York	James J. Mutrie	83	43	.659	1931	St. Louis[2]	Gabby Street	101	53	.656
1890	Brooklyn	Wm. H. McGunnigle	86	43	.667	1932	Chicago	Charles J. Grimm	90	64	.584
1891	Boston	Frank G. Selee	87	51	.630	1933	New York[2]	William H. Terry	91	61	.599
1892	Boston	Frank G. Selee	102	48	.680	1934	St. Louis[2]	Frank F. Frisch	95	58	.621
1893	Boston	Frank G. Selee	86	44	.662	1935	Chicago	Charles J. Grimm	100	54	.649
1894	Baltimore	Edward H. Hanlon	89	39	.695	1936	New York	William H. Terry	92	62	.597
1895	Baltimore	Edward H. Hanlon	87	43	.669	1937	New York	William H. Terry	95	57	.625
1896	Baltimore	Edward H. Hanlon	90	39	.698	1938	Chicago	Gabby Hartnett	89	63	.586
1897	Boston	Frank G. Selee	93	39	.705	1939	Cincinnati	Wm. B. McKechnie	97	57	.630
1898	Boston	Frank G. Selee	102	47	.685	1940	Cincinnati[2]	Wm. B. McKechnie	100	53	.654
1899	Brooklyn	Edward H. Hanlon	88	42	.677	1941	Brooklyn	Leo E. Durocher	100	54	.649
1900	Brooklyn	Edward H. Hanlon	82	54	.603	1942	St. Louis[2]	Wm. H. Southworth	106	48	.688
1901	Pittsburgh	Fred C. Clarke	90	49	.647	1943	St. Louis	Wm. H. Southworth	105	49	.682
1902	Pittsburgh	Fred C. Clarke	103	36	.741	1944	St. Louis[2]	Wm. H. Southworth	105	49	.682
1903	Pittsburgh	Fred C. Clarke	91	49	.650	1945	Chicago	Charles J. Grimm	98	56	.636
1904	New York[1]	John J. McGraw	106	47	.693	1946	St. Louis[2]	Edwin H. Dyer	98	58	.628
1905	New York[2]	John J. McGraw	105	48	.686	1947	Brooklyn	Burton E. Shotton	94	60	.610
1906	Chicago	Frank L. Chance	116	36	.763	1948	Boston	Wm. H. Southworth	91	62	.595
1907	Chicago[2]	Frank L. Chance	107	45	.704	1949	Brooklyn	Burton E. Shotton	97	57	.630
1908	Chicago[2]	Frank L. Chance	99	55	.643	1950	Philadelphia	Edwin M. Sawyer	91	63	.591
1909	Pittsburgh[2]	Fred C. Clarke	110	42	.724	1951	New York	Leo E. Durocher	98	59	.624
1910	Chicago	Frank L. Chance	104	50	.675	1952	Brooklyn	Charles W. Dressen	96	57	.630
1911	New York	John J. McGraw	99	54	.647	1953	Brooklyn	Charles W. Dressen	105	49	.682
1912	New York	John J. McGraw	103	48	.682	1954	New York[2]	Leo E. Durocher	97	57	.630
1913	New York	John J. McGraw	101	51	.664	1955	Brooklyn[2]	Walter Alston	98	55	.641
1914	Boston[2]	George T. Stallings	94	59	.614	1956	Brooklyn	Walter Alston	93	61	.604
1915	Philadelphia	Patrick J. Moran	90	62	.592	1957	Milwaukee[2]	Fred Haney	95	59	.617
1916	Brooklyn	Wilbert Robinson	94	60	.610	1958	Milwaukee	Fred Haney	92	62	.597
1917	New York	John J. McGraw	98	56	.636	1959	Los Angeles[2]	Walter Alston	88	68	.564

Year	Club	Manager	Won	Lost	Pct	Year	Club	Manager	Won	Lost	Pct
1960	Pittsburgh[2]	Danny Murtaugh	95	59	.617	1983	Philadelphia[10]	Paul Owens	90	72	.556
1961	Cincinnati	Fred Hutchinson	93	61	.604	1984	San Diego[11]	Dick Williams	92	70	.568
1962	San Francisco	Alvin Dark	103	62	.624	1985	St. Louis[11]	Whitey Herzog	101	61	.623
1963	Los Angeles[2]	Walter Alston	99	63	.611	1986	New York[2,8]	Dave Johnson	108	54	.667
1964	St. Louis[2]	Johnny Keane	93	69	.574	1987	St. Louis[5]	Whitey Herzog	95	67	.586
1965	Los Angeles[2]	Walter Alston	97	65	.599	1988	Los Angeles[2,12]	Tom Lasorda	94	67	.584
1966	Los Angeles	Walter Alston	95	67	.586	1989	San Francisco[12]	Roger Craig	92	70	.568
1967	St. Louis[2]	Red Schoendienst	101	60	.627	1990	Cincinnati[2,4]	Lou Piniella	91	71	.562
1968	St. Louis	Red Schoendienst	97	65	.599	1991	Atlanta[4]	Bobby Cox	94	68	.580
1969	New York[2,3]	Gil Hodges	100	62	.617	1992	Atlanta[4]	Bobby Cox	98	64	.605
1970	Cincinnati[4]	Sparky Anderson	102	60	.630	1993	Philadelphia[3]	Jim Fregosi	97	65	.599
1971	Pittsburgh[2,3]	Danny Murtaugh	97	65	.599	1994	Strike ended season Aug. 11. No playoffs, no pennant winner.				
1972	Cincinnati[4]	Sparky Anderson	95	59	.617						
1973	New York[6]	Yogi Berra	82	79	.509	1995	Atlanta[2,13]	Bobby Cox	90	54	.625
1974	Los Angeles[4]	Walter Alston	102	60	.630	1996	Atlanta[14]	Bobby Cox	96	66	.593
1975	Cincinnati[2,4]	Sparky Anderson	108	54	.667	1997	Florida[2,15]	Jim Leyland	92	70	.568
1976	Cincinnati[2,7]	Sparky Anderson	102	60	.630	1998	San Diego[16]	Bruce Bochy	98	64	.605
1977	Los Angeles[7]	Tom Lasorda	98	64	.605	1999	Atlanta[17]	Bobby Cox	103	59	.636
1978	Los Angeles[7]	Tom Lasorda	95	67	.586	2000	New York[18]	Bobby Valentine	94	68	.580
1979	Pittsburgh[2,6]	Chuck Tanner	98	64	.605	2001	Arizona[16]	Bob Brenly	92	70	.568
1980	Philadelphia[2,8]	Dallas Green	91	71	.562	2002	San Francisco[14]	Dusty Baker	95	66	.590
1981*	Los Angeles[2,9]	Tom Lasorda	63	47	.573	2003	Florida[19]	Jack McKeon	91	71	.562
1982	St. Louis[2,3]	Whitey Herzog	92	70	.568	2004	St. Louis[20]	Tony La Russa	105	57	.648

*Split season because of players' strike. 1. No World Series. 2. World Series winner. 3. Defeated Atlanta, Western Division winner, in playoff. 4. Defeated Pittsburgh, Eastern Division winner, in playoff. 5. Defeated San Francisco, Western Division winner, in playoff. 6. Defeated Cincinnati, Western Division winner, in playoff. 7. Defeated Philadelphia, Eastern Division winner, in playoff. 8. Defeated Houston, Western Division winner, in playoff. 9. Defeated Montreal, Eastern Division winner, in playoff. 10. Defeated Los Angeles, Western Division winner, in playoff. 11. Defeated Chicago, Eastern Division champion, in playoff. 12. Defeated New York, Eastern Division winner, in playoff. 13. Defeated Cincinnati, Central Division winner, in playoff. 14. Defeated St. Louis, Central Division winner, in playoff. 15. Eastern Division wildcard Florida defeated Atlanta, Eastern Division winner, in playoff. 16. Defeated Atlanta, Eastern Division winner, in playoff. 17. Defeated New York, Eastern Division wild card team, in playoff. 18. Eastern Division wild card New York defeated Central Division winner St. Louis in playoff. 19. Defeated Chicago, Central Division champion, in playoff. 20. Defeated Houston, Central Division wild card team, in playoff.

WORLD SERIES—2004

Boston Red Sox defeated St. Louis Cardinals, 4 games to 0.

1st Game—Boston, Oct. 23
Boston 11, St. Louis 9

St. Louis (N.L.)	AB	R	H	RBI	Boston (A.L.)	AB	R	H	RBI
Renteria ss	4	1	2	1	Damon cf	6	1	2	1
Walker rf	5	1	4	2	Cabrera ss	4	2	1	1
Pujols 1b	3	0	0	0	Ramirez lf	5	0	3	2
Rolen 3b	5	0	0	0	Ortiz dh	3	1	2	4
Edmonds cf	4	2	1	0	Millar 1b	5	1	1	0
Sanders dh	3	1	0	0	Mientkiewicz 1b	0	0	0	0
Womack 2b	1	1	0	0	Nixon rf	3	0	0	0
Anderson 2b	2	0	1	0	Kapler ph-rf	1	0	0	0
Matheny c	2	0	1	2	Mueller 3b	3	1	1	1
Marquis p	0	1	0	0	Mirabelli c	3	1	1	0
Molina c	1	0	0	0	Varitek ph-c	2	1	0	0
Taguchi lf	3	1	1	0	Bellhorn 2b	3	3	2	2
Cedeno ph-lf	2	1	1	0	Reese 2b	0	0	0	0
Totals	**35**	**9**	**11**	**6**	**Totals**	**38**	**11**	**13**	**11**

							R	H	E
St. Louis	0 1 1	3 0 2	0 2 0	—			9	11	1
Boston	4 0 3	0 0 0	2 2 x	—			11	13	4

HR—St. Louis: Walker; Boston: Ortiz, Bellhorn. LOB—St. Louis: 9, Boston: 12.

St. Louis	IP	H	R	ER	BB	SO	HR	ERA
Williams	2.1	8	7	7	3	1	1	27.00
Haren	3.2	2	0	0	3	1	0	0.00
Calero	0.1	1	2	2	2	0	0	54.00
King	0.1	1	0	0	0	0	0	0.00
Eldred	0.1	0	0	0	0	1	0	0.00
Tavarez (L, 0–1)	1.0	1	2	1	0	0	1	9.99
Boston								
Wakefield	3.2	3	5	5	5	2	1	12.27
Arroyo	2.1	4	2	2	0	4	0	7.71
Timlin	1.1	1	1	1	0	0	0	6.75
Embree	0.0	1	1	0	0	0	0	0.00
Foulke (W, 0–1)	1.2	2	0	0	1	3	0	0.00

2nd Game—Boston, Oct. 24
Boston 6, St. Louis 2

St. Louis (N.L.)	AB	R	H	RBI	Boston (A.L.)	AB	R	H	RBI
Renteria ss	3	1	0	0	Damon cf	5	1	1	0
Walker rf	4	0	0	0	Cabrera ss.	4	0	1	0
Pujols 2b	4	1	3	0	Ramirez lf	4	1	1	0
Rolen 3b	3	0	0	1	Kapler lf	0	0	0	0
Edmonds cf	4	0	0	0	Ortiz dh	3	1	0	0
Sanders lf	3	0	0	0	Varitek c	3	0	1	2
Womack 2b	4	0	1	0	Millar 1b	1	1	0	0
Matheny c	4	0	1	0	Mientkiewicz pr-1b	0	0	0	0
Anderson dh	2	0	0	0	Nixon rf	4	1	1	0
Taguchi ph-dh	1	0	0	0	Mueller 3b	3	1	2	0
					Bellhorn 2b	3	0	1	2
					Reese 2b	1	0	0	0
Totals	**32**	**2**	**5**	**1**	**Totals**	**31**	**6**	**8**	**6**

							R	H	E
St. Louis	0 0 0	1 0 0	0 1 0	—			2	5	0
Boston	2 0 0	2 0 2	0 0 x	—			6	8	4

LOB—St. Louis: 6, Boston: 9.

St. Louis	IP	H	R	ER	BB	SO	HR	ERA
Morris (L, 0–1)	4.1	4	4	4	3	0	0	8.31
Eldred	1.1	4	2	2	0	1	0	10.80
King	0.1	0	0	0	0	1	0	0.00
Marquis	1.0	0	0	0	2	0	0	0.00
Reyes	1.0	0	0	0	0	0	0	0.00
Boston								
Schilling (W, 1–0)	6.0	4	1	0	1	4	0	0.00
Embree	1.0	0	0	0	0	3	0	0.00
Timlin	0.2	1	1	1	1	0	0	9.00
Foulke	1.1	0	0	0	0	2	0	0.00

3rd Game—St. Louis, Oct. 26
Boston 4, St. Louis 1

Boston (A.L.)	AB	R	H	RBI		St. Louis (N.L.)	AB	R	H	RBI
Damon cf	5	1	1	0		Renteria ss	4	0	1	0
Cabrera ss	4	1	2	0		Walker rf	3	1	1	1
Ramirez lf	4	1	2	2		Pujols 1b	4	0	1	0
Ortiz 1b	4	0	1	0		Rolen 3b	3	0	0	0
Mientkiewicz 1b	0	0	0	0		Edmonds cf	3	0	0	0
Varitek c	3	0	0	0		Sanders lf	3	0	0	0
Mueller 3b	4	1	2	1		Womack 2b	3	0	0	0
Nixon rf	3	0	1	1		Matheny c	2	0	0	0
Kapler ph-rf	1	0	0	0		Cedeno ph	1	0	0	0
Bellhorn ss	3	0	0	0		Tavarez p	0	0	0	0
Reese 2b	0	0	0	0		Suppan p	1	0	1	0
P. Martinez p	2	0	0	0		Reyes p	0	0	0	0
Millar ph	1	0	0	0		Anderson ph	1	0	0	0
Timlin p	0	0	0	0		Calero p	0	0	0	0
Foulke p	0	0	0	0		King p	0	0	0	0
						Mabry ph	1	0	0	0
						Molina c	0	0	0	0
Totals	34	4	9	4		**Totals**	29	1	4	1

								R	H	E
Boston	100		120		000		—	4	9	0
St. Louis	000		000		001		—	1	4	0

HR—Boston: Ramirez; St. Louis: Walker. LOB—Boston: 8; St. Louis: 3.

	IP	H	R	ER	BB	SO	HR	ERA
Boston								
P. Martinez (W, 1–0)	7.0	3	0	0	2	6	0	0.00
Timlin	1.0	0	0	0	0	0	0	6.00
Foulke	1.0	1	1	1	0	2	1	2.25
St. Louis								
Suppan (L, 0–1)	4.2	8	4	4	1	4	1	7.71
Reyes	0.1	0	0	0	0	0	0	0.00
Calero	1.0	1	0	0	2	0	0	13.50
King	2.0	0	0	0	1	0	0	0.00
Tavarez	1.0	0	0	0	0	1	0	4.50

4th Game—St. Louis, Oct. 27
Boston 3, St. Louis 0

Boston (A.L.)	AB	R	H	RBI		St. Louis (N.L.)	AB	R	H	RBI
Damon cf	5	1	2	1		Womack 2b	3	0	1	0
Cabrera ss	5	0	0	0		Luna ph-2b	1	0	0	0
Ramirez lf	4	0	1	0		Walker rf	2	0	0	0
Ortiz 1b	3	1	1	0		Pujols 1b	4	0	1	0
Mientkiewicz 1b	1	0	0	0		Rolen 3b	4	0	0	0
Varitek c	5	1	1	0		Edmonds cf	4	0	0	0
Mueller 3b	4	0	1	0		Renteria ss	4	0	2	0
Nixon rf	4	0	3	2		Mabry lf	3	0	0	0
Kapler pr-rf	0	0	0	0		Isringhausen p	0	0	0	0
Bellhorn 2b	1	0	0	0		Molina c	2	0	0	0
Reese pr-2b	0	0	0	0		Cedeno ph	1	0	0	0
Lowe p	2	0	0	0		Matheny c	0	0	0	0
Millar ph	1	0	0	0		Marquis p	1	0	0	0
Arroyo p	0	0	0	0		Anderson ph	1	0	0	0
Embree p	0	0	0	0		Haren p	0	0	0	0
Foulke p	0	0	0	0		Sanders lf	0	0	0	0
Totals	35	3	9	3		**Totals**	30	0	4	0

								R	H	E
Boston	102		000		000		—	3	9	0
St. Louis	000		000		000		—	0	4	0

HR— Boston: Damon. LOB—Boston: 12; St. Louis: 6.

	IP	H	R	ER	BB	SO	HR	ERA
Boston								
Lowe (W, 1–0)	7.0	3	0	0	1	4	0	0.00
Arroyo	0.1	0	0	0	1	0	0	6.75
Embree	0.2	0	0	0	1	0	0	0.00
Foulke (S, 1)	1.0	1	0	0	0	1	0	1.80
St. Louis								
Marquis (L, 0–1)	6.0	6	3	3	5	4	1	3.86
Haren	1.0	2	0	0	0	1	0	0.00
Isringhausen	2.0	1	0	0	1	2	0	0.00

Series MVP: Manny Ramirez

Soccer

The early history of the sport is uncertain. A form of the game in which a leather ball was dribbled was played in China as early as the 4th century B.C. The Romans played a variation of soccer which eventually spread throughout Europe. British schools and universities played soccer (known as football) during the 1800s, however, each school used different sets of rules and the number of players varied. This difficulty was corrected on Oct. 26, 1863, when the Football Association (FA) was formed in London for the purpose of unifying the rules of the game.

The Federation of International Football Associations (FIFA) was created in 1913 as a world governing body to coordinate all of the national associations in the world. The FIFA held the first World Cup Championship tournament in 1930 in Montevideo, Uruguay. Today, soccer is the world's most popular sport. The first FIFA Women's World Cup was held in 1991 with the United States winning the title. The 2003 Women's World Cup was moved from China to the United States because of concern about a Chinese outbreak of Severe Acute Respiratory Syndrome.

WORLD CUP
(W) indicates Women's World Cup

1930	Uruguay	1954	West Germany	1978	Argentina	1995	Norway (W)
1934	Italy	1958	Brazil	1982	Italy	1998	France
1938	Italy	1962	Brazil	1986	Argentina	1999	United States (W)
1942	No competition	1966	England	1990	West Germany	2002	Brazil
1946	No competition	1970	Brazil	1991	United States (W)	2003	Germany (W)
1950	Uruguay	1974	West Germany	1994	Brazil		

WOMEN'S WORLD CUP—2003

SEMIFINALS
Germany 3, United States 0
Sweden 2, Canada 1

THIRD PLACE
United States 3, Canada 1

CHAMPIONSHIP
Germany 2, Sweden 1

WORLD CUP—2002

QUARTERFINALS
Brazil 2, England 1
Germany 1, United States 0
South Korea 0, Spain 0 (South Korea won 5–3 in shootout)
Turkey 1, Senegal 0

SEMIFINALS
Germany 1, South Korea 0
Brazil 1, Turkey 0
THIRD PLACE
Turkey 3, South Korea 2

CHAMPIONSHIP
Brazil 2, Germany 0
Goals scored: Ronaldo 2 (67th min and 79th min)

WORLD CUP
All-Time Top Ten

	Country	App	Gm	Record (W–L–T)	Pts	GF	GA		Country	App	Gm	Record (W–L–T)	Pts	GF	GA
1.	Brazil	17	87	60–13–14	141	191	82	7.	France	11	44	21–16–7	49	86	61
2.	Germany	15	85	50–17–18	123	176	106	8.	Sweden	10	42	15–16–10	42	71	65
3.	Italy	15	70	39–14–17	96	110	67	9.	Russia	9	37	17–14–6	41	64	44
4.	Argentina	13	60	30–19–11	72	102	71	10.	Yugoslavia	9	37	16–13–8	40	60	46
5.	England	11	50	26–13–15	61	68	45		Uruguay	10	40	15–15–10	40	65	57
6.	Spain	11	45	20–15–10	54	71	53								

MAJOR LEAGUE SOCCER 2004 STANDINGS

The GF and GA columns refer to Goals For and Goals Against in regulation play.

EASTERN CONFERENCE

Team	W	L	T	Pts	GF	GA	Team	W	L	T	Pts	GF	GA
Columbus Crew[1]	12	5	13	49	40	32	New England Revolution[1]	8	13	9	33	42	43
DC United[1]	11	10	9	42	43	42	Chicago Fire	8	13	9	33	36	44
MetroStars[1]	11	12	7	40	47	49							

1. Clinched playoffs.

WESTERN CONFERENCE

Team	W	L	T	Pts	GF	GA	Team	W	L	T	Pts	GF	GA
Kansas City Wizards[1]	14	9	7	49	38	30	San Jose Earthquake[1]	9	10	11	38	41	35
Los Angeles Galaxy[1]	11	9	10	43	42	40	Dallas Burn	10	14	6	36	34	45
Colorado Rapids[1]	10	9	11	41	29	32							

1. Clinched playoffs.

2004 REGULAR SEASON

LEADING SCORERS

	Gm	G	A	Pts
Amado Guevara, MetroStars	24	10	10	30
Pat Noonan, New England	29	11	8	30
Brian Ching, San Jose	25	12	4	28
Jaime Moreno, DC	27	7	14	28
Eddie Johnson, Dallas	26	12	3	27
Josh Wolff, Kansas City	26	10	7	27

LEADING GOALKEEPERS

	Gm	Shts	Svs	GA	GAA
Nick Rimando, DC	13	39	26	13	1.00
Tony Meola, Kansas City	21	98	76	22	1.05
Joe Cannon, Colorado	30	182	150	32	1.07
Jon Busch, Columbus	29	163	132	31	1.07
Pat Onstad, San Jose	25	130	98	32	1.28

GOAL SCORING LEADERS

	Gm	No
Brian Ching, San Jose	25	12
Eddie Johnson, Dallas	26	12
Edson Buddle, Columbus	24	11
Pat Noonan, New England	29	11
Damani Ralph, Chicago	26	11
Carlos Ruiz, Los Angeles	20	11

ASSIST LEADERS

	Gm	No
Jaime Moreno, DC	27	14
Jose Cancela, New England	25	10
Landon Donovan, San Jose	23	10
Simon Elliott, Columbus	27	10
Amado Guevara, MetroStars	24	10
Dema Kovalenko, D.C.	25	10
Ronnie O'Brien, Dallas	29	10

Extreme Sports

2004 SUMMER EXTREME GAMES
(Los Angeles, Calif., Aug. 5–8, 2004)

Skateboard: Paul Rodriguez (men's street), Bucky Lasek (men's vert), Elissa Steamer (women's street), Lyndsey Adams Hawkins (women's vert), Sandro Dias (men's vert best trick), Danny Way (men's big air)
Bike Stunt: Dave Mirra (vert), Dave Mirra (park), Corey Bohan (dirt)

Motocross: Chuck Carothers (best trick), Ben Bostrom (super moto), Jeremy McGrath (step up), Nate Adams (freestyle)
Wakeboarding: Dallas Friday (women), Phillip Soven (men)
Surfing: Team East

History of the Income Tax in the United States

Source: Sumeet Sagoo, staff economist, the Tax Foundation.

The nation had few taxes in its early history. From 1791 to 1802, the United States government was supported by internal taxes on distilled spirits, carriages, refined sugar, tobacco and snuff, property sold at auction, corporate bonds, and slaves. The high cost of the War of 1812 brought about the nation's first sales taxes on gold, silverware, jewelry, and watches. In 1817, however, Congress did away with all internal taxes, relying on tariffs on imported goods to provide sufficient funds for running the government.

In 1862, in order to support the Civil War effort, Congress enacted the nation's first income tax law. It was a forerunner of our modern income tax in that it was based on the principles of graduated, or progressive, taxation and of withholding income at the source. During the Civil War, a person earning from $600 to $10,000 per year paid tax at the rate of 3%. Those with incomes of more than $10,000 paid taxes at a higher rate. Additional sales and excise taxes were added, and an "inheritance" tax also made its debut. In 1866, internal revenue collections reached their highest point in the nation's 90-year history—more than $310 million, an amount not reached again until 1911.

The Act of 1862 established the office of Commissioner of Internal Revenue. The Commissioner was given the power to assess, levy, and collect taxes, and the right to enforce the tax laws through seizure of property and income and through prosecution. The powers and authority remain very much the same today.

In 1868, Congress again focused its taxation efforts on tobacco and distilled spirits and eliminated the income tax in 1872. It had a short-lived revival in 1894 and 1895. In the latter year, the U.S. Supreme Court decided that the income tax was unconstitutional because it was not apportioned among the states in conformity with the Constitution.

In 1913, the 16th Amendment to the Constitution made the income tax a permanent fixture in the U.S. tax system. The amendment gave Congress legal authority to tax income and resulted in a revenue law that taxed incomes of both individuals and corporations. In fiscal year 1918, annual internal revenue collections for the first time passed the billion-dollar mark, rising to $5.4 billion by 1920. With the advent of World War II, employment increased, as did tax collections—to $7.3 billion. The withholding tax on wages was introduced in 1943 and was instrumental in increasing the number of taxpayers to 60 million and tax collections to $43 billion by 1945.

In 1981, Congress enacted the largest tax cut in U.S. history, approximately $750 billion over six years. The tax reduction, however, was partially offset by two tax acts, in 1982 and 1984, that attempted to raise approximately $265 billion.

On Oct. 22, 1986, President Reagan signed into law the Tax Reform Act of 1986, one of the most far-reaching reforms of the United States tax system since the adoption of the income tax. In an attempt to remain revenue neutral, the act called for a $120 billion increase in business taxation and a corresponding decrease in individual taxation over a five-year period.

Following what seemed to be a yearly tradition of new tax acts that began in 1986, the Revenue Reconciliation Act of 1990 was signed into law on Nov. 5, 1990. As with the '87, '88, and '89 acts, the 1990 act, while providing a number of substantive provisions, was small in comparison with the 1986 act. The emphasis of the 1990 act was increased taxes on the wealthy.

On Aug. 10, 1993, President Clinton signed the Revenue Reconciliation Act of 1993 into law. The act's purpose was to reduce by approximately $496 billion the federal deficit that would otherwise accumulate in fiscal years 1994 through 1998. In 1997, Clinton signed another tax act. The act, which cut taxes by $152 billion, included a cut in capital-gains tax for individuals, a $500 per child tax credit, and tax incentives for education.

President George W. Bush signed tax acts in 2001, 2002, and 2003. The Job Creation and Workers Assistance Act of 2002 provided tax relief to businesses and included a 13-week extension on unemployment insurance and tax breaks for taxpayers affected by the Sept. 11, 2001, terrorist attacks. Overall, the act projected tax relief of $41.9 billion over the 2003–2012 period. The Jobs and Growth Tax Relief and Reconciliation Act of 2003, a ten-year $350 billion tax package—the third-largest tax cut in U.S. history—temporarily reduced dividend taxes, reduced capital-gains taxes, and increased child credit for most taxpayers.

Internal Revenue Service

The Internal Revenue Service (IRS), a bureau of the U.S. Treasury Department, is the federal agency charged with the administration of the tax laws passed by Congress.

Operations involving most taxpayers are carried out in district offices and service centers. District offices are organized into Resources Management, Examination, Collection, Taxpayer Service, Employee Plans and Exempt Organizations, and Criminal Investigation. All tax returns are filed with the service centers, where the IRS computer operations are located.

Prior to 1987, all tax return processing was performed by hand. In an attempt to improve the speed and efficiency of the manual processing procedure, the IRS began testing an electronic return filing system beginning with the filing of 1985 returns.

Internal Revenue Service

	2003	2000	1996	1995	1994	1970
U.S. population (in thousands)	291,837	283,212	266,210	263,717	261,348	204,878
Number of IRS employees	98,824	97,074	106,642	112,024	110,665	68,683
Cost to govt. of collecting $100 in taxes	$0.48	$0.39	$0.49	$0.54	$0.57	$0.45
Tax per capita	$6,691.86	$7,404.04	$5,584.11	$5,216.70	$4,884.17	$955.31
Collections by principal sources (in thousands of dollars)						
Total IRS collections	$1,952,929,045	$2,096,916,925	$1,486,546,674	$1,375,731,835	$1,276,466,776	$195,722,096
Income and profits taxes						
Individual	$987,208,878	1,137,077,702	$745,313,276	$675,779,337	$619,819,153	$103,651,585
Corporation	$194,146,298	$235,654,894	$189,054,791	$174,422,173	$154,204,684	$35,036,983
Employment taxes	$695,975,801	$639,651,814	$492,365,178	$465,405,305	$443,831,352	$37,449,188
Estate and gift taxes	$22,826,908	$29,721,620	$17,591,817	$15,144,394	$15,606,793	$3,680,076
Alcohol taxes	(1)	(1)	(1)	(1)	(1)	$4,746,382
Tobacco taxes	(1)	(1)	(1)	(1)	(1)	$2,094,212
Excise taxes	$52,771,160	$54,810,895	$42,221,611	$44,980,627	$43,004,794	$2,380,609

NOTE: For fiscal year ending Sept. 30th. 1. Alcohol and tobacco tax collections are now collected and reported by the Bureau of Alcohol, Tobacco, and Firearms. *Source:* 2003 IRS Data Book.

The two most significant results of the test were that refunds for the electronically filed returns were issued more quickly and the tax processing error rate was significantly lower when compared with paper returns. Electronic filing of individual income tax returns with refunds became an operational program in selected areas for the 1987 processing year.

Auditing Tax Returns

Most taxpayers' contacts with the IRS arise through the auditing of their tax returns. The service has been empowered by Congress to inquire about all persons who may be liable for any tax and to obtain for review the books and/or records pertinent to those taxpayers' returns.

In 2002 the IRS announced a new auditing policy that focuses less on wage earners—particularly those earning less than $100,000—and instead looks more closely at the very wealthy and business owners, as well as on complex business partnerships, tax shelters, and offshore accounts. A computer program will help to determine which returns have the potential for hidden or unreported income and thus merit an audit.

The Appeals Process

Taxpayers who, after audit of their tax returns, disagree with a proposed change in their tax liabilities are entitled to an independent review of their cases. Taxpayers are able to seek an immediate, informal appeal with the Appeals Office. If, however, the dispute arises from a field audit and the amount in question exceeds $10,000, a taxpayer must submit a written protest. Alternatively, the taxpayer can wait for the examiner's report and then request consideration by the Appeals Office and file a protest if necessary. Taxpayers may represent themselves or be represented by an attorney, accountant, or any other adviser authorized to practice before the IRS. Taxpayers can forgo their right to the above process and await receipt of a deficiency notice. At this juncture, taxpayers can either (1) not pay the deficiency and petition the Tax Court by a required deadline or (2) pay the deficiency and file a claim for refund with the District Director's office. If the claim is not allowed, a suit for refund may be brought either in the District Court or the Claims Court.

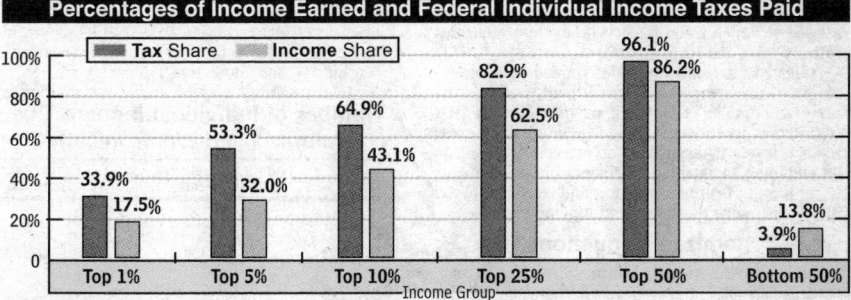

Percentages of Income Earned and Federal Individual Income Taxes Paid

■ Tax Share   ■ Income Share

Income Group	Tax Share	Income Share
Top 1%	33.9%	17.5%
Top 5%	53.3%	32.0%
Top 10%	64.9%	43.1%
Top 25%	82.9%	62.5%
Top 50%	96.1%	86.2%
Bottom 50%	13.8%	3.9%

NOTE: Figures for 2001. *Source:* Tax Foundation. Web: http://taxfoundation.org.

Federal Individual Income Tax

Tax Brackets—2004 Taxable Income

Joint return	Single taxpayer	Rate
$0–$14,000	$0–$7,000	10.0%
14,000–56,800	7,000–28,400	15.0
56,800–114,650	28,400–68,800	25.0
114,650 –174,700	68,800–143,500	28.0
174,700–311,950	143,500–311,950	33.0
311,950 and up	311,950 and up	35.0

Source: Tax Foundation.

The federal individual income tax is levied on the worldwide income of U.S. citizens and resident aliens and on certain types of U.S. source income of nonresidents. For a nonitemizer, "tax table income" is adjusted gross income less $3,000 for each personal exemption and the standard deduction. If a taxpayer itemizes, tax table income is adjusted gross income minus total itemized deductions and personal exemptions. In addition, individuals may also be subject to the alternative minimum tax.

Who Must File a Return[1]

If your filing status is:	Age at end of 2003	Gross income at least
Single	Under 65	$7,800
	65 or older	8,950
Married filing jointly	Under 65 (both spouses)	15,600
	65 or older (one spouse)	16,550
	65 or older (both spouses)	17,500
Married filing separately	Any age	3,050
Head of household	Under 65	10,050
	65 or older	11,200
Qualifying widower with dependent child	Under 65	12,550
	65 or older	13,500

1. In 2003.

Adjusted Gross Income

Gross income consists of wages and salaries, unemployment compensation, tips and gratuities, interest, dividends, annuities, rents and royalties, up to 85% of Social Security benefits if the recipient's income exceeds a base amount, and certain other types of income. Among the items excluded from gross income, and thus not subject to tax, are public assistance benefits and interest on exempt securities (mostly state and local bonds).

Adjusted gross income is determined by subtracting from gross income: alimony paid, penalties on early withdrawal of savings, payments to an IRA (reduced proportionately based upon adjusted gross income levels if taxpayer is an active participant in an employer maintained retirement plan), payments to a Keogh retirement plan, and self-employed health insurance payments and moving expenses.

Itemized Deductions

Taxpayers may itemize deductions or take the standard deduction. The standard deduction amounts for 2003 were as follows: $4,750 for single persons, $7,000 for heads of household, $9,500 for married filing jointly or qualifying widower, and $4,750 for married filing separately. Taxpayers 65 and older or blind are entitled to an additional standard deduction of $950.

In itemizing deductions, the following are major items that may be deducted in 2003: state and local income and property taxes, charitable contributions, employee moving expenses, medical expenses (exceeding 7.5% of adjusted gross income), casualty losses (only the amount over the $100 floor which exceeds 10% of adjusted gross income), mortgage interest, and miscellaneous deductions (deductible only to the extent by which cumulatively they exceed 2% of adjusted gross income).

Personal Exemptions

Personal exemptions are available to the taxpayer for himself, his spouse, and his dependents. The 2003 amount was $3,050 for each individual. No exemption is allowed to a taxpayer who can be claimed as a dependent on another taxpayer's return.

Credits

Taxpayers can reduce their income tax liability by claiming the benefit of certain tax credits. Each dollar of tax credit offsets a dollar of tax liability. The following are a few of the available tax credits.

Certain low income households may claim an Earned Income Credit. The maximum Earned Income Credit for 2003 was $382 for taxpayers with no qualifying children, $2,547 for taxpayers with one qualifying child, $4,204 for taxpayers with two or more qualifying children. The maximum credit is reduced if earned income or adjusted gross income exceeds $13,750 for taxpayers with one or more children, or exceeds $6,250 for taxpayers with no children. For families with no qualifying children, the credit is zero if earned income or adjusted gross income exceeds $11,230; for families with one qualifying child, the credit is zero if earned income or adjusted gross income exceeds $29,666; and for taxpayers with two or more qualifying children, the credit is zero if earned income or adjusted gross income exceeds $33,692. The earned income credit is a refundable credit.

A credit for Child and Dependent Care Expenses is available for amounts paid to care for a qualifying child or other dependent so that the taxpayer can work or look for work. The credit is up to 30% (depending on adjusted gross income) of up to $3,000 of employment-related expenses for one qualifying child or dependent and up to $6,000 of employment-related expenses for two qualifying individuals.

The elderly and those under 65 who are retired under total disability may be entitled to a credit of

Number of Individual Income Tax Returns Filed Electronically

Year	Number of returns (in thousands)	Percentage increase
1995	11,807	n.a.
1996	14,968	26.8%
1997	19,136	27.8
1998	24,580	28.4
1999	29,349	19.4
2000	35,394	20.6
2001	40,245	13.7
2002	46,890	16.5
2003	52,945	12.9

Source: 2003 IRS Data Book.

State Taxes on Individuals

(as of Jan. 1, 2004)

State	Sales/use tax (percent)[1]	Income tax (percent)[2]	State	Sales/use tax (percent)[1]	Income tax (percent)[2]
Alabama	4%	2.0% – 5.0%	Nebraska	5.5%	2.56% – 6.84%
Alaska	none	none	Nevada	6.5	none
Arizona	5.6	2.87 – 5.04	New Hampshire	none	([4])
Arkansas	5.125	1.0 – 7.0[3]	New Jersey	6	1.4 – 6.37
California	7.25	1.0 – 9.3[3]	New Mexico	5	1.7 – 6.8
Colorado	2.9	4.63	New York	4.25	4.0 – 7.70
Connecticut	6	3.0 – 5.0	North Carolina	4.5	6.0 – 8.25
Delaware	none	2.2 – 5.95	North Dakota	5	2.1 – 5.54
Florida	6	none	Ohio	6	0.743 – 7.5
Georgia	4	1.0 – 6.0	Oklahoma	4.5	0.5 – 6.75
Hawaii	4	1.4 – 8.25	Oregon	none	5.0 – 9.0
Idaho	6	1.6 – 7.8	Pennsylvania	6	3.07
Illinois	6.25	3.0	Rhode Island	7	25.0[5]
Indiana	6	3.4	South Carolina	5	2.5 – 7.0
Iowa	5	0.36 – 8.98	South Dakota	4	none
Kansas	5.3	3.5 – 6.45	Tennessee	7	([4])
Kentucky	6	2.0 – 6.0	Texas	6.25	none
Louisiana	4	2.0 – 6.0	Utah	4.75	2.3 – 7.0
Maine	5	2.0 – 8.5	Vermont	6	3.6 – 9.5
Maryland	5	2.0 – 4.75	Virginia	4.5	2.0 – 5.75
Massachusetts	5	5.3	Washington	6.5	none
Michigan	6	4.0	West Virginia	6	3.0 – 6.5
Minnesota	6.5	5.35 – 7.85	Wisconsin	5	4.6 – 6.75
Mississippi	7	3.0 – 5.0	Wyoming	4	none
Missouri	4.225	1.5 – 6.0	District of Columbia	5.75	5.0 – 9.5
Montana	none	2.0 – 11.0			

1. Local and county taxes, if any, are additional. 2. Tax rate for individuals; unless otherwise noted, range denotes progressive structure; higher income pays higher rate. 3. Indexed for inflation. 4. State income tax is limited to dividends and interest. 5. Percentage of federal tax liability. *Source:* The Federation of Tax Administrators.

up to $750 (if single) or $1,125 (if married and filing jointly). No credit is available if the taxpayer is single and has adjusted gross income of $17,500 or more. Similarly, the credit is unavailable to a married couple filing jointly if their adjusted gross income exceeds $25,000.

Effective for tax years beginning after Dec. 1, 1997, taxpayers who have qualifying children for whom the taxpayer may claim a dependency exemption and who are less than 17 years old as of the close of the tax year are entitled to the child tax credit. The amount of the credit for 2003 was $1,000. The child credit begins to phase out when AGI reaches $110,000 for joint filers and $75,000 for singles. Taxpayers who have three or more qualifying children may also be entitled to an additional credit.

Federal Estate and Gift Taxes

A Federal Estate Tax Return must generally be filed for the estate of every U.S. citizen or resident whose gross estate, taxable gifts, and specific exemptions exceed $1,000,000 for decedents dying in 2003, and according to the following table if dying in succeeding years:

Decedent dying in	Exclusion amount
2003	$1,000,000
2004 and 2005	1,500,000
2006, 2007, and 2008	2,000,000
2009	3,500,000

The Economic Growth and Tax Relief Reconciliation Act of 2001 completely phases out the federal estate and gift tax by 2010. The tax rates are lowered and the exemption is raised between 2002 and 2009, and the tax is completely eliminated in 2010. However, the post-act law will bring the Estate and Gift Tax back into existence in 2011.

A unified credit of $202,050 is available to offset both estate and gift taxes. Any part of the credit used to offset gift taxes is not available to offset estate taxes. As a result, although they are still taxable as gifts, lifetime taxable transfers no longer cushion the impact of progressive estate tax rates. Lifetime transfers and transfers made at death are combined for estate tax rate purposes.

Gift taxes are computed by applying the uniform rate schedule to lifetime taxable transfers (after deducting the unified credit) and subtracting the taxes payable for prior taxable periods. In general, estate taxes are computed by applying the uniform rate schedule to cumulative transfers and subtracting the gift taxes paid. An appropriate adjustment is made for taxes on lifetime transfers—such as certain gifts within three years of death—in a decedent's estate.

For 2004, an annual gift tax exclusion is provided that permits tax-free gifts to each donee of $11,000 for each year. A husband and wife who agree to treat gifts to third persons as joint gifts can exclude up to $22,000 a year to each donee. An unlimited exclusion for medical expenses and school tuition both paid directly to the institution for the benefit of any donee is also available in addition to the annual gift tax exclusion.

Federal Corporation Taxes

Corporations are taxed under a graduated tax rate structure. If a corporation has taxable income in excess of $100,000, the amount of tax shall be increased by the lesser of 5% of such excess or $11,750. When a corporation has taxable income in excess of $15,000,000, the amount of tax shall be increased by an additional amount equal to the lesser of 3% of such excess or $100,000.

If the corporation qualifies, it may elect to be an S corporation. If it makes this election, the corporation will not (with certain exceptions) pay corporate tax on its income. Its income is instead passed through and taxed to its shareholders. There are several requirements a corporation must meet to qualify as an S corporation, including having 75 or fewer shareholders and having only one class of stock.

Corporate Tax Rates

Taxable income	Tax rate
$0–$50,000	15%
$50,001–$75,000	25%
$75,001–$10,000,000	34%
$10,000,001 and up	35%

State Corporation Income and Franchise Taxes

All states except Texas, Nevada, South Dakota, Washington, and Wyoming impose a tax on corporation net income. The majority of states impose the tax at flat rates ranging from 2.3% to approximately 10.75%. Several states have adopted a graduated basis of rates for corporations.

Nearly all states follow the federal law in defining net income. However, many states provide for varying exclusions and adjustments.

A state is empowered to tax all of the net income of its domestic corporations. With regard to non-resident corporations, however, it may only tax the net income on business carried on within its boundaries. Corporations are, therefore, required to apportion their incomes among the states where they do business, and pay a tax to each of these states. Nearly all states provide an apportionment to their domestic corporations, too, in order that they not be unduly burdened. Several states tax unincorporated businesses separately.

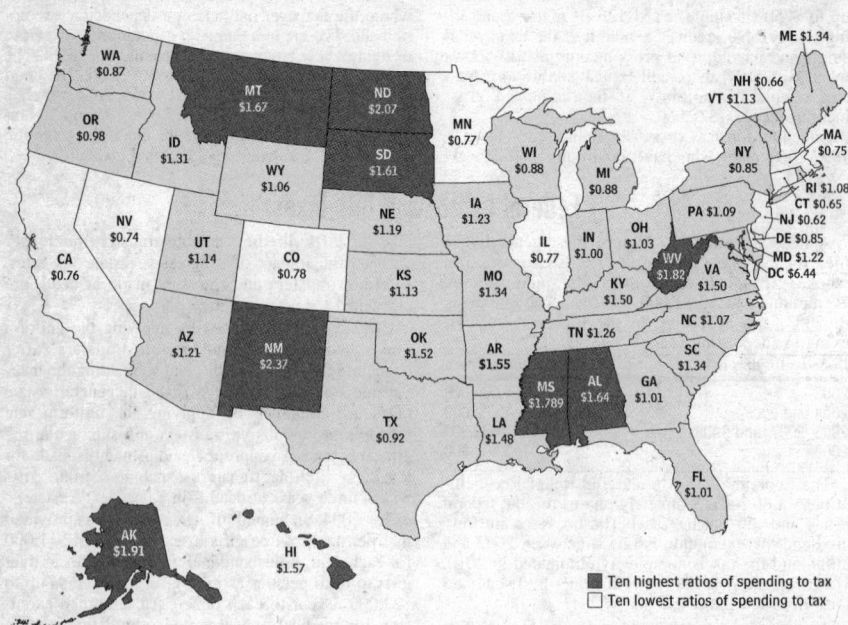

Federal Expenditures for Every Dollar of Taxes Sent to Washington

WA $0.87
MT $1.67
ND $2.07
ME $1.34
NH $0.66
VT $1.13
OR $0.98
ID $1.31
MN $0.77
MA $0.75
WY $1.06
SD $1.61
WI $0.88
MI $0.88
NY $0.85
RI $1.08
CT $0.65
NV $0.74
UT $1.14
NE $1.19
IA $1.23
IL $0.77
IN $1.00
OH $1.03
PA $1.09
NJ $0.62
DE $0.85
CA $0.76
CO $0.78
KS $1.13
MO $1.34
KY $1.50
WV $1.82
VA $1.50
MD $1.22
DC $6.44
AZ $1.21
NM $2.37
OK $1.52
AR $1.55
TN $1.26
NC $1.07
SC $1.34
MS $1.789
AL $1.64
GA $1.01
TX $0.92
LA $1.48
FL $1.01
AK $1.91
HI $1.57

■ Ten highest ratios of spending to tax
□ Ten lowest ratios of spending to tax

NOTE: For fiscal year 2002. *Source:* Tax Foundation. Web: http://taxfoundation.org/pr-fedtaxspendingratio.html.

The Person of the Year

How "Lucky Lindy"—and a slow week for news— gave birth to a memorable annual tradition

The founders of TIME Magazine, Henry Luce and Briton Haddon, were strong believers in the idea that history is shaped by the deeds of extraordinary men and women. This thesis, most memorably advanced by the British writer Thomas Carlyle, was well-suited to the American vision of the two Yale graduates, since it ran counter to the assertions of Karl Marx and others that history is made by impersonal economic and social forces.

TIME's insistence on the primacy of the individual finds its most memorable form in the magazine's annual designation of a Person of the Year—the individual whose actions most affected the course of the news within the last 12 months. But the magazine's signature annual tribute was not the result of high-level philosophizing: rather, it was driven by something far more important to journalists—a deadline.

The year was 1927; it was the last week in December. During the holiday season, the normal flow of public events had temporarily ebbed to a trickle. Looking to 1928, the editors at TIME were having trouble finding a newsworthy cover subject for the first issue of the new year. At the same time, they realized that they had passed up several opportunities during the year to put aviator Charles Lindbergh on its cover. Since his nonstop flight from New York to Paris in late May, the young pilot had been idolized—yet he had never appeared on the magazine's cover. So the editors came up with a new concept: instead of highlighting a personality of the week, it was decided that the cover for Jan. 2, 1928, would feature Lindbergh, and that beneath his likeness would be the words "Man of the Year."

A year later, the cover for TIME's first issue of 1929 revealed that its editors had named car magnate Walter P. Chrysler as Man of the Year for 1928—and it was obvious that an annual tradition had been born. Though TIME named a number of Women of the Year in the decades that followed, the editors eventually settled on the non-gender-specific term Person of the Year for the magazine's annual citation.

The term "Person of the Year"—redolent of countless Chamber of Commerce dinners—suggests to many people that it is awarded as an accolade. It is not. Rather, it designates the person who, in the editors' opinion, has most affected the course of history in the past twelve months—for good or for ill.

In 1938, for instance, Adolf Hitler completed his Anschluss of Austria and brokered the tragic agreement at Munich that put Czechoslovakia into his hands. However reluctantly, the editors concluded that Hitler's actions had most affected history's course, and he became the 1938 Man of the Year. Similarly, in 1979, Ayatullah Khomeini was named Man of the Year, even while he held Americans hostage in Teheran. TIME received more than 14,000 letters complaining about the choice.

After 75 years, the Person of the Year has become an institution: whereas in one sense it is a sort of intellectual parlor game, it also challenges TIME's editors and readers to reflect on the events of the past year critically, dispassionately, and rigorously. □

1927 Charles Lindbergh	1954 John Foster Dulles	1980 Ronald Reagan
1928 Walter P. Chrysler	1955 Harlow H. Curtice	1981 Lech Walesa
1929 Owen D. Young	1956 Hungarian Patriot	1982 The Personal Computer
1930 Mahatma Gandhi	1957 Nikita Khrushchev	1983 Ronald Reagan and
1931 Pierre Laval	1958 Charles DeGaulle	Yuri Andropov
1932 Franklin D. Roosevelt	1959 Dwight D. Eisenhower	1984 Peter Ueberroth
1933 Hugh S. Johnson	1960 U.S. Scientists	1985 Deng Xiaoping
1934 Franklin D. Roosevelt	1961 John F. Kennedy	1986 Corazon Aquino
1935 Haile Selassie	1962 Pope John XXIII	1987 Mikhail Gorbachev
1936 Wallis Warfield Simpson	1963 Rev. Martin Luther King, Jr.	1988 Endangered Earth
1937 Gen. and Mrs. Chiang	1964 Lyndon B. Johnson	1989 Mikhail Gorbachev
Kai-shek	1965 Gen. William Westmoreland	1990 George Bush
1938 Adolf Hitler	1966 Americans under 25	1991 Ted Turner
1939 Joseph Stalin	1967 Lyndon B. Johnson	1992 Bill Clinton
1940 Winston Churchill	1968 Astronauts Anders,	1993 The Peacemakers: Rabin,
1941 Franklin D. Roosevelt	Borman, Lovell	Arafat, Mandela, De Klerk
1942 Joseph Stalin	1969 The Middle Americans	1994 Pope John Paul II
1943 Gen. George C. Marshall	1970 Willy Brandt	1995 Newt Gingrich
1944 Gen. Dwight D. Eisenhower	1971 Richard M. Nixon	1996 Dr. David Ho
1945 Harry S. Truman	1972 Richard M. Nixon and	1997 Andrew Grove
1946 James F. Byrnes	Henry Kissinger	1998 Bill Clinton and
1947 Gen. George C. Marshall	1973 Judge John J. Sirica	Kenneth Starr
1948 Harry S. Truman	1974 King Faisal	1999 Jeff Bezos
1949 Winston Churchill	1975 American Women	2000 George W. Bush
1950 G.I. Joe	1976 Jimmy Carter	2001 Rudolph Giuliani
1951 Mohammed Mossadegh	1977 Anwar Sadat	2002 The Whistleblowers
1952 Queen Elizabeth II	1978 Deng Xiaoping	2003 The American Soldier
1953 Konrad Adenauer	1979 Ayatollah Khomeini	

People in the News, 2004

Freddy Adu, professional soccer player, became the youngest athlete to play in a major American sports league since 1887 in April, when, at age 14, he made his debut with Major League Soccer's D.C. United. Born in Ghana, Africa, Adu moved to Maryland with his family in 1997.

Iyad Allawi, Iraqi neurologist, was named prime minister of Iraq in May. A former exile and member of the Iraqi Governing Council, Allawi has close ties to the CIA and the Bush administration. With the financial backing of foreign governments and the CIA, Allawi formed the Iraqi National Accord, a group of former Baathists living in exile. The group attempted to overthrow Saddam Hussein in 1996. Allawi visited the U.S. in September and painted a rosy picture of Iraq—despite the growing instability and insurgency there.

Jean-Bertrand Aristide, president of Haiti, resigned in February, under intense pressure from the United States, France, and his political opponents, and went into exile. He was strongly criticized for failing to fight poverty and government corruption. Violent protests rocked Haiti during its January 2004 bicentennial celebrations, with armed rebels capturing major cities and demanding that Aristide step down.

Lance Armstrong, American bicyclist, proved once again in July that he is indeed the King of the Mountains, as he breezed past his rivals to win a record-breaking sixth consecutive Tour de France race. In 1996 Armstrong was diagnosed with cancer and given only a 50% chance to live.

Gloria Macapagal Arroyo, Philippine president, was condemned by the international community in July for giving in to the demands of Iraqi insurgents who kidnapped a Filipino truck driver. In May elections, President Arroyo narrowly defeated film star Fernando Poe, 39.5% to 36.6%.

José María Aznar, Spanish politician, was handed a stunning defeat in March elections, just three days after the terrorist attack in Madrid that killed about 202 people and injured about 1,400. His Popular Party lost to the Spanish Socialist Workers Party, headed by José Luis Rodríguez Zapatero, who took over as prime minister. Many Spaniards believe that al-Qaeda targeted Spain because Aznar supported the United States' war on Iraq.

Nicholas Berg, U.S. businessman from Pennsylvania, was decapitated in Iraq in May. The brutal murder was broadcast on an Islamist website, which said the killing was in retaliation for the torture of Iraqi prisoners by U.S. military personnel. His was the first of a number of horrific beheadings by militants in Iraq.

Sandy Berger, former national security adviser to President Clinton, stepped down as a senior adviser to Sen. John Kerry in July, after it was leaked that the Justice Department is investigating him for removing highly classified documents from the National Archives. He was reviewing the papers in 2003, while preparing for his testimony before the commission investigating the Sept. 11, 2001, terrorist attacks. Berger said the documents got mixed up with other papers in his portfolio.

Todd Bertuzzi, forward for the Vancouver Canucks, attacked Colorado Avalanche player Steve Moore during a National Hockey league game in March, breaking his neck. Bertuzzi punched Moore in the head from behind and then drove his head into the ice. He was suspended for the remainder of the season.

Conrad Black, founder and former CEO of Hollinger International, a media conglomerate that owns the Chicago Sun-Times, the Jerusalem Post, and other holdings, was accused by its board of stealing more than $400 million from the company. In August, the company outlined the excesses he lavished upon himself and his family at the company's expense. The list included "summer drinks" valued at more than $24,000 and two jets worth nearly $24 million.

William Boykin, U.S. Army general, violated military rules when he spoke in uniform at churches and before religious groups, portraying the war on terror in religious terms. He called the God of Islam "an idol," and said, "My God was a real God." He also declared that President Bush is in the White House because "God put him there." The deputy inspector general for the Defense Department said Boykin made 23 such speeches dating back to Jan. 2002.

Lakhdar Brahimi, the UN's special envoy to Iraq, selected a caretaker government to run Iraq until elections are held in January 2005. The temporary government replaced the U.S.-appointed Iraqi Governing Council in June.

L. Paul Bremer, former top civilian administrator of Iraq, formally transferred sovereignty back to the Iraqis in June, two days ahead of schedule. Iraqi prime minister Iyad Allawi requested the change to thwart attacks by insurgents. During Bremer's tenure in Iraq, the country slipped into lawlessness and violence. But he did manage to oversee the creation of the Iraqi Governing Council and the formation of the interim Iraqi government. In October, he said he didn't think enough troops were deployed to Iraq, angering the Bush administration.

Sergey Brin and Larry Page, founders of Google, the phenomenally popular search engine, positioned themselves to be billionaires several times over when in April they announced plans to take their company public. They offered the shares in an unconventional auction. When the company went public in August, the demand for shares was lower than expected, and the company reduced the number of shares offered. In addition, the price of shares—$85—was significantly lower than the $108–$135 range initially targeted.

Kobe Bryant, professional basketball player, pleaded not guilty in May to a charge of sexual assault. He was accused of raping a 19-year-old receptionist at a Vail, Colo., spa. He said he and the woman had consensual sex in June 2003. The woman dropped the charges against Bryant in August.

Ahmad Chalabi, Iraqi politician, lost his status as a favorite of the Pentagon and the Bush administration in May, when the U.S. ended a program in which it paid $335,000 a month to his Iraqi National Congress in exchange for intelligence gathering. A week later, U.S. troops and Iraqi police raided his home and his office, searching for evidence of corruption and fraud. Officials also accused Chalabi of telling Iranian officials that the U.S. had broken Iran's secret code used to send classified messages. The break was a long time coming; the White House justified its preemptive war on Iraq at least partially on assurances from Chalabi that Saddam Hussein had developed weapons of mass destruction, information that was deliberately misleading and in some cases, outright fabrication.

Hugo Chávez, leftist president of Venezuela, survived a recall referendum in August, with about 58% of voters opting to retain him. Over the past few years, the opposition has launched several national strikes against Chávez, claiming he's an ideologue who has stacked the courts and circumvented the legislative process to enact expensive social programs. He draws most of his support from the country's legion of poor.

Wesley Clark, retired four-star general, competed as an underdog candidate in the race for the Democratic presidential nomination, campaigning on his military background and his pragmatic approach to politics. He dropped out of the race in February. Clark led U.S. and allied troops in NATO's war in Kosovo in 1999, and retired from the military in 2000 after 34 years of service.

Richard Clarke, counterterrorism expert under four presidents—three of them Republican—created a furor in Washington with his unflinching criticism of the Bush administration's handling of the war on terror. On *60 Minutes* Clarke said Bush did a "terrible job on the war against terrorism." In his book, *Against All Enemies: Inside America's War on Terror,* released in March, Clarke said President Bush demanded Clarke find a link between the Sept. 11, 2001, terrorist attacks and Saddam Hussein—a link Clarke insists never existed. In addition, Clarke said that throughout 2001, Bush's inner circle failed to heed his warnings of an imminent terrorist attack. Instead, Clarke said, all eyes were focused on Iraq. After the book's release, Bush's team quickly shifted into damage-control mode, attempting to discredit Clarke. In his testimony before the commission investigating the Sept. 11, 2001, terrorist attacks, Clarke apologized to victims' families, saying, "Your government failed you. Those you entrusted with protecting you failed you. And I failed you."

Bill Clinton, former president, launched a national book tour in June with the publication of his much-anticipated memoir, *My Life.* More than 500,000 copies of the book were sold in its first day of publication, surpassing the all-time record set by Hillary Rodham Clinton's *Living History.* His book was more revealing than his wife's; he expresses contrition about his affair with Monica Lewinsky and attacks former independent counsel Kenneth Starr. Clinton underwent quadruple bypass surgery in September.

Joseph Darby, U.S. reservist military police officer in Iraq, turned over to U.S. Army officials the infamous CD containing the appalling photographs of fellow soldiers abusing and humiliating Iraqi inmates at the Abu Ghraib prison. The photos touched off a major scandal that reverberated around the world and seriously tainted perceptions of the U.S. occupation of Iraq.

Gavyn Davies and Greg Dyke, BBC executives, resigned in January, after British judge Lord Hutton concluded that British prime minister Tony Blair had not intentionally "sexed-up" the intelligence dossier about Iraq's weapons capabilities to justify war in Iraq, as reported by the BBC in May 2003. In 2003, Blair said intelligence reports indicated Saddam Hussein could launch biological and chemical weapons in 45 minutes. The BBC questioned the accuracy of the report and asserted that the Blair administration knew the information was unreliable but used it anyway to build a stronger case for war. Hutton censured the BBC for sloppy reporting and editing.

Howard Dean, former governor of Vermont, enjoyed frontrunner status in the crowded field of Democratic presidential hopefuls before the first primary. His star dimmed early, however, when he placed third in the Iowa caucuses and second in New Hampshire. He dropped out of the race in February. Throughout the campaign, Dean was an outspoken critic of the war in Iraq and of President Bush. He also revolutionized political campaigning, using the Internet as a fund-raising and organizational tool.

Tom DeLay, House majority leader, was rebuked three times in the course two weeks by the House Ethics Committee. He was criticized for pressuring another representative to vote in favor of the Medicare bill, for questionable fund-raising tactics, and for asking federal aviation officials to help find Texas Democratic legislators who fled the state rather than vote on a redistricting plan they deemed unfair.

Luis Echeverría, former president of Mexico, in July was charged with genocide in the 1971 massacre of 25 student protesters. The special prosecutor said Echeverría allowed a military-trained hit squad to brutally beat the demonstrators. A federal judge, however, dismissed the case the following day, claiming the statute of limitations had expired.

Bob Edwards, beloved radio show anchor, was reassigned from host of National Public Radio's "Morning Edition" to senior correspondent. Edwards hosted the popular early-morning show since its inception, 25 years ago. The move was widely criticized by listeners. NPR said his removal was part of an attempt to refresh its programming. In October, he made the leap to XM Satellite Radio, a pay service, hosting a one-hour morning program.

John Edwards, U.S. senator from North Carolina since 1999 and former trial attorney, frequently spoke of two Americas—one for the privileged and one for those left behind by the Bush administration—during his bid for the Democratic presidential nomination. As the other candidates attacked one another, Edwards remained positive and reserved his venom for the policies of the Bush administration. He dropped out of the race in March. Kerry selected Edwards as his running mate in July 2004, hoping Edwards's youthful charm and charisma would appeal to voters.

Michael Eisner, media executive, was dealt a stunning vote of no confidence by the shareholders of the Walt Disney Company in March, when they refused to reelect him as chairman of the company. He retained the title of chief executive, however. The shareholders named former senator George Mitchell as chairman. Investors have been highly critical of Eisner's leadership and the lackluster performance of the company's stock. In September he said he plans to step down in 2006.

Richard Foster, chief Medicare actuary, testified before members of the House Ways and Means Committee in March, telling them that he had informed the Bush administration in June 2003 that the Medicare prescription drug benefit would cost about $100 billion more than it had publicly estimated. The White House failed to tell Congress of Foster's concern until after Bush signed the bill in December. In addition, Foster said his boss, Thomas Scully, the administrator of Medicare, threatened to fire him if he revealed his concerns to Congress.

Sonia Gandhi, Italian-born Indian politician, stunned India in May when she refused to become the country's prime minister. She was widely expected to accept the post after her party, the Indian National Congress Party, prevailed over the ruling Bharatiya Janata Party (BJP) in parliamentary elections. The BJP vociferously protested Gandhi's expected elevation to prime minister, saying her foreign birth precluded her from assuming the position. The Congress Party instead chose former finance minister Manmohan Singh. Gandhi is part of India's powerful Gandhi dynasty.

Mel Gibson, actor and director, garnered intense buzz for his incendiary film, *The Passion of the Christ,* months before its February release. The film, in Latin and Aramaic with English subtitles, depicts the last 12 hours of Jesus's life in explicitly violent detail. Many derided the film as anti-Semitic, saying it cast blame on the Jews for Jesus Christ's crucifixion. A number of evangelical Christian and Catholic groups, however, praised the film for its portrayal of Jesus Christ's sacrifice. *New Yorker* film critic David Denby said Gibson's "obsession with pain, disguised by religious feelings, has now reached a frightening apotheosis."

Porter Goss, former U.S. congressman from Florida, became director of the CIA in September. Goss served as the chairman of the House Intelligence Committee and worked for the CIA as a spy during the cold war. He has been critical of the agency, saying it has "ignored its core mission" and is in "dysfunctional denial of any need for corrective action."

Paul Hamm, gymnast, found himself at the center of a controversy when Olympic judges erroneously awarded the gold medal in the all-around competition to him, when it should have gone to South Korean gymnast Yang Tae Young. Officials allowed Hamm to keep the medal. It was a bittersweet end to a stunning performance by Hamm, who stumbled early on in the competition, only to excel in later events to launch an astonishing comeback.

Abu Issa al-Hindi, senior member of al-Qaeda, was arrested in August by British authorities who think he had surveyed potential targets in New York in 2000 and 2001. He was detained after officials in Pakistan arrested Muhammad Naeem Noor Khan and confiscated his laptop, which included detailed surveillance reports on buildings in the U.S.

Jack Idema, vigilante, was convicted in September of entering Afghanistan illegally, operating an illegal jail, and taking hostages and torturing them. He was sentenced to 10 years in jail. Idema, a former Green Beret, said he was working for a secret counterterrorism unit sanctioned by the Pentagon. The Pentagon denied the claim. Brent Bennett and Edward Caraballo were also convicted and received sentences of 8 and 10 years, respectively. Caraballo is a television journalist who said he was in Iraq filming a documentary on the war against terrorism.

Janet Jackson and Justin Timberlake, pop stars, created an enormous scandal when Timberlake ripped the bodice of Jackson's costume during the halftime show of February's Super Bowl XXXVIII, exposing her right breast, which was pierced and adorned with a brooch. Timberlake promptly apologized for the "wardrobe malfunction." The Federal Communications Commission fined CBS, which broadcast the Super Bowl, $550,000 for the incident.

Michael Jackson, pop star, pleaded not guilty in January to nine felony counts—seven of allegedly engaging in lewd acts with a child under age 14 and two of giving an intoxicant to a child. After his court appearance, Jackson greeted hundreds of screaming fans outside the courthouse and danced on the top of an SUV. The charges were replaced in May with 10 similar felony charges. He's accused of molesting a child who was suffering from cancer at his Neverland ranch in California in 2003.

Jiang Yanyong, Chinese surgeon, was released after 45 days in military custody. He was detained for writing a letter to top members of the government that criticized the deadly crackdown on democracy protesters in Tiananmen Square in 1989. Upon his release, Jiang said, "The next thing I will direct my energies to is the problem of AIDS." In 2003, Jiang revealed that several hospitals in China had underreported the number SARS patients.

Paul Johnson, engineer, was beheaded in Saudi Arabia by members of al-Qaeda. An employee of Lockheed Martin, Johnson worked on Apache helicopters. Kenneth Scroggs, another Lockheed Martin employee, was killed at about the same time as Johnson's abduction. Hours after Johnson's murder was publicized, Saudi officials killed four leaders of al-Qaeda in Saudi Arabia.

David Kay, former chief weapons inspector, stepped down in January, after his Iraqi Survey Group, a 1,400-member team whose mission was to uncover Iraq's weapons of mass destruction, failed to find any evidence of chemical, biological, and nuclear weapons in Iraq. He stated that the team was "almost all wrong" about Iraq's weapons of mass destruction.

Thomas Kean and Lee Hamilton, chairman and vice chairman of the commission investigating the Sept. 11, 2001, terrorist attacks, who in July released a 500+ page report on the tragedy. It called for an overhaul of the intelligence community, including the creation of a cabinet-level intelligence director. The bipartisan report was widely praised for its clarity and detail. In October, it was nominated for a National Book Award.

John Kerry, U.S. senator from Massachusetts, was the Democratic candidate for president in 2004. Throughout the campaign, Kerry accused President Bush of mismanaging the war in Iraq and the war on terrorism and promised to roll back the Bush tax cuts. The president accused Kerry of being a "flip-flopper" and said he lacked the resolute leadership required to fight the war on terrorism. Kerry selected Sen. John Edwards as his running mate in July.

Abdul Qadeer Khan, Pakistani scientist considered the father of Pakistan's nuclear weapons program, admitted in February that he had passed on designs and technology for building nuclear weapons to other countries, including North Korea, Iran, and Libya. He emphatically denied that his government had sanctioned the transactions.

Muhammad Naeem Noor Khan, Pakistani computer engineer and al-Qaeda operative, was captured in Pakistan in July. The CIA found files on his laptop computer that indicated al-Qaeda had conducted detailed reconnaissance of several financial buildings in the U.S. The discovery prompted the Bush administration to raise the terror alert in areas of New York; Washington, DC; and New Jersey.

Dennis J. Kucinich, member of Congress, emerged as the most liberal candidate in the race for the Democratic presidential nomination. Prior to being elected to the House of Representatives, Kucinich served as an Ohio state senator and mayor of Cleveland. He won the mayoral race at age 31, becoming the youngest mayor elected to lead a major American city. He has lobbied for human rights, worker rights, and the environment, and is an outspoken critic of the war in Iraq and the policies of the World Trade Organization.

Brandon Mayfield, Oregon lawyer, was arrested in May on a material witness warrant in connection with the deadly train bombing in Madrid in March. The FBI identified him from a digital photograph taken from a plastic bag found near the scene. After being held for two weeks, Mayfield was released from prison when the FBI acknowledged that his fingerprints did not match those on the bag. Weeks before his arrest, Spanish authorities had expressed doubts about the fingerprints the FBI claimed were a 100% match.

James McGreevey, governor of New Jersey, announced in August that he would resign because he had had an affair with another man. "My truth is that I am a gay American," he said. Golan Cipel came forward and said he was the man with whom the governor had the relationship. Cipel said, however, the relationship was not consensual, and threatened, but did not follow through on, a sexual harassment lawsuit. McGreevey had given Cipel a number of government jobs for which he was clearly unqualified.

Mike Melvill, test pilot, became the first civilian to reach space in a privately financed and developed spacecraft. In June Melvill guided SpaceShipOne 62 miles above California, successfully overcoming technical problems that could have proven tragic. The entire flight out of Earth's atmosphere and back down lasted 90 minutes.

Zell Miller, Democratic senator from Georgia, delivered a vitriolic keynote address at the Republican National Convention in August, lambasting the Democratic nominee, Sen. John Kerry. "Our nation is being torn apart and made weaker because of the Democrats' manic obsession to bring down our commander in chief," he said. Republicans declared him their favorite Democrat; Democrats accused him of betrayal. In an interview after the speech, a clearly agitated Miller said he wished he could challenge MSNBC's Chris Matthews to a duel.

Michael Moore, filmmaker, gained an impassioned following with the release of *Fahrenheit 9/11,* a documentary harshly critical of President Bush, his administration, the war in Iraq, and Bush's handling of the war on terrorism. The film won the Palme d'Or (the top prize) at the Cannes International Film Festival. In its opening weekend in late June, *Fahrenheit 9/11* took in nearly $22 million at the box office to become the highest-grossing documentary of all time.

Ralph Nader, consumer advocate, declared his candidacy for president in February. The announcement outraged many Democrats who feared Nader would siphon votes away from the Democratic nominee and cost the party the White House—a scenario similar to the 2000 election.

Gavin Newsom, mayor of San Francisco, declared in February that the city would allow same-sex marriages, saying they are permitted under the equality provisions in the state constitution. Almost 3,200 same-sex couples were married within 10 days of Newsom's announcement. The state supreme court declared in August that the gay marriages that were performed in San Francisco are "void and of no legal effect from their inception." The unanimous ruling stated that Newsom did not have the authority to permit such unions.

Barack Obama, state senator from Illinois, delivered a rousing keynote speech at July's Democratic National Convention. "There's not a black America and white America and Latino America and Asian America; there's the United States of America," he said. Obama, whose black father was born in Kenya and white mother in Kansas, is running for a seat in the U.S. Senate. Obama won the Democratic primary in a landslide.

Paul O'Neill, President Bush's first treasury secretary, spoke out against the Bush administration during an interview in January on *60 Minutes.* He said the administration had been planning an attack against Iraq since the first days of Bush's presidency.

Rod Paige, U.S. secretary of education, stunned members of the National Education Association, the country's largest teachers union, when he compared it to a "terrorist organization." The union contends that the Bush administration has underfunded the No Child Left Behind Act and placed unrealistic demands on schools. Paige apologized for the comment.

Carly Patterson, gymnast, won the hearts of Americans and the gold medal in the all-around competition at the 2004 Summer Olympics in Athens. She's the second American woman to do so. She also took home silver medals in the team competition and the balance beam.

Michael Phelps, swimmer, entered the 2004 Summer Olympics poised to tie or break Mark Spitz's record seven gold medals. While he didn't accomplish the Olympian feat, he did bring home eight medals, tying with Russian gymnast Aleksandr Dityatin as the winningest athlete at a single Olympic Games.

Charles Pickering, Sr., trial judge, was appointed to the U.S. Court of Appeals by President Bush during the Congressional recess. The senate had blocked his nomination twice, with Democrats opposing him because of his decisions on racial issues in his 11 years as a judge in Hattiesburg, Miss.

Vladimir Putin, president of Russia, called for a broad overhaul of the government in September, after a series of terrorist attacks killed nearly 500 people, including 340 at a middle school in Beslan, in southern Russia. The world community expressed deep concern that Putin's plans would consolidate his power and roll back democracy in Russia.

Dan Rather, journalist, found himself at the center of a media storm in September, when he and his network, CBS, admitted that they could not definitively prove the authenticity of documents they used in a *60 Minutes* segment, which suggested President Bush received preferential treatment when he joined the National Guard and later when he served in it. Supporters of Bush immediately cast doubt on the documents, which were supposedly written by Bush's squadron commander, who has been dead for 20 years. The commander's secretary came forward to say that while the information in the memos was accurate, they appeared to have been forged. Finally, after a flurry of analysts examined the typeface of the memos and came up with conflicting conclusions, former Lt. Col. Bill Burkett, who handed the documents to CBS, admitted he lied about his source and did not say from whom he obtained them.

Ron Reagan, son of former president Ronald Reagan, angered many Republicans by speaking out against the Bush administration's stem-cell research policy. He spoke at the Democratic National Convention in July, urging voters to support new research using stem cells. "Surely we can distinguish between undifferentiated cells multiplying in a tissue culture and a living, breathing person," he said.

Condoleezza Rice, national security adviser, testified before the commission investigating the Sept. 11, 2001, terrorist attacks in April. During the often contentious questioning, she said that although the Bush administration had been warned that al-Qaeda might be planning an attack on U.S. soil, there was no concrete evidence that such an action was imminent. She said a classified document delivered to Bush on Aug. 6, 2001, titled "Bin Laden Determined to Attack Inside the United States," was historical and didn't provide new threat information.

Linda Ronstadt, singer, was ejected from Las Vegas's Aladdin Hotel in July after she dedicated the song "Desperado" to Michael Moore and encouraged the audience to see his new film, *Fahrenheit 9/11,* a documentary harshly critical of the Bush administration. Casino president William Timmins had her removed from the premises after some of the people in the audience booed her, ripped posters from the wall, and threw drinks.

Donald Rumsfeld, U.S. secretary of defense, was reprimanded by President Bush in May for his handling of the Abu Ghraib prison abuse scandal in Iraq. Although the Pentagon launched an investigation into the misconduct in January 2004, President Bush and Congress did not learn of the extent of the abuse until April, when photos documenting the humiliation and torture of Iraqi prisoners were broadcast on *60 Minutes II* and run in the *New Yorker.* Following the war in Iraq, Rumsfeld was repeatedly criticized by both Democrats and Republicans for a lack of prewar planning and for not deploying an adequate number of troops.

Moktada al-Sadr, radical Shiite cleric, ordered a bloody uprising against U.S. troops based in southern Iraq in early April, after authorities shuttered his newspaper, *Al Hawza,* alleging it incited violence. The insurgency lasted seven weeks and claimed hundreds of fighters in al-Sadr's Mahdi Army. Another violent uprising followed in August. Grand Ayatollah Ali al-Sistani negotiated a truce between al-Sadr and the U.S.

Ricardo Sanchez, U.S. Army general, served as top commander in Iraq for more than a year, until shortly after the Abu Ghraib prison-abuse scandal broke in April. Although Pentagon officials said the decision to replace him had nothing to do with the controversy,

Sanchez was widely criticized for not alerting Congress about the graphic photographs that detailed the abuse of Iraqi prisoners at the hands of U.S. troops. Two panels that investigated the abuse scandal released reports in August that criticized Sanchez, saying he initially approved interrogation techniques that violated the Geneva Convention and then revised his policy three times in a month in late 2003. The policy changes created confusion and led to the abuse, the panels said.

Antonin Scalia, Supreme Court justice, refused in March to recuse himself from a case involving Vice President Dick Cheney, a close friend with whom he went duck hunting just weeks after the court agreed to hear the case. The Sierra Club and Judicial Watch were seeking to force Cheney to reveal details about private meetings of his energy task force. In a 21-page memo, Scalia said, "If it is reasonable to think that a Supreme Court Justice can be bought so cheap, the nation is in deeper trouble than I had imagined."

Michael Scheuer, senior CIA officer, lashed out at the panel that investigated the Sept. 11, 2001, terrorist attacks. He called the panel and the CIA "bureaucratic cowards" for not holding an agency or individuals accountable for the tragedy. His invective was particularly critical of former CIA director George Tenet, saying he "starved and is starving the [Osama] bin Laden unit of officers while handling plenty of officers to staff his personal public relations office, as well as the staffs that handled diversity, multiculturalism, and employee newsletters." Scheuer also wrote a best-selling book, *Imperial Hubris,* published anonymously, that criticized President Bush's war on terror.

Ariel Sharon, Israeli prime minister, announced a plan to unilaterally disengage from the Gaza Strip. In February, he said he would order the evacuation of settlers and soldiers from the Gaza Strip. He later said he intended to enhance Israeli control of West Bank settlements. While President Bush and the majority of Israelis supported his plan, his Likud Party voted down his proposal in May. Sharon was spared a potentially devastating blow to his career when the attorney general dropped bribery charges against him in June. The charges stemmed from a failed real estate deal from the late 1990s involving a developer who sought Sharon's support for a project on a Greek island.

Al Sharpton, Jr., controversial civil rights activist and minister, ran a long-shot campaign for the Democratic presidential nomination. Sharpton was an outspoken critic of President Bush—and the other Democratic candidates, daring to utter blunt one-liners that the other candidates largely avoided. On Howard Dean's frightening howl after losing the Iowa caucuses, Sharpton said, "I wanted to say to Governor Dean, don't be hard on yourself about hooting and hollering. If I had spent the money you did and got 18%, I'd still be in Iowa hooting and hollering." And on President Bush, he quipped, "We've read Bush's lips. They lied." His campaign, however, failed to raise significant funds and lacked organizational structure. In addition, black voters, his assumed base of support, never rallied around his campaign.

Manmohan Singh, Indian economist, was sworn in as India's 13th prime minister in May, becoming the country's first Sikh premier. He accepted the post after the Indian National Congress prevailed over the ruling Bharatiya Janata Party (BJP) in parliamentary elections, and its leader, Sonia Gandhi, refused to become prime minister. As the former finance minister, Singh saved the country from potential financial ruin and initiated economic changes that have contributed to India's prospering economy.

Martha Stewart, diva of domesticity, was sentenced to five months in prison in July after being found guilty on four counts of obstruction of justice and lying to federal investigators. The judge stayed her sentence pending appeal, but Stewart opted to begin serving her sentence in October. She was also fined $30,000. The charges stem from her December 2001 sale of 3,928 shares of the biotech stock ImClone. She made the trade the day before the FDA announced it had declined to review ImClone's new cancer drug—news that sent shares tumbling.

Swift Boat Veterans for Truth, political advocacy group, sponsored several television commercials over the summer that questioned Sen. John Kerry's military record and said he lied about combat situations for which he earned medals. Although only one member of the group actually served on a Swift boat with Kerry and most of the group's allegations have been discredited, Kerry's poll ratings slipped in the wake of the ads. They also ran ads against Kerry's anti–Vietnam war protests, which many believe is the source of their animus against Kerry.

Maj. Gen. Antonio Taguba, Army official, investigated allegations of humiliating abuse endured by Iraqis at the hands of U.S. soldiers at the Abu Ghraib prison. His report, completed in March, said prisoners had been stripped, beaten, sexually assaulted, and threatened with rape between October and December 2003. Reservist military police told him that their superiors and CIA personnel encouraged the abuse to "set physical and mental conditions for favorable interrogation of witnesses."

George Tenet, former director of the CIA, resigned in June, citing "personal reasons." His resignation, however, came as the CIA faced withering attacks for not having prevented the Sept. 11, 2001, terrorist attacks and for distributing intelligence that Iraq possessed weapons of mass destruction—information that precipitated the U.S.-led war—when no such weapons have been found. Tenet admitted in February that the prewar intelligence on Iraq's nuclear weapons programs and capabilities could have overestimated the actual arsenal.

Sheik Ahmed Yassin, spiritual leader and founder of Hamas, was assassinated by Israeli forces in March. Israeli officials acknowledged they intended to kill Yassin, who they blame for organizing terrorist attacks and suicide bombings that have killed hundreds of Israeli citizens and soldiers. Israel troops also killed his successor, Abdel Aziz Rantisi.

Sheik Ghazi Ajil al-Yawar, Iraqi tribal leader, was named president of the interim Iraqi government in June. A Sunni and member of the Iraqi Governing Council, al-Yawar quickly moved to win the support of Iraqis, blaming the U.S. for the dismal situation in Iraq. The post of president is mostly ceremonial.

James Yee, U.S. Army chaplain at the terrorist detention center at Guantánamo Bay prison, was arrested in September 2003 on suspicion of espionage, mutiny, and sedition. The army later reduced the charges to mishandling classified information, but added charges of adultery and conduct unbecoming an officer. In March Yee, a Muslim, was convicted of the lesser charges. Yee appealed the decision, and in April was cleared of all charges.

Sheik Abu Musab al-Zarqawi, Jordanian militant and terrorist who has ties to al-Qaeda, was blamed for many of the bombings and beheadings in Iraq. In March authorities said they intercepted a letter from al-Zarqawi to the top leadership of al-Qaeda, in which he took responsibility for dozens of bombings in Iraq, including the August 2003 attack on UN headquarters in Baghdad, and outlined plans to further destabilize Iraq by inciting a civil war between the country's Shiite and Sunni populations.

2004 Deaths

(through October 21, 2004)

Abu Abbas, 55: former leader of the terrorist group Palestine Liberation Front who organized the 1985 hijacking of the *Achille Lauro,* an Italian cruise ship. During the operation, hijackers shot and killed an American passenger. Abbas was captured in Iraq in 2003 by U.S. Special Forces troops. March 8, 2004

Brock Adams, 77: politician from Washington who served six terms as a U.S. representative before becoming President Carter's transportation secretary in 1977. In 1986, he unseated Republican senator Slade Gorton. Dogged by allegations of sexual harassment, which he denied, Adams did not seek reelection. Sept. 10, 2004

Umberto Agnelli, 69: Italian businessman who took over as the chairman of Fiat after his brother's death in 2003. The Agnelli family's empire included not only the Fiat car company, but also holdings in publishing, telecommunications, and banking. May 27, 2004

Victor Argo, 69: film actor who played tough guys in dozens of films, including *Mean Streets* and *Taxi Driver.* April 6, 2004

Richard Avedon, 81: fashion and portrait photographer who captured his subjects at their most dramatic. Both experimental and stark, his work is known for its uncompromising realism. He was staff photographer for *Harper's Bazaar, Vogue,* and most recently *The New Yorker.* Oct. 1, 2004

Peter Barnes, 73: British playwright and screenwriter who penned the satirical play *The Ruling Class* and earned an Oscar nomination for his screenplay for *Enchanted April.* July 1, 2004

Emily Morison Beck, 88: editor of the 13th, 14th, and 15th editions of *Bartlett's Familiar Quotations.* March 28, 2004

Arnold O. Beckman, 104: scientist who invented several user-friendly scientific devices, including a tool to measure acidity and alkalinity and the quartz spectrophotometer, an instrument that pioneered automatic chemical analysis. May 18, 2004

Geoffrey Beene, 77: couturier whose innovative, modern designs emphasized the curves of women's bodies and often featured spiral seams. He also designed men's clothing. Sept. 28, 2004

Sune Bergström, 88: Swedish biochemist who was part of a team of scientists that discovered the structure and use of prostaglandins, compounds that affect blood pressure and body temperature, among other bodily functions. Bergström, along with I. Samuelsson and John R. Vane, won the 1982 Nobel Prize in Physiology or Medicine. Aug. 15, 2004

Elmer Bernstein, 82: Oscar-winning composer who scored more than 200 films, including *To Kill a Mockingbird.* Aug. 18, 2004

Jan Berry, 62: half of the surf-music duo Jan and Dean. The pair recorded the hits "Deadman's Curve" and "The Little Old Lady from Pasadena" and earned 10 gold records in the 1960s. Berry's career ended in a 1966 car accident that left him paralyzed and brain injured. March 26, 2004

Fanny Blankers-Koen, 85: Dutch sprinter who, as a 30-year-old mother of two, won four gold medals in track and field events at the 1948 Olympics. Jan. 25, 2004

Daniel Boorstin, 89: prolific writer and historian who won the 1973 Pulitzer Prize in History for *The Ameri-* *cans: The Democratic Experience,* a history of advances and inventions after the Civil War. He served as librarian of Congress from 1975 to 1987. Feb. 28, 2004

Phoebe Brand, 96: actress and theater teacher who was one of the founders of the influential Group Theatre. At age 86, she made her film debut in *Vanya on 42nd Street.* July 3, 2004

Marlon Brando, 80: Academy Award–winning actor considered a singular practitioner of Method acting. His inward-looking style and rough sex appeal established him as one of Hollywood's most respected actors. He's best known for two films made in 1972, *The Godfather* and *Last Tango in Paris.* He won the Best Actor Oscar for *The Godfather* but refused the award in protest of Hollywood's treatment of Native Americans. His other films include *On the Waterfront* and *Apocalypse Now.* July 1, 2004

Laura Branigan, 47: pop singer best known for her 1982 hit "Gloria." She died of a brain aneurysm. Aug. 26, 2004

Mary-Ellis Bunim, 57: television producer who, with her husband, Jonathan Murray, created *The Real World,* MTV's real-life soap opera, which ushered in the era of reality television. Jan. 29, 2004

R. W. Burchfield, 81: lexicographer who edited the four-volume supplement to the *Oxford English Dictionary.* July 5, 2004

Anne Burford, 62: head of the Environmental Protection Agency under President Reagan who was a target of environmentalists who opposed her cuts to the EPA budget and her policy of giving states a larger role in regulation. She resigned after 22 months on the job. July 18, 2004

Richard Butler, 86: white supremacist who established the Aryan Nations in the 1970s. Sept. 8, 2004

James Cantalupo, 60: chairman and chief executive of McDonald's who came out of retirement in 2003 to help revitalize the company. April 19, 2004

Henri Cartier-Bresson, 95: esteemed French photojournalist whose images chronicled momentous events and made art out of the otherwise mundane. He had a gift for capturing "the decisive moment," occurrences at their most significant point. Aug. 3, 2004

Ray Charles, 73: singer, pianist, and composer whose soulful tunes combined gospel, blues, pop, country, and jazz. A pioneer in rock music whose songs ranged from pop standards to love songs to bebop, Charles, who was blind since age 7, paved the way for such artists as Elvis Presley, Aretha Franklin, and Van Morrison. He won 12 Grammy Awards. His hits include "Georgia on My Mind," "Drown in My Own Tears," and "A Fool for You." June 10, 2004

Julia Child, 91: Emmy Award–winning chef and television personality whose breezy style demystified French cooking for a generation of Americans reared on tuna casserole rather than *boeuf bourguignon.* In 1961, Child, Simone Beck, and Louisette Bertholle wrote *Mastering the Art of French Cooking.* Her PBS show, *The French Chef,* followed in 1963. Aug. 13, 2004

Alistair Cooke, 95: British-born journalist and television and radio host whose commentary on American culture found a wide audience in both the U.S. and the UK. Cooke hosted the weekly BBC radio show *Letter* *from America* from 1946 until Feb. 2004. He also lent his sophisticated wit to *Masterpiece Theatre,* which he hosted from 1971 to 1992. March 30, 2004

Gordon Cooper, 77: pioneering NASA astronaut who ventured into orbit twice—in 1963 as the pilot of the last *Mercury* mission and in 1965 as commander of *Gemini 5.* Oct. 4, 2004

Marjorie Courtenay-Latimer, 97: South African naturalist who in 1938 discovered a coelacanth, a species of fish believed to have been extinct for 70 million years. May 17, 2004

Archibald Cox, 92: special prosecutor who was fired by the Nixon administration in the Oct. 1973 "Saturday Night Massacre." Two months after Cox joined the Watergate investigation, it was revealed that Nixon had secretly recorded phone conversations about the break-in. The White House refused Cox's repeated requests to relinquish the tapes, and Cox turned to the courts. Nixon defied a court order to surrender the tapes, and Cox was fired. May 29, 2004

Francis Crick, 88: molecular biologist who in 1959 with James Watson codiscovered the double-helical structure of deoxyribonucleic acid (DNA), the chemical that carries hereditary characteristics from generation to generation. They won the 1962 Nobel Prize in Physiology or Medicine for their work, along with Maurice Wilkins. Crick's later work included research on protein synthesis and embryonic development. July 28, 2004

Joseph Cullman, 92: former CEO of Philip Morris (1957 to 1978) who transformed the company into one of the biggest in the U.S. He led the fight against the government's ban on cigarette advertising, insisting that cigarettes posed no health risk. April 30, 2004

Agnes "Sis" Cunningham, 95: folk musician who cofounded the influential folk-song journal *Broadside* in 1962. June 27, 2004

Rodney Dangerfield, 82: comic and actor known for his self-deprecating humor and his catch phrase, "I don't get no respect." He appeared in the films *Caddyshack* and *Back to School.* Oct. 5, 2004

Paula Danziger, 59: author who wrote dozens of children's books, including *The Cat Ate My Gymsuit* and the *Amber Brown* series. July 8, 2004

Eileen Darby Lester, 87: photographer who took pictures of more than 500 Broadway shows and a long list of stars, including Marlon Brando, Tallulah Bankhead, and Katharine Hepburn. March 30, 2004

Samuel Dash, 79: attorney who as chief counsel for the Senate Select Committee on Presidential Campaign Activities investigated the Watergate break-in and the White House's secret audiotape system that ultimately proved the downfall of President Nixon. May 29, 2004

Marvin Davis, 79: businessman who made billions in the oil industry. He bought Fox studios in 1981 and later sold it to Rupert Murdoch. Sept. 25, 2004

Joel Dean, 73: co-founder of the SoHo upscale food market Dean & DeLuca, now a 19-store chain. May 24, 2004

Frances Dee, 96: striking movie star of Hollywood's golden era who starred in *An American Tragedy* and *Little Women.* She was married to actor Joel McCrea for 57 years. March 6, 2004

David Dellinger, 88: activist who organized several antiwar protests, including the 1967 demonstration at the Pentagon. As one of the Chicago Seven, Dellinger was tried for inciting a riot at the 1968 Democratic Convention. May 25, 2004

Jacques Derrida, 74: French philosopher who originated deconstruction, a controversial and widely influential movement that shaped literary theory and a variety of other disciplines, particularly in the 1970s and 1980s. In writings such as *Of Grammatology* and *Writing and Difference,* he argued that all broadly

philosophical claims have meaning only in the system of competing and opposing possibilities they wish to transcend. Oct. 8, 2004

Carmine De Sapio, 95: powerful politician who dominated New York City Democratic politics as the last Tammany Hall boss. His power and popularity plummeted in the 1960s, however, when he was criticized as corrupt and authoritarian and convicted of petty bribery. July 27, 2004

Larry Desmedt ("Indian Larry"), 55: biker and builder of custom motorcycles. He was often photographed by Robert Mapplethorpe. He died while performing a stunt. Aug. 28, 2004

Edmund DiGiulio, 76: inventor who developed the Steadicam, a system for keeping motion picture cameras stable during filming. He won several Oscars for his innovations in cinematography. June 4, 2004

Julius Dixon, 90: rock-and-roll songwriter who penned the pop hits "Lollipop" and "Dim, Dim the Lights (I Want Some Atmosphere)." Jan. 30, 2004

Dick Durrance, 89: ski racer who developed ski resorts in Sun Valley, Idaho, and Aspen, Colorado. He won 17 national titles. June 13, 2004

Fred Ebb, 76: lyricist who, with partner John Kander, penned some of Broadway's most memorable scores, including *Cabaret, Woman of the Year,* and *Kiss of the Spider Woman,* all of which earned the pair Tony Awards. Sept. 11, 2004

Maxime Faget, 83: innovative aerospace engineer who designed the *Mercury* space capsule and worked on all of NASA's manned spacecraft, including *Gemini, Apollo,* and the space shuttle. Oct. 9, 2004

Hiram L. Fong, 97: businessman and lawyer who was the first Asian American to serve in the U.S. Senate. Elected in 1959, he was one of Hawaii's first two senators. Aug. 18, 2004

Robert Fulton, Jr., 95: inventor and adventurer whose creations range from a flying car, the Airphibian, to a system to evacuate spies from enemy territory, called the Fulton Skyhook. May 7, 2004

Geneviève, 83: French chanteuse who frequently appeared on the *Tonight Show,* where she would flirt with host Jack Paar and endearingly mangle the English language. March 14, 2004

Nicolai Ghiaurov, 74: Bulgarian opera singer who used his rich bass voice in such productions as Gounod's *Faust* and Verdi's *Don Carlo.* June 2, 2004

Joe Gold, 82: bodybuilder who opened Gold's Gym in Venice Beach, California, in 1965. The 1977 film *Pumping Iron* was set at the gym. July 11, 2004

Thomas Gold, 84: astrophysicist known for his unconventional and often controversial theories, including the steady-state theory of the cosmology, which stated the universe is infinite and continuously creating new matter. June 22, 2004

Jerry Goldsmith, 75: prolific composer who wrote hundreds of film scores and television theme songs, including music for the films *Patton* and *Basic Instinct* and television's *The Twilight Zone.* July 21, 2004

Olivia Goldsmith, 54: writer whose satirical debut novel, *The First Wives Club,* about three women whose husbands left them for younger brides, became a bestseller and a hit movie. Jan. 15, 2004

Spalding Gray, 62: actor and monologuist whose autobiographical stories revealed a thoughtful, yet deeply troubled man. His acclaimed autobiographical performances include *Swimming to Cambodia* and *Monster in a Box.* He appeared in the films *The Killing Fields* and *Beaches.* He committed suicide. Jan. 2004

Virginia Grey, 87: versatile actress who appeared in about 100 films, including *Uncle Tom's Cabin* and *Portrait in Black.* July 31, 2004

Uta Hagen, 84: stage actress who won a Tony Award for her role as Martha in Edward Albee's *Who's Afraid of Virginia Woolf?* In a career that spanned seven decades, she starred in plays by Shakespeare, Chekhov, and Tennessee Williams. Jan. 14, 2004

Syd Hoff, 91: writer and illustrator whose children's book *Danny the Dinosaur* has sold more than 10 million copies. He wrote more than 60 children's books and contributed 571 cartoons to *The New Yorker*. May 12, 2004

Godfrey Newbold Hounsfield, 84: British electrical engineer who invented the first CAT scan machine. He won the 1979 Nobel Prize in Physiology or Medicine for his work. Aug. 12, 2004

Bart Howard, 88: songwriter who penned the tune "Fly Me to the Moon." Feb. 21, 2004

Ulrich Inderbinen, 103: Swiss mountain guide known as the King of the Alps who climbed the Matterhorn at least 370 times. June 14, 2004

J. J. Jackson, 62: broadcaster who was one of MTV's original video jockeys when the network debuted in 1981. March 17, 2004

Illinois Jacquet, 81: influential jazz tenor saxophonist and bandleader whose solo on the song "Flying Home," first recorded with Lionel Hampton's orchestra, made him a legend. July 22, 2004

Rick James, 56: musician who pioneered the "punk-funk" style of the late 1970s and early 1980s. His song "Super Freak" propelled him to fame. Aug. 6, 2004

Mildred Jeffrey, 93: activist who was an early leader in the women's, civil rights, and labor movements. She was awarded the Presidential Medal of Freedom in 2000. March 24, 2004

Elvin Jones, 76: jazz drummer whose explosive and complex style influenced scores of jazz and rock musicians. May 18, 2004

Princess Juliana, 94: queen of the Netherlands (1948–1980) who promoted social welfare programs and ended 346 years of colonial rule in Indonesia. In 1980, Juliana abdicated to her daughter Beatrix. March 20, 2004

M. M. Kaye, 95: British novelist whose best-selling historical novel *The Far Pavilions*, about a British orphan in pre-independence India who falls in love with a princess, has sold millions of copies. Jan. 29, 2004

Bob Keeshan, 76: television personality who for nearly 30 years played the gentle father-figure Captain Kangaroo. Jan. 23, 2004

John Kelley, 97: distance runner who ran the Boston Marathon a record 61 times, winning twice and placing second 7 times. Oct. 6, 2004

Alan King, 76: comedian with a decidedly borscht-belt sensibility. His shtick typically focused on the frustrations of middle-class Americans. He appeared on Broadway and in 30 films, including *Author! Author!* and *Bonfire of the Vanities*. May 9, 2004

Clayton Kirkpatrick, 89: newspaper editor who presided over the *Chicago Tribune* for 10 years. June 19, 2004

Paul Klebnikov, 41: editor of *Forbes Russia* and an investigative journalist who has written about politics, business, and corruption in Russia. He was shot as he was leaving his office in Moscow. July 9, 2004

Thomas Klestil, 71: two-term Austrian president who expressed regret for Austria's complicity with the Nazis during World War II and sympathy for Holocaust victims. He died two days before his second six-year term was to end. July 6, 2004

Whitman Knapp, 95: federal judge who led New York City's two-year police corruption investigation that began in 1970. The film *Serpico* was based on the scandal and the ensuing inquiry by the Knapp Commission. June 14, 2004

Pierre Koenig, 78: modern architect known for his industrial-style glass-and-steel homes, most of which grace southern California. His Case Study House #22 is one of the most photographed homes in the world. April 4, 2004

Elisabeth Kübler-Ross, 78: pioneering psychiatrist whose research helped terminally ill patients come to terms with death. Her 1969 bestseller, *On Death and Dying*, encouraged public discussion about a once taboo subject. Aug. 24, 2004

Karol Kennedy Kucher, 72: figure skater who, with her brother Peter, won a silver medal in pairs at the 1952 Olympics and a gold medal at the world championships in 1950. They also won five U.S. titles. June 25, 2004

Ryszard Kuklinski, 73: former Polish army colonel who spied for the CIA from 1972 to 1981, passing on to the agency more than 35,000 pages of documents. Feb. 10, 2004

Jacek Kuron, 70: Polish intellectual and politician who guided the country in its battle against Communist rule. He cofounded the Committee to Assist Workers (KOR), which joined forces with the Solidarity movement. Their protests throughout the 1980s ultimately led to the collapse of the Communist government. Kuron became labor minister in 1989, and lost a bid for the presidency in 1995. June 17, 2004

Al Lapin, Jr., 76: entrepreneur who cofounded the International House of Pancakes with his brother in 1958. By 1970 the company was worth $40 million. June 16, 2004

Fred LaRue, 75: aide to President Nixon who served 136 days in jail for his involvement in the Watergate scandal. He paid the burglars who broke into the Democratic National Committee headquarters $300,000 for their silence. July 24, 2004

Estée Lauder, 97: entrepreneur who, with her husband, developed a department-store line of cosmetics that grew into a multibillion-dollar business. The company also owns Clinique, Origins, Prescriptives, and Aramis. April 24, 2004

Jerome Lawrence, 88: playwright who, with writing partner Robert E. Lee, wrote nearly 40 plays, including *Inherit the Wind* and *Auntie Mame*. Feb. 29, 2004

Janet Leigh, 77: esteemed actress who gave compelling performances in dozens of films, including *The Manchurian Candidate* and *Touch of Evil*. She's best known as the larcenous office worker who was gruesomely stabbed to death in the shower in Hitchcock's *Pyscho*. Oct. 3, 2004

Edward Lewis, 86: geneticist who won a 1995 Nobel Prize in Medicine for his "discoveries concerning the genetic control of early embryonic development" in humans. July 21, 2004

José López Portillo, 83: Mexican politician who, as president from 1976 to 1982, led the country to near financial collapse with profligate spending and an allegedly corrupt government. Feb. 17, 2004

William Manchester, 82: writer whose biographies and histories meticulously detailed the lives of prominent political and military figures, including Gen. Douglas MacArthur and Winston Churchill. His book about the assassination of President Kennedy, *The Death of a President*, created a scandal with the Kennedy family. June 1, 2004

Nino Manfredi, 83: Italian actor who appeared in more than 100 films during his 54-year career, including *We All Loved Each Other So Much* and *Bread and Chocolate*. June 4, 2004

Alberta Martin, 97: one of the last-known Confederate widows. At age 21, she married civil-war veteran William Jasper Martin, then 81. Upon his death, she married his grandson from his first marriage. May 31, 2004

Brian Maxwell, 51: world-class marathon runner who developed the endurance-enhancing PowerBar. He began working on the bars in 1983 and launched the PowerBar company in 1986. He sold his company to Nestlé in 2000 for $375 million. March 19, 2004

Sir Richard May, 65: British judge who oversaw the war-crimes tribunal of former Yugoslav president Slobodan Milosevic. He presided over the trial for two years, frequently sparring with the obstinate defendant. July 1, 2004

Mercedes McCambridge, 87: film, stage, and television actress who often played strong-willed women. She won an Oscar for her role in *All the King's Men.* She provided the voice for the gravelly voiced possessed girl in *The Exorcist.* March 2, 2004

Tug McGraw, 59: left-handed relief pitcher who helped the New York Mets and the Philadelphia Phillies capture World Series championships. He tallied 180 saves in his 19-year career. Jan. 5, 2004

Mary McGrory, 85: liberal columnist who earned a national reputation for her coverage of 1954's McCarthy hearings for the Washington *Star.* Her commentary on the Kennedy assassination in 1963 made her one of the best-known print journalists in the country. McGrory won the Pulitzer Prize for Commentary in 1975 for her coverage of the Watergate scandal. April 21, 2004

Norris McWhirter, 78: journalist and sports announcer who, with his twin brother Ross, started the *Guinness Book of World Records* in 1955. More than 100 million of the books have been sold. In 1954, McWhirter was the announcer when Roger Bannister ran a mile in under four minutes. April 20, 2004

Russ Meyer, 82: filmmaker who crossed over from soft-core-porn "nudie" films to the mainstream with 1970's *Beyond the Valley of the Dolls.* His 1965 film *Faster, Pussycat! Kill! Kill!* was rereleased in 1995 to critical praise. Sept. 18, 2004

Ann Miller, 81: athletic tap dancer who appeared in a string of films in the 1940s and 1950s, including *Kiss Me Kate* and *On the Town.* She made a splash with her 1979 comeback, Broadway's *Sugar Babies,* opposite Mickey Rooney. Jan. 22, 2004

Czeslaw Milosz, 93: Polish essayist and poet who won the 1980 Nobel Prize in Literature. Many of his early poems poignantly recall the horrors of World War II and the Nazi occupation of Poland. His later poems drew on the Communist dictatorship in Poland. In his best-known work, *The Captive Mind,* Milosz critically analyzed the oppression of intellectuals under Communist totalitarianism. Aug. 14, 2004

Jan Miner, 86: actress best known for playing Madge the manicurist in Palmolive commercials. Feb. 15, 2004

Thomas Moorer, 91: navy admiral who served as chairman of the Joint Chiefs of Staff from 1970–1974 and as chief of naval operations during the Vietnam War. Feb. 5, 2004

Carl Mydans, 97: photographer who worked for *Life* magazine for 36 years. He shot his most memorable images during World War II. They include one of Gen. Douglas MacArthur walking through the water toward the shore in the Philippines. Aug. 16, 2004

Helmut Newton, 83: artistic fashion photographer known for his provocative, often explicit photos that frequently appeared in fashion magazines such as *Vogue.* January 23, 2004

Paul Nitze, 97: public official and nuclear expert who for more than 40 years was highly influential in shaping U.S. policy toward the Soviet Union. He was a member of the U.S. delegation to the Strategic Arms Limitation Talks and helped to negotiate the Intermediate Range Nuclear Forces (INF) treaty. He also served as Secretary of the Navy and Deputy Secretary of Defense. Oct. 19, 2004

Jack Paar, 85: comedian who was the unpredictable, intelligent host of the *Tonight Show* from 1957 to 1962. His guests included a mix of celebrities, politicians, and wits, including Richard Nixon, Jayne Mansfield, and Peter Ustinov. Jan. 27, 2004

Robert Pastorelli, 49: actor who played the screwball housepainter Eldin on the television series *Murphy Brown.* He also appeared in the films *Dances with Wolves* and *Get Shorty.* March 8, 2004

Daniel Petrie, 83: film and television director whose films include *A Raisin in the Sun* and *Resurrection.* Aug. 22, 2004

William Pickering, 93: former director of NASA's Jet Propulsion Laboratory (1954–1976) who oversaw many of the country's first exploits into space, including 1958's launch of the first spacecraft into orbit, *Explorer I,* and the first robotic missions to the Moon, Venus, and Mars. March 15, 2004

Maria Pintasilgo, 74: Portuguese engineer and politician who was the country's first and only female prime minister. July 10, 2004

Sir John Pople, 78: British-born scientist who won a Nobel Prize in Chemistry in 1998 for his work on a computer program that facilitates the study of the properties of molecules and how they work together in chemical reactions. March 15, 2004

Nuha al-Radi, 63: Iraqi artist and writer whose book, *Baghdad Diaries,* chronicles life during the first Gulf War. The book is equally critical of Saddam Hussein and the United States. She moved to Beirut after the book was published. Aug. 30, 2004

Johnny Ramone, 55: guitarist who cofounded the Ramones, a pioneering punk band whose influence extends from the Sex Pistols and the Clash to U2 and Nirvana. The band recorded 21 albums. Its hits include "Teenage Lobotomy" and "Rock 'n' Roll High School." He died of cancer. Sept. 15, 2004

Tony Randall, 84: actor best known for his role as the persnickety Felix Unger in the television series *The Odd Couple.* Randall had enjoyed a successful theater and film career long before the show debuted. He starred in films *Pillow Talk* and *Send Me No Flowers* and in dozens of stage productions. May 17, 2004

David Raskin, 92: composer who scored more than 100 films and 300 television shows. He's best known for the haunting theme song for the 1944 film *Laura.* Aug. 9, 2004

Ronald Reagan, 93: 40th president of the United States, remembered for his eloquence, his ability to connect with his constituency, and his unbridled optimism. Reagan won the presidency in 1980, promising moderate policies and a smaller government. Barely three months into his first term, Reagan was the target of a would-be assassin's bullet; his courageous comeback earned him public admiration. The president gained acclaim for his nomination of Sandra Day O'Connor as the first woman on the Supreme Court. He was reelected in a landslide in 1984. Congress passed his huge tax cut, but the growing budget deficit remained an issue with the public and members of Congress. Reagan's popularity dipped sharply in 1986 when the Iran-Contra scandal broke. Reagan's place in history will rest, perhaps, on the short- and intermediate-range missile treaty signed on a cordial visit to the Soviet Union. June 5, 2004

Christopher Reeve, 52: actor who became a movie icon with the title role in 1978's *Superman.* Vowing to "escape the cape," he starred in the period films *The Bostonians* and *The Remains of the Day.* A 1995 fall from a horse left Reeve paralyzed and wheelchairbound, but he continued to work, directing *In the Gloaming* for HBO and performing in the 1997 remake of Alfred Hitchcock's *Rear Window.* He was a tireless advocate for stem-cell research. Oct. 10, 2004

Alexandra Ripley, 70: writer who penned *Scarlett,* the sequel to *Gone with the Wind.* She was hired by the estate of Margaret Mitchell to write the book. Jan. 10, 2004

Laurance Rockefeller, 94: business executive and conservationist who was one of five grandsons of oil magnate John D. Rockefeller. He made his own fortune as a venture capitalist. July 11, 2004

Marvin Runyon, 79: former auto executive who served as postmaster general of the U.S. Postal Service from 1992 to 1998. He also served as chairman of the Tennessee Valley Authority. May 3, 2004

Françoise Sagan, 69: French novelist who wrote her first book, the best-selling *Bonjour Tristesse,* about France's sophisticated yet immoral society, at age 19. Sept. 24, 2004

Pierre Salinger, 79: award-winning journalist who served as President Kennedy's White House press secretary from 1961 to 1964. He oversaw the first live televised presidential news conference in 1961. After politics, Salinger returned to journalism and worked as chief foreign correspondent for ABC News. Oct. 16, 2004

Isabel Sanford, 86: actress who won an Emmy Award for her role as Louise on *The Jeffersons.* She made her film debut in 1967's *Guess Who's Coming to Dinner.* July 9, 2004

Francesco Scavullo, 82: photographer whose often provocative portraits appeared frequently on the covers of fashion magazines, particularly *Cosmopolitan.* Jan. 6, 2004

Marge Schott, 75: former owner of the Cincinnati Reds. She bought the team in 1984, becoming the first woman to buy a Major League team. Her downfall began in 1992, when colleagues complained that she used racial and ethnic slurs when referring to players. She was suspended from the team's operations in 1993 and again in 1996. She relinquished control of the team in 1999. March 2, 2004

Hubert Selby, 75: writer whose *Last Exit to Brooklyn* explicitly described the underbelly of Brooklyn during the 1950s, revealing an urban wasteland littered with drugs, gangs, and promiscuity. His other works include *The Room* and *The Demon.* April 26, 2004

Harold Shipman, 57: British doctor, known as "Dr. Death," who was convicted in 2000 of murdering 15 patients. An investigation later determined that he killed as many as 260 people in 23 years. His victims were mostly women whom he killed while making house calls. Jan. 13, 2004

Jeff Smith, 65: former minister who reinvented himself as public television's Frugal Gourmet. He wrote a series of best-selling cookbooks. His career came to an abrupt end in 1997, when seven men filed a lawsuit that accused him of sexual abuse. He was never charged with a crime. July 7, 2004

John Maynard Smith, 84: evolutionary biologist who applied gaming theory to his study of animal behavior, answering such questions as why animals sometimes raise their young while at other times they leave the responsibility to a mate. April 19, 2004

Carrie Snodgress, 57: actress who earned an Oscar nomination for her role as an unhappy homemaker in the film *Diary of a Mad Housewife.* April 1, 2004

Stephen Sprouse, 50: fashion designer whose punk-inspired, sophisticated creations were favored by rock stars as well as followers of haute couture. March 4, 2004

Ray Stark, 88: influential and prolific film producer who made more than 125 films, including *Funny Girl* and *Steel Magnolias.* Jan. 17, 2004

Jan Sterling, 82: cool, crafty actress who appeared in the films *Ace in the Hole* and *Caged.* She earned an Oscar nomination for 1954's *The High and the Mighty.* March 26, 2004

Roger Straus, 87: publisher who headed Farrar, Straus, & Giroux, one of the most respected publishing houses in the industry. The company remained the last of the independents until 1994, when Straus sold it to a German media company. The company published the works of Isaac Bashevis Singer, Flannery O'Connor, and Susan Sontag. May 25, 2004

June Taylor, 86: Emmy Award–winning choreographer whose Broadway-inspired numbers on *The Jackie Gleason Show* introduced TV audiences to the chorus line. May 16, 2004

Robert Teeter, 65: Republican pollster and consultant who developed the tracking poll, which monitored public opinion in daily polls. June 13, 2004

Ingrid Thulin, 77: aloof Swedish actress who frequently appeared in Ingmar Bergman films, including *Wild Strawberries.* Her other credits include *The Silence* and *Cries and Whispers.* Jan. 7, 2004

John Toland, 91: author and World War II historian whose book *The Rising Sun: The Decline and Fall of the Japanese Empire, 1936–1945,* won the Pulitzer Prize in 1971. Jan. 4, 2004

Boris Trajkovski, 47: former Methodist minister who was elected president of Macedonia in 1999. In 2001, he helped to prevent an uprising by minority Albanians by giving them broader rights and making Albanian one of the country's two official languages. He died in a plane crash. Feb. 26, 2004

Doris Troy, 67: pop singer who recorded the 1963 hit "Just One Look." Her life story inspired the musical *Mama, I Want to Sing.* Feb. 16, 2004

Peter Ustinov, 82: singular writer, director, and actor whose intelligence and charming wit graced his books, plays, and films. He wrote the plays *Romanoff and Juliet* and *The Unknown Soldier and His Wife* and the novel *Krumnagel.* He acted in the films *Quo Vadis* and *Spartacus,* for which he won a Best Supporting Actor Oscar. Ustinov acted in, wrote, and directed the films *Billy Budd* and *Lady L.* He played Agatha Christie's detective Hercule Poirot in several theatrical and television films. March 28, 2004

Walter Wager, 79: spy novelist who wrote more than 30 books, including *58 Minutes,* which was adapted for film and released as *Die Hard,* and *Teflon,* which also became a film. July 11, 2004

Rodger Ward, 83: race-car driver who won the Indianapolis 500 in 1959 and 1962. July 5, 2004

Eleanor Holm Whalen, 90?: swimmer who won a gold medal in 100-meter backstroke at the 1932 Olympics. She created an Olympic-sized scandal in 1936 when she was kicked off the U.S. swimming team for drinking champagne in public and shooting craps with journalists while on board a ship bringing athletes to the Berlin games. Jan. 31, 2004

Fred Whipple, 97: rocket scientist whose "dirty snowball theory" suggested that comets are made of ice and rock. He invented a thin shield of metal, called the Whipple shield, to protect spacecraft from high-speed particles. Aug. 30, 2004

John Whitehead, 55: R&B singer and songwriter who, with Gene McFadden, recorded a string of hits in the 1970s, including the No. 1 hit "Ain't No Stoppin' Us Now." May 11, 2004

Maurice Wilkins, 87: British biophysicist who contributed to the discovery of the double-helix structure of DNA, the chemical that carries hereditary characteristics from generation to generation. He won the 1962 Nobel Prize in Physiology or Medicine for his work, along with Francis Crick and James Watson. Oct. 6, 2004

Claude (Fiddler) Williams, 96: renowned musician who was a jazz violin virtuoso and Count Basie's first recorded guitarist. He played at President Clinton's second inauguration. April 25, 2004

Paul Winfield, 62: versatile actor who earned an Oscar nomination for his role in *Sounder* and an Emmy Award for his work on TV's *Picket Fences.* He also played Martin Luther King, Jr., in the miniseries *King.* March 7, 2004

Fay Wray, 96: plucky actress who confronted beasts and villains in several films, most famously 1933's *King Kong,* in which she let out a terrifying shriek as the ape put her atop the Empire State Building. Aug. 8, 2004